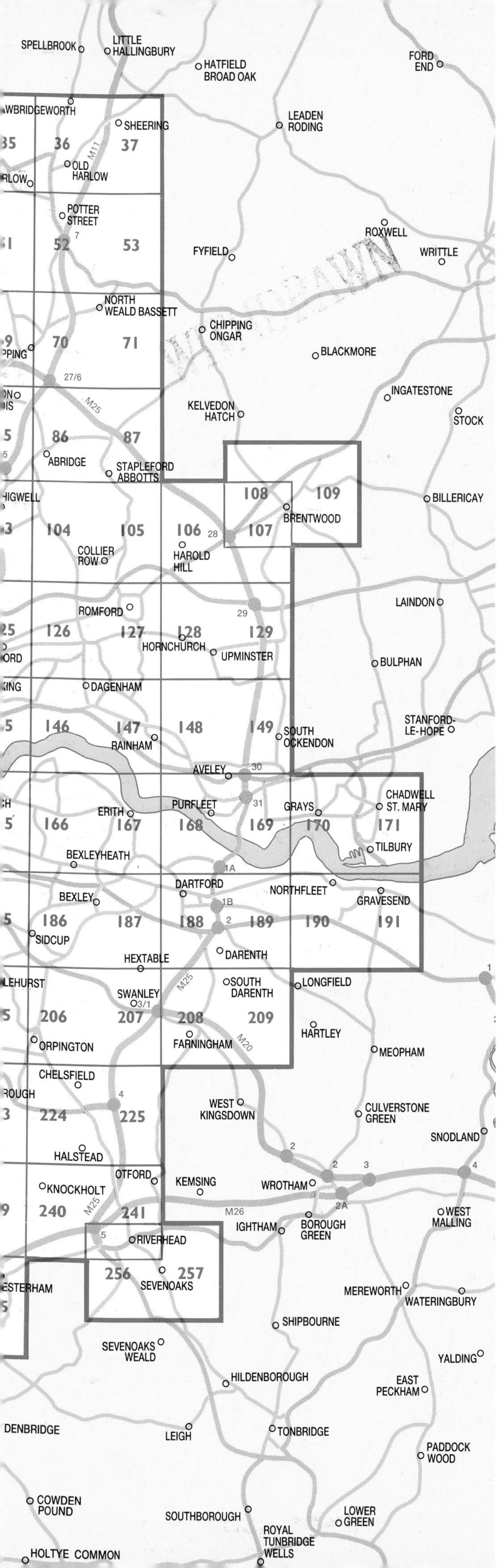

This edition produced for The Book People Ltd.,
Hall Wood Avenue, Haydock,
St. Helens WA11 9UL

Published by Collins
An imprint of HarperCollins *Publishers*
77-85 Fulham Palace Road
Hammersmith
London W6 8JB

The HarperCollins website address is: www.**fire**and**water**.com
© Copyright Nicholson 1999
First published by Geographia Ltd 1977
Fourteenth edition May 2000

TED SMART

All mapping and information is generated from the
Bartholomew digital databases
Bartholomew web site: www.bartholomewmaps.com

London Underground Map by permission of London
Regional Transport LRT Registered User No. 99/3054

All rights reserved. No part of this publication may be
reproduced, stored in a retrieval system, or transmitted,
in any form or by any means, electronic, mechanical,
photocopying, recording or otherwise, without the prior
written permission of the publisher and copyright owners.

The contents of this publication are believed correct at the
time of printing. Nevertheless, the publisher can accept
no responsibility for errors or omissions, changes in the
detail given, or for any expense or loss thereby caused.

The representation of a road, track or footpath is no
evidence of a right of way.

Printed in Italy

ISBN 0 583 33291 9

The maps in this product are also available for purchase
in digital format, from Bartholomew Data Sales

Tel: +44 (0)1242 233887
Fax: +44 (0)1242 222725

e-mail: bartholomew@harpercollins.co.uk

Queries concerning this product to be addressed to:
        The Publisher,
        HarperCollins*Cartographic*,
        4, Manchester Park,
        Tewkesbury Road,
        Cheltenham,
        GL51 9EJ

THE LIBRARY
GUILDFORD COLLEGE
of Further and Higher Education

REF 914.421 NIC
95645

NICHOLSON

GREATER LONDON STREET ATLAS

CONTENTS

TED SMART

M25 LONDON ORBITAL MOTORWAY

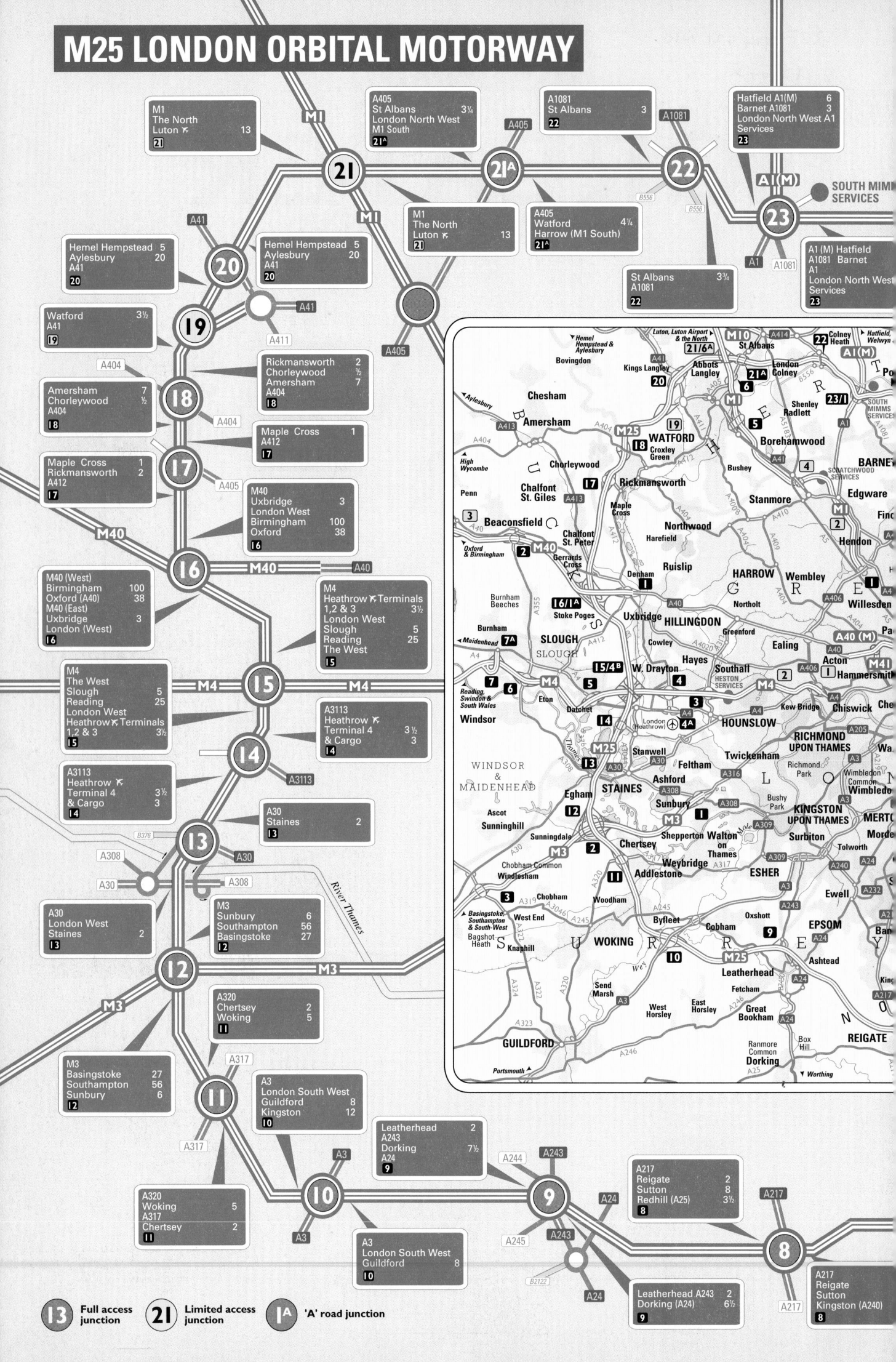

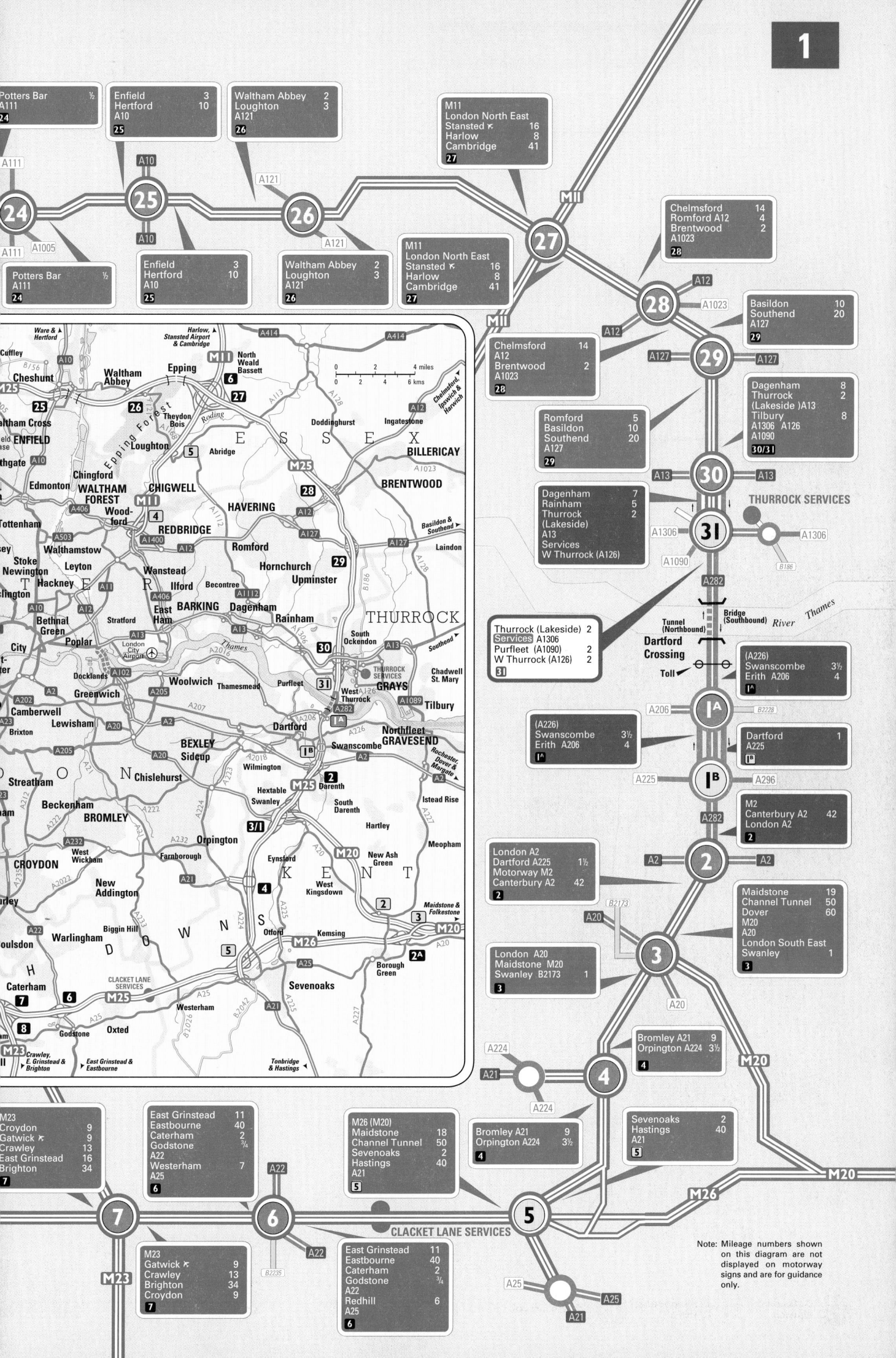

JUNCTION OF EXIT

JUNCTION OF ENTRY

Junction Number	Name
1	DARTFORD
2	A2
3	M20
4	A21
5	M26
6	A22
7	M23
8	REIGATE
9	LEATHERHEAD
10	A3
11	CHERTSEY
12	M3
13	A30
14	HEATHROW 4
15	M4, HEATHROW 1-3
16	M40
17	RICKMANSWORTH
18	A404
19	WATFORD
20	A41
21	M1
22	ST. ALBANS
23	A1 (M)
24	A111
25	A10
26	EPPING
27	M11
28	A12
29	A127
30	A13
31	A13

Mileage chart (shortest distance in miles between junctions of entry (rows) and exit (columns)):

Entry ↓ / Exit →	1	2	3	4	5	6	7	8	9	10	11	12	13	14	15	16	17	18	19	20	21	22	23	24	25	26	27	28	29	30	31
2	1																														
3	4	3																													
4	8	7	4																												
5	12	11	8	4																											
6	22	21	18	14	10																										
7	25	24	21	17	14	3																									
8	28	27	24	20	16	6	3																								
9	35	34	31	27	23	13	10	7																							
10	41	40	37	33	29	19	16	13	6																						
11	46	45	42	38	34	24	21	18	11	5																					
12	48	47	44	40	36	26	23	20	13	7	2																				
13	51	50	47	43	39	29	26	23	16	10	5	3																			
14	53	52	49	45	41	31	28	25	18	12	7	5	2																		
15	55	54	51	47	43	33	30	27	20	14	9	7	4	2																	
16	59	59	56	52	48	38	35	32	25	19	14	12	9	7	5																
17	53	54	57	58	54	44	41	38	31	25	20	18	15	13	11	6															
18	52	53	56	57	55	45	42	39	32	26	21	19	16	14	12	7	1														
19	49	50	53	57	58	59	46	43	40	33	28	24	22	19	14	10	4	3													
20	48	49	52	56	57	59	47	44	41	34	29	25	23	20	15	11	5	4	1												
21	45	46	49	53	57	59	49	46	43	36	31	27	24	21	19	14	11	8	5	4											
22	40	41	44	48	52	56	54	51	48	41	36	32	29	24	20	15	12	11	8	7	3										
23	37	38	41	45	49	59	57	54	51	44	39	34	31	27	24	19	16	15	12	9	6	3									
24	34	35	38	42	46	56	59	56	53	47	42	37	34	30	25	21	19	18	15	14	11	9	6								
25	28	29	32	36	40	50	53	59	56	46	40	38	34	30	25	21	20	20	17	15	12	7	9	6							
26	25	26	29	33	37	47	50	53	59	51	46	43	40	36	31	25	24	23	20	18	15	12	9	3	3						
27	21	22	25	29	33	43	46	49	56	57	52	50	47	43	38	32	31	27	24	23	20	16	13	7	4						
28	13	14	17	21	25	35	38	41	48	54	59	58	55	53	51	46	40	36	35	32	27	24	21	15	12	8	4				
29	10	11	14	18	22	32	35	38	45	51	56	59	58	56	54	49	43	39	38	35	30	27	24	18	15	11	7	3			
30	5	6	9	13	17	27	30	33	40	46	51	53	56	58	59	54	48	44	43	40	35	32	29	23	20	16	8	5	5		
31	4	5	8	12	16	26	29	32	39	45	50	52	55	57	59	55	49	48	45	44	41	36	33	30	24	21	17	9	6	1	

Mileage Clockwise

Mileage AntiClockwise

Note: This chart shows the shortest distance between junctions. The colours indicate whether the distance is clockwise or anticlockwise. The total distance around the M25 is approximately 117 miles.

KEY TO ROUTE PLANNING MAPS

3

KEY TO MAP PAGES

M4	Motorway
30 / 29	Motorway junction (full / limited)
off road	Motorway service areas (full / limited)
dual A48	Primary route
dual A30	'A' Road
dual B1403	'B' Road
	Minor road

Restricted access due to road condition or private ownership

29 Roads projected or under construction

⊗ Multi-level junction

Roundabout

24 / 25 10 / 10 Road distances (miles)

Road tunnel

➤ Steep hill (arrows point downhill)

Level crossing

Toll

Railway line and station

Railway tunnel

✈ Airport / Ⓗ Heliport

Built up areas

☐ ☐ ☐ Towns, villages and other settlements

Sevenoaks Primary route destination

County / Unitary Authority boundary

Danger Zone Military range

Woodland

468 ▲941 Height in metres

Lake, dam and river

Canal / Dry canal / Canal tunnel

Beach

Scale:
0 1 2 3 4 5 miles
0 1 2 3 4 5 km

Proposed millennium sites are shown as a red and yellow symbol of the relevant category i.e. ★

ℹ️ all year / ℹ️ seasonal — Tourist information office

Preserved railway — +++ 1738

Battlefield

Ancient monument

Ecclesiastical building

Castle

Historic house (with or without garden)

Garden

Museum / Art gallery

Theme park

Major sports venue

Motor racing circuit

Racecourse

Country park

Nature reserve

Wildlife park or Zoo

Other interesting feature

Golf course

(NT) National Trust property

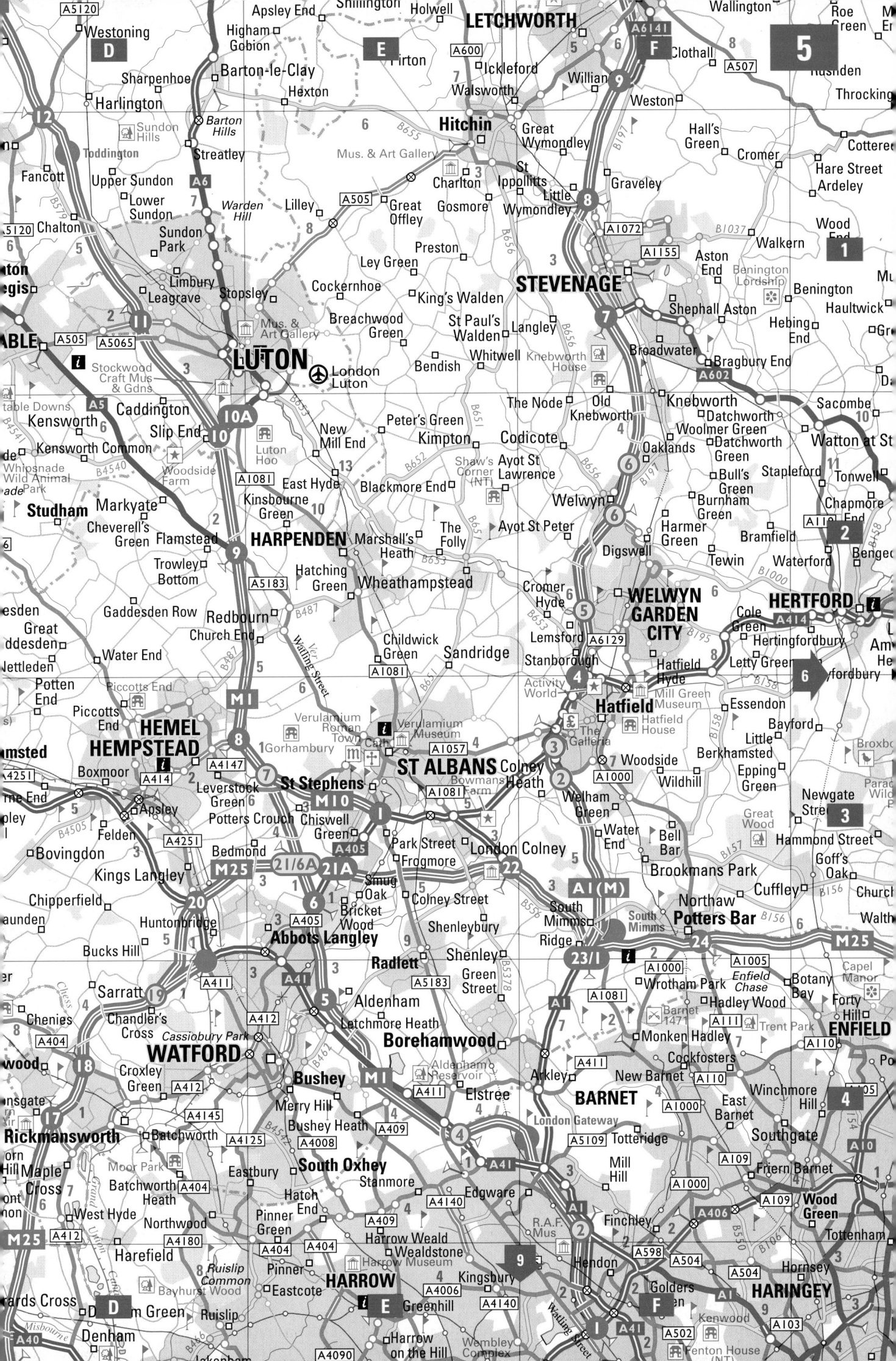

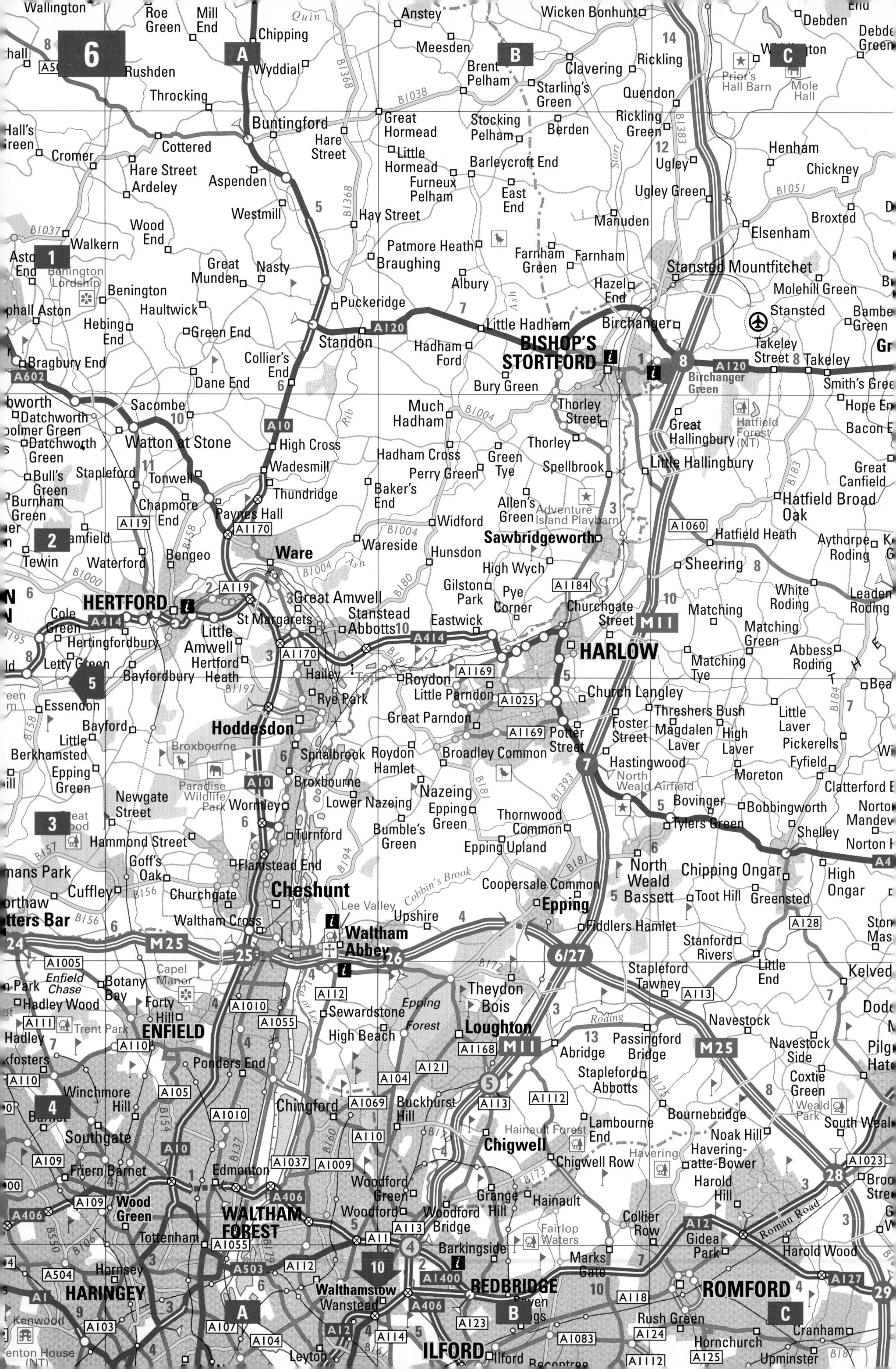

Wallington
Roe Green
Mill End
Quin
Anstey
Meesden
Wicken Bonhunt
End
Debden
Debden Green

A50
Rushden
Chipping
Wyddial
Brent Pelham
Starling's Green
Clavering
Rickling
14
Prior's Hall Barn
Mole Hall
C
Wellington

Throcking
Buntingford
Great Hormead
Stocking Pelham
Berden
Quendon
Rickling Green
12
Henham

Hall's Green
Cromer
Cottered
Hare Street
Little Hormead
Barleycroft End
Ugley
Chickney

B1037
Hare Street
Ardeley
Aspenden
Westmill
Furneux Pelham
East End
Manuden
Ugley Green
B1051
Broxted

Walkern
Wood End
5
Hay Street
Patmore Heath
Farnham Green
Farnham
Stansted Mountfitchet
Elsenham

Aston End
Benington Lordship
Great Munden
Nasty
Braughing
Albury
Hazel End
Birchanger
Molehill Green
Stansted
Bambers Green

Benington
Haultwick
Puckeridge
Little Hadham
BISHOP'S STORTFORD
Birchanger Green
8
A120
Takeley Street
8 Takeley
Gr

Hebing End
Green End
Standon
A120
Hadham Ford
Bury Green
Thorley Street
Great Hallingbury
Hatfield Forest (NT)
Smith's Green

Bragbury End
A602
Collier's End
6
Much Hadham
Thorley
Spellbrook
Little Hallingbury
Hope End
Bacon End

Datchworth
Bolmer Green
Datchworth Green
Sacombe
10
High Cross
B1004
Hadham Cross
Green Tye
Adventure Island Playbarn
3
Hatfield Heath
A1060
Great Canfield
Hatfield Broad Oak

Watton at Stone
Wadesmill
Perry Green
Allen's Green
Sawbridgeworth
Hatfield Heath
Aythorpe Roding

Bull's Green
Burnham Green
Stapleford
11
Tonwell
Thundridge
Baker's End
Widford
High Wych
A1184
Sheering
8
White Roding
Leaden Roding

Chapmore End
Paynes Hall
A1170
Wareside
Hunsdon
Pye Corner
Churchgate Street
10
M11
Matching
Matching Green
Abbess Roding

Tewin
Waterford
Bengeo
Ware
B1004
Ash
High Wych
Gilston Park
HARLOW
Matching Tye
White Roding

HERTFORD
A119
Great Amwell
Stanstead Abbotts
Eastwick
A414
A1025
Church Langley
Threshers Bush
Little Laver
B184

Cole Green
A414
St Margarets
10
A1170
Roydon
Little Parndon
A1169
5
Foster Street
Magdalen Laver
High Laver
Pickerells
Fyfield

Hertingfordbury
Little Amwell
Hailey
B197
Great Parndon
A1169
Potter Street
Hastingwood
North
Moreton
Clatterford End

Bayfordbury
Hertford Heath
Rye Park
Broadley Common
7
North Weald Airfield
Bovinger
Bobbingworth
Norton Mandeville

Essendon
Bayford
Hoddesdon
Spitalbrook
Roydon Hamlet
Nazeing
Thornwood Common
Tylers Green
Shelley
Norton H

Berkhamsted
Little Epping Green
Broxbourne
Paradise Wildlife Park
Wormley
Lower Nazeing
Epping Green
Epping Upland
6
North Weald
Chipping Ongar
High Ongar

Newgate Street
A10
Turnford
Bumble's Green
Epping
Bassett
Toot Hill
Greensted

Hammond Street
Goff's Oak
Flamstead End
Cobbin's Brook
Coopersale Common
B181
Fiddlers Hamlet
Stanford Rivers
A128

Cuffley
Churchgate
Cheshunt
Lee Valley
Upshire
4
Epping
Stapleford Tawney
Little End
Kelved

Potters Bar
B156
Waltham Cross
M25
25
Waltham Abbey
26
6/27
M25
A113
Navestock

Enfield Chase
Capel Manor
Botany Bay
Forty Hill
A112
Sewardstone
Epping Forest
Theydon Bois
3
Stapleford Abbotts
Navestock Side
Pilg

Hadley Wood
A1005
A1010
A1055
High Beach
Loughton
A1168
M11
13
Passingford Bridge
Coxtie Green
Dod
Hat

Hadley
A111
Trent Park
ENFIELD
A110
Ponders End
A104
A121
5
A113
Abridge
Lambourne End
Bournebridge
Weald Park
South Weald

Winchmore Hill
A105
Chingford
A1069
Buckhurst Hill
A112
Chigwell
Hainault Forest
Noak Hill
Havering-atte-Bower

Southgate
A154
A1010
A110
Chigwell Row
Havering
Harold Hill
A1023
28

Friern Barnet
Wood Green
Edmonton
A1037
A1009
Woodford Green
Hainault
Grange Hill
Collier Row
A12
Roman Road
Broo

A109
A406
A406
Woodford
Woodford Bridge
Fairlop Waters
A12
Gidea Park
Harold Wood

WALTHAM FOREST
A1055
A113
Barkingside
Marks Gate
A127

HARINGEY
A503
A502
10
A
4
2
A1400
B
REDBRIDGE
Rush Green
A118
ROMFORD
4
C
29

Kenwood
Fenton House (NT)
A103
A107
A104
WALTHAMSTOW
Wanstead
A406
ILFORD
A123
Seven
A1083
Hornchurch
A125
Upminster
B

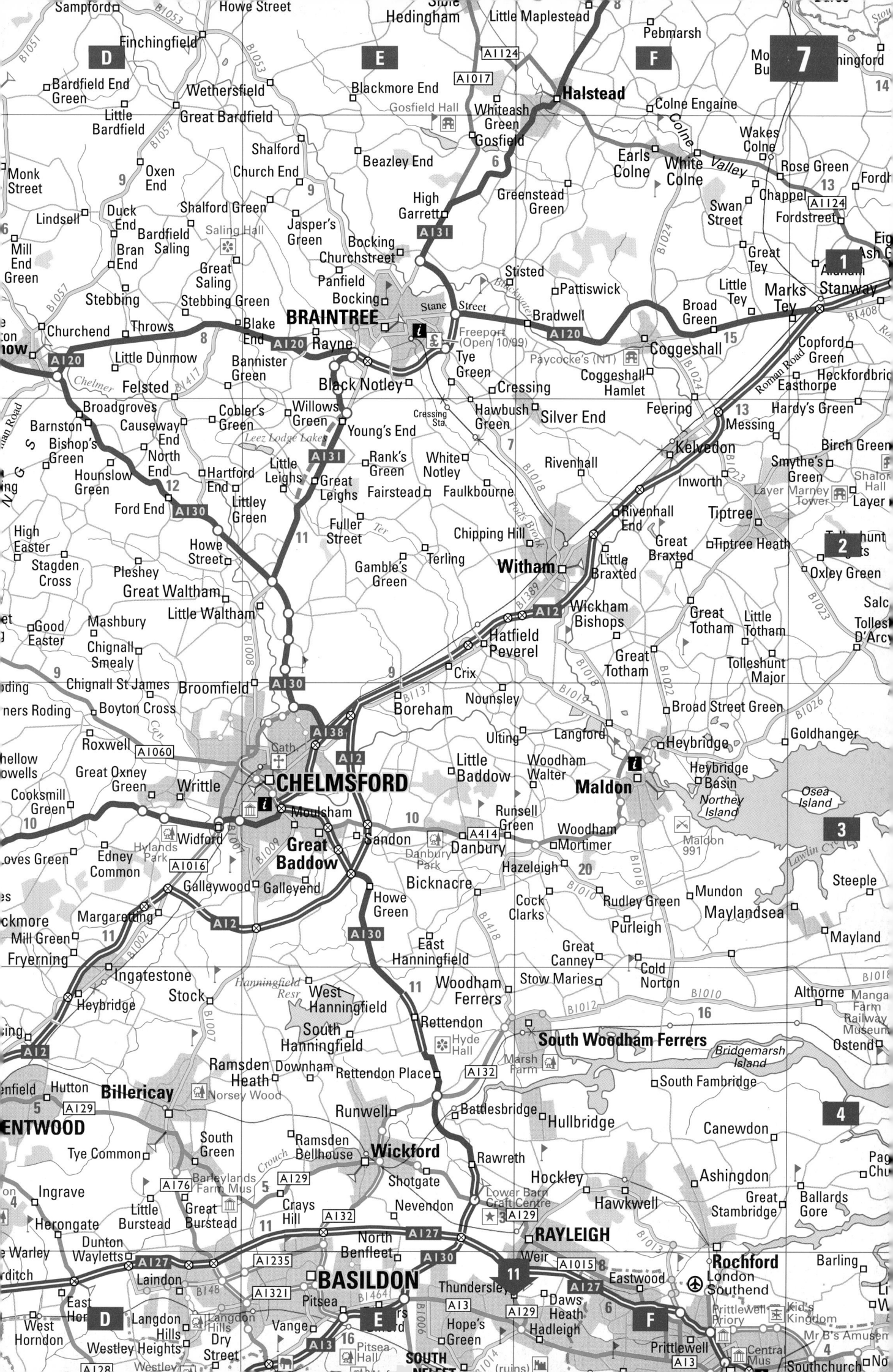

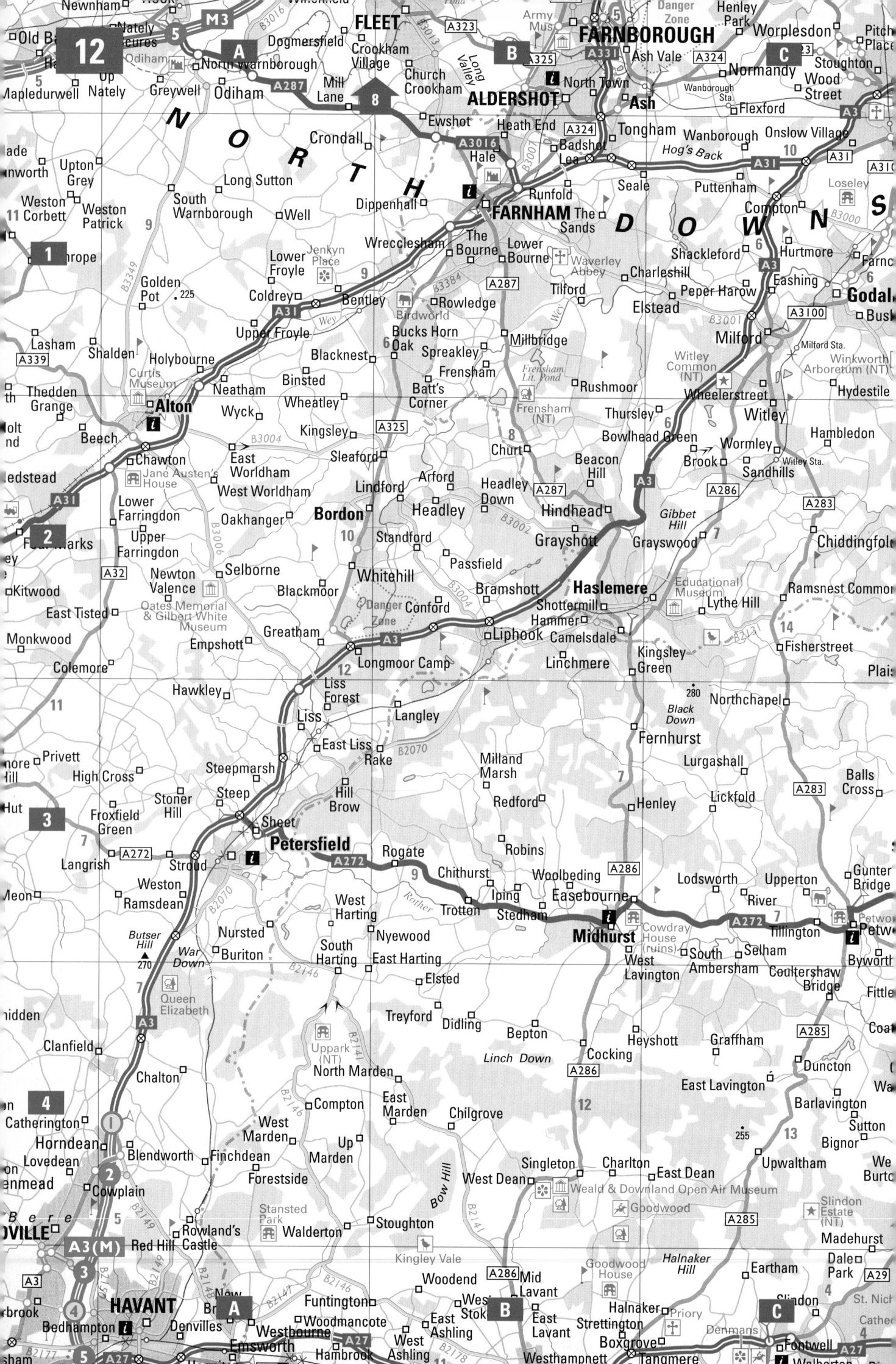

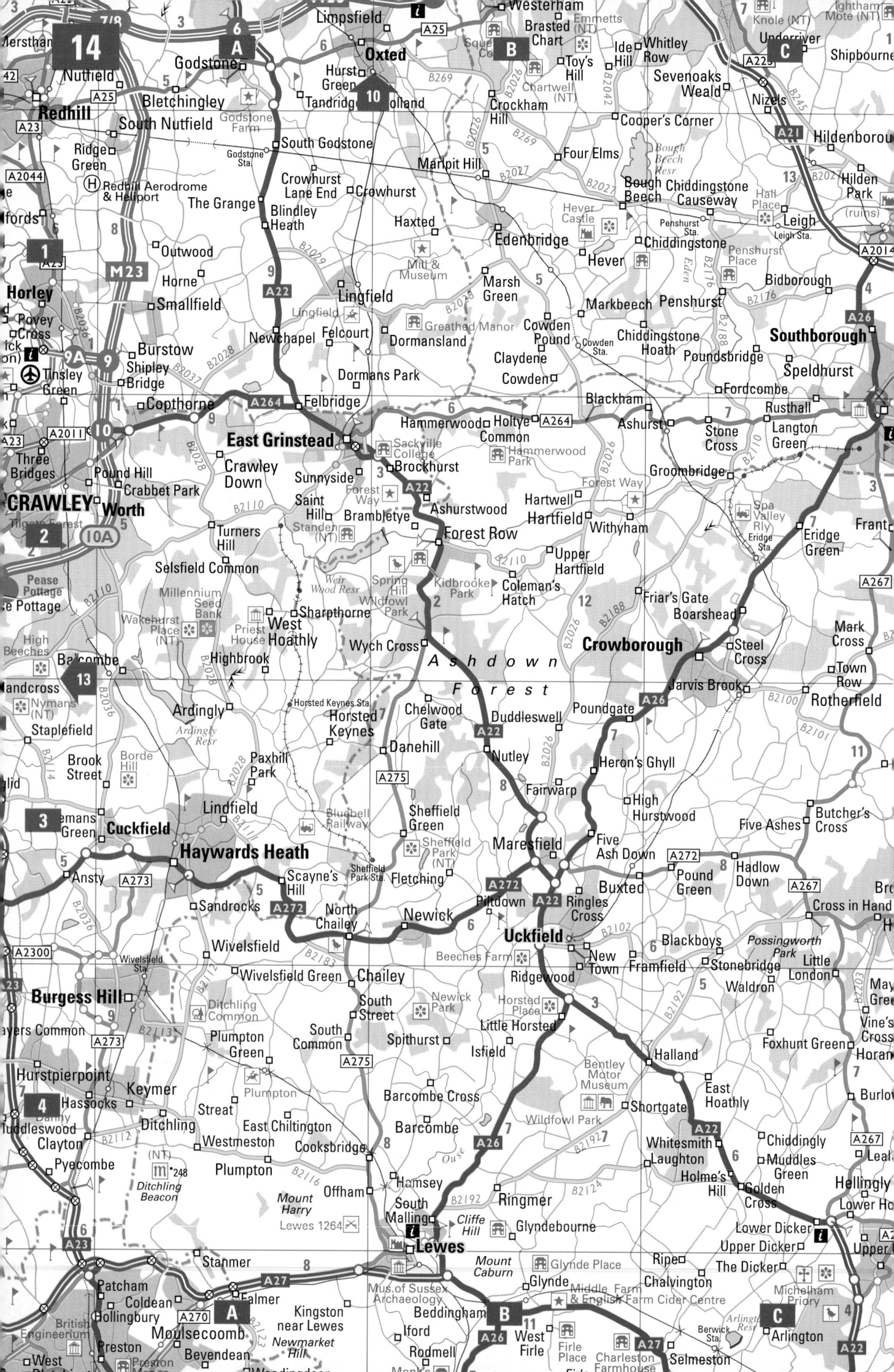

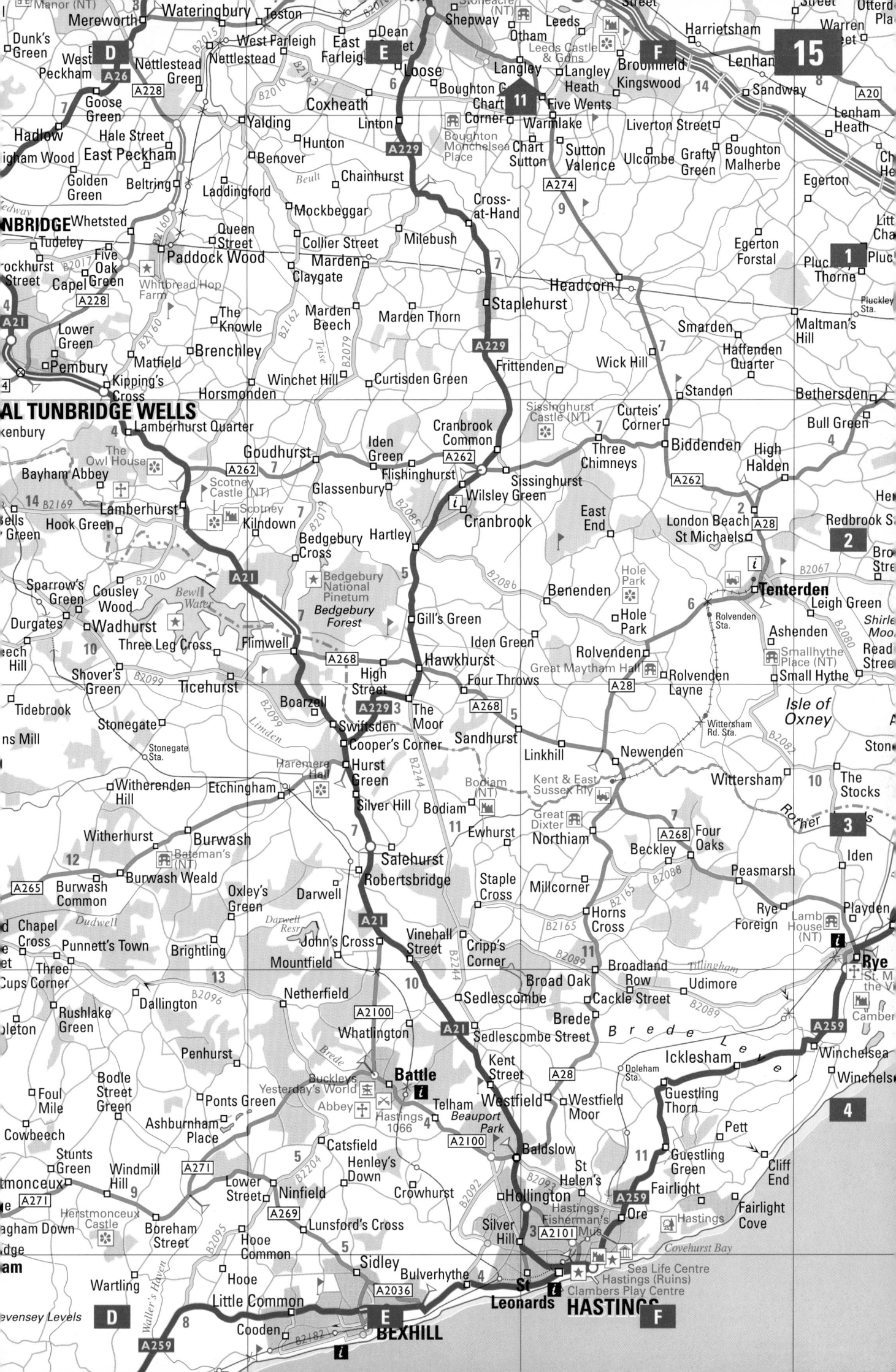

THE LIBRARY
GUILDFORD COLLEGE
of Further and Higher Education

KEY TO MAP SYMBOLS

- ⓘ Tourist information centre
- 🅿 Short stay car park
- 🅿 Long stay car park
- ⊛ Railway station
- ⊖ London underground station
- 🚌 Bus station

LUTON

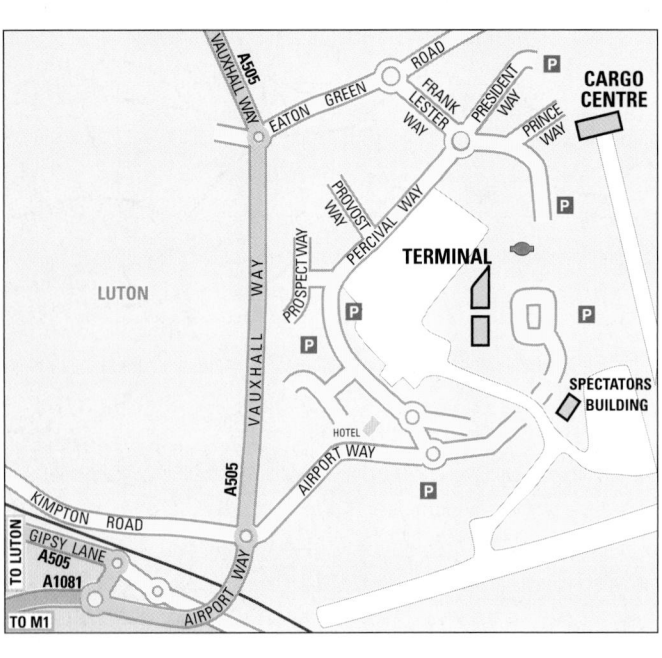

Tel. 01582 405100

STANSTED

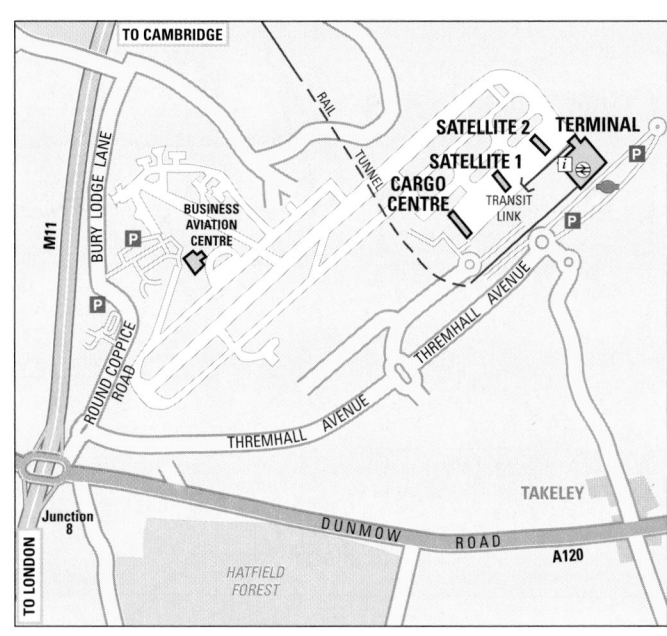

Tel. 01279 680500

HEATHROW

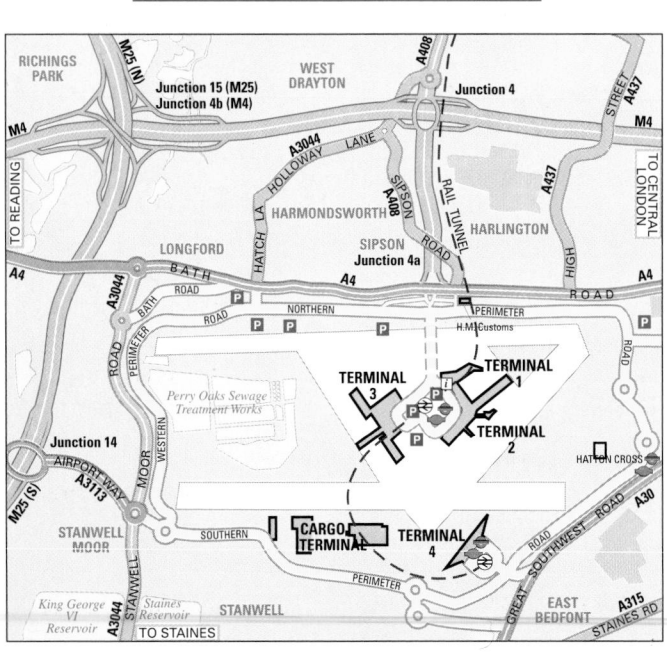

Tel. 020 8759 4321

GATWICK

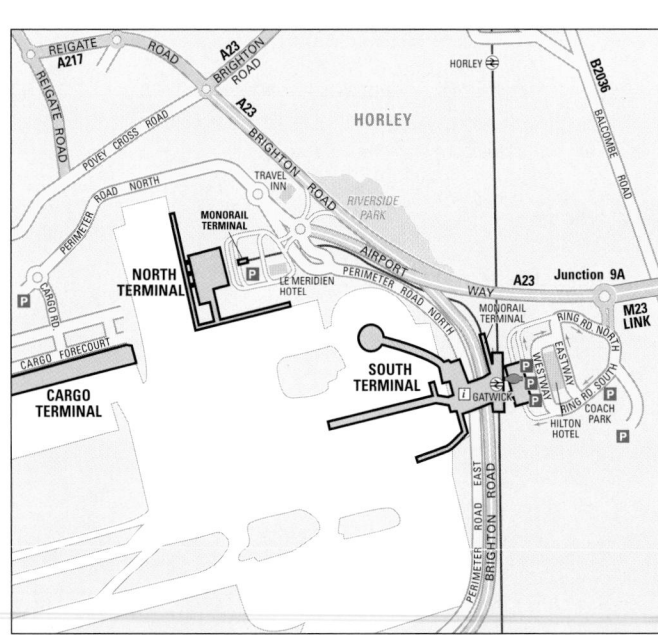

Tel. 01293 535353

KEY TO LONDON URBAN AREA MAPS

KEY TO MAP SYMBOLS

- tunnel M25 — motorway
- restricted access 9 21 — junction numbers
- dual A5 projected/under constr. — primary route
- dual A4251 projected/under constr. — 'A' road
- dual B652 projected/under constr. — 'B' road
- other road
- restricted access
- roundabouts
- tunnelled roads
- Toll — toll / one way street
- county / borough boundary
- car ferry
- canal
- tunnel — railway
- railway station
- London Regional Transport station
- light railway/ tramway station
- heliport
- 25 — page continuation number
- open space / park / sports ground
- woods
- golf course
- garden
- historic house
- museum
- cathedral
- castle
- information centre
- racecourse
- motor racing circuit
- ★ landmark public house

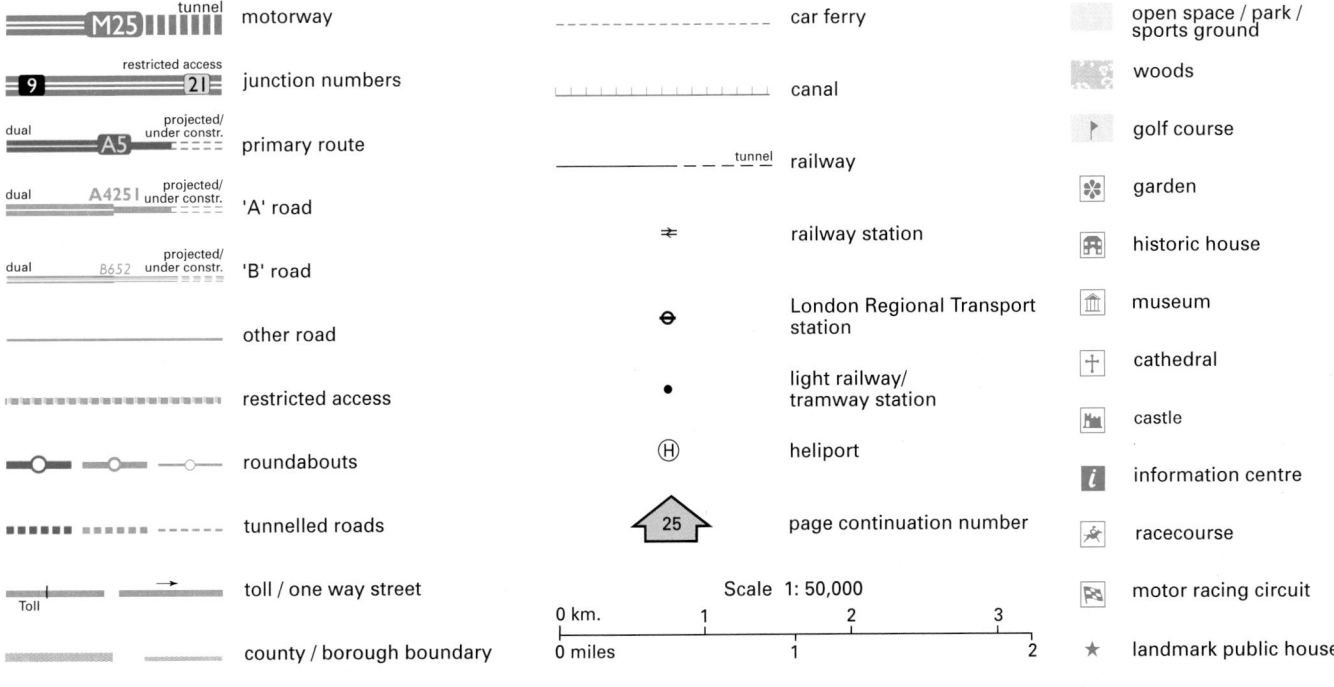

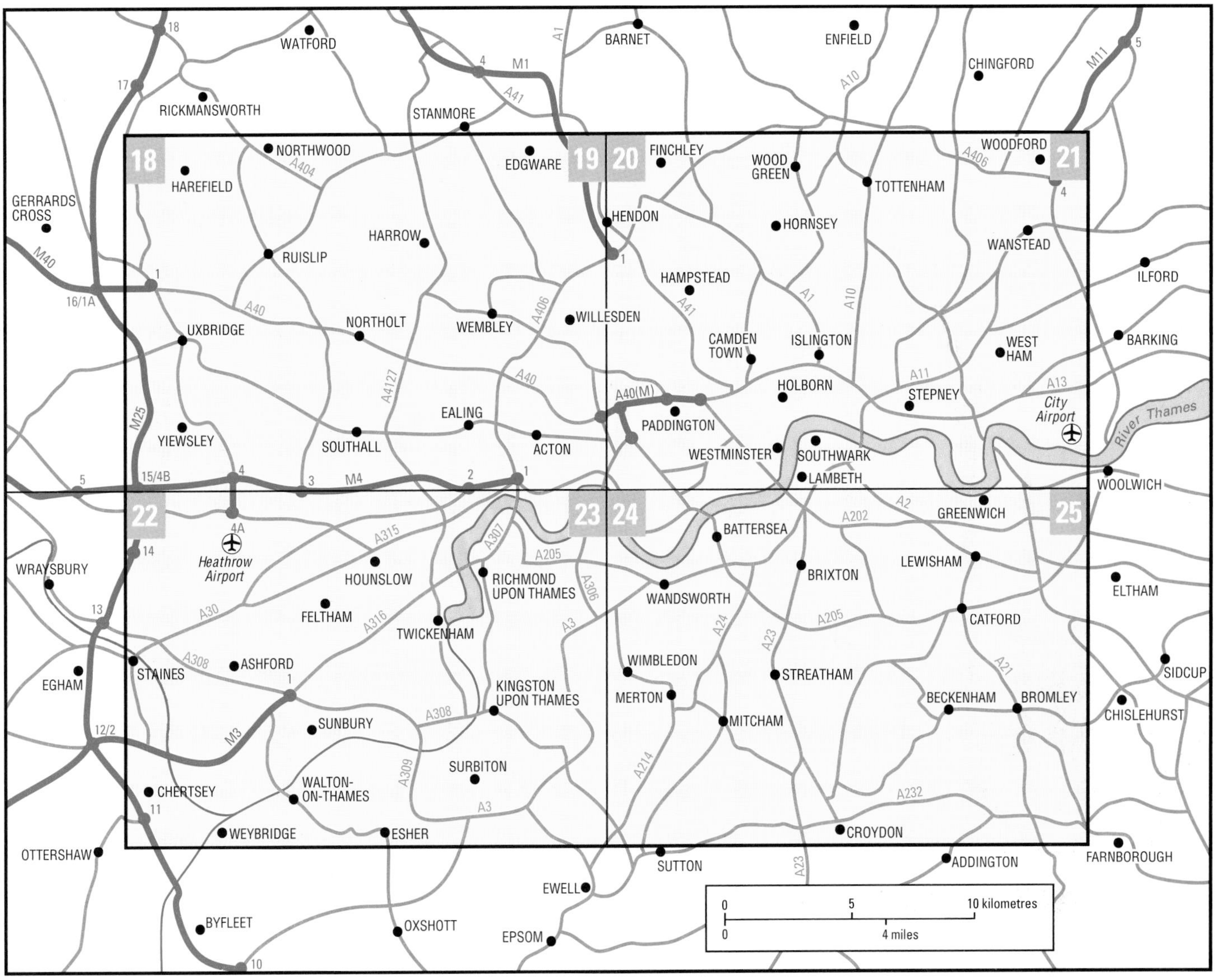

Scale 1: 50,000

0 km. 1 2 3

0 miles 1 2

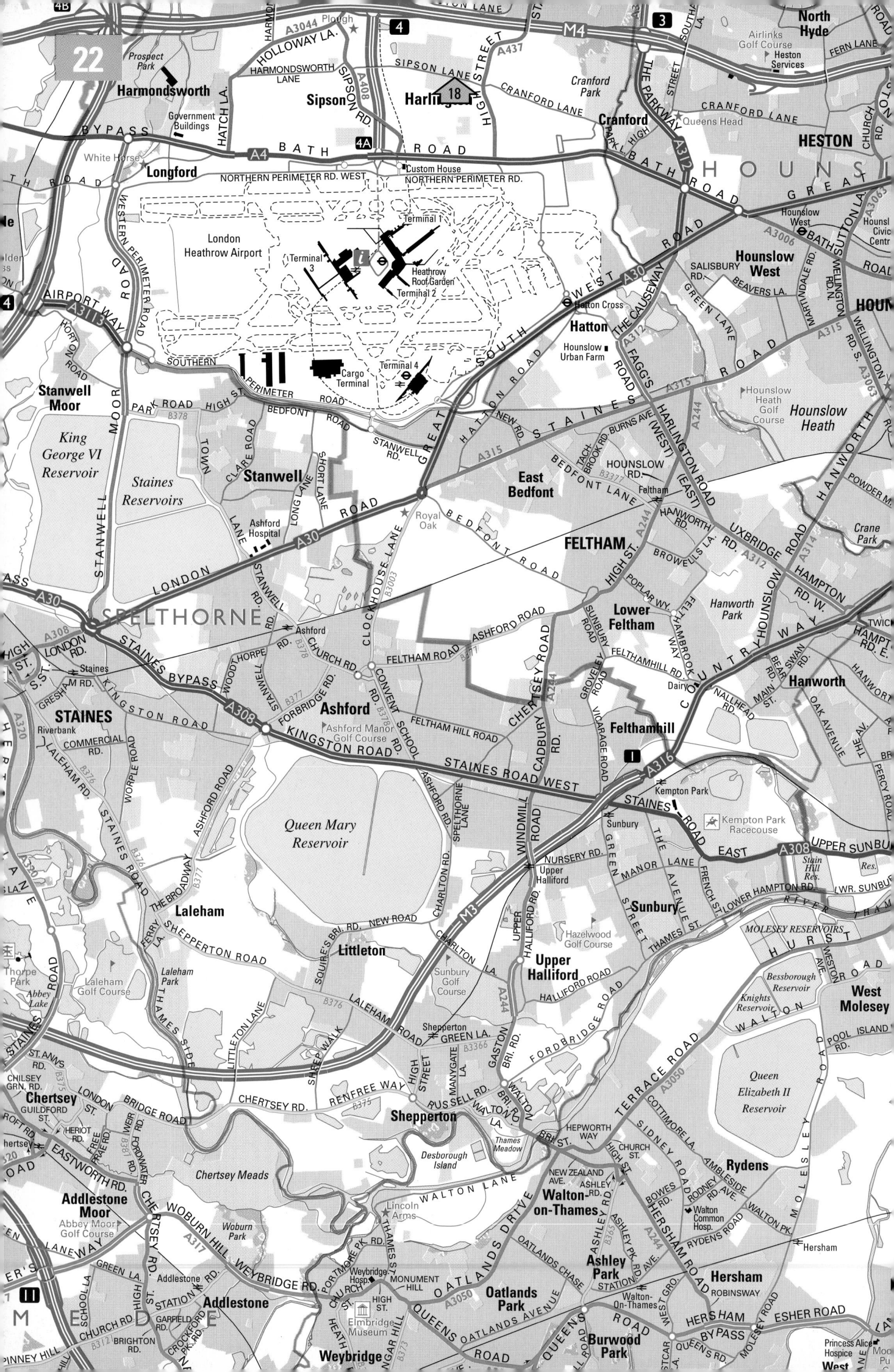

10 10A KIMPTON 6
THUNDRIDGE
STAPLEFORD
WELWYN 6
ASTON CLINTON
FLAMSTEAD HARPENDEN WHEATHAMPSTEAD WELWYN GARDEN CITY WARE
LITTLE GADDESDEN REDBOURN 28 29 30 31 32 33
TRING HERTFORD
STANSTE ABBOTT
NORTHCHURCH BERKHAMSTED HATFIELD HODDESDON
WENDOVER 38 39 40 41 42 43 44 45 46 47 48 49
HEMEL HEMPSTEAD St. ALBANS BROXBOURNE
BOURNE END M10 A1(M)

BOVINGDON 21/6A 21A 22 BROOKMANS PARK
WOOD GREAT MISSENDEN 54 56 57 58 59 60 61 62 63 64 65 66 67
CHESHAM CHIPPERFIELD ABBOTS LANGLEY LONDON COLNEY POTTERS BAR CUFFLEY CHESHUNT WA ABE
20 23/1 24

25
AMERSHAM LITTLE CHALFONT RADLETT
HAZLEMERE 55 72 73 74 75 76 77 78 79 80 81 82 83
HIGH WYCOMBE CHORLEYWOOD WATFORD BUSHEY BOREHAMWOOD BARNET EAST BARNET ENFIELD
18 19

TYLERS GREEN CHALFONT St. GILES RICKMANSWORTH 4 TOTTERIDGE SOUTHGATE CHINGFOR
88 89 90 91 92 93 94 95 96 97 98 99 100 101
LOUDWATER CHALFONT COMMON HAREFIELD NORTHWOOD STANMORE EDGWARE FINCHLEY WOOD GREEN TOTTENHAM
BEACONSFIELD 17 M1 2

FLACKWELL HEATH PINNER
WOOBURN GERRARDS CROSS KENTON HENDON HORNSEY WALTHAMSTOW
ARLOW 110 111 112 113 114 115 116 117 118 119 120 121 122 123
BOURNE END EGYPT DENHAM RUISLIP HARROW WEMBLEY HAMPSTEAD STOKE NEWINGTON LEYTON
M40 16/1A SUDBURY HACKNEY

FARNHAM COMMON STOKE POGES UXBRIDGE NORTHOLT WILLESDEN CAMDEN TOWN ISLINGTON
MAIDENHEAD 130 131 132 133 134 135 136 137 138 139 140 141 142 143
A404(M) BURNHAM IVER YIEWSLEY HAYES SOUTHALL EALING ACTON PADDINGTON HOLBORN STEPNEY
OLANDS 8/9 SLOUGH M4

7 LANGLEY WEST DRAYTON HAMMERSMITH WESTMINSTER SOUTHWARK
ETON WICK 6 15/4B 2 1 LAMBETH
150 151 152 153 154 155 156 157 158 159 160 161 162 163
HOLYPORT WINDSOR 4A 4 3 KEW BARNES BATTERSEA GREENWICH
M4 HEATHROW AIRPORT LONDON BRIXTON LEWISHAM
14 HOUNSLOW

OLD WINDSOR WRAYSBURY RICHMOND WANDSWORTH CATFORD
WINKFIELD 13 FELTHAM TWICKENHAM
172 173 174 175 176 177 178 179 180 181 182 183
FIELD EGHAM STAINES ASHFORD TEDDINGTON WIMBLEDON STREATHAM
ASCOT 1

BRACKNELL VIRGINIA WATER SUNBURY KINGSTON UPON THAMES MERTON MITCHAM BECKENHAM
192 193 194 195 196 197 198 199 200 201 202 203
12/2 M3 CHERTSEY WALTON-ON-THAMES SURBITON
BROOMHALL M25 11

OTTERSHAW WEYBRIDGE ESHER CROYDON ADDINGTO
BAGSHOT 3 SUTTON
LIGHTWATER 210 211 212 213 214 215 216 217 218 219 220 221
CAMBERLEY CHOBHAM BYFLEET OXSHOTT EWELL PURLEY SANDERSTEAD
EPSOM

BISLEY WOKING STOKE D'ABERNON ASHTEAD BANSTEAD COULSDON WARLINGHAM
FRIMLEY 10 9
226 227 228 229 230 231 232 233 234 235 236 237
MYTCHETT PIRBRIGHT RIPLEY OCKHAM FETCHAM LEATHERHEAD TADWORTH HOOLEY 7 CATERHAM
NBOROUGH MAYFORD

JACOBS WELL EAST HORSLEY GREAT BOOKHAM WALTON ON THE HILL 7/8 M25 6
242 243 244 245 246 247 248 249 250 251 252 253
LDERSHOT NORMANDY STOUGHTON EAST CLANDON HOOLEY 8 GODSTONE OXTE
REIGATE REDHILL

TONGHAM GUILDFORD WESTCOTT BROCKHAM EARLSWOOD SOUTH GODSTONE
LE GOMSHALL DORKING 258 259 260 261 262 263 264 265 266 267
SHACKLEFORD COMPTON SHALFORD ABINGER HAMMER NORTH HOLMWOOD LEIGH SALFORDS BLINDLEY HEATH
M23

SHAMLEY GREEN HOLMBURY St. MARY
ELSTEAD GODALMING BEARE GREEN HORLEY LINGF
MILFORD 268 269
GRAFHAM JAYES PARK CHARLWOOD GATWICK AIRPORT LONDON NEWCHAPEL
WITLEY 9A 9
CRANLEIGH

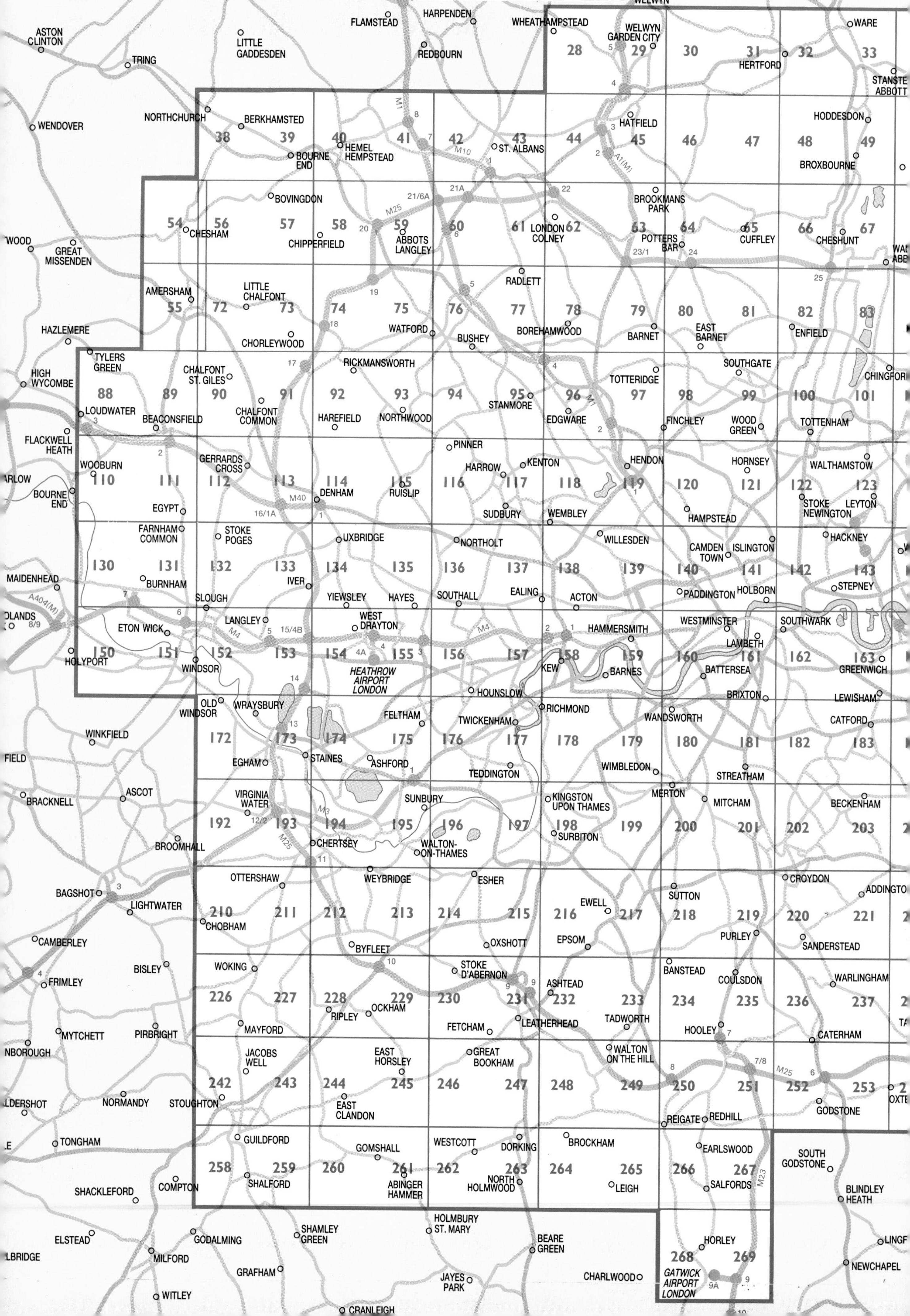

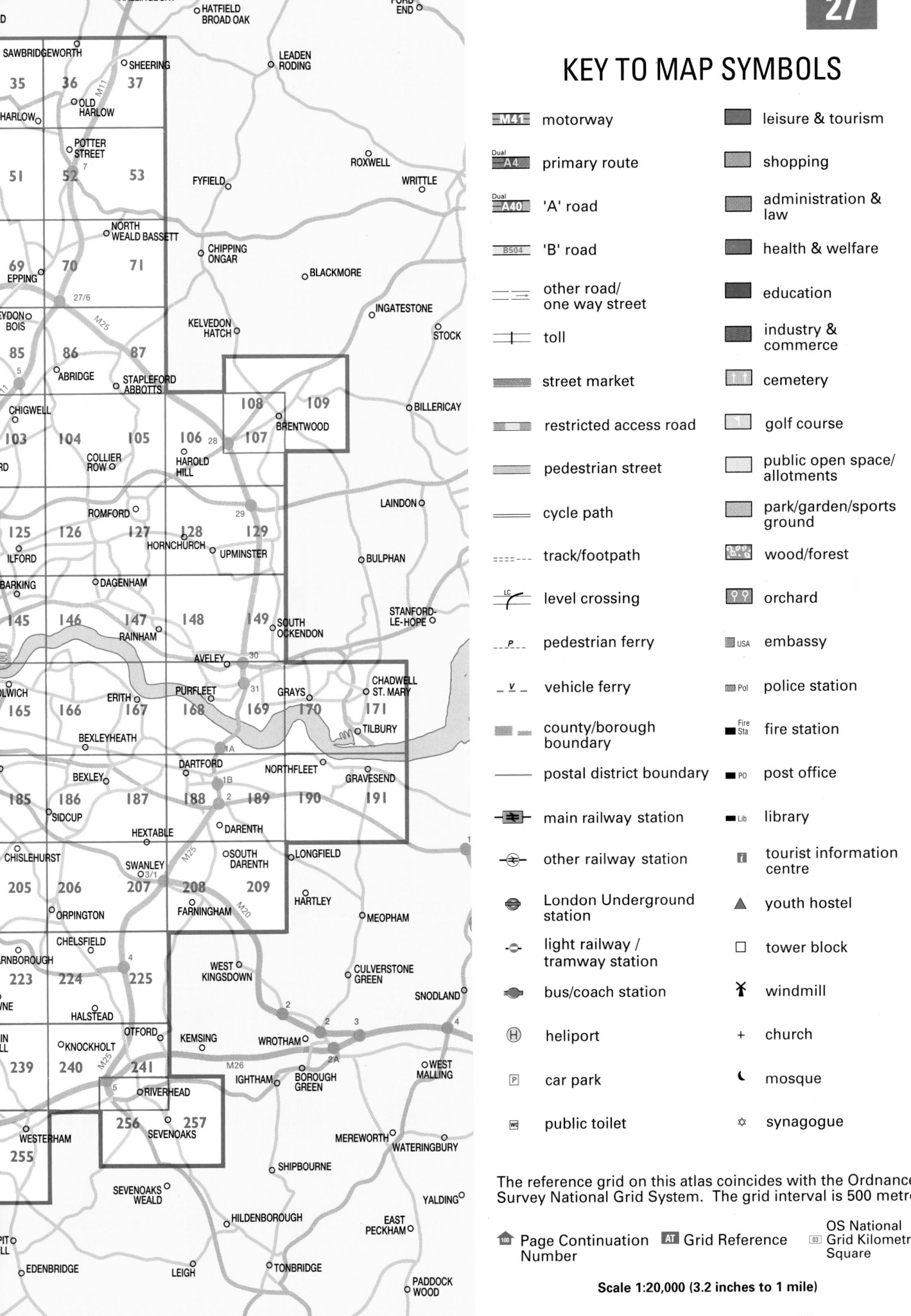

SPELLBROOK · LITTLE HALLINGBURY · HATFIELD BROAD OAK · FORD END
SAWBRIDGEWORTH · SHEERING
35 · 36 · 37
HARLOW · OLD HARLOW · LEADEN RODING · ROXWELL · WRITTLE
POTTER STREET
51 · 52 · 53 · FYFIELD
NORTH WEALD BASSETT · CHIPPING ONGAR · BLACKMORE · INGATESTONE
69 · 70 · 71
EPPING · KELVEDON HATCH · STOCK
THEYDON BOIS · 85 · 86 · 87 · BILLERICAY
ABRIDGE · STAPLEFORD ABBOTTS
CHIGWELL · 108 · 109
103 · 104 · 105 · 106 · 107 · BRENTWOOD
COLLIER ROW · HAROLD HILL
ROMFORD · LAINDON
125 · 126 · 127 · 128 · 129
ILFORD · HORNCHURCH · UPMINSTER · BULPHAN
BARKING · DAGENHAM
145 · 146 · 147 · 148 · 149 · SOUTH OCKENDON · STANFORD-LE-HOPE
RAINHAM · AVELEY
WOOLWICH · PURFLEET · GRAYS · CHADWELL ST. MARY
165 · 166 · 167 · 168 · 169 · 170 · 171 · TILBURY
ERITH · BEXLEYHEATH · DARTFORD · NORTHFLEET · GRAVESEND
185 · 186 · 187 · 188 · 189 · 190 · 191
BEXLEY · SIDCUP · HEXTABLE · DARENTH
CHISLEHURST · SWANLEY · SOUTH DARENTH · LONGFIELD
205 · 206 · 207 · 208 · 209 · HARTLEY
ORPINGTON · FARNINGHAM · MEOPHAM
CHELSFIELD · WEST KINGSDOWN · CULVERSTONE GREEN · SNODLAND
223 · 224 · 225
HALSTEAD · OTFORD · KEMSING · WROTHAM · WEST MALLING
239 · 240 · 241 · IGHTHAM · BOROUGH GREEN
RIVERHEAD
256 · 257
WESTERHAM · SEVENOAKS · MEREWORTH · WATERINGBURY
255 · SHIPBOURNE · YALDING
SEVENOAKS WEALD · HILDENBOROUGH · EAST PECKHAM
EDENBRIDGE · LEIGH · TONBRIDGE · PADDOCK WOOD
COWDEN POUND · SOUTHBOROUGH · ROYAL TUNBRIDGE WELLS · LOWER GREEN
HOLTYE COMMON

KEY TO MAP SYMBOLS

M41	motorway
Dual A4	primary route
Dual A40	'A' road
B504	'B' road
	other road/ one way street
	toll
	street market
	restricted access road
	pedestrian street
	cycle path
	track/footpath
LC	level crossing
P	pedestrian ferry
V	vehicle ferry
	county/borough boundary
	postal district boundary
	main railway station
	other railway station
	London Underground station
	light railway / tramway station
	bus/coach station
H	heliport
P	car park
wc	public toilet

	leisure & tourism
	shopping
	administration & law
	health & welfare
	education
	industry & commerce
	cemetery
	golf course
	public open space/ allotments
	park/garden/sports ground
	wood/forest
	orchard
USA	embassy
Pol	police station
Fire Sta	fire station
PO	post office
Lib	library
i	tourist information centre
▲	youth hostel
□	tower block
✗	windmill
+	church
☾	mosque
✡	synagogue

The reference grid on this atlas coincides with the Ordnance Survey National Grid System. The grid interval is 500 metres.

🏠 100 Page Continuation Number   AT Grid Reference   OS National 03 Grid Kilometre Square

Scale 1:20,000 (3.2 inches to 1 mile)

0 · 0.25 · 0.50 · 0.75 · 1 kilometre

0 · ¼ · ½ mile

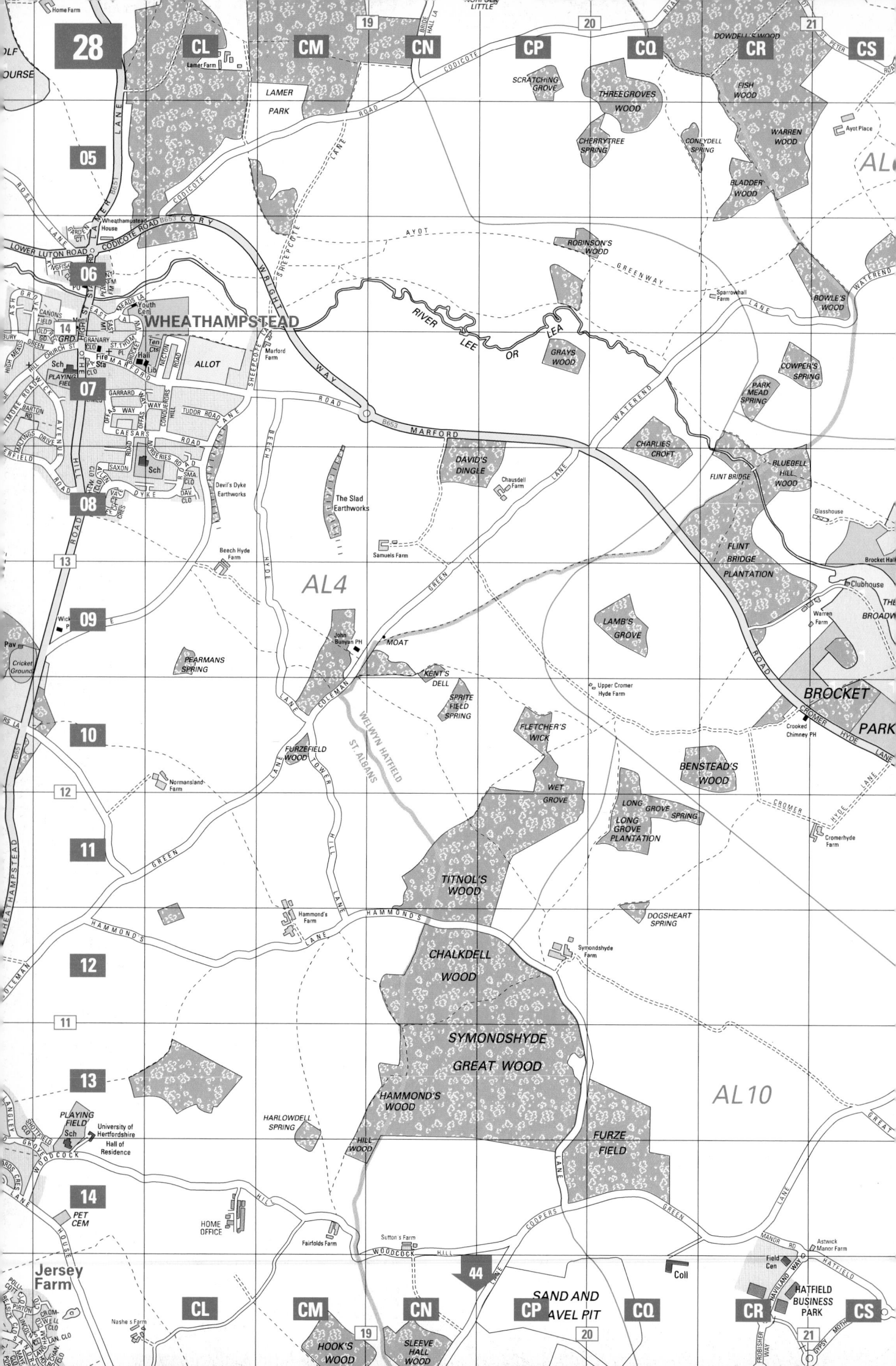

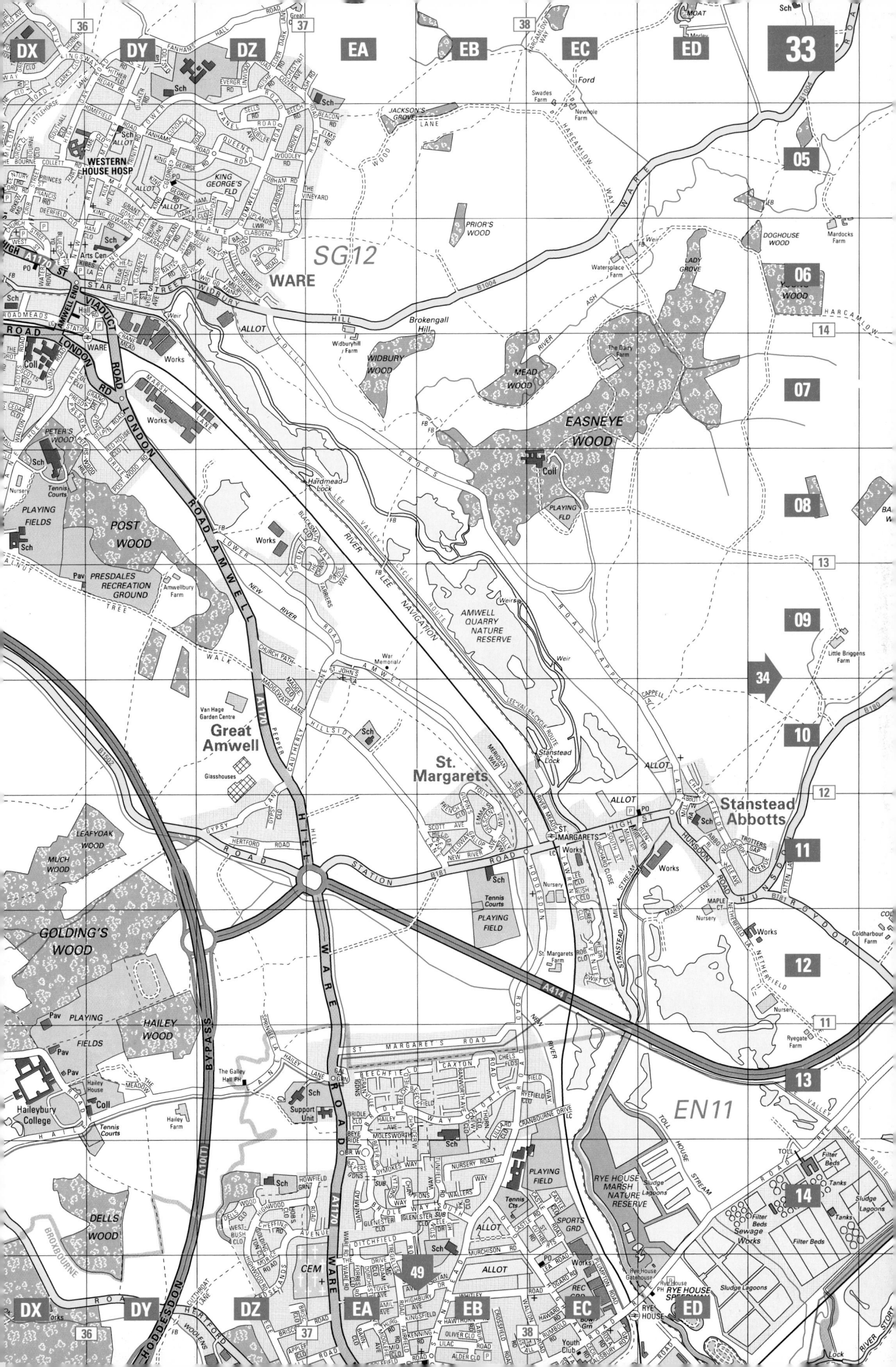

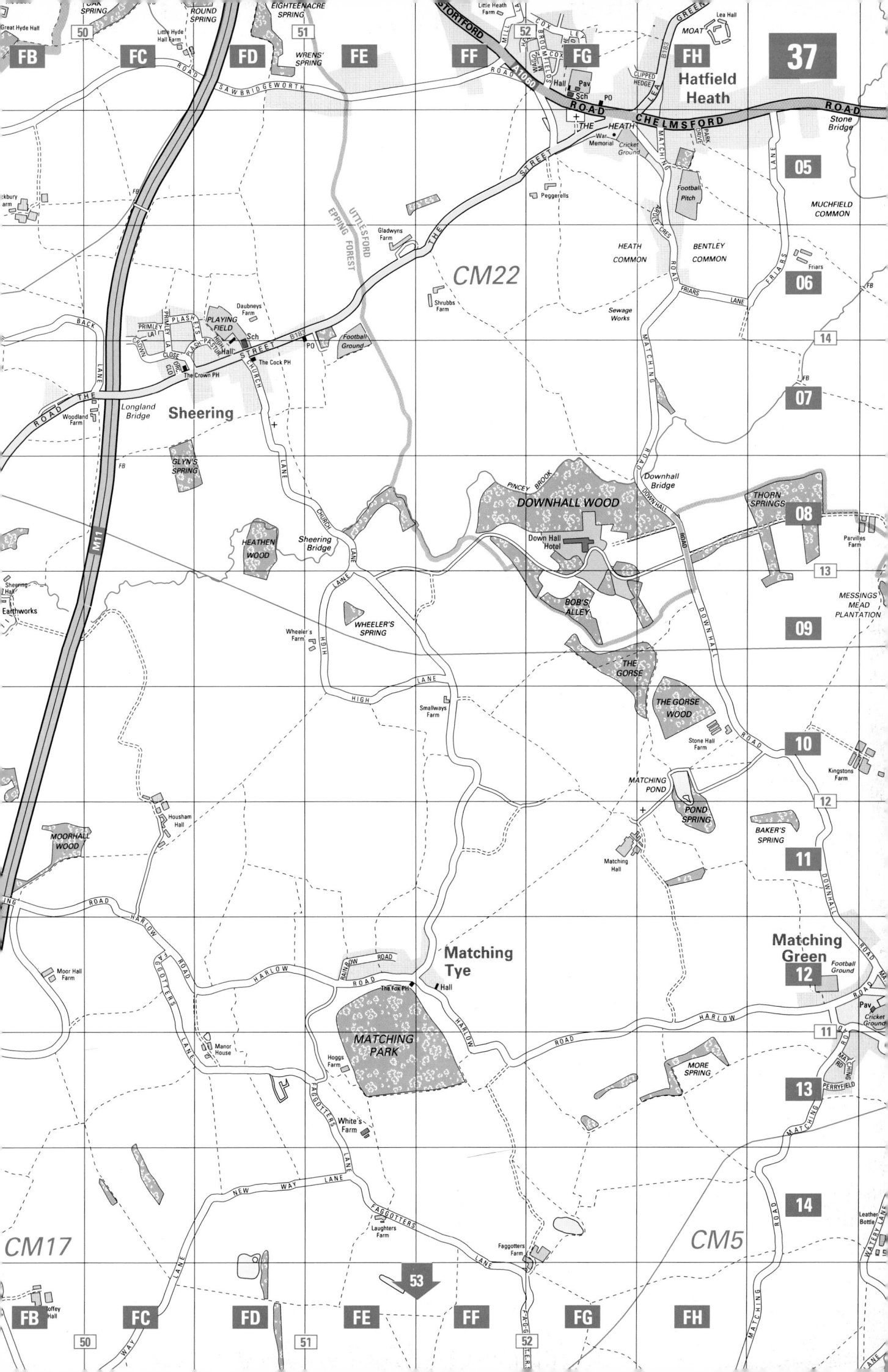

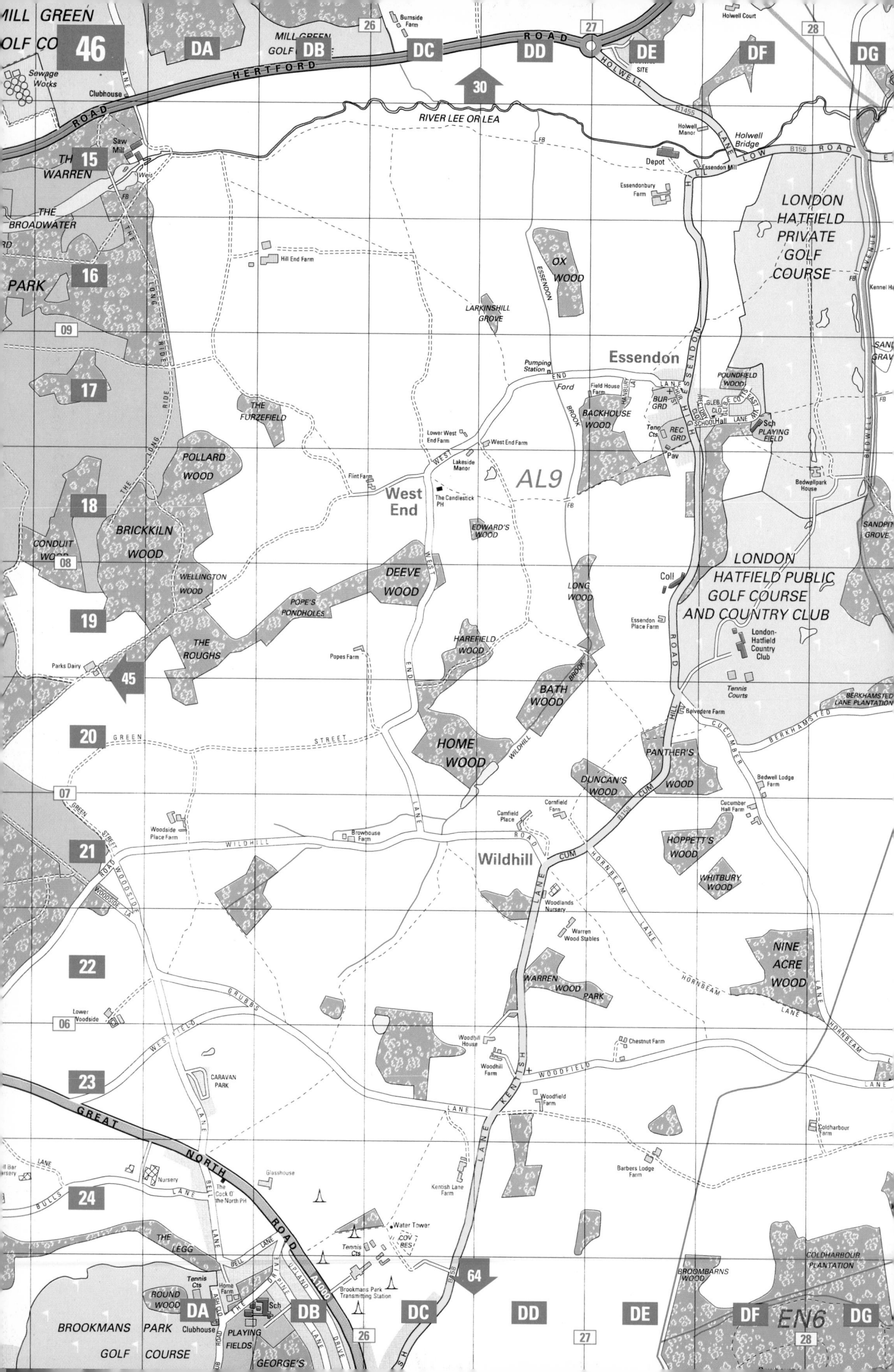

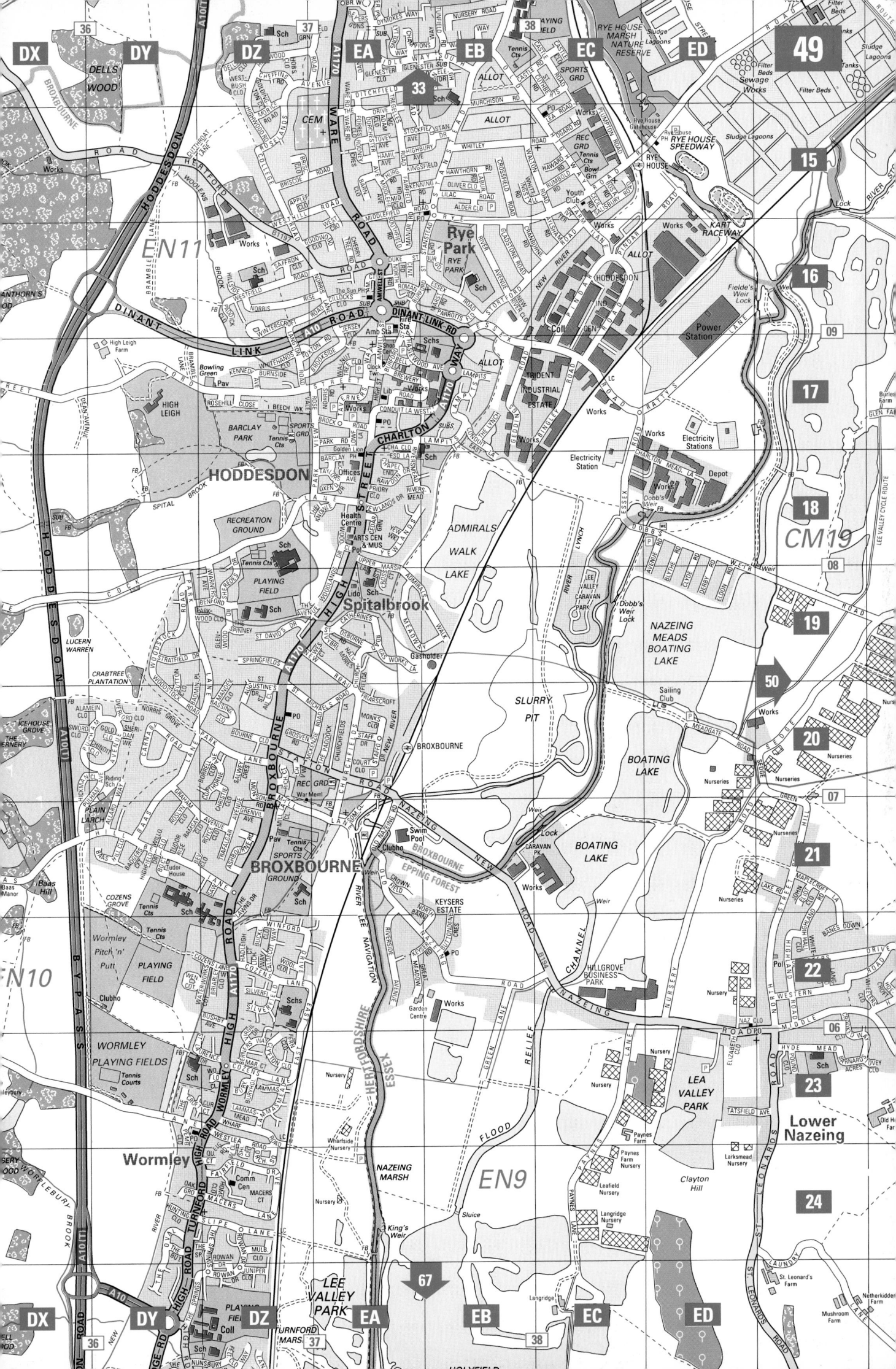

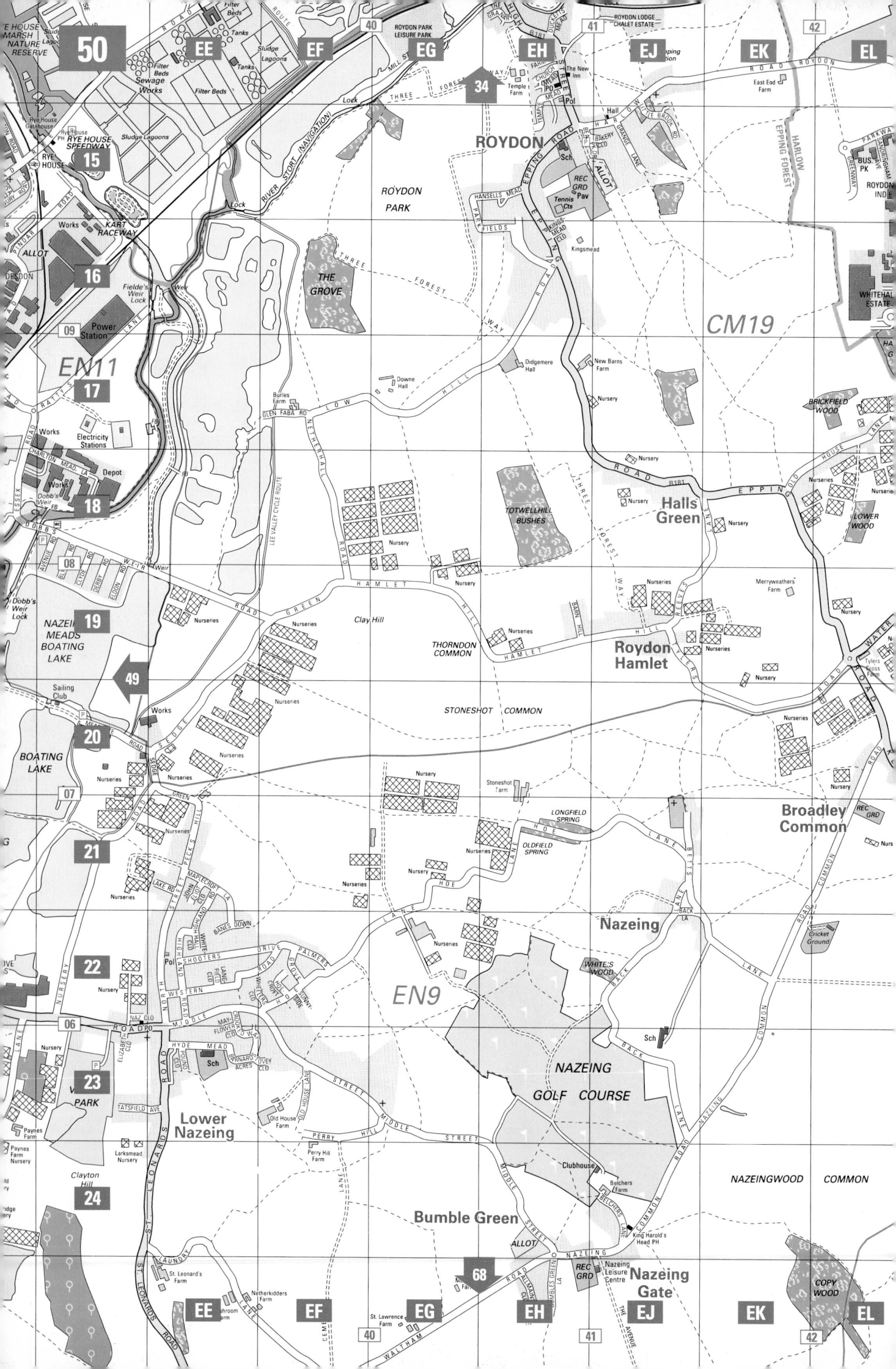

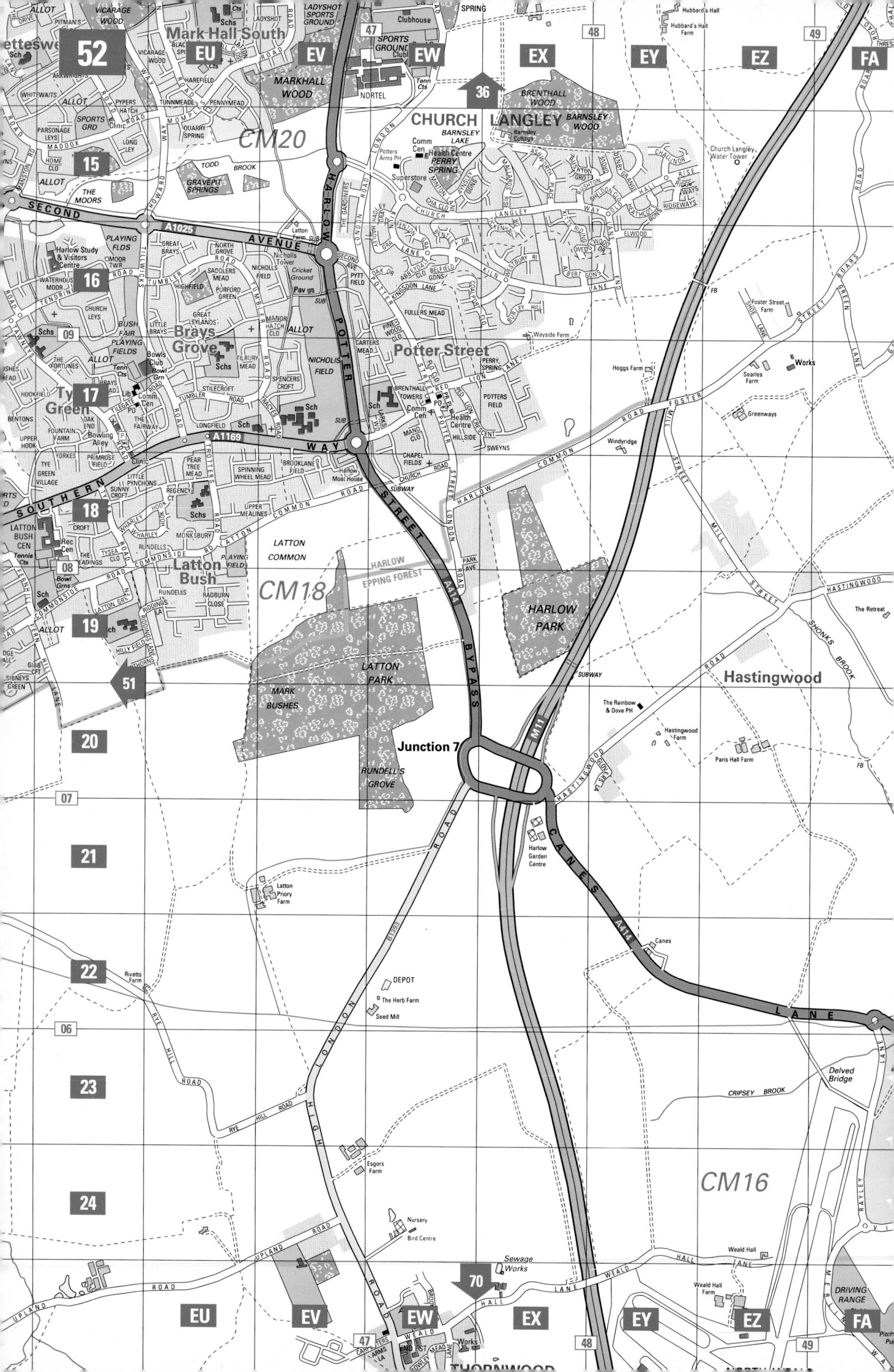

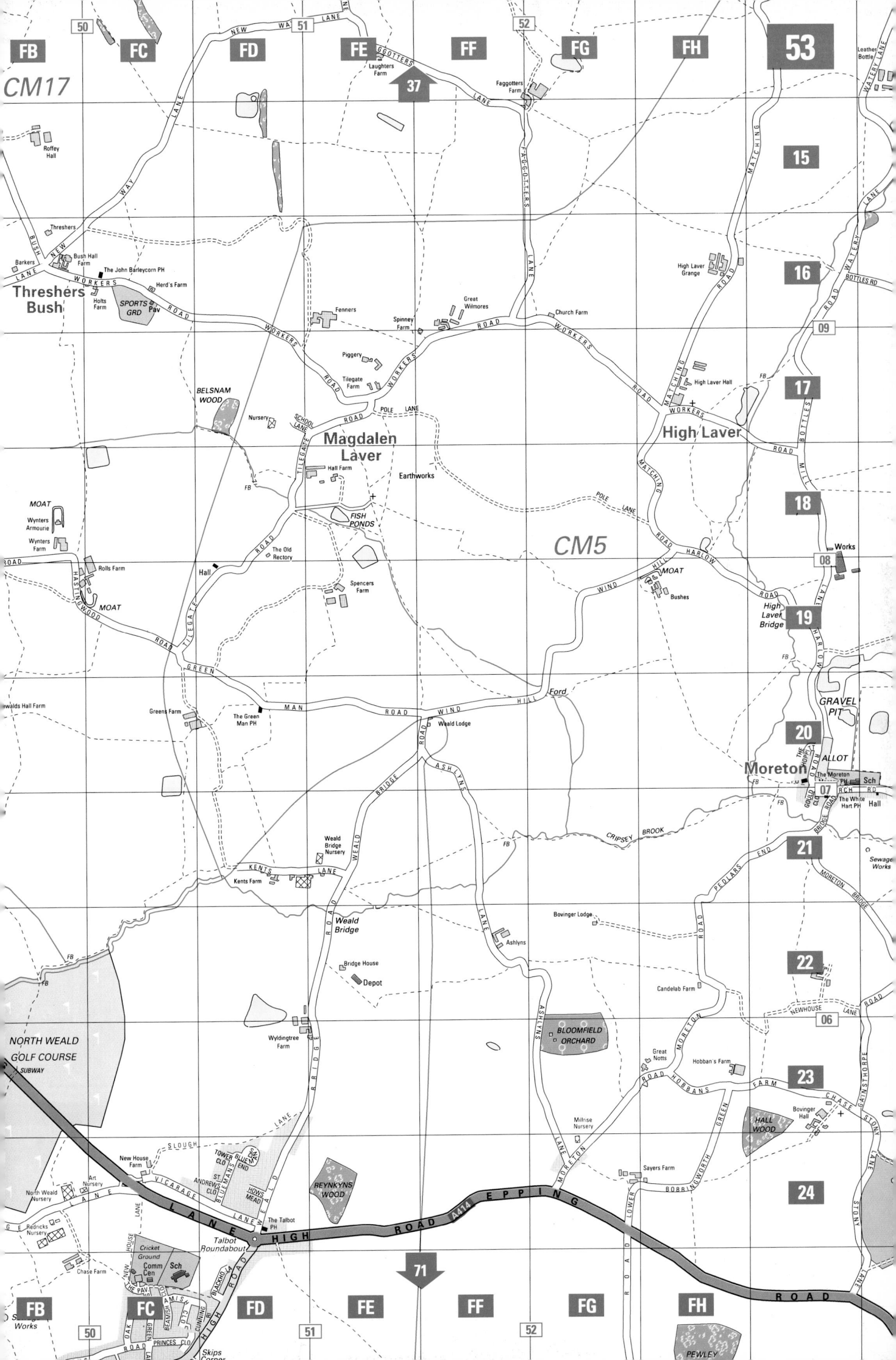

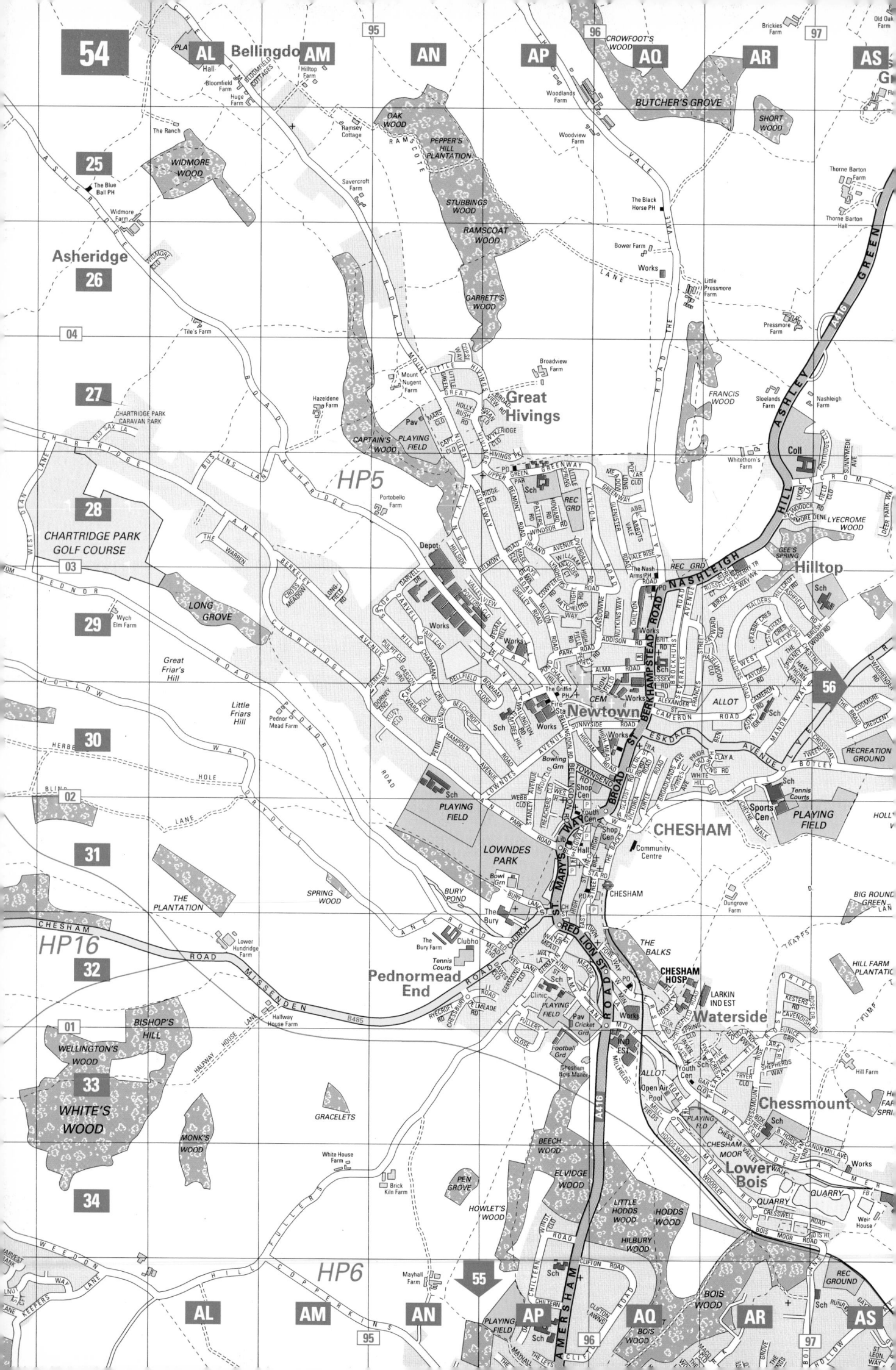

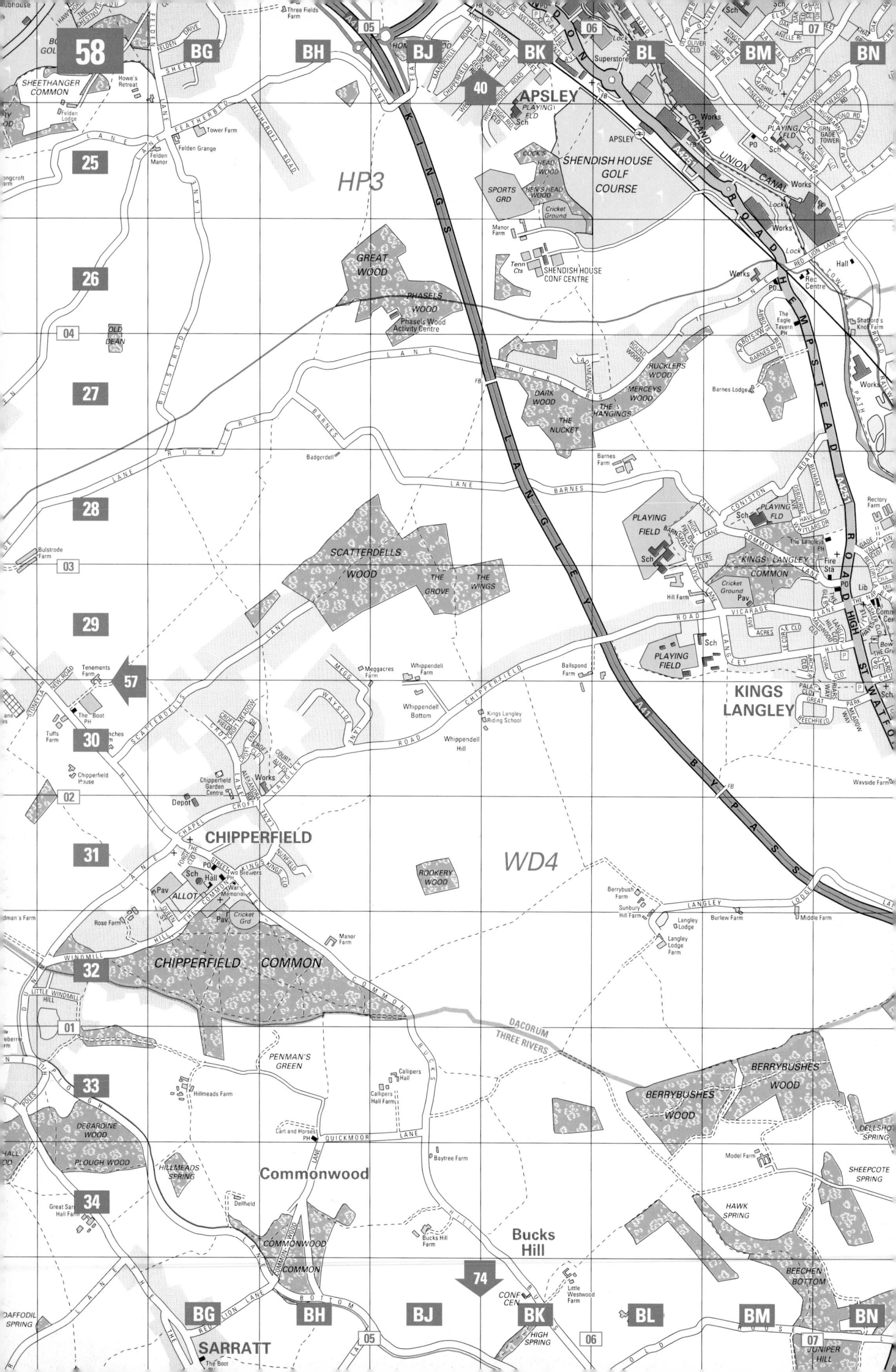

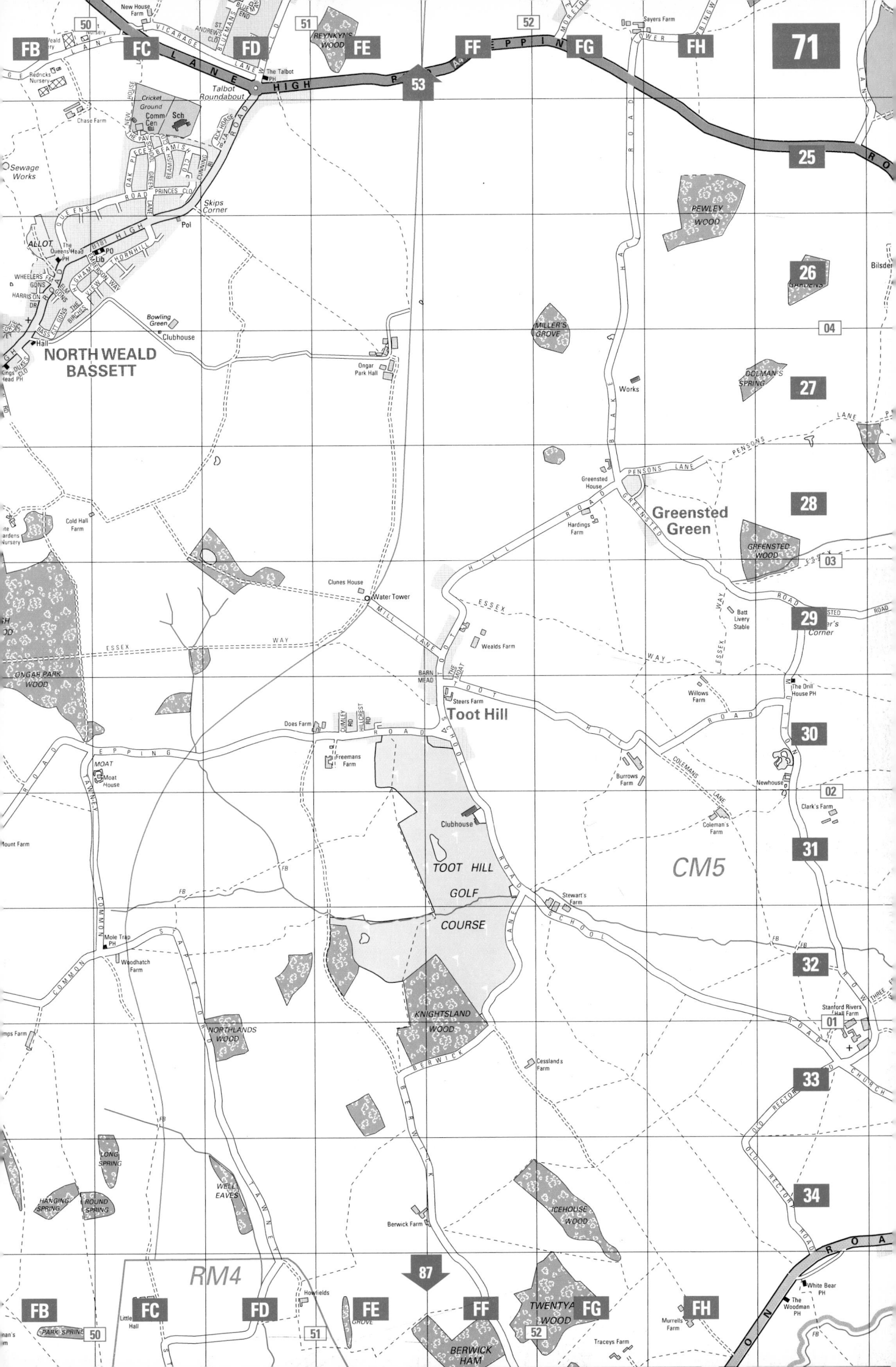

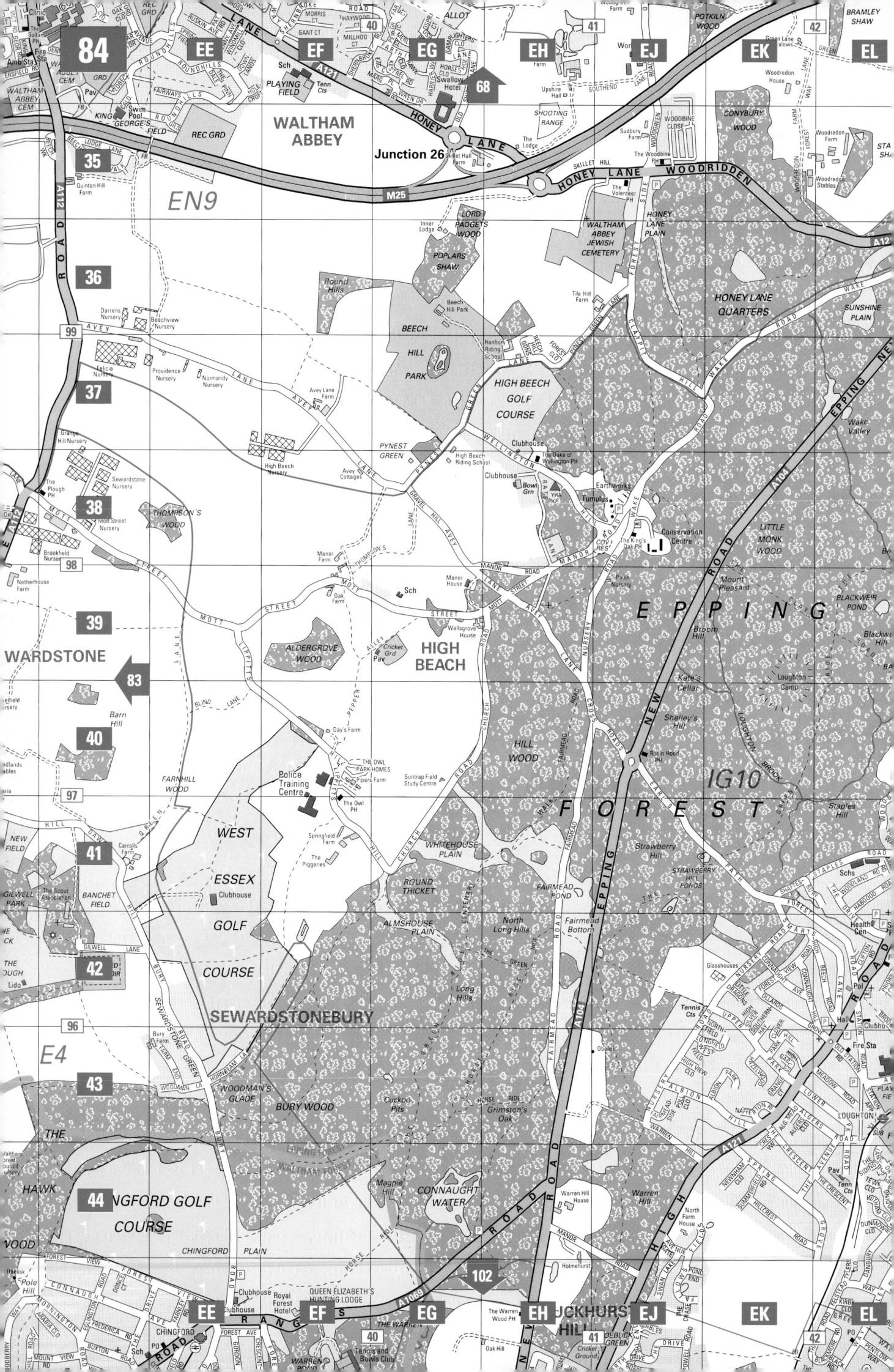

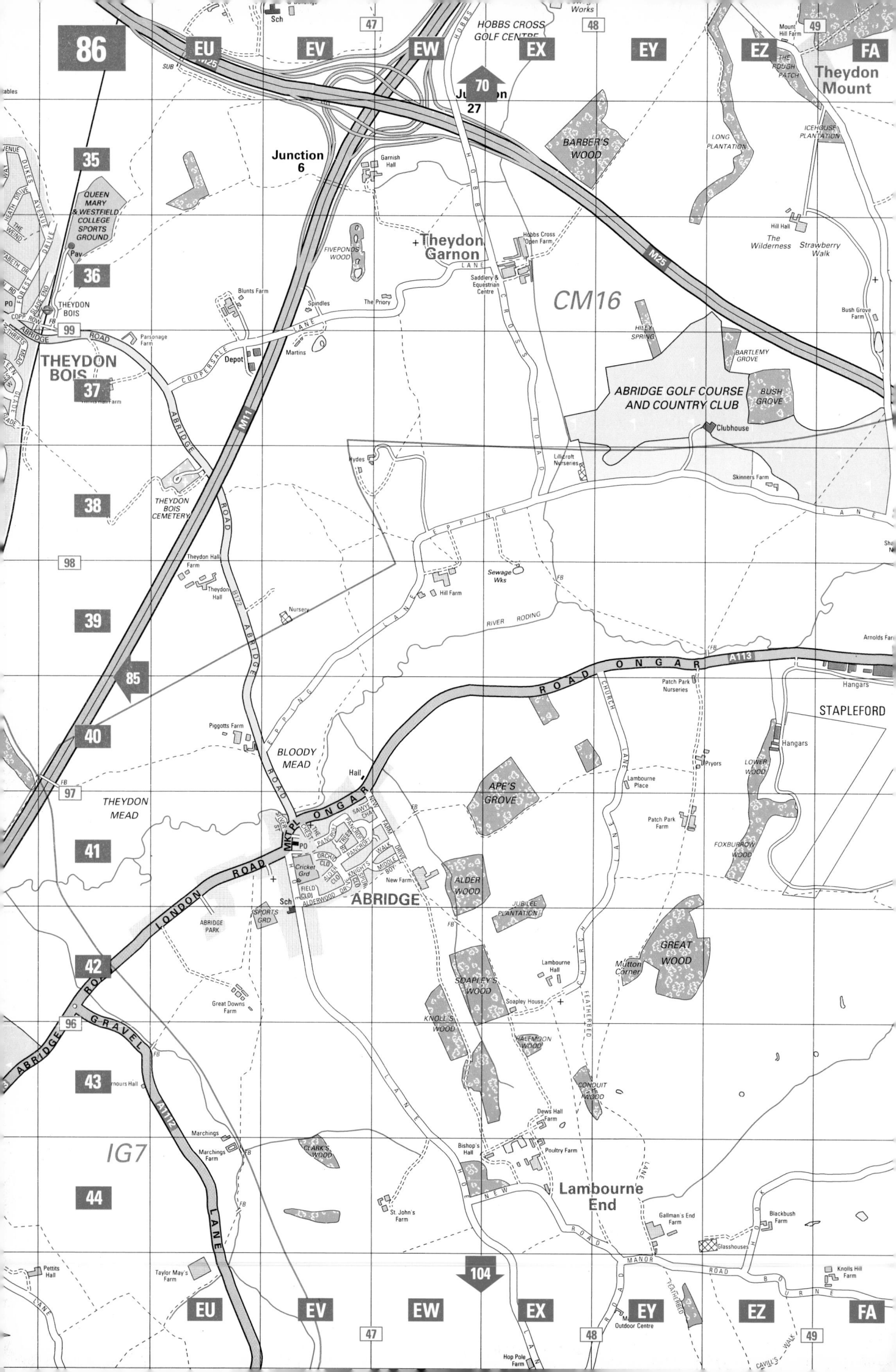

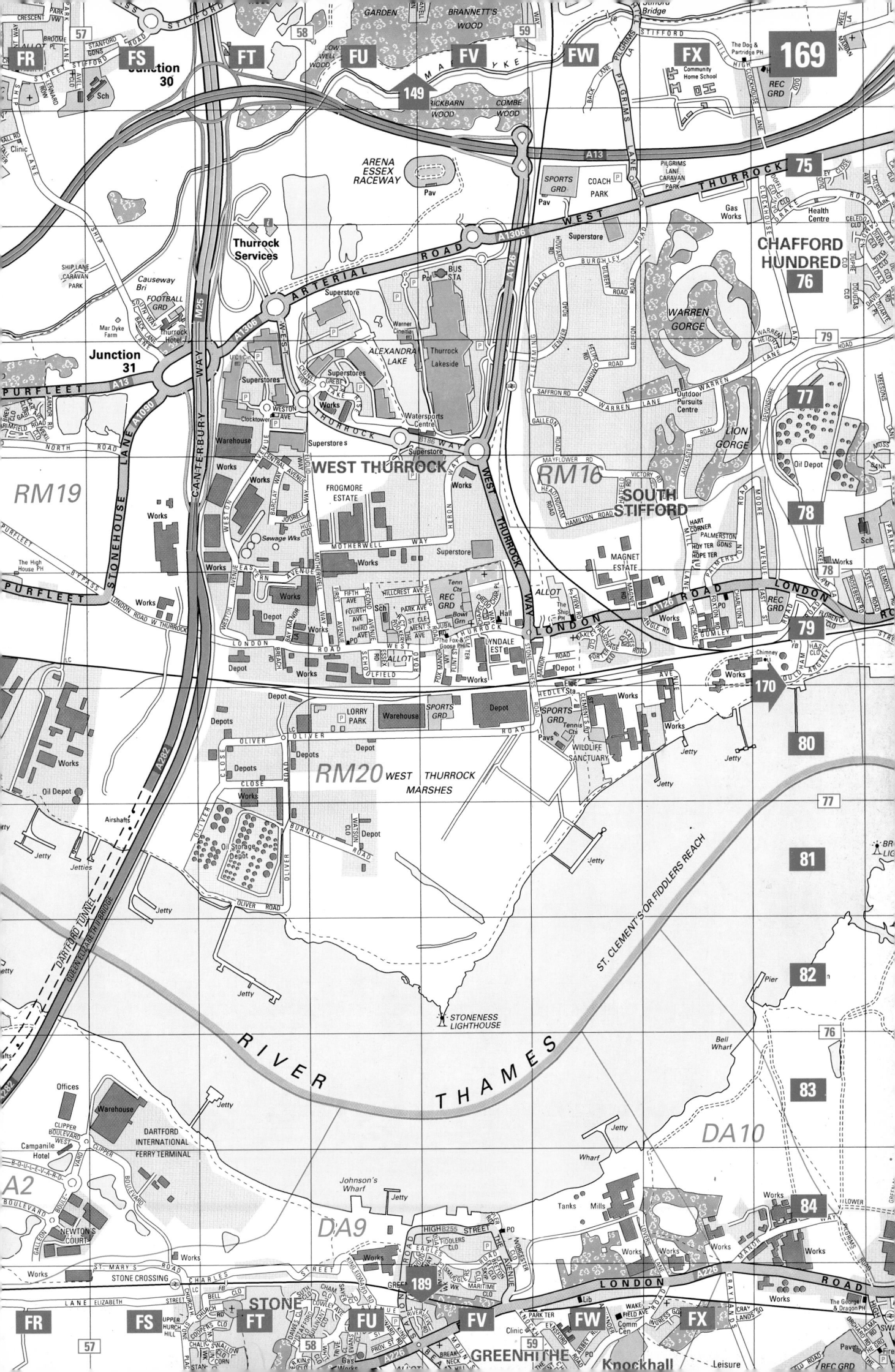

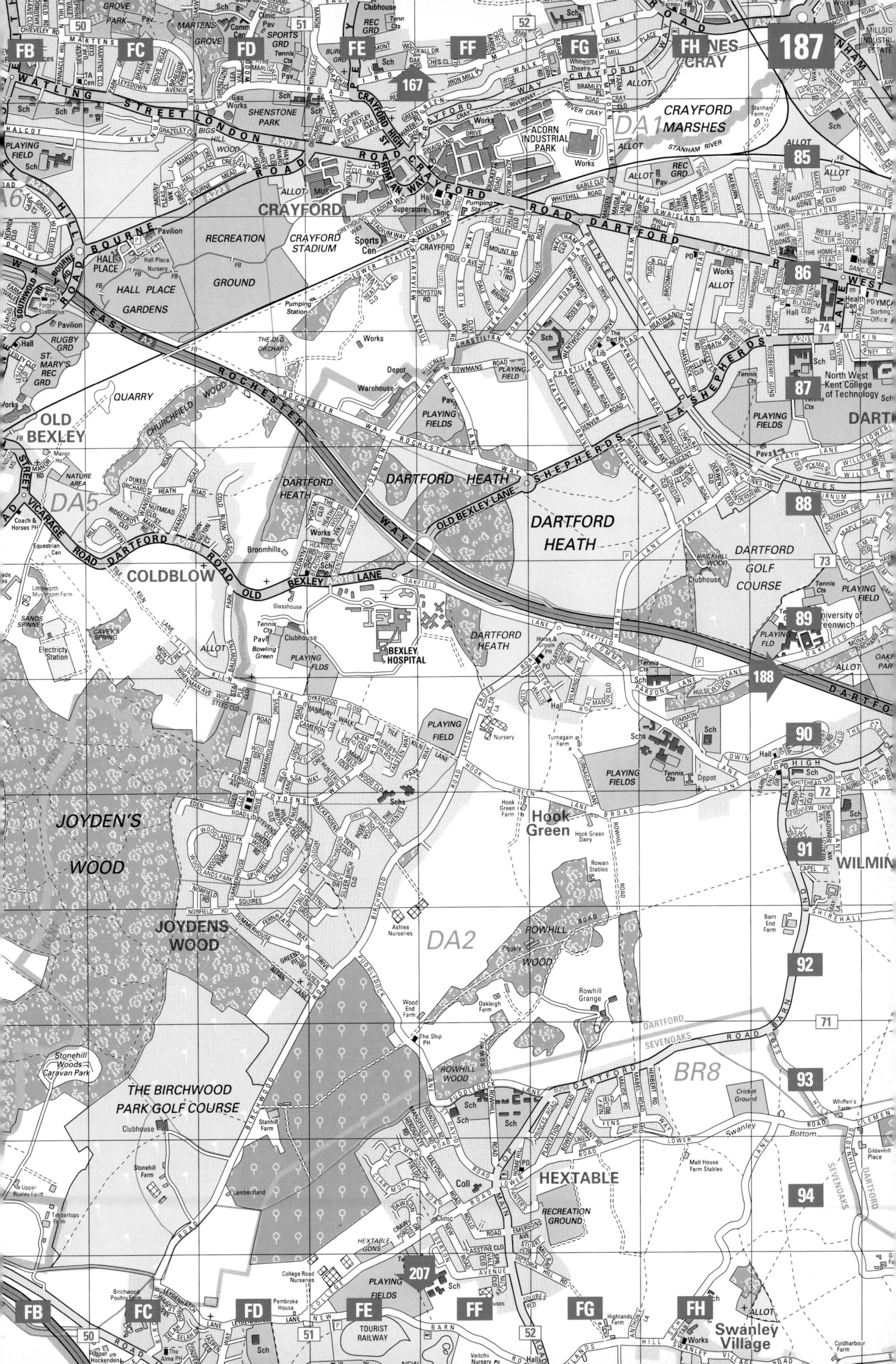

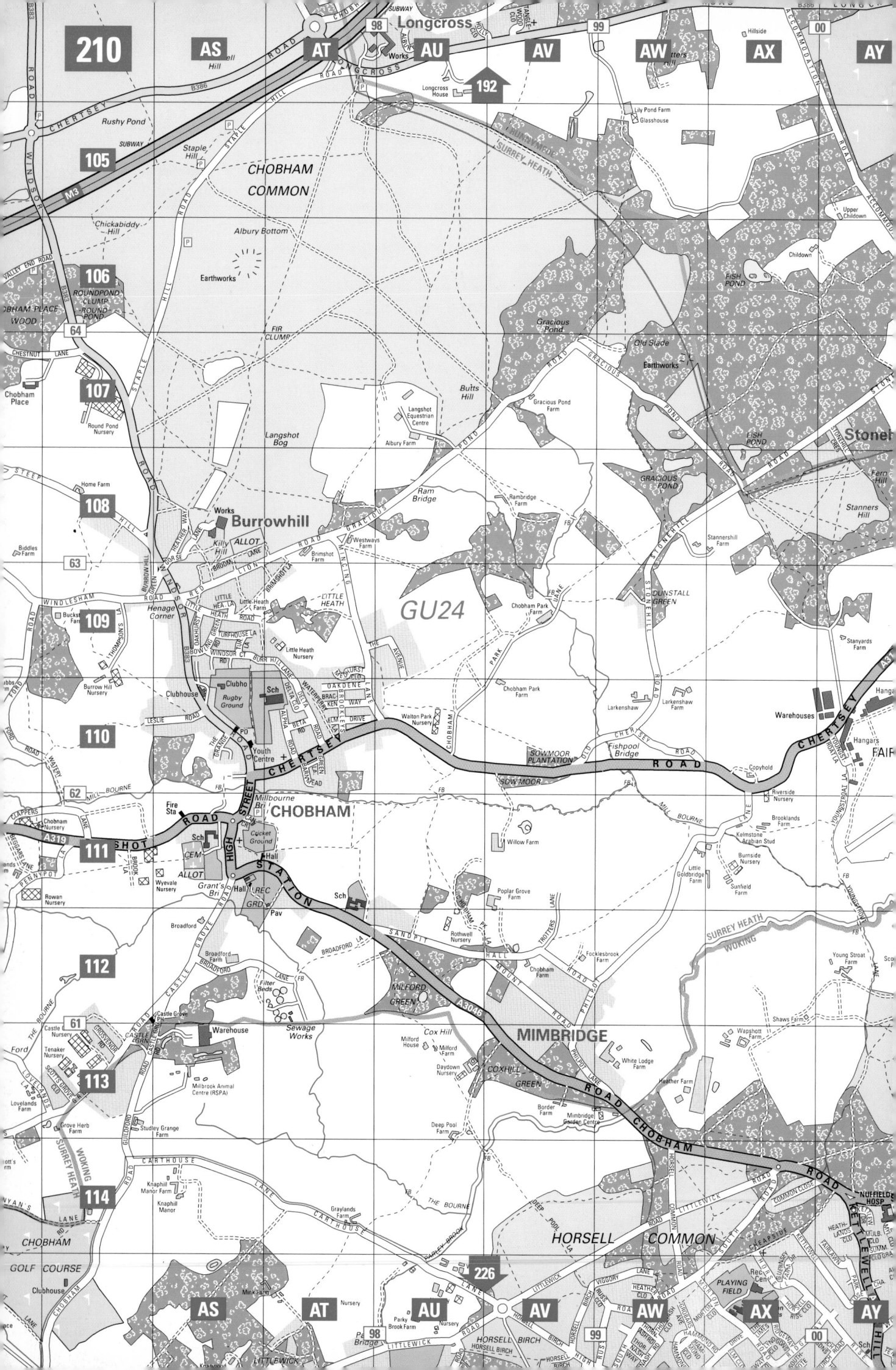

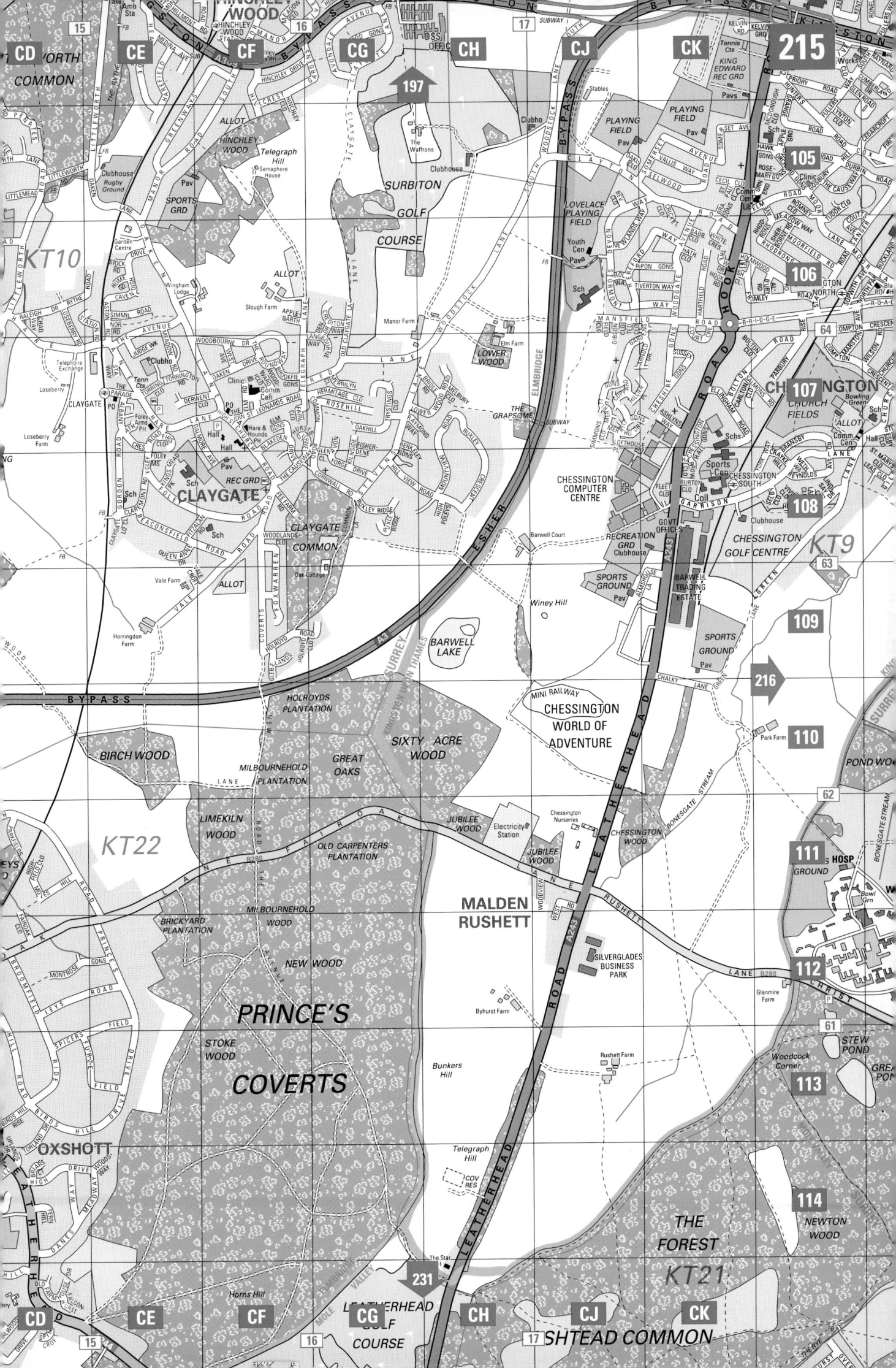

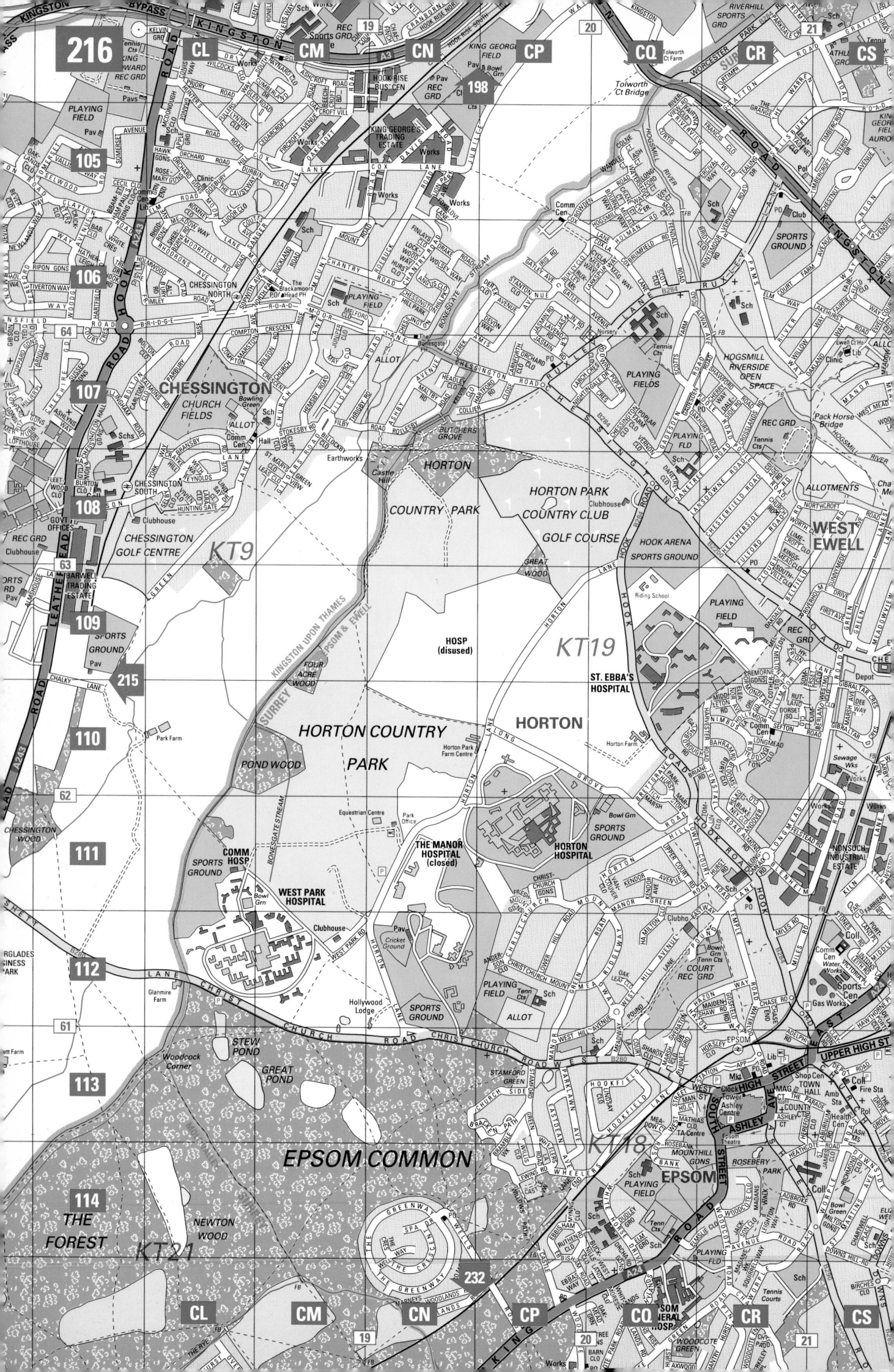

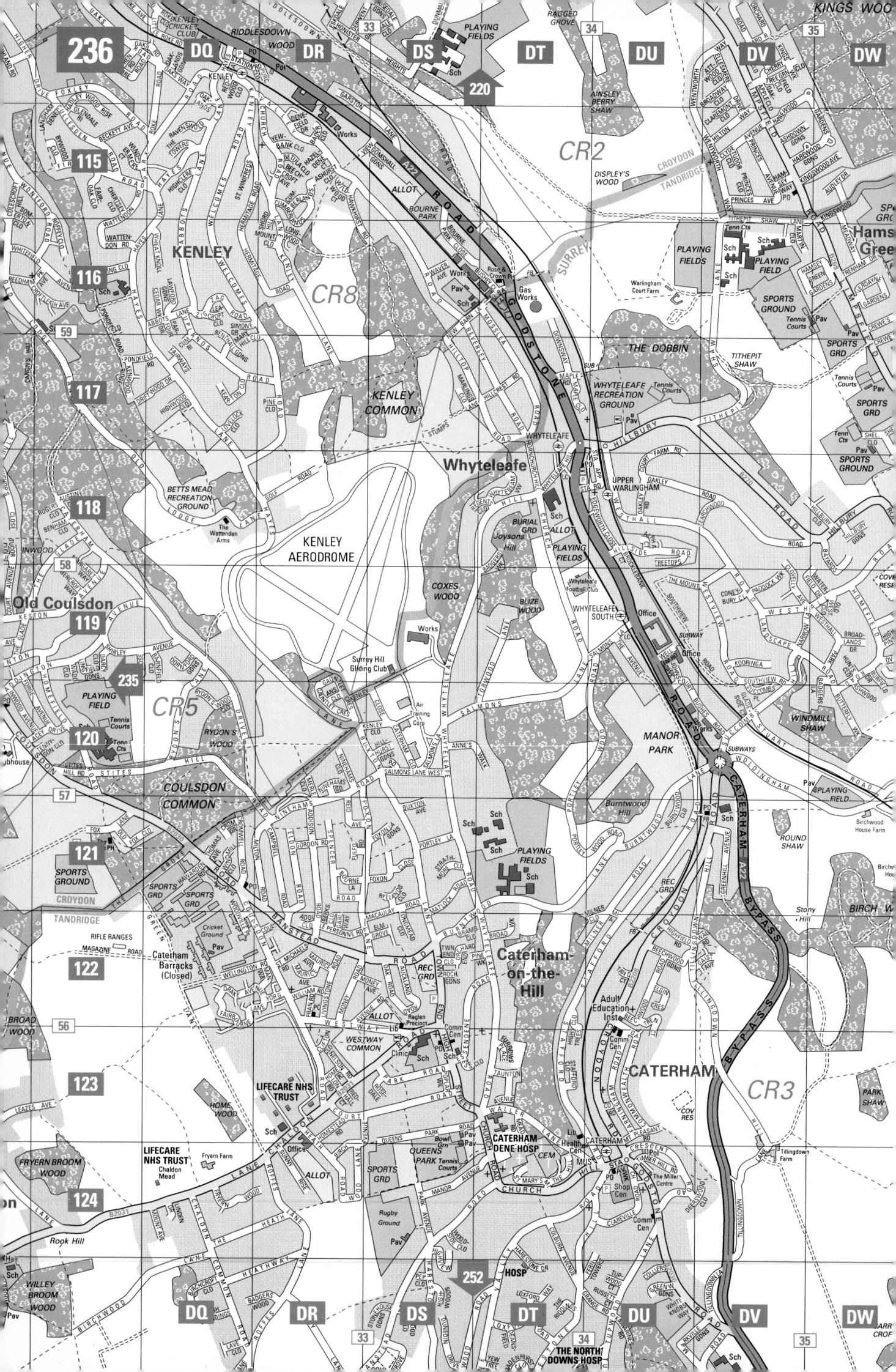

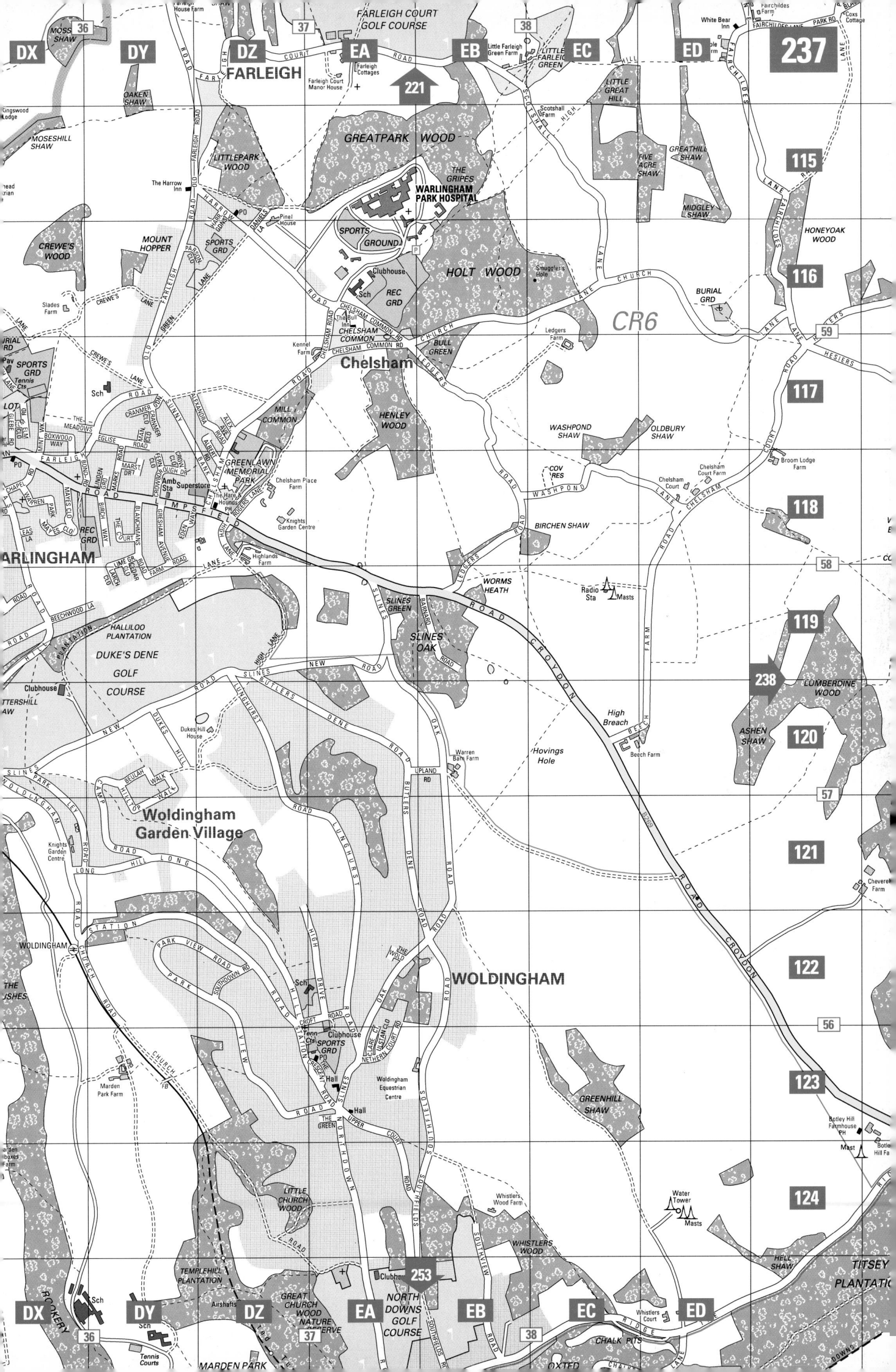

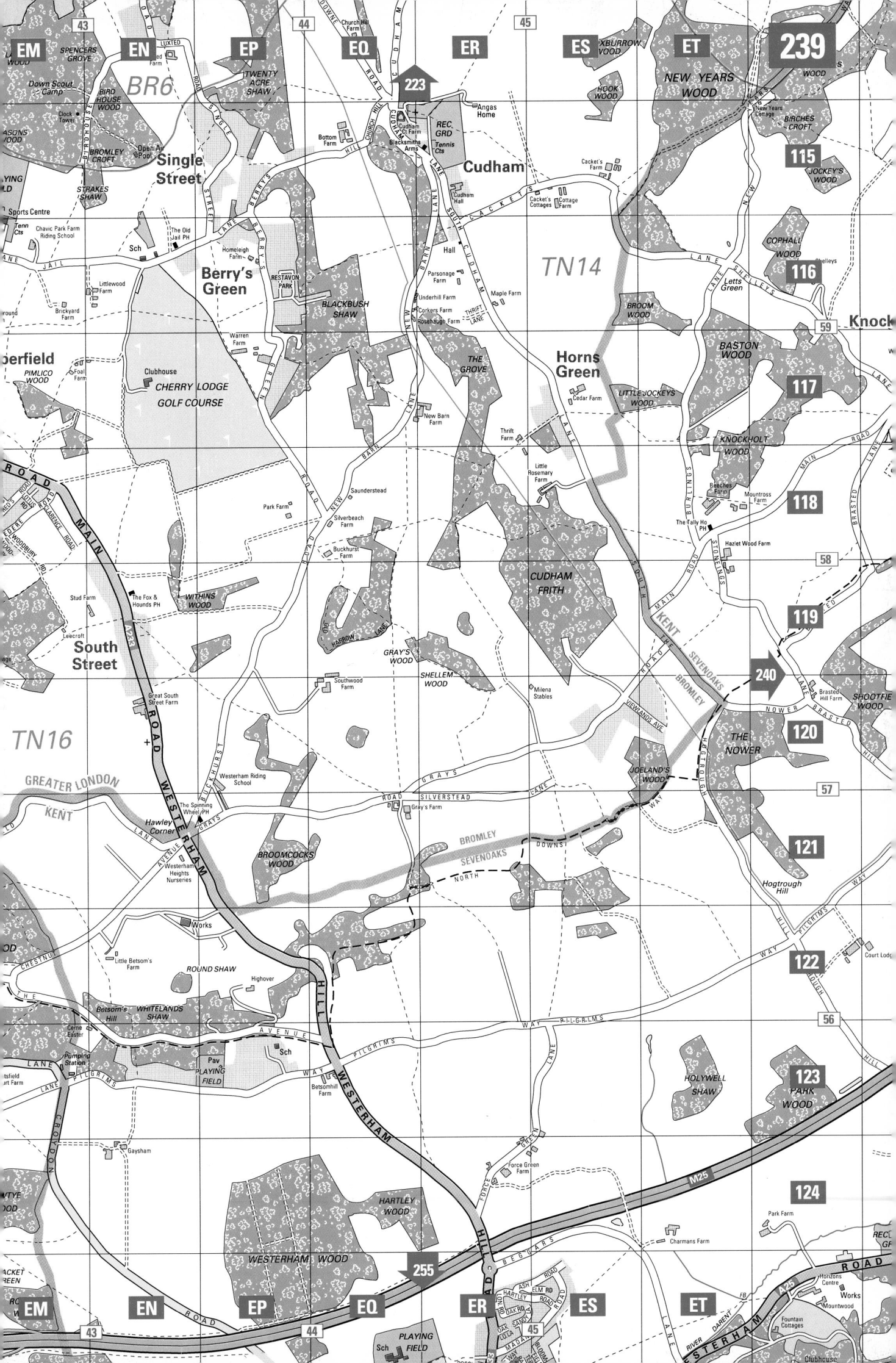

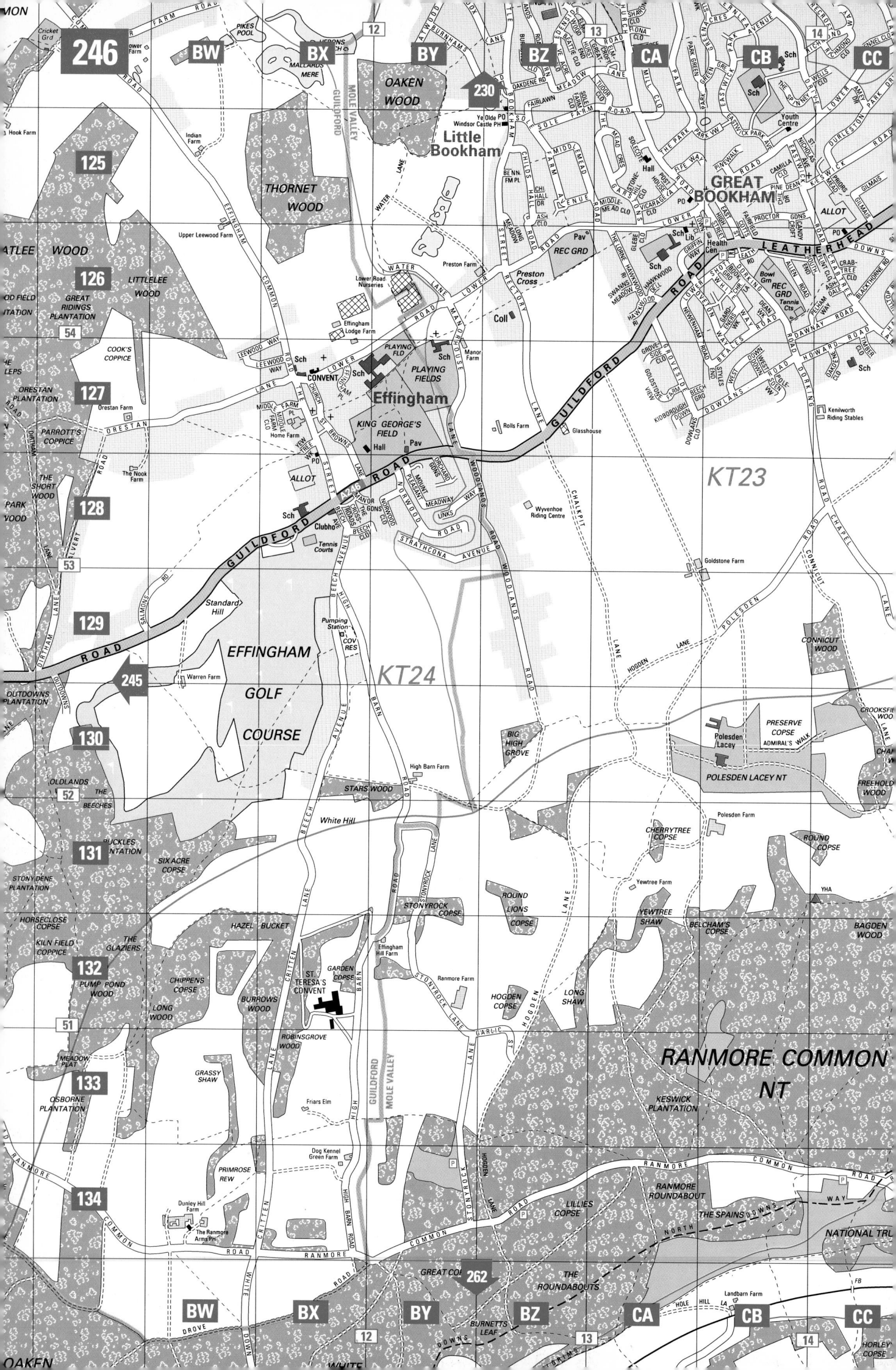

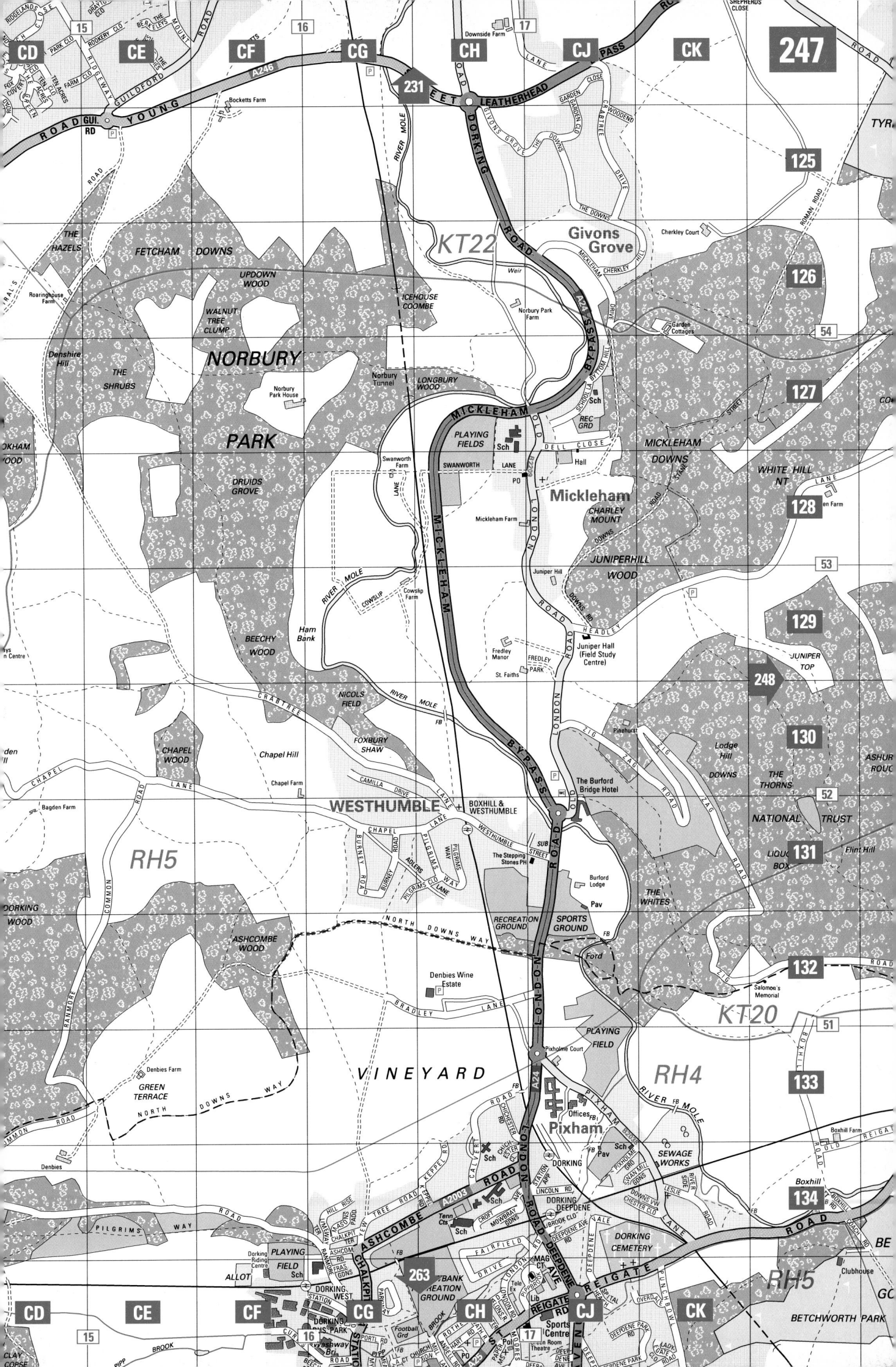

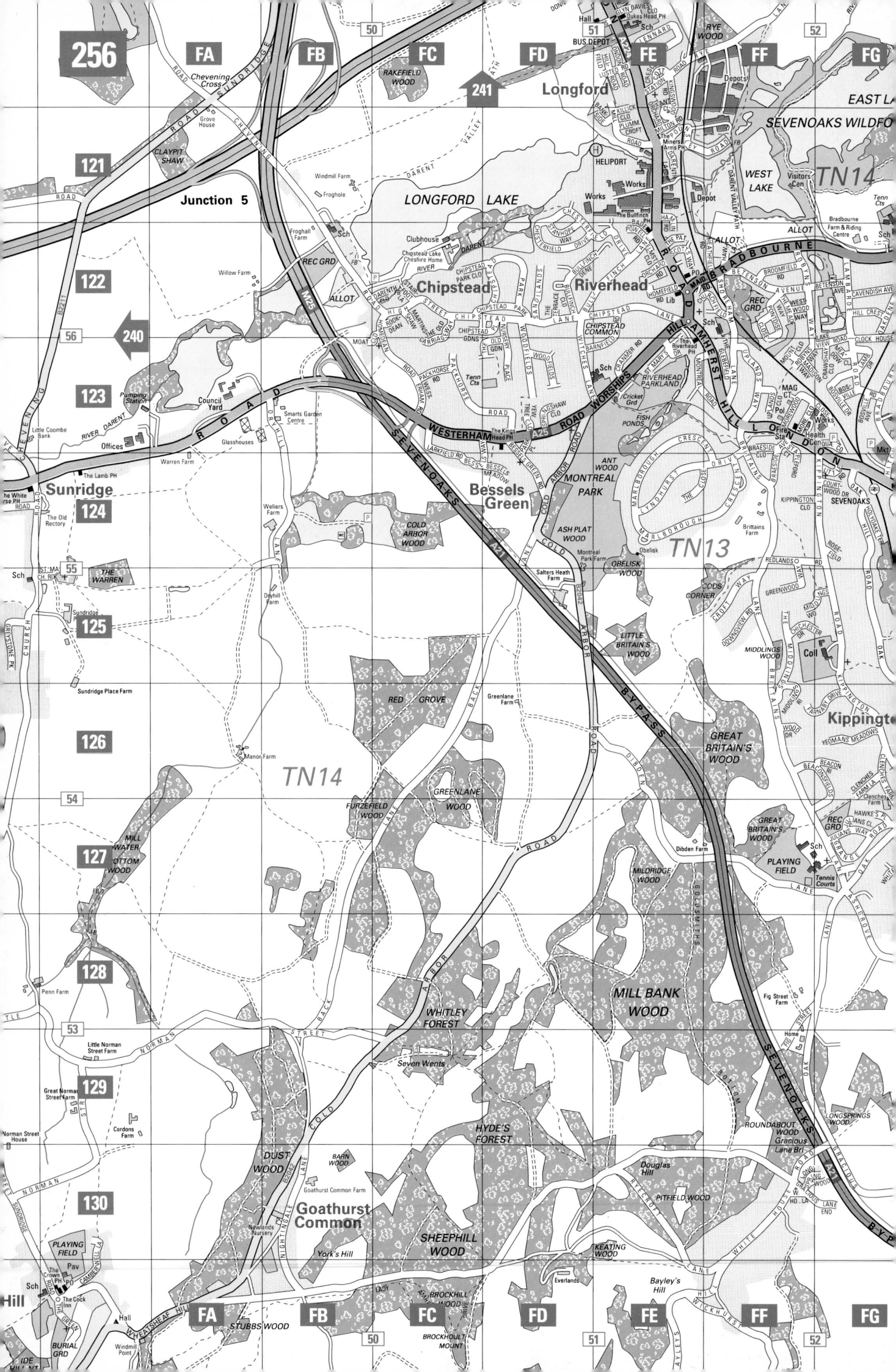

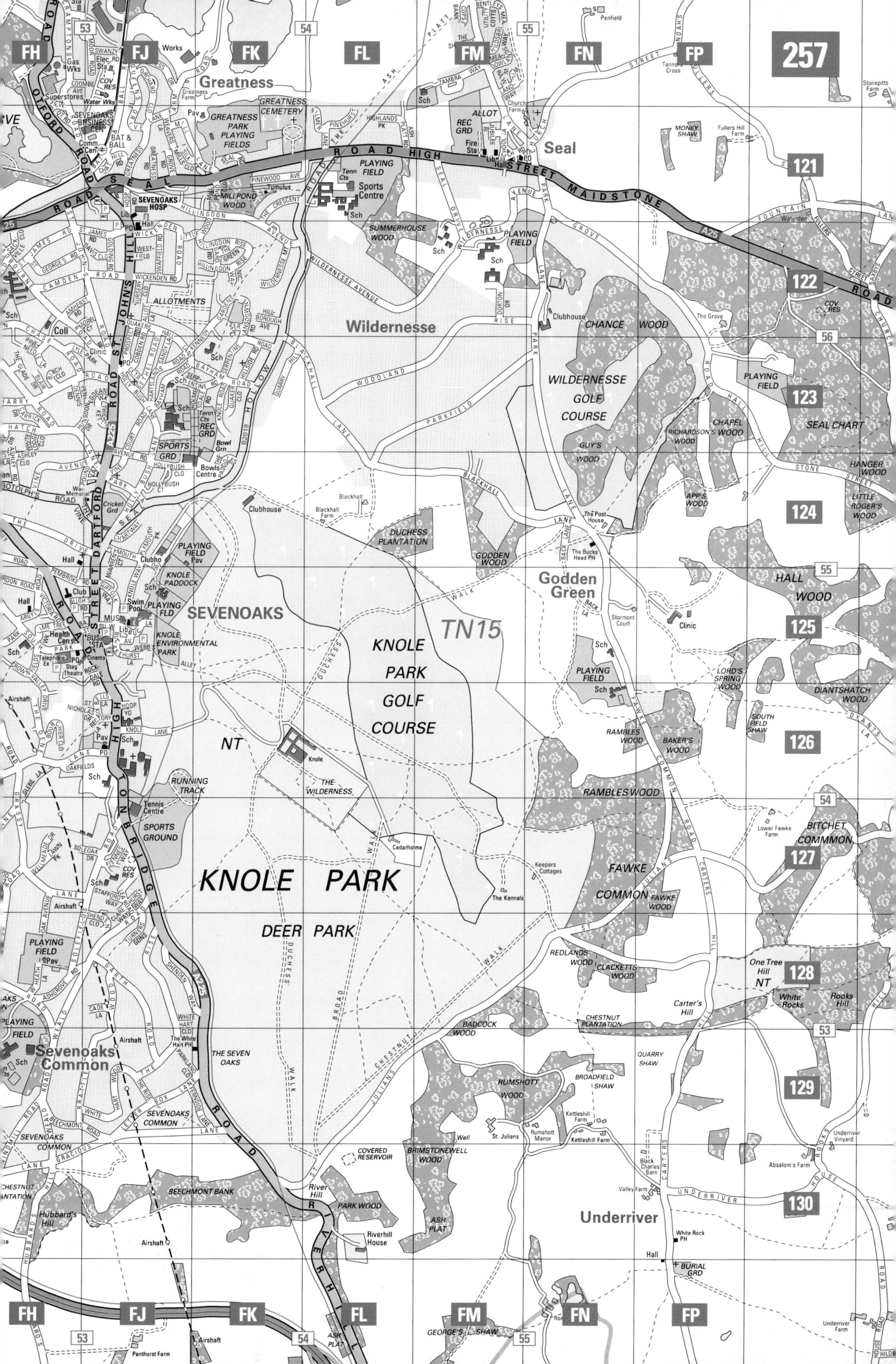

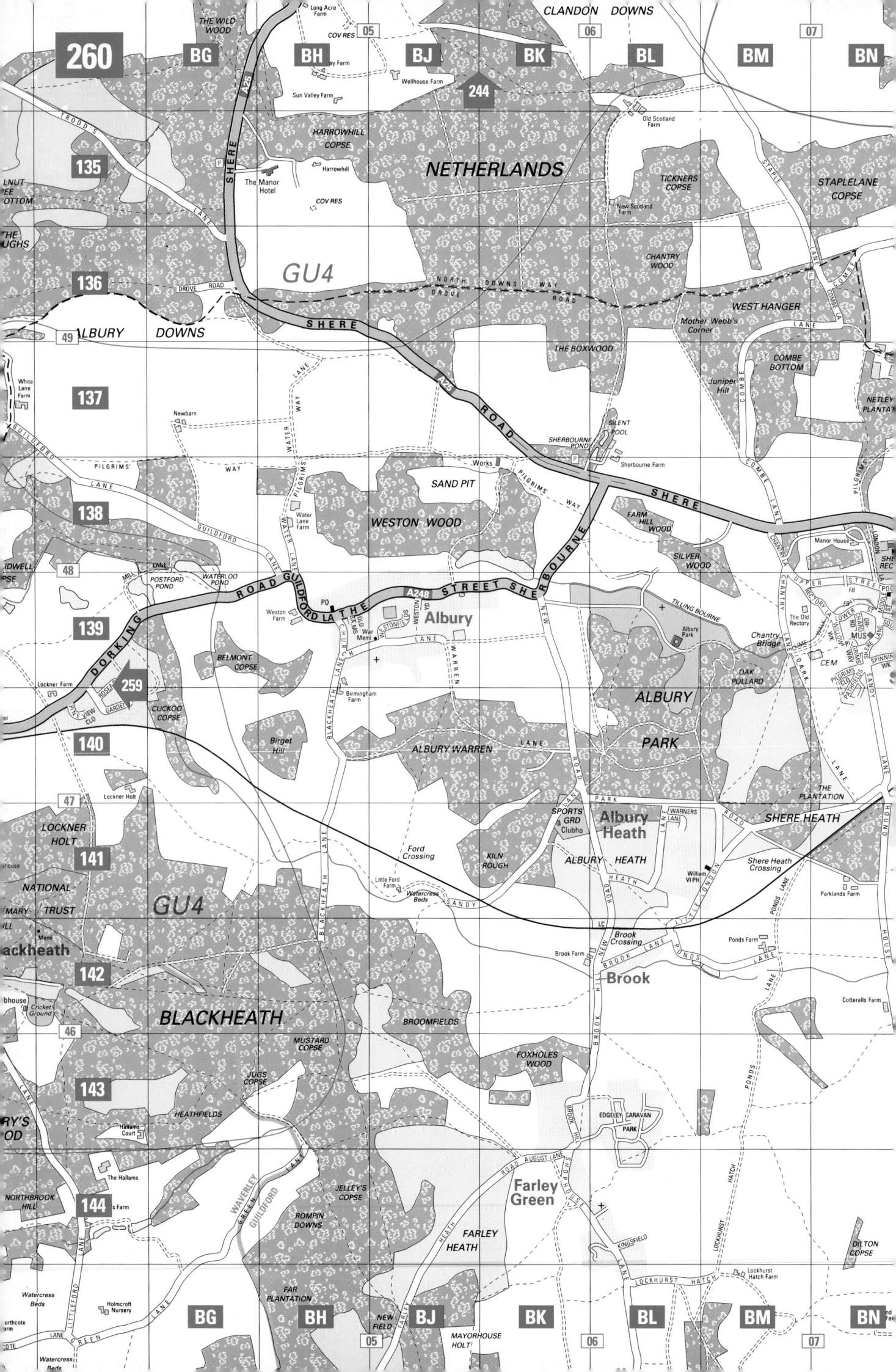

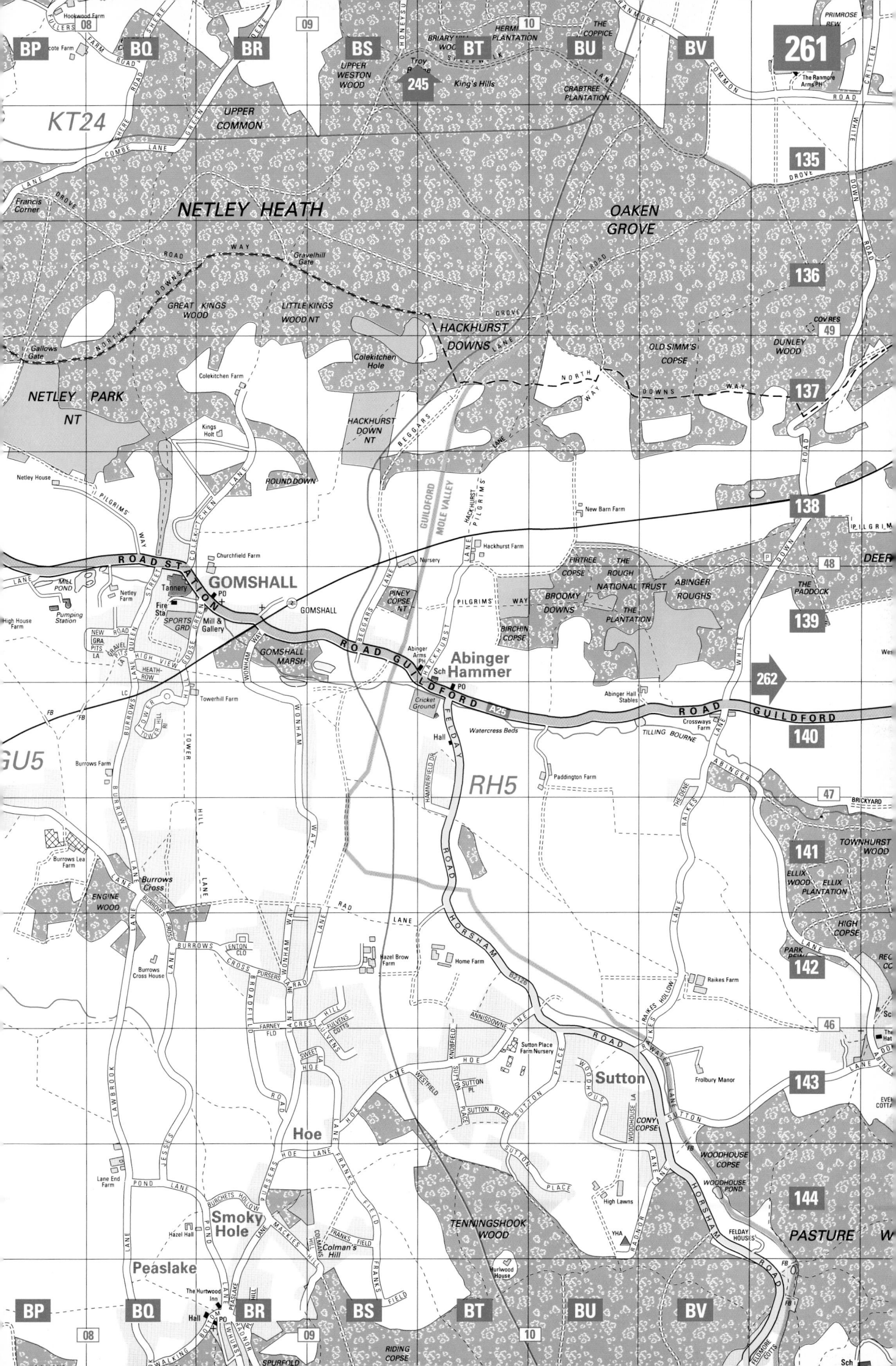

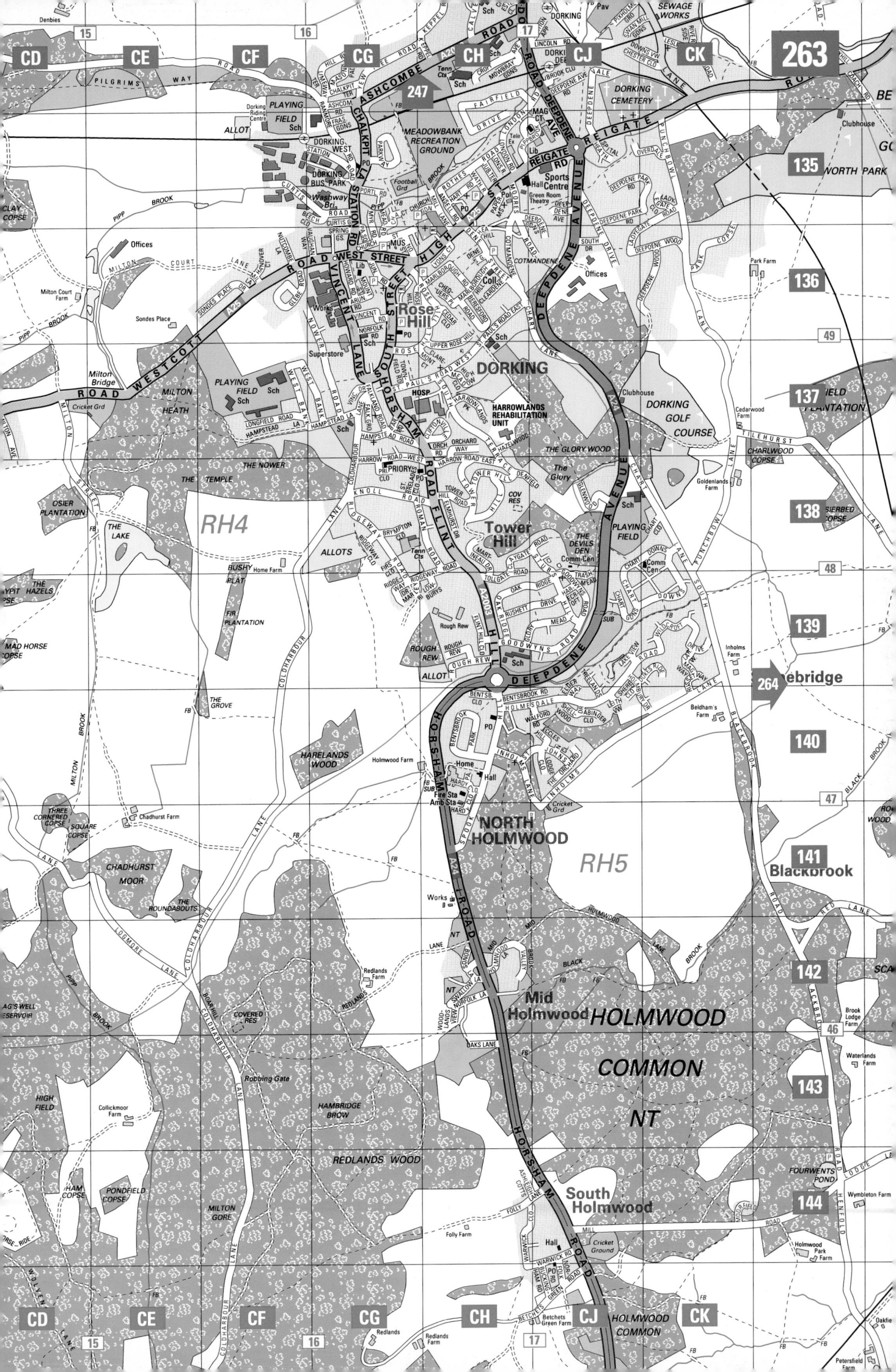

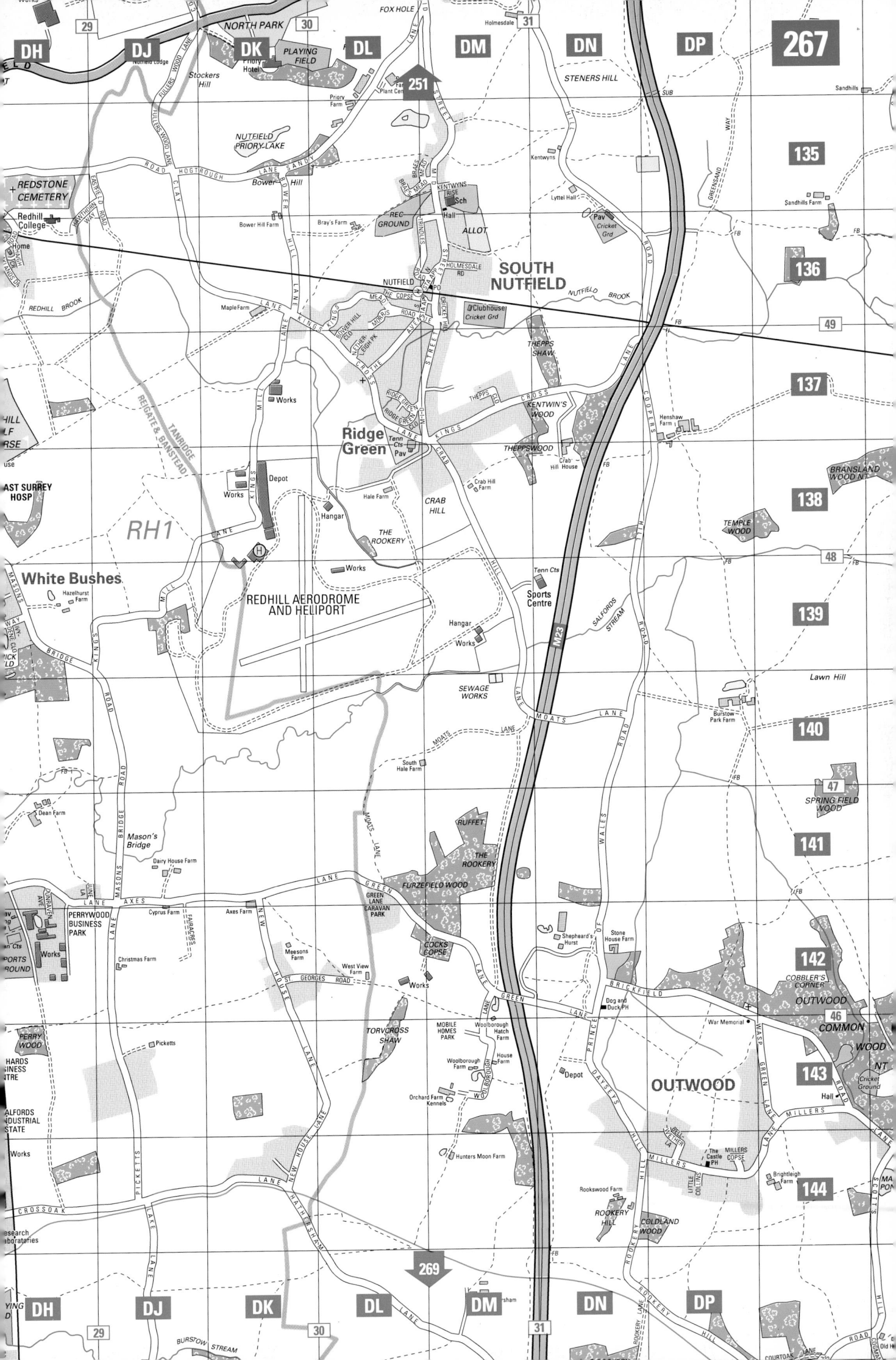

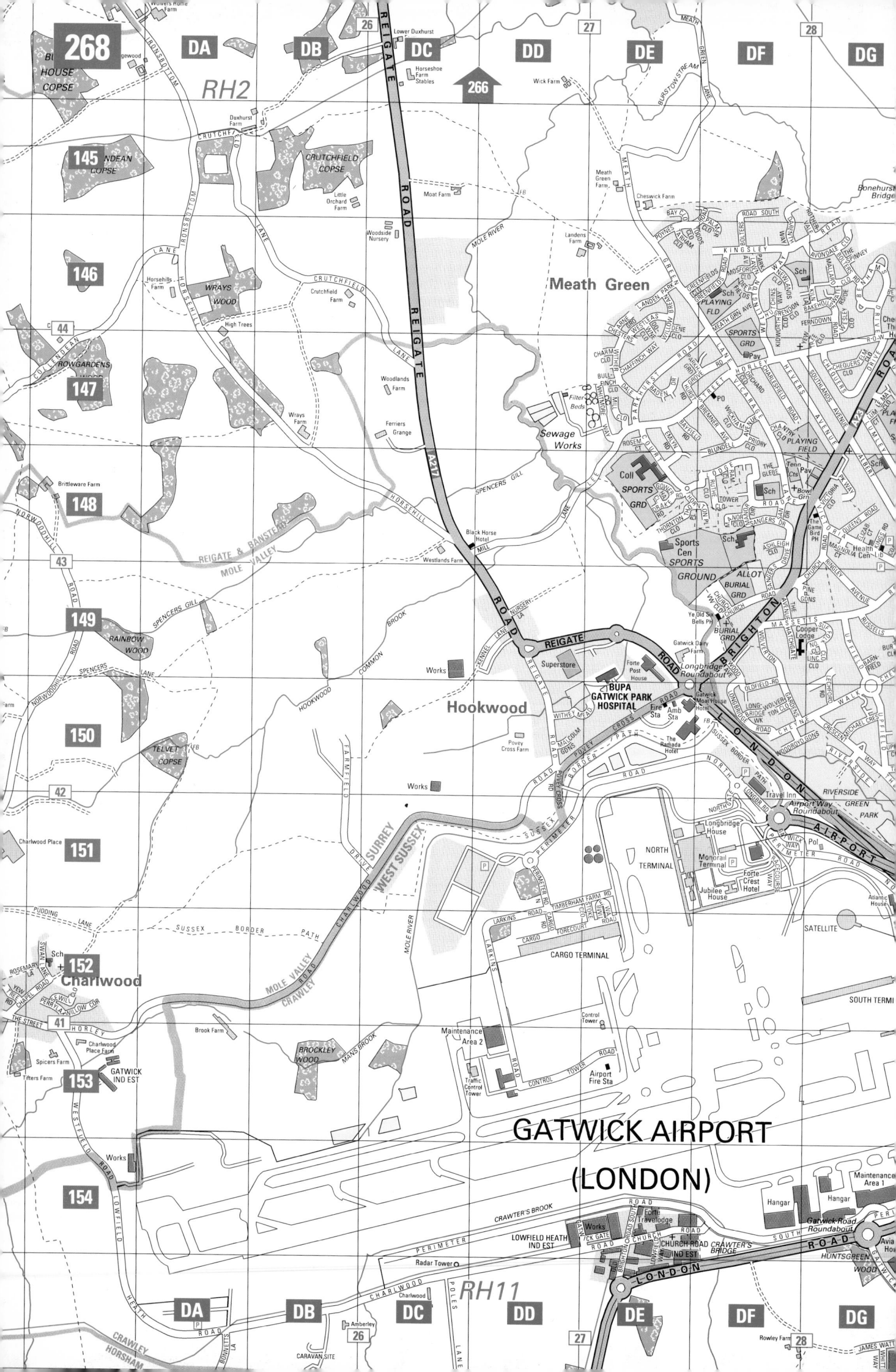

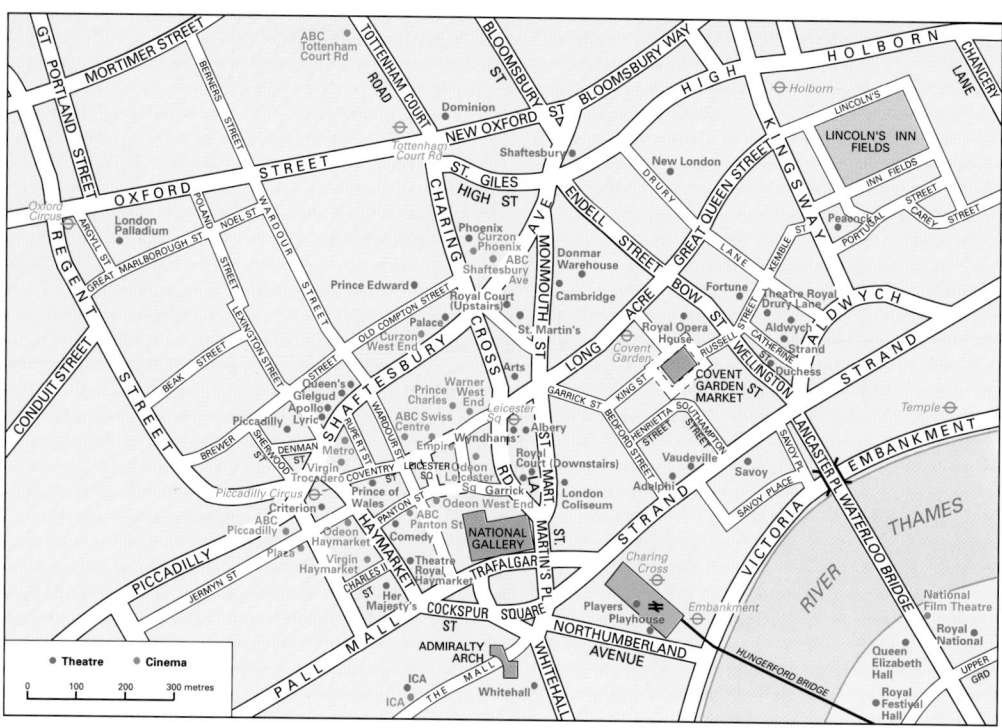

THEATRES

Adelphi 020 7344 0055
Albery 020 7369 1730
Aldwych 020 7416 6003
Apollo 020 7416 6022
Arts 020 7836 2132
Cambridge 020 7494 5054
Comedy 020 7369 1731
Criterion 020 7369 1747
Dominion 020 7656 1888
Donmar Warehouse 020 7369 1732
Duchess 020 7494 5075
Fortune 020 7836 2238
Garrick 020 7494 5085
Gielgud 020 7494 5065
Her Majesty's 020 7494 5400
ICA 020 7930 3647
London Coliseum 020 7632 8300
London Palladium 020 7494 5020
Lyric 020 7494 5045
New London 020 7405 0072
Palace 020 7434 0909
Peacock 020 7314 8800
Phoenix 020 7369 1733
Piccadilly 020 7369 1734
Players 020 7839 1134
Playhouse 020 7839 4401
Prince Edward 020 7734 8951
Prince of Wales 020 7839 5987
Queen Elizabeth Hall
    020 7960 4242
Queen's 020 7494 5041
Royal Court Theatre Downstairs
    020 7565 5000
Royal Court Theatre Upstairs
    020 7565 5000
Royal Festival Hall
    020 7960 4242
Royal National 020 7452 3000
Royal Opera House (CLOSED)
    020 7304 4000
St. Martin's 020 7836 1443
Savoy 020 7836 8888
Shaftesbury 020 7379 5399
Strand 020 7930 8800
Theatre Royal, Drury Lane
    020 7494 5550
Theatre Royal, Haymarket
    020 7930 8800
Vaudeville 020 7836 9987
Whitehall 020 7369 1735
Wyndhams 020 7369 1736

CINEMAS

ABC Panton St 020 7930 0631
ABC Piccadilly 020 7437 3561
ABC ShaftesburyAvenue
    020 7836 6279
ABC Swiss Centre
    020 7439 4470
ABC Tottenham Court Rd
    020 7636 6148
Curzon Phoenix 020 7369 1721

Curzon West End 020 7369 1722
Empire 020 7437 1234
ICA 020 7930 3647
Metro 020 7437 0757
National Film Theatre
    020 7928 3232
Odeon Haymarket
    0426 915353
Odeon Leicester Sq
    020 8315 4215

Odeon Mezzanine
(Odeon Leicester Sq)
    020 8315 4215
Odeon West End
    020 8315 4221
Plaza 020 7437 1234
Prince Charles 020 7437 8181
Virgin Haymarket 0870 907 0712
Virgin Trocadero 0870 907 0716
Warner West End 020 7437 4347

WEST END SHOPPING

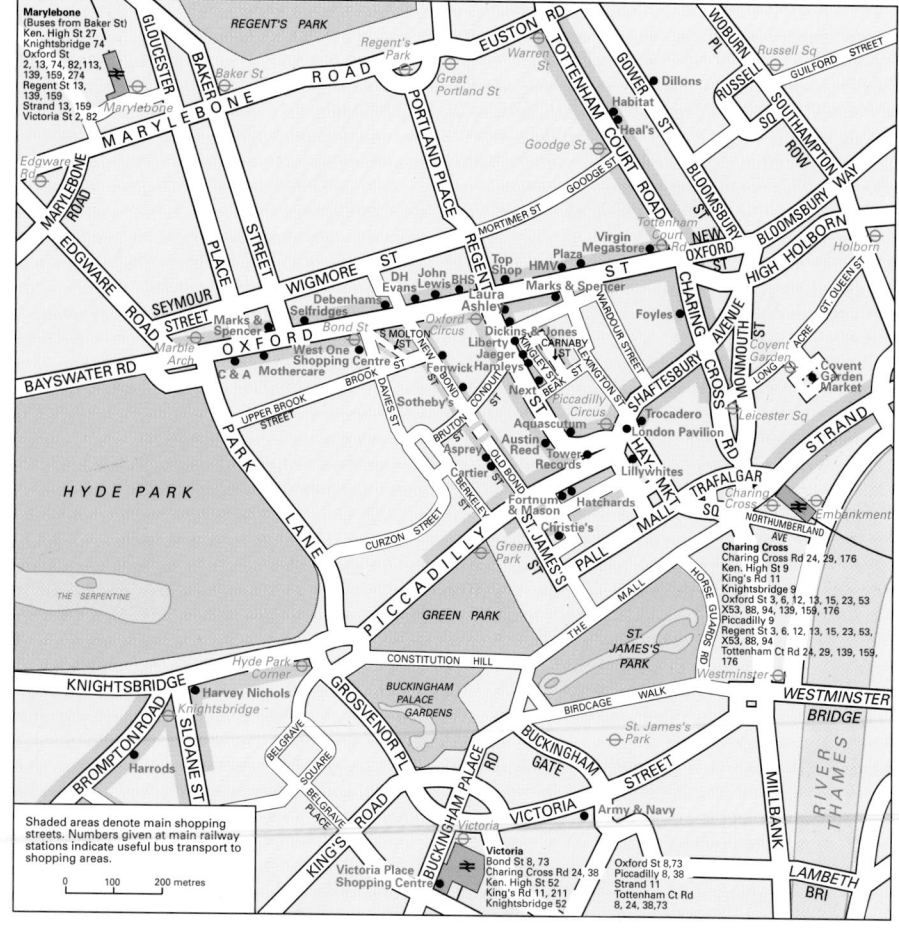

SHOPS

Aquascutum 020 7734 6090
Army & Navy 020 7834 1234
Asprey 020 7493 6767
Austin Reed 020 7734 6789
BHS (Oxford St) 020 7629 2011
C & A 020 7629 7272
Cartier 020 7493 6962
Christie's 020 7839 9060
Covent Garden Market 020 7836 9137
DH Evans 020 7629 8800
Debenhams 020 7580 3000
Dickins & Jones 020 7734 7070
Dillons 020 7636 1577
Fenwick 020 7629 9161
Fortnum & Mason 020 7734 8040
Foyles 020 7437 5660
Habitat (Tottenham Court Rd)
    020 7631 3880
Hamleys 020 7734 3161
Harrods 020 7730 1234
Harvey Nichols 020 7235 5000
Hatchards 020 7439 9921
Heal's 020 7636 1666
HMV 020 7631 3423
Jaeger 020 7200 4000
John Lewis 020 7629 7711
Laura Ashley (Regent St) 020 7355 1363
Liberty 020 7734 1234
Lillywhites 020 7930 3181
London Pavilion 020 7437 1838
Marks & Spencer
    (Marble Arch) 020 7935 7954
Marks & Spencer (Oxford St)
    020 7437 7722
Mothercare 020 7580 1688
Next (Regent St) 020 7434 2515
Plaza on Oxford St 020 7637 8811
Selfridges 020 7629 1234
Sotheby's 020 7493 8080
Top Shop & Top Man 020 7636 7700
Tower Records 020 7439 2500
Trocadero 020 7439 1791
Victoria Place Shopping Centre
    020 7931 8811
Virgin Megastore 020 7580 5822

Shoot Up Hill • Finchley Road • Haverstock Hill • Chalk Farm Rd • Kentish Town Rd • Camden Road • York Way • Caledonian Road • A503 • A5200 • A5203 • A1 • St. Paul's Road • A104 • A104 • Dalston La • Road • A104 • **Hackney** • Well Street • Victoria Park • Road • A106 • Maire Street

Kilburn • Primrose Hill • Road • **Camden Town** • Camden Road • Islington • Essex Road • New North Road • A1200 • Upper Street • A10 • Kingsland Road • Hackney Rd

272 • **St. John's Wood** • Prince Albert Road • Regent's Park • A41 • Albany St. • Euston Road • **273** **274** • ST. PANCRAS STA. • Road • EUSTON STA. • KINGS CROSS STA. • Pentonville Rd • City Road • A5201 • Goswell Rd. • A1 • Old Street • A10 • Bethnal Green Road • **275** • **Bethnal Green** • Mile End Road • A11

Maida Vale • Edgware Road • MARYLEBONE STA. • A501 • Marylebone • Road • Tottenham Court Road • **Bloomsbury** • Gray's Inn • Clerkenwell Road • A201 • City Road • London Wall • A1211 • LIVERPOOL STREET STA. • **Stepney** • Commercial Road • A13

Road • Westway • A404 • PADDINGTON STA. • A5 • Sussex Gardens • Oxford Street • **Soho** • Regent Street • **Covent Garden** • A4 • Fleet Street • Embankment • **St. Paul's** • **City**

Bayswater • Bayswater Road • Marble Arch • Park Lane • **Mayfair** • Piccadilly • The Mall • **276** • **Kensington** • Kensington Gardens • **Hyde Park** • Green Park • St. James's Park • Whitehall • CHARING CROSS STA. • **277** **278** • WATERLOO INT. STA. • WATERLOO STA. • Blackfriars Road • **Southwark** • The Tower • Tooley St. • LONDON BRIDGE STA. • **279** • **Wapping** • RIVER THAMES • Rotherhithe Tunnel • A1203 • The Highway

Holland Park • Kensington High St. • Kensington Road • A315 • **Knightsbridge** • Victoria Street • **Lambeth** • Kennington Road • Jamaica Road • **Bermondsey** • Southwark Park • Lower Road • A200

Cromwell Road • A4 • **Belgravia** • VICTORIA STA. • Vauxhall • **Westminster** • Lambeth Road • A2 • Tower Bridge Road • Old Kent Road • Rotherhithe New Road

Earls Court • Warwick Road • A308 • Brompton Road • **Chelsea** • A3213 • A202 Road • Albert Embankment • A3 • A201 • A215 Camberwell • Road

Old Brompton Road • King's Road • **THAMES** • RIVER • Nine Elms Lane • A3216 • Battersea Park Road • A3205 • A3031 • Battersea Park Road • Wandsworth Road • A203 • Clapham Road • A3 • Brixton Road • A23 • Camberwell New Road • A202 • **Kennington** • Kent Road • A2

Fulham Road • A308 • A304 • Battersea Park • **Peckham** • Peckham Road • A202 • Queens Road

0 ____ 1mile

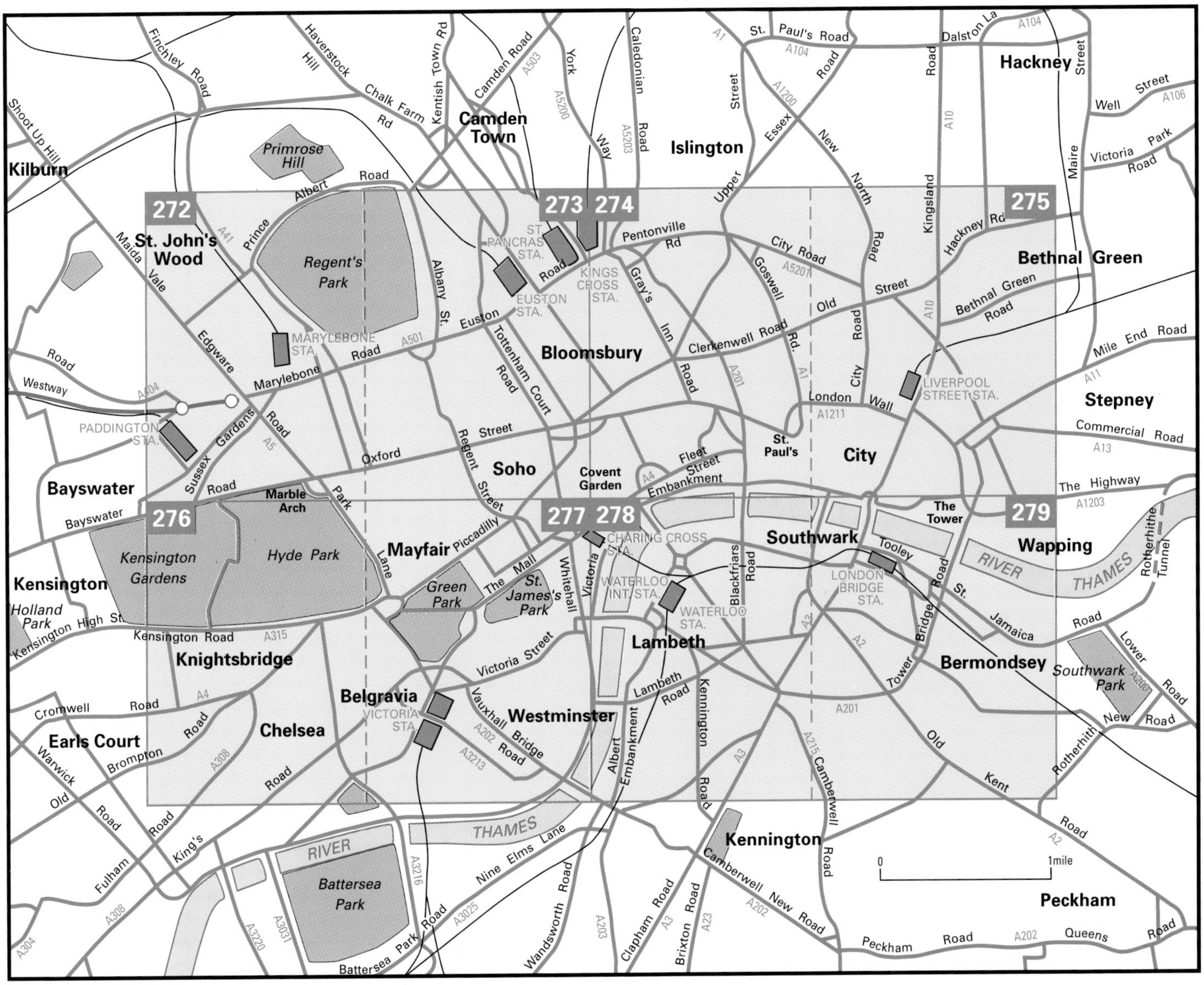

KEY TO MAP SYMBOLS

A40(M) — motorway
Dual A4 — primary route
Dual A40 — 'A' road
B504 — 'B' road
— other road/one way street
— street market
— pedestrian street
— access restriction
======== — track/footpath
— — — — ferry
CITY — borough boundary

EC2 — postal district boundary
🚉 — main railway station
🚉 — other railway station
Ⓤ — London Underground station
— Docklands Light Railway station
— bus/coach station
P — car park
i — tourist information centre
🎭 — theatre
⊠ — major hotel
⌐USA — embassy
10 — grid reference

■ POL — police station
■ Fire Sta — fire station
■ PO — post office
■ Lib — library
🎥 — cinema
+ — church
☾ — mosque
✡ — synagogue
Mormon ■ — other place of worship
WC — public toilet
□ — tower block
274 — page continuation number

■ leisure and tourism
■ shopping
■ administration and law
■ health and welfare
■ education
■ industry and commerce
public open space
park/garden/sports ground
† † cemetery

Scale 1 : 10,000 (6.3 inches to 1 mile)

0 ____ 0.25 ____ 0.50 ____ 0.75 ____ 1 kilometre
0 ____ 1/4 ____ 1/2 mile

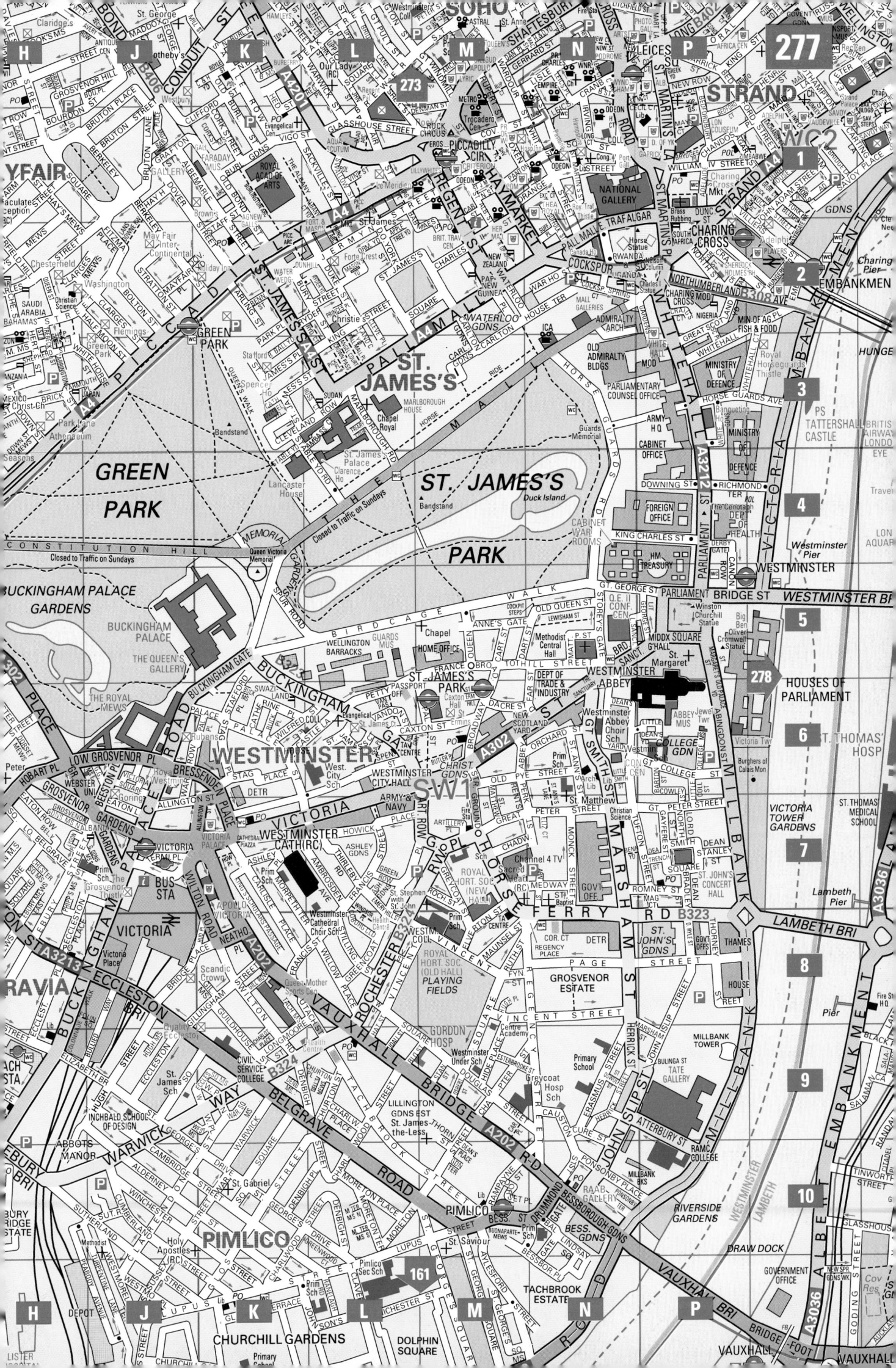

The following is a comprehensive listing of the places of interest which appear in this atlas. Bold references can be found within the Central London enlarged scale section (pages 272-279).

281

THE LIBRARY
GUILDFORD COLLEGE
of Further and Higher Education

The following is a comprehensive listing of all named places which appear in this atlas. Bold references can be found within the Central London enlarged scale section (pages 272-276). Postal information is in either London postal district or non-London post town form. For an explanation of post town abbreviations please consult page 287.

Leatherhead Common, Lthd.	231	CF119
Leavesden Grn., Wat.	59	BT34
Lee SE12	184	EF86
Leigh, Reig.	265	CU141
Lemsford, Welw.G.C.	29	CT10
Lessness Heath, Belv.	167	FB78
Letchmore Heath, Wat.	77	CD38
Letty Grn., Hert.	31	DH13
Leverstock Grn., Hem.H.	41	BQ21
Lewisham SE13	163	EB83
Leyton E11	123	EB60
Leytonstone E11	123	ED59
Limehouse E14	143	DY73
Limpsfield, Oxt.	254	EG128
Linford, S.le H.	171	GM75
Lisson Gro. NW8	**272**	**A4**
Little Berkhamsted, Hert.	47	DH18
Little Bookham, Lthd.	246	BY125
Little Chalfont, Ch.St.G.	72	AW40
Little Ealing W5	157	CJ77
Little Ilford E12	124	EL64
Little Parndon, Harl.	35	EP14
Little Thurrock, Grays	170	GD76
Little Woodcote, Cars.	218	DG112
Littleton, Guil.	258	AU140
Littleton, Shep.	195	BP97
London Colney, St.Alb.	61	CJ27
Long Ditton, Surb.	197	CJ102
Longcross, Cher.	192	AU104
Longford, Sev.	241	FD120
Longford, West Dr.	154	BH81
Longlands, Chis.	185	EQ90
Loudwater, H.Wyc.	88	AD53
Loudwater, Rick.	74	BK41
Loughton, Loug.	85	EM43
Low St., Til.	171	GM79
Lower Ashtead, Ash.	231	CJ119
Lower Bois, Chesh.	54	AR34
Lower Clapton E5	122	DW63
Lower Edmonton N9	100	DT46
Lower Feltham, Felt.	175	BS90
Lower Grn., Esher	196	CA103
Lower Holloway N7	121	DM64
Lower Kingswood, Tad.	250	DA127
Lower Nazeing, Wal.Abb.	50	EE23
Lower Sydenham SE26	183	DX91
Loxford, Ilf.	125	EQ64
Lye Grn., Chesh.	56	AT27
Lyne, Cher.	193	BA102
Magdalen Laver, Ong.	53	FE17
Maida Hill W9	139	CZ70
Maida Vale W9	140	DB70
Malden Rushett, Chess.	215	CH111
Manor Pk. E12	124	EL63
Manor Pk., Slou.	131	AQ70
Maple Cross, Rick.	91	BD49
Margery, Tad.	250	DA129
Mark Hall N., Harl.	36	EU12
Mark Hall S., Harl.	36	EU14
Mark's Gate, Rom.	104	EY54
Marshalswick, St.Alb.	43	CG17
Martyr's Grn., Wok.	229	BR120
Marylebone NW1	**272**	**D8**
Matching Tye, Harl.	37	FF12
Maybury, Wok.	227	BB117
Mayfair W1	**277**	**H1**
Mayford, Wok.	226	AW122
Maypole, Orp.	224	EZ107
Mead Vale, Red.	266	DD136
Meath Grn., Horl.	268	DD146
Merrow, Guil.	243	BB133
Merry Hill, Wat.	94	CB46
Merstham, Red.	251	DH128
Merton SW19	200	DA95
Merton Pk. SW19	200	DA96
Mickleham, Dor.	247	CJ128
Mid Holmwood, Dor.	263	CH142
Middle Grn., Slou.	132	AY73
Mile End E1	143	DY69
Mill End, Rick.	91	BF45
Mill Hill NW7	97	CU50
Millwall E14	163	EB76
Milton, Grav.	191	GK86
Mimbridge, Wok.	210	AV113
Mitcham, Mitch.	200	DG97
Mogador, Tad.	249	CY129
Moneyhill, Rick.	92	BH46
Monken Hadley, Barn.	79	CZ39
Monks Orchard, Croy.	203	DZ101
Moor Pk., Nthwd.	93	BQ49
Morden, Mord.	200	DA97
Morden Pk., Mord.	199	CY100
Mortlake SW14	158	CQ83
Motspur Pk., N.Mal.	199	CU100
Mottingham SE9	184	EJ89
Mount End, Epp.	70	EZ32
Mount Hermon, Wok.	226	AX118
Muckingford, S.le H.	171	GM76
Mugswell, Couls.	250	DB125
Muswell Hill N10	121	DH55
Nalderswood, Reig.	265	CW144
Nazeing, Wal.Abb.	50	EJ22
Nazeing Gate, Wal.Abb.	68	EJ25
Neasden NW2	118	CS62
Netteswell, Harl.	35	ES14

New Addington, Croy.	221	EC109
New Ash Grn., Long.	209	FX103
New Barnet, Barn.	80	DB42
New Beckenham, Beck.	183	DZ93
New Charlton SE7	164	EJ77
New Cross SE14	163	DY81
New Cross Gate SE14	163	DX81
New Eltham SE9	185	EN89
New Grns., St.Alb.	42	CC16
New Haw, Add.	212	BK108
New Malden, N.Mal.	198	CR97
New Southgate N11	99	DK49
New Town, Dart.	188	FN86
Newbury Pk., Ilf.	125	ER57
Newgate St., Hert.	47	DK24
Newington SE1	**279**	**H8**
Newtown, Chesh.	54	AP30
Newyears Grn., Uxb.	114	BM59
Nine Elms SW8	161	DJ80
Noak Hill, Rom.	106	FK47
Noel Pk. N22	99	DN54
Norbiton, Kings.T.	198	CP96
Norbury SW16	201	DM95
Nork, Bans.	233	CX115
North Acton W3	138	CR70
North Beckton E6	144	EL70
North Cheam, Sutt.	199	CX104
North Cray, Sid.	186	EZ90
North Finchley N12	98	DD50
North Harrow, Har.	116	CA58
North Hillingdon, Uxb.	135	BQ65
North Holmwood, Dor.	263	CH141
North Hyde, Sthl.	156	BY77
North Kensington W10	139	CW72
North Looe, Epsom	217	CW113
North Ockendon, Upmin.	129	FV64
North Sheen, Rich.	158	CN82
North Watford, Wat.	75	BV37
North Weald Bassett, Epp.	71	FB27
North Wembley, Wem.	117	CH61
North Woolwich E16	164	EL75
Northaw, Pot.B.	64	DF30
Northchurch, Berk.	38	AT17
Northfleet, Grav.	190	GD86
Northfleet Grn., Grav.	190	GC92
Northolt, Nthlt.	136	BY66
Northumberland Heath, Erith	167	FC80
Northwood, Nthwd.	93	BR51
Northwood Hills, Nthwd.	93	BT54
Norwood Grn., Sthl.	156	CA77
Norwood New Town SE19	182	DQ93
Notting Hill W11	139	CY72
Nunhead SE15	162	DW83
Nuper's Hatch, Rom.	105	FD45
Nutfield, Red.	251	DM133
Oakleigh Pk. N20	98	DD46
Oakley Grn., Wind.	150	AH82
Oakwood N14	81	DK44
Oatlands Pk., Wey.	213	BR105
Ockham, Wok.	228	BN121
Old Bexley, Bex.	187	FB87
Old Coulsdon, Couls.	235	DN119
Old Ford E3	143	DZ67
Old Harlow, Harl.	36	EX11
Old Hatfield, Hat.	45	CX17
Old Malden, Wor.Pk.	198	CR102
Old Oak Common NW10	138	CS71
Old Windsor, Wind.	172	AU86
Old Woking, Wok.	227	BA121
Onslow Village, Guil.	258	AS136
Orchard Leigh, Chesh.	56	AV28
Orpington, Orp.	205	ET102
Orsett Heath, Grays	171	GG75
Osidge N14	99	DH46
Osterley, Islw.	157	CD80
Otford, Sev.	241	FG116
Ottershaw, Cher.	211	BC106
Outwood, Red.	267	DP143
Oxhey, Wat.	76	BW44
Oxlease, Hat.	45	CV19
Oxshott, Lthd.	215	CD114
Oxted, Oxt.	253	ED129
Pachesham Pk., Lthd.	231	CG116
Paddington W2	140	DB71
Palmers Grn. N13	99	DN48
Panshanger, Welw.G.C.	30	DB09
Park Barn, Guil.	242	AS133
Park Langley, Beck.	203	EC99
Park Royal NW10	138	CN68
Park St., St.Alb.	61	CD26
Parrock Fm., Grav.	191	GK90
Parsons Grn. SW6	159	CZ81
Passmores, Harl.	51	ER17
Patchetts Grn., Wat.	76	CC39
Peartree, Welw.G.C.	29	CZ09
Peasmarsh, Guil.	258	AW142
Pebble Coombe, Tad.	248	CS128
Peckham SE15	162	DT80
Pednormead End, Chesh.	54	AN32
Penge SE20	182	DW94
Penn, H.Wyc.	88	AE48
Pentonville N1	**274**	**D1**
Perivale, Grnf.	137	CJ67
Perry St., Grav.	190	GE88
Petersham, Rich.	178	CL88

Petts Wd., Orp.	205	ER99
Piccotts End, Hem.H.	40	BJ16
Pilgrims Hatch, Brwd.	108	FV43
Pimlico SW1	**277**	**K10**
Pinnacles, Harl.	51	EN15
Pinner, Pnr.	116	BY56
Pinner Grn., Pnr.	94	BW54
Pinnerwood Pk., Pnr.	94	BW53
Pitch Pl., Guil.	242	AT129
Pixham, Dor.	247	CJ133
Plaistow E13	144	EF69
Plaistow, Brom.	184	EF93
Plumstead SE18	165	ES78
Ponders End, Enf.	83	DX43
Pooley Grn., Egh.	173	BC92
Poplar E14	143	EB73
Potten End, Berk.	39	BC16
Potter St., Harl.	52	EW17
Potters Bar, Pot.B.	64	DA32
Potters Crouch, St.Alb.	60	BW25
Poverest, Orp.	205	ET99
Poyle, Slou.	153	BE81
Pratt's Bottom, Orp.	224	EV110
Preston, Wem.	117	CK60
Primrose Hill NW8	140	DF67
Purfleet, Purf.	168	FP77
Purley, Pur.	219	DM111
Putney SW15	179	CW85
Putney Heath SW15	179	CW86
Putney Vale SW15	179	CT90
Pyrford, Wok.	227	BE115
Pyrford Grn., Wok.	228	BH117
Pyrford Village, Wok.	228	BG118
Queensbury, Har.	117	CK55
Radlett, Rad.	77	CH35
Rainham, Rain.	147	FG69
Ramsden, Orp.	206	EW102
Rayners La., Har.	116	BZ60
Raynes Pk. SW20	199	CV97
Redbridge, Ilf.	125	EM58
Redhill, Red.	250	DF134
Redstreet, Grav.	190	GB93
Regent's Pk. NW1	**273**	**H1**
Reigate, Reig.	250	DA134
Richings Pk., Iver	153	BD75
Richmond, Rich.	178	CL86
Rickmansworth, Rick.	92	BL45
Ridge, Pot.B.	62	CS34
Ridge Grn., Red.	267	DL137
Ripley, Wok.	228	BJ122
Ripley Springs, Egh.	172	AY93
Riverhead, Sev.	256	FD122
Riverview Pk., Grav.	190	GE92
Roe Grn., Hat.	45	CU18
Roehampton SW15	179	CU85
Roestock, St.Alb.	44	CR23
Romford, Rom.	127	FF57
Rose Hill, Dor.	263	CG136
Rosehill, Sutt.	200	DB102
Rosherville, Grav.	191	GF85
Rotherhithe SE16	163	DX76
Row Town, Add.	211	BF108
Rowley Grn., Barn.	79	CT42
Roxeth, Har.	117	CD61
Roydon, Harl.	50	EG15
Roydon Hamlet, Harl.	50	EJ19
Ruislip, Ruis.	115	BS59
Ruislip Common, Ruis.	115	BR57
Ruislip Gdns., Ruis.	115	BS63
Ruislip Manor, Ruis.	115	BU61
Rush Grn., Rom.	127	FC59
Ryde, The, Hat.	45	CW15
Rydens, Walt.	196	BW103
Rydeshill, Guil.	242	AS131
Rye Pk., Hodd.	49	EB16
St. Albans, St.Alb.	43	CE20
St. George's Hill, Wey.	213	BQ110
St. Helier, Cars.	200	DD101
St. James's SW1	**277**	**L3**
St. John's SE8	163	EA82
St. John's, Wok.	226	AV118
St. John's Wd. NW8	140	DC68
St. Julians, St.Alb.	43	CD22
St. Luke's EC1	**275**	**J4**
St. Margarets, Twick.	177	CG85
St. Margarets, Ware	33	EB10
St. Mary Cray, Orp.	206	EV99
St. Pancras WC1	**273**	**P3**
St. Paul's Cray, Orp.	206	EU96
St. Stephens, St.Alb.	42	CC22
St. Vincent's Hamlet, Brwd.	106	FP46
Salfords, Red.	266	DF142
Sanderstead, S.Croy.	220	DT111
Sands End SW6	160	DC81
Sarratt, Rick.	74	BG35
Sawbridgeworth, Saw.	36	EW05
Seal, Sev.	257	FN121
Seer Grn., Beac.	89	AR52
Selhurst SE25	202	DS100
Selsdon, S.Croy.	220	DW110
Send, Wok.	227	BC124
Send Marsh, Wok.	227	BF124
Sendgrove, Wok.	243	BC126
Seven Kings, Ilf.	125	ES59
Sevenoaks, Sev.	257	FJ125

285

Sevenoaks Common, Sev.	257	FH129
Sewardstone E4	83	EC39
Sewardstonebury E4	84	EE42
Shacklewell N16	122	DT63
Shadwell E1	142	DW73
Shalford, Guil.	258	AX141
Sheering, B.Stort.	37	FC07
Sheerwater, Wok.	211	BC113
Shenfield, Brwd.	109	FZ45
Shenley, Rad.	62	CN33
Shepherd's Bush W12	139	CW74
Shepperton, Shep.	195	BP101
Shere, Guil.	260	BN139
Sherrardspark, Welw.G.C.	29	CV07
Shirley, Croy.	203	DX104
Shooter's Hill SE18	165	EQ81
Shoreditch E1	**275**	**P5**
Shoreham, Sev.	225	FG111
Shortlands, Brom.	204	EE97
Shreding Grn., Iver	133	BC72
Sidcup, Sid.	185	ET91
Sidlow, Reig.	266	DB141
Silvertown E16	164	EJ75
Single St., West.	239	EN115
Singlewell, Grav.	191	GK93
Sipson, West Dr.	154	BN79
Slough, Slou.	132	AS74
Smallfield, Horl.	269	DP149
Smallford, St.Alb.	44	CP19
Smoky Hole, Guil.	261	BR144
Snaresbrook E11	124	EE57
Sockett's Heath, Grays	170	GD76
Soho W1	**273**	**M10**
Somers Town NW1	**273**	**N1**
South Acton W3	158	CP76
South Beddington, Wall.	219	DK107
South Chingford E4	101	DZ50
South Croydon, S.Croy.	220	DQ107
South Darenth, Dart.	209	FR95
South Hackney E9	142	DW67
South Hampstead NW6	140	DB66
South Harefield, Uxb.	114	BJ56
South Harrow, Har.	116	CB62
South Hatfield, Hat.	45	CU20
South Holmwood, Dor.	263	CJ144
South Hornchurch, Rain.	147	FE67
South Kensington SW7	160	DB76
South Lambeth SW8	161	DL81
South Merstham, Red.	251	DJ130
South Mimms, Pot.B.	63	CT32
South Norwood SE25	202	DT97
South Nutfield, Red.	267	DM136
South Ockendon, S.Ock.	149	FW70
South Oxhey, Wat.	94	BW48
South Pk., Reig.	266	DA138
South Ruislip, Ruis.	116	BW63
South Stifford, Grays	169	FX78
South St., West.	239	EM119
South Tottenham N15	122	DS57
South Weald, Brwd.	108	FS47
South Wimbledon SW19	180	DA94
South Woodford E18	102	EF54
Southall, Sthl.	136	BX74
Southborough, Brom.	205	EM100
Southend SE6	183	EC91
Southfields SW18	180	DA88
Southfleet, Grav.	190	GB93
Southgate N14	99	DJ47
Southlea, Slou.	152	AV82
Southwark SE1	**278**	**G3**
Spitalbrook, Hodd.	49	EA19
Spring Gro., Islw.	157	CE82
Staines, Stai.	174	BG93
Stamford Hill N16	122	DS60
Stanborough, Welw.G.C.	29	CT12
Stanmore, Stan.	95	CG50
Stanstead Abbotts, Ware	33	ED11
Stanwell, Stai.	174	BL87
Stanwell Moor, Stai.	174	BG85
Stapleford Abbotts, Rom.	87	FC43
Stapleford Tawney, Rom.	87	FC37
Stepney E1	142	DW71
Stewards, Harl.	51	ER19
Stockwell SW9	161	DK83
Stoke D'Abernon, Cob.	230	BZ116
Stoke Grn., Slou.	132	AU70
Stoke Newington N16	122	DS61
Stoke Poges, Slou.	132	AT66
Stone, Green.	189	FT85
Stonebridge NW10	138	CP67
Stonebridge, Dor.	264	CL139
Stonehill, Cher.	210	AY107
Stoneleigh, Epsom	217	CU106
Stoughton, Guil.	242	AV131
Strand WC2	**273**	**P10**
Stratford E15	143	EC65
Strawberry Hill, Twick.	177	CE90
Streatham SW16	181	DL91
Streatham Hill SW2	181	DM88
Streatham Pk. SW16	181	DJ91
Streatham Vale SW16	181	DK94
Strood Grn., Bet.	264	CP138
Stroud Grn. N4	121	DM58
Stroude, Vir.W.	193	AZ96
Sudbury, Wem.	117	CG64
Summerstown SW17	180	DB91
Sumners, Harl.	51	EN19
Sunbury, Sun.	195	BV97
Sundridge, Brom.	184	EJ93
Sundridge, Sev.	240	EZ124
Sunnymeads, Wind.	152	AY84
Surbiton, Surb.	198	CL101
Sutton, Dor.	261	BU143
Sutton, Sutt.	218	DA107
Sutton at Hone, Dart.	188	FN94
Sutton Grn., Guil.	243	AZ125
Swanley, Swan.	207	FE98
Swanley Village, Swan.	207	FH95
Swanscombe, Swans.	190	FZ86
Swillet, The, Rick.	73	BB44
Sydenham SE26	182	DV92
Tadworth, Tad.	233	CV122
Tandridge, Oxt.	253	EA133
Taplow, Maid.	130	AE70
Tatling End, Ger.Cr.	113	BB61
Tatsfield, West.	238	EL120
Tattenham Cor., Epsom	233	CV118
Teddington, Tedd.	177	CG93
Tewin, Welw.	30	DE05
Thames Ditton, T.Ditt.	197	CF100
Thamesmead SE28	146	EU74
Thamesmead N. SE28	146	EX72
Thamesmead W. SE18	165	EQ76
Theydon Bois, Epp.	85	ET37
Theydon Garnon, Epp.	86	EW36
Theydon Mt., Epp.	70	FA34
Thorney, Iver	154	BH76
Thornton Heath, Th.Hth.	201	DP98
Thornwood, Epp.	70	EW25
Thorpe, Egh.	193	BC97
Thorpe Grn., Egh.	193	BA98
Thorpe Lea, Egh.	173	BB93
Threshers Bush, Harl.	53	FB16
Tilbury, Til.	171	GG81
Titsey, Oxt.	254	EH125
Tokyngton, Wem.	138	CP65
Tolworth, Surb.	198	CN103
Toot Hill, Ong.	71	FF30
Tooting Graveney SW17	180	DE93
Tottenham N17	100	DS53
Tottenham Hale N17	122	DU55
Totteridge N20	97	CY46
Tower Hill, Dor.	263	CH138
Townsend, St.Alb.	43	CD17
Tufnell Pk. N7	121	DK63
Tulse Hill SE21	182	DQ88
Turnford, Brox.	67	DZ26
Twickenham, Twick.	177	CG89
Twitton, Sev.	241	FE116
Tye Grn., Harl.	51	ET17
Tylers Causeway, Hert.	47	DK22
Tyler's Grn., Gdse.	252	DV129
Tyrrell's Wd., Lthd.	232	CM123
Tyttenhanger, St.Alb.	44	CL23
Underhill, Barn.	80	DA43
Underriver, Sev.	257	FN130
Upminster, Upmin.	128	FQ62
Upper Clapton E5	122	DV60
Upper Edmonton N18	100	DU50
Upper Elmers End, Beck.	203	DZ99
Upper Halliford, Shep.	195	BS97
Upper Holloway N19	121	DJ62
Upper Norwood SE19	182	DR94
Upper Sydenham SE26	182	DU91
Upper Tooting SW17	180	DE90
Upper Walthamstow E17	123	EC56
Upshire, Wal.Abb.	68	EJ32
Upton E7	144	EH66
Upton, Slou.	152	AU76
Upton Pk. E6	144	EJ67
Upton Pk., Slou.	152	AT76
Uxbridge, Uxb.	134	BK66
Uxbridge Moor, Iver	134	BG67
Uxbridge Moor, Uxb.	134	BG67
Vauxhall SW8	161	DK79
Virginia Water, Vir.W.	192	AW97
Waddon, Croy.	201	DN103
Walham Grn. SW6	160	DB80
Wallington, Wall.	219	DJ106
Waltham Abbey, Wal.Abb.	84	EF35
Waltham Cross, Wal.Cr.	67	DZ33
Walthamstow E17	101	EB54
Walton on the Hill, Tad.	249	CT125
Walton-on-Thames, Walt.	195	BT103
Walworth SE17	**279**	**H10**
Wandsworth SW18	179	CZ85
Wanstead E11	124	EG59
Wapping E1	142	DU74
Ware, Ware	33	DZ06
Warley, Brwd.	108	FV50
Warlingham, Warl.	237	DX118
Warners End, Hem.H.	39	BE19
Warwick Wold, Red.	251	DN129
Water End, Hat.	63	CV26
Waterford, Hert.	31	DM05
Waterside, Chesh.	54	AR32
Watford, Wat.	75	BU41
Watford Heath, Wat.	94	BX46
Wealdstone, Har.	117	CF55
Welham Grn., Hat.	45	CV23
Well End, Borwd.	78	CR38
Well Hill, Orp.	225	FB107
Welling, Well.	166	EU83
Welwyn Gdn. City, Welw.G.C.	29	CX10
Wembley, Wem.	118	CL64
Wembley Pk., Wem.	118	CM61
Wennington, Rain.	148	FK73
Wentworth, Vir.W.	192	AS100
West Acton W3	138	CN72
West Barnes, N.Mal.	199	CV98
West Brompton SW10	160	DA79
West Byfleet, W.Byf.	212	BH113
West Clandon, Guil.	244	BH129
West Drayton, West Dr.	154	BK76
West Dulwich SE21	182	DR90
West End, Esher	214	BZ107
West End, Hat.	46	DC18
West Ewell, Epsom	216	CS108
West Grn. N15	122	DQ56
West Ham E15	144	EF66
West Hampstead NW6	120	DB64
West Harrow, Har.	116	CC59
West Heath SE2	166	EX79
West Hendon NW9	118	CS59
West Horsley, Lthd.	245	BP127
West Kilburn W9	139	CZ69
West Molesey, W.Mol.	196	BZ98
West Norwood SE27	182	DQ90
West Thurrock, Grays	169	FU78
West Tilbury, Til.	171	GL79
West Watford, Wat.	75	BU42
West Wickham, W.Wick.	203	EC103
Westbourne Grn. W2	140	DA71
Westcott, Dor.	262	CC138
Westcourt, Grav.	191	GL89
Westerham, West.	255	EQ126
Westfield, Wok.	227	AZ122
Westhumble, Dor.	247	CG131
Westminster SW1	**277**	**K6**
Weston Grn., T.Ditt.	197	CF102
Wexham St., Slou.	132	AW67
Weybridge, Wey.	212	BN105
Wheathampstead, St.Alb.	28	CL06
Whelpley Hill, Chesh.	56	AX26
Whetstone N20	98	DB47
White Bushes, Red.	267	DH139
Whitechapel E1	142	DU72
Whiteley Village, Walt.	213	BS110
Whitton, Twick.	176	CB87
Whyteleafe, Cat.	236	DS118
Widmore, Brom.	204	EJ97
Wildernesse, Sev.	257	FL122
Wildhill, Hat.	46	DD21
Willesden NW10	139	CT65
Willesden Grn. NW10	139	CV66
Wilmington, Dart.	188	FJ91
Wimbledon SW19	179	CY93
Wimbledon Pk. SW19	179	CZ90
Winchmore Hill N21	99	DM45
Winchmore Hill, Amer.	88	AJ45
Windmill Hill, Grav.	191	GG88
Windsor, Wind.	152	AS81
Wisley, Wok.	228	BL116
Woking, Wok.	227	AZ118
Woldingham, Cat.	237	EB122
Woldingham Gdn. Village, Cat.	237	DY121
Wombwell Pk., Grav.	190	GD89
Wonersh, Guil.	259	BB144
Wooburn, H.Wyc.	110	AD58
Wooburn Grn., H.Wyc.	110	AF56
Wood Grn. N22	99	DL53
Woodbridge Hill, Guil.	242	AU132
Woodcote, Epsom	232	CQ116
Woodcote, Pur.	219	DK111
Woodford, Wdf.Grn.	102	EH51
Woodford Bri., Wdf.Grn.	103	EM52
Woodford Grn., Wdf.Grn.	102	EG50
Woodford Wells, Wdf.Grn.	102	EH48
Woodhall, Welw.G.C.	29	CY11
Woodham, Add.	211	BF111
Woodhatch, Reig.	266	DC137
Woodlands, Islw.	157	CE82
Woodmansterne, Bans.	234	DE115
Woodside, Croy.	202	DT100
Woodside, Wat.	59	BU33
Woolwich SE18	165	EM78
Worcester Pk., Wor.Pk.	199	CT103
World's End, Enf.	81	DN41
Wormley, Brox.	49	DY24
Wormley W. End, Brox.	48	DS22
Wotton, Dor.	262	BZ139
Wraysbury, Stai.	173	AZ86
Wrythe, The, Cars.	200	DE103
Yeading, Hayes	135	BV69
Yiewsley, West Dr.	134	BL74

General Abbreviations

All	Alley	Conv	Convent	Gar	Garage	Ms	Mews	St.	Saint
Allot	Allotments	Cor	Corner	Gdn	Garden	Mt	Mount	Sta	Station
Amb	Ambulance	Cors	Corners	Gdns	Gardens	Mus	Museum	Sts	Streets
App	Approach	Coron	Coroners	Govt	Government	N	North	Sub	Subway
Arc	Arcade	Cotts	Cottages	Gra	Grange	PH	Public House	Swim	Swimming
Ave	Avenue	Cov	Covered	Grd	Ground	Par	Parade	TA	Territorial Army
Bdy	Broadway	Crem	Crematorium	Grds	Grounds	Pas	Passage	Tenn	Tennis
Bldgs	Buildings	Cres	Crescent	Grn	Green	Pav	Pavilion	Ter	Terrace
Boul	Boulevard	Ct	Court	Grns	Greens	Pk	Park	Thea	Theatre
Bowl	Bowling	Ctyd	Courtyard	Gro	Grove	Pl	Place	Trd	Trading
Bri	Bridge	Dep	Depot	Gros	Groves	Prec	Precinct	Twr	Tower
C of E	Church of England	Dr	Drive	Ho	House	Prom	Promenade	Twrs	Towers
Cath	Cathedral	Dws	Dwellings	Hos	Houses	Pt	Point	Vill	Villas
Cem	Cemetery	E	East	Hosp	Hospital	Quad	Quadrant	Vw	View
Cen	Central, Centre	Ed	Education	Ind	Industrial	RC	Roman Catholic	W	West
Cft	Croft	Elec	Electricity	Junct	Junction	Rd	Road	Wd	Wood
Cfts	Crofts	Emb	Embankment	La	Lane	Rds	Roads	Wds	Woods
Ch	Church	Est	Estate	Las	Lanes	Rec	Recreation	Wf	Wharf
Chyd	Churchyard	Ex	Exchange	Lo	Lodge	Res	Reservoir	Wk	Walk
Cin	Cinema	FB	Footbridge	Lwr	Lower	Ri	Rise	Wks	Walks
Circ	Circus	FC	Football Club	Mag	Magistrates	S	South	Yd	Yard
Clo	Close	Fld	Field	Mans	Mansions	Sch	School		
Co	County	Flds	Fields	Meml	Memorial	Shop	Shopping		
Coll	College	Fm	Farm	Mkt	Market	Sq	Square		
Comm	Community	Gall	Gallery	Mkts	Markets	St	Street		

Post Town Abbreviations

Abb.L.	Abbots Langley	Chig.	Chigwell	Hert.	Hertford	Rain.	Rainham	Twick.	Twickenham
Add.	Addlestone	Chis.	Chislehurst	Hmptn.	Hampton	Red.	Redhill	Upmin.	Upminster
Amer.	Amersham	Cob.	Cobham	Hodd.	Hoddesdon	Reig.	Reigate	Uxb.	Uxbridge
Ash.	Ashtead	Couls.	Coulsdon	Horl.	Horley	Rich.	Richmond	Vir.W.	Virginia Water
Ashf.	Ashford	Craw.	Crawley	Horn.	Hornchurch	Rick.	Rickmansworth	W.Byf.	West Byfleet
B.End	Bourne End	Croy.	Croydon	Houns.	Hounslow	Rom.	Romford	W.Mol.	West Molesey
B.Stort.	Bishop's Stortford	Dag.	Dagenham	Ilf.	Ilford	Ruis.	Ruislip	W.Wick.	West Wickham
Bans.	Banstead	Dart.	Dartford	Islw.	Isleworth	S.Croy.	South Croydon	Wal.Abb.	Waltham Abbey
Bark.	Barking	Dor.	Dorking	Ken.	Kenley	S.le H.	Stanford le Hope	Wal.Cr.	Waltham Cross
Barn.	Barnet	E.Mol.	East Molesey	Kes.	Keston	S.Ock.	South Ockendon	Wall.	Wallington
Beac.	Beaconsfield	Eden.	Edenbridge	Kings L.	Kings Langley	Saw.	Sawbridgeworth	Walt.	Walton-on-Thames
Beck.	Beckenham	Edg.	Edgware	Kings.T.	Kingston upon Thames	Sev.	Sevenoaks	Warl.	Warlingham
Belv.	Belvedere	Egh.	Egham	Long.	Longfield	Shep.	Shepperton	Wat.	Watford
Berk.	Berkhamsted	Enf.	Enfield	Loug.	Loughton	Sid.	Sidcup	Wdf.Grn.	Woodford Green
Bet.	Betchworth	Epp.	Epping	Lthd.	Leatherhead	Slou.	Slough	Well.	Welling
Bex.	Bexley	Felt.	Feltham	Maid.	Maidenhead	St.Alb.	St. Albans	Welw.	Welwyn
Bexh.	Bexleyheath	Gat.	Gatwick	Mitch.	Mitcham	Stai.	Staines	Welw.G.C.	Welwyn Garden City
Borwd.	Borehamwood	Gdmg.	Godalming	Mord.	Morden	Stan.	Stanmore	Wem.	Wembley
Brent.	Brentford	Gdse.	Godstone	N.Mal.	New Malden	Sthl.	Southall	West Dr.	West Drayton
Brom.	Bromley	Ger.Cr.	Gerrards Cross	Nthlt.	Northolt	Sun.	Sunbury-on-Thames	West.	Westerham
Brox.	Broxbourne	Grav.	Gravesend	Nthwd.	Northwood	Surb.	Surbiton	Wey.	Weybridge
Brwd.	Brentwood	Green.	Greenhithe	Ong.	Ongar	Sutt.	Sutton	Whyt.	Whyteleafe
Buck.H.	Buckhurst Hill	Grnf.	Greenford	Orp.	Orpington	Swan.	Swanley	Wind.	Windsor
Cars.	Carshalton	Guil.	Guildford	Oxt.	Oxted	Swans.	Swanscombe	Wok.	Woking
Cat.	Caterham	H.Wyc.	High Wycombe	Pnr.	Pinner	T.Ditt.	Thames Ditton	Wor.Pk.	Worcester Park
Ch.St.G.	Chalfont St. Giles	Har.	Harrow	Pot.B.	Potters Bar	Tad.	Tadworth		
Cher.	Chertsey	Harl.	Harlow	Pur.	Purley	Tedd.	Teddington		
Chesh.	Chesham	Hat.	Hatfield	Purf.	Purfleet	Th.Hth.	Thornton Heath		
Chess.	Chessington	Hem.H.	Hemel Hempstead	Rad.	Radlett	Til.	Tilbury		

Notes

A strict word-by-word alphabetical order is followed in the index whereby generic terms such as Avenue, Close, Gardens etc., although abbreviated, are ordered in their expanded form. So, for example, Abbot St. comes before Abbots Ave., and Abbots Ri. comes before Abbots Rd.

Street names preceded by a definite article (i.e. The) are indexed from their second word onwards with the article being placed at the end of the name,
e.g. Avenue, The, or Long Walk, The

The alphabetical order extends to include postal information so that where two or more streets have exactly the same name, London post town references are given first in alpha-numeric order and are followed by non-London post town references in alphabetic order,
e.g. Abbey Gdns. NW8 is followed by Abbey Gdns. W6 and then Abbey Gdns., Chertsey.

In some cases there are two or more streets of the same name in the same postal area. In order to aid correct location, extra information will be given in brackets,
e.g. High St., Epsom and High St. (Ewell), Epsom.

The street name and postal district or post town of an entry is followed by the page number and grid reference on which the name will be found, e.g. Abbey Road SW19 will be found on page 180 and in square DC94. Likewise, Norfolk Crescent, Sidcup will be found on page 185 and in square ES87 (within postal district DA15).

All streets within the Central London enlarged-scale section (pages 272-279) are shown in **bold type** when named in the index, e.g. **Abbey St. SE1** will be found on page **279** and in square **N6**. Certain streets may also be duplicated on parts of pages 140-142 and 160-162. In these cases the Central London section reference is always given first in bold type, followed by the same name in standard type, e.g.

Abbey Orchard St. SW1 277 M6
Abbey Orchard St. SW1 161 DK76

The index also contains some roads for which there is insufficient space to name on the map. The adjoining, or nearest named thoroughfare to such roads is shown in *italics*, and the reference indicates where the unnamed road is located off the named thoroughfare,
e.g. Oyster Catchers Close E16 is off *Freemasons Road* and is located off this road on page 144 in square EH72.

A.C. Ct., T.Ditt. 197 CG100
Harvest La.
A1(M) Business Pk., Hat. 45 CW23
Abberley Ms. SW4 161 DH83
Cedars Rd.
Abberton Wk., Rain. 147 FE66
Ongar Way
Abbess Clo. E6 144 EL71
Oliver Gdns.
Abbess Clo. SW2 181 DN88
Abbeville Rd. N8 121 DK56
Barrington Rd.
Abbeville Rd. SW4 181 DJ86
Abbey Ave., St.Alb. 42 CA23
Abbey Ave., Wem. 138 CL68
Abbey Clo., Hayes 135 BV74
Abbey Clo., Nthlt. 136 BZ69
Invicta Gro.
Abbey Clo., Pnr. 115 BV55
Abbey Clo., Rom. 127 FG58
Abbey Clo., Slou. 131 AL73
Abbey Clo., Wok. 227 BE116
Abbey Ct., Wal.Abb. 67 EB34
Abbey Cres., Belv. 166 FA77
Abbey Dr. SW17 180 DG92
Church La.
Abbey Dr., Abb.L. 59 BU32
Abbey Dr., Stai. 194 BJ97
Abbey Gdns. NW8 140 DC68
Abbey Gdns. SE16 162 DU77
Southwark Pk. Rd.
Abbey Gdns. W6 159 CY79
Abbey Gdns., Cher. 194 BG100
Abbey Grn., Cher. 194 BG100
Abbey Gro. SE2 166 EV77
Abbey La. E15 143 EC68
Abbey La., Beck. 183 EA94
Abbey Manufacturing Est., Wem. 138 CM67
Abbey Ms. E17 123 EA57
Leamington Ave.
Abbey Mill End, St.Alb. 42 CC21
Abbey Mill La., St.Alb. 42 CC21
Abbey Mills, St.Alb. 42 CC21
Abbey Orchard St. SW1 277 M6
Abbey Orchard St. SW1 161 DK76
Abbey Par. W5 138 CM69
Hanger La.
Abbey Pk., Beck. 183 EA94
Abbey Pk. La., Slou. 111 AL61
Abbey Pl., Dart. 188 FK85
Priory Rd.
Abbey Rd. E15 143 ED68
Abbey Rd. NW6 140 DB66
Abbey Rd. NW8 140 DB67
Abbey Rd. NW10 138 CP68
Abbey Rd. SE2 166 EX77
Abbey Rd. SW19 180 DC94
Abbey Rd., Bark. 145 EP66
Abbey Rd., Belv. 166 EX77
Abbey Rd., Bexh. 166 EY84
Abbey Rd., Cher. 194 BH101
Abbey Rd., Croy. 201 DP104
Abbey Rd., Enf. 82 DS43
Abbey Rd., Grav. 191 GL88
Abbey Rd., Green. 189 FW85
Abbey Rd., Ilf. 125 ER57
Abbey Rd., Shep. 194 BN102
Abbey Rd., S.Croy. 221 DX110
Abbey Rd., Vir.W. 192 AX99
Abbey Rd., Wal.Cr. 67 DY34
Abbey Rd., Wok. 226 AW117
Abbey Rd. Est. NW8 140 DB67
Abbey St. E13 144 EG70
Abbey St. SE1 279 N6
Abbey St. SE1 162 DT76
Abbey Ter. SE2 166 EW77
Abbey Vw. NW7 97 CT48
Abbey Vw., Wal.Abb. 67 EB33
Abbey Vw., Wat. 76 BX36
Abbey Vw. Rd., St.Alb. 42 CC20
Abbey Wk., W.Mol. 196 CB97
Abbey Way SE2 166 EX75
Wolvercote Rd.
Abbey Wf. Ind. Est., Bark. 145 ER68
Abbey Wd. La., Rain. 148 FK68
Abbey Wd. Rd. SE2 166 EV77
Abbeydale Clo., Harl. 52 EW16
Abbeydale Rd., Wem. 138 CN67
Abbeyfield Est. SE16 162 DW77
Abbeyfield Rd.
Abbeyfield Rd. SE16 162 DW77
Abbeyfields Clo. NW10 138 CN69
Abbeyhill Rd., Sid. 186 EW89
Abbot Clo., Stai. 174 BK94
Abbot Clo., W.Byf. 212 BK110
Abbot Rd., Guil. 258 AX136
Abbot St. E8 142 DT65
Abbots Ave., St.Alb. 43 CE23
Abbots Ave. W., St.Alb. 43 CD23
Abbots Clo. N1 142 DQ65
Alwyne Rd.
Abbots Clo., Brwd. 109 GA46
Abbots Clo., Guil. 258 AS137
Abbots Clo., Orp. 205 EQ102
Abbots Clo., Rain. 148 FJ68
Abbots Clo., Ruis. 116 BX62
Abbots Clo., Uxb. 134 BK71
Abbots Cres., Enf. 81 DP40
Abbots Dr., Har. 116 CA61
Abbots Dr., Vir.W. 192 AW98
Abbots Fld., Grav. 191 GJ93
Ruffets Wd.
Abbots Gdns. N2 120 DD56
Abbots Gdns. W8 160 DB76
St. Mary's Pl.
Abbots Grn., Croy. 221 DX107
Abbots La. SE1 279 N3
Abbots La., Ken. 236 DQ116
Abbots Manor Est. SW1 277 H10
Abbots Pk. SW2 181 DN88
Abbots Pk., St.Alb. 43 CF22
Abbot's Pl. NW6 140 DB67
Abbots Ri., Kings L. 58 BM26
Abbots Ri., Red. 250 DG132
Abbots Ri., Ware 33 ED11
Abbot's Rd. E6 144 EK67
Abbots Rd., Abb.L. 59 BQ31
Abbots Rd., Edg. 96 CQ52
Abbots Ter. N8 121 DL58
Abbots Tilt, Walt. 196 BY104
Abbots Vw., Kings L. 58 BM27
Abbots Wk. W8 160 DB76
St. Mary's Pl.
Abbots Wk., Cat. 236 DU122
Tillingdown Hill
Abbots Way, Beck. 203 DY99
Abbots Way, Guil. 243 BD133
Abbotsbury Clo. E15 143 EC68
Abbotsbury Clo. W14 159 CZ75
Abbotsbury Rd.
Abbotsbury Gdns., Pnr. 116 BW58
Abbotsbury Ms. SE15 162 DW83
Abbotsbury Rd. W14 159 CY75
Abbotsbury Rd., Brom. 204 EF103
Abbotsbury Rd., Mord. 200 DB99
Abbotsford Ave. N15 122 DQ56
Abbotsford Clo., Wok. 227 BA117
Onslow Cres.
Abbotsford Gdns., Wdf.Grn. 102 EG52
Abbotsford Lo., Nthwd. 93 BS50
Abbotsford Rd., Ilf. 126 EU61
Abbotshade Rd. SE16 143 DX74
Abbotshall Ave. N14 99 DJ48
Abbotshall Rd. SE6 183 ED88
Abbotsleigh Clo., Sutt. 218 DB108
Abbotsleigh Rd. SW16 181 DJ91
Abbotsmede Clo., Twick. 177 CF89
Abbotstone Rd. SW15 159 CW83
Abbotsweld, Harl. 51 ER18
Abbotswell Rd. SE4 183 DZ85
Abbotswood, Guil. 243 AZ132
Abbotswood Clo., Belv. 166 EY76
Coptefield Dr.
Abbotswood Clo., Guil. 243 AZ131
Abbotswood Dr., Wey. 213 BR110
Abbotswood Gdns., Ilf. 125 EM55
Abbotswood Rd. SE22 162 DS84
Abbotswood Rd. SW16 181 DK90
Abbotswood Way, Hayes 135 BV74
Abbott Ave. SW20 199 CX95
Abbott Clo., Hmptn. 176 BY93
Abbott Clo., Nthlt. 136 BZ65
Abbott Rd. E14 143 EC72
Abbotts Clo. SE28 146 EW73
Abbotts Clo., Rom. 127 FB55
Abbotts Clo., Swan. 207 FG98
Abbotts Cres. E4 101 ED49
Abbotts Dr., Wal.Abb. 68 EG33
Abbotts Dr., Wem. 117 CH61
Abbotts Pk. Rd. E10 123 EC59
Abbotts Pl., Chesh. 54 AQ28
Abbotts Rd., Barn. 80 DB42
Abbotts Rd., Mitch. 201 DJ98
Abbotts Rd., Sthl. 136 BY74
Abbotts Rd., Sutt. 217 CY105
Abbotts Vale, Chesh. 54 AQ28
Abbotts Wk., Bexh. 166 EX80
Abbotts Wk., Wind. 151 AL82
Abbotts Way, Slou. 131 AK74
Abbotts Way, Ware 33 ED11
Abbs Cross Gdns., Horn. 128 FJ60
Abbs Cross La., Horn. 128 FJ63
Abchurch La. EC4 275 L10
Abchurch La. EC4 142 DR73
Abchurch Yd. EC4 275 K10
Abdale Rd. W12 139 CV74
Abel Clo., Hem.H. 40 BN20
Abenberg Way, Brwd. 109 GB47
Abenglen Ind. Est., Hayes 155 BR75
Aberavon Rd. E3 143 DY69
Abercairn Rd. SW16 181 DJ94
Aberconway Rd., Mord. 200 DB97
Abercorn Clo. NW7 97 CY52
Abercorn Clo. NW8 140 DC69
Abercorn Clo., S.Croy. 221 DX112
Abercorn Cres., Har. 116 CB61
Abercorn Gdns., Har. 117 CK59
Abercorn Gdns., Rom. 126 EV58
Abercorn Gro., Ruis. 115 BR56
Abercorn Pl. NW8 140 DC69
Abercorn Rd. NW7 97 CY52
Abercorn Rd., Stan. 95 CJ52
Abercorn Way SE1 162 DU78
Abercorn Way, Wok. 226 AU118
Abercrombie Dr., Enf. 82 DU39
Abercrombie St. SW11 160 DE82
Abercrombie Way, Harl. 51 EQ17
Aberdale Gdns., Pot.B. 63 CY32
Aberdare Clo., W.Wick. 203 EC103
Aberdare Gdns. NW6 140 DB66
Aberdare Gdns. NW7 97 CX52
Aberdare Rd., Enf. 82 DW42
Aberdeen Ave., Slou. 131 AN73
Aberdeen La. N5 122 DQ64
Aberdeen Par. N18 100 DV50
Angel Rd.
Aberdeen Pk. N5 122 DQ64
Aberdeen Pk. Ms. N5 122 DQ63
Aberdeen Pl. NW8 140 DD70
Aberdeen Rd. N5 122 DQ63
Aberdeen Rd. N18 100 DV50
Aberdeen Rd. NW10 119 CT64
Aberdeen Rd., Croy. 220 DQ105
Aberdeen Rd., Har. 95 CF54
Aberdeen Sq. E14 143 DZ74
Westferry Circ.
Aberdeen Ter. SE3 163 ED82
Aberdour Rd., Ilf. 126 EV62
Aberdour St. SE1 279 M8
Aberdour St. SE1 162 DS77
Aberfeldy St. E14 143 EC72
Aberford Gdns. SE18 164 EL81
Aberford Rd., Borwd. 78 CN40
Aberfoyle Rd. SW16 181 DK93
Abergeldie Rd. SE12 184 EH86
Abernethy Rd. SE13 164 EE84
Abersham Rd. E8 122 DT64
Abery St. SE18 165 ES77
Abingdon Clo. NW1 141 DK65
Camden Sq.
Abingdon Clo. SE1 162 DT77
Bushwood Dr.
Abingdon Clo. SW19 180 DC93
Abingdon Clo., Uxb. 134 BM67
Abingdon Clo., Wok. 226 AV118
Abingdon Pl., Pot.B. 64 DB32
Abingdon Rd. N3 98 DC54
Abingdon Rd. SW16 201 DL96
Abingdon Rd. W8 160 DA76
Abingdon St. SW1 277 P6
Abingdon St. SW1 161 DL76
Abingdon Vill. W8 160 DA76
Abingdon Way, Orp. 224 EV105
Abinger Ave., Sutt. 217 CW109
Abinger Clo., Bark. 126 EU63
Abinger Clo., Brom. 204 EL97
Abinger Clo., Dor. 263 CJ140
Abinger Clo., Wall. 219 DL106
Garden Clo.
Abinger Common Rd., Dor. 262 BY144
Abinger Dr., Red. 266 DE136
Abinger Gdns., Islw. 157 CE83
Sussex Ave.
Abinger Gro. SE8 163 DZ79
Abinger La., Dor. 261 BV140
Abinger Ms. W9 140 DA70
Warlock Rd.
Abinger Rd. W4 158 CS76
Abinger Way, Guil. 243 BB129
Ablett St. SE16 162 DW78
Abney Gdns. N16 122 DT61
Stoke Newington High St.
Aboyne Dr. SW20 199 CU96
Aboyne Est. SW17 180 DD90
Aboyne Rd. NW10 118 CR62
Aboyne Rd. SW17 180 DD90
Abridge Clo., Wal.Cr. 83 DX35
Abridge Gdns., Rom. 104 FA51
Abridge Pk. (Abridge), Rom. 86 EU42
Abridge Rd., Chig. 85 ER44
Abridge Rd., Epp. 85 ES36
Abridge Rd. (Abridge), Rom. 86 EU39
Abridge Way, Bark. 146 EV68
Abyssinia Clo. SW11 160 DE84
Cairns Rd.
Acacia Ave. N17 100 DR52
Acacia Ave., Brent. 157 CH80
Acacia Ave., Hayes 135 BT72
Acacia Ave., Horn. 127 FF61
Acacia Ave., Mitch. 201 DH96
Acacia Ave., Ruis. 115 BU60
Acacia Ave., Shep. 194 BN99
Acacia Ave., Stai. 152 AY84
Acacia Ave., Wem. 118 CL64
Acacia Ave., West Dr. 134 BM73
Acacia Ave., Wok. 226 AX120
Acacia Clo. SE20 202 DU96
Selby Rd.
Acacia Clo., Add. 211 BF110
Acacia Clo., Orp. 205 ER99
Acacia Clo., Stan. 95 CE51
Acacia Clo., Wal.Cr. 66 DS27
Acacia Ct., Berk. 38 AV20
Acacia Dr., Add. 211 BF110
Acacia Dr., Bans. 217 CX114
Acacia Dr., Sutt. 199 CZ102
Acacia Dr., Upmin. 128 FN62
Acacia Gdns. NW8 140 DD68
Acacia Rd.
Acacia Gdns., Upmin. 129 FT59
Acacia Gdns., W.Wick. 203 EC103
Acacia Gro. SE21 182 DR89
Acacia Gro., N.Mal. 198 CS97
Acacia Ms., West Dr. 154 BK79
Acacia Pl. NW8 140 DD68
Acacia Rd. E11 124 EE61
Acacia Rd. E17 123 DY58
Acacia Rd. N22 99 DN53
Acacia Rd. NW8 140 DD68
Acacia Rd. SW16 201 DL95
Acacia Rd. W3 138 CQ73
Acacia Rd., Beck. 203 DZ97
Acacia Rd., Dart. 188 FK88
Acacia Rd., Enf. 82 DR39
Acacia Rd., Green. 189 FS86
Acacia Rd., Guil. 242 AX134
Acacia Rd., Hmptn. 176 CA93
Acacia Rd., Mitch. 200 DG96
Acacia Rd., Stai. 174 BH92
Acacia St., Hat. 45 CU21
Acacia Wk., Swan. 207 FD96
Walnut Way
Acacia Way, Sid. 185 ET88
Academy Gdns., Croy. 202 DT102
Academy Gdns., Nthlt. 136 BX68
Academy Pl. SE18 165 EM81
Academy Rd. SE18 165 EM81
Acanthus Dr. SE1 162 DU78
Acanthus Rd. SW11 160 DG83
Accommodation La., West Dr. 154 BG81
Accommodation Rd. NW11 119 CZ59
Accommodation Rd., Cher. 192 AX104
Acer Ave., Hayes 136 BY71
Acer Ave., Rain. 148 FK69
Acer Rd., West. 238 EK116
Acers, St.Alb. 60 CC28
Acfold Rd. SW6 160 DB81
Achilles Clo. SE1 162 DU78
Achilles Clo., Hem.H. 40 BM18
Achilles Pl., Wok. 226 AW117
Achilles Rd. NW6 120 DA64
Achilles St. SE14 163 DY80
Achilles Way W1 276 G3
Acklam Rd. W10 139 CZ71
St. Ervans Rd.
Acklington Dr. NW9 96 CS53
Ackmar Rd. SW6 160 DA81
Ackroyd Dr. E3 143 DZ71
Ackroyd Rd. SE23 183 DX87
Ackworth Clo. N9 100 DW45
Turin Rd.
Acland Clo. SE18 165 ER80
Clothworkers Rd.
Acland Cres. SE5 162 DR84
Acland Rd. NW2 139 CV65
Acme Rd., Wat. 75 BU38
Acol Cres., Ruis. 115 BV64
Acol Rd. NW6 140 DA66
Aconbury Rd., Dag. 146 EV67
Acorn Clo. E4 101 EB50
The Lawns
Acorn Clo., Chis. 185 EQ92
Acorn Clo., Enf. 81 DP39
Acorn Clo., Horl. 269 DJ147
Acorn Clo., Stan. 95 CH52
Acorn Ct., Ilf. 125 ES58
Acorn Gdns. SE19 202 DT95
Acorn Gdns. W3 138 CR71
Acorn Gro., Hayes 155 BT80
Acorn Gro., Ruis. 115 BT63
Acorn Gro., Tad. 233 CY124
Warren Lo. Dr.
Acorn Gro., Wok. 226 AY121
Old Sch. Pl.
Acorn Ind. Pk., Dart. 187 FG85
Acorn La. (Cuffley), Pot.B. 65 DL29
Acorn Par. SE15 162 DV80
Carlton Gro.
Acorn Pl., Wat. 75 BU37
Acorn Rd., Dart. 187 FF85
Acorn Rd., Hem.H. 40 BN21
Acorn St., Ware 34 EK08
Acorn Wk. SE16 143 DY74
Acorn Way SE23 183 DX90
Acorn Way, Orp. 223 EP105
Acorns, The, Chig. 103 ES49
Acorns, The, Horl. 269 DP148
Acorns Clo., Hmptn. 176 CB93
Acorns Way, Esher 214 CC106
Acre La. SW2 161 DL84
Acre La., Cars. 218 DG105
Acre La., Wall. 218 DG105
Acre Pas., Wind. 151 AR81
Madeira Wk.
Acre Path, Nthlt. 136 BY65
Arnold Rd.
Acre Rd. SW19 180 DD93
Acre Rd., Dag. 147 FB66
Acre Rd., Kings.T. 198 CL95
Acre Vw., Horn. 128 FL56
Acre Way, Nthwd. 93 BT53
Acre Wd., Hem.H. 40 BL20
Acrefield Rd., Ger.Cr. 112 AX55
Acres End, Amer. 55 AS39
Acres Gdns., Tad. 233 CX119
Acrewood Way, St.Alb. 44 CM20
Acris St. SW18 180 DC85
Acton Clo. N9 100 DU47
Acton Clo. (Cheshunt), Wal.Cr. 67 DY31
Acton La. NW10 138 CQ69
Acton La. W3 158 CQ75
Acton La. W4 158 CQ77
Acton Ms. E8 142 DT67
Acton Pk. Ind. Est. W3 158 CR75
Acton St. WC1 274 B3
Acton St. WC1 141 DM69
Acuba Rd. SW18 180 DB88
Acworth Clo. N9 100 DW45
Turin Rd.
Ada Gdns. E14 143 ED72
Ada Gdns. E15 144 EF67
Ada Pl. E2 142 DU67
Ada Rd. SE5 162 DS80
Ada Rd., Wem. 117 CJ62
Ada St. E8 142 DV67
Adair Clo. SE25 202 DV97
Adair Rd. W10 139 CY70
Adair Twr. W10 139 CY70
Appleford Rd.
Adam & Eve Ct. W1 273 L8
Adam & Eve Ms. W8 160 DA76
Adam Clo., Slou. 131 AN74
Telford Dr.
Adam Ct. SW7 160 DC77
Gloucester Rd.
Adam Pl. N16 122 DT61
Stoke Newington High St.
Adam Rd. E4 101 DZ51
Adam St. WC2 278 A1
Adam St. WC2 141 DL73
Adam Wk. SW6 159 CW80
Adams Clo. N3 98 DA52
Falkland Ave.
Adams Clo. NW9 118 CP61
Adams Clo., Surb. 198 CM100
Adams Ct. EC2 275 L8
Adams Gdns. Est. SE16 162 DW75
St. Marychurch St.
Adams Pl. E14 143 EB74
North Colonnade
Adams Pl. N7 121 DM64
George's Rd.
Adams Rd. N17 100 DR54
Adams Rd., Beck. 203 DY99
Adams Row W1 276 G1
Adams Row W1 140 DG73
Adams Sq., Bexh. 166 EY83
Regency Way
Adams Way, Croy. 202 DT100
Adamsfield, Wal.Cr. 66 DT26
Adamson Rd. E16 144 EG72
Adamson Rd. NW3 140 DD66
Adamsrill Clo., Enf. 82 DR43
Adamsrill Rd. SE26 183 DY91
Adare Wk. SW16 181 DM90
Adastral Est. NW9 96 CS53
Adcock Wk., Orp. 223 ET105
Borkwood Pk.
Adderley Gdns. SE9 185 EN91
Adderley Gro. SW11 180 DG85
Culmstock Rd.
Adderley Rd., Har. 95 CF53
Adderley St. E14 143 EC72
Addington Border, Croy. 221 DY110
Addington Clo., Wind. 151 AN83
Addington Ct. SW14 158 CR83
Addington Dr. N12 98 DC51
Addington Gro. SE26 183 DY91
Addington Rd. E3 143 EA69
Addington Rd. E16 144 EE70
Addington Rd. N4 121 DN58
Addington Rd., Croy. 201 DN102
Addington Rd., S.Croy. 220 DU112
Addington Rd., W.Wick. 221 EC105
Addington Sq. SE5 162 DR79
Addington St. SE1 278 C5
Addington Village Rd., Croy. 221 DZ107
Addis Clo., Enf. 83 DX39
Addiscombe Ave., Croy. 202 DU101
Addiscombe Clo., Har. 117 CJ57
Addiscombe Ct. Rd., Croy. 202 DS102
Addiscombe Gro., Croy. 202 DS103
Addiscombe Rd., Croy. 202 DS103
Addiscombe Rd., Wat. 75 BV42
Addison Ave. N14 81 DH44
Addison Ave. W11 139 CY74
Addison Ave., Houns. 156 CC81
Addison Bri. Pl. W14 159 CZ77
Addison Clo., Cat. 236 DR122
Addison Clo., Nthwd. 93 BU53
Addison Clo., Orp. 205 EQ100
Addison Cres. W14 159 CY76
Addison Dr. SE12 184 EH85
Eltham Rd.
Addison Gdns. W14 159 CX76
Addison Gdns., Grays 170 GC77
Palmers Dr.
Addison Gdns., Surb. 198 CM98
Addison Gro. W4 158 CS76
Addison Pl. W11 139 CY74
Addison Pl., Sthl. 136 CA73
Longford Ave.
Addison Rd. E11 124 EG58
Addison Rd. E17 123 EB57
Addison Rd. SE25 202 DU98
Addison Rd. W14 159 CY76
Addison Rd., Brom. 204 EJ99
Addison Rd., Cat. 236 DR121
Addison Rd., Chesh. 54 AQ29
Addison Rd., Enf. 82 DW39
Addison Rd., Guil. 258 AY135
Addison Rd., Ilf. 103 EQ53
Addison Rd., Tedd. 177 CH93
Addison Rd., Wok. 227 AZ117
Chertsey Rd.
Addison Way NW11 119 CZ56
Addison Way, Hayes 135 BU72
Addison Way, Nthwd. 93 BT53
Addison's Clo., Croy. 203 DZ103
Addle Hill EC4 274 G9
Addle St. EC2 275 J7
Addlestone Moor, Add. 194 BJ103
Addlestone Pk., Add. 212 BH106
Addlestone Rd., Add. 212 BL105
Adecroft Way, W.Mol. 196 CC97
Adela Ave., N.Mal. 199 CV99
Adela St. W10 139 CY70
Kensal Rd.
Adelaide Ave. SE4 163 DZ84
Adelaide Clo., Enf. 82 DS38
Adelaide Clo., Slou. 151 AN75
Amerden Way
Adelaide Clo., Stan. 95 CG49
Adelaide Cotts. W7 157 CF75
Adelaide Gdns., Rom. 126 EY57
Adelaide Gro. W12 139 CU74
Adelaide Pl., Wey. 213 BR105
Adelaide Rd. E10 123 EC62
Adelaide Rd. NW3 140 DD66
Adelaide Rd. SW18 180 DA85
Putney Bri. Rd.
Adelaide Rd. W13 137 CG74
Adelaide Rd., Ashf. 174 BK92
Adelaide Rd., Chis. 185 EP92
Adelaide Rd., Houns. 156 BY81
Adelaide Rd., Ilf. 125 EP61
Adelaide Rd., Rich. 158 CM84
Adelaide Rd., Sthl. 156 BY77
Adelaide Rd., Surb. 198 CL99
Adelaide Rd., Tedd. 177 CF93
Adelaide Rd., Til. 171 GF81
Adelaide Rd., Walt. 195 BU104
Adelaide Sq., Wind. 151 AR82
Adelaide St. WC2 277 P1
Adelaide St., St.Alb. 43 CD19
Adelaide Ter., Brent. 157 CK78
Adelaide Wk. SW9 161 DN84
Sussex Wk.
Adelina Gro. E1 142 DW71
Adelina Ms. SW12 181 DK88
King's Ave.
Adeline Pl. WC1 273 N7
Adeline Pl. WC1 141 DK71
Adelphi Cres., Hayes 135 BT69
Adelphi Cres., Horn. 127 FG61
Adelphi Gdns., Slou. 152 AS75
Adelphi Rd., Epsom 216 CR113
Adelphi Ter. WC2 278 A1
Adelphi Ter. WC2 141 DL73
Adelphi Way, Hayes 135 BT69
Aden Gro. N16 122 DR63
Aden Rd., Enf. 83 DY42
Aden Rd., Ilf. 125 EP59
Aden Ter. N16 122 DR63
Adeney Clo. W6 159 CX79
Adenmore Rd. SE6 183 EA87
Adeyfield Gdns., Hem.H. 40 BM19
Adeyfield Rd., Hem.H. 40 BK19
Adhern Ct., St.Alb. 43 CJ22
Adie Rd. W6 159 CW76
Adine Rd. E13 144 EH70
Adler St. E1 142 DU72
Adlers La., Dor. 247 CG131
Adley St. E5 123 DY63
Adlington Clo. N18 100 DS50
Admaston Rd. SE18 165 EQ79
Admiral Clo., Orp. 206 EX98
Admiral Pl. SE16 143 DY74
Admiral Seymour Rd. SE9 165 EM84
Admiral Sq. SW10 160 DC81
Admiral St. SE8 163 EA81
Admiral St., Hert. 32 DU09
Admiral Way, Berk. 38 AT17
Tortoiseshell Way
Admirals Clo. E18 124 EH56
Admirals Clo., St.Alb. 44 CS23
Admirals Ct., Guil. 243 BB133
Admiral's Rd., Lthd. 247 CD126
Admirals Wk. NW3 120 DC62
Admiral's Wk., Dor. 246 CB130
Admirals Wk., Green. 189 FV85
Admirals Wk., Hodd. 49 EA19
Admirals Wk., St.Alb. 43 CG23
Admiral's Wk., The, Couls. 235 DM120
Goodenough Way
Admirals Way E14 163 EA75
Admiralty Clo. SE8 163 EA80
Reginald Sq.
Admiralty Rd., Tedd. 177 CF93
Adnams Wk., Rain. 147 FF65
Lovell Wk.
Adolf St. SE6 183 EB91
Adolphus Rd. N4 121 DP61
Adolphus St. SE8 163 DZ80
Adomar Rd., Dag. 126 EX62
Adpar St. W2 140 DD71
Adrian Ave. NW2 119 CV60
North Circular Rd.
Adrian Clo., Uxb. 92 BK53
Adrian Ms. SW10 160 DB79
Adrian Rd., Abb.L. 59 BS31
Adrienne Ave., Sthl. 136 BZ69
Adstock Ms., Ger.Cr. 90 AX53
Church La.
Adstock Way, Grays 170 FZ77
Advance Rd. SE27 182 DQ91
Advent Way N18 101 DX50
Eley Rd.
Advice Ave., Grays 170 GA75
Adys Rd. SE15 162 DT83
Aerodrome Rd. NW4 119 CU55
Aerodrome Rd. NW9 119 CT55
Aerodrome Way, Houns. 156 BW79

Alexander Evans Ms. SE23 183 DX88
Sunderland Rd.
Alexander Godley Clo., Ash. 232 CM119
Alexander La., Brwd. 109 GB44
Alexander Ms. W2 140 DB72
Alexander St.
Alexander Pl. SW7 276 B8
Alexander Pl. SW7 160 DE77
Alexander Rd. N19 121 DL62
Alexander Rd., Bexh. 166 EX82
Alexander Rd., Chis. 185 EP92
Alexander Rd., Couls. 235 DH115
Alexander Rd., Egh. 173 BC92
Alexander Rd., Green. 189 FW85
Alexander Rd., Hert. 31 DN09
Alexander Rd., Reig. 266 DA137
Alexander Rd., St.Alb. 61 CJ25
Alexander Sq. SW3 276 B8
Alexander Sq. SW3 160 DE77
Alexander St. W2 140 DA72
Alexander St., Chesh. 54 AQ30
Alexanders Wk., Cat. 252 DT126
Alexandra Ave. N22 99 DK53
Alexandra Ave. SW11 160 DG81
Alexandra Ave. W4 158 CR80
Alexandra Ave., Har. 116 BZ60
Alexandra Ave., Sthl. 136 BZ73
Alexandra Ave., Sutt. 200 DA104
Alexandra Ave., Warl. 237 DZ117
Alexandra Clo., Ashf. 175 BR94
Alexandra Rd.
Alexandra Clo., Grays 171 GH75
Alexandra Clo., Har. 116 CA62
Alexandra Ave.
Alexandra Clo., Stai. 174 BK93
Alexandra Clo., Swan. 207 FE96
Alexandra Clo., Walt. 195 BU103
Alexandra Cotts. SE14 163 DZ81
Alexandra Ct. N14 81 DJ43
Alexandra Ct., Ashf. 175 BR93
Alexandra Rd.
Alexandra Ct., Wem. 118 CM63
Alexandra Cres., Brom. 184 EF93
Alexandra Dr. SE19 182 DS92
Alexandra Dr., Surb. 198 CN101
Alexandra Est. NW8 140 DB67
Alexandra Gdns. N10 121 DH56
Alexandra Gdns. W4 158 CS80
Alexandra Gdns., Cars. 218 DG109
Alexandra Gdns., Houns. 156 CB82
Alexandra Gro. N4 121 DP60
Alexandra Gro. N12 98 DB50
Alexandra Ms. N2 120 DF55
Fortis Grn.
Alexandra Ms. SW19 180 DA93
Alexandra Rd.
Alexandra Palace Way N22 121 DJ56
Alexandra Pk. Rd. N10 99 DH54
Alexandra Pk. Rd. N22 99 DJ53
Alexandra Pl. NW8 140 DC67
Alexandra Pl. SE25 202 DR99
Alexandra Pl., Croy. 202 DS102
Alexandra Rd.
Alexandra Pl., Guil. 259 AZ136
Alexandra Rd. E6 145 EN69
Alexandra Rd. E10 123 EC62
Alexandra Rd. E17 123 DZ58
Alexandra Rd. E18 124 EH55
Alexandra Rd. N8 121 DN55
Alexandra Rd. N9 100 DV45
Alexandra Rd. N10 99 DH53
Alexandra Rd. N15 122 DR57
Alexandra Rd. NW4 119 CX56
Alexandra Rd. NW8 140 DC66
Alexandra Rd. SE26 183 DX93
Alexandra Rd. SW14 158 CR83
Alexandra Rd. SW19 179 CZ93
Alexandra Rd. W4 158 CR75
Alexandra Rd., Add. 212 BK105
Alexandra Rd., Ashf. 175 BR94
Alexandra Rd., Borwd. 78 CR38
Alexandra Rd., Brent. 157 CK79
Alexandra Rd., Brwd. 108 FW48
Alexandra Rd., Croy. 202 DS102
Alexandra Rd., Egh. 172 AW93
Alexandra Rd., Enf. 83 DX42
Alexandra Rd., Epsom 217 CT113
Alexandra Rd., Erith 167 FF79
Alexandra Rd., Grav. 191 GL87
Alexandra Rd., Hem.H. 40 BK19
Alexandra Rd., Houns. 156 CB82
Alexandra Rd., Kings L. 58 BN29
Alexandra Rd. (Chipperfield), Kings L. 58 BG30
Alexandra Rd., Kings.T. 178 CN94
Alexandra Rd., Mitch. 180 DE94
Alexandra Rd., Rain. 147 FF67
Alexandra Rd., Rich. 158 CM82
Alexandra Rd., Rick. 74 BG36
Alexandra Rd., Rom. 127 FF58
Alexandra Rd. (Chadwell Heath), Rom. 126 EX58
Alexandra Rd., St.Alb. 43 CE20
Alexandra Rd., Slou. 151 AR76
Alexandra Rd., T.Ditt. 197 CF99
Alexandra Rd., Til. 171 GF82
Alexandra Rd., Twick. 177 CJ86
Alexandra Rd., Uxb. 134 BK68
Alexandra Rd., Warl. 237 DY117
Alexandra Rd., Wat. 75 BU40
Alexandra Rd., West. 238 EH119
Alexandra Rd., Wind. 151 AR82
Alexandra Sq., Mord. 200 DA99
Alexandra St. E16 144 EG71
Alexandra St. SE14 163 DY80
Alexandra Ter., Guil. 258 AY135
Alexandra Wk. SE19 182 DS92
Alexandra Way, Wal.Cr. 67 DZ34
Alexandria Rd. W13 137 CG73
Alexis St. SE16 162 DU77
Alfan La., Dart. 187 FD92
Alfearn Rd. E5 122 DW63
Alford Clo., Guil. 243 BB131
Alford Grn., Croy. 221 ED107
Alford Pl. N1 275 J1
Alford Rd. SW8 161 DK81
Alford Rd., Erith 167 FC78
Alfoxton Ave. N15 121 DP56
Alfred Gdns., Sthl. 136 BY73
Alfred Ms. W1 273 M6
Alfred Ms. W1 141 DK71
Alfred Pl. WC1 273 M6
Alfred Pl. WC1 141 DK71
Alfred Pl., Grav. 191 GF88
Alfred Prior Ho. E12 125 EN63
Alfred Rd. E15 124 EF64
Alfred Rd. SE25 202 DU99
Alfred Rd. W2 140 DA71
Alfred Rd. W3 138 CQ74
Alfred Rd., Belv. 166 EZ78
Alfred Rd., Brwd. 108 FX47
Alfred Rd., Buck.H. 102 EK47
Alfred Rd., Dart. 188 FL91
Alfred Rd., Felt. 176 BW89
Alfred Rd., Grav. 191 GH89
Alfred Rd., Kings.T. 198 CL97
Alfred Rd., S.Ock. 148 FQ74
Alfred Rd., Sutt. 218 DC106
Alfred St. E3 143 DZ69
Alfred St. E16 144 EF73
Alfred St., Grays 170 GC79
Alfreda St. SW11 161 DH81
Alfred's Gdns., Bark. 145 ES68
Alfreds Way, Bark. 145 EQ69
Alfreds Way Ind. Est., Bark. 146 EU67
Alfreton Clo. SW19 179 CX90
Alfriston Ave., Croy. 201 DL101
Alfriston Ave., Har. 116 CA58
Alfriston Clo., Surb. 198 CM99
Alfriston Rd. SW11 180 DF85
Algar Clo., Islw. 157 CG83
Algar Rd.
Algar Clo., Stan. 95 CF50
Algar Rd., Islw. 157 CG83
Algarve Rd. SW18 180 DB88
Algernon Rd. NW4 119 CU58
Algernon Rd. NW6 140 DA67
Algernon Rd. SE13 163 EB83
Algers Clo., Loug. 84 EK43
Algers Mead, Loug. 84 EK43
Algers Rd., Loug. 84 EK43
Algiers Rd. SE13 163 EA84
Alibon Gdns., Dag. 126 FA64
Alibon Rd., Dag. 126 EZ64
Alice Gilliatt Ct. W14 159 CZ78
Alice La. E3 143 DZ67
Alice La., Slou. 130 AH70
Alice Ms., Tedd. 177 CF92
Luther Rd.
Alice Ruston Pl., Wok. 226 AW119
Alice St. SE1 279 M7
Alice St. SE1 162 DS76
Alice Thompson Clo. SE12 184 EJ89
Alice Walker Clo. SE24 161 DP84
Shakespeare Rd.
Alice Way, Houns. 156 CB84
Alicia Ave., Har. 117 CH56
Alicia Clo., Har. 117 CJ56
Alicia Gdns., Har. 117 CH56
Alie St. E1 142 DT72
Alington Cres. NW9 118 CQ60
Alington Gro., Wall. 219 DJ109
Alison Clo. E6 145 EN72
Alison Clo., Croy. 203 DX102
Shirley Oaks Rd.
Alison Clo., Wok. 226 AY115
Aliwal Rd. SW11 160 DE84
Alkerden La., Green. 189 FW86
Alkerden La., Swans. 189 FX86
Alkerden Rd. W4 158 CS78
Alkham Rd. N16 122 DT60
All Hallows Rd. N17 100 DS53
All Saints Clo. N9 100 DU47
All Saints Clo., Chig. 104 EV48
All Saints Clo., Swans. 190 FZ85
High St.
All Saints Cres., Wat. 60 BX33
All Saints Dr. SE3 164 EE82
All Saints Dr., S.Croy. 220 DT112
All Saints La., Rick. 74 BN44
All Saints Ms., Stan. 95 CE51
Uxbridge Rd.
All Saints Pas. SW18 180 DB85
Wandsworth High St.
All Saints Rd. SW19 180 DC94
All Saints Rd. W3 158 CQ76
All Saints Rd. W11 139 CZ72
All Saints Rd., Grav. 191 GF88
All Saints Rd., Sutt. 200 DB104
All Saints St. N1 141 DM68
All Saints Twr. E10 123 EB59
All Souls Ave. NW10 139 CV68
All Souls Pl. W1 273 J7
Allan Barclay Clo. N15 122 DT58
High Rd.
Allan Clo., N.Mal. 198 CR99
Allan Way W3 138 CQ71
Allandale, Hem.H. 40 BK19
Allandale, St.Alb. 42 CB23
Allandale Ave. N3 119 CY55
Allandale Cres., Pot.B. 63 CZ32
Allandale Pl., Orp. 206 EX104
Allandale Rd., Enf. 83 DX36
Allandale Rd., Horn. 127 FF59
Allard Clo., Orp. 206 EW101
Allard Clo. (Cheshunt), Wal.Cr. 66 DT27
Allard Cres. (Bushey), Wat. 94 CC46
Allard Gdns. SW4 181 DK85
Allard Way, Brox. 49 DY21
Allardyce St. SW4 161 DM84
Allbrook Clo., Tedd. 177 CE92
Allcot Clo., Felt. 175 BT88
Allcroft Rd. NW5 120 DG64
Alldicks Rd., Hem.H. 40 BM22
Allen Clo., Mitch. 201 DH95
Allen Clo., Rad. 62 CL32
Russet Dr.
Allen Clo., Sun. 195 BV95
Allen Ct., Dor. 263 CH136
High St.
Allen Ct., Grnf. 117 CF64
Allen Ct., Hat. 45 CV20
Drakes Way
Allen Edwards Dr. SW8 161 DL81
Allen Ho. Pk., Wok. 226 AW120
Allen Pl., Twick. 177 CG88
Church St.
Allen Rd. E3 143 DZ68
Allen Rd. N16 122 DS63
Allen Rd., Beck. 203 DX96
Allen Rd., Croy. 201 DM102
Allen Rd., Lthd. 246 CB126
Allen Rd., Rain. 148 FJ69
Allen Rd., Sun. 195 BV95
Allen St. W8 160 DA76
Allenby Ave., S.Croy. 220 DQ109
Allenby Clo., Grnf. 136 CA69
Allenby Cres., Grays 170 GB78
Allenby Dr., Horn. 128 FL60
Allenby Rd. SE23 183 DY90
Allenby Rd., Sthl. 136 CA69
Allenby Rd., West. 238 EL117
Allendale Ave., Sthl. 136 CA72
Allendale Clo. SE5 162 DR81
Daneville Rd.
Allendale Clo. SE26 183 DX92
Allendale Clo., Dart. 189 FR88
Princes Rd.
Allendale Rd., Grnf. 137 CH65
Allende Ave., Harl. 35 EQ12
Allens Rd., Enf. 82 DW43
Allensbury Pl. NW1 141 DK66
Allenswood Rd. SE9 164 EL83
Allerds Rd., Slou. 131 AM67
Allerford Ct., Har. 116 CB57
Allerford Rd. SE6 183 EB90
Allerton Clo., Borwd. 78 CM38
Allerton Rd. N16 122 DQ61
Allerton Rd., Borwd. 78 CL38
Allerton Wk. N7 121 DM61
Durham Rd.
Allestree Rd. SW6 159 CY80
Alleyn Cres. SE21 182 DR89
Alleyn Pk. SE21 182 DR89
Alleyn Pk., Sthl. 156 CA78
Alleyn Rd. SE21 182 DR90
Alleyndale Rd., Dag. 126 EW61
Allfarthing La. SW18 180 DB86
Allgood Clo., Mord. 199 CX100
Allgood St. E2 142 DT68
Allhallows La. EC4 279 K1
Allhallows Rd. E6 144 EL71
Allhusen Gdns., Slou. 112 AY63
Alderbourne La.
Alliance Clo., Wem. 117 CK63
Milford Gdns.
Alliance Rd. E13 144 EJ70
Alliance Rd. SE18 166 EU79
Alliance Rd. W3 138 CP70
Allied Ind. Est. W3 158 CS75
Allied Way W3 158 CS75
Larden Rd.
Allingham Clo. W7 137 CF73
Allingham Ct., Gdmg. 258 AT144
Summers Rd.
Allingham Rd., Reig. 266 DA137
Allingham St. N1 142 DQ68
Allington Ave. N17 100 DS51
Allington Clo. SW19 179 CX92
High St. Wimbledon
Allington Clo., Grav. 191 GM88
Farley Rd.
Allington Clo., Grnf. 136 CC66
Allington Ct. SW19 179 CX92
High St. Wimbledon
Allington Ct., Enf. 83 DX43
Allington Ct., Slou. 132 AT73
Myrtle Cres.
Allington Rd. NW4 119 CV57
Allington Rd. W10 139 CY68
Allington Rd., Har. 116 CC57
Allington Rd., Orp. 205 ER103
Allington St. SW1 277 J7
Allington St. SW1 161 DH76
Allison Clo. SE10 163 EC81
Dartmouth Hill
Allison Clo., Wal.Abb. 68 EG33
Allison Gro. SE21 182 DS88
Allison Rd. N8 121 DN57
Allison Rd. W3 138 CQ72
Allitsen Rd. NW8 272 B1
Allitsen Rd. NW8 140 DE68
Allmains Clo., Wal.Abb. 68 EH25
Allnutt Way SW4 181 DK85
Allnutts Rd., Epp. 70 EU33
Alloa Rd. SE8 163 DY78
Alloa Rd., Ilf. 126 EU61
Allonby Dr., Ruis. 115 BP59
Allonby Gdns., Wem. 117 CJ60
Allotment La., Sev. 257 FJ122
Alloway Clo., Wok. 226 AV118
Inglewood
Alloway Rd. E3 143 DY69
Allsop Pl. NW1 272 E5
Allsop Pl. NW1 140 DF70
Allum Clo., Borwd. 78 CL42
Allum Gro., Tad. 233 CV121
Preston La.
Allum La., Borwd. 77 CK43
Allum Way N20 98 DC46
Allwood Clo. SE26 183 DX91
Allwood Rd., Wal.Cr. 66 DT27
Allyn Clo., Stai. 173 BF93
Penton Rd.
Alma Ave. E4 101 EC52
Alma Ave., Horn. 128 FL63
Alma Clo., Wok. 226 AS118
Alma Cres., Sutt. 217 CY106
Alma Cut, St.Alb. 43 CE21
Alma Gro. SE1 162 DT77
Alma Pl. NW10 139 CV69
Harrow Rd.
Alma Pl. SE19 182 DT94
Alma Pl., Th.Hth. 201 DN99
Alma Rd. N10 99 DH52
Alma Rd. SW18 160 DC84
Alma Rd., Berk. 38 AS17
Alma Rd., Cars. 218 DE106
Alma Rd., Chesh. 54 AQ29
Alma Rd., Enf. 83 DY41
Alma Rd., Esher 197 CE102
Alma Rd., Orp. 206 EX103
Alma Rd., Reig. 250 DB133
Alma Rd., St.Alb. 43 CE21
Alma Rd., Sid. 186 EU90
Alma Rd., Sthl. 136 BY73
Alma Rd., Swans. 190 FZ85
Alma Rd., Wind. 151 AQ82
Alma Rd. (Eton Wick), Wind. 151 AM77
Alma Row, Har. 95 CD53
Alma Sq. NW8 140 DC69
Alma St. E15 143 ED65
Alma St. NW5 141 DH65
Alma Ter. SW18 180 DD87
Almack Rd. E5 122 DW63
Almeida St. N1 141 DP66
Almer Rd. SW20 179 CU94
Almeric Rd. SW11 160 DF84
Almington St. N4 121 DL60
Almners Rd., Cher. 193 BA102
Almond Ave. W5 158 CL76
Almond Ave., Cars. 200 DF103
Almond Ave., Uxb. 115 BP62
Almond Ave., West Dr. 154 BN76
Almond Ave., Wok. 226 AX121
Almond Clo. SE15 162 DU82
Almond Clo., Brom. 205 EN101
Almond Clo., Egh. 172 AV93
Almond Clo., Grays 171 GG76
Almond Clo., Guil. 242 AX130
Almond Clo., Hayes 135 BS73
Almond Clo., Ruis. 115 BT62
The Roundways
Almond Clo., Shep. 195 BQ96
Almond Clo., Wind. 151 AP82
Almond Dr., Swan. 207 FD96
Almond Gro., Brent. 157 CH80
Almond Rd. N17 100 DU52
Almond Rd. SE16 162 DV77
Almond Rd., Dart. 188 FQ87
Almond Rd., Epsom 216 CR111
Almond Rd., Slou. 130 AH68
Almond Wk., Hat. 45 CU21
Southdown Rd.
Almond Way, Borwd. 78 CP42
Almond Way, Brom. 205 EN101
Almond Way, Har. 94 CB54
Almond Way, Mitch. 201 DK99
Almonds, The, St.Alb. 43 CH24
Almonds Ave., Buck.H. 102 EG47
Almons Way, Slou. 132 AV71
Almorah Rd. N1 142 DR66
Almorah Rd., Houns. 156 BX81
Alms Heath, Wok. 229 BP121
Almshouse La., Chess. 215 CJ109
Almshouse La., Enf. 82 DV37
Almshouses, The, Dor. 263 CH135
Cotmandene
Alnwick Gro., Mord. 200 DB98
Bordesley Rd.
Alnwick Rd. E16 144 EJ72
Alnwick Rd. SE12 184 EH87
Alperton La., Grnf. 137 CK68
Alperton La., Wem. 137 CK68
Alperton St. W10 139 CY70
Alpha Clo. NW1 272 C3
Alpha Ct., Whyt. 236 DU118
Alpha Gro. E14 163 EA75
Alpha Pl. NW6 140 DA68
Alpha Pl. SW3 160 DE79
Alpha Rd. E4 101 EA48
Alpha Rd. N18 100 DU51
Alpha Rd. SE14 163 DZ81
Alpha Rd., Brwd. 109 GD44
Alpha Rd., Croy. 202 DS102
Alpha Rd., Enf. 83 DY42
Alpha Rd., Surb. 198 CM100
Alpha Rd., Tedd. 177 CD92
Alpha Rd., Uxb. 135 BP70
Alpha Rd., Wok. 227 BB116
Alpha Rd. (Chobham), Wok. 210 AT110
Alpha St. SE15 162 DU82
Alpha St. N., Slou. 152 AU75
Alpha St. S., Slou. 152 AT76
Alpha Way, Egh. 193 BC95
Alphabet Gdns., Cars. 200 DD100
Alphabet Sq. E3 143 EA71
Hawgood St.
Alphea Clo. SW19 180 DE94
Courtney Rd.
Alpine Ave., Surb. 198 CQ103
Alpine Clo., Croy. 202 DS104
Alpine Copse, Brom. 205 EN96
Alpine Rd. SE16 162 DW77
Alpine Rd., Red. 250 DG131
Alpine Rd., Walt. 195 BU101
Alpine Vw., Sutt. 218 DE106
Alpine Wk., Stan. 95 CE47
Alpine Way E6 145 EN71
Alresford Rd., Guil. 258 AU135
Alric Ave. NW10 138 CR66
Alric Ave., N.Mal. 198 CS97
Alroy Rd. N4 121 DN59
Alsace Rd. SE17 279 M10
Alsace Rd. SE17 162 DS78
Alscot Rd. SE1 162 DT77
Alscot Way SE1 279 P8
Alscot Way SE1 162 DT77
Alsford Wf., Berk. 38 AW18
Alsike Rd. SE2 166 EX76
Alsike Rd., Erith 166 EY76
Alsom Ave., Wor.Pk. 217 CT105
Alston Clo., Surb. 197 CH101
Alston Rd. N18 100 DV50
Alston Rd. SW17 180 DD91
Alston Rd., Barn. 79 CY41
Alston Rd., Hem.H. 40 BG21
Alt Gro. SW19 179 CZ94
St. George's Rd.
Altair Clo. N17 100 DT51
Altair Way, Nthwd. 93 BT50
Altash Way SE9 185 EM89
Altenburg Ave. W13 157 CH76
Altenburg Gdns. SW11 160 DF84
Alterton Clo., Wok. 226 AU117
Altham Gro., Harl. 35 ET12
Altham Rd., Pnr. 94 BY52
Althea St. SW6 160 DB82
Althorne Gdns. E18 124 EF56
Althorne Rd., Red. 266 DG136
Althorne Way, Dag. 126 FA61
Althorp Rd. SW17 180 DF88
Althorp Rd., St.Alb. 43 CE19
Althorpe Gro. SW11 160 DD81
Westbridge Rd.
Althorpe Ms. SW11 160 DD81
Westbridge Rd.
Althorpe Rd., Har. 116 CC57
Altmore Ave. E6 145 EM66
Alton Ave., Stan. 95 CF52
Alton Clo., Bex. 186 EY88
Alton Clo., Islw. 157 CF82
Alton Ct., Stai. 193 BE95
Alton Gdns., Beck. 183 EA94
Alton Gdns., Twick. 177 CD86
Alton Rd. N17 122 DR55
Alton Rd. SW15 179 CU88
Alton Rd., Croy. 201 DN104
Alton Rd., Rich. 158 CL84
Alton St. E14 143 EB71
Altona Rd., H.Wyc. 88 AD52
Altona Way, Slou. 131 AP72
Altwood Clo., Slou. 131 AL71
Burnham La.
Altyre Clo., Beck. 203 DZ99
Altyre Rd., Croy. 202 DR103
Altyre Way, Beck. 203 DZ100
Aluric Clo., Grays 171 GH77
Alva Way, Wat. 94 BX47
Alvanley Gdns. NW6 120 DB64
Alverstoke Rd., Rom. 106 FL52
Alverston Gdns. SE25 202 DS99
Alverstone Ave. SW19 180 DA89
Alverstone Ave., Barn. 98 DE45
Alverstone Gdns. SE9 185 EQ88
Alverstone Rd. E12 125 EN63
Alverstone Rd. NW2 139 CW66
Alverstone Rd., N.Mal. 199 CT98
Alverstone Rd., Wem. 118 CM60
Alverton, St.Alb. 42 CC17
Green La.
Alverton St. SE8 163 DZ78
Alveston Ave., Har. 117 CH55
Alvey Est. SE17 279 M9
Alvey St. SE17 279 M10
Alvey St. SE17 162 DS78
Alvia Gdns., Sutt. 218 DC105
Alvington Cres. E8 122 DT64
Alvista Ave., Maid. 130 AH72
Alway Ave., Epsom 216 CQ106
Alwen Gro., S.Ock. 149 FV71
Alwold Cres. SE12 184 EH86
Alwyn Ave. W4 158 CR78
Alwyn Clo., Borwd. 78 CM44
Alwyn Clo., Croy. 221 EB108
Alwyn Gdns. NW4 119 CU56
Alwyn Gdns. W3 138 CP72
Alwyne Ave., Brwd. 109 GA44
Alwyne Ct., Wok. 226 AY116
Alwyne La. N1 141 DP66
Alwyne Vill.
Alwyne Pl. N1 142 DQ65
Alwyne Rd. N1 142 DQ66
Alwyne Rd. SW19 179 CZ93
Alwyne Rd. W7 137 CE73
Alwyne Sq. N1 142 DQ65
Alwyne Vill. N1 141 DP66
Alwyns Clo., Cher. 194 BG100
Alwyns La.
Alwyns La., Cher. 193 BF100
Alyngton, Berk. 38 AS16
Alyth Gdns. NW11 120 DA58
Alzette Ho. E2 143 DX68
Mace St.
Amalgamated Dr., Brent. 157 CG79
Amanda Clo., Ilf. 103 ER51
Amanda Ct., Slou. 152 AX76
Amazon St. E1 142 DV72
Hessel St.
Ambassador Clo., Houns. 156 BY82
Ambassador Gdns. E6 145 EM71
Ambassador Sq. E14 163 EB77
Ambassador's Ct. SW1 277 L3
Amber Ave. E17 101 DY53
Amber Gro. NW2 119 CX60
Prayle Gro.
Amber St. E15 143 ED65
Salway Rd.
Ambercroft Way, Couls. 235 DP119
Amberden Ave. N3 120 DA55
Ambergate St. SE17 278 G10
Ambergate St. SE17 161 DP78
Amberley Clo., Orp. 223 ET106
Warnford Rd.
Amberley Clo., Pnr. 116 BZ55
Amberley Clo., Wok. 243 BF125
Amberley Ct., Maid. 130 AC69
Amberley Ct., Sid. 186 EW92
Amberley Dr., Add. 211 BF110
Amberley Gdns., Enf. 100 DS45
Amberley Gdns., Epsom 217 CT105
Amberley Gro. SE26 182 DV92
Amberley Gro., Croy. 202 DT101
Amberley Rd. E10 123 EA59
Amberley Rd. N13 99 DM47
Amberley Rd. SE2 166 EX79
Amberley Rd. W9 140 DA71
Amberley Rd., Buck.H. 102 EJ46
Amberley Rd., Enf. 100 DT45
Amberley Rd., Slou. 131 AL71
Amberley Way, Houns. 176 BW85
Amberley Way, Mord. 199 CZ101
Amberley Way, Rom. 127 FB56
Amberley Way, Uxb. 134 BL69
Amberry Ct., Harl. 35 ER14
Amberside Clo., Islw. 177 CD86
Amberwood Ri., N.Mal. 198 CS100
Amblecote, Cob. 214 BY112
Amblecote Clo. SE12 184 EH90
Amblecote Meadows SE12 184 EH90
Amblecote Rd. SE12 184 EH90
Ambler Rd. N4 121 DP62
Ambleside, Brom. 183 ED93
Ambleside, Epp. 70 EU31
Ambleside Ave. SW16 181 DK91
Ambleside Ave., Beck. 203 DY99
Ambleside Ave., Horn. 127 FH64
Ambleside Ave., Walt. 196 BW102
Ambleside Clo. E9 122 DW64
Churchill Wk.
Ambleside Clo. E10 123 EB59
Ambleside Clo., Red. 267 DH139
Ambleside Cres., Enf. 83 DX41
Ambleside Dr., Felt. 175 BT88
Ambleside Gdns., Ilf. 124 EL56
Ambleside Gdns., S.Croy. 221 DX109
Ambleside Gdns., Sutt. 218 DC107
Ambleside Gdns., Wem. 117 CK60
Ambleside Rd. NW10 139 CT66
Ambleside Rd., Bexh. 166 FA82
Ambleside Way, Egh. 173 BB94
Ambrey Way, Wall. 219 DK109
Ambrooke Rd., Belv. 166 FA76
Ambrosden Ave. SW1 277 L7
Ambrosden Ave. SW1 161 DJ76
Ambrose Ave. NW11 119 CY59
Ambrose Clo. E6 144 EL71
Lovage App.
Ambrose Clo., Dart. 167 FF84
Ambrose Clo., Orp. 205 ET104
Stapleton Rd.
Ambrose Ms. SW11 160 DF82
Abercrombie St.
Ambrose St. SE16 162 DV77
Ambrose Wk. E3 143 EA68
Malmesbury Rd.
Amelia St. SE17 279 H10
Amelia St. SE17 161 DP78

Ashcroft Ri., Couls. 235 DL116
Ashcroft Rd. E3 143 DY69
Ashcroft Rd., Chess. 198 CM104
Ashcroft Sq. W6 159 CW77
King St.
Ashdale, Lthd. 246 CC126
Ashdale Clo., Stai. 174 BL89
Ashdale Clo., Twick. 176 CC87
Ashdale Gro., Stan. 95 CF51
Ashdale Rd. SE12 184 EH88
Ashdale Way, Twick. 176 CC87
Ashdale Clo.
Ashdales, St.Alb. 43 CD24
Ashdene SE15 162 DV81
Carlton Gro.
Ashdene, Pnr. 116 BW55
Ashdene Clo., Ashf. 175 BQ94
Ashdon Clo., Brwd. 109 GC44
Poplar Dr.
Ashdon Clo., Wdf.Grn. 102 EH51
Ashdon Rd. NW10 139 CT67
Ashdon Rd. (Bushey), Wat. 76 BX41
Ashdown Clo., Beck. 203 EB96
Ashdown Clo., Bex. 187 FC87
Ashdown Clo., Reig. 266 DB138
Ashdown Cres. NW5 120 DG64
Queens Cres.
Ashdown Cres. (Cheshunt), Wal.Cr. 67 DY28
Ashdown Dr., Borwd. 78 CM40
Ashdown Est. E11 124 EE63
High Rd. Leytonstone
Ashdown Gdns., S.Croy. 236 DV115
Ashdown Rd., Enf. 82 DW41
Ashdown Rd., Epsom 217 CT113
Ashdown Rd., Kings.T. 198 CL96
Ashdown Rd., Reig. 266 DB138
Ashdown Rd., Uxb. 134 BN68
Ashdown Wk. E14 163 EA77
Charnwood Gdns.
Ashdown Wk., Rom. 105 FB54
Ashdown Way SW17 180 DG89
Ashdown Way, Amer. 55 AR36
Chestnut La.
Ashen E6 145 EN72
Downings
Ashen Dr., Dart. 187 FG86
Ashen Gro. SW19 180 DA90
Ashen Vale, S.Croy. 221 DX109
Ashenden Rd. E5 123 DY64
Ashenden Rd., Guil. 242 AT134
Ashenden Wk., Slou. 111 AR63
Ashendene Rd., Hert. 47 DL20
Asher Way E1 142 DU74
Asheridge Rd., Chesh. 54 AM28
Ashfield Ave., Felt. 175 BV88
Ashfield Ave. (Bushey), Wat. 76 CB44
Ashfield Clo., Beck. 183 EA94
Brackley Rd.
Ashfield Clo., Rich. 178 CL88
Ashfield La., Chis. 185 EQ93
Ashfield Par. N14 99 DK46
Ashfield Rd. N4 122 DQ58
Ashfield Rd. N14 99 DJ48
Ashfield Rd. W3 139 CT74
Ashfield Rd., Chesh. 54 AR29
Ashfield St. E1 142 DV71
Ashfields, Loug. 85 EM40
Ashfields, Wat. 75 BT35
Ashford Ave. N8 121 DL56
Ashford Ave., Ashf. 175 BP93
Ashford Ave., Brwd. 108 FV48
Ashford Ave., Hayes 136 BX72
Ashford Clo. E17 123 DZ58
Ashford Clo., Ashf. 174 BL91
Ashford Cres., Ashf. 174 BL90
Ashford Cres., Enf. 82 DW40
Ashford Gdns., Cob. 230 BX116
Ashford Grn., Wat. 94 BX50
Ashford Ind. Est., Ashf. 175 BQ91
Ashford La., Maid. 150 AG75
Ashford La., Wind. 150 AH75
Ashford Rd. E6 145 EN65
Ashford Rd. E18 102 EH54
Ashford Rd. NW2 119 CX63
Ashford Rd., Ashf. 175 BP94
Ashford Rd., Felt. 175 BR91
Ashford Rd., Iver 133 BC67
Ashford Rd., Stai. 194 BK95
Ashford St. N1 275 M2
Ashgrove Rd., Ashf. 175 BQ92
Ashgrove Rd., Brom. 183 ED93
Ashgrove Rd., Ilf. 125 ET60
Ashgrove Rd., Sev. 256 FG127
Ashingdon Clo. E4 101 EC48
Ashington Rd. SW6 159 CZ82
Ashlake Rd. SW16 181 DL91
Ashland Pl. W1 272 F6
Ashland Pl. W1 140 DG71
Ashlar Pl. SE18 165 EP77
Masons Hill
Ashlea Rd., Ger.Cr. 90 AY54
Ashleigh Ave., Egh. 173 BC94
Ashleigh Clo., Amer. 55 AS39
Ashleigh Clo., Horl. 268 DF148
Ashleigh Cotts., Dor. 263 CH144
Ashleigh Gdns., Sutt. 200 DB103
Ashleigh Gdns., Upmin. 129 FR62
Ashleigh Rd. SE20 202 DV97
Ashleigh Rd. SW14 158 CS83
Ashley Ave., Epsom 216 CR113
Ashley Ave., Ilf. 103 EP54
Ashley Ave., Mord. 200 DA99
Chalgrove Ave.
Ashley Cen., Epsom 216 CR113
Ashley Clo. NW4 97 CW54
Ashley Clo., Lthd. 246 BZ125
Ashley Clo., Pnr. 93 BV54
Ashley Clo., Sev. 257 FH124
Ashley Clo., Walt. 195 BS102
Ashley Clo., Welw.G.C. 29 CW07
Ashley Ct., Epsom 216 CR113
Ashley Ct., Hat. 45 CV17
Ashley Ct., Wok. 226 AT118
Ashley Cres. N22 99 DN54
Ashley Cres. SW11 160 DG83
Ashley Dr., Bans. 218 DA114
Ashley Dr., Borwd. 78 CQ43
Ashley Dr., H.Wyc. 88 AC45
Ashley Dr., Islw. 157 CE79
Ashley Dr., Twick. 176 CB88
Ashley Dr., Walt. 195 BU104
Ashley Gdns. N13 100 DQ49
Ashley Gdns. SW1 277 L7
Ashley Gdns., Guil. 259 AZ141
Ashley Gdns., Orp. 223 ES106
Ashley Gdns., Rich. 177 CK89
Ashley Gdns., Wem. 118 CL61
Ashley Grn. La., Chesh. 54 AR27
Ashley Grn. Rd., Chesh. 54 AR27
Ashley Gro., Loug. 84 EL41
Staples Rd.
Ashley La. NW4 97 CW54
Ashley La., Croy. 219 DP105
Ashley Pk. Ave., Walt. 195 BT103
Ashley Pk. Cres., Walt. 195 BT102
Ashley Pk. Rd., Walt. 195 BU103
Ashley Pl. SW1 277 K7
Ashley Pl. SW1 161 DJ76
Ashley Ri., Walt. 213 BT105
Ashley Rd. E4 101 EA50
Ashley Rd. E7 144 EJ66
Ashley Rd. N17 122 DU55
Ashley Rd. N19 121 DL60
Ashley Rd. SW19 180 DB93
Ashley Rd., Dor. 262 CC137
Ashley Rd., Enf. 82 DW40
Ashley Rd., Epsom 216 CR113
Ashley Rd., Hmptn. 196 CA95
Ashley Rd., Hert. 31 DN10
Ashley Rd., Rich. 158 CL83
Jocelyn Rd.
Ashley Rd., St.Alb. 43 CJ20
Ashley Rd., Sev. 257 FH124
Ashley Rd., T.Ditt. 197 CF100
Ashley Rd., Th.Hth. 201 DM98
Ashley Rd., Uxb. 134 BH68
Ashley Rd., Walt. 195 BU102
Ashley Rd., Wok. 226 AT118
Ashley Wk. NW7 97 CW52
Ashleys, Rick. 91 BF45
Ashlin Rd. E15 123 ED63
Ashling Rd., Croy. 202 DU102
Ashlone Rd. SW15 159 CW83
Ashlyn Clo. (Bushey), Wat. 76 BY41
Ashlyn Gro., Horn. 128 FK55
Ashlyns Ct., Berk. 38 AV20
Ashlyns La., Ong. 53 FF20
Ashlyns Pk., Cob. 214 BY113
Ashlyns Rd., Berk. 38 AV20
Ashlyns Rd., Epp. 69 ET30
Ashlyns Way, Chess. 215 CK107
Ashmead N14 81 DJ43
Ashmead Dr., Uxb. 114 BG61
Ashmead Gate, Brom. 204 EJ95
Ashmead La., Uxb. 114 BG61
Ashmead Rd. SE8 163 EA82
Ashmead Rd., Felt. 175 BU88
Ashmeads Ct., Rad. 61 CK33
Ashmere Ave., Beck. 203 ED96
Ashmere Clo., Sutt. 217 CW106
Ashmere Gro. SW2 161 DL84
Ashmill St. NW1 272 B6
Ashmill St. NW1 140 DE71
Ashmole Pl. SW8 161 DM79
Ashmole St. SW8 161 DM79
Ashmore Ct., Houns. 156 CA79
Wheatlands
Ashmore Gdns., Hem.H. 41 BP21
Ashmore Gro., Well. 165 ER83
Ashmore La., Kes. 222 EJ111
Ashmore Rd. W9 139 CZ68
Ashmount Rd. N15 122 DT57
Ashmount Rd. N19 121 DJ59
Ashmount Ter. W5 157 CK77
Murray Rd.
Ashmour Gdns., Rom. 105 FD54
Ashneal Gdns., Har. 117 CD62
Ashness Gdns., Grnf. 137 CH65
Ashness Rd. SW11 180 DF85
Ashridge Clo., Har. 117 CJ58
Ashridge Clo., Hem.H. 57 BA28
Ashridge Cres. SE18 165 EQ80
Ashridge Dr., St.Alb. 60 BY30
Ashridge Dr., Wat. 93 BV50
Ashridge Gdns. N13 99 DK50
Ashridge Gdns., Pnr. 116 BY56
Ashridge Ri., Berk. 38 AT18
Ashridge Rd., Chesh. 56 AW31
Ashridge Way, Mord. 199 CZ97
Ashridge Way, Sun. 175 BU93
Ashtead Gap, Lthd. 231 CG116
Kingston Rd.
Ashtead Rd. E5 122 DU59
Ashtead Wds. Rd., Ash. 231 CJ116
Ashton Clo., Sutt. 218 DA105
Ashton Clo., Walt. 213 BV107
Ashton Gdns., Houns. 156 BZ84
Ashton Gdns., Rom. 126 EY58
Ashton Rd. E15 123 ED64
Ashton Rd., Enf. 83 DY36
Ashton Rd., Rom. 106 FK52
Ashton Rd., Wok. 226 AT117
Ashton St. E14 143 EC73
Ashtree Ave., Mitch. 200 DD96
Ashtree Clo., Orp. 223 EP105
Broadwater Gdns.
Ashtree Ct., St.Alb. 43 CF20
Granville Rd.
Ashtree Way, Hem.H. 40 BG21
Ashurst Clo. SE20 202 DV95
Ashurst Clo., Dart. 167 FF83
Ashurst Clo., Ken. 236 DR115
Ashurst Clo., Nthwd. 93 BS52
Ashurst Dr., Ilf. 125 EP58
Ashurst Dr., Shep. 194 BL99
Ashurst Dr., Tad. 248 CP130
Ashurst Rd. N12 98 DE50
Ashurst Rd., Barn. 80 DF43
Ashurst Rd., Tad. 233 CV121
Ashurst Wk., Croy. 202 DV103
Ashvale Dr., Upmin. 129 FS61
Ashvale Gdns., Rom. 105 FD50
Ashvale Gdns., Upmin. 129 FS61
Ashvale Rd. SW17 180 DF92
Ashville Rd. E11 123 ED61
Ashwater Rd. SE12 184 EG88
Ashwell Clo. E6 144 EL72
Northumberland Rd.
Ashwell St., St.Alb. 43 CD19
Ashwells Way, Ch.St.G. 90 AW47
Ashwin St. E8 142 DT65
Ashwindham Ct., Wok. 226 AT118
Raglan Rd.
Ashwood, Warl. 236 DW120
Ashwood Ave., Rain. 147 FH69
Ashwood Ave., Uxb. 134 BN72
Ashwood Gdns., Croy. 221 EB107
Ashwood Gdns., Hayes 155 BT77
Cranford Dr.
Ashwood Pk., Lthd. 230 CC123
Ashwood Pk., Wok. 227 BA118
Ashwood Rd. E4 101 ED48
Ashwood Rd., Egh. 172 AV93
Ashwood Rd., Pot.B. 64 DB33
Ashwood Rd., Wok. 227 AZ118
Ashworth Clo. SE5 162 DR82
Denmark Hill
Ashworth Pl., Guil. 242 AT134
Ashworth Pl., Harl. 52 EX15
Ashworth Rd. W9 140 DB69
Aske St. N1 275 M2
Askern Clo., Bexh. 166 EX84
Askew Cres. W12 159 CT75
Askew Fm. La., Grays 170 FY79
Askew Rd. W12 139 CT74
Askew Rd., Nthwd. 93 BR47
Askham Ct. W12 139 CU74
Askham Rd. W12 139 CU74
Askill Dr. SW15 179 CY85
Keswick Rd.
Askwith Rd., Rain. 147 FD69
Asland Rd. E15 143 ED67
Aslett St. SW18 180 DB87
Asmar Clo., Couls. 235 DL115
Asmara Rd. NW2 119 CY64
Asmuns Hill NW11 120 DA57
Asmuns Pl. NW11 119 CZ57
Aspasia Clo., St.Alb. 43 CF21
Aspdin Rd., Grav. 190 GD90
Aspen Clo. N19 121 DJ61
Hargrave Pk.
Aspen Clo. W5 158 CM75
Aspen Clo., Cob. 230 BY116
Aspen Clo., Guil. 243 BD131
Aspen Clo., Orp. 224 EU106
Aspen Clo., St.Alb. 60 BY30
Aspen Clo., Slou. 131 AP71
Birch Gro.
Aspen Clo., Stai. 173 BF90
Aspen Clo., Swan. 207 FD95
Aspen Clo., West Dr. 134 BM74
Aspen Copse, Brom. 205 EM96
Aspen Ct., Hayes 155 BS77
Clement Gdns.
Aspen Dr., Wem. 117 CG63
Aspen Gdns. W6 159 CV78
Aspen Gdns., Mitch. 200 DG99
Aspen Grn., Erith 166 EZ76
Aspen Gro., Upmin. 128 FN63
Aspen La., Nthlt. 136 BY69
Aspen Pk. Dr., Wat. 75 BV35
Aspen Sq., Wey. 195 BR104
Oatlands Dr.
Aspen Way E14 143 ED73
Aspen Way, Bans. 217 CX114
Aspen Way, Enf. 83 DX35
Aspen Way, Felt. 175 BV90
Aspen Way, Welw.G.C. 30 DC10
Aspenlea Rd. W6 159 CX79
Aspern Gro. NW3 120 DE64
Aspinall Rd. SE4 163 DX83
Aspinden Rd. SE16 162 DV77
Aspley Rd. SW18 180 DB85
Aspley Way NW2 119 CU61
Asplins Rd. N17 100 DU53
Asquith Clo., Dag. 126 EW60
Crystal Way
Ass Ho. La., Har. 94 CB49
Assam St. E1 142 DU72
White Ch. La.
Assata Ms. N1 141 DP65
St. Paul's Rd.
Assembly Pas. E1 142 DW71
Assembly Wk., Cars. 200 DE101
Assher Rd., Walt. 196 BY104
Assheton Rd., Beac. 89 AK51
Assurance Cotts., Belv. 166 EZ78
Heron Hill
Astall Clo., Har. 95 CE53
Sefton Ave.
Astbury Rd. SE15 162 DW81
Aste St. E14 163 EC75
Astell St. SW3 276 C10
Astell St. SW3 160 DE78
Asteys Row N1 141 DP66
River Pl.
Asthall Gdns., Ilf. 125 EQ56
Astle St. SW11 160 DG82
Astleham Rd., Shep. 194 BL97
Astley, Grays 170 FZ79
Astley Ave. NW2 119 CW64
Astley Rd., Hem.H. 40 BJ20
Aston Ave., Har. 117 CJ59
Aston Clo., Ash. 231 CJ118
Aston Clo., Sid. 186 EU90
Aston Clo., Wat. 76 BW40
Aston Clo. (Bushey), Wat. 76 CC44
Aston Grn., Houns. 156 BW82
Aston Mead, Wind. 151 AL81
Aston Ms., Rom. 126 EW59
Reynolds Ave.
Aston Rd. SW20 199 CW96
Aston Rd. W5 137 CK72
Aston Rd., Esher 215 CE106
Aston St. E14 143 DY72
Aston Way, Epsom 233 CT116
Aston Way, Pot.B. 64 DD32
Astons Rd., Nthwd. 93 BQ48
Astonville St. SW18 180 DA88
Astor Ave., Rom. 127 FC58
Astor Clo., Add. 212 BK105
Astor Clo., Kings.T. 178 CP93
Astoria Wk. SW9 161 DN83
Astra Clo., Horn. 147 FH65
Astra Dr., Grav. 191 GL92
Astrop Ms. W6 159 CW76
Astrop Ter. W6 159 CW75
Astwick Ave., Hat. 45 CT15
Astwood Ms. SW7 160 DB77
Asylum Arch Rd., Red. 266 DF137
Asylum Rd. SE15 162 DV80
Atalanta Clo., Pur. 219 DN110
Atalanta St. SW6 159 CX81
Atbara Ct., Tedd. 177 CH93
Atbara Rd., Tedd. 177 CH93
Atcham Rd., Houns. 156 CC84
Atcost Rd., Bark. 146 EU71
Atheldene Rd. SW18 180 DC87
Athelney St. SE6 183 EA90
Athelstan Clo., Rom. 106 FM54
Athelstan Rd.
Athelstan Rd., Kings.T. 198 CM98
Athelstan Rd., Rom. 106 FM53
Athelstan Wk. N., Welw.G.C. 29 CY10
Athelstan Wk. S., Welw.G.C. 29 CX10
Athelstan Way, Orp. 206 EU95
Athelstane Gro. E3 143 DZ68
Athelstane Ms. N4 121 DN60
Stroud Grn. Rd.
Athelstone Rd., Har. 95 CD54
Athelstone Rd., Hem.H. 40 BM23
Athena Clo., Har. 117 CE61
Byron Hill Rd.
Athena Clo., Kings.T. 198 CM97
Athena Pl., Nthwd. 93 BT53
The Dr.
Athenaeum Pl. N10 121 DH55
Fortis Grn. Rd.
Athenaeum Rd. N20 98 DC46
Athenlay Rd. SE15 183 DX85
Athens Gdns. W9 140 DA70
Elgin Ave.
Atherden Rd. E5 122 DW63
Atherfield Rd., Reig. 266 DC137
Atherfold Rd. SW9 161 DL83
Atherley Way, Houns. 176 BZ87
Atherstone Ms. SW7 160 DC77
Atherton Clo., Guil. 258 AY140
Atherton Clo., Stai. 174 BK86
Atherton Ct. (Eton), Wind. 151 AR80
Meadow La.
Atherton Dr. SW19 179 CX91
Atherton Gdns., Grays 171 GJ77
Atherton Heights, Wem. 137 CJ65
Atherton Ms. E7 144 EF65
Atherton Pl., Har. 117 CD55
Atherton Pl., Sthl. 136 CB73
Longford Ave.
Atherton Rd. E7 144 EF65
Atherton Rd. SW13 159 CU80
Atherton Rd., Ilf. 102 EL54
Atherton St. SW11 160 DE82
Athlon Rd., Wem. 137 CK68
Athlone, Esher 215 CE107
Athlone Clo. E5 122 DV63
Goulton Rd.
Athlone Clo., Rad. 77 CG36
Athlone Rd. SW2 181 DM87
Athlone Sq., Wind. 151 AQ81
Alma Rd.
Athlone St. NW5 140 DG65
Athol Clo., Pnr. 93 BV53
Athol Gdns., Pnr. 93 BV53
Athol Rd., Erith 167 FC78
Athol Sq. E14 143 EC72
Athol Way, Uxb. 134 BN69
Athole Gdns., Enf. 82 DS43
Atholl Rd., Ilf. 126 EU59
Atkins Clo., Wok. 226 AU118
Greythorne Rd.
Atkins Dr., W.Wick. 203 ED103
Atkins Rd. E10 123 EB58
Atkins Rd. SW12 181 DK87
Atkinson Clo., Orp. 224 EU106
Martindale Ave.
Atkinson Rd. E16 144 EJ71
Atlanta Boul., Rom. 127 FE58
Atlantic Rd. SW9 161 DN84
Atlas Gdns. SE7 164 EJ77
Atlas Ms. E8 142 DT65
Tyssen St.
Atlas Ms. N7 141 DM65
Atlas Rd. E13 144 EG68
Atlas Rd. NW10 138 CS69
Atlas Rd., Dart. 168 FM83
Cornwall Rd.
Atlas Rd., Wem. 118 CQ63
Atley Rd. E3 143 EA67
Atlip Rd., Wem. 138 CL67
Atney Rd. SW15 159 CY84
Atria Rd., Nthwd. 93 BU50
Attenborough Clo., Wat. 94 BY48
Harrow Way
Atterbury Clo., West. 255 ER126
Atterbury Rd. N4 121 DN58
Atterbury St. SW1 277 P9
Atterbury St. SW1 161 DL77
Attewood Ave. NW10 118 CS62
Attewood Rd., Nthlt. 136 BY65
Attfield Clo. N20 98 DD47
Attimore Clo., Welw.G.C. 29 CV10
Attimore Rd., Welw.G.C. 29 CV10
Attle Clo., Uxb. 134 BN68
Attlee Clo., Hayes 135 BV69
Attlee Clo., Th.Hth. 202 DQ100
Attlee Ct., Grays 170 GA76
Lucas Rd.
Attlee Dr., Dart. 188 FN85
Attlee Rd. SE28 146 EV73
Attlee Rd., Hayes 135 BU69
Attlee Ter. E17 123 EB56
Attneave St. WC1 274 D3
Attwood Clo., S.Croy. 220 DV114
Atwater Clo. SW2 181 DN88
Atwell Clo. E10 123 EB58
Belmont Pk. Rd.
Atwell Rd. SE15 162 DU82
Rye La.
Atwood, Lthd. 230 BY124
Atwood Ave., Rich. 158 CN82
Atwood Rd. W6 159 CV77
Aubert Pk. N5 121 DN63
Aubert Rd. N5 121 DP63
Aubretia Clo., Rom. 106 FL53
Aubrey Ave., St.Alb. 61 CJ26
Aubrey Pl. NW8 140 DC68
Violet Hill
Aubrey Rd. E17 123 EA55
Aubrey Rd. N8 121 DL57
Aubrey Rd. W8 139 CZ74
Aubrey Wk. W8 139 CZ74
Aubreys Rd., Hem.H. 39 BE20
Aubyn Hill SE27 182 DQ91
Aubyn Sq. SW15 159 CU84
Auckland Ave., Rain. 147 FF69
Auckland Clo. SE19 202 DT95
Auckland Clo., Enf. 82 DV37
Auckland Clo., Til. 171 GG82
Auckland Gdns. SE19 202 DS95
Auckland Hill SE27 182 DQ91
Auckland Ri. SE19 202 DS95
Auckland Rd. E10 123 EB62
Auckland Rd. SE19 202 DT95
Auckland Rd. SW11 160 DE84
Auckland Rd., Cat. 236 DS122
Auckland Rd., Ilf. 125 EP60
Auckland Rd., Kings.T. 198 CM98
Auckland Rd., Pot.B. 63 CX32
Auckland St. SE11 161 DM78
Kennington La.
Auden Pl. NW1 140 DG67
Manley St.
Audleigh Pl., Chig. 103 EN51
Audley Clo. N10 99 DH52
Audley Clo. SW11 160 DG83
Audley Clo., Add. 212 BH106
Audley Clo., Borwd. 78 CN41
Audley Ct. E18 124 EF56
Audley Ct., Pnr. 94 BW54
Audley Dr., Warl. 236 DW115
Audley Firs, Walt. 214 BW105
Audley Gdns., Ilf. 125 ET61
Audley Gdns., Loug. 85 EQ40
Audley Gdns., Wal.Abb. 67 EC34
Audley Pl., Sutt. 218 DB108
Audley Rd. NW4 119 CU58
Audley Rd. W5 138 CM71
Audley Rd., Enf. 81 DP40
Audley Rd., Rich. 178 CM85
Audley Sq. W1 276 G2
Audley Wk., Orp. 206 EW100
Audrey Clo., Beck. 203 EB100
Audrey Gdns., Wem. 117 CH61
Audrey Rd., Ilf. 125 EP62
Audrey St. E2 142 DU68
Audric Clo., Kings.T. 198 CN95
Audwick Clo. (Cheshunt), Wal.Cr. 67 DY28
Augur Clo., Stai. 173 BF92
Augurs La. E13 144 EH69
August End, Slou. 133 AY72
August La., Guil. 260 BK144
Augusta Clo., W.Mol. 196 BZ97
Freeman Dr.
Augusta Rd., Twick. 176 CC89
Augusta St. E14 143 EB72
Augustine Clo., Slou. 153 BE83
Augustine Rd. W14 159 CX76
Augustine Rd., Grav. 191 GJ87
Augustine Rd., Har. 94 CB53
Augustine Rd., Orp. 206 EX97
Augustus Clo., Brent. 157 CK80
Augustus Clo., St.Alb. 42 CA22
Augustus La., Orp. 206 EU103
Augustus Rd. SW19 179 CX88
Augustus St. NW1 273 J1
Augustus St. NW1 141 DH68
Aulton Pl. SE11 161 DN78
Milverton St.
Aultone Way, Cars. 200 DF104
Aultone Way, Sutt. 200 DB103
Aurelia Gdns., Croy. 201 DM99
Aurelia Rd., Croy. 201 DL100
Auriel Ave., Dag. 147 FD65
Auriga Ms. N16 122 DR64
Auriol Clo., Wor.Pk. 198 CS104
Auriol Pk. Rd.
Auriol Dr., Grnf. 137 CD66
Auriol Dr., Uxb. 135 BP65
Auriol Pk. Rd., Wor.Pk. 198 CS104
Auriol Rd. W14 159 CY77
Aurum Clo., Horl. 269 DH149
Austell Gdns. NW7 96 CS48
Austen Clo. SE28 146 EV74
Austen Clo., Green. 189 FW85
Austen Clo., Loug. 85 ER41
Austen Clo., Til. 171 GJ82
Coleridge Rd.
Austen Gdns., Dart. 168 FM84
Keyes Rd.
Austen Ho. NW6 140 DA69
Austen Rd., Erith 167 FB81
Belmont Rd.
Austen Rd., Guil. 259 AZ135
Austen Rd., Har. 116 CB61
Austenway, Ger.Cr. 112 AY55
Austenwood Clo., Ger.Cr. 90 AW54
Austenwood La., Ger.Cr. 90 AX54
Austin Ave., Brom. 204 EL99
Austin Clo. SE23 183 DZ87
Austin Clo., Couls. 235 DP118
Austin Clo., Twick. 177 CJ85
Austin Ct. E6 144 EJ67
Kings Rd.
Austin Friars EC2 275 L8
Austin Friars EC2 142 DR72
Austin Friars Pas. EC2 275 L8
Austin Friars Sq. EC2 275 L8
Austin Rd. SW11 160 DG81
Austin Rd., Grav. 191 GF88
Austin Rd., Hayes 155 BT75
Austin Rd., Orp. 206 EU100
Austin St. E2 275 P3
Austin St. E2 142 DT69
Austin Waye, Uxb. 134 BJ67
Austin's La., Uxb. 115 BQ62
Austins Mead, Hem.H. 57 BB28
Austins Pl., Hem.H. 40 BK19
St. Mary's Rd.
Austral Clo., Sid. 185 ET90
Austral Dr., Horn. 128 FK59
Austral St. SE11 278 F8
Austral St. SE11 161 DP77
Australia Rd. W12 139 CV73
Australia Rd., Slou. 132 AV74
Austyn Gdns., Surb. 198 CP102
Autumn Clo., Enf. 82 DU39
Autumn Clo., Slou. 131 AM74
Autumn Dr., Sutt. 218 DB109
Autumn Glades, Hem.H. 41 BQ22
Autumn Gro., Welw.G.C. 30 DB11
Autumn St. E3 143 EA67
Auxiliaries Way, Uxb. 113 BF57
Avalon Clo. SW20 199 CY96
Avalon Clo. W13 137 CG71
Avalon Clo., Enf. 81 DN40
Avalon Clo., Orp. 206 EX104
Avalon Clo., Wat. 60 BY32
Avalon Rd. SW6 160 DB81
Avalon Rd. W13 137 CG70
Avalon Rd., Orp. 206 EV103
Avard Gdns., Orp. 223 EQ105
Isabella Dr.
Avarn Rd. SW17 180 DF93
Ave Maria La. EC4 274 G9
Ave Maria La. EC4 141 DP72
Avebury, Slou. 131 AN74

Avebury Ct. N1 142 DR67
Poole St.
Avebury Ct., Hem.H. 40 BN18
Avebury Pk., Surb. 197 CK101
Avebury Rd. E11 123 ED60
Southwest Rd.
Avebury Rd. SW19 199 CZ95
Avebury Rd., Orp. 205 ER104
Avebury St. N1 142 DR67
Poole St.
Aveley Bypass, S.Ock. 148 FQ73
Aveley Clo., S.Ock. 149 FR74
Aveley Rd., Rom. 127 FD56
Aveley Rd., Upmin. 148 FP65
Aveline St. SE11 161 DN78
Aveling Clo., Pur. 219 DM113
Aveling Pk. Rd. E17 101 EA54
Avelon Rd., Rain. 147 FG67
Avelon Rd., Rom. 105 FD51
Avenell Rd. N5 121 DP62
Avening Rd. SW18 180 DA87
Brathway Rd.
Avening Ter. SW18 180 DA86
Avenons Rd. E13 144 EG70
Avenue, The E4 101 ED51
Avenue, The (Leytonstone) E11 124 EF61
Avenue, The (Wanstead) E11 124 EH58
Avenue, The N3 98 DA54
Sylvan Ave.
Avenue, The N8 121 DN55
Avenue, The N10 99 DJ54
Avenue, The N11 99 DH50
Avenue, The N17 100 DS54
Avenue, The NW6 139 CX67
Avenue, The SE7 164 EJ80
Avenue, The SE10 163 ED80
Avenue, The SW4 180 DG85
Avenue, The SW11 180 DF87
Bellevue Rd.
Avenue, The SW18 180 DE87
Avenue, The W4 158 CS76
Avenue, The W13 137 CH73
Avenue, The, Add. 212 BG110
Avenue, The, Amer. 55 AQ38
Avenue, The, Barn. 79 CY41
Avenue, The, Beck. 203 EB95
Avenue, The, Bet. 248 CN134
Avenue, The, Bex. 186 EX86
Avenue, The, Brwd. 109 FZ50
Avenue, The, Brom. 204 EK97
Avenue, The, Cars. 218 DG108
Avenue, The, Couls. 235 DK115
Avenue, The, Croy. 202 DS104
Avenue, The, Egh. 173 BB91
Avenue, The, Epsom 217 CV108
Avenue, The, Esher 215 CE107
Avenue, The, Grav. 191 GG88
Avenue, The, Green. 169 FV84
Avenue, The, Guil. 242 AS127
Avenue, The, Hmptn. 176 BZ93
Avenue, The, Har. 95 CF53
Avenue, The, Hem.H. 39 BE19
Avenue, The, Hert. 31 DP07
Avenue, The, Hodd. 49 DZ19
Avenue, The, Horl. 268 DF149
Avenue, The, Horn. 128 FJ61
Avenue, The, Houns. 176 CB85
Avenue, The (Cranford),Houns. 155 BU81
Avenue, The, Islw. 157 CD80
Jersey Rd.
Avenue, The, Kes. 204 EK104
Avenue, The, Lthd. 215 CF112
Avenue, The, Loug. 84 EK44
Avenue, The, Maid. 130 AC69
Avenue, The, Nthwd. 93 BQ51
Avenue, The, Orp. 205 ET103
Avenue, The (St. Paul's Cray), Orp. 186 EV94
Avenue, The, Pnr. 116 BZ58
Avenue, The (Hatch End), Pnr. 94 BZ51
Avenue, The, Pot.B. 63 CZ30
Avenue, The, Rad. 61 CG33
Avenue, The, Red. 267 DL137
Avenue, The, Rich. 158 CM82
Avenue, The, Rom. 127 FD56
Avenue, The, Slou. 111 AP63
Avenue, The (Datchet), Slou. 152 AV81
Avenue, The, Stai. 194 BH95
Avenue, The (Sunnymeads), Stai. 152 AX83
Avenue, The, Sun. 195 BV95
Avenue, The, Surb. 198 CM100
Avenue, The, Sutt. 217 CY109
Avenue, The (Cheam), Sutt. 217 CV108
Avenue, The, Tad. 233 CV122
Avenue, The, Twick. 177 CH85
Avenue, The (Cowley), Uxb. 134 BK70
Avenue, The (Ickenham), Uxb. 114 BN63
Avenue, The, Wal.Abb. 68 EJ25
Avenue, The, Wat. 75 BU40
Avenue, The (Bushey), Wat. 76 BZ42
Avenue, The, Wem. 118 CL60
Avenue, The, West Dr. 154 BL76
Avenue, The, W.Wick. 203 EC101
Avenue, The, West. 239 EM122
Avenue, The, Whyt. 236 DU119
Avenue, The, Wind. 172 AV85
Avenue, The, Wok. 210 AT109
Avenue, The, Wor.Pk. 199 CT103
Avenue App., Kings L. 58 BN30
Avenue Clo. N14 81 DJ44
Avenue Clo. NW8 140 DE67
Avenue Clo., Houns. 155 BU81
The Ave.
Avenue Clo., Rom. 106 FM52
Avenue Clo., Tad. 233 CV122
Avenue Clo., West Dr. 154 BK76
Avenue Cres. W3 158 CP75
Avenue Cres., Houns. 155 BV80
Avenue Dr., Slou. 133 AZ71
Avenue Elmers, Surb. 198 CL99
Avenue Gdns. SE25 202 DU97
Avenue Gdns. SW14 158 CS83
Avenue Gdns. W3 158 CP75
Avenue Gdns., Horl. 269 DJ149
Avenue Gdns., Houns. 155 BU80
The Ave.
Avenue Gdns., Tedd. 177 CF94
Avenue Gate, Loug. 84 EJ44
Avenue Ind. Est. E4 101 DZ51
Avenue Ms. N10 121 DH55
Avenue Pk. Rd. SE27 181 DP89
Avenue Ri. (Bushey), Wat. 76 CA43
Avenue Rd. E7 124 EH63
Avenue Rd. N6 121 DJ59
Avenue Rd. N12 98 DC49
Avenue Rd. N14 99 DH45
Avenue Rd. N15 122 DR57
Avenue Rd. NW3 140 DD66
Avenue Rd. NW8 140 DD66
Avenue Rd. NW10 139 CT68
Avenue Rd. SE20 202 DW95
Avenue Rd. SE25 202 DT96
Avenue Rd. SW16 201 DK96
Avenue Rd. SW20 199 CV96
Avenue Rd. W3 158 CP75
Avenue Rd., Bans. 234 DB115
Avenue Rd., Beck. 203 DX95
Avenue Rd., Belv. 167 FC77
Avenue Rd., Bexh. 166 EY84
Avenue Rd., Brent. 157 CJ78
Avenue Rd., Brwd. 108 FW49
Avenue Rd., Cat. 236 DR122
Avenue Rd., Cob. 230 BX116
Avenue Rd., Epp. 85 ER36
Avenue Rd., Epsom 216 CR114
Avenue Rd., Erith 167 FC80
Avenue Rd., Felt. 175 BT90
Avenue Rd., Hmptn. 196 CB95
Avenue Rd., Hodd. 49 ED19
Avenue Rd., Islw. 157 CF81
Avenue Rd., Kings.T. 198 CL97
Avenue Rd., N.Mal. 198 CS98
Avenue Rd., Pnr. 116 BY55
Avenue Rd. (Chadwell Heath), Rom. 126 EV60
Avenue Rd. (Harold Wd.), Rom. 106 FM52
Avenue Rd., St.Alb. 43 CE19
Avenue Rd., Sev. 257 FJ124
Avenue Rd., Sthl. 156 BZ75
Avenue Rd., Stai. 173 BD92
Avenue Rd., Sutt. 218 DA110
Avenue Rd., Tedd. 177 CG94
Avenue Rd., Wall. 219 DJ108
Avenue Rd., West. 238 EL120
Avenue Rd., Wdf.Grn. 102 EJ51
Avenue S., Surb. 198 CM101
Avenue Ter., N.Mal. 198 CQ97
Kingston Rd.
Avenue Ter., Wat. 76 BY44
Averil Ct., Maid. 130 AJ72
Averil Gro. SW16 181 DP93
Averill St. W6 159 CX79
Avern Gdns., W.Mol. 196 CB98
Avern Rd., W.Mol. 196 CB98
Avery Fm. Row SW1 277 H9
Avery Gdns., Ilf. 125 EM57
Avery Hill Rd. SE9 185 ER86
Avery Row W1 273 J10
Avery Row W1 141 DH73
Avey La., Loug. 84 EH39
Avey La., Wal.Abb. 83 ED36
Avia Clo., Hem.H. 40 BK24
Aviary Clo. E16 144 EF71
Aviary Rd., Wok. 228 BG116
Aviemore Clo., Beck. 203 DZ99
Aviemore Way, Beck. 203 DY99
Avignon Rd. SE4 163 DX83
Avington Clo., Guil. 242 AY134
London Rd.
Avington Ct. SE1 162 DS77
Old Kent Rd.
Avington Gro. SE20 182 DW94
Avington Way SE15 162 DT80
Daniel Gdns.
Avior Dr., Nthwd. 93 BT49
Avis Gro., Croy. 221 DY111
Avis Sq. E1 143 DX72
Avoca Rd. SW17 180 DG91
Avocet Ms. SE28 165 ER76
Avon Clo., Add. 212 BG107
Avon Clo., Grav. 191 GK89
Avon Clo., Hayes 136 BW70
Avon Clo., Slou. 131 AL73
Avon Clo., Sutt. 218 DC105
Avon Clo., Wat. 60 BW34
Avon Clo., Wor.Pk. 199 CU103
Avon Ct., Grnf. 136 CB70
Braund Ave.
Avon Grn., S.Ock. 149 FV72
Avon Ms., Pnr. 94 BZ53
Avon Path, S.Croy. 220 DQ107
Avon Pl. SE1 279 J5
Avon Rd. E17 123 ED55
Avon Rd. SE4 163 EA83
Avon Rd., Grnf. 136 CA70
Avon Rd., Sun. 175 BT94
Avon Rd., Upmin. 129 FR58
Avon Sq., Hem.H. 40 BM15
Avon Way E18 124 EG55
Avondale Ave. N12 98 DB50
Avondale Ave. NW2 118 CS62
Avondale Ave., Barn. 98 DF46
Avondale Ave., Esher 197 CG104
Avondale Ave., Stai. 173 BF94
Avondale Ave., Wor.Pk. 199 CT102
Avondale Clo., Horl. 268 DG146
Avondale Clo., Loug. 103 EM45
Avondale Clo., Walt. 214 BW106
Pleasant Pl.
Avondale Ct. E11 124 EE60
Avondale Ct. E16 144 EE71
Avondale Rd.
Avondale Ct. E18 102 EH53
Avondale Cres., Enf. 83 DY41
Avondale Cres., Ilf. 124 EK57
Avondale Dr., Hayes 135 BU74
Avondale Dr., Loug. 103 EM45
Avondale Gdns., Houns. 176 BZ85
Avondale Ms., Brom. 184 EG93
Avondale Rd.
Avondale Pk. Gdns. W11 139 CY73
Avondale Pk. Rd. W11 139 CY73
Avondale Pavement SE1 162 DU78
Avondale Sq.
Avondale Ri. SE15 162 DT83
Avondale Rd. E16 144 EE71
Avondale Rd. E17 123 EA59
Avondale Rd. N3 98 DC53
Avondale Rd. N13 99 DN47
Avondale Rd. N15 121 DP57
Avondale Rd. SE9 184 EL89
Avondale Rd. SW14 158 CR83
Avondale Rd. SW19 180 DB92
Avondale Rd., Ashf. 174 BK90
Avondale Rd., Brom. 184 EE93
Avondale Rd., Har. 117 CF55
Avondale Rd., S.Croy. 220 DQ108
Avondale Rd., Well. 166 EW82
Avondale Sq. SE1 162 DU78
Avonley Rd. SE14 162 DW80
Avonmead, Wok. 226 AW118
Silversmiths Way
Avonmore Ave., Guil. 243 AZ133
Avonmore Gdns. W14 159 CY77
Avonmore Rd.
Avonmore Pl. W14 159 CY77
Avonmore Rd.
Avonmore Rd. W14 159 CY77
Avonmouth Rd., Dart. 188 FK85
Avonmouth St. SE1 279 H6
Avonmouth St. SE1 162 DQ76
Avontar Rd., S.Ock. 149 FV70
Avonwick Rd., Houns. 156 CB82
Avril Way E4 101 EC50
Avro Way, Wall. 219 DL108
Avro Way, Wey. 212 BL111
Award Gdns., Orp. 223 EQ105
Awlfield Ave. N17 100 DR53
Awliscombe Rd., Well. 165 ET82
Axe St., Bark. 145 EQ67
Axes La., Red. 267 DJ141
Axholme Ave., Edg. 96 CN53
Axminster Cres., Well. 166 EW81
Axminster Rd. N7 121 DL62
Axtaine Rd., Orp. 206 EX101
Axtane, Grav. 190 FZ94
Axtane Clo. (Sutton at Hone), Dart. 208 FQ96
Axwood, Epsom 232 CQ115
Aybrook St. W1 272 F7
Aybrook St. W1 140 DG71
Aycliffe Clo., Brom. 205 EM98
Aycliffe Dr., Hem.H. 40 BL15
Aycliffe Rd. W12 139 CT74
Aycliffe Rd., Borwd. 78 CL39
Aylebridges Ave., Egh. 173 BC94
Aylands Clo., Wem. 118 CL61
Preston Rd.
Aylands Rd., Enf. 83 DX36
Ayles Rd., Hayes 135 BV69
Aylesbury Clo. E7 144 EF65
Atherton Rd.
Aylesbury Cres., Slou. 131 AR72
Aylesbury End, Beac. 89 AL54
Aylesbury Est. SE17 162 DR78
Villa St.
Aylesbury Rd. SE17 162 DR78
Aylesbury Rd., Brom. 204 EG97
Aylesbury St. EC1 274 F5
Aylesbury St. EC1 141 DP70
Aylesbury St. NW10 118 CR62
Aylesford Ave., Beck. 203 DY99
Aylesford St. SW1 161 DK78
Aylesham Clo. NW7 97 CU52
Aylesham Rd., Orp. 205 ET101
Aylestone Ave. NW6 139 CX66
Aylesworth Ave., Slou. 131 AN69
Doddsfield Rd.
Aylesworth Spur, Wind. 172 AV87
Aylets Fld., Harl. 51 ES18
Aylett Rd. SE25 202 DV98
Belfast Rd.
Aylett Rd., Islw. 157 CE82
Aylett Rd., Upmin. 128 FQ61
Ayley Cft., Enf. 82 DU43
Ayliffe Clo., Kings.T. 198 CN96
Cambridge Gdns.
Aylmer Clo., Stan. 95 CG49
Aylmer Dr., Stan. 95 CG49
Aylmer Par. N2 120 DF57
Aylmer Rd.
Aylmer Rd. E11 124 EF60
Aylmer Rd. N2 120 DE57
Aylmer Rd. W12 159 CT75
Aylmer Rd., Dag. 126 EY62
Ayloffe Rd., Dag. 146 EZ65
Ayloffs Clo., Horn. 128 FL57
Ayloffs Wk., Horn. 128 FK57
Aylsham Dr., Uxb. 115 BQ61
Aylsham La., Rom. 106 FJ49
Aylsham Rd., Hodd. 49 EC16
Aylton Est. SE16 162 DW75
Renforth St.
Aylward Gdns., Chesh. 54 AN30
Aylward Rd. SE23 183 DX89
Aylward Rd. SW20 199 CZ96
Aylward St. E1 142 DW72
Aylwards Ri., Stan. 95 CG49
Aylwyn Est. SE1 279 N6
Aylwyn Est. SE1 162 DS76
Aymer Clo., Stai. 193 BE95
Aymer Dr., Stai. 193 BE95
Aynho St., Wat. 75 BV43
Aynhoe Rd. W14 159 CX77
Aynscombe Angle, Orp. 206 EU101
Aynscombe La. SW14 158 CQ83
Aynscombe Path SW14 158 CQ82
Thames Bank
Aynsley Gdns., Harl. 52 EW15
Ayot Grn., Welw. 29 CU07
Ayot Greenway, St.Alb. 28 CN06
Ayot Little Grn., Welw. 29 CT06
Ayot Path, Borwd. 78 CN38
Walshford Way
Ayr Ct. W3 138 CN71
Monks Dr.
Ayr Grn., Rom. 105 FE52
Ayr Way, Rom. 105 FE52
Ayres Clo. E13 144 EG69
Ayres Cres. NW10 138 CR66
Ayres St. SE1 279 J4
Ayres St. SE1 162 DQ75
Ayron Rd., S.Ock. 149 FV70
Ayrsome Rd. N16 122 DS62
Ayrton Rd. SW7 160 DD76
Wells Way
Aysgarth Rd. SE21 182 DS86
Aytoun Pl. SW9 161 DM82
Aytoun Rd. SW9 161 DM82
Azalea Clo. W7 137 CF74
Azalea Clo., Ilf. 125 EP64
Lavender Pl.
Azalea Ct., Wok. 226 AX119
Azalea Ct., Wdf.Grn. 102 EE52
Bridle Path
Azalea Dr., Swan. 207 FD98
Azalea Wk., Pnr. 115 BV57
Azalea Wk., Sthl. 156 CC75
Navigator Dr.
Azalea Way, Slou. 132 AY72
Blinco La.
Azenby Rd. SE15 162 DT82
Azile Everitt Ho. SE18 165 EQ78
Vicarage Pk.
Azof St. SE10 164 EE77

B

Baalbec Rd. N5 121 DP64
Baas Hill, Brox. 49 DX21
Baas Hill Clo., Brox. 49 DY21
Baas La., Brox. 49 DY21
Babbacombe Clo., Chess. 215 CK106
Babbacombe Gdns., Ilf. 124 EL56
Babbacombe Rd., Brom. 204 EG95
Baber Dr., Felt. 176 BW86
Babington Ri., Wem. 138 CN65
Babington Rd. NW4 119 CV56
Babington Rd. SW16 181 DK92
Babington Rd., Dag. 126 EW64
Babington Rd., Horn. 127 FH60
Babmaes St. SW1 277 M2
Babylon La., Tad. 250 DA127
Bacchus Wk. N1 275 M1
Bachelors Acre, Wind. 151 AR81
Bachelor's La., Wok. 228 BM124
Baches St. N1 275 L3
Baches St. N1 142 DR69
Back, The, Berk. 39 BB16
Back Ch. La. E1 142 DU73
Back Grn., Walt. 214 BW107
Back Hill EC1 274 D5
Back Hill EC1 141 DN70
Back La. N8 121 DL57
Back La. NW3 120 DC63
Heath St.
Back La., Bex. 186 FA87
Back La., B.Stort. 36 FA06
Back La., Brent. 157 CK79
Back La., Ch.St.G. 90 AU48
Back La., Edg. 96 CQ53
Back La., Grays 149 FW74
Back La., Guil. 244 BK131
Back La., Hert. 48 DQ18
Back La., Purf. 169 FS76
Back La., Rich. 177 CJ90
Back La., Rick. 73 BB38
Back La., Rom. 126 EY59
St. Chad's Rd.
Back La. (Godden Grn.), Sev. 257 FN124
Back La. (Ide Hill), Sev. 256 FB128
Back La., Wal.Abb. 50 EJ22
Back La., Wat. 77 CE39
Back La., Welw. 30 DE05
Back Path, Red. 252 DQ133
Back Rd., Sid. 186 EU91
Back St., Harl. 36 EW11
Broadway Ave.
Backhouse Pl. SE17 279 N9
Backley Gdns. SE25 202 DU100
Backs, The, Chesh. 54 AQ31
Bacon Gro. SE1 279 P7
Bacon Gro. SE1 162 DT76
Bacon La. NW9 118 CP56
Bacon La., Edg. 96 CN53
Bacon Link, Rom. 105 FB51
Bacon St. E1 142 DT70
Bacon St. E2 142 DT70
Bacon Ter., Dag. 126 EV64
Fitzstephen Rd.
Bacons Dr. (Cuffley), Pot.B. 65 DL29
Bacons La. N6 120 DG60
Bacons Mead, Uxb. 114 BG61
Bacton NW5 120 DG64
Bacton St. E2 142 DW69
Roman Rd.
Badburgham Ct., Wal.Abb. 68 EF33
Baddow Clo., Dag. 146 FA67
Baddow Clo., Wdf.Grn. 102 EK51
Baden Clo., Stai. 174 BG94
Baden Dr., Horl. 268 DE147
Baden Pl. SE1 279 K4
Baden Powell Clo., Surb. 198 CM103
Baden Powell Rd., Sev. 256 FE122
Baden Rd. N8 121 DK56
Baden Rd., Guil. 242 AU132
Baden Rd., Ilf. 125 EP64
Bader Clo., Ken. 236 DR115
Bader Clo., Welw.G.C. 30 DC09
Bader Gdns., Slou. 151 AN75
Bader Wk., Grav. 190 GE90
Bader Way, Rain. 147 FG65
Badger Clo., Felt. 175 BU90
Sycamore Clo.
Badger Clo., Guil. 242 AV131
Badger Clo., Houns. 156 BW83
Badger Clo., Ilf. 125 EQ59
Badger Way, Hat. 45 CV20
Badgers Clo., Ashf. 174 BM92
Fordbridge Rd.
Badgers Clo., Borwd. 78 CM40
Kingsley Ave.
Badgers Clo., Enf. 81 DP41
Badgers Clo., Har. 117 CD58
Badgers Clo., Hayes 135 BS74
Badgers Clo., Hert. 32 DV09
Badgers Clo., Wok. 226 AW118
Badgers Copse, Orp. 205 ET103
Badgers Copse, Wor.Pk. 199 CT103
Badgers Cft. N20 97 CY46
Badgers Cft. SE9 185 EN90
Badgers Cft., Brox. 49 DY21
Badgers Cft., Hem.H. 41 BR21
Badgers Hill, Vir.W. 192 AW99
Badgers Hole, Croy. 221 DX105
Badgers La., Warl. 236 DW119
Badgers Mt., Grays 171 GF75
Badgers Ri., Sev. 224 FA110
Badgers Rd., Sev. 225 FB110
Badgers Wk., N.Mal. 198 CS96
Badgers Wk., Pur. 219 DJ111
Badgers Wk., Rick. 73 BF42
Badgers Wk., Whyt. 236 DT119
Badgers Wd., Cat. 252 DQ125
Badgers Wd., Slou. 111 AQ64
Badingham Dr., Lthd. 231 CE123
Badlis Rd. E17 101 EA54
Badlow Clo., Erith 167 FE80
Badminton Clo., Borwd. 78 CN40
Badminton Clo., Har. 117 CE56
Badminton Clo., Nthlt. 136 CA66
Badminton Ms. E16 144 EE72
Silvertown Way
Badminton Pl., Brox. 49 DY20
Badminton Rd. SW12 180 DG86
Badsworth Rd. SE5 162 DQ81
Baffin Way E14 143 ED73
Prestons Rd.
Bagden Hill, Dor. 247 CD130
Bagley Clo., West Dr. 154 BL75
Bagley's La. SW6 160 DB81
Bagleys Spring, Rom. 126 EY56
Bagot Clo., Ash. 232 CM116
Bagshot Ct. SE18 165 EN81
Prince Imperial Rd.
Bagshot Rd., Egh. 172 AW94
Bagshot Rd., Enf. 100 DT45
Bagshot St. SE17 162 DS78
Bahram Rd., Epsom 216 CR110
Baildon St. SE8 163 EA80
Watson's St.
Bailey Clo. E4 101 EC49
Bailey Clo., Purf. 169 FR77
Gabion Ave.
Bailey Clo., Wind. 151 AN82
Bailey Pl. SE26 183 DX93
Bailey Rd., Dor. 262 CC137
Baillie Clo., Rain. 147 FH70
Baillie Rd., Guil. 259 AZ135
Baillies Wk. W5 157 CK75
Liverpool Rd.
Bainbridge Rd., Dag. 126 EZ63
Bainbridge St. WC1 273 N8
Bainbridge St. WC1 141 DK72
Bainton Mead, Wok. 226 AU117
Baird Ave., Sthl. 136 CB73
Baird Clo. NW9 118 CQ58
Baird Clo., Slou. 151 AP75
Haig Dr.
Baird Clo. (Bushey), Wat. 76 CB44
Ashfield Ave.
Baird Gdns. SE19 182 DS91
Baird Rd., Enf. 82 DV42
Baird St. EC1 275 J4
Bairstow Clo., Borwd. 78 CL39
Baizdon Rd. SE3 164 EE82
Bakeham La., Egh. 192 AX95
Bakehouse Rd., Horl. 268 DF146
Baker Boy La., Croy. 221 DZ112
Baker Hill Clo., Grav. 191 GF91
Baker La., Mitch. 200 DG96
Baker Pas. NW10 138 CS67
Acton La.
Baker Rd. NW10 138 CS67
Baker Rd. SE18 164 EL81
Baker St. NW1 272 E5
Baker St. NW1 140 DF70
Baker St. W1 272 E6
Baker St. W1 140 DF71
Baker St., Enf. 82 DR41
Baker St., Hert. 32 DS09
Baker St., Pot.B. 79 CY36
Baker St., Wey. 212 BN105
Bakers Ave. E17 123 EB58
Bakers Ct. SE25 202 DS97
Bakers End SW20 199 CY96
Bakers Fld. N7 121 DK63
Crayford Rd.
Bakers Gdns., Cars. 200 DE103
Bakers Gro., Welw.G.C. 30 DC08
Bakers Hill E5 122 DV60
Bakers Hill, Barn. 80 DB40
Bakers La. N6 120 DF58
Bakers La., Epp. 69 ET30
Bakers La., Saw. 35 ES05
Bakers Mead, Gdse. 252 DW130
Baker's Ms. W1 272 F8
Bakers Ms., Orp. 223 ET107
Bakers Orchard, H.Wyc. 110 AE58
Bakers Pas. NW3 120 DC63
Heath St.
Baker's Rents E2 275 P3
Bakers Rd., Uxb. 134 BK66
Bakers Rd. (Cheshunt), Wal.Cr. 66 DV30
Bakers Row E15 144 EE68
Baker's Row EC1 274 D5
Baker's Row EC1 141 DN70
Bakers Wd., Uxb. 113 BD60
Baker's Yd. EC1 141 DN70
Baker's Row
Baker's Yd., Uxb. 134 BK66
Bakers Rd.
Bakery Clo. SW9 161 DM81
Bakery Clo., Harl. 50 EJ15
Bakery Path, Edg. 96 CP51
Station Rd.
Bakery Pl. SW11 160 DF84
Altenburg Gdns.
Bakewell Way, N.Mal. 198 CS96
Bala Gdn. NW9 118 CS58
Snowdon Dr.
Balaam St. E13 144 EG70
Balaams La. N14 99 DK47
Balaclava Rd. SE1 162 DT77
Balaclava Rd., Surb. 197 CJ101
Balben Path E9 143 DX66
Speldhurst Rd.
Balcaskie Rd. SE9 185 EM85
Balchen Rd. SE3 164 EK82
Balchier Rd. SE22 182 DV86
Balchins La., Dor. 262 CA138
Balcombe Clo., Bexh. 166 EX84
Balcombe Gdns., Horl. 269 DJ149
Balcombe Rd., Craw. 269 DK154
Balcombe Rd., Horl. 269 DH147
Balcombe St. NW1 272 D4
Balcombe St. NW1 140 DF70
Balcon Way, Borwd. 78 CQ39
Balcorne St. E9 142 DW66
Balder Ri. SE12 184 EH89
Balderton St. W1 272 G9
Balderton St. W1 140 DG72
Baldock St. E3 143 EB68
Baldock St., Ware 33 DX06
Baldock Way, Borwd. 78 CM39
Baldocks Rd., Epp. 85 ES35
Baldry Gdns. SW16 181 DL93
Baldwin Cres. SE5 162 DQ81

Baldwin Cres., Guil. 243 BC132
Baldwin Rd., Beac. 89 AP54
Baldwin Rd., Slou. 130 AJ69
Baldwin St. EC1 275 K3
Baldwin Ter. N1 142 DQ68
Baldwins, Welw.G.C. 30 DC09
Baldwin's Gdns. EC1 274 D6
Baldwin's Gdns. EC1 141 DN71
Baldwins Hill, Loug. 85 EM40
Baldwins La., Rick. 74 BN42
Baldwins Shore, Wind. 151 AR79
Baldwyn Gdns. W3 138 CR73
Baldwyns Pk., Bex. 187 FD89
Baldwyns Rd., Bex. 187 FD89
Balfe St. N1 274 A1
Balfe St. N1 141 DL68
Balfern Gro. W4 158 CS78
Balfern St. SW11 160 DE82
Balfont Clo., S.Croy. 220 DU113
Balfour Ave. W7 137 CF74
Balfour Ave., Wok. 226 AY122
Balfour Gro. N20 98 DF48
Balfour Ho. W10 139 CX71
St. Charles Sq.
Balfour Ms. N9 100 DU48
The Bdy.
Balfour Ms. W1 276 G2
Balfour Pl. SW15 159 CV84
Balfour Pl. W1 276 G1
Balfour Rd. N5 122 DQ63
Balfour Rd. SE25 202 DU99
Balfour Rd. SW19 180 DB94
Balfour Rd. W3 138 CQ71
Balfour Rd. W13 157 CG75
Balfour Rd., Brom. 204 EK99
Balfour Rd., Cars. 218 DF108
Balfour Rd., Grays 170 GC77
Balfour Rd., Har. 117 CD57
Balfour Rd., Houns. 156 CB83
Balfour Rd., Ilf. 125 EP61
Balfour Rd., Sthl. 156 BX76
Balfour Rd., Wey. 212 BN105
Balfour St. SE17 279 K8
Balfour St. SE17 162 DR77
Balfour St., Hert. 32 DQ08
Balgonie Rd. E4 101 ED46
Balgores Cres., Rom. 127 FH55
Balgores La., Rom. 127 FH55
Balgores Sq., Rom. 127 FH56
Balgowan Clo., N.Mal. 198 CS98
Balgowan Rd., Beck. 203 DY97
Balgowan St. SE18 165 ET77
Balham Gro. SW12 180 DG87
Balham High Rd. SW12 180 DG90
Balham High Rd. SW17 180 DG90
Balham Hill SW12 181 DH87
Balham New Rd. SW12 181 DH87
Balham Pk. Rd. SW12 180 DF88
Balham Rd. N9 100 DU47
Balham Sta. Rd. SW12 181 DH88
Balkan Wk. E1 142 DV73
Pennington St.
Balladier Wk. E14 143 EB71
Morris Rd.
Ballamore Rd., Brom. 184 EG90
Ballance Rd. E9 143 DX65
Ballands N., The, Lthd. 231 CE122
Ballands S., The, Lthd. 231 CE123
Ballantine St. SW18 160 DC84
Ballantyne Dr., Tad. 233 CZ121
Ballard Clo., Kings.T. 178 CR94
Ballard Grn., Wind. 151 AL80
Ballards Clo., Dag. 147 FB67
Ballards Fm. Rd., Croy. 220 DU107
Ballards Fm. Rd., S.Croy. 220 DU107
Ballards Grn., Tad. 233 CY119
Ballards La. N3 98 DA53
Ballards La. N12 98 DC51
Ballards La., Oxt. 254 EJ129
Ballards Ms., Edg. 96 CN51
Ballards Ri., S.Croy. 220 DU107
Ballards Rd. NW2 119 CU61
Ballards Rd., Dag. 147 FB68
Ballards Way, Croy. 220 DV107
Ballards Way, S.Croy. 220 DU107
Ballast Quay SE10 163 ED78
Ballater Clo., Wat. 94 BW49
Ballater Rd. SW2 161 DL84
Ballater Rd., S.Croy. 220 DT106
Ballenger Ct., Wat. 75 BV41
Ballina St. SE23 183 DX87
Ballingdon Rd. SW11 180 DG86
Ballinger Ct., Berk. 38 AV20
Ballinger Pt. E3 143 EB69
Bromley High St.
Balliol Ave. E4 102 EE49
Balliol Rd. N17 100 DS53
Balliol Rd. W10 139 CX72
Balliol Rd., Well. 166 EV82
Balloch Rd. SE6 183 ED88
Ballogie Ave. NW10 118 CS63
Ballow Clo. SE5 162 DS80
Harris St.
Balls Pond Pl. N1 142 DR65
Balls Pond Rd.
Balls Pond Rd. N1 142 DR65
Balmain Clo. W5 137 CK74
Balmer Rd. E3 143 DZ68
Balmes Rd. N1 142 DR67
Balmoral Ave. N11 98 DG50
Balmoral Ave., Beck. 203 DY98
Balmoral Clo. SW15 179 CX86
Westleigh Ave.
Balmoral Clo., Slou. 131 AL72
Balmoral Cres., W.Mol. 196 CA97
Balmoral Dr., Borwd. 78 CR43
Balmoral Dr., Hayes 135 BS70
Balmoral Dr., Sthl. 136 BZ70
Balmoral Dr., Wok. 227 BC116
Balmoral Gdns. W13 157 CG76
Balmoral Gdns., Bex. 186 EZ87
Balmoral Gdns., Ilf. 125 ET60
Balmoral Gdns., Wind. 151 AR83
Balmoral Gro. N7 141 DM65
Balmoral Ms. W12 159 CT76
Balmoral Rd. E7 124 EJ63
Balmoral Rd. E10 123 EB61
Balmoral Rd. NW2 139 CV65
Balmoral Rd., Abb.L. 59 BU32
Balmoral Rd., Brwd. 108 FV44
Balmoral Rd. (Sutton at Hone), Dart. 188 FP94
Balmoral Rd., Enf. 83 DX36
Balmoral Rd., Har. 116 CA63
Balmoral Rd., Horn. 128 FK62
Balmoral Rd., Kings.T. 198 CM98
Balmoral Rd., Rom. 127 FH57
Balmoral Rd., Wat. 76 BW38
Balmoral Rd., Wor.Pk. 199 CV104
Balmoral Way, Sutt. 218 DA110
Balmore Cres., Barn. 80 DG43
Balmore St. N19 121 DH61
Balmuir Gdns. SW15 159 CW84
Balnacraig Ave. NW10 118 CS63
Balniel Gate SW1 277 N10
Balniel Gate SW1 161 DK78
Balquhain Clo., Ash. 231 CK117
Balsams Clo., Hert. 32 DR11
Baltic Clo. SW19 180 DD94
Baltic Ct. SE16 163 DX75
Timber Pond Rd.
Baltic St. E. EC1 275 H5
Baltic St. E. EC1 142 DQ70
Baltic St. W. EC1 275 H5
Baltic St. W. EC1 142 DQ70
Baltimore Pl., Well. 165 ET82
Balvernie Gro. SW18 179 CZ87
Bamber Ho., Bark. 145 EQ67
St. Margarets
Bamborough Gdns. W12 159 CW75
Bamford Ave., Wem. 138 CM67
Bamford Ct. E15 123 EB64
Clays La.
Bamford Rd., Bark. 145 EQ65
Bamford Rd., Brom. 183 EC92
Bamford Way, Rom. 105 FB50
Bampfylde Clo., Wall. 201 DJ104
Bampton Rd. SE23 183 DX90
Bampton Rd., Rom. 106 FL52
Bampton Way, Wok. 226 AU118
Banavie Gdns., Beck. 203 EC95
Banbury Ave., Slou. 131 AM71
Banbury Clo., Enf. 81 DP39
Holtwhites Hill
Banbury Ct. WC2 273 P10
Banbury Ct., Sutt. 218 DA108
Banbury Enterprise Cen., Croy. 201 DP103
Factory La.
Banbury Rd. E9 143 DX66
Banbury Rd. E17 101 DY53
Banbury St. SW11 160 DE82
Banbury St., Wat. 75 BU43
Banbury Wk., Nthlt. 136 CA68
Brabazon Rd.
Banchory Rd. SE3 164 EH80
Bancroft Ave. N2 120 DE57
Bancroft Ave., Buck.H. 102 EG47
Bancroft Clo., Ashf. 174 BN92
Feltham Hill Rd.
Bancroft Ct., Nthlt. 136 BW67
Bancroft Ct., Reig. 250 DB134
Bancroft Gdns., Har. 94 CC53
Bancroft Gdns., Orp. 205 ET102
Bancroft Rd. E1 143 DX69
Bancroft Rd., Har. 94 CC53
Bancroft Rd., Reig. 250 DA134
Band La., Egh. 173 AZ92
Banders Ri., Guil. 243 BC133
Bandon Ri., Wall. 219 DK106
Banes Down, Wal.Abb. 50 EE22
Bangalore St. SW15 159 CW83
Bangor Clo., Nthlt. 116 CB64
Bangors Clo., Iver 133 BE72
Bangors Rd. N., Iver 133 BD67
Bangors Rd. S., Iver 133 BE69
Banim St. W6 159 CV77
Banister Rd. W10 139 CX69
Bank, The N6 121 DH60
Cholmeley Pk.
Bank Ave., Mitch. 200 DD96
Bank Ct., Dart. 188 FL86
High St.
Bank Ct., Hem.H. 40 BJ21
Marlowes
Bank End SE1 279 J2
Bank End SE1 142 DQ74
Bank La. SW15 178 CS85
Bank La., Kings.T. 178 CL94
Bank Ms., Sutt. 218 DA111
Sutton Ct. Rd.
Bank Mill, Berk. 38 AY19
Bank Mill La., Berk. 38 AY20
Bank Pl., Brwd. 108 FW47
High St.
Bank Rd., H.Wyc. 88 AC47
Bank St., Grav. 191 GH86
Bank St., Sev. 257 FH125
Bankfoot, Grays 170 FZ78
Bankfoot Rd., Brom. 184 EE91
Bankhurst Rd. SE6 183 DZ87
Banks La., Bexh. 166 EZ84
Banks La., Epp. 70 EY33
Bank's La., Lthd. 229 BV122
Banks Rd., Borwd. 78 CQ40
Banks Spur, Slou. 151 AP75
Cooper Way
Banks Way, Guil. 243 AZ131
Banksia Rd. N18 100 DW50
Banksian Wk., Islw. 157 CE81
The Gro.
Bankside SE1 279 H1
Bankside SE1 142 DQ73
Bankside, Enf. 81 DP39
Bankside, Grav. 190 GC86
Bankside, Sev. 256 FE121
Bankside, S.Croy. 220 DT107
Bankside, Sthl. 136 BX74
Bankside, Wok. 226 AV118
Wyndham Rd.
Bankside Ave., Nthlt. 135 BU68
Townson Ave.
Bankside Clo., Bex. 187 FD91
Bankside Clo., Cars. 218 DE107
Bankside Clo., Islw. 157 CF84
Bankside Clo., West. 238 EJ118
Bankside Dr., T.Ditt. 197 CH102
Bankside Way SE19 182 DS93
Lunham Rd.
Bankton Rd. SW2 161 DN84
Bankwell Rd. SE13 164 EE84
Bann Clo., S.Ock. 149 FV73
Banner Clo., Purf. 169 FR77
Brimfield Rd.
Banner St. EC1 275 J5
Banner St. EC1 142 DQ70
Bannerman Ho. SW8 161 DM79
Banning St. SE10 164 EE78
Bannister Clo. SW2 181 DN88
Ewen Cres.
Bannister Clo., Grnf. 117 CD64
Bannister Clo., Slou. 152 AY75
Bannister Dr., Brwd. 109 GC44
Bannister Gdns., Orp. 206 EW97
Main Rd.
Bannister Ho. E9 123 DX64
Homerton High St.
Bannister's Rd., Guil. 258 AT136
Bannockburn Rd. SE18 165 ES77
Banstead Gdns. N9 100 DS48
Banstead Rd., Bans. 217 CX112
Banstead Rd., Cars. 218 DE107
Banstead Rd., Cat. 236 DR122
Banstead Rd., Epsom 217 CV110
Banstead Rd., Pur. 219 DN111
Banstead Rd. S., Sutt. 218 DC111
Banstead St. SE15 162 DW83
Banstead Way, Wall. 219 DL106
Banstock Rd., Edg. 96 CP51
Banting Dr. N21 81 DM43
Banton Clo., Enf. 82 DV40
Central Ave.
Bantry St. SE5 162 DR80
Banwell Rd., Bex. 186 EX86
Woodside La.
Banyard Rd. SE16 162 DV76
Southwark Pk. Rd.
Banyards, Horn. 128 FL56
Bapchild Pl., Orp. 206 EW98
Okemore Gdns.
Baptist Gdns. NW5 140 DG65
Queens Cres.
Barandon Wk. W11 139 CX73
Whitchurch Rd.
Barb Ms. W6 159 CW76
Barbara Brosnan Ct. NW8 140 DD68
Grove End Rd.
Barbara Clo., Shep. 195 BP99
Barbara Hucklesby Clo. N22 99 DP54
The Sandlings
Barbauld Rd. N16 122 DS62
Barbel Clo., Wal.Cr. 67 EA34
Barber Clo. N21 99 DN45
Barberry Clo., Rom. 106 FJ51
Barberry Rd., Hem.H. 40 BG20
Barber's All. E13 144 EH69
Greengate St.
Barbers Rd. E15 143 EB68
Barbican, The EC2 275 H6
Barbican, The EC2 142 DQ71
Barbican Rd., Grnf. 136 CB72
Barbon Clo. WC1 274 A6
Barbot Clo. N9 100 DU48
Barchard St. SW18 180 DB85
Barchester Clo. W7 137 CF74
Barchester Clo., Uxb. 134 BJ70
Barchester Rd., Har. 95 CD54
Barchester Rd., Slou. 153 AZ75
Barchester St. E14 143 EB71
Barclay Clo. SW6 160 DA80
Barclay Clo., Hert. 32 DV11
Barclay Clo., Lthd. 230 CB123
Barclay Clo., Wat. 75 BU44
Barclay Ct., Hodd. 49 EA18
Barclay Ct., Slou. 151 AQ75
Barclay Oval, Wdf.Grn. 102 EG49
Barclay Path E17 123 EC57
Grove Rd.
Barclay Rd. E11 124 EE60
Barclay Rd. E13 144 EJ70
Barclay Rd. E17 123 EC57
Barclay Rd. N18 100 DR51
Barclay Rd. SW6 160 DA80
Barclay Rd., Croy. 202 DR104
Barclay Way SE22 182 DU87
Lordship La.
Barclay Way, Grays 169 FT78
Barcombe Ave. SW2 181 DL89
Barcombe Clo., Orp. 206 EU97
Bard Rd. W10 139 CX73
Barden Clo., Uxb. 92 BJ52
Barden St. SE18 165 ES80
Bardeswell Clo., Brwd. 108 FW47
Bardfield Ave., Rom. 126 EX55
Bardney Rd., Mord. 200 DB98
Bardolph Ave., Croy. 221 DY109
Bardolph Rd. N7 121 DL63
Bardolph Rd., Rich. 158 CM83
St. Georges Rd.
Bardon Wk., Wok. 226 AV117
Bampton Way
Bards Cor., Hem.H. 40 BH19
Laureate Way
Bardsey Pl. E1 142 DW71
Bardsey Wk. N1 142 DQ65
Clephane Rd.
Bardsley Clo., Croy. 202 DT104
Bardsley La. SE10 163 EC79
Bardwell Ct., St.Alb. 43 CD21
Bardwell Rd., St.Alb. 43 CD21
Barfett St. W10 139 CZ70
Barfield (Sutton at Hone), Dart. 188 FP94
Barfield Ave. N20 98 DF47
Barfield Rd. E11 124 EF60
Barfield Rd., Brom. 205 EN97
Barfields, Loug. 85 EN42
Barfields, Red. 251 DP133
Barfields Gdns., Loug. 85 EN42
Barfields
Barfields Path, Loug. 85 EN42
Barfolds, Hat. 45 CW23
Dixons Hill Rd.
Barford Clo. NW4 97 CU53
Barford St. N1 141 DN67
Barforth Rd. SE15 162 DV83
Barfreston Way SE20 202 DV95
Bargate Clo. SE18 165 ET78
Bargate Clo., N.Mal. 199 CU101
Bargate Ct., Guil. 242 AS134
Park Barn Dr.
Barge Ho. Rd. E16 165 EP75
Barge Ho. St. SE1 278 E2
Barge Wk., E.Mol. 197 CD97
Barge Wk., Kings.T. 197 CK96
Barge Wk., Walt. 196 BW97
Bargery Rd. SE6 183 EB88
Bargrove Ave., Hem.H. 40 BG21
Bargrove Clo. SE20 182 DU94
Bargrove Cres. SE6 183 DZ89
Elm La.
Barham Ave., Borwd. 78 CM41
Barham Clo., Brom. 204 EL102
Barham Clo., Chis. 185 EP92
Barham Clo., Grav. 191 GM88
Barham Clo., Rom. 105 FB54
Barham Clo., Wem. 137 CH65
Barham Clo., Wey. 213 BQ105
Barham Rd. SW20 179 CU94
Barham Rd., Chis. 185 EP92
Barham Rd., Dart. 188 FN87
Barham Rd., S.Croy. 220 DQ105
Baring Clo. SE12 184 EG89
Baring Cres., Beac. 88 AJ52
Baring Rd. SE12 184 EG87
Baring Rd., Barn. 80 DD42
Baring Rd., Beac. 88 AJ52
Baring Rd., Croy. 202 DU102
Baring St. N1 142 DR67
Bark Burr Rd., Grays 170 FZ75
Bark Hart Rd., Orp. 206 EV102
Bark Pl. W2 140 DB73
Barker Dr. NW1 141 DJ66
Barker Ms. SW4 161 DH84
Barker Rd., Cher. 193 BE101
Barker St. SW10 160 DC79
Barker Wk. SW16 181 DK90
Mount Ephraim Rd.
Barker Way SE22 182 DU88
Dulwich Common
Barkham Rd. N17 100 DR52
Barking Ind. Pk., Bark. 145 ET67
Barking Rd. E6 144 EK68
Barking Rd. E13 144 EG70
Barking Rd. E16 144 EE71
Barkis Way SE16 162 DV78
Egan Way
Barkston Gdns. SW5 160 DB77
Barkston Path, Borwd. 78 CN37
Walshford Way
Barkway Ct. N4 122 DQ62
Queens Dr.
Barkwood Clo., Rom. 127 FC57
Barkworth Rd. SE16 162 DV78
Credon Rd.
Barlborough St. SE14 163 DX80
Barlby Gdns. W10 139 CX70
Barlby Rd. W10 139 CW71
Barle Gdns., S.Ock. 149 FV72
Barlee Cres., Uxb. 134 BJ71
Barley Clo. (Bushey), Wat. 76 CB43
Barley Cft., Harl. 51 ES19
Barley Cft., Hem.H. 41 BQ20
Barley Cft., Hert. 32 DR07
Barley Flds., H.Wyc. 110 AE55
Barley La., Ilf. 126 EU59
Barley La., Rom. 126 EV56
Barley Mow Ct., Bet. 248 CQ134
Barley Mow La., St.Alb. 44 CL23
Barley Mow Pas. EC1 274 G7
Barley Mow Pas. W4 158 CR78
Heathfield Ter.
Barley Mow Rd., Egh. 172 AW91
Barley Mow Way, Shep. 194 BN98
Barley Ponds Clo., Ware 33 DZ06
Barley Ponds Rd., Ware 33 DZ06
Barley Shotts Business Pk. W10 139 CZ71
St. Ervans Rd.
Barleycorn Way E14 143 DZ73
Barleycorn Way, Horn. 128 FM58
Barleycroft Grn., Welw.G.C. 29 CW09
Barleycroft Rd., Welw.G.C. 29 CW10
Barleyfields Clo., Rom. 126 EV58
Barleymead, Horl. 269 DH147
Oatlands
Barlow Clo., Wall. 219 DL107
Cobham Clo.
Barlow Pl. W1 277 J1
Barlow Rd. NW6 139 CZ65
Barlow Rd. W3 138 CP74
Barlow Rd., Hmptn. 176 CA94
Barlow St. SE17 279 L9
Barlow Way, Rain. 147 FD71
Barmeston Rd. SE6 183 EB89
Barmor Clo., Har. 94 CB54
Barmouth Ave., Grnf. 137 CF68
Barmouth Rd. SW18 180 DC86
Barmouth Rd., Croy. 203 DX103
Barn Clo., Ashf. 175 BP92
Barn Clo., Bans. 234 DD115
Barn Clo., Epsom 232 CQ115
Barn Clo., Hem.H. 40 BM23
Barnfield
Barn Clo., Nthlt. 136 BW68
Barn Clo., Rad. 77 CG35
Barn Clo., Slou. 111 AP63
Barn Clo., Welw.G.C. 29 CW09
Barn Cres., Pur. 220 DR113
Barn Cres., Stan. 95 CJ51
Barn Elms Pk. SW15 159 CW82
Barn End Dr., Dart. 188 FJ90
Barn End La., Dart. 188 FJ93
Barn Hill, Harl. 50 EH19
Barn Hill, Wem. 118 CN60
Barn Lea, Rick. 92 BG46
Barn Mead, Epp. 85 ES36
Barn Mead, Harl. 51 ER17
Barn Mead, Ong. 71 FE29
Barn Meadow La., Lthd. 230 BZ124
Barn Ms., Har. 116 CA62
Barn Ri., Wem. 118 CN60
Barn St. N16 122 DS62
Stoke Newington Ch. St.
Barn Way, Wem. 118 CN60
Barnabas Ct. N21 81 DN43
Cheyne Wk.
Barnabas Rd. E9 123 DX64
Barnaby Clo., Har. 116 CC61
Barnaby Pl. SW7 160 DD77
Barnaby Way, Chig. 103 EN48
Barnacre Clo., Uxb. 134 BK72
New Peachey La.
Barnacres Rd., Hem.H. 58 BM25
Barnard Acres, Wal.Abb. 50 EE23
Barnard Clo. SE18 165 EN76
Barnard Clo., Chis. 205 ER95
Barnard Clo., Sun. 175 BV94
Oak Gro.
Barnard Clo., Wall. 219 DK108
Barnard Ct., Wok. 226 AS118
Raglan Rd.
Barnard Gdns., Hayes 135 BV70
Barnard Gdns., N.Mal. 199 CU98
Barnard Grn., Welw.G.C. 29 CZ10
Barnard Gro. E15 144 EF66
Vicarage La.
Barnard Hill N10 99 DH53
Barnard Ms. SW11 160 DE84
Barnard Rd. SW11 160 DE84
Barnard Rd., Enf. 82 DV40
Barnard Rd., Mitch. 200 DG97
Barnard Rd., Warl. 237 EB119
Barnard Way, Hem.H. 40 BL22
Barnardo Dr., Ilf. 125 EQ56
Civic Way
Barnardo St. E1 143 DX72
Devonport St.
Barnard's Inn EC1 274 D8
Barnards Pl., S.Croy. 219 DP109
Barnato Clo., W.Byf. 212 BL112
Viscount Gdns.
Barnby Sq. E15 144 EE67
Barnby St.
Barnby St. E15 144 EE67
Barnby St. NW1 273 L2
Barnby St. NW1 141 DJ69
Barncroft Clo., Loug. 85 EM43
Barncroft Clo., Uxb. 135 BP71
Harlington Rd.
Barncroft Grn., Loug. 85 EN43
Barncroft Rd., Berk. 38 AT20
Barncroft Rd., Loug. 85 EN43
Barncroft Way, St.Alb. 43 CG21
Barndicott, Welw.G.C. 30 DC09
Barnehurst Ave., Bexh. 167 FC81
Barnehurst Ave., Erith 167 FC81
Barnehurst Clo., Erith 167 FC81
Barnehurst Rd., Bexh. 167 FC82
Barnes All., Hmptn. 196 CC96
Hampton Ct. Rd.
Barnes Ave. SW13 159 CU80
Barnes Ave., Chesh. 54 AQ30
Barnes Ave., Sthl. 156 BZ77
Barnes Bri. SW13 158 CS82
Barnes Bri. W4 158 CS82
Barnes Clo. E12 124 EK63
Barnes Ct. E16 144 EJ71
Ridgwell Rd.
Barnes Ct., Wdf.Grn. 102 EK50
Barnes Cray Cotts., Dart. 187 FG85
Maiden La.
Barnes Cray Rd., Dart. 167 FG84
Barnes End, N.Mal. 199 CU99
Barnes High St. SW13 159 CT82
Barnes Ho., Bark. 145 ER67
St. Marys
Barnes La., Kings L. 58 BH27
Barnes Ri., Kings L. 58 BM27
Barnes Rd. N18 100 DW49
Barnes Rd., Gdmg. 258 AS143
Barnes Rd., Ilf. 125 EQ64
Barnes St. E14 143 DY72
Barnes Ter. SE8 163 DZ78
Barnes Wallis Dr., Wey. 212 BL111
Barnes Way, Iver 133 BF73
Barnesbury Ho. SW4 181 DK86
Barnesdale Cres., Orp. 206 EU100
Barnet Bypass, Barn. 78 CS39
Barnet Dr., Brom. 204 EL103
Barnet Gate La., Barn. 79 CT44
Barnet Gro. E2 142 DU69
Barnet Hill, Barn. 79 CZ42
Barnet Ho. N20 98 DC47
Barnet La. N20 97 CZ46
Barnet La., Barn. 80 DA44
Barnet La., Borwd. 77 CK44
Barnet Rd. (Arkley), Barn. 78 CR44
Barnet Rd., Pot.B. 64 DB34
Barnet Rd., St.Alb. 62 CL27
Barnet Trd. Est., Barn. 79 CZ41
Barnet Way NW7 96 CR48
Barnet Wd. Rd., Brom. 204 EH103
Barnett Clo., Erith 167 FF82
Barnett Clo., Guil. 259 BC143
Barnett Clo., Lthd. 231 CH119
Barnett La., Guil. 259 BB144
Barnett Row, Guil. 242 AX129
Barnett St. E1 142 DV72
Cannon St. Rd.
Barnett Wd. La., Ash. 231 CJ118
Barnett Wd. La., Lthd. 231 CH120
Barnetts Shaw, Oxt. 253 ED127
Barney Clo. SE7 164 EJ78
Barnfield, Bans. 218 DB114
Barnfield, Epp. 70 EU28
Barnfield, Grav. 191 GG89
Barnfield, Hem.H. 40 BM23
Barnfield, Horl. 268 DG149
Barnfield, Iver 133 BE72
Barnfield, N.Mal. 198 CS100
Barnfield, Slou. 131 AK74
Barnfield Ave., Croy. 202 DW103
Barnfield Ave., Kings.T. 178 CL92
Barnfield Ave., Mitch. 201 DH98
Barnfield Clo. N4 121 DL59
Crouch Hill
Barnfield Clo. SW17 180 DC90
Barnfield Clo., Couls. 236 DQ119
Barnfield Clo., Hodd. 49 EA15
Barnfield Clo., Swan. 207 FC101
Barnfield Clo., Wal.Abb. 50 EF22
Hoe La.
Barnfield Gdns. SE18 165 EP79
Plumstead Common Rd.
Barnfield Gdns., Kings.T. 178 CL92
Barnfield Pl. E14 163 EA77
Barnfield Rd. SE18 165 EP79
Barnfield Rd. W5 137 CJ70
Barnfield Rd., Belv. 166 EZ79
Barnfield Rd., Edg. 96 CQ53
Barnfield Rd., Orp. 206 EX97
Barnfield Rd., St.Alb. 43 CJ17
Barnfield Rd., Sev. 256 FD123
Barnfield Rd., S.Croy. 220 DS109
Barnfield Rd., Welw.G.C. 29 CY11
Barnfield Rd., West. 238 EK120
Barnfield Way, Oxt. 254 EG133
Barnfield Wd. Clo., Beck. 203 ED100
Barnfield Wd. Rd., Beck. 203 ED100
Barnham Rd., Grnf. 136 CC69
Barnham St. SE1 279 N4
Barnham St. SE1 162 DS75
Barnhill, Pnr. 116 BW57
Barnhill Ave., Brom. 204 EF99
Barnhill La., Hayes 135 BV70
Barnhill Rd., Hayes 135 BV70
Barnhill Rd., Wem. 118 CQ62
Barnhurst Path, Wat. 94 BW50

Barningham Way NW9 118 CR58
Barnlea Clo., Felt. 176 BY89
Barnmead, Wok. 210 AT110
Barnmead Gdns., Dag. 126 EZ64
Barnmead Rd., Beck. 203 DY95
Barnmead Rd., Dag. 126 EZ64
Barns Ct., Harl. 51 EN20
Barnsbury Clo., N.Mal. 198 CQ98
Barnsbury Cres., Surb. 198 CP102
Barnsbury Est. N1 141 DN67
Barnsbury Rd.
Barnsbury Gro. N7 141 DM65
Barnsbury La., Surb. 198 CP103
Barnsbury Pk. N1 141 DN66
Barnsbury Rd. N1 141 DN68
Barnsbury Sq. N1 141 DN66
Barnsbury St. N1 141 DN66
Barnsbury Ter. N1 141 DM66
Barnscroft SW20 199 CV97
Barnsdale Ave. E14 163 EB77
Barnsdale Clo., Borwd. 78 CM39
Barnsdale Rd. W9 139 CZ70
Barnsfield Pl., Uxb. 134 BJ67
Barnside Ct., Welw.G.C. 29 CW09
Barnsley Rd., Rom. 106 FM52
Barnsley St. E1 142 DV70
Barnstaple Path, Rom. 106 FJ50
Barnstaple Rd.
Barnstaple Rd., Rom. 106 FJ50
Barnstaple Rd., Ruis. 116 BW62
Barnston Wk. N1 142 DQ67
Popham St.
Barnston Way, Brwd. 109 GC43
Barnsway, Kings L. 58 BL28
Barnway, Egh. 172 AW92
Barnwell Rd. SW2 181 DN85
Barnwell Rd., Dart. 168 FM83
Barnwood Clo. W9 140 DB70
Barnwood Clo., Guil. 242 AS132
Barnwood Clo., Ruis. 115 BR61
Lysander Rd.
Barnwood Ct. E16 144 EG74
North Woolwich Rd.
Barnwood Rd., Guil. 242 AS133
Barnyard, The, Tad. 233 CU124
Baron Clo. N11 98 DG50
Balmoral Ave.
Baron Clo., Sutt. 218 DB110
Baron Gdns., Ilf. 125 EQ55
Baron Gro., Mitch. 200 DE98
Baron Rd., Dag. 126 EX60
Baron St. N1 274 D1
Baron St. N1 141 DN68
Baron Wk. E16 144 EF71
Baron Wk., Mitch. 200 DE98
Baroness Rd. E2 142 DT69
Diss St.
Baronet Gro. N17 100 DU53
St. Paul's Rd.
Baronet Rd. N17 100 DU53
Barons, The, Twick. 177 CH86
Barons Ct., Wall. 201 DK104
Whelan Way
Barons Ct. Rd. W14 159 CY78
Barons Gate, Barn. 80 DE44
Barons Hurst, Epsom 232 CQ116
Barons Keep W14 159 CY78
Barons Mead, Har. 117 CE56
Barons Pl. SE1 278 E5
Barons Pl. SE1 161 DN75
Barons Wk., Croy. 203 DY100
Barons Way, Egh. 173 BD93
Barons Way, Reig. 266 DA138
Baronsfield Rd., Twick. 177 CH86
Baronsmead Rd. SW13 159 CU81
Baronsmede W5 158 CM75
Baronsmere Rd. N2 120 DE56
Barque Ms. SE8 163 EA79
Watergate St.
Barr Rd., Grav. 191 GM89
Barr Rd., Pot.B. 64 DC33
Barra Clo., Hem.H. 41 BP23
Barra Hall Circ., Hayes 135 BS72
Barra Hall Rd., Hayes 135 BS73
Barrack La., Wind. 151 AR81
Barrack Path, Wok. 226 AT118
Barrack Rd., Guil. 242 AU132
Barrack Rd., Houns. 156 BX84
Barrack Row, Grav. 191 GH86
Barracks Hill, Amer. 89 AM45
Barracks La., Barn. 79 CY41
High St.
Barrards Way, Beac. 89 AQ51
Barratt Ave. N22 99 DM54
Barratt Ind. Pk., Sthl. 156 CA75
Barratt Way, Har. 117 CD55
Tudor Rd.
Barrenger Rd. N10 98 DF53
Barrens Brae, Wok. 227 BA118
Barrens Clo., Wok. 227 BA119
Barrens Pk., Wok. 227 BA118
Barrett Clo., Rom. 105 FH52
Barrett Rd. E17 123 EC56
Barrett Rd., Lthd. 231 CD124
Barrett St. W1 272 G9
Barrett St. W1 140 DG72
Barretts Grn. Rd. NW10 138 CQ69
Barretts Gro. N16 122 DS64
Barretts Rd., Sev. 241 FD120
Barrhill Rd. SW2 181 DL89
Barricane, Wok. 226 AV119
Barrie Clo., Couls. 235 DJ115
Barrie Est. W2 140 DD73
Craven Ter.
Barrie Twr. W3 158 CQ75
Barriedale SE14 163 DY82
Barrier App. SE7 164 EK76
Barringer Sq. SW17 180 DG91
Barrington Clo. NW5 120 DG64
Grafton Rd.
Barrington Clo., Ilf. 103 EM53
Hurstleigh Gdns.
Barrington Clo., Loug. 85 EQ42
Barrington Rd.
Barrington Ct., Brwd. 109 GC44
Barrington Ct., Dor. 263 CG137
Barrington Rd.
Barrington Dr., Uxb. 92 BG52
Park La.
Barrington Grn., Loug. 85 EQ42
Barrington Lo., Wey. 213 BQ106
Barrington Pk. Gdns., Ch.St.G. 90 AX46
Barrington Rd. E12 145 EN65
Barrington Rd. N8 121 DK57
Barrington Rd. SW9 161 DP83
Barrington Rd., Bexh. 166 EX82
Barrington Rd., Dor. 263 CG137
Barrington Rd., Loug. 85 EQ42
Barrington Rd., Pur. 219 DJ112
Barrington Rd., Sutt. 200 DA102
Barrington Vill. SE18 165 EN81
Barrow Ave., Cars. 218 DF108
Barrow Clo. N21 99 DP48
Barrow Grn. Rd., Oxt. 253 EA130
St. Margarets
Barrow Hedges Clo., Cars. 218 DE108
Barrow Hedges Way, Cars. 218 DE108
Barrow Hill, Wor.Pk. 198 CS103
Barrow Hill Clo., Wor.Pk. 198 CS103
Barrow Hill
Barrow Hill Rd. NW8 272 B1
Barrow Hill Rd. NW8 140 DE68
Barrow La. (Cheshunt), Wal.Cr. 66 DT30
Barrow Pt. Ave., Pnr. 94 BY54
Barrow Pt. La., Pnr. 94 BY54
Barrow Rd. SW16 181 DK93
Barrow Rd., Croy. 219 DN106
Barrow Wk., Brent. 157 CJ78
Glenhurst Rd.
Barrow Way N7 121 DM62
Barrowdene Clo., Pnr. 94 BY54
Paines La.
Barrowell Grn. N21 99 DP47
Barrowfield Clo. N9 100 DV48
Barrowgate Rd. W4 158 CQ78
Barrows Rd., Harl. 51 EM15
Barrowsfield, S.Croy. 220 DT112
Barrs Rd. NW10 138 CR66
Barry Ave. N15 122 DT58
Craven Pk. Rd.
Barry Ave., Bexh. 166 EY80
Barry Ave., Wind. 151 AQ80
Barry Clo., Grays 171 GG76
Barry Clo., Orp. 205 ES104
Barry Clo., St.Alb. 60 CB25
Barry Rd. E6 144 EL72
Barry Rd. NW10 138 CQ66
Barry Rd. SE22 182 DU86
Bars, The, Guil. 258 AX135
Barset Rd. SE15 162 DW83
Barson Clo. SE20 182 DW94
Barston Rd. SE27 182 DQ89
Barstow Cres. SW2 181 DM88
Bartel Clo., Hem.H. 41 BR22
Bartelotts Rd., Slou. 131 AK70
Barter St. WC1 274 A7
Barter St. WC1 141 DL71
Barters Wk., Pnr. 116 BY55
High St.
Barth Rd. SE18 165 ES77
Bartholomew Clo. EC1 275 H7
Bartholomew Clo. EC1 142 DQ71
Bartholomew Clo. SW18 160 DC84
Bartholomew Ct., Dor. 263 CG137
South St.
Bartholomew Dr., Rom. 106 FK54
Bartholomew La. EC2 275 L9
Bartholomew Pl. EC1 275 H7
Bartholomew Rd. NW5 141 DJ65
Bartholomew Sq. E1 142 DV70
Coventry Rd.
Bartholomew Sq. EC1 275 J4
Bartholomew Sq. EC1 142 DQ70
Bartholomew St. SE1 279 L7
Bartholomew St. SE1 162 DR76
Bartholomew Vill. NW5 141 DJ65
Bartholomew Way, Swan. 207 FE97
Bartle Ave. E6 144 EL68
Bartle Rd. W11 139 CY72
Bartlett Clo. E14 143 EA72
Bartlett Ct. EC4 274 E8
Bartlett Rd., Grav. 191 GG88
Bartlett Rd., West. 255 EQ126
Bartlett St., S.Croy. 220 DR106
Bartletts Mead, Hert. 32 DR06
Bartlow Gdns., Rom. 105 FD53
Barton, The, Cob. 214 BW112
Barton Ave., Rom. 127 FB60
Barton Clo. E6 145 EM72
Brandreth Rd.
Barton Clo. E9 122 DW64
Churchill Wk.
Barton Clo. SE15 162 DV83
Kirkwood Rd.
Barton Clo., Add. 212 BG107
Barton Clo., Bexh. 186 EY85
Barton Clo., Chig. 103 EQ47
Barton Clo., Shep. 195 BP100
Barton Grn., N.Mal. 198 CR96
Barton Meadows, Ilf. 125 EP56
Barton Rd. W14 159 CY78
Barton Rd. (Sutton at Hone), Dart. 188 FP94
Barton Rd., Guil. 259 BA144
Barton Rd., Horn. 127 FG60
Barton Rd., Sid. 186 EY93
Barton Rd., Slou. 153 AZ75
Barton St. SW1 277 P6
Barton Way, Borwd. 78 CN40
Barton Way, Rick. 75 BP43
Bartons, The, Borwd. 77 CK44
Bartonway NW8 140 DD68
Queen's Ter.
Bartram Clo., Uxb. 135 BP70
Lees Rd.
Bartram Rd. SE4 183 DY85
Bartrams La., Barn. 80 DC38
Bartrop Clo., Wal.Cr. 66 DR28
Poppy Wk.
Barville Clo. SE4 163 DY84
St. Norbert Rd.
Barwell Trd. Est., Chess. 215 CK109
Barwick Rd. E7 124 EH63
Barwood Ave., W.Wick. 203 EB102
Basden Gro., Felt. 176 CA89
Basedale Rd., Dag. 146 EV66
Baseing Clo. E6 145 EN73
Basford Way, Wind. 151 AK83
Bashley Rd. NW10 138 CR70
Basil Ave. E6 144 EL68
Basil Gdns., Croy. 203 DX102
Primrose La.
Basil St. SW3 276 D6
Basil St. SW3 160 DF76
Basildene Rd., Houns. 156 BX83
Basildon Ave., Ilf. 103 EN53
Basildon Clo., Sutt. 218 DB109
Basildon Rd. SE2 166 EU78
Basildon Rd., Bexh. 166 EY82
Basildon Sq., Hem.H. 40 BM16
Basin S. E16 145 EP74
Basing Clo., T.Ditt. 197 CF101
Basing Ct. SE15 162 DT81
Basing Dr., Bex. 186 EZ86
Basing Hill NW11 119 CZ60
Basing Hill, Wem. 118 CM61
Basing Ho., Bark. 145 ER67
St. Margarets
Basing Ho. Yd. E2 275 N2
Basing Pl. E2 275 N2
Basing Rd., Bans. 217 CZ114
Basing Rd., Rick. 91 BF46
Basing St. W11 139 CZ72
Basing Way N3 120 DA55
Basing Way, T.Ditt. 197 CF101
Basingdon Way SE5 162 DR84
Basingfield Rd., T.Ditt. 197 CF101
Basinghall Ave. EC2 275 K7
Basinghall Ave. EC2 142 DR71
Basinghall Gdns., Sutt. 218 DB109
Basinghall St. EC2 275 K8
Basinghall St. EC2 142 DQ71
Basire St. N1 142 DQ67
Baskerville Rd. SW18 180 DE87
Basket Gdns. SE9 184 EL85
Baslow Clo., Har. 95 CD53
Baslow Wk. E5 123 DX63
Overbury St.
Basnett Rd. SW11 160 DG83
Basque Ct. SE16 163 DX75
Poolmans St.
Bassano St. SE22 182 DT85
Bassant Rd. SE18 165 ET79
Bassein Pk. Rd. W12 159 CT75
Basset Clo., Add. 212 BH110
Basset Ho., Dag. 146 EV67
Bassett Clo., Sutt. 218 DB109
Bassett Gdns., Epp. 71 FB26
Bassett Gdns., Islw. 156 CC80
Bassett Rd. W10 139 CX72
Bassett Rd., Uxb. 134 BJ66
New Windsor St.
Bassett Rd., Wok. 227 BC116
Bassett St. NW5 140 DG65
Bassett Way, Grnf. 136 CB72
Bassett Way, Slou. 131 AL70
Pemberton Rd.
Bassetts Clo., Orp. 205 EP104
Bassetts Way, Orp. 223 EP105
Bassil Rd., Hem.H. 40 BK21
Bassingbourne Clo., Brox. 49 DZ20
Bassingburn Wk., Welw.G.C. 29 CZ10
Bassingham Rd. SW18 180 DC87
Bassingham Rd., Wem. 137 CK65
Bassishaw Highwalk EC2 142 DQ71
London Wall
Basswood Clo. SE15 162 DV83
Linden Gro.
Bastable Ave., Bark. 145 ES68
Bastion Highwalk EC2 142 DQ71
London Wall
Bastion Ho. EC2 142 DQ71
London Wall
Bastion Rd. SE2 166 EU78
Baston Manor Rd., Brom. 204 EH104
Baston Rd., Brom. 204 EH102
Bastwick St. EC1 275 H4
Bastwick St. EC1 142 DQ70
Basuto Rd. SW6 160 DA81
Bat & Ball Rd., Sev. 257 FJ121
Batavia Clo., Sun. 196 BW95
Batavia Ms. SE14 163 DY80
Goodwood Rd.
Batavia Rd. SE14 163 DY80
Batavia Rd., Sun. 195 BV95
Batchelor St. N1 141 DN68
Batchelors Way, Amer. 55 AR39
Batchelors Way, Chesh. 54 AP29
Batchwood Dr., St.Alb. 42 CB19
Batchwood Gdns., St.Alb. 43 CD17
Batchwood Grn., Orp. 206 EU97
Batchwood Vw., St.Alb. 42 CC18
Batchworth Heath Hill, Rick. 92 BN49
Batchworth Hill, Rick. 92 BM48
Batchworth La., Nthwd. 93 BP50
Batchworth Roundabout, Rick. 92 BK46
Bate St. E14 143 DZ73
Three Colt St.
Bateman Clo., Bark. 145 EQ65
Glenny Rd.
Bateman Ho. SE17 161 DP79
Otto St.
Bateman Rd. E4 101 EA51
Bateman Rd., Rick. 74 BN44
Bateman St. W1 273 M9
Bateman's Bldgs. W1 273 M9
Bateman's Row EC2 275 N4
Bateman's Row EC2 142 DS70
Bates Clo., Slou. 132 AY72
Bates Cres. SW16 181 DJ94
Bates Cres., Croy. 219 DN106
Bates Rd., Rom. 106 FN52
Bates Wk., Add. 212 BJ107
Bateson St. SE18 165 ES77
Gunning St.
Bateson Way, Wok. 211 BC114
Batford Clo., Welw.G.C. 30 DB10
Waterford Grn.
Bath Clo. SE15 162 DV80
Asylum Rd.
Bath Ct. EC1 274 D5
Bath Ho. Rd., Croy. 201 DL102
Bath Pas., Kings.T. 197 CK96
St. James Rd.
Bath Pl. EC2 142 DS69
Rivington St.
Bath Pl., Barn. 79 CZ41
Bath Rd. E7 144 EK65
Bath Rd. N9 100 DV47
Bath Rd. W4 158 CS77
Bath Rd., Dart. 187 FH87
Bath Rd., Hayes 155 BS81
Bath Rd., Houns. 156 BX82
Bath Rd., Maid. 130 AC72
Bath Rd., Mitch. 200 DD97
Bath Rd., Rom. 126 EY58
Bath Rd., Slou. 131 AK72
Bath Rd. (Colnbrook), Slou. 153 BB79
Bath Rd. (Poyle), Slou. 153 BE81
Bath Rd., West Dr. 154 BK81
Bath St. EC1 275 J3
Bath St. EC1 142 DQ69
Bath St., Grav. 191 GH86
Bath Ter. SE1 279 H7
Bath Ter. SE1 162 DQ76
Bathgate Rd. SW19 179 CX90
Baths Rd., Brom. 204 EK98
Bathurst Ave. SW19 200 DB95
Brisbane Ave.
Bathurst Clo., Iver 153 BF75
Bathurst Gdns. NW10 139 CV68
Bathurst Ms. W2 272 A10
Bathurst Rd., Hem.H. 40 BK17
Bathurst Rd., Ilf. 125 EP60
Bathurst St. W2 272 A10
Bathurst St. W2 140 DD73
Bathurst Wk., Iver 153 BE75
Bathway SE18 165 EN77
Batley Clo., Mitch. 200 DF101
Batley Pl. N16 122 DT62
Batley Rd. N16 122 DT62
Stoke Newington High St.
Batley Rd., Enf. 82 DR39
Batman Clo. W12 139 CV74
Baton Clo., Purf. 169 FR77
Brimfield Rd.
Batoum Gdns. W6 159 CW76
Batson St. W12 159 CU75
Batsworth Rd., Mitch. 200 DD97
Batten Ave., Wok. 226 AS119
Batten Clo. E6 145 EM72
Savage Gdns.
Batten St. SW11 160 DE83
Battenburg Wk. SE19 182 DS92
Brabourne Clo.
Batterdale, Hat. 45 CW17
Battersby Rd. SE6 183 ED89
Battersea Bri. SW3 160 DD80
Battersea Bri. SW11 160 DE80
Battersea Bri. Rd. SW11 160 DE80
Battersea Ch. Rd. SW11 160 DD81
Battersea High St. SW11 160 DD81
Battersea Pk. SW11 160 DF80
Battersea Pk. Rd. SW8 161 DH81
Battersea Pk. Rd. SW11 160 DE82
Battersea Ri. SW11 180 DD85
Battersea Sq. SW11 160 DD81
Battersea High St.
Battery Rd. SE28 165 ES75
Battis, The, Rom. 127 FE58
Waterloo Rd.
Battishill Gdns. N1 141 DP66
Waterloo Ter.
Battishill St. N1 141 DP66
Waterloo Ter.
Battle Bri. La. SE1 279 M3
Battle Bri. La. SE1 142 DS74
Battle Bri. Rd. NW1 273 P1
Battle Bri. Rd. NW1 141 DL68
Battle Clo. SW19 180 DC93
North Rd.
Battle Rd., Belv. 167 FC77
Battle Rd., Erith 167 FC77
Battlebridge La., Red. 251 DH130
Battledean Rd. N5 121 DP64
Battlefield Rd., St.Alb. 43 CF18
Battlemead Clo., Maid. 130 AC68
Battlers Grn. Dr., Rad. 77 CE37
Batts Hill, Red. 250 DE132
Batts Hill, Reig. 250 DD132
Batty St. E1 142 DU72
Baudwin Rd. SE6 184 EE89
Baugh Rd., Sid. 186 EW92
Baulk, The SW18 180 DA87
Bavant Rd. SW16 201 DM96
Bavaria Rd. N19 121 DL61
Bavent Rd. SE5 162 DQ82
Bawdale Rd. SE22 182 DT85
Bawdsey Ave., Ilf. 125 ET56
Bawtree Clo., Sutt. 218 DC110
Bawtree Rd. SE14 163 DY80
Bawtree Rd., Uxb. 134 BK65
Bawtry Rd. N20 98 DF48
Baxendale N20 98 DC47
Baxendale St. E2 142 DU69
Baxter Ave., Red. 250 DE134
Baxter Clo., Uxb. 135 BP69
Baxter Rd. E16 144 EJ72
Baxter Rd. N1 142 DR65
Baxter Rd. N18 100 DV49
Baxter Rd. NW10 138 CS70
Baxter Rd., Ilf. 125 EP64
Bay Clo., Horl. 268 DE145
Bay Ct. W5 158 CL76
Popes La.
Bay Manor La., Grays 169 FT79
Bay Tree Clo., Brom. 204 EJ95
Bay Tree Wk., Wat. 75 BT38
Bayards, Warl. 236 DW118
Baydon Ct., Brom. 204 EF97
Bayeaux, Tad. 233 CX122
Heathcote
Bayes Clo. SE26 182 DW92
Bayfield Rd. SE9 164 EK84
Bayfield Rd., Horl. 268 DE147
Bayford Clo., Hem.H. 41 BQ15
Bayford Clo., Hert. 32 DQ11
Bayford Grn., Hert. 47 DN17
Bayford La., Hert. 31 DM14
Bayford Ms. E8 142 DV66
Bayford St.
Bayford Rd. NW10 139 CX69
Bayford St. E8 142 DV66
Bayham Pl. NW1 141 DJ67
Bayham Rd. W4 158 CR76
Bayham Rd. W13 137 CH73
Bayham Rd., Mord. 200 DB98
Bayham Rd., Sev. 257 FJ123
Bayham St. NW1 141 DJ67
Bayhorne La., Horl. 269 DJ150
Bayhurst Dr., Nthwd. 93 BT51
Bayley Cres., Slou. 131 AG71
Bayley St. WC1 273 M7
Bayley St. WC1 141 DK71
Bayley Wk. SE2 166 EY78
Woolwich Rd.
Bayleys Mead, Brwd. 109 GC47
Baylie Ct., Hem.H. 40 BL19
Baylie La.
Baylie La., Hem.H. 40 BL19
Baylin Rd. SW18 180 DB86
Garratt La.
Baylis Par., Slou. 132 AS72
Oatlands Dr.
Baylis Rd. SE1 278 D5
Baylis Rd. SE1 161 DN75
Baylis Rd., Slou. 131 AR73
Bayliss Ave. SE28 146 EX73
Bayliss Clo. N21 81 DL43
Macleod Rd.
Bayly Rd., Dart. 188 FN86
Baymans Wd., Brwd. 109 FZ47
Bayne Clo. E6 145 EM72
Savage Gdns.
Bayne Hill, Beac. 89 AR52
Bayne Hill Clo., Beac. 89 AR52
Baynes Clo., Enf. 82 DU39
Baynes Ms. NW3 140 DD65
Belsize La.
Baynes St. NW1 141 DJ66
Baynham Clo., Bex. 186 EZ86
Bayonne Rd. W6 159 CY79
Bayshill Ri., Nthlt. 136 CB65
Bayston Rd. N16 122 DT62
Bayswater Rd. W2 140 DB73
Baythorne St. E3 143 DZ71
Baytree Clo., Sid. 185 ET88
Baytree Clo., Wal.Cr. 66 DT27
Baytree Ct., Slou. 130 AJ69
Baytree Rd. SW2 161 DM84
Baywood Sq., Chig. 104 EV49
Bazalgette Clo., N.Mal. 198 CR99
Bazalgette Gdns., N.Mal. 198 CR99
Bazely St. E14 143 EC73
Bazile Rd. N21 81 DN44
Beach Gro., Felt. 176 CA89
Beacham Clo. SE7 164 EK78
Beachborough Rd., Brom. 183 EC91
Beachcroft Rd. E11 124 EE62
Beachcroft Way N19 121 DK60
Beachy Rd. E3 143 EA66
Beacon Clo., Bans. 233 CX116
Beacon Clo., Ger.Cr. 90 AY52
Beacon Clo., Uxb. 114 BK64
Beacon Dr., Dart. 189 FV90
Beacon Gate SE14 163 DX82
Beacon Gro., Cars. 218 DG105
Beacon Hill N7 121 DL64
Beacon Hill, H.Wyc. 88 AD48
Beacon Hill, Purf. 168 FP78
Beacon Hill, Wok. 226 AV119
Beacon Ri., Sev. 256 FG126
Beacon Rd. SE13 183 ED86
Beacon Rd., Erith 167 FH80
Beacon Rd., Houns. 174 BN86
Beacon Rd., Ware 33 EA05
Beacon Way, Bans. 233 CX116
Beacon Way, Beac. 88 AG54
Holtspur Way
Beacon Way, Rick. 92 BG45
Beaconfield Ave., Epp. 69 ET29
Beaconfield Rd., Epp. 69 ET29
Beaconfield Way, Epp. 69 ET29
Beaconfields, Sev. 256 FF126
Beacons, The, Loug. 85 EN38
Beacons Clo. E6 144 EL71
Oliver Gdns.
Beaconsfield Clo. N11 98 DG50
Beaconsfield Clo. SE3 164 EG79
Beaconsfield Clo. W4 158 CQ78
Beaconsfield Clo., Hat. 45 CW17
Beaconsfield Common La., Slou. 111 AQ58
Beaconsfield Par. SE9 184 EL91
Beaconsfield Rd.
Beaconsfield Pl., Epsom 216 CS112
Beaconsfield Rd. E10 123 EC61
Beaconsfield Rd. E16 144 EF70
Beaconsfield Rd. E17 123 DZ58
Beaconsfield Rd. N9 100 DU48
Beaconsfield Rd. N11 98 DG48
Beaconsfield Rd. N15 122 DS56
Beaconsfield Rd. NW10 139 CT65
Beaconsfield Rd. SE3 164 EF80
Beaconsfield Rd. SE9 184 EL89
Beaconsfield Rd. SE17 162 DR79
Beaconsfield Rd. W4 158 CR76
Beaconsfield Rd. W5 157 CJ75
Beaconsfield Rd., Bex. 187 FD89
Beaconsfield Rd., Brom. 204 EK97
Beaconsfield Rd., Croy. 202 DR100
Beaconsfield Rd., Enf. 83 DX37
Beaconsfield Rd., Epsom 232 CR119
Beaconsfield Rd., Esher 215 CE108
Beaconsfield Rd., Hat. 45 CW17
Beaconsfield Rd., Hayes 136 BW74
Beaconsfield Rd., N.Mal. 198 CR96
Beaconsfield Rd., St.Alb. 43 CE20
Beaconsfield Rd., Slou. 131 AQ68
Beaconsfield Rd., Sthl. 136 BX74
Beaconsfield Rd., Surb. 198 CM101
Beaconsfield Rd., Twick. 177 CH86
Beaconsfield Rd., Wok. 227 AZ120
Beaconsfield Ter., Rom. 126 EX58
Beaconsfield Ter. Rd. W14 159 CY76
Beaconsfield Wk. E6 145 EN72
East Ham Manor Way
Beaconsfield Wk. SW6 159 CZ81
Parsons Grn. La.
Beacontree Ave. E17 101 ED53
Beacontree Rd. E11 124 EF59
Beadles La., Oxt. 253 ED130
Beadlow Clo., Cars. 200 DD100
Olveston Wk.
Beadman Pl. SE27 181 DP91
Norwood High St.
Beadman St. SE27 181 DP91
Beadnell Rd. SE23 183 DX88
Beadon Rd. W6 159 CW77
Beadon Rd., Brom. 204 EG98
Beads Hall La., Brwd. 108 FV42
Beaford Gro. SW20 199 CY97
Beagle Clo., Felt. 175 BV91
Beagle Clo., Rad. 77 CF37
Beagles Clo., Orp. 206 EX103
Beak St. W1 273 L10
Beak St. W1 141 DJ73
Beal Clo., Well. 166 EU81
Beal Rd., Ilf. 125 EN61
Beale Clo. N13 99 DP50
Beale Pl. E3 143 DZ68
Beale Rd. E3 143 DZ67
Beales La., Wey. 194 BN104
Beales Rd., Lthd. 246 CB127
Bealings End, Beac. 89 AK50
Beam Ave., Dag. 147 FB67
Beam Way, Dag. 147 FD66
Beaminster Gdns., Ilf. 103 EP54

Beamish Clo., Epp. 71 FC25
Beamish Dr. (Bushey), Wat. 94 CC46
Beamish Rd. N9 100 DU46
Beamish Rd., Orp. 206 EW101
Bean La., Dart. 189 FV89
Bean Rd., Bexh. 166 EX84
Bean Rd., Green. 189 FV85
Beanacre Clo. E9 143 DZ65
Beane Rd., Hert. 31 DP09
Beanshaw SE9 185 EN91
Beansland Gro., Rom. 104 EY54
Bear All. EC4 274 F8
Bear Clo., Rom. 127 FB58
Bear Gdns. SE1 279 H2
Bear Gdns. SE1 142 DQ74
Bear La. SE1 278 G3
Bear La. SE1 141 DP74
Bear Rd., Felt. 176 BX92
Bear St. WC2 273 N10
Beard Rd., Kings.T. 178 CM92
Beardell St. SE19 182 DT93
Beardow Gro. N14 81 DJ44
Beard's Hill, Hmptn. 196 CA95
Beard's Hill Clo., Hmptn. 196 CA95
Beard's Hill
Beards Rd., Ashf. 175 BS93
Beardsfield E13 144 EG67
Valetta Gro.
Beardsley Ter., Dag. 126 EV64
Fitzstephen Rd.
Beardsley Way W3 158 CR75
Bearfield Rd., Kings.T. 178 CL94
Bearing Clo., Chig. 104 EU49
Bearing Way, Chig. 104 EU49
Bears Den, Tad. 233 CZ122
Bearstead Ri. SE4 183 DZ85
Bearstead Ter., Beck. 203 EA95
Copers Cope Rd.
Bearswood End, Beac. 89 AL51
Bearwood Clo., Add. 212 BG107
Ongar Pl.
Bearwood Clo., Pot.B. 64 DD31
Beasley's Ait La., Sun. 195 BT100
Beasleys Yd., Uxb. 134 BJ66
Warwick Pl.
Beatrice Ave. SW16 201 DM96
Beatrice Ave., Wem. 118 CL64
Beatrice Clo. E13 144 EG70
Chargeable La.
Beatrice Clo., Pnr. 115 BU56
Reid Clo.
Beatrice Ct., Buck.H. 102 EK47
Beatrice Gdns., Grav. 190 GE89
Beatrice Pl. W8 160 DB76
Beatrice Rd. E17 123 EA57
Beatrice Rd. N4 121 DN59
Beatrice Rd. N9 100 DW45
Beatrice Rd. SE1 162 DU77
Beatrice Rd., Oxt. 254 EE129
Beatrice Rd., Rich. 178 CM85
Albert Rd.
Beatrice Rd., Sthl. 136 BZ74
Beatson Wk. SE16 143 DY74
Beattie Clo., Lthd. 230 BZ124
Beattock Ri. N10 121 DH56
Beatty Ave., Guil. 243 BA133
Beatty Rd. N16 122 DS63
Beatty Rd., Stan. 95 CJ51
Beatty St. NW1 141 DJ68
Beattyville Gdns., Ilf. 125 EN55
Beauchamp Clo. W4 158 CQ76
Church Path
Beauchamp Gdns., Rick. 92 BG46
Beauchamp Pl. SW3 276 C6
Beauchamp Pl. SW3 160 DE76
Beauchamp Rd. E7 144 EH66
Beauchamp Rd. SE19 202 DR95
Beauchamp Rd. SW11 160 DE84
Beauchamp Rd., E.Mol. 196 CB99
Beauchamp Rd., Sutt. 218 DA105
Beauchamp Rd., Twick. 177 CG87
Beauchamp Rd., W.Mol. 196 CB99
Beauchamp St. EC1 274 D7
Beauchamp Ter. SW15 159 CV83
Dryburgh Rd.
Beauclare Clo., Lthd. 231 CK121
Hatherwood
Beauclerc Rd. W6 159 CV76
Beauclerk Clo., Felt. 175 BV88
Florence Rd.
Beaudesert Ms., West Dr. 154 BL75
Beaufort E6 145 EN71
Newark Knok
Beaufort Ave., Har. 117 CG56
Beaufort Clo. E4 101 EB51
Higham Sta. Ave.
Beaufort Clo. SW15 179 CV87
Beaufort Clo. W5 138 CM71
Beaufort Clo., Epp. 70 FA26
Beaufort Clo., Grays 170 FZ76
Clifford Rd.
Beaufort Clo., Reig. 249 CZ133
Beaufort Clo., Rom. 127 FC56
Beaufort Clo., Wok. 227 BC116
Beaufort Ct., Rich. 177 CJ91
Beaufort Rd.
Beaufort Dr. NW11 120 DA56
Beaufort Gdns. NW4 119 CW58
Beaufort Gdns. SW3 276 C6
Beaufort Gdns. SW3 160 DE76
Beaufort Gdns. SW16 181 DM94
Beaufort Gdns., Houns. 156 BY81
Beaufort Gdns., Ilf. 125 EN60
Beaufort Ms. SW6 159 CZ79
Lillie Rd.
Beaufort Pk. NW11 120 DA56
Beaufort Pl., Maid. 150 AD75
Beaufort Rd. W5 138 CM71
Beaufort Rd., Kings.T. 198 CL98
Beaufort Rd., Reig. 249 CZ133
Beaufort Rd., Rich. 177 CJ91
Beaufort Rd., Ruis. 115 BR61
Lysander Rd.
Beaufort Rd., Twick. 177 CJ87
Beaufort Rd., Wok. 227 BC116
Beaufort St. SW3 160 DD79
Beaufort Way, Epsom 217 CU108
Beauforts, Egh. 172 AW92
Beaufoy Rd. N17 100 DS52
Beaufoy Wk. SE11 278 C9
Beaufoy Wk. SE11 161 DM77
Beaulieu Ave. SE26 182 DV91
Beaulieu Clo. NW9 118 CS55
Beaulieu Clo. SE5 162 DR83
Beaulieu Clo., Houns. 176 BZ85
Beaulieu Clo., Mitch. 200 DG95
Beaulieu Clo., Slou. 152 AV81
Beaulieu Clo., Twick. 177 CK86
Beaulieu Clo., Wat. 94 BW46
Beaulieu Dr., Pnr. 116 BX58
Beaulieu Gdns. N21 100 DQ45
Beaulieu Pl. W4 158 CQ76
Rothschild Rd.
Beauly Way, Rom. 105 FE53
Beaumanor Gdns. SE9 185 EN91
Beanshaw
Beaumaris Dr., Wdf.Grn. 102 EK52
Beaumayes Clo., Hem.H. 40 BH21
Beaumont Ave. W14 159 CZ78
Beaumont Ave., Har. 116 CB58
Beaumont Ave., Rich. 158 CM83
Beaumont Ave., St.Alb. 43 CH18
Beaumont Ave., Wem. 117 CJ64
Beaumont Clo., Kings.T. 178 CN94
Beaumont Clo., Rom. 106 FJ54
Beaumont Cres. W14 159 CZ78
Beaumont Cres., Rain. 147 FG65
Beaumont Dr., Ashf. 175 BR92
Beaumont Dr., Grav. 190 GE87
Beaumont Dr., St.Alb. 43 CE18
Beaumont Gdns. NW3 120 DA62
Beaumont Gdns., Brwd. 109 GC44
Bannister Dr.
Beaumont Gate, Rad. 77 CH35
Shenley Hill
Beaumont Gro. E1 143 DX70
Beaumont Ms. W1 272 G6
Beaumont Pk. Dr., Harl. 50 EH15
Beaumont Pl. W1 273 L4
Beaumont Pl. W1 141 DJ70
Beaumont Pl., Barn. 79 CZ39
Beaumont Pl., Islw. 177 CF85
Beaumont Ri. N19 121 DK59
Beaumont Rd. E10 123 EB59
Beaumont Rd. E13 144 EH69
Beaumont Rd. SE19 182 DQ93
Beaumont Rd. SW19 179 CY87
Beaumont Rd. W4 158 CQ76
Beaumont Rd., Brox. 48 DR24
Beaumont Rd., Orp. 205 ER100
Beaumont Rd., Pur. 219 DN113
Beaumont Rd., Slou. 131 AR70
Beaumont Rd., Wind. 151 AQ82
Beaumont Sq. E1 143 DX70
Beaumont St. W1 272 G6
Beaumont St. W1 140 DG71
Beaumont Vw. 66 DR26
(Cheshunt), Wal.Cr.
Beaumont Wk. NW3 140 DF66
Beaumonts, Red. 266 DF142
Beauvais Ter., Nthlt. 136 BX69
Beauval Rd. SE22 182 DT86
Beaver Clo. SE20 182 DU94
Lullington Rd.
Beaver Clo., Hmptn. 196 CB95
Beaver Gro., Nthlt. 136 BY69
Jetstar Way
Beaver Rd., Ilf. 104 EW50
Beaverbank Rd. SE9 185 ER88
Beavers Clo., Guil. 242 AS133
Beavers Cres., Houns. 156 BX84
Beavers La., Houns. 156 BW82
Beavers La. Camp, Houns. 156 BW83
Beaverwood Rd., Chis. 185 ES93
Beavor Gro. W6 159 CU77
Beavor La.
Beavor La. W6 159 CU77
Bebbington Rd. SE18 165 ES77
Beblets Clo., Orp. 223 ET106
Bec Clo., Ruis. 116 BX62
Beccles Dr., Bark. 145 ES65
Beccles St. E14 143 DZ73
Beck Clo. SE13 163 EB81
Beck Ct., Beck. 203 DX97
Beck La., Beck. 203 DX97
Beck River Pk., Beck. 203 EA95
Rectory Rd.
Beck Rd. E8 142 DV67
Beck Way, Beck. 203 DZ97
Beckenham Gdns. N9 100 DS48
Beckenham Gro., Brom. 203 ED96
Beckenham Hill Rd. SE6 183 EC92
Beckenham Hill Rd., 183 EB92
Beck.
Beckenham La., Brom. 204 EE96
Beckenham Pl. Pk., Beck. 183 EB94
Beckenham Rd., Beck. 203 DX95
Beckenham Rd., W.Wick. 203 EB101
Beckenshaw Gdns., Bans. 234 DD115
Beckers, The N16 122 DU62
Rectory Rd.
Becket Ave. E6 145 EN69
Becket Clo. SE25 202 DU100
Becket Clo., Brwd. 107 FW51
Becket Fold, Har. 117 CF57
Courtfield Cres.
Becket Rd. N18 100 DW49
Becket St. SE1 279 K6
Beckets Sq., Berk. 38 AU17
Bridle Way
Beckett Ave., Ken. 235 DP115
Beckett Clo. NW10 138 CR65
Beckett Clo. SW16 181 DK89
Beckett Clo., Belv. 166 EY76
Tunstock Way
Beckett Wk., Beck. 183 DY93
Becketts, Hert. 31 DN10
Becketts Ave., St.Alb. 42 CC17
Becketts Clo., Felt. 175 BV86
Becketts Clo., Orp. 205 ET104
Becketts Pl., Kings.T. 197 CK95
Beckford Dr., Orp. 205 ER101
Beckford Pl. SE17 162 DQ78
Walworth Rd.
Beckford Rd., Croy. 202 DT100
Beckingham Rd., Guil. 242 AU133
Beckings Way, H.Wyc. 110 AC56
Becklow Gdns. W12 159 CU75
Becklow Rd.
Becklow Rd. W12 159 CT75
Beckman Clo., Sev. 241 FC115
Becks Rd., Sid. 186 EU90
Beckton Pk. Roundabout 164 EK76
E16
Royal Albert Way
Beckton Retail Pk. E6 145 EN71
Beckton Rd. E16 144 EF71
Beckway Rd. SW16 201 DK96
Beckway St. SE17 279 M9
Beckway St. SE17 162 DR77
Beckwith Rd. SE24 182 DR86
Beclands Rd. SW17 180 DG93
Becmead Ave. SW16 181 DK91
Becmead Ave., Har. 117 CH57
Becondale Rd. SE19 182 DS92
Becontree Ave., Dag. 126 EV63
Bective Pl. SW15 159 CZ84
Bective Rd.
Bective Rd. E7 124 EG63
Bective Rd. SW15 159 CY84
Becton Pl., Erith 167 FB80
Bedale Rd., Enf. 82 DQ38
Bedale Rd., Rom. 106 FN50
Bedale St. SE1 279 K3
Bedale St. SE1 142 DR74
Bedale Wk., Dart. 188 FP88
Princes Ave.
Beddington Fm. Rd., Croy. 201 DL101
Beddington Gdns., Cars. 218 DG107
Beddington Gdns., Wall. 219 DH107
Beddington Grn., Orp. 205 ET95
Beddington Gro., Wall. 219 DK106
Beddington La., Croy. 201 DJ99
Beddington Path, Orp. 205 ET95
Beddington Rd., Ilf. 125 ET59
Beddington Rd., Orp. 205 ES95
Beddington Trd. Pk. W., 201 DL102
Croy.
Beddington Fm. Rd.
Beddlestead La., Warl. 238 EF117
Bede Clo., Pnr. 94 BX53
Bede Rd., Rom. 126 EW58
Bedenham Way SE15 162 DT80
Daniel Gdns.
Bedens Rd., Sid. 186 EY93
Bedfont Clo., Felt. 175 BQ86
Bedfont Clo., Mitch. 200 DG96
Bedfont Ct., Stai. 154 BH84
Bedfont Ct. Est., Stai. 154 BG83
Bedfont Grn. Clo., Felt. 175 BQ88
Bedfont La., Felt. 175 BS87
Bedfont Rd., Felt. 175 BQ88
Bedfont Rd., Stai. 174 BL86
Bedford Ave. WC1 273 N7
Bedford Ave. WC1 141 DK71
Bedford Ave., Amer. 72 AW39
Bedford Ave., Barn. 79 CZ43
Bedford Ave., Hayes 135 BV72
Bedford Ave., Slou. 131 AM72
Bedford Clo. N10 98 DG52
Bedford Clo. W4 158 CS79
Bedford Clo., Rick. 73 BB38
Bedford Clo., Wok. 226 AW115
Bedford Cor. W4 158 CS77
The Ave.
Bedford Ct. WC2 277 P1
Bedford Cres., Enf. 83 DY35
Bedford Dr., Slou. 111 AP64
Bedford Gdns. W8 140 DA74
Bedford Gdns., Horn. 128 FJ61
Bedford Hill SW12 181 DH88
Bedford Hill SW16 181 DH88
Bedford Ho. SW4 161 DL84
Bedford Pk., Croy. 202 DQ102
Bedford Pk. Rd., St.Alb. 43 CE20
Bedford Pas. SW6 159 CY80
Dawes Rd.
Bedford Pl. WC1 273 P6
Bedford Pl. WC1 141 DL71
Bedford Pl., Croy. 202 DR102
Bedford Rd. E6 145 EN67
Bedford Rd. E17 101 EA54
Bedford Rd. E18 102 EG54
Bedford Rd. N2 120 DE55
Bedford Rd. N8 121 DK58
Bedford Rd. N9 100 DV45
Bedford Rd. N15 122 DS56
Bedford Rd. N22 99 DL53
Bedford Rd. NW7 96 CS47
Bedford Rd. SW4 161 DL83
Bedford Rd. W4 158 CR76
Bedford Rd. W13 137 CH73
Bedford Rd., Dart. 188 FN87
Bedford Rd., Grav. 191 GF89
Bedford Rd., Grays 170 GB78
Bedford Rd., Guil. 258 AW135
Bedford Rd., Har. 116 CC58
Bedford Rd., Ilf. 125 EP62
Bedford Rd., Nthwd. 93 BQ48
Bedford Rd., Orp. 206 EV103
Bedford Rd., Ruis. 115 BT63
Bedford Rd., St.Alb. 43 CE21
Bedford Rd., Sid. 185 ES90
Bedford Rd., Twick. 177 CD90
Bedford Rd., Wor.Pk. 199 CW103
Bedford Row WC1 274 C6
Bedford Row WC1 141 DM71
Bedford Sq. WC1 273 N7
Bedford Sq. WC1 141 DK71
Bedford St. WC2 273 P10
Bedford St. WC2 141 DL73
Bedford St., Berk. 38 AX19
Bedford St., Wat. 75 BV39
Bedford Ter. SW2 181 DL85
Lyham Rd.
Bedford Way WC1 273 N5
Bedford Way WC1 141 DK70
Bedfordbury WC2 277 P1
Bedgebury Gdns. SW19 179 CY89
Bedgebury Rd. SE9 164 EK84
Bedivere Rd., Brom. 184 EG90
Bedlow Way, Croy. 219 DM105
Bedmond Grn., Abb.L. 59 BT27
Bedmond La., St.Alb. 42 BZ22
Bedmond La. (Potters 42 BW24
Crouch), St.Alb.
Bedmond Rd., Abb.L. 59 BT29
Bedmond Rd., Hem.H. 41 BQ21
Bedonwell Rd. SE2 166 EY79
Bedonwell Rd., Belv. 166 EY79
Bedonwell Rd., Bexh. 166 EZ81
Bedser Clo. SE11 161 DM79
Harleyford Rd.
Bedser Clo., Th.Hth. 202 DQ97
Bedser Dr., Grnf. 117 CD64
Bedster Gdns., W.Mol. 196 CB96
Bedwardine Rd. SE19 182 DS94
Bedwell Ave., Hat. 46 DG18
Bedwell Ave., Hert. 46 DG17
Bedwell Clo., Welw.G.C. 29 CY10
Bedwell Gdns., Hayes 155 BS78
Bedwell Rd. N17 100 DS53
Bedwell Rd., Belv. 166 FA78
Bedwin Way SE16 162 DV78
Catlin St.
Beeby Rd. E16 144 EH71
Beech Ave. N20 98 DE46
Beech Ave. W3 138 CS74
Beech Ave., Brent. 157 CH80
Beech Ave., Brwd. 109 FZ48
Beech Ave., Buck.H. 102 EH47
Beech Ave., Enf. 81 DN35
Beech Ave., Lthd. 246 BX128
Beech Ave., Rad. 61 CG33
Beech Ave., Ruis. 115 BV60
Beech Ave., Sid. 186 EU87
Beech Ave., S.Croy. 220 DR111
Beech Ave., Swan. 207 FF98
Beech Ave., Upmin. 128 FP62
Beech Ave., West. 238 EK119
Westmore Rd.
Beech Bottom, St.Alb. 43 CD17
Beech Clo. N9 82 DU44
Beech Clo. SE8 163 DZ79
Clyde St.
Beech Clo. SW15 179 CU87
Beech Clo. SW19 179 CW93
Beech Clo., Ashf. 175 BR92
Beech Clo., Cars. 200 DF103
Beech Clo., Cob. 214 CA112
Beech Clo., Dor. 263 CG135
Beech Clo., Hat. 45 CU19
Beech Clo., Horn. 127 FH62
Beech Clo., Lthd. 246 BX128
Beech Clo., Stai. 174 BK87
St. Marys Cres.
Beech Clo., Sun. 196 BX96
Harfield Rd.
Beech Clo., Walt. 214 BW105
Beech Clo., Ware 33 DX08
Beech Clo., W.Byf. 212 BL112
Beech Clo., West Dr. 154 BN76
Beech Clo. Ct., Cob. 214 BZ111
Beech Copse, Brom. 205 EM96
Beech Copse, S.Croy. 220 DS106
Beech Ct. E17 123 ED55
Beech Ct. SE9 184 EL86
Beech Ct., Ilf. 125 EN62
Riverdene Rd.
Beech Cres., Tad. 248 CQ130
Beech Dell, Kes. 223 EM105
Beech Dr. N2 98 DF54
Beech Dr., Berk. 38 AW20
Beech Dr., Borwd. 78 CM40
Beech Dr., Reig. 250 DD134
Beech Dr., Saw. 36 EW07
Beech Dr., Tad. 233 CZ122
Beech Dr., Wok. 228 BG124
Beech Fm. Rd., Warl. 237 EC120
Beech Gdns. EC2 142 DQ71
Aldersgate St.
Beech Gdns. W5 158 CL75
Beech Gdns., Dag. 147 FB66
Beech Gdns., Wok. 226 AY115
Beech Gro., Add. 212 BH105
Beech Gro., Amer. 55 AQ39
Beech Gro., Cat. 252 DS126
Beech Gro., Croy. 221 DY110
Beech Gro., Epsom 233 CV117
Beech Gro., Guil. 242 AT134
Beech Gro., Ilf. 103 ES51
Beech Gro., Lthd. 246 CA127
Beech Gro., Mitch. 201 DK99
Beech Gro., N.Mal. 198 CR97
Beech Gro., S.Ock. 148 FQ74
Beech Gro., Wok. 226 AX123
Beech Hall Cres. E4 101 ED52
Beech Hall Rd. E4 101 EC52
Beech Hill, Barn. 80 DD38
Beech Hill, Wok. 226 AX123
Beech Hill Ave., Barn. 80 DC39
Beech Hill Ct., Berk. 38 AX18
Beech Hill Gdns., Wal.Abb. 84 EH37
Beech Holt, Lthd. 231 CJ122
Beech Ho., Croy. 221 EB107
Beech Ho. Rd., Croy. 202 DR104
Beech Hyde La., St.Alb. 28 CM07
Beech La., Beac. 90 AS52
Beech La., Buck.H. 102 EH47
Beech La., Guil. 258 AW137
Beech Lawns N12 98 DD50
Beech Lo., Stai. 173 BE92
Beech Pk., Amer. 72 AV39
Beech Pl., Epp. 69 ET31
Beech Pl., St.Alb. 43 CD17
Beech Rd. N11 99 DL51
Beech Rd. SW16 201 DL96
Beech Rd., Dart. 188 FK88
Beech Rd., Epsom 233 CT115
Beech Rd., Felt. 175 BS87
Beech Rd., Orp. 224 EU108
Beech Rd., Red. 251 DJ126
Beech Rd., Reig. 250 DA131
Beech Rd., St.Alb. 43 CE17
Beech Rd., Sev. 257 FH125
Victoria Rd.
Beech Rd., Slou. 152 AY75
Beech Rd., Wat. 75 BU37
Beech Rd., West. 238 EH118
Beech Rd., Wey. 213 BR105
Beech Row, Rich. 178 CL91
Beech St. EC2 275 H6
Beech St. EC2 142 DQ71
Beech St., Rom. 127 FC56
Beech Tree Glade E4 102 EF46
Forest Side
Beech Wk. NW7 96 CS51
Beech Wk., Dart. 167 FG84
Beech Wk., Epsom 217 CU111
Beech Wk., Hodd. 49 DZ17
Beech Way NW10 138 CR66
Beech Way, Epsom 233 CT115
Beech Way, S.Croy. 221 DX113
Beech Way, Twick. 176 CA90
Beech Waye, Ger.Cr. 113 AZ59
Beechall, Cher. 211 BC108
Beechcroft, Ash. 232 CM119
Beechcroft, Chis. 185 EN94
Beechcroft Ave. NW11 119 CZ59
Beechcroft Ave., Bexh. 167 FD81
Beechcroft Ave., Har. 116 CA59
Beechcroft Ave., Ken. 236 DR115
Beechcroft Ave., N.Mal. 198 CQ95
Beechcroft Ave., Rick. 75 BQ44
Beechcroft Ave., Sthl. 136 BZ74
Beechcroft Clo., Houns. 156 BY80
Beechcroft Clo., Orp. 223 ER105
Beechcroft Gdns., Wem. 118 CM62
Beechcroft Manor, Wey. 195 BR104
Beechcroft Rd. E18 102 EH54
Beechcroft Rd. SW14 158 CQ83
Elm Rd.
Beechcroft Rd. SW17 180 DE89
Beechcroft Rd., Chesh. 54 AN30
Beechcroft Rd., Chess. 216 CM105
Beechcroft Rd., Orp. 223 ER105
Beechcroft Rd. 76 BY43
(Bushey), Wat.
Beechdale N21 99 DM47
Beechdale Rd. SW2 181 DM86
Beechdene, Tad. 233 CV122
Beechen Cliff Way, Islw. 157 CF81
Henley Clo.
Beechen Gro., Pnr. 116 BZ55
Beechen Gro., Wat. 75 BV41
Beechen La., Tad. 249 CZ125
Beechenlea La., Swan. 207 FG98
Beeches, The, Amer. 55 AN36
Woodfield Pk.
Beeches, The, Bans. 234 DB116
Beeches, The, Beac. 88 AH54
Beeches, The, Brwd. 108 FV48
Beeches, The, Guil. 259 AZ144
Beeches, The, Houns. 156 CB81
Beeches, The, Lthd. 231 CE124
Beeches, The, Rick. 73 BF43
Beeches, The, St.Alb. 61 CD27
Beeches, The, Til. 171 GH82
Beeches Ave., Cars. 218 DE108
Beeches Clo. SE20 202 DW95
Genoa Rd.
Beeches Clo., Tad. 234 DA123
Beeches Ct., Brom. 184 EG93
Avondale Rd.
Beeches Dr., Slou. 111 AP63
Beeches Pk., Beac. 89 AK53
Beeches Rd. SW17 180 DE90
Beeches Rd., Slou. 111 AP64
Beeches Rd., Sutt. 199 CY102
Beeches Wk., Cars. 218 DD109
Beeches Way, B.End 110 AD61
Harvest Hill
Beeches Wd., Tad. 234 DA122
Beechfield, Bans. 218 DB113
Beechfield, Hodd. 33 EA13
Beechfield, Kings L. 58 BM30
Beechfield, Saw. 36 EZ05
Beechfield Cotts., Brom. 204 EJ96
Widmore Rd.
Beechfield Gdns., Rom. 127 FC59
Beechfield Rd. N4 122 DQ58
Beechfield Rd. SE6 183 DZ88
Beechfield Rd., Brom. 204 EJ96
Beechfield Rd., Erith 167 FE80
Beechfield Rd., Hem.H. 40 BH21
Beechfield Rd., Ware 33 DZ05
Beechfield Rd., Welw.G.C. 29 CY10
Beechfield Wk., Wal.Abb. 83 ED35
Beechhill Rd. SE9 185 EN85
Beechlawn, Guil. 259 AZ135
Beechmeads, Cob. 214 BX113
Beechmont Ave., Vir.W. 192 AX99
Beechmont Clo., Brom. 184 EE92
Beechmont Rd., Sev. 257 FH129
Beechmore Gdns., Sutt. 199 CX103
Beechmore Rd. SW11 160 DF81
Beechmount Ave. W7 137 CD71
Beecholm Ms., Wal.Cr. 67 DX28
Beecholme, Bans. 217 CY114
Beecholme Ave., Mitch. 201 DH95
Beecholme Est. E5 122 DV62
Prout Rd.
Beechpark Way, Wat. 75 BS37
Beechtree Ave., Egh. 172 AV93
Beechtree Clo., Stan. 95 CJ50
Beechtree Pl., Sutt. 218 DB106
St. Nicholas Way
Beechvale Clo. N12 98 DE50
Beechway, Bex. 186 EX86
Beechway, Guil. 243 BB133
Beechway, S.Croy. 221 DX113
Beechwood Ave. N3 119 CZ55
Beechwood Ave., Amer. 72 AW38
Beechwood Ave., Couls. 235 DH115
Beechwood Ave., Grnf. 136 CB69
Beechwood Ave., Har. 116 CB62
Beechwood Ave., Hayes 135 BR73
Beechwood Ave., Orp. 223 ES106
Beechwood Ave., Pot.B. 64 DB33
Beechwood Ave., Rich. 158 CN81
Beechwood Ave., Rick. 73 BB42
Beechwood Ave., Ruis. 115 BT61
Beechwood Ave., St.Alb. 43 CH18
Beechwood Ave., Stai. 174 BH93
Beechwood Ave., Sun. 175 BU93
Beechwood Ave., Tad. 234 DA121
Beechwood Ave., Th.Hth. 201 DP98
Beechwood Ave., Uxb. 134 BM72
Beechwood Ave., Wey. 213 BS105
Beechwood Clo. NW7 96 CR50
Beechwood Clo., Amer. 72 AW39
Beechwood Clo., Hert. 32 DT09
Beechwood Clo., Surb. 197 CK101
Beechwood Clo. 66 DS26
(Cheshunt), Wal.Cr.
Beechwood Clo., Wey. 213 BS105
Beechwood Clo., Wok. 226 AS117
Beechwood Ct., Cars. 218 DF105
Beechwood Ct., Sun. 175 BU93
Beechwood Cres., Bexh. 166 EX83
Beechwood Dr., Cob. 214 CA111
Beechwood Dr., Kes. 222 EK105
Beechwood Dr., Wdf.Grn. 102 EF50
Beechwood Gdns. NW10 138 CM69
St. Annes Gdns.
Beechwood Gdns., Cat. 236 DU122
Beechwood Gdns., Har. 116 CB62
Beechwood Gdns., Ilf. 125 EM57
Beechwood Gdns., Rain. 147 FH71
Beechwood Gdns., Slou. 152 AS75
Beechwood Gro. W3 138 CS73
East Acton La.
Beechwood Gro., Surb. 197 CJ101
Beechwood La., Warl. 237 DX119
Beechwood Manor, Wey. 213 BS105
Beechwood Ms. N9 100 DU47
Beechwood Pk. E18 124 EG55
Beechwood Pk., Hem.H. 39 BF24
Beechwood Pk., Lthd. 231 CJ123
Beechwood Ri., Chis. 185 EP91

Beechwood Ri., Wat. 75 BV36
Beechwood Rd. E8 142 DT65
Beechwood Rd. N8 121 DK56
Beechwood Rd., Beac. 88 AJ53
Beechwood Rd., Cat. 236 DU122
Beechwood Rd., Slou. 131 AR71
Beechwood Rd., S.Croy. 220 DS110
Beechwood Rd., Vir.W. 192 AU101
Beechwood Rd., Wok. 226 AS117
Beechwood Vill., Red. 266 DG144
Beechwoods Ct. SE19 182 DT92
Crystal Palace Par.
Beechworth Clo. NW3 120 DA61
Beecot La., Walt. 196 BW103
Beecroft Rd. SE4 183 DY85
Beehive Clo. E8 142 DT66
Beehive Clo., Borwd. 77 CK44
Beehive Clo., Uxb. 134 BM66
Honey Hill
Beehive Grn., Welw.G.C. 30 DA11
Beehive La., Ilf. 125 EM57
Beehive La., Welw.G.C. 30 DA12
Beehive Pas. EC3 275 M9
Beehive Pl. SW9 161 DN83
Beehive Rd., Stai. 173 BF92
Beehive Rd. (Cheshunt), 65 DP28
Wal.Cr.
Beehive Way, Reig. 266 DB138
Beeken Dene, Orp. 223 EQ105
Isabella Dr.
Beel Clo., Amer. 72 AW39
Beeleigh Rd., Mord. 200 DB98
Beesfield La. 208 FN101
(Farningham), Dart.
Beeston Clo. E8 122 DU64
Ferncliff Rd.
Beeston Clo., Wat. 94 BX49
Beeston Dr., Wal.Cr. 67 DX27
Beeston Pl. SW1 277 J7
Beeston Pl. SW1 161 DH76
Beeston Rd., Barn. 80 DD44
Beeston Way, Felt. 176 BW86
Beethoven Rd., Borwd. 77 CJ44
Beethoven St. W10 139 CY69
Beeton Clo., Green. 189 FV85
Beeton Clo., Pnr. 94 CA52
Begbie Rd. SE3 164 EJ81
Beggars Bush La., Wat. 75 BR43
Beggars Hill, Epsom 216 CS107
Beggars Hollow, Enf. 82 DR37
Beggars La., Dor. 261 BS139
Beggars La., West. 255 ER125
Beggars Roost La., Sutt. 218 DA107
Begonia Clo. E6 144 EL71
Begonia Pl., Hmptn. 176 CA93
Gresham Rd.
Begonia Wk. W12 139 CT72
Du Cane Rd.
Beira St. SW12 181 DH87
Beken Ct., Wat. 76 BW35
Bekesbourne St. E14 143 DY72
Ratcliffe La.
Bekesbourne Twr., Orp. 206 EX102
Belcher Rd., Hodd. 49 EA16
Amwell St.
Belchers La., Wal.Abb. 50 EJ24
Belcroft Clo., Brom. 184 EF94
Hope Pk.
Beldam Haw, Sev. 224 FA112
Beldham Gdns., W.Mol. 196 CB97
Belfairs Dr., Rom. 126 EW59
Belfairs Grn., Wat. 94 BX50
Heysham Dr.
Belfast Ave., Slou. 131 AQ72
Belfast Rd. N16 122 DT61
Belfast Rd. SE25 202 DV98
Belfield Gdns., Harl. 52 EW16
Belfield Rd., Epsom 216 CR109
Belfont Wk. N7 121 DL63
Belford Gro. SE18 165 EN77
Belford Rd., Borwd. 78 CM38
Belfort Rd. SE15 162 DW82
Belfry Ave., Uxb. 92 BG53
Belfry La., Rick. 92 BJ46
Belgrade Rd. N16 122 DS63
Belgrade Rd., Hmptn. 196 CB95
Belgrave Ave., Rom. 128 FJ55
Belgrave Ave., Wat. 75 BT43
Belgrave Clo. N14 81 DJ43
Prince George Ave.
Belgrave Clo. W3 158 CQ75
Avenue Rd.
Belgrave Clo., Orp. 206 EW98
Belgrave Clo., St.Alb. 43 CJ16
Belgrave Clo., Walt. 213 BV105
Belgrave Cres., Sun. 195 BV95
Belgrave Dr., Kings L. 59 BQ28
Belgrave Gdns. N14 81 DK43
Belgrave Gdns. NW8 140 DB67
Belgrave Gdns., Stan. 95 CJ50
Copley Rd.
Belgrave Manor, Wok. 226 AY119
Belgrave Ms., Uxb. 134 BK70
Belgrave Ms. N. SW1 276 F5
Belgrave Ms. N. SW1 160 DG76
Belgrave Ms. S. SW1 276 G6
Belgrave Ms. S. SW1 160 DG76
Belgrave Ms. W. SW1 276 F6
Belgrave Ms. W. SW1 160 DG76
Belgrave Pl. SW1 276 G6
Belgrave Pl. SW1 160 DG76
Belgrave Pl., Slou. 152 AV75
Clifton Rd.
Belgrave Rd. E10 123 EC60
Belgrave Rd. E11 124 EG61
Belgrave Rd. E13 144 EJ69
Belgrave Rd. E17 123 EA57
Belgrave Rd. SE25 202 DU98
Belgrave Rd. SW1 277 K9
Belgrave Rd. SW1 161 DH77
Belgrave Rd. SW13 159 CT80
Belgrave Rd., Houns. 156 BZ83
Belgrave Rd., Ilf. 125 EM60
Belgrave Rd., Mitch. 200 DD97
Belgrave Rd., Slou. 132 AS73
Belgrave Rd., Sun. 195 BV95
Belgrave Sq. SW1 276 F6
Belgrave Sq. SW1 160 DG76
Belgrave St. E1 143 DX71
Belgrave Ter., Wdf.Grn. 102 EG48
Belgrave Wk., Mitch. 200 DD97
Belgrave Yd. SW1 277 H7
Belgravia Gdns., Brom. 184 EE93
Belgravia Ho. SW4 181 DK86
Belgravia Ms., Kings.T. 197 CK98
Belgrove St. WC1 274 A2
Belgrove St. WC1 141 DL69
Belham Rd., Kings L. 58 BM28
Belham Wk. SE5 162 DR81
D'Eynsford Rd.
Belhaven Ct., Borwd. 78 CM39
Belinda Rd. SW9 161 DP83
Belitha Vill. N1 141 DM66
Bell Ave., Rom. 105 FH53
Bell Ave., West Dr. 154 BM76
Bell Bri. Rd., Cher. 193 BF102
Bell Clo., Abb.L. 59 BT27
Bell Clo., Beac. 89 AM53
Bell Clo., Green. 189 FT85
Bell Clo., Pnr. 94 BW54
Bell Clo., Ruis. 115 BT62
Bell Clo., Slou. 132 AV71
Bell Common, Epp. 69 ES32
Bell Ct., Surb. 198 CP103
Barnsbury La.
Bell Cres., Couls. 235 DH121
Maple Way
Bell Dr. SW18 179 CY87
Bell Fm. Ave., Dag. 127 FC62
Bell Gdns. E17 123 DZ57
Markhouse Rd.
Bell Gdns., Orp. 206 EW99
Bell Gate, Hem.H. 40 BL17
Bell Grn. SE26 183 DZ90
Bell Grn., Hem.H. 57 BB27
Bell Grn. La. SE26 183 DZ92
Bell Hill, Croy. 202 DQ104
Surrey St.
Bell Ho. Rd., Rom. 127 FC60
Bell Inn Yd. EC3 275 L9
Bell La. E1 275 P7
Bell La. E1 142 DT71
Bell La. E16 144 EG74
Bell La. NW4 119 CW56
Bell La., Abb.L. 59 BT27
Bell La., Amer. 72 AV39
Bell La., Berk. 38 AS18
Bell La., Brox. 49 DY21
Bell La., Enf. 83 DX38
Bell La., Hat. 46 DA24
Bell La., Hert. 32 DR09
Bell La., Hodd. 49 EA17
Bell La., Lthd. 231 CD123
Bell La., St.Alb. 62 CL29
Bell La., Twick. 177 CG88
The Embk.
Bell La., Wem. 117 CK61
Magnet Rd.
Bell La. (Eton Wick), Wind. 151 AM77
Bell La. Clo., Lthd. 231 CD123
Bell Mead, Saw. 36 EY05
Bell Meadow SE19 182 DS91
Dulwich Wd. Ave.
Bell Meadow, Gdse. 252 DV132
Hickmans Clo.
Bell Par., Wind. 151 AM82
St. Andrews Ave.
Bell Rd., E.Mol. 197 CD99
Bell Rd., Enf. 82 DR39
Bell Rd., Houns. 156 CB83
Bell St. NW1 272 B6
Bell St. NW1 140 DE71
Bell St., Reig. 250 DA134
Bell St., Saw. 36 EY05
Bell Vw., Wind. 151 AM83
Bell Vw. Clo., Wind. 151 AM82
Bell Wk., Saw. 36 EY05
London Rd.
Bell Water Gate SE18 165 EN76
Bell Weir Clo., Stai. 173 BB89
Bell Wf. La. EC4 275 J10
Bell Yd. WC2 274 D9
Bell Yd. WC2 141 DN72
Bellamy Clo. W14 159 CZ78
Aisgill Ave.
Bellamy Clo., Edg. 96 CQ48
Bellamy Clo., Uxb. 114 BN62
Bellamy Clo., Wat. 75 BU39
Bellamy Dr., Stan. 95 CH53
Bellamy Rd. E4 101 EB51
Bellamy Rd., Enf. 82 DR40
Bellamy Rd. (Cheshunt), 67 DY29
Wal.Cr.
Bellamy St. SW12 181 DH87
Bellasis Ave. SW2 181 DL89
Bellclose Rd., West Dr. 154 BL75
Belle Staines Pleasaunce E4 101 EA47
Belle Vue, Grnf. 137 CD67
Belle Vue Clo., Stai. 194 BG95
Belle Vue Est. NW4 119 CW56
Bell La.
Belle Vue La. (Bushey), Wat. 95 CD46
Belle Vue Rd. E17 101 ED54
Belle Vue Rd. NW4 119 CW56
Bell La.
Belle Vue Rd., Orp. 223 EN110
Standard Rd.
Belle Vue Rd., Ware 33 DZ06
Bellefield Rd., Orp. 206 EV99
Bellefields Rd. SW9 161 DM83
Bellegrove Clo., Well. 165 ET82
Bellegrove Rd., Well. 165 ES82
Bellenden Rd. SE15 162 DT83
Belleville Rd. SW11 180 DE85
Bellevue Ms. N11 98 DG50
Bellevue Rd.
Bellevue Par. SW17 180 DE88
Bellevue Rd.
Bellevue Pk., Th.Hth. 202 DQ97
Bellevue Pl. E1 142 DW70
Bellevue Pl., Slou. 152 AT76
Albert St.
Bellevue Rd. N11 98 DG49
Bellevue Rd. SW13 159 CU82
Bellevue Rd. SW17 180 DE88
Bellevue Rd. W13 137 CH70
Bellevue Rd., Bexh. 186 EZ85
Bellevue Rd., Horn. 128 FM60
Bellevue Rd., Kings.T. 198 CL97
Bellevue Rd., Rom. 105 FC51
Bellew St. SW17 180 DC90
Bellfield, Croy. 221 DZ108
Bellfield Ave., Har. 95 CD50
Bellfields Ct., Guil. 242 AW130
Oak Tree Dr.
Bellfields Rd., Guil. 242 AX132
Bellflower Clo. E6 144 EL71
Sorrel Gdns.
Bellflower Path, Rom. 106 FJ52
Bellgate Ms. NW5 121 DH62
York Ri.
Bellhouse La., Brwd. 108 FS43
Bellingdon Rd., Chesh. 54 AP30
Bellingham Ct., Bark. 146 EV69
Renwick Rd.
Bellingham Grn. SE6 183 EA90
Bellingham Rd. SE6 183 EC90
Bellman Ave., Grav. 191 GL88
Bellmarsh Rd., Add. 212 BH105
Bellmount Wd. Ave., Wat. 75 BS39
Bello Clo. SE24 181 DP87
Bellot Gdns. SE10 164 EE78
Bellot St. SE10 164 EE78
Bellring Clo., Belv. 166 FA79
Bells All. SW6 160 DA82
Bells Gdn. Est. SE15 162 DU80
Buller Clo.
Bells Hill, Barn. 79 CX43
Bell's Hill, Slou. 132 AU67
Bells Hill Grn., Slou. 132 AU66
Bells La., Slou. 153 BB83
Bellswood La., Iver 133 BB71
Belltrees Gro. SW16 181 DM92
Bellwether La., Red. 267 DP143
Bellwood Rd. SE15 163 DX84
Belmarsh Rd. SE28 165 ES75
Western Way
Belmont, Slou. 131 AN71
Belmont Ave. N9 100 DU46
Belmont Ave. N13 99 DL50
Belmont Ave. N17 122 DQ55
Belmont Ave., Barn. 80 DF43
Belmont Ave., Guil. 242 AT131
Belmont Ave., N.Mal. 199 CU99
Belmont Ave., Sthl. 156 BY76
Belmont Ave., Upmin. 128 FM61
Belmont Ave., Well. 165 ES82
Belmont Ave., Wem. 138 CM67
Belmont Circle, Har. 95 CH54
Kenton La.
Belmont Clo. E4 101 ED50
Belmont Clo. N20 98 DB46
Belmont Clo. SW4 161 DJ83
Belmont Clo., Barn. 80 DF42
Belmont Clo., Uxb. 134 BK65
Belmont Clo., Wdf.Grn. 102 EH49
Belmont Ct. NW11 119 CZ57
Belmont Gro. SE13 163 ED83
Belmont Hall Ct. SE13 163 ED83
Belmont Gro.
Belmont Hill SE13 163 EC83
Belmont Hill, St.Alb. 43 CD21
Belmont La., Chis. 185 ER92
Belmont La., Stan. 95 CJ52
Belmont Pk. SE13 163 ED84
Belmont Pk. Clo. SE13 163 ED84
Belmont Pk.
Belmont Pk. Rd. E10 123 EB58
Belmont Ri., Sutt. 217 CZ107
Belmont Rd. N15 122 DQ56
Belmont Rd. N17 122 DQ55
Belmont Rd. SE25 202 DV99
Belmont Rd. SW4 161 DJ83
Belmont Rd. W4 158 CR77
Belmont Rd., Beck. 203 DZ96
Belmont Rd., Chesh. 54 AP28
Belmont Rd., Chis. 185 EP92
Belmont Rd., Erith 166 FA80
Belmont Rd., Grays 170 FZ79
Belmont Rd., Har. 117 CF55
Belmont Rd., Hem.H. 40 BL24
Belmont Rd., Horn. 128 FK62
Belmont Rd., Ilf. 125 EQ62
Belmont Rd., Lthd. 231 CG122
Belmont Rd., Reig. 266 DC135
Belmont Rd., Sutt. 218 DA110
Belmont Rd., Twick. 177 CD89
Belmont Rd., Uxb. 134 BK66
Belmont Rd., Wall. 219 DH106
Belmont Rd. (Bushey), Wat. 76 BY43
Belmont St. NW1 140 DG66
Belmont Ter. W4 158 CR77
Belmont Rd.
Belmor, Borwd. 78 CN43
Belmore Ave., Hayes 135 BU72
Belmore Ave., Wok. 227 BD116
Belmore La. N7 121 DK64
Belmore St. SW8 161 DK81
Beloe Clo. SW15 159 CU83
Belper Ct. E5 123 DX63
Pedro St.
Belsham St. E9 142 DW65
Belsize Ave. N13 99 DM51
Belsize Ave. NW3 140 DD65
Belsize Ave. W13 157 CH76
Belsize Clo., Hem.H. 40 BN21
Belsize Clo., St.Alb. 43 CJ15
Belsize Cres. NW3 120 DD64
Belsize Gdns., Sutt. 218 DB105
Belsize Gro. NW3 140 DE65
Belsize La. NW3 140 DD65
Belsize Ms. NW3 140 DD65
Belsize La.
Belsize Pk. NW3 140 DD65
Belsize Pk. Gdns. NW3 140 DE65
Belsize Pk. Ms. NW3 140 DD65
Belsize La.
Belsize Pl. NW3 140 DD65
Belsize La.
Belsize Rd. NW6 140 DB67
Belsize Rd., Har. 95 CD52
Belsize Rd., Hem.H. 40 BN21
Belsize Sq. NW3 140 DD65
Belsize Ter. NW3 140 DD65
Belson Rd. SE18 165 EM77
Belswains Grn., Hem.H. 40 BL23
Belswains La.
Belswains La., Hem.H. 40 BL23
Beltana Dr., Grav. 191 GL91
Beltane Dr. SW19 179 CX90
Belthorn Cres. SW12 181 DJ87
Beltinge Rd., Rom. 106 FM54
Belton Rd. E7 144 EH66
Belton Rd. E11 124 EE63
Belton Rd. N17 122 DS55
Belton Rd. NW2 139 CU65
Belton Rd., Berk. 38 AU18
Belton Rd., Sid. 186 EU91
Belton Way E3 143 EA71
Beltona Gdns. (Cheshunt), 67 DX27
Wal.Cr.
Beltran Rd. SW6 160 DB82
Beltwood Rd., Belv. 167 FC77
Belvedere Ave. SW19 179 CY92
Belvedere Ave., Ilf. 103 EP54
Belvedere Bldgs. SE1 278 G5
Belvedere Clo., Esher 214 CB106
Belvedere Clo., Grav. 191 GJ88
Belvedere Clo., Guil. 242 AV132
Belvedere Clo., Tedd. 177 CE92
Belvedere Clo., Wey. 212 BN106
Belvedere Ct. N2 120 DD57
Belvedere Dr. SW19 179 CY92
Belvedere Gdns., St.Alb. 60 CA27
Belvedere Gdns., W.Mol. 196 BZ99
Belvedere Gro. SW19 179 CY92
Belvedere Ho., Felt. 175 BU88
Belvedere Ind. Est., Belv. 167 FC76
Crabtree Manorway S.
Belvedere Ms. SE15 162 DW83
Belvedere Pl. SE1 278 G5
Belvedere Rd. E10 123 DY60
Belvedere Rd. SE1 278 C4
Belvedere Rd. SE1 161 DM75
Belvedere Rd. SE2 146 EX74
Belvedere Rd. SE19 182 DT94
Belvedere Rd. W7 157 CE76
Belvedere Rd., Bexh. 166 EZ83
Belvedere Rd., Brwd. 108 FT48
Belvedere Rd., West. 239 EM118
Belvedere Sq. SW19 179 CY92
Belvedere Strand NW9 97 CT54
Belvedere Way, Har. 118 CL58
Belvoir Clo. SE9 184 EL90
Belvoir Rd. SE22 182 DU87
Belvue Clo., Nthlt. 136 CA66
Belvue Rd., Nthlt. 136 CA66
Bembridge Clo. NW6 139 CY66
Bembridge Ct., Slou. 152 AT76
Park St.
Bembridge Gdns., Ruis. 115 BR61
Bemerton Est. N1 141 DL66
Bemerton St. N1 141 DM67
Bemish Rd. SW15 159 CX83
Bempton Dr., Ruis. 115 BV61
Bemsted Rd. E17 123 DZ55
Ben Hale Clo., Stan. 95 CH49
Ben Jonson Rd. E1 143 DX71
Ben Smith Way SE16 162 DU76
Jamaica Rd.
Ben Tillet Clo. E16 145 EM74
Newland St.
Ben Tillet Clo., Bark. 146 EU66
Benares Rd. SE18 165 ET77
Benbow Clo., St.Alb. 43 CH22
Benbow Rd. W6 159 CV76
Benbow St. SE8 163 EA79
Benbow Waye, Uxb. 134 BJ71
Benbrick Rd., Guil. 258 AU135
Benbury Clo., Brom. 183 EC92
Bence, The, Egh. 193 BB97
Bench Fld., S.Croy. 220 DT107
Bench Manor Cres., Ger.Cr. 90 AW54
Benchleys Rd., Hem.H. 39 BF21
Bencombe Rd., Pur. 219 DN114
Bencroft (Cheshunt), 66 DU26
Wal.Cr.
Bencroft Rd. SW16 181 DJ94
Bencroft Rd., Hem.H. 40 BL20
Bencurtis Pk., W.Wick. 203 ED104
Bendall Ms. NW1 272 C6
Bendemeer Rd. SW15 159 CX83
Bendish Rd. E6 144 EL66
Bendmore Ave. SE2 166 EU78
Bendon Valley SW18 180 DB87
Bendysh Rd. (Bushey), Wat. 76 BY41
Benedict Clo., Belv. 166 EY76
Tunstock Way
Benedict Clo., Orp. 205 ES104
Benedict Dr., Felt. 175 BR87
Benedict Rd. SW9 161 DM83
Benedict Rd., Mitch. 200 DD97
Benedict Way N2 120 DC55
Benedictine Gate, Wal.Cr. 67 DY27
Benenden Grn., Brom. 204 EF99
Benenstock Rd., Stai. 173 BF85
Benets Rd., Horn. 128 FN60
Benett Gdns. SW16 201 DL96
Benfleet Clo., Cob. 214 BY112
Benfleet Clo., Sutt. 200 DC104
Benford Rd., Hodd. 49 DZ19
Bengal Ct. EC3 142 DR72
Birchin La.
Bengal Rd., Ilf. 125 EP63
Bengarth Dr., Har. 95 CD54
Bengarth Rd., Nthlt. 136 BX67
Bengeo Meadows, Hert. 32 DR06
Bengeo Ms., Hert. 32 DQ06
Bengeo St.
Bengeo St., Hert. 32 DQ06
Bengeworth Rd. SE5 162 DQ83
Bengeworth Rd., Har. 117 CG61
Benham Clo. SW11 160 DD83
Benham Clo., Chesh. 54 AP29
Benham Clo., Chess. 215 CJ107
Merritt Gdns.
Benham Clo., Couls. 235 DP118
Benham Gdns., Houns. 156 BZ84
Benham Rd. W7 137 CE71
Benhams Clo., Horl. 268 DG146
Benhams Dr., Horl. 268 DG146
Benhams Pl. NW3 120 DC63
Holly Wk.
Benhill Ave., Sutt. 218 DB105
Benhill Rd. SE5 162 DR80
Benhill Rd., Sutt. 200 DC104
Benhill Wd. Rd., Sutt. 218 DC105
Benhilton Gdns., Sutt. 200 DB104
Benhurst Ave., Horn. 127 FH63
Benhurst Clo., S.Croy. 221 DX110
Benhurst Ct. SW16 181 DN92
Benhurst Gdns., S.Croy. 220 DW110
Benhurst La. SW16 181 DN92
Benin St. SE13 183 ED87
Benison Ct., Slou. 152 AT76
Osborne St.
Benjafield Clo. N18 100 DV49
Brettenham Rd.
Benjamin Clo. E8 142 DU67
Benjamin Clo., Horn. 127 FG58
Benjamin St. EC1 274 F6
Benjamin St. EC1 141 DP71
Benledi St. E14 143 ED72
Benn St. E9 143 DY65
Bennerley Rd. SW11 180 DE85
Bennet's Hill EC4 274 G10
Bennetsfield Rd., Uxb. 135 BP74
Bennett Clo., Cob. 213 BU113
Bennett Clo., Kings.T. 197 CJ95
Bennett Clo., Nthwd. 93 BT52
Bennett Clo., Well. 166 EU82
Bennett Clo., Welw.G.C. 29 CZ13
Bennett Gro. SE13 163 EB81
Bennett Pk. SE3 164 EF83
Bennett Rd. E13 144 EJ70
Bennett Rd. N16 122 DS63
Bennett Rd., Rom. 126 EY58
Bennett St. SW1 277 K2
Bennett St. W4 158 CS79
Bennett Way, Dart. 189 FR91
Bennett Way, Guil. 244 BG129
Bennetts, Chesh. 54 AR30
Bennetts Ave., Croy. 203 DY103
Bennetts Ave., Grnf. 137 CE67
Bennetts Castle La., Dag. 126 EW63
Bennetts Clo. N17 100 DT51
Bennetts Clo., Mitch. 201 DH95
Bennetts Clo., St.Alb. 44 CR23
Meadway
Bennetts Clo., Slou. 131 AN74
Bennetts Copse, Chis. 184 EL93
Bennetts End Clo., Hem.H. 40 BM22
Bennetts End Rd., Hem.H. 40 BM21
Bennetts Fm. Pl., Lthd. 246 BZ125
Bennetts Gate, Hem.H. 40 BN23
Bennetts End Rd.
Bennetts Way, Croy. 203 DY103
Bennetts Yd. SW1 277 N7
Benning Clo., Wind. 151 AK83
Benningholme Rd., Edg. 96 CS51
Bennington Rd. N17 100 DS53
Bennington Rd., Wdf.Grn. 102 EE52
Bennions Clo., Horn. 148 FK65
Franklin Rd.
Bennison Dr., Rom. 106 FK54
Benn's Wk., Rich. 158 CL84
Rosedale Rd.
Benrek Clo., Ilf. 103 EQ53
Bensbury Clo. SW15 179 CW87
Bensham Clo., Th.Hth. 202 DQ98
Bensham Gro., Th.Hth. 202 DQ96
Bensham La., Croy. 201 DP101
Bensham La., Th.Hth. 201 DP98
Bensham Manor Rd., 202 DQ98
Th.Hth.
Bensington Ct., Felt. 175 BR86
Benskin Rd., Wat. 75 BU43
Benskins La. 106 FK46
(Havering-atte-Bower), Rom.
Bensley Clo. N11 98 DF50
Benson Ave. E6 144 EJ68
Benson Clo., Houns. 156 CA84
Benson Clo., Slou. 132 AU74
Benson Clo., Uxb. 134 BL71
Benson Quay E1 142 DW73
Garnet St.
Benson Rd. SE23 182 DW88
Benson Rd., Croy. 201 DN104
Benson Rd., Grays 170 GB79
Bentfield Gdns. SE9 184 EJ90
Aldersgrove Ave.
Benthal Rd. N16 122 DU61
Benthall Gdns., Ken. 236 DQ116
Bentham Ave., Wok. 227 BC115
Bentham Rd. E9 143 DX65
Bentham Rd. SE28 146 EV73
Bentham Wk. NW10 118 CQ64
Bentinck Clo., Ger.Cr. 112 AX57
Bentinck Ms. W1 272 G8
Bentinck Pl. NW8 272 B1
Bentinck Rd., West Dr. 134 BK74
Bentinck St. W1 272 G8
Bentinck St. W1 140 DG72
Bentley Dr., Harl. 52 EW16
Bentley Dr., Ilf. 125 EQ58
Bentley Dr., Wey. 212 BN109
Bentley Heath La., Barn. 79 CZ35
Bentley Pk., Slou. 131 AK68
Bentley Rd. N1 142 DS65
Tottenham Rd.
Bentley Rd., Hert. 31 DL08
Bentley Rd., Slou. 131 AN74
Bentley St., Grav. 191 GJ86
Bentley Way, Stan. 95 CG50
Bentley Way, Wdf.Grn. 102 EG48
Benton Rd., Ilf. 125 ER60
Benton Rd., Wat. 94 BX50
Bentons, Harl. 51 ES17
Bentons La. SE27 182 DQ91
Bentons Ri. SE27 182 DR92
Bentry Clo., Dag. 126 EY61
Bentry Rd., Dag. 126 EY61
Bentsbrook Clo., Dor. 263 CH140
Bentsbrook Pk., Dor. 263 CH140
Bentsbrook Rd., Dor. 263 CH140
Bentsley Clo., St.Alb. 43 CJ16
Bentworth Rd. W12 139 CV72
Benwell Ct., Sun. 195 BU95
Benwell Rd. N7 121 DN63
Benwick Clo. SE16 162 DV77
Benworth St. E3 143 DZ69
Benyon Path, S.Ock. 149 FW68
Benyon Rd. N1 142 DR67
Southgate Rd.
Beomonds Row, Cher. 194 BG101
Berber Rd. SW11 180 DF85
Berberis Clo., Guil. 242 AW132
Berberis Wk., West Dr. 154 BL77
Berceau Wk., Wat. 75 BS39
Bercta Rd. SE9 185 EQ89
Berdens La., Brwd. 129 FT55
Bere St. E1 143 DX73
Cranford St.
Berecroft, Harl. 51 ER20
Beredens La., Brwd. 129 FT55
Berefield, Hem.H. 40 BK18
Berenger Wk. SW10 160 DD80
Blantyre St.
Berens Rd. NW10 139 CX69
Berens Rd., Orp. 206 EX99
Berens Way, Chis. 205 ET98
Beresford Ave. N20 98 DF47
Beresford Ave. W7 137 CD71
Beresford Ave., Slou. 132 AW73
Beresford Ave., Surb. 198 CP102
Beresford Ave., Twick. 177 CJ86
Beresford Ave., Wem. 138 CM67
Beresford Dr., Brom. 204 EL97
Beresford Dr., Wdf.Grn. 102 EJ49
Beresford Gdns., Enf. 82 DS42

Beresford Gdns., Houns. 176 BZ85
Beresford Gdns., Rom. 126 EY57
Beresford Rd. E4 102 EE46
Beresford Rd. E17 101 EB53
Beresford Rd. N2 120 DE55
Beresford Rd. N5 122 DR64
Beresford Rd. N8 121 DN57
Beresford Rd., Dor. 263 CH136
Beresford Rd., Grav. 190 GE87
Beresford Rd., Har. 117 CD57
Beresford Rd., Kings.T. 198 CM95
Beresford Rd., N.Mal. 198 CQ98
Beresford Rd., Rick. 91 BF46
Beresford Rd., St.Alb. 43 CH21
Beresford Rd., Sthl. 136 BX74
Beresford Rd., Sutt. 217 CZ108
Beresford Sq. SE18 165 EP77
Beresford St. SE18 165 EP76
Beresford Ter. N5 122 DQ64
Berestede Rd. W6 159 CT78
Bergen Sq. SE16 163 DY76
Norway Gate
Berger Clo., Orp. 205 ER100
Berger Rd. E9 143 DX65
Berghem Ms. W14 159 CX76
Blythe Rd.
Berghers Hill, H.Wyc. 110 AF59
Bergholt Ave., Ilf. 124 EL57
Bergholt Cres. N16 122 DS59
Bergholt Ms. NW1 141 DJ66
Rossendale Way
Bericot Way, Welw.G.C. 30 DC09
Bering Wk. E16 144 EK72
Berisford Ms. SW18 180 DC86
Berkeley Ave., Bexh. 166 EX81
Berkeley Ave., Chesh. 54 AM28
Berkeley Ave., Grnf. 137 CE65
Berkeley Ave., Houns. 155 BU81
Berkeley Ave., Ilf. 103 EN54
Berkeley Ave., Rom. 105 FC52
Berkeley Clo., Abb.L. 59 BT32
Berkeley Clo., Borwd. 78 CN43
Berkeley Clo., Chesh. 54 AN30
Berkeley Ave.
Berkeley Clo., Horn. 128 FP61
Berkeley Clo., Kings.T. 178 CL94
Berkeley Clo., Orp. 205 ES101
Berkeley Clo., Pot.B. 63 CY32
Berkeley Clo., Ruis. 115 BU62
Berkeley Clo., Stai. 173 BD89
Berkeley Clo., Ware 32 DW05
Berkeley Ct. N14 81 DJ44
Berkeley Ct., Guil. 242 AY134
London Rd.
Berkeley Ct., Wall. 201 DJ104
Berkeley Ct., Wey. 195 BR103
Berkeley Cres., Barn. 80 DD43
Berkeley Cres., Dart. 188 FM88
Berkeley Dr., Horn. 128 FN60
Berkeley Gdns. N21 100 DR45
Berkeley Gdns. W8 140 DA74
Brunswick Gdns.
Berkeley Gdns., Esher 215 CG107
Berkeley Gdns., Walt. 195 BT101
Berkeley Gdns., W.Byf. 211 BF114
Berkeley Ho. E3 143 EA69
Wellington Way
Berkeley Ms. W1 272 E9
Berkeley Pl. SW19 179 CX93
Berkeley Pl., Epsom 232 CR115
Berkeley Rd. E12 124 EL64
Berkeley Rd. N8 121 DK57
Berkeley Rd. N15 122 DR58
Berkeley Rd. NW9 118 CN56
Berkeley Rd. SW13 159 CU81
Berkeley Rd., Uxb. 135 BQ66
Berkeley Sq. W1 277 J1
Berkeley Sq. W1 141 DH73
Berkeley St. W1 277 J2
Berkeley St. W1 141 DH74
Berkeley Wk. N7 121 DM61
Durham Rd.
Berkeley Waye, Houns. 156 BX80
Berkeleys, The, Lthd. 231 CE124
Berkely Rd., H.Wyc. 88 AC53
Berkhampstead Rd., Belv. 166 FA78
Berkhampstead Rd., Chesh. 54 AQ30
Berkhamsted Ave., Wem. 138 CM65
Berkhamsted Bypass, Berk. 38 AV21
Berkhamsted Bypass, Hem.H. 39 BB23
Berkhamsted Hill, Berk. 38 AY17
Berkhamsted La., Hat. 46 DF20
Berkhamsted La., Hert. 47 DJ19
Berkhamsted Pl., Berk. 38 AW17
Berkhamsted Rd., Hem.H. 39 BD17
Berkley Ave., Wal.Cr. 67 DX34
Berkley Clo., St.Alb. 43 CJ16
Berkley Ct., Berk. 38 AW18
Mill St.
Berkley Ct., Guil. 242 AY134
London Rd.
Berkley Ct., Rick. 75 BR43
Mayfare
Berkley Dr., W.Mol. 196 BZ97
Berkley Gro. NW1 140 DF66
Berkley Rd.
Berkley Rd. NW1 140 DF66
Berkley Rd., Beac. 89 AK49
Berkley Rd., Grav. 191 GH86
Berks Hill, Rick. 73 BC43
Berkshire Ave., Slou. 131 AP72
Berkshire Clo., Cat. 236 DR122
Berkshire Gdns. N13 99 DN51
Berkshire Gdns. N18 100 DV50
Berkshire Rd. E9 143 DZ65
Berkshire Sq., Mitch. 201 DL98
Berkshire Way
Berkshire Way, Horn. 128 FN57
Berkshire Way, Mitch. 201 DL98
Bermans Clo., Brwd. 109 GB47
Hanging Hill La.
Bermans Way NW10 118 CS63
Bermondsey Sq. SE1 279 N6
Bermondsey St. SE1 279 M3
Bermondsey St. SE1 162 DS75
Bermondsey Wall E. SE16 162 DU75
Bermondsey Wall W. SE16 162 DU75
Bermuda Rd., Til. 171 GG82
Bernal Clo. SE28 146 EX73
Haldane Rd.
Bernard Ashley Dr. SE7 164 EH78
Bernard Ave. W13 157 CH76
Bernard Cassidy St. E16 144 EF71
Bernard Gdns. SW19 179 CZ92
Bernard Rd. N15 122 DT57
Bernard Rd., Rom. 127 FC59
Bernard Rd., Wall. 219 DH106
Bernard St. WC1 273 P5
Bernard St. WC1 141 DL70
Bernard St., Grav. 191 GH86
Bernard St., St.Alb. 43 CD19
Bernards Clo., Ilf. 103 EQ52
Bernato Clo., W.Byf. 212 BL112
Viscount Gdns.
Bernays Clo., Stan. 95 CJ51
Bernays Gro. SW9 161 DM84
Berne Rd., Th.Hth. 201 DP99
Bernel Dr., Croy. 203 DZ104
Berners Clo., Slou. 131 AL73
Berners Dr. W13 137 CG72
Berners Dr., Brox. 49 DZ23
Berners Way
Berners Dr., St.Alb. 43 CE23
Berners Ms. W1 273 L7
Berners Ms. W1 141 DJ71
Berners Pl. W1 273 L8
Berners Pl. W1 141 DJ72
Berners Rd. N1 141 DN67
Berners Rd. N22 99 DN53
Berners St. W1 273 L7
Berners St. W1 141 DJ71
Berners Way, Brox. 49 DZ23
Bernersmede SE3 164 EG83
Blackheath Pk.
Berney Rd., Croy. 202 DR101
Bernice Clo., Rain. 148 FJ70
Bernville Way, Har. 118 CM57
Kenton Rd.
Bernwell Rd. E4 102 EE48
Berridge Grn., Edg. 96 CP52
Berridge Rd. SE19 182 DS92
Berries, The, St.Alb. 43 CG16
Berriman Rd. N7 121 DM62
Berrington Dr., Lthd. 229 BT124
Berriton Rd., Har. 116 BZ60
Berry Ave., Wat. 75 BU36
Berry Clo. N21 99 DP46
Berry Clo. NW10 138 CS66
Berry Clo., Horn. 128 FJ64
Airfield Way
Berry Clo., Rick. 92 BH45
Berry Ct., Houns. 176 BZ85
Berry Fld. Pk., Amer. 55 AP37
Berry Gro. La. (Bushey), Wat. 76 BY38
Berry Hill, Maid. 130 AD70
Berry Hill, Stan. 95 CK49
Berry La. SE21 182 DR91
Berry La., Rick. 92 BH45
Berry Meade, Ash. 232 CM117
Berry Pl. EC1 274 G3
Berry St. EC1 274 G4
Berry St. EC1 141 DP70
Berry Wk., Ash. 232 CM119
Berry Way W5 158 CL76
Berry Way, Rick. 92 BH45
Berrybank Clo. E4 101 EC47
Greenbank Clo.
Berrydale Rd., Hayes 136 BY70
Berryfield, Slou. 132 AW72
Berryfield Clo. E17 123 EB56
Berryfield Clo., Brom. 204 EL95
Berryfield Rd. SE17 278 G10
Berryfield Rd. SE17 161 DP78
Berryhill SE9 165 EP84
Berryhill Gdns. SE9 165 EP84
Berrylands SW20 199 CW97
Berrylands, Orp. 206 EW104
Berrylands, Surb. 198 CM100
Berrylands Rd., Surb. 198 CM100
Berryman Clo., Dag. 126 EW62
Bennetts Castle La.
Berrymans La. SE26 183 DX91
Berrymead, Hem.H. 40 BM18
Berrymead Gdns. W3 158 CQ75
Berrymede Rd. W4 158 CR76
Berrys Grn. Rd., West. 239 EP115
Berrys Hill, West. 239 EP115
Berrys La., W.Byf. 212 BK111
Berryscroft Ct., Stai. 174 BJ94
Berryscroft Rd.
Berryscroft Rd., Stai. 174 BJ94
Bersham La., Grays 170 FZ77
Bert Rd., Th.Hth. 202 DQ99
Bertal Rd. SW17 180 DD91
Berther Rd., Horn. 128 FK59
Berthon St. SE8 163 EA80
Bertie Rd. NW10 139 CU65
Bertie Rd. SE26 183 DX93
Bertram Cotts. SW19 180 DA94
Hartfield Rd.
Bertram Rd. NW4 119 CU58
Bertram Rd., Enf. 82 DU42
Bertram Rd., Kings.T. 178 CN94
Bertram St. N19 121 DH61
Bertram Way, Enf. 82 DT42
Bertrand St. SE13 163 EB83
Bertrand Way SE28 146 EV73
Berwick Ave., Hayes 136 BX72
Berwick Ave., Slou. 131 AP72
Berwick Clo., Beac. 89 AP54
Berwick Clo., Stan. 95 CF52
Gordon Ave.
Berwick Clo., Wal.Cr. 67 EA34
Berwick Cres., Sid. 185 ES86
Berwick La., Ong. 71 FE33
Berwick Pond Clo., Rain. 148 FK68
Berwick Pond Rd., Rain. 148 FM68
Berwick Pond Rd., Upmin. 148 FM66
Berwick Rd. E16 144 EH72
Berwick Rd. N22 99 DP53
Berwick Rd., Borwd. 78 CL38
Berwick Rd., Rain. 148 FK68
Berwick Rd., Well. 166 EV81
Berwick St. W1 273 L8
Berwick St. W1 141 DJ72
Berwick Way, Orp. 206 EU102
Berwick Way, Sev. 257 FH121
Berwyn Ave., Houns. 156 CB81
Berwyn Rd. SE24 181 DP88
Berwyn Rd., Rich. 158 CP84
Beryl Ave. E6 144 EL71
Beryl Rd. W6 159 CX78
Berystede, Kings.T. 178 CP94
Besant Ct. N1 122 DR64
Newington Grn. Rd.
Besant Rd. NW2 119 CY63
Besant Wk. N7 121 DM61
Newington Barrow Way
Besant Way NW10 118 CQ64
Besley St. SW16 181 DJ94
Bessant Dr., Rich. 158 CP81
Bessborough Gdns. SW1 277 N10
Bessborough Gdns. SW1 161 DK78
Bessborough Pl. SW1 277 M10
Bessborough Pl. SW1 161 DK78
Bessborough Rd. SW15 179 CU88
Bessborough Rd., Har. 117 CD60
Bessborough St. SW1 277 M10
Bessborough St. SW1 161 DK78
Bessels Grn. Rd., Sev. 256 FD123
Bessels Meadow, Sev. 256 FD124
Bessels Way, Sev. 256 FC124
Bessemer Rd. SE5 162 DQ82
Bessemer Rd., Welw.G.C. 29 CY05
Bessie Lansbury Clo. E6 145 EN72
Bessingby Rd., Ruis. 115 BV61
Bessingham Wk. SE4 163 DX84
Frendsbury Rd.
Besson St. SE14 162 DW81
Bessy St. E2 142 DW69
Roman Rd.
Bestobell Rd., Slou. 131 AQ72
Bestwood St. SE8 163 DX77
Beswick Ms. NW6 140 DB65
Lymington Rd.
Beta Rd., Wok. 227 BB116
Beta Rd. (Chobham), Wok. 210 AT110
Beta Way, Egh. 193 BC95
Betam Rd., Hayes 155 BR75
Betchworth Clo., Sutt. 218 DD106
Turnpike La.
Betchworth Rd., Ilf. 125 ES61
Betchworth Way, Croy. 221 EC109
Betenson Ave., Sev. 256 FF122
Betham Rd., Grnf. 137 CD69
Bethany Waye, Felt. 175 BS87
Bethecar Rd., Har. 117 CE57
Bethel Rd., Sev. 257 FJ123
Bethel Rd., Well. 166 EW83
Bethell Ave. E16 144 EF70
Bethell Ave., Ilf. 125 EN59
Bethersden Clo., Beck. 183 DZ94
Bethnal Grn. Rd. E1 275 P4
Bethnal Grn. Rd. E1 142 DT70
Bethnal Grn. Rd. E2 142 DT70
Bethune Ave. N11 98 DF49
Bethune Rd. N16 122 DR59
Bethune Rd. NW10 138 CR70
Bethwin Rd. SE5 161 DP80
Betjeman Clo., Couls. 235 DM117
Betjeman Clo., Pnr. 116 CA56
Betjeman Clo., Wal.Cr. 66 DU28
Rosedale Way
Betjeman Way, Hem.H. 40 BH18
Betley Ct., Walt. 195 BV104
Betony Clo., Croy. 203 DX102
Primrose La.
Betony Rd., Rom. 106 FK51
Cloudberry Rd.
Betoyne Ave. E4 102 EE49
Betsham Rd., Erith 167 FF80
Betsham Rd., Grav. 189 FX92
Betsham Rd., Swans. 190 FY87
Betstyle Rd. N11 99 DH49
Betterton Dr., Sid. 186 EY89
Betterton Rd., Rain. 147 FE69
Betterton St. WC2 273 P9
Betterton St. WC2 141 DL72
Bettles Clo., Uxb. 134 BJ68
Westcott Way
Bettons Pk. E15 144 EE67
Bettridge Rd. SW6 159 CZ82
Betts Clo., Beck. 203 DY96
Kendall Rd.
Betts La., Wal.Abb. 50 EJ21
Betts Ms. E17 123 DZ58
Queen's Rd.
Betts Rd. E16 144 EH73
Victoria Dock Rd.
Betts St. E1 142 DV73
The Highway
Betts Way SE20 202 DV95
Betts Way, Surb. 197 CH102
Betula Clo., Ken. 236 DR115
Betula Wk., Rain. 148 FK69
Between Sts., Cob. 213 BU114
Beulah Ave., Th.Hth. 201 DM98
Beulah Rd.
Beulah Clo., Edg. 96 CP48
Beulah Cres., Th.Hth. 202 DQ96
Beulah Gro., Croy. 202 DQ100
Beulah Hill SE19 181 DP93
Beulah Path E17 123 EB57
Addison Rd.
Beulah Rd. E17 123 EB57
Beulah Rd. SW19 179 CZ94
Beulah Rd., Epp. 70 EU29
Beulah Rd., Horn. 128 FJ62
Beulah Rd., Sutt. 218 DA105
Beulah Rd., Th.Hth. 202 DQ97
Beulah Wk., Cat. 237 DY120
Beult Rd., Dart. 167 FG83
Bev Callender Clo. SW8 161 DH83
Daley Thompson Way
Bevan Ave., Bark. 146 EU66
Bevan Clo., Hem.H. 40 BK22
Bevan Ct., Croy. 219 DN106
Bevan Hill, Chesh. 54 AP29
Bevan Pl., Swan. 207 FE98
Bevan Rd. SE2 166 EV78
Bevan Rd., Barn. 80 DF42
Bevan St. N1 142 DQ67
Bevan Way, Horn. 128 FM63
Bevans Clo., Green. 189 FW86
Johnsons Way
Bevenden St. N1 275 L2
Bevenden St. N1 142 DR69
Bevercote Wk., Belv. 166 EZ79
Osborne Rd.
Beveridge Rd. NW10 138 CS66
Curzon Cres.
Beverley NW8 272 B3
Beverley Ave. SW20 199 CT95
Beverley Ave., Houns. 156 BZ84
Beverley Ave., Sid. 185 ET87
Beverley Clo. N21 100 DQ46
Beverley Clo. SW11 160 DD84
Maysoule Rd.
Beverley Clo. SW13 159 CT82
Beverley Clo., Add. 212 BK106
Beverley Clo., Brox. 49 DY21
Beverley Clo., Chess. 215 CJ105
Beverley Clo., Enf. 82 DS42
Beverley Clo., Epsom 217 CW111
Beverley Clo., Horn. 128 FM59
Beverley Clo., Wey. 195 BS103
Beverley Cotts. SW15 178 CR91
Kingston Vale
Beverley Ct. N14 99 DJ45
Beverley Ct. SE4 163 DZ83
Beverley Ct., Slou. 152 AV75
Dolphin Rd.
Beverley Cres., Wdf.Grn. 102 EH53
Beverley Dr., Edg. 118 CN55
Beverley Gdns. NW11 119 CY59
Beverley Gdns. SW13 159 CT83
Beverley Gdns., Horn. 128 FM59
Beverley Gdns., St.Alb. 43 CK16
Beverley Gdns., Stan. 95 CG53
Beverley Gdns. (Cheshunt), Wal.Cr. 66 DT30
Beverley Gdns., Welw.G.C. 30 DC09
Beverley Gdns., Wem. 118 CM60
Beverley Gdns., Wor.Pk. 199 CU102
Green La.
Beverley Heights, Reig. 250 DB132
Beverley La. SW15 179 CT90
Beverley La., Kings.T. 178 CS94
Beverley Ms. E4 101 ED51
Beverley Rd.
Beverley Path SW13 159 CT82
Beverley Rd. E4 101 ED51
Beverley Rd. E6 144 EK69
Beverley Rd. SE20 202 DV96
Wadhurst Clo.
Beverley Rd. SW13 159 CT83
Beverley Rd. W4 159 CT78
Beverley Rd., Bexh. 167 FC82
Beverley Rd., Brom. 204 EL103
Beverley Rd., Dag. 126 EY63
Beverley Rd., Kings.T. 197 CJ95
Beverley Rd., Mitch. 201 DK98
Beverley Rd., N.Mal. 199 CU98
Beverley Rd., Ruis. 115 BU61
Beverley Rd., Sthl. 156 BY77
Beverley Rd., Sun. 195 BT95
Beverley Rd., Whyt. 236 DS116
Beverley Rd., Wor.Pk. 199 CW103
Beverley Way SW20 199 CT95
Beverley Way, N.Mal. 199 CT95
Beversbrook Rd. N19 121 DK62
Beverston Ms. W1 140 DF71
Upper Montagu St.
Beverstone Rd. SW2 181 DM85
Beverstone Rd., Th.Hth. 201 DN98
Bevil Ct., Hodd. 33 EA14
Molesworth
Bevill Allen Clo. SW17 180 DF92
Bevill Clo. SE25 202 DU97
Bevin Clo. SE16 143 DY74
Bevin Ct. WC1 141 DN69
Holford St.
Bevin Rd., Hayes 135 BU69
Bevin Way WC1 274 D2
Bevington Rd. W10 139 CY71
Bevington Rd., Beck. 203 EB96
Bevington St. SE16 162 DU75
Bevis Clo., Dart. 188 FQ86
Bevis Marks EC3 275 N8
Bevis Marks EC3 142 DS72
Bewcastle Gdns., Enf. 81 DL42
Bewdley St. N1 141 DN66
Bewick St. SW8 161 DH82
Bewley Clo. (Cheshunt), Wal.Cr. 67 DX31
Bewley St. E1 142 DV73
Bewlys Rd. SE27 181 DP92
Bexhill Clo., Felt. 176 BY89
Bexhill Rd. N11 99 DK50
Bexhill Rd. SE4 183 DZ86
Bexhill Rd. SW14 158 CQ83
Bexhill Wk. E15 144 EE68
Mitre Rd.
Bexley Clo., Dart. 187 FE85
Bexley Gdns. N9 100 DR48
Bexley Gdns., Rom. 126 EV57
Bexley High St., Bex. 186 FA87
Bexley La., Dart. 187 FE85
Bexley La., Sid. 186 EW91
Bexley Rd. SE9 185 EP85
Bexley Rd., Erith 167 FC80
Bexley St., Wind. 151 AQ81
Beyers Gdns., Hodd. 33 EA14
Beyers Prospect, Hodd. 33 EA14
Beyers Ride, Hodd. 33 EA13
Beynon Rd., Cars. 218 DF106
Bianca Ho. N1 142 DS68
Crondall St.
Bianca Rd. SE15 162 DT79
Bibsworth Rd. N3 97 CZ54
Bibury Clo. SE15 162 DS79
Bicester Rd., Rich. 158 CN83
Bickenhall St. W1 272 E6
Bickenhall St. W1 140 DF71
Bickersteth Rd. SW17 180 DF93
Bickerton Rd. N19 121 DJ61
Bickley Cres., Brom. 204 EL98
Bickley Pk. Rd., Brom. 204 EL97
Bickley Rd. E10 123 EB59
Bickley Rd., Brom. 204 EK96
Bickley St. SW17 180 DE92
Bicknell Rd. SE5 162 DQ83
Bickney Way, Lthd. 230 CC122
Bicknoller Clo., Sutt. 218 DB110
Bicknoller Rd., Enf. 82 DS39
Bicknor Rd., Orp. 205 ES101
Bidborough Clo., Brom. 204 EF99
Bidborough St. WC1 273 P3
Bidborough St. WC1 141 DL69
Biddenden Way SE9 185 EN91
Biddenden Way, Grav. 190 GE94
Biddenham Turn, Wat. 76 BW35
Bidder St. E16 144 EE71
Biddestone Rd. N7 121 DM63
Biddles Clo., Slou. 131 AL74
Biddulph Rd. W9 140 DB69
Biddulph Rd., S.Croy. 220 DQ109
Bideford Ave., Grnf. 137 CH68
Bideford Clo., Edg. 96 CN53
Bideford Clo., Felt. 176 BZ90
Bideford Clo., Rom. 106 FJ53
Bideford Gdns., Enf. 100 DS45
Bideford Rd., Brom. 184 EF90
Bideford Rd., Enf. 83 DZ38
Bideford Rd., Ruis. 115 BV62
Bideford Rd., Well. 166 EV80
Bideford Spur, Slou. 131 AP69
Bidhams Cres., Tad. 233 CW121
Bidwell Gdns. N11 99 DJ52
Bidwell St. SE15 162 DV81
Big Common La., Red. 251 DP133
Big Hill E5 122 DV60
Bigbury Clo. N17 100 DR52
Weir Hall Rd.
Bigbury Rd. N17 100 DS52
Barkham Rd.
Biggerstaff Rd. E15 143 EC67
Biggerstaff St. N4 121 DN61
Biggin Ave., Mitch. 200 DF95
Biggin Hill SE19 201 DP95
Biggin Hill Clo., Kings.T. 177 CJ92
Biggin La., Grays 171 GH79
Biggin Way SE19 181 DP94
Bigginwood Rd. SW16 181 DP94
Biggs Row SW15 159 CX83
Felsham Rd.
Bigland St. E1 142 DV72
Bignell Rd. SE18 165 EP78
Bignold Rd. E7 124 EG63
Bigwood Rd. NW11 120 DB57
Biko Clo., Uxb. 134 BJ72
Sefton Way
Bill Hamling Clo. SE9 185 EM89
Billet Clo., Rom. 126 EX55
Billet La., Berk. 38 AU18
Billet La., Horn. 128 FK60
Billet La., Iver 133 BB69
Billet La., Slou. 133 BB69
Billet Rd. E17 101 DX53
Billet Rd., Rom. 126 EV56
Billet Rd., Stai. 174 BG90
Farnell Rd.
Billets Hart Clo. W7 157 CE75
Billing Pl. SW10 160 DB80
Billing Rd. SW10 160 DB80
Billing St. SW10 160 DB80
Billingford Clo. SE4 163 DX84
Billington Rd. SE14 163 DX80
Billiter Sq. EC3 275 N9
Billiter St. EC3 275 N9
Billiter St. EC3 142 DS72
Billockby Clo., Chess. 216 CM107
Billson St. E14 163 EC77
Billy Lows La., Pot.B. 64 DA31
Bilsby Gro. SE9 184 EK91
Bilton Clo., Slou. 153 BE82
Bilton Rd., Erith 167 FG80
Bilton Rd., Grnf. 137 CG67
Bilton Way, Enf. 83 DY39
Bilton Way, Hayes 155 BV75
Bina Gdns. SW5 160 DC77
Bincote Rd., Enf. 81 DM41
Binden Rd. W12 159 CT76
Bindon Grn., Mord. 200 DB98
Bayham Rd.
Binfield Rd. SW4 161 DL81
Binfield Rd., S.Croy. 220 DT106
Binfield Rd., W.Byf. 212 BL112
Bingfield St. N1 141 DL67
Bingham Clo., S.Ock. 149 FV72
Bingham Dr., Stai. 174 BK94
Bingham Dr., Wok. 226 AT118
Bingham Pl. W1 272 F6
Bingham Rd., Croy. 202 DU102
Bingham Rd., Slou. 130 AG71
Bingham St. N1 142 DR65
Bingley Rd. E16 144 EJ72
Bingley Rd., Grnf. 136 CC70
Bingley Rd., Hodd. 49 EC17
Bingley Rd., Sun. 175 BU94
Binney St. W1 272 G9
Binney St. W1 140 DG72
Binns Rd. W4 158 CS78
Binns Ter. W4 158 CS78
Binns Rd.
Binscombe Cres., Gdmg. 258 AS144
Binsey Wk. SE2 166 EW75
Binyon Cres., Stan. 95 CF50
Birbeck Gdns., Wdf.Grn. 102 EF47
Birbetts Rd. SE9 185 EM89
Birch Ave. N13 100 DQ48
Birch Ave., Cat. 236 DR124
Birch Ave., Lthd. 231 CF120
Birch Ave., West Dr. 134 BM72
Birch Circle, Gdmg. 258 AT143
Birch Clo. E16 144 EE71
Birch Clo. N19 121 DJ61
Hargrave Pk.
Birch Clo. SE15 162 DU82
Birch Clo., Add. 212 BK109
Birch Clo., Amer. 55 AS37
Birch Clo., Brent. 157 CH80
Birch Clo., Buck.H. 102 EK48
Birch Clo., Dart. 208 FK104
Birch Clo., Houns. 157 CD83
Birch Clo., Rom. 127 FB55
Birch Clo., Sev. 257 FH123
Birch Clo., Tedd. 177 CG92
Birch Clo., Wok. 226 AW119
Birch Clo. (Send Marsh), Wok. 243 BF125
Birch Copse, St.Alb. 60 BY30
Birch Ct., Nthwd. 93 BQ51
Rickmansworth Rd.
Birch Cres., Horn. 128 FL56
Birch Cres., S.Ock. 149 FX69
Birch Cres., Uxb. 134 BM67
Birch Dr., Hat. 45 CU19
Birch Dr., Rick. 91 BD50
Birch Gdns., Dag. 127 FC62
Birch Grn. NW9 96 CS52
Clayton Fld.
Birch Grn., Hem.H. 39 BF19
Birch Grn., Hert. 31 DJ11
Birch Grn., Stai. 173 BF90
Birch Gro. E11 124 EE62
Birch Gro. SE12 184 EF87
Birch Gro. W3 138 CN74
Birch Gro., Cob. 214 BW114
Birch Gro., Pot.B. 64 DA32
Birch Gro., Shep. 195 BS96
Birch Gro., Slou. 131 AP71
Birch Gro., Tad. 233 CY124
Birch Gro., Well. 166 EU84
Birch Gro., Wind. 151 AK81
Birch Gro., Wok. 227 BD115
Birch Hill, Croy. 221 DX106

Birch La., Hem.H. 57 BB33
Birch La., Pur. 219 DL111
Birch Leys, Hem.H. 41 BQ15
Hunters Oak
Birch Mead, Orp. 205 EN103
Birch Pk., Har. 94 CC52
Birch Pl., Green. 189 FS86
Birch Rd., Felt. 176 BX92
Birch Rd., Gdmg. 258 AT143
Birch Rd., Rom. 127 FB55
Birch Row, Brom. 205 EN101
Birch Tree Ave., W.Wick. 222 EF106
Birch Tree Clo., Chesh. 56 AV30
Birch Tree Wk., Wat. 75 BT37
Birch Tree Way, Croy. 202 DV103
Birch Vale, Cob. 214 CA113
Birch Vw., Epp. 70 EV29
Birch Wk., Borwd. 78 CN39
Grove Rd.
Birch Wk., Erith 167 FC79
Birch Wk., Mitch. 201 DH95
Birch Wk., W.Byf. 212 BG112
Birch Way, Chesh. 54 AR29
Birch Way, Hat. 45 CV16
Crawford Rd.
Birch Way, St.Alb. 61 CK27
Birch Way, Warl. 237 DY118
Birch Wd., Rad. 62 CN34
Birchall La., Hert. 30 DD11
Birchall La., Welw.G.C. 30 DD11
Birchall Wd., Welw.G.C. 30 DC10
Bircham Path SE4 163 DX84
St. Norbert Rd.
Birchanger Rd. SE25 202 DU99
Birchcroft Clo., Cat. 252 DQ125
Birchdale, Ger.Cr. 112 AX60
Birchdale Clo., W.Byf. 212 BJ111
Birchdale Gdns., Rom. 126 EX59
Birchdale Rd. E7 124 EJ64
Birchdene Dr. SE28 146 EU74
Birchen Clo. NW9 118 CR61
Birchen Gro. NW9 118 CR61
Birchend Clo., S.Croy. 220 DR107
Sussex Rd.
Bircherley Ct., Hert. 32 DR09
Priory St.
Bircherley St., Hert. 32 DR09
Railway St.
Birches, The N21 81 DM44
Birches, The SE7 164 EH79
Birches, The, Brwd. 108 FY48
Birches, The, Epp. 71 FB26
Birches, The, Hem.H. 39 BF23
Birches, The, Lthd. 245 BS126
Birches, The, Orp. 223 EN105
Birches, The, Swan. 207 FE96
Birches, The (Bushey), Wat. 76 CC43
Birches, The, Wok. 227 AZ118
Heathside Rd.
Birches Clo., Epsom 232 CS115
Birches Clo., Mitch. 200 DF97
Birches Clo., Pnr. 116 BY57
Birchfield Clo., Add. 212 BH105
Birchfield Clo., Couls. 235 DM116
Birchfield Gro., Epsom 217 CW110
Birchfield Rd. (Cheshunt), Wal.Cr. 66 DV29
Birchfield St. E14 143 EA73
Birchgate Ms., Tad. 233 CW121
Bidhams Cres.
Birchin La. EC3 275 L9
Birchin La. EC3 142 DR72
Birchington Clo., Bexh. 167 FB81
Birchington Clo., Orp. 206 EW102
Hart Dyke Rd.
Birchington Rd. N8 121 DK58
Birchington Rd. NW6 140 DA67
Birchington Rd., Surb. 198 CM101
Birchington Rd., Wind. 151 AN82
Birchlands Ave. SW12 180 DF87
Birchmead, Wat. 75 BT38
Birchmead Ave., Pnr. 116 BW56
Birchmead Clo., St.Alb. 43 CD17
Birchmere Row SE3 164 EF82
Birchmore Wk. N5 122 DQ62
Highbury Quad.
Birchville Ct. (Bushey), Wat. 95 CE46
Heathbourne Rd.
Birchway, Hat. 45 CV16
Crawford Rd.
Birchway, Hayes 135 BU74
Birchway, Red. 267 DH136
Birchwood, Wal.Abb. 68 EE34
Roundhills
Birchwood Ave. N10 120 DG55
Birchwood Ave., Beck. 203 DZ98
Birchwood Ave., Hat. 45 CU16
Birchwood Ave., Sid. 186 EV89
Birchwood Ave., Wall. 200 DG104
Birchwood Clo., Brwd. 107 FW51
Canterbury Way
Birchwood Clo., Hat. 45 CU16
Birchwood Clo., Horl. 269 DH147
Birchwood Clo., Mord. 200 DB98
Birchwood Ct. N13 99 DP50
Birchwood Ct., Edg. 96 CQ54
Birchwood Dr. NW3 120 DB62
Birchwood Dr., Dart. 187 FE91
Birchwood Dr., W.Byf. 212 BG112
Birchwood Gro., Hmptn. 176 CA93
Birchwood La., Cat. 251 DP125
Birchwood La., Esher 215 CD109
Birchwood La., Lthd. 215 CF110
Birchwood La., Sev. 240 EZ115
Birchwood Pk. Ave., Swan. 207 FE97
Birchwood Rd. SW17 181 DH92
Birchwood Rd., Dart. 187 FD93
Birchwood Rd., Orp. 205 ER98
Birchwood Rd., Swan. 207 FC95
Birchwood Rd., W.Byf. 212 BG112
Birchwood Ter., Swan. 207 FC95
Birchwood Rd.
Birchwood Way, St.Alb. 60 CB28
Bird in Bush Rd. SE15 162 DU80
Bird La., Brwd. 129 FW55
Bird La., Upmin. 129 FR57
Bird La., Uxb. 92 BJ54
Bird St. W1 272 G9
Bird Wk., Twick. 176 BZ88
Bird-in-Hand La., Brom. 204 EK96
Bird-in-Hand Pas. SE23 182 DW89
Dartmouth Rd.
Birdbrook Clo., Brwd. 109 GB44
Birdbrook Clo., Dag. 147 FC66
Birdbrook Rd. SE3 164 EJ83
Birdcage Wk. SW1 277 L5
Birdcage Wk. SW1 161 DJ75
Birdcage Wk., Harl. 35 EQ14
Birdcroft Rd., Welw.G.C. 29 CX10
Birdham Clo., Brom. 204 EL99
Birdhouse La., Orp. 239 EN115
Birdhurst Ave., S.Croy. 220 DR105
Birdhurst Gdns., S.Croy. 220 DR105
Birdhurst Ri., S.Croy. 220 DS106
Birdhurst Rd. SW18 160 DC84
Birdhurst Rd. SW19 180 DE93
Birdhurst Rd., S.Croy. 220 DS106
Birdie Way, Hert. 32 DV08
Birdlip Clo. SE15 162 DS79
Birds Clo., Welw.G.C. 30 DB11
Birds Fm. Ave., Rom. 105 FB53
Birds Hill Dr., Lthd. 215 CD113
Birds Hill Ri., Lthd. 215 CD113
Birds Hill Rd., Lthd. 215 CD112
Birdsfield La. E3 143 DZ67
Birdswood Dr., Wok. 226 AS120
Birdwood Clo., S.Croy. 220 DW111
Birdwood Clo., Tedd. 177 CE91
Birfield Rd., H.Wyc. 88 AC53
Birkbeck Ave. W3 138 CQ73
Birkbeck Ave., Grnf. 136 CC67
Birkbeck Gdns., Wdf.Grn. 102 EF47
Birkbeck Gro. W3 158 CR75
Birkbeck Hill SE21 181 DP89
Birkbeck Ms. E8 122 DT64
Sandringham Rd.
Birkbeck Pl. SE21 182 DQ88
Birkbeck Rd. E8 122 DT64
Birkbeck Rd. N8 121 DL56
Birkbeck Rd. N12 98 DC50
Birkbeck Rd. N17 100 DT53
Birkbeck Rd. NW7 97 CT50
Birkbeck Rd. SW19 180 DB92
Birkbeck Rd. W3 138 CR74
Birkbeck Rd. W5 157 CJ77
Birkbeck Rd., Beck. 202 DW96
Birkbeck Rd., Brwd. 109 GD44
Birkbeck Rd., Enf. 82 DR39
Birkbeck Rd., Ilf. 125 ER57
Birkbeck Rd., Rom. 127 FD60
Birkbeck Rd., Sid. 186 EU90
Birkbeck St. E2 142 DV69
Cambridge Heath Rd.
Birkbeck Way, Grnf. 136 CC67
Birkdale Ave., Pnr. 116 CA55
Birkdale Ave., Rom. 106 FM52
Birkdale Clo., Orp. 205 ER101
Birkdale Gdns., Croy. 221 DX105
Birkdale Gdns., Wat. 94 BX48
Birkdale Rd. SE2 166 EU77
Birkdale Rd. W5 138 CL70
Birken Ms., Nthwd. 93 BP50
Birkenhead Ave., Kings.T. 198 CM96
Birkenhead St. WC1 274 A2
Birkenhead St. WC1 141 DL69
Birkett Way, Ch.St.G. 72 AX41
Birkhall Rd. SE6 183 ED88
Birkheads Rd., Reig. 250 DA133
Birklands La., St.Alb. 43 CH24
Birklands Pk., St.Alb. 43 CH24
Birkwood Clo. SW12 181 DK87
Birley Rd. N20 98 DC47
Birley Rd., Slou. 131 AR72
Birley St. SW11 160 DG82
Birling Rd., Erith 167 FD80
Birnam Clo., Wok. 228 BG124
Birnam Rd. N4 121 DM61
Birse Cres. NW10 118 CS63
Birstall Grn., Wat. 94 BX49
Birstall Rd. N15 122 DS57
Birtley Path, Borwd. 78 CL39
Darrington Rd.
Biscay Rd. W6 159 CX78
Biscoe Clo., Houns. 156 CA79
Biscoe Way SE13 163 ED83
Bisenden Rd., Croy. 202 DS103
Bisham Clo., Cars. 200 DF101
Bisham Gdns. N6 120 DG60
Bishop Butt Clo., Orp. 205 ET104
Stapleton Rd.
Bishop Duppa's Pk., Shep. 195 BR101
Bishop Fox Way, W.Mol. 196 BZ98
Bishop Ken Rd., Har. 95 CF54
Bishop Kings Rd. W14 159 CY77
Bishop Rd. N14 99 DH45
Bishop Sq., Hat. 44 CS17
Bishop St. N1 142 DQ67
Bishop Way NW10 138 CS66
Bishop Wilfred Wd. Clo. SE15 162 DU82
Moncrieff St.
Bishop's Ave. E13 144 EH67
Bishop's Ave. SW6 159 CX82
Bishops Ave., Borwd. 78 CM43
Bishops Ave., Brom. 204 EJ96
Bishops Ave., Nthwd. 93 BS49
Bishops Ave., Rom. 126 EW58
Bishops Ave., The N2 120 DD59
Bishops Bri. W2 140 DC71
Bishops Bri. Rd. W2 140 DB72
Bishops Clo. E17 123 EB56
Bishops Clo. N19 121 DJ62
Wyndham Cres.
Bishops Clo. SE9 185 EQ89
Bishops Clo., Barn. 79 CX44
Bishop's Clo., Couls. 235 DN118
Bishops Clo., Enf. 82 DV40
Central Ave.
Bishops Clo., Hat. 45 CT18
Bishops Clo., Rich. 177 CK90
Bishops Clo., St.Alb. 43 CG16
Bishops Clo., Sutt. 200 DA104
Bishops Clo., Uxb. 134 BN68
Bishop's Ct. EC4 274 F8
Bishop's Ct. WC2 274 D8
Bishops Ct., Green. 189 FS85
Chalice Way
Bishops Dr., Felt. 175 BR86
Bishops Dr., Nthlt. 136 BY67
Bishops Fm. Clo., Wind. 150 AH82
Bishops Garth, St.Alb. 43 CG16
Bishops Clo.
Bishops Gro. N2 120 DD58
Bishops Gro., Hmptn. 176 BZ91
Bishop's Hall, Kings.T. 197 CK96
Bishops Hall Rd., Brwd. 108 FV44
Bishops Hill, Walt. 195 BU101
Bishops Mead, Hem.H. 40 BH22
Bishops Orchard, Slou. 131 AP69
Bishop's Pk. Rd. SW6 159 CX82
Bishops Pk. Rd. SW16 201 DL95
Bishops Ri., Hat. 45 CT18
Bishops Rd. N6 120 DG58
Bishops Rd. SW6 159 CY81
Bishops Rd. W7 157 CE75
Bishops Rd., Croy. 201 DP101
Bishops Rd., Hayes 135 BQ71
Bishops Rd., Slou. 152 AU75
Bishops Ter. SE11 278 E8
Bishops Ter. SE11 161 DN77
Bishops Wk., Chis. 205 EQ95
Bishops Wk., Croy. 221 DX106
Bishops Wk., H.Wyc. 110 AE58
Bishop's Wk., Pnr. 116 BY55
High St.
Bishops Way E2 142 DV68
Bishops Way, Egh. 173 BD93
Bishops Wd., Wok. 226 AT117
Bishopsfield, Harl. 51 ER18
Bishopsford Rd., Mord. 200 DC101
Bishopsgate EC2 275 M9
Bishopsgate EC2 142 DS72
Bishopsgate Arc. EC2 275 N7
Bishopsgate Chyd. EC2 275 M8
Bishopsgate Rd., Egh. 172 AT90
Bishopsmead Clo., Lthd. 245 BS128
Ockham Rd. S.
Bishopsmead Dr., Lthd. 245 BT129
Bishopsmead Par., Lthd. 245 BS129
Ockham Rd. S.
Bishopsthorpe Rd. SE26 183 DX91
Bishopswood Rd. N6 120 DF59
Biskra, Wat. 75 BU39
Bisley Clo., Wal.Cr. 67 DX33
Bisley Clo., Wor.Pk. 199 CW102
Bispham Rd. NW10 138 CM69
Bisson Rd. E15 143 EC68
Bisterne Ave. E17 123 ED55
Bitchet Rd., Sev. 257 FP127
Bittacy Clo. NW7 97 CX51
Bittacy Hill NW7 97 CX51
Bittacy Pk. Ave. NW7 97 CX51
Bittacy Ri. NW7 97 CW51
Bittacy Rd. NW7 97 CX51
Bittams La., Cher. 211 BD105
Bittern Clo., Hayes 136 BX71
Bittern St. SE1 279 H5
Bitterne Dr., Wok. 226 AT117
Bittoms, The, Kings.T. 197 CK97
Bixley Clo., Sthl. 156 BZ77
Black Acre Clo., Amer. 55 AS39
Black Boy La. N15 122 DQ57
Black Boy Wd., St.Alb. 60 CA30
Black Cut, St.Alb. 43 CE21
Black Eagle Clo., West. 255 EQ127
Black Fan Clo., Enf. 82 DQ39
Black Fan Rd., Welw.G.C. 30 DA08
Black Friars Ct. EC4 274 F10
Black Friars La. EC4 274 F10
Black Friars La. EC4 141 DP72
Black Gates, Pnr. 116 BZ55
Church La.
Black Horse Ave., Chesh. 54 AR33
Black Horse Clo., Wind. 151 AK82
Black Horse Ct. SE1 279 L6
Black Lake Clo., Egh. 193 BA95
Black Lion Ct., Harl. 36 EW11
Black Lion Hill, Rad. 62 CL32
Black Lion La. W6 159 CU77
Black Pk. Rd., Slou. 132 AY68
Black Path E10 123 DX59
Black Prince Clo., W.Byf. 212 BM114
Black Prince Rd. SE1 278 A9
Black Prince Rd. SE1 161 DM77
Black Prince Rd. SE11 278 C9
Black Prince Rd. SE11 161 DM77
Black Rod Clo., Hayes 155 BT76
Black Swan Ct., Ware 33 DX06
Baldock St.
Black Swan Yd. SE1 279 M4
Black Thorne Rd., West. 238 EK115
Blackacre Rd., Epp. 85 ER37
Blackall St. EC2 275 M4
Blackberry Clo., Guil. 242 AV131
Blackberry Clo., Shep. 195 BS98
Cherry Way
Blackberry Fm. Clo., Houns. 156 BY80
Blackberry Fld., Orp. 206 EU95
Blackbird Hill NW9 118 CQ61
Blackbird Yd. E2 142 DT69
Ravenscroft St.
Blackbirds La., Wat. 77 CD35
Blackborne Rd., Dag. 146 FA65
Blackborough Clo., Reig. 250 DC134
Blackborough Rd., Reig. 266 DB135
Blackbridge Rd., Wok. 226 AX119
Blackbrook La., Brom. 205 EN97
Blackbrook Rd., Dor. 263 CK140
Blackburn, The, Lthd. 230 BZ124
Little Bookham St.
Blackburn Rd. NW6 140 DB65
Blackburn Trd. Est., Stai. 174 BM86
Blackburne's Ms. W1 272 F10
Blackburne's Ms. W1 140 DG73
Blackbury Clo., Pot.B. 64 DC31
Blackbush Ave., Rom. 126 EX57
Blackbush Clo., Sutt. 218 DB108
Blackbush Spring, Harl. 36 EU14
Blackdale (Cheshunt), Wal.Cr. 66 DU27
Blackdown Ave., Wok. 227 BE115
Blackdown Clo. N2 98 DC54
Blackdown Clo., Wok. 227 BC116
Blackdown Ter. SE18 165 EN80
Prince Imperial Rd.
Blackett Clo., Stai. 193 BE96
Blackett St. SW15 159 CX83
Blacketts Wd. Dr., Rick. 73 BB43
Blackfen Rd., Sid. 185 ES86
Blackford Clo., S.Croy. 219 DP109
Blackford Rd., Wat. 94 BX50
Blackford's Path SW15 179 CU87
Roehampton High St.
Blackfriars Bri. EC4 278 F1
Blackfriars Bri. EC4 141 DP73
Blackfriars Bri. SE1 278 F1
Blackfriars Bri. SE1 141 DP73
Blackfriars Pas. EC4 274 F10
Blackfriars Rd. SE1 278 F2
Blackfriars Rd. SE1 141 DP74
Blackhall La., Sev. 257 FK123
Blackhall Pl., Sev. 257 FL124
Blackhall La.
Blackheath Ave. SE10 163 ED80
Blackheath Gro. SE3 164 EF82
Blackheath Gro., Guil. 259 BB143
Blackheath Hill SE10 163 EC81
Blackheath La., Guil. 259 BB143
Blackheath Pk. SE3 164 EF83
Blackheath Ri. SE13 163 EC82
Blackheath Rd. SE10 163 EB81
Blackheath Vale SE3 164 EE82
Blackheath Village SE3 164 EF82
Blackhills, Esher 214 BZ109
Blackhorse Clo., Amer. 72 AT38
Blackhorse Cres., Amer. 55 AS38
Blackhorse La. E17 123 DX56
Blackhorse La., Croy. 202 DU101
Blackhorse La., Epp. 71 FD25
Blackhorse La., Reig. 250 DB129
Blackhorse Ms. E17 123 DX55
Blackhorse Rd.
Blackhorse Rd. E17 123 DX56
Blackhorse Rd. SE8 163 DY78
Blackhorse Rd., Sid. 186 EU91
Blackhorse Rd., Wok. 226 AS122
Blacklands Dr., Hayes 135 BQ70
Blacklands Meadow, Red. 251 DL133
Blacklands Rd. SE6 183 EC91
Blacklands Ter. SW3 276 D9
Blacklands Ter. SW3 160 DF77
Blackley Clo., Wat. 75 BT37
Blackmans Clo., Dart. 188 FJ88
Blackmans La., Warl. 222 EE114
Blackmans Yd. E2 142 DU70
Cheshire St.
Blackmead, Sev. 241 FD119
London Rd.
Blackmoor La., Wat. 75 BQ44
Blackmore Ave., Sthl. 137 CD74
Blackmore Clo., Grays 170 GB78
Blackmore Ct., Wal.Abb. 68 EG33
Blackmore Cres., Wok. 211 BC114
Blackmore Rd., Buck.H. 102 EL45
Blackmore Way, Uxb. 134 BK65
Blackmores, Harl. 51 EP15
Blackmores Gro., Tedd. 177 CG93
Blackness La., Kes. 222 EK108
Blackness La., Wok. 226 AY119
Blacknest Rd., Vir.W. 192 AT97
Blackpond La., Slou. 131 AP65
Blackpool Gdns., Hayes 135 BS70
Blackpool Rd. SE15 162 DV82
Blacks Rd. W6 159 CW77
Queen Caroline St.
Blackshaw Pl. N1 142 DS66
Hertford Rd.
Blackshaw Rd. SW17 180 DC91
Blackshots La., Grays 170 GD75
Blacksmith Clo., Ash. 232 CM119
Rectory La.
Blacksmith Clo., Ware 33 DZ08
Blacksmith La., Guil. 259 BC139
Blacksmith Row, Slou. 153 BA77
Blacksmiths Clo., Rom. 126 EW58
Blacksmiths Hill, S.Croy. 220 DU113
Blacksmiths La., Cher. 194 BG101
Blacksmiths La., Orp. 206 EW99
Blacksmiths La., Rain. 147 FF67
Blacksmiths La., St.Alb. 42 CB20
Blacksmiths La., Stai. 194 BH97
Blacksmiths La., Uxb. 113 BC61
Blackstock Ms. N4 121 DP61
Blackstock Rd.
Blackstock Rd. N4 121 DP61
Blackstock Rd. N5 121 DP61
Blackstone Clo., Red. 266 DE135
Blackstone Est. E8 142 DU66
Blackstone Hill, Red. 250 DE134
Blackstone Rd. NW2 119 CW64
Blackthorn Ave., West Dr. 154 BN77
Blackthorn Clo., Reig. 266 DC136
Blackthorn Clo., St.Alb. 43 CJ17
Blackthorn Clo., Wat. 59 BV32
Blackthorn Ct., Houns. 156 BY80
Blackthorn Dell, Slou. 152 AW76
Blackthorn Gro., Bexh. 166 EY83
Blackthorn Rd., Reig. 266 DB136
Blackthorn Rd., Welw.G.C. 30 DA10
Blackthorn St. E3 143 EA70
Blackthorn Way, Brwd. 108 FX50
Blackthorne Ave., Croy. 202 DW102
Blackthorne Clo., Hat. 45 CT21
Blackthorne Dr. E4 101 ED49
Blackthorne Rd., Lthd. 246 CC126
Blackthorne Rd., Slou. 153 BE83
Blacktree Ms. SW9 161 DN83
Blackwall La. SE10 164 EE78
Blackwall Pier E14 144 EE73
Blackwall Tunnel E14 143 ED74
Blackwall Tunnel App. SE10 164 EE75
Blackwall Tunnel Northern App. E3 143 EA68
Blackwall Tunnel Northern App. E14 143 EC70
Blackwall Way E14 143 EC73
Blackwater Clo. E7 124 EF64
Tower Hamlets Rd.
Blackwater Clo., Rain. 147 FD71
Blackwater La., Hem.H. 41 BS23
Blackwater Rd., Sutt. 218 DB105
High St.
Blackwater St. SE22 182 DT85
Blackwell Clo. E5 123 DY63
Blackwell Clo., Har. 95 CD52
Blackwell Dr., Wat. 76 BW44
Blackwell Gdns., Edg. 96 CN48
Blackwell Hall La., Chesh. 72 AT35
Blackwell Rd., Kings L. 58 BN29
Blackwood Clo., W.Byf. 212 BJ112
Blackwood St. SE17 279 K10
Blackwood St. SE17 162 DR78
Blade Ms. SW15 159 CZ84
Deodar Rd.
Bladen Clo., Wey. 213 BR107
Blades Clo., Lthd. 231 CK120
Bladindon Dr., Bex. 186 EW87
Bladon Clo., Guil. 243 BA133
Bladon Gdns., Har. 116 CB58
Blagdens Clo. N14 99 DJ47
Blagdens La. N14 99 DK47
Blagdon Rd. SE13 183 EB86
Blagdon Rd., N.Mal. 199 CT98
Blagdon Wk., Tedd. 177 CJ93
Blagrove Rd. W10 139 CY71
Blair Ave. NW9 118 CS59
Blair Ave., Esher 196 CC103
Blair Clo. N1 142 DQ65
Blair Clo., Hayes 155 BU77
Blair Clo., Sid. 185 ES85
Blair Dr., Sev. 257 FH123
Blair Rd., Slou. 132 AS74
Blair St. E14 143 EC72
Blairderry Rd. SW2 181 DL89
Blairhead Dr., Wat. 93 BV48
Blake Ave., Bark. 145 ES67
Blake Clo. W10 139 CW71
Blake Clo., Cars. 200 DE101
Blake Clo., Rain. 147 FF67
Blake Clo., St.Alb. 43 CG23
Blake Clo., Well. 165 ES81
Blake Gdns. SW6 160 DB81
Blake Gdns., Dart. 168 FM84
Blake Hall Cres. E11 124 EG60
Blake Hall Rd. E11 124 EG59
Blake Hall Rd., Ong. 71 FG27
Blake Ho., Beck. 183 EA93
Blake Rd. E16 144 EF70
Blake Rd. N11 99 DJ52
Blake Rd., Croy. 202 DS103
Blake Rd., Mitch. 200 DE97
Blake St. SE8 163 EA79
Watergate St.
Blakeborough Dr., Rom. 106 FL54
Blakeden Dr., Esher 215 CF107
Blakehall Rd., Cars. 218 DF107
Blakeley Cotts. SE10 163 ED75
Tunnel Ave.
Blakemere Rd., Welw.G.C. 29 CX07
Blakemore Rd. SW16 181 DL90
Blakemore Rd., Th.Hth. 201 DM99
Blakemore Way, Belv. 166 EY76
Blakeney Ave., Beck. 203 DZ95
Blakeney Clo. E8 122 DU64
Ferncliff Rd.
Blakeney Clo. N20 98 DC46
Blakeney Clo. NW1 141 DK66
Rossendale Way
Blakeney Clo., Epsom 216 CR111
Blakeney Rd., Beck. 203 DZ95
Blakenham Rd. SW17 180 DF91
Blaker Ct. SE7 164 EJ80
Fairlawn
Blaker Rd. E15 143 EC67
Blakes Ave., N.Mal. 199 CT99
Blakes Ct., Saw. 36 EY05
Church St.
Blake's Grn., W.Wick. 203 EC102
Blakes La., Guil. 244 BL132
Blakes La., Lthd. 244 BN131
Blakes La., N.Mal. 199 CT99
Blakes Rd. SE15 162 DS80
Blakes Ter., N.Mal. 199 CU99
Blakes Way, Til. 171 GJ82
Coleridge Rd.
Blakesley Ave. W5 137 CJ72
Blakesley Wk. SW20 199 CZ96
Kingston Rd.
Blakesware Gdns. N9 100 DR45
Blakewood Clo., Felt. 176 BW91
Blanch Clo. SE15 162 DW80
Culmore Rd.
Blanchard Clo. SE9 184 EL90
Blanchard Way E8 142 DU65
Blanchards Hill, Guil. 242 AY126
Blanche La., Pot.B. 63 CU32
Blanche St. E16 144 EF70
Blanchedowne SE5 162 DR84
Blanchland Rd., Mord. 200 DB99
Blanchmans Rd., Warl. 237 DY118
Bland St. SE9 164 EK84
Blandfield Rd. SW12 180 DG86
Blandford Ave., Beck. 203 DY96
Blandford Ave., Twick. 176 CB88
Blandford Clo. N2 120 DC57
Blandford Clo., Croy. 201 DL104
Blandford Clo., Rom. 127 FB56
Blandford Clo., Slou. 152 AX76
Blandford Clo., Wok. 227 BB117
Blandford Ct., Slou. 152 AX76
Blandford Rd. S.
Blandford Cres. E4 101 EC45
Blandford Rd. W4 158 CS76
Blandford Rd. W5 157 CK75
Blandford Rd., Beck. 202 DW96
Blandford Rd., St.Alb. 43 CG20
Blandford Rd., Sthl. 156 CA77
Blandford Rd., Tedd. 177 CD92
Blandford Rd. N., Slou. 152 AX76
Blandford Rd. S., Slou. 152 AX76
Blandford Sq. NW1 272 C5
Blandford Sq. NW1 140 DE70
Blandford St. W1 272 E8
Blandford St. W1 140 DF72
Blandford Waye, Hayes 136 BW72
Blaney Cres. E6 145 EP69
Blanford Rd., Reig. 266 DC135
Blanmerle Rd. SE9 185 EP88
Blann Clo. SE9 184 EK86
Blantyre St. SW10 160 DD80
Blantyre Wk. SW10 160 DD80
Blantyre St.
Blashford NW3 140 DF66
Blashford St. SE13 183 ED87
Blasker Wk. E14 163 EA78
Blattner Clo., Borwd. 78 CL42
Blawith Rd., Har. 117 CE56
Blaydon Clo. N17 100 DV52
Blaydon Clo., Ruis. 115 BS59
Blaydon Wk. N17 100 DV52
Blays Clo., Egh. 172 AW93
Blays La., Egh. 172 AV94
Bleak Hill La. SE18 165 ET79
Blean Gro. SE20 182 DW94
Bleasdale Ave., Grnf. 137 CG68
Blechynden St. W10 139 CX73
Bramley Rd.
Bleddyn Clo., Sid. 186 EW86
Bledlow Clo. SE28 146 EW73
Bledlow Ri., Grnf. 136 CC68
Bleeding Heart Yd. EC1 274 E7
Blegborough Rd. SW16 181 DJ93
Blencarn Clo., Wok. 226 AT116
Blendon Dr., Bex. 186 EX86
Blendon Path, Brom. 184 EF94
Hope Pk.
Blendon Rd., Bex. 186 EW86
Blendon Ter. SE18 165 EQ78

Blendworth Way SE15 162 DS80
Daniel Gdns.
Blenheim Ave., Ilf. 125 EN58
Blenheim Clo. N21 100 DQ46
Elm Pk. Rd.
Blenheim Clo. SW20 199 CW97
Blenheim Clo., Dart. 188 FJ86
Blenheim Clo., Grnf. 137 CD68
Leaver Gdns.
Blenheim Clo., Rom. 127 FC56
Blenheim Clo., Saw. 36 EW07
Blenheim Clo., Slou. 133 AZ74
Blenheim Clo., Upmin. 129 FS60
Blenheim Clo., Wall. 219 DJ108
Blenheim Clo., Wat. 94 BX45
Blenheim Clo., W.Byf. 211 BF113
Madeira Rd.
Blenheim Ct. N19 121 DL61
Marlborough Rd.
Blenheim Ct., Sid. 185 ER90
Blenheim Cres. W11 139 CY73
Blenheim Cres., Ruis. 115 BR61
Blenheim Cres., S.Croy. 220 DQ108
Blenheim Dr., Well. 165 ET81
Blenheim Gdns. NW2 139 CW65
Blenheim Gdns. SW2 181 DM86
Blenheim Gdns., Kings.T. 178 CP94
Blenheim Gdns., S.Croy. 220 DU112
Blenheim Gdns., S.Ock. 148 FP74
Blenheim Gdns., Wall. 219 DJ107
Blenheim Gdns., Wem. 118 CL62
Blenheim Gdns., Wok. 226 AV119
Blenheim Gro. SE15 162 DU82
Blenheim Pk. Rd., S.Croy. 220 DQ109
Blenheim Pas. NW8 140 DC68
Blenheim Ter.
Blenheim Ri. N15 122 DT56
Talbot Rd.
Blenheim Rd. E6 144 EK69
Blenheim Rd. E15 124 EE63
Blenheim Rd. E17 123 DX55
Blenheim Rd. NW8 140 DC68
Blenheim Rd. SE20 182 DW94
Maple Rd.
Blenheim Rd. SW20 199 CW97
Blenheim Rd. W4 158 CS76
Blenheim Rd., Abb.L. 59 BU32
Blenheim Rd., Barn. 79 CX41
Blenheim Rd., Brwd. 108 FU44
Blenheim Rd., Brom. 204 EL98
Blenheim Rd., Dart. 188 FJ86
Blenheim Rd., Epsom 216 CR111
Blenheim Rd., Har. 116 CB58
Blenheim Rd., Nthlt. 136 CB65
Blenheim Rd., Orp. 206 EW103
Blenheim Rd., St.Alb. 43 CF19
Blenheim Rd., Sid. 186 EW88
Blenheim Rd., Slou. 152 AX77
Blenheim Rd., Sutt. 200 DA104
Blenheim St. W1 273 H9
Blenheim Ter. NW8 140 DC68
Blenheim Way, Epp. 70 FA27
Blenheim Way, Islw. 157 CG81
Blenkarne Rd. SW11 180 DF86
Blenkin Clo., St.Alb. 42 CC16
Bleriot Rd., Houns. 156 BW80
Blessbury Rd., Edg. 96 CQ53
Blessing Way, Bark. 146 EW69
Blessington Clo. SE13 163 ED83
Blessington Rd. SE13 163 ED84
Bletchingley Clo., Red. 251 DJ129
Bletchingley Clo., Th.Hth. 201 DP98
Bletchingley Rd., Gdse. 252 DU131
Bletchingley Rd. (Bletchingley), Red. 251 DN133
Bletchingley Rd. (South Merstham), Red. 251 DJ129
Bletchley Ct. N1 275 K1
Bletchley St. N1 275 J1
Bletchley St. N1 142 DQ68
Bletchmore Clo., Hayes 155 BR78
Bletsoe Wk. N1 142 DQ68
Cropley St.
Bligh Rd., Grav. 191 GG86
Blighs Rd., Sev. 257 FH125
Blinco La., Slou. 132 AY72
Blincoe Clo. SW19 179 CX89
Blind La., Bans. 234 DE115
Blind La., Bet. 264 CQ137
Wheelers La.
Blind La., H.Wyc. 110 AC56
Blind La., Loug. 84 EE40
Blind La., Wal.Abb. 68 EJ33
Blindman's La. (Cheshunt), Wal.Cr. 67 DX30
Bliss Cres. SE13 163 EB82
Coldbath St.
Blissett St. SE10 163 EC81
Blisworth Clo., Hayes 136 BY70
Braunston Dr.
Blithbury Rd., Dag. 146 EV65
Blithdale Rd. SE2 166 EU77
Blithfield St. W8 160 DB76
Blockhouse Rd., Grays 170 GC79
Blockley Rd., Wem. 117 CH61
Bloemfontein Ave. W12 139 CV74
Bloemfontein Rd. W12 139 CV73
Blomfield Rd. W9 140 DB71
Blomfield St. EC2 275 L7
Blomfield St. EC2 142 DR71
Blomfield Vill. W2 140 DB71
Blomville Rd., Dag. 126 EY62
Blondel St. SW11 160 DG82
Blondell Clo., West Dr. 154 BK79
Blondin Ave. W5 157 CJ77
Blondin St. E3 143 EA68
Bloom Gro. SE27 181 DP90
Bloom Pk. Rd. SW6 159 CZ80
Bloomburg St. SW1 277 L9
Bloomfield Clo., Wok. 226 AS118
Bloomfield Cres., Ilf. 125 EP58
Bloomfield Pl. W1 273 J10
Bloomfield Rd. N6 120 DG58
Bloomfield Rd. SE18 165 EP78
Bloomfield Rd., Brom. 204 EK99
Bloomfield Rd., Kings.T. 198 CL98
Bloomfield Ter. SW1 276 G10
Bloomfield Ter. SW1 160 DG78
Bloomfield Ter., West. 255 ES125
Bloomhall Rd. SE19 182 DR92
Bloomsbury Clo. W5 138 CM73
Bloomsbury Clo., Epsom 216 CR110
Bloomsbury Ct. WC1 274 A7
Bloomsbury Ct., Guil. 259 AZ135
St. Lukes Sq.
Bloomsbury Ct., Pnr. 116 BZ55
Bloomsbury Ho. SW4 181 DK86
Bloomsbury Pl. SW18 180 DC85
Fullerton Rd.
Bloomsbury Pl. WC1 274 A6
Bloomsbury Sq. WC1 274 A7
Bloomsbury Sq. WC1 141 DL71
Bloomsbury St. WC1 273 N7
Bloomsbury St. WC1 141 DK71
Bloomsbury Way WC1 273 P8
Bloomsbury Way WC1 141 DL71
Blore Clo. SW8 161 DK81
Thessaly Rd.
Blore Ct. W1 273 M10
Blossom Clo. W5 158 CL75
Almond Ave.
Blossom Clo., Dag. 146 EZ67
Blossom Clo., S.Croy. 220 DT106
Melville Ave.
Blossom La., Enf. 82 DQ39
Blossom St. E1 275 N5
Blossom St. E1 142 DS70
Blossom Way, Uxb. 134 BM66
Blossom Way, West Dr. 154 BN77
Blossom Waye, Houns. 156 BY80
Blount St. E14 143 DY71
Bloxam Gdns. SE9 184 EL85
Bloxhall Rd. E10 123 DZ60
Bloxham Cres., Hmptn. 176 BZ94
Bloxworth Clo., Wall. 201 DJ104
Blucher Rd. SE5 162 DQ80
Blucher St., Chesh. 54 AP31
Blue Anchor All., Rich. 158 CL84
Kew Rd.
Blue Anchor La. SE16 162 DU77
Blue Anchor La., Til. 171 GL77
Blue Anchor Yd. E1 142 DU73
Blue Ball La., Egh. 173 AZ92
Blue Ball Yd. SW1 277 K3
Blue Barn La., Wey. 212 BN111
Blue Cedars, Bans. 217 CX114
Bluebell Ave. E12 124 EL64
Bluebell Clo. SE26 182 DT91
Bluebell Clo., Hem.H. 39 BE21
Sundew Rd.
Bluebell Clo., Hert. 32 DU09
Bluebell Clo., Orp. 205 EQ103
Bluebell Clo., Wall. 201 DH102
Bluebell Ct., Wok. 226 AX119
Bluebell Dr., Abb.L. 59 BT27
Bluebell Dr., Wal.Cr. 66 DR28
St. James Rd.
Bluebell La., Lthd. 245 BS129
Bluebell Way, Ilf. 145 EP65
Blueberry Clo., St.Alb. 43 CD16
Blueberry Gdns., Couls. 235 DM116
Blueberry La., Sev. 240 EW116
Bluebridge Ave., Hat. 63 CY27
Bluebridge Rd., Hat. 63 CY26
Bluecoat Yd., Ware 33 DX06
Bluecoats Ave., Hert. 32 DR09
Bluefield Clo., Hmptn. 176 CA92
Bluegates, Epsom 217 CU108
Bluehouse Hill, St.Alb. 42 CA20
Bluehouse La., Oxt. 254 EE128
Bluehouse Rd. E4 102 EE48
Bluemans, Epp. 53 FD24
Bluemans End, Epp. 53 FD24
Bluett Rd., St.Alb. 61 CK27
Blumfield Ct., Slou. 131 AK71
Blumfield Cres., Slou. 131 AK70
Blundel La., Cob. 230 BZ116
Blundell Ave., Horl. 268 DF147
Blundell Clo., St.Alb. 43 CD16
Blundell Rd., Edg. 96 CR53
Blundell St. N7 141 DL66
Blunden Clo., Dag. 126 EW60
Blunesfield, Pot.B. 64 DD31
Blunt Rd., S.Croy. 220 DR106
Blunts Ave., West Dr. 154 BN80
Blunts La., St.Alb. 42 BX24
Blunts Rd. SE9 185 EN85
Blurton Rd. E5 122 DW63
Blyth Clo. E14 163 ED77
Manchester Rd.
Blyth Clo., Borwd. 78 CM39
Blyth Clo., Twick. 177 CF86
Grimwood Rd.
Blyth Rd. E17 123 DZ59
Blyth Rd. SE28 146 EW73
Blyth Rd., Brom. 204 EF95
Blyth Rd., Hayes 155 BS75
Blyth Wk., Upmin. 129 FS58
Blythe Clo. SE6 183 DZ87
Blythe Clo., Iver 133 BF72
Blythe Hill SE6 183 DZ87
Blythe Hill, Orp. 205 ET95
Blythe Hill La. SE6 183 DZ87
Blythe Rd. W14 159 CX76
Blythe Rd., Hodd. 49 ED19
Blythe St. E2 142 DV69
Blythe Vale SE6 183 DZ88
Blythswood Rd., Ilf. 126 EU60
Blythway, Welw.G.C. 29 CZ06
Blythwood Rd. N4 121 DL59
Blythwood Rd., Pnr. 94 BX53
Blyton Clo., Beac. 89 AK51
Boades Ms. NW3 120 DD63
New End
Boadicea St. N1 141 DM67
Copenhagen St.
Boakes Clo. NW9 118 CQ56
Roe Grn.
Boakes Meadow, Sev. 225 FF111
Boar Clo., Chig. 104 EU50
Board Sch. Rd., Wok. 227 AZ116
Boardman Ave. E4 83 EB43
Boardman Clo., Barn. 79 CY43
Boarlands Clo., Slou. 131 AM73
Boarlands Path, Slou. 131 AM73
Brook Path
Boar's Head Yd., Brent. 157 CK80
Brent Way
Boars Rd., Harl. 52 FA16
Boat Lifter Way SE16 163 DY77
Sweden Gate
Boathouse Wk. SE15 162 DT80
Boathouse Wk., Rich. 157 CK81
Kew Rd.
Bob Anker Clo. E13 144 EG69
Chesterton Rd.
Bob Marley Way SE24 161 DN84
Mayall Rd.
Bobbin Clo. SW4 161 DJ83
Bobs La., Rom. 105 FF53
Bocketts La., Lthd. 231 CF124
Bockhampton Rd., Kings.T. 178 CM94
Bocking St. E8 142 DV67
Boddicott Clo. SW19 179 CY89
Bodell Clo., Grays 170 GB75
Bodiam Clo., Enf. 82 DR40
Bodiam Rd. SW16 181 DK94
Bodle Ave., Swans. 190 FY87
Bodley Clo., Epp. 69 ET30
Bodley Clo., N.Mal. 198 CS99
Bodley Manor Way SW2 181 DN87
Papworth Way
Bodley Rd., N.Mal. 198 CR100
Bodmin Ave., Slou. 131 AN71
Bodmin Clo., Har. 116 BZ62
Bodmin Clo., Orp. 206 EW102
Bodmin Gro., Mord. 200 DB98
Bodmin St. SW18 180 DA88
Bodnant Gdns. SW20 199 CV97
Bodney Rd. E8 122 DV64
Bodwell Clo., Hem.H. 40 BG19
Boeing Way, Sthl. 155 BV76
Boevey Path, Belv. 166 EZ78
Orchard Ave.
Bogey La., Orp. 223 EM108
Bognor Gdns., Wat. 94 BW50
Bowring Grn.
Bognor Rd., Well. 166 EX81
Bohemia, Hem.H. 40 BL19
Bohemia Pl. E8 142 DW65
Bohun Gro., Barn. 80 DE44
Boileau Par. W5 138 CM72
Boileau Rd.
Boileau Rd. SW13 159 CU80
Boileau Rd. W5 138 CM72
Bois Ave., Amer. 55 AP36
Bois Hall Rd., Add. 212 BK106
Bois Hill, Chesh. 54 AS34
Bois La., Amer. 55 AR36
Bois Moor Rd., Chesh. 54 AQ33
Boissy Clo., St.Alb. 44 CL21
Bolden St. SE8 163 EB82
Bolderwood Way, W.Wick. 203 EB103
Boldmere Rd., Pnr. 116 BW59
Boleyn Ave., Enf. 82 DV39
Boleyn Ave., Epsom 217 CU110
Boleyn Clo. E17 123 EA56
Boleyn Clo., Grays 170 FZ76
Clifford Rd.
Boleyn Clo., Hem.H. 41 BQ15
Parr Cres.
Boleyn Clo., Loug. 84 EL44
Roding Gdns.
Boleyn Clo., Stai. 173 BE92
Chertsey La.
Boleyn Ct., Brox. 49 DY21
Boleyn Ct., Buck.H. 102 EG46
Boleyn Dr., Ruis. 116 BX61
Boleyn Dr., St.Alb. 43 CD22
Boleyn Dr., W.Mol. 196 BZ97
Boleyn Gdns., Brwd. 109 GA48
Boleyn Gdns., Dag. 147 FC66
Boleyn Gdns., W.Wick. 203 EB103
Boleyn Gro., W.Wick. 203 EC103
Boleyn Rd. E6 144 EK68
Boleyn Rd. E7 144 EG66
Boleyn Rd. N16 122 DS64
Boleyn Wk., Lthd. 231 CF120
Boleyn Way, Barn. 80 DC41
Boleyn Way, Ilf. 103 EQ51
Boleyn Way, Swans. 190 FY87
Bolina Rd. SE16 162 DW78
Bolingbroke Gro. SW11 180 DF86
Bolingbroke Rd. W14 159 CX76
Bolingbroke Wk. SW11 160 DD81
Bolingbroke Way, Hayes 135 BR74
Bolingbroke, St.Alb. 43 CG16
Bolliger Ct. NW10 138 CQ70
Park Royal Rd.
Bollo Bri. Rd. W3 158 CP76
Bollo La. W3 158 CP75
Bollo La. W4 158 CQ77
Bolney St. SW8 161 DM80
Bolney Way, Felt. 176 BY90
Bolsover Gro., Red. 251 DL129
Bolsover St. W1 273 J5
Bolsover St. W1 141 DH70
Bolstead Rd., Mitch. 201 DH95
Bolt Cellar La., Epp. 69 ES30
Bolt Ct. EC4 274 E9
Bolters La., Bans. 217 CZ114
Bolters Rd., Horl. 268 DG146
Bolters Rd. S., Horl. 268 DF146
Boltmore Clo. NW4 119 CX55
Bolton Ave., Wind. 151 AR83
Bolton Clo. SE20 202 DU96
Selby Rd.
Bolton Clo., Chess. 215 CK107
Bolton Cres. SE5 161 DP79
Bolton Cres., Wind. 151 AQ83
Bolton Gdns. NW10 139 CX68
Bolton Gdns. SW5 160 DB78
Bolton Gdns., Brom. 184 EF93
Bolton Gdns., Tedd. 177 CG93
Bolton Gdns. Ms. SW10 160 DB78
Bolton Rd. E15 144 EF65
Bolton Rd. N18 100 DT50
Bolton Rd. NW8 140 DB67
Bolton Rd. NW10 138 CS67
Bolton Rd. W4 158 CQ80
Bolton Rd., Chess. 215 CK107
Bolton Rd., Har. 116 CC56
Bolton Rd., Wind. 151 AQ83
Bolton St. W1 277 J2
Bolton St. W1 141 DH74
Bolton Wk. N7 121 DM61
Durham Rd.
Boltons, The SW10 160 DC78
Boltons, The, Wem. 117 CF63
Boltons, The, Wdf.Grn. 102 EG49
Boltons Clo., Wok. 228 BG116
Boltons La., Hayes 155 BQ81
Boltons La., Wok. 228 BG116
Boltons Pl. SW10 160 DC78
Bombay St. SE16 162 DV77
Bombers La., West. 239 ES120
Grays Rd.
Bomer Clo., West Dr. 154 BN80
Bomore Rd. W11 139 CY73
Bon Marche Ter. SE27 182 DS91
Gipsy Rd.
Bonar Pl., Chis. 184 EL94
Bonar Rd. SE15 162 DU80
Bonaventure Ct., Grav. 191 GM91
Bonchester Clo., Chis. 185 EN94
Bonchurch Clo., Sutt. 218 DB108
Bonchurch Rd. W10 139 CY71
Bonchurch Rd. W13 137 CH74
Bond Clo., Sev. 240 EX115
Bond Clo., West Dr. 134 BM72
Bond Ct. EC4 275 K9
Bond Gdns., Wall. 219 DJ105
Bond Rd., Mitch. 200 DE96
Bond Rd., Surb. 198 CM102
Bond Rd., Warl. 237 DX118
Bond St. E15 124 EE64
Bond St. W4 158 CS77
Chiswick Common Rd.
Bond St. W5 137 CK73
Bond St., Egh. 172 AV92
Bond St., Grays 170 GC79
Bondfield Rd. E6 144 EL71
Lovage App.
Bondfield Rd., Hayes 135 BU69
Bondfield Wk., Dart. 168 FM83
Joyce Grn. La.
Bonding Yd. Wk. SE16 163 DY76
Finland St.
Bonds La., Dor. 263 CH142
Bondway SW8 161 DL79
Bone Mill La., Gdse. 253 DY134
Eastbourne Rd.
Bonehurst Rd., Horl. 268 DG146
Bonehurst Rd., Red. 266 DG142
Boneta Rd. SE18 165 EM76
Bonfield Rd. SE13 163 EC84
Bonham Gdns., Dag. 126 EX61
Bonham Rd. SW2 181 DM85
Bonham Rd., Dag. 126 EX61
Bonheur Rd. W4 158 CR75
Bonhill St. EC2 275 L5
Bonhill St. EC2 142 DR70
Boniface Gdns., Har. 94 CB52
Boniface Rd., Uxb. 115 BP62
Boniface Wk., Har. 94 CB52
Bonks Hill, Saw. 36 EX06
Bonner Hill Rd., Kings.T. 198 CM97
Bonner Rd. E2 142 DW68
Bonner St. E2 142 DW68
Bonner Wk., Grays 170 FZ76
Clifford Rd.
Bonners Clo., Wok. 227 AZ122
Bonnersfield Clo., Har. 117 CF58
Bonnersfield La., Har. 117 CF58
Bonneville Gdns. SW4 181 DJ86
Bonney Gro. (Cheshunt), Wal.Cr. 66 DU30
Bonney Way, Swan. 207 FE96
Bonnington Rd., Horn. 128 FK64
Bonnington Sq. SW8 161 DM79
Bonnington Twr., Brom. 204 EL100
Bonningtons, Brwd. 109 GB48
Bonny St. NW1 141 DJ66
Bonny's Rd., Reig. 265 CX135
Bonser Rd., Twick. 177 CF89
Bonsey Clo., Wok. 226 AY121
Bonsey La., Wok. 226 AY121
Bonseys La., Wok. 211 AZ109
Bonsor Dr., Tad. 233 CY122
Bonsor St. SE5 162 DS80
Bonville Gdns. NW4 119 CU56
Handowe Clo.
Bonville Rd., Brom. 184 EF92
Book Ms. WC2 273 N9
Booker Clo. E14 143 DZ71
Wallwood St.
Booker Rd. N18 100 DU50
Bookham Ct., Lthd. 230 BZ123
Church Rd.
Bookham Gro., Lthd. 246 CB126
Bookham Ind. Pk., Lthd. 230 BZ123
Bookham Rd., Cob. 230 BW119
Boone Ct. N9 100 DW48
Boone St. SE13 164 EE84
Boones Rd. SE13 164 EE84
Boord St. SE10 164 EE76
Boot St. N1 275 M3
Boot St. N1 142 DS69
Booth Clo. SE28 146 EV73
Booth Dr., Stai. 174 BK93
Booth Rd. NW9 96 CR54
Booth Rd., Croy. 201 DP103
Waddon New Rd.
Boothby Rd. N19 121 DK61
Booths Clo., Hat. 45 CX24
Booth's Pl. W1 273 L7
Bordars Rd. W7 137 CE71
Bordars Wk. W7 137 CE71
Borden Ave., Enf. 82 DR44
Border Cres. SE26 182 DV92
Border Gdns., Croy. 221 EB105
Border Rd. SE26 182 DV92
Bordergate, Mitch. 200 DF95
Borders La., Loug. 85 EN42
Borderside, Slou. 132 AU72
Bordesley Rd., Mord. 200 DB98
Bordon Wk. SW15 179 CU87
Boreas Wk. N1 274 G1
Boreham Ave. E16 144 EG72
Boreham Clo. E11 123 EC60
Hainault Rd.
Boreham Holt, Borwd. 78 CM42
Boreham Rd. N22 100 DQ54
Borehamwood Ind. Pk., Borwd. 78 CR40
Borer's Pas. E1 275 N8
Borgard Rd. SE18 165 EM77
Borkwood Pk., Orp. 223 ET105
Borkwood Way, Orp. 223 ES105
Borland Clo., Green. 189 FU85
Steele Ave.
Borland Rd. SE15 162 DW84
Borland Rd., Tedd. 177 CH93
Born Wk., Slou. 130 AH69
Bornedene, Pot.B. 63 CY31
Borneo St. SW15 159 CW83
Borough, The, Bet. 264 CN135
Borough High St. SE1 279 J5
Borough High St. SE1 162 DQ75
Borough Hill, Croy. 201 DP104
Borough Rd. SE1 278 G6
Borough Rd. SE1 161 DP76
Borough Rd., Islw. 157 CE81
Borough Rd., Kings.T. 198 CN95
Borough Rd., Mitch. 200 DE96
Borough Rd., West. 238 EK121
Borough Sq. SE1 279 H5
Borough Way, Pot.B. 63 CY32
Borrell Clo., Brox. 49 DZ20
Borrett Clo. SE17 162 DQ78
Penrose St.
Borrodaile Rd. SW18 180 DB86
Borrowdale Ave., Har. 95 CG54
Borrowdale Clo., Egh. 173 BB94
Derwent Rd.
Borrowdale Clo., Ilf. 124 EL56
Borrowdale Clo., S.Croy. 220 DT113
Borrowdale Ct., Enf. 82 DQ39
Borrowdale Ct., Hem.H. 40 BL17
Borrowdale Dr., S.Croy. 220 DT112
Borthwick Ms. E15 124 EE63
Borthwick Rd.
Borthwick Rd. E15 124 EE63
Borthwick Rd. NW9 119 CT58
West Hendon Bdy.
Borthwick St. SE8 163 EA78
Borwick Ave. E17 123 DZ55
Bosanquet Clo., Uxb. 134 BK70
Bosanquet Rd., Hodd. 49 EC15
Bosbury Rd. SE6 183 EC90
Boscastle Rd. NW5 121 DH62
Bosco Clo., Orp. 223 ET105
Strickland Way
Boscobel Pl. SW1 276 G8
Boscobel Pl. SW1 160 DG77
Boscobel St. NW8 272 A5
Boscobel St. NW8 140 DD70
Boscombe Ave. E10 123 ED59
Boscombe Ave., Grays 170 GD77
Boscombe Ave., Horn. 128 FK60
Boscombe Clo. E5 123 DY64
Boscombe Clo., Egh. 193 BC95
Boscombe Gdns. SW16 181 DL93
Boscombe Rd. SW17 180 DG93
Boscombe Rd. SW19 200 DA95
Boscombe Rd. W12 139 CU74
Boscombe Rd., Wor.Pk. 199 CW102
Bosgrove E4 101 EC46
Boss St. SE1 279 P4
Bostal Row, Bexh. 166 EZ83
Harlington Rd.
Bostall Heath SE2 166 EV78
Bostall Hill SE2 166 EU78
Bostall La. SE2 166 EV78
Bostall Manorway SE2 166 EV77
Bostall Pk. Ave., Bexh. 166 EY80
Bostall Rd., Orp. 186 EV94
Boston Gdns. W4 158 CS79
Boston Gdns. W7 157 CG77
Boston Gro., Ruis. 115 BQ58
Boston Gro., Slou. 131 AQ72
Boston Manor Rd., Brent. 157 CH77
Boston Pk. Rd., Brent. 157 CJ78
Boston Pl. NW1 272 D5
Boston Pl. NW1 140 DF70
Boston Rd. E6 144 EL69
Boston Rd. E17 123 EA58
Boston Rd. W7 137 CE74
Boston Rd., Croy. 201 DM100
Boston Rd., Edg. 96 CQ52
Boston St. E2 142 DU68
Audrey St.
Boston Vale W7 157 CG77
Bostonthorpe Rd. W7 157 CE75
Bosville Ave., Sev. 256 FG123
Bosville Dr., Sev. 256 FG123
Bosville Rd., Sev. 256 FG123
Boswell Clo., Orp. 206 EW100
Killewarren Way
Boswell Ct. WC1 274 A6
Boswell Path, Hayes 155 BT77
Croyde Ave.
Boswell Rd., Th.Hth. 202 DQ98
Boswell St. WC1 274 A6
Boswell St. WC1 141 DL71
Bosworth Clo. E17 101 DZ53
Bosworth Cres., Rom. 106 FJ51
Bosworth Rd. N11 99 DK51
Bosworth Rd. W10 139 CY70
Bosworth Rd., Barn. 80 DA41
Bosworth Rd., Dag. 126 FA62
Botany Bay La., Chis. 205 EQ96
Botany Clo., Barn. 80 DE42
Botany Way, Purf. 168 FP78
Boteley Clo. E4 101 ED47
Botery's Cross, Red. 251 DP133
Botha Rd. E13 144 EH71
Botham Clo., Edg. 96 CQ52
Pavilion Way
Bothwell Clo. E16 144 EF71
Bothwell Rd., Croy. 221 EC110
Bothwell St. W6 159 CX79
Delorme St.
Botley La., Chesh. 56 AU30
Botley Rd., Chesh. 54 AR30
Botley Rd., Hem.H. 40 BN15
Botolph All. EC3 275 M10
Botolph La. EC3 275 M10
Botsford Rd. SW20 199 CY96
Bott Rd., Dart. 188 FM91
Bottom Ho. Fm. La., Ch.St.G. 89 AR47
Bottom La., Beac. 89 AP51
Bottom La., Chesh. 56 AT34
Bottom La., Kings L. 74 BH35
Bottrells Clo., Ch.St.G. 90 AT47
Bottrells La., Amer. 89 AP46
Bottrells La., Ch.St.G. 90 AT47
Botts Ms. W2 140 DA72
Chepstow Rd.
Botts Pas. W2 140 DA72
Chepstow Rd.
Botwell Common Rd., Hayes 135 BR73
Botwell Cres., Hayes 135 BS72
Botwell La., Hayes 135 BS73
Boucher Clo., Tedd. 177 CF92
Boucher Dr., Grav. 191 GF90
Bouchier Wk., Rain. 147 FG65
Deere Ave.
Boughton Ave., Brom. 204 EF101
Boughton Hall Ave., Wok. 227 BF124
Boughton Rd. SE28 165 ES76
Boughton Way, Amer. 72 AW38
Boulcott St. E1 143 DX72
Boulevard, The SW17 180 DG89
Balham High Rd.

Boulevard, The, Pnr. 116 CA56
Pinner Rd.
Boulevard, The, Wat. 75 BR43
Boulevard, The, Welw.G.C. 29 CZ07
Boulmer Rd., Uxb. 134 BJ69
Boulogne Rd., Croy. 202 DQ100
Boulter Gdns., Rain. 147 FG65
Boulters Clo., Maid. 130 AC70
Boulters Clo., Slou. 151 AN75
Amerden Way
Boulters Ct., Maid. 130 AC70
Boulters Gdns., Maid. 130 AC70
Boulters La., Maid. 130 AC70
Boulthurst Way, Oxt. 254 EH132
Boulton Ho., Brent. 158 CL78
Boulton Rd., Dag. 126 EY62
Boultwood Rd. E6 145 EM72
Bounce, The, Hem.H. 40 BK18
Bounce Hill (Navestock), Rom. 87 FH38
Mill La.
Bounces La. N9 100 DV47
Bounces Rd. N9 100 DV47
Boundaries Rd. SW12 180 DF89
Boundaries Rd., Felt. 176 BW88
Boundary Ave. E17 123 DZ59
Boundary Rd.
Boundary Clo. SE20 202 DU96
Haysleigh Gdns.
Boundary Clo., Ilf. 125 ES63
Loxford La.
Boundary Clo., Kings.T. 198 CP97
Boundary Clo., Sthl. 156 CA78
Boundary Ct., Welw.G.C. 29 CZ13
Boundary La.
Boundary Dr., Brwd. 109 GE45
Boundary Dr., Hert. 32 DR07
Boundary La. E13 144 EK69
Boundary La. SE17 162 DQ79
Boundary La., Welw.G.C. 29 CY12
Boundary Par. N8 121 DL58
Boundary Pas. E2 275 P4
Boundary Pl., H.Wyc. 110 AD55
Boundary Rd. E13 144 EJ68
Boundary Rd. E17 123 DZ59
Boundary Rd. N9 82 DW44
Boundary Rd. N22 121 DP55
Boundary Rd. NW8 140 DC67
Boundary Rd. SW19 180 DD93
Boundary Rd., Ashf. 174 BJ92
Boundary Rd., Bark. 145 ER67
Boundary Rd., Cars. 218 DG108
Boundary Rd., Ger.Cr. 90 AX52
Boundary Rd., H.Wyc. 88 AC54
Boundary Rd., Maid. 130 AE70
Boundary Rd., Pnr. 116 BX59
Boundary Rd., Rom. 127 FG58
Boundary Rd., St.Alb. 43 CE18
Boundary Rd., Sid. 185 ES85
Boundary Rd., Upmin. 128 FN62
Boundary Rd., Wall. 219 DH107
Boundary Rd., Wem. 118 CL62
Boundary Rd., Wok. 227 BA116
Boundary Row SE1 278 F4
Boundary St. E2 275 P3
Boundary St. E2 142 DT70
Boundary St., Erith 167 FF80
Boundary Way, Croy. 221 EA106
Boundary Way, Hem.H. 41 BQ17
Boundary Way, Wat. 59 BV32
Boundary Way, Wok. 227 BA115
Boundary Yd., Wok. 227 BA116
Boundary Rd.
Boundfield Rd. SE6 184 EE90
Bounds Grn. Rd. N11 99 DJ51
Bounds Grn. Rd. N22 99 DL52
Bourchier Clo., Sev. 257 FH126
Bourchier St. W1 273 M10
Bourdon Pl. W1 273 J10
Bourdon Rd. SE20 202 DW96
Bourdon St. W1 277 H1
Bourdon St. W1 141 DH73
Bourke Clo. NW10 138 CS65
Mayo Rd.
Bourke Clo. SW4 181 DL86
Bourke Hill, Couls. 234 DF118
Bourlet Clo. W1 273 K7
Bourn Ave. N15 122 DR56
Bourn Ave., Barn. 80 DD43
Bourn Ave., Uxb. 134 BN70
Bournbrook Rd. SE3 164 EK83
Bourne, The N14 99 DK46
Bourne, The, Hem.H. 57 BA27
Bourne, The, Ware 33 DX05
Bourne Ave. N14 99 DL47
Bourne Ave., Cher. 194 BG97
Eastern Ave.
Bourne Ave., Hayes 155 BQ76
Bourne Ave., Ruis. 116 BW64
Bourne Ave., Wind. 151 AQ84
Bourne Bri. La., Rom. 104 EZ45
Bourne Clo., Brox. 49 DZ20
Bourne Clo., Guil. 259 BB140
Bourne Clo., Ware 33 DX05
Bourne Clo., W.Byf. 212 BH113
Bourne Ct., Ruis. 115 BV64
Bourne Dr., Mitch. 200 DD96
Bourne End, Horn. 128 FN59
Bourne End La., Hem.H. 57 BA25
Bourne End Rd., Maid. 110 AD63
Bourne End Rd., Nthwd. 93 BS49
Bourne Est. EC1 274 D6
Bourne Est. EC1 141 DN71
Bourne Gdns. E4 101 EB49
Bourne Gro., Ash. 231 CK119
Bourne Hill N13 99 DM47
Bourne Ind. Pk., Dart. 187 FE85
Bourne Rd.
Bourne La., Cat. 236 DR121
Bourne Mead, Bex. 187 FC85
Bourne Meadow, Egh. 193 BB98
Bourne Pk. Clo., Ken. 236 DS116
Bourne Pl. W4 158 CR78
Dukes Ave.
Bourne Rd. E7 124 EF62
Bourne Rd. N8 121 DL58
Bourne Rd., Berk. 38 AT18
Bourne Rd., Bex. 187 FB87
Bourne Rd., Brom. 204 EK98
Bourne Rd., Dart. 187 FD85
Bourne Rd., Gdmg. 258 AT144
Bourne Rd., Grav. 191 GM89
Bourne Rd., Red. 251 DJ130
Bourne Rd., Slou. 151 AQ75
Bourne Rd., Vir.W. 192 AX99
Bourne Rd. (Bushey), Wat. 76 CA43
Bourne St. SW1 276 F9
Bourne St. SW1 160 DG77
Bourne St., Croy. 201 DP103
Waddon New Rd.
Bourne Ter. W2 140 DB71
Bourne Vale, Brom. 204 EF102
Bourne Vw., Grnf. 137 CF65
Bourne Vw., Ken. 236 DR115
Bourne Way, Add. 212 BJ106
Bourne Way, Brom. 204 EE103
Bourne Way, Epsom 216 CQ105
Bourne Way, Sutt. 217 CZ106
Bourne Way, Swan. 207 FC97
Bourne Way, Wok. 227 BA115
Bourne Way (Mayford), Wok. 226 AX122
Bournebridge Clo., Brwd. 109 GE45
Bournefield Rd., Whyt. 236 DT118
Godstone Rd.
Bournehall Ave. (Bushey), Wat. 76 CA43
Bournehall La. (Bushey), Wat. 76 CA44
Bournehall Rd. (Bushey), Wat. 76 CA44
Bournemead Ave., Nthlt. 135 BU68
Bournemead Clo., Nthlt. 135 BU69
Bournemead Way, Nthlt. 135 BV68
Bournemouth Rd. SE15 162 DU82
Bournemouth Rd. SW19 200 DA95
Bourneside, Vir.W. 192 AU101
Bourneside Cres. N14 99 DK46
Bourneside Gdns. SE6 183 EC92
Bourneside Rd., Add. 212 BK105
Bournevale Rd. SW16 181 DL91
Bournewood Rd. SE18 166 EU80
Bournewood Rd., Orp. 206 EV101
Bournville Rd. SE6 183 EA87
Bournwell Clo., Barn. 80 DF41
Bourton Clo., Hayes 135 BU74
Avondale Dr.
Bousfield Rd. SE14 163 DX82
Bousley Ri., Cher. 211 BD107
Boutflower Rd. SW11 160 DE84
Bouverie Gdns., Har. 117 CK58
Bouverie Ms. N16 122 DS61
Bouverie Rd.
Bouverie Pl. W2 272 A8
Bouverie Pl. W2 140 DD72
Bouverie Rd. N16 122 DS60
Bouverie Rd., Couls. 234 DG118
Bouverie Rd., Har. 116 CC58
Bouverie St. EC4 274 E9
Bouverie St. EC4 141 DN72
Bouverie Way, Slou. 152 AY78
Bouvier Rd., Enf. 82 DW38
Boveney Clo., Slou. 151 AN75
Amerden Way
Boveney New Rd. (Eton Wick), Wind. 151 AL77
Boveney Rd. SE23 183 DX87
Boveney Rd., Wind. 150 AJ77
Boveney Wd. La., Slou. 110 AJ62
Bovey Way, S.Ock. 149 FV71
Bovill Rd. SE23 183 DX87
Bovingdon Ave., Wem. 138 CN65
Bovingdon Clo. N19 121 DJ61
Junction Rd.
Bovingdon Cres., Wat. 60 BX34
Bovingdon Grn. La., Hem.H. 57 AZ28
Bovingdon La. NW9 96 CS53
Bovingdon Rd. SW6 160 DB81
Bovingdon Sq., Mitch. 201 DL98
Leicester Ave.
Bow Arrow La., Dart. 188 FN86
Bow Bri. Est. E3 143 EB68
Bow Chyd. EC4 275 J9
Bow Common La. E3 143 DY70
Bow Ind. Est. E15 143 EB66
Bow La. EC4 275 J9
Bow La. EC4 142 DQ72
Bow La. N12 98 DC52
Bow La., Mord. 199 CY100
Bow Rd. E3 143 DZ69
Bow St. E15 124 EE64
Bow St. WC2 274 A9
Bow St. WC2 141 DL72
Bowater Clo. NW9 118 CR57
Bowater Clo. SW2 181 DL86
Bowater Pl. SE3 164 EH80
Bowater Ridge, Wey. 213 BR110
Bowater Rd. SE18 164 EK76
Bowden Clo., Felt. 175 BS88
Bowden Dr., Horn. 128 FL60
Bowden St. SE11 278 E10
Bowden St. SE11 161 DN78
Bowditch SE8 163 DZ78
Bowdon Rd. E17 123 EA59
Bowen Dr. SE21 182 DS90
Bowen Rd., Har. 116 CC59
Bowen St. E14 143 EB72
Bowens Wd., Croy. 221 DZ109
Bower Ave. SE10 164 EE81
Bower Clo., Nthlt. 136 BW68
Bower Clo., Rom. 105 FD52
Bower Ct., Epp. 70 EU32
Bower Ct., Wok. 227 BB116
Princess Rd.
Bower Fm. Rd. (Havering-atte-Bower), Rom. 105 FC48
Bower Hill, Epp. 70 EU32
Bower Hill Clo., Red. 267 DL137
Bower Hill La., Red. 267 DK135
Bower La. (Eynsford), Dart. 208 FL103
Bower Rd., Swan. 187 FG94
Bower St. E1 143 DX72
Bower Ter., Epp. 70 EU32
Bower Hill
Bower Vale, Epp. 70 EU32
Bower Way, Slou. 131 AL73
Bowerdean St. SW6 160 DB81
Bowerman Ave. SE14 163 DY79
Bowerman Rd., Grays 171 GG77
Bowers Ave., Grav. 191 GF91
Bowers Clo., Guil. 243 BA130
Cotts Wd. Dr.
Bowers Fm. Dr., Guil. 243 BA130
Bowers La., Guil. 243 BA129
Bowers Rd., Sev. 225 FF111
Bowers Wk. E6 145 EM72
Northumberland Rd.
Bowes Clo., Sid. 186 EV86
Bowes Rd. N11 99 DH50
Bowes Rd. N13 99 DL50
Bowes Rd. W3 138 CS73
Bowes Rd., Dag. 126 EW63
Bowes Rd., Stai. 173 BE92
Bowes Rd., Walt. 195 BV103
Bowes-Lyon Clo., Wind. 151 AQ81
Alma Rd.
Bowes-Lyon Ms., St.Alb. 43 CD20
Lower Dagnall St.
Bowfell Rd. W6 159 CW79
Bowford Ave., Bexh. 166 EY81
Bowgate, St.Alb. 43 CE19
Bowhay, Brwd. 109 GA47
Bowhill Clo. SW9 161 DN80
Bowie Clo. SW4 181 DK87
Bowl Ct. EC2 275 N5
Bowl Ct. EC2 142 DS70
Bowland Rd. SW4 161 DK84
Bowland Rd., Wdf.Grn. 102 EJ51
Bowland Yd. SW1 276 E5
Bowlers Orchard, Ch.St.G. 90 AU48
Bowles Grn., Enf. 82 DV36
Bowles Rd. SE1 162 DU79
Old Kent Rd.
Bowley Clo. SE19 182 DT93
Bowley La. SE19 182 DT92
Bowling Ct., Wat. 75 BU42
Bowling Grn. Clo. SW15 179 CV87
Bowling Grn. La. EC1 274 E4
Bowling Grn. La. EC1 141 DN70
Bowling Grn. Pl. SE1 279 K4
Bowling Grn. Pl. SE1 162 DR75
Bowling Grn. Rd., Wok. 210 AS109
Bowling Grn. Row SE18 165 EM76
Samuel St.
Bowling Grn. St. SE11 161 DN79
Bowling Grn. Wk. N1 275 M2
Bowling Rd., Ware 33 DY06
Bowls, The, Chig. 103 ES48
Bowls Clo., Stan. 95 CH50
Bowman Ave. E16 144 EF73
Bowman Ms. SW18 179 CZ88
Bowmans Clo. W13 137 CH74
Bowmans Clo., Pot.B. 64 DD32
Bowmans Clo., Slou. 130 AH67
Bowmans Ct., Hem.H. 40 BK18
Bowmans Grn., Wat. 76 BX36
Bowmans Lea SE23 182 DW87
Bowmans Meadow, Wall. 201 DH104
Bowmans Ms. E1 142 DU72
Hooper St.
Bowmans Ms. N7 121 DL62
Seven Sisters Rd.
Bowmans Pl. N7 121 DL62
Holloway Rd.
Bowmans Rd., Dart. 187 FF87
Bowman's Trd. Est. NW9 118 CM55
Westmoreland Rd.
Bowmead SE9 185 EM89
Bowmont Clo., Brwd. 109 GB44
Bowmore Wk. NW1 141 DK66
St. Paul's Cres.
Bown Clo., Til. 171 GH83
Bowness Clo. E8 142 DT65
Beechwood Rd.
Bowness Cres. SW15 178 CS92
Bowness Dr., Houns. 156 BY84
Bowness Rd. SE6 183 EB87
Bowness Rd., Bexh. 167 FB82
Bowness Way, Horn. 127 FG64
Bowood Rd. SW11 180 DG85
Bowood Rd., Enf. 83 DX40
Bowring Grn., Wat. 94 BW50
Bowrons Ave., Wem. 137 CK66
Bowry Dr., Stai. 173 AZ86
Bowsprit, The, Cob. 230 BW115
Bowstridge La., Ch.St.G. 90 AW48
Bowyer Clo. E6 145 EM71
Bowyer Cres., Uxb. 113 BF58
Bowyer Dr., Slou. 131 AL74
Bowyer Pl. SE5 162 DQ80
Bowyer St. SE5 162 DQ80
Bowyers, Hem.H. 40 BK18
Bowyers Clo., Ash. 232 CM118
Box La., Bark. 146 EV68
Box La., Hem.H. 39 BE24
Box Ridge Ave., Pur. 219 DM112
Box Tree Clo., Chesh. 54 AR33
Box Wk., Lthd. 245 BS132
Boxall Rd. SE21 182 DS86
Boxfield, Welw.G.C. 30 DB12
Boxford Clo., S.Croy. 221 DX112
Boxgrove Ave., Guil. 243 BA132
Boxgrove La., Guil. 243 BA133
Boxgrove Rd. SE2 166 EV75
Boxgrove Rd., Guil. 243 BA133
Boxhill, Hem.H. 40 BK18
Boxhill Rd., Dor. 248 CL133
Boxhill Rd., Tad. 248 CM132
Boxhill Way, Bet. 264 CP138
Boxley Rd., Mord. 200 DC98
Boxley St. E16 144 EH74
Boxmoor Rd., Har. 117 CH56
Boxmoor Rd., Rom. 105 FC50
Boxoll Rd., Dag. 126 EZ63
Boxted Clo., Buck.H. 102 EL46
Boxted Rd., Hem.H. 39 BE18
Boxtree La., Har. 94 CC53
Boxtree Rd., Har. 95 CD52
Boxtree Wk., Orp. 206 EX102
Eldred Dr.
Boxwell Rd., Berk. 38 AV19
Boxwood Clo., West Dr. 154 BM75
Hawthorne Cres.
Boxwood Way, Warl. 237 DX117
Boxworth Clo. N12 98 DD50
Fenstanton Ave.
Boxworth Gro. N1 141 DM67
Richmond Ave.
Boyard Rd. SE18 165 EP78
Boyce Clo., Borwd. 78 CL39
Boyce St. SE1 278 B3
Boyce Way E13 144 EG70
Boycroft Ave. NW9 118 CQ58
Boyd Ave., Sthl. 136 BZ74
Boyd Clo., Kings.T. 178 CN94
Crescent Rd.
Boyd Rd. SW19 180 DD93
Boyd St. E1 142 DU72
Boydell Ct. NW8 140 DD66
St. John's Wd. Pk.
Boyfield St. SE1 278 G5
Boyfield St. SE1 161 DP75
Boyland Rd., Brom. 184 EF92
Boyle Ave., Stan. 95 CG51
Boyle Fm. Rd., T.Ditt. 197 CG100
Boyle St. W1 273 K10
Boyne Ave. NW4 119 CX56
Boyne Rd. SE13 163 EC83
Boyne Rd., Dag. 126 FA62
Boyne Ter. Ms. W11 139 CZ74
Boyseland Ct., Edg. 96 CQ47
Boyson Rd. SE17 162 DR79
Boythorn Way SE16 162 DV78
Credon Rd.
Boyton Clo. E1 143 DX70
Stayner's Rd.
Boyton Clo. N8 121 DL55
Boyton Rd. N8 121 DL55
Brabant Ct. EC3 275 M10
Brabant Rd. N22 99 DM54
Brabazon Ave., Wall. 219 DL108
Brabazon Rd., Houns. 156 BW80
Brabazon Rd., Nthlt. 136 CA68
Brabazon St. E14 143 EB72
Brabourn Gro. SE15 162 DW82
Brabourne Clo. SE19 182 DS92
Brabourne Cres., Bexh. 166 EZ79
Brabourne Heights NW7 96 CS48
Brabourne Ri., Beck. 203 EC99
Bracewell Ave., Grnf. 137 CG65
Bracewell Rd. W10 139 CW71
Bracewood Gdns., Croy. 202 DT104
Bracey Ms. N4 121 DL61
Bracey St.
Bracey St. N4 121 DL61
Bracken, The E4 101 EC47
Hortus Rd.
Bracken Ave. SW12 180 DG86
Bracken Ave., Croy. 203 EA104
Bracken Clo. E6 145 EM71
Bracken Clo., Borwd. 78 CN40
Hartforde Rd.
Bracken Clo., Lthd. 230 BZ124
Bracken Clo., Slou. 111 AR63
Bracken Clo., Sun. 175 BT93
Cavendish Rd.
Bracken Clo., Twick. 176 CA87
Hedley Rd.
Bracken Clo., Wok. 227 AZ118
Bracken Dr., Chig. 103 EP51
Bracken End, Islw. 177 CD85
Bracken Gdns. SW13 159 CU82
Bracken Hill Clo., Brom. 204 EF95
Bracken Hill La.
Bracken Hill La., Brom. 204 EF95
Bracken Ind. Est., Ilf. 103 ET52
Bracken Ms. E4 101 EC47
Hortus Rd.
Bracken Ms., Rom. 127 FB58
Bracken Path, Epsom 216 CN113
Bracken Way, Guil. 242 AS132
Bracken Way, Wok. 210 AT110
Brackenbridge Dr., Ruis. 116 BX62
Brackenbury Gdns. W6 159 CV76
Brackenbury Rd. N2 120 DC55
Brackenbury Rd. W6 159 CV76
Brackendale N21 99 DM47
Brackendale, Pot.B. 64 DA33
Brackendale Clo., Houns. 156 CB81
Brackendale Gdns., Upmin. 128 FQ63
Brackendene, Dart. 187 FE91
Brackendene, St.Alb. 60 BZ30
Brackendene Clo., Wok. 227 BA115
Brackenfield Clo. E5 122 DV63
Tiger Way
Brackenforde, Slou. 152 AW75
Brackenhill, Cob. 214 CA111
Brackens, The, Enf. 100 DS45
Brackens, The, Hem.H. 40 BK19
Heather Way
Brackens, The, Orp. 224 EU106
Brackens Dr., Brwd. 108 FW50
Brackenside, Horl. 269 DH147
Stockfield
Brackenwood, Sun. 195 BU95
Brackley, Wey. 213 BR106
Brackley Clo., Wall. 219 DL108
Brackley Rd. W4 158 CS78
Brackley Rd., Beck. 183 DZ94
Brackley Sq., Wdf.Grn. 102 EK52
Brackley St. EC1 275 J6
Brackley Ter. W4 158 CS78
Bracklyn Clo. N1 142 DR68
Parr St.
Bracklyn Ct. N1 142 DR68
Wimbourne St.
Bracklyn St. N1 142 DR68
Bracknell Clo. N22 99 DN53
Bracknell Gdns. NW3 120 DB63
Bracknell Gate NW3 120 DB64
Bracknell Pl., Hem.H. 40 BM16
Bracknell Way NW3 120 DB63
Bracondale, Esher 214 CC107
Bracondale Rd. SE2 166 EU77
Brad St. SE1 278 E3
Bradbery, Rick. 91 BD50
Bradbourne Pk. Rd., Sev. 256 FG123
Bradbourne Rd., Bex. 186 FA87
Bradbourne Rd., Grays 170 GB79
Bradbourne Rd., Sev. 257 FH122
Bradbourne St. SW6 160 DA82
Bradbourne Vale Rd., Sev. 256 FF122
Bradbury Clo., Borwd. 78 CP39
Bradbury Clo., Sthl. 156 BZ77
Bradbury Gdns., Slou. 112 AX63
Bradbury Ms. N16 122 DS64
Bradbury St.
Bradbury St. N16 122 DS64
Braddock Clo., Islw. 157 CF83
Braddon Rd., Rich. 158 CM83
Braddyll St. SE10 164 EE78
Braden St. W9 140 DB70
Shirland Rd.
Bradenham Ave., Well. 166 EU84
Bradenham Clo. SE17 162 DR79
Bradenham Rd., Har. 117 CH56
Bradenham Rd., Hayes 135 BS69
Bradenhurst Clo., Cat. 252 DT125
Bradfield Clo., Guil. 243 BA131
Bradfield Clo., Wok. 226 AY118
Bradfield Dr., Bark. 126 EU64
Bradfield Rd. E16 164 EG75
Bradfield Rd., Ruis. 116 BY64
Bradford Clo. SE26 182 DV91
Coombe Rd.
Bradford Clo., Brom. 205 EM102
Bradford Dr., Epsom 217 CT107
Bradford Rd. W3 158 CS75
Warple Way
Bradford Rd., Ilf. 125 ER60
Bradford Rd., Rick. 91 BC45
Bradford Rd., Slou. 131 AN72
Bradgate (Cuffley), Pot.B. 65 DK27
Bradgate Clo. (Cuffley), Pot.B. 65 DK28
Bradgate Rd. SE6 183 EA86
Brading Cres. E11 124 EH61
Brading Rd. SW2 181 DM87
Brading Rd., Croy. 201 DM100
Bradiston Rd. W9 139 CZ69
Bradleigh Ave., Grays 170 GB76
Bradley Clo. N7 141 DM65
Sutterton St.
Bradley Clo., Sutt. 218 DA110
Station Rd.
Bradley Gdns. W13 137 CH72
Bradley La., Dor. 247 CG132
Bradley Ms. SW17 180 DF88
Bellevue Rd.
Bradley Rd. N22 99 DM54
Bradley Rd. SE19 182 DQ93
Bradley Rd., Enf. 83 DY37
Bradley Rd., Slou. 131 AR73
Bradley Stone Rd. E6 145 EM71
Bradley's Clo. N1 141 DN68
White Lion St.
Bradman Row, Edg. 96 CQ52
Pavilion Way
Bradmead SW8 161 DH80
Bradmore Grn., Couls. 235 DM118
Coulsdon Rd.
Bradmore Grn., Hat. 63 CY26
Bradmore Ho. E1 142 DW71
Jamaica St.
Bradmore La., Hat. 63 CW27
Bradmore Pk. Rd. W6 159 CV77
Bradmore Way, Couls. 235 DL117
Bradmore Way, Hat. 63 CY26
Bradshaw Clo. SW19 180 DA93
Bradshaw Clo., Wind. 151 AL81
Bradshaw Rd., Wat. 76 BW39
Bradshawe Waye, Uxb. 134 BL71
Bradshaws, Hat. 45 CT22
Bradshaws Clo. SE25 202 DU97
Bradstock Rd. E9 143 DX65
Bradstock Rd., Epsom 217 CU106
Bradwell Ave., Dag. 126 FA61
Bradwell Clo. E18 124 EF56
Bradwell Clo., Horn. 147 FH65
Bradwell Grn., Brwd. 109 GC44
Bradwell Ms. N18 100 DU49
Lyndhurst Rd.
Bradwell Rd., Buck.H. 102 EL46
Bradwell St. E1 143 DX69
Brady Ave., Loug. 85 EQ40
Brady St. E1 142 DV70
Bradymead E6 145 EP72
Warwall
Braemar Ave. N22 99 DL53
Braemar Ave. NW10 118 CR62
Braemar Ave. SW19 180 DA89
Braemar Ave., Bexh. 167 FC84
Braemar Ave., S.Croy. 220 DQ110
Braemar Ave., Th.Hth. 201 DN97
Braemar Ave., Wem. 137 CK66
Braemar Gdns. NW9 96 CR53
Braemar Gdns., Horn. 128 FN58
Braemar Gdns., Sid. 185 ER90
Braemar Gdns., Slou. 151 AN75
Braemar Gdns., W.Wick. 203 EC102
Braemar Rd. E13 144 EF70
Braemar Rd. N15 122 DS57
Braemar Rd., Brent. 157 CK79
Braemar Rd., Wor.Pk. 199 CV104
Braes Mead, Red. 267 DL135
Braes St. N1 141 DP66
Braeside, Add. 212 BH111
Braeside, Beck. 183 EA92
Braeside Ave. SW19 199 CY95
Braeside Ave., Sev. 256 FF124
Braeside Clo., Pnr. 94 CA52
The Ave.
Braeside Clo., Sev. 256 FF123
Braeside Cres., Bexh. 167 FC84
Braeside Rd. SW16 181 DJ94
Braesyde Clo., Belv. 166 EZ77
Brafferton Rd., Croy. 220 DQ105
Braganza St. SE17 161 DP78
Bragmans La., Hem.H. 57 BB34
Bragmans La., Rick. 57 BD33
Braham St. E1 142 DT72
Braid, The, Chesh. 54 AS30
Braid Ave. W3 138 CS72
Braid Clo., Felt. 176 BZ89
Braidwood Rd. SE6 183 ED88
Braidwood St. SE1 279 M3
Brailsford Clo., Mitch. 180 DE94
Brailsford Rd. SW2 181 DN85
Brain Clo., Hat. 45 CV17
Brainton Ave., Felt. 175 BV87
Braintree Ave., Ilf. 124 EL56
Braintree Rd., Dag. 126 FA62
Braintree Rd., Ruis. 115 BV63
Braintree St. E2 142 DW70
Braithwaite Ave., Rom. 126 FA59
Braithwaite Gdns., Stan. 95 CJ53
Braithwaite Rd., Enf. 83 DZ41
Brakefield Rd., Grav. 190 GB93
Brakey Hill, Red. 252 DS134
Brakynbery, Berk. 38 AS16
Bramah Grn. SW9 161 DN81
Bramalea Clo. N6 120 DG58
Bramall Clo. E15 124 EF64
Idmiston Rd.
Bramber Ct. W5 158 CL77
Sterling Pl.
Bramber Ct., Slou. 131 AN74
Bramber Rd. N12 98 DE50
Bramber Rd. W14 159 CZ79
Bramble Ave., Dart. 189 FW90
Bramble Banks, Cars. 218 DG109
Bramble Clo., Cat. 236 DS122
Burntwood La.
Bramble Clo., Croy. 221 EA105
Bramble Clo., Guil. 242 AS132
Bramble Clo., Red. 266 DG136
Bramble Clo., Shep. 195 BR98
Halliford Clo.
Bramble Clo., Stan. 95 CK52
Bramble Clo., Uxb. 134 BM71

Broadwick St. W1 273 **L10**
Broadwick St. W1 141 DJ72
Broadwood, Grav. 191 GH92
Broadwood Ave., Ruis. 115 BS58
Brocas Clo. NW3 140 DE66
Fellows Rd.
Brocas St. (Eton), Wind. 151 AR80
Brock Grn., S.Ock. 149 FV72
Cam Grn.
Brock Pl. E3 143 EB70
Brock Rd. E13 144 EH71
Brock St. SE15 162 DW83
Evelina Rd.
Brock Way, Vir.W. 192 AW99
Brockdish Ave., Bark. 125 ET64
Brockenhurst, W.Mol. 196 BZ100
Brockenhurst Ave., Wor.Pk. 198 CS102
Brockenhurst Clo., Wok. 211 AZ114
Brockenhurst Gdns. NW7 96 CS51
Brockenhurst Gdns., Ilf. 125 EQ64
Brockenhurst Rd., Croy. 202 DV101
Brockenhurst Way SW16 201 DK96
Brocket Clo., Chig. 103 ET50
Burrow Rd.
Brocket Pk., Welw.G.C. 28 CR10
Brocket Rd., Grays 171 GG76
Brocket Rd., Hodd. 49 EA17
Brocket Rd., Welw.G.C. 29 CT11
Brocket Way, Chig. 103 ES50
Brockett Clo., Welw.G.C. 29 CV09
Brockham Clo. SW19 179 CZ92
Brockham Cres., Croy. 221 ED108
Brockham Dr. SW2 181 DM87
Fairview Pl.
Brockham Dr., Ilf. 125 EP58
Brockham Grn., Bet. 264 CP135
Brockham La., Bet. 248 CN134
Brockham Pk., Bet. 264 CQ139
Brockham St. SE1 279 **J6**
Brockham St. SE1 162 DQ76
Brockhamhill Pk., Tad. 248 CQ131
Brockhamhurst Rd., Bet. 264 CN141
Brockhurst Clo., Stan. 95 CF51
Brockhurst Rd., Chesh. 54 AQ29
Brockill Cres. SE4 163 DY84
Brocklebank Ct., Whyt. 236 DU118
Brocklebank Rd. SE7 164 EH77
Brocklebank Rd. SW18 180 DC87
Brocklehurst St. SE14 163 DX80
Brockles Mead, Harl. 51 EQ19
Brocklesbury Clo., Wat. 76 BW41
Brocklesby Rd. SE25 202 DV98
Brockley Ave., Stan. 96 CL48
Brockley Clo., Stan. 96 CL49
Brockley Combe, Wey. 213 BR105
Brockley Cres., Rom. 105 FC52
Brockley Cross SE4 163 DY83
Endwell Rd.
Brockley Footpath SE15 162 DW84
Brockley Gdns. SE4 163 DZ82
Brockley Gro. SE4 183 DZ85
Brockley Gro., Brwd. 109 GA46
Brockley Hall Rd. SE4 183 DY85
Brockley Hill, Stan. 95 CJ46
Brockley Ms. SE4 183 DY85
Brockley Pk. SE23 183 DY87
Brockley Ri. SE23 183 DY87
Brockley Rd. SE4 163 DZ83
Brockley Vw. SE23 183 DY87
Brockley Way SE4 183 DX85
Brockleyside, Stan. 96 CL49
Brockman Ri., Brom. 183 ED91
Brocks Dr., Sutt. 199 CY104
Brockshot Clo., Brent. 157 CK78
Brocksparkwood, Brwd. 109 GB48
Brockswood La., Welw.G.C. 29 CU08
Brockton Clo., Rom. 127 FF56
Brockway Clo. E11 124 EE61
Brockway Clo., Guil. 243 BB133
Brockway Ho., Slou. 153 BB78
Brockwell Clo., Orp. 205 ET98
Brockwell Pk. Gdns. SE24 181 DN87
Brockworth Clo. SE15 162 DS79
Broderick Gro., Lthd. 246 CA126
Lower Shott
Brodewater Rd., Borwd. 78 CP40
Brodia Rd. N16 122 DS62
Brodie Rd. E4 101 EC46
Brodie Rd., Enf. 82 DQ38
Brodie Rd., Guil. 258 AY135
Brodie St. SE1 162 DT78
Coopers Rd.
Brodlove La. E1 143 DX73
Brodrick Gro. SE2 166 EV77
Brodrick Rd. SW17 180 DE89
Brograve Gdns., Beck. 203 EB96
Broke Ct., Guil. 243 BC131
Speedwell Clo.
Broke Fm. Dr., Orp. 224 EX109
Broke Wk. E8 142 DU67
Marlborough Ave.
Broken Furlong (Eton), Wind. 151 AQ78
Broken Gate La., Uxb. 113 BC60
Broken Wf. EC4 275 **H10**
Brokes Cres., Reig. 250 DA132
Brokes Rd., Reig. 250 DA130
Brokesley St. E3 143 DZ69
Bromar Rd. SE5 162 DS83
Bromborough Grn., Wat. 94 BW50
Brome Rd. SE9 165 EM83
Bromefield, Stan. 95 CJ53
Bromefield Ct., Wal.Abb. 68 EG33
Bromehead Rd. E1 142 DW72
Commercial Rd.
Bromell's Rd. SW4 161 DJ84
Bromet Clo., Wat. 75 BT38
Hempstead Rd.
Bromfelde Rd. SW4 161 DK83
Bromfelde Wk. SW4 161 DL82
Bromfield St. N1 141 DN68
Bromford Clo., Oxt. 254 EG133
Bromhall Rd., Dag. 146 EV65
Bromhedge SE9 185 EM90
Bromholm Rd. SE2 166 EV76
Bromleigh Clo. (Cheshunt), Wal.Cr. 67 DY28
Martins Dr.
Bromleigh Ct. SE23 182 DV89
Lapse Wd. Wk.
Bromley, Grays 170 FZ79
Bromley Ave., Brom. 184 EE94
Bromley Common, Brom. 204 EJ98
Bromley Cres., Brom. 204 EF97
Bromley Cres., Ruis. 115 BT63
Bromley Gdns., Brom. 204 EF97
Bromley Gro., Brom. 203 ED96
Bromley Hall Rd. E14 143 EC71
Bromley High St. E3 143 EB69
Bromley Hill, Brom. 184 EE93
Bromley La., Chis. 185 EQ94
Bromley Pl. W1 273 **K6**
Bromley Rd. E10 123 EB58
Bromley Rd. E17 101 EA54
Bromley Rd. N17 100 DT53
Bromley Rd. N18 100 DR48
Bromley Rd. SE6 183 EB89
Bromley Rd., Beck. 203 EB96
Bromley Rd., Brom. 203 EB96
Bromley Rd. (Downham), Brom. 183 ED91
Bromley Rd., Chis. 205 EP95
Bromley St. E1 143 DX71
Brompton Arc. SW3 276 **D5**
Brompton Clo. SE20 202 DU96
Selby Rd.
Brompton Clo., Houns. 176 BZ85
Brompton Dr., Erith 167 FH80
Brompton Gro. N2 120 DE56
Brompton Pk. Cres. SW6 160 DB79
Brompton Pl. SW3 276 **C6**
Brompton Pl. SW3 160 DE76
Brompton Rd. SW1 276 **D5**
Brompton Rd. SW1 160 DF75
Brompton Rd. SW3 276 **B8**
Brompton Rd. SW3 160 DE77
Brompton Rd. SW7 276 **B7**
Brompton Rd. SW7 160 DE76
Brompton Sq. SW3 276 **B6**
Brompton Sq. SW3 160 DE76
Brompton Ter. SE18 165 EN81
Prince Imperial Rd.
Bromwich Ave. N6 120 DG61
Bromyard Ave. W3 138 CS73
Bromyard Ho. SE15 162 DV80
Commercial Way
Bromycroft, Slou. 131 AN69
Brondesbury Ct. NW2 139 CX65
Brondesbury Ms. NW6 140 DA66
Willesden La.
Brondesbury Pk. NW2 139 CW66
Brondesbury Pk. NW6 139 CX66
Brondesbury Rd. NW6 139 CZ68
Brondesbury Vill. NW6 139 CZ68
Bronsart Rd. SW6 159 CY80
Bronsdon Way, Uxb. 113 BF61
Bronson Rd. SW20 199 CX96
Bronte Clo. E7 124 EG63
Bective Rd.
Bronte Clo., Erith 167 FB81
Belmont Rd.
Bronte Clo., Ilf. 125 EN56
Bronte Clo., Til. 171 GJ82
Bronte Gro., Dart. 168 FM84
Bronte Ho. NW6 140 DA69
Bronte Vw., Grav. 191 GJ88
Bronti Clo. SE17 162 DQ78
Bronze St. SE8 163 EA80
Brook Ave., Dag. 147 FB66
Brook Ave., Edg. 96 CP51
Brook Ave., Wem. 118 CN62
Brook Clo. NW7 97 CY52
Frith Ct.
Brook Clo. SW20 199 CV97
Brook Clo. W3 138 CN74
West Lo. Ave.
Brook Clo., Borwd. 78 CP41
Brook Clo., Chis. 205 EN95
Brook Clo., Dor. 247 CJ134
Brook Clo., Rom. 105 FF53
Brook Clo., Ruis. 115 BS59
Brook Clo., Stai. 174 BM87
Brook Cres. E4 101 EA49
Brook Cres. N9 100 DV49
Brook Cres., Slou. 131 AL72
Brook Dr. SE11 278 **E7**
Brook Dr. SE11 161 DN76
Brook Dr., Har. 116 CC56
Brook Dr., Rad. 61 CF33
Brook Dr., Ruis. 115 BS58
Brook Dr., Sun. 175 BS92
Chertsey Rd.
Brook End, Saw. 36 EX05
Brook Fm. Rd., Cob. 230 BX115
Brook Gdns. E4 101 EB49
Brook Gdns. SW13 159 CT83
Brook Gdns., Kings.T. 198 CQ95
Brook Gate W1 276 **E1**
Brook Grn. W6 159 CW76
Brook Hill, Guil. 260 BK143
Brook Hill, Oxt. 253 EC130
Brook Ind. Est., Hayes 136 BX74
Brook La. SE3 164 EH82
Brook La., Berk. 38 AV18
Brook La., Bex. 186 EX86
Brook La., Brom. 184 EG93
Brook La., Guil. 260 BL142
Brook La., Saw. 36 EX05
Brook La., Wok. 227 BE122
Brook La. N., Brent. 157 CK78
Brook Mead, Epsom 216 CS107
Brook Meadow N12 98 DB48
Brook Meadow Clo., Wdf.Grn. 102 EE51
Brook Ms. N. W2 140 DD73
Craven Ter.
Brook Par., Chig. 103 EP48
High Rd.
Brook Pk. Clo. N21 81 DP44
Brook Path, Slou. 131 AM73
Brook Pl., Barn. 80 DA43
Brook Ri., Chig. 103 EN48
Brook Rd. N8 121 DL56
Brook Rd. N22 121 DM55
Brook Rd. NW2 119 CT61
Brook Rd., Borwd. 78 CN39
Brook Rd., Brwd. 108 FT48
Brook Rd., Buck.H. 102 EG47
Brook Rd., Epp. 70 EU33
Brook Rd., Grav. 190 GE88
Brook Rd., Guil. 259 BC140
Brook Rd., Ilf. 125 ES58
Brook Rd., Loug. 84 EL42
Brook Rd., Red. 266 DF135
Brook Rd. (Merstham), Red. 251 DJ129
Brook Rd., Rom. 105 FF53
Brook Rd., Saw. 36 EX06
Brook Rd., Surb. 198 CL103
Brook Rd., Swan. 207 FD97
Brook Rd., Th.Hth. 202 DQ98
Brook Rd., Twick. 177 CG86
Brook Rd., Wal.Cr. 67 DZ34
Brook Rd. S., Brent. 157 CK79
Brook St. N17 100 DT54
High Rd.
Brook St. W1 273 **H10**
Brook St. W1 140 DG73
Brook St. W2 272 **A10**
Brook St. W2 140 DD73
Brook St., Belv. 167 FB78
Brook St., Brwd. 107 FR50
Brook St., Erith 167 FB79
Brook St., Kings.T. 198 CL96
Brook St., Wind. 151 AR82
Brook Valley, Dor. 263 CH142
Brook Wk. N2 98 DD53
Old Fm. Rd.
Brook Wk., Edg. 96 CR51
Brook Way, Chig. 103 EN48
Brook Way, Lthd. 231 CG118
Brook Way, Rain. 147 FH71
Brookbank, H.Wyc. 110 AC60
Brookbank Ave. W7 137 CD71
Brookbank Rd. SE13 163 EA83
Brookdale N11 99 DJ49
Brookdale Ave., Upmin. 128 FN62
Brookdale Clo., Upmin. 128 FP62
Brookdale Rd. E17 123 EA55
Brookdale Rd. SE6 183 EB86
Brookdale Rd., Bex. 186 EY86
Brookdene Ave., Wat. 93 BV45
Brookdene Dr., Nthwd. 93 BT52
Brookdene Rd. SE18 165 ET77
Brooke Ave., Har. 116 CC62
Brooke Clo. (Bushey), Wat. 94 CC45
Brooke Rd. E5 122 DU62
Brooke Rd. E17 123 EC56
Brooke Rd. N16 122 DT62
Brooke Rd., Grays 170 GA78
Brooke St. EC1 274 **D7**
Brooke St. EC1 141 DN71
Brooke Way (Bushey), Wat. 94 CC45
Richfield Rd.
Brookehowse Rd. SE6 183 EA89
Brookend Rd., Sid. 185 ES88
Brooker Rd., Wal.Abb. 67 EC34
Brookers Clo., Ash. 231 CJ117
Brooke's Ct. EC1 274 **D6**
Brookes Mkt. EC1 274 **D6**
Brookfield N6 120 DG62
Brookfield, Epp. 70 EW25
Brookfield, Gdmg. 258 AU143
Brookfield, Wok. 226 AV116
Brookfield Ave. E17 123 EC56
Brookfield Ave. NW7 97 CV51
Brookfield Ave. W5 137 CK70
Brookfield Ave., Sutt. 218 DE105
Brookfield Clo. NW7 97 CV51
Brookfield Clo., Brwd. 109 GC44
Brookfield Clo., Cher. 211 BD107
Brookfield Clo., Red. 266 DG140
Brookfield Ct., Grnf. 136 CC69
Brookfield Ct., Har. 117 CK57
Brookfield Cres. NW7 97 CV51
Brookfield Cres., Har. 118 CL57
Brookfield Gdns., Esher 215 CF107
Brookfield Gdns. (Cheshunt), Wal.Cr. 67 DX27
Brookfield La. (Cheshunt), Wal.Cr. 66 DV28
Brookfield Pk. NW5 121 DH62
Brookfield Path, Wdf.Grn. 102 EE51
Brookfield Rd. E9 143 DY65
Brookfield Rd. N9 100 DU48
Brookfield Rd. W4 158 CR75
Brookfield Rd., H.Wyc. 110 AD60
Brookfields, Enf. 83 DX42
Brookfields, Saw. 36 EX05
Brookfields Ave., Mitch. 200 DE99
Brookhill Clo. SE18 165 EP78
Brookhill Clo., Barn. 80 DE43
Brookhill Rd. SE18 165 EP77
Brookhill Rd., Barn. 80 DD43
Brookhouse Dr., H.Wyc. 110 AC60
Brookhouse Gdns. E4 102 EE49
Brookhurst Rd., Add. 212 BH107
Brooking Rd. E7 124 EG64
Brookland Clo. NW11 120 DB56
Brookland Garth NW11 120 DB56
Brookland Hill NW11 120 DB56
Brookland Ri. NW11 120 DA56
Brooklands, Dart. 188 FL88
Brooklands App., Rom. 127 FD56
Brooklands Ave. SW19 180 DB89
Brooklands Ave., Sid. 185 ER89
Brooklands Clo., Cob. 230 BY115
Brooklands Clo., Rom. 127 FD56
Marshalls Rd.
Brooklands Clo., Sun. 195 BS95
Brooklands Ct., Add. 212 BK110
Brooklands Dr., Grnf. 137 CJ67
Brooklands Gdns., Horn. 128 FJ57
Brooklands Gdns., Pot.B. 63 CY32
Brooklands Ind. Est., Wey. 212 BL110
Brooklands La., Rom. 127 FD56
Brooklands La., Wey. 212 BM107
Brooklands Pk. SE3 164 EG83
Brooklands Rd., Rom. 127 FD56
Brooklands Rd., T.Ditt. 197 CF102
Brooklands Rd., Wey. 213 BP107
Brooklands Way, Red. 250 DE132
Brooklane Fld., Harl. 52 EV18
Brooklea Clo. NW9 96 CS53
Brookleys, Wok. 210 AT110
Brooklyn Ave. SE25 202 DV98
Brooklyn Ave., Loug. 84 EL42
Brooklyn Clo., Cars. 200 DE103
Brooklyn Clo., Wok. 226 AY119
Brooklyn Ct., Wok. 226 AY119
Brooklyn Rd.
Brooklyn Gro. SE25 202 DV98
Brooklyn Rd. SE25 202 DV98
Brooklyn Rd., Brom. 204 EK99
Brooklyn Rd., Wok. 226 AY118
Brooklyn Way, West Dr. 154 BK76
Brookmans Ave., Hat. 63 CY26
Brookmans Clo., Upmin. 129 FS59
Brookmarsh Ind. Est. SE10 163 EB80
Norman Rd.
Brookmead Ave., Brom. 205 EM99
Brookmead Clo., Orp. 206 EV101
Brookmead Rd., Croy. 201 DJ100
Brookmead Way, Orp. 206 EV100
Brookmeads Est., Mitch. 200 DE99
Brookmill Rd. SE8 163 EA81
Brooks Ave. E6 145 EM70
Brooks Clo. SE9 185 EN89
Brooks Clo., Wey. 212 BN110
Brooks Ct. E15 123 EB64
Clays La.
Brooks Ct., Hert. 31 DM08
Brooks La. W4 158 CN79
Brook's Ms. W1 273 **H10**
Brook's Ms. W1 141 DH73
Brooks Rd. E13 144 EG67
Brooks Rd. W4 158 CN78
Brooks Way, Orp. 206 EW96
Brooksbank St. E9 142 DW65
Brooksby Ms. N1 141 DN66
Brooksby St.
Brooksby St. N1 141 DN66
Brooksby's Wk. E9 123 DX64
Brookscroft, Croy. 221 DZ110
Brookscroft Rd. E17 101 EB53
Brooksfield, Welw.G.C. 30 DB08
Brookshill, Har. 95 CD50
Brookshill Ave., Har. 95 CD50
Brookshill Dr., Har. 95 CD50
Brookside N21 81 DM44
Brookside, Barn. 80 DE44
Brookside, Cars. 218 DG106
Brookside, Cher. 193 BE101
Brookside, Guil. 242 AX129
Brookside, Harl. 51 EM18
Brookside, Hat. 44 CR18
Brookside, Hert. 32 DS09
Brookside, Hodd. 49 EA17
Brookside, Horn. 128 FL57
Brookside, Ilf. 103 EQ51
Brookside, Orp. 205 ET101
Brookside, Pot.B. 63 CU32
Brookside, Slou. 153 BC80
Brookside, Uxb. 134 BM66
Brookside, Wal.Abb. 68 EE33
Broomstick Hall Rd.
Brookside Ave., Ashf. 174 BJ92
Brookside Ave., Stai. 152 AY83
Brookside Clo., Barn. 79 CY44
Brookside Clo., Felt. 175 BU90
Sycamore Clo.
Brookside Clo., Har. 117 CK57
Brookside Clo. (Kenton), Har. 116 BY63
Brookside Cres. (Cuffley), Pot.B. 65 DL27
Brookside Cres., Wor.Pk. 199 CU102
Green La.
Brookside Gdns., Enf. 82 DW37
Brookside Rd. N9 100 DV49
Brookside Rd. N19 121 DJ61
Junction Rd.
Brookside Rd. NW11 119 CY58
Brookside Rd., Grav. 191 GF94
Brookside Rd., Hayes 136 BW73
Brookside Rd., Wat. 93 BV45
Brookside S., Barn. 98 DG45
Brookside Wk. N3 119 CX55
Brookside Wk. N12 98 DA51
Brookside Wk. NW4 119 CY56
Brookside Wk. NW11 119 CY56
Brookside Way, Croy. 203 DX100
Brooksville Ave. NW6 139 CY67
Brookvale, Erith 167 FB81
Brookview Rd. SW16 181 DJ92
Brookville Rd. SW6 159 CZ80
Brookway SE3 164 EG83
Brookwood, Horl. 269 DH147
Stockfield
Brookwood Ave. SW13 159 CT83
Brookwood Clo., Brom. 204 EF98
Brookwood Rd. SW18 179 CZ88
Brookwood Rd., Houns. 156 CB81
Broom Ave., Orp. 206 EV96
Broom Clo., Brom. 204 EL100
Broom Clo., Esher 214 CB106
Broom Clo., Hat. 45 CT21
Broom Clo., Tedd. 177 CK94
Broom Clo. (Cheshunt), Wal.Cr. 66 DU27
Broom Gdns., Croy. 203 EA104
Broom Gro., Wat. 75 BU38
Bay Tree Wk.
Broom Hall, Lthd. 214 CC114
Broom Hill, Hem.H. 39 BE21
Broom Hill, Slou. 132 AU66
Broom La., Wok. 210 AS109
Broom Leys, St.Alb. 43 CK17
Broom Lock, Tedd. 177 CJ93
Broom Mead, Bexh. 186 FA85
Broom Pk., Tedd. 177 CK94
Broom Rd., Croy. 203 EA104
Broom Rd., Tedd. 177 CH92
Broom Water, Tedd. 177 CJ93
Broom Water W., Tedd. 177 CJ92
Broom Way, Wey. 213 BS105
Broomcroft Ave., Nthlt. 136 BW69
Broomcroft Clo., Wok. 227 BD116
Broomcroft Dr., Wok. 227 BD116
Broome Clo., Epsom 248 CQ126
Broome Pl., S.Ock. 149 FR74
Broome Rd., Hmptn. 176 BZ94
Broome Way SE5 162 DQ80
Broomer Pl., Wal.Cr. 66 DW29
Broomfield E17 123 DZ59
Broomfield, Guil. 242 AS133
Broomfield, Harl. 36 EV12
Broomfield, St.Alb. 60 CC27
Broomfield, Stai. 174 BG93
Broomfield, Sun. 195 BU95
Broomfield Ave. N13 99 DM50
Broomfield Ave., Brox. 67 DY26
Broomfield Ave., Loug. 85 EM44
Broomfield Clo., Guil. 242 AS132
Broomfield Clo., Rom. 105 FD52
Broomfield Ct., Wey. 213 BP107
Broomfield La. N13 99 DL49
Broomfield Pk., Dor. 262 CC137
Broomfield Pl. W13 137 CH74
Broomfield Rd.
Broomfield Ride, Lthd. 215 CD112
Broomfield Ri., Abb.L. 59 BR32
Broomfield Rd. N13 99 DL50
Broomfield Rd. W13 137 CH74
Broomfield Rd., Add. 212 BH111
Broomfield Rd., Beck. 203 DY98
Broomfield Rd., Bexh. 186 FA85
Broomfield Rd., Rich. 158 CM81
Broomfield Rd., Rom. 126 EX59
Broomfield Rd., Sev. 256 FF122
Broomfield Rd., Surb. 198 CM102
Broomfield Rd., Swans. 190 FY86
Broomfield Rd., Tedd. 177 CJ93
Melbourne Rd.
Broomfield St. E14 143 EA71
Broomfields, Esher 214 CC106
Broomgrove Gdns., Edg. 96 CN53
Broomgrove Rd. SW9 161 DM82
Broomhall End, Wok. 226 AY116
Broomhall La.
Broomhall La., Wok. 226 AY116
Broomhall Rd., S.Croy. 220 DR109
Broomhall Rd., Wok. 226 AY116
Broomhill Ri., Bexh. 186 FA85
Broomhill Rd. SW18 180 DA85
Broomhill Rd., Dart. 187 FH86
Broomhill Rd., Ilf. 126 EU61
Broomhill Rd., Orp. 206 EU101
Broomhill Rd., Wdf.Grn. 102 EG51
Broomhill Wk., Wdf.Grn. 102 EF52
Broomhills, Grav. 190 FY91
Betsham Rd.
Broomhills, Welw.G.C. 30 DA08
Broomhouse La. SW6 160 DA82
Broomhouse Rd. SW6 160 DA82
Broomlands La., Oxt. 254 EL127
Broomloan La., Sutt. 200 DA103
Brooms Clo., Welw.G.C. 29 CX06
Broomsleigh St. NW6 119 CZ64
Broomstick Hall Rd., Wal.Abb. 67 ED33
Broomstick La., Chesh. 56 AU30
Broomwood Clo., Croy. 203 DX99
Broomwood Gdns., Brwd. 108 FU44
Broomwood Rd. SW11 180 DF86
Broomwood Rd., Orp. 206 EV96
Broseley Gdns., Rom. 106 FL49
Broseley Gro. SE26 183 DY92
Broseley Rd., Rom. 106 FL49
Broster Gdns. SE25 202 DT97
Brough Clo. SW8 161 DL80
Kenchester Clo.
Brough Clo., Kings.T. 177 CK92
Brougham Rd. E8 142 DU67
Brougham Rd. W3 138 CQ72
Brougham St. SW11 160 DF82
Reform St.
Broughinge Rd., Borwd. 78 CN40
Broughton Ave. N3 119 CY55
Broughton Ave., Rich. 177 CH90
Broughton Dr. SW9 161 DN84
Broughton Gdns. N6 121 DJ58
Broughton Rd. SW6 160 DB82
Broughton Rd. W13 137 CH73
Broughton Rd., Orp. 205 ER103
Broughton Rd., Sev. 241 FG116
Broughton Rd., Th.Hth. 201 DN100
Broughton Rd. App. SW6 160 DB82
Wandsworth Bri. Rd.
Broughton St. SW8 160 DG82
Broughton Way, Rick. 92 BG45
Brouncker Rd. W3 158 CQ75
Brow, The, Ch.St.G. 90 AX48
Brow, The, Red. 266 DG139
Spencer Way
Brow, The, Wat. 59 BV33
Brow Clo., Orp. 206 EX101
Brow Cres.
Brow Cres., Orp. 206 EW102
Browells La., Felt. 175 BV89
Brown Clo., Wall. 219 DL108
Brown Hart Gdns. W1 272 **G10**
Brown Hart Gdns. W1 140 DG73
Brown Rd., Grav. 191 GL88
Brown St. W1 272 **D8**
Brown St. W1 140 DF72
Browne Clo., Brwd. 108 FV46
Browne Clo., Rom. 105 FB50
Bamford Way
Brownfield St. E14 143 EB72
Brownfields, Welw.G.C. 29 CZ08
Browngraves Rd., Hayes 155 BQ80
Brownhill Rd. SE6 183 EB87
Browning Ave. W7 137 CF72
Browning Ave., Sutt. 218 DE105
Browning Ave., Wor.Pk. 199 CV102
Browning Clo. E17 123 EC56
Greenacre Gdns.
Browning Clo. W9 140 DC70
Randolph Ave.
Browning Clo., Hmptn. 176 BZ91
Browning Clo., Rom. 104 EZ52
Browning Clo., Well. 165 ES81
Browning Est. SE17 279 **J10**
Browning Est. SE17 162 DQ78
Browning Ho. W12 139 CW72
Wood La.
Browning Ms. W1 272 **G7**
Browning Rd. E11 124 EF59
Browning Rd. E12 145 EM65
Browning Rd., Dart. 168 FM84
Browning Rd., Enf. 82 DR37
Browning Rd., Lthd. 247 CD125
Browning St. SE17 279 **J10**
Browning St. SE17 162 DQ78
Browning Wk., Til. 171 GJ82
Coleridge Rd.
Browning Way, Houns. 156 BX81
Brownlea Gdns., Ilf. 126 EU61
Brownlow Ms. WC1 274 **C5**
Brownlow Ms. WC1 141 DM70
Brownlow Rd. E7 124 EH63
Woodford Rd.
Brownlow Rd. E8 142 DT67
Brownlow Rd. N3 98 DB52
Brownlow Rd. N11 99 DL51
Brownlow Rd. NW10 138 CS66
Brownlow Rd. W13 137 CG74
Brownlow Rd., Berk. 38 AW18
Brownlow Rd., Borwd. 78 CN42
Brownlow Rd., Croy. 220 DS105
Brownlow Rd., Red. 250 DE134
Brownlow St. WC1 274 **C7**
Brownrigg Rd., Ashf. 174 BN91
Brown's Bldgs. EC3 275 **N9**
Browns La. NW5 121 DH64
Browns La., Lthd. 246 BX127
Browns Rd. E17 123 EA55
Browns Rd., Surb. 198 CM101
Browns Spring, Berk. 39 BC16

Burleigh Wk. SE6 183 EC88
Muirkirk Rd.
Burleigh Way, Enf. 82 DR41
Church St.
Burleigh Way (Cuffley), Pot.B. 65 DL30
Burley Clo. E4 101 EA50
Burley Clo. SW16 201 DK96
Burley Hill, Harl. 52 EX16
Burley Orchard, Cher. 194 BG100
Burley Rd. E16 144 EJ71
Burlingham Clo., Guil. 243 BD132
Gilliat Dr.
Burlings La., Sev. 239 ET118
Burlington Arc. W1 277 K1
Burlington Ave., Rich. 158 CN81
Burlington Ave., Rom. 127 FB58
Burlington Ave., Slou. 152 AS75
Burlington Clo. E6 144 EL72
Northumberland Rd.
Burlington Clo. W9 139 CZ70
Burlington Clo., Felt. 175 BR87
Burlington Clo., Orp. 205 EP103
Burlington Clo., Pnr. 115 BV55
Tolcarne Dr.
Burlington Gdns. W1 277 K1
Burlington Gdns. W1 141 DJ73
Burlington Gdns. W3 138 CQ74
Burlington Gdns. W4 158 CQ78
Burlington Gdns., Rom. 126 EY59
Burlington La. W4 158 CS80
Burlington Ms. W3 138 CQ74
Burlington Pl. SW6 159 CY82
Burlington Rd.
Burlington Pl., Wdf.Grn. 102 EH48
Burlington Ri., Barn. 98 DE46
Burlington Rd. N10 98 DG54
Tetherdown
Burlington Rd. N17 100 DU53
Burlington Rd. SW6 159 CY82
Burlington Rd. W4 158 CQ78
Burlington Rd., Enf. 82 DR39
Burlington Rd., Islw. 157 CD81
Burlington Rd., N.Mal. 199 CT98
Burlington Rd., Slou. 130 AH70
Burlington Rd., Th.Hth. 202 DQ96
Burma Rd. N16 122 DR63
Burma Rd., Wok. 192 AT103
Burman Clo., Dart. 188 FQ87
Burmester Rd. SW17 180 DC90
Burn Clo., Add. 212 BK105
Burn Side N9 100 DW48
Burn Wk., Slou. 130 AH69
Wilmot Rd.
Burnaby Cres. W4 158 CQ79
Burnaby Gdns. W4 158 CP79
Burnaby Rd., Grav. 190 GE87
Burnaby St. SW10 160 DC80
Burnbrae Clo. N12 98 DB51
Burnbury Rd. SW12 181 DJ88
Burncroft Ave., Enf. 82 DW40
Burne Jones Ho. W14 159 CZ77
Burne St. NW1 272 B6
Burne St. NW1 140 DE71
Burnell Ave., Rich. 177 CJ92
Burnell Ave., Well. 166 EU82
Burnell Gdns., Stan. 95 CK53
Burnell Rd., Sutt. 218 DB105
Burnell Wk. SE1 162 DT78
Cadet Dr.
Burnell Wk., Brwd. 107 FW51
Burnels Ave. E6 145 EN69
Burness Clo. N7 141 DM65
Roman Way
Burness Clo., Uxb. 134 BK68
Whitehall Rd.
Burnet Ave., Guil. 243 BB131
Woodruff Ave.
Burnet Clo., Hem.H. 40 BL21
Burnet Gro., Epsom 216 CQ113
Burnett Clo. E9 122 DW64
Burnett Pk., Harl. 51 EP20
Burnett Rd., Erith 168 FK79
Burnett Sq., Hert. 31 DM08
Burnetts Rd., Wind. 151 AL81
Burney Ave., Surb. 198 CM99
Burney Clo., Lthd. 246 CC125
Burney Dr., Loug. 85 EP40
Burney Rd., Dor. 247 CG131
Burney St. SE10 163 EC80
Burnfoot Ave. SW6 159 CY81
Burnfoot Ct. SE22 182 DV88
Burnham NW3 140 DE66
Burnham Ave., Beac. 111 AN55
Burnham Ave., Uxb. 115 BQ63
Burnham Clo. NW7 97 CU52
Burnham Clo. SE1 162 DT77
Cadet Dr.
Burnham Clo., Enf. 82 DS38
Burnham Clo., Wind. 151 AK82
Burnham Ct. NW4 119 CW56
Burnham Cres. E11 124 EJ56
Burnham Cres., Dart. 168 FJ84
Burnham Dr., Reig. 250 DA133
Burnham Dr., Wor.Pk. 199 CX103
Burnham Gdns., Croy. 202 DT101
Burnham Gdns., Hayes 155 BR76
Burnham Gdns., Houns. 155 BV81
Burnham La., Slou. 131 AL70
Burnham Rd. E4 101 DZ50
Burnham Rd., Dag. 146 EV66
Burnham Rd., Dart. 168 FJ84
Burnham Rd., Mord. 200 DB99
Burnham Rd., Rom. 127 FD55
Burnham Rd., St.Alb. 43 CG20
Burnham Rd., Sid. 186 EY89
Burnham St. E2 142 DW69
Burnham St., Kings.T. 198 CN95
Burnham Wk., Slou. 111 AN64
Burnham Way SE26 183 DZ92
Burnham Way W13 157 CH77
Burnhams Rd., Lthd. 230 BY124
Burnhill Rd., Beck. 203 EA96
Burnley Clo., Wat. 94 BW50
Burnley Rd. NW10 119 CT64
Burnley Rd. SW9 161 DM82
Burnley Rd., Grays 169 FT81
Burns Ave., Felt. 175 BU86
Burns Ave., Rom. 126 EW59
Burns Ave., Sid. 186 EU86
Burns Ave., Sthl. 136 CA73
Burns Clo. SW19 180 DD93
North Rd.
Burns Clo., Erith 167 FF81
Burns Clo., Hayes 135 BT71
Burns Clo., Well. 165 ET81
Burns Dr., Bans. 217 CY114
Burns Pl., Til. 171 GH81
Burns Rd. NW10 139 CT67
Burns Rd. SW11 160 DF82
Burns Rd. W13 157 CH75
Burns Rd., Wem. 138 CL68
Burns Way, Brwd. 109 GD45
Burns Way, Houns. 156 BX82
Burnsall St. SW3 276 C10
Burnsall St. SW3 160 DE78
Burnside, Ash. 232 CM118
Burnside, Hert. 31 DN10
Burnside, Hodd. 49 DZ17
Burnside, St.Alb. 43 CH22
Burnside, Saw. 36 EX05
Burnside Ave. E4 101 DZ51
Burnside Clo. SE16 143 DX74
Burnside Clo., Barn. 80 DA41
Burnside Clo., Hat. 45 CU15
Homestead Rd.
Burnside Clo., Twick. 177 CG86
Burnside Cres., Wem. 137 CK67
Burnside Rd., Dag. 126 EW61
Burnside Ter., Harl. 36 EZ12
Hobbs Cross Rd.
Burnt Ash Hill SE12 184 EF86
Burnt Ash La., Brom. 184 EG94
Burnt Ash Rd. SE12 184 EF85
Burnt Common Clo., Wok. 243 BF125
Burnt Fm. Ride, Enf. 65 DP34
Burnt Fm. Ride, Wal.Cr. 65 DP31
Burnt Mill, Harl. 35 EQ13
Burnt Mill Clo., Harl. 35 EQ12
Burntmill La.
Burnt Oak Bdy., Edg. 96 CP52
Burnt Oak Flds., Edg. 96 CQ53
Burnt Oak La., Sid. 186 EU89
Burntcommon La., Wok. 244 BG125
Burnthouse La., Dart. 188 FL91
Burnthwaite Rd. SW6 159 CZ80
Burntmill Cor., Harl. 35 EQ11
Eastwick Rd.
Burntmill La., Harl. 35 EQ12
Burntwood, Brwd. 108 FW48
Gerrard Cres.
Burntwood Ave., Horn. 128 FK58
Burntwood Clo. SW18 180 DD88
Burntwood Clo., Cat. 236 DU121
Burntwood Gra. Rd. SW18 180 DD88
Burntwood Gro., Sev. 257 FH127
Burntwood La. SW17 180 DC90
Burntwood La., Cat. 236 DS122
Burntwood Rd., Sev. 257 FH128
Burntwood Vw. SE19 182 DT92
Bowley La.
Burnway, Horn. 128 FL59
Buross St. E1 142 DV72
Commercial Rd.
Burpham La., Guil. 243 BA130
Burr Clo. E1 142 DU74
Burr Clo., Bexh. 166 EZ83
Burr Clo., St.Alb. 62 CL27
Burr Hill La., Wok. 210 AS109
Burr Rd. SW18 180 DA88
Burrage Gro. SE18 165 EQ77
Burrage Pl. SE18 165 EP78
Burrage Rd. SE18 165 EQ77
Burrard Rd. E16 144 EH72
Burrard Rd. NW6 120 DA64
Burrell, The, Dor. 262 CC137
Burrell Clo., Croy. 203 DY100
Burrell Clo., Edg. 96 CP47
Burrell Row, Beck. 203 EA96
High St.
Burrell St. SE1 278 F2
Burrell St. SE1 141 DP74
Burrell Twr. E10 123 EA59
Burrells Wf. Sq. E14 163 EB78
Burrfield Dr., Orp. 206 EX99
Burritt Rd., Kings.T. 198 CN96
Burroughs, The NW4 119 CV56
Burroughs Gdns. NW4 119 CV56
Burrow Clo., Chig. 103 ET50
Burrow Rd.
Burrow Grn., Chig. 103 ET50
Burrow Rd. SE22 162 DS84
Burrow Rd., Chig. 103 ET50
Burrow Wk. SE21 182 DQ87
Rosendale Rd.
Burroway Rd., Slou. 153 BB76
Burrowfield, Welw.G.C. 29 CX11
Burrowfield Ind. Est., Welw.G.C. 29 CX12
Burrows Clo., Guil. 242 AT133
Burrows Clo., H.Wyc. 88 AC45
Burrows Clo., Lthd. 230 BZ124
Burrows Cross, Guil. 261 BQ141
Burrows Hill Clo., Houns. 154 BJ84
Burrows Hill La., Houns. 154 BH84
Burrows La., Guil. 261 BQ140
Burrows Ms. SE1 278 F4
Burrows Rd. NW10 139 CW69
Bursdon Clo., Sid. 185 ET89
Burses Way, Brwd. 109 GB45
Bursland Rd., Enf. 83 DX42
Burslem Ave., Ilf. 104 EU51
Burslem St. E1 142 DU72
Burstead Clo., Cob. 214 BX112
Burstock Rd. SW15 159 CY84
Burston Dr., St.Alb. 60 CC28
Burston Rd. SW15 179 CX85
Burston Vill. SW15 179 CX85
St. John's Ave.
Burstow Rd. SW20 199 CY95
Burt Rd. E16 144 EJ74
Burtenshaw Rd., T.Ditt. 197 CG101
Burtley Clo. N4 122 DQ60
Burton Ave., Wat. 75 BU42
Burton Clo., Chess. 215 CK108
Burton Clo., Horl. 268 DG149
Burton Ct. SW3 160 DF78
Franklin's Row
Burton Gdns., Houns. 156 BZ81
Burton Gro. SE17 162 DR78
Portland St.
Burton La. SW9 161 DN82
Burton La. (Cheshunt), Wal.Cr. 66 DS29
Burton Ms. SW1 276 G9
Burton Pl. WC1 273 N3
Burton Rd. E18 124 EH55
Burton Rd. NW6 139 CZ66
Burton Rd. SW9 161 DP82
Burton Rd., Kings.T. 178 CL94
Burton Rd., Loug. 85 EQ42
Burton St. WC1 273 N3
Burton St. WC1 141 DK69
Burton Way, Wind. 151 AL82
Burtonhole Clo. NW7 97 CX49
Burtonhole La. NW7 97 CW50
Burtons La., Ch.St.G. 72 AW40
Burtons La., Rick. 73 BA43
Burtons Rd., Hmptn. 176 CB91
Burtons Way, Ch.St.G. 72 AW40
Burtwell La. SE27 182 DR91
Burwash Ct., Orp. 206 EW99
Rookery Gdns.
Burwash Ho. SE1 279 L5
Burwash Rd. SE18 165 ER78
Burway Cres., Cher. 194 BG97
Burwell Ave., Grnf. 137 CE65
Burwell Clo. E1 142 DV72
Bigland St.
Burwell Rd. E10 123 DY60
Burwell Wk. E3 143 EA70
Burwood Ave., Brom. 204 EH103
Burwood Ave., Ken. 219 DP114
Burwood Ave., Pnr. 115 BV57
Burwood Clo., Guil. 243 BD133
Burwood Clo., Reig. 250 DD134
Burwood Clo., Surb. 198 CN102
Burwood Clo., Walt. 214 BW107
Burwood Gdns., Rain. 147 FF69
Burwood Pk. Rd., Walt. 213 BV105
Burwood Pl. W2 272 C8
Burwood Pl. W2 140 DE72
Burwood Rd., Walt. 213 BS108
Bury Ave., Hayes 135 BS68
Bury Ave., Ruis. 115 BQ58
Bury Clo. SE16 143 DX74
Rotherhithe St.
Bury Clo., Wok. 226 AX116
Bury Ct. EC3 275 N8
Bury Flds., Guil. 258 AW136
Bury Grn., Hem.H. 40 BJ19
Bury Grn. Rd. (Cheshunt), Wal.Cr. 66 DU31
Bury Gro., Mord. 200 DB99
Bury Hill, Hem.H. 40 BH19
Bury Hill Clo., Hem.H. 40 BJ19
Bury Holme, Brox. 49 DZ23
Bury La., Chesh. 54 AP31
Bury La., Epp. 69 ER28
Bury La., Rick. 92 BK46
Bury La., Wok. 226 AW116
Bury Meadows, Rick. 92 BK46
Bury Pl. WC1 273 P7
Bury Pl. WC1 141 DL71
Bury Ri., Hem.H. 57 BD25
Bury Rd. E4 84 EE42
Bury Rd. N22 121 DN55
Bury Rd., Dag. 127 FB64
Bury Rd., Epp. 69 ES31
Bury Rd., Harl. 36 EW11
Bury Rd., Hat. 45 CW17
Bury Rd., Hem.H. 40 BJ19
Bury St. EC3 275 N9
Bury St. EC3 142 DS72
Bury St. N9 100 DT45
Bury St. SW1 277 K2
Bury St. SW1 141 DJ74
Bury St., Guil. 258 AW136
Bury St., Ruis. 115 BQ57
Bury St. W. N9 100 DR45
Bury Wk. SW3 276 B9
Bury Wk. SW3 160 DE77
Burycroft, Welw.G.C. 29 CY06
Burydell La., St.Alb. 61 CD27
Busbridge Ho. E14 143 EA71
Brabazon St.
Busby Ms. NW5 141 DK65
Busby Pl. NW5 141 DK65
Busby St. E2 142 DT70
Chilton St.
Bush Clo., Add. 212 BJ106
Bush Clo., Ilf. 125 ER57
Bush Cotts. SW18 180 DA85
Putney Bri. Rd.
Bush Ct. W12 159 CX75
Bush Elms Rd., Horn. 127 FG59
Bush Fair, Harl. 52 EU17
Tilegate Rd.
Bush Gro. NW9 118 CQ59
Bush Gro., Stan. 95 CK52
Bush Hall La., Hat. 45 CX15
Bush Hill N21 100 DQ45
Bush Hill Rd. N21 82 DR44
Bush Hill Rd., Har. 118 CM58
Bush Ind. Est. NW10 138 CR70
Bush La. EC4 275 K10
Bush La., Wok. 227 BD124
Bush Rd. E8 142 DV67
Bush Rd. E11 124 EF59
Bush Rd. SE8 163 DX77
Bush Rd., Buck.H. 102 EK49
Bush Rd., Rich. 158 CM79
Bush Rd., Shep. 194 BM99
Bushbaby Clo. SE1 279 M7
Bushbarns (Cheshunt), Wal.Cr. 66 DU29
Bushberry Rd. E9 143 DY65
Bushbury La., Bet. 264 CN139
Bushby Ave., Brox. 49 DZ22
Bushell Clo. SW2 181 DM89
Bushell Grn. (Bushey), Wat. 95 CD47
Bushell St. E1 142 DU74
Hermitage Wall
Bushell Way, Chis. 185 EN92
Bushetts Gro., Red. 251 DH128
Bushey Ave. E18 124 EF55
Bushey Ave., Orp. 205 ER101
Bushey Clo. E4 101 EC48
Bushey Clo., Pur. 236 DS116
Bushey Clo., Uxb. 114 BN61
Bushey Clo., Welw.G.C. 30 DB10
Bushey Ct. SW20 199 CV97
Bushey Cft., Harl. 51 ES17
Bushey Cft., Oxt. 253 EC130
Bushey Down SW12 181 DH89
Bedford Hill
Bushey Grn., Welw.G.C. 30 DB10
Bushey Gro. Rd. (Bushey), Wat. 76 BX42
Bushey Hall Dr. (Bushey), Wat. 76 BY42
Bushey Hall Rd. (Bushey), Wat. 76 BX42
Bushey Hill Rd. SE5 162 DS81
Bushey La., Sutt. 200 DA104
Bushey Lees, Sid. 185 ET86
Fen Gro.
Bushey Ley, Welw.G.C. 30 DB10
Bushey Mill Cres., Wat. 76 BW37
Bushey Mill La., Wat. 76 BW37
Bushey Mill La. (Bushey), Wat. 76 BY38
Bushey Rd. E13 144 EJ68
Bushey Rd. N15 122 DS58
Bushey Rd. SW20 199 CV97
Bushey Rd., Croy. 203 EA103
Bushey Rd., Hayes 155 BS77
Bushey Rd., Sutt. 218 DA105
Bushey Rd., Uxb. 114 BN61
Bushey Shaw, Ash. 231 CH117
Bushey Vw. Wk., Wat. 76 BW40
Raphael Dr.
Bushey Way, Beck. 203 ED100
Bushfield Clo., Edg. 96 CP47
Bushfield Cres., Edg. 96 CP47
Bushfield Dr., Red. 266 DG139
Bushfield Rd., Hem.H. 57 BC25
Bushfield Wk., Swans. 190 FY86
Bushfields, Loug. 85 EN43
Bushgrove Rd., Dag. 126 EX63
Bushmead Clo. N15 122 DT56
Copperfield Dr.
Bushmoor Cres. SE18 165 EQ80
Bushnell Rd. SW17 181 DH89
Bushrise, Wat. 75 BU36
Bushway, Dag. 126 EX63
Bushwood E11 124 EF60
Bushwood Clo., Hat. 45 CV23
Dellsome La.
Bushwood Dr. SE1 162 DT77
Bushwood Rd., Rich. 158 CN79
Bushy Hill Dr., Guil. 243 BB132
Bushy Pk., Hmptn. 197 CF95
Bushy Pk., Tedd. 197 CF95
Bushy Pk. Gdns., Tedd. 177 CD92
Bushy Pk. Rd., Tedd. 177 CH94
Bushy Rd., Lthd. 230 CB122
Bushy Rd., Tedd. 177 CF93
Buslins La., Chesh. 54 AL28
Butcher Row E1 143 DX73
Butcher Row E14 143 DX73
Butcher Wk., Swans. 190 FY87
Manor Rd.
Butchers La., Sev. 209 FX103
Butchers Rd. E16 144 EG72
Bute Ave., Rich. 178 CL89
Bute Ct., Wall. 219 DJ106
Bute Rd.
Bute Gdns. W6 159 CX77
Bute Gdns., Wall. 219 DJ106
Bute Gdns. W., Wall. 219 DJ106
Bute Rd., Croy. 201 DN102
Bute Rd., Ilf. 125 EP57
Bute Rd., Wall. 219 DJ105
Bute St. SW7 160 DD77
Bute Wk. N1 142 DR65
Marquess Rd.
Butler Ave., Har. 117 CD59
Butler Pl. SW1 277 M6
Butler Rd. NW10 139 CT66
Curzon Cres.
Butler Rd., Dag. 126 EV63
Butler Rd., Har. 116 CC59
Butler St. E2 142 DW69
Knottisford St.
Butler St., Uxb. 135 BP70
Butler Wk., Grays 170 GD77
Palmers Dr.
Butlers Clo., Amer. 55 AN37
Butlers Clo., Wind. 151 AK82
Butlers Ct. Rd., Beac. 89 AK54
Butlers Dene Rd., Cat. 237 DZ119
Butlers Dr. E4 83 EC38
Butlers Hill, Lthd. 245 BP130
Butlers Wf. SE1 162 DT75
Lafone St.
Butt Fld. Vw., St.Alb. 42 CC24
Butter Hill, Cars. 200 DG104
Butter Hill, Dor. 263 CG136
South St.
Butter Hill, Wall. 200 DG104
Buttercross La., Epp. 70 EU30
Buttercup Clo., Rom. 106 FK53
Copperfields Way
Buttercup Sq., Stai. 174 BK88
Diamedes Ave.
Butterfield, H.Wyc. 110 AD59
Butterfield Clo. SE16 162 DV75
Wilson Gro.
Butterfield Clo., Twick. 177 CF86
Rugby Rd.
Butterfield La., St.Alb. 43 CE24
Butterfield Sq. E6 145 EM72
Harper Rd.
Butterfields E17 123 EC57
Butterfly La. SE9 185 EP86
Butterfly La., Borwd. 77 CH41
Butterfly Wk. SE5 162 DR81
Denmark Hill
Butterfly Wk., Warl. 236 DW120
Butteridges Clo., Dag. 146 EZ67
Butterly Ave., Dart. 188 FM89
Buttermere Ave., Slou. 130 AJ71
Buttermere Clo. SE1 162 DT77
Willow Wk.
Buttermere Clo., Felt. 175 BT88
Buttermere Clo., Mord. 199 CX100
Buttermere Clo., St.Alb. 43 CH21
Buttermere Dr. SW15 179 CY85
Buttermere Gdns., Pur. 220 DR113
Buttermere Rd., Orp. 206 EX98
Buttermere Wk. E8 142 DT65
Buttermere Way, Egh. 173 BB94
Keswick Rd.
Buttersweet Ri., Saw. 36 EY06
Brook Rd.
Butterwick W6 159 CW77
Butterwick, Wat. 76 BY36
Butterworth Gdns., Wdf.Grn. 102 EG50
Harts Gro.
Buttesland St. N1 275 L2
Buttesland St. N1 142 DR69
Buttfield Clo., Dag. 147 FB65
Buttlehide, Rick. 91 BD50
Buttmarsh Clo. SE18 165 EP78
Button St., Swan. 208 FJ96
Buttondene Cres., Brox. 49 EB22
Butts, The, Brent. 157 CJ79
Butts, The, Brox. 49 DY24
Butts, The, Sev. 241 FH116
Butts, The, Sun. 196 BW97
Elizabeth Gdns.
Butts Cotts., Felt. 176 BZ90
Butts Cres., Felt. 176 CA90
Butts End, Hem.H. 40 BG18
Butts Grn. Rd., Horn. 128 FK58
Butts Piece, Nthlt. 135 BV68
Longhook Gdns.
Butts Rd., Brom. 184 EE92
Butts Rd., Wok. 226 AY117
Butts Rd. Ind. Est., Wok. 226 AY118
Buttsbury Rd., Ilf. 125 EQ64
Buttsmead, Nthwd. 93 BQ52
Buxted Rd. E8 142 DT66
Buxted Rd. N12 98 DE50
Buxted Rd. SE22 162 DS84
Buxton Ave., Cat. 236 DS121
Buxton Clo., St.Alb. 43 CK17
Buxton Clo., Wdf.Grn. 102 EK51
Buxton Ct. N1 275 J2
Buxton Cres., Sutt. 217 CY105
Buxton Dr. E11 124 EE56
Buxton Dr., N.Mal. 198 CR96
Buxton Gdns. W3 138 CP73
Buxton La., Cat. 236 DR120
Buxton Path, Wat. 94 BW48
Buxton Rd. E4 101 ED45
Buxton Rd. E6 144 EL69
Buxton Rd. E15 124 EE64
Buxton Rd. E17 123 DY56
Buxton Rd. N19 121 DK60
Buxton Rd. NW2 139 CV65
Buxton Rd. SW14 158 CS83
Buxton Rd., Ashf. 174 BK92
Buxton Rd., Epp. 85 ES36
Buxton Rd., Erith 167 FD80
Buxton Rd., Grays 170 GE75
Buxton Rd., Ilf. 125 ES58
Buxton Rd., Th.Hth. 201 DP99
Buxton Rd., Wal.Abb. 68 EG33
Buxton St. E1 142 DT70
Buzzard Creek Ind. Est., Bark. 145 ET71
By the Mt., Welw.G.C. 29 CX10
By the Wd., Wat. 94 BX47
By-Wood End, Ger.Cr. 91 AZ50
Byam St. SW6 160 DC82
Byards Cft. SW16 201 DK95
Byatt Wk., Hmptn. 176 BY93
Victors Dr.
Bybend Clo., Slou. 131 AP67
Bychurch End, Tedd. 177 CF92
Church Rd.
Bycliffe Ter., Grav. 191 GF87
Bycroft Rd., Sthl. 136 CA70
Bycroft St. SE20 183 DX94
Parish La.
Bycullah Ave., Enf. 81 DP41
Bycullah Rd., Enf. 81 DP40
Byde St., Hert. 32 DQ08
Bye, The W3 138 CS72
Bye Way, The, Har. 95 CF53
Bye Ways, Twick. 176 CB90
Byegrove Rd. SW19 180 DD93
Byers Clo., Pot.B. 64 DC34
Byeway, The SW14 158 CQ83
Byeway, The, Epsom 217 CT105
Byeway, The, Rick. 92 BL47
Byeways, The, Ash. 231 CK118
Skinners La.
Byeways, The, Surb. 198 CN99
Byfeld Gdns. SW13 159 CU81
Byfield, Welw.G.C. 29 CY06
Byfield Clo. SE16 163 DY75
Byfield Rd., Islw. 157 CG83
Byfleet Ind. Est., W.Byf. 212 BK111
Byfleet Rd., Add. 212 BK109
Byfleet Rd., Cob. 212 BN112
Byford Clo. E15 144 EE66
Bygrove, Croy. 221 EB107
Bygrove St. E14 143 EB72
Byland Clo. N21 99 DM45
Bylands, Wok. 227 BA119
Bylands Clo. SE2 166 EV76
Finchale Rd.
Bylands Clo. SE16 143 DX74
Rotherhithe St.
Byne Rd. SE26 182 DW93
Byne Rd., Cars. 200 DE103
Bynes Rd., S.Croy. 220 DR108
Byng Dr., Pot.B. 64 DA31
Byng Pl. WC1 273 M5
Byng Pl. WC1 141 DK70
Byng Rd., Barn. 79 CX41
Byng St. E14 163 EA75
Bynghams, Harl. 51 EM17
Bynon Ave., Bexh. 166 EZ83
Byre, The N14 81 DH44
Farm La.
Byre Rd. N14 80 DG44
Farm La.
Byrefield Rd., Guil. 242 AT131
Byrne Rd. SW12 181 DH88
Byron Ave. E12 144 EL65
Byron Ave. E18 124 EF55
Byron Ave. NW9 118 CP56
Byron Ave., Borwd. 78 CN43
Byron Ave., Couls. 235 DL115
Byron Ave., Houns. 155 BU82
Byron Ave., N.Mal. 199 CU99
Byron Ave., Sutt. 218 DD105
Byron Ave., Wat. 76 BX39
Byron Ave. E., Sutt. 218 DD105
Byron Clo. E8 142 DU67
Byron Clo. SE26 183 DY91
Porthcawe Rd.
Byron Clo. SE28 146 EW74
Byron Clo., Hmptn. 176 BZ91
Byron Clo., Wal.Cr. 66 DT27
Allard Clo.
Byron Clo., Walt. 196 BY102
Byron Clo., Wok. 226 AS117
Byron Ct. W9 140 DA70
Lanhill Rd.
Byron Ct., Enf. 81 DP40
Bycullah Rd.
Byron Dr. N2 120 DD58
Byron Dr., Erith 167 FB81
Belmont Rd.

Byr–Cam This index reads in the sequence: Street Name / Postal District or Post Town / Map Page Number / Grid Reference

Byron Gdns., Sutt. 218 DD105
Byron Gdns., Til. 171 GJ81
Byron Hill Rd., Har. 117 CD60
Byron Ho., Beck. 183 EB93
Byron Ho., Slou. 153 BB78
Byron Ms. NW3 120 DE63
Byron Ms. W9 140 DA70
Shirland Rd.
Byron Pl., Lthd. 231 CH122
Byron Rd. E10 123 EB60
Byron Rd. E17 123 EA55
Byron Rd. NW2 119 CV61
Byron Rd. NW7 97 CU50
Byron Rd. W5 138 CM74
Byron Rd., Add. 212 BK105
Byron Rd., Brwd. 109 GD45
Byron Rd., Dart. 168 FP84
Byron Rd., Har. 117 CE58
Byron Rd. (Wealdstone), Har. 95 CF54
Byron Rd., S.Croy. 220 DV110
Byron Rd., Wem. 117 CJ61
Byron St. E14 143 EC72
St. Leonards Rd.
Byron Ter. N9 100 DW45
Byron Way, Hayes 135 BS70
Byron Way, Nthlt. 136 BY69
Byron Way, Rom. 106 FJ53
Byron Way, West Dr. 154 BM77
Bysouth Clo., Ilf. 103 EP53
Bythorn St. SW9 161 DM84
Byton Rd. SW17 180 DF93
Byttom Hill, Dor. 247 CJ127
Byward Ave., Felt. 176 BW86
Byward St. EC3 279 N1
Byward St. EC3 142 DS73
Bywater Pl. SE16 143 DY74
Bywater St. SW3 276 D10
Bywater St. SW3 160 DF78
Byway, The, Pot.B. 64 DA33
Byway, The, Sutt. 218 DD109
Byways, Berk. 38 AY18
Byways, Slou. 130 AG71
Bywell Pl. W1 273 K7
Bywood Ave., Croy. 202 DW100
Bywood Clo., Ken. 235 DP115
Byworth Wk. N19 121 DK60
Courtauld Rd.

C

C.I. Twr., N.Mal. 198 CS97
Cabbell Pl., Add. 212 BJ105
Cabbell St. NW1 272 B7
Cabbell St. NW1 140 DE71
Cabell Rd., Guil. 242 AS133
Cabinet Way E4 101 DZ51
Cable Pl. SE10 163 EC81
Diamond Ter.
Cable St. E1 142 DU73
Cabot Sq. E14 143 EA74
Cabot Way E6 144 EK67
Parr Rd.
Cabrera Ave., Vir.W. 192 AW100
Cabrera Clo., Vir.W. 192 AX100
Cabul Rd. SW11 160 DE82
Cackets La., Sev. 239 ER115
Cactus Wk. W12 139 CT73
Du Cane Rd.
Cadbury Clo., Islw. 157 CG81
Cadbury Clo., Sun. 175 BS94
Cadbury Rd., Sun. 175 BS94
Cadbury Way SE16 162 DU76
Yalding Rd.
Caddington Clo., Barn. 80 DE43
Caddington Rd. NW2 119 CY62
Caddis Clo., Stan. 95 CF52
Daventer Dr.
Caddy Clo., Egh. 173 BA92
Cade La., Sev. 257 FJ128
Cade Rd. SE10 163 ED81
Cadell Clo. E2 142 DT69
Shipton St.
Cader Rd. SW18 180 DC86
Cadet Dr. SE1 162 DT78
Cadet Pl. SE10 164 EE78
Cadiz Rd., Dag. 147 FC66
Cadiz St. SE17 162 DQ78
Cadley Ter. SE23 182 DW89
Cadlocks Hill, Sev. 224 EZ110
Cadmer Clo., N.Mal. 198 CS98
Cadmore Ct., Hert. 31 DM07
The Ridgeway
Cadmore La. (Cheshunt), Wal.Cr. 67 DX28
Cadmus Clo. SW4 161 DK83
Aristotle Rd.
Cadogan Ave., Dart. 189 FR87
Cadogan Clo., Beck. 203 ED95
Albemarle Rd.
Cadogan Clo., Har. 116 CB63
Cadogan Clo., Tedd. 177 CE92
Cadogan Ct., Sutt. 218 DB107
Cadogan Gdns. E18 124 EH55
Cadogan Gdns. N3 98 DB53
Cadogan Gdns. N21 81 DN43
Cadogan Gdns. SW3 276 E8
Cadogan Gdns. SW3 160 DF77
Cadogan Gate SW1 276 E8
Cadogan Gate SW1 160 DF77
Cadogan La. SW1 276 F7
Cadogan La. SW1 160 DG76
Cadogan Pl. SW1 276 E6
Cadogan Pl. SW1 160 DF76
Cadogan Rd., Surb. 197 CK99
Cadogan Sq. SW1 276 E7
Cadogan Sq. SW1 160 DF76
Cadogan St. SW3 276 D9
Cadogan St. SW3 160 DF77
Cadogan Ter. E9 143 DZ65
Cadoxton Ave. N15 122 DT58
Cadwallon Rd. SE9 185 EP89
Caedmon Rd. N7 121 DM63
Caen Wd. Rd., Ash. 231 CJ118
Caenshill Rd., Wey. 212 BN108
Caenwood Clo., Wey. 212 BN107
Caerleon Clo., Sid. 186 EW92
Caerleon Ter. SE2 166 EV77
Blithdale Rd.
Caernarvon Clo., Hem.H. 40 BK20
Caernarvon Clo., Horn. 128 FN60
Caernarvon Clo., Mitch. 201 DL97
Caernarvon Dr., Ilf. 103 EN53
Caesars Wk., Mitch. 200 DF99
Caesars Way, Shep. 195 BR100
Cage Pond Rd., Rad. 62 CM33
Cage Rd. E16 144 EE71
Malmesbury Rd.
Cage Yd., Reig. 250 DA134
High St.
Cages Wd. Dr., Slou. 111 AP63
Cahill St. EC1 275 J5
Cahir St. E14 163 EB77
Caillard Rd., W.Byf. 212 BL111
Cains La., Felt. 175 BR85
Caird St. W10 139 CY69
Cairn Ave. W5 137 CK74
Cairn Way, Stan. 95 CF51
Cairndale Clo., Brom. 184 EF94
Cairnfield Ave. NW2 118 CS62
Cairngorm Clo., Tedd. 177 CG92
Vicarage Rd.
Cairngorm Pl., Slou. 131 AR70
Cairns Ave., Wdf.Grn. 102 EL51
Cairns Clo., Dart. 168 FK84
Cairns Clo., St.Alb. 43 CK21
Cairns Rd. SW11 180 DE85
Cairo New Rd., Croy. 201 DP103
Cairo Rd. E17 123 EA56
Caishowe Rd., Borwd. 78 CP39
Caister Clo., Hem.H. 40 BL21
Caistor Ms. SW12 181 DH87
Caistor Rd.
Caistor Pk. Rd. E15 144 EF67
Caistor Rd. SW12 181 DH87
Caithness Gdns., Sid. 185 ET86
Caithness Rd. W14 159 CX76
Caithness Rd., Mitch. 181 DH94
Calabria Rd. N5 141 DP65
Calais Gate SE5 161 DP81
Calais St.
Calais St. SE5 161 DP81
Calbourne Ave., Horn. 127 FH64
Calbourne Rd. SW12 180 DF87
Calbroke Rd., Slou. 131 AM70
Calcott Clo., Brwd. 108 FV46
Calcott Wk. SE9 184 EL91
Calcutta Rd., Til. 171 GF82
Caldbeck, Wal.Abb. 67 ED34
Caldbeck Ave., Wor.Pk. 199 CU103
Caldecot Ave., Wal.Cr. 66 DT29
Caldecot Rd. SE5 162 DQ82
Caldecot Way, Brox. 49 DZ22
Caldecote Gdns. (Bushey), Wat. 77 CE44
Caldecote La. (Bushey), Wat. 95 CF45
Caldecott Way E5 123 DX62
Calder Ave., Grnf. 137 CF68
Calder Ave., Hat. 64 DA26
Calder Clo., Enf. 82 DS41
Calder Ct., Slou. 153 AZ78
Calder Gdns., Edg. 118 CN55
Calder Rd., Mord. 200 DC99
Calder Way, Slou. 153 BE83
Calderon Pl. W10 139 CW71
St. Quintin Gdns.
Calderon Rd. E11 123 EC63
Caldervale Rd. SW4 181 DK85
Calderwood, Grav. 191 GL92
Calderwood St. SE18 165 EN77
Caldicot Grn. NW9 118 CS58
Snowdon Dr.
Caldwell Rd., Wat. 94 BX49
Caldwell St. SW9 161 DM80
Caldwell Yd. EC4 142 DQ73
Upper Thames St.
Caldy Rd., Belv. 167 FB76
Caldy Wk. N1 142 DQ65
Clephane Rd.
Cale St. SW3 276 B10
Cale St. SW3 160 DE78
Caleb St. SE1 279 H4
Caledon Clo., Beac. 89 AL52
Caledon Pl., Guil. 243 BA131
Darfield Rd.
Caledon Rd. E6 144 EL67
Caledon Rd., Beac. 89 AL52
Caledon Rd., St.Alb. 61 CJ26
Caledon Rd., Wall. 218 DG105
Caledon Rd., Stai. 174 BL87
Caledonia St. N1 274 A1
Caledonia St. N1 141 DL68
Caledonian Clo., Ilf. 126 EV60
Caledonian Rd. N1 274 A1
Caledonian Rd. N1 141 DL68
Caledonian Rd. N7 121 DM63
Caledonian Way, Gat. 269 DH151
Queen's Gate
Caledonian Wf. Rd. E14 163 ED77
Caletock Way SE10 164 EF78
Calfstock La. (South Darenth), Dart. 208 FL98
Calico Row SW11 160 DC83
York Pl.
Calidore Clo. SW2 181 DM86
Endymion Rd.
California La. (Bushey), Wat. 95 CD46
California Rd., N.Mal. 198 CQ97
Caliph Clo., Grav. 191 GM90
Callaby Ter. N1 142 DR65
Wakeham St.
Callaghan Clo. SE13 164 EE84
Glenton Rd.
Callan Gro., S.Ock. 149 FW73
Callander Rd. SE6 183 EB89
Callard Ave. N13 99 DP50
Callcott Rd. NW6 139 CZ66
Callcott St. W8 140 DA74
Hillgate Pl.
Callendar Rd. SW7 160 DD76
Calley Down Cres., Croy. 221 ED110
Callingham Clo. E14 143 DZ71
Wallwood St.
Callis Fm. Clo., Stai. 174 BL86
Bedfont Rd.
Callis Rd. E17 123 DZ58
Callisto Ct., Hem.H. 40 BM17
Jupiter Dr.
Callow Fld., Pur. 219 DN113
Callow Hill, Vir.W. 192 AW97
Callow St. SW3 160 DD79
Callowland Clo., Wat. 75 BV38
Calluna Ct., Wok. 227 AZ118
Heathside Rd.
Calmington Rd. SE5 162 DS78
Calmont Rd., Brom. 183 ED93
Calmore Clo., Horn. 128 FJ64
Calne Ave., Ilf. 103 EP53
Calonne Rd. SW19 179 CX91
Calshot Ave., Grays 170 FZ75
Calshot Rd., Houns. 154 BN82
Calshot St. N1 141 DM68
Calshot Way, Enf. 81 DP41
Calthorpe Gdns., Edg. 96 CL50
Jesmond Way
Calthorpe Gdns., Sutt. 200 DC104
Calthorpe St. WC1 274 C4
Calthorpe St. WC1 141 DM70
Calton Ave. SE21 182 DS86
Calton Ave., Hert. 31 DM08
Calton Rd., Barn. 80 DC44
Calverley Clo., Beck. 183 EB93
Calverley Cres., Dag. 126 FA61
Calverley Gdns., Har. 117 CK59
Calverley Gro. N19 121 DK60
Calverley Rd., Epsom 217 CU107
Calvert Ave. E2 275 N3
Calvert Ave. E2 142 DS69
Calvert Clo., Belv. 166 FA77
Calvert Clo., Sid. 186 EY93
Calvert Cres., Dor. 247 CH134
Calvert Rd.
Calvert Rd. SE10 164 EF78
Calvert Rd., Barn. 79 CX40
Calvert Rd., Dor. 247 CH134
Calvert Rd., Lthd. 245 BV128
Calvert St. NW1 140 DG67
Chalcot Rd.
Calverton SE5 162 DS79
Albany Rd.
Calverton Rd. E6 145 EN67
Calvert's Bldgs. SE1 279 K3
Calvin Clo., Orp. 206 EX97
Calvin St. E1 275 P5
Calvin St. E1 142 DT70
Calydon Rd. SE7 164 EH78
Calypso Way SE16 163 DZ77
Cam Grn., S.Ock. 149 FV72
Cam Rd. E15 143 ED67
Camac Rd., Twick. 177 CD88
Cambalt Rd. SW15 179 CX85
Camberley Ave. SW20 199 CV96
Camberley Ave., Enf. 82 DS42
Camberley Clo., Sutt. 199 CX104
Camberley Rd., Houns. 154 BN83
Cambert Way SE3 164 EH84
Camberwell Ch. St. SE5 162 DR81
Camberwell Glebe SE5 162 DS81
Camberwell Grn. SE5 162 DR81
Camberwell Gro. SE5 162 DR81
Camberwell New Rd. SE5 161 DN79
Camberwell Pas. SE5 162 DQ81
Camberwell Grn.
Camberwell Rd. SE5 162 DQ79
Camberwell Sta. Rd. SE5 162 DQ81
Cambeys Rd., Dag. 127 FB64
Camborne Ave. W13 157 CH75
Camborne Ave., Rom. 106 FK52
Camborne Dr., Hem.H. 40 BL16
Camborne Ms. W11 139 CY72
St. Marks Rd.
Camborne Rd. SW18 180 DA87
Camborne Rd., Croy. 202 DU101
Camborne Rd., Houns. 154 BN83
Camborne Rd., Mord. 199 CX99
Camborne Rd., Sid. 186 EW90
Camborne Rd., Sutt. 218 DA108
Camborne Rd., Well. 165 ET82
Camborne Way, Houns. 156 CA81
Camborne Way, Rom. 106 FL52
Cambourne Ave. N9 101 DX45
Cambray Rd. SW12 181 DJ88
Cambray Rd., Orp. 205 ET101
Cambria Clo., Houns. 156 CA84
Cambria Clo., Sid. 185 ER88
Cambria Ct., Felt. 175 BV87
Hounslow Rd.
Cambria Ct., Slou. 152 AW75
Turner Rd.
Cambria Cres., Grav. 191 GL91
Cambria Gdns., Stai. 174 BL87
Cambria Rd. SE5 162 DQ83
Cambria St. SW6 160 DB80
Cambrian Ave., Ilf. 125 ES57
Cambrian Clo. SE27 181 DP90
Cambrian Gro., Grav. 191 GG87
Cambrian Rd. E10 123 EA59
Cambrian Rd., Rich. 178 CM86
Cambrian Way, Hem.H. 40 BL17
Cambridge Ave. NW6 140 DA68
Cambridge Ave., Grnf. 117 CF64
Cambridge Ave., N.Mal. 198 CS96
Cambridge Ave., Rom. 128 FJ55
Cambridge Ave., Slou. 131 AM72
Cambridge Ave. (Burnham), Slou. 130 AH68
Cambridge Ave., Well. 165 ET84
Cambridge Barracks Rd. SE18 165 EM77
Cambridge Circ. WC2 273 N9
Cambridge Circ. WC2 141 DK72
Cambridge Clo. N22 99 DN53
Pellatt Gro.
Cambridge Clo. NW10 118 CQ62
Cambridge Clo. SW20 199 CV95
Cambridge Clo., Houns. 156 BY84
Cambridge Clo. (Cheshunt), Wal.Cr. 66 DW29
Cambridge Clo., West Dr. 154 BK79
Cambridge Clo., Wok. 226 AT118
Bingham Dr.
Cambridge Cotts., Rich. 158 CN79
Cambridge Cres. E2 142 DV68
Cambridge Cres., Tedd. 177 CG92
Cambridge Dr. SE12 184 EG85
Cambridge Dr., Pot.B. 63 CX31
Cambridge Dr., Ruis. 116 BX61
Cambridge Gdns. N10 98 DG53
Cambridge Gdns. N13 99 DN50
Cambridge Gdns. N17 100 DR52
Great Cambridge Rd.
Cambridge Gdns. N21 100 DR45
Cambridge Gdns. NW6 140 DA68
Cambridge Gdns. W10 139 CX72
Cambridge Gdns., Enf. 82 DU40
Cambridge Gdns., Grays 171 GG77
Cambridge Gdns., Kings.T. 198 CN96
Cambridge Gate NW1 273 J4
Cambridge Gate Ms. NW1 273 J4
Cambridge Grn. SE9 185 EP88
Cambridge Gro. SE20 202 DV95
Cambridge Gro. W6 159 CV77
Cambridge Gro. Rd., Kings.T. 198 CN97
Cambridge Heath Rd. E1 142 DV70
Cambridge Heath Rd. E2 142 DW70
Cambridge Mans. SW11 160 DF81
Cambridge Rd.
Cambridge Par., Enf. 82 DU39
Great Cambridge Rd.
Cambridge Pk. E11 124 EG59
Cambridge Pk., Twick. 177 CJ86
Cambridge Pk. Rd. E11 124 EF59
Cambridge Pl. W8 160 DB75
Cambridge Rd. E4 101 ED46
Cambridge Rd. E11 124 EF58
Cambridge Rd. NW6 140 DA69
Cambridge Rd. SE20 202 DV97
Cambridge Rd. SW11 160 DF81
Cambridge Rd. SW13 159 CT82
Cambridge Rd. SW20 199 CV95
Cambridge Rd. W7 157 CF75
Cambridge Rd., Ashf. 175 BQ94
Cambridge Rd., Bark. 145 EQ66
Cambridge Rd., Beac. 88 AJ53
Cambridge Rd., Brom. 184 EG94
Cambridge Rd., Cars. 218 DE107
Cambridge Rd., Hmptn. 176 BZ94
Cambridge Rd., Harl. 36 EW09
Cambridge Rd., Har. 116 CA57
Cambridge Rd., Houns. 156 BY84
Cambridge Rd., Ilf. 125 ES60
Cambridge Rd., Kings.T. 198 CN96
Cambridge Rd., Mitch. 201 DH97
Cambridge Rd., N.Mal. 198 CR98
Cambridge Rd., Rich. 158 CN80
Cambridge Rd., St.Alb. 43 CH21
Cambridge Rd., Sid. 185 ES91
Cambridge Rd., Sthl. 136 BZ74
Cambridge Rd., Tedd. 177 CF91
Cambridge Rd., Twick. 177 CK86
Cambridge Rd., Uxb. 134 BK65
Cambridge Rd., Walt. 195 BV100
Cambridge Rd., Wat. 76 BW42
Cambridge Rd., W.Mol. 196 BZ98
Cambridge Rd. Est., Kings.T. 198 CN96
Cambridge Rd. N. W4 158 CP78
Cambridge Rd. S. W4 158 CP78
Oxford Rd. S.
Cambridge Row SE18 165 EP78
Cambridge Sq. W2 272 B8
Cambridge Sq. W2 140 DE72
Cambridge St. SW1 277 J10
Cambridge St. SW1 161 DH77
Cambridge Ter. N13 99 DN50
Cambridge Ter. NW1 273 H3
Cambridge Ter., Berk. 38 AX19
Cambridge Ter. Ms. NW1 273 J3
Cambus Clo., Hayes 136 BY71
Cambus Rd. E16 144 EG71
Camdale Rd. SE18 165 ET80
Camden Ave., Felt. 176 BW89
Camden Ave., Hayes 136 BX73
Camden Clo., Chis. 205 EQ95
Camden Clo., Grav. 190 GC88
Camden Clo., Grays 171 GH77
Camden Est. SE15 162 DT81
Camden Gdns. NW1 141 DH66
Kentish Town Rd.
Camden Gdns., Sutt. 218 DB106
Camden Gdns., Th.Hth. 201 DP97
Camden Gro., Chis. 185 EP93
Camden High St. NW1 141 DH67
Camden Hill Rd. SE19 182 DS93
Camden La. N7 141 DK65
Camden Lock Pl. NW1 141 DH66
Chalk Fm. Rd.
Camden Ms. NW1 141 DJ66
Camden Pk. Rd. NW1 141 DK65
Camden Pk. Rd., Chis. 185 EM94
Camden Pas. N1 141 DP67
Camden Rd. E11 124 EH58
Camden Rd. E17 123 DZ58
Camden Rd. N7 121 DL63
Camden Rd. NW1 141 DJ66
Camden Rd., Bex. 186 EY88
Camden Rd., Cars. 218 DF105
Camden Rd., Grays 170 FZ76
Camden Rd., Sev. 257 FH122
Camden Rd., Sutt. 218 DA106
Camden Row SE3 164 EE82
Camden Sq. NW1 141 DK65
Camden Sq. SE15 162 DT81
Exeter Rd.
Camden St. NW1 141 DJ66
Camden Ter. NW1 141 DK65
North Vill.
Camden Wk. N1 141 DP67
Camden Way, Chis. 185 EM94
Camden Way, Th.Hth. 201 DP97
Camdenhurst St. E14 143 DY72
Camel Gro., Kings.T. 177 CK92
Camel Rd. E16 144 EK74
Camelford Wk. W11 139 CY72
Lancaster Rd.
Camellia Clo., Rom. 106 FL53
Columbine Way
Camellia Ct., Wdf.Grn. 102 EE52
Bridle Path
Camellia Pl., Twick. 176 CB87
Camellia St. SW8 161 DL80
Camelot Clo. SE28 165 ER75
Camelot Clo. SW19 180 DA91
Camelot Clo., West. 238 EJ116
Camelot St. SE15 162 DV80
Bird in Bush Rd.
Camera Pl. SW10 160 DD79
Cameron Clo. N18 100 DV49
Cameron Clo. N20 98 DE47
Myddelton Pk.
Cameron Clo., Bex. 187 FD90
Cameron Clo., Brwd. 108 FX49
Cameron Ct., Ware 33 DX05
Crib St.
Cameron Dr., Wal.Cr. 67 DX34
Cameron Pl. E1 142 DV72
Varden St.
Cameron Rd. SE6 183 DZ89
Cameron Rd., Brom. 204 EG98
Cameron Rd., Chesh. 54 AQ30
Cameron Rd., Croy. 201 DP100
Cameron Rd., Ilf. 125 ES60
Cameron Sq., Mitch. 200 DE95
Camerton Clo. E8 142 DT65
Buttermere Wk.
Camfield, Welw.G.C. 29 CZ13
Camgate Est., Stai. 174 BM86
Camilla Clo., Lthd. 246 CB125
Camilla Clo., Sun. 175 BS93
Camilla Dr., Dor. 247 CG130
Camilla Rd. SE16 162 DV77
Camille Clo. SE25 202 DU97
Camlan Rd., Brom. 184 EF91
Camlet St. E2 275 P4
Camlet St. E2 142 DT70
Camlet Way, Barn. 80 DA40
Camlet Way, St.Alb. 42 CB19
Camley St. NW1 141 DK66
Camm Ave., Wind. 151 AL83
Camm Gdns., Kings.T. 198 CM96
Church Rd.
Camm Gdns., T.Ditt. 197 CE101
Camomile Ave., Mitch. 200 DF95
Camomile St. EC3 275 M8
Camomile St. EC3 142 DS72
Camp End Rd., Wey. 213 BR110
Camp Rd. SW19 179 CV92
Camp Rd., Cat. 237 DY120
Camp Rd., Ger.Cr. 112 AW58
Camp Rd., St.Alb. 43 CF20
Camp Vw. SW19 179 CV92
Camp Vw. Rd., St.Alb. 43 CH21
Campana Rd. SW6 160 DA81
Campbell Ave., Ilf. 125 EP56
Campbell Ave., Wok. 227 AZ121
Campbell Clo. SE18 165 EN81
Moordown
Campbell Clo. SW16 181 DK92
Campbell Clo. (Havering-atte-Bower), Rom. 105 FE51
Campbell Clo., Ruis. 115 BU58
Campbell Clo., Twick. 177 CD89
Campbell Ct. N17 100 DT53
Campbell Cft., Edg. 96 CN50
Campbell Dr., Beac. 88 AJ50
Campbell Gordon Way NW2 119 CV63
Campbell Rd. E3 143 EA69
Campbell Rd. E6 144 EL67
Campbell Rd. E15 124 EF63
Trevelyan Rd.
Campbell Rd. E17 123 DZ56
Campbell Rd. N17 100 DT53
Campbell Rd. W7 137 CE73
Campbell Rd., Cat. 236 DR121
Campbell Rd., Croy. 201 DP101
Campbell Rd., E.Mol. 197 CF97
Hampton Ct. Rd.
Campbell Rd., Grav. 191 GF88
Campbell Rd., Twick. 177 CD88
Campbell Rd., Wey. 212 BN108
Campbell Wk. N1 141 DL67
Outram Pl.
Campbells Clo., Harl. 52 EV16
Carters Mead
Campdale Rd. N7 121 DK62
Campden Cres., Dag. 126 EV63
Campden Cres., Wem. 117 CH62
Campden Gro. W8 160 DA75
Campden Hill W8 160 DA75
Campden Hill Gdns. W8 140 DA74
Campden Hill Gate W8 160 DA75
Duchess of Bedford's Wk.
Campden Hill Pl. W11 139 CZ74
Holland Pk. Ave.
Campden Hill Rd. W8 140 DA74
Campden Hill Sq. W8 139 CZ74
Campden Ho. Clo. W8 160 DA75
Hornton St.
Campden Rd., S.Croy. 220 DS106
Campden Rd., Uxb. 114 BM62
Campden St. W8 140 DA74
Campen Clo. SW19 179 CY89
Queensmere Rd.
Camperdown St. E1 142 DT72
Leman St.
Campfield Rd. SE9 184 EK87
Campfield Rd., Hert. 31 DP09
Campfield Rd., St.Alb. 43 CG21
Camphill Ct., W.Byf. 212 BG112
Camphill Ind. Est., W.Byf. 212 BH111
Camphill Rd., W.Byf. 212 BG113
Campine Clo. (Cheshunt), Wal.Cr. 67 DX28
Welsummer Way
Campion Clo. E6 145 EM73
Campion Clo., Croy. 220 DS105
Campion Clo., Grav. 190 GE91
Campion Clo., Har. 118 CM58
Campion Clo. (Denham), Uxb. 114 BG62
Lindsey Rd.
Campion Clo. (Hillingdon), Uxb. 134 BM71
Campion Clo., Wat. 59 BU33
Campion Ct., Grays 170 GD79
Campion Dr., Tad. 233 CV120
Campion Gdns., Wdf.Grn. 102 EG50
Campion Pl. SE28 146 EV74
Campion Rd. SW15 159 CW84
Campion Rd., Hem.H. 39 BE21
Campion Rd., Islw. 157 CF81
Campion Ter. NW2 119 CX63
Campions, Epp. 70 EU28
Campions, Loug. 85 EN38
Campions, The, Borwd. 78 CM38
Campions Clo., Borwd. 78 CP37
Campions Ct., Berk. 38 AU19
Cample La., S.Ock. 149 FU73
Camplin Rd., Har. 118 CL57
Camplin St. SE14 163 DX80
Campsbourne, The N8 121 DL56
Rectory Gdns.
Campsbourne Rd. N8 121 DL55
Campsey Gdns., Dag. 146 EV66
Campsey Rd., Dag. 146 EV66
Campsfield Rd. N8 121 DL55
Campsbourne Rd.
Campshill Pl. SE13 183 EC85
Campshill Rd.
Campshill Rd. SE13 183 EC85
Campus, The, Welw.G.C. 29 CX08
Campus Rd. E17 123 DZ58
Camrose Ave., Edg. 96 CM54
Camrose Ave., Erith 167 FB79
Camrose Ave., Felt. 175 BV91

Camrose Clo., Croy. 203 DY101
Camrose Clo., Mord. 200 DA98
Camrose St. SE2 166 EU78
Can Hatch, Tad. 233 CY118
Canada Ave. N18 100 DQ51
Canada Ave., Red. 266 DG138
Canada Cres. W3 138 CQ70
Canada Dr., Red. 266 DG138
Canada Est. SE16 162 DW76
Canada Fm. Rd. (South Darenth), Dart. 209 FU98
Canada Fm. Rd., Long. 209 FV99
Canada Gdns. SE13 183 EC85
Canada La., Brox. 67 DY25
Great Cambridge Rd.
Canada Rd. W3 138 CQ71
Canada Rd., Cob. 214 BW113
Canada Rd., Erith 167 FH80
Canada Rd., Slou. 152 AV75
Canada Rd., W.Byf. 212 BK111
Canada Sq. E14 143 EB74
Canada St. SE16 163 DX75
Canada Way W12 139 CV73
Canada Yd. S. SE16 163 DX76
Canadas, The, Brox. 67 DY25
Canadian Ave. SE6 183 EB88
Canadian Memorial Ave., Egh. 192 AS96
Canal App. SE8 163 DY78
Canal Basin, Grav. 191 GK86
Canal Clo. E1 143 DY70
Canal Clo. W10 139 CX70
Canal Gro. SE15 162 DU79
Canal Head SE15 162 DU81
Peckham High St.
Canal Path E2 142 DT67
Canal Rd. E3 143 DY70
Canal Rd., Grav. 191 GJ86
Canal St. SE5 162 DR79
Canal Wk. N1 142 DR67
Canal Wk. SE26 182 DW92
Canal Wk., Croy. 202 DS100
Canal Way NW1 140 DG67
Regents Pk. Rd.
Canal Way NW10 138 CR68
Canal Way W10 139 CX70
Canal Way, Wem. 138 CM67
Canal Way Wk. W10 139 CY70
Kensal Rd.
Canal Wf., Slou. 153 BA75
Canary Wf. E14 143 EA74
Canberra Clo. NW4 119 CU55
Canberra Clo., Dag. 147 FD66
Canberra Clo., Horn. 128 FJ63
Canberra Clo., St.Alb. 43 CF16
Canberra Cres., Dag. 147 FD66
Canberra Dr., Nthlt. 136 BW69
Canberra Rd. E6 145 EM67
Barking Rd.
Canberra Rd. SE7 164 EJ79
Canberra Rd. W13 137 CG74
Canberra Rd., Bexh. 166 EX79
Canberra Rd., Houns. 154 BN83
Canberra Sq., Til. 171 GG82
Canbury Ave., Kings.T. 198 CM95
Canbury Ms. SE26 182 DU90
Wells Pk. Rd.
Canbury Pk. Rd., Kings.T. 198 CL95
Canbury Pas., Kings.T. 197 CK95
Canbury Path, Orp. 206 EU97
Cancell Rd. SW9 161 DN81
Candahar Rd. SW11 160 DE82
Cander Way, S.Ock. 149 FV73
Candlefield Clo., Hem.H. 40 BN23
Candlefield Rd.
Candlefield Rd., Hem.H. 40 BN23
Candlefield Wk., Hem.H. 40 BN23
Candlefield Rd.
Candlemas La., Beac. 89 AL53
Candlemas Mead, Beac. 89 AL53
Candler St. N15 122 DR58
Candover Clo., West Dr. 154 BK80
Candover Rd., Horn. 127 FH60
Candover St. W1 273 K7
Candy Cft., Lthd. 246 CB125
Candy St. E3 143 DZ67
Cane Clo., Wall. 219 DL108
Kingsford Ave.
Cane Hill, Rom. 106 FK54
Bennison Dr.
Caneland Ct., Wal.Abb. 68 EF34
Canes La., Epp. 52 FA22
Canes La., Harl. 52 EX21
Canewdan Clo., Wok. 226 AY119
Guildford Rd.
Caney Ms. NW2 119 CX61
Claremont Rd.
Canfield Dr., Ruis. 115 BV64
Canfield Gdns. NW6 140 DB66
Canfield Pl. NW6 140 DC65
Canfield Gdns.
Canfield Rd., Rain. 147 FF67
Canfield Rd., Wdf.Grn. 102 EL52
Canford Ave., Nthlt. 136 BY67
Canford Clo., Enf. 81 DN40
Canford Dr., Add. 194 BH103
Canford Gdns., N.Mal. 198 CS100
Canford Pl., Tedd. 177 CH93
Canford Rd. SW11 180 DG85
Cangels Clo., Hem.H. 39 BF22
Canham Rd. SE25 202 DS97
Canham Rd. W3 158 CS75
Canmore Gdns. SW16 181 DJ94
Cann Hall Rd. E11 124 EE63
Canning Cres. N22 99 DM53
Canning Cross SE5 162 DS82
Canning Pas. W8 160 DC75
Victoria Rd.
Canning Pl. W8 160 DC76
Canning Pl. Ms. W8 160 DC76
Canning Pl.
Canning Rd. E15 144 EE68
Canning Rd. E17 123 DY56
Canning Rd. N5 121 DP62
Canning Rd., Croy. 202 DT103
Canning Rd., Har. 117 CE55
Cannington Rd., Dag. 146 EW65
Cannizaro Rd. SW19 179 CW92
Cannon Clo. SW20 199 CW97
Cannon Clo., Hmptn. 176 CB93
Hanworth Rd.
Cannon Cres., Wok. 210 AS111
Cannon Dr. E14 143 EA73
Cannon Gro., Lthd. 231 CE122
Cannon Hill N14 99 DK48
Cannon Hill NW6 120 DA64
Cannon Hill Clo., Maid. 150 AC77
Cannon Hill La. SW20 199 CY97
Cannon La. NW3 120 DD62
Cannon La., Pnr. 116 BY57
Cannon Ms., Wal.Abb. 67 EB33
Cannon Mill Ave., Chesh. 54 AR33
Cannon Pl. NW3 120 DC62
Cannon Pl. SE7 164 EL78
Cannon Rd. N14 99 DL48
Cannon Rd., Bexh. 166 EY81
Cannon Rd., Wat. 76 BW43
Cannon St. EC4 275 H9
Cannon St. EC4 142 DQ72
Cannon St., St.Alb. 43 CD19
Cannon St. Rd. E1 142 DV72
Cannon Wk., Grav. 191 GJ87
Cannon Way, Lthd. 231 CE121
Cannon Way, W.Mol. 196 CA98
Cannonbury Ave., Pnr. 116 BX58
Cannons Meadow, Welw. 30 DE05
Cannonside, Lthd. 231 CE122
Canon Ave., Rom. 126 EW57
Canon Beck Rd. SE16 162 DW75
Canon Hill, Couls. 235 DN118
Canon Mohan Clo. N14 81 DH44
Farm La.
Canon Rd., Brom. 204 EJ97
Canon Row SW1 277 P4
Canon Row SW1 161 DL75
Canon St. N1 142 DQ67
Canon Trd. Est., The, Wem. 118 CP63
Canonbie Rd. SE23 182 DW87
Canonbury Cres. N1 142 DQ66
Canonbury Gro. N1 142 DQ66
Canonbury La. N1 141 DP66
Canonbury Pk. N. N1 142 DQ65
Canonbury Pk. S. N1 142 DQ65
Canonbury Pl. N1 141 DP65
Canonbury Rd. N1 141 DP65
Canonbury Rd., Enf. 82 DS39
Canonbury Sq. N1 141 DP66
Canonbury St. N1 142 DQ66
Canonbury Vill. N1 141 DP66
Canonbury Yd. N1 142 DQ67
New N. Rd.
Canons Brook, Harl. 51 EN15
Canons Clo. N2 120 DD59
Canons Clo., Edg. 96 CM51
Canons Clo., Rad. 77 CH35
Canons Clo., Reig. 249 CZ133
Canons Cor., Edg. 96 CL49
Canons Dr., Edg. 96 CL51
Canons Gate, Harl. 35 EN13
Canons Gate, Wal.Cr. 67 DZ26
Thomas Rochford Way
Canons Hatch, Tad. 233 CY118
Canon's Hill, Couls. 235 DN118
Canons La., Tad. 233 CY118
Canons Rd., Ware 32 DW05
Canons Wk., Croy. 203 DX104
Canonsleigh Rd., Dag. 146 EV66
Canopus Way, Nthwd. 93 BU49
Canopus Way, Stai. 174 BL87
Canrobert St. E2 142 DV69
Cantelowes Rd. NW1 141 DK65
Canterbury Ave., Ilf. 124 EL59
Canterbury Ave., Sid. 186 EW89
Canterbury Ave., Slou. 131 AQ70
Canterbury Ave., Upmin. 129 FT60
Canterbury Clo. E6 145 EM72
Harper Rd.
Canterbury Clo., Amer. 55 AS39
Canterbury Clo., Beck. 203 EB95
Canterbury Clo., Chig. 103 ET48
Canterbury Clo., Dart. 188 FN87
Canterbury Clo., Grnf. 136 CB72
Canterbury Clo., Nthwd. 93 BT51
Canterbury Cres. SW9 161 DN83
Canterbury Gro. SE27 181 DN91
Canterbury Par., S.Ock. 149 FW69
Canterbury Pl. SE17 278 G9
Canterbury Pl. SE17 161 DP77
Canterbury Rd. E10 123 EC59
Canterbury Rd. NW6 139 CZ68
Canterbury Rd., Borwd. 78 CN40
Canterbury Rd., Croy. 201 DN101
Canterbury Rd., Felt. 176 BY90
Canterbury Rd., Grav. 191 GJ89
Canterbury Rd., Guil. 242 AT132
Canterbury Rd., Har. 116 CB57
Canterbury Rd., Mord. 200 DB101
Canterbury Rd., Wat. 75 BV40
Canterbury Ter. NW6 140 DA68
Canterbury Way, Brwd. 107 FW51
Canterbury Way, Grays 169 FS78
Canterbury Way, Rick. 75 BQ41
Cantley Gdns. SE19 202 DT95
Cantley Gdns., Ilf. 125 EQ58
Cantley Rd. W7 157 CG76
Canton St. E14 143 EA72
Cantrell Rd. E3 143 DZ70
Cantwell Rd. SE18 165 EP80
Canute Gdns. SE16 163 DX77
Canvey St. SE1 278 G2
Cape Clo., Bark. 145 EQ65
North St.
Cape Rd. N17 122 DU55
High Cross Rd.
Cape Rd., St.Alb. 43 CH20
Cape Yd. E1 142 DU74
Asher Way
Capel Ave., Wall. 219 DM106
Capel Clo. N20 98 DC48
Capel Clo., Brom. 205 EM102
Capel Ct. EC2 275 L9
Capel Ct. SE20 202 DW95
Melvin Rd.
Capel Gdns., Ilf. 125 ET63
Capel Gdns., Pnr. 116 BZ56
Capel Pl., Dart. 188 FJ91
Capel Pt. E7 124 EH63
Capel Rd. E7 124 EH63
Capel Rd. E12 124 EK63
Capel Rd., Barn. 80 DE44
Capel Rd., Enf. 82 DV36
Capel Rd., Wat. 76 BY44
Capel Vere Wk., Wat. 75 BS39
Capell Ave., Rick. 73 BC43
Capell Rd., Rick. 73 BD43
Capell Way, Rick. 73 BD43
Capella Rd., Nthwd. 93 BT49
Capener's Clo. SW1 276 F5
Capern Rd. SW18 180 DC88
Cargill Rd.
Capital Business Cen., Wem. 137 CK67
Capital Interchange Way, Brent. 158 CN78
Capital Pl., Croy. 219 DM106
Stafford Rd.
Capitol Ind. Est. NW9 118 CQ55
Capitol Way NW9 118 CQ55
Capland St. NW8 272 A4
Capland St. NW8 140 DD70
Caple Rd. NW10 139 CT68
Capon Clo., Brwd. 108 FV46
Caponfield, Welw.G.C. 30 DB11
Cappell La., Ware 33 EC09
Capper St. WC1 273 L5
Capper St. WC1 141 DJ70
Caprea Clo., Hayes 136 BX71
Triandra Way
Capri Rd., Croy. 202 DT102
Capstan Clo., Rom. 126 EV58
Capstan Ct., Dart. 168 FQ84
Capstan Ride, Enf. 81 DN40
Crofton Way
Capstan Rd. SE8 163 DZ77
Capstan Sq. E14 163 EC75
Capstan Way SE16 143 DY74
Capstan's Wf., Wok. 226 AT118
Capstone Rd., Brom. 184 EF91
Captain Cook Clo., Ch.St.G. 90 AV49
Captains Clo., Chesh. 54 AN27
Captains Wk., Berk. 38 AX20
Capthorne Ave., Har. 116 BY60
Capuchin Clo., Stan. 95 CH51
Capulet Ms. E16 144 EE72
Silvertown Way
Capworth St. E10 123 EA60
Caractacus Cottage Vw., Wat. 93 BU45
Caractacus Grn., Wat. 75 BT44
Caradoc Clo. W2 140 DA72
Caradoc St. SE10 164 EE78
Caradon Clo. E11 124 EE61
Brockway Clo.
Caradon Clo., Wok. 226 AV118
Caradon Way N15 122 DR56
Caravan La., Rick. 92 BL45
Caravel Clo. E14 163 EA76
Tiller Rd.
Caravel Clo., Grays 170 FZ76
Caravel Ms. SE8 163 EA79
Watergate St.
Caravelle Gdns., Nthlt. 136 BX69
Javelin Way
Caraway Clo. E13 144 EH71
Caraway Pl., Guil. 242 AU129
Caraway Pl., Wall. 201 DH104
Carberry Rd. SE19 182 DS93
Carbery Ave. W3 158 CM75
Carbis Clo. E4 101 ED46
Carbis Rd. E14 143 DZ72
Carbone Hill, Hert. 65 DJ27
Carbone Hill (Cuffley), Pot.B. 65 DJ27
Carbuncle Pas. Way N17 100 DU54
Carburton St. W1 273 J6
Carburton St. W1 141 DH71
Carbury Clo., Horn. 148 FJ65
Cardale St. E14 163 EC76
Plevna St.
Cardamom Clo., Guil. 242 AU130
Carde Clo., Hert. 31 DM08
Carden Rd. SE15 162 DV83
Cardiff Rd. W7 157 CG76
Cardiff Rd., Enf. 82 DV42
Cardiff Rd., Wat. 75 BV44
Cardiff St. SE18 165 ES80
Cardiff Way, Abb.L. 59 BU32
Cardigan Clo., Slou. 131 AM73
Cardigan Clo., Wok. 226 AS118
Bingham Dr.
Cardigan Gdns., Ilf. 126 EU61
Cardigan Rd. E3 143 DZ68
Cardigan Rd. SW13 159 CU82
Cardigan Rd. SW19 180 DC93
Haydons Rd.
Cardigan Rd., Rich. 178 CL86
Cardigan St. SE11 278 D10
Cardigan St. SE11 161 DN78
Cardigan Wk. N1 142 DQ66
Ashby Gro.
Cardinal Ave., Borwd. 78 CP41
Cardinal Ave., Kings.T. 178 CL92
Cardinal Ave., Mord. 199 CY100
Cardinal Bourne St. SE1 279 L7
Cardinal Clo., Chis. 205 ER95
Cardinal Clo., Mord. 199 CY100
Cardinal Clo. (Cheshunt), Wal.Cr. 66 DT26
Adamsfield
Cardinal Clo., Wor.Pk. 217 CU105
Cardinal Cres., N.Mal. 198 CQ96
Cardinal Dr., Ilf. 103 EQ51
Cardinal Dr., Walt. 196 BX102
Cardinal Gro., St.Alb. 42 CB22
Cardinal Pl. SW15 159 CX84
Cardinal Rd., Felt. 175 BV88
Cardinal Rd., Ruis. 116 BX60
Cardinal Way, Har. 117 CE55
Wolseley Rd.
Cardinal Way, Rain. 148 FK68
Cardinals Wk., Hmptn. 176 CC94
Cardinals Wk., Maid. 130 AJ72
Cardinals Wk., Sun. 175 BS93
Cardinals Way N19 121 DK60
Cardine Ms. SE15 162 DV80
Cardingham, Wok. 226 AU117
Cardington Sq., Houns. 156 BX84
Cardington St. NW1 273 L2
Cardington St. NW1 141 DJ69
Cardozo Rd. N7 121 DL64
Cardrew Ave. N12 98 DD50
Cardrew Clo. N12 98 DD50
Cardross St. W6 159 CV76
Cardwell Rd. N7 121 DL63
Cardwell Rd. SE18 165 EM77
Cardwells Keep, Guil. 242 AU131
Cardy Rd., Hem.H. 40 BH20
Carew Clo. N7 121 DM61
Carew Clo., Couls. 235 DP119
Carew Rd. N17 100 DU54
Carew Rd. W13 157 CJ75
Carew Rd., Ashf. 175 BQ93
Carew Rd., Mitch. 200 DG96
Carew Rd., Nthwd. 93 BS51
Carew Rd., Th.Hth. 201 DP97
Carew Rd., Wall. 219 DJ107
Carew St. SE5 162 DQ82
Carey Clo., Wind. 151 AP83
Carey Ct., Bexh. 187 FB85
Carey Gdns. SW8 161 DJ81
Carey La. EC2 275 H8
Carey Pl. SW1 277 M9
Carey Rd., Dag. 126 EY63
Carey St. WC2 274 C9
Carey St. WC2 141 DM72
Carey Way, Wem. 118 CQ63
Fourth Way
Careys Cft., Berk. 38 AU16
Careys Wd., Horl. 269 DP148
Carfax Pl. SW4 161 DK84
Holwood Pl.
Carfax Rd., Hayes 155 BT78
Carfax Rd., Horn. 127 FF63
Carfree Clo. N1 141 DN66
Bewdley St.
Cargill Rd. SW18 180 DB88
Cargo Forecourt Rd., Gat. 268 DD152
Cargo Rd., Gat. 268 DD152
Cargreen Pl. SE25 202 DT98
Cargreen Rd.
Cargreen Rd. SE25 202 DT98
Carholme Rd. SE23 183 DZ88
Carisbrook Ave., Wat. 76 BX39
Carisbrook Clo., Stan. 95 CK54
Carisbrook Rd., St.Alb. 60 CB26
Carisbrooke Ave., Bex. 186 EX88
Carisbrooke Clo., Enf. 82 DT39
Carisbrooke Clo., Horn. 128 FN60
Carisbrooke Ct., Slou. 132 AT73
Carisbrooke Gdns. SE15 162 DT80
Commercial Way
Carisbrooke Rd. E17 123 DY56
Carisbrooke Rd., Brwd. 108 FV44
Carisbrooke Rd., Brom. 204 EJ98
Carisbrooke Rd., Mitch. 201 DK98
Carker's La. NW5 121 DH64
Carl Ekman Ho., Grav. 190 GD87
Carlbury Clo., St.Alb. 43 CH21
Carleton Ave., Wall. 219 DK108
Carleton Clo., Esher 197 CD102
Carleton Pl. (Horton Kirby), Dart. 208 FQ98
Carleton Rd. N7 121 DK64
Carleton Rd., Dart. 188 FN87
Carleton Rd. (Cheshunt), Wal.Cr. 67 DX27
Carleton Vill. NW5 121 DJ64
Leighton Gro.
Carlile Clo. E3 143 DZ68
Carlina Gdns., Wdf.Grn. 102 EH50
Carlingford Gdns., Mitch. 180 DF94
Carlingford Rd. N15 121 DP55
Carlingford Rd. NW3 120 DD63
Carlingford Rd., Mord. 199 CX100
Carlisle Ave. EC3 275 P9
Carlisle Ave. W3 138 CS72
Carlisle Ave., St.Alb. 43 CD18
Carlisle Clo., Kings.T. 198 CN95
Carlisle Gdns., Har. 117 CK59
Carlisle Gdns., Ilf. 124 EL58
Carlisle La. SE1 278 C7
Carlisle La. SE1 161 DM76
Carlisle Ms. NW8 272 A6
Carlisle Ms. NW8 140 DD71
Carlisle Pl. N11 99 DH49
Carlisle Pl. SW1 277 K7
Carlisle Pl. SW1 161 DJ76
Carlisle Rd. E10 123 EA60
Carlisle Rd. N4 121 DN59
Carlisle Rd. NW6 139 CY67
Carlisle Rd. NW9 118 CQ55
Carlisle Rd., Dart. 188 FN86
Carlisle Rd., Hmptn. 176 CB94
Carlisle Rd., Rom. 127 FF57
Carlisle Rd., Slou. 131 AR73
Carlisle Rd., Sutt. 217 CZ106
Carlisle St. W1 273 M9
Carlisle Wk. E8 142 DT65
Laurel St.
Carlisle Way SW17 180 DG92
Carlos Pl. W1 272 G10
Carlos Pl. W1 140 DG73
Carlow St. NW1 141 DJ68
Arlington Rd.
Carlton Ave. N14 81 DK43
Carlton Ave., Felt. 176 BW86
Carlton Ave., Green. 189 FS86
Carlton Ave., Har. 117 CH57
Carlton Ave., Hayes 155 BS77
Carlton Ave., S.Croy. 220 DS108
Carlton Ave. E., Wem. 117 CK61
Carlton Ave. W., Wem. 117 CH61
Carlton Clo. NW3 120 DA61
Carlton Clo., Borwd. 78 CR42
Carlton Clo., Chess. 215 CK107
Carlton Clo., Edg. 96 CN50
Carlton Clo., Upmin. 128 FP61
Carlton Clo., Wok. 211 AZ114
Carlton Ct. SW9 161 DP81
Carlton Ct., Ilf. 125 ER55
Carlton Ct., Uxb. 134 BK71
Carlton Cres., Sutt. 217 CY105
Carlton Dr. SW15 179 CX85
Carlton Dr., Ilf. 125 ER55
Carlton Gdns. SW1 277 M3
Carlton Gdns. SW1 141 DK74
Carlton Gdns. W5 137 CJ72
Carlton Grn., Red. 250 DE131
Carlton Gro. SE15 162 DV81
Carlton Hill NW8 140 DB68
Carlton Ho. Ter. SW1 277 M3
Carlton Ho. Ter. SW1 141 DK74
Carlton Par., Orp. 206 EV101
Carlton Par., Sev. 257 FJ122
St. John's Hill
Carlton Pk. Ave. SW20 199 CX96
Carlton Pl., Felt. 175 BT87
Carlton Pl., Nthwd. 93 BP50
Carlton Rd. E11 124 EF60
Carlton Rd. E12 124 EK63
Carlton Rd. E17 101 DY53
Carlton Rd. N4 121 DN59
Carlton Rd. N11 98 DG50
Carlton Rd. SW14 158 CQ83
Carlton Rd. W4 158 CR75
Carlton Rd. W5 137 CJ73
Carlton Rd., Erith 167 FB79
Carlton Rd., Grays 170 GE75
Carlton Rd., N.Mal. 198 CS96
Carlton Rd., Red. 250 DE131
Carlton Rd., Reig. 250 DD132
Carlton Rd., Rom. 127 FF57
Carlton Rd., Sid. 185 ET92
Carlton Rd., Slou. 132 AV73
Carlton Rd., S.Croy. 220 DR107
Carlton Rd., Sun. 175 BT94
Carlton Rd., Walt. 195 BV101
Carlton Rd., Well. 166 EV83
Carlton Rd., Wok. 211 BA114
Carlton Sq. E1 143 DX70
Argyle Rd.
Carlton St. SW1 277 M1
Carlton Ter. E11 124 EH57
Carlton Ter. N18 100 DR48
Carlton Ter. SE26 182 DW90
Carlton Twr. Pl. SW1 276 E6
Carlton Twr. Pl. SW1 160 DF76
Carlton Tye, Horl. 269 DJ147
Carlton Vale NW6 140 DA68
Carlton Vill. SW15 179 CW85
St. John's Ave.
Carlwell St. SW17 180 DE92
Carlyle Ave., Brom. 204 EK97
Carlyle Ave., Sthl. 136 BZ73
Carlyle Clo. N2 120 DC58
Carlyle Clo. NW10 138 CR67
Carlyle Clo., W.Mol. 196 CB96
Carlyle Gdns., Sthl. 136 BZ73
Carlyle Pl. SW15 159 CX84
Carlyle Rd. E12 124 EL63
Carlyle Rd. SE28 146 EV73
Carlyle Rd. W5 157 CJ77
Carlyle Rd., Croy. 202 DU103
Carlyle Rd., Stai. 173 BF94
Carlyle Sq. SW3 160 DD78
Carlyon Ave., Har. 116 BZ63
Carlyon Clo., Wem. 138 CL67
Carlyon Rd., Hayes 136 BW71
Carlyon Rd., Wem. 138 CL68
Carmalt Gdns. SW15 159 CW84
Carmalt Gdns., Walt. 214 BW106
Carmarthen Gdn. NW9 118 CS58
Snowdon Dr.
Carmarthen Rd., Slou. 132 AS73
Carmel Clo., Wok. 226 AY118
Carmel Ct. W8 160 DB75
Holland St.
Carmel Ct., Wem. 118 CP61
Carmelite Clo., Har. 94 CC53
Carmelite Rd., Har. 94 CC53
Carmelite St. EC4 274 E10
Carmelite St. EC4 141 DN73
Carmelite Wk., Har. 94 CC53
Carmelite Way, Har. 94 CC54
Hampden Rd.
Carmen Ct., Borwd. 78 CM38
Belford Rd.
Carmen St. E14 143 EB72
Carmichael Clo. SW11 160 DD83
Darien Rd.
Carmichael Clo., Ruis. 115 BU63
Carmichael Ms. SW18 180 DD86
Heathfield Rd.
Carmichael Rd. SE25 202 DU98
Carminia Rd. SW17 181 DH89
Carnaby Rd., Brox. 49 DY20
Carnaby St. W1 273 K9
Carnaby St. W1 141 DJ72
Carnac St. SE27 182 DR91
Carnach Grn., S.Ock. 149 FV73
Carnanton Rd. E17 101 ED53
Carnarvon Ave., Enf. 82 DT41
Carnarvon Dr., Hayes 155 BQ77
Carnarvon Rd. E10 123 EC58
Carnarvon Rd. E15 144 EF65
Carnarvon Rd. E18 102 EF54
Carnarvon Rd., Barn. 79 CY41
Carnation St. SE2 166 EV78
Carnbrook Rd. SE3 164 EK83
Carnecke Gdns. SE9 184 EL85
Carnegie Clo., Surb. 198 CM103
Fullers Ave.
Carnegie Pl. SW19 179 CX90
Carnegie Rd., St.Alb. 43 CD16
Carnegie St. N1 141 DM67
Carnforth Clo., Epsom 216 CP107
Carnforth Gdns., Horn. 127 FG64
Carnforth Rd. SW16 181 DK94
Carnie Lo. SW17 181 DH90
Manville Rd.
Carnoustie Dr. N1 141 DM66
Carnwath Rd. SW6 160 DA83
Caro La., Hem.H. 40 BN22
Carol St. NW1 141 DJ67
Carolina Clo. E15 124 EE64
Carolina Rd., Th.Hth. 201 DP96
Caroline Clo. N10 99 DH54
Alexandra Pk. Rd.
Caroline Clo. SW16 181 DM91
Caroline Clo. W2 140 DB73
Bayswater Rd.
Caroline Clo., Croy. 220 DS105
Brownlow Rd.
Caroline Clo., Islw. 157 CE80
Caroline Clo., West Dr. 154 BK75
Caroline Ct., Ashf. 175 BP93
Caroline Ct., Stan. 95 CG51
The Chase
Caroline Gdns. SE15 162 DV80
Caroline Pl. SW11 160 DG82
Caroline Pl. W2 140 DB73
Caroline Pl., Hayes 155 BS80
Caroline Pl., Wat. 76 BY44
Capel Rd.
Caroline Pl. Ms. W2 140 DB73
Orme La.
Caroline Rd. SW19 179 CZ94
Caroline St. E1 143 DX72
Caroline Ter. SW1 276 F9
Caroline Ter. SW1 160 DG77
Caroline Wk. W6 159 CY79
Laundry Rd.
Carolyn Clo., Wok. 226 AT119
Carolyn Dr., Orp. 206 EU104
Caroon Dr., Rick. 74 BH36
Carpenders Ave., Wat. 94 BY48
Carpenter Clo., Epsom 217 CT109
West St.
Carpenter Gdns. N21 99 DP47
Carpenter St. W1 277 H1

Carpenter Way, Pot.B. 64 DC33
Carpenters Arms La., Epp. 70 EV25
Carpenters Ct., Twick. 177 CE89
Carpenters Path, Brwd. 109 GD43
Carpenters Pl. SW4 161 DK84
Carpenters Rd. E15 143 EA65
Carpenters Rd., Enf. 82 DW36
Carpenters Wd. Dr., Rick. 73 BB42
Carr Gro. SE18 164 EL77
Carr Rd. E17 101 DZ54
Carr Rd., Nthlt. 136 CA65
Carr St. E14 143 DY71
Carrara Wk. SW9 161 DN84
Somerleyton Rd.
Carriage Dr. E. SW11 160 DG80
Carriage Dr. N. SW11 160 DF80
Carriage Dr. S. SW11 160 DF81
Carriage Dr. W. SW11 160 DF80
Carriageway, The, Sev. 240 EW124
Carrick Clo., Islw. 157 CG83
Carrick Dr., Ilf. 103 EQ53
Carrick Dr., Sev. 257 FH123
Carrick Gdns. N17 100 DS52
Flexmere Rd.
Carrick Gate, Esher 196 CC104
Carrick Ms. SE8 163 EA79
Watergate St.
Carriden Ct., Hert. 31 DM07
The Ridgeway
Carrill Way, Belv. 166 EX77
Carrington Ave., Borwd. 78 CP43
Carrington Ave., Houns. 176 CB85
Carrington Clo., Barn. 79 CU43
Carrington Clo., Borwd. 78 CQ43
Carrington Clo., Croy. 203 DY101
Carrington Clo., Kings.T. 178 CQ92
Carrington Clo., Red. 250 DF133
Carrington Gdns. E7 124 EH63
Woodford Rd.
Carrington Pl., Esher 214 CB106
Carrington Rd., Dart. 188 FM86
Carrington Rd., Rich. 158 CN84
Carrington Rd., Slou. 132 AS73
Carrington Sq., Har. 94 CC52
Carrington St. W1 277 H3
Carrol Clo. NW5 121 DH63
Carroll Ave., Guil. 243 BB134
Carroll Clo. E15 124 EF64
Carroll Hill, Loug. 85 EM41
Carron Clo. E14 143 EB72
Carronade Pl. SE28 165 EQ76
Carroun Rd. SW8 161 DM80
Carrow Rd., Dag. 146 EV66
Carrow Rd., Walt. 196 BX104
Kenilworth Dr.
Carroway La., Grnf. 137 CD69
Cowgate Rd.
Carrs La. N21 82 DQ43
Carshalton Gro., Sutt. 218 DD105
Carshalton Pk. Rd., Cars. 218 DF107
Carshalton Pl., Cars. 218 DG105
Carshalton Rd., Bans. 218 DF114
Carshalton Rd., Cars. 218 DE106
Carshalton Rd., Mitch. 200 DG98
Carshalton Rd., Sutt. 218 DC106
Carsington Gdns., Dart. 188 FK89
Carslake Rd. SW15 179 CW86
Carson Rd. E16 144 EG70
Carson Rd. SE21 182 DQ89
Carson Rd., Barn. 80 DF42
Carstairs Rd. SE6 183 EC90
Carston Clo. SE12 184 EF85
Carswell Clo., Brwd. 109 GD44
Carswell Clo., Ilf. 124 EK56
Roding La. S.
Carswell Rd. SE6 183 EC87
Cart La. E4 101 ED45
Cart Path, Wat. 60 BW33
Cartbridge Clo., Wok. 227 BB123
Send Rd.
Cartel Clo., Purf. 169 FR77
Carter Clo., Rom. 105 FB52
Carter Clo., Wall. 219 DK108
Carter Clo., Wind. 151 AN82
Carter Ct. EC4 141 DP72
Carter La.
Carter Dr., Rom. 105 FB52
Carter La. EC4 274 G9
Carter La. EC4 141 DP72
Carter Pl. SE17 162 DQ78
Carter Rd. E13 144 EH67
Carter Rd. SW19 180 DD93
Carter Rd., Slou. 131 AL73
Carter St. SE17 162 DQ79
Carter Wk., H.Wyc. 88 AC47
Carteret St. SW1 277 M5
Carteret St. SW1 161 DK75
Carteret Way SE8 163 DY77
Carterhatch La., Enf. 82 DT38
Carterhatch Rd., Enf. 82 DW39
Carters Clo., Wor.Pk. 199 CX103
Carters Cotts., Red. 266 DE136
Kings Ave.
Carters Hill, Sev. 257 FP127
Carters Hill Clo. SE9 184 EJ88
Carters La. SE23 183 DY89
Carters La., Epp. 51 EP24
Carters La., Wok. 227 BC120
Carters Mead, Harl. 52 EV17
Carters Rd., Epsom 233 CT115
Carters Row, Grav. 191 GF88
Carters Yd. SW18 180 DA85
Wandsworth High St.
Cartersfield Rd., Wal.Abb. 67 EC34
Cartersfield Rd. Est., Wal.Abb. 67 EC34
Cartersmeade Clo., Horl. 269 DH147
Wheatfield Way
Carthew Rd. W6 159 CV76
Carthew Vill. W6 159 CV76
Carthouse La., Wok. 210 AT114
Carthusian St. EC1 275 H6
Carthusian St. EC1 142 DQ71
Cartier Circle E14 143 EB74
Carting La. WC2 278 A1
Carting La. WC2 141 DL73
Cartmel Clo. N17 100 DV52
Heybourne Rd.
Cartmel Clo., Reig. 250 DE133
Cartmel Rd., Bexh. 166 FA81
Cartmell Gdns., Mord. 200 DC99
Carton St. W1 272 E8
Cartwright Gdns. WC1 273 P3
Cartwright Gdns. WC1 141 DL69
Cartwright Rd., Dag. 146 EY66
Cartwright St. E1 142 DT73
Cartwright Way SW13 159 CV80
Carve Ley, Welw.G.C. 30 DB10
Carver Rd. SE24 182 DQ86
Carville Cres., Brent. 158 CL77
Cary Rd. E11 124 EE63
Cary Wk., Rad. 61 CH34
Carysfort Rd. N8 121 DK57
Carysfort Rd. N16 122 DR62
Casband Ct., Abb.L. 59 BS31
Cascade Ave. N10 121 DJ56
Cascade Clo., Buck.H. 102 EK47
Cascade Rd.
Cascade Clo., Orp. 206 EW97
Cascade Rd., Buck.H. 102 EK47
Cascades, Croy. 221 DZ110
Caselden Clo., Add. 212 BJ106
Casella Rd. SE14 163 DX80
Casewick Rd. SE27 181 DN92
Casimir Rd. E5 122 DV62
Casino Ave. SE24 182 DR85
Caspian St. SE5 162 DR80
Caspian Wk. E16 144 EK72
King George Ave.
Caspian Wf. E3 143 EB71
Violet Rd.
Cassandra Clo., Nthlt. 117 CD63
Cassandra Gate, Wal.Cr. 67 DZ27
Casselden Rd. NW10 138 CR66
Cassidy Rd. SW6 160 DA80
Cassilda Rd. SE2 166 EU77
Cassilis Rd., Twick. 177 CH85
Cassio Rd., Wat. 75 BV41
Cassiobridge Rd., Wat. 75 BS42
Cassiobury Ave., Felt. 175 BT86
Cassiobury Ct., Wat. 75 BT40
Cassiobury Dr., Wat. 75 BS38
Cassiobury Pk. Ave., Wat. 75 BS41
Cassiobury Rd. E17 123 DX57
Cassis Ct., Loug. 85 EQ42
Cassland Rd. E9 143 DX66
Cassland Rd., Th.Hth. 202 DR98
Casslee Rd. SE6 183 DZ87
Cassocks Sq., Shep. 195 BR101
Casson St. E1 142 DU71
Casstine Clo., Swan. 187 FF94
Castalia Sq. E14 163 EC75
Roserton St.
Castalia St. E14 163 EC75
Plevna St.
Castano Ct., Abb.L. 59 BS31
Castell Rd., Loug. 85 EQ39
Castellain Rd. W9 140 DB70
Castellan Ave., Rom. 127 FH55
Castellane Clo., Stan. 95 CF52
Daventer Dr.
Castello Ave. SW15 179 CW85
Castelnau SW13 159 CU81
Castelnau Pl. SW13 159 CV79
Castelnau
Castelnau Row SW13 159 CV79
Lonsdale Rd.
Casterbridge NW6 140 DB67
Casterbridge Rd. SE3 164 EG83
Casterton St. E8 142 DV65
Wilton Way
Castile Rd. SE18 165 EN77
Castillon Rd. SE6 184 EE89
Castlands Rd. SE6 183 DZ89
Castle Ave. E4 101 ED50
Castle Ave., Epsom 217 CU109
Castle Ave., Rain. 147 FE66
Castle Ave., Slou. 152 AU79
Castle Ave., West Dr. 134 BL73
Castle Baynard St. EC4 274 G10
Castle Clo. E9 123 DY64
Swinnerton St.
Castle Clo. SW19 179 CX90
Castle Clo., Brom. 204 EE97
Castle Clo., Hodd. 33 EC14
Castle Clo., Red. 252 DQ133
Castle Clo., Reig. 266 DB138
Castle Clo., Rom. 106 FJ48
Castle Clo., Sun. 175 BS94
Mill Fm. Ave.
Castle Clo. (Bushey), Wat. 76 CB44
Castle Ct. EC3 275 L9
Castle Ct. SE26 183 DY91
Champion Rd.
Castle Dr., Horl. 269 DJ149
Castle Dr., Ilf. 124 EL58
Castle Dr., Reig. 266 DA138
Castle Fm. Rd., Sev. 225 FF109
Castle Gdns., Dor. 248 CM134
Castle Gate Way, Berk. 38 AW17
Castle Grn., Wey. 195 BS104
Castle Gro. Rd., Wok. 210 AS112
Castle Hill, Berk. 38 AW17
Castle Hill, Guil. 258 AX136
Castle Hill, Long. 209 FX99
Castle Hill, Wind. 151 AR81
Castle Hill Ave., Berk. 38 AW18
Castle Hill Ave., Croy. 221 EB109
Castle Hill Clo., Berk. 38 AV18
Castle Hill Rd., Egh. 172 AV90
Castle La. SW1 277 K6
Castle La. SW1 161 DJ76
Castle Mead, Hem.H. 40 BH22
Castle Ms. N12 98 DC50
Castle Rd.
Castle Ms. NW1 141 DH65
Castle Rd.
Castle Par., Epsom 217 CU108
Ewell Bypass
Castle Pl. NW1 141 DH65
Castle Rd.
Castle Pl. W4 158 CS77
Windmill Rd.
Castle Pt. E6 144 EJ68
Castle Rd. N12 98 DC50
Castle Rd. NW1 141 DH65
Castle Rd., Couls. 234 DE120
Castle Rd., Dag. 146 EV67
Castle Rd., Dart. 225 FH107
Castle Rd., Enf. 83 DY39
Castle Rd., Epsom 216 CP114
Castle Rd., Grays 170 FZ79
Castle Rd., Hodd. 33 EC14
Castle Rd., Islw. 157 CF82
Castle Rd., Nthlt. 136 CB65
Castle Rd., St.Alb. 43 CH20
Castle Rd., Sev. 225 FG108
Castle Rd., Sthl. 156 BZ76
Castle Rd., Swans. 190 FZ86
Castle Rd., Wey. 195 BR104
Castle Rd., Wok. 211 AZ114
Castle Sq., Guil. 258 AX136
Castle Sq., Red. 252 DQ133
Castle St. E6 144 EJ68
Castle St., Berk. 38 AW19
Castle St., Green. 189 FU85
Castle St., Guil. 258 AX136
Castle St., Hert. 32 DQ10
Castle St., Kings.T. 198 CL96
Castle St., Red. 251 DP133
Castle St., Slou. 152 AT76
Castle St., Swans. 190 FZ86
Castle Vw., Epsom 216 CP114
Castle Vw. Rd., Wey. 213 BP105
Castle Wk., Reig. 250 DA134
High St.
Castle Wk., Sun. 196 BW97
Elizabeth Gdns.
Castle Way SW19 179 CX90
Castle Way, Epsom 217 CU109
Castle Ave.
Castle Way, Felt. 176 BW91
Castle Yd. N6 120 DG59
North Rd.
Castle Yd. SE1 278 G2
Castle Yd., Rich. 177 CK85
Hill St.
Castlebar Hill W5 137 CH71
Castlebar Ms. W5 137 CJ71
Castlebar Pk. W5 137 CH70
Castlebar Rd. W5 137 CJ72
Castlecombe Dr. SW19 179 CX87
Castlecombe Rd. SE9 184 EL91
Castledine Rd. SE20 182 DV94
Castlefield Rd., Reig. 250 DA134
Castleford Ave. SE9 185 EP88
Castlegate, Rich. 158 CM83
Castlehaven Rd. NW1 141 DH66
Castleleigh Ct., Enf. 82 DR43
Castlemaine Ave., Epsom 217 CV109
Castlemaine Ave., S.Croy. 220 DT106
Castlemaine Twr. SW11 160 DF82
Castlereagh St. W1 272 C8
Castlereagh St. W1 140 DF72
Castleton Ave., Bexh. 167 FD81
Castleton Ave., Wem. 118 CL63
Castleton Clo., Bans. 234 DA115
Castleton Clo., Croy. 203 DY100
Castleton Dr., Bans. 234 DA115
Castleton Gdns., Wem. 118 CL62
Castleton Rd. E17 101 ED54
Castleton Rd. SE9 184 EK91
Castleton Rd., Ilf. 126 EU60
Castleton Rd., Mitch. 201 DK98
Castleton Rd., Ruis. 116 BX60
Castletown Rd. W14 159 CY78
Castleview Gdns., Ilf. 124 EL58
Castleview Rd., Slou. 152 AW77
Castlewood Dr. SE9 165 EM82
Castlewood Rd. N15 122 DU58
Castlewood Rd. N16 122 DU59
Castlewood Rd., Barn. 80 DD41
Castor La. E14 143 EB73
Cat Hill, Barn. 80 DF43
Catalpa Clo., Guil. 242 AW132
Cedar Way
Cater Gdns., Guil. 242 AT132
Caterham Ave., Ilf. 103 EM54
Caterham Bypass, Cat. 236 DV120
Caterham Clo., Cat. 236 DS120
Caterham Ct., Wal.Abb. 68 EF34
Shernbroke Rd.
Caterham Dr., Couls. 235 DP118
Caterham Rd. SE13 163 EC83
Catesby St. SE17 279 L9
Catesby St. SE17 162 DR77
Catford Bdy. SE6 183 EB87
Catford Hill SE6 183 DZ88
Catford Ms. SE6 183 EB87
Holbeach Rd.
Catford Rd. SE6 183 EA87
Cathall Rd. E11 123 ED61
Catham Clo., St.Alb. 43 CH22
Cathay St. SE16 162 DV75
Cathay Wk., Nthlt. 136 CA68
Brabazon Rd.
Cathcart Dr., Orp. 205 ES103
Cathcart Hill N19 121 DJ62
Cathcart Rd. SW10 160 DB79
Cathcart St. NW5 141 DH65
Cathedral Clo., Guil. 258 AV135
Cathedral Ct., St.Alb. 42 CB22
Cathedral Hill Ind. Est., Guil. 242 AU133
Cathedral Pl. EC4 275 H8
Cathedral St. SE1 279 K2
Cathedral St. SE1 142 DR74
Cathedral Vw., Guil. 242 AT134
Catherall Rd. N5 122 DQ62
Catherine Clo. SE16 143 DX74
Rotherhithe St.
Catherine Clo., Brwd. 108 FU43
Catherine Clo., Grays 170 FZ75
Catherine Clo., Hem.H. 41 BP15
Parr Cres.
Catherine Clo., W.Byf. 212 BL114
Catherine Ct. N14 81 DJ43
Conisbee Ct.
Catherine Dr., Rich. 158 CL84
Catherine Dr., Sun. 175 BT93
Catherine Gdns., Houns. 157 CD84
Catherine Gdns., Loug. 85 EM44
Roding Gdns.
Catherine Griffiths Ct. EC1 274 E4
Catherine Gro. SE10 163 EB81
Catherine Howard Ct., Wey. 195 BP104
Old Palace Rd.
Catherine Pl. SW1 277 K6
Catherine Pl. SW1 161 DJ76
Catherine Rd., Enf. 83 DY36
Catherine Rd., Rom. 127 FH57
Catherine Rd., Surb. 197 CK99
Catherine St. WC2 274 B10
Catherine St. WC2 141 DM73
Catherine St., St.Alb. 43 CD19
Catherine Wheel All. E1 275 N7
Catherine Wheel Rd., Brent. 157 CK80
Catherine Wheel Yd. SW1 277 K3
Catherine's Clo., West Dr. 154 BK76
Money La.
Cathles Rd. SW12 181 DH86
Cathnor Hill Ct. W12 159 CV76
Cathnor Rd. W12 159 CV75
Catisfield Rd., Enf. 83 DY37
Catkin Clo., Hem.H. 40 BH19
Catlin Cres., Shep. 195 BR99
Catlin Gdns., Gdse. 252 DV130
Catlin St. SE16 162 DU78
Catlin St., Hem.H. 40 BH23
Catling Clo. SE23 182 DW90
Catlins La., Pnr. 115 BV55
Cato Rd. SW4 161 DK83
Cato St. W1 272 C7
Cator Clo., Croy. 222 EE111
Cator Cres., Croy. 222 EE111
Cator La., Beck. 203 DZ95
Rectory Grn.
Cator Rd. SE26 183 DX93
Cator Rd., Cars. 218 DF106
Cator St. SE15 162 DT79
Catsey La. (Bushey), Wat. 94 CC45
Catsey Wds. (Bushey), Wat. 94 CC45
Catterick Way, Borwd. 78 CM39
Cattistock Rd. SE9 184 EL92
Cattlegate Rd., Enf. 65 DL34
Cattlegate Rd., Pot.B. 65 DK31
Cattley Clo., Barn. 79 CY42
Wood St.
Cattlins Clo., Wal.Cr. 66 DT29
Catton St. WC1 274 B7
Catton St. WC1 141 DM71
Cattsdell, Hem.H. 40 BL18
Caulfield Rd. E6 144 EL67
Caulfield Rd. SE15 162 DV82
Causeway, The N2 120 DE56
Causeway, The SW18 180 DB85
Causeway, The SW19 179 CW92
Causeway, The, Cars. 200 DG104
Causeway, The, Chess. 216 CL105
Causeway, The, Egh. 173 BC91
Causeway, The, Esher 215 CF108
Causeway, The, Felt. 155 BU84
Causeway, The, Maid. 150 AC75
Causeway, The, Pot.B. 64 DC31
Causeway, The, St.Alb. 42 CB22
King Harry La.
Causeway, The, Stai. 173 BC91
Causeway, The, Sutt. 218 DC109
Causeway, The, Tedd. 177 CF93
Broad St.
Causeway Clo., Pot.B. 64 DD31
Causeway Ct., Wok. 226 AT118
Bingham Dr.
Causeyware Rd. N9 100 DV45
Causton Rd. N6 121 DH59
Causton St. SW1 277 N9
Causton St. SW1 161 DK77
Cautherly La., Ware 33 DZ10
Cautley Ave. SW4 181 DJ85
Cavalier Clo., Rom. 126 EX56
Cavalier Gdns., Hayes 135 BR72
Hanover Circle
Cavalry Barracks, Houns. 156 BX83
Cavalry Cres., Houns. 156 BX84
Cavalry Cres., Wind. 151 AQ83
Cavalry Gdns. SW15 179 CZ85
Upper Richmond Rd.
Cavan Dr., St.Alb. 43 CD15
Cavaye Pl. SW10 160 DC78
Fulham Rd.
Cave Rd. E13 144 EH68
Cave Rd., Rich. 177 CJ91
Cave St. N1 141 DM68
Carnegie St.
Cavell Cres., Dart. 168 FN84
Cavell Cres., Rom. 106 FL54
Cavell Dr., Enf. 81 DN40
Cavell Rd. N17 100 DR52
Cavell Rd. (Cheshunt), Wal.Cr. 66 DT27
Cavell St. E1 142 DV71
Cavendish Ave. N3 98 DA54
Cavendish Ave. NW8 272 A1
Cavendish Ave. NW8 140 DD68
Cavendish Ave. W13 137 CG71
Cavendish Ave., Erith 167 FC80
Cavendish Ave., Har. 117 CD63
Cavendish Ave., Horn. 147 FH65
Cavendish Ave., N.Mal. 199 CU99
Cavendish Ave., Ruis. 115 BV64
Cavendish Ave., Sev. 256 FG122
Cavendish Ave., Sid. 186 EU87
Cavendish Ave., Well. 165 ET83
Cavendish Ave., Wdf.Grn. 102 EH53
Cavendish Clo. N18 100 DV50
Cavendish Rd.
Cavendish Clo. NW6 139 CZ66
Cavendish Rd.
Cavendish Clo. NW8 272 A2
Cavendish Clo. NW8 140 DD69
Cavendish Clo., Amer. 72 AV39
Cavendish Clo., Hayes 135 BS71
Westacott
Cavendish Clo., Maid. 130 AG72
Cavendish Clo., Sun. 175 BT93
Cavendish Ct. EC3 275 N8
Cavendish Ct., Rick. 75 BR43
Mayfare
Cavendish Ct., Sun. 175 BT93
Cavendish Cres., Borwd. 78 CN42
Cavendish Cres., Horn. 147 FH65
Cavendish Dr. E11 123 ED60
Cavendish Dr., Edg. 96 CM51
Cavendish Dr., Esher 215 CE106
Cavendish Gdns., Bark. 125 ES64
Cavendish Gdns., Ilf. 125 EN60
Cavendish Gdns., Red. 250 DG133
Cavendish Gdns., Rom. 126 EY57
Cavendish Ms. N. W1 273 J6
Cavendish Ms. S. W1 273 J7
Cavendish Pl. W1 273 J8
Cavendish Pl. W1 141 DH72
Cavendish Rd. E4 101 EC52
Cavendish Rd. N4 121 DN58
Cavendish Rd. N18 100 DV50
Cavendish Rd. NW6 139 CY66
Cavendish Rd. SW12 181 DH86
Cavendish Rd. SW19 180 DD94
Cavendish Rd. W4 158 CQ81
Cavendish Rd., Barn. 79 CW41
Cavendish Rd., Chesh. 54 AR32
Cavendish Rd., Croy. 201 DP102
Cavendish Rd., N.Mal. 198 CS99
Cavendish Rd., Red. 250 DG134
Cavendish Rd., St.Alb. 43 CF20
Cavendish Rd., Sun. 175 BT93
Cavendish Rd., Sutt. 218 DC108
Cavendish Rd., Wey. 213 BP109
Cavendish Rd., Wok. 226 AX119
Cavendish Sq. W1 273 J8
Cavendish Sq. W1 141 DH72
Cavendish Sq., Long. 209 FX97
Cavendish St. N1 275 K1
Cavendish St. N1 142 DR68
Cavendish Ter., Felt. 175 BU89
High St.
Cavendish Way, Hat. 45 CT18
Cavendish Way, W.Wick. 203 EB102
Cavenham Clo., Wok. 226 AY119
Cavenham Gdns., Horn. 128 FJ57
Cavenham Gdns., Ilf. 125 ER62
Caverleigh Way, Wor.Pk. 199 CU102
Caversham Ave. N13 99 DN48
Caversham Ave., Sutt. 199 CY103
Caversham Flats SW3 160 DF79
Caversham St.
Caversham Rd. N15 122 DQ56
Caversham Rd. NW5 141 DJ65
Caversham Rd., Kings.T. 198 CM96
Caversham St. SW3 160 DF79
Caverswall St. W12 139 CW72
Caveside Clo., Chis. 205 EN95
Cavill's Wk., Rom. 104 EW47
Cawcott Dr., Wind. 151 AL81
Cawdor Ave., S.Ock. 149 FU73
Cawdor Cres. W7 157 CG77
Cawley Hatch, Harl. 51 EM15
Cawnpore St. SE19 182 DS92
Cawsey Way, Wok. 226 AY117
Caxton Ave., Add. 212 BG107
Caxton Dr., Uxb. 134 BK68
Chiltern Vw. Rd.
Caxton Gdns., Guil. 242 AV133
Caxton Gro. E3 143 EA69
Caxton Hill, Hert. 32 DS09
Caxton Hill Extension Rd., Hert. 32 DT09
Caxton La., Oxt. 254 EL131
Caxton Ms., Brent. 157 CK79
The Butts
Caxton Ri., Red. 250 DG133
Caxton Rd. N22 99 DM54
Caxton Rd. SW19 180 DC92
Caxton Rd. W12 139 CX74
Caxton Rd., Hodd. 33 EB13
Caxton Rd., Sthl. 156 BX76
Caxton St. SW1 277 L6
Caxton St. SW1 161 DJ76
Caxton St. N. E16 144 EF73
Victoria Dock Rd.
Caxton Way, Wat. 93 BR45
Caxtons Ct., Guil. 243 BA132
Caygill Clo., Brom. 204 EF98
Cayley Clo., Wall. 219 DL108
Brabazon Ave.
Cayton Pl. EC1 275 K3
Cayton Rd., Grnf. 137 CE68
Cayton St. EC1 275 K3
Cazenove Rd. E17 101 EA53
Cazenove Rd. N16 122 DT61
Cearn Way, Couls. 235 DM115
Cearns Ho. E6 144 EK67
Cecil Ave., Bark. 145 ER66
Cecil Ave., Enf. 82 DT42
Cecil Ave., Grays 170 FZ75
Cecil Ave., Horn. 128 FK55
Cecil Ave., Wem. 118 CM64
Cecil Clo., Ashf. 175 BQ93
Cecil Clo., Chess. 215 CK105
Cecil Ct. WC2 277 P1
Cecil Ct., Barn. 79 CX41
Cecil Cres., Hat. 45 CV16
Cecil Pk., Pnr. 116 BY56
Cecil Pl., Mitch. 200 DF99
Cecil Rd. E11 124 EE62
Cecil Rd. E13 144 EG67
Cecil Rd. E17 101 EA53
Cecil Rd. N10 99 DH54
Cecil Rd. N14 99 DJ46
Cecil Rd. NW9 118 CR55
Cecil Rd. NW10 138 CS67
Cecil Rd. SW19 180 DB94
Cecil Rd. W3 138 CQ71
Cecil Rd., Ashf. 175 BQ94
Cecil Rd., Croy. 201 DL100
Cecil Rd., Enf. 82 DQ42
Cecil Rd., Grav. 191 GF88
Cecil Rd., Har. 117 CE55
Cecil Rd., Hert. 32 DQ12
Cecil Rd., Hodd. 49 EC15
Cecil Rd., Houns. 156 CC82
Cecil Rd., Ilf. 125 EP63
Cecil Rd., Iver 133 BE72
Cecil Rd., Pot.B. 63 CU32
Cecil Rd., Rom. 126 EX59
Cecil Rd., St.Alb. 43 CF20
Cecil Rd., Slou. 131 AM70
Cecil Rd., Sutt. 217 CZ107
Cecil Rd. (Cheshunt), Wal.Cr. 67 DX32
Cecil St., Wat. 75 BV38
Cecil Way, Brom. 204 EG102
Cecile Pk. N8 121 DL58
Cecilia Clo. N2 120 DC55
Cecilia Rd. E8 122 DT64
Cedar Ave., Barn. 98 DE45
Cedar Ave., Cob. 230 BW115
Cedar Ave., Enf. 82 DW40
Cedar Ave., Grav. 191 GJ91
Cedar Ave., Hayes 135 BU72
Acacia Ave.
Cedar Ave., Rom. 126 EY57
Cedar Ave., Ruis. 136 BW65
Cedar Ave., Sid. 186 EU87
Cedar Ave., Twick. 176 CB86
Cedar Ave., Upmin. 128 FN62
Cedar Ave., Wal.Cr. 67 DX33
Cedar Ave., West Dr. 134 BM74
Cedar Chase, Maid. 130 AD70
Cedar Clo. SE21 182 DQ88
Cedar Clo. SW15 178 CR91
Cedar Clo., Borwd. 78 CP42
Cedar Clo., Brwd. 109 GD45
Cedar Clo., Brom. 204 EL104
Cedar Clo., Buck.H. 102 EK47
Cedar Clo., Cars. 218 DF107
Cedar Clo., Dor. 263 CH136
Cedar Clo., E.Mol. 197 CE98
Cedar Rd.
Cedar Clo., Epsom 217 CT114
Cedar Clo., Esher 214 BZ108

Cedar Clo., Hert. 31 DP09
Cedar Clo., Pot.B. 64 DA30
Cedar Clo., Reig. 266 DC136
Cedar Clo., Rom. 127 FC56
Cedar Clo., Saw. 36 EY06
Cedar Clo., Stai. 194 BJ96
Cedar Clo., Swan. 207 FC96
Cedar Clo., Ware 33 DX07
Cedar Clo., Warl. 237 DY118
Cedar Copse, Brom. 205 EM96
Cedar Ct. E8 142 DT66
Cedar Ct. N1 142 DQ66
Essex Rd.
Cedar Ct. SE9 184 EL86
Cedar Ct. SW19 179 CX90
Cedar Ct., Egh. 173 BA91
Cedar Ct., Epp. 70 EU31
Cedar Ct., St.Alb. 43 CK20
Cedar Cres., Brom. 204 EL104
Cedar Dr. N2 120 DE56
Cedar Dr. 208 FP96
(Sutton at Hone), Dart.
Cedar Dr., Lthd. 231 CE122
Cedar Dr., Pnr. 94 CA52
Cedar Gdns., Sutt. 218 DC107
Cedar Gdns., Upmin. 128 FQ62
Cedar Gdns., Wok. 226 AV118
St. John's Rd.
Cedar Grn., Hodd. 49 EA18
Cedar Gro. W5 158 CL76
Cedar Gro., Amer. 55 AR39
Cedar Gro., Bex. 186 EW86
Cedar Gro., Sthl. 136 CA71
Cedar Gro., Wey. 213 BQ105
Cedar Heights, Rich. 178 CL88
Cedar Hill, Epsom 232 CQ116
Cedar Ho., Croy. 221 EB107
Cedar Ho., Sun. 175 BT94
Cedar Lawn Ave., Barn. 79 CY43
Cedar Mt. SE9 184 EK88
Cedar Pk. Gdns., Rom. 126 EX59
Cedar Pk. Rd., Enf. 82 DQ38
Cedar Pl. SE7 164 EJ78
Floyd Rd.
Cedar Pl., Nthwd. 93 BQ51
Cedar Ri. N14 98 DG45
Cedar Rd. N17 100 DT53
Cedar Rd. NW2 119 CW63
Cedar Rd., Berk. 38 AX20
Cedar Rd., Brwd. 109 GD44
Cedar Rd., Brom. 204 EJ96
Cedar Rd., Cob. 213 BV114
Cedar Rd., Croy. 202 DR103
Cedar Rd., Dart. 188 FK88
Cedar Rd., E.Mol. 197 CE98
Cedar Rd., Enf. 81 DP38
Cedar Rd., Erith 167 FG81
Cedar Rd., Felt. 175 BR88
Cedar Rd., Grays 171 GG76
Cedar Rd., Hat. 45 CU19
Cedar Rd., Horn. 128 FJ62
Cedar Rd., Houns. 156 BW82
Cedar Rd., Rom. 127 FC56
Cedar Rd., Sutt. 218 DC107
Cedar Rd., Tedd. 177 CG92
Cedar Rd., Wat. 76 BW44
Cedar Rd., Wey. 212 BN105
Cedar Rd., Wok. 226 AV120
Cedar Ter., Rich. 158 CL84
Cedar Ter. Rd., Sev. 257 FJ123
Cedar Tree Gro. SE27 181 DP92
Cedar Vista, Rich. 158 CL81
Kew Rd.
Cedar Wk., Hem.H. 40 BK22
Cedar Wk., Ken. 236 DQ116
Cedar Wk., Tad. 233 CY120
Cedar Wk., Wal.Abb. 67 ED34
Cypress Clo.
Cedar Wk., Welw.G.C. 30 DB10
Cedar Way NW1 141 DK66
Cedar Way, Berk. 38 AX20
Cedar Way, Guil. 242 AW132
Cedar Way, Slou. 152 AY78
Cedar Way, Sun. 175 BS94
Cedar Wd. Dr., Wat. 75 BV35
Cedarcroft Rd., Chess. 216 CM105
Cedarhurst, Brom. 184 EE94
Elstree Hill
Cedarhurst Dr. SE9 184 EJ85
Cedarne Rd. SW6 160 DB80
Cedars, Bans. 218 DF114
Cedars, The E15 144 EF67
Portway
Cedars, The W13 137 CJ72
Heronsforde
Cedars, The, Buck.H. 102 EG46
Cedars, The, Guil. 243 BA131
Cedars, The, Lthd. 231 CK121
Cedars, The, Reig. 250 DD134
Cedars, The, Tedd. 177 CF93
Adelaide Rd.
Cedars, The, W.Byf. 212 BM112
Cedars Ave. E17 123 EA57
Cedars Ave., Mitch. 200 DG98
Cedars Ave., Rick. 92 BJ46
Cedars Clo. NW4 119 CX55
Cedars Clo., Ger.Cr. 90 AY50
Cedars Ct. N9 100 DS47
Church St.
Cedars Dr., Uxb. 134 BM68
Cedars Ms. SW4 161 DH84
Cedars Rd.
Cedars Pl. SE7 164 EJ78
Floyd Rd.
Cedars Rd. E15 144 EE65
Cedars Rd. N9 100 DU47
Church St.
Cedars Rd. N21 99 DP47
Cedars Rd. SW4 161 DH83
Cedars Rd. SW13 159 CT82
Cedars Rd. W4 158 CQ79
Cedars Rd., Beck. 203 DY96
Cedars Rd., Croy. 201 DL104
Cedars Rd., Kings.T. 197 CJ95
Cedars Rd., Mord. 200 DA98
Cedars Wk., Rick. 73 BF42
Cedarville Gdns. SW16 181 DM93
Cedarwood Dr., St.Alb. 43 CK20
Cedra Ct. N16 122 DU60
Cedric Ave., Rom. 127 FE55
Cedric Rd. SE9 185 EQ90
Celadon Clo., Enf. 83 DY41
Celandine Clo. E14 143 EA71
Celandine Clo., S.Ock. 149 FW70
Celandine Dr. SE28 146 EV74
Celandine Rd., Walt. 214 BY105
Celandine Way E15 144 EE69
Celbridge Ms. W2 140 DB72
Porchester Rd.
Celedon Clo., Grays 170 FY75
Celestial Gdns. SE13 163 ED84
Celia Cres., Ashf. 174 BK93
Celia Rd. N19 121 DJ63
Cell Barnes Clo., St.Alb. 43 CH22
Cell Barnes La.
Cell Barnes La., St.Alb. 43 CG21
Cell Fm. Ave., Wind. 172 AV85
Celtic Ave., Brom. 204 EE97
Celtic Rd., W.Byf. 212 BL114
Celtic St. E14 143 EB71
Cement Block Cotts., Grays 170 GC78
Cemetery Hill, Hem.H. 40 BJ21
Cemetery La. SE7 164 EL79
Cemetery La., Shep. 195 BP101
Cemetery La., Wal.Abb. 68 EF25
Cemetery Rd. E7 124 EF63
Cemetery Rd. N17 100 DS52
Cemetery Rd. SE2 166 EV80
Cemmaes Ct. Rd., Hem.H. 40 BJ20
Cemmaes Meadow, Hem.H. 40 BJ20
Cenacle Clo. NW3 120 DA62
Centaur St. SE1 278 C6
Centaur St. SE1 161 DM76
Centaurs Business Pk., Islw. 157 CG79
Centaury Ct., Grays 170 GD79
Centenary Rd., Enf. 83 DZ42
Centenary Trd. Est., Enf. 83 DZ42
Centenary Way, Amer. 72 AT38
Central Ave. E11 123 ED61
Central Ave. N2 98 DD54
Central Ave. N9 100 DS48
Central Ave. SW11 160 DF80
Central Ave., Enf. 82 DV40
Central Ave., Grav. 191 GH89
Central Ave., Grays 169 FT77
Central Ave., Harl. 35 ER14
Central Ave., Hayes 135 BT74
Central Ave., Houns. 156 CC84
Central Ave., Pnr. 116 BZ58
Central Ave., S.Ock. 168 FQ75
Central Ave., Til. 171 GG81
Central Ave., Wall. 219 DL106
Central Ave., Wal.Cr. 67 DY33
Central Ave., Well. 165 ET82
Central Ave., W.Mol. 196 BZ98
Central Circ. NW4 119 CV57
Hendon Way
Central Dr., Horn. 128 FL62
Central Dr., St.Alb. 43 CJ19
Central Dr., Slou. 131 AM73
Central Dr., Welw.G.C. 29 CZ07
Central Gdns., Mord. 200 DC99
Central Hill SE19 182 DR92
Central Mkts. EC1 274 G7
Central Mkts. EC1 142 DQ71
Central Par., Croy. 221 EC110
Central Par., Felt. 176 BW87
Sparrow Fm. Dr.
Central Par., Surb. 198 CL100
St. Mark's Hill
Central Pk. Ave., Dag. 127 FB62
Central Pk. Est., Houns. 176 BX85
Central Pk. Rd. E6 144 EK68
Central Pl. SE25 202 DV98
Portland Rd.
Central Rd., Dart. 188 FL85
Central Rd., Harl. 36 EU11
Central Rd., Mord. 200 DA100
Central Rd., Wem. 117 CH64
Central Rd., Wor.Pk. 199 CU102
Central Sq. NW11 120 DA57
Central Sq., Wem. 118 CL64
Station Gro.
Central Sq., W.Mol. 196 BZ98
Central St. EC1 275 H2
Central St. EC1 142 DQ69
Central Way NW10 138 CQ69
Central Way SE28 146 EU74
Central Way, Cars. 218 DE108
Central Way, Felt. 175 BU85
Central Way, Oxt. 253 ED127
Centre, The, Felt. 175 BU89
Highfield Rd.
Centre, The, Walt. 195 BU102
Hepworth Way
Centre Ave. W3 138 CR74
Centre Ave. W10 139 CW69
Harrow Rd.
Centre Ave., Epp. 69 ET32
Centre Clo., Epp. 69 ET32
Centre Ave.
Centre Common Rd., Chis. 185 EQ93
Centre Dr., Epp. 69 ET32
Centre Grn., Epp. 69 ET32
Centre Ave.
Centre Rd. E7 124 EG61
Centre Rd. E11 124 EG61
Centre Rd., Dag. 147 FB68
Centre St. E2 142 DV68
Centre Way E17 101 EC52
Centre Way N9 100 DW47
Centreway NW7 97 CU52
Centreway, Ilf. 125 EQ61
Centric Clo. NW1 141 DH67
Oval Rd.
Centurion Clo. N7 141 DM66
Centurion Ct., Wall. 201 DH103
Wandle Rd.
Centurion La. E3 143 DZ68
Libra Rd.
Centurion Way, Erith 166 FA76
Centurion Way, Purf. 168 FM77
Century Rd. E17 123 DY55
Century Rd., Hodd. 49 EA16
Century Rd., Stai. 173 BC92
Century Rd., Ware 33 DX05
Cephas Ave. E1 142 DW70
Cephas St. E1 142 DW70
Ceres Rd. SE18 165 ET77
Cerise Rd. SE15 162 DU81
Cerne Clo., Hayes 136 BW73
Cerne Rd., Grav. 191 GL91
Cerne Rd., Mord. 200 DC100
Cerney Ms. W2 140 DD73
Gloucester Ter.
Cerotus Pl., Cher. 193 BF101
Cervantes Ct. W2 140 DB72
Inverness Ter.
Cervantes Ct., Nthwd. 93 BT52
Cervia Way, Grav. 191 GM90
Cester St. E2 142 DU67
Whiston Rd.
Cestreham Cres., Chesh. 54 AR29
Ceylon Rd. W14 159 CX76
Chace Ave., Pot.B. 64 DD32
Chadacre Ave., Ilf. 125 EM55
Chadacre Rd., Epsom 217 CV107
Chadbourn St. E14 143 EB71
Chadd Dr., Brom. 204 EL97
Chadd Grn. E13 144 EG67
Chadfields, Til. 171 GG80
Chadhurst Clo., Dor. 263 CK139
Wildcroft Dr.
Chadview Ct., Rom. 126 EX59
Chadville Gdns., Rom. 126 EX57
Chadway, Dag. 126 EW60
Chadwell, Ware 32 DW07
Chadwell Ave., Rom. 126 EV59
Chadwell Ave. 66 DW28
(Cheshunt), Wal.Cr.
Chadwell Bypass, Grays 171 GF78
Chadwell Heath La., Rom. 126 EV56
Chadwell Hill, Grays 171 GH79
Chadwell Ri., Ware 32 DW07
Chadwell Rd., Grays 170 GE77
Chadwell St. EC1 274 E2
Chadwell St. EC1 141 DN69
Chadwick Ave. E4 101 ED49
Chadwick Ave. SW19 180 DA93
Chadwick Clo., Grav. 190 GE89
Chadwick Clo., Tedd. 177 CG93
Chadwick Dr., Rom. 106 FK54
Chadwick Rd. E11 124 EE59
Chadwick Rd. NW10 139 CT67
Chadwick Rd. SE15 162 DT82
Chadwick Rd., Ilf. 125 EP62
Chadwick St. SW1 277 M7
Chadwick St. SW1 161 DK76
Chadwick Way SE28 146 EX73
Chadwin Rd. E13 144 EH71
Chadworth Way, Esher 215 CD106
Chaffers Mead, Ash. 232 CM116
Chaffinch Ave., Croy. 203 DX100
Chaffinch Clo. N9 101 DX46
Chaffinch Clo., Croy. 203 DX99
Chaffinch Clo., Surb. 198 CN104
Chaffinch La., Wat. 93 BT45
Chaffinch Rd., Beck. 203 DY95
Chaffinch Way, Horl. 268 DE147
Chaffinches Grn., Hem.H. 40 BN24
Chafford Wk., Rain. 148 FJ68
Chafford Way, Rom. 126 EW56
Chagford St. NW1 272 D5
Chagford St. NW1 140 DF70
Chailey Ave., Enf. 82 DT40
Chailey Clo., Houns. 156 BX81
Springwell Rd.
Chailey Pl., Walt. 214 BY105
Chailey St. E5 122 DW62
Chairmans Ave., Uxb. 113 BF58
Chalcombe Rd. SE2 166 EV76
Chalcot Clo., Sutt. 218 DA108
Chalcot Cres. NW1 140 DF67
Chalcot Gdns. NW3 140 DF65
Chalcot Ms. SW16 181 DL90
Chalcot Rd. NW1 140 DG66
Chalcot Sq. NW1 140 DG66
Chalcott Gdns., Surb. 197 CJ102
Chalcroft Rd. SE13 184 EE85
Chaldon Clo., Red. 266 DE136
Chaldon Common Rd., Cat. 236 DQ124
Chaldon Path, Th.Hth. 201 DP98
Chaldon Rd. SW6 159 CY80
Chaldon Rd., Cat. 236 DR124
Chaldon Way, Couls. 235 DL117
Chale Rd. SW2 181 DL86
Chale Wk., Sutt. 218 DB109
Hulverston Clo.
Chalet Clo., Berk. 38 AT19
Chalet Clo., Bex. 187 FD91
Chalet Est. NW7 97 CU49
Chalfont Ave., Amer. 72 AX39
Chalfont Ave., Wem. 138 CP65
Chalfont Clo., Hem.H. 41 BP15
Chalfont Ct. NW9 119 CT55
Chalfont Grn. N9 100 DS48
Chalfont La., Ger.Cr. 91 BC51
Chalfont La., Rick. 73 BB43
Chalfont La. 91 BE51
(Maple Cross), Rick.
Chalfont Rd. N9 100 DS48
Chalfont Rd. SE25 202 DT97
Chalfont Rd., Beac. 89 AR51
Chalfont Rd., Ger.Cr. 91 BB48
Chalfont Rd., Hayes 155 BU75
Chalfont Rd., Rick. 91 BD49
Chalfont Sta. Rd., Amer. 72 AX40
Chalfont Wk., Pnr. 94 BW54
Willows Clo.
Chalfont Way W13 157 CH76
Chalford Clo., W.Mol. 196 CA98
Chalford Flats, H.Wyc. 110 AE57
Chalford Rd. SE21 182 DR90
Chalford Wk., Wdf.Grn. 102 EK53
Chalforde Gdns., Rom. 127 FH56
Chalgrove, Welw.G.C. 30 DD09
Chalgrove Ave., Mord. 200 DA99
Chalgrove Cres., Ilf. 102 EL54
Chalgrove Gdns. N3 119 CY55
Chalgrove Rd. E9 142 DW65
Morning La.
Chalgrove Rd. N17 100 DV53
Chalgrove Rd., Sutt. 218 DD108
Chalice Clo., Wall. 219 DK107
Lavender Vale
Chalice Way, Green. 189 FS85
Chalk Cres. SE12 184 EH90
Chalk Fm. Rd. NW1 140 DG66
Chalk Hill, Amer. 89 AM45
Chalk Hill, Chesh. 54 AP29
Chalk Hill, Wat. 76 BX44
Chalk Hill Rd. W6 159 CX77
Shortlands
Chalk La., Ash. 232 CM119
Chalk La., Barn. 80 DF41
Chalk La., Epsom 232 CR115
Chalk La., Harl. 36 FA14
Chalk La., Lthd. 245 BT130
Chalk Paddock, Epsom 232 CR115
Chalk Pit Ave., Orp. 206 EW97
Chalk Pit La., Slou. 130 AH65
Dropmore Rd.
Chalk Pit Rd., Bans. 234 DA117
Chalk Pit Rd., Epsom 232 CQ119
Chalk Pit Way, Sutt. 218 DC106
Chalk Rd. E13 144 EH71
Chalk Wk., Sutt. 218 DB109
Hulverston Clo.
Chalkdale, Welw.G.C. 30 DB08
Chalkdell Flds., St.Alb. 43 CG16
Chalkdell Hill, Hem.H. 40 BL20
Chalkenden Clo. SE20 182 DV94
Chalkhill Rd., Wem. 118 CN62
Chalklands, The, Wem. 118 CQ62
The Leadings
Chalkley Clo., Mitch. 200 DF96
Chalkmill Rd., Enf. 82 DV41
Crown Rd.
Chalkpit La., Bet. 248 CP133
Chalkpit La., Dor. 247 CG134
Chalkpit La. 246 BZ128
(Great Bookham), Lthd.
Chalkpit La., Oxt. 253 EC126
Chalkpit Ter., Dor. 247 CG134
Chalkpit Wd., Oxt. 253 ED127
Chalkpits Caravan Pk., 110 AE57
H.Wyc.
Chalkstone Clo., Well. 166 EU81
Chalkwell Pk. Ave., Enf. 82 DS42
Chalky Bank, Grav. 191 GG91
Chalky La., Chess. 215 CK109
Challacombe Clo., Brwd. 109 GB46
Challenge Clo., Grav. 191 GM91
Challenge Rd., Ashf. 175 BR90
Challice Way SW2 181 DM88
Challin St. SE20 202 DW95
Challinor, Harl. 52 EY15
Challis Rd., Brent. 157 CK78
Challock Clo., West. 238 EJ116
Challoner Clo. N2 98 DD54
Challoner Cres. W14 159 CZ78
Challoner St.
Challoner St. W14 159 CZ78
Challoners Clo., E.Mol. 197 CD98
Chalmers Ct., Rick. 92 BM45
Chalmers Rd., Ashf. 175 BP91
Chalmers Rd., Bans. 234 DD115
Chalmers Rd. E., Ashf. 175 BP91
Chalmers Wk. SE17 161 DP79
Hillingdon St.
Chalmers Way, Felt. 175 BU85
Chaloner Ct. SE1 279 K4
Chalsey Rd. SE4 163 DZ84
Chalton Dr. N2 120 DC58
Chalton St. NW1 141 DJ68
Chalvey Gdns., Slou. 152 AS75
Chalvey Gro., Slou. 151 AP76
Chalvey Pk., Slou. 152 AS75
Chalvey Rd. E., Slou. 151 AR75
Chalvey Rd. W., Slou. 152 AS75
Chamber St. E1 142 DT73
Chamberlain Clo. SE28 165 ER76
Broadwater Rd.
Chamberlain Clo., Harl. 52 EW15
Chamberlain Cotts. SE5 162 DR81
Camberwell Gro.
Chamberlain Cres., W.Wick. 203 EB102
Chamberlain La., Pnr. 115 BU56
Chamberlain Pl. E17 123 DY55
Chamberlain Rd. N2 98 DC54
Chamberlain Rd. N9 100 DU48
Chamberlain Rd. W13 157 CG75
Midhurst Rd.
Chamberlain St. NW1 140 DF66
Regents Pk. Rd.
Chamberlain Wk., Felt. 176 BY91
Burgess Clo.
Chamberlain Way, Pnr. 115 BV55
Chamberlain Way, Surb. 198 CL101
Chamberlayne Rd. NW10 139 CW67
Chambers Clo., Green. 189 FU85
Chambers Gdns. N2 98 DD53
Strawberry Vale
Chambers La. NW10 139 CV66
Chambers Rd. N7 121 DL63
Chambers St. SE16 162 DU75
Chambers St., Hert. 32 DQ09
Chambersbury La., Hem.H. 40 BN24
Chambord St. E2 142 DT69
Champion Cres. SE26 183 DY91
Champion Gro. SE5 162 DR83
Champion Hill SE5 162 DR83
Champion Hill Est. SE5 162 DS83
Champion Pk. SE5 162 DR82
Champion Pk. Est. SE5 162 DR83
Denmark Hill
Champion Rd. SE26 183 DY91
Champion Rd., Upmin. 128 FP61
Champions Grn., Hodd. 33 EA14
Champions Way
Champions Way, Hodd. 33 EA14
Champness Clo. SE27 182 DR91
Rommany Rd.
Champneys Clo., Sutt. 217 CZ108
Chance Clo., Grays 170 FZ76
Chance St. E1 275 P4
Chance St. E1 142 DT70
Chance St. E2 275 P4
Chance St. E2 142 DT70
Chancel St. SE1 278 F3
Chancel St. SE1 141 DP74
Chancellor Gdns., S.Croy. 219 DP109
Chancellor Gro. SE21 182 DQ89
Chancellor Pas. E14 143 EA74
South Colonnade
Chancellor Pl. NW9 97 CT54
Chancellor Way, Sev. 256 FG122
Chancellors Rd. W6 159 CW78
Chancellors St. W6 159 CW78
Chancelot Rd. SE2 166 EV77
Chancery Clo., St.Alb. 43 CK15
Chancery Ct., Dart. 188 FN87
Downs Ave.
Chancery La. WC2 274 D8
Chancery La. WC2 141 DN72
Chancery La., Beck. 203 EB96
Chanctonbury Chase, Red. 251 DH134
Chanctonbury Clo. SE9 185 EP90
Chanctonbury Gdns., Sutt. 218 DB108
Chanctonbury Way N12 98 DA49
Chandler Ave. E16 144 EG71
Chandler Clo., Hmptn. 196 CA95
Chandler Rd., Loug. 85 EP39
Chandler St. E1 142 DV74
Wapping La.
Chandler Way SE15 162 DT80
Chandlers Clo., Felt. 175 BT87
Chandlers Dr., Erith 167 FD77
West St.
Chandler's La., Rick. 74 BL36
Chandlers Ms. E14 163 EA75
Chandlers Rd., St.Alb. 43 CJ17
Chandlers Way SW2 181 DN87
Chandlers Way, Hert. 31 DN09
Chandlers Way, Rom. 127 FE57
Chandos Ave. E17 101 EA54
Chandos Ave. N14 99 DJ48
Chandos Ave. N20 98 DC46
Chandos Ave. W5 157 CK77
Chandos Clo., Amer. 72 AW38
Chandos Clo., Buck.H. 102 EH47
Chandos Cres., Edg. 96 CM52
Chandos Mall, Slou. 152 AT75
High St.
Chandos Par., Edg. 96 CM52
Chandos Pl. WC2 277 P1
Chandos Pl. WC2 141 DL73
Chandos Rd. E15 123 ED64
Chandos Rd. N2 98 DD54
Chandos Rd. N17 100 DS54
Chandos Rd. NW2 119 CW64
Chandos Rd. NW10 138 CS70
Chandos Rd., Borwd. 78 CM40
Chandos Rd., Har. 116 CC57
Chandos Rd., Pnr. 116 BX59
Chandos Rd., Stai. 173 BD92
Chandos St. W1 273 J7
Chandos St. W1 141 DH71
Chandos Way NW11 120 DB60
Change All. EC3 275 L9
Chanlock Path, S.Ock. 149 FV73
Carnach Grn.
Channel Clo., Houns. 156 CA81
Channel Gate Rd. NW10 139 CT69
Old Oak La.
Channelsea Rd. E15 143 ED67
Channing Clo., Horn. 128 FM59
Channings, Wok. 226 AY115
Chant Sq. E15 143 ED66
Chant St. E15 143 ED66
Chanton Dr., Sutt. 217 CW110
Chantrey Clo., Ash. 231 CJ119
Chantrey Rd. SW9 161 DM83
Chantreywood, Brwd. 109 GA48
Chantry, The, Harl. 36 EU13
Chantry, The, Uxb. 134 BM69
Chantry Clo., Enf. 82 DQ38
Bedale Rd.
Chantry Clo., Har. 118 CM57
Chantry Clo., Horl. 268 DF147
Chantry Clo., Kings L. 58 BN29
Chantry Clo., Sid. 186 EY92
Ellenborough Rd.
Chantry Clo., West Dr. 134 BK73
Chantry Clo., Wind. 151 AN81
Chantry Cotts., Guil. 259 BB140
Chantry Rd.
Chantry Ct., Hat. 45 CU19
Chantry La.
Chantry Hurst, Epsom 232 CR115
Chantry La., Brom. 204 EK99
Bromley Common
Chantry La., Guil. 260 BM138
Chantry La., Hat. 45 CT19
Chantry La., St.Alb. 61 CK26
Chantry Pl., Har. 94 CB53
Chantry Pt. W9 139 CZ70
Chantry Rd., Cher. 194 BJ101
Chantry Rd., Chess. 216 CM106
Chantry Rd., Guil. 259 BB140
Chantry Rd., Har. 94 CB53
Chantry St. N1 141 DP67
Chantry Vw. Rd., Guil. 258 AX137
Chantry Way, Mitch. 200 DD97
Chantry Way, Rain. 147 FD68
Chapel Ave., Add. 212 BH105
Chapel Clo., Dart. 187 FE85
Chapel Clo., Grays 169 FV79
Chapel Clo., Hat. 64 DD27
Chapel Clo., Wat. 59 BT34
Chapel Cotts., Hem.H. 40 BK18
Chapel Ct. N2 120 DE55
Chapel Ct. SE1 279 K4
Chapel Ct., Dor. 263 CG135
Chapel Cft., Berk. 38 AS17
Chapel Cft., Kings L. 58 BG31
Chapel End, Ger.Cr. 90 AX54
Austenwood La.
Chapel End, Hodd. 49 EA18
Chapel Fm. Rd. SE9 185 EM90
Chapel Flds., Harl. 52 EW18
Chapel Gro., Add. 212 BH105
Chapel Gro., Epsom 233 CW119
Chapel High, Brwd. 108 FW47
High St.
Chapel Hill, Dart. 187 FE85
Chapel Hill, Lthd. 246 BX127
The St.
Chapel Ho. St. E14 163 EB78
Chapel La., Chig. 103 ET48
Chapel La. (Westcott), Dor. 262 CC137
Chapel La. (Westhumble), 247 CD130
Dor.
Chapel La., Hert. 31 DH13
Chapel La. 246 CC128
(Great Bookham), Lthd.
Chapel La., Pnr. 116 BX55
Chapel La., Rom. 126 EX59
Chapel La., Slou. 132 AV66
Chapel La., Uxb. 134 BN72
Chapel Mkt. N1 141 DN68
Chapel Pk. Rd., Add. 212 BH105
Chapel Path E11 124 EH58
Chapel Pl. EC2 275 M3
Chapel Pl. N1 141 DN68
Chapel Mkt.
Chapel Pl. N17 100 DT52
White Hart La.
Chapel Pl. W1 273 H9
Chapel Pl. W1 141 DH72
Chapel Rd. SE27 181 DP91
Chapel Rd. W13 137 CH74
Chapel Rd., Bexh. 166 FA84
Chapel Rd., Epp. 69 ET30
Chapel Rd. (Smallfield), 269 DP148
Horl.
Chapel Rd., Houns. 156 CB83
Chapel Rd., Ilf. 125 EN62
Chapel Rd., Oxt. 254 EJ131
Chapel Rd., Red. 250 DF134

Chapel Rd., Tad. 233 CW123
Chapel Rd., Twick. 177 CH87
Orleans Rd.
Chapel Rd., Warl. 237 DX118
Chapel Row, Uxb. 92 BJ53
Chapel Side W2 140 DB73
Chapel Sq., Vir.W. 192 AY98
Chapel Stones N17 100 DT53
King's Rd.
Chapel St. E15 143 ED66
Chapel St. NW1 272 B7
Chapel St. NW1 140 DE71
Chapel St. SW1 276 G5
Chapel St. SW1 160 DG76
Chapel St., Berk. 38 AW19
Chapel St., Enf. 82 DR41
Chapel St., Guil. 258 AX136
Castle St.
Chapel St., Hem.H. 40 BK19
Chapel St., Slou. 152 AT75
Chapel St., Uxb. 134 BJ67
Trumper Way
Chapel St., Wok. 227 BC121
Chapel Ter., Loug. 84 EL42
Forest Rd.
Chapel Vw., S.Croy. 220 DW107
Chapel Wk. NW4 119 CV56
Chapel Wk., Croy. 202 DQ103
Wellesley Rd.
Chapel Way N7 121 DM62
Sussex Way
Chapel Way, Epsom 233 CW119
Chapel Yd. SW18 180 DA85
Wandsworth High St.
Chapelfields, Ware 33 ED10
Chapelhouse Clo., Guil. 242 AS134
Park Barn Dr.
Chapelmount Rd., Wdf.Grn. 103 EM51
Chapels Clo., Slou. 131 AL74
Chaplaincy Gdns., Horn. 128 FL60
Chaplin Clo. SE1 278 E4
Chaplin Clo. SE1 161 DN75
Chaplin Cres., Sun. 175 BS93
Chaplin Rd. E15 144 EE67
Chaplin Rd. N17 122 DT55
Chaplin Rd. NW2 139 CU65
Chaplin Rd., Dag. 146 EY66
Chaplin Rd., Wem. 137 CJ65
Chaplin Sq. N12 98 DD52
Chapman Clo., West Dr. 154 BM76
Chapman Cres., Har. 118 CL57
Chapman Rd. E9 143 DZ65
Chapman Rd., Belv. 166 FA78
Chapman Rd., Croy. 201 DN102
Chapman St. E1 142 DV73
Chapmans Cres., Chesh. 54 AN29
Chapman's La. SE2 166 EW77
Chapmans La., Belv. 166 EX77
Chapmans La., Orp. 206 EW96
Chapmans Pk. Ind. Est. NW10 139 CT65
Chapmans Rd., Sev. 240 EY124
Chapmans Yd., Wat. 76 BW42
New Rd.
Chapone Pl. W1 273 M9
Chapter Clo. W4 158 CQ76
Beaumont Rd.
Chapter Clo., Uxb. 134 BM66
Chapter Ho. Ct. EC4 274 G9
Chapter Rd. NW2 119 CU64
Chapter Rd. SE17 161 DP78
Chapter St. SW1 277 M9
Chapter St. SW1 161 DK77
Chapter Way, Hmptn. 176 CA91
Chaptree Ms., Wind. 151 AR80
Chara Pl. W4 158 CR79
Charcroft Gdns., Enf. 83 DX42
Chardin Rd. W4 158 CS77
Elliott Rd.
Chardins Clo., Hem.H. 39 BF19
Chardmore Rd. N16 122 DU60
Chardwell Clo. E6 144 EL72
Northumberland Rd.
Charecroft Way W12 159 CX75
Charfield Ct. W9 140 DB70
Shirland Rd.
Charford Rd. E16 144 EG71
Chargate Clo., Walt. 213 BT107
Chargeable La. E13 144 EF70
Chargeable St. E16 144 EF70
Chargrove Clo. SE16 163 DX75
Marlow Way
Charing Clo., Orp. 223 ET105
Charing Cross WC2 277 P2
Charing Cross Rd. WC2 273 N9
Charing Cross Rd. WC2 141 DK72
Chariotts Pl., Wind. 151 AR81
Peascod St.
Charlbert St. NW8 140 DE68
Charlbury Ave., Stan. 95 CK50
Charlbury Clo., Rom. 106 FJ51
Charlbury Cres., Rom. 106 FJ51
Charlbury Gdns., Ilf. 125 ET61
Charlbury Gro. W5 137 CJ72
Charlbury Rd., Uxb. 114 BM62
Charldane Rd. SE9 185 EP90
Charlecote Gro. SE26 182 DV90
Charlecote Rd., Dag. 126 EY62
Charlemont Rd. E6 145 EM69
Charles Barry Clo. SW4 161 DJ83
Charles Burton Ct. E5 123 DY64
Ashenden Rd.
Charles Clo., Sid. 186 EV91
Charles Coveney Rd. SE15 162 DT81
Southampton Way
Charles Cres., Har. 117 CD59
Charles Dickens Ho. E2 142 DV69
Charles Gdns., Slou. 132 AV72
Borderside
Charles Grinling Wk. SE18 165 EN77
Charles Ho. N17 100 DT52
Charles Ho., Wind. 151 AQ81
Alma Rd.
Charles La. NW8 140 DD68
St. John's Wd. High St.
Charles Pl. NW1 273 L3
Charles Rd. E7 144 EJ66
Lens Rd.
Charles Rd. SW19 200 DA95
Charles Rd. W13 137 CG72
Charles Rd., Dag. 147 FD65
Charles Rd., Rom. 126 EX59
Charles Rd., Sev. 225 FB110
Charles Rd., Stai. 174 BK93
Charles II St. SW1 277 M2
Charles II St. SW1 141 DK74
Charles Sevright Dr. NW7 97 CX50
Charles Sq. N1 275 L3
Charles Sq. Est. N1 142 DR69
Pitfield St.
Charles St. E16 144 EK74
Charles St. SW13 158 CS82
Charles St. W1 277 H2
Charles St. W1 141 DH74
Charles St., Berk. 38 AV19
Charles St., Cher. 193 BF102
Charles St., Croy. 202 DQ104
Charles St., Enf. 82 DT43
Charles St., Epp. 70 EU32
Charles St., Grays 170 GB79
Charles St., Green. 189 FS85
Charles St., Hem.H. 40 BJ21
Charles St., Houns. 156 BY82
Charles St., Uxb. 135 BP70
Charles St., Wind. 151 AQ81
Charlesfield SE9 184 EJ90
Charlesfield Rd., Horl. 268 DF147
Charleston Clo., Felt. 175 BU90
Charleston St. SE17 279 J9
Charleston St. SE17 162 DQ77
Charlesworth Clo., Hem.H. 40 BK22
Charleville Circ. SE26 182 DU92
Charleville Rd. W14 159 CY78
Charlieville Rd., Erith 167 FC80
Northumberland Pk.
Charlmont Rd. SW17 180 DF93
Charlock Way, Guil. 243 BB131
Charlock Way, Wat. 75 BT44
Charlotte Clo., Bexh. 186 EY85
Charlotte Despard Ave. SW11 160 DG81
Charlotte Gdns., Rom. 105 FB51
Charlotte Gro., Horl. 269 DN147
Charlotte Ms. W1 273 L6
Charlotte Ms. W14 159 CY77
Munden St.
Charlotte Pl. NW9 118 CQ57
Uphill Dr.
Charlotte Pl. SW1 277 K9
Charlotte Pl. W1 273 L7
Charlotte Pl., Grays 169 FV79
Charlotte Rd. EC2 275 M3
Charlotte Rd. EC2 142 DS70
Charlotte Rd. SW13 159 CT81
Charlotte Rd., Dag. 147 FB65
Charlotte Rd., Wall. 219 DJ107
Charlotte Row SW4 161 DJ83
North St.
Charlotte Sq., Rich. 178 CM86
Greville Rd.
Charlotte St. W1 273 L6
Charlotte St. W1 141 DJ71
Charlotte Ter. N1 141 DM67
Charlow Clo. SW6 160 DC82
Townmead Rd.
Charlton Ave., Walt. 213 BV105
Charlton Ch. La. SE7 164 EJ78
Charlton Clo., Hodd. 49 EA17
Charlton Clo., Slou. 151 AP75
Haig Dr.
Charlton Clo., Uxb. 115 BP61
Charlton Cres., Bark. 145 ET68
Charlton Dene SE7 164 EJ80
Charlton Dr., West. 238 EK117
Charlton Gdns., Couls. 235 DJ118
Charlton Kings, Wey. 195 BS104
Charlton Kings Rd. NW5 121 DK64
Charlton La. SE7 164 EK78
Charlton La., Shep. 195 BQ97
Charlton Mead La., Hodd. 49 ED18
Charlton Mead La. S., Hodd. 49 ED18
Charlton Mead La.
Charlton Pk. La. SE7 164 EK80
Charlton Pk. Rd. SE7 164 EK79
Charlton Pl. N1 141 DP68
Charlton Pl., Wind. 150 AJ82
Charlton Row
Charlton Rd. N9 101 DX46
Charlton Rd. NW10 138 CS67
Charlton Rd. SE3 164 EH80
Charlton Rd. SE7 164 EJ79
Charlton Rd., Har. 117 CK57
Charlton Rd., Shep. 195 BQ97
Charlton Rd., Wem. 118 CM60
Charlton Row, Wind. 150 AJ82
Charlton Sq., Wind. 150 AJ82
Charlton Row
Charlton St., Grays 169 FX79
Charlton Wk., Wind. 150 AJ82
Charlton Row
Charlton Way SE3 164 EE81
Charlton Way, Hodd. 49 EA17
Charlton Way, Wind. 150 AJ82
Charlwood, Croy. 221 DZ109
Charlwood Clo., Har. 95 CE52
Kelvin Cres.
Charlwood Dr., Lthd. 231 CD115
Charlwood Pl. SW1 277 L9
Charlwood Pl. SW1 161 DJ77
Charlwood Rd. SW15 159 CX84
Charlwood Rd., Horl. 268 DB152
Charlwood Sq., Mitch. 200 DD97
Charlwood St. SW1 277 L10
Charlwood St. SW1 161 DJ78
Charlwood Ter. SW15 159 CX84
Cardinal Pl.
Charm Clo., Horl. 268 DE147
Charman Rd., Red. 250 DE134
Charmans La., Reig. 264 CS140
Charmian Ave., Stan. 117 CK55
Charminster Ave. SW19 200 DA96
Charminster Ct., Surb. 197 CK100
Charminster Rd. SE9 184 EK91
Charminster Rd., Wor.Pk. 199 CX102
Charmouth Ct., St.Alb. 43 CG17
Charmouth Rd., St.Alb. 43 CG18
Charmouth Rd., Well. 166 EV81
Charmwood La., Orp. 224 EV109
Charne, The, Sev. 241 FG117
Charnock, Swan. 207 FE98
Charnock Rd. E5 122 DV62
Charnwood Ave. SW19 200 DA96
Charnwood Clo., N.Mal. 198 CS98
Charnwood Dr. E18 124 EH55
Charnwood Gdns. E14 163 EA77
Charnwood Pl. N20 98 DC48
Charnwood Rd. SE25 202 DR99
Charnwood Rd., Enf. 82 DV36
Charnwood Rd., Uxb. 134 BN69
Charnwood St. E5 122 DV61
Charrington Rd., Croy. 201 DP103
Drayton Rd.
Charrington St. NW1 141 DK68
Charsley Clo., Amer. 72 AW39
Charsley Rd. SE6 183 EB89
Chart Clo., Brom. 204 EE95
Chart Clo., Croy. 202 DW100
Stockbury Rd.
Chart Clo., Dor. 263 CK140
Chart Downs, Dor. 263 CJ139
Chart Gdns., Dor. 263 CJ139
Chart La., Dor. 263 CH136
Chart La., Reig. 250 DB134
Chart La. S., Dor. 263 CJ138
Chart St. N1 275 L2
Chart St. N1 142 DR69
Charta Rd., Egh. 173 BC93
Charter Ave., Ilf. 125 ER60
Charter Clo., St.Alb. 43 CD20
Charter Clo., Slou. 152 AT76
Osborne St.
Charter Ct., N.Mal. 198 CS97
Charter Cres., Houns. 156 BY84
Charter Dr., Amer. 72 AT38
Charter Dr., Bex. 186 EY87
Charter Pl., Uxb. 134 BJ66
Charter Pl., Wat. 76 BW41
Beechen Gro.
Charter Rd., Kings.T. 198 CP97
Charter Rd., The, Wdf.Grn. 102 EE51
Charter Sq., Kings.T. 198 CP96
Charter Way N3 119 CZ56
Regents Pk. Rd.
Charter Way N14 81 DJ44
Charterhouse Ave., Wem. 117 CJ63
Charterhouse Bldgs. EC1 274 G5
Charterhouse Dr., Sev. 256 FG123
Charterhouse Ms. EC1 274 G6
Charterhouse Rd., Orp. 206 EU104
Charterhouse Sq. EC1 274 G6
Charterhouse Sq. EC1 141 DP71
Charterhouse St. EC1 274 F7
Charterhouse St. EC1 141 DN71
Charteris Rd. N4 121 DN60
Charteris Rd. NW6 139 CZ67
Charteris Rd., Wdf.Grn. 102 EH52
Charters Clo. SE19 182 DS92
Charters Cross, Harl. 51 ER18
Chartfield Ave. SW15 179 CV85
Chartfield Rd., Reig. 266 DC135
Chartfield Sq. SW15 179 CX85
Chartfield Ave.
Chartham Gro. SE27 181 DN90
Royal Circ.
Chartham Rd. SE25 202 DV97
Chartley Ave. NW2 118 CS62
Chartley Ave., Stan. 95 CF51
Charton Clo., Belv. 166 EZ79
Chartridge Clo., Barn. 79 CU43
Chartridge Clo., Wat. 76 CC44
Chartridge La., Chesh. 54 AM29
Chartridge Way, Hem.H. 41 BQ20
Chartway, Reig. 250 DB134
Chartway, Sev. 257 FJ124
Chartwell Clo. SE9 185 EQ89
Chartwell Clo., Croy. 202 DR102
Tavistock Rd.
Chartwell Clo., Grnf. 136 CB67
Chartwell Clo., Wal.Abb. 68 EE33
Chartwell Dr., Orp. 223 ER106
Chartwell Gdns., Sutt. 199 CZ104
Chartwell Gate, Beac. 89 AK53
Chartwell Pl., Epsom 216 CS114
Chartwell Pl., Har. 117 CD60
Chartwell Pl., Sutt. 199 CZ104
Chartwell Rd., Nthwd. 93 BT51
Chartwell Way SE20 202 DV95
Charville La., Hayes 135 BQ69
Charville La. W., Uxb. 135 BP69
Charwood SW16 181 DN91
Chasden Rd., Hem.H. 39 BF17
Chase, The E12 124 EK63
Chase, The SW4 161 DH83
Chase, The SW16 181 DM94
Chase, The SW20 199 CY95
Chase, The, Ash. 231 CJ118
Chase, The, Bexh. 167 FB83
Chase, The (Cromwell Rd.), Brwd. 108 FV49
Chase, The (Ingrave), Brwd. 109 GC50
Chase, The (Seven Arches Rd.), Brwd. 108 FX48
Chase, The (Woodman Rd.), Brwd. 108 FX50
Chase, The, Brom. 204 EH97
Chase, The, Chesh. 54 AP29
Chalk Hill
Chase, The, Chig. 103 EQ49
Chase, The, Couls. 219 DJ114
Chase, The, Edg. 96 CP53
Chase, The, Grays 169 FX79
Chase, The, Guil. 258 AU135
Chase, The, Hem.H. 40 BL21
Turners Hill
Chase, The (Tylers Grn.), H.Wyc. 88 AC46
Chase, The (Wooburn), H.Wyc. 110 AF59
Chase, The, Horn. 127 FF62
Chase, The (East Horsley), Lthd. 245 BT126
Chase, The (Oxshott), Lthd. 230 CC115
Chase, The, Loug. 102 EJ45
Chase, The, Pnr. 116 BZ56
Chase, The (Eastcote), Pnr. 116 BW58
Chase, The, Rad. 77 CF35
Chase, The, Reig. 250 DD134
Chase, The, Rom. 127 FE55
Chase, The (Chadwell Heath), Rom. 126 EY58
Chase, The (Rush Grn.), Rom. 127 FD62
Chase, The, Stan. 95 CG50
Chase, The, Sun. 195 BV95
Chase, The, Tad. 234 DA122
Chase, The, Upmin. 129 FS62
Chase, The, Uxb. 114 BN64
Chase, The, Wall. 219 DL106
Chase, The (Cheshunt), Wal.Cr. 65 DP28
Chase, The, Ware 33 EA09
Chase, The, Wat. 75 BS42
Chase Clo., Amer. 55 AN43
Chase Clo., H.Wyc. 88 AC46
Chase Ct. Gdns., Enf. 82 DQ41
Chase Cross Rd., Rom. 105 FC52
Chase End, Epsom 216 CR112
Chase Gdns. E4 101 EA49
Chase Gdns., Twick. 177 CD86
Chase Grn., Enf. 82 DQ41
Chase Grn. Ave., Enf. 81 DP40
Chase Hill, Enf. 82 DQ41
Chase Ho. Gdns., Horn. 128 FM57
Great Nelmes Chase
Chase La., Chig. 103 ET48
Chase La., Ilf. 125 ER57
Chase Ridings, Enf. 81 DN40
Chase Rd. N14 81 DJ43
Chase Rd. NW10 138 CR70
Chase Rd. W3 138 CR70
Chase Rd., Brwd. 108 FW48
Chase Rd., Epsom 216 CR112
Chase Side N14 80 DG43
Chase Side, Enf. 82 DQ41
Chase Side Ave. SW20 199 CY96
Chase Side Ave., Enf. 82 DQ40
Chase Side Cres., Enf. 82 DQ39
Chase Side Pl., Enf. 82 DQ41
Chase Side
Chase Sq., Grav. 191 GH86
Princes St.
Chase Way N14 99 DH47
Chasefield Clo., Guil. 243 BA131
Chasefield Rd. SW17 180 DF91
Chaseley Dr. W4 158 CP81
Wellesley Rd.
Chaseley Dr., S.Croy. 220 DR110
Chaseley St. E14 143 DY72
Chasemore Clo., Mitch. 200 DF101
Chasemore Gdns., Croy. 219 DP106
Thorneloe Gdns.
Chaseside Clo., Rom. 105 FE51
Chaseside Gdns., Cher. 194 BH101
Chaseville Pk. Rd. N21 81 DL43
Chaseways, Saw. 36 EW07
Chasewood Ave., Enf. 81 DP40
Chastilian Rd., Dart. 187 FF87
Chatelet Clo., Horl. 269 DH147
Chatfield, Slou. 131 AN71
Chatfield Ct., Cat. 236 DR122
York Gate
Chatfield Dr., Guil. 243 BC132
Kingfisher Dr.
Chatfield Rd. SW11 160 DC83
Chatfield Rd., Croy. 201 DP102
Chatham Ave., Brom. 204 EF101
Chatham Clo. NW11 120 DA57
Chatham Clo., Sutt. 199 CZ101
Chatham Hill Rd., Sev. 257 FJ121
Chatham Pl. E9 142 DW65
Chatham Rd. E17 123 DY55
Chatham Rd. E18 102 EF54
Grove Hill
Chatham Rd. SW11 180 DF86
Chatham Rd., Kings.T. 198 CN96
Chatham Rd., Orp. 223 EQ106
Chatham St. SE17 279 K8
Chatham St. SE17 162 DR77
Chatsfield, Epsom 217 CU110
Chatsfield Pl. W5 138 CL72
Chatsworth Ave. NW4 97 CW54
Chatsworth Ave. SW20 199 CY95
Chatsworth Ave., Brom. 184 EH92
Chatsworth Ave., Sid. 186 EU88
Chatsworth Ave., Wem. 118 CM64
Chatsworth Clo. NW4 97 CW54
Chatsworth Clo., Borwd. 78 CN41
Chatsworth Clo., W.Wick. 204 EF103
Chatsworth Ct. W8 160 DA77
Pembroke Rd.
Chatsworth Cres., Houns. 157 CD84
Chatsworth Dr., Enf. 100 DU45
Chatsworth Est. E5 123 DX63
Elderfield Rd.
Chatsworth Gdns. W3 138 CP74
Chatsworth Gdns., Har. 116 CB60
Chatsworth Gdns., N.Mal. 199 CT99
Chatsworth Pl., Lthd. 215 CD113
Chatsworth Pl., Mitch. 200 DF97
Chatsworth Pl., Tedd. 177 CG91
Chatsworth Ri. W5 138 CM70
Chatsworth Rd. E5 122 DW62
Chatsworth Rd. E15 124 EF64
Chatsworth Rd. NW2 139 CX65
Chatsworth Rd. W4 158 CQ79
Chatsworth Rd. W5 138 CM70
Chatsworth Rd., Croy. 220 DR105
Chatsworth Rd., Dart. 188 FJ85
Chatsworth Rd., Hayes 135 BV70
Chatsworth Rd., Sutt. 217 CX106
Chatsworth Way SE27 181 DP90
Chatteris Ave., Rom. 106 FJ51
Chattern Hill, Ashf. 175 BP91
Chattern Rd., Ashf. 175 BQ91
Chatterton Rd. N4 121 DP62
Chatterton Rd., Brom. 204 EK98
Chatto Rd. SW11 180 DF85
Chaucer Ave., Hayes 135 BU71
Chaucer Ave., Houns. 155 BV82
Chaucer Ave., Rich. 158 CN83
Chaucer Ave., Wey. 212 BN108
Chaucer Clo. N11 99 DJ50
Chaucer Clo., Bans. 217 CY114
Chaucer Clo., Berk. 38 AT18
Chaucer Clo., Til. 171 GJ82
Chaucer Ct. N16 122 DS63
Chaucer Ct., Guil. 258 AW137
Lawn Rd.
Chaucer Dr. SE1 162 DT77
Chaucer Gdns., Sutt. 200 DA104
Chaucer Grn., Croy. 202 DW101
Chaucer Pk., Dart. 188 FM87
Chaucer Rd. E7 144 EG65
Chaucer Rd. E11 124 EG58
Chaucer Rd. E17 101 EC54
Chaucer Rd. SE24 181 DN85
Chaucer Rd. W3 138 CQ74
Chaucer Rd., Ashf. 174 BL91
Chaucer Rd., Grav. 190 GD90
Chaucer Rd., Rom. 105 FH52
Chaucer Rd., Sid. 186 EW88
Chaucer Rd., Sutt. 218 DA105
Chaucer Rd., Well. 165 ET81
Chaucer Way SW19 180 DD93
Chaucer Way, Add. 212 BG107
Chaucer Way, Dart. 168 FN84
Chaucer Way, Hodd. 33 EA13
Chaulden Ho. Gdns., Hem.H. 39 BF21
Chaulden La., Hem.H. 39 BD22
Chaulden Ter., Hem.H. 39 BF21
Chauncey Clo. N9 100 DU48
Chauncy Ave., Pot.B. 64 DC33
Chaundrye Clo. SE9 184 EL86
Chauntler Clo. E16 144 EH72
Chauntry Clo., Maid. 130 AC73
Chave Rd., Dart. 188 FL90
Chavecroft Ter., Epsom 233 CW119
Chaworth Rd., Cher. 211 BC107
Cheam Clo., Tad. 233 CV121
Waterfield
Cheam Common Rd., Wor.Pk. 199 CV103
Cheam Mans., Sutt. 217 CY108
Cheam Pk. Way, Sutt. 217 CY107
Cheam Rd., Epsom 217 CU110
Cheam Rd., Sutt. 217 CZ107
Cheam Rd. (East Ewell), Sutt. 217 CX110
Cheam St. SE15 162 DV83
Evelina Rd.
Cheapside EC2 275 H9
Cheapside EC2 142 DQ72
Cheapside, Wok. 210 AX114
Cheapside La., Uxb. 113 BF62
Chedburgh, Welw.G.C. 30 DD08
Cheddar Rd., Houns. 154 BN82
Cromer Rd.
Cheddar Waye, Hayes 135 BV72
Cheddington Rd. N18 100 DS48
Chedworth Clo. E16 144 EF72
Hallsville Rd.
Cheelson Rd., S.Ock. 149 FW68
Cheeseman Clo., Hmptn. 176 BY93
Cheesemans Ter. W14 159 CZ78
Cheffins Rd., Hodd. 33 DZ14
Chelford Rd., Brom. 183 ED92
Chelmer Cres., Bark. 146 EV68
Chelmer Dr., Brwd. 109 GE44
Chelmer Rd. E9 123 DX64
Chelmer Rd., Grays 171 GG78
Chelmer Rd., Upmin. 129 FR58
Chelmsford Ave., Rom. 105 FD52
Chelmsford Clo. E6 145 EM72
Guildford Rd.
Chelmsford Clo. W6 159 CX79
Chelmsford Clo., Sutt. 218 DA109
Chelmsford Dr., Upmin. 128 FM62
Chelmsford Gdns., Ilf. 124 EL59
Chelmsford Rd. E11 123 ED60
Chelmsford Rd. E17 123 EA58
Chelmsford Rd. E18 102 EF53
Chelmsford Rd. N14 99 DJ45
Chelmsford Rd., B.Stort. 37 FH05
Chelmsford Rd., Brwd. 109 FZ44
Chelmsford Rd., Hert. 31 DN10
Chelmsford Sq. NW10 139 CW67
Chelsea Bri. SW1 161 DH79
Chelsea Bri. SW8 161 DH79
Chelsea Bri. Rd. SW1 276 F10
Chelsea Bri. Rd. SW1 160 DG78
Chelsea Cloisters SW3 160 DE77
Lucan Pl.
Chelsea Clo. NW10 138 CR67
Winchelsea Rd.
Chelsea Clo., Edg. 96 CN54
Chelsea Clo., Hmptn. 176 CC93
Chelsea Embk. SW3 160 DE79
Chelsea Flds., Hodd. 33 EB13
Chelsea Gdns., Sutt. 217 CY105
Chelsea Harbour SW10 160 DD81
Chelsea Harbour Dr. SW10 160 DC81
Chelsea Manor Gdns. SW3 160 DE78
Chelsea Manor St. SW3 160 DE78
Chelsea Pk. Gdns. SW3 160 DD79
Chelsea Sq. SW3 276 A10
Chelsea Sq. SW3 160 DD78
Chelsea Wf. SW10 160 DD80
Lots Rd.
Chelsfield Ave. N9 101 DX45
Chelsfield Gdns. SE26 182 DW90
Chelsfield Grn. N9 101 DX45
Chelsfield Ave.
Chelsfield Hill, Orp. 224 EW109
Chelsfield La., Orp. 224 FA108
Chelsfield La. (Chelsfield), Orp. 206 EX101
Chelsfield La., Sev. 225 FC109
Chelsfield Rd., Orp. 206 EW100
Chelsham Clo., Warl. 237 DY118
Limpsfield Rd.
Chelsham Common Rd., Warl. 237 EA117
Chelsham Ct. Rd., Warl. 237 ED118
Chelsham Rd. SW4 161 DK83
Chelsham Rd., S.Croy. 220 DR107
Chelsham Rd., Warl. 237 DZ118
Chelsing Ri., Hem.H. 41 BQ21
Chelston App., Ruis. 115 BU61
Chelston Rd., Ruis. 115 BU60
Chelsworth Clo., Rom. 106 FM53
Chelsworth Dr.
Chelsworth Dr. SE18 165 ER79
Chelsworth Dr., Rom. 106 FL53
Cheltenham Ave., Twick. 177 CG87
Cheltenham Clo., Grav. 191 GJ92
Cheltenham Clo., N.Mal. 198 CQ97
Northcote Rd.
Cheltenham Clo., Nthlt. 136 CB65
Cheltenham Gdns. E6 144 EL68
Cheltenham Gdns., Loug. 84 EL44
Cheltenham Pl. W3 138 CP74
Cheltenham Pl., Har. 118 CL56
Cheltenham Rd. E10 123 EC58
Cheltenham Rd. SE15 162 DW84
Cheltenham Rd., Orp. 206 EU104
Cheltenham Ter. SW3 276 E10
Cheltenham Ter. SW3 160 DF78
Cheltenham Vill., Stai. 173 BF86
Chelverton Rd. SW15 159 CX84
Chelveston, Welw.G.C. 30 DD08
Chelwood Ave., Hat. 45 CU16
Chelwood Clo. E4 83 EB44
Chelwood Clo., Epsom 217 CT112
Chelwood Clo., Nthwd. 93 BQ52
Chelwood Gdns., Rich. 158 CN82
Chelwood Wk. SE4 163 DY84
Chenappa Clo. E13 144 EG69

Chenduit Way, Stan. 95 CF50
Chene Dr., St.Alb. 43 CD18
Cheney Rd. NW1 273 P1
Cheney Rd. NW1 141 DL68
Cheney Row E17 101 DZ53
Cheney St., Pnr. 116 BW57
Cheneys Rd. E11 124 EE62
Chenies, The, Dart. 187 FE91
Chenies, The, Orp. 205 ES100
Chenies Ave., Amer. 72 AW39
Chenies Ct., Hem.H. 41 BP15
Datchet Clo.
Chenies Hill, Hem.H. 57 BB34
Chenies Ms. WC1 273 M5
Chenies Par., Amer. 72 AW40
Chenies Pl. NW1 141 DK68
Chenies Rd., Rick. 73 BD40
Chenies St. WC1 273 M6
Chenies St. WC1 141 DK71
Chenies Way, Wat. 93 BS45
Cheniston Clo., W.Byf. 212 BG113
Madeira Rd.
Cheniston Gdns. W8 160 DB76
Chennells, Hat. 45 CT19
Chepstow Ave., Horn. 128 FL62
Chepstow Clo. SW15 179 CY86
Lytton Gro.
Chepstow Cres. W11 140 DA73
Chepstow Cres., Ilf. 125 ES58
Chepstow Gdns., Sthl. 136 BZ72
Chepstow Pl. W2 140 DA72
Chepstow Ri., Croy. 202 DS104
Chepstow Rd. W2 140 DA72
Chepstow Rd. W7 157 CG76
Chepstow Rd., Croy. 202 DS104
Chepstow Vill. W11 139 CZ73
Chepstow Way SE15 162 DT80
Exeter Rd.
Chequer St. EC1 275 J5
Chequer St., St.Alb. 43 CD20
Chequer Tree Clo., Wok. 226 AS116
Chequers, Hat. 29 CX13
Chequers, Welw.G.C. 29 CX12
Chequers Clo., Horl. 268 DG147
Chequers Clo., Orp. 205 ET98
Chequers Clo., Tad. 249 CU125
Chequers Dr., Horl. 268 DG147
Chequers Fld., Welw.G.C. 29 CX12
Chequers Gdns. N13 99 DP50
Chequers Hill, Amer. 55 AR40
Chequers La., Dag. 146 EZ71
Chequers La., Tad. 249 CU125
Chequers La., Wat. 60 BW30
Chequers Orchard, Iver 133 BF72
Chequers Par. SE9 185 EM86
Eltham High St.
Chequers Pl., Dor. 263 CH136
Chequers Rd., Brwd. 106 FM46
Chequers Rd., Loug. 85 EN43
Chequers Rd., Rom. 106 FL47
Chequers Sq., Uxb. 134 BJ66
High St.
Chequers Wk., Wal.Abb. 68 EF33
Chartwell Clo.
Chequers Way N13 99 DP50
Chequers Yd., Dor. 263 CH136
Chequers Pl.
Cherbury Clo. SE28 146 EX72
Cherbury Ct. N1 142 DR68
Cherbury St.
Cherbury St. N1 275 L1
Cherbury St. N1 142 DR68
Cherchefelle Ms., Stan. 95 CH50
Cherimoya Gdns., W.Mol. 196 CB97
Kelvinbrook
Cherington Rd. W7 137 CF74
Cheriton Ave., Brom. 204 EF99
Cheriton Ave., Ilf. 103 EM54
Cheriton Clo. W5 137 CJ71
Cheriton Clo., Barn. 80 DG41
Cheriton Clo., St.Alb. 43 CK16
Cheriton Ct., Walt. 196 BW102
St. Johns Dr.
Cheriton Dr. SE18 165 ER80
Cheriton Sq. SW17 180 DG89
Cherkley Hill, Lthd. 247 CJ126
Cherries, The, Slou. 132 AV72
Cherry Acre, Ger.Cr. 90 AX49
Cherry Ave., Brwd. 109 FZ48
Cherry Ave., Slou. 152 AX75
Cherry Ave., Sthl. 136 BX74
Cherry Ave., Swan. 207 FD97
Cherry Bounce, Hem.H. 40 BK18
Cherry Clo. E17 123 EB57
Eden Rd.
Cherry Clo. SW2 181 DN87
Tulse Hill
Cherry Clo. W5 157 CK76
Cherry Clo., Bans. 217 CX114
Cherry Clo., Cars. 200 DF103
Cherry Clo., Mord. 199 CY98
Cherry Clo., Ruis. 115 BT62
The Roundways
Cherry Cres., Brent. 157 CH80
Cherry Cft., Welw.G.C. 29 CX05
Cherry Dr., Beac. 88 AH51
Cherry Gdn. St. SE16 162 DV75
Cherry Gdns., Dag. 126 EZ64
Cherry Gdns., Nthlt. 136 CB66
Cherry Garth, Brent. 157 CK78
Cherry Grn. Clo., Red. 267 DH136
Cherry Gro., Hayes 135 BV74
Cherry Gro., Uxb. 135 BP71
Cherry Hill, Barn. 80 DB44
Cherry Hill, Har. 95 CE52
Cherry Hill, Rick. 74 BH41
Cherry Hill, St.Alb. 60 CA25
Cherry Hill Gdns., Croy. 219 DM105
Cherry Hollow, Abb.L. 59 BT31
Cherry La., West Dr. 154 BM77
Cherry Laurel Wk. SW2 181 DM86
Beechdale Rd.
Cherry Orchard, Amer. 55 AS37
Cherry Orchard, Ash. 232 CP118
Cherry Orchard, Hem.H. 40 BG18
Cherry Orchard, Slou. 132 AV66
Cherry Orchard, Stai. 174 BG92
Cherry Orchard, West Dr. 154 BL75
Cherry Orchard Clo., Orp. 206 EW99
Cherry Orchard Gdns., Croy. 202 DR103
Oval Rd.
Cherry Orchard Gdns., W.Mol. 196 BZ97
Cherry Orchard Rd., Brom. 204 EL103
Cherry Orchard Rd., Croy. 202 DR103
Cherry Orchard Rd., W.Mol. 196 BZ97
Cherry Ri., Ch.St.G. 90 AX47
Cherry Rd., Enf. 82 DW38
Cherry St., Rom. 127 FD57
Cherry St., Wok. 226 AY118
Cherry Tree Ave., Guil. 242 AT134
Cherry Tree Ave., St.Alb. 61 CK26
Cherry Tree Ave., Stai. 174 BH93
Cherry Tree Ave., West Dr. 134 BM72
Cherry Tree Clo., Grays 170 GD79
Cherry Tree Clo., Rain. 147 FG68
Cherry Tree Clo., Wem. 117 CF63
Cherry Tree Ct. NW9 118 CQ56
Cherry Tree Ct., Couls. 235 DM117
Cherry Tree Dr. SW16 181 DL90
Cherry Tree Grn., Hert. 31 DM07
Cherry Tree Grn., S.Croy. 220 DV114
Cherry Tree La., Dart. 187 FF90
Cherry Tree La., Hem.H. 41 BQ15
Cherry Tree La., Pot.B. 64 DB34
Ashwood Rd.
Cherry Tree La., Rain. 147 FE69
Cherry Tree La., Rick. 91 BC46
Cherry Tree La., Slou. 133 AZ65
Cherry Tree Ri., Buck.H. 102 EJ49
Cherry Tree Rd. E15 124 EE63
Wingfield Rd.
Cherry Tree Rd. N2 120 DF56
Cherry Tree Rd., Beac. 110 AH55
Cherry Tree Rd., Hodd. 49 EA16
Cherry Tree Rd., Slou. 131 AQ66
Cherry Tree Rd., Wat. 75 BV36
Cherry Tree Wk. EC1 142 DQ70
Whitecross St.
Cherry Tree Wk., Beck. 203 DZ98
Cherry Tree Wk., Chesh. 54 AR29
Cherry Tree Wk., W.Wick. 222 EF105
Cherry Tree Way, H.Wyc. 88 AC46
Cherry Tree Way, Stan. 95 CH51
Cherry Wk., Brom. 204 EG102
Cherry Wk., Grays 171 GG76
Cherry Wk., Rain. 147 FF68
Cherry Wk., Rick. 74 BJ40
Cherry Way, Epsom 216 CR107
Cherry Way, Hat. 45 CU21
Cherry Way, Shep. 195 BR98
Cherry Way, Slou. 153 BC83
Cherry Wd. Clo., Beac. 89 AR50
Cherry Wd. Way W5 138 CN71
Hanger Vale La.
Cherrycot Hill, Orp. 223 ER105
Cherrycot Ri., Orp. 223 EQ105
Cherrycroft Gdns., Pnr. 94 BZ52
Westfield Pk.
Cherrydale, Wat. 75 BT42
Cherrydown Ave. E4 101 DZ48
Cherrydown Clo. E4 101 DZ48
Cherrydown Rd., Sid. 186 EX89
Cherrydown Wk., Rom. 105 FB54
Cherrytree La., Ger.Cr. 90 AX54
Cherrytree La., Iver 134 BG67
Cherrywood Ave., Egh. 172 AV94
Cherrywood Clo. E3 143 DY69
Cherrywood Clo., Kings.T. 178 CN94
Cherrywood Dr. SW15 179 CX85
Cherrywood Dr., Grav. 190 GE91
Cherrywood La., Mord. 199 CY98
Cherston Gdns., Loug. 85 EN42
Cherston Rd.
Cherston Rd., Loug. 85 EN42
Chertsey Bri. Rd., Cher. 194 BK101
Chertsey Clo., Ken. 235 DP115
Chertsey Cres., Croy. 221 EC110
Chertsey Dr., Sutt. 199 CY103
Chertsey La., Cher. 193 BF97
Chertsey La., Stai. 173 BE92
Chertsey Rd. E11 123 ED61
Chertsey Rd., Add. 194 BH103
Chertsey Rd., Ashf. 175 BR94
Chertsey Rd., Felt. 175 BS92
Chertsey Rd., Ilf. 125 ER63
Chertsey Rd., Shep. 194 BK101
Chertsey Rd., Sun. 175 BR94
Chertsey Rd., Twick. 177 CF86
Chertsey Rd., W.Byf. 212 BK111
Chertsey Rd., Wok. 227 AZ116
Chertsey Rd. (Chobham), Wok. 210 AT110
Chertsey St. SW17 180 DG92
Chertsey St., Guil. 258 AX135
Cherubs, The, Slou. 131 AQ65
Chervil Clo., Felt. 175 BU90
Chervil Ms. SE28 146 EV74
Cherwell Clo., Rick. 74 BN43
Cherwell Clo., Slou. 153 BB79
Tweed Rd.
Cherwell Ct., Epsom 216 CQ105
Cherwell Gro., S.Ock. 149 FU73
Cherwell Way, Ruis. 115 BQ58
Cheryls Clo. SW6 160 DB81
Cheselden Rd., Guil. 258 AY135
Cheseman St. SE26 182 DV90
Chesfield Rd., Kings.T. 178 CL94
Chesham Ave., Orp. 205 EP100
Chesham Clo. SW1 276 F7
Chesham Clo., Rom. 127 FD56
Chesham Clo., Sutt. 217 CY110
Chesham Ct., Nthwd. 93 BT51
Frithwood Ave.
Chesham Cres. SE20 202 DW96
Chesham La., Ch.St.G. 90 AY48
Chesham La., Ger.Cr. 90 AY49
Chesham Ms. SW1 276 F6
Chesham Ms. SW1 160 DG76
Chesham Ms., Guil. 259 AZ135
Chesham Rd.
Chesham Pl. SW1 276 F7
Chesham Pl. SW1 160 DG76
Chesham Rd. SE20 202 DW96
Chesham Rd. SW19 180 DD92
Chesham Rd., Amer. 55 AQ36
Chesham Rd., Berk. 38 AV21
Chesham Rd., Chesh. 54 AL32
Chesham Rd., Guil. 259 AZ135
Chesham Rd., Hem.H. 56 AY27
Chesham Rd., Kings.T. 198 CN96
Chesham St. NW10 118 CR62
Chesham St. SW1 276 F7
Chesham St. SW1 160 DG76
Chesham Ter. W13 157 CH75
Chesham Way, Wat. 75 BS44
Cheshire Clo. SE4 163 DZ82
Cheshire Clo., Cher. 211 BD107
Cheshire Clo., Horn. 128 FN57
Cheshire Clo., Mitch. 201 DL97
Cheshire Ct., Slou. 152 AV75
Clements Clo.
Cheshire Gdns., Chess. 215 CK107
Cheshire Rd. N22 99 DM51
Cheshire St. E2 142 DT70
Chesholm Rd. N16 122 DS62
Cheshunt Pk. (Cheshunt), Wal.Cr. 66 DV26
Cheshunt Rd. E7 144 EH65
Cheshunt Rd., Belv. 166 FA78
Cheshunt Wash (Cheshunt), Wal.Cr. 67 DY27
Chesil Ct. E2 142 DW68
Bonner Rd.
Chesil Way, Hayes 135 BT69
Chesilton Rd. SW6 159 CZ81
Chesley Gdns. E6 144 EK68
Cheslyn Gdns., Wat. 75 BT37
Chesney Cres., Croy. 221 EC108
Chesney St. SW11 160 DG81
Chesnut Est. N17 122 DT55
Chesnut Rd.
Chesnut Gro. N17 122 DT55
Chesnut Rd.
Chesnut Rd. N17 122 DT55
Chess Clo., Chesh. 72 AX36
Chess Clo., Rick. 74 BK42
Chess Hill, Rick. 74 BK42
Chess La., Rick. 74 BK42
Chess Vale Ri., Rick. 74 BM44
Chess Valley Wk., Chesh. 54 AR33
Chess Valley Wk., Rick. 73 AZ37
Chess Way, Rick. 74 BG41
Chessbury Rd., Chesh. 54 AN32
Chessfield Pk., Amer. 72 AY39
Chessholme Ct., Sun. 175 BS94
Scotts Ave.
Chessholme Rd., Ashf. 175 BQ93
Chessington Ave. N3 119 CY55
Chessington Ave., Bexh. 166 EY80
Chessington Clo., Epsom 216 CQ107
Chessington Ct., Pnr. 116 BZ56
Chessington Hall Gdns., Chess. 215 CK108
Chessington Hill Pk., Chess. 216 CN106
Chessington Lo. N3 119 CZ55
Chessington Rd., Epsom 216 CP107
Chessington Way, W.Wick. 203 EB103
Chessmount Ri., Chesh. 54 AR33
Chesson Rd. W14 159 CZ79
Chesswood Way, Pnr. 94 BX54
Chester Ave., Rich. 178 CM86
Chester Ave., Twick. 176 BZ88
Chester Ave., Upmin. 129 FS61
Chester Clo. SW1 277 H5
Chester Clo. SW1 161 DH75
Chester Clo. SW13 159 CV83
Chester Clo., Ashf. 175 BR92
Chester Clo., Dor. 247 CJ134
Chester Clo., Guil. 242 AT132
Chester Clo., Loug. 85 EQ39
Chester Clo., Pot.B. 64 DB29
Chester Clo., Sutt. 200 DA103
Broomloan La.
Chester Clo., Uxb. 135 BP72
Dawley Ave.
Chester Clo. N. NW1 273 J2
Chester Clo. S. NW1 273 J3
Chester Cotts. SW1 276 F9
Chester Ct. NW1 273 J2
Chester Ct. SE5 162 DR80
Chester Cres. E8 142 DT65
Ridley Rd.
Chester Dr., Har. 116 BZ58
Chester Gdns. W13 137 CH72
Chester Gdns., Enf. 82 DV44
Chester Gdns., Mord. 200 DC100
Chester Gate NW1 273 H3
Chester Gate NW1 141 DH69
Chester Grn., Loug. 85 EQ39
Chester Ms. SW1 277 H6
Chester Ms. SW1 161 DH76
Chester Path, Loug. 85 EQ39
Chester Pl. NW1 273 H2
Chester Rd. E7 144 EK66
Chester Rd. E11 124 EH58
Chester Rd. E16 144 EE70
Chester Rd. E17 123 DX57
Chester Rd. N9 100 DV46
Chester Rd. N17 122 DR55
Chester Rd. N19 121 DH61
Chester Rd. NW1 272 G3
Chester Rd. NW1 140 DG69
Chester Rd. SW19 179 CW93
Chester Rd., Borwd. 78 CQ41
Chester Rd., Chig. 103 EN47
Chester Rd., Houns. 155 BV83
Chester Rd. (Heathrow Airport), Houns. 154 BN83
Chester Rd., Ilf. 125 ET60
Chester Rd., Lthd. 245 BV129
Dirtham La.
Chester Rd., Loug. 85 EP40
Chester Rd., Nthwd. 93 BS52
Chester Rd., Sid. 185 ES85
Chester Rd., Slou. 131 AR72
Chester Rd., Wat. 75 BU43
Chester Row SW1 276 F9
Chester Row SW1 160 DG77
Chester Sq. SW1 276 G8
Chester Sq. SW1 160 DG77
Chester Sq. Ms. SW1 277 H7
Chester St. E2 142 DU70
Chester St. SW1 276 G6
Chester St. SW1 160 DG76
Chester Ter. NW1 273 H2
Chester Way SE11 278 E9
Chester Way SE11 161 DN77
Chesterfield Clo., Orp. 206 EX98
Chesterfield Dr., Dart. 187 FH85
Chesterfield Dr., Esher 197 CG103
Chesterfield Dr., Sev. 256 FD122
Chesterfield Gdns. N4 121 DP57
Chesterfield Gdns. SE10 163 ED80
Crooms Hill
Chesterfield Gdns. W1 277 H2
Chesterfield Gdns. W1 141 DH74
Chesterfield Gro. SE22 182 DT85
Chesterfield Hill W1 277 H2
Chesterfield Hill W1 141 DH74
Chesterfield Ms. N4 121 DP57
Chesterfield Gdns.
Chesterfield Ms., Ashf. 174 BL91
Chesterfield Rd.
Chesterfield Rd. E10 123 EC58
Chesterfield Rd. N3 98 DA51
Chesterfield Rd. W4 158 CQ79
Chesterfield Rd., Ashf. 174 BL91
Chesterfield Rd., Barn. 79 CX43
Chesterfield Rd., Enf. 83 DY37
Chesterfield Rd., Epsom 216 CR108
Chesterfield St. W1 277 H2
Chesterfield St. W1 141 DH74
Chesterfield Wk. SE10 163 ED81
Chesterfield Way SE15 162 DW80
Chesterfield Way, Hayes 155 BU75
Chesterford Gdns. NW3 120 DB63
Chesterford Ho. SE18 164 EK80
Shooter's Hill Rd.
Chesterford Rd. E12 125 EM64
Chesters, Horl. 268 DE146
Chesters, The, N.Mal. 198 CS95
Chesterton Clo. SW18 180 DA85
Ericcson Clo.
Chesterton Clo., Chesh. 54 AP29
Milton Rd.
Chesterton Clo., Grnf. 136 CB68
Chesterton Dr., Red. 251 DL128
Chesterton Dr., Stai. 174 BM88
Chesterton Grn., Beac. 89 AL52
Chesterton Rd. E13 144 EG69
Chesterton Rd. W10 139 CX71
Chesterton Ter. E13 144 EG69
Chesterton Ter., Kings.T. 198 CN96
Chesterton Way, Til. 171 GJ82
Chesthunte Rd. N17 100 DQ53
Chestnut All. SW6 159 CZ79
Lillie Rd.
Chestnut Ave. E7 124 EH63
Chestnut Ave. N8 121 DL57
Chestnut Ave. SW14 158 CR83
Thornton Rd.
Chestnut Ave., Brent. 157 CK77
Chestnut Ave., Brwd. 108 FS45
Chestnut Ave., Buck.H. 102 EK48
Chestnut Ave., Chesh. 54 AR29
Chestnut Ave., E.Mol. 197 CF97
Chestnut Ave., Edg. 96 CL51
Chestnut Ave., Epsom 216 CS105
Chestnut Ave., Esher 197 CD101
Chestnut Ave., Grays 170 GB75
Chestnut Ave., Guil. 258 AW137
Chestnut Ave., Hmptn. 176 CA94
Chestnut Ave., Horn. 127 FF61
Chestnut Ave., Nthwd. 93 BT54
Chestnut Ave., Rick. 74 BG43
Chestnut Ave., Slou. 152 AY75
Chestnut Ave., Tedd. 197 CF96
Chestnut Ave., Vir.W. 192 AT98
Chestnut Ave., Walt. 213 BS110
Chestnut Ave., Wem. 117 CH64
Chestnut Ave., West Dr. 134 BM73
Chestnut Ave., W.Wick. 222 EE106
Chestnut Ave., West. 238 EK123
Chestnut Ave., Wey. 213 BQ108
Chestnut Ave. N. E17 123 EC56
Chestnut Ave. S. E17 123 EC56
Chestnut Clo. N14 81 DJ43
Chestnut Clo. N16 122 DR61
Lordship Gro.
Chestnut Clo. SE6 183 EC92
Chestnut Clo. SE14 163 DZ83
Shardeloes Rd.
Chestnut Clo. SW16 181 DN91
Chestnut Clo., Add. 212 BK106
Chestnut Clo., Amer. 55 AR37
Chestnut Clo., Ashf. 175 BP91
Chestnut Clo., Berk. 39 BB17
Chestnut Clo., Buck.H. 102 EK48
Chestnut Clo., Cars. 200 DF102
Chestnut Clo., Egh. 172 AW93
Chestnut Clo., Ger.Cr. 91 AZ53
Chestnut Clo., Grav. 191 GF86
Burch Rd.
Chestnut Clo., Hayes 135 BS73
Chestnut Clo., Horn. 128 FJ63
Lancaster Dr.
Chestnut Clo., Orp. 224 EU106
Chestnut Clo., Red. 267 DH136
Haigh Cres.
Chestnut Clo., Sid. 186 EU88
Chestnut Clo., Sun. 175 BT93
Chestnut Clo., Tad. 234 DA123
Chestnut Clo., Ware 34 EK06
Chestnut Clo., West Dr. 155 BP80
Chestnut Clo., Wok. 228 BG124
Chestnut Copse, Oxt. 254 EH132
Chestnut Ct. SW6 159 CZ79
North End Rd.
Chestnut Ct., Amer. 55 AR37
Chestnut Dr. E11 124 EG58
Chestnut Dr., Berk. 38 AX20
Chestnut Dr., Bexh. 166 EX83
Chestnut Dr., Egh. 172 AX93
Chestnut Dr., Har. 95 CF52
Chestnut Dr., Pnr. 116 BX58
Chestnut Dr., St.Alb. 43 CH18
Chestnut Dr., Wind. 151 AL84
Chestnut Glen, Horn. 127 FG61
Chestnut Gro. SE20 182 DV94
Hawthorn Gro.
Chestnut Gro. SW12 180 DG87
Chestnut Gro. W5 157 CK76
Chestnut Gro., Barn. 80 DF43
Chestnut Gro., Brwd. 108 FW47
Chestnut Gro., Dart. 187 FD91
Chestnut Gro., Ilf. 103 ES51
Chestnut Gro., Islw. 157 CG84
Chestnut Gro., Mitch. 201 DK99
Chestnut Gro., N.Mal. 198 CR97
Chestnut Gro., S.Croy. 220 DV108
Chestnut Gro., Stai. 174 BJ93
Chestnut Gro., Wem. 117 CH64
Chestnut Gro., Wok. 226 AY120
Chestnut La. N20 97 CY46
Chestnut La., Amer. 55 AR36
Chestnut La., Sev. 257 FH124
Chestnut La., Wey. 213 BP106
Chestnut Manor Clo., Stai. 174 BH92
Chestnut Mead, Red. 250 DE133
Oxford Rd.
Chestnut Pl., Ash. 232 CL119
Chestnut Ri. SE18 165 ES78
Chestnut Ri. (Bushey), Wat. 94 CB45
Chestnut Rd. SE27 181 DP90
Chestnut Rd. SW20 199 CX96
Chestnut Rd., Ashf. 175 BP91
Chestnut Rd., Beac. 88 AH54
Chestnut Rd., Dart. 188 FK88
Chestnut Rd., Enf. 83 DY36
Chestnut Rd., Guil. 242 AX134
Chestnut Rd., Horl. 269 DH146
Chestnut Rd., Kings.T. 178 CL94
Chestnut Rd., Twick. 177 CE89
Chestnut Wk., Epp. 51 EP24
Epping Rd.
Chestnut Wk., Ger.Cr. 90 AY52
Chestnut Wk., Sev. 257 FL129
Chestnut Wk., Shep. 195 BS99
Chestnut Wk., Walt. 213 BS109
Octagon Rd.
Chestnut Wk., Wat. 75 BU37
Chestnut Wk., W.Byf. 212 BL112
Royston Rd.
Chestnut Wk., Wdf.Grn. 102 EG50
Chestnut Way, Felt. 175 BV90
Chestnuts, Brwd. 109 GB45
Chestnuts, The, Hem.H. 39 BF24
Chestnuts, The, Hert. 32 DR09
Chestnuts, The, Horl. 269 DH146
Chestnuts, The, Rom. 86 EV41
Chestnuts, The, Walt. 195 BU103
Cheston Ave., Croy. 203 DY103
Chestwood Gro., Uxb. 134 BM66
Cheswick Clo., Dart. 167 FF84
Chesworth Clo., Erith 167 FE81
Chettle Clo. SE1 279 K6
Chettle Ct. N8 121 DN58
Chetwode Dr., Epsom 233 CX118
Chetwode Rd. SW17 180 DF90
Chetwode Rd., Tad. 233 CW119
Chetwood Wk. E6 144 EL71
Oliver Gdns.
Chetwynd Ave., Barn. 98 DF46
Chetwynd Dr., Uxb. 134 BM68
Chetwynd Rd. NW5 121 DH63
Cheval Pl. SW7 276 C6
Cheval Pl. SW7 160 DE76
Cheval St. E14 163 EA76
Cheveley Clo., Rom. 106 FM53
Chelsworth Dr.
Cheveley Gdns., Slou. 130 AJ68
Chevely Clo., Epp. 70 EX29
Cheveney Wk., Brom. 204 EG97
Marina Clo.
Chevening La., Sev. 240 EY116
Chevening Rd. NW6 139 CX68
Chevening Rd. SE10 164 EF78
Chevening Rd. SE19 182 DR93
Chevening Rd., Sev. 240 EZ119
Chevenings, The, Sid. 186 EW90
Cheverton Rd. N19 121 DK60
Chevet St. E9 123 DY64
Kenworthy Rd.
Chevington Way, Horn. 128 FK63
Cheviot Clo., Bans. 234 DB115
Cheviot Clo., Bexh. 167 FE82
Cheviot Clo., Enf. 82 DR40
Cheviot Clo., Hayes 155 BR80
Cheviot Clo., Sutt. 218 DD109
Cheviot Clo. (Bushey), Wat. 76 CC44
Cheviot Gdns. NW2 119 CX61
Cheviot Gate NW2 119 CY61
Cheviot Rd. SE27 181 DN92
Cheviot Rd., Horn. 127 FG59
Cheviot Rd., Slou. 153 BA78
Cheviot Way, Ilf. 125 ES56
Cheviots, Hat. 45 CU21
Cheviots, Hem.H. 40 BM17
Chevron Clo. E16 144 EG72
Chevy Rd., Sthl. 156 CC75
Chewton Rd. E17 123 DY56
Cheyham Gdns., Sutt. 217 CX110
Cheyham Way, Sutt. 217 CY110
Cheyne Ave. E18 124 EF55
Cheyne Ave., Twick. 176 BZ88
Cheyne Clo. NW4 119 CW58
Cheyne Wk.
Cheyne Clo., Amer. 55 AR36
Cheyne Clo., Brom. 204 EL104
Cedar Cres.
Cheyne Clo., Ger.Cr. 112 AY60
Cheyne Clo., Ware 33 DX05
Cheyne Ct. SW3 160 DF79
Flood St.
Cheyne Ct., Bans. 234 DB115
Park Rd.
Cheyne Gdns. SW3 160 DE79
Cheyne Hill, Surb. 198 CM98
Cheyne Ms. SW3 160 DE79
Cheyne Wk.
Cheyne Path W7 137 CF72
Copley Clo.
Cheyne Pl. SW3 160 DF79
Royal Hospital Rd.
Cheyne Rd., Ashf. 175 BR93
Cheyne Row SW3 160 DE79
Cheyne Wk. N21 81 DP43
Cheyne Wk. NW4 119 CW58
Cheyne Wk. SW3 160 DE79
Cheyne Wk. SW10 160 DD80
Cheyne Wk., Chesh. 54 AR31
Cheyne Wk., Croy. 202 DU103
Cheyne Wk., Horl. 268 DF150
Cheyne Wk., Long. 209 FX97
Cavendish Sq.
Cheyney Rd., Ashf. 175 BR93
Cheyneys Ave., Edg. 95 CK51
Chichele Gdns., Croy. 220 DT105
Brownlow Rd.
Chichele Rd. NW2 119 CX64
Chichele Rd., Oxt. 254 EE128
Chicheley Gdns., Har. 94 CC52
Chicheley Rd., Har. 94 CC52
Chicheley St. SE1 278 C4
Chicheley St. SE1 161 DM75
Chichester Ave., Ruis. 115 BR61
Chichester Clo. E6 144 EL72
Chichester Clo. SE3 164 EJ81
Chichester Clo., Dor. 247 CH134
Chichester Clo., Hmptn. 176 BZ93
Maple Clo.
Chichester Clo., S.Ock. 148 FQ74
Chichester Ct., Epsom 217 CT109
Chichester Ct., Slou. 152 AV75
Chichester Ct., Stan. 118 CL55

Chichester Dr., Pur. 219 DM112
Chichester Dr., Sev. 256 FF125
Chichester Gdns., Ilf. 124 EL59
Chichester Ms. SE27 181 DN91
Chichester Rents WC2 274 D8
Chichester Ri., Grav. 191 GK91
Chichester Rd. E11 124 EE62
Chichester Rd. N9 100 DU47
Chichester Rd. NW6 140 DA68
Chichester Rd. W2 140 DB71
Chichester Rd., Croy. 202 DS104
Chichester Rd., Dor. 247 CH133
Chichester Rd., Green. 189 FT85
Chichester Row, Amer. 55 AR38
Chichester St. SW1 161 DJ78
Chichester Way E14 163 ED77
Chichester Way, Felt. 176 BW87
Chichester Way, Wat. 60 BY33
Chicksand St. E1 142 DT71
Chiddingfold N12 98 DA48
Chiddingstone Ave., Bexh. 166 EZ80
Chiddingstone Clo., Sutt. 218 DA110
Chiddingstone St. SW6 160 DA82
Chieftan Dr., Purf. 168 FM77
Chieveley Rd., Bexh. 167 FB84
Chiffinch Gdns., Grav. 190 GE90
Chignell Pl. W13 137 CG74
The Bdy.
Chigwell Hill E1 142 DV73
Pennington St.
Chigwell Hurst Ct., Pnr. 94 BX54
Chigwell La., Loug. 85 EQ42
Chigwell Pk. Dr., Chig. 103 EN48
Chigwell Ri., Chig. 103 EN47
Chigwell Rd. E18 124 EH55
Chigwell Rd., Wdf.Grn. 102 EK52
Chigwell Vw., Rom. 104 FA51
Lodge La.
Chilberton Dr., Red. 251 DJ130
Chilbrook Rd., Cob. 229 BU118
Chilcot Clo. E14 143 EB72
Grundy St.
Chilcote La., Amer. 72 AV39
Chilcott Rd., Wat. 75 BS36
Childebert Rd. SW17 181 DH89
Childeric Rd. SE14 163 DY80
Childerley St. SW6 159 CX81
Fulham Palace Rd.
Childers, The, Wdf.Grn. 103 EM50
Childers St. SE8 163 DY79
Childs Ave., Uxb. 92 BJ54
Childs Clo., Horn. 128 FJ58
Childs Cres., Swans. 189 FX86
Childs Hall Clo., Lthd. 246 BZ125
Childs Hall Rd.
Childs Hall Dr., Lthd. 246 BZ125
Childs Hall Rd., Lthd. 246 BZ125
Childs Hill Wk. NW2 119 CZ62
Church Wk.
Childs La. SE19 182 DS93
Westow St.
Child's Pl. SW5 160 DA77
Child's St. SW5 160 DA77
Child's Wk. SW5 160 DA77
Child's Pl.
Childs Way NW11 119 CZ57
Childwick Ct., Hem.H. 40 BN23
Rumballs Rd.
Chilham Clo., Bex. 186 EZ87
Chilham Clo., Grnf. 137 CG68
Chilham Clo., Hem.H. 40 BL21
Chilham Rd. SE9 184 EL91
Chilham Way, Brom. 204 EG101
Chillerton Rd. SW17 180 DG92
Chillingworth Gdns., Twick. 177 CF90
Tower Rd.
Chillingworth Rd. N7 121 DN64
Liverpool Rd.
Chilmans Dr., Lthd. 246 CB125
Chilmark Gdns., N.Mal. 199 CT101
Chilmark Gdns., Red. 251 DL129
Chilmark Rd. SW16 201 DK96
Chilmead La., Red. 251 DK132
Chilsey Grn. Rd., Cher. 193 BE100
Chiltern Ave., Amer. 55 AR38
Chiltern Ave., Twick. 176 CA88
Chiltern Ave. (Bushey), Wat. 76 CC44
Chiltern Clo., Berk. 38 AT18
Chiltern Clo., Bexh. 167 FE81
Cumbrian Ave.
Chiltern Clo., Borwd. 78 CM40
Chiltern Clo., Croy. 202 DS104
Chiltern Clo., Uxb. 114 BN61
Chiltern Clo. (Cheshunt), Wal.Cr. 65 DP27
Chiltern Clo. (Bushey), Wat. 76 CB44
Chiltern Clo., Wok. 226 AW122
Chiltern Clo., Wor.Pk. 199 CW103
Cotswold Way
Chiltern Dene, Enf. 81 DM42
Chiltern Dr., Rick. 91 BF45
Chiltern Dr., Surb. 198 CN100
Chiltern Gdns. NW2 119 CX62
Chiltern Gdns., Brom. 204 EF98
Chiltern Gdns., Horn. 128 FJ62
Chiltern Hill, Ger.Cr. 90 AY53
Chiltern Hills Rd., Beac. 88 AJ53
Chiltern Par., Amer. 55 AQ37
Chiltern Pk. Ave., Berk. 38 AU17
Chiltern Rd. E3 143 EA70
Knapp Rd.
Chiltern Rd., Amer. 55 AP35
Chiltern Rd., Grav. 190 GE90
Chiltern Rd., Ilf. 125 ES56
Chiltern Rd., Pnr. 116 BW57
Chiltern Rd., St.Alb. 43 CJ15
Chiltern Rd., Slou. 130 AH71
Chiltern Rd., Sutt. 218 DB109
Chiltern St. W1 272 F6
Chiltern St. W1 140 DG71
Chiltern Vw. Rd., Uxb. 134 BJ68
Chiltern Way, Wdf.Grn. 102 EG48
Chilterns, Berk. 38 AT17
Chilterns, Hat. 45 CU21
Chilterns, Hem.H. 40 BL18
Chilterns, The, Sutt. 218 DB109
Gatton Clo.
Chilthorne Clo. SE6 183 DZ87
Ravensbourne Pk. Cres.
Chilton Ave. W5 157 CK77
Chilton Clo., H.Wyc. 88 AC45
Chilton Ct., Hert. 31 DM07
The Ridgeway
Chilton Ct., Walt. 213 BU105
Chilton Grn., Welw.G.C. 30 DC09
Chilton Gro. SE8 163 DX77
Chilton Rd., Chesh. 54 AQ29
Chilton Rd., Edg. 96 CN51
Manor Pk. Cres.
Chilton Rd., Grays 171 GG76
Chilton Rd., Rich. 158 CN83
Chilton St. E2 142 DT70
Chiltonian Ind. Est. SE12 184 EF86
Chiltons, The E18 102 EG54
Grove Hill
Chiltons Clo., Bans. 234 DB115
High St.
Chilver St. SE10 164 EF78
Chilwell Gdns., Wat. 94 BW49
Chilwick, Slou. 131 AM69
Chilworth Ct. SW19 179 CX88
Chilworth Gdns., Sutt. 200 DC104
Chilworth Ms. W2 140 DD72
Chilworth Rd., Guil. 260 BG139
Chilworth St. W2 140 DC72
Chimes Ave. N13 99 DN50
Chinbrook Cres. SE12 184 EH90
Chinbrook Rd.
Chinbrook Est. SE9 184 EK90
Chinbrook Rd. SE12 184 EH90
Chinchilla Dr., Houns. 156 BW82
Chindit Clo., Brox. 49 DY20
Chindits La., Brwd. 108 FW50
Chine, The N10 121 DJ56
Chine, The N21 81 DP44
Chine, The, Dor. 263 CH135
High St.
Chine, The, Wem. 117 CH64
Ching Ct. WC2 273 P9
Ching Way E4 101 DZ51
Chingdale Rd. E4 102 EE48
Chingford Ave. E4 101 EA48
Chingford Hall Est. E4 101 DZ51
Chingford Ind. Est. E4 101 DY50
Chingford La., Wdf.Grn. 102 EE49
Chingford Mt. Rd. E4 101 EA49
Chingford Rd. E4 101 EA51
Chingford Rd. E17 101 EB53
Chingley Clo., Brom. 184 EE93
Chinnery Clo., Enf. 82 DT39
Garnault Rd.
Chinnor Cres., Grnf. 136 CB68
Chinthurst La., Guil. 258 AY141
Chinthurst Pk., Guil. 258 AY142
Chip St. SW4 161 DK84
Prescott Pl.
Chipka St. E14 163 EC75
Chipley St. SE14 163 DY79
Nynehead St.
Chipmunk Gro., Nthlt. 136 BY69
Argus Way
Chippendale All., Uxb. 134 BK66
Chippendale Waye
Chippendale St. E5 123 DX62
Chippendale Waye, Uxb. 134 BK66
Chippenham Ave., Wem. 118 CP64
Chippenham Clo., Pnr. 115 BT56
Chippenham Clo., Rom. 106 FK50
Chippenham Rd.
Chippenham Gdns. NW6 140 DA69
Chippenham Gdns., Rom. 106 FK50
Chippenham Ms. W9 140 DA70
Chippenham Rd. W9 140 DA70
Chippenham Rd., Rom. 106 FK51
Chippenham Wk., Rom. 106 FK51
Chippenham Rd.
Chipperfield Clo., Upmin. 129 FS60
Chipperfield Rd., Hem.H. 40 BJ24
Chipperfield Rd. (Bovingdon), Hem.H. 57 BB27
Chipperfield Rd., Kings L. 58 BJ30
Chipperfield Rd., Orp. 206 EU95
Chipping Clo., Barn. 79 CY41
St. Albans Rd.
Chippingfield, Harl. 36 EW12
Chipstead Ave., Th.Hth. 201 DP98
Chipstead Clo. SE19 182 DT94
Chipstead Clo., Couls. 234 DG116
Chipstead Clo., Ger.Cr. 90 AW53
Chipstead Clo., Red. 266 DG136
Chipstead Clo., Sutt. 218 DB109
Chipstead Ct., Wok. 226 AS117
Creston Ave.
Chipstead Gdns. NW2 119 CV61
Chipstead Gate, Couls. 235 DJ119
Woodfield Clo.
Chipstead La., Couls. 234 DB124
Chipstead La., Sev. 256 FC122
Chipstead La., Tad. 249 CZ125
Chipstead Pk., Sev. 256 FD122
Chipstead Pk. Clo., Sev. 256 FC122
Chipstead Pl. Gdns., Sev. 256 FC122
Chipstead Rd., Bans. 233 CZ117
Chipstead Rd., Erith 167 FE80
Chipstead Rd., Houns. 154 BN83
Chipstead Sta. Par., Couls. 234 DF118
Station App.
Chipstead St. SW6 160 DA81
Chipstead Valley Rd., Couls. 234 DG116
Chipstead Way, Bans. 234 DF115
Chirk Clo., Hayes 136 BY70
Braunston Dr.
Chirton Wk., Wok. 226 AU118
Shilburn Way
Chisenhale Rd. E3 143 DY68
Chisholm Rd., Croy. 202 DS103
Chisholm Rd., Rich. 178 CM86
Chisledon Wk. E9 143 DZ65
Osborne Rd.
Chislehurst Ave. N12 98 DC52
Chislehurst Rd., Brom. 204 EK96
Chislehurst Rd., Chis. 204 EK96
Chislehurst Rd., Orp. 205 ES100
Chislehurst Rd., Rich. 178 CL85
Chislehurst Rd., Sid. 186 EU92
Chislet Clo., Beck. 183 EA94
Abbey La.
Chisley Rd. N15 122 DS58
Chiswell Ct., Wat. 76 BW38
Chiswell Grn. La., St.Alb. 60 BY25
Chiswell Sq. SE3 164 EH82
Brook La.
Chiswell St. EC1 275 K6
Chiswell St. EC1 142 DR71
Chiswick Bri. SW14 158 CQ82
Chiswick Bri. W4 158 CQ82
Chiswick Clo., Croy. 201 DM104
Chiswick Common Rd. W4 158 CR77
Chiswick Ct., Pnr. 116 BZ55
Chiswick Gdns. W4 158 CQ81
Hartington Rd.
Chiswick High Rd. W4 158 CN78
Chiswick High Rd., Brent. 158 CN78
Chiswick Ho. Grds. W4 158 CR79
Chiswick La. W4 158 CS78
Chiswick La. S. W4 159 CT78
Chiswick Mall W4 159 CT79
Chiswick Mall W6 159 CU78
Chiswick Quay W4 158 CQ81
Chiswick Rd. N9 100 DU47
Chiswick Rd. W4 158 CQ77
Chiswick Sq. W4 158 CS79
Hogarth Roundabout
Chiswick Staithe W4 158 CQ81
Chiswick Ter. W4 158 CQ77
Acton La.
Chiswick Village W4 158 CP79
Chiswick Wf. W4 159 CT79
Chittenden Cotts., Wok. 228 BL116
Chitterfield Gate, West Dr. 154 BN80
Chitty St. W1 273 L6
Chitty St. W1 141 DJ71
Chittys Common, Guil. 242 AT130
Chitty's La., Dag. 126 EX61
Chittys Wk., Guil. 242 AT130
Chivalry Rd. SW11 180 DE85
Chivenor Gro., Kings.T. 177 CK92
Chivers Rd. E4 101 EB49
Choats Manor Way, Bark. 146 EV70
Renwick Rd.
Choats Rd., Bark. 146 EW68
Choats Rd., Dag. 146 EY69
Chobham Clo., Cher. 211 BB107
Chobham Gdns. SW19 179 CX89
Chobham La., Wok. 192 AT104
Chobham Pk. La., Wok. 210 AU110
Chobham Rd. E15 123 ED64
Chobham Rd., Cher. 211 BA108
Chobham Rd., Wok. 226 AY116
Chobham Rd. (Horsell), Wok. 210 AW113
Choir Grn., Wok. 226 AS117
Semper Clo.
Cholmeley Cres. N6 121 DH59
Cholmeley Pk. N6 121 DH60
Cholmley Gdns. NW6 120 DA64
Fortune Grn. Rd.
Cholmley Rd., T.Ditt. 197 CH100
Cholmondeley Ave. NW10 139 CU68
Cholmondeley Wk., Rich. 177 CJ85
Choppins Ct. E1 142 DV74
Wapping La.
Chopwell Clo. E15 143 ED66
Bryant St.
Chorleywood Bottom, Rick. 73 BD43
Chorleywood Clo., Rick. 92 BK45
Chorleywood Cres., Orp. 205 ET96
Chorleywood Lo. La., Rick. 73 BF41
Rickmansworth Rd.
Chorleywood Rd., Rick. 74 BG42
Choumert Gro. SE15 162 DU82
Choumert Rd. SE15 162 DT83
Choumert Sq. SE15 162 DU82
Chow Sq. E8 122 DT64
Arcola St.
Chrislaine Clo. (Stanwell), Stai. 174 BK86
High St.
Chrisp St. E14 143 EB71
Christ Ch. Ave., Erith 167 FD79
Christ Ch. Pas. EC1 274 G8
Christ Ch. Rd. SW14 178 CP85
Christ Ch. Rd., Beck. 203 EA96
Fairfield Rd.
Christ Ch. Rd., Epsom 216 CL112
Christ Ch. Rd., Surb. 198 CM101
Christchurch Ave. N12 98 DC51
Christchurch Ave. NW6 139 CX67
Christchurch Ave., Har. 117 CF56
Christchurch Ave., Rain. 147 FF68
Christchurch Ave., Tedd. 177 CG92
Christchurch Ave., Wem. 138 CL65
Christchurch Clo. SW19 180 DD94
Christchurch Clo., St.Alb. 42 CC19
Christchurch Cres., Grav. 191 GJ87
Christchurch Rd.
Christchurch Cres., Rad. 77 CG36
Christchurch Gdns., Epsom 216 CP111
Christchurch Gdns., Har. 117 CG56
Christchurch Grn., Wem. 138 CL65
Christchurch Hill NW3 120 DD62
Christchurch Ind. Cen., Har. 117 CF56
Christchurch La., Barn. 79 CY40
Christchurch Mt., Epsom 216 CP112
Christchurch Pk., Sutt. 218 DC108
Christchurch Pas. NW3 120 DD62
Christchurch Hill
Christchurch Pas., Barn. 79 CY41
Christchurch La.
Christchurch Rd. N8 121 DL58
Christchurch Rd. SW2 181 DM88
Christchurch Rd. SW19 200 DD95
Christchurch Rd., Dart. 188 FJ86
Christchurch Rd., Grav. 191 GJ88
Christchurch Rd., Hem.H. 40 BK19
Christchurch Rd., Houns. 154 BN82
Christchurch Rd., Ilf. 125 EP60
Christchurch Rd., Pur. 219 DP110
Christchurch Rd., Sid. 185 ET91
Christchurch Rd., Til. 171 GG81
Christchurch Rd., Vir.W. 192 AU97
Christchurch Sq. E9 142 DW67
Victoria Pk. Rd.
Christchurch St. SW3 160 DF79
Christchurch Ter. SW3 160 DF79
Christchurch St.
Christchurch Way SE10 164 EE78
Christchurch Way, Wok. 227 AZ117
Church St. E.
Christian Ct. SE16 143 DZ74
Christian Flds. SW16 181 DN94
Christian Flds. Ave., Grav. 191 GJ91
Christian Sq., Wind. 151 AQ81
Alma Rd.
Christian St. E1 142 DU72
Christie Clo., Brox. 49 DZ21
Christie Dr., Croy. 202 DT100
Christie Gdns., Rom. 126 EV58
Christie Rd. E9 143 DY65
Christie Wk., Cat. 236 DQ121
Coulsdon Rd.
Christies Ave., Sev. 224 FA110
Christina Sq. N4 121 DP60
Adolphus Rd.
Christina St. EC2 275 M4
Christmas La., Slou. 111 AQ62
Christopher Ave. W7 157 CG76
Christopher Clo. SE16 163 DX75
Christopher Clo., Horn. 128 FK63
Chevington Way
Christopher Clo., Sid. 185 ET85
Christopher Clo., Tad. 233 CW123
High St.
Christopher Ct., Hem.H. 40 BK23
Seaton Rd.
Christopher Ct., Tad. 233 CW123
Christopher Gdns., Dag. 126 EX64
Wren Rd.
Christopher Pl. NW1 273 N3
Christopher Pl., St.Alb. 43 CD20
Market Pl.
Christopher Rd., Sthl. 155 BV77
Christopher St. EC2 275 L5
Christopher St. EC2 142 DR70
Christopher's Ms. W11 139 CY74
Penzance St.
Christy Rd., West. 238 EJ115
Chryssell Rd. SW9 161 DN80
Chrystie La., Lthd. 246 CB126
Chubworthy St. SE14 163 DY79
Chucks La., Tad. 233 CV124
Chudleigh Cres., Ilf. 125 ES63
Chudleigh Gdns., Sutt. 200 DC104
Chudleigh Rd. NW6 139 CX66
Chudleigh Rd. SE4 183 DZ85
Chudleigh Rd., Rom. 106 FL49
Chudleigh Rd., Twick. 177 CE86
Chudleigh St. E1 143 DX72
Chudleigh Way, Ruis. 115 BU60
Chulsa Rd. SE26 182 DV92
Chumleigh St. SE5 162 DS79
Chumleigh Wk., Surb. 198 CM98
Church All., Croy. 201 DP101
Handcroft Rd.
Church All., Wat. 76 CC38
Church App. SE21 182 DR90
Church App., Egh. 193 BC97
Church App., Sev. 239 EQ115
Cudham La. S.
Church App., Stai. 174 BK86
Church Ave. E4 101 ED51
Church Ave. NW1 141 DH65
Kentish Town Rd.
Church Ave. SW14 158 CR83
Church Ave., Beck. 203 EA95
Church Ave., Nthlt. 136 BZ66
Church Ave., Pnr. 116 BY58
Church Ave., Ruis. 115 BR60
Church Ave., Sid. 186 EU92
Church Ave., Sthl. 156 BY76
Church Clo. N20 98 DE48
Church Clo. W8 160 DB75
Kensington Ch. St.
Church Clo., Add. 212 BH105
Church Clo., Edg. 96 CQ50
Church Clo., Hayes 135 BR71
Church Clo., Hert. 47 DJ19
Goddards Clo.
Church Clo., Lthd. 231 CD124
Church Clo., Loug. 85 EM40
Church Clo., Nthwd. 93 BT52
Church Clo. (Cuffley), Pot.B. 65 DL29
Church Clo., Rad. 77 CG36
Church Clo., Stai. 194 BJ97
The Bdy.
Church Clo., Tad. 249 CZ127
Buckland Rd.
Church Clo., Uxb. 134 BH68
Church Clo., West Dr. 154 BL76
Church Clo., Wind. 151 AR79
Church Clo., Wok. 226 AX116
Church Ct., Reig. 250 DB134
Church Ct., Rich. 177 CK85
George St.
Church Cres. E9 143 DX66
Church Cres. N3 97 CZ53
Church Cres. N10 121 DH56
Church Cres. N20 98 DE48
Church Cres., St.Alb. 42 CC19
Church Cres., Saw. 36 EZ05
Forebury Ave.
Church Cres., S.Ock. 149 FW69
Church Cft., St.Alb. 43 CJ23
Church Dr. NW9 118 CR60
Church Dr., Har. 116 BZ58
Church Dr., Maid. 150 AC75
Church Dr., W.Wick. 204 EE104
Church Elm La., Dag. 146 FA65
Church End E17 123 EB56
Church End NW4 119 CV55
Church End, Harl. 51 EN17
Church Entry EC4 141 DP72
Carter La.
Church Fm. Clo., Swan. 207 FC100
Church Fm. La., Sutt. 217 CY107
Church Fld., Dart. 188 FK89
Church Fld., Epp. 70 EU29
Church Fld., Rad. 77 CG36
Church Fld., Sev. 256 FE122
Church Gdns. W5 157 CK75
Church Gdns., Dor. 263 CG135
Church Gdns., Wem. 117 CG63
Church Gate SW6 159 CY83
Church Grn., Hayes 135 BT72
Church Grn., St.Alb. 43 CD19
Hatfield Rd.
Church Grn., Walt. 214 BW107
Church Gro. SE13 163 EB84
Church Gro., Amer. 72 AY39
Church Gro., Kings.T. 197 CJ95
Church Gro., Slou. 132 AW71
Church Hill E17 123 EA56
Church Hill N21 99 DM45
Church Hill SE18 165 EM76
Church Hill SW19 179 CZ92
Church Hill, Abb.L. 59 BT26
Church Hill, Cars. 218 DF106
Church Hill, Cat. 236 DT124
Church Hill, Dart. 188 FK90
Church Hill (Crayford), Dart. 167 FE84
Church Hill, Epp. 70 EU30
Church Hill, Green. 189 FS85
Church Hill, Guil. 260 BN139
Church Hill, Har. 117 CE60
Church Hill, Hert. 32 DV11
Church Hill, Loug. 85 EM41
Church Hill, Orp. 206 EU101
Church Hill, Pur. 219 DL110
Church Hill (Merstham), Red. 251 DH126
Church Hill (Nutfield), Red. 251 DM133
Church Hill, Sev. 239 EQ115
Church Hill, Uxb. 114 BJ55
Church Hill, Welw.G.C. 29 CU10
Church Hill, West. 238 EK122
Church Hill (Horsell), Wok. 226 AX116
Church Hill (Pyrford), Wok. 227 BF117
Church Hill Rd. E17 123 EB56
Church Hill Rd., Barn. 80 DE44
Church Hill Rd., Surb. 198 CL99
Church Hill Rd., Sutt. 217 CX105
Church Hill Wd., Orp. 206 EU99
Church Hollow, Purf. 168 FN78
Church Hyde SE18 165 ES79
Old Mill Rd.
Church Island, Stai. 173 BD91
Church La. E11 124 EE60
Church La. E17 123 EB56
Church La. N2 120 DC55
Church La. N8 121 DM56
Church La. N9 100 DU47
Church La. N17 100 DS53
Church La. NW9 118 CQ58
Church La. SW17 181 DH92
Church La. SW19 199 CZ95
Church La. W5 157 CJ75
Church La. (Nork), Bans. 233 CX117
Reigate Rd.
Church La., Berk. 38 AW19
Church La., B.Stort. 37 FD07
Church La. (Hutton), Brwd. 109 GE46
Church La., Brom. 204 EL102
Church La., Brox. 48 DV21
Church La., Cat. 235 DN123
Church La., Chess. 216 CM107
Church La., Chis. 205 EQ95
Church La., Couls. 234 DG122
Church La., Dag. 147 FB65
Church La., Enf. 82 DR41
Church La., Epp. 71 FB27
Church La., Epsom 233 CX117
Reigate Rd.
Church La. (Headley), Epsom 232 CQ124
Church La., Ger.Cr. 90 AX53
Church La., Gdse. 253 DX132
Church La., Guil. 260 BH139
Church La. (Worplesdon), Guil. 242 AS127
Church La., Har. 95 CF53
Church La., Hat. 45 CW18
Church La., Hem.H. 57 BB27
Church La., Hert. 47 DM17
Church La., Horl. 269 DL153
Church La., Kings L. 58 BN29
Church La., Loug. 85 EM41
Church La., Maid. 150 AC75
Church La., Oxt. 253 ED130
Church La., Pnr. 116 BY55
Church La., Pot.B. 64 DG30
Church La., Purf. 168 FN78
London Rd. Purfleet
Church La. (Wennington), Rain. 148 FK72
Church La., Red. 252 DR133
Church La., Rich. 178 CL88
Petersham Rd.
Church La. (Mill End), Rick. 92 BG46
Church La. (Sarratt), Rick. 73 BF38
Church La., Rom. 127 FE56
Church La. (Abridge), Rom. 86 EY40
Church La. (Stapleford Abbotts), Rom. 87 FC42
Church La., St.Alb. 44 CP22
Church La. (Stoke Poges), Slou. 132 AT70
Church La. (Wexham), Slou. 132 AV70
Church La., Tedd. 177 CF92
Church La., T.Ditt. 197 CF100
Church La., Twick. 177 CG88
Church La., Upmin. 129 FV64
Church La., Uxb. 134 BH68
Church La., Wall. 201 DK104
Church La. (Cheshunt), Wal.Cr. 66 DV29
Church La., Warl. 237 DX117
Church La. (Chelsham), Warl. 237 EB117
Church La., Wat. 76 CB38
Church La., West. 238 EK122
Church La., Wind. 151 AR81
Church La. (Send), Wok. 243 BB126
Church La. Ave., Couls. 235 DH122
Church La. Dr., Couls. 235 DH122
Church Langley Way, Harl. 52 EW15
Church Leys, Harl. 51 ET16
Church Manor Est. SW9 161 DN80
Vassall Rd.
Church Manorway SE2 166 EU78
Church Manorway, Erith 167 FD76
Church Mead, Harl. 34 EH14
Church Meadow, Surb. 197 CJ103
Church Ms., Ware 33 DX06
Church St.
Church Mill Gra., Harl. 36 EY11
Church Mt. N2 120 DD57
Church Pas. EC2 142 DQ72
Gresham St.
Church Pas., Barn. 79 CZ42
Wood St.
Church Pas., Surb. 198 CL99
Adelaide Rd.
Church Path E11 124 EG57
Church Path E17 123 EB56
St. Mary Rd.
Church Path N12 98 DC50
Church Path N17 100 DS52
White Hart La.
Church Path N20 98 DC49
Church Path NW10 138 CS66
Church Path SW14 158 CR83
North Worple Way
Church Path SW19 199 CZ96
Church Path W4 158 CQ76
Church Path W7 137 CE74
Station Rd.
Church Path, Cob. 213 BU114

Church Path, Couls. 235 DN118
Canon's Hill
Church Path, Croy. 202 DQ103
Keeley Rd.
Church Path, Grav. 190 GC86
Church Path, Grays 170 GA79
Church Path, Green. 189 FT86
London Rd.
Church Path, Hert. 32 DR10
Church Path, Maid. 150 AC75
Church Path, Mitch. 200 DE97
Church Path, Sthl. 156 BZ76
Church Path, Ware 33 DZ09
Church Path, Wok. 227 AZ117
High St.
Church Pl. SW1 277 L1
Church Pl. W5 157 CK75
Church Pl., Mitch. 200 DE97
Church Pl., Twick. 177 CH88
Church St.
Church Pl., Uxb. 115 BQ62
Church Ri. SE23 183 DX89
Church Ri., Chess. 216 CM107
Church Rd. E10 123 EA60
Church Rd. E12 124 EL64
Church Rd. E17 101 DY54
Church Rd. N6 120 DG58
Church Rd. N17 100 DS53
Church Rd. NW4 119 CV56
Church Rd. NW10 138 CS66
Church Rd. SE19 202 DS95
Church Rd. SW13 159 CT82
Church Rd. (Wimbledon) SW19 179 CY92
Church Rd. W3 138 CQ74
Church Rd. W7 137 CD73
Church Rd., Add. 212 BG106
Church Rd., Ashf. 174 BM90
Church Rd., Ash. 231 CK117
Church Rd., Bark. 145 EQ65
Church Rd., Beac. 89 AR51
Church Rd., Berk. 39 BB16
Church Rd., Bexh. 166 EZ83
Church Rd., B.End 110 AD62
Church Rd., Brom. 204 EG96
Church Rd. (Shortlands), Brom. 204 EE97
Church Rd., Buck.H. 102 EH46
Church Rd., Cat. 236 DT123
Church Rd. (Woldingham), Cat. 237 DX122
Church Rd., Craw. 268 DE154
Church Rd., Croy. 201 DP103
Church Rd. (Sutton at Hone), Dart. 188 FL94
Church Rd., E.Mol. 197 CD98
Church Rd., Egh. 173 AZ92
Church Rd., Enf. 82 DW44
Church Rd., Epsom 216 CS112
Church Rd. (West Ewell), Epsom 216 CR108
Church Rd., Erith 167 FC78
Church Rd., Esher 215 CF107
Church Rd., Felt. 176 BX92
Church Rd., Grav. 191 GJ94
Church Rd., Green. 189 FS85
Church Rd., Guil. 258 AX135
Church Rd., Harl. 52 EW18
Church Rd., Hayes 135 BT74
Church Rd., Hem.H. 41 BQ21
Church Rd., Hert. 32 DQ08
Church Rd. (Little Berkhamsted), Hert. 47 DJ19
Church Rd. (Penn), H.Wyc. 88 AD47
Church Rd., Horl. 268 DF149
Church Rd. (Smallfield), Horl. 269 DN152
Church Rd. (Cranford), Houns. 155 BV78
Church Rd. (Heston), Houns. 156 CA80
Church Rd., Ilf. 125 ES58
Church Rd., Islw. 157 CD81
Church Rd., Iver 133 BC69
Church Rd., Ken. 236 DR115
Church Rd., Kes. 222 EK108
Church Rd., Kings.T. 198 CM96
Church Rd., Lthd. 231 CH122
Church Rd. (Great Bookham), Lthd. 230 BZ123
Church Rd., Loug. 84 EG41
Church Rd., Mitch. 200 DD97
Church Rd., Nthlt. 136 BX68
Church Rd., Nthwd. 93 BT52
Church Rd. (Chelsfield), Orp. 224 EW108
Church Rd. (Farnborough), Orp. 223 EQ106
Church Rd., Pot.B. 64 DA30
Church Rd., Pur. 219 DL110
Church Rd., Red. 266 DE136
Church Rd., Reig. 266 DA136
Church Rd., Rich. 158 CL84
Church Rd. (Ham), Rich. 177 CK91
Church Rd. (Harold Wd.), Rom. 106 FN53
Church Rd. (Havering-atte-Bower), Rom. 106 FJ46
Church Rd. (Halstead), Sev. 224 EY111
Church Rd. (Seal), Sev. 257 FM121
Church Rd., Shep. 195 BP101
Church Rd., Sid. 186 EU91
Church Rd., Slou. 131 AQ69
Church Rd., Sthl. 156 BZ76
Church Rd., Stan. 95 CH50
Church Rd., Surb. 197 CJ102
Church Rd., Sutt. 217 CY107
Church Rd., Swan. 208 FK95
Church Rd. (Crockenhill), Swan. 207 FD101
Church Rd., Swans. 190 FZ86
Church Rd., Tedd. 177 CE91
Church Rd., Til. 171 GF81
Church Rd. (West Tilbury), Til. 171 GL79
Church Rd. (Cowley), Uxb. 134 BK70
Church Rd. (Harefield), Uxb. 114 BJ55
Church Rd., Wall. 201 DJ104
Church Rd., Warl. 237 DX117
Church Rd., Wat. 75 BU39
Church Rd., Well. 166 EV82
Church Rd., Welw.G.C. 29 CX09
Church Rd., W.Byf. 212 BL114
Church Rd., West Dr. 154 BK76
Church Rd. (Biggin Hill), West. 238 EK117
Church Rd. (Brasted), West. 240 EV124
Church Rd., Whyt. 236 DT118
Church Rd., Wind. 172 AV85
Church Rd. (Horsell), Wok. 226 AY116
Church Rd. (St. John's), Wok. 226 AU119
Church Rd., Wor.Pk. 198 CS103
Church Rd. Ind. Est., Craw. 268 DE154
Church Rd. Merton SW19 200 DD95
Church Row NW3 120 DC63
Church Row, Chis. 205 EQ95
Church Row Ms., Ware 33 DX06
Church St.
Church Side, Epsom 216 CP113
Church Sq., Shep. 195 BP101
Church St. E15 144 EE68
Church St. E16 145 EP74
Church St. N9 100 DT47
Church St. NW8 272 A6
Church St. NW8 140 DD71
Church St. W2 272 A6
Church St. W2 140 DD71
Church St. W4 159 CT79
Church St., Amer. 55 AP40
Church St., Bet. 264 CS135
Church St., Chesh. 54 AP31
Church St., Cob. 229 BV115
Church St., Croy. 202 DQ103
Church St., Dag. 147 FB65
Church St., Dor. 263 CG136
Church St., Enf. 82 DQ41
Church St., Epsom 216 CS113
Church St. (Ewell), Epsom 217 CU109
Church St., Esher 214 CB105
Church St., Grav. 191 GH86
Church St. (Southfleet), Grav. 190 GA92
Church St., Grays 170 GC79
Church St., Hmptn. 196 CC96
Church St., Hat. 45 CW18
Church St. (Essendon), Hat. 46 DE17
Church St., Hem.H. 40 BK18
Church St. (Bovingdon), Hem.H. 57 BB27
Church St., Hert. 32 DR09
Church St., Islw. 157 CH83
Church St., Kings.T. 197 CK96
Church St., Lthd. 231 CH122
Church St. (Effingham), Lthd. 246 BX127
Church St., Reig. 250 DA134
Church St., Rick. 92 BL46
Church St., St.Alb. 43 CD19
Church St., Saw. 36 EY05
Church St. (Seal), Sev. 257 FN121
Church St. (Shoreham), Sev. 225 FF111
Church St., Slou. 152 AT75
Church St. (Burnham), Slou. 130 AJ70
Church St. (Chalvey), Slou. 151 AQ75
Church St., Stai. 173 BE91
Church St., Sun. 195 BU97
Church St., Sutt. 218 DB106
High St.
Church St., Twick. 177 CG88
Church St., Wal.Abb. 67 EC33
Church St., Walt. 195 BU102
Church St., Ware 33 DX06
Church St., Wat. 76 BW42
Church St., Wey. 212 BN105
Church St., Wind. 151 AR81
Castle Hill
Church St., Wok. 227 AZ117
Church St. E., Wok. 227 AZ117
Church St. Est. NW8 272 A5
Church St. Est. NW8 140 DD70
Church St. N. E15 144 EE67
Church St. Pas. E15 144 EE67
Church St.
Church St. W., Wok. 226 AY117
Church Stretton Rd., Houns. 176 CC85
Church Ter. NW4 119 CV55
Church Ter. SE13 164 EE83
Church Ter. SW8 161 DK82
Church Ter., Rich. 177 CK85
Church Ter., Wind. 151 AL82
Church Vale N2 120 DF55
Church Vale SE23 182 DW89
Church Vw., Brox. 49 DZ20
Church Vw., S.Ock. 168 FQ75
Church Vw., Swan. 207 FD97
Lime Rd.
Church Vw., Upmin. 128 FN61
Church Vw. Clo., Horl. 268 DF149
Church Vill., Sev. 256 FE122
Church Fld.
Church Wk. N6 120 DG62
Swains La.
Church Wk. N16 122 DR63
Church Wk. NW2 119 CZ62
Church Wk. NW4 119 CW55
Church Wk. NW9 118 CR61
Church Wk. SW13 159 CU81
Church Wk. SW15 179 CV85
St. Margarets Cres.
Church Wk. SW16 201 DJ96
Church Wk. SW20 199 CW97
Church Wk., Brent. 157 CJ79
Church Wk., Cat. 236 DU124
Church Wk., Cher. 194 BG100
Church Wk., Dart. 188 FK90
Church Wk., Grav. 191 GK88
Church Wk., Hayes 135 BS72
Church Wk., Horl. 268 DF149
Woodroyd Ave.
Church Wk., Lthd. 231 CH122
The Cres.
Church Wk., Red. 252 DQ133
Church Wk., Reig. 250 DC134
Reigate Rd.
Church Wk., Rich. 177 CK85
Red Lion St.
Church Wk., Saw. 36 EZ05
Church Wk., Slou. 130 AH70
Church Wk., T.Ditt. 197 CF100
Church Wk., Walt. 195 BU102
Church Wk., Wey. 195 BP103
Beales La.
Church Way N20 98 DD48
Church Way, Barn. 80 DF42
Mount Pleasant
Church Way, Edg. 96 CN51
Station Rd.
Church Way, Oxt. 254 EF132
Church Way, S.Croy. 220 DT110
Churchbury Clo., Enf. 82 DS40
Churchbury La., Enf. 82 DR41
Churchbury Rd. SE9 184 EK87
Churchbury Rd., Enf. 82 DR40
Churchcroft Clo. SW12 180 DG87
Endlesham Rd.
Churchdown, Brom. 184 EE91
Churchfield, Harl. 36 EV13
Churchfield Ave. N12 98 DC51
Churchfield Clo., Har. 116 CC56
Churchfield Clo., Hayes 135 BT73
West Ave.
Churchfield Ms., Slou. 132 AU72
Churchfield Path (Cheshunt), Wal.Cr. 66 DW29
Churchfield Rd. W3 138 CQ74
Churchfield Rd. W7 157 CE75
Churchfield Rd. W13 137 CH74
Churchfield Rd., Ger.Cr. 90 AX53
Churchfield Rd., Reig. 249 CZ133
Churchfield Rd., Walt. 195 BU102
Churchfield Rd., Well. 166 EU83
Churchfield Rd., Welw. 30 DC06
Churchfield Rd., Wey. 212 BN105
Churchfields E18 102 EG53
Churchfields SE10 163 EC79
Roan St.
Churchfields, Brox. 49 EA20
Churchfields, Guil. 243 BA130
Burpham La.
Churchfields, Loug. 84 EL42
Churchfields, W.Mol. 196 CA97
Churchfields, Wok. 226 AY116
Churchfields Ave., Felt. 176 BZ90
Churchfields Ave., Wey. 213 BP105
Churchfields La., Brox. 49 EA20
Churchfields Rd., Beck. 203 DX96
Churchfields Rd., Wat. 75 BT36
Churchgate (Cheshunt), Wal.Cr. 66 DV30
Churchgate Gdns., Harl. 36 EZ11
Sheering Rd.
Churchgate Rd. (Cheshunt), Wal.Cr. 66 DV29
Churchgate St., Harl. 36 EY11
Churchill Ave., Har. 117 CH58
Churchill Ave., Uxb. 135 BP69
Churchill Clo., Dart. 188 FP88
Churchill Clo., Felt. 175 BT88
Churchill Clo., Lthd. 231 CE123
Churchill Clo., Uxb. 135 BP69
Churchill Clo., Warl. 236 DW117
Churchill Ct. W5 138 CM70
Churchill Ct., Nthlt. 116 CA64
Churchill Ct., Stai. 174 BJ93
Churchill Cres., Hat. 45 CW23
Dixons Hill Rd.
Churchill Dr., Beac. 88 AJ50
Churchill Dr., Wey. 195 BQ104
Churchill Gdns. SW1 161 DJ78
Churchill Gdns. W3 138 CN72
Churchill Gdns. Rd. SW1 161 DH78
Churchill Ms., Wdf.Grn. 102 EF51
High Rd. Woodford Grn.
Churchill Pl. E14 143 EB74
Churchill Pl., Har. 117 CE56
Sandridge Clo.
Churchill Rd. E16 144 EJ72
Churchill Rd. NW2 139 CV65
Churchill Rd. NW5 121 DH63
Churchill Rd. (Horton Kirby), Dart. 208 FQ98
Churchill Rd., Edg. 96 CM51
Churchill Rd., Grav. 191 GF88
Churchill Rd., Grays 170 GD79
Churchill Rd., Guil. 258 AY135
Churchill Rd., Horl. 269 DP148
Churchill Rd., St.Alb. 43 CG18
Churchill Rd., Slou. 153 AZ77
Churchill Rd., S.Croy. 220 DQ109
Churchill Ter. E4 101 EA49
Churchill Wk. E9 122 DW64
Churchill Way, Brom. 204 EG97
Ethelbert Rd.
Churchill Way, Sun. 175 BU92
Churchill Way, West. 222 EL114
Churchley Rd. SE26 182 DV91
Churchmead Clo., Barn. 80 DE44
Churchmead Rd. NW10 139 CU65
Churchmore Rd. SW16 201 DJ95
Churchside Clo., West. 238 EJ117
Churchview Rd., Twick. 177 CD88
Churchway NW1 273 N2
Churchway NW1 141 DK69
Churchwell Path E9 142 DW65
Morning La.
Churchwood Gdns., Wdf.Grn. 102 EG49
Churchyard Row SE11 278 G8
Churston Ave. E13 144 EH67
Churston Clo. SW2 181 DP88
Tulse Hill
Churston Dr., Mord. 199 CX99
Churston Gdns. N11 99 DJ51
Churton Pl. SW1 277 L9
Churton St. SW1 277 L9
Churton St. SW1 161 DJ77
Chusan Pl. E14 143 DZ72
Commercial Rd.
Chuters Clo., W.Byf. 212 BL112
Chuters Gro., Epsom 217 CT112
Chyne, The, Ger.Cr. 113 AZ57
Chyngton Clo., Sid. 185 ET90
Cibber Rd. SE23 183 DX89
Cicada Rd. SW18 180 DC86
Cicely Rd. SE15 162 DU81
Cillocks Clo., Hodd. 49 EA16
Cimba Wd., Grav. 191 GL91
Cinder Path, Wok. 226 AW119
Cinderford Way, Brom. 184 EE91
Cinema Par. W5 138 CM70
Ashbourne Rd.
Cinnamon Clo., Croy. 201 DL101
Cinnamon Gdns., Guil. 242 AU129
Cinnamon Row SW11 160 DC83
Cinnamon St. E1 142 DV74
Cintra Pk. SE19 182 DT94
Cippenham Clo., Slou. 131 AM73
Cippenham La., Slou. 131 AM73
Circle, The NW2 118 CS62
Circle, The NW7 96 CR50
Circle, The, Til. 171 GG81
Toronto Rd.
Circle Gdns. SW19 200 DA96
Circle Gdns., W.Byf. 212 BM112
High Rd.
Circle Rd., Walt. 213 BS110
Circuits, The, Pnr. 116 BW56
Circular Rd. N17 122 DT55
Circular Way SE18 165 EM79
Circus Ms. W1 272 D6
Circus Pl. EC2 275 L7
Circus Rd. NW8 140 DD69
Circus St. SE10 163 EC80
Cirencester St. W2 140 DB71
Cirrus Cres., Grav. 191 GL92
Cissbury Ring N. N12 97 CZ50
Cissbury Ring S. N12 97 CZ50
Cissbury Rd. N15 122 DR57
Citadel Pl. SE11 278 B10
Citizen Rd. N7 121 DN62
Citron Ter. SE15 162 DV83
Nunhead La.
City Gdn. Row N1 274 G1
City Gdn. Row N1 141 DP68
City Rd. EC1 274 F1
City Rd. EC1 141 DP68
Civic Clo., St.Alb. 43 CD20
Civic Offices, St.Alb. 43 CD20
Civic Sq., Til. 171 GG82
Civic Way, Ilf. 125 EQ56
Civic Way, Ruis. 116 BX64
Clabon Ms. SW1 276 D7
Clabon Ms. SW1 160 DF76
Clack St. SE16 162 DW75
Clacket La., West. 238 EL124
Clacton Rd. E6 144 EK69
Clacton Rd. E17 123 DY58
Clacton Rd. N17 100 DT54
Sperling Rd.
Claigmar Gdns. N3 98 DB53
Claire Ct. N12 98 DC48
Claire Ct., Pnr. 94 BZ52
Westfield Pk.
Claire Ct., Wat. 95 CD46
Claire Pl. E14 163 EA76
Clairvale, Horn. 128 FL59
Clairvale Rd., Houns. 156 BX81
Clairview Rd. SW16 181 DH92
Clairville Gdns. W7 137 CE74
Clairville Pt. SE23 183 DX90
Clammas Way, Uxb. 134 BJ71
Clamp Hill, Stan. 95 CD49
Clancarty Rd. SW6 160 DA82
Clandon Ave., Egh. 173 BC94
Clandon Clo. W3 158 CP75
Avenue Rd.
Clandon Clo., Epsom 217 CT107
Clandon Gdns. N3 120 DA55
Clandon Pk., Guil. 244 BG130
Clandon Rd., Guil. 258 AY135
Clandon Rd. (West Clandon), Guil. 244 BG128
Clandon Rd., Ilf. 125 ES61
Clandon Rd., Wok. 243 BF125
Clandon St. SE8 163 EA82
Clandon Way, Wok. 243 BF125
Clandon Rd.
Clanfield Way SE15 162 DS80
Diamond St.
Clanricarde Gdns. W2 140 DA73
Clap La., Dag. 127 FB62
Clapgate Rd. (Bushey), Wat. 76 CB44
Clapham Common N. Side SW4 160 DF84
Clapham Common S. Side SW4 181 DH86
Clapham Common W. Side SW4 160 DF84
Clapham Cres. SW4 161 DK84
Clapham High St. SW4 161 DK84
Clapham Junct. Est. SW11 160 DE84
Clapham Manor St. SW4 161 DJ83
Clapham Pk. Est. SW4 181 DK86
Clapham Pk. Rd. SW4 161 DK84
Clapham Rd. SW9 161 DL83
Clapham Rd. Est. SW4 161 DK83
Claps Gate La. E6 145 EP70
Royal Docks Rd.
Claps Gate La., Bark. 145 EP70
Royal Docks Rd.
Clapton App., H.Wyc. 110 AD55
Clapton Common E5 122 DT59
Clapton Pk. Est. E5 123 DY63
Blackwell Clo.
Clapton Pas. E5 122 DW64
Lower Clapton Rd.
Clapton Sq. E5 122 DW64
Clapton Ter. N16 122 DU60
Oldhill St.
Clapton Way E5 122 DU63
Clara Pl. SE18 165 EN77
Clare Clo. N2 120 DC55
Thomas More Way
Clare Clo., Borwd. 78 CM44
Clare Clo., W.Byf. 212 BG113
Clare Cor. SE9 185 EP87
Clare Cotts., Red. 251 DP133
Clare Ct., Cat. 237 EA123
Clare Ct., Nthwd. 93 BS50
Clare Cres., Lthd. 231 CG119
Clare Dr., Slou. 111 AP63
Clare Gdns. E7 124 EG63
Clare Gdns. W11 139 CY72
Westbourne Pk. Rd.
Clare Gdns., Bark. 145 ET65
Clare Gdns., Egh. 173 BA92
Mowbray Cres.
Clare Gdns., Stan. 95 CJ50
Clare Hill, Esher 214 CB107
Clare La. N1 142 DQ66
Clare Lawn Ave. SW14 178 CR85
Clare Mkt. WC2 274 B9
Clare Ms. SW6 160 DB80
Waterford Rd.
Clare Pk., Amer. 55 AS40
Clare Pl. SW15 179 CT86
Minstead Gdns.
Clare Rd. E11 123 ED58
Clare Rd. NW10 139 CU66
Clare Rd. SE14 163 DZ82
Clare Rd., Grnf. 137 CD65
Clare Rd., Houns. 156 BZ83
Clare Rd., Maid. 130 AJ72
Clare Rd., Stai. 174 BK88
Clare St. E2 142 DV68
Clare Way, Bexh. 166 EY81
Clare Way, Sev. 257 FJ128
Clare Wd., Lthd. 231 CH118
Claredale, Wok. 226 AY119
Claremont Ave.
Claredale St. E2 142 DV68
Claremont, St.Alb. 60 CA31
Claremont (Cheshunt), Wal.Cr. 66 DT29
Claremont Ave., Esher 214 BZ107
Claremont Ave., Har. 118 CL57
Claremont Ave., N.Mal. 199 CV99
Claremont Ave., Sun. 195 BV95
Claremont Ave., Walt. 214 BX105
Claremont Ave., Wok. 226 AY119
Claremont Clo. E16 145 EN74
Claremont Clo. N1 274 D1
Claremont Clo. N1 141 DN68
Claremont Clo. SW2 181 DL88
Streatham Hill
Claremont Clo., Grays 170 GC76
Premier Ave.
Claremont Clo., Orp. 223 EN105
Claremont Clo., S.Croy. 236 DV115
Claremont Clo., Walt. 214 BW106
Claremont Ct., Dor. 263 CH137
Claremont Cres., Dart. 167 FE84
Claremont Cres., Rick. 75 BQ43
Claremont Dr., Esher 214 CB108
Claremont Dr., Shep. 195 BP100
Claremont Dr., Wok. 226 AY119
Claremont End, Esher 214 CB107
Claremont Gdns., Ilf. 125 ES61
Claremont Gdns., Surb. 198 CL99
Claremont Gdns., Upmin. 129 FR60
Claremont Gro. W4 158 CS80
Edensor Gdns.
Claremont Gro., Wdf.Grn. 102 EJ51
Claremont La., Esher 214 CB105
Claremont Pk. N3 97 CY53
Claremont Pk. Rd., Esher 214 CB107
Claremont Pl., Grav. 191 GH87
Cutmore St.
Claremont Rd. E7 124 EH64
Claremont Rd. E17 101 DY54
Claremont Rd. N6 121 DH59
Claremont Rd. NW2 119 CW59
Claremont Rd. W9 139 CZ68
Claremont Rd. W13 137 CG71
Claremont Rd., Barn. 80 DD37
Claremont Rd., Brom. 204 EL98
Claremont Rd., Croy. 202 DU102
Claremont Rd., Esher 215 CE108
Claremont Rd., Har. 95 CE54
Claremont Rd., Horn. 127 FG58
Claremont Rd., Red. 250 DG131
Claremont Rd., Stai. 173 BD92
Claremont Rd., Surb. 198 CL100
Claremont Rd., Swan. 187 FE94
Claremont Rd., Tedd. 177 CF92
Claremont Rd., Twick. 177 CH86
Claremont Rd., W.Byf. 212 BG112
Claremont Rd., Wind. 151 AQ82
Claremont Sq. N1 274 D1
Claremont Sq. N1 141 DN68
Claremont St. E16 145 EN74
Claremont St. N18 100 DU51
Claremont St. SE10 163 EB79
Claremont Way NW2 119 CW60
Claremount Clo., Epsom 233 CW117
Claremount Gdns., Epsom 233 CW117
Clarence Ave. SW4 181 DK87
Clarence Ave., Brom. 204 EL98
Clarence Ave., Ilf. 125 EN58
Clarence Ave., N.Mal. 198 CQ96
Clarence Ave., Upmin. 128 FN61
Clarence Clo., Walt. 213 BV105
Clarence Clo. (Bushey), Wat. 95 CF45
Clarence Ct., Egh. 173 AZ93
Clarence St.
Clarence Ct., Horl. 269 DK147
Clarence Way
Clarence Cres. SW4 181 DK86
Clarence Cres., Sid. 186 EV90
Clarence Cres., Wind. 151 AQ81
Clarence Dr., Egh. 172 AW91
Clarence Gdns. NW1 273 J3
Clarence Gdns. NW1 141 DH69
Clarence La. SW15 178 CS86
Clarence Ms. E5 122 DV64
Clarence Ms. SE16 143 DX74
Clarence Pas. NW1 273 P1
Clarence Pl. E5 122 DV64
Clarence Pl., Grav. 191 GH87
Clarence Rd. E5 122 DV63
Clarence Rd. E12 124 EK64
Clarence Rd. E16 144 EE70
Clarence Rd. E17 101 DX54
Clarence Rd. N15 122 DQ57
Clarence Rd. N22 99 DL52
Clarence Rd. NW6 139 CZ66
Clarence Rd. SE9 184 EL89
Clarence Rd. SW19 180 DB93
Clarence Rd. W4 158 CN78
Clarence Rd., Berk. 38 AW19
Clarence Rd., Bexh. 166 EY84
Clarence Rd., Brwd. 108 FV44
Clarence Rd., Brom. 204 EK97
Clarence Rd., Croy. 202 DR101
Clarence Rd., Enf. 82 DV43
Clarence Rd., Grays 170 GB78
Clarence Rd., Red. 266 DD137
Clarence Rd., Rich. 158 CM81
Clarence Rd., St.Alb. 43 CF20
Clarence Rd., Sid. 186 EV90
Clarence Rd., Sutt. 218 DB105
Clarence Rd., Tedd. 177 CF93
Clarence Rd., Wall. 219 DH106
Clarence Rd., Walt. 213 BV105
Clarence Rd., West. 239 EM118
Clarence Rd., Wind. 151 AN81
Clarence Row, Grav. 191 GH87
Clarence St., Egh. 173 AZ93
Clarence St., Kings.T. 198 CL96
Clarence St., Rich. 158 CL84
Clarence St., Sthl. 156 BX76
Clarence St., Stai. 173 BE91
Clarence Ter. NW1 272 E4
Clarence Ter., Houns. 156 CB84
Clarence Wk. SW4 161 DL82
Clarence Wk., Red. 266 DD137
Clarence Way NW1 141 DH66

Clarence Way, Horl. 269 DK147
Clarence Way Est. NW1 141 DH66
Clarenden Pl., Dart. 187 FE92
Clarendon Clo. W2 272 B10
Clarendon Clo., Orp. 206 EU97
Clarendon Ct., Slou. 132 AV73
Clarendon Cres. W11 139 CY73
Clarendon Rd.
Clarendon Cres., Twick. 177 CD90
Clarendon Cross W11 139 CY73
Portland Rd.
Clarendon Dr. SW15 159 CW83
Clarendon Gdns. NW4 119 CU55
Clarendon Gdns. W9 140 DC70
Clarendon Gdns., Dart. 189 FR87
Clarendon Gdns., Ilf. 125 EM60
Clarendon Gdns., Wem. 117 CK62
Clarendon Gate, Cher. 211 BC107
Murray Rd.
Clarendon Grn., Orp. 206 EU97
Clarendon Gro. NW1 273 M2
Clarendon Gro., Mitch. 200 DF97
Clarendon Gro., Orp. 206 EU98
Clarendon Ms. W2 272 B10
Clarendon Ms., Bex. 187 FB88
Clarendon Ms., Borwd. 78 CN41
Clarendon Rd.
Clarendon Path, Orp. 206 EU97
Clarendon Pl. W2 272 B10
Clarendon Pl. W2 140 DE73
Clarendon Ri. SE13 163 EC83
Clarendon Rd. E11 123 ED60
Clarendon Rd. E17 123 EB58
Clarendon Rd. E18 124 EG55
Clarendon Rd. N8 121 DM55
Clarendon Rd. N15 121 DP56
Clarendon Rd. N18 100 DU51
Clarendon Rd. N22 99 DM54
Clarendon Rd. SW19 180 DE94
Clarendon Rd. W5 138 CL70
Clarendon Rd. W11 139 CY73
Clarendon Rd., Ashf. 174 BM91
Clarendon Rd., Borwd. 78 CN41
Clarendon Rd., Croy. 201 DP103
Clarendon Rd., Grav. 191 GJ86
Clarendon Rd., Har. 117 CE58
Clarendon Rd., Hayes 155 BT75
Clarendon Rd., Red. 250 DF133
Clarendon Rd., Sev. 256 FG124
Clarendon Rd., Wall. 219 DJ107
Clarendon Rd. (Cheshunt), Wal.Cr. 67 DX29
Clarendon Rd., Wat. 75 BV40
Clarendon St. SW1 277 J10
Clarendon St. SW1 161 DH78
Clarendon Ter. W9 140 DC70
Lanark Pl.
Clarendon Wk. W11 139 CY72
Lancaster Rd.
Clarendon Way N21 82 DQ44
Clarendon Way, Chis. 205 ET97
Clarendon Way, Orp. 206 EU97
Clarens St. SE6 183 DZ89
Clares, The, Cat. 236 DU124
Clareville Rd.
Claret Gdns. SE25 202 DS97
Clareville Gro. SW7 160 DC77
Clareville Rd., Cat. 236 DU124
Clareville Rd., Orp. 205 EQ103
Clareville St. SW7 160 DC77
Clarewood Wk. SW9 161 DN84
Somerleyton Rd.
Clarges Ms. W1 277 H2
Clarges Ms. W1 141 DH74
Clarges St. W1 277 J2
Clarges St. W1 141 DH74
Claribel Rd. SW9 161 DP82
Clarice Way, Wall. 219 DL109
Claridge Rd., Dag. 126 EX60
Clarina Rd. SE20 183 DX94
Evelina Rd.
Clarissa Rd., Rom. 126 EX59
Clarissa St. E8 142 DT67
Clark Clo., Erith 167 FG81
Forest Rd.
Clark St. E1 142 DV71
Clark Way, Houns. 156 BX80
Clarke Grn., Wat. 75 BU35
Clarke Path N16 122 DU60
Braydon Rd.
Clarke Way, Wat. 75 BU35
Clarkebourne Dr., Grays 170 GD79
Clarkes Ave., Wor.Pk. 199 CX102
Clarkes Dr., Uxb. 134 BL71
Clarke's Ms. W1 272 G6
Clarkes Rd., Hat. 45 CV17
Clarkfield, Rick. 92 BH46
Clarks La., Epp. 69 ET31
Clarks La., Sev. 224 EZ112
Clarks La., Warl. 238 EF123
Clarks La., West. 238 EJ123
Clarks Mead (Bushey), Wat. 94 CC45
Clarks Pl. EC2 275 M8
Clarks Pl. EC2 142 DS72
Clarks Rd., Ilf. 125 ER61
Clarkson Rd. E16 144 EF72
Clarkson St. E2 142 DV69
Clarksons, The, Bark. 145 EQ68
Classon Clo., West Dr. 154 BL75
Claston Clo., Dart. 167 FE84
Iron Mill La.
Claude Rd. E10 123 EC61
Claude Rd. E13 144 EH67
Claude Rd. SE15 162 DV82
Claude St. E14 163 EA77
Claudia Jones Way SW2 181 DL86
Claudia Pl. SW19 179 CY88
Claudian Pl., St.Alb. 42 CA21
Claudian Way, Grays 171 GH76
Claughton Rd. E13 144 EJ68
Claughton Way, Brwd. 109 GD44
Clauson Ave., Nthlt. 116 CB64
Clave St. E1 142 DV74
Cinnamon St.
Clavell St. SE10 163 EC79
Claverdale Rd. SW2 181 DM87
Claverhambury Rd., Wal.Abb. 68 EF29
Clavering Ave. SW13 159 CV79
Clavering Clo., Twick. 177 CG91
Clavering Rd. E12 124 EK60
Clavering Way, Brwd. 109 GC44
Poplar Dr.
Claverings Ind. Est. N9 101 DX47
Claverley Gro. N3 98 DB53
Claverley Vill. N3 98 DB52
Claverley Gro.
Claverton Clo., Hem.H. 40 BK19
Claverton St. SW1 161 DJ78
Claxton Gro. W6 159 CX78
Clay Acre, Chesh. 54 AR30
Clay Ave., Mitch. 201 DH96
Clay Hill, Enf. 81 DP37
Clay La., Edg. 96 CP47
Clay La., Epsom 232 CP124
Clay La., Guil. 243 BA129
Clay La., Red. 267 DJ135
Clay La., Stai. 174 BM87
Clay La. (Bushey), Wat. 95 CE45
Clay Rd., The, Loug. 84 EK39
Clay St. W1 272 E7
Clay St., Beac. 88 AJ48
Clay Tye Rd., Upmin. 129 FW64
Claybank Gro. SE13 163 EB83
Algernon Rd.
Claybourne Ms. SE19 182 DS94
Church Rd.
Claybridge Rd. SE12 184 EJ91
Claybrook Clo. N2 120 DD55
Long La.
Claybrook Rd. W6 159 CX79
Clayburn Gdns., S.Ock. 149 FV73
Claybury (Bushey), Wat. 94 CB45
Claybury Bdy., Ilf. 124 EL55
Claybury Rd., Wdf.Grn. 102 EL52
Claycroft, Welw.G.C. 30 DB08
Claydon Dr., Croy. 219 DL105
Claydon End, Ger.Cr. 112 AY55
Claydon La., Ger.Cr. 112 AY55
Claydon Rd., Wok. 226 AU116
Clayfarm Rd. SE9 185 EQ89
Clayfields, H.Wyc. 88 AC45
Claygate Clo., Horn. 127 FG63
Claygate Cres., Croy. 221 EC107
Claygate La., Esher 197 CG104
Claygate La., T.Ditt. 197 CG102
Claygate La., Wal.Abb. 67 EC30
Claygate Lo. Clo., Esher 215 CE108
Claygate Rd. W13 157 CH76
Claygate Rd., Dor. 263 CH139
Clayhall Ave., Ilf. 124 EL55
Clayhall La., Reig. 265 CX138
Clayhall La., Wind. 172 AT85
Clayhanger, Guil. 243 BC132
Kingfisher Dr.
Clayhill, Surb. 198 CN99
Clayhill Clo., Reig. 265 CU141
Clayhill Cres. SE9 184 EK91
Clayhill Rd., Reig. 264 CS143
Claylands Pl. SW8 161 DN80
Claylands Rd. SW8 161 DM79
Claymill Ho. SE18 165 EQ78
Claymore, Hem.H. 40 BL16
Claymore Clo., Mord. 200 DA101
Claypit Hill, Wal.Abb. 84 EJ36
Claypole Dr., Houns. 156 BY81
Claypole Rd. E15 143 EC68
Clayponds Ave., Brent. 158 CL77
Clayponds Gdns. W5 157 CK77
Clayponds La., Brent. 158 CL78
Clays La. E15 123 EB64
Clay's La., Loug. 85 EN39
Clays La. Clo. E15 123 EB64
Clayside, Chig. 103 EQ50
Clayton Ave., Upmin. 128 FP64
Clayton Ave., Wem. 138 CL66
Clayton Clo. E6 145 EM72
Brandreth Rd.
Clayton Cres., Brent. 157 CK78
Clayton Cft. Rd., Dart. 187 FG89
Clayton Dr., Guil. 242 AT131
Clayton Fld. NW9 96 CS52
Clayton Mead, Gdse. 252 DV130
Clayton Ms. SE10 163 ED81
Clayton Rd. SE15 162 DU81
Clayton Rd., Chess. 215 CJ105
Clayton Rd., Epsom 216 CS113
Clayton Rd., Hayes 155 BS75
Clayton Rd., Islw. 157 CE83
Clayton Rd., Rom. 127 FC60
Clayton St. SE11 161 DN79
Clayton Ter., Hayes 136 BX71
Jollys La.
Clayton Wk., Amer. 72 AW39
Clayton Way, Uxb. 134 BK70
Claywood Clo., Orp. 205 ES101
Claywood La., Dart. 189 FX90
Clayworth Clo., Sid. 186 EV86
Cleall Ave., Wal.Abb. 67 EC34
Quaker La.
Cleanthus Clo. SE18 165 EP81
Cleanthus Rd.
Cleanthus Rd. SE18 165 EP81
Clearbrook Way E1 143 DX72
West Arbour St.
Cleardene, Dor. 263 CH136
Cleardown, Wok. 227 BB118
Clears, The, Reig. 249 CY132
Clearwater Ter. W11 159 CX75
Lorne Gdns.
Clearwell Dr. W9 140 DB70
Cleave Ave., Hayes 155 BS77
Cleave Ave., Orp. 223 ES107
Cleave Prior, Couls. 234 DE119
Cleaveland Rd., Surb. 197 CK99
Cleaver Sq. SE11 278 E10
Cleaver Sq. SE11 161 DN78
Cleaver St. SE11 278 E10
Cleaver St. SE11 161 DN78
Cleaverholme Clo. SE25 202 DV100
Cleeve, The, Guil. 243 BA134
Cleeve Ct., Felt. 175 BS88
Kilross Rd.
Cleeve Hill SE23 182 DV88
Cleeve Pk. Gdns., Sid. 186 EV89
Cleeve Rd., Lthd. 231 CF120
Clegg St. E1 142 DV74
Prusom St.
Clegg St. E13 144 EG68
Cleland Path, Loug. 85 EP39
Cleland Rd., Ger.Cr. 90 AX54
Clem Attlee Ct. SW6 159 CZ79
Clem Attlee Par. SW6 159 CZ79
Clem Attlee Ct.
Clematis Clo., Rom. 106 FJ52
Clematis Gdns., Wdf.Grn. 102 EG50
Clematis St. W12 139 CU73
Clemence St. E14 143 DZ71
Clement Atlee Sq., Harl. 51 ER15
South Gate
Clement Ave. SW4 161 DK84
Clement Clo. NW6 139 CW66
Clement Clo. W4 158 CR77
Acton La.
Clement Clo., Pur. 235 DP116
Croftleigh Ave.
Clement Gdns., Hayes 155 BS77
Clement Rd. SW19 179 CY92
Clement Rd., Beck. 203 DX96
Clement Rd. (Cheshunt), Wal.Cr. 67 DY27
Clement St., Swan. 188 FJ93
Clement Way, Upmin. 128 FM62
Clementhorpe Rd., Dag. 146 EW65
Clementina Rd. E10 123 DZ60
Clementine Clo. W13 157 CH75
Balfour Rd.
Clements Ave. E16 144 EG73
Clements Clo., Slou. 152 AV75
Clements Ct., Houns. 156 BX84
Clements Ct., Ilf. 125 EP62
Clements La.
Clement's Inn WC2 274 C9
Clement's Inn WC2 141 DM72
Clement's Inn Pas. WC2 274 C9
Clements La. EC4 275 L10
Clements La. EC4 142 DR73
Clements La., Ilf. 125 EP62
Clements Mead, Lthd. 231 CG119
Clements Pl., Brent. 157 CK78
Clements Rd. E6 144 EL66
Clements Rd. SE16 162 DU76
Clements Rd., Ilf. 125 EP62
Clements Rd., Rick. 73 BD43
Clements Rd., Walt. 195 BV103
Clements St., Ware 33 DY06
Clenches Fm. La., Sev. 256 FG126
Clenches Fm. Rd., Sev. 256 FG126
Clendon Way SE18 165 ER77
Polthorne Gro.
Clennam St. SE1 162 DQ75
Southwark Bri. Rd.
Clensham La., Sutt. 200 DA103
Clenston Ms. W1 272 D8
Clephane Rd. N1 142 DQ65
Clere St. EC2 275 L4
Clerics Wk., Shep. 195 BR100
Gordon Rd.
Clerkenwell Clo. EC1 274 E4
Clerkenwell Clo. EC1 141 DN70
Clerkenwell Grn. EC1 274 E5
Clerkenwell Grn. EC1 141 DN70
Clerkenwell Rd. EC1 274 D5
Clerkenwell Rd. EC1 141 DN70
Clerks Cft., Red. 252 DR133
Clerks Piece, Loug. 85 EM41
Clermont Rd. E9 142 DW67
Cleve Rd. NW6 140 DA66
Cleve Rd., Sid. 186 EX90
Clevedon, Wey. 213 BR106
Clevedon Clo. N16 122 DT62
Smalley Clo.
Clevedon Gdns., Hayes 155 BR76
Clevedon Gdns., Houns. 155 BV81
Clevedon Rd. SE20 203 DX95
Clevedon Rd., Kings.T. 198 CN96
Clevedon Rd., Twick. 177 CK86
Clevehurst Clo., Slou. 132 AU65
Cleveland, Hem.H. 41 BP18
Cleveland Ave. SW20 199 CZ96
Cleveland Ave. W4 159 CT77
Cleveland Ave., Hmptn. 176 BZ94
Cleveland Clo., H.Wyc. 110 AE55
Wootton Way
Cleveland Clo., Walt. 195 BV104
Cleveland Cres., Borwd. 78 CQ43
Cleveland Dr., Stai. 194 BH96
Cleveland Gdns. N4 122 DQ57
Cleveland Gdns. NW2 119 CX61
Cleveland Gdns. SW13 159 CT82
Cleveland Gdns. W2 140 DC72
Cleveland Gdns., Wor.Pk. 198 CS103
Cleveland Gro. E1 142 DW70
Cleveland Way
Cleveland Ms. W1 273 K6
Cleveland Pk., Stai. 174 BL86
Northumberland Clo.
Cleveland Pk. Ave. E17 123 EA56
Cleveland Pk. Cres. E17 123 EA56
Cleveland Pl. SW1 277 L2
Cleveland Ri., Mord. 199 CX101
Cleveland Rd. E18 124 EG55
Cleveland Rd. N1 142 DR66
Cleveland Rd. N9 100 DV45
Cleveland Rd. SW13 159 CT82
Cleveland Rd. W4 158 CQ76
Antrobus Rd.
Cleveland Rd. W13 137 CG71
Cleveland Rd., Ilf. 125 EP62
Cleveland Rd., Islw. 157 CG84
Cleveland Rd., N.Mal. 198 CS98
Cleveland Rd., Uxb. 134 BK68
Cleveland Rd., Well. 165 ET82
Cleveland Rd., Wor.Pk. 198 CS103
Cleveland Row SW1 277 K3
Cleveland Row SW1 141 DJ74
Cleveland Sq. W2 140 DC72
Cleveland St. W1 273 J5
Cleveland St. W1 141 DH70
Cleveland Ter. W2 140 DC72
Cleveland Way E1 142 DW70
Cleveley Clo. SE7 164 EK77
Cleveley Cres. W5 138 CL68
Cleveleys Rd. E5 122 DV62
Cleverley Est. W12 139 CU74
Cleves Ave., Brwd. 108 FV46
Cleves Ave., Epsom 217 CV109
Cleves Clo., Cob. 213 BV114
Cleves Clo., Loug. 84 EL44
Cleves Ct., Wind. 151 AM83
Cleves Cres., Croy. 221 EC111
Cleves Rd. E6 144 EK67
Cleves Rd., Hem.H. 41 BP15
Cleves Rd., Rich. 177 CJ90
Cleves Wk., Ilf. 103 EQ52
Cleves Way, Hmptn. 176 BZ94
Cleves Way, Ruis. 116 BX60
Cleves Way, Sun. 175 BT93
Cleves Wd., Wey. 213 BS105
Clewer Ave., Wind. 151 AN82
Clewer Ct. Rd., Wind. 151 AN80
Clewer Cres., Har. 95 CD53
Clewer Flds., Wind. 151 AQ81
Clewer Hill Rd., Wind. 151 AL82
Clewer New Town, Wind. 151 AN82
Clewer Pk., Wind. 151 AN80
Clichy Est. E1 142 DW71
Clifden Rd. E5 122 DW64
Clifden Rd., Brent. 157 CK79
Clifden Rd., Twick. 177 CF88
Cliff End, Pur. 219 DP112
Cliff Pl., S.Ock. 149 FX69
Cliff Rd. NW1 141 DK65
Cliff Ter. SE8 163 EA82
Cliff Vill. NW1 141 DK65
Cliff Wk. E16 144 EF70
Cliffe Rd., S.Croy. 220 DR106
Cliffe Wk., Sutt. 218 DC106
Turnpike La.
Clifford Ave. SW14 158 CP83
Clifford Ave., Chis. 185 EM93
Clifford Ave., Ilf. 103 EP53
Clifford Ave., Wall. 219 DJ105
Clifford Clo., Nthlt. 136 BY67
Clifford Dr. SW9 161 DP84
Clifford Gdns. NW10 139 CW68
Clifford Gro., Ashf. 174 BN91
Clifford Manor Rd., Guil. 258 AY138
Clifford Rd. E16 144 EF70
Clifford Rd. E17 101 EC54
Clifford Rd. N9 82 DW44
Clifford Rd. SE25 202 DU98
Clifford Rd., Barn. 80 DB41
Clifford Rd., Grays 170 FZ76
Clifford Rd., Houns. 156 BX83
Clifford Rd., Rich. 177 CK89
Clifford Rd., Wem. 137 CK67
Clifford St. W1 277 K1
Clifford St. W1 141 DJ73
Clifford Way NW10 119 CT63
Clifford's Inn Pas. EC4 274 D9
Cliffview Rd. SE13 163 EA83
Clifton Ave. E17 123 DX55
Clifton Ave. N3 97 CZ53
Clifton Ave. W12 159 CT75
Clifton Ave., Felt. 176 BW90
Clifton Ave., Stan. 95 CH54
Clifton Ave., Sutt. 218 DB111
Clifton Ave., Wem. 138 CM65
Clifton Clo., Add. 194 BH103
Clifton Clo., Cat. 236 DR123
Clifton Clo., Orp. 223 EQ106
Clifton Clo. (Cheshunt), Wal.Cr. 67 DY29
Clifton Ct. N4 121 DN61
Playford Rd.
Clifton Ct. NW8 140 DD70
Edgware Rd.
Clifton Cres. SE15 162 DV80
Clifton Est. SE15 162 DV81
Consort Rd.
Clifton Gdns. N15 122 DT58
Clifton Gdns. NW11 119 CZ58
Clifton Gdns. W4 158 CR77
Chiswick High Rd.
Clifton Gdns. W9 140 DC70
Clifton Gdns., Enf. 81 DL42
Clifton Gdns., Uxb. 135 BP68
Clifton Gro. E8 142 DU65
Clifton Gro., Grav. 191 GH87
Clifton Hill NW8 140 DB68
Clifton Lawns, Amer. 55 AQ35
Clifton Marine Par., Grav. 191 GF86
Clifton Pk. Ave. SW20 199 CW96
Clifton Pl. SE16 162 DW75
Canon Beck Rd.
Clifton Pl. W2 272 A9
Clifton Pl. W2 140 DD72
Clifton Pl., Bans. 234 DA116
Court Rd.
Clifton Ri. SE14 163 DY80
Clifton Ri., Wind. 151 AK81
Clifton Rd. E7 144 EK65
Clifton Rd. E16 144 EE71
Clifton Rd. N3 98 DC53
Clifton Rd. N8 121 DK58
Clifton Rd. N22 99 DJ53
Clifton Rd. NW10 139 CU68
Clifton Rd. SE25 202 DR98
Clifton Rd. SW19 179 CX93
Clifton Rd. W9 140 DC70
Clifton Rd., Amer. 55 AP35
Clifton Rd., Couls. 235 DH115
Clifton Rd., Grav. 191 GG86
Clifton Rd., Grnf. 136 CC70
Clifton Rd., Har. 118 CM57
Clifton Rd., Horn. 127 FG58
Clifton Rd., Ilf. 125 ER58
Clifton Rd., Islw. 157 CD82
Clifton Rd., Kings.T. 178 CM94
Clifton Rd., Loug. 84 EL42
Clifton Rd., Sid. 185 ES91
Clifton Rd., Slou. 152 AV75
Clifton Rd., Sthl. 156 BY77
Clifton Rd., Tedd. 177 CE91
Clifton Rd., Wall. 219 DH106
Clifton Rd., Wat. 75 BV43
Clifton Rd., Well. 166 EW83
Clifton St. EC2 275 M6
Clifton St. EC2 142 DS71
Clifton St., St.Alb. 43 CE19
Clifton Ter. N4 121 DN61
Clifton Vill. W9 140 DC71
Clifton Wk. E6 144 EL71
Tollgate Rd.
Clifton Wk., Dart. 188 FP86
Osbourne Rd.
Clifton Way SE15 162 DW80
Clifton Way, Borwd. 78 CN39
Clifton Way, Brwd. 109 GD46
Clifton Way, Wem. 138 CL67
Clifton Way, Wok. 226 AT117
Cliftons La., Reig. 249 CX133
Cliftonville, Dor. 263 CH137
Climb, The, Rick. 74 BH44
Clinch Ct. E16 144 EG71
Brent Rd.
Cline Rd. N11 99 DJ51
Cline Rd., Guil. 259 AZ136
Clinger Ct. N1 142 DS67
Pitfield St.
Clink St. SE1 279 K2
Clink St. SE1 142 DQ74
Clinton Ave., E.Mol. 196 CC98
Clinton Ave., Well. 166 EU84
Clinton Cres., Ilf. 103 ES51
Clinton End, Hem.H. 41 BQ20
Clinton Rd. E3 143 DY69
Clinton Rd. E7 124 EG63
Clinton Rd. N15 122 DR56
Clinton Rd., Lthd. 231 CJ123
Clipper Boul., Dart. 169 FS83
Clipper Boul. W., Dart. 169 FR83
Clipper Clo. SE16 163 DX75
Kinburn St.
Clipper Cres., Grav. 191 GM91
Clipper Way SE13 163 EC84
Clippesby Clo., Chess. 216 CM107
Clipstone Ms. W1 273 K5
Clipstone Ms. W1 141 DJ71
Clipstone Rd., Houns. 156 CA83
Clipstone St. W1 273 J6
Clipstone St. W1 141 DH71
Clissold Clo. N2 120 DF55
Clissold Ct. N4 122 DQ61
Clissold Cres. N16 122 DR63
Clissold Rd. N16 122 DR62
Clitheroe Ave., Har. 116 CA60
Clitheroe Gdns., Wat. 94 BX48
Clitheroe Rd. SW9 161 DL82
Clitheroe Rd., Rom. 105 FC50
Clitherow Ave. W7 157 CG76
Clitherow Pas., Brent. 157 CH78
Clitherow Rd.
Clitherow Rd., Brent. 157 CH78
Clitterhouse Cres. NW2 119 CW60
Clitterhouse Rd. NW2 119 CW60
Clive Ave. N18 100 DU51
Claremont St.
Clive Ave., Dart. 187 FF86
Clive Clo., Pot.B. 63 CZ31
Clive Ct. W9 140 DC70
Maida Vale
Clive Ct., Slou. 151 AR75
Clive Par., Nthwd. 93 BS52
Maxwell Rd.
Clive Pas. SE21 182 DR90
Clive Rd.
Clive Rd. SE21 182 DR90
Clive Rd. SW19 180 DE93
Clive Rd., Belv. 166 FA77
Clive Rd., Brwd. 107 FW52
Clive Rd., Enf. 82 DU42
Clive Rd., Esher 214 CB105
Clive Rd., Felt. 175 BU86
Clive Rd., Grav. 191 GH86
Clive Rd., Rom. 127 FH57
Clive Rd., Twick. 177 CF91
Clive Way, Enf. 82 DU42
Clive Way, Wat. 76 BW39
Cliveden Clo. N12 98 DC49
Woodside Ave.
Cliveden Clo., Brwd. 109 FZ45
Cliveden Pl. SW1 276 F8
Cliveden Pl. SW1 160 DG77
Cliveden Pl., Shep. 195 BQ100
Cliveden Rd. SW19 199 CZ95
Cliveden Rd., Maid. 130 AD69
Clivedon Ct. W13 137 CH71
Clivedon Rd. E4 102 EE50
Clivedon Rd., Slou. 110 AE64
Clivesdale Dr., Hayes 135 BU74
Cloak La. EC4 275 K10
Cloak La. EC4 142 DQ73
Clock Ho. La., Sev. 256 FG123
Clock Ho. Mead, Lthd. 214 CB114
Clock Ho. Rd., Beck. 203 DY97
Clock Twr. Ms. N1 142 DQ67
Arlington Ave.
Clock Twr. Pl. N7 141 DL65
Clock Twr. Rd., Islw. 157 CF83
Clockhouse Ave., Bark. 145 EQ67
Clockhouse Clo. SW19 179 CW90
Clockhouse Clo., W.Byf. 212 BM112
Clockhouse La., Ashf. 174 BN91
Clockhouse La., Felt. 175 BP90
Clockhouse La., Grays 170 FY75
Clockhouse La., Rom. 105 FB52
Clockhouse La. E., Egh. 173 BB94
Clockhouse La. W., Egh. 173 BA94
Cloister Clo., Rain. 147 FH70
Cloister Clo., Tedd. 177 CH92
Cloister Gdns. SE25 202 DV100
Cloister Gdns., Edg. 96 CQ50
Cloister Garth, Berk. 38 AW19
Cloister Garth, St.Alb. 43 CE24
Cloister Rd. NW2 119 CZ62
Cloister Rd. W3 138 CQ71
Cloister Wk., Hem.H. 40 BK18
Townsend
Cloisters, The, Rick. 92 BL45
Cloisters, The (Bushey), Wat. 76 CB44
Cloisters, The, Welw.G.C. 29 CX09
Cloisters, The, Wok. 227 BB121
Cloisters Ave., Brom. 205 EM99
Cloisters Mall, Kings.T. 197 CK96
Union St.
Clonard Way, Pnr. 94 CA51
Clonbrock Rd. N16 122 DS63
Cloncurry St. SW6 159 CX82
Clonmel Clo., Har. 117 CD61
Clonmel Rd. SW6 159 CZ80
Clonmel Rd., Tedd. 177 CD91
Clonmel Way, Slou. 130 AH69
Clonmell Rd. N17 122 DR55
Clonmore St. SW18 179 CZ88
Cloonmore Ave., Orp. 223 ET105
Clorane Gdns. NW3 120 DA62
Close, The E4 101 EC52
Beech Hall Rd.
Close, The N14 99 DK47
Close, The N20 97 CZ47
Close, The SE3 163 ED82
Heath La.
Close, The, Barn. 80 DF44
Close, The, Beck. 203 DY98
Close, The, Bet. 264 CP138
Close, The, Bex. 186 FA86
Close, The, Brwd. 108 FX48
Close, The, Cars. 218 DE109
Close, The, Dart. 188 FJ90
Close, The, Grays 170 GC75
Close, The, Guil. 259 BB144
Close, The, Har. 94 CC54
Harrow Vw.
Close, The, Hat. 63 CY26
Close, The, Horl. 269 DJ150
Close, The, Islw. 157 CD82
Close, The, Iver 133 BC69
Close, The, Mitch. 200 DF98

Close, The, N.Mal. 198 CQ96
Close, The, Orp. 205 ES100
Close, The (Eastcote), Pnr. 116 BW59
Close, The (Rayners La.), Pnr. 116 BZ59
Close, The, Pot.B. 64 DA32
Close, The (Pampisford Rd.), Pur. 219 DP110
Close, The (Russell Hill), Pur. 219 DM110
Close, The, Rad. 61 CF33
Close, The, Reig. 266 DB135
Close, The, Rich. 158 CP83
Close, The, Rick. 92 BJ46
Mount Vw.
Close, The, Rom. 126 EY58
Close, The, Sev. 256 FE124
Close, The, Sid. 186 EV91
Close, The, Slou. 131 AK73
St. George's Cres.
Close, The, Sutt. 199 CZ101
Close, The, Uxb. 134 BL66
Close, The (Hillingdon), Uxb. 134 BN67
Close, The, Vir.W. 192 AX99
Close, The, Ware 33 DY06
Close, The (Bushey), Wat. 76 CB43
Close, The (Barnhill Rd.), Wem. 118 CQ62
Close, The (Lyon Pk. Ave.), Wem. 138 CL65
Close, The, W.Byf. 212 BG113
Closemead Clo., Nthwd. 93 BQ51
Cloth Ct. EC1 274 G7
Cloth Fair EC1 274 G7
Cloth Fair EC1 141 DP71
Cloth St. EC1 275 H6
Clothier St. E1 275 N8
Clothworkers Rd. SE18 165 ER80
Cloudberry Rd., Rom. 106 FK51
Cloudesdale Rd. SW17 181 DH89
Cloudesley Pl. N1 141 DN67
Cloudesley Rd. N1 141 DN67
Cloudesley Rd., Bexh. 166 EZ81
Cloudesley Rd., Erith 167 FF81
Cloudesley Sq. N1 141 DN67
Cloudesley St. N1 141 DN67
Clouston Clo., Wall. 219 DL106
Clova Rd. E7 144 EF65
Clove Cres. E14 143 ED73
Clove Hitch Quay SW11 160 DC83
Cotton Row
Clove St. E13 144 EG70
Barking Rd.
Clovelly Ave. NW9 119 CT56
Clovelly Ave., Uxb. 115 BQ63
Clovelly Ave., Warl. 236 DV118
Clovelly Clo., Pnr. 115 BV55
Clovelly Clo., Uxb. 115 BQ63
Clovelly Ct., Horn. 128 FM61
Clovelly Gdns. SE19 202 DT95
Clovelly Gdns., Enf. 100 DS45
Clovelly Gdns., Rom. 105 FB53
Clovelly Rd. N8 121 DK56
Clovelly Rd. W4 158 CR75
Clovelly Rd. W5 157 CJ75
Clovelly Rd., Bexh. 166 EY79
Clovelly Rd., Houns. 156 BZ82
Clovelly Way E1 142 DW72
Jamaica St.
Clovelly Way, Har. 116 BZ61
Clovelly Way, Orp. 205 ET100
Clover Clo. E11 123 ED61
Clover Ct., Grays 170 GD79
Churchill Rd.
Clover Ct., Wok. 226 AX118
Clover Hill, Couls. 235 DH121
Clover Lea, Gdmg. 258 AS143
Clover Leas, Epp. 69 ET30
Clover Ms. SW3 160 DF79
Dilke St.
Clover Rd., Guil. 242 AS133
Clover Way, Hem.H. 40 BH19
Clover Way, Wall. 200 DG102
Cloverdale Gdns., Sid. 185 ET86
Cloverfield, Welw.G.C. 29 CZ06
Cloverfields, Horl. 269 DH147
Cloverland, Hat. 45 CT21
Cloverleys, Loug. 84 EK43
Clovers, The, Grav. 190 GE91
Clowders Rd. SE6 183 DZ90
Clowser Clo., Sutt. 218 DC106
Turnpike La.
Cloyster Wd., Edg. 95 CK52
Cloysters Grn. E1 142 DU74
Thomas More St.
Club Gdns. Rd., Brom. 204 EG101
Club Row E1 275 P4
Club Row E1 142 DT70
Club Row E2 275 P4
Club Row E2 142 DT70
Clump, The, Rick. 74 BG43
Clump Ave., Tad. 248 CQ131
Clumps, The, Ashf. 175 BR91
Clumps, The, Felt. 175 BR91
Clunas Gdns., Rom. 128 FK55
Clunbury Ave., Sthl. 156 BZ78
Clunbury St. N1 275 L1
Clunbury St. N1 142 DR68
Cluny Est. SE1 279 M6
Cluny Ms. SW5 160 DA77
Cluny Pl. SE1 279 M6
Cluse Ct. N1 142 DQ68
Dame St.
Clutterbucks, Rick. 74 BG36
Clutton St. E14 143 EB71
Clydach Rd., Enf. 82 DT42
Clyde Ave., S.Croy. 236 DV115
Clyde Circ. N15 122 DS56
Clyde Clo., Red. 250 DG133
Clyde Ct., Red. 250 DG133
Clyde Clo.
Clyde Cres., Upmin. 129 FS58
Clyde Pl. E10 123 EB59
Clyde Rd. N15 122 DS56
Clyde Rd. N22 99 DK53
Clyde Rd., Croy. 202 DT103
Clyde Rd., Hodd. 49 ED19
Clyde Rd., Stai. 174 BK88
Clyde Rd., Sutt. 218 DA106
Clyde Rd., Wall. 219 DJ107
Clyde Sq., Hem.H. 40 BM15
Clyde St. SE8 163 DZ79
Clyde Ter. SE23 182 DW89
Clyde Ter., Hert. 32 DU09
Clyde Vale SE23 182 DW89
Clyde Way, Rom. 105 FE52
Clyde Way, Stai. 193 BE95
Clydesdale, Enf. 83 DX42
Clydesdale Ave., Stan. 117 CK55
Clydesdale Clo., Borwd. 78 CR43
Clydesdale Clo., Islw. 157 CF83
Clydesdale Gdns., Rich. 158 CP84
Clydesdale Rd. W11 139 CZ72
Clydesdale Rd., Horn. 127 FF59
Clydesdale Wk., Brox. 67 DZ25
Tarpan Way
Clydon Clo., Erith 167 FE79
Clyfford Rd., Ruis. 115 BT63
Clyfton Clo., Brox. 49 DZ23
Clymping Dene, Felt. 175 BV87
Clyston Rd., Wat. 75 BT44
Clyston St. SW8 161 DJ82
Clyve Way, Stai. 193 BE95
Coach All., H.Wyc. 110 AF60
Coach & Horses Yd. W1 273 K10
Coach Ho. La. N5 121 DP63
Highbury Hill
Coach Ho. La. SW19 179 CX91
Coach Ho. Ms. SE23 182 DW86
Coach Ho. Yd. SW18 160 DB84
Ebner St.
Coach Rd., Bet. 248 CL134
Coach Rd., Cher. 211 BC107
Coachhouse Ms. SE20 182 DV94
Coachlands Ave., Guil. 242 AT134
Coal Rd., Grays 171 GL77
Coal Wf. Rd. W12 159 CX75
Shepherds Bush Pl.
Coaldale Wk. SE21 182 DQ87
Lairdale Clo.
Coalecroft Rd. SW15 159 CW84
Coalport Clo., Harl. 52 EW16
Coast Hill, Dor. 262 BZ139
Coast Hill La., Dor. 262 CA138
Coat Wicks, Beac. 89 AQ51
Coate St. E2 142 DU68
Coates Dell, Wat. 60 BY33
Coates Hill Rd., Brom. 205 EN96
Coates Rd., Borwd. 95 CK45
Coates Wk., Brent. 158 CL78
Burford Rd.
Coates Way, Wat. 60 BX32
Cob Mead, Hat. 45 CV16
Cobb Clo., Borwd. 78 CQ43
Cobb Clo., Slou. 152 AX81
Cobb Grn., Wat. 59 BV32
Cobb Rd., Berk. 38 AT19
Cobb St. E1 275 P7
Cobb St. E1 142 DT71
Cobbett Clo., Enf. 82 DW36
Cobbett Rd. SE9 164 EL83
Cobbett Rd., Guil. 242 AT133
Cobbett Rd., Twick. 176 CA88
Cobbett St. SW8 161 DM80
Cobbetts Ave., Ilf. 124 EK57
Cobbetts Clo., Wok. 226 AV117
Cobbetts Hill, Wey. 213 BP107
Cobbins, The, Wal.Abb. 68 EE33
Cobbins Way, Harl. 36 EY11
Cobbinsend Rd., Wal.Abb. 68 EK29
Cobblers Clo., Slou. 131 AP68
Cobblers Wk., E.Mol. 197 CH95
Cobblers Wk., Hmptn. 196 CC95
High St.
Cobblers Wk., Kings.T. 197 CG95
Cobblers Wk., Tedd. 177 CD94
Cobbles, The, Brwd. 108 FY47
Cobbles, The, Upmin. 129 FT59
Cobblestone Pl., Croy. 202 DQ102
Oakfield Rd.
Cobbold Est. NW10 139 CT65
Cobbold Ms. W12 159 CT75
Cobbold Rd.
Cobbold Rd. E11 124 EF62
Cobbold Rd. NW10 139 CT65
Cobbold Rd. W12 159 CT75
Cobb's Ct. EC4 141 DP72
Carter La.
Cobb's Rd., Houns. 156 BZ84
Cobden Clo., Uxb. 134 BJ67
Cobden Hill, Rad. 77 CH36
Cobden Rd. E11 124 EE62
Cobden Rd. SE25 202 DU99
Cobden Rd., Orp. 223 ER105
Cobden Rd., Sev. 257 FJ123
Cobham, Grays 170 GB75
Cobham Ave., N.Mal. 199 CU99
Cobham Clo. SW11 180 DE86
Cobham Clo., Brom. 204 EL101
Cobham Clo., Sid. 186 EV86
Park Mead
Cobham Clo., Slou. 131 AN74
Cippenham La.
Cobham Clo., Wall. 219 DL107
Cobham Gate, Cob. 213 BV114
Cobham Ho., Bark. 145 EQ67
St. Margarets
Cobham Pk. Rd., Cob. 229 BV117
Cobham Pl., Bexh. 186 EY85
Cobham Rd. E17 101 EC53
Cobham Rd. N22 121 DP55
Cobham Rd., Cob. 230 CA117
Cobham Rd., Houns. 156 BW80
Cobham Rd., Ilf. 125 ES61
Cobham Rd., Kings.T. 198 CN96
Cobham Rd., Lthd. 230 CC121
Cobham Rd., Ware 33 DZ05
Cobham St., Grav. 191 GG87
Cobham Way, Lthd. 245 BS126
Cobill Clo., Horn. 128 FJ56
Cobland Rd. SE12 184 EJ91
Coborn Rd. E3 143 DZ69
Coborn St. E3 143 DZ69
Cobourg Rd. SE5 162 DT79
Cobourg St. NW1 273 L3
Cobourg St. NW1 141 DJ69
Cobs Way, Add. 212 BJ110
Cobsdene, Grav. 191 GK93
Coburg Clo. SW1 277 L8
Coburg Cres. SW2 181 DM88
Coburg Gdns., Ilf. 102 EK54
Coburg Rd. N22 121 DM55
Cochrane Ms. NW8 272 A1
Cochrane Rd. SW19 179 CZ94
Cochrane St. NW8 272 A1
Cochrane St. NW8 140 DD68
Cock Grn., Harl. 51 EP17
Cock Hill E1 275 N7
Cock La. EC1 274 F7
Cock La. EC1 141 DP71
Cock La., Brox. 48 DU20
Cock La., Hodd. 49 DY19
Cock La., Lthd. 230 CC122
Cockayne Way SE8 163 DY77
Windlass Pl.
Cockbush Ave., Hert. 32 DU08
Cocker Rd., Enf. 82 DW36
Cockerell Rd. E17 123 DY58
Cockerhurst Rd., Sev. 225 FD107
Cockett Rd., Slou. 152 AY76
Cockfosters Rd., Barn. 80 DF41
Cockle Way, Rad. 62 CL33
Cockmannings La., Orp. 206 EX102
Cockmannings Rd., Orp. 206 EX101
Cockpit Steps SW1 277 N5
Cockpit Yd. WC1 274 C6
Cockrobin La., Harl. 35 EN08
Cockrobin La., Ware 35 EN05
Cocks Cres., N.Mal. 199 CT98
Cock's Yd., Uxb. 134 BJ66
Bakers Rd.
Cocksett Ave., Orp. 223 ES107
Cockshot Hill, Reig. 266 DB136
Cockshot Rd., Reig. 266 DB135
Cockspur Ct. SW1 277 N2
Cockspur St. SW1 277 N2
Cockspur St. SW1 141 DK74
Cocksure La., Sid. 186 FA90
Code St. E1 142 DT70
Codham Hall La., Brwd. 129 FV56
Codicote Dr., Wat. 60 BX34
Codicote Rd., St.Alb. 28 CL05
Codicote Row, Hem.H. 40 BN15
Codicote Ter. N4 122 DQ61
Green Las.
Codling Clo. E1 142 DU74
Torrington Pl.
Codling Way, Wem. 117 CK63
Codmore Cres., Chesh. 54 AS30
Codmore Wd. Rd., Chesh. 56 AX33
Codrington Ct., Wok. 226 AS118
Raglan Rd.
Codrington Cres., Grav. 191 GJ92
Codrington Gdns., Grav. 191 GK92
Codrington Hill SE23 183 DY87
Codrington Ms. W11 139 CY72
Blenheim Cres.
Cody Clo., Har. 117 CK55
Cody Clo., Wall. 219 DK108
Alcock Clo.
Cody Rd. E16 143 ED70
Coe Ave. SE25 202 DU100
Coe Spur, Slou. 151 AP75
Coe's All., Barn. 79 CY42
Wood St.
Cofers Circle, Wem. 118 CP62
Coftards, Slou. 132 AW72
Cogan Ave. E17 101 DY53
Coin St. SE1 278 D2
Coin St. SE1 141 DN74
Coity Rd. NW5 140 DG65
Coke St. E1 142 DU72
Cokers La. SE21 182 DR88
Perifield
Coke's Fm. La., Ch.St.G. 72 AV41
Coke's La., Amer. 72 AX40
Coke's La., Ch.St.G. 72 AW41
Colas Ms. NW6 140 DA67
Birchington Rd.
Colbeck Ms. SW7 160 DB77
Colbeck Rd., Har. 116 CC59
Colberg Pl. N16 122 DS59
Colborne Way, Wor.Pk. 199 CW104
Colbrook Ave., Hayes 155 BR76
Colbrook Clo., Hayes 155 BR76
Colburn Ave., Cat. 236 DT124
Colburn Ave., Pnr. 94 BY51
Colburn Cres., Guil. 243 BA131
Sutherland Dr.
Colburn Way, Sutt. 200 DD104
Colby Rd. SE19 182 DS92
Colby Rd., Walt. 195 BU102
Winchester Rd.
Colchester Ave. E12 125 EM62
Colchester Dr., Pnr. 116 BX57
Colchester Rd. E10 123 EC59
Colchester Rd. E17 123 EA58
Colchester Rd., Edg. 96 CQ52
Colchester Rd., Nthwd. 93 BU54
Colchester Rd., Rom. 106 FK53
Colchester St. E1 142 DT72
Braham St.
Colcokes Rd., Bans. 234 DA116
Cold Arbor Rd., Sev. 256 FB129
Cold Blow Cres., Bex. 187 FD88
Cold Blow La. SE14 163 DX80
Cold Blows, Mitch. 200 DF97
Cold Harbour E14 163 EC75
Coldbath Sq. EC1 274 D4
Coldbath St. SE13 163 EB81
Coldershaw Rd. W13 137 CG74
Coldfall Ave. N10 98 DF54
Coldham Gro., Enf. 83 DY37
Coldharbour Clo., Egh. 193 BC97
Coldharbour La. SE5 162 DQ83
Coldharbour La. SW9 161 DN84
Coldharbour La., Dor. 263 CE142
Coldharbour La., Egh. 193 BC97
Coldharbour La., Hayes 155 BT75
Coldharbour La., Pur. 219 DN110
Coldharbour La., Rain. 147 FE72
Coldharbour La., Red. 252 DT134
Coldharbour La. (Bushey), Wat. 76 CB44
Coldharbour La., Wok. 227 BF115
Coldharbour Pl. SE5 162 DQ82
Denmark Hill
Coldharbour Rd., Croy. 219 DN106
Coldharbour Rd., Grav. 190 GE89
Coldharbour Rd., Harl. 51 EM16
Coldharbour Rd., W.Byf. 211 BF114
Coldharbour Rd., Wok. 227 BF115
Coldharbour Way, Croy. 219 DN106
Coldmoreham Yd., Amer. 55 AN39
Coldshott, Oxt. 254 EG133
Coldstream Gdns. SW18 179 CZ86
Cole Ave., Grays 171 GH77
Linford Rd.
Cole Clo. SE28 146 EV74
Cole Gdns., Houns. 155 BU80
Cole Grn. Bypass, Hert. 30 DF13
Cole Grn. La., Welw.G.C. 29 CY11
Cole Grn. Way, Hert. 30 DF13
Cole Pk. Gdns., Twick. 177 CG86
Cole Pk. Rd., Twick. 177 CG87
Cole Pk. Vw., Twick. 177 CG86
Hill Vw. Rd.
Cole Rd., Twick. 177 CG86
Cole Rd., Wat. 75 BV39
Stamford Rd.
Cole St. SE1 279 J5
Cole St. SE1 162 DQ75
Colebeck Ms. N1 141 DP65
Colebert Ave. E1 142 DW70
Colebrook, Cher. 211 BD107
Colebrook Clo. SW15 179 CX87
West Hill
Colebrook Gdns., Loug. 85 EP40
Colebrook Ho. E14 143 EB72
Brabazon St.
Colebrook La., Loug. 85 EP40
Colebrook Path, Loug. 85 EP40
Colebrook La.
Colebrook Pl., Cher. 211 BB108
Colebrook Rd. SW16 201 DL95
Colebrook Way N11 99 DH50
Colebrooke Ave. W13 137 CH72
Colebrooke Dr. E11 124 EH59
Colebrooke Pl. N1 141 DP67
St. Peters St.
Colebrooke Ri., Brom. 204 EE96
Colebrooke Rd., Red. 250 DE132
Colebrooke Row N1 274 F1
Colebrooke Row N1 141 DP68
Coleby Path SE5 162 DR80
Harris St.
Coledale Dr., Stan. 95 CJ53
Coleford Rd. SW18 180 DC85
Colegrave Rd. E15 123 ED64
Colegrove Rd. SE15 162 DT79
Coleherne Ct. SW5 160 DB78
Coleherne Ms. SW10 160 DB78
Coleherne Rd. SW10 160 DB78
Colehill Gdns. SW6 159 CY82
Fulham Palace Rd.
Colehill La. SW6 159 CY81
Colekitchen La., Guil. 261 BQ138
Coleman Clo. SE25 202 DU96
Warminster Rd.
Coleman Flds. N1 142 DQ67
Coleman Grn. La., St.Alb. 28 CM10
Coleman Rd. SE5 162 DS80
Coleman Rd., Belv. 166 FA77
Coleman Rd., Dag. 146 EY65
Coleman St. EC2 275 K8
Coleman St. EC2 142 DR72
Colemans Heath SE9 185 EN90
Colemans La., Ong. 71 FH30
Coleman's La., Wal.Abb. 67 ED26
Colenorton Cres. (Eton Wick), Wind. 151 AL77
Colenso Rd. E5 122 DW63
Colenso Rd., Ilf. 125 ES60
Colepits Wd. Rd. SE9 185 ER85
Coleraine Rd. N8 121 DN55
Coleraine Rd. SE3 164 EF79
Coleridge Ave. E12 144 EL65
Coleridge Ave., Sutt. 218 DE105
Coleridge Clo. SW8 161 DH82
Coleridge Clo. (Cheshunt), Wal.Cr. 66 DT27
Peakes La.
Coleridge Cres., Slou. 153 BE81
Coleridge Gdns. NW6 140 DC66
Fairhazel Gdns.
Coleridge La. N8 121 DL58
Coleridge Rd.
Coleridge Rd. E17 123 DZ56
Coleridge Rd. N4 121 DN61
Coleridge Rd. N8 121 DK58
Coleridge Rd. N12 98 DC50
Coleridge Rd., Ashf. 174 BL91
Coleridge Rd., Croy. 202 DW100
Coleridge Rd., Dart. 168 FN84
Coleridge Rd., Rom. 105 FH52
Coleridge Rd., Til. 171 GJ82
Coleridge Sq. W13 137 CG72
Berners Dr.
Coleridge Wk. NW11 120 DA56
Coleridge Wk., Brwd. 109 GC45
Coleridge Way, Hayes 135 BU72
Coleridge Way, Orp. 206 EU100
Coleridge Way, West Dr. 154 BL77
Coles Cres., Har. 116 CB61
Coles Grn., Loug. 85 EN39
Coles Grn. (Bushey), Wat. 94 CC46
Coles Grn. Ct. NW2 119 CU61
Coles Grn. Rd. NW2 119 CU60
Coles Hill, Hem.H. 40 BG18
Coles La., West. 240 EW123
Colesburg Rd., Beck. 203 DZ97
Colescroft Hill, Pur. 235 DN115
Colesdale (Cuffley), Pot.B. 65 DL30
Coleshill La., Amer. 88 AJ45
Coleshill Rd., Tedd. 177 CE93
Colesmead Rd., Red. 250 DF131
Colestown St. SW11 160 DE82
Colet Clo. N13 99 DP51
Colet Gdns. W14 159 CX78
Colet Rd., Brwd. 109 GC43
Colets Orchard, Sev. 241 FH116
Coley Ave., Wok. 227 BA118
Coley St. WC1 274 C5
Coley St. WC1 141 DM70
Colfe Rd. SE23 183 DY88
Colgrove, Welw.G.C. 29 CW10
Colham Ave., West Dr. 134 BL74
Colham Grn. Rd., Uxb. 134 BN71
Colham Mill Rd., West Dr. 154 BK75
Colham Rd., Uxb. 134 BM70
Colin Clo. NW9 118 CS56
Colin Clo., Croy. 203 DZ104
Colin Clo., Dart. 188 FP86
Colin Clo., W.Wick. 204 EF104
Colin Cres. NW9 119 CT56
Colin Dr. NW9 119 CT57
Colin Gdns. NW9 119 CT57
Colin Par. NW9 118 CS56
Edgware Rd.
Colin Pk. Rd. NW9 118 CS55
Colin Rd. NW10 139 CU65
Colin Rd., Cat. 236 DU123
Colin Way, Slou. 151 AP76
Colina Ms. N15 121 DP57
Harringay Rd.
Colina Rd. N15 121 DP57
Colindale Ave. NW9 118 CR55
Colindale Ave., St.Alb. 43 CF21
Colindale Business Pk. NW9 118 CQ55
Colindeep Gdns. NW4 119 CU57
Colindeep La. NW4 119 CU56
Colindeep La. NW9 118 CS55
Colinette Rd. SW15 159 CW84
Colinswood Rd., Slou. 111 AP61
Colinton Rd., Ilf. 126 EV61
Coliston Pas. SW18 180 DA87
Coliston Rd.
Coliston Rd. SW18 180 DA87
Collamore Ave. SW18 180 DE88
Collapit Clo., Har. 116 CB58
Collard Ave., Loug. 85 EQ40
Collard Grn., Loug. 85 EQ40
Collard Ave.
College App. SE10 163 EC79
College Ave., Egh. 173 BB93
College Ave., Epsom 217 CT114
College Ave., Grays 170 GB77
College Ave., Har. 95 CE53
College Ave., Slou. 152 AS76
College Clo. E9 122 DW64
Median Rd.
College Clo. N18 100 DT50
College Clo., Add. 194 BK104
College Clo., Grays 170 GC77
College Clo., Har. 95 CE52
College Clo., Twick. 177 CD88
Meadway
College Clo., Ware 33 DX07
College Ct. (Cheshunt), Wal.Cr. 66 DW30
College Cres. NW3 140 DD65
College Cres., Red. 250 DG131
College Cres., Wind. 151 AP82
College Cross N1 141 DN66
College Dr., Ruis. 115 BU59
College Gdns. E4 101 EB45
College Gdns. N18 100 DT50
College Gdns. SE21 182 DS88
College Gdns. SW17 180 DE89
College Gdns., Enf. 82 DR39
College Gdns., Ilf. 124 EL57
College Gdns., N.Mal. 199 CT99
College Gate, Harl. 51 EQ15
College Grn. SE19 182 DS94
College Gro. NW1 141 DK67
St. Pancras Way
College Hill EC4 275 J10
College Hill Rd., Har. 95 CE52
College La. NW5 121 DH63
College La., Hat. 44 CS20
College La., Wok. 226 AW119
College Ms. SW1 277 P6
College Ms. SW18 180 DB85
St. Ann's Hill
College Pk. Clo. SE13 163 ED84
College Pk. Rd. N17 100 DT51
College Rd.
College Pl. E17 124 EE56
College Pl. NW1 141 DJ67
College Pl. SW10 160 DC80
Hortensia Rd.
College Pl., St.Alb. 42 CC20
College Pt. E15 144 EF65
Wolffe Gdns.
College Rd. E17 123 EC57
College Rd. N17 100 DT51
College Rd. N21 99 DN47
College Rd. NW10 139 CW68
College Rd. SE19 182 DT92
College Rd. SE21 182 DS87
College Rd. SW19 180 DD93
College Rd. W13 137 CH72
College Rd., Abb.L. 59 BT31
College Rd., Brom. 204 EG95
College Rd., Croy. 202 DR103
College Rd., Enf. 82 DR39
College Rd., Epsom 217 CU114
College Rd., Grav. 190 GB85
College Rd., Grays 170 GC77
College Rd., Guil. 258 AX135
College Rd. (Harrow on the Hill), Har. 117 CE58
College Rd. (Harrow Weald), Har. 95 CE53
College Rd., Hert. 32 DW13
College Rd., Hodd. 49 DZ15
College Rd., Islw. 157 CF81
College Rd., St.Alb. 43 CH21
College Rd., Slou. 131 AM74
College Rd., Swan. 207 FE95
College Rd. (Cheshunt), Wal.Cr. 66 DW30
College Rd., Wem. 117 CK60
College Rd., Wok. 227 BB116
College Row E9 123 DX64
Homerton High St.
College Slip, Brom. 204 EG95
College St. EC4 275 K10
College St., St.Alb. 43 CD20
College Ter. E3 143 DZ69
College Ter. N3 97 CZ54
Hendon La.
College Vw. SE9 184 EK88
College Wk., Kings.T. 198 CL96
Grange Rd.
College Way, Ashf. 174 BM91
College Way, Nthwd. 93 BR51
College Way, Welw.G.C. 29 CX08
College Yd. NW5 121 DH63
College La.
Collent St. E9 142 DW65
Coller Cres., Dart. 189 FS91
Colless Rd. N15 122 DT57
Collet Clo. (Cheshunt), Wal.Cr. 67 DX28
Collet Gdns. (Cheshunt), Wal.Cr. 67 DX28
Collet Clo.
Collett Rd. SE16 162 DU76
Collett Rd., Hem.H. 40 BJ20
Collett Rd., Ware 33 DX05
Collett Way, Sthl. 136 CB74
Colley Hill La., Slou. 112 AT62
Colley La., Reig. 249 CY133
Colley Manor Dr., Reig. 249 CX133
Colley Way, Reig. 249 CY131
Colleyland, Rick. 73 BD42
Collier Clo. E6 145 EP72
Trader Rd.
Collier Clo., Epsom 216 CN107

Consul Gdns., Swan. 187 FG93
Princes Rd.
Content St. SE17 279 J9
Content St. SE17 162 DQ77
Contessa Clo., Orp. 223 ES106
Control Twr. Rd., Gat. 268 DD153
Control Twr. Rd., Houns. 154 BN83
Convair Wk., Nthlt. 136 BX69
Kittiwake Rd.
Convent Clo., Beck. 183 EC94
Convent Gdns. W5 157 CJ77
Convent Gdns. W11 139 CZ72
Kensington Pk. Rd.
Convent Hill SE19 182 DQ93
Convent La., Cob. 213 BS111
Seven Hills Rd.
Convent Rd., Ashf. 174 BN92
Convent Rd., Wind. 151 AN82
Convent Way, Sthl. 156 BW77
Conway Clo., H.Wyc. 88 AC53
Conway Clo., Rain. 147 FG66
Conway Clo., Stan. 95 CG51
Conway Cres., Grnf. 137 CE68
Conway Cres., Rom. 126 EW58
Conway Dr., Ashf. 175 BQ93
Conway Dr., Hayes 155 BQ76
Conway Dr., Sutt. 218 DB107
Conway Gdns., Enf. 82 DS38
Conway Gdns., Grays 170 GB80
Conway Gdns., Mitch. 201 DK98
Conway Gdns., Wem. 117 CJ59
Conway Gro. W3 138 CR71
Conway Ms. W1 273 K5
Conway Rd. N14 99 DL48
Conway Rd. N15 121 DP57
Conway Rd. NW2 119 CW61
Conway Rd. SE18 165 ER77
Conway Rd. SW20 199 CW95
Conway Rd., Felt. 176 BX92
Conway Rd., Houns. 176 BZ87
Conway Rd. (Heathrow Airport), Houns. 155 BP83
Conway Rd., Maid. 130 AH72
Conway St. E13 144 EG70
Conway St. W1 273 K5
Conway St. W1 141 DJ70
Conway Wk., Hmptn. 176 BZ93
Fearnley Cres.
Conybeare NW3 140 DE66
King Henry's Rd.
Conybury Clo., Wal.Abb. 68 EG32
Conyer St. E3 143 DY68
Conyers, Harl. 35 EQ13
Conyers Clo., Walt. 214 BX106
Conyers Clo., Wdf.Grn. 102 EE51
Conyers Rd. SW16 181 DK92
Conyers Way, Loug. 85 EP41
Cooden Clo., Brom. 184 EH94
Plaistow La.
Cooderidge Clo. N17 100 DT51
Brantwood Rd.
Cook Ct. SE16 142 DW74
Rotherhithe St.
Cook Rd., Dag. 146 EY67
Cook Sq., Erith 167 FF80
Cooke Clo. E14 143 EA74
Cabot Sq.
Cookes Clo. E11 124 EF61
Cookes La., Sutt. 217 CY107
Cookham Cres. SE16 163 DX75
Marlow Way
Cookham Dene Clo., Chis. 205 ER95
Cookham Hill, Orp. 206 FA104
Cookham Rd., Sid. 206 FA95
Cookham Rd., Swan. 206 FA95
Cookhill Rd. SE2 166 EV75
Cooks Clo., Rom. 105 FC53
Cook's Hole Rd., Enf. 81 DP38
Cooks Mead (Bushey), Wat. 76 CB44
Cook's Rd. E15 143 EB68
Cooks Rd. SE17 161 DP79
Cooks Spinney, Harl. 36 EU13
Cooks Vennel, Hem.H. 40 BG18
Cooks Way, Hat. 45 CV20
Cookson Gro., Erith 167 FB80
Sussex Rd.
Cool Oak La. NW9 118 CS59
Coolfin Rd. E16 144 EG72
Coolgardie Ave. E4 101 ED50
Coolgardie Ave., Chig. 103 EN48
Coolgardie Rd., Ashf. 175 BQ92
Coolhurst Rd. N8 121 DK58
Coomassie Rd. W9 139 CZ70
Bravington Rd.
Coombe, The, Bet. 248 CR131
Coombe Ave., Croy. 220 DS105
Coombe Ave., Sev. 241 FH120
Coombe Bank, Kings.T. 198 CS95
Coombe Clo., Edg. 96 CM54
Coombe Clo., Houns. 156 CA84
Coombe Cor. N21 99 DP46
Coombe Cres., Hmptn. 176 BY94
Coombe Dr., Add. 211 BF107
Coombe Dr., Kings.T. 178 CR94
Coombe Dr., Ruis. 115 BV60
Coombe End, Kings.T. 178 CR94
Coombe Gdns. SW20 199 CU96
Coombe Gdns., Berk. 38 AT18
Coombe Gdns., N.Mal. 199 CT98
Coombe Heights, Kings.T. 178 CS94
Coombe Hill Ct., Wind. 151 AL83
Coombe Hill Glade, Kings.T. 178 CS94
Coombe Hill Rd., Kings.T. 178 CS94
Coombe Hill Rd., Rick. 92 BG45
Coombe Ho. Chase, N.Mal. 198 CR95
Coombe La. SW20 199 CT95
Coombe La., Croy. 220 DV106
Coombe La. W., Kings.T. 198 CP95
Coombe Lea, Brom. 204 EL97
Coombe Neville, Kings.T. 178 CR94
Coombe Pk., Kings.T. 178 CR92
Coombe Ridings, Kings.T. 178 CQ92
Coombe Ri., Brwd. 109 FZ46
Coombe Ri., Kings.T. 198 CQ95
Coombe Rd. N22 99 DN54
Coombe Rd. NW10 118 CR62
Coombe Rd. SE26 182 DV91
Coombe Rd. W4 158 CS78
Coombe Rd. W13 157 CH76
Northcroft Rd.
Coombe Rd., Croy. 220 DQ105
Coombe Rd., Grav. 191 GJ89
Coombe Rd., Hmptn. 176 BZ93
Coombe Rd., Kings.T. 198 CN95
Coombe Rd., N.Mal. 198 CS96
Coombe Rd., Rom. 128 FM55
Coombe Rd. (Bushey), Wat. 94 CC45
Coombe Vale, Ger.Cr. 112 AY60
Coombe Wk., Sutt. 200 DB104
Coombe Way, W.Byf. 212 BM112
Coombe Wd. Hill, Pur. 220 DQ112
Coombe Wd. Rd., Kings.T. 178 CQ92
Coombefield Clo., N.Mal. 198 CS99
Coombehurst Clo., Barn. 80 DF40
Coombelands La., Add. 212 BG107
Coomber Way, Croy. 201 DK101
Coombermere Clo., Wind. 151 AP82
Coombes Rd., Dag. 146 EZ67
Coombes Rd., St.Alb. 61 CJ26
Coombewood Dr., Rom. 126 FA58
Coombfield Dr., Dart. 189 FR91
Coombs St. N1 274 G1
Coombs St. N1 141 DP68
Coomer Ms. SW6 159 CZ79
Coomer Pl.
Coomer Pl. SW6 159 CZ79
Coomer Rd. SW6 159 CZ79
Coomer Pl.
Cooms Wk., Edg. 96 CQ53
East Rd.
Cooper Ave. E17 101 DY53
Cooper Clo. SE1 278 E5
Cooper Clo., Green. 189 FS85
Cooper Clo., Horl. 269 DN148
Cooper Ct. E15 123 EB64
Clays La.
Cooper Cres., Cars. 200 DF104
Cooper Rd. NW10 119 CU64
Cooper Rd., Croy. 219 DP105
Cooper Rd., Guil. 258 AY136
Cooper St. E16 144 EF71
Lawrence St.
Cooper Way, Slou. 151 AP76
Cooperage Clo. N17 100 DT51
Brantwood Rd.
Coopers Clo. E1 142 DW70
Coopers Clo., Chig. 104 EV47
Coopers Clo., Dag. 147 FB65
Coopers Clo. (South Darenth), Dart. 209 FR95
Coopers Clo., Stai. 173 BE92
Coopers Cres., Borwd. 78 CQ39
Coopers Grn. La., Hat. 28 CR14
Coopers Grn. La., St.Alb. 44 CL17
Coopers Grn. La., Welw.G.C. 29 CU12
Coopers Hill La., Egh. 172 AW90
Coopers Hill Rd., Red. 251 DM133
Coopers La. E10 123 EB60
Coopers La. NW1 273 N1
Coopers La. NW1 141 DK68
Cooper's La. SE12 184 EH89
Coopers La., Pot.B. 64 DD31
Coopers La. Rd., Pot.B. 64 DE31
Coopers Rd. SE1 162 DT78
Coopers Rd., Grav. 190 GE88
Coopers Rd., Pot.B. 64 DC30
Cooper's Row EC3 275 P10
Coopers Row, Iver 133 BD70
Coopers Shaw Rd., Til. 171 GK80
Coopers Wk. (Cheshunt), Wal.Cr. 67 DX28
Cooper's Yd. SE19 182 DS93
Westow Hill
Coopersale Clo., Wdf.Grn. 102 EJ52
Navestock Cres.
Coopersale Common, Epp. 70 EX28
Coopersale La., Epp. 86 EU37
Coopersale Rd. E9 123 DX64
Coopersale St., Epp. 70 EW32
Coote Gdns., Dag. 126 EZ62
Nicholas Rd.
Coote Rd., Bexh. 166 EZ81
Coote Rd., Dag. 126 EZ62
Cope Pl. W8 160 DA76
Cope St. SE16 163 DX77
Copeland Dr. E14 163 EA77
Copeland Rd. E17 123 EB57
Copeland Rd. SE15 162 DU82
Copeman Clo. SE26 182 DW92
Copeman Rd., Brwd. 109 GD45
Copenhagen Gdns. W4 158 CR75
Copenhagen Pl. E14 143 DZ72
Copenhagen St. N1 141 DL67
Copenhagen Way, Walt. 195 BV104
Copers Cope Rd., Beck. 183 DZ94
Copeswood Rd., Wat. 75 BV39
Copford Clo., Wdf.Grn. 102 EL51
Copford Wk. N1 142 DQ67
Popham St.
Copinger Wk., Edg. 96 CP53
North Rd.
Copland Ave., Wem. 117 CK64
Copland Clo., Wem. 117 CJ64
Copland Ms., Wem. 138 CL65
Copland Rd.
Copland Rd., Wem. 138 CL65
Copleigh Dr., Tad. 233 CY120
Copleston Ms. SE15 162 DT82
Copleston Rd.
Copleston Pas. SE15 162 DT82
Copleston Rd. SE15 162 DT83
Copley Clo. SE17 161 DP79
Hillingdon St.
Copley Clo. W7 137 CF70
Copley Clo., Red. 250 DE132
Copley Clo., Wok. 226 AS119
Copley Dene, Brom. 204 EK95
Copley Pk. SW16 181 DM93
Copley Rd., Stan. 95 CJ50
Copley St. E1 143 DX71
Stepney Grn.
Copley Way, Tad. 233 CX120
Copmans Wick, Rick. 73 BD43
Copnor Way SE15 162 DS80
Diamond St.
Coppard Gdns., Chess. 215 CJ107
Copped Hall SE21 182 DR89
Glazebrook Clo.
Coppelia Rd. SE3 164 EF84
Coppen Rd., Dag. 126 EZ59
Copper Beech Clo. NW3 140 DD65
Daleham Ms.
Copper Beech Clo., Grav. 191 GK87
Copper Beech Clo., Hem.H. 39 BF23
Copper Beech Clo., Ilf. 103 EN53
Copper Beech Clo., Orp. 206 EW99
Rookery Gdns.
Copper Beech Clo., Wind. 151 AK81
Copper Beech Clo., Wok. 226 AV121
Copper Beech Ct., Loug. 85 EN39
Copper Beech Rd., S.Ock. 149 FW69
Copper Beeches, Islw. 157 CD81
Eversley Cres.
Copper Clo. SE19 182 DT94
Copper Mead Clo. NW2 119 CW62
Copper Mill Dr., Islw. 157 CF82
Copper Mill La. SW17 180 DC91
Copper Ridge, Ger.Cr. 91 AZ50
Copper Row SE1 142 DT74
Horselydown La.
Copperas St. SE8 163 EB79
Copperbeech Clo. NW3 120 DD64
Akenside Rd.
Copperdale Rd., Hayes 155 BU75
Copperfield, Chig. 103 ER50
Copperfield App., Chig. 103 ER51
Copperfield Ave., Uxb. 134 BN71
Copperfield Clo., S.Croy. 220 DQ111
Copperfield Ct., Lthd. 231 CG121
Kingston Rd.
Copperfield Ct., Pnr. 116 BZ56
Copperfield Dr. N15 122 DT56
Copperfield Gdns., Brwd. 108 FV46
Copperfield Ms. N18 100 DS50
Copperfield Ri., Add. 211 BF106
Copperfield Rd. E3 143 DY70
Copperfield Rd. SE28 146 EW72
Copperfield St. SE1 278 G4
Copperfield St. SE1 161 DP75
Copperfield Way, Chis. 185 EQ93
Copperfield Way, Pnr. 116 BZ56
Copperfields, Beac. 89 AL50
Copperfields, Lthd. 230 CC122
Copperfields, Welw.G.C. 30 DC10
Forresters Dr.
Copperfields Way, Rom. 106 FK53
Coppergate Clo., Brom. 204 EH95
Copperkins Gro., Amer. 55 AP36
Copperkins La., Amer. 55 AM35
Coppermill La. E17 122 DW58
Coppermill La., Rick. 91 BE52
Coppermill La., Uxb. 91 BE52
Coppermill Rd., Stai. 173 BB86
Copperwood, Hert. 32 DT09
Coppetts Clo. N12 98 DE52
Coppetts Rd. N10 98 DF52
Coppice, The, Ashf. 175 BP93
School Rd.
Coppice, The, Beac. 89 AR51
School La.
Coppice, The, Enf. 81 DP42
Coppice, The, Hem.H. 41 BP19
Coppice, The, Wat. 76 BW44
Coppice, The, West Dr. 134 BL72
Coppice Clo. SW20 199 CW97
Coppice Clo., Hat. 45 CT22
Coppice Clo., Ruis. 115 BR58
Coppice Clo., Stan. 95 CF51
Coppice Dr. SW15 179 CU86
Coppice Dr., Stai. 172 AX87
Coppice End, Wok. 227 BE116
Coppice Fm. Rd., H.Wyc. 88 AC45
Coppice La., Reig. 249 CZ132
Coppice Path, Chig. 104 EV49
Coppice Row, Epp. 85 EN36
Coppice Wk. N20 98 DA48
Coppice Way E18 124 EF56
Coppice Way, Slou. 111 AR61
Coppies Gro. N11 99 DH49
Copping Clo., Croy. 220 DS105
Tipton Dr.
Coppings, The, Hodd. 33 EA14
Danemead
Coppins, The, Croy. 221 EB107
Coppins, The, Har. 95 CE51
Coppins Clo., Berk. 38 AS19
Coppins La., Iver 133 BF71
Coppock Clo. SW11 160 DE82
Coppsfield, W.Mol. 196 CA97
Hurst Rd.
Copse, The E4 102 EF46
Copse, The, Amer. 55 AQ38
Copse, The, Beac. 88 AJ51
Copse, The, Cat. 252 DU126
Tupwood La.
Copse, The, Hem.H. 39 BE18
Copse, The, Hert. 32 DU09
Copse, The, Lthd. 230 CB123
Copse, The, Red. 267 DL136
Copse Ave., W.Wick. 203 EB104
Copse Clo. SE7 164 EH79
Copse Clo., Guil. 259 BC140
Copse Clo., Nthwd. 93 BQ54
Copse Clo., Slou. 131 AM74
Copse Clo., West Dr. 154 BK76
Copse Edge Ave., Epsom 217 CT113
Copse Glade, Surb. 197 CK102
Copse Hill SW20 199 CU95
Copse Hill, Harl. 51 EP18
Copse Hill, Pur. 219 DL113
Copse Hill, Sutt. 218 DB108
Copse La., Beac. 90 AS52
Copse La., Horl. 269 DJ147
Copse Rd., Cob. 213 BV113
Copse Rd., Red. 266 DC136
Copse Rd., Wok. 226 AT118
Copse Vw., S.Croy. 221 DX109
Copse Way, Chesh. 54 AN27
Copse Wd., Iver 133 BD67
Copse Wd. Clo., Reig. 250 DE132
Green La.
Copse Wd. Way, Nthwd. 93 BP53
Copsem Dr., Esher 214 CB107
Copsem La., Esher 214 CB107
Copsem La., Lthd. 214 CC111
Copsem Way, Esher 214 CC107
Copsen Wd., Lthd. 214 CC111
Copsewood Clo., Sid. 185 ES86
Parish Gate Dr.
Copshall Clo., Harl. 51 ES19
Copsleigh Ave., Red. 266 DG141
Copsleigh Clo., Red. 266 DG140
Copsleigh Way, Red. 266 DG140
Copt Hill La., Tad. 233 CY120
Coptefield Dr., Belv. 166 EX76
Coptfold Rd., Brwd. 108 FW47
Copthall Ave. EC2 275 L8
Copthall Ave. EC2 142 DR72
Copthall Bldgs. EC2 275 L8
Copthall Clo. EC2 275 K8
Copthall Clo., Ger.Cr. 91 AZ52
Copthall Cor., Ger.Cr. 90 AY52
Copthall Dr. NW7 97 CU52
Copthall Gdns. NW7 97 CU52
Copthall Gdns., Twick. 177 CF88
Copthall La., Ger.Cr. 90 AY52
Copthall Rd. E., Uxb. 114 BN61
Copthall Rd. W., Uxb. 114 BN61
Copthall Way, Add. 211 BF110
Copthorne Ave. SW12 181 DK87
Copthorne Ave., Brom. 205 EM103
Copthorne Ave., Brox. 49 DZ20
Copthorne Ave., Ilf. 103 EP51
Copthorne Chase, Ashf. 174 BM91
Ford Rd.
Copthorne Clo., Rick. 74 BM43
Copthorne Clo., Shep. 195 BQ100
Copthorne Gdns., Horn. 128 FN57
Copthorne Ms., Hayes 155 BS77
Copthorne Ri., S.Croy. 220 DR113
Copthorne Rd., Lthd. 231 CH120
Copthorne Rd., Rick. 74 BM44
Coptic St. WC1 273 P7
Coptic St. WC1 141 DL71
Copwood Clo. N12 98 DD49
Coral Clo., Rom. 126 EW55
Coral Row SW11 160 DC83
Gartons Way
Coral St. SE1 278 E5
Coral St. SE1 161 DN75
Coraline Clo., Sthl. 136 BZ69
Coralline Wk. SE2 166 EW75
Corals Mead, Welw.G.C. 29 CX10
Coram Clo., Berk. 38 AW20
Coram Grn., Brwd. 109 GD44
Coram St. WC1 273 P5
Coram St. WC1 141 DL70
Coran Clo. N9 101 DX45
Corban Rd., Houns. 156 CA83
Corbar Clo., Barn. 80 DD39
Corbet Clo., Wall. 200 DG102
Corbet Ct. EC3 275 L9
Corbet Pl. E1 275 P6
Corbet Rd., Epsom 216 CS110
Corbets Ave., Upmin. 128 FP64
Corbets Tey Rd., Upmin. 128 FP63
Corbett Clo., Croy. 221 ED112
Corbett Gro. N22 99 DL52
Bounds Grn. Rd.
Corbett Ho., Wat. 94 BW48
Corbett Rd. E11 124 EJ58
Corbett Rd. E17 123 EC55
Corbetts La. SE16 162 DW77
Rotherhithe New Rd.
Corbetts Pas. SE16 162 DW77
Rotherhithe New Rd.
Corbicum E11 124 EE59
Corbiere Ct. SW19 179 CX93
Thornton Rd.
Corbiere Ho. N1 142 DS67
Corbins La., Har. 116 CB62
Corbridge Cres. E2 142 DV68
Corby Clo., Egh. 172 AW93
Corby Clo., St.Alb. 60 CA25
Corby Cres., Enf. 81 DL42
Corby Dr., Egh. 172 AV93
Corby Rd. NW10 138 CR68
Corby Way E3 143 EA70
Knapp Rd.
Corbylands Rd., Sid. 185 ES87
Corbyn St. N4 121 DL60
Corcorans, Brwd. 108 FV44
Cord Way E14 163 EA76
Mellish St.
Corde Way, Slou. 151 AQ75
Cordelia Clo. SE24 161 DP84
Cordelia Gdns., Stai. 174 BL87
Cordelia Rd., Stai. 174 BL87
Cordelia St. E14 143 EB72
Cordell Clo. (Cheshunt), Wal.Cr. 67 DY28
Corder Clo., St.Alb. 42 CA23
Corderoy Pl., Cher. 193 BE100
Cording St. E14 143 EB71
Chrisp St.
Cordingley Rd., Ruis. 115 BR61
Cordons Clo., Ger.Cr. 90 AX53
Cordova Rd. E3 143 DY69
Cordrey Gdns., Couls. 235 DL115
Cordwainers Wk. E13 144 EG68
Clegg St.
Cordwell Rd. SE13 184 EE85
Corelli Rd. SE3 164 EL81
Corfe Ave., Har. 116 CA63
Corfe Clo., Ash. 231 CJ118
Corfe Clo., Hayes 136 BW72
Corfe Clo., Hem.H. 40 BL21
Corfe Gdns., Slou. 131 AN73
Avebury
Corfe Twr. W3 158 CQ75
Corfield Rd. N21 81 DM43
Corfield St. E2 142 DV69
Corfton Rd. W5 138 CL72
Coriander Ave. E14 143 ED72
Coriander Cres., Guil. 242 AU129
Cories Clo., Dag. 126 EX61
Corinium Clo., Wem. 118 CM63
Corinium Gate, St.Alb. 42 CA22
Corinne Rd. N19 121 DJ63
Corinth Par., Hayes 135 BT71
Corinthian Manorway, Erith 167 FD77
Corinthian Rd., Erith 167 FD77
Cork Sq. E1 142 DV74
Smeaton St.
Cork St. W1 277 K1
Cork St. W1 141 DJ73
Cork St. Ms. W1 277 K1
Cork Tree Way E4 101 DY50
Corker Wk. N7 121 DM61
Corkran Rd., Surb. 197 CK101
Corkscrew Hill, W.Wick. 203 EC103
Corlett St. NW1 272 B6
Cormongers La., Red. 251 DJ134
Cormont Rd. SE5 161 DP81
Cormorant Clo. E17 101 DX53
Banbury Rd.
Cormorant Rd. E7 124 EF64
Cormorant Wk., Horn. 147 FH65
Heron Flight Ave.
Corn Cft., Hat. 45 CV16
Corn Mead, Welw.G.C. 29 CW06
Corn Mill Dr., Orp. 206 EU101
Corn Way E11 123 ED62
Cornbury Rd., Edg. 95 CK52
Cornelia Pl., Erith 167 FE79
Queen St.
Cornelia St. N7 141 DM65
Cornell Clo., Sid. 186 EY93
Cornell Way, Rom. 104 FA50
Corner, The, W.Byf. 212 BG113
Old Woking Rd.
Corner Grn. SE3 164 EG82
Corner Hall, Hem.H. 40 BJ22
Corner Hall Ave., Hem.H. 40 BK22
Corner Ho. St. WC2 277 P2
Corner Mead NW9 97 CT52
Corner Vw., Hat. 45 CW24
Cornerfield, Hat. 45 CV15
Corners, Welw.G.C. 30 DA07
Cornerside, Ashf. 175 BQ94
Corney Reach Way W4 158 CS80
Corney Rd. W4 158 CS79
Cornfield Clo., Uxb. 134 BK68
The Greenway
Cornfield Rd., Reig. 266 DC135
Cornfield Rd. (Bushey), Wat. 76 CB42
Cornfields, Gdmg. 258 AU143
Cornfields, Hem.H. 40 BH21
Cornflower La., Croy. 203 DX102
Cornflower Ter. SE22 182 DV86
Cornflower Way, Rom. 106 FL53
Cornford Clo., Brom. 204 EG99
Cornford Gro. SW12 181 DH89
Cornhill EC3 275 L9
Cornhill EC3 142 DR72
Cornhill Clo., Add. 194 BH103
Cornish Ct. N9 100 DV45
Cornish Gro. SE20 202 DV95
Cornish Ho. SE17 161 DP79
Otto St.
Cornish Ho., Brent. 158 CM78
Cornmill, Wal.Abb. 67 EB33
Cornmill La. SE13 163 EC83
Cornmow Dr. NW10 119 CU63
Cornshaw Rd., Dag. 126 EX60
Cornsland, Brwd. 108 FX48
Cornsland Ct., Brwd. 108 FV48
Cornthwaite Rd. E5 122 DW62
Cornwall Ave. E2 142 DW69
Cornwall Ave. N3 98 DA52
Cornwall Ave. N22 99 DL53
Cornwall Ave., Esher 215 CF108
The Causeway
Cornwall Ave., Slou. 131 AQ70
Cornwall Ave., Sthl. 136 BZ71
Cornwall Ave., Well. 165 ES83
Cornwall Ave., W.Byf. 212 BM114
Cornwall Clo., Bark. 145 ET65
Cornwall Clo., Horn. 128 FN56
Cornwall Clo., Wal.Cr. 67 DY33
Cornwall Clo. (Eton Wick), Wind. 151 AL78
Cornwall Cres. W11 139 CY72
Cornwall Dr., Orp. 186 EW94
Cornwall Gdns. NW10 139 CV65
Cornwall Gdns. SW7 160 DB76
Cornwall Gdns. Wk. SW7 160 DB76
Cornwall Gdns.
Cornwall Gate, Purf. 168 FN77
Fanns Ri.
Cornwall Gro. W4 158 CS78
Cornwall Ms. S. SW7 160 DC76
Cornwall Ms. W. SW7 160 DB76
Cornwall Gdns.
Cornwall Rd. N4 121 DN59
Cornwall Rd. N15 122 DR57
Cornwall Rd. N18 100 DU50
Fairfield Rd.
Cornwall Rd. SE1 278 D2
Cornwall Rd. SE1 141 DN74
Cornwall Rd., Brwd. 108 FV43
Cornwall Rd., Croy. 201 DP103
Cornwall Rd., Dart. 168 FM83
Cornwall Rd., Esher 215 CG108
Cornwall Rd., Har. 116 CC58
Cornwall Rd., Pnr. 94 BZ52
Cornwall Rd., Ruis. 115 BT62
Cornwall Rd., St.Alb. 43 CE22
Cornwall Rd., Sutt. 217 CZ108
Cornwall Rd., Twick. 177 CG87
Cornwall Rd., Uxb. 134 BK65
Cornwall Rd., Wind. 172 AU86
Cornwall St. E1 142 DV73
Watney St.
Cornwall Ter. NW1 272 E5
Cornwall Ter. Ms. NW1 272 E5
Cornwall Way, Stai. 173 BE93
Cornwallis Ave. N9 100 DV47
Cornwallis Ave. SE9 185 ER89
Cornwallis Clo., Erith 167 FF79
Cornwallis Gro. N9 100 DV47
Cornwallis Rd. E17 123 DX56
Cornwallis Rd. N9 100 DV47
Cornwallis Rd. N19 121 DL61
Cornwallis Rd., Dag. 126 EX63
Cornwallis Sq. N19 121 DL61
Cornwallis Wk. SE9 165 EM83
Cornwell Ave., Grav. 191 GJ90
Cornwood Clo. N2 120 DD57
Cornwood Dr. E1 142 DW72
Cornworthy Rd., Dag. 126 EW64
Corona Rd. SE12 184 EG87
Coronation Ave. N16 122 DT62
Victorian Rd.
Coronation Ave., Slou. 132 AY71
Coronation Ave., Wind. 152 AT82
Coronation Clo., Bex. 186 EX86
Coronation Clo., Ilf. 125 EQ56
Coronation Dr., Horn. 127 FH63
Coronation Hill, Epp. 69 ET30
Coronation Rd. E13 144 EJ69
Coronation Rd. NW10 138 CM69
Coronation Rd., Hayes 155 BT77
Coronation Rd., Ware 33 DX05
Coronation Wk., Twick. 176 CA88
Coronet, The, Horl. 269 DJ150
Coronet St. N1 275 M3
Coronet St. N1 142 DS69
Corporation Ave., Houns. 156 BY84
Corporation Row EC1 274 E4
Corporation Row EC1 141 DN70
Corporation St. E15 144 EE68
Corporation St. N7 121 DL64
Corral Gdns., Hem.H. 40 BM19
Corran Way, S.Ock. 149 FV73
Corrance Rd. SW2 161 DL84
Corri Ave. N14 99 DK49
Corrib Dr., Sutt. 218 DE106

Cranbrook Dr., Esher 196 CC102
Cranbrook Dr., Rom. 127 FH56
Cranbrook Dr., St.Alb. 44 CL20
Cranbrook Dr., Twick. 176 CB88
Cranbrook Est. E2 143 DX68
Cranbrook Ms. E17 123 DZ57
Cranbrook Pk. N22 99 DM53
Cranbrook Pt. E16 144 EG74
Cranbrook Ri., Ilf. 125 EM58
Cranbrook Rd. SE8 163 EA81
Cranbrook Rd. SW19 179 CY94
Cranbrook Rd. W4 158 CS78
Cranbrook Rd., Barn. 80 DD44
Cranbrook Rd., Bexh. 166 EZ81
Cranbrook Rd., Houns. 156 BZ84
Cranbrook Rd., Ilf. 125 EN57
Cranbrook Rd., Th.Hth. 202 DQ96
Cranbrook St. E2 143 DX68
Roman Rd.
Cranbury Rd. SW6 160 DB82
Crane Ave. W3 138 CQ73
Crane Ave., Islw. 177 CG85
Crane Clo., Dag. 146 FA65
Crane Clo., Har. 116 CC62
Crane Ct. EC4 274 E9
Crane Ct., Epsom 216 CQ105
Crane Gdns., Hayes 155 BT77
Crane Gro. N7 141 DN65
Crane Lo. Rd., Houns. 155 BV79
Crane Mead SE16 163 DX77
Crane Mead, Ware 33 DY07
Crane Pk. Rd., Twick. 176 CB89
Crane Rd., Twick. 177 CE88
Crane St. SE10 163 ED78
Crane St. SE15 162 DT81
Southampton Way
Crane Way, Twick. 176 CC87
Cranebrook, Twick. 176 CC89
Manor Rd.
Craneford Clo., Twick. 177 CF87
Craneford Way, Twick. 177 CE87
Cranell Grn., S.Ock. 149 FV74
Cranes Dr., Surb. 198 CL98
Cranes Pk., Surb. 198 CL98
Cranes Pk. Ave., Surb. 198 CL98
Cranes Pk. Cres., Surb. 198 CM98
Cranes Way, Borwd. 78 CQ43
Craneswater, Hayes 155 BT80
Craneswater Pk., Sthl. 156 BZ78
Cranfield Clo. SE27 182 DQ90
Dunelm Gro.
Cranfield Ct., Wok. 226 AU118
Martindale Rd.
Cranfield Cres. (Cuffley), Pot.B. 65 DL29
Cranfield Dr. NW9 96 CS52
Cranfield Dr., Wat. 80 BY32
Cranfield Rd. SE4 163 DZ83
Cranfield Rd. E., Cars. 218 DG109
Cranfield Rd. W., Cars. 218 DF109
Cranfield Row SE1 278 E6
Cranford Ave. N13 99 DL50
Cranford Ave., Stai. 174 BL87
Cranford Clo. SW20 179 CV94
Cranford Clo., Pur. 220 DQ113
Cranford Clo., Stai. 174 BL87
Canopus Way
Cranford Cotts. E1 143 DX73
Cranford St.
Cranford Ct., Hert. 31 DM07
The Ridgeway
Cranford Dr., Hayes 155 BT77
Cranford La., Hayes 155 BR79
Cranford La. (Cranford), Houns. 155 BT81
Cranford La. (Hatton Cross), Houns. 155 BT83
Cranford La. (Heston), Houns. 155 BV80
Cranford Pk. Rd., Hayes 155 BT77
Cranford Ri., Esher 214 CC106
Cranford Rd., Dart. 188 FL88
Cranford St. E1 143 DX73
Cranford Way N8 121 DM57
Cranham Gdns., Upmin. 129 FS60
Cranham Rd., Horn. 127 FH58
Cranhurst Rd. NW2 119 CW64
Cranleigh Clo. SE20 202 DV96
Cranleigh Clo., Bex. 187 FB86
Cranleigh Clo., Orp. 206 EU104
Cranleigh Clo., S.Croy. 220 DU112
Cranleigh Clo. (Cheshunt), Wal.Cr. 66 DU28
Cranleigh Dr., Swan. 207 FE99
Cranleigh Gdns. N21 81 DN43
Cranleigh Gdns. SE25 202 DS97
Cranleigh Gdns., Bark. 145 ER66
Cranleigh Gdns., Har. 118 CL57
Cranleigh Gdns., Kings.T. 178 CM93
Cranleigh Gdns., Loug. 85 EM44
Cranleigh Gdns., S.Croy. 220 DU112
Cranleigh Gdns., Sthl. 136 BZ72
Cranleigh Gdns., Sutt. 200 DB103
Cranleigh Ms. SW11 160 DE82
Cranleigh Rd. N15 122 DQ57
Cranleigh Rd. SW19 199 CZ97
Cranleigh Rd., Esher 196 CC102
Cranleigh Rd., Felt. 175 BT91
Cranleigh Rd., Guil. 259 BB144
Cranleigh St. NW1 273 L1
Cranleigh St. NW1 141 DJ68
Cranley Clo., Guil. 243 BA134
Cranley Dene Ct. N10 121 DH56
Cranley Dr., Ilf. 125 EQ59
Cranley Dr., Ruis. 115 BT61
Cranley Gdns. N10 121 DH56
Cranley Gdns. N13 99 DM48
Cranley Gdns. SW7 160 DC78
Cranley Gdns., Wall. 219 DJ108
Cranley Ms. SW7 160 DC78
Cranley Par. SE9 184 EL91
Beaconsfield Rd.
Cranley Pl. SW7 160 DD77
Cranley Rd. E13 144 EH71
Cranley Rd., Guil. 243 AZ134
Cranley Rd., Ilf. 125 EQ58
Cranley Rd., Walt. 213 BS106
Cranmer Ave. W13 157 CH76
Cranmer Clo., Mord. 199 CX100
Cranmer Clo., Pot.B. 64 DB30
Cranmer Clo., Ruis. 116 BX60
Cranmer Clo., Stan. 95 CJ52
Cranmer Clo., Warl. 237 DY117
Cranmer Clo., Wey. 213 BR108
Cranmer Ct. SW3 276 C9
Cranmer Ct. SW4 161 DK83
Cranmer Ct., Hmptn. 176 CB92
Cranmer Rd.
Cranmer Fm. Clo., Mitch. 200 DF98
Cranmer Gdns., Dag. 127 FC63
Cranmer Gdns., Warl. 237 DY117
Cranmer Rd. E7 124 EH63
Cranmer Rd. SW9 161 DN80
Cranmer Rd., Croy. 201 DP104
Cranmer Rd., Edg. 96 CP48
Cranmer Rd., Hmptn. 176 CB92
Cranmer Rd., Hayes 135 BR72
Cranmer Rd., Kings.T. 178 CL92
Cranmer Rd., Mitch. 200 DF98
Cranmer Rd., Sev. 256 FE123
Cranmer Ter. SW17 180 DD92
Cranmore Ave., Islw. 156 CC80
Cranmore Cotts., Lthd. 245 BP129
Cranmore Ct., St.Alb. 43 CF19
Cranmore La., Lthd. 245 BP129
Cranmore Rd., Brom. 184 EF90
Cranmore Rd., Chis. 185 EM92
Cranmore Way N10 121 DJ56
Cranston Clo., Houns. 156 BY82
Cranston Clo., Reig. 266 DB135
Cranston Clo., Uxb. 115 BR61
Cranston Est. N1 275 L1
Cranston Est. N1 142 DR68
Cranston Gdns. E4 101 EB50
Cranston Pk. Ave., Upmin. 128 FP63
Cranston Rd. SE23 183 DY88
Cranstoun Clo., Guil. 242 AT130
Cranswick Rd. SE16 162 DV78
Crantock Rd. SE6 183 EB89
Cranwell Clo. E3 143 EB70
Cranwell Gro., Shep. 194 BM98
Cranwell Rd., Houns. 155 BP82
Cranwich Ave. N21 100 DR45
Cranwich Rd. N16 122 DR59
Cranwood St. EC1 275 L3
Cranwood St. EC1 142 DR69
Cranworth Cres. E4 101 ED46
Cranworth Gdns. SW9 161 DN81
Craster Rd. SW2 181 DM87
Crathie Rd. SE12 184 EH86
Crathorn St. SE13 163 EC83
Loampit Vale
Cravan Ave., Felt. 175 BU89
Craven Ave. W5 137 CJ73
Craven Ave., Sthl. 136 BZ71
Craven Clo., Hayes 135 BU72
Craven Gdns. SW19 180 DA92
Craven Gdns., Bark. 145 ES68
Craven Gdns., Ilf. 103 ER54
Craven Gdns. (Collier Row), Rom. 104 FA50
Craven Gdns. (Harold Wd.), Rom. 106 FQ51
Craven Hill W2 140 DC73
Craven Hill Gdns. W2 140 DC73
Craven Hill Ms. W2 140 DC73
Craven Ms. SW11 160 DG83
Taybridge Rd.
Craven Pk. NW10 138 CS67
Craven Pk. Ms. NW10 138 CS67
Craven Pk. Rd. N15 122 DT58
Craven Pk. Rd. NW10 138 CS67
Craven Pas. WC2 277 P2
Craven Rd. NW10 138 CR67
Craven Rd. W2 140 DC72
Craven Rd. W5 137 CJ73
Craven Rd., Croy. 202 DV102
Craven Rd., Kings.T. 198 CM95
Craven Rd., Orp. 206 EX104
Craven St. WC2 277 P2
Craven St. WC2 141 DL74
Craven Ter. W2 140 DC73
Craven Wk. N16 122 DU59
Cravens, The, Horl. 269 DN148
Crawford Ave., Wem. 117 CK64
Crawford Clo., Islw. 157 CE82
Crawford Compton Clo., Horn. 148 FJ65
Crawford Est. SE5 162 DQ82
Crawford Gdns. N13 99 DP48
Crawford Gdns., Nthlt. 136 BZ69
Crawford Ms. W1 272 D7
Crawford Pas. EC1 274 D5
Crawford Pl. W1 272 C8
Crawford Pl. W1 140 DE72
Crawford Rd. SE5 162 DQ81
Crawford Rd., Hat. 45 CU16
Crawford St. W1 272 C7
Crawford St. W1 140 DF71
Crawfords, Swan. 187 FE94
Crawley Dr., Hem.H. 40 BM16
Crawley Rd. E10 123 EB60
Crawley Rd. N22 100 DQ54
Crawley Rd., Enf. 100 DS45
Crawshaw Ct. SW9 161 DN81
Eythorne Rd.
Crawshaw Rd., Cher. 211 BD107
Crawshay Clo., Sev. 256 FG123
Crawthew Gro. SE22 162 DT84
Cray Ave., Ash. 232 CL116
Cray Ave., Orp. 206 EV100
Cray Clo., Dart. 167 FG84
Cray Riverway, Dart. 187 FF85
Cray Rd., Belv. 166 FA79
Cray Rd., Sid. 186 EW94
Cray Rd., Swan. 207 FB100
Cray Valley Rd., Orp. 206 EU99
Craybrooke Rd., Sid. 186 EV91
Crayburne, Grav. 190 FZ92
Craybury End SE9 185 EQ89
Craydene Rd., Erith 167 FF81
Crayford Clo. E6 144 EL71
Neatscourt Rd.
Crayford High St., Dart. 187 FE85
Crayford Rd. N7 121 DK63
Crayford Rd., Dart. 187 FE85
Crayford Way, Dart. 187 FF85
Crayke Hill, Chess. 216 CL108
Craylands, Orp. 206 EW97
Craylands La., Swans. 189 FX85
Craylands Sq., Swans. 189 FX85
Crayle St., Slou. 131 AN69
Craymill Sq., Dart. 167 FG83
Norris Way
Crayonne Clo., Sun. 195 BS95
Crayside Ind. Est., Dart. 167 FH84
Thames Rd.
Crealock Gro., Wdf.Grn. 102 EF50
Crealock St. SW18 180 DB86
Creasey Clo., Horn. 127 FH61
St. Leonards Way
Creasy Clo., Abb.L. 59 BT31
Creasy Est. SE1 279 M7
Crebor St. SE22 182 DU86
Credenhall Dr., Brom. 205 EM102
Credenhill St. SW16 181 DJ93
Crediton Hill NW6 120 DB64
Crediton Rd. E16 144 EG72
Pacific Rd.
Crediton Rd. NW10 139 CX67
Crediton Way, Esher 215 CG106
Credo Way, Grays 169 FV79
Credon Rd. E13 144 EJ68
Credon Rd. SE16 162 DV78
Cree Way, Rom. 105 FE52
Creechurch La. EC3 275 N9
Creechurch La. EC3 142 DS72
Creechurch Pl. EC3 275 N9
Creed Ct. EC4 141 DP72
Ludgate Hill
Creed La. EC4 274 G9
Creek, The, Grav. 190 GB85
Creek, The, Sun. 195 BU99
Creek Rd. SE8 163 EA79
Creek Rd. SE10 163 EB79
Creek Rd., Bark. 145 ET69
Creek Rd., E.Mol. 197 CE98
Creekside SE8 163 EB80
Creekside, Rain. 147 FE70
Creeland Gro. SE6 183 DZ88
Catford Hill
Crefeld Clo. W6 159 CX79
Creffield Rd. W3 138 CM73
Creffield Rd. W5 138 CM73
Creighton Ave. E6 144 EK68
Creighton Ave. N2 120 DE55
Creighton Ave. N10 98 DF54
Creighton Ave., St.Alb. 43 CD24
Creighton Clo. W12 139 CV73
Bloemfontein Rd.
Creighton Rd. N17 100 DS52
Creighton Rd. NW6 139 CX68
Creighton Rd. W5 157 CK76
Cremer St. E2 275 P1
Cremer St. E2 142 DT68
Cremorne Est. SW10 160 DD79
Milman's St.
Cremorne Gdns., Epsom 216 CR109
Cremorne Rd. SW10 160 DC80
Cremorne Rd., Grav. 191 GF87
Crescent, The E17 123 DY57
Crescent, The EC3 275 P10
Crescent, The N11 98 DG49
Crescent, The NW2 119 CV62
Crescent, The SW13 159 CT82
Crescent, The SW19 180 DA90
Crescent, The W3 138 CS72
Crescent, The, Abb.L. 59 BT30
Crescent, The, Ashf. 174 BM92
Crescent, The, Barn. 80 DB41
Crescent, The, Beck. 203 EA95
Crescent, The, Bex. 186 EW87
Crescent, The, Cat. 237 EA123
Crescent, The, Cher. 194 BG97
Western Ave.
Crescent, The, Croy. 202 DR99
Crescent, The, Egh. 172 AY93
Crescent, The, Epp. 69 ET32
Crescent, The, Epsom 216 CN114
Crescent, The, Grav. 191 GF89
Crescent, The, Green. 189 FW85
Crescent, The, Guil. 242 AU133
Crescent, The, Harl. 36 EW09
Crescent, The, Har. 116 CC60
Crescent, The, Hayes 155 BQ80
Crescent, The, Horl. 268 DG150
Crescent, The, Ilf. 125 EN58
Crescent, The, Lthd. 231 CH122
Crescent, The, Loug. 84 EK43
Crescent, The, N.Mal. 198 CQ96
Crescent, The, Reig. 250 DB134
Chartway
Crescent, The, Rick. 75 BP44
Crescent, The, St.Alb. 60 CA30
Crescent, The, Sev. 257 FK121
Crescent, The, Shep. 195 BT101
Crescent, The, Sid. 185 ET91
Crescent, The, Slou. 152 AS75
Crescent, The, Sthl. 156 BZ75
Crescent, The, Surb. 198 CL99
Crescent, The, Sutt. 218 DD106
Crescent, The (Belmont), Sutt. 218 DA111
Crescent, The, Upmin. 129 FS59
Crescent, The, Wat. 76 BW42
Crescent, The (Aldenham), Wat. 94 CB47
Crescent, The, Wem. 117 CG61
Crescent, The, W.Mol. 196 CA98
Crescent, The, W.Wick. 204 EE100
Crescent, The, Wey. 194 BN104
Crescent Ave., Grays 170 GD78
Crescent Ave., Horn. 127 FF61
Crescent Cotts., Sev. 241 FE120
Crescent Dr., Brwd. 108 FY46
Crescent Dr., Orp. 205 EP100
Crescent E., Barn. 80 DC38
Crescent Gdns. SW19 180 DA90
Crescent Gdns., Ruis. 115 BV59
Crescent Gdns., Swan. 207 FC96
Crescent Gro. SW4 161 DJ84
Crescent Gro., Mitch. 200 DE98
Crescent La. SW4 161 DJ84
Crescent Pl. SW3 276 B8
Crescent Pl. SW3 160 DE77
Crescent Ri. N22 99 DK53
Crescent Ri., Barn. 80 DE43
Crescent Rd. E4 102 EE45
Crescent Rd. E6 144 EJ67
Crescent Rd. E10 123 EB61
Crescent Rd. E13 144 EG67
Crescent Rd. E18 102 EJ54
Crescent Rd. N3 97 CZ53
Crescent Rd. N8 121 DK58
Crescent Rd. N9 100 DU46
Crescent Rd. N11 98 DF49
Crescent Rd. N15 121 DP55
Carlingford Rd.
Crescent Rd. N22 99 DK53
Crescent Rd. SE18 165 EP78
Crescent Rd. SW20 199 CX95
Crescent Rd., Barn. 80 DD42
Crescent Rd., Beck. 203 EB96
Crescent Rd., Brwd. 108 FV49
Crescent Rd., Brom. 184 EG94
Crescent Rd., Cat. 236 DU124
Crescent Rd., Dag. 127 FB62
Crescent Rd., Enf. 81 DP42
Crescent Rd., Erith 167 FF79
Crescent Rd., Hem.H. 40 BK20
Crescent Rd., Kings.T. 178 CN94
Crescent Rd., Red. 252 DQ133
Crescent Rd., Reig. 266 DA136
Crescent Rd., Shep. 195 BQ99
Crescent Rd., Sid. 185 ET90
Crescent Rd., S.Ock. 168 FQ75
Crescent Row EC1 275 H5
Crescent Stables SW15 159 CY84
Upper Richmond Rd.
Crescent St. N1 141 DM66
Crescent Vw., Loug. 84 EK43
Crescent Wk., S.Ock. 168 FQ75
Crescent Way N12 98 DE51
Crescent Way SE4 163 EA83
Crescent Way SW16 181 DM93
Crescent Way, Horl. 268 DG150
Crescent Way, Orp. 223 ES106
Crescent Way, S.Ock. 149 FR74
Crescent W., Barn. 80 DC39
Crescent Wd. Rd. SE26 182 DU90
Cresford Rd. SW6 160 DB81
Crespigny Rd. NW4 119 CV58
Cress End, Rick. 92 BG46
Springwell Ave.
Cress Rd., Slou. 151 AP75
Cressage Clo., Sthl. 136 CA70
Cressall Clo., Lthd. 231 CH120
Cresset Clo., Ware 33 EC12
Cresset Rd. E9 142 DW65
Cresset St. SW4 161 DK83
Cressfield Clo. NW5 120 DG64
Cressida Rd. N19 121 DJ60
Cressingham Gro., Sutt. 218 DC105
Cressingham Rd. SE13 163 EC83
Cressingham Rd., Edg. 96 CR51
Cressington Clo. N16 122 DS64
Wordsworth Rd.
Cresswell Gdns. SW5 160 DC78
Cresswell Pk. SE3 164 EF83
Cresswell Pl. SW10 160 DC78
Cresswell Rd. SE25 202 DU98
Cresswell Rd., Chesh. 54 AR34
Cresswell Rd., Felt. 176 BY91
Cresswell Rd., Twick. 177 CK86
Cresswell Way N21 99 DN45
Cressy Ct. E1 142 DW71
Cressy Pl.
Cressy Ct. W6 159 CV76
Cressy Pl. E1 142 DW71
Cressy Rd. NW3 120 DF64
Crest, The N13 99 DN49
Crest, The NW4 119 CW57
Crest, The, Saw. 36 EX05
Crest, The, Surb. 198 CN99
Crest, The (Cheshunt), Wal.Cr. 65 DP27
Orchard Way
Crest Ave., Grays 170 GB80
Crest Clo., Sev. 225 FB111
Crest Dr., Enf. 82 DW38
Crest Gdns., Ruis. 116 BW62
Crest Hill, Guil. 261 BR142
Crest Pk., Hem.H. 41 BQ19
Crest Rd. NW2 119 CT62
Crest Rd., Brom. 204 EF101
Crest Rd., S.Croy. 220 DV108
Crest Vw., Green. 169 FU84
Woodland Way
Crest Vw., Pnr. 116 BX56
Crest Vw. Dr., Orp. 205 EP99
Cresta Dr., Add. 211 BF110
Crestbrook Ave. N13 99 DP48
Crestfield St. WC1 274 A2
Crestfield St. WC1 141 DL69
Cresthill Ave., Grays 170 GC77
Creston Ave., Wok. 226 AS116
Creston Way, Wor.Pk. 199 CX102
Crestway SW15 179 CU86
Crestwood Way, Houns. 176 BZ85
Creswick Ct., Welw.G.C. 29 CX10
Creswick Rd. W3 138 CP73
Creswick Wk. E3 143 EA69
Malmesbury Rd.
Creswick Wk. NW11 119 CZ56
Crete Hall Rd., Grav. 190 GD86
Creton St. SE18 165 EN76
Crew Curve, Berk. 38 AT16
Crewdson Rd. SW9 161 DN80
Crewdson Rd., Horl. 269 DH148
Crewe Pl. NW10 139 CT69
Crewe's Ave., Warl. 236 DW116
Crewe's Clo., Warl. 236 DW117
Crewe's La., Warl. 236 DW117
Crews St. E14 163 EA77
Crewys Rd. NW2 119 CZ61
Crewys Rd. SE15 162 DV82
Crib St., Ware 33 DX05
Crichton Ave., Wall. 219 DK106
Crichton Rd., Cars. 218 DF108
Cricket Fld. Rd., Uxb. 134 BK67
Cricket Grn., Mitch. 200 DF97
Cricket Grd. Rd., Chis. 205 EP95
Cricket Hill, Red. 267 DM136
Cricket La., Beck. 183 DY92
Cricket Way, Wey. 195 BS103
Cricketers Arms Rd., Enf. 82 DQ40
Cricketers Clo. N14 99 DJ45
Cricketers Clo., Chess. 215 CK105
Cricketers Clo., Erith 167 FE78
Cricketers Clo., St.Alb. 43 CE19
Stonecross
Cricketers Ct. SE11 278 F9
Cricketers Ter., Cars. 200 DE104
Wrythe La.
Cricketfield Rd. E5 122 DV63
Cricketfield Rd., West Dr. 154 BJ77
Cricklade Ave. SW2 181 DL89
Cricklade Ave., Rom. 106 FK51
Cricklewood Bdy. NW2 119 CW62
Cricklewood La. NW2 119 CX63
Cricklewood Trd. Est. NW2 119 CY62
Cridland St. E15 144 EF67
Church St.
Crieff Ct., Tedd. 177 CJ94
Crieff Rd. SW18 180 DC86
Criffel Ave. SW2 181 DK89
Crimp Hill Rd., Egh. 172 AU90
Crimp Hill Rd., Wind. 172 AT87
Crimscott St. SE1 279 N7
Crimscott St. SE1 162 DS76
Crimsworth Rd. SW8 161 DK81
Crinan St. N1 141 DL68
Cringle St. SW8 161 DJ80
Cripplegate St. EC2 275 H6
Crisp Rd. W6 159 CW78
Crispe Ho., Bark. 145 ER68
Dovehouse Mead
Crispen Rd., Felt. 176 BY91
Crispian Clo. NW10 118 CS63
Crispin Clo., Ash. 232 CM118
Crispin Clo., Croy. 201 DL103
Harrington Clo.
Crispin Cres., Croy. 201 DK103
Crispin Rd., Edg. 96 CQ51
Crispin St. E1 275 P7
Crispin St. E1 142 DT71
Crispin Way, Slou. 111 AR63
Criss Cres., Ger.Cr. 90 AW54
Criss Gro., Ger.Cr. 90 AW54
Cristowe Rd. SW6 159 CZ82
Criterion Ms. N19 121 DK61
Critten La., Dor. 246 BX134
Crockenhall Way, Grav. 190 GE94
Crockenhill La., Dart. 208 FJ102
Crockenhill La., Swan. 207 FG101
Crockenhill Rd., Orp. 206 EX99
Crockenhill Rd., Swan. 206 EZ100
Crockerton Rd. SW17 180 DF89
Crockery La., Guil. 244 BL129
Crockford Clo., Add. 212 BJ105
Crockford Pk. Rd., Add. 212 BJ106
Crockham Way SE9 185 EN91
Crocknorth Rd., Lthd. 245 BT132
Crocus Clo., Croy. 203 DX102
Cornflower La.
Crocus Fld., Barn. 79 CZ44
Croffets, Tad. 233 CX121
Croft, The NW10 139 CT68
Croft, The W5 138 CL71
Croft, The, Barn. 79 CY42
Croft, The, Brox. 49 DY23
Croft, The, Houns. 156 BY79
Croft, The, Loug. 85 EN40
Croft, The, Pnr. 116 BZ59
Rayners La.
Croft, The, Ruis. 116 BW63
Croft, The, St.Alb. 60 CA25
Croft, The, Swan. 207 FC97
Croft, The, Welw.G.C. 29 CZ12
Croft, The, Wem. 117 CJ64
Croft Ave., Dor. 247 CH134
Croft Ave., W.Wick. 203 EC102
Croft Clo. NW7 96 CS48
Croft Clo., Belv. 166 EZ78
Croft Clo., Chis. 185 EM91
Croft Clo., Hayes 155 BQ80
Croft Clo., Kings L. 58 BG30
Croft Clo., Uxb. 134 BN66
Croft End Rd., Kings L. 58 BG30
Croft Fld., Hat. 45 CU18
Croft Fld., Kings L. 58 BG30
Croft Gdns. W7 157 CG75
Croft Gdns., Ruis. 115 BS60
Croft La., Kings L. 58 BG30
Croft Lo. Clo., Wdf.Grn. 102 EH51
Croft Meadow, Kings L. 58 BG30
Croft Ms. N12 98 DC48
Croft Rd. SW16 201 DN95
Croft Rd. SW19 180 DC94
Croft Rd., Brom. 184 EG93
Croft Rd., Cat. 237 DZ122
Croft Rd., Enf. 83 DY39
Croft Rd., Ger.Cr. 90 AY54
Croft Rd., Sutt. 218 DE106
Croft Rd., Ware 32 DW05
Croft Rd., West. 255 EP126
Croft St. SE8 163 DY77
Croft Wk., Brox. 49 DZ23
The Cft.
Croft Way NW3 120 DA63
Ferncroft Ave.
Croft Way, Sev. 256 FF125
Croft Way, Sid. 185 ES90
Croftdown Rd. NW5 120 DG62
Crofters, The, Wind. 172 AU86
Crofters Clo., Islw. 177 CD85
Ploughmans End
Crofters Ct. SE8 163 DY77
Crofters Mead, Croy. 221 DZ109
Crofters Rd., Nthwd. 93 BS49
Crofters Way NW1 141 DK67
Crofthill Rd., Slou. 131 AP70
Croftleigh Ave., Pur. 235 DP116
Crofton, Ash. 232 CL118
Crofton Ave. W4 158 CQ80
Crofton Ave., Bex. 186 EX87
Crofton Ave., Orp. 205 EQ103
Crofton Ave., Walt. 196 BW104
Crofton Clo., Cher. 211 BC108
Crofton Gro. E4 101 ED49
Crofton La., Orp. 205 ER103
Crofton Pk. Rd. SE4 183 DZ86
Crofton Rd. E13 144 EH70
Crofton Rd. SE5 162 DS81
Crofton Rd., Grays 170 GE75
Crofton Rd., Orp. 205 EN104
Crofton Ter. E5 123 DY64
Studley Clo.
Crofton Ter., Rich. 158 CM84
Crofton Way, Barn. 80 DB44
Wycherley Cres.
Crofton Way, Enf. 81 DN40
Croftongate Way SE4 183 DY85
Crofts, The, Hem.H. 41 BP21
Crofts, The, Shep. 195 BS98
Crofts La. N22 99 DN52
Glendale Ave.
Crofts Path, Hem.H. 40 BN22
Crofts Rd., Har. 117 CG58
Crofts St. E1 142 DU73
Croftside SE25 202 DU97
Sunny Bank
Croftway NW3 120 DA63
Croftway, Rich. 177 CH90
Crogsland Rd. NW1 140 DG66
Croham Clo., S.Croy. 220 DS108
Croham Manor Rd., S.Croy. 220 DS108
Croham Mt., S.Croy. 220 DS108
Croham Pk. Ave., S.Croy. 220 DS106

Croham Rd., S.Croy. 220 DR106
Croham Valley Rd., S.Croy. 220 DT107
Croindene Rd. SW16 201 DL95
Cromartie Rd. N19 121 DK59
Cromarty Rd., Edg. 96 CP47
Crombie Clo., Ilf. 125 EM57
Crombie Rd., Sid. 185 ER88
Cromer Clo., Uxb. 135 BQ72
Dawley Ave.
Cromer Hyde La., Welw.G.C. 28 CR10
Cromer Pl., Orp. 205 ER102
Andover Rd.
Cromer Rd. E10 123 ED58
James La.
Cromer Rd. N17 100 DU54
Cromer Rd. SE25 202 DV97
Cromer Rd. SW17 180 DG93
Cromer Rd., Barn. 80 DC42
Cromer Rd., Horn. 128 FK59
Cromer Rd., Houns. 154 BN83
Cromer Rd., Rom. 127 FC58
Cromer Rd. (Chadwell Heath), Rom. 126 EY58
Cromer Rd., Wat. 76 BW38
Cromer Rd., Wdf.Grn. 102 EG49
Cromer Rd. W., Houns. 154 BN83
Cromer St. WC1 274 A3
Cromer St. WC1 141 DL69
Cromer Ter. E8 122 DU64
Ferncliff Rd.
Cromer Vill. Rd. SW18 179 CZ86
Cromford Clo., Orp. 205 ES104
Cromford Path E5 123 DX63
Overbury St.
Cromford Rd. SW18 180 DA85
Cromford Way, N.Mal. 198 CR95
Cromlix Clo., Chis. 205 EP96
Crompton St. W2 140 DD70
Cromwell Ave. N6 121 DH60
Cromwell Ave. W6 159 CV77
Cromwell Ave., Brom. 204 EH97
Cromwell Ave., N.Mal. 199 CT99
Cromwell Ave. (Cheshunt), Wal.Cr. 66 DU30
Cromwell Clo. E1 142 DU74
Vaughan Way
Cromwell Clo. N2 120 DD56
Cromwell Clo. W3 138 CQ74
High St.
Cromwell Clo., Brom. 204 EH98
Cromwell Clo., Ch.St.G. 90 AW48
Cromwell Clo., St.Alb. 43 CK15
Cromwell Clo., Walt. 195 BV102
Cromwell Cres. SW5 160 DA77
Cromwell Dr., Slou. 132 AS72
Cromwell Gdns. SW7 276 A7
Cromwell Gdns. SW7 160 DD76
Cromwell Gro. W6 159 CW76
Cromwell Gro., Cat. 236 DQ121
Cromwell Ind. Est. E10 123 DY60
Cromwell Ms. SW7 276 A8
Cromwell Ms. SW7 160 DD77
Cromwell Pl. N6 121 DH60
Cromwell Ave.
Cromwell Pl. SW7 276 A8
Cromwell Pl. SW7 160 DD77
Cromwell Pl. SW14 158 CQ83
Cromwell Pl. W3 138 CQ74
Grove Pl.
Cromwell Rd. E7 144 EJ66
Cromwell Rd. E17 123 EC57
Cromwell Rd. N3 98 DC54
Cromwell Rd. N10 98 DG52
Cromwell Rd. SW5 160 DB77
Cromwell Rd. SW7 160 DB77
Cromwell Rd. SW9 161 DP81
Cromwell Rd. SW19 180 DA92
Cromwell Rd., Beck. 203 DY96
Cromwell Rd., Borwd. 78 CL39
Cromwell Rd., Brwd. 108 FV49
Cromwell Rd., Cat. 236 DQ121
Cromwell Rd., Croy. 202 DR101
Cromwell Rd., Felt. 175 BV88
Cromwell Rd., Grays 170 GA77
Cromwell Rd., Hayes 135 BR72
Cromwell Rd., Hert. 32 DT08
Cromwell Rd., Houns. 156 CA84
Cromwell Rd., Kings.T. 198 CL95
Cromwell Rd., Red. 250 DF133
Cromwell Rd., Tedd. 177 CG93
Cromwell Rd. (Cheshunt), Wal.Cr. 66 DV28
Cromwell Rd., Walt. 196 BW102
Cromwell Rd., Ware 33 DZ05
Cromwell Rd., Wem. 138 CL68
Cromwell Rd., Wor.Pk. 198 CR104
Cromwell St., Houns. 156 CA84
Cromwell Twr. EC2 142 DQ71
Whitecross St.
Cromwell Wk., Red. 250 DF134
Cromwells Mere, Rom. 105 FD51
Havering Rd.
Crondace Rd. SW6 160 DA81
Crondall St. N1 275 M1
Crondall St. N1 142 DR68
Cronks Hill, Red. 266 DC136
Cronks Hill, Reig. 266 DC136
Cronks Hill Clo., Red. 266 DD136
Cronks Hill Rd., Red. 266 DD136
Crook Log, Bexh. 166 EX83
Crooke Rd. SE8 163 DY78
Crooked Billet SW19 179 CW93
Woodhayes Rd.
Crooked Billet Roundabout E17 101 EA52
Crooked Billet Yd. E2 142 DS69
Kingsland Rd.
Crooked La., Grav. 191 GH86
Crooked Mile, Wal.Abb. 67 EC33
Crooked Usage N3 119 CY55
Crooked Way, Wal.Abb. 50 EE22
Crookham Rd. SW6 159 CZ81
Crookhams, Welw.G.C. 30 DA07
Crookston Rd. SE9 165 EN83
Croombs Rd. E16 144 EJ71
Crooms Hill SE10 163 EC80
Crooms Hill Gro. SE10 163 EC80
Crop Common, Hat. 45 CV16
Cropley Ct. N1 142 DR68
Cropley St.
Cropley St. N1 142 DR68
Croppath Rd., Dag. 126 FA63
Cropthorne Ct. W9 140 DC69
Maida Vale
Crosby Clo., Beac. 111 AM55
Crosby Clo., Felt. 176 BY91
Crosby Clo., St.Alb. 43 CJ23
Crosby Ct. SE1 279 K4
Crosby Rd. E7 144 EG65
Crosby Rd., Dag. 147 FB68
Crosby Row SE1 279 K4
Crosby Row SE1 162 DR75
Crosby Sq. EC3 275 M9
Crosby Wk. E8 142 DT65
Laurel St.
Crosby Wk. SW2 181 DN87
Crosier Rd., Uxb. 115 BQ63
Crosier Way, Ruis. 115 BS62
Crosland Pl. SW11 160 DG83
Taybridge Rd.
Cross Ave. SE10 163 ED79
Cross Deep, Twick. 177 CF90
Cross Deep Gdns., Twick. 177 CF89
Cross Keys Clo. W1 272 G7
Cross Keys Clo., Sev. 256 FG127
Brittains La.
Cross Keys Sq. EC1 275 H7
Cross Lances Rd., Houns. 156 CB84
Cross La. EC3 279 M1
Cross La. N8 121 DM55
Cross La., Beac. 111 AM55
Cross La., Bex. 186 EZ87
Cross La., Cher. 211 BB107
Chobham Rd.
Cross La., Hert. 31 DP09
Cross La. E., Grav. 191 GH89
Cross La. Footpath, Cher. 211 BB107
Cross La. W., Grav. 191 GH89
Cross Las., Ger.Cr. 91 AZ50
Cross Las., Guil. 243 AZ134
Cross Las. Clo., Ger.Cr. 91 AZ50
Cross Las.
Cross Meadow, Chesh. 54 AM29
Cross Oak, Wind. 151 AN82
Cross Oak Rd., Berk. 38 AU20
Cross Rd. E4 102 EE46
Cross Rd. N11 99 DH50
Cross Rd. N22 99 DN52
Cross Rd. SE5 162 DS82
Cross Rd. SW19 180 DA94
Cross Rd., Brom. 204 EL103
Cross Rd., Croy. 202 DR102
Cross Rd., Dart. 188 FJ86
Cross Rd. (Hawley), Dart. 188 FM91
Cross Rd., Enf. 82 DT42
Cross Rd., Felt. 176 BY91
Cross Rd., Grav. 191 GF86
Cross Rd., Har. 117 CD56
Cross Rd. (South Harrow), Har. 116 CB62
Cross Rd. (Wealdstone), Har. 95 CG54
Cross Rd., Hert. 32 DQ08
Cross Rd., Kings.T. 178 CM94
Cross Rd., Orp. 206 EV99
Cross Rd., Pur. 219 DP113
Cross Rd., Rom. 126 FA56
Cross Rd. (Chadwell Heath), Rom. 126 EW59
Cross Rd., Sid. 186 EV91
Sidcup Hill
Cross Rd., Sutt. 218 DD106
Cross Rd. (Belmont), Sutt. 218 DA110
Cross Rd., Tad. 233 CW122
Cross Rd., Uxb. 134 BJ66
New Windsor St.
Cross Rd., Wal.Cr. 67 DY33
Cross Rd., Wat. 76 BY44
Cross Rd., Wey. 195 BR104
Cross Rd., Wdf.Grn. 103 EM51
Cross Rds., Loug. 84 EH40
Cross St. N1 141 DP67
Cross St. SW13 158 CS82
Cross St., Erith 167 FE78
Bexley Rd.
Cross St., Hmptn. 176 CC92
Cross St., Harl. 51 ER15
Cross St., St.Alb. 43 CD20
Spencer St.
Cross St., Uxb. 134 BJ66
Cross St., Ware 33 DY06
Cross St., Wat. 76 BW41
Cross Way, Pnr. 93 BV54
Cross Way, The, Har. 95 CE54
Cross Ways, Hem.H. 41 BP20
Crossacres, Wok. 227 BE116
Crossbow Rd., Chig. 103 ET50
Crossbrook, Hat. 44 CS19
Crossbrook Rd. SE3 164 EL82
Crossbrook St. (Cheshunt), Wal.Cr. 67 DX31
Crossett Grn., Hem.H. 41 BQ22
Crossfell Rd., Hem.H. 41 BQ22
Crossfield Clo., Berk. 38 AT19
Crossfield Pl., Wey. 213 BP108
Crossfield Rd. N17 122 DQ55
Crossfield Rd. NW3 140 DD65
Crossfield Rd., Hodd. 49 EB15
Crossfield St. SE8 163 EA80
Crossfields, Loug. 85 EP43
Crossfields, St.Alb. 42 CB23
Crossford St. SW9 161 DL82
Crossgate, Edg. 96 CN48
Crossgate, Grnf. 137 CH65
Crossing Rd., Epp. 70 EU32
Crossland Rd., Red. 250 DG134
Crossland Rd., Th.Hth. 201 DP99
Crosslands, Cher. 211 BE105
Crosslands Ave. W5 138 CM74
Crosslands Ave., Sthl. 156 BZ78
Crosslands Rd., Epsom 216 CR107
Crosslet St. SE17 279 L8
Crosslet Vale SE10 163 EB81
Blackheath Rd.
Crossley Clo., West. 238 EK115
Crossley St. N7 141 DN65
Crossleys, Ch.St.G. 90 AW49
Crossmead SE9 185 EM88
Crossmead, Wat. 75 BV44
Crossmead Ave., Grnf. 136 CA69
Crossmount Ho. SE5 162 DQ80
Bowyer St.
Crossness La. SE28 146 EX73
Bayliss Ave.
Crossness Rd., Bark. 145 ET69
Crossoak La., Red. 266 DG144
Crossoaks La., Borwd. 78 CR35
Crossoaks La. (South Mimms), Pot.B. 62 CS34
Crosspath, The, Rad. 77 CG35
Crossroads, The, Lthd. 246 BX128
Crossthwaite Ave. SE5 162 DR84
Crosswall EC3 275 P10
Crosswall EC3 142 DT73
Crossway N12 98 DD51
Crossway N16 122 DS64
Crossway N22 99 DP52
Crossway NW9 119 CT56
Crossway SE28 146 EW72
Crossway SW20 199 CW98
Crossway W13 137 CG70
Crossway, Chesh. 54 AS30
Crossway, Dag. 126 EW62
Crossway, Enf. 100 DS45
Crossway, Hayes 135 BU74
Crossway, Orp. 205 ER98
Crossway, Ruis. 116 BW63
Crossway, Walt. 195 BV103
Crossway, Welw.G.C. 29 CW05
Crossway, Wdf.Grn. 102 EJ49
Crossway, The SE9 184 EK89
Crossway, The, Uxb. 134 BM68
Crossways N21 82 DQ44
Crossways, Beac. 89 AM54
Crossways, Berk. 38 AT20
Crossways, Brwd. 109 GA44
Crossways, Egh. 173 BD93
Crossways, Lthd. 246 BX127
The St.
Crossways, Rom. 127 FH55
Crossways, S.Croy. 221 DY108
Crossways, Sun. 175 BT94
Crossways, Sutt. 218 DD109
Crossways, West. 238 EJ120
Crossways, The, Couls. 235 DM119
Crossways, The, Guil. 258 AT136
Crossways, The, Houns. 156 BZ80
Crossways, The, Red. 251 DJ130
Crossways, The, Wem. 118 CN61
Crossways Boul., Dart. 168 FQ84
Crossways Business Pk., Dart. 168 FQ84
Crossways La., Reig. 250 DC128
Crossways Rd., Beck. 203 EA98
Crossways Rd., Mitch. 201 DH97
Crosswell Clo., Shep. 195 BQ96
Crosthwaite Way, Slou. 131 AK71
Croston St. E8 142 DU67
Crothall Clo. N13 99 DM48
Crouch Ave., Bark. 146 EV68
Crouch Clo., Beck. 183 EA93
Abbey La.
Crouch Cft. SE9 185 EN90
Crouch End Hill N8 121 DK59
Crouch Hall Rd. N8 121 DK58
Crouch Hill N4 121 DL59
Crouch Hill N8 121 DL58
Crouch La. (Cheshunt), Wal.Cr. 66 DQ28
Crouch Oak La., Add. 212 BJ105
Crouch Rd. NW10 138 CR66
Crouch Rd., Grays 171 GG78
Crouch Valley, Upmin. 129 FR59
Crouchfield, Hem.H. 40 BH21
Crouchfield, Hert. 32 DQ06
Crouchman's Clo. SE26 182 DT90
Crow Clo., Warl. 237 DY118
Crow Dr., Sev. 241 FC115
Crow Grn. La., Brwd. 108 FU43
Crow Grn. Rd., Brwd. 108 FT43
Crow La., Rom. 126 EZ59
Crow Piece La., Slou. 131 AM66
Crowborough Clo., Warl. 237 DY118
Crowborough Dr., Warl. 237 DY118
Crowborough Path, Wat. 94 BX49
Prestwick Rd.
Crowborough Rd. SW17 180 DG93
Crowden Way SE28 146 EW73
Crowder St. E1 142 DV73
Crowfoot Clo. E9 123 DZ64
Lee Conservancy Rd.
Crowhurst Clo. SW9 161 DN82
Crowhurst Mead, Gdse. 252 DW130
Crowhurst Way, Orp. 206 EW99
Crowland Ave., Hayes 155 BS77
Crowland Gdns. N14 99 DL45
Crowland Rd. N15 122 DT57
Crowland Rd., Th.Hth. 202 DR98
Crowland Ter. N1 142 DR66
Crowland Wk., Mord. 200 DB100
Crowlands Ave., Rom. 127 FB58
Crowley Cres., Croy. 219 DN106
Crowline Wk. N1 142 DR65
Clephane Rd.
Crowmarsh Gdns. SE23 182 DW87
Tyson Rd.
Crown Arc., Kings.T. 197 CK96
Union St.
Crown Ash Hill, West. 222 EH114
Crown Ash La., West. 238 EG116
Crown Clo. E3 143 EA67
Crown Clo. NW6 140 DB65
Crown Clo. NW7 97 CT47
Crown Clo., B.Stort. 37 FC07
Crown Clo., Hayes 155 BT75
Station Rd.
Crown Clo., Orp. 224 EU105
Crown Clo., Walt. 196 BW101
Crown Ct. EC2 275 J9
Crown Ct. SE12 184 EH86
Crown Ct. WC2 274 A9
Crown Ct., Brom. 204 EK99
Victoria Rd.
Crown Dale SE19 181 DP93
Crown Gate, Harl. 51 ER15
Crown Heights, Guil. 258 AY137
Crown Hill, Croy. 202 DQ103
Crown Hill, Epp. 69 EN34
Crown Hill, Wal.Abb. 68 EL33
Crown La. N14 99 DJ46
Crown La. SW16 181 DN92
Crown La., Brom. 204 EK99
Crown La., Chis. 205 EQ95
Crown La., H.Wyc. 88 AF48
Crown La., Mord. 200 DA97
Crown La., Slou. 131 AN67
Crown La., Vir.W. 192 AX100
Crown La. Gdns. SW16 181 DN92
Crown La.
Crown La. Spur, Brom. 204 EK100
Crown Meadow, Slou. 153 BB80
Crown Ms. E13 144 EJ67
Waghorn Rd.
Crown Ms. W6 159 CU77
Crown Office Row EC4 274 D10
Crown Par., Hayes 135 BT71
Crown Pas. SW1 277 L3
Crown Pas., Wat. 76 BW42
The Cres.
Crown Pl. NW5 141 DH65
Kentish Town Rd.
Crown Pt. Par. SE19 181 DP93
Beulah Hill
Crown Ri., Cher. 193 BF102
Crown Ri., Wat. 60 BW34
Crown Rd. N10 98 DG52
Crown Rd., Borwd. 78 CN39
Crown Rd., Enf. 82 DU41
Crown Rd., Grays 170 GA79
Crown Rd., Ilf. 125 ER56
Crown Rd., Mord. 200 DA98
Crown Rd., N.Mal. 198 CQ95
Crown Rd., Orp. 224 EU106
Crown Rd., Ruis. 116 BX64
Crown Rd., Sev. 225 FF110
Crown Rd., Slou. 153 BB80
Crown Rd., Sutt. 218 DA105
Crown Rd., Twick. 177 CH86
Crown Rd., Vir.W. 192 AW100
Crown Sq., Wok. 227 AZ117
Commercial Way
Crown St. SE5 162 DQ80
Crown St. W3 138 CP74
Crown St., Brwd. 108 FW47
Crown St., Dag. 147 FC65
Crown St., Egh. 173 BA91
Crown St., Har. 117 CD60
Crown Ter., Rich. 158 CM84
Crown Wk., Uxb. 134 BJ66
Oxford Rd.
Crown Wk., Wem. 118 CM62
Crown Way, West Dr. 134 BM74
Crown Wds. La. SE9 165 EQ82
Crown Wds. La. SE18 165 EP82
Crown Wds. Way SE9 185 ER85
Crown Yd., Houns. 156 CC83
High St.
Crowndale Rd. NW1 141 DJ68
Crownfield, Brox. 49 EA21
Crownfield Ave., Ilf. 125 ES58
Crownfield Rd. E15 123 ED63
Crownfields, Sev. 257 FH125
Crownhill Rd. NW10 139 CT67
Crownhill Rd., Wdf.Grn. 102 EL52
Crownmead Way, Rom. 127 FB56
Crownstone Rd. SW2 181 DN85
Crowntree Clo., Islw. 157 CF79
Crows Rd. E15 143 ED69
Crows Rd., Epp. 69 ET30
Crowshott Ave., Stan. 95 CJ54
Crowstone Rd., Grays 170 GC75
Crowther Ave., Brent. 158 CL77
Crowther Rd. SE25 202 DU98
Crowthorne Clo. SW18 179 CZ88
Crowthorne Rd. W10 139 CX72
Croxdale Rd., Borwd. 78 CM40
Croxden Clo., Edg. 118 CM55
Croxden Wk., Mord. 200 DC100
Croxford Gdns. N22 99 DP52
Croxford Way, Rom. 127 FD60
Horace Ave.
Croxley Clo., Orp. 206 EV96
Croxley Grn., Orp. 206 EV95
Croxley Rd. W9 139 CZ69
Croxley Vw., Wat. 75 BS44
Croxted Clo. SE21 182 DQ87
Croxted Rd. SE21 182 DQ87
Croxted Rd. SE24 182 DQ87
Croyde Ave., Grnf. 136 CC69
Croyde Ave., Hayes 155 BS77
Croyde Clo., Sid. 185 ER87
Croydon Flyover, The, Croy. 219 DP105
Duppas Hill Rd.
Croydon Gro., Croy. 201 DP102
Croydon La., Bans. 218 DB114
Croydon La. S., Bans. 218 DB114
Croydon Rd. E13 144 EF70
Croydon Rd. SE20 202 DV96
Croydon Rd., Beck. 203 DY97
Croydon Rd., Brom. 204 EJ104
Croydon Rd., Cat. 236 DU122
Croydon Rd., Croy. 219 DH105
Croydon Rd., Houns. 155 BP82
Croydon Rd., Kes. 205 EM104
Croydon Rd., Mitch. 200 DG98
Croydon Rd., Reig. 250 DB134
Croydon Rd., Wall. 219 DH105
Croydon Rd., Warl. 237 EC119
Croydon Rd., W.Wick. 204 EE104
Croydon Rd., West. 239 EM123
Croyland Rd. N9 100 DU46
Croylands Dr., Surb. 198 CL101
Croysdale Ave., Sun. 195 BU97
Crozier Dr., S.Croy. 220 DV109
Crozier Ter. E9 123 DX64
Crucible Clo., Rom. 126 EV58
Crucifix La. SE1 279 M4
Crucifix La. SE1 162 DS75
Cruden Ho. SE17 161 DP79
Hillingdon St.
Cruden Rd., Grav. 191 GM90
Cruden St. N1 141 DP67
Cruick Ave., S.Ock. 149 FW73
Cruikshank Rd. E15 124 EE63
Cruikshank St. WC1 274 D2
Cruikshank St. WC1 141 DN69
Crum Clo., Slou. 130 AJ72
Crummock Gdns. NW9 118 CS57
Crumpsall St. SE2 166 EW77
Crundale Ave. NW9 118 CN57
Crundale Twr., Orp. 206 EW102
Crunden Rd., S.Croy. 220 DR108
Crusader Clo., Purf. 168 FN77
Centurion Way
Crusader Gdns., Croy. 202 DS104
Cotelands
Crusader Way, Wat. 75 BT44
Crushes Clo., Brwd. 109 GE44
Crusoe Rd., Erith 167 FD78
Crusoe Rd., Mitch. 180 DF94
Crutched Friars EC3 275 N10
Crutched Friars EC3 142 DS73
Crutches La., Beac. 90 AS51
Crutchfield La., Horl. 268 DA145
Crutchfield La., Walt. 195 BV103
Crutchley Rd. SE6 184 EE89
Crystal Ave., Horn. 128 FL63
Crystal Ct. SE19 182 DT92
College Rd.
Crystal Palace Par. SE19 182 DT93
Crystal Palace Pk. Rd. SE26 182 DU92
Crystal Palace Rd. SE22 182 DT86
Crystal Palace Sta. Rd. SE19 182 DU93
Anerley Hill
Crystal Ter. SE19 182 DR93
Crystal Vw. Ct., Brom. 183 ED91
Winlaton Rd.
Crystal Way, Dag. 126 EW60
Crystal Way, Har. 117 CF57
Cuba Dr., Enf. 82 DW40
Cuba St. E14 163 EA75
Cubitt Sq., Sthl. 136 CC74
Windmill Ave.
Cubitt Steps E14 143 EA74
Cabot Sq.
Cubitt St. WC1 274 C3
Cubitt St. WC1 141 DM69
Cubitt St., Croy. 219 DM106
Cubitt Ter. SW4 161 DJ83
Cubitts Yd. WC2 274 A10
Cublands, Hert. 32 DV09
Cuckmans Dr., St.Alb. 60 CA25
Cuckoo Ave. W7 137 CE70
Cuckoo Dene W7 137 CD71
Cuckoo Hall La. N9 100 DW45
Cuckoo Hill, Pnr. 116 BW55
Cuckoo Hill Dr., Pnr. 116 BW55
Cuckoo Hill Rd., Pnr. 116 BW56
Cuckoo La. W7 137 CE73
Cuckoo Pound, Shep. 195 BS99
Cucumber La., Hat. 46 DF20
Cudas Clo., Epsom 217 CT105
Cuddington Ave., Wor.Pk. 199 CT104
Cuddington Clo., Tad. 233 CW120
Cuddington Pk. Clo., Bans. 217 CZ113
Cuddington Way, Sutt. 217 CX112
Cudham Clo., Sutt. 218 DA110
Cudham Dr., Croy. 221 EC110
Cudham La. N., Orp. 223 ES110
Cudham La. N., Sev. 223 EQ114
Cudham La. S., Sev. 239 ER116
Cudham Pk. Rd., Sev. 223 ES110
Cudham Rd., Orp. 223 EN111
Cudham Rd., West. 238 EL120
Cudham St. SE6 183 EC87
Cudworth St. E1 142 DV70
Cuff Cres. SE9 184 EK86
Cuff Pt. E2 275 P2
Cuffley Ave., Wat. 60 BX34
Cuffley Ct., Hem.H. 41 BQ15
Cuffley Hill (Cheshunt), Wal.Cr. 65 DM29
Cugley Rd., Dart. 188 FQ87
Culford Gdns. SW3 276 E9
Culford Gdns. SW3 160 DF77
Culford Gro. N1 142 DS65
Culford Ms. N1 142 DS65
Southgate Rd.
Culford Rd. N1 142 DS66
Culford Rd., Grays 170 GC75
Culgaith Gdns., Enf. 81 DL42
Cullen Sq., S.Ock. 149 FW73
Cullen Way NW10 138 CQ70
Cullera Clo., Nthwd. 93 BT51
Cullerne Clo., Epsom 217 CT110
Cullesden Rd., Ken. 235 DP115
Culling Rd. SE16 162 DW76
Lower Rd.
Cullings Ct., Wal.Abb. 68 EF33
Cullington Clo., Har. 117 CG56
Cullingworth Rd. NW10 119 CU64
Culloden Clo. SE16 162 DU78
Culloden Rd., Enf. 81 DP40
Culloden St. E14 143 EC72
Cullum St. EC3 275 M10
Culmington Rd. W13 137 CJ74
Culmington Rd., S.Croy. 220 DQ108
Culmore Cross SW12 181 DH88
Culmore Rd. SE15 162 DV80
Culmstock Rd. SW11 180 DG85
Culpeper Clo., Ilf. 103 EP51
Culross Clo. N15 122 DQ56
Culross St. W1 276 F1
Culross St. W1 140 DG73
Culsac Rd., Surb. 198 CL103
Culver Dr., Oxt. 254 EE130
Culver Gro., Stan. 95 CJ54
Culver Rd., St.Alb. 43 CE19
Culverden Rd. SW12 181 DJ89
Culverden Rd., Wat. 93 BV48
Culverhay, Ash. 232 CL116
Culverhouse Gdns. SW16 181 DM90
Culverlands Clo., Stan. 95 CH49
Culverley Rd. SE6 183 EB88
Culvers Ave., Cars. 200 DE103
Culvers Cft., Beac. 89 AQ51
Culvers Retreat, Cars. 200 DF102
Culvers Way, Cars. 200 DF104
Culverstone Clo., Brom. 204 EF100
Culvert La., Uxb. 134 BH68
Culvert Pl. SW11 160 DG82
Culvert Rd. N15 122 DS57
Culvert Rd. SW11 160 DF81
Culworth St. NW8 272 B1
Cum Cum Hill, Hat. 46 DD21
Cumberland Ave. NW10 138 CP69
Cumberland Ave., Grav. 191 GJ87
Cumberland Ave., Guil. 242 AU129
Cumberland Ave., Horn. 128 FL62
Cumberland Ave., Slou. 131 AQ70
Cumberland Ave., Well. 165 ES83
Cumberland Clo. E8 142 DT65
Cumberland Clo. SW20 179 CX94
Lansdowne Rd.
Cumberland Clo., Amer. 72 AV39
Cumberland Clo., Epsom 216 CS110
Cumberland Clo., Hem.H. 41 BS24
Cumberland Clo., Hert. 31 DP06
Cumberland Clo., Horn. 128 FL62
Cumberland Clo., Ilf. 103 EQ53
Carrick Dr.
Cumberland Clo., Twick. 177 CH86
Westmorland Clo.
Cumberland Cres. W14 159 CY77
Cumberland Dr., Bexh. 166 EY80
Cumberland Dr., Chess. 198 CM104
Cumberland Dr., Dart. 188 FM87

Cumberland Dr., Esher 197 CG103
Cumberland Gdns. NW4 97 CX54
Cumberland Gdns. WC1 274 C2
Cumberland Gate W1 272 D10
Cumberland Gate W1 140 DF73
Cumberland Mkt. NW1 273 J2
Cumberland Mkt. NW1 141 DH69
Cumberland Mkt. Est. NW1 273 J2
Cumberland Mills Sq. E14 163 ED78
Saunders Ness Rd.
Cumberland Pk. W3 138 CQ73
Cumberland Pl. NW1 273 H2
Cumberland Pl. SE6 184 EF88
Cumberland Pl., Sun. 195 BU98
Cumberland Rd. E12 124 EK63
Cumberland Rd. E13 144 EH71
Cumberland Rd. E17 101 DY54
Cumberland Rd. N9 100 DW46
Cumberland Rd. N22 99 DM54
Cumberland Rd. SE25 202 DV100
Cumberland Rd. SW13 159 CT81
Cumberland Rd. W3 138 CQ73
Cumberland Rd. W7 157 CF75
Cumberland Rd., Ashf. 174 BK90
Cumberland Rd., Brom. 204 EE98
Cumberland Rd., Har. 116 CB57
Cumberland Rd., Rich. 158 CN80
Cumberland Rd., Stan. 118 CM55
Cumberland St. SW1 277 J10
Cumberland St. SW1 161 DH78
Cumberland St., Stai. 173 BD92
Cumberland Ter. NW1 273 H1
Cumberland Ter. Ms. NW1 273 H1
Cumberland Vill. W3 138 CQ73
Cumberland Rd.
Cumberlands, Ken. 236 DR115
Cumberlow Ave. SE25 202 DT97
Cumberlow Pl., Hem.H. 41 BQ21
Cumbernauld Gdns., Sun. 175 BT92
Cumberton Rd. N17 100 DR53
Cumbrae Gdns., Surb. 197 CJ102
Cumbrian Ave., Bexh. 167 FE81
Cumbrian Gdns. NW2 119 CX61
Cumbrian Way, Uxb. 134 BK66
Chippendale Waye
Cumley Rd., Ong. 71 FE30
Cumming St. N1 274 C1
Cumming St. N1 141 DM68
Cummings Hall La., Rom. 106 FJ48
Cumnor Gdns., Epsom 217 CU107
Cumnor Ri., Ken. 236 DQ117
Cumnor Rd., Sutt. 218 DC107
Cunard Cres. N21 82 DR44
Cunard Pl. EC3 275 N9
Cunard Rd. NW10 138 CR69
Cunard St. SE5 162 DS79
Albany Rd.
Cunard Wk. SE16 163 DX77
Trident St.
Cundalls Rd., Ware 33 DY05
Cundy Rd. E16 144 EJ72
Cundy St. SW1 276 G9
Cundy St. SW1 160 DG77
Cundy St. Est. SW1 276 G9
Cunliffe Clo., Epsom 232 CP124
Cunliffe Rd., Wor.Pk. 217 CT105
Cunliffe St. SW16 181 DJ93
Cunningham Ave., Enf. 83 DY36
Cunningham Ave., Guil. 243 BA133
Cunningham Ave., St.Alb. 43 CF22
Cunningham Clo., Rom. 126 EW57
Chadwell Heath La.
Cunningham Clo., W.Wick. 203 EB103
Cunningham Hill Rd., 43 CF22
St.Alb.
Cunningham Pk., Har. 116 CC57
Cunningham Pl. NW8 140 DD70
Cunningham Ri., Epp. 71 FC25
Cunningham Rd. N15 122 DU56
Cunningham Rd., Bans. 234 DD115
Cunningham Rd. 67 DY27
(Cheshunt), Wal.Cr.
Cunnington St. W4 158 CQ77
Cupar Rd. SW11 161 DH81
Cupola Clo., Brom. 184 EH92
Cureton St. SW1 277 N9
Cureton St. SW1 161 DK77
Curfew Bell Rd., Cher. 193 BF101
Curfew Ho., Bark. 145 EQ67
St. Ann's
Curfew Yd., Wind. 151 AR80
Thames St.
Curlew Clo. SE28 146 EX73
Curlew Clo., Berk. 38 AW20
Curlew Clo., S.Croy. 221 DX111
Curlew Ct., Brox. 49 DZ23
Curlew Ct., Surb. 198 CM104
Curlew Gdns., Guil. 243 BD132
Curlew St. SE1 279 P4
Curlew St. SE1 162 DT75
Curlew Way, Hayes 136 BX71
Curlews, The, Grav. 191 GK89
Curling Clo., Couls. 235 DM120
Curling La., Grays 170 FZ78
Curling Vale, Guil. 258 AU136
Curnick's La. SE27 182 DQ91
Chapel Rd.
Curnock Est. NW1 141 DJ67
Plender St.
Curran Ave., Sid. 185 ET85
Curran Ave., Wall. 200 DG104
Curran Clo., Uxb. 134 BJ70
Currey Rd., Grnf. 136 CC65
Curricle St. W3 138 CS74
Currie Hill Clo. SW19 179 CZ91
Currie St., Hert. 32 DS09
Curries La., Slou. 111 AK64
Curry Ri. NW7 97 CX51
Cursitor St. EC4 274 D8
Cursitor St. EC4 141 DN72
Curtain Pl. EC2 142 DS69
Curtain Rd.
Curtain Rd. EC2 275 N3
Curtain Rd. EC2 142 DS69
Curteys, Harl. 36 EX10
Curthwaite Gdns., Enf. 81 DK42
Curtis Clo., Rick. 92 BG46
Curtis Dr. W3 138 CR72
Curtis Fld. Rd. SW16 181 DM91
Curtis Gdns., Dor. 263 CG135
Curtis La., Wem. 138 CL65
Montrose Cres.
Curtis Mill Grn., Rom. 87 FE42
Curtis Mill La., Rom. 87 FE42
Curtis Rd., Dor. 263 CF135
Curtis Rd., Epsom 216 CQ105
Curtis Rd., Hem.H. 41 BR21
Curtis Rd., Horn. 128 FM60
Curtis Rd., Houns. 176 BY87
Curtis St. SE1 279 P8
Curtis St. SE1 162 DT77
Curtis Way SE1 279 P8
Curtis Way SE1 162 DT77
Curtis Way SE28 146 EV73
Tawney Rd.
Curtis Way, Berk. 38 AX20
Curtismill Clo., Orp. 206 EV97
Curtismill Way, Orp. 206 EV97
Curvan Clo., Epsom 217 CT110
Curve, The W12 139 CU73
Curwen Ave. E7 124 EH63
Woodford Rd.
Curwen Rd. W12 159 CU75
Curzon Ave., Beac. 89 AK51
Curzon Ave., Enf. 83 DX43
Curzon Ave., H.Wyc. 88 AC45
Curzon Ave., Stan. 95 CG53
Curzon Clo., H.Wyc. 88 AC45
Curzon Clo., Orp. 223 ER105
Curzon Clo., Wey. 212 BN105
Curzon Rd.
Curzon Cres. NW10 138 CS66
Curzon Cres., Bark. 145 ET68
Curzon Dr., Grays 170 GC80
Curzon Gate W1 276 G3
Curzon Mall, Slou. 152 AT75
High St.
Curzon Pl. W1 276 G3
Curzon Pl., Pnr. 116 BW57
Curzon Rd. N10 99 DH54
Curzon Rd. W5 137 CH70
Curzon Rd., Th.Hth. 201 DN100
Curzon Rd., Wey. 212 BN105
Curzon St. W1 276 G3
Curzon St. W1 140 DG74
Cusack Clo., Twick. 177 CF91
Waldegrave Rd.
Cussons Clo. (Cheshunt), 66 DU29
Wal.Cr.
Custom Ho. Quay EC3 142 DS73
Lower Thames St.
Custom Ho. Reach SE16 163 DZ75
Odessa St.
Custom Ho. Wk. EC3 142 DS73
Lower Thames St.
Cut, The SE1 278 E4
Cut, The SE1 161 DN75
Cut, The, Slou. 131 AN70
Long Furlong Dr.
Cut Hills, Egh. 192 AU97
Cutcombe Rd. SE5 162 DQ82
Cuthbert Gdns. SE25 202 DS97
Cuthbert Rd. E17 123 EC55
Cuthbert Rd. N18 100 DU50
Fairfield Rd.
Cuthbert Rd., Croy. 201 DP103
Cuthbert St. W2 140 DD70
Cuthberts Clo., Wal.Cr. 66 DT29
Cuthill Wk. SE5 162 DR81
Kerfield Pl.
Cutler St. E1 275 N8
Cutler St. E1 142 DS72
Cutlers Gdns. E1 275 N8
Cutlers Gdns. Arc. EC2 142 DS72
Cutler St.
Cutlers Sq. E14 163 EA77
Britannia Rd.
Cutmore Dr., St.Alb. 44 CP22
Cutmore St., Grav. 191 GH87
Cutthroat All., Rich. 177 CJ89
Ham St.
Cutthroat La., Hodd. 49 DY15
Cutting, The, Red. 266 DF136
Cuttsfield Ter., Hem.H. 39 BF21
Cutty Sark Ct., Green. 189 FU85
Low Clo.
Cuxton Clo., Bexh. 186 EY85
Cwmbran Ct., Hem.H. 40 BM16
Cyclamen Clo., Hmptn. 176 CA93
Gresham Rd.
Cyclamen Rd., Swan. 207 FD98
Cyclamen Way, Epsom 216 CQ106
Cyclops Ms. E14 163 EA77
Cygnet Ave., Felt. 176 BW87
Cygnet Clo. NW10 118 CR64
Cygnet Clo., Borwd. 78 CQ39
Cygnet Clo., Nthwd. 93 BQ52
Cygnet Clo., Wok. 226 AV116
Cygnet Gdns., Grav. 191 GF89
Cygnet St. E1 142 DT70
Sclater St.
Cygnet Vw., Grays 169 FT77
Cygnet Way, Hayes 136 BX71
Cygnets, The, Felt. 176 BY91
Cygnets Clo., Red. 250 DG132
Cymbeline Ct., Har. 117 CF58
Cynthia St. N1 274 C1
Cynthia St. N1 141 DM68
Cyntra Pl. E8 142 DV66
Mare St.
Cypress Ave., Enf. 81 DN35
Cypress Ave., Twick. 176 CC87
Cypress Ave., Welw.G.C. 30 DC10
Cypress Clo., Wal.Abb. 67 ED34
Cypress Gro., Ilf. 103 ES51
Cypress Path, Rom. 106 FK52
Cypress Pl. W1 273 L5
Cypress Rd. SE25 202 DS96
Cypress Rd., Guil. 242 AW132
Cypress Rd., Har. 95 CD54
Cypress Tree Clo., Sid. 185 ET87
Whiteoak Gdns.
Cypress Wk., Egh. 172 AV93
Cypress Wk., Wat. 75 BV35
Cedar Wd. Dr.
Cypress Way, Bans. 217 CX114
Cyprus Ave. N3 97 CY54
Cyprus Clo. N4 121 DP58
Atterbury Rd.
Cyprus Gdns. N3 97 CY54
Cyprus Pl. E2 142 DW68
Cyprus Pl. E6 145 EN73
Cyprus Rd. N3 97 CZ54
Cyprus Rd. N9 100 DT47
Cyprus Roundabout E16 164 EK77
Royal Albert Way
Cyprus St. E2 142 DW68
Cyrena Rd. SE22 182 DT86
Cyril Mans. SW11 160 DF81
Cyril Rd., Bexh. 166 EY82
Cyril Rd., Orp. 206 EU101
Cyrils Way, St.Alb. 43 CD23
Maynard Dr.
Cyrus St. EC1 274 G4
Cyrus St. EC1 141 DP70
Czar St. SE8 163 EA79

D

Dabbling Clo., Erith 167 FH80
Dabbs Hill La., Nthlt. 116 CA64
D'Abernon Clo., Esher 214 CA105
D'Abernon Dr., Cob. 230 BY116
Dabin Cres. SE10 163 EC81
Dacca St. SE8 163 DZ79
Dace Rd. E3 143 EA67
Dacorum Way, Hem.H. 40 BJ20
Dacre Ave., Ilf. 103 EN54
Dacre Ave., S.Ock. 149 FR74
Dacre Clo., Chig. 103 EQ49
Dacre Clo., Grnf. 136 CB68
Dacre Cres., S.Ock. 149 FR74
Dacre Gdns. SE13 164 EE84
Dacre Gdns., Borwd. 78 CR43
Dacre Gdns., Chig. 103 EQ49
Dacre Pk. SE13 164 EE83
Dacre Pl. SE13 164 EE83
Dacre Rd. E11 124 EF60
Dacre Rd. E13 144 EH67
Dacre Rd., Croy. 201 DL101
Dacre St. SW1 277 M6
Dacre St. SW1 161 DK76
Dacres Rd. SE23 183 DX90
Dade Way, Sthl. 156 BZ78
Daerwood Clo., Brom. 205 EM102
Daffodil Ave., Brwd. 108 FV43
Daffodil Clo., Croy. 203 DX102
Primrose La.
Daffodil Gdns., Ilf. 125 EP64
Daffodil Pl., Hmptn. 176 CA93
Gresham Rd.
Daffodil St. W12 139 CT73
Dafforne Rd. SW17 180 DF90
Dagden Rd., Guil. 258 AY140
Dagenham Ave., Dag. 146 EY67
Dagenham Rd. E10 123 DZ60
Dagenham Rd., Dag. 127 FB63
Dagenham Rd., Rain. 147 FD66
Dagenham Rd., Rom. 127 FD59
Dagger La., Borwd. 77 CG44
Daggs Dell Rd., Hem.H. 39 BE18
Dagley Fm. Caravan Pk., 258 AX140
Guil.
Dagley La., Guil. 258 AX141
Dagmar Ave., Wem. 118 CM63
Dagmar Gdns. NW10 139 CX68
Dagmar Pas. N1 141 DP67
Cross St.
Dagmar Rd. N4 121 DN59
Dagmar Rd. N15 122 DR56
Cornwall Rd.
Dagmar Rd. N22 99 DK53
Dagmar Rd. SE5 162 DS81
Dagmar Rd. SE25 202 DS99
Dagmar Rd., Dag. 147 FC66
Dagmar Rd., Kings.T. 198 CM95
Dagmar Rd., Sthl. 156 BY76
Dagmar Rd., Wind. 151 AR82
Dagmar Ter. N1 141 DP67
Dagnall Cres., Uxb. 134 BJ71
Dagnall Pk. SE25 202 DS100
Dagnall Rd. SE25 202 DS99
Dagnall St. SW11 160 DF82
Dagnam Pk. Clo., Rom. 106 FN50
Dagnam Pk. Dr., Rom. 106 FL50
Dagnam Pk. Gdns., Rom. 106 FN51
Dagnam Pk. Sq., Rom. 106 FP51
Dagnan Rd. SW12 181 DH87
Dagonet Gdns., Brom. 184 EG90
Shroffold Rd.
Dagonet Rd., Brom. 184 EG90
Dahlia Dr., Swan. 207 FF96
Dahlia Gdns., Ilf. 145 EP65
Dahlia Gdns., Mitch. 201 DK98
Dahlia Rd. SE2 166 EV77
Dahomey Rd. SW16 181 DJ93
Daiglen Dr., S.Ock. 149 FU72
Daimler Way, Wall. 219 DL108
Daines Clo. E12 125 EM62
Colchester Ave.
Daines Clo., S.Ock. 149 FU70
Dainford Clo., Brom. 183 ED92
Dainton Clo., Brom. 204 EH95
Daintry Clo., Har. 117 CG56
Daintry Lo., Nthwd. 93 BT52
Daintry Way E9 143 DZ65
Eastway
Dairsie Rd. SE9 165 EN83
Dairy Clo. 188 FP94
(Sutton at Hone), Dart.
Dairy Clo., Th.Hth. 202 DQ96
Dairy La. SE18 165 EM77
Rideout St.
Dairy La., Eden. 255 EN134
Dairy Ms. SW9 161 DL83
Dairy Wk. SW19 179 CY91
Dairy Way, Abb.L. 59 BT29
Tithe Barn Ct.
Dairyman's Wk., Guil. 243 BB129
Daisy Clo., Croy. 203 DX102
Primrose La.
Daisy Dobbins Wk. N19 121 DL59
Hillrise Rd.
Daisy La. SW6 160 DA83
Daisy Rd. E16 144 EE70
Cranberry La.
Daisy Rd. E18 102 EH54
Dakota Gdns. E6 144 EL70
Dakota Gdns., Nthlt. 136 BY69
Argus Way
Dalberg Rd. SW2 181 DN85
Dalberg Way SE2 166 EX76
Lanridge Rd.
Dalby Rd. SW18 160 DC84
Dalby St. NW5 141 DH65
Dalcross Rd., Houns. 156 BY82
Dale, The, Kes. 222 EK105
Dale, The, Wal.Abb. 68 EE34
Dale Ave., Edg. 96 CM53
Dale Ave., Houns. 156 BY83
Dale Clo. SE3 164 EG83
Dale Clo., Add. 212 BH106
Dale Clo., Barn. 80 DB44
Dale Clo., Dart. 187 FF86
Dale Clo., Pnr. 93 BV53
Dale Clo., S.Ock. 149 FU72
Dale Ct., Saw. 36 EX06
The Crest
Dale Ct., Slou. 151 AQ75
Tuns La.
Dale Dr., Hayes 135 BT70
Dale End, Dart. 187 FF86
Dale Rd.
Dale Gdns., Wdf.Grn. 102 EH49
Dale Grn. Rd. N11 99 DH48
Dale Gro. N12 98 DC50
Dale Pk. Ave., Cars. 200 DF103
Dale Pk. Rd. SE19 202 DQ95
Dale Rd. NW5 120 DG64
Grafton Rd.
Dale Rd. SE17 161 DP79
Dale Rd., Dart. 187 FF86
Dale Rd., Grav. 190 GA91
Dale Rd., Grnf. 136 CB71
Dale Rd., Pur. 219 DN112
Dale Rd., Sun. 175 BT94
Dale Rd., Sutt. 217 CZ105
Dale Rd., Swan. 207 FC96
Dale Rd., Walt. 195 BT101
Dale Row W11 139 CY72
St. Marks Rd.
Dale Side, Ger.Cr. 112 AY60
Dale St. W4 158 CS78
Dale Vw., Epsom 232 CP123
Dale Vw., Erith 167 FF82
Dale Vw., Wok. 226 AV118
Dale Vw. Ave. E4 101 EC47
Dale Vw. Cres. E4 101 EC47
Dale Vw. Gdns. E4 101 ED48
Dale Wk., Dart. 188 FP88
Princes Ave.
Dale Wd. Rd., Orp. 205 ES101
Dalebury Rd. SW17 180 DE89
Dalegarth Gdns., Pur. 220 DR113
Daleham Ave., Egh. 173 BA93
Daleham Dr., Uxb. 135 BP72
Daleham Gdns. NW3 120 DD64
Daleham Ms. NW3 140 DD65
Dalehead NW1 273 K1
Dalehead NW1 141 DJ68
Dalemain Ms. E16 144 EE72
Silvertown Way
Dales Path, Borwd. 78 CR43
Farriers Way
Dales Rd., Borwd. 78 CR43
Daleside, Orp. 224 EU106
Daleside Clo., Orp. 224 EU107
Daleside Dr., Pot.B. 63 CZ32
Daleside Gdns., Chig. 103 EQ48
Daleside Rd. SW16 181 DH92
Daleside Rd., Epsom 216 CR107
Dalestone Ms., Rom. 105 FH51
Daleview Rd. N15 122 DS58
Dalewood, Welw.G.C. 30 DD10
Dalewood Clo., Horn. 128 FL59
Dalewood Gdns., Wor.Pk. 199 CV103
Daley St. E9 143 DX65
Daley Thompson Way SW8 161 DH83
Dalgarno Gdns. W10 139 CW71
Dalgarno Gdns. Est. W10 139 CW70
Dalgarno Way W10 139 CW70
Dalgleish St. E14 143 DY72
Daling Way E3 143 DY68
Dalkeith Gro., Stan. 95 CK50
Dalkeith Rd. SE21 182 DQ88
Dalkeith Rd., Ilf. 125 EQ62
Dallas Rd. NW4 119 CU59
Dallas Rd. SE26 182 DV91
Dallas Rd. W5 138 CM71
Dallas Rd., Sutt. 217 CY107
Dallas Ter., Hayes 155 BT76
Dallega Clo., Hayes 135 BR73
Dawley Rd.
Dallin Rd. SE18 165 EP80
Dallin Rd., Bexh. 166 EX84
Dalling Rd. W6 159 CV77
Dallinger Rd. SE12 184 EF86
Dallington Clo., Walt. 214 BW107
Dallington St. EC1 274 G4
Dallington St. EC1 141 DP70
Dalmain Rd. SE23 183 DX88
Dalmally Rd., Croy. 202 DT101
Dalmeny Ave. N7 121 DK63
Dalmeny Ave. SW16 201 DN96
Dalmeny Clo., Wem. 137 CJ65
Dalmeny Cres., Houns. 157 CD84
Dalmeny Rd. N7 121 DK62
Dalmeny Rd., Barn. 80 DC44
Dalmeny Rd., Cars. 218 DG108
Dalmeny Rd., Erith 167 FB81
Dalmeny Rd., Wor.Pk. 199 CV104
Dalmeyer Rd. NW10 139 CT65
Dalmore Ave., Esher 215 CF107
Dalmore Rd. SE21 182 DQ89
Dalroy Clo., S.Ock. 149 FU72
Dalrymple Clo. N14 99 DK45
Dalrymple Rd. SE4 163 DY84
Dalston Cross Shop. Cen. 142 DT65
E8
Kingsland High St.
Dalston Gdns., Stan. 96 CL53
Dalston La. E8 142 DT65
Dalton Ave., Mitch. 200 DE96
Dalton Clo., Hayes 135 BR70
Dalton Clo., Orp. 205 ES104
Dalton Clo., Pur. 220 DQ112
Dalton Rd., Har. 95 CD54
Athelstone Rd.
Dalton St. SE27 181 DP89
Dalton St., St.Alb. 43 CD19
Daltons Rd., Orp. 225 FB105
Daltons Rd., Swan. 207 FC102
Dalwood St. SE5 162 DS81
Daly Ct. E15 123 EC64
Clays La.
Dalyell Rd. SW9 161 DM83
Damascene Wk. SE21 182 DQ88
Lovelace Rd.
Damask Cres. E16 144 EE70
Cranberry La.
Damask Grn., Hem.H. 39 BE21
Dame St. N1 142 DQ68
Damer Ter. SW10 160 DC80
Tadema Rd.
Dames Rd. E7 124 EG62
Dameswick Vw., St.Alb. 60 CA27
Damien St. E1 142 DV72
Damigos Rd., Grav. 191 GM88
Damon Clo., Sid. 186 EV90
Damphurst La., Dor. 262 BZ139
Sheephouse La.
Damson Ct., Swan. 207 FD98
Damson Gro., Slou. 151 AQ75
Damson Way, Cars. 218 DF110
Damsonwood Clo., Sthl. 156 CA76
Dan Leno Wk. SW6 160 DB80
Britannia Rd.
Danbrook Rd. SW16 201 DL95
Danbury Clo., Brwd. 108 FT43
Danbury Clo., Rom. 126 EX55
Danbury Ms., Wall. 219 DH105
Danbury Rd., Loug. 102 EL45
Danbury Rd., Rain. 147 FF67
Danbury St. N1 141 DP68
Danbury Way, Wdf.Grn. 102 EJ51
Danby St. SE15 162 DT83
Dancer Rd. SW6 159 CZ81
Dancer Rd., Rich. 158 CN83
Dancers Hill Rd., Barn. 79 CW36
Dancers La., Barn. 79 CW35
Dando Cres. SE3 164 EH83
Dandridge Clo. SE10 164 EF78
Dandridge Clo., Slou. 152 AX77
Dandridge Dr., B.End 110 AC60
Millside
Dane Clo., Amer. 72 AT41
Dane Clo., Bex. 186 FA87
Dane Clo., Orp. 223 ER106
Dane Ct., Hert. 32 DS09
Dane Ct., Wok. 227 BF115
Dane Pl. E3 143 DY68
Roman Rd.
Dane Rd. N18 100 DW49
Dane Rd. SW19 200 DC95
Dane Rd. W13 137 CJ74
Dane Rd., Ashf. 175 BQ93
Dane Rd., Ilf. 125 EQ64
Dane Rd., Sev. 241 FE117
Dane Rd., Sthl. 136 BY73
Dane Rd., Warl. 237 DX117
Dane St. WC1 274 B7
Danebury, Croy. 221 EB107
Danebury Ave. SW15 178 CS86
Daneby Rd. SE6 183 EB90
Danecourt Gdns., Croy. 202 DT104
Danecroft Rd. SE24 182 DQ85
Danehill Wk., Sid. 186 EU90
Hatherley Rd.
Danehurst Gdns., Ilf. 124 EL57
Danehurst St. SW6 159 CY81
Daneland, Barn. 80 DF43
Danemead, Hodd. 33 EA14
Danemead Gro., Nthlt. 116 CB64
Danemere St. SW15 159 CW83
Danes, The, St.Alb. 60 CC28
Danes Clo., Grav. 190 GC90
Danes Clo., Lthd. 214 CC114
Danes Ct., Wem. 118 CP62
Danes Gate, Har. 117 CE55
Danes Hill, Wok. 227 BA118
Danes Rd., Rom. 127 FC59
Danes Way, Brwd. 108 FU43
Danes Way, Lthd. 215 CD114
Danesbury Pk., Hert. 32 DR08
Danesbury Rd., Felt. 175 BV88
Danescombe SE12 184 EG88
Winn Rd.
Danescourt Cres., Sutt. 200 DC103
Danescroft NW4 119 CX57
Danescroft Ave. NW4 119 CX57
Danescroft Gdns. NW4 119 CX57
Danesdale Rd. E9 143 DY65
Danesfield SE5 162 DS79
Albany Rd.
Daneshill, Red. 250 DE133
Daneshill Clo., Red. 250 DE133
Danesrood, Guil. 259 AZ135
Lower Edgeborough Rd.
Daneswood Ave. SE6 183 EC90
Daneswood Clo., Wey. 213 BP106
Danethorpe Rd., Wem. 137 CK65
Danetree Clo., Epsom 216 CQ108
Danetree Rd., Epsom 216 CQ108
Danette Gdns., Dag. 126 EZ61
Daneville Rd. SE5 162 DR81
Dangan Rd. E11 124 EG58
Daniel Bolt Clo. E14 143 EB71
Uamvar St.
Daniel Clo. N18 100 DW49
Daniel Clo. SW17 180 DE93
Daniel Clo., Grays 171 GH76
Daniel Clo. 170 FY75
(Chafford Hundred), Grays
Daniel Gdns. SE15 162 DT80
Daniel Pl. NW4 119 CV58
Daniel Rd. W5 138 CM73
Daniel Way, Bans. 218 DB114
Daniell Way, Croy. 201 DM102
Daniells, Welw.G.C. 30 DA08
Daniels La., Warl. 237 DZ116
Daniels Ms. SE4 163 DZ84
Daniels Rd. SE15 162 DW83
Danley Rd., Grays 170 GB79
Derby Rd.
Danses Clo., Guil. 243 BD132
Dansey Pl. W1 273 M10
Dansington Rd., Well. 166 EU84
Danson Cres., Well. 166 EV83
Danson La., Well. 166 EU84
Danson Mead, Well. 166 EW83
Danson Pk., Bexh. 166 EW84
Danson Rd., Bex. 186 EX85
Danson Rd., Bexh. 186 EX85
Dante Pl. SE11 278 G9
Dante Rd. SE11 278 F8
Dante Rd. SE11 161 DP77
Danube St. SW3 276 C10
Danvers Rd. N8 121 DK56
Danvers St. SW3 160 DD79
Danvers Way, Cat. 236 DQ121
Coulsdon Rd.
Danyon Clo., Rain. 148 FJ68
Danziger Way, Borwd. 78 CQ39
Dapdune Ct., Guil. 242 AW134
Dapdune Rd., Guil. 242 AX134
Dapdune Wf., Guil. 242 AW134
Daphne Gdns. E4 101 EC48
Gunners Gro.

Daphne St. SW18 180 DC86
Daplyn St. E1 142 DU71
Hanbury St.
D'Arblay St. W1 273 L9
D'Arblay St. W1 141 DJ72
Darby Clo., Cat. 236 DQ122
Fairbourne La.
Darby Cres., Sun. 196 BW96
Darby Dr., Wal.Abb. 67 EC33
Darby Gdns., Sun. 196 BW96
Darcy Ave., Wall. 219 DJ105
Darcy Clo. N20 98 DD47
D'Arcy Clo., Brwd. 109 GB45
Darcy Clo., Couls. 235 DP119
Darcy Clo. (Cheshunt), Wal.Cr. 67 DY31
D'Arcy Dr., Har. 117 CK56
Darcy Gdns., Dag. 146 EZ67
D'Arcy Gdns., Har. 118 CL56
D'Arcy Pl., Ash. 232 CM117
Darcy Rd. SW16 201 DL96
D'Arcy Rd., Ash. 232 CM117
Darcy Rd., Islw. 157 CG81
London Rd.
D'Arcy Rd., Sutt. 217 CX105
Dare Gdns., Dag. 126 EY62
Grafton Rd.
Darell Rd., Rich. 158 CN83
Darent Mead (Sutton at Hone), Dart. 208 FP95
Darent Valley Path, Dart. 188 FM89
Darent Valley Path, Sev. 256 FC121
Darenth Clo., Sev. 256 FC122
Darenth Gdns., West. 255 ER126
Quebec Ave.
Darenth Hill, Dart. 188 FP92
Darenth La., Sev. 256 FE121
Darenth La., S.Ock. 149 FU72
Darenth Rd. N16 122 DT59
Darenth Rd., Dart. 188 FM87
Darenth Rd. (Darenth), Dart. 188 FP91
Darenth Rd., Well. 166 EU81
Darenth Way, Horl. 268 DF145
Darenth Way, Sev. 225 FG111
Darenth Wd. Rd., Dart. 189 FS90
Darfield Rd. SE4 183 DZ85
Darfield Rd., Guil. 243 BA131
Darfield Way W10 139 CX72
Darfur St. SW15 159 CX83
Dargate Clo. SE19 182 DT94
Chipstead Clo.
Darien Rd. SW11 160 DD83
Dark La., Brwd. 108 FT50
Dark La., Guil. 260 BM139
Dark La. (Cheshunt), Wal.Cr. 66 DU31
Dark La., Ware 33 DY05
Darkes La., Pot.B. 63 CZ32
Darkhole Ride, Wind. 150 AG84
Darlan Rd. SW6 159 CZ80
Darlaston Rd. SW19 179 CX94
Darley Clo., Add. 212 BJ106
Darley Clo., Croy. 203 DY100
Darley Dr., N.Mal. 198 CR96
Darley Gdns., Mord. 200 DC100
Darley Rd. N9 100 DT46
Darley Rd. SW11 180 DF86
Darling Rd. SE4 163 EA83
Darling Row E1 142 DV70
Darlington Clo., Amer. 55 AR38
King George V Rd.
Darlington Gdns., Rom. 106 FK50
Darlington Path, Rom. 106 FK50
Darlington Gdns.
Darlington Rd. SE27 181 DP92
Darlton Clo., Dart. 167 FF83
Darmaine Clo., S.Croy. 220 DQ108
Churchill Rd.
Darndale Clo. E17 101 DZ54
Darnets Fld., Sev. 241 FF117
Darnhills, Rad. 77 CF35
Darnicle Hill (Cheshunt), Wal.Cr. 65 DM25
Darnley Ho. E14 143 DY72
Camdenhurst St.
Darnley Pk., Wey. 195 BP104
Darnley Rd. E9 142 DW65
Darnley Rd., Grav. 191 GG88
Darnley Rd., Grays 170 GB79
Stanley Rd.
Darnley Rd., Wdf.Grn. 102 EG53
Darnley St., Grav. 191 GG87
Darnley Ter. W11 139 CY74
St. James Gdns.
Darns Hill, Swan. 207 FC101
Darrell Clo., Slou. 153 AZ77
Darrell Rd. SE22 182 DU85
Darren Clo. N4 121 DM59
Darrick Wd. Rd., Orp. 205 ER103
Darrington Rd., Borwd. 78 CL39
Darris Clo., Hayes 136 BY70
Darrs La., Berk. 38 AS17
Darsley Dr. SW8 161 DL81
Dart, The, Hem.H. 40 BN15
Dart Clo., Slou. 153 BB79
Dart Clo., Upmin. 129 FR58
Dart Grn., S.Ock. 149 FV72
Dart St. W10 139 CY69
Dartfields, Rom. 106 FK51
Dartford Ave. N9 82 DW44
Dartford Bypass, Dart. 188 FJ90
Dartford Ind. Trd. Est., Dart. 188 FM89
Dartford Rd., Bex. 187 FC88
Dartford Rd., Dart. 187 FG86
Dartford Rd. (Farningham), Dart. 208 FM100
Dartford Rd. (Wilmington), Dart. 187 FH93
Dartford Rd., Sev. 257 FJ124
Dartford St. SE17 162 DQ79
Dartford Tunnel, Dart. 169 FR82
Dartford Tunnel, Grays 169 FR82
Dartford Tunnel App., Grays 169 FR82
Dartford Tunnel App. Rd., Dart. 188 FP86
Dartmoor Wk. E14 163 EA77
Charnwood Gdns.
Dartmouth Ave., Wok. 211 BC114
Dartmouth Clo. W11 140 DA72
Dartmouth Grn., Wok. 211 BD114
St. Michael's Rd.
Dartmouth Gro. SE10 163 EC81
Dartmouth Hill SE10 163 EC81
Dartmouth Pk. Ave. NW5 121 DH62
Dartmouth Pk. Hill N19 121 DH60
Dartmouth Pk. Hill NW5 121 DJ62
Dartmouth Pk. Rd. NW5 121 DH63
Dartmouth Path, Wok. 211 BD114
Dartmouth Ave.
Dartmouth Pl. SE23 182 DW89
Dartmouth Rd.
Dartmouth Pl. W4 158 CS79
Dartmouth Rd. E16 144 EG72
Fords Pk. Rd.
Dartmouth Rd. NW2 139 CX65
Dartmouth Rd. NW4 119 CU58
Dartmouth Rd. SE23 182 DW89
Dartmouth Rd. SE26 182 DV90
Dartmouth Rd., Brom. 204 EG101
Dartmouth Rd., Ruis. 115 BU62
Dartmouth Row SE10 163 EC81
Dartmouth St. SW1 277 N5
Dartmouth St. SW1 161 DK75
Dartmouth Ter. SE10 163 ED81
Dartnell Ave., W.Byf. 212 BH112
Dartnell Clo., W.Byf. 212 BH112
Dartnell Ct., W.Byf. 212 BJ112
Dartnell Cres., W.Byf. 212 BH112
Dartnell Keep, W.Byf. 212 BH112
Dartnell Pk. Rd., W.Byf. 212 BH112
Dartnell Pl., W.Byf. 212 BH112
Dartnell Rd., Croy. 202 DT101
Dartrey Wk. SW10 160 DD80
World's End Est.
Dartview Clo., Grays 170 GE77
Darvel Clo., Wok. 226 AU116
Darvell Dr., Chesh. 54 AN29
Darville Rd. N16 122 DT62
Darvills La., Slou. 151 AR75
Darwell Clo. E6 145 EN68
Darwin Clo. N11 99 DH48
Darwin Clo., Orp. 223 ER106
Darwin Clo., St.Alb. 43 CE16
Darwin Dr., Sthl. 136 CB72
Darwin Gdns., Wat. 94 BW50
Darwin Rd. N22 99 DP53
Darwin Rd. W5 157 CJ78
Darwin Rd., Slou. 153 AZ75
Darwin Rd., Til. 171 GF81
Darwin Rd., Well. 165 ET83
Darwin St. SE17 279 L8
Darwin St. SE17 162 DR77
Daryngton Dr., Grnf. 137 CD68
Daryngton Dr., Guil. 243 BB134
Dashes, The, Harl. 35 ES14
Dashwood Clo., Bexh. 186 FA85
Dashwood Clo., Slou. 152 AW77
Dashwood Clo., W.Byf. 212 BJ112
Dashwood Rd. N8 121 DM58
Dashwood Rd., Grav. 191 GG89
Dassett Rd. SE27 181 DP92
Datchelor Pl. SE5 162 DR81
Datchet Clo., Hem.H. 41 BP15
Datchet Pl., Slou. 152 AV81
Datchet Rd. SE6 183 DZ90
Datchet Rd., Slou. 152 AT77
Datchet Rd. (Horton), Slou. 153 AZ83
Datchet Rd., Wind. 151 AR80
Datchet Rd. (Old Windsor), Wind. 152 AU84
Datchworth Ct. N4 122 DQ62
Queens Dr.
Datchworth Turn, Hem.H. 41 BQ20
Date St. SE17 162 DQ78
Daubeney Gdns. N17 100 DQ52
Daubeney Rd. E5 123 DY63
Daubeney Rd. N17 100 DQ52
Daubeney Twr. SE8 163 DZ77
Dault Rd. SW18 180 DC86
Davema Clo., Chis. 205 EN95
Davenant Rd. N19 121 DK61
Davenant Rd., Croy. 219 DP105
Duppas Hill Rd.
Davenant St. E1 142 DU71
Davenham Ave., Nthwd. 93 BT49
Davenport Clo., Tedd. 177 CG93
Davenport Rd. SE6 183 EC86
Davenport Rd., Sid. 186 EX89
Daventer Dr., Stan. 95 CF52
Daventry Ave. E17 123 EA57
Daventry Clo., Slou. 153 BF81
Daventry Gdns., Rom. 106 FJ50
Daventry Grn., Rom. 106 FJ50
Hailsham Rd.
Daventry Rd., Rom. 106 FJ50
Daventry St. NW1 272 B6
Daventry St. NW1 140 DE71
Davern Clo. SE10 164 EF77
Davey Clo. N7 141 DM65
Davey Rd. E9 143 EA66
Davey St. SE15 162 DT79
David Ave., Grnf. 137 CE69
David Clo., Hayes 155 BR80
David Dr., Rom. 106 FN51
David Ms. W1 272 F6
David Rd., Dag. 126 EY61
David Rd., Slou. 153 BF82
David St. E15 143 ED65
Davidge St. SE1 278 G5
Davidge St. SE1 161 DP75
Davids Rd. SE23 182 DW88
David's Way, Ilf. 103 ES52
Davidson Gdns. SW8 161 DL80
Davidson La., Har. 117 CF59
Grove Hill
Davidson Rd., Croy. 202 DS102
Davidson Way, Rom. 127 FE58
Davies Clo., Croy. 202 DT100
Davies Clo., Rain. 148 FJ69
Davies La. E11 124 EE61
Davies Ms. W1 273 H10
Davies St. W1 273 H10
Davies St. W1 141 DH73
Davies St., Hert. 32 DS09
Davies Way, H.Wyc. 88 AC54
Davington Gdns., Dag. 126 EV64
Davington Rd., Dag. 146 EV65
Davinia Clo., Wdf.Grn. 103 EM51
Deacon Way
Davis Ave., Grav. 190 GE88
Davis Clo., Sev. 257 FJ122
Davis Rd. W3 139 CT74
Davis Rd., Chess. 216 CN105
Davis Rd., Grays 170 FZ76
Davis Rd., S.Ock. 149 FR74
Davis Rd., Wey. 212 BM110
Davis St. E13 144 EH68
Davison Clo., Wal.Cr. 67 DX28
Davison Dr. (Cheshunt), Wal.Cr. 67 DX28
Davisville Rd. W12 159 CU75
Davos Clo., Wok. 226 AY119
Davys Clo., St.Alb. 28 CL08
Davys Pl., Grav. 191 GL93
Dawell Dr., West. 238 EJ117
Dawes Ave., Horn. 128 FK62
Dawes Ave., Islw. 177 CG85
Dawes Clo., Chesh. 54 AP32
Dawes Clo., Green. 189 FT85
Dawes Ct., Esher 214 CB105
Dawes E. Rd., Slou. 130 AJ70
Dawes Ho. SE17 279 K9
Dawes La., Rick. 73 BE37
Dawes Moor Clo., Slou. 132 AW72
Dawes Rd. SW6 159 CY80
Dawes Rd., Uxb. 134 BL68
Dawes St. SE17 279 L10
Dawes St. SE17 162 DR78
Dawley, Welw.G.C. 29 CZ06
Dawley Ave., Uxb. 135 BQ72
Dawley Ct., Hem.H. 40 BN16
Dawley Grn., S.Ock. 149 FU72
Dawley Par., Hayes 135 BQ73
Dawley Rd.
Dawley Ride, Slou. 153 BE81
Dawley Rd., Hayes 135 BQ73
Dawlish Ave. N13 99 DL49
Dawlish Ave. SW18 180 DB89
Dawlish Ave., Grnf. 137 CG68
Dawlish Dr., Ilf. 125 ES63
Dawlish Dr., Pnr. 116 BY57
Dawlish Dr., Ruis. 115 BU61
Dawlish Rd. E10 123 EC60
Dawlish Rd. N17 122 DU55
Dawlish Rd. NW2 139 CX65
Dawlish Wk., Rom. 106 FJ53
Neave Cres.
Dawn Clo., Houns. 156 BY83
Dawn Redwood Clo., Slou. 153 BA83
Dawnay Gdns. SW18 180 DD89
Dawnay Rd. SW18 180 DC89
Dawnay Rd., Lthd. 246 CB126
Dawpool Rd. NW2 119 CT61
Daws Hill E4 83 EC40
Daws La. NW7 97 CT50
Dawson Ave., Bark. 145 ET66
Dawson Ave., Orp. 206 EV96
Dawson Clo. SE18 165 EQ77
Dawson Clo., Hayes 135 BR71
Dawson Clo., Wind. 151 AN82
Dawson Dr., Rain. 147 FH66
Dawson Dr., Swan. 187 FE93
Dawson Gdns., Bark. 145 ET66
Dawson Ave.
Dawson Heights Est. SE22 182 DU87
Dawson Pl. W2 140 DA73
Dawson Rd. NW2 119 CW64
Dawson Rd., Kings.T. 198 CM97
Dawson Rd., W.Byf. 212 BK111
Dawson St. E2 142 DT68
Dax Ct., Sun. 196 BW97
Thames St.
Day Spring, Guil. 242 AV130
Daybrook Rd. SW19 200 DB96
Daye Mead, Welw.G.C. 30 DB12
Daylesford Ave. SW15 159 CU84
Daylop Dr., Chig. 104 EV48
Daymer Gdns., Pnr. 115 BV56
Daymerslea Ridge, Lthd. 231 CJ121
Days Acre, S.Croy. 220 DT110
Days Clo., Hat. 45 CT18
Days La., Brwd. 108 FU42
Days La., Sid. 185 ES87
Days Mead, Hat. 45 CT18
Daysbrook Rd. SW2 181 DM89
Dayseys Hill, Red. 267 DN143
Dayton Dr., Erith 168 FK78
Dayton Gro. SE15 162 DW81
De Barowe Ms. N5 121 DP63
Leigh Rd.
De Beauvoir Cres. N1 142 DS67
De Beauvoir Est. N1 142 DR67
De Beauvoir Rd. N1 142 DS67
De Beauvoir Sq. N1 142 DS66
De Bohun Ave. N14 81 DH44
De Brome Rd., Felt. 176 BW88
De Burgh Pk., Bans. 234 DB115
De Crespigny Pk. SE5 162 DR82
De Frene Rd. SE26 183 DX91
De Havilland Ave., Hat. 44 CS17
De Havilland Clo., Hat. 45 CT17
De Havilland Ct., Rad. 62 CL32
Armstrong Gdns.
De Havilland Dr., Wey. 212 BL111
De Havilland Rd., Edg. 96 CN54
De Havilland Rd., Houns. 156 BW80
De Havilland Rd., Wall. 219 DL108
De Havilland Way, Abb.L. 59 BT32
De Havilland Way, Stai. 174 BK86
De Lapre Clo., Orp. 206 EX101
De Lara Way, Wok. 226 AX118
De Laune St. SE17 161 DP78
De Luci Rd., Erith 167 FC78
De Lucy St. SE2 166 EV77
De Mandeville Gate, Enf. 82 DU42
Southbury Rd.
De Montfort Rd. SW16 181 DL90
De Morgan Rd. SW6 160 DB83
De Quincey Ms. E16 144 EE72
Silvertown Way
De Quincey Rd. N17 100 DR53
De Ros Pl., Egh. 173 BA93
De Salis Rd., Uxb. 135 BQ70
De Tany Ct., St.Alb. 43 CD21
De Vere Cotts. W8 160 DC76
Canning Pl.
De Vere Gdns. W8 160 DC75
De Vere Gdns., Ilf. 125 EM61
De Vere Ms. W8 160 DC76
Canning Pl.
De Vere Wk., Wat. 75 BS40
De Walden St. W1 272 G7
Deacon Clo., Cob. 229 BV119
Deacon Clo., Pur. 219 DL109
Deacon Clo., St.Alb. 43 CD24
Creighton Ave.
Deacon Fld., Guil. 242 AV133
Midleton Rd.
Deacon Ms. N1 142 DR66
Deacon Pl., Cat. 236 DQ121
Coulsdon Rd.
Deacon Rd. NW2 119 CU64
Deacon Rd., Kings.T. 198 CM95
Deacon Way SE17 279 H8
Deacon Way SE17 162 DQ77
Deacon Way, Wdf.Grn. 103 EM52
Deacons Clo., Borwd. 78 CN42
Deacons Clo., Pnr. 93 BV54
Deacons Hill, Wat. 76 BW44
Deacon's Hill Rd., Borwd. 78 CM42
Deacons Leas, Orp. 223 ER105
Deacons Wk., Hmptn. 176 BZ91
Bishops Gro.
Deaconsfield Rd., Hem.H. 40 BK23
Deadfield La., Hert. 30 DF13
Deadhearn La., Ch.St.G. 90 AY46
Deadman's Ash La., Rick. 74 BH36
Deakin Clo., Wat. 93 BS45
Chenies Way
Deal Ave., Slou. 131 AM72
Deal Porters Way SE16 162 DW76
Deal Rd. SW17 180 DG93
Deal St. E1 142 DU71
Deal's Gateway SE10 163 EB81
Blackheath Rd.
Dealtry Rd. SW15 159 CW84
Dean Ave., Hodd. 49 DX17
Dean Bradley St. SW1 277 P7
Dean Bradley St. SW1 161 DL76
Dean Clo. E9 122 DW64
Churchill Wk.
Dean Clo. SE16 143 DX74
Surrey Water Rd.
Dean Clo., Uxb. 134 BM66
Dean Clo., Wind. 151 AK83
Dean Clo., Wok. 227 BE115
Dean Ct., Wem. 117 CH62
Dean Dr., Stan. 96 CL54
Dean Farrar St. SW1 277 N6
Dean Farrar St. SW1 161 DK76
Dean Fld., Hem.H. 57 BA27
Dean Gdns. E17 123 ED56
Dean Gdns. W13 137 CH74
Northfield Ave.
Dean La., Red. 235 DH123
Dean Oak La., Reig. 265 CW144
Dean Rd. NW2 139 CW65
Dean Rd., Croy. 220 DR105
Dean Rd., Hmptn. 176 BZ92
Dean Rd., Houns. 176 CB85
Dean Ryle St. SW1 277 P8
Dean Ryle St. SW1 161 DL77
Dean Stanley St. SW1 277 P7
Dean Stanley St. SW1 161 DL76
Dean St. E7 124 EG64
Dean St. W1 273 M8
Dean St. W1 141 DK72
Dean Trench St. SW1 277 P7
Dean Wk., Edg. 96 CQ51
Deansbrook Rd.
Dean Wk., Lthd. 246 CB126
Dean Way, Ch.St.G. 90 AU48
Dean Way, Sthl. 156 CB75
Dean Wd. Rd., Beac. 89 AR52
Deanacre Clo., Ger.Cr. 90 AY51
Deancroft Rd., Ger.Cr. 90 AY51
Deancross St. E1 142 DW72
Deane Ave., Ruis. 115 BV64
Deane Cft. Rd., Pnr. 116 BW58
Deane Way, Ruis. 115 BV58
Deanery Clo. N2 120 DE56
Deanery Ms. W1 276 G2
Deanery Rd. E15 144 EE65
Deanery Rd., Eden. 255 EQ134
Deanery St. W1 276 G2
Deanery St. W1 140 DG74
Deanhill Rd. SW14 158 CP84
Deans Bldgs. SE17 279 L9
Deans Bldgs. SE17 162 DR77
Deans Clo. W4 158 CP79
Deans Clo., Abb.L. 59 BR32
Deans Clo., Amer. 72 AT37
Park Rd.
Dean's Clo., Croy. 202 DT104
Deans Clo., Edg. 96 CQ51
Deans Clo., Slou. 132 AV67
Deans Clo., Tad. 233 CV124
Deans La.
Deans Ct. EC4 274 G9
Deans Dr. N13 99 DP51
Deans Dr., Edg. 96 CR50
Deans Gdns., St.Alb. 43 CG16
Dean's Gate Clo. SE23 183 DX90
Deans La., Edg. 96 CQ51
Deans La., Red. 251 DN133
Deans La., Tad. 233 CV124
Deans Ms. W1 273 J8
Dean's Pl. SW1 277 M10
Dean's Pl. SW1 161 DK78
Deans Rd. W7 137 CF74
Deans Rd., Brwd. 108 FV48
Deans Rd., Red. 251 DJ130
Deans Rd., Sutt. 200 DB104
Deans Wk., Couls. 235 DN118
Deans Way, Edg. 96 CQ50
Dean's Yd. SW1 277 N6
Deansbrook Clo., Edg. 96 CQ51
Deansbrook Rd., Edg. 96 CP52
Deanscroft Ave. NW9 118 CQ61
Deansfield, Cat. 252 DT125
Deansway N2 120 DD56
Deansway N9 100 DS48
Deansway, Chesh. 54 AP29
Deansway, Hem.H. 40 BM23
Dearn Gdns., Mitch. 200 DE97
Dearne Clo., Stan. 95 CG50
Dearsley Ho., Rain. 147 FD68
Dearsley Rd., Enf. 82 DV41
Baird Rd.
Deason St. E15 143 EC67
High St.
Debden Clo., Kings.T. 177 CK92
Debden Clo., Wdf.Grn. 102 EK52
Debden Ind. Group, Loug. 85 ER42
Debden La., Loug. 85 EP38
Debden Rd., Loug. 85 EP38
Debden Wk., Horn. 147 FH65
Tangmere Cres.
Debenham Rd. (Cheshunt), Wal.Cr. 66 DV27
Debnams Rd. SE16 162 DW77
Rotherhithe New Rd.
Deborah Clo., Islw. 157 CE81
Deborah Cres., Ruis. 115 BR59
Debrabant Clo., Erith 167 FD79
Deburgh Rd. SW19 180 DC94
Decies Way, Slou. 132 AU67
Decima St. SE1 279 M6
Decima St. SE1 162 DS76
Deck Clo. SE16 163 DX75
Thame Rd.
Decoy Ave. NW11 119 CY57
Dedswell Dr., Guil. 244 BG129
Dedworth Dr., Wind. 151 AM81
Dedworth Rd., Wind. 150 AJ82
Dee, The, Hem.H. 40 BM15
Dee Clo., Upmin. 129 FS58
Dee Rd., Rich. 158 CM84
Dee St. E14 143 EC72
Dee Way, Epsom 216 CS110
Dee Way, Rom. 105 FE52
Deeley Rd. SW8 161 DK81
Deena Clo. W3 138 CM72
Deena Clo., Slou. 131 AL73
Deep Acres, Amer. 55 AN36
Deep Fld., Slou. 152 AV80
Deep Pool La., Wok. 210 AV114
Deepdale SW19 179 CX91
Deepdale Ave., Brom. 204 EF98
Deepdene W5 138 CM70
Deepdene, Pot.B. 63 CX31
Deepdene Ave., Croy. 202 DT104
Deepdene Ave., Dor. 263 CH139
Deepdene Ave. Rd., Dor. 247 CJ134
Deepdene Clo. E11 124 EG56
Deepdene Ct. N21 81 DP44
Deepdene Dr., Dor. 263 CJ135
Deepdene Gdns. SW2 181 DM87
Deepdene Gdns., Dor. 263 CH135
Deepdene Pk. Rd., Dor. 263 CJ135
Deepdene Path, Loug. 85 EN42
Deepdene Rd. SE5 162 DR84
Deepdene Rd., Loug. 85 EN42
Deepdene Rd., Well. 166 EU83
Deepdene Vale, Dor. 263 CJ135
Deepdene Wd., Dor. 263 CJ136
Deepfield Way, Couls. 235 DL116
Deepfields, Horl. 268 DF146
Deepwell Clo., Islw. 157 CG81
Deepwood La., Grnf. 137 CD69
Cowgate Rd.
Deer Pk., Harl. 51 EN18
Deer Pk. Clo., Kings.T. 178 CP94
Deer Pk. Gdns., Mitch. 200 DD97
Deer Pk. Rd. SW19 200 DB96
Deer Pk. Wk., Chesh. 54 AS28
Deer Pk. Way, W.Wick. 204 EE103
Deerbarn Rd., Guil. 242 AV133
Deerbrook Rd. SE24 181 DP88
Deerdale Rd. SE24 162 DQ84
Deere Ave., Rain. 147 FG65
Deerfield Clo., Ware 33 DX05
Deerhurst Clo., Felt. 175 BU91
Deerhurst Cres., Hmptn. 176 CC92
Deerhurst Rd. NW2 139 CX65
Deerhurst Rd. SW16 181 DM92
Deerings Dr., Pnr. 115 BU57
Deerings Rd., Reig. 250 DB134
Deerleap Gro. E4 83 EB43
Deerleap La., Sev. 224 EX113
Deerleap Rd., Dor. 262 CB137
Deers Fm. Clo., Wok. 228 BL116
Deerswood Ave., Hat. 45 CV20
Deerswood Clo., Cat. 236 DU124
Deeside Rd. SW17 180 DD90
Deeves Hall La., Pot.B. 62 CS32
Defiance Wk. SE18 165 EM76
Antelope Rd.
Defiant Way, Wall. 219 DL108
Defoe Ave., Rich. 158 CN80
Defoe Clo. SE16 163 DZ75
Vaughan St.
Defoe Clo. SW17 180 DE93
Defoe Clo., Erith 167 FE81
Selkirk Dr.
Defoe Ho. EC2 142 DQ71
Beech St.
Defoe Par., Grays 171 GH76
Defoe Rd. N16 122 DS61
Defoe Way, Rom. 104 FA51
Degema Rd., Chis. 185 EP92
Dehar Cres. NW9 119 CT59
Deimos Dr., Hem.H. 40 BN17
Dekker Rd. SE21 182 DS86
Delabole Rd., Red. 251 DL129
Delacourt Rd. SE3 164 EH80
Old Dover Rd.
Delafield Rd. SE7 164 EH78
Delafield Rd., Grays 170 GD78
Delaford Clo., Iver 134 BG72
Delaford Rd. SE16 162 DV78
Delaford St. SW6 159 CY80
Delagarde Rd., West. 255 EQ126
Delahay Ri., Berk. 38 AV17
Delamare Rd. (Cheshunt), Wal.Cr. 67 DY30
Delamere Cres., Croy. 202 DW100
Delamere Gdns. NW7 96 CR51
Delamere Rd. SW20 199 CX95
Delamere Rd. W5 138 CL74
Delamere Rd., Borwd. 78 CP39
Delamere Rd., Hayes 136 BX73
Delamere Rd., Reig. 266 DB138
Delamere Ter. W2 140 DB71
Delancey Pas. NW1 141 DH67
Delancey St.
Delancey St. NW1 141 DH67
Delaporte, Epsom 216 CS112
Delargy Clo., Grays 171 GH76
Delaware Rd. W9 140 DB70
Delawyk Cres. SE24 182 DQ86
Delcombe Ave., Wor.Pk. 199 CW102
Delderfield, Lthd. 231 CK120
Delfcroft, Ware 32 DW05
Delft Way SE22 182 DS85
East Dulwich Gro.
Delhi Rd., Enf. 100 DT45
Delhi St. N1 141 DL67
Delia St. SW18 180 DB87
Delius Clo., Borwd. 77 CJ44
Delius Gro. E15 143 EC68
Dell, The SE2 166 EU78
Dell, The SE19 202 DT95
Dell, The, Bex. 187 FE88
Dell, The, Brent. 157 CJ79
Dell, The, Brwd. 107 FV51
Dell, The, Felt. 175 BV87
Harlington Rd. W.
Dell, The, Ger.Cr. 90 AY51

Diceland Rd., Bans. 233 CZ116
Dicey Ave. NW2 119 CW63
Dick Turpin Way, Felt. 155 BT84
Dickens Ave. N3 98 DC53
Dickens Ave., Dart. 168 FN84
Dickens Ave., Til. 171 GH81
Dickens Ave., Uxb. 135 BP72
Dickens Clo., Erith 167 FB81
Belmont Rd.
Dickens Clo., Hayes 155 BS77
Croyde Ave.
Dickens Clo., Rich. 178 CL89
Dickens Clo., St.Alb. 43 CD19
Dickens Clo., Wal.Cr. 66 DU26
Dickens Ct., Hat. 45 CV16
Ground La.
Dickens Dr., Add. 211 BF107
Dickens Dr., Chis. 185 EQ93
Dickens Est. SE1 162 DT75
Dickens Est. SE16 162 DT75
Dickens La. N18 100 DS50
Dickens Ri., Chig. 103 EP48
Dickens Rd. E6 144 EK68
Dickens Rd., Grav. 191 GL88
Dickens Sq. SE1 279 J6
Dickens Sq. SE1 162 DQ76
Dickens St. SW8 161 DH82
Dickenson Clo. N9 100 DU46
Croyland Rd.
Dickenson Rd. N8 121 DL59
Dickenson Rd., Felt. 176 BX92
Dickenson St. NW5 141 DH65
Dalby St.
Dickensons La. SE25 202 DU99
Dickensons Pl. SE25 202 DU100
Dickerage La., N.Mal. 198 CQ97
Dickerage Rd., Kings.T. 198 CQ95
Dickerage Rd., N.Mal. 198 CQ95
Dickinson Ave., Rick. 74 BN44
Dickinson Sq., Rick. 74 BN44
Dickson (Cheshunt), Wal.Cr. 66 DT27
Dickson Fold, Pnr. 116 BX56
Dickson Rd. SE9 164 EL83
Didsbury Clo. E6 145 EM67
Barking Rd.
Dig Dag Hill (Cheshunt), Wal.Cr. 66 DT27
Digby Cres. N4 122 DQ61
Digby Gdns., Dag. 146 FA67
Digby Pl., Croy. 202 DT104
Digby Rd. E9 123 DX64
Digby Rd., Bark. 145 ET66
Digby St. E2 142 DW69
Digby Wk., Horn. 148 FJ65
Pembrey Way
Digby Way, W.Byf. 212 BM112
High Rd.
Digdens Ri., Epsom 232 CQ115
Dighton Ct. SE5 162 DQ79
Hillingdon St.
Dighton Rd. SW18 180 DC85
Digswell Clo., Borwd. 78 CN38
Digswell Hill, Welw.G.C. 29 CX08
Digswell Ho., Welw.G.C. 29 CX05
Digswell Ho. Ms., Welw.G.C. 29 CX05
Monks Ri.
Digswell La., Welw.G.C. 29 CZ05
Digswell Ri., Welw.G.C. 29 CX07
Digswell Rd., Welw.G.C. 29 CY06
Digswell St. N7 141 DN65
Holloway Rd.
Dilhorne Clo. SE12 184 EH90
Dilke St. SW3 160 DF79
Dillwyn Clo. SE26 183 DY91
Dilston Clo., Nthlt. 136 BW69
Yeading La.
Dilston Gro. SE16 162 DW77
Abbeyfield Rd.
Dilston Rd., Lthd. 231 CG119
Dilton Gdns. SW15 179 CV88
Dimes Pl. W6 159 CV77
King St.
Dimmock Dr., Grnf. 117 CD64
Dimmocks La., Rick. 74 BH36
Dimond Clo. E7 124 EG63
Dimsdale Dr. NW9 118 CQ60
Dimsdale Dr., Enf. 82 DU44
Dimsdale Dr., Slou. 111 AM64
Dimsdale St., Hert. 32 DQ09
Dimsdale Wk. E13 144 EG67
Stratford Rd.
Dimson Cres. E3 143 EA70
Wellington Way
Dinant Link Rd., Hodd. 49 DY16
Dingle, The, Uxb. 135 BP69
Dingle Clo., Barn. 79 CT44
Dingle Gdns. E14 143 EA73
Dingle Rd., Ashf. 175 BP92
Dingley La. SW16 181 DK89
Dingley Pl. EC1 275 J3
Dingley Pl. EC1 142 DQ69
Dingley Rd. EC1 275 H3
Dingley Rd. EC1 142 DQ69
Dingwall Ave., Croy. 202 DQ103
Dingwall Gdns. NW11 120 DA58
Dingwall Pl., Croy. 202 DR103
Dingwall Rd.
Dingwall Rd. SW18 180 DC87
Dingwall Rd., Cars. 218 DF109
Dingwall Rd., Croy. 202 DR102
Dinmont St. E2 142 DV68
Coate St.
Dinmore, Hem.H. 57 AZ28
Dinsdale Clo., Wok. 227 BA118
Dinsdale Gdns. SE25 202 DS99
Dinsdale Gdns., Barn. 80 DB43
Dinsdale Rd. SE3 164 EF79
Dinsmore Rd. SW12 181 DH87
Dinton Rd. SW19 180 DD93
Dinton Rd., Kings.T. 178 CM94
Dione Rd., Hem.H. 40 BM17
Saturn Way
Diploma Ave. N2 120 DE56
Dirdene Clo., Epsom 217 CT112
Dirdene Gdns., Epsom 217 CT112
Dirdene Gro., Epsom 217 CT112
Dirleton Rd. E15 144 EF67
Dirtham La., Lthd. 245 BV129
Disbrowe Rd. W6 159 CY79
Discovery Wk. E1 142 DV74
Wapping La.
Dishforth La. NW9 96 CS53
Disney Ms. N4 121 DP57
Chesterfield Gdns.
Disney Pl. SE1 279 J4
Disney St. SE1 279 J4
Dison Clo., Enf. 83 DX39
Disraeli Clo. SE28 146 EW74
Disraeli Clo. W4 158 CR77
Acton La.
Disraeli Ct., Slou. 153 BB79
Sutton Pl.
Disraeli Gdns. SW15 159 CZ84
Fawe Pk. Rd.
Disraeli Pk., Beac. 89 AK51
Disraeli Rd. E7 144 EG65
Disraeli Rd. NW10 138 CR68
Disraeli Rd. SW15 159 CY84
Disraeli Rd. W5 137 CK74
Diss St. E2 275 P2
Diss St. E2 142 DT69
Distaff La. EC4 275 H10
Distaff La. EC4 142 DQ73
Distillery La. W6 159 CW78
Fulham Palace Rd.
Distillery Rd. W6 159 CW78
Distillery Wk., Brent. 158 CL79
Pottery Rd.
Distin St. SE11 278 D9
District Rd., Wem. 117 CH64
Ditch All. SE10 163 EB81
Ditchburn St. E14 143 EC73
Ditches La., Couls. 235 DL120
Ditchfield Rd., Hayes 136 BY70
Ditchfield Rd., Hodd. 33 EA14
Dittisham Rd. SE9 184 EL91
Ditton Clo., T.Ditt. 197 CG101
Watts Rd.
Ditton Gra. Clo., Surb. 197 CK102
Ditton Gra. Dr., Surb. 197 CK102
Ditton Hill, Surb. 197 CJ102
Ditton Hill Rd., Surb. 197 CJ102
Ditton Lawn, T.Ditt. 197 CG102
Ditton Pk. Rd., Slou. 152 AY79
Ditton Pl. SE20 202 DV95
Hartfield Gro.
Ditton Reach, T.Ditt. 197 CH100
Ditton Rd., Bexh. 186 EX85
Ditton Rd., Slou. 153 AZ79
Ditton Rd. (Datchet), Slou. 152 AX81
Ditton Rd., Sthl. 156 BZ78
Ditton Rd., Surb. 197 CK103
Divis Way SW15 179 CV86
Dover Pk. Dr.
Divot Pl., Hert. 32 DV08
Dixon Clark Ct. N1 141 DP65
Canonbury Rd.
Dixon Clo. E6 145 EM72
Brandreth Rd.
Dixon Dr., Wey. 212 BM110
Dixon Pl., W.Wick. 203 EB102
Dixon Rd. SE14 163 DY81
Dixon Rd. SE25 202 DS97
Dixon's All. SE16 162 DV75
West La.
Dixons Hill Clo., Hat. 63 CV25
Dixons Hill Rd., Hat. 63 CU25
Dobbin Clo., Har. 95 CG54
Dobb's Weir Rd., Hodd. 49 EC18
Dobell Rd. SE9 185 EM85
Dobree Ave. NW10 139 CV66
Dobson Clo. NW6 140 DD66
Dobson Rd., Grav. 191 GL92
Dock Hill Ave. SE16 163 DX75
Dock Rd. E16 144 EF73
Dock Rd., Brent. 157 CK80
Dock Rd., Grays 170 GD79
Dock Rd., Til. 170 GE81
Dock St. E1 142 DU73
Dockers Tanner Rd. E14 163 EA77
Dockett Eddy La., Shep. 194 BM102
Dockhead SE1 162 DT75
Dockland St. E16 145 EN74
Dockley Rd. SE16 162 DU76
Dockwell Clo., Felt. 155 BU84
Doctor Johnson Ave. SW17 181 DH90
Doctors Clo. SE26 182 DW92
Doctors Commons Rd., Berk. 38 AV19
Doctors La., Cat. 235 DN123
Docwra's Bldgs. N1 142 DS65
Dod St. E14 143 EA72
Dodbrooke Rd. SE27 181 DN90
Doddinghurst Rd., Brwd. 108 FW44
Doddington Gro. SE17 161 DP79
Doddington Pl. SE17 161 DP79
Dodd's Cres., W.Byf. 212 BH114
Dodds La., Ch.St.G. 90 AU47
Dodds La., Hem.H. 40 BJ16
Dodd's La., Wok. 212 BG114
Dodds Pk., Bet. 264 CP136
Doddsfield Rd., Slou. 131 AN69
Dodsley Pl. N9 100 DW48
Dodson St. SE1 278 E5
Dodson St. SE1 161 DN75
Dodwood, Welw.G.C. 30 DB10
Doebury Wk. SE18 166 EU79
Prestwood Clo.
Doel Clo. SW19 180 DC94
Dog Kennel Hill SE22 162 DS83
Dog Kennel Hill Est. SE22 162 DS83
Dog Kennel La., Hat. 45 CU17
Dog Kennel La., Rick. 73 BF43
Dog La. NW10 118 CS63
Doggets Ct., Barn. 80 DE43
Doggett Rd. SE6 183 EA87
Doggetts Fm. Rd., Uxb. 113 BC59
Doggetts Way, St.Alb. 42 CC22
Doggetts Wd. Clo., Ch.St.G. 72 AV42
Doggetts Wd. La., Ch.St.G. 72 AV41
Doghurst Ave., Hayes 155 BP80
Doghurst Dr., West Dr. 155 BP80
Doghurst La., Couls. 234 DF120
Dognell Grn., Welw.G.C. 29 CV08
Dogwood Clo., Grav. 191 GF91
Doherty Rd. E13 144 EG70
Dolben St. SE1 278 G3
Dolben St. SE1 141 DP74
Dolby Ct. EC4 142 DQ73
Garlick Hill
Dolby Rd. SW6 159 CZ82
Dolland St. SE11 161 DM78
Dollis Ave. N3 97 CZ53
Dollis Brook Wk., Barn. 79 CY44
Dollis Cres., Ruis. 116 BW60
Dollis Hill Ave. NW2 119 CV62
Dollis Hill Est. NW2 119 CU62
Dollis Hill La. NW2 119 CT63
Dollis Ms. N3 97 CZ53
Dollis Pk.
Dollis Pk. N3 97 CZ53
Dollis Rd. N3 97 CY53
Dollis Rd. NW7 97 CY52
Dollis Valley Grn. Wk. N20 98 DC47
Totteridge La.
Dollis Valley Grn. Wk., Barn. 79 CY44
Leeside
Dollis Valley Way, Barn. 79 CZ43
Dolman Clo. N3 98 DC54
Avondale Rd.
Dolman Rd. W4 158 CR77
Dolman St. SW4 161 DM84
Dolphin App., Rom. 127 FF56
Dolphin Clo. SE16 163 DX75
Kinburn St.
Dolphin Clo. SE28 146 EX72
Dolphin Clo., Surb. 197 CK100
Dolphin Ct. NW11 119 CY58
Dolphin Ct., Slou. 152 AV75
Dolphin Rd.
Dolphin Ct., Stai. 174 BG90
Bremer Rd.
Dolphin Ct. N., Stai. 174 BG90
Bremer Rd.
Dolphin Est., The, Sun. 195 BS95
Dolphin La. E14 143 EB73
Dolphin Rd., Nthlt. 136 BZ67
Dolphin Rd., Slou. 152 AV75
Dolphin Rd., Sun. 195 BS95
Dolphin Rd. N., Sun. 195 BS95
Dolphin Rd. S., Sun. 195 BR95
Dolphin Rd. W., Sun. 195 BS95
Dolphin Sq. SW1 161 DJ78
Dolphin Sq. W4 158 CS80
Dolphin St., Kings.T. 198 CL95
Dolphin Yd., St.Alb. 43 CD20
Dolphin Yd., Ware 33 DX06
East St.
Dombey St. WC1 274 B6
Dombey St. WC1 141 DM71
Dome Hill, Cat. 252 DS127
Dome Hill Pk. SE26 182 DT91
Dome Hill Peak, Cat. 252 DS126
Dome Way, Red. 250 DF133
Domett Clo. SE5 162 DR84
Domfe Pl. E5 122 DW63
Rushmore Rd.
Domingo St. EC1 275 H4
Dominion Dr., Rom. 105 FB51
Dominion Rd., Croy. 202 DT101
Dominion Rd., Sthl. 156 BY76
Dominion St. EC2 275 L6
Dominion Way, Rain. 147 FG69
Domonic Dr. SE9 185 EP91
Domville Clo. N20 98 DD47
Don Phelan Clo. SE5 162 DR81
Don Way, Rom. 105 FE52
Donald Biggs Dr., Grav. 191 GK87
Donald Dr., Rom. 126 EW57
Donald Rd. E13 144 EH67
Donald Rd., Croy. 201 DM100
Donald Wds. Gdns., Surb. 198 CP103
Donaldson Rd. NW6 139 CZ67
Donaldson Rd. SE18 165 EN81
Doncaster Dr., Nthlt. 116 BZ64
Doncaster Gdns. N4 122 DQ58
Stanhope Gdns.
Doncaster Gdns., Nthlt. 116 BZ64
Doncaster Grn., Wat. 94 BW50
Doncaster Rd. N9 100 DV45
Doncaster Way, Upmin. 128 FM62
Doncel Ct. E4 101 ED45
Donegal St. N1 274 C1
Donegal St. N1 141 DM68
Doneraile St. SW6 159 CX82
Dongola Rd. E13 144 EH69
Dongola Rd. N17 122 DS55
Dongola Rd. W. E13 144 EH69
Balaam St.
Donington Ave., Ilf. 125 EQ57
Donkey All. SE22 182 DU87
Donkey La. (Farningham), Dart. 208 FP103
Donkey La., Dor. 262 BX143
Donkey La., Enf. 82 DU40
Donkey La., Horl. 269 DK153
Donnay Clo., Ger.Cr. 112 AX58
Donne Ct. SE24 182 DQ86
Donne Gdns., Wok. 227 BE115
Donne Pl. SW3 276 C8
Donne Pl. SW3 160 DE77
Donne Pl., Mitch. 201 DH98
Donne Rd., Dag. 126 EW61
Donnefield Ave., Edg. 96 CL52
Donnington Rd. NW10 139 CV66
Donnington Rd., Har. 117 CJ57
Donnington Rd., Sev. 241 FD120
Donnington Rd., Wor.Pk. 199 CU103
Donnybrook Rd. SW16 181 DJ94
Donovan Ave. N10 121 DH55
Donovan Clo., Epsom 216 CR110
Nimbus Rd.
Doods Pk. Rd., Reig. 250 DC133
Doods Rd., Reig. 250 DC133
Doods Way, Reig. 250 DC133
Doon St. SE1 278 D2
Doone Clo., Tedd. 177 CG93
Doone Gdns., Wok. 227 BE115
Dora Rd. SW19 180 DA92
Dora St. E14 143 DZ72
Dorado Gdns., Orp. 206 EX104
Doral Way, Cars. 218 DF106
Doran Dr., Red. 250 DD134
Doran Gdns., Red. 250 DD134
Doran Gro. SE18 165 ES80
Doran Mans. N2 120 DF57
Great N. Rd.
Doran Wk. E15 143 EC66
Dorcas Ct., St.Alb. 43 CE21
Dorchester Ave. N13 100 DQ49
Dorchester Ave., Bex. 186 EX88
Dorchester Ave., Har. 116 CC58
Dorchester Ave., Hodd. 49 EA15
Dorchester Clo., Dart. 188 FM87
Dorchester Clo., Nthlt. 116 CB64
Dorchester Clo., Orp. 186 EU94
Grovelands Rd.
Dorchester Ct. N14 99 DH45
Dorchester Ct. SE24 182 DQ85
Dorchester Ct., Rick. 75 BR43
Mayfare
Dorchester Ct., Wok. 227 BA116
Dorchester Dr. SE24 182 DQ85
Dorchester Dr., Felt. 175 BS86
Dorchester Gdns. E4 101 EA49
Dorchester Gdns. NW11 120 DA56
Dorchester Gro. W4 158 CS78
Dorchester Ms., N.Mal. 198 CR98
Elm Rd.
Dorchester Ms., Twick. 177 CJ87
Dorchester Rd., Grav. 191 GK90
Dorchester Rd., Mord. 200 DB101
Dorchester Rd., Nthlt. 116 CB64
Dorchester Rd., Wey. 195 BP104
Dorchester Rd., Wor.Pk. 199 CW102
Dorchester Way, Har. 118 CM58
Dorchester Waye, Hayes 135 BV72
Dorcis Ave., Bexh. 166 EY82
Dordrecht Rd. W3 138 CS74
Dore Ave. E12 125 EN64
Dore Gdns., Mord. 200 DB101
Doreen Ave. NW9 118 CR60
Dorell Clo., Sthl. 136 BZ71
Doria Dr., Grav. 191 GL90
Doria Rd. SW6 159 CZ82
Dorian Rd., Horn. 127 FG60
Doric Dr., Tad. 233 CZ120
Doric Way NW1 273 M2
Doric Way NW1 141 DK69
Dorien Rd. SW20 199 CX96
Dorincourt, Wok. 227 BE115
Doris Ave., Erith 167 FC81
Doris Rd. E7 144 EG66
Doris Rd., Ashf. 175 BR93
Dorking Business Pk., Dor. 263 CG135
Dorking Clo. SE8 163 DZ79
Dorking Clo., Wor.Pk. 199 CX103
Dorking Gdns., Rom. 106 FK50
Dorking Glen, Rom. 106 FK49
Dorking Ri., Rom. 106 FK49
Dorking Rd., Epsom 232 CN116
Dorking Rd., Guil. 259 BD140
Dorking Rd., Lthd. 247 CH125
Dorking Rd. (Great Bookham), Lthd. 246 CB126
Dorking Rd., Rom. 106 FK49
Dorking Rd., Tad. 233 CX123
Dorking Wk., Rom. 106 FK49
Dorkins Way, Upmin. 129 FS59
Dorlcote Rd. SW18 180 DE87
Dorling Dr., Epsom 217 CT112
Dorly Clo., Shep. 195 BS98
Dorma Trd. Est. E10 123 DX60
Dorman Pl. N9 100 DU47
Balham Rd.
Dorman Wk. NW10 118 CR64
Garden Way
Dorman Way NW8 140 DD67
Dormans Clo., Nthwd. 93 BR52
Dormay St. SW18 180 DB85
Dormer Clo. E15 144 EF65
Dormer Clo., Barn. 79 CX43
Dormers Ave., Sthl. 136 CA72
Dormers Ri., Sthl. 136 CB73
Dormers Wells La., Sthl. 136 CA72
Dormie Clo., St.Alb. 42 CC18
Dormywood, Ruis. 115 BT57
Dornberg Clo. SE3 164 EG80
Dornberg Rd. SE3 164 EH80
Banchory Rd.
Dorncliffe Rd. SW6 159 CY82
Dornels, Slou. 132 AW72
Dorney NW3 140 DE66
Dorney End, Chesh. 54 AN30
Dorney Gro., Wey. 195 BP103
Dorney Reach Rd., Maid. 150 AF76
Dorney Ri., Orp. 205 ET98
Dorney Way, Houns. 176 BY85
Dorney Wd. Rd., Slou. 110 AJ62
Dornfell St. NW6 119 CZ64
Dornford Gdns., Couls. 236 DQ119
Dornton Rd. SW12 181 DH89
Dornton Rd., S.Croy. 220 DR106
Dorothy Ave., Wem. 138 CL66
Dorothy Evans Clo., Bexh. 167 FB84
Dorothy Gdns., Dag. 126 EV63
Dorothy Rd. SW11 160 DF83
Dorrell Pl. SW9 161 DN84
Brixton Rd.
Dorrien Wk. SW16 181 DK89
Dingley La.
Dorriens Cft., Berk. 38 AT16
Dorrington Ct. SE25 202 DS96
Dorrington Gdns., Horn. 128 FK60
Dorrington Pt. E3 143 EB69
Bromley High St.
Dorrington St. EC1 274 D6
Dorrington St. EC1 141 DN71
Dorrit Cres., Guil. 242 AS132
Dorrit Ms. N18 100 DS50
Dorrit Way, Chis. 185 EQ93
Dorrofield Clo., Rick. 75 BQ43
Dors Clo. NW9 118 CR60
Dorset Ave., Hayes 135 BS69
Dorset Ave., Rom. 127 FD56
Dorset Ave., Sthl. 156 CA77
Dorset Ave., Well. 165 ET84
Dorset Bldgs. EC4 274 F9
Dorset Clo. NW1 272 D6
Dorset Clo., Berk. 38 AT18
Dorset Clo., Hayes 135 BS69
Dorset Cres., Grav. 191 GL91
Dorset Dr., Edg. 96 CM51
Dorset Dr., Wok. 227 BB117
Dorset Est. E2 142 DT69
Dorset Gdns., Mitch. 201 DM98
Dorset Ms. N3 98 DA53
Dorset Ms. SW1 277 H6
Dorset Pl. E15 143 ED65
Dorset Pl. SW1 277 M10
Dorset Ri. EC4 274 F9
Dorset Ri. EC4 141 DP72
Dorset Rd. E7 144 EJ66
Dorset Rd. N15 122 DR56
Dorset Rd. N22 99 DL53
Dorset Rd. SE9 184 EL89
Dorset Rd. SW8 161 DL80
Dorset Rd. SW19 200 DA95
Dorset Rd. W5 157 CJ76
Dorset Rd., Ashf. 174 BK90
Dorset Rd., Beck. 203 DX97
Dorset Rd., Har. 116 CC58
Dorset Rd., Mitch. 200 DE96
Dorset Rd., Sutt. 218 DA110
Dorset Rd., Wind. 151 AQ82
Dorset Sq. NW1 272 D5
Dorset Sq. NW1 140 DF70
Dorset Sq., Epsom 216 CR110
Dorset St. W1 272 E7
Dorset St. W1 140 DF71
Dorset St., Sev. 257 FH125
High St.
Dorset Way, Twick. 177 CD88
Dorset Way, Uxb. 134 BM68
Dorset Way, W.Byf. 212 BK110
Dorset Waye, Houns. 156 BZ80
Dorton Dr., Sev. 257 FM122
Dorville Cres. W6 159 CV76
Dorville Rd. SE12 184 EF85
Dothill Rd. SE18 165 ER80
Douai Gro., Hmptn. 196 CC95
Doubleday Rd., Loug. 85 EQ41
Doug Siddons Ct., Grays 170 GC79
Elm Rd.
Doughty Ms. WC1 274 B5
Doughty Ms. WC1 141 DM70
Doughty St. WC1 274 B4
Doughty St. WC1 141 DM70
Douglas Ave. E17 101 EA53
Douglas Ave., N.Mal. 199 CV98
Douglas Ave., Rom. 106 FL54
Douglas Ave., Wat. 76 BX37
Douglas Ave., Wem. 138 CL66
Douglas Clo., Grays 170 FY76
Douglas Clo., Guil. 242 AX128
Douglas Clo., Stan. 95 CG50
Douglas Clo., Wall. 219 DL107
Douglas Ct., Cat. 236 DQ122
Fairbourne La.
Douglas Ct., West. 238 EL117
Douglas Cres., Hayes 136 BW70
Douglas Dr., Croy. 203 EA104
Douglas Est. N1 142 DQ65
Douglas Gdns., Berk. 38 AT18
Douglas La., Stai. 173 AZ85
Douglas Ms. NW2 119 CY62
Douglas Pl. E14 163 EC78
Manchester Rd.
Douglas Rd. E4 102 EE45
Douglas Rd. E16 144 EG71
Douglas Rd. N1 142 DQ66
Douglas Rd. N22 99 DN53
Douglas Rd. NW6 139 CZ67
Douglas Rd., Add. 194 BH104
Douglas Rd., Esher 196 CB103
Douglas Rd., Horn. 127 FF58
Douglas Rd., Houns. 156 CB83
Douglas Rd., Ilf. 126 EU59
Douglas Rd., Kings.T. 198 CP96
Douglas Rd., Reig. 250 DA133
Douglas Rd., Slou. 131 AR71
Douglas Rd., Stai. 174 BK86
Douglas Rd., Surb. 198 CM103
Douglas Rd., Well. 166 EV81
Douglas Sq., Mord. 200 DA100
Douglas St. SW1 277 M9
Douglas St. SW1 161 DK77
Douglas Ter. E17 101 EA53
Douglas Ave.
Douglas Way SE8 163 DZ80
Douglas Way, Welw.G.C. 30 DC09
Doulton Ms. NW6 140 DB65
Lymington Rd.
Doultons, The, Stai. 174 BG94
Dounesforth Gdns. SW18 180 DB88
Dounsell Ct., Brwd. 108 FU44
Ongar Rd.
Douro Pl. W8 160 DB76
Douro St. E3 143 EA68
Douthwaite Sq. E1 142 DU74
Torrington Pl.
Dove App. E6 144 EL71
Dove Clo., Nthlt. 136 BX70
Wayfarer Rd.
Dove Clo., S.Croy. 221 DX111
Dove Ct. EC2 275 K9
Dove Ct., Beac. 89 AK52
Dove Ct., Hat. 45 CU19
Dove Ho. Cres., Slou. 131 AL69
Dove Ho. Gdns. E4 101 EA47
Dove La., Pot.B. 64 DB34
Dove Ms. SW5 160 DC77
Dove Pk., Pnr. 94 CA52
Dove Pk., Rick. 73 BB44
Dove Rd. N1 142 DR65
Dove Row E2 142 DU67
Dove Wk. SW1 276 F10
Dove Wk., Horn. 147 FH65
Heron Flight Ave.
Dovecot Clo., Pnr. 115 BV57
Dovecote Ave. N22 121 DN55
Dovecote Clo., Wey. 195 BP104
Dovecote Gdns. SW14 158 CR83
Avondale Rd.
Dovecott Gdns. SW14 158 CR83
North Worple Way
Dovedale Ave., Har. 117 CJ58
Dovedale Ave., Ilf. 103 EN54
Dovedale Clo., Guil. 243 BA131
Weylea Ave.
Dovedale Clo., Uxb. 92 BJ54
Dovedale Clo., Well. 166 EU81
Dovedale Ri., Mitch. 180 DF94
Dovedale Rd. SE22 182 DV85
Dovedale Rd., Dart. 188 FQ88
Dovedon Clo. N14 99 DL47
Dovehouse Cft., Harl. 36 EU13
Mistley Rd.
Dovehouse Grn., Wey. 213 BR105
Rosslyn Pk.
Dovehouse Mead, Bark. 145 ER68
Dovehouse St. SW3 276 B10
Dovehouse St. SW3 160 DD78
Doveney Clo., Orp. 206 EW97
Dover Clo. NW2 119 CX61
Brent Ter.
Dover Clo., Rom. 105 FC54
Dover Flats SE1 162 DS77
Old Kent Rd.
Dover Gdns., Cars. 200 DF104
Dover Ho. Rd. SW15 159 CU84
Dover Pk. Dr. SW15 179 CV86
Dover Rd. E12 124 EJ61
Dover Rd. N9 100 DW47
Dover Rd. SE19 182 DR93
Dover Rd., Grav. 190 GD86
Dover Rd., Rom. 126 EY58
Dover Rd., Slou. 131 AM72
Dover Rd. E., Grav. 190 GE87
Dover St. W1 277 J1

Dukes Ave., N.Mal. 199 CT97
Dukes Ave., Nthlt. 136 BY66
Dukes Ave., Rich. 177 CJ91
Dukes Clo., Ashf. 175 BQ91
Dukes Clo., Epp. 71 FB27
Dukes Clo., Ger.Cr. 112 AX60
Dukes Clo., Hmptn. 176 BZ92
Dukes Clo., Kings.T. 177 CK91
Dukes Ct. E6 145 EN67
Dukes Ct., Wok. 227 AZ117
Dukes Dr., Slou. 111 AM64
Dukes Grn. Ave., Felt. 175 BU85
Dukes Hill, Cat. 237 DY120
Dukes Kiln Dr., Ger.Cr. 112 AW60
Dukes La. W8 160 DB75
Dukes La., Ger.Cr. 112 AY60
Dukes Lo., Nthwd. 93 BS50
Eastbury Ave.
Duke's Meadows W4 158 CQ82
Great Chertsey Rd.
Dukes Ms. N10 121 DH55
Dukes Ave.
Duke's Ms. W1 272 G8
Dukes Orchard, Bex. 187 FC88
Duke's Pas. E17 123 EC55
Marlowe Rd.
Dukes Pl. EC3 275 N9
Dukes Pl. EC3 142 DS72
Dukes Ride, Dor. 263 CK139
Dukes Ride, Ger.Cr. 112 AY60
Dukes Ride, Uxb. 114 BL63
Dukes Rd. E6 145 EN67
Dukes Rd. W3 138 CN70
Duke's Rd. WC1 273 N3
Duke's Rd. WC1 141 DK69
Dukes Rd., Walt. 214 BX106
Dukes Valley, Ger.Cr. 112 AV61
Dukes Way, Berk. 38 AU17
Dukes Way, W.Wick. 204 EE104
Dukes Wd. Ave., Ger.Cr. 112 AY59
Dukes Wd. Dr., Ger.Cr. 112 AX60
Duke's Yd. W1 272 G10
Dukesthorpe Rd. SE26 183 DX91
Dulas St. N4 121 DM60
Everleigh St.
Dulford St. W11 139 CY73
Dulka Rd. SW11 180 DF85
Dulverton Rd. SE9 185 EQ89
Dulverton Rd., Rom. 106 FK51
Dulverton Rd., Ruis. 115 BU60
Dulverton Rd., S.Croy. 220 DW110
Dulwich Common SE21 182 DS88
Dulwich Common SE22 182 DT88
Dulwich Lawn Clo. SE22 182 DT85
Melbourne Gro.
Dulwich Oaks, The SE21 182 DT90
Dulwich Rd. SE24 181 DN85
Dulwich Village SE21 182 DS86
Dulwich Way, Rick. 74 BN43
Dulwich Wd. Ave. SE19 182 DS91
Dulwich Wd. Pk. SE19 182 DS91
Dumbarton Ave., Wal.Cr. 67 DX34
Dumbarton Rd. SW2 181 DL86
Dumbleton Clo., Kings.T. 198 CP95
Gloucester Rd.
Dumbreck Rd. SE9 165 EM84
Dumfries Clo., Wat. 93 BT48
Dumont Rd. N16 122 DS62
Dumpton Pl. NW1 140 DG66
Gloucester Ave.
Dumville Dr., Gdse. 252 DV131
Dunally Pk., Shep. 195 BR101
Dunbar Ave. SW16 201 DN96
Dunbar Ave., Beck. 203 DY98
Dunbar Ave., Dag. 126 FA62
Dunbar Clo., Hayes 135 BU71
Dunbar Clo., Slou. 132 AU72
Dunbar Ct., Sutt. 218 DD106
Dunbar Ct., Walt. 195 BV103
Dunbar Gdns., Dag. 126 FA64
Dunbar Rd. E7 144 EG65
Dunbar Rd. N22 99 DN53
Dunbar Rd., N.Mal. 198 CQ98
Dunbar St. SE27 182 DQ90
Dunblane Clo., Edg. 96 CP47
Tayside Dr.
Dunblane Rd. SE9 164 EL82
Dunboe Pl., Shep. 195 BQ101
Dunboyne Rd. NW3 120 DF64
Dunbridge St. E2 142 DU70
Duncan Clo., Barn. 80 DC42
Duncan Clo., Welw.G.C. 29 CY10
Duncan Dr., Guil. 243 BA133
Duncan Gro. W3 138 CS72
Duncan Rd. E8 142 DV67
Duncan Rd., Rich. 158 CL84
Duncan Rd., Tad. 233 CY119
Duncan St. N1 141 DP68
Duncan Ter. N1 274 F1
Duncan Ter. N1 141 DP68
Duncan Way (Bushey), Wat. 76 BZ40
Duncannon Cres., Wind. 151 AK83
Duncannon St. WC2 277 P1
Duncannon St. WC2 141 DL73
Dunch St. E1 142 DV72
Watney St.
Duncombe Clo., Amer. 55 AS38
Duncombe Clo., Hert. 32 DQ07
Duncombe Ct., Stai. 173 BF94
Duncombe Hill SE23 183 DY87
Duncombe Rd. N19 121 DK60
Duncombe Rd., Berk. 38 AS17
Duncombe Rd., Hert. 32 DQ08
Duncrievie Rd. SE13 183 ED86
Duncroft SE18 165 ES80
Duncroft, Wind. 151 AM83
Duncroft Clo., Reig. 249 CZ133
Dundalk Rd. SE4 163 DY83
Dundas Gdns., W.Mol. 196 CB97
Dundas Rd. SE15 162 DW82
Dundee Rd. E13 144 EH68
Dundee Rd. SE25 202 DV99
Dundee Rd., Slou. 131 AM72
Dundee St. E1 142 DV74
Dundela Gdns., Wor.Pk. 217 CV105
Dundonald Clo. E6 144 EL72
Northumberland Rd.
Dundonald Rd. NW10 139 CX67
Dundonald Rd. SW19 179 CY94
Dundrey Cres., Red. 251 DL129
Dunedin Dr., Cat. 252 DS125
Dunedin Rd. E10 123 EB62
Dunedin Rd., Ilf. 125 EQ60
Dunedin Rd., Rain. 147 FE69
Dunedin Way, Hayes 136 BW70
Dunelm Gro. SE27 182 DQ91
Dunelm St. E1 143 DX72
Dunfee Way, W.Byf. 212 BL112
Dunfield Gdns. SE6 183 EB92
Dunfield Rd. SE6 183 EB92
Dunford Rd. N7 121 DM63
Dungarvan Ave. SW15 159 CU84
Dungates La., Bet. 249 CU133
Dunheved Clo., Th.Hth. 201 DN100
Dunheved Rd. N., Th.Hth. 201 DN100
Dunheved Rd. S., Th.Hth. 201 DN100
Dunheved Rd. W., Th.Hth. 201 DN100
Dunholme Grn. N9 100 DT48
Dunholme La. N9 100 DT48
Dunholme Rd.
Dunholme Rd. N9 100 DT48
Dunkeld Rd. SE25 202 DR98
Dunkeld Rd., Dag. 126 EV61
Dunkellin Gro., S.Ock. 149 FU72
Dunkellin Way
Dunkellin Way, S.Ock. 149 FU72
Dunkery Rd. SE9 184 EK91
Dunkin Rd., Dart. 168 FN84
Dunkirk Clo., Grav. 191 GJ92
Christian Flds. Ave.
Dunkirk St. SE27 182 DQ91
Waring St.
Dunlace Rd. E5 122 DW63
Dunleary Clo., Houns. 176 BZ87
Dunley Dr., Croy. 221 EB108
Dunlin Clo., Red. 266 DE139
Dunlin Ho. W13 137 CF70
Dunlin Ri., Guil. 243 BD132
Dunlin Rd., Hem.H. 40 BL15
Dunloe Ave. N17 122 DR55
Dunloe St. E2 142 DT68
Dunlop Pl. SE16 162 DT76
Spa Rd.
Dunlop Pt. E16 144 EG74
Dunlop Rd., Til. 171 GF81
Dunmail Dr., Pur. 220 DS114
Dunmore Pt. E2 275 P3
Dunmore Rd. NW6 139 CY67
Dunmore Rd. SW20 199 CW95
Dunmow Clo., Felt. 176 BX91
Dunmow Clo., Loug. 84 EL44
Dunmow Clo., Rom. 126 EW57
Dunmow Dr., Rain. 147 FF67
Dunmow Ho., Dag. 146 EV67
Dunmow Rd. E15 123 ED63
Dunmow Wk. N1 142 DQ67
Popham St.
Dunn Mead NW9 97 CT52
Field Mead
Dunn St. E8 122 DT64
Dunnale Cres. SE16 163 DY77
Plough Way
Dunnets, Wok. 226 AS117
Dunning Clo., S.Ock. 149 FU72
Dent Clo.
Dunningford Clo., Horn. 127 FF64
Dunnock Clo. N9 101 DX46
Dunnock Clo., Borwd. 78 CN42
Dunnock Rd. E6 144 EL72
Dunns Pas. WC1 274 A8
Dunny La., Kings L. 57 BE32
Dunnymans Rd., Bans. 233 CZ115
Dunollie Pl. NW5 121 DJ64
Dunollie Rd.
Dunollie Rd. NW5 121 DJ64
Dunoon Rd. SE23 182 DW87
Dunottar Clo., Red. 266 DD136
Dunraven Ave., Red. 267 DH141
Dunraven Dr., Enf. 81 DN40
Dunraven Rd. W12 139 CU74
Dunraven St. W1 272 E10
Dunsany Rd. W14 159 CX76
Dunsborough Pk., Wok. 228 BJ120
Dunsbury Clo., Sutt. 218 DB109
Nettlecombe Clo.
Dunsdon Ave., Guil. 258 AV135
Dunsfold Ri., Couls. 219 DK113
Dunsfold Way, Croy. 221 EB108
Dunsford Way SW15 179 CV86
Dover Pk. Dr.
Dunsmore Clo., Hayes 136 BY70
Kingsash Dr.
Dunsmore Clo. (Bushey), Wat. 77 CD44
Dunsmore Rd., Walt. 195 BV100
Dunsmore Way (Bushey), Wat. 77 CD44
Dunsmure Rd. N16 122 DS60
Dunspring La., Ilf. 103 EP54
Dunstable Clo., Rom. 106 FK51
Dunstable Rd.
Dunstable Ms. W1 272 G6
Dunstable Rd., Rich. 158 CL84
Dunstable Rd., Rom. 106 FK51
Dunstable Rd., W.Mol. 196 BZ98
Dunstall Grn., Wok. 210 AW109
Dunstall Rd. SW20 179 CV93
Dunstall Way, W.Mol. 196 CB97
Dunstalls, Harl. 51 EN19
Dunstan Clo. N2 120 DC55
Thomas More Way
Dunstan Rd. NW11 119 CZ60
Dunstan Rd., Couls. 235 DK117
Dunstans Gro. SE22 182 DV86
Dunstans Rd. SE22 182 DU87
Dunster Ave., Mord. 199 CX102
Dunster Clo., Barn. 79 CX42
Dunster Clo., Rom. 105 FC54
Dunster Clo., Uxb. 92 BH53
Dunster Ct. EC3 275 M10
Dunster Cres., Horn. 128 FN61
Dunster Dr. NW9 118 CQ60
Dunster Gdns. NW6 139 CZ66
Dunster Gdns., Slou. 131 AN73
Avebury
Dunster Way, Har. 116 BY62
Dunsters Mead, Welw.G.C. 30 DA11
Dunsterville Way SE1 279 L5
Dunston Rd. E8 142 DT67
Dunston Rd. SW11 160 DG83
Dunston St. E8 142 DT67
Dunton Clo., Surb. 198 CL102
Dunton Rd. E10 123 EB59
Dunton Rd. SE1 279 P9
Dunton Rd. SE1 162 DT77
Dunton Rd., Rom. 127 FE56
Duntshill Rd. SW18 180 DB88
Dunvegan Clo., W.Mol. 196 CB98
Dunvegan Rd. SE9 165 EM84
Dunwich Rd., Bexh. 166 EZ81
Dunworth Ms. W11 139 CZ72
Portobello Rd.
Duplex Ride SW1 276 E5
Dupont Rd. SW20 199 CX96
Dupont St. E14 143 DY71
Maroon St.
Duppas Ave., Croy. 219 DP105
Violet La.
Duppas Clo., Shep. 195 BR99
Green La.
Duppas Hill La., Croy. 219 DP105
Duppas Hill Rd.
Duppas Hill Rd., Croy. 219 DN105
Duppas Hill Ter., Croy. 201 DP104
Duppas Rd., Croy. 201 DN104
Dupre Clo., Grays 170 FY76
Dupre Cres., Beac. 89 AP54
Dupre Wk., H.Wyc. 110 AD59
Stratford Dr.
Dupree Rd. SE7 164 EH78
Dura Den Clo., Beck. 183 EB94
Durand Clo., Cars. 200 DF102
Durand Gdns. SW9 161 DM81
Durand Way NW10 138 CQ66
Durands Wk. SE16 163 DY75
Salter Rd.
Durant Rd., Swan. 187 FG93
Durant St. E2 142 DU69
Durants Pk. Ave., Enf. 83 DX42
Durants Rd., Enf. 82 DW42
Durban Gdns., Dag. 147 FC66
Durban Rd. E15 144 EE69
Durban Rd. E17 101 DZ53
Durban Rd. N17 100 DS51
Durban Rd. SE27 182 DQ91
Durban Rd., Beck. 203 DZ96
Durban Rd., Ilf. 125 ES60
Durban Rd. E., Wat. 75 BU42
Durban Rd. W., Wat. 75 BU42
Durbin Rd., Chess. 216 CL105
Durdans Rd., Sthl. 136 BZ72
Durell Gdns., Dag. 126 EX64
Durell Rd., Dag. 126 EX64
Durfold Dr., Reig. 250 DC134
Durford Cres. SW15 179 CV88
Durham Ave., Brom. 204 EF98
Durham Ave., Houns. 156 BZ79
Durham Ave., Rom. 128 FJ56
Durham Ave., Slou. 131 AN72
Durham Ave., Wdf.Grn. 102 EK50
Durham Clo. SW20 199 CV96
Durham Rd.
Durham Clo., Guil. 242 AT132
Durham Clo., Saw. 36 EW06
Durham Clo., Ware 33 EB10
Durham Hill, Brom. 184 EF91
Durham Ho. St. WC2 278 A1
Durham Pl. SW3 160 DF78
Smith St.
Durham Pl., Ilf. 125 EQ63
Eton Rd.
Durham Ri. SE18 165 EQ78
Durham Rd. E12 124 EK63
Durham Rd. E16 144 EE70
Durham Rd. N2 120 DE55
Durham Rd. N7 121 DM61
Durham Rd. N9 100 DU47
Durham Rd. SW20 199 CV95
Durham Rd. W5 157 CK76
Durham Rd., Borwd. 78 CQ41
Durham Rd., Brom. 204 EF97
Durham Rd., Dag. 127 FC64
Durham Rd., Felt. 176 BW87
Durham Rd., Har. 116 CB57
Durham Rd., Sid. 186 EV92
Durham Row E1 143 DY71
Durham St. SE11 161 DM78
Durham Ter. W2 140 DB72
Durham Wf., Brent. 157 CJ80
High St.
Durham Yd. E2 142 DV69
Teesdale St.
Durian Way, Erith 167 FH80
Durleston Pk. Dr., Lthd. 246 CC125
Durley Ave., Pnr. 116 BY59
Durley Gdns., Orp. 224 EV105
Durley Rd. N16 122 DS59
Durlston Rd. E5 122 DU61
Durlston Rd., Kings.T. 178 CL93
Durndale La., Grav. 190 GE91
Durnell Way, Loug. 85 EN41
Durnford St. N15 122 DS57
Durnford St. SE10 163 EC79
Greenwich Ch. St.
Durning Rd. SE19 182 DR92
Durnsford Ave. SW19 180 DA89
Durnsford Rd. N11 99 DK53
Durnsford Rd. SW19 180 DA89
Durrant Pl., Chesh. 54 AN27
Great Hivings
Durrant Way, Orp. 223 ER106
Durrant Way, Swans. 190 FY87
Durrants Clo., Rain. 148 FJ68
Durrants Dr., Rick. 75 BQ41
Durrants Hill Rd., Hem.H. 40 BK23
Durrants La., Berk. 38 AS19
Durrants Rd., Berk. 38 AT18
Durrell Rd. SW6 159 CZ81
Durrell Way, Shep. 195 BR100
Durrington Ave. SW20 199 CW95
Durrington Pk. Rd. SW20 199 CW95
Durrington Rd. E5 123 DY63
Dursley Clo. SE3 164 EJ82
Dursley Gdns. SE3 164 EK81
Dursley Rd. SE3 164 EJ82
Durward St. E1 142 DV71
Durweston Ms. W1 272 E6
Durweston St. W1 272 E7
Dury Falls Clo., Horn. 128 FM60
Dury Rd., Barn. 79 CZ40
Dutch Barn Clo., Stai. 174 BK86
Dutch Elm Ave., Wind. 152 AT80
Dutch Gdns., Kings.T. 178 CP93
Windmill Ri.
Dutch Yd. SW18 180 DA85
Wandsworth High St.
Duthie St. E14 143 EC73
Prestons Rd.
Dutton St. SE10 163 EC81
Dutton Way, Iver 133 BE72
Duxberry Clo., Brom. 204 EL99
Southborough La.
Duxford Clo., Horn. 147 FH65
Duxons Turn, Hem.H. 41 BP19
Maylands Ave.
Dwight Ct. SW6 159 CY82
Burlington Rd.
Dwight Rd., Wat. 93 BR45
Dye Ho. La. E3 143 EA67
Dyer's Bldgs. EC1 274 D7
Dyers Fld., Horl. 269 DP148
Dyers Hall Rd. E11 124 EE61
Dyers La. SW15 159 CV84
Dyers Way, Rom. 105 FH52
Dyke Dr., Orp. 206 EW102
Dykes Path, Wok. 227 BC115
Bentham Ave.
Dykes Way, Brom. 204 EF97
Dykewood Clo., Bex. 187 FE90
Dylan Clo., Borwd. 95 CK45
Coates Rd.
Dylan Rd. SE24 161 DP84
Dylan Rd., Belv. 166 FA76
Dylan Thomas Ho. N8 121 DM56
Dylways SE5 162 DR84
Dymchurch Clo., Ilf. 125 EN55
Dymchurch Clo., Orp. 223 ES105
Dymes Path SW19 179 CX89
Queensmere Rd.
Dymock St. SW6 160 DB83
Dymoke Grn., St.Alb. 43 CG16
Dymoke Rd., Horn. 127 FF59
Dymokes Way, Hodd. 33 EA14
Dymond Est. SW17 180 DE90
Glenburnie Rd.
Dyne Rd. NW6 139 CY66
Dyneley Rd. SE12 184 EJ91
Dynevor Rd. N16 122 DT62
Dynevor Rd., Rich. 178 CL85
Dynham Rd. NW6 140 DA66
Dyott St. WC1 273 N8
Dyott St. WC1 141 DK72
Dyrham La., Barn. 79 CU36
Dysart Ave., Kings.T. 177 CJ92
Dysart St. EC2 275 M5
Dyson Clo., Wind. 151 AP83
Dyson Rd. E11 124 EE58
Dyson Rd. E15 144 EF65
Dysons Clo., Wal.Cr. 67 DX33
Dysons Rd. N18 100 DV50

E

Eade Rd. N4 122 DQ59
Eagans Clo. N2 120 DE55
Market Pl.
Eagle Ave., Rom. 126 EY58
Eagle Clo. SE16 162 DW78
Varcoe Rd.
Eagle Clo., Enf. 82 DW42
Eagle Clo., Horn. 147 FH65
Eagle Clo., Wall. 219 DL107
Eagle Clo., Wal.Abb. 68 EG34
Eagle Ct. EC1 274 F6
Eagle Ct. EC1 141 DP71
Eagle Ct., Hert. 32 DV08
Eagle Dr. NW9 96 CS54
Eagle Hill SE19 182 DR93
Eagle La. E11 124 EG56
Eagle Ms. N1 142 DS65
Tottenham Rd.
Eagle Pl. SW1 277 L1
Eagle Pl. SW7 160 DC78
Old Brompton Rd.
Eagle Rd., Guil. 242 AX134
Eagle Rd., Wem. 137 CK66
Eagle St. WC1 274 B7
Eagle St. WC1 141 DM71
Eagle Ter., Wdf.Grn. 102 EH52
Eagle Way, Brwd. 107 FV51
Eagle Way, Grav. 190 GA85
Eagle Way, Hat. 45 CU20
Eagle Wf. E14 143 EB71
Broomfield St.
Eagle Wf. Rd. N1 142 DQ68
Eagles Dr., West. 238 EK118
Eagles Rd., Green. 169 FU84
Eaglesfield Rd. SE18 165 EP82
Ealdham Sq. SE9 164 EJ84
Ealing Clo., Borwd. 78 CR39
Ealing Downs Ct., Grnf. 137 CG69
Perivale La.
Ealing Grn. W5 137 CK74
Ealing Pk. Gdns. W5 157 CJ77
Ealing Rd., Brent. 157 CK77
Ealing Rd., Nthlt. 136 CA67
Ealing Rd., Wem. 138 CL65
Ealing Village W5 138 CL72
Eamont Clo., Ruis. 115 BP59
Allonby Dr.
Eamont St. NW8 140 DE68
Eardemont Clo., Dart. 167 FF84
Eardley Cres. SW5 160 DA78
Eardley Pt. SE18 165 EP77
Wilmount St.
Eardley Rd. SW16 181 DJ92
Eardley Rd., Belv. 166 FA78
Eardley Rd., Sev. 257 FH124
Earl Clo. N11 99 DH50
Earl Ri. SE18 165 ER77
Earl Rd. SE1 279 P10
Earl Rd. SE1 162 DT78
Earl Rd. SW14 158 CQ84
Elm Rd.
Earl Rd., Grav. 190 GE89
Earl St. EC2 275 L6
Earl St. EC2 142 DR71
Earl St., Wat. 76 BW41
Earldom Rd. SW15 159 CW84
Earle Gdns., Kings.T. 178 CL94
Earleswood, Cob. 214 BX112
Earlham Gro. E7 124 EF64
Earlham Gro. N22 99 DM52
Earlham St. WC2 273 N9
Earlham St. WC2 141 DK72
Earls Ct. Gdns. SW5 160 DB77
Earls Ct. Rd. SW5 160 DA77
Earls Ct. Rd. W8 160 DA77
Earls Ct. Sq. SW5 160 DB78
Earls Cres., Har. 117 CE56
Earls La., Pot.B. 62 CS32
Earls La., Slou. 131 AL74
Earl's Path, Loug. 84 EJ40
Earls Ter. W8 159 CZ76
Earls Wk. W8 160 DA76
Earls Wk., Dag. 126 EV63
Earls Way, Orp. 205 ET103
Station Rd.
Earlsbrook Rd., Red. 266 DF136
Earlsdown Ho., Bark. 145 ER68
Wheelers Cross
Earlsferry Way N1 141 DM66
Earlsfield, Maid. 150 AC77
Earlsfield Rd. SW18 180 DC88
Earlshall Rd. SE9 165 EM84
Earlsmead, Har. 116 BZ63
Earlsmead Rd. N15 122 DT57
Earlsmead Rd. NW10 139 CW69
Earlsthorpe Ms. SW12 180 DG86
Earlsthorpe Rd. SE26 183 DX91
Earlstoke St. EC1 274 F2
Earlston Gro. E9 142 DV67
Earlswood Ave., Th.Hth. 201 DN99
Earlswood Clo. SE10 164 EE78
Earlswood St.
Earlswood Gdns., Ilf. 125 EN55
Earlswood Rd., Red. 266 DF136
Earlswood St. SE10 164 EE78
Early Ms. NW1 141 DH67
Arlington Rd.
Earnshaw St. WC2 273 N8
Earnshaw St. WC2 141 DK72
Earsby St. W14 159 CY77
Easby Cres., Mord. 200 DB100
Easebourne Rd., Dag. 126 EW64
Easedale Dr., Horn. 127 FG64
Easedale Ho., Islw. 177 CF85
Easington Pl., Guil. 259 AZ135
Maori Rd.
Easington Way, S.Ock. 149 FU71
Easley's Ms. W1 272 G8
East Acton La. W3 138 CS73
East Arbour St. E1 143 DX72
East Ave. E12 144 EL66
East Ave. E17 123 EB56
East Ave., Hayes 155 BT75
East Ave., Sthl. 136 BZ73
East Ave., Wall. 219 DM106
East Ave., Walt. 213 BT110
Octagon Rd.
East Bank N16 122 DS59
East Barnet Rd., Barn. 80 DD42
East Burnham La., Slou. 131 AN67
East Burrow Fld., Welw.G.C. 29 CX11
East Churchfield Rd. W3 138 CR74
East Clo. W5 138 CN70
East Clo., Barn. 80 DG42
East Clo., Grnf. 136 CC68
East Clo., Rain. 147 FH70
East Clo., St.Alb. 60 CB25
East Common, Ger.Cr. 112 AY58
East Ct., Wem. 117 CJ61
East Cres. N11 98 DF49
East Cres., Enf. 82 DS43
East Cres., Wind. 151 AM81
East Cres. Rd., Grav. 191 GJ86
East Cross Route E3 143 DZ66
East Dene Dr., Rom. 106 FK50
East Dr., Cars. 218 DE109
East Dr., Nthwd. 93 BS47
East Dr., Orp. 206 EV100
East Dr., St.Alb. 44 CL19
East Dr., Saw. 36 EY06
East Dr., Slou. 132 AS69
East Dr., Vir.W. 192 AV100
East Dr., Wat. 75 BV35
East Duck Lees La., Enf. 83 DY42
Duck Lees La.
East Dulwich Gro. SE22 182 DS85
East Dulwich Rd. SE15 162 DU84
East Dulwich Rd. SE22 162 DT84
East End Rd. N2 120 DB55
East End Rd. N3 97 CZ54
East End Way, Pnr. 116 BY55
East Entrance, Dag. 147 FB68
East Ferry Rd. E14 163 EB77
East Flint, Hem.H. 39 BF19
East Gdns. SW17 180 DE93
East Gdns., Wok. 227 BC117
East Gate, Harl. 35 ER14
East Gorse, Croy. 221 DY112
East Grn., Hem.H. 58 BM25
East Hall La., Rain. 148 FK72
East Hall Rd., Orp. 206 EY101
East Ham Ind. Est. E6 144 EK70
East Ham Manor Way E6 145 EN72
East Harding St. EC4 274 E8
East Heath Rd. NW3 120 DC62
East Hill SW18 180 DB85
East Hill, Dart. 188 FM87
East Hill (South Darenth), Dart. 208 FQ95
East Hill, Oxt. 254 EE129
East Hill, S.Croy. 220 DS110
East Hill, Wem. 118 CN61
East Hill, West. 238 EH118
East Hill, Wok. 227 BC116
East Hill Dr., Dart. 188 FM87
East Hill Rd., Oxt. 254 EE129
East Holme, Erith 167 FD81
East Holme, Hayes 135 BU74
East India Dock Rd. E14 143 EA72
East India Dock Wall Rd. E14 143 ED73
East Kent Ave., Grav. 190 GC86
East La. SE16 162 DU75
East La., Abb.L. 59 BT28
East La., Dart. 209 FR96
East Hill
East La., Kings.T. 197 CK97
East La., Lthd. 245 BQ126
East La., Wem. 117 CH62
East Lo. La., Enf. 81 DK36
East Mascalls SE7 164 EJ79
Mascalls Rd.
East Mead, Ruis. 116 BX62
East Mead, Welw.G.C. 30 DB12
East Meads, Guil. 258 AT135
East Mill, Grav. 191 GF86
East Milton Rd., Grav. 191 GK87
East Mimms, Hem.H. 40 BL19
East Mt. St. E1 142 DV71
East Pk., Harl. 36 EW12
East Pk., Saw. 36 EY06
East Pk. Clo., Rom. 126 EX57
East Pas. EC1 275 H6

Elm Tree Clo. NW8 140 DD69
Elm Tree Clo., Ashf. 175 BP92
Convent Rd.
Elm Tree Clo., Cher. 193 BE103
Green La.
Elm Tree Clo., Horl. 268 DG147
Elm Tree Clo., Nthlt. 136 BZ68
Elm Tree Rd. NW8 140 DD69
Elm Wk. NW3 120 DA61
Elm Wk. SW20 199 CW98
Elm Wk., Orp. 205 EM104
Elm Wk., Rad. 77 CF36
Elm Wk., Rom. 127 FG55
Elm Way N11 98 DG51
Elm Way NW10 118 CS63
Elm Way, Brwd. 108 FU49
Elm Way, Epsom 216 CR106
Elm Way, Rick. 92 BH46
Elm Way, Wor.Pk. 199 CW104
Elmar Grn., Slou. 131 AN69
Elmar Rd. N15 122 DR56
Elmbank Ave., Barn. 79 CW42
Elmbank Ave., Egh. 172 AV93
Elmbank Ave., Guil. 258 AU135
Elmbank Way W7 137 CD71
Elmbourne Dr., Belv. 167 FB77
Elmbourne Rd. SW17 180 DG90
Elmbridge, Harl. 36 EZ12
Elmbridge Ave., Surb. 198 CP99
Elmbridge Clo., Ruis. 115 BU58
Elmbridge Dr., Ruis. 115 BT57
Elmbridge La., Wok. 227 AZ119
Elmbridge Rd., Ilf. 104 EU51
Elmbridge Wk. E8 142 DU66
Wilman Gro.
Elmbrook Clo., Sun. 195 BV95
Elmbrook Gdns. SE9 164 EL84
Elmbrook Rd., Sutt. 217 CZ105
Elmcote Way, Rick. 74 BM44
Elmcourt Rd. SE27 181 DP89
Elmcroft, Lthd. 230 CA124
Elmcroft Ave. E11 124 EH57
Elmcroft Ave. N9 82 DV44
Elmcroft Ave. NW11 119 CZ59
Elmcroft Ave., Sid. 185 ET87
Elmcroft Clo. E11 124 EH56
Elmcroft Clo. N8 121 DM57
Elmcroft Clo. W5 137 CK72
Elmcroft Clo., Chess. 198 CL104
Elmcroft Clo., Felt. 175 BT86
Elmcroft Cres. NW11 119 CX59
Elmcroft Cres., Har. 116 CA55
Elmcroft Dr., Ashf. 174 BN92
Elmcroft Dr., Chess. 198 CL104
Elmcroft Gdns. NW9 118 CN57
Elmcroft Rd., Orp. 206 EU101
Elmcroft St. E5 122 DW63
Elmdale Rd. N13 99 DM50
Elmdene, Surb. 198 CQ102
Elmdene Ave., Horn. 128 FM57
Elmdene Clo., Beck. 203 DZ99
Elmdene Rd. SE18 165 EP78
Elmdon Rd., Houns. 156 BX82
Elmdon Rd. 155 BT83
(Hatton Cross), Houns.
Elmer Ave. 105 FE48
(Havering-atte-Bower), Rom.
Elmer Clo., Enf. 81 DM41
Elmer Clo., Rain. 147 FG66
Elmer Cotts., Lthd. 231 CG123
Elmer Gdns., Edg. 96 CP52
Elmer Gdns., Islw. 157 CD83
Elmer Gdns., Rain. 147 FG66
Elmer Ms., Lthd. 231 CG122
Elmer Rd. SE6 183 EC87
Elmers Dr., Tedd. 177 CH93
Kingston Rd.
Elmers End Rd. SE20 202 DW96
Elmers End Rd., Beck. 202 DW96
Elmers Rd. SE25 202 DU101
Elmerside Rd., Beck. 203 DY98
Elmfield, Lthd. 230 CA123
Elmfield Ave. N8 121 DL57
Elmfield Ave., Mitch. 200 DG95
Elmfield Ave., Tedd. 177 CF92
Elmfield Clo., Grav. 191 GH88
Elmfield Clo., Har. 117 CE61
Elmfield Clo., Pot.B. 63 CY33
Elmfield Pk., Brom. 204 EG97
Elmfield Rd. E4 101 EC47
Elmfield Rd. E17 123 DX57
Elmfield Rd. N2 120 DD55
Elmfield Rd. SW17 180 DG89
Elmfield Rd., Brom. 204 EG97
Elmfield Rd., Pot.B. 63 CY32
Elmfield Rd., Sthl. 156 BY76
Elmfield Way W9 140 DA71
Elmfield Way, S.Croy. 220 DT109
Elmgate Ave., Felt. 175 BV90
Elmgate Gdns., Edg. 96 CR50
Elmgreen Clo. E15 144 EE67
Church St. N.
Elmgrove Cres., Har. 117 CF57
Elmgrove Gdns., Har. 117 CG57
Elmgrove Rd., Croy. 202 DV101
Elmgrove Rd., Har. 117 CF57
Elmgrove Rd., Wey. 212 BN105
Elmhurst, Belv. 166 EY79
Elmhurst Ave. N2 120 DD55
Elmhurst Ave., Mitch. 180 DG94
Elmhurst Ct., Guil. 259 AZ135
Lower Edgeborough Rd.
Elmhurst Dr. E18 102 EG54
Elmhurst Dr., Dor. 263 CH138
Elmhurst Dr., Horn. 128 FJ60
Elmhurst Gdns. E18 102 EH53
Elmhurst Rd. E7 144 EH66
Elmhurst Rd. N17 100 DS54
Elmhurst Rd. SE9 184 EL89
Elmhurst Rd., Enf. 82 DW37
Elmhurst Rd., Slou. 153 BA76
Elmhurst St. SW4 161 DK83
Elmhurst Way, Loug. 103 EM45
Elmington Clo., Bex. 187 FB86
Elmington Est. SE5 162 DR80
Elmington Rd. SE5 162 DR81
Elmira St. SE13 163 EB83
Elmlea Dr., Hayes 135 BS71
Grange Rd.
Elmlee Clo., Chis. 185 EM93
Elmley Clo. E6 144 EL71
Northumberland Rd.
Elmley St. SE18 165 ER77
Elmore Clo., Wem. 138 CL68
Elmore Rd. E11 123 EC62
Elmore Rd., Couls. 234 DF121
Elmore Rd., Enf. 83 DX38
Elmore St. N1 142 DR66
Elmores, Loug. 85 EN41
Elmpark Gdns., S.Croy. 220 DW110
Elmroyd Ave., Pot.B. 63 CZ33
Elmroyd Clo., Pot.B. 63 CZ33
Elms, The SW13 159 CT83
Elms, The, Hert. 32 DU09
Elms Ave. N10 121 DH55
Elms Ave. NW4 119 CX57
Elms Ct., Wem. 117 CG63
Elms Cres. SW4 181 DJ86
Elms Fm. Rd., Horn. 128 FJ64
Elms Gdns., Dag. 126 EZ63
Elms Gdns., Wem. 117 CG63
Elms Ind. Est., Rom. 106 FP52
Elms La., Wem. 117 CG62
Elms Ms. W2 140 DD73
Elms Pk. Ave., Wem. 117 CG63
Elms Rd. SW4 181 DJ85
Elms Rd., Ger.Cr. 90 AY52
Elms Rd., Har. 95 CE52
Elms Rd., Ware 33 EA05
Elms Wk. SE3 164 EF84
Elmscott Gdns. N21 82 DQ44
Elmscott Rd., Brom. 184 EE92
Elmscroft N8 121 DM57
Tottenham La.
Elmscroft Gdns., Pot.B. 63 CZ32
Elmsdale Rd. E17 123 DZ56
Elmshaw Rd. SW15 179 CU85
Elmshorn, Epsom 233 CW116
Elmshott La., Slou. 131 AL73
Elmshurst Cres. N2 120 DC56
Elmside, Croy. 221 EB107
Elmside, Guil. 258 AU135
Elmside Rd., Wem. 118 CN62
Elmsleigh Ave., Har. 117 CH56
Elmsleigh Cen., The, Stai. 173 BF91
Elmsleigh Rd., Stai. 173 BF92
Thames St.
Elmsleigh Rd., Twick. 177 CD89
Elmslie Clo., Epsom 216 CQ114
Elmslie Clo., Wdf.Grn. 103 EM51
Gwynne Pk. Ave.
Elmslie Pt. E3 143 DZ71
Ackroyd Dr.
Elmstead Ave., Chis. 185 EM92
Elmstead Ave., Wem. 118 CL60
Elmstead Clo. N20 98 DA47
Elmstead Clo., Epsom 216 CS106
Elmstead Clo., Sev. 256 FE122
Elmstead Cres., Well. 166 EW79
Elmstead Gdns., Wor.Pk. 199 CU104
Elmstead Glade, Chis. 185 EM93
Elmstead La., Chis. 184 EL94
Elmstead Rd., Erith 167 FE81
Elmstead Rd., Ilf. 125 ES61
Elmstead Rd., W.Byf. 212 BG113
Elmstone Rd. SW6 160 DA81
Elmsway, Ashf. 174 BM92
Elmswood, Lthd. 230 BZ124
Elmsworth Ave., Houns. 156 CB82
Elmton Way E5 122 DU62
Rendlesham Rd.
Elmtree Clo., W.Byf. 212 BL113
Elmtree Hill, Chesh. 54 AP30
Elmtree Rd., Tedd. 177 CE91
Elmwood, Saw. 36 EZ06
Elmwood, Welw.G.C. 29 CV10
Elmwood Ave. N13 99 DL50
Elmwood Ave., Borwd. 78 CP42
Elmwood Ave., Felt. 175 BU89
Elmwood Ave., Har. 117 CG57
Elmwood Clo., Ash. 231 CK117
Elmwood Clo., Epsom 217 CU108
Elmwood Clo., Wall. 200 DG103
Elmwood Ct., Ash. 231 CK117
Elmwood Clo.
Elmwood Ct., Wem. 117 CG62
Elmwood Cres. NW9 118 CQ56
Elmwood Dr., Bex. 186 EY87
Elmwood Dr., Epsom 217 CU107
Elmwood Gdns. W7 137 CE72
Elmwood Pk., Ger.Cr. 112 AY60
Elmwood Rd. SE24 182 DR85
Elmwood Rd. W4 158 CQ79
Elmwood Rd., Croy. 201 DP101
Elmwood Rd., Mitch. 200 DF97
Elmwood Rd., Red. 250 DG130
Elmwood Rd., Slou. 132 AV73
Elmworth Gro. SE21 182 DR89
Elnathan Ms. W9 140 DB70
Shirland Rd.
Elphinstone Rd. E17 101 DZ54
Elphinstone St. N5 121 DP63
Avenell Rd.
Elrick Clo., Erith 167 FE79
Elrington Rd. E8 142 DU65
Elrington Rd., Wdf.Grn. 102 EG50
Elruge Clo., West Dr. 154 BK76
Elsa Rd., Well. 166 EV82
Elsa St. E1 143 DY71
Elsdale St. E9 142 DW65
Elsden Ms. E2 142 DW68
Old Ford Rd.
Elsden Rd. N17 100 DT53
Elsdon Rd., Wok. 226 AU118
Elsenham Rd. E12 125 EN64
Elsenham St. SW18 179 CZ88
Elsham Rd. E11 124 EE62
Elsham Rd. W14 159 CY75
Elsham Ter. W14 159 CY75
Elsie Rd. SE22 162 DT84
Elsiedene Rd. N21 100 DQ45
Elsiemaud Rd. SE4 183 DZ85
Elsinge Rd., Enf. 82 DV36
Elsinore Ave., Stai. 174 BL87
Elsinore Gdns. NW2 119 CY62
Elsinore Rd. SE23 183 DY88
Elsinore Way, Rich. 158 CP83
Lower Richmond Rd.
Elsley Rd. SW11 160 DF83
Elspeth Rd. SW11 160 DF84
Elspeth Rd., Wem. 118 CL64
Elsrick Ave., Mord. 200 DA99
Chalgrove Ave.
Elstan Way, Croy. 203 DY101
Elsted St. SE17 279 L9
Elsted St. SE17 162 DR77
Elston La., Sev. 241 FF117
Elstow Clo. SE9 185 EN85
Elstow Clo., Ruis. 116 BX59
Elstow Gdns., Dag. 146 EY67
Elstow Rd., Dag. 146 EY66
Elstree Gdns. N9 100 DV46
Elstree Gdns., Belv. 166 EY77
Elstree Gdns., Ilf. 125 EQ64
Elstree Hill, Brom. 184 EE94
Elstree Hill N., Borwd. 77 CK44
Elstree Hill S., Borwd. 95 CJ45
Elstree Rd., Borwd. 77 CH44
Elstree Rd. (Bushey), Wat. 95 CD45
Elstree Way, Borwd. 78 CP41
Elswell Ct., Hert. 31 DM08
Elswick Rd. SE13 163 EB82
Elswick St. SW6 160 DC82
Elsworth Clo., Felt. 175 BS88
Elsworthy, T.Ditt. 197 CE100
Elsworthy Ri. NW3 140 DE66
Elsworthy Rd. NW3 140 DD67
Elsworthy Ter. NW3 140 DE66
Elsynge Rd. SW18 180 DD85
Eltham Ave., Slou. 151 AL75
Eltham Grn. SE9 184 EJ85
Eltham Grn. Rd. SE9 164 EJ84
Eltham High St. SE9 185 EM86
Eltham Hill SE9 184 EK85
Eltham Palace Rd. SE9 184 EJ86
Eltham Pk. Gdns. SE9 165 EN84
Eltham Pl., Guil. 242 AT132
Canterbury Rd.
Eltham Rd. SE9 184 EJ85
Eltham Rd. SE12 184 EG85
Elthiron Rd. SW6 160 DA81
Elthorne Ave. W7 157 CF75
Elthorne Ct., Felt. 176 BW88
Elthorne Pk. Rd. W7 157 CF75
Elthorne Rd. N19 121 DK61
Elthorne Rd. NW9 118 CR59
Elthorne Rd., Uxb. 134 BK68
Elthorne Way NW9 118 CR58
Elthruda Rd. SE13 183 ED86
Eltisley Rd., Ilf. 125 EP63
Elton Ave., Barn. 79 CZ43
Elton Ave., Grnf. 137 CE65
Elton Ave., Wem. 117 CH64
Elton Clo., Kings.T. 177 CJ94
Elton Ho. E3 143 DZ67
Elton Pk., Wat. 75 BV40
Elton Pl. N16 122 DS64
Elton Rd., Hert. 32 DQ08
Elton Rd., Kings.T. 198 CM95
Elton Rd., Pur. 219 DJ112
Elton Way (Bushey), Wat. 76 CB40
Eltringham St. SW18 160 DC84
Elvaston Ms. SW7 160 DC76
Elvaston Pl. SW7 160 DC76
Elveden Clo., Wok. 228 BH117
Elveden Pl. NW10 138 CN68
Elveden Rd. NW10 138 CN68
Elvedon Rd., Cob. 213 BV111
Elvendon Rd. N13 99 DL51
Elver Gdns. E2 142 DU68
St. Peter's Clo.
Elverson Rd. SE8 163 EB82
Elverton St. SW1 277 M8
Elverton St. SW1 161 DK77
Elvet Ave., Rom. 128 FJ56
Elvington Grn., Brom. 204 EF99
Elvington La. NW9 96 CS53
Elvino Rd. SE26 183 DX92
Elvis Rd. NW2 139 CW65
Elwell Clo., Egh. 173 BA92
Mowbray Cres.
Elwick Rd., S.Ock. 149 FW72
Elwill Way, Beck. 203 EC98
Elwin St. E2 142 DU69
Elwood, Harl. 52 EY16
Elwood Rd., Beac. 88 AH54
Elwood St. N5 121 DP62
Elwyn Gdns. SE12 184 EG87
Ely Ave., Slou. 131 AQ71
Ely Clo., Amer. 55 AS39
Ely Clo., Erith 167 FF82
Ely Clo., Hat. 45 CT17
Ely Clo., N.Mal. 199 CT96
Ely Ct. EC1 274 E7
Ely Gdns., Borwd. 78 CR43
Ely Gdns., Dag. 127 FC62
Ely Gdns., Ilf. 124 EL59
Canterbury Ave.
Ely Pl. EC1 274 E7
Ely Pl., Guil. 242 AT132
Canterbury Rd.
Ely Pl., Wdf.Grn. 103 EN51
Ely Rd. E10 123 EC59
Ely Rd., Croy. 202 DR99
Ely Rd. 155 BT82
(Heathrow Airport), Houns.
Eastern Perimeter Rd.
Ely Rd. (Hounslow W.), 156 BW83
Houns.
Ely Rd., St.Alb. 43 CH21
Elyne Rd. N4 121 DN58
Elysian Ave., Orp. 205 ES100
Elysium Pl. SW6 159 CZ82
Fulham Pk. Gdns.
Elysium St. SW6 159 CZ82
Fulham Pk. Gdns.
Elystan Clo., Wall. 219 DH109
Elystan Pl. SW3 276 C10
Elystan Pl. SW3 160 DE78
Elystan St. SW3 276 B9
Elystan St. SW3 160 DE77
Elystan Wk. N1 141 DN67
Cloudesley Rd.
Emanuel Ave. W3 138 CQ72
Emanuel Dr., Hmptn. 176 BZ92
Emba St. SE16 162 DU75
Embankment SW15 159 CX82
Embankment, The, Stai. 172 AW87
Embankment, The, Twick. 177 CG88
Embankment Gdns. SW3 160 DF79
Embankment Pl. WC2 278 A2
Embankment Pl. WC2 141 DL74
Embassy Ct., Sid. 186 EV90
Embassy Ct., Well. 166 EV83
Ember Clo., Add. 212 BK106
Ember Clo., Orp. 205 EQ101
Ember Fm. Ave., E.Mol. 197 CD100
Ember Fm. Way, E.Mol. 197 CD100
Ember Gdns., T.Ditt. 197 CE101
Ember La., E.Mol. 197 CD100
Ember La., Esher 197 CD101
Ember Rd., Slou. 153 BB76
Embercourt Rd., T.Ditt. 197 CE100
Emberson Way, Epp. 71 FC26
Emberton SE5 162 DS79
Albany Rd.
Embleton Rd. SE13 163 EB84
Embleton Rd., Wat. 93 BU48
Embleton Wk., Hmptn. 176 BZ93
Fearnley Cres.
Embley Pt. E5 122 DV63
Tiger Way
Embry Clo., Stan. 95 CG49
Embry Dr., Stan. 95 CG51
Embry Way, Stan. 95 CG49
Emden Clo., West Dr. 154 BN75
Emden St. SW6 160 DB81
Emerald Clo. E16 144 EL72
Emerald Ct., Slou. 152 AS75
Emerald Gdns., Dag. 126 FA60
Emerald St. WC1 274 B6
Emerald St. WC1 141 DM71
Emerson Dr., Horn. 128 FK59
Emerson Gdns., Har. 118 CM58
Emerson Rd., Ilf. 125 EN59
Emerson St. SE1 279 H2
Emerson St. SE1 142 DQ74
Emersons Ave., Swan. 187 FF94
Emerton Clo., Bexh. 166 EY84
Emerton Ct., Berk. 38 AS16
Emerton Garth
Emerton Garth, Berk. 38 AS16
Emerton Rd., Lthd. 230 CC120
Emery Hill St. SW1 277 L7
Emery Hill St. SW1 161 DJ76
Emery St. SE1 278 E6
Emes Rd., Erith 167 FC80
Emily Jackson Clo., Sev. 257 FH124
Emily Pl. N7 121 DN63
Emley Rd., Add. 194 BG104
Emlyn Gdns. W12 158 CS75
Emlyn La., Lthd. 231 CG122
Emlyn Rd. W12 158 CS75
Emlyn Rd., Horl. 268 DE147
Emlyn Rd., Red. 266 DG136
Emma Rd. E13 144 EF68
Emma St. E2 142 DV68
Emmanuel Clo., Guil. 242 AU131
Emmanuel Clo., Nthwd. 93 BT52
Emmanuel Rd.
Emmanuel Lo., Wal.Cr. 66 DW30
College Rd.
Emmanuel Rd. SW12 181 DJ88
Emmanuel Rd., Nthwd. 93 BT52
Emma's Cres., Ware 33 EB11
Emmaus Way, Chig. 103 EN50
Emmetts Clo., Wok. 226 AX117
Emmott Ave., Ilf. 125 EQ57
Emmott Clo. E1 143 DY70
Emmott Clo. NW11 120 DC58
Emms Pas., Kings.T. 197 CK96
High St.
Emperor Clo., Berk. 38 AT16
Springfield Rd.
Emperor's Gate SW7 160 DB76
Empire Ave. N18 100 DQ50
Empire Cen., Wat. 76 BW39
Empire Ct., Wem. 118 CP62
Empire Rd., Grnf. 137 CH67
Empire Vill., Red. 266 DG144
Empire Way, Wem. 118 CM63
Empire Wf. Rd. E14 163 ED77
Empire Yd. N7 121 DL62
Holloway Rd.
Empress Ave. E4 101 EB52
Empress Ave. E12 124 EJ61
Empress Ave., Ilf. 125 EM61
Empress Ave., Wdf.Grn. 102 EF52
Empress Dr., Chis. 185 EP93
Empress Pl. SW6 160 DA78
Empress Rd., Grav. 191 GL87
Empress St. SE17 162 DQ79
Empson St. E3 143 EB70
Emsworth Clo. N9 100 DW46
Emsworth Rd., Ilf. 103 EP54
Emsworth St. SW2 181 DL89
Emu Rd. SW8 161 DH82
Ena Rd. SW16 201 DL97
Enborne Grn., S.Ock. 149 FU71
Elan Rd.
Enbrook St. W10 139 CY69
End Way, Surb. 198 CN101
Endale Clo., Cars. 200 DF103
Endeavour Rd. 67 DY27
(Cheshunt), Wal.Cr.
Endeavour Way SW19 180 DB91
Endeavour Way, Bark. 146 EU68
Endeavour Way, Croy. 201 DK101
Endell St. WC2 273 P8
Endell St. WC2 141 DL72
Enderby St. SE10 164 EE78
Enderley Clo., Har. 95 CE53
Enderley Rd., Har. 95 CE53
Endersby Rd., Barn. 79 CW43
Endersleigh Gdns. NW4 119 CU56
Endlebury Rd. E4 101 EC47
Endlesham Rd. SW12 180 DG87
Endsleigh Clo., S.Croy. 220 DW110
Endsleigh Gdns. WC1 273 M4
Endsleigh Gdns. WC1 141 DK70
Endsleigh Gdns., Ilf. 125 EM61
Endsleigh Gdns., Surb. 197 CJ100
Endsleigh Gdns., Walt. 214 BW106
Endsleigh Pl. WC1 273 N4
Endsleigh Pl. WC1 141 DK70
Endsleigh Rd. W13 137 CG73
Endsleigh Rd., Red. 251 DJ129
Endsleigh Rd., Sthl. 156 BY77
Endsleigh St. WC1 273 N4
Endsleigh St. WC1 141 DK70
Endwell Rd. SE4 163 DY82
Endymion Clo., Hat. 45 CW17
Endymion Rd.
Endymion Ms., Hat. 45 CW17
Endymion Rd.
Endymion Rd. N4 121 DN59
Endymion Rd. SW2 181 DM86
Endymion Rd., Hat. 45 CW17
Enfield Clo., Uxb. 134 BK68
Villier St.
Enfield Retail Pk., Enf. 82 DU41
Crown Rd.
Enfield Rd. N1 142 DS66
Enfield Rd. W3 158 CP75
Enfield Rd., Brent. 157 CK78
Enfield Rd., Enf. 81 DL42
Enfield Rd., Houns. 155 BS82
Eastern Perimeter Rd.
Enfield Wk., Brent. 157 CK78
Enfield Rd.
Enford St. W1 272 D6
Enford St. W1 140 DF71
Engadine Clo., Croy. 202 DT104
Engadine St. SW18 179 CZ88
Engate St. SE13 163 EC84
Engayne Gdns., Upmin. 128 FP60
Engel Pk. NW7 97 CW51
Engineer Clo. SE18 165 EN79
Engineers Way, Wem. 118 CN63
Englands La. NW3 140 DF65
Englands La., Loug. 85 EN40
Englefield Clo., Croy. 202 DQ100
Queen's Rd.
Englefield Clo., Enf. 81 DN40
Englefield Clo., Orp. 205 ET98
Englefield Cres., Orp. 205 ET98
Englefield Grn., Egh. 172 AW91
Englefield Path, Orp. 206 EU98
Englefield Rd. N1 142 DR66
Englefield Rd., Orp. 206 EU98
Engleheart Dr., Felt. 175 BT86
Engleheart Rd. SE6 183 EB87
Englehurst, Egh. 172 AW93
Englewood Rd. SW12 181 DH86
Engliff La., Wok. 227 BF116
English Gdns., Stai. 172 AX85
English Grds. SE1 279 M3
English St. E3 143 DZ70
Enid Clo., St.Alb. 60 BZ31
Enid St. SE16 162 DT76
Enmore Ave. SE25 202 DU99
Enmore Gdns. SW14 178 CR85
Enmore Rd. SE25 202 DU99
Enmore Rd. SW15 159 CW84
Enmore Rd., Sthl. 136 CA70
Enndale Cres., Slou. 130 AJ71
Ennerdale Ave., Horn. 127 FG64
Ennerdale Ave., Stan. 117 CJ55
Ennerdale Clo., Felt. 175 BT88
Ennerdale Clo., St.Alb. 43 CH22
Ennerdale Clo. (Cheam), 217 CZ105
Sutt.
Ennerdale Dr. NW9 118 CS57
Ennerdale Gdns., Wem. 117 CJ60
Ennerdale Ho. E3 143 DZ70
Ennerdale Rd., Bexh. 166 FA81
Ennerdale Rd., Rich. 158 CM82
Ennersdale Rd. SE13 183 ED85
Ennis Rd. N4 121 DN60
Ennis Rd. SE18 165 EQ79
Ennismore Ave. W4 159 CT77
Ennismore Ave., Grnf. 137 CE65
Ennismore Ave., Guil. 243 AZ134
Ennismore Gdns. SW7 276 B6
Ennismore Gdns. SW7 160 DE75
Ennismore Gdns., T.Ditt. 197 CE100
Ennismore Gdns. Ms. SW7 276 B6
Ennismore Gdns. Ms. SW7 160 DE76
Ennismore Ms. SW7 276 B6
Ennismore Ms. SW7 160 DE76
Ennismore St. SW7 276 B6
Ennismore St. SW7 160 DE76
Ensign Clo., Pur. 219 DN110
Ensign Clo., Stai. 174 BL88
Ensign Dr. N13 100 DQ48
Ensign St. E1 142 DU73
Ensign Way, Stai. 174 BK88
Enslin Rd. SE9 185 EN87
Ensor Ms. SW7 160 DD78
Cranley Gdns.
Enstone Rd., Enf. 83 DY41
Enstone Rd., Uxb. 114 BM62
Enterdent Rd., Gdse. 252 DW134
Enterprise Clo., Croy. 201 DN102
Enterprise Way NW10 139 CU69
Enterprise Way SW18 160 DA84
Enterprise Way, Tedd. 177 CF92
Enterprize Way SE8 163 DZ77
Epirus Ms. SW6 160 DA80
Epirus Rd.
Epirus Rd. SW6 159 CZ80
Epping Clo. E14 163 EA77
Epping Clo., Rom. 127 FB55
Epping Glade E4 83 EC44
Epping Grn., Hem.H. 40 BN15
Epping La., Rom. 86 EV40
Epping New Rd., Buck.H. 102 EG48
Epping New Rd., Loug. 84 EJ41
Epping Pl. N1 141 DN65
Liverpool Rd.
Epping Rd., Epp. 85 EM35
Epping Rd. (Epping Grn.), 51 EP24
Epp.
Epping Rd. 70 EW28
(North Weald Bassett), Epp.
Epping Rd., Harl. 50 EH15
Epping Rd., Ong. 53 FF24
Epping Rd. (Toot Hill), Ong. 71 FC30
Epping Rd., Wal.Abb. 50 EL19
Epping Way E4 83 EB44
Epple Rd. SW6 159 CZ81
Epsom Clo., Bexh. 167 FB83
Epsom Clo., Nthlt. 116 BZ64
Epsom Downs, Epsom 233 CT118
Epsom Gap, Lthd. 231 CH115
Kingston Rd.
Epsom La. N., Epsom 233 CV118
Epsom La. S., Tad. 233 CW121
Epsom Rd. E10 123 EC58
Epsom Rd., Ash. 232 CM118
Epsom Rd., Croy. 219 DN105
Epsom Rd., Epsom 217 CT111
Epsom Rd., Guil. 258 AY135
Epsom Rd. 244 BH132
(East Clandon), Guil.
Epsom Rd., Ilf. 125 ET58
Epsom Rd., Lthd. 231 CH121
Epsom Rd. 245 BP130
(West Horsley), Lthd.
Epsom Rd., Mord. 200 DA100
Epsom Rd., Sutt. 199 CZ101
Epsom Sq., Houns. 155 BT82
Eastern Perimeter Rd.
Epsom Way, Horn. 128 FM63
Epstein Rd. SE28 146 EU74
Epworth Rd., Islw. 157 CH81
Epworth St. EC2 275 L5
Epworth St. EC2 142 DR70
Equity Sq. E2 142 DT69
Shacklewell St.

Erasmus St. SW1 277 N9
Erasmus St. SW1 161 DK77
Erconwald St. W12 139 CT72
Eresby Dr., Beck. 203 EA102
Eresby Pl. NW6 140 DA66
Eric Clo. E7 124 EG63
Eric Rd. E7 124 EG63
Eric Rd. NW10 139 CT65
Church Rd.
Eric Rd., Rom. 126 EX59
Eric Steele Ho., St.Alb. 60 CB27
Eric St. E3 143 DZ70
Erica Clo., Slou. 131 AL73
Erica Ct., Swan. 207 FE98
Azalea Dr.
Erica Ct., Wok. 226 AX118
Erica Gdns., Croy. 203 EA104
Erica St. W12 139 CU73
Ericcson Clo. SW18 180 DA85
Eridge Grn. Clo., Orp. 206 EW102
Petten Gro.
Eridge Rd. W4 158 CR76
Erin Clo., Brom. 184 EE94
Erindale SE18 165 ER79
Erindale Ter. SE18 165 ER79
Eriswell Cres., Walt. 213 BS107
Eriswell Rd., Walt. 213 BT105
Erith Ct., Purf. 168 FN77
Thamley
Erith Cres., Rom. 105 FC53
Erith High St., Erith 167 FE78
Erith Rd., Belv. 166 FA78
Erith Rd., Bexh. 167 FB84
Erith Rd., Erith 167 FC81
Erkenwald Clo., Cher. 193 BE101
Erlanger Rd. SE14 163 DX81
Erlesmere Gdns. W13 157 CG76
Ermine Clo., Houns. 156 BW82
Ermine Clo., St.Alb. 42 CA21
Ermine Clo. (Cheshunt), Wal.Cr. 66 DV31
Ermine Ho. N17 100 DT52
Ermine Rd. N15 122 DT58
Ermine Rd. SE13 163 EB84
Ermine Side, Enf. 82 DU43
Ermine St., Hert. 48 DV16
Ermington Rd. SE9 185 EQ89
Ermyn Clo., Lthd. 231 CK121
Ermyn Way, Lthd. 231 CK121
Ernald Ave. E6 144 EL68
Ernan Clo., S.Ock. 149 FU71
Ernan Rd., S.Ock. 149 FU71
Erncroft Way, Twick. 177 CF86
Ernest Ave. SE27 181 DP91
Ernest Clo., Beck. 203 EA99
Ernest Gdns. W4 158 CP79
Ernest Gro., Beck. 203 DZ99
Ernest Rd., Horn. 128 FL58
Ernest Rd., Kings.T. 198 CP96
Ernest Sq., Kings.T. 198 CP96
Ernest St. E1 143 DX70
Ernle Rd. SW20 179 CV94
Ernshaw Pl. SW15 179 CY85
Carlton Dr.
Erpingham Rd. SW15 159 CW83
Erridge Rd. SW19 200 DA96
Erriff Dr., S.Ock. 149 FT71
Errington Clo., Grays 171 GH76
Cedar Rd.
Errington Dr., Wind. 151 AN81
Errington Rd. W9 139 CZ70
Errol Gdns., Hayes 135 BV70
Errol Gdns., N.Mal. 199 CU98
Errol St. EC1 275 J5
Errol St. EC1 142 DQ70
Erroll Rd., Rom. 127 FF56
Erskine Clo., Sutt. 200 DE104
Erskine Cres. N17 122 DV56
Erskine Hill NW11 120 DA57
Erskine Ms. NW3 140 DF66
Erskine Rd.
Erskine Rd. E17 123 DZ56
Erskine Rd. NW3 140 DF66
Erskine Rd., Sutt. 218 DD105
Erskine Rd., Wat. 94 BW48
Erwood Rd. SE7 164 EL78
Esam Way SW16 181 DN92
Escombe Dr., Guil. 242 AV129
Escot Way, Barn. 79 CW43
Escott Gdns. SE9 184 EL91
Escott Pl., Cher. 211 BC107
Escreet Gro. SE18 165 EN77
Esdaile Gdns., Upmin. 129 FR59
Esdaile La., Hodd. 49 EA17
Esher Ave., Rom. 127 FC58
Esher Ave., Sutt. 199 CX104
Esher Ave., Walt. 195 BU100
Esher Bypass, Chess. 215 CJ105
Esher Bypass, Cob. 213 BU112
Esher Bypass, Esher 215 CH108
Esher Clo., Bex. 186 EY88
Esher Clo., Esher 214 CB106
Esher Cres., Houns. 155 BS82
Eastern Perimeter Rd.
Esher Gdns. SW19 179 CX89
Esher Grn., Esher 214 CB105
Esher Ms., Mitch. 200 DF97
Esher Pk. Ave., Esher 214 CC105
Esher Pl. Ave., Esher 214 CA105
Esher Rd., E.Mol. 197 CD100
Esher Rd., Ilf. 125 ES62
Esher Rd., Walt. 214 BX106
Esk Rd. E13 144 EG70
Esk Way, Rom. 105 FD52
Eskdale, St.Alb. 62 CM27
Eskdale Ave., Chesh. 54 AQ30
Eskdale Ave., Nthlt. 136 BZ67
Eskdale Clo., Dart. 188 FQ88
Eskdale Clo., Wem. 117 CK61
Eskdale Ct., Hem.H. 40 BL17
Lonsdale
Eskdale Gdns., Pur. 220 DR114
Eskdale Rd., Bexh. 166 FA82
Eskdale Rd., Uxb. 134 BH68
Eskley Gdns., S.Ock. 149 FV71
Eskmont Ridge SE19 182 DS94
Esmar Cres. NW9 119 CU59
Esme Ho. SW15 159 CT84
Ludovick Wk.
Esmeralda Rd. SE1 162 DU77
Esmond Clo., Rain. 147 FH66
Dawson Dr.
Esmond Rd. NW6 139 CZ67
Esmond Rd. W4 158 CR77
Esmond St. SW15 159 CY84
Esparto St. SW18 180 DB87
Essenden Rd., Belv. 166 FA78
Essenden Rd., S.Croy. 220 DS108
Essendene Clo., Cat. 236 DS123
Essendene Rd., Cat. 236 DS123
Essendine Rd. W9 140 DA69
Essendon Gdns., Welw.G.C. 29 CZ09
Essendon Hill, Hat. 46 DE17
Essendon Rd., Hert. 46 DG15
Essex Ave., Islw. 157 CE83
Essex Ave., Slou. 131 AQ71
Essex Clo. E17 123 DY56
Essex Clo., Add. 212 BJ105
Essex Clo., Mord. 199 CX101
Essex Clo., Rom. 127 FB56
Essex Clo., Ruis. 116 BX60
Essex Ct. EC4 274 D9
Essex Ct. SW13 159 CT82
Essex Gdns. N4 121 DP58
Essex Gdns., Horn. 128 FM57
Essex Gro. SE19 182 DR93
Essex Ho. E14 143 EB72
Giraud St.
Essex La., Kings L. 59 BR33
Essex Pk. N3 98 DB51
Essex Pk. Ms. W3 138 CS74
Essex Pl. W4 158 CQ77
Essex Rd. E4 102 EE46
Essex Rd. E10 123 EC58
Essex Rd. E12 124 EL64
Essex Rd. E17 123 DY58
Essex Rd. E18 102 EH54
Essex Rd. N1 141 DP67
Essex Rd. NW10 138 CS66
Essex Rd. W3 138 CQ73
Essex Rd. W4 158 CR77
Belmont Rd.
Essex Rd., Bark. 145 ER66
Essex Rd., Borwd. 78 CN41
Essex Rd., Chesh. 54 AQ29
Essex Rd., Dag. 127 FC64
Essex Rd., Dart. 188 FK86
Essex Rd., Enf. 82 DR42
Essex Rd., Grav. 191 GG88
Essex Rd., Grays 169 FU79
Essex Rd., Hodd. 49 EB16
Essex Rd., Long. 209 FX96
Essex Rd., Rom. 126 FA56
Essex Rd. (Chadwell Heath), Rom. 126 EW59
Essex Rd., Wat. 75 BU40
Essex Rd. S. E11 123 ED59
Essex St. E7 124 EG64
Essex St. WC2 274 D10
Essex St., St.Alb. 43 CE19
Essex Twr. SE20 202 DV95
Essex Vill. W8 160 DA75
Essex Way, Brwd. 107 FW51
Essex Way, Epp. 70 EV32
Essex Way, Ong. 71 FF29
Essex Wf. E5 122 DW61
Essian St. E1 143 DY71
Essoldo Way, Edg. 118 CM55
Estate Way E10 123 DZ60
Estcourt Rd. SE25 202 DV100
Estcourt Rd. SW6 159 CZ80
Estcourt Rd., Wat. 76 BW41
Este Rd. SW11 160 DE83
Estella Ave., N.Mal. 199 CV98
Estelle Rd. NW3 120 DF63
Esterbrooke St. SW1 277 M9
Esterbrooke St. SW1 161 DK77
Esther Clo. N21 99 DN45
Esther Rd. E11 124 EE59
Estreham Rd. SW16 181 DK93
Estridge Clo., Houns. 156 CA84
Estuary Clo., Bark. 146 EV69
Eswyn Rd. SW17 180 DF91
Etchingham Pk. Rd. N3 98 DB52
Etchingham Rd. E15 123 EC63
Eternit Wk. SW6 159 CW81
Etfield Gro., Sid. 186 EV92
Ethel Rd. E16 144 EH72
Ethel Rd., Ashf. 174 BL92
Ethel St. SE17 279 J9
Ethel Ter., Orp. 224 EW109
Ethelbert Clo., Brom. 204 EG97
Ethelbert Gdns., Ilf. 125 EM57
Ethelbert Rd. SW20 199 CX95
Ethelbert Rd., Brom. 204 EG97
Ethelbert Rd., Dart. 188 FL91
Ethelbert Rd., Erith 167 FC80
Ethelbert Rd., Orp. 206 EX97
Ethelbert St. SW12 181 DH88
Fernlea Rd.
Ethelburga Rd., Rom. 106 FM53
Ethelburga St. SW11 160 DE81
Ethelden Rd. W12 139 CV74
Ethelene Ave. N10 121 DJ56
Ethelred Clo., Welw.G.C. 29 CZ10
Ethelwine Pl., Abb.L. 59 BT30
The Cres.
Etheridge Grn., Loug. 85 EQ41
Etheridge Rd.
Etheridge Rd. NW2 119 CW59
Etheridge Rd., Loug. 85 EP40
Etherley Rd. N15 122 DQ57
Etherow St. SE22 182 DU86
Etherstone Grn. SW16 181 DN91
Etherstone Rd.
Etherstone Rd. SW16 181 DN91
Ethnard Rd. SE15 162 DV79
Ethorpe Clo., Ger.Cr. 112 AY57
Ethorpe Cres., Ger.Cr. 112 AY57
Ethronvi Rd., Bexh. 166 EY83
Etloe Rd. E10 123 EA61
Etna Rd., St.Alb. 43 CD19
Eton Ave. N12 98 DC52
Eton Ave. NW3 140 DD66
Eton Ave., Barn. 80 DE44
Eton Ave., Houns. 156 BZ79
Eton Ave., N.Mal. 198 CR99
Eton Ave., Wem. 117 CH64
Eton Clo., Slou. 152 AU79
Eton College Rd. NW3 140 DF65
Eton Ct. NW3 140 DD66
Eton Ave.
Eton Ct., Stai. 173 BF92
Richmond Rd.
Eton Ct., Wem. 117 CJ63
Eton Ave.
Eton Ct. (Eton), Wind. 151 AR80
Eton Garages NW3 140 DE65
Lambolle Pl.
Eton Gro. NW9 118 CN55
Eton Gro. SE13 164 EE83
Eton Hall NW3 140 DF65
Eton College Rd.
Eton Pl. NW3 140 DG66
Haverstock Hill
Eton Ri. NW3 140 DF65
Eton College Rd.
Eton Rd. NW3 140 DF66
Eton Rd., Hayes 155 BT80
Eton Rd., Ilf. 125 EQ64
Eton Rd., Orp. 224 EV105
Eton Rd., Slou. 152 AT78
Eton Sq. (Eton), Wind. 151 AR80
Eton St., Rich. 178 CL85
Eton Vill. NW3 140 DF65
Eton Way, Dart. 168 FJ84
Eton Wick Rd. (Eton Wick), Wind. 151 AL77
Etta St. SE8 163 DY79
Etton Clo., Horn. 128 FL61
Ettrick St. E14 143 EC72
Etwell Pl., Surb. 198 CM100
Euclid Way, Grays 169 FT78
Eugene Clo., Rom. 128 FJ56
Eugenia Rd. SE16 162 DW77
Eunice Gro., Chesh. 54 AR33
Eureka Rd., Kings.T. 198 CN96
Washington Rd.
Europa Pk. Rd., Guil. 242 AW133
Europa Pl. EC1 275 H3
Europa Rd., Hem.H. 40 BM17
Jupiter Dr.
Europe Rd. SE18 165 EM76
Eustace Rd. E6 144 EL69
Eustace Rd. SW6 160 DA80
Eustace Rd., Guil. 243 BD132
Eustace Rd., Rom. 126 EX59
Euston Ave., Wat. 75 BT43
Euston Cen. NW1 141 DJ70
Triton Sq.
Euston Gro. NW1 273 M3
Euston Gro. NW1 141 DK69
Euston Rd. N1 141 DH70
Euston Rd. NW1 273 J5
Euston Rd. NW1 141 DH70
Euston Rd., Croy. 201 DN102
Euston Sq. NW1 273 M3
Euston Sq. NW1 141 DK69
Euston Sta. Colonnade NW1 273 M3
Euston St. NW1 273 L3
Euston St. NW1 141 DJ69
Eva Rd., Rom. 126 EW59
Evandale Rd. SW9 161 DN82
Evangelist Rd. NW5 121 DH63
Evans Ave., Wat. 75 BT35
Evans Clo. E8 142 DT65
Buttermere Wk.
Evans Clo., Green. 189 FU85
Evans Clo., Rick. 74 BN43
New Rd.
Evans Gro., Felt. 176 CA89
Evans Gro., St.Alb. 43 CJ16
Evans Rd. SE6 184 EE89
Evansdale, Rain. 147 FF69
New Zealand Way
Evanston Ave. E4 101 EC52
Evanston Gdns., Ilf. 124 EL58
Eve Rd. E11 124 EE63
Eve Rd. E15 144 EE68
Eve Rd. N17 122 DS55
Eve Rd., Islw. 157 CG84
Eve Rd., Wok. 227 BB115
Evelina Rd. SE15 162 DW83
Evelina Rd. SE20 183 DX94
Eveline Lowe Est. SE16 162 DU76
Eveline Rd., Mitch. 200 DF95
Evelyn Ave. NW9 118 CR55
Evelyn Ave., Ruis. 115 BT59
Evelyn Clo., Twick. 176 CB87
Evelyn Clo., Wok. 226 AX120
Evelyn Ct. N1 275 K1
Evelyn Cres., Sun. 195 BT95
Evelyn Denington Rd. E6 145 EM71
Evelyn Dr., Pnr. 94 BX52
Evelyn Fox Ct. W10 139 CW71
Evelyn Gdns. SW7 160 DD78
Evelyn Gdns., Gdse. 252 DW130
Evelyn Gdns., Rich. 158 CL84
Kew Rd.
Evelyn Gro. W5 138 CM74
Evelyn Gro., Sthl. 136 BZ72
Evelyn Rd. E16 144 EH74
Evelyn Rd. E17 123 EC56
Evelyn Rd. SW19 180 DB92
Evelyn Rd. W4 158 CR76
Evelyn Rd., Barn. 80 DF42
Evelyn Rd., Rich. 158 CL83
Evelyn Rd. (Ham), Rich. 177 CJ90
Evelyn Sharp Clo., Rom. 128 FK55
Amery Gdns.
Evelyn St. SE8 163 DY78
Evelyn Ter., Rich. 158 CL83
Evelyn Wk. N1 275 K1
Evelyn Wk. N1 142 DR68
Evelyn Wk., Brwd. 107 FW51
Wilmot Grn.
Evelyn Way, Cob. 230 BZ116
Evelyn Way, Sun. 195 BT95
Evelyn Way, Wall. 219 DK105
Evelyn Yd. W1 273 M8
Evelyns Clo., Uxb. 134 BN72
Evening Hill, Beck. 183 EC94
Evenwood Clo. SW15 179 CY85
Everard Ave., Brom. 204 EG102
Everard Ave., Slou. 152 AS75
Everard Clo., St.Alb. 43 CD22
Everard La., Cat. 236 DU122
Tillingdown Hill
Everard Way, Wem. 118 CL62
Everatt Clo. SW18 179 CZ86
Amerland Rd.
Everdon Rd. SW13 159 CU79
Everest Clo., Grav. 190 GE90
Everest Ct., Wok. 226 AS116
Langmans Way
Everest Pl. E14 143 EC71
Everest Pl., Swan. 207 FD98
Everest Rd. SE9 185 EM85
Everest Rd., Stai. 174 BK87
Everest Way, Hem.H. 40 BN19
Everett Clo., Pnr. 115 BT55
Everett Clo., Wat. 95 CE46
Everett Wk., Belv. 166 EZ78
Osborne Rd.
Everglade, West. 238 EK118
Everglade Strand NW9 97 CT53
Evergreen Ct., Stai. 174 BK87
Evergreen Oak Ave., Wind. 152 AU83
Evergreen Wk., Hem.H. 40 BL22
Redwood Dr.
Evergreen Way, Hayes 135 BT73
Evergreen Way, Stai. 174 BK87
Everilda St. N1 141 DM67
Evering Rd. E5 122 DU62
Evering Rd. N16 122 DU62
Everington Rd. N10 98 DF54
Everington St. W6 159 CX79
Everitt Rd. NW10 138 CR69
Everlands Clo., Wok. 226 AY118
Everlasting La., St.Alb. 42 CC18
Everleigh St. N4 121 DM60
Eversfield Gdns. NW7 96 CS51
Eversfield Rd., Reig. 250 DB134
Eversfield Rd., Rich. 158 CM82
Evershed Wk. W4 158 CR76
Eversholt St. NW1 141 DJ68
Evershot Rd. N4 121 DM60
Eversleigh Gdns., Upmin. 129 FR60
Eversleigh Rd. E6 144 EK67
Eversleigh Rd. N3 97 CZ52
Eversleigh Rd. SW11 160 DF83
Eversleigh Rd., Barn. 80 DC43
Eversley Ave., Bexh. 167 FD82
Eversley Ave., Wem. 118 CN61
Eversley Clo. N21 81 DM44
Eversley Cres. N21 81 DM44
Eversley Cres., Islw. 157 CD81
Eversley Cres., Ruis. 115 BS61
Eversley Cross, Bexh. 167 FE82
Eversley Mt. N21 81 DM44
Eversley Pk. SW19 179 CV92
Eversley Pk. Rd. N21 81 DM44
Eversley Rd. SE7 164 EH79
Eversley Rd. SE19 182 DR94
Eversley Rd., Surb. 198 CM98
Eversley Way, Croy. 221 EA105
Eversley Way, Egh. 193 BC96
Everthorpe Rd. SE15 162 DT83
Everton Bldgs. NW1 273 K3
Everton Dr., Stan. 118 CM55
Everton Rd., Croy. 202 DU102
Evesham Ave. E17 101 EA54
Evesham Clo., Grnf. 136 CB68
Evesham Clo., Reig. 249 CZ133
Evesham Clo., Sutt. 218 DA108
Evesham Grn., Mord. 200 DB100
Evesham Rd. E15 144 EF66
Evesham Rd. N11 99 DJ50
Evesham Rd., Felt. 176 BW87
Sparrow Fm. Dr.
Evesham Rd., Grav. 191 GK89
Evesham Rd., Mord. 200 DB100
Evesham Rd., Reig. 249 CZ134
Evesham Rd. N., Reig. 249 CZ133
Evesham St. W11 139 CX73
Evesham Wk. SE5 162 DR82
Love Wk.
Evesham Wk. SW9 161 DN82
Evesham Way SW11 160 DG83
Evesham Way, Ilf. 125 EN55
Evreham Rd., Iver 133 BE72
Evry Rd., Sid. 186 EW93
Ewald Rd. SW6 159 CZ82
Ewan Rd., Rom. 106 FK54
Ewanrigg Ter., Wdf.Grn. 102 EJ50
Ewart Gro. N22 99 DN53
Ewart Pl. E3 143 DZ68
Ewart Rd. SE23 183 DX87
Ewe Clo. N7 141 DL65
Ewelands, Horl. 269 DJ147
Ewell Bypass, Epsom 217 CU107
Ewell Ct. Ave., Epsom 216 CS106
Ewell Downs Rd., Epsom 217 CU111
Ewell Ho. Gro., Epsom 217 CT110
Ewell Pk. Way, Epsom 217 CU107
Ewell Rd., Surb. 198 CL99
Ewell Rd. (Long Ditton), Surb. 197 CH101
Ewell Rd., Sutt. 217 CX108
Ewellhurst Rd., Ilf. 102 EL54
Ewelme Rd. SE23 182 DW88
Ewen Cres. SW2 181 DN87
Ewer St. SE1 279 H3
Ewer St. SE1 142 DQ74
Ewhurst Ave., S.Croy. 220 DT109
Ewhurst Clo., Sutt. 217 CW109
Ewhurst Ho. E1 142 DW71
Jamaica St.
Ewhurst Rd. SE4 183 DZ86
Exbury Rd. SE6 183 EA89
Excel Ct. WC2 277 N1
Excelsior Clo., Kings.T. 198 CN96
Washington Rd.
Excelsior Gdns. SE13 163 EC82
Exchange Arc. EC2 275 N6
Exchange Arc. EC2 142 DS71
Exchange Bldgs. E1 142 DS72
Cutler St.
Exchange Ct. WC2 278 A1
Exchange Pl. EC2 275 M6
Exchange Pl. EC2 142 DS71
Exchange Rd., Wat. 75 BV41
Exchange Sq. EC2 275 M6
Exchange Sq. EC2 142 DS71
Exchange St., Rom. 127 FE57
Exeforde Ave., Ashf. 174 BN91
Exeter Clo. E6 145 EM72
Harper Rd.
Exeter Clo., Wat. 76 BW40
Exeter Gdns., Ilf. 124 EL60
Exeter Ho. SW15 179 CW86
Putney Heath
Exeter Ms. NW6 140 DB65
West Hampstead Ms.
Exeter Pl., Guil. 242 AT132
Exeter Rd. E16 144 EG71
Exeter Rd. E17 123 EA57
Exeter Rd. N9 100 DW47
Exeter Rd. N14 99 DH46
Exeter Rd. NW2 119 CY64
Exeter Rd. SE15 162 DT81
Exeter Rd., Croy. 202 DS101
Exeter Rd., Dag. 147 FB65
Exeter Rd., Enf. 83 DX41
Exeter Rd., Felt. 176 BZ90
Exeter Rd., Grav. 191 GK90
Exeter Rd., Har. 116 BY61
Exeter Rd., Well. 165 ET82
Exeter St. WC2 274 A10
Exeter St. WC2 141 DL73
Exeter Way SE14 163 DZ80
Exford Gdns. SE12 184 EH88
Exford Rd. SE12 184 EH89
Exhibition Clo. W12 139 CW73
Exhibition Rd. SW7 276 A6
Exhibition Rd. SW7 160 DD75
Exmoor Clo., Ilf. 103 EQ53
Exmoor St. W10 139 CX71
Exmouth Mkt. EC1 274 D4
Exmouth Mkt. EC1 141 DN70
Exmouth Ms. NW1 273 L3
Exmouth Pl. E8 142 DV66
Exmouth Rd. E17 123 DZ57
Exmouth Rd., Brom. 204 EH97
Exmouth Rd., Grays 170 GB79
Exmouth Rd., Hayes 135 BS69
Exmouth Rd., Ruis. 116 BW62
Exmouth Rd., Well. 166 EW81
Exmouth St. E1 142 DW72
Commercial Rd.
Exning Rd. E16 144 EF70
Exon St. SE17 279 M9
Exon St. SE17 162 DS77
Explorer Ave., Stai. 174 BL87
Explorer Dr., Wat. 75 BT44
Express Dr., Ilf. 126 EV60
Exton Cres. NW10 138 CQ66
Exton Gdns., Dag. 126 EW64
Exton St. SE1 278 D3
Exton St. SE1 141 DN74
Eyebright Clo., Croy. 203 DX102
Primrose La.
Eyhurst Ave., Horn. 127 FG62
Eyhurst Clo. NW2 119 CU61
Eyhurst Clo., Tad. 233 CZ123
Eyhurst Spur, Tad. 233 CZ124
Eylewood Rd. SE27 182 DQ92
Eynella Rd. SE22 182 DT87
Eynham Rd. W12 139 CW72
Eynsford Clo., Orp. 205 EQ101
Eynsford Cres., Bex. 186 EW88
Eynsford Rd., Green. 189 FW85
Eynsford Rd., Ilf. 125 ES61
Eynsford Rd., Sev. 225 FH110
Eynsford Rd., Swan. 207 FD100
Eynsham Dr. SE2 166 EU77
Eynswood Dr., Sid. 186 EV92
Eyot Gdns. W6 159 CT78
Eyot Grn. W4 159 CT79
Chiswick Mall
Eyre Clo., Rom. 127 FH56
Eyre Ct. NW8 140 DD68
Finchley Rd.
Eyre St. Hill EC1 274 D5
Eyston Dr., Wey. 212 BN110
Eythorne Rd. SW9 161 DN81
Eywood Rd., St.Alb. 42 CC22
Ezra St. E2 142 DT69

F

Faber Gdns. NW4 119 CU57
Fabian Rd. SW6 159 CZ80
Fabian St. E6 145 EM70
Fackenden La., Sev. 225 FH113
Factory La. N17 100 DT54
Factory La., Croy. 201 DN102
Factory Path, Stai. 173 BE91
Mustard Mill Rd.
Factory Pl. E14 163 EB78
Factory Rd. E16 144 EL74
Factory Rd., Grav. 190 GC86
Factory Sq. SW16 181 DL93
Factory Yd. W7 137 CE74
Uxbridge Rd.
Faesten Way, Bex. 187 FE90
Faggotters La., Harl. 37 FC12
Faggotters La., Ong. 53 FG16
Faggotts Clo., Rad. 77 CJ35
Faggs Rd., Felt. 175 BU85
Fagnall La., Amer. 88 AJ45
Fagus Ave., Rain. 148 FK69
Faints Clo., Wal.Cr. 66 DT29
Fair Acres, Brom. 204 EG99
Fair Clo. (Bushey), Wat. 94 CB45
Claybury
Fair Grn., Saw. 36 EY05
The Sq.
Fair La., Couls. 250 DC125
Fair Leas, Chesh. 54 AN29
Fair St. SE1 279 N4
Fair St., Houns. 156 CC83
High St.
Fairacre, Hem.H. 40 BM24
Fairacre, N.Mal. 198 CS97
Fairacres SW15 179 CU85
Fairacres, Cob. 214 BX112
Fairacres, Croy. 221 DZ109
Fairacres, Ruis. 115 BT59
Fairacres, Tad. 233 CW121
Fairacres, Wind. 151 AK82
Fairacres Clo., Pot.B. 63 CZ33
Fairbairn Clo., Pur. 219 DN113
Fairbairn Grn. SW9 161 DN81
Fairbank Ave., Orp. 205 EP103
Fairbanks Rd. N17 122 DT55
Fairborne Way, Guil. 242 AU131
Fairbourne, Cob. 214 BX113
Fairbourne Clo., Wok. 226 AU118
Abercorn Way
Fairbourne La., Cat. 236 DQ122
Fairbourne Rd. N17 122 DS55
Fairbridge Rd. N19 121 DK61
Fairbrook Clo. N13 99 DN50
Fairbrook Rd. N13 99 DN51
Fairburn Clo., Borwd. 78 CN39
Fairburn Ct. SW15 179 CY85
Mercier Rd.
Fairby Rd. SE12 184 EH85
Fairchild Clo. SW11 160 DD82
Wye St.
Fairchild Pl. EC2 275 N5
Fairchild St. EC2 275 N5
Fairchildes Ave., Croy. 221 ED112
Fairchildes La., Warl. 221 ED114

Fairclough St. E1 142 DU72
Faircroft, Slou. 131 AP70
Faircross Ave., Bark. 145 EQ65
Faircross Ave., Rom. 105 FD52
Faircross Way, St.Alb. 43 CG18
Fairdale Gdns. SW15 159 CV84
Fairdale Gdns., Hayes 155 BU75
Fairdene Rd., Couls. 235 DK118
Fairey Ave., Hayes 155 BT77
Fairfax Ave., Epsom 217 CV110
Fairfax Ave., Red. 250 DE133
Fairfax Clo., Walt. 195 BV102
Fairfax Gdns. SE3 164 EJ81
Fairfax Ms., Amer. 55 AN40
Fairfax Pl. NW6 140 DC66
Fairfax Rd. N8 121 DN56
Fairfax Rd. NW6 140 DC66
Fairfax Rd. W4 158 CS76
Fairfax Rd., Grays 170 GB78
Fairfax Rd., Hert. 32 DT08
Fairfax Rd., Tedd. 177 CG93
Fairfax Rd., Til. 171 GF81
Fairfax Rd., Wok. 227 BB120
Fairfax Way N10 98 DG52
Cromwell Rd.
Fairfield App., Stai. 172 AX86
Fairfield Ave. NW4 119 CV58
Fairfield Ave., Edg. 96 CP51
Fairfield Ave., Horl. 268 DG149
Fairfield Ave., Ruis. 115 BQ59
Fairfield Ave., Slou. 152 AW80
Fairfield Ave., Stai. 173 BF91
Fairfield Ave., Twick. 176 CB88
Fairfield Ave., Upmin. 128 FQ62
Fairfield Ave., Wat. 94 BW48
Fairfield Clo. N12 98 DC49
Fairfield Clo., Dor. 247 CH134
Fairfield Dr.
Fairfield Clo., Enf. 83 DY42
Scotland Grn. Rd. N.
Fairfield Clo., Epsom 216 CS106
Fairfield Clo., Hat. 45 CW15
Fairfield Clo., Horn. 127 FG60
Fairfield Clo., Mitch. 180 DE94
Fairfield Clo., Nthwd. 93 BP50
Thirlmere Gdns.
Fairfield Clo., Rad. 77 CE37
Fairfield Clo., Sid. 185 ET86
Fairfield Clo., Slou. 152 AX80
Fairfield Cotts., Lthd. 246 CB125
Fairfield Ct. NW10 139 CU67
Fairfield Cres., Edg. 96 CP51
Fairfield Dr. SW18 180 DB85
Fairfield Dr., Brox. 49 DZ24
Fairfield Dr., Dor. 247 CH134
Fairfield Dr., Grnf. 137 CJ67
Fairfield Dr., Har. 116 CC55
Fairfield Dr., Slou. 130 AJ69
Fairfield E., Kings.T. 198 CL96
Fairfield Gdns. N8 121 DL57
Elder Ave.
Fairfield Gro. SE7 164 EK79
Fairfield Ind. Est., Kings.T. 198 CN97
Fairfield La., Slou. 131 AP68
Fairfield N., Kings.T. 198 CL96
Fairfield Pk., Cob. 214 BX114
Fairfield Path, Croy. 202 DR104
Fairfield Pl., Kings.T. 198 CL97
Fairfield Ri., Guil. 242 AT133
Fairfield Rd. E3 143 EA68
Fairfield Rd. E17 101 DY54
Fairfield Rd. N8 121 DL57
Fairfield Rd. N18 100 DU49
Fairfield Rd. W7 157 CG76
Southdown Ave.
Fairfield Rd., Beck. 203 EA96
Fairfield Rd., Bexh. 166 EZ82
Fairfield Rd., Brwd. 108 FW48
Fairfield Rd., Brom. 184 EG94
Fairfield Rd., Croy. 202 DS104
Fairfield Rd., Epp. 70 EV29
Fairfield Rd., Hodd. 49 EA15
Fairfield Rd., Ilf. 145 EP65
Fairfield Rd., Kings.T. 198 CL96
Fairfield Rd., Lthd. 231 CH121
Fairfield Rd., Orp. 205 ER100
Fairfield Rd., Sthl. 136 BZ72
Fairfield Rd., Stai. 172 AX86
Fairfield Rd., Uxb. 134 BK65
Fairfield Rd., West Dr. 134 BL73
Fairfield Rd., Wdf.Grn. 102 EG51
Fairfield S., Kings.T. 198 CL97
Fairfield St. SW18 180 DB85
Fairfield Wk., Lthd. 231 CH121
Fairfield Rd.
Fairfield Wk. (Cheshunt), Wal.Cr. 67 DY28
Martins Dr.
Fairfield Way, Barn. 80 DA43
Fairfield Way, Couls. 219 DK114
Fairfield Way, Epsom 216 CS106
Fairfield W., Kings.T. 198 CL96
Fairfields, Cher. 194 BG102
Fairfields, Grav. 191 GL92
Fairfields Clo. NW9 118 CQ57
Fairfields Cres. NW9 118 CQ57
Fairfields Rd., Houns. 156 CC83
Fairfolds, Wat. 76 BY35
Fairfoot Rd. E3 143 EA70
Fairford Ave., Bexh. 167 FD81
Fairford Ave., Croy. 203 DX99
Fairford Clo., Croy. 203 DX99
Fairford Clo., Reig. 250 DC132
Fairford Clo., Rom. 106 FP51
Fairford Way
Fairford Clo., W.Byf. 211 BF114
Fairford Gdns., Wor.Pk. 199 CT103
Fairford Way, Rom. 106 FP51
Fairgreen, Barn. 80 DF41
Fairgreen E., Barn. 80 DF41
Fairgreen Rd., Th.Hth. 201 DP99
Fairham Ave., S.Ock. 149 FU73
Fairhaven, Egh. 173 AZ92
Fairhaven Ave., Croy. 203 DX100
Fairhaven Cres., Wat. 93 BU48
Fairhaven Rd., Red. 250 DG130
Fairhazel Gdns. NW6 140 DB65
Fairhill, Hem.H. 40 BM24
Fairholme, Felt. 175 BR87
Fairholme Ave., Rom. 127 FG57
Fairholme Clo. N3 119 CY56
Fairholme Cres., Ash. 231 CJ117
Fairholme Cres., Hayes 135 BT70
Fairholme Gdns. N3 119 CY55
Fairholme Gdns., Upmin. 129 FT59
Fairholme Rd. W14 159 CY78
Fairholme Rd., Ashf. 174 BL92
Fairholme Rd., Croy. 201 DN101
Fairholme Rd., Har. 117 CF57
Fairholme Rd., Ilf. 125 EM59
Fairholme Rd., Sutt. 217 CZ107
Fairholt Clo. N16 122 DS60
Fairholt Rd. N16 122 DR60
Fairholt St. SW7 276 C6
Fairkytes Ave., Horn. 128 FK60
Fairland Rd. E15 144 EF65
Fairlands Ave., Buck.H. 102 EG47
Fairlands Ave., Sutt. 200 DA103
Fairlands Ave., Th.Hth. 201 DM98
Fairlands Ct. SE9 185 EN86
North Pk.
Fairlawn SE7 164 EJ79
Fairlawn, Lthd. 230 BZ124
Fairlawn Ave. N2 120 DE56
Fairlawn Ave. W4 158 CQ77
Fairlawn Ave., Bexh. 166 EX82
Fairlawn Clo. N14 81 DJ44
Fairlawn Clo., Esher 215 CF107
Fairlawn Clo., Felt. 176 BZ91
Fairlawn Clo., Kings.T. 178 CQ93
Fairlawn Dr., Red. 266 DE136
Fairlawn Dr., Wdf.Grn. 102 EG52
Fairlawn Gdns., Sthl. 136 BZ73
Fairlawn Gro. W4 158 CQ77
Fairlawn Gro., Bans. 218 DD113
Fairlawn Pk. SE26 183 DY92
Fairlawn Pk., Wind. 151 AL84
Fairlawn Pk., Wok. 210 AY114
Fairlawn Rd. SW19 179 CZ94
Fairlawn Rd., Cars. 218 DC111
Fairlawns, Add. 211 BF111
Fairlawns, Brwd. 108 FU48
Fairlawns, Horl. 269 DH149
Fairlawns, Pnr. 94 BW54
Fairlawns, Sun. 195 BU97
Fairlawns, Twick. 177 CJ86
Fairlawns, Wat. 75 BT38
Langley Rd.
Fairlawns, Wey. 213 BS106
Fairlawns Clo., Horn. 128 FM59
Fairlawns Clo., Stai. 174 BH93
Fairlea Pl. W5 137 CJ71
Fairley Way (Cheshunt), Wal.Cr. 66 DV28
Fairlie Gdns. SE23 182 DW87
Fairlie Rd., Slou. 131 AN72
Fairlight Ave. E4 101 ED47
Fairlight Ave. NW10 138 CS68
Fairlight Ave., Wind. 151 AR82
Fairlight Ave., Wdf.Grn. 102 EG51
Fairlight Clo. E4 101 ED47
Fairlight Clo., Wor.Pk. 217 CW105
Fairlight Dr., Uxb. 134 BK65
Fairlight Rd. SW17 180 DD91
Fairlop Clo., Horn. 147 FH65
Fairlop Gdns., Ilf. 103 EQ52
Fairlop Rd. E11 123 ED59
Fairlop Rd., Ilf. 103 EQ54
Fairmark Dr., Uxb. 134 BN65
Fairmead, Brom. 205 EM98
Fairmead, Surb. 198 CP102
Fairmead, Wok. 226 AW118
Fairmead Clo., Brom. 205 EM98
Fairmead Clo., Houns. 156 BX80
Fairmead Clo., N.Mal. 198 CR97
Fairmead Cres., Edg. 96 CQ48
Fairmead Gdns., Ilf. 124 EL57
Fairmead Rd. N19 121 DK62
Fairmead Rd., Croy. 201 DM102
Fairmead Rd., Loug. 84 EH43
Fairmead Side, Loug. 84 EJ43
Fairmeads, Cob. 214 BZ113
Fairmeads, Loug. 85 EP40
Fairmile Ave. SW16 181 DK92
Fairmile Ave., Cob. 214 BY114
Fairmile La., Cob. 214 BX112
Fairmile Pk. Copse, Cob. 214 BZ112
Fairmile Pk. Rd., Cob. 214 BZ113
Fairmont Clo., Belv. 166 EZ78
Lullingstone Rd.
Fairmount Rd. SW2 181 DM86
Fairoak Clo., Ken. 235 DP115
Fairoak Clo., Lthd. 215 CD112
Fairoak Clo., Orp. 205 EP101
Fairoak Dr. SE9 185 ER85
Fairoak Gdns., Rom. 105 FE54
Fairoak La., Chess. 215 CH111
Fairoak La., Lthd. 215 CC113
Fairs Rd., Lthd. 231 CG119
Fairseat Clo. (Bushey), Wat. 95 CE47
Hive Rd.
Fairstead Wk. N1 142 DQ67
Popham Rd.
Fairstone Ct., Horl. 269 DH147
Tanyard Way
Fairthorn Rd. SE7 164 EG78
Fairtrough Rd., Orp. 224 EV113
Fairview, Epsom 217 CW111
Fairview, Erith 167 FF80
Guild Rd.
Fairview, Pot.B. 64 DB29
Hawkshead Rd.
Fairview Ave., Brwd. 109 GE45
Fairview Ave., Rain. 148 FK68
Fairview Ave., Wem. 137 CK65
Fairview Ave., Wok. 227 AZ118
Fairview Clo. E17 101 DY53
Fairview Clo., Chig. 103 ES49
Fairview Clo., Wok. 227 AZ118
Fairview Ave.
Fairview Ct., Ashf. 174 BN92
Fairview Cres., Har. 116 CA60
Fairview Dr., Chig. 103 ES49
Fairview Dr., Orp. 223 ER105
Fairview Dr., Shep. 194 BM99
Fairview Dr., Wat. 75 BS36
Fairview Gdns., Wdf.Grn. 102 EH53
Fairview Ind. Pk., Rain. 147 FD71
Fairview Pl. SW2 181 DM87
Fairview Rd. N15 122 DT57
Fairview Rd. SW16 201 DM95
Fairview Rd., Chig. 103 ES49
Fairview Rd., Enf. 81 DN39
Fairview Rd., Epsom 217 CT111
Fairview Rd., Grav. 190 GD94
Fairview Rd., Maid. 130 AG72
Fairview Rd., Slou. 131 AM70
Fairview Rd., Sutt. 218 DD106
Fairview Way, Edg. 96 CN49
Fairwater Ave., Well. 166 EU84
Fairwater Dr., Add. 212 BK109
Fairway SW20 199 CW97
Fairway, Bexh. 186 EY85
Fairway, Cars. 218 DC111
Fairway, Cher. 194 BH102
Fairway, Guil. 243 BD134
Fairway, Hem.H. 40 BM24
Fairway, Orp. 205 ER99
Fairway, Saw. 36 EY05
Fairway, Vir.W. 192 AW100
Fairway, Ware 32 DW07
Fairway, Wdf.Grn. 102 EJ50
Fairway, The N13 100 DQ48
Fairway, The N14 81 DH44
Fairway, The NW7 96 CR48
Fairway, The W3 138 CS72
Fairway, The, Abb.L. 59 BR32
Fairway, The, Barn. 80 DB44
Fairway, The, Brom. 205 EM99
Fairway, The, Grav. 191 GG89
Fairway, The, Harl. 51 ET17
Fairway, The, H.Wyc. 110 AC56
Fairway, The, Lthd. 231 CG118
Fairway, The, N.Mal. 198 CR95
Fairway, The, Nthlt. 136 CC65
Fairway, The, Nthwd. 93 BS49
Fairway, The, Ruis. 116 BW63
Fairway, The, Slou. 130 AJ69
Fairway, The, Upmin. 128 FQ59
Fairway, The, Uxb. 134 BM69
Fairway, The, Wem. 117 CH62
Fairway, The, W.Mol. 196 CB97
Fairway, The, Wey. 212 BN111
Fairway Ave. NW9 118 CP55
Fairway Ave., Borwd. 78 CP40
Fairway Ave., West Dr. 134 BJ74
Fairway Clo. NW11 120 DC59
Fairway Clo., Croy. 203 DY99
Fairway Clo., Epsom 216 CQ105
Fairway Clo., Houns. 176 BW85
Fairway Clo., St.Alb. 60 CC27
Fairway Clo., West Dr. 134 BK74
Fairway Ave.
Fairway Clo., Wok. 226 AV119
Fairway Ct. NW7 96 CR48
The Fairway
Fairway Ct., Hem.H. 40 BM24
Fairway
Fairway Dr. SE28 146 EX72
Summerton Way
Fairway Dr., Dart. 188 FP87
Fairway Dr., Grnf. 136 CB66
Fairway Est., Grnf. 136 CC66
Fairway Gdns., Beck. 203 ED100
Fairway Gdns., Ilf. 125 EQ64
Fairways, Ashf. 175 BP93
Fairways, Ken. 236 DQ117
Fairways, Stan. 96 CL54
Fairways, Tedd. 177 CK94
Fairways, Wal.Abb. 68 EE34
Fairways, Wal.Cr. 67 DX26
Fairweather Clo. N15 122 DS56
Fairweather Rd. N16 122 DU58
Fairwell La., Lthd. 245 BP128
Fairwyn Rd. SE26 183 DY91
Fakenham Clo. NW7 97 CU52
Fakenham Clo., Nthlt. 136 CA65
Goodwood Dr.
Fakruddin St. E1 142 DU70
Falaise, Egh. 172 AY92
Falcon Ave., Brom. 204 EL98
Falcon Ave., Grays 170 GB80
Falcon Clo. SE1 278 G2
Falcon Clo. W4 158 CQ79
Sutton La. S.
Falcon Clo., Dart. 188 FM85
Falcon Clo., Hat. 45 CU20
Falcon Clo., Nthwd. 93 BS52
Falcon Clo., Saw. 36 EW06
Falcon Clo., Wal.Abb. 68 EG34
Kestrel Rd.
Falcon Ct., Wok. 211 BC114
Blackmore Cres.
Falcon Cres., Enf. 83 DX43
Falcon Dr., Stai. 174 BK86
Falcon Gro. SW11 160 DE83
Falcon Ho. W13 137 CF70
Falcon La. SW11 160 DE83
Falcon Ms., Grav. 190 GE88
Falcon Ridge, Berk. 38 AW20
Falcon Rd. SW11 160 DE82
Falcon Rd., Enf. 83 DX43
Falcon Rd., Guil. 258 AX135
Falcon Rd., Hmptn. 176 BZ94
Falcon St. E13 144 EF70
Falcon Ter. SW11 160 DE83
Falcon Trd. Est. NW10 118 CS63
Falcon Way E11 124 EG56
Falcon Way E14 163 EB77
Falcon Way NW9 96 CS54
Falcon Way, Felt. 175 BV85
Falcon Way, Har. 118 CL57
Falcon Way, Horn. 147 FG66
Falcon Way, Sun. 195 BS96
Falcon Way, Wat. 60 BY34
Falcon Way, Welw.G.C. 29 CY07
Falconberg Ct. W1 273 N8
Falconberg Ms. W1 273 M8
Falconer Rd., Ilf. 104 EV50
Falconer Rd. (Bushey), Wat. 76 BZ44
Falconer Wk. N7 121 DM61
Newington Barrow Way
Falconers Pk., Saw. 36 EX06
Falconhurst, Lthd. 231 CD115
Falcons Cft., H.Wyc. 110 AE55
Falconwood, Egh. 172 AY92
Falconwood, Lthd. 229 BT124
Falconwood Ave., Well. 165 ER82
Falconwood Par., Well. 165 ES84
Falconwood Rd., Croy. 221 DZ109
Falcourt Clo., Sutt. 218 DB106
Falkirk Clo., Horn. 128 FN60
Falkirk Gdns., Wat. 94 BX50
Blackford Rd.
Falkirk Ho. W9 140 DB69
Falkirk St. N1 275 N1
Falkirk St. N1 142 DS68
Falkland Ave. N3 98 DA52
Falkland Ave. N11 98 DG49
Falkland Gdns., Dor. 263 CG137
Harrow Rd. W.
Falkland Gro., Dor. 263 CG137
Falkland Pk. Ave. SE25 202 DS97
Falkland Pl. NW5 121 DJ64
Falkland Rd.
Falkland Rd. N8 121 DN56
Falkland Rd. NW5 121 DJ64
Falkland Rd., Barn. 79 CY40
Falkland Rd., Dor. 263 CG137
Fallaize Ave., Ilf. 125 EP63
Riverdene Rd.
Falling La., West Dr. 134 BL73
Falloden Way NW11 120 DA56
Fallow Clo., Chig. 103 ET50
Fallow Ct. SE16 162 DU78
Argyle Way
Fallow Ct. Ave. N12 98 DC52
Fallow Flds., Loug. 84 EJ44
Fallowfield, Stan. 95 CG49
Fallowfield, Welw.G.C. 29 CZ06
Fallowfield Clo., Uxb. 92 BJ53
Fallowfield Ct., Stan. 95 CG48
Stanmore Hill
Fallowfield Wk., Hem.H. 40 BG17
Tollpit End
Fallowfield Way, Horl. 269 DH147
Fallowfields Dr. N12 98 DE51
Fallows Clo. N2 98 DC54
Fallsbrook Rd. SW16 181 DH93
Falmer Rd. E17 123 EB55
Falmer Rd. N15 122 DQ57
Falmer Rd., Enf. 82 DS42
Falmouth Ave. E4 101 ED50
Falmouth Clo. N22 99 DM52
Truro Rd.
Falmouth Clo. SE12 184 EF85
Falmouth Gdns., Ilf. 124 EK56
Falmouth Rd. SE1 279 J7
Falmouth Rd. SE1 162 DQ76
Falmouth Rd., Slou. 131 AN72
Falmouth Rd., Walt. 214 BW105
Falmouth St. E15 123 ED64
Falstaff Gdns., St.Alb. 42 CC23
Falstaff Ms., Hmptn. 177 CD92
Hampton Rd.
Falstone, Wok. 226 AV118
Fambridge Clo. SE26 183 DZ91
Fambridge Rd., Dag. 126 FA60
Famet Ave., Pur. 220 DQ113
Famet Clo., Pur. 220 DQ113
Famet Wk., Pur. 220 DQ113
Fane St. W14 159 CZ79
North End Rd.
Fanhams Rd., Ware 33 DY05
Fann St. EC1 275 H5
Fann St. EC1 142 DQ70
Fann St. EC2 275 H5
Fann St. EC2 142 DQ70
Fanns Ri., Purf. 168 FN77
Fanshaw St. N1 275 M2
Fanshaw St. N1 142 DS69
Fanshawe Ave., Bark. 145 EQ65
Fanshawe Cres., Dag. 126 EY64
Fanshawe Cres., Horn. 128 FK58
Fanshawe Cres., Ware 32 DW05
Fanshawe Rd., Grays 171 GG76
Fanshawe Rd., Rich. 177 CJ91
Fanshawe St., Hert. 31 DP08
Fanshaws La., Hert. 48 DQ18
Fanthorpe St. SW15 159 CW83
Far End, Hat. 45 CV21
Faraday Ave., Sid. 186 EU89
Faraday Clo. N7 141 DM65
Bride St.
Faraday Clo., Slou. 131 AP71
Faraday Clo., Wat. 75 BR44
Faraday Rd. E15 144 EF65
Faraday Rd. SW19 180 DA93
Faraday Rd. W3 138 CQ73
Faraday Rd. W10 139 CY71
Faraday Rd., Slou. 131 AP71
Faraday Rd., Sthl. 136 CB73
Faraday Rd., Well. 166 EU83
Faraday Rd., W.Mol. 196 CA98
Faraday Way SE18 164 EK76
Faraday Way, Croy. 201 DM102
Ampere Way
Faraday Way, Orp. 206 EV98
Fareham Rd., Felt. 176 BW87
Fareham St. W1 273 M8
Farewell Pl., Mitch. 200 DE95
Faringdon Ave., Brom. 205 EN101
Faringdon Ave., Rom. 106 FJ53
Faringford Clo., Pot.B. 64 DD31
Faringford Rd. E15 144 EE66
Farington Acres, Wey. 195 BR104
Faris Barn Dr., Add. 211 BF112
Faris La., Add. 211 BF111
Farjeon Rd. SE3 164 EK81
Farland Rd., Hem.H. 41 BP20
Farleton Clo., Wey. 213 BR107
Farleigh Ave., Brom. 204 EF100
Farleigh Border, Croy. 221 DX112
Farleigh Ct., Guil. 242 AS134
Park Barn Dr.
Farleigh Ct. Rd., Warl. 221 DZ114
Farleigh Dean Cres., Croy. 221 EB111
Farleigh Pl. N16 122 DT63
Farleigh Rd.
Farleigh Rd. N16 122 DT63
Farleigh Rd., Add. 212 BG111
Farleigh Rd., Warl. 237 DX118
Farley Dr., Ilf. 125 ES60
Farley Heath, Guil. 260 BJ144
Farley La., West. 255 EP127
Farley Nursery, West. 255 EQ127
Farley Pk., Oxt. 253 ED130
Farley Pl. SE25 202 DU98
Farley Rd. SE6 183 EC87
Farley Rd., Grav. 191 GM88
Farley Rd., S.Croy. 220 DU108
Farleycroft, West. 255 EQ126
Farleys Clo., Lthd. 245 BQ126
Farlington Pl. SW15 179 CV87
Roehampton La.
Farlow Clo., Grav. 191 GF90
Farlow Rd. SW15 159 CW83
Farlton Rd. SW18 180 DB87
Farm Ave. NW2 119 CY62
Farm Ave. SW16 181 DL91
Farm Ave., Har. 116 BZ59
Farm Ave., Swan. 207 FC97
Farm Ave., Wem. 137 CJ65
Farm Clo., Amer. 72 AX39
Farm Clo., Barn. 79 CV43
Farm Clo., Borwd. 77 CK38
Farm Clo., Brwd. 109 GC45
Farm Clo., Buck.H. 102 EJ48
Farm Clo., Cher. 193 BA100
Farm Clo., Couls. 234 DF120
Farm Clo., Dag. 147 FC66
Farm Clo., Guil. 242 AX131
Waterside Rd.
Farm Clo., Harl. 34 EH14
Farm Clo., Hert. 31 DN09
Farm Clo. (East Horsley), Lthd. 245 BT128
Farm Clo. (Fetcham), Lthd. 231 CD124
Farm Clo., Maid. 150 AC78
Farm Clo. (Cuffley), Pot.B. 65 DK27
Farm Clo., Shep. 194 BN101
Farm Clo., Sthl. 136 CB73
Farm Clo., Stai. 173 BE92
Farm Clo., Sutt. 218 DD108
Farm Clo., Uxb. 115 BP61
Farm Clo., Wall. 219 DJ110
Farm Clo. (Cheshunt), Wal.Cr. 66 DW30
Farm Clo., Welw.G.C. 29 CW09
Farm Clo., W.Byf. 212 BM112
Farm Clo., W.Wick. 204 EE104
Farm Ct. NW4 119 CU55
Farm Cres., Slou. 132 AV71
Farm Dr., Croy. 203 DZ103
Farm Dr., Pur. 219 DK112
Farm End E4 84 EE43
Farm End, Nthwd. 93 BP53
Drakes Dr.
Farm Fld., Wat. 75 BS38
Farm Flds., S.Croy. 220 DS111
Farm Gro., Beac. 88 AJ50
Farm Hill Rd., Wal.Abb. 67 ED33
Farm La. N14 80 DG44
Farm La. SW6 160 DA79
Farm La., Add. 212 BG107
Farm La., Ash. 232 CN116
Farm La., Beac. 89 AR52
Farm La., Cars. 218 DF110
Farm La., Croy. 203 DZ103
Farm La., Epsom 232 CP120
Farm La., Hodd. 49 EC15
Farm La., Lthd. 245 BT128
Farm La., Pur. 219 DJ110
Farm La., Rick. 74 BH41
Farm La., Slou. 131 AR73
Whitby Rd.
Farm La., Wok. 227 BC123
Farm Lea, H.Wyc. 110 AF56
Farm Pl. W8 140 DA74
Uxbridge St.
Farm Pl., Berk. 38 AT18
Farm Pl., Dart. 167 FG84
Farm Rd. N21 100 DQ46
Farm Rd., Edg. 96 CP51
Farm Rd., Esher 196 CB102
Farm Rd., Grays 171 GF75
Farm Rd., Houns. 176 BY88
Farm Rd., Maid. 130 AG72
Farm Rd., Mord. 200 DB99
Farm Rd., Nthwd. 93 BQ50
Farm Rd., Rain. 148 FJ69
Farm Rd., Rick. 73 BA42
Farm Rd., St.Alb. 43 CH19
Farm Rd., Sev. 257 FJ121
Farm Rd., Stai. 174 BH93
Farm Rd., Sutt. 218 DD108
Farm Rd., Warl. 237 DY119
Farm Rd., Wok. 227 BB120
Farm St. W1 277 H1
Farm St. W1 141 DH73
Farm Vale, Bex. 187 FB86
Farm Vw., Tad. 249 CZ127
Farm Wk. NW11 119 CZ57
Farm Wk., Guil. 258 AT136
Wilderness Rd.
Farm Wk., Horl. 268 DF148
Court Lo. Rd.
Farm Way, Buck.H. 102 EJ49
Farm Way, Horn. 127 FH63
Farm Way, Nthwd. 93 BS49
Farm Way, Stai. 173 BF86
Farm Way (Bushey), Wat. 76 CB42
Farm Way, Wor.Pk. 199 CW104
Farm Yd., Wind. 151 AR80
Farman Gro., Nthlt. 136 BX69
Wayfarer Rd.
Farmborough Clo., Har. 117 CD59
Pool Rd.
Farmcote Rd. SE12 184 EG88
Farmcroft, Grav. 191 GG89
Farmdale Rd. SE10 164 EG78
Farmdale Rd., Cars. 218 DE108
Farmer Rd. E10 123 EB60
Farmer St. W8 140 DA74
Uxbridge St.
Farmers Clo., Wat. 59 BV33
Farmers Ct., Wal.Abb. 68 EG33
Winters Way
Farmers Rd. SE5 161 DP80
Farmers Rd., Stai. 173 BE92
Farmers Way, Beac. 89 AQ51
Farmfield Dr., Horl. 268 DB150
Farmfield Rd., Brom. 184 EE92
Farmhouse Clo., Brox. 67 DZ25
Farmhouse Clo., Wok. 227 BD115
Farmhouse La., Hem.H. 40 BN18
Farmhouse Rd. SW16 181 DJ94
Farmilo Rd. E17 123 DZ59
Farmington Ave., Sutt. 200 DD104
Farmland Wk., Chis. 185 EP92
Farmlands, Enf. 81 DN39
Farmlands, Pnr. 115 BU56
Farmlands, The, Nthlt. 136 CA65
Moat Fm. Rd.
Farmleigh N14 99 DJ45
Farmleigh Gro., Walt. 213 BS106
Farmstead Rd. SE6 183 EB91
Farmstead Rd., Har. 95 CD53
Farmview, Cob. 230 BX116
Farmway, Dag. 126 EW62
Farnaby Dr., Sev. 256 FF126
Farnaby Rd. SE9 164 EJ84
Farnaby Rd., Brom. 183 ED94
Farnan Ave. E17 101 EA54
Farnan Rd. SW16 181 DL92
Farnborough Ave. E17 123 DY55
Farnborough Ave., S.Croy. 221 DX108
Farnborough Clo., Wem. 118 CP61
Chalkhill Rd.

Farnborough Common, Orp. 205 EM104
Farnborough Cres., Brom. 204 EF102
Saville Row
Farnborough Cres., S.Croy. 221 DY109
Farnborough Hill, Orp. 223 ER106
Farnborough Way SE15 162 DS80
Daniel Gdns.
Farnborough Way, Orp. 223 EP106
Farnburn Ave., Slou. 131 AP71
Farncombe St. SE16 162 DU75
Farncombe St., Gdmg. 258 AS144
Farndale Ave. N13 99 DP48
Farndale Cres., Grnf. 136 CC69
Farnell Ms. SW5 160 DB78
Earls Ct. Sq.
Farnell Rd., Islw. 157 CD84
Farnell Rd., Stai. 174 BG90
Farnes Dr., Rom. 106 FJ54
Farney Fld., Guil. 261 BR142
Farnham Clo. N20 98 DC45
Farnham Clo., Hem.H. 57 BA28
Farnham Clo., Saw. 36 EW06
Farnham Gdns. SW20 199 CV96
Farnham La., Slou. 131 AL69
Farnham Pk. La., Slou. 131 AQ66
Farnham Pl. SE1 278 G3
Farnham Rd., Guil. 258 AS137
Farnham Rd., Ilf. 125 ET59
Farnham Rd., Rom. 106 FK50
Farnham Rd., Slou. 131 AQ71
Farnham Rd., Well. 166 EW82
Farnham Royal SE11 161 DM78
Farningham Cres., Cat. 236 DU123
Commonwealth Rd.
Farningham Hill Rd. (Farningham), Dart. 208 FJ99
Farningham Rd. N17 100 DU52
Farningham Rd., Cat. 236 DU123
Farnley, Wok. 226 AT117
Farnley Rd. E4 102 EE45
Farnley Rd. SE25 202 DR98
Farnol Rd., Dart. 188 FN85
Faro Clo., Brom. 205 EN96
Faroe Rd. W14 159 CX76
Farorna Wk., Enf. 81 DN39
Farquhar Rd. SE19 182 DT92
Farquhar Rd. SW19 180 DA90
Farquhar St., Hert. 32 DQ08
Farquharson Rd., Croy. 202 DQ102
Farr Ave., Bark. 146 EU68
Farr Rd., Enf. 82 DR39
Farraline Rd., Wat. 75 BV42
Farrance Rd., Rom. 126 EY58
Farrance St. E14 143 EA72
Farrans Ct., Har. 117 CH59
Farrant Ave. N22 99 DN54
Farrant Clo., Orp. 224 EU108
Farrant Way, Borwd. 78 CL39
Farrell Ho. E1 142 DW72
Devonport St.
Farren Rd. SE23 183 DY89
Farrer Ms. N8 121 DJ56
Farrer Rd.
Farrer Rd. N8 121 DJ56
Farrer Rd., Har. 118 CL57
Farriday Clo., St.Alb. 43 CE16
Farrier Clo., Sun. 195 BU98
Farrier Rd., Nthlt. 136 CA68
Farrier St. NW1 141 DH66
Farrier Wk. SW10 160 DC79
Farriers, Ware 33 EA09
Farriers Clo., Epsom 216 CS112
Farriers Clo., Grav. 191 GM88
Farriers Ct., Wat. 59 BV32
Farriers End, Brox. 67 DZ26
Farriers Rd., Epsom 216 CS111
Farriers Way, Borwd. 78 CR43
Farringdon La. EC1 274 E5
Farringdon La. EC1 141 DN70
Farringdon Rd. EC1 274 D4
Farringdon Rd. EC1 141 DN70
Farringdon St. EC4 274 F8
Farringdon St. EC4 141 DP71
Farringford Clo., St.Alb. 60 CA26
Farrington Ave., Orp. 206 EV97
Farrington Pl., Chis. 185 ER94
Farrins Rents SE16 143 DY74
Farrow La. SE14 162 DW80
Farrow Pl. SE16 163 DY76
Ropemaker Rd.
Farthing All. SE1 162 DU75
Wolseley St.
Farthing Clo., Dart. 168 FM84
Trevithick Dr.
Farthing Flds. E1 142 DV74
Raine St.
Farthing Grn. La., Slou. 132 AU68
Farthing St., Orp. 223 EM108
Farthingale Ct., Wal.Abb. 68 EG34
Farthingale La., Wal.Abb. 68 EG34
Farthingale Wk. E15 143 ED66
Great Eastern Rd.
Farthings, Wok. 226 AS116
Farthings, The, Hem.H. 40 BH20
Farthings, The, Kings.T. 198 CN95
Brunswick Rd.
Farthings Clo. E4 102 EE48
Farthings Clo., Pnr. 115 BV58
Farwell Rd., Sid. 186 EV90
Farwig La., Brom. 204 EF95
Fashion St. E1 142 DT71
Fashoda Rd., Brom. 204 EJ98
Fassett Rd. E8 142 DU65
Fassett Rd., Kings.T. 198 CL98
Fassett Sq. E8 142 DU65
Fassnidge Way, Uxb. 134 BJ66
Oxford Rd.
Fauconberg Rd. W4 158 CQ79
Faulkner Clo., Dag. 126 EX59
Faulkner St. SE14 162 DW81
Faulkner's All. EC1 274 F6
Faulkners Rd., Walt. 214 BW106
Fauna Clo., Rom. 126 EW58
Faunce St. SE17 161 DP78
Harmsworth St.
Favart Rd. SW6 160 DA81
Faverolle Grn., Wal.Cr. 67 DX28
Faversham Ave. E4 102 EE46
Faversham Ave., Enf. 82 DR44
Faversham Clo., Chig. 104 EV47
Faversham Rd. SE6 183 DZ87
Faversham Rd., Beck. 203 DZ96
Faversham Rd., Mord. 200 DB100
Fawcett Clo. SW11 160 DD82
Fawcett Est. E5 122 DU60
Fawcett Rd. NW10 139 CT66
Fawcett Rd., Croy. 202 DQ104
Fawcett Rd., Wind. 151 AP81
Fawcett St. SW10 160 DB79
Fawcus Clo., Esher 215 CF107
Dalmore Ave.
Fawe Pk. Rd. SW15 159 CZ84
Fawe St. E14 143 EB71
Fawke Common Rd., Sev. 257 FN126
Fawkes Ave., Dart. 188 FM89
Fawkham Grn. Rd. (Fawkham Grn.), Long. 209 FV104
Fawkham Rd., Long. 209 FX98
Fawkon Wk., Hodd. 49 EA18
Taverners Way
Fawley Rd. NW6 120 DB64
Fawn Ct., Hat. 45 CW16
Fawn Rd. E13 144 EJ68
Fawn Rd., Chig. 103 ET50
Fawnbrake Ave. SE24 181 DP85
Fawns Manor Clo., Felt. 175 BQ88
Fawns Manor Rd., Felt. 175 BR88
Fawood Ave. NW10 138 CR66
Fawsley Clo., Slou. 153 BE80
Fawters Clo., Brwd. 109 GD44
Fay Grn., Abb.L. 59 BR33
Fayerfield, Pot.B. 64 DD31
Faygate Cres., Bexh. 186 FA85
Faygate Rd. SW2 181 DM89
Fayland Ave. SW16 181 DJ92
Faymore Gdns., S.Ock. 149 FU72
Feacey Down, Hem.H. 40 BH18
Fearn Clo., Lthd. 245 BS129
Fearney Mead, Rick. 92 BG46
Fearnley Cres., Hmptn. 176 BY92
Fearnley Rd., Welw.G.C. 29 CW10
Fearnley St., Wat. 75 BV42
Fearns Mead, Brwd. 108 FW50
Bucklers Ct.
Fearon St. SE10 164 EG78
Feather Dell, Hat. 45 CT18
Featherbed La., Abb.L. 59 BV26
Sergehill La.
Featherbed La., Croy. 221 DZ108
Featherbed La., Hem.H. 58 BG25
Featherbed La., Rom. 86 EX42
Featherbed La., Warl. 221 EB111
Feathers La., Stai. 173 BA89
Feathers Pl. SE10 163 ED79
Featherstone Ave. SE23 182 DV89
Featherstone Clo., Pot.B. 64 DD32
Featherstone Gdns., Borwd. 78 CQ42
Featherstone Ind. Est., Sthl. 156 BY75
Featherstone Rd. NW7 97 CV51
Featherstone Rd., Sthl. 156 BY76
Featherstone St. EC1 275 K4
Featherstone St. EC1 142 DR70
Featherstone Ter., Sthl. 156 BY76
Featley Rd. SW9 161 DP83
Federal Rd., Grnf. 137 CJ68
Federal Way, Wat. 76 BW39
Federation Rd. SE2 166 EV77
Fee Fm. Rd., Esher 215 CF108
Feenan Highway, Til. 171 GG80
Felbridge Ave., Stan. 95 CG53
Felbridge Clo. SW16 181 DN91
Felbridge Clo., Sutt. 218 DB109
Felbrigge Rd., Ilf. 125 ET61
Felcott Clo., Walt. 196 BW104
Felcott Rd., Walt. 196 BW104
Felday Hos., Dor. 261 BV144
Felday Rd. SE13 183 EB86
Felday Rd., Dor. 261 BT140
Felden Clo., Pnr. 94 BY52
Felden Clo., Wat. 60 BX34
Felden Dr., Hem.H. 40 BG24
Felden La., Hem.H. 40 BG24
Felden Rd., Hem.H. 39 BF23
Felden St. SW6 159 CZ81
Feldman Clo. N16 122 DU60
Felgate Ms. W6 159 CV77
Felhampton Rd. SE9 185 EP89
Felhurst Cres., Dag. 127 FB63
Felicia Way, Grays 171 GH77
Felipe Rd., Grays 169 FW77
Felix Ave. N8 121 DL58
Felix Dr., Guil. 244 BG128
Felix La., Shep. 195 BS100
Felix Rd. W13 137 CG73
Felix Rd., Walt. 195 BU100
Felix St. E2 142 DV68
Hackney Rd.
Felixstowe Rd. N9 100 DU48
Felixstowe Rd. N17 122 DT55
Felixstowe Rd. NW10 139 CV69
Felixstowe Rd. SE2 166 EV76
Fell Rd., Croy. 202 DQ104
Fell Wk., Edg. 96 CP53
East Rd.
Felland Way, Reig. 266 DD138
Fellbrigg Rd. SE22 182 DT85
Fellbrigg St. E1 142 DV70
Headlam St.
Fellbrook, Rich. 177 CH90
Fellowes Clo., Hayes 136 BX70
Paddington Clo.
Fellowes La., St.Alb. 44 CR23
Fellowes Rd., Cars. 200 DE104
Fellows Ct. E2 275 P1
Fellows Rd. NW3 140 DD66
Felltram Way SE7 164 EG77
Felmersham Clo. SW4 161 DK84
Haselrigge Rd.
Felmingham Rd. SE20 202 DW96
Felmongers, Harl. 36 EV13
Fels Clo., Dag. 127 FB62
Fels Fm. Ave., Dag. 127 FC62
Felsberg Rd. SW2 181 DL86
Felsham Rd. SW15 159 CX83
Felspar Clo. SE18 165 ET78
Felstead Ave., Ilf. 103 EN53
Felstead Clo., Brwd. 109 GC44
Felstead Gdns. E14 163 EC78
Ferry St.
Felstead Rd. E11 124 EG59
Felstead Rd., Epsom 216 CR111
Felstead Rd., Loug. 102 EL45
Felstead Rd., Orp. 206 EU103
Felstead Rd., Rom. 105 FC51
Felstead Rd., Wal.Cr. 67 DY32
Felstead St. E9 143 DZ65
Felsted Rd. E16 144 EK72
Feltham Ave., E.Mol. 197 CE98
Feltham Hill Rd., Ashf. 175 BP92
Feltham Hill Rd., Felt. 175 BU91
Feltham Rd., Ashf. 175 BP91
Feltham Rd., Mitch. 200 DF96
Feltham Rd., Red. 266 DF139
Feltham Wk., Red. 266 DF139
Felthambrook Ind. Est., Felt. 175 BV90
Felthambrook Way, Felt. 175 BV90
Felton Clo., Borwd. 78 CL38
Felton Clo., Brox. 67 DZ25
Felton Clo., Orp. 205 EP100
Felton Gdns., Bark. 145 ES67
Sutton Rd.
Felton Lea, Sid. 185 ET92
Felton Rd. W13 157 CJ75
Camborne Ave.
Felton Rd., Bark. 145 ES68
Sutton Rd.
Felton St. N1 142 DR67
Fen Clo., Brwd. 109 GC42
Fen Ct. EC3 275 M10
Fen Gro., Sid. 185 ET86
Fen La., Upmin. 149 FW65
Fen St. E16 144 EF73
Victoria Dock Rd.
Fencepiece Rd., Chig. 103 EQ50
Fencepiece Rd., Ilf. 103 EQ51
Fenchurch Ave. EC3 275 M9
Fenchurch Ave. EC3 142 DS72
Fenchurch Bldgs. EC3 275 N9
Fenchurch Pl. EC3 275 N10
Fenchurch St. EC3 275 M10
Fenchurch St. EC3 142 DS73
Fendall Rd., Epsom 216 CQ106
Fendall St. SE1 279 N7
Fendall St. SE1 162 DS76
Fendt Clo. E16 144 EF73
Bowman Ave.
Fendyke Rd., Belv. 166 EX76
Fenelon Pl. W14 159 CZ77
Fengates Rd., Red. 250 DE134
Fenham Rd. SE15 162 DU80
Fenman Ct. N17 100 DV53
Shelbourne Rd.
Fenman Gdns., Ilf. 126 EV60
Fenn Clo., Brom. 184 EG93
Fenn St. E9 122 DW64
Fennel Clo. E16 144 EE70
Cranberry La.
Fennel Clo., Croy. 203 DX102
Primrose La.
Fennel Clo., Guil. 243 BB131
Fennel St. SE18 165 EN79
Fennells Mead, Epsom 217 CT109
Fennels, Harl. 51 EQ20
Fenner Clo. SE16 162 DV77
Layard Rd.
Fenner Ho., Walt. 213 BU105
Fenner Rd., Grays 169 FW77
Fenner Sq. SW11 160 DD83
Thomas Baines Rd.
Fenning St. SE1 279 M4
Fennings, The, Amer. 55 AR36
Fenns Way, Wok. 226 AY115
Fennycroft Rd., Hem.H. 39 BF17
Fens Way, Swan. 187 FG93
Fensomes All., Hem.H. 40 BK19
Queensway
Fenstanton Ave. N12 98 DD51
Fenswood Clo., Bex. 186 FA86
Fentiman Rd. SW8 161 DL79
Fentiman Way, Horn. 128 FL60
Fenton Ave., Stai. 174 BJ93
Fenton Clo. E8 142 DT65
Laurel St.
Fenton Clo. SW9 161 DM82
Fenton Clo., Chis. 185 EM92
Fenton Clo., Red. 250 DG134
Fenton Gra., Harl. 52 EW16
Fenton Rd. N17 100 DQ52
Fenton Rd., Red. 250 DG134
Fentons Ave. E13 144 EH68
Fentum Rd., Guil. 242 AU132
Fenwick Clo. SE18 165 EN79
Ritter St.
Fenwick Clo., Wok. 226 AV118
Fenwick Gro. SE15 162 DU83
Fenwick Path, Borwd. 78 CM38
Berwick Rd.
Fenwick Pl. SW9 161 DL83
Fenwick Rd. SE15 162 DU83
Ferdinand Pl. NW1 140 DG66
Ferdinand St.
Ferdinand St. NW1 140 DG66
Fergus Rd. N5 121 DP64
Calabria Rd.
Ferguson Ave., Grav. 191 GJ91
Ferguson Ave., Rom. 106 FJ54
Ferguson Ave., Surb. 198 CM99
Ferguson Clo. E14 163 EA77
Ferguson Clo., Brom. 203 ED97
Ferguson Ct., Rom. 106 FK54
Ferguson Dr. W3 138 CR72
Ferme Pk. Rd. N4 121 DM59
Ferme Pk. Rd. N8 121 DL57
Fermor Rd. SE23 183 DY88
Fermoy Rd. W9 139 CZ70
Fermoy Rd., Grnf. 136 CB70
Fern Ave., Mitch. 201 DK98
Fern Clo., Brox. 49 DZ23
Fern Clo., Erith 167 FH81
Hollywood Way
Fern Clo., Warl. 237 DY118
Fern Dells, Hat. 45 CT19
Fern Dene W13 137 CH71
Templewood
Fern Dr., Hem.H. 40 BL21
Fern Gro., Felt. 175 BV87
Fern Gro., Welw.G.C. 29 CX05
Fern Hill, Lthd. 215 CD114
Fern Hill La., Harl. 51 ES19
Fern La., Houns. 156 BZ78
Fern Leys, St.Alb. 43 CJ17
Fern Rd., Maid. 130 AH72
Fern St. E3 143 EA70
Fern Twrs., Cat. 252 DU125
Fern Wk., Ashf. 174 BK92
Ferndale Rd.
Fern Way, Wat. 75 BV35
Fernbank, Buck.H. 102 EH46
Fernbank Ave., Horn. 128 FJ63
Fernbank Ave., Walt. 196 BY101
Fernbank Ave., Wem. 117 CF63
Fernbank Rd., Add. 212 BG106
Fernbrook Ave., Sid. 185 ES85
Blackfen Rd.
Fernbrook Cres. SE13 184 EE86
Fernbrook Rd.
Fernbrook Dr., Har. 116 CB59
Fernbrook Rd. SE13 184 EE86
Ferncliff Rd. E8 122 DU64
Ferncroft Ave. N12 98 DE51
Ferncroft Ave. NW3 120 DA62
Ferncroft Ave., Ruis. 116 BW61
Ferndale, Brom. 204 EJ96
Ferndale, Guil. 242 AS132
Ferndale Ave. E17 123 ED57
Ferndale Ave., Cher. 193 BE104
Ferndale Ave., Houns. 156 BY83
Ferndale Ct. SE3 164 EF80
Ferndale Cres., Uxb. 134 BJ69
Ferndale Rd. E7 144 EH66
Ferndale Rd. E11 124 EE61
Ferndale Rd. N15 122 DT58
Ferndale Rd. SE25 202 DV99
Ferndale Rd. SW4 161 DM84
Ferndale Rd. SW9 161 DL84
Ferndale Rd., Ashf. 174 BK92
Ferndale Rd., Bans. 233 CZ116
Ferndale Rd., Enf. 83 DY36
Ferndale Rd., Grav. 191 GH89
Ferndale Rd., Rom. 105 FC54
Ferndale Rd., Wok. 227 AZ116
Ferndale St. E6 145 EP73
Ferndale Ter., Har. 117 CF56
Ferndale Way, Orp. 223 ER106
Ferndell Ave., Bex. 187 FD90
Fernden Ri., Gdmg. 258 AS144
Fernden Way, Rom. 127 FB58
Ferndene, St.Alb. 60 BZ31
Ferndene Rd. SE24 162 DQ84
Ferndown, Horl. 268 DF146
Ferndown, Horn. 128 FM58
Ferndown, Nthwd. 93 BU54
Ferndown Ave., Orp. 205 ER102
Ferndown Clo., Guil. 259 BA135
Ferndown Clo., Pnr. 94 BY52
Ferndown Clo., Sutt. 218 DD107
Ferndown Ct., Guil. 242 AW133
Ferndown Gdns., Cob. 214 BW113
Ferndown Rd. SE9 184 EK87
Ferndown Rd., Wat. 94 BW48
Fernecroft, St.Alb. 42 CC23
Fernery, The, Stai. 173 BE92
Fernes Clo., Uxb. 134 BJ72
Ferney Ct., W.Byf. 212 BK112
Ferney Rd.
Ferney Meade Way, Islw. 157 CG82
Ferney Rd., Barn. 98 DG45
Ferney Rd., W.Byf. 212 BK112
Fernhall Dr., Ilf. 124 EK57
Fernhall La., Wal.Abb. 68 EK31
Fernham Rd., Th.Hth. 202 DQ97
Fernhead Rd. W9 139 CZ69
Fernheath Way, Dart. 187 FD92
Fernhill, Harl. 51 ES19
Fernhill Clo., Wok. 226 AW120
Fernhill Ct. E17 101 ED54
Fernhill Gdns., Kings.T. 177 CK92
Fernhill La., Wok. 226 AW120
Fernhill Pk., Wok. 226 AW120
Fernhill Rd., Horl. 269 DK152
Fernhill St. E16 145 EM74
Fernhills, Kings L. 59 BR34
Fernholme Rd. SE15 183 DX85
Fernhurst Clo., Beac. 89 AM53
Fernhurst Gdns., Edg. 96 CN51
Fernhurst Rd. SW6 159 CY81
Fernhurst Rd., Ashf. 175 BQ91
Fernhurst Rd., Croy. 202 DU101
Fernie Clo., Chig. 104 EU50
Fernihough Clo., Wey. 212 BN111
Fernlands Clo., Cher. 193 BE104
Fernlea, Lthd. 230 CB124
Fernlea Rd. SW12 181 DH88
Fernlea Rd., Mitch. 200 DG96
Fernleigh Clo., Croy. 219 DN105
Stafford Rd.
Fernleigh Ct., Har. 94 CB54
Fernleigh Ct., Wem. 118 CL61
Fernleigh Rd. N21 99 DN47
Ferns, The, Beac. 89 AM54
Ferns Clo., Enf. 83 DY36
Ferns Clo., S.Croy. 220 DV110
Ferns Rd. E15 144 EF65
Fernsbury St. WC1 274 D3
Fernsham Wk., Slou. 111 AQ64
Fernshaw Rd. SW10 160 DC79
Fernside NW11 120 DA61
Finchley Rd.
Fernside, Buck.H. 102 EH46
Fernside Ave. NW7 96 CR48
Fernside Ave., Felt. 175 BV91
Fernside La., Sev. 257 FJ129
Fernside Rd. SW12 180 DF88
Fernsleigh Clo., Ger.Cr. 90 AY51
Fernthorpe Rd. SW16 181 DJ93
Ferntower Rd. N5 122 DR64
Fernville La., Hem.H. 40 BK20
Midland Rd.
Fernways, Ilf. 125 EP63
Cecil Rd.
Fernwood, Croy. 221 DY109
Fernwood Ave. SW16 181 DK91
Fernwood Ave., Wem. 117 CJ64
Bridgewater Rd.
Fernwood Clo., Brom. 204 EJ96
Fernwood Cres. N20 98 DF48
Ferny Hill, Barn. 80 DF38
Ferranti Clo. SE18 164 EK76
Ferraro Clo., Houns. 156 CA79
Ferrers Ave., Wall. 219 DK105
Ferrers Ave., West Dr. 154 BK75
Ferrers Rd. SW16 181 DK92
Ferrestone Rd. N8 121 DM56
Ferriby Clo. N1 141 DN66
Bewdley St.
Ferrier Pt. E16 144 EH71
Forty Acre La.
Ferrier St. SW18 160 DB84
Ferriers Way, Epsom 233 CW118
Ferring Clo., Har. 116 CC60
Ferrings SE21 182 DS89
Ferris Ave., Croy. 203 DZ104
Ferris Rd. SE22 162 DU84
Ferro Rd., Rain. 147 FG70
Ferron Rd. E5 122 DV62
Ferry Ave., Stai. 173 BE94
Ferry La. N17 122 DV56
Ferry La. SW13 159 CT79
Ferry La., Brent. 158 CL79
Ferry La., Cher. 194 BG100
Ferry La., Guil. 258 AW138
Portsmouth Rd.
Ferry La., Rain. 147 FE72
Ferry La., Rich. 158 CM79
Ferry La., Shep. 194 BN102
Ferry La. (Hythe End), Stai. 173 BB89
Ferry La. (Laleham), Stai. 194 BJ97
Ferry Pl. SE18 165 EN76
Woolwich High St.
Ferry Rd. SW13 159 CU80
Ferry Rd., Maid. 150 AC75
Ferry Rd., Tedd. 177 CH92
Ferry Rd., T.Ditt. 197 CH100
Ferry Rd., Til. 171 GG83
Ferry Rd., Twick. 177 CH88
Ferry Rd., W.Mol. 196 CA97
Ferry Sq., Brent. 157 CK79
Ferry Sq., Shep. 195 BP101
Ferry St. E14 163 EC78
Ferryhills Clo., Wat. 94 BW48
Ferrymead Ave., Grnf. 136 CA69
Ferrymead Dr., Grnf. 136 CA69
Ferrymead Gdns., Grnf. 136 CC68
Ferrymoor, Rich. 177 CH90
Feryby Rd., Grays 171 GH76
Feryngs Clo., Harl. 36 EX11
Watlington Rd.
Fesants Cft., Harl. 36 EV12
Festing Rd. SW15 159 CX83
Festival Clo., Bex. 186 EX88
Festival Clo., Erith 167 FF80
Betsham Rd.
Festival Clo., Uxb. 135 BP67
Festival Path, Wok. 226 AT119
Fetcham Common La., Lthd. 230 CB121
Fetcham Pk. Dr., Lthd. 231 CE123
Fetter La. EC4 274 E9
Fetter La. EC4 141 DN72
Ffinch St. SE8 163 EA80
Fiddicroft Ave., Bans. 218 DB114
Fiddle Bri. La., Hat. 45 CT17
Fiddlers Clo., Green. 169 FV84
Fidler Pl. (Bushey), Wat. 76 CB44
Ashfield Ave.
Field Clo. E4 101 EB51
Field Clo., Brom. 204 EJ96
Field Clo., Buck.H. 102 EJ48
Field Clo., Chesh. 54 AS28
Field Clo., Chess. 215 CJ106
Field Clo., Guil. 243 BD132
Field Clo., Hayes 155 BQ80
Field Clo., Houns. 155 BV81
Field Clo., Rom. 86 EV41
Field Clo., Ruis. 115 BQ60
Field Way
Field Clo., St.Alb. 43 CG16
Field Clo., S.Croy. 220 DV114
Field Clo., W.Mol. 196 CB99
Field Ct. WC1 274 C7
Field Ct., Oxt. 254 EE127
Field End, Barn. 79 CV42
Field End, Couls. 219 DK114
Field End, Nthlt. 136 BX65
Field End, Ruis. 136 BW65
Field End, Twick. 177 CF91
Field End Clo., Wat. 94 BY45
Field End Rd., Pnr. 115 BV57
Field End Rd., Ruis. 116 BW60
Field La., Brent. 157 CJ80
Field La., Gdmg. 258 AT144
The Oval
Field La., Tedd. 177 CG92
Field Mead NW7 96 CS52
Field Mead NW9 96 CS52
Field Pl., Gdmg. 258 AS144
George Rd.
Field Pl., N.Mal. 199 CT100
Field Rd. E7 124 EG63
Field Rd. N17 122 DR55
Field Rd. W6 159 CY78
Field Rd., Felt. 175 BV86
Field Rd., Hem.H. 40 BN21
Field Rd., S.Ock. 148 FQ74
Field Rd., Uxb. 113 BD63
Field Rd., Wat. 76 BY44
Field St. WC1 274 B2
Field St. WC1 141 DM69
Field Vw., Egh. 173 BC92
Field Vw., Felt. 175 BR91
Field Vw. Ri., St.Alb. 60 BY29
Field Vw. Rd., Pot.B. 64 DA33
Field Way NW10 138 CQ66
Twybridge Way
Field Way, Berk. 38 AY21
Field Way, Croy. 221 EB108
Field Way, Ger.Cr. 90 AX52
Field Way, Grnf. 136 CB67
Field Way, Hem.H. 57 BA27
Field Way, Hodd. 33 EC13
Field Way, Rick. 92 BH46
Field Way, Ruis. 115 BQ60
Field Way, Uxb. 134 BK70
Field Way, Wok. 243 BF125
Fieldcommon La., Walt. 196 BY102
Fieldend Rd. SW16 201 DJ95
Fielders Clo., Enf. 82 DS42
Woodfield Clo.
Fielders Clo., Har. 116 CC60
Fielders Grn., Guil. 243 BA134
Fieldfare Rd. SE28 146 EW73
Fieldgate La., Mitch. 200 DE97
Fieldgate St. E1 142 DU71
Fieldhouse Rd. SW12 181 DJ88
Fieldhurst, Slou. 153 AZ78
Fieldhurst Clo., Add. 212 BH106
Fielding Ave., Til. 171 GH81
Fielding Ave., Twick. 176 CC90
Fielding Ho. NW6 140 DA69
Fielding Ms. SW13 159 CV79
Castelnau
Fielding Rd. W4 158 CR76
Fielding Rd. W14 159 CX76
Fielding St. SE17 162 DQ79
Fielding Way, Brwd. 109 GC44
Fieldings, The SE23 182 DW88
Fieldings, The, Horl. 269 DJ147
Fieldings, The, Wok. 226 AT116
Fieldings Rd. (Cheshunt), Wal.Cr. 67 DZ28

Fields Ct., Pot.B. 64 DD33
Fields End La., Hem.H. 39 BD18
Fields Est. E8 142 DU66
Fields Pk. Cres., Rom. 126 EW57
Fieldsend Rd., Sutt. 217 CY106
Fieldside Clo., Orp. 223 EQ105
State Fm. Ave.
Fieldside Rd., Brom. 183 ED92
Fieldview SW18 180 DD88
Fieldview, Horl. 269 DH147
Stockfield
Fieldway, Amer. 55 AP41
Fieldway, Dag. 126 EW62
Fieldway, Orp. 205 ER100
Fieldway, Ware 33 EB11
Fieldway Cres. N5 121 DN64
Fiennes Clo., Dag. 126 EW60
Fiennes Way, Sev. 257 FJ127
Fiesta Dr., Dag. 147 FC70
Fife Rd. E16 144 EG71
Fife Rd. N22 99 DP52
Fife Rd. SW14 178 CQ85
Fife Rd., Kings.T. 198 CL96
Fife Ter. N1 141 DM68
Wynford Rd.
Fifehead Clo., Ashf. 174 BL93
Fifeway, Lthd. 246 CA125
Fifield La., Wind. 150 AD84
Fifield Path SE23 183 DX90
Bampton Rd.
Fifield Rd., Maid. 150 AD80
Fifth Ave. E12 125 EM63
Fifth Ave. W10 139 CY69
Fifth Ave., Grays 169 FU79
Fifth Ave., Harl. 35 EQ12
Fifth Ave., Hayes 135 BT74
Fifth Ave., Wat. 76 BW35
Fifth Cross Rd., Twick. 177 CD89
Fifth Way, Wem. 118 CP63
Fig St., Sev. 256 FF129
Fig Tree Clo. NW10 138 CS67
Craven Pk.
Fig Tree Hill, Hem.H. 40 BK19
Figges Rd., Mitch. 180 DG94
Filby Rd., Chess. 216 CM107
Filey Ave. N16 122 DU60
Filey Clo., Sutt. 218 DC108
Filey Clo., West. 238 EH119
Filey Spur, Slou. 151 AP75
Filey Waye, Ruis. 115 BU61
Fillebrook Ave., Enf. 82 DS40
Fillebrook Rd. E11 123 ED60
Filmer La., Sev. 257 FL121
Filmer Rd. SW6 159 CY81
Filmer Rd., Wind. 151 AK82
Filston La., Sev. 241 FD116
Filston Rd., Erith 167 FB78
Riverdale Rd.
Finborough Rd. SW10 160 DB78
Finborough Rd. SW17 180 DF93
Finch Ave. SE27 182 DR91
Finch Clo. NW10 118 CR64
Finch Clo., Barn. 80 DA43
Brent Pl.
Finch Clo., Hat. 45 CU20
Eagle Way
Finch Dr., Felt. 176 BX87
Finch End, H.Wyc. 88 AC47
Finch Grn., Rick. 73 BF42
Finch La. EC3 275 L9
Finch La., Amer. 72 AT42
Finch La., Beac. 88 AJ50
Finch La. (Bushey), Wat. 76 CA43
Finch Ms. SE15 162 DT81
Southampton Way
Finch Rd., Berk. 38 AU19
Finch Rd., Guil. 242 AX134
Finchale Rd. SE2 166 EU76
Fincham Clo., Uxb. 115 BQ61
Aylsham Dr.
Finchdale, Hem.H. 40 BG20
Finchdale Rd. SE2 166 EU76
Finchdean Way SE15 162 DT80
Daniel Gdns.
Finches, The, Hert. 32 DV09
Finches Ri., Guil. 243 BC132
Finchingfield Ave., Wdf.Grn. 102 EJ52
Finchley Clo., Dart. 188 FN86
Finchley Ct. N3 98 DB51
Finchley La. NW4 119 CW56
Finchley Pk. N12 98 DC49
Finchley Pl. NW8 140 DD68
Finchley Rd. NW2 120 DA62
Finchley Rd. NW3 120 DB64
Finchley Rd. NW8 140 DD66
Finchley Rd. NW11 119 CZ56
Finchley Rd., Grays 170 GB79
Finchley Way N3 98 DA52
Finchmoor, Harl. 51 ER18
Finck St. SE1 278 C5
Finck St. SE1 161 DM75
Finden Rd. E7 124 EH64
Findhorn Ave., Hayes 135 BV71
Findhorn St. E14 143 EC72
Findlay Dr., Guil. 242 AT130
Findon Clo. SW18 180 DA86
Wimbledon Pk. Rd.
Findon Clo., Har. 116 CB62
Findon Gdns., Rain. 147 FG71
Findon Rd. N9 100 DV46
Findon Rd. W12 159 CU75
Fine Bush La., Uxb. 115 BP58
Fingal St. SE10 164 EF78
Finglesham Clo., Orp. 206 EX102
Westwell Clo.
Finians Clo., Uxb. 134 BM66
Finland Quay SE16 163 DY76
Finland Rd. SE4 163 DY83
Finland St. SE16 163 DY76
Finlay Gdns., Add. 212 BJ105
Finlay St. SW6 159 CX81
Finlays Clo., Chess. 216 CN106
Finnart Clo., Wey. 213 BQ105
Finnart Ho. Dr., Wey. 213 BQ105
Vaillant Rd.
Finnis St. E2 142 DV69
Finnymore Rd., Dag. 146 EY66
Finsbury Ave. EC2 275 L7
Finsbury Circ. EC2 275 L7
Finsbury Circ. EC2 142 DR71
Finsbury Cotts. N22 99 DL52
Clarence Rd.
Finsbury Est. EC1 274 E3
Finsbury Est. EC1 141 DN69
Finsbury Ho. N22 99 DL53
Finsbury Mkt. EC2 275 M5
Finsbury Mkt. EC2 142 DS70
Finsbury Pk. Ave. N4 122 DQ58
Finsbury Pk. Rd. N4 121 DP61
Finsbury Pavement EC2 275 L6
Finsbury Pavement EC2 142 DR71
Finsbury Rd. N22 99 DM53
Finsbury Sq. EC2 275 L5
Finsbury Sq. EC2 142 DR71
Finsbury St. EC2 275 K6
Finsbury St. EC2 142 DR71
Finsbury Way, Bex. 186 EZ86
Finsen Rd. SE5 162 DQ83
Finstock Rd. W10 139 CX72
Finucane Dr., Orp. 206 EW101
Finucane Gdns., Rain. 147 FG65
Finucane Ri. (Bushey), Wat. 94 CC47
Finway Ct., Wat. 75 BT43
Whippendell Rd.
Finway Rd., Hem.H. 41 BP16
Fiona Clo., Lthd. 230 CA124
Fir Clo., Walt. 195 BU101
Fir Dene, Orp. 205 EM104
Fir Gra. Ave., Wey. 213 BP106
Fir Gro., N.Mal. 199 CT100
Fir Gro., Wok. 226 AU119
Fir Pk., Harl. 51 EP18
Fir Rd., Felt. 176 BX92
Fir Rd., Sutt. 199 CZ102
Fir Tree Ave., Slou. 132 AT70
Fir Tree Ave., West Dr. 154 BN76
Fir Tree Clo. SW16 181 DJ92
Fir Tree Clo. W5 138 CL72
Fir Tree Clo., Epsom 217 CT105
Fir Tree Clo., Esher 214 CC106
Fir Tree Clo., Grays 170 GD79
Fir Tree Clo., Hem.H. 40 BN21
Fir Tree Clo., Lthd. 231 CJ123
Fir Tree Clo., Orp. 223 ET106
Highfield Ave.
Fir Tree Clo., Rom. 127 FD55
Fir Tree Gdns., Croy. 221 EA105
Fir Tree Gro., Cars. 218 DF108
Fir Tree Hill, Rick. 74 BM38
Fir Tree Pl., Ashf. 174 BN92
Percy Ave.
Fir Tree Rd., Bans. 217 CW114
Fir Tree Rd., Epsom 233 CV116
Fir Tree Rd., Guil. 242 AX131
Fir Tree Rd., Houns. 156 BY84
Fir Tree Rd., Lthd. 231 CJ123
Fir Tree Wk., Dag. 127 FC62
Wheel Fm. Dr.
Fir Tree Wk., Enf. 82 DR41
Fir Tree Wk., Reig. 250 DD134
Fir Trees, Rom. 86 EV41
Fir Trees Clo. SE16 143 DY74
Firbank Clo. E16 144 EK71
Firbank Clo., Enf. 82 DQ42
Gladbeck Way
Firbank Dr., Wat. 94 BY45
Firbank Dr., Wok. 226 AV119
Firbank La., Wok. 226 AV119
Firbank Pl., Egh. 172 AV93
Firbank Rd. SE15 162 DV82
Firbank Rd., Rom. 105 FB50
Firbank Rd., St.Alb. 43 CF16
Fircroft Ave., Chess. 216 CM105
Fircroft Clo., Slou. 132 AU65
Fircroft Clo., Wok. 227 AZ118
Fircroft Ct., Wok. 227 AZ118
Fircroft Clo.
Fircroft Gdns., Har. 117 CE62
Fircroft Rd. SW17 180 DF89
Firdene, Surb. 198 CQ102
Fire Bell All., Surb. 198 CL100
Fire Sta. All., Barn. 79 CZ40
Christchurch La.
Firecrest Dr. NW3 120 DB62
Firefly Clo., Wall. 219 DL108
Defiant Way
Firefly Gdns. E6 144 EL70
Jack Dash Way
Firfield Rd., Add. 212 BG105
Firfields, Wey. 213 BP107
Firham Pk. Ave., Rom. 106 FN52
Firhill Rd. SE6 183 EA91
Firlands, Horl. 269 DH147
Stockfield
Firlands, Wey. 213 BS107
Firmin Rd., Dart. 188 FJ85
Firmingers Rd., Orp. 225 FB106
Firs, The N20 98 DD46
Firs, The W5 137 CK71
Firs, The, Bex. 187 FD88
Dartford Rd.
Firs, The, Brwd. 108 FU44
Firs, The, Cat. 236 DR122
York Gate
Firs, The, Guil. 258 AV138
Firs, The, St.Alb. 43 CH24
Firs, The, Tad. 249 CZ126
Brighton Rd.
Firs, The, Wal.Cr. 66 DS27
Firs, The, Welw.G.C. 29 CW05
Firs Ave. N10 120 DG55
Firs Ave. N11 98 DF51
Firs Ave. SW14 158 CQ84
Firs Ave., Wind. 151 AM83
Firs Clo. N10 120 DG55
Firs Ave.
Firs Clo. SE23 183 DX87
Firs Clo., Dor. 263 CG138
Firs Clo., Esher 215 CE107
Firs Clo., Hat. 45 CV19
Firs Clo., Mitch. 201 DH96
Firs Dr., Houns. 155 BV81
Firs Dr., Loug. 85 EN39
Firs Dr., Slou. 133 AZ74
Firs End, Ger.Cr. 112 AY55
Southside
Firs La. N13 100 DQ48
Firs La. N21 100 DQ47
Firs La., Pot.B. 64 DB33
Firs Pk. Ave. N21 100 DR46
Firs Pk. Gdns. N21 100 DQ46
Firs Rd., Ken. 235 DP115
Firs Wk., Nthwd. 93 BR51
Firs Wk., Wdf.Grn. 102 EG50
Firs Way, Guil. 242 AT133
Firs Wd. Clo., Pot.B. 64 DF32
Firsby Ave., Croy. 203 DX102
Firsby Rd. N16 122 DT60
Firscroft N13 100 DQ48
Firsdene Clo., Cher. 211 BD107
Slade Rd.
Firsgrove Cres., Brwd. 108 FV49
Firsgrove Rd., Brwd. 108 FV49
Firside Gro., Sid. 185 ET88
First Ave. E12 124 EL63
First Ave. E13 144 EG69
First Ave. E17 123 EA57
First Ave. N18 100 DW49
First Ave. NW4 119 CW56
First Ave. SW14 158 CS83
First Ave. W3 139 CT74
First Ave. W10 139 CZ70
First Ave., Amer. 55 AQ40
First Ave., Bexh. 166 EW80
First Ave., Dag. 147 FB68
First Ave., Enf. 82 DT43
First Ave., Epsom 216 CS109
First Ave., Grav. 190 GE88
First Ave., Grays 169 FU79
First Ave., Hayes 135 BT74
First Ave., Rom. 126 EW57
First Ave., Walt. 195 BV100
First Ave., Wat. 76 BW35
First Ave., Wem. 117 CK61
First Ave., W.Mol. 196 BZ98
First Avenue-Mandela Ave., Harl. 35 ET13
First Clo., W.Mol. 196 CC97
First Cres., Slou. 131 AQ71
First Cross Rd., Twick. 177 CE89
First Slip, Lthd. 231 CG118
First St. SW3 276 C8
First St. SW3 160 DE77
First Way, Wem. 118 CP63
Firstway SW20 199 CW96
Firswood Ave., Epsom 217 CT106
Firth Gdns. SW6 159 CY81
Firtree Ave., Mitch. 200 DG96
Firtree Clo. (Stoneleigh), Epsom 233 CV116
Firtree Ct., Borwd. 78 CM42
Firwood Ave., St.Alb. 44 CL20
Firwood Clo., Wok. 226 AS119
Firwood Rd., Vir.W. 192 AS100
Fish St. Hill EC3 279 L1
Fish St. Hill EC3 142 DR73
Fisher Clo., Croy. 202 DT102
Grant Rd.
Fisher Clo., Grnf. 136 CA69
Gosling Clo.
Fisher Clo., Kings L. 58 BN29
Fisher Clo., Walt. 213 BV105
Fisher Rd., Har. 95 CF54
Fisher St. E16 144 EG71
Fisher St. WC1 274 B7
Fisher St. WC1 141 DM71
Fisherman Clo., Rich. 177 CJ91
Locksmeade Rd.
Fishermans Dr. SE16 163 DX75
Fishermans Hill, Grav. 190 GB85
Fisherman's Wk. E14 143 EA74
Cabot Sq.
Fishers, Horl. 269 DJ147
Ewelands
Fishers Clo., Wal.Cr. 67 EA34
Fishers Ct. SE14 163 DX81
Besson St.
Fishers Hatch, Harl. 35 ES14
School La.
Fishers La. W4 158 CR77
Fishers La., Epp. 69 ES32
Fishers Way, Belv. 147 FC74
Fishersdene, Esher 215 CG107
Fisherton Est. NW8 272 A4
Fisherton St. NW8 140 DD70
Fisherton St. Est. NW8 140 DD70
Fishery Pas., Hem.H. 40 BG22
Fishery Rd.
Fishery Rd., Hem.H. 40 BG22
Fishery Rd., Maid. 130 AC74
Fishponds Rd. SW17 180 DE91
Fishponds Rd., Kes. 222 EK106
Fishpool St., St.Alb. 42 CB20
Fisons Rd. E16 144 EG74
Fitzalan Rd. N3 119 CY55
Fitzalan Rd., Esher 215 CE108
Fitzalan St. SE11 278 D8
Fitzalan St. SE11 161 DM77
Fitzgeorge Ave. W14 159 CY77
Fitzgeorge Ave., N.Mal. 198 CR95
Fitzgerald Ave. SW14 158 CS83
Fitzgerald Clo. E11 124 EG57
Fitzgerald Rd.
Fitzgerald Ho. E14 143 EB72
Kerbey St.
Fitzgerald Ho., Hayes 135 BV74
Fitzgerald Rd. E11 124 EG57
Fitzgerald Rd. SW14 158 CR83
Fitzgerald Rd., T.Ditt. 197 CG100
Fitzhardinge St. W1 272 F8
Fitzhardinge St. W1 140 DG72
Fitzhugh Gro. SW18 180 DD86
Fitzhugh Gro. Est. SW18 180 DD86
Fitzilian Ave., Rom. 106 FM53
Fitzjames Ave. W14 159 CY77
Fitzjames Ave., Croy. 202 DU103
Fitzjohn Ave., Barn. 79 CY43
Fitzjohn Clo., Guil. 243 BC131
Fitzjohn's Ave. NW3 120 DD64
Fitzmaurice Pl. W1 277 J2
Fitzmaurice Pl. W1 141 DH74
Fitzneal St. W12 139 CT72
Fitzrobert Pl., Egh. 173 BA93
Fitzroy Clo. N6 120 DF60
Fitzroy Ct. W1 273 L5
Fitzroy Cres. W4 158 CR80
Fitzroy Gdns. SE19 182 DS94
Fitzroy Ms. W1 273 K5
Fitzroy Pk. N6 120 DF61
Fitzroy Rd. NW1 140 DG67
Fitzroy Sq. W1 273 K5
Fitzroy Sq. W1 141 DJ70
Fitzroy St. W1 273 K5
Fitzroy St. W1 141 DJ70
Fitzroy Yd. NW1 140 DG67
Fitzroy Rd.
Fitzstephen Rd., Dag. 126 EV64
Fitzwarren Gdns. N19 121 DJ60
Fitzwilliam Ave., Rich. 158 CM82
Fitzwilliam Ct., Harl. 36 EY11
Fitzwilliam Ms. E16 144 EE72
Silvertown Way
Fitzwilliam Rd. SW4 161 DJ83
Fitzwygram Clo., Hmptn. 176 CC92
Five Acre NW9 97 CT53
Five Acres, Chesh. 54 AR33
Five Acres, Harl. 51 ES18
Five Acres, H.Wyc. 110 AE56
Five Acres, Kings L. 58 BM29
Five Acres, St.Alb. 61 CK25
Five Acres Ave., St.Alb. 60 BZ29
Five Bell All. E14 143 DZ73
Three Colt St.
Five Elms Rd., Brom. 204 EH104
Five Elms Rd., Dag. 126 EZ62
Five Oaks, Add. 211 BF107
Five Oaks La., Chig. 104 EY51
Five Wents, Swan. 207 FG96
Fiveacre Clo., Th.Hth. 201 DN100
Fiveash Rd., Grav. 191 GF87
Fiveways Rd. SW9 161 DN82
Fladbury Rd. N15 122 DR58
Fladgate Rd. E11 124 EE58
Flag Clo., Croy. 203 DX102
Flag Wk., Pnr. 115 BU58
Eastcote Rd.
Flags, The, Hem.H. 41 BP20
Flagstaff Clo., Wal.Abb. 67 EB33
Flagstaff Rd., Wal.Abb. 67 EB33
Flambard Rd., Har. 117 CG58
Flamborough Clo., West. 238 EH119
Flamborough Rd., Ruis. 115 BU62
Flamborough Spur, Slou. 151 AN75
Flamborough St. E14 143 DY72
Flamingo Gdns., Nthlt. 136 BY69
Jetstar Way
Flamingo Wk., Horn. 147 FG66
Flamstead End Rd. (Cheshunt), Wal.Cr. 66 DV28
Flamstead Gdns., Dag. 146 EW66
Flamstead Rd.
Flamstead Rd., Dag. 146 EW66
Flamsted Ave., Wem. 138 CN65
Flamsteed Rd. SE7 164 EL78
Flanchford Rd. W12 159 CT76
Flanchford Rd., Reig. 265 CT140
Flanders Ct., Egh. 173 BC92
Flanders Cres. SW17 180 DF94
Flanders Rd. E6 145 EM68
Flanders Rd. W4 158 CS77
Flanders Way E9 143 DX65
Flank St. E1 142 DU73
Dock St.
Flash La., Enf. 81 DP37
Flask Cotts. NW3 120 DD63
New End Sq.
Flask Wk. NW3 120 DC63
Flatfield Rd., Hem.H. 40 BN22
Flaunden Bottom, Chesh. 72 AY36
Flaunden Bottom, Hem.H. 57 AZ34
Flaunden Hill, Hem.H. 57 AZ33
Flaunden La., Hem.H. 57 BB32
Flaunden La., Rick. 57 BD33
Flaunden Pk., Hem.H. 57 BA32
Flavell Ms. SE10 164 EE78
Flavian Clo., St.Alb. 42 BZ22
Flaxen Clo. E4 101 EB48
Flaxen Rd.
Flaxen Rd. E4 101 EB48
Flaxley Rd., Mord. 200 DB100
Flaxman Ct. W1 273 M9
Flaxman Rd. SE5 161 DP83
Flaxman Ter. WC1 273 N3
Flaxman Ter. WC1 141 DK69
Flaxmore Pl., Beck. 203 ED100
Flaxton Rd. SE18 165 ER80
Flecker Clo., Stan. 95 CF50
Fleece Dr. N9 100 DU49
Fleece Rd., Surb. 197 CJ102
Fleece Wk. N7 141 DL65
Manger Rd.
Fleeming Clo. E17 101 DZ54
Pennant Ter.
Fleeming Rd. E17 101 DZ54
Fleet Ave., Dart. 188 FQ88
Fleet Ave., Upmin. 129 FR58
Fleet Clo., Ruis. 115 BQ58
Fleet Clo., Upmin. 129 FR58
Fleet Clo., W.Mol. 196 CA99
Fleet La., W.Mol. 196 BZ100
Fleet Pl. EC4 141 DN72
Farringdon St.
Fleet Rd. NW3 120 DE64
Fleet Rd., Dart. 188 FP88
Fleet Rd., Grav. 190 GC90
Fleet Sq. WC1 274 C3
Fleet St. EC4 274 E9
Fleet St. EC4 141 DN72
Fleet St. Hill E1 142 DU70
Weaver St.
Fleetdale Par., Dart. 188 FQ88
Fleet Ave.
Fleetside, W.Mol. 196 BZ99
Fleetway, Egh. 193 BC97
Fleetway W. Business Pk., Grnf. 137 CH68
Fleetwood Clo. E16 144 EK71
Fleetwood Clo., Ch.St.G. 90 AU49
Fleetwood Clo., Chess. 215 CK108
Fleetwood Clo., Croy. 202 DS104
Chepstow Ri.
Fleetwood Clo., Tad. 233 CX120
Fleetwood Ct. E6 145 EM71
Evelyn Denington Rd.
Fleetwood Ct., W.Byf. 212 BG113
Fleetwood Gro. W3 138 CS73
East Acton La.
Fleetwood Rd. NW10 119 CU64
Fleetwood Rd., Kings.T. 198 CP97
Fleetwood Rd., Slou. 132 AT74
Fleetwood Sq., Kings.T. 198 CP97
Fleetwood St. N16 122 DS61
Stoke Newington Ch. St.
Fleetwood Way, Wat. 94 BW49
Fleming Ave., Ruis. 115 BV61
Fleming Clo. (Cheshunt), Wal.Cr. 66 DU26
Fleming Ct. W2 140 DD71
St. Marys Ter.
Fleming Ct., Croy. 219 DN106
Fleming Cres., Hert. 31 DN09
Windsor Dr.
Fleming Gdns., Rom. 106 FK54
Bartholomew Dr.
Fleming Gdns., Til. 171 GJ81
Fielding Ave.
Fleming Mead, Mitch. 180 DE94
Fleming Rd. SE17 161 DP79
Fleming Rd., Grays 169 FV77
Fleming Rd., Sthl. 136 CB72
Fleming Way SE28 146 EX73
Fleming Way, Islw. 157 CF83
Flemings, Brwd. 107 FW51
Flemish Flds., Cher. 194 BG101
Flempton Rd. E10 123 DY60
Fletcher Clo. E6 145 EP72
Trader Rd.
Fletcher Clo., Cher. 211 BE107
Fletcher La. E10 123 EC59
Fletcher Path SE8 163 EA80
New Butt La.
Fletcher Rd. W4 158 CQ76
Fletcher Rd., Cher. 211 BD107
Fletcher Rd., Chig. 103 ET50
Fletcher St. E1 142 DU73
Fletcher Way, Hem.H. 40 BJ18
Fletchers Clo., Brom. 204 EH98
Fletching Rd. E5 122 DW62
Fletching Rd. SE7 164 EJ79
Fletton Rd. N11 99 DL52
Fleur de Lis St. E1 275 N5
Fleur de Lis St. E1 142 DS70
Fleur Gates SW19 179 CX87
Princes Way
Flex Meadow, Harl. 50 EL16
Flexley Wd., Welw.G.C. 29 CZ06
Flexmere Gdns. N17 100 DR53
Flexmere Rd.
Flexmere Rd. N17 100 DR53
Flight App. NW9 97 CT54
Lanacre Ave.
Flimwell Clo., Brom. 184 EE92
Flinders Clo., St.Alb. 43 CG22
Flint Clo., Lthd. 246 CC126
Flint Clo., Red. 250 DF133
Flint Clo., Sutt. 218 DB114
Flint Down Clo., Orp. 206 EU95
Flint Hill, Dor. 263 CH138
Flint Hill Clo., Dor. 263 CH139
Flint St. SE17 279 L9
Flint St. SE17 162 DR77
Flint St., Grays 169 FV79
Flint Way, St.Alb. 42 CC16
Flintlock Clo., Stai. 154 BG84
Flintmill Cres. SE3 164 EL82
Flinton St. SE17 279 N10
Flinton St. SE17 162 DS78
Flitcroft St. WC2 273 N9
Flock Mill Pl. SW18 180 DB88
Flockton St. SE16 162 DU75
George Row
Flodden Rd. SE5 162 DQ81
Flood La., Twick. 177 CG88
Church La.
Flood Pas. SE18 165 EM77
Samuel St.
Flood St. SW3 160 DE78
Flood Wk. SW3 160 DE79
Flora Clo. E14 143 EB72
Flora Clo., Croy. 221 EC111
Flora Gdns. W6 159 CV77
Ravenscourt Rd.
Flora Gdns., Rom. 126 EW58
Flora Gro., St.Alb. 43 CF21
Flora St., Belv. 166 EZ78
Victoria St.
Floral Ct., Ash. 231 CJ118
Rosedale
Floral Dr., St.Alb. 61 CK26
Floral St. WC2 273 P10
Floral St. WC2 141 DL73
Florence Ave., Add. 212 BG111
Florence Ave., Enf. 82 DQ41
Florence Ave., Mord. 200 DC99
Florence Cantwell Wk. N19 121 DL59
Hillrise Rd.
Florence Clo., Grays 170 FY79
Florence Clo., Harl. 52 EW17
Florence Clo., Horn. 128 FL61
Florence Clo., Walt. 195 BV101
Florence Rd.
Florence Clo., Wat. 75 BU35
Florence Dr., Enf. 82 DQ41
Florence Gdns. W4 158 CQ79
Florence Gdns., Stai. 174 BH94
Florence Nightingale Ho. N1 142 DR65
Clephane Rd.
Florence Rd. E6 144 EJ67
Florence Rd. E13 144 EF68
Florence Rd. N4 121 DN60
Florence Rd. SE2 166 EW76
Florence Rd. SE14 163 DZ81
Florence Rd. SW19 180 DB93
Florence Rd. W4 158 CR76
Florence Rd. W5 138 CL73
Florence Rd., Beck. 203 DY96
Florence Rd., Brom. 204 EG95
Florence Rd., Felt. 175 BV88
Florence Rd., Kings.T. 178 CM94
Florence Rd., S.Croy. 220 DR109
Florence Rd., Sthl. 156 BX77
Florence Rd., Walt. 195 BV101
Florence St. E16 144 EF70
Florence St. N1 141 DP66
Florence St. NW4 119 CW56
Florence Ter. SE14 163 DZ81
Florence Way SW12 180 DF88
Florfield Pas. E8 142 DV65
Reading La.
Florfield Rd. E8 142 DV65
Reading La.
Florian Ave., Sutt. 218 DD105
Florian Rd. SW15 159 CY84
Florida Clo. (Bushey), Wat. 95 CD47
Florida Rd., Guil. 258 AY140
Florida Rd., Th.Hth. 201 DP95
Florida St. E2 142 DU69
Floriston Ave., Uxb. 135 BQ66
Floriston Clo., Stan. 95 CH53
Floriston Gdns., Stan. 95 CH53
Floss St. SW15 159 CW82
Flower & Dean Wk. E1 142 DT71
Thrawl St.
Flower Cres., Cher. 211 BB107
Flower La. NW7 97 CT50
Flower La., Gdse. 253 DX131

Flower Wk., Guil. 258 AW137
Flower Wk., The SW7 160 DC75
Flowerfield, Sev. 241 FF117
Flowerhill Way, Grav. 190 GE94
Flowers Ms. N19 121 DJ61
Tollhouse Way
Flowersmead SW17 180 DG89
Floyd Rd. SE7 164 EJ78
Floyds La., Wok. 228 BG116
Fludyer St. SE13 164 EE84
Flyer's Way, The, West. 255 ER126
Folair Way SE16 162 DV78
Catlin St.
Fold Cft., Harl. 35 EN14
Foley Clo., Beac. 88 AJ51
Foley Ms., Esher 215 CE107
Foley Rd., Esher 215 CE108
Foley Rd., West. 238 EK118
Foley St. W1 273 K7
Foley St. W1 141 DJ71
Folgate St. E1 275 N6
Folgate St. E1 142 DS71
Foliot St. W12 139 CT72
Folkes La., Upmin. 129 FS57
Folkestone Ct., Slou. 153 BA78
Folkestone Rd. E6 145 EN68
Folkestone Rd. E17 123 EB56
Folkestone Rd. N18 100 DU49
Folkingham La. NW9 96 CR53
Folkington Cor. N12 97 CZ50
Follet Dr., Abb.L. 59 BT31
Follett Clo., Wind. 172 AV86
Follett St. E14 143 EC72
Folly, The, Hert. 32 DR09
Folly Ave., St.Alb. 42 CC19
Folly Clo., Rad. 77 CF36
Folly La. E4 101 DY53
Folly La. E17 101 DY53
Folly La., Dor. 263 CH144
Folly La., St.Alb. 42 CC19
Folly Ms. W11 139 CZ72
Portobello Rd.
Folly Pathway, Rad. 77 CF35
Folly Vw., Ware 33 EB10
Folly Wall E14 163 EC75
Follyfield Rd., Bans. 218 DA114
Font Hills N2 98 DC54
Fontaine Rd. SW16 181 DM94
Fontarabia Rd. SW11 160 DG84
Fontayne Ave., Chig. 103 EQ49
Fontayne Ave., Rain. 147 FE66
Fontayne Ave., Rom. 127 FE55
Fontenoy Rd. SW12 181 DH89
Fonteyne Gdns., Wdf.Grn. 102 EK54
Lechmere Ave.
Fonthill Clo. SE20 202 DU96
Selby Rd.
Fonthill Ms. N4 121 DN61
Lennox Rd.
Fonthill Rd. N4 121 DM60
Fontley Way SW15 179 CU87
Fontmell Clo., Ashf. 174 BN92
Fontmell Clo., St.Alb. 43 CE18
Fontmell Pk., Ashf. 174 BM92
Fontwell Clo., Har. 95 CE52
Fontwell Clo., Nthlt. 136 CA65
Fontwell Dr., Brom. 205 EN99
Fontwell Pk. Gdns., Horn. 128 FL63
Football La., Har. 117 CE60
Footbury Hill Rd., Orp. 206 EU101
Footpath, The SW15 179 CU85
Parkstead Rd.
Foots Cray High St., Sid. 186 EW93
Foots Cray La., Sid. 186 EW88
Footscray Rd. SE9 185 EN86
Footway, The SE9 185 EQ87
Forbench Clo., Wok. 228 BH122
Forbes Ave., Pot.B. 64 DD33
Forbes Clo. NW2 119 CU61
Forbes Clo., Horn. 127 FH60
St. Leonards Way
Forbes Ct. SE19 182 DS92
Forbes St. E1 142 DU72
Ellen St.
Forbes Way, Ruis. 115 BV61
Forburg Rd. N16 122 DU60
Force Grn. La., West. 239 ER124
Ford Clo. E3 143 DY68
Roman Rd.
Ford Clo., Ashf. 174 BL93
Ford Clo., Har. 117 CD59
Ford Clo., Rain. 147 FF66
Ford Clo., Shep. 194 BN98
Ford Clo., Th.Hth. 201 DP99
Ford Clo. (Bushey), Wat. 76 CC42
Ford End, Uxb. 113 BF61
Ford End, Wdf.Grn. 102 EH51
Ford La., Iver 134 BG72
Ford La., Rain. 147 FF66
Ford Rd. E3 143 DY67
Ford Rd., Ashf. 174 BM91
Ford Rd., Cher. 194 BH102
Ford Rd., Dag. 146 EZ66
Ford Rd., Grav. 190 GB85
Ford Rd. (Old Woking), Wok. 227 BB120
Ford Sq. E1 142 DV71
Ford St. E16 144 EF72
Fordbridge Clo., Cher. 194 BH102
Fordbridge Rd., Ashf. 174 BL93
Fordbridge Rd., Shep. 195 BS100
Fordbridge Rd., Sun. 195 BS100
Fordcroft Rd., Orp. 206 EV99
Forde Ave., Brom. 204 EJ97
Fordel Rd. SE6 183 ED88
Fordham Clo., Barn. 80 DE41
Fordham Clo., Horn. 128 FN59
Fordham Rd., Barn. 80 DD41
Fordham St. E1 142 DU72
Fordhook Ave. W5 138 CM73
Fordingley Rd. W9 139 CZ69
Fordington Rd. N6 120 DF57
Fordmill Rd. SE6 183 EA89
Fords Gro. N21 100 DQ46
Fords Pk. Rd. E16 144 EG72
Fordwater Rd., Cher. 194 BH102
Fordwater Trd. Est., Cher. 194 BH102
Fordwich Clo., Hert. 31 DN09
Fordwich Clo., Orp. 205 ET101
Fordwich Hill, Hert. 31 DN09
Fordwich Ri., Hert. 31 DN09
Fordwich Rd., Welw.G.C. 29 CW10
Fordwych Rd. NW2 119 CY63
Fordyce Clo., Horn. 128 FM59
Fordyce Rd. SE13 183 EC86
Fordyke Rd., Dag. 126 EZ61
Fore St. EC2 275 J7
Fore St. EC2 142 DQ71
Fore St. N9 100 DU49
Fore St. N18 100 DT51
Fore St., Harl. 36 EW11
Fore St., Hat. 45 CW17
Fore St., Hert. 32 DR09
Fore St., Pnr. 115 BU57
Fore St. Ave. EC2 275 K7
Forebury, The, Saw. 36 EY05
Forebury Ave., Saw. 36 EZ05
Forebury Cres., Saw. 36 EZ05
Forefield, St.Alb. 60 CA27
Foreland Ct. NW4 97 CX53
Foreland St. SE18 165 ER77
Plumstead Rd.
Forelands Way, Chesh. 54 AQ32
Foreman Ct. W6 159 CW77
Hammersmith Bdy.
Foremark Clo., Ilf. 103 ET51
Foreshore SE8 163 DZ77
Forest, The E11 124 EE56
Forest App. E4 102 EE45
Forest App., Wdf.Grn. 102 EG52
Forest Ave. E4 102 EE45
Forest Ave., Chig. 103 EN50
Forest Ave., Hem.H. 40 BK22
Forest Business Pk. E17 123 DY59
Forest Clo. E11 124 EF57
Forest Clo., Chis. 205 EN95
Forest Clo., Lthd. 245 BT125
Forest Clo., Wal.Abb. 84 EH37
Forest Clo., Wok. 227 BD115
Forest Clo., Wdf.Grn. 102 EH49
Forest Ct. E4 102 EF46
Forest Ct. E11 124 EE56
Forest Cres., Ash. 232 CN116
Forest Cft. SE23 182 DV89
Forest Dr. E12 124 EK62
Forest Dr., Epp. 85 ES36
Forest Dr., Kes. 222 EL105
Forest Dr., Sun. 175 BT94
Forest Dr., Tad. 233 CY121
Forest Dr., Wdf.Grn. 101 ED52
Forest Dr. E. E11 123 ED59
Forest Dr. W. E11 123 EC59
Forest Edge, Buck.H. 102 EJ49
Forest Gdns. N17 100 DT54
Forest Gate NW9 118 CS57
Forest Glade E4 102 EE49
Forest Glade E11 124 EE58
Forest Glade, Epp. 70 EY28
Forest Grn. Rd., Maid. 150 AD82
Forest Grn. Rd., Wind. 150 AD82
Forest Gro. E8 142 DT65
Forest Heights, Buck.H. 102 EG47
Forest Hill Rd. SE22 182 DV85
Forest Hill Rd. SE23 182 DW86
Forest Ind. Est., Ilf. 103 ES53
Forest La. E7 124 EG64
Forest La. E15 144 EE65
Forest La., Chig. 103 EN50
Forest La., Lthd. 229 BT124
Forest Mt. Rd., Wdf.Grn. 101 ED52
Forest Ridge, Beck. 203 EA97
Forest Ridge, Kes. 222 EL105
Forest Ri. E17 123 ED57
Forest Rd. E7 124 EG63
Forest Rd. E8 142 DT65
Forest Rd. E11 123 ED59
Forest Rd. E17 122 DW56
Forest Rd. N9 100 DV46
Forest Rd. N17 122 DW56
Forest Rd., Enf. 83 DY36
Forest Rd., Erith 167 FG81
Forest Rd., Felt. 176 BW89
Forest Rd., Ilf. 103 ES53
Forest Rd., Lthd. 229 BU123
Forest Rd., Loug. 84 EK41
Forest Rd., Rich. 158 CN80
Forest Rd., Rom. 127 FB55
Forest Rd., Sutt. 200 DA102
Forest Rd. (Cheshunt), Wal.Cr. 67 DX29
Forest Rd., Wat. 59 BV33
Forest Rd., Wind. 151 AL82
Forest Rd., Wok. 227 BD115
Forest Rd., Wdf.Grn. 102 EG48
Forest Side E4 102 EF45
Forest Side E7 124 EH63
Capel Rd.
Forest Side, Buck.H. 102 EH46
Forest Side, Epp. 69 ER33
Forest Side, Wal.Abb. 84 EJ36
Forest Side, Wor.Pk. 199 CT102
Forest St. E7 124 EG64
Forest Vw. E4 101 ED45
Forest Vw. E11 124 EF59
Forest Vw. Ave. E10 123 ED57
Forest Vw. Rd. E12 124 EL63
Forest Vw. Rd. E17 101 EC53
Forest Vw. Rd., Loug. 84 EK42
Forest Wk. (Bushey), Wat. 76 BZ39
Millbrook Rd.
Forest Way N19 121 DJ61
Hargrave Pk.
Forest Way, Ash. 232 CM117
Forest Way, Loug. 84 EL41
Forest Way, Orp. 205 ET99
Forest Way, Sid. 185 ER87
Forest Way, Wal.Abb. 68 EK33
Forest Way, Wdf.Grn. 102 EH49
Forestdale N14 99 DK49
Forester Rd. SE15 162 DV84
Foresters Clo., Wall. 219 DK108
Foresters Clo., Wal.Cr. 66 DS27
Foresters Clo., Wok. 226 AT118
Foresters Cres., Bexh. 167 FB84
Foresters Dr. E17 123 ED56
Foresters Dr., Wall. 219 DK107
Forestholme Clo. SE23 182 DW89
Forfar Rd. N22 99 DP53
Forfar Rd. SW11 160 DG81
Forge Ave., Couls. 235 DN120
Forge Clo., Brom. 204 EG102
Forge Clo., Hayes 155 BR79
High St.
Forge Clo., Kings L. 58 BG31
Forge Cotts. W5 137 CK74
Ealing Grn.
Forge Dr., Esher 215 CG108
Forge Dr., Slou. 131 AQ65
Forge End, Amer. 55 AP40
Forge End, St.Alb. 60 CA26
Forge La. (Horton Kirby), Dart. 208 FQ98
Forge La., Felt. 176 BY92
Forge La., Grav. 191 GM89
Forge La., Nthwd. 93 BS52
Forge La., Sun. 195 BU97
Forge La., Sutt. 217 CY108
Forge Pl. NW1 140 DG65
Malden Cres.
Forge Way, Sev. 225 FF111
Forgefield, West. 238 EK116
Main Rd.
Forman Pl. N16 122 DT63
Farleigh Rd.
Formby Ave., Stan. 117 CJ55
Formosa St. W9 140 DB70
Formunt Clo. E16 144 EF71
Vincent St.
Forres Clo., Hodd. 49 EA15
Forres Gdns. NW11 120 DA58
Forrest Gdns. SW16 201 DM97
Forrester Path SE26 182 DW91
Forresters Dr., Welw.G.C. 30 DC10
Forris Ave., Hayes 135 BT74
Forset St. W1 272 C8
Forset St. W1 140 DE72
Forstal Clo., Brom. 204 EG97
Ridley Rd.
Forster Rd. E17 123 DY58
Forster Rd. N17 122 DT55
Forster Rd. SW2 181 DL87
Forster Rd., Beck. 203 DY97
Forster Rd., Croy. 202 DQ101
Windmill Rd.
Forsters Clo., Rom. 126 EZ58
Forsters Way, Hayes 135 BV72
Forston St. N1 142 DR68
Cropley St.
Forsyte Cres. SE19 202 DS95
Forsyth Gdns. SE17 161 DP79
Forsyth Path, Wok. 211 BD113
Forsyth Pl., Enf. 82 DS43
Forsyth Rd., Wok. 211 BC114
Forsythia Clo., Ilf. 125 EP64
Forsythia Pl., Guil. 242 AW132
Larch Ave.
Fort La., Reig. 250 DB130
Reigate Hill
Fort Rd. SE1 162 DT77
Fort Rd., Guil. 258 AY137
Fort Rd., Nthlt. 136 CA66
Fort Rd., Sev. 241 FC115
Fort Rd., Tad. 248 CP131
Boxhill Rd.
Fort Rd., Til. 171 GH84
Fort St. E1 275 N7
Fort St. E1 142 DS71
Fort St. E16 144 EH74
Forterie Gdns., Ilf. 126 EU62
Fortescue Ave. E8 142 DV66
Mentmore Ter.
Fortescue Ave., Twick. 176 CC90
Fortescue Rd. SW19 180 DD94
Fortescue Rd., Edg. 96 CQ53
Fortescue Rd., Wey. 212 BM105
Fortess Gro. NW5 121 DH64
Fortess Rd.
Fortess Rd. NW5 121 DH64
Fortess Wk. NW5 121 DH64
Fortess Rd.
Forth Rd., Upmin. 129 FR58
Forthbridge Rd. SW11 160 DG84
Fortin Clo., S.Ock. 149 FU73
Fortin Path, S.Ock. 149 FU73
Fortin Way
Fortin Way, S.Ock. 149 FU73
Fortis Clo. E16 144 EJ72
Fortis Grn. N2 120 DE56
Fortis Grn. N10 120 DG55
Fortis Grn. Ave. N2 120 DF55
Fortis Grn. Rd. N10 120 DG55
Fortismere Ave. N10 120 DG55
Fortnam Rd. N19 121 DK61
Fortnums Acre, Stan. 95 CF51
Fortrose Gdns. SW2 181 DK88
New Pk. Rd.
Fortrye Clo., Grav. 190 GE89
Fortuna Clo. N7 141 DM65
Vulcan Way
Fortune Gate Rd. NW10 138 CS67
Fortune Grn. Rd. NW6 120 DA63
Fortune La., Borwd. 77 CK44
Fortune St. EC1 275 J5
Fortune St. EC1 142 DQ70
Fortune Wk. SE28 165 ER76
Broadwater Rd.
Fortune Way NW10 139 CU69
Fortunes, The, Harl. 51 ET17
Fortunes Mead, Nthlt. 136 BY65
Forty Acre La. E16 144 EG71
Forty Ave., Wem. 118 CM62
Forty Clo., Wem. 118 CM62
Forty Grn. Rd., Beac. 88 AH51
Forty Hill, Enf. 82 DS38
Forty La., Wem. 118 CP61
Fortyfoot Rd., Lthd. 231 CJ121
Forum, The, W.Mol. 196 CB98
Forum Pl., Hat. 45 CU17
Forum Way, Edg. 96 CN51
High St.
Forumside, Edg. 96 CN51
High St.
Forval Clo., Mitch. 200 DF99
Forward Dr., Har. 117 CF56
Fosbury Ms. W2 140 DB73
Inverness Ter.
Foscote Ms. W9 140 DA71
Amberley Rd.
Foscote Rd. NW4 119 CV57
Foskett Rd. SW6 159 CZ82
Foss Ave., Croy. 219 DN106
Foss Rd. SW17 180 DD91
Fossdene Rd. SE7 164 EH78
Fossdyke Clo., Hayes 136 BY71
Fosse Way W13 137 CG71
Fosse Way, W.Byf. 211 BF113
Brantwood Dr.
Fossil Rd. SE13 163 EA83
Fossington Rd., Belv. 166 EX77
Fossway, Dag. 126 EW61
Foster Ave., Wind. 151 AL83
Foster Clo. (Cheshunt), Wal.Cr. 67 DY30
Windmill La.
Foster La. EC2 275 H8
Foster La. EC2 142 DQ72
Foster Rd. E13 144 EG70
Foster Rd. W3 138 CS73
Foster Rd. W4 158 CR78
Foster Rd., Hem.H. 40 BG22
Foster St. NW4 119 CW56
Foster St., Harl. 52 EY17
Foster Wk. NW4 119 CW56
New Brent St.
Fosterdown, Gdse. 252 DV129
Fosters Clo. E18 102 EH53
Fosters Clo., Chis. 185 EM92
Fosters Path, Slou. 131 AM70
Vermont Rd.
Fothergill Clo. E13 144 EG68
Fothergill Dr. N21 81 DM43
Fotheringay Gdns., Slou. 131 AN73
Fotheringham Rd., Enf. 82 DT42
Fotherley Rd., Rick. 91 BF47
Foubert's Pl. W1 273 K9
Foubert's Pl. W1 141 DJ72
Foulden Rd. N16 122 DT63
Foulden Ter. N16 122 DT63
Foulden Rd.
Foulis Ter. SW7 276 A10
Foulis Ter. SW7 160 DD78
Foulser Rd. SW17 180 DF90
Foulsham Rd., Th.Hth. 202 DQ97
Founder Clo. E6 145 EP72
Trader Rd.
Founders Ct. EC2 275 K8
Founders Dr., Uxb. 113 BF58
Founders Gdns. SE19 182 DQ94
Foundry Clo. SE16 143 DY74
Foundry La., Slou. 153 BB83
Foundry Ms. NW1 273 L4
Fount St. SW8 161 DK80
Fountain Clo., Uxb. 135 BQ71
New Rd.
Fountain Ct. EC4 274 D10
Fountain Dr. SE19 182 DT91
Fountain Dr., Cars. 218 DF108
Fountain Fm., Harl. 51 ET17
Fountain Gdns., Wind. 151 AR83
Fountain Grn. Sq. SE16 162 DU75
Bermondsey Wall E.
Fountain Ms. N5 122 DQ63
Kelross Rd.
Fountain Pl. SW9 161 DN81
Fountain Pl., Wal.Abb. 67 EC34
Fountain Rd. SW17 180 DD92
Fountain Rd., Red. 266 DE136
Fountain Rd., Th.Hth. 202 DQ96
Fountain Sq. SW1 277 H8
Fountain St. E2 142 DT69
Columbia Rd.
Fountain Wk., Grav. 190 GE86
Fountains Ave., Felt. 176 BZ90
Fountains Clo., Felt. 176 BZ89
Fountains Cres. N14 99 DL45
Fountayne Rd. N15 122 DU56
Fountayne Rd. N16 122 DU61
Four Acres, Cob. 214 BY113
Four Acres, Guil. 243 BC132
Four Acres, Welw.G.C. 29 CZ11
Four Acres, The, Saw. 36 EZ06
Four Acres Dr., Hem.H. 40 BM22
Four Acres Wk., Hem.H. 40 BM22
Four Seasons Cres., Sutt. 199 CZ103
Kimpton Rd.
Four Seasons Ind. Est., Sthl. 156 CB76
Four Tubs, The (Bushey), Wat. 95 CD45
Four Wents, Cob. 214 BW114
Four Wents, The E4 101 ED47
Kings Rd.
Fouracres SW12 181 DH89
Little Dimocks
Fouracres, Enf. 83 DY39
Fourland Wk., Edg. 96 CQ51
Fournier St. E1 142 DT71
Fourth Ave. E12 125 EM63
Fourth Ave. W10 139 CY69
Fourth Ave., Grays 169 FU79
Fourth Ave., Harl. 51 EM15
Fourth Ave., Hayes 135 BT74
Fourth Ave., Rom. 127 FC60
Fourth Ave., Wat. 76 BX35
Fourth Cross Rd., Twick. 177 CD89
Fourth Dr., Couls. 235 DK116
Fourth Way, Wem. 118 CQ63
Fourways, St.Alb. 44 CM20
Hatfield Rd.
Fowey Ave., Ilf. 124 EK57
Fowey Clo. E1 142 DV74
Kennet St.
Fowler Clo. SW11 160 DD83
Fowler Rd. E7 124 EG63
Fowler Rd. N1 141 DP66
Halton Rd.
Fowler Rd., Ilf. 104 EV51
Fowler Rd., Mitch. 200 DG96
Fowlers Clo., Sid. 186 EY92
Thursland Rd.
Fowlers Mead, Wok. 210 AS109
Windsor Rd.
Fowlers Wk. W5 137 CK70
Fowley Clo., Wal.Cr. 67 DZ34
Fowley Mead Caravan Pk., Wal.Cr. 67 EA34
Fownes St. SW11 160 DE83
Fox and Knot St. EC1 274 G6
Fox Clo. E1 142 DW70
Fox Clo. E16 144 EG71
Fox Clo., Borwd. 77 CK44
Rodgers Clo.
Fox Clo., Orp. 224 EU106
Fox Clo., Rom. 105 FB50
Fox Clo. (Bushey), Wat. 76 CB42
Fox Clo., Wey. 213 BR106
Fox Clo., Wok. 227 BD115
Fox Covert, Lthd. 231 CD124
Fox Hill SE19 182 DT94
Fox Hill, Kes. 222 EH106
Fox Hill Gdns. SE19 182 DT94
Fox Hills Clo., Cher. 211 BB107
Fox Hollow Dr., Bexh. 166 EX83
Fox Ho. Rd., Belv. 167 FB77
Fox La. N13 99 DL47
Fox La. W5 138 CL70
Fox La., Cat. 235 DP121
Fox La., Kes. 222 EH106
Fox La., Lthd. 230 BY124
Fox La. N., Cher. 193 BF102
Fox La. S., Cher. 193 BF102
Guildford St.
Fox Manor Way, Grays 169 FV79
Fox Rd. E16 144 EF71
Fox Rd., Slou. 152 AX77
Foxacre, Cat. 236 DS122
Town End Clo.
Foxberry Rd. SE4 163 DY83
Foxborough Clo., Slou. 153 BA78
Foxborough Gdns. SE4 183 EA86
Foxborough Hill Rd., Guil. 258 AX144
Foxbourne Rd. SW17 180 DG89
Foxburrow Rd., Chig. 104 EX49
Foxburrows Ave., Guil. 242 AT134
Foxbury Ave., Chis. 185 ER93
Foxbury Clo., Brom. 184 EH93
Foxbury Clo., Orp. 224 EU106
Foxbury Dr.
Foxbury Dr., Orp. 224 EU107
Foxbury Rd., Brom. 184 EG93
Foxcombe, Croy. 221 EB107
Foxcombe Clo. E6 144 EK68
Boleyn Rd.
Foxcombe Rd. SW15 179 CU88
Alton Rd.
Foxcote SE5 162 DS78
Albany Rd.
Foxcroft, St.Alb. 43 CG22
Foxcroft Rd. SE18 165 EP81
Foxdell, Nthwd. 93 BR51
Foxdell Way, Ger.Cr. 90 AY50
Foxdells, Hert. 31 DJ12
Foxearth Clo., West. 238 EL118
Foxearth Rd., S.Croy. 220 DV110
Foxearth Spur, S.Croy. 220 DW109
Foxenden Rd., Guil. 258 AY135
Foxes Clo., Hert. 32 DV09
Foxes Dale SE3 164 EG83
Foxes Dale, Brom. 203 ED97
Foxes Dr., Wal.Cr. 66 DU29
Foxes Grn., Grays 171 GG75
Foxfield Clo., Nthwd. 93 BT51
Foxfield Rd., Orp. 205 ER103
Foxglove Clo., Hat. 45 CV19
Foxglove Clo., Sthl. 136 BY73
Foxglove Clo., Stai. 174 BK88
Foxglove Gdns. E11 124 EJ56
Foxglove Gdns., Guil. 243 BC132
Foxglove Gdns., Pur. 219 DL111
Foxglove La., Chess. 216 CN105
Foxglove Rd., S.Ock. 149 FW71
Foxglove St. W12 139 CT73
Foxglove Way, Wall. 201 DH102
Foxgloves, The, Hem.H. 39 BE21
Foxgrove N14 99 DL48
Foxgrove Ave., Beck. 183 EB94
Foxgrove Dr., Wok. 227 BA115
Foxgrove Path, Wat. 94 BX50
Foxgrove Rd., Beck. 183 EB94
Foxhall Rd., Upmin. 128 FQ64
Foxham Rd. N19 121 DK62
Foxhanger Gdns., Wok. 227 BA116
Oriental Rd.
Foxherne, Slou. 152 AW75
Foxhill, Wat. 75 BU36
Foxhills, Wok. 226 AW117
Foxhills Rd., Cher. 211 BA105
Foxhole Rd. SE9 184 EL85
Foxholes, Wey. 213 BR106
Foxholes Ave., Hert. 32 DT09
Foxholes Business Pk., Hert. 32 DT09
Foxhollow Dr., Slou. 111 AQ64
Foxhollows, Hat. 45 CV16
Foxholt Gdns. NW10 138 CQ66
Foxhome Clo., Chis. 185 EN93
Foxhounds La., Grav. 190 GA90
Foxlake Rd., W.Byf. 212 BM112
Foxlands Clo., Wat. 59 BU34
Foxlands Cres., Dag. 127 FC64
Foxlands La., Dag. 127 FD64
Rainham Rd. S.
Foxlands Rd., Dag. 127 FC64
Foxlees, Wem. 117 CG63
Foxley Clo. E8 122 DU64
Ferncliff Rd.
Foxley Clo., Loug. 85 EP40
Foxley Clo., Red. 266 DG139
Foxley Gdns., Pur. 219 DP113
Foxley Hill Rd., Pur. 219 DN112
Foxley La., Pur. 219 DJ111
Foxley Rd. SW9 161 DN80
Foxley Rd., Ken. 219 DP114
Foxley Rd., Th.Hth. 201 DP98
Foxley Sq. SW9 161 DP80
Cancell Rd.
Foxleys, Wat. 94 BY47
Foxmead Clo., Enf. 81 DM41
Foxmoor Ct., Uxb. 114 BG58
North Orbital Rd.
Foxmore St. SW11 160 DF81
Foxon Clo., Cat. 236 DS121
Foxon La., Cat. 236 DR121
Foxon La. Gdns., Cat. 236 DS121
Foxs La., Hat. 45 CY23
Fox's Path, Mitch. 200 DE96
Foxton Gro., Mitch. 200 DD96
Foxton Rd., Grays 169 FX79
Foxton Rd., Hodd. 49 DZ17
Foxwarren, Esher 215 CF109
Foxwell Clo. SE4 163 DY83
Foxwell St.
Foxwell Ms. SE4 163 DY83
Foxwell St.
Foxwell St. SE4 163 DY83
Foxwood Clo. NW7 96 CS49
Foxwood Clo., Felt. 175 BV90
Foxwood Grn. Clo., Enf. 82 DS44
Foxwood Gro., Orp. 224 EW110
Foxwood Rd. SE3 164 EF84
Foxwood Rd., Dart. 189 FV90
Foyle Dr., S.Ock. 149 FU71
Foyle Rd. N17 100 DU53
Foyle Rd. SE3 164 EF79
Frailey Clo., Wok. 227 BB116
Frailey Hill, Wok. 227 BB116
Framewood Rd., Slou. 132 AW66
Framfield Clo. N12 98 DA48
Framfield Ct., Enf. 82 DS44

Framfield Rd. N5 121 DP64
Framfield Rd. W7 137 CF72
Framfield Rd., Mitch. 180 DG94
Framlingham Clo. E5 122 DW61
Detmold Rd.
Framlingham Cres. SE9 184 EL91
Frampton Clo., Sutt. 218 DA108
Frampton Pk. Est. E9 142 DW66
Frampton Pk. Rd. E9 142 DW65
Frampton Rd., Epp. 70 EU28
Frampton Rd., Houns. 176 BY85
Frampton Rd., Pot.B. 64 DC30
Frampton St. NW8 272 A5
Frampton St. NW8 140 DD70
Frampton St., Hert. 32 DR09
Francemary Rd. SE4 183 EA85
Frances Ave., Maid. 130 AC70
Frances Gdns., S.Ock. 149 FT72
Garron La.
Frances Rd. E4 101 EA51
Frances Rd., Wind. 151 AQ83
Frances St. SE18 165 EM77
Frances St., Chesh. 54 AQ30
Franche Ct. Rd. SW17 180 DC90
Franchise St., Chesh. 54 AQ30
Francis Ave., Bexh. 166 FA82
Francis Ave., Felt. 175 BU90
Francis Ave., Ilf. 125 ER61
Francis Ave., St.Alb. 42 CC17
Francis Barber Clo. SW16 181 DM91
Well Clo.
Francis Chichester Way SW11 160 DG81
Francis Clo. E14 163 ED77
Saunders Ness Rd.
Francis Clo., Epsom 216 CR105
Francis Clo., Shep. 194 BN98
Francis Gro. SW19 179 CZ93
Francis Rd. E10 123 EC60
Francis Rd. N2 120 DF56
Lynmouth Rd.
Francis Rd., Cat. 236 DR122
Francis Rd., Croy. 201 DP101
Francis Rd., Dart. 188 FK85
Francis Rd., Grnf. 137 CH68
Francis Rd., Har. 117 CG57
Francis Rd., Houns. 156 BX82
Francis Rd., Ilf. 125 ER61
Francis Rd., Orp. 206 EX97
Francis Rd., Pnr. 116 BW57
Francis Rd., Wall. 219 DJ107
Francis Rd., Ware 33 DX05
Francis Rd., Wat. 75 BV42
Francis St. E15 124 EE64
Francis St. SW1 277 K8
Francis St. SW1 161 DJ77
Francis St., Ilf. 125 ER61
Francis Ter. N19 121 DJ62
Junction Rd.
Francis Wk. N1 141 DM67
Bingfield St.
Francis Way, Slou. 131 AK73
Franciscan Rd. SW17 180 DF92
Francklyn Gdns., Edg. 96 CN48
Francombe Gdns., Rom. 127 FG58
Franconia Rd. SW4 181 DK85
Frank Bailey Wk. E12 125 EN64
Gainsborough Ave.
Frank Burton Clo. SE7 164 EH78
Victoria Way
Frank Dixon Clo. SE21 182 DS88
Frank Dixon Way SE21 182 DS88
Frank Lunnon Clo., B.End 110 AC60
Frank Martin Ct., Wal.Cr. 66 DU30
Frank St. E13 144 EG70
Frank Trowell Ct., Felt. 175 BU88
Frankfurt Rd. SE24 182 DQ85
Frankham St. SE8 163 EA80
Frankland Clo. SE16 162 DW77
Frankland Clo., Rick. 92 BN45
Frankland Clo., Wdf.Grn. 102 EJ50
Frankland Rd. E4 101 EA50
Frankland Rd. SW7 160 DD76
Frankland Rd., Rick. 75 BP44
Franklands Dr., Add. 211 BF108
Franklin Ave., Slou. 131 AP71
Franklin Ave. (Cheshunt), Wal.Cr. 66 DU30
Franklin Clo. N20 98 DC45
Franklin Clo. SE13 163 EB81
Franklin Clo. SE27 181 DP90
Franklin Clo., Hem.H. 40 BL23
Franklin Clo., Kings.T. 198 CN97
Franklin Clo., St.Alb. 44 CS22
Franklin Cres., Mitch. 201 DJ98
Franklin Ho. NW9 119 CT59
Franklin Pas. SE9 164 EL83
Phineas Pett Rd.
Franklin Rd. SE20 182 DW94
Franklin Rd., Bexh. 166 EY81
Franklin Rd., Grav. 191 GK92
Franklin Rd., Horn. 148 FJ65
Franklin Rd., Wat. 75 BV40
Franklin Sq. W14 159 CZ78
Marchbank Rd.
Franklin St. E3 143 EB69
St. Leonards St.
Franklin St. N15 122 DS58
Franklin Way, Croy. 201 DL102
Franklins Ms., Har. 116 CC61
Franklin's Row SW3 276 E10
Franklin's Row SW3 160 DF78
Franklyn Cres., Wind. 151 AK83
Franklyn Gdns., Ilf. 103 ER51
Franklyn Rd. NW10 139 CT66
Franklyn Rd., Walt. 195 BU100
Franks Ave., N.Mal. 198 CQ98
Franks Fld., Guil. 261 BS144
Franks La. (Horton Kirby), Dart. 228 FN99
Franks Rd., Guil. 242 AU131
Frankswood Ave., Orp. 205 EP99
Frankswood Ave., West Dr. 134 BM72
Franlaw Cres. N13 100 DQ49
Franmil Rd., Horn. 127 FG60
Fransfield Gro. SE26 182 DV90
Frant Clo. SE20 182 DW94
Frant Rd., Th.Hth. 201 DP99
Franthorne Way SE6 183 EB89
Fraser Clo. E6 144 EL72
Linton Gdns.
Fraser Clo., Bex. 187 FC88
Dartford Rd.
Fraser Gdns., Dor. 263 CG135
Fraser Ho., Brent. 158 CM78
Fraser Rd. E17 123 EB57
Fraser Rd. N9 100 DV48
Fraser Rd., Erith 167 FC78
Fraser Rd., Grnf. 137 CH67
Fraser Rd. (Cheshunt), Wal.Cr. 67 DY28
Fraser St. W4 158 CS78
Frating Cres., Wdf.Grn. 102 EG51
Frays Ave., West Dr. 154 BK75
Frays Clo., West Dr. 154 BK76
Frays Lea, Uxb. 134 BJ68
Frays Waye, Uxb. 134 BJ67
Frazer Ave., Ruis. 116 BW64
Frazer Clo., Rom. 127 FF59
Frazier St. SE1 278 D5
Frazier St. SE1 161 DN75
Frean St. SE16 162 DU76
Fred Wigg Twr. E11 124 EF61
Freda Corbett Clo. SE15 162 DU80
Bird in Bush Rd.
Frederic Ms. SW1 276 E5
Frederic St. E17 123 DY57
Frederica Rd. E4 101 ED45
Frederica St. N7 141 DM66
Caledonian Rd.
Frederick Andrews Ct., Grays 170 GD79
Frederick Clo. W2 272 C10
Frederick Clo. W2 140 DE73
Frederick Clo., Sutt. 217 CZ105
Frederick Ct. NW2 119 CY62
Douglas Ms.
Frederick Cres. SW9 161 DP80
Frederick Cres., Enf. 82 DW40
Frederick Gdns., Sutt. 217 CZ106
Frederick Pl. SE18 165 EP78
Frederick Rd. SE17 161 DP78
Chapter Rd.
Frederick Rd., Rain. 147 FD68
Frederick Rd., Sutt. 217 CZ106
Frederick Sq. SE16 143 DY73
Rotherhithe St.
Frederick St. WC1 274 B3
Frederick St. WC1 141 DM69
Frederick Ter. E8 142 DT67
Haggerston Rd.
Frederick's Pl. EC2 275 K9
Fredericks Pl. N12 98 DC49
Frederick's Row EC1 274 F2
Fredley Pk., Dor. 247 CJ129
Fredora Ave., Hayes 135 BT70
Free Prae Rd., Cher. 194 BG102
Freeborne Gdns., Rain. 147 FG65
Mungo Pk. Rd.
Freedom Clo. E17 123 DY56
Freedom Rd. N17 100 DR54
Freedom St. SW11 160 DF82
Freedown La., Sutt. 218 DB113
Freegrove Rd. N7 121 DL64
Freeland Pk. NW4 97 CY54
Freeland Rd. W5 138 CM73
Freeland Way, Erith 167 FG81
Slade Grn. Rd.
Freelands Ave., S.Croy. 221 DX109
Freelands Gro., Brom. 204 EH95
Freelands Rd., Brom. 204 EH95
Freelands Rd., Cob. 213 BV114
Freeling St. N1 141 DM66
Caledonian Rd.
Freeman Clo., Nthlt. 136 BY66
Freeman Ct., Chesh. 54 AQ30
Barnes Ave.
Freeman Dr., W.Mol. 196 BZ97
Freeman Rd., Grav. 191 GL90
Freeman Rd., Mord. 200 DD99
Freeman Way, Horn. 128 FL58
Freemans Clo., Shep. 195 BS98
Freemans Clo., Slou. 132 AT65
Freemans La., Hayes 135 BS73
Freemantle Ave., Enf. 83 DX43
Freemasons Rd. E16 144 EH71
Freemasons Rd., Croy. 202 DS102
Freesia Clo., Orp. 223 ET106
Briarswood Way
Freethorpe Clo. SE19 202 DS95
Freezeland Way, Uxb. 134 BN65
Western Ave.
Freke Rd. SW11 160 DG83
Fremantle Rd., Belv. 166 FA77
Fremantle Rd., Ilf. 103 EQ54
Fremantle St. SE17 279 M10
Fremantle St. SE17 162 DS78
Fremont St. E9 142 DW67
French Gdns., Cob. 214 BW114
French Horn La., Hat. 45 CV17
French Ordinary Ct. EC3 142 DS73
Crutched Friars
French Pl. E1 275 N4
French Row, St.Alb. 43 CD20
Market Pl.
French St., Sun. 196 BW96
French St., West. 255 ES128
Frenchaye, Add. 212 BJ106
Frenches, The, Red. 250 DG132
Frenches Ct., Red. 250 DG132
Frenches Rd.
Frenches Dr., Red. 250 DG132
The Frenches
Frenches Rd., Red. 250 DG132
Frenchlands Hatch, Lthd. 245 BS127
French's Clo., Ware 33 EB11
French's Wells, Wok. 226 AV117
Frenchum Gdns., Slou. 131 AL73
Frendsbury Rd. SE4 163 DY84
Frensham (Cheshunt), Wal.Cr. 66 DT27
Frensham Clo., Sthl. 136 BZ70
Frensham Ct., Mitch. 200 DD97
Phipps Bri. Rd.
Frensham Dr. SW15 179 CT90
Frensham Dr., Croy. 221 EC108
Frensham Rd. SE9 185 ER89
Frensham Rd., Ken. 219 DP114
Frensham St. SE15 162 DU79
Frensham Way, Epsom 233 CW116
Frere St. SW11 160 DE82
Fresh Wf. Rd., Bark. 145 EP67
Freshborough Ct., Guil. 259 AZ135
Lower Edgeborough Rd.
Freshfield Ave. E8 142 DT66
Freshfield Clo. SE13 163 ED84
Marischal Rd.
Freshfield Dr. N14 99 DH45
Freshfields, Croy. 203 DZ101
Freshfields Ave., Upmin. 128 FP64
Freshford St. SW18 180 DC90
Freshmount Gdns., Epsom 216 CP111
Freshwater Clo. SW17 180 DG93
Freshwater Rd. SW17 180 DG93
Freshwater Rd., Dag. 126 EX60
Freshwaters, Harl. 35 ES14
School La.
Freshwell Ave., Rom. 126 EW56
Freshwood Clo., Beck. 203 EB95
Freshwood Way, Wall. 219 DH109
Freston Gdns., Barn. 80 DF43
Freston Pk. N3 97 CZ54
Freston Rd. W10 139 CX73
Freston Rd. W11 139 CX73
Freta Rd., Bexh. 186 EZ85
Fretherne Rd., Welw.G.C. 29 CX09
Frewin Rd. SW18 180 DD88
Friar Ms. SE27 181 DP90
Prioress Rd.
Friar Rd., Hayes 136 BX70
Friar Rd., Orp. 206 EU99
Friar St. EC4 274 G9
Friars, The, Chig. 103 ES49
Friars, The, Harl. 51 EN17
Friars Ave. N20 98 DE48
Friars Ave. SW15 179 CT90
Friars Ave., Brwd. 109 GA46
Friars Clo. E4 101 EC48
Friars Clo. N2 120 DD56
Friars Clo., Brwd. 109 GA45
Friars Clo., Nthlt. 136 BX69
Broomcroft Ave.
Friars Fld., Berk. 38 AS16
Heron Elm
Friars Gdns. W3 138 CR72
St. Dunstans Ave.
Friars Gate, Guil. 258 AU136
Friars Gate Clo., Wdf.Grn. 102 EG49
Friars La., B.Stort. 37 FH06
Friars La., Rich. 177 CK85
Friars Mead E14 163 EC76
Friars Ms. SE9 185 EN85
Friars Orchard, Lthd. 231 CD121
Friars Pl. La. W3 138 CR73
Friars Ri., Wok. 227 BA118
Friars Rd. E6 144 EK67
Friars Rd., Vir.W. 192 AX98
Friars Stile Pl., Rich. 178 CL86
Friars Stile Rd.
Friars Stile Rd., Rich. 178 CL86
Friars Wk. N14 99 DH45
Friars Wk. SE2 166 EX78
Friars Way W3 138 CR72
Friars Way, Cher. 194 BG99
Friars Way, Kings L. 58 BN30
Friars Way (Bushey), Wat. 76 BZ39
Friars Wd., Croy. 221 DY109
Friarscroft, Brox. 49 EA20
Friary, The, Wind. 172 AW86
Friary Bri., Guil. 258 AW136
Friary Clo. N12 98 DE50
Friary Ct. SW1 277 L3
Friary Ct., Wok. 226 AT118
Friary Est. SE15 162 DU79
Friary Island, Stai. 172 AW86
Friary La., Wdf.Grn. 102 EG49
Friary Pas., Guil. 258 AW136
Friary St.
Friary Rd. N12 98 DD49
Friary Rd. SE15 162 DU80
Friary Rd. W3 138 CQ72
Friary Rd., Stai. 172 AW87
Friary St., Guil. 258 AW136
Friary Way N12 98 DE49
Friday Hill E4 102 EE47
Friday Hill E. E4 102 EE48
Friday Hill W. E4 102 EE47
Friday Rd., Erith 167 FD78
Friday Rd., Mitch. 180 DF94
Friday St. EC4 275 H9
Friday St. EC4 142 DQ73
Friday St., Dor. 262 BY143
Frideswide Pl. NW5 121 DJ64
Islip St.
Friend St. EC1 274 F2
Friend St. EC1 141 DP69
Friendly Pl. SE13 163 EB81
Lewisham Rd.
Friendly St. SE8 163 EA82
Friendly St. Ms. SE8 163 EA82
Friendly St.
Friends Ave., Wal.Cr. 67 DX31
Friends Rd., Croy. 202 DR104
Friends Rd., Pur. 219 DP112
Friends Wk., Stai. 173 BF92
South St.
Friends Wk., Uxb. 134 BK66
Bakers Rd.
Friendship Wk., Nthlt. 136 BX69
Wayfarer Rd.
Friern Barnet La. N11 98 DF49
Friern Barnet La. N20 98 DC47
Friern Barnet Rd. N11 98 DF50
Friern Ct. N20 98 DD48
Friern Mt. Dr. N20 98 DC45
Friern Pk. N12 98 DC50
Friern Rd. SE22 182 DU87
Friern Watch Ave. N12 98 DC49
Frigate Ms. SE8 163 EA79
Watergate St.
Frimley Ave., Horn. 128 FN60
Frimley Clo. SW19 179 CY89
Frimley Clo., Croy. 221 EC108
Frimley Ct., Sid. 186 EW92
Frimley Cres., Croy. 221 EC108
Frimley Gdns., Mitch. 200 DE97
Frimley Rd., Chess. 215 CK106
Frimley Rd., Hem.H. 39 BE19
Frimley Rd., Ilf. 125 ES62
Frimley Vw., Wind. 151 AK81
Frimley Way E1 143 DX70
Frimley Way, Wall. 219 DL106
Fringewood Clo., Nthwd. 93 BP53
Frinsted Clo., Orp. 206 EX98
Frinsted Rd., Erith 167 FD80
Frinton Clo., Wat. 93 BV47
Frinton Dr., Wdf.Grn. 101 ED52
Frinton Ms., Ilf. 125 EN58
Bramley Cres.
Frinton Rd. E6 144 EK69
Frinton Rd. N15 122 DS58
Frinton Rd. SW17 180 DG93
Frinton Rd., Rom. 104 EZ52
Frinton Rd., Sid. 186 EY89
Friston Path, Chig. 103 ES50
Manford Way
Friston St. SW6 160 DB82
Friswell Pl., Bexh. 166 FA84
Frith Ct. NW7 97 CY52
Frith Knowle, Walt. 213 BV106
Frith La. NW7 97 CY52
Frith Rd. E11 123 EC63
Frith Rd., Croy. 202 DQ103
Frith St. W1 273 M9
Frith St. W1 141 DK72
Fritham Clo., N.Mal. 198 CS100
Frithe, The, Slou. 132 AV72
Friths Dr., Reig. 250 DB131
Frithsden Copse, Berk. 39 AZ15
Frithsden Rd., Berk. 38 AY17
Frithville Gdns. W12 139 CW74
Frithwald Rd., Cher. 193 BF101
Frithwood Ave., Nthwd. 93 BS51
Frizlands La., Dag. 127 FB63
Frobisher Clo., Ken. 236 DR117
Hayes La.
Frobisher Clo., Pnr. 116 BX59
Frobisher Cres., Stai. 174 BL87
Frobisher Gdns., Guil. 243 BA133
Frobisher Gdns., Stai. 174 BL87
Frobisher Cres.
Frobisher Pas. E14 143 EA74
North Colonnade
Frobisher Rd. E6 145 EM72
Frobisher Rd. N8 121 DN56
Frobisher Rd., Erith 167 FF80
Frobisher Rd., St.Alb. 43 CJ22
Frobisher St. SE10 164 EE79
Frobisher Way, Grav. 191 GL92
Frobisher Way, Hat. 44 CR15
Frog La., Guil. 242 AY125
Frog La., Rain. 147 FD71
Froggy La., Uxb. 113 BD61
Froghall La., Chig. 103 ER49
Froghole La., Eden. 255 ER132
Frogley Rd. SE22 162 DT84
Frogmoor La., Rick. 92 BK47
Frogmore SW18 180 DA85
Frogmore, St.Alb. 61 CD27
Frogmore Ave., Hayes 135 BS70
Frogmore Clo., Slou. 151 AN75
Frogmore Clo., Sutt. 199 CX104
Frogmore Dr., Wind. 152 AS81
Frogmore Gdns., Hayes 135 BS70
Frogmore Gdns., Sutt. 217 CY105
Frogmore Mobile Home Pk., St.Alb. 61 CD27
Frogmore Rd., Hem.H. 40 BK23
Frognal NW3 120 DC64
Frognal Ave., Har. 117 CF56
Frognal Ave., Sid. 186 EU92
Frognal Clo. NW3 120 DC64
Frognal Ct. NW3 140 DC65
Frognal Gdns. NW3 120 DC63
Frognal La. NW3 120 DB64
Frognal Par. NW3 140 DC65
Frognal Ct.
Frognal Pl., Sid. 186 EU93
Frognal Ri. NW3 120 DC62
Frognal Way NW3 120 DC63
Froissart Rd. SE9 184 EK85
Frome Rd. N22 121 DP55
Westbury Ave.
Frome Sq., Hem.H. 40 BN15
Waveney
Frome St. N1 142 DQ68
Fromer Rd., H.Wyc. 110 AD59
Fromondes Rd., Sutt. 217 CY106
Front, The, Berk. 39 BB16
Front La., Upmin. 129 FS61
Frostic Wk. E1 142 DU71
Chicksand St.
Froude St. SW8 161 DH82
Frowick Clo., Hat. 45 CV23
Frowyke Cres., Pot.B. 63 CU32
Fruen Rd., Felt. 175 BT87
Fry Clo., Rom. 104 FA50
Fry Rd. E6 144 EK66
Fry Rd. NW10 139 CT67
Fryatt Rd. N17 100 DR52
Fryatt St. E14 144 EE72
Orchard Pl.
Fryent Clo. NW9 118 CN57
Fryent Cres. NW9 118 CS58
Fryent Flds. NW9 118 CS58
Fryent Gro. NW9 118 CS58
Fryent Way NW9 118 CN57
Fryer Clo., Chesh. 54 AR33
Fryern Wd., Cat. 236 DQ124
Frye's Bldgs. N1 141 DN68
Upper St.
Frying Pan All. E1 275 P7
Fryston Ave., Couls. 219 DH114
Fryston Ave., Croy. 202 DU103
Fryth Mead, St.Alb. 42 CB19
Fuchsia St. SE2 166 EV78
Fulbeck Dr. NW9 96 CS53
Fulbeck Way, Har. 94 CC54
Fulbourne Clo., Red. 250 DE132
Dennis Clo.
Fulbourne Rd. E17 101 EC53
Fulbourne St. E1 142 DV71
Durward St.
Fulbrook Ave., Add. 212 BG111
Fulbrook La., S.Ock. 149 FT73
Fulbrook Ms. N19 121 DJ63
Junction Rd.
Fulbrook Rd. N19 121 DJ63
Junction Rd.
Fulbrooks Ave., Wor.Pk. 199 CT102
Fulford Gro., Wat. 93 BV47
Fulford Rd., Cat. 236 DR121
Fulford Rd., Epsom 216 CR108
Fulford St. SE16 162 DV75
Paradise St.
Fulham Bdy. SW6 160 DA80
Fulham Clo., Uxb. 135 BQ70
Uxbridge Rd.
Fulham Ct. SW6 160 DA80
Fulham Rd.
Fulham High St. SW6 159 CY82
Fulham Palace Rd. SW6 159 CX79
Fulham Palace Rd. W6 159 CW78
Fulham Pk. Gdns. SW6 159 CZ82
Fulham Pk. Rd. SW6 159 CZ82
Fulham Rd. SW3 160 DD78
Fulham Rd. SW6 159 CY82
Fulham Rd. SW10 160 DD78
Fulkes Cotts., Lthd. 245 BP128
Fullarton Cres., S.Ock. 149 FT72
Fuller Clo. E2 142 DU70
St. Matthew's Row
Fuller Clo., Orp. 223 ET106
Fuller Gdns., Wat. 75 BV37
Fuller Rd.
Fuller Rd., Dag. 126 EV62
Fuller Rd., Wat. 75 BV37
Fuller St. NW4 119 CW56
Fuller Ter., Ilf. 125 EQ64
Loxford La.
Fuller Way, Hayes 155 BT78
Fuller Way, Rick. 74 BN43
Fullers Ave., Surb. 198 CM103
Fullers Ave., Wdf.Grn. 102 EF52
Fullers Clo., Chesh. 54 AP32
Fullers Clo., Rom. 105 FC52
Fullers Clo., Wal.Abb. 68 EF33
Fullers Fm. Rd., Lthd. 245 BP134
Fullers Hill, Amer. 54 AM34
Fullers Hill, Chesh. 54 AM34
Fullers Hill, West. 255 ER126
High St.
Fullers La., Rom. 105 FC52
Fullers Mead, Harl. 52 EW16
Fullers Rd. E18 102 EF53
Fullers Way N., Surb. 198 CM104
Fullers Way S., Chess. 216 CL105
Fullers Wd., Croy. 221 EA106
Fullers Wd. La., Red. 251 DJ134
Fullerton Clo., W.Byf. 212 BM114
Fullerton Dr., W.Byf. 212 BL114
Fullerton Rd. SW18 180 DC85
Fullerton Rd., Cars. 218 DE109
Fullerton Rd., Croy. 202 DT101
Fullerton Rd., W.Byf. 212 BL114
Fullerton Way, W.Byf. 212 BL114
Fullmer Way, Add. 211 BF110
Fullwell Ave., Ilf. 103 EM53
Fullwoods Ms. N1 275 L2
Fulmar Ct., Surb. 198 CM100
Fulmar Cres., Hem.H. 40 BG21
Fulmar Rd., Horn. 147 FG66
Fulmead St. SW6 160 DB81
Fulmer Clo., Hmptn. 176 BY92
Fulmer Common Rd., Iver 133 BA65
Fulmer Common Rd., Slou. 112 AX64
Fulmer Dr., Ger.Cr. 112 AX61
Fulmer La., Ger.Cr. 113 BA62
Fulmer La., Slou. 112 AY62
Fulmer Ri. Est., Slou. 133 AZ65
Fulmer Rd. E16 144 EK71
Fulmer Rd., Ger.Cr. 112 AY59
Fulmer Rd., Slou. 112 AX63
Fulmer Way W13 157 CH76
Fulmer Way, Ger.Cr. 112 AY58
Fulready Rd. E10 123 ED57
Fulstone Clo., Houns. 156 BZ84
Fulthorp Rd. SE3 164 EF82
Fulton Ms. W2 140 DC73
Porchester Ter.
Fulton Rd., Wem. 118 CN62
Fulvens, Guil. 261 BS142
Fulvens Cotts., Guil. 261 BS142
Fulwell Cross Roundabout, Ilf. 103 ER54
Fencepiece Rd.
Fulwell Pk. Ave., Twick. 176 CB89
Fulwell Rd., Tedd. 177 CD91
Fulwich Rd., Dart. 188 FM86
Fulwood Ave., Wem. 138 CM68
Fulwood Clo., Hayes 135 BT72
Fulwood Gdns., Twick. 177 CF86
Fulwood Pl. WC1 274 C7
Fulwood Wk. SW19 179 CY88
Furber St. W6 159 CV76
Furham Feild, Pnr. 94 CA52
Furley Rd. SE15 162 DU80
Furlong Clo., Wall. 200 DG102
Furlong Rd. N7 141 DN65
Furlong Rd., Dor. 262 CC137
Furlong Way, Ware 33 DZ09
Furlongs, Hem.H. 40 BG19
Furlough, The, Wok. 227 BA117
Pembroke Rd.
Furmage St. SW18 180 DB87
Furmingers Rd., Orp. 225 FB106
Furneaux Ave. SE27 181 DP92
Furner Clo., Dart. 167 FF83
Furness Clo., Grays 171 GH78
Furness Pl., Wind. 150 AJ82
Furness Row
Furness Rd. NW10 139 CU68
Furness Rd. SW6 160 DB82
Furness Rd., Har. 116 CB59
Furness Rd., Mord. 200 DB101
Furness Row, Wind. 150 AJ82
Furness Sq., Wind. 150 AJ82
Furness Row
Furness Wk., Wind. 150 AJ82
Furness Row
Furness Way, Horn. 127 FG64
Furness Way, Wind. 150 AJ82
Furnival Ave., Slou. 131 AP71
Furnival Clo., Vir.W. 192 AX100
Furnival St. EC4 274 D8
Furnival St. EC4 141 DN72
Furrow La. E9 122 DW64
Furrowfield, Hat. 45 CV16
Cob Mead
Furrows, The, Uxb. 114 BJ57
Furrows, The, Walt. 196 BW103
Furrows Pl., Cat. 236 DT123
Fursby Ave. N3 98 DA51
Furse Ave., St.Alb. 43 CG17
Further Acre NW9 97 CT54
Further Grn. Rd. SE6 184 EE87
Furtherfield, Abb.L. 59 BS32
Furtherfield Clo., Croy. 201 DN100
Furtherground, Hem.H. 40 BL21
Furze Clo., Red. 250 DF133
Furze Clo., Wat. 94 BW50
Furze Fm. Clo., Rom. 104 EY54
Furze Fld., Lthd. 215 CD113
Furze Gro., Tad. 233 CZ121
Furze Hill, Pur. 219 DL111
Furze Hill, Red. 250 DE133
Linkfield La.
Furze Hill, Tad. 233 CZ120

Furze La., Gdmg. 258 AT143
Furze La., Pur. 219 DL111
Furze Rd., Add. 211 BF107
Furze Rd., Hem.H. 39 BE21
Furze Rd., Th.Hth. 202 DQ97
Furze St. E3 143 EA71
Furze Vw., Rick. 73 BC44
Furzebushes La., St.Alb. 60 BY25
Furzedown Dr. SW17 181 DH92
Furzedown Rd. SW17 181 DH92
Furzedown Rd., Sutt. 218 DC111
Furzefield (Cheshunt), Wal.Cr. 66 DV28
Furzefield Clo., Chis. 185 EP93
Furzefield Cres., Reig. 266 DC136
Furzefield Rd. SE3 164 EH80
Furzefield Rd., Beac. 88 AJ52
Furzefield Rd., Reig. 266 DC136
Furzefield Rd., Welw.G.C. 29 CY10
Furzeground Way, Uxb. 135 BQ74
Furzeham Rd., West Dr. 154 BL75
Furzehill Rd., Borwd. 78 CN41
Furzen Clo., Slou. 131 AN69
Furzen Cres., Hat. 45 CT21
Furzewood, Sun. 195 BU95
Fuschia Ct., Wdf.Grn. 102 EE52
Bridle Path
Fusedale Way, S.Ock. 149 FT73
Fuzzens Wk., Wind. 151 AL82
Fyfe Way, Brom. 204 EG96
Fyfield Clo., Brom. 203 ED98
Fyfield Ct. E7 144 EG65
Fyfield Rd. E17 123 ED55
Fyfield Rd. SW9 161 DN83
Fyfield Rd., Enf. 82 DS41
Fyfield Rd., Rain. 147 FF67
Fyfield Rd., Wdf.Grn. 102 EJ52
Fynes St. SW1 277 M8
Fynes St. SW1 161 DK77

G

Gabion Ave., Purf. 169 FR77
Gable Clo. SE26 182 DV91
Lawrie Pk. Ave.
Gable Clo., Abb.L. 59 BS32
Gable Clo., Dart. 187 FG85
Gable Clo., Pnr. 94 CA52
Gable Ct. SE26 182 DV92
Lawrie Pk. Ave.
Gables, The, Bans. 233 CZ117
Gables, The, Hem.H. 40 BK19
Chapel St.
Gables, The, Lthd. 214 CC112
Gables, The, Wem. 118 CM63
Gables Ave., Ashf. 174 BM92
Gables Ave., Borwd. 78 CM41
Gables Clo. SE5 162 DS81
Gables Clo. SE12 184 EG88
Gables Clo., Ger.Cr. 90 AY49
Gables Clo., Slou. 152 AU79
Gables Clo., Wok. 227 AZ120
Kingfield Rd.
Gabriel Clo., Felt. 176 BX91
Gabriel Clo., Rom. 105 FC52
Gabriel Spring Rd. (Fawkham Grn.), Long. 209 FR103
Gabriel Spring Rd. (East), Long. 209 FS103
Gabriel St. SE23 183 DX87
Gabrielle Clo., Wem. 118 CM62
Gabrielle Ct. NW3 140 DD65
Gabriels Gdns., Grav. 191 GL92
Gad Clo. E13 144 EH69
Gadbrook Rd., Bet. 264 CQ140
Gaddesden Ave., Wem. 138 CM65
Gaddesden Cres., Wat. 60 BX34
Gaddesdon Gro., Welw.G.C. 30 DC09
Widford Rd.
Gade Ave., Wat. 75 BS42
Gade Bank, Rick. 75 BR42
Rousebarn La.
Gade Clo., Hayes 135 BV74
Gade Clo., Hem.H. 40 BH17
Gade Clo., Wat. 75 BS42
Gade Twr., Hem.H. 58 BN25
Gade Valley Clo., Kings L. 58 BN28
Gade Vw. Gdns., Kings L. 59 BQ32
Gade Vw. Rd., Hem.H. 40 BK24
Gadebridge La., Hem.H. 40 BH18
Gadebridge Rd., Hem.H. 40 BG18
Gadesden Rd., Epsom 216 CQ107
Gadsbury Clo. NW9 119 CT58
Gadsden Clo., Upmin. 129 FS58
Gadswell Clo., Wat. 76 BX36
Gadwall Clo. E16 144 EH72
Freemasons Rd.
Gadwall Way SE28 165 ER75
Goldfinch Rd.
Gage Rd. E16 144 EE71
Malmesbury Rd.
Gage St. WC1 274 A6
Gainford St. N1 141 DN67
Richmond Ave.
Gainsborough Ave. E12 125 EN64
Gainsborough Ave., Dart. 188 FJ85
Gainsborough Ave., St.Alb. 43 CF19
Gainsborough Ave., Til. 171 GG81
Gainsborough Clo., Beck. 183 EA94
Gainsborough Clo., Esher 197 CE102
Lime Tree Ave.
Gainsborough Ct. N12 98 DB50
Gainsborough Ct. W12 159 CW75
Lime Gro.
Gainsborough Ct., Walt. 213 BU105
Gainsborough Dr., Grav. 190 GD90
Gainsborough Dr., S.Croy. 220 DU113
Gainsborough Gdns. NW3 120 DD62
Gainsborough Gdns. NW11 119 CZ59
Gainsborough Gdns., Edg. 96 CM54
Gainsborough Gdns., Grnf. 117 CE64
Gainsborough Gdns., Islw. 177 CD85
Gainsborough Ms. SE26 182 DV90
Panmure Rd.
Gainsborough Pl., Chig. 103 ET48
Gainsborough Rd. E11 124 EE59
Gainsborough Rd. E15 144 EE69
Gainsborough Rd. N12 98 DB50
Gainsborough Rd. W4 159 CT77
Gainsborough Rd., Dag. 126 EV63
Gainsborough Rd., Epsom 216 CQ110
Gainsborough Rd., Hayes 135 BQ68
Gainsborough Rd., N.Mal. 198 CR100
Gainsborough Rd., Rain. 147 FG67
Gainsborough Rd., Rich. 158 CM82
Gainsborough Rd., Wdf.Grn. 102 EL51
Gainsborough Sq., Bexh. 166 EX83
Regency Way
Gainsford Rd. E17 123 DZ56
Gainsford St. SE1 279 P4
Gainsford St. SE1 162 DT75
Gainswood, Welw.G.C. 29 CY10
Mill Grn. Rd.
Gairloch Rd. SE5 162 DS82
Gaisford St. NW5 141 DJ65
Gaist Ave., Cat. 236 DV122
Gaitskell Rd. SE9 185 EQ88
Galahad Clo., Slou. 151 AN75
Mitchell Clo.
Galahad Rd., Brom. 184 EG90
Galata Rd. SW13 159 CU80
Galatea Sq. SE15 162 DV83
Scylla Rd.
Galbraith St. E14 163 EC76
Galdana Ave., Barn. 80 DC41
Gale Clo., Hmptn. 176 BY93
Stewart Clo.
Gale Clo., Mitch. 200 DD97
Gale Cres., Bans. 234 DA117
Gale St. E3 143 EA71
Gale St., Dag. 126 EW64
Galeborough Ave., Wdf.Grn. 101 ED52
Galen Pl. WC1 274 A7
Galena Rd. W6 159 CV77
Gales Clo., Guil. 243 BD132
Gilliat Dr.
Gales Gdns. E2 142 DV69
Gales Way, Wdf.Grn. 102 EL52
Galesbury Rd. SW18 180 DC86
Galey Grn., S.Ock. 149 FV71
Bovey Way
Galgate Clo. SW19 179 CY88
Gallants Fm. Rd., Barn. 98 DE45
Galleon Boul., Dart. 169 FR84
Galleon Clo. SE16 163 DX75
Kinburn St.
Galleon Rd., Grays 169 FW77
Galleons La., Slou. 132 AW70
Gallery Gdns., Nthlt. 136 BX68
Gallery Rd. SE21 182 DR88
Galley Grn., Hert. 33 EA13
Galley Hill, Hem.H. 39 BF18
Galley Hill Rd., Grav. 190 FZ85
Galley La., Barn. 79 CT38
Galleyhill Rd., Wal.Abb. 68 EE32
Galleymead Rd., Slou. 153 BF81
Galleywall Rd. SE16 162 DV77
Galleywood Cres., Rom. 105 FD51
Gallia Rd. N5 121 DP64
Galliard Clo. N9 82 DW44
Galliard Rd. N9 100 DU46
Gallions Clo., Bark. 146 EU69
Gallions Rd. E16 145 EP73
Gallions Rd. SE7 164 EH77
Gallions Roundabout E16 164 EK78
Royal Albert Way
Gallon Clo. SE7 164 EJ77
Gallop, The, S.Croy. 220 DV108
Gallop, The, Sutt. 218 DD110
Gallosson Rd. SE18 165 ES77
Galloway Clo., Brox. 67 DZ25
Galloway Path, Croy. 220 DR105
St. Peter's Rd.
Galloway Rd. W12 139 CU74
Gallows Cor., Rom. 106 FJ53
Gallows Hill, Kings L. 59 BQ31
Gallows Hill La., Abb.L. 59 BQ32
Gallus Clo. N21 81 DM44
Gallus Sq. SE3 164 EH83
Gallys Rd., Wind. 151 AK82
Galpins Rd., Th.Hth. 201 DL99
Galsworthy Ave., Rom. 126 EV59
Galsworthy Clo. SE28 146 EV74
Galsworthy Cres. SE3 164 EJ81
Merriman Rd.
Galsworthy Rd. NW2 119 CY63
Galsworthy Rd., Cher. 194 BG101
Galsworthy Rd., Kings.T. 178 CP94
Galsworthy Rd., Til. 171 GJ81
Galsworthy Ter. N16 122 DS62
Hawksley Rd.
Galton St. W10 139 CY69
Galva Clo., Barn. 80 DG42
Galvani Way, Croy. 201 DM102
Ampere Way
Galveston Rd. SW15 179 CZ85
Galvin Rd., Slou. 131 AQ74
Galvins Clo., Guil. 242 AU131
Galway St. EC1 275 J3
Galway St. EC1 142 DQ69
Gambetta St. SW8 161 DH82
Gambia St. SE1 278 G3
Gambles La., Wok. 228 BJ124
Gambole Rd. SW17 180 DE91
Games Rd., Barn. 80 DF41
Gamlen Rd. SW15 159 CX84
Gammon Clo., Hem.H. 40 BN21
Gammons Fm. Clo., Wat. 75 BT36
Gammons La., Brox. 66 DS25
Gammons La., Wat. 75 BS36
Gamuel Clo. E17 123 EA58
Gander Grn. La., Sutt. 199 CY103
Ganders Ash, Wat. 59 BU33
Gandhi Clo. E17 123 EA58
Gane Clo., Wall. 219 DL108
Kingsford Ave.
Gangers Hill, Gdse. 253 DY128
Ganghill, Guil. 243 BA132
Gant Ct., Wal.Abb. 68 EF34
Ganton St. W1 273 K10
Ganton Wk., Wat. 94 BY49
Woodhall La.
Gantshill Cres., Ilf. 125 EN57
Gantshill Cross, Ilf. 125 EN58
Eastern Ave.
Ganymede Pl., Hem.H. 40 BM18
Jupiter Dr.
Gap Rd. SW19 180 DA92
Garage Rd. W3 138 CN72
Garbrand Wk., Epsom 217 CT109
Garbutt Pl. W1 272 G6
Garbutt Rd., Upmin. 128 FQ61
Gard St. EC1 274 G2
Garden Ave., Bexh. 166 FA83
Garden Ave., Hat. 45 CU22
Garden Ave., Mitch. 181 DH94
Garden City, Edg. 96 CN51
Garden Clo. E4 101 EA50
Garden Clo. SE12 184 EH90
Garden Clo. SW15 179 CV87
Garden Clo., Add. 212 BK105
Garden Clo., Ashf. 175 BQ93
Garden Clo., Bans. 234 DA115
Garden Clo., Barn. 79 CV42
Garden Clo., Hmptn. 176 BZ92
Garden Clo., Lthd. 231 CJ124
Garden Clo., Nthlt. 136 BY67
Garden Clo., Ruis. 115 BS61
Garden Clo., St.Alb. 43 CH19
Garden Clo., Wall. 219 DL106
Garden Clo., Wat. 75 BT40
Garden Cotts., Orp. 206 EW96
Main Rd.
Garden Ct. EC4 274 D10
Garden Ct. SE15 162 DT81
Sumner Est.
Garden Ct., Rich. 158 CM81
Lichfield Rd.
Garden Ct., Welw.G.C. 29 CZ08
Tewin Rd.
Garden Ct., W.Mol. 196 CB98
Avern Rd.
Garden End, Amer. 55 AS37
Garden Fld. La., Berk. 39 AZ21
Garden La. SW2 181 DM88
Christchurch Rd.
Garden La., Brom. 184 EH93
Garden Ms. W2 140 DA73
Linden Gdns.
Garden Ms., Slou. 132 AT74
Littledown Rd.
Garden Pl., Dart. 188 FK90
Garden Reach, Ch.St.G. 72 AX41
Garden Rd. NW8 140 DC69
Garden Rd. SE20 202 DW95
Garden Rd., Abb.L. 59 BS31
Garden Rd., Brom. 184 EH94
Garden Rd., Rich. 158 CN83
Garden Rd., Sev. 257 FK122
Garden Rd., Walt. 195 BV100
Garden Row SE1 278 F7
Garden Row SE1 161 DP76
Garden Row, Grav. 191 GF90
Garden St. E1 143 DX71
Garden Ter. SW1 277 M10
Garden Ter. Rd., Harl. 36 EW11
Garden Wk. EC2 275 M3
Garden Wk., Beck. 203 DZ95
Hayne Rd.
Garden Wk., Couls. 235 DH123
Garden Way NW10 138 CQ65
Garden Way, Loug. 85 EN38
Gardeners Clo. N11 98 DG49
Gardeners Rd., Croy. 201 DP102
Gardeners Wk., Lthd. 246 CB126
Gardenia Rd., Enf. 82 DS44
Gardenia Way, Wdf.Grn. 102 EH50
Harts Gro.
Gardens, The SE22 162 DU84
Gardens, The, Beck. 203 EC95
Gardens, The, Esher 214 CA105
Gardens, The, Felt. 175 BR86
Gardens, The, Har. 116 CC58
Gardens, The, Hat. 63 CY27
Gardens, The, Pnr. 116 BZ58
Gardens, The, Wat. 75 BT40
Gardiner Ave. NW2 119 CW64
Gardiner Clo., Dag. 126 EX63
Gardiner Clo., Orp. 206 EW96
Gardiners, The, Harl. 52 EV16
Gardner Clo. E11 124 EH58
Gardner Gro., Felt. 176 BZ89
Gardner Rd. E13 144 EH70
Gardner Rd., Guil. 242 AX134
Gardners La. EC4 275 H10
Gardnor Rd. NW3 120 DD63
Flask Wk.
Garendon Gdns., Mord. 200 DB101
Garendon Rd., Mord. 200 DA101
Gareth Clo., Wor.Pk. 199 CX103
Burnham Dr.
Gareth Gro., Brom. 184 EG91
Garfield Pl., Wind. 151 AR82
Albany Rd.
Garfield Rd. E4 101 ED46
Garfield Rd. E13 144 EF70
Garfield Rd. SW11 160 DG83
Garfield Rd. SW19 180 DC92
Garfield Rd., Add. 212 BJ106
Garfield Rd., Enf. 82 DW42
Garfield Rd., Twick. 177 CG88
York St.
Garfield St., Wat. 75 BV38
Garford St. E14 143 EA73
Garganey Wk. SE28 146 EW73
Gargles Clo., Green. 189 FU85
Cowley Ave.
Garibaldi Rd., Red. 266 DF135
Garibaldi St. SE18 165 ES77
Garland Clo., Hem.H. 40 BK19
Garland Clo., Wal.Cr. 67 DY31
Garland Rd. SE18 165 ER80
Garland Rd., Stan. 96 CL53
Garland Rd., Ware 33 DY06
Garland Way, Cat. 236 DR122
Garland Way, Horn. 128 FL56
Garlands Ct., Croy. 220 DR105
Chatsworth Rd.
Garlands Rd., Lthd. 231 CH121
Garlands Rd., Red. 266 DF135
Garlic St., Dor. 246 BZ132
Garlichill Rd., Epsom 233 CV117
Garlick Hill EC4 275 J10
Garlick Hill EC4 142 DQ73
Garlies Rd. SE23 183 DY90
Garlinge Rd. NW2 139 CZ65
Garman Clo. N18 100 DR50
Garman Rd. N17 100 DW52
Garnault Ms. EC1 274 E3
Garnault Pl. EC1 274 E3
Garnault Rd., Enf. 82 DT38
Garner Dr., Brox. 67 DY26
Garner Rd. E17 101 EC53
Garner St. E2 142 DU68
Coate St.
Garners Clo., Ger.Cr. 91 AZ51
Garners End, Ger.Cr. 90 AY51
Garners Rd., Ger.Cr. 90 AY51
Garnet Clo., Slou. 151 AN75
Mitchell Clo.
Garnet Rd. NW10 138 CS65
Garnet Rd., Th.Hth. 202 DQ98
Garnet St. E1 142 DW73
Garnet Wk. E6 144 EL71
Kingfisher St.
Garnett Clo. SE9 165 EM83
Garnett Clo., Wat. 76 BX37
Garnett Dr., St.Alb. 60 BZ29
Garnett Rd. NW3 120 DF64
Garnett Way E17 101 DY53
McEntee Ave.
Garnham Clo. N16 122 DT61
Garnham St.
Garnham St. N16 122 DT61
Garnies Clo. SE15 162 DT80
Daniel Gdns.
Garnon Mead, Epp. 70 EX28
Garrad's Rd. SW16 181 DK90
Garrard Clo., Bexh. 166 FA83
Garrard Clo., Chis. 185 EP92
Garrard Rd., Bans. 234 DA116
Garrard Rd., Slou. 131 AL70
Garrard Wk. NW10 138 CS65
Garnet Rd.
Garratt Clo., Croy. 219 DL105
Garratt La. SW17 180 DD91
Garratt La. SW18 180 DB85
Garratt Rd., Edg. 96 CN52
Garratt Ter. SW17 180 DE91
Garratts La., Bans. 233 CZ116
Garratts Rd. (Bushey), Wat. 94 CC45
Garrett Clo. W3 138 CR71
Jenner Ave.
Garrett Clo., Chesh. 54 AR33
Garrett St. EC1 275 J4
Garrick Ave. NW11 119 CY58
Garrick Clo. SW18 160 DC84
Garrick Clo. W5 138 CL70
Garrick Clo., Rich. 177 CK85
The Grn.
Garrick Clo., Stai. 174 BG94
Garrick Clo., Walt. 213 BV105
Garrick Cres., Croy. 202 DS103
Garrick Dr. NW4 97 CW54
Garrick Dr. SE28 165 ER76
Broadwater Rd.
Garrick Gdns., W.Mol. 196 CA97
Garrick Pk. NW4 97 CX54
Garrick Rd. NW9 119 CT58
Garrick Rd., Grnf. 136 CB70
Garrick Rd., Rich. 158 CN82
Garrick St. WC2 273 P10
Garrick St. WC2 141 DL73
Garrick St., Grav. 191 GH86
Barrack Row
Garrick Way NW4 119 CX56
Garrison Clo. SE18 165 EN80
Red Lion La.
Garrison La., Chess. 215 CK108
Garrison Par., Purf. 168 FN77
Comet Clo.
Garrolds Clo., Swan. 207 FD96
Garron La., S.Ock. 149 FT72
Garry Clo., Rom. 105 FE52
Garry Way, Rom. 105 FE52
Garside Clo. SE28 165 ER76
Goosander Way
Garside Clo., Hmptn. 176 CB93
Garsington Ms. SE4 163 DZ83
Garsmouth Way, Wat. 76 BX36
Garson Gro., Chesh. 54 AN29
Garson La., Stai. 172 AX87
Garson Mead, Esher 214 BZ106
Garson Rd., Esher 214 BZ107
Garston Cres., Wat. 60 BW34
Garston Dr., Wat. 60 BW34
Garston La., Ken. 220 DR114
Garston La., Wat. 60 BX34
Garston Pk. Par., Wat. 60 BX34
Garstons, The, Lthd. 246 CA125
Garter Way SE16 163 DX75
Poolmans St.
Garth, The, Abb.L. 59 BR33
Garth, The, Cob. 214 BY113
Garth, The, Hmptn. 176 CB93
Uxbridge Rd.
Garth, The, Har. 118 CM58
Garth Clo. W4 158 CR78
Garth Clo., Kings.T. 178 CM92
Garth Clo., Mord. 199 CX101
Garth Clo., Ruis. 116 BX60
Garth Ct. W4 158 CR78
Garth Rd.
Garth Ms. W5 138 CL70
Greystoke Gdns.
Garth Rd. NW2 119 CZ61
Garth Rd. W4 158 CR79
Garth Rd., Kings.T. 178 CM92
Garth Rd., Mord. 199 CW100
Garth Rd., Sev. 257 FJ128
Garth Rd., S.Ock. 149 FW70
Garth Rd. Ind. Est., Mord. 199 CX101
Garthland Dr., Barn. 79 CV43
Garthorne Rd. SE23 183 DX87
Garthside, Rich. 178 CL92
Garthway N12 98 DE51
Gartlett Rd., Wat. 76 BW41
Gartmoor Gdns. SW19 179 CZ88
Gartmore Rd., Ilf. 125 ET61
Garton Pl. SW18 180 DC86
Gartons Clo., Enf. 82 DW42
Gartons Way SW11 160 DC83
Garvary Rd. E16 144 EH72
Garvin Ave., Beac. 89 AL53
Garvock Dr., Sev. 256 FG126
Garway Rd. W2 140 DB72
Gas Wks. La., Brox. 49 EA19
Gascoigne Gdns., Wdf.Grn. 102 EE52
Gascoigne Pl. E2 275 P2
Gascoigne Pl. E2 142 DT69
Gascoigne Rd., Bark. 145 EQ67
Gascoigne Rd., Croy. 221 EC110
Gascoigne Rd., Wey. 195 BP104
Gascons Gro., Slou. 131 AN70
Gascony Ave. NW6 140 DA66
Gascoyne Clo., Pot.B. 63 CU32
Gascoyne Clo., Rom. 106 FK52
Gascoyne Dr., Dart. 167 FF82
Gascoyne Rd. E9 143 DX66
Gascoyne Way, Hert. 32 DQ09
Gaselee St. E14 143 EC73
Gasholder Pl. SE11 161 DM78
Kennington La.
Gaskarth Rd. SW12 181 DH86
Gaskarth Rd., Edg. 96 CQ53
Gaskell Rd. N6 120 DF58
Gaskell St. SW4 161 DL82
Gaskin St. N1 141 DP67
Gaspar Clo. SW5 160 DB77
Courtfield Gdns.
Gaspar Ms. SW5 160 DB77
Courtfield Gdns.
Gassiot Rd. SW17 180 DF91
Gassiot Way, Sutt. 200 DD104
Gasson Rd., Swans. 190 FY86
Gastein Rd. W6 159 CX79
Gaston Bell Clo., Rich. 158 CM83
Gaston Bri. Rd., Shep. 195 BR100
Gaston Rd., Mitch. 200 DG97
Gaston Way, Shep. 195 BQ99
Gataker St. SE16 162 DV76
Gatcombe Rd. E16 144 EE72
Silvertown Way
Gatcombe Rd. N19 121 DK62
Gatcombe Way, Barn. 80 DF41
Gate Clo., Borwd. 78 CQ39
Gate End, Nthwd. 93 BU52
Gate Ho. Sq. SE1 142 DQ74
Southwark Bri. Rd.
Gate Ms. SW7 276 C5
Gate Ms. SW7 160 DE75
Gate St. WC2 274 B8
Gatecroft, Hem.H. 40 BM22
Gateforth St. NW8 272 B5
Gateforth St. NW8 140 DE70
Gatehill Rd., Nthwd. 93 BT52
Gatehope Dr., S.Ock. 149 FT72
Gatehouse Clo., Kings.T. 178 CQ94
Gateley Rd. SW9 161 DM83
Gater Dr., Enf. 82 DR39
Gates Grn. Rd., Kes. 222 EH105
Gates Grn. Rd., W.Wick. 204 EF104
Gatesborough St. EC2 275 M4
Gatesden Rd., Lthd. 230 CC123
Gateshead Rd., Borwd. 78 CM40
Gateside Rd. SW17 180 DF90
Gatestone Rd. SE19 182 DS93
Gateway SE17 162 DQ79
Gateway, Wey. 195 BP104
Palace Dr.
Gateway, The, Wok. 211 BB114
Gateway Arc. N1 141 DP68
Islington High St.
Gateway Clo., Nthwd. 93 BQ51
Gateway Ind. Est. NW10 139 CT69
Gateway Ms. E8 122 DT64
Shacklewell La.
Gateways, Guil. 243 BA134
Gateways, The SW3 276 C9
Gateways, The, Wal.Cr. 66 DS28
Burton La.
Gatewick Clo., Slou. 132 AW74
Gatfield Gro., Felt. 176 CA89
Gathorne Rd. N22 99 DN54
Gathorne St. E2 143 DX68
Mace St.
Gatley Ave., Epsom 216 CP106
Gatley Dr., Guil. 243 AZ131
Gatliff Rd. SW1 161 DH78
Gatling Rd. SE2 166 EU78
Gatting Clo., Edg. 96 CQ52
Pavilion Way
Gatting Way, Uxb. 134 BL65
Gatton Bottom, Red. 250 DG127
Gatton Bottom, Reig. 250 DC130
Gatton Clo., Reig. 250 DC131
Gatton Clo., Sutt. 218 DB109
Gatton Pk., Reig. 250 DG128
Gatton Pk. Rd., Red. 250 DD132
Gatton Pk. Rd., Reig. 250 DD132
Gatton Rd. SW17 180 DE91
Gatton Rd., Reig. 250 DC132
Gattons Way, Sid. 186 EZ91
Gatward Clo. N21 81 DP44
Gatward Grn. N9 100 DT47
Gatwick Gate, Craw. 268 DE154
Gatwick Rd. SW18 179 CZ87
Gatwick Rd., Gat. 268 DG154
Gatwick Rd., Grav. 191 GH90
Gatwick Way, Gat. 268 DF151
Gatwick Way, Horn. 128 FM63
Haydock Clo.
Gauden Clo. SW4 161 DK83
Gauden Rd. SW4 161 DK82
Gaumont App., Wat. 75 BV41
Gaumont Ter. W12 159 CW75
Lime Gro.
Gaunt St. SE1 278 G6
Gaunt St. SE1 162 DQ76
Gauntlet Clo., Nthlt. 136 BY66
Gauntlet Cres., Ken. 236 DR120
Gauntlett Ct., Wem. 117 CH64
Gauntlett Rd., Sutt. 218 DD106
Gautrey Rd. SE15 162 DW82
Gautrey Sq. E6 145 EM72
Truesdale Rd.
Gavel St. SE17 279 L8
Gavell Rd., Cob. 213 BU113
Gavenny Path, S.Ock. 149 FT72
Gaverick St. E14 163 EA77
Gaveston Dr., Berk. 38 AV17
Gaveston Rd., Lthd. 231 CG120
Gaveston Rd., Slou. 131 AM69
Gavestone Clo., W.Byf. 212 BM113
Gavestone Cres. SE12 184 EH87
Gavestone Rd. SE12 184 EH87
Gaviller Pl. E5 122 DV63
Clarence Rd.
Gavin St. SE18 165 ES77
Gavina Clo., Mord. 200 DD99
Gaviots Clo., Ger.Cr. 113 AZ60
Gaviots Grn., Ger.Cr. 112 AY60
Gaviots Way, Ger.Cr. 112 AY59
Gawber St. E2 142 DW69
Gawsworth Clo. E15 124 EE64
Ash Rd.
Gawthorne Ave. NW7 97 CY50
Lane App.
Gawthorne Ct. E3 143 EA68
Mostyn Gro.
Gay Clo. NW2 119 CV64
Gay Gdns., Dag. 127 FC63
Gay Rd. E15 143 ED68
Gay St. SW15 159 CX83
Waterman St.

Name	Page	Grid
Gaydon Ho. W2	140	DB71
Gaydon La. NW9	96	CS53
Gayfere Rd., Epsom	217	CU106
Gayfere Rd., Ilf.	125	EM55
Gayfere St. SW1	**277**	**P7**
Gayfere St. SW1	161	DL76
Gayford Rd. W12	159	CT75
Gayhurst SE17	162	DR79
Hopwood Rd.		
Gayhurst Rd. E8	142	DU66
Gayler Clo., Red.	252	DT133
Gaylor Rd., Nthlt.	116	BZ64
Gaylor Rd., Til.	170	GE81
Gaynes Ct., Upmin.	128	FP63
Gaynes Hill Rd., Wdf.Grn.	102	EL51
Gaynes Pk. Rd., Upmin.	128	FN63
Gaynes Rd., Upmin.	128	FP61
Gaynesford Rd. SE23	183	DX89
Gaynesford Rd., Cars.	218	DF108
Gaysham Ave., Ilf.	125	EN57
Gaysham Hall, Ilf.	125	EP55
Longwood Gdns.		
Gayton Clo., Amer.	55	AS35
Gayton Clo., Ash.	232	CL118
Gayton Ct., Har.	117	CF58
Gayton Cres. NW3	120	DD63
Gayton Rd. NW3	120	DD63
Gayton Rd. SE2	166	EW76
Gayton Rd., Har.	117	CF58
Gayville Rd. SW11	180	DF86
Gaywood Ave. (Cheshunt), Wal.Cr.	67	DX30
Gaywood Clo. SW2	181	DM88
Gaywood Est. SE1	**278**	**G7**
Gaywood Rd. E17	123	EA55
Gaywood Rd., Ash.	232	CM118
Gaywood St. SE1	**278**	**G7**
Gaza St. SE17	161	DP78
Braganza St.		
Gazelda Vill., Wat.	76	BX43
Lower High St.		
Gazelle Glade, Grav.	191	GM92
Gean Wk., Hat.	45	CU21
Southdown Rd.		
Geariesville Gdns., Ilf.	125	EP56
Geary Clo., Horl.	269	DP150
Geary Dr., Brwd.	108	FW46
Geary Rd. NW10	119	CU64
Geary St. N7	121	DM64
GEC Est., Wem.	117	CK62
Geddes Pl., Bexh.	166	FA84
Market Pl.		
Geddes Rd. (Bushey), Wat.	76	CC42
Geddings Rd., Hodd.	49	EB17
Gedeney Rd. N17	100	DQ53
Gedling Pl. SE1	162	DT76
Gee St. EC1	**275**	**H4**
Gee St. EC1	142	DQ70
Geere Rd. E15	144	EF67
Gees Ct. W1	**272**	**G9**
Geffrye Ct. N1	**275**	**N1**
Geffrye Est. N1	142	DS68
Stanway St.		
Geffrye St. E2	**275**	**P1**
Geffrye St. E2	142	DT68
Geisthorp Ct., Wal.Abb.	68	EG33
Winters Way		
Geldart Rd. SE15	162	DV80
Geldeston Rd. E5	122	DU61
Gell Clo., Uxb.	114	BM62
Gellatly Rd. SE14	162	DW82
Gelsthorpe Rd., Rom.	105	FB52
Gemini Gro., Nthlt.	136	BY69
Javelin Way		
General Gordon Pl. SE18	165	EP77
General Wolfe Rd. SE10	163	ED81
Generals Wk., The, Enf.	83	DY37
Genesis Business Pk., Wok.	227	BC115
Genesta Rd. SE18	165	EP79
Geneva Clo., Shep.	195	BS96
Geneva Dr. SW9	161	DN84
Geneva Gdns., Rom.	126	EY57
Geneva Rd., Kings.T.	198	CL98
Geneva Rd., Th.Hth.	202	DQ99
Genever Clo. E4	101	EA50
Genista Rd. N18	100	DV50
Genoa Ave. SW15	179	CW85
Genoa Rd. SE20	202	DW95
Genotin Rd., Enf.	82	DR41
Genotin Ter., Enf.	82	DR41
Genotin Rd.		
Gentian Row SE13	163	EC81
Sparta St.		
Gentlemans Row, Enf.	82	DQ41
Gentry Gdns. E13	144	EG70
Whitwell Rd.		
Genyn Rd., Guil.	258	AV135
Geoffrey Ave., Rom.	106	FN51
Geoffrey Clo. SE5	162	DQ82
Geoffrey Gdns. E6	144	EL68
Geoffrey Rd. SE4	163	DZ83
George Avey Cft., Epp.	71	FB26
George Beard Rd. SE8	163	DZ77
George Comberton Wk. E12	125	EN64
Gainsborough Ave.		
George Ct. WC2	**278**	**A1**
George Cres. N10	98	DG52
George Downing Est. N16	122	DT61
Cazenove Rd.		
George V Ave., Pnr.	94	BZ53
George V Clo., Pnr.	116	CA55
George V Ave.		
George V Way, Grnf.	137	CH67
George V Way, Rick.	74	BG36
George Gange Way, Har.	117	CE55
George Grn. Dr., Slou.	133	AZ72
George Grn. Rd., Slou.	132	AX72
George Gro. Rd. SE20	202	DU95
George Inn Yd. SE1	**279**	**K3**
George La. E18	102	EG54
George La. SE13	183	EC86
George La., Brom.	204	EH102
George Lansbury Ho. N22	99	DN53
Progress Way		
George Loveless Ho. E2	142	DT69
Diss St.		
George Lowe Ct. W2	140	DB71
Bourne Ter.		
George Ms. NW1	**273**	**K3**
George Ms., Enf.	82	DR41
Sydney Rd.		
George Pl. N17	122	DS55
Dongola Rd.		
George Rd. E4	101	EA51
George Rd., Gdmg.	258	AS144
George Rd., Guil.	242	AX134
George Rd., Kings.T.	178	CQ94
George Rd., N.Mal.	199	CT98
George Row SE16	162	DU75
George Sq. SW19	199	CZ97
Mostyn Rd.		
George St. E16	144	EF72
George St. W1	**272**	**D8**
George St. W1	140	DF72
George St. W7	137	CE74
The Bdy.		
George St., Bark.	145	EQ66
George St., Berk.	38	AX19
George St., Chesh.	54	AQ30
Berkhampstead Rd.		
George St., Croy.	202	DQ103
George St., Grays	170	GA79
George St., Hem.H.	40	BK19
George St., Hert.	32	DQ09
George St., Houns.	156	BZ82
George St., Rich.	177	CK85
George St., Rom.	127	FF58
George St., St.Alb.	43	CD20
George St., Sthl.	156	BY77
George St., Stai.	173	BF91
George St., Sutt.	218	DB106
George St., Uxb.	134	BK66
George St., Wat.	76	BW42
George Wyver Clo. SW19	179	CY87
Beaumont Rd.		
George Yd. EC3	**275**	**L9**
George Yd. W1	**272**	**G10**
George Yd. W1	140	DG73
Georgelands (Ripley), Wok.	228	BH121
Georges Clo., Orp.	206	EW97
Georges Dr., Brwd.	108	FT43
Georges Dr., H.Wyc.	110	AC56
Georges Mead, Borwd.	77	CK44
George's Rd. N7	121	DM64
Georges Rd., Brom.	205	EM97
Georges Rd., West.	238	EK120
Georges Sq. SW6	159	CZ79
North End Rd.		
Georges Ter., Cat.	236	DQ122
Coulsdon La.		
George's Wd. Rd., Hat.	64	DA26
Georgetown Clo. SE19	182	DR92
St. Kitts Ter.		
Georgette Pl. SE10	163	EC80
King George St.		
Georgeville Gdns., Ilf.	125	EP56
Georgewood Rd., Hem.H.	58	BM25
Georgia Rd., N.Mal.	198	CQ98
Georgia Rd., Th.Hth.	201	DP95
Georgian Clo., Brom.	204	EH101
Georgian Clo., Stai.	174	BH91
Georgian Clo., Stan.	95	CG52
Georgian Clo., Uxb.	114	BL63
Georgian Ct. SW16	181	DL91
Gleneldon Rd.		
Georgian Ct., Wem.	138	CN65
Georgian Way, Har.	117	CD61
Georgiana St. NW1	141	DJ67
Georgina Gdns. E2	142	DT69
Columbia Rd.		
Geraint Rd., Brom.	184	EG91
Gerald Ms. SW1	**276**	**G8**
Gerald Rd. E16	144	EF70
Gerald Rd. SW1	**276**	**G8**
Gerald Rd. SW1	160	DG77
Gerald Rd., Dag.	126	EZ61
Gerald Rd., Grav.	191	GL87
Gerald Sq. SW1	160	DG77
Eccleston St.		
Geraldine Rd. SW18	180	DC85
Geraldine Rd. W4	158	CN79
Geraldine St. SE11	**278**	**F7**
Geraldine St. SE11	161	DP76
Geralds Gro., Bans.	217	CX114
Redfern Ave.		
Gerard Ave., Houns.	176	CA87
Gerard Rd. SW13	159	CT81
Gerard Rd., Har.	117	CG58
Gerards Clo. SE16	162	DW78
Gerda Rd. SE9	185	EQ89
Gerdview Dr., Dart.	188	FJ91
Germain St., Chesh.	54	AP32
Germains Clo., Chesh.	54	AP32
Germander Way E15	144	EE69
Gernon Clo., Rain.	148	FK68
Jordans Way		
Gernon Rd. E3	143	DY68
Geron Way NW2	119	CV61
Gerpins La., Upmin.	148	FM68
Gerrard Cres., Brwd.	108	FW48
Gerrard Gdns., Pnr.	115	BU57
Gerrard Pl. W1	**273**	**N10**
Gerrard Rd. N1	141	DP68
Gerrard St. W1	**273**	**N10**
Gerrard St. W1	141	DK73
Gerrards Clo. N14	81	DJ43
Gerrards Cross Rd., Slou.	132	AU66
Gerrards Mead, Bans.	233	CZ117
Garratts La.		
Gerridge St. SE1	**278**	**E6**
Gerridge St. SE1	161	DN76
Gerry Raffles Sq. E15	143	ED65
Salway Rd.		
Gertrude Rd., Belv.	166	FA77
Gertrude St. SW10	160	DC79
Gervaise Clo., Slou.	131	AM74
Gervase Clo., Wem.	118	CQ62
Gervase Rd., Edg.	96	CQ53
Gervase St. SE15	162	DV80
Gews Cor. (Cheshunt), Wal.Cr.	67	DX29
Ghent St. SE6	183	EA89
Ghent Way E8	142	DT65
Giant Arches Rd. SE24	182	DQ87
Giant Tree Hill (Bushey), Wat.	95	CD46
Gibb Cft., Harl.	51	ES19
Gibbard Ms. SW19	179	CX92
Gibbfield Clo., Rom.	126	EY55
Gibbins Rd. E15	143	EC66
Gibbon Rd. SE15	162	DW82
Gibbon Rd. W3	138	CS73
Gibbon Rd., Kings.T.	198	CL95
Gibbon Wk. SW15	159	CU84
Swinburne Rd.		
Gibbons Clo., Borwd.	78	CL39
Gibbons Rd. NW10	138	CS65
Gibbs Ave. SE19	182	DR92
Gibbs Clo. SE19	182	DR92
Gibbs Clo. (Cheshunt), Wal.Cr.	67	DX29
Gibbs Couch, Wat.	94	BX48
Gibbs Grn. W14	159	CZ78
Gibbs Grn., Edg.	96	CQ50
Gibbs Rd. N18	100	DW49
Gibbs Sq. SE19	182	DR92
Gibraltar Clo., Brwd.	107	FW51
Essex Way		
Gibraltar Cres., Epsom	216	CS110
Gibraltar Ho., Brwd.	107	FW51
Gibraltar Wk. E2	142	DT69
Colebert Ave.		
Gibson Clo. E1	142	DW70
Gibson Clo. N21	81	DN44
Gibson Clo., Chess.	215	CJ107
Gibson Clo., Epp.	71	FC25
Beamish Clo.		
Gibson Clo., Grav.	191	GF90
Gibson Clo., Islw.	157	CD83
Gibson Ct., Slou.	153	AZ78
Gibson Gdns. N16	122	DT61
Northwold Rd.		
Gibson Pl., Stai.	174	BJ86
Gibson Rd. SE11	**278**	**C9**
Gibson Rd. SE11	161	DM77
Gibson Rd., Dag.	126	EW60
Gibson Rd., Sutt.	218	DB106
Gibson Rd., Uxb.	114	BM63
Gibson Sq. N1	141	DN67
Gibson St. SE10	164	EE78
Gibson's Hill SW16	181	DN94
Gidd Hill, Couls.	234	DG116
Gidea Ave., Rom.	127	FG55
Gidea Clo., Rom.	127	FG55
Gidea Clo., S.Ock.	149	FW69
Tyssen Pl.		
Gideon Clo., Belv.	167	FB77
Gideon Rd. SW11	160	DG84
Gidian Ct., St.Alb.	61	CD27
Giesbach Rd. N19	121	DJ61
Giffard Rd. N18	100	DS50
Giffard Way, Guil.	242	AU131
Giffin St. SE8	163	EA80
Gifford Gdns. W7	137	CD71
Gifford Pl., Brwd.	108	FX50
Blackthorn Way		
Gifford St. N1	141	DL66
Giffordside, Grays	171	GH78
Gift La. E15	144	EF67
Giggs Hill, Orp.	206	EU96
Giggs Hill Gdns., T.Ditt.	197	CG102
Giggs Hill Rd., T.Ditt.	197	CG101
Gilbert Clo. SE18	165	EM81
Gilbert Clo., Swans.	189	FX86
Gilbert Gro., Edg.	96	CR53
Gilbert Ho. EC2	142	DQ71
Fore St.		
Gilbert Ho. SE8	163	EA79
McMillan St.		
Gilbert Pl. WC1	**273**	**P7**
Gilbert Rd. SE11	**278**	**E9**
Gilbert Rd. SE11	161	DN77
Gilbert Rd. SW19	180	DC94
Gilbert Rd., Belv.	166	FA76
Gilbert Rd., Brom.	184	EG94
Gilbert Rd., Grays	169	FW76
Gilbert Rd., Pnr.	116	BX56
Gilbert Rd., Rom.	127	FF56
Gilbert Rd., Uxb.	92	BK54
Gilbert St. E15	124	EE63
Gilbert St. W1	**272**	**G9**
Gilbert St., W1	140	DG72
Gilbert St., Enf.	82	DW37
Gilbert St., Houns.	156	CC83
High St.		
Gilbey Way, Berk.	38	AU19
Gilbey Clo., Uxb.	115	BP63
Gilbey Rd. SW17	180	DE91
Gilbey Wk., H.Wyc.	110	AD59
Stratford Dr.		
Gilbeys Yd. NW1	141	DH67
Oval Rd.		
Gilbourne Rd. SE18	165	ET79
Gilda Ave., Enf.	83	DY43
Gilda Cres. N16	122	DU60
Gildea St. W1	**273**	**J7**
Gilden Clo., Harl.	36	EY11
Gilden Cres. NW5	120	DG64
Gilden Way, Harl.	36	EW12
Gildenhill Rd., Swan.	188	FJ93
Gilders, Saw.	36	EX05
Gilders Rd., Chess.	216	CM108
Gildersome St. SE18	165	EN79
Nightingale Vale		
Giles Clo., Rain.	148	FK68
Giles Coppice SE19	182	DT91
Giles Travers Clo., Egh.	193	BC97
Gilfrid Clo., Uxb.	135	BP72
Craig Dr.		
Gilhams Ave., Bans.	217	CX112
Gilkes Cres. SE21	182	DS86
Gilkes Pl. SE21	182	DS86
Gill Ave. E16	144	EG72
Gill Cres., Grav.	191	GF90
Gill St. E14	143	DZ73
Gillam Way, Rain.	147	FG65
Gillan Grn. (Bushey), Wat.	94	CC47
Gillards Ms. E17	123	EA56
Gillards Way		
Gillards Way E17	123	EA56
Gillender St. E3	143	EC70
Gillender St. E14	143	EC70
Gillespie Rd. N5	121	DN62
Gillett Ave. E6	144	EL68
Gillett Pl. N16	122	DS64
Gillett St.		
Gillett Rd., Th.Hth.	202	DR98
Gillett St. N16	122	DS64
Gillfoot NW1	**273**	**K1**
Gillfoot NW1	141	DJ68
Gillham Ter. N17	100	DU51
Gillian Gro., Pur.	220	DN110
Gillian Cres., Rom.	106	FJ54
Gillian Ave., St.Alb.	42	CC24
Gillian Pk. Rd., Sutt.	199	CZ102
Gillian St. SE13	183	EB85
Gilliat Clo., Iver	133	BE72
Dutton Way		
Gilliat Dr., Guil.	243	BD132
Gilliat Rd., Slou.	132	AS73
Gilliat's Grn., Rick.	73	BD42
Gillies St. NW5	120	DG64
Gilling Ct. NW3	140	DE66
Gillingham Ms. SW1	**277**	**K8**
Gillingham Rd. NW2	119	CY62
Gillingham Row SW1	**277**	**K8**
Gillingham St. SW1	**277**	**J8**
Gillingham St. SW1	161	DJ77
Gillison Wk. SE16	162	DU76
Tranton Rd.		
Gillman Dr. E15	144	EF67
Gillmans Rd., Orp.	206	EV102
Gills Hill, Rad.	77	CF35
Gills Hill La., Rad.	77	CF36
Gills Hollow, Rad.	77	CF36
Gill's Rd., Dart.	209	FS95
Gillum Clo., Barn.	98	DF46
Gilmais, Lthd.	246	CC125
Gilman Cres., Wind.	151	AK83
Gilmore Clo., Slou.	152	AW75
Gilmore Clo., Uxb.	114	BN62
Gilmore Cres., Ashf.	174	BN92
Gilmore Rd. SE13	163	ED84
Gilmour Clo., Wal.Cr.	82	DU35
Gilpin Ave. SW14	158	CR84
Gilpin Clo., Mitch.	200	DE96
Gilpin Cres. N18	100	DT50
Gilpin Cres., Twick.	176	CB87
Gilpin Rd. E5	123	DY63
Gilpin Rd., Ware	33	DY07
Gilpin Way, Hayes	155	BR80
Gilpin's Gallop, Ware	33	EB11
Gilpins Ride, Berk.	38	AX18
Gilroy Clo., Rain.	147	FF65
Gilroy Way, Orp.	206	EV101
Gilsland, Wal.Abb.	84	EE35
Gilsland Rd., Th.Hth.	202	DR98
Gilstead Ho., Bark.	146	EV68
Gilstead Rd. SW6	160	DB82
Gilston Rd. SW10	160	DC78
Giltspur St. EC1	**274**	**G8**
Giltspur St. EC1	141	DP72
Gilwell Clo. E4	83	EB42
Antlers Hill		
Gilwell La. E4	83	ED42
Gilwell Pk. E4	83	EC41
Gimcrack Hill, Lthd.	231	CH123
Dorking Rd.		
Gippeswyck Clo., Pnr.	94	BX53
Uxbridge Rd.		
Gipsy Hill SE19	182	DS92
Gipsy La. SW15	159	CU83
Gipsy La., Grays	170	GC79
Gipsy Rd. SE27	182	DQ91
Gipsy Rd., Well.	166	EX81
Gipsy Rd. Gdns. SE27	182	DQ91
Giralda Clo. E16	144	EK71
Fulmer Rd.		
Giraud St. E14	143	EB72
Girdlers Rd. W14	159	CX77
Girdlestone Wk. N19	121	DJ61
Girdwood Rd. SW18	179	CY87
Girling Way, Felt.	155	BU83
Gironde Rd. SW6	159	CZ80
Girtin Rd. (Bushey), Wat.	76	CB43
Girton Ave. NW9	118	CN55
Girton Clo., Nthlt.	136	CC65
Girton Ct., Wal.Cr.	67	DY30
Girton Gdns., Croy.	203	EA104
Girton Rd. SE26	183	DX92
Girton Rd., Nthlt.	136	CC65
Girton Vill. W10	139	CX72
Cambridge Gdns.		
Girton Way, Rick.	75	BQ43
Gisborne Gdns., Rain.	147	FF69
Gisbourne Clo., Wall.	201	DK104
Gisburn Rd. N8	121	DM56
Gisburne Ho., Wat.	75	BU37
Gisburne Way, Wat.	75	BU37
Gissing Wk. N1	141	DN66
Lofting Rd.		
Gittens Clo., Brom.	184	EF91
Given Wilson Wk. E13	144	EF68
Stride Rd.		
Givons Gro., Lthd.	247	CH125
Glacier Way, Wem.	137	CK68
Gladbeck Way, Enf.	81	DP43
Gladding Rd. E12	124	EK63
Glade, The N21	81	DM44
Glade, The SE7	164	EJ80
Glade, The, Brwd.	109	GA46
Glade, The, Brom.	204	EK96
Glade, The, Couls.	235	DN119
Glade, The, Croy.	203	DX99
Glade, The, Enf.	81	DN41
Glade, The, Epsom	217	CU106
Glade, The, Ger.Cr.	112	AX60
Glade, The, H.Wyc.	88	AC46
Glade, The, Ilf.	103	EM53
Glade, The, Lthd.	230	CA122
Glade, The, Sev.	257	FH123
Glade, The, Stai.	174	BH94
Glade, The, Sutt.	217	CY109
Glade, The, Tad.	234	DA121
Glade, The, Upmin.	128	FQ64
Glade, The, W.Byf.	211	BE113
Glade, The, W.Wick.	203	EB104
Glade, The, Wdf.Grn.	102	EH48
Glade Clo., Surb.	197	CK100
Glade Ct., Ilf.	103	EM53
The Glade		
Glade Gdns., Croy.	203	DY101
Glade La., Sthl.	156	CB75
Glade Spur, Tad.	234	DB121
Glades, The, Grav.	191	GK93
Glades Pl., Brom.	204	EG96
Glades Shop. Cen., The, Brom.	204	EG96
Gladeside N21	99	DM45
Gladeside, Croy.	203	DX101
Gladeside, St.Alb.	43	CK17
Gladeside Clo., Chess.	215	CK108
Leatherhead Rd.		
Gladeside Ct., Warl.	236	DV120
Gladesmore Rd. N15	122	DT58
Gladeswood Rd., Belv.	167	FB77
Gladeway, The, Wal.Abb.	67	ED33
Gladiator St. SE23	183	DY87
Glading Ter. N16	122	DT62
Gladioli Clo., Hmptn.	176	CA93
Gresham Rd.		
Gladsdale Dr., Pnr.	115	BV56
Gladsmuir Clo., Walt.	196	BW103
Gladsmuir Rd. N19	121	DJ60
Gladsmuir Rd., Barn.	79	CY40
Gladstone Ave. E12	144	EL66
Gladstone Ave. N22	99	DN54
Gladstone Ave., Felt.	175	BU86
Gladstone Ave., Twick.	177	CD87
Gladstone Clo., Ware	33	DX05
High Oak Rd.		
Gladstone Ms. NW6	139	CZ66
Cavendish Rd.		
Gladstone Ms. SE20	182	DW94
Gladstone Pk. Gdns. NW2	119	CV63
Gladstone Pl. E3	143	DZ68
Roman Rd.		
Gladstone Pl., Barn.	79	CX42
Gladstone Rd. SW19	180	DA94
Gladstone Rd. W4	158	CR76
Acton La.		
Gladstone Rd., Ash.	231	CK118
Gladstone Rd., Buck.H.	102	EH46
Gladstone Rd., Chesh.	54	AQ31
Gladstone Rd., Croy.	202	DR101
Gladstone Rd., Dart.	188	FM86
Gladstone Rd., Hodd.	49	EB16
Gladstone Rd., Kings.T.	198	CN97
Gladstone Rd., Orp.	223	EQ106
Gladstone Rd., Sthl.	156	BY75
Gladstone Rd., Surb.	197	CK103
Gladstone Rd., Ware	33	DX05
Gladstone Rd., Wat.	76	BW41
Gladstone St. SE1	**278**	**F6**
Gladstone St. SE1	161	DP76
Gladstone Ter. SE27	182	DQ91
Gladstone Ter. SW8	161	DH81
Gladstone Way, Har.	117	CE55
Gladstone Way, Slou.	131	AN74
Gladwell Rd. N8	121	DM58
Gladwell Rd., Brom.	184	EG93
Gladwyn Rd. SW15	159	CX83
Gladys Rd. NW6	140	DA66
Glaisher St. SE10	163	EC80
Straightsmouth		
Glaisyer Way, Iver	133	BC68
Glamis Clo. (Cheshunt), Wal.Cr.	66	DU29
Glamis Cres., Hayes	155	BQ76
Glamis Dr., Horn.	128	FL60
Glamis Pl. E1	142	DW73
Glamis Rd. E1	142	DW73
Glamis Way, Nthlt.	136	CC65
Glamorgan Clo., Mitch.	201	DL97
Glamorgan Rd., Kings.T.	177	CJ94
Glanfield, Hem.H.	40	BL17
Bathurst Rd.		
Glanfield Rd., Beck.	203	DZ98
Glanleam Rd., Stan.	95	CK49
Glanmead, Brwd.	108	FY46
Glanmor Rd., Slou.	132	AV73
Glanthams Clo., Brwd.	109	FZ47
Glanthams Rd., Brwd.	109	FZ47
Glanty, The, Egh.	173	BB91
Glanville Dr., Horn.	128	FM60
Glanville Rd. SW2	181	DL85
Glanville Rd., Brom.	204	EH97
Glasbrook Ave., Twick.	176	BZ88
Glasbrook Rd. SE9	184	EK87
Glaserton Rd. N16	122	DS59
Glasford St. SW17	180	DF93
Glasgow Ho. W9	140	DB68
Glasgow Rd. E13	144	EH68
Glasgow Rd. N18	100	DV50
Aberdeen Rd.		
Glasgow Rd., Slou.	131	AN72
Glasgow Ter. SW1	161	DJ78
Glass St. E2	142	DV70
Coventry Rd.		
Glass Yd. SE18	165	EN76
Glasse Clo. W13	137	CG73
Glasshill St. SE1	**278**	**G4**
Glasshill St. SE1	161	DP75
Glasshouse All. EC4	**274**	**E9**
Glasshouse Flds. E1	143	DX73
Glasshouse St. W1	**277**	**L1**
Glasshouse St. W1	141	DJ73
Glasshouse Wk. SE11	**278**	**A10**
Glasshouse Wk. SE11	161	DL78
Glasshouse Yd. EC1	**275**	**H5**
Glasslyn Rd. N8	121	DK57
Glassmill La., Brom.	204	EF96
Glastonbury Ave., Wdf.Grn.	102	EK52
Glastonbury Clo., Orp.	206	EW102
Glastonbury Rd. N9	100	DT46
Glastonbury Rd., Mord.	200	DA101
Glastonbury St. NW6	119	CZ64
Glaucus St. E3	143	EB71
Glazbury Rd. W14	159	CY77
Glazebrook Clo. SE21	182	DR89
Glazebrook Rd., Tedd.	177	CF94
Glean Wk., Hat.	45	CU21
Southdown Rd.		
Gleave Clo., St.Alb.	43	CH19
Glebe, The SE3	164	EE83
Glebe, The SW16	181	DK91
Glebe, The, Chis.	205	EQ95
Glebe, The, Horl.	268	DF148
Glebe, The, Kings L.	58	BN29
Glebe, The, Reig.	265	CU141
Glebe, The, Wat.	60	BX33
Glebe, The, West Dr.	154	BM77
Glebe, The, Wor.Pk.	199	CT102
Glebe Ave., Enf.	81	DP41
Glebe Ave., Har.	118	CL55
Glebe Ave., Mitch.	200	DE96
Glebe Ave., Ruis.	133	BV65
Glebe Ave., Uxb.	115	BQ63
Glebe Ave., Wdf.Grn.	102	EG51
Glebe Clo. W4	158	CS78
Glebe St.		
Glebe Clo., Ger.Cr.	90	AX52
Glebe Clo., Hat.	46	DF17
Glebe Clo., Hem.H.	40	BL23
Glebe Clo., Lthd.	246	CA126
Glebe Clo., S.Croy.	220	DT111
Glebe Clo., Uxb.	115	BQ63
Glebe Cotts., Guil.	244	BH132
Glebe Cotts., Hat.	46	DF17
Glebe Cotts., Sutt.	218	DB105
Vale Rd.		
Glebe Cotts., West.	240	EV123

Glebe Ct. W7 137 CD73
Glebe Ct., Guil. 243 AZ134
Glebe Ct., Mitch. 200 DF97
Glebe Ct., Stan. 95 CJ50
Glebe Rd.
Glebe Cres. NW4 119 CW56
Glebe Cres., Har. 118 CL55
Glebe Gdns., N.Mal. 198 CS101
Glebe Gdns., W.Byf. 212 BK114
Glebe Ho. Dr., Brom. 204 EH102
Glebe Hyrst SE19 182 DT91
Giles Coppice
Glebe Hyrst, S.Croy. 220 DT112
Glebe La., Barn. 79 CU43
Glebe La., Dor. 262 BX143
Glebe La., Har. 118 CL56
Glebe La., Sev. 257 FH126
Glebe Path, Mitch. 200 DE97
Glebe Pl. SW3 160 DE79
Glebe Pl. (Horton Kirby), Dart. 208 FQ98
Glebe Rd. E8 142 DT66
Middleton Rd.
Glebe Rd. N3 98 DC53
Glebe Rd. N8 121 DM56
Glebe Rd. NW10 139 CT65
Glebe Rd. SW13 159 CU82
Glebe Rd., Ash. 231 CK118
Glebe Rd., Brom. 204 EG95
Glebe Rd., Cars. 218 DF107
Glebe Rd., Dag. 147 FB65
Glebe Rd., Dor. 263 CF136
Glebe Rd., Egh. 173 BC93
Glebe Rd., Ger.Cr. 90 AW53
Glebe Rd., Grav. 191 GF88
Glebe Rd., Hayes 135 BT74
Glebe Rd., Hert. 32 DR07
Glebe Rd., Rain. 147 FH69
Glebe Rd., Red. 235 DH124
Glebe Rd., Stai. 174 BH92
Glebe Rd., Stan. 95 CJ50
Glebe Rd., Sutt. 217 CY109
Glebe Rd., Uxb. 134 BJ68
Glebe Rd., Warl. 237 DX117
Glebe Rd., Wind. 172 AV85
Glebe Side, Twick. 177 CF87
Glebe St. W4 158 CS78
Glebe Ter. E3 143 EA69
Bow Rd.
Glebe Way, Amer. 55 AR36
Glebe Way, Erith 167 FE79
Glebe Way, Felt. 176 CA90
Glebe Way, Horn. 128 FL59
Glebe Way, S.Croy. 220 DT112
Glebe Way, W.Wick. 203 EC103
Glebefield, The, Sev. 256 FF123
Glebeland, Hat. 45 CW18
St. Ethelreda's Dr.
Glebeland Gdns., Shep. 195 BQ100
Glebelands, Chig. 104 EV48
Glebelands, Dart. 167 FF84
Glebelands, Esher 215 CF109
Glebelands, Harl. 35 ET12
Glebelands, H.Wyc. 88 AC47
Glebelands, W.Mol. 196 CB99
Glebelands Ave. E18 102 EG54
Glebelands Ave., Ilf. 125 ER59
Glebelands Clo. SE5 162 DS83
Grove Hill Rd.
Glebelands Rd., Felt. 175 BU87
Glebeway, Wdf.Grn. 102 EJ50
Gledhow Gdns. SW5 160 DC77
Gledhow Wd., Tad. 234 DB121
Gledstanes Rd. W14 159 CY78
Gledwood Ave., Hayes 135 BT71
Gledwood Cres., Hayes 135 BT71
Gledwood Dr., Hayes 135 BT71
Gledwood Gdns., Hayes 135 BT71
Gleed Ave. (Bushey), Wat. 95 CD47
Gleeson Dr., Orp. 223 ET106
Glegg Pl. SW15 159 CX84
Glen, The, Add. 211 BF106
Glen, The, Brom. 204 EE96
Glen, The, Croy. 203 DX104
Glen, The, Enf. 81 DP42
Glen, The, Hem.H. 40 BM15
Glen, The, Nthwd. 93 BR52
Glen, The, Orp. 205 EM104
Glen, The, Pnr. 116 BY59
Glen, The (Eastcote), Pnr. 115 BV57
Glen, The, Rain. 148 FJ70
Glen, The, Slou. 152 AW77
Glen, The, Sthl. 156 BZ78
Glen, The, Wem. 117 CK63
Glen Albyn Rd. SW19 179 CX89
Glen Ave., Ashf. 174 BN91
Glen Clo., Shep. 194 BN98
Glen Clo., Tad. 233 CY123
Glen Cres., Wdf.Grn. 102 EH51
Glen Faba Rd., Harl. 50 EF17
Glen Gdns., Croy. 201 DP104
Glen Ri., Wdf.Grn. 102 EH51
Glen Rd. E13 144 EJ70
Glen Rd. E17 123 DZ57
Glen Rd., Chess. 198 CL104
Glen Rd. End, Wall. 219 DH109
Glen Ter. E14 163 EC75
Manchester Rd.
Glen Vw., Grav. 191 GJ88
Glen Wk., Islw. 177 CD85
Glen Way, Wat. 75 BS38
Glena Mt., Sutt. 218 DC105
Glenaffric Ave. E14 163 ED77
Glenalla Rd., Ruis. 115 BT59
Glenalmond Rd., Har. 118 CL56
Glenalvon Way SE18 164 EL77
Glenarm Rd. E5 122 DW64
Glenavon Clo., Esher 215 CG107
Glenavon Gdns., Slou. 152 AW77
Glenavon Rd. E15 144 EE66
Glenbarr Clo. SE9 165 EP83
Dumbreck Rd.
Glenbow Rd., Brom. 184 EE93
Glenbrook N., Enf. 81 DM42
Glenbrook Rd. NW6 120 DA64
Glenbrook S., Enf. 81 DM42
Glenbuck Ct., Surb. 197 CK100
Glenbuck Rd.
Glenbuck Rd., Surb. 197 CK100
Glenburnie Rd. SW17 180 DE90
Glencairn Dr. W5 137 CJ70
Glencairn Rd. SW16 181 DL94
Glencairne Clo. E16 144 EK71
Glencoe Ave., Ilf. 125 ER59
Glencoe Dr., Dag. 126 FA63
Glencoe Rd., Hayes 136 BX70
Glencoe Rd. (Bushey), Wat. 76 CA44
Glencoe Rd., Wey. 194 BN104
Glencourse Grn., Wat. 94 BX49
Caldwell Rd.
Glendale, Hem.H. 40 BH20
Glendale, Swan. 207 FF99
Glendale Ave. N22 99 DN52
Glendale Ave., Edg. 96 CN49
Glendale Ave., Rom. 126 EW59
Glendale Clo. SE9 165 EN83
Dumbreck Rd.
Glendale Clo., Brwd. 108 FY46
Glendale Clo., Wok. 226 AW118
Glendale Dr. SW19 179 CZ92
Glendale Dr., Guil. 243 BC131
Glendale Gdns., Wem. 117 CK60
Glendale Ms., Beck. 203 EB95
Glendale Ri., Ken. 235 DP115
Glendale Rd., Erith 167 FC77
Glendale Rd., Grav. 190 GE91
Glendale Wk. (Cheshunt), Wal.Cr. 67 DY30
Glendale Way SE28 146 EW73
Glendall St. SW9 161 DM84
Glendarvon St. SW15 159 CX83
Glendene Ave., Lthd. 245 BS126
Glendevon Clo., Edg. 96 CP48
Tayside Dr.
Glendish Rd. N17 100 DU53
Glendor Gdns. NW7 96 CR49
Glendower Cres., Orp. 206 EU100
Glendower Gdns. SW14 158 CR83
Glendower Rd.
Glendower Pl. SW7 160 DD77
Glendower Rd. E4 101 ED46
Glendower Rd. SW14 158 CR83
Glendown Rd. SE2 166 EU78
Glendun Rd. W3 138 CS73
Gleneagle Ms. SW16 181 DK92
Ambleside Ave.
Gleneagle Rd. SW16 181 DK93
Gleneagles, Stan. 95 CH51
Gleneagles Clo. SE16 162 DV78
Ryder Dr.
Gleneagles Clo., Orp. 205 ER102
Gleneagles Clo., Rom. 106 FM52
Gleneagles Clo., Stai. 174 BK86
Gleneagles Clo., Stan. 95 CH51
Gleneagles Clo., Wat. 94 BX49
Gleneagles Grn., Orp. 205 ER102
Tandridge Dr.
Gleneagles Twr., Sthl. 136 CC72
Gleneldon Ms. SW16 181 DL91
Gleneldon Rd. SW16 181 DL91
Glenelg Rd. SW2 181 DL85
Glenesk Rd. SE9 165 EN83
Glenester Clo., Hodd. 33 EA14
Glenfarg Rd. SE6 183 ED88
Glenferrie Rd., St.Alb. 43 CG20
Glenfield Clo., Bet. 264 CP138
Glenfield Cres., Ruis. 115 BR59
Glenfield Rd. SW12 181 DJ88
Glenfield Rd. W13 157 CH75
Glenfield Rd., Ashf. 175 BP93
Glenfield Rd., Bans. 234 DB115
Glenfield Rd., Bet. 264 CP138
Glenfield Ter. W13 137 CH74
Glenfinlas Way SE5 161 DP80
Glenforth St. SE10 164 EF78
Glengall Causeway E14 163 EA76
Glengall Gro. E14 163 EC76
Glengall Rd. NW6 139 CZ67
Glengall Rd. SE15 162 DT78
Glengall Rd., Bexh. 166 EY83
Glengall Rd., Edg. 96 CP48
Glengall Rd., Wdf.Grn. 102 EG51
Glengall Ter. SE15 162 DT79
Glengarnock Ave. E14 163 EC77
Glengarry Rd. SE22 182 DS85
Glenham Dr., Ilf. 125 EP57
Glenhaven Ave., Borwd. 78 CN41
Glenhead Clo. SE9 165 EP83
Dumbreck Rd.
Glenheadon Clo., Lthd. 231 CK123
Glenheadon Ri.
Glenheadon Ri., Lthd. 231 CK123
Glenhill Clo. N3 98 DA54
Glenhouse Rd. SE9 185 EN85
Glenhurst Ave. NW5 120 DG63
Glenhurst Ave., Bex. 186 EZ88
Glenhurst Ave., Ruis. 115 BQ59
Glenhurst Ct. SE19 182 DT92
Glenhurst Ri. SE19 182 DQ94
Glenhurst Rd. N12 98 DD50
Glenhurst Rd., Brent. 157 CJ79
Glenilla Rd. NW3 140 DE65
Glenister Ho., Hayes 135 BV74
Glenister Pk. Rd. SW16 181 DK94
Glenister Rd. SE10 164 EF78
Glenister Rd., Chesh. 54 AQ28
Glenister St. E16 145 EN74
Glenlea Rd. SE9 185 EN85
Glenlion Ct., Wey. 195 BR104
Glenloch Rd. NW3 140 DE65
Glenloch Rd., Enf. 82 DW40
Glenluce Rd. SE3 164 EG79
Glenlyn Ave., St.Alb. 43 CH21
Glenlyon Rd. SE9 185 EN85
Glenmere Ave. NW7 97 CU52
Glenmill, Hmptn. 176 BZ92
Glenmire Ter., Ware 33 ED11
Glenmore Clo., Add. 194 BH104
Glenmore Gdns., Abb.L. 59 BU32
Stewart Clo.
Glenmore Rd. NW3 140 DE65
Glenmore Rd., Well. 165 ET80
Glenmore Way, Bark. 146 EU69
Glenmount Path SE18 165 EQ78
Raglan Rd.
Glenn Ave., Pur. 219 DP111
Glennie Rd. SE27 181 DN90
Glenny Rd., Bark. 145 EQ65
Glenorchy Clo., Hayes 136 BY71
Glenparke Rd. E7 144 EH65
Glenrosa Gdns., Grav. 191 GM92
Glenrosa St. SW6 160 DC82
Glenrose Ct., Sid. 186 EV92
Glenroy St. W12 139 CW72
Glensdale Rd. SE4 163 DZ83
Glenshee Clo., Nthwd. 93 BQ51
Merrows Clo.
Glenshiel Rd. SE9 185 EN85
Glenside, Chig. 103 EP51
Glenside Cotts., Slou. 152 AT76
Upton Pk.
Glentanner Way SW17 180 DD90
Aboyne Rd.
Glentham Gdns. SW13 159 CV79
Glentham Rd.
Glentham Rd. SW13 159 CU79
Glenthorne Ave., Croy. 202 DV102
Glenthorne Clo., Sutt. 200 DA102
Glenthorne Clo., Uxb. 134 BN69
Uxbridge Rd.
Glenthorne Gdns., Ilf. 125 EN55
Glenthorne Gdns., Sutt. 200 DA102
Glenthorne Ms. W6 159 CV77
Glenthorne Rd.
Glenthorne Rd. E17 123 DY57
Glenthorne Rd. N11 98 DF50
Glenthorne Rd. W6 159 CV77
Glenthorne Rd., Kings.T. 198 CM98
Glenthorpe Rd., Mord. 199 CX99
Glenton Clo., Rom. 105 FE51
Glenton Rd. SE13 164 EE84
Glenton Way, Rom. 105 FE52
Glentrammon Ave., Orp. 223 ET107
Glentrammon Clo., Orp. 223 ET106
Glentrammon Gdns., Orp. 223 ET107
Glentrammon Rd., Orp. 223 ET107
Glentworth St. NW1 272 E5
Glentworth St. NW1 140 DF70
Glenure Rd. SE9 185 EN85
Glenview SE2 166 EX79
Glenview Gdns., Hem.H. 40 BH20
Glenview Rd.
Glenview Rd., Brom. 204 EK96
Glenview Rd., Hem.H. 40 BH20
Glenville Ave., Enf. 82 DQ38
Glenville Gro. SE8 163 DZ80
Glenville Ms. SW18 180 DB87
Glenville Rd., Kings.T. 198 CN95
Glenwood, Brox. 49 DZ19
Glenwood, Dor. 263 CJ138
Glenwood, Welw.G.C. 30 DD10
Glenwood Ave. NW9 118 CS60
Glenwood Ave., Rain. 147 FG70
Glenwood Clo., Har. 117 CF57
Glenwood Dr., Rom. 127 FG57
Glenwood Gdns., Ilf. 125 EN57
Glenwood Gro. NW9 118 CQ60
Glenwood Rd. N15 121 DP57
Glenwood Rd. NW7 96 CS48
Glenwood Rd. SE6 183 DZ88
Glenwood Rd., Epsom 217 CU107
Glenwood Rd., Houns. 157 CD83
Glenwood Way, Croy. 203 DX100
Glenworth Ave. E14 163 ED77
Glenworth Pl., Slou. 131 AQ74
Glevum Clo., St.Alb. 42 BZ22
Gliddon Rd. W14 159 CY77
Glimpsing Grn., Erith 166 EY76
Glisson Rd., Uxb. 134 BN68
Gload Cres., Orp. 206 EX103
Global App. E3 143 EB68
Hancock Rd.
Globe Ct., Hert. 32 DQ07
Grove Wk.
Globe Ind. Estates, Grays 170 GC78
Globe Pond Rd. SE16 143 DY74
Globe Rd. E1 143 DX70
Globe Rd. E2 142 DW69
Globe Rd. E15 124 EF64
Globe Rd., Horn. 127 FG58
Globe Rd., Wdf.Grn. 102 EJ51
Globe Rope Wk. E14 163 EC77
Stebondale St.
Globe St. SE1 279 K5
Globe St. SE1 162 DR75
Globe Ter. E2 142 DW69
Globe Rd.
Globe Yd. W1 273 H9
Glory Clo., H.Wyc. 110 AF56
Glory Mead, Dor. 263 CH139
Glory Mill La., H.Wyc. 110 AE56
Glossop Rd., S.Croy. 220 DR109
Gloster Rd., N.Mal. 198 CS98
Gloster Rd., Wok. 227 BA121
Gloucester Ave. NW1 140 DG66
Gloucester Ave., Grays 170 GC75
Gloucester Ave., Horn. 128 FN56
Gloucester Ave., Sid. 185 ES89
Gloucester Ave., Slou. 131 AQ71
Gloucester Ave., Wal.Cr. 67 DY33
Gloucester Ave., Well. 165 ET84
Gloucester Circ. SE10 163 EC80
Gloucester Clo. NW10 138 CR66
Gloucester Clo., S.Ock. 149 FW69
South Rd.
Gloucester Clo., T.Ditt. 197 CG102
Gloucester Ct. EC3 279 N1
Gloucester Ct., Rich. 158 CN80
Gloucester Ct., Til. 171 GF82
Dock Rd.
Gloucester Ct., Uxb. 114 BG58
Moorfield Rd.
Gloucester Cres. NW1 141 DH67
Gloucester Cres., Stai. 174 BK93
Gloucester Dr. N4 121 DP61
Gloucester Dr. NW11 120 DA56
Gloucester Dr., Stai. 173 BC90
Gloucester Gdns. NW11 119 CZ59
Gloucester Gdns. W2 140 DC72
Bishops Bri. Rd.
Gloucester Gdns., Barn. 80 DG42
Gloucester Gdns., Ilf. 124 EL59
Gloucester Gdns., Sutt. 200 DB103
Gloucester Gate NW1 141 DH68
Gloucester Gate Ms. NW1 141 DH68
Gloucester Gate
Gloucester Gro., Edg. 96 CR53
Gloucester Gro. Est. SE15 162 DS79
Gloucester Ho. N7 121 DL62
Gloucester Ho. NW6 140 DA68
Gloucester Ms. E10 123 EA59
Gloucester Rd.
Gloucester Ms. W2 140 DC72
Gloucester Ms. W. W2 140 DC72
Cleveland Ter.
Gloucester Par., Sid. 186 EU85
Gloucester Pl. NW1 272 D4
Gloucester Pl. NW1 140 DF70
Gloucester Pl. W1 272 E6
Gloucester Pl. W1 140 DF71
Gloucester Pl., Wind. 151 AR82
Gloucester Pl. Ms. W1 272 E7
Gloucester Rd. E10 123 EA59
Gloucester Rd. E11 124 EH57
Gloucester Rd. E12 125 EM62
Gloucester Rd. E17 101 DX54
Gloucester Rd. N17 122 DR55
Gloucester Rd. N18 100 DT50
Gloucester Rd. SW7 160 DC76
Gloucester Rd. W3 158 CQ75
Gloucester Rd. W5 157 CJ75
Gloucester Rd., Barn. 80 DB43
Gloucester Rd., Belv. 166 EZ78
Gloucester Rd., Brwd. 108 FV43
Gloucester Rd., Croy. 202 DR102
Gloucester Rd., Dart. 187 FH87
Gloucester Rd., Enf. 82 DQ38
Gloucester Rd., Felt. 176 BW88
Gloucester Rd., Grav. 191 GJ91
Gloucester Rd., Guil. 242 AT132
Gloucester Rd., Hmptn. 176 CB94
Gloucester Rd., Har. 116 CB57
Gloucester Rd., Houns. 156 BY84
Gloucester Rd., Kings.T. 198 CN96
Gloucester Rd., Red. 250 DF133
Gloucester Rd., Rich. 158 CN80
Gloucester Rd., Rom. 127 FE58
Gloucester Rd., Tedd. 177 CE92
Gloucester Rd., Twick. 176 CC88
Gloucester Sq. E2 142 DU67
Whiston Rd.
Gloucester Sq. W2 272 A9
Gloucester Sq. W2 140 DD72
Gloucester Sq., Wok. 226 AY117
Church St. E.
Gloucester St. SW1 161 DJ78
Gloucester Ter. W2 140 DB72
Gloucester Wk. W8 160 DA75
Gloucester Wk., Wok. 227 AZ117
Church St. E.
Gloucester Way EC1 274 E3
Gloucester Way EC1 141 DN69
Glover Clo. SE2 166 EW77
Glover Clo., Wal.Cr. 66 DT27
Allwood Rd.
Glover Dr. N18 100 DW51
Glover Rd., Pnr. 116 BX58
Glovers Clo., Hert. 32 DQ11
Glovers Gro., Ruis. 115 BP59
Glovers La., Harl. 52 EY20
Glovers Rd., Reig. 266 DB135
Gloxinia Rd., Grav. 190 GB93
Gloxinia Wk., Hmptn. 176 CA93
The Ave.
Glycena Rd. SW11 160 DF83
Glyn Ave., Barn. 80 DD42
Glyn Clo. SE25 202 DS96
Glyn Clo., Epsom 217 CU109
Glyn Ct. SW16 181 DN90
Glyn Davies Clo., Sev. 241 FE120
Glyn Dr., Sid. 186 EV91
Glyn Rd. E5 123 DX63
Glyn Rd., Enf. 82 DW42
Glyn Rd., Wor.Pk. 199 CX103
Glyn St. SE11 161 DM78
Kennington La.
Glynde Ms. SW3 276 C7
Glynde Rd., Bexh. 166 EX83
Glynde St. SE4 183 DZ86
Glyndebourne Pk., Orp. 205 EP103
Glyndon Rd. SE18 165 EQ77
Glynfield Rd. NW10 138 CS66
Glynne Rd. N22 99 DN54
Glynswood, Ger.Cr. 91 AZ52
Glynwood Ct. SE23 182 DW90
Goat La., Enf. 82 DT38
Goat La., Surb. 197 CH103
Goat Rd., Mitch. 200 DF101
Goat St. SE1 279 P4
Goat Wf., Brent. 158 CL79
Goaters All. SW6 159 CZ80
Dawes Rd.
Goatsfield Rd., West. 238 EJ120
Goatswood La., Rom. 105 FH45
Gobions Ave., Rom. 105 FD52
Gobions Way, Pot.B. 64 DB28
Swanley Bar La.
Goblins Grn., Welw.G.C. 29 CX10
Godalming Ave., Wall. 219 DL106
Godalming Rd. E14 143 EB71
Godbold Rd. E15 144 EE69
Goddard Clo., Shep. 194 BM97
Magdalene Rd.
Goddard Rd., Beck. 203 DX98
Goddards Clo., Hert. 47 DJ19
Goddards Way, Ilf. 125 ER60
Goddington Chase, Orp. 224 EV105
Goddington La., Orp. 206 EU104
Godfrey Ave., Nthlt. 136 BY67
Godfrey Ave., Twick. 177 CD87
Godfrey Hill SE18 164 EL77
Godfrey Rd. SE18 165 EM77
Godfrey St. E15 143 EC68
Godfrey St. SW3 276 C10
Godfrey St. SW3 160 DE78
Godfrey Way, Houns. 176 BZ87
Goding St. SE11 161 DL78
Godley Rd. SW18 180 DD88
Godley Rd., W.Byf. 212 BM114
Godliman St. EC4 275 H9
Godliman St. EC4 142 DQ72
Godman Rd. SE15 162 DV82
Godman Rd., Grays 171 GG76
Godolphin Clo. N13 99 DP51
Godolphin Clo., Sutt. 217 CZ110
Godolphin Pl. W3 138 CR73
Vyner Rd.
Godolphin Rd. W12 139 CV74
Godolphin Rd., Beac. 89 AQ51
Godolphin Rd., Slou. 131 AR73
Godolphin Rd., Wey. 213 BR107
Godric Cres., Croy. 221 ED110
Godson Rd., Croy. 201 DN104
Godson St. N1 141 DN68
White Lion St.
Godstone Bypass, Gdse. 252 DW129
Godstone Grn., Gdse. 252 DV131
Godstone Grn. Rd., Gdse. 252 DV131
Godstone Hill, Gdse. 252 DV127
Godstone Rd., Cat. 236 DU124
Godstone Rd., Ken. 219 DN112
Godstone Rd., Oxt. 253 EA131
Godstone Rd., Pur. 219 DN112
Godstone Rd., Red. 252 DR133
Godstone Rd., Sutt. 218 DC105
Godstone Rd., Twick. 177 CG86
Godstone Rd., Whyt. 236 DT116
Godstow Rd. SE2 166 EV75
Godwin Clo. E4 83 EC38
Godwin Clo. N1 142 DQ68
Napier Gro.
Godwin Clo., Epsom 216 CQ107
Godwin Ct. NW1 141 DJ68
Crowndale Rd.
Godwin Rd. E7 124 EH63
Godwin Rd., Brom. 204 EJ97
Goffers Rd. SE3 164 EE82
Goffs Cres. (Cheshunt), Wal.Cr. 66 DQ29
Goffs La. (Cheshunt), Wal.Cr. 66 DR29
Goffs Oak Ave. (Cheshunt), Wal.Cr. 65 DP28
Goffs Rd., Ashf. 175 BR93
Gogmore Fm. Clo., Cher. 193 BF101
Gogmore La., Cher. 193 BF101
Goidel Clo., Wall. 219 DK105
Golborne Gdns. W10 139 CZ70
Golborne Rd.
Golborne Ms. W10 139 CY71
Portobello Rd.
Golborne Rd. W10 139 CY71
Gold Clo., Brox. 49 DY20
Gold Cft., Hem.H. 40 BN22
Gold Hill, Edg. 96 CR51
Gold Hill E., Ger.Cr. 90 AX54
Gold Hill N., Ger.Cr. 90 AW53
Gold Hill W., Ger.Cr. 90 AW54
Gold La., Edg. 96 CR51
Golda Clo., Barn. 79 CX44
Goldace, Grays 170 FZ79
Goldbeaters Gro., Edg. 96 CS51
Goldcliff Clo., Mord. 200 DA101
Goldcrest Clo. E16 144 EK71
Sheerwater Rd.
Goldcrest Clo. SE28 146 EW73
Goldcrest Clo., Horl. 268 DE147
Wither Dale
Goldcrest Ms. W5 137 CK71
Montpelier Ave.
Goldcrest Way, Croy. 221 ED109
Goldcrest Way, Pur. 219 DK110
Goldcrest Way (Bushey), Wat. 94 CC46
Golden Ct., Rich. 177 CK85
George St.
Golden Cres., Hayes 135 BS74
Golden Cross Ms. W11 139 CZ72
Basing St.
Golden Dell, Welw.G.C. 29 CZ13
Golden La. EC1 275 H5
Golden La. EC1 142 DQ70
Golden La. Est. EC1 275 H5
Golden Manor W7 137 CE73
Golden Oak Clo., Slou. 131 AQ65
Golden Plover Clo. E16 144 EH72
Maplin Rd.
Golden Sq. W1 273 L10
Golden Sq. W1 141 DJ73
Golden Yd. NW3 120 DC63
Heath St.
Golders Clo., Edg. 96 CP50
Golders Gdns. NW11 119 CY59
Golders Grn. Cres. NW11 119 CZ59
Golders Grn. Rd. NW11 119 CY58
Golders Manor Dr. NW11 119 CX58
Golders Pk. Clo. NW11 120 DA60
Golders Ri. NW4 119 CX57
Golders Way NW11 119 CZ59
Goldfinch Clo., Orp. 224 EU106
Goldfinch Gdns., Guil. 243 BD133
Goldfinch Rd. SE28 165 ER76
Goldfinch Rd., S.Croy. 221 DX110
Goldfinch Way, Borwd. 78 CN42
Siskin Clo.
Goldfort Wk., Wok. 226 AS116
Langmans Way
Goldhawk Ms. W12 159 CV75
Devonport Rd.
Goldhawk Rd. W6 159 CT77
Goldhawk Rd. W12 159 CU76
Goldhaze Clo., Wdf.Grn. 102 EK52
Goldhurst Ter. NW6 140 DB66
Golding Clo., Chess. 215 CJ107
Coppard Gdns.
Golding Rd., Sev. 257 FJ122
Golding St. E1 142 DU72
Goldingham Ave., Loug. 85 EQ40
Goldings, The, Wok. 226 AT116
Goldings Cres., Hat. 45 CV17
Goldings Hill, Loug. 85 EM37
Goldings La., Hert. 31 DN06
Goldings Ri., Loug. 85 EN39
Goldings Rd., Loug. 85 EN39
Goldington Clo., Hodd. 33 DZ14
Goldington Cres. NW1 141 DK68
Goldington Cres. Gdns. NW1 141 DK68
Goldington St. NW1 141 DK68
Goldman Clo. E2 142 DU70
Goldney Rd. W9 140 DA70
Goldrings Rd., Lthd. 214 CB113
Goldsborough Cres. E4 101 EB47
Goldsborough Rd. SW8 161 DK81
Goldsdown Clo., Enf. 83 DY40
Goldsdown Rd., Enf. 83 DX40
Goldsel Rd., Swan. 207 FD99
Goldsel Rd. Ind. Est., Swan. 207 FE98
Goldsmid St. SE18 165 ES78
Sladedale Rd.
Goldsmith, Grays 170 FZ79
Goldsmith Ave. E12 144 EL65
Goldsmith Ave. NW9 118 CS57
Goldsmith Ave. W3 138 CR73
Goldsmith Ave., Rom. 126 FA59
Goldsmith Clo. W3 138 CS74
East Acton La.
Goldsmith Clo., Har. 116 CB60
Goldsmith La. NW9 118 CP56
Goldsmith Rd. E10 123 EA60
Goldsmith Rd. E17 101 DX54
Goldsmith Rd. N11 98 DF50
Goldsmith Rd. SE15 162 DU81
Goldsmith Rd. W3 138 CR74
Goldsmith St. EC2 275 J8
Goldsmiths Clo., Wok. 226 AW118
Goldsmith's Row E2 142 DU68
Goldsmith's Sq. E2 142 DU68
Goldstone Clo., Ware 33 DX05
High Oak Rd.

Goldstone Fm. Vw., Lthd. 246 CA127
Goldsworth Orchard, Wok. 226 AU118
St. John's Rd.
Goldsworth Pk. Trd. Est., Wok. 226 AU116
Goldsworth Rd., Wok. 226 AW118
Goldsworthy Gdns. SE16 162 DW77
Goldsworthy Way, Slou. 130 AJ72
Goldwell Rd., Th.Hth. 201 DM98
Goldwin Clo. SE14 162 DW81
Goldwing Clo. E16 144 EG72
Golf Clo., Stan. 95 CJ52
Golf Clo. (Bushey), Wat. 76 BX41
Golf Clo., Wok. 211 BE114
Golf Club Dr., Kings.T. 178 CR94
Golf Club Rd., Hat. 64 DA26
Golf Club Rd., Wey. 213 BP109
Golf Club Rd., Wok. 226 AU120
Golf Ho. Rd., Oxt. 254 EJ129
Golf Links Ave., Grav. 191 GH92
Golf Ride, Enf. 81 DN35
Golf Rd. W5 138 CM72
Boileau Rd.
Golf Rd., Brom. 205 EN97
Golf Rd., Ken. 236 DR118
Golf Side, Sutt. 217 CY111
Golf Side, Twick. 177 CD90
Golfe Rd., Ilf. 125 ER62
Golfside Clo. N20 98 DE48
Golfside Clo., N.Mal. 198 CS96
Goliath Clo., Wall. 219 DL108
Avro Way
Gollogly Ter. SE7 164 EJ78
Gombards, St.Alb. 43 CD19
Gombards All., St.Alb. 43 CD20
Worley Rd.
Gomer Gdns., Tedd. 177 CG93
Gomer Pl., Tedd. 177 CG93
Gomm Rd. SE16 162 DW76
Gomms Wd. Clo., Beac. 88 AH51
Gomshall Ave., Wall. 219 DL106
Gomshall Gdns., Ken. 236 DS115
Gomshall La., Guil. 260 BN139
Gomshall Rd., Sutt. 217 CW110
Gondar Gdns. NW6 119 CZ64
Gonnerston, St.Alb. 42 CC19
Kings Rd.
Gonson Pl. SE8 163 EA79
Gonson St. SE8 163 EB79
Gonston Clo. SW19 179 CY89
Boddicott Clo.
Gonville Ave., Rick. 75 BP44
Gonville Cres., Nthlt. 136 CB65
Gonville Rd., Th.Hth. 201 DM99
Gonville St. SW6 159 CY83
Putney Bri. App.
Goodall Rd. E11 123 EC62
Gooden Ct., Har. 117 CE62
Goodenough Clo., Couls. 235 DN120
Goodenough Rd. SW19 179 CZ94
Goodenough Way, Couls. 235 DM120
Goodge Pl. W1 273 L7
Goodge St. W1 273 L7
Goodge St. W1 141 DJ71
Goodhall St. NW10 138 CS69
Goodhart Pl. E14 143 DY73
Goodhart Way, W.Wick. 204 EE101
Goodhew Rd., Croy. 202 DU100
Gooding Clo., N.Mal. 198 CQ98
Goodinge Clo. N7 141 DL65
Goodlake Ct., Uxb. 113 BF59
Goodley Stock Rd., Eden. 255 EP131
Goodley Stock Rd., West. 255 EP128
Goodman Cres. SW2 181 DK89
Goodman Pk., Slou. 132 AW74
Goodman Pl., Stai. 173 BF91
High St.
Goodman Rd. E10 123 EC59
Goodmans Ct., Wem. 117 CK63
Goodman's Flds. E1 142 DU72
Goodman's Stile
Goodman's Stile E1 142 DU72
Goodmans Yd. E1 275 P10
Goodmans Yd. E1 142 DT73
Goodmayes Ave., Ilf. 126 EU60
Goodmayes La., Ilf. 126 EU61
Goodmayes Rd., Ilf. 126 EU60
Goodmead Rd., Orp. 206 EU101
Goodrich Clo., Wat. 75 BU35
Goodrich Rd. SE22 182 DT86
Goods Way NW1 141 DL68
Goodson Rd. NW10 138 CS66
Goodway Gdns. E14 143 ED72
Goodwin Ave., Brwd. 109 GE44
Goodwin Clo. SE16 162 DU76
Goodwin Clo., Mitch. 200 DD97
Goodwin Ct., Wal.Cr. 67 DY28
Goodwin Dr., Sid. 186 EX90
Goodwin Gdns., Croy. 219 DP107
Goodwin Meadows, H.Wyc. 110 AE57
Goodwin Rd. N9 100 DW46
Goodwin Rd. W12 159 CU75
Goodwin Rd., Croy. 219 DP106
Goodwin Rd., Slou. 131 AM69
Goodwin St. N4 121 DN61
Fonthill Rd.
Goodwins Ct. WC2 273 P10
Goodwood Ave., Enf. 82 DW37
Goodwood Ave., Horn. 128 FL63
Goodwood Ave., Wat. 75 BS35
Goodwood Clo., Hodd. 49 EA16
Goodwood Clo., Mord. 200 DA98
Goodwood Clo., Stan. 95 CJ50
Goodwood Cres., Grav. 191 GJ92
Goodwood Dr., Nthlt. 136 CA65
Goodwood Path, Borwd. 78 CN41
Stratfield Rd.
Goodwood Rd. SE14 163 DY80
Goodwood Rd., Red. 250 DF132
Goodwyn Ave. NW7 96 CS50
Goodwyns Rd., Dor. 263 CH139
Goodwyns Vale N10 98 DG53
Goodyers Ave., Rad. 61 CF33
Goodyers Gdns. NW4 119 CX57
Gooseander Way SE28 165 ER76
Goose Acre, Chesh. 56 AT30
Goose Acre, Welw.G.C. 29 CZ11
Goose Cft., Hem.H. 39 BF19
Goose Grn., Cob. 229 BU119
Goose Grn., Guil. 261 BQ139
Goose Grn., Hodd. 49 DY17
Lord St.
Goose Grn., Slou. 131 AP68
Goose Grn. Clo., Orp. 206 EU96
Goose La., Wok. 226 AV122
Goose Rye Rd., Guil. 242 AT125
Goose Sq. E6 145 EM72
Harper Rd.
Gooseacre La., Har. 117 CK57
Gooseley La. E6 145 EN69
Gooshays Dr., Rom. 106 FL50
Gooshays Gdns., Rom. 106 FL51
Goossens Clo., Sutt. 218 DC106
Turnpike La.
Gophir La. EC4 275 K10
Gopsall St. N1 142 DR67
Goral Mead, Rick. 92 BK46
Gordon Ave. E4 102 EE51
Gordon Ave. SW14 158 CS84
Gordon Ave., Horn. 127 FF61
Gordon Ave., S.Croy. 220 DQ110
Gordon Ave., Stan. 95 CF52
Gordon Ave., Twick. 177 CG85
Gordon Clo. E17 123 EA58
Gordon Clo. N19 121 DJ60
Highgate Hill
Gordon Clo., Cher. 193 BE104
Gordon Clo., St.Alb. 43 CH21
Kitchener Clo.
Gordon Clo., Stai. 174 BH93
Gordon Ct. W12 139 CV72
Gordon Cres., Croy. 202 DS102
Gordon Cres., Hayes 155 BU76
Gordon Dr., Cher. 193 BE104
Gordon Dr., Shep. 195 BR100
Gordon Gdns., Edg. 96 CP54
Gordon Gro. SE5 161 DP82
Gordon Hill, Enf. 82 DQ39
Gordon Ho. Rd. NW5 120 DG63
Gordon Pl. W8 160 DA75
Gordon Pl., Grav. 191 GJ86
East Ter.
Gordon Prom., Grav. 191 GJ86
Gordon Prom. E., Grav. 191 GJ86
Gordon Rd. E4 102 EE45
Gordon Rd. E11 124 EG58
Gordon Rd. E15 123 EC63
Gordon Rd. E18 102 EH53
Gordon Rd. N3 97 CZ52
Gordon Rd. N9 100 DV47
Gordon Rd. N11 99 DK52
Gordon Rd. SE15 162 DV82
Gordon Rd. W4 158 CP79
Gordon Rd. W5 137 CJ73
Gordon Rd. W13 137 CH73
Gordon Rd., Ashf. 174 BL90
Gordon Rd., Bark. 145 ES67
Gordon Rd., Beck. 203 DZ97
Gordon Rd., Belv. 167 FC77
Gordon Rd., Brwd. 109 GA46
Gordon Rd., Cars. 218 DF107
Gordon Rd., Cat. 236 DR121
Gordon Rd., Chesh. 54 AQ32
Gordon Rd., Dart. 188 FK87
Gordon Rd., Enf. 82 DR39
Gordon Rd., Esher 215 CE108
Gordon Rd., Grav. 190 GE87
Gordon Rd., Grays 170 GE75
Gordon Rd., Har. 117 CE55
Gordon Rd., Houns. 156 CC84
Gordon Rd., Ilf. 125 ER62
Gordon Rd., Kings.T. 198 CM95
Gordon Rd., Red. 250 DG131
Gordon Rd., Rich. 158 CM82
Gordon Rd., Rom. 126 EZ58
Gordon Rd., Sev. 257 FH125
Gordon Rd., Shep. 195 BR100
Gordon Rd., Sid. 185 ES85
Gordon Rd., Sthl. 156 BY77
Gordon Rd., Stai. 173 BC91
Gordon Rd., Surb. 198 CM101
Gordon Rd., Wal.Abb. 67 EA34
Gordon Rd., West Dr. 134 BL73
Gordon Rd., Wind. 151 AM82
Gordon Sq. WC1 273 M4
Gordon Sq. WC1 141 DK70
Gordon St. E13 144 EG69
Grange Rd.
Gordon St. WC1 273 M4
Gordon St. WC1 141 DK70
Gordon Way, Barn. 79 CZ42
Gordon Way, Brom. 204 EG95
Gordon Way, Ch.St.G. 90 AV48
Gordonbrock Rd. SE4 183 EA85
Gordondale Rd. SW19 180 DA89
Gordons Way, Oxt. 253 ED128
Gore Ct. NW9 118 CN57
Gore Hill, Amer. 55 AP43
Gore Rd. E9 142 DW67
Gore Rd. SW20 199 CW96
Gore Rd., Dart. 188 FQ90
Gore Rd., Slou. 130 AH69
Gore St. SW7 160 DC76
Gorefield Pl. NW6 140 DA68
Gorelands La., Ch.St.G. 90 AX46
Gorell Rd., Beac. 89 AP54
Goresbrook Rd., Dag. 146 EV67
Goresbrook Village, Dag. 146 EV67
Goresbrook Rd.
Gorham Dr., St.Alb. 43 CE23
Gorham Pl. W11 139 CY73
Mary Pl.
Gorhambury Dr., St.Alb. 42 BZ19
Goring Clo., Rom. 105 FC53
Goring Gdns., Dag. 126 EW63
Goring Rd. N11 99 DL51
Goring Rd., Dag. 147 FD65
Goring Rd., Stai. 173 BD92
Goring St. EC3 275 N8
Goring St. EC3 142 DS72
Goring Way, Grnf. 136 CC68
Gorings Sq., Stai. 173 BE91
Gorle Clo., Wat. 59 BU34
Gorleston Rd. N15 122 DR57
Gorleston St. W14 159 CY77
Gorman Rd. SE18 165 EM77
Gorringe Ave. (South Darenth), Dart. 209 FR96
Gorringe Pk. Ave., Mitch. 180 DF94
Gorse Clo. E16 144 EG72
Gorse Clo., Hat. 45 CT21
Gorse Clo., Tad. 233 CV120
Gorse Ct., Guil. 243 BC132
Kingfisher Dr.
Gorse Hill (Farningham), Dart. 208 FN101
Gorse Hill La., Vir.W. 192 AX98
Gorse Hill Rd., Vir.W. 192 AX98
Gorse La., Wok. 210 AS108
Gorse Mead, Slou. 131 AP74
Gorse Ri. SW17 180 DG92
Gorse Rd., Croy. 203 EA104
Gorse Rd., Orp. 206 EZ102
Gorse Wk., West Dr. 134 BL72
Gorselands Clo., W.Byf. 212 BJ111
Gorseway, Rom. 127 FD61
Gorsewood Rd., Wok. 226 AS119
Gorst Rd. NW10 138 CQ70
Gorst Rd. SW11 180 DF86
Gorsuch Pl. E2 275 P2
Gorsuch St. E2 275 P2
Gorsuch St. E2 142 DT69
Gosberton Rd. SW12 180 DF88
Gosbury Hill, Chess. 216 CL105
Gosden Common, Guil. 258 AY143
Gosden Hill Rd., Guil. 243 BC130
Gosfield Rd., Dag. 126 FA61
Gosfield Rd., Epsom 216 CR112
Gosfield St. W1 273 K6
Gosfield St. W1 141 DJ71
Gosford Gdns., Ilf. 125 EM57
Gosforth La., Wat. 93 BU48
Gosforth Path, Wat. 93 BU48
Gosforth La.
Goshawk Gdns., Hayes 135 BS69
Goslar Way, Wind. 151 AP82
Goslett Yd. WC2 273 N9
Gosling Clo., Grnf. 136 CA69
Gosling Grn., Slou. 152 AY76
Gosling Rd., Slou. 152 AY76
Gosling Way SW9 161 DN81
Gospatrick Rd. N17 100 DQ52
Gospel Oak Est. NW5 120 DF64
Gosport Dr., Horn. 148 FJ65
Gosport Rd. E17 123 DZ57
Gosport Wk. N17 122 DV57
Yarmouth Cres.
Gosport Way SE15 162 DT80
Pentridge St.
Goss Hill, Dart. 188 FJ93
Goss Hill, Swan. 188 FJ93
Gossage Rd. SE18 165 ER78
Ancona Rd.
Gossage Rd., Uxb. 134 BM66
Gossamers, The, Wat. 76 BY35
Gosselin Rd., Hert. 32 DQ07
Gosset St. E2 142 DT69
Gosshill Rd., Chis. 205 EN96
Gossington Clo., Chis. 185 EP91
Beechwood Ri.
Gossoms End, Berk. 38 AU18
Gossoms Ryde, Berk. 38 AU18
Gosterwood St. SE8 163 DY79
Gostling Rd., Twick. 176 CA88
Goston Gdns., Th.Hth. 201 DN97
Goswell Hill, Wind. 151 AR81
Goswell Rd. EC1 274 F1
Goswell Rd. EC1 141 DP68
Goswell Rd., Wind. 151 AR80
Gothic Clo., Dart. 188 FK90
Gothic Ct., Hayes 155 BR79
Sipson La.
Gothic Rd., Twick. 177 CD89
Gottfried Ms. NW5 121 DJ63
Fortess Rd.
Goudhurst Rd., Brom. 184 EE92
Gouge Ave., Grav. 190 GE88
Gough Rd. E15 124 EF63
Gough Rd., Enf. 82 DV40
Gough Sq. EC4 274 E8
Gough St. WC1 274 C4
Gough St. WC1 141 DM70
Gough Wk. E14 143 EA72
Saracen St.
Gould Clo., Hat. 45 CV24
Gould Ct. SE19 182 DS92
Gould Ct., Guil. 243 BD132
Eustace Rd.
Gould Rd., Felt. 175 BS87
Gould Rd., Twick. 177 CE88
Gould Ter. E8 122 DV64
Kenmure Rd.
Goulds Grn., Uxb. 135 BP72
Goulston St. E1 275 P8
Goulston St. E1 142 DT72
Goulton Rd. E5 122 DV63
Gourley Pl. N15 122 DS57
Gourley St.
Gourley St. N15 122 DS57
Gourock Rd. SE9 185 EN85
Govan St. E2 142 DU67
Whiston Rd.
Government Row, Enf. 83 EA38
Governors Ave., Uxb. 113 BF57
Governors Clo., Amer. 72 AT37
Govett Ave., Shep. 195 BQ99
Govier Clo. E15 144 EE66
Gowan Ave. SW6 159 CY81
Gowan Rd. NW10 139 CV65
Gowar Fld., Pot.B. 63 CU32
Gower, The, Egh. 193 BB97
Gower Clo. SW4 181 DJ86
Gower Ct. WC1 273 M4
Gower Ms. WC1 273 N7
Gower Ms. WC1 141 DK71
Gower Pl. WC1 273 L4
Gower Pl. WC1 141 DJ70
Gower Rd. E7 144 EG65
Gower Rd., Horl. 268 DE148
Gower Rd., Islw. 157 CF79
Gower Rd., Wey. 213 BR107
Gower St. WC1 273 M5
Gower St. WC1 141 DJ70
Gowers, The, Amer. 55 AS36
Gowers, The, Harl. 36 EU13
Gowers La., Grays 171 GF75
Gower's Wk. E1 142 DU72
Gowland Pl., Beck. 203 DZ96
Gowlett Rd. SE15 162 DU83
Gowrie Rd. SW11 160 DG83
Graburn Way, E.Mol. 197 CD97
Grace Ave., Bexh. 166 EZ82
Grace Clo. SE9 184 EK90
Grace Clo., Borwd. 78 CR39
Grace Clo., Edg. 96 CQ52
Pavilion Way
Grace Clo., Ilf. 103 ET51
Grace Ct., Slou. 131 AQ74
Grace Jones Clo. E8 142 DU65
Parkholme Rd.
Grace Path SE26 182 DW91
Silverdale
Grace Rd., Croy. 202 DQ100
Grace St. E3 143 EB69
Gracechurch St. EC3 275 L10
Gracechurch St. EC3 142 DR73
Gracedale Rd. SW16 181 DH92
Gracefield Gdns. SW16 181 DL90
Grace's All. E1 142 DU73
Ensign St.
Graces Ms. SE5 162 DR82
Graces Rd. SE5 162 DS82
Gracious La., Sev. 256 FG130
Gracious La. End, Sev. 256 FF130
Gracious Pond Rd., Wok. 210 AT108
Gradient, The SE26 182 DU91
Graeme Rd., Enf. 82 DR40
Graemesdyke Ave. SW14 158 CP83
Graemesdyke Rd., Berk. 38 AU20
Grafton Clo. W13 137 CG72
Grafton Clo., Houns. 176 BY88
Grafton Clo., Slou. 132 AY72
Grafton Clo., W.Byf. 211 BF113
Madeira Rd.
Grafton Clo., Wor.Pk. 198 CS104
Grafton Ct., Felt. 175 BR88
Loxwood Clo.
Grafton Cres. NW1 141 DH65
Grafton Gdns. N4 122 DQ58
Grafton Gdns., Dag. 126 EY61
Grafton Ho. E3 143 EA69
Wellington Way
Grafton Ms. N1 142 DQ68
Frome St.
Grafton Ms. W1 273 K5
Grafton Pk. Rd., Wor.Pk. 198 CS103
Grafton Pl. NW1 273 M3
Grafton Pl. NW1 141 DK69
Grafton Rd. NW5 120 DG64
Grafton Rd. W3 138 CQ73
Grafton Rd., Croy. 201 DN102
Grafton Rd., Dag. 126 EY60
Grafton Rd., Enf. 81 DM41
Grafton Rd., Har. 116 CC57
Grafton Rd., N.Mal. 198 CS97
Grafton Rd., Wor.Pk. 216 CR105
Grafton Sq. SW4 161 DJ83
Grafton St. W1 277 J1
Grafton St. W1 141 DH73
Grafton Ter. NW5 120 DF64
Grafton Way W1 273 K5
Grafton Way W1 141 DJ70
Grafton Way WC1 273 L5
Grafton Way WC1 141 DJ70
Grafton Way, W.Mol. 196 BZ98
Grafton Yd. NW5 141 DH65
Prince of Wales Rd.
Graftons, The NW2 120 DA62
Hermitage La.
Graham Ave. W13 157 CH75
Graham Ave., Brox. 49 DY20
Graham Ave., Mitch. 200 DG95
Graham Clo., Brwd. 109 GC43
Graham Clo., Croy. 203 EA103
Graham Clo., St.Alb. 43 CD22
Graham Gdns., Surb. 198 CL102
Graham Rd. E8 142 DU65
Graham Rd. E13 144 EG69
Graham Rd. N15 121 DP55
Graham Rd. NW4 119 CV58
Graham Rd. SW19 179 CZ94
Graham Rd. W4 158 CR76
Graham Rd., Bexh. 166 FA84
Graham Rd., Hmptn. 176 CA91
Graham Rd., Har. 117 CE55
Graham Rd., Mitch. 200 DG95
Graham Rd., Pur. 219 DN113
Graham St. N1 274 G1
Graham St. N1 141 DP68
Graham Ter. SW1 276 F9
Graham Ter. SW1 160 DG77
Grahame Pk. Est. NW9 97 CT52
Grahame Pk. Way NW7 97 CT52
Grahame Pk. Way NW9 97 CT54
Grainger Clo., Nthlt. 116 CC64
Lancaster Rd.
Grainger Rd. N22 100 DQ53
Grainger Rd., Islw. 157 CF82
Grainge's Yd., Uxb. 134 BJ66
Cross St.
Gramer Clo. E11 123 ED61
Grampian Clo., Orp. 205 ET100
Cotswold Ri.
Grampian Gdns. NW2 119 CY60
Grampian Way, Hayes 155 BR80
Grampian Way, Slou. 153 BA78
Granard Ave. SW15 179 CV85
Granard Rd. SW12 180 DF87
Granaries, The, Wal.Abb. 68 EE33
Granary, The, Harl. 34 EH14
Granary Clo. N9 100 DW45
Turin Rd.
Granary Clo., Horl. 268 DG146
Waterside
Granary Rd. E1 142 DV70
Granary St. NW1 141 DK67
Granby Bldgs. SE11 278 B9
Granby Pk. Rd. (Cheshunt), Wal.Cr. 66 DT28
Granby Rd. SE9 165 EM82
Granby Rd., Grav. 190 GC86
Granby St. E2 142 DT70
Granby Ter. NW1 273 K1
Granby Ter. NW1 141 DJ68
Grand Ave. EC1 274 G6
Grand Ave. N10 120 DG56
Grand Ave., Surb. 198 CP99
Grand Ave., Wem. 118 CN64
Grand Ave. E., Wem. 138 CN65
Victoria Ave.
Grand Depot Rd. SE18 165 EN78
Grand Dr. SW20 199 CW96
Grand Dr., Sthl. 156 CC75
Grand Par. Ms. SW15 179 CY85
Upper Richmond Rd.
Grand Stand Rd., Epsom 233 CT117
Grand Union Cres. E8 142 DU67
Grand Union Ind. Est. NW10 138 CP68
Grand Union Wk. NW1 141 DH66
Grand Vw. Ave., West. 238 EJ117
Grand Wk. E1 143 DY70
Solebay St.
Granden Rd. SW16 201 DL96
Grandfield Ave., Wat. 75 BT39
Grandis Cotts., Wok. 228 BH122
Grandison Rd. SW11 180 DF85
Grandison Rd., Wor.Pk. 199 CW103
Granfield St. SW11 160 DD81
Grange, The N2 98 DD54
Central Ave.
Grange, The N20 98 DC46
Grange, The SE1 279 P6
Grange, The SE1 162 DT76
Grange, The SW19 179 CX93
Grange, The, Croy. 203 DZ103
Grange, The, Dart. 209 FR95
Grange, The, Walt. 195 BV103
Grange, The, Wem. 138 CN66
Grange, The, Wind. 172 AV85
Grange, The, Wok. 210 AS110
Grange, The, Wor.Pk. 198 CR104
Grange Ave. N12 98 DC50
Grange Ave. N20 97 CY45
Grange Ave. SE25 202 DS96
Grange Ave., Barn. 98 DE46
Grange Ave., Stan. 95 CH54
Grange Ave., Twick. 177 CE89
Grange Ave., Wdf.Grn. 102 EG51
Grange Clo., Brwd. 109 GC50
Grange Clo., Edg. 96 CQ50
Grange Clo., Ger.Cr. 90 AY53
Grange Clo., Grav. 191 GF91
Grange Clo., Guil. 242 AV130
Grange Clo., Hayes 135 BS71
Grange Clo., Hem.H. 40 BN21
Grange Clo., Hert. 31 DP09
Grange Clo., Houns. 156 BZ79
Grange Clo., Lthd. 231 CK120
Grange Clo. (Bletchingley), Red. 252 DR133
Grange Clo. (Merstham), Red. 251 DH128
Grange Clo., Sid. 186 EU90
Grange Clo., Stai. 172 AY86
Grange Clo., W.Mol. 196 CB98
Grange Clo., West. 255 EQ126
Grange Clo., Wdf.Grn. 102 EG52
Grange Ct. E8 142 DT66
Queensbridge Rd.
Grange Ct. WC2 274 C9
Grange Ct., Chig. 103 EQ47
Grange Ct., Loug. 84 EK43
Grange Ct., Nthlt. 136 BW68
Grange Ct., Stai. 174 BG92
Grange Ct., Wal.Abb. 67 EC34
Grange Ct., Walt. 195 BU103
Grange Cres. SE28 146 EW72
Grange Cres., Chig. 103 ER50
Grange Cres., Dart. 188 FP86
Grange Dr., Chis. 184 EL93
Grange Dr., H.Wyc. 110 AD60
Grange Dr., Orp. 224 EW109
Rushmore Hill
Grange Dr., Red. 251 DH128
London Rd. S.
Grange Dr., Wok. 210 AY114
Grange End, Horl. 269 DN148
Grange Fm. Clo., Har. 116 CC61
Grange Flds., Ger.Cr. 90 AY53
Lower Rd.
Grange Gdns. N14 99 DK46
Grange Gdns. NW3 120 DB62
Grange Gdns. SE25 202 DS96
Grange Gdns., Bans. 218 DB113
Grange Gdns., Pnr. 116 BY55
Grange Gdns., Slou. 111 AR64
Grange Gdns., Ware 33 DY07
Grange Gro. N1 142 DQ65
Grange Hill SE25 202 DS96
Grange Hill, Edg. 96 CQ50
Grange Ho., Bark. 145 ER67
St. Margarets
Grange La. SE21 182 DT89
Grange La., Harl. 50 EJ15
Grange La., Wat. 77 CD39
Grange Mans., Epsom 217 CT108
Grange Meadow, Bans. 218 DB113
Grange Ms. SE10 163 ED80
Crooms Hill
Grange Par., Hayes 135 BT71
Grange Pk. W5 138 CL74
Grange Pk., Wok. 210 AY114
Grange Pk. Ave. N21 82 DQ44
Grange Pk. Pl. SW20 179 CV94
Grange Pk. Rd. E10 123 EB60
Grange Pk. Rd., Th.Hth. 202 DR98
Grange Pl. NW6 140 DA66
Grange Pl., Stai. 194 BJ96
Grange Rd. E10 123 EA60
Grange Rd. E13 144 EF69
Grange Rd. E17 123 DY57
Grange Rd. N6 120 DG58
Grange Rd. N17 100 DU51
Grange Rd. N18 100 DU51
Grange Rd. NW10 139 CV65
Grange Rd. SE1 279 N7
Grange Rd. SE1 162 DS76
Grange Rd. SE19 202 DR96
Grange Rd. SE25 202 DR97
Grange Rd. SW13 159 CU81
Grange Rd. W4 158 CP78
Grange Rd. W5 137 CK74
Grange Rd., Add. 212 BG110
Grange Rd., Borwd. 78 CM43
Grange Rd., Cat. 252 DU125
Grange Rd., Chess. 198 CL104
Grange Rd., Edg. 96 CR51
Grange Rd., Egh. 173 AZ92
Grange Rd., Ger.Cr. 90 AY53
Grange Rd., Grav. 191 GG87
Grange Rd., Grays 170 GB79
Grange Rd., Guil. 242 AV129
Grange Rd., Har. 117 CG58
Grange Rd. (South Harrow), Har. 117 CD61
Grange Rd., Hayes 135 BS72
Grange Rd., Ilf. 125 EP63
Grange Rd., Kings.T. 198 CL97
Grange Rd., Lthd. 231 CK120
Grange Rd., Orp. 205 EQ103
Grange Rd., Rom. 105 FH52
Grange Rd., Sev. 256 FG127
Grange Rd., S.Croy. 220 DQ110
Grange Rd., S.Ock. 148 FQ74
Grange Rd., Sthl. 156 BY75
Grange Rd., Sutt. 218 DA108
Grange Rd., Th.Hth. 202 DR98
Grange Rd., Walt. 214 BY105
Grange Rd. (Bushey), Wat. 76 BY43
Grange Rd., W.Mol. 196 CB98

Grange Rd., Wok. 210 AY114
Grange St. N1 142 DR68
Bridport Pl.
Grange St., St.Alb. 43 CD19
Grange Vale, Sutt. 218 DB108
Grange Wk. SE1 279 N6
Grange Wk. SE1 162 DS76
Grange Way N12 98 DB49
Grange Way, Erith 167 FH80
Grange Way, Iver 133 BF72
Grange Yd. SE1 279 P7
Grange Yd. SE1 162 DT76
Grangecliffe Gdns. SE25 202 DS96
Grangecourt Rd. N16 122 DS60
Grangedale Clo., Nthwd. 93 BS53
Grangefields Rd., Guil. 242 AX128
Grangehill Pl. SE9 165 EM83
Westmount Rd.
Grangehill Rd. SE9 165 EM84
Grangemill Rd. SE6 183 EA90
Grangemill Way SE6 183 EA89
Grangemount, Lthd. 231 CK120
Granger Way, Rom. 127 FG58
Grangeview Rd. N20 98 DC46
Grangeway NW6 140 DA66
Messina Ave.
Grangeway, Horl. 269 DN148
Grangeway, Wdf.Grn. 102 EJ49
Grangeway, The N21 81 DP44
Grangeway Gdns., Ilf. 124 EL57
Grangeways Clo., Grav. 191 GF91
Grangewood, Bex. 186 EZ88
Hurst Rd.
Grangewood, Pot.B. 64 DB30
Grangewood, Slou. 132 AW71
Grangewood Ave., Grays 170 GE76
Grangewood Ave., Rain. 148 FJ70
Grangewood Clo., Brwd. 109 GA48
Knight's Way
Grangewood Clo., Pnr. 115 BU57
Grangewood Dr., Sun. 175 BT94
Forest Dr.
Grangewood La., Beck. 183 DZ93
Grangewood St. E6 144 EK67
Granham Gdns. N9 100 DT47
Granite St. SE18 165 ET78
Granleigh Rd. E11 124 EE61
Gransden Ave. E8 142 DV66
Gransden Rd. W12 159 CT75
Wendell Rd.
Grant Ave., Slou. 132 AS72
Grant Clo. N14 99 DJ45
Grant Clo., Shep. 195 BP100
Grant Pl., Croy. 202 DT102
Grant Rd. SW11 160 DD84
Grant Rd., Croy. 202 DT102
Grant Rd., Har. 117 CE55
Grant St. E13 144 EG69
Grant St. N1 141 DN68
Chapel Mkt.
Grant Way, Islw. 157 CG80
Grantbridge St. N1 141 DP68
Grantchester Clo., Har. 117 CF62
Grantham Clo., Edg. 96 CL48
Grantham Gdns., Rom. 126 EZ58
Grantham Gdns., Ware 33 DY05
Grantham Grn., Borwd. 78 CQ43
Grantham Pl. W1 277 H3
Grantham Rd. E12 125 EN63
Grantham Rd. SW9 161 DL83
Grantham Rd. W4 158 CS80
Grantley Clo., Guil. 258 AY141
Grantley Gdns., Guil. 242 AU133
Grantley Rd., Guil. 242 AU133
Grantley Rd., Houns. 156 BW82
Grantley St. E1 143 DX69
Grantock Rd. E17 101 ED53
Granton Ave., Upmin. 128 FM61
Granton Rd. SW16 201 DJ95
Granton Rd., Ilf. 126 EU60
Granton Rd., Sid. 186 EW93
Grants Clo. NW7 97 CW52
Grants La., Oxt. 254 EJ133
Grantully Rd. W9 140 DB69
Grantwood Clo., Red. 267 DH139
Bushfield Dr.
Granville Ave. N9 100 DW48
Granville Ave., Felt. 175 BU89
Granville Ave., Houns. 176 CA85
Granville Ave., Slou. 131 AR71
Granville Clo., Croy. 202 DS103
Granville Clo., W.Byf. 212 BM113
Church Rd.
Granville Clo., Wey. 213 BQ107
Granville Ct. N1 142 DR67
Granville Dene, Hem.H. 57 BA27
Granville Gdns. SW16 201 DM95
Granville Gdns. W5 138 CM74
Granville Gdns., Hodd. 33 EA13
Granville Gro. SE13 163 EC83
Granville Ms., Sid. 186 EU91
Granville Pk. SE13 163 EC83
Granville Pl. 98 DC52
(North Finchley) N12
High Rd.
Granville Pl. W1 272 F9
Granville Pl. W1 140 DG72
Granville Pl., Pnr. 94 BX54
Elm Pk. Rd.
Granville Rd. E17 123 EB58
Granville Rd. E18 102 EH54
Granville Rd. N4 121 DM58
Granville Rd. N12 98 DB51
Granville Rd. N13 99 DM51
Russell Rd.
Granville Rd. N22 99 DP53
Granville Rd. NW2 119 CZ61
Granville Rd. NW6 140 DA68
Granville Rd. SW18 179 CZ87
Granville Rd. SW19 180 DA94
Russell Rd.
Granville Rd., Barn. 79 CW42
Granville Rd., Berk. 38 AS17
Granville Rd., Epp. 70 EV29
Granville Rd., Grav. 191 GF88
Granville Rd., Hayes 155 BT77
Granville Rd., Ilf. 125 EP60
Granville Rd., Oxt. 254 EF129
Granville Rd., St.Alb. 43 CF20
Granville Rd., Sev. 256 FG124
Granville Rd., Sid. 186 EU91
Granville Rd., Uxb. 135 BP65
Granville Rd., Wat. 76 BW42
Granville Rd., Well. 166 EW83
Granville Rd., West. 255 EQ126
Granville Rd., Wey. 213 BQ108
Granville Rd., Wok. 227 AZ120
Granville Sq. SE15 162 DS80
Blakes Rd.
Granville Sq. WC1 274 C3
Granville Sq. WC1 141 DM69
Granville St. WC1 274 C3
Granville St. WC1 141 DM69
Grape St. WC2 273 P8
Graphite Sq. SE11 278 B10
Grasdene Rd. SE18 166 EU80
Grasmere Ave. SW15 178 CR91
Grasmere Ave. SW19 200 DA97
Grasmere Ave. W3 138 CR73
Grasmere Ave., Houns. 176 CB86
Grasmere Ave., Orp. 205 EP104
Grasmere Ave., Ruis. 115 BQ59
Grasmere Ave., Slou. 132 AU73
Grasmere Ave., Wem. 117 CJ59
Grasmere Clo., Felt. 175 BT88
Grasmere Clo., Guil. 243 BB133
Grasmere Clo., Hem.H. 41 BP22
Grasmere Clo., Loug. 85 EM40
Grasmere Clo., Wat. 59 BV32
Grasmere Ct. N22 99 DM51
Palmerston Rd.
Grasmere Gdns., Har. 95 CG54
Grasmere Gdns., Ilf. 125 EM57
Grasmere Gdns., Orp. 205 EP104
Grasmere Rd. E13 144 EG68
Grasmere Rd. N10 99 DH53
Grasmere Rd. N17 100 DU51
Grasmere Rd. SE25 202 DV100
Grasmere Rd. SW16 181 DM92
Grasmere Rd., Bexh. 167 FC81
Grasmere Rd., Brom. 204 EF95
Grasmere Rd., Orp. 205 EP104
Grasmere Rd., Pur. 219 DP111
Grasmere Rd., St.Alb. 43 CH22
Grasmere Way, W.Byf. 212 BM112
Grass Pk. N3 97 CZ53
Grass Warren, Welw. 30 DE06
Grassfield Clo., Couls. 235 DJ119
Grassingham End, Ger.Cr. 90 AY52
Grassingham Rd., Ger.Cr. 90 AY52
Grassington Clo., St.Alb. 60 CA30
Grassington Rd., Sid. 186 EU91
Grasslands, Horl. 269 DN148
Grassmere, Horl. 269 DJ147
Grassmere Clo., Egh. 173 BB94
Keswick Rd.
Grassmere Rd., Horn. 128 FM56
Grassmount SE23 182 DV89
Grassmount, Pur. 219 DJ110
Grassway, Wall. 219 DJ105
Grassy Clo., Hem.H. 40 BG19
Grassy La., Sev. 257 FH126
Grasvenor Ave., Barn. 80 DB44
Grately Way SE15 162 DT80
Daniel Gdns.
Gratton Dr., Wind. 151 AL84
Gratton Rd. W14 159 CY76
Gratton Ter. NW2 119 CX62
Gravel Clo., Chig. 104 EU47
Gravel Hill N3 97 CZ54
Gravel Hill, Bexh. 187 FB85
Gravel Hill, Croy. 221 DX107
Gravel Hill, Ger.Cr. 90 AY51
Gravel Hill, Hem.H. 40 BH20
Gravel Hill, Lthd. 231 CH121
North St.
Gravel Hill, Loug. 84 EG38
Gravel Hill, Uxb. 114 BK64
Gravel Hill Clo., Bexh. 187 FB85
Gravel Hill Ter., Hem.H. 40 BG21
Gravel La. E1 275 P8
Gravel La., Chig. 85 ET42
Gravel La., Hem.H. 40 BG21
Gravel Path, Berk. 38 AX19
Gravel Path, Hem.H. 40 BG20
Gravel La.
Gravel Pit La. SE9 185 EQ85
Gravel Pit Way, Orp. 206 EU103
Gravel Pits La., Guil. 261 BQ139
Gravel Rd., Brom. 204 EL104
Gravel Rd., Dart. 188 FP94
Gravel Rd., Twick. 177 CE88
Graveley Ave., Borwd. 78 CQ42
Graveley Ct., Hem.H. 41 BQ21
Graveley Dell, Welw.G.C. 30 DB10
Waterford Grn.
Gravelly Hill, Cat. 252 DS128
Gravelly Ride SW19 179 CT91
Gravelwood Clo., Chis. 185 EQ90
Gravely Way, H.Wyc. 88 AF45
Graveney Gro. SE20 182 DW94
Graveney Rd. SW17 180 DE91
Gravesend Rd. W12 139 CU73
Gravetts La., Guil. 242 AS131
Gray Ave., Dag. 126 EZ60
Gray Gdns., Rain. 127 FG64
Gray Pl., Cher. 211 BC107
Murray Rd.
Gray St. SE1 278 E5
Grayburn Clo., Ch.St.G. 90 AU47
Grayham Cres., N.Mal. 198 CR98
Grayham Rd., N.Mal. 198 CR98
Grayland Clo., Brom. 204 EK95
Graylands, Epp. 85 ER37
Graylands, Wok. 226 AY116
Graylands Clo., Wok. 226 AY116
Grayling Clo. E16 144 EE70
Cranberry La.
Grayling Ct., Berk. 38 AT17
Tortoiseshell Way
Grayling Rd. N16 122 DR61
Grayling Sq. E2 142 DU69
Nelson Gdns.
Graylings, The, Abb.L. 59 BR33
Grays End Clo., Grays 170 GA76
Grays Fm. Rd., Orp. 206 EV95
Gray's Inn WC1 274 C6
Gray's Inn WC1 141 DM71
Gray's Inn Pl. WC1 274 C7
Gray's Inn Rd. WC1 274 A2
Gray's Inn Rd. WC1 141 DL69
Gray's Inn Sq. WC1 274 D6
Grays La., Ashf. 175 BP91
Gray's La., Ash. 232 CM119
Gray's La., Epsom 232 CP121
Shepherds' Wk.
Grays Pk. Rd., Slou. 132 AU68
Grays Pl., Slou. 132 AT74
Grays Rd., Gdmg. 258 AT144
Grays Rd., Slou. 132 AT74
Grays Rd., Uxb. 134 BL67
Grays Rd., West. 239 EP121
Grays Wk., Brwd. 109 GD45
Grays Wk., Chesh. 54 AP29
Grays Wd., Horl. 269 DJ148
Gray's Yd. W1 272 G8
Grayscroft Rd. SW16 181 DK94
Graysfield, Welw.G.C. 30 DA12
Grayshott Rd. SW11 160 DG82
Grayswood Gdns. SW20 199 CV96
Farnham Gdns.
Graywood Ct. N12 98 DC52
Grazebrook Rd. N16 122 DR61
Grazeley Clo., Bexh. 187 FC85
Grazeley Ct. SE19 182 DS91
Gipsy Hill
Grazings, The, Hem.H. 40 BM18
Great Acre Ct. SW4 161 DK84
St. Alphonsus Rd.
Great Bell All. EC2 275 K8
Great Benty, West Dr. 154 BL77
Great Bois Wd., Amer. 55 AP36
Bois Ave.
Great Braitch La., Hat. 28 CS13
Great Brays, Harl. 52 EU16
Great Break, Welw.G.C. 30 DB10
Great Brownings SE21 182 DT91
Great Bushey Dr. N20 98 DB46
Great Cambridge Rd. N9 100 DR48
Great Cambridge Rd. N17 100 DR52
Great Cambridge Rd. N18 100 DR49
Great Cambridge Rd., Brox. 67 DY26
Great Cambridge Rd., Enf. 82 DU41
Great Cambridge Rd. 66 DW32
(Cheshunt), Wal.Cr.
Great Castle St. W1 273 J8
Great Castle St. W1 141 DH72
Great Cen. Ave., Ruis. 116 BW64
Great Cen. St. NW1 272 D6
Great Cen. St. NW1 140 DF71
Great Cen. Way NW10 118 CQ63
Great Chapel St. W1 273 M8
Great Chapel St. W1 141 DK72
Great Chertsey Rd. W4 158 CQ82
Great Chertsey Rd., Felt. 176 CA90
Great Ch. La. W6 159 CX78
Great College St. SW1 277 P6
Great College St. SW1 161 DL76
Great Conduit, Welw.G.C. 30 DC08
Great Cross Ave. SE10 164 EE80
Great Cullings, Rom. 127 FE61
Great Cumberland Ms. W1 272 D9
Great Cumberland Pl. W1 272 E8
Great Cumberland Pl. W1 140 DF72
Great Dell, Welw.G.C. 29 CX07
Great Dover St. SE1 279 K5
Great Dover St. SE1 162 DR75
Great Eastern Rd. E15 143 ED66
Great Eastern Rd., Brwd. 108 FW49
Great Eastern St. EC2 275 M3
Great Eastern St. EC2 142 DS69
Great Eastern Wk. EC2 275 M7
Great Ellshams, Bans. 234 DA116
Great Elms Rd., Brom. 204 EJ98
Great Elms Rd., Hem.H. 40 BM24
Great Fld. NW9 96 CS53
Great Fleete Way, Bark. 146 EW68
Great Galley Clo., Bark. 146 EV69
Great Ganett, Welw.G.C. 30 DB11
Great Gdns. Rd., Horn. 127 FH58
Great George St. SW1 277 N5
Great George St. SW1 161 DK75
Great Goodwin Dr., Guil. 243 BB132
Great Gregories La., Epp. 69 ES33
Great Gro. (Bushey), Wat. 76 CB42
Great Guildford St. SE1 279 H2
Great Guildford St. SE1 142 DQ74
Great Harry Dr. SE9 185 EN90
Great Heath, Hat. 45 CV15
Great Hivings, Chesh. 54 AN27
Great James St. WC1 274 B6
Great James St. WC1 141 DM71
Great Julians, Rick. 74 BN42
Grove Cres.
Great Lake Ct., Horl. 269 DH147
Tanyard Way
Great Ley, Welw.G.C. 29 CY11
Great Leylands, Harl. 52 EU16
Great Marlborough St. W1 273 K9
Great Marlborough St. W1 141 DJ72
Great Maze Pond SE1 279 L4
Great Maze Pond SE1 142 DR74
Great Meadow, Brox. 49 EA22
Great Molewood, Hert. 31 DP06
Great Nelmes Chase, Horn. 128 FM57
Great New St. EC4 274 E8
Great Newport St. WC2 273 N10
Great N. Rd. N2 120 DE56
Great N. Rd. N6 120 DF57
Great N. Rd., Barn. 79 CZ40
Great N. Rd. 80 DB43
(New Barnet), Barn.
Great N. Rd., Hat. 64 DB27
Great N. Rd., Pot.B. 64 DB27
Great N. Rd., Welw. 29 CV05
Great N. Rd., Welw.G.C. 29 CU08
Great N. Way NW4 97 CV53
Great Oaks, Brwd. 109 GB44
Great Oaks, Chig. 103 EQ49
Great Oaks Pk., Guil. 243 BB129
Great Ormond St. WC1 274 A6
Great Ormond St. WC1 141 DL71
Great Owl Rd., Chig. 103 EN48
Great Palmers, Hem.H. 40 BM15
Great Pk., Kings L. 58 BM30
Great Percy St. WC1 274 C2
Great Percy St. WC1 141 DM69
Great Peter St. SW1 277 M7
Great Peter St. SW1 161 DK76
Great Plumtree, Harl. 35 ET13
Great Portland St. W1 273 J6
Great Portland St. W1 141 DH70
Great Pulteney St. W1 273 L10
Great Pulteney St. W1 141 DJ73
Great Quarry, Guil. 258 AX137
Great Queen St. WC2 274 A9
Great Queen St. WC2 141 DL72
Great Queen St., Dart. 188 FM87
Great Rd., Hem.H. 40 BM19
Great Ropers La., Brwd. 107 FU51
Great Russell St. WC1 273 N8
Great Russell St. WC1 141 DK72
Great St. Helens EC3 275 M8
Great St. Thomas Apostle EC4 275 J10
Great Scotland Yd. SW1 277 P2
Great Scotland Yd. SW1 141 DL74
Great Slades, Pot.B. 63 CZ33
Great Smith St. SW1 277 N6
Great Smith St. SW1 161 DK76
Great South-West Rd., Felt. 175 BQ87
Great South-West Rd., 155 BV83
Houns.
Great Spilmans SE22 182 DS85
Great Strand NW9 97 CT53
Great Sturgess Rd., 39 BF20
Hem.H.
Great Suffolk St. SE1 278 G3
Great Suffolk St. SE1 141 DP74
Great Sutton St. EC1 274 G5
Great Sutton St. EC1 141 DP70
Great Swan All. EC2 275 K8
Great Tattenhams, Epsom 233 CV118
Great Thrift, Orp. 205 EQ98
Great Till Clo., Sev. 241 FE116
Great Titchfield St. W1 273 K6
Great Titchfield St. W1 141 DJ71
Great Twr. St. EC3 275 M10
Great Twr. St. EC3 142 DS73
Great Trinity La. EC4 275 J10
Great Turnstile WC1 274 C7
Great Warley St., Brwd. 107 FU53
Great W. Rd. W4 158 CP78
Great W. Rd. W6 159 CU78
Great W. Rd., Brent. 158 CP78
Great W. Rd., Houns. 156 BY82
Great W. Rd., Islw. 157 CD80
Great Western Ind. Pk., Sthl. 156 CB75
Great Western Rd. W9 139 CZ71
Great Western Rd. W11 139 CZ71
Great Wf. Rd. E14 143 EB74
Churchill Pl.
Great Whites Rd., Hem.H. 40 BM22
Great Winchester St. EC2 275 L8
Great Winchester St. EC2 142 DR72
Great Windmill St. W1 273 M10
Great Windmill St. W1 141 DK73
Great Woodcote Dr., Pur. 219 DK110
Great Woodcote Pk., Pur. 219 DK110
Great Yd. SE1 279 N4
Greatdown Rd. W7 137 CF70
Greatfield Ave. E6 145 EM70
Greatfield Clo. N19 121 DJ63
Warrender Rd.
Greatfield Clo. SE4 163 EA84
Greatfields Dr., Uxb. 134 BN71
Greatfields Rd., Bark. 145 ER67
Greatford Dr., Guil. 243 BD134
Greatham Rd. 76 BX41
(Bushey), Wat.
Greatham Wk. SW15 179 CU88
Bessborough Rd.
Greatheart, Hem.H. 40 BL18
Greathurst End, Lthd. 230 BZ124
Greatness La., Sev. 257 FJ121
Greatness Rd., Sev. 257 FJ121
Greatorex St. E1 142 DU71
Greatwood, Chis. 185 EN94
Greatwood Clo., Cher. 211 BC109
Greaves Clo., Bark. 145 ES66
Norfolk Rd.
Greaves Pl. SW17 180 DE91
Grebe Ave., Hayes 136 BX72
Cygnet Way
Grebe Clo. E7 124 EF64
Cormorant Rd.
Grebe Clo. E17 101 DY52
Grebe Crest, Grays 169 FU77
Grecian Cres. SE19 181 DP93
Greding Wk., Brwd. 109 GB47
Gredo Ho., Bark. 146 EV69
Greek Ct. W1 273 N9
Greek St. W1 273 N9
Greek St. W1 141 DK72
Greek Yd. WC2 273 P10
Green, The E4 101 EC46
Green, The E11 124 EH58
Green, The E15 144 EE65
Green, The N9 100 DU47
Green, The N14 99 DK48
Green, The N21 99 DN45
Green, The SW14 158 CQ83
Green, The SW19 179 CX92
Green, The W3 138 CS72
Green, The W5 137 CK74
The Gro.
Green, The, Amer. 55 AR38
Batchelors Way
Green, The, Berk. 39 BB17
Green, The, Bexh. 166 FA81
Green, The, Brom. 204 EG101
Green, The, Cars. 218 DG105
Green, The, Cat. 237 EA123
Green, The, Ch.St.G. 90 AW47
High St.
Green, The, Croy. 221 DZ109
Green, The, Epp. 85 ES36
Green, The, Epsom 217 CU112
Green, The, Esher 215 CF107
Green, The, Felt. 175 BV89
Green, The, Hayes 135 BS72
Wood End
Green, The, Hem.H. 57 BA27
Green, The, H.Wyc. 110 AE57
Green, The, Houns. 156 CA79
Heston Rd.
Green, The, Lthd. 231 CD124
Green, The, Mord. 199 CY98
Green, The, N.Mal. 198 CQ97
Green, The 224 EW110
(Pratt's Bottom), Orp.
Rushmore Hill
Green, The 186 EV94
(St. Paul's Cray), Orp.
The Ave.
Green, The, Rain. 148 FL73
Green, The, Rich. 177 CK85
Green, The 74 BM44
(Croxley Grn.), Rick.
Green, The (Sarratt), Rick. 74 BG35
Green, The, Sev. 257 FK122
Green, The, Shep. 195 BS98
Green, The, Sid. 186 EU91
Green, The, Slou. 130 AH70
Green, The (Chalvey), 151 AR75
Slou.
Green, The (Datchet), 152 AV80
Slou.
Green, The, S.Ock. 149 FW69
Green, The, Sthl. 156 BY76
Green, The, Stai. 172 AY86
Green, The, Sutt. 200 DB104
Green, The, Tad. 233 CY119
Green, The, Til. 171 GL79
Green, The, Twick. 177 CE89
Green, The, Uxb. 115 BQ61
Green, The, Wal.Abb. 67 EC34
Sewardstone Rd.
Green, The (Cheshunt), 66 DW28
Wal.Cr.
Green, The, Walt. 213 BS110
Octagon Rd.
Green, The, Warl. 237 DX117
Green, The, Wat. 77 CE39
Green, The, Well. 165 ES84
Green, The, Wem. 117 CG61
Green, The, West Dr. 154 BK76
Green, The, West. 255 ER126
Green, The, Wdf.Grn. 102 EG50
Green Acres, Croy. 202 DT104
Green Acres, Hem.H. 41 BR21
Green Acres, Welw.G.C. 29 CZ12
Green Arbour Ct. EC1 274 F8
Green Ave. NW7 96 CR49
Green Ave. W13 157 CH76
Green Bank E1 142 DV74
Green Bank N12 98 DB49
Green Banks, Upmin. 129 FS60
Green Clo. NW9 118 CQ58
Green Clo. NW11 120 DC59
Green Clo., Brom. 204 EE97
Green Clo., Cars. 200 DF103
Green Clo., Epp. 51 EP24
Green Clo., Felt. 176 BY92
Green Clo., Hat. 63 CY26
Station Rd.
Green Clo., Maid. 130 AH72
Green Clo. (Cheshunt), 67 DY31
Wal.Cr.
Green Common La., H.Wyc. 110 AG59
Green Ct. Rd., Swan. 207 FD100
Green Cres., H.Wyc. 110 AC56
Green Cft., Edg. 96 CQ50
Deans La.
Green Cft., Hat. 45 CU15
Talbot Rd.
Green Curve, Bans. 217 CZ114
Green Dale SE5 162 DR84
Wanley Rd.
Green Dale SE22 182 DS85
Green Dale Clo. SE22 182 DS85
Green Dale
Green Dell Way, Hem.H. 41 BQ21
Green Dene, Lthd. 245 BT131
Green Dragon Ct. SE1 279 K2
Green Dragon La. N21 81 DN43
Green Dragon La., Brent. 158 CL78
Green Dragon Yd. E1 142 DU71
Old Montague St.
Green Dr., Slou. 152 AY77
London Rd.
Green Dr., Sthl. 136 CA74
Green Dr., Wok. 227 BF123
Green E. Rd., Beac. 90 AS52
Green End N21 99 DP47
Green End, Chess. 216 CL105
Green End Gdns., Hem.H. 40 BG21
Green End La., Hem.H. 39 BF20
Green End Rd., Hem.H. 40 BG22
Green Gdns., Orp. 223 EQ106
Green Glade, Epp. 85 ES37
Green Glades, Horn. 128 FM58
Green Hill, Buck.H. 102 EJ46
Green Hill, Orp. 223 EM112
Green Hill La., Warl. 237 DY117
Sunny Bank
Green Hill Ter. SE18 165 EM78
Green Hill Way, Croy. 221 DX112
Green Hundred Rd. SE15 162 DU79
Green La. E4 83 ED41
Green La. NW4 119 CX56
Green La. SE9 185 EP88
Green La. SE20 183 DX94
Green La. SW16 181 DM94
Green La. W7 157 CE75
Green La., Add. 194 BG104
Green La., Amer. 55 AS38
Green La. 55 AR35
(Chesham Bois), Amer.
Green La., Ash. 231 CJ117
Green La., Brwd. 108 FU46
Greenshaw
Green La. 108 FV43
(Pilgrims Hatch), Brwd.
Green La. (Warley), Brwd. 107 FU52
Green La., Brox. 49 EB23
Green La., Cher. 193 BE103
Green La., Chesh. 56 AV34
Green La., Chess. 216 CL109
Green La., Chig. 103 ES46
Green La., Chis. 185 EP90
Green La., Cob. 214 BY112
Green La., Couls. 250 DA125
Green La., Dag. 126 EX61
Green La., Edg. 96 CM49
Green La., Egh. 173 BB92
Green La. (Thorpe), Egh. 193 BD95
Green La., Felt. 176 BY92
Green La., Guil. 243 BB134
Green La. (Shamley Grn.), 260 BG144
Guil.
Green La. (West Clandon), 244 BG127
Guil.
Green La., Harl. 52 FA16
Green La., Har. 117 CE62
Green La., Hem.H. 41 BQ21
Green La. (Bovingdon), 57 BA28
Hem.H.
Green La., Horl. 269 DM152
Green La., Houns. 155 BV83
Green La., Ilf. 125 EQ61
Green La., Lthd. 231 CK121
Green La. (Fifield), Maid. 150 AC81
Green La., Mord. 200 DA100
Green La., N.Mal. 198 CQ99
Green La., Nthwd. 93 BR52
Green La., Pur. 219 DJ111
Green La., Red. 250 DE132
Green La. (Bletchingley), 252 DS131
Red.

Grimwade Cres. SE15 162 DW83
Evelina Rd.
Grimwood Rd., Twick. 177 CF87
Grindal St. SE1 278 D5
Grindall Clo., Croy. 219 DP105
Hillside Rd.
Grindcobbe, St.Alb. 43 CD23
Grindley Gdns., Croy. 202 DT100
Grinling Pl. SE8 163 EA79
Grinstead Rd. SE8 163 DY78
Grisedale Clo., Pur. 220 DR114
Grisedale Gdns., Pur. 220 DS114
Grittleton Ave., Wem. 138 CP65
Grittleton Rd. W9 140 DA70
Grizedale Ter. SE23 182 DV89
Eliot Bank
Grobars Ave., Wok. 226 AW115
Grocer's Hall Ct. EC2 275 K9
Grogan Clo., Hmptn. 176 BZ93
Groom Cres. SW18 180 DD87
Groom Pl. SW1 276 G6
Groom Pl. SW1 160 DG76
Groom Rd., Brox. 67 DZ26
Groom Wk., Guil. 242 AY130
Slyfield Grn.
Groombridge Clo., Walt. 213 BV106
Groombridge Clo., Well. 186 EU85
Groombridge Rd. E9 143 DX66
Groomfield Clo. SW17 180 DG91
Grooms Cotts., Chesh. 56 AV30
Grooms Dr., Pnr. 115 BU57
Grosmont Rd. SE18 165 ET79
Grosse Way SW15 179 CV86
Grosvenor Ave. N5 122 DQ64
Grosvenor Ave. SW14 158 CS83
Grosvenor Ave., Cars. 218 DF107
Grosvenor Ave., Har. 116 CB58
Grosvenor Ave., Hayes 135 BS68
Grosvenor Ave., Kings L. 59 BQ28
Grosvenor Ave., Rich. 178 CL85
Grosvenor Rd.
Grosvenor Clo., Iver 133 BD69
Grosvenor Clo., Loug. 85 EP39
Grosvenor Cotts. SW1 276 F8
Grosvenor Ct. N14 99 DJ45
Grosvenor Ct., Guil. 243 BA132
London Rd.
Grosvenor Ct., Rick. 75 BR43
Mayfare
Grosvenor Ct., Slou. 132 AS72
Stoke Poges La.
Grosvenor Cres. NW9 118 CN56
Grosvenor Cres. SW1 276 G5
Grosvenor Cres. SW1 160 DG75
Grosvenor Cres., Dart. 188 FK85
Grosvenor Cres., Uxb. 135 BP66
Grosvenor Cres. Ms. SW1 276 F5
Grosvenor Cres. Ms. SW1 160 DG75
Grosvenor Dr., Horn. 128 FJ60
Grosvenor Dr., Loug. 85 EP40
Grosvenor Dr., Maid. 130 AC71
Grosvenor Est. SW1 277 N8
Grosvenor Est. SW1 161 DK77
Grosvenor Gdns. E6 144 EK69
Grosvenor Gdns. N10 121 DJ55
Grosvenor Gdns. N14 81 DK42
Grosvenor Gdns. NW2 119 CW64
Grosvenor Gdns. NW11 119 CZ58
Grosvenor Gdns. SW1 277 J7
Grosvenor Gdns. SW1 161 DH76
Grosvenor Gdns. SW14 158 CS83
Grosvenor Gdns., Kings.T. 177 CK93
Grosvenor Gdns., Upmin. 129 FR60
Grosvenor Gdns., Wall. 219 DJ108
Grosvenor Gdns., Wdf.Grn. 102 EG51
Grosvenor Gdns. Ms. E. SW1 277 J6
Grosvenor Gdns. Ms. N. SW1 277 H7
Grosvenor Gdns. Ms. S. SW1 277 J7
Grosvenor Gate W1 276 E1
Grosvenor Hill SW19 179 CY93
Grosvenor Hill W1 273 H10
Grosvenor Hill W1 141 DH73
Grosvenor Pk. SE5 162 DQ80
Grosvenor Pk. Rd. E17 123 EA57
Grosvenor Path, Loug. 85 EP39
Grosvenor Pl. SW1 276 G5
Grosvenor Pl. SW1 160 DG75
Grosvenor Pl., Wey. 195 BR104
Vale Rd.
Grosvenor Ri. E. E17 123 EB57
Grosvenor Rd. E6 144 EK67
Grosvenor Rd. E7 144 EH65
Grosvenor Rd. E10 123 EC60
Grosvenor Rd. E11 124 EG57
Grosvenor Rd. N3 97 CZ52
Grosvenor Rd. N9 100 DV46
Grosvenor Rd. N10 99 DH53
Grosvenor Rd. SE25 202 DU98
Grosvenor Rd. SW1 161 DH79
Grosvenor Rd. W4 158 CP78
Grosvenor Rd. W7 137 CG74
Grosvenor Rd., Belv. 166 FA79
Grosvenor Rd., Bexh. 186 EX85
Grosvenor Rd., Borwd. 78 CN41
Grosvenor Rd., Brent. 157 CK79
Grosvenor Rd., Brox. 49 DZ20
Grosvenor Rd., Dag. 126 EZ60
Grosvenor Rd., Epsom 232 CR119
Grosvenor Rd., Houns. 156 BZ83
Grosvenor Rd., Ilf. 125 EQ62
Grosvenor Rd., Nthwd. 93 BT50
Grosvenor Rd., Orp. 205 ES100
Grosvenor Rd., Rich. 178 CL85
Grosvenor Rd., Rom. 127 FD59
Grosvenor Rd., St.Alb. 43 CE21
Grosvenor Rd., Sthl. 156 BZ76
Grosvenor Rd., Stai. 174 BG94
Grosvenor Rd., Twick. 177 CG87
Grosvenor Rd., Wall. 219 DH107
Grosvenor Rd., Wat. 76 BW41
Grosvenor Rd., W.Wick. 203 EB102
Grosvenor Sq. W1 272 G10
Grosvenor Sq. W1 140 DG73
Grosvenor St. W1 273 H10
Grosvenor St. W1 141 DH73
Grosvenor Ter. SE5 162 DQ79
Grosvenor Ter., Hem.H. 40 BG21
Grosvenor Vale, Ruis. 115 BT61
Grosvenor Way E5 122 DW61
Grosvenor Wf. Rd. E14 163 ED77
Grote's Bldgs. SE3 164 EE82
Grote's Pl. SE3 164 EE82
Groton Rd. SW18 180 DB89
Grotto, The, Ware 33 DX07
Grotto Pas. W1 272 G6
Grotto Rd., Twick. 177 CF89
Grotto Rd., Wey. 195 BP104
Ground La., Hat. 45 CV16
Grove, The E15 144 EE65
Grove, The N3 98 DA53
Grove, The N4 121 DM59
Grove, The N6 120 DG60
Grove, The N8 121 DK57
Grove, The N13 99 DN50
Grove, The N14 81 DJ43
Grove, The NW9 118 CR57
Grove, The NW11 119 CY59
Grove, The W5 137 CK74
Grove, The, Add. 212 BH106
Grove, The, Amer. 55 AR36
Grove, The, Bexh. 166 EX84
Grove, The, Brwd. 108 FT49
Grove, The, Cat. 235 DP121
Grove, The, Chesh. 72 AX36
Grove, The, Couls. 235 DK115
Grove, The, Edg. 96 CP49
Grove, The, Egh. 173 BA92
Grove, The, Enf. 81 DN40
Grove, The, Epsom 216 CS113
Grove, The (Ewell), Epsom 217 CT110
West St.
Grove, The, Esher 196 CB102
Grove, The, Grav. 191 GH87
Grove, The, Grnf. 136 CC72
Grove, The, Hat. 64 DA26
Grove, The, Horl. 269 DH149
Grove, The, Islw. 157 CE81
Grove, The, Pot.B. 64 DD32
Grove, The, Rad. 61 CG34
Grove, The, Sid. 186 EY92
Grove, The, Slou. 152 AU75
Grove, The, Swan. 207 FF97
Grove, The, Swans. 190 FZ85
Grove, The, Tedd. 177 CG91
Grove, The, Twick. 177 CH86
Bridge Rd.
Grove, The, Upmin. 128 FP63
Grove, The, Uxb. 114 BN64
Grove, The, Walt. 195 BV101
Grove, The, W.Wick. 203 EB104
Grove, The, West. 238 EK118
Grove, The, Wok. 227 AZ116
Grove Ave. N3 98 DA52
Grove Ave. N10 99 DJ54
Grove Ave. W7 137 CE72
Grove Ave., Epsom 216 CS113
Grove Ave., Pnr. 116 BY57
Grove Ave., Sutt. 218 DA107
Grove Rd.
Grove Ave., Twick. 177 CF88
Grove Clo. N14 99 DH45
Avenue Rd.
Grove Clo. SE23 183 DY88
Grove Clo., Brom. 204 EG103
Grove Clo., Felt. 176 BY91
Grove Clo., Ger.Cr. 90 AW53
Grove La.
Grove Clo., Kings.T. 198 CM98
Grove Clo., Slou. 152 AU76
Alpha St. S.
Grove Clo., Uxb. 114 BN64
Grove Clo., Wind. 172 AV87
Grove Cor., Lthd. 246 CA126
Lower Shott
Grove Cotts. SW3 160 DE79
Grove Ct. SE3 164 EG81
Grove Ct., E.Mol. 197 CD99
Walton Rd.
Grove Ct., Wal.Abb. 67 EB33
Grove Cres. E18 102 EF54
Grove Cres. NW9 118 CQ56
Grove Cres. SE5 162 DS82
Grove Cres., Felt. 176 BY91
Grove Cres., Kings.T. 198 CL97
Grove Cres., Rick. 74 BN42
Grove Cres., Walt. 195 BV101
Grove Cres. Rd. E15 143 ED65
Grove End E18 102 EF54
Grove Hill
Grove End, Ger.Cr. 90 AW53
Grove End La., Esher 197 CD102
Grove End Rd. NW8 140 DD68
Grove Fm. Ind. Est., Mitch. 200 DF99
Grove Fm. Pk., Nthwd. 93 BR50
Grove Footpath, Surb. 198 CL98
Grove Gdns. E15 144 EE65
Grove Gdns. NW4 119 CU57
Grove Gdns. NW8 272 C3
Grove Gdns., Dag. 127 FC62
Grove Gdns., Enf. 83 DX38
Grove Gdns., Tedd. 177 CG91
Grove Grn. Rd. E11 123 EC62
Grove Hall Ct. NW8 140 DC69
Hall Rd.
Grove Hall Rd., Wat. 76 BY42
Grove Heath Ct., Wok. 228 BJ124
Grove Heath N., Wok. 228 BH122
Grove Heath Rd. (Ripley), Wok. 228 BH123
Grove Hill E18 102 EF54
Grove Hill, Ger.Cr. 90 AW52
Grove Hill, Har. 117 CE59
Grove Hill Rd. SE5 162 DS83
Grove Hill Rd., Har. 117 CE59
Grove Ho. Rd. N8 121 DL56
Grove La. SE5 162 DS82
Grove La., Beac. 89 AL53
Grove La., Chesh. 56 AU27
Grove La., Chig. 103 ET48
Grove La., Couls. 219 DH114
Grove La., Epp. 70 EU30
High St.
Grove La., Ger.Cr. 90 AV53
Grove La., Kings.T. 198 CL98
Grove La., Uxb. 134 BM70
Grove Lea, Hat. 45 CU21
Grove Mkt. Pl. SE9 185 EM86
Grove Mead, Hat. 45 CT18
Grove Meadow, Welw.G.C. 30 DC09
Grove Ms. W6 159 CW76
Grove Ms. W11 139 CZ72
Portobello Rd.
Grove Mill La., Wat. 75 BP37
Grove Pk. E11 124 EH58
Grove Pk. NW9 118 CQ56
Grove Pk. SE5 162 DS82
Grove Pk. Ave. E4 101 EB52
Grove Pk. Bri. W4 158 CQ80
Grove Pk. Gdns. W4 158 CQ80
Grove Pk. Ms. W4 158 CQ80
Grove Pk. Rd. N15 122 DS56
Grove Pk. Rd. SE9 184 EJ90
Grove Pk. Rd. W4 158 CP80
Grove Pk. Rd., Rain. 147 FG67
Grove Pk. Ter. W4 158 CP80
Grove Pas. E2 142 DV68
The Oval
Grove Pas., Tedd. 177 CG92
Grove Path (Cheshunt), Wal.Cr. 66 DU31
Tudor Ave.
Grove Pl. NW3 120 DD63
Christchurch Hill
Grove Pl. W3 138 CQ74
Grove Pl. W5 137 CK74
The Gro.
Grove Pl., Bark. 145 EQ67
Clockhouse Ave.
Grove Pl., Hat. 45 CW24
Dixons Hill Rd.
Grove Pl., Wat. 76 CB39
Hartspring La.
Grove Pl., Wey. 213 BQ106
Princes Rd.
Grove Rd. E3 143 DX67
Grove Rd. E4 101 EC49
Grove Rd. E11 124 EF59
Grove Rd. E17 123 EB58
Grove Rd. E18 102 EF54
Grove Rd. N11 99 DH50
Grove Rd. N12 98 DD50
Grove Rd. N15 122 DS57
Grove Rd. NW2 139 CW65
Grove Rd. SW13 159 CT82
Grove Rd. SW19 180 DC94
Grove Rd. W3 138 CQ74
Grove Rd. W5 137 CK73
Grove Rd., Amer. 72 AT37
Grove Rd., Ash. 232 CM118
Grove Rd., Barn. 80 DE41
Grove Rd., Beac. 89 AK53
Grove Rd., Belv. 166 EZ79
Grove Rd., Bexh. 167 FC84
Grove Rd., Borwd. 78 CN39
Grove Rd., Brent. 157 CJ78
Grove Rd., Cher. 193 BF100
Grove Rd., E.Mol. 197 CD98
Grove Rd., Edg. 96 CN51
Grove Rd., Epsom 216 CS113
Grove Rd., Grav. 190 GB85
Grove Rd., Grays 170 GB79
Grove Rd., Guil. 243 BC134
Grove Rd., Hem.H. 40 BG22
Grove Rd., Horl. 268 DE147
Grove Rd., Houns. 156 CA84
Grove Rd., Islw. 157 CE81
Grove Rd., Mitch. 200 DG97
Grove Rd., Nthwd. 93 BR50
Grove Rd., Oxt. 253 EC134
Southlands La.
Grove Rd., Pnr. 116 BZ57
Grove Rd., Rich. 178 CM86
Grove Rd., Rick. 92 BG47
Grove Rd., Rom. 126 EV59
Grove Rd., St.Alb. 43 CD21
Grove Rd., Sev. 257 FJ121
Grove Rd. (Seal), Sev. 257 FN122
Grove Rd., Shep. 195 BQ100
Grove Rd., Slou. 131 AK68
Grove Rd., Surb. 197 CK99
Grove Rd., Sutt. 218 DA107
Grove Rd., Th.Hth. 201 DN98
Grove Rd., Twick. 177 CD90
Grove Rd., Uxb. 134 BK66
Grove Rd., Ware 33 DZ05
Grove Rd., West. 238 EJ120
Grove Rd., Wind. 151 AQ82
Grove Rd., Wok. 227 AZ116
Grove Rd. W., Enf. 82 DW37
Grove Shaw, Tad. 233 CY124
Grove St. N18 100 DT50
Grove St. SE8 163 DZ77
Grove Ter. NW5 121 DH62
Grove Ter., Tedd. 177 CG91
Grove Vale SE22 162 DS84
Grove Vale, Chis. 185 EN93
Grove Vill. E14 143 EB73
Grove Wk., Hert. 32 DQ07
Grove Way, Esher 196 CC101
Grove Way, Rick. 73 BB43
Grove Way, Uxb. 134 BK66
Grove Wd. Hill, Couls. 219 DJ114
Grovebarns, Stai. 174 BG93
Grovebury Clo., Erith 167 FD79
Grovebury Gdns., St.Alb. 60 CC27
Grovebury Rd. SE2 166 EV75
Grovedale Clo. (Cheshunt), Wal.Cr. 66 DT30
Grovedale Rd. N19 121 DK61
Grovehall Rd. (Bushey), Wat. 76 BY42
Grovehill Rd., Red. 250 DE134
Groveland Ave. SW16 181 DM94
Groveland Ct. EC4 275 J9
Groveland Rd., Beck. 203 DZ97
Groveland Way, N.Mal. 198 CQ99
Grovelands, Hem.H. 41 BQ18
Grovelands, St.Alb. 60 CB27
Grovelands, W.Mol. 196 CA98
Grovelands Clo. SE5 162 DS82
Grovelands Clo., Har. 116 CB62
Grovelands Ct. N14 99 DK45
Grovelands Rd. N13 99 DM49
Grovelands Rd. N15 122 DU58
Grovelands Rd., Orp. 186 EU94
Grovelands Rd., Pur. 219 DL112
Grovelands Way, Grays 170 FZ78
Groveley Rd., Sun. 175 BS92
Grover Clo., Hem.H. 40 BK18
Grover Rd., Wat. 76 BX44
Groves Clo., B.End 110 AC60
Groveside, Lthd. 246 CA127
Groveside Clo. W3 138 CP72
Groveside Clo., Cars. 200 DE103
Groveside Clo., Lthd. 246 CA127
Groveside Rd. E4 102 EE47
Grovestile Waye, Felt. 175 BR87
Groveway SW9 161 DM81
Groveway, Dag. 126 EX63
Groveway, Wem. 118 CQ64
Grovewood, Rich. 158 CN81
Sandycoombe Rd.
Grovewood Clo., Rick. 73 BB43
Grovewood Pl., Wdf.Grn. 103 EM51
Grubb St., Oxt. 254 EJ128
Grubbs La., Hat. 46 DA22
Grummant Rd. SE15 162 DT81
Grundy St. E14 143 EB72
Gruneisen Rd. N3 98 DB52
Guardian Clo., Horn. 127 FH60
Guards Club Rd., Maid. 130 AC72
Guards Rd., Wind. 150 AJ82
Guards Wk., Wind. 150 AJ82
Guards Rd.
Guardsman Clo., Brwd. 108 FX50
Gubbins La., Rom. 106 FM52
Gubyon Ave. SE24 181 DP85
Guerin Sq. E3 143 DZ69
Malmesbury Rd.
Guernsey Clo., Guil. 243 BA129
Cotts Wd. Dr.
Guernsey Clo., Houns. 156 CA81
Guernsey Fm. Dr., Wok. 226 AX115
Guernsey Gro. SE24 182 DQ87
Guernsey Rd. E11 123 ED60
Guessens Ct., Welw.G.C. 29 CW09
Guessens Gro., Welw.G.C. 29 CW09
Guessens Rd., Welw.G.C. 29 CW09
Guessens Wk., Welw.G.C. 29 CW08
Guibal Rd. SE12 184 EH87
Guild Rd. SE7 164 EK78
Guild Rd., Erith 167 FF80
Guildcroft, Guil. 243 BA134
Guildersfield Rd. SW16 181 DL94
Guildford & Godalming Bypass, Guil. 258 AS137
Guildford Ave., Felt. 175 BT89
Guildford Business Pk., Guil. 242 AV133
Guildford Bypass, Guil. 243 AZ131
Guildford Gdns., Rom. 106 FL51
Guildford Gro. SE10 163 EB81
Guildford La., Guil. 260 BH139
Guildford La., Wok. 226 AX120
Guildford Lo. Dr., Lthd. 245 BT129
Guildford Pk. Ave., Guil. 258 AV135
Guildford Pk. Rd., Guil. 258 AV135
Guildford Rd. E6 145 EM72
Guildford Rd. E17 101 EC53
Guildford Rd. SW8 161 DL81
Guildford Rd., Cher. 193 BE102
Guildford Rd., Croy. 202 DR100
Guildford Rd. (Abinger Hammer), Dor. 261 BS139
Guildford Rd. (Westcott), Dor. 262 CA138
Guildford Rd., Gdmg. 258 AU144
Guildford Rd., Guil. 242 AX127
Guildford Rd., Ilf. 125 ES61
Guildford Rd., Lthd. 247 CE125
Guildford Rd. (East Horsley), Lthd. 245 BT130
Guildford Rd. (Great Bookham), Lthd. 246 BZ127
Guildford Rd., Rom. 106 FL51
Guildford Rd., St.Alb. 43 CH21
Guildford Rd., Wok. 226 AY119
Guildford Rd. (Mayford), Wok. 226 AX122
Guildford St., Cher. 193 BF102
Guildford St., Stai. 174 BG93
Guildford Way, Wall. 219 DL106
Guildhall Bldgs. EC2 275 K8
Guildhall Yd. EC2 142 DR72
Gresham St.
Guildhouse St. SW1 277 K8
Guildhouse St. SW1 161 DJ77
Guildown Ave. N12 98 DB49
Guildown Ave., Guil. 258 AV137
Guildown Rd., Guil. 258 AV137
Guildsway E17 101 DZ53
Guileshill La., Wok. 228 BL123
Guilford Ave., Surb. 198 CM99
Guilford Pl. WC1 274 B5
Guilford Pl. WC1 141 DM70
Guilford St. WC1 274 A5
Guilford St. WC1 141 DL70
Guilford Vill., Surb. 198 CM100
Alpha Rd.
Guilfords, Harl. 36 EX10
Guilsborough Clo. NW10 138 CS66
Guinevere Gdns., Wal.Cr. 67 DX31
Guinness Bldgs. SE1 279 M7
Guinness Bldgs. SE1 162 DS77
Guinness Clo. E9 143 DY66
Guinness Clo., Hayes 155 BR76
Guinness Ct., Wok. 226 AT118
Iveagh Rd.
Guinness Sq. SE1 279 M8
Guinness Trust Bldgs. SE11 278 F10
Guinness Trust Bldgs. SE11 161 DP78
Guinness Trust Bldgs. SW3 276 D9
Guinness Trust Est. N16 122 DS60
Holmleigh Rd.
Guinness Trust Est. SW9 161 DP84
Guion Rd. SW6 159 CZ82
Gull Clo., Wall. 219 DL108
Gull Wk., Horn. 147 FH66
Heron Flight Ave.
Gulland Clo. (Bushey), Wat. 76 CC43
Gulland Wk. N1 142 DQ65
Clephane Rd.
Gullbrook, Hem.H. 40 BG20
Gullet Wd. Rd., Wat. 75 BU35
Gulliver Clo., Nthlt. 136 BZ67
Gulliver Rd., Sid. 185 ES89
Gulliver St. SE16 163 DZ76
Gulphs, The, Hert. 32 DR09
Gulston Wk. SW3 160 DF77
Blacklands Ter.
Gumleigh Rd. W5 157 CJ77
Gumley Gdns., Islw. 157 CG83
Gumley Rd., Grays 169 FX79
Gumping Rd., Orp. 205 EQ102
Gun Hill, Til. 171 GK79
Gun St. E1 275 P7
Gun St. E1 142 DT71
Gundulph Rd., Brom. 204 EJ97
Gunfleet Clo., Grav. 191 GL87
Gunmakers La. E3 143 DY67
Gunn Rd., Swans. 190 FY86
Gunnell Clo. SE26 182 DU91
Gunnell Clo., Croy. 202 DU100
Gunner La. SE18 165 EN78
Gunners Gro. E4 101 EC48
Gunners Rd. SW18 180 DD89
Gunnersbury Ave. W3 138 CM74
Gunnersbury Ave. W4 138 CM74
Gunnersbury Ave. W5 138 CM74
Gunnersbury Clo. W4 158 CP78
Grange Rd.
Gunnersbury Ct. W3 158 CP75
Bollo La.
Gunnersbury Cres. W3 158 CN75
Gunnersbury Dr. W5 158 CM75
Gunnersbury Gdns. W3 158 CN75
Gunnersbury La. W3 158 CN76
Gunnersbury Ms. W4 158 CP78
Chiswick High Rd.
Gunnersbury Pk. W3 158 CM77
Gunnersbury Pk. W5 158 CM77
Gunning St. SE18 165 ES77
Gunpowder Sq. EC4 274 E8
Gunpowder Sq. EC4 141 DN72
Gunstor Rd. N16 122 DS63
Gunter Gro. SW10 160 DC79
Gunter Gro., Edg. 96 CR53
Gunterstone Rd. W14 159 CY77
Gunthorpe St. E1 142 DT71
Gunton Rd. E5 122 DV61
Gunton Rd. SW17 180 DG93
Gunwhale Clo. SE16 143 DX74
Gurdon Rd. SE7 164 EG78
Gurnard Clo., West Dr. 134 BK73
Trout Rd.
Gurnell Gro. W13 137 CF70
Gurnells Rd., Beac. 89 AQ50
Gurney Clo. E15 124 EE64
Gurney Rd.
Gurney Clo. E17 101 DX53
Gurney Clo., Bark. 145 EP65
Gurney Ct. Rd., St.Alb. 43 CF18
Gurney Cres., Croy. 201 DM102
Gurney Dr. N2 120 DC56
Gurney Rd. E15 124 EE64
Gurney Rd., Cars. 200 DG104
Gurney Rd., Nthlt. 135 BV69
Gurney's Clo., Red. 266 DF135
Guthrie St. SW3 276 B10
Gutter La. EC2 275 J8
Gutter La. EC2 142 DQ72
Gutteridge La., Rom. 87 FC44
Guy Barnett Clo. SE3 164 EG83
Casterbridge Rd.
Guy Rd., Wall. 201 DK104
Guy St. SE1 279 L4
Guy St. SE1 162 DR75
Guyatt Gdns., Mitch. 200 DG96
Ormerod Gdns.
Guyscliff Rd. SE13 183 EC85
Guysfield Clo., Rain. 147 FG67
Guysfield Dr., Rain. 147 FG67
Gwalior Rd. SW15 159 CX83
Felsham Rd.
Gwendolen Ave. SW15 159 CX84
Gwendolen Clo. SW15 179 CX85
Gwendoline Ave. E13 144 EH67
Gwendwr Rd. W14 159 CY78
Gwent Clo., Wat. 60 BX34
Gwillim Clo., Sid. 186 EU85
Gwydor Rd., Beck. 203 DX98
Gwydyr Rd., Brom. 204 EF97
Gwyn Clo. SW6 160 DC80
Gwynn Rd., Grav. 190 GC89
Gwynne Ave., Croy. 203 DX101
Gwynne Clo. W4 159 CT79
Gwynne Clo., Wind. 151 AL81
Gwynne Pk. Ave., Wdf.Grn. 103 EM51
Gwynne Pl. WC1 274 C3
Gwynne Rd. SW11 160 DD82
Gwynne Rd., Cat. 236 DQ121
Coulsdon Rd.
Gwynne Vaughan Ave., Guil. 242 AU130
Gwynns Wk., Hert. 32 DS09
Gyfford Wk., Wal.Cr. 66 DV31
Hawthorne Clo.
Gylcote Clo. SE5 162 DR84
Gyles Pk., Stan. 95 CJ52
Gyllyngdune Gdns., Ilf. 125 ET62
Gypsy Clo., Ware 33 DZ11
Gypsy La., Hat. 29 CZ13
Gypsy La., Kings L. 59 BR33
Gypsy La., Slou. 112 AS62
Gypsy La., Ware 33 DZ11
Gypsy Moth Ave., Hat. 44 CS15

H

Ha-Ha Rd. SE18 165 EM79
Haarlem Rd. W14 159 CX76
Haberdasher Pl. N1 275 L2
Haberdasher St. N1 275 L2
Haberdasher St. N1 142 DR69
Habgood Rd., Loug. 84 EL41
Haccombe Rd. SW19 180 DC93
Haydons Rd.
Hackbridge Grn., Wall. 200 DG103
Hackbridge Pk. Gdns., Cars. 200 DG103
Hackbridge Rd., Wall. 200 DG103
Hackett La., Saw. 35 ET05
Hacketts La., Wok. 211 BF114
Hackford Rd. SW9 161 DM81
Hackforth Clo., Barn. 79 CV43
Hackhurst La., Dor. 261 BT139
Hackington Cres., Beck. 183 EA93
Hackney Clo., Borwd. 78 CR43
Hackney Gro. E8 142 DV65
Reading La.
Hackney Rd. E2 275 P2
Hackney Rd. E2 142 DT69
Hacton Dr., Horn. 128 FK63
Hacton La., Horn. 128 FM61
Hacton La., Upmin. 128 FM64
Hadden Rd. SE28 165 ES76
Hadden Way, Grnf. 137 CD65
Haddington Rd., Brom. 183 ED91
Haddo St. SE10 163 EC79
Haddon Clo., Borwd. 78 CN40
Haddon Clo., Enf. 82 DU44
Haddon Clo., Hem.H. 40 BN21
Haddon Clo., N.Mal. 199 CT99

Haddon Clo., Wey. 195 BR104
Haddon Gro., Sid. 185 ET87
Haddon Rd., Orp. 206 EW99
Haddon Rd., Rick. 73 BC43
Haddon Rd., Sutt. 218 DB105
Haddonfield SE8 163 DX77
Hadfield Clo., Sthl. 136 BZ69
Adrienne Ave.
Hadfield Rd., Stai. 174 BK86
Hadleigh Clo. E1 142 DW70
Mantus Rd.
Hadleigh Clo. SW20 199 CZ96
Hadleigh Ct., Brox. 49 DZ22
Hadleigh Dr., Sutt. 218 DA109
Hadleigh Rd. N9 100 DV45
Hadleigh St. E2 142 DW69
Hadleigh Wk. E6 144 EL72
Kirkham Rd.
Hadley Clo. N21 81 DN44
Hadley Clo., Borwd. 78 CM43
Hadley Common, Barn. 80 DA40
Hadley Gdns. W4 158 CR78
Hadley Gdns., Sthl. 156 BZ78
Hadley Gra., Harl. 52 EW15
Hadley Grn., Barn. 79 CZ40
Hadley Grn. Rd., Barn. 79 CZ40
Hadley Grn. W., Barn. 79 CY40
Hadley Gro., Barn. 79 CY40
Hadley Highstone, Barn. 79 CZ39
Hadley Pl., Wey. 212 BN108
Hadley Ridge, Barn. 79 CZ41
Hadley Rd. (Hadley Wd.), Barn. 80 DG38
Hadley Rd. (New Barnet), Barn. 80 DB41
Hadley Rd., Belv. 166 EZ77
Hadley Rd., Enf. 81 DL38
Hadley Rd., Mitch. 201 DK98
Hadley St. NW1 141 DH65
Hadley Way N21 81 DN44
Hadley Wd. Ri., Ken. 235 DP115
Hadlow Ct., Slou. 131 AQ73
Hadlow Pl. SE19 182 DU94
Hadlow Rd., Sid. 186 EU91
Hadlow Rd., Well. 166 EW80
Hadlow Way, Grav. 190 GE94
Hadrian Clo., St.Alb. 42 CA22
Hadrian Clo., Stai. 174 BL88
Hadrian Way
Hadrian Clo., Wall. 219 DL108
De Havilland Rd.
Hadrian Est. E2 142 DU68
Hackney Rd.
Hadrian St. SE10 164 EE78
Hadrian Way, Stai. 174 BK87
Hadrians Ride, Enf. 82 DT43
Hadyn Pk. Rd. W12 159 CU75
Hafer Rd. SW11 160 DF84
Hafton Rd. SE6 184 EE88
Hag Hill La., Maid. 130 AG72
Hag Hill Ri., Maid. 130 AG72
Hagden La., Wat. 75 BT43
Haggard Rd., Twick. 177 CG87
Haggerston Rd. E8 142 DT66
Haggerston Rd., Borwd. 78 CL38
Hagsdell La., Hert. 32 DR09
Hagsdell Rd., Hert. 32 DR09
Hague St. E2 142 DU69
Derbyshire St.
Haig Clo., St.Alb. 43 CH21
Kitchener Clo.
Haig Dr., Slou. 151 AP75
Haig Gdns., Grav. 191 GJ87
Haig Rd., Grays 171 GG76
Haig Rd., Stan. 95 CJ50
Haig Rd., Uxb. 135 BP71
Haig Rd., West. 238 EL117
Haig Rd. E. E13 144 EJ69
Haig Rd. W. E13 144 EJ69
Haigh Cres., Red. 267 DH136
Haigville Gdns., Ilf. 125 EP56
Hailes Clo. SW19 180 DC93
North Rd.
Hailey Ave., Hodd. 33 EA13
Hailey La., Hert. 33 DX13
Hailey Rd., Erith 166 FA75
Haileybury Ave., Enf. 82 DT44
Haileybury Rd., Orp. 224 EU105
Hailsham Ave. SW2 181 DM89
Hailsham Clo., Rom. 106 FJ50
Hailsham Clo., Surb. 197 CK101
Hailsham Dr., Har. 117 CD55
Hailsham Gdns., Rom. 106 FJ50
Hailsham Rd. SW17 180 DG93
Hailsham Rd., Rom. 106 FJ50
Hailsham Ter. N18 100 DQ50
Haimo Rd. SE9 184 EK85
Hainault Ct. E17 123 ED56
Hainault Gore, Rom. 126 EY57
Hainault Gro., Chig. 103 EQ49
Hainault Rd. E11 123 EC60
Hainault Rd., Chig. 103 EP48
Hainault Rd., Rom. 105 FC54
Hainault Rd. (Chadwell Heath), Rom. 126 EZ58
Hainault Rd. (Hainault), Rom. 126 EV55
Hainault St. SE9 185 EP88
Hainault St., Ilf. 125 EQ61
Haines Ct., Wey. 213 BR106
St. George's Lo.
Haines Way, Wat. 59 BU34
Hainford Clo. SE4 163 DX84
Haining Clo. W4 158 CN78
Wellesley Rd.
Hainthorpe Rd. SE27 181 DP90
Hainton Clo. E1 142 DV72
Halberd Ms. E5 122 DV61
Knightland Rd.
Halbutt Gdns., Dag. 126 EZ62
Halbutt St., Dag. 126 EZ63
Halcomb St. N1 142 DS67
Halcot Ave., Bexh. 187 FB85
Halcrow St. E1 142 DV71
Newark St.
Halcyon Way, Horn. 128 FM60
Haldan Rd. E4 101 EC51
Haldane Clo. N10 99 DH52
Haldane Gdns., Grav. 190 GC88
Haldane Pl. SW18 180 DB88
Haldane Rd. E6 144 EK69
Haldane Rd. SE28 146 EX73
Haldane Rd. SW6 159 CZ80
Haldane Rd., Sthl. 136 CC73
Haldens, Welw.G.C. 29 CZ06
Haldon Clo., Chig. 103 ES50
Haldon Rd. SW18 179 CZ85
Hale, The E4 101 ED52
Hale, The N17 122 DU55
Hale Clo. E4 101 EC48
Hale Clo., Edg. 96 CQ50
Hale Clo., Orp. 223 EQ105
Hale Dr. NW7 96 CQ51
Hale End, Rom. 105 FH51
Hale End, Wok. 226 AV121
Hale End Clo., Ruis. 115 BU58
Hale End Rd. E4 101 ED51
Hale End Rd. E17 101 ED53
Hale End Rd., Wdf.Grn. 101 ED52
Hale Gdns. N17 122 DU55
Hale Gdns. W3 138 CN74
Hale Gro. Gdns. NW7 96 CR50
Hale La. NW7 96 CR50
Hale La., Edg. 96 CP50
Hale La., Sev. 241 FE117
Hale Path SE27 181 DP91
Hale Pit Rd., Lthd. 246 CC126
Hale Rd. E6 144 EL70
Hale Rd. N17 122 DU55
Hale Rd., Hert. 32 DR10
Hale St. E14 143 EB73
Hale St., Stai. 173 BE91
Hale Wk. W7 137 CE71
Benham Rd.
Halefield Rd. N17 100 DU53
Hales Oak, Lthd. 246 CC126
Hales Pk., Hem.H. 41 BQ19
Hales Pk. Clo., Hem.H. 41 BQ19
Hales St. SE8 163 EA80
Deptford High St.
Halesowen Rd., Mord. 200 DB101
Haleswood, Cob. 213 BV114
Haleswood Rd., Hem.H. 41 BP19
Halesworth Clo. E5 122 DW61
Theydon Rd.
Halesworth Clo., Rom. 106 FL52
Halesworth Rd. SE13 163 EB83
Halesworth Rd., Rom. 106 FL51
Haley Rd. NW4 119 CW58
Half Acre, Brent. 157 CK79
Half Acre Rd. W7 137 CE74
Half Moon Ct. EC1 275 H7
Half Moon Cres. N1 141 DM68
Half Moon La. SE24 182 DQ86
Half Moon La., Epp. 69 ET31
Half Moon Meadow, Hem.H. 41 BP15
Half Moon Pas. E1 142 DT72
Braham St.
Half Moon St. W1 277 J2
Half Moon St. W1 141 DH74
Half Moon Yd., St.Alb. 43 CD20
Chequer St.
Halfacre Hill, Ger.Cr. 91 AZ53
Halfhide La. (Cheshunt), Wal.Cr. 67 DX27
Halfhides, Wal.Abb. 67 ED33
Halford Rd. E10 123 ED57
Halford Rd. SW6 160 DA79
Halford Rd., Rich. 178 CL85
Halford Rd., Uxb. 114 BN64
Halfpenny Clo., Guil. 259 BD140
Halfpenny La., Guil. 259 BC136
Halfway Ct., Purf. 168 FN77
Thamley
Halfway Grn., Walt. 195 BV104
Halfway Ho. La., Amer. 54 AL33
Halfway St., Sid. 185 ER87
Haliburton Rd., Twick. 177 CG85
Haliday Wk. N1 142 DR65
Balls Pond Rd.
Halidon Clo. E9 122 DW64
Urswick Rd.
Halidon Ri., Rom. 106 FP51
Halifax Rd., Enf. 82 DQ40
Halifax Rd., Grnf. 136 CB67
Halifax Rd., Rick. 91 BC45
Halifax St. SE26 182 DV91
Halifax Way, Welw.G.C. 30 DE09
Halifield Dr., Belv. 166 EY76
Haling Down Pas., S.Croy. 220 DQ109
Kingsdown Ave.
Haling Gro., S.Croy. 220 DQ108
Haling Pk. Gdns., S.Croy. 219 DP107
Haling Pk. Rd., S.Croy. 219 DP107
Haling Rd., S.Croy. 220 DR107
Halings La., Uxb. 113 BD56
Halkin Arc. SW1 276 F6
Halkin Ms. SW1 276 F6
Halkin Pl. SW1 276 F6
Halkin Pl. SW1 160 DG76
Halkin St. SW1 276 G5
Halkin St. SW1 160 DG75
Halkingcroft, Slou. 152 AW75
Hall, The SE3 164 EG83
Hall Ave. N18 100 DR51
Weir Hall Ave.
Hall Ave., S.Ock. 148 FQ74
Hall Clo. W5 138 CL71
Hall Clo., Gdmg. 258 AS144
Hall Clo., Rick. 92 BG46
Hall Ct., Slou. 152 AV80
Hall Ct., Tedd. 177 CF92
Teddington Pk.
Hall Cres., S.Ock. 168 FQ75
Hall Dene Clo., Guil. 243 BC133
Hall Dr. SE26 182 DW92
Hall Dr. W7 137 CE72
Hall Dr., Uxb. 92 BJ53
Hall Fm. Clo., Stan. 95 CH49
Hall Fm. Dr., Twick. 177 CD87
Hall Gdns. E4 101 DZ49
Hall Gdns., St.Alb. 44 CR23
Hall Gate NW8 140 DC69
Hall Rd.
Hall Grn. La., Brwd. 109 GC45
Hall Gro., Welw.G.C. 30 DB11
Hall Heath Clo., St.Alb. 43 CH18
Hall Hill, Oxt. 253 ED131
Hall Hill, Sev. 257 FP123
Hall La. E4 101 DY50
Hall La. NW4 97 CU53
Hall La., Brwd. 109 FZ44
Hall La., Hayes 155 BR80
Hall La., S.Ock. 149 FW68
Hall La., Upmin. 106 FQ54
Hall Meadow, Slou. 130 AJ68
Hall Oak Wk. NW6 139 CZ65
Maygrove Rd.
Hall Pk., Berk. 38 AY20
Hall Pk. Gate, Berk. 38 AY21
Hall Pk. Hill, Berk. 38 AY21
Hall Pk. Rd., Upmin. 128 FQ64
Hall Pl. W2 140 DD70
Hall Pl., Wok. 227 BA116
Hall Pl. Clo., St.Alb. 43 CE19
Hall Pl. Cres., Bex. 187 FC85
Hall Pl. Dr., Wey. 213 BS106
Hall Pl. Gdns., St.Alb. 43 CE19
Hall Rd. E6 145 EM67
Hall Rd. E15 123 ED63
Hall Rd. NW8 140 DC69
Hall Rd., Dart. 168 FM84
Hall Rd., Grav. 190 GC90
Hall Rd., Hem.H. 41 BP18
Hall Rd., Islw. 177 CD85
Hall Rd., Rom. 126 EW58
Hall Rd. (Gidea Pk.), Rom. 127 FH55
Hall Rd., S.Ock. 168 FQ75
Hall Rd., Wall. 219 DH109
Hall St. EC1 274 G2
Hall St. EC1 141 DP69
Hall St. N12 98 DC50
Hall Ter., Rom. 106 FN52
Hall Ter., S.Ock. 169 FR75
Hall Vw. SE9 184 EK89
Hall Way, Pur. 219 DP113
Downs Ct. Rd.
Hallam Clo., Chis. 185 EM92
Hallam Clo., Wat. 76 BW40
Hallam Gdns., Pnr. 94 BY52
Hallam Ms. W1 273 J6
Hallam Rd. N15 121 DP56
Hallam Rd. SW13 159 CV83
Hallam St. W1 273 J5
Hallam St. W1 141 DH71
Halland Way, Nthwd. 93 BR51
Halley Gdns. SE13 163 ED84
Halley Rd. E7 144 EJ65
Halley Rd. E12 144 EK65
Halley St. E14 143 DY71
Halleys App., Wok. 226 AU118
Halleys Ct., Wok. 226 AU118
Halleys App.
Halleys Ridge, Hert. 31 DN10
Halleys Wk., Add. 212 BJ108
Hallfield Est. W2 140 DC72
Cleveland Ter.
Hallford Way, Dart. 188 FJ85
Halliards, The, Walt. 195 BU100
Felix Rd.
Halliday Sq., Sthl. 137 CD74
Halliford Clo., Shep. 195 BR98
Halliford Rd., Shep. 195 BS99
Halliford Rd., Sun. 195 BT99
Halliford St. N1 142 DQ66
Halling Hill, Harl. 35 ET13
Hallingbury Ct. E17 123 EB55
Hallington Clo., Wok. 226 AV117
Halliwell Rd. SW2 181 DM86
Halliwick Rd. N10 98 DG53
Hallmark Trd. Est. NW10 118 CQ63
Great Cen. Way
Hallmead Rd., Sutt. 200 DB104
Hallmores, Brox. 49 EA19
Hallowell Ave., Croy. 219 DL105
Hallowell Clo., Mitch. 200 DG97
Hallowell Rd., Nthwd. 93 BS52
Hallowes Cres., Wat. 93 BU48
Hayling Rd.
Hallowfield Way, Mitch. 200 DD97
Hallside Rd., Enf. 82 DT38
Hallsland Way, Oxt. 254 EF132
Hallsville Rd. E16 144 EF72
Hallswelle Rd. NW11 119 CZ57
Hallwood Cres., Brwd. 108 FY45
Hallywell Cres. E6 145 EM71
Halons Rd. SE9 185 EN87
Halpin Pl. SE17 279 L9
Halsbrook Rd. SE3 164 EJ83
Halsbury Clo., Stan. 95 CH49
Halsbury Rd. W12 139 CU74
Halsbury Rd. E., Nthlt. 116 CC63
Halsbury Rd. W., Nthlt. 116 CB64
Halse Dr., Slou. 111 AM63
Halsend, Hayes 135 BV74
Halsey Ms. SW3 276 D8
Halsey Pk., St.Alb. 62 CM27
Halsey Pl., Wat. 75 BV38
Halsey Rd., Wat. 75 BV41
Halsey St. SW3 276 D8
Halsey St. SW3 160 DF77
Halsford Bri. Ind. Est., Brwd. 108 FW47
Halsham Cres., Bark. 145 ET65
Halsmere Rd. SE5 161 DP81
Halstead Clo., Croy. 202 DQ104
Charles St.
Halstead Ct. N1 275 L1
Halstead Gdns. N21 100 DR46
Halstead Hill (Cheshunt), Wal.Cr. 66 DS29
Halstead La., Sev. 224 EZ114
Halstead Rd. E11 124 EG57
Halstead Rd. N21 100 DR46
Halstead Rd., Enf. 82 DS42
Halstead Rd., Erith 167 FE81
Halstead Way, Brwd. 109 GC44
Halston Clo. SW11 180 DF86
Halstow Rd. NW10 139 CX69
Halstow Rd. SE10 164 EG78
Halsway, Hayes 135 BU74
Halt Robin La., Belv. 167 FB77
Halt Robin Rd.
Halt Robin Rd., Belv. 166 FA77
Halter Clo., Borwd. 78 CR43
Clydesdale Clo.
Halton Cross St. N1 141 DP67
Halton Rd.
Halton Rd. N1 141 DP66
Halton Rd., Grays 171 GH76
Haltside, Hat. 44 CS19
Halwick Clo., Hem.H. 40 BH21
Ham, The, Brent. 157 CJ80
Ham Clo., Rich. 177 CJ90
Ham Common, Rich. 177 CK90
Ham Fm. Rd., Rich. 177 CK91
Ham Gate Ave., Rich. 178 CL91
Ham La., Egh. 172 AV91
Ham La., Wind. 152 AW84
Ham Pk. Rd. E7 144 EG66
Ham Pk. Rd. E15 144 EF66
Ham Ridings, Rich. 178 CM92
Ham St., Rich. 177 CH88
Ham Vw., Croy. 203 DY100
Ham Yd. W1 273 M10
Hambalt Rd. SW4 181 DJ85
Hamble Clo., Ruis. 115 BS61
Chichester Ave.
Hamble Clo., Wok. 226 AU117
Hamble Ct., Kings.T. 177 CK94
Hamble La., S.Ock. 149 FT71
Hamble St. SW6 160 DB83
Hamble Wk., Nthlt. 136 CA68
Brabazon Rd.
Hamble Wk., Wok. 226 AU118
Denton Way
Hambledon Clo., Uxb. 135 BP71
Aldenham Dr.
Hambledon Gdns. SE25 202 DT97
Hambledon Hill, Epsom 232 CQ116
Hambledon Pl. SE21 182 DS88
Hambledon Rd. SW18 179 CZ87
Hambledon Rd., Cat. 236 DQ121
Coulsdon Rd.
Hambledon Vale, Epsom 232 CQ116
Hambledown Rd., Sid. 185 ER87
Hambleton Clo., Wor.Pk. 199 CW103
Cotswold Way
Hamblings Clo., Rad. 61 CK33
Hambridge Way SW2 181 DN87
Hambro Ave., Brom. 204 EG102
Hambro Rd. SW16 181 DK93
Hambro Rd., Brwd. 108 FX47
Hambrook Rd. SE25 202 DV97
Hambrough Rd., Sthl. 136 BY74
Hamburgh Ct., Wal.Cr. 67 DX28
Hamden Cres., Dag. 127 FB62
Hamel Clo., Har. 117 CK55
Hamelin St. E14 143 EC72
St. Leonards Rd.
Hamels Dr., Hert. 32 DV08
Hamer Clo., Hem.H. 57 BA28
Hamerton Rd., Grav. 190 GB85
Hameway E6 145 EN70
Hamfield Clo., Oxt. 253 EC127
Hamfrith Rd. E15 144 EF65
Hamhaugh Island, Shep. 194 BN103
Hamilton Ave. N9 100 DU45
Hamilton Ave., Cob. 213 BU113
Hamilton Ave., Hodd. 49 EA15
Hamilton Ave., Ilf. 125 EP56
Hamilton Ave., Rom. 105 FD54
Hamilton Ave., Surb. 198 CN103
Hamilton Ave., Sutt. 199 CY102
Hamilton Ave., Wok. 227 BE115
Hamilton Clo. N17 122 DT55
Hamilton Clo. NW8 140 DD69
Hamilton Clo. SE16 163 DY75
Somerford Way
Hamilton Clo., Barn. 80 DE42
Hamilton Clo., Cher. 193 BF102
Hamilton Clo., Epsom 216 CQ112
Hamilton Clo., Felt. 175 BT92
Hamilton Clo., Guil. 242 AU129
Hamilton Clo., Pot.B. 63 CU33
Hamilton Clo., Pur. 219 DP112
Hamilton Clo., St.Alb. 60 CA31
Hamilton Clo., Stan. 95 CF47
Hamilton Ct. W5 138 CM73
Hamilton Ct. W9 140 DC69
Maida Vale
Hamilton Ct., Hat. 45 CV20
Cooks Way
Hamilton Ct., Lthd. 246 CB125
Eastwick Pk. Ave.
Hamilton Cres. N13 99 DN49
Hamilton Cres., Brwd. 108 FW49
Hamilton Cres., Har. 116 BZ62
Hamilton Cres., Houns. 176 CB85
Hamilton Dr., Guil. 242 AU129
Hamilton Dr., Rom. 106 FL54
Hamilton Gdns. NW8 140 DC69
Hamilton Gdns., Slou. 130 AH69
Hamilton Gordon Ct., Guil. 242 AW133
Langley Clo.
Hamilton La. N5 121 DP63
Hamilton Pk.
Hamilton Mead, Hem.H. 57 BA27
Hamilton Ms. W1 277 H4
Hamilton Pk. N5 121 DP63
Hamilton Pk. W. N5 121 DP63
Hamilton Pl. W1 276 G3
Hamilton Pl. W1 140 DG74
Hamilton Pl., Guil. 242 AU129
Hamilton Pl., Sun. 175 BV94
Hamilton Pl., Tad. 233 CZ122
Hamilton Rd. E15 144 EE69
Hamilton Rd. E17 101 DY54
Hamilton Rd. N2 120 DC55
Hamilton Rd. N9 100 DU45
Hamilton Rd. NW10 119 CU64
Hamilton Rd. NW11 119 CX59
Hamilton Rd. SE27 182 DR91
Hamilton Rd. SW19 180 DB94
Hamilton Rd. W4 158 CS75
Hamilton Rd. W5 138 CL73
Hamilton Rd., Barn. 80 DE42
Hamilton Rd., Berk. 38 AV19
Hamilton Rd., Bexh. 166 EY82
Hamilton Rd., Brent. 157 CK79
Hamilton Rd., Felt. 175 BT91
Hamilton Rd., Grays 169 FW78
Hamilton Rd., Har. 117 CE57
Hamilton Rd., Hayes 135 BV73
Hamilton Rd., Ilf. 125 EP63
Hamilton Rd., Kings L. 59 BQ33
Hamilton Rd., Rom. 127 FH57
Hamilton Rd., St.Alb. 43 CG19
Hamilton Rd., Sid. 186 EU91
Hamilton Rd., Slou. 131 AN72
Hamilton Rd., Sthl. 136 BZ74
Hamilton Rd., Th.Hth. 202 DR97
Hamilton Rd., Twick. 177 CE88
Hamilton Rd., Uxb. 134 BK70
Hamilton Rd., Wat. 93 BV48
Hamilton Sq. SE1 279 L4
Hamilton St. SE8 163 EA79
Deptford High St.
Hamilton St., Wat. 76 BW43
Hamilton Ter. NW8 140 DB68
Hamilton Wk., Erith 167 FF80
Frobisher Rd.
Hamilton Way N3 98 DA51
Hamilton Way N13 99 DP49
Hamilton Way, Wall. 219 DK109
Hamlea Clo. SE12 184 EG85
Hamlet, The SE5 162 DR83
Hamlet, The, Berk. 39 BA16
Hamlet Clo. SE13 164 EE84
Old Rd.
Hamlet Clo., Rom. 104 FA52
Hamlet Gdns. W6 159 CU77
Hamlet Hill, Harl. 50 EF19
Hamlet Rd. SE19 182 DT94
Hamlet Rd., Rom. 104 FA52
Hamlet Sq. NW2 119 CY62
Cricklewood Trd. Est.
Hamlet Sq. NW11 119 CY62
The Vale
Hamlet Way SE1 279 L4
Hamlets Way E3 143 DZ70
Hamlin Cres., Pnr. 116 BW57
Hamlin Rd., Sev. 256 FE121
Hamlyn Clo., Edg. 96 CL48
Hamlyn Gdns. SE19 182 DS94
Hamm Ct., Wey. 194 BM104
Hamm Moor La., Add. 212 BL106
Hammarskjold Rd., Harl. 35 ER13
Hammelton Grn. SW9 161 DP81
Cromwell Rd.
Hammelton Rd., Brom. 204 EF95
Hammer La., Hem.H. 40 BM19
Hammer Par., Wat. 59 BT33
Hammerfield Dr., Dor. 261 BT141
Hammers Gate, St.Alb. 60 CA25
Hammers La. NW7 97 CU50
Hammersley La., H.Wyc. 88 AC49
Hammersmith Bri. SW13 159 CV78
Hammersmith Bri. Rd. W6 159 CW78
Hammersmith Bdy. W6 159 CW77
Hammersmith Flyover W6 159 CW78
Hammersmith Gro. W6 159 CW75
Hammersmith Rd. W6 159 CX77
Hammersmith Rd. W14 159 CX77
Hammersmith Ter. W6 159 CU78
Hammet Clo., Hayes 136 BX71
Willow Tree La.
Hammett St. EC3 275 P10
Hammond Ave., Mitch. 201 DH96
Hammond Clo., Barn. 79 CY43
Hammond Clo., Grnf. 117 CD64
Lilian Board Way
Hammond Clo., Hmptn. 196 CA95
Hammond Clo. (Cheshunt), Wal.Cr. 66 DS26
Hammond Clo., Wok. 226 AW115
Hammond End, Slou. 111 AP63
Hammond Rd., Enf. 82 DV40
Hammond Rd., Sthl. 156 BY76
Hammond Rd., Wok. 226 AW115
Hammond St. NW5 141 DJ65
Hammond Way SE28 146 EV73
Oriole Way
Hammonds Clo., Dag. 126 EW62
Hammonds La., Brwd. 107 FV51
Hammond's La., Hat. 28 CN12
Hammond's La., St.Alb. 28 CN12
Hammondstreet Rd. (Cheshunt), Wal.Cr. 65 DP25
Hamond Clo., S.Croy. 219 DP109
Hamonde Clo., Edg. 96 CP47
Hampden Ave., Beck. 203 DY96
Hampden Ave., Chesh. 54 AN30
Hampden Clo. NW1 273 N1
Hampden Clo., Epp. 70 FA27
Hampden Clo., Slou. 132 AU69
Hampden Cres., Brwd. 108 FW49
Hampden Cres. (Cheshunt), Wal.Cr. 66 DV31
Hampden Gurney St. W1 272 D9
Hampden Hill, Beac. 88 AH53
Hampden Hill, Ware 33 DZ05
Hampden Hill Clo., Ware 33 DZ05
Hampden Hill
Hampden La. N17 100 DT53
Hampden Pl., St.Alb. 61 CE29
Hampden Rd. N8 121 DN56
Hampden Rd. N10 98 DG52
Hampden Rd. N17 100 DU53
Hampden Rd. N19 121 DK61
Holloway Rd.
Hampden Rd., Beck. 203 DY96
Hampden Rd., Ger.Cr. 90 AX53
Hampden Rd., Grays 170 GB78
Hampden Rd., Har. 94 CC53
Hampden Rd., Kings.T. 198 CN97
Hampden Rd., Rom. 105 FB52
Hampden Rd., Slou. 153 AZ76
Hampden Sq. N14 99 DH46
Osidge La.
Hampden Way N14 99 DH47
Hampden Way, Wat. 75 BS36
Hampermill La., Wat. 93 BT47
Hampshire Ave., Slou. 131 AQ71
Hampshire Clo. N18 100 DV50
Hampshire Hog La. W6 159 CV77
King St.
Hampshire Rd. N22 99 DM52
Hampshire Rd., Horn. 128 FN56
Hampshire St. NW5 141 DK65
Torriano Ave.
Hampson Way SW8 161 DM81
Hampstead Clo. SE28 146 EV74
Hampstead Gdns. NW11 120 DA58
Hampstead Gdns., Rom. 126 EV57
Hampstead Grn. NW3 120 DE64
Hampstead Gro. NW3 120 DC62
Hampstead High St. NW3 120 DC63
Hampstead Hill Gdns. NW3 120 DD63
Hampstead La. N6 120 DD59
Hampstead La. NW3 120 DD60
Hampstead La., Dor. 263 CG137
Hampstead Rd. NW1 273 K1
Hampstead Rd. NW1 141 DJ68
Hampstead Rd., Dor. 263 CG137
Hampstead Sq. NW3 120 DC62
Hampstead Wk. E3 143 DZ67
Parnell Rd.
Hampstead Way NW11 119 CZ57
Hampton Clo. N11 99 DH50
Balmoral Ave.
Hampton Clo. NW6 140 DA69
Hampton Clo. SW20 179 CW94
Hampton Ct. N1 141 DP65
Upper St.
Hampton Ct. Ave., E.Mol. 197 CD99
Hampton Ct. Cres., E.Mol. 197 CD97
Hampton Ct. Palace, E.Mol. 197 CE97
Hampton Ct. Par., E.Mol. 197 CE98
Creek Rd.

Harrison Rd., Dag. 147 FB65
Harrison St. WC1 274 A3
Harrison St. WC1 141 DL69
Harrison Wk. (Cheshunt), Wal.Cr. 67 DX30
Harrison Way, Sev. 256 FG122
Harrison Way, Slou. 131 AK74
Harrisons Ri., Croy. 201 DP104
Harris's La., Ware 32 DW05
Harrogate Ct., Slou. 153 BA78
Harrogate Rd., Wat. 94 BW48
Harrold Rd., Dag. 126 EV64
Harrow Ave., Enf. 82 DT44
Harrow Bottom Rd., Vir.W. 193 AZ100
Harrow Clo., Add. 194 BH103
Harrow Clo., Chess. 215 CK108
Harrow Clo., Dor. 263 CG137
Harrow Rd. W.
Harrow Cres., Rom. 105 FH52
Harrow Dr. N9 100 DT46
Harrow Dr., Horn. 127 FH58
Harrow Flds. Gdns., Har. 117 CE62
Harrow Gdns., Orp. 224 EV105
Harrow Gdns., Warl. 237 DZ116
Harrow Gate Gdns., Dor. 263 CH138
Horsham Rd.
Harrow Grn. E11 124 EE62
Harrow Rd.
Harrow La. E14 143 EC73
Harrow La., Gdmg. 258 AS144
Farncombe St.
Harrow Manorway SE2 166 EW76
Harrow Pk., Har. 117 CE61
Harrow Pas., Kings.T. 197 CK96
Market Pl.
Harrow Pl. E1 275 P8
Harrow Pl. E1 142 DS72
Harrow Rd. E6 144 EL67
Harrow Rd. E11 124 EE62
Harrow Rd. NW10 139 CV69
Harrow Rd. W2 139 CX69
Harrow Rd. W9 139 CX69
Harrow Rd. W10 139 CX69
Harrow Rd., Bark. 145 ES67
Harrow Rd., Cars. 218 DE106
Harrow Rd., Felt. 174 BN88
Harrow Rd., Ilf. 125 EQ63
Harrow Rd., Sev. 240 EY115
Harrow Rd., Slou. 153 AZ76
Harrow Rd., Warl. 237 DZ115
Harrow Rd., Wem. 117 CF63
Harrow Rd. (Tokyngton), Wem. 118 CN64
Harrow Rd. E., Dor. 263 CH138
Harrow Rd. W., Dor. 263 CG138
Harrow Vw., Har. 94 CC53
Harrow Vw., Hayes 135 BU72
Harrow Vw., Uxb. 135 BQ69
Harrow Vw. Rd. W5 137 CH70
Harrow Way, Shep. 195 BQ96
Harrow Way, Wat. 94 BY48
Harrow Weald Pk., Har. 95 CD51
Harroway Rd. SW11 160 DD82
Harrowby Gdns., Grav. 190 GE89
Harrowby St. W1 272 C8
Harrowby St. W1 140 DE72
Harrowdene Clo., Wem. 117 CK63
Harrowdene Gdns., Tedd. 177 CG93
Harrowdene Rd., Wem. 117 CK64
Harrowes Meade, Edg. 96 CN48
Harrowgate Rd. E9 143 DY65
Harrowlands Pk., Dor. 263 CH137
Harrowsley Ct., Horl. 269 DH147
Tanyard Way
Harrowsley Grn. La., Horl. 269 DJ149
Hart Clo., Red. 252 DT134
Hart Cor., Grays 169 FX78
Mill La.
Hart Cres., Chig. 103 ET50
Hart Dyke Cres., Swan. 207 FD97
Hart Dyke Rd.
Hart Dyke Rd., Orp. 206 EW102
Hart Dyke Rd., Swan. 207 FD96
Hart Gdns., Dor. 263 CH135
Hart Rd.
Hart Gro. W5 138 CN74
Hart Gro., Sthl. 136 CA71
Hart Rd., Dor. 263 CH135
Hart Rd., Harl. 36 EW10
Hart Rd., St.Alb. 43 CD21
Hart Rd., W.Byf. 212 BL113
Hart St. EC3 275 N10
Hart St., Brwd. 108 FW47
Harte Rd., Houns. 156 BZ82
Hartfield Ave., Borwd. 78 CN43
Hartfield Ave., Nthlt. 135 BV68
Hartfield Clo., Borwd. 78 CN43
Hartfield Ct., Ware 33 DX05
Hartfield Cres. SW19 179 CZ94
Hartfield Cres., W.Wick. 204 EG104
Hartfield Gro. SE20 202 DW95
Hartfield Pl., Grav. 190 GD87
Hartfield Rd. SW19 179 CZ93
Hartfield Rd., Chess. 215 CK106
Hartfield Rd., W.Wick. 222 EG105
Hartfield Ter. E3 143 EA68
Hartford Ave., Har. 117 CG55
Hartford Rd., Bex. 186 FA86
Hartford Rd., Epsom 216 CN107
Hartforde Rd., Borwd. 78 CN40
Harthall La., Hem.H. 59 BP28
Hartham Clo. N7 121 DL64
Hartham Clo., Islw. 157 CG81
Hartham La., Hert. 32 DQ09
Hartham Rd. N7 121 DL64
Hartham Rd. N17 100 DT54
Hartham Rd., Islw. 157 CF81
Harting Rd. SE9 184 EL91
Hartington Clo., Har. 117 CE63
Hartington Ct. W4 158 CP80
Hartington Pl., Reig. 250 DA132
Reigate Hill
Hartington Rd. E16 144 EH72
Hartington Rd. E17 123 DY58
Hartington Rd. SW8 161 DL81
Hartington Rd. W4 158 CP80
Hartington Rd. W13 137 CH73
Hartington Rd., Sthl. 156 BY76
Hartington Rd., Twick. 177 CH87
Hartismere Rd. SW6 159 CZ80
Hartlake Rd. E9 143 DX65
Hartland Clo. N21 82 DQ44
Elmscott Gdns.
Hartland Clo., Add. 212 BJ109
Hartland Clo., Edg. 96 CN47
Hartland Clo., Slou. 131 AR74
Hartland Dr., Edg. 96 CN47
Hartland Dr., Ruis. 115 BV62
Hartland Rd. E15 144 EF66
Hartland Rd. N11 98 DF50
Hartland Rd. NW1 141 DH66
Hartland Rd. NW6 139 CZ68
Hartland Rd., Add. 212 BG108
Hartland Rd., Epp. 70 EU31
Hartland Rd., Hmptn. 176 CB91
Hartland Rd., Horn. 127 FG61
Hartland Rd., Islw. 157 CG83
Hartland Rd., Mord. 200 DA101
Hartland Rd. (Cheshunt), Wal.Cr. 67 DX30
Hartland Way, Croy. 203 DY103
Hartland Way, Mord. 199 CZ101
Hartlands Clo., Bex. 186 EZ86
Hartley Ave. E6 144 EL67
Hartley Ave. NW7 97 CT50
Hartley Clo. NW7 97 CT50
Hartley Clo., Brom. 205 EM96
Hartley Clo., Slou. 132 AW67
Hartley Copse, Wind. 172 AU86
Hartley Down, Pur. 235 DM115
Hartley Fm. Est., Pur. 235 DM115
Hartley Hill, Pur. 235 DM115
Hartley Old Rd., Pur. 235 DM115
Hartley Rd. E11 124 EF60
Hartley Rd., Croy. 201 DP101
Hartley Rd., Well. 166 EW80
Hartley Rd., West. 255 ER125
Hartley St. E2 142 DW69
Hartley Way, Pur. 235 DM115
Hartmann Rd. E16 144 EK74
Hartmoor Ms., Enf. 83 DX37
Ordnance Rd.
Hartnoll St. N7 121 DM64
Eden Gro.
Harton Clo., Brom. 204 EK95
Harton Rd. N9 100 DV47
Harton St. SE8 163 EA81
Harts Clo. (Bushey), Wat. 76 CA39
Harts Gdns., Guil. 242 AV131
Harts Gro., Wdf.Grn. 102 EG50
Harts Hill Clo., Uxb. 134 BN65
Harts La. SE14 163 DY80
Harts La., Bark. 145 EP65
Hartsbourne Ave. (Bushey), Wat. 94 CC47
Hartsbourne Clo. (Bushey), Wat. 95 CD47
Hartsbourne Rd. (Bushey), Wat. 95 CD47
Hartsbourne Way, Hem.H. 41 BQ21
Hartscroft, Croy. 221 DY109
Hartshill Rd., Grav. 191 GF89
Hartshill Wk., Wok. 226 AV116
Sythwood
Hartshorn All. EC3 275 N9
Hartshorn Gdns. E6 145 EN70
Hartslands Rd., Sev. 257 FJ123
Hartslock Dr. SE2 166 EX75
Hartsmead Rd. SE9 185 EM89
Hartsmoor Ms., Enf. 83 DX37
Hartspiece Rd., Red. 266 DG136
Hartspring Ind. Est., Wat. 76 CA40
Hartspring La. (Bushey), Wat. 76 CA40
Hartsway, Enf. 82 DW42
Hartswood, Dor. 263 CK139
Wildcroft Dr.
Hartswood Ave., Reig. 266 DA138
Hartswood Clo., Brwd. 108 FY49
Hartswood Grn. (Bushey), Wat. 95 CD47
Hartswood Rd. W12 159 CT75
Hartswood Rd., Brwd. 108 FY49
Hartsworth Clo. E13 144 EF68
Hartville Rd. SE18 165 ES77
Hartwell Clo., H.Wyc. 88 AC45
Hartwell Dr. E4 101 EC51
Hartwell Dr., Beac. 89 AK52
Hartwell St. E8 142 DT65
Dalston La.
Harvard Hill W4 158 CP79
Harvard La. W4 158 CP78
Harvard Rd.
Harvard Rd. SE13 183 EC85
Harvard Rd. W4 158 CP78
Harvard Rd., Islw. 157 CE81
Harvard Wk., Horn. 127 FG63
Harvel Clo., Orp. 206 EU97
Harvel Cres. SE2 166 EX78
Harvest Bank Rd., W.Wick. 204 EF104
Harvest Ct., Shep. 194 BN98
Harvest End, Wat. 76 BX36
Harvest Hill, B.End 110 AC61
Harvest La., T.Ditt. 197 CG100
Harvest Mead, Hat. 45 CV17
Harvest Rd., Egh. 172 AX92
Harvest Rd., Felt. 175 BU91
Harvest Rd. (Bushey), Wat. 76 CB42
Harvest Way, Swan. 207 FD101
Harvester Rd., Epsom 216 CR110
Harvesters, St.Alb. 43 CK16
Harvesters Clo., Islw. 177 CD85
Harvestside, Horl. 269 DJ147
Harvey, Grays 170 GB75
Harvey Cen., Harl. 51 EQ15
Harvey Gdns. E11 124 EF60
Harvey Rd.
Harvey Gdns. SE7 164 EJ78
Harvey Gdns., Loug. 85 EP41
Harvey Ho., Brent. 158 CL78
Harvey Orchard, Beac. 88 AJ52
Harvey Pt. E16 144 EH71
Fife Rd.
Harvey Rd. E11 124 EE60
Harvey Rd. N8 121 DM57
Harvey Rd. SE5 162 DR81
Harvey Rd., Guil. 258 AY136
Harvey Rd., Houns. 176 BZ87
Harvey Rd., Ilf. 125 EP64
Harvey Rd., Nthlt. 136 BW66
Harvey Rd., Rick. 74 BN44
Harvey Rd., St.Alb. 61 CJ26
Harvey Rd., Slou. 153 BB76
Harvey Rd., Uxb. 134 BN68
Harvey Rd., Walt. 195 BU101
Harvey St. N1 142 DR67
Harveyfields, Wal.Abb. 67 EC34
Harveys La., Rom. 127 FD61
Harvil Rd. (Harefield), Uxb. 114 BJ56
Harvil Rd. (Ickenham), Uxb. 114 BL60
Harvill Rd., Sid. 186 EX92
Harvington Wk. E8 142 DU66
Wilman Gro.
Harvist Est. N7 121 DN63
Harvist Rd. NW6 139 CX68
Harwater Dr., Loug. 85 EM40
Harwell Clo., Ruis. 115 BR60
Harwell Pas. N2 120 DF56
Harwich La. EC2 275 N6
Harwich La. EC2 142 DS71
Harwich Rd., Slou. 131 AN72
Harwood Ave., Brom. 204 EH96
Harwood Ave., Horn. 128 FL55
Harwood Ave., Mitch. 200 DE97
Harwood Clo. N12 98 DE51
Summerfields Ave.
Harwood Clo., Welw. 30 DE05
Harwood Clo., Welw.G.C. 29 CY05
Harwood Clo., Wem. 117 CK63
Harrowdene Rd.
Harwood Dr., Uxb. 134 BM67
Harwood Gdns., Wind. 172 AV87
Harwood Hall La., Upmin. 148 FP65
Harwood Hill, Welw.G.C. 29 CY06
Harwood Pk., Red. 266 DG143
Harwood Rd. SW6 160 DA80
Harwood Ter. SW6 160 DB81
Harwoods Rd., Wat. 75 BU42
Harwoods Yd. N21 99 DN45
Wades Hill
Hascombe Ter. SE5 162 DR82
Hasedines Rd., Hem.H. 40 BG19
Haselbury Rd. N9 100 DS48
Haselbury Rd. N18 100 DS49
Haseldine Meadows, Hat. 45 CT19
Haseldine Rd., St.Alb. 61 CK26
Haseley End SE23 182 DW87
Tyson Rd.
Haselrigge Rd. SW4 161 DK84
Haseltine Rd. SE26 183 DZ91
Haselwood Dr., Enf. 81 DP42
Haskard Rd., Dag. 126 EX63
Haskell Ho. NW10 138 CR67
Hasker St. SW3 276 C8
Hasker St. SW3 160 DE77
Haslam Ave., Sutt. 199 CY102
Haslam Clo. N1 141 DN66
Haslam Clo., Uxb. 115 BQ61
Haslemere Ave. NW4 119 CX58
Haslemere Ave. SW18 180 DB89
Haslemere Ave. W7 157 CG76
Haslemere Ave. W13 157 CG76
Haslemere Ave., Barn. 98 DF46
Haslemere Ave., Houns. 156 BW82
Haslemere Ave., Mitch. 200 DD96
Haslemere Clo., Hmptn. 176 BZ92
Haslemere Clo., Wall. 219 DL106
Stafford Rd.
Haslemere Est., Harl. 51 EM15
Haslemere Gdns. N3 119 CZ55
Haslemere Heathrow Est., Houns. 155 BV82
Haslemere Pinnacles Est., Harl. 51 EN16
Haslemere Rd. N8 121 DK59
Haslemere Rd. N21 99 DP47
Haslemere Rd., Bexh. 166 EZ82
Haslemere Rd., Ilf. 125 ET61
Haslemere Rd., Th.Hth. 201 DP99
Haslemere Rd., Wind. 151 AN81
Hasler Clo. SE28 146 EV73
Haslett Rd., Shep. 195 BS96
Haslewood Ave., Hodd. 49 EA17
Hasluck Gdns., Barn. 80 DB44
Hassard St. E2 142 DT68
Hackney Rd.
Hassendean Rd. SE3 164 EH79
Hassett Rd. E9 143 DX65
Hassock Wd., Kes. 222 EK105
Hassocks Clo. SE26 182 DV90
Hassocks Rd. SW16 201 DJ95
Hassop Rd. NW2 119 CX63
Hassop Wk. SE9 184 EL91
Hasted Clo., Green. 189 FW86
Hasted Rd. SE7 164 EK78
Hastings Ave., Ilf. 125 EQ56
Hastings Clo. SE15 162 DU80
Hastings Clo., Barn. 80 DC42
Leicester Rd.
Hastings Clo., Grays 170 FY79
Hastings Clo., Maid. 150 AC77
Hastings Dr., Surb. 197 CJ100
Hastings Ho. SE18 165 EM77
Cardwell Rd.
Hastings Rd. N11 99 DJ50
Hastings Rd. N17 122 DR55
Hastings Rd. W13 137 CH73
Hastings Rd., Brom. 204 EL102
Hastings Rd., Croy. 202 DT102
Hastings Rd., Rom. 127 FH57
Hastings St. WC1 273 P3
Hastings St. WC1 141 DL69
Hastings Wk., Rick. 75 BQ42
Hastings Way (Bushey), Wat. 76 BY42
Hastingwood Rd., Harl. 52 EX20
Hastoe Clo., Hayes 136 BY70
Kingsash Dr.
Hat and Mitre Ct. EC1 274 G5
Hatch, The, Enf. 83 DX39
Hatch, The, Wind. 150 AJ80
Hatch Clo., Add. 194 BH104
Hatch Gdns., Tad. 233 CX120
Hatch Gro., Rom. 126 EY56
Hatch La. E4 101 ED49
Hatch La., Bans. 234 DF115
Rectory La.
Hatch La., Couls. 234 DG115
Hatch La., West Dr. 154 BK80
Hatch La., Wind. 151 AN83
Hatch La., Wok. 229 BP120
Hatch Pl., Kings.T. 178 CM92
Hatch Rd. SW16 201 DL96
Hatch Rd., Brwd. 108 FU43
Hatch Side, Chig. 103 EN50
Hatcham Pk. Ms. SE14 163 DX81
Hatcham Pk. Rd.
Hatcham Pk. Rd. SE14 163 DX81
Hatcham Rd. SE15 162 DW79
Hatchard Rd. N19 121 DK61
Hatchcroft NW4 119 CV55
Hatchett Rd., Felt. 175 BQ88
Hatchgate, Horl. 268 DF149
Hatchgate Gdns., Slou. 131 AK69
Hatchlands Rd., Red. 250 DE134
Hatchwood Clo., Wdf.Grn. 102 EF49
Sunset Ave.
Hatcliffe Clo. SE3 164 EF83
Hatcliffe St. SE10 164 EF78
Woolwich Rd.
Hatfield Ave., Hat. 44 CS15
Hatfield Clo. SE14 163 DX80
Reaston St.
Hatfield Clo., Brwd. 109 GD45
Hatfield Clo., Horn. 128 FK64
Hatfield Clo., Ilf. 125 EP55
Hatfield Clo., Mitch. 200 DD98
Hatfield Clo., Sutt. 218 DB109
Hatfield Clo., W.Byf. 212 BH112
Hatfield Cres., Hem.H. 40 BM16
Hatfield Ho., Hat. 45 CX18
Hatfield Mead, Mord. 200 DA99
Central Rd.
Hatfield Pk., Hat. 45 CV18
Hatfield Rd. E15 124 EE64
Hatfield Rd. W4 158 CR75
Hatfield Rd. W13 137 CG74
Hatfield Rd., Ash. 232 CM119
Hatfield Rd., Dag. 146 EY65
Hatfield Rd., Grays 169 FW78
Hatfield Rd., Hert. 30 DF12
Hatfield Rd., Pot.B. 64 DC30
Hatfield Rd., St.Alb. 43 CE20
Hatfield Rd., Slou. 152 AU75
Hatfield Rd., Wat. 75 BV39
Hatfields SE1 278 E2
Hatfields SE1 141 DN74
Hatfields, Loug. 85 EP41
Hathaway Clo., Brom. 205 EM102
Hathaway Clo., Ruis. 115 BT63
Stafford Rd.
Hathaway Clo., Stan. 95 CG50
Hathaway Ct., St.Alb. 44 CL20
Hathaway Cres. E12 145 EM65
Hathaway Gdns. W13 137 CF71
Hathaway Gdns., Grays 170 GB76
Hathaway Rd.
Hathaway Gdns., Rom. 126 EX57
Hathaway Rd., Croy. 201 DP101
Hathaway Rd., Grays 170 GB77
Hatherleigh Clo., Chess. 215 CK106
Hatherleigh Clo., Mord. 200 DA98
Hatherleigh Gdns., Pot.B. 64 DD31
Hatherleigh Rd., Ruis. 115 BU61
Hatherleigh Way, Rom. 106 FK53
Hatherley Cres., Sid. 186 EU89
Hatherley Gdns. E6 144 EK68
Hatherley Gdns. N8 121 DL58
Hatherley Gro. W2 140 DB72
Hatherley Ms. E17 123 EA56
Hatherley Rd. E17 123 DZ56
Hatherley Rd., Rich. 158 CM81
Hatherley Rd., Sid. 186 EU91
Hatherley St. SW1 277 L9
Hathern Gdns. SE9 185 EN91
The Knole
Hatherop Rd., Hmptn. 176 BZ94
Hathersham Clo., Horl. 269 DN147
Hathersham La., Horl. 267 DL144
Hatherwood, Lthd. 231 CK121
Hathorne Clo. SE15 162 DV82
Hathway St. SE15 162 DW82
Gibbon Rd.
Hathway Ter. SE14 162 DW82
Gibbon Rd.
Hatley Ave., Ilf. 125 EQ56
Hatley Clo. N11 98 DF50
Hatley Rd. N4 121 DM61
Hatteraick St. SE16 162 DW75
Brunel Rd.
Hatters La., Wat. 75 BR44
Hattersfield Clo., Belv. 166 EZ77
Hatton Ave., Slou. 131 AR70
Hatton Clo. SE18 165 ER80
Hatton Clo., Grav. 190 GE90
Hatton Ct. E5 123 DY63
Gilpin Rd.
Hatton Gdn. EC1 274 E6
Hatton Gdn. EC1 141 DN70
Hatton Gdns., Mitch. 200 DF99
Hatton Grn., Felt. 155 BU84
Hatton Gro., West Dr. 154 BK75
Hatton Ho. E1 142 DU73
Wellclose Sq.
Hatton Pl. EC1 274 E6
Hatton Pl. EC1 141 DN70
Hatton Rd., Croy. 201 DN102
Hatton Rd., Felt. 175 BQ87
Hatton Rd. (Cheshunt), Wal.Cr. 67 DX29
Hatton Row NW8 272 A5
Hatton St. NW8 272 A5
Hatton Wall EC1 274 D6
Hatton Wall EC1 141 DN71
Haunch of Venison Yd. W1 273 H9
Havana Clo., Rom. 127 FE57
Havana Rd. SW19 180 DA89
Havannah St. E14 163 EA75
Havant Rd. E17 123 EC55
Havant Way SE15 162 DT80
Daniel Gdns.
Havelock Pl., Har. 117 CE58
Havelock Rd. N17 100 DU54
Havelock Rd. SW19 180 DC92
Havelock Rd., Belv. 166 EZ77
Havelock Rd., Brom. 204 EJ98
Havelock Rd., Croy. 202 DT103
Havelock Rd., Dart. 187 FH87
Havelock Rd., Grav. 191 GF88
Havelock Rd., Har. 117 CE55
Havelock Rd., Kings L. 58 BM28
Havelock Rd., Sthl. 156 BY76
Havelock St. N1 141 DL67
Havelock St., Ilf. 125 EP61
Havelock Ter. SW8 161 DH80
Havelock Wk. SE23 182 DW88
Haven, The SE26 182 DV92
Springfield Rd.
Haven, The, Grays 171 GG77
Haven, The, Rich. 158 CN83
Haven Clo. SE9 185 EM90
Haven Clo. SW19 179 CX90
Haven Clo., Grav. 191 GF94
Haven Clo., Hat. 45 CT17
Haven Clo., Hayes 135 BS71
Haven Clo., Sid. 186 EW93
Haven Clo., Swan. 207 FF96
Haven Grn. W5 137 CK72
Haven Grn. Ct. W5 137 CK72
Haven La. W5 138 CL72
Haven Pl. W5 137 CK73
The Bdy.
Haven Pl., Grays 170 GC75
Haven Rd., Ashf. 175 BP91
Haven St. NW1 141 DH66
Castlehaven Rd.
Haven Ter. W5 138 CM73
The Bdy.
Havengore Ave., Grav. 191 GL87
Havenhurst Ri., Enf. 81 DN40
Havensfield, Kings L. 58 BH31
Nunfield
Havenwood, Wem. 118 CP62
Havenwood Clo., Brwd. 107 FW51
Wilmot Grn.
Havercroft Clo., St.Alb. 42 CB22
King Harry La.
Haverfield Gdns., Rich. 158 CN80
Haverfield Rd. E3 143 DY69
Haverford Way, Edg. 96 CM53
Haverhill Rd. E4 101 EC46
Haverhill Rd. SW12 181 DJ88
Havering Dr., Rom. 127 FE56
Havering Gdns., Rom. 126 EW57
Havering Rd., Rom. 127 FD55
Havering St. E1 143 DX72
Devonport St.
Havering Way, Bark. 146 EV69
Havers Ave., Walt. 214 BX106
Haversfield Est., Brent. 158 CL78
Haversham Clo., Twick. 177 CK86
Haversham Pl. N6 120 DF61
Haverstock Hill NW3 140 DF65
Haverstock Rd. NW5 120 DG64
Haverstock St. N1 274 G1
Haverstock St. N1 141 DP68
Haverthwaite Rd., Orp. 205 ER103
Havil St. SE5 162 DS80
Havisham Pl. SE19 181 DP93
Haward Rd., Hodd. 49 EC15
Hawarden Gro. SE24 182 DQ87
Hawarden Hill NW2 119 CU62
Hawarden Rd. E17 123 DX56
Hawarden Rd., Cat. 236 DQ121
Hawbridge Rd. E11 123 ED60
Hawes Clo., Nthwd. 93 BT52
Hawes La. E4 83 EC38
Hawes La., W.Wick. 203 EC102
Hawes Rd. N18 100 DV51
Hawes Rd., Brom. 204 EH95
Hawes Rd., Tad. 233 CX120
Hatch Gdns.
Hawes St. N1 141 DP66
Haweswater Dr., Wat. 60 BW33
Haweswater Ho., Islw. 177 CF85
Hawfield Bank, Orp. 206 EX104
Hawfield Gdns., St.Alb. 61 CD26
Hawgood St. E3 143 EA71
Hawk Clo., Wal.Abb. 68 EG34
Hawkdene E4 83 EB44
Hawke Pk. Rd. N22 121 DP55
Hawke Pl. SE16 163 DX75
Middleton Dr.
Hawke Rd. SE19 182 DS93
Hawkenbury, Harl. 51 EN17
Hawker Clo., Wall. 219 DL108
Kingsford Ave.
Hawkes Clo., Grays 170 GB79
New Rd.
Hawke's Pl., Sev. 256 FG127
Hawkes Rd., Mitch. 200 DE95
Hawkesbury Rd. SW15 179 CV85
Hawkesfield Rd. SE23 183 DY89
Hawkesley Clo., Twick. 177 CG91
Hawkesworth Clo., Nthwd. 93 BS52
Hawkewood Rd., Sun. 195 BU97
Hawkhirst Rd., Ken. 236 DR115
Hawkhurst, Cob. 214 CA114
Hawkhurst Gdns., Chess. 216 CL105
Hawkhurst Gdns., Rom. 105 FD51
Hawkhurst Rd. SW16 201 DK95
Hawkhurst Way, N.Mal. 198 CR99
Hawkhurst Way, W.Wick. 203 EB103
Hawkinge Wk., Orp. 206 EV97
Farrington Ave.
Hawkinge Way, Horn. 148 FJ65
Hawkins Ave., Grav. 191 GJ91
Hawkins Clo. NW7 96 CR50
Hale La.
Hawkins Clo., Borwd. 78 CQ40
Banks Rd.
Hawkins Clo., Har. 117 CD59
Hawkins Rd., Tedd. 177 CH93
Hawkins Way SE6 183 EA91
Hawkley Gdns. SE27 181 DP89
Hawkridge Clo., Rom. 126 EW58
Hawks Hill, B.End 110 AC61
Hawks Hill, Lthd. 231 CF123
Guildford Rd.
Hawks Hill Clo., Lthd. 231 CF123
Hawks Ms. SE10 163 EC80
Luton Pl.
Hawks Rd., Kings.T. 198 CM96
Hawksbrook La., Beck. 203 EB100
Hawkshaw Clo. SW2 181 DL87
Tierney Rd.
Hawkshead Clo., Brom. 184 EE94
Hawkshead La., Hat. 63 CW28
Hawkshead Rd. NW10 139 CT66
Hawkshead Rd. W4 158 CS75
Hawkshead Rd., Pot.B. 63 CZ28
Hawkshill, St.Alb. 43 CG21
Hawkshill Clo., Esher 214 CA107
Hawkshill Dr., Hem.H. 39 BE23
Hawkshill Rd., Slou. 131 AN69
Hawkshill Way, Esher 214 BZ107
Hawkslade Rd. SE15 183 DX85
Hawksley Rd. N16 122 DR62
Hawksmead Clo., Enf. 82 DX35
Hawksmoor, Rad. 62 CN33
Hawksmoor Clo. E6 144 EL72
Allhallows Rd.
Hawksmoor Clo. SE18 165 ES78
Hawksmoor Grn., Brwd. 109 GD43
Hawksmoor Ms. E1 142 DV73
Cable St.
Hawksmoor St. W6 159 CX79
Hawksmouth E4 101 EB45
Hawkstone Rd. SE16 162 DW77
Hawksview, Cob. 214 BZ113
Hawksway, Stai. 173 BF90

Hawkswell Clo., Wok. 226 AT117
Hawkswell Wk., Wok. 226 AS117
Lockfield Dr.
Hawkswood Gro., Slou. 133 AZ65
Hawkswood La., Ger.Cr. 113 AZ64
Hawkwell Ct. E4 101 EC48
Colvin Gdns.
Hawkwell Wk. N1 142 DQ67
Basire St.
Hawkwood Cres. E4 83 EB44
Hawkwood Dell, Lthd. 246 CA126
Hawkwood La., Chis. 205 EQ95
Hawkwood Mt. E5 122 DV60
Hawkwood Ri., Lthd. 246 CA126
Hawlands Dr., Pnr. 116 BY59
Hawley Clo., Hmptn. 176 BZ93
Hawley Cres. NW1 141 DH66
Hawley Ms. NW1 141 DH66
Hawley St.
Hawley Rd. N18 101 DX50
Hawley Rd. NW1 141 DH66
Hawley Rd., Dart. 188 FL89
Hawley St. NW1 141 DH66
Hawley Way, Ashf. 174 BN92
Haws La., Stai. 174 BG86
Hawstead La., Orp. 224 EZ106
Hawstead Rd. SE6 183 EB86
Hawsted, Buck.H. 102 EH45
Hawthorn Ave. N13 99 DL50
Hawthorn Ave., Brwd. 109 FZ48
Hawthorn Ave., Cars. 218 DG108
Hawthorn Ave., Rain. 147 FH70
Hawthorn Ave., Rich. 158 CL82
Kew Rd.
Hawthorn Ave., Th.Hth. 201 DP95
Hawthorn Cen., Har. 117 CF56
Hawthorn Clo., Abb.L. 59 BU32
Magnolia Ave.
Hawthorn Clo., Bans. 217 CY114
Hawthorn Clo., Grav. 191 GH87
Hawthorn Clo., Hmptn. 176 CA92
Hawthorn Clo., Hert. 31 DN08
Hawthorn Clo., Houns. 155 BV80
Hawthorn Clo., Orp. 205 ER100
Hawthorn Clo., Red. 266 DG139
Bushfield Dr.
Hawthorn Clo., Wat. 75 BT38
Hawthorn Clo., Wok. 226 AY120
Hawthorn Cotts., Well. 166 EU83
Hook La.
Hawthorn Ct., Rich. 158 CP81
West Hall Rd.
Hawthorn Cres. SW17 180 DG92
Hawthorn Dr., Har. 116 CA58
Hawthorn Dr., Uxb. 134 BJ65
Hawthorn Dr., W.Wick. 222 EE105
Hawthorn Gdns. W5 157 CK76
Hawthorn Gro. SE20 182 DV94
Hawthorn Gro., Barn. 79 CT44
Hawthorn Gro., Enf. 82 DR38
Hawthorn Hatch, Brent. 157 CH80
Hawthorn La., Hem.H. 39 BF19
Hawthorn La., Sev. 256 FF122
Hawthorn La., Slou. 131 AL66
Hawthorn Ms. NW7 97 CY53
Holders Hill Rd.
Hawthorn Pl., Erith 167 FC78
Hawthorn Pl., Hayes 135 BT73
Central Ave.
Hawthorn Pl., H.Wyc. 88 AC47
Hawthorn Rd. N8 121 DK55
Hawthorn Rd. N18 100 DT51
Hawthorn Rd. NW10 139 CU66
Hawthorn Rd., Bexh. 166 EZ84
Hawthorn Rd., Brent. 157 CH80
Hawthorn Rd., Buck.H. 102 EK49
Hawthorn Rd., Dart. 188 FK88
Hawthorn Rd., Hodd. 49 EB15
Hawthorn Rd., Stai. 173 BC91
Hawthorn Rd., Sutt. 218 DE106
Hawthorn Rd., Wall. 219 DH108
Hawthorn Rd., Wok. 226 AX120
Hawthorn Rd. (Send Marsh), Wok. 227 BF124
Hawthorn Wk. W10 139 CY70
Droop St.
Hawthorn Way N9 100 DS47
Hawthorn Way, Add. 212 BJ110
Hawthorn Way, Chesh. 54 AR29
Hawthorn Way, Red. 267 DH136
Hawthorn Way, St.Alb. 42 CA24
Hawthorn Way, Stai. 174 BK87
Hawthornden Clo. N12 98 DE51
Fallowfields Dr.
Hawthorndene Clo., Brom. 204 EF103
Hawthorndene Rd., Brom. 204 EF103
Hawthorne Ave., Har. 117 CG58
Hawthorne Ave., Mitch. 200 DD96
Hawthorne Ave., Ruis. 115 BV59
Hawthorne Ave. (Cheshunt), Wal.Cr. 66 DV30
Hawthorne Ave., West. 238 EK115
Hawthorne Clo. N1 142 DS65
Hawthorne Clo., Brom. 205 EM97
Hawthorne Clo., Sutt. 200 DB103
Aultone Way
Hawthorne Clo. (Cheshunt), Wal.Cr. 66 DV31
Hawthorne Ct., Walt. 196 BX103
Ambleside Ave.
Hawthorne Cres., Slou. 132 AS72
Hawthorne Cres., S.Croy. 220 DW111
Hawthorne Cres., West Dr. 154 BM75
Hawthorne Fm. Ave., Nthlt. 136 BY67
Hawthorne Gro. NW9 118 CQ59
Hawthorne Ms., Grnf. 136 CC72
Greenford Rd.
Hawthorne Pl., Epsom 216 CS112
Hawthorne Rd. E17 123 EA55
Hawthorne Rd., Brom. 205 EM97
Hawthorne Rd., Rad. 61 CG34
Hawthorne Way, Guil. 243 BB130
Hawthorne Way, Shep. 195 BR98
Hawthornes, Hat. 45 CT20
Hazel Gro.
Hawthornes Cen., Har. 117 CF56
Hawthorns, Harl. 51 ET19
Hawthorns, Welw.G.C. 29 CX07
Hawthorns, Wdf.Grn. 102 EG48
Hawthorns, The, Berk. 38 AU18
Hawthorns, The, Epsom 217 CT107
Ewell Bypass
Hawthorns, The, Hem.H. 39 BF24
Hawthorns, The, Loug. 85 EN42
Hawthorns, The, Oxt. 254 EG132
Hawthorns, The, Rick. 91 BD50
Hawthorns, The, Slou. 153 BF81
Hawtrees, Rad. 77 CF35
Hawtrey Ave., Nthlt. 136 BX68
Hawtrey Clo., Slou. 152 AV75
Hawtrey Dr., Ruis. 115 BU59
Hawtrey Rd. NW3 140 DE66
Hawtrey Rd., Wind. 151 AQ82
Haxted Rd., Brom. 204 EH95
North Rd.
Hay Clo. E15 144 EE66
Hay Clo., Borwd. 78 CQ40
Hay Currie St. E14 143 EB72
Hay Hill W1 277 J1
Hay Hill W1 141 DH73
Hay La. NW9 118 CQ56
Hay La., Slou. 112 AX63
Hay St. E2 142 DU67
Haybourn Mead, Hem.H. 40 BH21
Hayburn Way, Horn. 127 FF60
Haycroft Clo., Couls. 235 DP118
Caterham Dr.
Haycroft Gdns. NW10 139 CU67
Haycroft Rd. SW2 181 DL85
Haycroft Rd., Surb. 197 CK104
Hayday Rd. E16 144 EG71
Hayden Ct., Add. 212 BH111
Hayden Way, Rom. 105 FC54
Haydens Clo., Orp. 206 EW100
Haydens Pl. W11 139 CZ72
Portobello Rd.
Haydens Rd., Harl. 51 EQ15
Haydn Ave., Pur. 219 DN114
Haydns Ms. W3 138 CQ72
Emanuel Ave.
Haydock Ave., Nthlt. 136 CA65
Haydock Clo., Horn. 128 FM63
Haydock Grn., Nthlt. 136 CA65
Haydock Ave.
Haydon Clo. NW9 118 CQ56
Haydon Clo., Enf. 82 DS44
Mortimer Dr.
Haydon Dr., Pnr. 115 BV56
Haydon Pk. Rd. SW19 180 DA92
Haydon Pl., Guil. 258 AX135
Haydon Rd., Dag. 126 EW61
Haydon Rd., Wat. 76 BY44
Haydon St. EC3 275 P10
Haydon Wk. E1 142 DT73
Mansell St.
Haydon Way SW11 160 DD84
St. John's Hill
Haydons Rd. SW19 180 DB92
Hayes, The, Epsom 232 CR119
Hayes Barton, Wok. 227 BD116
Hayes Chase, W.Wick. 203 ED100
Hayes Clo., Brom. 204 EG103
Hayes Clo., Grays 169 FW79
Hayes Ct. SW2 181 DL88
Hayes Cres. NW11 119 CZ57
Hayes Cres., Sutt. 217 CX105
Hayes Dr., Rain. 147 FH66
Hayes End Clo., Hayes 135 BR70
Hayes End Dr., Hayes 135 BR70
Hayes End Rd., Hayes 135 BR70
Hayes Gdn., Brom. 204 EG103
Hayes Hill, Brom. 204 EE102
Hayes Hill Rd., Brom. 204 EF102
Hayes La., Beck. 203 EC97
Hayes La., Brom. 204 EG99
Hayes La., Ken. 235 DP116
Hayes Mead Rd., Brom. 204 EE102
Hayes Pl. NW1 272 C5
Hayes Rd., Brom. 204 EG98
Hayes Rd., Green. 189 FS87
Hayes Rd., Sthl. 155 BV77
Hayes St., Brom. 204 EH102
Hayes Wk., Brox. 67 DZ25
Landau Way
Hayes Wk., Horl. 269 DN147
Hayes Wk., Pot.B. 64 DB33
Hyde Ave.
Hayes Way, Beck. 203 EC98
Hayes Wd. Ave., Brom. 204 EH102
Hayesford Pk. Dr., Brom. 204 EF99
Hayfield Clo. (Bushey), Wat. 76 CB42
Hayfield Pas. E1 142 DW70
Stepney Grn.
Hayfield Rd., Orp. 206 EU99
Hayfield Yd. E1 142 DW70
Mile End Rd.
Hayfields, Horl. 269 DJ147
Ryelands
Haygarth Pl. SW19 179 CX92
Haygreen Clo., Kings.T. 178 CP93
Hayland Clo. NW9 118 CR56
Hayles St. SE11 278 F8
Hayles St. SE11 161 DP77
Haylett Gdns., Kings.T. 197 CK98
Anglesea Rd.
Hayling Ave., Felt. 175 BU90
Hayling Clo. N16 122 DS64
Pellerin Rd.
Hayling Rd., Wat. 93 BT48
Haymaker Clo., Uxb. 134 BM66
Honey Hill
Hayman Cres., Hayes 135 BR68
Hayman St. N1 141 DP66
Cross St.
Haymarket SW1 277 M1
Haymarket SW1 141 DK73
Haymarket Arc. SW1 277 M1
Haymeads, Welw.G.C. 29 CY06
Haymeads Dr., Esher 214 CC107
Haymer Gdns., Wor.Pk. 199 CU104
Haymerle Rd. SE15 162 DU79
Haymill Clo., Grnf. 137 CF69
Haymill Rd., Slou. 131 AK70
Hayne Rd., Beck. 203 DZ96
Hayne St. EC1 274 G6
Haynes Clo. N11 98 DG48
Haynes Clo. N17 100 DV52
Haynes Clo. SE3 164 EE83
Haynes Clo., Slou. 153 AZ77
Haynes Clo., Welw.G.C. 30 DA10
Haynes Clo., Wok. 228 BH122
Haynes La. SE19 182 DS93
Haynes Mead, Berk. 38 AU17
Haynes Rd., Grav. 191 GF90
Haynes Rd., Horn. 128 FK57
Haynes Rd., Wem. 138 CL66
Haynt Wk. SW20 199 CY97
Hay's La. SE1 279 M3
Hay's Ms. W1 277 H2
Hay's Ms. W1 141 DH74
Hays Wk., Sutt. 217 CX110
Hayse Hill, Wind. 151 AK81
Haysleigh Gdns. SE20 202 DU96
Haysoms Clo., Rom. 127 FE56
Haystall Clo., Hayes 135 BS68
Hayter Rd. SW2 181 DL85
Hayton Clo. E8 142 DT65
Buttermere Wk.
Haywain, Oxt. 253 ED130
Hayward Clo. SW19 180 DB94
Hayward Clo., Bex. 187 FD85
Hayward Clo., Dart. 187 FD85
Hayward Dr., Dart. 188 FM90
Hayward Gdns. SW15 179 CW86
Hayward Rd. N20 98 DC47
Haywards Clo., Brwd. 109 GE44
Haywards Mead (Eton Wick), Wind. 151 AM78
Hayward's Pl. EC1 274 F5
Haywood Clo., Pnr. 94 BX54
Haywood Ct., Wal.Abb. 68 EF34
Haywood Dr., Hem.H. 39 BF23
Haywood Pk., Rick. 73 BF43
Haywood Ri., Orp. 223 ES105
Haywood Rd., Brom. 204 EK98
Hayworth Clo., Enf. 83 DY40
Green St.
Hazel Ave., Guil. 242 AW130
Hazel Ave., West Dr. 154 BN76
Hazel Bank, Surb. 198 CQ102
Hazel Clo. N13 100 DR48
Hazel Clo. N19 121 DJ61
Hargrave Pk.
Hazel Clo. SE15 162 DU82
Copeland Rd.
Hazel Clo., Brent. 157 CH80
Hazel Clo., Croy. 203 DX101
Hazel Clo., Egh. 172 AV93
Hazel Clo., Horn. 127 FH62
Hazel Clo., Mitch. 201 DK98
Hazel Clo., Reig. 266 DC136
Hazel Clo., Twick. 176 CC87
Hazel Clo., Wal.Cr. 66 DS26
The Laurels
Hazel Dr., Erith 167 FG81
Hazel Dr., S.Ock. 149 FX69
Hazel Dr., Wok. 243 BF125
Hazel End, Swan. 207 FE99
Hazel Gdns., Edg. 96 CP49
Hazel Gdns., Grays 170 GE76
Hazel Gdns., Saw. 36 EZ06
Sun St.
Hazel Gro. SE26 183 DX91
Hazel Gro., Enf. 82 DU44
Dimsdale Dr.
Hazel Gro., Hat. 45 CT21
Hazel Gro., Orp. 205 EP103
Hazel Gro., Rom. 126 EY55
Hazel Gro., Stai. 174 BH93
Hazel Gro., Wat. 75 BV35
Cedar Wd. Dr.
Hazel Gro., Welw.G.C. 30 DB08
Hazel Gro., Wem. 138 CL67
Carlyon Rd.
Hazel Gro. Est. SE26 183 DX91
Hazel La., Rich. 178 CL89
Hazel Mead, Barn. 79 CV43
Hazel Mead, Epsom 217 CU110
Hazel Ri., Horn. 128 FJ58
Hazel Rd. E15 124 EE64
Wingfield Rd.
Hazel Rd. NW10 139 CV69
Hazel Rd., Berk. 38 AX20
Hazel Rd., Dart. 188 FK89
Hazel Rd., Erith 167 FG81
Hazel Rd., Reig. 266 DC136
Hazel Rd., St.Alb. 60 CB28
Hazel Rd., W.Byf. 212 BG114
Hazel Tree Rd., Wat. 75 BV37
Hazel Wk., Brom. 205 EN100
Hazel Wk., Dor. 263 CJ139
Lake Vw.
Hazel Way E4 101 DZ51
Hazel Way SE1 279 P8
Hazel Way, Couls. 234 DF119
Hazel Way, Lthd. 230 CC122
Hazelbank Ct., Cher. 194 BJ102
Hazelbank Rd. SE6 183 ED89
Hazelbank Rd., Cher. 194 BJ101
Hazelbourne Rd. SW12 181 DH86
Hazelbrouck Gdns., Ilf. 103 ER52
Hazelbury Ave., Abb.L. 59 BQ32
Hazelbury Clo. SW19 200 DA96
Hazelbury Grn. N9 100 DS48
Hazelbury La. N9 100 DS48
Hazelcroft, Pnr. 94 CB51
Hazelcroft Clo., Uxb. 134 BM66
Hazeldean Rd. NW10 138 CR66
Hazeldell Link, Hem.H. 39 BF21
Hazeldell Rd., Hem.H. 39 BF21
Hazeldene, Add. 212 BJ106
Hazeldene, Wal.Cr. 67 DY32
Hazeldene Ct., Ken. 236 DR115
Hazeldene Dr., Pnr. 116 BW55
Hazeldene Gdns., Uxb. 135 BQ67
Hazeldene Rd., Ilf. 126 EV61
Hazeldene Rd., Well. 166 EW82
Hazeldon Rd. SE4 183 DY85
Hazeleigh, Brwd. 109 GB48
Hazeleigh Gdns., Wdf.Grn. 102 EL50
Hazelgreen Clo. N21 99 DP46
Hazelhurst, Beck. 203 ED95
Hazelhurst, Horl. 269 DJ147
Hazelhurst Clo., Guil. 243 BB129
Weybrook Dr.
Hazelhurst Rd. SW17 180 DC91
Hazelhurst Rd., Slou. 130 AJ68
Hazell Cres., Rom. 105 FB53
Hazell Pk., Amer. 55 AR39
Hazell Way, Slou. 132 AT66
Hazells Rd., Grav. 190 GD92
Hazellville Rd. N19 121 DK59
Hazelmere Clo., Felt. 175 BR86
Hazelmere Clo., Lthd. 231 CH119
Hazelmere Clo., Nthlt. 136 BZ68
Hazelmere Dr., Nthlt. 136 BZ68
Hazelmere Gdns., Horn. 127 FH57
Hazelmere Rd. NW6 139 CZ67
Hazelmere Rd., Nthlt. 136 BZ68
Hazelmere Rd., Orp. 205 EQ98
Hazelmere Rd., St.Alb. 43 CJ17
Hazelmere Wk., Nthlt. 136 BZ68
Hazelmere Way, Brom. 204 EG100
Hazels, The, Welw. 30 DE05
Hazeltree La., Nthlt. 136 BY69
Hazelwood, Dor. 263 CH137
Hazelwood, Loug. 84 EK43
Hazelwood Ave., Mord. 200 DB98
Hazelwood Clo. W5 158 CL75
Hazelwood Clo., Chesh. 54 AR29
Hazelwood Clo., Har. 116 CB56
Hazelwood Ct. NW10 118 CS62
Neasden La. N.
Hazelwood Cres. N13 99 DN49
Hazelwood Cft., Surb. 198 CL100
Hazelwood Dr., Pnr. 93 BV54
Hazelwood Dr., St.Alb. 43 CJ18
Hazelwood Gdns., Brwd. 108 FU43
Hazelwood Gro., S.Croy. 220 DV113
Hazelwood Heights, Oxt. 254 EG131
Hazelwood La. N13 99 DN49
Hazelwood La., Abb.L. 59 BR31
Hazelwood La., Couls. 234 DE118
Hazelwood Pk. Clo., Chig. 103 ES50
Hazelwood Rd. E17 123 DY57
Hazelwood Rd., Enf. 82 DT44
Hazelwood Rd., Oxt. 254 EH132
Hazelwood Rd., Rick. 75 BQ44
Hazelwood Rd., Sev. 223 ER112
Hazelwood Rd., Wok. 226 AS118
Hazlebury Rd. SW6 160 DB82
Hazledean Rd., Croy. 202 DR103
Hazledene Rd. W4 158 CQ79
Hazlemere Gdns., Wor.Pk. 199 CU102
Hazlemere Rd., H.Wyc. 88 AC45
Hazlemere Rd., Slou. 132 AV74
Hazlewell Rd. SW15 179 CV85
Hazlewood Clo. E5 123 DY62
Mandeville St.
Hazlewood Cres. W10 139 CY70
Hazlitt Ms. W14 159 CY76
Hazlitt Rd.
Hazlitt Rd. W14 159 CY76
Hazon Way, Epsom 216 CQ112
Heacham Ave., Uxb. 115 BQ62
Head St. E1 143 DX72
Headcorn Pl., Th.Hth. 201 DM98
Headcorn Rd.
Headcorn Rd. N17 100 DT52
Headcorn Rd., Brom. 184 EG92
Headcorn Rd., Th.Hth. 201 DM98
Headfort Pl. SW1 276 G5
Headfort Pl. SW1 160 DG75
Headingley Clo., Ilf. 103 ET51
Headingley Clo., Rad. 62 CL32
Headingley Clo. (Cheshunt), Wal.Cr. 66 DT26
Headington Rd. SW18 180 DC89
Headlam Rd. SW4 181 DK86
Headlam St. E1 142 DV70
Headley App., Ilf. 125 EP57
Headley Ave., Wall. 219 DM106
Headley Chase, Brwd. 108 FW49
Headley Clo., Epsom 216 CN107
Headley Common, Brwd. 107 FV52
Warley Gap
Headley Common Rd., Epsom 248 CR126
Headley Common Rd., Tad. 248 CS128
Headley Ct. SE26 182 DW92
Headley Dr., Croy. 221 EB108
Headley Dr., Epsom 233 CV119
Headley Dr., Ilf. 125 EP58
Headley Gro., Tad. 233 CV120
Headley Heath App., Dor. 248 CP130
Ashurst Dr.
Headley Heath App., Tad. 248 CP130
Headley La., Dor. 247 CJ129
Headley Rd. (Ashtead Pk.), Epsom 232 CP118
Headley Rd. (Tyrrell's Wd.), Epsom 232 CN122
Headley Rd., Lthd. 231 CJ122
Head's Ms. W11 140 DA72
Artesian Rd.
Headstone Dr., Har. 117 CD55
Headstone Gdns., Har. 116 CC56
Headstone La., Har. 94 CB52
Headstone Rd., Har. 117 CE57
Headway, The, Epsom 217 CT109
Headway Clo., Rich. 177 CJ91
Locksmeade Rd.
Heald St. SE14 163 DZ81
Healey Dr., Orp. 223 ET105
Healey Rd., Wat. 75 BT44
Healey St. NW1 141 DH65
Heanor Ct. E5 123 DX62
Pedro St.
Heards La., Brwd. 109 FZ41
Hearn Ri., Nthlt. 136 BX67
Hearn Rd., Rom. 127 FF58
Hearn St. EC2 275 N5
Hearn St. EC2 142 DS70
Hearne Ct., Ch.St.G. 90 AV48
Gordon Way
Hearne Rd. W4 158 CN79
Hearnes Clo., Beac. 89 AR50
Hearnes Mead, Beac. 89 AR50
Hearn's Bldgs. SE17 279 L9
Hearn's Ri., Orp. 206 EX98
Hearn's Rd., Orp. 206 EW98
Hearnville Rd. SW12 180 DG88
Heath, The W7 137 CE74
Lower Boston Rd.
Heath, The, B.Stort. 37 FG05
Heath, The, Cat. 236 DQ124
Heath, The, Rad. 61 CG33
Heath Ave., Bexh. 166 EX79
Heath Ave., St.Alb. 43 CD18
Heath Brow NW3 120 DC62
North End Way
Heath Brow, Hem.H. 40 BJ22
Heath Clo. NW11 120 DB59
Heath Clo. W5 138 CM70
Heath Clo., Bans. 218 DB114
Heath Clo., Guil. 242 AV132
Heath Clo., Hayes 155 BR80
Heath Clo., Hem.H. 40 BJ21
Heath Clo., Orp. 206 EW100
Sussex Rd.
Heath Clo., Pot.B. 64 DB30
Heath Clo., Rom. 127 FG55
Heath Clo., Stai. 174 BJ86
Heath Clo., Vir.W. 192 AX98
Heath Cotts., Pot.B. 64 DB30
Heath Rd.
Heath Ct., Houns. 156 BZ84
Heath Ct., Uxb. 134 BL66
Heath Dr. NW3 120 DB63
Heath Dr. SW20 199 CW98
Heath Dr., Epp. 85 ES36
Heath Dr., Pot.B. 64 DA30
Heath Dr., Rom. 105 FG53
Heath Dr., Sutt. 218 DC109
Heath Dr., Tad. 249 CU125
Heath Dr., Wok. 227 BB122
Heath End Rd., Bex. 187 FE88
Heath Fm. Ct., Wat. 75 BR37
Grove Mill La.
Heath Fm. La., St.Alb. 43 CE18
Heath Gdns., Twick. 177 CF88
Heath Gro. SE20 182 DW94
Maple Rd.
Heath Gro., Sun. 175 BT94
Heath Hill, Dor. 263 CH135
Heath Hurst Rd. NW3 120 DE63
Heath La. SE3 163 ED82
Heath La., Dart. 187 FG89
Heath La., Guil. 260 BL141
Heath La., Hem.H. 40 BJ22
Heath La., Hert. 32 DW13
Heath La. Lwr., Dart. 188 FJ88
Heath La. Upper, Dart. 187 FH88
Heath Mead SW19 179 CX90
Heath Pk. Ct., Rom. 127 FG57
Heath Pk. Rd.
Heath Pk. Dr., Brom. 204 EL97
Heath Pk. Rd., Rom. 127 FG57
Heath Ridge Grn., Cob. 214 CA113
Heath Ri. SW15 179 CX86
Heath Ri., Brom. 204 EF100
Heath Ri., Dor. 262 CC138
Heath Ri., Vir.W. 192 AX98
Heath Ri., Wok. 228 BH123
Heath Rd. SW8 161 DH82
Heath Rd., Beac. 88 AG54
Heath Rd., Bex. 187 FC88
Heath Rd., Cat. 236 DR123
Heath Rd., Dart. 187 FF86
Heath Rd., Grays 171 GG75
Heath Rd., Har. 116 CC59
Heath Rd., Houns. 156 CB84
Heath Rd., Lthd. 214 CC112
Heath Rd., Pot.B. 64 DA30
Heath Rd., Rom. 126 EX59
Heath Rd., St.Alb. 43 CE19
Heath Rd., Th.Hth. 202 DQ97
Heath Rd., Twick. 177 CF88
Heath Rd., Uxb. 135 BQ70
Heath Rd., Wat. 94 BX45
Heath Rd., Wey. 212 BN105
Heath Rd., Wok. 227 AZ115
Heath Side NW3 120 DD63
Heath Side, Orp. 205 EQ102
Heath St. NW3 120 DC62
Heath St., Dart. 188 FK87
Heath Vw. N2 120 DC56
Heath Vw., Lthd. 245 BT125
Heath Vw. Clo. N2 120 DC56
Heath Vw. Gdns., Grays 170 GC75
Heath Vw. Rd., Grays 170 GC75
Heath Vill. SE18 165 ET78
Heath Vill. SW18 180 DC88
Cargill Rd.
Heath Way, Erith 167 FC81
Heatham Pk., Twick. 177 CF87
Heathbourne Rd. (Bushey), Wat. 95 CE46
Heathbridge, Wey. 212 BN108
Heathclose Ave., Dart. 187 FH87
Heathclose Rd., Dart. 187 FG88
Heathcock Ct. WC2 141 DL73
Strand
Heathcote, Tad. 233 CX121
Heathcote Ave., Hat. 45 CU16
Heathcote Ave., Ilf. 103 EM54
Heathcote Gdns., Harl. 52 EY15
Heathcote Gro. E4 101 EC48
Heathcote Rd., Epsom 216 CR114
Heathcote Rd., Twick. 177 CH86
Heathcote St. WC1 274 B4
Heathcote St. WC1 141 DM70
Heathcote Way, West Dr. 134 BK74
Tavistock Rd.
Heathcroft NW11 120 DB60
Heathcroft W5 138 CM70
Heathcroft Ave., Sun. 175 BT94
Heathdale Ave., Houns. 156 BY83
Heathdene, Tad. 233 CY119
Canons La.
Heathdene Dr., Belv. 167 FB77
Heathdene Rd. SW16 181 DM94
Heathdene Rd., Wall. 218 DG108
Heathdown Rd., Wok. 227 BD115
Heathedge SE26 182 DV89
Heathend Rd., Bex. 187 FE88
Heather Ave., Rom. 105 FD54
Heather Clo. E6 145 EP72
Heather Clo. SE13 183 ED87
Heather Clo. SW8 161 DH83
Heather Clo., Abb.L. 59 BU32
Magnolia Ave.
Heather Clo., Add. 212 BH110
Heather Clo., Brwd. 108 FV43
Heather Clo., Guil. 242 AV132
Heather Clo., Hmptn. 196 BZ95
Heather Clo., Islw. 177 CD85
Harvesters Clo.
Heather Clo., Red. 251 DH130
Heather Clo., Rom. 105 FD53
Heather Clo., Tad. 233 CY122
Heather Clo., Uxb. 134 BM71
Violet Ave.
Heather Clo., Wok. 226 AW115
Heather Dr., Dart. 187 FG87
Heather Dr., Enf. 81 DP40
Chasewood Ave.
Heather Dr., Rom. 105 FD54
Heather End, Swan. 207 FD98
Heather Gdns. NW11 119 CY58
Heather Gdns., Rom. 105 FD54
Heather Gdns., Sutt. 218 DA107
Heather Glen, Rom. 105 FD54
Heather La., Wat. 75 BT35
Heather La., West Dr. 134 BL72
Heather Pk. Dr., Wem. 138 CN66
Heather Pl., Esher 214 CB105
Park Rd.

Heather Ri. (Bushey), Wat. 76 BZ40
Heather Rd. E4 101 DZ51
Silver Birch Ave.
Heather Rd. NW2 119 CT61
Heather Rd. SE12 184 EG89
Heather Rd., Welw.G.C. 29 CW11
Heather Wk. W10 139 CY70
Droop St.
Heather Wk., Edg. 96 CP50
Heather Wk., Twick. 176 CA87
Stephenson Rd.
Heather Wk., Walt. 213 BT110
Octagon Rd.
Heather Way, Hem.H. 40 BK19
Heather Way, Pot.B. 63 CZ32
Heather Way, Rom. 105 FD54
Heather Way, S.Croy. 221 DX109
Heather Way, Stan. 95 CF51
Heather Way, Wok. 210 AS108
Heatherbank SE9 165 EM82
Heatherbank, Chis. 205 EN96
Heatherbank Clo., Dart. 187 FE86
Heatherdale Clo., Kings.T. 178 CP94
Heatherden Grn., Iver 133 BC67
Heatherdene, Lthd. 245 BR125
Heatherdene Clo. N12 98 DC53
Bow La.
Heatherdene Clo., Mitch. 200 DE98
Heatherfields, Add. 212 BH110
Heatherlands, Horl. 269 DH147
Stockfield
Heatherlands, Sun. 175 BU93
Heatherley Dr., Ilf. 124 EL55
Heathers, The, Stai. 174 BM87
Heatherset Gdns. SW16 181 DM94
Heatherside Dr., Vir.W. 192 AU100
Heatherside Gdns., Slou. 111 AR62
Heatherside Rd., Epsom 216 CR108
Heatherside Rd., Sid. 186 EX90
Wren Rd.
Heathersland, Dor. 263 CJ139
Goodwyns Rd.
Heatherton Pk., Amer. 55 AP36
Heathervale Caravan Pk., Add. 212 BJ110
Heathervale Rd., Add. 212 BH110
Heatherwood Clo. E12 124 EJ61
Heatherwood Dr., Hayes 135 BR68
Charville La.
Heathfield E4 101 EC48
Heathfield, Chis. 185 EQ93
Heathfield, Cob. 214 CA114
Heathfield Ave. SW18 180 DD87
Heathfield Rd.
Heathfield Ave., S.Croy. 221 DY109
Heathfield Clo. E16 144 EK71
Heathfield Clo., Kes. 222 EJ106
Heathfield Clo., Pot.B. 64 DB30
Heathfield Clo., Wok. 227 BA118
Heathfield Ct., St.Alb. 43 CE19
Avenue Rd.
Heathfield Dr., Mitch. 200 DE95
Heathfield Dr., Red. 266 DE139
Heathfield Gdns. NW11 119 CX58
Heathfield Gdns. SW18 180 DD86
Heathfield Rd.
Heathfield Gdns. W4 158 CQ78
Heathfield Gdns., Croy. 220 DR105
Coombe Rd.
Heathfield La., Chis. 185 EP93
Heathfield N., Twick. 177 CF87
Heathfield Pk. NW2 139 CW65
Heathfield Pk. Dr., Rom. 126 EV57
Barley La.
Heathfield Ri., Ruis. 115 BQ59
Heathfield Rd. SW18 180 DC86
Heathfield Rd. W3 158 CP75
Heathfield Rd., Bexh. 166 EZ84
Heathfield Rd., Brom. 184 EF94
Heathfield Rd., Croy. 220 DR105
Heathfield Rd., Kes. 222 EJ106
Heathfield Rd., Sev. 256 FF122
Heathfield Rd., Slou. 110 AF63
Heathfield Rd., Walt. 214 BY105
Heathfield Rd. (Bushey), Wat. 76 BY42
Heathfield Rd., Wok. 227 BA118
Heathfield S., Twick. 177 CF87
Heathfield Sq. SW18 180 DD87
Heathfield St. W11 139 CY73
Portland Rd.
Heathfield Ter. SE18 165 ES79
Heathfield Ter. W4 158 CQ78
Heathfield Vale, S.Croy. 221 DX109
Heathfield Way, Ger.Cr. 112 AX58
Heathfields Ct., Houns. 176 BY85
Frampton Rd.
Heathgate NW11 120 DB58
Heathgate, Hert. 32 DV13
Heathland Rd. N16 122 DS60
Heathlands, Tad. 233 CX122
Heathlands Clo., Sun. 195 BT96
Heathlands Clo., Twick. 177 CF88
Heathlands Clo., Wok. 210 AY114
Heathlands Dr., St.Alb. 43 CE18
Heathlands Ri., Dart. 187 FH86
Heathlands Way, Houns. 176 BY85
Frampton Rd.
Heathlee Rd. SE3 164 EF84
Heathlee Rd., Dart. 187 FE86
Heathley End, Chis. 185 EQ93
Heathmans Rd. SW6 159 CZ81
Heathrow, Guil. 261 BQ139
Heathrow Clo., West Dr. 154 BH81
Heathrow International Trd. Est., Houns. 155 BV83
Heathrow W. Business Pk., Slou. 153 BB77
Heaths Clo., Enf. 82 DS40
Heathside, Esher 197 CE104
Heathside, Houns. 176 BZ87
Heathside, St.Alb. 43 CE18
Heathside, Wey. 213 BP106
Heathside Ave., Bexh. 166 EY82
Heathside Clo., Esher 197 CE104
Heathside Clo., Nthwd. 93 BR50
Heathside Ct., Tad. 233 CV123
Heathside Cres., Wok. 227 AZ117
Heathside Gdns., Wok. 227 BA117
Heathside Pk. Rd., Wok. 227 AZ118
Heathside Pl., Epsom 233 CX118
Heathside Rd., Nthwd. 93 BR49
Heathside Rd., Wok. 227 AZ118
Heathstan Rd. W12 139 CU72
Heathurst Rd., S.Croy. 220 DS109
Heathview Ave., Dart. 187 FE86
Heathview Ct. SW19 179 CX89
Heathview Cres., Dart. 187 FG87
Heathview Dr. SE2 166 EX79
Heathview Gdns. SW15 179 CW87
Heathview Rd., Th.Hth. 201 DN98
Heathville Rd. N19 121 DL59
Heathwall St. SW11 160 DF83
Heathway SE3 164 EG80
Heathway, Cat. 252 DQ125
Heathway, Croy. 203 DZ104
Heathway, Dag. 126 EZ62
Heathway, Iver 133 BD68
Heathway, Lthd. 229 BT124
Heathway, Wdf.Grn. 102 EJ49
Heathwood Gdns. SE7 164 EL77
Heathwood Gdns., Swan. 207 FC96
Heathwood Wk., Bex. 187 FE88
Heaton Ave., Rom. 105 FH52
Heaton Clo. E4 101 EC48
Friars Clo.
Heaton Clo., Rom. 106 FJ52
Heaton Ct., Wal.Cr. 67 DX29
Heaton Gra. Rd., Rom. 105 FF54
Heaton Rd. SE15 162 DU83
Heaton Rd., Mitch. 180 DG94
Heaton Way, Rom. 106 FJ52
Heavens Lea, B.End 110 AC61
Heaver Rd. SW11 160 DD83
Wye St.
Heavitree Clo. SE18 165 ER78
Heavitree Rd. SE18 165 ER78
Heayfield, Welw.G.C. 30 DC08
Hebden Ct. E2 142 DT67
Laburnum St.
Hebden Ter. N17 100 DS51
Commercial Rd.
Hebdon Rd. SW17 180 DE90
Heber Rd. NW2 119 CX64
Heber Rd. SE22 182 DT86
Hebron Rd. W6 159 CV76
Hecham Clo. E17 101 DY54
Heckfield Pl. SW6 160 DA80
Fulham Rd.
Heckford St. E1 143 DX73
The Highway
Hector St. SE18 165 ES77
Heddington Gro. N7 121 DM64
Heddon Clo., Islw. 157 CG84
Heddon Ct. Ave., Barn. 80 DF43
Heddon Rd., Barn. 80 DF43
Heddon St. W1 273 K10
Heddon St. W1 141 DJ73
Hedge Hill, Enf. 81 DP39
Hedge La. N13 99 DP48
Hedge Lea, H.Wyc. 110 AD55
Hedge Pl. Rd., Green. 189 FT86
Hedge Row, Hem.H. 40 BG18
Hedge Wk. SE6 183 EB92
Lushington Rd.
Hedgebrooms, Welw.G.C. 30 DC08
Hedgeley, Ilf. 125 EM56
Hedgemans Rd., Dag. 146 EX66
Hedgemans Way, Dag. 146 EY65
Hedgerley Ct., Wok. 226 AW117
Hedgerley Gdns., Grnf. 136 CC68
Hedgerley Hill, Slou. 111 AR62
Hedgerley La., Beac. 111 AN56
Hedgerley La., Ger.Cr. 112 AV59
Hedgerley La., Slou. 112 AS58
Hedgerow, Ger.Cr. 90 AY54
Hedgerow Wk., Wal.Cr. 67 DX30
Hedgerows, Saw. 36 EZ05
Hedgerows, The, Grav. 190 GE89
Hedgers Gro. E9 143 DY65
Hedges, The, St.Alb. 42 CC16
Hedges Clo., Hat. 45 CV17
Hedgeside, Berk. 39 BA16
Hedgeside Rd., Nthwd. 93 BQ50
Hedgeway, Guil. 258 AU136
Hedgewood Gdns., Ilf. 125 EN56
Hedgley St. SE12 184 EF85
Hedingham Clo. N1 142 DQ66
Popham Rd.
Hedingham Clo., Horl. 269 DJ147
Hedingham Rd., Dag. 126 EV64
Hedingham Rd., Grays 169 FW78
Hedingham Rd., Horn. 128 FN60
Hedley Ave., Grays 169 FW80
Hedley Rd., St.Alb. 43 CH20
Hedley Rd., Twick. 176 CA87
Hedley Row N5 122 DR64
Poets Rd.
Hedley Vw., H.Wyc. 88 AD54
Hedsor Hill, B.End 110 AC61
Hedsor La., H.Wyc. 110 AF60
Hedworth Ave., Wal.Cr. 67 DX33
Heenan Clo., Bark. 145 EQ65
Glenny Rd.
Heene Rd., Enf. 82 DR39
Heideck Gdns., Brwd. 109 GB47
Victors Cres.
Heidegger Cres. SW13 159 CV79
Trinity Ch. Rd.
Heigham Rd. E6 144 EL66
Heighams, Harl. 51 EM18
Heighton Gdns., Croy. 219 DP106
Heights, The SE7 164 EJ78
Heights, The, Beck. 183 EC94
Heights, The, Hem.H. 40 BM18
Saturn Way
Heights, The, Loug. 85 EM40
Heights, The, Nthlt. 116 BZ64
Heights, The, Wal.Abb. 68 EH25
Heights, The, Wey. 212 BN110
Heights Clo. SW20 179 CV94
Heights Clo., Bans. 233 CY116
Heiron St. SE17 161 DP79
Helby Rd. SW4 181 DK86
Helder Gro. SE12 184 EF87
Helder St., S.Croy. 220 DR107
Heldmann Clo., Houns. 157 CD84
Helen Ave., Felt. 175 BV87
Helen Clo. N2 120 DC55
Thomas More Way
Helen Clo., Dart. 187 FH87
Helen Clo., W.Mol. 196 CB98
Helen Rd., Horn. 128 FK55
Helen St. SE18 165 EP77
Wilmount St.
Helena Clo., Barn. 80 DD38
Helena Clo., Wall. 219 DL108
Kingsford Ave.
Helena Pl. E9 142 DW67
Fremont St.
Helena Rd. E13 144 EF68
Helena Rd. E17 123 EA57
Helena Rd. NW10 119 CV64
Helena Rd. W5 137 CK71
Helena Rd., Wind. 151 AR82
Helena Sq. SE16 143 DY73
Rotherhithe St.
Helens Gate, Wal.Cr. 67 DZ26
Helen's Pl. E2 142 DW69
Roman Rd.
Helenslea Ave. NW11 119 CZ60
Helford Clo., Ruis. 115 BS61
Chichester Ave.
Helford Wk., Wok. 226 AU118
Helford Way, Upmin. 129 FR58
Helgiford Gdns., Sun. 175 BS94
Helions Rd., Harl. 51 EP15
Helix Gdns. SW2 181 DM86
Helix Rd.
Helix Rd. SW2 181 DM86
Helleborine, Grays 170 FZ78
Hellings St. E1 142 DU74
Wapping High St.
Helme Clo. SW19 179 CZ92
Helmet Row EC1 275 J4
Helmet Row EC1 142 DQ70
Helmsdale, Wok. 226 AV118
Winnington Way
Helmsdale Clo., Hayes 136 BY70
Berrydale Rd.
Helmsdale Clo., Rom. 105 FE52
Helmsdale Rd. SW16 201 DK95
Helmsdale Rd., Rom. 105 FE52
Helmsley Pl. E8 142 DV66
Helsinki Sq. SE16 163 DY76
Finland St.
Helston Clo., Pnr. 94 BZ52
Helston Gro., Hem.H. 40 BK15
Helston La., Wind. 151 AP81
Helston Pl., Abb.L. 59 BT32
Shirley Rd.
Helvellyn Clo., Egh. 173 BB94
Helvetia St. SE6 183 DZ89
Hemans St. SW8 161 DK80
Hemberton Rd. SW9 161 DL83
Hemel Hempstead Rd., Hem.H. 41 BR22
Hemel Hempstead Rd., St.Alb. 42 BW22
Hemel Hempstead Rd. (Redbourn), St.Alb. 41 BQ15
Hemery Rd., Grnf. 117 CD64
Heming Rd., Edg. 96 CP52
Hemingford Clo. N12 98 DD50
Fenstanton Ave.
Hemingford Rd. N1 141 DM67
Hemingford Rd., Sutt. 217 CW105
Hemingford Rd., Wat. 75 BS36
Hemington Ave. N11 98 DF50
Hemlock Clo., Tad. 233 CY124
Warren Lo. Dr.
Hemlock Rd. W12 139 CT73
Hemmen La., Hayes 135 BT72
Hemming Clo., Hmptn. 196 CA95
Chandler Clo.
Hemming St. E1 142 DU70
Hemming Way, Wat. 75 BU35
Hemmings, The, Berk. 38 AT20
Hemmings Clo., Sid. 186 EV89
Hemnall St., Epp. 69 ET31
Hemp Wk. SE17 279 L8
Hempshaw Ave., Bans. 234 DF116
Hempson Ave., Slou. 152 AW76
Hempstall, Welw.G.C. 30 DB11
Linces Way
Hempstead Clo., Buck.H. 102 EG47
Hempstead La., Berk. 39 BB17
Hempstead Rd. E17 101 ED54
Hempstead Rd., Hem.H. 57 BA27
Hempstead Rd., Kings L. 58 BM26
Hempstead Rd., Wat. 75 BR36
Hemsby Rd., Chess. 216 CM107
Hemstal Rd. NW6 140 DA66
Hemsted Rd., Erith 167 FE80
Hemswell Dr. NW9 96 CS53
Hemsworth Ct. N1 142 DS68
Hemsworth St.
Hemsworth St. N1 142 DS68
Hemus Pl. SW3 160 DE78
Chelsea Manor St.
Hemwood Rd., Wind. 151 AK83
Hen & Chicken Ct. EC4 141 DN72
Fleet St.
Henbane Path, Rom. 106 FK52
Clematis Clo.
Henbit Clo., Tad. 233 CV119
Henbury Way, Wat. 94 BX48
Henchley Dene, Guil. 243 BD131
Henchman St. W12 139 CT72
Hencroft St. N., Slou. 152 AT75
Hencroft St. S., Slou. 152 AT76
Osborne St.
Hendale Ave. NW4 119 CU55
Henderson Ave., Guil. 242 AV129
Henderson Clo. NW10 138 CQ65
Henderson Clo., Horn. 127 FH61
St. Leonards Way
Henderson Clo., St.Alb. 42 CC16
Henderson Dr. NW8 140 DD70
Cunningham Pl.
Henderson Dr., Dart. 168 FM84
Henderson Pl., Abb.L. 59 BT27
Henderson Rd. E7 144 EJ65
Henderson Rd. N9 100 DV46
Henderson Rd. SW18 180 DE87
Henderson Rd., Croy. 202 DR100
Henderson Rd., Hayes 135 BU69
Henderson Rd., West. 222 EJ112
Hendham Rd. SW17 180 DE89
Hendon Ave. N3 97 CY53
Hendon Gdns., Rom. 105 FC51
Hendon La. N3 119 CY55
Hendon Pk. Row NW11 119 CZ58
Hendon Rd. N9 100 DU47
Hendon Way NW2 119 CX59
Hendon Way NW4 119 CV58
Hendon Way, Stai. 174 BK86
Hendon Wd. La. NW7 97 CT45
Hendre Rd. SE1 279 N9
Hendren Clo., Grnf. 117 CD64
Dimmock Dr.
Hendrick Ave. SW12 180 DF87
Heneage Cres., Croy. 221 EC110
Heneage La. EC3 275 N9
Heneage St. E1 142 DT71
Henfield Clo. N19 121 DJ60
Henfield Clo., Bex. 186 FA86
Henfield Rd. SW19 199 CZ95
Henfold La., Dor. 264 CL144
Hengelo Gdns., Mitch. 200 DD98
Hengist Rd. SE12 184 EH87
Hengist Rd., Erith 167 FB80
Hengist Way, Brom. 203 ED98
Hengrave Rd. SE23 182 DW87
Hengrove Ct., Bex. 186 EY88
Hurst Rd.
Hengrove Cres., Ashf. 174 BK90
Henhurst Rd., Grav. 191 GL94
Henley Ave., Sutt. 199 CY104
Henley Bank, Guil. 258 AU136
Henley Clo., Grnf. 136 CC68
Henley Clo., Islw. 157 CF81
Henley Ct. N14 99 DJ45
Henley Ct., Wok. 227 BA120
Henley Deane, Grav. 190 GE91
Henley Dr. SE1 162 DT77
Henley Dr., Kings.T. 179 CT94
Henley Gdns., Pnr. 115 BV55
Henley Gdns., Rom. 126 EY57
Henley Rd. E16 165 EM75
Henley Rd. N18 100 DS49
Henley Rd. NW10 139 CW67
Henley Rd., Ilf. 125 EQ63
Henley Rd., Slou. 131 AL72
Henley St. SW11 160 DG82
Henley Way, Felt. 176 BX92
Henlow Pl., Rich. 177 CK89
Sandpits Rd.
Hennel Clo. SE23 182 DW90
Hennessy Ct., Wok. 211 BC113
Henniker Gdns. E6 144 EK69
Henniker Ms. SW3 160 DD79
Callow St.
Henniker Pt. E15 124 EE64
Henniker Rd. E15 123 ED64
Henning St. SW11 160 DE81
Henningham Rd. N17 100 DR53
Henrietta Ms. WC1 274 A4
Henrietta Pl. W1 273 H8
Henrietta Pl. W1 141 DH72
Henrietta St. E15 123 EC64
Henrietta St. WC2 274 A10
Henrietta St. WC2 141 DL73
Henriques St. E1 142 DU72
Henry Clo., Enf. 82 DS38
Henry Cooper Way SE9 184 EK90
Henry Darlot Dr. NW7 97 CX50
Henry Dickens Ct. W11 139 CX73
Henry Jackson Rd. SW15 159 CX83
Henry Rd. E6 144 EL68
Henry Rd. N4 122 DQ60
Henry Rd., Barn. 80 DD43
Henry Rd., Slou. 151 AR75
Henry St., Brom. 204 EH95
Henry St., Grays 170 GC79
East Thurrock Rd.
Henry St., Hem.H. 40 BK24
Henry Wells Sq., Hem.H. 40 BL16
Aycliffe Dr.
Henry's Ave., Wdf.Grn. 102 EF50
Henry's Wk., Ilf. 103 ER52
Henryson Rd. SE4 183 EA85
Hensford Gdns. SE26 182 DV91
Wells Pk. Rd.
Henshall St. N1 142 DR65
Henshaw St. SE17 279 K8
Henshaw St. SE17 162 DR77
Henshawe Rd., Dag. 126 EX62
Henshill Pt. E3 143 EB69
Bromley High St.
Henslow Way, Wok. 211 BD114
Henslowe Rd. SE22 182 DU85
Henson Ave. NW2 119 CW64
Henson Clo., Orp. 205 EP103
Henson Path, Har. 117 CK55
Brancker Rd.
Henson Pl., Nthlt. 136 BW67
Henstridge Pl. NW8 140 DE68
Hensworth Rd., Ashf. 174 BK92
Henty Clo. SW11 160 DE80
Henty Wk. SW15 179 CV85
Henville Rd., Brom. 204 EJ95
Henwick Rd. SE9 164 EK83
Henwood Rd. SE16 162 DW76
Gomm Rd.
Henwood Side, Wdf.Grn. 103 EM51
Love La.
Hepburn Gdns., Brom. 204 EE102
Hepburn Ms. SW11 180 DF85
Webbs Rd.
Hepple Clo., Islw. 157 CH82
Hepplestone Clo. SW15 179 CV86
Dover Pk. Dr.
Hepscott Rd. E9 143 EA65
Hepworth Ct., Bark. 126 EU64
Hepworth Gdns., Bark. 126 EU64
Hepworth Rd. SW16 181 DL94
Hepworth Wk. NW3 120 DE64
Haverstock Hill
Hepworth Way, Walt. 195 BT102
Heracles Clo., Wall. 219 DL108
Gull Clo.
Herald Gdns., Wall. 201 DH104
Herald St. E2 142 DV70
Three Colts La.
Herald Wk., Dart. 188 FM85
Temple Hill Sq.
Herald's Ct. SE11 278 F9
Herald's Pl. SE11 278 E8
Herbal Hill EC1 274 E5
Herbal Hill EC1 141 DN70
Herbert Cres. SW1 276 E6
Herbert Cres., Wok. 226 AS118
Herbert Gdns. NW10 139 CV67
Herbert Gdns. W4 158 CP79
Magnolia Rd.
Herbert Gdns., Rom. 126 EX59
Herbert Pl. SE18 165 EP79
Plumstead Common Rd.
Herbert Rd. E12 124 EL63
Herbert Rd. E17 123 DZ59
Herbert Rd. N11 99 DL52
Herbert Rd. N15 122 DT57
Herbert Rd. NW9 119 CU58
Herbert Rd. SE18 165 EN80
Herbert Rd. SW19 179 CZ94
Herbert Rd., Bexh. 166 EY82
Herbert Rd., Brom. 204 EK99
Herbert Rd., Horn. 128 FL59
Herbert Rd., Ilf. 125 ES61
Herbert Rd., Kings.T. 198 CM97
Herbert Rd., Sthl. 136 BZ74
Herbert Rd., Swan. 187 FH93
Herbert Rd., Swans. 190 FZ86
Herbert St. E13 144 EG68
Herbert St. NW5 140 DG65
Herbert St., Hem.H. 40 BK19
St. Mary's Rd.
Herbert Ter. SE18 165 EP79
Herbert Rd.
Herbrand St. WC1 273 P4
Herbrand St. WC1 141 DL70
Hercies Rd., Uxb. 134 BM66
Hercules Pl. N7 121 DL62
Hercules St.
Hercules Rd. SE1 278 C7
Hercules Rd. SE1 161 DM76
Hercules St. N7 121 DL62
Hercules Twr. SE14 163 DY79
Milton Ct. Rd.
Hereford Ave., Barn. 98 DF46
Hereford Clo., Epsom 216 CR113
Hereford Clo., Guil. 242 AT132
Hereford Clo., Stai. 194 BH95
Hereford Copse, Wok. 226 AV119
Hereford Gdns. SE13 184 EE85
Longhurst Rd.
Hereford Gdns., Ilf. 124 EL59
Hereford Gdns., Pnr. 116 BY57
Hereford Gdns., Twick. 176 CC88
Hereford Ho. NW6 140 DA68
Hereford Ms. W2 140 DA72
Hereford Rd.
Hereford Pl. SE14 163 DZ80
Hereford Retreat SE15 162 DU80
Bird in Bush Rd.
Hereford Rd. E11 124 EH57
Hereford Rd. W2 140 DA72
Hereford Rd. W3 138 CP73
Hereford Rd. W5 157 CJ76
Hereford Rd., Felt. 176 BW88
Hereford Sq. SW7 160 DC77
Hereford St. E2 142 DU70
Hereford Way, Chess. 215 CJ106
Herent Dr., Ilf. 124 EL56
Hereward Ave., Pur. 219 DN111
Hereward Clo., Wal.Abb. 67 EC32
Hereward Gdns. N13 99 DN50
Hereward Grn., Loug. 85 EQ39
Hereward Rd. SW17 180 DE91
Herga Ct., Har. 117 CE62
Herga Ct., Wat. 75 BU40
Herga Rd., Har. 117 CF56
Herington Gro., Brwd. 109 GA45
Heriot Ave. E4 101 EA47
Heriot Rd. NW4 119 CW57
Heriot Rd., Cher. 194 BG101
Heriots Clo., Stan. 95 CG49
Heritage Clo., Uxb. 134 BJ70
Heritage Hill, Kes. 222 EJ106
Heritage Lawn, Horl. 269 DJ147
Heritage Vw., Har. 117 CF62
Heritage Wk., Rick. 73 BE41
Chenies Rd.
Herkomer Clo. (Bushey), Wat. 76 CB44
Herkomer Rd. (Bushey), Wat. 76 CA43
Herlwyn Ave., Ruis. 115 BS61
Herlwyn Gdns. SW17 180 DF91
Hermes Pt. W9 140 DA70
Harrow Rd.
Hermes St. N1 274 D1
Hermes Wk., Nthlt. 136 CA68
Hotspur Rd.
Hermes Way, Wall. 219 DK108
Hermiston Ave. N8 121 DL57
Hermit Pl. NW6 140 DB67
Belsize Rd.
Hermit Rd. E16 144 EF70
Hermit St. EC1 274 F2
Hermit St. EC1 141 DP69
Hermitage, The SE23 182 DW88
Hermitage, The SW13 159 CT81
Hermitage, The, Felt. 175 BT90
Hermitage, The, Rich. 178 CL85
Hermitage, The, Uxb. 134 BK65
Hermitage Clo. E18 124 EF56
Hermitage Clo., Enf. 81 DP40
Hermitage Clo., Esher 215 CG107
Hermitage Clo., Shep. 194 BN98
Hermitage Clo., Slou. 152 AW76
Hermitage Ct. E18 124 EG56
Hermitage Ct. NW2 120 DA62
Hermitage La.
Hermitage Ct., Pot.B. 64 DC33
Southgate Rd.
Hermitage Gdns. NW2 120 DA62
Hermitage Gdns. SE19 182 DQ94
Hermitage La. N18 100 DR50
Hermitage La. NW2 120 DA62
Hermitage La. SE25 202 DU100
Hermitage La. SW16 181 DM94
Hermitage La., Croy. 202 DU100
Hermitage La., Wind. 151 AN83
Hermitage Path SW16 201 DL95
Hermitage Rd. N4 121 DP59
Hermitage Rd. N15 121 DP59
Hermitage Rd. SE19 182 DQ94
Hermitage Rd., Ken. 236 DQ116
Hermitage Row E8 122 DU64
Hermitage St. W2 140 DD71
Harrow Rd.
Hermitage Wk. E18 124 EF56
Hermitage Wall E1 142 DU74
Hermitage Way, Stan. 95 CG53
Hermitage Wds. Cres., Wok. 226 AS119
Hermon Gro., Hayes 135 BU74
Hermon Hill E11 124 EG57
Hermon Hill E18 124 EH55
Herndon Clo., Egh. 173 BA91
Herndon Rd. SW18 180 DC85
Herne Clo. NW10 118 CR64
North Circular Rd.
Herne Ct., Ch.St.G. 90 AV48
Herne Hill SE24 182 DQ85
Herne Hill Rd. SE24 162 DQ83
Herne Ms. N18 100 DU49
Lyndhurst Rd.

Herne Pl. SE24 181 DP85
Herne Rd., Surb. 197 CK103
Herne Rd. (Bushey), Wat. 76 CB44
Herneshaw, Hat. 45 CT20
Hazel Gro.
Herns La., Welw.G.C. 30 DB08
Herns Way, Welw.G.C. 30 DA07
Heron Clo. E17 101 DZ54
Heron Clo. NW10 138 CS65
Heron Clo., Buck.H. 102 EG46
Heron Clo., Guil. 242 AV131
Heron Clo., Rick. 92 BK47
Heron Clo., Saw. 36 EX06
Heron Clo., Uxb. 134 BK65
Heron Ct., Brom. 204 EJ98
Heron Cres., Sid. 185 ES90
Heron Dale, Add. 212 BK106
Heron Dr., Slou. 153 BB77
Heron Dr., Ware 33 EC12
Heron Elm, Berk. 38 AS16
Heron Flight Ave., Horn. 147 FH66
Heron Hill, Belv. 166 EZ78
Heron Ms., Ilf. 125 EP61
Balfour Rd.
Heron Pl. SE16 143 DY74
Heron Quay E14 143 EA74
Heron Rd. SE24 162 DQ84
Heron Rd., Croy. 202 DS103
Tunstall Rd.
Heron Rd., Twick. 157 CG84
Heron Sq., Rich. 177 CK85
Bridge St.
Heron Wk., Nthwd. 93 BS49
Heron Wk., Wok. 211 BC114
Blackmore Cres.
Heron Way, Grays 169 FV78
Heron Way, Hat. 45 CU19
Heron Way, Upmin. 129 FS60
Herondale, S.Croy. 221 DX109
Herondale Ave. SW18 180 DD88
Heronfield, Egh. 172 AV93
Heronfield, Pot.B. 64 DC30
Herongate Rd. E12 124 EJ61
Herongate Rd., Swan. 187 FE93
Herongate Rd. (Cheshunt), Wal.Cr. 67 DY27
Heronry, The, Walt. 213 BU107
Herons, The E11 124 EF58
Herons Cft., Wey. 213 BR107
Heron's Pl., Islw. 157 CH83
Herons Ri., Barn. 80 DE42
Herons Way, St.Alb. 43 CG24
Herons Wd., Harl. 35 EP13
Herons Wd. Ct., Horl. 269 DH147
Tanyard Way
Heronsforde W13 137 CJ72
Heronsgate, Edg. 96 CN50
Heronsgate Rd., Rick. 73 BB44
Heronslea, Wat. 76 BW36
Heronslea Dr., Stan. 96 CL50
Heronswood, Wal.Abb. 68 EE34
Roundhills
Heronswood Pl., Welw.G.C. 30 DA10
Heronswood Rd., Welw.G.C. 30 DA09
Heronway, Brwd. 109 GB46
Heronway, Wdf.Grn. 102 EJ49
Herrick Rd. N5 122 DQ62
Herrick St. SW1 277 N9
Herrick St. SW1 161 DK77
Herries St. W10 139 CY68
Herringham Rd. SE7 164 EJ76
Herrings La., Cher. 194 BG100
Herrongate Clo., Enf. 82 DT40
Hersant Clo. NW10 139 CU67
Herschel Pk. Dr., Slou. 152 AT75
Herschel St., Slou. 152 AT75
Herschell Rd. SE23 183 DY87
Hersham Bypass, Walt. 213 BV106
Hersham Clo. SW15 179 CU87
Hersham Gdns., Walt. 214 BW105
Hersham Rd., Walt. 195 BU102
Hersham Trd. Est., Walt. 196 BY103
Hertford Ave. SW14 178 CR85
Hertford Clo., Barn. 80 DD41
Hertford Pl. W1 273 K5
Hertford Rd. N1 142 DS67
Hertford Rd. N2 120 DE55
Hertford Rd. N9 100 DU47
Hertford Rd., Bark. 145 EP66
Hertford Rd., Barn. 80 DC41
Hertford Rd., Enf. 82 DW40
Hertford Rd., Hat. 30 DA14
Hertford Rd., Hert. 30 DF08
Hertford Rd. (Hertford Heath), Hert. 32 DW13
Hertford Rd. (Marden Hill), Hert. 30 DG06
Hertford Rd., Hodd. 49 DY15
Hertford Rd., Ilf. 125 ES58
Hertford Rd., Wal.Cr. 83 DY35
Hertford Rd., Ware 32 DW07
Hertford Rd. (Great Amwell), Ware 33 DZ11
Hertford Rd., Welw. 30 DA05
Hertford Rd. (Tewin), Welw. 30 DE05
Hertford Sq., Mitch. 201 DL98
Hertford Way
Hertford St. W1 276 G3
Hertford St. W1 140 DG74
Hertford Wk., Belv. 166 FA78
Hoddesdon Rd.
Hertford Way, Mitch. 201 DL98
Hertingfordbury Rd., Hert. 31 DM10
Hertslet Rd. N7 121 DM62
Hertsmere Rd. E14 143 EA73
Hervey Clo. N3 98 DA53
Hervey Pk. Rd. E17 123 DY56
Hervey Rd. SE3 164 EH81
Hervines Ct., Amer. 55 AQ37
Hervines Rd., Amer. 55 AP37
Hesa Rd., Hayes 135 BU72
Hesiers Hill, Warl. 238 EE117
Hesiers Rd., Warl. 238 EE117
Hesketh Ave., Dart. 188 FP88
Hesketh Pl. W11 139 CY73
Hesketh Rd. E7 124 EG62
Heslop Rd. SW12 180 DF88
Hesper Ms. SW5 160 DB78
Hesperus Cres. E14 163 EB77
Hessel Rd. W13 157 CG75
Hessel St. E1 142 DV72
Hesselyn Dr., Rain. 147 FH66
Hessle Gro., Epsom 217 CT111
Hester Rd. N18 100 DU50
Hester Rd. SW11 160 DE80
Hester Ter., Rich. 158 CN83
Chilton Rd.
Hestercombe Ave. SW6 159 CY82
Hesterman Way, Croy. 201 DL102
Heston Ave., Houns. 156 BY79
Heston Gra. La., Houns. 156 BZ79
Heston Ind. Cen., Houns. 156 BW79
Heston Ind. Mall, Houns. 156 BZ80
Heston Rd., Houns. 156 CA79
Heston Rd., Red. 266 DF138
Heston St. SE14 163 EA81
Heston Wk., Red. 266 DF138
Heswell Grn., Wat. 93 BU48
Fairhaven Cres.
Hetchleys, Hem.H. 40 BG17
Hetherington Clo., Slou. 131 AM69
Hetherington Rd. SW4 161 DL84
Hetherington Rd., Shep. 195 BQ96
Hetherington Way, Uxb. 114 BL63
Hethersett Clo., Reig. 250 DC131
Hetley Gdns. SE19 182 DT94
Fox Hill
Hetley Rd. W12 139 CV74
Heton Gdns. NW4 119 CU56
Heusden Way, Ger.Cr. 113 AZ60
Hevelius Clo. SE10 164 EF78
Hever Ct. Rd., Grav. 191 GJ93
Hever Cft. SE9 185 EN91
Hever Gdns., Brom. 205 EN96
Heverham Rd. SE18 165 ES77
Hevers Ave., Horl. 268 DF147
Heversham Rd., Bexh. 166 FA82
Hewens Rd., Hayes 135 BQ70
Hewens Rd., Uxb. 135 BQ70
Hewer St. W10 139 CX71
Hewers Way, Tad. 233 CV120
Hewett Clo., Stan. 95 CH49
Hewett Pl., Swan. 207 FD98
Hewett Rd., Dag. 126 EW64
Hewett St. EC2 275 N5
Hewins Clo., Wal.Abb. 68 EE33
Broomstick Hall Rd.
Hewish Rd. N18 100 DS49
Hewison St. E3 143 DZ68
Hewitt Ave. N22 99 DP54
Hewitt Clo., Croy. 203 EA104
Hewitt Rd. N8 121 DN57
Hewitts Rd., Orp. 224 EZ108
Hewlett Rd. E3 143 DY68
Hexagon, The N6 120 DF60
Hexal Rd. SE6 184 EE90
Hexham Gdns., Islw. 157 CG80
Hexham Rd. SE27 182 DQ89
Hexham Rd., Barn. 80 DB42
Hexham Rd., Mord. 200 DB102
Hextalls La., Red. 252 DR128
Heybourne Rd. N17 100 DV52
Heybridge Ave. SW16 181 DL94
Heybridge Dr., Ilf. 103 ER54
Heybridge Way E10 123 DY59
Heydons Clo., St.Alb. 43 CD18
Heyford Ave. SW8 161 DL80
Heyford Ave. SW20 199 CZ97
Heyford Rd., Mitch. 200 DE96
Heyford Rd., Rad. 77 CF37
Heyford Way, Hat. 45 CW16
Heygate St. SE17 279 H9
Heygate St. SE17 162 DQ77
Heylyn Sq. E3 143 DZ69
Malmesbury Rd.
Heymede, Lthd. 231 CJ123
Heynes Rd., Dag. 126 EW63
Heysham Dr., Wat. 94 BW50
Heysham La. NW3 120 DB62
Heysham Rd. N15 122 DR58
Heythorp St. SW18 179 CZ88
Heythorpe Clo., Wok. 226 AT117
Kenton Way
Heythrop Dr., Uxb. 114 BM63
Heywood Ave. NW9 96 CS53
Heyworth Rd. E5 122 DV63
Heyworth Rd. E15 124 EF63
Hibbert Ave., Wat. 76 BX38
Hibbert Lo., Ger.Cr. 90 AX54
Gold Hill E.
Hibbert Rd. E17 123 DZ59
Hibbert Rd., Har. 95 CF54
Hibbert St. SW11 160 DC83
Hibberts All., Wind. 151 AR81
Peascod St.
Hibberts Way, Ger.Cr. 112 AY56
North Pk.
Hibbs Clo., Swan. 207 FD96
Hibernia Dr., Grav. 191 GM90
Hibernia Gdns., Houns. 156 CA84
Hibernia Rd., Houns. 156 CA84
Hichisson Rd. SE15 182 DW85
Hickin Clo. SE7 164 EK77
Hickin St. E14 163 EC76
Plevna St.
Hickling Rd., Ilf. 125 EP64
Hickman Ave. E4 101 EC51
Hickman Clo. E16 144 EK71
Hickman Clo., Brox. 49 DX20
Hickman Rd., Rom. 126 EW59
Hickmans Clo., Gdse. 252 DW132
Hickmore Wk. SW4 161 DJ83
Hickory Clo. N9 100 DU45
Hicks Ave., Grnf. 137 CD68
Hicks Clo. SW11 160 DE83
Hicks St. SE8 163 DY78
Hidalgo Ct., Hem.H. 40 BM18
Hidcote Clo., Wok. 227 BB116
Hidcote Gdns. SW20 199 CV97
Hide E6 145 EN72
Downings
Hide Pl. SW1 277 M9
Hide Pl. SW1 161 DK77
Hide Rd., Har. 116 CC56
Hideaway, The, Abb.L. 59 BU31
Hides, The, Harl. 35 ER14
Hides St. N7 141 DM65
Sheringham Rd.
Higgins Wk., Hmptn. 176 BY93
Abbott Clo.
High, The, Harl. 51 ER15
High Acres, Abb.L. 59 BR32
High Barn La., Dor. 246 BX134
High Barn Rd., Lthd. 246 BX129
High Beech, S.Croy. 220 DS108
High Beech Rd., Loug. 84 EL42
High Beeches, Bans. 217 CW114
High Beeches, Ger.Cr. 112 AX60
High Beeches, Orp. 224 EU107
High Beeches, Sid. 186 EY92
High Beeches Clo., Pur. 219 DK110
High Bois La., Amer. 55 AR35
Bois La.
High Bri. SE10 163 ED78
High Bri. Wf. SE10 163 ED78
High Bri.
High Broom Cres., W.Wick. 203 EB101
High Canons, Borwd. 78 CQ37
High Cedar Dr. SW20 179 CV94
High Clandon, Guil. 244 BL133
High Clo., Rick. 74 BJ43
High Coombe Pl., Kings.T. 178 CR94
High Coppice, Amer. 55 AQ39
High Cross, Wat. 77 CD37
High Cross Cen. N15 122 DU56
High Cross Rd. N17 122 DU55
High Dells, Hat. 45 CT19
High Dr., Cat. 237 EA122
High Dr., Lthd. 215 CD114
High Dr., N.Mal. 198 CQ95
High Elms, Chig. 103 ES49
High Elms, Upmin. 129 FS60
High Elms, Wdf.Grn. 102 EG50
High Elms Clo., Nthwd. 93 BR51
High Elms La., Wat. 59 BV31
High Elms Rd., Orp. 223 EN111
High Fld., Bans. 234 DE117
High Firs, Rad. 77 CF35
High Firs, Swan. 207 FE98
High Foleys, Esher 215 CH108
High Gables, Loug. 84 EK43
High Garth, Esher 214 CC107
High Gro. SE18 165 ER80
High Gro., Brom. 204 EJ95
High Gro., St.Alb. 43 CD18
High Gro., Welw.G.C. 29 CW08
High Hill Est. E5 122 DV60
Mount Pleasant La.
High Hill Ferry E5 122 DV60
High Hill Rd., Warl. 237 EC115
High Holborn WC1 273 P8
High Holborn WC1 141 DL72
High Ho. La., Til. 171 GK77
High Lands, Hat. 45 CW15
High La. W7 137 CD71
High La., B.Stort. 37 FE09
High La., Cat. 237 DZ119
High La., Warl. 237 DZ118
High Lawns, Har. 117 CE62
High Level Dr. SE26 182 DU91
High Mead, Chig. 103 EQ47
High Mead, Har. 117 CE57
High Mead, W.Wick. 203 ED103
High Meadow Clo., Dor. 263 CH137
High Meadow Clo., Pnr. 115 BV56
Daymer Gdns.
High Meadow Cres. NW9 118 CR57
High Meadow Pl., Cher. 193 BF100
High Meadows, Chig. 103 ER50
High Meads Rd. E16 144 EK72
Fulmer Rd.
High Mt. NW4 119 CU58
High Oak Rd., Ware 33 DX05
High Oaks, Enf. 81 DM38
High Oaks, St.Alb. 42 CC15
High Oaks Rd., Welw.G.C. 29 CV08
High Pk. Ave., Lthd. 245 BT126
High Pk. Ave., Rich. 158 CN81
High Pk. Rd., Rich. 158 CN81
High Pastures, B.Stort. 37 FD07
High Path SW19 200 DB95
High Path Rd., Guil. 243 BC134
High Pewley, Guil. 258 AY136
High Pine Clo., Wey. 213 BQ106
High Pines, Warl. 236 DW119
High Pt. N6 120 DG59
High Pt. SE9 185 EP90
High Ridge (Cuffley), Pot.B. 65 DL27
High Ridge Clo., Hem.H. 58 BK25
High Ridge Rd., Hem.H. 58 BK25
High Rd. N2 98 DD53
High Rd. N11 99 DH50
High Rd. N12 98 DC49
High Rd. N15 122 DT58
High Rd. N17 122 DT55
High Rd. N20 98 DC47
High Rd. N22 99 DM51
High Rd. (Willesden) NW10 139 CT65
High Rd., Brox. 49 DZ23
High Rd., Buck.H. 102 EH48
High Rd., Chig. 103 EN50
High Rd., Couls. 234 DE124
High Rd. (Wilmington), Dart. 188 FJ90
High Rd., Epp. 69 ER32
High Rd. (North Weald Bassett), Epp. 71 FB27
High Rd. (Thornwood), Epp. 70 EV28
High Rd. (Harrow Weald), Har. 95 CE52
High Rd., Hat. 46 DD17
High Rd., Ilf. 125 EQ61
High Rd. (Goodmayes), Ilf. 126 EU60
High Rd. (Seven Kings), Ilf. 125 ET60
High Rd., Loug. 84 EJ44
High Rd., Pnr. 115 BV57
High Rd., Reig. 250 DC127
High Rd. (Chadwell Heath), Rom. 126 EU60
High Rd., Uxb. 134 BJ71
High Rd. (Ickenham), Uxb. 115 BP62
High Rd. (Bushey), Wat. 95 CD46
High Rd. (Leavesden Grn.), Wat. 75 BT35
High Rd., Wem. 118 CL64
High Rd., W.Byf. 212 BK112
High Rd. Leyton E10 123 EB58
High Rd. Leyton E15 123 EC63
High Rd. Leytonstone E11 124 EE63
High Rd. Leytonstone E15 124 EE63
High Rd. Turnford, Brox. 67 DY25
High Rd. Woodford Grn. E18 102 EF53
High Rd. Woodford Grn., Wdf.Grn. 102 EF51
High Rd. Wormley (Turnford), Brox. 49 DY24
High Silver, Loug. 84 EK42
High Standing, Cat. 252 DQ125
High St. E11 124 EG57
High St. E13 144 EG68
High St. E15 143 EC68
High St. E17 123 DY57
High St. N8 121 DL56
High St. N14 99 DK47
High St. NW7 97 CV50
High St. (Harlesden) NW10 139 CT68
High St. SE20 182 DW94
High St. (South Norwood) SE25 202 DT98
High St. SW6 159 CY83
High St. W3 138 CP74
High St. W5 137 CK73
High St., Abb.L. 59 BS31
High St. (Bedmond), Abb.L. 59 BT27
High St., Add. 212 BH105
High St., Amer. 55 AM38
High St., Bans. 234 DA115
High St., Barn. 79 CY41
High St., Beck. 203 EA96
High St., Berk. 38 AW19
High St. (Elstree), Borwd. 77 CK44
High St., Brent. 158 CL79
High St., Brwd. 108 FW47
High St., Brom. 204 EG96
High St., Brox. 49 DZ21
High St., Cars. 218 DF105
High St., Cat. 236 DS123
High St., Ch.St.G. 90 AW48
High St., Chesh. 54 AP31
High St., Chis. 185 EP93
High St., Cob. 213 BV114
High St., Croy. 202 DQ104
High St., Dart. 188 FL87
High St. (Bean), Dart. 189 FV90
High St. (Eynsford), Dart. 208 FL103
High St. (Farningham), Dart. 208 FL100
High St., Dor. 263 CH136
High St., Edg. 96 CN51
High St., Egh. 173 BA92
High St. (Ponders End), Enf. 82 DW42
High St., Epp. 69 ET31
High St., Epsom 216 CR113
High St. (Ewell), Epsom 217 CT109
High St., Esher 214 CB105
High St. (Claygate), Esher 215 CF107
High St., Felt. 175 BT90
High St., Ger.Cr. 90 AY53
High St., Gdse. 252 DV131
High St., Grav. 191 GH86
High St. (Northfleet), Grav. 190 GB86
High St., Grays 170 GA79
High St., Green. 169 FU84
High St., Guil. 258 AX135
High St., Hmptn. 196 CB95
High St., Harl. 36 EW11
High St. (Roydon), Harl. 34 EH14
High St., Har. 117 CE60
High St. (Wealdstone), Har. 95 CE54
High St., Hayes 155 BR79
High St., Hem.H. 40 BK19
High St. (Bovingdon), Hem.H. 57 BA27
High St., Hodd. 49 EA17
High St., Horl. 269 DH148
High St., Horn. 128 FK60
High St., Houns. 156 CB83
High St. (Cranford), Houns. 155 BU80
High St., Ilf. 125 EQ55
High St., Iver 133 BE72
High St., Kings L. 58 BN29
High St., Kings.T. 197 CK97
High St. (Hampton Wick), Kings.T. 197 CJ95
High St., Lthd. 231 CH122
High St. (Great Bookham), Lthd. 246 CB125
High St. (Oxshott), Lthd. 215 CD113
High St. (Bray), Maid. 150 AC75
High St. (Taplow), Maid. 130 AE70
High St., N.Mal. 198 CS98
High St., Nthwd. 93 BT53
High St., Orp. 206 EU103
High St. (Downe), Orp. 223 EN111
High St. (Farnborough), Orp. 223 EP106
High St. (Green St. Grn.), Orp. 223 ET108
High St. (St. Mary Cray), Orp. 206 EW100
High St., Oxt. 253 ED130
High St. (Limpsfield), Oxt. 254 EG128
High St., Pnr. 116 BY55
High St., Pot.B. 64 DC33
High St., Purf. 168 FN78
London Rd. Purfleet
High St., Pur. 219 DN111
High St., Red. 250 DF134
High St. (Bletchingley), Red. 252 DQ133
High St. (Merstham), Red. 251 DH128
High St. (Nutfield), Red. 251 DM133
High St., Reig. 250 DA134
High St., Rick. 92 BK46
High St., Rom. 127 FE57
High St., Ruis. 115 BS59
High St. (Colney Heath), St.Alb. 44 CP22
High St. (London Colney), St.Alb. 61 CJ25
High St., Sev. 257 FJ126
High St. (Chipstead), Sev. 256 FC122
High St. (Otford), Sev. 241 FF116
High St. (Seal), Sev. 257 FL121
High St. (Shoreham), Sev. 225 FF110
High St., Shep. 195 BP101
High St., Slou. 152 AT75
High St. (Burnham), Slou. 130 AJ69
High St. (Chalvey), Slou. 151 AQ76
High St. (Colnbrook), Slou. 153 BC80
High St. (Datchet), Slou. 152 AV81
High St. (Langley), Slou. 153 AZ78
High St., S.Ock. 148 FQ74
High St., Sthl. 136 BZ74
High St., Stai. 173 BF91
High St. (Stanwell), Stai. 174 BK86
High St. (Wraysbury), Stai. 172 AY86
High St., Sutt. 218 DB105
High St. (Cheam), Sutt. 217 CY107
High St., Swan. 207 FF97
High St., Swans. 190 FZ85
High St., Tad. 233 CW123
High St., Tedd. 177 CF92
High St., T.Ditt. 197 CG101
High St., Th.Hth. 202 DQ98
High St. (Whitton), Twick. 176 CC87
High St., Uxb. 134 BJ66
High St. (Cowley), Uxb. 134 BJ69
High St. (Harefield), Uxb. 92 BJ54
High St., Wal.Cr. 67 DX33
High St. (Cheshunt), Wal.Cr. 67 DX29
High St., Walt. 195 BU102
High St., Ware 33 DX06
High St. (Hunsdon), Ware 34 EK06
High St. (Stanstead Abbotts), Ware 33 EC11
High St., Wat. 75 BV41
High St. (Bushey), Wat. 76 BZ44
High St., Wem. 118 CM63
High St., West Dr. 154 BK79
High St. (Yiewsley), West Dr. 134 BK73
High St., W.Mol. 196 CA98
High St., W.Wick. 203 EB102
High St., West. 255 EQ127
High St. (Brasted), West. 240 EV124
High St., Wey. 212 BN105
High St., Wind. 151 AR81
High St. (Eton), Wind. 151 AR79
High St., Wok. 227 AZ117
High St. (Chobham), Wok. 210 AS111
High St. (Horsell), Wok. 226 AV115
High St. (Old Woking), Wok. 227 BA121
High St. (Ripley), Wok. 228 BH122
High St. Colliers Wd. SW19 180 DD94
High St. Grn., Hem.H. 40 BN18
High St. Ms. SW19 179 CY92
High St. N. E6 144 EL66
High St. N. E12 124 EL64
High St. S. E6 145 EM68
High St. Wimbledon SW19 179 CX92
High Timber St. EC4 275 H10
High Timber St. EC4 142 DQ73
High Tor Clo., Brom. 184 EH94
Babbacombe Rd.
High Tree Clo., Add. 211 BF106
High Tree Clo., Saw. 36 EX06
High Tree Ct. W7 137 CE73
High Trees SW2 181 DN88
High Trees, Barn. 80 DE43
High Trees, Croy. 203 DY102
High Trees Clo., Cat. 236 DT123
High Trees Ct., Brwd. 108 FW49
Warley Mt.
High Trees Rd., Reig. 266 DC135
High Vw., Guil. 261 BQ139
High Vw., Hat. 45 CT20
High Vw., Pnr. 116 BW55
High Vw., Rick. 74 BG42
High Vw., Sutt. 217 CZ111
High Vw., Wat. 75 BT44
High Vw. Ave., Grays 170 GC78
High Vw. Clo. SE19 202 DT96
High Vw. Clo., Loug. 84 EJ43
High Vw. Rd. E18 124 EF55
High Vw. Rd., Guil. 258 AS137
High Vw. Rd., Sid. 186 EV91
High Wickfield, Welw.G.C. 30 DC10
Amwell Common
High Worple, Har. 116 BY59
High Wych La., Saw. 36 EU05
High Wych Rd., Saw. 35 ES09
Higham Hill Rd. E17 101 DY53
Higham Mead, Chesh. 54 AQ30
Higham Pl. E17 123 DY55
Higham Rd. N17 122 DR55
Higham Rd., Chesh. 54 AP30
Higham Rd., Wdf.Grn. 102 EG51
Higham Sta. Ave. E4 101 EA51
Higham St. E17 123 DY55
Higham Vw., Epp. 71 FB26
Highams Lo. Business Cen. E17 123 DX55
Highams Pk. Ind. Est. E4 101 EC51
Highbank Way N8 121 DN58
Highbanks Clo., Well. 166 EV80
Highbanks Rd., Pnr. 94 CA51
Highbarns Rd., Hem.H. 58 BN25
Highbarrow Rd., Croy. 202 DU101
Highbridge SE10 163 ED78
Highbridge Rd., Bark. 145 EP67
Highbridge St., Wal.Abb. 67 EB33
Highbrook Rd. SE3 164 EK83
Highbury Ave., Hodd. 49 EA15
Highbury Ave., Th.Hth. 201 DN96
Highbury Clo., N.Mal. 198 CQ98
Highbury Clo., W.Wick. 203 EB103
Highbury Cor. N5 141 DP65
Highbury Cres. N5 121 DP64
Highbury Est. N5 122 DQ64
Highbury Gdns., Ilf. 125 ES61
Highbury Gra. N5 122 DQ63
Highbury Gro. N5 141 DP65
Highbury Hill N5 121 DN62
Highbury Ms. N7 141 DN65
Holloway Rd.
Highbury New Pk. N5 122 DQ64
Highbury Pk. N5 121 DP63
Highbury Pk. Ms. N5 122 DQ63
Highbury Gra.
Highbury Pl. N5 141 DP65
Highbury Quad. N5 122 DQ62
Highbury Rd. SW19 179 CY92
Highbury Sta. Rd. N1 141 DN65
Highbury Ter. N5 121 DP64
Highbury Ter. Ms. N5 121 DP64
Highclere, Guil. 243 BA132
Highclere Clo., Ken. 236 DQ115
Highclere Ct., St.Alb. 43 CE19
Avenue Rd.
Highclere Dr., Hem.H. 40 BN24
Highclere Rd., N.Mal. 198 CR97
Highclere St. SE26 183 DY91
Highcliffe Dr. SW15 179 CT86
Highcliffe Gdns., Ilf. 124 EL57
Highcombe SE7 164 EH79
Highcombe Clo. SE9 184 EK88
Highcotts La., Guil. 243 BF126
Highcotts La., Wok. 243 BF125
Highcroft NW9 118 CS57
Highcroft Ave., Wem. 138 CN67
Highcroft Ct., Lthd. 230 CA123
Highcroft Gdns. NW11 119 CZ58

Highcroft Rd. N19 121 DL59
Highcroft Rd., Hem.H. 58 BG25
Highcross Rd., Grav. 189 FX92
Highcross Way SW15 179 CU88
Highdaun Dr. SW16 201 DM98
Highdown, Wor.Pk. 198 CS103
Highdown La., Sutt. 218 DB111
Highdown Rd. SW15 179 CV86
Higher Dr., Bans. 217 CX112
Higher Dr., Lthd. 245 BS127
Higher Dr., Pur. 219 DN113
Higher Grn., Epsom 217 CU113
Highfield, Ch.St.G. 90 AX47
Highfield, Felt. 175 BU88
Highfield, Guil. 258 AY142
Highfield, Harl. 52 EU16
Highfield, Kings L. 58 BL28
Highfield Ave. NW9 118 CQ57
Highfield Ave. NW11 119 CX59
Highfield Ave., Erith 167 FB79
Highfield Ave., Grnf. 117 CE64
Highfield Ave., Orp. 223 ET106
Highfield Ave., Pnr. 116 BZ57
Highfield Ave., Wem. 118 CL62
Highfield Clo. N22 99 DN53
Highfield Clo. NW9 118 CQ57
Highfield Clo. SE13 183 ED87
Highfield Clo., Amer. 55 AR37
Highfield Clo., Egh. 172 AW93
Highfield Clo., Lthd. 215 CD111
Highfield Clo., Nthwd. 93 BS53
Highfield Clo., Rom. 105 FC51
Highfield Clo., Surb. 197 CJ102
Highfield Clo., W.Byf. 212 BG113
Highfield Ct. N14 81 DJ44
Highfield Cres., Horn. 128 FM61
Highfield Cres., Nthwd. 93 BS53
Highfield Dr., Brom. 204 EE98
Highfield Dr., Brox. 49 DY21
Highfield Dr., Epsom 217 CT108
Highfield Dr., Uxb. 114 BL62
Highfield Dr., W.Wick. 203 EB103
Highfield Gdns. NW11 119 CY58
Highfield Gdns., Grays 170 GD75
Highfield Grn., Epp. 69 ES31
Highfield Hill SE19 182 DR94
Highfield La., Hem.H. 40 BM18
Highfield La., St.Alb. 43 CJ22
Highfield Link, Rom. 105 FD51
Highfield Pk. Dr., St.Alb. 43 CH23
Highfield Pl., Epp. 69 ES31
Highfield Rd. N21 99 DP47
Highfield Rd. NW11 119 CY58
Highfield Rd. W3 138 CP71
Highfield Rd., Berk. 38 AX20
Highfield Rd., Bexh. 186 EZ85
Highfield Rd., Brom. 205 EM98
Highfield Rd., Cat. 236 DU122
Highfield Rd., Cher. 194 BG102
Highfield Rd., Chesh. 54 AP29
Highfield Rd., Chis. 205 ET97
Highfield Rd., Dart. 188 FK87
Highfield Rd., Felt. 175 BU88
Highfield Rd., Hert. 32 DR11
Highfield Rd., Horn. 128 FM61
Highfield Rd., Islw. 157 CF81
Highfield Rd., Nthwd. 93 BS53
Highfield Rd., Pur. 219 DM110
Highfield Rd., Rom. 105 FC52
Highfield Rd., Sun. 195 BT98
Highfield Rd., Surb. 198 CQ101
Highfield Rd., Sutt. 218 DE106
Highfield Rd. (Cheshunt), Wal.Cr. 66 DS26
Highfield Rd., Walt. 195 BU102
Highfield Rd. (Bushey), Wat. 76 BY43
Highfield Rd., W.Byf. 212 BG113
Highfield Rd., West. 238 EJ117
Highfield Rd., Wind. 151 AM83
Highfield Rd., Wdf.Grn. 102 EL52
Highfield Rd. S., Dart. 188 FK87
Highfield Twrs., Rom. 105 FD50
Highfield Way, Horn. 128 FM61
Highfield Way, Pot.B. 64 DB32
Highfield Way, Rick. 74 BG44
Highfields, Ash. 231 CK119
Highfields, Lthd. 231 CD124
Highfields (East Horsley), Lthd. 245 BS128
Highfields (Cuffley), Pot.B. 65 DL28
Highfields, Rad. 77 CF35
Highfields Gro. N6 120 DF60
Highgate Ave. N6 121 DH59
Highgate Clo. N6 120 DG59
Highgate Gro., Saw. 36 EX05
Highgate High St. N6 120 DG60
Highgate Hill N6 121 DH60
Highgâte Hill N19 121 DH60
Highgate Rd. NW5 121 DH63
Highgate Wk. SE23 182 DW89
Highgate W. Hill N6 120 DG60
Highgrove, Brwd. 108 FV44
Highgrove Clo. N11 98 DG50
Balmoral Ave.
Highgrove Clo., Chis. 204 EL95
Highgrove Ct., Beck. 183 EA94
Park Rd.
Highgrove Ms., Cars. 200 DF104
Highgrove Ms., Grays 170 GC78
Highgrove Rd., Dag. 126 EW64
Highgrove Way, Ruis. 115 BU58
Highland Ave. W7 137 CE72
Highland Ave., Brwd. 108 FW46
Highland Ave., Dag. 127 FC62
Highland Ave., Loug. 84 EL44
Highland Cotts., Wall. 219 DH105
Highland Ct. E18 102 EH53
Highland Cft., Beck. 183 EB92
Highland Dr., Hem.H. 41 BP20
Highland Dr. (Bushey), Wat. 94 CC45
Highland Pk., Felt. 175 BT91
Highland Rd. SE19 182 DS93
Highland Rd., Amer. 55 AR39
Highland Rd., Bexh. 186 FA85
Highland Rd., Brom. 204 EF95
Highland Rd., Nthwd. 93 BT54
Highland Rd., Pur. 219 DN114
Highland Rd., Sev. 225 FB110
Highland Rd., Wal.Abb. 50 EE22
Highlands, Ash. 231 CJ119
Highlands, Wat. 94 BW46
Highlands, The, Edg. 96 CP54
Highlands, The, Lthd. 245 BS125
Highlands, The, Pot.B. 64 DC30
Highlands, The, Rick. 92 BH45
Highlands Ave. W3 138 CQ73
Highlands Ave., Lthd. 231 CJ122
Highlands Clo. N4 121 DL59
Mount Vw. Rd.
Highlands Clo., Ger.Cr. 90 AY52
Highlands Clo., Houns. 156 CB81
Highlands Clo., Lthd. 231 CH122
Highlands End, Ger.Cr. 91 AZ52
Highlands Gdns., Ilf. 125 EM60
Highlands Heath SW15 179 CW87
Highlands Hill, Swan. 207 FG96
Highlands La., Ger.Cr. 91 AZ51
Highlands La., Wok. 226 AY122
Highlands Pk., Lthd. 231 CK123
Highlands Pk., Sev. 257 FL121
Highlands Rd., Barn. 80 DA43
Highlands Rd., Beac. 89 AQ50
Highlands Rd., Lthd. 231 CH122
Highlands Rd., Orp. 206 EV101
Highlands Rd., Reig. 250 DD133
Highlea Clo. NW9 96 CS53
Highlever Rd. W10 139 CW71
Highmead SE18 165 ET80
Highmead Cres., Wem. 138 CM66
Highmoor, Amer. 55 AR39
Highmore Rd. SE3 164 EE80
Highover Pk., Amer. 55 AQ40
Highpoint, Wey. 212 BN106
Highridge Clo., Epsom 232 CS115
Highridge La., Bet. 264 CP140
Highshore Rd. SE15 162 DT82
Highstead Cres., Erith 167 FE80
Highstone Ave. E11 124 EG58
Highview, Cat. 236 DS124
Highview Ave., Edg. 96 CQ49
Highview Ave., Wall. 219 DM106
Highview Clo., Pot.B. 64 DC33
Highview Gdns.
Highview Cres., Brwd. 109 GC44
Highview Gdns. N3 119 CY56
Highview Gdns. N11 99 DJ50
Highview Gdns., Edg. 96 CQ50
Highview Gdns., Pot.B. 64 DC33
Highview Gdns., St.Alb. 43 CJ15
Highview Gdns., Upmin. 128 FP61
Highview Ho., Rom. 126 EY56
Highview Rd. SE19 182 DR93
Highview Rd. W13 137 CG71
Highway, The E1 142 DU73
Highway, The E14 143 DX73
Highway, The, Orp. 224 EV106
Highway, The, Stan. 95 CF53
Highway, The, Sutt. 218 DC109
Highwold, Couls. 234 DG118
Highwood, Brom. 203 ED97
Highwood Ave. N12 98 DC49
Highwood Ave. (Bushey), Wat. 76 BZ39
Highwood Clo., Brwd. 108 FV45
Highwood Clo., Ken. 236 DQ117
Highwood Clo., Orp. 205 EQ103
Highwood Dr., Orp. 205 EQ103
Highwood Gdns., Ilf. 125 EM57
Highwood Gro. NW7 96 CR50
Highwood Hall La., Hem.H. 59 BQ25
Highwood Hill NW7 97 CT47
Highwood La., Loug. 85 EN43
Highwood Rd. N19 121 DL62
Highwood Rd., Hodd. 33 DZ14
Highwoods, Cat. 252 DS125
Highwoods, Lthd. 231 CJ121
Highworth Rd. N11 99 DK51
Hilary Ave., Mitch. 200 DG97
Hilary Clo. SW6 160 DB80
Hilary Clo., Erith 167 FB81
Hilary Clo., Horn. 128 FK64
Hilary Rd. W12 139 CT72
Hilary Rd., Slou. 152 AY75
Hilbert Rd., Sutt. 199 CX104
Hilborough Way, Orp. 223 ER106
Hilbury Clo., Amer. 55 AQ35
Hilda May Ave., Swan. 207 FD97
Hilda Rd. E6 144 EK66
Hilda Rd. E16 144 EE70
Hilda Ter. SW9 161 DN82
Hilda Vale Clo., Orp. 223 EP105
Hilda Vale Rd., Orp. 223 EN105
Hilden Dr., Erith 167 FH80
Hildenborough Gdns., Brom. 184 EE93
Hildenlea Pl., Brom. 204 EE96
Hildenley Clo., Red. 251 DK128
Malmstone Ave.
Hildens, The, Dor. 262 CB138
Hilders, The, Ash. 232 CP117
Hildreth St. SW12 181 DH88
Hildyard Rd. SW6 160 DA79
Hiley Rd. NW10 139 CW69
Hilfield La., Wat. 76 CB39
Hilfield La. S. (Bushey), Wat. 77 CF44
Hilgay, Guil. 243 AZ134
Hilgay Clo., Guil. 243 AZ134
Hilgrove Rd. NW6 140 DC66
Hiliary Gdns., Stan. 95 CJ54
Hiljon Cres., Ger.Cr. 90 AY53
Hill, The, Cat. 236 DT124
Hill, The, Grav. 190 GC86
Hill, The, Harl. 36 EW11
Hill Ave., Amer. 55 AQ38
Hill Barn, S.Croy. 220 DS111
Hill Brow, Brom. 204 EK95
Hill Brow, Dart. 187 FF86
Hill Brow Clo., Bex. 187 FD91
Hill Clo. NW2 119 CV62
Hill Clo. NW11 120 DA58
Hill Clo., Barn. 79 CW43
Hill Clo., Chis. 185 EP92
Hill Clo., Grav. 190 GE94
Hill Clo., Har. 117 CE62
Hill Clo., H.Wyc. 110 AF56
Hill Clo., Pur. 220 DQ112
Hill Clo., Stan. 95 CH49
Hill Clo., Wok. 226 AX115
Hill Common, Hem.H. 40 BN24
Hill Ct., Gdmg. 258 AS144
Hill Ct., Nthlt. 116 CA64
Hill Cres. N20 98 DB47
Hill Cres., Bex. 187 FC88
Hill Cres., Har. 117 CG57
Hill Cres., Horn. 128 FJ58
Hill Cres., Surb. 198 CM99
Hill Cres., Wor.Pk. 199 CW103
Hill Crest, Pot.B. 64 DC34
Hill Crest, Sev. 256 FG122
Hill Crest, Sid. 186 EU87
Hill Crest Gdns. N3 119 CY56
Hill Dr. NW9 118 CQ60
Hill Dr. SW16 201 DM97
Hill End, Orp. 205 ET103
The App.
Hill End La., St.Alb. 43 CJ23
Hill End Rd., Uxb. 92 BJ52
Hill Fm. App., H.Wyc. 110 AE55
Hill Fm. Ave., Wat. 59 BU33
Hill Fm. Clo., Wat. 59 BU33
Hill Fm. La., Ch.St.G. 90 AT46
Hill Fm. Rd. W10 139 CW71
Hill Fm. Rd., Chesh. 54 AR34
Hill Fm. Rd., Ger.Cr. 90 AY52
Hill Fm. Rd., Maid. 130 AD68
Hill Gro., Rom. 127 FE55
Hill Ho. Ave., Stan. 95 CF52
Hill Ho. Clo. N21 99 DN45
Hill Ho. Clo., Ger.Cr. 90 AY52
Rickmansworth La.
Hill Ho. Dr., Reig. 266 DB136
Hill Ho. Dr., Wey. 212 BN111
Hill Ho. Rd. SW16 181 DM92
Hill Ho. Rd., Dart. 188 FQ87
Hill La., Orp. 207 FB104
Hill La., Ruis. 115 BQ60
Hill La., Tad. 233 CY121
Hill Ley, Hat. 45 CT18
Hill Leys (Cuffley), Pot.B. 65 DL28
Hill Meadow, Amer. 55 AM43
Hill Pk. Dr., Lthd. 231 CF119
Hill Path SW16 181 DM92
Valley Rd.
Hill Pl., Slou. 131 AP66
Hill Ri. N9 82 DV44
Hill Ri. NW11 120 DB56
Hill Ri. SE23 182 DV88
London Rd.
Hill Ri., Dart. 189 FR92
Hill Ri., Dor. 247 CG134
Hill Ri., Esher 197 CH103
Hill Ri., Ger.Cr. 90 AX54
Hill Ri., Grnf. 136 CC66
Hill Ri., Pot.B. 64 DC34
Hill Ri. (Cuffley), Pot.B. 65 DL28
Hill Ri., Rich. 177 CK85
Hill Ri., Rick. 92 BH45
Hill Ri., Ruis. 115 BQ60
Hill Ri., Slou. 153 BA79
Hill Ri., Upmin. 128 FN61
Hill Ri., Walt. 195 BT101
Hill Ri. Cres., Ger.Cr. 90 AX54
Hill Rd. N10 98 DF53
Hill Rd. NW8 140 DC68
Hill Rd., Brwd. 108 FU48
Hill Rd., Cars. 218 DE107
Hill Rd., Dart. 188 FL89
Hill Rd., Epp. 85 ES38
Hill Rd., Har. 117 CG57
Hill Rd., Hem.H. 39 BE21
Hill Rd., Lthd. 230 CB122
Hill Rd., Mitch. 201 DH95
Hill Rd., Nthwd. 93 BR51
Hill Rd., Pnr. 116 BY58
Hill Rd., Pur. 219 DM112
Hill Rd., Sutt. 218 DB106
Hill Rd., Wem. 117 CH62
Hill St. W1 276 G2
Hill St. W1 140 DG74
Hill St., Rich. 177 CK85
Hill St., St.Alb. 42 CC20
Hill Top NW11 120 DB56
Hill Top, Loug. 85 EN40
Hill Top, Mord. 200 DB100
Hill Top Clo., Loug. 85 EN41
Hill Top Pl., Loug. 85 EN41
Hill Top Vw., Wdf.Grn. 103 EM51
Hill Vw., Berk. 38 AU17
Hill Vw. Clo., Tad. 233 CW121
Shelvers Way
Hill Vw. Cres., Guil. 242 AT132
Hill Vw. Cres., Orp. 205 ET102
Hill Vw. Dr., Well. 165 ES82
Hill Vw. Gdns. NW9 118 CR57
Hill Vw. Rd., Esher 215 CG108
Hill Vw. Rd., Orp. 205 ET102
Hill Vw. Rd., Stai. 172 AX86
Hill Vw. Rd., Twick. 177 CG86
Hill Vw. Rd., Wok. 227 AZ118
Hill Waye, Ger.Cr. 113 AZ58
Hillars Heath Rd., Couls. 235 DL115
Hillary Ave., Grav. 190 GE90
Hillary Cres., Walt. 196 BW102
Hillary Ri., Barn. 80 DA42
Hillary Rd., Hem.H. 40 BN20
Hillary Rd., Sthl. 156 CA76
Hillbeck Clo. SE15 162 DW80
Hillbeck Way, Grnf. 137 CD67
Hillborne Clo., Hayes 155 BU78
Hillborough Ave., Sev. 257 FK122
Hillborough Clo. SW19 180 DC94
Hillbrook Gdns., Wey. 212 BN108
Hillbrook Rd. SW17 180 DF90
Hillbrow, N.Mal. 199 CT97
Hillbrow Cotts., Gdse. 252 DW132
Hillbrow Ct., Gdse. 252 DW132
Hillbrow Rd., Brom. 184 EE94
Hillbrow Rd., Esher 214 CC105
Hillbury, Hat. 45 CT19
Hillbury Ave., Har. 117 CH57
Hillbury Clo., Warl. 236 DW118
Hillbury Gdns., Warl. 236 DW118
Hillbury Rd. SW17 181 DH90
Hillbury Rd., Warl. 236 DU117
Hillbury Rd., Whyt. 236 DU117
Hillcote Ave. SW16 181 DN94
Hillcourt Ave. N12 98 DB51
Hillcourt Est. N16 122 DR60
Hillcourt Rd. SE22 182 DV86
Hillcrest N6 120 DG59
Hillcrest N21 99 DN45
Hillcrest, Hat. 45 CU18
Hillcrest, St.Alb. 42 CB22
Hillcrest, Wey. 213 BP105
Hillcrest Ave. NW11 119 CY57
Hillcrest Ave., Cher. 211 BE105
Hillcrest Ave., Edg. 96 CP49
Hillcrest Ave., Grays 169 FU79
Hillcrest Ave., Pnr. 116 BX56
Hillcrest Clo. SE26 182 DU91
Hillcrest Clo., Beck. 203 DZ99
Hillcrest Clo., Epsom 233 CT115
Hillcrest Dr., Green. 189 FV85
Riverview Rd.
Hillcrest Gdns. NW2 119 CU62
Hillcrest Gdns., Esher 197 CF104
Hillcrest Par., Couls. 219 DH114
Hillcrest Rd. E17 101 ED54
Hillcrest Rd. E18 102 EF54
Hillcrest Rd. W3 138 CN74
Hillcrest Rd. W5 138 CL71
Hillcrest Rd., Brom. 184 EG91
Hillcrest Rd., Dart. 187 FF87
Hillcrest Rd., Guil. 242 AT133
Hillcrest Rd., Horn. 127 FG59
Hillcrest Rd., Loug. 84 EK44
Hillcrest Rd., Ong. 71 FE30
Hillcrest Rd., Orp. 206 EU103
Hillcrest Rd., Pur. 219 DM110
Hillcrest Rd., Rad. 62 CN33
Hillcrest Rd., West. 238 EK116
Hillcrest Rd., Whyt. 236 DT117
Hillcrest Vw., Beck. 203 DZ100
Hillcrest Way, Epp. 70 EU31
Hillcrest Waye, Ger.Cr. 113 AZ58
Hillcroft, Loug. 85 EN40
Hillcroft Ave., Pnr. 116 BZ58
Hillcroft Ave., Pur. 219 DJ113
Hillcroft Cres. W5 137 CK72
Hillcroft Cres., Ruis. 116 BX62
Hillcroft Cres., Wat. 93 BU46
Hillcroft Cres., Wem. 118 CM63
Hillcroft Rd. E6 145 EP71
Hillcroft Rd., Chesh. 54 AR29
Hillcroft Rd., H.Wyc. 88 AC46
Hillcroome Rd., Sutt. 218 DD107
Hillcross Ave., Mord. 199 CX100
Hilldale Rd., Sutt. 217 CZ105
Hilldeane Rd., Pur. 219 DN109
Hilldene Ave., Rom. 106 FJ51
Hilldene Clo., Rom. 106 FK50
Hilldown Rd. SW16 181 DL94
Hilldown Rd., Brom. 204 EE102
Hilldown Rd., Hem.H. 40 BG18
Hilldrop Cres. N7 121 DK64
Hilldrop Est. N7 121 DK64
Hilldrop La. N7 121 DK64
Hilldrop Rd. N7 121 DK64
Hilldrop Rd., Brom. 184 EG93
Hillend SE18 165 EP81
Hillersdon, Slou. 132 AV71
Hillersdon Ave. SW13 159 CU82
Hillersdon Ave., Edg. 96 CM50
Hillery Clo. SE17 279 L9
Hilley Fld. La., Lthd. 230 CC122
Hillfield, Hat. 45 CV15
Hillfield Ave. N8 121 DL57
Hillfield Ave. NW9 118 CS57
Hillfield Ave., Mord. 200 DE100
Hillfield Ave., Wem. 138 CL66
Hillfield Clo., Guil. 243 BC132
Hillfield Clo., Har. 116 CC56
Hillfield Clo., Red. 250 DG134
Hillfield Ct. NW3 120 DE64
Hillfield Ct., Hem.H. 40 BL20
Hillfield Pk. N10 121 DH55
Hillfield Pk. N21 99 DN47
Hillfield Pk. Ms. N10 121 DH56
Hillfield Rd. NW6 119 CZ64
Hillfield Rd., Ger.Cr. 90 AY52
Hillfield Rd., Hmptn. 176 BZ94
Hillfield Rd., Hem.H. 40 BK20
Hillfield Rd., Red. 250 DG134
Hillfield Rd., Sev. 241 FE120
Hillfield Sq., Ger.Cr. 90 AY52
Hillfoot Ave., Rom. 105 FC53
Hillfoot Rd., Rom. 105 FC53
Hillford Pl., Red. 266 DG140
Hillgate Pl. SW12 181 DH87
Hillgate Pl. W8 140 DA74
Hillgate St. W8 140 DA74
Hillgrove, Ger.Cr. 90 AY53
Hillgrove Business Pk., Wal.Abb. 49 EC22
Hillhouse, Wal.Abb. 68 EF33
Hillhurst Gdns., Cat. 236 DS120
Hilliard Rd., Nthwd. 93 BT53
Hilliards Ct. E1 142 DV74
Wapping High St.
Hilliards Rd., Uxb. 134 BK72
Hilliards St. E1 142 DW74
Wapping High St.
Hillier Clo., Barn. 80 DB44
Hillier Gdns., Croy. 219 DN106
Crowley Cres.
Hillier Pl., Chess. 215 CJ107
Hillier Rd. SW11 180 DF86
Hillier Rd., Guil. 243 BA134
Hilliers Ave., Uxb. 134 BN69
Harlington Rd.
Hilliers La., Croy. 201 DL104
Hillingdale, West. 238 EH118
Hillingdon Ave., Sev. 257 FJ121
Hillingdon Ave., Stai. 174 BL88
Hillingdon Hill, Uxb. 134 BL69
Hillingdon Ri., Sev. 257 FK122
Hillingdon Rd., Bexh. 167 FC82
Hillingdon Rd., Grav. 191 GG89
Hillingdon Rd., Uxb. 134 BJ67
Hillingdon Rd., Wat. 59 BU34
Hillingdon St. SE5 161 DP79
Hillingdon St. SE17 161 DP79
Hillington Gdns., Wdf.Grn. 102 EK54
Hillman Clo., Horn. 128 FK55
Hillman Clo., Uxb. 114 BL64
Hillman Dr. W10 139 CW70
Hillman St. E8 142 DV65
Hillmarton Rd. N7 121 DL64
Hillmay Dr., Hem.H. 40 BJ21
Hillmead, Berk. 38 AU20
Hillmead Ct., Maid. 130 AF71
Hillmead Dr. SW9 161 DP84
Hillmont Rd., Esher 197 CE104
Hillmore Gro. SE26 183 DX92
Hillreach SE18 165 EM78
Hillrise Ave., Wat. 76 BX38
Hillrise Rd. N19 121 DL59
Hillrise Rd., Rom. 105 FC51
Hills Chase, Brwd. 108 FW49
Hills La., Nthwd. 93 BS53
Hills Ms. W5 138 CL73
Hills Pl. W1 273 K9
Hills Rd., Buck.H. 102 EH46
Hillsboro Rd. SE22 182 DS85
Hillsborough Grn., Wat. 93 BU48
Ashburnham Dr.
Hillsgrove Clo., Well. 166 EW80
Hillside NW9 118 CR56
Hillside NW10 138 CQ66
Hillside SW19 179 CX93
Hillside, Bans. 233 CY115
Hillside, Barn. 80 DC43
Hillside, Chesh. 54 AN28
Hillside, Dart. 189 FS92
Hillside (Farningham), Dart. 208 FM101
Hillside, Erith 167 FD77
Hillside, Grays 170 GD77
Hillside, Harl. 52 EW17
Hillside, Hat. 45 CU18
Hillside, Hodd. 49 DZ16
Hillside, Slou. 152 AS75
Hillside, Uxb. 114 BJ57
Hillside, Vir.W. 192 AW100
Hillside, Ware 32 DW07
Hillside, Welw.G.C. 30 DB12
Hillside, Wok. 226 AX120
Hillside, The, Orp. 224 EV109
Hillside Ave. N11 98 DF51
Hillside Ave., Borwd. 78 CP42
Hillside Ave., Grav. 191 GK89
Hillside Ave., Pur. 219 DP113
Hillside Ave. (Cheshunt), Wal.Cr. 67 DX31
Hillside Ave., Wem. 118 CM63
Hillside Ave., Wdf.Grn. 102 EJ50
Hillside Clo. NW8 140 DB68
Hillside Clo., Abb.L. 59 BS32
Hillside Clo., Bans. 233 CY116
Hillside Clo., Bet. 264 CN135
Hillside Clo., Ch.St.G. 90 AV48
Hillside Clo., Ger.Cr. 90 AY51
Hillside Clo., Mord. 199 CY98
Hillside Clo., Wdf.Grn. 102 EJ50
Hillside Ct., St.Alb. 43 CE19
Hillside Rd.
Hillside Ct., Swan. 207 FG98
Hillside Cres., Enf. 82 DR38
Hillside Cres., Har. 116 CC60
Hillside Cres., Nthwd. 93 BU53
Hillside Cres. (Cheshunt), Wal.Cr. 67 DX31
Hillside Cres., Ware 33 EB11
Hillside Cres., Wat. 76 BY44
Pinner Rd.
Hillside Dr., Edg. 96 CN51
Hillside Dr., Grav. 191 GK89
Hillside Est. N15 122 DT58
Hillside Gdns. E17 123 ED55
Hillside Gdns. N6 120 DG58
Hillside Gdns. SW2 181 DN89
Hillside Gdns., Add. 211 BF106
Hillside Gdns., Barn. 79 CY42
Hillside Gdns., Berk. 38 AX20
Hillside Gdns., Bet. 248 CN134
Hillside Gdns., Edg. 96 CM49
Hillside Gdns., Har. 118 CL59
Hillside Gdns., Nthwd. 93 BU52
Hillside Gdns., Wall. 219 DJ108
Hillside Gate, St.Alb. 43 CE19
Hillside Gro. N14 99 DK45
Hillside Gro. NW7 97 CU52
Hillside La., Brom. 204 EG103
Hillside La., Ware 33 EA10
Hillside Pas. SW2 181 DM89
Hillside Ri., Nthwd. 93 BU52
Hillside Rd. N15 122 DS58
Hillside Rd. SW2 181 DM89
Hillside Rd. W5 138 CL71
Hillside Rd., Ash. 232 CM117
Hillside Rd., Brom. 204 EF97
Hillside Rd., Couls. 235 DL118
Hillside Rd., Croy. 219 DP106
Hillside Rd., Dart. 187 FG86
Hillside Rd., Epsom 217 CV110
Hillside Rd., Nthwd. 93 BU52
Hillside Rd., Rad. 77 CH35
Hillside Rd., Rick. 73 BC43
Hillside Rd., St.Alb. 43 CE19
Hillside Rd., Sev. 257 FK123
Hillside Rd., Sthl. 136 CA70
Hillside Rd., Surb. 198 CM98
Hillside Rd., Sutt. 217 CZ108
Hillside Rd. (Bushey), Wat. 76 BY43
Hillside Rd., West. 238 EL119
Hillside Rd., Whyt. 236 DU118
Hillside Ter., Hert. 32 DQ11
Hillside Wk., Brwd. 108 FU48
Hillsleigh Rd. W8 139 CZ74
Hillsmead Way, S.Croy. 220 DU113
Hillspur Clo., Guil. 242 AT133
Hillspur Rd., Guil. 242 AT133
Hillstowe St. E5 122 DW62
Hilltop, Sutt. 199 CZ101
Hilltop Clo., Guil. 242 AT130
Hilltop Clo., Lthd. 231 CJ123
Hilltop Clo. (Cheshunt), Wal.Cr. 66 DT26
Hilltop Gdns. NW4 97 CV53
Great N. Way
Hilltop Gdns., Dart. 188 FM85
Hilltop Gdns., Orp. 205 ES103
Hilltop La., Cat. 251 DN126
Hilltop La., Red. 251 DN126
Hilltop Ri., Lthd. 246 CC126
Hilltop Rd. NW6 140 DA66
Hilltop Rd., Berk. 38 AW20
Hilltop Rd., Grays 169 FV79
Hilltop Rd., Kings L. 59 BR27
Hilltop Rd., Reig. 266 DB136
Hilltop Rd., Whyt. 236 DS117
Hilltop Wk., Cat. 237 DY120
Hilltop Way, Stan. 95 CG48
Hillview SW20 179 CV94
Hillview, Mitch. 201 DL98
Hillview Ave., Har. 118 CL57
Hillview Ave., Horn. 128 FJ58
Hillview Clo., Pnr. 94 BZ51
Hillview Clo., Pur. 219 DP111
Hillview Ct., Wok. 227 AZ118
Hillview Cres., Ilf. 125 EM58
Hillview Dr., Red. 266 DG135
Philanthropic Rd.
Hillview Gdns. NW4 119 CX56
Hillview Gdns., Har. 116 CA55
Hillview Gdns. (Cheshunt), Wal.Cr. 67 DX27
Hillview Rd. NW7 97 CX49

Hillview Rd., Chis. 185 EN92
Hillview Rd., Pnr. 94 BZ52
Hillview Rd., Sutt. 200 DC104
Hillway N6 120 DG60
Hillway NW9 118 CS59
Hillway, Amer. 55 AP41
Hillwood Clo., Brwd. 109 GB46
Hillwood Gro., Brwd. 109 GB46
Hillworth Rd. SW2 181 DN87
Hilly Fld., Harl. 51 ET19
Hilly Flds. Cres. SE4 163 EA83
Hillyard Rd. W7 137 CE71
Hillyard St. SW9 161 DN81
Hillyfield E17 123 DY55
Hillyfields, Loug. 85 EN40
Hillyfields, Welw.G.C. 30 DC08
Hilperton Rd., Slou. 152 AS75
Hilsea St. E5 122 DW63
Hilton Ave. N12 98 DD50
Hilton Clo., Uxb. 134 BH68
Hilton Ct., Horl. 269 DK147
Clarence Way
Hilton Way, S.Croy. 236 DV115
Hilversum Cres. SE22 182 DS85
East Dulwich Gro.
Himalayan Way, Wat. 75 BT43
Himley Rd. SW17 180 DE92
Hinchcliffe Clo., Wall. 219 DM108
Roe Way
Hinchley Clo., Esher 197 CF104
Hinchley Dr., Esher 197 CF104
Hinchley Way, Esher 197 CG104
Hinckler Clo., Wall. 219 DL108
Kingsford Ave.
Hinckley Rd. SE15 162 DU84
Hind Clo., Chig. 103 ET50
Hind Ct. EC4 274 E9
Hind Cres., Erith 167 FD79
Hind Gro. E14 143 EA72
Hind Ter., Grays 169 FX78
Mill La.
Hinde Ms. W1 140 DG72
Marylebone La.
Hinde St. W1 272 G8
Hinde St. W1 140 DG72
Hindes Rd., Har. 117 CD57
Hindhead Clo. N16 122 DS60
Hindhead Clo., Uxb. 135 BP71
Aldenham Dr.
Hindhead Gdns., Nthlt. 136 BY67
Hindhead Grn., Wat. 94 BW50
Hindhead Way, Wall. 219 DL106
Hindmans Rd. SE22 182 DU85
Hindmans Way, Dag. 146 EZ70
Hindmarsh Clo. E1 142 DU73
Cable St.
Hindrey Rd. E5 122 DV64
Hindsley's Pl. SE23 182 DW89
Hinkler Rd., Har. 117 CK55
Hinkley Clo., Uxb. 114 BJ56
Hinksey Clo., Slou. 153 BB76
Hinksey Path SE2 166 EX75
Hinstock Rd. SE18 165 EQ79
Hinton Ave., Houns. 156 BX84
Hinton Clo. SE9 184 EL88
Hinton Rd. N18 100 DS49
Hinton Rd. SE24 161 DP83
Hinton Rd., Slou. 131 AL73
Hinton Rd., Uxb. 134 BJ67
Hinton Rd., Wall. 219 DJ107
Hintons, Harl. 51 EM19
Hipley Ct., Guil. 259 BA135
Warren Rd.
Hipley St., Wok. 227 BB121
Hippodrome Ms. W11 139 CY73
Portland Rd.
Hippodrome Pl. W11 139 CY73
Hiroshima Wk. SE7 164 EH76
Hiscocks Ho. NW10 138 CQ66
Hitcham La., Slou. 130 AE69
Hitcham Rd. E17 123 DZ59
Hitcham Rd., Maid. 130 AF72
Hitcham Rd., Slou. 130 AF70
Hitchcock Clo., Shep. 194 BM97
Hitchen Hatch La., Sev. 256 FG124
Hitchens Clo., Hem.H. 39 BF19
Hitchin Clo., Rom. 106 FJ49
Hitchin Sq. E3 143 DY68
Hitchings Way, Reig. 266 DA138
Hither Grn. La. SE13 183 EC85
Hither Meadow, Ger.Cr. 90 AY53
Lower Rd.
Hitherbaulk, Welw.G.C. 29 CY11
Hitherbroom Rd., Hayes 135 BU74
Hitherbury Clo., Guil. 258 AW137
Hitherfield Rd. SW16 181 DM89
Hitherfield Rd., Dag. 126 EY61
Hitherlands SW12 181 DH89
Hithermoor Rd., Stai. 174 BG86
Hitherway, Welw.G.C. 29 CX05
Hitherwell Dr., Har. 95 CD53
Hitherwood Clo., Horn. 128 FK63
Swanbourne Dr.
Hitherwood Clo., Reig. 250 DE132
Hitherwood Dr. SE19 182 DT91
Hive Clo. 95 CD47
(Bushey), Wat.
Hive La., Grav. 190 GB86
Hive Rd. (Bushey), Wat. 95 CD47
Hivings Hill, Chesh. 54 AN28
Hivings Pk., Chesh. 54 AP28
Hixberry La., St.Alb. 43 CK21
Hoadly Rd. SW16 181 DK90
Hobart Clo. N20 98 DE47
Hobart Clo., Hayes 136 BX70
Hobart Dr., Hayes 136 BX70
Hobart Gdns., Th.Hth. 202 DR97
Hobart La., Hayes 136 BX70
Hobart Pl. SW1 277 H6
Hobart Pl. SW1 161 DH76
Hobart Pl., Rich. 178 CM86
Chisholm Rd.
Hobart Rd., Dag. 126 EX63
Hobart Rd., Hayes 136 BX70
Hobart Rd., Ilf. 103 EQ54
Hobart Rd., Til. 171 GG81
Hobart Rd., Wor.Pk. 199 CV104
Hobart Wk., St.Alb. 43 CF16
Valley Rd.
Hobarts Dr., Uxb. 113 BF58
Hobbans Fm. Chase, Ong. 53 FH23
Hobbayne Rd. W7 137 CD72
Hobbes Wk. SW15 179 CV85
Hobbs Clo., St.Alb. 44 CL21
Hobbs Clo. (Cheshunt), 67 DX29
Wal.Cr.
Hobbs Clo., W.Byf. 212 BH113
Hobbs Cross Rd., Epp. 86 EW35
Hobbs Cross Rd., Harl. 36 EY12
Hobbs Grn. N2 120 DC55
Hobbs Hill, Hem.H. 40 BM23
Hobbs Hill Rd., Hem.H. 40 BL24
Hobbs Ms., Ilf. 125 ET61
Ripley Rd.
Hobbs Pl. Est. N1 142 DS67
Pitfield St.
Hobbs Rd. SE27 182 DQ91
Hobbs Way, Welw.G.C. 29 CW10
Hobday St. E14 143 EB71
Hobill Wk., Surb. 198 CM100
Hoblands End, Chis. 185 ES93
Hobletts Rd., Hem.H. 40 BM19
Hobsons Clo., Hodd. 33 DZ14
Hobsons Pl. E1 142 DU71
Hanbury St.
Hobtoe Rd., Harl. 35 EN14
Hobury St. SW10 160 DC79
Hockenden La., Swan. 206 FA97
Hocker St. E2 275 P3
Hockeridge Bottom, Berk. 38 AT21
Hockering Gdns., Wok. 227 BA118
Hockering Rd., Wok. 227 BA118
Hockett Clo. SE8 163 DY77
Hocklands, Welw.G.C. 30 DC08
Hockley Ave. E6 144 EL68
Hockley Dr., Rom. 105 FH54
Hockley La., Slou. 132 AV67
Hocroft Ave. NW2 119 CZ62
Hocroft Rd. NW2 119 CZ63
Hocroft Wk. NW2 119 CZ62
Hodder Dr., Grnf. 137 CF68
Hoddesdon Bypass, Brox. 49 DX24
Hoddesdon Bypass, Hert. 33 DZ13
Hoddesdon Ind. Cen., Hodd. 49 EC16
Hoddesdon Rd., Belv. 166 FA78
Hoddesdon Rd., Brox. 67 DX26
Hoddesdon Rd., Hodd. 49 DY15
Hoddesdon Rd., Ware 33 EC11
Hodds Wd. Rd., Chesh. 54 AQ33
Hodford Rd. NW11 119 CZ60
Hodges Way, Wat. 75 BU44
Hodgkin Clo. SE28 146 EX73
Fleming Way
Hodgson Gdns., Guil. 243 AZ131
Sutherland Dr.
Hodings Rd., Harl. 35 EP14
Hodnet Gro. SE16 163 DX77
Hawkstone Rd.
Hodsoll Ct., Orp. 206 EX99
Hodson Clo., Har. 116 BZ62
Hodson Cres., Orp. 206 EX99
Hoe, The, Wat. 94 BX47
Hoe La., Dor. 261 BT143
Hoe La., Enf. 82 DU38
Hoe La., Guil. 261 BR144
Hoe La., Rom. 86 EV41
Hoe La., Wal.Abb. 50 EF22
Hoe La., Ware 33 DX09
Hoe Meadow, Beac. 88 AJ51
Hoe St. E17 123 EA57
Hoebrook Clo., Wok. 226 AX121
Hoecroft, Wal.Abb. 50 EF22
Hoestock Rd., Saw. 36 EX05
Hofland Rd. W14 159 CX76
Hog Hill Rd., Rom. 104 EZ52
Hog Pits, Hem.H. 57 BB32
Hogan Ms. W2 140 DD71
Porteus Rd.
Hogan Way E5 122 DU61
Geldeston Rd.
Hogarth Ave., Ashf. 175 BQ93
Hogarth Ave., Brwd. 108 FY48
Hogarth Clo. E16 144 EK71
Hogarth Clo. W5 138 CL71
Hogarth Clo., Slou. 131 AL73
Hogarth Ct. EC3 275 N10
Hogarth Ct. SE19 182 DT91
Fountain Dr.
Hogarth Ct. (Bushey), Wat. 94 CB45
Steeplands
Hogarth Cres. SW19 200 DD95
Hogarth Cres., Croy. 202 DQ101
Hogarth Gdns., Houns. 156 CA80
Hogarth Hill NW11 119 CZ56
Hogarth La. W4 158 CS79
Hogarth Pl. SW5 160 DB77
Hogarth Rd.
Hogarth Reach, Loug. 85 EM43
Hogarth Rd. SW5 160 DB77
Hogarth Rd., Dag. 126 EV64
Hogarth Rd., Edg. 96 CN54
Hogarth Roundabout W4 158 CS79
Hogarth Way, Hmptn. 196 CC95
Hogback Wd. Rd., Beac. 88 AH51
Hogden La., Dor. 246 BZ134
Hogden La., Lthd. 246 CA129
Hogfair La., Slou. 130 AJ69
Hogg End La., Hem.H. 41 BR17
Hogg End La., St.Alb. 41 BT17
Hogg La., Borwd. 77 CG42
Hogg La., Grays 170 GA76
Hogpits Bottom, Hem.H. 57 BA32
Hogs Back, Guil. 258 AS137
Hogs La., Grav. 190 GD90
Hogs Orchard, Swan. 207 FH95
School La.
Hogscross La., Couls. 234 DF123
Hogshead Pas. E1 142 DV73
Pennington St.
Hogshill La., Cob. 213 BV114
Hogsmill Way, Epsom 216 CQ106
Hogtrough Hill, West. 239 ET120
Hogtrough La., Oxt. 253 EA128
Hogtrough La., Red. 267 DJ135
Holbeach Gdns., Sid. 185 ES86
Holbeach Ms. SW12 181 DH88
Harberson Rd.
Holbeach Rd. SE6 183 EA87
Holbeck La. (Cheshunt), 66 DT26
Wal.Cr.
Holbeck Row SE15 162 DU80
Holbein Gate, Nthwd. 93 BS50
Holbein Ms. SW1 276 F10
Holbein Ms. SW1 160 DG78
Holbein Pl. SW1 276 F9
Holbein Pl. SW1 160 DG77
Holbein Ter., Dag. 126 EV63
Marlborough Rd.
Holberton Gdns. NW10 139 CV69
Holborn EC1 274 D7
Holborn EC1 141 DN71
Holborn Circ. EC1 274 E7
Holborn Clo., St.Alb. 43 CK15
Holborn Pl. WC1 274 B7
Holborn Rd. E13 144 EH70
Holborn Viaduct EC1 274 E7
Holborn Viaduct EC1 141 DN71
Holborn Way, Mitch. 200 DF96
Holbreck Pl., Wok. 227 AZ118
Heathside Rd.
Holbrook Clo. N19 121 DH60
Dartmouth Pk. Hill
Holbrook Clo., Enf. 82 DT39
Holbrook La., Chis. 185 ER94
Holbrook Meadow, 173 BC93
Egh.
Holbrook Rd. E15 144 EF68
Holbrook Way, Brom. 205 EM100
Holbrooke Ct. N7 121 DL62
Holbrooke Pl., Rich. 177 CK85
Hill Ri.
Holburne Clo. SE3 164 EJ81
Holburne Gdns. SE3 164 EK81
Holburne Rd. SE3 164 EJ81
Holcombe Hill NW7 97 CU48
Highwood Hill
Holcombe Rd. N17 122 DT55
Holcombe Rd., Ilf. 125 EN59
Holcombe St. W6 159 CV78
Holcon Ct., Red. 250 DG131
Holcote Clo., Belv. 166 EY76
Blakemore Way
Holcroft Rd. E9 142 DW66
Holdbrook, Wal.Cr. 67 EA34
Holdbrook N., Wal.Cr. 67 DZ34
Holdbrook S., Wal.Cr. 67 DZ34
Queens Way
Holdbrook Way, Rom. 106 FM54
Holden Ave. N12 98 DB50
Holden Ave. NW9 118 CQ60
Holden Clo., Dag. 126 EV62
Holden Clo., Hert. 32 DS08
Holden Gdns., Brwd. 108 FX50
Holden Pt. E15 143 ED65
Waddington Rd.
Holden Rd. N12 98 DB50
Holden St. SW11 160 DG82
Holden Way, Upmin. 129 FR60
Holdenby Rd. SE4 183 DY85
Holdenhurst Ave. N12 98 DB52
Holder Clo. N3 98 DB52
Holderness Way SE27 181 DP92
Holdernesse Clo., Islw. 157 CG81
Blenheim Way
Holdernesse Rd. SW17 180 DF90
Holders Hill Ave. NW4 97 CX54
Holders Hill Circ. NW7 97 CY52
Dollis Rd.
Holders Hill Cres. NW4 97 CX54
Holders Hill Dr. NW4 119 CX55
Holders Hill Gdns. NW4 97 CY54
Holders Hill Rd. NW4 97 CX54
Holders Hill Rd. NW7 97 CY53
Holdgate St. SE7 164 EK76
Westmoor St.
Holdings, The, Hat. 45 CX16
Hole Fm. La., Brwd. 107 FU53
Hole Hill La., Dor. 262 CB136
Holecroft, Wal.Abb. 68 EE34
Holford Pl. WC1 274 C2
Holford Rd. NW3 120 DC62
Holford Rd., Grays 171 GK77
Holford Rd., Guil. 243 BC134
Holford Rd., S.le H. 171 GL75
Holford St. WC1 274 D2
Holford St. WC1 141 DN69
Holgate Ave. SW11 160 DD83
Holgate Gdns., Dag. 146 FA65
Holgate Rd., Dag. 126 FA64
Holland Ave. SW20 199 CT95
Holland Ave., Sutt. 218 DA108
Holland Clo., Barn. 98 DD45
Holland Clo., Brom. 204 EF103
Holland Clo., Red. 250 DF134
Holland Clo., Rom. 127 FC57
Holland Clo., Stan. 95 CH50
Holland Cres., Oxt. 254 EG133
Holland Dr. SE23 183 DY90
Holland Gdns. W14 159 CY76
Holland Gdns., Egh. 193 BF96
Holland Gdns., Wat. 76 BW35
Holland Gro. SW9 161 DN80
Holland La., Oxt. 254 EG133
Holland Pk. W8 159 CZ75
Holland Pk. W11 139 CY74
Holland Pk. Ave. W11 139 CY74
Holland Pk. Ave., Ilf. 125 ES58
Holland Pk. Gdns. W14 159 CY75
Holland Pk. Ms. W11 139 CZ74
Holland Pk. Rd. W14 159 CZ76
Holland Pas. N1 142 DQ67
Basire St.
Holland Pl. W8 160 DB75
Kensington Ch. St.
Holland Rd. E6 145 EM67
Holland Rd. E15 144 EE69
Holland Rd. NW10 139 CU67
Holland Rd. SE25 202 DU99
Holland Rd. W14 159 CX75
Holland Rd., Oxt. 254 EG133
Holland Rd., Wem. 137 CK65
Holland St. SE1 278 G2
Holland St. SE1 141 DP74
Holland St. W8 160 DA75
Holland Vill. Rd. W14 159 CY75
Holland Wk. N19 121 DK60
Duncombe Rd.
Holland Wk. W8 159 CZ75
Holland Wk., Stan. 95 CG50
Holland Way, Brom. 204 EF103
Hollands, The, Felt. 176 BX91
Hollands, The, Wor.Pk. 199 CT102
Hollands Cft., Ware 34 EK06
Hollar Rd. N16 122 DT62
Stoke Newington High St.
Hollen St. W1 273 L8
Hollen St. W1 141 DK72
Holles Clo., Hmptn. 176 CA93
Holles St. W1 273 J8
Holles St. W1 141 DH72
Holley Rd. W3 158 CS75
Hollickwood Ave. N12 98 DF51
Holliday Sq. SW11 160 DD83
Fowler Clo.
Holliday St., Berk. 38 AX19
Hollidge Way, Dag. 147 FB65
Hollier Ct., Hat. 45 CV17
Holliers Way, Hat. 45 CU18
Hollies, The E11 124 EG57
Hollies, The N20 98 DD46
Hollies, The, Grav. 191 GK93
Hollies, The, Har. 117 CG56
Hollies, The, Hem.H. 57 BA29
Hollies, The, Welw.G.C. 29 CV13
Hollies Ave., Sid. 185 ET89
Hollies Ave., W.Byf. 211 BF113
Hollies Clo. SW16 181 DN93
Hollies Clo., Twick. 177 CF89
Hollies Ct., Add. 212 BJ106
Hollies End NW7 97 CV50
Hollies Rd. W5 157 CJ77
Hollies Way SW12 180 DG87
Bracken Ave.
Hollies Way, Pot.B. 64 DC31
Holligrave Rd., Brom. 204 EG95
Hollingbourne Ave., Bexh. 166 EZ80
Hollingbourne Gdns. W13 137 CH71
Hollingbourne Rd. SE24 182 DQ85
Hollingbourne Twr., Orp. 206 EX102
Hollingsworth Rd., Croy. 220 DV107
Hollington Cres., N.Mal. 199 CT100
Hollington Rd. E6 145 EM69
Hollington Rd. N17 100 DU54
Hollingworth Clo., W.Mol. 196 BZ98
Hollingworth Rd., Orp. 205 EP101
Hollingworth Way, West. 255 ER126
Hollis Pl., Grays 170 GA77
Ward Ave.
Hollman Gdns. SW16 181 DP93
Hollow, The, Wdf.Grn. 102 EF49
Hollow Clo., Guil. 258 AV135
Lynwood
Hollow Cotts., Purf. 168 FN78
Hollow Hill La., Iver 133 BB73
Hollow La., Dor. 262 BX140
Hollow La., Vir.W. 192 AW97
Hollow Wk., Rich. 158 CL80
Kew Rd.
Hollow Way La., Amer. 55 AS35
Hollow Way La., Chesh. 72 AT35
Holloway Dr., Vir.W. 192 AY98
Holloway Hill, Cher. 193 BC104
Holloway La., Rick. 73 BB38
Holloway La., West Dr. 154 BK79
Holloway Rd. E6 145 EM69
Holloway Rd. E11 124 EE62
Holloway Rd. N7 121 DL62
Holloway Rd. N19 121 DJ61
Holloway St., Houns. 156 CB83
Holloways La., Hat. 45 CX23
Hollowfield Ave., Grays 170 GD77
Hollowfield Wk., Nthlt. 136 BY65
Hollows, The, Brent. 158 CM79
Kew Bri. Rd.
Holly Ave., Add. 212 BG110
Holly Ave., Stan. 96 CL54
Holly Ave., Walt. 196 BX102
Holly Bank Rd., Wok. 226 AV119
Holly Bush Hill NW3 120 DC63
Holly Bush La., Hmptn. 176 BZ94
Holly Bush La., Sev. 257 FJ124
Holly Bush Steps NW3 120 DC63
Heath St.
Holly Bush Vale NW3 120 DC63
Heath St.
Holly Clo. NW10 138 CS66
Holly Clo., Buck.H. 102 EK48
Holly Clo., Cher. 192 AU104
Holly Clo., Egh. 172 AV93
Holly Clo., Felt. 176 BY92
Holly Clo., Hat. 45 CT19
Holly Clo., Slou. 111 AQ63
Holly Clo., Wall. 219 DH108
Holly Clo., Wok. 226 AV119
Holly Cres., Beck. 203 DZ99
Holly Cres., Wind. 151 AK82
Holly Cres., Wdf.Grn. 101 ED52
Holly Cft., Hert. 31 DN08
Holly Cross Rd., Ware 33 DZ07
Holly Dr. E4 101 EB45
Holly Dr., Berk. 38 AX20
Holly Dr., Brent. 157 CG79
Holly Dr., Pot.B. 64 DB33
Holly Dr., Wind. 172 AS85
Holly Fm. Rd., Sthl. 156 BY78
Holly Fld., Harl. 51 EQ18
Holly Gdns., West Dr. 154 BM75
Holly Grn., Wey. 213 BR105
Holly Gro. NW9 118 CQ59
Holly Gro. SE15 162 DT82
Holly Gro., Pnr. 94 BY53
Holly Gro. (Bushey), Wat. 95 CD45
Holly Gro. Rd., Hert. 31 DH07
Holly Hedge Ter. SE13 183 ED85
Holly Hedges La., Hem.H. 57 BC30
Holly Hedges La., Rick. 57 BD32
Holly Hill N21 81 DM44
Holly Hill NW3 120 DC63
Holly Hill Dr., Bans. 234 DA116
Holly Hill Rd., Belv. 167 FB78
Holly Hill Rd., Erith 167 FC78
Holly Ho., Brwd. 108 FX46
Sawyers Hall La.
Holly La., Bans. 234 DA116
Holly La. E., Bans. 234 DB116
Holly La. W., Bans. 234 DB117
Holly Lea, Guil. 242 AX128
Holly Lo. Gdns. N6 120 DG60
Holly Ms. SW10 160 DC78
Drayton Gdns.
Holly Mt. NW3 120 DC63
Holly Bush Hill
Holly Pk. N3 119 CZ55
Holly Pk. N4 121 DL59
Holly Pk. Est. N4 121 DM59
Blythwood Rd.
Holly Pk. Gdns. N3 120 DA55
Holly Pk. Rd. N11 98 DG50
Holly Pk. Rd. W7 137 CF74
Holly Rd. E11 124 EF59
Holly Rd. W4 158 CR77
Dolman Rd.
Holly Rd., Dart. 188 FK88
Holly Rd., Enf. 83 DX36
Holly Rd., Hmptn. 176 CC93
Holly Rd., Houns. 156 CB84
Holly Rd., Orp. 224 EU108
Holly Rd., Reig. 266 DB136
Holly Rd., Twick. 177 CG88
Holly St. E8 142 DT65
Holly St. Est. E8 142 DT66
Holly St.
Holly Ter. N20 98 DC47
Holly Tree Ave., Swan. 207 FE96
Holly Tree Clo., Chesh. 56 AV31
Holly Tree Rd., Cat. 236 DS122
Elm Gro.
Holly Vw. Clo. NW4 119 CU58
Holly Wk. NW3 120 DC63
Holly Wk., Enf. 82 DQ41
Gentlemans Row
Holly Wk., Rich. 158 CL82
Holly Wk., Welw.G.C. 29 CW05
Holly Way, Mitch. 201 DK98
Hollybank Clo., Hmptn. 176 CA92
Hollybank Rd., W.Byf. 212 BG114
Hollyberry La. NW3 120 DC63
Holly Wk.
Hollybrake Clo., Chis. 185 ER94
Hollybush Ave., St.Alb. 42 CA24
Hollybush Clo. E11 124 EG57
Hollybush Clo., Berk. 39 BD16
Hollybush Clo., Har. 95 CE53
Hollybush Clo., Sev. 257 FJ124
Hollybush Clo., Wat. 94 BW45
Hollybush Ct., Sev. 257 FJ124
Hollybush Gdns. E2 142 DV69
Hollybush Hill E11 124 EF59
Hollybush Hill, Slou. 132 AU66
Hollybush La., Amer. 55 AR36
Hollybush La., Hem.H. 39 BF19
Hollybush La., Iver 133 BB72
Hollybush La., Orp. 224 FA107
Hollybush La., Uxb. 113 BC61
Hollybush La., Welw.G.C. 29 CZ12
Hollybush La., Wok. 228 BK119
Hollybush Pl. E2 142 DV69
Bethnal Grn. Rd.
Hollybush Rd., Chesh. 54 AN27
Hollybush Rd., Grav. 191 GJ89
Hollybush Rd., Kings.T. 178 CL92
Hollybush St. E13 144 EH69
Hollybush Wk. SW9 161 DP84
Hollybush Way, Wal.Cr. 66 DU28
Hollycombe, Egh. 172 AW91
Hollycroft Ave. NW3 120 DA62
Hollycroft Ave., Wem. 118 CM61
Hollycroft Clo., West Dr. 154 BN79
Hollycroft Gdns., West Dr. 154 BN79
Hollydale Dr., Brom. 205 EM104
Hollydale Rd. SE15 162 DW81
Hollydell, Hert. 32 DQ11
Hollydene SE15 162 DV81
Hollydown Way E11 123 ED62
Hollyfield, Hat. 45 CU21
Hollyfield Ave. N11 98 DF50
Hollyfield Rd., Surb. 198 CM101
Hollyfields, Brox. 67 DY26
Hollyhedge Rd., Cob. 213 BV114
Hollyhock Clo., Hem.H. 39 BE19
Hollymead, Cars. 200 DF104
Hollymead Rd., Couls. 234 DG118
Hollymeoak Rd., Couls. 235 DH119
Hollymoor La., Epsom 216 CR110
Hollymount Clo. SE10 163 EC81
Hollytree Clo. SW19 179 CX88
Hollytree Clo., Ger.Cr. 90 AY50
Hollywood Ct., Borwd. 78 CM42
Deacon's Hill Rd.
Hollywood Gdns., Hayes 135 BV72
Hollywood Ms. SW10 160 DC79
Hollywood Rd.
Hollywood Rd. E4 101 DY50
Hollywood Rd. SW10 160 DC79
Hollywood Way, Erith 167 FH81
Hollywood Way, Wdf.Grn. 101 ED52
Hollywoods, Croy. 221 DZ109
Holm Clo., Add. 211 BE112
Holm Gro., Uxb. 134 BN66
Holm Oak Clo. SW15 179 CZ86
West Hill
Holm Oak Ms. SW4 181 DL85
King's Ave.
Holm Wk. SE3 164 EG82
Blackheath Pk.
Holman Rd. SW11 160 DD82
Holman Rd., Epsom 216 CQ106
Holmbank Dr., Shep. 195 BS98
Holmbridge Gdns., Enf. 83 DX42
Holmbrook Dr. NW4 119 CX57
Holmbury Ct. SW17 180 DF90
Holmbury Ct. SW19 180 DE94
Cavendish Rd.
Holmbury Dr., Dor. 263 CJ139
Holmbury Gdns., Hayes 135 BT74
Church Rd.
Holmbury Gro., Croy. 221 DZ108
Holmbury Pk., Brom. 184 EL94
Holmbury Vw. E5 122 DV60
Holmbush Rd. SW15 179 CY86
Holmcote Gdns. N5 122 DQ64
Holmcroft, Tad. 249 CV125
Holmcroft Way, Brom. 205 EM99
Holmdale Clo., Borwd. 78 CM40
Holmdale Gdns. NW4 119 CX57
Holmdale Rd. NW6 120 DA64
Holmdale Rd., Chis. 185 EQ92
Holmdale Ter. N15 122 DS59
Holmdene Ave. NW7 97 CU51
Holmdene Ave. SE24 182 DQ85
Holmdene Ave., Har. 116 CB55
Holmdene Clo., Beck. 203 EC96
Holme Chase, Wey. 213 BQ107
Holme Clo., Hat. 45 CT15
Holme Clo. (Cheshunt), 67 DY31
Wal.Cr.
Holme Lacey Rd. SE12 184 EF86
Holme Lea, Wat. 60 BW34
Kingsway
Holme Pk., Borwd. 78 CM40
Holme Rd. E6 144 EL67
Holme Rd., Hat. 45 CT15
Holme Rd., Horn. 128 FN60
Holme Way, Stan. 95 CF51
Holmead Rd. SW6 160 DB80
Holmebury Clo. (Bushey), 95 CE47
Wat.
Holmedale, Slou. 132 AW73
Holmefield Ct. NW3 140 DE65
Holmes Ave. E17 123 DZ55

Holmes Ave. NW7 97 CY50
Holmes Meadow, Harl. 51 EP21
Holmes Pl. SW10 160 DC79
Fulham Rd.
Holmes Rd. NW5 141 DH65
Holmes Rd. SW19 180 DC94
Holmes Rd., Twick. 177 CF89
Holmes Ter. SE1 278 D4
Holmes Ter. SE1 161 DN75
Holmesdale, Wal.Cr. 82 DW35
Holmesdale Ave. SW14 158 CP83
Holmesdale Clo. SE25 202 DT97
Holmesdale Clo., Guil. 243 BB133
Holmesdale Hill (South Darenth), Dart. 208 FQ95
Holmesdale Rd. N6 121 DH59
Holmesdale Rd. SE25 202 DR99
Holmesdale Rd., Bexh. 166 EX82
Holmesdale Rd., Croy. 202 DR99
Holmesdale Rd. (South Darenth), Dart. 208 FQ95
Holmesdale Rd., Dor. 263 CH140
Holmesdale Rd., Red. 267 DM136
Holmesdale Rd., Reig. 250 DA133
Holmesdale Rd., Rich. 158 CM81
Holmesdale Rd., Tedd. 177 CJ94
Holmesdale Ter., Dor. 263 CH140
Holmesdale Rd.
Holmesley Rd. SE23 183 DY86
Holmethorpe Ave., Red. 251 DH131
Holmethorpe Ind. Est., Red. 251 DH131
Holmewood Gdns. SW2 181 DM87
Holmewood Rd. SE25 202 DS97
Holmewood Rd. SW2 181 DL87
Holmfield Ave. NW4 119 CX57
Holmhurst Rd., Belv. 167 FB78
Holmlea Rd., Slou. 152 AX81
Holmlea Wk., Slou. 152 AW81
Holmleigh Ave., Dart. 168 FJ84
Holmleigh Rd. N16 122 DS60
Holmleigh Rd. Est. N16 122 DT60
Holmleigh Rd.
Holms St. E2 142 DU68
Audrey St.
Holmsdale Clo., Iver 133 BF72
Holmsdale Gro., Bexh. 167 FE82
Holmsdale Rd., Sev. 257 FJ123
Holmshaw Clo. SE26 183 DY91
Holmshill La., Borwd. 78 CS36
Holmside Ri., Wat. 93 BV48
Holmside Rd. SW12 180 DG86
Holmsley Clo., N.Mal. 199 CT100
Holmstall Ave., Edg. 118 CQ55
Holmwood Ave., Brwd. 109 GA43
Holmwood Ave., S.Croy. 220 DT113
Holmwood Clo., Add. 212 BG106
Holmwood Clo., Har. 116 CC55
Holmwood Clo., Lthd. 245 BS128
Holmwood Clo., Nthlt. 136 CB65
Holmwood Clo., Sutt. 217 CX109
Holmwood Gdns. N3 98 DA54
Holmwood Gdns., Wall. 219 DH107
Holmwood Gro. NW7 96 CR50
Holmwood Rd., Chess. 215 CK106
Holmwood Rd., Enf. 83 DX36
Holmwood Rd., Ilf. 125 ES61
Holmwood Rd., Sutt. 217 CW110
Holmwood Vw. Rd., Dor. 263 CH142
Horsham Rd.
Holmwood Vill. SE7 164 EG78
Holne Chase N2 120 DC58
Holne Chase, Mord. 199 CZ100
Holness Rd. E15 144 EF65
Holroyd Clo., Esher 215 CF109
Holroyd Rd. SW15 159 CW84
Holroyd Rd., Esher 215 CF109
Holstein Ave., Wey. 212 BN105
Holstein Way, Erith 166 EX76
Holstock Rd., Ilf. 125 EQ61
Holsworth Clo., Har. 116 CC57
Holsworthy Sq. WC1 274 C5
Holsworthy Way, Chess. 215 CJ106
Holt, The, Hem.H. 40 BL21
Turners Hill
Holt, The, Ilf. 103 EQ51
Holt, The, Wall. 219 DJ105
Holt, The, Welw.G.C. 30 DD10
Holt Clo. N10 120 DG56
Holt Clo. SE28 146 EV73
Holt Clo., Borwd. 78 CM42
Holt Clo., Chig. 103 ET50
Holt Ct. E15 123 EC64
Clays La.
Holt Rd. E16 144 EL74
Holt Rd., Wem. 117 CH62
Holt Way, Chig. 103 ET50
Holton St. E1 143 DX70
Holtsmere Clo., Wat. 76 BW35
Holtspur Ave., H.Wyc. 110 AE56
Holtspur Clo., Beac. 88 AG54
Holtspur La., H.Wyc. 110 AE57
Holtspur Top La., Beac. 88 AG54
Holtspur Way, Beac. 88 AG54
Holtwhite Ave., Enf. 82 DQ40
Holtwhites Hill, Enf. 81 DP39
Holtwood Rd., Lthd. 214 CC114
Holwell Caravan Site, Hat. 30 DE14
Holwell Hyde, Welw.G.C. 30 DC11
Holwell Hyde La., Welw.G.C. 30 DC12
Holwell La., Hat. 30 DE14
Holwell Pl., Pnr. 116 BY56
Holwell Rd., Welw.G.C. 29 CY10
Holwood Clo., Walt. 196 BW103
Holwood Pk. Ave., Orp. 223 EM105
Holwood Pl. SW4 161 DK84
Holy Cross Hill, Brox. 48 DU24
Holy Wk., Brox. 49 EA19
St. Catherines Rd.
Holybourne Ave. SW15 179 CU87
Holyfield Rd., Wal.Abb. 67 EC29
Holyhead Clo. E3 143 EA69
Holyhead Clo. E6 145 EM71
Valiant Way
Holyoak Rd. SE11 278 F8
Holyoake Ave., Wok. 226 AW117
Holyoake Ct. SE16 163 DZ75
Bryan Rd.
Holyoake Cres., Wok. 226 AW117
Holyoake Ter., Sev. 256 FG124
Holyoake Wk. N2 120 DC55
Holyoake Wk. W5 137 CJ70
Holyport Rd. SW6 159 CW80
Holyrood Ave., Har. 116 BY63
Holyrood Cres., St.Alb. 43 CD24
Holyrood Gdns., Edg. 118 CP55
Holyrood Gdns., Grays 171 GJ77
Holyrood Rd., Barn. 80 DC44
Holyrood St. SE1 279 M3
Holywell Clo. SE3 164 EG79
Holywell Clo., Stai. 174 BL88
Holywell Hill, St.Alb. 43 CD21
Holywell Ind. Est., Wat. 75 BR44
Holywell La. EC2 275 N4
Holywell La. EC2 142 DS70
Holywell Rd., Wat. 75 BU43
Holywell Row EC2 275 M5
Holywell Row EC2 142 DS70
Holywell Way, Stai. 174 BL88
Home Barn Ct., Lthd. 246 BX127
The St.
Home Clo., Brox. 49 DZ24
Home Clo., Cars. 200 DF103
Home Clo., Harl. 35 ET14
Home Clo., Lthd. 231 CD121
Home Clo., Nthlt. 136 BZ69
Home Ct., Felt. 175 BU88
Home Fm. Clo., Bet. 264 CS135
Home Fm. Clo., Epsom 233 CX117
Home Fm. Clo., Esher 214 CB107
Home Fm. Clo., Shep. 195 BS98
Home Fm. Clo., T.Ditt. 197 CF101
Home Fm. Gdns., Walt. 196 BW103
Home Fm. Rd., Rick. 92 BM49
Home Fm. Way, Slou. 132 AW67
Home Fld., Berk. 39 BB16
Home Gdns., Dag. 127 FC62
Home Gdns., Dart. 188 FL86
Home Hill, Swan. 187 FF94
Home Lea, Orp. 223 ET106
Home Ley, Welw.G.C. 29 CY09
Home Mead, Stan. 95 CJ53
Home Mead Clo., Grav. 191 GH87
Home Meadow, Bans. 234 DA116
Holly La.
Home Meadow, Slou. 131 AQ68
Home Meadow, Welw.G.C. 29 CZ09
Home Orchard, Dart. 188 FL86
Home Pk., Oxt. 254 EG131
Home Pk. Mill Link Rd., Kings L. 59 BP31
Home Pk. Rd. SW19 179 CZ91
Home Pk. Wk., Kings.T. 197 CK98
Home Rd. SW11 160 DE82
Home Way, Rick. 91 BF46
Homecroft Gdns., Loug. 85 EP42
Homecroft Rd. N22 99 DP53
Homecroft Rd. SE26 182 DW92
Homedean Rd., Sev. 256 FC122
Homefarm Clo., Cher. 211 BA108
Homefarm Rd. W7 137 CE72
Homefield, Hem.H. 57 BB28
Homefield, Wal.Abb. 68 EG32
Homefield, Walt. 214 BX105
Homefield Ave., Ilf. 125 ES57
Homefield Clo. NW10 138 CQ65
Homefield Clo., Add. 211 BE112
Homefield Clo., Epp. 70 EU30
Homefield Clo., Hayes 136 BX70
Homefield Clo., Horl. 269 DH147
Tanyard Way
Homefield Clo., Lthd. 231 CJ121
Homefield Clo., Orp. 206 EV98
Homefield Clo., Swan. 207 FF97
Homefield Gdns. N2 120 DD55
Homefield Gdns., Mitch. 200 DC96
Homefield Gdns., Tad. 233 CW120
Homefield Ms., Beck. 203 EA95
Homefield Pk., Sutt. 218 DB107
Homefield Ri., Orp. 206 EU102
Homefield Rd. SW19 179 CX93
Homefield Rd. W4 159 CT78
Homefield Rd., Brom. 204 EJ95
Homefield Rd., Couls. 235 DP119
Homefield Rd., Edg. 96 CR51
Homefield Rd., Hem.H. 40 BN20
Homefield Rd., Rad. 77 CF37
Homefield Rd., Rick. 73 BC42
Green St.
Homefield Rd., Sev. 256 FE122
Homefield Rd., Walt. 196 BY101
Homefield Rd., Ware 33 DY05
Homefield Rd., Warl. 236 DW119
Homefield Rd. (Bushey), Wat. 76 CA42
Homefield Rd., Wem. 117 CG63
Homefield St. N1 275 M1
Homeland Dr., Sutt. 218 DB109
Homelands, Lthd. 231 CJ121
Homelands Dr. SE19 182 DS94
Homeleigh Ct., Wal.Cr. 66 DV29
Homeleigh Rd. SE15 183 DX85
Homemead SW12 181 DH89
Homemead Rd., Brom. 205 EM99
Homemead Rd., Croy. 202 DW100
Homer Clo., Bexh. 167 FC81
Homer Dr. E14 163 EA77
Homer Rd. E9 143 DY65
Homer Rd., Croy. 203 DX100
Homer Row W1 272 C7
Homer Row W1 140 DE71
Homer St. W1 272 C7
Homer St. W1 140 DE71
Homerfield, Welw.G.C. 29 CW08
Homers Rd., Wind. 151 AK81
Homersham Rd., Kings.T. 198 CN96
Homerswood La., Welw. 29 CU05
Homerton Gro. E9 123 DX64
Homerton High St. E9 122 DW64
Homerton Rd. E9 123 DY64
Homerton Row E9 122 DW64
Homerton Ter. E9 142 DW65
Morning La.
Homesdale Clo. E11 124 EG57
Homesdale Rd., Brom. 204 EJ98
Homesdale Rd., Cat. 236 DR123
Homesdale Rd., Orp. 205 ES101
Homesfield NW11 120 DA57
Homestall Rd. SE22 182 DW85
Homestead, The N11 99 DH49
Homestead, The, Dart. 188 FJ86
Homestead Clo., St.Alb. 60 CC27
Homestead Clo., Welw.G.C. 29 CZ11
Homestead Gdns., Esher 215 CE106
Homestead La., Welw.G.C. 29 CZ12
Homestead Paddock N14 81 DH43
Homestead Pk. NW2 119 CT62
Homestead Rd. SW6 159 CZ80
Homestead Rd., Cat. 236 DR123
Homestead Rd., Dag. 126 EZ61
Homestead Rd., Hat. 45 CU15
Homestead Rd., Orp. 224 EV108
Homestead Rd., Rick. 92 BK45
Park Rd.
Homestead Rd., Stai. 174 BH93
Homestead Way, Croy. 221 EC111
Homesteads, The, Ware 34 EK07
Hunsdon Rd.
Homewaters Ave., Sun. 195 BT95
Homeway, Rom. 106 FP51
Homewillow Clo. N21 81 DP44
Homewood, Slou. 132 AX72
Homewood Ave. (Cuffley), Pot.B. 65 DL27
Homewood Clo., Hmptn. 176 BZ93
Fearnley Cres.
Homewood Cres., Chis. 185 ES93
Homewood La., Pot.B. 65 DJ27
Homewood Rd., St.Alb. 43 CH17
Honduras St. EC1 275 H4
Honey Clo., Dag. 147 FB65
Honey Hill, Uxb. 134 BM66
Honey La. EC2 275 J9
Honey La., Wal.Abb. 68 EE33
Honeybourne Rd. NW6 120 DB64
Honeybourne Way, Orp. 205 ER102
Honeybrook, Wal.Abb. 68 EE33
Honeybrook Rd. SW12 181 DJ87
Honeycrock La., Red. 266 DG141
Honeycroft, Loug. 85 EN42
Honeycroft, Welw.G.C. 29 CW10
Honeycroft Dr., St.Alb. 43 CJ22
Honeycroft Hill, Uxb. 134 BL66
Honeycross Rd., Hem.H. 39 BE21
Honeyden Rd., Sid. 186 EY93
Honeyman Clo. NW6 139 CX66
Honeymeade, Saw. 36 EW08
Honeypot Clo. NW9 118 CM56
Honeypot La. NW9 118 CL55
Honeypot La., Brwd. 108 FU48
Honeypot La., Stan. 118 CL55
Honeypots Rd., Wok. 226 AX122
Honeysett Rd. N17 100 DT54
Reform Row
Honeysuckle Bottom, Lthd. 245 BS134
Honeysuckle Clo., Brwd. 108 FV43
Honeysuckle Clo., Hert. 32 DU09
Honeysuckle Clo., Horl. 269 DJ147
Briars Wd.
Honeysuckle Clo., Iver 133 BC72
Honeysuckle Clo., Rom. 106 FK51
Cloudberry Rd.
Honeysuckle Clo., Sthl. 136 BY73
Honeysuckle Fld., Chesh. 54 AQ30
Honeysuckle Gdns., Croy. 203 DX102
Primrose La.
Honeysuckle Gdns., Hat. 45 CV19
Honeysuckle La., Dor. 263 CJ139
Treelands
Honeywell Rd. SW11 180 DE86
Honeywood Clo., Pot.B. 64 DD33
Honeywood Rd. NW10 139 CT68
Honeywood Rd., Islw. 157 CG84
Honeywood Wk., Cars. 218 DF105
Honister Clo., Stan. 95 CH53
Honister Gdns., Stan. 95 CH53
Honister Heights, Pur. 220 DR114
Honister Pl., Stan. 95 CH53
Honiton Rd. NW6 139 CZ68
Honiton Rd., Rom. 127 FD58
Honiton Rd., Well. 165 ET82
Honley Rd. SE6 183 EB87
Honnor Rd., Stai. 174 BK94
Honor Oak Pk. SE23 183 DX86
Honor Oak Ri. SE23 182 DW86
Honor Oak Rd. SE23 182 DW88
Hoo, The, Harl. 36 EW10
Hood Ave. N14 81 DH44
Hood Ave. SW14 178 CQ85
Hood Ave., Orp. 206 EV99
Hood Clo., Croy. 201 DP102
Parson's Mead
Hood Ct. EC4 274 E9
Hood Rd. SW20 179 CT94
Hood Rd., Rain. 147 FE68
Hood Wk., Rom. 105 FB53
Hoodcote Gdns. N21 99 DP45
Hook, The, Barn. 80 DD44
Hook Fm. Rd., Brom. 204 EK99
Hook Gate, Enf. 82 DV36
Hook Grn. La., Dart. 187 FF90
Hook Grn. Rd., Grav. 190 FY94
Hook Heath Ave., Wok. 226 AV119
Hook Heath Gdns., Wok. 226 AT121
Hook Heath Rd., Wok. 226 AT121
Hook Hill, S.Croy. 220 DS110
Hook Hill La., Wok. 226 AV121
Hook Hill Pk., Wok. 226 AV121
Hook La., Guil. 260 BN140
Hook La., Pot.B. 64 DF32
Hook La., Rom. 86 EZ44
Hook La., Well. 165 ET84
Hook Ri. N., Surb. 198 CN104
Hook Ri. S., Surb. 198 CN104
Hook Rd., Chess. 215 CK106
Hook Rd., Epsom 216 CQ108
Hook Rd., Surb. 198 CL104
Hook Wk., Edg. 96 CQ51
Hooke Rd., Lthd. 245 BT125
Hookers Rd. E17 123 DX55
Hookfield, Epsom 216 CQ113
Hookfield, Harl. 51 ES17
Hookfields, Grav. 190 GE90
Hooking Grn., Har. 116 CB57
Hooks Clo. SE15 162 DV81
Woods Rd.
Hooks Hall Dr., Dag. 127 FC62
Hooks Way SE22 182 DU88
Dulwich Common
Hookstone Way, Wdf.Grn. 102 EK52
Hookwood Cor., Oxt. 254 EH128
Hookwood La.
Hookwood La., Oxt. 254 EH128
Hookwood Rd., Orp. 224 EW111
Hooley La., Red. 266 DF135
Hoop La. NW11 119 CZ59
Hooper Rd. E16 144 EG72
Hooper Sq. E1 142 DU73
Hooper St.
Hooper St. E1 142 DU73
Hooper's Ct. SW3 276 D5
Hoopers Yd., Sev. 257 FJ126
Hop Gdns. WC2 141 DL73
St. Martin's La.
Hope Clo. N1 142 DQ65
Wallace Rd.
Hope Clo. SE12 184 EH90
Hope Clo., Sutt. 218 DC106
Hope Clo., Wdf.Grn. 102 EJ51
West Gro.
Hope Grn., Wat. 59 BU33
Hope Pk., Brom. 184 EF94
Hope Rd., Swans. 190 FZ86
High St.
Hope St. SW11 160 DD83
Hope Ter., Grays 169 FX78
Hopedale Rd. SE7 164 EH79
Hopefield Ave. NW6 139 CY68
Hopes Clo., Houns. 156 CA79
Old Cote Dr.
Hopetown St. E1 142 DT71
Brick La.
Hopewell Dr., Grav. 191 GM92
Hopewell St. SE5 162 DR80
Hopewell Yd. SE5 162 DR80
Hopewell St.
Hopfield, Wok. 226 AY116
Hopfield Ave., W.Byf. 212 BL112
Hopgarden La., Sev. 256 FG128
Hopgood St. W12 139 CW74
Macfarlane Rd.
Hopground Clo., St.Alb. 43 CG22
Hopkins Clo. N10 98 DG52
Cromwell Rd.
Hopkins Clo., Rom. 128 FJ55
Hopkins Ms. E15 144 EF67
West Rd.
Hopkins St. W1 273 L9
Hopkinsons Pl. NW1 140 DG67
Fitzroy Rd.
Hoppers Rd. N13 99 DN47
Hoppers Rd. N21 99 DN47
Hoppett Rd. E4 102 EE47
Hoppety, The, Tad. 233 CX122
Hopping La. N1 141 DP65
St. Mary's Gro.
Hoppingwood Ave., N.Mal. 198 CS97
Hoppit Rd., Wal.Abb. 67 EB33
Hoppner Rd., Hayes 135 BQ68
Hopton Ct., Guil. 242 AS134
Park Barn Dr.
Hopton Gdns. SE1 278 G2
Hopton Gdns., N.Mal. 199 CU100
Hopton Rd. SW16 181 DL92
Hopton St. SE1 278 G2
Hopton St. SE1 141 DP74
Hopwood Clo. SW17 180 DC90
Hopwood Rd. SE17 162 DR79
Hopwood Wk. E8 142 DU66
Wilman Gro.
Horace Ave., Rom. 127 FC60
Horace Rd. E7 124 EH63
Horace Rd., Ilf. 125 EQ55
Horace Rd., Kings.T. 198 CM97
Horatio Ct. SE16 142 DW74
Rotherhithe St.
Horatio Pl. E14 163 EC75
Cold Harbour
Horatio Pl. SW19 180 DA94
Kingston Rd.
Horatio St. E2 142 DU68
Horatius Way, Croy. 219 DM106
Horbury Cres. W11 140 DA73
Horbury Ms. W11 139 CZ73
Ladbroke Rd.
Horder Rd. SW6 159 CY81
Hordle Gdns., St.Alb. 43 CF21
Hordle Prom. E. SE15 162 DT80
Daniel Gdns.
Hordle Prom. N. SE15 162 DT80
Daniel Gdns.
Hordle Prom. S. SE15 162 DT80
Pentridge St.
Hordle Prom. W. SE15 162 DS80
Diamond St.
Horizon Way SE7 164 EH77
Horksley Gdns., Brwd. 109 GC44
Bannister Dr.
Horley Clo., Bexh. 186 FA85
Horley Lo. La., Red. 266 DF143
Horley Rd. SE9 184 EL91
Horley Rd., Red. 266 DF136
Horley Row, Horl. 268 DF147
Hormead Rd. W9 139 CZ70
Horn Clo., Hert. 32 DQ11
Horn La. SE10 164 EG77
Horn La. W3 138 CQ74
Horn La., Bexh. 167 FC82
Horn La., Wdf.Grn. 102 EG51
Horn Pk. Clo. SE12 184 EH85
Horn Pk. La. SE12 184 EH85
Hornbeam Ave., Upmin. 128 FN63
Hornbeam Clo. SE11 278 D8
Hornbeam Clo., Borwd. 78 CN39
Hornbeam Clo., Brwd. 109 GB48
Hornbeam Clo., Buck.H. 102 EK48
Hornbeam Rd.
Hornbeam Clo., Epp. 85 ER37
Hornbeam Clo., Hert. 31 DP08
Hornbeam Clo., Nthlt. 116 BZ64
Hornbeam Cres., Brent. 157 CH80
Hornbeam Gdns., Slou. 152 AU76
Upton Rd.
Hornbeam Gro. E4 102 EE48
Hornbeam La. E4 84 EE43
Hornbeam La., Bexh. 167 FC82
Hornbeam La., Hat. 46 DE21
Hornbeam La., Hert. 46 DG23
Hornbeam Rd., Buck.H. 102 EK48
Hornbeam Rd., Epp. 85 ER37
Hornbeam Rd., Guil. 242 AW131
Hornbeam Rd., Hayes 136 BW71
Hornbeam Rd., Reig. 266 DB137
Hornbeam Ter., Cars. 200 DE102
Hornbeam Twr. E11 123 ED62
Hollydown Way
Hornbeam Wk., Rich. 178 CM89
Hornbeam Wk., Walt. 213 BT109
Octagon Rd.
Hornbeam Way, Brom. 205 EN100
Hornbeam Way, Wal.Cr. 66 DT29
Hornbeams, St.Alb. 60 BZ30
Hornbeams, The, Harl. 35 EQ13
Hornbeams Ave., Enf. 82 DW35
Hornbeams Ri. N11 98 DG51
Hornbill Clo., Uxb. 134 BK72
Hornblower Clo. SE16 163 DY77
Greenland Quay
Hornbuckle Clo., Har. 117 CD61
Hornby Clo. NW3 140 DD66
Horncastle Clo. SE12 184 EG87
Horncastle Rd. SE12 184 EG87
Hornchurch Clo., Kings.T. 177 CK91
Hornchurch Hill, Whyt. 236 DT117
Hornchurch Rd., Horn. 127 FF60
Horndean Clo. SW15 179 CU88
Bessborough Rd.
Horndon Clo., Rom. 105 FC53
Horndon Grn., Rom. 105 FC53
Horndon Rd., Rom. 105 FC53
Horne Rd., Shep. 194 BM98
Horne Way SW15 159 CW82
Horner La., Mitch. 200 DD96
Hornets, The, Wat. 75 BV42
Hornfair Rd. SE7 164 EJ79
Hornford Way, Rom. 127 FE59
Hornhatch, Guil. 259 BB140
Hornhatch Clo., Guil. 259 BB140
Hornhatch La., Guil. 259 BA140
Hornhill Rd., Ger.Cr. 91 BB50
Hornhill Rd., Rick. 91 BD50
Horniman Dr. SE23 182 DV88
Horning Clo. SE9 184 EL91
Hornminster Glen, Horn. 128 FN61
Horns End, Pnr. 116 BW56
Horns Mill Rd., Hert. 32 DQ12
Horns Rd., Hert. 32 DQ10
Horns Rd., Ilf. 125 ER58
Hornsby La., Grays 171 GG75
Hornsey La. N6 121 DH60
Hornsey La. N19 121 DH60
Hornsey La. Est. N19 121 DK59
Hornsey La.
Hornsey La. Gdns. N6 121 DJ59
Hornsey Pk. Rd. N8 121 DM55
Hornsey Ri. N19 121 DK59
Hornsey Ri. Gdns. N19 121 DK59
Hornsey Rd. N7 121 DM62
Hornsey Rd. N19 121 DL60
Hornsey St. N7 121 DM64
Hornsfield, Welw.G.C. 30 DC08
Hornshay St. SE15 162 DW79
Hornton Pl. W8 160 DB75
Hornton St.
Hornton St. W8 160 DA75
Horsa Clo., Wall. 219 DL108
Kingsford Ave.
Horsa Rd. SE12 184 EJ87
Horsa Rd., Erith 167 FB80
Horse and Dolphin Yd. W1 273 N10
Horse Fair, Kings.T. 197 CK96
Wood St.
Horse Guards Ave. SW1 277 P3
Horse Guards Ave. SW1 141 DL74
Horse Guards Rd. SW1 277 N3
Horse Guards Rd. SW1 141 DK74
Horse Hill, Chesh. 56 AX32
Horse Leaze E6 145 EN72
Horse Ride SW1 277 M3
Horse Ride, Cars. 218 DF112
Horse Ride, Dor. 263 CD144
Wolvens La.
Horse Ride, Lthd. 245 BQ132
Epsom Rd.
Horse Rd. E7 124 EH62
Centre Rd.
Horse Shoe Cres., Nthlt. 136 CA68
Horse Shoe Yd. W1 273 J10
Horse Yd. N1 141 DP67
Essex Rd.
Horsebridges Clo., Dag. 146 EY67
Horsecroft, Bans. 233 CZ117
Lyme Regis Rd.
Horsecroft Clo., Orp. 206 EV102
Horsecroft Pl., Harl. 50 EL16
Horsecroft Rd., Edg. 96 CR52
Horsecroft Rd., Harl. 50 EL16
Horsecroft Rd., Hem.H. 40 BG22
Horseferry Pl. SE10 163 EC79
Horseferry Rd. E14 143 DX73
Horseferry Rd. SW1 277 M7
Horseferry Rd. SW1 161 DK77
Horsehill, Horl. 268 DA146
Horselers, Hem.H. 40 BN23
Horsell Birch, Wok. 226 AV115
Horsell Common, Wok. 210 AV114
Horsell Common Rd., Wok. 210 AW114
Horsell Ct., Cher. 194 BH101
Stepgates
Horsell Moor, Wok. 226 AX117
Horsell Pk., Wok. 226 AX116
Horsell Pk. Clo., Wok. 226 AX116
Horsell Ri., Wok. 226 AX115
Horsell Ri. Clo., Wok. 226 AX115
Horsell Rd. N5 121 DN64
Horsell Rd., Orp. 206 EV95
Horsell Vale, Wok. 226 AY115
Horsell Way, Wok. 226 AW116
Horselydown La. SE1 279 P4
Horselydown La. SE1 162 DT75
Horseman Side, Brwd. 105 FH46
Horsemans Ride, St.Alb. 60 CA25
Horsemoor Clo., Slou. 153 BA77
Parlaunt Rd.
Horsenden Ave., Grnf. 117 CE64
Horsenden Cres., Grnf. 117 CF64
Horsenden La. N., Grnf. 137 CF65
Horsenden La. S., Grnf. 137 CG67
Horseshoe, The, Bans. 233 CZ115
Horseshoe, The, Couls. 219 DK113
Horseshoe, The, Hem.H. 41 BQ22
Horseshoe Clo. E14 163 EC78
Ferry St.
Horseshoe Clo. NW2 119 CV61
Horseshoe Clo., Wal.Abb. 68 EG34
Horseshoe Cres., Beac. 89 AL54
Horseshoe Grn., Sutt. 200 DB103
Aultone Way
Horseshoe Hill, Slou. 110 AJ63
Horseshoe Hill, Wal.Abb. 68 EH33
Horseshoe La. N20 97 CX46
Horseshoe La., Enf. 82 DQ41
Chase Side
Horseshoe La., Wat. 59 BV32
Horseshoe La. E., Guil. 243 BB133
Horseshoe La. W., Guil. 243 BB133
Horseshoe Ridge, Wey. 213 BQ111
Horsfeld Gdns. SE9 184 EL85
Horsfeld Rd. SE9 184 EK85
Horsfield Clo., Dart. 188 FQ87

Horsford Rd. SW2 181 DM85
Horsham Ave. N12 98 DE50
Horsham Rd., Bexh. 186 FA86
Horsham Rd., Dor. 263 CG137
Horsham Rd. 263 CH140
(North Holmwood), Dor.
Horsham Rd. 261 BT142
(Sutton), Dor.
Horsham Rd., Felt. 175 BQ86
Horsham Rd., Guil. 258 AX142
Horsley Clo., Epsom 216 CR113
Horsley Dr., Croy. 221 EC108
Horsley Dr., Kings.T. 177 CK92
Horsley Rd. E4 101 EC47
Horsley Rd., Brom. 204 EH95
Palace Rd.
Horsley Rd., Cob. 229 BU122
Horsley St. SE17 162 DR79
Horsleys, Rick. 91 BD50
Horsmonden Clo., Orp. 205 ET101
Horsmonden Rd. SE4 183 DZ85
Hortensia Rd. SW10 160 DC80
Horticultural Pl. W4 158 CR78
Heathfield Ter.
Horton Ave. NW2 119 CY63
Horton Bri. Rd., West Dr. 134 BM74
Horton Clo., Maid. 130 AC70
Horton Clo., West Dr. 134 BM74
Horton Gdns., Epsom 216 CQ111
Horton Hill
Horton Hill, Epsom 216 CQ111
Horton Ind. Pk., West Dr. 134 BM74
Horton La., Epsom 216 CP109
Horton Rd. E8 142 DV65
Horton Rd. 208 FQ98
(Horton Kirby), Dart.
Horton Rd., Slou. 153 BA82
Horton Rd. (Datchet), Slou. 152 AV80
Horton Rd. (Poyle), Slou. 153 BE83
Horton Rd., Stai. 174 BG85
Horton Rd., West Dr. 134 BL74
Horton St. SE13 163 EB83
Horton Way, Croy. 203 DX99
Horton Way 208 FM101
(Farningham), Dart.
Hortons Way, West. 255 ER126
Hortus Rd. E4 101 EC47
Hortus Rd., Sthl. 156 BZ75
Horvath Clo., Wey. 213 BR105
Horwood Clo., Rick. 92 BG45
Thellusson Way
Horwood Ct., Wat. 76 BX37
Hosack Rd. SW17 180 DF88
Hoser Ave. SE12 184 EG89
Hosey Common Rd., 255 EQ133
Eden.
Hosey Common Rd., West. 255 ER130
Hosey Hill, West. 255 ER127
Hosier La. EC1 274 F7
Hosier La. EC1 141 DP71
Hoskins Clo. E16 144 EJ72
Hoskins Clo., Hayes 155 BT78
Cranford Dr.
Hoskins Rd., Oxt. 254 EE129
Hoskins St. SE10 163 ED78
Hoskins Wk., Oxt. 254 EE129
Hospital Bri. Rd., Twick. 176 CB87
Hospital Hill, Chesh. 54 AQ32
Hospital La., Islw. 177 CF85
Hospital Rd. E9 123 DX64
Homerton Row
Hospital Rd., Houns. 156 CA83
Hospital Rd., Sev. 257 FJ121
Hotham Clo. 188 FN94
(Sutton at Hone), Dart.
Hotham Clo., Swan. 207 FH95
Hotham Clo., W.Mol. 196 CA97
Garrick Gdns.
Hotham Rd. SW15 159 CW83
Hotham Rd. SW19 180 DC94
Hotham Rd. Ms. SW19 180 DC94
Haydons Rd.
Hotham St. E15 144 EE67
Hothfield Pl. SE16 162 DW76
Lower Rd.
Hotspur Rd., Nthlt. 136 CA68
Hotspur St. SE11 278 D10
Hotspur St. SE11 161 DN78
Houblon Rd., Rich. 178 CL85
Houblons Hill, Epp. 70 EW31
Houghton Clo. E8 142 DT65
Buttermere Wk.
Houghton Clo., Hmptn. 176 BY93
Houghton Rd. N15 122 DT57
West Grn. Rd.
Houghton St. WC2 274 C9
Houlder Cres., Croy. 219 DP107
Hound Ho. Rd., Guil. 260 BN141
Houndsden Rd. N21 81 DM44
Houndsditch EC3 275 N8
Houndsditch EC3 142 DS72
Houndsfield Rd. N9 100 DV45
Hounslow Ave., Houns. 176 CB85
Hounslow Gdns., Houns. 176 CB85
Hounslow Rd. 175 BV88
(Feltham), Felt.
Hounslow Rd. 176 BX91
(Hanworth), Felt.
Hounslow Rd., Twick. 176 CB86
House La., St.Alb. 43 CK16
Housefield Way, St.Alb. 43 CJ23
Houseman Way SE5 162 DR80
Hopewell St.
Housewood End, Hem.H. 40 BH17
Houston Pl., Esher 197 CE102
Lime Tree Ave.
Houston Rd. SE23 183 DY89
Hove Ave. E17 123 DZ57
Hove Clo., Brwd. 109 GC47
Hove Gdns., Sutt. 200 DB102
Hoveden Rd. NW2 119 CY64
Hoveton Rd. SE28 146 EW72
How La., Couls. 234 DF119
How Wd., St.Alb. 60 CB28
Howard Agne Clo., Hem.H. 57 BA27
Howard Ave., Bex. 186 EW88
Howard Ave., Epsom 217 CU110
Howard Ave., Slou. 131 AR71
Howard Business Pk., 67 ED33
Wal.Abb.
Howard Clo.
Howard Clo. N11 98 DG47
Howard Clo. NW2 119 CY63
Howard Clo. W3 138 CP72
Howard Clo., Ash. 232 CM118
Howard Clo., Hmptn. 176 CC93
Howard Clo., Lthd. 231 CJ123
Windmill Dr.
Howard Clo. 245 BR125
(West Horsley), Lthd.
Howard Clo., Loug. 84 EL44
Howard Clo., St.Alb. 43 CH22
Howard Clo., Sun. 175 BT93
Catherine Dr.
Howard Clo., Tad. 249 CT125
Howard Clo., Wal.Abb. 67 ED33
Howard Clo., Wat. 75 BU37
Howard Clo. (Bushey), Wat. 95 CE45
Howard Cres., Beac. 89 AQ50
Howard Dr., Borwd. 78 CR42
Howard Gdns., Guil. 243 BA133
Howard Ms. N5 121 DP63
Hamilton Pk.
Howard Pl. SW1 277 K7
Howard Ridge, Guil. 243 BA130
Howard Rd. E6 145 EM68
Howard Rd. E11 124 EE62
Howard Rd. E17 123 EA55
Howard Rd. N15 122 DS58
Howard Rd. N16 122 DR63
Howard Rd. NW2 119 CX63
Howard Rd. SE20 202 DW95
Howard Rd. SE25 202 DU99
Howard Rd., Bark. 145 ER67
Howard Rd., Beac. 89 AQ50
Howard Rd., Brom. 184 EG94
Howard Rd., Chesh. 54 AP28
Howard Rd., Couls. 235 DJ115
Howard Rd., Dart. 188 FN86
Howard Rd., Dor. 263 CG136
Howard Rd. (North 263 CJ140
Holmwood), Dor.
Holmesdale Rd.
Howard Rd., Grays 169 FW76
Howard Rd., Ilf. 125 EP63
Howard Rd., Islw. 157 CF83
Howard Rd., Lthd. 229 BU122
Howard Rd. (Great 246 CB127
Bookham), Lthd.
Howard Rd., N.Mal. 198 CS97
Howard Rd., Reig. 266 DB135
Howard Rd., Sthl. 136 CB72
Howard Rd., Surb. 198 CM100
Howard Rd., Upmin. 128 FQ61
Howard St., T.Ditt. 197 CH101
Howard Wk. N2 120 DC56
Howard Way, Barn. 79 CX43
Howard Way, Harl. 35 ET12
Howards Clo., Pnr. 93 BV54
Howards Clo., Wok. 227 BA120
Howards Crest Clo., Beck. 203 EC96
Howards Dr., Hem.H. 39 BF17
Howards La. SW15 179 CV85
Howards La., Add. 211 BE107
Howards Rd. E13 144 EG69
Howards Rd., Wok. 227 AZ120
Howards Thicket, Ger.Cr. 112 AW61
Howards Wd. Dr., Ger.Cr. 112 AX61
Howardsgate, Welw.G.C. 29 CX08
Howarth Ct. E15 123 EC64
Taylor Ct.
Howarth Rd. SE2 166 EU78
Howberry Clo., Edg. 95 CK51
Howberry Rd., Edg. 95 CK51
Howberry Rd., Stan. 95 CK51
Howberry Rd., Th.Hth. 202 DR95
Howbury La., Erith 167 FG82
Howbury Rd. SE15 162 DW83
Howcroft Cres. N3 98 DA52
Howcroft La., Grnf. 137 CD69
Cowgate Rd.
Howden Clo. SE28 146 EX73
Howden Rd. SE25 202 DT96
Howden St. SE15 162 DU83
Howe Clo., Rad. 62 CL32
Howe Clo., Rom. 104 FA53
Howe Dell, Hat. 45 CV18
Howe Dr., Beac. 89 AK50
Howe Dr., Cat. 236 DR122
York Gate
Howe Rd., Hem.H. 40 BN22
Howell Clo., Rom. 126 EX57
Howell Hill Clo., Epsom 217 CW111
Howell Hill Gro., Epsom 217 CW110
Howell Wk. SE1 278 G9
Howes Clo. N3 120 DA55
Howfield Grn., Hodd. 33 DZ14
Howgate Rd. SW14 158 CR83
Howick Pl. SW1 277 L7
Howick Pl. SW1 161 DJ76
Howicks Grn., Welw.G.C. 30 DA12
Howie St. SW11 160 DE80
Howitt Rd. NW3 140 DE65
Howland Est. SE16 162 DW76
Lower Rd.
Howland Garth, St.Alb. 42 CC24
Howland Ms. E. W1 273 L6
Howland St. W1 273 K6
Howland St. W1 141 DJ71
Howland Way SE16 163 DY75
Howlands, Welw.G.C. 29 CX12
Howletts La., Ruis. 115 BQ57
Howletts Rd. SE24 182 DQ86
Howley Pl. W2 140 DC71
Howley Rd., Croy. 201 DP104
Hows Clo., Uxb. 134 BJ67
Hows Rd.
Hows Mead, Epp. 53 FD24
Hows Rd., Uxb. 134 BJ67
Hows St. E2 142 DT68
Howsman Rd. SW13 159 CU79
Howson Rd. SE4 163 DY84
Howson Ter., Rich. 178 CL86
Howton Pl. (Bushey), Wat. 95 CD46
Hoxton Mkt. N1 275 M3
Hoxton Sq. N1 275 M3
Hoxton Sq. N1 142 DS69
Hoxton St. N1 142 DS67
Hoy St. E16 144 EF72
Hoy Ter., Grays 169 FX78
Hoylake Cres., Uxb. 114 BN61
Hoylake Gdns., Mitch. 201 DJ97
Hoylake Gdns., Rom. 106 FN52
Hoylake Gdns., Ruis. 115 BV60
Hoylake Gdns., Wat. 94 BX49
Hoylake Rd. W3 138 CS72
Hoyland Clo. SE15 162 DV80
Commercial Way
Hoyle Rd. SW17 180 DE92
Hubbard Dr., Chess. 215 CJ107
Hubbard Rd. SE27 182 DQ91
Hubbard St. E15 144 EE67
Hubbards Chase, Horn. 128 FN57
Hubbards Clo., Horn. 128 FN57
Hubbard's Hill, Sev. 257 FH130
Hubbards Rd., Rick. 73 BD43
Hubbinet Ind. Est., Rom. 127 FC55
Hubert Day Clo., Beac. 89 AK52
Seeleys Rd.
Hubert Gro. SW9 161 DL83
Hubert Rd. E6 144 EK69
Hubert Rd., Brwd. 108 FV48
Hubert Rd., Rain. 147 FF69
Hubert Rd., Slou. 152 AX76
Hubert Rd. Ind. Est., Brwd. 108 FV48
Hucknall Clo., Rom. 106 FM51
Huddart St. E3 143 DZ71
Huddleston Clo. E2 142 DW68
Huddleston Rd. N7 121 DJ62
Huddlestone Cres., Red. 251 DK128
Huddlestone Rd. E7 124 EF63
Huddlestone Rd. NW2 139 CV65
Hudson Ave., Uxb. 113 BF58
Hudson Clo., St.Alb. 43 CD22
Hudson Clo., Wat. 75 BT36
Hudson Ct. SW19 180 DB94
Hudson Ct., Guil. 242 AT133
Cobbett Rd.
Hudson Gdns., Orp. 223 ET107
Superior Dr.
Hudson Pl. SE18 165 EQ78
Hudson Rd., Bexh. 166 EZ82
Hudson Rd., Hayes 155 BR79
Hudsons, Tad. 233 CX121
Hudson's Pl. SW1 277 K8
Huggin Ct. EC4 275 J10
Huggin Hill EC4 275 J10
Huggins La., Hat. 45 CW23
Huggins Pl. SW2 181 DM88
Roupell Rd.
Hugh Dalton Ave. SW6 159 CZ79
Rylston Rd.
Hugh Gaitskell Clo. SW6 159 CZ79
Rylston Rd.
Hugh Ms. SW1 277 J9
Hugh Pl. SW1 277 M8
Hugh St. SW1 277 J9
Hugh St. SW1 161 DH77
Hughan Rd. E15 123 ED64
Hughenden Ave., Har. 117 CH57
Hughenden Gdns., Nthlt. 136 BW69
Hughenden Rd., St.Alb. 43 CH17
Hughenden Rd., Slou. 131 AR72
Hughenden Rd., Wor.Pk. 199 CU101
Hughendon Ter. E15 123 EC63
Westdown Rd.
Hughes Rd., Ashf. 175 BQ94
Hughes Rd., Grays 171 GG76
Hughes Rd., Hayes 135 BU73
Hughes Wk., Croy. 202 DQ101
St. Saviours Rd.
Hugh's Twr., Harl. 35 ER14
Hugo Gdns., Rain. 147 FF65
Hugo Rd. N19 121 DJ63
Hugon Rd. SW6 160 DB83
Huguenot Pl. E1 142 DT71
Huguenot Pl. SW18 180 DC85
Huguenot Sq. SE15 162 DV83
Scylla Rd.
Hull Clo. SE16 163 DX75
Hull Clo., Slou. 151 AQ75
Hull Clo., Sutt. 218 DB110
Yardbridge Clo.
Hull Gro., Harl. 51 EN20
Hull St. EC1 275 H3
Hullbridge Ms. N1 142 DR67
Sherborne St.
Hulletts La., Brwd. 108 FT43
Hulse Ave., Bark. 145 ER65
Hulse Ave., Rom. 105 FB53
Hulse Ter., Ilf. 125 EQ64
Loxford La.
Hulsewood Clo., Dart. 187 FH90
Hulton Clo., Lthd. 231 CJ123
Windmill Dr.
Hulverston Clo., Sutt. 218 DB110
Humber Ave., S.Ock. 149 FT72
Humber Dr. W10 139 CX70
Humber Dr., Upmin. 129 FR58
Humber Rd. NW2 119 CV61
Humber Rd. SE3 164 EF79
Humber Rd., Dart. 188 FK85
Humber Way, Slou. 153 BA77
Humberstone Rd. E13 144 EJ69
Humberton Clo. E9 123 DY64
Marsh Hill
Humbolt Clo., Guil. 242 AS134
Humbolt Rd. W6 159 CY79
Hume Ave., Til. 171 GG83
Hume Ter. E16 144 EJ72
Prince Regent La.
Hume Way, Ruis. 115 BU58
Humes Ave. W7 157 CE76
Hummer Rd., Egh. 173 BA91
Humphrey Clo., Ilf. 103 EM53
Humphrey Clo., Lthd. 230 CC122
Humphrey St. SE1 279 P10
Humphrey St. SE1 162 DT78
Humphries Clo., Dag. 126 EZ63
Hundred Acre NW9 97 CT54
Hundred Acres La., Amer. 55 AR40
Hungerdown E4 101 EC46
Hungerford Ave., Slou. 132 AS71
Hungerford Bri. SE1 278 B3
Hungerford Bri. SE1 141 DM74
Hungerford Bri. WC2 278 B3
Hungerford Bri. WC2 141 DM74
Hungerford La. WC2 278 A2
Hungerford Rd. N7 141 DK65
Hungerford Sq., Wey. 213 BR105
Rosslyn Pk.
Hungerford St. E1 142 DV72
Commercial Rd.
Hungry Hill, Wok. 228 BK124
Hungry Hill La.
Hungry Hill La., Wok. 228 BK124
Hunsdon, Welw.G.C. 30 DD09
Hunsdon Clo., Dag. 146 EY65
Hunsdon Dr., Sev. 257 FH123
Hunsdon Rd. SE14 163 DX80
Hunsdon Rd. 33 ED11
(Stanstead Abbotts), Ware
Hunslett St. E2 142 DW68
Royston St.
Hunston Rd., Mord. 200 DB102
Hunt Clo., St.Alb. 43 CK17
Villiers Cres.
Hunt Rd., Grav. 190 GE90
Hunt Rd., Sthl. 156 CA76
Hunt St. W11 139 CX74
Hunt Way SE22 182 DU88
Dulwich Common
Hunter Ave., Brwd. 109 GA44
Hunter Clo. SE1 279 L7
Hunter Clo. SW12 180 DG88
Balham Pk. Rd.
Hunter Clo., Borwd. 78 CQ43
Hunter Clo., Pot.B. 64 DB33
Hunter Dr., Horn. 128 FJ63
Hunter Ho., Felt. 175 BU88
Hunter Rd. SW20 199 CW95
Hunter Rd., Guil. 258 AY135
Hunter Rd., Ilf. 125 EP64
Hunter Rd., Th.Hth. 202 DR97
Hunter St. WC1 274 A4
Hunter St. WC1 141 DL70
Hunter Wk. E13 144 EG67
Stratford Rd.
Hunter Wk., Borwd. 78 CQ43
Ashley Dr.
Huntercombe Clo., Maid. 130 AH72
Huntercombe La., Slou. 130 AJ71
Huntercombe La. N., Maid. 130 AJ72
Huntercombe La. S., Maid. 130 AH74
Huntercombe Spur, Slou. 130 AJ73
Huntercrombe Gdns., Wat. 94 BW50
Hunters, The, Beck. 203 EC95
Hunters Clo., Bex. 187 FE90
Hunters Clo., Chesh. 54 AN30
Hunters Clo., Epsom 216 CQ113
Marshalls Clo.
Hunters Clo., Hem.H. 57 BA29
Hunters Ct., Rich. 177 CK85
Friars La.
Hunters Gro., Har. 117 CJ56
Hunters Gro., Hayes 135 BU74
Hunters Gro., Orp. 223 EP105
Hunters Gro., Rom. 105 FB50
Hunters Hall Rd., Dag. 126 FA63
Hunters Hill, Ruis. 116 BW62
Hunters La., Wat. 59 BT33
Hunters Meadow SE19 182 DS91
Dulwich Wd. Ave.
Hunters Oak, Hem.H. 41 BP15
Hunters Pk., Berk. 38 AY18
Hunters Reach, Wal.Cr. 66 DT29
Hunters Ride, St.Alb. 60 CA31
Hunters Rd., Chess. 198 CL104
Hunters Sq., Dag. 126 FA63
Hunters Wk., Sev. 224 EY114
Hunters Way, Croy. 220 DS105
Brownlow Rd.
Hunters Way, Enf. 81 DN39
Hunters Way, Welw.G.C. 29 CZ12
Huntersfield Clo., Reig. 250 DB131
Hunting Clo., Esher 214 CA105
Hunting Gate, Hem.H. 40 BL16
Hunting Gate Clo., Enf. 81 DN41
Hunting Gate Dr., Chess. 216 CL108
Hunting Gate Ms., Sutt. 200 DB104
Hunting Gate Ms., Twick. 177 CE88
Colne Rd.
Huntingdon Clo., Brox. 49 DY24
Huntingdon Clo., Mitch. 201 DL98
Huntingdon Gdns. W4 158 CQ80
Huntingdon Gdns., Wor.Pk. 199 CW104
Huntingdon Rd. N2 120 DE55
Huntingdon Rd. N9 100 DW46
Huntingdon Rd., Red. 250 DF134
Huntingdon Rd., Wok. 226 AT117
Huntingdon St. E16 144 EF72
Huntingdon St. N1 141 DM66
Huntingfield, Croy. 221 DZ108
Huntingfield Rd. SW15 159 CU84
Huntingfield Way, Egh. 173 BD93
Huntings Rd., Dag. 146 FA65
Huntland Clo., Rain. 147 FH71
Huntley Ave., Grav. 190 GB86
Huntley Dr. N3 98 DA51
Huntley St. WC1 273 L5
Huntley St. WC1 141 DJ70
Huntley Way SW20 199 CU96
Huntly Rd. SE25 202 DS98
Hunton Bri. Hill, Kings L. 59 BQ33
Hunton Bri. Ind. Est., 59 BQ33
Kings L.
Hunton St. E1 142 DU71
Hunt's Clo. SE3 164 EG82
Hunt's Ct. WC2 277 N1
Hunts La. E15 143 EC68
Hunts La., Maid. 130 AE68
Hunts Mead, Enf. 83 DX41
Hunts Mead Clo., Chis. 185 EM94
Hunts Slip Rd. SE21 182 DS90
Huntsman Clo., Warl. 236 DW119
Huntsman Rd., Ilf. 104 EU51
Huntsman St. SE17 279 L9
Huntsman St. SE17 162 DS77
Huntsmans Clo., Felt. 175 BV91
Huntsmans Clo., Lthd. 231 CD124
The Grn.
Huntsmans Dr., Upmin. 128 FQ64
Huntsmill Rd., Hem.H. 39 BE21
Huntsmoor Rd., Epsom 216 CR106
Huntspill St. SW17 180 DC90
Huntswood La., Maid. 130 AE66
Huntsworth La., Slou. 130 AF67
Huntsworth Ms. NW1 272 D5
Hurley Clo., Walt. 195 BV103
Hurley Cres. SE16 163 DX75
Marlow Way
Hurley Gdns., Guil. 243 BA130
Hurley Rd., Grnf. 136 CB72
Hurlfield, Dart. 188 FJ90
Hurlford, Wok. 226 AU117
Hurlingham Ct. SW6 159 CZ83
Hurlingham Gdns. SW6 159 CZ83
Hurlingham Rd. SW6 159 CZ82
Hurlingham Rd., Bexh. 166 EZ80
Hurlingham Sq. SW6 160 DB83
Peterborough Rd.
Hurlock St. N5 121 DP62
Hurlstone Rd. SE25 202 DR99
Hurn Ct. Rd., Houns. 156 BX82
Renfrew Rd.
Hurnford Clo., S.Croy. 220 DS110
Huron Clo., Orp. 223 ET107
Winnipeg Dr.
Huron Rd. SW17 180 DG89
Hurren Clo. SE3 164 EE83
Hurricane Way, Abb.L. 59 BU32
Abbey Dr.
Hurricane Way, Epp. 70 FA27
Hurry Clo. E15 144 EE66
Hursley Rd., Chig. 103 ET50
Tufter Rd.
Hurst Ave. E4 101 EA49
Hurst Ave. N6 121 DJ58
Hurst Clo. E4 101 EA48
Hurst Clo. NW11 120 DB58
Hurst Clo., Brom. 204 EF102
Hurst Clo., Chess. 216 CN106
Hurst Clo., Nthlt. 136 BZ65
Hurst Clo., Welw.G.C. 30 DC10
Hurst Clo., Wok. 226 AW120
Hurst Cft., Guil. 258 AY137
Hurst Dr., Tad. 249 CU126
Hurst Dr., Wal.Cr. 67 DX34
Hurst Est. SE2 166 EX78
Hurst Grn. Clo., Oxt. 254 EG132
Hurst Grn. Rd., Oxt. 254 EF132
Hurst Gro., Walt. 195 BT102
Hurst La. SE2 166 EX78
Hurst La., E.Mol. 196 CC98
Hurst La., Egh. 193 BA96
Hurst La., Epsom 232 CQ124
Hurst Pk. Ave., Horn. 128 FL63
Newmarket Way
Hurst Pl., Nthwd. 93 BP53
Hurst Ri., Barn. 80 DA41
Hurst Rd. E17 123 EB55
Hurst Rd. N21 99 DN46
Hurst Rd., Bex. 186 EW88
Hurst Rd., Buck.H. 102 EK46
Hurst Rd., Croy. 220 DR106
Hurst Rd., E.Mol. 196 CA97
Hurst Rd., Epsom 216 CR111
Hurst Rd. 232 CR123
(Headley), Epsom
Hurst Rd., Erith 167 FC81
Hurst Rd., Horl. 268 DE147
Hurst Rd., Sid. 186 EU89
Hurst Rd., Slou. 131 AK71
Hurst Rd., Tad. 233 CU123
Hurst Rd., Walt. 196 BW99
Hurst Rd., W.Mol. 196 CA97
Hurst Springs, Bex. 186 EY88
Hurst St. SE24 181 DP86
Hurst Vw. Rd., S.Croy. 220 DS108
Hurst Way, Sev. 257 FJ127
Hurst Way, S.Croy. 220 DS107
Hurst Way, Wok. 211 BE114
Hurstbourne, Esher 215 CF107
Hurstbourne Gdns., Bark. 145 ES65
Hurstbourne Rd. SE23 183 DY88
Hurstcourt Rd., Sutt. 200 DB102
Hurstdene Ave., Brom. 204 EF102
Hurstdene Ave., Stai. 174 BH93
Hurstdene Gdns. N15 122 DS59
Hurstfield, Brom. 204 EG99
Hurstfield Cres., Hayes 135 BS70
Hurstfield Dr., Maid. 130 AH72
Hurstfield Rd., W.Mol. 196 CA97
Hurstlands, Oxt. 254 EG132
Hurstlands Clo., Horn. 128 FJ59
Hurstleigh Clo., Red. 250 DF132
Hurstleigh Dr., Red. 250 DF132
Hurstleigh Gdns., Ilf. 103 EM53
Hurstlings, Welw.G.C. 30 DB10
Hurstmead Ct., Edg. 96 CP49
Hurstway Wk. W11 139 CX73
Whitchurch Rd.
Hurstwood Ave. E18 124 EH56
Hurstwood Ave., Bex. 186 EY88
Hurstwood Ave., Bexh. 167 FE81
Hurstwood Ave., Brwd. 108 FV45
Ongar Rd.
Hurstwood Ave., Erith 167 FE81
Hurstwood Ct., Upmin. 128 FP60
Hurstwood Dr., Brom. 205 EM97
Hurstwood Rd. NW11 119 CY56
Hurtwood Rd., Walt. 196 BZ101
Hurworth Rd., Slou. 152 AW76
Huson Clo. NW3 140 DE66
Hussars Clo., Houns. 156 BY83
Husseywell Cres., Brom. 204 EG102
Hutchings Clo., Horn. 128 FL62
Hutchings Rd., Beac. 89 AK50
Hutchings St. E14 163 EA75
Hutchings Wk. NW11 120 DB56
Hutchingsons Rd., Croy. 221 EC111
Hutchins Clo. E15 143 EC66
Gibbins Rd.
Hutchins Way, Horl. 268 DF146
Hutchinson Ter., Wem. 117 CK62
Hutton Clo., Grnf. 117 CD64
Mary Peters Dr.
Hutton Clo., Hert. 31 DN09
Hutton Clo., Wdf.Grn. 102 EH51
Hutton Dr., Brwd. 109 GC45
Hutton Gdns., Har. 94 CC52
Hutton Wk.
Hutton Gate, Brwd. 109 GB45
Hutton Gro. N12 98 DB50
Hutton Ind. Est., Brwd. 109 GE43
Hutton La., Har. 94 CC52
Hutton Rd., Brwd. 109 FZ45
Hutton Row, Edg. 96 CQ52
Pavilion Way
Hutton St. EC4 274 E9
Hutton Village, Brwd. 109 GE44
Hutton Wk., Har. 94 CC52
Huxbear St. SE4 183 DZ85
Huxley Clo., Nthlt. 136 BY67
Huxley Clo., Uxb. 134 BK70
Huxley Dr., Rom. 126 EV59
Huxley Gdns. NW10 138 CM69
Huxley Par. N18 100 DQ50
Huxley Pl. N13 99 DP48
Huxley Rd. E10 123 EC61
Huxley Rd. N18 100 DR49
Huxley Rd., Well. 165 ET83
Huxley Sayze N18 100 DQ50
Huxley St. W10 139 CY69
Hyacinth Clo., Hmptn. 176 CA93
Gresham Rd.
Hyacinth Ct., Pnr. 116 BW55
Tulip Ct.
Hyacinth Dr., Uxb. 134 BL66
Hyacinth Rd. SW15 179 CU88

Hyburn Clo., Hem.H. 41 BP21
Hyburn Clo., St.Alb. 60 BZ30
Hycliffe Gdns., Chig. 103 EQ49
Hyde, The NW9 118 CS56
Hyde, The, Ware 32 DV05
Hyde Ave., Pot.B. 64 DB33
Hyde Clo. E13 144 EG68
Pelly Rd.
Hyde Clo., Ashf. 175 BS93
Hyde Ter.
Hyde Clo., Barn. 79 CZ41
Hyde Ct. N20 98 DD48
Hyde Cres. NW9 118 CS57
Hyde Dr., Orp. 206 EV98
Hyde Grn., Beac. 89 AM52
Hyde Ho. NW9 118 CS57
The Hyde
Hyde La. SW11 160 DE81
Battersea Bri. Rd.
Hyde La., Hem.H. 58 BN27
Hyde La. (Bovingdon), Hem.H. 57 AZ27
Hyde La., St.Alb. 61 CE28
Hyde La., Wok. 228 BN120
Hyde Mead, Wal.Abb. 50 EE23
Hyde Meadows, Hem.H. 57 BA28
Hyde Pk. SW7 276 B2
Hyde Pk. SW7 140 DE74
Hyde Pk. W1 276 B2
Hyde Pk. W1 140 DE74
Hyde Pk. W2 276 B2
Hyde Pk. W2 140 DE74
Hyde Pk. Ave. N21 100 DQ47
Hyde Pk. Cor. W1 276 G4
Hyde Pk. Cor. W1 160 DG75
Hyde Pk. Cres. W2 272 B9
Hyde Pk. Cres. W2 140 DE72
Hyde Pk. Gdns. N21 100 DQ46
Hyde Pk. Gdns. W2 272 A10
Hyde Pk. Gdns. W2 140 DD73
Hyde Pk. Gdns. Ms. W2 272 A10
Hyde Pk. Gate SW7 160 DC75
Hyde Pk. Gate Ms. SW7 160 DC75
Hyde Pk. Gate
Hyde Pk. Pl. W2 272 C10
Hyde Pk. Sq. W2 272 B9
Hyde Pk. Sq. W2 140 DE72
Hyde Pk. Sq. Ms. W2 272 B9
Hyde Pk. St. W2 272 B9
Hyde Pk. St. W2 140 DE72
Hyde Rd. N1 142 DS67
Hyde Rd., Bexh. 166 EZ82
Hyde Rd., Rich. 178 CM85
Albert Rd.
Hyde Rd., S.Croy. 220 DR113
Hyde Rd., Wat. 75 BU40
Hyde St. SE8 163 EA79
Deptford High St.
Hyde Ter., Ashf. 175 BS93
Hyde Vale SE10 163 ED81
Hyde Valley, Welw.G.C. 29 CZ11
Hyde Wk., Mord. 200 DA101
Glastonbury Rd.
Hyde Way N9 100 DT47
Hyde Way, Hayes 155 BT77
Hyde Way, Welw.G.C. 29 CY09
Hydefield Clo. N21 100 DR46
Hydefield Ct. N9 100 DS47
Hyder Rd., Grays 171 GJ76
Hyderabad Way E15 144 EE66
Hydes Pl. N1 141 DP66
Compton Ave.
Hydeside Gdns. N9 100 DT47
Hydethorpe Ave. N9 100 DT47
Hydethorpe Rd. SW12 181 DJ88
Hyland Clo., Horn. 127 FH59
Hyland Way, Horn. 127 FH59
Hylands Clo., Epsom 232 CQ115
Hylands Ms., Epsom 232 CQ115
Hylands Rd. E17 101 ED54
Hylands Rd., Epsom 232 CQ115
Hylle Clo., Wind. 151 AL81
Hylton St. SE18 165 ET77
Hyndewood SE23 183 DX90
Hyndman St. SE15 162 DV79
Hynton Rd., Dag. 126 EW61
Hyperion Ct., Hem.H. 40 BM17
Saturn Way
Hyperion Pl., Epsom 216 CR109
Hyperion Wk., Horl. 269 DH150
Hyrons Clo., Amer. 55 AS38
Hyrons La., Amer. 55 AR38
Hyrstdene, S.Croy. 219 DP105
Hyson Rd. SE16 162 DV77
Galleywall Rd.
Hythe, The, Stai. 173 BE92
Hythe Ave., Bexh. 166 EY80
Hythe Clo. N18 100 DU49
Hythe Clo., Orp. 206 EW98
Sandway Rd.
Hythe End Rd., Stai. 173 AZ89
Hythe Fld. Ave., Egh. 173 BD93
Hythe Pk. Rd., Egh. 173 BC92
Hythe Path, Th.Hth. 202 DR97
Buller Rd.
Hythe Rd. NW10 139 CU70
Hythe Rd., Stai. 173 BD92
Hythe Rd., Th.Hth. 202 DR96
Hythe St., Dart. 188 FL86
Hythe St. Lwr., Dart. 188 FL85
Hyver Hill NW7 78 CR44

I

Ian Sq., Enf. 83 DX39
Lansbury Rd.
Ibbetson Path, Loug. 85 EP41
Ibbotson Ave. E16 144 EF72
Ibbott St. E1 142 DW70
Mantus Rd.
Iberian Ave., Wall. 219 DK105
Ibis La. W4 158 CQ81
Ibis Way, Hayes 136 BX72
Cygnet Way
Ibscott Clo., Dag. 147 FC65
Ibsley Gdns. SW15 179 CU88
Ibsley Way, Barn. 80 DE43
Icehouse Wd., Oxt. 254 EE131
Iceland Rd. E3 143 EA67
Ickburgh Est. E5 122 DV62
Ickburgh Rd.
Ickburgh Rd. E5 122 DV62
Ickenham Clo., Ruis. 115 BR61
Ickenham Rd., Ruis. 115 BQ61
Ickenham Rd., Uxb. 115 BQ61
Ickleton Rd. SE9 184 EL91
Icklingham Gate, Cob. 214 BW112
Icklingham Rd.
Icklingham Rd., Cob. 214 BW112
Icknield Clo., St.Alb. 42 BZ22
Icknield Dr., Ilf. 125 EP57
Ickworth Pk. Rd. E17 123 DY56
Ida Rd. N15 122 DR57
Ida St. E14 143 EC72
Iden Clo., Brom. 204 EE97
Idlecombe Rd. SW17 180 DG93
Idmiston Rd. E15 124 EF64
Idmiston Rd. SE27 182 DQ90
Idmiston Rd., Wor.Pk. 199 CT101
Idmiston Sq., Wor.Pk. 199 CT102
Idol La. EC3 279 M1
Idonia St. SE8 163 EA80
Iffley Clo., Uxb. 134 BK66
Iffley Rd. W6 159 CV76
Ifield Clo., Red. 266 DE137
Ifield Rd. SW10 160 DB79
Ifield Way, Grav. 191 GK93
Ifold Rd., Red. 266 DG136
Ifor Evans Pl. E1 143 DX70
Mile End Rd.
Ightham Rd., Erith 166 FA80
Ikea Twr. NW10 118 CR64
Ikona Ct., Wey. 213 BQ106
Ilbert St. W10 139 CX69
Ilchester Gdns. W2 140 DB73
Ilchester Pl. W14 159 CZ76
Ilchester Rd., Dag. 126 EV64
Ildersly Gro. SE21 182 DR89
Ilderton Rd. SE15 162 DW80
Ilderton Rd. SE16 162 DV78
Ilex Clo., Egh. 172 AV94
Ilex Clo., Sun. 196 BW96
Oakington Dr.
Ilex Ct., Berk. 38 AV19
Ilex Ho. N4 121 DM59
Ilex Rd. NW10 139 CT65
Ilex Way SW16 181 DN92
Ilford Hill, Ilf. 125 EN62
Ilford La., Ilf. 125 EP62
Ilfracombe Cres., Horn. 128 FJ63
Ilfracombe Gdns., Rom. 126 EV59
Ilfracombe Rd., Brom. 184 EF90
Iliffe St. SE17 278 G10
Iliffe St. SE17 161 DP78
Iliffe Yd. SE17 278 G10
Ilkeston Ct. E5 123 DX63
Overbury St.
Ilkley Clo. SE19 182 DR93
Ilkley Rd. E16 144 EJ71
Ilkley Rd., Wat. 94 BX50
Illingworth, Wind. 151 AL83
Illingworth Clo., Mitch. 200 DD97
Illingworth Way, Enf. 82 DS42
Ilmington Rd., Har. 117 CK58
Ilminster Gdns. SW11 160 DE84
Imber Clo. N14 99 DJ45
Imber Clo., Esher 197 CD102
Ember La.
Imber Ct. Ind. Est., E.Mol. 197 CD100
Imber Gro., Esher 197 CD101
Imber Pk. Rd., Esher 197 CD102
Imber St. N1 142 DR67
Imer Pl., T.Ditt. 197 CF101
Imperial Ave. N16 122 DT62
Victorian Rd.
Imperial Business & Retail Pk., Grav. 191 GF86
Imperial Clo., Har. 116 CA58
Imperial College Rd. SW7 160 DD76
Imperial Cres., Wey. 195 BQ104
Churchill Dr.
Imperial Dr., Grav. 191 GM92
Imperial Dr., Har. 116 CA59
Imperial Gdns., Mitch. 201 DH97
Imperial Ms. E6 144 EJ68
Central Pk. Rd.
Imperial Rd. N22 99 DL53
Imperial Rd. SW6 160 DB81
Imperial Rd., Felt. 175 BS87
Imperial Rd., Wind. 151 AN83
Imperial Sq. SW6 160 DB81
Imperial St. E3 143 EC69
Imperial Way, Chis. 185 EQ90
Imperial Way, Croy. 219 DN107
Imperial Way, Har. 118 CL58
Imperial Way, Wat. 76 BW39
Inca Dr. SE9 185 EP87
Ince Rd., Walt. 213 BS108
Inchmery Rd. SE6 183 EB89
Inchwood, Croy. 221 EB105
Indells, Hat. 45 CT19
Independent Pl. E8 122 DT64
Downs Pk. Rd.
Independents Rd. SE3 164 EF83
Blackheath Village
Inderwick Rd. N8 121 DM57
Indescon Ct. E14 163 EA75
India Pl. WC2 274 B10
India Rd., Slou. 152 AV75
India St. EC3 275 P9
India Way W12 139 CV73
Indus Rd. SE7 164 EJ80
Industry Ter. SW9 161 DN83
Canterbury Cres.
Ingal Rd. E13 144 EG70
Ingate Pl. SW8 161 DH81
Ingatestone Rd. E12 124 EJ60
Ingatestone Rd. SE25 202 DV99
Ingatestone Rd., Wdf.Grn. 102 EH52
Ingelow Rd. SW8 161 DH82
Ingels Mead, Epp. 69 ET29
Ingersoll Rd. W12 139 CV74
Ingersoll Rd., Enf. 82 DW38
Ingestre Pl. W1 273 L9
Ingestre Rd. E7 124 EG63
Ingestre Rd. NW5 121 DH63
Ingham Clo., S.Croy. 221 DX109
Ingham Rd. NW6 120 DA63
Ingham Rd., S.Croy. 220 DW109
Ingle Clo., Pnr. 116 BZ55
Inglebert St. EC1 274 D2
Ingleboro Dr., Pur. 220 DQ113
Ingleborough St. SW9 161 DN82
Ingleby Clo., Dag. 147 FB65
Ingleby Dr., Har. 117 CD62
Ingleby Gdns., Chig. 104 EV48
Ingleby Rd. N7 121 DL62
Ingleby Rd., Dag. 147 FB65
Ingleby Rd., Grays 171 GH76
Ingleby Rd., Ilf. 125 EP60
Ingleby Way, Chis. 185 EN92
Ingleby Way, Wall. 219 DJ109
Ingledew Rd. SE18 165 ER78
Inglefield, Pot.B. 64 DA30
Ingleglen, Horn. 128 FN59
Ingleglen, Slou. 111 AP64
Inglehurst, Add. 212 BH110
Inglehurst Gdns., Ilf. 125 EM57
Inglemere Rd. SE23 183 DX90
Inglemere Rd., Mitch. 180 DF94
Ingles, Welw.G.C. 29 CX06
Inglesham Wk. E9 143 DZ65
Beanacre Clo.
Ingleside, Slou. 153 BE81
Ingleside Clo., Beck. 183 EA94
Ingleside Gro. SE3 164 EF79
Inglethorpe St. SW6 159 CX81
Ingleton Ave., Well. 186 EU85
Ingleton Rd. N18 100 DU51
Ingleton Rd., Cars. 218 DE109
Ingleton St. SW9 161 DN82
Ingleway N12 98 DD51
Inglewood, Cher. 193 BF104
Inglewood, Croy. 221 DY109
Middlefields
Inglewood, Wok. 226 AV118
Inglewood Clo. E14 163 EA77
Inglewood Clo., Horn. 128 FK63
Inglewood Clo., Ilf. 103 ET51
Inglewood Copse, Brom. 204 EL96
Inglewood Rd. NW6 120 DA64
Inglewood Rd., Bexh. 167 FD84
Inglis Barracks NW7 97 CY50
Inglis Rd. W5 138 CM73
Inglis Rd., Croy. 202 DT102
Inglis St. SE5 161 DP81
Ingoldsby Rd., Grav. 191 GL88
Ingram Ave. NW11 120 DC59
Ingram Clo. SE11 278 C8
Ingram Clo., Stan. 95 CJ50
Ingram Rd. N2 120 DE56
Ingram Rd., Dart. 188 FL88
Ingram Rd., Grays 170 GC77
Ingram Rd., Th.Hth. 202 DQ95
Ingram Way, Grnf. 137 CD67
Ingrams Clo., Walt. 214 BW106
Ingrave Ho., Dag. 146 EV67
Ingrave Rd., Brwd. 108 FX47
Ingrave Rd., Rom. 127 FD56
Ingrave St. SW11 160 DD83
Ingrebourne Gdns., Upmin. 128 FQ60
Ingrebourne Rd., Rain. 147 FH70
Ingress Gdns., Green. 189 FX85
Ingress St. W4 158 CS78
Devonshire Rd.
Ingreway, Rom. 106 FP51
Inholms La., Dor. 263 CH140
Inigo Jones Rd. SE7 164 EL80
Inigo Pl. WC2 273 P10
Inkerman Rd. NW5 141 DH65
Inkerman Rd., St.Alb. 43 CE21
Inkerman Rd. (Eton Wick), Wind. 151 AM77
Inkerman Rd., Wok. 226 AS118
Inkerman Ter., Chesh. 54 AQ33
Inkerman Way, Wok. 226 AS118
Inks Grn. E4 101 EB50
Inman Rd. NW10 138 CS67
Inman Rd. SW18 180 DC87
Inmans Row, Wdf.Grn. 102 EG49
Inner Circle NW1 272 F3
Inner Circle NW1 140 DG69
Inner Pk. Rd. SW19 179 CX88
Inner Ring E., Houns. 155 BP83
Inner Ring W., Houns. 154 BN83
Inner Temple La. EC4 274 D9
Innes Clo. SW20 199 CY96
Innes Ct., Hem.H. 40 BK22
Innes Gdns. SW15 179 CV86
Innes Yd., Croy. 202 DQ104
High St.
Inniskilling Rd. E13 144 EJ68
Inskip Clo. E10 123 EB61
Inskip Dr., Horn. 128 FL60
Inskip Rd., Dag. 126 EX60
Institute Pl. E8 122 DV64
Amhurst Rd.
Institute Rd., Dor. 262 CC137
Guildford Rd.
Institute Rd., Epp. 70 EX29
Institute Rd., Maid. 130 AF72
Instone Clo., Wall. 219 DL108
De Havilland Rd.
Instone Rd., Dart. 188 FK87
Integer Gdns. E11 123 ED59
Forest Rd.
Interchange E. Ind. Est. E5 122 DW60
Theydon Rd.
International Ave., Houns. 156 BW78
International Trd. Est., Sthl. 155 BV76
Inver Clo. E5 122 DW61
Theydon Rd.
Inver Ct. W2 140 DB72
Inverness Ter.
Inveraray Pl. SE18 165 ER79
Old Mill Rd.
Inverclyde Gdns., Rom. 126 EX56
Inveresk Gdns., Wor.Pk. 199 CT104
Inverforth Clo. NW3 120 DC61
North End Way
Inverforth Rd. N11 99 DH50
Inverine Rd. SE7 164 EH78
Invermore Pl. SE18 165 EQ77
Inverness Ave., Enf. 82 DS39
Inverness Dr., Ilf. 103 ES51
Inverness Gdns. W8 140 DB74
Vicarage Gate
Inverness Ms. W2 140 DB73
Inverness Ter.
Inverness Pl. W2 140 DB73
Inverness Rd. N18 100 DV50
Aberdeen Rd.
Inverness Rd., Houns. 156 BZ84
Inverness Rd., Sthl. 156 BY77
Inverness Rd., Wor.Pk. 199 CX102
Inverness St. NW1 141 DH67
Inverness Ter. W2 140 DB72
Inverton Rd. SE15 163 DX84
Invicta Clo., Chis. 185 EN92
Invicta Gro., Nthlt. 136 BZ69
Invicta Plaza SE1 141 DP74
Southwark St.
Invicta Rd. SE3 164 EG80
Invicta Rd., Dart. 188 FP86
Inville Rd. SE17 162 DR78
Inwen Ct. SE8 163 DY78
Inwood Ave., Couls. 235 DN120
Inwood Ave., Houns. 156 CC83
Inwood Clo., Croy. 203 DY103
Inwood Ct., Walt. 196 BW103
Inwood Rd., Houns. 156 CB84
Inworth St. SW11 160 DE82
Inworth Wk. N1 142 DQ67
Popham St.
Ion Sq. E2 142 DU68
Hackney Rd.
Iona Clo. SE6 183 EA87
Iona Cres., Slou. 131 AL72
Ionian Way, Hem.H. 40 BM18
Jupiter Dr.
Ipswich Rd. SW17 180 DG93
Ipswich Rd., Slou. 131 AN73
Ireland Clo. E6 145 EM71
Bradley Stone Rd.
Ireland Pl. N22 99 DL52
Whittington Rd.
Ireland Row E14 143 DZ72
Commercial Rd.
Ireland Yd. EC4 274 G9
Irene Rd. SW6 160 DA81
Irene Rd., Cob. 214 CB114
Irene Rd., Orp. 205 ET101
Ireton Ave., Walt. 195 BS103
Ireton Clo. N10 98 DG52
Cromwell Rd.
Ireton Pl., Grays 170 GA77
Russell Rd.
Ireton St. E3 143 EA70
Tidworth Rd.
Iris Ave., Bex. 186 EY86
Iris Clo. E6 144 EL71
Iris Clo., Brwd. 108 FV43
Iris Clo., Croy. 203 DX102
Iris Clo., Surb. 198 CM101
Iris Ct., Pnr. 116 BW55
Iris Cres., Bexh. 166 EZ79
Iris Path, Rom. 106 FJ52
Clematis Clo.
Iris Rd., Epsom 216 CP106
Iris Way E4 101 DZ51
Irkdale Ave., Enf. 82 DT39
Iron Bri. Clo. NW10 118 CS64
Iron Bri. Clo., Sthl. 136 CC74
Iron Bri. Rd., Uxb. 154 BN75
Iron Bri. Rd., West Dr. 154 BN75
Iron Dr., Hert. 32 DV08
Iron Mill La., Dart. 167 FE84
Iron Mill Pl. SW18 180 DB86
Garratt La.
Iron Mill Pl., Dart. 167 FF84
Iron Mill Rd. SW18 180 DB86
Ironmonger La. EC2 275 K9
Ironmonger Pas. EC1 275 J3
Ironmonger Row EC1 275 J3
Ironmonger Row EC1 142 DQ69
Ironmongers Pl. E14 163 EA77
Spindrift Ave.
Irons Bottom, Horl. 268 DA146
Irons Way, Rom. 105 FC52
Ironsbottom, Reig. 265 CZ143
Ironside Clo. SE16 163 DX75
Kinburn St.
Irvine Ave., Har. 117 CG55
Irvine Clo. N20 98 DE47
Irvine Gdns., S.Ock. 149 FT72
Irvine Pl., Vir.W. 192 AY99
Irvine Way, Orp. 205 ET101
Irving Ave., Nthlt. 136 BX67
Irving Gro. SW9 161 DM82
Irving Rd. W14 159 CX76
Irving St. WC2 277 N1
Irving St. WC2 141 DK73
Irving Wk., Swans. 190 FY87
Durrant Way
Irving Way NW9 119 CT57
Irving Way, Swan. 207 FD96
Irwin Ave. SE18 165 ES80
Irwin Gdns. NW10 139 CV67
Irwin Rd., Guil. 258 AU136
Isabel St. SW9 161 DM81
Isabella Clo. N14 99 DJ45
Isabella Dr., Orp. 223 EQ105
Isabella Rd. E9 122 DW64
Isabella St. SE1 278 F3
Isabella St. SE1 141 DP74
Isabelle Clo., Wal.Cr. 66 DQ29
Doverfield
Isambard Clo., Uxb. 134 BK70
Isambard Ms. E14 163 EC76
Isambard Pl. SE16 142 DW74
Rotherhithe St.
Isbell Gdns., Rom. 105 FE52
Isbells Dr., Reig. 266 DB136
Isel Way SE22 182 DS85
East Dulwich Gro.
Isenburg Way, Hem.H. 40 BK15
Isham Rd. SW16 201 DL96
Isis Clo. SW15 159 CW84
Isis Clo., Ruis. 115 BQ58
Isis Dr., Upmin. 129 FS58
Isis St. SW18 180 DC89
Isla Rd. SE18 165 EQ79
Island, The, Stai. 173 BA90
Island Clo., Stai. 173 BE91
Island Fm. Ave., W.Mol. 196 BZ99
Island Fm. Rd., W.Mol. 196 BZ99
Island Rd., Mitch. 180 DF94
Island Row E14 143 DY72
Commercial Rd.
Islay Gdns., Houns. 176 BX85
Islay Wk. N1 142 DQ66
Douglas Rd.
Isledon Rd. N7 121 DN62
Islehurst Clo., Chis. 205 EN95
Islet Pk. Dr., Maid. 130 AC68
Islet Pk. Rd., Maid. 130 AC68
Islington Grn. N1 141 DP67
Islington High St. N1 141 DN68
Islington Pk. Ms. N1 141 DN66
Islington Pk. St.
Islington Pk. St. N1 141 DN66
Islip Gdns., Edg. 96 CR52
Islip Gdns., Nthlt. 136 BY66
Islip Manor Rd., Nthlt. 136 BY66
Islip St. NW5 121 DJ64
Ismailia Rd. E7 144 EH66
Ismay Ct., Slou. 132 AS73
Elliman Ave.
Isom Clo. E13 144 EJ70
Belgrave Rd.
Istead Ri., Grav. 191 GF94
Itchingwood Common Rd., Oxt. 254 EJ133
Ivanhoe Clo., Uxb. 134 BK71
Ivanhoe Dr., Har. 117 CG55
Ivanhoe Rd. SE5 162 DT83
Ivanhoe Rd., Houns. 156 BX83
Ivatt Pl. W14 159 CZ78
Ivatt Way N17 121 DP55
Ive Fm. Clo. E10 123 EA61
Ive Fm. La. E10 123 EA61
Iveagh Ave. NW10 138 CN68
Iveagh Clo. E9 143 DX67
Iveagh Clo. NW10 138 CN68
Iveagh Clo., Nthwd. 93 BP53
Iveagh Rd., Guil. 258 AV135
Iveagh Rd., Wok. 226 AT118
Iveagh Ter. NW10 138 CN68
Iveagh Ave.
Ivedon Rd., Well. 166 EW82
Iveley Rd. SW4 161 DJ82
Iver La., Iver 134 BG72
Iver La., Uxb. 134 BH70
Iver Rd., Brwd. 108 FV44
Iver Rd., Iver 134 BG72
Iverdale Clo., Iver 133 BC73
Ivere Dr., Barn. 80 DB44
Iverhurst Clo., Bexh. 186 EX85
Iverna Ct. W8 160 DA76
Iverna Gdns. W8 160 DA76
Iverna Gdns., Felt. 175 BR85
Ivers Way, Croy. 221 EB108
Iverson Rd. NW6 139 CZ65
Ives Gdns., Rom. 127 FF56
Sims Clo.
Ives Rd. E16 144 EE71
Ives Rd., Hert. 31 DP08
Ives Rd., Slou. 153 AZ76
Ives St. SW3 276 C8
Ives St. SW3 160 DE77
Ivestor Ter. SE23 182 DW87
Ivimey St. E2 142 DU69
Ivinghoe Clo., Enf. 82 DS39
Ivinghoe Clo., St.Alb. 43 CJ15
Highview Gdns.
Ivinghoe Clo., Wat. 76 BX35
Ivinghoe Rd., Dag. 126 EV64
Ivinghoe Rd., Rick. 92 BG45
Ivinghoe Rd. (Bushey), Wat. 95 CD45
Ivins Rd., Beac. 88 AG54
Ivor Clo., Guil. 259 AZ135
Ivor Gro. SE9 185 EP88
Ivor Pl. NW1 272 D5
Ivor Pl. NW1 140 DF70
Ivor St. NW1 141 DJ66
Ivory Ct., Hem.H. 40 BL23
Ivory Sq. SW11 160 DC83
Gartons Way
Ivorydown, Brom. 184 EG91
Ivy Bower Clo., Green. 189 FV85
Riverview Rd.
Ivy Chimneys Rd., Epp. 69 ES32
Ivy Clo., Dart. 188 FN87
Ivy Clo., Grav. 191 GJ90
Ivy Clo., Har. 116 BZ63
Ivy Clo., Pnr. 116 BW59
Ivy Clo., Sun. 196 BW96
Ivy Cotts. E14 143 EB73
Grove Vill.
Ivy Ct. SE16 162 DU78
Argyle Way
Ivy Cres. W4 158 CQ77
Ivy Cres., Slou. 131 AM73
Ivy Gdns. N8 121 DL58
Ivy Gdns., Mitch. 201 DK97
Ivy Ho. La., Berk. 38 AY19
Ivy Ho. La., Sev. 241 FD118
Ivy La., Houns. 156 BZ84
Ivy La., Sev. 240 EY116
Ivy La., Wok. 227 BB117
Ivy Lea, Rick. 92 BG46
Springwell Ave.
Ivy Mill Clo., Gdse. 252 DV132
Ivy Mill La., Gdse. 252 DU132
Ivy Pl., Surb. 198 CM100
Alpha Rd.
Ivy Rd. E16 144 EG72
Pacific Rd.
Ivy Rd. E17 123 EA58
Ivy Rd. N14 99 DJ45
Ivy Rd. NW2 119 CW63
Ivy Rd. SE4 163 DZ84
Ivy Rd. SW17 180 DE92
Tooting High St.
Ivy Rd., Houns. 156 CB84
Ivy Rd., Surb. 198 CN103
Ivy St. N1 142 DS68
Ivy Ter., Hodd. 49 EC15
Ivy Wk., Dag. 146 EY65
Ivybridge, Brox. 49 EA19
Ivybridge Clo., Twick. 177 CG87
Ivybridge Clo., Uxb. 134 BL69
Ivybridge Est., Islw. 177 CF85
Ivybridge La. WC2 278 A1
Ivychurch Clo. SE20 182 DW94
Ivychurch La. SE17 279 N10
Ivydale Rd. SE15 163 DX83
Ivydale Rd., Cars. 200 DF103
Ivyday Gro. SW16 181 DM90
Ivydene, W.Mol. 196 BZ99
Ivydene Clo., Red. 267 DH139
Ivydene Clo., Sutt. 218 DC105
Ivyhouse Rd., Dag. 146 EX65
Ivyhouse Rd., Uxb. 115 BP63
Ivymount Rd. SE27 181 DN90
Ixworth Pl. SW3 276 B10
Ixworth Pl. SW3 160 DE78
Izane Rd., Bexh. 166 EZ84

J

Jacaranda Clo., N.Mal. 198 CS97
Jack Barnett Way N22 99 DM54
Mayes Rd.
Jack Clow Rd. E15 144 EE68

Jack Cornwell St. E12 125 EN63
Jack Dash Way E6 144 EL70
Jack Stevens Clo., Harl. 52 EW17
Hillside
Jack Walker Ct. N5 121 DP63
Jackass La., Kes. 222 EH106
Jackass La., Oxt. 253 DZ131
Jackdaws, Welw.G.C. 30 DC09
Jackets La., Nthwd. 93 BP53
Jacketts Fld., Abb.L. 59 BT31
Jacklin Grn., Wdf.Grn. 102 EG49
Jackman Ms. NW10 118 CS62
Jackman St. E8 142 DV67
Jackmans La., Wok. 226 AU119
Jacks La., Uxb. 92 BG52
Jackson Clo., Epsom 216 CR114
Jackson Clo., Green. 189 FU85
Cowley Ave.
Jackson Clo., Uxb. 134 BL66
Jackson Rd.
Jackson Rd. N7 121 DM63
Jackson Rd., Bark. 145 ER67
Jackson Rd., Barn. 80 DD44
Jackson Rd., Brom. 204 EL103
Jackson Rd., Uxb. 134 BL66
Jackson St. SE18 165 EN79
Jackson Way, Sthl. 156 CB75
Jacksons Dr., Wal.Cr. 66 DU28
Jacksons La. N6 120 DG59
Jacksons Pl., Croy. 202 DR102
Cross Rd.
Jacksons Way, Croy. 203 EA104
Jacob St. SE1 162 DT75
Jacobs Ave., Rom. 106 FL54
Jacobs Clo., Dag. 127 FB63
Jacobs Clo., Wind. 151 AL81
Jacobs Ho. E13 144 EJ69
Jacobs Ladder, Hat. 45 CW18
The Bdy.
Jacobs La., Dart. 208 FQ97
Jacob's Well Ms. W1 272 G8
Jacob's Well Rd., Guil. 242 AX129
Jacqueline Clo., Nthlt. 136 BZ67
Canford Ave.
Jade Clo. E16 144 EK72
Jade Clo. NW2 119 CX59
Marble Dr.
Jade Clo., Dag. 126 EW60
Jaffe Rd., Ilf. 125 ER60
Jaffray Pl. SE27 181 DP91
Chapel Rd.
Jaffray Rd., Brom. 204 EK98
Jaggard Way SW12 180 DF87
Jagger Clo., Dart. 188 FQ87
Jago Clo. SE18 165 EQ79
Jago Wk. SE5 162 DR80
Lomond Gro.
Jail La. (Biggin Hill), West. 238 EK115
Jamaica Rd. SE1 162 DT75
Jamaica Rd. SE16 162 DU76
Jamaica Rd., Th.Hth. 201 DP100
Jamaica St. E1 142 DW71
James Ave. NW2 119 CW64
James Ave., Dag. 126 EZ60
James Bedford Clo., Pnr. 94 BW54
James Boswell Clo. SW16 181 DN91
Curtis Fld. Rd.
James Clo. E13 144 EG68
Richmond St.
James Clo. NW11 119 CY58
Woodlands
James Clo., Rom. 127 FG57
James Clo. (Bushey), Wat. 76 BY43
Aldenham Rd.
James Collins Clo. W9 139 CZ70
Fermoy Rd.
James Ct. N1 142 DQ66
Morton Rd.
James Dudson Ct. NW10 138 CQ66
James Gdns. N22 99 DP52
James Hammett Ho. E2 142 DT69
Ravenscroft St.
James Joyce Wk. SE24 161 DP84
Shakespeare Rd.
James La. E10 123 ED59
James La. E11 123 ED58
James Martin Clo., Uxb. 114 BG58
James Newman Ct. SE9 185 EN90
Great Harry Dr.
James Pl. N17 100 DT53
Ruskin Rd.
James Rd., Dart. 187 FF87
James Rd., Guil. 258 AW142
James Sinclair Pt. E13 144 EJ67
James St. W1 272 G8
James St. W1 140 DG72
James St. WC2 274 A10
James St., Bark. 145 EQ66
James St., Enf. 82 DT43
James St., Epp. 69 ET28
James St., Houns. 157 CD83
James St., Wind. 151 AR81
James Ter. SW14 158 CR83
Addington Ct.
James Yd. E4 101 ED51
Larkshall Rd.
Jameson Clo. W3 158 CQ75
Acton La.
Jameson Ct., St.Alb. 43 CF19
Avenue Rd.
Jameson St. W8 140 DA74
James's Cotts., Rich. 158 CN80
Kew Rd.
Jamestown Rd. NW1 141 DH67
Jamieson Ho., Houns. 176 BZ86
Jamnagar Clo., Stai. 173 BF93
Jane St. E1 142 DV72
Commercial Rd.
Janet St. E14 163 EA76
Janeway Pl. SE16 162 DV75
Janeway St.
Janeway St. SE16 162 DU75
Janice Ms., Ilf. 125 EP62
Oakfield Rd.
Janmead, Brwd. 109 GB45
Janoway Hill La., Wok. 226 AW119
Firbank La.
Jansen Wk. SW11 160 DD84
Hope St.
Janson Clo. E15 124 EE64
Janson Rd.
Janson Clo. NW10 118 CS62
Janson Rd. E15 124 EE64
Jansons Rd. N15 122 DS55
Japan Cres. N4 121 DM59
Japan Rd., Rom. 126 EX58
Japonica Clo., Wok. 226 AW118
Jardine Rd. E1 143 DX73
Jarman Clo., Hem.H. 40 BL22
Jarmans Way, Hem.H. 40 BM21
Jarrah Cotts., Purf. 169 FR79
London Rd. Purfleet
Jarrett Clo. SW2 181 DP88
Jarrow Clo., Mord. 200 DB99
Jarrow Rd. N17 122 DV56
Jarrow Rd. SE16 162 DW77
Jarrow Rd., Rom. 126 EW58
Jarrow Way E9 123 DZ64
Jarvis Cleys (Cheshunt), Wal.Cr. 66 DT26
Roundcroft
Jarvis Clo., Barn. 79 CX43
Jarvis Rd. SE22 162 DS84
Melbourne Gro.
Jarvis Rd., S.Croy. 220 DR107
Jarvis Way, Rom. 106 FL54
Jasmin Clo., Nthwd. 93 BT53
Jasmin Rd., Epsom 216 CP107
Jasmin Way, Hem.H. 39 BE19
Jasmine Clo., Ilf. 125 EP64
Jasmine Clo., Orp. 205 EP103
Jasmine Clo., Red. 266 DG139
Spencer Way
Jasmine Clo., Sthl. 136 BY73
Jasmine Clo., Wok. 226 AT116
Jasmine Dr., Hert. 32 DU09
Jasmine Gdns., Croy. 203 EA104
Jasmine Gdns., Har. 116 CA61
Jasmine Gdns., Hat. 45 CU16
Jasmine Gro. SE20 202 DV95
Jasmine Ter., West Dr. 154 BN75
Jasmine Way, E.Mol. 197 CE98
Hampton Ct. Way
Jason Clo., Brwd. 108 FT49
Jason Clo., Red. 266 DE139
Jason Clo., Wey. 213 BQ106
Jason Ct. W1 140 DG72
Marylebone La.
Jason Wk. SE9 185 EN91
Jasons Dr., Guil. 243 BC131
Jasons Hill, Chesh. 56 AV30
Jasper Clo., Enf. 82 DW38
Jasper Pas. SE19 182 DT93
Jasper Rd. E16 144 EK72
Jasper Rd. SE19 182 DT93
Jasper Wk. N1 275 K2
Javelin Way, Nthlt. 136 BX69
Jay Gdns., Chis. 185 EM91
Jay Ms. SW7 160 DC75
Jaycroft, Enf. 81 DN39
The Ridgeway
Jays Covert, Couls. 234 DG120
Jebb Ave. SW2 181 DL86
Jebb St. E3 143 EA68
Jedburgh Rd. E13 144 EJ69
Jedburgh St. SW11 160 DG84
Jeddo Rd. W12 159 CT75
Jefferies Ho. NW10 138 CR66
Jefferson Clo. W13 157 CH76
Jefferson Clo., Ilf. 125 EP57
Jefferson Clo., Slou. 153 BA77
Jefferson Wk. SE18 165 EN79
Kempt St.
Jeffreys Pl. NW1 141 DJ66
Jeffreys St.
Jeffreys Rd. SW4 161 DL82
Jeffreys Rd., Enf. 83 DZ41
Jeffreys St. NW1 141 DJ66
Jeffreys Wk. SW4 161 DL82
Jeffries Pas., Guil. 258 AX135
High St.
Jeffries Rd., Lthd. 245 BP131
Jeffries Rd., Ware 33 DY06
Jeffs Clo., Hmptn. 176 CB93
Uxbridge Rd.
Jeffs Rd., Sutt. 217 CZ105
Jeger Ave. E2 142 DT67
Jeken Rd. SE9 164 EJ84
Jelf Rd. SW2 181 DN85
Jellicoe Ave., Grav. 191 GJ90
Jellicoe Ave. W., Grav. 191 GJ90
Kitchener Ave.
Jellicoe Clo., Slou. 151 AP75
Jellicoe Gdns., Stan. 95 CF51
Jellicoe Rd. E13 144 EG70
Jutland Rd.
Jellicoe Rd. N17 100 DR52
Jellicoe Rd., Wat. 75 BU44
Jengar Clo., Sutt. 218 DB105
Jenkins Ave., St.Alb. 60 BY30
Jenkins La. E6 145 EN68
Jenkins La., Bark. 145 EP68
Jenkins Rd. E13 144 EH70
Jenner Ave. W3 138 CR71
Jenner Ho. SE3 164 EE79
Jenner Pl. SW13 159 CV79
Jenner Rd. N16 122 DT62
Jenner Rd., Guil. 258 AY135
Jennery La., Slou. 130 AJ69
Jennett Rd., Croy. 201 DN104
Jennifer Rd., Brom. 184 EF90
Jennings Clo., Add. 212 BJ109
Woodham La.
Jennings Fld., H.Wyc. 110 AC56
Jennings Rd. SE22 182 DT86
Jennings Rd., St.Alb. 43 CF19
Jennings Way, Barn. 79 CW41
Jennings Way, Hem.H. 40 BL22
Jenningtree Rd., Erith 167 FH80
Jenningtree Way, Belv. 167 FC75
Jenny Hammond Clo. E11 124 EF62
Newcomen Rd.
Jenny Path, Rom. 106 FK52
Jenson Way SE19 182 DT94
Jenton Ave., Bexh. 166 EY81
Jephson Rd. E7 144 EJ66
Jephson St. SE5 162 DR81
Grove La.
Jephtha Rd. SW18 180 DA86
Jeppos La., Mitch. 200 DF98
Jerdan Pl. SW6 160 DA80
Fulham Bdy.
Jeremiah St. E14 143 EB72
Jeremys Grn. N18 100 DV49
Jermyn St. SW1 277 L2
Jermyn St. SW1 141 DJ74
Jerningham Ave., Ilf. 103 EP54
Jerningham Rd. SE14 163 DY82
Jerome Cres. NW8 272 B4
Jerome Cres. NW8 140 DE70
Jerome Dr., St.Alb. 42 CA22
Jerome St. E1 275 P5
Jerounds, Harl. 51 EP17
Jerrard St. N1 275 N1
Jerrard St. SE13 163 EB83
Jersey Ave., Stan. 95 CH54
Jersey Clo., Cher. 193 BF104
Jersey Clo., Guil. 243 BB129
Weybrook Dr.
Jersey Clo., Hodd. 49 EA16
Jersey Dr., Orp. 205 ER100
Jersey La., St.Alb. 43 CH18
Jersey Par., Houns. 156 CB81
Jersey Rd. E11 123 ED60
Jersey Rd. E16 144 EJ72
Prince Regent La.
Jersey Rd. SW17 181 DH93
Jersey Rd. W7 157 CG75
Jersey Rd., Houns. 156 CB81
Jersey Rd., Ilf. 125 EP63
Jersey Rd., Islw. 157 CD80
Jersey Rd., Rain. 147 FG66
Jersey St. E2 142 DV69
Bethnal Grn. Rd.
Jerusalem Pas. EC1 274 F5
Jervis Ave., Enf. 83 DY36
Jervis Ct. W1 273 J9
Jerviston Gdns. SW16 181 DN92
Jesmond Ave., Wem. 138 CM65
Jesmond Clo., Mitch. 200 DG97
Jesmond Rd., Croy. 202 DT101
Jesmond Way, Stan. 96 CL50
Jessam Ave. E5 122 DV60
Jessamine Pl., Dart. 188 FQ87
Jessamine Rd. W7 137 CE74
Jessamine Ter., Swan. 207 FC95
Birchwood Rd.
Jessamy Rd., Wey. 195 BP103
Jesse Rd. E10 123 EC60
Jessel Dr., Loug. 85 EQ39
Jesses La., Guil. 261 BQ144
Jessett Clo., Erith 167 FD77
West St.
Jessica Rd. SW18 180 DC86
Jessie Blythe La. N19 121 DL59
Hillrise Rd.
Jessiman Ter., Shep. 194 BN99
Jessop Ave., Sthl. 156 BZ77
Jessop Rd. SE24 161 DP84
Milkwood Rd.
Jessops Way, Croy. 201 DJ100
Jessup Clo. SE18 165 EQ77
Jetstar Way, Nthlt. 136 BY69
Jetty Wk., Grays 170 GA79
Jevington Way SE12 184 EH88
Jewel Rd. E17 123 EA55
Jewels Hill, West. 222 EG112
Jewry St. EC3 275 P9
Jewry St. EC3 142 DT72
Jew's Row SW18 160 DB84
Jews Wk. SE26 182 DV91
Jeymer Ave. NW2 119 CV64
Jeymer Dr., Grnf. 136 CC67
Jeypore Rd. SW18 180 DC87
Jillian Clo., Hmptn. 176 CA94
Jim Bradley Clo. SE18 165 EN77
John Wilson St.
Jim Desormeaux Bungalows, Harl. 35 ES13
School La.
Jinnings, The, Welw.G.C. 30 DA12
Joan Cres. SE9 184 EK87
Joan Gdns., Dag. 126 EY61
Joan Rd., Dag. 126 EY60
Joan St. SE1 278 F3
Joan St. SE1 141 DP74
Jocelyn Rd., Rich. 158 CL83
Jocelyn St. SE15 162 DU81
Jocelyns, Harl. 36 EW11
Jocketts Hill, Hem.H. 39 BF20
Jocketts Rd., Hem.H. 39 BF21
Jockey's Flds. WC1 274 C6
Jockey's Flds. WC1 141 DM71
Jodane St. SE8 163 DZ77
Jodrell Clo., Islw. 157 CG81
Blenheim Way
Jodrell Rd. E3 143 DZ67
Jodrell Way, Grays 169 FT78
Joel St., Nthwd. 115 BU55
Joel St., Pnr. 115 BU55
Johanna St. SE1 278 D5
John Adam St. WC2 278 A1
John Adam St. WC2 141 DL73
John Aird Ct. W2 140 DC71
Howley Pl.
John Ashby Clo. SW2 181 DL86
John Barnes Wk. E15 144 EF65
Hamfrith Rd.
John Bradshaw Rd. N14 99 DK46
High St.
John Burns Dr., Bark. 145 ES66
John Campbell Rd. N16 122 DS64
John Carpenter St. EC4 274 E10
John Carpenter St. EC4 141 DP73
John Cobb Rd., Wey. 212 BN108
John Cornwall VC Ho. E12 125 EN63
John Ct., Hodd. 33 EA14
Molesworth
John Deed Ind. Est., Mitch. 200 DF100
John Eliot Clo., Wal.Abb. 50 EE21
John Felton Rd. SE16 162 DU75
John Fisher St. E1 142 DU73
John Gooch Dr., Enf. 81 DP39
John Groom's Est., Edg. 96 CQ49
John Islip St. SW1 277 N10
John Islip St. SW1 161 DK78
John Keats Ho. N22 99 DM52
John Maurice Clo. SE17 162 DR77
John McKenna Wk. SE16 162 DU76
Tranton Rd.
John Newton Ct., Well. 166 EV83
Danson La.
John Parker Clo., Dag. 147 FB66
John Parker Sq. SW11 160 DD83
Thomas Baines Rd.
John Penn St. SE13 163 EB81
John Perrin Pl., Har. 118 CL59
John Princes St. W1 273 J8
John Princes St. W1 141 DH72
John Rennie Wk. E1 142 DV74
Wine Clo.
John Roll Way SE16 162 DU76
John Ruskin St. SE5 161 DP80
John Russell Clo., Guil. 242 AU131
John Silkin La. SE8 163 DX78
John Smith Ave. SW6 159 CZ80
John Spencer Sq. N1 141 DP65
John St. E15 144 EF67
John St. SE25 202 DU98
John St. WC1 274 C5
John St. WC1 141 DM70
John St., Enf. 82 DT43
John St., Grays 170 GC79
John St., Houns. 156 BY82
John Tate Rd., Hert. 32 DT10
John Taylor Ct., Slou. 131 AQ74
John Trundle Ct. EC2 142 DQ71
Beech St.
John Walsh Twr. E11 124 EF61
John Williams Clo. SE14 163 DX79
John Wilson St. SE18 165 EN76
John Woolley Clo. SE13 163 ED84
Johnby Clo., Enf. 83 DY37
Manly Dixon Dr.
Johns Ave. NW4 119 CW56
Johns Clo., Ashf. 175 BQ91
John's La., Berk. 38 AT21
Johns La., Mord. 200 DC99
John's Ms. WC1 274 C5
John's Ms. WC1 141 DM70
John's Pl. E1 142 DV72
Damien St.
Johns Rd., West. 238 EK120
John's Ter., Croy. 202 DS102
John's Ter., Rom. 106 FP51
Johns Wk., Whyt. 236 DU119
Johnsdale, Oxt. 254 EF129
Johnson Clo. E8 142 DU67
Johnson Clo., Grav. 190 GD90
Johnson Ct., Hem.H. 40 BL22
Johnson Rd., Brom. 204 EK99
Johnson Rd., Croy. 202 DR101
Johnson Rd., Houns. 156 BW80
Johnson St. E1 142 DW73
Cable St.
Johnson St., Sthl. 156 BW76
Johnsons Ave., Sev. 225 FB110
Johnsons Clo., Cars. 200 DE104
Johnson's Ct. EC4 141 DN72
Fleet St.
Johnsons Ct., Sev. 257 FM121
School La.
Johnsons Dr., Hmptn. 196 CC95
Johnson's Pl. SW1 161 DJ78
Johnsons Way NW10 138 CP70
Johnsons Way, Green. 189 FW86
Johnsons Yd., Uxb. 134 BJ66
Redford Way
Johnston Clo. SW9 161 DM81
Hackford Rd.
Johnston Grn., Guil. 242 AU130
Johnston Rd., Wdf.Grn. 102 EG50
Johnston Ter. NW2 119 CX62
Campion Ter.
Johnston Wk., Guil. 242 AU130
Johnstone Rd. E6 145 EM69
Joiner St. SE1 279 L3
Joiner's Arms Yd. SE5 162 DR81
Denmark Hill
Joiners Clo., Chesh. 56 AV30
Joiners Clo., Ger.Cr. 91 AZ52
Joiners La., Ger.Cr. 90 AY53
Joiners Way, Ger.Cr. 90 AY52
Joinville Pl., Add. 212 BK105
Jolliffe Rd., Red. 251 DJ126
Jollys La., Har. 117 CD60
Lower Rd.
Jollys La., Hayes 136 BX71
Jonathan St. SE11 278 B10
Jonathan St. SE11 161 DM78
Jones Rd. E13 144 EH70
Holborn Rd.
Jones Rd. (Cheshunt), Wal.Cr. 65 DP30
Jones St. W1 277 H1
Jones Wk., Rich. 178 CM86
Pyrland Rd.
Jones Way, Slou. 111 AR61
Jonquil Clo., Welw.G.C. 30 DB11
Jonquil Gdns., Hmptn. 176 BZ93
Partridge Rd.
Jonson Clo., Hayes 135 BU71
Jonson Clo., Mitch. 201 DH98
Joram Way SE16 162 DV78
Egan Way
Jordan Clo., Dag. 127 FB63
Muggeridge Rd.
Jordan Clo., Har. 116 BZ62
Hamilton Cres.
Jordan Clo., S.Croy. 220 DT111
Jordan Clo., Wat. 75 BT35
Jordan Rd., Grnf. 137 CH67
Jordans Clo., Guil. 243 BA133
Beatty Ave.
Jordans Clo., Islw. 157 CE81
Jordans Clo., Red. 266 DG139
Spencer Way
Jordans Clo., Stai. 174 BJ87
Jordans La., Beac. 90 AS53
Jordans Rd., Rick. 92 BG45
Jordans Way, Beac. 90 AT51
Jordans Way, Rain. 148 FK68
Jordans Way, St.Alb. 60 BZ30
Joseph Ave. W3 138 CR72
Joseph Locke Way, Esher 196 CA103
Mill Rd.
Joseph Powell Clo. SW12 181 DH86
Hazelbourne Rd.
Joseph Ray Rd. E11 124 EE61
High Rd. Leytonstone
Joseph St. E3 143 DZ70
Josephine Ave. SW2 181 DM85
Josephine Ave., Tad. 249 CZ126
Josephine Clo., Tad. 249 CZ127
Joseph's Rd., Guil. 242 AW133
Joshua St. E14 143 EC72
St. Leonards Rd.
Joslin Rd., Purf. 168 FQ78
Joubert St. SW11 160 DF82
Journeys End, Slou. 132 AS71
Jowett St. SE15 162 DT80
Joy Rd., Grav. 191 GJ88
Joyce Ave. N18 100 DT50
Joyce Ct., Wal.Abb. 67 ED34
Joyce Dawson Way SE28 146 EU73
Thamesmere Dr.
Joyce Grn. La., Dart. 168 FM84
Joyce Grn. Wk., Dart. 168 FM84
Joyce Page Clo. SE7 164 EK79
Lansdowne La.
Joyce Wk. SW2 181 DN86
Joydens Wd. Rd., Bex. 187 FD91
Joydon Dr., Rom. 126 EV58
Joyes Clo., Rom. 106 FK49
Joyners Clo., Dag. 126 EZ63
Joyners Fld., Harl. 51 EQ19
Jubb Powell Ho. N15 122 DS58
Jubilee Ave. E4 101 EC51
Jubilee Ave., Rom. 127 FB57
Jubilee Ave., St.Alb. 61 CK26
Jubilee Ave., Twick. 176 CC87
Jubilee Ave., Ware 33 DZ05
Jubilee Clo. NW9 118 CR58
Jubilee Clo., Green. 189 FW86
Jubilee Clo., Pnr. 94 BW54
Jubilee Clo., Rom. 127 FB57
Jubilee Clo., Stai. 174 BJ87
Jubilee Ct., Hat. 45 CV15
Jubilee Ct., Stai. 174 BG92
Leacroft
Jubilee Cres. E14 163 EC76
Jubilee Cres. N9 100 DU46
Jubilee Cres., Add. 212 BK106
Jubilee Cres., Grav. 191 GL89
Jubilee Dr., Ruis. 116 BX63
Jubilee Gdns., Sthl. 136 CA72
Jubilee Pl. SW3 276 C10
Jubilee Pl. SW3 160 DE78
Jubilee Ri., Sev. 257 FM121
Jubilee Rd., Grays 169 FV79
Jubilee Rd., Grnf. 137 CH67
Jubilee Rd., Orp. 224 FA107
Jubilee Rd., Sutt. 217 CX108
Jubilee Rd., Wat. 75 BU38
Jubilee St. E1 142 DW72
Jubilee Ter., Bet. 264 CP138
Jubilee Ter., Dor. 263 CH135
Jubilee Wk., Wat. 93 BV49
Muirfield Rd.
Jubilee Way SW19 200 DB95
Jubilee Way, Chess. 216 CN105
Jubilee Way, Felt. 175 BT88
Jubilee Way, Sid. 186 EU89
Judd St. WC1 273 P3
Judd St. WC1 141 DL69
Jude St. E16 144 EF72
Judeth Gdns., Grav. 191 GL92
Judge Heath La., Hayes 135 BQ72
Judge St., Wat. 75 BV38
Judge Wk., Esher 215 CE107
Judges Hill, Pot.B. 64 DE29
Judith Ave., Rom. 105 FB51
Juer St. SW11 160 DE80
Juglans Rd., Orp. 206 EU102
Julia Gdns., Bark. 146 EX68
Julia St. NW5 120 DG63
Oak Village
Julian Ave. W3 138 CP73
Julian Clo., Barn. 80 DB41
Julian Clo., Wok. 226 AW118
Julian Hill, Har. 117 CE61
Julian Hill, Wey. 212 BN108
Julian Pl. E14 163 EB78
Julian Rd., Orp. 224 EU107
Juliana Clo. N2 120 DB55
East End Rd.
Julians Clo., Sev. 256 FG127
Julians Way, Sev. 256 FG127
Julien Rd. W5 157 CJ77
Julien Rd., Couls. 235 DK115
Juliette Rd. E13 144 EF68
Juliette Way, S.Ock. 168 FM75
Junction App. SE13 163 EC83
Loampit Vale
Junction App. SW11 160 DE83
Junction Ave. W10 139 CW69
Harrow Rd.
Junction Ms. W2 272 B8
Junction Pl. W2 272 A8
Junction Rd. E13 144 EH68
Junction Rd. N9 100 DU46
Junction Rd. N17 122 DU55
Junction Rd. N19 121 DJ63
Junction Rd. W5 157 CK77
Junction Rd., Ashf. 175 BQ92
Junction Rd., Brwd. 108 FW49
Junction Rd., Dart. 188 FK86
Junction Rd., Dor. 263 CG136
Junction Rd., Har. 117 CE58
Junction Rd., Rom. 127 FF56
Junction Rd., S.Croy. 220 DR106
Junction Rd. E., Rom. 126 EY59
Kenneth Rd.
Junction Rd. W., Rom. 126 EY59
Junction Wf. N1 275 H1
Junction Wf. N1 142 DQ68
June Clo., Couls. 219 DH114
June La., Red. 267 DH141
Junewood Clo., Add. 211 BF111
Juniper Ave., St.Alb. 60 CA31
Juniper Clo., Barn. 79 CX43
Juniper Clo., Brox. 67 DZ25
Juniper Clo., Chess. 216 CM107
Juniper Clo., Guil. 242 AV129
Juniper Clo., Reig. 266 DC136
Juniper Clo., Rick. 92 BK48
Juniper Clo., Wem. 118 CN64
Juniper Clo., West. 238 EL117
Juniper Ct., Slou. 152 AU75
Nixey Clo.
Juniper Cres. NW1 140 DG66
Juniper Gdns. SW16 201 DJ95
Leonard Rd.
Juniper Gdns., Sun. 175 BT93
Juniper Gate, Rick. 92 BK47
Juniper Grn., Hem.H. 39 BE20
Juniper Gro., Wat. 75 BU38
Bay Tree Wk.
Juniper La. E6 144 EL71
Juniper La., H.Wyc. 110 AD56
Juniper Rd., Ilf. 125 EP63
Juniper Rd., Reig. 266 DC136
Juniper St. E1 142 DW73
Juniper Wk., Bet. 264 CQ136
Warrenne Rd.
Juniper Wk., Swan. 207 FD96
Pear Tree Clo.
Juniper Way, Hayes 135 BR73
Juniper Way, Rom. 106 FL53

Juno Rd., Hem.H. 40 BM17
Saturn Way
Juno Way SE14 163 DX79
Jupiter Dr., Hem.H. 40 BM18
Jupiter Way N7 141 DM65
Jupp Rd. E15 143 ED66
Jupp Rd. W. E15 143 EC67
Jurgens Rd., Purf. 169 FR79
London Rd. Purfleet
Justice Wk. SW3 160 DE79
Lawrence St.
Justin Clo., Brent. 157 CK80
Justin Rd. E4 101 DZ51
Jute La., Enf. 83 DY40
Jutland Clo. N19 121 DL60
Sussex Way
Jutland Gdns., Couls. 235 DL120
Goodenough Way
Jutland Pl., Egh. 173 BC92
Mullens Rd.
Jutland Rd. E13 144 EG70
Jutland Rd. SE6 183 EC87
Jutsums Ave., Rom. 127 FB58
Jutsums La., Rom. 127 FB58
Juxon Clo., Har. 94 CB53
Augustine Rd.
Juxon St. SE11 278 C8
Juxon St. SE11 161 DM77

K

Kaduna Clo., Pnr. 115 BV57
Kale Rd., Erith 166 EY75
Kambala Rd. SW11 160 DD83
Kandlewood, Brwd. 109 GB45
Kangley Bri. Rd. SE26 183 DZ91
Karen Clo., Brwd. 108 FW45
Karen Clo., Rain. 147 FE68
Karen Ct. SE4 163 DZ82
Wickham Rd.
Karen Ct., Brom. 204 EF95
Blyth Rd.
Karen Ter. E11 124 EF61
Montague Rd.
Karoline Gdns., Grnf. 137 CD68
Oldfield La. N.
Kashgar Rd. SE18 165 ET77
Kashmir Clo., Add. 212 BK109
Kashmir Rd. SE7 164 EK80
Kassala Rd. SW11 160 DF81
Katella Trd. Est., Bark. 145 ES69
Kates Clo., Barn. 79 CU43
Kates Cft., Welw.G.C. 29 CY13
Katharine St., Croy. 202 DQ104
Katherine Clo., Add. 212 BG107
Katherine Clo., Hem.H. 40 BL23
Katherine Clo., H.Wyc. 88 AC47
Katherine Gdns. SE9 164 EK84
Katherine Gdns., Ilf. 103 EQ52
Katherine Rd. E6 144 EK66
Katherine Rd. E7 144 EJ65
Katherine Rd., Twick. 177 CG88
London Rd.
Katherine Sq. W11 139 CY74
Wilsham St.
Katherines Way, Harl. 51 EN18
Kathleen Ave. W3 138 CQ71
Kathleen Ave., Wem. 138 CL66
Kathleen Rd. SW11 160 DF83
Katrine Sq., Hem.H. 40 BK16
Kavanaghs Rd., Brwd. 108 FU48
Kavanaghs Ter., Brwd. 108 FV48
Kavanaghs Rd.
Kay Rd. SW9 161 DL82
Kay St. E2 142 DU68
Kay St. E15 143 ED66
Kay St., Well. 166 EV81
Kaye Ct., Guil. 242 AW131
Kaye Don Way, Wey. 212 BN111
Kayemoor Rd., Sutt. 218 DE108
Kaywood Clo., Slou. 152 AW76
Kean St. WC2 274 B9
Kean St. WC2 141 DM72
Kearton Clo., Ken. 236 DQ117
Keary Rd., Swans. 190 FY87
Keatley Grn. E4 101 DZ51
Keats Ave., Red. 250 DG132
Keats Ave., Rom. 105 FH52
Keats Clo. E11 124 EH57
Nightingale La.
Keats Clo. NW3 120 DE63
Keats Gro.
Keats Clo. SE1 279 P9
Keats Clo. SW19 180 DD93
North Rd.
Keats Clo., Chig. 103 EQ51
Keats Clo., Enf. 83 DX43
Keats Clo., Hayes 135 BU71
Keats Gdns., Til. 171 GH82
Keats Gro. NW3 120 DE63
Keats Ho., Beck. 183 EA93
Keats La., Wind. 151 AR79
Keats Pl. EC2 275 K7
Keats Rd., Belv. 167 FC76
Keats Rd., Well. 165 ES81
Keats Wk., Brwd. 109 GD45
Byron Rd.
Keats Way, Croy. 202 DW100
Keats Way, Grnf. 136 CB71
Keats Way, West Dr. 154 BM77
Keble Clo., Nthlt. 116 CC64
Keble Clo., Wor.Pk. 199 CT102
Keble St. SW17 180 DC91
Keble Ter., Abb.L. 59 BT32
Kechill Gdns., Brom. 204 EG101
Kedelston Ct. E5 123 DX63
Redwald Rd.
Kedleston Dr., Orp. 205 ET100
Kedleston Wk. E2 142 DV69
Middleton St.
Keedonwood Rd., Brom. 184 EE92
Keefield, Harl. 51 EP20
Keel Clo. SE16 143 DX74
Keel Clo., Bark. 146 EY69
Choats Rd.
Keel Dr., Slou. 151 AP75
Keele Clo., Wat. 76 BW40
Keeler Clo., Wind. 151 AL83
Keeley Rd., Croy. 202 DQ103
Keeley St. WC2 274 B9
Keeley St. WC2 141 DM72
Keeling Rd. SE9 184 EK85
Keely Clo., Barn. 80 DE43
Keemor Clo. SE18 165 EN80
Llanover Rd.
Keens Clo. SW16 181 DK92
Keens La., Guil. 242 AT130
Keens Pk. Rd., Guil. 242 AT130
Keens Rd., Croy. 220 DQ105
Keens Yd. N1 141 DP65
St. Paul's Rd.
Keensacre, Iver 133 BD68
Keep, The SE3 164 EG82
Keep, The, Kings.T. 178 CM93
Keep La. N11 98 DG49
Gardeners Clo.
Keepers Clo., Guil. 243 BD131
Keepers Fm. Clo., Wind. 151 AL82
Keepers Ms., Tedd. 177 CJ93
Keepers Wk., Vir.W. 192 AX99
Keesey St. SE17 162 DR79
Keetons Rd. SE16 162 DV76
Keevil Dr. SW19 179 CX87
Keighley Clo. N7 121 DL64
Penn Rd.
Keighley Rd., Rom. 106 FL52
Keightley Dr. SE9 185 EQ88
Keilder Clo., Uxb. 134 BN68
Charnwood Rd.
Keildon Rd. SW11 160 DF84
Keir, The SW19 179 CW92
West Side Common
Keir Hardie Est. E5 122 DV60
Springfield
Keir Hardie Ho. W6 159 CW79
Lochaline St.
Keir Hardie Way, Bark. 146 EU66
Keir Hardie Way, Hayes 135 BU69
Keith Ave. (Sutton at Hone), Dart. 188 FP93
Keith Connor Clo. SW8 161 DH83
Daley Thompson Way
Keith Gro. W12 159 CU75
Keith Pk. Cres., West. 222 EH113
Keith Pk. Rd., Uxb. 134 BM66
Keith Rd. E17 101 DZ53
Keith Rd., Bark. 145 ER68
Keith Rd., Hayes 155 BS76
Keith Way, Horn. 128 FL59
Keiths Rd., Hem.H. 40 BN21
Kelbrook Rd. SE3 164 EL82
Kelburn Way, Rain. 147 FG69
Dominion Way
Kelby Path SE9 185 EP90
Kelbys, Welw.G.C. 30 DC08
Kelceda Clo. NW2 119 CU61
Kelf Gro., Hayes 135 BT72
Kelfield Gdns. W10 139 CW72
Kelfield Ms. W10 139 CX72
Kelfield Gdns.
Kell St. SE1 278 G6
Kelland Clo. N8 121 DK57
Palace Rd.
Kelland Rd. E13 144 EG70
Kellaway Rd. SE3 164 EJ82
Keller Cres. E12 124 EK63
Kellerton Rd. SE13 184 EE85
Kellett Rd. SW2 161 DN84
Kelling Gdns., Croy. 201 DP101
Kellino St. SW17 180 DF91
Kellner Rd. SE28 165 ET76
Kelly Clo., Shep. 195 BS96
Kelly Ct., Borwd. 78 CR40
Kelly Rd. NW7 97 CY51
Kelly St. NW1 141 DH65
Kelly Way, Rom. 126 EY57
Kelman Clo. SW4 161 DK82
Kelman Clo., Wal.Cr. 67 DX31
Kelmore Gro. SE22 162 DU84
Kelmscott Clo. E17 101 DZ54
Kelmscott Clo., Wat. 75 BU43
Kelmscott Cres., Wat. 75 BU43
Kelmscott Gdns. W12 159 CU76
Kelmscott Rd. SW11 180 DE85
Kelpatrick Rd., Slou. 131 AK72
Kelross Pas. N5 122 DQ63
Kelross Rd.
Kelross Rd. N5 122 DQ63
Kelsall Clo. SE3 164 EH82
Kelsey Clo., Horl. 268 DF148
Court Lo. Rd.
Kelsey La., Beck. 203 EA97
Kelsey Pk. Ave., Beck. 203 EB96
Kelsey Pk. Rd., Beck. 203 EA96
Kelsey Rd., Orp. 206 EV96
Kelsey Sq., Beck. 203 EA96
High St.
Kelsey St. E2 142 DU70
Kelsey Way, Beck. 203 EA97
Kelshall, Wat. 76 BY36
Kelshall Ct. N4 122 DQ61
Brownswood Rd.
Kelsie Way, Ilf. 103 ES51
Kelso Dr., Grav. 191 GM91
Kelso Pl. W8 160 DB76
Kelso Rd., Cars. 200 DC101
Kelson Ho. E14 163 EC76
Kelston Rd., Ilf. 103 EP54
Kelvedon Ave., Walt. 213 BS108
Kelvedon Clo., Brwd. 109 GE44
Kelvedon Clo., Kings.T. 178 CN93
Kelvedon Rd. SW6 159 CZ80
Kelvedon Wk., Rain. 147 FE67
Ongar Way
Kelvedon Way, Wdf.Grn. 103 EM51
Kelvin Ave. N13 99 DM51
Kelvin Ave., Lthd. 231 CF119
Kelvin Ave., Tedd. 177 CE93
Kelvin Clo., Epsom 216 CN107
Kelvin Cres., Har. 95 CE52
Kelvin Dr., Twick. 177 CH86
Kelvin Gdns., Croy. 201 DL101
Kelvin Gdns., Sthl. 136 CA72
Kelvin Gro. SE26 182 DV90
Kelvin Gro., Chess. 198 CL104
Kelvin Ind. Est., Grnf. 136 CB66
Kelvin Par., Orp. 205 ES102
Kelvin Rd. N5 121 DP63
Kelvin Rd., Til. 171 GG82
Kelvin Rd., Well. 166 EU83
Kelvinbrook, W.Mol. 196 CB97
Kelvington Clo., Croy. 203 DY101
Kelvington Rd. SE15 183 DX85
Kember St. N1 141 DM66
Carnoustie Dr.
Kemble Clo., Pot.B. 64 DD33
Kemble Clo., Wey. 213 BR105
Kemble Cotts., Add. 194 BG104
Emley Rd.
Kemble Dr., Brom. 204 EL104
Kemble Par., Pot.B. 64 DC32
High St.
Kemble Rd. N17 100 DU53
Kemble Rd. SE23 183 DX88
Kemble Rd., Croy. 201 DN104
Kemble St. WC2 274 B9
Kemble St. WC2 141 DM72
Kembleside Rd., West. 238 EJ118
Kemerton Rd. SE5 162 DQ83
Kemerton Rd., Beck. 203 EB96
Kemerton Rd., Croy. 202 DT101
Kemeys St. E9 123 DY64
Kemishford, Wok. 226 AU123
Kemnal Rd., Chis. 185 EQ94
Kemp Gdns., Croy. 202 DQ100
St. Saviours Rd.
Kemp Pl. (Bushey), Wat. 76 CA44
Kemp Rd., Dag. 126 EX60
Kempe Clo., St.Alb. 42 CC24
Kempe Rd. NW6 139 CX68
Kempe Rd., Enf. 82 DV36
Kempis Way SE22 182 DS85
East Dulwich Gro.
Kemplay Rd. NW3 120 DD63
Kemprow, Wat. 77 CD36
Kemp's Ct. W1 273 L9
Kemps Dr. E14 143 EA73
Morant St.
Kemps Dr., Nthwd. 93 BT52
Kemps Gdns. SE13 183 EC85
Thornford Rd.
Kempsford Gdns. SW5 160 DA78
Kempsford Rd. SE11 278 F9
Kempsford Rd. SE11 161 DN77
Kempshott Rd. SW16 181 DK94
Kempson Rd. SW6 160 DA81
Kempt St. SE18 165 EN79
Kempthorne Rd. SE8 163 DY77
Kempton Ave., Horn. 128 FM63
Kempton Ave., Nthlt. 136 CA65
Kempton Ave., Sun. 195 BV95
Kempton Clo., Erith 167 FC79
Kempton Clo., Uxb. 115 BQ63
Kempton Ct., Sun. 195 BV95
Kempton Rd. E6 145 EM67
Kempton Rd., Hmptn. 196 BZ96
Kempton Wk., Croy. 203 DY100
Kemsing Clo., Bex. 186 EY87
Kemsing Clo., Brom. 204 EF103
Bourne Way
Kemsing Clo., Th.Hth. 202 DQ98
Kemsing Rd. SE10 164 EG78
Kemsley Clo., Grav. 191 GF91
Kemsley Clo., Green. 189 FV86
Kemsley Rd., West. 238 EK119
Ken Way, Wem. 118 CQ61
Kenbury Clo., Uxb. 114 BN62
Kenbury Gdns. SE5 162 DQ82
Kenbury St.
Kenbury St. SE5 162 DQ82
Kenchester Clo. SW8 161 DL80
Kencot Way, Erith 166 EZ75
Kendal Ave. N18 100 DR49
Kendal Ave. W3 138 CN70
Kendal Ave., Bark. 145 ES66
Kendal Ave., Epp. 70 EU30
Kendal Clo. SW9 161 DP80
Kendal Clo., Felt. 175 BT88
Ambleside Dr.
Kendal Clo., Hayes 135 BS68
Kendal Clo., Reig. 250 DD133
Kendal Clo., Slou. 132 AU73
Kendal Clo., Wdf.Grn. 102 EF47
Kendal Cft., Horn. 127 FG64
Kendal Dr., Slou. 132 AU73
Kendal Gdns. N18 100 DR49
Kendal Gdns., Sutt. 200 DC103
Kendal Par. N18 100 DR49
Great Cambridge Rd.
Kendal Pl. SW15 179 CZ85
Upper Richmond Rd.
Kendal Rd. NW10 119 CU63
Kendal St. W2 272 C9
Kendal St. W2 140 DE72
Kendale, Grays 171 GH76
Kendale, Hem.H. 41 BP21
Kendale Rd., Brom. 184 EE92
Kendall Ave., Beck. 203 DY96
Kendall Ave., S.Croy. 220 DR109
Kendall Ave. S., S.Croy. 220 DQ110
Kendall Clo., Welw.G.C. 29 CZ13
Kendall Ct. SW19 180 DD93
Byegrove Rd.
Kendall Pl. W1 272 F7
Kendall Rd., Beck. 203 DY96
Kendall Rd., Islw. 157 CG82
Kendalmere Clo. N10 99 DH53
Kendals Clo., Rad. 77 CE36
Kender St. SE14 162 DW81
Kendoa Rd. SW4 161 DK84
Kendon Clo. E11 124 EH57
The Ave.
Kendor Ave., Epsom 216 CQ111
Kendra Hall Rd., S.Croy. 219 DP108
Kendrey Gdns., Twick. 177 CE86
Kendrick Ms. SW7 160 DD77
Reece Ms.
Kendrick Pl. SW7 160 DD77
Kendrick Rd., Slou. 152 AV76
Kenelm Clo., Har. 117 CG62
Kenerne Dr., Barn. 79 CY43
Kenford Clo., Wat. 59 BV32
Kenia Wk., Grav. 191 GM90
Cervia Way
Kenilford Rd. SW12 181 DH87
Kenilworth Ave. E17 101 EA54
Kenilworth Ave. SW19 180 DA92
Kenilworth Ave., Cob. 214 CB114
Kenilworth Ave., Har. 116 BZ63
Kenilworth Ave., Rom. 106 FP51
Kenilworth Clo., Bans. 234 DB116
Kenilworth Clo., Borwd. 78 CQ41
Kenilworth Clo., Hem.H. 40 BL21
Kenilworth Clo., Slou. 152 AT76
Kenilworth Ct. SW15 159 CX83
Kenilworth Ct., Wat. 75 BU39
Hempstead Rd.
Kenilworth Cres., Enf. 82 DS39
Kenilworth Dr., Borwd. 78 CQ41
Kenilworth Dr., Rick. 75 BP42
Kenilworth Dr., Walt. 196 BX104
Kenilworth Gdns. SE18 165 EP82
Kenilworth Gdns., Hayes 135 BT71
Kenilworth Gdns., Horn. 128 FJ62
Kenilworth Gdns., Ilf. 125 ET61
Kenilworth Gdns., Loug. 85 EM44
Kenilworth Gdns., Sthl. 136 BZ69
Kenilworth Gdns., Stai. 174 BJ92
Kenilworth Gdns., Wat. 94 BW50
Kenilworth Rd. E3 143 DY68
Kenilworth Rd. NW6 139 CZ67
Kenilworth Rd. SE20 203 DX95
Kenilworth Rd. W5 138 CL74
Kenilworth Rd., Ashf. 174 BK90
Kenilworth Rd., Edg. 96 CQ48
Kenilworth Rd., Epsom 217 CU106
Kenilworth Rd., Orp. 205 EQ100
Kenley Ave. NW9 96 CS53
Kenley Clo., Bex. 186 FA87
Kenley Clo., Cat. 236 DR120
Kenley Clo., Chis. 205 ES97
Kenley Gdns., Horn. 128 FM61
Kenley Gdns., Th.Hth. 201 DP98
Kenley La., Ken. 220 DQ114
Kenley Rd. SW19 199 CZ96
Kenley Rd., Kings.T. 198 CP96
Kenley Rd., Twick. 177 CG86
Kenley Wk. W11 139 CY73
Princedale Rd.
Kenley Wk., Sutt. 217 CX105
Kenlor Rd. SW17 180 DD92
Kenmare Dr., Mitch. 180 DF94
Kenmare Gdns. N13 100 DQ49
Kenmare Rd., Th.Hth. 201 DN100
Kenmere Gdns., Wem. 138 CN67
Kenmere Rd., Well. 166 EW82
Kenmont Gdns. NW10 139 CV69
Kenmore Ave., Har. 117 CG56
Kenmore Clo., Rich. 158 CN80
Kent Rd.
Kenmore Cres., Hayes 135 BT69
Kenmore Gdns., Edg. 96 CP54
Kenmore Rd., Har. 117 CK55
Kenmore Rd., Ken. 219 DP114
Kenmure Rd. E8 122 DV64
Kenmure Yd. E8 122 DV64
Kenmure Rd.
Kennard Rd. E15 143 ED66
Kennard Rd. N11 98 DF50
Kennard St. E16 145 EM74
Kennard St. SW11 160 DG81
Kenneally Clo., Wind. 150 AJ82
Kenneally Row
Kenneally Pl., Wind. 150 AJ82
Kenneally Row
Kenneally Rd., Wind. 150 AJ82
Kenneally Row
Kenneally Row, Wind. 150 AJ82
Kenneally Wk., Wind. 150 AJ82
Kenneally Row
Kennedy Ave., Enf. 82 DW44
Kennedy Ave., Hodd. 49 DZ17
Kennedy Clo. E13 144 EG68
Kennedy Clo., Mitch. 200 DG95
Kennedy Clo., Orp. 205 ER102
Kennedy Clo., Pnr. 94 BZ51
Kennedy Clo., Slou. 131 AQ65
Kennedy Clo. (Cheshunt), Wal.Cr. 67 DY28
Kennedy Gdns., Sev. 257 FJ123
Kennedy Path W7 137 CF70
Harp Rd.
Kennedy Rd. W7 137 CE71
Kennedy Rd., Bark. 145 ES67
Kennedy Wk. SE17 162 DR77
Flint St.
Kennel Clo., Lthd. 230 CC124
Kennel Hill SE22 162 DS83
Kennel La., Horl. 268 DD149
Kennel La., Lthd. 230 CC122
Kennelwood Cres., Croy. 221 ED111
Kennelwood La., Hat. 45 CV17
Kenners La., Wal.Abb. 50 EL20
Kennet Clo. SW11 160 DD84
Maysoule Rd.
Kennet Clo., Upmin. 129 FS58
Kennet Grn., S.Ock. 149 FV73
Cawdor Ave.
Kennet Rd. W9 139 CZ70
Kennet Rd., Dart. 167 FG83
Kennet Rd., Islw. 157 CF83
Kennet Sq., Mitch. 200 DE95
Kennet St. E1 142 DU74
Kennet Wf. La. EC4 275 J10
Kenneth Ave., Ilf. 125 EP63
Kenneth Cres. NW2 119 CV64
Kenneth Gdns., Stan. 95 CG51
Kenneth More Rd., Ilf. 125 EP62
Oakfield Rd.
Kenneth Rd., Bans. 234 DD115
Kenneth Rd., Rom. 126 EX59
Kenneth Robbins Ho. N17 100 DV52
Kennett Ct., Swan. 207 FE97
Kennett Dr., Hayes 136 BY71
Kennett Rd., Slou. 153 BB76
Kenning Rd., Hodd. 49 EA15
Kenning St. SE16 162 DW75
Railway Ave.
Kenning Ter. N1 142 DS67
Kenninghall Rd. E5 122 DU62
Kenninghall Rd. N18 100 DW50
Kennings Way SE11 278 F10
Kennings Way SE11 161 DN78
Kennington Grn. SE11 161 DN78
Montford Pl.
Kennington Gro. SE11 161 DM79
Oval Way
Kennington La. SE11 161 DL78
Kennington Oval SE11 161 DM79
Kennington Pk. Est. SE11 161 DN79
Harleyford St.
Kennington Pk. Gdns. SE11 161 DN79
Montford Pl.
Kennington Pk. Pl. SE11 161 DN79
Kennington Pk. Rd. SE11 161 DN79
Kennington Rd. SE1 278 D6
Kennington Rd. SE1 161 DN76
Kennington Rd. SE11 278 D8
Kennington Rd. SE11 161 DN76
Kenny Rd. NW7 97 CY50
Kennylands Rd., Ilf. 104 EU52
Kenrick Pl. W1 272 F7
Kenrick Sq., Red. 252 DS133
Kensal Rd. W10 139 CX70
Kensington Ave. E12 144 EL65
Kensington Ave., Th.Hth. 201 DN95
Kensington Ave., Wat. 75 BT42
Kensington Ch. Ct. W8 160 DB75
Kensington Ch. St. W8 140 DA74
Kensington Ch. Wk. W8 160 DB75
Kensington Clo. N11 98 DG51
Kensington Ct. W8 160 DB75
Kensington Ct. Gdns. W8 160 DB76
Kensington Ct. Pl.
Kensington Ct. Ms. W8 160 DB75
Kensington Ct. Pl.
Kensington Ct. Pl. W8 160 DB76
Kensington Dr., Wdf.Grn. 102 EK54
Kensington Gdns. W2 140 DB74
Kensington Gdns., Ilf. 125 EM60
Kensington Gdns., Kings.T. 197 CK97
Portsmouth Rd.
Kensington Gdns. Sq. W2 140 DB72
Kensington Gate W8 160 DC76
Kensington Gore SW7 160 DC75
Kensington Hall Gdns. W14 159 CZ78
Beaumont Ave.
Kensington High St. W8 160 DA76
Kensington High St. W14 159 CZ76
Kensington Mall W8 140 DA74
Kensington Palace Gdns. W8 140 DB74
Kensington Pk. Gdns. W11 139 CZ73
Kensington Pk. Ms. W11 139 CZ72
Kensington Pk. Rd.
Kensington Pk. Rd. W11 139 CZ72
Kensington Pl. W8 140 DA74
Kensington Rd. SW7 160 DC75
Kensington Rd. W8 160 DB75
Kensington Rd., Brwd. 108 FU44
Kensington Rd., Nthlt. 136 CA69
Kensington Rd., Rom. 127 FC58
Kensington Sq. W8 160 DB75
Kensington Ter., S.Croy. 220 DR108
Sanderstead Rd.
Kensley Chase, Slou. 131 AQ67
Kent Ave. W13 137 CH71
Kent Ave., Dag. 146 FA70
Kent Ave., Slou. 131 AQ71
Kent Ave., Well. 185 ET85
Kent Clo., Borwd. 78 CR38
Kent Clo., Mitch. 201 DL98
Kent Clo., Orp. 223 ES107
Kent Clo., Stai. 174 BK93
Kent Clo., Uxb. 134 BJ65
Kent Dr., Barn. 80 DG42
Kent Dr., Horn. 128 FK63
Kent Dr., Tedd. 177 CE92
Kent Gdns. W13 137 CH71
Kent Gdns., Ruis. 115 BV58
Kent Gate Way, Croy. 221 DZ107
Kent Hatch Rd., Eden. 255 EM131
Kent Hatch Rd., Oxt. 254 EJ129
Kent Ho. La., Beck. 183 DY92
Kent Ho. Rd. SE20 183 DX94
Kent Ho. Rd. SE26 183 DY92
Kent Ho. Rd., Beck. 183 DX94
Kent Pas. NW1 272 D4
Kent Rd. N21 100 DR46
Kent Rd. W4 158 CQ76
Kent Rd., Dag. 127 FB64
Kent Rd., Dart. 188 FK86
Kent Rd., E.Mol. 196 CC98
Kent Rd., Grav. 191 GG88
Kent Rd., Grays 170 GC79
Kent Rd., Kings.T. 197 CK97
Kent Rd., Long. 209 FX96
Kent Rd., Orp. 206 EV100
Kent Rd., Rich. 158 CN80
Kent Rd., W.Wick. 203 EB102
Kent Rd., Wok. 227 BB116
Kent St. E2 142 DT68
Kent St. E13 144 EH69
Kent Ter. NW1 272 C3
Kent Ter. NW1 140 DE69
Kent Twrs. SE20 182 DV94
Kent Vw., S.Ock. 168 FQ75
Kent Vw. Gdns., Ilf. 125 ES61
Kent Wk. SW9 161 DP84
Moorland Rd.
Kent Way SE15 162 DT81
Sumner Est.
Kent Way, Surb. 198 CL104
Kent Yd. SW7 276 C5
Kentford Way, Nthlt. 136 BY67
Kentish Bldgs. SE1 279 K4
Kentish La., Hat. 64 DC26
Kentish Rd., Belv. 166 FA77
Kentish Town Rd. NW1 141 DH66
Kentish Town Rd. NW5 141 DH65
Kentish Way, Brom. 204 EG96
Kentmere Rd. SE18 165 ES77
Kenton Ave., Har. 117 CF59
Kenton Ave., Sthl. 136 CA73
Kenton Ave., Sun. 196 BX96
Kenton Ct. W14 159 CZ76
Kensington High St.
Kenton Gdns., Har. 117 CJ57
Kenton Gdns., St.Alb. 43 CF21
Kenton La., Har. 95 CF51
Kenton Pk. Ave., Har. 117 CK56
Kenton Pk. Clo., Har. 117 CJ56
Kenton Pk. Cres., Har. 117 CK56
Kenton Pk. Rd., Har. 117 CJ56
Kenton Rd. E9 143 DX65
Kenton Rd., Har. 117 CF59
Kenton St. WC1 273 P4
Kenton St. WC1 141 DL70
Kenton Way, Hayes 135 BS69
Exmouth Rd.
Kenton Way, Wok. 226 AT117
Kentons La., Wind. 151 AL82
Kents Ave., Hem.H. 40 BK24
Kents La., Epp. 53 FD21
Kents Pas., Hmptn. 196 BZ95
Kentwode Grn. SW13 159 CU80
Kentwyns Ri., Red. 267 DM135
Kenver Ave. N12 98 DD51
Kenward Rd. SE9 184 EJ85
Kenway, Rain. 148 FJ69
Kenway, Rom. 105 FC54
Kenway Clo., Rain. 148 FJ69
Kenway
Kenway Dr., Amer. 72 AV39
Kenway Rd. SW5 160 DB77
Kenway Wk., Rain. 148 FK69
Kenway

Kings Lynn Path, Rom. 106 FK51
Kings Lynn Dr.
Kings Mead, Horl. 269 DP148
Kings Mead, Red. 267 DL136
Kings Mead Pk., Esher 215 CE108
Kings Meadow, Kings L. 58 BN28
Kings Ms. SW4 181 DL85
King's Ave.
King's Ms. WC1 274 C5
King's Ms. WC1 141 DM70
Kings Ms., Chig. 103 EQ47
Kings Mill La., Red. 267 DJ139
King's Orchard SE9 184 EL86
Kings Paddock, Hmptn. 196 CC95
Kings Par., Cars. 200 DE104
Wrythe La.
King's Pas. E11 124 EE59
Kings Pas., Kings.T. 197 CK96
Kings Pl. SE1 279 H5
Kings Pl. W4 158 CQ77
Chiswick High Rd.
Kings Pl., Buck.H. 102 EK47
King's Reach Twr. SE1 278 E2
Kings Ride Gate, Rich. 158 CN84
Kings Rd. E4 101 ED46
Kings Rd. E6 144 EJ67
Kings Rd. E11 124 EE59
King's Rd. N17 100 DT53
Kings Rd. N18 100 DU50
Kings Rd. N22 99 DM53
Kings Rd. NW10 139 CV66
Kings Rd. SE25 202 DU97
King's Rd. SW1 160 DD79
King's Rd. SW3 160 DD79
King's Rd. SW6 160 DB80
King's Rd. SW10 160 DC80
Kings Rd. SW14 158 CR83
Kings Rd. SW19 180 DA93
Kings Rd. W5 137 CK71
Kings Rd., Add. 212 BH110
Kings Rd., Bark. 145 EQ66
North St.
Kings Rd., Barn. 79 CW41
Kings Rd., Berk. 38 AU20
Kings Rd., Brwd. 108 FW47
Kings Rd., Ch.St.G. 90 AW47
Kings Rd., Egh. 173 BA91
Kings Rd., Felt. 176 BW88
Kings Rd., Guil. 242 AX134
Kings Rd. (Shalford), Guil. 258 AY141
Kings Rd., Har. 116 BZ61
Kings Rd., Hert. 32 DU08
Kings Rd., Horl. 268 DG148
Kings Rd., Kings.T. 178 CL94
Kings Rd., Mitch. 200 DG97
Kings Rd., Orp. 223 ET105
Kings Rd., Rich. 178 CM86
Kings Rd., Rom. 127 FG57
Kings Rd., St.Alb. 42 CC20
Kings Rd. 61 CJ26
(London Colney), St.Alb.
Kings Rd., Slou. 152 AS76
Kings Rd., Surb. 197 CJ102
Kings Rd., Sutt. 218 DA110
Kings Rd., Tedd. 177 CD92
Kings Rd., Twick. 177 CH86
Kings Rd., Uxb. 134 BK68
Kings Rd., Wal.Cr. 67 DY34
Kings Rd., Walt. 195 BV103
Kings Rd., West Dr. 154 BM75
Kings Rd., West. 238 EH118
Kings Rd., Wind. 151 AR84
Kings Rd., Wok. 227 BA116
King's Scholars' Pas. SW1 277 K7
King's Ter. NW1 141 DJ67
Plender St.
Kings Ter., Islw. 157 CG83
Worple Rd.
Kings Wk., Grays 170 GA79
Kings Wk., Kings.T. 197 CK95
Kings Wk., S.Croy. 220 DV114
Kings Way, Har. 117 CE56
Kingsand Rd. SE12 184 EG89
Kingsash Dr., Hayes 136 BY70
Kingsbridge Ave. W3 158 CM75
Kingsbridge Circ., Rom. 106 FL52
Kingsbridge Clo., Rom. 106 FL51
Kingsbridge Cres., Sthl. 136 BZ71
Kingsbridge Rd. W10 139 CW72
Kingsbridge Rd., Bark. 145 ER68
Kingsbridge Rd., Mord. 199 CX101
Kingsbridge Rd., Rom. 106 FL51
Kingsbridge Rd., Sthl. 156 BZ77
Kingsbridge Rd., Walt. 195 BV101
Kingsbridge Way, Hayes 135 BS69
Bradenham Rd.
Kingsbrook, Lthd. 231 CG118
Ryebrook Rd.
Kingsbury Ave., St.Alb. 42 CC19
Kingsbury Circle NW9 118 CN57
Kingsbury Cres., Stai. 173 BD91
Kingsbury Dr., Wind. 172 AU87
Kingsbury Rd. N1 142 DS65
Kingsbury Rd. NW9 118 CN57
Kingsbury Ter. N1 142 DS65
Kingsbury Trd. Est. NW9 118 CR58
Kingsclere Clo. SW15 179 CU87
Kingscliffe Gdns. SW19 179 CZ88
Kingscote Rd. W4 158 CR76
Kingscote Rd., Croy. 202 DV101
Kingscote Rd., N.Mal. 198 CR97
Kingscote St. EC4 274 F10
Kingscourt Rd. SW16 181 DK90
Kingscroft, Welw.G.C. 30 DB08
Kingscroft Rd. NW2 139 CZ65
Kingscroft Rd., Bans. 234 DD115
Kingscroft Rd., Lthd. 231 CH120
Kingsdale Gdns. W11 139 CX74
Kingsdale Rd. SE18 165 ET79
Kingsdale Rd. SE20 183 DX94
Kingsdale Rd., Berk. 38 AU20
Kingsdene, Tad. 233 CV121
Kingsdon La., Harl. 52 EW16
Kingsdown Ave. W3 138 CS73
Kingsdown Ave. W13 157 CH75
Kingsdown Ave., S.Croy. 219 DP109
Kingsdown Clo. W10 139 CX72
Kingsdown Clo., Grav. 191 GM88
Farley Rd.
Kingsdown Rd. E11 124 EE62
Kingsdown Rd. N19 121 DL62
Kingsdown Rd., Epsom 217 CU113
Kingsdown Rd., Sutt. 217 CY106
Kingsdown Way, Brom. 204 EG101
Kingsdowne Rd., Surb. 198 CL101
Kingsend, Ruis. 115 BR60
Kingsfield, Guil. 260 BL144
Kingsfield, Hodd. 49 EA15
Kingsfield, Wind. 151 AK81
Kingsfield Ave., Har. 116 CB56
Kingsfield Ct., Wat. 94 BX45
Kingsfield Dr., Enf. 83 DX35
Kingsfield Ho. SE9 184 EK90
Kingsfield Rd., Har. 117 CD59
Kingsfield Rd., Wat. 94 BX45
Kingsfield Ter., Dart. 188 FK86
Priory Rd.
Kingsfield Way, Enf. 83 DX35
Kingsford Ave., Wall. 219 DL108
Kingsford St. NW5 120 DF64
Kingsford Way E6 145 EM71
Kingsgate, Wem. 118 CQ62
Kingsgate Ave. N3 120 DA55
Kingsgate Clo., Bexh. 166 EY81
Kingsgate Clo., Orp. 206 EW97
Main Rd.
Kingsgate Pl. NW6 140 DA66
Kingsgate Rd. NW6 140 DA66
Kingsgate Rd., Kings.T. 198 CL95
Kingsground SE9 184 EL87
Kingshall Ms. SE13 163 EC83
Lewisham Rd.
Kingshill Ave., Har. 117 CH56
Kingshill Ave., Hayes 135 BS69
Kingshill Ave., Nthlt. 135 BU69
Kingshill Ave., Rom. 105 FC51
Kingshill Ave., St.Alb. 43 CH17
Kingshill Ave., Wor.Pk. 199 CU101
Kingshill Dr., Har. 95 CH54
Kingshill Way, Berk. 38 AU21
Kingshold Rd. E9 142 DW66
Kingsholm Gdns. SE9 164 EK84
Kingshurst Rd. SE12 184 EG87
Kingsland NW8 140 DE67
Broxwood Way
Kingsland, Harl. 51 EQ17
Kingsland, Pot.B. 63 CZ33
Kingsland Grn. E8 142 DS65
Kingsland High St. E8 142 DT65
Kingsland Pas. E8 142 DS65
Kingsland Grn.
Kingsland Rd. E2 275 N2
Kingsland Rd. E2 142 DS69
Kingsland Rd. E8 142 DS67
Kingsland Rd. E13 144 EJ69
Kingsland Rd., Hem.H. 40 BG22
Kingslawn Clo. SW15 179 CV85
Howards La.
Kingslea, Lthd. 231 CG120
Kingsleigh Pl., Mitch. 200 DF97
Chatsworth Pl.
Kingsleigh Wk., Brom. 204 EF98
Stamford Dr.
Kingsley Ave. W13 137 CG72
Kingsley Ave., Bans. 234 DA115
Kingsley Ave., Borwd. 78 CM40
Kingsley Ave., Dart. 188 FN85
Kingsley Ave., Egh. 172 AV93
Kingsley Ave., Houns. 156 CC82
Kingsley Ave., Sthl. 136 CA73
Kingsley Ave., Sutt. 218 DD105
Kingsley Ave. (Cheshunt), 66 DV29
Wal.Cr.
Kingsley Clo. N2 120 DC57
Kingsley Clo., Dag. 127 FB63
Kingsley Clo., Horl. 268 DF146
Kingsley Rd.
Kingsley Ct., Edg. 96 CP47
Kingsley Ct., Welw.G.C. 29 CZ13
Kingsley Dr., Wor.Pk. 199 CT103
Badgers Copse
Kingsley Flats SE1 162 DS77
Old Kent Rd.
Kingsley Gdns. E4 101 EA50
Kingsley Gdns., Horn. 128 FK56
Kingsley Gro., Reig. 266 DA137
Kingsley Ms. E1 142 DV73
Wapping La.
Kingsley Ms. W8 160 DB76
Stanford Rd.
Kingsley Ms., Chis. 185 EP93
Kingsley Path, Slou. 131 AK70
Wordsworth Rd.
Kingsley Pl. N6 120 DG59
Kingsley Rd. E7 144 EG66
Kingsley Rd. E17 101 EC54
Kingsley Rd. N13 99 DN49
Kingsley Rd. NW6 139 CZ67
Kingsley Rd. SW19 180 DB92
Kingsley Rd., Brwd. 109 GD45
Kingsley Rd., Croy. 201 DN102
Kingsley Rd., Har. 116 CC63
Kingsley Rd., Horl. 268 DF146
Kingsley Rd., Houns. 156 CB81
Kingsley Rd., Ilf. 103 EQ53
Kingsley Rd., Loug. 85 ER41
Kingsley Rd., Orp. 223 ET107
Kingsley Rd., Pnr. 116 BZ56
Kingsley St. SW11 160 DF83
Kingsley Wk., Grays 171 GG77
Kingsley Way N2 120 DC57
Kingsley Wd. Dr. SE9 185 EM90
Kingslyn Cres. SE19 202 DS95
Kingsman Par. SE18 165 EM76
Woolwich Ch. St.
Kingsman St. SE18 165 EM76
Kingsmead, Barn. 80 DA42
Kingsmead (Cuffley), Pot.B. 65 DL28
Kingsmead, Rich. 178 CM86
Kingsmead, St.Alb. 43 CK17
Kingsmead, Saw. 36 EY06
Kingsmead, Wal.Cr. 67 DX28
Kingsmead, West. 238 EK116
Kingsmead Ave. N9 100 DV46
Kingsmead Ave. NW9 118 CR59
Kingsmead Ave., Mitch. 201 DJ97
Kingsmead Ave., Rom. 127 FE58
Kingsmead Ave., Sun. 196 BW96
Kingsmead Ave., Surb. 198 CN103
Kingsmead Ave., Wor.Pk. 199 CV103
Kingsmead Clo., Epsom 216 CR108
Kingsmead Clo., Harl. 50 EH16
Kingsmead Clo., Sid. 186 EU89
Kingsmead Clo., Tedd. 177 CH93
Kingsmead Dr., Nthlt. 136 BZ66
Kingsmead Est. E9 123 DY63
Kingsmead Way
Kingsmead Rd. SW2 181 DN89
Kingsmead Way E9 123 DY63
Kingsmere Clo. SW15 159 CY83
Felsham Rd.
Kingsmere Pk. NW9 118 CP60
Kingsmere Rd. SW19 179 CX89
Kingsmill Ct., Hat. 45 CV20
Drakes Way
Kingsmill Gdns., Dag. 126 EZ64
Kingsmill Rd., Dag. 126 EZ64
Kingsmill Ter. NW8 140 DD68
Kingsmoor Rd., Harl. 51 EP17
Kingsnympton Pk., 178 CP94
Kings.T.
Kingspark Ct. E18 124 EG55
Kingsridge SW19 179 CY89
Kingsridge Gdns., Dart. 188 FK86
Kingsthorpe Rd. SE26 183 DX91
Kingston Ave., Felt. 175 BS86
Kingston Ave., Lthd. 231 CH121
Kingston Ave. 245 BS126
(East Horsley), Lthd.
Kingston Ave., Sutt. 199 CY104
Kingston Ave., West Dr. 134 BM73
Kingston Bri., Kings.T. 197 CK96
Kingston Bypass SW15 178 CS91
Kingston Bypass SW20 178 CS93
Kingston Bypass, Esher 197 CE103
Kingston Bypass, N.Mal. 199 CU98
Kingston Bypass, Surb. 197 CH104
Kingston Clo., Nthlt. 136 BZ66
Kingston Clo., Rom. 126 EY55
Kingston Clo., Tedd. 177 CH93
Kingston Ct. N4 122 DQ58
Wiltshire Gdns.
Kingston Ct., Grav. 190 GB85
Kingston Cres., Ashf. 174 BJ92
Kingston Cres., Beck. 203 DZ95
Kingston Gdns., Croy. 201 DL104
Wandle Rd.
Kingston Hall Rd., Kings.T. 197 CK97
Kingston Hill, Kings.T. 198 CN95
Kingston Hill Ave., Rom. 126 EY55
Kingston Hill Pl., Kings.T. 178 CQ91
Kingston Ho. Gdns., Lthd. 231 CG121
Upper Fairfield Rd.
Kingston La., Lthd. 244 BM127
Kingston La., Tedd. 177 CG92
Kingston La., Uxb. 134 BL69
Kingston La., West Dr. 154 BM75
Kingston Pk. Est., Kings.T. 178 CP93
Kingston Pl., Har. 95 CF52
Richmond Gdns.
Kingston Ri., Add. 212 BG110
Kingston Rd. N9 100 DU47
Kingston Rd. SW15 179 CU89
Kingston Rd. SW19 199 CY96
Kingston Rd. SW20 199 CW96
Kingston Rd., Ashf. 174 BL93
Kingston Rd., Barn. 80 DD43
Kingston Rd., Epsom 216 CS105
Kingston Rd., Ilf. 125 EP63
Kingston Rd., Kings.T. 198 CP97
Kingston Rd., Lthd. 231 CG121
Kingston Rd., N.Mal. 198 CR98
Kingston Rd., Rom. 127 FF56
Kingston Rd., Sthl. 156 BZ75
Kingston Rd., Stai. 173 BF91
Kingston Rd., Surb. 198 CP103
Kingston Rd., Tedd. 177 CH92
Kingston Rd., Wor.Pk. 198 CQ104
Kingston Sq. SE19 182 DR92
Kingston Vale SW15 178 CR91
Kingstown St. NW1 140 DG67
Kingswater Pl. SW11 160 DE80
Battersea Ch. Rd.
Kingsway N12 98 DC51
Kingsway SW14 158 CP83
Kingsway WC2 274 B8
Kingsway WC2 141 DM72
Kingsway, Croy. 219 DM106
Kingsway, Enf. 82 DV43
Kingsway, Ger.Cr. 112 AY55
Kingsway, Hayes 135 BQ71
Kingsway, Iver 133 BE72
High St.
Kingsway, N.Mal. 199 CW98
Kingsway, Orp. 205 EQ99
Kingsway (Cuffley), Pot.B. 65 DL30
Kingsway, Slou. 131 AP65
Kingsway, Stai. 174 BK88
Kingsway, Wat. 75 BT35
Kingsway, Wem. 118 CL63
Kingsway, W.Wick. 204 EE104
Kingsway, Wok. 226 AX118
Kingsway, Wdf.Grn. 102 EJ50
Kingsway, The, Epsom 216 CS111
Kingsway Ave., S.Croy. 220 DW109
Kingsway Ave., Wok. 226 AX118
Kingsway Business Pk., 196 BZ95
Hmptn.
Kingsway Cres., Har. 116 CC56
Kingsway Ind. Est. N18 101 DX51
Kingsway Rd., Sutt. 217 CY107
Kingswear Rd. NW5 121 DH62
Kingswear Rd., Ruis. 115 BU61
Kingswell Ride (Cuffley), 65 DL30
Pot.B.
Kingswood Ave. NW6 139 CY67
Kingswood Ave., Belv. 166 EZ77
Kingswood Ave., Brom. 204 EE97
Kingswood Ave., Hmptn. 176 CB93
Kingswood Ave., Houns. 156 BZ81
Kingswood Ave., S.Croy. 236 DV115
Kingswood Ave., Swan. 207 FF98
Kingswood Ave., Th.Hth. 201 DN99
Kingswood Clo. N20 98 DC45
Kingswood Clo. SW8 161 DL80
Kenchester Clo.
Kingswood Clo., Dart. 188 FJ85
Kingswood Clo., Egh. 172 AX91
Kingswood Clo., Enf. 82 DS43
Kingswood Clo., Guil. 243 BC133
Kingswood Clo., N.Mal. 199 CT100
Motspur Pk.
Kingswood Clo., Orp. 205 ER101
Kingswood Clo., Surb. 198 CL101
Kingswood Clo., Wey. 213 BP108
Kingswood Creek, Stai. 172 AX85
Kingswood Dr. SE19 182 DS91
Kingswood Dr., Cars. 200 DF102
Kingswood Dr., Sutt. 218 DB109
Kingswood Est. SE21 182 DS91
Bowen Dr.
Kingswood La., Warl. 236 DW115
Kingswood Pk. N3 97 CZ54
Kingswood Pl. SE13 164 EE84
Kingswood Ri., Egh. 172 AX92
Kingswood Rd. SE20 182 DW93
Kingswood Rd. SW2 181 DL86
Kingswood Rd. SW19 179 CZ94
Kingswood Rd. W4 158 CQ76
Kingswood Rd., Brom. 203 ED98
Kingswood Rd., Ilf. 126 EU60
Kingswood Rd., Sev. 241 FE120
Kingswood Rd., Tad. 233 CV121
Kingswood Rd., Wat. 59 BV34
Kingswood Rd., Wem. 118 CN62
Kingswood Ter. W4 158 CQ76
Kingswood Rd.
Kingswood Way, S.Croy. 220 DW113
Kingswood Way, Wall. 219 DL106
Kingsworth Clo., Beck. 203 DY99
Shirley Cres.
Kingsworthy Clo., 198 CM97
Kings.T.
Kingthorpe Rd. NW10 138 CR66
Kingthorpe Ter. NW10 138 CR65
Kingwell Rd., Barn. 80 DD38
Kingwood Rd. SW6 159 CY80
Kinlet Rd. SE18 165 EQ81
Kinloch Dr. NW9 118 CR59
Kinloch St. N7 121 DM62
Hornsey Rd.
Kinloss Gdns. N3 119 CZ55
Kinloss Rd., Cars. 200 DC101
Kinnaird Ave. W4 158 CQ80
Kinnaird Ave., Brom. 184 EF93
Kinnaird Clo., Brom. 184 EF93
Kinnaird Clo., Slou. 130 AJ72
Kinnaird Way, Wdf.Grn. 103 EM51
Kinnear Rd. W12 159 CT75
Kinnersley Manor, Reig. 266 DC142
Kinnersley Wk., Reig. 266 DB139
Castle Dr.
Kinnerton Pl. N. SW1 276 E5
Kinnerton Pl. S. SW1 276 E5
Kinnerton St. SW1 276 F5
Kinnerton St. SW1 160 DG75
Kinnerton Yd. SW1 276 E5
Kinnoul Rd. W6 159 CY79
Kinross Ave., Wor.Pk. 199 CU103
Kinross Clo., Edg. 96 CP47
Tayside Dr.
Kinross Clo., Har. 118 CL57
Kinross Clo., Sun. 175 BT92
Kinross Dr., Sun. 175 BT92
Kinsale Rd. SE15 162 DU83
Kintore Way SE1 279 P8
Kintyre Clo. SW16 201 DM96
Kinveachy Gdns. SE7 164 EL78
Kinver Rd. SE26 182 DW91
Kipings, Tad. 233 CX122
Heathcote
Kipling Ave., Til. 171 GH81
Kipling Dr. SW19 180 DD93
Kipling Est. SE1 279 L5
Kipling Est. SE1 162 DR75
Kipling Pl., Stan. 95 CF51
Uxbridge Rd.
Kipling Rd., Bexh. 166 EY81
Kipling Rd., Dart. 188 FP85
Kipling St. SE1 279 L5
Kipling St. SE1 162 DR75
Kipling Ter. N9 100 DR48
Kipling Twrs., Rom. 105 FH52
Kippington Clo., Sev. 256 FF124
Kippington Dr. SE9 184 EK88
Kippington Rd., Sev. 256 FG124
Kirby Clo., Epsom 217 CT106
Kirby Clo., Ilf. 103 ES51
Kirby Clo., Loug. 102 EL45
Kirby Clo., Nthwd. 93 BT51
Kirby Clo., Rom. 106 FN50
Kirby Est. SE16 162 DV76
Kirby Gro. SE1 279 M4
Kirby Gro. SE1 162 DS75
Kirby Rd., Dart. 188 FQ87
Kirby Rd., Wok. 226 AW117
Kirby St. EC1 274 E6
Kirby Way, Walt. 196 BW100
Kirchen Rd. W13 137 CH73
Kirk Ct., Sev. 256 FG123
Kirk La. SE18 165 EQ79
Kirk Ri., Sutt. 200 DB104
Kirk Rd. E17 123 DZ58
Kirkcaldy Grn., Wat. 94 BW48
Trevose Way
Kirkdale SE26 182 DW91
Kirkdale Rd. E11 124 EE60
Kirkefields, Guil. 242 AU131
Kirkfield Clo. W13 137 CH74
Broomfield Rd.
Kirkham Rd. E6 144 EL72
Kirkham St. SE18 165 ES79
Kirkland Ave., Ilf. 103 EN54
Kirkland Ave., Wok. 226 AS116
Kirkland Clo., Sid. 185 ES86
Kirkland Wk. E8 142 DT65
Laurel St.
Kirklands, Welw.G.C. 29 CX05
Kirkleas Rd., Surb. 198 CL102
Kirklees Rd., Dag. 126 EW64
Kirklees Rd., Th.Hth. 201 DN99
Kirkley Rd. SW19 200 DA95
Kirkly Clo., S.Croy. 220 DS109
Kirkman Pl. W1 273 M7
Kirkmichael Rd. E14 143 EC72
Dee St.
Kirks Pl. E14 143 DZ71
Rhodeswell Rd.
Kirkside Rd. SE3 164 EG79
Kirkstall Ave. N17 122 DR56
Kirkstall Gdns. SW2 181 DK88
Kirkstall Rd. SW2 181 DK88
Kirkstead Ct. E5 123 DY62
Mandeville St.
Kirksted Rd., Mord. 200 DB102
Kirkstone Way, Brom. 184 EE93
Kirkton Rd. N15 122 DS56
Kirkwall Pl. E2 142 DW69
Kirkwall Spur, Slou. 132 AS71
Kirkwood Rd. SE15 162 DV82
Kirn Rd. W13 137 CH73
Kirchen Rd.
Kirrane Clo., N.Mal. 199 CT99
Kirtle Rd., Chesh. 54 AQ31
Kirtley Rd. SE26 183 DY91
Kirtling St. SW8 161 DJ80
Kirton Clo. W4 158 CR77
Dolman Rd.
Kirton Clo., Horn. 148 FJ65
Kirton Gdns. E2 142 DT69
Chambord St.
Kirton Rd. E13 144 EJ68
Kirton Wk., Edg. 96 CQ52
Kirwyn Way SE5 161 DP80
Kitcat Ter. E3 143 EA69
Kitchener Ave., Grav. 191 GJ90
Kitchener Clo., St.Alb. 43 CH21
Kitchener Rd. E7 144 EH65
Kitchener Rd. E17 101 EB53
Kitchener Rd. N2 120 DE55
Kitchener Rd. N17 122 DR55
Kitchener Rd., Dag. 147 FB65
Kitchener Rd., Th.Hth. 202 DR97
Kitcheners Mead, St.Alb. 42 CC20
Kite Fld., Berk. 38 AS16
Kite Yd. SW11 160 DF81
Cambridge Rd.
Kitley Gdns. SE19 202 DT95
Kitsbury Rd., Berk. 38 AV19
Kitsbury Ter., Berk. 38 AV19
Kitsmead La., Cher. 192 AW102
Kitson Rd. SE5 162 DR80
Kitson Rd. SW13 159 CU81
Kitson Way, Harl. 35 EQ14
Kitswell Way, Rad. 61 CF33
Kitten La., Ware 34 EE11
Kitters Grn., Abb.L. 59 BS31
High St.
Kittiwake Clo., S.Croy. 221 DY110
Kittiwake Rd., Nthlt. 136 BX69
Kittiwake Way, Hayes 136 BX71
Kitto Rd. SE14 163 DX82
Kitt's End Rd., Barn. 79 CX36
Kitts Riding, Harl. 52 EX15
Kiver Rd. N19 121 DK61
Kiwi Clo., Twick. 177 CH86
Crown Rd.
Klea Ave. SW4 181 DJ86
Knapdale Clo. SE23 182 DV89
Knapmill Rd. SE6 183 EA89
Knapmill Way SE6 183 EB89
Knapp Clo. NW10 138 CS65
Knapp Rd. E3 143 EA70
Knapp Rd., Ashf. 174 BM91
Knapton Ms. SW17 180 DG93
Seely Rd.
Knaresborough Dr. SW18 180 DB88
Knaresborough Pl. SW5 160 DB77
Knatchbull Rd. NW10 138 CR67
Knatchbull Rd. SE5 161 DP82
Knaves Beech, H.Wyc. 88 AD53
Knaves Beech Business 88 AC54
Cen., H.Wyc.
Knaves Beech Way, H.Wyc. 88 AC54
Knebworth Ave. E17 101 EA53
Knebworth Path, Borwd. 78 CR42
Knebworth Rd. N16 122 DS63
Nevill Rd.
Knee Hill SE2 166 EW77
Knee Hill Cres. SE2 166 EW77
Knella Grn., Welw.G.C. 30 DA09
Knella Rd., Welw.G.C. 29 CZ10
Kneller Gdns., Islw. 177 CD86
Kneller Rd. SE4 163 DY84
Kneller Rd., N.Mal. 198 CS101
Kneller Rd., Twick. 176 CC86
Knight St., Saw. 36 EY05
Knighten St. E1 142 DU74
Knightland Rd. E5 122 DV61
Knighton Clo., Rom. 127 FD58
Knighton Clo., S.Croy. 219 DP108
Knighton Clo., Wdf.Grn. 102 EH49
Knighton Dr., Wdf.Grn. 102 EH49
Knighton La., Buck.H. 102 EH47
Knighton Pk. Rd. SE26 183 DX92
Knighton Rd. E7 124 EG62
Knighton Rd., Red. 266 DG136
Knighton Rd., Rom. 127 FC58
Knighton Rd., Sev. 241 FF116
Knighton St. E1 142 DU74
Knighton Way La., Uxb. 134 BH65
Knightrider Ct. EC4 142 DQ73
Godliman St.
Knightrider St. EC4 142 DQ73
Godliman St.
Knights Arc. SW1 276 D5
Knights Ave. W5 158 CL75
Knights Clo. E9 122 DW64
Churchill Wk.
Knights Clo., Egh. 173 BD93
Knights Clo., Wind. 151 AK81
Knights Ct., Kings.T. 198 CL97
Knights Ct., Rom. 126 EY58
Knights Hill SE27 181 DP92
Knights Hill Sq. SE27 181 DP91
Knights Hill
Knights La. N9 100 DU48
Knights Manor Way, Dart. 188 FM85
Knights Orchard, Hem.H. 39 BF18
Knights Pk., Kings.T. 198 CL97
Knights Pl., Wind. 151 AQ83
Frances Rd.
Knights Ridge, Orp. 224 EV106
Stirling Dr.
Knights Rd. E16 164 EG75
Knights Rd., Stan. 95 CJ49
Knights Wk. SE11 278 F9
Knights Wk., Rom. 86 EV41
Knight's Way, Brwd. 109 GA48
Knights Way, Ilf. 103 EQ51
Knightsbridge SW1 276 E4
Knightsbridge SW1 160 DF75
Knightsbridge SW7 276 C5
Knightsbridge SW7 160 DE75
Knightsbridge Cres., Stai. 174 BH93
Knightsbridge Gdns., 127 FD57
Rom.
Knightsbridge Grn. SW1 276 D5
Knightsbridge Grn. SW1 160 DF75
Knightsbridge Way, 40 BL19
Hem.H.
Knightsfield, Welw.G.C. 29 CY06
Knightswood, Wok. 226 AT118
Knightswood Clo., Edg. 96 CQ47
Knightwood Clo., Reig. 266 DA136
Knightwood Cres., N.Mal. 198 CS100
Knipp Hill, Cob. 214 BZ113
Knivet Rd. SW6 160 DA79
Knobfield, Dor. 261 BT143
Knobs Hill Rd. E15 143 EB67

Knockhall Chase, Green. 189 FV85
Knockhall Rd., Green. 189 FV86
Knockholt Clo., Sutt. 218 DB110
Knockholt Main Rd., Sev. 240 EY115
Knockholt Rd. SE9 184 EK85
Knockholt Rd., Sev. 224 EZ113
Knole, The SE9 185 EN91
Knole, The, Grav. 190 GD94
Knole Clo., Croy. 202 DW100
Stockbury Rd.
Knole Gate, Sid. 185 ES90
Woodside Cres.
Knole La., Sev. 257 FJ126
Knole Rd., Dart. 187 FG87
Knole Rd., Sev. 257 FK123
Knole Way, Sev. 257 FJ125
Knoll, The W13 137 CJ71
Knoll, The, Beck. 203 EB95
Knoll, The, Brom. 204 EG102
Knoll, The, Cher. 193 BF102
Knoll, The, Cob. 214 CA113
Knoll, The, Hert. 32 DV08
Knoll, The, Lthd. 231 CJ121
Knoll Ct. SE19 182 DT92
Knoll Cres., Nthwd. 93 BS54
Knoll Dr. N14 98 DG45
Knoll Pk. Rd., Cher. 193 BF102
Knoll Ri., Orp. 205 ET102
Knoll Rd. SW18 180 DC85
Knoll Rd., Bex. 186 FA87
Knoll Rd., Dor. 263 CG138
Knoll Rd., Sid. 186 EV92
Knolles Cres., Hat. 45 CV23
Knollmead, Surb. 198 CQ102
Knolls, The, Epsom 233 CW116
Knolls Clo., Wor.Pk. 199 CV104
Knollys Clo. SW16 181 DN90
Knollys Rd. SW16 181 DM90
Knolton Way, Slou. 132 AV72
Knottisford St. E2 142 DW69
Knottocks Clo., Beac. 89 AK50
Knottocks Dr., Beac. 88 AJ50
Knottocks End, Beac. 89 AK50
Knotts Grn. Ms. E10 123 EB58
Knotts Grn. Rd.
Knotts Grn. Rd. E10 123 EB58
Knotts Pl., Sev. 256 FG124
Knowl Hill, Wok. 227 BB118
Knowl Pk., Borwd. 78 CL43
Knowl Way, Borwd. 78 CM43
Knowland Way, Uxb. 113 BF58
Knowle, The, Hodd. 49 EA18
Knowle, The, Tad. 233 CW121
Knowle Ave., Bexh. 166 EY80
Knowle Clo. SW9 161 DN83
Knowle Gdns., W.Byf. 211 BF113
Madeira Rd.
Knowle Grn., Stai. 174 BG92
Knowle Gro., Vir.W. 192 AW101
Knowle Gro. Clo., Vir.W. 192 AW101
Knowle Hill, Vir.W. 192 AV101
Knowle Pk., Cob. 230 BY115
Knowle Pk. Ave., Stai. 174 BH93
Knowle Rd., Brom. 204 EL103
Knowle Rd., Twick. 177 CE88
Knowles Clo., West Dr. 134 BL74
Knowles Hill Cres. SE13 183 ED85
Knowles Wk. SW4 161 DJ83
Knowlton Grn., Brom. 204 EF99
Knowsley Ave., Sthl. 136 CB74
Knowsley Rd. SW11 160 DF82
Knox Rd. E7 144 EF65
Knox Rd., Guil. 242 AV130
Knox St. W1 272 D6
Knox St. W1 140 DF71
Knoyle St. SE14 163 DY79
Chubworthy St.
Knutsford Ave., Wat. 76 BX38
Kodak Ho., Hem.H. 40 BJ22
Koh-i-noor Ave. (Bushey), Wat. 76 CA44
Kohat Rd. SW19 180 DB92
Koonowla Clo., West. 238 EK115
Kooringa, Warl. 236 DV119
Korda Clo., Shep. 194 BM97
Kossuth St. SE10 164 EE78
Kotree Way SE1 162 DU77
Beatrice Rd.
Kramer Ms. SW5 160 DA78
Kempsford Gdns.
Kreedman Wk. E8 122 DU64
Kreisel Wk., Rich. 158 CM79
Kuala Gdns. SW16 201 DM95
Kuhn Way E7 124 EG64
Forest La.
Kydbrook Clo., Orp. 205 EQ101
Kylemore Clo. E6 144 EK68
Parr Rd.
Kylemore Rd. NW6 140 DA66
Kymberley Rd., Har. 117 CE58
Kyme Rd., Horn. 127 FF58
Kynance Clo., Rom. 106 FJ48
Kynance Gdns., Stan. 95 CJ53
Kynance Ms. SW7 160 DC76
Kynance Pl. SW7 160 DC76
Kynaston Ave. N16 122 DT62
Dynevor Rd.
Kynaston Ave., Th.Hth. 202 DQ99
Kynaston Clo., Har. 95 CD52
Kynaston Cres., Th.Hth. 202 DQ99
Kynaston Rd. N16 122 DS62
Kynaston Rd., Brom. 184 EG92
Kynaston Rd., Enf. 82 DR39
Kynaston Rd., Orp. 206 EV101
Kynaston Rd., Th.Hth. 202 DQ99
Kynaston Wd., Har. 95 CD52
Kynock Rd. N18 100 DW49
Kyrle Rd. SW11 180 DF86
Kytes Dr., Wat. 60 BX33
Kytes Est., Wat. 60 BX33
Kyverdale Rd. N16 122 DT59

L

La Plata Gro., Brwd. 108 FV48
La Roche Clo., Slou. 152 AW76
La Tourne Gdns., Orp. 205 EQ104
Laburnham Ave., West Dr. 134 BM73
Laburnham Clo., Upmin. 129 FU59
Laburnham Gdns., Upmin. 129 FT59
Laburnum Ave. N9 100 DS47
Laburnum Ave. N17 100 DR52
Laburnum Ave., Dart. 188 FJ88
Laburnum Ave., Horn. 127 FF62
Laburnum Ave., Sutt. 200 DE104
Laburnum Ave., Swan. 207 FC97
Laburnum Clo. E4 101 DZ51
Laburnum Clo. N11 98 DG51
Laburnum Clo. SE15 162 DW80
Clifton Way
Laburnum Clo., Guil. 242 AW131
Laburnum Clo. (Cheshunt), Wal.Cr. 67 DX31
Laburnum Ct. E2 142 DT67
Laburnum St.
Laburnum Ct., Stan. 95 CJ49
Laburnum Cres., Sun. 195 BV95
Batavia Rd.
Laburnum Gdns. N21 100 DQ47
Laburnum Gdns., Croy. 203 DX101
Laburnum Gro. N21 100 DQ47
Laburnum Gro. NW9 118 CQ59
Laburnum Gro., Grav. 190 GD87
Laburnum Gro., Houns. 156 BZ84
Laburnum Gro., N.Mal. 198 CR96
Laburnum Gro., Ruis. 115 BR58
Laburnum Gro., St.Alb. 60 CB25
Laburnum Gro., Slou. 153 BB79
Laburnum Gro., S.Ock. 149 FW69
Laburnum Gro., Sthl. 136 BZ70
Laburnum Ho., Dag. 126 FA61
Althorne Way
Laburnum Pl., Egh. 172 AV93
Laburnum Rd. SW19 180 DC94
Laburnum Rd., Cher. 194 BG102
Laburnum Rd., Epp. 70 EW29
Laburnum Rd., Epsom 216 CS113
Laburnum Rd., Hayes 155 BT77
Laburnum Rd., Hodd. 49 EB15
Laburnum Rd., Mitch. 200 DG96
Laburnum Rd., Wok. 226 AX119
Laburnum St. E2 142 DT67
Laburnum Wk., Horn. 128 FJ64
Laburnum Way, Brom. 205 EN101
Laburnum Way, Stai. 174 BM88
Laburnum Way (Cheshunt), Wal.Cr. 65 DP28
Millcrest Rd.
Lacebark Clo., Sid. 185 ET87
Lacey Ave., Couls. 235 DN120
Lacey Clo. N9 100 DU47
Lacey Clo., Egh. 173 BD94
Lacey Dr., Couls. 235 DN120
Lacey Dr., Dag. 126 EV63
Lacey Dr., Edg. 96 CL49
Lacey Dr., Hmptn. 196 BZ95
Lacey Grn., Couls. 235 DN120
Lacey Wk. E3 143 EA68
Lackford Rd., Couls. 234 DF118
Lackington St. EC2 275 L6
Lackington St. EC2 142 DR71
Lackmore Rd., Enf. 82 DW35
Lacock Clo. SW19 180 DC93
Lacon Rd. SE22 162 DU84
Lacy Rd. SW15 159 CX84
Ladas Rd. SE27 182 DQ91
Ladbroke Cres. W11 139 CY72
Ladbroke Gro.
Ladbroke Gdns. W11 139 CZ73
Ladbroke Gro. W10 139 CX70
Ladbroke Gro. W11 139 CY72
Ladbroke Gro., Red. 250 DG133
Ladbroke Ms. W11 139 CY74
Ladbroke Rd.
Ladbroke Rd. W11 139 CZ74
Ladbroke Rd., Enf. 82 DT44
Ladbroke Rd., Epsom 216 CR114
Ladbroke Rd., Horl. 269 DH146
Ladbroke Rd., Red. 250 DG133
Ladbroke Sq. W11 139 CZ73
Ladbroke Ter. W11 139 CZ73
Ladbroke Wk. W11 139 CZ74
Ladbrook Clo., Pnr. 116 BZ57
Ladbrook Rd. SE25 202 DR97
Ladbrooke Clo., Pot.B. 64 DA32
Strafford Gate
Ladbrooke Cres., Sid. 186 EX90
Ladbrooke Dr., Pot.B. 64 DA32
Ladbrooke Rd., Slou. 151 AQ76
Ladderstile Ride, Kings.T. 178 CQ92
Ladderswood Way N11 99 DJ50
Ladds Way, Swan. 207 FD98
Ladies Gro., St.Alb. 42 CB19
Lady Booth Rd., Kings.T. 198 CL96
Lady Gro., Welw.G.C. 29 CY13
Lady Hay, Wor.Pk. 199 CT103
Lady Margaret Rd. N19 121 DJ63
Lady Margaret Rd. NW5 121 DJ64
Lady Margaret Rd., Sthl. 136 BZ71
Lady Somerset Rd. NW5 121 DH63
Ladybower Ct. E5 123 DY63
Gilpin Rd.
Ladycroft Gdns., Orp. 223 EQ106
Ladycroft Rd. SE13 163 EB83
Ladycroft Wk., Stan. 95 CK53
Ladycroft Way, Orp. 223 EQ106
Ladyday Pl., Slou. 131 AQ74
Glenworth Pl.
Ladyegate Clo., Dor. 263 CK135
Ladyegate Rd., Dor. 263 CJ136
Ladyfield Clo., Loug. 85 EP42
Ladyfields, Grav. 191 GF91
Ladyfields, Loug. 85 EP42
Ladygate La., Ruis. 115 BP58
Ladygrove, Croy. 221 DY109
Ladygrove Dr., Guil. 243 BA129
Ladymead, Guil. 242 AW133
Ladymeadow, Kings L. 58 BK27
Lady's Clo., Wat. 75 BV42
Ladyshot, Harl. 36 EU14
Ladysmith Ave. E6 144 EL68
Ladysmith Ave., Ilf. 125 ER59
Ladysmith Rd. E16 144 EF69
Ladysmith Rd. N17 100 DU54
Ladysmith Rd. N18 100 DV50
Ladysmith Rd. SE9 185 EN86
Ladysmith Rd., Enf. 82 DS41
Ladysmith Rd., Har. 95 CE54
Ladysmith Rd., St.Alb. 43 CD19
Ladythorpe Clo., Add. 212 BH105
Church Rd.
Ladywalk, Rick. 91 BE50
Ladywell Clo. SE4 163 DZ84
Adelaide Ave.
Ladywell Heights SE4 183 DZ86
Ladywell Prospect, Saw. 36 FA06
Ladywell Rd. SE13 183 EB85
Ladywell St. E15 144 EF67
Plaistow Gro.
Ladywood Ave., Orp. 205 ES99
Ladywood Clo., Rick. 74 BH41
Ladywood Rd., Dart. 189 FS92
Ladywood Rd., Hert. 31 DM09
Ladywood Rd., Surb. 198 CN103
Lafone Ave., Felt. 176 BW88
Alfred Rd.
Lafone St. SE1 279 P4
Lafone St. SE1 162 DT75
Lagado Ms. SE16 143 DX74
Lagger, The, Ch.St.G. 90 AV48
Lagger Clo., Ch.St.G. 90 AV48
Laglands Clo., Reig. 250 DC132
Lagonda Ave., Ilf. 103 ET51
Lagonda Way, Dart. 168 FJ84
Arundel Rd.
Lagoon Rd., Orp. 206 EV99
Laidon Sq., Hem.H. 40 BK16
Laing Clo., Ilf. 103 ER51
Laing Dean, Nthlt. 136 BW67
Laings Ave., Mitch. 200 DF96
Lainlock Pl., Houns. 156 CB81
Spring Gro. Rd.
Lainson St. SW18 180 DA87
Laird Ave., Grays 170 GD75
Laird Ho. SE5 162 DQ80
Redcar St.
Lairdale Clo. SE21 182 DQ88
Lairs Clo. N7 141 DL65
Manger Rd.
Laitwood Rd. SW12 181 DH88
Lake, The (Bushey), Wat. 94 CC46
Lake Ave., Brom. 184 EG93
Lake Ave., Rain. 148 FK68
Lake Ave., Slou. 131 AR73
Lake Clo. SW19 179 CZ92
Lake Rd.
Lake Clo., W.Byf. 212 BK112
Lake Dr. (Bushey), Wat. 94 CC47
Lake End Ct., Maid. 130 AH72
Taplow Rd.
Lake End Rd., Maid. 130 AH73
Lake End Rd., Wind. 150 AH75
Lake Gdns., Dag. 126 FA64
Lake Gdns., Rich. 177 CH89
Lake Gdns., Wall. 201 DH104
Lake Ho. Rd. E11 124 EG62
Lake La., Horl. 267 DJ144
Lake Ri., Grays 169 FU77
Lake Ri., Rom. 105 FF54
Lake Rd. SW19 179 CZ92
Lake Rd., Croy. 203 DZ103
Lake Rd., Rom. 126 EX56
Lake Rd., Vir.W. 192 AV98
Lake Rd., Wal.Abb. 50 EE21
Lake Vw., Dor. 263 CJ139
Lake Vw., Edg. 96 CM50
Lake Vw., Pot.B. 64 DC33
Lake Vw. Rd., Sev. 256 FG123
Lakedale Rd. SE18 165 ES78
Lakefield Rd. N22 99 DP54
Lakefields Clo., Rain. 148 FK68
Lakehall Gdns., Th.Hth. 201 DP99
Lakehall Rd., Th.Hth. 201 DP99
Lakehurst Rd., Epsom 216 CS106
Lakeland Clo., Chig. 104 EV49
Lakeland Clo., Har. 95 CD51
Lakenheath N14 81 DJ43
Laker Pl. SW15 179 CY86
Lakers Ri., Bans. 234 DE116
Lakes Clo., Guil. 259 BB140
Lakes La., Beac. 89 AM54
Lakes Rd., Kes. 222 EJ106
Lakeside N3 98 DB54
Lakeside W13 137 CJ72
Edgehill Rd.
Lakeside, Beck. 203 EB97
Lakeside, Enf. 81 DK42
Lakeside, Rain. 148 FL68
Lakeside, Red. 250 DG132
Lakeside, Wall. 201 DH104
Derek Ave.
Lakeside, Wey. 195 BS103
Lakeside, Wok. 226 AS119
Lakeside Ave. SE28 146 EU74
Lakeside Ave., Ilf. 124 EK56
Lakeside Clo. SE25 202 DU96
Lakeside Clo., Chig. 103 ET49
Lakeside Clo., Ruis. 115 BR56
Lakeside Clo., Sid. 186 EW85
Lakeside Clo., Wok. 226 AS119
Lakeside Ct. N4 121 DP61
Lakeside Ct., Borwd. 78 CN43
Cavendish Cres.
Lakeside Cres., Barn. 80 DF43
Lakeside Cres., Brwd. 108 FX48
Lakeside Cres., Wey. 195 BQ104
Churchill Dr.
Lakeside Dr., Brom. 204 EL104
Lakeside Dr., Esher 214 CC107
Lakeside Dr., Slou. 132 AS67
Lakeside Pl., St.Alb. 61 CK27
Lakeside Rd. N13 99 DM49
Lakeside Rd. W14 159 CX76
Lakeside Rd., Slou. 153 BF80
Lakeside Rd. (Cheshunt), Wal.Cr. 66 DW28
Lakeside Way, Wem. 118 CN63
Lakeswood Rd., Orp. 205 EP99
Lakeview Ct. SW19 179 CY89
Victoria Dr.
Lakeview Rd. SE27 181 DN92
Lakeview Rd., Well. 166 EV84
Lakis Clo. NW3 120 DC63
Flask Wk.
Laleham Ave. NW7 96 CR48
Laleham Ct., Wok. 226 AY116
Laleham Pk., Stai. 194 BJ99
Laleham Reach, Cher. 194 BH96
Laleham Rd. SE6 183 EC87
Laleham Rd., Shep. 194 BL98
Laleham Rd., Stai. 173 BF92
Lalor St. SW6 159 CY82
Lamb Clo., Hat. 45 CV19
Lamb Clo., Til. 171 GJ82
Coleridge Rd.
Lamb Clo., Wat. 60 BW34
Lamb La. E8 142 DV66
Lamb St. E1 275 P6
Lamb St. E1 142 DT71
Lamb Wk. SE1 279 M5
Lamb Yd., Wat. 76 BX43
Lambarde Ave. SE9 185 EN91
Lambarde Dr., Sev. 256 FG123
Lambarde Rd., Sev. 256 FG122
Lambardes Clo., Orp. 224 EW110
Lamberhurst Clo., Orp. 206 EX102
Lamberhurst Rd. SE27 181 DN91
Lamberhurst Rd., Dag. 126 EY60
Lambert Ave., Rich. 158 CN83
Lambert Ave., Slou. 152 AY75
Lambert Clo., West. 238 EK116
Lambert Ct. (Bushey), Wat. 76 BX42
Lambert Jones Ms. EC2 142 DQ71
Beech St.
Lambert Rd. E16 144 EH72
Lambert Rd. N12 98 DC50
Lambert Rd. SW2 181 DL85
Lambert Rd., Bans. 218 DA114
Lambert St. N1 141 DN66
Lambert Wk., Wem. 117 CK62
Clarendon Gdns.
Lambert Way N12 98 DC50
Woodhouse Rd.
Lamberts Pl., Croy. 202 DR102
Lamberts Rd., Surb. 198 CL99
Lambeth Bri. SE1 278 A8
Lambeth Bri. SE1 161 DL77
Lambeth Bri. SW1 278 A8
Lambeth Bri. SW1 161 DL77
Lambeth High St. SE1 278 B8
Lambeth High St. SE1 161 DM77
Lambeth Hill EC4 275 H10
Lambeth Hill EC4 142 DQ73
Lambeth Palace Rd. SE1 278 B7
Lambeth Palace Rd. SE1 161 DM76
Lambeth Rd. SE1 278 D7
Lambeth Rd. SE1 161 DM76
Lambeth Rd. SE11 161 DM76
Lambeth Rd., Croy. 201 DN101
Lambeth Wk. SE11 278 C8
Lambeth Wk. SE11 161 DM77
Lamble St. NW5 120 DG64
Lambley Rd., Dag. 146 EV65
Lambly Hill, Vir.W. 192 AY97
Lambolle Pl. NW3 140 DE65
Lambolle Rd. NW3 140 DE65
Lambourn Chase, Rad. 77 CF36
Lambourn Clo. W7 157 CF75
Lambourn Rd. SW4 161 DH83
Lambourne Ave. SW19 179 CZ91
Lambourne Clo., Chig. 104 EV47
Lambourne Rd.
Lambourne Cres., Chig. 104 EV47
Lambourne Cres., Wok. 211 BD113
Lambourne Dr., Brwd. 109 GE45
Lambourne Dr., Cob. 230 BX115
Lambourne Gdns. E4 101 EA47
Lambourne Gdns., Bark. 145 ET66
Lambourne Rd.
Lambourne Gdns., Enf. 82 DT40
Lambourne Gdns., Horn. 128 FK61
Lambourne Gro., Kings.T. 198 CP96
Kenley Rd.
Lambourne Pl. SE3 164 EH81
Shooter's Hill Rd.
Lambourne Rd. E11 123 ED59
Lambourne Rd., Bark. 145 ES66
Lambourne Rd., Chig. 103 ET49
Lambourne Rd., Ilf. 125 ES61
Lambrook Ter. SW6 159 CY81
Lamb's Bldgs. EC1 275 K5
Lambs Clo. (Cuffley), Pot.B. 65 DM29
Lambs Conduit Pas. WC1 274 B6
Lamb's Conduit St. WC1 274 B5
Lamb's Conduit St. WC1 141 DM70
Lambs La., Rain. 147 FH71
Lambs Meadow, Wdf.Grn. 102 EK54
Lambs Ms. N1 141 DP67
Colebrooke Row
Lamb's Pas. EC1 275 K6
Lamb's Pas. EC1 142 DR71
Lambs Ter. N9 100 DR47
Lambs Wk., Enf. 82 DQ40
Lambscroft Ave. SE9 184 EJ90
Lambscroft Way, Ger.Cr. 90 AY54
Lambton Ave., Wal.Cr. 67 DX32
Lambton Pl. W11 139 CZ72
Westbourne Gro.
Lambton Rd. N19 121 DL60
Lambton Rd. SW20 199 CW95
Lambyn Cft., Horl. 269 DJ147
Lamerock Rd., Brom. 184 EF91
Lamerton Rd., Ilf. 103 EP54
Lamerton St. SE8 163 EA79
Lamford Clo. N17 100 DR52
Lamington St. W6 159 CV77
Lamlash St. SE11 278 F8
Lammas Ave., Mitch. 200 DG96
Lammas Ct., Wind. 151 AQ82
Lammas Dr., Stai. 173 BD91
Lammas Grn. SE26 182 DV90
Lammas La., Esher 214 CA106
Lammas Mead, Brox. 49 DZ23
Lammas Pk. W5 157 CJ75
Lammas Pk. Gdns. W5 137 CJ74
Lammas Pk. Rd. W5 137 CJ74
Lammas Rd. E9 143 DX66
Lammas Rd. E10 123 DY61
Lammas Rd., Rich. 177 CJ91
Lammas Rd., Slou. 131 AK71
Lammas Rd., Wat. 76 BW43
Lammas Way, H.Wyc. 88 AC54
Lammermoor Rd. SW12 181 DH87
Lamont Rd. SW10 160 DC79
Lamont Rd. Pas. SW10 160 DD79
Lamont Rd.
Lamorbey Clo., Sid. 185 ET88
Lamorna Ave., Grav. 191 GK89
Lamorna Clo. E17 101 EC54
Lamorna Clo., Orp. 206 EU101
Lamorna Clo., Rad. 61 CH34
Lamorna Gro., Stan. 95 CK53
Lampard Gro. N16 122 DT60
Lampern Sq. E2 142 DU69
Nelson Gdns.
Lampeter Clo., Wok. 226 AY118
Lampeter Sq. W6 159 CY79
Humbolt Rd.
Lampits, Hodd. 49 EB17
Lamplighter Clo. E1 142 DW70
Cleveland Way
Lamplighters Clo., Dart. 188 FM86
Lamplighters Clo., Wal.Abb. 68 EG34
Lampmead Rd. SE12 184 EF85
Lamport Clo. SE18 165 EM77
Lampton Ave., Houns. 156 CB81
Lampton Ho. Clo. SW19 179 CX91
Lampton Pk. Rd., Houns. 156 CB82
Lampton Rd., Houns. 156 CB82
Lamsey Rd., Hem.H. 40 BK22
Lamson Rd., Rain. 147 FF70
Lanacre Ave. NW9 96 CR53
Lanark Clo. W5 137 CJ71
Lanark Pl. W9 140 DC70
Lanark Rd. W9 140 DB68
Lanark Sq. E14 163 EB76
Lanata Wk., Hayes 136 BX70
Ramulis Dr.
Lanbury Rd. SE15 163 DX84
Lancashire Ct. W1 273 J10
Lancaster Ave. E18 124 EH56
Lancaster Ave. SE27 181 DP89
Lancaster Ave. SW19 179 CX92
Lancaster Ave., Bark. 145 ES66
Lancaster Ave., Barn. 80 DC38
Lancaster Ave., Mitch. 201 DL99
Lancaster Ave., Slou. 131 AQ70
Lancaster Clo. N1 142 DS66
Hertford Rd.
Lancaster Clo. N17 100 DU52
Park La.
Lancaster Clo. NW9 97 CT52
Corner Mead
Lancaster Clo., Brwd. 108 FU43
Lancaster Clo., Brom. 204 EF98
Lancaster Clo., Egh. 172 AX92
Lancaster Clo., Kings.T. 177 CK92
Lancaster Clo., Wok. 227 BA116
Lancaster Cotts., Rich. 178 CL86
Lancaster Pk.
Lancaster Ct. SE27 181 DP89
Lancaster Ct. SW6 159 CZ80
Lancaster Ct. W2 140 DC73
Lancaster Gate
Lancaster Ct., Bans. 217 CZ114
Lancaster Ct., Walt. 195 BU101
Lancaster Dr. E14 143 EC74
Prestons Rd.
Lancaster Dr. NW3 140 DE65
Lancaster Dr., Hem.H. 57 AZ27
Lancaster Dr., Horn. 127 FH64
Lancaster Dr., Loug. 84 EL44
Lancaster Gdns. SW19 179 CY92
Lancaster Gdns. W13 157 CH75
Lancaster Gdns., Kings.T. 177 CK92
Lancaster Gate W2 140 DC73
Lancaster Gro. NW3 140 DD65
Lancaster Ms. SW18 180 DB85
East Hill
Lancaster Ms. W2 140 DC73
Lancaster Ms., Rich. 178 CL86
Richmond Hill
Lancaster Pk., Rich. 178 CL85
Lancaster Pl. SW19 179 CX92
Lancaster Rd.
Lancaster Pl. WC2 274 B10
Lancaster Pl. WC2 141 DM73
Lancaster Pl., Houns. 156 BW82
Lancaster Pl., Ilf. 125 EQ64
Staines Rd.
Lancaster Pl., Twick. 177 CG86
Lancaster Rd. E7 144 EG66
Lancaster Rd. E11 124 EE61
Lancaster Rd. E17 101 DX54
Lancaster Rd. N4 121 DM59
Lancaster Rd. N11 99 DK51
Lancaster Rd. N18 100 DT50
Lancaster Rd. NW10 119 CU64
Lancaster Rd. SE25 202 DT96
Lancaster Rd. SW19 179 CX92
Lancaster Rd. W11 139 CY72
Lancaster Rd., Barn. 80 DD43
Lancaster Rd., Enf. 82 DR39
Lancaster Rd., Epp. 70 FA26
Lancaster Rd., Grays 169 FX78
Lancaster Rd., Har. 116 CA57
Lancaster Rd., Nthlt. 136 CC65
Lancaster Rd., St.Alb. 43 CF18
Lancaster Rd., Sthl. 136 BY73
Lancaster Rd., Uxb. 134 BK65
Lancaster St. SE1 278 G5
Lancaster St. SE1 161 DP75
Lancaster Ter. W2 140 DD73
Lancaster Wk. W2 140 DD74
Lancaster Wk., Hayes 135 BQ72
Lancaster Way, Abb.L. 59 BT31
Lance Rd., Har. 116 CC59
Lancefield St. W10 139 CZ69
Lancell St. N16 122 DS61
Stoke Newington Ch. St.
Lancelot Ave., Wem. 117 CK63
Lancelot Clo., Slou. 151 AN75
Mitchell Clo.
Lancelot Cres., Wem. 117 CK63
Lancelot Gdns., Barn. 98 DG45
Lancelot Pl. SW7 276 D5
Lancelot Pl. SW7 160 DF75
Lancelot Rd., Ilf. 103 ES51
Lancelot Rd., Well. 166 EU84
Lancelot Rd., Wem. 117 CK63
Lancer Sq. W8 160 DB75
Old Ct. Pl.
Lancey Clo. SE7 164 EK77
Cleveley Clo.
Lanchester Rd. N6 120 DF57
Lancing Gdns. N9 100 DT46
Lancing Rd. W13 137 CH73
Drayton Grn. Rd.
Lancing Rd., Croy. 201 DM100
Lancing Rd., Felt. 175 BT89
Lancing Rd., Ilf. 125 ER58
Lancing Rd., Orp. 206 EU103
Lancing Rd., Rom. 106 FL52
Lancing St. NW1 273 M3
Lancing Way, Rick. 75 BP43
Lancresse Clo., Uxb. 134 BK65
Lancresse Ct. N1 142 DS67
Landau Way, Brox. 67 DZ25
Landau Way, Erith 168 FK78
Landcroft Rd. SE22 182 DT85
Landells Rd. SE22 182 DT86
Landen Pk., Horl. 268 DE146
Lander Rd., Grays 170 GD78
Landford Clo., Rick. 92 BL47
Landford Rd. SW15 159 CW83
Landgrove Rd. SW19 180 DA92
Landmann Way SE14 163 DX79

Landmead Rd. (Cheshunt), Wal.Cr. 67 DY29
Landon Pl. SW1 276 D6
Landon Pl. SW1 160 DF76
Landon Wk. E14 143 EB73
Cottage St.
Landon Way, Ashf. 175 BP93
Courtfield Rd.
Landons Clo. E14 143 EC74
Landor Rd. SW9 161 DL83
Landor Wk. W12 159 CU75
Landport Way SE15 162 DT80
Daniel Gdns.
Landra Gdns. N21 81 DP44
Landridge Rd. SW6 159 CZ82
Landrock Rd. N8 121 DL58
Lands End, Borwd. 77 CK44
Landscape Rd., Warl. 236 DV119
Landscape Rd., Wdf.Grn. 102 EH52
Landseer Ave. E12 125 EN64
Landseer Ave., Grav. 190 GD90
Landseer Clo. SW19 200 DC95
Brangwyn Cres.
Landseer Clo., Edg. 96 CN54
Landseer Clo., Horn. 127 FH60
Landseer Rd. N19 121 DL62
Landseer Rd., Enf. 82 DU43
Landseer Rd., N.Mal. 198 CR101
Landseer Rd., Sutt. 218 DA107
Landstead Rd. SE18 165 ER80
Landway, The, Orp. 206 EW97
Lane, The NW8 140 DC68
Marlborough Pl.
Lane, The SE3 164 EG83
Lane, The, Cher. 194 BG97
Lane, The, Vir.W. 192 AY97
Lane App. NW7 97 CY50
Lane Ave., Green. 189 FW86
Lane Clo. NW2 119 CV62
Lane Clo., Add. 212 BH106
Lane End, Bexh. 167 FB83
Lane End, Epsom 216 CP114
Lane End, Harl. 52 EY15
Lane End, Hat. 45 CT21
Lane Gdns. (Bushey), Wat. 95 CE45
Lane Ms. E12 125 EM62
Colchester Ave.
Lane Wd. Clo., Amer. 72 AT39
Lanefield Wk., Welw.G.C. 29 CW09
Lanercost Clo. SW2 181 DN89
Lanercost Gdns. N14 99 DL45
Lanercost Rd. SW2 181 DN89
Lanes Ave., Grav. 191 GG91
Lanesborough Pl. SW1 276 G4
Laneside, Chis. 185 EP92
Laneside, Edg. 96 CQ50
Laneside Ave., Dag. 126 EZ59
Laneway SW15 179 CV85
Sunnymead Rd.
Lanfranc Rd. E3 143 DY68
Lanfrey Pl. W14 159 CZ78
North End Rd.
Lang Clo., Lthd. 230 CB123
Lang St. E1 142 DW70
Langaller La., Lthd. 230 CB122
Langbourne Ave. N6 120 DG61
Langbourne Way, Esher 215 CG107
Langbrook Rd. SE3 164 EK83
Langcroft Clo., Cars. 200 DF104
Langdale Ave., Mitch. 200 DF97
Langdale Clo. SE17 162 DQ79
Langdale Clo. SW14 158 CP84
Clifford Ave.
Langdale Clo., Dag. 126 EW60
Langdale Clo., Orp. 205 EP104
Grasmere Rd.
Langdale Clo., Wok. 226 AW116
Langdale Ct., Hem.H. 40 BL17
Wharfedale
Langdale Cres., Bexh. 166 FA80
Langdale Dr., Hayes 135 BS68
Langdale Gdns., Grnf. 137 CH69
Langdale Gdns., Horn. 127 FG64
Langdale Gdns., Wal.Cr. 83 DX35
Langdale Rd. SE10 163 EC80
Langdale Rd., Th.Hth. 201 DN98
Langdale St. E1 142 DV72
Burslem St.
Langdale Wk., Grav. 190 GE90
Landseer Ave.
Langdon Ct. NW10 138 CS67
Langdon Cres. E6 145 EN68
Langdon Dr. NW9 118 CQ60
Langdon Pk. Rd. N6 121 DJ59
Langdon Pl. SW14 158 CQ83
Rosemary La.
Langdon Rd. E6 145 EN67
Langdon Rd., Brom. 204 EH97
Langdon Rd., Mord. 200 DC99
Langdon Shaw, Sid. 185 ET92
Langdon Wk., Mord. 200 DC99
Langdon Rd.
Langdon Way SE1 162 DU77
Simms Rd.
Langfield Clo., Wal.Abb. 50 EE22
Langford Clo. E8 122 DU64
Langford Clo. N15 122 DS58
Langford Clo. NW8 140 DC68
Langford Pl.
Langford Ct. NW8 140 DC68
Langford Pl.
Langford Cres., Barn. 80 DF42
Langford Grn. SE5 162 DS83
Langford Grn., Brwd. 109 GC44
Langford Pl. NW8 140 DC68
Langford Pl., Sid. 186 EU90
Langford Rd. SW6 160 DB82
Gilstead Rd.
Langford Rd., Barn. 80 DE42
Langford Rd., Wdf.Grn. 102 EJ51
Langfords, Buck.H. 102 EK47
Langfords Way, Croy. 221 DY111
Langham Clo. N15 121 DP55
Langham Rd.
Langham Clo., St.Alb. 43 CK15
Langham Ct., Horn. 128 FK59
Langham Dene, Ken. 235 DP115
Langham Dr., Rom. 126 EV58
Langham Gdns. N21 81 DN43
Langham Gdns. W13 137 CH73
Langham Gdns., Edg. 96 CQ52
Langham Gdns., Rich. 177 CJ91
Langham Gdns., Wem. 117 CJ61
Langham Ho. Clo., Rich. 177 CK91
Langham Pl. N15 121 DP55
Langham Pl. W1 273 J7
Langham Pl. W1 141 DH71
Langham Pl. W4 158 CS79
Hogarth Roundabout
Langham Pl., Egh. 173 AZ92
Langham Rd. N15 121 DP55
Langham Rd. SW20 199 CW95
Langham Rd., Edg. 96 CQ51
Langham Rd., Tedd. 177 CH92
Langham St. W1 273 J7
Langham St. W1 141 DH71
Langhedge Clo. N18 100 DT51
Langhedge La.
Langhedge La. N18 100 DT51
Langhedge La. Ind. Est. N18 100 DT51
Langholm Clo. SW12 181 DK87
King's Ave.
Langholme (Bushey), Wat. 94 CC46
Langhorne Rd., Dag. 146 FA66
Langland Ct., Nthwd. 93 BQ52
Langland Cres., Stan. 95 CK54
Langland Dr., Pnr. 94 BY52
Langland Gdns. NW3 120 DB64
Langland Gdns., Croy. 203 DZ103
Langlands Dr., Dart. 189 FS92
Langlands Ri., Epsom 216 CQ113
Burnet Gro.
Langler Rd. NW10 139 CW68
Langley Ave., Hem.H. 40 BL23
Langley Ave., Ruis. 115 BV61
Langley Ave., Surb. 197 CK102
Langley Ave., Wor.Pk. 199 CX102
Langley Broom, Slou. 153 AZ78
Langley Business Cen., Slou. 153 BA75
Langley Clo., Epsom 232 CR119
Langley Clo., Guil. 242 AW133
Langley Clo., Rom. 106 FK52
Langley Ct. SE9 185 EN86
Langley Ct. WC2 273 P10
Langley Ct., Beck. 203 EB99
Langley Cres. E11 124 EH59
Langley Cres., Dag. 146 EW66
Langley Cres., Edg. 96 CQ48
Langley Cres., Hayes 155 BT80
Langley Cres., Kings L. 58 BN30
Langley Cres., St.Alb. 42 CC18
Langley Dr. E11 124 EH59
Langley Dr. W3 158 CP75
Langley Dr., Brwd. 108 FU48
Langley Gdns., Brom. 204 EJ98
Langley Gdns., Dag. 146 EX66
Langley Gdns., Orp. 205 EP100
Langley Gro., N.Mal. 198 CS96
Langley Hill, Kings L. 58 BM29
Langley Hill Clo., Kings L. 58 BN29
Langley La. SW8 161 DL79
Langley La., Abb.L. 59 BT31
Langley La., Epsom 248 CQ125
Tumber St.
Langley Lo. La., Kings L. 58 BL31
Langley Meadow, Loug. 85 ER40
Langley Oaks Ave., S.Croy. 220 DU110
Langley Pk. NW7 96 CS51
Langley Pk. Rd., Iver 133 BC72
Langley Pk. Rd., Slou. 153 BA75
Langley Pk. Rd., Sutt. 218 DC106
Langley Quay, Slou. 153 BA75
Langley Rd. SW19 199 CZ95
Langley Rd., Abb.L. 59 BS31
Langley Rd., Beck. 203 DY98
Langley Rd., Islw. 157 CF82
Langley Rd., Kings L. 58 BH30
Langley Rd., Slou. 152 AW76
Langley Rd., S.Croy. 221 DX109
Langley Rd., Stai. 173 BF93
Langley Rd., Surb. 198 CL101
Langley Rd., Wat. 75 BT39
Langley Rd., Well. 166 EW79
Langley Row, Barn. 79 CZ39
Langley St. WC2 273 P9
Langley St. WC2 141 DL72
Langley Vale Rd., Epsom 232 CP120
Langley Wk., Wok. 226 AY119
Midhope Rd.
Langley Way, Wat. 75 BS40
Langley Way, W.Wick. 203 ED102
Langleybury La., Kings L. 75 BP37
Langmans La., Wok. 226 AV118
Langmans Way, Wok. 226 AS116
Langmead Dr. (Bushey), Wat. 95 CD45
Langmead St. SE27 181 DP91
Beadman St.
Langmore Ct., Bexh. 166 EX83
Regency Way
Langport Ct., Walt. 196 BW102
Langridge Ms., Hmptn. 176 BZ93
Oak Ave.
Langroyd Rd. SW17 180 DF89
Langshott, Horl. 269 DH146
Langshott Clo., Add. 211 BE111
Langshott La., Horl. 269 DH148
Langside Ave. SW15 159 CU84
Langside Cres. N14 99 DK48
Langston Hughes Clo. SE24 161 DP84
Shakespeare Rd.
Langston Rd., Loug. 85 EQ43
Langthorn Ct. EC2 275 L8
Langthorne Cres., Grays 170 GC77
Langthorne Rd. E11 123 EC62
Langthorne St. SW6 159 CX81
Langton Ave. E6 145 EN69
Langton Ave. N20 98 DC45
Langton Ave., Epsom 217 CT111
Langton Clo. WC1 274 C4
Langton Clo., Add. 194 BH104
Langton Clo., Wok. 226 AT117
Kenton Way
Langton Gro., Nthwd. 93 BQ50
Langton Ri. SE23 182 DV87
Langton Rd. NW2 119 CW62
Langton Rd. SW9 161 DP80
Langton Rd., Har. 94 CC52
Langton Rd., Hodd. 49 DZ17
Langton Rd., W.Mol. 196 CC99
Langton St. SW10 160 DC79
Langton Way SE3 164 EF81
Langton Way, Croy. 202 DS104
Langton Way, Egh. 173 BC93
Langton Way, Grays 171 GJ77
Langton's Meadow, Slou. 131 AQ65
Langtry Rd. NW8 140 DB67
Langtry Rd., Nthlt. 136 BX68
Langtry Wk. NW8 140 DC66
Alexandra Pl.
Langwood Chase, Tedd. 177 CJ93
Langwood Gdns., Wat. 75 BU39
Langworth Clo., Dart. 188 FK90
Langworth Dr., Hayes 135 BU72
Lanhill Rd. W9 140 DA70
Lanier Rd. SE13 183 EC86
Lanigan Dr., Houns. 176 CB85
Lankaster Gdns. N2 98 DD53
Lankers Dr., Har. 116 BZ58
Lankton Clo., Beck. 203 EC95
Lannock Rd., Hayes 135 BS74
Lannoy Rd. SE9 185 EQ88
Lanrick Copse, Berk. 38 AY18
Lanrick Rd. E14 143 ED72
Lanridge Rd. SE2 166 EX76
Lansbury Ave. N18 100 DR50
Lansbury Ave., Bark. 146 EU66
Lansbury Ave., Felt. 175 BV86
Lansbury Ave., Rom. 126 EY57
Lansbury Clo. NW10 118 CQ64
Lansbury Cres., Dart. 188 FN85
Lansbury Dr., Hayes 135 BS68
Lansbury Est. E14 143 EB72
Lansbury Gdns. E14 143 EC72
Lansbury Gdns., Til. 171 GG81
Lansbury Rd., Enf. 83 DX39
Lansbury Way N18 100 DS50
Lansbury Ave.
Lansdell Rd., Mitch. 200 DG96
Lansdown, Guil. 243 BA134
Lansdown Clo., Walt. 196 BW102
St. Johns Dr.
Lansdown Clo., Wok. 226 AT119
Lansdown Pl., Grav. 191 GF88
Lansdown Rd. E7 144 EJ66
Lansdown Rd., Ger.Cr. 90 AX53
Lansdown Rd., Sid. 186 EV90
Lansdowne Ave., Bexh. 166 EW80
Lansdowne Ave., Orp. 205 EP102
Lansdowne Ave., Slou. 132 AS74
Lansdowne Clo. SW20 179 CX94
Lansdowne Clo., Surb. 198 CP103
Kingston Rd.
Lansdowne Clo., Twick. 177 CF88
Lion Rd.
Lansdowne Clo., Wat. 76 BX35
Lansdowne Ct., Slou. 132 AS74
Lansdowne Ct., Wor.Pk. 199 CU103
Lansdowne Cres. W11 139 CZ73
Lansdowne Dr. E8 142 DU65
Lansdowne Gdns. SW8 161 DL81
Lansdowne Grn. SW8 161 DL81
Hartington Rd.
Lansdowne Gro. NW10 118 CS63
Lansdowne Hill SE27 181 DP90
Lansdowne La. SE7 164 EK78
Lansdowne Ms. SE7 164 EK78
Lansdowne Ms. W11 139 CZ74
Lansdowne Rd.
Lansdowne Pl. SE1 279 L6
Lansdowne Pl. SE19 182 DT94
Lansdowne Ri. W11 139 CY73
Lansdowne Rd. E4 101 EA47
Lansdowne Rd. E11 124 EF61
Lansdowne Rd. E17 123 EA58
Lansdowne Rd. E18 124 EG55
Lansdowne Rd. N3 97 CZ52
Lansdowne Rd. N10 99 DJ54
Lansdowne Rd. N17 100 DU53
Lansdowne Rd. SW20 179 CW94
Lansdowne Rd. W11 139 CY73
Lansdowne Rd., Brom. 184 EG94
Lansdowne Rd., Chesh. 54 AQ29
Lansdowne Rd., Croy. 202 DQ103
Lansdowne Rd., Epsom 216 CQ108
Lansdowne Rd., Har. 117 CE59
Lansdowne Rd., Houns. 156 CB83
Lansdowne Rd., Ilf. 125 ET60
Lansdowne Rd., Pur. 219 DN112
Lansdowne Rd., Sev. 257 FK122
Lansdowne Rd., Stai. 174 BH94
Lansdowne Rd., Stan. 95 CJ51
Lansdowne Rd., Til. 171 GF82
Lansdowne Rd., Uxb. 135 BP72
Lansdowne Row W1 277 J2
Lansdowne Sq., Grav. 191 GF86
Lansdowne Ter. WC1 274 A5
Lansdowne Ter. WC1 141 DL70
Lansdowne Wk. W11 139 CZ74
Lansdowne Way SW8 161 DK81
Lansdowne Wd. Clo. SE27 181 DP90
Lansfield Ave. N18 100 DU49
Lant St. SE1 279 H4
Lant St. SE1 162 DQ75
Lantern Clo. SW15 159 CU84
Lantern Clo., Wem. 117 CK64
Lanterns Ct. E14 163 EA75
Lanvanor Rd. SE15 162 DW82
Lapford Clo. W9 139 CZ70
Lapponum Wk., Hayes 136 BX71
Lochan Clo.
Lapse Wd. Wk. SE23 182 DV89
Lapstone Gdns., Har. 117 CJ58
Lapwing Clo., Erith 167 FH80
Lapwing Clo., Hem.H. 40 BL16
Lapwing Clo., S.Croy. 221 DY110
Lapwing Ct., Surb. 198 CN104
Chaffinch Clo.
Lapwing Gro., Guil. 243 BD132
Lapwing Way, Abb.L. 59 BU31
College Rd.
Lapwing Way, Hayes 136 BX72
Lapwings, The, Grav. 191 GK89
Lapworth Clo., Orp. 206 EW103
Lara Clo. SE13 183 EC86
Lara Clo., Chess. 216 CL108
Larbert Rd. SW16 181 DJ94
Larby Pl., Epsom 216 CS110
Larch Ave. W3 138 CS74
Larch Ave., Guil. 242 AW132
Larch Ave., St.Alb. 60 BY30
Larch Clo. E13 144 EH70
Larch Clo. N11 98 DG52
Larch Clo. N19 121 DJ61
Bredgar Rd.
Larch Clo. SE8 163 DZ79
Clyde St.
Larch Clo. SW12 181 DH88
Larch Clo., H.Wyc. 88 AC45
Larch Clo., Red. 266 DC136
Larch Clo., Slou. 131 AP71
Larch Clo., Tad. 234 DC121
Larch Clo., Wal.Cr. 66 DS27
The Firs
Larch Clo., Warl. 237 DY119
Larch Cres., Epsom 216 CP107
Larch Cres., Hayes 136 BW70
Larch Dr. W4 158 CN78
Gunnersbury Ave.
Larch Grn. NW9 96 CS53
Clayton Fld.
Larch Gro., Sid. 185 ET88
Larch Ms. N19 121 DJ61
Bredgar Rd.
Larch Ri., Berk. 38 AU18
Larch Rd. E10 123 EA61
Walnut Rd.
Larch Rd. NW2 119 CW63
Larch Rd., Dart. 188 FK87
Larch Tree Way, Croy. 203 EA104
Larch Wk., Swan. 207 FD96
Larch Way, Brom. 205 EN101
Larchdene, Orp. 205 EN103
Larches, The N13 100 DQ48
Larches, The, Nthwd. 93 BQ51
Larches, The, St.Alb. 43 CK16
Larches, The, Uxb. 135 BP68
Larches, The, Wat. 76 BY43
Larches, The, Wok. 226 AY116
Larches Ave. SW14 158 CR84
Larches Ave., Enf. 82 DW35
Larchlands, The, H.Wyc. 88 AD46
Larchwood Ave., Rom. 105 FB51
Larchwood Clo., Bans. 233 CY115
Larchwood Clo., Rom. 105 FC51
Larchwood Dr., Egh. 172 AV93
Larchwood Gdns., Brwd. 108 FU44
Larchwood Rd. SE9 185 EP89
Larchwood Rd., Hem.H. 40 BM18
Larcom St. SE17 279 J9
Larcom St. SE17 162 DQ77
Larcombe Clo., Croy. 220 DT105
Larden Rd. W3 138 CS74
Largewood Ave., Surb. 198 CM103
Largo Wk., Erith 167 FE81
Selkirk Dr.
Larissa St. SE17 279 L10
Lark Ave., Stai. 173 BF90
Kestrel Ave.
Lark Ri., Hat. 45 CU20
Lark Ri., Lthd. 245 BS131
Lark Row E2 142 DW67
Lark Way, Cars. 200 DE101
Larkbere Rd. SE26 183 DY91
Larken Dr. (Bushey), Wat. 94 CC46
Larkfield, Cob. 213 BU113
Larkfield Ave., Har. 117 CH55
Larkfield Clo., Brom. 204 EF103
Larkfield Ct., Horl. 269 DN148
Cooper Clo.
Larkfield Rd., Rich. 158 CL84
Larkfield Rd., Sev. 256 FC123
Larkfield Rd., Sid. 185 ET90
Larkfields, Grav. 190 GE90
Larkhall Clo., Walt. 214 BW107
Larkhall Ct., Rom. 105 FC54
Larkhall La. SW4 161 DK82
Larkhall Ri. SW4 161 DJ83
Larkham Clo., Felt. 175 BS90
Larkhill Ter. SE18 165 EN80
Larkin Clo., Brwd. 109 GC45
Larkin Clo., Couls. 235 DM117
Larkin Ind. Est., Chesh. 54 AR32
Larkings La., Slou. 132 AV67
Larkins Rd., Gat. 268 DD152
Larks Gro., Bark. 145 ES66
Larks Ri., Chesh. 54 AR33
Larks Wd., Harl. 52 EW17
Larksfield, Egh. 172 AW94
Larksfield, Horl. 269 DH147
Larksfield Gro., Enf. 82 DV39
Larkshall Cres. E4 101 EC49
Larkshall Rd. E4 101 EC50
Larkspur Clo. E6 144 EL71
Larkspur Clo. N17 100 DR52
Fryatt Rd.
Larkspur Clo. NW9 118 CP57
Old Kenton La.
Larkspur Clo., Hem.H. 39 BE19
Larkspur Clo., Orp. 206 EW103
Larkspur Clo., Ruis. 115 BQ59
Glovers Gro.
Larkspur Clo., S.Ock. 149 FW69
Larkspur Way, Dor. 263 CK139
Larkspur Way, Epsom 216 CP106
Larkswood Clo., Erith 167 FG81
Larkswood Ct. E4 101 ED50
Larkswood Ri., Pnr. 116 BW56
Larkswood Ri., St.Alb. 43 CJ15
Larkswood Rd. E4 101 EA49
Larkway Clo. NW9 118 CR56
Larmans Rd., Enf. 82 DW36
Larnach Rd. W6 159 CX79
Larne Rd., Ruis. 115 BT59
Larner Rd., Erith 167 FE80
Larpent Ave. SW15 179 CW85
Larsen Dr., Wal.Abb. 67 ED34
Larwood Clo., Grnf. 117 CD64
Las Palmas Est., Shep. 195 BQ101
Lascelles Ave., Har. 117 CD59
Lascelles Clo. E11 123 ED61
Lascelles Clo., Brwd. 108 FU43
Lascelles Rd., Slou. 152 AV76
Lascotts Rd. N22 99 DM51
Lassa Rd. SE9 184 EL85
Lassell St. SE10 163 ED78
Lasseter Pl. SE3 164 EF79
Vanbrugh Hill
Lasswade Rd., Cher. 193 BF101
Lasterton St. E8 142 DV65
Wilton Way
Latchett Rd. E18 102 EH53
Latchford Pl., Chig. 104 EV49
Manford Way
Latching Clo., Rom. 106 FK49
Troopers Dr.
Latchingdon Ct. E17 123 DX56
Latchingdon Gdns., Wdf.Grn. 102 EL51
Latchmere Clo., Rich. 178 CL92
Latchmere La., Kings.T. 178 CM93
Latchmere Pas. SW11 160 DE82
Cabul Rd.
Latchmere Rd. SW11 160 DF82
Latchmere Rd., Kings.T. 178 CL94
Latchmere St. SW11 160 DF82
Latchmoor Ave., Ger.Cr. 112 AX56
Latchmoor Way, Ger.Cr. 112 AX55
Lateward Rd., Brent. 157 CK79
Latham Clo. E6 144 EL72
Oliver Gdns.
Latham Clo., Twick. 177 CG87
Latham Clo., West. 238 EJ116
Latham Ho. E1 143 DX72
Latham Rd., Bexh. 186 FA85
Latham Rd., Twick. 177 CF87
Lathams Way, Croy. 201 DM102
Lathkill Clo., Enf. 100 DT45
Lathom Rd. E6 144 EL66
Latimer SE17 162 DS78
Beaconsfield Rd.
Latimer Ave. E6 145 EM67
Latimer Clo., Amer. 72 AW39
Latimer Clo., Hem.H. 40 BN15
Latimer Clo., Pnr. 94 BW53
Latimer Clo., Wat. 93 BS45
Latimer Clo., Wok. 227 BB116
Latimer Clo., Wor.Pk. 217 CV105
Latimer Dr., Horn. 128 FK62
Latimer Gdns., Pnr. 94 BW53
Latimer Gdns., Welw.G.C. 30 DB09
Latimer Ms., Chesh. 72 AY36
Latimer Pl. W10 139 CW72
Latimer Rd. E7 124 EH63
Latimer Rd. N15 122 DS58
Latimer Rd. SW19 180 DB93
Latimer Rd. W10 139 CW71
Latimer Rd., Barn. 80 DB41
Latimer Rd., Chesh. 54 AR34
Latimer Rd., Croy. 201 DP104
Abbey Rd.
Latimer Rd., Rick. 73 AZ38
Latimer Rd., Tedd. 177 CF92
Latimer St. E1 143 DX71
Stepney Way
Latimer Way, Beac. 88 AJ49
Latium Clo., St.Alb. 43 CD21
Latona Dr., Grav. 191 GM92
Latona Rd. SE15 162 DU79
Lattimer Pl. W4 159 CT80
Lattimore Rd., St.Alb. 43 CE21
Latton Clo., Esher 214 CB105
Latton Clo., Walt. 196 BY101
Latton Common Rd., Harl. 52 EU18
Latton Grn., Harl. 51 ET19
Latton Hall Clo., Harl. 36 EU14
Latton St., Harl. 36 EU14
Latymer Clo., Wey. 213 BQ105
Latymer Ct. W6 159 CX77
Latymer Rd. N9 100 DT47
Latymer Way N9 100 DR47
Laud St. SE11 278 B10
Laud St., Croy. 202 DQ104
Lauder Clo., Nthlt. 136 BX68
Lauderdale Dr., Rich. 177 CK90
Lauderdale Pl. EC2 142 DQ71
Aldersgate St.
Lauderdale Rd. W9 140 DB69
Lauderdale Rd., Kings L. 59 BQ33
Lauderdale Twr. EC2 142 DQ71
Beech St.
Laughton Ct., Borwd. 78 CR40
Banks Rd.
Laughton Rd., Nthlt. 136 BX67
Launcelot Rd., Brom. 184 EG91
Launcelot St. SE1 278 D5
Launceston Clo., Rom. 106 FJ53
Launceston Gdns., Grnf. 137 CJ67
Launceston Pl. W8 160 DC76
Launceston Rd., Grnf. 137 CJ67
Launch St. E14 163 EC76
Launders La., Rain. 148 FM69
Laundress La. N16 122 DU62
Laundry La. N1 142 DQ67
Greenman St.
Laundry La., Wal.Abb. 68 EE25
Laundry Rd. W6 159 CY79
Laundry Rd., Guil. 258 AW135
Laura Clo. E11 124 EJ57
Laura Clo., Enf. 82 DS43
Laura Dr., Swan. 187 FG94
Laura Pl. E5 122 DW63
Lauradale Rd. N2 120 DF56
Laureate Way, Hem.H. 40 BG18
Laurel Ave., Egh. 172 AV92
Laurel Ave., Grav. 191 GJ89
Laurel Ave., Pot.B. 63 CZ32
Laurel Ave., Slou. 152 AY75
Laurel Ave., Twick. 177 CF88
Laurel Bank Gdns. SW6 159 CZ82
New Kings Rd.
Laurel Bank Rd., Enf. 82 DQ39
Laurel Bank Vill. W7 137 CE74
Lower Boston Rd.
Laurel Clo. N19 121 DJ61
Hargrave Pk.
Laurel Clo. SW17 180 DE92
Laurel Clo., Brwd. 109 GB43
Laurel Clo., Dart. 188 FJ88
Willow Rd.
Laurel Clo., Hem.H. 40 BM19
Laurel Clo., Ilf. 103 EQ51
Laurel Clo., Sid. 186 EU90
Laurel Clo., Slou. 153 BE80
Laurel Clo., Wok. 211 BD113
Laurel Cres., Croy. 203 EA104
Laurel Cres., Rom. 127 FE60
Laurel Cres., Wok. 211 BC113
Laurel Dr. N21 99 DN45
Laurel Dr., Oxt. 254 EF131
Laurel Flds., Pot.B. 63 CZ31
Laurel Gdns. E4 101 EB45
Laurel Gdns. NW7 96 CR48
Laurel Gdns. W7 137 CE74
Laurel Gdns., Houns. 156 BY84
Laurel Gro. SE20 182 DV94
Laurel Gro. SE26 183 DX91
Laurel La., West Dr. 154 BL77
Laurel Lo. La., Barn. 79 CW36
Dancers La.
Laurel Pk., Har. 95 CF52
Laurel Rd. SW13 159 CU82
Laurel Rd. SW20 199 CV95
Laurel Rd., Ger.Cr. 90 AX53
Laurel Rd., Hmptn. 177 CD92

Laurel Rd., St.Alb. 43 CF20
Laurel St. E8 142 DT65
Laurel Vw. N12 98 DB48
Laurel Way E18 124 EF56
Laurel Way N20 98 DA48
Laurels, The, Bans. 233 CZ117
Laurels, The, Berk. 39 BC17
Laurels, The, Cob. 230 BY115
Laurels, The, Dart. 188 FJ90
Laurels, The, Wal.Cr. 66 DS27
Laurels, The, Wey. 195 BR104
Laurels Rd., Iver 133 BD68
Laurelsfield, St.Alb. 42 CB23
Laurence Ms. W12 159 CU75
Askew Rd.
Laurence Pountney Hill EC4 275 K10
Laurence Pountney La. EC4 275 K10
Laurie Gro. SE14 163 DY81
Laurie Rd. W7 137 CE71
Laurie Wk., Rom. 127 FE56
Laurier Rd. NW5 121 DH62
Laurier Rd., Croy. 202 DT101
Lauries Clo., Hem.H. 39 BB22
Laurimel Clo., Stan. 95 CH51
September Way
Laurino Pl. (Bushey), Wat. 94 CC47
Lauriston Rd. E9 143 DX67
Lauriston Rd. SW19 179 CX93
Lausanne Rd. N8 121 DN56
Lausanne Rd. SE15 162 DW81
Lauser Rd., Stai. 174 BJ87
Laustan Clo., Guil. 243 BC134
Lavell St. N16 122 DR63
Lavender Ave. NW9 118 CQ60
Lavender Ave., Brwd. 108 FV43
Lavender Ave., Mitch. 200 DE95
Lavender Ave., Wor.Pk. 199 CW104
Lavender Clo. SW3 160 DD79
Danvers St.
Lavender Clo., Brom. 204 EL100
Lavender Clo., Cars. 219 DH105
Lavender Clo., Cat. 252 DQ125
Lavender Clo., Couls. 235 DJ119
Lavender Clo., Red. 267 DH139
Lavender Clo., Rom. 106 FK52
Lavender Clo. (Cheshunt), Wal.Cr. 66 DT27
Lavender Ct., W.Mol. 196 CB97
Molesham Way
Lavender Gdns. SW11 160 DF84
Lavender Gdns., Enf. 81 DP39
Lavender Gdns., Har. 95 CE51
Uxbridge Rd.
Lavender Gro. E8 142 DU66
Lavender Gro., Mitch. 200 DE95
Lavender Hill SW11 160 DF84
Lavender Hill, Enf. 81 DN39
Lavender Hill, Swan. 207 FD97
Lavender Ms., Wall. 219 DL107
Lavender Pk. Rd., W.Byf. 212 BG112
Lavender Pl., Ilf. 125 EP64
Lavender Ri., West Dr. 154 BN75
Lavender Rd. SE16 143 DY74
Lavender Rd. SW11 160 DD83
Lavender Rd., Cars. 218 DG105
Lavender Rd., Croy. 201 DM100
Lavender Rd., Enf. 82 DR39
Lavender Rd., Epsom 216 CP106
Lavender Rd., Sutt. 218 DD105
Lavender Rd., Uxb. 134 BM71
Lavender Rd., Wok. 227 BB116
Lavender Sq. E11 123 ED62
Anglian Rd.
Lavender St. E15 144 EE65
Manbey Gro.
Lavender Sweep SW11 160 DF84
Lavender Ter. SW11 160 DE83
Falcon Rd.
Lavender Vale, Wall. 219 DK107
Lavender Wk. SW11 160 DF84
Lavender Wk., Hem.H. 40 BK18
Townsend
Lavender Wk., Mitch. 200 DG97
Lavender Way, Croy. 203 DX100
Lavengro Rd. SE27 182 DQ89
Lavenham Rd. SW18 179 CZ89
Lavernock Rd., Bexh. 166 FA82
Lavers Rd. N16 122 DS62
Laverstoke Gdns. SW15 179 CT87
Laverton Ms. SW5 160 DB77
Laverton Pl.
Laverton Pl. SW5 160 DB77
Lavidge Rd. SE9 184 EL89
Lavina Gro. N1 141 DM68
Wharfdale Rd.
Lavington Rd. W13 137 CH74
Lavington Rd., Croy. 201 DM104
Lavington St. SE1 278 G3
Lavington St. SE1 141 DP74
Lavinia Ave., Wat. 60 BX34
Lavinia Rd., Dart. 188 FM86
Lavrock La., Rick. 92 BM45
Law Ho., Bark. 146 EU68
Law St. SE1 279 L6
Law St. SE1 162 DR76
Lawbrook La., Guil. 261 BQ143
Lawdons Gdns., Croy. 219 DP105
Lawford Ave., Rick. 73 BC44
Lawford Clo., Horn. 128 FJ63
Lawford Clo., Rick. 73 BC44
Lawford Clo., Wall. 219 DL109
Lawford Gdns., Dart. 188 FJ85
Lawford Gdns., Ken. 236 DQ116
Lawford Rd. N1 142 DS66
Lawford Rd. NW5 141 DJ65
Lawford Rd. W4 158 CQ80
Lawkland, Slou. 131 AQ69
Lawless St. E14 143 EB73
Lawley Rd. N14 99 DH45
Lawley St. E5 122 DW63
Lawn, The, Harl. 36 EV12
Lawn, The, Sthl. 156 CA78
Lawn Ave., West Dr. 154 BJ75
Lawn Clo. N9 100 DT45
Lawn Clo., Brom. 184 EH93
Lawn Clo., N.Mal. 198 CS96
Lawn Clo., Ruis. 115 BT62
Lawn Clo., Slou. 152 AW80
Lawn Clo., Swan. 207 FC96
Lawn Cres., Rich. 158 CN82
Lawn Fm. Gro., Rom. 126 EY56
Lawn Gdns. W7 137 CE74
Lawn Ho. Clo. E14 163 EC75
Lawn La. SW8 161 DL79
Lawn La., Hem.H. 40 BK22
Lawn Pk., Sev. 257 FH127
Lawn Pl. SE15 162 DT81
Sumner Est.
Lawn Rd. NW3 120 DF64
Lawn Rd., Beck. 183 DZ94
Lawn Rd., Grav. 190 GC86
Lawn Rd., Guil. 258 AW137
Lawn Rd., Uxb. 134 BJ66
New Windsor St.
Lawn Ter. SE3 164 EE83
Lawn Vale, Pnr. 94 BY54
Lawnfield NW2 139 CX66
Coverdale Rd.
Lawns, The E4 101 EA50
Lawns, The SE3 164 EE83
Lee Ter.
Lawns, The SE19 202 DR95
Lawns, The, Hem.H. 39 BE19
Lawns, The, Pnr. 94 CB52
Lawns, The, St.Alb. 42 CC19
Lawns, The, Sid. 186 EV91
Lawns, The, Sutt. 217 CY108
Lawns, The, Welw.G.C. 29 CX06
Lawns Cres., Grays 170 GD79
Lawns Dr., The, Brox. 49 DZ21
Lawnside SE3 164 EF84
Lawnsway, Rom. 105 FC52
Lawrance Gdns. (Cheshunt), Wal.Cr. 67 DX28
Lawrance Rd., St.Alb. 42 CC16
Lawrence Ave. E12 125 EN63
Lawrence Ave. E17 101 DX53
Lawrence Ave. N13 99 DP49
Lawrence Ave. NW7 96 CS49
Lawrence Ave., N.Mal. 198 CR100
Lawrence Ave., Ware 33 EC11
Lawrence Bldgs. N16 122 DT62
Lawrence Campe Clo. N20 98 DD48
Friern Barnet La.
Lawrence Clo. E3 143 EA69
Lawrence Clo. N15 122 DS55
Lawrence Rd.
Lawrence Clo., Guil. 243 BB129
Ladygrove Dr.
Lawrence Clo., Hert. 31 DL08
Lawrence Ct. NW7 96 CS50
Lawrence Cres., Dag. 127 FB62
Lawrence Cres., Edg. 96 CN54
Lawrence Dr., Uxb. 115 BQ63
Lawrence Est., Houns. 156 BW84
Lawrence Gdns. NW7 97 CT48
Lawrence Gdns., Til. 171 GH80
Lawrence Hill E4 101 EA47
Lawrence Hill Gdns., Dart. 188 FJ86
Lawrence Hill Rd., Dart. 188 FJ86
Lawrence La. EC2 275 J9
Lawrence La., Bet. 249 CV132
Lawrence Moorings, Saw. 36 EZ06
Lawrence Pl. N1 141 DL67
Outram Pl.
Lawrence Rd. E6 144 EL67
Lawrence Rd. E13 144 EH67
Lawrence Rd. N15 122 DS56
Lawrence Rd. N18 100 DV49
Lawrence Rd. SE25 202 DT98
Lawrence Rd. W5 157 CK77
Lawrence Rd., Erith 167 FB80
Sussex Rd.
Lawrence Rd., Hmptn. 176 BZ94
Lawrence Rd., Hayes 135 BQ68
Lawrence Rd., Houns. 156 BW84
Lawrence Rd., Pnr. 116 BX58
Lawrence Rd., Rich. 177 CJ91
Lawrence Rd., Rom. 127 FH57
Lawrence Rd., W.Wick. 222 EG105
Lawrence Sq., Grav. 191 GF90
Haynes Rd.
Lawrence St. E16 144 EF71
Lawrence St. NW7 97 CT50
Lawrence St. SW3 160 DE79
Lawrence Way NW10 118 CQ63
Lawrence Way, Slou. 131 AK71
Lawrence Weaver Clo., Mord. 200 DB100
Green La.
Lawrie Pk. Ave. SE26 182 DV92
Lawrie Pk. Cres. SE26 182 DV92
Lawrie Pk. Gdns. SE26 182 DV91
Lawrie Pk. Rd. SE26 182 DV93
Lawson Clo. E16 144 EJ71
Lawson Clo. SW19 179 CX90
Lawson Est. SE1 279 K7
Lawson Gdns., Dart. 188 FK85
Lawson Gdns., Pnr. 115 BV55
Lawson Rd., Dart. 168 FK84
Lawson Rd., Enf. 82 DW39
Lawson Rd., Sthl. 136 BZ70
Lawton Rd. E3 143 DY69
Lawton Rd. E10 123 ED60
Lawton Rd., Barn. 80 DD41
Lawton Rd., Loug. 85 EP40
Laxcon Clo. NW10 118 CQ64
Laxey Rd., Orp. 223 ET107
Laxley Clo. SE5 161 DP80
Laxton Gdns., Red. 251 DK128
Laxton Pl. NW1 273 J4
Layard Rd. SE16 162 DV77
Layard Rd., Enf. 82 DT39
Layard Rd., Th.Hth. 202 DR96
Layard Sq. SE16 162 DV77
Laybrook, St.Alb. 43 CG16
Layburn Cres., Slou. 153 BB79
Laycock St. N1 141 DN65
Layer Gdns. W3 138 CN73
Layfield Clo. NW4 119 CV59
Layfield Cres. NW4 119 CV59
Layfield Rd. NW4 119 CV59
Layhams Rd., Kes. 222 EF106
Layhams Rd., W.Wick. 203 ED104
Layhill, Hem.H. 40 BK18
Laymarsh Clo., Belv. 166 EZ76
Laymead Clo., Nthlt. 136 BY65
Laystall St. EC1 274 D5
Laystall St. EC1 141 DN70
Layters Ave., Ger.Cr. 90 AW54
Layters Ave. S., Ger.Cr. 90 AW54
Layters Clo., Ger.Cr. 90 AW54
Layters End, Ger.Cr. 90 AW54
Layters Grn. La., Ger.Cr. 112 AU55
Layters Way, Ger.Cr. 112 AX56
Layton Ct., Wey. 213 BP105
Castle Vw. Rd.
Layton Cres., Croy. 219 DN106
Layton Rd. N1 141 DN68
Parkfield St.
Layton Rd., Brent. 157 CK78
Layton Rd., Houns. 156 CB84
Laytons Bldgs. SE1 279 K4
Laytons La., Sun. 195 BT96
Layzell Wk. SE9 184 EK88
Mottingham La.
Lazar Wk. N7 121 DM61
Briset Way
Le Corte Clo., Kings L. 58 BM29
Le May Ave. SE12 184 EH90
Le May Clo., Horl. 268 DG147
Le Personne Rd., Cat. 236 DR122
Lea, The, Egh. 173 BC94
Lea Bri. Rd. E5 122 DV62
Lea Bri. Rd. E10 123 EA59
Lea Bri. Rd. E17 123 ED57
Lea Bushes, Wat. 76 CA35
Lea Clo. (Bushey), Wat. 76 CB43
Lea Cres., Ruis. 115 BT63
Lea Gdns., Wem. 118 CM63
Lea Hall Rd. E10 123 EA60
Lea Mt., Wal.Cr. 66 DS28
Lea Rd., Beck. 203 EA96
Fairfield Rd.
Lea Rd., Enf. 82 DR39
Lea Rd., Grays 171 GG78
Lea Rd., Hodd. 49 EC15
Lea Rd., Sev. 257 FJ127
Lea Rd., Sthl. 156 BY77
Lea Rd., Wal.Abb. 67 EA34
Lea Rd. Trd. Est., Wal.Abb. 67 EA34
Lea Side Ind. Est., Enf. 83 DZ41
Lea Vale, Dart. 167 FD84
Lea Valley Rd. E4 83 DX43
Lea Valley Rd., Enf. 83 DX43
Lea Valley Viaduct E4 101 DX50
Lea Valley Viaduct N18 101 DX50
Lea Vw. Hos. E5 122 DV60
Springfield
Leabank Clo., Har. 117 CE62
Leabank Sq. E9 143 EA65
Leabank Vw. N15 122 DU58
Leabourne Rd. N16 122 DU58
Leach Gro., Lthd. 231 CJ122
Leachcroft, Ger.Cr. 90 AV53
Leacroft, Stai. 174 BG92
Leacroft Ave. SW12 180 DF87
Leacroft Clo., Ken. 236 DQ116
Leacroft Clo., Stai. 174 BH91
Leacroft Clo., West Dr. 134 BL72
Leacroft Rd., Iver 133 BD72
Leadale Ave. E4 101 DZ47
Leadale Rd. N15 122 DU58
Leadale Rd. N16 122 DU58
Leadbeaters Clo. N11 98 DF50
Goldsmith Rd.
Leadenhall Mkt. EC3 275 M9
Leadenhall Pl. EC3 275 M9
Leadenhall St. EC3 275 M9
Leadenhall St. EC3 142 DS72
Leader Ave. E12 125 EN64
Leadings, The, Wem. 118 CQ62
Leaf Clo., Nthwd. 93 BR52
Leaf Clo., T.Ditt. 197 CE99
Leaf Gro. SE27 181 DN92
Leafield Clo. SW16 181 DP93
Leafield Clo., Wok. 226 AV118
Winnington Way
Leafield La., Sid. 186 EZ91
Leafield Rd. SW20 199 CZ97
Leafield Rd., Sutt. 200 DA103
Leaford Cres., Wat. 75 BT37
Leaforis Rd., Wal.Cr. 66 DU28
Leafy Gro., Kes. 222 EJ106
Leafy Oak Rd. SE12 184 EJ91
Leafy Way, Brwd. 109 GD46
Leafy Way, Croy. 202 DT103
Leagrave St. E5 122 DW62
Leahoe Gdns., Hert. 32 DQ10
Leaholme Gdns., Slou. 130 AJ71
Leaholme Way, Ruis. 115 BQ58
Leahurst Rd. SE13 183 ED85
Leake Ct. SE1 278 C4
Leake St. SE1 278 C4
Leake St. SE1 161 DM75
Lealand Rd. N15 122 DT58
Leamington Ave. E17 123 EA57
Leamington Ave., Brom. 184 EJ92
Leamington Ave., Mord. 199 CY98
Leamington Ave., Orp. 223 ES105
Leamington Clo. E12 125 EM64
Leamington Clo., Brom. 184 EJ92
Leamington Clo., Houns. 176 CC85
Leamington Clo., Rom. 106 FN51
Leamington Rd.
Leamington Cres., Har. 116 BY62
Leamington Gdns., Ilf. 125 ET61
Leamington Pk. W3 138 CR71
Leamington Pl., Hayes 135 BT70
Leamington Rd., Rom. 106 FN50
Leamington Rd., Sthl. 156 BX77
Leamington Rd. Vill. W11 139 CZ71
Leamore St. W6 159 CV77
Leamouth Rd. E6 144 EL72
Leamouth Rd. E14 143 ED72
Leander Ct. SE8 163 EA81
Leander Dr., Grav. 191 GM91
Leander Gdns., Wat. 76 BY37
Leander Rd. SW2 181 DM87
Leander Rd., Nthlt. 136 CA68
Leander Rd., Th.Hth. 201 DM98
Leapale La., Guil. 258 AX135
Leapale Rd., Guil. 258 AX135
Learoyd Gdns. E6 145 EN73
Leas, The, Hem.H. 40 BN24
Leas, The, Stai. 174 BG91
Leas, The, Upmin. 129 FR59
Leas, The (Bushey), Wat. 76 BZ39
Leas Clo., Chess. 216 CM108
Leas Dale SE9 185 EN90
Leas Dr., Iver 133 BE72
Leas Grn., Chis. 185 ET93
Leas La., Warl. 237 DX118
Leas Rd., Guil. 258 AW135
Leas Rd., Warl. 237 DX118
Leaside, Hem.H. 41 BQ21
Leaside, Lthd. 230 CA123
Leaside Ave. N10 120 DG55
Leaside Ct., Uxb. 135 BP69
The Larches
Leaside Rd. E5 122 DW60
Leasowes Rd. E10 123 EA60
Leasway, Brwd. 108 FX48
Leasway, Upmin. 128 FQ62
Leathart Clo., Horn. 147 FH66
Dowding Way
Leather Bottle La., Belv. 166 EZ77
St. Augustine's Rd.
Leather Clo., Mitch. 200 DG96
Leather Gdns. E15 144 EE67
Abbey Rd.
Leather La. EC1 274 D6
Leather La. EC1 141 DN70
Leather La., Horn. 128 FK60
North St.
Leatherbottle Grn., Erith 166 EZ76
Leatherdale St. E1 142 DW70
Portelet Rd.
Leatherhead Bypass Rd., Lthd. 231 CH120
Leatherhead Clo. N16 122 DS60
Leatherhead Ind. Est., Lthd. 231 CG121
Station Rd.
Leatherhead Rd., Ash. 231 CK121
Leatherhead Rd., Chess. 215 CJ111
Leatherhead Rd., Lthd. 246 CB126
Leatherhead Rd. (Great Bookham), Lthd. 231 CK121
Leatherhead Rd. (Oxshott), Lthd. 215 CD114
Leathermarket Ct. SE1 162 DS75
Leathermarket St. SE1 279 M5
Leathermarket St. SE1 162 DS75
Leathersellers Clo., Barn. 79 CY42
The Ave.
Leathsail Rd., Har. 116 CB62
Leathwaite Rd. SW11 160 DF84
Leathwell Rd. SE8 163 EB82
Leaveland Clo., Beck. 203 EA98
Leaver Gdns., Grnf. 137 CD68
Leaves Grn. Cres., Kes. 222 EJ111
Leaves Grn. Rd., Kes. 222 EK111
Leavesden Rd., Stan. 95 CG51
Leavesden Rd., Wat. 75 BV38
Leavesden Rd., Wey. 213 BP106
Leaview, Wal.Abb. 67 EB33
Leaway E10 123 DX60
Leazes Ave., Cat. 235 DN124
Lebanon Ave., Felt. 176 BX92
Lebanon Clo., Wat. 75 BR36
Lebanon Ct., Twick. 177 CH87
Lebanon Dr., Cob. 214 CA113
Lebanon Gdns. SW18 180 DA85
Lebanon Gdns., West. 238 EK117
Lebanon Pk., Twick. 177 CH87
Lebanon Rd. SW18 180 DA85
Lebanon Rd., Croy. 202 DS102
Lebrun Sq. SE3 164 EH83
Lechford Rd., Horl. 268 DG149
Lechmere App., Wdf.Grn. 102 EJ54
Lechmere Ave., Chig. 103 EQ49
Lechmere Ave., Wdf.Grn. 102 EK54
Lechmere Rd. NW2 139 CV65
Leckford Rd. SW18 180 DC89
Leckwith Ave., Bexh. 166 EY79
Lecky St. SW7 160 DD78
Leconfield Ave. SW13 159 CT83
Leconfield Rd. N5 122 DR63
Leconfield Wk., Horn. 148 FJ65
Airfield Way
Lectern La., St.Alb. 43 CD24
Leda Ave., Enf. 83 DX38
Leda Rd. SE18 165 EM76
Ledborough La., Beac. 89 AK52
Ledborough Wd., Beac. 89 AL51
Ledbury Est. SE15 162 DV80
Ledbury Ms. N. W11 140 DA73
Ledbury Rd.
Ledbury Ms. W. W11 140 DA73
Ledbury Rd.
Ledbury Pl., Croy. 220 DQ105
Ledbury Rd.
Ledbury Rd. W11 139 CZ72
Ledbury Rd., Croy. 220 DQ105
Ledbury Rd., Reig. 249 CZ133
Ledbury St. SE15 162 DU80
Ledger Clo., Guil. 243 BB132
Ledger Dr., Add. 211 BF107
Ledger La., Maid. 150 AD82
Ledgers Rd., Slou. 151 AR75
Ledgers Rd., Warl. 237 EB119
Ledrington Rd. SE19 182 DU93
Anerley Hill
Ledway Dr., Wem. 118 CM59
Lee Ave., Rom. 126 EY58
Lee Bri. SE13 163 EC83
Lee Ch. St. SE13 164 EE84
Lee Clo. E17 101 DX53
Lee Clo., Barn. 80 DC42
Lee Clo., Hert. 32 DQ11
Lee Clo., Ware 33 EC11
Lee Conservancy Rd. E9 123 DZ64
Lee Fm. Clo., Chesh. 56 AU30
Lee Gdns. Ave., Horn. 128 FN60
Lee Grn. SE12 184 EF85
Lee Grn., Orp. 206 EU99
Lee Grn. La., Epsom 232 CP124
Lee Gro., Chig. 103 EN47
Lee High Rd. SE12 164 EF84
Lee High Rd. SE13 163 ED84
Lee Pk. SE3 164 EF84
Lee Pk. Way N9 101 DY48
Lee Pk. Way N18 101 DX50
Lee Rd. NW7 97 CX52
Lee Rd. SE3 164 EF83
Lee Rd. SW19 200 DB95
Lee Rd., Enf. 82 DU44
Lee Rd., Grnf. 137 CJ67
Lee St. E8 142 DT67
Lee St., Horl. 268 DE148
Lee Ter. SE3 164 EE83
Lee Ter. SE13 164 EE83
Lee Valley Trd. Est. N18 101 DX50
Lee Vw., Enf. 81 DP39
Leech La., Epsom 248 CQ126
Leech La., Lthd. 248 CP126
Leechcroft Ave., Sid. 185 ET85
Leechcroft Ave., Swan. 207 FF97
Leechcroft Rd., Wall. 200 DG104
Leecroft Rd., Barn. 79 CY43
Leeds Clo., Orp. 206 EX103
Leeds Pl. N4 121 DM61
Tollington Pk.
Leeds Rd., Ilf. 125 ER60
Leeds Rd., Slou. 132 AS73
Leeds St. N18 100 DU50
Leefe Way, Pot.B. 65 DK28
Leefern Rd. W12 159 CU75
Leegate SE12 184 EF85
Leegate Clo., Wok. 226 AV116
Sythwood
Leeke St. WC1 274 B2
Leeke St. WC1 141 DM69
Leeland Rd. W13 137 CG74
Leeland Ter. W13 137 CG74
Leeland Way NW10 119 CT63
Leeming Rd., Borwd. 78 CM39
Leerdam Dr. E14 163 EC76
Lees, The, Croy. 203 DZ103
Lees Ave., Nthwd. 93 BT54
Lees Pl. W1 272 F10
Lees Pl. W1 140 DG73
Lees Rd., Uxb. 135 BP70
Leeside, Barn. 79 CY43
Leeside, Pot.B. 64 DD31
Wayside
Leeside Cres. NW11 119 CY58
Leeside Rd. N17 100 DV51
Leeson Rd. SE24 161 DN84
Leesons Hill, Chis. 205 ES97
Leesons Hill, Orp. 206 EU97
Leesons Way, Orp. 205 ET96
Leeward Gdns. SW19 179 CZ92
Leeway SE8 163 DZ78
Leeway Clo., Pnr. 94 BZ52
Leewood Clo. SE12 184 EF86
Upwood Rd.
Leewood Pl., Swan. 207 FD98
Leewood Way, Lthd. 246 BW127
Lefevre Wk. E3 143 DZ67
Old Ford Rd.
Lefroy Rd. W12 159 CT75
Legard Rd. N5 121 DP62
Legatt Rd. SE9 184 EK85
Leggatt Rd. E15 143 EC68
Leggatts Clo., Wat. 75 BT36
Leggatts Ri., Wat. 75 BU35
Leggatts Way, Wat. 75 BT36
Leggatts Wd. Ave., Wat. 75 BV36
Legge St. SE13 183 EC85
Leggfield Ter., Hem.H. 39 BF20
Leghorn Rd. NW10 139 CT68
Leghorn Rd. SE18 165 ER78
Legion Clo. N1 141 DN66
Legion Ct., Mord. 200 DA100
Legion Rd., Grnf. 136 CC67
Legion Way N12 98 DE52
Downway
Legon Ave., Rom. 127 FC60
Legrace Ave., Houns. 156 BX82
Leicester Ave., Mitch. 201 DL98
Leicester Clo., Wor.Pk. 217 CW105
Leicester Ct. WC2 273 N10
Leicester Gdns., Ilf. 125 ES59
Leicester Pl. WC2 273 N10
Leicester Rd. E11 124 EH57
Leicester Rd. N2 120 DE55
Leicester Rd. NW10 138 CR66
Leicester Rd., Barn. 80 DB43
Leicester Rd., Croy. 202 DS101
Leicester Rd., Til. 171 GF81
Leicester Sq. WC2 277 N1
Leicester Sq. WC2 141 DK73
Leicester St. WC2 273 N10
Leigh Ave., Ilf. 124 EK56
Leigh Clo., Add. 211 BF108
Leigh Clo., N.Mal. 198 CR98
Leigh Common, Welw.G.C. 29 CY11
Leigh Cor., Cob. 214 BW114
Leigh Hill Rd.
Leigh Ct., Borwd. 78 CR40
Banks Rd.
Leigh Ct., Har. 117 CE60
Leigh Ct. Clo., Cob. 214 BW114
Leigh Cres., Croy. 221 EB108
Leigh Dr., Rom. 106 FK49
Leigh Gdns. NW10 139 CW68
Leigh Hill Rd., Cob. 214 BW114
Leigh Hunt Dr. N14 99 DK46
Leigh Hunt St. SE1 279 H4
Leigh Orchard Clo. SW16 181 DM90
Leigh Pk., Slou. 152 AW80
Leigh Pl. EC1 141 DN71
Baldwin's Gdns.
Leigh Pl., Cob. 214 BW114
Leigh Pl., Well. 166 EU82
Leigh Pl. La., Gdse. 253 DY132
Leigh Pl. Rd., Reig. 265 CU140
Leigh Rd. E6 145 EN65
Leigh Rd. E10 123 EC59
Leigh Rd. N5 121 DP63
Leigh Rd., Cob. 213 BV113
Leigh Rd., Grav. 191 GH89
Leigh Rd., Houns. 157 CD84
Leigh Rd., Slou. 131 AP73
Leigh Rodd, Wat. 94 BZ48
Leigh Sq., Wind. 151 AK82
Leigh St. WC1 273 P4
Leigh St. WC1 141 DL70
Leigh Ter., Orp. 206 EV97
Saxville Rd.
Leigham Ave. SW16 181 DL90
Leigham Ct. Rd. SW16 181 DL89
Leigham Dr., Islw. 157 CE80
Leigham Vale SW2 181 DN89
Leigham Vale SW16 181 DM90
Leighton Ave. E12 125 EN64
Leighton Ave., Pnr. 116 BY55
Leighton Buzzard Rd., Hem.H. 40 BJ19
Leighton Clo., Edg. 96 CN54
Leighton Cres. NW5 121 DJ64
Leighton Gro.
Leighton Gdns. NW10 139 CV68
Leighton Gdns., S.Croy. 220 DV113
Leighton Gdns., Til. 171 GG80
Leighton Gro. NW5 121 DJ64
Leighton Pl. NW5 121 DJ64
Leighton Rd. NW5 121 DJ64
Leighton Rd. W13 157 CG75
Leighton Rd., Enf. 82 DT43
Leighton Rd., Har. 95 CD54
Leighton St., Croy. 201 DP102
Leighton Way, Epsom 216 CR114

Leila Parnell Pl. SE7 164 EJ79
Leinster Ave. SW14 158 CQ83
Leinster Gdns. W2 140 DC72
Leinster Ms. W2 140 DC73
Leinster Pl. W2 140 DC72
Leinster Rd. N10 121 DH56
Leinster Rd. NW6 140 DA69
Stafford Rd.
Leinster Sq. W2 140 DA72
Leinster Ter. W2 140 DC73
Leiston Spur, Slou. 132 AS72
Leisure La., W.Byf. 212 BH112
Leith Clo. NW9 118 CR60
Leith Hill, Orp. 206 EU95
Leith Hill Grn., Orp. 206 EU95
Leith Hill
Leith Hill La., Dor. 262 BY144
Leith Pk. Rd., Grav. 191 GH88
Leith Rd. N22 99 DP53
Leith Rd., Epsom 216 CS112
Leith Vw., Dor. 263 CJ140
Leith Yd. NW6 140 DA67
Quex Rd.
Leithcote Gdns. SW16 181 DM91
Leithcote Path SW16 181 DM90
Lela Ave., Houns. 156 BW82
Lelitia Clo. E8 142 DU67
Pownall Rd.
Leman St. E1 142 DT72
Lemark Clo., Stan. 95 CJ50
Lemmon Rd. SE10 164 EE79
Lemna Rd. E11 124 EE59
Lemonfield Dr., Wat. 60 BY33
Lemonwell Ct. SE9 185 EQ85
Lemonwell Dr.
Lemonwell Dr. SE9 185 EQ85
Lemsford Clo. N15 122 DU57
Lemsford Ct. N4 122 DQ61
Brownswood Rd.
Lemsford Ct., Borwd. 78 CQ42
Lemsford La., Welw.G.C. 29 CV10
Lemsford Rd., Hat. 45 CT16
Lemsford Rd., St.Alb. 43 CF20
Lemsford Rd., Welw.G.C. 29 CT11
Lemsford Village Rd., Welw.G.C. 29 CU10
Lemuel St. SW18 180 DB86
St. Ann's Hill
Len Freeman Pl. SW6 159 CZ80
John Smith Ave.
Lena Gdns. W6 159 CW76
Lena Kennedy Clo. E4 101 EC51
Lenanton Steps E14 163 EA75
Manilla St.
Lendal Ter. SW4 161 DK83
Lenelby Rd., Surb. 198 CN102
Lenham Rd. SE12 164 EF84
Lenham Rd., Bexh. 166 EZ79
Lenham Rd., Sutt. 218 DB105
Lenham Rd., Th.Hth. 202 DR96
Lenmore Ave., Grays 170 GC76
Lennard Ave., W.Wick. 204 EE103
Lennard Clo., W.Wick. 204 EE103
Lennard Rd. SE20 183 DX93
Lennard Rd., Beck. 183 DY94
Lennard Rd., Brom. 205 EM102
Lennard Rd., Croy. 202 DQ102
Lennard Rd., Sev. 241 FE120
Lennard Row, S.Ock. 149 FR74
Lennon Rd. NW2 139 CW65
Lennox Ave., Grav. 191 GF86
Lennox Clo., Rom. 127 FF58
Lennox Gdns. NW10 119 CT63
Lennox Gdns. SW1 276 D7
Lennox Gdns. SW1 160 DF76
Lennox Gdns., Croy. 219 DP105
Lennox Gdns., Ilf. 125 EM60
Lennox Gdns. Ms. SW1 276 D7
Lennox Gdns. Ms. SW1 160 DF76
Lennox Rd. E17 123 DZ58
Lennox Rd. N4 121 DM61
Lennox Rd., Grav. 191 GF86
Lennox Rd. E., Grav. 191 GG87
Lenor Clo., Bexh. 166 EY84
Lens Rd. E7 144 EJ66
Lensbury Clo. (Cheshunt), Wal.Cr. 67 DY28
Ashdown Cres.
Lensbury Way SE2 166 EW76
Lent Grn. La., Slou. 130 AH70
Lent Ri. Rd., Slou. 130 AH69
Lenthall Ave., Grays 170 GA75
Lenthall Pl. SW7 160 DC77
Gloucester Rd.
Lenthall Rd. E8 142 DT66
Lenthall Rd., Loug. 85 ER42
Lenthorp Rd. SE10 164 EF77
Lentmead Rd., Brom. 184 EF90
Lenton Clo., Guil. 261 BR142
Lenton Ri., Rich. 158 CL83
Evelyn Ter.
Lenton St. SE18 165 ER77
Lenville Way SE16 162 DU78
Catlin St.
Leo St. SE15 162 DV80
Leo Yd. EC1 274 G5
Leof Cres. SE6 183 EB92
Leominster Rd., Mord. 200 DC100
Leominster Wk., Mord. 200 DC100
Leonard Ave., Mord. 200 DC99
Leonard Ave., Rom. 127 FD60
Leonard Ave., Sev. 241 FH116
Leonard Ave., Swans. 190 FY87
Leonard Rd. E4 101 EA51
Leonard Rd. E7 124 EG63
Leonard Rd. N9 100 DT48
Leonard Rd. SW16 201 DJ95
Leonard Rd., Sthl. 156 BX76
Leonard Robbins Path SE28 146 EV73
Tawney Rd.
Leonard St. E16 144 EL74
Leonard St. EC2 275 L4
Leonard St. EC2 142 DR70
Leonard Way, Brwd. 108 FS49
Leontine Clo. SE15 162 DU80
Leopards Ct. EC1 274 D6
Leopold Ave. SW19 179 CZ92
Leopold Ms. E9 142 DW67
Fremont St.
Leopold Rd. E17 123 EA57
Leopold Rd. N2 120 DD55
Leopold Rd. N18 100 DV50
Leopold Rd. NW10 138 CS66
Leopold Rd. SW19 179 CZ91
Leopold Rd. W5 138 CM74
Leopold St. E3 143 DZ71
Leopold Ter. SW19 180 DA92
Dora Rd.
Lepe Clo., Brom. 184 EE91
Winlaton Rd.
Leppoc Rd. SW4 181 DK85
Leret Way, Lthd. 231 CG121
Leroy St. SE1 279 M7
Leroy St. SE1 162 DS77
Lerwick Dr., Slou. 132 AS71
Lesbourne Rd., Reig. 266 DB135
Lescombe Clo. SE23 183 DY90
Lescombe Rd. SE23 183 DY90
Lesley Clo., Bex. 187 FB87
Lesley Clo., Grav. 191 GF94
Lesley Clo., Swan. 207 FD97
Leslie Gdns., Sutt. 218 DA107
Leslie Gro., Croy. 202 DR102
Leslie Gro. Pl., Croy. 202 DR102
Leslie Gro.
Leslie Pk. Rd., Croy. 202 DS102
Leslie Rd. E11 123 EC63
Leslie Rd. E16 144 EH72
Leslie Rd. N2 120 DD55
Leslie Rd., Dor. 247 CK134
Leslie Rd., Wok. 210 AS110
Leslie Smith Sq. SE18 165 EN79
Nightingale Vale
Lesney Fm. Est., Erith 167 FD80
Lesney Pk., Erith 167 FD79
Lesney Pk. Rd., Erith 167 FD79
Lessar Ave. SW4 181 DH85
Lessing St. SE23 183 DY87
Lessingham Ave. SW17 180 DF91
Lessingham Ave., Ilf. 125 EN55
Lessington Ave., Rom. 127 FC58
Lessness Ave., Bexh. 166 EX80
Lessness Pk., Belv. 166 EZ78
Lessness Rd., Belv. 166 FA78
Stapley Rd.
Lessness Rd., Mord. 200 DC100
Lester Ave. E15 144 EE70
Leston Clo., Rain. 147 FG69
Leswin Pl. N16 122 DT62
Leswin Rd.
Leswin Rd. N16 122 DT62
Letchfield, Chesh. 56 AV31
Letchford Gdns. NW10 139 CU69
Letchford Ms. NW10 139 CU69
Letchford Gdns.
Letchford Ter., Har. 94 CB53
Letchmore Rd., Rad. 77 CG36
Letchworth Ave., Felt. 175 BT87
Letchworth Clo., Brom. 204 EG99
Letchworth Clo., Wat. 94 BX50
Letchworth Dr., Brom. 204 EG99
Letchworth St. SW17 180 DF91
Lethbridge Clo. SE13 163 EC81
Lett Rd. E15 143 ED66
Letter Box La., Sev. 257 FJ129
Letterstone Rd. SW6 159 CZ80
Varna Rd.
Lettice St. SW6 159 CZ81
Lettsom St. SE5 162 DS82
Lettsom Wk. E13 144 EG68
Stratford Rd.
Leucha Rd. E17 123 DY57
Levana Clo. SW19 179 CY88
Levehurst Way SW4 161 DL82
Leven Clo., Wal.Cr. 67 DX33
Leven Clo., Wat. 94 BX50
Leven Dr., Wal.Cr. 67 DX33
Leven Rd. E14 143 EC71
Leven Way, Hayes 135 BS72
Leven Way, Hem.H. 40 BK16
Levendale Rd. SE23 183 DY89
Lever Sq., Grays 171 GG77
Lever St. EC1 274 G3
Lever St. EC1 141 DP69
Leveret Clo., Croy. 221 ED111
Leveret Clo., Wat. 59 BU34
Leverett St. SW3 276 C8
Leverholme Gdns. SE9 185 EN90
Leverson St. SW16 181 DJ93
Leverstock Grn. Rd., Hem.H. 41 BQ21
Leverstock Grn. Way, Hem.H. 41 BQ20
Leverton Pl. NW5 121 DJ64
Leverton St.
Leverton St. NW5 121 DJ64
Leverton Way, Wal.Abb. 67 EC33
Leveson Rd., Grays 171 GH76
Levett Gdns., Ilf. 125 ET63
Levett Rd., Bark. 145 ES65
Levett Rd., Lthd. 231 CH120
Levine Gdns., Bark. 146 EX68
Levison Way N19 121 DK61
Grovedale Rd.
Levylsdene, Guil. 243 BD134
Lewes Clo., Nthlt. 136 CA65
Lewes Rd. N12 98 DE50
Lewes Rd., Brom. 204 EK96
Lewes Rd., Rom. 106 FK49
Lewes Way, Rick. 75 BQ42
Lewesdon Clo. SW19 179 CX88
Leweston Pl. N16 122 DT59
Lewey Ho. E3 143 DZ70
Lewgars Ave. NW9 118 CQ58
Lewin Rd. SW14 158 CR83
Lewin Rd. SW16 181 DK93
Lewin Rd., Bexh. 186 EY85
Lewins Rd., Epsom 216 CP114
Lewins Rd., Ger.Cr. 112 AX55
Lewins Way, Slou. 131 AM73
Lewis Ave. E17 101 EA53
Lewis Clo. N14 99 DJ45
Orchid Rd.
Lewis Clo., Add. 212 BJ105
Lewis Clo., Brwd. 109 FZ45
Lewis Clo., Uxb. 92 BJ54
Lewis Cres. NW10 118 CQ64
Lewis Gdns. N2 98 DD54
Lewis Gro. SE13 163 EC83
Lewis La., Ger.Cr. 90 AY53
Lewis Rd., Horn. 128 FJ58
Lewis Rd., Mitch. 200 DD96
Lewis Rd., Rich. 177 CK85
Red Lion St.
Lewis Rd., Sid. 186 EW90
Lewis Rd., Sthl. 156 BY75
Lewis Rd., Sutt. 218 DB105
Lewis Rd., Swans. 190 FY86
Lewis Rd., Well. 166 EW83
Lewis St. NW1 141 DH65
Lewis Way, Dag. 147 FB65
Lewisham High St. SE13 183 EB86
Lewisham Hill SE13 163 EC82
Lewisham Pk. SE13 183 EC85
Lewisham Rd. SE13 163 EB81
Lewisham St. SW1 277 N5
Lewisham Way SE4 163 EA82
Lewisham Way SE14 163 DZ81
Lexden Dr., Rom. 126 EV58
Lexden Rd. W3 138 CP74
Lexden Rd., Mitch. 201 DK98
Lexham Gdns. W8 160 DA77
Lexham Gdns., Amer. 55 AQ37
Lexham Gdns. Ms. W8 160 DB76
Lexham Gdns.
Lexham Ho., Bark. 145 ER67
St. Margarets
Lexham Ms. W8 160 DA77
Lexham Wk. W8 160 DB76
Lexham Gdns.
Lexington Clo., Borwd. 78 CM41
Lexington Ct., Pur. 220 DQ110
Lexington St. W1 273 L10
Lexington St. W1 141 DJ73
Lexington Way, Barn. 79 CX42
Lexington Way, Upmin. 129 FT58
Lexton Gdns. SW12 181 DK88
Ley Hill Rd., Hem.H. 56 AX30
Ley St., Ilf. 125 EP61
Ley Wk., Welw.G.C. 30 DC09
Leyborne Ave. W13 157 CH75
Leyborne Pk., Rich. 158 CN81
Leybourne Ave., W.Byf. 212 BM113
Leybourne Clo., Brom. 204 EG100
Leybourne Clo., W.Byf. 212 BM113
Leybourne Ave.
Leybourne Rd. E11 124 EF60
Leybourne Rd. NW1 141 DH66
Leybourne Rd. NW9 118 CN57
Leybourne Rd., Uxb. 135 BQ67
Leybourne St. NW1 141 DH66
Hawley St.
Leybridge Ct. SE12 184 EG85
Leyburn Clo. E17 123 EC56
Leyburn Cres., Rom. 106 FL52
Leyburn Gdns., Croy. 202 DT103
Leyburn Gro. N18 100 DU51
Leyburn Rd. N18 100 DU51
Leyburn Rd., Rom. 106 FL52
Leycroft Clo., Loug. 85 EN43
Leycroft Gdns., Erith 167 FG81
Leyden St. E1 275 P7
Leydenhatch La., Swan. 207 FC95
Leydon Clo. SE16 143 DX74
Lagado Ms.
Leyes Rd. E16 144 EJ72
Leyfield, Wor.Pk. 198 CS102
Leyhill Clo., Swan. 207 FE99
Leyland Ave., Enf. 83 DY40
Leyland Ave., St.Alb. 43 CD22
Leyland Clo. (Cheshunt), Wal.Cr. 66 DW28
Leyland Gdns., Wdf.Grn. 102 EJ50
Leyland Rd. SE12 184 EF85
Leylands La., Stai. 153 BF84
Leylang Rd. SE14 163 DX80
Leys, The N2 120 DC56
Leys, The, Amer. 55 AP35
Leys, The, Har. 118 CL58
Leys, The, St.Alb. 43 CK17
Leys Ave., Dag. 147 FC67
Leys Clo., Dag. 147 FC66
Leys Clo., Har. 117 CD57
Leys Clo., Uxb. 92 BK53
Leys Gdns., Barn. 80 DG43
Leys Rd., Hem.H. 40 BL22
Leys Rd., Lthd. 215 CD112
Leys Rd. E., Enf. 83 DY39
Leys Rd. W., Enf. 83 DY39
Leysdown, Welw.G.C. 30 DD09
Leysdown Ave., Bexh. 167 FC84
Leysdown Rd. SE9 184 EL89
Leysfield Rd. W12 159 CU76
Leyspring Rd. E11 124 EF60
Leyswood Dr., Ilf. 125 ES57
Leythe Rd. W3 158 CQ75
Leyton Business Cen. E10 123 EA61
Leyton Cross Rd., Dart. 187 FF90
Leyton Gra. E10 123 EB60
Leyton Gra. Est. E10 123 EA60
Leyton Grn. Rd. E10 123 EC58
Leyton Ind. Village E10 123 DX59
Leyton Pk. Rd. E10 123 EC62
Leyton Rd. E15 123 ED64
Leyton Rd. SW19 180 DC94
Leyton Way E11 124 EE59
Leytonstone Rd. E15 144 EE65
Leywick St. E15 144 EE68
Lezayre Rd., Orp. 223 ET107
Liardet St. SE14 163 DY79
Liberia Rd. N5 141 DP65
Liberty, The, Rom. 127 FE57
Liberty Ave. SW19 200 DC95
Liberty Clo., Hert. 32 DQ12
Liberty Hall Rd., Add. 212 BG106
Liberty La., Add. 212 BG106
Liberty Ms. SW12 181 DH86
Liberty Ri., Add. 212 BG107
Liberty St. SW9 161 DM81
Libra Rd. E3 143 DZ67
Libra Rd. E13 144 EG68
Library Hill, Brwd. 108 FX47
Coptfold Rd.
Library Pl. E1 142 DV73
Cable St.
Library St. SE1 278 F5
Library St. SE1 161 DP75
Library Way, Twick. 176 CC87
Nelson Rd.
Lichfield Clo., Barn. 80 DG41
Lichfield Gdns., Rich. 158 CL84
Lichfield Gro. N3 98 DA53
Lichfield Rd. E3 143 DY69
Lichfield Rd. E6 144 EK69
Lichfield Rd. N9 100 DU47
Winchester Rd.
Lichfield Rd. NW2 119 CY63
Lichfield Rd., Dag. 126 EV63
Lichfield Rd., Houns. 156 BW83
Lichfield Rd., Nthwd. 115 BU55
Lichfield Rd., Rich. 158 CM81
Lichfield Rd., Wdf.Grn. 102 EE49
Lichfield Sq., Rich. 158 CL84
Lichfield Gdns.
Lichfield Ter., Upmin. 129 FS61
Lichfield Way, Brox. 49 DZ22
Lichfield Way, S.Croy. 221 DX110
Lichlade Clo., Orp. 223 ET105
Lidbury Rd. NW7 97 CY51
Lidcote Gdns. SW9 161 DN82
Liddall Way, West Dr. 134 BM74
Liddell Clo., Har. 117 CK55
Liddell Gdns. NW10 139 CW68
Liddell Pl., Wind. 150 AJ83
Liddell Way
Liddell Rd. NW6 140 DA65
Liddell Sq., Wind. 150 AJ83
Liddell Way
Liddell Way, Wind. 150 AJ83
Lidding Rd., Har. 117 CK57
Liddington Hall Dr., Guil. 242 AS131
Liddington New Rd., Guil. 242 AS131
Liddington Rd. E15 144 EF67
Liddon Rd. E13 144 EH69
Liddon Rd., Brom. 204 EJ97
Liden Clo. E17 123 DZ60
Hitcham Rd.
Lidfield Rd. N16 122 DR63
Lidgate Rd. SE15 162 DT80
Chandler Way
Lidiard Rd. SW18 180 DC89
Lidlington Pl. NW1 273 L1
Lidlington Pl. NW1 141 DJ68
Lido Sq. N17 100 DR53
Lidstone Clo., Wok. 226 AV117
Lidyard Rd. N19 121 DJ60
Lieutenant Ellis Way, Wal.Cr. 66 DU29
Liffler Rd. SE18 165 ES78
Lifford St. SW15 159 CX84
Liffords Pl. SW13 159 CT82
Lightcliffe Rd. N13 99 DN49
Lighter Clo. SE16 163 DY77
Lighterman Ms. E1 143 DX72
Belgrave St.
Lightermans Rd. E14 163 EA75
Lightermans Wk. SW18 160 DA84
Lightfoot Rd. N8 121 DL57
Lightley Clo., Wem. 138 CM66
Stanley Ave.
Ligonier St. E2 275 P4
Lila Pl., Swan. 207 FE98
Lilac Ave., Wok. 226 AX120
Lilac Clo. E4 101 DZ51
Lilac Clo., Brwd. 108 FV43
Magnolia Way
Lilac Clo., Guil. 242 AW130
Lilac Clo. (Cheshunt), Wal.Cr. 66 DV31
Greenwood Ave.
Lilac Gdns. W5 157 CK76
Lilac Gdns., Croy. 203 EA104
Lilac Gdns., Hayes 135 BS72
Lilac Gdns., Rom. 127 FE60
Lilac Gdns., Swan. 207 FD97
Lilac Pl. SE11 278 B9
Lilac Pl. SE11 161 DM77
Lilac Pl., West Dr. 134 BM73
Cedar Ave.
Lilac Rd., Hodd. 49 EB15
Lilac St. W12 139 CU73
Lilacs Ave., Enf. 82 DW36
Lilburne Gdns. SE9 184 EL85
Lilburne Rd. SE9 184 EL85
Lilburne Wk. NW10 138 CQ65
Pitfield Way
Lile Cres. W7 137 CE71
Lilestone Est. NW8 140 DD70
Fisherton St.
Lilestone St. NW8 272 B4
Lilestone St. NW8 140 DE70
Lilford Rd. SE5 161 DP82
Lilian Barker Clo. SE12 184 EG85
Lilian Board Way, Grnf. 117 CD64
Lilian Clo. N16 122 DS62
Barbauld Rd.
Lilian Cres., Brwd. 109 GC47
Lilian Gdns., Wdf.Grn. 102 EH53
Lilian Rd. SW16 201 DJ95
Lillechurch Rd., Dag. 146 EV65
Lilleshall Rd., Mord. 200 DD99
Lilley Clo. E1 142 DU74
Hermitage Wall
Lilley Clo., Brwd. 108 FT49
Lilley Dr., Tad. 234 DB122
Lilley La. NW7 96 CR50
Lillian Ave. W3 158 CN75
Lillian Rd. SW13 159 CU79
Lilliard Clo., Hodd. 33 EB13
Lillie Rd. SW6 159 CX79
Lillie Rd., West. 238 EK118
Lillie Yd. SW6 160 DA79
Lillieshall Rd. SW4 161 DH83
Lillington Gdns. Est. SW1 277 L9
Lilliots La., Lthd. 231 CG119
Kingston Rd.
Lilliput Ave., Nthlt. 136 BY67
Lilliput Rd., Rom. 127 FD59
Lily Clo. W14 159 CX77
Gliddon Rd.
Lily Gdns., Wem. 137 CJ68
Lily Pl. EC1 274 E6
Lily Pl. EC1 141 DN71
Lily Rd. E17 123 EA58
Lilyville Rd. SW6 159 CZ81
Limbourne Ave., Dag. 126 EZ59
Limburg Rd. SW11 160 DF84
Lime Ave., Brwd. 109 FZ48
Lime Ave., Grav. 190 GD87
Lime Ave., Upmin. 128 FN63
Lime Ave., West Dr. 134 BM73
Lime Ave., Wind. 152 AT80
Lime Clo. E1 142 DU74
Lime Clo., Brom. 204 EL98
Lime Clo., Buck.H. 102 EK48
Lime Clo., Cars. 200 DF103
Lime Clo., Guil. 244 BH128
Lime Clo., Har. 95 CG54
Lime Clo., Pnr. 115 BT55
Lime Clo., Reig. 266 DB137
Lime Clo., Rom. 127 FC56
Lime Clo., S.Ock. 149 FW69
Lime Clo., Ware 33 DY05
Lime Clo., Wat. 94 BX45
Lime Ct., Mitch. 200 DD96
Lewis Rd.
Lime Cres., Sun. 196 BW96
Lime Gro. N20 97 CZ46
Lime Gro. W12 159 CW75
Lime Gro., Add. 212 BG105
Lime Gro., Guil. 242 AV130
Lime Gro. (West Clandon), Guil. 244 BG128
Lime Gro., Hayes 135 BR73
Lime Gro., Ilf. 103 ET51
Lime Gro., N.Mal. 198 CR97
Lime Gro., Orp. 205 EP103
Lime Gro., Ruis. 115 BV58
Lime Gro., Sid. 185 ET86
Lime Gro., Twick. 177 CF86
Lime Gro., Warl. 237 DY118
Lime Gro., Wok. 226 AY121
Lime Meadow Ave., S.Croy. 220 DU113
Lime Pit La., Sev. 241 FC117
Lime Rd., Epp. 69 ET31
Lime Rd., Rich. 158 CM84
St. Mary's Gro.
Lime Rd., Swan. 207 FD97
Lime Row, Erith 166 EZ76
Northwood Pl.
Lime St. E17 123 DY56
Lime St. EC3 275 M10
Lime St. EC3 142 DS73
Lime St. Pas. EC3 275 M10
Lime Ter. W7 137 CE73
Manor Ct. Rd.
Lime Tree Ave., Esher 197 CD102
Lime Tree Ave., T.Ditt. 197 CD102
Lime Tree Clo., Lthd. 230 CA124
Lime Tree Gro., Croy. 203 DZ104
Lime Tree Pl., Mitch. 201 DH95
Lime Tree Pl., St.Alb. 43 CF21
Lime Tree Rd., Houns. 156 CB81
Lime Tree Ter. SE6 183 DZ88
Winterstoke Rd.
Lime Tree Wk., Amer. 72 AT39
Lime Tree Wk., Enf. 82 DQ38
Lime Tree Wk., Rick. 74 BH43
Lime Tree Wk., Sev. 257 FH125
Lime Tree Wk., Vir.W. 192 AY98
Lime Tree Wk. (Bushey), Wat. 95 CE46
Lime Tree Wk., W.Wick. 222 EF105
Lime Wk. E15 144 EE67
Church St. N.
Lime Wk., Guil. 260 BM139
Lime Wk., Hem.H. 40 BM22
Lime Wk., Uxb. 114 BJ64
Lime Wks. Rd., Red. 251 DJ126
Limeburner La. EC4 274 F9
Limeburner La. EC4 141 DP72
Limebush Clo., Add. 212 BJ109
Limecroft Clo., Epsom 216 CR108
Limedene Clo., Pnr. 94 BX53
Limeharbour E14 163 EB76
Limehouse Causeway E14 143 DZ73
Limehouse Flds. Est. E14 143 DY71
Limekiln Dr. SE7 164 EH79
Limerick Clo. SW12 181 DJ87
Limerick Gdns., Upmin. 129 FT59
Limerston St. SW10 160 DC79
Limes, The W2 140 DA73
Linden Gdns.
Limes, The, Amer. 55 AP35
Limes, The, Brwd. 109 FZ48
Limes, The, Brom. 204 EL103
Limes, The, Purf. 168 FN78
Tank Hill Rd.
Limes, The, St.Alb. 43 CE18
Limes, The, Welw.G.C. 30 DA11
Limes, The, Wok. 226 AX115
Limes Ave. E11 124 EH56
Limes Ave. N12 98 DC49
Limes Ave. NW7 96 CS51
Limes Ave. NW11 119 CY59
Limes Ave. SE20 182 DV94
Limes Ave. SW13 159 CT82
Limes Ave., Cars. 200 DF102
Limes Ave., Chig. 103 EQ50
Limes Ave., Croy. 201 DN104
Limes Ave., Horl. 269 DH150
Limes Ave., The N11 99 DH50
Limes Clo., Ashf. 174 BN92
Limes Ct., Brwd. 108 FX46
Sawyers Hall La.
Limes Ct., Hodd. 49 EA17
Charlton Way
Limes Fld. Rd. SW14 158 CS83
White Hart La.
Limes Gdns. SW18 180 DA86
Limes Gro. SE13 163 EC84
Limes Pl., Croy. 202 DR101
Limes Rd., Beck. 203 EB96
Limes Rd., Croy. 202 DR100
Limes Rd., Egh. 173 AZ92
Limes Rd. (Cheshunt), Wal.Cr. 67 DX32
Limes Rd., Wey. 212 BN105
Limes Row, Orp. 223 EP106
Orchard Rd.
Limes Wk. SE15 162 DV84
Limes Wk. W5 157 CK75
Chestnut Gro.
Limesdale Gdns., Edg. 96 CQ54
Limesford Rd. SE15 163 DX84
Limestone Wk., Erith 166 EX76
Alsike Rd.
Limetree Clo. SW2 181 DM88
Limetree Ter., Well. 166 EU83
Hook La.
Limetree Wk. SW17 180 DG92
Church La.
Limeway Ter., Dor. 247 CG134
Limewood Clo. W13 137 CH72
St. Stephens Rd.
Limewood Ct., Ilf. 125 EM57
Beehive La.
Limewood Rd., Erith 167 FC80
Limpsfield Ave. SW19 179 CX89
Limpsfield Ave., Th.Hth. 201 DM99
Limpsfield Rd., S.Croy. 220 DU112
Limpsfield Rd., Warl. 236 DW116
Linacre Ct. W6 159 CX78
Linacre Rd. NW2 139 CV65
Linberry Wk. SE8 163 DY77
Carteret Way
Lince La., Dor. 263 CD137
Guildford Rd.

Linces Way, Welw.G.C. 30 DB11
Linchfield Rd., Slou. 152 AW81
Linchmere Rd. SE12 184 EF87
Lincoln Ave. N14 99 DJ48
Lincoln Ave. SW19 179 CX90
Lincoln Ave., Rom. 127 FD60
Lincoln Ave., Twick. 176 CB89
Lincoln Clo. SE25 202 DU100
Woodside Grn.
Lincoln Clo., Erith 167 FF82
Lincoln Clo., Grnf. 136 CC67
Lincoln Clo., Har. 116 BZ57
Lincoln Clo., Horl. 268 DG149
Lincoln Clo., Horn. 128 FN57
Lincoln Clo., Welw.G.C. 30 DC08
Lincoln Ct. N16 122 DR59
Lincoln Ct., Berk. 38 AV19
Lincoln Ct., Borwd. 78 CR43
Lincoln Cres., Enf. 82 DS43
Lincoln Dr., Rick. 75 BP44
Lincoln Dr., Wat. 94 BW48
Lincoln Dr., Wok. 227 BE115
Lincoln Gdns., Ilf. 124 EL59
Lincoln Grn. Rd., Orp. 205 ET99
Lincoln Hatch La., Slou. 130 AJ70
Lincoln Ms. NW6 139 CZ67
Willesden La.
Lincoln Ms. SE21 182 DR88
Lincoln Pk., Amer. 55 AS39
Lincoln Rd. E7 144 EK65
Lincoln Rd. E13 144 EH70
Lincoln Rd. E18 102 EG53
Grove Rd.
Lincoln Rd. N2 120 DE55
Lincoln Rd. SE25 202 DV97
Lincoln Rd., Dor. 247 CJ134
Lincoln Rd., Enf. 82 DS42
Lincoln Rd., Erith 167 FF82
Lincoln Rd., Felt. 176 BZ90
Lincoln Rd., Ger.Cr. 90 AY53
Lincoln Rd., Guil. 242 AT132
Lincoln Rd., Har. 116 BZ57
Lincoln Rd., Mitch. 201 DL99
Lincoln Rd., N.Mal. 198 CQ97
Lincoln Rd., Nthwd. 93 BT54
Lincoln Rd., Sid. 186 EV92
Lincoln Rd., Wem. 137 CK65
Lincoln Rd., Wor.Pk. 199 CV102
Lincoln St. E11 124 EE61
Lincoln St. SW3 276 D9
Lincoln St. SW3 160 DF77
Lincoln Wk., Epsom 216 CR110
Hollymoor La.
Lincoln Way, Enf. 82 DV43
Lincoln Way, Rick. 75 BP44
Lincoln Way, Slou. 131 AK73
Lincoln Way, Sun. 195 BS95
Lincolns, The NW7 97 CT48
Lincolns Clo., St.Alb. 43 CJ15
Lincolns Fld., Epp. 69 ET29
Lincoln's Inn WC2 141 DM72
Chancery La.
Lincoln's Inn Flds. WC2 274 B8
Lincoln's Inn Flds. WC2 141 DM72
Lincolnshott, Grav. 190 GA92
Lincombe Rd., Brom. 184 EF90
Lind Rd., Sutt. 218 DC106
Lind St. SE8 163 EA82
Lindal Cres., Enf. 81 DL43
Lindal Rd. SE4 183 DZ85
Lindale Clo., Vir.W. 192 AT98
Lindales, The N17 100 DT51
Brantwood Rd.
Lindbergh, Welw.G.C. 30 DC09
Lindbergh Rd., Wall. 219 DL108
Linden Ave. NW10 139 CX68
Linden Ave., Couls. 235 DH116
Linden Ave., Dart. 188 FJ88
Linden Ave., Enf. 82 DU39
Linden Ave., Houns. 176 CB85
Linden Ave., Ruis. 115 BU60
Linden Ave., Th.Hth. 201 DP98
Linden Ave., Wem. 118 CM64
Linden Chase Rd., Sev. 257 FH122
Linden Clo. N14 81 DJ44
Linden Clo., Add. 212 BG111
Linden Clo., Orp. 224 EU106
Linden Clo., Purf. 168 FQ79
Linden Clo., Ruis. 115 BU60
Linden Clo., Stan. 95 CH50
Linden Clo., Tad. 233 CX120
Linden Clo., T.Ditt. 197 CF101
Linden Clo., Wal.Cr. 66 DV30
Linden Ct. W12 139 CW74
Linden Ct., Egh. 172 AV93
Linden Ct., Lthd. 231 CH121
Linden Cres., Grnf. 137 CF65
Linden Cres., Kings.T. 198 CM96
Linden Cres., St.Alb. 43 CJ20
Linden Cres., Wdf.Grn. 102 EH51
Linden Dr., Cat. 236 DQ124
Linden Dr., Ger.Cr. 90 AY54
Woodside Hill
Linden Dr., Slou. 131 AQ67
Linden Gdns. W2 140 DA73
Linden Gdns. W4 158 CS78
Linden Gdns., Enf. 82 DU39
Linden Gdns., Lthd. 231 CJ121
Linden Glade, Hem.H. 40 BG21
Linden Gro. SE15 162 DV83
Linden Gro. SE26 182 DW93
Linden Gro., N.Mal. 198 CS97
Linden Gro., Tedd. 177 CF92
Waldegrave Rd.
Linden Gro., Walt. 195 BT103
Linden Gro., Warl. 237 DY118
Linden Ho., Slou. 153 BB78
Linden Lawns, Wem. 118 CM63
Linden Lea N2 120 DC57
Linden Lea, Wat. 59 BU33
Linden Leas, W.Wick. 203 ED103
Linden Ms. N1 122 DR64
Mildmay Gro. N.
Linden Ms. W2 140 DA73
Linden Pit Path, Lthd. 231 CH121
Linden Pl., Epsom 216 CS112
East St.
Linden Pl., Lthd. 245 BS126
Station App.
Linden Pl., Mitch. 200 DE98
Linden Ri., Brwd. 108 FX50
Linden Rd. E17 123 DZ57
High St.
Linden Rd. N10 121 DH56
Linden Rd. N11 98 DF47
Linden Rd. N15 122 DQ56
Linden Rd., Guil. 242 AX134
Linden Rd., Hmptn. 176 CA94
Linden Rd., Lthd. 231 CH121
Linden Rd., Wey. 213 BQ109
Linden Sq., Sev. 256 FE122
London Rd.
Linden St., Rom. 127 FD56
Linden Wk. N19 121 DJ61
Hargrave Pk.
Linden Way N14 81 DJ44
Linden Way, Pur. 219 DJ110
Linden Way, Shep. 195 BQ99
Linden Way, Wok. 227 AZ121
St. Martha's Ave.
Linden Way (Send Marsh), Wok. 227 BF124
Lindenfield, Chis. 205 EP96
Lindens, The N12 98 DD50
Lindens, The W4 158 CQ81
Hartington Rd.
Lindens, The, Croy. 221 EC107
Lindens, The, Hem.H. 39 BF23
Lindens, The, Loug. 85 EM43
Lindens Clo., Lthd. 246 BY128
Mount Pleasant
Lindeth Clo., Stan. 95 CJ51
Old Ch. La.
Lindfield Gdns. NW3 120 DC64
Lindfield Gdns., Guil. 243 AZ133
Applecroft Rd.
Lindfield Rd. W5 137 CJ70
Lindfield Rd., Croy. 202 DT100
Lindfield Rd., Rom. 106 FL50
Lindfield St. E14 143 EA72
Lindisfarne Clo., Grav. 191 GL89
St. Benedict's Ave.
Lindisfarne Rd. SW20 179 CU94
Lindisfarne Rd., Dag. 126 EW62
Lindisfarne Way E9 123 DY63
Lindley Est. SE15 162 DU80
Bird in Bush Rd.
Lindley Rd. E10 123 EB61
Lindley Rd., Gdse. 252 DW130
Lindley Rd., Walt. 196 BX104
Lindley St. E1 142 DW71
Lindlings, Hem.H. 39 BE21
Lindo Clo., Chesh. 54 AP30
Lindo St. SE15 162 DW82
Selden Rd.
Lindore Rd. SW11 160 DF84
Lindores Rd., Cars. 200 DC101
Lindrop St. SW6 160 DC82
Lindsay Clo., Chess. 216 CL108
Lindsay Clo., Epsom 216 CQ113
Lindsay Clo., Stai. 174 BK85
Lindsay Dr., Har. 118 CL58
Lindsay Dr., Shep. 195 BR100
Lindsay Pl., Wal.Cr. 66 DV30
Lindsay Rd., Add. 212 BG110
Lindsay Rd., Hmptn. 176 CB91
Lindsay Rd., Wor.Pk. 199 CV103
Lindsay Sq. SW1 161 DK78
Lindsell St. SE10 163 EC81
Lindsey Clo., Brwd. 108 FU49
Lindsey Clo., Brom. 204 EK97
Lindsey Clo., Mitch. 201 DL98
Lindsey Gdns., Felt. 175 BR87
Lindsey Ms. N1 142 DQ66
Lindsey Rd., Dag. 126 EW63
Lindsey Rd., Uxb. 114 BG62
Lindsey Smith Ho., Vir.W. 192 AY99
Lindsey St. EC1 274 G6
Lindsey St. EC1 141 DP71
Lindsey St., Epp. 69 ER28
Lindsey Way, Horn. 128 FJ57
Lindum Pl., St.Alb. 42 BZ22
Lindum Rd., Tedd. 177 CJ94
Lindvale, Wok. 226 AY115
Lindway SE27 181 DP92
Lindwood Clo. E6 144 EL71
Northumberland Rd.
Linfield Clo. NW4 119 CW55
Linfield Clo., Walt. 213 BV106
Linfields, Amer. 72 AW40
Linford Clo., Harl. 51 EP17
Linford End, Harl. 51 EP17
Linford Rd. E17 123 EC55
Linford Rd., Grays 171 GH77
Linford St. SW8 161 DJ81
Ling Rd. E16 144 EG71
Ling Rd., Erith 167 FC79
Lingards Rd. SE13 163 EC84
Lingey Clo., Sid. 185 ET89
Lingfield Ave., Dart. 188 FP87
Lingfield Ave., Kings.T. 198 CL98
Lingfield Ave., Upmin. 128 FM62
Lingfield Clo., Enf. 82 DS44
Lingfield Clo., Nthwd. 93 BS52
Lingfield Cres. SE9 165 ER84
Lingfield Gdns. N9 100 DV45
Lingfield Gdns., Couls. 235 DP119
Lingfield Rd. SW19 179 CX93
Lingfield Rd., Grav. 191 GH89
Lingfield Rd., Wor.Pk. 199 CW104
Lingham St. SW9 161 DL82
Lingholm Way, Barn. 79 CX42
Lingmere Clo., Chig. 103 EQ47
Lingmoor Dr., Wat. 60 BW33
Lingrove Gdns., Buck.H. 102 EH47
Beech La.
Lings Coppice SE21 182 DR89
Lingwell Rd. SW17 180 DE90
Lingwood Gdns., Islw. 157 CE80
Lingwood Rd. E5 122 DU59
Linhope St. NW1 272 D4
Linhope St. NW1 140 DF70
Link, The SE9 185 EN90
Sandling Ri.
Link, The W3 138 CP72
Link, The, Enf. 83 DY39
Link, The, Nthlt. 116 BZ64
Eastcote La.
Link, The, Pnr. 116 BW59
Link, The, Slou. 132 AV72
Link, The, Wem. 117 CJ60
Nathans Rd.
Link Ave., Wok. 227 BD115
Link Clo., Hat. 45 CV18
Link Dr., Hat. 45 CV18
Link La., Wall. 219 DK107
Link Rd. N11 98 DG49
Link Rd., Add. 212 BL105
Weybridge Rd.
Link Rd., Dag. 147 FB68
Link Rd., Felt. 175 BT87
Link Rd., Slou. 152 AW80
Link Rd., Wall. 200 DG102
Link Rd. (Bushey), Wat. 76 BX40
Link St. E9 122 DW64
Link Wk., Hat. 45 CV17
Link Way, Brom. 204 EL101
Link Way, Dag. 126 EW63
Link Way, Horn. 128 FL60
Link Way, Pnr. 94 BX53
Link Way, Stai. 174 BH93
Link Way, Uxb. 114 BG58
Link Way, Wok. 227 BC117
Linkfield, Brom. 204 EG100
Linkfield, Welw.G.C. 29 CY13
Linkfield, W.Mol. 196 CB97
Linkfield Cor., Red. 250 DE133
Hatchlands Rd.
Linkfield Gdns., Red. 250 DE134
Hatchlands Rd.
Linkfield La., Red. 250 DE133
Linkfield Rd., Islw. 157 CF82
Linkfield St., Red. 250 DE134
Linklea Clo. NW9 96 CS52
Links, The E17 123 DY56
Links, The (Cheshunt), Wal.Cr. 67 DX26
Links, The, Walt. 195 BU103
Links, The, Welw.G.C. 29 CV09
Applecroft Rd.
Links Ave., Hert. 32 DV08
Links Ave., Mord. 200 DA98
Links Ave., Rom. 127 FH55
Links Brow, Lthd. 231 CE124
Links Clo., Ash. 231 CJ117
Links Dr. N20 98 DA46
Links Dr., Borwd. 78 CM41
Links Dr., Rad. 61 CF33
Links Gdns. SW16 181 DN94
Links Grn. Way, Cob. 214 CA114
Links Pl., Ash. 231 CK117
Links Rd. NW2 119 CT61
Links Rd. SW17 180 DG93
Links Rd. W3 138 CN72
Links Rd., Ashf. 174 BL92
Links Rd., Ash. 231 CJ118
Links Rd., Epsom 217 CU113
Links Rd., Guil. 258 AY144
Links Rd., H.Wyc. 110 AC55
Links Rd., W.Wick. 203 EC102
Links Rd., Wdf.Grn. 102 EG50
Links Side, Enf. 81 DM41
Links Vw. N3 97 CZ52
Links Vw., Dart. 187 FH88
Links Vw., St.Alb. 42 CB18
Links Vw. Ave., Bet. 248 CN134
Links Vw. Clo., Stan. 95 CG51
Links Vw. Rd., Croy. 203 EA104
Links Vw. Rd., Hmptn. 176 CC92
Links Way, Beck. 203 EA100
Links Way, Lthd. 246 BY128
Links Way, Nthwd. 93 BQ52
Links Way, Rick. 75 BQ41
Links Yd. E1 142 DU71
Spelman St.
Linkscroft Ave., Ashf. 175 BP93
Linkside N12 97 CZ51
Linkside, Chig. 103 EQ50
Linkside, N.Mal. 198 CS96
Linkside Clo., Enf. 81 DM41
Linkside Gdns., Enf. 81 DM41
Linksway NW4 97 CX54
Linkswood Rd., Slou. 130 AJ68
Linkway N4 122 DQ59
Linkway SW20 199 CV97
Linkway, Guil. 242 AT133
Linkway, Rich. 177 CH90
Linkway, The, Barn. 80 DB44
Linkway, The, Sutt. 218 DC109
Linkway Rd., Brwd. 108 FT48
Linkwood Wk. NW1 141 DK66
Maiden La.
Linley Cres., Rom. 127 FB55
Linley Rd. N17 100 DS54
Linnell Clo. NW11 120 DB58
Linnell Dr. NW11 120 DB58
Linnell Rd. N18 100 DU50
Fairfield Rd.
Linnell Rd. SE5 162 DS82
Linnell Rd., Red. 266 DG135
Linnet Clo. N9 101 DX46
Linnet Clo. SE28 146 EW73
Linnet Clo., S.Croy. 221 DX110
Linnet Clo. (Bushey), Wat. 94 CC45
Linnet Gro., Guil. 243 BD132
Partridge Way
Linnet Ms. SW12 180 DG87
Linnet Rd., Abb.L. 59 BU31
College Rd.
Linnet Wk., Hat. 45 CU20
Lark Ri.
Linnet Way, Purf. 168 FP78
Linnett Clo. E4 101 EC49
Linnington Ave., Chesh. 56 AU30
Linom Rd. SW4 161 DL84
Linscott Rd. E5 122 DW63
Linsdell Rd., Bark. 145 EQ67
Linsey Clo., Hem.H. 40 BN24
Linsey St. SE16 162 DU77
Linslade Clo., Houns. 176 BY85
Frampton Rd.
Linslade Clo., Pnr. 115 BV55
Linslade Rd., Orp. 224 EU107
Linstead Ct. SE9 185 ES86
Linstead St. NW6 140 DA66
Linstead Way SW18 179 CY87
Linster Gro., Borwd. 78 CQ43
Lintaine Clo. W6 159 CY79
Moylan Rd.
Linthorpe Ave., Wem. 137 CJ65
Linthorpe Rd. N16 122 DS59
Linthorpe Rd., Barn. 80 DE41
Linton Ave., Borwd. 78 CM39
Linton Clo., Mitch. 200 DF101
Linton Clo., Well. 166 EV81
Anthony Rd.
Linton Gdns. E6 144 EL72
Linton Glade, Croy. 221 DY109
Linton Gro. SE27 181 DP92
Linton Rd., Bark. 145 EQ66
Linton St. N1 142 DQ67
Lintons, The, Bark. 145 EQ66
Lintons La., Epsom 216 CS112
Lintott Ct., Stai. 174 BK86
Linver Rd. SW6 159 CZ82
Linwood, Saw. 36 EY05
Linwood Clo. E6 144 EL71
Northumberland Rd.
Linwood Clo. SE5 162 DT82
Linwood Cres., Enf. 82 DU39
Linwood Way SE15 162 DT80
Daniel Gdns.
Linzee Rd. N8 121 DL56
Lion Ave., Twick. 177 CF88
Lion Rd.
Lion Clo. SE4 183 EA86
Lion Clo., Shep. 194 BL97
Lion Ct., Borwd. 78 CQ39
Lion Gate Gdns., Rich. 158 CM83
Lion Grn. Rd., Couls. 235 DK115
Lion La., Red. 250 DF133
Lion Pk. Ave., Chess. 216 CN105
Lion Rd. E6 145 EM71
Lion Rd. N9 100 DU47
Lion Rd., Bexh. 166 EZ84
Lion Rd., Croy. 202 DQ99
Pawson's Rd.
Lion Rd., Twick. 177 CF88
Lion Way, Brent. 157 CK80
Lion Wf. Rd., Islw. 157 CH83
Lion Yd. SW4 161 DK84
Tremadoc Rd.
Lionel Gdns. SE9 184 EK85
Lionel Ms. W10 139 CY71
Telford Rd.
Lionel Rd. SE9 184 EK85
Lionel Rd., Brent. 158 CL76
Lions Clo. SE9 184 EJ90
Liphook Clo., Horn. 127 FF63
Petworth Way
Liphook Cres. SE23 182 DW87
Liphook Rd., Wat. 94 BX49
Lippitts Hill, Loug. 84 EE39
Lipsham Clo., Bans. 218 DD113
Lipton Clo. SE28 146 EW73
Aisher Rd.
Lipton Rd. E1 143 DX72
Bower St.
Lisbon Ave., Twick. 176 CC89
Lisburne Rd. NW3 120 DF63
Lisford St. SE15 162 DT81
Lisgar Ter. W14 159 CZ77
Liskeard Clo., Chis. 185 EQ93
Liskeard Gdns. SE3 164 EG81
Liskeard Lo., Cat. 252 DU126
Lisle Pl., Grays 170 GA76
Lisle St. WC2 273 N10
Lisle St. WC2 141 DK73
Lismore, Hem.H. 41 BQ22
Lismore Circ. NW5 120 DG64
Wellesley Rd.
Lismore Clo., Islw. 157 CG82
Lismore Pk., Slou. 132 AT72
Lismore Rd. N17 122 DR55
Lismore Rd., S.Croy. 220 DS107
Lismore Wk. N1 142 DQ65
Clephane Rd.
Liss Way SE15 162 DT80
Pentridge St.
Lissenden Gdns. NW5 120 DG63
Lissoms Rd., Couls. 234 DG118
Lisson Grn. Est. NW8 272 B3
Lisson Grn. Est. NW8 140 DE69
Lisson Gro. NW1 272 A4
Lisson Gro. NW1 140 DE70
Lisson Gro. NW8 272 A4
Lisson Gro. NW8 140 DD70
Lisson St. NW1 272 B6
Lisson St. NW1 140 DE71
Lister Ave., Rom. 106 FK54
Lister Clo. W3 138 CR71
Lister Clo., Mitch. 200 DE95
Lister Gdns. N18 100 DQ50
Lister Ho. SE3 164 EE79
Lister Rd. E11 124 EE60
Lister Rd., Til. 171 GG82
Lister St. E13 144 EG69
Sewell St.
Lister Wk. SE28 146 EX73
Haldane Rd.
Liston Rd. N17 100 DU53
Tern Way
Liston Rd. SW4 161 DJ83
Liston Way, Wdf.Grn. 102 EJ52
Listowel Clo. SW9 161 DN80
Mandela St.
Listowel Rd., Dag. 126 FA62
Listria Pk. N16 122 DS61
Litcham Spur, Slou. 131 AR72
Litchfield Ave. E15 144 EE65
Litchfield Ave., Mord. 199 CZ101
Litchfield Gdns. NW10 139 CU65
Litchfield Rd., Sutt. 218 DC105
Litchfield St. WC2 273 N10
Litchfield St. WC2 141 DK73
Litchfield Way NW11 120 DB57
Litchfield Way, Guil. 258 AT136
Lithos Rd. NW3 140 DC65
Little Acre, Beck. 203 EA97
Little Acre, St.Alb. 43 CD17
Little Acres, Ware 33 DX07
Little Albany St. NW1 273 J3
Little Argyll St. W1 273 K9
Little Aston Rd., Rom. 106 FN52
Little Belhus Clo., S.Ock. 149 FU70
Little Benty, West Dr. 154 BK77
Little Birch Clo., Add. 212 BK109
Little Birches, Sid. 185 ES89
Little Boltons, The SW5 160 DB78
Little Boltons, The SW10 160 DB78
Little Bookham St., Lthd. 230 BZ123
Little Bornes SE21 182 DS91
Little Borough, Bet. 264 CN135
Little Brays, Harl. 52 EU16
Little Bri. Rd., Berk. 38 AX19
Little Britain EC1 274 G7
Little Britain EC1 141 DP71
Little Brook Rd., Harl. 50 EJ15
Little Brownings SE23 182 DV89
Little Buntings, Wind. 151 AM83
Little Burrow, Welw.G.C. 29 CX11
Little Bury St. N9 100 DR46
Little Bushey La. (Bushey), Wat. 76 CA41
Little Catherells, Hem.H. 39 BF18
Little Cattins, Harl. 51 EM19
Little Cedars N12 98 DC49
Woodside Ave.
Little Chapels Way, Slou. 151 AN75
Little Chester St. SW1 277 H6
Little Chester St. SW1 161 DH76
Little College La. EC4 142 DR73
Garlick Hill
Little College St. SW1 277 P6
Little Collins, Red. 267 DP144
Little Common La., Red. 251 DP132
Little Ct., W.Wick. 204 EE103
Little Cranmore La., Lthd. 245 BP128
Little Dean's Yd. SW1 277 P6
Little Dell, Welw.G.C. 29 CX07
Little Dimocks SW12 181 DH89
Little Dormers, Ger.Cr. 113 AZ56
Little Dorrit Ct. SE1 279 J4
Little Dorrit Ct. SE1 162 DQ75
Little Dragons, Loug. 84 EK42
Little Ealing La. W5 157 CJ77
Little Edward St. NW1 273 J2
Little Elms, Hayes 155 BR80
Little Essex St. WC2 274 D10
Little Ferry Rd., Twick. 177 CH88
Ferry Rd.
Little Friday Rd. E4 102 EE47
Little Ganett, Welw.G.C. 30 DB11
Little Gaynes Gdns., Upmin. 128 FP63
Little Gaynes La., Upmin. 128 FM63
Little Gearies, Ilf. 125 EP56
Little George St. SW1 277 P5
Little Gerpins La., Upmin. 148 FM67
Little Gra., Grnf. 137 CG69
Perivale La.
Little Graylings, Abb.L. 59 BS33
Little Grn., Chesh. 54 AN27
Little Grn., Rich. 157 CK84
Little Grn. La., Cher. 193 BE104
Little Grn. La., Rick. 74 BM41
Little Grn. St. NW5 121 DH63
College La.
Little Gregories La., Epp. 85 ER35
Little Gro. (Bushey), Wat. 76 CB42
Little Gro. Fld., Harl. 51 EQ15
Little Halliards, Walt. 195 BU100
Felix Rd.
Little Hardings, Welw.G.C. 30 DC08
Little Hayes, Kings L. 58 BN29
Little Heath SE7 164 EL78
Little Heath, Rom. 126 EV56
Little Heath La., Berk. 39 BB21
Little Heath Rd., Bexh. 166 EY81
Little Heath Rd., Wok. 210 AS109
Little Henleys, Ware 34 EK06
Little Hide, Guil. 243 BB132
Little Hill, Rick. 73 BC44
Little Hivings, Chesh. 54 AN27
Little How Cft., Abb.L. 59 BQ31
Little Ilford La. E12 125 EM63
Little Julians Hill, Sev. 256 FG128
Little Kiln, Gdmg. 258 AS143
Little Lake, Welw.G.C. 30 DB12
Little Ley, Welw.G.C. 29 CY12
Little London, Guil. 260 BL142
Little Marlborough St. W1 273 K9
Little Martins (Bushey), Wat. 76 CB43
Little Mead, Hat. 45 CV15
Little Mead, Wok. 226 AT116
Little Mimms, Hem.H. 40 BK19
Little Moreton Clo., W.Byf. 212 BH112
Little Moss La., Pnr. 94 BY54
Little Mundells, Welw.G.C. 29 CZ07
Little New St. EC4 274 E8
Little Newport St. WC2 273 N10
Little Newport St. WC2 141 DK73
Little Orchard, Add. 211 BF111
Little Orchard, Hem.H. 40 BN18
Little Orchard, Wok. 211 BA114
Little Orchard Clo., Abb.L. 59 BR31
Little Orchard Clo., Pnr. 94 BY54
Barrow Pt. La.
Little Orchard Way, Guil. 258 AY142
Little Oxhey La., Wat. 94 BX50
Little Pk., Hem.H. 57 BA28
Little Pk. Dr., Felt. 176 BX89
Little Pk. Gdns., Enf. 82 DQ41
Little Pastures, Brwd. 108 FT49
Tern Way
Little Pipers Clo. (Cheshunt), Wal.Cr. 65 DP29
Little Pluckets Way, Buck.H. 102 EJ46
Little Port Spur, Slou. 132 AS72
Little Portland St. W1 273 J8
Little Portland St. W1 141 DJ72
Little Potters (Bushey), Wat. 95 CD45
Little Pynchons, Harl. 51 ET18
Little Queen St., Dart. 188 FM87
Little Queens Rd., Tedd. 177 CF93
Little Redlands, Brom. 204 EL96
Little Reeves Ave., Amer. 72 AT39
Little Ridge, Welw.G.C. 30 DA09
Little Rivers, Welw.G.C. 30 DA08
Little Rd., Croy. 202 DS102
Lower Addiscombe Rd.
Little Rd., Hayes 155 BT75
Little Rd., Hem.H. 40 BM19
Little Roke Ave., Ken. 219 DP113
Little Roke Rd., Ken. 220 DQ114
Little Russell St. WC1 273 P7
Little Russell St. WC1 141 DL71
Little Russets, Brwd. 109 GE45
Hutton Village
Little St. James's St. SW1 277 K3
Little St. James's St. SW1 141 DJ74
Little St. Leonards SW14 158 CQ83
Little Sanctuary SW1 277 N5
Little Shardeloes, Amer. 55 AN40
Little Smith St. SW1 277 N6
Little Somerset St. E1 275 P9
Little Spring, Chesh. 54 AP28
Little Strand NW9 97 CT54
Little Stream Clo., Nthwd. 93 BS50
Little St., Guil. 242 AV130
Little Sutton La., Slou. 153 BC78
Little Thistle, Welw.G.C. 30 DC11
Little Thrift, Orp. 205 EQ98
Little Titchfield St. W1 273 K7
Little Trinity La. EC4 275 J10
Little Turnstile WC1 274 B7
Little Wade, Welw.G.C. 29 CZ12
Little Wk., Harl. 51 EQ15
Little Warren Clo., Guil. 259 BB136

Little Widbury, Ware 33 DZ06
Little Widbury La., Ware 33 DZ06
Little Windmill Hill, Kings L. 57 BE32
Little Wd. Clo., Orp. 206 EU95
Little Woodcote La., Cars. 218 DG112
Little Woodcote La., Pur. 218 DG112
Little Woodcote La., Wall. 218 DG112
Little Woodlands, Wind. 151 AM83
Little Youngs, Welw.G.C. 29 CW09
Littlebrook Ave., Slou. 131 AL70
Littlebrook Clo., Croy. 203 DX100
Littlebrook Gdns. (Cheshunt), Wal.Cr. 66 DW30
Littlebrook Manor Way, Dart. 168 FN84
Littlebury Rd. SW4 161 DK83
Littlecombe SE7 164 EH79
Littlecombe Clo. SW15 179 CX86
Littlecote Clo. SW19 179 CX87
Littlecote Pl., Pnr. 94 BZ53
Littlecourt Rd., Sev. 256 FG124
Littlecroft SE9 165 EN83
Littlecroft, Grav. 190 GE94
Littlecroft Rd., Egh. 173 AZ92
Littledale SE2 166 EU79
Littledale, Dart. 188 FQ90
Littledown Rd., Slou. 132 AT74
Littlefield Clo. N19 121 DJ63
Tufnell Pk. Rd.
Littlefield Clo., Kings.T. 198 CL96
Fairfield W.
Littlefield Rd., Edg. 96 CQ52
Littleford La., Guil. 259 BE142
Littlegrove, Barn. 80 DE44
Littleheath La., Cob. 214 BZ114
Littleheath La., Wok. 210 AS109
Littleheath Rd., S.Croy. 220 DV108
Littlehorse La., Ware 33 DX05
Littlejohn Rd. W7 137 CF72
Littlejohn Rd., Orp. 206 EU100
Littlemead, Esher 215 CD105
Littlemede SE9 185 EM90
Littlemoor Rd., Ilf. 125 ER62
Littlemore Rd. SE2 166 EU75
Littlers Clo. SW19 200 DD95
Runnymede
Littlestone Clo., Beck. 183 EA93
Abbey La.
Littleton Ave. E4 102 EF46
Littleton Cres., Har. 117 CF61
Littleton La., Guil. 258 AU139
Littleton La., Reig. 265 CX136
Littleton La., Shep. 194 BK101
Littleton Rd., Ashf. 175 BQ94
Littleton Rd., Har. 117 CF61
Littleton St. SW18 180 DC89
Littlewick Rd., Wok. 210 AW114
Littlewood SE13 183 EC85
Littlewood, Sev. 257 FJ122
Littlewood Clo. W13 157 CH76
Littleworth Ave., Esher 215 CD106
Littleworth Common Rd., Esher 197 CD104
Littleworth La., Esher 215 CD105
Littleworth Pl., Esher 215 CD105
Littleworth Rd., Esher 215 CD106
Littleworth Rd., Slou. 110 AJ63
Litton Ct., H.Wyc. 88 AC53
Livermere Rd. E8 142 DT67
Liverpool Gro. SE17 162 DR78
Liverpool Rd. E10 123 EC58
Liverpool Rd. E16 144 EE71
Liverpool Rd. N1 141 DN66
Liverpool Rd. N7 121 DN64
Liverpool Rd. W5 157 CK75
Liverpool Rd., Kings.T. 178 CN94
Liverpool Rd., St.Alb. 43 CE20
Liverpool Rd., Slou. 131 AP72
Liverpool Rd., Th.Hth. 202 DQ97
Liverpool Rd., Wat. 75 BV43
Liverpool St. EC2 275 M7
Liverpool St. EC2 142 DS71
Livesey Clo., Kings.T. 198 CM97
Livesey Pl. SE15 162 DU79
Peckham Pk. Rd.
Livingston College Twrs. E10 123 EC58
Livingstone Gdns., Grav. 191 GK92
Livingstone Pl. E14 163 EC78
Ferry St.
Livingstone Rd. E15 143 EC67
Livingstone Rd. E17 123 EB58
Livingstone Rd. N13 99 DL51
Livingstone Rd. SW11 160 DD83
Winstanley Rd.
Livingstone Rd., Cat. 236 DR122
Livingstone Rd., Grav. 191 GK92
Livingstone Rd., Houns. 156 CC84
Livingstone Rd., Sthl. 136 BX73
Livingstone Rd., Th.Hth. 202 DQ96
Livingstone Ter., Rain. 147 FE67
Stanley Rd. N.
Livingstone Wk. SW11 160 DD83
Livingstone Wk., Hem.H. 40 BM16
Livonia St. W1 273 L9
Lizard St. EC1 275 J3
Lizard St. EC1 142 DQ69
Lizban St. SE3 164 EH80
Llanbury Clo., Ger.Cr. 90 AY52
Llanelly Rd. NW2 119 CZ61
Llanover Rd. SE18 165 EN79
Llanover Rd., Wem. 117 CK62
Llanthony Rd., Mord. 200 DD100
Llanvanor Rd. NW2 119 CZ61
Llewellyn St. SE16 162 DU75
Chambers St.
Lloyd Ave. SW16 201 DL95
Lloyd Ave., Couls. 218 DG114
Lloyd Baker St. WC1 274 C3
Lloyd Baker St. WC1 141 DM69
Lloyd Ct., Pnr. 116 BX57
Lloyd Pk. Ave., Croy. 220 DT105
Lloyd Rd. E6 145 EM67
Lloyd Rd. E17 123 DX56
Lloyd Rd., Dag. 146 EZ65
Lloyd Rd., Wor.Pk. 199 CW104
Lloyd Sq. WC1 274 D2
Lloyd Sq. WC1 141 DN69
Lloyd St. WC1 274 D2
Lloyd St. WC1 141 DN69
Lloyd's Ave. EC3 275 N9
Lloyd's Ave. EC3 142 DS72
Lloyds Pl. SE3 164 EE82
Lloyd's Row EC1 274 F3
Lloyds Way, Beck. 203 DY99
Loampit Hill SE13 163 EA82
Loampit Vale SE13 163 EB83
Loanda Clo. E8 142 DT67
Clarissa St.
Loates La., Wat. 76 BW41
Loats Rd. SW2 181 DL86
Lobelia Clo. E6 144 EL71
Sorrel Gdns.
Local Board Rd., Wat. 76 BW43
Locarno Rd. W3 138 CQ74
High St.
Locarno Rd., Grnf. 136 CC70
Lochaber Rd. SE13 164 EE84
Lochaline St. W6 159 CW79
Lochan Clo., Hayes 136 BY70
Lochinvar Clo., Slou. 151 AP75
Haig Dr.
Lochinvar St. SW12 181 DH87
Lochmere Clo., Erith 167 FB79
Lochnagar St. E14 143 EC71
Lochnell, Berk. 38 AT17
Lock Ave., Maid. 130 AC69
Lock Chase SE3 164 EE83
Lock Clo., Add. 211 BE112
Lock Clo., Sthl. 156 CC75
Navigator Dr.
Lock Island, Shep. 194 BN103
Lock La., Wok. 228 BH116
Lock Path, Wind. 151 AK79
Lock Rd., Guil. 242 AX131
Lock Rd., Rich. 177 CJ91
Locke Clo., Rain. 147 FF65
Locke Gdns., Slou. 152 AW75
Locke King Clo., Wey. 212 BN108
Locke King Rd., Wey. 212 BN108
Locke Way, Wok. 227 AZ117
Broadway
Lockers Pk. La., Hem.H. 40 BH20
Lockesfield Pl. E14 163 EB78
Lockesley Dr., Orp. 205 ET100
Lockesley Sq., Surb. 197 CK100
Locket Rd., Har. 117 CE55
Lockets Clo., Wind. 151 AL81
Lockfield Ave., Enf. 83 DY40
Lockfield Dr., Wok. 226 AS116
Lockgate Clo. E9 123 DZ64
Lee Conservancy Rd.
Lockhart Clo. N7 141 DM65
Lockhart Clo., Enf. 82 DV43
Derby Rd.
Lockhart Rd., Cob. 214 BW113
Lockhart St. E3 143 DZ70
Lockhurst St. E5 123 DX63
Lockie Pl. SE25 202 DU97
Lockier Wk., Wem. 117 CK62
Hutchinson Ter.
Lockington Rd. SW8 161 DH81
Lockley Cres., Hat. 45 CV16
Lockmead Rd. N15 122 DU58
Lockmead Rd. SE13 163 EC83
Lockner Holt, Guil. 259 BF141
Locks La., Mitch. 200 DF95
Lockside E14 143 DY73
Northey St.
Locksley Dr., Wok. 226 AT118
Robin Hood Rd.
Locksley Est. E14 143 DZ72
Locksley St. E14 143 DZ71
Locksmeade Rd., Rich. 177 CJ91
Lockswood Clo., Barn. 80 DG41
Lockwood Clo. SE26 183 DX91
Lockwood Ind. Pk. N17 122 DV55
Lockwood Path, Wok. 211 BE113
Lockwood Sq. SE16 162 DV76
Lockwood Wk., Rom. 127 FE57
Lockwood Way E17 101 DX54
Lockwood Way, Chess. 216 CN106
Lockyer Est. SE1 279 L4
Lockyer Rd., Purf. 168 FQ79
Lockyer St. SE1 279 L5
Loddiges Rd. E9 142 DW66
Loddon Spur, Slou. 132 AS73
Loder Clo., Wok. 211 BD113
Loder St. SE15 162 DW80
Lodge Ave. SW14 158 CS83
Lodge Ave., Borwd. 78 CM43
Lodge Ave., Croy. 201 DN104
Lodge Ave., Dag. 146 EU67
Lodge Ave., Dart. 188 FJ86
Lodge Ave., Har. 118 CL56
Lodge Ave., Rom. 127 FG57
Lodge Clo. N18 100 DQ50
Lodge Clo., Chig. 104 EU48
Lodge Clo., Cob. 230 BZ116
Lodge Clo., Dor. 263 CJ140
Lodge Clo., Edg. 96 CM51
Lodge Clo., Egh. 172 AX92
Lodge Clo., Epsom 217 CW110
Howell Hill Gro.
Lodge Clo., Hert. 32 DQ07
Lodge Clo., Islw. 157 CH81
Lodge Clo., Lthd. 231 CD122
Lodge Clo., Orp. 206 EV102
Lodge Clo., Slou. 151 AQ75
Lodge Clo., Uxb. 134 BJ70
Lodge Clo., Wall. 200 DG102
Lodge Ct., Horn. 128 FL61
Lodge Cres., Orp. 206 EV102
Lodge Cres., Wal.Cr. 67 DX34
Lodge Dr. N13 99 DN49
Lodge Dr., Hat. 45 CX15
Lodge Dr., Rick. 74 BJ42
Lodge Dr., The, Beac. 89 AL54
Lodge End, Rad. 61 CH34
Lodge End, Rick. 75 BR41
Lodge Fld., Welw.G.C. 29 CY06
Lodge Gdns., Beck. 203 DZ99
Lodge Hall, Harl. 51 ES19
Lodge Hill SE2 166 EV80
Lodge Hill, Ilf. 124 EL56
Lodge Hill, Pur. 235 DN115
Lodge Hill, Well. 166 EV80
Lodge La. N12 98 DC50
Lodge La., Bex. 186 EX86
Lodge La., Ch.St.G. 73 AZ43
Lodge La., Croy. 221 EA107
Lodge La., Dor. 264 CL144
Lodge La., Grays 170 GC76
Lodge La., Red. 266 DE143
Lodge La., Rom. 104 FA52
Lodge La., Wal.Abb. 83 ED35
Lodge La., West. 255 EQ127
Lodge Pl., Sutt. 218 DB106
Lodge Rd. NW4 119 CW56
Lodge Rd. NW8 272 A3
Lodge Rd. NW8 140 DD69
Lodge Rd., Brom. 184 EH94
Lodge Rd., Croy. 201 DP100
Lodge Rd., Lthd. 230 CC122
Lodge Rd., Sutt. 218 DB106
Throwley Way
Lodge Rd., Wall. 219 DH106
Lodge Vill., Wdf.Grn. 102 EF52
Lodge Way, Ashf. 174 BL89
Lodge Way, Shep. 195 BQ96
Lodge Way, Wind. 151 AL83
Lodgebottom Rd., Lthd. 248 CN127
Lodgehill Pk. Clo., Har. 116 CB61
Lodore Gdns. NW9 118 CS57
Lodore Grn., Uxb. 114 BL62
Lodore St. E14 143 EC72
Loewen Rd., Grays 171 GG76
Lofthouse Pl., Chess. 215 CJ107
Loftie St. SE16 162 DU75
Lofting Rd. N1 141 DM66
Loftus Rd. W12 139 CV74
Logan Clo., Enf. 83 DX39
Logan Clo., Houns. 156 BZ83
Logan Ms. W8 160 DA77
Logan Pl. W8 160 DA77
Logan Rd. N9 100 DV47
Logan Rd., Wem. 118 CL61
Loggetts, The SE21 182 DR90
Logmore La., Dor. 262 CB138
Logs Hill, Chis. 184 EL94
Logs Hill Clo., Chis. 204 EL95
Lois Dr., Shep. 195 BP99
Lolesworth Clo. E1 142 DT71
Commercial St.
Lollard St. SE11 278 C8
Lollard St. SE11 161 DN77
Lollards Clo., Amer. 55 AQ37
Lollesworth La., Lthd. 245 BQ126
Loman Path, S.Ock. 149 FT72
Loman St. SE1 278 G4
Loman St. SE1 161 DP75
Lomas Clo., Croy. 221 EC108
Lomas Ct. E8 142 DT66
Lomas St. E1 142 DU71
Lombard Ave., Enf. 82 DW39
Lombard Ave., Ilf. 125 ES60
Lombard Business Pk. SW19 200 DB96
Lombard Ct. EC3 275 L10
Lombard La. EC4 274 E9
Lombard Rd. N11 99 DH50
Lombard Rd. SW11 160 DD82
Lombard Rd. SW19 200 DB96
Lombard St. EC3 275 L9
Lombard St. EC3 142 DR72
Lombard St., Dart. 208 FQ99
Lombard Wall SE7 164 EH76
Lombards, The, Horn. 128 FM59
Lombardy Clo., Hem.H. 41 BR21
Lombardy Clo., Wok. 226 AT117
Nethercote Ave.
Lombardy Dr., Berk. 38 AX20
Lombardy Pl. W2 140 DB73
Bark Pl.
Lombardy Way, Borwd. 78 CL39
Lomond Clo. N15 122 DS57
Lomond Clo., Wem. 138 CM66
Lomond Gdns., S.Croy. 221 DY108
Lomond Gro. SE5 162 DR80
Lomond Ho. SE5 162 DR81
Lomond Gro.
Lomond Rd., Hem.H. 40 BK16
Loncin Mead Ave., Add. 212 BJ109
Loncroft Rd. SE5 162 DS79
Londesborough Rd. N16 122 DS63
London Bri. EC4 279 L2
London Bri. EC4 142 DR73
London Bri. SE1 279 L2
London Bri. SE1 142 DR74
London Bri. St. SE1 279 L3
London Bri. St. SE1 142 DR74
London Bri. Wk. SE1 279 L2
London City Airport E16 144 EL74
London Colney Bypass, St.Alb. 61 CK25
London Colney Ind. Est., St.Alb. 62 CL27
London End, Beac. 89 AM54
London Flds. E8 142 DV66
London Flds. E. Side E8 142 DV66
London Flds. W. Side E8 142 DU66
London Hollow, H.Wyc. 88 AD54
London Ind. Pk. E6 145 EP71
London La. E8 142 DV66
London La., Brom. 184 EF94
London La., Guil. 260 BN138
London La., Lthd. 245 BU131
London Ms. W2 272 A9
London Rd. E13 144 EG68
London Rd. SE1 278 F6
London Rd. SE1 161 DP76
London Rd. SE23 182 DV88
London Rd. SW16 201 DM95
London Rd. SW17 180 DF94
London Rd., Amer. 55 AQ40
London Rd., Ashf. 174 BJ90
London Rd., Bark. 145 EP66
London Rd., Beac. 89 AM54
London Rd., Berk. 38 AX20
London Rd., Borwd. 78 CQ36
London Rd., Brent. 157 CF82
London Rd., Brwd. 108 FT49
London Rd., Brom. 184 EF94
London Rd., Cat. 236 DR123
London Rd., Ch.St.G. 90 AW47
London Rd., Croy. 201 DP102
London Rd., Dart. 188 FP87
London Rd. (Crayford), Dart. 187 FD85
London Rd. (Farningham), Dart. 208 FL100
London Rd., Dor. 247 CH133
London Rd., Egh. 192 AW95
London Rd., Enf. 82 DR42
London Rd., Epp. 52 EV23
London Rd., Epsom 217 CU108
London Rd., Felt. 174 BH90
London Rd., Gat. 268 DF150
London Rd., Grav. 190 GD86
London Rd., Grays 169 FW79
London Rd., Green. 189 FT86
London Rd., Guil. 258 AY135
London Rd. (Old Harlow), Harl. 52 EV16
London Rd. (Potter St.), Harl. 52 EW18
London Rd. (Thornwood), Harl. 52 EV22
London Rd., Har. 117 CE61
London Rd., Hem.H. 40 BG22
London Rd., Hert. 32 DS09
London Rd., H.Wyc. 88 AD54
London Rd., Houns. 156 CC83
London Rd., Islw. 157 CF82
London Rd., Kings.T. 198 CM96
London Rd., Mitch. 200 DE98
London Rd. (Beddington Cor.), Mitch. 200 DG101
London Rd., Mord. 200 DA99
London Rd., Ong. 87 FH36
London Rd., Rad. 62 CM33
London Rd., Red. 250 DG133
London Rd., Reig. 250 DA134
London Rd., Rick. 92 BM47
London Rd., Rom. 126 FA58
London Rd. (Abridge), Rom. 86 EU42
London Rd. (Stapleford Tawney), Rom. 87 FC40
London Rd., St.Alb. 43 CD20
London Rd., Saw. 36 EY05
London Rd., Sev. 256 FF123
London Rd. (Halstead), Sev. 225 FB112
London Rd. (Longford), Sev. 241 FD119
London Rd., Slou. 152 AW76
London Rd. (Datchet), Slou. 152 AV80
London Rd., S.Ock. 148 FM74
London Rd., Stai. 173 BF91
London Rd., Stan. 95 CJ50
London Rd., Sutt. 199 CW104
London Rd., Swan. 207 FC95
London Rd., Swans. 189 FX85
London Rd., Th.Hth. 201 DN99
London Rd., Til. 171 GH82
London Rd., Twick. 177 CG87
London Rd., Vir.W. 192 AT97
London Rd., Wall. 219 DH105
London Rd., Ware 33 DX07
London Rd. (Bushey), Wat. 76 BY44
London Rd., Wem. 118 CL64
London Rd., West. 255 ER126
London Rd., Wok. 243 BD128
London Rd. E., Amer. 55 AR41
London Rd. N., Red. 251 DH126
London Rd. Purfleet, Purf. 168 FN78
London Rd. S., Red. 250 DG130
London Rd. W., Amer. 55 AQ40
London Rd. W. Thurrock, Grays 169 FS79
London Sq., Guil. 242 AY134
London Stile W4 158 CN78
Wellesley Rd.
London St. EC3 275 N10
London St. W2 140 DD72
London St., Cher. 194 BG101
London Wall EC2 275 J7
London Wall EC2 142 DQ71
London Wall Bldgs. EC2 275 L7
Londons Clo., Upmin. 128 FQ64
Londrina Ter., Berk. 38 AX19
Lone Oak, Horl. 269 DP150
Lonesome La., Reig. 266 DB138
Lonesome Way SW16 201 DH95
Long Acre WC2 273 P10
Long Acre WC2 141 DL73
Long Acre, Orp. 206 EX103
Long Arrotts, Hem.H. 40 BH18
Long Banks, Harl. 51 ER19
Long Barn Clo., Wat. 59 BU32
Long Bottom La., Beac. 89 AN51
Long Chaulden, Hem.H. 39 BE20
Long Clo., Slou. 131 AP66
Long Copse Clo., Lthd. 230 CB123
Long Ct. WC2 277 N1
Long Ct., Purf. 168 FN77
Thamley
Long Cross Rd., Wok. 192 AT104
Long Deacon Rd. E4 102 EE46
Long Dr. W3 138 CS72
Long Dr., Grnf. 136 CB67
Long Dr., Ruis. 116 BX63
Long Dr., Slou. 130 AJ69
Long Dyke, Guil. 243 BB132
Long Elmes, Har. 94 CB53
Long Elms, Abb.L. 59 BR33
Long Elms Clo., Abb.L. 59 BR33
Long Elms
Long Fallow, St.Alb. 60 CA27
Long Fld. NW9 96 CS52
Long Furlong Dr., Slou. 131 AK70
Long Gore, Gdmg. 258 AS142
Long Grn., Chig. 103 ES49
Long Gro., Rom. 106 FL54
Long Gro. Rd., Epsom 216 CP110
Long Hedges, Houns. 156 CA81
Great W. Rd.
Long Hill, Cat. 237 DX121
Long John, Hem.H. 40 BM22
Long La. EC1 274 G6
Long La. EC1 141 DP71
Long La. N2 98 DC54
Long La. N3 98 DB52
Long La. SE1 279 K5
Long La. SE1 162 DR75
Long La., Bexh. 166 EX80
Long La., Croy. 202 DV100
Long La., Grays 170 GA75
Long La., Hem.H. 57 AZ31
Long La., Rick. 91 BF46
Long La. (Heronsgate), Rick. 73 BC44
Long La., Stai. 174 BM89
Long La., Uxb. 135 BP67
Long Ley, Harl. 51 ET15
Long Ley, Welw.G.C. 30 DC09
Long Leys E4 101 EB51
Long Lo. Dr., Walt. 196 BW104
Long Mark Rd. E16 144 EK71
Fulmer Rd.
Long Mead NW9 97 CT53
Long Meadow NW5 121 DK64
Torriano Ave.
Long Meadow, Brwd. 109 GC47
Long Meadow, Chesh. 54 AQ28
Long Meadow, Lthd. 246 BZ126
Long Meadow, Sev. 241 FD119
London Rd.
Long Meadow Clo., W.Wick. 203 EC101
Long Mimms, Hem.H. 40 BL19
Long Pk., Amer. 55 AQ36
Long Pk. Clo., Amer. 55 AQ36
Long Pk. Way, Amer. 55 AQ35
Long Pond Rd. SE3 164 EE81
Long Reach, Lthd. 245 BP125
Long Reach, Wok. 228 BN123
Long Reach Ct., Bark. 145 ER68
Long Reach Rd., Bark. 145 ET70
Long Readings La., Slou. 131 AP70
Long Ride, The, Hat. 45 CZ16
Long Ridings Ave., Brwd. 109 GB43
Long Rd. SW4 161 DH84
Long Shaw, Lthd. 231 CG120
Long Spring, St.Alb. 43 CF16
Long St. E2 275 P2
Long St. E2 142 DT69
Long St., Wal.Abb. 68 EL32
Long Vw., Berk. 38 AU17
Long Wk. SE1 279 N6
Long Wk. SE18 165 EP79
Long Wk. SW13 158 CS82
The Ter.
Long Wk., Ch.St.G. 72 AX41
Long Wk., Epsom 233 CW119
Long Wk., Lthd. 244 BN128
Long Wk., N.Mal. 198 CQ97
Long Wk., Wal.Abb. 67 EA30
Long Wk., W.Byf. 212 BJ114
Long Wk., The, Wind. 151 AR83
Long Wk. Rd., Uxb. 135 BP74
Long Wd. Dr., Beac. 90 AT51
Long Yd. WC1 274 B5
Long Yd. WC1 141 DM70
Longacre, Harl. 36 EV11
Longacre Pl., Cars. 218 DG107
Beddington Gdns.
Longacre Rd. E17 101 ED53
Longacres, St.Alb. 43 CK20
Longaford Way, Brwd. 109 GC46
Longbeach Rd. SW11 160 DF83
Longberrys NW2 119 CZ62
Longboat Row, Sthl. 136 BZ72
Longbottom La., Beac. 89 AR52
Longbourne Grn., Gdmg. 258 AS143
Barnes Rd.
Longbourne Way, Cher. 193 BF100
Longboyds, Cob. 213 BV114
Longbridge Rd., Bark. 145 ER65
Longbridge Rd., Dag. 126 EU63
Longbridge Rd., Gat. 268 DF150
Longbridge Rd., Horl. 268 DF150
Longbridge Roundabout, Horl. 268 DE149
Longbridge Wk., Horl. 268 DF150
Longbridge Way SE13 183 EC85
Longbridge Way, Uxb. 134 BH68
Longbury Clo., Orp. 206 EV97
Longbury Dr., Orp. 206 EV97
Longchamp Clo., Horl. 269 DJ148
Carlton Tye
Longcliffe Path, Wat. 93 BU48
Gosforth La.
Longcroft SE9 185 EM90
Longcroft, Wat. 93 BV45
Longcroft Ave., Bans. 218 DC114
Longcroft Dr., Wal.Cr. 67 DZ34
Longcroft Gdns., Welw.G.C. 29 CX10
Longcroft Grn., Welw.G.C. 29 CX11
Stanborough Rd.
Longcroft La., Hem.H. 57 BC28
Longcroft La., Welw.G.C. 29 CX10
Longcroft Ri., Loug. 85 EN43
Longcroft Rd., Rick. 91 BD50
Longcrofte Rd., Edg. 95 CK52
Longcrofts, Wal.Abb. 68 EE34
Roundhills
Longcross Rd., Cher. 192 AY104
Longdean Pk., Hem.H. 40 BN24
Longdon Wd., Kes. 204 EL104
Longdown La. N., Epsom 217 CU114
Longdown La. S., Epsom 217 CU114
Longdown Rd. SE6 183 EA91
Longdown Rd., Epsom 217 CU114
Longdown Rd., Guil. 259 BB137
Longfellow Dr., Brwd. 109 GC45
Longfellow Rd. E17 123 DZ58
Longfellow Rd., Wor.Pk. 199 CU102
Longfellow Way SE1 162 DT77
Chaucer Dr.
Longfield, Brom. 204 EF95
Longfield, Harl. 52 EU17
Longfield, Hem.H. 41 BP22
Longfield, Loug. 84 EJ43
Longfield, Slou. 111 AR62
Hedgerley Hill
Longfield Ave. E17 123 DY56
Longfield Ave. NW7 97 CU52
Longfield Ave. W5 137 CJ73
Longfield Ave., Enf. 82 DW37
Longfield Ave., Horn. 127 FF59
Longfield Ave., Wall. 200 DG102
Longfield Ave., Wem. 118 CL60
Longfield Cres. SE26 182 DW90
Longfield Cres., Tad. 233 CW120
Longfield Dr. SW14 178 CP85
Longfield Dr., Amer. 55 AP38
Longfield Dr., Mitch. 180 DE94
Longfield Est. SE1 162 DT77
Longfield La. (Cheshunt), Wal.Cr. 66 DT27
Longfield Rd. W5 137 CJ72
Longfield Rd., Chesh. 54 AM29
Longfield Rd., Dor. 263 CF137
Longfield St. SW18 180 DA87
Longfield Wk. W5 137 CJ72
Longford Ave., Felt. 175 BS86
Longford Ave., Sthl. 136 CA73
Longford Ave., Stai. 174 BL88
Longford Clo., Hmptn. 176 CA91
Longford Clo., Hayes 136 BX73
Longford Gdns.
Longford Ct. E5 123 DX63
Pedro St.
Longford Ct. NW4 119 CX56
Longford Ct., Epsom 216 CQ105
Longford Gdns., Hayes 136 BX73
Longford Gdns., Sutt. 200 DC104
Longford Rd., Twick. 176 CA88

Lon–Lud This index reads in the sequence: Street Name / Postal District or Post Town / Map Page Number / Grid Reference

Longford St. NW1 273 J4
Longford St. NW1 141 DH70
Longford Wk. SW2 181 DN87
Papworth Way
Longford Way, Stai. 174 BL88
Longhayes Ave., Rom. 126 EX56
Longheath Gdns., Croy. 202 DW99
Longhedge Ho. SE26 182 DT91
Longhedge St. SW11 160 DG82
Longhill Rd. SE6 183 ED89
Longhook Gdns., Nthlt. 135 BU68
Longhope Clo. SE15 162 DS79
Longhouse Rd., Grays 171 GH76
Longhurst Rd. SE13 183 ED85
Longhurst Rd., Croy. 202 DV100
Longhurst Rd., Lthd. 245 BS129
Longland Bri., B.Stort. 37 FC07
Longland Ct. SE1 162 DU78
Rolls Rd.
Longland Dr. N20 98 DB48
Longlands, Hem.H. 40 BM20
Longlands Ave., Couls. 218 DG114
Longlands Clo. (Cheshunt), Wal.Cr. 67 DX32
Longlands Ct. W11 139 CZ73
Portobello Rd.
Longlands Ct., Mitch. 200 DG95
Summerhill Way
Longlands Pk. Cres., Sid. 185 ES90
Longlands Rd., Sid. 185 ES90
Longlands Rd., Welw.G.C. 29 CZ10
Longleat Ms., Orp. 206 EW98
High St.
Longleat Rd., Enf. 82 DS43
Longleat Way, Felt. 175 BR87
Longlees, Rick. 91 BD50
Longleigh La. SE2 166 EW79
Longleigh La., Bexh. 166 EW79
Longlents Ho. NW10 138 CR67
Shrewsbury Cres.
Longley Ave., Wem. 138 CM67
Longley Rd. SW17 180 DE93
Longley Rd., Croy. 201 DP101
Longley Rd., Har. 116 CC57
Longley St. SE1 162 DU77
Longley Way NW2 119 CW62
Longmarsh Vw. (Sutton at Hone), Dart. 208 FP95
Longmead, Chis. 205 EN96
Longmead, Epsom 216 CR110
Longmead, Guil. 243 BC134
Longmead, Hat. 45 CV15
Longmead, Wind. 151 AL81
Longmead Clo., Brwd. 108 FY46
Longmead Clo., Cat. 236 DS122
Longmead Dr., Sid. 186 EX89
Longmead La., Slou. 131 AK66
Longmead Rd. SW17 180 DF92
Longmead Rd., Epsom 216 CR111
Longmead Rd., Hayes 135 BT73
Longmead Rd., T.Ditt. 197 CE101
Longmeadow Rd., Sid. 185 ES88
Longmere Gdns., Tad. 233 CW119
Longmoor, Wal.Cr. 67 DY29
Longmoor Pt. SW15 179 CV88
Norley Vale
Longmoore St. SW1 277 K9
Longmoore St. SW1 161 DJ77
Longmore Ave., Barn. 80 DC44
Longmore Clo., Rick. 91 BF49
Longmore Gdns., Welw.G.C. 29 CZ09
Longmore Rd., Walt. 214 BY105
Longnor Rd. E1 143 DX69
Longport Clo., Ilf. 104 EU51
Longreach Rd., Erith 167 FH80
Longridge Gro., Wok. 211 BE114
Old Woking Rd.
Longridge La., Sthl. 136 CB72
Longridge Rd. SW5 160 DA77
Longs Clo., Wok. 228 BG116
Longs Ct., Rich. 158 CM84
Crown Ter.
Longshaw Rd. E4 101 ED48
Longshore SE8 163 DZ77
Longside Clo., Egh. 193 BC95
Longspring, Wat. 75 BV38
Longspring Wd., Sev. 256 FF130
Longstaff Cres. SW18 180 DA86
Longstaff Rd. SW18 180 DA86
Longstone Ave. NW10 139 CT66
Longstone Rd. SW17 181 DH92
Longstone Rd., Iver 133 BC68
Longthornton Rd. SW16 201 DJ96
Longton Ave. SE26 182 DU91
Longton Gro. SE26 182 DV91
Longtown Clo., Rom. 106 FJ50
Longtown Rd., Rom. 106 FJ50
Longview, Beac. 110 AF55
Longview Way, Rom. 105 FD53
Longville Rd. SE11 278 G8
Longwalk Rd., Uxb. 135 BP74
Longwood, Harl. 51 ER20
Longwood Clo., Upmin. 128 FQ64
Longwood Dr. SW15 179 CU86
Longwood Gdns., Ilf. 125 EM56
Longwood La., Amer. 55 AR39
Longwood Rd., Hert. 31 DM07
Longwood Rd., Ken. 236 DR116
Longworth Clo. SE28 146 EX72
Longworth Dr., Maid. 130 AC70
Loning, The NW9 118 CS56
Loning, The, Enf. 82 DW38
Lonsdale, Hem.H. 40 BL17
Lonsdale Ave. E6 144 EK69
Lonsdale Ave., Brwd. 109 GD44
Lonsdale Ave., Rom. 127 FC58
Lonsdale Ave., Wem. 118 CL64
Lonsdale Clo. E6 144 EL70
Lonsdale Ave.
Lonsdale Clo. SE9 184 EK90
Lonsdale Clo., Edg. 96 CM50
Orchard Dr.
Lonsdale Clo., Pnr. 94 BY52
Lonsdale Clo., Uxb. 135 BQ71
Dawley Ave.
Lonsdale Cres., Dart. 188 FQ89
Lonsdale Cres., Ilf. 125 EP58
Lonsdale Dr., Enf. 81 DK42
Lonsdale Gdns., Th.Hth. 201 DM98
Lonsdale Ms., Rich. 158 CN81
Elizabeth Cotts.
Lonsdale Pl. N1 141 DN66
Barnsbury St.
Lonsdale Rd. E11 124 EF59
Lonsdale Rd. NW6 139 CZ67
Lonsdale Rd. SE25 202 DV98
Lonsdale Rd. SW13 159 CU79
Lonsdale Rd. W4 159 CT77
Lonsdale Rd. W11 139 CZ72
Lonsdale Rd., Bexh. 166 EZ82
Lonsdale Rd., Dor. 263 CH135
Lonsdale Rd., Sthl. 156 BX76
Lonsdale Rd., Wey. 212 BN108
Lonsdale Sq. N1 141 DN67
Lonsdale Way, Maid. 150 AC78
Loobert Rd. N15 122 DS55
Looe Gdns., Ilf. 125 EP55
Loom La., Rad. 77 CF37
Loom Pl., Rad. 77 CG36
Loop Rd., Chis. 185 EQ93
Loop Rd., Epsom 232 CQ116
Woodcote Side
Loop Rd., Wal.Abb. 67 EB32
Loop Rd., Wok. 227 AZ120
Lopen Rd. N18 100 DS49
Loraine Clo., Enf. 82 DW43
Loraine Gdns., Ash. 232 CL117
Loraine Rd. N7 121 DM63
Loraine Rd. W4 158 CP79
Lorane Ct., Wat. 75 BU40
Stratford Rd.
Lord Ave., Ilf. 125 EM56
Lord Chancellor Wk., Kings.T. 198 CQ95
Lord Gdns., Ilf. 124 EL56
Lord Hills Bri. W2 140 DB71
Porchester Rd.
Lord Hills Rd. W2 140 DB71
Lord Holland La. SW9 161 DN81
Myatt's Flds. S.
Lord Knyvett Clo., Stai. 174 BK86
Lord Mayors Dr., Slou. 131 AM65
Lord Napier Pl. W6 159 CU78
Upper Mall
Lord N. St. SW1 277 P7
Lord N. St. SW1 161 DL76
Lord Roberts Ms. SW6 160 DB80
Moore Pk. Rd.
Lord Roberts Ter. SE18 165 EN78
Lord St. E16 144 EL74
Lord St., Grav. 191 GH87
Lord St., Hodd. 48 DV17
Lord St., Wat. 76 BW41
Lord Warwick St. SE18 165 EM76
Lordell Pl. SW19 179 CW93
Lorden Wk. E2 142 DU69
Turin St.
Lord's Clo. SE21 182 DQ89
Lords Clo., Felt. 176 BY89
Lords Clo., Rad. 62 CL32
Lord's Vw. NW8 272 A3
Lords Wd., Welw.G.C. 30 DC09
Lordsbury Fld., Wall. 219 DJ110
Lordsgrove Clo., Tad. 233 CV120
Whitegate Way
Lordship Clo., Brwd. 109 GD46
Lordship Gro. N16 122 DR61
Lordship La. N17 100 DQ53
Lordship La. N22 99 DN54
Lordship La. SE22 182 DT86
Lordship La. Est. SE22 182 DU88
Lordship Pk. N16 122 DQ61
Lordship Pk. Ms. N16 122 DQ61
Allerton Rd.
Lordship Pl. SW3 160 DE79
Cheyne Row
Lordship Rd. N16 122 DR60
Lordship Rd., Nthlt. 136 BY66
Lordship Rd. (Cheshunt), Wal.Cr. 66 DV30
Lordship Ter. N16 122 DR61
Lordsmead Rd. N17 100 DS53
Lordswood Clo., Dart. 189 FS91
Lorenzo St. WC1 274 B1
Lorenzo St. WC1 141 DM69
Loretto Gdns., Har. 118 CL56
Lorian Clo. N12 98 DB49
Lorian Dr., Reig. 250 DC133
Loring Rd. N20 98 DE47
Loring Rd., Berk. 38 AW20
Loring Rd., Islw. 157 CF82
Loring Rd., Wind. 151 AM81
Loris Rd. W6 159 CW76
Lorn Ct. SW9 161 DN82
Lorn Rd.
Lorn Rd. SW9 161 DM82
Lorne, The, Lthd. 246 CA126
Lorne Ave., Croy. 203 DX101
Lorne Clo. NW8 272 C3
Lorne Clo., Slou. 151 AP76
Lorne Gdns. E11 124 EJ56
Lorne Gdns. W11 159 CX75
Lorne Gdns., Croy. 203 DX101
Lorne Rd. E7 124 EH63
Lorne Rd. E17 123 EA57
Lorne Rd. N4 121 DM60
Lorne Rd., Brwd. 108 FW49
Lorne Rd., Har. 95 CF54
Lorne Rd., Rich. 178 CM85
Albert Rd.
Lorraine Chase, S.Ock. 168 FM75
Lorraine Pk., Har. 95 CE52
Lorrimore Rd. SE17 161 DP79
Lorrimore Sq. SE17 161 DP79
Lorton Clo., Grav. 191 GL89
Losberne Way SE16 162 DU78
Catlin St.
Loseberry Rd., Esher 215 CD106
Loseley Pk., Guil. 258 AS140
Loseley Rd., Gdmg. 258 AS143
Losfield Rd., Wind. 151 AL81
Lossie Dr., Iver 133 BB73
Lothair Rd. W5 157 CK75
Lothair Rd. N. N4 121 DP58
Lothair Rd. S. N4 121 DN59
Lothbury EC2 275 K8
Lothbury EC2 142 DR72
Lothian Ave., Hayes 135 BV71
Lothian Clo., Wem. 117 CG63
Lothian Rd. SW9 161 DP81
Lothian Wd., Tad. 233 CV122
Lothrop St. W10 139 CY69
Lots Rd. SW10 160 DC80
Lotus Clo. SE21 182 DQ90
Lotus Rd., West. 239 EM118
Loubet St. SW17 180 DF93
Loudhams Rd., Amer. 72 AW39
Loudhams Wd. La., Ch.St.G. 72 AX40
Loudoun Ave., Ilf. 125 EP57
Loudoun Rd. NW8 140 DC66
Loudoun Rd. Ms. NW8 140 DC67
Loudoun Rd.
Loudwater Clo., Sun. 195 BU98
Loudwater Dr., Rick. 74 BJ42
Loudwater Heights, Rick. 74 BH41
Loudwater La., Rick. 74 BK42
Loudwater Ridge, Rick. 74 BJ42
Loudwater Rd., Sun. 195 BU98
Lough Rd. N7 121 DM64
Loughborough Est. SW9 161 DP82
Loughborough Rd.
Loughborough Pk. SW9 161 DP84
Loughborough Rd. SW9 161 DN82
Loughborough St. SE11 161 DM78
Loughton Ct., Wal.Abb. 68 EH33
Stanway Rd.
Loughton La., Epp. 85 ER38
Loughton Way, Buck.H. 102 EK46
Louis Ms. N10 99 DH53
Louisa Gdns. E1 143 DX70
Louisa St.
Louisa Ho. SW15 159 CT84
Arabella Dr.
Louisa St. E1 143 DX70
Louise Aumonier Wk. N19 121 DL59
Hillrise Rd.
Louise Bennett Clo. SE24 161 DP84
Shakespeare Rd.
Louise Gdns., Rain. 147 FE69
Louise Rd. E15 144 EE65
Louisville Rd. SW17 180 DG90
Louvain Rd., Green. 189 FS87
Louvain Way, Wat. 59 BV32
Louvaine Rd. SW11 160 DD84
Lovage App. E6 144 EL71
Lovat Clo. NW2 119 CT62
Lovat La. EC3 279 M1
Lovat Wk., Houns. 156 BY80
Cranford La.
Lovatt Clo., Edg. 96 CP51
Lovatt Dr., Ruis. 115 BT57
Lovatts, Rick. 74 BN42
Love Grn. La., Iver 133 BD71
Love Hill La., Slou. 133 BA73
Love La. EC2 275 J8
Love La. EC2 142 DQ72
Love La. N17 100 DT52
Love La. SE18 165 EP77
Love La. SE25 202 DV97
Love La., Abb.L. 59 BT30
Love La., Bex. 186 EZ86
Love La., Gdse. 252 DW132
Love La., Grav. 191 GJ87
Love La., Iver 133 BD72
Love La., Kings L. 58 BL28
Love La., Mitch. 200 DE97
Love La., Mord. 200 DA101
Love La., Pnr. 116 BY55
Love La., S.Ock. 148 FQ74
Love La., Surb. 197 CJ103
Love La., Sutt. 217 CY107
Love La., Tad. 249 CT127
Love La., Wdf.Grn. 103 EM51
Love Wk. SE5 162 DR82
Loveday Rd. W13 137 CH74
Lovegrove St. SE1 162 DU78
Lovegrove Wk. E14 143 EC74
Lovejoy La., Wind. 151 AK82
Lovekyn Clo., Kings.T. 198 CM96
Queen Elizabeth Rd.
Lovel Ave., Well. 166 EU82
Lovel Clo., Hem.H. 40 BG20
Lovel End, Ger.Cr. 90 AW52
Lovel Mead, Ger.Cr. 90 AW52
Lovel Rd., Ger.Cr. 90 AW52
Lovelace Ave., Brom. 205 EN100
Lovelace Clo., Lthd. 229 BU123
Lovelace Dr., Wok. 227 BE116
Lovelace Gdns., Bark. 126 EU63
Lovelace Gdns., Surb. 197 CK101
Lovelace Gdns., Walt. 214 BW106
Lovelace Grn. SE9 165 EM83
Lovelace Rd. SE21 182 DQ89
Lovelace Rd., Barn. 98 DE45
Lovelace Rd., Surb. 197 CJ101
Lovelands La., Tad. 250 DB127
Lovelinch Clo. SE15 162 DW79
Lovell Ho. E8 142 DU67
Lovell Pl. SE16 163 DY76
Ropemaker Rd.
Lovell Rd., Enf. 82 DV35
Lovell Rd., Rich. 177 CJ90
Lovell Rd., Sthl. 136 CB72
Lovell Wk., Rain. 147 FG65
Lovelock Clo., Ken. 236 DQ117
Loveridge Ms. NW6 139 CZ65
Loveridge Rd.
Loveridge Rd. NW6 139 CZ65
Lovers La., Green. 169 FX84
Lovers Wk. N3 98 DA52
Lovers Wk. NW7 97 CY51
Lovers Wk. SE10 164 EE80
Lover's Wk. W1 276 F2
Lover's Wk. W1 140 DG74
Lovet Rd., Harl. 51 EN16
Lovett Dr., Cars. 200 DC101
Lovett Rd., Stai. 173 BB91
Lovett Rd., Uxb. 114 BJ55
Lovett Way NW10 118 CQ64
Lovett's Pl. SW18 160 DB84
Old York Rd.
Lovibonds Ave., Orp. 223 EP105
Lovibonds Ave., West Dr. 134 BM72
Low Clo., Green. 189 FU85
Low Cross Wd. La. SE21 182 DT90
Low Hall Clo. E4 101 EA45
Low Hall La. E17 123 DY58
Low Hill Rd., Harl. 50 EF17
Low Rd., Hat. 46 DF15
Low St. La., Til. 171 GM77
Lowbell La., St.Alb. 62 CL27
Lowbrook Rd., Ilf. 125 EP63
Lowburys, Dor. 263 CH139
Lowdell Clo., West Dr. 134 BL72
Lowden Rd. N9 100 DV46
Lowden Rd. SE24 162 DQ84
Lowden Rd., Sthl. 136 BY73
Lowe, The, Chig. 104 EU49
Lowe Ave. E16 144 EG71
Charford Rd.
Lowe Clo., Chig. 104 EU50
Lowell St. E14 143 DY72
Lowen Rd., Rain. 147 FD68
Lower Aberdeen Wf. E14 143 DZ74
Westferry Rd.
Lower Addiscombe Rd., Croy. 202 DS102
Lower Addison Gdns. W14 159 CY75
Lower Alderton Hall La., Loug. 85 EN43
Lower Barn, Hem.H. 40 BM23
Lower Barn Rd., Pur. 220 DR113
Lower Bedfords Rd., Rom. 105 FE51
Lower Belgrave St. SW1 277 H7
Lower Belgrave St. SW1 161 DH76
Lower Bobbingworth Grn., Ong. 53 FG24
Lower Boston Rd. W7 137 CE74
Lower Bri. Rd., Red. 250 DF134
Lower Britwell Rd., Slou. 131 AK70
Lower Broad St., Dag. 146 FA67
Lower Bury La., Epp. 69 ES31
Lower Camden, Chis. 185 EM94
Lower Ch. Hill, Green. 189 FS85
Church Hill
Lower Ch. St., Croy. 201 DP103
Waddon New Rd.
Lower Cippenham La., Slou. 131 AL74
Lower Clabdens, Ware 33 DZ06
Lower Clapton Rd. E5 122 DW64
Lower Clarendon Wk. W11 139 CY72
Lancaster Rd.
Lower Common S. SW15 159 CV83
Lower Cookham Rd., Maid. 130 AC67
Lower Coombe St., Croy. 220 DQ105
Lower Ct. Rd., Epsom 216 CQ111
Lower Cft., Swan. 207 FF98
Lower Dagnall St., St.Alb. 42 CC20
Lower Downs Rd. SW20 199 CX95
Lower Drayton Pl., Croy. 201 DP103
Drayton Rd.
Lower Dr., Beac. 89 AK50
Lower Dunnymans, Bans. 217 CZ114
Basing Rd.
Lower Edgeborough Rd., Guil. 259 AZ135
Lower Emms, Hem.H. 41 BP15
Lower Fm. Rd., Lthd. 229 BV124
Lower George St., Rich. 177 CK85
George St.
Lower Gravel Rd., Brom. 204 EL102
Lower Grn., Welw. 30 DE05
Lower Grn. Rd., Esher 196 CB103
Lower Grn. W., Mitch. 200 DE97
Lower Grosvenor Pl. SW1 277 H6
Lower Grosvenor Pl. SW1 161 DH76
Lower Gro. Rd., Rich. 178 CM86
Lower Hall La. E4 101 DY50
Lower Ham Rd., Kings.T. 177 CK93
Lower Hampton Rd., Sun. 196 BW97
Lower Hatfield Rd., Hert. 47 DK15
Lower High St., Wat. 76 BW42
Lower Higham Rd., Grav. 191 GM88
Lower Hill Rd., Epsom 216 CP112
Lower James St. W1 273 L10
Lower John St. W1 273 L10
Lower Kenwood Ave., Enf. 81 DK43
Lower Kings Rd., Berk. 38 AW19
Lower Lea Crossing E14 144 EE73
Lower Lees Rd., Slou. 131 AN69
Lower Maidstone Rd. N11 99 DJ51
Telford Rd.
Lower Mall W6 159 CV78
Lower Mardyke Ave., Rain. 147 FC68
Lower Marsh SE1 278 D5
Lower Marsh SE1 161 DM75
Lower Marsh La., Kings.T. 198 CM98
Lower Mead, Iver 133 BD69
Lower Meadow, Harl. 51 ES19
Lower Meadow, Wal.Cr. 67 DX27
Lower Merton Ri. NW3 140 DE66
Lower Morden La., Mord. 199 CX100
Lower Mortlake Rd., Rich. 158 CL84
Lower Noke Clo., Brwd. 106 FM47
Lower Northfield, Bans. 217 CZ114
Lower Paddock Rd., Wat. 76 BY44
Lower Pk. Rd. N11 99 DJ50
Lower Pk. Rd., Belv. 166 FA76
Lower Pk. Rd., Couls. 234 DE118
Lower Pk. Rd., Loug. 84 EK43
Lower Paxton Rd., St.Alb. 43 CE21
Lower Peryers, Lthd. 245 BS128
Lower Plantation, Rick. 74 BJ41
Lower Queens Rd., Buck.H. 102 EK47
Lower Range Rd., Grav. 191 GL87
Lower Richmond Rd. SW14 158 CP83
Lower Richmond Rd. SW15 159 CV83
Lower Richmond Rd., Rich. 158 CN83
Lower Riding, Beac. 88 AH53
Lower Rd. SE8 163 DX77
Lower Rd. SE16 162 DW76
Lower Rd., Belv. 167 FB76
Lower Rd., Brwd. 109 GD41
Lower Rd., Erith 167 FD77
Lower Rd., Ger.Cr. 90 AY53
Lower Rd., Grav. 170 GA84
Lower Rd., Har. 117 CD60
Lower Rd., Hem.H. 58 BN25
Lower Rd., Ken. 219 DP113
Lower Rd., Lthd. 231 CD123
Lower Rd., Loug. 85 EN39
Lower Rd., Orp. 206 EV100
Lower Rd., Red. 266 DD136
Lower Rd., Rick. 73 BC42
Lower Rd., Sutt. 218 DC105
Lower Rd., Swan. 187 FF94
Lower Rd., Til. 171 GG84
Lower Rd., Uxb. 113 BC59
Lower Rd., Ware 33 DZ08
Lower Robert St. WC2 278 A1
Lower Sales, Hem.H. 39 BF21
Lower Sandfields, Wok. 227 BD124
Lower Sawley Wd., Bans. 217 CZ114
Upper Sawley Wd.
Lower Shott, Lthd. 246 CA126
Lower Shott (Cheshunt), Wal.Cr. 66 DT26
Lower Sloane St. SW1 276 F9
Lower Sloane St. SW1 160 DG77
Lower Sq., Islw. 157 CH83
Lower Sta. Rd. (Crayford), Dart. 187 FE86
Lower Strand NW9 97 CT54
Lower St., Guil. 260 BN139
Lower Sunbury Rd., Hmptn. 196 BZ96
Lower Swaines, Epp. 69 ES30
Lower Sydenham Ind. Est. SE26 183 DZ92
Lower Tail, Wat. 94 BY48
Lower Talbot Wk. W11 139 CY72
Lancaster Rd.
Lower Teddington Rd., Kings.T. 177 CK94
Lower Ter. NW3 120 DC62
Lower Thames St. EC3 279 L1
Lower Thames St. EC3 142 DR73
Lower Tub (Bushey), Wat. 95 CD45
Lower Wd. Rd., Esher 215 CG107
Lower Yott, Hem.H. 40 BM21
Lowerfield, Welw.G.C. 30 DA10
Lowestoft Clo. E5 122 DW61
Theydon Rd.
Lowestoft Dr., Slou. 130 AJ72
Lowestoft Rd., Wat. 75 BV39
Loweswater Clo., Wat. 60 BW33
Loweswater Clo., Wem. 117 CK61
Lowfield, Saw. 36 EX06
Lowfield Heath Ind. Est., Craw. 268 DD154
Lowfield La., Hodd. 49 EA17
Lowfield Rd. NW6 140 DA66
Lowfield Rd. W3 138 CQ72
Lowfield St., Dart. 188 FL89
Lowick Rd., Har. 117 CE56
Lowlands, Hat. 45 CW15
Lowlands Dr., Stai. 174 BK85
Lowlands Gdns., Rom. 127 FB58
Lowlands Rd., Har. 117 CE58
Lowlands Rd., Pnr. 116 BW58
Lowlands Rd., S.Ock. 148 FP74
Lowman Rd. N7 121 DM63
Lowndes Ave., Chesh. 54 AP30
Lowndes Clo. SW1 276 G7
Lowndes Clo. SW1 160 DG76
Lowndes Pl. SW1 276 F7
Lowndes Pl. SW1 160 DG76
Lowndes Sq. SW1 276 E5
Lowndes Sq. SW1 160 DF75
Lowndes St. SW1 276 E6
Lowndes St. SW1 160 DF76
Lowood Ct. SE19 182 DT92
Lowood St. E1 142 DV73
Dellow St.
Lowry Cres., Mitch. 200 DE96
Lowry Rd., Dag. 126 EV64
Lowshoe La., Rom. 104 FA53
Lowson Gro., Wat. 94 BY45
Lowswood Clo., Nthwd. 93 BQ53
Lowth Rd. SE5 162 DQ82
Lowther Clo., Borwd. 78 CM43
Lowther Dr., Enf. 81 DL42
Lowther Gdns. SW7 160 DD75
Prince Consort Rd.
Lowther Hill SE23 183 DY87
Lowther Rd. E17 101 DY54
Lowther Rd. N7 121 DN64
Mackenzie Rd.
Lowther Rd. SW13 159 CT81
Lowther Rd., Kings.T. 198 CM95
Lowther Rd., Stan. 118 CM55
Lowthorpe, Wok. 226 AU118
Shilburn Way
Loxford Ave. E6 144 EK68
Loxford La., Ilf. 125 EQ64
Loxford Rd., Bark. 145 EP65
Loxford Rd., Cat. 252 DT125
Loxford Way, Cat. 252 DT125
Loxham Rd. E4 101 EA52
Loxham St. WC1 274 A3
Loxley Clo. SE26 183 DX92
Loxley Rd. SW18 180 DD88
Loxley Rd., Berk. 38 AS17
Loxley Rd., Hmptn. 176 BZ91
Loxton Rd. SE23 183 DX88
Loxwood Clo., Felt. 175 BR88
Loxwood Clo., Orp. 206 EX103
Loxwood Rd. N17 122 DS55
Lubbock Rd., Chis. 185 EM94
Lubbock St. SE14 162 DW80
Lucan Dr., Stai. 174 BK94
Lucan Pl. SW3 276 B9
Lucan Pl. SW3 160 DE77
Lucan Rd., Barn. 79 CY41
Lucas Ave. E13 144 EH67
Lucas Ave., Har. 116 CA61
Lucas Ct., Har. 116 CA60
Lucas Ct., Wal.Abb. 68 EF33
Lucas Rd. SE20 182 DW93
Lucas Rd., Grays 170 GA76
Lucas Sq. NW11 120 DA58
Hampstead Way
Lucas St. SE8 163 EA81
Lucerne Clo. N13 99 DL48
Lucerne Clo., Wok. 226 AY119
Claremont Ave.
Lucerne Ct., Erith 166 EY76
Middle Way
Lucerne Gro. E17 123 ED56
Lucerne Ms. W8 140 DA74
Kensington Mall
Lucerne Rd. N5 121 DP63
Lucerne Rd., Orp. 205 ET102
Lucerne Rd., Th.Hth. 201 DP99
Lucerne Way, Rom. 106 FK51
Lucey Rd. SE16 162 DU76
Lucey Way SE16 162 DU76
Linsey St.
Lucie Ave., Ashf. 175 BP93
Lucien Rd. SW17 180 DG91
Lucien Rd. SW19 180 DB89
Lucknow St. SE18 165 ES80
Lucks Hill, Hem.H. 39 BE20
Lucorn Clo. SE12 184 EF86
Lucton Ms., Loug. 85 EP42
Luctons Ave., Buck.H. 102 EJ46
Lucy Cres. W3 138 CQ71
Lucy Gdns., Dag. 126 EY62
Grafton Rd.
Luddesdon Rd., Erith 166 FA79
Luddington Ave., Vir.W. 193 AZ96
Ludford Clo. NW9 96 CS54

Ludford Clo., Croy. 219 DP105
Warrington Rd.
Ludgate Bdy. EC4 274 F9
Ludgate Bdy. EC4 141 DP72
Ludgate Circ. EC4 274 F9
Ludgate Hill EC4 274 F9
Ludgate Hill EC4 141 DP72
Ludgate Sq. EC4 274 G9
Ludham Clo. SE28 146 EW72
Rollesby Way
Ludlow Clo., Brom. 204 EG97
Ludlow Clo., Har. 116 BZ63
Ludlow Mead, Wat. 93 BV48
Ludlow Pl., Grays 170 GB76
Ludlow Rd. W5 137 CJ70
Ludlow Rd., Felt. 175 BU91
Ludlow Rd., Guil. 258 AV135
Ludlow St. EC1 275 H4
Ludlow Way N2 120 DC56
Ludlow Way, Rick. 75 BQ42
Ludovick Wk. SW15 158 CS84
Ludwick Clo., Welw.G.C. 29 CZ11
Ludwick Grn., Welw.G.C. 29 CZ10
Ludwick Ms. SE14 163 DY80
Ludwick Way, Welw.G.C. 29 CZ09
Luff Clo., Wind. 151 AL83
Luffield Rd. SE2 166 EV76
Luffman Rd. SE12 184 EH90
Lugard Rd. SE15 162 DV82
Lugg App. E12 125 EN62
Luke Ho. E1 142 DV72
Luke St. EC2 275 M4
Luke St. EC2 142 DS70
Lukin Cres. E4 101 ED48
Lukin St. E1 142 DW72
Lukintone Clo., Loug. 84 EL44
Lullarook Clo., West. 238 EJ116
Lullingstone Ave., Swan. 207 FF97
Lullingstone Clo., Orp. 186 EV94
Lullingstone Cres.
Lullingstone Cres., Orp. 186 EU94
Lullingstone La. SE13 183 ED86
Lullingstone La. (Eynsford), Dart. 208 FJ104
Lullingstone Rd., Belv. 166 EZ79
Lullington Garth N12 97 CZ50
Lullington Garth, Borwd. 78 CP43
Lullington Garth, Brom. 184 EE94
Lullington Rd. SE20 182 DU94
Lullington Rd., Dag. 146 EY66
Lulot Gdns. N19 121 DH61
Dartmouth Pk. Hill
Lulworth SE17 279 K10
Lulworth Ave., Houns. 156 CB80
Lulworth Ave. (Cheshunt), Wal.Cr. 65 DP29
Lulworth Ave., Wem. 117 CJ59
Lulworth Clo., Har. 116 BZ62
Lulworth Cres., Mitch. 200 DE96
Lulworth Dr., Pnr. 116 BX59
Lulworth Dr., Rom. 105 FB50
Lulworth Gdns., Har. 116 BY61
Lulworth Rd. SE9 184 EL89
Lulworth Rd. SE15 162 DV82
Lulworth Rd., Well. 165 ET82
Lulworth Waye, Hayes 135 BV72
Lumbards, Welw.G.C. 30 DA06
Lumen Rd., Wem. 117 CK61
Lumley Clo., Belv. 166 FA79
Lumley Ct. WC2 278 A1
Lumley Ct., Horl. 268 DG147
Lumley Gdns., Sutt. 217 CY106
Lumley Rd., Horl. 268 DG147
Lumley Rd., Sutt. 217 CY107
Lumley St. W1 272 G9
Lumley St. W1 140 DG72
Luna Rd., Th.Hth. 202 DQ97
Lunar Clo., West. 238 EK116
Lunar Ho., Croy. 202 DQ102
Lundin Wk., Wat. 94 BX49
Woodhall La.
Lundy Dr., Hayes 155 BS77
Lundy Wk. N1 142 DQ65
Clephane Rd.
Lunedale Rd., Dart. 188 FP89
Lunedale Wk., Dart. 188 FP88
Lunedale Rd.
Lunghurst Rd., Cat. 237 DZ120
Lunham Rd. SE19 182 DS93
Lupin Clo. SW2 181 DP89
Palace Rd.
Lupin Clo., Croy. 203 DX102
Primrose La.
Lupin Clo., West Dr. 154 BK78
Magnolia St.
Lupin Cres., Ilf. 125 EP62
Ilford La.
Luppit Clo., Brwd. 109 GA46
Lupton Clo. SE12 184 EH91
Lupton St. NW5 121 DJ63
Lupus St. SW1 161 DH78
Luralda Gdns. E14 163 EC78
Saunders Ness Rd.
Lurgan Ave. W6 159 CX79
Lurline Gdns. SW11 160 DG81
Luscombe Ct., Brom. 204 EE96
Luscombe Way SW8 161 DL80
Lushes Ct., Loug. 85 EP43
Lushes Rd.
Lushes Rd., Loug. 85 EP43
Lushington Dr., Cob. 213 BV114
Lushington Rd. NW10 139 CV68
Lushington Rd. SE6 183 EB92
Lushington Ter. E8 122 DU64
Wayland Ave.
Lusted Hall La., West. 238 EJ120
Lusted Rd., Sev. 241 FE120
Lusteds Clo., Dor. 263 CJ139
Glory Mead
Luther Clo., Edg. 96 CQ47
Luther King Clo. E17 123 DY58
Luther King Rd., Harl. 51 ER15
Luther Rd., Tedd. 177 CF92
Luton Pl. SE10 163 EC80
Luton Rd. E17 123 DZ55
Luton Rd., Sid. 186 EW90
Luton St. NW8 272 A5
Luton St. NW8 140 DD70
Lutton Ter. NW3 120 DD63
Flask Wk.
Luttrell Ave. SW15 179 CV85
Lutwyche Rd. SE6 183 DZ89
Luxborough La., Chig. 102 EL48
Luxborough St. W1 272 F5
Luxborough St. W1 140 DG71
Luxemburg Gdns. W6 159 CX77
Luxfield Rd. SE9 184 EL88
Luxford St. SE16 163 DX77
Luxmore Gdns. SE4 163 DZ81
Luxmore St.
Luxmore St. SE4 163 DZ81
Luxor St. SE5 162 DQ83
Luxted Rd., Orp. 223 EN112
Lyal Rd. E3 143 DY68
Lyall Ave. SE21 182 DS90
Lyall Ms. SW1 276 F7
Lyall Ms. SW1 160 DG76
Lyall Ms. W. SW1 276 F7
Lyall St. SW1 276 F7
Lyall St. SW1 160 DG76
Lycaste Clo., St.Alb. 43 CG21
Lycett Pl. W12 159 CU75
Becklow Rd.
Lych Gate, Wat. 60 BX33
Lych Gate Rd., Orp. 206 EU102
Lych Gate Wk., Hayes 135 BT73
Lych Way, Wok. 226 AX116
Lyconby Gdns., Croy. 203 DY101
Lycrome La., Chesh. 54 AR28
Lycrome Rd., Chesh. 54 AR28
Lydd Clo., Sid. 185 ES90
Lydd Rd., Bexh. 166 EZ80
Lydden Ct. SE9 185 ES86
Lydden Gro. SW18 180 DB87
Lydden Rd. SW18 180 DB87
Lydeard Rd. E6 145 EM66
Lydele Clo., Wok. 227 AZ115
Lydford Ave., Slou. 131 AR70
Lydford Clo. N16 122 DS64
Pellerin Rd.
Lydford Rd. N15 122 DR57
Lydford Rd. NW2 139 CW65
Lydford Rd. W9 139 CZ70
Lydhurst Ave. SW2 181 DM89
Lydia Ms., Hat. 45 CW24
Lydia Rd., Erith 167 FF79
Lydney Clo. SE15 162 DS80
Blakes Rd.
Lydney Clo. SW19 179 CY89
Princes Way
Lydon Rd. SW4 161 DJ83
Lydsey Clo., Slou. 131 AN69
Lydstep Rd., Chis. 185 EN91
Lye, The, Tad. 233 CW122
Lye Grn. Rd., Chesh. 54 AR30
Lye La., St.Alb. 60 CA28
Lyell Pl. E., Wind. 150 AJ83
Lyell Pl. W., Wind. 150 AJ83
Lyell Pl. E.
Lyell Wk. E., Wind. 150 AJ83
Lyell Pl. E.
Lyell Wk. W., Wind. 150 AJ83
Lyell Pl. E.
Lyfield, Lthd. 214 CB114
Lyford Rd. SW18 180 DD87
Lygean Ave., Ware 33 DY06
Lygon Pl. SW1 277 H7
Lyham Clo. SW2 181 DL86
Lyham Rd. SW2 181 DL85
Lyle Clo., Mitch. 200 DG101
Lyle Pk., Sev. 257 FH123
Lymbourne Clo., Sutt. 218 DA110
Lymden Gdns., Reig. 266 DB135
Lyme Fm. Rd. SE12 164 EG84
Lyme Gro. E9 142 DW66
St. Thomas's Sq.
Lyme Regis Rd., Bans. 233 CZ117
Lyme Rd., Well. 166 EV81
Lyme St. NW1 141 DJ66
Lyme Ter. NW1 141 DJ66
Royal College St.
Lymer Ave. SE19 182 DT92
Lymescote Gdns., Sutt. 200 DA103
Lyminge Clo., Sid. 185 ET91
Lyminge Gdns. SW18 180 DE88
Lymington Ave. N22 99 DN54
Lymington Clo. E6 145 EM71
Valiant Way
Lymington Clo. SW16 201 DK96
Lymington Dr., Ruis. 115 BR61
Lymington Gdns., Epsom 217 CT106
Lymington Rd. NW6 140 DB65
Lymington Rd., Dag. 126 EX60
Lympstone Gdns. SE15 162 DU80
Lyn Ms. E3 143 DZ69
Tredegar Sq.
Lynbridge Gdns. N13 99 DP49
Lynbrook Clo. SE15 162 DS80
Blakes Rd.
Lynbrook Clo., Rain. 147 FD68
Lynceley Gra., Epp. 70 EU29
Lynch, The, Hodd. 49 EB17
Lynch, The, Uxb. 134 BJ67
New Windsor St.
Lynch Clo., Uxb. 134 BJ66
New Windsor St.
Lynch Hill La., Slou. 131 AL70
Lynch Wk. SE8 163 DZ79
Prince St.
Lynchen Clo., Houns. 155 BU81
The Ave.
Lyncott Cres. SW4 161 DH84
Lyncroft Ave., Pnr. 116 BY57
Lyncroft Gdns. NW6 120 DA64
Lyncroft Gdns. W13 157 CJ75
Lyncroft Gdns., Epsom 217 CT109
Lyncroft Gdns., Houns. 176 CC85
Lyndale NW2 119 CZ63
Lyndale Ave. NW2 119 CZ62
Lyndale Clo. SE3 164 EF79
Lyndale Ct., W.Byf. 212 BG113
Parvis Rd.
Lyndale Rd., Red. 250 DF131
Lynden Way, Swan. 207 FC97
Lyndhurst Ave. N12 98 DF51
Lyndhurst Ave. NW7 96 CS51
Lyndhurst Ave. SW16 201 DK96
Lyndhurst Ave., Pnr. 93 BV53
Lyndhurst Ave., Sthl. 136 CB74
Lyndhurst Ave., Sun. 195 BU97
Lyndhurst Ave., Surb. 198 CP102
Lyndhurst Ave., Twick. 176 BZ88
Lyndhurst Clo. NW10 118 CR62
Lyndhurst Clo., Bexh. 167 FB83
Lyndhurst Clo., Croy. 202 DT104
Lyndhurst Clo., Orp. 223 EP105
Lyndhurst Clo., Wok. 226 AX115
Lyndhurst Dr. E10 123 EC59
Lyndhurst Dr., Horn. 128 FJ60
Lyndhurst Dr., N.Mal. 198 CS100
Lyndhurst Dr., Sev. 256 FE124
Lyndhurst Gdns. N3 97 CY53
Lyndhurst Gdns. NW3 120 DD64
Lyndhurst Gdns., Bark. 145 ES65
Lyndhurst Gdns., Enf. 82 DS42
Lyndhurst Gdns., Ilf. 125 ER58
Lyndhurst Gdns., Pnr. 93 BV53
Lyndhurst Gro. SE15 162 DS82
Lyndhurst Ri., Chig. 103 EN49
Lyndhurst Rd. E4 101 EC52
Lyndhurst Rd. N18 100 DU49
Lyndhurst Rd. N22 99 DM51
Lyndhurst Rd. NW3 120 DD64
Lyndhurst Rd., Bexh. 167 FB83
Lyndhurst Rd., Chesh. 54 AP28
Lyndhurst Rd., Couls. 234 DG116
Lyndhurst Rd., Grnf. 136 CB70
Lyndhurst Rd., Reig. 266 DA137
Lyndhurst Rd., Th.Hth. 201 DN98
Lyndhurst Sq. SE15 162 DT81
Lyndhurst Ter. NW3 120 DD64
Lyndhurst Way SE15 162 DT81
Lyndhurst Way, Brwd. 109 GC45
Lyndhurst Way, Cher. 193 BE104
Lyndhurst Way, Sutt. 218 DA108
Lyndon Ave., Pnr. 94 BY51
Lyndon Ave., Sid. 185 ET85
Lyndon Ave., Wall. 200 DG104
Lyndon Rd., Belv. 166 FA77
Lyndwood Dr., Wind. 172 AU86
Lyne Clo., Vir.W. 193 AZ100
Lyne Cres. E17 101 DZ53
Lyne Crossing Rd., Cher. 193 BA100
Lyne La., Cher. 193 BA100
Lyne La., Egh. 193 BA98
Lyne La., Vir.W. 193 BA100
Lyne Rd., Vir.W. 192 AX100
Lyne Way, Hem.H. 39 BF18
Lynegrove Ave., Ashf. 175 BQ92
Lyneham Wk. E5 123 DY64
Ashenden Rd.
Lyneham Wk., Pnr. 115 BT55
Wiltshire La.
Lynett Rd., Dag. 126 EX61
Lynette Ave. SW4 181 DH86
Lynford Clo., Edg. 96 CQ53
Lynford Gdns., Edg. 96 CP48
Lynford Gdns., Ilf. 125 ET61
Lynhurst Cres., Uxb. 135 BQ66
Lynhurst Rd., Uxb. 135 BQ66
Lynmere Rd., Well. 166 EV82
Lynmouth Ave., Enf. 82 DT44
Lynmouth Ave., Mord. 199 CX101
Lynmouth Dr., Ruis. 115 BV61
Lynmouth Gdns., Grnf. 137 CH67
Lynmouth Gdns., Houns. 156 BX81
Lynmouth Ri., Orp. 206 EV98
Lynmouth Rd. E17 123 DY58
Lynmouth Rd. N2 120 DF56
Lynmouth Rd. N16 122 DT60
Lynmouth Rd., Grnf. 137 CH67
Lynmouth Rd., Welw.G.C. 29 CZ09
Lynn Clo., Ashf. 175 BR92
Goffs Rd.
Lynn Clo., Har. 95 CD54
Lynn Ms. E11 124 EE61
Lynn Rd.
Lynn Rd. E11 124 EE61
Lynn Rd. SW12 181 DH87
Lynn Rd., Ilf. 125 ER59
Lynn St., Enf. 82 DR39
Lynn Wk., Reig. 266 DB137
Lynne Clo., Orp. 223 ET107
Lynne Clo., S.Croy. 220 DW111
Lynne Wk., Esher 214 CC106
Lynne Way NW10 138 CS65
Lynne Way, Nthlt. 136 BX68
Lynross Clo., Rom. 106 FM54
Lynscott Way, S.Croy. 219 DP109
Lynsted Clo., Bexh. 187 FB85
Lynsted Clo., Brom. 204 EJ96
Lynsted Ct., Beck. 203 DY96
Churchfields Rd.
Lynsted Gdns. SE9 164 EK83
Lynton Ave. N12 98 DD49
Lynton Ave. NW9 119 CT56
Lynton Ave. W13 137 CG72
Lynton Ave., Orp. 206 EV98
Lynton Ave., Rom. 104 FA53
Lynton Ave., St.Alb. 43 CJ21
Lynton Clo. NW10 118 CS64
Lynton Clo., Chess. 216 CL105
Lynton Clo., Islw. 157 CF84
Lynton Cres., Ilf. 125 EP58
Lynton Crest, Pot.B. 64 DA32
Strafford Gate
Lynton Est. SE1 162 DU77
Lynton Rd.
Lynton Gdns. N11 99 DK51
Lynton Gdns., Enf. 100 DS45
Lynton Mead N20 98 DA48
Lynton Par., Wal.Cr. 67 DX30
Turners Hill
Lynton Rd. E4 101 EB50
Lynton Rd. N8 121 DK57
Lynton Rd. NW6 139 CZ67
Lynton Rd. SE1 162 DT77
Lynton Rd. W3 138 CN73
Lynton Rd., Chesh. 54 AP28
Lynton Rd., Croy. 201 DN100
Lynton Rd., Grav. 191 GG88
Lynton Rd., Har. 116 BY61
Lynton Rd., N.Mal. 198 CR99
Lynton Rd. S., Grav. 191 GG88
Lynton Wk., Hayes 135 BS69
Exmouth Rd.
Lynwood, Guil. 258 AV135
Lynwood Ave., Couls. 235 DH115
Lynwood Ave., Egh. 172 AY93
Lynwood Ave., Epsom 217 CT114
Lynwood Ave., Slou. 152 AX76
Lynwood Clo. E18 102 EJ53
Gordon Rd.
Lynwood Clo., Har. 116 BY62
Lynwood Clo., Rom. 105 FB51
Lynwood Clo., Wok. 211 BD113
Lynwood Dr., Nthwd. 93 BS53
Lynwood Dr., Rom. 105 FB51
Lynwood Dr., Wor.Pk. 199 CU103
Lynwood Gdns., Croy. 219 DM105
Lynwood Gdns., Sthl. 136 BZ71
Lynwood Gro. N21 99 DN46
Lynwood Gro., Orp. 205 ES101
Lynwood Heights, Rick. 74 BH43
Lynwood Rd. SW17 180 DF90
Lynwood Rd. W5 138 CL70
Lynwood Rd., Epsom 217 CT114
Lynwood Rd., Red. 250 DG132
Lynwood Rd., T.Ditt. 197 CF103
Lynx Hill, Lthd. 245 BS128
Lyon Business Pk., Bark. 145 ES68
Lyon Meade, Stan. 95 CJ53
Lyon Pk. Ave., Wem. 138 CL65
Lyon Rd. SW19 200 DC95
Lyon Rd., Har. 117 CF58
Lyon Rd., Rom. 127 FF59
Lyon Rd., Walt. 196 BY103
Lyon St. N1 141 DM66
Caledonian Rd.
Lyon Way, Grnf. 137 CE67
Lyon Way, St.Alb. 44 CN20
Lyons Ct., Dor. 263 CH136
Lyons Dr., Guil. 242 AU129
Lyons Pl. NW8 140 DD70
Lyons Wk. W14 159 CY77
Lyonsdene, Tad. 249 CZ127
Smithy La.
Lyonsdown Ave., Barn. 80 DC44
Lyonsdown Rd., Barn. 80 DB44
Lyoth Rd., Orp. 205 EQ103
Lyric Dr., Grnf. 136 CB70
Lyric Rd. SW13 159 CT81
Lys Hill Gdns., Hert. 31 DP07
Lysander Clo., Hem.H. 57 AZ27
Lysander Gdns., Surb. 198 CM100
Ewell Rd.
Lysander Gro. N19 121 DK60
Lysander Rd., Croy. 219 DM107
Lysander Rd., Ruis. 115 BR61
Lysander Way, Abb.L. 59 BU32
Lysander Way, Orp. 205 EQ104
Lysander Way, Welw.G.C. 30 DD08
Lysia St. SW6 159 CX80
Lysias Rd. SW12 181 DH86
Lysons Wk. SW15 179 CU85
Swinburne Rd.
Lytchet Rd., Brom. 184 EH94
Lytchet Way, Enf. 82 DW39
Lytchgate Clo., S.Croy. 220 DS108
Lytcott Dr., W.Mol. 196 BZ97
Freeman Dr.
Lytcott Gro. SE22 182 DT85
Lyte St. E2 142 DW68
Bishops Way
Lytham Ave., Wat. 94 BX50
Lytham Gro. W5 138 CM69
Lytham St. SE17 162 DR78
Lyttelton Clo. NW3 140 DE66
Hawtrey Rd.
Lyttelton Rd. E10 123 EB62
Lyttelton Rd. N2 120 DC57
Lyttleton Rd. N8 121 DN55
Lytton Ave. N13 99 DN47
Lytton Ave., Enf. 83 DY38
Lytton Clo. N2 120 DC58
Lytton Clo., Loug. 85 ER41
Lytton Clo., Nthlt. 136 BZ66
Lytton Gdns., Wall. 219 DK105
Lytton Gdns., Welw.G.C. 29 CX09
Lytton Gro. SW15 179 CX85
Lytton Rd. E11 124 EE59
Lytton Rd., Barn. 80 DC42
Lytton Rd., Grays 171 GG77
Lytton Rd., Pnr. 94 BY52
Lytton Rd., Rom. 127 FH57
Lytton Rd., Wok. 227 BB116
Lytton Strachey Path SE28 146 EV73
Titmuss Ave.
Lyttons Way, Hodd. 33 EA14
Lyveden Rd. SE3 164 EH80
Lyveden Rd. SW17 180 DE93
Lywood Clo., Tad. 233 CW122

M

Mabbotts, Tad. 233 CX121
Mabbutt Clo., St.Alb. 60 BY30
Mabel Rd., Swan. 187 FG93
Mabel St., Wok. 226 AX117
Maberley Cres. SE19 182 DU94
Maberley Rd. SE19 202 DT95
Maberley Rd., Beck. 203 DX97
Mabeys Wk., Saw. 36 EV06
Mabledon Pl. WC1 273 N3
Mabledon Pl. WC1 141 DK69
Mablethorpe Rd. SW6 159 CY80
Mabley St. E9 123 DY64
Macaret Clo. N20 98 DC45
MacArthur Clo. E7 144 EG65
Macarthur Ter. SE7 164 EK79
Macaulay Ave., Esher 197 CE103
Macaulay Ct. SW4 161 DH83
Macaulay Rd. E6 144 EK68
Macaulay Rd. SW4 161 DH83
Macaulay Rd., Cat. 236 DS122
Macaulay Sq. SW4 161 DH84
Macaulay Way SE28 146 EV73
Booth Clo.
Macauley Ms. SE13 163 EC81
Macbean St. SE18 165 EP76
Macbeth St. W6 159 CV78
Macclesfield Bri. NW1 140 DE68
Macclesfield Rd. EC1 275 H2
Macclesfield Rd. EC1 142 DQ69
Macclesfield Rd. SE25 202 DV99
Macclesfield St. W1 273 N10
Macdonald Ave., Dag. 127 FB62
Macdonald Ave., Horn. 128 FL55
Macdonald Clo., Amer. 55 AR35
Macdonald Rd. E7 124 EG63
Macdonald Rd. E17 101 EC54
Macdonald Rd. N11 98 DF50
Macdonald Rd. N19 121 DJ61
Macdonald Way, Horn. 128 FL56
Macdonnell Gdns., Wat. 75 BT35
High Rd.
Macduff Rd. SW11 160 DG81
Mace Clo. E1 142 DV74
Kennet St.
Mace Ct., Grays 170 GE79
Mace La., Sev. 223 ER113
Mace St. E2 143 DX68
Macers Ct., Brox. 49 DZ24
Macers La., Brox. 49 DZ24
MacFarlane La., Islw. 157 CF79
Macfarlane Rd. W12 139 CW74
Macfarren Pl. NW1 272 G5
Macgregor Rd. E16 144 EJ71
Machell Rd. SE15 162 DW83
Macintosh Clo., Wal.Cr. 65 DP25
Hammondstreet Rd.
Mackay Rd. SW4 161 DH83
Mackennal St. NW8 140 DE68
Mackenzie Mall, Slou. 152 AT75
High St.
Mackenzie Rd. N7 141 DM65
Mackenzie Rd., Beck. 202 DW96
Mackenzie St., Slou. 132 AT74
Mackenzie Wk. E14 143 EA74
South Colonnade
Mackenzie Way, Grav. 191 GK93
Mackeson Rd. NW3 120 DF63
Mackie Rd. SW2 181 DN87
Mackies Hill, Guil. 261 BR144
Mackintosh La. E9 123 DX64
Homerton High St.
Macklin St. WC2 274 A8
Macklin St. WC2 141 DL72
Mackrells, Red. 266 DC137
Mackrow Wk. E14 143 EC73
Robin Hood La.
Macks Rd. SE16 162 DU77
Mackworth St. NW1 273 K2
Mackworth St. NW1 141 DJ69
Maclaren Ms. SW15 159 CW84
Clarendon Dr.
Maclean Rd. SE23 183 DY86
Maclennan Ave., Rain. 148 FK69
Macleod Clo., Grays 170 GD77
Macleod Rd. N21 81 DL43
Macleod St. SE17 162 DQ78
Maclise Rd. W14 159 CY76
Macmillan Gdns., Dart. 168 FN84
Keyes Rd.
Macoma Rd. SE18 165 ER79
Macoma Ter. SE18 165 ER79
Macon Way, Upmin. 129 FS59
Maconochies Rd. E14 163 EB78
Macquarie Way E14 163 EB77
Macready Pl. N7 121 DL63
Warlters Rd.
Macroom Rd. W9 139 CZ69
Mada Rd., Orp. 205 EP103
Madan Rd., West. 255 ER125
Madans Wk., Epsom 232 CR115
Maddams St. E3 143 EB70
Madden Clo., Swans. 189 FX86
Maddison Clo., Tedd. 177 CF93
Maddock Way SE17 161 DP79
Cooks Rd.
Maddocks Clo., Sid. 186 EX92
Maddox La., Lthd. 230 BY123
Maddox Pk., Lthd. 230 BY123
Maddox Rd., Harl. 35 ES14
Maddox Rd., Hem.H. 41 BP20
Maddox St. W1 273 J10
Maddox St. W1 141 DH73
Madeira Ave., Brom. 184 EE94
Madeira Clo., W.Byf. 212 BG113
Brantwood Gdns.
Madeira Cres., W.Byf. 212 BG113
Brantwood Gdns.
Madeira Gro., Wdf.Grn. 102 EJ51
Madeira Rd. E11 123 ED60
Madeira Rd. N13 99 DP49
Madeira Rd. SW16 181 DL92
Madeira Rd., Mitch. 200 DF98
Madeira Rd., W.Byf. 211 BF113
Madeira Wk., Brwd. 108 FY48
Madeira Wk., Reig. 250 DD133
Madeira Wk., Wind. 151 AR81
Madeley Clo., Amer. 55 AR36
Madeley Rd. W5 138 CL72
Madeline Gro., Ilf. 125 ER64
Madeline Rd. SE20 182 DU94
Madells, Epp. 69 ET31
Madge Gill Way E6 144 EL67
Ron Leighton Way
Madgeways Clo., Ware 33 DZ10
Madgeways La., Ware 33 DZ10
Madinah Rd. E8 142 DU65
Madison Cres., Bexh. 166 EW80
Madison Gdns., Bexh. 166 EW80
Madison Gdns., Brom. 204 EF97
Madison Way, Sev. 256 FF123
Madras Pl. N7 141 DN65
Madras Rd., Ilf. 125 EP63
Madresfield Ct., Rad. 62 CL32
Russet Dr.
Madrid Rd. SW13 159 CU81
Madrid Rd., Guil. 258 AV135
Madrigal La. SE5 161 DP80
Madron St. SE17 279 N10
Madron St. SE17 162 DS78
Maesmaur Rd., West. 238 EK121
Mafeking Ave. E6 144 EL68
Mafeking Ave., Brent. 158 CL79
Mafeking Ave., Ilf. 125 ER59
Mafeking Rd. E16 144 EF70
Mafeking Rd. N17 100 DU54
Mafeking Rd., Enf. 82 DT41
Mafeking Rd., Stai. 173 BB89
Mag Ct., Beac. 111 AM55
Magazine Pl., Lthd. 231 CH122
Magazine Rd., Cat. 235 DP122
Magdala Ave. N19 121 DH61
Magdala Rd., Islw. 157 CG83
Magdala Rd., S.Croy. 220 DR108
Napier Rd.
Magdalen Clo., W.Byf. 212 BL114
Magdalen Cres., W.Byf. 212 BL114
Magdalen Gdns., Brwd. 109 GE44
Magdalen Gro., Orp. 224 EV105
Magdalen Pas. E1 142 DT73
Prescot St.
Magdalen Rd. SW18 180 DC88
Magdalen St. SE1 279 M3
Magdalen St. SE1 142 DS74
Magdalene Clo. SE15 162 DV82
Heaton Rd.
Magdalene Gdns. E6 145 EN70
Magdalene Rd., Shep. 194 BM97
Magee St. SE11 161 DN79
Maggie Blake's Cause SE1 279 P3
Magna Carta La., Stai. 172 AX88
Magna Rd., Egh. 172 AV93
Magnaville Rd. (Bushey), Wat. 95 CE45

Magnet Rd., Grays 169 FW79
Magnet Rd., Wem. 117 CK61
Magnin Clo. E8 142 DU67
Wilde Clo.
Magnolia Ave., Abb.L. 59 BU32
Magnolia Clo., Hert. 32 DU09
Magnolia Clo., Kings.T. 178 CP93
Magnolia Clo., St.Alb. 61 CD27
Magnolia Ct., Har. 118 CM59
Magnolia Ct., Horl. 268 DG148
Magnolia Ct., Rich. 158 CP81
West Hall Rd.
Magnolia Dr., West. 238 EK116
Magnolia Gdns. E10 123 EB61
Oliver Rd.
Magnolia Gdns., Slou. 152 AW76
Magnolia Pl. SW4 181 DL85
Magnolia Pl. W5 138 CL71
Montpelier Rd.
Magnolia Rd. W4 158 CP79
Magnolia St., West Dr. 154 BK77
Magnolia Way, Brwd. 108 FV43
Magnolia Way, Dor. 263 CK139
Magnolia Way, Epsom 216 CQ106
Magnum Clo., Rain. 148 FJ70
Magpie All. EC4 274 E9
Magpie Clo. E7 124 EF64
Magpie Clo. NW9 96 CS54
Eagle Dr.
Magpie Clo., Couls. 235 DJ118
Ashbourne Clo.
Magpie Clo., Enf. 82 DU39
Magpie Hall Clo., Brom. 204 EL100
Magpie Hall La., Brom. 204 EL101
Magpie Hall Rd. (Bushey), Wat. 95 CE47
Magpie La., Amer. 89 AM45
Magpie La., Brwd. 107 FW54
Magpie Pl. SE14 163 DY79
Milton Ct. Rd.
Magpie Wk., Hat. 45 CU20
Lark Ri.
Magpie Way, Slou. 131 AL70
Pemberton Rd.
Magpies, The, Epp. 51 EP24
Magri Wk. E1 142 DW71
Ashfield St.
Maguire Dr., Rich. 177 CJ91
Maguire St. SE1 162 DT75
Mahatma Gandhi Ho., Wem. 118 CM64
Mahlon Ave., Ruis. 115 BV64
Mahogany Clo. SE16 143 DY74
Mahon Clo., Enf. 82 DT39
Maida Ave. E4 101 EB45
Maida Ave. W2 140 DC71
Maida Rd., Belv. 166 FA76
Maida Vale W9 140 DB68
Maida Vale Rd., Dart. 187 FG85
Maida Way E4 101 EB45
Maiden Erlegh Ave., Bex. 186 EY88
Maiden La. NW1 141 DK66
Maiden La. SE1 279 J2
Maiden La. WC2 274 A10
Maiden La. WC2 141 DL73
Maiden La., Dart. 167 FG83
Maiden Rd. E15 144 EE66
Maidenhead Rd., Wind. 151 AK80
Maidenhead St., Hert. 32 DR09
Broadway
Maidenshaw Rd., Epsom 216 CR112
Maidenstone Hill SE10 163 EC81
Maids of Honour Row, Rich. 177 CK85
The Grn.
Maidstone Ave., Rom. 105 FC54
Maidstone Bldgs. SE1 279 K3
Maidstone Ho. E14 143 EB72
Carmen St.
Maidstone Rd. N11 99 DJ51
Maidstone Rd., Grays 170 GA79
Maidstone Rd., Sev. 256 FE122
Maidstone Rd. (Seal), Sev. 257 FN121
Maidstone Rd., Sid. 186 EX93
Maidstone Rd., Swan. 207 FC95
Maidstone St. E2 142 DU68
Audrey St.
Main Ave., Enf. 82 DT43
Main Ave., Nthwd. 93 BQ48
Main Dr., Ger.Cr. 112 AW57
Main Dr., Iver 153 BE77
Main Dr., Wem. 117 CK62
Main Par., Rick. 73 BC42
Whitelands Ave.
Main Rd. (Farningham), Dart. 208 FM100
Main Rd. 188 FP93
(Sutton at Hone), Dart.
Main Rd., Eden. 255 EQ134
Main Rd., Kes. 222 EJ112
Main Rd., Long. 209 FX96
Main Rd., Orp. 206 EW98
Main Rd., Rom. 127 FF56
Main Rd. (Knockholt), Sev. 239 ET119
Main Rd. (Sundridge), Sev. 240 EX124
Main Rd., Sid. 185 ES90
Main Rd., Swan. 187 FF94
Main Rd. (Crockenhill), Swan. 207 FC100
Main Rd., West. 222 EJ114
Main St., Felt. 176 BX92
Mainridge Rd., Chis. 185 EN91
Maisemore St. SE15 162 DU80
Peckham Pk. Rd.
Maisie Webster Clo., Stai. 174 BK87
Lauser Rd.
Maitland Clo. SE10 163 EB80
Maitland Clo., Houns. 156 BZ83
Maitland Clo., W.Byf. 212 BG113
Maitland Pk. Est. NW3 140 DF65
Maitland Pk. Rd. NW3 140 DF65
Maitland Pk. Vill. NW3 140 DF65
Maitland Pl. E5 122 DV63
Clarence Rd.
Maitland Rd. E15 144 EF65
Maitland Rd. SE26 183 DX93
Maize Row E14 143 DZ73
Commercial Rd.
Maizecroft, Horl. 269 DJ147
Oatlands
Maizey Ct., Brwd. 108 FU43
Danes Way
Majendie Rd. SE18 165 ER78
Majestic Way, Mitch. 200 DF96
Major Rd. E15 123 ED64
Major Rd. SE16 162 DU76
Jamaica Rd.
Majors Fm. Rd., Slou. 152 AX80
Makepeace Ave. N6 120 DG61
Makepeace Rd. E11 124 EG56
Makepeace Rd., Nthlt. 136 BY67
Makins St. SW3 276 C9
Makins St. SW3 160 DE77
Malabar St. E14 163 EA75
Malacca Fm., Guil. 244 BH128
Malam Gdns. E14 143 EB73
Wades Pl.
Malan Clo., West. 238 EL117
Malan Sq., Rain. 147 FH65
Malbrook Rd. SW15 159 CV84
Malcolm Ct., Stan. 95 CJ50
Malcolm Cres. NW4 119 CU58
Malcolm Dr., Surb. 197 CK102
Malcolm Gdns., Horl. 268 DD150
Malcolm Pl. E2 142 DW70
Malcolm Rd. E1 142 DW70
Malcolm Rd. SE20 182 DW94
Malcolm Rd. SE25 202 DU100
Malcolm Rd. SW19 179 CY93
Malcolm Rd., Couls. 235 DK115
Malcolm Rd., Uxb. 114 BM63
Malcolm Way E11 124 EG57
Malcolms Way N14 81 DJ43
Malden Ave. SE25 202 DV97
Malden Ave., Grnf. 117 CE64
Malden Clo., Amer. 72 AT38
Malden Cres. NW1 140 DG65
Malden Grn. Ave., Wor.Pk. 199 CT102
Malden Hill, N.Mal. 199 CT97
Malden Hill Gdns., N.Mal. 199 CT97
Malden Pk., N.Mal. 199 CT100
Malden Pl. NW5 120 DG64
Grafton Ter.
Malden Rd. NW5 120 DF64
Malden Rd., Borwd. 78 CN41
Malden Rd., N.Mal. 198 CS99
Malden Rd., Sutt. 199 CW104
Malden Rd., Wat. 75 BU40
Malden Rd., Wor.Pk. 199 CT101
Malden Way, N.Mal. 198 CR100
Maldon Clo. E15 123 ED64
David St.
Maldon Clo. N1 142 DQ67
Maldon Clo. SE5 162 DS83
Maldon Rd. N9 100 DT48
Maldon Rd. W3 138 CQ73
Maldon Rd., Rom. 127 FC59
Maldon Rd., Wall. 219 DH106
Maldon Wk., Wdf.Grn. 102 EJ51
Malet Clo., Egh. 173 BD93
Malet Pl. WC1 273 M5
Malet Pl. WC1 141 DK70
Malet St. WC1 273 M5
Malet St. WC1 141 DK70
Maley Ave. SE27 181 DP89
Malford Ct. E18 102 EG54
Malford Gro. E18 124 EF56
Malfort Rd. SE5 162 DS83
Malham Rd. SE23 183 DX88
Malins Clo., Barn. 79 CV43
Malkin Dr., Beac. 88 AJ52
Mall, The E15 143 ED66
Broadway
Mall, The N14 99 DL48
Mall, The SW1 277 L4
Mall, The SW1 161 DJ75
Mall, The SW14 178 CQ85
Mall, The W5 138 CL73
Mall, The, Brom. 204 EG97
High St.
Mall, The, Croy. 202 DQ102
Poplar Wk.
Mall, The, Har. 118 CM58
Mall, The, Horn. 127 FH60
Mall, The, St.Alb. 60 CC27
Mall, The, Surb. 197 CK99
Mall Rd. W6 159 CV78
Mallams Ms. SW9 161 DP83
St. James's Cres.
Mallard Clo. E9 143 DZ65
Mallard Clo. W7 157 CE75
Mallard Clo., Barn. 80 DD44
The Hook
Mallard Clo., Dart. 188 FM85
Mallard Clo., Horl. 268 DG146
Mallard Clo., Red. 250 DG131
Mallard Clo., Twick. 176 CA87
Stephenson Rd.
Mallard Clo., Upmin. 129 FT59
Mallard Dr., Slou. 131 AM73
Mallard Path SE28 165 ER76
Tom Cribb Rd.
Mallard Pl., Twick. 177 CH90
Mallard Rd., Abb.L. 59 BU31
College Rd.
Mallard Rd., S.Croy. 221 DX110
Mallard Wk. SE28 165 ER76
Goosander Way
Mallard Wk., Beck. 203 DX99
Mallard Wk., Sid. 186 EW93
Cray Rd.
Mallard Way NW9 118 CQ59
Mallard Way, Brwd. 109 GB45
Mallard Way, Nthwd. 93 BQ52
Mallard Way, Wall. 219 DJ109
Mallard Way, Wat. 76 BY36
Mallards, The, Stai. 194 BH96
Thames Side
Mallards Reach, Wey. 195 BR103
Mallards Ri., Harl. 52 EX15
Mallards Rd., Wdf.Grn. 102 EH52
Mallet Dr., Nthlt. 116 BZ64
Mallet Rd. SE13 183 ED86
Malling Clo., Croy. 202 DW100
Malling Gdns., Mord. 200 DC100
Malling Way, Brom. 204 EF101
Mallinson Clo., Horn. 128 FJ64
Mallinson Rd. SW11 180 DE85
Mallinson Rd., Croy. 201 DK104
Mallion Ct., Wal.Abb. 68 EF33
Mallord St. SW3 160 DD79
Mallory Clo. SE4 163 DY84
Mallory Gdns., Barn. 98 DG45
Mallory St. NW8 272 B5
Mallory St. NW8 140 DE70
Mallow Clo., Croy. 203 DX102
Marigold Way
Mallow Clo., Grav. 190 GE91
Mallow Clo., Tad. 233 CV119
Mallow Ct., Grays 170 GD79
Mallow Cres., Guil. 243 BB131
Mallow Cft., Hat. 45 CV19
Oxlease Dr.
Mallow Mead NW7 97 CY52
Mallow St. EC1 275 K4
Mallow Wk., Wal.Cr. 66 DR28
Mallows, The, Uxb. 115 BP62
Mallows Grn., Harl. 51 EN20
Mallys Pl., Dart. 208 FQ95
Malm Clo., Rick. 92 BK47
Malmains Clo., Beck. 203 ED98
Malmains Way, Beck. 203 EC98
Malmesbury Clo., Pnr. 115 BT56
Malmesbury Rd. E3 143 DZ69
Malmesbury Rd. E16 144 EE71
Malmesbury Rd. E18 102 EF53
Malmesbury Rd., Mord. 200 DC101
Malmesbury Ter. E16 144 EF71
Malmescroft, Hem.H. 41 BQ22
Malmsdale, Welw.G.C. 29 CX05
Malmstone Ave., Red. 251 DJ128
Malpas Dr., Pnr. 116 BX57
Malpas Rd. E8 142 DV65
Malpas Rd. SE4 163 DZ82
Malpas Rd., Dag. 146 EX65
Malpas Rd., Grays 171 GJ76
Malpas Rd., Slou. 132 AV73
Malt Hill, Egh. 172 AY92
Malt Ho. Clo., Wind. 172 AV87
Malt La., Rad. 77 CG35
Newlands Ave.
Malt St. SE1 162 DU79
Malta Rd. E10 123 EA60
Malta Rd., Til. 171 GF82
Malta St. EC1 274 G4
Maltby Clo., Orp. 206 EU102
Vinson Clo.
Maltby Dr., Enf. 82 DV38
Maltby Rd., Chess. 216 CN107
Maltby St. SE1 279 P5
Maltby St. SE1 162 DT76
Malthouse Dr. W4 158 CS79
Malthouse Dr., Felt. 176 BX92
Malthouse Pas. SW13 158 CS82
The Ter.
Malthouse Pl., Rad. 61 CG34
Malthouse Sq., Beac. 111 AM55
Malthus Path SE28 146 EW74
Owen Clo.
Malting Ho. E14 143 DZ73
Oak La.
Malting Way, Islw. 157 CF83
Maltings, The, Harl. 36 EW11
Maltings, The, Kings L. 59 BQ33
Maltings, The, Orp. 205 ET102
Maltings, The, Oxt. 254 EF131
Maltings, The, St.Alb. 43 CD20
Chequer St.
Maltings, The, W.Byf. 212 BM113
Maltings Clo. SW13 158 CS82
Cleveland Gdns.
Maltings Dr., Epp. 70 EU29
Palmers Hill
Maltings La., Epp. 70 EU29
Maltings Ms., Amer. 55 AP40
Maltings Ms., Sid. 186 EU90
Station Rd.
Maltings Pl. SW6 160 DB81
Maltmans La., Ger.Cr. 112 AW55
Malton Ave., Slou. 131 AP72
Malton Ms. SE18 165 ES79
Malton St.
Malton Ms. W10 139 CY72
Cambridge Gdns.
Malton Rd. W10 139 CY72
St. Marks Rd.
Malton St. SE18 165 ES79
Maltravers St. WC2 274 C10
Malus Clo., Add. 211 BF108
Malus Clo., Hem.H. 40 BN19
Malus Dr., Add. 211 BF107
Malva Clo. SW18 180 DB85
St. Ann's Hill
Malvern Ave. E4 101 ED52
Malvern Ave., Bexh. 166 EY80
Malvern Ave., Har. 116 BY62
Malvern Clo. SE20 202 DU96
Derwent Rd.
Malvern Clo. W10 139 CZ71
Malvern Clo., Cher. 211 BC107
Malvern Clo., Hat. 45 CT17
Malvern Clo., Mitch. 201 DJ97
Malvern Clo., St.Alb. 43 CJ16
Malvern Clo., Surb. 198 CL102
Malvern Clo., Uxb. 114 BN61
Malvern Ct. SE14 162 DW80
Avonley Rd.
Malvern Ct. SW7 276 A8
Malvern Ct. SW7 160 DD77
Malvern Ct., Slou. 153 BA79
Hill Ri.
Malvern Dr., Felt. 176 BX92
Malvern Dr., Ilf. 125 ET63
Malvern Dr., Wdf.Grn. 102 EJ50
Malvern Gdns. NW2 119 CY61
Malvern Gdns. NW6 139 CZ68
Malvern Gdns., Har. 118 CL56
Malvern Gdns., Loug. 85 EM44
Malvern Ms. NW6 140 DA69
Malvern Rd.
Malvern Pl. NW6 139 CZ69
Malvern Rd. E6 144 EL67
Malvern Rd. E8 142 DU66
Malvern Rd. E11 124 EE61
Malvern Rd. N8 121 DM55
Malvern Rd. N17 122 DU55
Malvern Rd. NW6 140 DA69
Malvern Rd., Enf. 83 DY36
Malvern Rd., Grays 170 GD77
Malvern Rd., Hmptn. 176 CA94
Malvern Rd., Hayes 155 BS80
Malvern Rd., Horn. 127 FG58
Malvern Rd., Orp. 224 EV105
Malvern Rd., Surb. 198 CL103
Malvern Rd., Th.Hth. 201 DN98
Malvern Ter. N1 141 DN67
Malvern Ter. N9 100 DT46
Malvern Way W13 137 CH71
Templewood
Malvern Way, Hem.H. 40 BM18
Malvern Way, Rick. 75 BP43
Malvina Ave., Grav. 191 GH89
Malwood Rd. SW12 181 DH86
Malyons, The, Shep. 195 BR100
Gordon Rd.
Malyons Rd. SE13 183 EB86
Malyons Rd., Swan. 187 FF94
Malyons Ter. SE13 183 EB85
Managers St. E14 143 EC74
Prestons Rd.
Manan Clo., Hem.H. 41 BQ22
Manatee Pl., Wall. 201 DK104
Croydon Rd.
Manaton Clo. SE15 162 DV83
Manaton Cres., Sthl. 136 CA72
Manbey Gro. E15 144 EE65
Manbey Pk. Rd. E15 144 EE65
Manbey Rd. E15 144 EE65
Manbey St. E15 144 EE65
Manborough Ave. E6 145 EM69
Manbre Rd. W6 159 CW79
Manchester Dr. W10 139 CY70
Manchester Gro. E14 163 EC78
Manchester Ms. W1 272 F7
Manchester Rd. E14 163 EC78
Manchester Rd. N15 122 DR58
Manchester Rd., Th.Hth. 202 DQ97
Manchester Row, Dart. 187 FE85
Manchester Sq. W1 272 F8
Manchester Sq. W1 140 DG72
Manchester St. W1 272 F7
Manchester St. W1 140 DG71
Manchester Way, Dag. 127 FB63
Manchuria Rd. SW11 180 DG86
Manciple St. SE1 279 L5
Manciple St. SE1 162 DR75
Mandalay Rd. SW4 181 DJ85
Mandarin St. E14 143 EA73
Salter St.
Mandarin Way, Hayes 136 BX72
Mandela Avenue-First Ave., Harl. 35 ES13
Mandela Clo. NW10 138 CQ66
Mandela Rd. E16 144 EG72
Mandela St. NW1 141 DJ67
Mandela St. SW9 161 DN80
Mandela Way SE1 279 N8
Mandela Way SE1 162 DS77
Mandelyns, Berk. 38 AS16
Mandeville Clo. SE3 164 EF80
Vanbrugh Pk.
Mandeville Clo. SW20 199 CY95
Mandeville Clo., Brox. 49 DZ20
Mandeville Clo., Guil. 242 AU131
Mandeville Clo., Harl. 52 EW17
Mandeville Clo., Hert. 32 DQ12
Mandeville Clo., Wat. 75 BT38
Mandeville Ct. E4 101 DY49
Mandeville Ct., Egh. 173 BA91
Mandeville Dr., St.Alb. 43 CD23
Mandeville Dr., Surb. 197 CK102
Mandeville Pl. W1 272 G8
Mandeville Pl. W1 140 DG72
Mandeville Ri., Welw.G.C. 29 CX07
Mandeville Rd. N14 99 DH47
Mandeville Rd., Enf. 83 DY36
Mandeville Rd., Hert. 32 DQ12
Mandeville Rd., Islw. 157 CG82
Mandeville Rd., Nthlt. 136 BZ66
Mandeville Rd., Pot.B. 64 DC32
Mandeville Rd., Shep. 194 BN99
Mandeville St. E5 123 DY62
Mandeville Wk., Brwd. 109 GE44
Kelvedon Clo.
Mandrake Rd. SW17 180 DF89
Mandrake Way E15 144 EE66
Elliot Clo.
Mandrell Rd. SW2 181 DL85
Manette St. W1 273 N9
Manette St. W1 141 DK72
Manfield Clo., Slou. 131 AN69
Manford Clo., Chig. 104 EU49
Manford Cross, Chig. 104 EU50
Manford Way, Chig. 103 ES49
Manfred Rd. SW15 179 CZ85
Manger Rd. N7 141 DL65
Mangles Rd., Guil. 242 AX132
Mangold Way, Erith 166 EY76
Mangrove Dr., Hert. 32 DS11
Mangrove La., Hert. 32 DS11
Mangrove Rd., Hert. 32 DS10
Manhattan Ct., Nthlt. 136 BX69
Manhattan Wf. E16 164 EG75
Manilla St. E14 163 EA75
Manister Rd. SE2 166 EU76
Manitoba Ct. SE16 162 DW75
Renforth St.
Manitoba Gdns., Orp. 223 ET107
Superior Dr.
Manley Ct. N16 122 DT62
Stoke Newington High St.
Manley Rd., Hem.H. 40 BL19
Knightsbridge Way
Manley St. NW1 140 DG67
Manly Dixon Dr., Enf. 83 DY37
Mann Clo., Croy. 202 DQ104
Salem Pl.
Mannamead, Epsom 232 CS119
Mannamead Clo., Epsom 232 CS119
Mannamead
Mannicotts, Welw.G.C. 29 CV09
Mannin Rd., Rom. 126 EV59
Manning Gdns., Har. 117 CK59
Manning Pl., Rich. 178 CM86
Grove Rd.
Manning Rd. E17 123 DY57
Southcote Rd.
Manning Rd., Dag. 146 FA65
Manning Rd., Orp. 206 EX99
Manning St., S.Ock. 148 FQ74
Manningford Clo. EC1 274 F2
Manningtree Clo. SW19 179 CY88
Manningtree Rd., Ruis. 115 BV63
Manningtree St. E1 142 DU72
White Ch. La.
Mannock Dr., Loug. 85 EQ40
Mannock Rd. N22 121 DP55
Mannock Rd., Dart. 168 FM83
Barnwell Rd.
Manns Clo., Islw. 177 CF85
Manns Rd., Edg. 96 CN51
Manoel Rd., Twick. 176 CC89
Manor Ave. SE4 163 DZ82
Manor Ave., Cat. 236 DS124
Manor Ave., Hem.H. 40 BK23
Manor Ave., Horn. 128 FJ57
Manor Ave., Houns. 156 BX83
Manor Ave., Nthlt. 136 BZ66
Manor Chase, Wey. 213 BP106
Manor Clo. E17 101 DY54
Manor Rd.
Manor Clo. NW7 96 CR50
Manor Dr.
Manor Clo. NW9 118 CP57
Manor Clo. SE28 146 EW73
Manor Clo., Barn. 79 CY42
Manor Clo., Berk. 38 AW19
Manor Clo., Dag. 147 FD65
Manor Clo. (Crayford), Dart. 167 FD84
Manor Clo. (Wilmington), Dart. 187 FG90
Manor Clo., Hat. 45 CT15
Manor Clo., Hert. 32 DR07
Manor Clo., Horl. 268 DF148
Manor Clo., Lthd. 245 BS128
Manor Clo., Rom. 127 FG57
Manor Rd.
Manor Clo., Ruis. 115 BT60
Manor Clo., S.Ock. 148 FQ74
Manor Clo., Warl. 237 DY117
Manor Clo., Wok. 227 BF116
Manor Clo., Wor.Pk. 198 CS102
Manor Clo. S., S.Ock. 148 FQ74
Manor Clo.
Manor Cotts., Nthwd. 93 BT53
Manor Cotts. App. N2 98 DC54
Manor Ct. E10 123 EB60
Grange Pk. Rd.
Manor Ct. N2 120 DF57
Manor Ct. SW6 160 DB81
Bagley's La.
Manor Ct., Enf. 82 DV36
Manor Rd.
Manor Ct., Rad. 77 CF38
Manor Ct., Slou. 131 AM74
Richards Way
Manor Ct., Twick. 176 CC89
Manor Ct., Wem. 118 CL64
Manor Ct., Wey. 213 BP105
Manor Ct. Rd. W7 137 CE73
Manor Cres., Beac. 89 AR50
Manor Cres., Guil. 242 AV132
Manor Cres., Horn. 128 FJ57
Manor Cres., Surb. 198 CN100
Manor Cres., W.Byf. 212 BM113
Manor Dr. N14 99 DH45
Manor Dr. N20 98 DE48
Manor Dr. NW7 96 CR50
Manor Dr., Add. 212 BG110
Manor Dr., Amer. 55 AP36
Manor Dr., Epsom 216 CS107
Manor Dr., Esher 197 CF104
Manor Dr., Felt. 176 BX92
Lebanon Ave.
Manor Dr., Horl. 268 DF148
Manor Dr., St.Alb. 60 CA27
Manor Dr., Sun. 195 BU96
Manor Dr., Surb. 198 CM100
Manor Dr., Wem. 118 CM63
Manor Dr., The, Wor.Pk. 198 CS102
Manor Dr. N., N.Mal. 198 CR100
Manor Dr. N., Wor.Pk. 198 CS102
Manor Est. SE16 162 DV77
Manor Fm. (Farningham), Dart. 208 FM101
Manor Fm. Ave., Shep. 195 BP100
Manor Fm. Clo., Wind. 151 AM83
Manor Fm. Clo., Wor.Pk. 198 CS102
Manor Fm. Dr. E4 102 EE48
Manor Fm. Est., Stai. 172 AW86
Manor Fm. La., Egh. 173 BA92
Manor Fm. Rd., Enf. 82 DV36
Manor Fm. Rd., Th.Hth. 201 DN96
Manor Fm. Rd., Wem. 137 CK67
Manor Fm. Way, Beac. 89 AR51
Orchard Rd.
Manor Flds. SW15 179 CX86
Manor Gdns. N7 121 DL62
Manor Gdns. SW20 199 CZ96
Manor Gdns. W3 158 CN77
Manor Gdns., Gdmg. 258 AS144
Farncombe St.
Manor Gdns., Guil. 242 AV132
Manor Gdns., Hmptn. 176 CB94
Manor Gdns., H.Wyc. 110 AE58
Manor Gdns., Lthd. 246 BX128
Manor Gdns., Rich. 158 CM84
Manor Gdns., Ruis. 116 BW64
Manor Gdns., S.Croy. 220 DT107
Manor Gdns., Sun. 195 BU95
Manor Gate, Nthlt. 136 BY66
Manor Grn. Rd., Epsom 216 CP113
Manor Gro. SE15 162 DW79
Manor Gro., Beck. 203 EB96
Manor Gro., Maid. 150 AD80
Manor Gro., Rich. 158 CN84
Manor Hall Ave. NW4 97 CW54
Manor Hall Dr. NW4 97 CX54
Manor Hatch Clo., Harl. 52 EV16
Manor Ho. Ct., Epsom 216 CQ113
Manor Ho. Ct., Shep. 195 BP101
Manor Ho. Dr. NW6 139 CX66
Manor Ho. Dr., Nthwd. 93 BP52
Manor Ho. Gdns., Abb.L. 59 BR31
Manor Ho. La., Slou. 152 AV80
Horton Rd.
Manor Ho. Way, Islw. 157 CH83
Manor La. SE12 184 EE86
Manor La. SE13 184 EE85
Manor La., Felt. 175 BU89
High St.
Manor La., Ger.Cr. 112 AX59
Manor La., Hayes 155 BR79
Manor La. 209 FW101
(Fawkham Grn.), Long.
Manor La., Sev. 209 FW103
Manor La., Sun. 195 BU96
Manor La., Sutt. 218 DC106
Manor La., Tad. 250 DA129
Manor La. Ter. SE13 164 EE84
Manor Leaze, Egh. 173 BB92
Manor Lo., Guil. 242 AV132
Manor Ms. NW6 140 DA68
Cambridge Ave.
Manor Ms. SE4 163 DZ82
Manor Mt. SE23 182 DW88
Manor Par. NW10 139 CT68
Station Rd.
Manor Par., Hat. 45 CT15
Green Las.

Manor Pk. SE13 183 ED85
Manor Pk., Chis. 205 ER96
Manor Pk., Rich. 158 CM84
Manor Pk. Clo., W.Wick. 203 EB102
Manor Pk. Cres., Edg. 96 CN51
Manor Pk. Dr., Har. 116 CB55
Manor Pk. Gdns., Edg. 96 CN50
Manor Pk. Par. SE13 163 ED84
Lee High Rd.
Manor Pk. Rd. E12 124 EK63
Manor Pk. Rd. N2 120 DC55
Manor Pk. Rd. NW10 139 CT67
Manor Pk. Rd., Chis. 205 EQ95
Manor Pk. Rd., Sutt. 218 DC106
Manor Pk. Rd., W.Wick. 203 EB102
Manor Pl. SE17 279 H10
Manor Pl. SE17 161 DP78
Manor Pl., Chis. 205 ER96
Manor Pl., Dart. 188 FL88
Highfield Rd. S.
Manor Pl., Felt. 175 BU88
Manor Pl., Mitch. 201 DJ97
Manor Pl., Stai. 174 BH92
Manor Pl., Sutt. 218 DB106
Manor Pl., Walt. 195 BT101
Manor Rd.
Manor Rd. E10 123 EA59
Manor Rd. E15 144 EE68
Manor Rd. E16 144 EE70
Manor Rd. E17 101 DY54
Manor Rd. N16 122 DR61
Manor Rd. N17 100 DU53
Manor Rd. N22 99 DL51
Manor Rd. SE25 202 DU98
Manor Rd. SW20 199 CZ96
Manor Rd. W13 137 CG73
Manor Rd., Ashf. 174 BM92
Manor Rd., Bark. 145 ET65
Manor Rd., Barn. 79 CY43
Manor Rd., Beac. 89 AR50
Manor Rd., Beck. 203 EA96
Manor Rd., Bex. 187 FB88
Manor Rd., Chesh. 54 AP29
Lansdowne Rd.
Manor Rd., Chig. 103 EN51
Manor Rd., Dag. 147 FC65
Manor Rd., Dart. 167 FE84
Manor Rd., E.Mol. 197 CD98
Manor Rd., Enf. 82 DQ40
Manor Rd., Erith 167 FF79
Manor Rd., Grav. 191 GH86
Manor Rd., Grays 170 GC79
Manor Rd. (West Thurrock), Grays 169 FW79
Manor Rd., Guil. 242 AV131
Manor Rd., Harl. 36 EW10
Manor Rd., Har. 117 CG58
Manor Rd., Hat. 28 CR14
Manor Rd., Hayes 135 BU72
Manor Rd., Hodd. 49 EA16
Manor Rd., Loug. 84 EH44
Manor Rd. (High Beach), Loug. 84 EH39
Manor Rd., Mitch. 201 DJ98
Manor Rd., Pot.B. 63 CZ31
Manor Rd., Red. 251 DJ129
Manor Rd., Reig. 249 CZ132
Manor Rd., Rich. 158 CM83
Manor Rd., Rom. 127 FG57
Manor Rd. (Chadwell Heath), Rom. 126 EX58
Manor Rd. (Lambourne End), Rom. 104 EW47
Manor Rd., Ruis. 115 BR60
Manor Rd., St.Alb. 43 CE19
Manor Rd. (London Colney), St.Alb. 61 CJ26
Manor Rd., Sev. 240 EX124
Manor Rd., Sid. 186 EU90
Manor Rd., Sutt. 217 CZ108
Manor Rd., Swans. 189 FX86
Manor Rd., Tedd. 177 CG92
Manor Rd., Til. 171 GG82
Manor Rd., Twick. 176 CC89
Manor Rd., Wall. 219 DH105
Manor Rd., Wal.Abb. 67 ED33
Manor Rd., Walt. 195 BT101
Manor Rd., Wat. 75 BU39
Manor Rd., W.Wick. 203 EB103
Manor Rd., West. 238 EL120
Manor Rd., Wind. 151 AL82
Manor Rd., Wok. 226 AW116
Manor Rd. (Send Marsh), Wok. 227 BF123
Manor Rd., Wdf.Grn. 103 EM51
Manor Rd. N., Esher 197 CF104
Manor Rd. N., T.Ditt. 197 CG103
Manor Rd. N., Wall. 219 DH105
Manor Rd. S., Esher 215 CE105
Manor Sq., Dag. 126 EW61
Manor St., Berk. 38 AW19
Manor Vale, Brent. 157 CJ78
Manor Vw. N3 98 DB54
Manor Wk., Wey. 213 BP106
Manor Way E4 101 ED49
Manor Way NW9 118 CS56
Manor Way SE3 164 EF84
Manor Way, Amer. 55 AM44
Manor Way, Bans. 234 DF116
Manor Way, Beck. 203 EA96
Manor Way, Bex. 186 FA88
Manor Way, Bexh. 167 FD83
Manor Way, Borwd. 78 CQ40
Manor Way, Brwd. 108 FU48
Manor Way, Brom. 204 EL100
Manor Way, Chesh. 54 AR30
Manor Way, Egh. 173 AZ93
Manor Way, Grays 170 GB80
Manor Way (Little Thurrock Marshes), Grays 170 GD80
Manor Way, Guil. 258 AS137
Manor Way, Har. 116 CB56
Manor Way, Lthd. 230 CC115
Manor Way, Mitch. 201 DJ97
Manor Way, Orp. 205 EQ99
Manor Way, Pot.B. 64 DA30
Manor Way, Pur. 219 DL112
Manor Way, Rain. 147 FE72
Manor Way, Rick. 74 BN42
Manor Way, Ruis. 115 BS59
Manor Way, S.Croy. 220 DS107
Manor Way, Sthl. 156 BX77
Manor Way, Swans. 169 FX84
Manor Way, Til. 170 GC80
Manor Way (Cheshunt), Wal.Cr. 67 DY31
Russells Ride
Manor Way, Wok. 227 BB121
Manor Way, Wor.Pk. 198 CS102
Manor Way, The, Wall. 219 DH105
Manor Way Ind. Est., Grays 170 GC80
Manor Waye, Uxb. 134 BK67
Manor Wd. Rd., Pur. 219 DL113
Manorbrook SE3 164 EG84
Manorcrofts Rd., Egh. 173 BA93
Manordene Clo., T.Ditt. 197 CG102
Manordene Rd. SE28 146 EW72
Manorfield Clo. N19 121 DJ63
Tufnell Pk. Rd.
Manorfields Clo., Chis. 205 ET97
Manorgate Rd., Kings.T. 198 CN95
Manorhall Gdns. E10 123 EA60
Manorhouse La., Lthd. 246 BY126
Manorside, Barn. 79 CY42
Manorside Clo. SE2 166 EW77
Manorville Rd., Hem.H. 40 BJ24
Manorway, Enf. 100 DS45
Manorway, Wdf.Grn. 102 EJ50
Manpreet Ct. E12 125 EM64
Morris Ave.
Manresa Rd. SW3 160 DE78
Mansard Beeches SW17 180 DG92
Mansard Clo., Horn. 127 FG61
Mansard Clo., Pnr. 116 BX55
Mansards, The, St.Alb. 43 CE19
Avenue Rd.
Manscroft Rd., Hem.H. 40 BH18
Manse Clo., Hayes 155 BR79
Manse Rd. N16 122 DT62
Manse Way, Swan. 207 FG98
Mansel Clo., Guil. 242 AV129
Mansel Clo., Slou. 132 AV71
Mansel Gro. E17 101 EA53
Mansel Rd. SW19 179 CY93
Mansell Clo., Wind. 151 AL82
Mansell Rd. W3 158 CR75
Mansell Rd., Grnf. 136 CB71
Mansell St. E1 142 DT72
Mansell Way, Cat. 236 DR122
Manser Rd., Rain. 147 FE69
Mansergh Clo. SE18 164 EL80
Mansfield, Saw. 36 EU06
Mansfield Ave. N15 122 DR56
Mansfield Ave., Barn. 80 DF44
Mansfield Ave., Ruis. 115 BV60
Mansfield Clo. N9 82 DU44
Mansfield Clo., Orp. 206 EX101
Mansfield Clo., Wey. 213 BP106
Mansfield Dr., Hayes 135 BS70
Mansfield Dr., Red. 251 DK128
Mansfield Gdns., Hert. 32 DQ07
Mansfield Gdns., Horn. 128 FK61
Mansfield Hill E4 101 EB46
Mansfield Ms. W1 273 H7
Mansfield Pl. NW3 120 DC63
New End
Mansfield Rd. E11 124 EH58
Mansfield Rd. E17 123 DZ56
Mansfield Rd. NW3 120 DF64
Mansfield Rd. W3 138 CP70
Mansfield Rd., Chess. 215 CJ106
Mansfield Rd., Ilf. 125 EN61
Mansfield Rd., S.Croy. 220 DR107
Mansfield Rd., Swan. 187 FE93
Mansfield St. W1 273 H7
Mansfield St. W1 141 DH71
Mansford St. E2 142 DU68
Manship Rd., Mitch. 180 DG94
Mansion Gdns. NW3 120 DB62
Mansion Ho. EC4 275 K9
Mansion Ho. Pl. EC4 275 K9
Mansion La., Iver 133 BC74
Manson Ms. SW7 160 DC77
Manson Pl. SW7 160 DD77
Manstead Gdns., Rain. 147 FH72
Mansted Gdns., Rom. 126 EW59
Manston Ave., Sthl. 156 CA77
Manston Clo. SE20 202 DW95
Garden Rd.
Manston Clo. (Cheshunt), Wal.Cr. 66 DW30
Manston Gro., Kings.T. 177 CK92
Manston Rd., Guil. 243 BA130
Manston Rd., Harl. 51 ES15
Manston Way, Horn. 147 FH65
Manstone Rd. NW2 119 CY64
Manthorp Rd. SE18 165 EQ78
Mantilla Rd. SW17 180 DG91
Mantle Rd. SE4 163 DY83
Mantle Way E15 144 EE66
Romford Rd.
Mantlet Clo. SW16 181 DJ94
Manton Ave. W7 157 CF75
Manton Clo., Hayes 135 BS73
Manton Rd. SE2 166 EU77
Mantua St. SW11 160 DD83
Mantus Clo. E1 142 DW70
Mantus Rd.
Mantus Rd. E1 142 DW70
Manus Way N20 98 DC47
Blakeney Clo.
Manville Gdns. SW17 181 DH89
Manville Rd. SW17 180 DG89
Manwood Rd. SE4 183 DZ85
Manwood St. E16 145 EM74
Manygate La., Shep. 195 BQ101
Manygates SW12 181 DH89
Maori Rd., Guil. 243 AZ134
Mape St. E2 142 DV70
Mapesbury Rd. NW2 139 CY66
Mapeshill Pl. NW2 139 CW65
Maple Ave. E4 101 DZ50
Maple Ave. W3 138 CS74
Maple Ave., Har. 116 CB61
Maple Ave., St.Alb. 42 CC16
Maple Ave., Upmin. 128 FP62
Maple Ave., West Dr. 134 BL73
Maple Clo. N16 122 DU58
Maple Clo. SW4 181 DK86
Maple Clo., Brwd. 109 FZ48
Cherry Ave.
Maple Clo., Buck.H. 102 EK48
Maple Clo., Epp. 85 ER37
Loughton La.
Maple Clo., Hmptn. 176 BZ93
Maple Clo., Hat. 45 CU19
Elm Dr.
Maple Clo., Hayes 136 BX69
Maple Clo., Horn. 127 FH62
Maple Clo., Ilf. 103 ES50
Maple Clo., Mitch. 201 DH95
Maple Clo., Orp. 205 ER99
Maple Clo., Ruis. 115 BV58
Maple Clo., Swan. 207 FE96
Maple Clo. (Bushey), Wat. 76 BY40
Maple Clo., Whyt. 236 DT117
Maple Ct., Egh. 172 AV93
Ashwood Rd.
Maple Ct., N.Mal. 198 CR97
Maple Ct., Ware 33 ED11
Maple Cres., Sid. 186 EU86
Maple Cres., Slou. 132 AV73
Maple Cross Ind. Est., Rick. 91 BF49
Maple Gdns., Edg. 96 CS52
Maple Gdns., Stai. 174 BL89
Maple Gate, Loug. 85 EN40
Maple Grn., Hem.H. 39 BE18
Maple Gro. NW9 118 CQ59
Maple Gro. W5 157 CJ76
Maple Gro., Brent. 157 CH80
Maple Gro., Guil. 242 AX132
Maple Gro., Sthl. 136 BZ71
Maple Gro., Wat. 75 BU39
Maple Gro., Welw.G.C. 29 CZ06
Maple Gro., Wok. 226 AY121
Maple Hill, Hem.H. 56 AX30
Ley Hill Rd.
Maple Ind. Est., Felt. 175 BU90
Maple Leaf Clo., Abb.L. 59 BU32
Magnolia Ave.
Maple Leaf Clo., West. 238 EK116
Main Rd.
Maple Leaf Dr., Sid. 185 ET88
Maple Leaf Sq. SE16 163 DX75
St. Elmos Rd.
Maple Lo. Clo., Rick. 91 BE49
Maple Ms. NW6 140 DB68
Kilburn Pk. Rd.
Maple Ms. SW16 181 DM92
Maple Pl. W1 273 L5
Maple Pl., Bans. 233 CX115
Maple Pl., West Dr. 134 BM73
Maple Ave.
Maple River Ind. Est., Harl. 36 EV09
Maple Rd. E11 124 EE58
Maple Rd. SE20 202 DV95
Maple Rd., Ash. 231 CK119
Maple Rd., Dart. 188 FJ88
Maple Rd., Grav. 191 GJ91
Maple Rd., Grays 170 GC79
Maple Rd., Hayes 136 BW69
Maple Rd., Red. 266 DF138
Maple Rd., Surb. 197 CK100
Maple Rd., Whyt. 236 DT117
Maple Rd., Wok. 228 BG124
Maple Springs, Wal.Abb. 68 EG33
Maple St. W1 273 K6
Maple St. W1 141 DJ71
Maple St., Rom. 127 FC56
Maple Wk. W10 139 CX70
Droop St.
Maple Wk., Sutt. 218 DB110
Maple Way, Couls. 235 DH121
Maple Way, Felt. 175 BU90
Maplecourt Wk., Wind. 151 AN77
Common Rd.
Maplecroft Clo. E6 144 EL72
Allhallows Rd.
Maplecroft La., Wal.Abb. 50 EE21
Mapledale Ave., Croy. 202 DU103
Mapledene, Chis. 185 EQ92
Kemnal Rd.
Mapledene Rd. E8 142 DU66
Maplefield, St.Alb. 60 CB29
Maplefield La., Ch.St.G. 72 AV41
Maplehurst, Lthd. 231 CD123
Maplehurst Clo., Kings.T. 198 CL98
Mapleleafe Gdns., Ilf. 125 EP55
Maples, The, Bans. 218 DB114
Maples, The, Cher. 211 BC107
Maples, The, Harl. 51 EP20
Maples, The, Wal.Cr. 66 DS28
Burton La.
Maples Pl. E1 142 DV71
Raven Row
Maplescombe La. (Farningham), Dart. 208 FN104
Maplestead Rd. SW2 181 DM87
Maplestead Rd., Dag. 146 EV67
Maplethorpe Rd., Th.Hth. 201 DN98
Mapleton Clo., Brom. 204 EG100
Mapleton Cres. SW18 180 DB86
Mapleton Cres., Enf. 82 DW38
Mapleton Rd. E4 101 EC48
Mapleton Rd. SW18 180 DA86
Mapleton Rd., Eden. 255 ET133
Mapleton Rd., Enf. 82 DV40
Mapleton Rd., West. 255 ES131
Maplin Clo. N21 81 DM44
Maplin Pk., Slou. 153 BB75
Maplin Rd. E16 144 EG72
Maplin St. E3 143 DZ69
Mapperley Dr., Wdf.Grn. 102 EE52
Forest Dr.
Mar Rd., S.Ock. 149 FW70
Maran Way, Erith 166 EX75
Marban Rd. W9 139 CZ69
Marbeck Clo., Wind. 151 AK81
Marble Arch W1 272 D10
Marble Arch W1 140 DF73
Marble Clo. W3 138 CP74
Marble Dr. NW2 119 CX60
Marble Hill Clo., Twick. 177 CH87
Marble Hill Gdns., Twick. 177 CH87
Marble Quay E1 142 DU74
Marbles Way, Tad. 233 CX119
Marbrook Ct. SE12 184 EJ90
Marcellina Way, Orp. 205 ES104
Marcet Rd., Dart. 188 FJ85
March Rd., Twick. 177 CG87
March Rd., Wey. 212 BN106
Marchant Rd. E11 123 ED61
Marchant St. SE14 163 DY79
Sanford St.
Marchbank Rd. W14 159 CZ79
Marchmant Clo., Horn. 128 FJ62
Marchmont Gdns., Rich. 178 CM85
Marchmont Rd.
Marchmont Grn., Hem.H. 40 BK18
Paston Rd.
Marchmont Rd., Rich. 178 CM85
Marchmont Rd., Wall. 219 DJ108
Marchmont St. WC1 273 P4
Marchmont St. WC1 141 DL70
Marchside Clo., Houns. 156 BX81
Springwell Rd.
Marchwood Clo. SE5 162 DS80
Marchwood Cres. W5 137 CJ72
Marcia Ct., Slou. 131 AM74
Richards Way
Marcia Rd. SE1 279 N9
Marcia Rd. SE1 162 DS77
Marcilly Rd. SW18 180 DD85
Marco Rd. W6 159 CV76
Marcon Pl. E8 122 DV64
Marconi Rd. E10 123 EA60
Marconi Rd., Grav. 190 GD90
Marconi Way, Sthl. 136 CB72
Marcourt Lawns W5 138 CL70
Marcus Ct. E15 144 EE67
Marcus Garvey Way SE24 161 DN84
Marcus Rd., Dart. 187 FG87
Marcus St. E15 144 EE67
Marcus St. SW18 180 DB86
Marcus Ter. SW18 180 DB86
Marcuse Rd., Cat. 236 DQ121
Coulsdon Rd.
Mardale Dr. NW9 118 CR57
Mardell Rd., Croy. 203 DX99
Marden Ave., Brom. 204 EF100
Marden Clo., Chig. 104 EV47
Marden Cres., Bex. 187 FC85
Marden Cres., Croy. 201 DM100
Marden Pk., Cat. 253 DZ125
Marden Rd. N17 122 DS55
Marden Rd., Croy. 201 DM100
Marden Rd., Rom. 127 FE58
Kingsmead Ave.
Marden Sq. SE16 162 DV76
Marder Rd. W13 157 CG75
Mardon St. E14 143 DY71
Mardyke Rd., Harl. 36 EU13
Mare St. E8 142 DV67
Marechal Niel Ave., Sid. 185 ER90
Mares Fld., Croy. 202 DS104
Mareschal Rd., Guil. 258 AW136
Marescroft Rd., Slou. 131 AL70
Maresfield Gdns. NW3 120 DC64
Marfleet Clo., Cars. 200 DE103
Marford Rd., St.Alb. 28 CN07
Marford Rd., Welw.G.C. 28 CR09
Margaret Ave. E4 83 EB44
Margaret Ave., Brwd. 109 FZ45
Margaret Ave., St.Alb. 43 CD18
Margaret Bondfield Ave., Bark. 146 EU66
Margaret Bldgs. N16 122 DT60
Margaret Rd.
Margaret Clo., Abb.L. 59 BT32
Margaret Clo., Epp. 70 EU29
Margaret Rd.
Margaret Clo., Pot.B. 64 DC33
Margaret Clo., Rom. 127 FH57
Margaret Rd.
Margaret Clo., Stai. 174 BK93
Charles Rd.
Margaret Clo., Wal.Abb. 67 EC33
Margaret Ct. W1 273 K8
Margaret Dr., Horn. 128 FM60
Margaret Gardner Dr. SE9 185 EM89
Margaret Ingram Clo. SW6 159 CZ79
Rylston Rd.
Margaret Rd. N16 122 DT60
Margaret Rd., Barn. 80 DD42
Margaret Rd., Bex. 186 EX86
Margaret Rd., Epp. 70 EU29
Margaret Rd., Guil. 258 AW135
Margaret Rd., Rom. 127 FH57
Margaret Sq., Uxb. 134 BJ67
Margaret St. W1 273 J8
Margaret St. W1 141 DH72
Margaret Way, Couls. 235 DP118
Margaret Way, Ilf. 124 EL58
Margaretta Ter. SW3 160 DE79
Margaretting Rd. E12 124 EJ60
Margate Rd. SW2 181 DL85
Margeholes, Wat. 94 BY47
Margery Gro., Tad. 249 CY129
Margery La., Tad. 249 CZ129
Margery Pk. Rd. E7 144 EG65
Margery Rd., Dag. 126 EX62
Margery St. WC1 274 D3
Margery St. WC1 141 DN69
Margery Wd., Welw.G.C. 30 DA06
Margherita Pl., Wal.Abb. 68 EG34
Margherita Rd., Wal.Abb. 68 EG34
Margin Dr. SW19 179 CX92
Margravine Gdns. W6 159 CX78
Margravine Rd. W6 159 CX78
Marham Gdns. SW18 180 DE88
Marham Gdns., Mord. 200 DC100
Maria Clo. SE1 162 DU77
Beatrice Rd.
Maria Ter. E1 143 DX70
Maria Theresa Clo., N.Mal. 198 CR99
Mariam Gdns., Horn. 128 FM61
Marian Clo., Hayes 136 BX70
Marian Ct., Sutt. 218 DB106
Marian Pl. E2 142 DV68
Marian Rd. SW16 201 DJ95
Marian Sq. E2 142 DU68
Pritchard's Rd.
Marian St. E2 142 DV68
Hackney Rd.
Marian Way NW10 139 CT66
Maricas Ave., Har. 95 CD52
Marie Lloyd Gdns. N19 121 DL59
Hornsey Ri. Gdns.
Marie Lloyd Wk. E8 142 DU65
Forest Rd.
Mariette Way, Wall. 219 DL109
Marigold All. SE1 278 F1
Marigold Clo., Sthl. 136 BY73
Lancaster Rd.
Marigold Pl., Harl. 36 EV11
Broadway Ave.
Marigold Rd. N17 100 DW52
Marigold St. SE16 162 DV75
Marigold Way E4 101 DZ51
Silver Birch Ave.
Marigold Way, Croy. 203 DX102
Marina App., Hayes 136 BY71
Marina Ave., N.Mal. 199 CV99
Marina Clo., Brom. 204 EG97
Marina Clo., Cher. 194 BH102
Marina Dr., Dart. 188 FN88
Marina Dr., Grav. 191 GF87
Marina Dr., Well. 165 ES82
Marina Gdns., Rom. 127 FB57
Marina Gdns. (Cheshunt), Wal.Cr. 66 DW30
Marina Way, Iver 133 BF73
Marina Way, Slou. 131 AK73
Marina Way, Tedd. 177 CK94
Fairways
Marine Dr. SE18 165 EM77
Marine St. SE16 162 DU76
Enid St.
Marinefield Rd. SW6 160 DB82
Mariner Gdns., Rich. 177 CJ90
Mariner Rd. E12 125 EM63
Dersingham Ave.
Mariner Way, Hem.H. 40 BN21
Mariners Ms. E14 163 ED77
Mariners Wk., Erith 167 FF79
Frobisher Rd.
Marion Ave., Shep. 195 BP99
Marion Clo., Ilf. 103 ER52
Marion Clo. (Bushey), Wat. 76 BZ39
Marion Cres., Orp. 206 EU99
Marion Gro., Wdf.Grn. 102 EE50
Marion Rd. NW7 97 CU50
Marion Rd., Th.Hth. 202 DQ99
Marischal Rd. SE13 163 ED83
Marisco Clo., Grays 171 GH77
Marish La., Uxb. 113 BC56
Marish Wf., Slou. 152 AY75
Maritime Clo., Green. 189 FV85
Maritime St. E3 143 DZ70
Marius Pas. SW17 180 DG89
Marius Rd.
Marius Rd. SW17 180 DG89
Marjoram Clo., Guil. 242 AU130
Marjorams Ave., Loug. 85 EM40
Marjorie Gro. SW11 160 DF84
Marjorie Ms. E1 143 DX72
Arbour Sq.
Mark Ave. E4 83 EB44
Mark Clo., Bexh. 166 EY81
Mark Clo., Sthl. 136 CB74
Longford Ave.
Mark Dr., Ger.Cr. 90 AX49
Mark Hall Moors, Harl. 36 EV12
Mark La. EC3 275 N10
Mark La. EC3 142 DS73
Mark La., Grav. 191 GL87
Mark Oak La., Lthd. 230 CA122
Mark Rd. N22 99 DP54
Mark Rd., Hem.H. 40 BN18
Mark St. E15 144 EE66
West Ham La.
Mark St. EC2 275 M4
Mark Way, Swan. 207 FG99
Markab Rd., Nthwd. 93 BT50
Marke Clo., Kes. 222 EL105
Markedge La., Couls. 234 DE124
Markedge La., Red. 250 DF125
Markenfield Rd., Guil. 242 AX134
Markeston Grn., Wat. 94 BX49
Market Ct. W1 273 K8
Market Est. N7 141 DL65
Clock Twr. Pl.
Market Hill SE18 165 EN76
Market La., Edg. 96 CQ53
Market La., Iver 153 BC75
Market La., Slou. 153 BC76
Market Link, Rom. 127 FE56
Market Meadow, Orp. 206 EW98
Market Ms. W1 277 H3
Market Oak La., Hem.H. 40 BN24
Market Par. SE15 162 DU82
Rye La.
Market Pl. N2 120 DE55
Market Pl. NW11 120 DC56
Market Pl. SE16 162 DU77
Southwark Pk. Rd.
Market Pl. W1 273 K8
Market Pl. W3 138 CQ74
Market Pl., Bexh. 166 FA84
Market Pl., Brent. 157 CK80
Lion Way
Market Pl., Dart. 188 FL87
Market St.
Market Pl., Enf. 82 DR41
The Town
Market Pl., Ger.Cr. 90 AX53
Market Pl., Hat. 45 CU17
Dog Kennel La.
Market Pl., Hert. 32 DR09
Fore St.
Market Pl., Kings.T. 197 CK96
Market Pl., Rom. 127 FE57
Market Pl. (Abridge), Rom. 86 EV41
Market Pl., St.Alb. 43 CD20
Market Pl., Til. 171 GG82
Market Rd. N7 141 DL65
Market Rd., Rich. 158 CN83
Market Row SW9 161 DN84
Atlantic Rd.
Market Sq. E14 143 EB72
Chrisp St.
Market Sq. N9 100 DU47
New Rd.
Market Sq., Amer. 54 AP32
High St.
Market Sq., Brom. 204 EG96
Market Sq., Harl. 35 ER14
Post Office Rd.
Market Sq., Stai. 173 BE91
Clarence St.
Market Sq., Uxb. 134 BJ66
High St.
Market Sq., Wal.Abb. 67 EC33
Leverton Way
Market Sq., West. 255 EQ127
Market Sq., Wok. 226 AY117
Cawsey Way
Market St. E6 145 EM68
Market St. SE18 165 EN77
Market St., Dart. 188 FL87
Market St., Guil. 258 AX135
Market St., Harl. 36 EW11
Market St., Hert. 32 DR09
Market St., Wat. 75 BV42
Market St., Wind. 151 AR81
Castle Hill
Market Way E14 143 EB72
Kerbey St.
Market Way, West. 255 ER126
Costell's Meadow

Marketfield Rd., Red. 250 DF134
Marketfield Way, Red. 250 DF134
Markfield, Croy. 221 DZ110
Markfield Gdns. E4 101 EB45
Markfield Rd. N15 122 DU56
Markfield Rd., Cat. 252 DV126
Markham Pl. SW3 276 D10
Markham Pl. SW3 160 DF78
Markham Sq. SW3 276 D10
Markham Sq. SW3 160 DF78
Markham St. SW3 276 C10
Markham St. SW3 160 DE78
Markhole Clo., Hmptn. 176 BZ94
Priory Rd.
Markhouse Ave. E17 123 DY58
Markhouse Rd. E17 123 DZ57
Markmanor Ave. E17 123 DY59
Marks Rd., Rom. 127 FC57
Marks Rd., Warl. 237 DY118
Marks Sq., Grav. 191 GF91
Mark's St., Reig. 250 DB133
Marksbury Ave., Rich. 158 CN83
Markville Gdns., Cat. 252 DU125
Markway, The, Sun. 196 BW96
Markwell Clo. SE26 182 DV91
Longton Gro.
Markwell Clo., W.Wick. 204 EE103
Deer Pk. Way
Markwell Wd., Harl. 51 EP21
Markyate Rd., Dag. 126 EV64
Marl Rd. SW18 160 DB84
Marl St. SW18 160 DC84
Marl Rd.
Marlands Rd., Ilf. 124 EL55
Marlborough Ave. E8 142 DU67
Marlborough Ave. N14 99 DJ48
Marlborough Ave., Edg. 96 CP48
Marlborough Ave., Ruis. 115 BQ58
Marlborough Bldgs. SW3 276 C8
Marlborough Bldgs. SW3 160 DE77
Marlborough Clo. N20 98 DF48
Marlborough Gdns.
Marlborough Clo. SE17 279 H9
Marlborough Clo. SW19 180 DE94
Marlborough Clo., Grays 170 GC75
Marlborough Clo., Orp. 205 ET101
Aylesham Rd.
Marlborough Clo., Upmin. 129 FS60
Marlborough Clo., Walt. 196 BX104
Arch Rd.
Marlborough Ct. W8 160 DA77
Marlborough Ct., Dor. 263 CH136
Marlborough Rd.
Marlborough Cres. W4 158 CR76
Marlborough Cres., Sev. 256 FE124
Marlborough Dr., Ilf. 124 EL55
Marlborough Dr., Wey. 195 BQ104
Marlborough Gdns. N20 98 DF48
Marlborough Gdns., Upmin. 129 FR60
Marlborough Gate, St.Alb. 43 CE20
Marlborough Gate Ho. W2 140 DD73
Elms Ms.
Marlborough Gro. SE1 162 DU78
Marlborough Hill NW8 140 DC67
Marlborough Hill, Dor. 263 CH136
Marlborough Hill, Har. 117 CD56
Marlborough La. SE7 164 EJ79
Marlborough Pk. Ave., Sid. 186 EU88
Marlborough Pl. NW8 140 DC68
Marlborough Ri., Hem.H. 40 BL17
Marlborough Rd. E4 101 EA51
Marlborough Rd. E7 144 EJ66
Marlborough Rd. E15 124 EE63
Borthwick Rd.
Marlborough Rd. E18 124 EG55
Marlborough Rd. N9 100 DT46
Marlborough Rd. N19 121 DK61
Marlborough Rd. N22 99 DL52
Marlborough Rd. SW1 277 L3
Marlborough Rd. SW1 141 DJ74
Marlborough Rd. SW19 180 DE93
Marlborough Rd. W4 158 CQ78
Marlborough Rd. W5 157 CK75
Marlborough Rd., Ashf. 174 BK92
Marlborough Rd., Bexh. 166 EX83
Marlborough Rd., Brwd. 108 FU44
Marlborough Rd., Brom. 204 EJ98
Marlborough Rd., Dag. 126 EV63
Marlborough Rd., Dart. 188 FJ86
Marlborough Rd., Dor. 263 CH136
Marlborough Rd., Felt. 176 BX89
Marlborough Rd., Hmptn. 176 CA93
Marlborough Rd., Islw. 157 CH81
Marlborough Rd., Rich. 178 CL86
Marlborough Rd., Rom. 126 FA56
Marlborough Rd., St.Alb. 43 CE20
Marlborough Rd., Slou. 152 AX77
Marlborough Rd., S.Croy. 220 DQ108
Marlborough Rd., Sthl. 156 BW76
Marlborough Rd., Sutt. 200 DA104
Marlborough Rd., Uxb. 135 BP70
Marlborough Rd., Wat. 75 BV42
Marlborough Rd., Wok. 227 BA116
Marlborough St. SW3 276 B9
Marlborough St. SW3 160 DE77
Marlborough Yd. N19 121 DK61
Marlborough Rd.
Marld, The, Ash. 232 CM118
Marle Gdns., Wal.Abb. 67 EC32
Marler Rd. SE23 183 DY88
Marlescroft Way, Loug. 85 EP43
Marley Ave., Bexh. 166 EX79
Marley Clo. N15 121 DP56
Stanmore Rd.
Marley Clo., Add. 211 BF107
Marley Clo., Grnf. 136 CA69
Marley Ct., Brox. 49 DZ23
Marley Ri., Dor. 263 CG138
Marley Rd., Welw.G.C. 30 DA11
Marley Wk. NW2 119 CW64
Lennon Rd.
Marlin Clo., Berk. 38 AT18
Marlin Clo., Sun. 175 BS93
Marlin Copse, Berk. 38 AU20
Marlin Sq., Abb.L. 59 BT31
Marling Way, Grav. 191 GL92
Marlingdene Clo., Hmptn. 176 CA93
Marlings Clo., Chis. 205 ES98
Marlings Clo., Whyt. 236 DS117
Marlings Pk. Ave., Chis. 205 ES98
Marlins, The, Nthwd. 93 BT50
Marlins Clo., Rick. 73 BE40
Marlins Clo., Sutt. 218 DC106
Turnpike La.
Marlins Meadow, Wat. 75 BR44
Marlins Turn, Hem.H. 40 BH17
Marloes Clo., Wem. 117 CK63
Marloes Rd. W8 160 DB76
Marlow Ave., Purf. 168 FN77
Marlow Clo. SE20 202 DV97
Marlow Ct. NW6 139 CX66
Marlow Ct. NW9 118 CS55
Marlow Cres., Twick. 177 CF86
Marlow Dr., Sutt. 199 CX103
Marlow Gdns., Hayes 155 BR76
Marlow Rd. E6 145 EM69
Marlow Rd. SE20 202 DV97
Marlow Rd., Sthl. 156 BZ76
Marlow Way SE16 163 DX75
Marlowe Clo., Chis. 185 ER93
Marlowe Clo., Ilf. 103 EQ53
Marlowe Gdns. SE9 185 EN86
Marlowe Gdns., Rom. 106 FJ53
Shenstone Gdns.
Marlowe Rd. E17 123 EC56
Marlowe Sq., Mitch. 201 DJ98
Marlowe Way, Croy. 201 DL103
Marlowes, Hem.H. 40 BK21
Marlowes, The NW8 140 DD67
Marlowes, The, Dart. 167 FD84
Marlpit Ave., Couls. 235 DL117
Marlpit La., Couls. 235 DK116
Marlton St. SE10 164 EF78
Woolwich Rd.
Marlwood Clo., Sid. 185 ES89
Marlyns Clo., Guil. 243 BA130
Marlyns Dr., Guil. 243 BA130
Marlyon Rd., Ilf. 104 EV50
Marmadon Rd. SE18 165 ET77
Marmion App. E4 101 EA49
Marmion Ave. E4 101 DZ49
Marmion Clo. E4 101 DZ49
Marmion Ms. SW11 160 DG83
Taybridge Rd.
Marmion Rd. SW11 160 DG84
Marmont Rd. SE15 162 DU81
Marmora Rd. SE22 182 DW86
Marmot Rd., Houns. 156 BX83
Marne Ave. N11 99 DH49
Marne Ave., Well. 166 EU83
Marne St. W10 139 CY69
Marnell Way, Houns. 156 BX83
Marney Rd. SW11 160 DG84
Marneys Clo., Epsom 232 CN115
Marnham Ave. NW2 119 CY63
Marnham Cres., Grnf. 136 CB69
Marnham Ri., Hem.H. 40 BG18
Marnock Rd. SE4 183 DZ85
Maroon St. E14 143 DY71
Maroons Way SE6 183 EA92
Marquess Rd. N1 142 DR65
Marquis Clo., Wem. 138 CM66
Marquis Rd. N4 121 DM60
Marquis Rd. N22 99 DM51
Marquis Rd. NW1 141 DK65
Marrabon Clo., Sid. 186 EU88
Marram Ct., Grays 170 GE79
Medlar Rd.
Marrick Clo. SW15 159 CU84
Marrilyne Ave., Enf. 83 DZ38
Marriot Ter., Rick. 73 BF42
Marriots Clo. NW9 119 CT58
Marriots Way, Hem.H. 40 BK22
Marriott Clo., Felt. 175 BR86
Marriott Lo. Clo., Add. 212 BJ105
Marriott Rd. E15 144 EE67
Marriott Rd. N4 121 DM60
Marriott Rd. N10 98 DF53
Marriott Rd., Barn. 79 CX41
Marriott Rd., Dart. 188 FM87
Marriotts, Harl. 36 EW10
Old Rd.
Marrods Bottom, Beac. 88 AJ47
Marrowells, Wey. 195 BS104
Marryat Pl. SW19 179 CY91
Marryat Rd. SW19 179 CX92
Marryat Rd., Enf. 82 DV35
Marryat Sq. SW6 159 CY81
Marsala Rd. SE13 163 EB84
Marsden Clo., Welw.G.C. 29 CV11
Marsden Grn., Welw.G.C. 29 CV10
Marsden Rd. N9 100 DV47
Marsden Rd. SE15 162 DT83
Marsden Rd., Welw.G.C. 29 CV10
Marsden St. NW5 140 DG65
Marsden Way, Orp. 205 ES104
Marsh Ave., Epsom 216 CS110
Marsh Ave., Mitch. 200 DF96
Marsh Clo. NW7 97 CT48
Marsh Clo., Wal.Cr. 67 DY33
Marsh Ct. SW19 200 DC95
High Path
Marsh Dr. NW9 119 CT58
Marsh Fm. Rd., Twick. 177 CF88
Marsh Grn. Rd., Dag. 146 FA67
Marsh Hill E9 123 DY64
Marsh La. E10 123 EA61
Marsh La. N17 100 DV53
Marsh La. NW7 96 CR49
Marsh La., Add. 212 BH105
Marsh La., Harl. 36 EY10
Marsh La., Maid. 150 AF75
Marsh La., Stan. 95 CJ50
Marsh La., Ware 33 DY07
Marsh La. (Stanstead Abbotts), Ware 33 ED12
Marsh Rd., Pnr. 116 BY56
Marsh Rd., Wem. 137 CK69
Marsh St. E14 163 EB77
Harbinger Rd.
Marsh St., Dart. 168 FN83
Marsh Ter., Orp. 206 EX98
Buttermere Rd.
Marsh Wall E14 143 EA74
Marsh Way, Rain. 147 FD72
Marshall Ave., St.Alb. 43 CE17
Marshall Clo. SW18 180 DC86
Allfarthing La.
Marshall Clo., Har. 117 CD59
Bowen Rd.
Marshall Clo., Houns. 176 BZ85
Marshall Clo., S.Croy. 220 DU113
Marshall Dr., Hayes 135 BT71
Marshall Path SE28 146 EV73
Attlee Rd.
Marshall Pl., Add. 212 BJ109
Marshall Rd. N17 100 DR53
Marshall St. W1 273 L9
Marshall St. W1 141 DJ72
Marshalls Clo. N11 99 DH49
Marshalls Clo., Epsom 216 CQ113
Marshalls Dr., Rom. 127 FE55
Marshall's Gro. SE18 164 EL77
Marshalls Pl. SE16 162 DT76
Spa Rd.
Marshalls Rd., Rom. 127 FD56
Marshall's Rd., Sutt. 218 DB105
Marshals Dr., St.Alb. 43 CF17
Marshalsea Rd. SE1 279 J4
Marshalsea Rd. SE1 162 DQ75
Marshalswick La., St.Alb. 43 CF17
Marsham Clo., Chis. 185 EP92
Marsham La., Ger.Cr. 112 AY58
Marsham Lo., Ger.Cr. 112 AY58
Marsham St. SW1 277 N7
Marsham St. SW1 161 DK76
Marsham Way, Ger.Cr. 112 AY57
Marshbrook Clo. SE3 164 EK83
Marshcroft Dr. (Cheshunt), Wal.Cr. 67 DY30
Marshe Clo., Pot.B. 64 DD32
Marshfield, Slou. 152 AW81
Marshfield St. E14 163 EC76
Marshfoot Rd., Grays 170 GE78
Marshgate, Harl. 35 ES12
School La.
Marshgate Dr., Hert. 32 DS08
Marshgate La. E15 143 EB66
Marshgate Path SE28 165 EQ77
Tom Cribb Rd.
Marshgate Sidings E15 143 EB66
Marshgate La.
Marshmoor Cres., Hat. 45 CX22
Marshmoor La.
Marshmoor Cres. Caravan Pk., Hat. 45 CX22
Marshmoor La., Hat. 45 CW22
Marshside Clo. N9 100 DW46
Marsland Clo. SE17 161 DP78
Marston, Epsom 216 CQ110
Marston Ave., Chess. 216 CL107
Marston Ave., Dag. 126 FA61
Marston Clo. NW6 140 DC66
Fairfax Rd.
Marston Clo., Chesh. 54 AN27
Marston Clo., Dag. 126 FA62
Marston Clo., Hem.H. 40 BN21
Marston Ct., Walt. 196 BW102
St. Johns Dr.
Marston Dr., Warl. 237 DY118
Marston Rd., Hodd. 49 EB16
Marston Rd., Ilf. 102 EL53
Marston Rd., Tedd. 177 CH92
Kingston Rd.
Marston Rd., Wok. 226 AV117
Marston Way SE19 181 DP94
Marsworth Ave., Pnr. 94 BX53
Marsworth Clo., Hayes 136 BY71
Marsworth Clo., Wat. 75 BS44
Mart St. WC2 274 A10
Martaban Rd. N16 122 DT61
Martel Pl. E8 142 DT65
Dalston La.
Martell Rd. SE21 182 DR90
Martello St. E8 142 DV66
Martello Ter. E8 142 DV66
Marten Gate, St.Alb. 43 CG16
Marten Rd. E17 101 EA54
Martens Ave., Bexh. 167 FB84
Martens Clo., Bexh. 167 FC84
Martha Ct. E2 142 DV68
Cambridge Heath Rd.
Martha Rd. E4 101 DZ51
Martha Rd. E15 144 EE65
Martha St. E1 142 DV72
Martham Clo. SE28 146 EX73
Marthorne Cres., Har. 95 CD54
Martian Ave., Hem.H. 40 BM17
Martin Bowes Rd. SE9 165 EM83
Martin Clo. N9 101 DX46
Martin Clo., Hat. 45 CU20
Martin Clo., S.Croy. 221 DX111
Martin Clo., Uxb. 134 BL68
Valley Rd.
Martin Clo., Warl. 236 DV116
Martin Clo., Wind. 150 AJ81
Martin Cres., Croy. 201 DN102
Martin Dale Ind. Est., Enf. 82 DV41
Martin Dene, Bexh. 186 EZ85
Martin Dr., Nthlt. 116 BZ64
Martin Dr., Rain. 147 FH70
Martin Gdns., Dag. 126 EW63
Martin Gro., Mord. 200 DA97
Martin La. EC4 275 L10
Martin Ri., Bexh. 186 EZ85
Martin Rd., Dag. 126 EW63
Martin Rd., Dart. 188 FJ90
Martin Rd., Guil. 242 AU132
Martin Rd., Slou. 152 AS76
Martin Rd., S.Ock. 149 FR74
Martin Way SW20 199 CX96
Martin Way, Mord. 200 DA97
Martin Way, Wok. 226 AU118
Martinbridge Trd. Est., Enf. 82 DU42
Martindale SW14 178 CQ85
Martindale, Iver 133 BD70
Martindale Ave. E16 144 EG73
Martindale Ave., Orp. 224 EU106
Martindale Clo., Guil. 243 BD132
Gilliat Dr.
Martindale Rd. SW12 181 DH87
Martindale Rd., Hem.H. 39 BF19
Martindale Rd., Houns. 156 BY84
Martindale Rd., Wok. 226 AT118
Martineau Clo., Esher 215 CD105
Martineau Dr., Dor. 263 CH138
Martineau Est. E1 142 DW73
Martineau Ms. N5 121 DP63
Martineau Rd.
Martineau Rd. N5 121 DP63
Martineau St. E1 142 DW73
Lukin St.
Martinfield, Welw.G.C. 29 CZ08
Martingale Clo., Sun. 195 BU98
Martingales Clo., Rich. 177 CK90
Martins Clo., Guil. 243 BC133
Martins Clo., Orp. 206 EX97
Martins Clo., Rad. 77 CE36
Martins Clo., W.Wick. 203 ED103
Martins Ct., St.Alb. 43 CH23
Cell Barnes La.
Martins Dr., Hert. 32 DV09
Martins Dr. (Cheshunt), Wal.Cr. 67 DY28
Martins Mt., Barn. 80 DA42
Martins Rd., Brom. 204 EE96
Martins Shaw, Sev. 256 FC122
Martins Wk. N10 98 DG53
Martins Wk., Borwd. 78 CN42
Siskin Clo.
Martinsfield Clo., Chig. 103 ES49
Martinstown Clo., Horn. 128 FN58
Martinsyde, Wok. 227 BC117
Martlesham, Welw.G.C. 30 DE09
Martlesham Clo., Horn. 128 FJ64
Martlet Gro., Nthlt. 136 BX69
Javelin Way
Martlett Ct. WC2 274 A9
Martley Dr., Ilf. 125 EP57
Martock Clo., Har. 117 CG56
Marton Clo. SE6 183 EA90
Marton Rd. N16 122 DS61
Martyr Clo., St.Alb. 43 CD24
Creighton Ave.
Martyr Rd., Guil. 258 AX135
Martyrs La., Wok. 211 BB112
Martys Yd. NW3 120 DD63
Hampstead High St.
Marunde Grn., Slou. 131 AM69
Marvell Ave., Hayes 135 BU71
Marvels Clo. SE12 184 EH89
Marvels La. SE12 184 EH89
Marville Rd. SW6 159 CZ80
Marvin St. E8 142 DV65
Sylvester Rd.
Marwell, West. 255 EP126
Marwell Clo., Rom. 127 FG58
Marwell Clo., W.Wick. 204 EF103
Deer Pk. Way
Marwood Clo., Kings L. 58 BN29
Marwood Clo., Well. 166 EV83
Marwood Way SE16 162 DV78
Catlin St.
Mary Adelaide Clo. SW15 178 CS91
Mary Ann Gdns. SE8 163 EA79
Mary Clo., Stan. 118 CM56
Mary Datchelor Clo. SE5 162 DR81
Mary Gardener Dr. SE9 185 EM89
Mary Grn. NW8 140 DB67
Mary Hill Clo., Ken. 236 DQ117
Mary Kingsley Ct. N19 121 DL59
Hillrise Rd.
Mary Lawrenson Pl. SE3 164 EG80
Heathway
Mary Macarthur Ho. W6 159 CY79
Field Rd.
Mary Morgan Ct., Slou. 131 AR71
Douglas Rd.
Mary Peters Dr., Grnf. 117 CD64
Mary Pl. W11 139 CY73
Mary Rd., Guil. 258 AW135
Mary Rose Clo., Hmptn. 196 CA95
Ashley Rd.
Mary Rose Mall E6 145 EN71
Frobisher Rd.
Mary Rose Way N20 98 DD46
Mary Seacole Clo. E8 142 DT67
Clarissa St.
Mary St. E16 144 EF71
Barking Rd.
Mary St. N1 142 DQ67
Mary Ter. NW1 141 DH67
Arlington Rd.
Maryatt Ave., Har. 116 CB61
Marybank SE18 165 EM77
Maryfield Clo., Bex. 187 FE90
Marygold Wk., Amer. 72 AV39
Maryland, Hat. 45 CT18
Maryland Convent, St.Alb. 43 CD18
Maryland Pk. E15 124 EE64
Maryland Pt. E15 144 EE65
Leytonstone Rd.
Maryland Rd. E15 123 ED64
Maryland Rd. N22 99 DM51
Maryland Rd., Th.Hth. 201 DP95
Maryland Sq. E15 124 EE64
Maryland St. E15 123 ED64
Maryland Wk. N1 142 DQ67
Popham St.
Maryland Way, Sun. 195 BU96
Marylands Rd. W9 140 DA70
Marylebone Flyover NW1 272 B7
Marylebone Flyover W2 272 A7
Marylebone High St. W1 272 G6
Marylebone High St. W1 140 DG71
Marylebone La. W1 272 G7
Marylebone La. W1 140 DG72
Marylebone Ms. W1 273 H7
Marylebone Ms. W1 141 DH71
Marylebone Pas. W1 273 L8
Marylebone Rd. NW1 272 E6
Marylebone Rd. NW1 140 DE71
Marylebone St. W1 272 G7
Marylebone St. W1 140 DG71
Marylee Way SE11 278 C10
Marylee Way SE11 161 DM77
Maryon Gro. SE7 164 EL77
Maryon Ms. NW3 120 DE63
South End Rd.
Maryon Rd. SE7 164 EL77
Maryon Rd. SE18 164 EL77
Mary's Clo. N17 100 DT53
Kemble Rd.
Mary's Ter., Twick. 177 CG87
Maryside, Slou. 152 AY75
Masbro Rd. W14 159 CX76
Mascalls Ct. SE7 164 EJ79
Victoria Way
Mascalls Gdns., Brwd. 108 FT49
Mascalls La., Brwd. 108 FT49
Mascalls Rd. SE7 164 EJ79
Mascotte Rd. SW15 159 CX84
Mascotts Clo. NW2 119 CV62
Masefield Ave., Borwd. 78 CP43
Masefield Ave., Sthl. 136 CA73
Masefield Ave., Stan. 95 CF50
Masefield Clo., Chesh. 54 AP28
Masefield Clo., Erith 167 FF81
Masefield Clo., Rom. 106 FJ53
Masefield Ct., Brwd. 108 FW49
Masefield Cres. N14 81 DJ43
Masefield Cres., Rom. 106 FJ53
Masefield Dr., Upmin. 128 FQ59
Masefield Gdns. E6 145 EN70
Masefield La., Hayes 135 BV70
Masefield Rd., Dart. 188 FP85
Masefield Rd., Grav. 190 GD90
Masefield Rd., Grays 170 GE75
Masefield Rd., Hmptn. 176 BZ91
Wordsworth Rd.
Masefield Vw., Orp. 205 EQ104
Masefield Way, Stai. 174 BM88
Mashie Rd. W3 138 CS72
Mashiters Hill, Rom. 105 FD54
Mashiters Wk., Rom. 127 FE55
Maskall Clo. SW2 181 DN88
Maskani Wk. SW16 181 DJ94
Bates Cres.
Maskell Rd. SW17 180 DC90
Maskelyne Clo. SW11 160 DE81
Mason Bradbear Ct. N1 142 DR65
St. Paul's Rd.
Mason Clo. E16 144 EG73
Mason Clo. SE16 162 DU78
Stevenson Cres.
Mason Clo. SW20 199 CX95
Mason Clo., Bexh. 167 FB83
Mason Clo., Borwd. 78 CR40
Mason Clo., Hmptn. 196 BZ95
Mason Ct., Slou. 131 AL73
Mason Dr., Rom. 106 FL54
Whitmore Ave.
Mason Rd., Wdf.Grn. 102 EE49
Mason St. SE17 279 L8
Mason St. SE17 162 DR77
Mason Way, Wal.Abb. 68 EE33
Masonic Hall Rd., Cher. 193 BF100
Masons Arms Ms. W1 273 J10
Masons Ave. EC2 275 K8
Masons Ave., Croy. 202 DQ104
Masons Ave., Har. 117 CF56
Masons Bri. Rd., Red. 267 DH139
Masons Ct., Wem. 118 CN61
Mayfields
Masons Grn. La. W3 138 CN70
Dukes Rd.
Masons Hill SE18 165 EP77
Masons Hill, Brom. 204 EG97
Masons Paddock, Dor. 247 CG134
Mason's Pl. EC1 275 H2
Mason's Pl. EC1 142 DQ69
Masons Pl., Mitch. 200 DF95
Masons Rd., Enf. 82 DV36
Masons Rd., Hem.H. 41 BP19
Masons Rd., Slou. 131 AL73
Mason's Yd. SW1 277 L2
Mason's Yd. SW19 179 CX92
High St. Wimbledon
Massetts Rd., Horl. 268 DF149
Massey Clo. N11 99 DH50
Grove Rd.
Massie Rd. E8 142 DU65
Graham Rd.
Massinger St. SE17 279 M9
Massingham St. E1 143 DX70
Masson Ave., Ruis. 136 BW65
Mast Ho. Ter. E14 163 EA77
Master Clo., Oxt. 254 EE129
Church La.
Master Gunner Pl. SE18 164 EL80
Masterman Ho. SE5 162 DR80
Lomond Gro.
Masterman Rd. E6 144 EL69
Masters St. E1 143 DX71
Masthead Clo., Dart. 168 FQ84
Mastmaker Rd. E14 163 EA75
Maswell Pk. Cres., Houns. 176 CC85
Maswell Pk. Rd., Houns. 176 CB85
Matcham Rd. E11 124 EE62
Matching Rd., B.Stort. 37 FH05
Matching Rd. (Old Harlow), Harl. 37 FB11
Matching Rd., Ong. 53 FH17
Matchless Dr. SE18 165 EN80
Matfield Clo., Brom. 204 EG99
Matfield Rd., Belv. 166 FA79
Matham Gro. SE22 162 DT84
Matham Rd., E.Mol. 197 CD99
Matheson Rd. W14 159 CZ77
Mathews Pk. Ave. E15 144 EF65
Mathias Clo., Epsom 216 CQ113
Mathisen Way, Slou. 153 BE81
Mathon Ct., Guil. 243 AZ134
Cross Las.
Matilda St. N1 141 DM67
Matlock Clo. SE24 162 DQ84
Matlock Clo., Barn. 79 CX44
Matlock Ct. SE5 162 DR84
Denmark Hill Est.
Matlock Cres., Sutt. 217 CY105
Matlock Cres., Wat. 94 BW48
Matlock Gdns., Horn. 128 FL62
Matlock Gdns., Sutt. 217 CY105
Matlock Pl., Sutt. 217 CY105
Matlock Rd. E10 123 EC58
Matlock Rd., Cat. 236 DS121
Matlock St. E14 143 DY72
Matlock Way, N.Mal. 198 CR95
Matrimony Pl. SW8 161 DJ82
Wandsworth Rd.
Matson Ct., Wdf.Grn. 102 EE52
Bridle Path
Matthew Arnold Clo., Cob. 213 BU114
Matthew Arnold Clo., Stai. 174 BJ93
Elizabeth Ave.
Matthew Clo. W10 139 CX70
Matthew Ct., Mitch. 201 DK99
Matthew Parker St. SW1 277 N5
Matthew Parker St. SW1 161 DK75
Matthew Rd., Red. 250 DF133
Matthews Ave. E6 145 EN68
Matthews Clo. (Havering-atte-Bower), Rom. 106 FM53
Oak Rd.
Matthews Gdns., Croy. 221 ED111
Matthews Rd., Grnf. 117 CD64
Matthews St. SW11 160 DF82
Matthews St., Reig. 266 DA138
Matthews Yd. WC2 273 P9
Matthias Rd. N16 122 DR64
Mattingley Way SE15 162 DT80
Daniel Gdns.
Mattison Rd. N4 121 DN58
Mattock La. W5 137 CJ74
Mattock La. W13 137 CH74
Maud Cashmore Way SE18 165 EM76

Maud Gdns. E13 144 EF67
Maud Gdns., Bark. 145 ET68
Maud Rd. E10 123 EC62
Maud Rd. E13 144 EF68
Maud St. E16 144 EF71
Maude Cres., Wat. 75 BV37
Maude Rd. E17 123 DY57
Maude Rd. SE5 162 DS81
Maude Rd., Beac. 89 AN54
Maude Rd., Swan. 187 FG93
Maude Ter. E17 123 DY56
Maudlin's Grn. E1 142 DU74
Marble Quay
Maudslay Rd. SE9 165 EM83
Maudsley Ho., Brent. 158 CL78
Mauleverer Rd. SW2 181 DL85
Maundeby Wk. NW10 138 CS65
Neasden La.
Maunder Rd. W7 137 CE74
Maunsel St. SW1 277 M8
Maunsel St. SW1 161 DK77
Maurice Ave. N22 99 DP54
Maurice Ave., Cat. 236 DR122
Maurice Brown Clo. NW7 97 CX50
Maurice St. W12 139 CV72
Maurice Wk. NW11 120 DC56
Maurier Clo., Nthlt. 136 BW67
Mauritius Rd. SE10 164 EE77
Maury Rd. N16 122 DU61
Mavelstone Clo., Brom. 204 EL95
Mavelstone Rd., Brom. 204 EK95
Maverton Rd. E3 143 EA67
Mavis Ave., Epsom 216 CS106
Mavis Clo., Epsom 216 CS106
Mavis Gro., Horn. 128 FL61
Mavis Wk. E6 144 EL71
Tollgate Rd.
Mawbey Est. SE1 162 DT78
Mawbey Pl. SE1 162 DT78
Mawbey Rd. SE1 162 DT78
Old Kent Rd.
Mawbey Rd., Cher. 211 BD107
Mawbey St. SW8 161 DL80
Mawney Clo., Rom. 105 FB54
Mawney Rd., Rom. 105 FB54
Mawson Clo. SW20 199 CY96
Mawson La. W4 159 CT79
Great W. Rd.
Maxey Gdns., Dag. 126 EY63
Maxey Rd. SE18 165 EQ77
Maxey Rd., Dag. 126 EY64
Maxfield Clo. N20 98 DC45
Maxilla Gdns. W10 139 CX72
Cambridge Gdns.
Maxilla Wk. W10 139 CX72
Kingsdown Clo.
Maxim Rd. N21 81 DN44
Maxim Rd., Dart. 187 FE85
Maxim Rd., Erith 167 FE77
Maximfeldt Rd., Erith 167 FE78
Maxted Clo., Hem.H. 41 BQ18
Maxted Pk., Har. 117 CE59
Maxted Rd. SE15 162 DT83
Maxted Rd., Hem.H. 41 BP17
Maxwell Clo., Croy. 201 DL101
Maxwell Clo., Rick. 92 BG47
Maxwell Dr., W.Byf. 212 BJ111
Maxwell Gdns., Orp. 205 ET104
Maxwell Ri., Wat. 94 BY45
Maxwell Rd. SW6 160 DB80
Maxwell Rd., Ashf. 175 BQ93
Maxwell Rd., Beac. 89 AK52
Maxwell Rd., Borwd. 78 CP41
Maxwell Rd., Nthwd. 93 BR52
Maxwell Rd., St.Alb. 43 CH21
Maxwell Rd., Well. 166 EU83
Maxwell Rd., West Dr. 154 BM77
Maxwelton Ave. NW7 96 CR50
Maxwelton Clo. NW7 96 CR50
May Ave., Grav. 191 GF88
Dover Rd. E.
May Ave., Orp. 206 EV99
May Clo., Chess. 216 CM107
May Clo., St.Alb. 43 CD18
May Cotts., Wat. 76 BW43
Watford Fld. Rd.
May Ct. SW19 200 DB95
May Ct., Grays 170 GE79
Medlar Rd.
May Gdns., Wem. 137 CJ69
May Rd. E4 101 EA51
May Rd. E13 144 EG68
May Rd., Dart. 188 FM91
May Rd., Twick. 177 CE88
May St. W14 159 CZ78
North End Rd.
May Tree La., Stan. 95 CF52
May Wk. E13 144 EH68
Queens Rd. W.
Maya Rd. N2 120 DC56
Mayall Rd. SE24 181 DP85
Maybank Ave. E18 102 EH54
Maybank Ave., Horn. 128 FJ64
Maybank Ave., Wem. 117 CF64
Maybank Gdns., Pnr. 115 BU57
Maybank Lo., Horn. 128 FJ64
Maybank Rd. E18 102 EH53
Maybells Commercial Est., Bark. 146 EX68
Mayberry Pl., Surb. 198 CM101
Maybourne Clo. SE26 182 DV92
Maybourne Ri., Wok. 226 AX124
Maybrick Rd., Horn. 128 FJ57
Maybrook Meadow Est., Bark. 126 EU64
Maybury Ave., Dart. 188 FQ88
Maybury Ave. (Cheshunt), Wal.Cr. 66 DV28
Maybury Clo., Loug. 85 EP42
Maybury Clo., Orp. 205 EP99
Maybury Clo., Slou. 131 AK72
Maybury Clo., Tad. 233 CY119
Ballards Grn.
Maybury Gdns. NW10 139 CV65
Maybury Hill, Wok. 227 BB116
Maybury Ms. N6 121 DJ59
Maybury Rd. E13 144 EJ70
Maybury Rd., Bark. 145 ET68
Maybury Rd., Wok. 227 AZ117
Maybury St. SW17 180 DE92
Maybush Rd., Horn. 128 FL59
Maychurch Clo., Stan. 95 CK52
Maycock Gro., Nthwd. 93 BT51
Maycroft, Pnr. 93 BV54
Maycroft Ave., Grays 170 GD78
Maycroft Gdns., Grays 170 GD78
Maycroft Rd. (Cheshunt), Wal.Cr. 66 DS26
Maycross Ave., Mord. 199 CZ97
Mayday Gdns. SE3 164 EL82
Mayday Rd., Th.Hth. 201 DP100
Maydwell Lo., Borwd. 78 CM40
Mayell Clo., Lthd. 231 CJ123
Mayerne Rd. SE9 184 EK85
Mayes Clo., Swan. 207 FG98
Mayes Clo., Warl. 237 DX118
Mayes Rd. N22 99 DM54
Mayesbrook Rd., Bark. 145 ET67
Mayesbrook Rd., Dag. 126 EV62
Mayesbrook Rd., Ilf. 126 EU62
Mayesford Rd., Rom. 126 EW59
Mayeswood Rd. SE12 184 EJ90
Mayfair Ave., Bexh. 166 EX83
Mayfair Ave., Ilf. 125 EM61
Mayfair Ave., Rom. 126 EX58
Mayfair Ave., Twick. 176 CC87
Mayfair Ave., Wor.Pk. 199 CT102
Mayfair Clo., Beck. 203 EB95
Mayfair Clo., St.Alb. 43 CJ15
Mayfair Clo., Surb. 198 CL102
Mayfair Gdns. N17 100 DQ51
Mayfair Gdns., Wdf.Grn. 102 EG52
Mayfair Ms. NW1 140 DF66
Regents Pk. Rd.
Mayfair Pl. W1 277 J2
Mayfair Pl. W1 141 DH74
Mayfair Rd., Dart. 188 FK85
Mayfair Ter. N14 99 DK45
Mayfare, Rick. 75 BR43
Mayfield, Bexh. 166 EZ83
Mayfield, Wal.Abb. 67 ED34
Roundhills
Mayfield, Welw.G.C. 29 CW05
Mayfield Ave. N12 98 DC49
Mayfield Ave. N14 99 DJ47
Mayfield Ave. W4 158 CS77
Mayfield Ave. W13 157 CH76
Mayfield Ave., Add. 212 BH110
Mayfield Ave., Ger.Cr. 112 AX56
Mayfield Ave., Har. 117 CH57
Mayfield Ave., Orp. 205 ET101
Mayfield Ave., Wdf.Grn. 102 EG51
Mayfield Clo. E8 142 DT65
Forest Rd.
Mayfield Clo. SW4 181 DK85
Mayfield Clo., Add. 212 BJ110
Mayfield Clo., Ashf. 175 BP93
Mayfield Clo., Harl. 36 EZ11
Mayfield Clo., Red. 266 DG140
Brookfield Clo.
Mayfield Clo., T.Ditt. 197 CH102
Mayfield Clo., Uxb. 135 BP69
Mayfield Clo., Walt. 213 BU105
Mayfield Cres. N9 82 DV44
Mayfield Cres., Th.Hth. 201 DM98
Mayfield Dr., Pnr. 116 BZ56
Mayfield Gdns. NW4 119 CX58
Mayfield Gdns. W7 137 CD72
Mayfield Gdns., Brwd. 108 FV46
Mayfield Gdns., Stai. 173 BF93
Mayfield Gdns., Walt. 213 BU105
Mayfield Rd. E4 101 EC47
Mayfield Rd. E8 142 DT66
Mayfield Rd. E13 144 EF70
Mayfield Rd. E17 101 DY54
Mayfield Rd. N8 121 DM57
Mayfield Rd. SW19 199 CZ95
Mayfield Rd. W3 138 CP73
Mayfield Rd. W12 158 CS75
Mayfield Rd., Belv. 167 FC77
Mayfield Rd., Brom. 204 EL99
Mayfield Rd., Dag. 126 EW60
Mayfield Rd., Enf. 83 DX40
Mayfield Rd., Grav. 191 GF87
Mayfield Rd., H.Wyc. 110 AE57
Mayfield Rd., S.Croy. 220 DR109
Mayfield Rd., Sutt. 218 DD107
Mayfield Rd., Th.Hth. 201 DM98
Mayfield Rd., Walt. 213 BU105
Mayfield Rd., Wey. 212 BM106
Mayfields, Grays 170 GC75
Mayfields, Swans. 190 FY86
Madden Clo.
Mayfields, Wem. 118 CN61
Mayfields Clo., Wem. 118 CN61
Mayflower Ave., Hem.H. 40 BK20
Mayflower Clo. SE16 163 DX77
Greenland Quay
Mayflower Clo., Hert. 31 DL11
Mayflower Clo., S.Ock. 149 FW70
Mayflower Clo., Wal.Abb. 50 EE22
Mayflower Ct. SE16 162 DW75
St. Marychurch St.
Mayflower Path, Brwd. 107 FW51
Eagle Way
Mayflower Rd. SW9 161 DL83
Mayflower Rd., Grays 169 FW78
Mayflower Rd., St.Alb. 60 CB27
Mayflower St. SE16 162 DW75
Mayflower Way, Beac. 110 AG55
Mayflower Way, Slou. 111 AR63
Mayfly Clo., Pnr. 116 BW59
Mayfly Gdns., Nthlt. 136 BX69
Ruislip Rd.
Mayford Clo. SW12 180 DF87
Mayford Clo., Beck. 203 DX97
Mayford Clo., Wok. 226 AX122
Mayford Rd. SW12 180 DF87
Maygood St. N1 141 DM68
Maygoods Clo., Uxb. 134 BK71
Maygoods Grn., Uxb. 134 BK71
Worcester Rd.
Maygoods La., Uxb. 134 BK71
Maygoods Vw., Uxb. 134 BJ71
Benbow Waye
Maygreen Cres., Horn. 127 FG59
Maygrove Rd. NW6 139 CZ65
Mayhall La., Amer. 55 AP35
Mayhew Clo. E4 101 EA48
Mayhill Rd. SE7 164 EH79
Mayhill Rd., Barn. 79 CY43
Maylands Ave., Hem.H. 41 BP17
Maylands Ave., Horn. 127 FH63
Maylands Dr., Sid. 186 EX90
Maylands Dr., Uxb. 134 BK65
Maylands Rd., Wat. 94 BW49
Maylands Way, Rom. 106 FQ51
Maylins Dr., Saw. 36 EX05
Maynard Clo. N15 122 DS56
Brunswick Rd.
Maynard Clo. SW6 160 DB80
Cambria St.
Maynard Clo., Erith 167 FF80
Maynard Ct., Wal.Abb. 68 EF34
Maynard Dr., St.Alb. 43 CD23
Maynard Path E17 123 EC57
Maynard Rd.
Maynard Pl., Pot.B. 65 DM29
Maynard Rd. E17 123 EC57
Maynard Rd., Hem.H. 40 BK21
Maynards, Horn. 128 FL59
Maynards Quay E1 142 DW73
Garnet St.
Mayne Ave., St.Alb. 42 BZ22
Maynooth Gdns., Cars. 200 DF101
Middleton Rd.
Mayo Clo. (Cheshunt), Wal.Cr. 66 DV28
Mayo Rd. NW10 138 CS65
Mayo Rd., Croy. 202 DR99
Mayo Rd., Walt. 195 BT101
Mayola Rd. E5 122 DW63
Mayor's La., Dart. 188 FJ92
Mayow Rd. SE23 183 DX90
Mayow Rd. SE26 183 DX91
Mayplace Ave., Dart. 167 FG84
Mayplace Clo., Bexh. 167 FB83
Mayplace La. SE18 165 EP80
Mayplace Rd. E., Bexh. 167 FB83
Mayplace Rd. E., Dart. 167 FE84
Mayplace Rd. W., Bexh. 166 FA84
Maypole Cres., Erith 168 FK79
Maypole Cres., Ilf. 103 ER52
Maypole Dr., Chig. 104 EU48
Maypole Rd., Grav. 191 GM88
Maypole Rd., Maid. 130 AG71
Maypole Rd., Orp. 224 EZ106
Mayroyd Ave., Surb. 198 CN103
Mays Clo., Wey. 212 BM110
Mays Ct. WC2 277 P1
Mays Gro., Wok. 227 BD123
Mays Hill Rd., Brom. 204 EE96
Mays La. E4 101 ED47
Mays La., Barn. 97 CU45
Mays Rd., Tedd. 177 CD92
Maysfield Rd., Wok. 227 BD123
Maysoule Rd. SW11 160 DD84
Mayswood Gdns., Dag. 147 FC65
Maythorne Clo., Wat. 75 BS42
Mayton St. N7 121 DM62
Maytree Clo., Edg. 96 CQ48
Maytree Clo., Guil. 242 AW131
Maytree Clo., Rain. 147 FE68
Maytree Cres., Wat. 75 BT35
Maytree Wk. SW2 181 DN89
Kingsmead Rd.
Maytrees, Rad. 77 CG37
Mayville Est. N16 122 DS64
King Henry St.
Mayville Rd. E11 124 EE61
Mayville Rd., Ilf. 125 EP64
Maywater Clo., S.Croy. 220 DR111
Maywin Dr., Horn. 128 FM60
Maywood Clo., Beck. 183 EB94
Maze Hill SE3 164 EE80
Maze Hill SE10 164 EE79
Maze Rd., Rich. 158 CN80
Mazenod Ave. NW6 140 DA66
McAdam Clo., Hodd. 49 EA15
McAdam Dr., Enf. 81 DP40
Rowantree Rd.
McAuley Clo. SE1 278 D6
McAuley Clo. SE1 161 DN76
McAuley Clo. SE9 185 EP85
McAuliffe Dr., Slou. 111 AM63
McCall Clo. SW4 161 DL82
Jeffreys Rd.
McCall Cres. SE7 164 EL78
McCarthy Rd., Felt. 176 BX92
McCoid Way SE1 279 H5
McCrone Ms. NW3 140 DD65
Belsize La.
McCudden Rd., Dart. 168 FM83
Cornwall Rd.
McCullum Rd. E3 143 DZ67
McDermott Clo. SW11 160 DE83
McDermott Rd. SE15 162 DU83
McDonald Ct., Hat. 45 CU20
McDonough Clo., Chess. 216 CL105
McDowall Rd. SE5 162 DQ81
McDowell Clo. E16 144 EF71
McEntee Ave. E17 101 DY53
McEwan Way E15 143 ED67
McGrath Rd. E15 124 EF64
McGredy (Cheshunt), Wal.Cr. 66 DV29
McGregor Rd. W11 139 CZ71
McIntosh Clo., Rom. 127 FE55
McIntosh Clo., Wall. 219 DL108
McIntosh Rd., Rom. 127 FE55
McKay Rd. SW20 179 CV94
McKay Trd. Est., Slou. 153 BE82
McKellar Clo. (Bushey), Wat. 94 CC47
McKenzie Rd., Brox. 49 DZ20
McKerrell Rd. SE15 162 DU81
McLeod Rd. SE2 166 EU77
McLeod's Ms. SW7 160 DB77
McMillan Clo., Grav. 191 GJ91
McMillan St. SE8 163 EA79
McNeil Rd. SE5 162 DS82
McNicol Dr. NW10 138 CQ68
McRae La., Mitch. 200 DF101
Mead, The N2 98 DC54
Mead, The W13 137 CH71
Mead, The, Ash. 232 CL119
Mead, The, Beac. 89 AL53
Mead, The, Beck. 203 EC95
Mead, The, Stan. 95 CJ53
Mead, The, Uxb. 114 BN61
Mead, The, Wall. 219 DK107
Mead, The (Cheshunt), Wal.Cr. 66 DW29
Mead, The, Wat. 94 BY48
Mead, The, W.Wick. 203 ED102
Mead Ave., Red. 266 DG142
Mead Ave., Slou. 153 BB75
Mead Business Pk., Hert. 32 DS08
Mead Clo., Egh. 173 BB93
Mead Clo., Grays 170 GB75
Mead Clo., Har. 95 CD53
Mead Clo., Loug. 85 EP40
Mead Clo., Red. 250 DG131
Mead Clo., Rom. 105 FG54
Mead Clo., Slou. 153 BB75
Mead Clo., Swan. 207 FG99
Mead Clo., Uxb. 114 BG61
Mead Ct. NW9 118 CQ57
Mead Ct., Egh. 173 BC93
Holbrook Meadow
Mead Ct., Wal.Abb. 67 EB34
Mead Ct., Wok. 226 AS116
Mead Cres. E4 101 EC49
Mead Cres., Dart. 188 FK88
Beech Rd.
Mead Cres., Lthd. 246 CA125
Mead Cres., Sutt. 218 DE105
Mead End, Ash. 232 CM117
Mead Gro., Rom. 126 EX55
Mead Ho. Rd., Hayes 135 BR70
Mead La., Cher. 194 BJ102
Mead La., Hert. 32 DS08
Mead La. Caravan Pk., Cher. 194 BJ102
Mead Pk. Est., Harl. 35 ET11
Mead Path SW17 180 DC91
Mead Pl. E9 142 DW65
Mead Pl., Croy. 201 DP102
Mead Pl., Rick. 92 BH46
Mead Plat NW10 138 CQ65
Mead Rd., Cat. 236 DT123
Mead Rd., Chis. 185 EQ93
Mead Rd., Dart. 188 FK88
Mead Rd., Edg. 96 CN51
Mead Rd., Grav. 191 GH89
Mead Rd., Rad. 62 CN33
Mead Rd., Rich. 177 CJ90
Mead Rd., Uxb. 134 BK65
Mead Rd., Walt. 214 BY105
Mead Row SE1 278 D6
Mead Wk., Slou. 153 BB75
Mead Way, Brom. 204 EE100
Mead Way, Couls. 235 DL118
Mead Way, Croy. 203 DY103
Mead Way, Slou. 131 AK71
Mead Way (Bushey), Wat. 76 BY40
Meadcroft Rd. SE11 161 DP79
Meade Clo. W4 158 CN79
Meade Ct., Tad. 233 CU124
Meades, The, Wey. 213 BR107
Meades La., Chesh. 54 AP32
Meadfield, Edg. 96 CP47
Meadfield Ave., Slou. 153 BA75
Meadfield Grn., Edg. 96 CP47
Meadfield Rd., Slou. 153 BA76
Meadfoot Rd. SW16 181 DJ94
Meadgate Ave., Wdf.Grn. 102 EL50
Meadgate Rd., Brox. 49 ED20
Meadhurst Rd., Cher. 194 BH102
Meadlands Dr., Rich. 177 CK89
Meadow, The, Chis. 185 EQ93
Meadow, The, Hert. 33 DY13
Meadow Ave., Croy. 203 DX100
Meadow Bank N21 81 DM44
Meadow Bungalows, Guil. 259 BB140
Meadow Clo. E4 101 EB46
Mount Echo Ave.
Meadow Clo. E9 123 DZ64
Meadow Clo. SE6 183 EA92
Meadow Clo. SW20 199 CW98
Meadow Clo., Barn. 79 CZ44
Meadow Clo., Bexh. 186 EZ85
Meadow Clo., Chesh. 54 AN27
Little Hivings
Meadow Clo., Chis. 185 EP92
Meadow Clo., Enf. 83 DY38
Meadow Clo., Esher 197 CF104
Meadow Clo., Gdmg. 258 AS144
Meadow Clo., Hat. 45 CX24
Meadow Clo., Hert. 32 DT08
Meadow Clo., Houns. 176 CA86
Meadow Clo., Nthlt. 136 CA68
Meadow Clo., Pur. 219 DK113
Meadow Clo., Rich. 178 CL88
Meadow Clo., Ruis. 115 BT58
Meadow Clo., St.Alb. 43 CJ17
Meadow Clo. (Bricket Wd.), St.Alb. 60 CA29
Meadow Clo. (London Colney), St.Alb. 61 CK27
Meadow Clo., Sev. 256 FG123
Meadow Clo., Sutt. 200 DB103
Aultone Way
Meadow Clo., Walt. 214 BZ105
Meadow Clo., Wind. 172 AV86
Meadow Cotts., Beac. 89 AL54
Meadow Ct., Epsom 216 CQ113
Meadow Ct., Harl. 51 ES19
Lodge Hall
Meadow Ct., Stai. 173 BE90
Moor La.
Meadow Cft., Hat. 45 CT18
Meadow Dell, Hat. 45 CT18
Meadow Dr. N10 120 DG55
Meadow Dr. NW4 97 CW54
Meadow Dr., Amer. 55 AS37
Meadow Dr., Wok. 227 BF123
Meadow Gdns., Edg. 96 CP51
Meadow Gdns., Stai. 173 BD92
Meadow Garth NW10 138 CQ65
Meadow Grn., Welw.G.C. 29 CW09
Meadow Hill, N.Mal. 198 CS100
Meadow Hill, Pur. 219 DJ113
Meadow La., Beac. 89 AM53
Meadow La., Cars. 200 DE103
Meadow La., Lthd. 230 CC121
Meadow La. (Eton), Wind. 151 AQ80
Meadow Ms. SW8 161 DM79
Meadow Pl. SW8 161 DL80
Meadow Pl. W4 158 CS80
Edensor Rd.
Meadow Ri., Couls. 219 DK113
Meadow Rd. SW8 161 DM80
Meadow Rd. SW19 180 DC94
Meadow Rd., Ashf. 175 BR92
Meadow Rd., Ash. 232 CL117
Meadow Rd., Bark. 145 ET66
Meadow Rd., Berk. 38 AU17
Meadow Rd., Borwd. 78 CP40
Meadow Rd., Brom. 204 EE95
Meadow Rd., Dag. 146 EZ65
Meadow Rd., Epp. 69 ET29
Meadow Rd., Esher 215 CE106
Meadow Rd., Felt. 176 BY89
Meadow Rd., Grav. 191 GG89
Meadow Rd., Guil. 243 BA130
Meadow Rd., Hem.H. 40 BN24
Meadow Rd., Loug. 84 EL43
Meadow Rd., Pnr. 116 BX56
Meadow Rd., Rom. 127 FC60
Meadow Rd., Slou. 152 AY76
Meadow Rd., Sthl. 136 BZ73
Meadow Rd., Sutt. 218 DE106
Meadow Rd., Vir.W. 192 AS99
Meadow Rd., Wat. 59 BU34
Meadow Rd. (Bushey), Wat. 76 CB43
Meadow Row SE1 279 H7
Meadow Row SE1 162 DQ76
Meadow Stile, Croy. 202 DQ104
High St.
Meadow Vw., Ch.St.G. 90 AU48
Meadow Vw., Har. 117 CE60
Meadow Vw., Sid. 186 EV87
Meadow Vw., Stai. 173 BF85
Meadow Vw. Rd., Hayes 135 BQ70
Meadow Vw. Rd., Th.Hth. 201 DP99
Meadow Wk. E18 124 EG56
Meadow Wk., Dag. 146 EZ65
Meadow Wk., Dart. 188 FJ91
Meadow Wk., Epsom 216 CS107
Meadow Wk., H.Wyc. 88 AC46
Meadow Wk., Tad. 233 CV124
Meadow Wk., Wall. 201 DH104
Meadow Way NW9 118 CR57
Meadow Way, Abb.L. 59 BT27
Meadow Way, Add. 212 BH105
Meadow Way, Chess. 216 CL106
Meadow Way, Chig. 103 EQ48
Meadow Way, Dart. 188 FQ87
Meadow Way, Hem.H. 39 BF23
Meadow Way, Kings L. 58 BN30
Meadow Way (Great Bookham), Lthd. 230 CB123
Meadow Way (West Horsley), Lthd. 245 BR125
Meadow Way (Dorney Reach), Maid. 150 AF75
Meadow Way (Fifield), Maid. 150 AD81
Meadow Way, Orp. 205 EN104
Meadow Way, Pot.B. 64 DA34
Meadow Way, Reig. 266 DB138
Meadow Way, Rick. 92 BJ45
Meadow Way, Ruis. 115 BV58
Meadow Way, Saw. 36 FA06
Meadow Way, Tad. 233 CY117
Meadow Way, Upmin. 128 FQ62
Meadow Way, Wem. 117 CK63
Meadow Way, Wind. 172 AV86
Meadow Way, The, Har. 95 CE53
Meadow Waye, Houns. 156 BY79
Meadowbank NW3 140 DF66
Meadowbank SE3 164 EF83
Meadowbank, Kings L. 58 BN30
Meadowbank, Lthd. 245 BS127
Meadowbank, Surb. 198 CM100
Meadowbank, Wat. 94 BW45
Meadowbank Clo. SW6 159 CW80
Meadowbank Clo., Barn. 79 CT43
Meadowbank Gdns., Houns. 155 BU81
Meadowbank Rd. NW9 118 CR59
Meadowbanks, Barn. 79 CU43
Barnet Rd.
Meadowbrook, Oxt. 253 EC130
Meadowbrook Clo., Slou. 153 BF81
Meadowbrook Rd., Dor. 263 CG135
Meadowcot La., Amer. 55 AM44
Meadowcourt Rd. SE3 164 EF84
Meadowcroft, Brom. 205 EM97
Meadowcroft, Ger.Cr. 90 AX54
Meadowcroft, St.Alb. 43 CG23
Meadowcroft (Bushey), Wat. 76 CB44
Meadowcroft Clo., Horl. 269 DJ151
Meadowcroft Rd. N13 99 DN47
Meadowcross, Wal.Abb. 68 EE34
Meadowlands, Cob. 213 BU113
Meadowlands, Guil. 244 BH130
Meadowlands, Horn. 128 FL59
Meadowlands, Oxt. 254 EG134
Meadowlands Pk., Add. 194 BL104
Meadowlea Clo., West Dr. 154 BK79
Meadows, The, Amer. 55 AS39
Meadows, The, Guil. 258 AW137
Meadows, The, Hem.H. 39 BE19
Meadows, The, Orp. 224 EW107
Meadows, The, Saw. 36 FA05
Meadows, The, Sev. 224 EZ113
Meadows, The, Warl. 237 DX117
Meadows, The, Welw.G.C. 30 DC09
Meadows Clo. E10 123 EA61
Meadows End, Sun. 195 BU95
Meadows Leigh Clo., Wey. 195 BQ104
Meadowside SE9 164 EJ84
Meadowside, Beac. 90 AT52
Meadowside, Dart. 188 FK88
Meadowside, Horl. 269 DH147
Stockfield
Meadowside, Lthd. 230 CA123
Meadowside, Walt. 196 BW103
Meadowside Rd., Sutt. 217 CY109
Meadowside Rd., Upmin. 128 FQ64
Meadowsweet Clo. E16 144 EK71
Monarch Dr.
Meadowview, Orp. 206 EW97
Meadowview Rd. SE6 183 EA91
Meadowview Rd., Bex. 186 EY86
Meadowview Rd., Epsom 216 CS109
Meads, The, Berk. 38 AS17
Meads, The, Edg. 96 CR51
Meads, The, St.Alb. 60 BZ29
Meads, The, Sutt. 199 CY104
Meads, The, Upmin. 129 FS61
Meads, The, Uxb. 134 BL70
Meads La., Ilf. 125 ES59
Meads Rd. N22 99 DP54
Meads Rd., Enf. 83 DY39
Meads Rd., Guil. 243 BA134
Meadsway, Brwd. 107 FV51
Meadvale Rd. W5 137 CH70
Meadvale Rd., Croy. 202 DT101
Meadview Rd., Ware 33 DX07
Meadway N14 99 DK47
Meadway NW11 120 DB58
Meadway SW20 199 CW98
Meadway, Ashf. 174 BN91
Meadway, Barn. 79 CZ42
Meadway, Beck. 203 EC95
Meadway, Berk. 38 AY18

Meadway, Enf. 82 DW37
Meadway, Epsom 216 CQ113
Meadway, Esher 214 CB109
Meadway, Grays 170 GD77
Meadway, Guil. 243 BC129
Meadway, Hodd. 49 EA19
Meadway, Ilf. 125 ES63
Meadway (Effingham), Lthd. 246 BY128
Meadway (Oxshott), Lthd. 215 CD114
Meadway, Rom. 105 FG54
Meadway, Ruis. 115 BR58
Meadway, St.Alb. 44 CR23
Meadway, Sev. 224 EZ113
Meadway, Stai. 174 BG94
Meadway, Surb. 198 CQ102
Meadway, Twick. 177 CD88
Meadway, Warl. 236 DW116
Meadway, Welw.G.C. 29 CZ11
Meadway, Wdf.Grn. 102 EJ50
Meadway, The SE3 163 ED82
Heath La.
Meadway, The, Buck.H. 102 EK46
Meadway, The, Horl. 269 DJ148
Meadway, The, Loug. 85 EM44
Meadway, The, Orp. 224 EV106
Meadway, The (Cuffley), Pot.B. 65 DM28
Meadway, The, Sev. 256 FF122
Meadway Clo. NW11 120 DB58
Meadway Clo., Barn. 80 DA42
Meadway Clo., Pnr. 94 CB51
Highbanks Rd.
Meadway Clo., Stai. 173 BF94
Meadway Ct. NW11 120 DB58
Meadway Dr., Add. 212 BJ108
Meadway Dr., Wok. 226 AW116
Meadway Gdns., Ruis. 115 BR58
Meadway Gate NW11 120 DA58
Meadway Pk., Ger.Cr. 112 AX60
Meaford Way SE20 182 DV94
Meakin Est. SE1 279 M6
Meakin Est. SE1 162 DS76
Meanley Rd. E12 124 EL63
Meard St. W1 273 M9
Meard St. W1 141 DK72
Meare Clo., Tad. 233 CW123
Meare Est., H.Wyc. 110 AD55
Meath Clo., Orp. 206 EV99
Meath Grn. Ave., Horl. 268 DF146
Meath Grn. La., Horl. 266 DE143
Meath Rd. E15 144 EF68
Meath Rd., Ilf. 125 EQ62
Meath St. SW11 161 DH81
Meautys, St.Alb. 42 BZ22
Mechanics Path SE8 163 EA80
Deptford High St.
Mecklenburgh Pl. WC1 274 B4
Mecklenburgh Pl. WC1 141 DM70
Mecklenburgh Sq. WC1 274 B4
Mecklenburgh Sq. WC1 141 DM70
Mecklenburgh St. WC1 274 B4
Mecklenburgh St. WC1 141 DM69
Medburn St. NW1 141 DK68
Medbury Rd., Grav. 191 GM88
Medcalf Rd., Enf. 83 DZ37
Medcroft Gdns. SW14 158 CQ84
Mede Clo., Stai. 172 AX88
Mede Fld., Lthd. 231 CD124
Medebourne Clo. SE3 164 EG83
Medesenge Way N13 99 DP51
Medfield St. SW15 179 CU87
Medhurst Clo. E3 143 DY68
Arbery Rd.
Medhurst Clo., Wok. 210 AT109
Medhurst Cres., Grav. 191 GL90
Medhurst Gdns., Grav. 191 GM90
Medhurst Rd. E3 143 DY68
Arbery Rd.
Median Rd. E5 122 DW64
Medick Ct., Grays 170 GE79
Medina Ave., Esher 197 CE104
Medina Gro. N7 121 DN62
Medina Rd.
Medina Rd. N7 121 DN62
Medina Rd., Grays 170 GD77
Medlake Rd., Egh. 173 BC93
Medland Clo., Wall. 200 DG102
Medlar Clo., Guil. 242 AW132
Medlar Clo., Nthlt. 136 BY68
Parkfield Ave.
Medlar Ct., Slou. 132 AW74
Medlar Rd., Grays 170 GD79
Medlar St. SE5 162 DQ81
Medley Rd. NW6 140 DA65
Medman Clo., Uxb. 134 BJ68
Chiltern Vw. Rd.
Medora Rd. SW2 181 DM87
Medora Rd., Rom. 127 FD56
Medow Mead, Rad. 61 CF33
Medusa Rd. SE6 183 EB86
Medway Bldgs. E3 143 DY68
Medway Rd.
Medway Clo., Croy. 202 DW100
Medway Clo., Ilf. 125 EQ64
Loxford La.
Medway Clo., Wat. 60 BW34
Medway Dr., Grnf. 137 CF68
Medway Gdns., Wem. 117 CG63
Medway Ms. E3 143 DY68
Medway Rd.
Medway Par., Grnf. 137 CF68
Medway Rd. E3 143 DY68
Medway Rd., Dart. 167 FG83
Medway Rd., Hem.H. 40 BM15
Medway St. SW1 277 N7
Medway St. SW1 161 DK76
Medwick Ms., Hem.H. 41 BP15
Hunters Oak
Medwin St. SW4 161 DM84
Meerbrook Rd. SE3 164 EJ83
Meeson Rd. E15 144 EF67
Meeson St. E5 123 DY63
Meesons La., Grays 170 FZ77
Meeting Flds. Path E9 142 DW65
Morning La.
Meeting Ho. La. SE15 162 DV81
Meetinghouse All. E1 142 DV74
Wapping La.
Megg La., Kings L. 58 BH29
Mehetabel Rd. E9 142 DW65
Meister Clo., Ilf. 125 ER60
Melancholy Wk., Rich. 177 CJ89
Melanda Clo., Chis. 185 EM92
Melanie Clo., Bexh. 166 EY81
Melba Gdns., Til. 171 GG80
Melba Way SE13 163 EB81
Melbourne Ave. N13 99 DM51
Melbourne Ave. W13 137 CG74
Melbourne Ave., Pnr. 116 CB55
Melbourne Ave., Slou. 131 AQ72
Melbourne Clo., Orp. 205 ES101
Melbourne Clo., St.Alb. 43 CF16
Melbourne Clo., Uxb. 114 BN63
Melbourne Clo., Wall. 219 DJ106
Melbourne Rd.
Melbourne Ct. E5 123 DY63
Daubeney Rd.
Melbourne Ct. N10 99 DH52
Sydney Rd.
Melbourne Ct. SE20 182 DU94
Melbourne Ct., Welw.G.C. 29 CV10
Melbourne Gdns., Rom. 126 EY57
Melbourne Gro. SE22 162 DS84
Melbourne Ho., Hayes 136 BW70
Melbourne Ms. SE6 183 EC87
Melbourne Ms. SW9 161 DN81
Melbourne Pl. WC2 274 C9
Melbourne Pl. WC2 141 DM73
Melbourne Rd. E6 145 EM67
Melbourne Rd. E10 123 EB59
Melbourne Rd. E17 123 DY56
Melbourne Rd. SW19 200 DA95
Melbourne Rd., Ilf. 125 EP60
Melbourne Rd., Tedd. 177 CJ93
Melbourne Rd., Til. 170 GE81
Melbourne Rd., Wall. 219 DH106
Melbourne Rd. (Bushey), Wat. 76 CB43
Melbourne Sq. SW9 161 DN81
Melbourne Ms.
Melbourne Ter. SW6 160 DB80
Waterford Rd.
Melbourne Way, Enf. 82 DT44
Melbury Ave., Sthl. 156 CB76
Melbury Clo., Cher. 194 BG101
Melbury Clo., Chis. 184 EL93
Melbury Clo., Esher 215 CH107
Melbury Clo., W.Byf. 212 BG114
Melbury Ct. W8 159 CZ76
Melbury Dr. SE5 162 DS80
Sedgmoor Pl.
Melbury Gdns. SW20 199 CV95
Melbury Rd. W14 159 CZ76
Melbury Rd., Har. 118 CM57
Melbury Ter. NW1 272 C5
Melbury Ter. NW1 140 DE70
Melcombe Gdns., Har. 118 CM58
Melcombe Pl. NW1 272 D6
Melcombe Pl. NW1 140 DF71
Melcombe St. NW1 272 E5
Melcombe St. NW1 140 DF70
Meldex Clo. NW7 97 CW51
Meldon Clo. SW6 160 DB81
Bagley's La.
Meldone Clo., Surb. 198 CP100
Meldrum Clo., Orp. 206 EW100
Killewarren Way
Meldrum Clo., Oxt. 254 EF132
Meldrum Rd., Ilf. 126 EU61
Melfield Gdns. SE6 183 EB91
Melford Ave., Bark. 145 ES65
Melford Clo., Chess. 216 CM106
Melford Rd. E6 145 EM70
Melford Rd. E11 124 EE61
Melford Rd. E17 123 DY56
Melford Rd. SE22 182 DU87
Melford Rd., Ilf. 125 ER61
Melfort Ave., Th.Hth. 201 DP97
Melfort Rd., Th.Hth. 201 DP97
Melgund Rd. N5 121 DN64
Melina Clo., Hayes 135 BR71
Middleton Rd.
Melina Pl. NW8 140 DD69
Melina Rd. W12 159 CV75
Melior Pl. SE1 279 M4
Melior St. SE1 279 M4
Melior St. SE1 162 DR75
Meliot Rd. SE6 183 ED89
Melksham Clo., Rom. 106 FM52
Melksham Dr., Rom. 106 FM52
Melksham Gdns.
Melksham Gdns., Rom. 106 FL52
Melksham Grn., Rom. 106 FM52
Melksham Gdns.
Mell St. SE10 164 EE78
Trafalgar Rd.
Meller Clo., Croy. 201 DL104
Melling Dr., Enf. 82 DU39
Melling St. SE18 165 ES79
Mellings, The, Hem.H. 41 BP15
Mellish Clo., Bark. 145 ET67
Mellish Gdns., Wdf.Grn. 102 EG50
Harts Gro.
Mellish St. E14 163 EA76
Mellison Rd. SW17 180 DE92
Mellitus St. W12 139 CT72
Mellor Clo., Walt. 196 BZ101
Mellor Wk., Wind. 151 AR81
Bachelors Acre
Mellow Clo., Bans. 218 DB114
Mellow La. E., Hayes 135 BQ69
Mellow La. W., Uxb. 135 BQ69
Mellows Rd., Ilf. 125 EM55
Mellows Rd., Wall. 219 DK106
Mells Cres. SE9 185 EM91
Melody La. N5 121 DP64
Highbury Gro.
Melody Rd. SW18 180 DC85
Melody Rd., West. 238 EJ118
Melon Pl. W8 160 DB75
Kensington Ch. St.
Melon Rd. E11 124 EE62
Melon Rd. SE15 162 DU81
Melrose Ave. N22 99 DP53
Melrose Ave. NW2 119 CV64
Melrose Ave. SW16 201 DM97
Melrose Ave. SW19 179 CZ89
Melrose Ave., Borwd. 78 CP43
Melrose Ave., Grnf. 136 CB68
Melrose Ave., Mitch. 181 DH94
Melrose Ave., Pot.B. 64 DB32
Melrose Ave., Twick. 176 CB87
Melrose Clo. SE12 184 EG88
Melrose Clo., Grnf. 136 CB68
Melrose Clo., Hayes 135 BU71
Melrose Cres., Orp. 223 ER105
Melrose Dr., Sthl. 136 CA74
Melrose Gdns. W6 159 CW76
Melrose Gdns., Edg. 96 CP54
Melrose Gdns., N.Mal. 198 CR97
Melrose Gdns., Walt. 214 BW106
Melrose Pl., Wat. 75 BT38
Wentworth Clo.
Melrose Rd. SW13 159 CT82
Melrose Rd. SW18 179 CZ86
Melrose Rd. SW19 200 DA96
Melrose Rd. W3 158 CQ76
Stanley Rd.
Melrose Rd., Couls. 235 DH115
Melrose Rd., Pnr. 116 BZ56
Melrose Rd., West. 238 EJ116
Melrose Rd., Wey. 212 BN106
Melrose Ter. W6 159 CW75
Melsa Rd., Mord. 200 DC100
Melsted Rd., Hem.H. 40 BH20
Melstock Ave., Upmin. 128 FQ63
Meltham Way SE16 162 DV78
Egan Way
Melthorne Dr., Ruis. 116 BW62
Melthorpe Gdns. SE3 164 EK81
Melton Clo., Ruis. 116 BW60
Melton Ct. SW7 276 A9
Melton Ct. SW7 160 DD77
Melton Flds., Epsom 216 CR109
Melton Gdns., Rom. 127 FF59
Melton Pl., Epsom 216 CR109
Melton Rd., Red. 251 DJ130
Melton St. NW1 273 L3
Melton St. NW1 141 DJ69
Melville Ave. SW20 179 CU94
Melville Ave., Grnf. 117 CF64
Melville Ave., S.Croy. 220 DT106
Melville Clo., Uxb. 115 BR62
Melville Gdns. N13 99 DN50
Melville Rd. E17 123 DZ55
Melville Rd. NW10 138 CR66
Melville Rd. SW13 159 CU81
Melville Rd., Rain. 147 FG70
Melville Rd., Rom. 105 FB52
Melville Rd., Sid. 186 EW89
Melville Vill. Rd. W3 138 CR74
High St.
Melvin Rd. SE20 202 DW95
Melvinshaw, Lthd. 231 CJ121
Melvyn Clo. (Cheshunt), Wal.Cr. 65 DP28
Melyn Clo. N7 121 DJ63
Anson Rd.
Memel Ct. EC1 275 H5
Memel St. EC1 275 H5
Memess Path SE18 165 EN79
Engineer Clo.
Memorial Ave. E15 144 EE69
Memorial Clo., Houns. 156 BZ79
Mendip Clo. SE26 182 DW91
Mendip Clo. SW19 179 CY89
Queensmere Rd.
Mendip Clo., Hayes 155 BR80
Mendip Clo., St.Alb. 43 CJ15
Mendip Clo., Slou. 153 BA78
Mendip Clo., Wor.Pk. 199 CW103
Cotswold Way
Mendip Dr. NW2 119 CY61
Mendip Rd. SW11 160 DC83
Mendip Rd., Bexh. 167 FE81
Mendip Rd., Horn. 127 FG59
Mendip Rd., Ilf. 125 ES57
Mendip Rd. (Bushey), Wat. 76 CC44
Mendip Way, Hem.H. 40 BL17
Mendlesham, Welw.G.C. 30 DE09
Mendora Rd. SW6 159 CY80
Mendoza Clo., Horn. 128 FL57
Menelik Rd. NW2 119 CY63
Menlo Gdns. SE19 182 DR94
Menotti St. E2 142 DU70
Dunbridge St.
Menthone Pl., Horn. 128 FK59
Mentmore Clo., Har. 117 CJ58
Mentmore Rd., St.Alb. 43 CD22
Mentmore Ter. E8 142 DV66
Meon Clo., Tad. 233 CV122
Meon Ct., Islw. 157 CE82
Meon Rd. W3 158 CQ75
Meopham Rd., Mitch. 201 DJ95
Mepham Cres., Har. 94 CC52
Mepham Gdns., Har. 94 CC52
Mepham St. SE1 278 D3
Mepham St. SE1 141 DM74
Mera Dr., Bexh. 166 FA84
Merantun Way SW19 200 DC95
Merbury Clo. SE13 183 ED85
Merbury Rd. SE28 165 ES75
Mercator Rd. SE13 163 ED84
Mercer Clo., T.Ditt. 197 CF101
Mercer Pl., Pnr. 94 BW54
Cross Way
Mercer St. WC2 273 P9
Mercer St. WC2 141 DL72
Mercer Wk., Uxb. 134 BJ66
High St.
Merceron St. E1 142 DV70
Mercers, Harl. 51 EN17
Mercers, Hem.H. 40 BL18
Mercers Clo. SE10 164 EF77
Mercers Pl. W6 159 CW77
Mercers Rd. N19 121 DK62
Mercers Row, St.Alb. 42 CC22
Merchant Dr., Hert. 32 DT08
Merchant St. E3 143 DZ69
Merchiston Rd. SE6 183 ED89
Merchland Rd. SE9 185 EQ88
Mercia Gro. SE13 163 EC84
Mercia Wk., Wok. 227 AZ117
Church St. W.
Mercian Way, Slou. 131 AK74
Mercier Rd. SW15 179 CY85
Mercury Cen. Ind. Est., Felt. 175 BU85
Mercury Gdns., Rom. 127 FE56
Mercury Wk., Hem.H. 40 BM17
Mercury Way SE14 163 DX79
Mercy Ter. SE13 163 EB84
Mere Clo. SW15 179 CX87
Mere Clo., Orp. 205 EN103
Mere End, Croy. 203 DX101
Mere Rd., Shep. 195 BP100
Mere Rd., Slou. 152 AT76
Mere Rd., Tad. 233 CV124
Mere Rd., Wey. 195 BR104
Mere Side, Orp. 205 EN103
Merebank La., Croy. 219 DM106
Meredith Ave. NW2 119 CW64
Meredith Clo., Pnr. 94 BX52
Meredith Rd., Grays 171 GG77
Meredith St. E13 144 EG69
Meredith St. EC1 274 F3
Meredyth Rd. SW13 159 CU82
Merefield, Saw. 36 EY06
Merefield Gdns., Tad. 233 CX119
Mereside Pl., Vir.W. 192 AX100
Meretone Clo. SE4 163 DY84
Merevale Cres., Mord. 200 DC100
Mereway Rd., Twick. 177 CD88
Merewood Clo., Brom. 205 EN96
Merewood Rd., Bexh. 167 FC82
Mereworth Clo., Brom. 204 EF99
Mereworth Dr. SE18 165 EP80
Merganser Gdns. SE28 165 ER76
Avocet Ms.
Meriden Clo., Brom. 184 EK94
Meriden Clo., Ilf. 103 EQ53
Meriden Way, Wat. 76 BY36
Meridian Gate E14 163 EC75
Meridian Gro., Horl. 269 DJ147
Wheatfield Way
Meridian Rd. SE7 164 EK80
Meridian Trd. Est. SE7 164 EH77
Meridian Wk. N17 100 DS51
Commercial Rd.
Meridian Way N9 101 DX47
Meridian Way N18 100 DW51
Meridian Way, Enf. 83 DX44
Meridian Way, Ware 33 EB10
Merifield Rd. SE9 164 EJ84
Merino Clo. E11 124 EJ56
Merino Pl., Sid. 186 EU86
Blackfen Rd.
Merivale Rd. SW15 159 CY84
Merivale Rd., Har. 116 CC59
Merland Clo., Tad. 233 CW120
Merland Grn., Tad. 233 CW120
Merland Ri.
Merland Ri., Epsom 233 CW119
Merland Ri., Tad. 233 CW120
Merle Ave., Uxb. 92 BH54
Merle Clo., Cat. 236 DR120
Merlewood, Sev. 257 FH123
Merlewood Clo., Cat. 236 DR120
Merlewood Dr., Chis. 205 EM95
Merley Ct. NW9 118 CQ60
Merlin Clo., Croy. 220 DS105
Minster Dr.
Merlin Clo., Ilf. 104 EW50
Merlin Clo., Mitch. 200 DE97
Merlin Clo., Nthlt. 136 BW69
Merlin Clo., Rom. 105 FD51
Merlin Clo., Slou. 153 BB79
Merlin Clo., Wal.Abb. 68 EG34
Merlin Ct., Wok. 211 BC114
Blackmore Cres.
Merlin Cres., Edg. 96 CM53
Merlin Gdns., Brom. 184 EG90
Merlin Gdns., Rom. 105 FD51
Merlin Gro., Beck. 203 DZ98
Merlin Gro., Ilf. 103 EP51
Merlin Rd. E12 124 EK61
Merlin Rd., Rom. 105 FD51
Merlin Rd., Well. 166 EU84
Merlin Rd. N., Well. 166 EU84
Merlin St. WC1 274 D3
Merlin Way, Epp. 70 FA25
Merling Clo., Chess. 215 CK106
Coppard Gdns.
Merling Cft., Berk. 38 AS17
Merlins Ave., Har. 116 BZ62
Mermagen Dr., Rain. 147 FH66
Mermaid Ct. SE1 279 K4
Mermaid Ct. SE1 162 DR75
Mermaid Ct. SE16 143 DZ74
Mermerus Gdns., Grav. 191 GM91
Merredene St. SW2 181 DM86
Merriam Clo. E4 101 EC50
Merrick Rd., Sthl. 156 BZ75
Merrick Sq. SE1 279 K6
Merrick Sq. SE1 162 DQ76
Merridene N21 81 DP44
Merrielands Cres., Dag. 146 EZ67
Merrilands Rd., Wor.Pk. 199 CW102
Merrilees Rd., Sid. 185 ES88
Merrilyn Clo., Esher 215 CG107
Merriman Rd. SE3 164 EJ81
Merrington Rd. SW6 160 DA79
Merrion Ave., Stan. 95 CK50
Merrion Wk. SE17 162 DR78
Dawes St.
Merritt Gdns., Chess. 215 CJ107
Merritt Rd. SE4 183 DZ85
Merritt Wk., Hat. 45 CV23
Merrivale N14 81 DK44
Merrivale Ave., Ilf. 124 EK56
Merrivale Gdns., Wok. 226 AW117
Merrow Business Cen., Guil. 243 BC131
Merrow La.
Merrow Chase, Guil. 243 BC134
Merrow Common Rd., Guil. 243 BD131
Merrow Copse, Guil. 243 BB133
Merrow Ct., Guil. 243 BD134
Levylsdene
Merrow Cft., Guil. 243 BC133
Merrow Downs, Guil. 259 BD135
Merrow Dr., Hem.H. 39 BE19
Merrow La., Guil. 243 BC129
Merrow Rd., Sutt. 217 CX109
Merrow St. SE17 162 DQ79
Merrow St., Guil. 243 BD132
Merrow Wk. SE17 279 L10
Merrow Way, Croy. 221 EC107
Merrow Way, Guil. 243 BD133
Merrow Wds., Guil. 243 BB132
Merrows Clo., Nthwd. 93 BQ51
Merry Hill Mt. (Bushey) Wat. 94 CB46
Merry Hill Rd. (Bushey), Wat. 76 BZ44
Merry Meet, Bans. 218 DF114
Merrydown Way, Chis. 204 EL95
Merryfield SE3 164 EF82
Merryfield Gdns., Stan. 95 CJ50
Merryfields, Uxb. 134 BL68
The Greenway
Merryfields Way SE6 183 EB87
Merryhill Clo. E4 101 EB45
Merryhills Clo., West. 238 EK116
Merryhills Ct. N14 81 DJ43
Merryhills Dr., Enf. 81 DK42
Merrylands, Cher. 193 BE104
Merrylands Rd., Lthd. 230 BZ123
Merryweather Clo., Dart. 188 FM86
Merrywood Gro., Tad. 249 CX130
Merrywood Pk., Reig. 250 DB132
Merrywood Pk., Tad. 248 CP130
Mersea Ho., Bark. 145 EP65
Mersey Ave., Upmin. 129 FR58
Mersey Pl., Hem.H. 40 BM15
Colne Way
Mersey Rd. E17 123 DZ55
Mersey Wk., Nthlt. 136 CA68
Brabazon Rd.
Mersham Dr. NW9 118 CN57
Mersham Pl. SE20 202 DV95
Jasmine Gro.
Mersham Rd., Th.Hth. 202 DR97
Merstham Rd., Red. 251 DM129
Merten Rd., Rom. 126 EY59
Merthyr Ter. SW13 159 CV79
Merton Ave. W4 159 CT77
Merton Ave., Nthlt. 116 CC64
Merton Ave., Uxb. 135 BP66
Merton Gdns., Orp. 205 EP99
Merton Gdns., Tad. 233 CX120
Marbles Way
Merton Hall Gdns. SW20 199 CY95
Merton Hall Rd. SW19 179 CY94
Merton High St. SW19 180 DC94
Merton Ind. Pk. SW19 200 DC95
Merton La. N6 120 DF61
Merton Mans. SW20 199 CX96
Merton Pk. Par. SW19 199 CZ95
Kingston Rd.
Merton Pl., Grays 171 GG77
Merton Ri. NW3 140 DE66
Merton Rd. E17 123 EC57
Merton Rd. SE25 202 DU99
Merton Rd. SW18 180 DA85
Merton Rd. SW19 180 DB94
Merton Rd., Bark. 145 ET66
Merton Rd., Enf. 82 DR38
Merton Rd., Har. 116 CC60
Merton Rd., Ilf. 125 ET59
Merton Rd., Slou. 152 AU76
Merton Rd., Wat. 75 BV42
Merton Wk., Lthd. 231 CG118
Merton Way
Merton Way, Lthd. 231 CG119
Merton Way, Uxb. 135 BP66
Merton Way, W.Mol. 196 CB98
Merttins Rd. SE15 183 DX85
Meru Clo. NW5 120 DG63
Kiln Pl.
Mervan Rd. SW2 161 DN84
Mervyn Ave. SE9 185 EQ90
Mervyn Rd. W13 157 CG76
Mervyn Rd., Shep. 195 BQ101
Merwin Way, Wind. 151 AK83
Meryfield Clo., Borwd. 78 CM40
Mesne Way, Sev. 225 FF112
Messaline Ave. W3 138 CQ72
Messant Clo., Rom. 106 FK54
Messent Rd. SE9 184 EJ85
Messeter Pl. SE9 185 EN86
Messina Ave. NW6 140 DA66
Metcalf Rd., Ashf. 175 BP92
Metcalfe Wk., Felt. 176 BY91
Gabriel Clo.
Meteor St. SW11 160 DG84
Meteor Way, Wall. 219 DL108
Metheringham Way NW9 96 CS53
Methley St. SE11 161 DN78
Methuen Clo., Edg. 96 CN52
Methuen Pk. N10 99 DH54
Methuen Rd., Belv. 167 FB77
Methuen Rd., Bexh. 166 EZ84
Methuen Rd., Edg. 96 CN52
Methwold Rd. W10 139 CX71
Metro Ind. Cen., Islw. 157 CE82
Metropolitan Cen., The, Grnf. 136 CB67
Meux Clo. (Cheshunt), Wal.Cr. 66 DU31
Mews, The N1 142 DQ67
St. Paul St.
Mews, The, Grays 170 GC77
Mews, The, Guil. 258 AW135
Walnut Tree Clo.
Mews, The, Harl. 51 ES19
Commonside Rd.
Mews, The, Ilf. 124 EK57
Mews, The, Rom. 127 FE56
Market Link
Mews, The, Sev. 256 FG123
Mews, The, Twick. 177 CH86
Bridge Rd.
Mews Deck E1 142 DV73
Sovereign Clo.
Mews End, West. 238 EK118
Mews Pl., Wdf.Grn. 102 EG49
Mews St. E1 142 DU74
Mexfield Rd. SW15 179 CZ85
Meyer Gro., Enf. 82 DU38
Meyer Rd., Erith 167 FC79
Meymott St. SE1 278 F3
Meymott St. SE1 141 DP74
Meynell Cres. E9 143 DX66
Meynell Gdns. E9 143 DX66
Meynell Rd. E9 143 DX66
Meynell Rd., Rom. 105 FH52
Meyrick Clo., Wok. 226 AS116
Meyrick Rd. NW10 139 CU65
Meyrick Rd. SW11 160 DD83
Mezen Clo., Nthwd. 93 BR50
Miah Ter. E1 142 DU74
Wapping High St.
Miall Wk. SE26 183 DY91
Micawber Ave., Uxb. 134 BN70
Micawber St. N1 275 J2
Micawber St. N1 142 DQ69
Michael Cres., Horl. 268 DG150
Michael Faraday Ho. SE17 162 DS78
Beaconsfield Rd.
Michael Gdns., Grav. 191 GL93
Michael Gdns., Horn. 128 FK56
Michael Gaynor Clo. W7 137 CF74
Michael Rd. E11 124 EE60
Michael Rd. SE25 202 DS97
Michael Rd. SW6 160 DD81
Michaelmas Clo. SW20 199 CW97
Michaels Clo. SE13 164 EE84

Michaels La. (Fawkham Grn.), Long. 209 FV103
Michaels La., Sev. 209 FV103
Micheldever Rd. SE12 184 EE86
Michelham Gdns., Tad. 233 CW121
Waterfield
Michelham Gdns., Twick. 177 CG90
Michels Row, Rich. 158 CL84
Kew Foot Rd.
Michigan Ave. E12 125 EM63
Michleham Down N12 97 CZ49
Micholls Ave., Ger.Cr. 90 AY49
Micklefield Rd., Hem.H. 41 BQ20
Micklefield Way, Borwd. 78 CL38
Mickleham Bypass, Dor. 247 CH128
Mickleham Clo., Orp. 205 ET96
Mickleham Downs, Dor. 247 CK127
Mickleham Dr., Lthd. 247 CJ126
Mickleham Gdns., Sutt. 217 CY107
Mickleham Rd., Orp. 205 ET95
Mickleham Way, Croy. 221 ED108
Micklem Dr., Hem.H. 39 BF19
Micklethwaite Rd. SW6 160 DA79
Mid Cross La., Ger.Cr. 91 AZ50
Mid Holmwood La., Dor. 263 CH142
Mid St., Red. 251 DM134
Midas Metropolitan Ind. Est., The, Mord. 199 CX102
Garth Rd.
Midcot Way, Berk. 38 AT17
Midcroft, Ruis. 115 BS60
Midcroft, Slou. 131 AP70
Middle Boy, Rom. 86 EW41
Middle Clo., Amer. 72 AT37
Middle Clo., Couls. 235 DN120
Middle Clo., Epsom 216 CS112
Middle La.
Middle Cres., Uxb. 113 BD59
Middle Dene NW7 96 CR48
Middle Dr., Beac. 89 AK50
Middle Fm. Clo., Lthd. 246 BX127
Middle Fm. Pl., Lthd. 246 BW127
Middle Fld. NW8 140 DD67
Middle Furlong (Bushey), Wat. 76 CB42
Middle Gorse, Croy. 221 DY112
Middle Grn., Bet. 264 CP136
Middle Grn., Slou. 132 AY74
Middle Grn., Stai. 174 BK94
Honnor Rd.
Middle Grn. Clo., Surb. 198 CM100
Alpha Rd.
Middle Hill, Egh. 172 AW91
Middle Hill, Hem.H. 39 BE20
Middle La. N8 121 DL57
Middle La., Epsom 216 CS112
Middle La., Hem.H. 57 BA29
Middle La., Sev. 257 FM121
Church Rd.
Middle La., Tedd. 177 CF93
Middle La. Ms. N8 121 DL57
Middle La.
Middle Meadow, Ch.St.G. 90 AW48
Middle Ope, Wat. 75 BV37
The Thrums
Middle Pk. Ave. SE9 184 EK86
Middle Path, Har. 117 CD60
Middle Rd.
Middle Rd. E13 144 EG68
London Rd.
Middle Rd. SW16 201 DJ96
Middle Rd., Barn. 80 DE44
Middle Rd., Berk. 38 AV19
Middle Rd., Brwd. 109 GC50
Middle Rd., Har. 117 CD61
Middle Rd., Lthd. 231 CH121
Middle Rd., Uxb. 113 BC59
Middle Rd., Wal.Abb. 67 EB32
Middle Row W10 139 CY70
Middle St. EC1 275 H6
Middle St., Bet. 264 CP136
Middle St., Croy. 202 DQ104
Surrey St.
Middle St., Guil. 260 BN139
Middle St., Wal.Abb. 50 EE22
Middle Temple EC4 274 D10
Middle Temple La. EC4 274 D9
Middle Temple La. EC4 141 DN72
Middle Wk., Slou. 130 AH69
Middle Wk., Wok. 226 AY117
Commercial Way
Middle Way SW16 201 DK96
Middle Way, Erith 166 EY76
Middle Way, Hayes 136 BX70
Douglas Cres.
Middle Way, Wat. 75 BV37
Middle Way, The, Har. 95 CF54
Middle Yd. SE1 279 M2
Middlefield, Hat. 45 CU17
Middlefield, Horl. 269 DJ147
Middlefield, Welw.G.C. 29 CY13
Middlefield Ave., Hodd. 49 EA15
Middlefield Clo., Hodd. 49 EA15
Middlefield Clo., St.Alb. 43 CJ17
Middlefield Gdns., Ilf. 125 EP58
Middlefield Rd., Hodd. 49 EA15
Middlefielde W13 137 CH71
Middlefields, Croy. 221 DY109
Middlegreen Rd., Slou. 152 AX75
Middleham Gdns. N18 100 DU51
Middleham Rd. N18 100 DU51
Middleknights Hill, Hem.H. 40 BG17
Middlemead Clo., Lthd. 246 CA125
Middlemead Rd., Lthd. 246 BZ125
Middlesborough Rd. N18 100 DU51
Middlesex Business Cen., The, Sthl. 156 BZ75
Middlesex Ct. W4 159 CT77
British Gro.
Middlesex Pas. EC1 274 G7
Middlesex Rd., Mitch. 201 DL98
Middlesex St. E1 275 N7
Middlesex St. E1 142 DS71
Middlesex Wf. E5 122 DW61
Middleton Ave. E4 101 DZ49
Middleton Ave., Grnf. 137 CD68
Middleton Ave., Sid. 186 EW93
Middleton Bldgs. W1 273 K7
Middleton Clo. E4 101 DZ48
Middleton Dr. SE16 163 DX75
Middleton Dr., Pnr. 115 BU55
Middleton Gdns., Ilf. 125 EP58
Middleton Gro. N7 121 DL64
Middleton Hall La., Brwd. 108 FY46
Middleton Ms. N7 121 DL64
Middleton Gro.
Middleton Rd. E8 142 DT66
Middleton Rd. NW11 120 DA59
Middleton Rd., Brwd. 108 FY46
Middleton Rd., Cars. 200 DD101
Middleton Rd., Cob. 229 BV119
Middleton Rd., Epsom 216 CR110
Middleton Rd., Hayes 135 BR71
Middleton Rd., Mord. 200 DB100
Middleton Rd., Rick. 92 BG46
Middleton St. E2 142 DV69
Middleton Way SE13 163 ED84
Middleway NW11 120 DB57
Middlings, The, Sev. 256 FF125
Middlings Ri., Sev. 256 FF126
Middlings Wd., Sev. 256 FF125
Midfield Ave., Bexh. 167 FC83
Midfield Ave., Swan. 187 FG93
Midfield Way, Orp. 206 EU95
Midford Pl. W1 273 L5
Midgarth Clo., Lthd. 214 CC114
Midholm NW11 120 DB56
Midholm, Wem. 118 CN60
Midholm Clo. NW11 120 DB56
Midholm Rd., Croy. 203 DY103
Midhope Clo., Wok. 226 AY119
Midhope Gdns., Wok. 226 AY119
Midhope Rd.
Midhope Rd., Wok. 226 AY119
Midhope St. WC1 274 A3
Midhurst Ave. N10 120 DG55
Midhurst Ave., Croy. 201 DN101
Midhurst Clo., Horn. 127 FG63
Midhurst Gdns., Uxb. 135 BQ66
Midhurst Hill, Bexh. 186 FA86
Midhurst Rd. W13 157 CG75
Midland Pl. E14 163 EC78
Ferry St.
Midland Rd. E10 123 EC59
Midland Rd. NW1 273 N1
Midland Rd. NW1 141 DK68
Midland Rd., Hem.H. 40 BK20
Midland Ter. NW2 119 CX62
Midland Ter. NW10 138 CS70
Shaftesbury Gdns.
Midleton Ind. Est. Rd., Guil. 242 AV133
Midleton Rd., Guil. 242 AV133
Midleton Rd., N.Mal. 198 CQ96
Midlothian Rd. E3 143 DY71
Midmoor Rd. SW12 181 DJ88
Midmoor Rd. SW19 199 CX95
Midship Clo. SE16 143 DX74
Surrey Water Rd.
Midstrath Rd. NW10 118 CS63
Midsummer Ave., Houns. 156 BZ84
Midway, St.Alb. 42 CB23
Midway, Sutt. 199 CZ101
Midway, Walt. 195 BV103
Midway Ave., Cher. 194 BG97
Eastern Ave.
Midway Ave., Egh. 193 BB97
Midwinter Clo., Well. 166 EU83
Hook La.
Midwood Clo. NW2 119 CV62
Miena Way, Ash. 231 CK117
Miers Clo. E6 145 EN67
Mighell Ave., Ilf. 124 EK57
Mike Spring Ct., Grav. 191 GK93
Milborne Gro. SW10 160 DC78
Milborne St. E9 142 DW65
Milborough Cres. SE12 184 EE86
Milbourne La., Esher 214 CC107
Milbrook, Esher 214 CC107
Milburn Dr., West Dr. 134 BL73
Milburn Wk., Epsom 232 CS115
Milcombe Clo., Wok. 226 AV118
Inglewood
Milcote St. SE1 278 F5
Milcote St. SE1 161 DP75
Mildenhall Rd. E5 122 DW63
Mildenhall Rd., Slou. 132 AS72
Mildmay Ave. N1 142 DR65
Mildmay Gro. N. N1 122 DR64
Mildmay Gro. S. N1 122 DR64
Mildmay Pk. N1 122 DR64
Mildmay Pl., Sev. 225 FF111
Mildmay Rd. N1 122 DR64
Mildmay Rd., Ilf. 125 EP62
Winston Way
Mildmay Rd., Rom. 127 FC57
Mildmay St. N1 142 DR65
Mildred Ave., Borwd. 78 CN42
Mildred Ave., Hayes 155 BR77
Mildred Ave., Nthlt. 116 CB64
Mildred Ave., Wat. 75 BT42
Mildred Clo., Dart. 188 FN86
Mildred Rd., Erith 167 FE78
Mile Clo., Wal.Abb. 67 EC33
Mile End, The E17 101 DX53
Mile End Pl. E1 143 DX70
Mile End Rd. E1 142 DW71
Mile End Rd. E3 143 DY70
Mile Ho. Clo., St.Alb. 43 CG23
Mile Ho. La., St.Alb. 43 CG23
Mile Path, Wok. 226 AV120
Mile Rd., Wall. 201 DH102
Miles Clo., Harl. 51 EP16
Miles La., Cob. 214 BY113
Miles Pl. NW1 272 B6
Miles Pl., Surb. 198 CM98
Villiers Ave.
Miles Rd. N8 121 DL55
Miles Rd., Epsom 216 CR112
Miles Rd., Mitch. 200 DD97
Miles St. SW8 161 DL79
Miles Way N20 98 DE47
Milespit Hill NW7 97 CV50
Milestone Clo. N9 100 DU47
Chichester Rd.
Milestone Clo., Sutt. 218 DD107
Milestone Clo., Wok. 228 BG122
Milestone Rd. SE19 182 DT93
Milestone Rd., Dart. 188 FP86
Milfoil St. W12 139 CU73
Milford Clo. SE2 166 EY79
Milford Clo., St.Alb. 43 CK16
Milford Gdns., Croy. 203 DX99
Tannery Clo.
Milford Gdns., Edg. 96 CN52
Milford Gdns., Wem. 117 CK63
Milford Gro., Sutt. 218 DC105
Milford La. WC2 274 D10
Milford La. WC2 141 DM73
Milford Ms. SW16 181 DM90
Milford Rd. W13 137 CH74
Milford Rd., Sthl. 136 CA73
Milford Way SE15 162 DT81
Sumner Est.
Milk St. E16 145 EP74
Milk St. EC2 275 J8
Milk St., Brom. 184 EH93
Milk Yd. E1 142 DW73
Milking La., Kes. 222 EK112
Milking La., Orp. 222 EL112
Milkwell Gdns., Wdf.Grn. 102 EH52
Milkwell Yd. SE5 162 DQ81
Milkwood Rd. SE24 181 DP85
Mill Ave., Uxb. 134 BJ68
Mill Bri., Hert. 32 DQ09
Mill Brook Rd., Orp. 206 EW98
Mill Clo., Cars. 200 DG103
Mill Clo., Chesh. 54 AS34
Mill Clo., Hem.H. 58 BN25
Mill Clo. (Piccotts End), Hem.H. 40 BH16
Mill Clo., Horl. 268 DE147
Mill Clo., Lthd. 230 CA124
Mill Clo., Ware 33 DX06
Mill Clo., Welw.G.C. 29 CU10
Mill Clo., West Dr. 154 BK76
Mill Cor., Barn. 79 CZ39
Mill Ct. E10 123 EC62
Mill Fm. Ave., Sun. 175 BS94
Mill Fm. Clo., Pnr. 94 BW54
Mill Fm. Cres., Houns. 176 BY88
Mill Fld., Harl. 36 EW11
Mill Gdns. SE26 182 DV91
Mill Grn. La., Hat. 45 CY15
Mill Grn. Rd., Mitch. 200 DF101
Mill Grn. Rd., Welw.G.C. 29 CY10
Mill Hill SW13 159 CU82
Mill Hill Rd.
Mill Hill, Brwd. 108 FY45
Mill Hill Circ. NW7 97 CT50
Watford Way
Mill Hill Gro. W3 138 CP74
Mill Hill Rd.
Mill Hill La., Bet. 248 CP134
Mill Hill Rd. SW13 159 CU82
Mill Hill Rd. W3 158 CP75
Mill Ho. Clo. (Eynsford), Dart. 208 FL102
Mill La.
Mill Ho. La., Cher. 193 BD98
Mill Ho. La., Egh. 193 BB98
Mill La. E4 83 EB41
Mill La. NW6 119 CY64
Mill La. SE18 165 EN78
Mill La., Amer. 55 AN39
Mill La., Beac. 89 AL54
Mill La., Brox. 49 DZ21
Mill La., Cars. 218 DF105
Mill La., Ch.St.G. 90 AU47
Mill La., Croy. 201 DM104
Mill La. (Eynsford), Dart. 208 FL102
Mill La., Dor. 263 CH135
Mill La., Egh. 193 BC98
Mill La., Epsom 217 CT109
Mill La., Ger.Cr. 113 AZ58
Mill La., Grays 169 FX78
Mill La., Guil. 258 AV142
Mill La. (Chilworth), Guil. 259 BF139
Dorking Rd.
Mill La., Harl. 36 EY11
Mill La., Horl. 268 DD148
Mill La., Kings L. 58 BN29
Mill La., Lthd. 231 CG122
Mill La. (Taplow), Maid. 130 AC72
Mill La. (Toot Hill), Ong. 71 FE29
Mill La. (Downe), Orp. 223 EN110
Mill La., Oxt. 254 EF132
Mill La. (The Chart), Oxt. 255 EM131
Mill La., Red. 251 DJ131
Mill La., Rick. 75 BQ44
Watford Rd.
Mill La. (Chadwell Heath), Rom. 126 EY58
Mill La. (Navestock), Rom. 87 FH38
Mill La., Sev. 257 FJ121
Mill La. (Shoreham), Sev. 225 FF110
Mill La., Slou. 153 BB83
Mill La., Wal.Cr. 67 DY28
Mill La., W.Byf. 212 BM113
Mill La., West. 255 EQ127
Mill La., Wind. 151 AN80
Mill La., Wok. 228 BK119
Mill La., Wdf.Grn. 102 EF50
Mill La. Clo., Brox. 49 DZ21
Mill Mead, Stai. 173 BF91
Mill Mead Ind. Cen. N17 100 DV54
Mill Mead Rd. N17 122 DV55
Mill Pk. Ave., Horn. 128 FL61
Mill Pl. E14 143 DZ72
East India Dock Rd.
Mill Pl., Chis. 205 EP95
Mill Pl., Dart. 167 FG84
Mill Pl., Kings.T. 198 CM97
Mill Pl., Slou. 152 AX82
Mill Pl. Caravan Pk., Slou. 152 AW82
Mill Plat, Islw. 157 CG82
Mill Plat Ave., Islw. 157 CG82
Mill Pond Clo., Sev. 257 FK121
Mill Pond Rd., Dart. 188 FL86
Mill Race, St.Alb. 42 BY15
Mill Race, Ware 33 ED11
Mill Ridge, Edg. 96 CM50
Mill Rd. E16 144 EH74
Mill Rd. SE13 163 EC83
Loampit Vale
Mill Rd. SW19 180 DC94
Mill Rd., Cob. 230 BW115
Mill Rd., Dart. 188 FM91
Mill Rd., Dor. 263 CJ144
Mill Rd., Epsom 217 CT112
Mill Rd., Erith 167 FC80
Mill Rd., Esher 196 CA103
Mill Rd., Grav. 190 GE87
Mill Rd., Hert. 32 DR09
Mill Rd., Ilf. 125 EN62
Mill Rd., Purf. 168 FP79
Mill Rd., Sev. 256 FE121
Mill Rd., S.Ock. 148 FQ73
Mill Rd., Tad. 233 CX123
Mill Rd., Twick. 176 CC89
Mill Rd., West Dr. 154 BJ76
Mill Row N1 142 DS67
Mill Shaw, Oxt. 254 EF132
Mill Shot Clo. SW6 159 CW81
Mill Stream Clo., Hert. 31 DP09
Mill St. SE1 162 DT75
Mill St. W1 273 K10
Mill St. W1 141 DJ73
Mill St., Berk. 38 AW19
Mill St., Harl. 52 EY17
Mill St., Hem.H. 40 BK24
Mill St., Kings.T. 198 CL97
Mill St., Red. 266 DE135
Mill St., Slou. 132 AT74
Mill St. (Colnbrook), Slou. 153 BD80
Mill St., West. 255 ER127
Mill Trd. Est., The NW10 138 CQ69
Mill Vale, Brom. 204 EF96
Mill Vw. Clo., Epsom 217 CT108
Mill Vw. Gdns., Croy. 203 DX104
Mill Way, Felt. 175 BV85
Mill Way, Lthd. 232 CM124
Mill Way, Rick. 91 BF46
Mill Way (Bushey), Wat. 76 BY40
Mill Yd. E1 142 DU73
Cable St.
Millacres, Ware 33 DX06
Station Rd.
Millais Ave. E12 125 EN64
Millais Gdns., Edg. 96 CN54
Millais Pl., Til. 171 GG80
Millais Rd. E11 123 EC63
Millais Rd., Enf. 82 DT43
Millais Rd., N.Mal. 198 CS101
Millais Way, Epsom 216 CQ105
Millan Clo., Add. 212 BH110
Milland Ct., Borwd. 78 CR39
Millard Clo. N16 122 DS64
Boleyn Rd.
Millard Ter., Dag. 146 FA65
Church Elm La.
Millbank SW1 277 P6
Millbank SW1 161 DL77
Millbank, Stai. 174 BH92
Millbank Twr. SW1 277 P9
Millbank Twr. SW1 161 DL77
Millbank Way SE12 184 EG85
Millbourne Rd., Felt. 176 BY91
Millbro, Swan. 187 FG94
Millbrook, Guil. 258 AX136
Millbrook, Wey. 213 BS105
Millbrook Ave., Well. 165 ER84
Millbrook Gdns., Rom. 105 FE54
Millbrook Gdns. (Chadwell Heath), Rom. 126 EZ58
Millbrook Rd. N9 100 DV46
Millbrook Rd. SW9 161 DP83
Millbrook Rd. (Bushey), Wat. 76 BZ39
Millbrook Way, Slou. 153 BE82
Millcrest Rd. (Cheshunt), Wal.Cr. 65 DP28
Millender Wk. SE16 162 DW77
Millennium Pl. E2 142 DV68
Millennium Sq. SE1 162 DT75
Tooley St.
Miller Clo., Mitch. 200 DF101
Miller Clo., Pnr. 94 BW54
Miller Pl., Ger.Cr. 112 AX57
Miller Rd. SW19 180 DD93
Miller Rd., Croy. 201 DM102
Miller Rd., Guil. 243 BC131
Miller St. NW1 141 DJ68
Miller Wk. SE1 141 DN74
Coin St.
Miller's Ave. E8 122 DT64
Millers Clo. NW7 97 CU49
Millers Clo., Chig. 104 EV46
Millers Clo., Rick. 73 BE41
Millers Clo., Stai. 174 BH92
Millers Copse, Epsom 232 CR119
Millers Copse, Red. 267 DP144
Millers Ct. W4 159 CT78
Chiswick Mall
Millers Ct., Hert. 32 DR10
Parliament Sq.
Millers Grn. Clo., Enf. 81 DP41
Miller's La., Chig. 104 EV46
Millers La., Red. 267 DP144
Millers La., Ware 33 EC11
Millers La., Wind. 172 AT86
Millers Meadow Clo. SE3 184 EF85
Meadowcourt Rd.
Millers Ri., St.Alb. 43 CE21
Miller's Ter. E8 122 DT64
Millers Way W6 159 CW75
Millersdale, Harl. 51 EP19
Millet Rd., Grnf. 136 CB69
Millfield, Berk. 38 AX18
Millfield, Sun. 195 BR95
Millfield, Welw.G.C. 30 DC08
Millfield Ave. E17 101 DY53
Millfield Dr., Grav. 190 GE89
Millfield La. N6 120 DF61
Millfield La., Tad. 249 CZ125
Millfield Pl. N6 120 DG61
Millfield Rd., Edg. 96 CQ54
Millfield Rd., Houns. 176 BY88
Millfield Wk., Hem.H. 40 BN22
Millfields, Chesh. 54 AQ33
Millfields Clo., Orp. 206 EV98
Millfields Est. E5 123 DX62
Denton Way
Millfields Rd. E5 122 DW63
Millford, Wok. 226 AV117
Millgrove St. SW11 160 DG81
Millharbour E14 163 EB76
Millhaven Clo., Rom. 126 EV58
Millhedge Clo., Cob. 230 BY116
Millhoo Ct., Wal.Abb. 68 EF34
Millhouse La., Abb.L. 59 BU27
Millhouse Pl. SE27 181 DP91
Millicent Rd. E10 123 DZ60
Milligan St. E14 143 DZ73
Milliners Ct., Loug. 85 EN40
The Cft.
Milling Rd., Edg. 96 CR52
Millington Rd., Hayes 155 BS76
Millman Ms. WC1 274 B5
Millman Ms. WC1 141 DM70
Millman Pl. WC1 274 B5
Millman St. WC1 274 B5
Millman St. WC1 141 DM70
Millmark Gro. SE14 163 DY82
Millmarsh La., Enf. 83 DY40
Millmead, Guil. 258 AW136
Millmead, W.Byf. 212 BM112
Millmead Ter., Guil. 258 AW136
Millpond Ct., Add. 212 BL106
Millpond Est. SE16 162 DV75
West La.
Mills Clo., Uxb. 134 BN68
Mills Ct. EC2 275 M4
Mills Gro. E14 143 EC71
Dewberry St.
Mills Gro. NW4 119 CX55
Mills Rd., Walt. 214 BW106
Mills Row W4 158 CR77
Bridge St.
Mills Spur, Wind. 172 AV87
Mills Way, Brwd. 109 GC46
Millshot Dr., Amer. 55 AQ40
Millside, B.End 110 AC60
Millside, Cars. 200 DF103
Millside Ind. Est., Dart. 168 FK84
Millside Pl., Islw. 157 CH82
Millsmead Way, Loug. 85 EM40
Millson Clo. N20 98 DD47
Millstead Clo., Tad. 233 CV122
Millstone Clo. (South Darenth), Dart. 208 FQ96
Millstone Ms., Dart. 208 FQ95
Millstream Clo. N13 99 DN50
Millstream La., Slou. 131 AL74
Millstream Rd. SE1 279 P5
Millstream Rd. SE1 162 DT75
Millthorn Clo., Rick. 74 BM43
Millview Clo., Reig. 250 DD132
Millwall Dock Rd. E14 163 EA76
Millwards, Hat. 45 CV21
Millway NW7 96 CS50
Millway, Reig. 250 DD134
Millway Gdns., Nthlt. 136 BZ65
Millwell Cres., Chig. 103 ER50
Millwood Rd., Houns. 176 CC85
Millwood Rd., Orp. 206 EW97
Millwood St. W10 139 CY71
St. Charles Sq.
Milman Clo., Pnr. 116 BX55
Milman Rd. NW6 139 CX68
Milman's St. SW10 160 DD79
Milne Feild, Pnr. 94 CA52
Milne Gdns. SE9 184 EL85
Milne Pk. E., Croy. 221 ED111
Milne Pk. W., Croy. 221 ED111
Milne Way, Uxb. 92 BH53
Milner App., Cat. 236 DU121
Milner Clo., Cat. 236 DU121
Milner Clo., Wat. 59 BV34
Milner Ct. (Bushey), Wat. 76 CB44
Milner Dr., Cob. 214 BZ112
Milner Dr., Twick. 177 CD87
Milner Pl. N1 141 DN67
Milner Pl., Cars. 218 DG105
High St.
Milner Rd. E15 144 EE69
Milner Rd. SW19 200 DB95
Milner Rd., Cat. 236 DU122
Milner Rd., Dag. 126 EW61
Milner Rd., Kings.T. 197 CK97
Milner Rd., Mord. 200 DD99
Milner Rd., Slou. 130 AG71
Milner Rd., Th.Hth. 202 DR97
Milner Sq. N1 141 DP66
Milner St. SW3 276 D8
Milner St. SW3 160 DF77
Milnthorpe Rd. W4 158 CR79
Milo Rd. SE22 182 DT86
Milroy Ave., Grav. 190 GE89
Milroy Wk. SE1 278 F2
Milson Rd. W14 159 CX76
Milstream Way, H.Wyc. 110 AD55
Milton Ave. E6 144 EK66
Milton Ave. N6 121 DJ59
Milton Ave. NW9 118 CQ55
Milton Ave. NW10 138 CQ67
Milton Ave., Barn. 79 CZ43
Milton Ave., Croy. 202 DR101
Milton Ave., Dor. 263 CD137
Milton Ave., Ger.Cr. 112 AX56
Milton Ave., Grav. 191 GJ88
Milton Ave., Horn. 127 FF61
Milton Ave., Sev. 225 FB110
Milton Ave., Sutt. 200 DD104
Milton Clo. N2 120 DC57
Milton Clo. SE1 279 P9
Milton Clo. SE1 162 DT77
Milton Clo., Hayes 135 BU72
Milton Clo., Slou. 153 BA83
Milton Clo., Sutt. 200 DD104
Milton Ct. EC2 275 K6
Milton Ct., Uxb. 115 BP62
Milton Ct., Wal.Abb. 67 EC34
Milton Ct. La., Dor. 263 CE136
Milton Ct. Rd. SE14 163 DY79
Milton Cres., Ilf. 125 EQ59
Milton Dene, Hem.H. 41 BP15
Milton Dr., Borwd. 78 CP43
Milton Dr., Shep. 194 BL98
Milton Flds., Ch.St.G. 90 AV48
Milton Gdn. Est. N16 122 DS63
Milton Gro.
Milton Gdns., Epsom 216 CS114
Milton Gdns., Stai. 174 BM88
Milton Gdns., Til. 171 GH81
Milton Gro. N11 99 DJ50
Milton Gro. N16 122 DR63
Milton Hall Rd., Grav. 191 GK88
Milton Hill, Ch.St.G. 90 AV48
Milton Flds.
Milton Lawns, Amer. 55 AR36
Milton Pk. N6 121 DJ59
Milton Pl. N7 121 DN64
George's Rd.
Milton Pl., Grav. 191 GJ86
Milton Rd. E17 123 EA56
Milton Rd. N6 121 DJ59
Milton Rd. N15 121 DP56
Milton Rd. NW7 97 CU50
Milton Rd. NW9 119 CU59
West Hendon Bdy.
Milton Rd. SE24 181 DP86
Milton Rd. SW14 158 CR83
Milton Rd. SW19 180 DC93
Milton Rd. W3 138 CR74
Milton Rd. W7 137 CF73
Milton Rd., Add. 212 BG107
Milton Rd., Belv. 166 FA77
Milton Rd., Brwd. 108 FW49
Milton Rd., Cat. 236 DR121

Milton Rd., Chesh. 54 AP29
Milton Rd., Croy. 202 DR102
Milton Rd., Egh. 173 AZ92
Milton Rd., Grav. 191 GH86
Milton Rd., Grays 170 GB78
Milton Rd., Hmptn. 176 CA94
Milton Rd., Har. 117 CE56
Milton Rd., Mitch. 180 DG94
Milton Rd., Rom. 127 FG58
Milton Rd., Sev. 256 FE121
Milton Rd., Slou. 131 AR70
Milton Rd., Sutt. 200 DA104
Milton Rd., Swans. 190 FY86
Milton Rd., Uxb. 114 BN63
Milton Rd., Wall. 219 DJ107
Milton Rd., Walt. 196 BX104
Milton Rd., Ware 33 DX05
Milton Rd., Well. 165 ET81
Milton St. EC2 275 K6
Milton St. EC2 142 DR71
Milton St., Dor. 263 CD137
Milton St., Swans. 189 FX86
Milton St., Wal.Abb. 67 EC34
Milton St., Wat. 75 BV38
Milton Way, Lthd. 246 CC125
Milton Way, West Dr. 154 BM77
Milverton Dr., Uxb. 115 BQ63
Milverton Gdns., Ilf. 125 ET61
Milverton Rd. NW6 139 CW66
Milverton St. SE11 161 DN78
Milverton Way SE9 185 EN91
Milward St. E1 142 DV71
Stepney Way
Milward Wk. SE18 165 EN79
Spearman St.
Milwards, Harl. 51 EP19
Mimas Rd., Hem.H. 40 BM17
Saturn Way
Mimms Hall Rd., Pot.B. 63 CX31
Mimms La., Pot.B. 62 CQ33
Mimms La., Rad. 62 CN33
Mimosa Clo., Brwd. 108 FV43
Mimosa Clo., Orp. 206 EW104
Berrylands
Mimosa Clo., Rom. 106 FJ52
Mimosa Rd., Hayes 136 BW71
Mimosa St. SW6 159 CZ81
Mimran Rd., Hert. 31 DP10
Mina Ave., Slou. 152 AX75
Mina Rd. SE17 162 DS78
Mina Rd. SW19 200 DA95
Minard Rd. SE6 184 EE87
Minchen Rd., Harl. 35 ET13
Minchenden Cres. N14 99 DJ48
Minchin Clo., Lthd. 231 CG122
Mincing La. EC3 275 M10
Mincing La. EC3 142 DS73
Mincing La., Wok. 210 AT108
Minden Rd. SE20 202 DV95
Minden Rd., Sutt. 199 CZ103
Minehead Rd. SW16 181 DM92
Minehead Rd., Har. 116 CA62
Minera Ms. SW1 276 G8
Minera Ms. SW1 160 DG77
Mineral St. SE18 165 ES77
Minerva Clo. SW9 161 DN80
Minerva Clo., Sid. 185 ES90
Minerva Dr., Wat. 75 BS36
Minerva Rd. E4 101 EB52
Minerva Rd. NW10 138 CQ69
Minerva Rd., Kings.T. 198 CM96
Minerva St. E2 142 DV68
Minerva Way, Beac. 89 AM54
Minet Ave. NW10 138 CS68
Minet Dr., Hayes 135 BU74
Minet Gdns. NW10 138 CS68
Minet Gdns., Hayes 135 BU74
Minet Rd. SW9 161 DP82
Minford Gdns. W14 159 CX75
Ming St. E14 143 EA73
Mingard Wk. N7 121 DM61
Hornsey Rd.
Minims, The, Hat. 45 CU17
Ministry Way SE9 185 EM89
Miniver Pl. EC4 142 DQ73
Garlick Hill
Mink Ct., Houns. 156 BW82
Minniecroft Rd., Slou. 130 AH69
Minniedale, Surb. 198 CM99
Minnow St. SE17 162 DS77
East St.
Minnow Wk. SE17 279 N9
Minorca Rd., Wey. 212 BN105
Minories EC3 275 P9
Minories EC3 142 DT72
Minshull Pl., Beck. 183 EA94
Minshull St. SW8 161 DK81
Wandsworth Rd.
Minson Rd. E9 143 DX67
Minstead Gdns. SW15 179 CT87
Minstead Way, N.Mal. 198 CS100
Minster Ave., Sutt. 200 DA103
Leafield Rd.
Minster Clo., Hat. 45 CU20
Minster Ct. EC3 142 DR73
Mincing La.
Minster Dr., Croy. 220 DS105
Minster Gdns., W.Mol. 196 BZ99
Molesey Ave.
Minster Pavement EC3 142 DR73
Mincing La.
Minster Rd. NW2 119 CY64
Minster Rd., Brom. 184 EH94
Minster Wk. N8 121 DL56
Lightfoot Rd.
Minster Way, Horn. 128 FM60
Minster Way, Slou. 153 AZ75
Minsterley Ave., Shep. 195 BS98
Minstrel Clo., Hem.H. 40 BH19
Minstrel Gdns., Surb. 198 CM99
Mint Clo., Uxb. 135 BP69
Mint Gdns., Dor. 263 CG135
Church St.
Mint Rd., Bans. 234 DC116
Mint Rd., Wall. 219 DH105
Mint St. SE1 279 H4
Mint Wk., Croy. 202 DQ104
High St.
Mint Wk., Warl. 237 DX117
Mint Wk., Wok. 226 AS117
Mintern Clo. N13 99 DP48
Mintern St. N1 142 DR68
Minterne Ave., Sthl. 156 CA77
Minterne Rd., Har. 118 CM57
Minterne Waye, Hayes 136 BW72
Minton La., Harl. 52 EW15
Minton Ms. NW6 140 DB65
Lymington Rd.
Minton Ri., Maid. 130 AH72
Mirabel Rd. SW6 159 CZ80
Mirador Cres., Slou. 132 AV73
Miramar Way, Horn. 128 FK64
Miranda Clo. E1 142 DW71
Sidney St.
Miranda Ct. W3 138 CM72
Queens Dr.
Miranda Rd. N19 121 DJ60
Mirfield St. SE7 164 EK76
Miriam Rd. SE18 165 ES78
Mirrie La., Uxb. 113 BC57
Mirror Path SE9 184 EJ90
Lambscroft Ave.
Misbourne Ave., Ger.Cr. 90 AX50
Misbourne Clo., Ger.Cr. 90 AY50
Misbourne Ct., Slou. 153 BA77
High St.
Misbourne Rd., Uxb. 134 BN67
Misbourne Vale, Ger.Cr. 90 AX50
Miskin Rd., Dart. 188 FJ87
Miskin Way, Grav. 191 GK93
Missden Dr., Hem.H. 41 BQ22
Missenden Clo., Felt. 175 BT88
Missenden Gdns., Mord. 200 DC100
Missenden Gdns., Slou. 130 AH72
Missenden Rd., Chesh. 54 AL32
Mission Gro. E17 123 DY57
Mission Pl. SE15 162 DU81
Mission Sq., Brent. 158 CL79
Netley Rd.
Mistletoe Clo., Croy. 203 DX102
Marigold Way
Mistley Rd., Harl. 36 EU13
Misty's Fld., Walt. 196 BW102
Mitali Pas. E1 142 DU72
Back Ch. La.
Mitcham Gdn. Village, Mitch. 200 DG99
Mitcham Ind. Est., Mitch. 200 DG95
Mitcham La. SW16 181 DH93
Mitcham Pk., Mitch. 200 DE98
Mitcham Rd. E6 144 EL69
Mitcham Rd. SW17 180 DF92
Mitcham Rd., Croy. 201 DL100
Mitcham Rd., Ilf. 125 ET59
Mitchell Ave., Grav. 190 GD89
Mitchell Clo. SE2 166 EW77
Mitchell Clo., Abb.L. 59 BU32
Mitchell Clo., Belv. 167 FC76
Mitchell Clo., Dart. 188 FL89
Mitchell Clo., Hem.H. 57 AZ27
Mitchell Clo., Rain. 148 FJ68
Mitchell Clo., St.Alb. 43 CD24
Mitchell Clo., Slou. 151 AN75
Mitchell Clo., Welw.G.C. 30 DC09
Mitchell Rd. N13 99 DP50
Mitchell Rd., Orp. 223 ET105
Mitchell St. EC1 275 H4
Mitchell St. EC1 142 DQ70
Mitchell Wk. E6 144 EL71
Oliver Gdns.
Mitchell Wk., Amer. 55 AS38
Mitchell Wk., Swans. 190 FY87
Mitchell Way NW10 138 CQ65
Mitchell Way, Brom. 204 EG95
Mitchellbrook Way NW10 138 CR65
Mitchells Clo., Guil. 258 AY140
Station Rd.
Mitchison Rd. N1 142 DR65
Mitchley Ave., Pur. 220 DQ113
Mitchley Ave., S.Croy. 220 DS113
Mitchley Gro., S.Croy. 220 DU113
Mitchley Hill, S.Croy. 220 DS113
Mitchley Rd. N17 122 DU55
Mitchley Vw., S.Croy. 220 DU113
Mitford Clo., Chess. 215 CJ107
Merritt Gdns.
Mitford Rd. N19 121 DL61
Mitre, The E14 143 DZ73
Three Colt St.
Mitre Ave. E17 123 DZ55
Greenleaf Rd.
Mitre Clo., Brom. 204 EF96
Beckenham La.
Mitre Clo., Shep. 195 BR100
Gordon Dr.
Mitre Clo., Sutt. 218 DC108
Mitre Ct. EC2 275 J8
Mitre Ct. EC4 274 E9
Mitre Rd. E15 144 EE68
Mitre Rd. SE1 278 E4
Mitre Rd. SE1 161 DN75
Mitre Sq. EC3 275 N9
Mitre St. EC3 275 N9
Mitre St. EC3 142 DS72
Mitre Way NW10 139 CV70
Mixbury Gro., Wey. 213 BR107
Mixnams La., Cher. 193 BF97
Mizen Clo., Cob. 214 BX114
Mizen Way, Cob. 230 BW115
Moat, The, N.Mal. 198 CS95
Moat, The, Ong. 71 FF29
Moat Clo., Orp. 223 ET107
Moat Clo., Sev. 256 FB123
Moat Clo. (Bushey), Wat. 76 CB43
Moat Ct., Ash. 232 CL117
Moat Cres. N3 120 DB55
Moat Cft., Well. 166 EW83
Moat Dr. E13 144 EJ68
Boundary Rd.
Moat Dr., Har. 116 CC56
Moat Dr., Ruis. 115 BS59
Moat Dr., Slou. 132 AW71
Moat Fm. Rd., Nthlt. 136 BZ65
Moat La., Erith 167 FG81
Moat Pl. SW9 161 DM83
Moat Pl. W3 138 CP72
Moat Pl., Uxb. 114 BH63
Moatfield Rd. (Bushey), Wat. 76 CB43
Moats La., Red. 267 DN140
Moatside, Enf. 82 DW42
Moatside, Felt. 176 BW91
Moatview Ct. (Bushey), Wat. 76 CB43
Palmer Ave.
Moatwood Grn., Welw.G.C. 29 CY10
Moberley Rd. SW4 181 DK87
Modbury Gdns. NW5 140 DG65
Queens Cres.
Modder Pl. SW15 159 CX84
Cardinal Pl.
Model Cotts. SW14 158 CQ84
Upper Richmond Rd. W.
Model Fm. Clo. SE9 184 EL90
Modling Ho. E2 143 DX69
Mace St.
Moelwyn Hughes Ct. N7 121 DK64
Hilldrop Cres.
Moelyn Ms., Har. 117 CG57
Moffat Rd. N13 99 DL51
Moffat Rd. SW17 180 DE91
Moffat Rd., Th.Hth. 202 DQ96
Moffats Clo., Hat. 64 DA26
Moffats La., Hat. 63 CY27
Mogador Cotts., Tad. 249 CX128
Mogador Rd.
Mogador Rd., Tad. 249 CY128
Mogden La., Islw. 177 CE85
Mohmmad Khan Rd. E11 124 EF60
Harvey Rd.
Moiety Rd. E14 163 EA75
Moir Clo., S.Croy. 220 DU109
Moira Clo. N17 100 DS54
Moira Rd. SE9 165 EM84
Moland Mead SE16 163 DX78
Crane Mead
Molash Rd., Orp. 206 EX98
Molasses Row SW11 160 DC83
Cinnamon Row
Mole Abbey Gdns., W.Mol. 196 CA97
New Rd.
Mole Business Pk., Lthd. 231 CG121
Mole Ct., Epsom 216 CQ105
Mole Rd., Lthd. 231 CD121
Mole Rd., Walt. 214 BX106
Mole Valley Pl., Ash. 231 CK119
Molember Ct., E.Mol. 197 CE99
Molember Rd., E.Mol. 197 CD99
Moles Hill, Lthd. 215 CD111
Molescroft SE9 185 EQ90
Molesey Ave., W.Mol. 196 BZ99
Molesey Clo., Walt. 214 BX106
Molesey Dr., Sutt. 199 CY103
Molesey Pk. Ave., W.Mol. 196 CB99
Molesey Pk. Clo., E.Mol. 196 CC99
Molesey Pk. Rd., E.Mol. 196 CB99
Molesey Pk. Rd., W.Mol. 196 CB99
Molesey Rd., Walt. 196 BY101
Molesey Rd., W.Mol. 196 BY99
Molesford Rd. SW6 160 DA81
Molesham Clo., W.Mol. 196 CB97
Molesham Way, W.Mol. 196 CB97
Molesworth, Hodd. 33 EA13
Molesworth Rd., Cob. 213 BU113
Molesworth St. SE13 163 EC84
Molewood Rd., Hert. 31 DP08
Molineaux Pl., Tedd. 177 CG92
Mollands La., S.Ock. 149 FW70
Mollison Ave., Enf. 83 DY43
Mollison Dr., Wall. 219 DK108
Mollison Ri., Grav. 191 GL92
Mollison Way, Edg. 96 CM54
Molloy Ct., Wok. 227 BA116
Courtenay Rd.
Molly Huggins Clo. SW12 181 DJ87
Molteno Rd., Wat. 75 BU39
Molyneaux Ave., Hem.H. 57 AZ27
Molyneux Rd., Gdmg. 258 AT144
Molyneux Rd., Wey. 212 BN106
Molyneux St. W1 272 C7
Molyneux St. W1 140 DE71
Momples Rd., Harl. 36 EV13
Mona Rd. SE15 162 DW82
Mona St. E16 144 EF71
Monahan Ave., Pur. 219 DM112
Monarch Clo., Felt. 175 BS87
Monarch Clo., Til. 171 GH82
Monarch Clo., W.Wick. 222 EF105
Monarch Dr. E16 144 EK71
Monarch Ms. E17 123 EB57
Monarch Ms. SW16 181 DN92
Monarch Pl., Buck.H. 102 EJ47
Monarch Rd., Belv. 166 FA76
Monarchs Way, Ruis. 115 BR60
Monarchs Way, Wal.Cr. 67 DY33
Monastery Gdns., Enf. 82 DR40
Monaveen Gdns., W.Mol. 196 CA97
Monck St. SW1 277 N7
Monck St. SW1 161 DK76
Monclar Rd. SE5 162 DR84
Moncorvo Clo. SW7 276 B5
Moncrieff Clo. E6 144 EL72
Linton Gdns.
Moncrieff Pl. SE15 162 DU82
Moncrieff St.
Moncrieff St. SE15 162 DU82
Mondial Way, Hayes 155 BQ80
Monega Rd. E7 144 EJ65
Monega Rd. E12 144 EK65
Money Ave., Cat. 236 DR122
Money Hill Rd., Rick. 92 BJ45
Money Hole La., Welw.G.C. 30 DE08
Money La., West Dr. 154 BK76
Money Rd., Cat. 236 DR122
Moneyhill Par., Rick. 92 BH46
Uxbridge Rd.
Mongers La., Epsom 217 CT110
Monica Clo., Wat. 76 BW40
Monier Rd. E3 143 EA66
Monivea Rd., Beck. 183 DZ94
Monk Dr. E16 144 EG72
Monk Pas. E16 144 EG73
Monk Dr.
Monk St. SE18 165 EN77
Monkchester Clo., Loug. 85 EN39
Monkey Island La., Maid. 150 AE78
Monkfrith Ave. N14 81 DH44
Monkfrith Clo. N14 99 DH45
Monkfrith Way N14 98 DG45
Monkhams Ave., Wdf.Grn. 102 EG50
Monkhams Dr., Wdf.Grn. 102 EH50
Monkhams La., Buck.H. 102 EH48
Monkhams La., Wdf.Grn. 102 EG50
Monkleigh Rd., Mord. 199 CY97
Monks Ave., Barn. 80 DC44
Monks Ave., W.Mol. 196 BZ99
Monks Chase, Brwd. 109 GC50
Monks Clo. SE2 166 EX77
Monks Clo., Brox. 49 EA20
Monks Clo., Enf. 82 DQ40
Monks Clo., Har. 116 CB61
Monks Clo., Ruis. 116 BX63
Monks Clo., St.Alb. 43 CE22
Monks Cres., Add. 212 BH106
Monks Cres., Walt. 195 BV102
Monks Dr. W3 138 CN71
Monks Grn., Lthd. 230 CC121
Monks Horton Way, St.Alb. 43 CH19
Monks Orchard, Dart. 188 FJ89
Monks Orchard Rd., Beck. 203 EA102
Monks Pk., Wem. 138 CP65
Monks Pk. Gdns., Wem. 138 CP66
Monks Pl., Cat. 236 DU122
Tillingdown Hill
Monks Ri., Welw.G.C. 29 CX05
Monks Rd., Bans. 234 DA116
Monks Rd., Enf. 82 DQ40
Monks Rd., Vir.W. 192 AX98
Monks Rd., Wind. 151 AK82
Monks Wk., Grav. 190 GA93
Monk's Wk., Reig. 250 DB134
Monks Way NW11 119 CZ56
Hurstwood Rd.
Monks Way, Beck. 203 EA100
Monks Way, Orp. 205 EQ102
Monks Way, Stai. 174 BK94
Monks Way, West Dr. 154 BL79
Harmondsworth La.
Monksbury, Harl. 52 EU18
Monksdene Gdns., Sutt. 200 DB104
Monksfield Way, Slou. 131 AN70
Monksgrove, Loug. 85 EN43
Monksmead, Borwd. 78 CQ42
Monkswell Ct. N10 98 DG53
Pembroke Rd.
Monkswell La., Couls. 234 DB124
Monkswick Rd., Harl. 35 ET13
Monkswood, Welw.G.C. 29 CW05
Monkswood Ave., Wal.Abb. 67 ED33
Monkswood Gdns., Borwd. 78 CR43
Monkswood Gdns., Ilf. 125 EN55
Monkton Rd., Well. 165 ET82
Monkton St. SE11 278 E8
Monkton St. SE11 161 DN77
Monkville Ave. NW11 119 CZ56
Monkwell Sq. EC2 275 J7
Monmouth Ave. E18 124 EH55
Monmouth Ave., Kings.T. 177 CJ94
Monmouth Clo. W4 158 CR76
Beaumont Rd.
Monmouth Clo., Mitch. 201 DL98
Recreation Way
Monmouth Clo., Well. 166 EU84
Monmouth Gro. W5 158 CL77
Sterling Pl.
Monmouth Pl. W2 140 DA72
Monmouth Rd.
Monmouth Rd. E6 145 EM69
Monmouth Rd. N9 100 DV47
Monmouth Rd. W2 140 DA72
Monmouth Rd., Dag. 126 EZ64
Monmouth Rd., Hayes 155 BS77
Monmouth Rd., Wat. 75 BV41
Monmouth St. WC2 273 P10
Monmouth St. WC2 141 DL72
Monnery Rd. N19 121 DJ62
Monnow Grn., S.Ock. 148 FQ73
Monnow Rd.
Monnow Rd. SE1 162 DU78
Monnow Rd., S.Ock. 148 FQ73
Mono La., Felt. 175 BV89
Monoux Gro. E17 101 EA53
Monro Dr., Guil. 242 AV131
Monro Gdns., Har. 95 CE52
Monroe Cres., Enf. 82 DV39
Monroe Dr. SW14 178 CP85
Mons Wk., Egh. 173 BC92
Mons Way, Brom. 204 EL100
Monsal Ct. E5 123 DX63
Redwald Rd.
Monsell Gdns., Stai. 173 BE92
Monsell Rd. N4 121 DP62
Monson Rd. NW10 139 CU68
Monson Rd. SE14 163 DX80
Monson Rd., Brox. 49 DZ20
Monson Rd., Red. 250 DF131
Montacute Rd. SE6 183 DZ87
Montacute Rd., Croy. 221 EC109
Montacute Rd., Mord. 200 DC100
Montacute Rd. (Bushey), Wat. 95 CE45
Montagu Cres. N18 100 DV49
Montagu Gdns. N18 100 DV49
Montagu Gdns., Wall. 219 DJ105
Montagu Mans. W1 272 E6
Montagu Ms. N. W1 272 E7
Montagu Ms. N. W1 140 DF71
Montagu Ms. S. W1 272 E8
Montagu Ms. W. W1 272 E8
Montagu Pl. W1 272 D7
Montagu Pl. W1 140 DF71
Montagu Rd. N9 100 DW48
Montagu Rd. N18 100 DV50
Montagu Rd. NW4 119 CU58
Montagu Rd. Ind. Est. N18 100 DW49
Montagu Row W1 272 E7
Montagu Sq. W1 272 E7
Montagu Sq. W1 140 DF71
Montagu St. W1 272 E8
Montagu St. W1 140 DF72
Montague Ave. SE4 163 DZ84
Montague Ave. W7 137 CF74
Montague Ave., S.Croy. 220 DS112
Montague Clo. SE1 279 K2
Montague Clo. SE1 142 DR74
Montague Clo., Walt. 195 BU101
Montague Dr., Cat. 236 DQ122
Drake Ave.
Montague Gdns. W3 138 CN73
Montague Pl. WC1 273 N6
Montague Pl. WC1 141 DK71
Montague Rd. E8 122 DU64
Montague Rd. E11 124 EF62
Montague Rd. N8 121 DM57
Montague Rd. N15 122 DU56
Montague Rd. SW19 180 DB94
Montague Rd. W7 157 CF75
Montague Rd. W13 137 CH72
Montague Rd., Berk. 38 AV19
Montague Rd., Croy. 201 DP102
Montague Rd., Houns. 156 CB83
Montague Rd., Rich. 178 CL86
Montague Rd., Slou. 132 AT73
Montague Rd. (Datchet), Slou. 152 AV81
Montague Rd., Sthl. 156 BY77
Montague Rd., Uxb. 134 BK66
Montague Sq. SE15 162 DW80
Clifton Way
Montague St. EC1 275 H7
Montague St. EC1 142 DQ71
Montague St. WC1 273 P6
Montague St. WC1 141 DL71
Montague Waye, Sthl. 156 BY76
Montalt Rd., Wdf.Grn. 102 EF50
Montana Clo., S.Croy. 220 DQ110
Montana Gdns., Sutt. 218 DC106
Lind Rd.
Montana Rd. SW17 180 DG91
Montana Rd. SW20 199 CW95
Montayne Rd. (Cheshunt), Wal.Cr. 67 DX32
Montbelle Rd. SE9 185 EP90
Montbretia Clo., Orp. 206 EW98
Montcalm Clo., Brom. 204 EG100
Montcalm Clo., Hayes 135 BV69
Ayles Rd.
Montcalm Rd. SE7 164 EK80
Montclare St. E2 275 P4
Monteagle Ave., Bark. 145 EQ65
Monteagle Way E5 122 DU62
Rendlesham Rd.
Monteagle Way SE15 162 DV83
Montefiore St. SW8 161 DH82
Montego Clo. SE24 161 DN84
Railton Rd.
Monteith Rd. E3 143 DZ67
Montem La., Slou. 131 AR74
Montem Rd. SE23 183 DZ87
Montem Rd., N.Mal. 198 CS98
Montem St. N4 121 DM60
Thorpedale Rd.
Montenotte Rd. N8 121 DJ57
Monterey Clo., Bex. 187 FC89
Montesole Ct., Pnr. 94 BW54
Pinner Hill Rd.
Montford Pl. SE11 161 DN78
Montford Rd., Sun. 195 BU98
Montfort Gdns., Ilf. 103 EQ51
Montfort Pl. SW19 179 CX88
Montfort Ri., Red. 266 DF142
Montgolfier Wk., Nthlt. 136 BY69
Jetstar Way
Montgomerie Clo., Berk. 38 AU17
Mortain Dr.
Montgomerie Dr., Guil. 242 AU129
Montgomery Ave., Esher 197 CE104
Montgomery Ave., Hem.H. 40 BN19
Montgomery Clo., Grays 170 GC75
Montgomery Clo., Mitch. 201 DL98
Montgomery Clo., Sid. 185 ET86
Montgomery Cres., Rom. 106 FJ50
Montgomery Dr. (Cheshunt), Wal.Cr. 67 DY28
Montgomery Rd. W4 158 CQ77
Montgomery Rd. (South Darenth), Dart. 209 FR95
Montgomery Rd., Edg. 96 CM51
Montgomery Rd., Wok. 226 AY118
Montholme Rd. SW11 180 DF86
Monthope Rd. E1 142 DU71
Casson St.
Montolieu Gdns. SW15 179 CV85
Montpelier Ave. W5 137 CJ71
Montpelier Ave., Bex. 186 EX87
Montpelier Clo., Uxb. 134 BN67
Montpelier Ct., Wind. 151 AQ82
St. Leonards Rd.
Montpelier Gdns. E6 144 EK69
Montpelier Gdns., Rom. 126 EW59
Montpelier Gro. NW5 121 DJ64
Montpelier Ms. SW7 276 C6
Montpelier Pl. E1 142 DW72
Sutton St.
Montpelier Pl. SW7 276 C6
Montpelier Pl. SW7 160 DE76
Montpelier Ri. NW11 119 CY59
Montpelier Ri., Wem. 117 CK60
Montpelier Rd. N3 98 DC53
Montpelier Rd. SE15 162 DV81
Montpelier Rd. W5 137 CK71
Montpelier Rd., Pur. 219 DP110
Montpelier Rd., Sutt. 218 DC105
Montpelier Row SE3 164 EF82
Montpelier Row, Twick. 177 CH87
Montpelier Sq. SW7 276 C6
Montpelier Sq. SW7 160 DE75
Montpelier St. SW7 276 C5
Montpelier St. SW7 160 DE76
Montpelier Ter. SW7 276 C5
Montpelier Vale SE3 164 EF82
Montpelier Wk. SW7 276 B6
Montpelier Wk. SW7 160 DE76
Montpelier Way NW11 119 CY59
Montrave Rd. SE20 182 DW94
Montreal Pl. WC2 274 B10
Montreal Rd., Ilf. 125 EQ59
Montreal Rd., Sev. 256 FE123
Montreal Rd., Til. 171 GG83
Montrell Rd. SW2 181 DL88
Montrose Ave. NW6 139 CY68
Montrose Ave., Edg. 96 CQ54
Montrose Ave., Rom. 106 FJ54
Montrose Ave., Sid. 186 EU87
Montrose Ave., Slou. 131 AP72
Montrose Ave. (Datchet), Slou. 152 AW80
Montrose Ave., Twick. 176 CB87
Montrose Ave., Well. 165 ER83
Montrose Clo., Ashf. 175 BQ93
Montrose Clo., Well. 165 ET83
Montrose Clo., Wdf.Grn. 102 EG49
Montrose Ct. SW7 276 A5
Montrose Ct. SW7 160 DD75
Montrose Cres. N12 98 DC51
Montrose Cres., Wem. 138 CL65
Montrose Gdns., Lthd. 215 CD112
Montrose Gdns., Mitch. 200 DF97
Montrose Gdns., Sutt. 200 DA103
Montrose Pl. SW1 276 G5
Montrose Pl. SW1 160 DG75
Montrose Rd., Felt. 175 BR87
Montrose Rd., Har. 95 CE54
Montrose Wk., Wey. 195 BP104
Montrose Way SE23 183 DX88
Montrose Way, Slou. 152 AX81
Montrouge Cres., Epsom 233 CW116

Mount Pleasant Wk., Bex. 187 FC85
Mount Ri., Red. 266 DD136
Mount Rd. NW2 119 CV62
Mount Rd. NW4 119 CU58
Mount Rd. SE19 182 DR93
Mount Rd. SW19 180 DA89
Mount Rd., Barn. 80 DE43
Mount Rd., Bexh. 186 EX85
Mount Rd., Chess. 216 CM106
Mount Rd., Dag. 126 EZ60
Mount Rd., Dart. 187 FF86
Mount Rd., Epp. 70 EW32
Mount Rd., Felt. 176 BY90
Mount Rd., Hayes 155 BT75
Mount Rd., Hert. 31 DN10
Mount Rd., Ilf. 125 EP64
Mount Rd., Mitch. 200 DD96
Mount Rd., N.Mal. 198 CR97
Mount Rd., Wok. 226 AV121
Mount Rd. (Chobham), Wok. 210 AV112
Mount Row W1 277 H1
Mount Row W1 141 DH73
Mount Sorrel, Hert. 32 DT09
Mount Sq., The NW3 120 DC62
Heath St.
Mount Stewart Ave., Har. 117 CK58
Mount St. W1 276 F1
Mount St. W1 140 DG73
Mount St., Dor. 263 CG136
Mount Ter. E1 142 DV71
New Rd.
Mount Vernon NW3 120 DC63
Mount Vw. NW7 96 CR48
Mount Vw. W5 137 CK70
Mount Vw., Enf. 81 DM38
Mount Vw., Rick. 92 BH46
Mount Vw., St.Alb. 62 CL27
Mount Vw. Rd. E4 101 EC45
Mount Vw. Rd. N4 121 DL59
Mount Vw. Rd. NW9 118 CR57
Mount Vill. SE27 181 DP90
Mount Way, Cars. 218 DG109
Mountacre Clo. SE26 182 DT91
Mountague Pl. E14 143 EC73
Mountain Ct. (Eynsford), Dart. 208 FL103
Pollyhaugh
Mountbatten Clo. SE18 165 ES79
Mountbatten Clo. SE19 182 DS92
Mountbatten Clo., St.Alb. 43 CH23
Mountbatten Clo., Slou. 152 AU75
Mountbatten Ct. SE16 142 DW74
Rotherhithe St.
Mountbatten Ct., Buck.H. 102 EK47
Mountbatten Gdns., Beck. 203 DY98
Balmoral Ave.
Mountbatten Ms. SW18 180 DC88
Inman Rd.
Mountbatten Sq., Wind. 151 AQ81
Alma Rd.
Mountbel Rd., Stan. 95 CG53
Mountcombe Clo., Surb. 198 CL101
Mountearl Gdns. SW16 181 DM90
Mountfield Clo. SE6 183 ED87
Mountfield Rd. E6 145 EN68
Mountfield Rd. N3 119 CZ55
Mountfield Rd. W5 137 CK72
Mountfield Rd., Hem.H. 40 BL20
Mountfield Way, Orp. 206 EW98
Mountford St. E1 142 DU72
Adler St.
Mountfort Cres. N1 141 DN66
Barnsbury Sq.
Mountfort Ter. N1 141 DN66
Barnsbury Sq.
Mountgrove Rd. N5 121 DP62
Mounthurst Rd., Brom. 204 EF101
Mountington Pk. Clo., Har. 117 CK58
Mountjoy Clo. SE2 166 EV75
Mountjoy Ho. EC2 142 DQ71
The Barbican
Mountnessing Bypass, Brwd. 109 GD41
Mounts Pond Rd. SE3 163 ED82
Mounts Rd., Green. 189 FV85
Mountsfield Clo., Stai. 174 BG85
Mountsfield Ct. SE13 183 ED86
Mountside, Felt. 176 BY90
Mountside, Guil. 258 AV136
Mountside, Stan. 95 CF53
Mountview, Nthwd. 93 BT51
Mountview Clo., Red. 266 DE136
Mountview Ct. N8 121 DP56
Green Las.
Mountview Ct., Wat. 76 CB43
Mountview Dr., Red. 266 DE136
Mountview Rd., Esher 215 CH108
Mountview Rd., Orp. 206 EU101
Mountview Rd. (Cheshunt), Wal.Cr. 66 DS26
Mountway, Pot.B. 64 DA30
Mountway, Welw.G.C. 29 CZ12
Mountway Clo., Welw.G.C. 29 CZ12
Mountwood, W.Mol. 196 CA97
Mountwood Clo., S.Croy. 220 DV110
Movers La., Bark. 145 ER67
Mowatt Clo. N19 121 DK60
Mowbray Ave., W.Byf. 212 BL113
Mowbray Cres., Egh. 173 BA92
Mowbray Gdns., Dor. 247 CH134
Mowbray Rd. NW6 139 CY66
Mowbray Rd. SE19 202 DT95
Mowbray Rd., Barn. 80 DC42
Mowbray Rd., Edg. 96 CN49
Mowbray Rd., Harl. 35 ET13
Mowbray Rd., Rich. 177 CJ90
Mowbrays Clo., Rom. 105 FC53
Mowbrays Rd., Rom. 105 FC54
Mowbrey Gdns., Loug. 85 EQ39
Mowlem St. E2 142 DV68
Mowlem Trd. Est. N17 100 DW52
Mowll St. SW9 161 DN80
Moxom Ave. (Cheshunt), Wal.Cr. 67 DY30
Windmill La.
Moxon Clo. E13 144 EF68
Whitelegg Rd.
Moxon St. W1 272 F7
Moxon St. W1 140 DG71
Moxon St., Barn. 79 CZ41
Moye Clo. E2 142 DU67
Dove Row
Moyers Rd. E10 123 EC59
Moylan Rd. W6 159 CY79
Moyne Ct., Wok. 226 AT118
Iveagh Rd.
Moyne Pl. NW10 138 CN68
Moynihan Dr. N21 81 DL43
Moys Clo., Croy. 201 DL100
Moyser Rd. SW16 181 DH92
Mozart St. W10 139 CZ69
Mozart Ter. SW1 276 G9
Muchelney Rd., Mord. 200 DC100
Muckhatch La., Egh. 193 BB97
Muckingford Rd., Til. 171 GL77
Mud La. W5 137 CK71
Muddy La., Slou. 132 AS71
Mudlarks Way SE7 164 EH76
Mudlarks Way SE10 164 EF76
Muggeridge Rd., Dag. 127 FB63
Muir Rd. E5 122 DU63
Muir St. E16 145 EM74
Newland St.
Muirdown Ave. SW14 158 CR84
Muirfield W3 138 CS72
Muirfield Clo. SE16 162 DV78
Ryder Dr.
Muirfield Clo., Wat. 94 BW50
Muirfield Cres. E14 163 EB76
Millharbour
Muirfield Grn., Wat. 94 BW49
Muirfield Rd., Wat. 93 BV49
Muirfield Rd., Wok. 226 AU118
Muirkirk Rd. SE6 183 EC88
Mulberry Ave., Stai. 174 BL88
Mulberry Ave., Wind. 152 AT82
Mulberry Clo. E4 101 EA47
Mulberry Clo. N8 121 DL57
Mulberry Clo. NW3 120 DD63
Hampstead High St.
Mulberry Clo. NW4 119 CW55
Mulberry Clo. SE7 164 EK79
Mulberry Clo. SE22 182 DU86
Mulberry Clo. SW3 160 DD79
Beaufort St.
Mulberry Clo. SW16 181 DJ91
Mulberry Clo., Amer. 72 AT39
Mulberry Clo., Barn. 80 DD42
Mulberry Clo., Brox. 49 DZ24
Mulberry Clo., Nthlt. 136 BY68
Parkfield Ave.
Mulberry Clo., Rom. 127 FH56
Mulberry Clo., St.Alb. 60 CB28
Mulberry Clo., Wey. 195 BP104
Mulberry Clo., Wok. 210 AY114
Mulberry Ct., Bark. 145 ET66
Westrow Dr.
Mulberry Ct., Beac. 89 AM54
Mulberry Ct., Guil. 243 BD131
Gilliat Dr.
Mulberry Cres., Brent. 157 CH80
Mulberry Cres., West Dr. 154 BN75
Mulberry Dr., Purf. 168 FM77
Mulberry Dr., Slou. 152 AY78
Mulberry Grn., Harl. 36 EX11
Mulberry Hill, Brwd. 109 FZ45
Mulberry La., Croy. 202 DT102
Mulberry Ms., Wall. 219 DJ107
Ross Rd.
Mulberry Par., West Dr. 154 BN76
Mulberry Pl. W6 159 CU78
Chiswick Mall
Mulberry Rd. E8 142 DT66
Mulberry Rd., Grav. 190 GE90
Mulberry St. E1 142 DU72
Adler St.
Mulberry Trees, Shep. 195 BR101
Mulberry Wk. SW3 160 DD79
Mulberry Way E18 102 EH54
Mulberry Way, Belv. 167 FC75
Mulberry Way, Ilf. 125 EQ56
Mulgrave Rd. NW10 119 CT63
Mulgrave Rd. SW6 159 CZ79
Mulgrave Rd. W5 137 CK70
Mulgrave Rd., Croy. 202 DR104
Mulgrave Rd., Har. 117 CG61
Mulgrave Rd., Sutt. 217 CZ108
Mulgrave Way, Wok. 226 AS118
Mulholland Clo., Mitch. 201 DH96
Mulkern Rd. N19 121 DK60
Mull Wk. N1 142 DQ65
Clephane Rd.
Mullards Clo., Mitch. 200 DF102
Mullein Ct., Grays 170 GD79
Mullens Rd., Egh. 173 BB92
Muller Rd. SW4 181 DK86
Mullet Gdns. E2 142 DU68
St. Peter's Clo.
Mullins Path SW14 158 CR83
Mullion Clo., Har. 94 CB53
Mullion Wk., Wat. 94 BX49
Ormskirk Rd.
Mulready St. NW8 272 B5
Multi Way W3 158 CS75
Valetta Rd.
Multon Rd. SW18 180 DD87
Mulvaney Way SE1 279 L5
Mulvaney Way SE1 162 DR75
Mumford Ct. EC2 275 J8
Mumford Rd. SE24 181 DP85
Railton Rd.
Mumfords La., Ger.Cr. 112 AU55
Muncaster Clo., Ashf. 174 BN91
Muncaster Rd. SW11 180 DF85
Muncaster Rd., Ashf. 175 BP92
Muncies Ms. SE6 183 EC89
Mund St. W14 159 CZ78
Mundania Rd. SE22 182 DV86
Munday Rd. E16 144 EG72
Mundells, Wal.Cr. 66 DU27
Mundells, Welw.G.C. 29 CZ07
Mundells Ct., Welw.G.C. 29 CZ07
Munden Dr., Wat. 76 BY37
Colne Way
Munden Gro., Wat. 76 BW38
Munden St. W14 159 CY77
Munden Vw., Wat. 76 BX36
Mundesley Clo., Wat. 94 BW49
Mundesley Spur, Slou. 132 AS72
Mundford Rd. E5 122 DW61
Mundon Gdns., Ilf. 125 ER60
Mundy St. N1 275 N2
Mundy St. N1 142 DS69
Munford Dr., Swans. 190 FY87
Mungo Pk. Clo. (Bushey), Wat. 94 CC47
Mungo Pk. Rd., Grav. 191 GK92
Mungo Pk. Rd., Rain. 147 FG65
Mungo Pk. Way, Orp. 206 EW100
Munnery Way, Orp. 205 EN103
Munnings Gdns., Islw. 177 CD85
Munro Dr. N11 99 DJ51
Munro Ms. W10 139 CY71
Munro Rd. (Bushey), Wat. 76 CB43
Munro Ter. SW10 160 DD79
Munslow Gdns., Sutt. 218 DC105
Munstead Vw., Guil. 258 AV138
Munster Ave., Houns. 156 BY84
Munster Ct., Tedd. 177 CJ93
Munster Gdns. N13 99 DP49
Munster Ms. SW6 159 CY80
Munster Rd.
Munster Rd. SW6 159 CY80
Munster Rd., Tedd. 177 CH93
Munster Sq. NW1 273 J3
Munster Sq. NW1 141 DH69
Munton Rd. SE17 279 J8
Munton Rd. SE17 162 DQ77
Murchison Ave., Bex. 186 EX88
Murchison Rd. E10 123 EC61
Murchison Rd., Hodd. 33 EB14
Murdoch Clo., Stai. 174 BG92
Murdock Clo. E16 144 EF72
Rogers Rd.
Murdock St. SE15 162 DV79
Murfett Clo. SW19 179 CY89
Murfitt Way, Upmin. 128 FN63
Muriel Ave., Wat. 76 BW43
Muriel St. N1 141 DM67
Murillo Rd. SE13 163 ED84
Murphy St. SE1 278 D5
Murphy St. SE1 161 DN75
Murray Ave., Brom. 204 EH97
Murray Ave., Houns. 176 CB85
Murray Cres., Pnr. 94 BX53
Murray Grn., Wok. 211 BC114
Bunyard Dr.
Murray Gro. N1 275 J1
Murray Gro. N1 142 DQ68
Murray Ms. NW1 141 DK66
Murray Rd. SW19 179 CX93
Murray Rd. W5 157 CJ77
Murray Rd., Berk. 38 AV18
Murray Rd., Cher. 211 BC107
Murray Rd., Nthwd. 93 BS53
Murray Rd., Orp. 206 EV97
Murray Rd., Rich. 177 CH89
Murray Sq. E16 144 EG72
Murray St. NW1 141 DK66
Murray Ter. NW3 120 DD63
Flask Wk.
Murray Ter. W5 157 CK77
Murray Rd.
Murrays La., W.Byf. 212 BK114
Murrells Wk., Lthd. 230 CA123
Murreys, The, Ash. 231 CK118
Mursell Est. SW8 161 DM81
Murthering La., Rom. 105 FF45
Murton Ct., St.Alb. 43 CE19
Murtwell Dr., Chig. 103 EQ51
Musard Rd. W6 159 CY79
Musbury St. E1 142 DW72
Muscal W6 159 CY79
Muscatel Pl. SE5 162 DS81
Dalwood St.
Muschamp Rd. SE15 162 DT83
Muschamp Rd., Cars. 200 DE103
Muscovy St. EC3 279 N1
Museum La. SW7 276 A7
Museum Pas. E2 142 DV69
Victoria Pk. Sq.
Museum St. WC1 273 P7
Museum St. WC1 141 DL71
Musgrave Clo., Barn. 80 DC39
Musgrave Clo., Wal.Cr. 66 DT27
Allwood Rd.
Musgrave Cres. SW6 160 DA80
Musgrave Rd., Islw. 157 CF81
Musgrove Rd. SE14 163 DX81
Musjid Rd. SW11 160 DD82
Kambala Rd.
Musk Hill, Hem.H. 39 BE21
Muskalls Clo. (Cheshunt), Wal.Cr. 66 DU27
Muskham Rd., Harl. 36 EU12
Musleigh Manor, Ware 33 DZ06
Musley Hill, Ware 33 DY05
Musley La., Ware 33 DY05
Musquash Way, Houns. 156 BW82
Mussenden La. (Horton Kirby), Dart. 208 FQ99
Mussenden La. (Fawkham Grn.), Long. 209 FT101
Mustard Mill Rd., Stai. 173 BE91
Muston Rd. E5 122 DV61
Mustow Pl. SW6 159 CZ82
Munster Rd.
Muswell Ave. N10 99 DH53
Muswell Hill N10 121 DH55
Muswell Hill Bdy. N10 121 DH55
Muswell Hill Pl. N10 121 DH56
Muswell Hill Rd. N6 120 DG58
Muswell Hill Rd. N10 120 DG58
Muswell Ms. N10 121 DH55
Muswell Rd.
Muswell Rd. N10 121 DH55
Mutchetts Clo., Wat. 60 BY33
Mutrix Rd. NW6 140 DA67
Mutton La., Pot.B. 63 CW31
Mutton Pl. NW1 141 DH65
Harmood St.
Muybridge Rd., N.Mal. 198 CQ96
Myatt Rd. SW9 161 DP81
Myatt's Flds. N. SW9 161 DN81
Eythorne Rd.
Myatt's Flds. S. SW9 161 DN82
Mycenae Rd. SE3 164 EG80
Myddelton Ave., Enf. 82 DS38
Myddelton Clo., Enf. 82 DT39
Myddelton Gdns. N21 99 DP45
Myddelton Pk. N20 98 DD48
Myddelton Pas. EC1 274 E2
Myddelton Rd. N8 121 DL56
Myddelton Sq. EC1 274 E2
Myddelton Sq. EC1 141 DN69
Myddelton St. EC1 274 E3
Myddelton St. EC1 141 DN69
Myddleton Ms. N22 99 DL52
Myddleton Path (Cheshunt), Wal.Cr. 66 DV31
Hawthorne Clo.
Myddleton Rd. N22 99 DL52
Myddleton Rd., Uxb. 134 BJ67
Myddleton Rd., Ware 33 DX07
Myers Dr., Slou. 111 AP64
Myers La. SE14 163 DX79
Mygrove Clo., Rain. 148 FK68
Mygrove Gdns., Rain. 148 FK68
Mygrove Rd., Rain. 148 FK68
Myles Ct., Wal.Cr. 66 DQ29
Mylis Clo. SE26 182 DV91
Mylius Clo. SE14 162 DW81
Kender St.
Mylne Clo., Wal.Cr. 66 DW27
Mylne St. EC1 274 D1
Mylne St. EC1 141 DN68
Mylor Clo., Wok. 210 AY114
Mymms Dr., Hat. 64 DA26
Mynchen Clo., Beac. 89 AK49
Mynchen End, Beac. 89 AK49
Mynchen Rd., Beac. 89 AK50
Mynns Clo., Epsom 216 CP114
Myra St. SE2 166 EU77
Myrdle St. E1 142 DU71
Myrke, The, Slou. 152 AT77
Myrna Clo. SW19 180 DE94
Myron Pl. SE13 163 EC83
Myrtle Ave., Felt. 155 BS84
Myrtle Ave., Ruis. 115 BU59
Myrtle Clo., Barn. 98 DF46
Myrtle Clo., Erith 167 FE81
Myrtle Clo., Slou. 153 BE81
Myrtle Clo., Uxb. 134 BM71
Violet Ave.
Myrtle Clo., West Dr. 154 BM76
Myrtle Cres., Slou. 132 AT73
Myrtle Gdns. W7 137 CE74
Myrtle Grn., Hem.H. 39 BE20
Newlands Rd.
Myrtle Gro., Enf. 82 DR38
Myrtle Gro., N.Mal. 198 CQ96
Myrtle Gro., S.Ock. 168 FQ75
Myrtle Pl., Dart. 189 FR87
Myrtle Rd. E6 144 EL67
Myrtle Rd. E17 123 DY58
Myrtle Rd. N13 100 DQ48
Myrtle Rd. W3 138 CQ74
Myrtle Rd., Brwd. 108 FW48
Myrtle Rd., Croy. 203 EA104
Myrtle Rd., Dart. 188 FK88
Myrtle Rd., Dor. 263 CG135
Myrtle Rd., Hmptn. 176 CC93
Myrtle Rd., Houns. 156 CC82
Myrtle Rd., Ilf. 125 EP61
Myrtle Rd., Rom. 106 FJ51
Myrtle Rd., Sutt. 218 DC106
Myrtle Wk. N1 275 M1
Myrtle Wk. N1 142 DS68
Myrtleberry Clo. E8 142 DT65
Beechwood Rd.
Myrtledene Rd. SE2 166 EU78
Myrtleside Clo., Nthwd. 93 BR52
Mysore Rd. SW11 160 DF83
Myth Clo., Upmin. 129 FR58
Myton Rd. SE21 182 DR90

N

Nadine St. SE7 164 EJ78
Nafferton Ri., Loug. 84 EK43
Nagasaki Wk. SE7 164 EJ76
Nagle Clo. E17 101 ED54
Nag's Head Ct. EC1 275 J5
Nags Head La., Brwd. 107 FS51
Nags Head La., Upmin. 106 FQ54
Nags Head La., Well. 166 EV83
Nags Head Rd., Enf. 82 DW42
Nailsworth Cres., Red. 251 DK129
Nailzee Clo., Ger.Cr. 112 AY59
Nairn Ct., Til. 171 GF82
Dock Rd.
Nairn Grn., Wat. 93 BU48
Nairn Rd., Ruis. 136 BW65
Nairn St. E14 143 EC71
Nairne Gro. SE24 182 DR85
Naish Ct. N1 141 DL67
Nalders Rd., Chesh. 54 AR30
Nallhead Rd., Felt. 176 BW92
Namton Dr., Th.Hth. 201 DM98
Nan Clark's La. NW7 97 CT47
Nancy Downs, Wat. 94 BW45
Nankin St. E14 143 EA72
Nansen Rd. SW11 160 DG84
Nansen Rd., Grav. 191 GK92
Nant Rd. NW2 119 CZ61
Nant St. E2 142 DV69
Cambridge Heath Rd.
Nantes Clo. SW18 160 DC84
Nantes Pas. E1 275 P6
Naoroji St. WC1 274 D3
Nap, The, Kings L. 58 BN29
Napier Ave. E14 163 EA78
Napier Ave. SW6 159 CZ83
Napier Clo. SE8 163 DZ80
Amersham Vale
Napier Clo. W14 159 CZ76
Napier Rd.
Napier Clo., Horn. 127 FH60
St. Leonards Way
Napier Clo., St.Alb. 61 CK25
Napier Clo., West Dr. 154 BM76
Napier Ct. SW6 159 CZ83
Ranelagh Gdns.
Napier Ct. (Cheshunt), Wal.Cr. 66 DV28
Flamstead End Rd.
Napier Dr. (Bushey), Wat. 76 BY42
Napier Gdns., Guil. 243 BB133
Napier Gro. N1 142 DQ68
Napier Ho., Rain. 147 FF69
Napier Pl. W14 159 CZ76
Napier Rd. E6 145 EN67
Napier Rd. E11 124 EE63
Napier Rd. E15 144 EE68
Napier Rd. N17 122 DS55
Napier Rd. NW10 139 CV69
Napier Rd. SE25 202 DV98
Napier Rd. W14 159 CY76
Napier Rd., Ashf. 175 BR94
Napier Rd., Belv. 166 EZ77
Napier Rd., Brom. 204 EH98
Napier Rd., Enf. 83 DX43
Napier Rd., Grav. 191 GF88
Napier Rd., Houns. 154 BK81
Napier Rd., Islw. 157 CG84
Napier Rd., S.Croy. 220 DR108
Napier Rd., Wem. 117 CK64
Napier Ter. N1 141 DP65
Napoleon Rd. E5 122 DV62
Napoleon Rd., Twick. 177 CH87
Napsbury Ave., St.Alb. 61 CJ26
Napsbury La., St.Alb. 43 CG23
Napton Clo., Hayes 136 BY70
Kingsash Dr.
Narbonne Ave. SW4 181 DJ85
Narboro Ct., Rom. 127 FG57
Manor Rd.
Narborough Clo., Uxb. 115 BQ61
Aylsham Dr.
Narborough St. SW6 160 DB82
Narcissus Rd. NW6 120 DA64
Narcot La., Ch.St.G. 90 AU48
Narcot La., Ger.Cr. 90 AW52
Narcot Rd., Ch.St.G. 90 AU48
Narcot Way, Ch.St.G. 90 AU49
Nare Rd., S.Ock. 148 FQ73
Naresby Fold, Stan. 95 CJ51
Narford Rd. E5 122 DU62
Narrow La., Warl. 236 DV119
Narrow St. E14 143 DY73
Narrow Way, Brom. 204 EL100
Nascot Pl., Wat. 75 BV40
Stamford Rd.
Nascot Rd., Wat. 75 BV40
Nascot St. W12 139 CW72
Nascot St., Wat. 75 BV40
Nascot Wd. Rd., Wat. 75 BT37
Naseby Clo. NW6 140 DC66
Fairfax Rd.
Naseby Clo., Islw. 157 CE81
Naseby Ct., Walt. 196 BW103
Clements Rd.
Naseby Rd. SE19 182 DR93
Naseby Rd., Dag. 126 FA62
Naseby Rd., Ilf. 103 EM53
Nash Clo., Borwd. 78 CM42
Nash Clo., Hat. 45 CX23
Nash Cft., Grav. 190 GE91
Nash Dr., Red. 250 DF132
Nash Gdns., Red. 250 DF132
Nash Grn., Brom. 184 EG93
Nash Grn., Hem.H. 58 BM25
Nash La., Kes. 222 EG108
Nash Pl. E14 143 EB74
South Colonnade
Nash Rd. N9 100 DW47
Nash Rd. SE4 163 DY84
Nash Rd., Rom. 126 EX56
Nash Rd., Slou. 153 AZ77
Nash St. NW1 273 J2
Nashdom La., Slou. 130 AF66
Nashleigh Hill, Chesh. 54 AQ29
Nash's Yd., Uxb. 134 BK66
Bakers Rd.
Nasmyth St. W6 159 CV76
Nassau Path SE28 146 EW74
Disraeli Clo.
Nassau Rd. SW13 159 CT81
Nassau St. W1 273 K7
Nassau St. W1 141 DJ71
Nassington Rd. NW3 120 DE63
Natal Rd. N11 99 DL51
Natal Rd. SW16 181 DK93
Natal Rd., Ilf. 125 EP63
Natal Rd., Th.Hth. 202 DR97
Natalie Clo., Felt. 175 BR87
Natalie Ms., Twick. 177 CD90
Sixth Cross Rd.
Nathan Clo., Upmin. 129 FS60
Nathan Way SE28 165 ES76
Nathaniel Clo. E1 142 DT71
Thrawl St.
Nathans Rd., Wem. 117 CJ60
Nation Way E4 101 EC46
Natwoke Clo., Beac. 89 AK50
Naunton Way, Horn. 128 FK62
Naval Row E14 143 EC73
Naval Wk., Brom. 204 EG97
High St.
Navarino Gro. E8 142 DU65
Navarino Rd. E8 142 DU65
Navarre Gdns., Rom. 105 FB50
Navarre Rd. E6 144 EL68
Navarre St. E2 275 P4
Navarre St. E2 142 DT70
Navenby Wk. E3 143 EA70
Rounton Rd.
Navestock Clo. E4 101 EC48
Mapleton Rd.
Navestock Cres., Wdf.Grn. 102 EJ53
Navestock Ho., Bark. 146 EV68
Navigator Dr., Sthl. 156 CC75
Navy St. SW4 161 DK83
Naylor Gro., Enf. 83 DX43
South St.
Naylor Rd. N20 98 DC47
Naylor Rd. SE15 162 DV80
Nazareth Gdns. SE15 162 DV82
Nazeing Common Rd., Wal.Abb. 50 EH24
Nazeing New Rd., Brox. 49 EA21
Nazeing Rd., Wal.Abb. 49 EC22
Nazeing Wk., Rain. 147 FE67
Ongar Way
Nazeingbury Clo., Wal.Abb. 49 ED22
Nazeingbury Par., Wal.Abb. 49 ED22
Nazeing Rd.
Nazrul St. E2 275 P2
Nazrul St. E2 142 DT69
Neagle Clo., Borwd. 78 CQ39
Balcon Way
Neal Ave., Sthl. 136 BZ69
Neal Clo., Ger.Cr. 113 BB60
Neal Clo., Nthwd. 93 BU53
Neal Ct., Hert. 32 DQ09
Neal Ct., Wal.Abb. 68 EF33
Neal St. WC2 273 P9
Neal St. WC2 141 DL72
Neal St., Wat. 76 BW43
Nealden St. SW9 161 DM83
Neale Clo. N2 120 DC55
Neal's Yd. WC2 273 P9
Near Acre NW9 97 CT53
Neasden Clo. NW10 118 CS64
Neasden La. NW10 118 CS62
Neasden La. N. NW10 118 CR62
Neasden Underpass NW10 118 CR62

Neasham Rd., Dag. 126 EV64
Neate St. SE5 162 DS79
Neath Gdns., Mord. 200 DC100
Neathouse Pl. SW1 277 K8
Neats Acre, Ruis. 115 BR59
Neatscourt Rd. E6 144 EK71
Neave Cres., Rom. 106 FJ53
Neb Cor. Rd., Oxt. 253 EC131
Nebraska St. SE1 279 K5
Neckinger SE16 162 DT76
Neckinger Est. SE16 162 DT76
Neckinger St. SE1 162 DT75
Nectarine Way SE13 163 EB82
Necton Rd., St.Alb. 28 CL07
Needham Clo., Wind. 151 AL81
Needham Rd. W11 140 DA72
Westbourne Gro.
Needham Ter. NW2 119 CX62
Needleman St. SE16 163 DX75
Needles Bank, Gdse. 252 DV131
Neela Clo., Uxb. 115 BP63
Neeld Cres. NW4 119 CV57
Neeld Cres., Wem. 118 CN64
Neil Clo., Ashf. 175 BQ92
Neil Wates Cres. SW2 181 DN88
Nelgarde Rd. SE6 183 EA87
Nell Gwynn Clo., Rad. 62 CL32
Nell Gwynne Ave., Shep. 195 BR100
Nella Rd. W6 159 CX79
Nelldale Rd. SE16 162 DW77
Nellgrove Rd., Uxb. 135 BP70
Nello James Gdns. SE27 182 DR91
Nelmes Clo., Horn. 128 FM57
Nelmes Cres., Horn. 128 FL57
Nelmes Rd., Horn. 128 FL59
Nelmes Way, Horn. 128 FK56
Nelson Ave., St.Alb. 43 CH23
Nelson Clo., Brwd. 108 FX50
Nelson Clo., Croy. 201 DP102
Nelson Clo., Felt. 175 BT88
Nelson Clo., Rom. 105 FB53
Nelson Clo., Slou. 152 AX77
Nelson Clo., Uxb. 135 BP69
Nelson Clo., Walt. 195 BV102
Nelson Clo., West. 238 EL117
Nelson Ct. SE16 142 DW74
Brunel Rd.
Nelson Gdns. E2 142 DU69
Nelson Gdns., Guil. 243 BA133
Nelson Gdns., Houns. 176 CA86
Nelson Gro. Rd. SW19 200 DB95
Nelson La., Uxb. 135 BP69
Nelson Rd.
Nelson Mandela Clo. N10 98 DG54
Nelson Mandela Rd. SE3 164 EJ83
Nelson Pas. EC1 275 J3
Nelson Pas. EC1 142 DQ69
Nelson Pl. N1 274 G1
Nelson Pl. N1 141 DP68
Nelson Pl., Sid. 186 EU91
Nelson Rd. E4 101 EA51
Nelson Rd. E11 124 EG56
Nelson Rd. N8 121 DM57
Nelson Rd. N9 100 DV47
Nelson Rd. N15 122 DS56
Nelson Rd. SE10 163 EC79
Nelson Rd. SW19 180 DB94
Nelson Rd., Ashf. 174 BL92
Nelson Rd., Belv. 166 EZ78
Nelson Rd., Brom. 204 EJ98
Nelson Rd., Cat. 236 DR123
Nelson Rd., Dart. 188 FJ86
Nelson Rd., Enf. 83 DX44
Nelson Rd., Grav. 191 GF89
Nelson Rd., Har. 117 CD60
Nelson Rd., Houns. 176 CA86
Nelson Rd. 154 BM81
(Heathrow Airport), Houns.
Nelson Rd., N.Mal. 198 CR99
Nelson Rd., Rain. 147 FF68
Nelson Rd., Sid. 186 EU91
Nelson Rd., S.Ock. 149 FW68
Nelson Rd., Stan. 95 CJ51
Nelson Rd., Twick. 176 CB87
Nelson Rd., Uxb. 135 BP69
Nelson Rd., Wind. 151 AM83
Nelson Sq. SE1 278 F4
Nelson Sq. SE1 161 DP75
Nelson St. E1 142 DV72
Nelson St. E6 145 EM68
Nelson St. E16 144 EF73
Huntingdon St.
Nelson St., Hert. 31 DP08
Nelson Ter. N1 274 G1
Nelson Ter. N1 141 DP68
Nelson Trd. Est. SW19 200 DB95
Nelson Wk. SE16 143 DY74
Rotherhithe St.
Nelson's Row SW4 161 DK84
Nelsons Yd. NW1 141 DJ68
Mornington Cres.
Nelwyn Ave., Horn. 128 FM57
Nemoure Rd. W3 138 CQ73
Nene Gdns., Felt. 176 BZ89
Nene Rd., Houns. 155 BP81
Nepaul Rd. SW11 160 DE82
Afghan Rd.
Nepean St. SW15 179 CU86
Neptune Dr., Hem.H. 40 BL18
Neptune Rd., Har. 117 CD58
Neptune Rd. 155 BR81
(Heathrow Airport), Houns.
Neptune St. SE16 162 DW76
Nesbit Rd. SE9 164 EK84
Nesbitt Clo. SE3 164 EE83
Hurren Clo.
Nesbitt Sq. SE19 182 DS94
Coxwell Rd.
Nesbitts All., Barn. 79 CZ41
Bath Pl.
Nesham St. E1 142 DU74
Ness Rd., Erith 168 FK79
Ness St. SE16 162 DU76
Spa Rd.
Nesta Rd., Wdf.Grn. 102 EE51
Nestles Ave., Hayes 155 BT76
Neston Rd., Wat. 76 BW37
Nestor Ave. N21 81 DP44
Nethan Dr., S.Ock. 148 FQ73
Nether Clo. N3 98 DA52
Nether Mt., Guil. 258 AV136
Nether St. N3 98 DA53
Nether St. N12 98 DB51
Netheravon Rd. W7 137 CF74
Netheravon Rd. N. W4 159 CT77
Netheravon Rd. S. W4 159 CT78
Netherbury Rd. W5 157 CK76
Netherby Gdns., Enf. 81 DL42
Netherby Pk., Wey. 213 BR106
Netherby Rd. SE23 182 DW87
Nethercote Ave., Wok. 226 AT117
Nethercourt Ave. N3 98 DA51
Netherfield Gdns., Bark. 145 ER65
Netherfield La., Ware 33 ED12
Netherfield Rd. N12 98 DB50
Netherfield Rd. SW17 180 DG90
Netherford Rd. SW4 161 DJ82
Netherhall Gdns. NW3 140 DC65
Netherhall Rd., Harl. 50 EF17
Netherhall Way NW3 120 DC64
Netherhall Gdns.
Netherlands, The, Couls. 235 DJ119
Netherlands Rd., Barn. 80 DD44
Netherleigh Clo. N6 121 DH60
Hornsey La.
Netherleigh Pk., Red. 267 DL137
Nethern Ct. Rd., Cat. 237 EA123
Netherne La., Couls. 235 DJ123
Netherne La., Red. 235 DJ123
Netherpark Dr., Rom. 105 FF54
Netherton Gro. SW10 160 DC79
Netherton Rd. N15 122 DR58
Seven Sisters Rd.
Netherton Rd., Twick. 177 CG85
Netherway, St.Alb. 42 CA23
Netherwood N2 98 DD54
Netherwood Pl. W14 159 CX76
Netherwood Rd.
Netherwood Rd. W14 159 CX76
Netherwood Rd., Beac. 89 AK50
Netherwood St. NW6 139 CZ66
Netley Clo., Croy. 221 EC108
Netley Clo., Sutt. 217 CX106
Netley Dr., Walt. 196 BZ101
Netley Gdns., Mord. 200 DC101
Netley Rd. E17 123 DZ57
Netley Rd., Brent. 158 CL79
Netley Rd. 155 BR81
(Heathrow Airport), Houns.
Netley Rd., Ilf. 125 ER57
Netley Rd., Mord. 200 DC101
Netley St. NW1 273 K3
Netteswell Orchard, Harl. 35 ER14
Netteswell Rd., Harl. 35 ES13
Netteswell Twr., Harl. 35 ER14
Nettlecombe Clo., Sutt. 218 DB109
Nettlecroft, Hem.H. 40 BH21
Nettlecroft, Welw.G.C. 30 DB08
Nettleden Ave., Wem. 138 CN65
Nettleden Rd., Berk. 39 AZ17
Nettlefold Pl. SE27 181 DP90
Nettles Ter., Guil. 242 AX134
Nettlestead Clo., Beck. 183 DZ94
Copers Cope Rd.
Nettleton Rd. SE14 163 DX81
Nettleton Rd., Houns. 155 BP81
Nettleton Rd., Uxb. 114 BM63
Nettlewood Rd. SW16 181 DK94
Neuchatel Rd. SE6 183 DZ89
Nevada Clo., N.Mal. 198 CQ98
Georgia Rd.
Nevada St. SE10 163 EC79
Nevell Rd., Grays 171 GH76
Nevern Pl. SW5 160 DA77
Nevern Rd. SW5 160 DA77
Nevern Sq. SW5 160 DA77
Nevil Clo., Nthwd. 93 BR50
Nevill Clo. W3 158 CQ75
Acton La.
Nevill Gro., Wat. 75 BV39
Nevill Rd. N16 122 DS63
Nevill Way, Loug. 102 EL45
Valley Hill
Neville Ave., N.Mal. 198 CR95
Neville Clo. E11 124 EF62
Neville Clo. NW1 273 N1
Neville Clo. NW6 139 CZ68
Neville Clo. SE15 162 DU80
Neville Clo., Bans. 218 DB114
Neville Clo., Esher 214 BZ107
Neville Clo., Houns. 156 CB82
Neville Clo., Pot.B. 63 CZ31
Neville Clo., Sid. 185 ET91
Neville Clo., Slou. 132 AT65
Neville Ct., Slou. 130 AJ69
Dropmore Rd.
Neville Dr. N2 120 DC58
Neville Gdns., Dag. 126 EX62
Neville Gill Clo. SW18 180 DB86
Neville Pl. N22 99 DM53
Neville Rd. E7 144 EG66
Neville Rd. NW6 139 CZ68
Neville Rd. W5 137 CK70
Neville Rd., Croy. 202 DR101
Neville Rd., Dag. 126 EX61
Neville Rd., Ilf. 103 EQ53
Neville Rd., Kings.T. 198 CN96
Neville Rd., Rich. 177 CJ89
Neville St. SW7 160 DD78
Neville Ter. SW7 160 DD78
Neville Wk., Cars. 200 DE101
Green Wrythe La.
Nevilles Ct. NW2 119 CU62
Nevin Dr. E4 101 EB46
Nevis Clo., Rom. 105 FE51
Nevis Rd. SW17 180 DG89
New Ash Clo. N2 120 DD55
Oakridge Dr.
New Barn La., Beac. 90 AS49
New Barn La., Sev. 239 EQ116
New Barn La., West. 239 EQ118
New Barn La., Whyt. 236 DS116
New Barn Rd., Grav. 190 GC92
New Barn Rd., Swan. 207 FE95
New Barn St. E13 144 EG70
New Barnes Ave., St.Alb. 43 CG23
New Barns Ave., Mitch. 201 DK98
New Barns Way, Chig. 103 EP48
New Battlebridge La., Red. 251 DH130
New Berry La., Walt. 214 BX106
New Bond St. W1 273 H9
New Bond St. W1 141 DH72
New Brent St. NW4 119 CW57
New Bri. St. EC4 274 F9
New Bri. St. EC4 141 DP72
New Broad St. EC2 275 M7
New Bdy. W5 137 CJ73
New Bdy., Hmptn. 177 CD92
Hampton Rd.
New Burlington Ms. W1 273 K10
New Burlington Pl. W1 273 K10
New Burlington St. W1 273 K10
New Burlington St. W1 141 DJ73
New Butt La. SE8 163 EA80
New Butt La. N. SE8 163 EA80
Reginald Rd.
New Causeway, Reig. 266 DB137
New Cavendish St. W1 272 G7
New Cavendish St. W1 140 DG71
New Change EC4 275 H9
New Change EC4 142 DQ72
New Chapel Sq., Felt. 175 BV88
New Charles St. EC1 274 G2
New Ch. Rd. SE5 162 DR80
New City Rd. E13 144 EJ69
New Clo. SW19 200 DC97
New Clo., Felt. 176 BY92
New College Ms. N1 141 DN66
Islington Pk. St.
New Compton St. WC2 273 N9
New Compton St. WC2 141 DK72
New Coppice, Wok. 226 AT119
New Ct. EC4 274 D10
New Ct., Add. 194 BJ104
New Covent Gdn. Mkt. SW8 161 DK80
New Coventry St. W1 277 N1
New Crane Pl. E1 142 DW74
Garnet St.
New Cross Rd. SE14 162 DW80
New Cross Rd., Guil. 242 AU132
New End NW3 120 DC63
New End Sq. NW3 120 DD63
New England St., St.Alb. 42 CC20
New Era Est. N1 142 DS67
Phillipp St.
New Fm. Ave., Brom. 204 EG98
New Fm. Dr., Rom. 86 EW41
New Fm. La., Nthwd. 93 BS53
New Ferry App. SE18 165 EN76
New Fetter La. EC4 274 E8
New Fetter La. EC4 141 DN72
New Ford Rd., Wal.Cr. 67 DZ34
New Forest La., Chig. 103 EN51
New Frontiers Science Pk., Harl. 51 EM16
New Gdn. Dr., West Dr. 154 BL75
Drayton Gdns.
New Globe Wk. SE1 279 H2
New Globe Wk. SE1 142 DQ74
New Goulston St. E1 275 P8
New Grns. Ave., St.Alb. 43 CD15
New Hall Dr., Rom. 106 FL53
New Haw Rd., Add. 212 BJ106
New Heston Rd., Houns. 156 BZ80
New Horizon Ct., Brent. 157 CG79
Shield Dr.
New Ho. La., Epp. 71 FC25
New Ho. La., Grav. 191 GF90
New Ho. La., Red. 267 DK142
New Ho. Pk., St.Alb. 43 CG23
New Inn Bdy. EC2 275 N4
New Inn La., Guil. 243 BB130
New Inn Pas. WC2 274 C9
New Inn St. EC2 275 N4
New Inn Yd. EC2 275 N4
New Inn Yd. EC2 142 DS70
New James Ct. SE15 162 DV83
Nunhead La.
New Kent Rd. SE1 279 H7
New Kent Rd. SE1 162 DQ76
New Kent Rd., St.Alb. 43 CD20
New King St. SE8 163 EA79
New Kings Rd. SW6 159 CZ82
New La., Guil. 227 AZ124
New La., Wok. 226 AY122
New Lo. Dr., Oxt. 254 EF128
New London St. EC3 275 N10
New Lydenburgh St. SE7 164 EJ76
New Mill Rd., Orp. 206 EW95
New Mt. St. E15 143 ED66
New N. Pl. EC2 275 M5
New N. Rd. N1 142 DQ66
New N. Rd., Ilf. 103 ER52
New N. Rd., Reig. 249 CZ134
New N. St. WC1 274 B6
New N. St. WC1 141 DM71
New Oak Rd. N2 98 DC54
New Orleans Wk. N19 121 DK59
New Oxford St. WC1 273 N8
New Oxford St. WC1 141 DK72
New Par., Ashf. 174 BM91
Church Rd.
New Par., Rick. 73 BC42
Whitelands Ave.
New Pk. Ave. N13 100 DQ48
New Pk. Clo., Nthlt. 136 BY65
New Pk. Ct. SW2 181 DL87
New Pk. Dr., Hem.H. 41 BP19
New Pk. Par. SW2 181 DL86
Doverfield Rd.
New Pk. Rd. SW2 181 DK88
New Pk. Rd., Ashf. 175 BQ92
New Pk. Rd., Hert. 47 DK24
New Pk. Rd., Uxb. 92 BJ53
New Peachey La., Uxb. 134 BK72
New Pl. Gdns., Upmin. 129 FR61
New Pl. Sq. SE16 162 DV76
New Plaistow Rd. E15 144 EE67
New Printing Ho. Sq. WC1 141 DM70
Gray's Inn Rd.
New Priory Ct. NW6 140 DA66
Mazenod Ave.
New Quebec St. W1 272 E9
New Quebec St. W1 140 DF72
New Ride SW7 276 B4
New River Ave., Ware 33 EB11
New River Clo., Hodd. 49 EB16
New River Ct. (Cheshunt), Wal.Cr. 66 DV30
Pengelly Clo.
New River Cres. N13 99 DP49
New River Wk. N1 142 DQ65
St. Paul's Rd.
New Rd. E1 142 DV71
New Rd. E4 101 EB49
New Rd. N8 121 DL57
New Rd. N9 100 DU48
New Rd. N17 100 DT53
New Rd. N22 100 DQ53
New Rd. NW7 97 CY52
New Rd. (Barnet Gate) NW7 97 CT45
New Rd. SE2 166 EX77
New Rd., Amer. 55 AS37
New Rd. (Coleshill), Amer. 55 AM42
New Rd., Berk. 38 AX18
New Rd. (Northchurch), Berk. 38 AS17
New Rd., Borwd. 77 CK44
New Rd., Brent. 157 CK78
New Rd., Brwd. 108 FX47
New Rd., Brox. 49 DZ19
New Rd., Ch.St.G. 72 AY41
New Rd., Dag. 146 FA67
New Rd. (South Darenth), Dart. 208 FQ96
New Rd., Dor. 263 CJ137
Deepdene Ave.
New Rd., Epp. 70 FA32
New Rd., Esher 196 CC104
New Rd. (Claygate), Esher 215 CF110
New Rd., Felt. 175 BR86
New Rd. (East Bedfont), Felt. 175 BV88
New Rd. (Hanworth), Felt. 176 BY92
New Rd., Grav. 191 GH86
New Rd., Grays 170 GA79
New Rd. (Manor Way), Grays 170 GB79
New Rd., Guil. 244 BL131
New Rd. (Albury), Guil. 260 BK139
New Rd. (Chilworth), Guil. 259 BB141
New Rd. (Gomshall), Guil. 261 BQ139
New Rd. (Wonersh), Guil. 259 BB143
New Rd., Harl. 36 EX11
New Rd., Har. 117 CF63
New Rd., Hayes 155 BQ80
New Rd., Hert. 32 DQ07
New Rd., Horl. 269 DP148
New Rd., Houns. 156 CB84
Station Rd.
New Rd., Ilf. 125 ES61
New Rd., Kings L. 57 BF30
New Rd., Kings.T. 178 CN94
New Rd., Lthd. 215 CF110
New Rd., Mitch. 200 DF102
New Rd., Orp. 206 EU101
New Rd. (Limpsfield), Oxt. 254 EH130
New Rd., Pot.B. 63 CU33
New Rd., Rad. 77 CE36
New Rd. (Shenley), Rad. 62 CN34
New Rd., Rain. 147 FC68
New Rd., Rich. 177 CJ91
New Rd., Rick. 74 BN43
New Rd. (Church End), Rick. 73 BF39
New Rd., Rom. 86 EX44
New Rd., Sev. 240 EX124
New Rd., Shep. 194 BN97
New Rd. (Datchet), Slou. 152 AX81
New Rd. (Langley), Slou. 153 BA76
New Rd., Stai. 173 BC92
New Rd., Swan. 207 FF97
New Rd. (Hextable), Swan. 187 FF94
New Rd., Tad. 233 CW123
New Rd., Uxb. 135 BQ70
New Rd., Ware 33 DX06
New Rd., Wat. 76 BW42
New Rd. (Letchmore Heath), Wat. 77 CE39
New Rd., Well. 166 EV82
New Rd. (Stanborough), Welw.G.C. 29 CU12
New Rd., W.Mol. 196 CA97
New Rd., Wey. 213 BQ106
New Rd. Hill, Kes. 222 EL109
New Rd. Hill, Orp. 222 EL109
New Row WC2 273 P10
New Row WC2 141 DL73
New Spring Gdns. Wk. SE11 161 DL78
Goding St.
New Sq. E6 145 EM72
Porter Rd.
New Sq. WC2 274 C8
New Sq. WC2 141 DM72
New Sq., Felt. 175 BQ88
New Sq., Slou. 152 AT75
New Sq. Pas. WC2 141 DM72
New Sq.
New St. EC2 275 N7
New St. EC2 142 DS71
New St., Berk. 38 AX19
New St., Stai. 174 BG91
New St., Wat. 76 BW42
New St., West. 255 EQ127
New St. Hill, Brom. 184 EH92
New St. Sq. EC4 274 E8
New Swan Yd., Grav. 191 GH86
Bank St.
New Trinity Rd. N2 120 DD55
New Turnstile WC1 274 B7
New Union Clo. E14 163 EC76
New Union St. EC2 275 K7
New Union St. EC2 142 DR71
New Wanstead E11 124 EF58
New Way La., Harl. 53 FB16
New Way Rd. NW9 118 CS56
New Wf. Rd. N1 141 DL68
New Wickham La., Egh. 173 BA94
New Windsor St., Uxb. 134 BJ66
New Wd., Welw.G.C. 30 DC08
New Years Grn. La., Uxb. 114 BL58
New Years La., Orp. 239 ET115
New Years La., Sev. 239 ET115
New Zealand Ave., Walt. 195 BT102
New Zealand Way W12 139 CV73
India Way
New Zealand Way, Rain. 147 FF69
Newall Rd., Houns. 155 BQ81
Newark Clo., Guil. 243 BB129
Dairyman's Wk.
Newark Clo., Wok. 228 BG121
Newark Cotts., Wok. 228 BG121
Newark Ct., Walt. 196 BW102
St. Johns Dr.
Newark Cres. NW10 138 CR69
Newark Grn., Borwd. 78 CR41
Newark Knok E6 145 EN72
Newark La., Wok. 227 BF118
Newark Rd., S.Croy. 220 DR107
Newark St. E1 142 DV71
Newark Way NW4 119 CU56
Newberries Ave., Rad. 77 CH35
Newberry Cres., Wind. 151 AK82
Newbery Rd., Erith 167 FF81
Newbery Way, Slou. 151 AR75
Newbiggin Path, Wat. 94 BW49
Newbolt Ave., Sutt. 217 CW106
Newbolt Rd., Stan. 95 CF50
Newborough Grn., N.Mal. 198 CR98
Newburgh Rd. W3 138 CQ74
Newburgh St. W1 273 K9
Newburgh St. W1 141 DJ72
Newburn St. SE11 161 DM78
Newbury Ave., Enf. 83 DZ38
Newbury Clo., Nthlt. 136 BZ65
Newbury Clo., Rom. 106 FK51
Newbury Gdns., Epsom 217 CT105
Newbury Gdns., Rom. 106 FK51
Newbury Gdns., Upmin. 128 FM62
Newbury Ho. N22 99 DL53
Newbury Ms. NW5 140 DG65
Malden Rd.
Newbury Rd. E4 101 EC51
Newbury Rd., Brom. 204 EG97
Newbury Rd., Houns. 154 BM81
Newbury Rd., Ilf. 125 ES58
Newbury Rd., Rom. 106 FK50
Newbury St. EC1 275 H6
Newbury Wk., Rom. 106 FK50
Newbury Way, Nthlt. 136 BZ65
Newby Clo., Enf. 82 DS40
Newby Pl. E14 143 EC73
Newby St. SW8 161 DH83
Newcastle Ave., Ilf. 104 EU51
Newcastle Clo. EC4 274 F8
Newcastle Pl. W2 272 A7
Newcastle Pl. W2 140 DD71
Newcastle Row EC1 274 E5
Newchurch Rd., Slou. 131 AM71
Newcombe Gdns. SW16 181 DL91
Newcombe Pk. NW7 96 CS50
Newcombe Pk., Wem. 138 CM67
Newcombe Ri., West Dr. 134 BL72
Newcombe St. W8 140 DA74
Kensington Pl.
Newcome Path, Rad. 62 CN34
Newcome Rd.
Newcome Rd., Rad. 62 CN34
Newcomen Rd. E11 124 EF62
Newcomen Rd. SW11 160 DD83
Newcomen St. SE1 279 K4
Newcomen St. SE1 162 DR75
Newcourt, Uxb. 134 BJ71
Newcourt St. NW8 272 B1
Newcourt St. NW8 140 DE68
Newcroft Clo., Uxb. 134 BM71
Newdales Clo. N9 100 DU47
Balham Rd.
Newdene Ave., Nthlt. 136 BX68
Newdigate Grn., Uxb. 92 BK53
Newdigate Rd., Uxb. 92 BJ53
Newdigate Rd. E., Uxb. 92 BK53
Newell Rd., Hem.H. 40 BL23
Newell St. E14 143 DZ72
Newenham Rd., Lthd. 246 CA126
Newent Clo. SE15 162 DS80
Newent Clo., Cars. 200 DF102
Newfield Clo., Hmptn. 196 CA95
Percy Rd.
Newfield La., Hem.H. 40 BL20
Newfield Ri. NW2 119 CV62
Newfield Way, St.Alb. 43 CJ22
Newfields, Welw.G.C. 29 CV10
Newford Clo., Hem.H. 41 BP19
Newgale Gdns., Edg. 96 CM53
Newgate, Croy. 202 DQ102
Newgate Clo., Felt. 176 BY89
Newgate Clo., St.Alb. 43 CK17
Newgate St. E4 102 EF48
Newgate St. EC1 274 G8
Newgate St. EC1 141 DP72
Newgate St., Hert. 47 DK21
Newgate St. Village, Hert. 65 DL25
Newgatestreet Rd. (Cheshunt), Wal.Cr. 65 DP25
Newhall Clo., Hem.H. 57 BA27
Newhall Ct., Wal.Abb. 68 EF33
Newham Way E6 145 EN70
Newham Way E16 144 EF71
Newhams Clo., Brom. 205 EM97
Newhams Row SE1 279 N5
Newhaven Clo., Hayes 155 BT77
Newhaven Cres., Ashf. 175 BR92
Newhaven Gdns. SE9 164 EK84
Newhaven La. E16 144 EF70
Newhaven Rd. SE25 202 DR99
Newhaven Spur, Slou. 131 AP70
Newhouse Ave., Rom. 126 EX55
Newhouse Clo., N.Mal. 198 CS101
Newhouse Cres., Wat. 59 BV32
Newhouse Rd., Hem.H. 57 BA26
Newhouse Wk., Mord. 200 DC101
Newick Clo., Bex. 187 FB86
Newick Rd. E5 122 DV62
Newing Grn., Brom. 184 EK94
Newington Barrow Way N7 121 DM62
Newington Butts SE1 278 G9
Newington Butts SE1 161 DP77
Newington Butts SE11 278 G9
Newington Butts SE11 161 DP77
Newington Causeway SE1 278 G7
Newington Causeway SE1 161 DP76
Newington Grn. N1 122 DR64
Newington Grn. N16 122 DR64
Newington Grn. Rd. N1 142 DR65
Newington Way N7 121 DM61
Hornsey Rd.
Newland Clo., Pnr. 94 BY51
Newland Clo., St.Alb. 43 CG23
Newland Ct., Wem. 118 CN61
Forty Ave.
Newland Dr., Enf. 82 DV39
Newland Gdns. W13 157 CG75
Newland Rd. N8 121 DL55
Newland St. E16 144 EL74
Newlands, Hat. 45 CW16
Newlands, The, Wall. 219 DJ108
Newlands Ave., Rad. 61 CF34
Newlands Ave., T.Ditt. 197 CE102
Newlands Ave., Wok. 227 AZ121
Newlands Clo., Brwd. 109 GD45
Newlands Clo., Edg. 96 CL48
Newlands Clo., Horl. 268 DF146
Newlands Clo., Sthl. 156 BY78
Newlands Clo., Walt. 214 BY105
Newlands Clo., Wem. 137 CJ65

Newlands Cor., Guil. 260 BG136
Shere Rd.
Newlands Ct. SE9 185 EN86
Newlands Dr., Slou. 153 BE83
Newlands Mobile Home Pk., Abb.L. 59 BT26
Newlands Pk. SE26 183 DX92
Newlands Pl., Barn. 79 CX43
Newlands Quay E1 142 DW73
Newlands Rd. SW16 201 DL96
Newlands Rd., Hem.H. 39 BE19
Newlands Rd., Wdf.Grn. 102 EF47
Newlands Wk., Wat. 60 BX33
Trevellance Way
Newlands Way, Chess. 215 CJ106
Newlands Way, Pot.B. 64 DB30
Newlands Wd., Croy. 221 DZ109
Newling Clo. E6 145 EM72
Porter Rd.
Newlyn Clo., St.Alb. 60 BY30
Newlyn Clo., Uxb. 134 BN71
Newlyn Gdns., Har. 116 BZ59
Newlyn Rd. N17 100 DT53
Newlyn Rd. NW2 119 CW60
Tilling Rd.
Newlyn Rd., Barn. 79 CZ42
Newlyn Rd., Well. 165 ET82
Newman Clo., Horn. 128 FL57
Newman Pas. W1 273 L7
Newman Rd. E13 144 EH69
Newman Rd. E17 123 DX57
Southcote Rd.
Newman Rd., Brom. 204 EG95
Newman Rd., Croy. 201 DM102
Newman Rd., Hayes 135 BV73
Newman St. W1 273 L7
Newman St. W1 141 DJ71
Newman Yd. W1 273 L8
Newmans Clo., Loug. 85 EP41
Newman's Ct. EC3 275 L9
Newmans Dr., Brwd. 109 GC45
Newmans La., Loug. 85 EN41
Newmans La., Surb. 197 CK100
Newmans Rd., Grav. 191 GF89
Newman's Row WC2 274 C7
Newmans Way, Barn. 80 DC39
Newmarket Ave., Nthlt. 116 CB64
Newmarket Grn. SE9 184 EK87
Middle Pk. Ave.
Newmarket Way, Horn. 128 FL63
Newminster Rd., Mord. 200 DC100
Newnes Path SW15 159 CV84
Putney Pk. La.
Newnham Ave., Ruis. 116 BW60
Newnham Clo., Loug. 84 EK44
Newnham Clo., Nthlt. 116 CC64
Newnham Clo., Slou. 132 AU74
Newnham Clo., Th.Hth. 202 DQ96
Newnham Gdns., Nthlt. 136 CC65
Newnham Ms. N22 99 DM53
Newnham Rd.
Newnham Pl., Grays 171 GG77
Newnham Rd. N22 99 DM53
Newnham Ter. SE1 278 D6
Newnham Way, Har. 118 CL57
Newnhams Clo., Brom. 205 EM97
Newnton Clo. N4 122 DR59
Newpiece, Loug. 85 EP41
Newport Ave. E13 144 EH70
Palmer Rd.
Newport Clo., Enf. 83 DY37
Newport Ct. WC2 273 N10
Newport Mead, Wat. 94 BX49
Kilmarnock Rd.
Newport Pl. WC2 273 N10
Newport Pl. WC2 141 DK73
Newport Rd. E10 123 EC61
Newport Rd. E17 123 DY56
Newport Rd. SW13 159 CU81
Newport Rd., Hayes 135 BR71
Uxbridge Rd.
Newport Rd., Houns. 154 BN81
Newport Rd., Slou. 131 AL70
Newport St. SE11 278 B9
Newport St. SE11 161 DM77
Newports, Saw. 36 EW06
Newports, Swan. 207 FD101
Newquay Cres., Har. 116 BY61
Newquay Gdns., Wat. 93 BV47
Fulford Gro.
Newquay Rd. SE6 183 EB89
Newry Rd., Twick. 177 CG85
Newsam Ave. N15 122 DR57
Newsham Rd., Wok. 226 AT117
Newstead, Hat. 45 CT21
Newstead Ave., Orp. 205 ER104
Newstead Clo. N12 98 DE51
Summerfields Ave.
Newstead Ri., Cat. 252 DV126
Newstead Rd. SE12 184 EF87
Newstead Wk., Cars. 200 DC101
Newstead Way SW19 179 CX91
Newteswell Dr., Wal.Abb. 67 ED32
Newton Abbot Rd., Grav. 191 GF89
Newton Ave. N10 98 DG53
Newton Ave. W3 158 CQ75
Newton Clo. E17 123 DY58
Newton Clo., Hodd. 33 EB13
Newton Clo., Slou. 153 AZ75
Newton Ct., Wind. 172 AU86
Newton Cres., Borwd. 78 CQ42
Newton Dr., Saw. 36 EX06
Newton Gro. W4 158 CS77
Newton La., Wind. 172 AV86
Newton Rd. E15 123 ED64
Newton Rd. N15 122 DT57
Newton Rd. NW2 119 CW62
Newton Rd. SW19 179 CY94
Newton Rd. W2 140 DB72
Newton Rd., Chig. 104 EV50
Newton Rd., Har. 95 CE54
Newton Rd., Islw. 157 CF82
Newton Rd., Pur. 219 DJ112
Newton Rd., Til. 171 GG82
Newton Rd., Well. 166 EU83
Newton Rd., Wem. 138 CM66
Newton St. WC2 274 A8
Newton St. WC2 141 DL72
Newton Wk., Edg. 96 CP53
North Rd.
Newton Way N18 100 DQ50
Newton Wd. Rd., Ash. 232 CM116
Newtons Clo., Rain. 147 FF66
Newtons Ct., Dart. 169 FR84
Newtons Yd. SW18 180 DB85
Wandsworth High St.
Newtonside Orchard, Wind. 172 AU86
Newtown Rd., Uxb. 134 BH65
Newtown St. SW11 161 DH81
Strasburg Rd.
Niagara Ave. W5 157 CJ77
Niagara Clo. N1 142 DR68
Cropley St.
Niagara Clo. (Cheshunt), Wal.Cr. 67 DX29
Nibthwaite Rd., Har. 117 CE57
Nichol Clo. N14 99 DK46
Nichol La., Brom. 184 EG94
Nicholas Clo., Grnf. 136 CB68
Nicholas Clo., St.Alb. 43 CD17
Nicholas Clo., S.Ock. 149 FW69
Nicholas Clo., Wat. 75 BV37
Nicholas Ct. E13 144 EH69
Tunmarsh La.
Nicholas Dr., Sev. 257 FH126
Nicholas Gdns. W5 157 CK75
Nicholas Gdns., Wok. 227 BE116
Nicholas La. EC4 275 L10
Nicholas La., Hert. 32 DQ09
Old Cross
Nicholas Pas. EC4 142 DR72
Lombard St.
Nicholas Rd. E1 142 DW70
Nicholas Rd., Borwd. 78 CM44
Nicholas Rd., Croy. 219 DL105
Nicholas Rd., Dag. 126 EZ61
Nicholas Wk., Grays 171 GH75
Godman Rd.
Nicholas Way, Hem.H. 40 BM18
Nicholas Way, Nthwd. 93 BQ53
Nicholay Rd. N19 121 DK61
Fairbridge Rd.
Nicholes Rd., Houns. 156 CA84
Nicholl Rd., Epp. 69 ET31
Nicholl St. E2 142 DU67
Nicholls Ave., Uxb. 134 BN70
Nicholls Fld., Harl. 52 EU16
Nicholls Wk., Wind. 150 AJ83
Nichollsfield Wk. N7 121 DM64
Hillmarton Rd.
Nichols Clo. N4 121 DM60
Osborne Rd.
Nichols Clo., Chess. 215 CJ107
Merritt Gdns.
Nichols Grn. W5 138 CL71
Montpelier Rd.
Nicholson Dr. (Bushey), Wat. 94 CC46
Nicholson Ms., Egh. 173 BA92
Nicholson Wk.
Nicholson Rd., Croy. 202 DT102
Nicholson St. SE1 278 F3
Nicholson St. SE1 141 DP74
Nicholson Wk., Egh. 173 BA92
Nicholson Way, Sev. 257 FK122
Nickelby Clo. SE28 146 EW72
Nickelby Clo., Uxb. 135 BP72
Dickens Ave.
Nicol Clo., Ger.Cr. 90 AX53
Nicol Clo., Twick. 177 CH86
Cassilis Rd.
Nicol End, Ger.Cr. 90 AW53
Nicol Rd., Ger.Cr. 90 AW53
Nicola Clo., Har. 95 CD54
Nicola Clo., S.Croy. 220 DQ107
Nicola Ms., Ilf. 103 EP52
Nicoll Pl. NW4 119 CV58
Nicoll Rd. NW10 138 CS67
Nicoll Way, Borwd. 78 CR43
Nicolson Rd., Orp. 206 EX101
Nicosia Rd. SW18 180 DE87
Nidderdale, Hem.H. 40 BM17
Wharfedale
Niederwald Rd. SE26 183 DY91
Nield Rd., Hayes 155 BT75
Nigel Clo., Nthlt. 136 BY67
Church Rd.
Nigel Ms., Ilf. 125 EP63
Nigel Playfair Ave. W6 159 CV77
King St.
Nigel Rd. E7 124 EJ64
Nigel Rd. SE15 162 DU83
Nigeria Rd. SE7 164 EJ80
Nightingale, St.Alb. 43 CJ23
Nightingale Ave. E4 102 EE50
Nightingale Ave., Lthd. 229 BR124
Nightingale Ave., Upmin. 129 FT60
Nightingale Clo. E4 102 EE49
Nightingale Clo. W4 158 CQ79
Grove Pk. Ter.
Nightingale Clo., Abb.L. 59 BU31
College Rd.
Nightingale Clo., Cars. 200 DG103
Nightingale Clo., Cob. 214 BX111
Nightingale Clo., Grav. 190 GE91
Nightingale Clo., Pnr. 116 BW57
Nightingale Clo., Rad. 77 CF36
Nightingale Clo., Red. 252 DS134
Nightingale Cres., Lthd. 245 BQ125
Nightingale Dr., Epsom 216 CP107
Nightingale Est. E5 122 DU62
Nightingale Gro. SE13 183 ED85
Nightingale Gro., Dart. 168 FN84
Keyes Rd.
Nightingale La. E11 124 EH57
Nightingale La. N6 120 DE59
Nightingale La. N8 121 DL56
Nightingale La. SW4 181 DH86
Nightingale La. SW12 180 DF87
Nightingale La., Brom. 204 EJ96
Nightingale La., Rich. 178 CL87
Nightingale La., St.Alb. 43 CJ24
Nightingale La., Sev. 256 FB130
Nightingale Ms. E3 143 DY68
Chisenhale Rd.
Nightingale Ms., Kings.T. 197 CK97
South La.
Nightingale Pk., Slou. 131 AM66
Nightingale Pl. SE18 165 EN79
Nightingale Pl. SW10 160 DC79
Fulham Rd.
Nightingale Pl., Rick. 92 BK45
Nightingale Rd. E5 122 DV62
Nightingale Rd. N9 82 DW44
Nightingale Rd. N22 99 DL53
Nightingale Rd. NW10 139 CT68
Nightingale Rd. W7 137 CF74
Nightingale Rd., Cars. 200 DF104
Nightingale Rd., Chesh. 54 AP29
Nightingale Rd., Esher 214 BZ106
Nightingale Rd., Guil. 242 AX134
Nightingale Rd., Hmptn. 176 CA92
Nightingale Rd., Lthd. 245 BT125
Nightingale Rd., Orp. 205 EQ100
Nightingale Rd., Rick. 92 BJ45
Nightingale Rd., S.Croy. 221 DX111
Nightingale Rd., Walt. 195 BV101
Nightingale Rd. (Bushey), Wat. 76 CA43
Nightingale Rd., W.Mol. 196 CB99
Nightingale Sq. SW12 180 DG87
Nightingale Vale SE18 165 EN79
Nightingale Wk. SW4 181 DH86
Nightingale Way E6 144 EL71
Nightingale Way, Swan. 207 FE97
Nightingale Way, Uxb. 113 BF59
Nightingales, Wal.Abb. 68 EE34
Roundhills
Nightingales, The, Stai. 174 BM87
Nightingales La., Ch.St.G. 90 AX46
Nile Path SE18 165 EN79
Jackson St.
Nile Rd. E13 144 EJ68
Nile St. N1 275 J2
Nile St. N1 142 DR69
Nile Ter. SE15 162 DT78
Nimbus Rd., Epsom 216 CR110
Nimegen Way SE22 182 DS85
East Dulwich Gro.
Nimmo Dr. (Bushey), Wat. 95 CD45
Nimrod Clo., Nthlt. 136 BX69
Britannia Clo.
Nimrod Pas. N1 142 DS65
Tottenham Rd.
Nimrod Rd. SW16 181 DH93
Nimrod Rd., Houns. 154 BN81
Northern Perimeter Rd.
Nine Acres, Slou. 131 AN74
Cippenham La.
Nine Acres Clo. E12 124 EL64
Nine Ashes, Ware 34 EK08
Acorn St.
Nine Elms Ave., Uxb. 134 BK71
Nine Elms Clo., Felt. 175 BT88
Nine Elms Clo., Uxb. 134 BK72
Nine Elms Gro., Grav. 191 GG87
Nine Elms La. SW8 161 DJ80
Nine Stiles Clo., Uxb. 134 BH65
Nineacres Way, Couls. 235 DL116
Ninefields, Wal.Abb. 68 EF33
Ninehams Clo., Cat. 236 DR120
Ninehams Gdns., Cat. 236 DR120
Ninehams Rd., Cat. 236 DR121
Ninehams Rd., West. 238 EJ121
Nineteenth Rd., Mitch. 201 DL98
Ninhams Wd., Orp. 223 EN105
Ninian Rd., Hem.H. 40 BL15
Ninnings Rd., Ger.Cr. 91 AZ52
Ninnings Way, Ger.Cr. 91 AZ52
Ninth Ave., Hayes 135 BU73
Nisbet Ho. E9 123 DX64
Homerton High St.
Nita Rd., Brwd. 108 FW50
Nithdale Rd. SE18 165 EP80
Nithsdale Gro., Uxb. 115 BQ62
Tweeddale Gro.
Niton Clo., Barn. 79 CX44
Niton Rd., Rich. 158 CN83
Niton St. SW6 159 CX80
Niven Clo., Borwd. 78 CQ39
Nixey Clo., Slou. 152 AU75
Noak Hill Rd., Rom. 106 FJ49
Nobel Dr., Hayes 155 BR80
Nobel Rd. N18 100 DW49
Noble St. EC2 275 H8
Noble St. EC2 142 DQ72
Noble St., Walt. 195 BV104
Nobles Way, Egh. 172 AY93
Noel Pk. Rd. N22 99 DN54
Noel Rd. E6 144 EL70
Noel Rd. N1 141 DP68
Noel Rd. W3 138 CN72
Noel Sq., Dag. 126 EW63
Noel St. W1 273 L9
Noel St. W1 141 DJ72
Noel Ter. SE23 182 DW89
Dartmouth Rd.
Noke Dr., Red. 250 DG133
Noke La., St.Alb. 60 BY26
Noke Side, St.Alb. 60 CA27
Nokes, The, Hem.H. 40 BG18
Nolan Way E5 122 DU63
Nolton Pl., Edg. 96 CM53
Nonsuch Clo., Ilf. 103 EP51
Nonsuch Ct. Ave., Epsom 217 CV110
Nonsuch Wk., Sutt. 217 CW110
Noons Cor. Rd., Dor. 262 BZ143
Nora Gdns. NW4 119 CX56
Norbiton Ave., Kings.T. 198 CN95
Norbiton Common Rd., Kings.T. 198 CP97
Norbiton Rd. E14 143 DZ72
Norbreck Gdns. NW10 138 CM69
Lytham Gro.
Norbreck Par. NW10 138 CM69
Lytham Gro.
Norbroke St. W12 139 CT73
Norburn St. W10 139 CY71
Chesterton Rd.
Norbury Ave. SW16 201 DM95
Norbury Ave., Houns. 157 CD84
Norbury Ave., Th.Hth. 201 DN96
Norbury Ave., Wat. 76 BW39
Norbury Clo. SW16 201 DN95
Norbury Ct. Rd. SW16 201 DL97
Norbury Cres. SW16 201 DM95
Norbury Cross SW16 201 DL97
Norbury Gdns., Rom. 126 EX57
Norbury Gro. NW7 96 CS48
Norbury Hill SW16 181 DN94
Norbury Pk., Dor. 247 CF127
Norbury Ri. SW16 201 DL97
Norbury Rd. E4 101 EA50
Norbury Rd., Reig. 249 CZ134
Norbury Rd., Th.Hth. 202 DQ96
Norbury Way, Lthd. 246 CC125
Norcombe Gdns., Har. 117 CJ58
Norcott Clo., Hayes 136 BW70
Willow Tree La.
Norcott Rd. N16 122 DU61
Norcroft Gdns. SE22 182 DU87
Norcutt Rd., Twick. 177 CE88
Nordenfeldt Rd., Erith 167 FD78
Nordmann Pl., S.Ock. 149 FX70
Norelands Dr., Slou. 130 AJ68
Norfield Rd., Dart. 187 FC91
Norfolk Ave. N13 99 DP51
Norfolk Ave. N15 122 DT58
Norfolk Ave., Slou. 131 AQ71
Norfolk Ave., S.Croy. 220 DT110
Norfolk Ave., Wat. 76 BW38
Norfolk Clo. N2 120 DE55
Park Rd.
Norfolk Clo. N13 99 DP51
Norfolk Clo., Barn. 80 DG42
Norfolk Clo., Dart. 188 FN86
Norfolk Clo., Horl. 268 DG149
Norfolk Clo., Twick. 177 CH86
Cassilis Rd.
Norfolk Cres. W2 272 B8
Norfolk Cres. W2 140 DE72
Norfolk Cres., Sid. 185 ES87
Norfolk Fm. Clo., Wok. 227 BD116
Norfolk Fm. Rd., Wok. 227 BD115
Norfolk Gdns., Bexh. 166 EZ81
Norfolk Gdns., Borwd. 78 CR42
Norfolk Ho. SE3 164 EE79
Norfolk Ho. Rd. SW16 181 DK90
Norfolk La., Dor. 263 CH142
Norfolk Pl. W2 272 A8
Norfolk Pl. W2 140 DD72
Norfolk Pl., Well. 166 EU82
Norfolk Rd. E6 145 EM67
Norfolk Rd. E17 101 DX54
Norfolk Rd. NW8 140 DD67
Norfolk Rd. NW10 138 CS66
Norfolk Rd. SW19 180 DE94
Norfolk Rd., Bark. 145 ES66
Norfolk Rd., Barn. 80 DA41
Norfolk Rd., Dag. 127 FB64
Norfolk Rd., Dor. 263 CG136
Norfolk Rd. (South Holmwood), Dor. 263 CJ144
Norfolk Rd., Enf. 82 DV44
Norfolk Rd., Esher 215 CE106
Norfolk Rd., Felt. 176 BW88
Norfolk Rd., Grav. 191 GK86
Norfolk Rd., Har. 116 CB57
Norfolk Rd., Ilf. 125 ES60
Norfolk Rd., Rick. 92 BL46
Norfolk Rd., Rom. 127 FC58
Norfolk Rd., Th.Hth. 202 DQ97
Norfolk Rd., Upmin. 128 FN62
Norfolk Rd., Uxb. 134 BK65
Norfolk Row SE1 278 B8
Norfolk Row SE1 161 DM76
Norfolk Sq. W2 272 A9
Norfolk Sq. W2 140 DD72
Norfolk Sq. Ms. W2 272 A9
Norfolk St. E7 124 EG64
Norfolk Ter. W6 159 CY78
Field Rd.
Norgrove Pk., Ger.Cr. 112 AY56
Norgrove St. SW12 180 DG88
Norheads La., Warl. 238 EG119
Norheads La., West. 238 EH117
Norhyrst Ave. SE25 202 DT97
Nork Gdns., Bans. 217 CY114
Nork Ri., Bans. 233 CX115
Nork Way, Bans. 217 CY114
Norland Pl. W11 139 CY74
Norland Rd. W11 139 CX74
Norland Sq. W11 139 CY74
Norlands Cres., Chis. 205 EP95
Norlands Gate, Chis. 205 EP95
Norlands La., Egh. 193 BE97
Norley Vale SW15 179 CU88
Norlington Rd. E10 123 EC60
Norlington Rd. E11 123 ED60
Norman Ave. N22 99 DP53
Norman Ave., Epsom 217 CT112
Norman Ave., Felt. 176 BY89
Norman Ave., S.Croy. 220 DQ110
Norman Ave., Sthl. 136 BY73
Norman Ave., Twick. 177 CH87
Norman Clo., Orp. 205 EQ104
Norman Clo., Rom. 105 FB54
Norman Clo., Wal.Abb. 67 ED33
Norman Ct., Ilf. 125 ER59
Norman Ct., Pot.B. 64 DC30
Norman Cres., Brwd. 109 GA48
Norman Cres., Houns. 156 BX80
Norman Cres., Pnr. 94 BW53
Norman Gro. E3 143 DY68
Norman Rd. E6 145 EM70
Norman Rd. E11 123 ED61
Norman Rd. N15 122 DT57
Norman Rd. SE10 163 EB80
Norman Rd. SW19 180 DC94
Norman Rd., Ashf. 175 BR93
Norman Rd., Belv. 167 FB76
Norman Rd., Dart. 188 FL88
Norman Rd., Horn. 127 FG59
Norman Rd., Ilf. 125 EP64
Norman Rd., Sutt. 218 DA106
Norman Rd., Th.Hth. 201 DP99
Norman St. EC1 275 H3
Norman Way N14 99 DL47
Norman Way W3 138 CP71
Normanby Clo. SW15 179 CZ85
Manfred Rd.
Normanby Rd. NW10 119 CT63
Normand Gdns. W14 159 CY79
Greyhound Rd.
Normand Ms. W14 159 CY79
Normand Rd.
Normand Rd. W14 159 CZ79
Normandy Ave., Barn. 79 CZ43
Normandy Dr., Berk. 38 AV17
Normandy Dr., Hayes 135 BQ72
Normandy Rd. SW9 161 DN81
Normandy Rd., St.Alb. 43 CD18
Normandy Ter. E16 144 EH72
Normandy Wk., Egh. 173 BC92
Mullens Rd.
Normandy Way, Erith 167 FE81
Normanhurst, Ashf. 174 BN92
Normanhurst, Brwd. 109 GC44
Normanhurst Ave., Bexh. 166 EX81
Normanhurst Dr., Twick. 177 CH85
St. Margarets Rd.
Normanhurst Rd. SW2 181 DM89
Normanhurst Rd., Orp. 206 EV96
Normanhurst Rd., Walt. 196 BX103
Normans, The, Slou. 132 AV72
Norman's Bldgs. EC1 142 DQ69
Ironmonger Row
Normans Clo. NW10 138 CR65
Normans Clo., Grav. 191 GG87
Normans Clo., Uxb. 134 BM71
Normans Mead NW10 138 CR65
Normansfield Ave., Tedd. 177 CJ94
Normansfield Clo. (Bushey), Wat. 94 CB45
Normanshire Ave. E4 101 EC49
Normanshire Dr.
Normanshire Dr. E4 101 EA49
Normanton Ave. SW19 180 DA89
Normanton Pk. E4 102 EE48
Normanton Rd., S.Croy. 220 DS106
Normanton St. SE23 183 DX89
Normington Clo. SW16 181 DN92
Norrels Dr., Lthd. 245 BT126
Norrels Ride, Lthd. 245 BT125
Norrice Lea N2 120 DD57
Norris Gro., Brox. 49 DY20
Norris La., Hodd. 49 EA16
Norris Ri., Hodd. 49 DZ16
Norris Rd., Hodd. 49 EA17
Norris Rd., Stai. 173 BF91
Norris St. SW1 277 M1
Norris Way, Dart. 167 FF83
Norroy Rd. SW15 159 CX84
Norrys Clo., Barn. 80 DF42
Norrys Rd., Barn. 80 DF42
Norseman Clo., Ilf. 126 EV60
Norseman Way, Grnf. 136 CB67
Olympic Way
Norstead Pl. SW15 179 CU89
Norsted La., Orp. 224 EU112
North Access Rd. E17 123 DX58
North Acre NW9 96 CS53
North Acre, Bans. 233 CZ116
North Acton Rd. NW10 138 CR68
North App., Nthwd. 93 BQ47
North App., Wat. 75 BT35
North Audley St. W1 272 F9
North Audley St. W1 140 DG73
North Ave. N18 100 DU49
North Ave. W13 137 CH71
North Ave., Brwd. 106 FQ45
North Ave., Cars. 218 DG108
North Ave., Har. 116 CB58
North Ave., Hayes 135 BU73
North Ave., Rad. 62 CL32
North Ave., Rich. 158 CN81
Sandycoombe Rd.
North Ave., Sthl. 136 BZ73
North Ave., Walt. 213 BS109
North Bank NW8 272 B3
North Bank NW8 140 DE69
North Barn, Brox. 49 EA21
North Birkbeck Rd. E11 123 ED62
North Branch Ave. W10 139 CW69
Harrow Rd.
North Burnham Clo., Slou. 130 AH68
Wyndham Cres.
North Carriage Dr. W2 272 B10
North Carriage Dr. W2 140 DE73
North Circular Rd. E4 101 DZ52
North Circular Rd. E18 102 EH53
North Circular Rd. N3 119 CZ56
North Circular Rd. N12 98 DD53
North Circular Rd. N13 99 DN50
North Circular Rd. NW2 118 CS62
North Circular Rd. NW10 118 CS63
North Circular Rd. NW11 119 CX58
North Clo., Barn. 79 CW43
North Clo., Bexh. 166 EX84
North Clo., Chig. 104 EU50
North Clo., Dag. 146 FA67
North Clo., Dor. 263 CJ140
North Clo., Felt. 175 BR86
North Rd.
North Clo., Mord. 199 CY98
North Clo., St.Alb. 60 CB25
North Clo., Wind. 151 AM81
North Colonnade E14 143 EA74
North Common, Wey. 213 BP105
North Common Rd. W5 138 CL73
North Common Rd., Uxb. 114 BK64
North Cotts., St.Alb. 61 CG25
North Countess Rd. E17 101 DZ54
North Ct. W1 273 L6
North Ct., Rick. 92 BG46
Hall Clo.
North Cray Rd., Bex. 186 FA89
North Cray Rd., Sid. 186 EY93
North Cres. E16 143 EC70
North Cres. N3 97 CZ54
North Cres. WC1 273 M6
North Cross Rd. SE22 182 DT85
North Cross Rd., Ilf. 125 EQ56
North Dene NW7 96 CR48
North Dene, Houns. 156 CB81
North Down, S.Croy. 220 DS111
North Downs Cres., Croy. 221 EB110
North Downs Rd., Croy. 221 EB109
North Downs Way, Bet. 248 CQ132
North Downs Way, Dor. 261 BU137
North Downs Way, Guil. 258 AT138
North Downs Way (Albury), Guil. 260 BJ136
North Downs Way, Oxt. 254 EE126
North Downs Way, Sev. 241 FD118
North Downs Way, Tad. 248 CQ132
North Downs Way, West. 239 ER121
North Dr. SW16 181 DJ91
North Dr., Beac. 110 AG55
North Dr., Houns. 156 CC82
North Dr., Orp. 223 ES105
North Dr., Rom. 128 FJ55
North Dr., Ruis. 115 BS59
North Dr., Slou. 132 AS69
North Dr., Vir.W. 192 AS100
North End NW3 120 DC61
North End, Buck.H. 102 EJ45
North End, Croy. 202 DQ103
North End Ave. NW3 120 DC61
North End Cres. W14 159 CZ77
North End Ho. W14 159 CY77
North End La., Orp. 223 EN111
North End Par. W14 159 CY77
North End Rd.
North End Rd. NW11 120 DA60
North End Rd. SW6 159 CZ79
North End Rd. W14 159 CY77
North End Rd., Wem. 118 CN62
North End Way NW3 120 DC61

Nutfield Clo., Cars. 200 DE104
Nutfield Gdns., Ilf. 125 ET61
Nutfield Gdns., Nthlt. 136 BW68
Nutfield Marsh Rd., Red. 251 DK131
Nutfield Rd. E15 123 EC63
Nutfield Rd. NW2 119 CU61
Nutfield Rd. SE22 182 DT85
Nutfield Rd., Couls. 234 DG116
Nutfield Rd., Red. 250 DG134
Nutfield Rd. 251 DJ129
(South Merstham), Red.
Nutfield Rd., Th.Hth. 201 DP98
Nutfield Way, Orp. 205 EN103
Nutford Pl. W1 272 C8
Nutford Pl. W1 140 DE72
Nuthatch Clo., Stai. 174 BM88
Nuthatch Gdns. SE28 165 ER75
Nuthatch Gdns., Reig. 266 DC138
Nuthurst Ave. SW2 181 DM89
Nutkins Way, Chesh. 54 AQ29
Nutley Clo., Swan. 207 FF95
Nutley Ct., Reig. 249 CZ134
Nutley La.
Nutley La., Reig. 249 CZ133
Nutley Ter. NW3 140 DC65
Nutmead Clo., Bex. 187 FC88
Nutmeg Clo. E16 144 EE70
Cranberry La.
Nutmeg La. E14 143 ED72
Nutt Gro., Edg. 95 CK47
Nutt St. SE15 162 DT80
Nuttall St. N1 142 DS68
Nutter La. E11 124 EJ58
Nuttfield Clo., Rick. 75 BP44
Nutty La., Shep. 195 BQ97
Nutwell St. SW17 180 DE92
Nutwood Ave., Bet. 264 CQ135
Nutwood Clo., Bet. 264 CQ135
Nuxley Rd., Belv. 166 EZ79
Nyanza St. SE18 165 ER79
Nye Bevan Est. E5 123 DX62
Nye Way, Hem.H. 57 BA28
Nyefield Pk., Tad. 249 CU126
Nylands Ave., Rich. 158 CN81
Nymans Gdns. SW20 199 CV97
Hidcote Gdns.
Nynehead St. SE14 163 DY80
Nyon Gro. SE6 183 DZ89
Nyssa Clo., Wdf.Grn. 103 EM51
Gwynne Pk. Ave.
Nyth Clo., Upmin. 129 FR58
Nyton Clo. N19 121 DL60
Courtauld Rd.

O

Oak Apple Ct. SE12 184 EG89
Oak Ave. N8 121 DL56
Oak Ave. N10 99 DH52
Oak Ave. N17 100 DR52
Oak Ave., Croy. 203 EA102
Oak Ave., Egh. 173 BC94
Oak Ave., Enf. 81 DM39
Oak Ave., Hmptn. 176 BY92
Oak Ave., Houns. 156 BY80
Oak Ave., St.Alb. 60 CA30
Oak Ave., Sev. 257 FH128
Oak Ave., Upmin. 128 FP62
Oak Ave., Uxb. 115 BP61
Oak Ave., West Dr. 154 BN76
Oak Bank, Croy. 221 EC107
Oak Bank, Wok. 226 AY119
Oak Clo. N14 99 DH45
Oak Clo., Dart. 167 FE84
Oak Clo., Gdmg. 258 AS143
Oak Clo., Hem.H. 40 BM24
Oak Clo., Sutt. 200 DC103
Oak Clo., Wal.Abb. 67 ED34
Oak Cottage Clo. SE6 184 EF88
Oak Cres. E16 144 EE71
Oak Dene W13 137 CH71
The Dene
Oak Dr., Berk. 38 AX20
Oak Dr., Saw. 36 EW07
Oak Dr., Tad. 248 CP130
Oak End, Harl. 51 ET17
Oak End Dr., Iver 133 BC68
Oak End Way, Add. 211 BE112
Oak End Way, Ger.Cr. 113 AZ57
Oak Gdns., Croy. 203 EA103
Oak Gdns., Edg. 96 CQ54
Oak Glade, Epp. 70 EX29
Coopersale Common
Oak Glade, Nthwd. 93 BP53
Oak Glen, Horn. 128 FL55
Oak Gra. Rd., Guil. 244 BG129
Oak Grn., Abb.L. 59 BS31
Oak Grn. Way, Abb.L. 59 BS32
Oak Grn.
Oak Gro. NW2 119 CX63
Oak Gro., Hat. 45 CT18
Oak Gro., Hert. 32 DS11
Oak Gro., Ruis. 115 BV59
Oak Gro., Sun. 175 BV94
Oak Gro., W.Wick. 203 EC103
Oak Gro. Rd. SE20 202 DW96
Oak Hill, Epsom 232 CR116
Oak Hill, Guil. 243 BC129
Oak Hill, Wdf.Grn. 101 ED52
Oak Hill Clo., Wdf.Grn. 101 ED52
Oak Hill Ct. SW19 179 CX94
Oak Hill Cres., Wdf.Grn. 101 ED52
Oak Hill Gdns., Wdf.Grn. 102 EE53
Oak Hill Pk. NW3 120 DB63
Oak Hill Pk. Ms. NW3 120 DC63
Oak Hill Rd., Rom. 105 FD45
Oak Hill Rd., Sev. 256 FG124
Oak Hill Way NW3 120 DC63
Oak La. E14 143 DZ73
Oak La. N2 98 DD54
Oak La. N11 99 DK51
Oak La., Egh. 172 AW90
Oak La., Islw. 157 CE84
Oak La. (Cuffley), Pot.B. 65 DM28
Oak La., Sev. 256 FF129
Oak La., Twick. 177 CG87
Oak La., Wind. 151 AN81
Oak La., Wok. 227 BC116
Beaufort Rd.
Oak La., Wdf.Grn. 102 EF49
Oak Leaf Clo., Epsom 216 CQ112
Oak Lo. Ave., Chig. 103 ER50
Oak Lo. Clo., Stan. 95 CJ50
Dennis La.
Oak Lo. Clo., Walt. 214 BW106
Oak Lo. Dr., Red. 266 DG142
Oak Lo. Dr., W.Wick. 203 EB101
Oak Lo. La., West. 255 ER125
Oak Manor Dr., Wem. 118 CM64
Oakington Manor Dr.
Oak Pk., W.Byf. 211 BE113
Oak Pk. Gdns. SW19 179 CX87
Oak Path (Bushey), Wat. 76 CB44
Ashfield Ave.
Oak Piece, Epp. 71 FC25
Oak Pl. SW18 180 DB85
East Hill
Oak Ridge, Dor. 263 CH139
Oak Ri., Buck.H. 102 EK48
Oak Rd. W5 137 CK73
The Bdy.
Oak Rd., Cat. 236 DS122
Oak Rd., Cob. 230 BX115
Oak Rd., Epp. 69 ET30
Oak Rd. 167 FC80
(Northumberland Heath), Erith
Oak Rd. (Slade Grn.), Erith 167 FG81
Oak Rd., Grav. 191 GJ90
Oak Rd., Grays 170 GC79
Oak Rd., Green. 189 FS86
Oak Rd., Lthd. 231 CG119
Oak Rd., N.Mal. 198 CR96
Oak Rd., Orp. 224 EU108
Oak Rd., Reig. 250 DB133
Oak Rd., Rom. 106 FM53
Oak Rd., West. 255 ER125
Oak Row SW16 201 DJ96
Oak Side, Uxb. 134 BH65
Oak St., Hem.H. 40 BM24
Oak St., Rom. 127 FC57
Oak Stubbs La., Maid. 150 AF75
Oak Tree Clo. W5 137 CJ72
Pinewood Gro.
Oak Tree Clo., Abb.L. 59 BR32
Oak Tree Clo. (Burpham), 243 BC129
Guil.
Oak Tree Clo. 242 AX128
(Jacobs Well), Guil.
Oak Tree Clo., Hat. 45 CU17
Oak Tree Clo., Hert. 32 DW12
Oak Tree Clo., Loug. 85 EQ39
Oak Tree Clo., Stan. 95 CH52
Oak Tree Clo., Vir.W. 192 AX100
Oak Tree Ct., Borwd. 77 CK44
Barnet La.
Oak Tree Dell NW9 118 CQ57
Oak Tree Dr. N20 98 DB46
Oak Tree Dr., Egh. 172 AW92
Oak Tree Dr., Guil. 242 AW130
Oak Tree Gdns., Brom. 184 EH92
Oak Tree Rd. NW8 272 A3
Oak Tree Rd. NW8 140 DE69
Oak Village NW5 120 DG63
Oak Wk., Saw. 36 EX07
Oak Way N14 99 DH45
Oak Way W3 138 CS74
Oak Way, Ash. 232 CN116
Oak Way, Croy. 203 DX100
Oak Way, Felt. 175 BS88
Oak Way, Reig. 266 DD135
Oakapple Clo., S.Croy. 220 DV114
Oakbank, Brwd. 109 GE43
Oakbank, Lthd. 230 CC123
Oakbank Ave., Walt. 196 BZ101
Oakbank Gro. SE24 162 DQ84
Oakbrook Clo., Brom. 184 EH91
Oakbury Rd. SW6 160 DB82
Oakcombe Clo., N.Mal. 198 CS95
Traps La.
Oakcroft Clo., Pnr. 93 BV54
Oakcroft Clo., W.Byf. 211 BF114
Oakcroft Rd. SE13 163 ED82
Oakcroft Rd., Chess. 216 CM105
Oakcroft Rd., W.Byf. 211 BF114
Oakcroft Vill., Chess. 216 CM105
Oakdale N14 99 DH46
Oakdale, Welw.G.C. 29 CX05
Oakdale Ave., Har. 118 CL57
Oakdale Ave., Nthwd. 93 BU54
Oakdale Clo., Wat. 94 BW49
Oakdale Ct. E4 101 EC50
Oakdale Gdns. E4 101 EC50
Oakdale La., Eden. 255 EQ133
Oakdale Rd. E7 144 EH66
Oakdale Rd. E11 123 ED61
Oakdale Rd. E18 102 EH54
Oakdale Rd. N4 122 DQ58
Oakdale Rd. SE15 162 DW83
Oakdale Rd. SW16 181 DL92
Oakdale Rd., Epsom 216 CR109
Oakdale Rd., Wat. 94 BW48
Oakdale Rd., Wey. 194 BN104
Oakdale Way, Mitch. 200 DG101
Wolseley Rd.
Oakden St. SE11 278 E8
Oakden St. SE11 161 DN77
Oakdene SE15 162 DV81
Carlton Gro.
Oakdene, Beac. 89 AL52
Oakdene, Tad. 233 CY120
Oakdene (Cheshunt), 67 DY30
Wal.Cr.
Oakdene, Wok. 210 AT110
Oakdene Ave., Chis. 185 EN92
Oakdene Ave., Erith 167 FC79
Oakdene Ave., T.Ditt. 197 CG102
Oakdene Clo., Bet. 264 CQ136
Oakdene Clo., Horn. 127 FH58
Oakdene Clo., Lthd. 246 CC127
Oakdene Clo., Pnr. 94 BZ52
Oakdene Dr., Surb. 198 CQ101
Oakdene Ms., Sutt. 199 CZ102
Oakdene Pk. N3 97 CZ52
Oakdene Rd., Bet. 264 CP136
Oakdene Rd., Cob. 213 BV114
Oakdene Rd., Guil. 258 AW142
Oakdene Rd., Hem.H. 40 BM24
Oakdene Rd., Lthd. 230 BZ124
Oakdene Rd., Orp. 205 ET99
Oakdene Rd., Red. 250 DE134
Oakdene Rd., Sev. 256 FG122
Oakdene Rd., Uxb. 135 BP68
Oakdene Rd., Wat. 75 BV36
Oakdene Way, St.Alb. 43 CJ20
Oake Ct. SW15 179 CY85
Oaken Coppice, Ash. 232 CN119
Oaken Dr., Esher 215 CF107
Oaken Gro., Welw.G.C. 29 CY11
Oaken La., Esher 215 CE105
Oakenshaw Clo., Surb. 198 CL101
Oakes Clo. E6 145 EM72
Savage Gdns.
Oakeshott Ave. N6 120 DG61
Oakey La. SE1 278 D6
Oakfield E4 101 EB50
Oakfield, Rick. 91 BF45
Oakfield, Wok. 226 AS116
Oakfield Ave., Har. 117 CH55
Oakfield Ave., Slou. 131 AP74
Oakfield Clo., N.Mal. 199 CT99
Blakes La.
Oakfield Clo., Pot.B. 63 CZ31
Oakfield Clo., Ruis. 115 BT58
Evelyn Ave.
Oakfield Clo., Wey. 213 BQ105
Oakfield Ct. N8 121 DL59
Oakfield Ct. NW2 119 CX59
Hendon Way
Oakfield Dr., Reig. 250 DA132
Oakfield Gdns. N18 100 DS49
Oakfield Gdns. SE19 182 DT92
Oakfield Gdns., Beck. 203 EA99
Oakfield Gdns., Cars. 200 DE102
Oakfield Gdns., Grnf. 137 CD70
Oakfield Glade, Wey. 213 BQ105
Oakfield La., Bex. 187 FE89
Oakfield La., Dart. 187 FG89
Oakfield La., Kes. 222 EJ105
Oakfield Pk. Rd., Dart. 188 FK89
Oakfield Pl., Dart. 188 FK89
Oakfield Rd. E6 144 EL67
Oakfield Rd. E17 101 DY54
Oakfield Rd. N3 98 DB53
Oakfield Rd. N4 121 DN58
Oakfield Rd. N14 99 DL48
Oakfield Rd. SE20 202 DV95
Oakfield Rd. SW19 179 CX90
Oakfield Rd., Ashf. 175 BP91
Oakfield Rd., Ash. 231 CK117
Oakfield Rd., Cob. 213 BV113
Oakfield Rd., Croy. 202 DQ102
Oakfield Rd., Ilf. 125 EP61
Oakfield Rd., Orp. 206 EU101
Goodmead Rd.
Oakfield St. SW10 160 DC79
Oakfields, Guil. 242 AS133
Oakfields, Sev. 257 FH126
Oakfields, Walt. 195 BU102
Oakfields, W.Byf. 212 BH114
Oakfields Rd. NW11 119 CY58
Oakford Rd. NW5 121 DJ63
Oakhall Ct. E11 124 EH58
Oakhall Dr., Sun. 175 BT92
Oakhall Rd. E11 124 EH58
Oakham Clo. SE6 183 DZ89
Rutland Wk.
Oakham Clo., Barn. 80 DG41
Oakham Dr., Brom. 204 EF98
Oakhampton Rd. NW7 97 CX52
Oakhill, Esher 215 CG107
Oakhill, Surb. 198 CL101
Oakhill Ave. NW3 120 DB63
Oakhill Ave., Pnr. 94 BY54
Oakhill Clo., Ash. 231 CJ118
Oakhill Clo., Rick. 91 BE49
Oakhill Ct. E11 124 EH58
Eastern Ave.
Oakhill Ct. SW19 179 CX94
Edge Hill
Oakhill Cres., Surb. 198 CL101
Oakhill Dr., Surb. 198 CL101
Oakhill Gdns., Wey. 195 BS103
Oatlands Dr.
Oakhill Gro., Surb. 198 CL100
Oakhill Path, Surb. 198 CL100
Glenbuck Rd.
Oakhill Pl. SW15 180 DA85
Oakhill Rd.
Oakhill Rd. SW15 179 CZ85
Oakhill Rd. SW16 201 DL95
Oakhill Rd., Add. 211 BF107
Oakhill Rd., Ash. 231 CJ118
Oakhill Rd., Beck. 203 EC96
Oakhill Rd., Orp. 205 ET102
Oakhill Rd., Purf. 168 FP78
Oakhill Rd., Reig. 266 DB135
Oakhill Rd., Rick. 91 BD49
Oakhill Rd., Surb. 198 CL100
Oakhill Rd., Sutt. 200 DB104
Oakhouse Rd., Bexh. 186 FA85
Oakhurst, Wok. 210 AS109
Oakhurst Ave., Barn. 98 DE45
Oakhurst Ave., Bexh. 166 EY80
Oakhurst Clo. E17 124 EE56
Oakhurst Clo., Ilf. 103 EQ53
Oakhurst Clo., Tedd. 177 CE92
Oakhurst Gdns. E4 102 EF46
Oakhurst Gdns. E17 124 EE56
Oakhurst Gdns., Bexh. 166 EY80
Oakhurst Gro. SE22 162 DU84
Oakhurst Ri., Cars. 218 DE110
Oakhurst Rd., Enf. 83 DX36
Oakhurst Rd., Epsom 216 CQ107
Oakington, Welw.G.C. 30 DD09
Oakington Ave., Amer. 72 AX39
Oakington Ave., Har. 116 CA59
Oakington Ave., Hayes 155 BR77
Oakington Ave., Wem. 118 CM62
Oakington Dr., Sun. 196 BW96
Oakington Manor Dr., Wem. 118 CN64
Oakington Rd. W9 140 DA70
Oakington Way N8 121 DL58
Oakland Gdns., Brwd. 109 GC43
Oakland Pl., Buck.H. 102 EG47
Oakland Rd. E15 124 EE63
Crownfield Rd.
Oakland Way, Epsom 216 CR107
Oaklands N21 99 DM47
Oaklands, Berk. 38 AU19
Oaklands, Horl. 269 DJ147
Oaklands, Ken. 220 DQ114
Oaklands, Lthd. 231 CD124
Oaklands, Twick. 176 CC87
Oaklands Ave. N9 82 DV44
Oaklands Ave., Esher 197 CD102
Oaklands Ave., Hat. 63 CY26
Oaklands Ave., Islw. 157 CF79
Oaklands Ave., Rom. 127 FE55
Oaklands Ave., Sid. 185 ET87
Oaklands Ave., Th.Hth. 201 DN98
Oaklands Ave., Wat. 93 BV46
Oaklands Ave., W.Wick. 203 EB104
Oaklands Clo., Bexh. 186 EZ85
Oaklands Clo., Chess. 215 CJ105
Oaklands Clo., Guil. 258 AY142
Oaklands Clo., Orp. 205 ES100
Oaklands Ct., Add. 194 BH104
Oaklands Ct., Wat. 75 BT39
Oaklands Ct., Wem. 117 CK64
Oaklands Dr., Harl. 52 EW16
Oaklands Dr., Red. 267 DH136
Oaklands Dr., S.Ock. 149 FW71
Oaklands Est. SW4 181 DJ86
Oaklands Gdns., Ken. 220 DQ114
Oaklands Gate, Nthwd. 93 BS51
Green La.
Oaklands Gro. W12 139 CU74
Oaklands Gro., Brox. 49 DY24
Oaklands La., Barn. 79 CV42
Oaklands La., St.Alb. 44 CL18
Oaklands La., West. 222 EH113
Oaklands Pk. Ave., Ilf. 125 ER61
High Rd.
Oaklands Pl. SW4 161 DJ84
St. Alphonsus Rd.
Oaklands Rd. N20 97 CZ45
Oaklands Rd. NW2 119 CX63
Oaklands Rd. SW14 158 CR83
Oaklands Rd. W7 157 CF75
Oaklands Rd., Bexh. 166 EZ84
Oaklands Rd., Brom. 184 EE94
Oaklands Rd., Dart. 188 FP88
Oaklands Rd., Grav. 191 GF91
Oaklands Rd. (Cheshunt), 66 DS26
Wal.Cr.
Oaklands Way, Tad. 233 CW122
Oaklands Way, Wall. 219 DK108
Oaklawn Rd., Lthd. 231 CE118
Oaklea Pas., Kings.T. 197 CK97
Oakleafe Gdns., Ilf. 125 EP55
Oakleigh Ave. N20 98 DD47
Oakleigh Ave., Edg. 96 CP54
Oakleigh Ave., Surb. 198 CN102
Oakleigh Clo. N20 98 DF48
Oakleigh Clo., Swan. 207 FE97
Oakleigh Ct., Barn. 80 DE44
Church Hill Rd.
Oakleigh Ct., Edg. 96 CQ54
Oakleigh Cres. N20 98 DE47
Oakleigh Dr., Rick. 75 BQ44
Oakleigh Gdns. N20 98 DC46
Oakleigh Gdns., Edg. 96 CM50
Oakleigh Gdns., Orp. 223 ES105
Oakleigh Ms. N20 98 DC47
Oakleigh Rd. N.
Oakleigh Pk. Ave., Chis. 205 EN96
Oakleigh Pk. N. N20 98 DD46
Oakleigh Pk. S. N20 98 DE45
Oakleigh Ri., Epp. 70 EU32
Bower Hill
Oakleigh Rd., Pnr. 94 BZ51
Oakleigh Rd., Uxb. 135 BQ66
Oakleigh Rd. N. N20 98 DE47
Oakleigh Rd. S. N11 98 DG48
Oakleigh Way, Mitch. 201 DH95
Oakleigh Way, Surb. 198 CN102
Oakley Ave. W5 138 CN73
Oakley Ave., Bark. 145 ET66
Oakley Ave., Croy. 219 DM105
Oakley Clo. E4 101 EC48
Mapleton Rd.
Oakley Clo. E6 144 EL72
Northumberland Rd.
Oakley Clo. W7 137 CE73
Oakley Clo., Add. 212 BK105
Oakley Clo., Grays 169 FW79
Oakley Clo., Islw. 157 CD81
Oakley Ct., Mitch. 200 DG102
London Rd.
Oakley Cres. EC1 274 G1
Oakley Cres., Slou. 132 AS73
Oakley Dell, Guil. 243 BC132
Oakley Dr. SE9 185 ER88
Oakley Dr. SE13 183 EC85
Hither Grn. La.
Oakley Dr., Brom. 204 EL104
Oakley Dr., Rom. 106 FN50
Oakley Gdns. N8 121 DM57
Oakley Gdns. SW3 160 DE79
Oakley Gdns., Bans. 234 DB115
Oakley Grn. Rd., Wind. 150 AG82
Oakley Pk., Bex. 186 EW87
Oakley Pl. SE1 162 DT78
Oakley Rd. N1 142 DR66
Oakley Rd. SE25 202 DV99
Oakley Rd., Brom. 204 EL104
Oakley Rd., Har. 117 CE58
Oakley Rd., Warl. 236 DU118
Oakley Sq. NW1 141 DJ68
Oakley St. SW3 160 DE79
Oakley Wk. W6 159 CX79
Greyhound Rd.
Oakley Yd. E2 142 DT70
Bacon St.
Oaklodge Way NW7 97 CT51
Oakmead Ave., Brom. 204 EG100
Oakmead Gdns., Edg. 96 CR49
Oakmead Grn., Epsom 232 CQ115
Oakmead Pl., Mitch. 200 DE95
Oakmead Rd. SW12 180 DG88
Oakmead Rd., Croy. 201 DK100
Oakmeade, Pnr. 94 CA51
Oakmere Ave., Pot.B. 64 DC33
Oakmere Clo., Pot.B. 64 DD31
Oakmere La., Pot.B. 64 DC32
Oakmere Rd. SE2 166 EU79
Oakmoor Way, Chig. 103 ES50
Oakmount Pl., Orp. 205 ER102
Oakridge, St.Alb. 60 BZ29
Oakridge Ave., Rad. 61 CF34
Oakridge Dr. N2 120 DD55
Oakridge La., Brom. 183 ED92
Downham Way
Oakridge La., Wat. 77 CD35
Oakridge Rd., Brom. 183 ED91
Oakroyd Ave., Pot.B. 63 CZ33
Oakroyd Clo., Pot.B. 63 CZ33
Oaks, The N12 98 DB49
Oaks, The SE18 165 EQ78
Oaks, The, Berk. 38 AU19
Oaks, The, Epsom 217 CT114
Oaks, The, Hayes 135 BQ68
Charville La.
Oaks, The, Ruis. 115 BS59
Oaks, The, Stai. 173 BF91
Moormede Cres.
Oaks, The, Swan. 207 FE96
Oaks, The, Wat. 94 BW46
Oaks, The, W.Byf. 212 BG114
Oaks, The, Wdf.Grn. 102 EE52
Oaks Ave. SE19 182 DS92
Oaks Ave., Felt. 176 BY89
Oaks Ave., Rom. 105 FC54
Oaks Ave., Wor.Pk. 199 CV104
Oaks Clo., Lthd. 231 CG121
Oaks Clo., Rad. 77 CF35
Oaks Gro. E4 102 EE47
Oaks La., Croy. 202 DW104
Oaks La., Dor. 263 CH143
Oaks La., Ilf. 125 ES57
Oaks Rd., Croy. 220 DV106
Oaks Rd., Ken. 219 DP114
Oaks Rd., Reig. 250 DD133
Oaks Rd., Stai. 174 BK86
Oaks Rd., Wok. 226 AY117
Oaks Track, Cars. 218 DF111
Oaks Track, Wall. 219 DH110
Oaks Way, Cars. 218 DF108
Oaks Way, Epsom 233 CV119
Epsom La. N.
Oaks Way, Ken. 220 DQ114
Oaks Way, Surb. 197 CK103
Oaksford Ave. SE26 182 DV90
Oakshade Rd., Brom. 183 ED91
Oakshade Rd., Lthd. 214 CC114
Oakshaw, Oxt. 253 ED127
Oakshaw Rd. SW18 180 DB87
Oakside, Uxb. 134 BH65
Oakside Ct., Horl. 269 DJ147
Oakside La.
Oakside La., Horl. 269 DJ147
Oakthorpe Rd. N13 99 DN50
Oaktree Ave. N13 99 DP48
Oaktree Clo., Brwd. 109 FZ49
Hawthorn Ave.
Oaktree Clo., Wal.Cr. 65 DP28
Oaktree Garth, Welw.G.C. 29 CY10
Oaktree Gro., Ilf. 125 ER64
Oakview Clo., Wal.Cr. 66 DV28
Oakview Gdns. N2 120 DD56
Oakview Gro., Croy. 203 DY102
Oakview Rd. SE6 183 EB92
Oakway SW20 199 CW98
Oakway, Amer. 55 AP35
Oakway, Brom. 203 ED96
Oakway, Wok. 226 AS119
Oakway Clo., Bex. 186 EY86
Oakways SE9 185 EP86
Oakwood, Berk. 38 AT20
Oakwood, Guil. 242 AU129
Oakwood, Wall. 219 DH109
Oakwood, Wal.Abb. 83 ED35
Roundhills
Oakwood Ave. N14 99 DK45
Oakwood Ave., Beck. 203 EC96
Oakwood Ave., Borwd. 78 CP42
Oakwood Ave., Brwd. 109 GE44
Oakwood Ave., Brom. 204 EH97
Oakwood Ave., Mitch. 200 DD96
Oakwood Ave., Pur. 219 DP112
Oakwood Ave., Sthl. 136 CA73
Oakwood Chase, Horn. 128 FM58
Oakwood Clo. N14 81 DJ44
Oakwood Clo., Chis. 185 EM93
Oakwood Clo., Dart. 188 FP88
Oakwood Clo., Lthd. 245 BS127
Oakwood Clo., Red. 250 DG134
Oakwood Clo. 267 DM136
(South Nutfield), Red.
The Ave.
Oakwood Clo., Wdf.Grn. 102 EL51
Green Wk.
Oakwood Ct. W14 159 CZ76
Oakwood Cres. N21 81 DL44
Oakwood Cres., Grnf. 137 CG65
Oakwood Dr. SE19 182 DR93
Oakwood Dr., Bexh. 167 FD84
Oakwood Dr., Edg. 96 CQ51
Oakwood Dr., Lthd. 245 BS127
Oakwood Dr., St.Alb. 43 CJ19
Oakwood Dr., Sev. 257 FH123
Oakwood Gdns., Ilf. 125 ET61
Oakwood Gdns., Orp. 205 EQ103
Oakwood Gdns., Sutt. 200 DA103
Oakwood Hill, Loug. 85 EM44
Oakwood Hill Ind. Est., 85 EP43
Loug.
Oakwood La. W14 159 CZ76
Oakwood Pk. Rd. N14 99 DK45
Oakwood Pl., Croy. 201 DN100
Oakwood Rd. NW11 120 DA56
Oakwood Rd. SW20 199 CU95
Oakwood Rd., Croy. 201 DN100
Oakwood Rd., Horl. 268 DG147
Oakwood Rd., Orp. 205 EQ103
Oakwood Rd., Pnr. 93 BV54
Oakwood Rd., Red. 251 DN129
Oakwood Rd., St.Alb. 60 BY29
Oakwood Rd., Vir.W. 192 AW99
Oakwood Rd., Wok. 226 AS119
Oakwood Vw. N14 81 DK43
Oakworth Rd. W10 139 CW71
Oast Ho. Clo., Stai. 172 AY87
Oast Rd., Oxt. 254 EF131
Oasthouse Way, Orp. 206 EV98
Oat La. EC2 275 J8
Oat La. EC2 142 DQ72
Oates Clo., Brom. 203 ED97
Oates Rd., Rom. 105 FB50
Oatfield Rd., Orp. 205 ET102
Oatfield Rd., Tad. 233 CV121
Oatland Ri. E17 101 DY54
Oatlands, Horl. 269 DH147
Oatlands Ave., Wey. 213 BQ106
Oatlands Chase, Wey. 195 BS104
Oatlands Clo., Wey. 213 BQ105
Oatlands Dr., Slou. 131 AR72
Oatlands Dr., Wey. 195 BR104
Oatlands Grn., Wey. 195 BR104
Oatlands Dr.
Oatlands Mere, Wey. 195 BR104
Oatlands Rd., Enf. 82 DW39
Oatlands Rd., Tad. 233 CY119
Oban Clo. E13 144 EJ70
Oban Ct., Slou. 151 AR75
Montem La.
Oban Ho., Bark. 145 ER68
Wheelers Cross

Oban Rd. E13 144 EJ69
Oban Rd. SE25 202 DR98
Oban St. E14 143 ED72
Obelisk Ride, Egh. 172 AS93
Oberon Clo., Borwd. 78 CQ39
Oberon Way, Shep. 194 BL97
Oberstein Rd. SW11 160 DD84
Oborne Clo. SE24 181 DP85
Observatory Gdns. W8 160 DA75
Observatory Rd. SW14 158 CQ84
Observatory Wk., Red. 250 DF134
Lower Bri. Rd.
Occupation La. SE18 165 EP81
Occupation La. W5 157 CK77
Occupation Rd. SE17 279 H10
Occupation Rd. SE17 162 DQ78
Occupation Rd. W13 157 CH75
Occupation Rd., Wat. 75 BV43
Ocean Est. E1 143 DX70
Ocean St. E1 143 DX71
Ockenden Clo., Wok. 227 AZ118
Ockenden Rd.
Ockenden Gdns., Wok. 227 AZ118
Ockenden Rd.
Ockenden Rd., Wok. 227 AZ118
Ockendon Rd. N1 142 DR65
Ockendon Rd., Upmin. 128 FQ64
Ockham Dr., Lthd. 229 BR124
Ockham Dr., Orp. 186 EU94
Ockham La., Cob. 229 BR120
Ockham La., Wok. 228 BN121
Ockham Rd. N., Lthd. 229 BQ123
Ockham Rd. N., Wok. 228 BL120
Ockham Rd. S., Lthd. 245 BS126
Ockley Ct., Guil. 243 BB129
Cotts Wd. Dr.
Ockley Rd. SW16 181 DL91
Ockley Rd., Croy. 201 DM101
Ockleys Mead, Gdse. 252 DW130
Octagon Arc. EC2 275 M7
Octagon Rd., Walt. 213 BS109
Octavia Clo., Mitch. 200 DE99
Octavia Rd., Islw. 157 CF83
Octavia St. SW11 160 DE81
Octavia Way SE28 146 EV73
Booth Clo.
Octavia Way, Stai. 174 BG93
Octavius St. SE8 163 EA80
Odard Rd., W.Mol. 196 CA98
Down St.
Oddesey Rd., Borwd. 78 CP39
Odencroft, Slou. 131 AN69
Odessa Rd. E7 124 EF63
Odessa Rd. NW10 139 CU68
Odessa St. SE16 163 DZ75
Odger St. SW11 160 DF82
Odhams Wk. WC2 273 P9
Odyssey Business Pk., Ruis. 115 BV64
Offa Rd., St.Alb. 42 CC20
Offas Mead E9 123 DY63
Lindisfarne Way
Offenbach Ho. E2 143 DX68
Mace St.
Offenham Rd. SE9 185 EM91
Offerton Rd. SW4 161 DJ83
Offham Slope N12 97 CZ50
Offley Rd. SW9 161 DN80
Offord Clo. N17 100 DU52
Offord Rd. N1 141 DM66
Offord St. N1 141 DM66
Ogard Rd., Hodd. 49 EC15
Ogilby St. SE18 165 EM77
Oglander Rd. SE15 162 DT84
Ogle St. W1 273 K6
Ogle St. W1 141 DJ71
Oglethorpe Rd., Dag. 126 EZ62
Ohio Rd. E13 144 EF70
Oil Mill La. W6 159 CU78
Okeburn Rd. SW17 180 DG92
Okehampton Clo. N12 98 DD50
Okehampton Cres., Well. 166 EV81
Okehampton Rd. NW10 139 CW67
Okehampton Rd., Rom. 106 FJ51
Okehampton Sq., Rom. 106 FJ51
Okemore Gdns., Orp. 206 EW98
Olaf St. W11 139 CX73
Old Acre, Wok. 212 BG114
Old Ave., W.Byf. 211 BE113
Old Ave., Wey. 213 BQ108
Old Ave. Clo., W.Byf. 211 BE113
Old Bailey EC4 274 G9
Old Bailey EC4 141 DP72
Old Bakery Ms., Guil. 260 BH139
Old Barn Clo., Sutt. 217 CY108
Old Barn La., Pur. 236 DT116
Old Barn La., Rick. 74 BM43
Old Barn Rd., Epsom 232 CQ117
Old Barn Way, Bexh. 167 FD83
Old Barrack Yd. SW1 276 F5
Old Barrowfield E15 144 EE67
New Plaistow Rd.
Old Bethnal Grn. Rd. E2 142 DU69
Old Bexley La., Bex. 187 FD89
Old Bexley La., Dart. 187 FF88
Old Bond St. W1 277 K1
Old Bond St. W1 141 DJ73
Old Brewers Yd. WC2 273 P9
Old Brewery Ms. NW3 120 DD63
Hampstead High St.
Old Bri. Clo., Nthlt. 136 CA68
Old Bri. St., Kings.T. 197 CK96
Old Broad St. EC2 275 L9
Old Broad St. EC2 142 DR72
Old Bromley Rd., Brom. 183 ED92
Old Brompton Rd. SW5 160 DB78
Old Brompton Rd. SW7 160 DB78
Old Bldgs. WC2 274 D8
Old Burlington St. W1 273 K10
Old Burlington St. W1 141 DJ73
Old Carriageway, The, Sev. 256 FC122
Old Castle St. E1 275 P8
Old Castle St. E1 142 DT72
Old Cavendish St. W1 273 H8
Old Cavendish St. W1 141 DH72
Old Change Ct. EC4 142 DQ72
Carter La.
Old Chapel Rd., Swan. 207 FC101
Old Charlton Rd., Shep. 195 BQ99
Old Chelsea Ms. SW3 160 DD79
Danvers St.
Old Chertsey Rd., Wok. 210 AV110
Old Chestnut Ave., Esher 214 CA107
Old Ch. La. NW9 118 CR61
Old Ch. La., Brwd. 109 GE42
Old Ch. La., Grnf. 137 CG69
Perivale La.
Old Ch. La., Stan. 95 CH50
Old Ch. Path, Esher 214 CB105
High St.
Old Ch. Rd. E1 143 DX72
Old Ch. Rd. E4 101 EA49
Old Ch. St. SW3 160 DD78
Old Claygate La., Esher 215 CG107
Old Clem Sq. SE18 165 EN79
Kempt St.
Old Coach Rd., Cher. 193 BD99
Old Common Rd., Cob. 213 BU112
Old Compton St. W1 273 M10
Old Compton St. W1 141 DK73
Old Cote Dr., Houns. 156 CA79
Old Ct., Ash. 232 CL119
Old Ct. Grn., Berk. 39 BC17
Hempstead La.
Old Ct. Pl. W8 160 DB75
Old Ct. Rd., Guil. 258 AU135
Old Crabtree La., Hem.H. 40 BL21
Old Cross, Hert. 32 DQ09
Old Dartford Rd. (Farningham), Dart. 208 FM100
Old Dean, Hem.H. 57 BA28
Old Deer Pk. Gdns., Rich. 158 CL83
Old Devonshire Rd. SW12 181 DH87
Old Dock App. Rd., Grays 170 GE77
Old Dock Clo., Rich. 158 CN79
Watcombe Cotts.
Old Dover Rd. SE3 164 EG80
Old Dr., The, Welw.G.C. 29 CV10
Old Epsom Rd., Guil. 244 BK131
Old Esher Clo., Walt. 214 BX106
Old Esher Rd.
Old Esher Rd., Walt. 214 BX106
Old Farleigh Rd., S.Croy. 220 DW110
Old Farleigh Rd., Warl. 237 DY117
Old Fm. Ave. N14 99 DJ45
Old Fm. Ave., Sid. 185 ER88
Old Fm. Clo., Beac. 88 AJ50
Old Fm. Clo., Houns. 156 BZ84
Old Fm. Gdns., Swan. 207 FF97
Old Fm. Pas., Hmptn. 196 CC95
Old Fm. Rd. N2 98 DD53
Old Fm. Rd., Guil. 242 AX131
Old Fm. Rd., Hmptn. 176 BZ93
Old Fm. Rd., West Dr. 154 BK75
Old Fm. Rd. E., Sid. 186 EU89
Old Fm. Rd. W., Sid. 185 ET89
Old Farmhouse Dr., Lthd. 231 CD115
Old Ferry Dr., Stai. 172 AW86
Old Fld. Clo., Amer. 72 AY39
Old Fish St. Hill EC4 275 H10
Old Fishery La., Hem.H. 39 BF22
Old Fives Ct., Slou. 130 AH69
Old Fleet La. EC4 274 F8
Old Fold Clo., Barn. 79 CZ39
Old Fold La.
Old Fold La., Barn. 79 CZ39
Old Fold Vw., Barn. 79 CW41
Old Ford Rd. E2 142 DW68
Old Ford Rd. E3 143 DX68
Old Forge Clo., Stan. 95 CG49
Old Forge Clo., Wat. 59 BU33
Old Forge Clo., Welw.G.C. 29 CZ05
Old Forge Cres., Shep. 195 BP100
Old Forge Ms. W12 159 CV75
Goodwin Rd.
Old Forge Rd., Enf. 82 DT38
Old Forge Way, Sid. 186 EV91
Old Fox Clo., Cat. 235 DP121
Old Fox Footpath, S.Croy. 220 DS108
Essenden Rd.
Old French Horn La., Hat. 45 CW17
Old Gannon Clo., Nthwd. 93 BQ50
Old Gdn., The, Sev. 256 FD123
Old Gdn. Ct., St.Alb. 42 CC20
Old Gloucester St. WC1 274 A6
Old Gloucester St. WC1 141 DL71
Old Hall Clo., Pnr. 94 BY53
Old Hall Dr., Pnr. 94 BY53
Old Hall Ri., Harl. 52 EY15
Old Hall St., Hert. 32 DR09
Old Harpenden Rd., St.Alb. 43 CE17
Old Harrow La., West. 239 EQ119
Old Hatch Manor, Ruis. 115 BT59
Old Herns La., Welw.G.C. 30 DC07
Herns La.
Old Hertford Rd., Hat. 45 CW16
Old Highway, Hodd. 33 EB14
Old Hill, Chis. 205 EN95
Old Hill, Orp. 223 ER107
Old Hill, Wok. 226 AX120
Old Homesdale Rd., Brom. 204 EJ98
Old Hospital Clo. SW12 180 DF88
Old Ho. Clo. SW19 179 CY92
Old Ho. Clo., Epsom 217 CT110
Old Ho. Ct., Hem.H. 40 BM20
Old Ho. Rd.
Old Ho. Gdns., Twick. 177 CJ86
Old Ho. La., Harl. 50 EK18
Old Ho. La., Kings L. 74 BL35
Old Ho. La., Wal.Abb. 50 EF23
Old Ho. Rd., Hem.H. 40 BM20
Old Howlett's La., Ruis. 115 BR58
Bury St.
Old Jamaica Rd. SE16 162 DU76
Old James St. SE15 162 DV83
Old Jewry EC2 275 K9
Old Jewry EC2 142 DR72
Old Kent Rd. SE1 279 M8
Old Kent Rd. SE1 162 DS77
Old Kent Rd. SE15 162 DV79
Old Kenton La. NW9 118 CP57
Old Kiln La., Bet. 264 CQ135
Old Kiln Rd. (Tylers Grn.), H.Wyc. 88 AC45
Old Kingston Rd., Wor.Pk. 198 CQ104
Old La., Cob. 229 BP117
Old La., West. 238 EK121
Old La. Gdns., Cob. 229 BT122
Old Leys, Hat. 45 CU21
Old Lo. La., Ken. 235 DN116
Old Lo. La., Pur. 219 DM113
Old Lo. Pl., Twick. 177 CH86
St. Margarets Rd.
Old Lo. Way, Stan. 95 CG50
Old London Rd., Dor. 247 CJ127
Old London Rd., Epsom 233 CU118
Old London Rd., Hert. 32 DS09
Old London Rd., Lthd. 245 BU126
Old London Rd., St.Alb. 43 CD21
Old London Rd., Sev. 224 EY109
Old London Rd. (Knockholt Pound), Sev. 240 EY115
Old Long Gro., Beac. 89 AQ51
Old Maidstone Rd., Sid. 186 EZ94
Old Malden La., Wor.Pk. 198 CR104
Old Malt Way, Wok. 226 AX117
Old Manor Dr., Grav. 191 GJ88
Old Manor Dr., Islw. 176 CC86
Old Manor Gdns., Guil. 259 BC140
Old Manor Ho. Ms., Shep. 194 BN97
Squires Bri. Rd.
Old Manor La., Guil. 259 BC140
Old Manor Way, Bexh. 167 FD82
Old Manor Way, Chis. 185 EM92
Old Manor Yd. SW5 160 DB77
Earls Ct. Rd.
Old Marsh La., Maid. 150 AF75
Old Marylebone Rd. NW1 272 C7
Old Marylebone Rd. NW1 140 DE71
Old Mead, Ger.Cr. 90 AY51
Old Meadow Clo., Berk. 38 AU21
Old Merrow St., Guil. 243 BC131
Old Ms., Har. 117 CE57
Hindes Rd.
Old Mill Clo. (Eynsford), Dart. 208 FL102
Old Mill Ct. E18 124 EJ55
Old Mill Gdns., Berk. 38 AX20
London Rd.
Old Mill La. W6 159 CU78
Old Mill La., Maid. 150 AC75
Old Mill La., Red. 251 DH128
Old Mill La., Uxb. 134 BH71
Old Mill Pl., Rom. 127 FD58
Old Mill Rd. SE18 165 ER79
Old Mill Rd., Kings L. 59 BQ34
Old Mill Rd., Uxb. 114 BG62
Old Mitre Ct. EC4 141 DN72
Fleet St.
Old Montague St. E1 142 DU71
Old Moor La., H.Wyc. 110 AE55
Old Nazeing Rd., Brox. 49 EA21
Old Nichol St. E2 275 P4
Old Nichol St. E2 142 DT70
Old N. St. WC1 274 B6
Old Nursery Ct., Slou. 111 AQ61
Old Oak Ave., Couls. 234 DE119
Old Oak Common La. NW10 138 CS70
Old Oak Common La. W3 138 CS71
Old Oak La. NW10 139 CT69
Old Oak Rd. W3 139 CT73
Old Oaks, Wal.Abb. 68 EE32
Old Orchard, Harl. 51 ER17
Old Orchard, St.Alb. 60 CC26
Old Orchard, Sun. 196 BW96
Old Orchard, W.Byf. 212 BM112
Old Orchard, The NW3 120 DF63
Nassington Rd.
Old Orchard Clo., Barn. 80 DD38
Old Orchard Clo., Uxb. 134 BN72
Old Orchard Ms., Berk. 38 AW20
Old Otford Rd., Sev. 241 FH117
Old Palace, The, Hat. 45 CX18
Old Palace La., Rich. 177 CJ85
Old Palace Rd., Croy. 201 DP104
Old Palace Rd., Guil. 258 AU135
Old Palace Rd., Wey. 195 BP104
Old Palace Ter., Rich. 177 CK85
King St.
Old Palace Yd. SW1 277 P6
Old Palace Yd. SW1 161 DL76
Old Palace Yd., Rich. 177 CK85
Old Paradise St. SE11 278 B8
Old Paradise St. SE11 161 DM77
Old Pk. Ave. SW12 180 DG86
Old Pk. Ave., Enf. 82 DQ42
Old Pk. Gro., Enf. 82 DQ42
Old Pk. La. W1 276 G3
Old Pk. La. W1 140 DG74
Old Pk. Ms., Houns. 156 BZ80
Old Pk. Ride, Wal.Cr. 65 DP31
Old Pk. Ridings N21 81 DP44
Old Pk. Rd. N13 99 DM49
Old Pk. Rd. SE2 166 EU78
Old Pk. Rd., Enf. 81 DP41
Old Pk. Rd. S., Enf. 81 DP42
Old Pk. Vw., Enf. 81 DN41
Old Parkbury La., St.Alb. 61 CF29
Old Parvis Rd., W.Byf. 212 BJ112
Old Perry St., Chis. 185 ES93
Old Perry St., Grav. 190 GE89
Old Polhill, Sev. 239 ET115
Old Portsmouth Rd., Gdmg. 258 AV143
Old Portsmouth Rd., Guil. 258 AV143
Old Pottery Clo., Reig. 266 DB136
Old Pound Clo., Islw. 157 CG81
Old Pye St. SW1 277 M6
Old Pye St. SW1 161 DK76
Old Quebec St. W1 272 E9
Old Quebec St. W1 140 DF72
Old Queen St. SW1 277 N5
Old Queen St. SW1 161 DK75
Old Rectory Clo., Tad. 233 CU124
Old Rectory Dr., Hat. 45 CV18
Old Rectory Gdns., Edg. 96 CN51
Old Rectory La., Lthd. 245 BS126
Old Rectory La., Uxb. 113 BE59
Old Rectory Rd., Ong. 71 FH34
Old Redding, Har. 94 CB50
Old Redstone Dr., Red. 266 DG135
Philanthropic Rd.
Old Reigate Rd., Bet. 248 CP134
Old Reigate Rd., Dor. 248 CL134
Old Rd. SE13 164 EE84
Old Rd., Add. 211 BF108
Old Rd., Bet. 248 CR134
Old Rd., Dart. 187 FD85
Old Rd., Enf. 82 DW39
Old Rd., Harl. 36 EW09
Old Rd. E., Grav. 191 GH88
Old Rd. W., Grav. 191 GF88
Old Rope Wk., Sun. 195 BV97
The Ave.
Old Royal Free Pl. N1 141 DN67
Liverpool Rd.
Old Royal Free Sq. N1 141 DN67
Old Ruislip Rd., Nthlt. 136 BW68
Old St. Mary's, Lthd. 245 BP129
Ripley La.
Old Savill's Cotts., Chig. 103 EQ49
The Chase
Old Sch. Clo. SW19 200 DA96
Old Sch. Clo., Beck. 203 DX96
Old Sch. Ct., Stai. 172 AY87
Old Sch. La., Bet. 264 CN138
Old Sch. Ms., Wey. 213 BR105
Old Sch. Pl., Wok. 226 AY121
Old Schools La., Epsom 217 CT109
Old Seacoal La. EC4 274 F9
Old Shire La., Ger.Cr. 91 BA46
Old Shire La., Rick. 73 BB44
Old Shire La., Wal.Abb. 84 EG35
Old Slade La., Iver 153 BE76
Old Sopwell Gdns., St.Alb. 43 CE22
Old S. Clo., Pnr. 94 BX53
Old S. Lambeth Rd. SW8 161 DL80
Old Sq. WC2 274 C8
Old Sq. WC2 141 DM72
Old Sta. App., Lthd. 231 CG121
Old Sta. Rd., Hayes 155 BT76
Old Sta. Rd., Loug. 84 EL43
Old Sta. Way, H.Wyc. 110 AE58
Old Stockley Rd., West Dr. 155 BP75
Old St. E13 144 EH68
Old St. EC1 275 H5
Old St. EC1 142 DQ70
Old Swan Yd., Cars. 218 DF105
Old Tilburstow Rd., Gdse. 252 DW134
Old Town SW4 161 DJ83
Old Town, Croy. 201 DP104
Old Town Clo., Beac. 89 AL54
Old Town Hall Arts Cen., Hem.H. 40 BJ19
Old Tram Yd. SE18 165 ES77
Lakedale Rd.
Old Tye Ave., West. 238 EL116
Old Uxbridge Rd., Rick. 91 BE50
Old Vicarage Way, H.Wyc. 110 AE59
Old Wk., The, Sev. 241 FH117
Old Watery La., H.Wyc. 110 AE55
Old Watford Rd., St.Alb. 60 BY30
Old Watling St., Grav. 191 GG92
Old Westhall Clo., Warl. 236 DW119
Old Woking Rd., W.Byf. 211 BF113
Old Woking Rd., Wok. 227 BB118
Old Woolwich Rd. SE10 163 ED78
Old York Rd. SW18 180 DB85
Oldacre Ms. SW12 181 DH87
Balham Gro.
Oldberry Rd., Edg. 96 CR51
Oldborough Rd., Wem. 117 CJ61
Oldbury Clo., Cher. 193 BE101
Oldbury Rd.
Oldbury Clo., Orp. 206 EX98
Oldbury Gro., Beac. 89 AK50
Oldbury Pl. W1 272 G6
Oldbury Pl. W1 140 DG71
Oldbury Rd., Cher. 193 BE101
Oldbury Rd., Enf. 82 DU40
Oldchurch Gdns., Rom. 127 FD59
Oldchurch Ri., Rom. 127 FD59
Oldchurch Rd., Rom. 127 FE58
Olden La., Pur. 219 DN112
Oldfield Circ., Nthlt. 136 CC65
The Fairway
Oldfield Clo., Brom. 205 EM98
Oldfield Clo., Grnf. 117 CE64
Oldfield Clo., Horl. 268 DF150
Oldfield Rd.
Oldfield Clo., Stan. 95 CG50
Oldfield Clo. (Cheshunt), Wal.Cr. 67 DY28
Oldfield Dr. (Cheshunt), Wal.Cr. 67 DY28
Oldfield Fm. Gdns., Grnf. 137 CD67
Oldfield Gdns., Ash. 231 CK119
Oldfield Gro. SE16 163 DX77
Oldfield La. N., Grnf. 137 CD68
Oldfield La. S., Grnf. 136 CC69
Oldfield Ms. N6 121 DJ59
Oldfield Rd. N16 122 DS62
Oldfield Rd. NW10 139 CT66
Oldfield Rd. SW19 179 CY93
Oldfield Rd. W3 159 CT75
Valetta Rd.
Oldfield Rd., Bexh. 166 EY82
Oldfield Rd., Brom. 204 EL98
Oldfield Rd., Hmptn. 196 BZ95
Oldfield Rd., Hem.H. 39 BE21
Oldfield Rd., Horl. 268 DF150
Oldfield Rd., St.Alb. 61 CK25
Oldfield Wd., Wok. 227 BB117
Maybury Hill
Oldfields Rd., Sutt. 199 CZ104
Oldforge Rd., H.Wyc. 88 AC53
Oldham Ter. W3 138 CQ74
Oldhill St. N16 122 DU60
Oldhouse Cft., Harl. 35 ES13
Oldridge Rd. SW12 180 DG87
Olds App., Wat. 93 BP46
Olds Clo., Wat. 93 BP46
Oldstead Rd., Brom. 183 ED91
Oldway La., Slou. 131 AK74
Oleander Clo., Orp. 223 ER106
O'Leary Sq. E1 142 DW71
Oley Pl. E1 143 DX71
Redman's Rd.
Olinda Rd. N16 122 DT58
Oliphant St. W10 139 CX69
Olive Rd. E13 144 EJ69
Olive Rd. NW2 119 CW63
Olive Rd. SW19 180 DC94
Norman Rd.
Olive Rd. W5 157 CK76
Olive Rd., Dart. 188 FK88
Olive St., Rom. 127 FD57
Oliver Ave. SE25 202 DT97
Oliver Clo. W4 158 CP79
Oliver Clo., Add. 212 BG105
Oliver Clo., Grays 169 FT80
Oliver Clo., Hem.H. 40 BL24
Oliver Clo., Hodd. 49 EB15
Oliver Clo., St.Alb. 61 CD27
Oliver Cres. (Farningham), Dart. 208 FM101
Oliver Gdns. E6 144 EL72
Oliver Goldsmith Est. SE15 162 DU81
Goldsmith Rd.
Oliver Gro. SE25 202 DT98
Oliver Ri., Hem.H. 40 BL24
Oliver Rd. E10 123 EB61
Oliver Rd. E17 123 EC57
Oliver Rd., Brwd. 109 GA43
Oliver Rd., Grays 169 FT81
Oliver Rd., Hem.H. 40 BL24
Oliver Rd., N.Mal. 198 CQ96
Oliver Rd., Rain. 147 FF67
Oliver Rd., Sutt. 218 DD105
Oliver Rd., Swan. 207 FD97
Olivers Clo., Berk. 39 BC16
Olivers Yd. EC1 275 L4
Olivette St. SW15 159 CX83
Felsham Rd.
Olivia Gdns., Uxb. 92 BJ53
Ollards Gro., Loug. 84 EK42
Olleberrie La., Rick. 57 BD32
Ollerton Grn. E3 143 DZ67
Ollerton Rd. N11 99 DK50
Olley Clo., Wall. 219 DL107
Ollgar Clo. W12 139 CT74
Olliffe St. E14 163 EC76
Olmar St. SE1 162 DU79
Olney Rd. SE17 161 DP79
Olron Cres., Bexh. 186 EX85
Olven Rd. SE18 165 EQ79
Olveston Wk., Cars. 200 DD100
Olwen Ms., Pnr. 94 BX54
Olyffe Ave., Well. 166 EU81
Olyffe Dr., Beck. 203 EC95
Olympia Ms. W2 140 DB73
Queensway
Olympia Way W14 159 CY76
Olympic Way, Grnf. 136 CB67
Olympic Way, Wem. 118 CN62
Olympus Sq. E5 122 DU63
Nolan Way
Oman Ave. NW2 119 CV63
O'Meara St. SE1 279 J3
O'Meara St. SE1 142 DQ74
Omega Clo. E14 163 EB76
Tiller Rd.
Omega Ct., Ware 33 DX06
Crib St.
Omega Pl. N1 274 A1
Omega Rd., Wok. 227 BA115
Omega St. SE14 163 EA81
Omega Way, Egh. 193 BC95
Ommaney Rd. SE14 163 DX81
Omnibus Way E17 101 EA54
On The Hill, Wat. 94 BY47
Ondine Rd. SE15 162 DT84
One Pin La., Slou. 111 AQ63
One Tree Clo. SE23 182 DW86
One Tree Hill Rd., Guil. 259 BB135
One Tree La., Beac. 89 AL52
Onega Gate SE16 163 DY76
O'Neill Path SE18 165 EN79
Kempt St.
Ongar Clo., Add. 211 BF107
Ongar Clo., Rom. 126 EW57
Ongar Hill, Add. 211 BF107
Ongar Pl., Add. 212 BG107
Ongar Rd. SW6 160 DA79
Ongar Rd., Add. 212 BG106
Ongar Rd., Brwd. 108 FV45
Ongar Rd., Rom. 86 EV41
Ongar Way, Rain. 147 FE67
Onra Rd. E17 123 EA59
Onslow Ave., Rich. 178 CL85
Onslow Ave., Sutt. 217 CZ110
Onslow Clo. E4 101 ED47
Onslow Clo., Hat. 45 CV18
Onslow Clo., T.Ditt. 197 CE102
Onslow Clo., Wok. 227 BA117
Onslow Cres.
Onslow Cres., Chis. 205 EP95
Onslow Cres., Wok. 227 BA117
Onslow Dr., Sid. 186 EX90
Onslow Gdns. E18 124 EH55
Onslow Gdns. N10 121 DH57
Onslow Gdns. N21 81 DN43
Onslow Gdns. SW7 160 DD78
Onslow Gdns., S.Croy. 220 DU112
Onslow Gdns., T.Ditt. 197 CE102
Onslow Gdns., Wall. 219 DJ107
Onslow Ms., Cher. 194 BG100
Onslow Ms. E. SW7 160 DD77
Cranley Pl.
Onslow Ms. W. SW7 160 DD77
Cranley Pl.
Onslow Rd., Croy. 201 DN102
Onslow Rd., Guil. 242 AX134
Onslow Rd., N.Mal. 199 CU98
Onslow Rd., Rich. 178 CL85
Onslow Rd., Walt. 213 BT105
Onslow Sq. SW7 276 A9
Onslow Sq. SW7 160 DD77
Onslow St. EC1 274 E5
Onslow St., Guil. 258 AW136
Onslow Way, T.Ditt. 197 CE102
Onslow Way, Wok. 227 BF115
Ontario Clo., Horl. 269 DN149
Ontario St. SE1 278 G7
Ontario Way E14 143 EA73
Opal Clo. E16 144 EK72
Opal Ct., Slou. 132 AV70
Wexham St.
Opal Ms. NW6 139 CZ67
Priory Pk. Rd.
Opal Ms., Ilf. 125 EP61
Ley St.
Opal St. SE11 278 F10
Opal St. SE11 161 DP77
Opendale Rd., Slou. 130 AH71
Openshaw Rd. SE2 166 EV77
Openview SW18 180 DC88
Ophelia Gdns. NW2 119 CY62
The Vale
Ophir Ter. SE15 162 DU81
Opossum Way, Houns. 156 BW82
Oppenheim Rd. SE13 163 EC82
Oppidans Ms. NW3 140 DF66
Meadowbank
Oppidans Rd. NW3 140 DF66
Orange Ct. E1 142 DU74
Hermitage Wall
Orange Ct. La., Orp. 223 EM109
Orange Gro. E11 124 EE62
Orange Hill Rd., Edg. 96 CQ52
Orange Pl. SE16 162 DW76
Lower Rd.
Orange St. WC2 277 N1
Orange St. WC2 141 DK73
Orange Tree Hill (Havering-atte-Bower), Rom. 105 FD50
Orange Yd. W1 273 N9
Orangery, The, Rich. 177 CJ89

Orangery La. SE9 185 EM85
Oratory La. SW3 276 A10
Orb St. SE17 279 K9
Orb St. SE17 162 DR77
Orbain Rd. SW6 159 CY80
Orbel St. SW11 160 DE81
Orbital Cres., Wat. 75 BT35
Orbital One, Dart. 188 FP89
Orchard, The N14 81 DH43
Orchard, The N21 82 DR44
Orchard, The NW11 120 DA57
Orchard, The SE3 163 ED82
Orchard, The W4 158 CR77
Orchard, The W5 137 CK71
Orchard, The, Bans. 234 DA115
Orchard, The, Dor. 263 CJ140
Orchard, The, Epsom 217 CT108
Orchard, The, Houns. 156 CC82
Orchard, The, Kings L. 58 BN29
Orchard, The, Sev. 256 FE121
Orchard, The, Swan. 207 FD96
Orchard, The, Vir.W. 192 AY99
Orchard, The, Welw.G.C. 29 CX07
Orchard, The, Wey. 213 BP105
Orchard, The, Wok. 226 AY122
Orchard Ave. N3 120 DA55
Orchard Ave. N14 81 DJ44
Orchard Ave. N20 98 DD47
Orchard Ave., Add. 211 BF111
Orchard Ave., Ashf. 175 BQ93
Orchard Ave., Belv. 166 EY79
Orchard Ave., Berk. 38 AU19
Orchard Ave., Brwd. 109 FZ48
Orchard Ave., Croy. 203 DY103
Orchard Ave., Dart. 187 FH87
Orchard Ave., Felt. 175 BR85
Orchard Ave., Grav. 191 GH92
Orchard Ave., Houns. 156 BY80
Orchard Ave., Mitch. 200 DG102
Orchard Ave., N.Mal. 198 CS96
Orchard Ave., Rain. 148 FJ70
Orchard Ave., Slou. 131 AK71
Orchard Ave., Sthl. 136 BY74
Orchard Ave., T.Ditt. 197 CG102
Orchard Ave., Wat. 59 BV31
Orchard Ave., Wind. 151 AN81
Orchard Bungalow Caravan Site, Slou. 131 AM66
Orchard Clo. E4 101 EA49
Chingford Mt. Rd.
Orchard Clo. E11 124 EH56
Orchard Clo. N1 142 DQ66
Morton Rd.
Orchard Clo. NW2 119 CU62
Orchard Clo. SE23 182 DW86
Brenchley Gdns.
Orchard Clo. SW20 199 CW98
Grand Dr.
Orchard Clo. W10 139 CY71
Orchard Clo., Ashf. 175 BQ93
Orchard Clo., Bans. 218 DB114
Orchard Clo., Beac. 89 AK52
Seeleys Rd.
Orchard Clo., Bexh. 166 EY81
Orchard Clo., B.Stort. 37 FC07
Orchard Clo., Borwd. 78 CM42
Orchard Clo., Edg. 96 CL51
Orchard Clo., Egh. 173 BB92
Orchard Clo., Epsom 216 CP107
Orchard Clo., Guil. 243 BB134
Orchard Clo., Hem.H. 40 BM18
Orchard Clo., Hert. 47 DJ19
Orchard Clo., Horl. 268 DF147
Orchard Clo., Lthd. 231 CF119
Orchard Clo. (Effingham), Lthd. 229 BT124
Orchard Clo. (Fetcham), Lthd. 231 CD122
Orchard Clo., Nthlt. 116 CC64
Orchard Clo. (Cuffley), Pot.B. 65 DL28
Orchard Clo., Rad. 77 CE37
Orchard Clo., Rick. 73 BD42
Orchard Clo., Ruis. 115 BQ59
Orchard Clo., St.Alb. 43 CF21
Orchard Clo., S.Ock. 149 FW70
Orchard Clo., Surb. 197 CH101
Orchard Clo., Uxb. 134 BH65
Orchard Clo., Walt. 195 BV101
Garden Rd.
Orchard Clo., Ware 33 DX05
Orchard Clo. (Stanstead Abbotts), Ware 33 EC11
Orchard Clo., Wat. 75 BT40
Orchard Clo. (Bushey), Wat. 95 CD46
Orchard Clo., Wem. 138 CL67
Orchard Clo., Wok. 227 BB116
Orchard Ct., Hem.H. 57 BA27
Orchard Ct., Islw. 157 CD81
Orchard Ct., Twick. 177 CD89
Orchard Ct., Wor.Pk. 199 CU102
Orchard Cres., Edg. 96 CQ50
Orchard Cres., Enf. 82 DT39
Orchard Cft., Harl. 36 EU13
Orchard Dr. SE3 164 EE82
Orchard Dr., Ash. 231 CK120
Orchard Dr., Edg. 96 CM50
Orchard Dr., Epp. 85 ES36
Orchard Dr., Grays 170 GA75
Orchard Dr. (Wooburn), H.Wyc. 110 AD59
Orchard Dr., Rick. 73 BC41
Orchard Dr., St.Alb. 60 CB27
Orchard Dr., Uxb. 134 BK70
Orchard Dr., Wat. 75 BT39
Orchard Dr., Wok. 226 AY115
Orchard End, Cat. 236 DS122
Orchard End, Lthd. 230 CC124
Orchard End, Wey. 195 BS103
Orchard End Ave., Amer. 72 AT39
Orchard End Clo., Amer. 72 AT39
Orchard Fld. Rd., Gdmg. 258 AT144
Orchard Gdns., Chess. 216 CL105
Orchard Gdns., Epsom 216 CQ114
Orchard Gdns., Lthd. 246 BY128
Orchard Gdns., Sutt. 218 DA106
Orchard Gdns., Wal.Abb. 67 EC34
Orchard Gate NW9 118 CS56
Orchard Gate, Esher 197 CD102
Orchard Gate, Grnf. 117 CH64
Orchard Gate, Slou. 111 AQ64
Orchard Grn., Orp. 205 ES103
Orchard Gro. SE20 182 DU94
Orchard Gro., Croy. 203 DY101
Orchard Gro., Edg. 96 CN53
Orchard Gro., Ger.Cr. 90 AW53
Orchard Gro., Har. 118 CM57
Orchard Gro., Orp. 205 ET103
Orchard Hill SE13 163 EB82
Coldbath St.
Orchard Hill, Cars. 218 DF106
Orchard Hill, Dart. 187 FE85
Orchard Ho. La., St.Alb. 43 CD21
Orchard La. SW20 199 CV95
Durham Rd.
Orchard La., Amer. 55 AR38
Orchard La., Brwd. 108 FT43
Orchard La., E.Mol. 197 CD100
Orchard La., Harl. 36 EY11
Orchard La., Wdf.Grn. 102 EJ49
Orchard Lea Clo., Wok. 227 BE115
Orchard Leigh, Chesh. 56 AT28
Orchard Mains, Wok. 226 AW119
Orchard Mead, Hat. 45 CT18
Days Mead
Orchard Ms. N1 142 DR66
Southgate Gro.
Orchard Ms., Beac. 89 AQ50
Orchard Rd.
Orchard Path, Slou. 133 BA72
Orchard Pl. E14 144 EE73
Orchard Pl. N17 100 DT52
Orchard Pl., Sev. 240 EY124
Orchard Ri., Croy. 203 DY102
Orchard Ri., Kings.T. 198 CQ95
Orchard Ri., Pnr. 115 BT55
Orchard Ri., Rich. 158 CP84
Orchard Ri. E, Sid. 185 ES85
Orchard Ri. W., Sid. 185 ES85
Orchard Rd. N6 121 DH59
Orchard Rd. SE3 164 EE82
Eliot Pl.
Orchard Rd. SE18 165 ER77
Orchard Rd., Barn. 79 CY42
Orchard Rd., Beac. 89 AM54
Orchard Rd. (Seer Grn.), Beac. 89 AQ50
Orchard Rd., Belv. 166 FA77
Orchard Rd., Brent. 157 CJ79
Orchard Rd., Brom. 204 EJ95
Orchard Rd., Ch.St.G. 90 AW47
Orchard Rd., Chess. 216 CL105
Orchard Rd., Dag. 146 FA67
Orchard Rd., Dor. 263 CH137
Orchard Rd., Enf. 82 DW43
Orchard Rd., Grav. 190 GC89
Orchard Rd., Guil. 258 AT136
Orchard Rd. (Burpham), Guil. 243 BB130
Orchard Rd. (Shalford), Guil. 258 AY140
Orchard Rd. (Shere), Guil. 260 BN139
Orchard Rd., Hmptn. 176 BZ94
Orchard Rd., Hayes 135 BT73
Orchard Rd., Houns. 176 BZ85
Orchard Rd., Kings.T. 198 CL96
Orchard Rd., Mitch. 200 DG102
Orchard Rd. (Farnborough), Orp. 223 EP106
Orchard Rd. (Pratt's Bottom), Orp. 224 EW110
Orchard Rd., Reig. 250 DB134
Orchard Rd., Rich. 158 CN83
Orchard Rd., Rom. 105 FB54
Orchard Rd. (Otford), Sev. 241 FF116
Orchard Rd. (Riverhead), Sev. 256 FE122
Orchard Rd., Sid. 185 ES91
Orchard Rd., S.Croy. 220 DV114
Orchard Rd., S.Ock. 149 FW70
Orchard Rd., Sun. 175 BV94
Hanworth Rd.
Orchard Rd., Sutt. 218 DA105
Orchard Rd., Swans. 190 FY85
Orchard Rd., Twick. 177 CG85
Orchard Rd., Well. 166 EV83
Orchard Rd., Wind. 172 AV86
Orchard Sq. W14 159 CZ78
Sun Rd.
Orchard Sq., Brox. 49 DZ24
Orchard St. E17 123 DY56
Orchard St. W1 272 F9
Orchard St. W1 140 DG72
Orchard St., Dart. 188 FL86
Orchard St., Hem.H. 40 BJ24
Orchard St., St.Alb. 42 CC21
Orchard Ter., Enf. 82 DU44
Great Cambridge Rd.
Orchard Vw., Uxb. 134 BK70
Orchard Way, Add. 212 BH106
Orchard Way, Ashf. 174 BM89
Orchard Way, Beck. 203 DY99
Orchard Way, Chig. 104 EU48
Orchard Way, Croy. 203 DY102
Orchard Way, Dart. 188 FK90
Orchard Way, Dor. 263 CH137
Orchard Way, Enf. 82 DS41
Orchard Way, Esher 214 CC107
Orchard Way, Hem.H. 57 BA28
Orchard Way, Oxt. 254 EG133
Orchard Way, Pot.B. 64 DB28
Orchard Way, Reig. 266 DB138
Orchard Way, Rick. 92 BG45
Orchard Way, Slou. 132 AY74
Orchard Way, Sutt. 218 DD105
Orchard Way, Tad. 249 CZ126
Orchard Way (Cheshunt), Wal.Cr. 65 DP27
Orchard Way, Wok. 243 BC125
Orchard Waye, Uxb. 134 BK68
Orchardleigh, Lthd. 231 CH122
Orchardleigh Ave., Enf. 82 DW40
Orchardmede N21 82 DR44
Orchards, The, Epp. 70 EU32
Orchards, The, Hert. 32 DQ06
Orchards Business Cen., Red. 267 DH143
Orchardson St. NW8 140 DD70
Orchardville, Slou. 130 AH70
Orchehill Ave., Ger.Cr. 112 AX56
Orchehill Ct., Ger.Cr. 112 AY57
Orchehill Ri., Ger.Cr. 112 AY57
Orchid Clo. E6 144 EL71
Orchid Clo., Rom. 86 EV41
Orchid Clo., Sthl. 136 BY72
Orchid Ct., Egh. 173 BB91
Orchid Rd. N14 99 DJ45
Orchid St. W12 139 CU73
Orchis Gro., Grays 170 FZ78
Orchis Way, Rom. 106 FM51
Orde Hall St. WC1 274 B6
Orde Hall St. WC1 141 DM71
Ordell Rd. E3 143 DZ68
Ordnance Clo., Felt. 175 BU90
Ordnance Cres. SE10 164 EE75
Ordnance Hill NW8 140 DD67
Ordnance Ms. NW8 140 DD68
St. Ann's Ter.
Ordnance Rd. E16 144 EF71
Ordnance Rd. SE18 165 EN79
Ordnance Rd., Enf. 83 DX37
Ordnance Rd., Grav. 191 GJ86
Oregano Dr. E14 143 ED72
Oregano Way, Guil. 242 AU129
Oregon Ave. E12 125 EM63
Oregon Clo., N.Mal. 198 CQ98
Georgia Rd.
Oregon Sq., Orp. 205 ER102
Orestan La., Lthd. 245 BV127
Orestes Ms. NW6 120 DA64
Aldred Rd.
Oreston Rd., Rain. 148 FK69
Orewell Gdns., Reig. 266 DB136
Orford Ct. SE27 181 DP89
Orford Gdns., Twick. 177 CF89
Orford Rd. E17 123 EA57
Orford Rd. E18 124 EH55
Orford Rd. SE6 183 EB90
Organ Hall Rd., Borwd. 77 CK39
Organ La. E4 101 EC47
Oriel Clo., Mitch. 201 DK98
Oriel Ct. NW3 120 DC63
Heath St.
Oriel Gdns., Ilf. 125 EM55
Oriel Pl. NW3 120 DC63
Heath St.
Oriel Rd. E9 143 DX65
Oriel Way, Nthlt. 136 CB66
Orient Clo., St.Alb. 43 CE22
Orient Ind. Pk. E10 123 EA61
Orient St. SE11 278 F8
Orient Way E5 123 DX62
Oriental Clo., Wok. 227 BA117
Oriental Rd.
Oriental Rd. E16 144 EK74
Oriental Rd., Wok. 227 AZ117
Oriental St. E14 143 EA73
Morant St.
Oriole Clo., Abb.L. 59 BU31
College Rd.
Oriole Way SE28 146 EV73
Orion Way, Nthwd. 93 BT49
Orissa Rd. SE18 165 ES78
Orkney St. SW11 160 DG82
Orlando Gdns., Epsom 216 CR110
Orlando Rd. SW4 161 DJ83
Orleans Clo., Esher 197 CD103
Orleans Rd. SE19 182 DR93
Orleans Rd., Twick. 177 CH87
Orleston Ms. N7 141 DN65
Orleston Rd. N7 141 DN65
Orlestone Gdns., Orp. 224 EY106
Orley Fm. Rd., Har. 117 CE62
Orlop St. SE10 164 EE78
Ormanton Rd. SE26 182 DU91
Orme Ct. W2 140 DB73
Orme Ct. Ms. W2 140 DB73
Orme La.
Orme La. W2 140 DB73
Orme Rd., Kings.T. 198 CP96
Orme Sq. W2 140 DB73
Bayswater Rd.
Ormeley Rd. SW12 181 DH87
Ormerod Gdns., Mitch. 200 DG96
Ormesby Clo. SE28 146 EX73
Wroxham Rd.
Ormesby Dr., Pot.B. 63 CX32
Ormesby Way, Har. 118 CM58
Ormiston Gro. W12 139 CV74
Ormiston Rd. SE10 164 EG78
Ormond Ave., Hmptn. 196 CB95
Ormond Ave., Rich. 177 CK85
Ormond Rd.
Ormond Clo. WC1 274 A6
Ormond Clo., Rom. 106 FK54
Chadwick Dr.
Ormond Cres., Hmptn. 196 CB95
Ormond Dr., Hmptn. 176 CB94
Ormond Ms. WC1 274 A5
Ormond Rd. N19 121 DL60
Ormond Rd., Rich. 177 CK85
Ormond Yd. SW1 277 L2
Ormonde Ave., Epsom 216 CR109
Ormonde Ave., Orp. 205 EQ103
Ormonde Gate SW3 160 DF78
Ormonde Pl. SW1 276 F9
Ormonde Ri., Buck.H. 102 EJ46
Ormonde Rd. SW14 158 CQ83
Ormonde Rd., Nthwd. 93 BR49
Ormonde Rd., Wok. 226 AW116
Ormonde Ter. NW8 140 DF67
Ormsby Gdns., Grnf. 136 CC68
Ormsby Pl. N16 122 DT62
Victorian Gro.
Ormsby Pt. SE18 165 EP77
Troy Ct.
Ormsby St. E2 275 P1
Ormsby St. E2 142 DT68
Ormside St. SE15 162 DW79
Ormside Way, Red. 251 DH130
Ormskirk Rd., Wat. 94 BX49
Ornan Rd. NW3 120 DE64
Oronsay, Hem.H. 41 BP22
Northend
Oronsay Wk. N1 142 DQ65
Clephane Rd.
Orpen Wk. N16 122 DS62
Orphanage Rd., Wat. 76 BW40
Orpheus St. SE5 162 DR81
Orpin Rd., Red. 251 DH130
Orpington Bypass, Orp. 224 EX106
Orpington Bypass, Sev. 224 EZ109
Orpington Gdns. N18 100 DS48
Orpington Rd. N21 99 DN46
Orpington Rd., Chis. 205 ES97
Orpwood Clo., Hmptn. 176 BZ93
Orsett Heath Cres., Grays 171 GG76
Orsett Rd., Grays 170 GA78
Orsett St. SE11 278 C10
Orsett St. SE11 161 DM78
Orsett Ter. W2 140 DB72
Orsett Ter., Wdf.Grn. 102 EJ52
Orsman Rd. N1 142 DS67
Orton Clo., St.Alb. 43 CH16
Orton St. E1 142 DU74
Hermitage Wall
Orville Rd. SW11 160 DD82
Orwell Clo., Rain. 147 FD71
Orwell Clo., Wind. 151 AR83
Orwell Ct. N5 122 DQ63
Orwell Rd. E13 144 EJ67
Osbaldeston Rd. N16 122 DU61
Osbert St. SW1 277 M9
Osberton Rd. SE12 184 EG85
Osborn Clo. E8 142 DU67
Osborn Gdns. NW7 97 CX52
Osborn La. SE23 183 DY87
Osborn St. E1 142 DT71
Osborn Ter. SE3 164 EF84
Lee Rd.
Osborn Way, Welw.G.C. 29 CX10
Osborne Ave., Stai. 174 BL87
Osborne Clo., Barn. 80 DG41
Osborne Clo., Beck. 203 DY98
Osborne Clo., Felt. 176 BX92
Osborne Clo., Horn. 127 FH58
Osborne Ct., Pot.B. 64 DB30
Osborne Rd.
Osborne Ct., Wind. 151 AQ82
Osborne Rd.
Osborne Gdns., Pot.B. 64 DB30
Osborne Gdns., Th.Hth. 202 DQ96
Osborne Gro. E17 123 DZ56
Osborne Gro. N4 121 DN60
Osborne Ms. E17 123 DZ56
Osborne Gro.
Osborne Ms., Wind. 151 AQ82
Osborne Pl., Sutt. 218 DD106
Osborne Rd. E7 124 EH64
Osborne Rd. E9 143 DZ65
Osborne Rd. E10 123 EB62
Osborne Rd. N4 121 DN60
Osborne Rd. N13 99 DN48
Osborne Rd. NW2 139 CV65
Osborne Rd. W3 158 CP75
Osborne Rd., Belv. 166 EZ78
Osborne Rd., Brwd. 108 FU44
Osborne Rd., Brox. 49 EA19
Osborne Rd., Buck.H. 102 EH46
Osborne Rd., Dag. 126 EZ64
Osborne Rd., Egh. 173 AZ93
Osborne Rd., Enf. 83 DY40
Osborne Rd., Horn. 127 FH58
Osborne Rd., Houns. 156 BZ83
Osborne Rd., Kings.T. 178 CL94
Osborne Rd., Pot.B. 64 DB30
Osborne Rd., Red. 250 DG131
Osborne Rd., Sthl. 136 CC72
Osborne Rd., Th.Hth. 202 DQ96
Osborne Rd., Uxb. 134 BJ66
Oxford Rd.
Osborne Rd., Wal.Cr. 67 DY27
Osborne Rd., Walt. 195 BU102
Osborne Rd., Wat. 76 BW38
Osborne Rd., Wind. 151 AQ82
Osborne Sq., Dag. 126 EZ63
Osborne St., Slou. 152 AT75
Osborne Ter. SW17 180 DG92
Church La.
Osbourne Ave., Kings L. 58 BM28
Osbourne Rd., Dart. 188 FP86
Oscar St. SE8 163 EA81
Oseney Cres. NW5 141 DJ65
Osgood Ave., Orp. 223 ET106
Osgood Gdns., Orp. 223 ET106
O'Shea Gro. E3 143 DZ67
Osidge La. N14 98 DG46
Osier Ms. W4 159 CT79
Osier Pl., Egh. 173 BC93
Osier St. E1 142 DW70
Osier Way E10 123 EB62
Osier Way, Bans. 217 CY114
Osier Way, Mitch. 200 DE99
Osiers Rd. SW18 160 DA84
Oslac Rd. SE6 183 EB92
Oslo Ct. NW8 272 B1
Oslo Sq. SE16 163 DY76
Norway Gate
Osman Clo. N15 122 DR58
Tewkesbury Rd.
Osman Rd. N9 100 DU48
Osman Rd. W6 159 CW76
Batoum Gdns.
Osmond Clo., Har. 116 CC61
Osmond Gdns., Wall. 219 DJ106
Osmund St. W12 139 CT72
Braybrook St.
Osnaburgh St. NW1 273 J4
Osnaburgh St. NW1 141 DH70
Osnaburgh Ter. NW1 273 J4
Osney Wk., Cars. 200 DD100
Osney Way, Grav. 191 GM89
Osprey Clo. E6 144 EL71
Dove App.
Osprey Clo. E11 124 EG56
Osprey Clo. E17 101 DY52
Osprey Clo., Wat. 60 BY34
Osprey Clo., West Dr. 154 BK75
Osprey Ct., Wal.Abb. 68 EG34
Osprey Gdns., S.Croy. 221 DX110
Osprey Ms., Enf. 82 DV43
Osprey Rd., Wal.Abb. 68 EG34
Ospringe Clo. SE20 182 DW94
Ospringe Ct. SE9 185 ER86
Ospringe Rd. NW5 121 DJ63
Osram Rd., Wem. 117 CK62
Osric Path N1 275 M1
Ossian Ms. N4 121 DM59
Ossian Rd. N4 121 DM59
Ossington Bldgs. W1 272 F6
Ossington Clo. W2 140 DB73
Ossington St.
Ossington St. W2 140 DB73
Ossory Rd. SE1 162 DU79
Ossulston St. NW1 273 M1
Ossulston St. NW1 141 DK68
Ossulton Pl. N2 120 DC55
East End Rd.
Ossulton Way N2 120 DC56
Ostade Rd. SW2 181 DM87
Osten Ms. SW7 160 DB76
McLeod's Ms.
Oster St., St.Alb. 42 CC19
Oster Ter. E17 123 DX57
Southcote Rd.
Osterberg Rd., Dart. 168 FM84
Osterley Ave., Islw. 157 CD80
Osterley Clo., Orp. 206 EU95
Leith Hill
Osterley Ct., Islw. 157 CD81
Osterley Cres., Islw. 157 CE81
Osterley Gdns., Th.Hth. 202 DQ96
Osterley Ho. E14 143 EB72
Giraud St.
Osterley La., Islw. 156 CC78
Osterley La., Sthl. 156 CA78
Osterley Pk., Islw. 157 CD78
Osterley Pk. Rd., Sthl. 156 BZ76
Osterley Pk. Vw. Rd. W7 157 CE75
Osterley Rd. N16 122 DS63
Osterley Rd., Islw. 157 CE80
Osterley Views, Sthl. 136 CC74
West Pk. Rd.
Ostliffe Rd. N13 99 DP50
Oswald Clo., Lthd. 230 CC122
Oswald Rd., Lthd. 230 CC122
Oswald Rd., St.Alb. 43 CE21
Oswald Rd., Sthl. 136 BY74
Oswald St. E5 123 DX62
Oswald Ter. NW2 119 CW62
Temple Rd.
Oswalds Mead E9 123 DY63
Lindisfarne Way
Osward, Croy. 221 DZ109
Osward Pl. N9 100 DV47
Osward Rd. SW17 180 DF89
Oswell Ho. E1 142 DV74
Penang St.
Oswin St. SE11 278 G8
Oswin St. SE11 161 DP77
Oswyth Rd. SE5 162 DS82
Otford Clo. SE20 202 DW95
Otford Clo., Bex. 187 FB86
Southwold Rd.
Otford Clo., Brom. 205 EN97
Otford Cres. SE4 183 DZ86
Otford La., Sev. 224 EZ112
Otford Rd., Sev. 241 FH118
Othello Clo. SE11 278 F10
Otis St. E3 143 EC69
Otley App., Ilf. 125 EP58
Otley Dr., Ilf. 125 EP58
Otley Rd. E16 144 EJ72
Otley Ter. E5 123 DX62
Otley Way, Wat. 94 BW48
Otlinge Clo., Orp. 206 EX98
Ottawa Gdns., Dag. 147 FD66
Ottawa Rd., Til. 171 GG82
Ottaway St. E5 122 DU62
Stellman Clo.
Ottenden Clo., Orp. 223 ES105
Southfleet Rd.
Otter Clo., Cher. 211 BB107
Otter Gdns., Hat. 45 CV19
Otter Meadow, Lthd. 231 CF119
Otter Rd., Grnf. 136 CC70
Otterbourne Rd. E4 101 ED48
Otterbourne Rd., Croy. 201 DP103
Otterburn Gdns., Islw. 157 CG80
Otterburn Ho. SE5 162 DQ80
Sultan St.
Otterburn St. SW17 180 DF93
Otterden St. SE6 183 EA91
Otterfield Rd., West Dr. 134 BL73
Ottermead La., Cher. 211 BC107
Otters Clo., Orp. 206 EX98
Otterspool La., Wat. 76 BY38
Otterspool Service Rd., Wat. 76 BZ38
Otterspool Way, Wat. 76 BZ38
Otto Clo. SE26 182 DV90
Otto St. SE17 161 DP79
Ottoman Ter., Wat. 76 BW41
Ebury Rd.
Ottways Ave., Ash. 231 CK119
Ottways La., Ash. 231 CK120
Otway Gdns., Wat. 95 CE45
Otways Clo., Pot.B. 64 DB32
Oulton Clo. E5 122 DW61
Mundford Rd.
Oulton Clo. SE28 146 EW72
Rollesby Way
Oulton Cres., Bark. 145 ET65
Oulton Cres., Pot.B. 63 CX32
Oulton Rd. N15 122 DR57
Oulton Way, Wat. 94 BY49
Oundle Ave. (Bushey), Wat. 76 CC44
Ousden Clo. (Cheshunt), Wal.Cr. 67 DY30
Ousden Dr. (Cheshunt), Wal.Cr. 67 DY30
Ouseley Rd. SW12 180 DF88
Ouseley Rd., Stai. 172 AW87
Ouseley Rd., Wind. 172 AW87
Outdowns, Lthd. 245 BV129
Outer Circle NW1 272 F5
Outer Circle NW1 140 DG70
Outfield Rd., Ger.Cr. 90 AX52
Outgate Rd. NW10 139 CT66
Outlook Dr., Ch.St.G. 90 AX48
Outram Pl. N1 141 DL67
Outram Pl., Wey. 213 BQ106
Outram Rd. E6 144 EL67
Outram Rd. N22 99 DK53
Outram Rd., Croy. 202 DT103
Outwich St. EC3 275 N8
Outwich St. EC3 142 DS72
Outwood La., Couls. 234 DE120
Outwood La., Red. 252 DR134
Outwood La., Tad. 234 DB122
Oval, The E2 142 DV68
Oval, The, Bans. 218 DA114
Oval, The, Brox. 67 DY25
Oval, The, Gdmg. 258 AT144
Oval, The, Guil. 258 AU135
Oval, The, Sid. 186 EU87
Oval Gdns., Grays 170 GC76
Oval Pl. SW8 161 DM80
Oval Rd. NW1 141 DH67
Oval Rd., Croy. 202 DR103
Oval Rd. N., Dag. 147 FB67
Oval Rd. S., Dag. 147 FB68
Oval Way SE11 161 DM78
Oval Way, Ger.Cr. 112 AY56
Ovenden Rd., Sev. 240 EX120
Over The Misbourne, Ger.Cr. 113 BA58
Over The Misbourne, Uxb. 113 BB58

Overbrae, Beck. 183 EA93
Overbrook, Lthd. 245 BP129
Overbrook Wk., Edg. 96 CN52
Overbury Ave., Beck. 203 EB97
Overbury Cres., Croy. 221 EC110
Overbury Rd. N15 122 DR58
Overbury St. E5 123 DX63
Overcliff Rd. SE13 163 EA83
Overcliff Rd., Grays 170 GD78
Overcliffe, Grav. 191 GF86
Overcourt Clo., Sid. 186 EV86
Overdale, Ash. 232 CL116
Overdale, Dor. 263 CK135
Overdale, Red. 252 DQ133
Overdale Ave., N.Mal. 198 CQ96
Overdale Rd. W5 157 CJ76
Overdale Rd., Chesh. 54 AP28
Overdown Rd. SE6 183 EA91
Overhill, Warl. 236 DW119
Overhill Rd. SE22 182 DU87
Overhill Rd., Pur. 219 DN109
Overhill Way, Beck. 203 EC99
Overlea Rd. E5 122 DU59
Overlord Clo., Brox. 49 DY20
Overmead, Sid. 185 ER87
Overmead, Swan. 207 FE99
Oversley Ho. W2 140 DA71
Overstand Clo., Beck. 203 EA99
Overstone Gdns., Croy. 203 DZ101
Overstone Rd. W6 159 CW76
Overstream, Rick. 74 BH42
Overthorpe Clo., Wok. 226 AS117
Overton Clo. NW10 138 CQ65
Overton Clo., Islw. 157 CF81
Avenue Rd.
Overton Ct. E11 124 EG59
Overton Dr. E11 124 EG59
Overton Dr., Rom. 126 EW59
Overton Rd. E10 123 DY60
Overton Rd. N14 81 DL43
Overton Rd. SE2 166 EW76
Overton Rd. SW9 161 DN82
Overton Rd., Sutt. 218 DA107
Overton Rd. E. SE2 166 EX76
Overtons Yd., Croy. 202 DQ104
Overy St., Dart. 188 FL86
Ovesdon Ave., Har. 116 BZ60
Oveton Way, Lthd. 246 CA126
Ovett Clo. SE19 182 DS93
Ovex Clo. E14 163 EC75
Ovington Ct., Wok. 226 AT116
Roundthorn Way
Ovington Gdns. SW3 276 C7
Ovington Gdns. SW3 160 DE76
Ovington Ms. SW3 276 C7
Ovington Ms. SW3 160 DE76
Ovington Sq. SW3 276 C7
Ovington Sq. SW3 160 DE76
Ovington St. SW3 276 C7
Ovington St. SW3 160 DE77
Owen Clo. SE28 146 EW74
Owen Clo., Hayes 135 BV69
Owen Gdns., Wdf.Grn. 102 EL51
Owen Pl., Lthd. 231 CH122
Church Rd.
Owen Rd. N13 100 DQ49
Owen Rd., Hayes 135 BV69
Owen St. EC1 274 E1
Owen Wk. SE20 182 DU94
Sycamore Gro.
Owen Waters Ho., Ilf. 103 EN53
Owen Way NW10 118 CQ64
Owenite St. SE2 166 EV77
Owen's Ct. EC1 274 F2
Owen's Row EC1 274 F2
Owens Way SE23 183 DY87
Owens Way, Rick. 74 BN43
Owgan Clo. SE5 162 DR80
Benhill Rd.
Owl Clo., S.Croy. 221 DX110
Owlets Hall Clo., Horn. 128 FM55
Prospect Rd.
Owlsears Clo., Beac. 89 AK51
Ownstead Gdns., S.Croy. 220 DT111
Ownsted Hill, Croy. 221 EC110
Ox La., Epsom 217 CU109
Church St.
Oxberry Ave. SW6 159 CY82
Oxdowne Clo., Cob. 214 CB114
Oxenden Dr., Hodd. 49 EA18
Oxenden Wd. Rd., Orp. 224 EW108
Oxendon St. SW1 277 M1
Oxendon St. SW1 141 DK73
Oxenford St. SE15 162 DT83
Oxenholme NW1 273 L1
Oxenholme NW1 141 DJ68
Oxenpark Ave., Wem. 118 CL60
Oxestalls Rd. SE8 163 DY78
Oxfield Clo., Berk. 38 AU20
Oxford Ave. SW20 199 CY96
Oxford Ave., Grays 171 GG77
Oxford Ave., Hayes 155 BT80
Oxford Ave., Horn. 128 FN56
Oxford Ave., Houns. 156 CA78
Oxford Ave., St.Alb. 43 CJ21
Oxford Ave., Slou. 131 AM71
Oxford Ave. (Burnham), Slou. 130 AH68
Oxford Circ. Ave. W1 273 K9
Oxford Clo. N9 100 DV47
Oxford Clo., Ashf. 175 BQ94
Oxford Clo., Grav. 191 GM89
Oxford Clo., Mitch. 201 DJ97
Oxford Clo., Nthwd. 93 BQ49
Oxford Clo. (Cheshunt), Wal.Cr. 66 DW29
Oxford Ct. EC4 275 K10
Oxford Ct. W3 138 CN72
Queens Dr.
Oxford Ct., Brwd. 108 FX49
Oxford Ct., Felt. 176 BX91
Oxford Way
Oxford Cres., N.Mal. 198 CR100
Oxford Dr., Ruis. 116 BW61
Oxford Gdns. N20 98 DD46
Oxford Gdns. N21 100 DQ45
Oxford Gdns. W4 158 CN78
Oxford Gdns. W10 139 CX72
Oxford Gdns., Uxb. 114 BG62
Oxford Rd.
Oxford Gate W6 159 CX77
Oxford La., Guil. 258 AX136
Sydenham Rd.
Oxford Ms., Bex. 186 FA87
Bexley High St.
Oxford Pl. NW10 118 CR62
Neasden La. N.
Oxford Rd. E15 143 ED65
Oxford Rd. N4 121 DN60
Oxford Rd. N9 100 DV47
Oxford Rd. NW6 140 DA68
Oxford Rd. SE19 182 DR93
Oxford Rd. SW15 159 CY84
Oxford Rd. W5 137 CK73
Oxford Rd., Beac. 111 AP55
Oxford Rd. (Holtspur), Beac. 88 AE54
Oxford Rd., Cars. 218 DE107
Oxford Rd., Enf. 82 DV43
Oxford Rd., Ger.Cr. 112 AT56
Oxford Rd., Guil. 258 AX136
Oxford Rd., Har. 116 CC58
Oxford Rd. (Wealdstone), Har. 117 CF55
Oxford Rd., H.Wyc. 88 AE54
Oxford Rd., Ilf. 125 EQ64
Oxford Rd., Red. 250 DE133
Oxford Rd., Rom. 106 FM51
Oxford Rd., Sid. 186 EV92
Oxford Rd., Tedd. 177 CD92
Oxford Rd., Uxb. 134 BJ65
Oxford Rd., Wall. 219 DJ106
Oxford Rd., Wind. 151 AQ81
Oxford Rd., Wdf.Grn. 102 EK50
Oxford Rd. E., Wind. 151 AQ81
Oxford Rd. N. W4 158 CP78
Oxford Rd. S. W4 158 CN78
Oxford Sq. W2 272 C9
Oxford Sq. W2 140 DE72
Oxford St. W1 272 F9
Oxford St. W1 140 DG72
Oxford St., Wat. 75 BV43
Oxford Ter., Guil. 258 AX136
Pewley Hill
Oxford Wk., Sthl. 136 BZ74
Oxford Way, Felt. 176 BX91
Oxgate Gdns. NW2 119 CV62
Oxgate La. NW2 119 CV61
Oxhawth Cres., Brom. 205 EN99
Oxhey Ave., Wat. 94 BX45
Oxhey Dr., Nthwd. 93 BV49
Oxhey Dr., Wat. 94 BW48
Oxhey Dr. S., Nthwd. 93 BV50
Oxhey La., Pnr. 94 CA50
Oxhey La., Wat. 94 BY46
Oxhey Ridge Clo., Nthwd. 93 BU50
Oxhey Rd., Wat. 76 BW44
Oxleas E6 145 EP72
Oxleas Clo., Well. 165 ER82
Oxlease Dr., Hat. 45 CV19
Oxleay Ct., Har. 116 CA60
Oxleay Rd., Har. 116 CA60
Oxleigh Clo., N.Mal. 198 CS99
Oxley Clo. SE1 162 DT78
Oxley Clo., Rom. 106 FJ54
Oxleys, The, Harl. 36 EY11
Oxleys Rd. NW2 119 CV62
Oxleys Rd., Wal.Abb. 68 EG33
Oxlip Clo., Croy. 203 DX102
Marigold Way
Oxlow La., Dag. 126 EZ63
Oxonian St. SE22 162 DT84
Oxshott Ri., Cob. 214 BX113
Oxshott Rd., Lthd. 231 CE116
Oxshott Way, Cob. 230 BY115
Oxted Clo., Mitch. 200 DD97
Oxted Rd., Gdse. 252 DW130
Oxtoby Way SW16 201 DK95
Oyster Catchers Clo. E16 144 EH72
Freemasons Rd.
Oyster La., W.Byf. 212 BK110
Oyster Row E1 142 DW72
Lukin St.
Oysterfields, St.Alb. 42 CB19
Ozolins Way E16 144 EG72

P

Pablo Neruda Clo. SE24 161 DP84
Shakespeare Rd.
Pace Pl. E1 142 DV72
Bigland St.
Paceheath Clo., Rom. 105 FD51
Pachesham Dr., Lthd. 231 CF116
Oxshott Rd.
Pachesham Pk., Lthd. 231 CF117
Pacific Clo., Felt. 175 BT88
Pacific Rd. E16 144 EG72
Packet Boat La., Uxb. 134 BH72
Packham Clo., Orp. 206 EW104
Berrylands
Packham Rd., Grav. 191 GF91
Packhorse Clo., St.Alb. 43 CJ17
Packhorse La., Borwd. 78 CS37
Buckettsland La.
Packhorse La., Pot.B. 62 CR32
Packhorse Rd., Ger.Cr. 112 AY55
Packhorse Rd., Sev. 256 FC123
Packington Rd. W3 158 CQ76
Packington Sq. N1 142 DQ67
Packington St. N1 141 DP67
Packmores Rd. SE9 185 ER85
Padbrook, Oxt. 254 EG129
Padbrook Clo., Oxt. 254 EG129
Padbury SE17 162 DS78
Bagshot St.
Padbury Clo., Felt. 175 BR88
Padbury Ct. E2 142 DT69
Padcroft Rd., West Dr. 134 BK74
Paddenswick Rd. W6 159 CU76
Paddick Clo., Hodd. 49 DZ16
Paddington Clo., Hayes 136 BX70
Paddington Grn. W2 272 A6
Paddington Grn. W2 140 DD71
Paddington St. W1 272 F6
Paddington St. W1 140 DG71
Paddock, The, Brox. 49 EA20
Paddock, The, Dor. 262 CB137
Paddock, The, Ger.Cr. 90 AY50
Paddock, The, Guil. 243 BD133
Paddock, The, Hat. 45 CU16
Paddock, The, Slou. 152 AV81
Paddock, The, Uxb. 115 BP63
Paddock, The, West. 255 EQ126
Paddock Clo. SE3 164 EG83
Paddock Clo. SE26 183 DX91
Paddock Clo. (South Darenth), Dart. 208 FQ95
Paddock Clo., Nthlt. 136 CA68
Paddock Clo., Orp. 223 EP105
State Fm. Ave.
Paddock Clo., Oxt. 254 EF131
Paddock Clo., Ware 34 EK06
Paddock Clo., Wor.Pk. 198 CS102
Paddock Gdns. SE19 182 DS93
Westow St.
Paddock Mead, Harl. 51 EQ20
Paddock Rd. NW2 119 CU62
Paddock Rd., Bexh. 166 EY84
Paddock Rd., Ruis. 116 BX62
Paddock Wk., Warl. 236 DV119
Paddock Way, Chis. 185 ER94
Paddock Way, Hem.H. 39 BE20
Paddock Way, Oxt. 254 EF131
Paddock Way, Wok. 211 BB114
Paddocks, The, Add. 212 BH110
Paddocks, The, Barn. 80 DF41
Paddocks, The, Lthd. 246 CB126
Leatherhead Rd.
Paddocks, The, Rick. 73 BF42
Paddocks, The, Rom. 87 FF44
Paddocks, The, Sev. 257 FK124
Paddocks, The, Vir.W. 192 AY100
Paddocks, The, Welw.G.C. 30 DB08
Paddocks, The, Wem. 118 CP61
Paddocks, The, Wey. 195 BS104
Paddocks Clo., Ash. 232 CL118
Paddocks Clo., Cob. 214 BW114
Paddocks Clo., Har. 116 CB63
Paddocks Clo., Orp. 206 EX103
Paddocks Mead, Wok. 226 AS116
Paddocks Rd., Guil. 243 BA130
Paddocks Way, Ash. 232 CL118
Paddocks Way, Cher. 194 BH102
Padfield Rd. SE5 162 DQ83
Padnall Rd., Rom. 126 EX55
Padstow Clo., Slou. 152 AY76
Padstow Rd., Enf. 81 DP40
Padstow Wk., Felt. 175 BT88
Padua Rd. SE20 202 DW95
Pagden St. SW8 161 DH81
Page Clo., Dag. 126 EY64
Page Clo., Dart. 189 FW90
Page Clo., Hmptn. 176 BY93
Page Clo., Har. 118 CM58
Page Cres., Croy. 219 DN106
Page Cres., Erith 167 FF80
Page Grn. Rd. N15 122 DU57
Page Grn. Ter. N15 122 DT57
Page Heath La., Brom. 204 EK97
Page Heath Vill., Brom. 204 EK97
Page Hill, Ware 32 DW05
Page Meadow NW7 97 CU52
Page Rd., Felt. 175 BR86
Page Rd., Hert. 32 DU09
Page St. NW7 97 CU51
Page St. SW1 277 N8
Page St. SW1 161 DK77
Pageant Ave. NW9 96 CR53
Pageant Clo., Til. 171 GJ81
Pageant Rd., St.Alb. 43 CD21
Pageant Wk., Croy. 202 DS104
Pageantmaster Ct. EC4 274 F9
Pagehurst Rd., Croy. 202 DV101
Pages Cft., Berk. 38 AU17
Pages Hill N10 98 DG54
Pages La. N10 98 DG54
Pages La., Rom. 106 FP54
Pages La., Uxb. 134 BJ65
Pages Wk. SE1 279 M8
Pages Wk. SE1 162 DS77
Pages Yd. W4 158 CS79
Church St.
Paget Ave., Sutt. 200 DD104
Paget Clo., Hmptn. 177 CD91
Paget Gdns., Chis. 205 EP95
Paget La., Islw. 157 CD83
Paget Pl., Kings.T. 178 CQ93
Paget Pl., T.Ditt. 197 CG102
Brooklands Rd.
Paget Ri. SE18 165 EN79
Paget Rd. N16 122 DR60
Paget Rd., Ilf. 125 EP63
Paget Rd., Slou. 153 AZ77
Paget Rd., Uxb. 135 BQ70
Paget St. EC1 274 F2
Paget Ter. SE18 165 EN79
Pagette Way, Grays 170 GA77
Pagitts Gro., Barn. 80 DB39
Paglesfield, Brwd. 109 GC44
Pagnell St. SE14 163 DZ80
Pagoda Ave., Rich. 158 CM83
Pagoda Gdns. SE3 163 ED82
Paignton Rd. N15 122 DS58
Paignton Rd., Ruis. 115 BU62
Paines Brook Rd., Rom. 106 FM51
Paines Brook Way
Paines Brook Way, Rom. 106 FM51
Paines Clo., Pnr. 94 BY54
Paines La., Pnr. 94 BY53
Pains Clo., Mitch. 201 DH96
Pains Hill, Oxt. 254 EJ132
Painsthorpe Rd. N16 122 DS62
Oldfield Rd.
Painters Ash La., Grav. 190 GD90
Painters La., Enf. 83 DY35
Painters Rd., Ilf. 125 ET55
Paisley Rd. N22 99 DP53
Paisley Rd., Cars. 200 DD102
Pakeman St. N7 121 DM62
Pakenham Clo. SW12 180 DG88
Balham Pk. Rd.
Pakenham St. WC1 274 C3
Pakenham St. WC1 141 DM69
Pakes Way, Epp. 85 ES37
Palace Ave. W8 140 DB74
Palace Clo., Kings L. 58 BM30
Palace Clo., Slou. 131 AM74
Palace Ct. NW3 120 DB64
Palace Ct. W2 140 DB73
Palace Ct., Brom. 204 EH95
Palace Gro.
Palace Ct., Har. 118 CL58
Palace Ct. Gdns. N10 121 DJ55
Palace Dr., Wey. 195 BP104
Palace Gdns., Buck.H. 102 EK46
Palace Gdns., Enf. 82 DR42
Sydney Rd.
Palace Gdns. Ms. W8 140 DA74
Palace Gdns. Ter. W8 140 DA74
Palace Gate W8 160 DC75
Palace Gates Rd. N22 99 DK54
Palace Grn. W8 160 DB75
Palace Grn., Croy. 221 DZ108
Palace Gro. SE19 182 DT94
Palace Gro., Brom. 204 EH95
Palace Ms. E17 123 DZ56
Palace Ms. SW1 276 G9
Palace Ms. SW6 159 CZ80
Hartismere Rd.
Palace Pl. SW1 277 K6
Palace Rd. N8 121 DK57
Palace Rd. N11 99 DK52
Palace Rd. SE19 182 DT94
Palace Rd. SW2 181 DM88
Palace Rd., Brom. 204 EH95
Palace Rd., E.Mol. 197 CD97
Palace Rd., Kings.T. 197 CK98
Palace Rd., Ruis. 116 BY63
Palace Rd., West. 239 EN121
Chestnut Ave.
Palace Rd. Est. SW2 181 DM88
Palace Sq. SE19 182 DT94
Palace St. SW1 277 K6
Palace St. SW1 161 DJ76
Palace Vw. SE12 184 EG89
Palace Vw., Brom. 204 EH97
Palace Vw., Croy. 221 DZ105
Palace Vw. Rd. E4 101 EB50
Palace Way, Wey. 195 BP104
Palace Dr.
Palamos Rd. E10 123 EA60
Palatine Ave. N16 122 DT63
Stoke Newington Rd.
Palatine Rd. N16 122 DS63
Palermo Rd. NW10 139 CU68
Palestine Gro. SW19 200 DD95
Palewell Clo., Orp. 206 EV96
Palewell Common Dr. SW14 178 CR85
Palewell Pk. SW14 178 CR85
Paley Gdns., Loug. 85 EP41
Palfrey Clo., St.Alb. 43 CD18
Palfrey Pl. SW8 161 DM80
Palgrave Ave., Sthl. 136 CA73
Palgrave Rd. W12 159 CT76
Palissy St. E2 275 P3
Pall Mall SW1 277 L3
Pall Mall SW1 141 DJ74
Pall Mall E. SW1 277 N2
Pall Mall E. SW1 141 DK74
Pall Mall Pl. SW1 277 L3
Pallant Way, Orp. 205 EN104
Pallas Rd., Hem.H. 40 BM18
Pallet Way SE18 164 EL81
Palliser Dr., Rain. 147 FG71
Palliser Rd. W14 159 CY78
Palliser Rd., Ch.St.G. 90 AV48
Palm Ave., Sid. 186 EX93
Palm Clo. E10 123 EB62
Palm Gro. W5 158 CL76
Palm Gro., Guil. 242 AW129
Palm Rd., Rom. 127 FC57
Palmar Cres., Bexh. 166 FA83
Palmar Rd., Bexh. 166 FA82
Palmarsh Clo., Orp. 206 EX98
Wotton Grn.
Palmeira Rd., Bexh. 166 EX83
Palmer Ave., Grav. 191 GK92
Palmer Ave., Sutt. 217 CW105
Palmer Ave. (Bushey), Wat. 76 CB43
Palmer Clo., Hert. 32 DQ07
Palmer Clo., Horl. 268 DF146
Palmer Clo., Houns. 156 CA81
Palmer Clo., Red. 266 DG135
Palmer Clo., W.Wick. 203 ED104
Palmer Cres., Cher. 211 BD107
Palmer Cres., Kings.T. 198 CL97
Palmer Gdns., Barn. 79 CX43
Palmer Pl. N7 121 DN64
Palmer Rd. E13 144 EH70
Palmer Rd., Dag. 126 EX60
Palmer Rd., Hert. 32 DR07
Palmer St. SW1 277 M6
Palmer St. SW1 161 DK76
Palmers Ave., Grays 170 GC78
Palmers Dr., Grays 170 GC77
Palmers Gro., Wal.Abb. 50 EF22
Palmers Gro., W.Mol. 196 CA98
Palmers Hill, Epp. 70 EU29
Palmers La., Enf. 82 DW39
Palmer's Lo., Guil. 258 AU135
Old Palace Rd.
Palmers Moor La., Iver 134 BG70
Palmers Orchard, Sev. 225 FF111
Palmers Pas. SW14 158 CQ83
Palmers Rd.
Palmers Rd. E2 143 DX68
Palmers Rd. N11 99 DJ50
Palmers Rd. SW14 158 CQ83
Palmers Rd. SW16 201 DM96
Palmers Rd., Borwd. 78 CP39
Palmers Way (Cheshunt), Wal.Cr. 67 DY29
Palmersfield Rd., Bans. 218 DA114
Palmerston Ave., Slou. 152 AV76
Palmerston Clo., Welw.G.C. 29 CW09
Palmerston Clo., Wok. 211 BA114
Palmerston Cres. N13 99 DM50
Palmerston Cres. SE18 165 EQ79
Palmerston Gdns., Grays 169 FX78
Palmerston Gro. SW19 180 DA94
Palmerston Rd. E7 124 EH64
Palmerston Rd. E17 123 DZ55
Palmerston Rd. N22 99 DM52
Palmerston Rd. NW6 139 CZ66
Palmerston Rd. SW14 158 CQ84
Palmerston Rd. SW19 180 DA94
Palmerston Rd. W3 158 CQ76
Palmerston Rd., Buck.H. 102 EH47
Palmerston Rd., Cars. 218 DF105
Palmerston Rd., Grays 169 FX79
Palmerston Rd., Har. 117 CE55
Palmerston Rd., Orp. 223 EQ105
Palmerston Rd., Rain. 148 FJ68
Palmerston Rd., Sutt. 218 DC105
Vernon Rd.
Palmerston Rd., Th.Hth. 202 DR99
Palmerston Rd., Twick. 177 CE86
Palmerston Way SW8 161 DH80
Bradmead
Pamela Ave., Hem.H. 40 BM23
Pamela Gdns., Pnr. 115 BV57
Pamela Wk. E8 142 DU67
Marlborough Ave.
Pampisford Rd., Pur. 219 DN111
Pampisford Rd., S.Croy. 220 DQ107
Pams Way, Epsom 216 CR106
Pancake La., Hem.H. 41 BR21
Pancras La. EC4 275 J9
Pancras Rd. NW1 273 P1
Pancras Rd. NW1 141 DK68
Pancroft, Rom. 86 EV41
Pandora Rd. NW6 140 DA65
Panel Rd., Ware 33 DZ05
Panfield Ms., Ilf. 125 EN58
Cranbrook Rd.
Panfield Rd. SE2 166 EU76
Pangbourne Ave. W10 139 CW71
Pangbourne Dr., Stan. 95 CK50
Pankhurst Clo. SE14 163 DX80
Briant St.
Pankhurst Clo., Islw. 157 CF83
Pankhurst Rd., Walt. 196 BW101
Panmuir Rd. SW20 199 CV95
Panmure Clo. N5 121 DP63
Panmure Rd. SE26 182 DV90
Pannard Pl., Sthl. 136 CB73
Pannells Clo., Cher. 193 BF102
Pannells Ct., Guil. 258 AX135
Panshanger Dr., Welw.G.C. 30 DB09
Panshanger La., Hert. 30 DF09
Pansy Gdns. W12 139 CU73
Panters, Swan. 187 FF94
Pantile Rd., Wey. 213 BR105
Pantile Row, Slou. 153 BA77
Pantile Wk., Uxb. 134 BJ66
High St.
Pantiles, The NW11 119 CZ57
Willifield Way
Pantiles, The, Bexh. 166 EZ80
Pantiles, The, Brom. 204 EL97
Pantiles, The (Bushey), Wat. 95 CD45
Pantiles Clo. N13 99 DP50
Princes Ave.
Pantiles Clo., Wok. 226 AV118
Panton St. SW1 277 M1
Panxworth Rd., Hem.H. 40 BL22
Panyer All. EC4 275 H8
Paper Ms., Dor. 263 CH135
Papercourt La., Wok. 227 BF122
Papermill Clo., Cars. 218 DG105
Papillons Wk. SE3 164 EG83
Papworth Gdns. N7 121 DM64
Liverpool Rd.
Papworth Way SW2 181 DN87
Parade, The SW11 160 DF80
Parade, The, Brwd. 108 FW48
Parade, The, Dart. 187 FF85
Crayford Way
Parade, The, Epsom 216 CR113
Parade, The, Esher 215 CE107
Parade, The, Rom. 106 FP51
Parade, The, S.Ock. 168 FQ75
Parade, The, Sun. 175 BT94
Parade, The, Vir.W. 192 AX100
Parade, The, Wat. 75 BV41
Parade, The (Carpenders Pk.), Wat. 94 BY48
Parade, The, Wind. 151 AK81
Parade Ms. SE27 181 DP89
Norwood Rd.
Paradise Clo. (Cheshunt), Wal.Cr. 66 DV28
Paradise Pas. N7 141 DN65
Sheringham Rd.
Paradise Pl. SE18 164 EL77
Woodhill
Paradise Rd. SW4 161 DL82
Paradise Rd., Rich. 178 CL85
Paradise Rd., Wal.Abb. 67 EC34
Paradise Row E2 142 DV69
Bethnal Grn. Rd.
Paradise St. SE16 162 DV75
Paradise Wk. SW3 160 DF79
Paradise Wd. La., Hem.H. 40 BK21
Paragon, The SE3 164 EF82
Paragon Clo. E16 144 EG72
Paragon Gro., Surb. 198 CM100
Paragon Ms. SE1 279 L8
Paragon Pl. SE3 164 EF82
Paragon Pl., Surb. 198 CM100
Berrylands Rd.
Paragon Rd. E9 142 DW65
Parbury Ri., Chess. 216 CL107
Parbury Rd. SE23 183 DY86
Parchment Clo., Amer. 55 AS37
Parchmore Rd., Th.Hth. 201 DP96
Parchmore Way, Th.Hth. 201 DP96
Pardon St. EC1 274 G4
Pardoner St. SE1 279 L6
Pardoner St. SE1 162 DR76
Pares Clo., Wok. 226 AX116
Parfett St. E1 142 DU71
Parfitt Clo. NW3 120 DC61
North End
Parfour Dr., Ken. 236 DQ116
Parfrey St. W6 159 CW79
Parham Dr., Ilf. 125 EP58
Parham Way N10 99 DJ54
Paringdon Rd., Harl. 51 EP19
Paris Gdns. SE1 278 F2
Paris Gdns. SE1 141 DP74
Parish Clo., Horn. 127 FH61
St. Leonards Way
Parish Gate Dr., Sid. 185 ES86
Parish La. SE20 183 DX93
Parish La., Slou. 111 AP61
Parish Ms. SE20 183 DX94
Parish Wf. Pl. SE18 164 EL77
Woodhill
Park, The N6 120 DG58
Park, The NW11 120 DB60
Park, The SE19 182 DS94
Park, The SE23 182 DV88
Park Hill
Park, The W5 137 CK74
Park, The, Cars. 218 DF106
Park, The, Lthd. 230 CA123
Park, The, St.Alb. 43 CG18
Park, The, Sid. 186 EU91
Park App., Well. 166 EV84
Park Ave. E6 145 EN67

Park Ave. E15 144 EE65
Park Ave. N3 98 DB53
Park Ave. N13 99 DN48
Park Ave. N18 100 DU49
Park Ave. N22 99 DL54
Park Ave. NW2 139 CV65
Park Ave. NW10 138 CM68
Park Ave. NW11 120 DB60
Park Ave. SW14 158 CR84
Park Ave., Bark. 145 EQ65
Park Ave., Barn. 80 DC43
Park Ave., Brwd. 109 GC46
Park Ave., Brom. 184 EF94
Park Ave., Cars. 218 DG107
Park Ave., Cat. 236 DS124
Park Ave., Chis. 205 ES97
Park Ave., Egh. 173 BC93
Park Ave., Enf. 82 DR43
Park Ave., Grav. 191 GJ88
Park Ave. (Perry St.), Grav. 190 GE88
Park Ave., Grays 169 FU79
Park Ave., Harl. 52 EW18
Park Ave., Houns. 176 CB86
Park Ave., Ilf. 125 EN60
Park Ave., Mitch. 181 DH94
Park Ave., Orp. 206 EU103
Park Ave. (Farnborough), Orp. 205 EM104
Park Ave., Pot.B. 64 DC34
Park Ave., Rad. 61 CH34
Park Ave., Red. 266 DF142
Park Ave., Rick. 74 BG43
Park Ave., Ruis. 115 BR58
Park Ave., St.Alb. 43 CG19
Park Ave., Sthl. 156 BZ75
Park Ave., Stai. 173 BF93
Park Ave. (Sunnymeads), Stai. 172 AX85
Park Ave., Upmin. 129 FS59
Park Ave., Wat. 75 BU41
Park Ave. (Bushey), Wat. 76 BX41
Park Ave., W.Wick. 203 EC103
Park Ave., Wdf.Grn. 102 EH50
Park Ave. E., Epsom 217 CU107
Park Ave. Ms., Mitch. 181 DH94
Park Ave.
Park Ave. N. N8 121 DK55
Park Ave. N. NW10 119 CV64
Park Ave. Rd. N17 100 DV52
Park Ave. S. N8 121 DK56
Park Ave. W., Epsom 217 CU107
Park Barn Dr., Guil. 242 AS132
Park Barn E., Guil. 242 AT133
Park Boul., Rom. 105 FF53
Park Chase, Guil. 242 AY134
Park Chase, Wem. 118 CM63
Park Clo. E9 142 DW67
Skipworth Rd.
Park Clo. NW2 119 CV62
Park Clo. NW10 138 CM69
Park Clo. SW1 276 D5
Park Clo. W4 158 CR78
Park Clo. W14 159 CZ76
Park Clo., Add. 212 BH110
Park Clo., Bet. 264 CP138
Park Clo., Cars. 218 DF107
Park Clo., Epp. 70 FA27
Park Clo., Esher 214 BZ107
Park Clo., Hmptn. 196 CC95
Park Clo., Har. 95 CE53
Park Clo., Hat. 63 CZ26
Park Clo. (Brookmans Pk.), Hat. 45 CW17
Park Clo., Houns. 176 CC85
Park Clo., Kings.T. 198 CN95
Park Clo., Lthd. 231 CD124
Park Clo., Rick. 93 BP49
Park Clo., Walt. 195 BT103
Park Clo. (Bushey), Wat. 76 BX41
Park Clo., Wind. 151 AR82
Park Copse, Dor. 263 CK136
Park Cor., Wind. 151 AL83
Park Cor. Dr., Lthd. 245 BS128
Park Cor. Rd., Grav. 190 FZ90
Park Ct. SE26 182 DV93
Park Ct., Harl. 35 ER13
Park Ct., Kings.T. 197 CJ95
Park Ct., N.Mal. 198 CR98
Park Ct., Wem. 118 CL64
Park Ct., W.Byf. 212 BG113
Park Ct., Wok. 227 AZ118
Park Dr.
Park Cres. N3 98 DB52
Park Cres. W1 273 H5
Park Cres. W1 141 DH70
Park Cres., Borwd. 78 CM41
Park Cres., Enf. 82 DR42
Park Cres., Erith 167 FC79
Park Cres., Har. 95 CE53
Park Cres., Horn. 127 FG59
Park Cres., Twick. 177 CD88
Park Cres. Ms. E. W1 273 J5
Park Cres. Ms. W. W1 273 H5
Park Cres. Rd., Erith 167 FD79
Park Cft., Edg. 96 CQ53
Park Dale N11 99 DK51
Bounds Grn. Rd.
Park Dr. N21 82 DQ44
Park Dr. NW11 120 DB60
Park Dr. SE7 164 EL79
Park Dr. SW14 158 CR84
Park Dr. W3 158 CN76
Park Dr., B.Stort. 37 FH05
Park Dr., Dag. 127 FC62
Park Dr., Har. 116 CA59
Park Dr. (Harrow Weald), Har. 95 CE51
Park Dr., Pot.B. 64 DA31
Park Dr., Rom. 127 FD56
Park Dr., Upmin. 128 FP63
Park Dr., Wey. 213 BP106
Park Dr., Wok. 227 AZ118
Park Dr. Clo. SE7 164 EL78
Park End NW3 120 DE63
South Hill Pk.
Park End, Brom. 204 EF95
Park End Rd., Rom. 127 FE56
Park Fm. Clo. N2 120 DC55
Park Fm. Clo., Pnr. 115 BV57
Field End Rd.
Park Fm. Rd., Brom. 204 EK95
Park Fm. Rd., Kings.T. 178 CL94
Park Fm. Rd., Upmin. 128 FM64
Park Gdn. Pl. W2 272 A9
Park Gdns. NW9 118 CP55
Park Gdns., Erith 167 FD77
Valley Rd.
Park Gdns., Kings.T. 178 CM92
Park Gate N2 120 DD55
Park Gate N21 99 DM45
Park Gate W5 137 CK71
Mount Ave.
Park Gra. Gdns., Sev. 257 FJ127
Solefields Rd.
Park Grn., Lthd. 230 CA124
Park Gro. E15 144 EG67
Park Gro. N11 99 DK52
Park Gro., Bexh. 167 FC84
Park Gro., Brom. 204 EH95
Park Gro., Ch.St.G. 72 AX41
Park Gro., Edg. 96 CM50
Park Gro. Rd. E11 124 EE61
Park Hall Rd. N2 120 DE56
Park Hall Rd. SE21 182 DR90
Park Hall Rd., Reig. 250 DA132
Park Hill SE23 182 DV89
Park Hill SW4 181 DK85
Park Hill W5 137 CK71
Park Hill, Brom. 204 EL98
Park Hill, Cars. 218 DE107
Park Hill, Harl. 36 EV12
Park Hill, Loug. 84 EK43
Park Hill, Rich. 178 CM86
Park Hill Clo., Cars. 218 DE106
Park Hill Ct. SW17 180 DF90
Beeches Rd.
Park Hill Ri., Croy. 202 DS103
Park Hill Rd., Brom. 204 EE96
Park Hill Rd., Croy. 202 DS103
Park Hill Rd., Hem.H. 40 BH20
Park Hill Rd., Sid. 185 ES90
Park Hill Rd., Wall. 219 DH107
Park Horsley, Lthd. 245 BU129
Park Ho. N21 99 DM45
Park Ho. Dr., Reig. 265 CZ136
Park Ho. Gdns., Twick. 177 CJ86
Park Ind. Est., St.Alb. 61 CE27
Park La. E15 143 ED67
High St.
Park La. N9 100 DS48
Park La. N17 100 DT52
Park La. N18 100 DS49
Sheldon Rd.
Park La. W1 272 E10
Park La. W1 140 DF73
Park La., Ash. 232 CM118
Park La., Bans. 234 DD118
Park La., Beac. 89 AM54
Park La., Brox. 49 DY19
Park La. (Wormley), Brox. 48 DV22
Park La., Cars. 218 DG105
Park La., Couls. 235 DK121
Park La., Croy. 202 DR104
Park La., Guil. 243 BC131
Park La., Harl. 35 ER13
Park La., Har. 116 CB62
Park La., Hayes 135 BS71
Park La., Hem.H. 40 BK21
Park La., Horn. 127 FF58
Park La. (Elm Pk.), Horn. 147 FH65
Park La., Houns. 155 BU80
Park La., Reig. 265 CY135
Park La., Rich. 157 CK84
Park La. (Chadwell Heath), Rom. 126 EX58
Park La., St.Alb. 44 CP23
Park La., Sev. 257 FJ124
Park La. (Seal), Sev. 257 FN121
Park La., Slou. 152 AV76
Park La. (Burnham), Slou. 111 AL64
Park La. (Horton), Slou. 153 BA83
Park La., S.Ock. 149 FR73
Park La., Stan. 95 CG48
Park La., Sutt. 217 CY107
Park La., Swan. 208 FJ96
Park La., Tedd. 177 CF93
Park La., Uxb. 92 BG53
Park La., Wal.Cr. 66 DW33
Park La. (Cheshunt), Wal.Cr. 66 DU26
Park La., Wem. 118 CL64
Park La. Clo. N17 100 DU52
Park La. E., Reig. 265 CZ137
Park La. Paradise (Cheshunt), Wal.Cr. 66 DU25
Park Lawn Rd., Wey. 213 BQ105
Park Lawns, Wem. 118 CM63
Park Ley Rd., Cat. 237 DX120
Park Mead, Harl. 35 EP14
Park Mead, Har. 116 CB62
Park Mead, Sid. 186 EV85
Park Meadow, Hat. 45 CW17
Park Ms. SE24 182 DQ86
Croxted Rd.
Park Ms., Chis. 185 EP93
Park Ms., E.Mol. 196 CC98
Park Ms., Hmptn. 176 CC92
Park Rd.
Park Ms., Hat. 45 CW16
Park Nook Gdns., Enf. 82 DR37
Park Par. NW10 139 CT68
Park Pl. E14 143 EA74
Park Pl. SW1 277 K3
Park Pl. SW1 141 DJ74
Park Pl. W3 158 CN77
Park Pl. W5 137 CK74
Park Pl., Amer. 72 AT38
Park Pl., Grav. 191 GJ86
Park Pl., Hmptn. 176 CC93
Park Pl., St.Alb. 61 CD27
Park Pl., Sev. 256 FD123
Park Pl., Wem. 118 CM63
Park Pl., Wok. 227 AZ118
Park Dr.
Park Pl. Vill. W2 140 DC71
Park Ridings N8 121 DN55
Park Ri. SE23 183 DY88
Park Ri., Berk. 38 AS17
Park Ri., Har. 95 CE53
Park Ri., Lthd. 231 CH121
Park Ri. Clo., Lthd. 231 CH121
Park Ri. Rd. SE23 183 DY88
Park Rd. E6 144 EJ67
Park Rd. E10 123 EA60
Park Rd. E12 124 EH60
Park Rd. E15 144 EG67
Park Rd. E17 123 DZ57
Park Rd. N2 120 DD55
Park Rd. N8 121 DJ56
Park Rd. N11 99 DK52
Park Rd. N14 99 DK45
Park Rd. N15 121 DP56
Park Rd. N18 100 DT49
Park Rd. NW1 272 D4
Park Rd. NW1 140 DF70
Park Rd. NW4 119 CU59
Park Rd. NW8 272 B2
Park Rd. NW8 140 DE69
Park Rd. NW9 118 CR59
Park Rd. NW10 138 CS67
Park Rd. SE25 202 DS98
Park Rd. SW19 180 DD94
Park Rd. W4 158 CQ80
Park Rd. W7 137 CF73
Park Rd., Amer. 72 AT37
Park Rd., Ashf. 175 BP92
Park Rd., Ash. 232 CL118
Park Rd., Bans. 234 DB115
Park Rd., Barn. 79 CZ42
Park Rd. (New Barnet), Barn. 80 DD42
Park Rd., Beck. 183 DZ94
Park Rd., Brwd. 108 FV46
Park Rd., Brom. 204 EH95
Park Rd., Cat. 236 DS123
Park Rd., Chesh. 54 AP31
Park Rd., Chis. 185 EP93
Park Rd., Dart. 188 FN87
Park Rd., E.Mol. 196 CC98
Park Rd., Egh. 173 BA91
Park Rd., Enf. 83 DY36
Park Rd., Esher 214 CB105
Park Rd., Felt. 176 BX91
Park Rd., Grav. 191 GH88
Park Rd., Grays 170 GB78
Park Rd., Guil. 242 AX134
Park Rd. (Albury), Guil. 260 BL140
Park Rd., Hmptn. 176 CB91
Park Rd., Hayes 135 BS71
Park Rd., Hem.H. 40 BJ22
Park Rd., Hert. 32 DS09
Park Rd., Hodd. 49 EA17
Park Rd., Houns. 176 CB85
Park Rd., Ilf. 125 ER62
Park Rd., Islw. 157 CH81
Park Rd., Ken. 235 DP115
Park Rd., Kings.T. 178 CM92
Park Rd. (Hampton Wick), Kings.T. 197 CJ95
Park Rd., N.Mal. 198 CR98
Park Rd., Orp. 206 EW99
Park Rd., Oxt. 254 EF128
Park Rd., Pot.B. 64 DG30
Park Rd., Rad. 77 CG35
Park Rd., Red. 250 DF132
Park Rd., Rich. 178 CM86
Park Rd., Rick. 92 BK45
Park Rd., Shep. 194 BN102
Park Rd., Slou. 131 AQ68
Park Rd., Stai. 174 BH86
Park Rd., Sun. 175 BV94
Park Rd., Surb. 198 CM100
Park Rd., Sutt. 217 CY107
Park Rd., Swan. 207 FF98
Park Rd., Swans. 190 FY86
Park Rd., Tedd. 177 CF94
Park Rd., Twick. 177 CJ86
Park Rd., Uxb. 134 BL66
Park Rd., Wall. 219 DH106
Park Rd. (Hackbridge), Wall. 201 DH103
Park Rd., Wal.Cr. 67 DX33
Park Rd., Ware 32 DV05
Park Rd., Warl. 222 EE114
Park Rd., Wat. 75 BV39
Park Rd. (Bushey), Wat. 76 CA44
Park Rd., Wem. 138 CL65
Park Rd., Wok. 227 AZ117
Park Rd. E. W3 158 CP75
Park Rd. E., Uxb. 134 BK68
Hillingdon Rd.
Park Rd. N. W3 158 CP75
Park Rd. N. W4 158 CR78
Park Rd. W., Kings.T. 197 CJ95
Park Row SE10 163 ED79
Park Royal Rd. NW10 138 CQ70
Park Royal Rd. W3 138 CQ70
Park Side, Add. 212 BH111
Park Side, Sutt. 217 CY107
Park Sq., Esher 214 CB105
Park Rd.
Park Sq. E. NW1 273 H4
Park Sq. E. NW1 141 DH70
Park Sq. Ms. NW1 273 H5
Park Sq. Ms. NW1 141 DH70
Park Sq. W. NW1 273 H4
Park Sq. W. NW1 141 DH70
Park St. SE1 279 H2
Park St. SE1 142 DQ74
Park St. W1 272 F10
Park St. W1 140 DG73
Park St., Berk. 38 AV18
Park St., Croy. 202 DQ103
Park St., Guil. 258 AW136
Park St., Hat. 45 CW17
Park St., St.Alb. 61 CD26
Park St., Slou. 152 AT76
Park St. (Colnbrook), Slou. 153 BD80
Park St., Tedd. 177 CE93
Park St., Wind. 151 AR81
Park St. La., St.Alb. 60 CB30
Park Ter., Green. 189 FV85
Park Ter. (Sundridge), Sev. 240 EX124
Main Rd.
Park Ter., Wor.Pk. 199 CU102
Park Vw. N21 99 DM45
Park Vw. W3 138 CQ71
Park Vw., Hat. 45 CW16
Park Vw., Hodd. 49 EA18
Park Vw., Horl. 268 DG148
Brighton Rd.
Park Vw., Lthd. 246 CA125
Park Vw., N.Mal. 199 CT97
Park Vw., Pnr. 94 BZ53
Park Vw., Pot.B. 64 DC33
Park Vw., S.Ock. 149 FR74
Park Vw., Wem. 118 CP64
Park Vw. Clo., St.Alb. 43 CG21
Park Vw. Ct., Ilf. 125 ES58
Brancaster Rd.
Park Vw. Ct., Wok. 227 AZ119
Park Vw. Cres. N11 99 DH49
Park Vw. Est. E2 143 DX68
Sewardstone Rd.
Park Vw. Gdns. NW4 119 CX58
Park Vw. Gdns., Bark. 145 ES68
River Rd.
Park Vw. Gdns., Grays 170 GB78
Park Vw. Gdns., Ilf. 125 EM56
Woodford Ave.
Park Vw. Rd. N3 98 DB53
Park Vw. Rd. N17 122 DU55
Park Vw. Rd. NW10 119 CT63
Park Vw. Rd. W5 138 CL71
Park Vw. Rd., Berk. 38 AV19
Park Vw. Rd., Cat. 237 DY122
Park Vw. Rd., Pnr. 93 BV52
Park Vw. Rd., Red. 266 DG141
Park Vw. Rd., Sthl. 136 CA74
Park Vw. Rd., Uxb. 134 BM72
Park Vw. Rd., Well. 166 EV83
Park Village E. NW1 141 DH68
Park Village W. NW1 141 DH68
Park Vill., Rom. 126 EX58
Park Vista SE10 163 ED79
Park Wk. N6 120 DG59
North Rd.
Park Wk. SW10 160 DC79
Park Wk., Ash. 232 CM119
Rectory La.
Park Way N20 98 DF49
Park Way NW11 119 CY57
Park Way, Bex. 187 FE90
Park Way, Brwd. 109 FZ46
Park Way, Edg. 96 CP53
Park Way, Enf. 81 DN40
Park Way, Felt. 175 BV87
Park Way, Horl. 268 DG148
Park Way, Ilf. 125 ET62
Park Way, Lthd. 230 CA123
Park Way, Rick. 92 BJ46
Park Way, Ruis. 115 BU60
Park Way, W.Mol. 196 CB97
Park W. W2 272 A9
Park W. Pl. W2 272 C8
Park Wks. Rd., Red. 251 DM133
Parkcroft Rd. SE12 184 EF87
Parkdale Cres., Wor.Pk. 198 CR104
Parkdale Rd. SE18 165 ES78
Parke Rd. SW13 159 CU81
Parke Rd., Sun. 195 BU98
Parker Ave., Hert. 32 DR07
Parker Ave., Til. 171 GJ81
Parker Clo. E16 144 EL74
Parker Ms. WC2 274 A8
Parker Rd., Croy. 220 DQ105
Parker Rd., Grays 170 FZ78
Parker St. E16 144 EL74
Parker St. WC2 274 A8
Parker St. WC2 141 DL72
Parker St., Wat. 75 BV39
Parkers Clo., Ash. 232 CL119
Parkers Hill, Ash. 232 CL119
Parkers La., Ash. 232 CL119
Parkers Row SE1 162 DT75
Jamaica Rd.
Parkes Rd., Chig. 103 ES50
Parkfield, Rick. 73 BF42
Parkfield, Sev. 257 FM123
Parkfield Ave. SW14 158 CS84
Parkfield Ave., Amer. 55 AR37
Parkfield Ave., Felt. 175 BU90
Parkfield Ave., Har. 94 CC54
Parkfield Ave., Nthlt. 136 BX68
Parkfield Ave., Uxb. 135 BP69
Parkfield Clo., Edg. 96 CP51
Parkfield Clo., Nthlt. 136 BY68
Parkfield Cres., Felt. 175 BU90
Parkfield Cres., Har. 94 CC54
Parkfield Cres., Ruis. 116 BY62
Parkfield Dr., Nthlt. 136 BX68
Parkfield Gdns., Har. 116 CB55
Parkfield Rd. NW10 139 CU66
Parkfield Rd. SE14 163 DZ81
Parkfield Rd., Felt. 175 BU90
Parkfield Rd., Har. 116 CC62
Parkfield Rd., Nthlt. 136 BY68
Parkfield Rd., Uxb. 115 BP61
Parkfield St. N1 141 DN68
Parkfield Way, Brom. 205 EM100
Parkfields SW15 159 CW84
Parkfields, Croy. 203 DZ102
Parkfields, Harl. 50 EG15
Parkfields, Lthd. 215 CD111
Parkfields, Welw.G.C. 29 CX09
Parkfields Ave. NW9 118 CR60
Parkfields Ave. SW20 199 CV96
Parkfields Clo., Cars. 218 DG105
Devonshire Rd.
Parkfields Rd., Kings.T. 178 CM92
Parkgate SE3 164 EF83
Parkgate, Slou. 130 AJ70
Parkgate Ave., Barn. 80 DC39
Parkgate Clo., Kings.T. 178 CP93
Warboys App.
Parkgate Cres., Barn. 80 DC39
Parkgate Gdns. SW14 178 CR85
Parkgate Rd. SW11 160 DE80
Parkgate Rd., Orp. 225 FB105
Parkgate Rd., Reig. 266 DB135
Parkgate Rd., Wall. 218 DG106
Parkgate Rd., Wat. 76 BW37
Parkham Ct., Brom. 204 EE96
Parkham St. SW11 160 DD81
Parkhill Clo., Horn. 128 FJ62
Parkhill Rd. E4 101 EC46
Parkhill Rd. NW3 120 DF64
Parkhill Rd., Bex. 186 EZ87
Parkhill Rd., Epsom 217 CT111
Parkhill Wk. NW3 120 DF64
Parkholme Rd. E8 142 DU65
Parkhouse St. SE5 162 DR80
Parkhurst, Epsom 216 CQ110
Parkhurst Gdns., Bex. 186 FA87
Parkhurst Gro., Horl. 268 DE147
Parkhurst Rd. E12 125 EN63
Parkhurst Rd. E17 123 DY56
Parkhurst Rd. N7 121 DL63
Parkhurst Rd. N11 98 DG49
Parkhurst Rd. N17 100 DU54
Parkhurst Rd. N22 99 DM51
Parkhurst Rd., Bex. 186 FA87
Parkhurst Rd., Guil. 242 AU133
Parkhurst Rd., Hert. 31 DP08
Parkhurst Rd., Horl. 268 DE147
Parkhurst Rd., Sutt. 218 DD105
Parkland Ave., Rom. 127 FE55
Parkland Ave., Slou. 152 AX77
Parkland Ave., Upmin. 128 FP64
Parkland Clo., Chig. 103 EQ48
Parkland Clo., Hodd. 33 EB14
Parkland Clo., Sev. 257 FJ129
Parkland Dr., St.Alb. 42 CA21
Parkland Gdns. SW19 179 CX88
Parkland Gro., Ashf. 174 BN91
Parkland Rd. N22 99 DM54
Parkland Rd., Ashf. 174 BN91
Parkland Rd., Wdf.Grn. 102 EG52
Parkland Wk. N4 121 DN59
Parkland Wk. N6 121 DJ59
Parkland Wk. N10 121 DH56
Parklands N6 121 DH59
Parklands, Add. 212 BJ106
Parklands, Chig. 103 EQ48
Parklands, Dor. 263 CH140
Parklands, Epp. 70 EX29
Parklands, Lthd. 230 CA123
Parklands, Oxt. 254 EE131
Parklands, Surb. 198 CM99
Parklands, Wal.Abb. 67 EC33
Parklands Clo. SW14 178 CQ85
Parklands Clo., Barn. 80 DD38
Parklands Ct., Houns. 156 BX82
Parklands Dr. N3 119 CY55
Parklands Pl., Guil. 243 BB134
Parklands Rd. SW16 181 DH92
Parklands Way, Wor.Pk. 198 CS103
Parklawn Ave., Epsom 216 CP113
Parklawn Ave., Horl. 268 DF146
Parklea Clo. NW9 96 CS53
Parkleigh Rd. SW19 200 DB96
Parkleys, Rich. 177 CK91
Parkmead SW15 179 CV86
Parkmead, Loug. 85 EN43
Parkmead Gdns. NW7 97 CT51
Parkmore Clo., Wdf.Grn. 102 EG49
Parkpale La., Bet. 264 CN139
Parkshot, Rich. 158 CL84
Parkside N3 98 DB53
Parkside NW2 119 CU62
Parkside NW7 97 CU51
Parkside SE3 164 EF80
Parkside SW19 179 CX91
Parkside, Buck.H. 102 EH47
Parkside, Ger.Cr. 113 AZ56
Lower Rd.
Parkside, Grays 170 GD76
Parkside, Hmptn. 177 CD92
Parkside, Pot.B. 64 DC32
High St.
Parkside, Sev. 224 EZ113
Parkside, Sid. 186 EV89
Parkside, Wal.Cr. 67 DY34
Parkside, Wat. 76 BW44
Parkside Ave. SW19 179 CX92
Parkside Ave., Bexh. 167 FD82
Parkside Ave., Brom. 204 EL98
Parkside Ave., Rom. 127 FD55
Parkside Ave., Til. 171 GH82
Parkside Clo. SE20 182 DW94
Parkside Clo., Lthd. 245 BT125
Parkside Ct., Wey. 212 BN105
Parkside Cres. N7 121 DN62
Parkside Cres., Surb. 198 CQ100
Parkside Cross, Bexh. 167 FE82
Parkside Dr., Edg. 96 CN48
Parkside Dr., Wat. 75 BS40
Parkside Est. E9 142 DW67
Rutland Rd.
Parkside Gdns. SW19 179 CX91
Parkside Gdns., Barn. 98 DF46
Parkside Gdns., Couls. 235 DH117
Parkside Ho., Dag. 127 FC62
Parkside Pl., Lthd. 245 BT125
Parkside Rd. SW11 160 DG81
Parkside Rd., Belv. 167 FB77
Parkside Rd., Houns. 176 CB85
Parkside Rd., Nthwd. 93 BT50
Parkside Ter. N18 100 DR49
Great Cambridge Rd.
Parkside Way, Har. 116 CB56
Parkstead Rd. SW15 179 CU85
Parkstone Ave. N18 100 DT50
Parkstone Ave., Horn. 128 FK58
Parkstone Rd. E17 123 EC55
Parkstone Rd. SE15 162 DU82
Rye La.
Parkthorne Clo., Har. 116 CB58
Parkthorne Dr., Har. 116 CA58
Parkthorne Rd. SW12 181 DK87
Parkview, St.Alb. 43 CG21
Parkview Chase, Slou. 131 AL72
Parkview Ct. SW18 180 DA86
Broomhill Rd.
Parkview Dr. SW19 200 DD96
Parkview Rd. SE9 185 EP88
Parkview Rd., Croy. 202 DU102
Parkview Vale, Guil. 243 BC132
Foxglove Gdns.
Parkville Rd. SW6 159 CZ80
Parkway N14 99 DL47
Parkway NW1 141 DH67
Parkway SW20 199 CX98
Parkway, Croy. 221 EB109
Parkway, Dor. 263 CG135
Parkway, Erith 166 EY76
Parkway, Guil. 242 AY133
Parkway, Harl. 50 EL15
Parkway, Rain. 147 FG70
Upminster Rd. S.
Parkway, Rom. 105 FF54
Parkway, Saw. 36 EY06
Parkway, Uxb. 134 BN66
Parkway, Welw.G.C. 29 CW11
Parkway, Wey. 213 BR105
Parkway, Wdf.Grn. 102 EJ50
Parkway, The, Hayes 136 BW72
Parkway, The (Cranford), Houns. 155 BU79
Parkway, The, Iver 133 BC67
Parkway Clo., Welw.G.C. 29 CW09
Parkway Ct., St.Alb. 43 CH23
Parkway Gdns., Welw.G.C. 29 CW10
Parkway Ms., Mitch. 181 DH94
Park Ave.
Parkway Trd. Est., Houns. 156 BW79
Parkwood N20 98 DF48
Parkwood, Beck. 203 EA95
Parkwood Ave., Esher 196 CC102
Parkwood Clo., Bans. 233 CX115

Parkwood Clo., Hodd. 49 DZ19
Parkwood Dr., Hem.H. 39 BF20
Parkwood Gro., Sun. 195 BU97
Parkwood Ms. N6 121 DH58
Parkwood Rd. SW19 179 CZ92
Parkwood Rd., Bans. 233 CX115
Parkwood Rd., Bex. 186 EZ87
Parkwood Rd., Islw. 157 CF81
Parkwood Rd., Red. 251 DL133
Parkwood Rd., West. 238 EL121
Parkwood Vw., Bans. 233 CW116
Parlaunt Rd., Iver 153 BC76
Parlaunt Rd., Slou. 153 BA77
Parley Dr., Wok. 226 AW117
Parliament Ct. E1 142 DS71
Sandy's Row
Parliament Hill NW3 120 DE63
Parliament La., Slou. 130 AF66
Parliament Ms. SW14 158 CQ82
Thames Bank
Parliament Sq. SW1 277 P5
Parliament Sq. SW1 161 DL75
Parliament Sq., Hert. 32 DR10
Parliament St. SW1 277 P5
Parliament St. SW1 161 DL75
Parma Cres. SW11 160 DF84
Parmiter St. E2 142 DV68
Parnall Rd., Harl. 51 ER18
Parndon Mill La., Harl. 35 EP12
Parndon Wd. Rd., Harl. 51 EQ20
Parnell Clo., Abb.L. 59 BT30
Parnell Clo., Edg. 96 CP49
Parnell Rd. E3 143 DZ67
Parnham St. E14 143 DY72
Blount St.
Parolles Rd. N19 121 DJ60
Paroma Rd., Belv. 166 FA76
Parr Ave., Epsom 217 CV109
Parr Clo. N9 100 DV49
Parr Clo., Lthd. 231 CF120
Parr Ct., Felt. 176 BW91
Parr Cres., Hem.H. 41 BP15
Parr Rd. E6 144 EK67
Parr Rd., Stan. 95 CK53
Parr St. N1 142 DR68
Parris Cft., Dor. 263 CJ139
Goodwyns Rd.
Parrock, The, Grav. 191 GJ88
Parrock Ave., Grav. 191 GJ88
Parrock Rd., Grav. 191 GJ88
Parrock St., Grav. 191 GH87
Parrotts Clo., Rick. 74 BN42
Parrotts Fld., Hodd. 49 EB16
Parrs Clo., S.Croy. 220 DR109
Florence Rd.
Parrs Pl., Hmptn. 176 CA94
Parry Ave. E6 145 EM72
Parry Clo., Epsom 217 CU107
Parry Dr., Wey. 212 BN110
Parry Grn. N., Slou. 153 AZ77
Parry Grn. S., Slou. 153 AZ77
Parry Pl. SE18 165 EP77
Parry Rd. SE25 202 DS97
Parry Rd. W10 139 CY69
Parry St. SW8 161 DL79
Parsifal Rd. NW6 120 DA64
Parsley Gdns., Croy. 203 DX102
Primrose La.
Parsloe Rd., Epp. 51 EN21
Parsloe Rd., Harl. 51 EP20
Parsloes Ave., Dag. 126 EX63
Parson St. NW4 119 CW56
Parsonage Clo., Abb.L. 59 BS30
Parsonage Clo., Dor. 262 CC138
Parsonage La.
Parsonage Clo., Hayes 135 BT72
Parsonage Clo., Warl. 237 DY116
Parsonage Gdns., Enf. 82 DQ40
Parsonage La. (South Darenth), Dart. 188 FP93
Parsonage La., Dor. 262 CC137
Parsonage La., Enf. 82 DR40
Parsonage La., Hat. 45 CV23
Parsonage La., Sid. 186 EZ91
Parsonage La., Slou. 131 AQ68
Parsonage La., Wind. 151 AN81
Parsonage Leys, Harl. 51 ET15
Parsonage Manorway, Belv. 166 FA79
Parsonage Rd., Ch.St.G. 90 AV48
Parsonage Rd., Egh. 172 AX92
Parsonage Rd., Grays 169 FW79
Parsonage Rd., Hat. 45 CV23
Parsonage Rd., Rain. 148 FJ69
Parsonage Rd., Rick. 92 BK45
Parsonage Sq., Dor. 263 CG135
Parsonage St. E14 163 EC77
Parsons Clo., Horl. 268 DE147
Baden Dr.
Parsons Cres., Edg. 96 CN48
Parsons Grn. SW6 160 DA82
Parsons Grn., Guil. 242 AX132
Bellfields Rd.
Parsons Grn. Ct., Guil. 242 AX132
Bellfields Rd.
Parsons Grn. La. SW6 160 DA81
Parsons Gro., Edg. 96 CN48
Parsons Hill SE18 165 EN76
Powis St.
Parson's Ho. W2 140 DD70
Edgware Rd.
Parsons La., Dart. 187 FG90
Parson's Mead, Croy. 201 DP102
Parsons Mead, E.Mol. 196 CC97
Parsons Pightle, Couls. 235 DN120
Coulsdon Rd.
Parsons Rd. E13 144 EJ68
Old St.
Parsons Wd., Slou. 131 AQ65
Parsonsfield Clo., Bans. 233 CX115
Parsonsfield Rd., Bans. 233 CX115
Parthenia Rd. SW6 160 DA81
Parthia Clo., Tad. 233 CV119
Partingdale La. NW7 97 CX50
Partington Clo. N19 121 DK60
Partridge Clo. E16 144 EK71
Fulmer Rd.
Partridge Clo., Barn. 79 CW44
Partridge Clo., Chesh. 54 AS28
Partridge Clo. (Bushey), Wat. 94 CB46
Partridge Ct. EC1 141 DP70
Percival St.
Partridge Dr., Orp. 205 EQ104
Partridge Grn. SE9 185 EN90
Partridge Knoll, Pur. 219 DP112
Partridge Mead, Bans. 233 CW116
Partridge Rd., Hmptn. 176 BZ93
Partridge Rd., Harl. 51 ER17
Partridge Rd., St.Alb. 43 CD16
Partridge Rd., Sid. 185 ES90
Partridge Sq. E6 144 EL71
Nightingale Way
Partridge Way N22 99 DL53
Partridge Way, Guil. 243 BD132
Parvills Rd., Wal.Abb. 67 ED32
Parvin St. SW8 161 DK81
Parvis Rd., W.Byf. 212 BG113
Pasadena Clo., Hayes 155 BU75
Pascal St. SW8 161 DK80
Pascoe Rd. SE13 183 ED85
Pasfield, Wal.Abb. 67 ED33
Pasley Clo. SE17 162 DQ78
Penrose St.
Pasquier Rd. E17 123 DY55
Passey Pl. SE9 185 EM86
Passfield Dr. E14 143 EB71
Uamvar St.
Passfield Path SE28 146 EV73
Booth Clo.
Passing All. EC1 274 F5
Passmore Gdns. N11 99 DK51
Passmore St. SW1 276 F9
Passmore St. SW1 160 DG78
Pastens Rd., Oxt. 254 EJ131
Pasteur Clo. NW9 96 CS54
Pasteur Dr., Rom. 106 FK54
Pasteur Gdns. N18 99 DP50
Paston Clo. E5 123 DX62
Caldecott Way
Paston Cres. SE12 184 EH87
Paston Rd., Hem.H. 40 BK18
Pastor St. SE11 278 G8
Pastor St. SE11 161 DP77
Pasture, The, St.Alb. 42 CA24
Pasture Clo. (Bushey), Wat. 94 CC45
Pasture Clo., Wem. 117 CH62
Pasture Rd. SE6 184 EE88
Pasture Rd., Dag. 126 EZ63
Pasture Rd., Wem. 117 CH61
Pastures, The N20 97 CZ46
Pastures, The, Hat. 45 CV19
Pastures, The, Hem.H. 39 BE19
Pastures, The, Wat. 94 BW45
Pastures, The, Welw.G.C. 30 DA11
Pastures Mead, Uxb. 134 BN65
Patch, The, Sev. 256 FE122
Patcham Ct., Sutt. 218 DC109
Patcham Ter. SW8 161 DH81
Pater St. W8 160 DA76
Paternoster Clo., Wal.Abb. 68 EF32
Paternoster Hill, Wal.Abb. 68 EF32
Paternoster Row EC4 275 H9
Paternoster Row (Havering-atte-Bower), Rom. 106 FJ47
Paternoster Sq. EC4 274 G8
Paterson Rd., Ashf. 174 BK92
Pates Manor Dr., Felt. 175 BR87
Path, The SW19 200 DB95
Pathfield Rd. SW16 181 DK93
Pathfields, Guil. 260 BN140
Pathway, The, Rad. 77 CF36
Pathway, The, Wat. 94 BX46
Anthony Clo.
Pathway, The, Wok. 243 BF125
Patience Rd. SW11 160 DE82
Patio Clo. SW4 181 DK86
Patmore Est. SW8 161 DJ81
Patmore La., Walt. 213 BT107
Patmore Link Rd., Hem.H. 41 BQ20
Patmore Rd., Wal.Abb. 68 EE34
Patmore St. SW8 161 DJ81
Patmore Way, Rom. 105 FB50
Patmos Rd. SW9 161 DP80
Paton Clo. E3 143 EA69
Paton St. EC1 275 H3
Patricia Clo., Slou. 131 AL73
Patricia Ct., Chis. 205 ER95
Manor Pk. Rd.
Patricia Ct., Well. 166 EV80
Patricia Dr., Horn. 128 FL60
Patricia Gdns., Sutt. 218 DA111
The Cres.
Patrick Connolly Gdns. E3 143 EB69
Talwin St.
Patrick Pas. SW11 160 DE82
Patrick Rd. E13 144 EJ69
Patrington Clo., Uxb. 134 BJ69
Boulmer Rd.
Patriot Sq. E2 142 DV68
Patrol Pl. SE6 183 EB86
Patrons Dr., Uxb. 113 BF58
Patshull Pl. NW5 141 DJ65
Patshull Rd.
Patshull Rd. NW5 141 DJ65
Patten All., Rich. 177 CK85
The Hermitage
Patten Rd. SW18 180 DE87
Pattenden Rd. SE6 183 DZ88
Patterdale Clo., Brom. 184 EF93
Patterdale Rd. SE15 162 DW80
Patterdale Rd., Dart. 189 FR88
Patterson Ct. SE19 182 DT94
Patterson Rd. SE19 182 DT93
Patterson Rd., Chesh. 54 AP28
Pattinson Pt. E16 144 EG71
Fife Rd.
Pattison Rd. NW2 120 DA62
Pattison Wk. SE18 165 EQ78
Sandbach Pl.
Paul Clo. E15 144 EE66
Paul St.
Paul Gdns., Croy. 202 DT103
Paul Robeson Clo. E6 145 EN69
Eastbourne Rd.
Paul St. E15 144 EE67
Paul St. EC2 275 L5
Paul St. EC2 142 DR70
Paulet Rd. SE5 161 DP82
Paulhan Rd., Har. 117 CJ56
Paulin Dr. N21 99 DN45
Pauline Cres., Twick. 176 CC88
Paulinus Clo., Orp. 206 EW96
Pauls Grn., Wal.Cr. 67 DY33
Eleanor Rd.
Pauls Hill, H.Wyc. 88 AF48
Pauls La., Hodd. 49 EA17
Taverners Way
Paul's Pl., Ash. 232 CP119
Pauls Wk. EC4 142 DQ73
Upper Thames St.
Paultons Sq. SW3 160 DD79
Paultons St. SW3 160 DD79
Pauntley St. N19 121 DJ60
Paved Ct., Rich. 177 CK85
King St.
Paveley Dr. SW11 160 DE80
Paveley St. NW8 272 C3
Paveley St. NW8 140 DE70
Pavement, The SW4 161 DJ84
Pavement, The W5 158 CL76
Popes La.
Pavement Ms., Rom. 126 EX59
Clarissa Rd.
Pavement Sq., Croy. 202 DU102
Pavet Clo., Dag. 147 FB65
Pavilion Gdns., Stai. 174 BH94
Pavilion Ms. N3 98 DA54
Windermere Ave.
Pavilion Rd. SW1 276 E5
Pavilion Rd. SW1 160 DF76
Pavilion Rd., Ilf. 125 EM59
Pavilion St. SW1 276 E7
Pavilion Ter., E.Mol. 197 CF98
Pavilion Ter., Ilf. 125 ES57
Southdown Cres.
Pavilion Way, Amer. 72 AW39
Pavilion Way, Edg. 96 CP52
Pavilion Way, Ruis. 116 BW61
Pavilions, The, Epp. 71 FC25
Pawleyne Clo. SE20 182 DW94
Pawsey Clo. E13 144 EG67
Plashet Rd.
Pawson's Rd., Croy. 202 DQ100
Paxford Rd., Wem. 117 CH61
Paxton Ave., Slou. 151 AQ76
Paxton Clo., Rich. 158 CM82
Paxton Clo., Walt. 196 BW101
Shaw Dr.
Paxton Gdns., Wok. 211 BE112
Paxton Pl. SE27 182 DS91
Paxton Rd. N17 100 DT52
Paxton Rd. SE23 183 DY90
Paxton Rd. W4 158 CS79
Paxton Rd., Berk. 38 AX19
Paxton Rd., Brom. 184 EG94
Paxton Rd., St.Alb. 43 CE21
Paxton Ter. SW1 161 DH79
Paycock Rd., Harl. 51 EN17
Payne Rd. E3 143 EB68
Payne St. SE8 163 DZ79
Paynell Ct. SE3 164 EE83
Lawn Ter.
Paynes La., Wal.Abb. 49 EC24
Paynes Wk. W6 159 CY79
Ancill Clo.
Paynesfield Ave. SW14 158 CR83
Paynesfield Rd. (Bushey), Wat. 95 CF45
Paynesfield Rd., West. 238 EJ121
Pea La., Upmin. 149 FU65
Peabody Ave. SW1 161 DH78
Sutherland St.
Peabody Clo. SE10 163 EB81
Devonshire Dr.
Peabody Dws. WC1 273 P4
Peabody Est. EC1 275 J5
Peabody Est. N17 100 DS53
Peabody Est. SE1 278 E3
Peabody Est. SE24 182 DQ87
Peabody Est. SW3 160 DE79
Margaretta Ter.
Peabody Est. W6 159 CW78
Peabody Est. W10 139 CW70
Peabody Hill SE21 181 DP88
Peabody Hill Est. SE21 181 DP88
Peabody Sq. N1 141 DP67
Essex Rd.
Peabody Sq. SE1 278 F5
Peabody Sq. SE1 161 DP75
Peabody Trust SE1 279 H3
Peabody Yd. N1 142 DQ67
Greenman St.
Peace Clo. N14 81 DH43
Peace Clo. SE25 202 DS98
Peace Clo., Wal.Cr. 66 DU29
Goffs La.
Peace Gro., Wem. 118 CP61
Peace Rd., Iver 133 BB67
Peace Rd., Slou. 133 BA68
Peace St. SE18 165 EP79
Nightingale Vale
Peach Cft., Grav. 190 GE90
Peach Rd. W10 139 CX69
Peach Tree Ave., West Dr. 134 BM72
Pear Tree Ave.
Peaches Clo., Sutt. 217 CY108
Peachey La., Uxb. 134 BK71
Peachum Rd. SE3 164 EF79
Peacock Ave., Felt. 175 BR88
Peacock Clo., Horn. 128 FL56
Peacock Gdns., S.Croy. 221 DY110
Peacock St. SE17 278 G9
Peacock St., Grav. 191 GJ87
Peacock Wk. E16 144 EH72
Sophia Rd.
Peacock Wk., Abb.L. 59 BU31
College Rd.
Peacock Wk., Dor. 263 CG137
Rose Hill
Peacock Yd. SE17 278 G9
Peacocks, Harl. 51 EM17
Peacocks Cen., Wok. 226 AY117
Victoria Way
Peacocks Clo., Berk. 38 AT17
Tortoiseshell Way
Peak, The SE26 182 DW90
Peak Hill SE26 182 DW91
Peak Hill Ave. SE26 182 DW91
Peak Hill Gdns. SE26 182 DW91
Peak Rd., Guil. 242 AU131
Peakes La. (Cheshunt), Wal.Cr. 66 DT27
Peakes Way (Cheshunt), Wal.Cr. 66 DT27
Peaketon Ave., Ilf. 124 EK56
Peaks Hill, Pur. 219 DK110
Peaks Hill Ri., Pur. 219 DL110
Peal Gdns. W13 137 CG70
Ruislip Rd. E.
Peall Rd., Croy. 201 DM100
Pear Clo. NW9 118 CR56
Pear Clo. SE14 163 DY80
Southerngate Way
Pear Pl. SE1 278 D4
Pear Rd. E11 123 ED62
Pear Tree Ave., West Dr. 134 BM72
Pear Tree Clo. E2 142 DT67
Pear Tree Clo., Add. 212 BG106
Pear Tree Rd.
Pear Tree Clo., Beac. 89 AQ51
Pear Tree Clo., Slou. 131 AM74
Pear Tree Clo., Swan. 207 FD96
Furtherfield
Pear Tree Ct. EC1 274 E5
Pear Tree Ct. EC1 141 DN70
Pear Tree Hill, Red. 266 DG143
Pear Tree Mead, Harl. 52 EU18
Pear Tree Rd., Add. 212 BG106
Pear Tree Rd., Ashf. 175 BQ92
Pear Tree Wk. (Cheshunt), Wal.Cr. 66 DR26
Pearce Clo., Mitch. 200 DG96
Pearce Rd., Chesh. 54 AP29
Pearce Rd., W.Mol. 196 CB97
Pearcefield Ave. SE23 182 DW88
Pearces Wk., St.Alb. 43 CD21
Albert St.
Pearcroft Rd. E11 123 ED61
Peardon St. SW8 161 DH82
Peareswood Gdns., Stan. 95 CK53
Peareswood Rd., Erith 167 FF81
Pearfield Rd. SE23 183 DY90
Pearl Clo. E6 145 EN72
Pearl Clo. NW2 119 CX59
Marble Dr.
Pearl Ct., Wok. 226 AS116
Langmans Way
Pearl Gdns., Slou. 131 AP74
Pearl Rd. E17 123 EA55
Pearl St. E1 142 DV74
Penang St.
Pearmain Clo., Shep. 195 BP99
Laleham Rd.
Pearman St. SE1 278 E6
Pearman St. SE1 161 DN76
Pears Rd., Houns. 156 CC83
Pearscroft Ct. SW6 160 DB81
Pearscroft Rd. SW6 160 DB81
Pearson Ave., Hert. 32 DQ11
Pearson Clo., Hert. 32 DQ11
Pearson Ave.
Pearson St. E2 142 DT68
Pearson Way, Dart. 188 FM89
Pearsons Ave. SE14 163 EA81
Tanners Hill
Peartree Ave. SW17 180 DC90
Peartree Clo., Amer. 72 AT39
Orchard End Ave.
Peartree Clo., Erith 167 FD81
Peartree Clo., Hem.H. 40 BG19
Peartree Clo., Mitch. 200 DE96
Peartree Clo., S.Croy. 220 DV114
Peartree Clo., S.Ock. 149 FW68
Peartree Clo., Welw.G.C. 29 CY09
Peartree Ct., Welw.G.C. 29 CY10
Peartree Fm., Welw.G.C. 29 CY09
Peartree Gdns., Dag. 126 EV63
Peartree Gdns., Rom. 105 FB54
Peartree La. E1 142 DW73
Glamis Rd.
Peartree La., Welw.G.C. 29 CY10
Peartree Rd., Enf. 82 DS41
Peartree Rd., Hem.H. 40 BG19
Peartree St. EC1 274 G4
Peartree St. EC1 141 DP70
Peary Pl. E2 142 DW69
Kirkwall Pl.
Peascod Pl., Wind. 151 AR81
Peascod St.
Peascod St., Wind. 151 AQ81
Peascroft Rd., Hem.H. 40 BN23
Pease Clo., Horn. 147 FH66
Dowding Way
Peatfield Clo., Sid. 185 ES90
Woodside Rd.
Peatmore Ave., Wok. 228 BG116
Peatmore Clo., Wok. 228 BG116
Pebble Clo., Tad. 248 CS128
Pebble Hill, Lthd. 245 BQ133
Pebble Hill Rd., Bet. 248 CS131
Pebble Hill Rd., Tad. 248 CS128
Pebworth Rd., Har. 117 CG61
Peckarmans Wd. SE26 182 DT90
Peckett Sq. N5 122 DQ63
Highbury Gra.
Peckford Pl. SW9 161 DN82
Peckham Gro. SE15 162 DS80
Peckham High St. SE15 162 DU81
Peckham Hill St. SE15 162 DU80
Peckham Pk. Rd. SE15 162 DU80
Peckham Rd. SE5 162 DS81
Peckham Rd. SE15 162 DT81
Peckham Rye SE15 162 DU83
Peckham Rye SE22 162 DU84
Pecks Hill, Wal.Abb. 50 EE21
Peckwater St. NW5 121 DJ64
Pedham Pl. Est., Swan. 207 FG99
Pedlars End, Ong. 53 FH21
Pedlars Wk. N7 141 DL65
Pedley Rd., Dag. 126 EW60
Pedley St. E1 142 DU70
Pednor Rd., Chesh. 54 AM30
Pednormead End, Chesh. 54 AP32
Pedro St. E5 123 DX62
Pedworth Gdns. SE16 162 DW77
Rotherhithe New Rd.
Peek Cres. SW19 179 CX92
Peeks Brook La., Horl. 269 DL153
Peel Clo. E4 101 EB47
Peel Clo. N9 100 DU48
Plevna Rd.
Peel Clo., Wind. 151 AP83
Peel Ct., Slou. 131 AQ71
Farnburn Ave.
Peel Cres., Hert. 31 DP06
Peel Dr. NW9 119 CT55
Peel Dr., Ilf. 124 EL55
Peel Gro. E2 142 DW68
Peel Pas. W8 140 DA74
Peel St.
Peel Pl., Ilf. 102 EL54
Peel Prec. NW6 140 DA68
Peel Rd. E18 102 EF53
Peel Rd. NW6 139 CZ69
Peel Rd., Har. 117 CF55
Peel Rd., Orp. 223 EQ106
Peel Rd., Wem. 117 CK62
Peel St. W8 140 DA74
Peel Way, Rom. 106 FM54
Peel Way, Uxb. 134 BL70
Peerage Way, Horn. 128 FL59
Peerless Dr., Uxb. 114 BJ56
Peerless St. EC1 275 K3
Peerless St. EC1 142 DR69
Pegamoid Rd. N18 100 DW48
Pegasus Ct., Abb.L. 59 BT32
Furtherfield
Pegasus Ct., Grav. 191 GJ90
Pegasus Pl. SE11 161 DN79
Clayton St.
Pegelm Gdns., Horn. 128 FM59
Pegg Rd., Houns. 156 BX80
Peggotty Way, Uxb. 135 BP72
Dickens Ave.
Pegley Gdns. SE12 184 EG89
Pegmire La., Wat. 76 CC39
Pegrams Rd., Harl. 51 EQ18
Pegs La., Hert. 32 DR10
Pegwell St. SE18 165 ES80
Peket Clo., Stai. 193 BE95
Pekin Clo. E14 143 EA72
Pekin St.
Pekin St. E14 143 EA72
Peldon Ct., Rich. 158 CM84
Peldon Rd., Harl. 51 EN17
Peldon Wk. N1 141 DP67
Britannia Row
Pelham Ave., Bark. 145 ET67
Pelham Clo. SE5 162 DS83
Pelham Ct., Hem.H. 41 BQ20
Pelham Ct., Welw.G.C. 30 DC10
Amwell Common
Pelham Cres. SW7 276 B9
Pelham Cres. SW7 160 DE77
Pelham Pl. SW7 276 B8
Pelham Pl. SW7 160 DE77
Pelham Rd. E18 124 EH55
Pelham Rd. N15 122 DT56
Pelham Rd. N22 99 DN54
Pelham Rd. SW19 180 DA94
Pelham Rd., Beck. 202 DW96
Pelham Rd., Bexh. 166 FA83
Pelham Rd., Grav. 191 GF88
Pelham Rd., Ilf. 125 ER61
Pelham Rd. S., Grav. 191 GF88
Pelham St. SW7 276 A8
Pelham St. SW7 160 DD77
Pelham Ter., Grav. 191 GF87
Campbell Rd.
Pelham Way, Lthd. 246 CB126
Pelhams, The, Wat. 76 BX35
Pelhams Clo., Esher 214 CA105
Pelhams Wk., Esher 196 CA104
Pelican Est. SE15 162 DT81
Pelican Pas. E1 142 DW70
Cambridge Heath Rd.
Pelican Wk. SW9 161 DP84
Loughborough Pk.
Pelier St. SE17 162 DQ79
Langdale Clo.
Pelinore Rd. SE6 184 EE89
Pellant Rd. SW6 159 CY80
Pellatt Gro. N22 99 DN53
Pellatt Rd. SE22 182 DT85
Pellatt Rd., Wem. 117 CK61
Pellerin Rd. N16 122 DS64
Pelling Hill, Wind. 172 AV87
Pelling St. E14 143 EA72
Pellipar Clo. N13 99 DN48
Pellipar Gdns. SE18 165 EM78
Pelly Rd. E13 144 EG67
Pelter St. E2 275 P2
Pelter St. E2 142 DT69
Pelton Ave., Sutt. 218 DB110
Pelton Rd. SE10 164 EE78
Pembar Ave. E17 123 DY55
Pember Rd. NW10 139 CX69
Pemberton Ave., Rom. 128 FJ55
Pemberton Clo., St.Alb. 43 CD23
Pemberton Gdns. N19 121 DJ62
Pemberton Gdns., Rom. 126 EY57
Pemberton Gdns., Swan. 207 FE97
Pemberton Ho. SE26 182 DU91
High Level Dr.
Pemberton Pl. E8 142 DV66
Mare St.
Pemberton Pl., Esher 196 CC104
Carrick Gate
Pemberton Rd. N4 121 DN57
Pemberton Rd., E.Mol. 196 CC98
Pemberton Rd., Slou. 131 AL70
Pemberton Row EC4 274 E8
Pemberton Ter. N19 121 DJ62
Pembrey Way, Horn. 148 FJ65
Pembridge Ave., Twick. 176 BZ88
Pembridge Chase, Hem.H. 57 BA28
Pembridge Clo.
Pembridge Clo., Hem.H. 57 AZ28
Pembridge Cres. W11 140 DA73
Pembridge Gdns. W2 140 DA73
Pembridge La., Brox. 48 DR21
Pembridge La., Hert. 48 DQ19
Pembridge Ms. W11 140 DA73
Pembridge Pl. W2 140 DA73
Pembridge Rd. W11 140 DA73
Pembridge Rd., Hem.H. 57 BA28
Pembridge Sq. W2 140 DA73
Pembridge Vill. W11 140 DA73
Pembroke Ave., Enf. 82 DV38
Pembroke Ave., Har. 117 CG55
Pembroke Ave., Surb. 198 CP99
Pembroke Ave., Walt. 214 BX105
Pembroke Clo. SW1 276 G5
Pembroke Clo. SW1 160 DG75
Pembroke Clo., Bans. 234 DB117
Pembroke Clo., Brox. 49 DY23
Pembroke Clo., Erith 167 FD77
Pembroke Clo., Horn. 128 FM56
Pembroke Dr. (Cheshunt), Wal.Cr. 65 DP29
Pembroke Gdns. W8 159 CZ77
Pembroke Gdns., Dag. 127 FB62
Pembroke Gdns., Wok. 227 BA118
Pembroke Gdns. Clo. W8 159 CZ76
Pembroke Ms. E3 143 DY69
Morgan St.
Pembroke Ms. N10 98 DG53
Pembroke Rd.
Pembroke Ms. W8 160 DA76
Earls Wk.

Pembroke Ms., Sev. 257 FH125
Pembroke Rd.
Pembroke Pl. W8 160 DA76
Pembroke Pl. 208 FP95
(Sutton at Hone), Dart.
Pembroke Pl., Edg. 96 CN52
Pembroke Rd. E6 145 EM71
Pembroke Rd. E17 123 EB57
Pembroke Rd. N8 121 DL56
Pembroke Rd. N10 98 DG53
Pembroke Rd. N13 100 DQ48
Pembroke Rd. N15 122 DT57
Pembroke Rd. SE25 202 DS98
Pembroke Rd. W8 160 DA77
Pembroke Rd., Brom. 204 EJ96
Pembroke Rd., Erith 167 FC78
Pembroke Rd., Grnf. 136 CB69
Pembroke Rd., Ilf. 125 ET60
Pembroke Rd., Mitch. 200 DG96
Pembroke Rd., Nthwd. 93 BQ48
Pembroke Rd., Ruis. 115 BS60
Pembroke Rd., Sev. 257 FH125
Pembroke Rd., Wem. 117 CK62
Pembroke Rd., Wok. 227 BA118
Pembroke Sq. W8 160 DA76
Pembroke St. N1 141 DL66
Pembroke Studios W8 159 CZ76
Pembroke Vill. W8 160 DA77
Pembroke Vill., Rich. 157 CK84
Pembroke Wk. W8 160 DA77
Pembroke Way, Hayes 155 BQ76
Pembury Ave., Wor.Pk. 199 CU102
Pembury Clo., Brom. 204 EF101
Pembury Clo., Couls. 218 DG114
Pembury Ct., Hayes 155 BR79
Pembury Cres., Sid. 186 EY90
Pembury Pl. E5 122 DV64
Pembury Rd. E5 122 DV64
Pembury Rd. N17 100 DT53
Pembury Rd. SE25 202 DU98
Pembury Rd., Bexh. 166 EY80
Pemdevon Rd., Croy. 201 DN101
Pemell Clo. E1 142 DW70
Colebert Ave.
Pemerich Clo., Hayes 155 BT78
Pempath Pl., Wem. 117 CK61
Pemsel Ct., Hem.H. 40 BK22
Crabtree La.
Penally Pl. N1 142 DR67
Shepperton Rd.
Penang St. E1 142 DV74
Penarth St. SE15 162 DW79
Penates, Esher 215 CD105
Penberth Rd. SE6 183 EC88
Penbury Rd., Sthl. 156 BZ77
Pencombe Ms. W11 139 CZ73
Denbigh Rd.
Pencraig Way SE15 162 DV79
Pencroft Dr., Dart. 188 FJ87
Shepherds La.
Penda Rd., Erith 167 FB80
Pendarves Rd. SW20 199 CW95
Penda's Mead E9 123 DY63
Lindisfarne Way
Pendell Ave., Hayes 155 BT80
Pendell Rd., Red. 251 DP131
Pendennis Clo., W.Byf. 212 BG114
Pendennis Rd. N17 122 DR55
Pendennis Rd. SW16 181 DL91
Pendennis Rd., Orp. 206 EW103
Pendennis Rd., Sev. 257 FH123
Penderel Rd., Houns. 176 CA85
Penderry Ri. SE6 183 ED89
Penderyn Way N7 121 DK63
Pendle Rd. SW16 181 DH93
Pendlestone Rd. E17 123 EB57
Pendleton Clo., Red. 266 DF136
Pendleton Rd., Red. 266 DC137
Pendleton Rd., Reig. 266 DC137
Pendragon Rd., Brom. 184 EF90
Pendragon Wk. NW9 118 CS58
Pendrell Rd. SE4 163 DY82
Pendrell St. SE18 165 ER79
Pendula Dr., Hayes 136 BX70
Pendulum Ms. E8 122 DT64
Birkbeck Rd.
Penerley Rd. SE6 183 EB88
Penerley Rd., Rain. 147 FH71
Penfold Clo., Croy. 201 DN104
Epsom Rd.
Penfold La., Bex. 186 EX88
Carisbrooke Ave.
Penfold Pl. NW1 272 B6
Penfold Pl. NW1 140 DE71
Penfold Rd. N9 101 DX46
Penfold St. NW1 272 A5
Penfold St. NW1 140 DD70
Penfold St. NW8 272 A5
Penfold St. NW8 140 DD70
Penford Gdns. SE9 164 EK83
Penford St. SE5 161 DP82
Pengarth Rd., Bex. 186 EX85
Penge Ho. SW11 160 DD83
Wye St.
Penge La. SE20 182 DW94
Penge Rd. E13 144 EJ67
Penge Rd. SE20 202 DU97
Penge Rd. SE25 202 DU97
Pengelly Clo. (Cheshunt), 66 DV30
Wal.Cr.
Penhall Rd. SE7 164 EK77
Penhill Rd., Bex. 186 EW86
Penhurst, Wok. 211 AZ114
Penhurst Rd., Ilf. 103 EP52
Penifather La., Grnf. 137 CD69
Peninsular Clo., Felt. 175 BR86
Penistone Rd. SW16 181 DL94
Penistone Wk., Rom. 106 FJ51
Okehampton Rd.
Penketh Dr., Har. 117 CD62
Penlow Rd., Harl. 51 EQ18
Penman Clo., St.Alb. 60 CA27
Penmon Rd. SE2 166 EU76
Penn Ave., Chesh. 54 AN30
Penn Bottom, H.Wyc. 88 AG45
Penn Clo., Grnf. 136 CB68
Penn Clo., Har. 117 CJ56
Penn Clo., Rick. 73 BD44
Penn Clo., Uxb. 134 BK70
Penn Dr., Uxb. 113 BF58
Penn Gdns., Chis. 205 EP96
Penn Gdns., Rom. 104 FA52
Penn Gaskell La., Ger.Cr. 91 AZ50
Penn La., Bex. 186 EX86
Penn Meadow, Slou. 132 AT67
Penn Pl., Rick. 92 BK45
Northway
Penn Rd. N7 121 DL64
Penn Rd., Beac. 88 AJ48
Penn Rd., Ger.Cr. 90 AX53
Penn Rd., Rick. 91 BF46
Penn Rd., St.Alb. 60 CC27
Penn Rd., Slou. 131 AR70
Penn Rd. (Datchet), Slou. 152 AX81
Penn Rd., Wat. 75 BV39
Penn St. N1 142 DR67
Penn Way, Rick. 73 BD44
Pennack Rd. SE15 162 DT79
Pennant Ms. W8 160 DB77
Pennant Ter. E17 101 DZ54
Pennard Rd. W12 159 CW75
Pennards, The, Sun. 196 BW96
Penne Clo., Rad. 61 CF34
Penner Clo. SW19 179 CY89
Victoria Dr.
Pennethorne Clo. E9 142 DW67
Victoria Pk. Rd.
Pennethorne Rd. SE15 162 DV80
Penney Clo., Dart. 188 FK87
Pennine Dr. NW2 119 CX61
Pennine La. NW2 119 CY61
Pennine Dr.
Pennine Rd., Slou. 131 AN71
Pennine Way, Bexh. 167 FE81
Pennine Way, Grav. 190 GE90
Pennine Way, Hayes 155 BR80
Pennine Way, Hem.H. 40 BM17
Pennings Ave., Guil. 242 AT132
Pennington Clo. SE27 182 DR91
Hamilton Rd.
Pennington Clo., Rom. 104 FA51
Pennington Dr. N21 81 DL43
Pennington Dr., Wey. 195 BS104
Pennington Rd., Beac. 110 AH55
Pennington Rd., Ger.Cr. 90 AX52
Pennington St. E1 142 DU73
Pennington Way SE12 184 EJ89
Penningtons, The, Amer. 55 AS37
Pennis La. 209 FW100
(Fawkham Grn.), Long.
Penniston Clo. N17 100 DQ54
Penny Clo., Rain. 147 FH69
Penny La., Shep. 195 BS101
Penny Ms. SW12 181 DH87
Caistor Rd.
Penny Rd. NW10 138 CP69
Pennycroft, Croy. 221 DY109
Pennyfield, Cob. 213 BU113
Pennyfields E14 143 EA73
Pennyfields, Brwd. 108 FW49
Pennylets Grn., Slou. 132 AT66
Pennymead, Harl. 36 EU14
Pennymead Dr., Lthd. 245 BT127
Pennymead Ri., Lthd. 245 BT127
Pennymoor Wk. W9 139 CZ69
Ashmore Rd.
Pennyroyal Ave. E6 145 EN72
Pennys La., Saw. 35 ER05
Penpoll Rd. E8 142 DV65
Penpool La., Well. 166 EV83
Penrhyn Ave. E17 101 DZ53
Penrhyn Cres. E17 101 EA53
Penrhyn Cres. SW14 158 CQ84
Penrhyn Gro. E17 101 EA53
Penrhyn Rd., Kings.T. 198 CL98
Penrith Clo. SW15 179 CY85
Penrith Clo., Beck. 203 EB95
Albemarle Rd.
Penrith Clo., Reig. 250 DE133
Penrith Clo., Uxb. 134 BK66
Chippendale Waye
Penrith Cres., Rain. 127 FG64
Penrith Pl. SE27 181 DP89
Harpenden Rd.
Penrith Rd. N15 122 DR57
Penrith Rd., Ilf. 103 ET51
Penrith Rd., N.Mal. 198 CR98
Penrith Rd., Rom. 106 FN51
Penrith Rd., Th.Hth. 202 DQ96
Penrith St. SW16 181 DJ93
Penrose Ave., Wat. 94 BX47
Penrose Ct., Hem.H. 40 BL16
Penrose Gro. SE17 162 DQ78
Penrose Ho. SE17 162 DQ78
Penrose St.
Penrose Rd., Lthd. 230 CC122
Penrose St. SE17 162 DQ78
Penry St. SE1 279 N9
Penryn St. NW1 141 DK68
Pensbury Pl. SW8 161 DJ82
Pensbury St. SW8 161 DJ82
Penscroft Gdns., Borwd. 78 CR42
Pensford Ave., Rich. 158 CN82
Penshurst, Harl. 36 EV12
Penshurst Ave., Sid. 186 EU86
Penshurst Clo., Ger.Cr. 90 AX54
Penshurst Gdns., Edg. 96 CP50
Penshurst Grn., Brom. 204 EF99
Penshurst Rd. E9 143 DX66
Penshurst Rd. N17 100 DT52
Penshurst Rd., Bexh. 166 EZ81
Penshurst Rd., Pot.B. 64 DD31
Penshurst Rd., Th.Hth. 201 DP99
Penshurst Wk., Brom. 204 EF99
Hayesford Pk. Dr.
Penshurst Way, Orp. 206 EW98
Star La.
Penshurst Way, Sutt. 218 DA108
Pensons La., Ong. 71 FG28
Penstemon Clo. N3 98 DA51
Penstock Footpath N22 121 DL55
Pentavia Retail Pk. NW7 97 CT52
Bunns La.
Pentelowe Gdns., Felt. 175 BU86
Pentire Clo., Upmin. 129 FS58
Pentire Rd. E17 101 ED53
Pentland, Hem.H. 40 BM17
Mendip Way
Pentland Ave., Edg. 96 CP47
Pentland Ave., Shep. 194 BN99
Pentland Clo. NW11 119 CY61
Pentland Gdns. SW18 180 DC86
St. Ann's Hill
Pentland Pl., Nthlt. 136 BY67
Pentland Rd., Slou. 131 AN71
Pentland Rd. (Bushey), 76 CC44
Wat.
Pentland St. SW18 180 DC86
Pentland Way, Uxb. 115 BQ62
Pentlands Clo., Mitch. 201 DH97
Pentley Clo., Welw.G.C. 29 CX06
Pentley Pk., Welw.G.C. 29 CX07
Pentlow St. SW15 159 CW83
Pentlow Way, Buck.H. 102 EL45
Pentney Rd. E4 101 ED46
Pentney Rd. SW12 181 DJ88
Pentney Rd. SW19 199 CY95
Midmoor Rd.
Penton Ave., Stai. 173 BF94
Penton Dr. (Cheshunt), 67 DX29
Wal.Cr.
Penton Gro. N1 274 D1
Penton Hall Dr., Stai. 194 BG95
Penton Hook Rd., Stai. 174 BG94
Penton Pk. Est., Cher. 194 BH97
Penton Pl. SE17 278 G10
Penton Pl. SE17 161 DP78
Penton Ri. WC1 274 C2
Penton Ri. WC1 141 DM69
Penton Rd., Stai. 173 BF94
Penton St. N1 274 D1
Penton St. N1 141 DN68
Pentonville Rd. N1 274 B1
Pentonville Rd. N1 141 DM68
Pentrich Ave., Enf. 82 DU38
Pentridge St. SE15 162 DT80
Pentyre Ave. N18 100 DR50
Penwerris Ave., Islw. 156 CC80
Penwith Rd. SW18 180 DA89
Penwith Wk., Wok. 226 AX119
Wych Hill Pk.
Penwood End, Wok. 226 AV121
Penwortham Rd. SW16 181 DH93
Penwortham Rd., S.Croy. 220 DQ110
Penylan Pl., Edg. 96 CN52
Penywern Rd. SW5 160 DA78
Penzance Clo., Uxb. 92 BK53
Penzance Gdns., Rom. 106 FN51
Penzance Pl. W11 139 CY74
Penzance Rd., Rom. 106 FN51
Penzance Spur, Slou. 131 AP70
Penzance St. W11 139 CY74
Peony Clo., Brwd. 108 FV44
Peony Ct., Wdf.Grn. 102 EE52
Bridle Path
Peony Gdns. W12 139 CU73
Peplins Clo., Hat. 63 CY26
Peplins Way, Hat. 63 CY25
Peploe Rd. NW6 139 CX68
Peplow Clo., West Dr. 134 BK74
Tavistock Rd.
Pepper All., Loug. 84 EF40
Pepper Clo. E6 145 EM71
Pepper Clo., Cat. 252 DS125
Pepper Hill, Grav. 190 GC90
Pepper Hill, Ware 33 DZ10
Pepper St. E14 163 EB76
Pepper St. SE1 279 H4
Pepperhill La., Grav. 190 GC90
Peppermead Sq. SE13 183 EA85
Peppermint Clo., Croy. 201 DL101
Peppermint Pl. E11 124 EE62
Birch Gro.
Peppie Clo. N16 122 DS61
Bouverie Rd.
Pepys Clo., Ash. 232 CN117
Pepys Clo., Dart. 168 FN84
Keyes Rd.
Pepys Clo., Grav. 190 GD90
Pepys Clo., Slou. 153 BB79
Pepys Clo., Til. 171 GJ81
Pepys Clo., Uxb. 115 BP63
Pepys Cres. E16 144 EE72
Silvertown Way
Pepys Cres., Barn. 79 CW43
Pepys Ri., Orp. 205 ET102
Pepys Rd. SE14 163 DX81
Pepys Rd. SW20 199 CW96
Pepys St. EC3 275 N10
Pepys St. EC3 142 DS73
Perceval Ave. NW3 120 DE64
Perch St. E8 122 DT63
Percheron Clo., Islw. 157 CG83
Percheron Rd., Borwd. 78 CR44
Percival Ct. N17 100 DT52
High Rd.
Percival Ct., Nthlt. 116 CA64
Percival Gdns., Rom. 126 EW58
Percival Rd. SW14 158 CQ84
Percival Rd., Enf. 82 DT42
Percival Rd., Felt. 175 BT89
Percival Rd., Horn. 128 FJ58
Percival Rd., Orp. 205 EP103
Percival St. EC1 274 F4
Percival St. EC1 141 DP70
Percival Way, Epsom 216 CQ105
Percy Ave., Ashf. 174 BN92
Percy Bryant Rd., Sun. 175 BS94
Percy Bush Rd., West Dr. 154 BM76
Percy Circ. WC1 274 C2
Percy Circ. WC1 141 DM69
Percy Gdns., Enf. 83 DX43
Percy Gdns., Hayes 135 BS69
Percy Gdns., Islw. 157 CG83
Percy Gdns., Wor.Pk. 198 CS102
Percy Ms. W1 273 M7
Percy Pas. W1 273 L7
Percy Pl., Slou. 152 AV81
Percy Rd. E11 124 EE59
Percy Rd. E16 144 EE71
Percy Rd. N12 98 DC50
Percy Rd. N21 100 DQ45
Percy Rd. NW6 140 DA69
Stafford Rd.
Percy Rd. SE20 203 DX95
Percy Rd. SE25 202 DU99
Percy Rd. W12 159 CU75
Percy Rd., Bexh. 166 EY82
Percy Rd., Guil. 242 AV132
Percy Rd., Hmptn. 176 CA94
Percy Rd., Ilf. 126 EU59
Percy Rd., Islw. 157 CG84
Percy Rd., Mitch. 200 DG101
Percy Rd., Rom. 127 FB55
Percy Rd., Twick. 176 CB88
Percy Rd., Wat. 75 BV42
Percy St. W1 273 M7
Percy St. W1 141 DK71
Percy St., Grays 170 GC79
Percy Ter., Ch.St.G. 90 AU48
Sycamore Rd.
Percy Way, Twick. 176 CC88
Percy Yd. WC1 274 C2
Peregrin Rd., Wal.Abb. 68 EG34
Peregrine Clo. NW10 118 CR64
Peregrine Clo., Wat. 60 BY34
Peregrine Ct. SW16 181 DM91
Leithcote Gdns.
Peregrine Ct., Well. 165 ET81
Peregrine Gdns., Croy. 203 DY103
Peregrine Ho. EC1 274 G2
Peregrine Ho. EC1 141 DP69
Peregrine Rd., Ilf. 104 EV50
Peregrine Rd., Sun. 195 BT96
Peregrine Wk., Horn. 147 FH65
Heron Flight Ave.
Peregrine Way SW19 179 CW94
Perham Rd. W14 159 CY78
Perham Way, St.Alb. 61 CK26
Peridot St. E6 144 EL71
Perifield SE21 182 DQ88
Perimeade Rd., Grnf. 137 CJ68
Perimeter Rd. E., Gat. 268 DG154
Perimeter Rd. N., Gat. 268 DD151
Perimeter Rd. S., Gat. 268 DC154
Periton Rd. SE9 164 EK84
Perivale Gdns. W13 137 CH70
Bellevue Rd.
Perivale Gdns., Wat. 59 BV34
Perivale Gra., Grnf. 137 CG69
Perivale Ind. Pk., Grnf. 137 CG67
Perivale La., Grnf. 137 CG69
Perivale New Business 137 CH68
Cen., Grnf.
Perkins Clo., Green. 189 FT85
Perkins Clo., Wem. 117 CH64
Perkins Ct., Ashf. 174 BM92
Perkin's Rents SW1 277 M6
Perkin's Rents SW1 161 DK76
Perkins Rd., Ilf. 125 ER57
Perkins Sq. SE1 279 J2
Perks Clo. SE3 164 EE83
Hurren Clo.
Perleybrooke La., Wok. 226 AU117
Bampton Way
Perpins Rd. SE9 185 ER86
Perram Clo., Brox. 67 DY26
Perran Rd. SW2 181 DP89
Christchurch Rd.
Perran Wk., Brent. 158 CL78
Burford Rd.
Perren St. NW5 141 DH65
Ryland Rd.
Perrers Rd. W6 159 CV77
Perrin Clo., Ashf. 174 BM92
Fordbridge Rd.
Perrin Ct., Wok. 227 BB115
Blackmore Cres.
Perrin Rd., Wem. 117 CG63
Perrins Ct. NW3 120 DC63
Hampstead High St.
Perrins La. NW3 120 DC63
Perrin's Wk. NW3 120 DC63
Perrior Rd., Gdmg. 258 AS144
Perriors Clo. (Cheshunt), 66 DU27
Wal.Cr.
Perrott St. SE18 165 EQ77
Perry Ave. W3 138 CR72
Perry Clo., Rain. 147 FD68
Lowen Rd.
Perry Clo., Uxb. 135 BQ72
Harlington Rd.
Perry Ct. N15 122 DS58
Albert Rd.
Perry Cft., Wind. 151 AL83
Perry Gdns. N9 100 DS48
Deansway
Perry Garth, Nthlt. 136 BW67
Perry Gro., Dart. 168 FN84
Perry Hall Clo., Orp. 206 EU101
Perry Hall Rd., Orp. 205 ET100
Perry Hill SE6 183 DZ90
Perry Hill, Guil. 242 AS128
Perry Hill, Wal.Abb. 50 EF23
Perry How, Wor.Pk. 199 CT102
Perry Mead, Enf. 81 DP40
Perry Mead (Bushey), 94 CB45
Wat.
Perry Oaks Dr. 154 BH82
(Heathrow Airport), Houns.
Perry Ri. SE23 183 DY90
Perry Rd., Dag. 146 EZ70
Perry Rd., Harl. 51 EQ18
Perry Spring, Harl. 52 EX17
Perry St., Chis. 185 ER93
Perry St., Dart. 167 FE84
Perry St., Grav. 190 GE88
Perry St. Gdns., Chis. 185 ES93
Old Perry St.
Perry Vale SE23 182 DW89
Perry Way, S.Ock. 148 FQ73
Perryfield Way NW9 119 CT58
Perryfield Way, Rich. 177 CH89
Perryfields Way, Slou. 130 AH70
Perrylands La., Horl. 269 DM149
Perryman Ho., Bark. 145 EQ67
Perryman Way, Slou. 131 AM69
Perrymans Fm. Rd., Ilf. 125 ER58
Perrymead St. SW6 160 DA81
Perryn Rd. SE16 162 DV76
Drummond Rd.
Perryn Rd. W3 138 CR74
Perrys La., Sev. 224 EV113
Perrys Pl. W1 273 M8
Perrysfield Rd. 67 DY26
(Cheshunt), Wal.Cr.
Perrywood Business Pk., 267 DH142
Red.
Persant Rd. SE6 184 EE90
Perseverance Pl. SW9 161 DN80
Perseverance Pl., Rich. 158 CL83
Shaftesbury Rd.
Persfield Clo., Epsom 217 CT110
Pershore Clo., Ilf. 125 EP57
Pershore Gro., Cars. 200 DD100
Pert Clo. N10 99 DH51
Perth Ave. NW9 118 CR59
Perth Ave., Hayes 136 BW70
Perth Ave., Slou. 131 AP72
Perth Clo. SW20 199 CU96
Perth Rd. E10 123 DY60
Perth Rd. E13 144 EH68
Perth Rd. N4 121 DN60
Perth Rd. N22 99 DP53
Perth Rd., Bark. 145 ER67
Perth Rd., Beck. 203 EC96
Perth Rd., Ilf. 125 EN58
Perth Ter., Ilf. 125 EQ59
Perwell Ave., Har. 116 BZ60
Perwell Ct., Har. 116 BZ60
Pescot Hill, Hem.H. 40 BH18
Peter Ave. NW10 139 CV66
Peter Ave., Oxt. 253 ED129
Peter Ms., Slou. 153 BA78
Grampian Way
Peter St. W1 273 M10
Peter St. W1 141 DK73
Peter St., Grav. 191 GH87
Peterboat Clo. SE10 164 EE77
Tunnel Ave.
Peterborough Ave., Upmin. 129 FS60
Peterborough Gdns., Ilf. 124 EL59
Peterborough Ms. SW6 160 DA82
Peterborough Rd. E10 123 EC57
Peterborough Rd. SW6 160 DA82
Peterborough Rd., Cars. 200 DE100
Peterborough Rd., Guil. 242 AT132
Peterborough Rd., Har. 117 CE60
Peterborough Vill. SW6 160 DB81
Peterchurch Ho. SE15 162 DV79
Commercial Way
Petergate SW11 160 DC84
Peterhead Ms., Slou. 153 BA78
Peterhill Clo., Ger.Cr. 90 AY50
Peterlee Ct., Hem.H. 40 BM16
Peters Ave., St.Alb. 61 CJ26
Peters Clo., Dag. 126 EX60
Peters Clo., Stan. 95 CK51
Peters Clo., Well. 165 ES82
Peters Hill EC4 275 H9
Peter's La. EC1 274 F6
Peters Path SE26 182 DV91
Peters Pl., Berk. 38 AS17
Peters Wd. Hill, Ware 33 DX07
Petersfield Ave., Rom. 106 FL51
Petersfield Ave., Slou. 132 AU74
Petersfield Ave., Stai. 174 BJ92
Petersfield Clo. N18 100 DQ50
Petersfield Clo., Rom. 106 FN51
Petersfield Cres., Couls. 235 DL115
Petersfield Ri. SW15 179 CV88
Petersfield Rd. W3 158 CQ75
Petersfield Rd., Stai. 174 BJ92
Petersham Ave., W.Byf. 212 BL112
Petersham Clo., Rich. 177 CK89
Petersham Clo., Sutt. 217 CZ106
Petersham Clo., W.Byf. 212 BL112
Petersham Dr., Orp. 205 ET96
Petersham Gdns., Orp. 205 ET96
Petersham La. SW7 160 DC76
Petersham Ms. SW7 160 DC76
Petersham Pl. SW7 160 DC76
Petersham Rd., Rich. 177 CK86
Petersham Ter., Croy. 201 DL104
Richmond Grn.
Peterstone Rd. SE2 166 EV76
Peterstow Clo. SW19 179 CY89
Peterstowe, Wok. 227 BB117
Peterswood, Harl. 51 ER19
Parnall Rd.
Peterwood Way, Croy. 201 DM103
Petherton Rd. N5 122 DQ64
Petley Rd. W6 159 CW79
Peto Pl. NW1 273 J4
Peto Pl. NW1 141 DH70
Peto St. N. E16 144 EF73
Victoria Dock Rd.
Petridge Rd., Red. 266 DF139
Petrie Clo. NW2 139 CY65
Pett Clo., Horn. 127 FH61
St. Leonards Way
Pett St. SE18 164 EL77
Petten Clo., Orp. 206 EX102
Petten Gro., Orp. 206 EW102
Petters Rd., Ash. 232 CM116
Petticoat Sq. E1 275 P8
Pettits Boul., Rom. 105 FE53
Pettits Clo., Rom. 105 FE54
Pettits La., Rom. 105 FE54
Pettits La. N., Rom. 105 FD53
Pettits Pl., Dag. 126 FA64
Pettits Rd., Dag. 126 FA64
Pettiward Clo. SW15 159 CW84
Pettley Gdns., Rom. 127 FD57
Pettman Cres. SE28 165 ER76
Petts Hill, Nthlt. 116 CB64
Petts La., Shep. 194 BN98
Petts Wd. Rd., Orp. 205 EQ99
Pettsgrove Ave., Wem. 117 CJ64
Petty France SW1 277 L6
Petty France SW1 161 DJ76
Petworth Clo., Couls. 235 DJ119
Petworth Clo., Nthlt. 136 BZ66
Petworth Ct., Wind. 151 AP81
Petworth Gdns. SW20 199 CV97
Hidcote Gdns.
Petworth Gdns., Uxb. 135 BQ67
Petworth Rd. N12 98 DE50
Petworth Rd., Bexh. 186 FA85
Petworth St. SW11 160 DE81
Petworth Way, Horn. 127 FF63
Petyt Pl. SW3 160 DE79
Old Ch. St.
Petyward SW3 276 C9
Petyward SW3 160 DE77
Pevel Ho., Dag. 126 FA61
Pevensey Ave. N11 99 DK50
Pevensey Ave., Enf. 82 DR40
Pevensey Clo., Islw. 156 CC80
Pevensey Rd. E7 124 EF63
Pevensey Rd. SW17 180 DD91
Pevensey Rd., Felt. 176 BY88
Pevensey Rd., Slou. 131 AN71
Peverel E6 145 EN72
Downings
Peveret Clo. N11 99 DH50
Woodland Rd.
Peveril Dr., Tedd. 177 CD92
Pewley Bank, Guil. 258 AY136
Pewley Hill, Guil. 258 AX136
Pewley Pt., Guil. 258 AY136
Pewley Way, Guil. 258 AY136
Pewsey Clo. E4 101 EA50
Peyton Pl. SE10 163 EC80
Peytons Cotts., Red. 251 DM132
Nutfield Marsh Rd.
Pharaoh Clo., Mitch. 200 DF101
Pharaoh's Island, Shep. 194 BM103
Pheasant Clo. E16 144 EG72
Maplin Rd.

Pheasant Clo., Berk. 38 AW20
Pheasant Clo., Pur. 219 DP113
Pheasant Hill, Ch.St.G. 90 AW47
Pheasant Ri., Chesh. 54 AR33
Pheasant Wk., Ger.Cr. 90 AX49
Pheasants Way, Rick. 92 BH45
Phelips Rd., Harl. 51 EN20
Phelp St. SE17 162 DR79
Phelps Way, Hayes 155 BT77
Phene St. SW3 160 DE79
Phil Brown Pl. SW8 161 DH82
Heath Rd.
Philan Way, Rom. 105 FD51
Philanthropic Rd., Red. 266 DG135
Philbeach Gdns. SW5 160 DA78
Philchurch Pl. E1 142 DU72
Ellen St.
Philip Ave., Rom. 127 FD60
Philip Ave., Swan. 207 FD98
Philip Clo., Brwd. 108 FW44
Philip Clo., Rom. 127 FD60
Philip Ave.
Philip Gdns., Croy. 203 DZ103
Philip La. N15 122 DR56
Philip Rd. SE15 162 DU83
Peckham Rye
Philip Rd., Rain. 147 FE69
Philip Rd., Stai. 174 BK93
Philip St. E13 144 EG70
Philip Wk. SE15 162 DV83
Philipot Path SE9 185 EM86
Court Yd.
Philippa Gdns. SE9 184 EK85
Philippa Way, Grays 171 GH77
Philips Clo., Cars. 200 DG102
Phillida Rd., Rom. 106 FN54
Phillimore Gdns. NW10 139 CW67
Phillimore Gdns. W8 160 DA75
Phillimore Gdns. Clo. W8 160 DA76
Phillimore Gdns.
Phillimore Pl. W8 160 DA75
Phillimore Pl., Rad. 77 CE36
Phillimore Wk. W8 160 DA76
Phillip Dr., H.Wyc. 110 AC56
Phillipers, Wat. 76 BX36
Phillipp St. N1 142 DS67
Phillips Clo., Dart. 187 FH86
Phillips Hatch, Guil. 259 BC143
Philpot La. EC3 275 M10
Philpot La., Wok. 210 AV113
Philpot Path, Ilf. 125 EQ62
Sunnyside Rd.
Philpot Sq. SW6 160 DB83
Peterborough Rd.
Philpot St. E1 142 DV72
Philpots Clo., West Dr. 134 BK73
Phineas Pett Rd. SE9 164 EL83
Phipp St. EC2 275 M4
Phipp St. EC2 142 DS70
Phipps Bri. Rd. SW19 200 DC96
Phipps Bri. Rd., Mitch. 200 DC96
Phipps Hatch La., Enf. 82 DQ38
Phipp's Ms. SW1 277 H7
Phipps Rd., Slou. 131 AL71
Phoebe Rd., Hem.H. 40 BM17
Phoebeth Rd. SE4 183 EA85
Phoenix Clo. E8 142 DT67
Stean St.
Phoenix Clo., Nthwd. 93 BT49
Phoenix Clo., W.Wick. 203 ED103
Phoenix Ct., Guil. 258 AX136
High St.
Phoenix Dr., Kes. 204 EK104
Phoenix Pk., Brent. 157 CK78
Phoenix Pl. WC1 274 C4
Phoenix Pl. WC1 141 DM70
Phoenix Pl., Dart. 188 FK87
Phoenix Rd. NW1 141 DK69
Phoenix Rd. SE20 182 DW93
Phoenix St. WC2 273 N9
Phoenix Way, Houns. 156 BW79
Phoenix Wf. SE10 164 EF75
Phygtle, The, Ger.Cr. 90 AY51
Phyllis Ave., N.Mal. 199 CV99
Physic Pl. SW3 160 DF79
Royal Hospital Rd.
Piazza, The WC2 141 DL73
Covent Gdn.
Picardy Manorway, Belv. 167 FB76
Picardy Rd., Belv. 166 FA78
Picardy St., Belv. 166 FA76
Piccadilly W1 277 J3
Piccadilly W1 141 DH74
Piccadilly Arc. SW1 277 K2
Piccadilly Circ. W1 277 M1
Piccadilly Circ. W1 141 DJ73
Piccadilly Pl. W1 277 L1
Piccards, The, Guil. 258 AW138
Chestnut Ave.
Piccotts End La., Hem.H. 40 BJ17
Piccotts End Rd., Hem.H. 40 BH16
Pick Hill, Wal.Abb. 68 EF32
Pickard St. EC1 274 G2
Pickering Ave. E6 145 EN68
Pickering Gdns., Croy. 202 DT100
Pickering Ms. W2 140 DB72
Bishops Bri. Rd.
Pickering Pl. SW1 277 L3
Pickering St. N1 141 DP67
Essex Rd.
Pickets Clo. (Bushey), Wat. 95 CD46
Pickets St. SW12 181 DH87
Pickett Cft., Stan. 95 CK53
Picketts, Welw.G.C. 29 CX06
Picketts La., Red. 267 DJ144
Picketts Lock La. N9 100 DW47
Pickford Clo., Bexh. 166 EY82
Pickford Dr., Slou. 133 AZ74
Pickford La., Bexh. 166 EY82
Pickford Rd., Bexh. 166 EY84
Pickford Rd., St.Alb. 43 CH20
Pickford Wf. N1 275 H1
Pickford Wf. N1 142 DQ68
Pickhurst Grn., Brom. 204 EF101
Pickhurst La., Brom. 204 EF101
Pickhurst La., W.Wick. 204 EE99
Pickhurst Mead, Brom. 204 EF101
Pickhurst Pk., Brom. 204 EE99
Pickhurst Ri., W.Wick. 203 EC101
Pickins Piece, Slou. 153 BA82
Pickle Herring St. SE1 142 DS74
Tooley St.
Pickmoss La., Sev. 241 FH116
Pickwick Clo., Houns. 176 BY85
Dorney Way
Pickwick Ct. SE9 184 EL88
West Pk.
Pickwick Gdns., Grav. 190 GD90
Pickwick Ms. N18 100 DS50
Pickwick Pl., Har. 117 CE59
Pickwick Rd. SE21 182 DR87
Pickwick St. SE1 279 H5
Pickwick Way, Chis. 185 EQ93
Pickworth Clo. SW8 161 DL80
Kenchester Clo.
Picquets Way, Bans. 233 CZ117
Picton Pl. W1 272 G9
Picton St. SE5 162 DR80
Piedmont Rd. SE18 165 ER78
Pield Heath Ave., Uxb. 134 BN70
Pield Heath Rd., Uxb. 134 BL70
Pier Head E1 142 DV74
Wapping High St.
Pier Par. E16 165 EN75
Pier Rd.
Pier Rd. E16 165 EN75
Pier Rd., Erith 167 FE79
Pier Rd., Felt. 175 BV85
Pier Rd., Grav. 191 GF86
Pier Rd., Green. 169 FV84
Pier St. E14 163 EC77
Pier Ter. SW18 160 DC84
Jew's Row
Pier Wk., Grays 170 GA79
Columbia Wf. Rd.
Pier Way SE28 165 ER76
Piercing Hill, Epp. 85 ER35
Piermont Grn. SE22 182 DV85
Piermont Pl., Brom. 204 EL96
Piermont Rd. SE22 182 DV85
Pierrepoint Arc. N1 141 DP68
Islington High St.
Pierrepoint Rd. W3 138 CP73
Pierrepoint Row N1 141 DP68
Islington High St.
Pierson Rd., Wind. 151 AK82
Pigeon La., Hmptn. 176 CA91
Pigeonhouse La., Couls. 250 DC125
Piggotts End, Amer. 55 AP40
Piggotts Orchard, Amer. 55 AP40
Piggs Cor., Grays 170 GC76
Piggy La., Rick. 73 BB44
Bullsland La.
Pigott St. E14 143 EA72
Pike Clo., Brom. 184 EH92
Pike La., Upmin. 129 FT64
Pike Rd. NW7 96 CR49
Ellesmere Ave.
Pike Way, Epp. 70 FA27
Pikes End, Pnr. 115 BV56
Pikes Hill, Epsom 216 CS113
Pikestone Clo., Hayes 136 BY70
Berrydale Rd.
Pilgrim Clo., Mord. 200 DB101
Pilgrim Clo., St.Alb. 60 CC27
Pilgrim Hill SE27 182 DQ91
Pilgrim Hill, Orp. 206 EX96
Pilgrim St. EC4 274 F9
Pilgrim St. EC4 141 DP72
Pilgrimage St. SE1 279 K5
Pilgrimage St. SE1 162 DR75
Pilgrims Clo. N13 99 DM49
Pilgrims Clo., Brwd. 108 FT43
Pilgrims Clo., Dor. 247 CG131
Pilgrims Clo., Guil. 260 BN139
Pilgrims Clo., Nthlt. 116 CC64
Pilgrims Clo., Wat. 60 BX33
Kytes Dr.
Pilgrims Ct. SE3 164 EG81
Pilgrim's La. NW3 120 DD63
Pilgrims La., Cat. 251 DM125
Pilgrims La., Oxt. 254 EH125
Pilgrims La., West. 238 EL123
Pilgrims Pl. NW3 120 DD63
Hampstead High St.
Pilgrims Pl., Reig. 250 DA132
Pilgrims Ri., Barn. 80 DE43
Pilgrims Rd., Swans. 170 FY84
Pilgrims Vw., Green. 189 FW86
Pilgrims Way E6 144 EL67
High St. N.
Pilgrims Way N19 121 DK60
Pilgrims' Way, Bet. 248 CQ133
Chalkpit La.
Pilgrims Way, Dart. 188 FN88
Pilgrims' Way, Dor. 261 BT139
Pilgrims Way (Westhumble), Dor. 247 CH131
Pilgrims Way, Guil. 258 AX138
Pilgrims' Way (Albury), Guil. 259 BF138
Pilgrims Way (Shere), Guil. 260 BN139
Pilgrims' Way, Reig. 249 CZ133
Pilgrims Way (Sundridge), Sev. 240 EV121
Pilgrims Way, S.Croy. 220 DT107
Bench Fld.
Pilgrim's Way, Wem. 118 CP60
Pilgrims Way, West. 239 EM123
Pilgrims Way W., Sev. 241 FD116
Pilkington Rd. SE15 162 DV82
Pilkington Rd., Orp. 205 EQ103
Pilkingtons, Harl. 52 EX16
Kitts Riding
Pilot Ind. Est. NW10 138 CR70
Pilots Pl., Grav. 191 GJ86
Pilsdon Clo. SW19 179 CX88
Inner Pk. Rd.
Piltdown Rd., Wat. 94 BX49
Pimlico Rd. SW1 276 F10
Pimlico Rd. SW1 160 DG78
Pimlico Wk. N1 275 M2
Pimms Clo., Guil. 243 BA130
Pimpernel Way, Rom. 106 FK51
Pinceybrook Rd., Harl. 51 EQ19
Pinchbeck Rd., Orp. 223 ET107
Pinchfield, Rick. 91 BD50
Pinchin St. E1 142 DU73
Pincott La., Lthd. 245 BP129
Pincott Pl. SE4 163 DX83
Billingford Clo.
Pincott Rd. SW19 180 DC94
Pincott Rd., Bexh. 186 FA85
Pindar Rd., Hodd. 49 EC16
Pindar St. EC2 275 M6
Pindar St. EC2 142 DS71
Pindock Ms. W9 140 DB70
Warwick Ave.
Pine Ave. E15 123 ED64
Pine Ave., Grav. 191 GK88
Pine Ave., W.Wick. 203 EB102
Pine Clo. E10 123 EB61
Walnut Rd.
Pine Clo. N14 99 DJ45
Pine Clo. N19 121 DJ61
Hargrave Pk.
Pine Clo. SE20 182 DW94
Graveney Gro.
Pine Clo., Add. 212 BH111
Pine Clo., Berk. 38 AV19
Pine Clo., Ken. 236 DR117
Pine Clo., Stan. 95 CH49
Pine Clo., Swan. 207 FF98
Pine Clo. (Cheshunt), Wal.Cr. 67 DX28
Pine Clo., Wok. 226 AW117
Pine Coombe, Croy. 221 DX105
Pine Ct., Upmin. 128 FN63
Pine Cres., Brwd. 109 GD42
Pine Cres., Cars. 218 DD111
Pine Dean, Lthd. 246 CB125
Pine Gdns., Horl. 268 DF149
Pine Gdns., Ruis. 115 BV60
Pine Gdns., Surb. 198 CN100
Pine Glade, Orp. 223 EM105
Pine Gro. N4 121 DL61
Pine Gro. N20 97 CZ46
Pine Gro. SW19 179 CZ92
Pine Gro., Hat. 64 DB25
Pine Gro., St.Alb. 60 BZ30
Pine Gro. (Bushey), Wat. 76 BZ40
Pine Gro., Wey. 213 BP106
Pine Gro. Ms., Wey. 213 BQ106
Pine Hill, Epsom 232 CR115
Pine Pl., Bans. 217 CX114
Pine Pl., Hayes 135 BT70
Pine Ridge, Cars. 218 DG109
Pine Rd. N11 98 DG47
Pine Rd. NW2 119 CW63
Pine Rd., Wok. 226 AW120
Pine St. EC1 274 D4
Pine St. EC1 141 DN70
Pine Tree Clo., Hem.H. 40 BK19
Christchurch Rd.
Pine Tree Clo., Houns. 155 BV81
Pine Tree Hill, Wok. 227 BD116
Pine Trees Dr., Uxb. 114 BL63
Pine Vw. Clo., Guil. 259 BF140
Pine Vw. Manor, Epp. 70 EU30
Pine Wk., Bans. 234 DF117
Pine Wk., Cars. 218 DD110
Pine Wk., Cat. 236 DS122
Pine Wk., Cob. 214 BX114
Pine Wk. (East Horsley), Lthd. 245 BT128
Pine Wk., Surb. 198 CN100
Pine Wk. E., Cars. 218 DD111
Pine Wk. W., Cars. 218 DD111
Pine Way, Egh. 172 AV93
Ashwood Rd.
Pine Wd., Sun. 195 BU95
Pineapple Ct. SW1 277 K6
Pineapple Rd., Amer. 72 AT39
Pinecrest Gdns., Orp. 223 EP105
Pinecroft, Brwd. 109 GB45
Pinecroft, Hem.H. 40 BM24
Pinecroft, Rom. 128 FJ56
Pinecroft Cres., Barn. 79 CY42
Hillside Gdns.
Pinedene SE15 162 DV81
Meeting Ho. La.
Pinefield Clo. E14 143 EA73
Pinehurst, Sev. 257 FL121
Pinehurst Clo., Abb.L. 59 BS32
Pinehurst Clo., Tad. 234 DA122
Pinehurst Wk., Orp. 205 ES102
Andover Rd.
Pinel Clo., Vir.W. 192 AY98
Pinelands Clo. SE3 164 EF80
St. John's Pk.
Pinemartin Clo. NW2 119 CW62
Pineneedle La., Sev. 257 FH123
Pines, The N14 81 DJ43
Pines, The, Borwd. 78 CM40
Anthony Rd.
Pines, The, Dor. 263 CH137
Pines, The, Hem.H. 39 BF24
Pines, The, Pur. 220 DQ113
Pines, The, Sun. 195 BU97
Pines, The, Wok. 211 AZ114
Pines, The, Wdf.Grn. 102 EG48
Pines Ave., Enf. 82 DV36
Pines Clo., Amer. 55 AP36
Pines Clo., Nthwd. 93 BS51
Pines Rd., Brom. 204 EL96
Pinetree Clo., Ger.Cr. 90 AW52
Pinewalk (Great Bookham), Lthd. 246 CB125
Pinewood, Welw.G.C. 29 CY11
Pinewood Ave., Add. 212 BJ109
Pinewood Ave., Pnr. 94 CB51
Pinewood Ave., Rain. 147 FH70
Pinewood Ave., Sev. 257 FK121
Pinewood Ave., Sid. 185 ES88
Pinewood Ave., Uxb. 134 BM72
Pinewood Clo., Borwd. 78 CR39
Pinewood Clo., Croy. 203 DY104
Pinewood Clo., Ger.Cr. 112 AY59
Dukes Wd. Ave.
Pinewood Clo., Harl. 52 EW16
Pinewood Clo., Iver 133 BC66
Pinewood Clo., Nthwd. 93 BV50
Oxhey Dr. S.
Pinewood Clo., Orp. 205 ER102
Pinewood Clo., Pnr. 94 CB51
Pinewood Clo., St.Alb. 43 CJ20
Pinewood Clo., Wat. 75 BU39
Pinewood Clo., Wok. 227 BA115
Pinewood Dr., Orp. 223 ES106
Pinewood Dr., Pot.B. 63 CZ31
Pinewood Dr., Stai. 174 BG92
Cotswold Clo.
Pinewood Gdns., Hem.H. 40 BH20
Pinewood Grn., Iver 133 BC66
Pinewood Gro. W5 137 CJ72
Pinewood Gro., Add. 212 BH110
Pinewood Pk., Add. 212 BH111
Pinewood Ride, Iver 133 BB65
Pinewood Ride, Slou. 133 BA65
Fulmer Common Rd.
Pinewood Rd. SE2 166 EX79
Pinewood Rd., Brom. 204 EG98
Pinewood Rd., Felt. 175 BV90
Pinewood Rd., Iver 133 BA65
Pinewood Rd. (Havering-atte-Bower), Rom. 105 FD49
Pinewood Rd., Vir.W. 192 AU98
Pinewood Way, Brwd. 109 GD43
Pinfold Rd. SW16 181 DL91
Pinfold Rd. (Bushey), Wat. 76 BZ40
Pinglestone Clo., West Dr. 154 BL80
Pink La., Slou. 130 AH68
Pinkcoat Clo., Felt. 175 BV90
Tanglewood Way
Pinkerton Pl. SW16 181 DK91
Riggindale Rd.
Pinkham Way N11 98 DG52
Pinkneys Ct., Maid. 130 AG72
Pinks Hill, Swan. 207 FE99
Pinkwell Ave., Hayes 155 BR77
Pinkwell La., Hayes 155 BQ77
Pinley Gdns., Dag. 146 EV67
Stamford Rd.
Pinn Clo., Uxb. 134 BK72
High Rd.
Pinn Way, Ruis. 115 BR59
Pinnacle Hill, Bexh. 167 FB84
Pinnacle Hill N., Bexh. 167 FB83
Pinnacles, Wal.Abb. 68 EE34
Pinnacles Ind. Est., Harl. 51 EM16
Pinnate Pl., Welw.G.C. 29 CY13
Pinnell Pl. SE9 164 EK84
Pinnell Rd. SE9 164 EK84
Pinner Ct., Pnr. 116 CA56
Pinner Grn., Pnr. 94 BW54
Pinner Gro., Pnr. 116 BY56
Pinner Hill, Pnr. 93 BV52
Pinner Hill Rd., Pnr. 94 BW53
Pinner Pk. Ave., Har. 116 CB55
Pinner Pk. Gdns., Har. 94 CC54
Pinner Rd., Har. 116 CB57
Pinner Rd., Nthwd. 93 BT53
Pinner Rd., Pnr. 116 BZ56
Pinner Rd., Wat. 76 BX44
Pinner Vw., Har. 116 CC56
Pinnocks Ave., Grav. 191 GH88
Pinstone Way, Ger.Cr. 113 BB61
Pintail Clo. E6 144 EL71
Swan App.
Pintail Rd., Wdf.Grn. 102 EH52
Pintail Way, Hayes 136 BX71
Pinto Clo., Borwd. 78 CR44
Percheron Rd.
Pinto Way SE3 164 EH84
Pioneer Pl., Croy. 221 EA109
Featherbed La.
Pioneer St. SE15 162 DU81
Pioneer Way W12 139 CV72
Du Cane Rd.
Pioneer Way, Swan. 207 FE97
Pioneer Way, Wat. 75 BT44
Piper Clo. N7 121 DM64
Piper Rd., Kings.T. 198 CN97
Pipers Clo., Cob. 230 BX115
Pipers Clo., Slou. 130 AJ69
Pipers End, Hert. 31 DJ13
Pipers End, Vir.W. 192 AX97
Piper's Gdns., Croy. 203 DY101
Pipers Grn. NW9 118 CQ57
Pipers Grn. La., Edg. 96 CL48
Pipewell Rd., Cars. 200 DE100
Pippbrook, Dor. 263 CH135
Pippbrook Gdns., Dor. 263 CH135
London Rd.
Pippens, Welw.G.C. 29 CY06
Pippin Clo. NW2 119 CV62
Pippin Clo., Croy. 203 DZ102
Pippins, The, Slou. 133 AZ74
Pickford Dr.
Pippins Clo., West Dr. 154 BK76
Pippins Ct., Ashf. 175 BP93
Piquet Rd. SE20 202 DW96
Pirbright Cres., Croy. 221 EC107
Pirbright Rd. SW18 179 CZ88
Pirie Clo. SE5 162 DR83
Denmark Hill
Pirie St. E16 144 EH74
Pirrip Clo., Grav. 191 GM89
Pirton Clo., St.Alb. 43 CJ15
Pishiobury Dr., Saw. 36 EW07
Pishiobury Ms., Saw. 36 EX08
Pit Fm. Rd., Guil. 243 BA134
Pitcairn Clo., Rom. 126 FA56
Pitcairn Rd., Mitch. 180 DF94
Pitch Pond Clo., Beac. 88 AH50
Pitchfont La., Oxt. 238 EF124
Pitchford St. E15 143 ED66
Pitfield Cres. SE28 146 EU74
Pitfield Est. N1 275 M2
Pitfield St. N1 275 M3
Pitfield St. N1 142 DS69
Pitfield Way NW10 138 CQ65
Pitfield Way, Enf. 82 DW39
Pitfold Clo. SE12 184 EG86
Pitfold Rd. SE12 184 EG86
Pitlake, Croy. 201 DP103
Pitman St. SE5 162 DQ80
Pitman's Fld., Harl. 35 ET14
Pitsea Pl. E1 143 DX72
Pitsea St.
Pitsea St. E1 143 DX72
Pitsfield, Welw.G.C. 29 CX06
Pitshanger La. W5 137 CH70
Pitshanger Pk. W13 137 CG70
Pitson Clo., Add. 212 BK105
Pitstone Clo., St.Alb. 43 CJ15
Highview Gdns.
Pitt Cres. SW19 180 DB91
Pitt Pl., Epsom 216 CS114
Pitt Rd., Epsom 216 CS114
Pitt Rd., Orp. 223 EQ105
Pitt Rd., Th.Hth. 202 DQ99
Pitt St. SE15 162 DT80
Pitt St. W8 160 DA75
Pittman Clo., Brwd. 109 GC50
Pittman Gdns., Ilf. 125 EQ64
Pitt's Head Ms. W1 276 G3
Pitt's Head Ms. W1 140 DG74
Pitts Rd., Slou. 131 AQ74
Pittsmead Ave., Brom. 204 EG101
Pittville Gdns. SE25 202 DU97
Pittwood, Brwd. 109 GA46
Pitwood Grn., Tad. 233 CW120
Pix Fm. La., Hem.H. 39 BB21
Pixfield Ct., Brom. 204 EF96
Beckenham La.
Pixham La., Dor. 247 CJ133
Pixholme Gro., Dor. 247 CJ134
Pixies Hill Cres., Hem.H. 39 BF22
Pixies Hill Rd., Hem.H. 39 BF21
Pixley St. E14 143 DZ72
Pixton Way, Croy. 221 DY109
Place Fm. Ave., Orp. 205 ER102
Place Fm. Rd., Red. 252 DR130
Placehouse La., Couls. 235 DM119
Placket Way, Slou. 131 AK74
Plain, The, Epp. 70 EV29
Plaines Clo., Slou. 131 AN74
Cippenham La.
Plaistow Gro. E15 144 EF67
Plaistow Gro., Brom. 184 EH94
Plaistow La., Brom. 184 EG94
Plaistow Pk. Rd. E13 144 EH68
Plaistow Rd. E13 144 EF67
Plaistow Rd. E15 144 EF67
Plaitford Clo., Rick. 92 BL47
Plane Ave., Grav. 190 GD87
Plane St. SE26 182 DV90
Plane Tree Cres., Felt. 175 BV90
Plane Tree Wk. SE19 182 DS93
Central Hill
Planes, The, Cher. 194 BJ101
Plantaganet Pl., Wal.Abb. 67 EB33
Plantagenet Clo., Wor.Pk. 216 CR105
Plantagenet Gdns., Rom. 126 EX59
Broomfield Rd.
Plantagenet Pl., Rom. 126 EX59
Broomfield Rd.
Plantagenet Rd., Barn. 80 DC42
Plantain Gdns. E11 123 ED62
Hollydown Way
Plantain Pl. SE1 279 K4
Plantation, The SE3 164 EG82
Plantation Dr., Orp. 206 EX102
Plantation La., Warl. 237 DX119
Plantation Rd., Amer. 55 AS37
Plantation Rd., Erith 167 FG81
Plantation Rd., Swan. 187 FG94
Plantation Wk., Hem.H. 40 BG17
Plantation Way, Amer. 55 AS37
Plantation Wf. SW11 160 DC83
Plasel Ct. E13 144 EG67
Plashet Rd.
Plashet Gdns., Brwd. 109 GA49
Plashet Gro. E6 144 EJ67
Plashet Rd. E13 144 EG67
Plashets, B.Stort. 37 FC06
Plassy Rd. SE6 183 EB87
Platford Grn., Horn. 128 FL55
Platina St. EC2 275 L4
Plato Rd. SW2 161 DL84
Platt, The SW15 159 CX83
Platt Meadow, Guil. 243 BD131
Eustace Rd.
Platt St. NW1 141 DK68
Platts Ave., Wat. 75 BV41
Platt's Eyot, Hmptn. 196 CA96
Platt's La. NW3 120 DA63
Platts Rd., Enf. 82 DW39
Plawsfield Rd., Beck. 203 DX95
Plaxtol Clo., Brom. 204 EJ95
Plaxtol Rd., Erith 166 FA79
Playfair St. W6 159 CW78
Winslow Rd.
Playfield Ave., Rom. 105 FC53
Playfield Cres. SE22 182 DT85
Playfield Rd., Edg. 96 CQ54
Playford Rd. N4 121 DM61
Playgreen Way SE6 183 EA90
Playground Clo., Beck. 203 DX96
Churchfields Rd.
Playhouse Yd. EC4 274 F9
Plaza W., Houns. 156 CB81
Pleasance, The SW15 159 CV84
Pleasance Rd. SW15 179 CV85
Pleasance Rd., Orp. 206 EV96
Pleasant Gro., Croy. 203 DZ104
Pleasant Pl. N1 141 DP66
Pleasant Pl., Rick. 91 BE52
Pleasant Pl., Walt. 214 BW107
Pleasant Ri., Hat. 45 CW15
Pleasant Rd., Kings.T. 198 CQ97
Pleasant Row NW1 141 DH67
Camden High St.
Pleasant Vw., Erith 167 FE78
Pleasant Vw. Pl., Orp. 223 EP106
High St.
Pleasant Way, Wem. 137 CJ68
Pleasure Pit Rd., Ash. 232 CP118
Plender St. NW1 141 DJ67
Plender St. Est. NW1 141 DJ67
Plender St.
Pleshey Rd. N7 121 DK63
Plesman Way, Wall. 219 DL109
Plevna Cres. N15 122 DS58
Plevna Rd. N9 100 DU48
Plevna Rd., Hmptn. 196 CB95
Plevna St. E14 163 EC76
Pleydell Ave. SE19 182 DT94
Pleydell Ave. W6 159 CT77
Pleydell Ct. EC4 141 DN72
Fleet St.
Pleydell Est. EC1 142 DQ69
Radnor St.
Pleydell St. EC4 274 E9
Plimsoll Clo. E14 143 EB72
Grundy St.
Plimsoll Rd. N4 121 DN62
Plough Ct. EC3 275 L10
Plough Fm. Clo., Ruis. 115 BR58
Plough Hill (Cuffley), Pot.B. 65 DL28
Plough Ind. Est., Lthd. 231 CG120
Kingston Rd.
Plough La. SE22 182 DT86
Plough La. SW17 180 DC91
Plough La. SW19 180 DB92
Plough La., Berk. 39 BB16
Plough La., Cob. 229 BU117
Plough La., Pur. 219 DM109
Plough La,, Rick. 57 BF33
Plough La., Slou. 132 AV67
Plough La., Tedd. 177 CG92
High St.
Plough La., Uxb. 92 BJ51
Plough La., Wall. 219 DL105
Plough La. Clo., Wall. 219 DL106
Plough Lees La., Slou. 132 AS73

Plo–Pow This index reads in the sequence: Street Name / Postal District or Post Town / Map Page Number / Grid Reference

Plough Ms. SW11 160 DD84
Plough Ter.
Plough Pl. EC4 274 E8
Plough Ri., Upmin. 129 FS59
Plough Rd. SW11 160 DD83
Plough Rd., Epsom 216 CR109
Plough Rd., Horl. 269 DP148
Plough St. E1 142 DT72
Leman St.
Plough Ter. SW11 160 DD84
Plough Way SE16 163 DX77
Plough Yd. EC2 275 N5
Plough Yd. EC2 142 DS70
Ploughmans Clo. NW1 141 DK67
Crofters Way
Ploughmans End, Islw. 177 CD85
Ploughmans End, Welw.G.C. 30 DC10
Plover Clo., Berk. 38 AW20
Plover Clo., Stai. 173 BF90
Waters Dr.
Plover Gdns., Upmin. 129 FT60
Plover Way SE16 163 DY76
Plover Way, Hayes 136 BX72
Plowden Bldgs. EC4 141 DN72
Middle Temple La.
Plowman Clo. N18 100 DR50
Plowman Way, Dag. 126 EW60
Ployters Rd., Harl. 51 EQ18
Plum Garth, Brent. 157 CK77
Plum La. SE18 165 EP80
Plumbers Row E1 142 DU71
Plumbridge St. SE10 163 EC81
Blackheath Hill
Plummer La., Mitch. 200 DF96
Plummer Rd. SW4 181 DK87
Plummers Cft., Sev. 256 FE121
Plumpton Ave., Horn. 128 FL63
Plumpton Clo., Nthlt. 136 CA65
Plumpton Rd., Hodd. 49 EC15
Plumpton Way, Cars. 200 DE104
Plumstead Common Rd. SE18 165 EP79
Plumstead High St. SE18 165 ER77
Plumstead Rd. SE18 165 EP77
Plumtree Clo., Dag. 147 FC65
Plumtree Clo., Wall. 219 DK108
Plumtree Ct. EC4 274 F8
Plumtree Mead, Loug. 85 EN41
Pluto Ri., Hem.H. 40 BL18
Plymouth Dr., Sev. 257 FJ124
Plymouth Ho., Rain. 147 FF69
Plymouth Pk., Sev. 257 FJ124
Plymouth Rd. E16 144 EG71
Plymouth Rd., Brom. 204 EH95
Plymouth Rd., Slou. 131 AL71
Plymouth Wf. E14 163 ED77
Plympton Ave. NW6 139 CZ66
Plympton Clo., Belv. 166 EY76
Halifield Dr.
Plympton Pl. NW8 272 B5
Plympton Rd. NW6 139 CZ66
Plympton St. NW8 272 B5
Plympton St. NW8 140 DE70
Plymstock Rd., Well. 166 EW80
Pocketsdell La., Hem.H. 56 AX28
Pocklington Clo. NW9 96 CS54
Pocock Ave., West Dr. 154 BM76
Brickfields Way
Pocock St. SE1 278 F4
Pocock St. SE1 161 DP75
Pococks La. (Eton), Wind. 152 AS78
Podmore Rd. SW18 160 DC84
Poets Chase, Hem.H. 40 BH18
Laureate Way
Poets Gate, Wal.Cr. 66 DQ28
St. James Rd.
Poets Rd. N5 122 DR64
Poets Way, Har. 117 CE56
Blawith Rd.
Point, The, Ruis. 115 BU63
Bedford Rd.
Point Clo. SE10 163 EC81
Point Hill
Point Hill SE10 163 EC80
Point of Thomas Path E1 142 DW73
Glamis Rd.
Point Pl., Wem. 138 CP66
Point Pleasant SW18 160 DA84
Pointalls Clo. N3 98 DC54
Pointer Clo. SE28 146 EX72
Pointers, The, Ash. 232 CL120
Pointers Clo. E14 163 EB78
Pointers Hill, Dor. 262 CC138
Pointers Rd., Cob. 229 BQ116
Poland St. W1 273 L8
Poland St. W1 141 DJ72
Polayn Garth, Welw.G.C. 29 CW08
Pole Cat All., Brom. 204 EF103
Pole Hanger La., Hem.H. 39 BE18
Pole Hill Rd. E4 101 EC45
Pole Hill Rd., Uxb. 135 BP70
Pole La., Ong. 53 FE17
Polebrook Rd. SE3 164 EJ83
Polecroft La. SE6 183 DZ89
Polehamptons, The, Hmptn. 176 CC94
High St.
Poles Hill, Chesh. 54 AN29
Poles Hill, Rick. 57 BE33
Polesden Gdns. SW20 199 CV96
Polesden Lacey, Dor. 246 CB130
Polesden La., Wok. 227 BF122
Polesden Rd., Lthd. 246 CB129
Polesden Vw., Lthd. 246 CB127
Polesteeple Hill, West. 238 EK117
Polesworth Ho. W2 140 DA71
Polesworth Rd., Dag. 146 EX66
Polhill, Sev. 225 FC114
Police Sta. La. (Bushey), Wat. 94 CB45
Sparrows Herne
Police Sta. Rd., Walt. 214 BW107
Pollard Ave., Uxb. 113 BF58
Pollard Clo. E16 144 EG73
Pollard Clo. N7 121 DM63
Pollard Clo., Chig. 104 EU50
Pollard Clo., Wind. 172 AV85
Pollard Hatch, Harl. 51 EP18
Pollard Rd. N20 98 DE47
Pollard Rd., Mord. 200 DD99
Pollard Rd., Wok. 227 BB116
Pollard Row E2 142 DU69
Pollard St. E2 142 DU69
Pollard Wk., Sid. 186 EW93
Evry Rd.
Pollards, Rick. 91 BD50
Pollards Clo., Loug. 84 EJ43
Pollards Clo. (Cheshunt), Wal.Cr. 66 DQ29
Pollards Cres. SW16 201 DL97
Pollards Hill E. SW16 201 DM97
Pollards Hill N. SW16 201 DL97
Pollards Hill S. SW16 201 DL97
Pollards Hill W. SW16 201 DL97
Pollards Oak Cres., Oxt. 254 EG132
Pollards Oak Rd., Oxt. 254 EG132
Pollards Wd. Hill, Oxt. 254 EH130
Pollards Wd. Rd. SW16 201 DL96
Pollards Wd. Rd., Oxt. 254 EH131
Pollen St. W1 273 K9
Pollicott Clo., St.Alb. 43 CJ15
Pollitt Dr. NW8 272 A4
Pollyhaugh (Eynsford), Dart. 208 FK104
Polperro Clo., Orp. 205 ET100
Cotswold Ri.
Polsted Rd. SE6 183 DZ87
Polthorne Est. SE18 165 EQ77
Polthorne Gro.
Polthorne Gro. SE18 165 EQ77
Poltimore Rd., Guil. 258 AU136
Polworth Rd. SW16 181 DL92
Polygon, The SW4 161 DJ84
Old Town
Polygon Rd. NW1 273 M1
Polygon Rd. NW1 141 DK68
Polytechnic St. SE18 165 EN77
Pomell Way E1 142 DT72
Commercial St.
Pomeroy Clo., Amer. 55 AR39
Pomeroy Cres., Wat. 75 BV36
Pomeroy St. SE14 162 DW81
Pomfret Rd. SE5 161 DP83
Flaxman Rd.
Pomoja La. N19 121 DK61
Pompadour Clo., Brwd. 108 FW50
Queen St.
Pond Clo. SE3 164 EF82
Pond Clo., Ash. 232 CL117
Pond Clo., Uxb. 92 BJ54
Pond Clo., Walt. 213 BT107
Pond Cottage La., W.Wick. 203 EA102
Pond Cotts. SE21 182 DS88
Pond Cft., Hat. 45 CT18
Pond Cft., Welw.G.C. 29 CY10
Pond Fld., Welw.G.C. 30 DA06
Pond Fld. End, Loug. 102 EJ45
Pond Grn., Ruis. 115 BS61
Pond Hill Gdns., Sutt. 217 CY107
Pond La., Ger.Cr. 90 AV53
Pond La., Guil. 261 BQ144
Pond Mead SE21 182 DR86
Pond Meadow, Guil. 242 AS134
Pond Pk. Rd., Chesh. 54 AP29
Pond Path, Chis. 185 EP93
Heathfield La.
Pond Piece, Lthd. 214 CB113
Pond Pl. SW3 276 B9
Pond Pl. SW3 160 DE77
Pond Rd. E15 144 EE68
Pond Rd. SE3 164 EF82
Pond Rd., Egh. 173 BC93
Pond Rd., Hem.H. 58 BN25
Pond Rd., Wok. 226 AU120
Pond Sq. N6 120 DG60
South Gro.
Pond St. NW3 120 DE64
Pond Wk., Upmin. 129 FS61
Pond Way, Tedd. 177 CJ93
Holmesdale Rd.
Ponder St. N7 141 DM66
Ponders End Ind. Est., Enf. 83 DZ42
Pondfield Cres., St.Alb. 43 CH16
Pondfield La., Brwd. 109 GA49
Pondfield Rd., Brom. 204 EE102
Pondfield Rd., Dag. 127 FB64
Pondfield Rd., Gdmg. 258 AT144
Pondfield Rd., Ken. 235 DP117
Pondfield Rd., Orp. 205 EP104
Ponds, The, Wey. 213 BS107
Ellesmere Rd.
Ponds La., Guil. 260 BL142
Pondside Clo., Hayes 155 BR80
Providence La.
Pondwicks, Amer. 55 AP39
Pondwicks Clo., St.Alb. 42 CC21
Pondwood Ri., Orp. 205 ES101
Ponler St. E1 142 DV72
Ponsard Rd. NW10 139 CV69
Ponsbourne Ho., Hert. 47 DL23
Ponsford St. E9 122 DW64
Ponsonby Pl. SW1 277 N10
Ponsonby Pl. SW1 161 DK78
Ponsonby Rd. SW15 179 CV87
Ponsonby Ter. SW1 277 N10
Ponsonby Ter. SW1 161 DK78
Pont St. SW1 276 D7
Pont St. SW1 160 DF76
Pont St. Ms. SW1 276 D7
Pont St. Ms. SW1 160 DF76
Pontefract Rd., Brom. 184 EF92
Pontoise Clo., Sev. 256 FF122
Ponton Rd. SW8 161 DK79
Pontypool Pl. SE1 278 F4
Pontypool Wk., Rom. 106 FJ51
Saddleworth Rd.
Pony Chase, Cob. 214 BZ113
Pool Clo., Beck. 183 EA92
Pool Clo., W.Mol. 196 BZ99
Pool Ct. SE6 183 EA89
Pool End Clo., Shep. 194 BN99
Pool Gro., Croy. 221 DY112
Pool La., Slou. 132 AS73
Pool Rd., Har. 117 CD59
Pool Rd., W.Mol. 196 BZ99
Poole Clo., Ruis. 115 BS61
Chichester Ave.
Poole Ct. Rd., Houns. 156 BY82
Vicarage Fm. Rd.
Poole Rd. E9 143 DX65
Poole Rd., Epsom 216 CR107
Poole Rd., Horn. 128 FM59
Poole Rd., Wok. 226 AY117
Poole St. N1 142 DR67
Poole Way, Hayes 135 BR69
Pooles Bldgs. EC1 274 D5
Pooles La. SW10 160 DC80
Lots Rd.
Pooles La., Dag. 146 EY68
Pooles Pk. N4 121 DN61
Seven Sisters Rd.
Pooley Ave., Egh. 173 BB92
Pooley Grn. Clo., Egh. 173 BC92
Pooley Grn. Rd., Egh. 173 BB92
Pooleys La., Hat. 45 CV23
Poolmans Rd., Wind. 151 AK83
Poolmans St. SE16 163 DX75
Poolsford Rd. NW9 118 CS56
Poonah St. E1 142 DW72
Hardinge St.
Pootings Rd., Eden. 255 ER134
Pope Clo. SW19 180 DD93
Shelley Way
Pope Clo., Felt. 175 BT88
Pope Rd., Brom. 204 EK99
Pope St. SE1 279 N5
Pope St. SE1 162 DS75
Popes Ave., Twick. 177 CE89
Popes Clo., Amer. 72 AT37
Popes Clo., Slou. 153 BB80
Popes Dr. N3 98 DA53
Popes Gro., Croy. 203 DZ104
Popes Gro., Twick. 177 CE89
Pope's Head All. EC3 142 DR72
Cornhill
Popes La. W5 157 CK76
Popes La., Oxt. 254 EE134
Popes La., Wat. 75 BV37
Popes Rd. SW9 161 DN83
Popes Rd., Abb.L. 59 BS31
Popham Clo., Felt. 176 BZ90
Popham Rd. N1 142 DQ67
Popham St. N1 142 DQ67
Poplar Ave., Amer. 72 AT39
Poplar Ave., Grav. 191 GJ91
Poplar Ave., Lthd. 231 CH122
Poplar Ave., Mitch. 200 DF95
Poplar Ave., Orp. 205 EP103
Poplar Ave., Sthl. 156 CB76
Poplar Ave., West Dr. 134 BM73
Poplar Bath St. E14 143 EB73
Lawless St.
Poplar Clo. E9 123 DZ64
Lee Conservancy Rd.
Poplar Clo., Chesh. 54 AQ28
Poplar Clo., Pnr. 94 BX53
Poplar Clo., Slou. 153 BE81
Poplar Ct. SW19 180 DA92
Poplar Cres., Epsom 216 CQ107
Poplar Dr., Bans. 217 CY114
Poplar Dr., Brwd. 109 GC44
Poplar Fm. Clo., Epsom 216 CQ107
Poplar Gdns., N.Mal. 198 CR96
Poplar Gro. N11 98 DG51
Poplar Gro. W6 159 CW75
Poplar Gro., N.Mal. 198 CR97
Poplar Gro., Wem. 118 CQ62
Poplar Gro., Wok. 226 AY119
Poplar High St. E14 143 EB73
Poplar Mt., Belv. 167 FB77
Poplar Pl. SE28 146 EW73
Poplar Pl. W2 140 DB73
Poplar Pl., Hayes 135 BU73
Central Ave.
Poplar Rd. SE24 162 DQ84
Poplar Rd. SW19 200 DA96
Poplar Rd., Ashf. 175 BQ93
Poplar Rd., Guil. 258 AY141
Poplar Rd., Lthd. 231 CH122
Poplar Rd., Sutt. 199 CZ102
Poplar Rd., Uxb. 114 BJ64
Poplar Rd. S. SW19 200 DA97
Poplar Row, Epp. 85 ES37
Poplar Shaw, Wal.Abb. 68 EF33
Poplar St., Rom. 127 FC56
Poplar Vw., Wem. 117 CK61
Magnet Rd.
Poplar Wk. SE24 162 DQ84
Poplar Wk., Cat. 236 DS123
Poplar Wk., Croy. 202 DQ103
Poplar Way, Felt. 175 BU90
Poplar Way, Ilf. 125 EQ56
Poplars, Welw.G.C. 30 DB08
Poplars, The N14 81 DH43
Poplars, The, Hem.H. 40 BH21
Poplars, The, Rom. 86 EV41
Hoe La.
Poplars, The, St.Alb. 43 CH24
Poplars, The, Wal.Cr. 66 DS27
The Laurels
Poplars Ave. NW10 139 CW65
Poplars Ave., Hat. 44 CR18
Poplars Clo., Hat. 44 CQ18
Poplars Clo., Ruis. 115 BS60
Poplars Clo., Wat. 59 BV32
Poplars Rd. E17 123 EB58
Poppins Ct. EC4 274 F9
Poppleton Rd. E11 124 EE58
Poppy Clo., Brwd. 108 FV43
Poppy Clo., Hem.H. 39 BE19
Poppy Clo., Wall. 200 DG102
Poppy La., Croy. 202 DW101
Poppy Wk., Wal.Cr. 66 DR28
Poppyfields, Welw.G.C. 30 DC09
Porch Way N20 98 DF48
Porchester Clo., Horn. 128 FL58
Porchester Gdns. W2 140 DB73
Porchester Gdns. Ms. W2 140 DB72
Porchester Gdns.
Porchester Mead, Beck. 183 EA93
Porchester Ms. W2 140 DB72
Porchester Sq.
Porchester Pl. W2 272 C9
Porchester Pl. W2 140 DE72
Porchester Rd. W2 140 DB71
Porchester Rd., Kings.T. 198 CP96
Porchester Sq. W2 140 DB72
Porchester Ter. W2 140 DC73
Porchester Ter. N. W2 140 DB72
Porchfield Clo., Grav. 191 GJ89
Whitehill Rd.
Porchfield Clo., Sutt. 218 DB110
Porcupine Clo. SE9 184 EL89
Porden Rd. SW2 161 DM84
Porlock Ave., Har. 116 CC60
Porlock Rd. W10 139 CX70
Ladbroke Gro.
Porlock Rd., Enf. 100 DT45
Porlock St. SE1 279 L4
Porlock St. SE1 162 DR75
Porridge Pot All., Guil. 258 AW136
Bury Flds.
Porrington Clo., Chis. 205 EN95
Port Ave., Green. 189 FV86
Port Cres. E13 144 EH70
Jenkins Rd.
Port Hill, Hert. 32 DQ09
Port Hill, Orp. 224 EV112
Port Vale, Hert. 31 DP08
Portal Clo. SE27 181 DN90
Portal Clo., Ruis. 115 BU63
Portal Clo., Uxb. 134 BL66
Portbury Clo. SE15 162 DU81
Clayton Rd.
Portchester Clo. SE5 162 DR84
Portcullis Lo. Rd., Enf. 82 DR41
Portelet Rd. E1 143 DX69
Porten Rd. W14 159 CY76
Porter Clo., Grays 169 FW79
Porter Rd. E6 145 EM72
Porter Sq. N19 121 DL60
Hornsey Rd.
Porter St. SE1 279 J2
Porter St. W1 272 E6
Porters Ave., Dag. 146 EV65
Porters Clo., Brwd. 108 FU46
Greenshaw
Porters Pk. Dr., Rad. 61 CK33
Porters Wk. E1 142 DV73
Pennington St.
Porters Way, West Dr. 154 BM76
Porters Wd., St.Alb. 43 CE16
Portersfield Rd., Enf. 82 DS42
Porteus Rd. W2 140 DC71
Portgate Clo. W9 139 CZ70
Porthcawe Rd. SE26 183 DY91
Porthkerry Ave., Well. 166 EU84
Portia Way E3 143 DZ70
Portinscale Rd. SW15 179 CY85
Portland Ave. N16 122 DT59
Portland Ave., Grav. 191 GH89
Portland Ave., N.Mal. 199 CT101
Portland Ave., Sid. 186 EU86
Portland Clo., Rom. 126 EY57
Portland Clo., Slou. 131 AK70
Portland Cres. SE9 184 EL89
Portland Cres., Felt. 175 BR91
Portland Cres., Grnf. 136 CB70
Portland Cres., Stan. 95 CK54
Portland Dr., Enf. 82 DS38
Clay Hill
Portland Dr., Red. 251 DK129
Portland Dr. (Cheshunt), Wal.Cr. 66 DU31
Portland Gdns. N4 121 DP58
Portland Gdns., Rom. 126 EX57
Portland Gro. SW8 161 DM81
Portland Heights, Nthwd. 93 BT49
Portland Ms. W1 273 L9
Portland Pl. W1 273 H5
Portland Pl. W1 141 DH71
Portland Pl., Epsom 216 CS112
Portland Pl., Hert. 32 DW11
Portland Ri. N4 121 DP60
Portland Ri. Est. N4 122 DQ60
Portland Rd. N15 122 DT56
Portland Rd. SE9 184 EL89
Portland Rd. SE25 202 DU98
Portland Rd. W11 139 CY73
Portland Rd., Ashf. 174 BL90
Portland Rd., Brom. 184 EJ91
Portland Rd., Dor. 263 CG135
Portland Rd., Grav. 191 GH88
Portland Rd., Hayes 135 BS69
Portland Rd., Kings.T. 198 CL97
Portland Rd., Mitch. 200 DE96
Portland Rd., Sthl. 156 BZ76
Portland Sq. E1 142 DV74
Watts St.
Portland St. SE17 279 K10
Portland St. SE17 162 DR78
Portland St., St.Alb. 42 CC20
Portland Ter., Rich. 157 CK84
Portland Wk. SE17 162 DR79
Portland St.
Portley La., Cat. 236 DS121
Portley Wd. Rd., Whyt. 236 DT121
Portman Ave. SW14 158 CR83
Portman Clo. W1 272 E8
Portman Clo. W1 140 DF72
Portman Clo., Bex. 187 FE88
Portman Clo., Bexh. 166 EX83
Queen Anne's Gate
Portman Clo., St.Alb. 43 CJ15
Portman Dr., Wdf.Grn. 102 EK54
Portman Gdns. NW9 96 CR54
Portman Gdns., Uxb. 134 BN66
Portman Gate NW1 272 C5
Portman Ho., St.Alb. 43 CD17
Portman Ms. S. W1 272 F9
Portman Ms. S. W1 140 DG72
Portman Pl. E2 142 DW69
Portman Rd., Kings.T. 198 CM96
Portman Sq. W1 272 F8
Portman Sq. W1 140 DG72
Portman St. W1 272 F9
Portman St. W1 140 DG72
Portmeadow Wk. SE2 166 EX75
Portmeers Clo. E17 123 DZ58
Lennox Rd.
Portmore Gdns., Rom. 104 FA50
Portmore Pk. Rd., Wey. 212 BN105
Portmore Quays, Wey. 212 BM105
Bridge Rd.
Portmore Way, Wey. 194 BN104
Portnall Dr., Vir.W. 192 AT99
Portnall Ri., Vir.W. 192 AT99
Portnall Rd. W9 139 CZ68
Portnall Rd., Vir.W. 192 AT99
Portnalls Clo., Couls. 235 DH116
Portnalls Ri., Couls. 235 DH116
Portnalls Rd., Couls. 235 DH118
Portnoi Clo., Rom. 105 FD54
Portobello Clo., Chesh. 54 AN29
Portobello Ct. W11 139 CZ73
Westbourne Gro.
Portobello Ms. W11 140 DA73
Portobello Rd.
Portobello Rd. W10 139 CY71
Portobello Rd. W11 139 CZ72
Porton Ct., Surb. 197 CJ100
Portpool La. EC1 274 D6
Portpool La. EC1 141 DN71
Portree Clo. N22 99 DM52
Nightingale Rd.
Portree St. E14 143 ED72
Portsdown, Edg. 96 CN50
Rectory La.
Portsdown Ave. NW11 119 CZ58
Portsdown Ms. NW11 119 CZ58
Portsea Ms. W2 272 C9
Portsea Pl. W2 272 C9
Portsea Rd., Til. 171 GJ81
Portslade Rd. SW8 161 DJ82
Portsmouth Ave., T.Ditt. 197 CG101
Portsmouth Ct., Slou. 132 AS73
Portsmouth Rd. SW15 179 CV87
Portsmouth Rd., Cob. 229 BQ115
Portsmouth Rd., Esher 214 BZ108
Portsmouth Rd., Guil. 258 AV141
Portsmouth Rd., Kings.T. 197 CK98
Portsmouth Rd., Surb. 197 CJ100
Portsmouth Rd., T.Ditt. 197 CE103
Portsmouth Rd., Wok. 228 BM119
Portsmouth St. WC2 274 B9
Portsoken St. E1 275 P10
Portsoken St. E1 142 DT73
Portswood Pl. SW15 179 CT87
Danebury Ave.
Portugal Gdns., Twick. 176 CC89
Fulwell Pk. Ave.
Portugal Rd., Wok. 227 AZ116
Portugal St. WC2 274 B9
Portugal St. WC2 141 DM72
Portway E15 144 EF67
Portway, Epsom 217 CU110
Portway Cres., Epsom 217 CU109
Portway Gdns. SE18 164 EK80
Shooter's Hill Rd.
Post Ho. La., Lthd. 246 CA125
Post La., Twick. 177 CD88
Post Meadow, Iver 133 BD69
Post Office App. E7 124 EH64
Post Office Ct. EC3 275 L9
Post Office La., Beac. 89 AK52
Post Office La., Slou. 132 AX72
Post Office Rd., Harl. 35 ER14
Post Office Row, Oxt. 254 EL131
Post Office Way SW8 161 DK80
Post Wd. Rd., Ware 33 DY08
Postern Grn., Enf. 81 DN40
Postfield, Welw.G.C. 30 DA06
Postmill Clo., Croy. 203 DX104
Postway Ms., Ilf. 125 EP62
Clements Rd.
Postwood Grn., Hert. 32 DW12
Potier St. SE1 279 L7
Potier St. SE1 162 DR76
Potkiln La., Beac. 111 AQ55
Pott St. E2 142 DV69
Potten End Hill, Berk. 39 BD16
Potten End Hill, Hem.H. 39 BE15
Potter Clo., Mitch. 201 DH96
Potter St., Harl. 52 EW16
Potter St., Nthwd. 93 BU53
Potter St., Pnr. 93 BV53
Potter St. Hill, Pnr. 93 BV51
Potterne Clo. SW19 179 CX87
Castlecombe Dr.
Potters Clo., Croy. 203 DY102
Potters Clo., Loug. 84 EL40
Potters Cross, Iver 133 BE69
Potters Fld., Harl. 52 EX17
Potters Fld., St.Alb. 43 CE16
Potters Flds. SE1 142 DS74
Tooley St.
Potters Gro., N.Mal. 198 CQ98
Potters Heights Clo., Pnr. 93 BV52
Potters La. SW16 181 DK93
Potters La., Barn. 80 DA42
Potters La., Borwd. 78 CQ39
Potters La., Wok. 227 BB123
Potters Rd. SW6 160 DC82
Potters Rd., Barn. 80 DB42
Potters Way, Reig. 266 DC138
Pottery La. W11 139 CY73
Portland Rd.
Pottery Rd., Bex. 187 FC89
Pottery Rd., Brent. 158 CL79
Pottery St. SE16 162 DV75
Pouchen End La., Hem.H. 39 BD17
Poulcott, Stai. 172 AY86
Poulett Gdns., Twick. 177 CF88
Poulett Rd. E6 145 EM68
Poulner Way SE15 162 DT80
Daniel Gdns.
Poulters Wd., Kes. 222 EK106
Poultney Clo., Rad. 62 CM32
Poulton Ave., Sutt. 200 DD104
Poulton Clo. E8 122 DV64
Spurstowe Ter.
Poultry EC2 275 K9
Poultry EC2 142 DR72
Pound, The, Slou. 130 AJ70
Hogfair La.
Pound Clo., Orp. 205 ER103
Pound Clo., Surb. 197 CJ102
Pound Clo., Wal.Abb. 50 EE23
Pound Ct., Ash. 232 CM118
Pound Ct. Dr., Orp. 205 ER103
Pound Cres., Lthd. 231 CD121
Pound Fld., Guil. 242 AX133
Pound Fld., Wat. 75 BT35
Ashfields
Pound La. NW10 139 CU65
Pound La., Epsom 216 CQ112
Pound La., Rad. 62 CM33
Pound La., Sev. 240 EX115
Pound La. (Knockholt Pound), Sev. 257 FJ124
Pound Pk. Rd. SE7 164 EK77
Pound Pl. SE9 185 EN86
Pound Pl., Guil. 259 AZ140
Pound Pl. Clo., Guil. 259 AZ140
Pound Rd., Bans. 233 CZ117
Pound Rd., Cher. 194 BH101
Pound St., Cars. 218 DF106
Pound Way, Chis. 185 EQ94
Royal Par.
Poundfield Gdns., Wok. 227 BC120
Poundfield Rd., Loug. 85 EN43
Poundwell, Welw.G.C. 30 DA10
Pounsley Rd., Sev. 256 FE121
Pountney Rd. SW11 160 DG83
Povest Rd., Orp. 205 EV102
Povey Cross Rd., Horl. 268 DD150
Powder Mill La., Dart. 188 FL89
Powder Mill La., Twick. 176 BZ87
Powdermill La., Wal.Abb. 67 EB33

Powdermill Ms., Wal.Abb. 67 EB33
Powdermill La.
Powdermill Way, Wal.Abb. 67 EB32
Powell Clo., Chess. 215 CK106
Coppard Gdns.
Powell Clo., Edg. 96 CM51
Powell Clo., Guil. 258 AT136
Powell Clo., Horl. 268 DE147
Baden Dr.
Powell Clo., Wall. 219 DK108
Hermes Way
Powell Gdns., Dag. 126 FA63
Powell Rd. E5 122 DV62
Powell Rd., Buck.H. 102 EJ45
Powells Clo., Dor. 263 CJ139
Goodwyns Rd.
Powell's Wk. W4 158 CS79
Power Rd. W4 158 CN77
Powers Ct., Twick. 177 CK87
Powerscroft Rd. E5 122 DW63
Powerscroft Rd., Sid. 186 EW93
Powis Ct., Pot.B. 64 DC34
Powis Gdns. NW11 119 CZ59
Powis Gdns. W11 139 CZ72
Powis Ms. W11 139 CZ72
Westbourne Pk. Rd.
Powis Pl. WC1 274 A5
Powis Pl. WC1 141 DL70
Powis Rd. E3 143 EB69
Powis Sq. W11 139 CZ72
Powis St. SE18 165 EN76
Powis Ter. W11 139 CZ72
Powle Ter., Ilf. 125 EQ64
Loxford La.
Powlett Pl. NW1 141 DH65
Harmood St.
Pownall Gdns., Houns. 156 CB84
Pownall Rd. E8 142 DU67
Pownall Rd., Houns. 156 CB84
Pownsett Ter., Ilf. 125 EQ64
Powster Rd., Brom. 184 EH92
Powys Clo., Bexh. 166 EX79
Powys La. N13 99 DL49
Powys La. N14 99 DL49
Poyle Ind. Est., Slou. 153 BE82
Poyle La., Slou. 130 AH67
Poyle Rd., Guil. 258 AY136
Poyle Rd., Slou. 153 BE83
Poyle Ter., Guil. 258 AX136
Sydenham Rd.
Poynder Rd., Til. 171 GH81
Poynders Ct. SW4 181 DJ86
Poynders Rd.
Poynders Gdns. SW4 181 DJ87
Poynders Hill, Hem.H. 41 BQ21
Poynders Rd. SW4 181 DJ86
Poynes Rd., Horl. 268 DE146
Poynings, The, Iver 153 BF77
Poynings Clo., Orp. 206 EW103
Poynings Rd. N19 121 DJ62
Poynings Way N12 98 DA50
Poynings Way, Rom. 106 FL53
Arlington Gdns.
Poyntell Cres., Chis. 205 ER95
Poynter Rd., Enf. 82 DU43
Poynton Rd. N17 100 DU54
Poyntz Rd. SW11 160 DF82
Poyser St. E2 142 DV68
Prae, The, Wok. 227 BF118
Prae Clo., St.Alb. 42 CB20
Praed Ms. W2 272 A8
Praed St. W2 272 A8
Praed St. W2 140 DD72
Praetorian Ct., St.Alb. 42 CC23
Pragel St. E13 144 EH68
Pragnell Rd. SE12 184 EH89
Prague Pl. SW2 181 DL85
Prah Rd. N4 121 DN61
Prairie Clo., Add. 194 BH104
Prairie Rd., Add. 194 BH104
Prairie St. SW8 160 DG82
Pratt Ms. NW1 141 DJ67
Pratt St.
Pratt St. NW1 141 DJ67
Pratt Wk. SE11 278 C8
Pratt Wk. SE11 161 DM77
Pratts La., Walt. 214 BX105
Molesey Rd.
Pratts Pas., Kings.T. 198 CL96
Eden St.
Prayle Gro. NW2 119 CX60
Prebend Gdns. W4 159 CT77
Prebend Gdns. W6 159 CT77
Prebend St. N1 142 DQ67
Precinct, The, W.Mol. 196 CB97
Victoria Ave.
Precinct Rd., Hayes 135 BU73
Precincts, The, Mord. 200 DB100
Green La.
Precincts, The, Slou. 130 AH70
Premier Ave., Grays 170 GC75
Premier Cor. W9 139 CZ68
Kilburn La.
Premier Pl. SW15 159 CY84
Putney High St.
Premiere Pl. E14 143 EA73
Garford St.
Prendergast Rd. SE3 164 EE83
Prentice Pl., Harl. 52 EW17
Prentis Rd. SW16 181 DK91
Prentiss Ct. SE7 164 EK77
Presburg Rd., N.Mal. 198 CS99
Presburg St. E5 123 DX62
Glyn Rd.
Prescelly Pl., Edg. 96 CM53
Prescot Rd., Slou. 153 BE82
Prescot St. E1 142 DT73
Prescott Ave., Orp. 205 EP100
Prescott Clo. SW16 181 DL94
Prescott Clo., Horn. 127 FH60
St. Leonards Way
Prescott Grn., Loug. 85 EQ41
Prescott Ho. SE17 161 DP79
Hillingdon St.
Prescott Pl. SW4 161 DK83
Prescott Rd. (Cheshunt), Wal.Cr. 67 DY27
Presdale Dr., Ware 33 DX07
Presentation Ms. SW2 181 DM88
Palace Rd.
President Dr. E1 142 DV74
Waterman Way
President St. EC1 275 H2
Press Rd. NW10 118 CR62
Press Rd., Uxb. 134 BK65
Prestage Way E14 143 EC73
Prestbury Ct., Wok. 226 AU118
Muirfield Rd.
Prestbury Cres., Bans. 234 DF116
Prestbury Rd. E7 144 EJ66
Prestbury Sq. SE9 185 EM91
Prested Rd. SW11 160 DE84
St. John's Hill
Preston Ave. E4 101 ED51
Preston Clo. SE1 279 M8
Preston Clo., Ash. 231 CJ116
Preston Clo., Twick. 177 CE90
Preston Ct., Walt. 196 BW102
St. Johns Dr.
Preston Dr. E11 124 EJ57
Preston Dr., Bexh. 166 EX81
Preston Dr., Epsom 216 CS107
Preston Gdns. NW10 138 CS65
Church Rd.
Preston Gdns., Enf. 83 DY37
Preston Gdns., Ilf. 124 EL58
Preston Gro., Ash. 231 CJ117
Preston Hill, Chesh. 54 AR29
Preston Hill, Har. 118 CL59
Preston La., Tad. 233 CV121
Preston Pl. NW2 139 CU65
Preston Pl., Rich. 178 CL85
Preston Rd. E11 124 EE58
Preston Rd. SE19 181 DP93
Preston Rd. SW20 179 CT94
Preston Rd., Grav. 190 GE88
Preston Rd., Har. 118 CL59
Preston Rd., Rom. 106 FK49
Preston Rd., Shep. 194 BN99
Preston Rd., Slou. 132 AW73
Preston Rd., Wem. 118 CL61
Preston Waye, Har. 118 CL60
Prestons Rd. E14 163 EC75
Prestons Rd., Brom. 204 EG104
Prestwick Clo., Sthl. 156 BY78
Ringway
Prestwick Rd., Wat. 94 BW46
Prestwood, Slou. 132 AV72
Prestwood Ave., Har. 117 CH56
Prestwood Clo. SE18 166 EU80
Prestwood Clo., Har. 117 CH56
Prestwood Dr., Rom. 105 FC50
Prestwood Gdns., Croy. 202 DQ101
Prestwood St. N1 275 J1
Pretoria Ave. E17 123 DY56
Pretoria Clo. N17 100 DT52
Pretoria Rd.
Pretoria Cres. E4 101 EC46
Pretoria Rd. E4 101 EC46
Pretoria Rd. E11 123 ED60
Pretoria Rd. E16 144 EF70
Pretoria Rd. N17 100 DT52
Pretoria Rd. SW16 181 DH93
Pretoria Rd., Cher. 193 BF102
Pretoria Rd., Ilf. 125 EP64
Pretoria Rd., Rom. 127 FC56
Pretoria Rd., Wat. 75 BU42
Pretoria Rd. N. N18 100 DT51
Prevost Rd. N11 98 DG47
Prey Heath, Wok. 226 AV123
Prey Heath Clo., Wok. 226 AW124
Prey Heath Rd., Wok. 226 AV124
Price Clo. NW7 97 CY51
Price Clo. SW17 180 DF90
Price Rd., Croy. 219 DP105
Price Way, Hmptn. 176 BY93
Victors Dr.
Prices La., Reig. 266 DA137
Price's Yd. N1 141 DM67
Pricklers Hill, Barn. 80 DB44
Prickley Wd., Brom. 204 EF102
Priddy's Yd., Croy. 202 DQ103
Crown Hill
Prideaux Pl. W3 138 CR73
Friars Pl. La.
Prideaux Pl. WC1 274 C2
Prideaux Pl. WC1 141 DM69
Prideaux Rd. SW9 161 DL83
Pridham Rd., Th.Hth. 202 DR98
Priest Ct. EC2 275 H8
Priest Hill, Egh. 172 AW90
Priest Hill, Wind. 172 AW88
Priest Pk. Ave., Har. 116 CA61
Priestfield Rd. SE23 183 DY90
Priestlands Pk. Rd., Sid. 185 ET90
Priestley Clo. N16 122 DT59
Ravensdale Rd.
Priestley Gdns., Rom. 126 EV58
Priestley Rd., Mitch. 200 DG96
Priestley Way E17 123 DX55
Priestley Way NW2 119 CU60
Priestly Gdns., Wok. 227 BA120
Priests Ave., Rom. 105 FD54
Priests Bri. SW14 158 CS83
Priests Bri. SW15 158 CS83
Priests Fld., Brwd. 109 GC50
Priests La., Brwd. 108 FY47
Prima Rd. SW9 161 DN80
Primley La., B.Stort. 37 FC06
Primrose Ave., Enf. 82 DR39
Primrose Ave., Horl. 269 DH149
Primrose Ave., Rom. 126 EU59
Primrose Clo. SE6 183 EC92
Primrose Clo., Har. 116 BZ62
Primrose Clo., Hat. 45 CV19
Primrose Clo., Hem.H. 39 BE21
Primrose Clo., Wall. 201 DH101
Primrose Dr., Hert. 32 DV09
Primrose Fld., Harl. 51 ET18
Primrose Gdns. NW3 140 DE65
Primrose Gdns., Ruis. 116 BW64
Primrose Gdns. (Bushey), Wat. 94 CB45
Primrose Glen, Horn. 128 FL56
Primrose Hill EC4 274 E9
Primrose Hill, Brwd. 108 FW48
Primrose Hill, Kings L. 59 BP28
Primrose Hill Ct. NW3 140 DF66
Primrose Hill Rd. NW3 140 DF66
Primrose Hill Studios NW1 140 DG67
Fitzroy Rd.
Primrose La., Croy. 202 DW102
Primrose Ms. NW1 140 DF66
Sharpleshall St.
Primrose Ms. SE3 164 EH80
Primrose Path (Cheshunt), Wal.Cr. 66 DU31
Primrose Rd. E10 123 EB60
Primrose Rd. E18 102 EH54
Primrose Rd., Walt. 214 BW106
Broomfield Rd.
Primrose St. EC2 275 M6
Primrose St. EC2 142 DS71
Primrose Wk., Epsom 217 CT108
Primrose Way, Wem. 137 CK68
Primula St. W12 139 CU72
Prince Albert Rd. NW1 272 C1
Prince Albert Rd. NW1 140 DF68
Prince Albert Rd. NW8 272 C1
Prince Albert Rd. NW8 140 DE69
Prince Albert Sq., Red. 266 DF139
Prince Alberts Wk., Wind. 152 AU81
Prince Arthur Ms. NW3 120 DC63
Perrins La.
Prince Arthur Rd. NW3 120 DC64
Prince Charles Ave. (South Darenth), Dart. 209 FR96
Prince Charles Dr. NW4 119 CW59
Prince Charles Rd. SE3 164 EF82
Prince Charles Way, Wall. 201 DH104
Prince Consort Cotts., Wind. 151 AR82
Prince Consort Dr., Chis. 205 ER95
Prince Consort Rd. SW7 160 DC76
Prince Edward Rd. E9 143 DZ65
Prince Edward St., Berk. 38 AW19
Prince George Ave. N14 81 DJ42
Prince George Duke of Kent Ct., Chis. 185 ER94
Holbrook La.
Prince George Rd. N16 122 DS63
Prince George's Ave. SW20 199 CW96
Prince George's Rd. SW19 200 DD95
Prince Henry Rd. SE7 164 EK80
Prince Imperial Rd. SE18 165 EM81
Prince Imperial Rd., Chis. 185 EP94
Prince John Rd. SE9 184 EL85
Prince of Orange La. SE10 163 EC80
Greenwich High Rd.
Prince of Wales Clo. NW4 119 CV56
Church Ter.
Prince of Wales Dr. SW8 161 DH80
Prince of Wales Dr. SW11 160 DE81
Prince of Wales Footpath, Enf. 83 DX37
St. Stephens Rd.
Prince of Wales Gate SW7 276 B5
Prince of Wales Gate SW7 160 DE75
Prince of Wales Pas. NW1 273 K3
Prince of Wales Rd. E16 144 EJ72
Prince of Wales Rd. NW5 140 DG65
Prince of Wales Rd. SE3 164 EF81
Prince of Wales Rd., Red. 267 DN143
Prince of Wales Rd., Sutt. 200 DD103
Prince of Wales Ter. W4 158 CS78
Prince of Wales Ter. W8 160 DB75
Kensington Rd.
Prince Pk., Hem.H. 40 BG21
Prince Regent Ct. SE16 143 DY74
Rotherhithe St.
Prince Regent La. E13 144 EH69
Prince Regent La. E16 144 EJ71
Prince Regent Rd., Houns. 156 CC83
Prince Rd. SE25 202 DS99
Prince Rupert Rd. SE9 165 EM84
Prince St. SE8 163 DZ79
Prince St., Wat. 76 BW41
Princedale Rd. W11 139 CY74
Princelet St. E1 142 DT71
Prince's Arc. SW1 277 L2
Princes Ave. N3 98 DA53
Princes Ave. N10 121 DH55
Princes Ave. N13 99 DN50
Princes Ave. N22 99 DK53
Princes Ave. NW9 118 CN56
Princes Ave. W3 158 CN76
Princes Ave., Cars. 218 DF108
Princes Ave., Dart. 188 FP88
Princes Ave., Enf. 83 DY36
Princes Ave., Grnf. 136 CB72
Princes Ave., Orp. 205 ES99
Princes Ave., S.Croy. 236 DV115
Princes Ave., Surb. 198 CN102
Princes Ave., Wat. 75 BT43
Princes Ave., Wdf.Grn. 102 EH49
Princes Clo. N4 121 DP60
Princes Clo. NW9 118 CN56
Princes Clo. SW4 161 DJ83
Old Town
Princes Clo., Berk. 38 AU17
Princes Clo., Edg. 96 CN50
Princes Clo., Epp. 71 FC25
Princes Clo., Sid. 186 EX90
Princes Clo., S.Croy. 236 DV115
Princes Clo., Tedd. 177 CD91
Princes Clo., Wind. 151 AM78
Princes Ct. E1 142 DV73
Princes Ct., Hem.H. 40 BH23
Roughdown Rd.
Princes Ct., Wem. 118 CL64
Princes Dr., Har. 117 CE55
Prince's Dr., Lthd. 215 CE112
Princes Gdns. SW7 276 A6
Princes Gdns. SW7 160 DD76
Princes Gdns. W3 138 CN71
Princes Gdns. W5 137 CJ70
Princes Gate SW7 276 A5
Princes Gate SW7 160 DE75
Princes Gate Ct. SW7 276 A5
Princes Gate Ms. SW7 276 A6
Princes Gate Ms. SW7 160 DD76
Princes La. N10 121 DH55
Princes Ms. W2 140 DA73
Hereford Rd.
Princes Par., Pot.B. 64 DC32
High St.
Princes Pk., Rain. 147 FG66
Princes Pk. Ave. NW11 119 CY58
Princes Pk. Ave., Hayes 135 BR73
Princes Pk. Circle, Hayes 135 BR73
Princes Pk. Clo., Hayes 135 BR73
Princes Pk. La., Hayes 135 BR73
Princes Pk. Par., Hayes 135 BR73
Princes Pk. La.
Princes Pl. SW1 277 L2
Princes Pl. W11 139 CY74
Princes Plain, Brom. 204 EL101
Princes Ri. SE13 163 EC82
Princes Riverside Rd. SE16 143 DX74
Princes Rd. N18 100 DW49
Princes Rd. SE20 183 DX93
Princes Rd. SW14 158 CR83
Princes Rd. SW19 180 DA93
Princes Rd. W13 137 CH74
Broomfield Rd.
Princes Rd., Ashf. 174 BM92
Princes Rd., B.End 110 AC60
Princes Rd., Buck.H. 102 EJ47
Princes Rd., Dart. 187 FG86
Princes Rd., Egh. 173 AZ93
Princes Rd., Felt. 175 BT89
Princes Rd., Grav. 191 GJ91
Princes Rd., Ilf. 125 ER56
Princes Rd., Kings.T. 198 CN95
Princes Rd., Red. 266 DF136
Princes Rd., Rich. 178 CM85
Princes Rd. (Kew), Rich. 158 CM81
Princes Rd., Rom. 127 FG57
Princes Rd., Swan. 187 FG93
Princes Rd., Tedd. 177 CD91
Princes Rd., Wey. 213 BP106
Princes Sq. W2 140 DB73
Princes St. EC2 275 K9
Princes St. EC2 142 DR72
Princes St. N17 100 DS51
Queen St.
Princes St. W1 273 J9
Princes St. W1 141 DH72
Princes St., Bexh. 166 EZ84
Princes St., Grav. 191 GH86
Princes St., Rich. 178 CL85
Sheen Rd.
Princes St., Slou. 152 AV75
Princes St., Sutt. 218 DD105
Princes St., Ware 33 DX05
Princes Ter. E13 144 EH67
Princes Vw., Dart. 188 FN88
Princes Way SW19 179 CX87
Princes Way, Brwd. 109 GA46
Princes Way, Buck.H. 102 EJ47
Princes Way, Croy. 219 DM106
Princes Way, Ruis. 116 BY63
Princes Way, W.Wick. 222 EF105
Princes Yd. W11 139 CY74
Princedale Rd.
Princesfield Rd., Wal.Abb. 68 EH33
Princess Ave., Wem. 118 CL61
Princess Ave., Wind. 151 AP83
Princess Ct. SE16 163 DZ76
Princess Cres. N4 121 DP61
Princess Diana Dr., St.Alb. 43 CJ21
Princess Gdns., Wok. 227 BB116
Princess La., Ruis. 115 BS60
Princess Mary's Rd., Add. 212 BJ105
Princess May Rd. N16 122 DS63
Princess Ms. NW3 140 DD65
Belsize Cres.
Princess Par., Orp. 205 EN104
Crofton Rd.
Princess Prec., Horl. 269 DH148
High St.
Princess Rd. NW1 140 DG67
Princess Rd. NW6 140 DA68
Princess Rd., Croy. 202 DQ100
Princess Rd., Wok. 227 BB116
Princess St. SE1 278 G7
Princess St. SE1 161 DP76
Princess Way, Red. 250 DG133
Princesses Wk., Rich. 158 CL80
Kew Rd.
Princethorpe Ho. W2 140 DB71
Princethorpe Rd. SE26 183 DX91
Princeton Ct. SW15 159 CX83
Felsham Rd.
Princeton St. WC1 274 B7
Princeton St. WC1 141 DM71
Pringle Gdns. SW16 181 DJ91
Print Village SE15 162 DT82
Chadwick Rd.
Printer St. EC4 274 E8
Printers Inn Ct. EC4 274 D8
Printers Way, Harl. 36 EU10
Printing Ho. Yd. E2 275 N3
Printinghouse La., Hayes 155 BS75
Priolo Rd. SE7 164 EJ78
Prior Ave., Sutt. 218 DE108
Prior Bolton St. N1 141 DP65
Prior Chase, Grays 170 FZ77
Prior Gro., Chesh. 54 AQ30
Prior Rd., Ilf. 125 EN62
Prior St. SE10 163 EC80
Prioress Rd. SE27 181 DP90
Prioress St. SE1 279 L7
Prioress St. SE1 162 DR76
Priors, The, Ash. 231 CK119
Priors Clo., Hert. 32 DV12
Priors Clo., Slou. 152 AU76
Priors Ct., Wok. 226 AU118
Priors Cft. E17 101 DY54
Priors Cft., Wok. 227 BA120
Priors Fld., Nthlt. 136 BY65
Arnold Rd.
Priors Gdns., Ruis. 116 BW64
Priors Mead, Enf. 82 DS39
Priors Mead, Lthd. 246 CC125
Priors Pk., Horn. 128 FJ62
Priors Rd., Wind. 151 AK83
Priors Wd. Rd., Hert. 32 DW12
Priorsford Ave., Orp. 206 EU98
Priory, The SE3 164 EF84
Priory, The, Gdse. 252 DV131
Priory Ave. E4 101 DZ48
Priory Ave. E17 123 EA57
Priory Ave. N8 121 DK56
Priory Ave. W4 158 CS77
Priory Ave., Harl. 36 EW10
Priory Ave., Orp. 205 ER100
Priory Ave., Sutt. 217 CX105
Priory Ave., Uxb. 114 BJ56
Priory Ave., Wem. 117 CF63
Priory Clo. E4 101 DZ48
Priory Clo. E18 102 EG53
Priory Clo. N3 97 CZ53
Church Cres.
Priory Clo. N14 81 DH43
Priory Clo. N20 97 CZ45
Priory Clo. SW19 200 DB95
High Path
Priory Clo., Beck. 203 DY97
Priory Clo., Brwd. 108 FU43
Priory Clo., Brox. 49 DY24
High Rd. Turnford
Priory Clo., Chis. 205 EM95
Priory Clo., Dart. 188 FJ85
Priory Clo., Dor. 263 CG138
Priory Clo., Hmptn. 196 BZ95
Priory Gdns.
Priory Clo., Hayes 135 BV73
Priory Clo., Hodd. 49 EA18
Priory Clo., Horl. 268 DF147
Priory Clo., Ruis. 115 BT60
Priory Clo., Stan. 95 CF48
Priory Clo., Sun. 175 BU94
Priory Clo. (Denham), Uxb. 114 BG62
Priory Clo. (Harefield), Uxb. 114 BH56
Priory Clo., Walt. 195 BU104
Priory Clo. (Sudbury), Wem. 117 CF63
Priory Clo., Wok. 211 BD113
Priory Ct. E17 101 DZ54
Priory Ct. EC4 141 DP72
Pilgrim St.
Priory Ct. SW8 161 DK81
Priory Ct., Berk. 38 AW19
Priory Ct., Guil. 258 AW137
Portsmouth Rd.
Priory Ct., Harl. 52 EV18
Southern Way
Priory Ct. (Bushey), Wat. 94 CC46
Sparrows Herne
Priory Ct. Est. E17 101 DZ54
Priory Cres. SE19 182 DQ94
Priory Cres., Sutt. 217 CX105
Priory Cres., Wem. 117 CG62
Priory Dr. SE2 166 EX78
Priory Dr., Reig. 266 DA136
Priory Dr., Stan. 95 CF48
Priory Fld. Dr., Edg. 96 CP49
Priory Flds. (Farningham), Dart. 208 FM103
Priory Gdns. N6 121 DH58
Priory Gdns. SE25 202 DT98
Priory Gdns. SW13 159 CT83
Priory Gdns. W4 158 CS77
Priory Gdns. W5 138 CL69
Hanger La.
Priory Gdns., Ashf. 175 BR92
Priory Gdns., Berk. 38 AW19
Priory Gdns., Dart. 188 FK85
Priory Gdns., Hmptn. 176 BZ94
Priory Gdns., Uxb. 114 BJ56
Priory Gdns., Wem. 117 CG63
Priory Gate, Wal.Cr. 67 DZ27
Priory Grn., Stai. 174 BH92
Priory Grn. Est. N1 141 DM68
Priory Gro. SW8 161 DL81
Priory Gro., Rom. 106 FL48
Priory Hill, Dart. 188 FK85
Priory Hill, Wem. 117 CG63
Priory La. SW15 178 CS86
Priory La. (Farningham), Dart. 208 FM102
Priory La., Rich. 158 CN80
Forest Rd.
Priory La., W.Mol. 196 CA98
Priory Ms. SW8 161 DL81
Priory Ms., Stai. 174 BH92
Chestnut Manor Clo.
Priory Pk. SE3 164 EF83
Priory Pk. Rd. NW6 139 CZ67
Priory Pk. Rd., Wem. 117 CG63
Priory Path, Rom. 106 FL48
Priory Pl., Dart. 188 FK86
Priory Pl., Walt. 195 BU104
Priory Rd. E6 144 EK67
Priory Rd. N8 121 DJ56
Priory Rd. NW6 140 DB67
Priory Rd. SW19 180 DD94
Priory Rd. W4 158 CR76
Priory Rd., Bark. 145 ER66
Priory Rd., Chess. 198 CL104
Priory Rd., Croy. 201 DN101
Priory Rd., Dart. 188 FK86
Priory Rd., Ger.Cr. 112 AX55
Priory Rd., Hmptn. 176 BZ94
Priory Rd., Houns. 176 CC85
Priory Rd., Loug. 84 EL42
Priory Rd., Reig. 266 DA136
Priory Rd., Rich. 158 CN80
Priory Rd., Rom. 106 FL48
Priory Rd., Slou. 130 AJ71
Priory Rd., Sutt. 217 CX105
Priory St. E3 143 EB69
St. Leonards St.
Priory St., Hert. 32 DR09
Priory St., Ware 32 DW06
Priory Ter. NW6 140 DB67
Priory Ter., Sun. 175 BU94
Priory Clo.
Priory Vw. (Bushey), Wat. 95 CE45
Priory Wk. SW10 160 DC78
Priory Wk., St.Alb. 43 CE23
Priory Way, Ger.Cr. 112 AX55
Priory Way, Har. 116 CB56
Priory Way, Slou. 152 AV80
Priory Way, Sthl. 156 BX76
Western Rd.
Priory Way, West Dr. 154 BL79
Pritchard's Rd. E2 142 DU68
Priter Rd. SE16 162 DU76
Priter Way SE16 162 DU76
Dockley Rd.
Private Rd., Enf. 82 DR43
Probert Rd. SW2 181 DN85
Probyn Rd. SW2 181 DP89
Procter St. WC1 274 B7
Procter St. WC1 141 DM71
Proctor Clo., Mitch. 200 DG95
Proctor Gdns., Lthd. 246 CB125
Proctors Clo., Felt. 175 BU88
Profumo Rd., Walt. 214 BX106
Progress Business Pk., The, Croy. 201 DM103
Progress Way N22 99 DN53
Progress Way, Croy. 201 DM103
Progress Way, Enf. 82 DU43
Promenade, The W4 158 CS81
Promenade App. Rd. W4 158 CS80
Promenade de Verdun, Pur. 219 DK111
Prospect Business Pk., Loug. 85 ER42
Langston Rd.
Prospect Clo. SE26 182 DV91
Prospect Clo., Belv. 166 FA77
Prospect Clo., Houns. 156 BZ81
Prospect Clo., Ruis. 116 BX59
Prospect Cotts. SW18 160 DA84
Point Pleasant

Queensborough Studios W2 140 DC73
Porchester Ter.
Queensborough Ter. W2 140 DB73
Queensbridge Pk., Islw. 177 CE85
Queensbridge Rd. E2 142 DT67
Queensbridge Rd. E8 142 DT66
Queensbury Circle Par., Har. 118 CL55
Streatfield Rd.
Queensbury Pl., Rich. 177 CK85
Friars La.
Queensbury Rd. NW9 118 CR59
Queensbury Rd., Wem. 138 CM68
Queensbury Sta. Par., Edg. 118 CM55
Queensbury St. N1 142 DQ66
Queenscourt, Wem. 118 CL63
Queenscroft Rd. SE9 184 EK86
Queensdale Cres. W11 139 CX74
Queensdale Pl. W11 139 CY74
Queensdale Rd. W11 139 CX74
Queensdale Wk. W11 139 CY74
Queensdown Rd. E5 122 DV63
Queensferry Wk. N17 122 DV56
Jarrow Rd.
Queensgate, Cob. 214 BX112
Queensgate Gdns., Chis. 205 ER95
Queensgate Pl. NW6 140 DA66
Queensland Ave. N18 100 DQ51
Queensland Ave. SW19 200 DB95
Queensland Pl. N7 121 DN63
Queensland Rd.
Queensland Rd. N7 121 DN63
Queensmead NW8 140 DD67
Queensmead, Lthd. 214 CC111
Queensmead, Slou. 152 AV81
Queensmead Ave., Epsom 217 CV110
Queensmead Rd., Brom. 204 EF96
Queensmere, Slou. 152 AT75
High St.
Queensmere Clo. SW19 179 CX89
Queensmere Rd. SW19 179 CX89
Queensmere Rd., Slou. 152 AU75
Wellington St.
Queensmill Rd. SW6 159 CX80
Queensthorpe Rd. SE26 183 DX91
Queenstown Gdns., Rain. 147 FF69
Queenstown Ms. SW8 161 DH82
Queenstown Rd.
Queenstown Rd. SW8 161 DH79
Queensville Rd. SW12 181 DK87
Queensway W2 140 DB72
Queensway, Croy. 219 DM107
Queensway, Enf. 82 DV42
Queensway, Hat. 45 CU17
Queensway, Hem.H. 40 BK19
Queensway, Orp. 205 EQ99
Queensway, Red. 250 DF133
Queensway, Sun. 195 BV96
Queensway, W.Wick. 204 EE104
Queensway, The, Ger.Cr. 112 AX56
Queensway N., Walt. 214 BW105
Robinsway
Queensway S., Walt. 214 BW106
Trenchard Clo.
Queenswood Ave. E17 101 EC53
Queenswood Ave., Brwd. 109 GD42
Queenswood Ave., Hmptn. 176 CB93
Queenswood Ave., Houns. 156 BZ82
Queenswood Ave., Th.Hth. 201 DN99
Queenswood Ave., Wall. 219 DK105
Queenswood Cres., Wat. 59 BU33
Queenswood Gdns. E11 124 EH60
Queenswood Pk. N3 97 CY54
Queenswood Rd. SE23 183 DX90
Queenswood Rd., Sid. 185 ET85
Quemerford Rd. N7 121 DM64
Quendell Wk., Hem.H. 40 BL20
Quendon Dr., Wal.Abb. 67 ED33
Quennel Way, Brwd. 109 GC45
Quennell Clo., Ash. 232 CL119
Parkers La.
Quentin Pl. SE13 164 EE83
Quentin Rd. SE13 164 EE83
Quentin Way, Vir.W. 192 AV98
Quernmore Clo., Brom. 184 EG93
Quernmore Rd. N4 121 DN58
Quernmore Rd., Brom. 184 EG93
Querrin St. SW6 160 DC82
Quex Ms. NW6 140 DA67
Quex Rd.
Quex Rd. NW6 140 DA67
Quick Pl. N1 141 DP67
Quick Rd. W4 158 CS78
Quick St. N1 274 G1
Quick St. N1 141 DP68
Quick St. Ms. N1 141 DP68
Quick St.
Quickbeams, Welw.G.C. 30 DA06
Quickberry Pl., Amer. 55 AQ39
Quickley La., Rick. 73 BB44
Quickley Ri., Rick. 73 BC44
Quickmoor La., Kings L. 58 BH33
Quicks Rd. SW19 180 DB94
Quickswood NW3 140 DE66
King Henry's Rd.
Quickwood Clo., Rick. 74 BG44
Quiet Clo., Add. 212 BG105
Quiet Nook, Kes. 204 EK104
Croydon Rd.
Quill Hall La., Amer. 55 AS37
Quill La. SW15 159 CX84
Quill St. N4 121 DN62
Quill St. W5 138 CL69
Quillot, The, Walt. 213 BT106
Quilp St. SE1 279 H4
Quilter Gdns., Orp. 206 EW102
Tintagel Rd.
Quilter Rd., Orp. 206 EW102
Quilter St. E2 142 DU69
Quilter St. SE18 165 ET78
Quinbrookes, Slou. 132 AW72
Quince Tree Clo., S.Ock. 149 FW70
Quinces Ct., Hem.H. 40 BG18
Quincy Rd., Egh. 173 BA92
Quinta Dr., Barn. 79 CV43
Quintin Ave. SW20 199 CZ95
Quintin Clo., Pnr. 115 BV57
Eastcote High Rd.
Quinton Clo., Beck. 203 EC97
Quinton Clo., Houns. 155 BV80
Quinton Clo., Wall. 219 DH105
Quinton Rd., T.Ditt. 197 CG102
Quinton St. SW18 180 DC89
Quintrell Clo., Wok. 226 AV117
Quixley St. E14 143 ED73
Quorn Rd. SE22 162 DS84

R

Raans Rd., Amer. 72 AT38
Rabbit La., Walt. 213 BU108
Rabbit Row W8 140 DA74
Kensington Mall
Rabbits Rd. E12 124 EL63
Rabbits Rd. (South Darenth), Dart. 209 FR96
Rabies Heath Rd., Gdse. 252 DU134
Rabies Heath Rd., Red. 252 DS133
Rabournmead Dr., Nthlt. 116 BY64
Raby Rd., N.Mal. 198 CR98
Raby St. E14 143 DY72
Salmon La.
Raccoon Way, Houns. 156 BW82
Racecourse Way, Gat. 268 DF151
Rachel Pt. E5 122 DU63
Muir Rd.
Rachels Way, Chesh. 54 AR34
Cresswell Rd.
Rackham Ms. SW16 181 DJ93
Westcote Rd.
Racks Ct., Guil. 258 AX136
Racton Rd. SW6 160 DA79
Rad La., Dor. 261 BS142
Horsham Rd.
Rad La., Guil. 261 BR142
Radbourne Ave. W5 157 CJ77
Radbourne Clo. E5 123 DX63
Overbury St.
Radbourne Cres. E17 101 ED54
Radbourne Rd. SW12 181 DJ87
Radburn Clo., Harl. 52 EU19
Radcliffe Ave. NW10 139 CU68
Radcliffe Ave., Enf. 82 DQ39
Radcliffe Gdns., Cars. 218 DE108
Radcliffe Ms., Hmptn. 176 CC92
Taylor Clo.
Radcliffe Path SW8 161 DJ82
St. Rule St.
Radcliffe Rd. N21 99 DP46
Radcliffe Rd., Croy. 202 DT103
Radcliffe Rd., Har. 95 CG54
Radcliffe Sq. SW15 179 CX86
Radcliffe Way, Nthlt. 136 BX69
Radcot Ave., Slou. 153 BB76
Radcot Pt. SE23 183 DX90
Radcot St. SE11 161 DN78
Methley St.
Raddington Rd. W10 139 CY71
Radfield Way, Sid. 185 ER87
Radford Rd. SE13 183 EC85
Radford Way, Bark. 145 ET69
Radipole Rd. SW6 159 CZ81
Radland Rd. E16 144 EF72
Radlet Ave. SE26 182 DV90
Radlett Clo. E7 144 EF65
Radlett La., Rad. 77 CK35
Radlett Pk. Rd., Rad. 61 CG34
Radlett Pl. NW8 140 DE67
Radlett Rd., St.Alb. 61 CE28
Radlett Rd., Wat. 76 BW41
Radlett Rd. (Aldenham), Wat. 76 CB39
Radley Ave., Ilf. 125 ET63
Radley Clo., Felt. 175 BT88
Radley Ct. SE16 163 DX75
Thame Rd.
Radley Gdns., Har. 118 CL56
Radley Ms. W8 160 DA76
Radley Rd. N17 100 DS54
Radley's La. E18 102 EG54
Radleys Mead, Dag. 147 FB65
Radlix Rd. E10 123 EA60
Radnor Ave., Har. 117 CE57
Radnor Ave., Well. 186 EV85
Radnor Clo., Chis. 185 ES93
Homewood Cres.
Radnor Clo., Mitch. 201 DL98
Radnor Cres. SE18 166 EU80
Radnor Cres., Ilf. 125 EM57
Radnor Gdns., Enf. 82 DS39
Radnor Gdns., Twick. 177 CF89
Radnor Gro., Uxb. 134 BN68
Charnwood Rd.
Radnor La., Dor. 261 BU144
Radnor Ms. W2 272 A9
Radnor Pl. W2 272 B9
Radnor Pl. W2 140 DE72
Radnor Rd. NW6 139 CY67
Radnor Rd. SE15 162 DU80
Radnor Rd., Har. 117 CD57
Radnor Rd., Twick. 177 CF88
Radnor Rd., Wey. 194 BN104
Radnor St. EC1 275 J3
Radnor St. EC1 142 DQ69
Radnor Ter. W14 159 CZ77
Radnor Wk. E14 163 EA77
Copeland Dr.
Radnor Wk. SW3 160 DE78
Radnor Wk., Croy. 203 DY100
Radnor Way NW10 138 CP70
Radnor Way, Slou. 152 AY77
Radolphs, Tad. 233 CX122
Heathcote
Radstock Ave., Har. 117 CG55
Radstock St. SW11 160 DE80
Radstock Way, Red. 251 DK128
Radstone Ct., Wok. 227 AZ118
Radwell Path, Borwd. 78 CL39
Cromwell Rd.
Raebarn Gdns., Barn. 79 CV43
Raeburn Ave., Dart. 187 FH85
Raeburn Ave., Surb. 198 CP102
Raeburn Clo. NW11 120 DC58
Raeburn Clo., Kings.T. 177 CK94
Raeburn Rd., Edg. 96 CN54
Raeburn Rd., Hayes 135 BR68
Raeburn Rd., Sid. 185 ES86
Raeburn St. SW2 161 DL84
Raeside Clo., Beac. 89 AQ50
Rafford Way, Brom. 204 EH96
Raft Rd. SW18 160 DA84
North Pas.
Rag Hill Clo., West. 238 EL121
Rag Hill Rd., West. 238 EK121
Ragged Hall La., St.Alb. 42 BX24
Raggleswood, Chis. 205 EN95
Raglan Ave., Wal.Cr. 67 DX34
Raglan Clo., Houns. 176 BY85
Vickers Way
Raglan Clo., Reig. 250 DC132
Raglan Ct. SE12 184 EG85
Raglan Ct., S.Croy. 219 DP106
Raglan Ct., Wem. 118 CM63
Raglan Gdns., Wat. 93 BV46
Raglan Rd. E17 123 EC57
Raglan Rd. SE18 165 EQ78
Raglan Rd., Belv. 166 EZ78
Raglan Rd., Brom. 204 EJ98
Raglan Rd., Enf. 100 DS45
Raglan Rd., Reig. 250 DB131
Raglan Rd., Wok. 226 AS118
Raglan St. NW5 141 DH65
Raglan Ter., Har. 116 CB63
Raglan Way, Nthlt. 136 CC65
Ragley Clo. W3 158 CQ75
Church Rd.
Rags La. (Cheshunt), Wal.Cr. 66 DS28
Ragstone Rd., Slou. 151 AR76
Rahn Rd., Epp. 70 EU31
Raider Clo., Rom. 104 FA53
Raikes Hollow, Dor. 261 BV142
Raikes La., Dor. 261 BV143
Railey Ms. NW5 121 DJ64
Railpit La., Warl. 238 EE115
Railshead Rd., Islw. 157 CH84
Railton Rd. SE24 161 DN84
Railway App. N4 121 DN58
Wightman Rd.
Railway App. SE1 279 L3
Railway App. SE1 142 DR74
Railway App., Har. 117 CF56
Railway App., Hert. 32 DQ09
Railway App., Twick. 177 CG87
Railway App., Wall. 219 DH107
Railway Ave. SE16 162 DW75
Railway Cotts., Hat. 44 CS19
Ellenbrook La.
Railway Cotts., Wat. 75 BV39
Railway Ms. E3 143 EA69
Wellington Way
Railway Ms. W10 139 CY72
Ladbroke Gro.
Railway Pas., Tedd. 177 CG93
Victoria Rd.
Railway Pl. SW19 179 CZ93
Hartfield Rd.
Railway Pl., Belv. 166 FA76
Railway Pl., Hert. 32 DS09
Railway Ri. SE22 162 DS84
Grove Vale
Railway Rd., Tedd. 177 CF91
Railway Rd., Wal.Cr. 67 DY33
Railway Side SW13 158 CS83
Railway Sq., Brwd. 108 FW48
Fairfield Rd.
Railway St. N1 274 A1
Railway St. N1 141 DL68
Railway St., Grav. 190 GA85
Railway St., Hert. 32 DR09
Railway St., Rom. 126 EW60
Railway Ter. SE13 183 EB85
Ladywell Rd.
Railway Ter., Felt. 175 BU88
Railway Ter., Hem.H. 58 BN27
Railway Ter., Slou. 132 AT74
Railway Ter., Stai. 173 BD92
Railway Ter., West. 255 ER125
Rainborough Clo. NW10 138 CQ65
Rainbow Ave. E14 163 EB78
Rainbow Ct., Wat. 76 BW44
Oxhey Rd.
Rainbow Ct., Wok. 226 AS116
Langmans Way
Rainbow Ind. Est., West Dr. 134 BK73
Rainbow Quay SE16 163 DY76
Rope St.
Rainbow Rd., Grays 169 FW77
Rainbow Rd., Harl. 37 FE12
Rainbow St. SE5 162 DS80
Raine St. E1 142 DV74
Rainer Clo. (Cheshunt), Wal.Cr. 67 DX29
Rainham Clo. SE9 185 ER86
Rainham Clo. SW11 180 DE86
Rainham Rd. NW10 139 CW69
Rainham Rd., Rain. 147 FG69
Rainham Rd. N., Dag. 126 FA61
Rainham Rd. S., Dag. 127 FB63
Rainhill Way E3 143 EA69
Rainsborough Ave. SE8 163 DY77
Rainsford Clo., Stan. 95 CJ50
Rainsford Rd. NW10 138 CP68
Rainsford St. W2 272 B8
Rainsford Way, Horn. 127 FG60
Rainton Rd. SE7 164 EG78
Rainville Rd. W6 159 CW79
Raisins Hill, Pnr. 116 BW55
Raith Ave. N14 99 DK48
Raleana Rd. E14 143 EC74
Raleigh Ave., Hayes 135 BV71
Raleigh Ave., Wall. 219 DK105
Raleigh Clo. NW4 119 CW57
Raleigh Clo., Erith 167 FF79
Raleigh Clo., Pnr. 116 BX59
Raleigh Clo., Ruis. 115 BT61
Raleigh Clo., Slou. 131 AN74
Raleigh Ct. SE16 143 DX74
Rotherhithe St.
Raleigh Ct., Stai. 174 BG91
Raleigh Ct., Wall. 219 DH107
Raleigh Dr. N20 98 DE48
Raleigh Dr., Esher 215 CD106
Raleigh Dr., Horl. 269 DN148
Raleigh Dr., Surb. 198 CQ102
Raleigh Gdns. SW2 181 DM86
Brixton Hill
Raleigh Gdns., Mitch. 200 DF97
Raleigh Ms. N1 141 DP67
Queen's Head St.
Raleigh Ms., Orp. 223 ET106
Osgood Ave.
Raleigh Rd. N8 121 DN56
Raleigh Rd. SE20 183 DX94
Raleigh Rd., Enf. 82 DR42
Raleigh Rd., Felt. 175 BT90
Raleigh Rd., Rich. 158 CM83
Raleigh Rd., Sthl. 156 BY78
Raleigh St. N1 141 DP67
Raleigh Way N14 99 DK46
Raleigh Way, Felt. 176 BW91
Ralliwood Rd., Ash. 232 CN119
Ralph Ct. W2 140 DB72
Queensway
Ralph Perring Ct., Beck. 203 EA98
Ralston St. SW3 160 DF78
Tedworth Sq.
Ralston Way, Wat. 94 BX47
Ram Gorse, Harl. 35 EP13
Ram Pas., Kings.T. 197 CK96
High St.
Ram Pl. E9 142 DW65
Chatham Pl.
Ram St. SW18 180 DB85
Rama Clo. SW16 181 DL94
Rama Ct., Har. 117 CE61
Ramac Ind. Est. SE7 164 EG77
Ramac Way SE7 164 EH78
Rambler Clo. SW16 181 DJ91
Rambler Clo., Maid. 130 AH72
Rambler La., Slou. 152 AW76
Ramblers Way, Welw.G.C. 30 DC10
Rambling Way, Berk. 39 BC16
Rame Clo. SW17 180 DG92
Ramilles Clo. SW2 181 DL86
Ramillies Pl. W1 273 K9
Ramillies Pl. W1 141 DJ72
Ramillies Rd. NW7 96 CS47
Ramillies Rd. W4 158 CR77
Ramillies Rd., Sid. 186 EV86
Ramillies St. W1 273 K9
Ramin Ct., Guil. 242 AW131
Rowan Clo.
Ramney Dr., Enf. 83 DY36
Ramornie Clo., Walt. 214 BZ106
Rampart St. E1 142 DV72
Commercial Rd.
Ramparts, The, St.Alb. 42 CB21
Rampayne St. SW1 277 M10
Rampayne St. SW1 161 DK78
Rampton Clo. E4 101 EA48
Rams Gro., Rom. 126 EY56
Ramsay Clo., Brox. 49 DY21
Ramsay Gdns., Rom. 106 FJ53
Ramsay Pl., Har. 117 CE60
Ramsay Rd. E7 124 EE63
Ramsay Rd. W3 158 CQ76
Ramsbury Rd., St.Alb. 43 CE21
Ramscote La., Chesh. 54 AN25
Ramscroft Clo. N9 100 DS45
Ramsdale Rd. SW17 180 DG92
Ramsden Clo., Orp. 206 EW102
Ramsden Dr., Rom. 104 FA52
Ramsden Rd. N11 98 DF50
Ramsden Rd. SW12 180 DG86
Ramsden Rd., Erith 167 FD80
Ramsden Rd., Orp. 206 EV101
Ramsey Clo. NW9 119 CT58
West Hendon Bdy.
Ramsey Clo., Grnf. 117 CD64
Ramsey Clo., Hat. 64 DD27
Ramsey Clo., Horl. 268 DF148
Ramsey Clo., St.Alb. 43 CG22
Ramsey Ct., Slou. 131 AK70
Lower Britwell Rd.
Ramsey Ho., Wem. 138 CL65
Ramsey Lo. Ct., St.Alb. 43 CE19
Hillside Rd.
Ramsey Ms. SW3 160 DE79
King's Rd.
Ramsey Rd., Th.Hth. 201 DM100
Ramsey St. E2 142 DU70
Ramsey Wk. N1 142 DR65
Clephane Rd.
Ramsey Way N14 99 DJ45
Ramsgate St. E8 142 DT65
Dalston La.
Ramsgill App., Ilf. 125 ET56
Ramsgill Dr., Ilf. 125 ET57
Ramson Ri., Hem.H. 39 BE21
Ramulis Dr., Hayes 136 BX70
Ramus Wd. Ave., Orp. 223 ES106
Rancliffe Gdns. SE9 164 EL84
Rancliffe Rd. E6 144 EL68
Randal Cres., Reig. 266 DA136
Randall Ave. NW2 118 CS61
Randall Clo. SW11 160 DE81
Randall Clo., Erith 167 FC79
Randall Clo., Slou. 153 AZ78
Randall Dr., Horn. 128 FJ63
Randall Pl. SE10 163 EC80
Randall Rd. SE11 278 B9
Randall Rd. SE11 161 DM78
Randall Row SE11 278 B9
Randalls Cres., Lthd. 231 CG120
Randalls Dr., Brwd. 109 GE44
Randalls Pk. Ave., Lthd. 231 CG120
Randalls Pk. Dr., Lthd. 231 CG121
Randalls Rd.
Randalls Ride, Hem.H. 40 BL18
Randalls Rd., Lthd. 231 CE119
Randalls Way, Lthd. 231 CG121
Randell's Rd. N1 141 DL67
Randle Rd., Rich. 177 CJ91
Randles La., Sev. 240 EX115
Randlesdown Rd. SE6 183 EA91
Randolph App. E16 144 EJ72
Baxter Rd.
Randolph Ave. W9 140 DB68
Randolph Clo., Bexh. 167 FC83
Randolph Clo., Cob. 230 CA115
Randolph Clo., Kings.T. 178 CQ92
Randolph Clo., Wok. 226 AS117
Creston Ave.
Randolph Cres. W9 140 DC70
Randolph Gdns. NW6 140 DB68
Randolph Gro., Rom. 126 EW57
Donald Dr.
Randolph Ho., Croy. 202 DQ102
Randolph Ms. W9 140 DC70
Randolph Rd. E17 123 EB57
Randolph Rd. W9 140 DC70
Randolph Rd., Epsom 217 CT114
Randolph Rd., Slou. 152 AY77
Randolph Rd., Sthl. 156 BZ75
Randolph St. NW1 141 DJ66
Randolph's La., West. 255 EP126
Randon Clo., Har. 94 CB54
Ranelagh Ave. SW6 159 CZ83
Ranelagh Ave. SW13 159 CU82
Ranelagh Bri. W2 140 DB71
Gloucester Ter.
Ranelagh Clo., Edg. 96 CN49
Ranelagh Dr., Edg. 96 CN49
Ranelagh Dr., Twick. 157 CH84
Ranelagh Gdns. E11 124 EJ57
Ranelagh Gdns. SW6 159 CZ83
Ranelagh Gdns. W4 158 CQ80
Grove Pk. Gdns.
Ranelagh Gdns. W6 159 CT76
Ranelagh Gdns., Grav. 191 GF87
Ranelagh Gdns., Ilf. 125 EM60
Ranelagh Gro. SW1 276 G10
Ranelagh Gro. SW1 160 DG78
Ranelagh Ms. W5 157 CK75
Ranelagh Rd.
Ranelagh Pl., N.Mal. 198 CS99
Rodney Rd.
Ranelagh Rd. E6 145 EN67
Ranelagh Rd. E11 124 EE63
Ranelagh Rd. E15 144 EE67
Ranelagh Rd. N17 122 DS55
Ranelagh Rd. N22 99 DM53
Ranelagh Rd. NW10 139 CT68
Ranelagh Rd. SW1 161 DJ78
Lupus St.
Ranelagh Rd. W5 157 CK75
Ranelagh Rd., Hem.H. 41 BP20
Ranelagh Rd., Red. 250 DE134
Ranelagh Rd., Sthl. 136 BX74
Ranelagh Rd., Wem. 137 CK65
Ranfurly Rd., Sutt. 200 DA103
Range Rd., Grav. 191 GL87
Range Way, Shep. 194 BN101
Rangefield Rd., Brom. 184 EE92
Rangemoor Rd. N15 122 DT57
Ranger Wk., Add. 212 BH106
Monks Cres.
Rangers Rd. E4 102 EE45
Rangers Rd., Loug. 102 EG45
Rangers Sq. SE10 163 ED81
Rangeworth Pl., Sid. 185 ET90
Priestlands Pk. Rd.
Rangoon St. EC3 142 DT72
Northumberland All.
Rank Ho., Harl. 51 EQ15
Rankin Clo. NW9 118 CS55
Ranleigh Gdns., Bexh. 166 EZ80
Ranmere St. SW12 181 DH88
Ormeley Rd.
Ranmoor Clo., Har. 117 CD56
Ranmoor Gdns., Har. 117 CD56
Ranmore Ave., Croy. 202 DT104
Ranmore Clo., Red. 250 DG131
Ranmore Common, Dor. 246 CA133
Ranmore Common Rd., Dor. 245 BU134
Ranmore Common Rd., Lthd. 245 BU134
Ranmore Path, Orp. 206 EU98
Ranmore Rd., Dor. 246 CC134
Ranmore Rd., Sutt. 217 CX109
Rannoch Clo., Edg. 96 CP47
Rannoch Rd. W6 159 CW79
Rannoch Wk., Hem.H. 40 BK16
Rannock Ave. NW9 118 CR59
Ranskill Rd., Borwd. 78 CN39
Ransom Clo., Wat. 94 BW45
Ransom Rd. SE7 164 EJ78
Harvey Gdns.
Ransom Wk. SE7 164 EJ78
Woolwich Rd.
Ranston Clo., Uxb. 113 BF58
Nightingale Way
Ranston St. NW1 272 B6
Rant Meadow, Hem.H. 40 BN22
Ranulf Rd. NW2 119 CZ63
Ranwell Clo. E3 143 DZ67
Beale Rd.
Ranwell St. E3 143 DZ67
Ranworth Ave., Hodd. 33 EB13
Ranworth Clo., Erith 167 FE82
Ranworth Clo., Hem.H. 40 BK22
Panxworth Rd.
Ranworth Rd. N9 100 DW47
Ranyard Clo., Chess. 198 CM104
Raphael Ave., Rom. 105 FF54
Raphael Ave., Til. 171 GG80
Raphael Clo., Rad. 62 CL32
Raphael Dr., Wat. 76 BW40
Raphael Rd., Grav. 191 GK87
Raphael St. SW7 276 D5
Raphael St. SW7 160 DF75
Rapier Clo., Purf. 168 FM77
Rasehill Clo., Rick. 74 BJ43
Rashleigh St. SW8 161 DH82
Peardon St.
Rashleigh Way (Horton Kirby), Dart. 208 FQ98
Rasper Rd. N20 98 DC47
Rastell Ave. SW2 181 DK89
Ratcliff Rd. E7 124 EJ64
Ratcliffe Clo. SE12 184 EG87
Ratcliffe Clo., Uxb. 134 BK69
Ratcliffe Cross St. E1 143 DX72
Ratcliffe La. E14 143 DY72
Ratcliffe Orchard E1 143 DX73
Rathbone Mkt. E16 144 EF71
Barking Rd.
Rathbone Pl. W1 273 M7
Rathbone Pl. W1 141 DK71
Rathbone Pt. E5 122 DU63
Nolan Way
Rathbone St. E16 144 EF71
Rathbone St. W1 273 L7
Rathbone St. W1 141 DJ71
Rathcoole Ave. N8 121 DM57
Rathcoole Gdns. N8 121 DM57
Rathfern Rd. SE6 183 DZ88
Rathgar Ave. W13 137 CH74
Rathgar Clo. N3 97 CZ54
Rathgar Clo., Red. 266 DG139
Rathgar Rd. SW9 161 DP83
Coldharbour La.
Rathlin, Hem.H. 41 BP22
Rathlin Wk. N1 142 DQ65
Clephane Rd.
Rathmell Dr. SW4 181 DK86
Rathmore Rd. SE7 164 EH78
Rathmore Rd., Grav. 191 GH87
Rathwell Path, Borwd. 78 CL39
Cromwell Rd.
Rats La., Loug. 84 EH38
Rattray Rd. SW2 161 DN84
Ratty's La., Hodd. 49 ED17
Raul Rd. SE15 162 DU81

Ravel Gdns., S.Ock. 148 FQ72
Ravel Rd., S.Ock. 148 FQ72
Raveley St. NW5 121 DJ63
Raven Clo. NW9 96 CS54
Eagle Dr.
Raven Clo., Rick. 92 BK45
Raven Ct. E5 122 DU62
Stellman Clo.
Raven Ct., Hat. 45 CU19
Raven Rd. E18 102 EJ54
Raven Row E1 142 DV71
Ravencroft, Grays 171 GH75
Alexandra Clo.
Ravendale Rd., Sun. 195 BT96
Ravenet St. SW11 161 DH81
Strasburg Rd.
Ravenfield, Egh. 172 AW93
Ravenfield Rd. SW17 180 DF90
Ravenfield Rd., Welw.G.C. 29 CZ09
Ravenhill Rd. E13 144 EJ68
Ravenna Rd. SW15 179 CX85
Ravenor Pk. Rd., Grnf. 136 CB69
Ravens Clo., Brom. 204 EF96
Ravens Clo., Enf. 82 DS40
Ravens Clo., Red. 250 DF133
Ravens La., Berk. 38 AX19
Ravens Ms. SE12 184 EG85
Ravens Way
Ravens Way SE12 184 EG85
Ravens Wf., Berk. 38 AX19
Ravensbourne Ave., Brom. 183 ED94
Ravensbourne Ave., Stai. 174 BL88
Ravensbourne Cres., Rom. 128 FM55
Ravensbourne Gdns. W13 137 CH71
Ravensbourne Gdns., Ilf. 103 EN53
Ravensbourne Pk. SE6 183 EA87
Ravensbourne Pk. Cres. SE6 183 DZ87
Ravensbourne Pl. SE13 163 EB82
Ravensbourne Rd. SE6 183 DZ88
Ravensbourne Rd., Brom. 204 EG97
Ravensbourne Rd., Dart. 167 FG83
Ravensbourne Rd., Twick. 177 CJ86
Ravensbury Ave., Mord. 200 DC99
Ravensbury Gro., Mitch. 200 DD98
Ravensbury La., Mitch. 200 DD98
Ravensbury Path, Mitch. 200 DD98
Ravensbury Rd. SW18 180 DA89
Ravensbury Rd., Orp. 205 ET97
Ravensbury Ter. SW18 180 DB88
Ravenscar Rd., Brom. 184 EE91
Ravenscar Rd., Surb. 198 CM103
Ravenscourt, Sun. 195 BT95
Ravenscourt Ave. W6 159 CU77
Ravenscourt Clo., Horn. 128 FL62
Ravenscourt Dr.
Ravenscourt Clo., Ruis. 115 BQ59
Ravenscourt Dr., Horn. 128 FL62
Ravenscourt Gdns. W6 159 CU77
Ravenscourt Gro., Horn. 128 FL61
Ravenscourt Pk. W6 159 CU76
Ravenscourt Pl. W6 159 CV77
Ravenscourt Rd. W6 159 CV77
Ravenscourt Rd., Orp. 206 EU97
Ravenscourt Sq. W6 159 CU76
Ravenscraig Rd. N11 99 DH49
Ravenscroft, Wat. 60 BY34
Ravenscroft Ave. NW11 119 CZ59
Ravenscroft Ave., Wem. 118 CL60
Ravenscroft Clo. E16 144 EG71
Ravenscroft Cres. SE9 185 EM90
Ravenscroft Pk., Barn. 79 CX42
Ravenscroft Rd. E16 144 EG71
Ravenscroft Rd. W4 158 CQ77
Ravenscroft Rd., Beck. 202 DW96
Ravenscroft Rd., Wey. 213 BQ111
Ravenscroft St. E2 142 DT68
Ravensdale Ave. N12 98 DC49
Ravensdale Gdns. SE19 182 DR94
Ravensdale Ms., Stai. 174 BH93
Ravensdale Rd. N16 122 DT59
Ravensdale Rd., Houns. 156 BY83
Ravensdell, Hem.H. 39 BF19
Ravensdon St. SE11 161 DN78
Ravensfield, Slou. 152 AX75
Ravensfield Clo., Dag. 126 EX63
Ravensfield Gdns., Epsom 216 CS106
Ravenshaw St. NW6 119 CZ64
Ravenshead Clo., S.Croy. 220 DW111
Ravenshill, Chis. 205 EP95
Ravenshurst Ave. NW4 119 CW56
Ravenside Clo. N18 101 DX50
Ravenside Retail Pk. N18 101 DX50
Angel Rd.
Ravenslea Rd. SW12 180 DF87
Ravensmead, Ger.Cr. 91 AZ50
Ravensmead Rd., Brom. 183 ED94
Ravensmede Way W4 159 CT77
Ravensmere, Epp. 70 EU31
Ravenstone SE17 162 DS78
Bagshot St.
Ravenstone Rd. N8 121 DN55
Ravenstone Rd. NW9 119 CT58
West Hendon Bdy.
Ravenstone St. SW12 180 DG88
Ravenswold, Ken. 236 DQ115
Ravenswood, Bex. 186 EY88
Ravenswood Ave., Surb. 198 CM103
Ravenswood Ave., W.Wick. 203 EC102
Ravenswood Clo., Cob. 230 BX115
Ravenswood Clo., Rom. 105 FB50
Ravenswood Ct., Kings.T. 178 CP93
Ravenswood Ct., Wok. 227 AZ118
Ravenswood Cres., Har. 116 BZ61
Ravenswood Cres., W.Wick. 203 EC102
Ravenswood Gdns., Islw. 157 CE81
Ravenswood Pk., Nthwd. 93 BU51
Ravenswood Rd. E17 123 EC56
Ravenswood Rd. SW12 181 DH87
Ravenswood Rd., Croy. 201 DP104
Ravensworth Rd. NW10 139 CV69
Ravensworth Rd. SE9 185 EM90
Ravensworth Rd., Slou. 131 AN69
Wentworth Ave.
Ravent Rd. SE11 278 C8
Ravent Rd. SE11 161 DM77
Ravey St. EC2 275 M4
Ravine Gro. SE18 165 ES79
Rawdon Dr., Hodd. 49 EA18
Rawlings Clo., Orp. 223 ET106
Rawlings La., Beac. 89 AQ48
Rawlings St. SW3 276 D8
Rawlings St. SW3 160 DF77
Rawlins Clo. N3 119 CY55
Rawlins Clo., S.Croy. 221 DY108
Rawnsley Ave., Mitch. 200 DD99
Raworth Ave., Hodd. 33 EB13
Rawreth Wk. N1 142 DQ67
Basire St.
Rawson St. SW11 160 DG81
Strasburg Rd.
Rawsthorne Clo. E16 145 EM74
Kennard St.
Rawstone Wk. E13 144 EG68
Clegg St.
Rawstorne Pl. EC1 274 F2
Rawstorne St. EC1 274 F2
Rawstorne St. EC1 141 DP69
Ray Clo., Chess. 215 CJ107
Merritt Gdns.
Ray Fld., Welw.G.C. 29 CX06
Ray Gdns., Bark. 146 EU68
Ray Gdns., Stan. 95 CH50
Ray Lo. Rd., Wdf.Grn. 102 EJ51
Ray Massey Way E6 144 EL67
Ron Leighton Way
Ray Mead Ct., Maid. 130 AC70
Boulters La.
Ray Mead Rd., Maid. 130 AC72
Ray Rd., Rom. 105 FB50
Ray Rd., W.Mol. 196 CB99
Ray St. EC1 274 E5
Ray St. EC1 141 DN70
Ray St. Bri. EC1 274 E5
Ray Wk. N7 121 DM61
Andover Rd.
Raybarn Rd., Hem.H. 40 BG18
Rayburn Rd., Horn. 128 FN59
Raydean Rd., Barn. 80 DB43
Raydon Rd. (Cheshunt), Wal.Cr. 67 DX32
Raydon St. N19 121 DH61
Raydons Gdns., Dag. 126 EY64
Raydons Rd., Dag. 126 EY64
Rayfield, Epp. 70 EU29
Rayfield Clo., Brom. 204 EL100
Rayford Ave. SE12 184 EF87
Rayford Clo., Dart. 188 FJ85
Raylands Mead, Ger.Cr. 112 AW57
Bull La.
Rayleas Clo. SE18 165 EP81
Rayleigh Ave., Tedd. 177 CE93
Rayleigh Clo. N13 100 DR48
Rayleigh Rd.
Rayleigh Clo., Brwd. 109 GC44
Rayleigh Ct., Kings.T. 198 CM96
Rayleigh Ri., S.Croy. 220 DS107
Rayleigh Rd. N13 100 DQ48
Rayleigh Rd. SW19 199 CZ95
Rayleigh Rd., Brwd. 109 GB44
Rayleigh Rd., Wdf.Grn. 102 EJ51
Rayley La., Epp. 52 FA24
Raymead Ave., Th.Hth. 201 DN99
Raymead Clo., Lthd. 231 CE122
Raymead Way, Lthd. 231 CE122
Raymer Clo., St.Alb. 43 CE19
Raymer Wk., Horl. 269 DJ147
Raymere Gdns. SE18 165 ER80
Raymond Ave. E18 124 EF55
Raymond Ave. W13 157 CG76
Raymond Bldgs. WC1 274 C6
Raymond Clo. SE26 182 DW92
Raymond Clo., Abb.L. 59 BR32
Raymond Clo., Slou. 153 BE81
Raymond Ct. N10 98 DG52
Pembroke Rd.
Raymond Cres., Guil. 258 AT135
Raymond Gdns., Chig. 104 EV48
Raymond Rd. E13 144 EJ66
Raymond Rd. SW19 179 CY93
Raymond Rd., Beck. 203 DY98
Raymond Rd., Ilf. 125 ER59
Raymond Rd., Slou. 153 BA76
Raymond Way, Esher 215 CG107
Raymonds Clo., Welw.G.C. 29 CY11
Raymonds Plain, Welw.G.C. 29 CY11
Raymouth Rd. SE16 162 DV77
Rayne Ct. E18 124 EF56
Rayner Twr. E10 123 EA59
Rayners Clo., Slou. 153 BC80
Rayners Clo., Wem. 117 CK64
Rayners Ct., Grav. 190 GB86
Rayners Ct., Har. 116 CA60
Rayners Cres., Nthlt. 135 BV69
Rayners Gdns., Nthlt. 135 BV68
Rayners La., Har. 116 CA60
Rayners La., Pnr. 116 BZ57
Rayners Rd. SW15 179 CY85
Raynes Ave. E11 124 EJ59
Raynham Ave. N18 100 DU51
Raynham Rd. N18 100 DU50
Raynham Rd. W6 159 CV77
Raynham St., Hert. 32 DS08
Raynham Ter. N18 100 DU50
Raynor Clo., Sthl. 136 BZ74
Raynor Pl. N1 142 DQ67
Elizabeth Ave.
Raynsford Rd., Ware 33 DY06
Raynton Clo., Har. 116 BY60
Raynton Clo., Hayes 135 BT70
Raynton Dr., Hayes 135 BT70
Raynton Rd., Enf. 83 DX37
Rays Ave. N18 100 DW49
Rays Ave., Wind. 151 AM80
Rays Hill, Dart. 208 FP98
Rays La., H.Wyc. 88 AC46
Rays Rd. N18 100 DW49
Rays Rd., W.Wick. 203 EC101
Raywood Clo., Hayes 155 BQ80
Raywood St. SW8 161 DH81
Gladstone Ter.
Reachview Clo. NW1 141 DJ66
Baynes St.
Read Ct., Wal.Abb. 68 EG33
Read Rd., Ash. 231 CK117
Read Way, Grav. 191 GK92
Reade Ct., Slou. 132 AV72
Victoria Rd.
Reade Wk. NW10 138 CS66
Denbigh Clo.
Readens, The, Bans. 234 DE116
Reading Arch Rd., Red. 250 DF134
Reading La. E8 142 DV65
Reading Rd., Nthlt. 116 CB64
Reading Rd., Sutt. 218 DC106
Reading Way NW7 97 CX50
Readings, The, Harl. 51 ET18
Readings, The, Rick. 73 BF41
Reads Clo., Ilf. 125 EP62
Chapel Rd.
Reads Rest La., Tad. 233 CZ119
Canons La.
Reapers Clo. NW1 141 DK67
Crofters Way
Reapers Way, Islw. 177 CD85
Hall Rd.
Reardon Path E1 142 DV74
Reardon St. E1 142 DV74
Reaston St. SE14 163 DX80
Rebecca Ter. SE16 162 DW76
Gomm Rd.
Reckitt Rd. W4 158 CS78
Record St. SE15 162 DW79
Recovery St. SW17 180 DE92
Recreation Ave., Rom. 127 FC57
Recreation Ave. (Harold Wd.), Rom. 106 FM54
Recreation Rd. SE26 183 DX91
Recreation Rd., Brom. 204 EF96
Recreation Rd., Guil. 242 AW134
Recreation Rd., Sid. 185 ET90
Recreation Rd., Sthl. 156 BY77
Recreation Way, Mitch. 201 DL97
Rector St. N1 142 DQ67
Rectory Chase, Brwd. 129 FX56
Rectory Clo. E4 101 EA48
Rectory Clo. N3 97 CZ54
Rectory Clo. SW20 199 CW97
Rectory Clo., Ash. 232 CM119
Rectory Clo., Dart. 167 FE84
Rectory Clo., Guil. 243 BD132
Rectory Clo., Hat. 46 DF17
Rectory Clo., Shep. 194 BN97
Rectory Clo., Sid. 186 EV91
Rectory Clo., Slou. 131 AQ69
Rectory Clo., Stan. 95 CH50
Rectory Clo., Surb. 197 CJ102
Rectory Clo., Ware 34 EK07
Rectory Clo., W.Byf. 212 BK113
Rectory Clo., Wind. 151 AN81
Rectory Cres. E11 124 EJ58
Rectory Fm. Rd., Enf. 81 DM38
Rectory Fld., Harl. 51 EP17
Rectory Fld. Cres. SE7 164 EJ80
Rectory Gdns. N8 121 DL56
Rectory Gdns. SW4 161 DJ83
Rectory Gdns., Ch.St.G. 90 AV48
Rectory Gdns., Hat. 45 CV18
Rectory Gdns., Nthlt. 136 BZ67
Rectory Gdns., Upmin. 129 FR61
Rectory Grn., Beck. 203 DZ95
Rectory Gro. SW4 161 DJ83
Rectory Gro., Croy. 201 DP103
Rectory Gro., Hmptn. 176 BZ91
Rectory Hill, Amer. 55 AP39
Rectory La. SW17 180 DG93
Rectory La., Ash. 232 CM118
Rectory La., Bans. 218 DF114
Rectory La., Berk. 38 AW19
Rectory La., Bet. 249 CT131
Rectory La., Edg. 96 CN51
Rectory La., Guil. 260 BM139
Rectory La., Harl. 51 EP17
Rectory La., Kings L. 58 BN28
Rectory La., Lthd. 246 BZ126
Rectory La., Loug. 85 EN40
Rectory La., Rad. 62 CM33
Rectory La., Rick. 92 BK46
Rectory La., Sev. 257 FJ126
Rectory La., Sid. 186 EV91
Rectory La., Stan. 95 CH50
Rectory La., Surb. 197 CH102
Rectory La., Wall. 201 DJ104
Rectory La., W.Byf. 212 BL113
Rectory La., West. 238 EL123
Rectory La. (Brasted), West. 240 EW123
Rectory Meadow, Grav. 190 GA92
Rectory Orchard SW19 179 CY91
Rectory Pk., S.Croy. 220 DS113
Rectory Pk. Ave., Nthlt. 136 BY69
Rectory Pl. SE18 165 EN77
Rectory Rd. E12 125 EM64
Rectory Rd. E17 123 EB55
Rectory Rd. N16 122 DT61
Rectory Rd. SW13 159 CU82
Rectory Rd. W3 138 CP74
Rectory Rd., Beck. 203 EA95
Rectory Rd., Couls. 250 DB125
Rectory Rd., Dag. 146 FA65
Rectory Rd., Grays 170 GD76
Rectory Rd., Hayes 135 BU72
Rectory Rd., Houns. 155 BV81
Rectory Rd., Kes. 222 EK108
Rectory Rd., Maid. 130 AD70
Rectory Rd., Rick. 92 BK46
Rectory Rd., Sthl. 156 BZ76
Rectory Rd., Sutt. 200 DA104
Rectory Rd., Swans. 190 FY87
Rectory Rd., Til. 171 GK79
Rectory Rd., Welw.G.C. 29 CV06
Rectory Sq. E1 143 DX71
Rectory Way, Amer. 55 AP40
Rectory Way, Uxb. 115 BP61
Rectory Wd., Harl. 35 EQ14
Reculver Ms. N18 100 DU49
Lyndhurst Rd.
Reculver Rd. SE16 163 DX78
Red Anchor Clo. SW3 160 DE79
Old Ch. St.
Red Barracks Rd. SE18 165 EM77
Red Cedars Rd., Orp. 205 ES101
Red Cottage Ms., Slou. 152 AW76
Red Ct., Slou. 132 AS74
Red Hill, Chis. 185 EP92
Red Hills, Hodd. 48 DV19
Red Ho. Clo., Beac. 88 AH51
Red Ho. Clo., Ware 33 DY07
Red Ho. La., Bexh. 166 EX84
Red Ho. La., Walt. 195 BU103
Red Ho. Rd., Croy. 201 DK100
Red Ho. Sq. N1 142 DQ65
Clephane Rd.
Red La., Dor. 264 CL141
Red La., Esher 215 CG107
Red La., Oxt. 254 EH134
Red Leaf Clo., Slou. 133 AZ74
Pickford Dr.
Red Lion Clo. SE17 162 DQ79
Red Lion Row
Red Lion Clo., Orp. 206 EW100
Red Lion Ct. EC4 274 E9
Red Lion Ct. EC4 141 DN72
Red Lion Cres., Harl. 52 EW17
Red Lion Hill N2 98 DD54
Red Lion La. SE18 165 EN81
Red Lion La., Harl. 52 EW17
Red Lion La., Hem.H. 58 BM26
Red Lion La., Rick. 74 BG35
Red Lion La., Wok. 210 AS109
Red Lion Rd.
Red Lion Pl. SE18 165 EN81
Shooter's Hill Rd.
Red Lion Rd., Surb. 198 CM103
Red Lion Rd., Wok. 210 AS109
Red Lion Row SE17 162 DQ79
Red Lion Sq. SW18 180 DA85
Wandsworth High St.
Red Lion Sq. WC1 274 B7
Red Lion Sq. WC1 141 DM71
Red Lion St. WC1 274 B6
Red Lion St. WC1 141 DM71
Red Lion St., Chesh. 54 AP32
Red Lion St., Rich. 177 CK85
Red Lion Way, H.Wyc. 110 AE57
Red Lion Yd. W1 276 G2
Red Lion Yd., Wat. 76 BW42
High St.
Red Lo. Cres., Bex. 187 FD90
Red Lo. Gdns., Berk. 38 AU20
Red Lo. Rd., Bex. 187 FD90
Red Lo. Rd., W.Wick. 203 EC102
Red Oak Clo., Orp. 205 EP104
Red Oaks Mead, Epp. 85 ER37
Red Path E9 143 DZ65
Eastway
Red Pl. W1 272 F10
Red Post Hill SE21 182 DR85
Red Post Hill SE24 162 DR84
Red Rd., Borwd. 78 CM40
Red Rd., Brwd. 108 FV49
Red St., Grav. 190 GA93
Red Willow, Harl. 51 EM18
Redan Pl. W2 140 DB72
Redan St. W14 159 CX76
Redan Ter. SE5 162 DQ82
Flaxman Rd.
Redbarn Clo., Pur. 219 DP111
Whytecliffe Rd. S.
Redberry Gro. SE26 182 DW90
Redbourn Rd., Hem.H. 40 BN16
Redbourn Rd., St.Alb. 42 CA18
Redbourne Ave. N3 98 DA53
Redbridge Gdns. SE5 162 DS80
Redbridge La. E., Ilf. 124 EK58
Redbridge La. W. E11 124 EH58
Redburn St. SW3 160 DF79
Redbury Clo., Rain. 147 FH70
Deri Ave.
Redcar Clo., Nthlt. 136 CB65
Redcar Rd., Rom. 106 FM50
Redcar St. SE5 162 DQ80
Redcastle Clo. E1 142 DW73
Redchurch St. E2 275 P4
Redchurch St. E2 142 DT70
Redcliffe Clo. SW5 160 DB78
Warwick Rd.
Redcliffe Gdns. SW5 160 DB78
Redcliffe Gdns. SW10 160 DB78
Redcliffe Gdns., Ilf. 125 EN60
Redcliffe Ms. SW10 160 DB78
Redcliffe Pl. SW10 160 DC79
Redcliffe Rd. SW10 160 DC78
Redcliffe Sq. SW10 160 DB78
Redcliffe St. SW10 160 DB79
Redclose Ave., Mord. 200 DA99
Chalgrove Ave.
Redclyffe Rd. E6 144 EJ67
Redcourt, Wok. 227 BD115
Redcroft Rd., Sthl. 136 CC73
Redcross Way SE1 279 J4
Redcross Way SE1 162 DQ75
Redden Ct. Rd., Rom. 128 FL55
Redding Dr., Amer. 55 AN37
Reddings, Hem.H. 40 BN22
Reddings, Welw.G.C. 29 CW07
Reddings, The NW7 97 CT48
Reddings, The, Borwd. 78 CM41
Reddings Ave. (Bushey), Wat. 76 CB43
Reddings Clo. NW7 97 CT49
Reddington Clo., S.Croy. 220 DS109
Beechwood Rd.
Reddington Dr., Slou. 152 AY76
Reddins Rd. SE15 162 DU79
Redditch Ct., Hem.H. 40 BM16
Reddons Rd., Beck. 183 DY94
Reddown Rd., Couls. 235 DK118
Reddy Rd., Erith 167 FF79
Rede Ct., Wey. 195 BP104
Old Palace Rd.
Rede Pl. W2 140 DA72
Chepstow Pl.
Redehall Rd., Horl. 269 DP148
Redesdale Gdns., Islw. 157 CG80
Redesdale St. SW3 160 DE79
Redfern Ave., Houns. 176 CA87
Redfern Clo., Uxb. 134 BJ67
Redfern Gdns., Rom. 106 FK54
Redfern Rd. NW10 138 CS66
Redfern Rd. SE6 183 EC87
Redfield La. SW5 160 DA77
Redford Ave., Couls. 219 DH114
Redford Ave., Th.Hth. 201 DM98
Redford Ave., Wall. 219 DL107
Redford Clo., Felt. 175 BT90
Redford Rd., Wind. 151 AK81
Redford Wk. N1 141 DP67
Britannia Row
Redford Way, Uxb. 134 BJ66
Redgate Dr., Brom. 204 EH103
Redgate Ter. SW15 179 CX86
Lytton Gro.
Redgrave Clo., Croy. 202 DT100
Redgrave Rd. SW15 159 CX83
Redhall Clo., Hat. 45 CT21
Redhall Ct., Cat. 236 DR123
Redhall Dr., Hat. 45 CT21
Redhall La., Rick. 74 BL39
Redheath Clo., Wat. 75 BT35
Redhill, Uxb. 113 BC60
Redhill Common, Red. 266 DE135
Redhill Dr., Edg. 96 CQ54
Redhill Rd., Cob. 213 BP112
Redhill St. NW1 273 J2
Redhill St. NW1 141 DH68
Redhouse Rd., West. 238 EJ121
Redington Gdns. NW3 120 DB63
Redington Rd. NW3 120 DB63
Redlands, Couls. 235 DL116
Redlands Ct., Brom. 184 EF94
Redlands Gdns., W.Mol. 196 BZ98
Dunstable Rd.
Redlands La., Dor. 263 CG142
Redlands Rd., Enf. 83 DY39
Redlands Rd., Sev. 256 FF124
Redlands Way SW2 181 DM87
Redlaw Way SE16 162 DU78
Catlin St.
Redleaf Clo., Belv. 166 FA79
Redleaves Ave., Ashf. 175 BP92
Redlees Clo., Islw. 157 CG84
Redman Clo., Nthlt. 136 BW68
Redmans La., Sev. 225 FD107
Redman's Rd. E1 142 DW71
Redmead La. E1 142 DU74
Wapping High St.
Redmead Rd., Hayes 155 BS77
Redmore Rd. W6 159 CV77
Redpoll Way, Erith 166 EX75
Redricks La., Harl. 35 ET09
Redriff Est. SE16 163 DY76
Redriff Rd. SE16 163 DX76
Redriff Rd., Rom. 105 FB54
Redriffe Rd. E13 144 EF67
Redroofs Clo., Beck. 203 EB95
Redruth Clo. N22 99 DM52
Palmerston Rd.
Redruth Gdns., Rom. 106 FM50
Redruth Rd. E9 142 DW67
Redruth Rd., Rom. 106 FM50
Redruth Wk., Rom. 106 FM50
Redruth Rd.
Redstart Clo. E6 144 EL71
Columbine Ave.
Redstart Clo. SE14 163 DY80
Southerngate Way
Redstart Clo., Croy. 221 ED110
Redston Rd. N8 121 DJ56
Redstone Hill, Red. 250 DG133
Redstone Hollow, Red. 266 DG135
Redstone Manor, Red. 250 DG134
Redstone Pk., Red. 250 DG134
Redstone Rd., Red. 266 DG135
Redvers Rd. N22 99 DN54
Redvers Rd., Warl. 237 DX118
Redvers St. N1 275 N2
Redwald Rd. E5 123 DX63
Redway Dr., Twick. 176 CC87
Redwing Clo., S.Croy. 221 DX111
Redwing Gro., Abb.L. 59 BU31
College Rd.
Redwing Path SE28 165 ER75
Whinchat Rd.
Redwing Ri., Guil. 243 BD132
Redwood, Egh. 193 BE96
Redwood, Slou. 130 AH68
Redwood Clo. N14 99 DK45
The Vale
Redwood Clo. SE16 143 DY74
Redwood Clo., Ken. 220 DQ114
Redwood Clo., Uxb. 135 BP68
The Larches
Redwood Clo., Wat. 94 BW49
Redwood Ct., Hem.H. 40 BL22
Redwood Est., Houns. 155 BV79
Redwood Gdns. E4 83 EB44
Sewardstone Rd.
Redwood Gdns., Chig. 104 EU50
Redwood Gdns., Slou. 131 AR73
Godolphin Rd.
Redwood Gro., Guil. 259 BC140
Redwood Mt., Reig. 250 DA131
Redwood Ri., Borwd. 78 CN37
Redwood Twr. E11 123 ED62
Hollydown Way
Redwood Wk., Surb. 197 CK102
Redwood Way, Barn. 79 CX43
Redwoods SW15 179 CU88
Redwoods, Hert. 32 DQ08
Redwoods Clo., Buck.H. 102 EH47
Beech La.
Reece Ms. SW7 160 DD77
Reed Ave., Orp. 205 ES104
Reed Clo. E16 144 EG71
Reed Clo. SE12 184 EG85
Reed Clo., Iver 133 BE72
Reed Clo., St.Alb. 62 CL27
Reed Pl., Shep. 194 BM102
Reed Pl., W.Byf. 211 BE113
Reed Pond Wk., Rom. 105 FF54
Reed Rd. N17 100 DT54
Reede Gdns., Dag. 127 FB64
Reede Rd.
Reede Rd., Dag. 146 FA65
Reede Way, Dag. 147 FB65
Reedham Clo. N17 122 DV56
Reedham Clo., St.Alb. 60 CA29
Reedham Dr., Pur. 219 DM113
Reedham Pk. Ave., Pur. 235 DN116
Reedham St. SE15 162 DU82
Reedholm Vill. N16 122 DR63
Winston Rd.
Reeds, The, Welw.G.C. 29 CX10
Reeds Cres., Wat. 76 BW40
Reeds Pl. NW1 141 DJ66
Royal College St.
Reeds Rest La., Tad. 233 CZ119
Reeds Wk., Wat. 76 BW40
Orphanage Rd.
Reedsfield Clo., Ashf. 175 BP91
The Yews
Reedsfield Rd., Ashf. 175 BP91
Reedworth St. SE11 278 E9
Reedworth St. SE11 161 DN77
Reenglass Rd., Stan. 95 CK49
Rees Gdns., Croy. 202 DT100
Rees St. N1 142 DQ67
Reesland Clo. E12 145 EN65
Reets Fm. Clo. NW9 118 CS58
Reeve Rd., Reig. 266 DC138
Reeves Ave. NW9 118 CR59
Reeves Cor., Croy. 201 DP103
Roman Way
Reeves Cres., Swan. 207 FD97
Reeves La., Harl. 50 EJ19

Reeves Ms. W1 276 F1
Reeves Ms. W1 140 DG73
Reeves Rd. E3 143 EB70
Reeves Rd. SE18 165 EP79
Reform Row N17 100 DT54
Reform St. SW11 160 DF82
Regal Clo. E1 142 DU71
Old Montague St.
Regal Clo. W5 137 CK71
Regal Ct. N18 100 DT50
College Clo.
Regal Cres., Wall. 201 DH104
Regal Dr. N11 99 DH50
Regal La. NW1 140 DG67
Regents Pk. Rd.
Regal Row SE15 162 DW81
Queens Rd.
Regal Way, Har. 118 CL58
Regal Way, Wat. 76 BW38
Regalfield Clo., Guil. 242 AT130
Regan Clo., Guil. 242 AV129
Regan Way N1 275 M1
Regan Way N1 142 DS68
Regarder Rd., Chig. 104 EU50
Regarth Ave., Rom. 127 FE58
Regency Clo. W5 138 CL72
Regency Clo., Chig. 103 EQ50
Regency Clo., Hmptn. 176 BZ92
Regency Ct., Brwd. 108 FW47
Regency Ct., Brox. 49 DZ23
Berners Way
Regency Ct., Harl. 52 EU18
Regency Cres. NW4 97 CX54
Regency Dr., Ruis. 115 BS60
Regency Dr., W.Byf. 211 BF113
Madeira Rd.
Regency Gdns., Horn. 128 FJ59
Regency Gdns., Walt. 196 BW102
Regency Lo., Buck.H. 102 EK47
Regency Ms. NW10 139 CU65
High Rd.
Regency Ms., Beck. 203 EC95
Regency Ms., Islw. 177 CE85
Queensbridge Pk.
Regency Pl. SW1 277 N8
Regency St. SW1 277 N8
Regency St. SW1 161 DK77
Regency Ter. SW3 160 DD78
Fulham Rd.
Regency Wk., Croy. 203 DY100
Regency Wk., Rich. 178 CL86
Friars Stile Rd.
Regency Way, Bexh. 166 EX83
Regency Way, Wok. 227 BD115
Regent Ave., Uxb. 135 BP66
Regent Clo. N12 98 DC50
Nether St.
Regent Clo., Add. 212 BK109
Regent Clo., Grays 170 GC75
Regent Clo., Har. 118 CL58
Regent Clo., Houns. 155 BV81
Regent Clo., St.Alb. 43 CJ16
Regent Ct., Slou. 132 AS72
Stoke Poges La.
Regent Ct., Wind. 151 AR81
Regent Cres., Red. 250 DF132
Regent Gdns., Ilf. 126 EU58
Regent Pk. Ind. Est., Lthd. 231 CG118
Regent Pl. SW19 180 DB92
Haydons Rd.
Regent Pl. W1 273 L10
Regent Pl., Croy. 202 DT102
Grant Rd.
Regent Rd. SE24 181 DP86
Regent Rd., Epp. 69 ET30
Regent Rd., Surb. 198 CM99
Regent Sq. E3 143 EB69
Regent Sq. WC1 274 A3
Regent Sq. WC1 141 DL69
Regent Sq., Belv. 167 FB77
Regent St. NW10 139 CX69
Wellington Rd.
Regent St. SW1 277 M1
Regent St. SW1 141 DK73
Regent St. W1 273 J8
Regent St. W1 141 DH72
Regent St. W4 158 CN78
Regent St., Wat. 75 BV38
Regents Ave. N13 99 DN50
Regents Bri. Gdns. SW8 161 DL80
Regents Clo., Hayes 135 BS71
Grange Par.
Regents Clo., Rad. 61 CG34
Regents Clo., S.Croy. 220 DS107
Regents Clo., Whyt. 236 DS118
Regents Dr., Kes. 222 EK106
Regents Ms. NW8 140 DC68
Langford Pl.
Regent's Pk. NW1 272 D1
Regent's Pk. NW1 140 DF68
Regent's Pk. Est. NW1 273 K3
Regents Pk. Rd. N3 119 CZ56
Regents Pk. Rd. NW1 140 DF67
Regents Pk. Ter. NW1 141 DH67
Oval Rd.
Regent's Pl. NW1 141 DJ70
Hampstead Rd.
Regent's Pl. SE3 164 EG82
Regents Row E8 142 DU67
Regina Clo., Barn. 79 CX41
Regina Rd. N4 121 DM60
Regina Rd. SE25 202 DU97
Regina Rd. W13 137 CG74
Regina Rd., Sthl. 156 BY77
Regina Ter. W13 137 CH74
Reginald Rd. E7 144 EG65
Reginald Rd. SE8 163 EA80
Reginald Rd., Nthwd. 93 BT53
Reginald Rd., Rom. 106 FN53
Reginald Sq. SE8 163 EA80
Regis Rd. NW5 121 DH64
Regnart Bldgs. NW1 273 L4
Reid Ave., Cat. 236 DR121
Reid Clo., Pnr. 115 BU56
Reidhaven Rd. SE18 165 ES77
Reigate Ave., Sutt. 200 DA103
Reigate Heath, Reig. 265 CX135
Reigate Hill, Reig. 250 DA133
Reigate Hill Clo., Reig. 250 DA131
Reigate Rd., Bet. 248 CN133
Reigate Rd., Brom. 184 EF90
Reigate Rd., Dor. 263 CJ135
Reigate Rd., Epsom 217 CU110
Reigate Rd., Horl. 268 DC146
Reigate Rd., Ilf. 125 ET61
Reigate Rd., Lthd. 231 CJ122
Reigate Rd., Red. 250 DD134
Reigate Rd., Reig. 250 DB134
Reigate Rd. (Sidlow), Reig. 266 DB141
Reigate Rd., Tad. 233 CY119
Reigate Way, Wall. 219 DL106
Reighton Rd. E5 122 DU62
Relay Rd. W12 139 CW74
Relf Rd. SE15 162 DU83
Relko Ct., Epsom 216 CR111
Relko Gdns., Sutt. 218 DD106
Relton Ms. SW7 276 C6
Rembrandt Clo. E14 163 ED76
Rembrandt Clo. SW1 276 F9
Rembrandt Dr., Grav. 190 GD90
Rembrandt Rd. SE13 164 EE84
Rembrandt Rd., Edg. 96 CN54
Rembrandt Way, Walt. 195 BV103
Remington Rd. E6 144 EL72
Remington Rd. N15 122 DR58
Remington St. N1 274 G1
Remington St. N1 141 DP68
Remnant St. WC2 274 B8
Rempstone Ms. N1 142 DR68
Mintern St.
Remus Rd. E3 143 EA66
Monier Rd.
Rendle Clo., Croy. 202 DT99
Rendle Clo., Ware 32 DV05
Rendlesham Ave., Rad. 77 CF37
Rendlesham Rd. E5 122 DU63
Rendlesham Rd., Enf. 81 DP39
Rendlesham Way, Rick. 73 BC44
Renforth St. SE16 162 DW75
Renfree Way, Shep. 194 BM101
Renfrew Clo. E6 145 EN73
Renfrew Rd. SE11 278 F8
Renfrew Rd. SE11 161 DP77
Renfrew Rd., Houns. 156 BX82
Renfrew Rd., Kings.T. 178 CP94
Renmans, The, Ash. 232 CM116
Renmuir St. SW17 180 DF93
Rennell St. SE13 163 EC83
Lewisham High St.
Rennels Way, Islw. 157 CE82
St. John's Rd.
Renness Rd. E17 123 DY55
Rennets Clo. SE9 185 ES85
Rennets Wd. Rd. SE9 185 ER85
Rennie Clo., Ashf. 174 BK90
Rennie Est. SE16 162 DV77
Rennie St. SE1 278 F2
Rennie St. SE1 141 DP74
Rennie Ter., Red. 266 DG135
Rennison Clo., Wal.Cr. 66 DT27
Allwood Rd.
Renown Clo., Croy. 201 DP102
Renown Clo., Rom. 104 FA53
Rensburg Rd. E17 123 DX57
Renshaw Clo., Belv. 166 EZ79
Grove Rd.
Renters Ave. NW4 119 CW58
Renton Dr., Orp. 206 EX101
Renwick Ind. Est., Bark. 146 EV67
Renwick Rd., Bark. 146 EV70
Repens Way, Hayes 136 BX70
Stipularis Dr.
Rephidim St. SE1 279 L7
Replingham Rd. SW18 179 CZ88
Reporton Rd. SW6 159 CY81
Repository Rd. SE18 165 EM79
Repton Ave., Hayes 155 BR77
Repton Ave., Rom. 127 FG55
Repton Ave., Wem. 117 CJ63
Repton Clo., Cars. 218 DE106
Repton Ct., Beck. 203 EB95
Repton Dr., Rom. 127 FG56
Repton Gdns., Rom. 127 FG55
Repton Grn., St.Alb. 43 CD17
Repton Gro., Ilf. 103 EM53
Repton Pl., Amer. 72 AU39
Repton Rd., Har. 118 CM56
Repton Rd., Orp. 206 EU104
Repton St. E14 143 DY72
Repton Way, Rick. 74 BN43
Repulse Clo., Rom. 105 FB53
Reservoir Rd. N14 81 DJ43
Reservoir Rd. SE4 163 DY82
Reservoir Rd., Ruis. 115 BQ57
Resolution Wk. SE18 165 EM76
Venus Rd.
Reson Way, Hem.H. 40 BH21
Restell Clo. SE3 164 EE79
Reston Clo., Borwd. 78 CN38
Reston Path, Borwd. 78 CN38
Reston Clo.
Reston Pl. SW7 160 DC75
Hyde Pk. Gate
Restons Cres. SE9 185 ER86
Restormel Clo., Houns. 176 CA85
Retcar Clo. N19 121 DH61
Dartmouth Pk. Hill
Retcar Pl. N19 121 DH61
Dartmouth Pk. Hill
Retford Clo., Borwd. 78 CN38
The Campions
Retford Clo., Rom. 106 FN51
Retford Path, Rom. 106 FN51
Retford Rd., Rom. 106 FM51
Retingham Way E4 101 EB47
Retreat, The NW9 118 CR57
Retreat, The SW14 158 CS83
South Worple Way
Retreat, The, Abb.L. 59 BQ31
Abbots Rd.
Retreat, The, Add. 212 BK106
Retreat, The, Amer. 72 AY39
Retreat, The, Brwd. 108 FV46
Costead Manor Rd.
Retreat, The (Hutton), Brwd. 109 GB44
Retreat, The, Egh. 172 AX92
Retreat, The, Grays 170 GB79
Retreat, The, Har. 116 CA59
Retreat, The, Maid. 150 AD80
Retreat, The, Orp. 224 EV107
Retreat, The, Surb. 198 CM100
Retreat, The, Th.Hth. 202 DR98
Retreat, The, Wor.Pk. 199 CV103
Retreat Clo., Har. 117 CJ57
Retreat Pl. E9 142 DW65
Retreat Rd., Rich. 177 CK85
Retreat Way, Chig. 104 EV48
Reubens Rd., Brwd. 109 GB44
Reunion Row E1 142 DV73
Pennington St.
Revel Rd., H.Wyc. 110 AD55
Reveley Sq. SE16 163 DY75
Howland Way
Revell Clo., Lthd. 230 CB122
Revell Dr., Lthd. 230 CB122
Revell Ri. SE18 165 ET79
Revell Rd., Kings.T. 198 CP96
Revell Rd., Sutt. 217 CZ107
Revelon Rd. SE4 163 DY83
Revels Clo., Hert. 32 DR07
Revels Rd., Hert. 32 DR07
Revelstoke Rd. SW18 179 CZ89
Reventlow Rd. SE9 185 EQ88
Reverdy Rd. SE1 162 DU77
Reverend Clo., Har. 116 CB62
Revesby Rd., Cars. 200 DD100
Review Rd. NW2 119 CT61
Review Rd., Dag. 147 FB67
Rewell St. SW6 160 DC80
Rewley Rd., Cars. 200 DD100
Rex Ave., Ashf. 174 BN93
Rex Clo., Rom. 105 FB52
Rex Pl. W1 276 G1
Reydon Ave. E11 124 EJ58
Reynard Clo. SE4 163 DY83
Foxwell St.
Reynard Clo., Brom. 205 EM97
Reynard Dr. SE19 182 DT94
Reynard Pl. SE14 163 DY79
Milton Ct. Rd.
Reynard Way, Hert. 32 DV09
Reynards Way, St.Alb. 60 BZ30
Reynardson Rd. N17 100 DQ52
Reynold Wk., Chesh. 54 AN27
Great Hivings
Reynolds Ave. E12 125 EN64
Reynolds Ave., Chess. 216 CL108
Reynolds Ave., Rom. 126 EW59
Reynolds Clo. NW11 120 DB59
Reynolds Clo. SW19 200 DD95
Reynolds Clo., Cars. 200 DF102
Reynolds Clo., Hem.H. 40 BG19
Reynolds Ct. E11 124 EF62
Cobbold Rd.
Reynolds Dr., Edg. 118 CM55
Reynolds Pl. SE3 164 EH80
Reynolds Pl., Rich. 178 CM86
Cambrian Rd.
Reynolds Rd. SE15 182 DW85
Reynolds Rd. W4 158 CQ76
Reynolds Rd., Beac. 88 AJ52
Reynolds Rd., Hayes 136 BW70
Reynolds Rd., N.Mal. 198 CR101
Reynolds Way, Croy. 220 DS105
Rheidol Ms. N1 142 DQ68
Rheidol Ter.
Rheidol Ter. N1 142 DQ67
Rheingold Way, Wall. 219 DL109
Rheola Clo. N17 100 DT53
Rhoda St. E2 142 DT70
Brick La.
Rhodes Ave. N22 99 DJ53
Rhodes Clo., Egh. 173 BC92
Mullens Rd.
Rhodes Moorhouse Ct., Mord. 200 DA100
Rhodes St. N7 121 DM64
Mackenzie Rd.
Rhodes Way, Wat. 76 BX40
Rhodesia Rd. E11 123 ED61
Rhodesia Rd. SW9 161 DL82
Rhodeswell Rd. E14 143 DY71
Rhododendron Ride, Egh. 172 AT93
Rhododendron Ride, Slou. 133 AZ69
Rhodrons Ave., Chess. 216 CL106
Rhondda Gro. E3 143 DY69
Rhyl Rd., Grnf. 137 CF68
Rhyl St. NW5 140 DG65
Rhys Ave. N11 99 DK52
Rialto Rd., Mitch. 200 DG96
Rib Vale, Hert. 32 DR06
Ribble Clo., Wdf.Grn. 102 EJ51
Prospect Rd.
Ribbledale, St.Alb. 62 CM27
Ribblesdale, Dor. 263 CH138
Roman Rd.
Ribblesdale, Hem.H. 40 BL17
Ribblesdale Ave., Nthlt. 136 CB65
Ribblesdale Rd. N8 121 DM56
Ribblesdale Rd. SW16 181 DH93
Ribblesdale Rd., Dart. 188 FQ88
Ribbon Dance Ms. SE5 162 DR81
Camberwell Gro.
Ribchester Ave., Grnf. 137 CF69
Ribston Clo., Brom. 205 EM102
Ribston Clo., Rad. 61 CK33
Wayside
Ricardo Path SE28 146 EW74
Byron Clo.
Ricardo Rd., Wind. 172 AV86
Meadow Way
Ricardo St. E14 143 EB72
Ricards Rd. SW19 179 CZ92
Rice Clo., Hem.H. 40 BM19
Ricebridge La., Reig. 265 CU137
Rich La. SW5 160 DB78
Warwick Rd.
Rich St. E14 143 DZ73
Richard Clo. SE18 164 EL77
Richard Foster Clo. E17 123 DZ59
Richard Stagg Clo., St.Alb. 43 CJ22
Richard St. E1 142 DV72
Commercial Rd.
Richards Ave., Rom. 127 FC57
Richards Clo., Har. 117 CG57
Richards Clo., Hayes 155 BR79
Richards Clo., Uxb. 134 BN67
Richards Clo. (Bushey), Wat. 95 CD45
Richards Pl. E17 123 EA55
Richards Pl. SW3 276 C8
Richards Rd., Cob. 214 CB114
Richards Way, Slou. 131 AL74
Richardson Clo. E8 142 DT67
Clarissa St.
Richardson Clo., Green. 189 FU85
Steele Ave.
Richardson Clo., St.Alb. 62 CL27
Richardson Pl., St.Alb. 44 CP22
Richardson Rd. E15 144 EE68
Richardson's Ms. W1 273 K5
Richbell Clo., Ash. 231 CK118
Richbell Pl. WC1 274 B6
Richborne Ter. SW8 161 DM80
Richborough Clo., Orp. 206 EX98
Richborough Rd. NW2 119 CY63
Riches Rd., Ilf. 125 EQ61
Richfield Rd. (Bushey), Wat. 94 CC45
Richford Rd. E15 144 EF67
Richford St. W6 159 CW75
Richings Way, Iver 153 BE76
Richland Ave., Couls. 218 DG114
Richlands Ave., Epsom 217 CU105
Richmer Rd., Erith 167 FG80
Richmond Ave. E4 101 ED50
Richmond Ave. N1 141 DM67
Richmond Ave. NW10 139 CW65
Richmond Ave. SW20 199 CY95
Richmond Ave., Felt. 175 BS86
Richmond Ave., Uxb. 135 BP65
Richmond Bri., Rich. 177 CK85
Richmond Bri., Twick. 177 CK86
Richmond Bldgs. W1 273 M9
Richmond Clo. E17 123 DZ58
Richmond Clo., Amer. 72 AT38
Richmond Clo., Borwd. 78 CQ43
Ripon Way
Richmond Clo., Epsom 216 CS114
Richmond Clo., Lthd. 230 CC124
Richmond Clo. (Cheshunt), Wal.Cr. 66 DW29
Richmond Clo., West. 238 EH119
Richmond Ct., Brox. 49 DZ20
Richmond Ct., Hat. 45 CV20
Cooks Way
Richmond Ct., Pot.B. 64 DC31
Richmond Cres. E4 101 ED50
Richmond Cres. N1 141 DM67
Richmond Cres. N9 100 DU46
Richmond Cres., Slou. 132 AU74
Richmond Cres., Stai. 173 BF92
Richmond Dr., Grav. 191 GL89
Richmond Dr., Shep. 195 BQ100
Richmond Dr., Wat. 75 BS40
Richmond Gdns. NW4 119 CU57
Richmond Gdns., Har. 95 CF52
Richmond Grn., Croy. 201 DL104
Richmond Gro. N1 141 DP66
Richmond Gro., Surb. 198 CM100
Ewell Rd.
Richmond Hill, Rich. 178 CL86
Richmond Hill Ct., Rich. 178 CL86
Richmond Ms. W1 273 M9
Richmond Ms., Tedd. 177 CF93
Broad St.
Richmond Pk., Kings.T. 178 CN88
Richmond Pk., Rich. 178 CN88
Richmond Pk. Rd. SW14 178 CQ85
Richmond Pk. Rd., Kings.T. 198 CL95
Richmond Pl. SE18 165 EQ77
Richmond Retail Pk., Rich. 158 CP81
Richmond Rd. E4 101 ED46
Richmond Rd. E7 124 EH64
Richmond Rd. E8 142 DT66
Richmond Rd. E11 123 ED61
Richmond Rd. N2 98 DC54
Richmond Rd. N11 99 DL51
Richmond Rd. N15 122 DS58
Richmond Rd. SW20 199 CV95
Richmond Rd. W5 158 CL75
Richmond Rd., Barn. 80 DB43
Richmond Rd., Couls. 235 DH115
Richmond Rd., Croy. 201 DL104
Richmond Rd., Grays 170 GC79
Richmond Rd., Ilf. 125 EQ62
Richmond Rd., Islw. 157 CG83
Richmond Rd., Kings.T. 177 CK92
Richmond Rd., Pot.B. 64 DC31
Richmond Rd., Rom. 127 FF58
Richmond Rd., Stai. 173 BF92
Richmond Rd., Th.Hth. 201 DP97
Richmond Rd., Twick. 177 CG88
Richmond St. E13 144 EG68
Richmond Ter. SW1 277 P4
Richmond Ter. SW1 161 DL75
Richmond Ter. Ms. SW1 161 DL75
Parliament St.
Richmond Wk., St.Alb. 43 CK16
Richmond Way E11 124 EG61
Richmond Way W12 159 CX75
Richmond Way W14 159 CX75
Richmond Way, Lthd. 230 CB124
Richmond Way, Rick. 75 BQ42
Richmount Gdns. SE3 164 EG83
Rick Roberts Way E15 143 EC67
Rickard Clo. NW4 119 CU56
Rickard Clo. SW2 181 DN88
Rickard Clo., West Dr. 154 BK76
Rickards Clo., Surb. 198 CL102
Rickett St. SW6 160 DA79
Ricketts Hill Rd., West. 238 EK121
Rickfield Clo., Hat. 45 CU20
Rickman Cres., Add. 194 BH104
Rickman Hill, Couls. 235 DH117
Rickman Hill Rd., Couls. 235 DH118
Rickman St. E1 142 DW69
Mantus Rd.
Rickmans La., Slou. 112 AS64
Rickmansworth Bypass, Rick. 73 BF42
Rickmansworth La., Ger.Cr. 90 AY52
Rickmansworth Rd., Amer. 55 AQ37
Rickmansworth Rd., Nthwd. 93 BP50
Rickmansworth Rd., Pnr. 93 BV54
Rickmansworth Rd., Rick. 73 BE41
Rickmansworth Rd., Uxb. 92 BJ53
Rickmansworth Rd., Wat. 75 BS42
Ricksons La., Lthd. 245 BP127
Rickthorne Rd. N19 121 DL61
Landseer Rd.
Rickwood, Horl. 269 DH147
Woodhayes
Rickyard Path SE9 164 EL84
Ridding La., Grnf. 117 CF64
Riddings, The, Cat. 252 DT125
Riddings La., Harl. 51 ET19
Riddlesdown Ave., Pur. 220 DQ111
Riddlesdown Rd., Pur. 220 DQ110
Riddons Rd. SE12 184 EJ90
Ride, The, Brent. 157 CH78
Ride, The, Enf. 82 DW41
Rideout St. SE18 165 EM77
Rider Clo., Sid. 185 ES86
Riders Way, Gdse. 252 DW131
Ridgdale St. E3 143 EA68
Ridge, The, Bex. 186 EZ87
Ridge, The, Cat. 253 EB126
Ridge, The, Couls. 219 DL114
Ridge, The, Epsom 232 CQ118
Ridge, The, Lthd. 231 CD124
Ridge, The, Orp. 205 ER103
Ridge, The, Pur. 219 DJ110
Ridge, The, Surb. 198 CN99
Ridge, The, Twick. 177 CD87
Ridge, The, Wok. 227 BB117
Ridge Ave. N21 100 DQ45
Ridge Ave., Dart. 187 FF86
Ridge Clo. NW4 97 CX54
Ridge Clo. NW9 118 CR56
Ridge Clo., Bet. 264 CP138
Ridge Clo., Wok. 226 AV121
Ridge Crest, Enf. 81 DM39
Ridge Grn., Red. 267 DL137
Ridge Grn. Clo., Red. 267 DL137
Ridge Hill NW11 119 CY60
Ridge La., Wat. 75 BS38
Ridge Langley, S.Croy. 220 DU109
Ridge Lea, Hem.H. 39 BF20
Ridge Pk., Pur. 219 DK110
Ridge Rd. N8 121 DM58
Ridge Rd. N21 100 DQ46
Ridge Rd. NW2 119 CZ62
Ridge Rd., Mitch. 181 DH94
Ridge Rd., Sutt. 199 CY102
Ridge St., Wat. 75 BV38
Ridge Way SE19 182 DS93
Central Hill
Ridge Way, Dart. 187 FF86
Ridge Way, Felt. 176 BY90
Ridge Way, Iver 133 BE73
Ridge Way, Rick. 92 BH45
Ridge Way, The, S.Croy. 220 DS109
Ridgebank, Slou. 131 AM73
Ridgebrook Rd. SE3 164 EJ83
Ridgecroft Clo., Bex. 187 FC88
Ridgefield, Wat. 75 BS37
Ridgegate Clo., Reig. 250 DD132
Ridgehurst Ave., Wat. 59 BT34
Ridgelands, Lthd. 231 CD124
Ridgemead Rd., Egh. 172 AU90
Ridgemont Gdns., Edg. 96 CQ49
Ridgemount, Guil. 258 AV135
Ridgemount, Wey. 195 BS103
Ridgemount Ave., Couls. 235 DH117
Ridgemount Ave., Croy. 203 DX103
Ridgemount Clo. SE20 182 DV94
Anerley Pk.
Ridgemount End, Ger.Cr. 90 AY50
Ridgemount Gdns., Enf. 81 DP41
Ridgemount Way, Red. 266 DD136
Ridges, The, Guil. 258 AW139
Ridgeview, St.Alb. 62 CM28
Ridgeview Clo., Barn. 79 CX44
Ridgeview Rd. N20 98 DB48
Ridgeway, Berk. 38 AT19
Ridgeway, Brwd. 109 GB46
Ridgeway, Brom. 204 EG103
Ridgeway, Dart. 189 FS92
Ridgeway, Epsom 216 CQ112
Ridgeway, Grays 170 GE77
Ridgeway, Welw.G.C. 30 DB09
Ridgeway, Wok. 226 AX115
Ridgeway, Wdf.Grn. 102 EJ49
Ridgeway, The E4 101 EB47
Ridgeway, The N3 98 DB52
Ridgeway, The N11 98 DF49
Ridgeway, The N14 99 DL47
Ridgeway, The NW7 97 CU48
Ridgeway, The NW9 118 CS56
Ridgeway, The NW11 119 CZ60
Ridgeway, The W3 158 CN76
Ridgeway, The, Amer. 55 AR40
Ridgeway, The, Croy. 201 DM104
Ridgeway, The, Enf. 81 DN39
Ridgeway, The, Ger.Cr. 112 AY55
Ridgeway, The, Guil. 259 BA135
Ridgeway, The, Har. 116 BZ57
Ridgeway, The (Kenton), Har. 117 CJ58
Ridgeway, The, Hert. 31 DM08
Ridgeway, The, Horl. 268 DG150
Ridgeway, The, Lthd. 214 CC114
Ridgeway, The (Oxshott), Lthd. 231 CD123
Ridgeway, The, Pot.B. 64 DD34
Ridgeway, The (Cuffley), Pot.B. 64 DE28
Ridgeway, The, Rad. 77 CF37
Ridgeway, The (Gidea Pk.), Rom. 127 FG56
Ridgeway, The (Harold Wd.), Rom. 106 FM53
Ridgeway, The, Ruis. 115 BU59
Ridgeway, The, St.Alb. 43 CG17
Ridgeway, The, Stan. 95 CJ51
Ridgeway, The, Sutt. 218 DD107
Ridgeway, The, Wat. 75 BS37
Ridgeway Ave., Barn. 80 DF44
Ridgeway Ave., Grav. 191 GH90
Ridgeway Clo., Chesh. 54 AP28
Ridgeway Clo., Dor. 263 CG138
Ridgeway Clo., Hem.H. 58 BM26
London Rd.
Ridgeway Clo., Lthd. 214 CC114
Ridgeway Clo., Wok. 226 AX115
Ridgeway Ct., Red. 250 DF134
Ridgeway Rd.
Ridgeway Cres., Orp. 205 ES104
Ridgeway Cres. Gdns., Orp. 205 ES103
Ridgeway Dr., Brom. 184 EH92
Ridgeway Dr., Dor. 263 CG139
Ridgeway E., Sid. 185 ET85
Ridgeway Gdns. N6 121 DJ59
Ridgeway Gdns., Ilf. 124 EL57
Ridgeway Gdns., Wok. 226 AX115
Ridgeway Ind. Est., Iver 133 BF73
Ridgeway Rd. SW9 161 DP83
Ridgeway Rd., Chesh. 54 AN28
Ridgeway Rd., Dor. 263 CG138
Ridgeway Rd., Islw. 157 CE80
Ridgeway Rd., Red. 250 DE134
Ridgeway Rd. N., Islw. 157 CE79
Ridgeway Wk., Nthlt. 136 BY65
Fortunes Mead

Rochford Way, Croy. 201 DL100
Rochford Way, Maid. 130 AG72
Rochfords Gdns., Slou. 132 AW74
Rock Ave. SW14 158 CR83
South Worple Way
Rock Gdns., Dag. 127 FB64
Rockwell Rd.
Rock Gro. Way SE16 162 DV77
Blue Anchor La.
Rock Hill SE26 182 DT91
Rock Hill, Orp. 224 FA107
Rock St. N4 121 DN61
Rockall Ct., Slou. 153 BB76
Rockbourne Rd. SE23 183 DX88
Rockchase Gdns., Horn. 128 FL58
Rockcliffe Ave., Kings L. 58 BN30
Rockdale Rd., Sev. 257 FH126
Rockells Pl. SE22 182 DV86
Rockfield Clo., Oxt. 254 EF131
Rockfield Rd., Oxt. 254 EF129
Rockford Ave., Grnf. 137 CG68
Rockhall Rd. NW2 119 CX63
Rockhampton Clo. SE27 181 DN91
Rockhampton Rd.
Rockhampton Rd. SE27 181 DN91
Rockhampton Rd., S.Croy. 220 DS107
Rockingham Ave., Horn. 127 FH58
Rockingham Clo. SW15 159 CT84
Rockingham Clo., Uxb. 134 BJ67
Rockingham Est. SE1 279 H7
Rockingham Est. SE1 162 DQ76
Rockingham Par., Uxb. 134 BJ66
Rockingham Rd., Uxb. 134 BH67
Rockingham St. SE1 279 H7
Rockingham St. SE1 162 DQ76
Rockland Rd. SW15 159 CY84
Rocklands Dr., Stan. 95 CH54
Rockleigh Ct., Brwd. 109 GA45
Hutton Rd.
Rockley Rd. W14 159 CX75
Rockmount Rd. SE18 165 ET78
Rockmount Rd. SE19 182 DR93
Rocks La. SW13 159 CU83
Rockshaw Rd., Red. 251 DJ127
Rockware Ave., Grnf. 137 CD67
Rockways, Barn. 79 CT44
Rockwell Gdns. SE19 182 DS91
Rockwell Rd., Dag. 127 FB64
Rockwood Pl. W12 159 CW75
Shepherds Bush Grn.
Rocky La., Reig. 250 DF128
Rocliffe St. N1 274 G1
Rocmoale Way SE8 163 EA80
Octavius St.
Rocombe Cres. SE23 182 DW87
Rocque La. SE3 164 EF83
Rodborough Rd. NW11 120 DA60
Roden Clo., Harl. 36 EZ11
Roden Ct. N6 121 DK59
Hornsey La.
Roden Gdns., Croy. 202 DS100
Roden St. N7 121 DM62
Roden St., Ilf. 125 EN62
Rodenhurst Rd. SW4 181 DJ86
Rodeo Clo., Erith 167 FH81
Hollywood Way
Roderick Rd. NW3 120 DF63
Rodgers Clo., Borwd. 77 CK44
Roding Ave., Wdf.Grn. 102 EL51
Roding Gdns., Loug. 84 EL44
Roding La., Buck.H. 102 EK46
Roding La., Chig. 103 EP47
Roding La. N., Wdf.Grn. 102 EL51
Roding La. S., Ilf. 124 EK56
Roding La. S., Wdf.Grn. 124 EK55
Roding Ms. E1 142 DU74
Kennet St.
Roding Rd. E5 123 DY63
Roding Rd. E6 145 EP71
Roding Rd., Loug. 84 EL43
Roding Trd. Est., Bark. 145 EP66
Roding Vw., Buck.H. 102 EK46
Roding Way, Rain. 148 FK68
Rodings, The, Upmin. 129 FR58
Rodings, The, Wdf.Grn. 102 EJ51
Rodings Row, Barn. 79 CY43
Leecroft Rd.
Rodmarton St. W1 272 E7
Rodmarton St. W1 140 DF71
Rodmell Clo., Hayes 136 BY70
Rodmell Slope N12 97 CZ50
Rodmere St. SE10 164 EE78
Trafalgar Rd.
Rodmill La. SW2 181 DL87
Rodney Ave., St.Alb. 43 CG22
Rodney Clo., Croy. 201 DP102
Rodney Clo., N.Mal. 198 CS99
Rodney Clo., Pnr. 116 BY59
Rodney Clo., Walt. 196 BW102
Rodney Rd.
Rodney Ct. W9 140 DC70
Maida Vale
Rodney Cres., Hodd. 49 EA15
Rodney Gdns., Pnr. 115 BV57
Rodney Gdns., W.Wick. 222 EG105
Rodney Grn., Walt. 196 BW103
Rodney Pl. E17 101 DY54
Rodney Pl. SE17 279 J8
Rodney Pl. SE17 162 DQ77
Rodney Pl. SW19 200 DC95
Rodney Rd. E11 124 EH56
Rodney Rd. SE17 279 J8
Rodney Rd. SE17 162 DQ77
Rodney Rd., Mitch. 200 DE96
Rodney Rd., N.Mal. 198 CS99
Rodney Rd., Twick. 176 CA87
Rodney Rd., Walt. 196 BW103
Rodney St. N1 141 DM68
Rodney Way, Guil. 243 BA133
Rodney Way, Rom. 104 FA53
Rodney Way, Slou. 153 BE81
Rodona Rd., Wey. 213 BR111
Rodway Rd. SW15 179 CU87
Rodway Rd., Brom. 204 EH95
Rodwell Clo., Ruis. 116 BW60
Rodwell Ct., Add. 212 BJ105
Garfield Rd.
Rodwell Pl., Edg. 96 CN51
Whitchurch La.
Rodwell Rd. SE22 182 DT86
Roe End NW9 118 CQ56
Roe Grn. NW9 118 CQ57
Roe Grn. Clo., Hat. 44 CS19
Roe Grn. La., Hat. 45 CT18
Roe Hill Clo., Hat. 45 CT19
Roe La. NW9 118 CP56
Roe Way, Wall. 219 DL108
Roebourne Way E16 165 EN75
Roebuck Clo., Ash. 232 CL120
Roebuck Clo., Felt. 175 BV91
Roebuck Clo., Reig. 250 DA134
Roebuck Grn., Slou. 131 AL74
Roebuck La. N17 100 DT51
High Rd.
Roebuck La., Buck.H. 102 EJ45
Roebuck Rd., Chess. 216 CN106
Roebuck Rd., Ilf. 104 EV50
Roedean Ave., Enf. 82 DW39
Roedean Clo., Enf. 82 DW39
Roedean Clo., Orp. 224 EV105
Roedean Cres. SW15 178 CS86
Roefields Clo., Hem.H. 40 BG24
Roehampton Clo. SW15 159 CU84
Roehampton Clo., Grav. 191 GL87
Roehampton Dr., Chis. 185 EQ93
Roehampton Gate SW15 178 CS86
Roehampton High St. SW15 179 CU87
Roehampton La. SW15 159 CU84
Roehampton Vale SW15 179 CT90
Roehyde Way, Hat. 44 CS20
Roestock Gdns., St.Alb. 44 CS22
Roestock La., St.Alb. 44 CR23
Rofant Rd., Nthwd. 93 BS51
Roffes La., Cat. 236 DR124
Roffey Clo., Horl. 268 DF148
Court Lo. Rd.
Roffey Clo., Pur. 235 DP116
Roffey St. E14 163 EC75
Roffords, Wok. 226 AV117
Rogate Ho. E5 122 DU62
Muir Rd.
Roger St. WC1 274 C5
Roger St. WC1 141 DM70
Rogers Clo., Cat. 236 DV122
Tillingdown Hill
Rogers Clo., Couls. 235 DP118
Rogers Ct., Swan. 207 FG98
Rogers Gdns., Dag. 126 FA64
Rogers La., Slou. 132 AT67
Rogers La., Warl. 237 DZ118
Rogers Mead, Gdse. 252 DV132
Ivy Mill La.
Rogers Rd. E16 144 EF72
Rogers Rd. SW17 180 DD91
Rogers Rd., Dag. 126 FA64
Rogers Rd., Grays 170 GC77
Rogers Ruff, Nthwd. 93 BQ53
Rogers Wk. N12 98 DB48
Brook Meadow
Rojack Rd. SE23 183 DX88
Roke Clo., Ken. 220 DQ114
Roke Lo. Rd., Ken. 219 DP113
Roke Rd., Ken. 236 DQ115
Rokeby Ct., Wok. 226 AT117
Rokeby Gdns., Wdf.Grn. 102 EG53
Rokeby Pl. SW20 179 CV94
Rokeby Rd. SE4 163 DZ82
Rokeby St. E15 143 ED67
Roker Pk. Ave., Uxb. 114 BL63
Rokesby Clo., Well. 165 ER82
Rokesby Pl., Wem. 117 CK64
Rokesby Rd., Slou. 131 AM69
Rokesly Ave. N8 121 DL57
Rokewood Ms., Ware 33 DX05
Roland Gdns. SW7 160 DC78
Roland Gdns., Felt. 176 BZ90
Roland Ms. E1 143 DX71
Stepney Grn.
Roland Rd. E17 123 ED56
Roland St., St.Alb. 43 CG20
Roland Way SE17 162 DR78
Roland Way SW7 160 DC78
Roland Gdns.
Roland Way, Wor.Pk. 199 CT103
Roles Gro., Rom. 126 EX56
Rolfe Clo., Barn. 80 DE42
Rolfe Clo., Beac. 89 AL54
Rolinsden Way, Kes. 222 EK105
Roll Gdns., Ilf. 125 EN57
Rollesby Rd., Chess. 216 CN107
Rollesby Way SE28 146 EW73
Rolleston Ave., Orp. 205 EP100
Rolleston Clo., Orp. 205 EP101
Rolleston Rd., S.Croy. 220 DR108
Rollins St. SE15 162 DW79
Rollit Cres., Houns. 176 CA85
Rollit St. N7 121 DM64
Hornsey Rd.
Rollo Rd., Swan. 187 FF94
Rolls Bldgs. EC4 274 D8
Rolls Pk. Ave. E4 101 EA51
Rolls Pk. Rd. E4 101 EB50
Rolls Pas. EC4 274 D8
Rolls Rd. SE1 162 DT78
Rollscourt Ave. SE24 182 DQ85
Rollswood, Welw.G.C. 29 CY12
Rolt St. SE8 163 DY79
Rolvenden Gdns., Brom. 184 EK94
Rolvenden Pl. N17 100 DU53
Manor Rd.
Rom Cres., Rom. 127 FF59
Rom Valley Way, Rom. 127 FE58
Roma Read Clo. SW15 179 CV87
Bessborough Rd.
Roma Rd. E17 123 DY55
Roman Clo. W3 158 CP75
Avenue Gdns.
Roman Clo., Felt. 176 BW85
Roman Clo., Rain. 147 FD68
Roman Clo., Uxb. 92 BG53
Roman Gdns., Kings L. 59 BP30
Roman Ms., Hodd. 49 EA16
North Rd.
Roman Ri. SE19 182 DR93
Roman Rd. E2 142 DW69
Roman Rd. E3 143 DY68
Roman Rd. E6 144 EK70
Roman Rd. N10 99 DH52
Roman Rd. NW2 119 CW62
Roman Rd. W4 159 CT77
Roman Rd., Brwd. 109 GC41
Roman Rd., Dor. 263 CG138
Roman Rd., Grav. 190 GC90
Roman Rd., Hert. 32 DV14
Roman Rd., Ilf. 145 EP65
Roman Sq. SE28 146 EU74
Roman St., Hodd. 49 EA16
Roman Vale, Harl. 36 EW10
Roman Vill. Rd. 188 FQ92
(South Darenth), Dart.
Roman Way N7 141 DM65
Roman Way SE15 162 DW80
Clifton Way
Roman Way, Croy. 201 DP103
Roman Way, Dart. 187 FE85
Roman Way, Enf. 82 DT43
Roman Way, Slou. 131 AP71
Roman Way Ind. Est. N1 141 DM66
Offord St.
Romanhurst Ave., Brom. 204 EE98
Romanhurst Gdns., Brom. 204 EE98
Romans End, St.Alb. 42 CC22
Romans Way, Wok. 228 BG115
Romany Gdns. E17 101 DY53
McEntee Ave.
Romany Gdns., Sutt. 200 DA101
Romany Ri., Orp. 205 EQ102
Romberg Rd. SW17 180 DG90
Romborough Gdns. SE13 183 EC85
Romborough Way SE13 183 EC85
Romeland, Borwd. 77 CK44
Romeland, Wal.Abb. 67 EC33
Romeland Hill, St.Alb. 42 CC20
Romero Clo. SW9 161 DM83
Stockwell Rd.
Romero Sq. SE3 164 EJ84
Romeyn Rd. SW16 181 DM90
Romford Rd. E7 124 EH64
Romford Rd. E12 124 EL63
Romford Rd. E15 144 EE65
Romford Rd., Chig. 104 EU48
Romford Rd., Rom. 104 EY52
Romford Rd., S.Ock. 148 FQ69
Romford St. E1 142 DU71
Romilly Dr., Wat. 94 BY49
Romilly Rd. N4 121 DP61
Romilly St. W1 273 M10
Romilly St. W1 141 DK73
Rommany Rd. SE27 182 DR91
Romney Chase, Horn. 128 FM58
Romney Clo. N17 100 DV53
Romney Clo. NW11 120 DC60
Romney Clo. SE14 162 DW80
Kender St.
Romney Clo., Ashf. 175 BQ92
Romney Clo., Chess. 216 CL105
Romney Clo., Har. 116 CA59
Romney Dr., Brom. 184 EK94
Romney Dr., Har. 116 CA59
Romney Gdns., Bexh. 166 EZ81
Romney Lock Rd., Wind. 151 AR80
Romney Ms. W1 272 F6
Romney Par., Hayes 135 BR68
Romney Rd.
Romney Rd. SE10 163 EC79
Romney Rd., Grav. 190 GE90
Romney Rd., Hayes 135 BR68
Romney Rd., N.Mal. 198 CR100
Romney Row NW2 119 CX61
Brent Ter.
Romney St. SW1 277 P7
Romney St. SW1 161 DL76
Romola Rd. SE24 181 DP88
Romsey Clo., Orp. 223 EP105
Romsey Clo., Slou. 153 AZ76
Romsey Dr., Slou. 111 AR62
Romsey Gdns., Dag. 146 EX67
Romsey Rd. W13 137 CG73
Romsey Rd., Dag. 146 EX67
Ron Leighton Way E6 144 EL67
Rona Rd. NW3 120 DG63
Rona Wk. N1 142 DR65
Clephane Rd.
Ronald Ave. E15 144 EE69
Ronald Clo., Beck. 203 DZ98
Ronald Rd., Beac. 89 AM53
Ronald Rd., Rom. 106 FN53
Ronald St. E1 142 DW72
Devonport St.
Ronalds Rd. N5 121 DN64
Ronalds Rd., Brom. 204 EG95
Ronaldsay Spur, Slou. 132 AS71
Ronaldstone Rd., Sid. 185 ES86
Ronart St., Har. 117 CF55
Stuart Rd.
Rondu Rd. NW2 119 CY64
Ronelean Rd., Surb. 198 CM104
Roneo Cor., Horn. 127 FF60
Hornchurch Rd.
Roneo Link, Horn. 127 FF60
Ronfearn Ave., Orp. 206 EX99
Ronneby Clo., Wey. 195 BS104
Ronson Way, Lthd. 231 CG121
Randalls Rd.
Ronver Rd. SE12 184 EG88
Baring Rd.
Rood La. EC3 275 M10
Rood La. EC3 142 DS73
Rook Clo., Horn. 147 FG66
Rook La., Cat. 235 DM124
Rook Rd., H.Wyc. 110 AD59
Rook Wk. E6 144 EL72
Allhallows Rd.
Rookdean, Sev. 256 FC122
Rooke Way SE10 164 EF78
Rookeries Clo., Felt. 175 BV90
Rookery, The, Dor. 262 CA138
Rookery, The, Grays 169 FU79
Rookery Clo. NW9 119 CT57
Rookery Clo., Lthd. 231 CE124
Rookery Ct., Grays 169 FU79
Rookery Cres., Dag. 147 FB66
Rookery Dr., Chis. 205 EN95
Rookery Dr., Dor. 262 CA138
Rookery Gdns., Orp. 206 EW99
Rookery Hill, Ash. 232 CN118
Rookery Hill, Red. 269 DN145
Rookery La., Brom. 204 EK100
Rookery La., Grays 170 GE78
Rookery La., Horl. 269 DN146
Rookery Rd. SW4 161 DJ84
Rookery Rd., Orp. 223 EM110
Rookery Rd., Stai. 174 BH92
Rookery Vw., Grays 170 GD78
Rookery Way NW9 119 CT57
Rookery Way, Tad. 249 CZ127
Rookes All., Hert. 32 DR09
Gascoyne Way
Rookesley Rd., Orp. 206 EX101
Rookfield Ave. N10 121 DJ56
Rookfield Clo. N10 121 DJ56
Cranmore Way
Rookley Clo., Sutt. 218 DB110
Rooks Clo., Welw.G.C. 29 CX10
Rooks Hill, Rick. 74 BK42
Rooks Hill, Welw.G.C. 29 CW10
Rooksmead Rd., Sun. 195 BT96
Rookstone Rd. SW17 180 DF92
Rookwood Ave., Loug. 85 EQ41
Rookwood Ave., N.Mal. 199 CU98
Rookwood Ave., Wall. 219 DK105
Rookwood Clo., Grays 170 GB77
Rookwood Clo., Red. 251 DH129
Rookwood Ct., Guil. 258 AW137
Rookwood Gdns. E4 102 EF46
Whitehall Rd.
Rookwood Gdns., Loug. 85 EQ41
Rookwood Ho., Bark. 145 ER68
St. Marys
Rookwood Rd. N16 122 DT59
Roosevelt Way, Dag. 147 FD65
Rootes Dr. W10 139 CX70
Roothill La., Bet. 264 CN140
Rope St. SE16 163 DY76
Rope Wk., Sun. 196 BW97
Rope Wk. Gdns. E1 142 DU72
Commercial Rd.
Rope Yd. Rails SE18 165 EP76
Ropemaker Rd. SE16 163 DY75
Ropemaker St. EC2 275 K6
Ropemaker St. EC2 142 DR71
Ropemakers Flds. E14 143 DZ73
Narrow St.
Roper La. SE1 279 N5
Roper St. SE9 185 EM86
Roper Way, Mitch. 200 DG96
Ropers Ave. E4 101 EB50
Ropers Wk. SW2 181 DN87
Brockwell Pk. Gdns.
Ropery St. E3 143 DZ70
Ropley St. E2 142 DU68
Rosa Alba Ms. N5 122 DQ63
Kelross Rd.
Rosa Ave., Ashf. 174 BN91
Rosaline Rd. SW6 159 CY80
Rosamond St. SE26 182 DV90
Rosamund Clo., S.Croy. 220 DR105
Rosary, The, Egh. 193 BE96
Rosary Clo., Houns. 156 BY82
Rosary Ct., Pot.B. 64 DB30
Rosary Gdns. SW7 160 DC77
Rosary Gdns., Ashf. 175 BP91
Rosaville Rd. SW6 159 CZ80
Roscoe St. EC1 275 J5
Roscoff Clo., Edg. 96 CQ53
Rose All. SE1 279 J2
Rose All. SE1 142 DQ74
Rose & Crown Ct. EC2 275 H8
Rose & Crown Yd. SW1 277 L2
Rose Ave. E18 102 EH54
Rose Ave., Grav. 191 GL88
Rose Ave., Mitch. 200 DF95
Rose Ave., Mord. 200 DC99
Rose Bank, Brwd. 108 FX48
Rose Bank Cotts., Wok. 226 AY122
Rose Bates Dr. NW9 118 CN56
Rose Bushes, Epsom 233 CV116
Rose Ct. E1 142 DS71
Sandy's Row
Rose Ct. SE26 182 DV89
Rose Ct., Pnr. 116 BW55
Nursery Rd.
Rose Ct., Wal.Cr. 66 DU27
Rose Dale, Orp. 205 EP103
Rose Dr., Chesh. 54 AR33
Rose End, Wor.Pk. 199 CX102
Rose Gdn. Clo., Edg. 96 CL51
Rose Gdns. W5 157 CK76
Rose Gdns., Felt. 175 BU89
Rose Gdns., Sthl. 136 CA70
Rose Gdns., Stai. 174 BK87
Diamedes Ave.
Rose Gdns., Wat. 75 BU43
Rose Glen NW9 118 CR56
Rose Glen, Rom. 127 FE60
Rose Hill, Dor. 263 CG137
Rose Hill, Slou. 130 AG67
Rose Hill, Sutt. 200 DB104
Rose La., Rom. 126 EX55
Rose La., Wok. 228 BJ121
Rose Lawn (Bushey), Wat. 94 CC46
Rose St. WC2 273 P10
Rose St., Grav. 190 GB86
Rose Vale, Hodd. 49 EA17
Rose Valley, Brwd. 108 FW48
Rose Vill., Dart. 188 FP87
Rose Wk., Pur. 219 DK111
Rose Wk., St.Alb. 43 CJ18
Rose Wk., Slou. 131 AP71
Birch Gro.
Rose Wk., Surb. 198 CP99
Rose Wk., W.Wick. 203 EC103
Rose Wk., The, Rad. 77 CH37
Rose Way SE12 184 EG85
Roseacre, Oxt. 254 EG134
Roseacre Clo. W13 137 CH71
Middlefielde
Roseacre Clo., Horn. 128 FM60
Roseacre Clo., Shep. 194 BN99
Roseacre Gdns., Guil. 259 BF140
Roseacre Gdns., 30 DD09
Welw.G.C.
Roseacre Rd., Well. 166 EV83
Roseary Clo., West Dr. 154 BK77
Rosebank SE20 182 DV94
Rosebank, Epsom 216 CQ114
Rosebank, Wal.Abb. 68 EE33
Rosebank Ave., Horn. 128 FJ64
Rosebank Ave., Wem. 117 CF63
Rosebank Clo. N12 98 DE50
Rosebank Clo., Tedd. 177 CG93
Rosebank Gdns. E3 143 DZ68
Rosebank Gro. E17 123 DZ55
Rosebank Rd. E17 123 EB58
Rosebank Rd. W7 157 CE75
Rosebank Vill. E17 123 EA56
Rosebank Wk. NW1 141 DK66
Maiden La.
Rosebank Wk. SE18 164 EL77
Woodhill
Rosebank Way W3 138 CR72
Roseberry Clo., Upmin. 129 FT58
Roseberry Ct., Wat. 75 BU39
Grandfield Ave.
Roseberry Gdns. N4 121 DP58
Roseberry Gdns., Dart. 188 FJ87
Roseberry Gdns., Orp. 205 ES104
Roseberry Gdns., Upmin. 129 FS58
Roseberry Pl. E8 142 DT65
Roseberry St. SE16 162 DV77
Rosebery Ave. E12 144 EL65
Rosebery Ave. EC1 274 D4
Rosebery Ave. EC1 141 DN70
Rosebery Ave. N17 100 DU54
Rosebery Ave., Epsom 216 CS114
Rosebery Ave., Har. 116 BY63
Rosebery Ave., N.Mal. 199 CT96
Rosebery Ave., Sid. 185 ES87
Rosebery Ave., Th.Hth. 202 DQ96
Rosebery Clo., Mord. 199 CX100
Rosebery Ct. EC1 141 DN70
Rosebery Ave.
Rosebery Ct., Grav. 191 GF88
Rosebery Cres., Wok. 227 AZ121
Rosebery Gdns. N8 121 DL57
Rosebery Gdns. W13 137 CG72
Rosebery Gdns., Sutt. 218 DB105
Rosebery Ms. N10 99 DJ54
Rosebery Ms. SW2 181 DL86
Rosebery Rd.
Rosebery Rd. N9 100 DU48
Rosebery Rd. N10 99 DJ54
Rosebery Rd. SW2 181 DL86
Rosebery Rd., Epsom 232 CR119
Rosebery Rd., Grays 170 FY79
Rosebery Rd., Houns. 176 CC85
Rosebery Rd., Kings.T. 198 CP96
Rosebery Rd., Sutt. 217 CZ107
Rosebery Rd. (Bushey), 94 CB45
Wat.
Rosebery Sq. EC1 274 D5
Rosebery Sq., Kings.T. 198 CP96
Rosebine Ave., Twick. 177 CD87
Rosebriar Clo., Wok. 228 BG116
Rosebriar Wk., Wat. 75 BT36
Rosebriars, Cat. 236 DS120
Salmons La. W.
Rosebriars, Esher 214 CC106
Rosebury Rd. SW6 160 DB82
Rosebury Vale, Ruis. 115 BU61
Rosecourt Rd., Croy. 201 DM100
Rosecroft Ave. NW3 120 DA62
Rosecroft Clo., Orp. 206 EW100
Rosecroft Clo., West. 239 EM118
Lotus Rd.
Rosecroft Dr., Wat. 75 BS36
Rosecroft Gdns. NW2 119 CU62
Rosecroft Gdns., Twick. 177 CD88
Rosecroft Rd., Sthl. 136 CA70
Rosecroft Wk., Pnr. 116 BX57
Rosecroft Wk., Wem. 117 CK64
Rosedale, Ash. 231 CJ118
Rosedale, Cat. 236 DS123
Rosedale, Welw.G.C. 29 CZ05
Rosedale Ave., Hayes 135 BR71
Rosedale Ave. 66 DT29
(Cheshunt), Wal.Cr.
Rosedale Clo. SE2 166 EV76
Finchale Rd.
Rosedale Clo. W7 157 CF75
Boston Rd.
Rosedale Clo., Dart. 188 FP87
Rosedale Clo., St.Alb. 60 BY30
Rosedale Clo., Stan. 95 CH51
Rosedale Ct. N5 121 DP63
Panmure Clo.
Rosedale Gdns., Dag. 146 EV66
Rosedale Rd. E7 124 EJ64
Rosedale Rd., Dag. 146 EV66
Rosedale Rd., Epsom 217 CU106
Rosedale Rd., Grays 170 GD78
Rosedale Rd., Rich. 158 CL84
Rosedale Rd., Rom. 105 FC54
Rosedale Ter. W6 159 CV76
Dalling Rd.
Rosedale Way 66 DU27
(Cheshunt), Wal.Cr.
Rosedene NW6 139 CX67
Rosedene Ave. SW16 181 DM90
Rosedene Ave., Croy. 201 DL101
Rosedene Ave., Grnf. 136 CA69
Rosedene Ave., Mord. 200 DA99
Rosedene Ct., Dart. 188 FJ87
Shepherds La.
Rosedene Ct., Ruis. 115 BS60
Rosedene Gdns., Ilf. 125 EN56
Rosedene Ter. E10 123 EB61
Rosedew Rd. W6 159 CX79
Rosefield, Sev. 256 FG124
Rosefield Clo., Cars. 218 DE106
Alma Rd.
Rosefield Gdns. E14 143 EA73
Rosefield Gdns., Cher. 211 BD107
Rosefield Rd., Stai. 174 BG91
Roseford Ct. W12 159 CX75
Shepherds Bush Grn.
Rosehart Ms. W11 140 DA72
Westbourne Gro.
Rosehatch Ave., Rom. 126 EX55
Roseheath, Hem.H. 39 BF19
Roseheath Rd., Houns. 176 BZ85
Rosehill, Esher 215 CG107
Rosehill, Hmptn. 196 CA95
Rosehill Ave., Sutt. 200 DC102
Rosehill Ave., Wok. 226 AW116
Rosehill Clo., Hodd. 49 DZ17
Rosehill Ct., Slou. 152 AU76
Yew Tree Rd.
Rosehill Fm. Meadow, 234 DB115
Bans.
The Tracery
Rosehill Gdns., Abb.L. 59 BQ32
Rosehill Gdns., Grnf. 117 CF64
Rosehill Gdns., Sutt. 200 DB103
Rosehill Pk. W., Sutt. 200 DB102
Rosehill Rd. SW18 180 DC86
Rosehill Rd., West. 238 EJ117
Roseland Clo. N17 100 DR52
Cavell Rd.
Roselands Ave., Hodd. 49 DZ15
Roseleigh Ave. N5 121 DP63
Roseleigh Clo., Twick. 177 CK86
Roseley Cotts., Harl. 35 EP11
Rosemary Ave. N3 98 DB54
Rosemary Ave. N9 100 DV46
Rosemary Ave., Enf. 82 DR39
Rosemary Ave., Houns. 156 BX82
Rosemary Ave., Rom. 127 FF55
Rosemary Ave., W.Mol. 196 CA97
Rosemary Clo., Croy. 201 DL101

Rosemary Clo., Harl. 36 EW11
Rosemary Clo., Oxt. 254 EG133
Rosemary Clo., S.Ock. 149 FW69
Rosemary Clo., Uxb. 134 BN71
Rosemary Ct., Horl. 268 DE147
Rosemary Cres., Guil. 242 AT130
Rosemary Dr. E14 143 ED72
Rosemary Dr., Ilf. 124 EK57
Rosemary Gdns. SW14 158 CQ83
Rosemary La.
Rosemary Gdns., Chess. 216 CL105
Rosemary Gdns., Dag. 126 EZ60
Rosemary La. SW14 158 CQ83
Rosemary La., Egh. 193 BB97
Rosemary La., Horl. 269 DH149
Rosemary Pl. N1 142 DR67
Shepperton Rd.
Rosemary Rd. SE15 162 DT80
Rosemary Rd. SW17 180 DC90
Rosemary Rd., Well. 165 ET81
Rosemary St. N1 142 DR67
Shepperton Rd.
Rosemead NW9 119 CT59
Rosemead, Cher. 194 BH101
Rosemead, Pot.B. 64 DC30
Rosemead Ave., Felt. 175 BT89
Rosemead Ave., Mitch. 201 DJ96
Rosemead Ave., Wem. 118 CL64
Rosemead Clo., Red. 266 DD136
Rosemead Gdns., Brwd. 109 GD42
Rosemont Ave. N12 98 DC51
Rosemont Rd. NW3 140 DC65
Rosemont Rd. W3 138 CP73
Rosemont Rd., Kings.T. 198 CQ97
Rosemont Rd., N.Mal. 198 CQ97
Rosemont Rd., Rich. 178 CL86
Rosemont Rd., Wem. 138 CL67
Rosemoor St. SW3 276 D9
Rosemoor St. SW3 160 DF77
Rosemount, Harl. 51 EP18
Rosemount Ave., W.Byf. 212 BG113
Rosemount Clo., Wdf.Grn. 103 EM51
Chapelmount Rd.
Rosemount Dr., Brom. 205 EM98
Rosemount Rd. W13 137 CG72
Rosenau Cres. SW11 160 DE81
Rosenau Rd. SW11 160 DE81
Rosendale Rd. SE21 182 DQ87
Rosendale Rd. SE24 182 DQ87
Roseneath Ave. N21 99 DP46
Roseneath Clo., Orp. 224 EW108
Roseneath Rd. SW11 180 DG86
Roseneath Wk., Enf. 82 DR42
Rosens Wk., Edg. 96 CP48
Rosenthal Rd. SE6 183 EB86
Rosenthorpe Rd. SE15 183 DX85
Roserton St. E14 163 EC75
Rosery, The, Croy. 203 DX100
Roses, The, Wdf.Grn. 102 EF52
Roses La., Wind. 151 AK82
Rosethorn Clo. SW12 181 DK87
Rosetrees, Guil. 259 BA135
Rosetta Clo. SW8 161 DL80
Kenchester Clo.
Rosetti Ter., Dag. 126 EV63
Marlborough Rd.
Roseveare Rd. SE12 184 EJ91
Roseville Ave., Houns. 176 CA85
Roseville Rd., Hayes 155 BU78
Rosevine Rd. SW20 199 CW95
Rosewarne Clo., Wok. 226 AU118
Muirfield Rd.
Roseway SE21 182 DR86
Rosewell Clo. SE20 182 DV94
Rosewood, Dart. 187 FE91
Rosewood, Esher 197 CG103
Rosewood, Sutt. 218 DC110
Rosewood, Wok. 227 BA119
Rosewood Ave., Grnf. 117 CG64
Rosewood Ave., Horn. 127 FG64
Rosewood Clo., Sid. 186 EW90
Rosewood Ct., Brom. 204 EJ95
Rosewood Ct., Hem.H. 39 BE19
Rosewood Ct., Rom. 126 EW57
Tendring Way
Rosewood Dr., Enf. 81 DN35
Rosewood Dr., Shep. 194 BM99
Rosewood Gdns. SE13 163 EC82
Lewisham Rd.
Rosewood Gro., Sutt. 200 DC103
Rosewood Sq. W12 139 CU72
Primula St.
Rosewood Ter. SE20 182 DW94
Laurel Gro.
Rosewood Way, Slou. 111 AQ64
Rosher Clo. E15 143 ED66
Rosherville Way, Grav. 190 GE87
Rosina St. E9 123 DX64
Roskell Rd. SW15 159 CX83
Rosken Dr., Slou. 131 AP68
Roslin Rd. W3 158 CP76
Roslin Way, Brom. 184 EG92
Roslyn Clo., Brox. 49 DY21
Roslyn Clo., Mitch. 200 DD96
Roslyn Ct., Wok. 226 AU118
St. John's Rd.
Roslyn Gdns., Rom. 105 FE54
Roslyn Rd. N15 122 DR57
Rosmead Rd. W11 139 CY73
Rosoman Pl. EC1 274 E4
Rosoman St. EC1 274 E3
Rosoman St. EC1 141 DN69
Ross Ave. NW7 97 CY50
Ross Ave., Dag. 126 EZ61
Ross Clo., Har. 94 CC52
Ross Clo., Hat. 45 CU15
Homestead Rd.
Ross Clo., Hayes 155 BR76
Ross Ct. SW15 179 CX87
Ross Cres., Wat. 75 BU35
Ross Par., Wall. 219 DH107
Ross Rd. SE25 202 DR97
Ross Rd., Cob. 214 BW113
Ross Rd., Dart. 187 FG86
Ross Rd., Twick. 176 CB88
Ross Rd., Wall. 219 DJ106
Ross Way SE9 164 EL83
Ross Way, Nthwd. 93 BT49
Rossall Clo., Horn. 127 FG58
Rossall Cres. NW10 138 CM69
Rossdale, Sutt. 218 DE106
Rossdale Dr. N9 82 DW44
Rossdale Dr. NW9 118 CQ60
Rossdale Rd. SW15 159 CW84
Rosse Ms. SE3 164 EH81
Rossendale St. E5 122 DV61
Rossendale Way NW1 141 DJ67
Rossetti Gdns., Couls. 235 DM118
Rossetti Rd. SE16 162 DV78
Rossgate, Hem.H. 40 BG18
Galley Hill
Rossignol Gdns., Cars. 200 DG103
Rossindel Rd., Houns. 176 CA85
Rossington Ave., Borwd. 78 CL38
Rossington St. E5 122 DU61
Rossiter Clo., Slou. 152 AY77
Rossiter Flds., Barn. 79 CY44
Rossiter Rd. SW12 181 DH88
Rossland Clo., Bexh. 187 FB85
Rosslare Clo., West. 255 ER125
Rosslyn Ave. E4 102 EF47
Rosslyn Ave. SW13 158 CS83
Rosslyn Ave., Barn. 80 DE44
Rosslyn Ave., Dag. 126 EZ59
Rosslyn Ave., Felt. 175 BU86
Rosslyn Ave., Rom. 106 FM54
Rosslyn Clo., Hayes 135 BR71
Morgans La.
Rosslyn Clo., Sun. 175 BS93
Cadbury Rd.
Rosslyn Clo., W.Wick. 204 EF104
Rosslyn Cres., Har. 117 CF56
Rosslyn Cres., Wem. 118 CL63
Rosslyn Hill NW3 120 DD63
Rosslyn Ms. NW3 120 DD63
Rosslyn Hill
Rosslyn Pk., Wey. 213 BR105
Rosslyn Pk. Ms. NW3 120 DD64
Lyndhurst Rd.
Rosslyn Rd. E17 123 EC56
Rosslyn Rd., Bark. 145 ER66
Rosslyn Rd., Twick. 177 CJ86
Rosslyn Rd., Wat. 75 BV41
Rossmore Rd. NW1 272 C5
Rossmore Rd. NW1 140 DE70
Rossway Dr. (Bushey), Wat. 76 CC43
Rosswood Gdns., Wall. 219 DH107
Rostella Rd. SW17 180 DD91
Rostrevor Ave. N15 122 DT58
Rostrevor Gdns., Hayes 135 BS74
Rostrevor Gdns., Iver 133 BD68
Rostrevor Gdns., Sthl. 156 BY78
Rostrevor Ms. SW6 159 CZ81
Rostrevor Rd.
Rostrevor Rd. SW6 159 CZ81
Rostrevor Rd. SW19 180 DA92
Roswell Clo. (Cheshunt), Wal.Cr. 67 DY30
Rotary St. SE1 278 F6
Roth Dr., Brwd. 109 GB47
Roth Wk. N7 121 DM62
Durham Rd.
Rothbury Ave., Rain. 147 FH71
Rothbury Gdns., Islw. 157 CG80
Rothbury Rd. E9 143 DZ66
Rothbury Wk. N17 100 DU52
Northumberland Gro.
Rother Clo., Wat. 60 BW34
Rotherfield Rd., Cars. 218 DG105
Rotherfield Rd., Enf. 83 DX37
Rotherfield St. N1 142 DQ66
Rotherham Wk. SE1 278 F3
Rotherhill Ave. SW16 181 DK93
Rotherhithe New Rd. SE16 162 DV78
Rotherhithe Old Rd. SE16 163 DX77
Rotherhithe St. SE16 162 DW75
Rotherhithe Tunnel E1 143 DX74
Rotherhithe Tunnel App. E14 143 DY73
Rotherhithe Tunnel App. SE16 162 DW75
Rothermere Rd., Croy. 219 DM106
Rothervale, Horl. 268 DG145
Rotherwick Hill W5 138 CM70
Rotherwick Rd. NW11 120 DA59
Rotherwood Clo. SW20 199 CY95
Rotherwood Rd. SW15 159 CX83
Rothery St. N1 141 DP67
Gaskin St.
Rothery Ter. SW9 161 DP80
Foxley Rd.
Rothes Rd., Dor. 263 CH135
Rothesay Ave. SW20 199 CY96
Rothesay Ave., Grnf. 137 CD65
Rothesay Ave., Rich. 158 CP84
Rothesay Rd. SE25 202 DR98
Rothsay Rd. E7 144 EJ66
Rothsay St. SE1 279 M6
Rothsay St. SE1 162 DS76
Rothsay Wk. E14 163 EA77
Charnwood Gdns.
Rothschild Rd. W4 158 CQ76
Rothschild St. SE27 181 DP91
Rothwell Gdns., Dag. 146 EW66
Rothwell Rd., Dag. 146 EW67
Rothwell St. NW1 140 DF67
Rotten Row SW1 276 D4
Rotten Row SW7 276 C4
Rotten Row SW7 160 DE75
Rotterdam Dr. E14 163 EC76
Rouel Rd. SE16 162 DU76
Rouge La., Grav. 191 GH88
Rougemont Ave., Mord. 200 DA100
Rough Lands, Wok. 227 BE115
Rough Rew, Dor. 263 CH139
Roughdown Ave., Hem.H. 40 BG23
Roughdown Rd., Hem.H. 40 BH23
Roughdown Vill. Rd., Hem.H. 40 BG23
Roughetts La., Cat. 252 DT129
Roughetts La., Red. 252 DS129
Roughlands, Wok. 227 BE115
Roughs, The, Nthwd. 93 BS48
Roughtallys, Epp. 70 EZ27
Roughwood Clo., Wat. 75 BS38
Roughwood La., Ch.St.G. 90 AY45
Round Gro., Croy. 203 DX101
Round Hill SE26 182 DW90
Round Oak Rd., Wey. 212 BM105
Roundacre SW19 179 CX89
Inner Pk. Rd.
Roundaway Rd., Ilf. 103 EM53
Roundcroft (Cheshunt), Wal.Cr. 66 DT26
Roundel Clo. SE4 163 DZ84
Adelaide Ave.
Roundhay Clo. SE23 183 DX89
Roundheads End, Beac. 88 AH51
Roundhedge Way, Enf. 81 DM38
Roundhill, Wok. 227 BB119
Old Woking Rd.
Roundhill Dr., Enf. 81 DM42
Roundhill Dr., Wok. 227 BB118
Old Woking Rd.
Roundhill Way, Cob. 214 CB112
Roundhill Way, Guil. 242 AT134
Roundhills, Wal.Abb. 67 ED34
Roundings, The, Hert. 32 DV14
Roundmead Ave., Loug. 85 EN40
Roundmead Clo., Loug. 85 EN41
Roundmoor Dr. (Cheshunt), Wal.Cr. 67 DX29
Roundtable Rd., Brom. 184 EF90
Roundthorn Way, Wok. 226 AT116
Roundtree Rd., Wem. 117 CH64
Roundway, Egh. 173 BC92
Roundway, West. 238 EK116
Norheads La.
Roundway, The N17 100 DQ53
Roundway, The, Esher 215 CF107
Roundway, The, Wat. 75 BT44
Roundways, The, Ruis. 115 BT62
Roundwood, Chis. 205 EP96
Roundwood, Kings L. 58 BL27
Roundwood Ave., Brwd. 109 GA45
Roundwood Ave., Uxb. 135 BQ74
Roundwood Clo., Ruis. 115 BR59
Roundwood Dr., Welw.G.C. 29 CW08
Roundwood Gro., Brwd. 109 GB45
Roundwood Rd. NW10 139 CT65
Roundwood Rd., Amer. 55 AS38
Roundwood Vw., Bans. 233 CX115
Roundwood Way, Bans. 233 CX115
Rounton Rd. E3 143 EA70
Rounton Rd., Wal.Abb. 68 EE33
Roupell Rd. SW2 181 DM88
Roupell St. SE1 278 E3
Roupell St. SE1 141 DN74
Rous Rd., Buck.H. 102 EL46
Rousden St. NW1 141 DJ66
Rouse Gdns. SE21 182 DS91
Rousebarn La., Rick. 74 BM38
Routemaster Clo. E13 144 EH69
Routh Ct., Felt. 175 BS88
Loxwood Clo.
Routh Rd. SW18 180 DE87
Routh St. E6 145 EM71
Routledge Clo. N19 121 DK60
Rover Ave., Ilf. 103 ET51
Rowallan Rd. SW6 159 CY80
Rowan Ave. E4 101 DZ51
Rowan Ave., Egh. 173 BC92
Rowan Clo. SW16 201 DJ95
Rowan Clo. W5 158 CL75
Rowan Clo., Beac. 88 AH54
Rowan Clo., Guil. 242 AW131
Rowan Clo., N.Mal. 198 CS96
Rowan Clo., Reig. 266 DC136
Rowan Clo., St.Alb. 44 CL20
Rowan Clo. (Bricket Wd.), St.Alb. 60 CA31
Rowan Clo., Stan. 95 CF51
Woodlands Dr.
Rowan Clo., Wem. 117 CG62
Rowan Ct., Borwd. 78 CL39
Theobald St.
Rowan Cres. SW16 201 DJ95
Rowan Cres., Dart. 188 FJ88
Rowan Dr. NW9 119 CU55
Rowan Dr., Brox. 49 DZ24
Rowan Gdns., Croy. 202 DT104
Radcliffe Rd.
Rowan Gdns., Iver 133 BC68
Rowan Grn., Couls. 235 DH121
Rowan Grn., Wey. 213 BR105
Rowan Grn. E., Brwd. 109 FZ49
Rowan Grn. W., Brwd. 109 FZ48
Rowan Gro., Couls. 235 DH121
Rowan Ind. Est., Croy. 202 DS101
Rowan Pl., Amer. 72 AT38
Rowan Pl., Hayes 135 BT73
West Ave.
Rowan Rd. SW16 201 DJ96
Rowan Rd. W6 159 CX77
Rowan Rd., Bexh. 166 EY83
Rowan Rd., Brent. 157 CH80
Rowan Rd., Swan. 207 FD97
Rowan Rd., West Dr. 154 BK77
Rowan Ter. W6 159 CX77
Bute Gdns.
Rowan Wk. N2 120 DC57
Rowan Wk. N19 121 DJ61
Bredgar Rd.
Rowan Wk. W10 139 CY70
Droop St.
Rowan Wk., Brom. 205 EM104
Rowan Wk., Hat. 45 CU21
Rowan Wk., Horn. 128 FK56
Rowan Way, Rom. 126 EW55
Rowanhurst Dr., Slou. 111 AQ64
Rowans, Welw.G.C. 30 DA06
Rowans, The N13 99 DP48
Rowans, The, Ger.Cr. 112 AX55
Rowans, The, Hem.H. 40 BG20
Rowans, The, Sun. 175 BT92
Rowans, The, Wok. 226 AY118
Rowans Way, Loug. 85 EM42
Rowantree Clo. N21 100 DR46
Rowantree Rd. N21 100 DR46
Rowantree Rd., Enf. 81 DP40
Rowanwood Ave., Sid. 186 EU88
Rowbarns Way, Lthd. 245 BT130
Rowben Clo. N20 98 DB46
Rowberry Clo. SW6 159 CW80
Rowbury, Gdmg. 258 AU143
Rowcroft, Hem.H. 39 BE21
Rowcross St. SE1 162 DT78
Rowdell Rd., Nthlt. 136 CA67
Rowden Pk. Gdns. E4 101 EA51
Rowden Rd.
Rowden Rd. E4 101 EA51
Rowden Rd., Beck. 203 DY95
Rowden Rd., Epsom 216 CP105
Rowditch La. SW11 160 DG82
Rowdon Ave. NW10 139 CV66
Rowdown Cres., Croy. 221 ED109
Rowdowns Rd., Dag. 146 EZ67
Rowe Gdns., Bark. 145 ET68
Rowe La. E9 122 DW64
Rowe Wk., Har. 116 CA62
Rowena Cres. SW11 160 DE82
Rowfant Rd. SW17 180 DG88
Rowhedge, Brwd. 109 GA48
Rowhill, Add. 211 BF107
Rowhill Rd. E5 122 DV63
Rowhill Rd., Dart. 187 FF93
Rowhill Rd., Swan. 187 FF93
Rowhurst Ave., Add. 212 BH107
Rowhurst Ave., Lthd. 231 CF117
Rowington Clo. W2 140 DB71
Rowland Ave., Har. 117 CJ55
Rowland Clo., Wind. 151 AK83
Rowland Ct. E16 144 EF70
Rowland Cres., Chig. 103 ES49
Rowland Gro. SE26 182 DV90
Dallas Rd.
Rowland Hill Ave. N17 100 DQ52
Rowland Hill St. NW3 120 DE64
Rowland Wk. (Havering-atte-Bower), Rom. 105 FE48
Rowland Way SW19 200 DB95
Hayward Clo.
Rowland Way, Ashf. 175 BQ94
Rowlands Ave., Pnr. 94 CA50
Rowlands Clo. N6 120 DG58
North Hill
Rowlands Clo. NW7 97 CU52
Rowlands Clo. (Cheshunt), Wal.Cr. 67 DX30
Rowlands Flds. (Cheshunt), Wal.Cr. 67 DX29
Rowlands Rd., Dag. 126 EZ61
Rowlatt Clo., Dart. 188 FJ91
Rowlatt Dr., St.Alb. 42 CA22
Rowlatt Rd., Dart. 188 FJ91
Whitehead Clo.
Rowley Ave., Sid. 186 EV87
Rowley Clo., Wat. 76 BY44
Lower Paddock Rd.
Rowley Clo., Wem. 138 CM66
Rowley Clo., Wok. 228 BG116
Rowley Ct., Cat. 236 DR122
Fairbourne La.
Rowley Gdns. N4 122 DQ59
Rowley Gdns. (Cheshunt), Wal.Cr. 67 DX28
Warwick Dr.
Rowley Grn. Rd., Barn. 79 CT43
Rowley Ind. Est. W3 158 CP76
Rowley La., Barn. 78 CS42
Rowley La., Borwd. 78 CR39
Rowley La., Slou. 132 AW67
Rowley Mead, Epp. 70 EW25
Rowley Rd. N15 122 DQ57
Rowley Way NW8 140 DB67
Rowleys Rd., Hert. 32 DT08
Rowlheys Pl., West Dr. 154 BL76
Rowlls Rd., Kings.T. 198 CM97
Rowney Gdns., Dag. 146 EW65
Rowney Gdns., Saw. 36 EW07
Rowney Rd., Dag. 146 EV65
Rowney Wd., Saw. 36 EW06
Rowntree Clifford Clo. E13 144 EH69
Liddon Rd.
Rowntree Path SE28 146 EV73
Booth Clo.
Rowntree Rd., Twick. 177 CE88
Rowse Clo. E15 143 EC67
Rowsley Ave. NW4 119 CW55
Rowstock Gdns. N7 121 DK64
Rowton Rd. SE18 165 EQ80
Rowtown, Add. 211 BF109
Rowzill Rd., Swan. 187 FF93
Roxborough Ave., Har. 117 CE59
Roxborough Ave., Islw. 157 CF80
Roxborough Pk., Har. 117 CE59
Roxborough Rd., Har. 117 CD57
Roxbourne Clo., Nthlt. 136 BX65
Roxburgh Ave., Upmin. 128 FQ62
Roxburgh Rd. SE27 181 DP92
Roxburn Way, Ruis. 115 BT62
Roxby Pl. SW6 160 DA79
Roxeth Ct., Ashf. 174 BN92
Roxeth Grn. Ave., Har. 116 CB62
Roxeth Gro., Har. 116 CB63
Roxeth Hill, Har. 117 CD61
Roxford Clo., Shep. 195 BS99
Roxley Rd. SE13 183 EB86
Roxton Gdns., Croy. 221 EA106
Roxwell Clo., Slou. 131 AL74
Roxwell Gdns., Brwd. 109 GC43
Roxwell Rd. W12 159 CU75
Roxwell Rd., Bark. 146 EU68
Roxwell Trd. Pk. E10 123 DY59
Roxwell Way, Wdf.Grn. 102 EJ52
Roxy Ave., Rom. 126 EW59
Roy Gdns., Ilf. 125 ES56
Roy Gro., Hmptn. 176 CB93
Roy Rd., Nthwd. 93 BT52
Roy Sq. E14 143 DY73
Narrow St.
Royal Albert Dock E16 144 EL73
Royal Albert Roundabout E16 164 EK75
Royal Albert Way
Royal Albert Way E16 144 EJ73
Royal Arc. W1 277 K1
Royal Ave. SW3 276 D10
Royal Ave. SW3 160 DF78
Royal Ave., Wal.Cr. 67 DY33
Royal Ave., Wor.Pk. 198 CS103
Royal Circ. SE27 181 DN90
Royal Clo. N16 122 DS60
Manor Rd.
Royal Clo., Ilf. 126 EU59
Royal Clo., Uxb. 134 BM72
Royal Clo., Wor.Pk. 198 CS103
Royal College St. NW1 141 DJ66
Royal Ct. EC3 142 DR72
Cornhill
Royal Ct. SE16 163 DZ76
Finland St.
Royal Ct., Hem.H. 40 BL23
Royal Cres. W11 139 CX74
Royal Cres., Ruis. 116 BY63
Royal Cres. Ms. W11 139 CX74
Queensdale Rd.
Royal Docks Rd. E6 145 EP72
Royal Docks Rd., Bark. 145 EP72
Royal Dr., Epsom 233 CV118
Royal Ex. EC3 275 L9
Royal Ex. EC3 142 DR72
Royal Ex. Ave. EC3 275 L9
Royal Ex. Bldgs. EC3 275 L9
Royal Ex. Steps EC3 142 DR72
Cornhill
Royal Hill SE10 163 EC80
Royal Hospital Rd. SW3 160 DF79
Royal La., Uxb. 134 BM71
Royal La., West Dr. 134 BM72
Royal London Est., The N17 100 DU51
Royal London Ind. Est. NW10 138 CR68
North Acton Rd.
Royal Mint Ct. EC3 142 DT73
Royal Mint Pl. E1 142 DT73
Blue Anchor Yd.
Royal Mint St. E1 142 DT73
Royal Mt. Ct., Twick. 177 CE90
Royal Naval Pl. SE14 163 DZ80
Royal Oak Ct. N1 142 DS69
Pitfield St.
Royal Oak Pl. SE22 182 DV86
Royal Oak Rd. E8 142 DV65
Royal Oak Rd., Bexh. 186 EZ85
Royal Oak Rd., Wok. 226 AW118
Royal Opera Arc. SW1 277 M2
Royal Orchard Clo. SW18 179 CY87
Royal Par. SE3 164 EF82
Royal Par. SW6 159 CY80
Dawes Rd.
Royal Par. W5 138 CL69
Western Ave.
Royal Par., Chis. 185 EQ94
Royal Par. Ms. SE3 164 EF82
Royal Par.
Royal Par. Ms., Chis. 185 EQ94
Royal Pier Ms., Grav. 191 GH86
Royal Pier Rd.
Royal Pier Rd., Grav. 191 GH86
Royal Pl. SE10 163 EC80
Royal Rd. E16 144 EJ72
Royal Rd. SE17 161 DP79
Royal Rd., Dart. 188 FN92
Royal Rd., St.Alb. 43 CH20
Royal Rd., Sid. 186 EX90
Royal Rd., Tedd. 177 CD92
Royal Route, Wem. 118 CN63
Royal St. SE1 278 C6
Royal St. SE1 161 DM76
Royal Victor Pl. E3 143 DX68
Royal Victoria Dock E16 144 EG73
Royal Wk., Wall. 201 DH104
Prince Charles Way
Royal Windsor Ct., Surb. 198 CN102
Royalty Ms. W1 273 M9
Royce Clo., Brox. 49 DZ21
Roycraft Ave., Bark. 145 ET68
Roycraft Clo., Bark. 145 ET68
Roycroft Clo. E18 102 EH53
Roycroft Clo. SW2 181 DN88
Roydene Rd. SE18 165 ES79
Roydon Clo. SW11 161 DH81
Reform St.
Roydon Clo., Loug. 102 EL45
Roydon Ct., Walt. 213 BU105
Roydon Rd., Harl. 34 EK14
Roydon Rd., Ware 34 EE12
Roydon St. SW11 161 DH81
Southolm St.
Roydonbury Ind. Est., Harl. 50 EL15
Royle Clo., Ger.Cr. 90 AY52
Royle Clo., Rom. 127 FH57
Royle Cres. W13 137 CG70
Royston Ave. E4 101 EA50
Royston Ave., Sutt. 200 DD104
Royston Ave., Wall. 219 DK105
Royston Ave., W.Byf. 212 BL112
Royston Clo., Hert. 31 DP09
Royston Clo., Houns. 155 BV81
Royston Clo., Walt. 195 BU102
Royston Ct. SE24 182 DQ86
Burbage Rd.
Royston Ct., Rich. 158 CM81
Lichfield Rd.
Royston Ct., Surb. 198 CN104
Hook Ri. N.
Royston Gdns., Ilf. 124 EK58
Royston Gro., Pnr. 94 CA51
Royston Par., Ilf. 124 EK58
Royston Pk. Rd., Pnr. 94 BZ51
Royston Rd. SE20 203 DX95
Royston Rd., Dart. 187 FF86
Royston Rd., Rich. 178 CL85
Royston Rd., Rom. 106 FN52
Royston Rd., St.Alb. 43 CH21
Royston Rd., W.Byf. 212 BL112
Royston St. E2 142 DW68
Royston Way, Slou. 130 AJ71
Roystons, The, Surb. 198 CP99
Rozel Ct. N1 142 DS67
Rozel Rd. SW4 161 DJ83
Rubastic Rd., Sthl. 156 BW76
Rubens Rd., Nthlt. 136 BW68
Rubens St. SE6 183 DZ89
Ruberoid Rd., Enf. 83 DZ41
Ruby Clo., Slou. 151 AN75
Ruby Ms. E17 123 EA55
Ruby Rd.
Ruby Rd. E17 123 EA55
Ruby St. SE15 162 DV79
Ruby Triangle SE15 162 DV79
Sandgate St.
Ruckholt Clo. E10 123 EB62
Ruckholt Rd. E10 123 EB63
Rucklers La., Kings L. 58 BG28
Ruckles Way, Amer. 55 AQ40
Rucklidge Ave. NW10 139 CT68
Rudall Cres. NW3 120 DD63
Willoughby Rd.
Ruddington Clo. E5 123 DY63
Ruddlesway, Wind. 151 AK81
Ruddstreet Clo. SE18 165 EP77
Ruddy Way NW7 97 CU51
Flower La.
Ruden Way, Epsom 233 CV116
Rudge Ri., Add. 211 BF106
Rudland Rd., Bexh. 167 FB83
Rudloe Rd. SW12 181 DJ87
Rudolf Pl. SW8 161 DL79
Miles St.
Rudolph Ct. SE22 182 DU87
Rudolph Rd. E13 144 EF68
Rudolph Rd. NW6 140 DA68
Rudolph Rd. (Bushey), Wat. 76 CA44
Rudsworth Clo., Slou. 153 BD80
Rudyard Gro. NW7 96 CQ51

Rue de St. Lawrence, Wal.Abb. 67 EC34
Quaker La.
Ruffets Wd., Grav. 191 GJ93
Ruffetts, The, S.Croy. 220 DV108
Ruffetts Clo., S.Croy. 220 DV108
Ruffetts Way, Tad. 233 CY118
Rufford Clo., Har. 117 CG58
Rufford St. N1 141 DL67
Rufford Twr. W3 138 CP74
Rufus Clo., Ruis. 116 BY62
Rufus St. N1 275 M3
Rugby Ave. N9 100 DT46
Rugby Ave., Grnf. 137 CD65
Rugby Ave., Wem. 117 CH64
Rugby Clo., Har. 117 CE57
Rugby Gdns., Dag. 146 EW65
Rugby La., Sutt. 217 CX109
Nonsuch Wk.
Rugby Rd. NW9 118 CN56
Rugby Rd. W4 158 CS75
Rugby Rd., Dag. 146 EV65
Rugby Rd., Islw. 177 CE85
Rugby Rd., Twick. 177 CE85
Rugby St. WC1 274 B5
Rugby St. WC1 141 DM70
Rugby Wk., Sutt. 217 CX109
Nonsuch Wk.
Rugby Way, Rick. 75 BP43
Rugg St. E14 143 EA73
Rugged La., Wal.Abb. 68 EK33
Ruggles-Brise Rd., Ashf. 174 BK92
Ruislip Clo., Grnf. 136 CB70
Ruislip Rd., Grnf. 136 CA69
Ruislip Rd., Nthlt. 136 BX69
Ruislip Rd. E. W7 137 CD70
Ruislip Rd. E. W13 137 CD70
Ruislip Rd. E., Grnf. 137 CD70
Ruislip St. SW17 180 DF91
Rum Clo. E1 142 DW73
Rumania Wk., Grav. 191 GM90
Cervia Way
Rumballs Clo., Hem.H. 40 BN23
Rumballs Rd., Hem.H. 40 BN23
Rumbold Rd. SW6 160 DB80
Rumbold Rd., Hodd. 49 EC15
Rumsey Clo., Hmptn. 176 BZ93
Rumsey Ms. N4 121 DP62
Monsell Rd.
Rumsey Rd. SW9 161 DM83
Rumsley, Wal.Cr. 66 DU27
Runbury Circ. NW9 118 CR61
Runcie Clo., St.Alb. 43 CG16
Runciman Clo., Orp. 224 EW110
Runcorn Clo. N17 122 DV56
Runcorn Cres., Hem.H. 40 BM16
Runcorn Pl. W11 139 CY73
Rundell Cres. NW4 119 CV57
Rundells, Harl. 51 ET18
Runes Clo., Mitch. 200 DD98
Runham Rd., Hem.H. 40 BL22
Runnel Fld., Har. 117 CE62
Runnemede Rd., Egh. 173 BA92
Running Horse Yd., Brent. 158 CL79
Pottery Rd.
Running Waters, Brwd. 109 GA49
Runnymede SW19 200 DC95
Runnymede Clo., Twick. 176 CB87
Runnymede Ct., Croy. 202 DT103
Runnymede Ct., Egh. 173 BA91
Runnymede Cres. SW16 201 DK95
Runnymede Gdns., Grnf. 137 CD68
Runnymede Gdns., Twick. 176 CB87
Runnymede Rd., Twick. 176 CB86
Runrig Hill, Amer. 55 AS35
Runsley, Welw.G.C. 30 DA06
Runtley Wd. La., Guil. 243 AZ125
Runway, The, Ruis. 115 BV64
Rupack St. SE16 162 DW75
St. Marychurch St.
Rupert Ave., Wem. 118 CL64
Rupert Ct. W1 273 M10
Rupert Gdns. SW9 161 DP82
Rupert Rd. N19 121 DK62
Holloway Rd.
Rupert Rd. NW6 139 CZ68
Rupert Rd. W4 158 CS76
Rupert Rd., Guil. 258 AV135
Rupert St. W1 273 M10
Rupert St. W1 141 DK73
Rural Clo., Horn. 127 FH60
Rural Vale, Grav. 190 GE87
Rural Way SW16 181 DH94
Rural Way, Red. 250 DG134
Ruscoe Dr., Wok. 227 BA117
Pembroke Rd.
Ruscoe Rd. E16 144 EF72
Ruscombe Dr., St.Alb. 60 CB26
Ruscombe Gdns., Slou. 152 AU80
Ruscombe Way, Felt. 175 BT87
Rush, The SW19 199 CZ95
Kingston Rd.
Rush Clo., Ware 33 EC11
Rush Cft., Gdmg. 258 AU143
Rush Grn. Gdns., Rom. 127 FC60
Rush Grn. Rd., Rom. 127 FC60
Rush Gro. St. SE18 165 EM77
Rush Hill Ms. SW11 160 DG83
Rush Hill Rd.
Rush Hill Rd. SW11 160 DG83
Rusham Pk. Ave., Egh. 173 AZ93
Rusham Rd. SW12 180 DF86
Rusham Rd., Egh. 173 AZ93
Rushbrook Cres. E17 101 DZ53
Rushbrook Rd. SE9 185 EQ89
Rushburn, H.Wyc. 110 AF56
Rushcroft Rd. E4 101 EA52
Rushcroft Rd. SW2 161 DN84
Rushden Clo. SE19 182 DR94
Rushden Gdns. NW7 97 CW51
Rushden Gdns., Ilf. 103 EN54
Rushdene SE2 166 EW76
Rushdene Ave., Barn. 98 DE45
Rushdene Clo., Nthlt. 136 BW68
Rushdene Cres., Nthlt. 136 BW68
Rushdene Rd., Brwd. 108 FW45
Rushdene Rd., Pnr. 116 BX58
Rushdene Wk., West. 238 EK117
Rushdon Clo., Grays 170 GA76
Rushdon Clo., Rom. 127 FG57
Rushen Dr., Hert. 32 DW12
Rushen Wk., Cars. 200 DD102
Paisley Rd.
Rushes Mead, Harl. 51 ES17
Rushes Mead, Uxb. 134 BJ67
Frays Waye
Rushet Rd., Orp. 206 EU96
Rushett Clo., T.Ditt. 197 CH102
Rushett Dr., Dor. 263 CH139
Rushett La., Chess. 215 CJ111
Rushett Rd., T.Ditt. 197 CH101
Rushetts Rd., Reig. 266 DC138
Rushey Clo., N.Mal. 198 CR98
Rushey Grn. SE6 183 EB87
Rushey Hill, Enf. 81 DM42
Rushey Mead SE4 183 EA85
Rushfield, Pot.B. 63 CX32
Rushfield, Saw. 36 EY05
Rushford Rd. SE4 183 DZ86
Rushgrove Ave. NW9 118 CS57
Rushleigh Ave. (Cheshunt), Wal.Cr. 67 DX31
Rushley Clo., Kes. 222 EK105
Rushmead E2 142 DV69
Florida St.
Rushmead, Rich. 177 CH90
Rushmead Clo., Croy. 220 DT105
Rushmere Ave., Upmin. 128 FQ62
Rushmere Ct., Wor.Pk. 199 CU103
The Ave.
Rushmere La., Chesh. 56 AU28
Rushmere La., Hem.H. 56 AX27
Rushmere Pl. SW19 179 CX92
Rushmoor Clo., Guil. 242 AT131
Rushmoor Clo., Pnr. 115 BV56
Rushmoor Clo., Rick. 92 BK47
Rushmore Clo., Brom. 204 EL97
Rushmore Cres. E5 123 DX63
Rushmore Rd.
Rushmore Hill, Orp. 224 EW109
Rushmore Hill, Sev. 224 EX112
Rushmore Rd. E5 122 DW63
Rusholme Ave., Dag. 126 FA62
Rusholme Gro. SE19 182 DS92
Rusholme Rd. SW15 179 CX86
Rushout Ave., Har. 117 CH58
Rushton Ave., Wat. 75 BU35
Rushton Gro., Harl. 52 EX15
Rushton St. N1 142 DR68
Rushworth Ave. NW4 119 CU55
Rushworth Gdns.
Rushworth Gdns. NW4 119 CU55
Rushworth Rd., Reig. 250 DA133
Rushworth St. SE1 278 G4
Rushworth St. SE1 161 DP75
Rushy Meadow La., Cars. 200 DE103
Ruskin Ave. E12 144 EL65
Ruskin Ave., Felt. 175 BT86
Ruskin Ave., Rich. 158 CN80
Ruskin Ave., Upmin. 128 FQ59
Ruskin Ave., Wal.Abb. 68 EE34
Ruskin Ave., Well. 166 EU82
Ruskin Clo. NW11 120 DB58
Ruskin Clo. (Cheshunt), Wal.Cr. 66 DS26
Ruskin Dr., Orp. 205 ES104
Ruskin Dr., Well. 166 EU83
Ruskin Dr., Wor.Pk. 199 CV103
Ruskin Gdns. W5 137 CK70
Ruskin Gdns., Har. 118 CM56
Ruskin Gdns., Rom. 105 FH52
Ruskin Gro., Dart. 188 FN85
Ruskin Gro., Well. 166 EU82
Ruskin Pk. Ho. SE5 162 DR83
Ruskin Rd. N17 100 DT53
Ruskin Rd., Belv. 166 FA77
Ruskin Rd., Cars. 218 DF106
Ruskin Rd., Croy. 201 DP103
Ruskin Rd., Grays 171 GG77
Ruskin Rd., Islw. 157 CF83
Ruskin Rd., Sthl. 136 BY73
Ruskin Rd., Stai. 173 BF94
Ruskin Wk. N9 100 DU47
Durham Rd.
Ruskin Wk. SE24 182 DQ85
Ruskin Wk., Brom. 204 EL100
Ruskin Way SW19 200 DD95
Rusland Ave., Orp. 205 ER104
Rusland Pk. Rd., Har. 117 CE56
Rusper Clo. NW2 119 CW62
Rusper Clo., Stan. 95 CJ49
Rusper Rd. N22 99 DP54
Rusper Rd., Dag. 146 EW65
Russelcroft Rd., Welw.G.C. 29 CW08
Russell Ave. N22 99 DN54
Russell Ave., St.Alb. 43 CD20
Russell Clo. NW10 138 CQ66
Russell Clo. SE7 164 EJ80
Russell Clo. W4 159 CT79
Russell Clo., Amer. 72 AX39
Russell Clo., Beck. 203 EB97
Russell Clo., Bexh. 166 FA84
Russell Clo., Brwd. 108 FV45
Russell Clo., Dart. 167 FG83
Russell Clo., Nthwd. 93 BQ50
Russell Clo., Ruis. 116 BW61
Russell Clo., Tad. 249 CU125
Russell Clo., Wok. 226 AW115
Russell Ct. SW1 277 L3
Russell Ct., Chesh. 54 AR29
Russell Ct., Guil. 242 AW131
Rowan Clo.
Russell Ct., Lthd. 231 CH122
Russell Ct., St.Alb. 60 CA30
Russell Cres., Wat. 75 BT35
High Rd.
Russell Dr., Stai. 174 BK86
Russell Gdns. N20 98 DE47
Russell Gdns. NW11 119 CY58
Russell Gdns. W14 159 CY76
Russell Gdns., Rich. 177 CJ89
Russell Gdns., West Dr. 154 BN78
Russell Gdns. Ms. W14 159 CY75
Russell Grn. Clo., Pur. 219 DN110
Russell Gro. NW7 96 CS50
Russell Gro. SW9 161 DN81
Russell Hill, Pur. 219 DM110
Russell Hill Pl., Pur. 219 DN111
Purley Way
Russell Hill Rd., Pur. 219 DN110
Russell Kerr Clo. W4 158 CQ80
Burlington La.
Russell La. N20 98 DE47
Russell La., Wat. 75 BR36
Russell Mead, Har. 95 CF52
Russell Pl. NW3 120 DE64
Aspern Gro.
Russell Pl. SE16 163 DY76
Onega Gate
Russell Pl. (Sutton at Hone), Dart. 208 FN95
Russell Pl., Hem.H. 40 BH23
Russell Rd. E4 101 DZ49
Russell Rd. E10 123 EB58
Russell Rd. E16 144 EG72
Russell Rd. E17 123 DZ55
Russell Rd. N8 121 DK58
Russell Rd. N13 99 DM51
Russell Rd. N15 122 DS57
Russell Rd. N20 98 DE47
Russell Rd. NW9 119 CT58
Russell Rd. SW19 180 DA94
Russell Rd. W14 159 CY76
Russell Rd., Buck.H. 102 EH46
Russell Rd., Enf. 82 DT38
Russell Rd., Grav. 191 GK86
Russell Rd., Grays 170 GA77
Russell Rd., Mitch. 200 DE97
Russell Rd., Nthlt. 116 CC64
Russell Rd., Nthwd. 93 BQ48
Russell Rd., Shep. 195 BP101
Russell Rd., Til. 170 GE81
Russell Rd., Twick. 177 CF86
Russell Rd., Walt. 195 BU100
Russell Rd., Wok. 226 AW115
Russell Sq. WC1 273 P5
Russell Sq. WC1 141 DL70
Russell Sq., Long. 209 FX97
Cavendish Sq.
Russell St. WC2 274 A10
Russell St. WC2 141 DL73
Russell St., Hert. 32 DQ09
Russell St., Wind. 151 AR81
Russell Wk., Rich. 178 CM86
Park Hill
Russell Way, Sutt. 218 DA106
Russell Way, Wat. 93 BV45
Russells, Tad. 233 CX122
Russells Cres., Horl. 268 DG149
Russell's Footpath SW16 181 DL92
Russells Ride (Cheshunt), Wal.Cr. 67 DY30
Russet Clo., Horl. 269 DJ148
Carlton Tye
Russet Clo., Stai. 173 BF86
Russet Clo., Uxb. 135 BQ70
Uxbridge Rd.
Russet Clo., Walt. 196 BX104
Russet Cres. N7 121 DM64
Stock Orchard Cres.
Russet Dr., Croy. 203 DY102
Russet Dr., Rad. 62 CL32
Russet Dr., St.Alb. 43 CJ21
Russet Way, Dor. 263 CK140
Russets, The, Ger.Cr. 90 AX54
Austenwood Clo.
Russets Clo. E4 101 ED49
Larkshall Rd.
Russett Clo., Orp. 224 EV106
Russett Clo., Wal.Cr. 66 DS26
Russett Ct., Cat. 252 DU125
Russett Hill, Ger.Cr. 112 AY55
Russett Way SE13 163 EB82
Conington Rd.
Russett Way, Swan. 207 FD96
Russett Wd., Welw.G.C. 30 DD10
Russetts, The, Horn. 128 FL56
Russetts Clo., Wok. 227 AZ115
Orchard Dr.
Russia Ct. EC2 275 J9
Russia Dock Rd. SE16 143 DY74
Russia La. E2 142 DW68
Russia Row EC2 275 J9
Russia Wk. SE16 163 DX75
Archangel St.
Russington Rd., Shep. 195 BR100
Rust Sq. SE5 162 DR80
Rusthall Ave. W4 158 CR77
Rusthall Clo., Croy. 202 DW100
Rustic Ave. SW16 181 DH94
Rustic Clo., Upmin. 129 FS60
Rustic Pl., Wem. 117 CK63
Rustic Wk. E16 144 EH72
Lambert Rd.
Rustington Wk., Mord. 199 CZ101
Ruston Ave., Surb. 198 CP101
Ruston Gdns. N14 80 DG44
Farm La.
Ruston Ms. W11 139 CY72
St. Marks Rd.
Ruston St. E3 143 DZ67
Rutford Rd. SW16 181 DL92
Ruth Clo., Stan. 118 CM56
Ruthen Clo., Epsom 216 CP114
Rutherford Clo., Borwd. 78 CQ40
Rutherford Clo., Sutt. 218 DD107
Rutherford Clo., Wind. 151 AM81
Rutherford St. SW1 277 M8
Rutherford St. SW1 161 DK77
Rutherford Twr., Sthl. 136 CB72
Rutherford Way (Bushey), Wat. 95 CD46
Rutherford Way, Wem. 118 CN62
Rutherglen Rd. SE2 166 EU79
Rutherwick Clo., Horl. 268 DF148
Rutherwick Ri., Couls. 235 DL117
Rutherwick Twr., Horl. 268 DF148
Rutherwyk Rd., Cher. 193 BE101
Rutherwyke Clo., Epsom 217 CU107
Ruthin Clo. NW9 118 CS58
Ruthin Rd. SE3 164 EG79
Ruthven Ave., Wal.Cr. 67 DX33
Ruthven St. E9 143 DX67
Lauriston Rd.
Rutland App., Horn. 128 FN57
Rutland Ave., Sid. 186 EU87
Rutland Ave., Slou. 131 AQ71
Rutland Clo. SW14 158 CP83
Rutland Clo. SW19 180 DE94
Rutland Rd.
Rutland Clo., Ash. 232 CL117
Rutland Clo., Bex. 186 EX88
Rutland Clo., Chess. 216 CM107
Rutland Clo., Dart. 188 FK87
Rutland Clo., Epsom 216 CR110
Rutland Clo., Red. 250 DF133
Rutland Ct., Enf. 82 DV43
Rutland Dr., Horn. 128 FN57
Rutland Dr., Mord. 199 CZ100
Rutland Dr., Rich. 177 CK88
Rutland Gdns. N4 121 DP58
Rutland Gdns. SW7 276 C5
Rutland Gdns. SW7 160 DE75
Rutland Gdns. W13 137 CG71
Rutland Gdns., Croy. 220 DS105
Rutland Gdns., Dag. 126 EW64
Rutland Gdns., Hem.H. 40 BM19
Rutland Gdns. Ms. SW7 276 C5
Rutland Gate SW7 276 C5
Rutland Gate SW7 160 DE75
Rutland Gate, Belv. 167 FB78
Rutland Gate, Brom. 204 EF98
Rutland Gate Ms. SW7 276 B5
Rutland Gro. W6 159 CV78
Rutland Ms. NW8 140 DB67
Boundary Rd.
Rutland Ms. E. SW7 276 B6
Rutland Ms. S. SW7 276 B6
Rutland Pk. NW2 139 CW65
Rutland Pk. SE6 183 DZ89
Rutland Pl. EC1 274 G6
Rutland Pl. (Bushey), Wat. 95 CD46
The Rutts
Rutland Rd. E7 144 EK66
Rutland Rd. E9 142 DW67
Rutland Rd. E11 124 EH57
Rutland Rd. E17 123 EA58
Rutland Rd. SW19 180 DE94
Rutland Rd., Har. 116 CC58
Rutland Rd., Hayes 155 BR77
Rutland Rd., Ilf. 125 EP63
Rutland Rd., Sthl. 136 CA70
Rutland Rd., Twick. 177 CD89
Rutland St. SW7 276 C6
Rutland St. SW7 160 DE76
Rutland Wk. SE6 183 DZ89
Rutland Way, Orp. 206 EW100
Rutley Clo. SE17 161 DP79
Royal Rd.
Rutley Clo., Rom. 106 FK54
Pasteur Dr.
Rutlish Rd. SW19 200 DA95
Rutson Rd., W.Byf. 212 BM114
Rutter Gdns., Mitch. 200 DD98
Rutters Clo., West Dr. 154 BN75
Rutts, The (Bushey), Wat. 95 CD46
Rutts Ter. SE14 163 DX81
Ruvigny Gdns. SW15 159 CX83
Ruxbury Rd., Cher. 193 BC100
Ruxley Clo., Epsom 216 CP106
Ruxley Clo., Sid. 186 EY93
Ruxley Cor. Ind. Est., Sid. 186 EX93
Ruxley Cres., Esher 215 CH107
Ruxley La., Epsom 216 CP107
Ruxley Ms., Epsom 216 CP106
Ruxley Ridge, Esher 215 CG108
Ruxton Clo., Swan. 207 FE97
Ryall Clo., St.Alb. 60 BY29
Ryalls Ct. N20 98 DF48
Ryan Clo. SE3 164 EJ84
Ryan Clo., Ruis. 115 BV60
Ryan Dr., Brent. 157 CG79
Ryan Way, Wat. 76 BW39
Ryarsh Cres., Orp. 223 ES105
Rycott Path SE22 182 DU87
Lordship La.
Rycroft La., Sev. 256 FE130
Rycroft Way N17 122 DT55
Ryculff Sq. SE3 164 EF82
Rydal Clo. NW4 97 CX53
Rydal Clo., Pur. 220 DR113
Rydal Ct., Wat. 59 BV32
Grasmere Clo.
Rydal Cres., Grnf. 137 CH69
Rydal Dr., Bexh. 166 EZ82
Rydal Dr., W.Wick. 204 EE103
Rydal Gdns. NW9 118 CS57
Rydal Gdns. SW15 178 CS92
Rydal Gdns., Houns. 176 CB86
Rydal Gdns., Wem. 117 CJ60
Rydal Rd. SW16 181 DK91
Rydal Way, Egh. 173 BB94
Rydal Way, Enf. 82 DW44
Rydal Way, Ruis. 116 BW63
Ryde, The, Hat. 45 CW15
Ryde, The, Stai. 194 BH95
Ryde Clo., Wok. 228 BJ121
Ryde Heron, Wok. 226 AS117
Robin Hood Rd.
Ryde Pl., Twick. 177 CJ86
Ryde Vale Rd. SW12 181 DH89
Rydens Ave., Walt. 195 BV103
Rydens Clo., Walt. 196 BW103
Rydens Gro., Walt. 214 BX105
Rydens Pk., Walt. 196 BX103
Rydens Rd.
Rydens Rd., Walt. 195 BV104
Rydens Way, Wok. 227 BA120
Ryder Ave., Hat. 44 CS20
Ryder Clo., Brom. 184 EH92
Ryder Clo., Hem.H. 57 BA28
Ryder Clo., Hert. 32 DV08
Ryder Clo. (Bushey), Wat. 76 CB44
Ryder Ct. SW1 277 L2
Ryder Dr. SE16 162 DV78
Ryder Gdns., Rain. 147 FF65
Ryder Ms. E9 122 DW64
Homerton High St.
Ryder St. SW1 277 L2
Ryder St. SW1 141 DJ74
Ryder Yd. SW1 277 L2
Ryders Ter. NW8 140 DC68
Blenheim Ter.
Rydes Ave., Guil. 242 AT131
Rydes Clo., Wok. 227 BC120
Rydes Hill Cres., Guil. 242 AT130
Rydes Hill Rd., Guil. 242 AT132
Rydings, Wind. 151 AM83
Rydon St. N1 142 DQ67
St. Paul St.
Rydons Clo. SE9 164 EL83
Rydon's La., Couls. 236 DQ120
Rydons Pk., Walt. 195 BT102
Rydon's Wd. Clo., Couls. 236 DQ120
Rydston Clo. N7 141 DM66
Sutterton St.
Rye, The N14 99 DJ45
Rye Clo., Bex. 187 FB86
Rye Clo., Guil. 242 AS132
Rye Clo., Horn. 128 FJ64
Rye Cres., Orp. 206 EW102
Rye Fld., Orp. 206 EX103
Rye Hill Est. SE15 162 DW84
Rye Hill Pk. SE15 162 DW84
Rye Hill Rd., Epp. 52 EU22
Rye Hill Rd., Harl. 51 ER20
Rye La. SE15 162 DU82
Rye La., Sev. 241 FE120
Rye Pas. SE15 162 DU83
Rye Rd. SE15 163 DX84
Rye Rd., Hodd. 49 EB15
Rye Wk. SW15 179 CX85
Chartfield Ave.
Rye Way, Edg. 96 CM51
Canons Dr.
Ryebridge Clo., Lthd. 231 CG118
Ryebrook Rd., Lthd. 231 CG118
Ryecotes Mead SE21 182 DS88
Ryecroft, Grav. 191 GL92
Ryecroft, Harl. 51 EP15
Ryecroft, Hat. 45 CT20
Hazel Gro.
Ryecroft, Wind. 151 AM83
Ryecroft Ave., Ilf. 103 EP54
Ryecroft Ave., Twick. 176 CB87
Ryecroft Clo., Hem.H. 41 BQ21
Poynders Hill
Ryecroft Ct., St.Alb. 44 CM20
Ryecroft Cres., Barn. 79 CV43
Ryecroft Rd. SE13 183 EC85
Ryecroft Rd. SW16 181 DN93
Ryecroft Rd., Chesh. 54 AN32
Ryecroft Rd., Orp. 205 ER100
Ryecroft Rd., Sev. 241 FG116
Ryecroft St. SW6 160 DB81
Ryedale SE22 182 DV86
Ryefield Ave., Uxb. 135 BP66
Ryefield Clo., Hodd. 33 EB13
Ryefield Path SW15 179 CU88
Ryefield Rd. SE19 182 DQ93
Ryeland Clo., West Dr. 134 BL72
Ryelands, Horl. 269 DJ147
Ryelands, Welw.G.C. 29 CZ12
Ryelands Clo., Cat. 236 DS121
Ryelands Ct., Lthd. 231 CG118
Ryelands Cres. SE12 184 EJ86
Ryelands Pl., Wey. 195 BS104
Ryfold Rd. SW19 180 DA90
Ryhope Rd. N11 99 DH49
Rykhill, Grays 171 GH76
Ryland Clo., Felt. 175 BT91
Ryland Ho., Croy. 202 DQ104
Ryland Rd. NW5 141 DH65
Rylandes Rd. NW2 119 CU62
Rylandes Rd., S.Croy. 220 DV109
Rylett Cres. W12 159 CT75
Rylett Rd. W12 159 CT76
Rylston Rd. N13 100 DR48
Rylston Rd. SW6 159 CZ79
Rymer Rd., Croy. 202 DS101
Rymer St. SE24 181 DP86
Rymill Clo., Hem.H. 57 BA28
Rymill St. E16 145 EN74
Rysbrack St. SW3 276 D6
Rysbrack St. SW3 160 DF76
Rysted La., West. 255 EQ126
Rythe Ct., T.Ditt. 197 CG101
Rythe Rd., Esher 215 CD106
Ryvers Rd., Slou. 153 AZ76

S

Sabah Ct., Ashf. 174 BN91
Sabbarton St. E16 144 EF72
Victoria Dock Rd.
Sabella Ct. E3 143 DZ68
Mostyn Gro.
Sabina Rd., Grays 171 GJ77
Sabine Rd. SW11 160 DF83
Sable Clo., Houns. 156 BW83
Sable St. N1 141 DP66
Canonbury Rd.
Sach Rd. E5 122 DV61
Sackville Ave., Brom. 204 EG102
Sackville Clo., Har. 117 CD62
Sackville Clo., Sev. 257 FH122
Sackville Ct., Rom. 106 FL53
Sackville Cres.
Sackville Cres., Rom. 106 FL53
Sackville Est. SW16 181 DL90
Sackville Gdns., Ilf. 125 EM60
Sackville Rd., Dart. 188 FK89
Sackville Rd., Sutt. 218 DA108
Sackville St. W1 277 L1
Sackville St. W1 141 DJ73
Sackville Way SE22 182 DU88
Dulwich Common
Sacombe Rd., Hem.H. 39 BF18
Saddington St., Grav. 191 GH87
Saddle Yd. W1 141 DH74
Hay's Ms.
Saddlebrook Pk., Sun. 175 BS94
Saddlers Clo., Borwd. 78 CR44
Farriers Way
Saddlers Clo., Pnr. 94 CA51
Saddlers Mead, Harl. 52 EU16
Saddlers Ms., Wem. 117 CF63
The Boltons
Saddler's Pk. (Eynsford), Dart. 208 FK104
Saddlers Way, Epsom 232 CR119
Saddlescombe Way N12 98 DA50
Saddleworth Rd., Rom. 106 FJ51
Saddleworth Sq., Rom. 106 FJ51
Sadler Clo., Mitch. 200 DF96
Sadlers Clo., Guil. 243 BD133
Sadlers Ride, W.Mol. 196 CB97
Sadlers Way, Hert. 31 DN09
Sadlier Rd., St.Alb. 43 CE22
Saffron Ave. E14 143 ED73
Saffron Clo. NW11 119 CZ57
Saffron Clo., Croy. 201 DL100
Saffron Clo., Hodd. 49 DZ16
Saffron Clo., Slou. 152 AV81
Saffron Ct., Felt. 175 BQ87
Staines Rd.
Saffron Hill EC1 274 E6
Saffron Hill EC1 141 DN70
Saffron La., Hem.H. 40 BH19
Saffron Platt, Guil. 242 AU130
Saffron Rd., Grays 169 FW77
Saffron Rd., Rom. 105 FC54
Saffron St. EC1 274 E6
Saffron Way, Surb. 197 CK102
Sage Clo. E6 145 EM71
Bradley Stone Rd.

Sage St. E1 142 DW73
Cable St.
Sage Way WC1 274 B3
Saigasso Clo. E16 144 EK72
Royal Rd.
Sail St. SE11 278 C8
Sail St. SE11 161 DM77
Sainfoin Rd. SW17 180 DG89
Sainsbury Rd. SE19 182 DS92
St. Agatha's Dr., Kings.T. 178 CM93
St. Agathas Gro., Cars. 200 DF102
St. Agnells Ct., Hem.H. 40 BN16
St. Agnells La., Hem.H. 40 BM15
St. Agnes Clo. E9 142 DW67
Gore Rd.
St. Agnes Pl. SE11 161 DP79
St. Agnes Well EC1 142 DR70
Old St.
St. Aidans Ct., Bark. 146 EV69
Choats Rd.
St. Aidan's Rd. SE22 182 DV86
St. Aidans Rd. W13 157 CH75
St. Aidan's Way, Grav. 191 GK90
St. Albans Ave. E6 145 EM69
St. Alban's Ave. W4 158 CR76
St. Albans Ave., Felt. 176 BX92
St. Albans Ave., Upmin. 129 FS60
St. Albans Ave., Wey. 194 BN104
St. Albans Clo. NW11 120 DA60
St. Albans Clo., Grav. 191 GK90
St. Albans Cres. N22 99 DN53
St. Alban's Cres., Wdf.Grn. 102 EG52
St. Albans Gdns., Grav. 191 GK90
St. Alban's Gdns., Tedd. 177 CG92
St. Albans Gro. W8 160 DB76
St. Alban's Gro., Cars. 200 DE101
St. Albans Hill, Hem.H. 40 BL23
St. Albans La. NW11 120 DA60
West Heath Dr.
St. Albans La., Abb.L. 59 BT26
St. Alban's Pl. N1 141 DP67
St. Albans Rd. NW5 120 DG62
St. Albans Rd. NW10 138 CS67
St. Albans Rd., Barn. 79 CW35
St. Albans Rd., Dart. 188 FM87
St. Albans Rd., Epp. 70 EX29
St. Albans Rd., Hem.H. 40 BK22
St. Albans Rd., Ilf. 125 ET60
St. Alban's Rd., Kings.T. 178 CL93
St. Albans Rd. (Dancers Hill), Pot.B. 79 CV35
St. Albans Rd. (South Mimms), Pot.B. 62 CS30
St. Albans Rd., Rad. 62 CN28
St. Albans Rd., Reig. 250 DA133
St. Albans Rd., St.Alb. 43 CF17
St. Albans Rd. (London Colney), St.Alb. 62 CN28
St. Alban's Rd., Sutt. 217 CZ105
St. Albans Rd., Wat. 75 BV40
St. Alban's Rd., Wdf.Grn. 102 EG52
St. Albans Rd. E., Hat. 45 CV17
St. Albans Rd. W., Hat. 44 CQ18
St. Albans Rd. W. (Roe Grn.), Hat. 45 CT17
St. Albans St. SW1 277 M1
St. Alban's St., Wind. 151 AR81
St. Albans Ter. W6 159 CY79
Margravine Rd.
St. Albans Twr. E4 101 DZ51
St. Alfege Pas. SE10 163 EC79
St. Alfege Rd. SE7 164 EK79
St. Alphage Gdns. EC2 275 J7
St. Alphage Highwalk EC2 142 DR71
London Wall
St. Alphage Wk., Edg. 96 CQ54
St. Alphege Rd. N9 100 DW45
St. Alphonsus Rd. SW4 161 DK84
St. Amunds Clo. SE6 183 EA91
St. Andrew Ms., Hert. 32 DQ09
St. Andrew St. EC4 274 E7
St. Andrew St. EC4 141 DN71
St. Andrew St., Hert. 32 DQ09
St. Andrews Ave., Horn. 127 FF64
St. Andrews Ave., Wem. 117 CG63
St. Andrews Ave., Wind. 151 AM82
St. Andrew's Clo. N12 98 DC49
Woodside Ave.
St. Andrews Clo. NW2 119 CV62
St. Andrews Clo. SE16 162 DV78
Ryder Dr.
St. Andrews Clo., Epp. 53 FD24
St. Andrew's Clo., Islw. 157 CD81
St. Andrews Clo., Reig. 266 DB135
St. Marys Rd.
St. Andrews Clo., Ruis. 116 BX61
St. Andrew's Clo., Shep. 195 BR98
St. Andrews Clo., Stai. 172 AY87
St. Andrews Clo., Stan. 95 CJ54
St. Andrews Clo., Wind. 172 AU86
St. Andrews Clo., Wok. 226 AW117
St. Mary's Rd.
St. Andrew's Ct. SW18 180 DC89
Waynflete St.
St. Andrews Ct., Wat. 75 BV39
St. Andrews Cres., Wind. 151 AM82
St. Andrews Dr., Orp. 206 EV100
St. Andrews Dr., Stan. 95 CJ53
St. Andrews Gdns., Cob. 214 BW113
St. Andrew's Gro. N16 122 DR60
St. Andrew's Hill EC4 274 G10
St. Andrew's Hill EC4 141 DP73
St. Andrew's Ms. N16 122 DS60
St. Andrews Ms. SE3 164 EG80
Mycenae Rd.
St. Andrews Pl. NW1 273 J4
St. Andrews Pl., Brwd. 109 FZ47
St. Andrews Rd. E11 124 EE58
St. Andrews Rd. E13 144 EH69
St. Andrews Rd. E17 101 DX54
St. Andrews Rd. N9 100 DW45
St. Andrews Rd. NW9 118 CR60
St. Andrews Rd. NW10 139 CV65
St. Andrews Rd. NW11 119 CZ58
St. Andrews Rd. W3 138 CS72
St. Andrews Rd. W7 157 CE75
Church Rd.
St. Andrews Rd. W14 159 CY79
St. Andrews Rd., Cars. 200 DE104
St. Andrews Rd., Couls. 235 DH116
St. Andrews Rd., Croy. 220 DQ105
Lower Coombe St.
St. Andrews Rd., Enf. 82 DR41
St. Andrew's Rd., Grav. 191 GH87
St. Andrews Rd., Hem.H. 40 BJ24
West Valley Rd.
St. Andrews Rd., Ilf. 125 EM59
St. Andrews Rd., Rom. 127 FD58
St. Andrews Rd., Sid. 186 EX90
St. Andrew's Rd., Surb. 197 CK100
St. Andrews Rd., Til. 170 GE81
St. Andrews Rd., Uxb. 134 BL67
St. Andrews Rd., Wat. 94 BX48
Bridlington Rd.
St. Andrews Sq. W11 139 CY72
St. Marks Rd.
St. Andrew's Sq., Surb. 197 CK100
St. Andrews Twr., Sthl. 136 CC73
St. Andrews Wk., Cob. 229 BV115
St. Andrews Way E3 143 EB70
St. Andrews Way, Oxt. 255 EM130
St. Andrews Way, Slou. 131 AK73
St. Anna Rd., Barn. 79 CX43
Sampson Ave.
St. Annes Ave., Stai. 174 BK87
St. Anne's Clo. N6 120 DG62
Highgate W. Hill
St. Annes Clo. (Cheshunt), Wal.Cr. 66 DU28
St. Anne's Clo., Wat. 94 BW49
St. Anne's Ct. W1 273 M9
St. Anne's Dr., Red. 250 DG133
St. Annes Gdns. NW10 138 CM69
St. Anne's Ho. N16 122 DS60
St. Anne's Mt., Red. 250 DG133
St. Annes Pk., Brox. 49 EA20
Friarscroft
St. Annes Pas. E14 143 DZ72
Newell St.
St. Annes Ri., Red. 250 DG133
St. Annes Rd. E11 123 ED61
St. Annes Rd., St.Alb. 61 CK27
St. Anne's Rd., Uxb. 114 BJ55
St. Anne's Rd., Wem. 117 CK64
St. Anne's Row E14 143 DZ72
St. Anne's St. E14 143 DZ72
Commercial Rd.
St. Anne's Way, Red. 250 DG133
St. Anne's Dr.
St. Ann's, Bark. 145 EQ67
St. Anns Clo., Cher. 193 BF100
St. Ann's Cres. SW18 180 DB86
St. Ann's Gdns. NW5 140 DG65
Queens Cres.
St. Ann's Hill SW18 180 DB85
St. Anns Hill Rd., Cher. 193 BC100
St. Ann's La. SW1 277 N6
St. Ann's Pk. Rd. SW18 180 DC86
St. Ann's Pas. SW13 158 CS83
Cross St.
St. Anns Rd. N9 100 DT47
St. Ann's Rd. N15 121 DP57
St. Ann's Rd. SW13 159 CT82
St. Anns Rd. W11 139 CX73
St. Ann's Rd., Bark. 145 EQ67
Axe St.
St. Anns Rd., Cher. 193 BF100
St. Ann's Rd., Har. 117 CE58
St. Ann's St. SW1 277 N6
St. Ann's St. SW1 161 DK76
St. Ann's Ter. NW8 140 DD68
St. Anns Vill. W11 139 CX74
St. Anns Way, S.Croy. 219 DP107
St. Anselm's Pl. W1 273 H9
St. Anselms Rd., Hayes 155 BT75
St. Anthonys Ave., Hem.H. 41 BP22
St. Anthonys Ave., Wdf.Grn. 102 EJ51
St. Anthonys Clo. E1 142 DU74
St. Anthonys Clo. SW17 180 DE89
College Gdns.
St. Anthony's Way, Felt. 155 BT84
St. Antony's Rd. E7 144 EH66
St. Arvans Clo., Croy. 202 DS104
St. Asaph Rd. SE4 163 DX83
St. Aubyn's Ave. SW19 179 CZ92
St. Aubyns Ave., Houns. 176 CA85
St. Aubyns Clo., Orp. 205 ET104
St. Aubyns Gdns., Orp. 205 ET103
St. Aubyn's Rd. SE19 182 DT93
St. Audrey Ave., Bexh. 166 FA82
St. Audreys Clo., Hat. 45 CV21
St. Audreys Grn., Welw.G.C. 29 CZ10
St. Augustine Rd., Grays 171 GH77
St. Augustine's Ave. W5 138 CL68
St. Augustines Ave., Brom. 204 EL99
St. Augustine's Ave., S.Croy. 220 DQ107
St. Augustines Ave., Wem. 118 CL62
St. Augustines Clo., Brox. 49 DZ20
St. Augustines Dr., Brox. 49 DZ19
St. Augustine's Path N5 121 DP64
St. Augustines Rd. NW1 141 DK66
St. Augustine's Rd., Belv. 166 EZ77
St. Austell Clo., Edg. 96 CM54
St. Austell Rd. SE13 163 EC82
St. Awdry's Rd., Bark. 145 ER66
St. Awdry's Wk., Bark. 145 EQ66
Station Par.
St. Barnabas Clo., Beck. 203 EC96
St. Barnabas Ct., Har. 94 CC53
St. Barnabas Rd. E17 123 EA58
St. Barnabas Rd., Mitch. 180 DG94
St. Barnabas Rd., Sutt. 218 DD106
St. Barnabas Rd., Wdf.Grn. 102 EH53
St. Barnabas St. SW1 276 G10
St. Barnabas St. SW1 160 DG78
St. Barnabas Ter. E9 123 DX64
St. Barnabas Vill. SW8 161 DL81
St. Bartholomews Clo. SE26 182 DV91
St. Bartholomews Ct., Guil. 259 AZ136
St. Bartholomew's Rd. E6 145 EM68
St. Bart's Clo., St.Alb. 43 CK21
St. Bejamins Dr., Orp. 224 EW109
St. Benedict's Ave., Grav. 191 GL89
St. Benedict's Clo. SW17 180 DG92
Church La.
St. Benet's Clo. SW17 180 DE89
College Gdns.
St. Benet's Gro., Cars. 200 DC101
St. Benet's Pl. EC3 275 L10
St. Bernards, Croy. 202 DS104
St. Bernard's Clo. SE27 182 DR91
St. Gothard Rd.
St. Bernard's Rd. E6 144 EK67
St. Bernards Rd., St.Alb. 43 CE19
St. Bernards Rd., Slou. 152 AW76
St. Blaise Ave., Brom. 204 EH96
St. Botolph Rd., Grav. 190 GD90
St. Botolph Row EC3 275 P9
St. Botolph St. EC3 275 P8
St. Botolph St. EC3 142 DT72
St. Botolph's Ave., Sev. 256 FG124
St. Botolph's Rd., Sev. 256 FG124
St. Brelades Clo., Dor. 263 CG138
St. Brelades Pl., St.Alb. 43 CK16
Harvesters
St. Bride St. EC4 274 F8
St. Bride St. EC4 141 DP72
St. Bride's Ave. EC4 141 DP72
New Bri. St.
St. Brides Ave., Edg. 96 CM53
St. Brides Clo., Erith 166 EX75
St. Katherines Rd.
St. Bride's Pas. EC4 274 F9
St. Catherines, Wok. 226 AW119
St. Catherines Clo. SW17 180 DE89
College Gdns.
St. Catherines Cross, Red. 252 DS134
St. Catherines Dr. SE14 163 DX82
Kitto Rd.
St. Catherines Dr., Guil. 258 AV138
St. Catherines Fm. Ct., Ruis. 115 BQ58
St. Catherines Hill, Guil. 258 AW138
Portsmouth Rd.
St. Catherine's Ms. SW3 276 D8
St. Catherines Pk., Guil. 259 AZ136
St. Catherines Rd. E4 101 EA47
St. Catherines Rd., Brox. 49 EA19
St. Catherines Rd., Ruis. 115 BR57
St. Cecilia Rd., Grays 171 GH77
St. Chads Clo., Surb. 197 CJ101
St. Chad's Dr., Grav. 191 GL90
St. Chad's Gdns., Rom. 126 EY59
St. Chad's Pl. WC1 274 A2
St. Chad's Pl. WC1 141 DL69
St. Chad's Rd., Rom. 126 EY58
St. Chad's Rd., Til. 171 GG82
St. Chad's St. WC1 274 A2
St. Chad's St. WC1 141 DL69
St. Charles Ct., Wey. 212 BN106
St. Charles Pl. W10 139 CY71
Chesterton Rd.
St. Charles Pl., Wey. 212 BN106
St. Charles Rd., Brwd. 108 FV46
St. Charles Sq. W10 139 CY71
St. Christopher Rd., Uxb. 134 BK71
St. Christopher's Clo., Islw. 157 CE81
St. Christopher's Dr., Hayes 135 BV73
St. Christophers Gdns., Th.Hth. 201 DN97
St. Christophers Ms., Wall. 219 DJ106
St. Christopher's Pl. W1 272 G8
St. Clair Clo., Oxt. 253 EC130
St. Clair Clo., Reig. 250 DC134
St. Clair Dr., Wor.Pk. 199 CV104
St. Clair Rd. E13 144 EH68
St. Claire Clo., Ilf. 103 EM54
St. Clair's Rd., Croy. 202 DT103
St. Clare St. EC3 275 P9
St. Clement Clo., Uxb. 134 BK72
St. Clements Ave., Grays 169 FU79
St. Clement's Clo., Grav. 191 GF90
Coldharbour Rd.
St. Clements Ct. EC4 142 DR73
Clements La.
St. Clements Ct. N7 141 DN65
Arundel Sq.
St. Clements Ct., Purf. 168 FN77
Thamley
St. Clements Heights SE26 182 DU90
St. Clement's La. WC2 274 C9
St. Clements Rd., Grays 169 FW80
St. Clements St. N1 141 DN65
St. Clements St. N7 141 DN65
St. Cloud Rd. SE27 182 DQ91
St. Columba's Clo., Grav. 191 GL90
St. Crispins Clo. NW3 120 DE63
St. Crispins Clo., Sthl. 136 BZ72
St. Crispins Way, Cher. 211 BC109
St. Cross Ct., Hodd. 49 EA19
St. Cross St. EC1 274 E6
St. Cross St. EC1 141 DN71
St. Cuthberts Clo., Egh. 172 AX93
St. Cuthberts Gdns., Pnr. 94 BZ52
Westfield Pk.
St. Cuthberts Rd. N13 99 DN51
St. Cuthberts Rd. NW2 139 CZ65
St. Cuthberts Rd., Hodd. 33 EC14
St. Cyprian's St. SW17 180 DF91
St. David Clo., Uxb. 134 BK71
St. Davids, Couls. 235 DM117
St. Davids Clo., Hem.H. 41 BR21
St. Davids Clo., Iver 133 BD67
St. David's Clo., Reig. 250 DC133
St. Davids Clo., Wem. 118 CQ62
St. David's Clo., W.Wick. 203 EB101
St. David's Ct. E17 123 EC55
St. David's Cres., Grav. 191 GK91
St. David's Dr., Brox. 49 DZ19
St. Davids Dr., Edg. 96 CM53
St. Davids Pl. NW4 119 CV59
St. Davids Rd., Swan. 187 FF93
St. Denis Rd. SE27 182 DR91
St. Dionis Rd. SW6 159 CZ82
St. Donatts Rd. SE14 163 DZ81
St. Dunstan's All. EC3 279 M1
St. Dunstans Ave. W3 138 CR73
St. Dunstans Clo., Hayes 155 BT77
St. Dunstan's Ct. EC4 141 DN72
Fleet St.
St. Dunstan's Dr., Grav. 191 GL91
St. Dunstans Gdns. W3 138 CR73
St. Dunstans Ave.
St. Dunstan's Hill EC3 279 M1
St. Dunstan's Hill EC3 142 DS73
St. Dunstan's Hill, Sutt. 217 CY106
St. Dunstan's La. EC3 279 M1
St. Dunstan's La., Beck. 203 EC100
St. Dunstan's Rd. E7 144 EJ65
St. Dunstans Rd. SE25 202 DT98
St. Dunstans Rd. W6 159 CX78
St. Dunstans Rd. W7 157 CE75
St. Dunstan's Rd., Felt. 175 BT90
St. Dunstans Rd., Houns. 155 BV82
St. Dunstans Rd., Ware 34 EK07
St. Edith Clo., Epsom 232 CN116
Dorking Rd.
St. Edmunds, Berk. 38 AW20
St. Edmunds Ave., Ruis. 115 BR58
St. Edmunds Clo. NW8 140 DF67
St. Edmunds Ter.
St. Edmunds Clo. SW17 180 DE89
College Gdns.
St. Edmunds Clo., Erith 166 EX75
St. Katherines Rd.
St. Edmunds Dr., Stan. 95 CG53
St. Edmund's La., Twick. 176 CB87
St. Edmunds Rd. N9 100 DU45
St. Edmunds Rd., Dart. 168 FM84
St. Edmunds Rd., Ilf. 125 EM58
St. Edmunds Ter. NW8 140 DE68
St. Edmunds Wk., St.Alb. 43 CJ21
St. Edmunds Way, Harl. 36 EW11
St. Edwards Clo. NW11 120 DA58
St. Edwards Clo., Croy. 221 ED111
St. Edwards Way, Rom. 127 FD57
St. Egberts Way E4 101 EC46
St. Elizabeth Dr., Epsom 232 CN116
Dorking Rd.
St. Elmo Clo., Slou. 131 AR70
St. Elmo Cres.
St. Elmo Cres., Slou. 131 AR70
St. Elmo Rd. W12 139 CT74
St. Elmos Rd. SE16 163 DX75
St. Erkenwald Ms., Bark. 145 ER67
St. Erkenwald Rd.
St. Erkenwald Rd., Bark. 145 ER67
St. Ermin's Hill SW1 277 M6
St. Ervans Rd. W10 139 CZ71
St. Ethelreda's Dr., Hat. 45 CW18
St. Fabian Twr. E4 101 DZ51
St. Faiths Clo., Enf. 82 DQ39
St. Faith's Rd. SE21 181 DP88
St. Fidelis Rd., Erith 167 FD77
St. Fillans Rd. SE6 183 EC88
St. Francis Ave., Grav. 191 GL91
St. Francis Clo., Orp. 205 ES100
St. Francis Clo., Pot.B. 64 DC33
St. Francis Clo., Wat. 93 BV46
St. Francis Rd. SE22 162 DS84
St. Francis Rd., Erith 167 FD77
West St.
St. Francis Rd., Uxb. 113 BF58
St. Francis Twr. E4 101 DZ51
St. Francis Way, Grays 171 GJ77
St. Gabriel's Clo. E11 124 EH60
St. Gabriels Rd. NW2 119 CX64
St. George St. W1 273 J10
St. George St. W1 141 DH73
St. Georges Ave. E7 144 EH66
St. Georges Ave. N7 121 DK63
St. Georges Ave. NW9 118 CQ56
St. George's Ave. W5 157 CK75
St. Georges Ave., Grays 170 GC77
St. Georges Ave., Horn. 128 FM59
St. Georges Ave., Sthl. 136 BZ73
St. George's Ave., Wey. 213 BP107
St. Georges Circ. SE1 278 F6
St. Georges Circ. SE1 161 DP76
St. Georges Clo. NW11 119 CZ58
St. George's Clo. SW8 161 DJ81
Patmore Est.
St. Georges Clo., Horl. 269 DH148
St. Georges Clo., Wem. 117 CG62
St. George's Clo., Wey. 213 BQ106
St. Georges Clo., Wind. 151 AL81
St. Georges Ct. E6 145 EM70
St. Georges Ct. EC4 274 F8
St. Georges Ct. SW7 160 DC76
Gloucester Rd.
St. Georges Cres., Grav. 191 GK91
St. George's Cres., Slou. 131 AK73
St. George's Dr. SW1 277 J9
St. George's Dr. SW1 161 DH77
St. Georges Dr., Uxb. 114 BM62
St. Georges Dr., Wat. 94 BY48
St. George's Est., Amer. 72 AU39
St. Georges Flds. W2 272 C9
St. Georges Flds. W2 140 DE72
St. Georges Gdns., Epsom 217 CT114
Lynwood Rd.
St. George's Gdns., Surb. 198 CP103
Hamilton Ave.
St. Georges Gro. SW17 180 DD90
St. Georges Gro. Est. SW17 180 DD90
St. Georges Ind. Est. N17 99 DP52
St. Georges La. EC3 275 L10
St. George's Lo., Wey. 213 BR106
St. Georges Ms. NW1 140 DF66
Regents Pk. Rd.
St. Georges Pl., Twick. 177 CG88
Church St.
St. Georges Rd. E7 144 EH65
St. Georges Rd. E10 123 EC62
St. Georges Rd. N9 100 DU48
St. Georges Rd. N13 99 DM48
St. Georges Rd. NW11 119 CZ58
St. Georges Rd. SE1 278 E6
St. Georges Rd. SE1 161 DN76
St. George's Rd. SW19 179 CZ94
St. Georges Rd. W4 158 CR75
St. Georges Rd. W7 137 CF74
St. Georges Rd., Add. 212 BJ105
St. George's Rd., Beck. 203 EB95
St. Georges Rd., Brom. 205 EM96
St. Georges Rd., Dag. 126 EY64
St. Georges Rd., Enf. 82 DT38
St. George's Rd., Felt. 176 BX91
St. Georges Rd., Hem.H. 40 BJ24
St. Georges Rd., Ilf. 125 EM59
St. George's Rd., Kings.T. 178 CN94
St. George's Rd., Mitch. 201 DH97
St. Georges Rd., Orp. 205 ER100
St. Georges Rd., Red. 267 DK142
St. Georges Rd., Rich. 158 CM83
St. George's Rd., Sev. 257 FH122
St. George's Rd., Sid. 186 EX93
St. Georges Rd., Swan. 207 FF98
St. Georges Rd., Twick. 177 CH85
St. Georges Rd., Wall. 219 DH106
St. Georges Rd., Wat. 75 BV38
St. George's Rd., Wey. 213 BR107
St. Georges Rd. W., Brom. 204 EL95
St. Georges Sq. E7 144 EH66
St. Georges Sq. E14 143 DY73
St. Georges Sq. SE8 163 DZ77
St. George's Sq. SW1 161 DK78
St. George's Sq., N.Mal. 198 CS97
High St.
St. George's Sq. Ms. SW1 161 DK78
St. Georges Ter. NW1 140 DF66
Regents Pk. Rd.
St. Georges Wk., Croy. 202 DQ104
St. Georges Way SE15 162 DS79
St. Gerards Clo. SW4 181 DJ85
St. German's Pl. SE3 164 EG81
St. Germans Rd. SE23 183 DY88
St. Giles Ave., Dag. 147 FB66
St. Giles Ave., Pot.B. 63 CV32
St. Giles Ave., Uxb. 115 BQ63
St. Giles Clo., Dag. 147 FB66
St. Giles Ave.
St. Giles Clo., Orp. 223 ER106
St. Giles High St. WC2 273 N8
St. Giles High St. WC2 141 DK72
St. Giles Pas. WC2 273 N9
St. Giles Rd. SE5 162 DS80
St. Gilles Ho. E2 143 DX68
Mace St.
St. Gothard Rd. SE27 182 DR91
St. Gregory Clo., Ruis. 116 BW63
St. Gregorys Cres., Grav. 191 GL89
St. Helena Rd. SE16 163 DX77
St. Helena St. WC1 274 D3
St. Helens Clo., Uxb. 134 BK71
St. Helens Ct., Epp. 70 EU30
Hemnall St.
St. Helens Ct., Rain. 147 FG70
St. Helens Cres. SW16 201 DM95
St. Helens Rd.
St. Helens Gdns. W10 139 CX71
St. Helens Pl. EC3 275 M8
St. Helens Rd. SW16 201 DM95
St. Helen's Rd. W13 137 CH74
Dane Rd.
St. Helens Rd., Erith 166 EX75
St. Helens Rd., Ilf. 125 EM58
St. Helier Ave., Mord. 200 DC101
St. Heliers Ave., Houns. 176 CA85
St. Heliers Rd. E10 123 EC58
St. Heliers Rd., St.Alb. 43 CH15
St. Hildas Ave., Ashf. 174 BL92
St. Hildas Clo. NW6 139 CX67
St. Hildas Clo. SW17 180 DE89
St. Hildas Clo., Horl. 269 DH148
St. Hilda's Rd. SW13 159 CV79
St. Hilda's Way, Grav. 191 GK91
St. Huberts Clo., Ger.Cr. 112 AY61
St. Huberts La., Ger.Cr. 113 AZ61
St. Hughe's Clo. SW17 180 DE89
College Gdns.
St. Hughs Rd. SE20 202 DV95
Ridsdale Rd.
St. Ives Clo., Rom. 106 FM52
St. Ivians Dr., Rom. 127 FG55
St. James Ave. E2 142 DW68
St. James Ave. N20 98 DE48
St. James Ave. W13 137 CG74
St. James Ave., Epsom 217 CT111
St. James Ave., Sutt. 218 DA106
St. James Clo. N20 98 DE48
St. James Clo. SE18 165 EQ78
Congleton Gro.
St. James Clo., Barn. 80 DD42
St. James Clo., Epsom 216 CS114
St. James Clo., N.Mal. 199 CT99
St. James Clo., Ruis. 116 BW61
St. James Clo., Wok. 226 AU118
St. James Gdns. W11 139 CY74
St. James Gdns., Wem. 137 CK66
St. James Gate NW1 141 DK66
St. Paul's Cres.
St. James Gro. SW11 160 DF82
Reform St.
St. James La., Green. 189 FS88
St. James Ms. E14 163 EC76
St. James Ms., Wey. 213 BP105
St. James Pl., Dart. 188 FK86
Spital St.
St. James Pl., Slou. 130 AJ72
Greenfern Ave.
St. James Rd. E15 124 EF64
St. James Rd. N9 100 DV47
Queens Rd.
St. James Rd., Cars. 200 DE104
St. James Rd., Kings.T. 197 CK96
St. James Rd., Mitch. 180 DG94
St. James Rd., Pur. 219 DP113
St. James Rd., Sev. 257 FH122
St. James Rd., Surb. 197 CK100
St. James Rd., Sutt. 218 DA106
St. James Rd. (Cheshunt), Wal.Cr. 66 DQ28
St. James Rd., Wat. 75 BV43
St. James St. W6 159 CW78
St. James Wk. EC1 274 F4
St. James Wk. SE15 162 DT80
Commercial Way
St. James Wk., Iver 153 BE75
St. James Way, Sid. 186 EY92
St. James's SE14 163 DY81
St. James's Ave., Beck. 203 DY97
St. James's Ave., Grav. 191 GG87
St. James's Ave., Hmptn. 176 CC92
St. James's Clo. SW17 180 DF89
St. James's Dr.
St. James's Cotts., Rich. 177 CK85
Paradise Rd.
St. James's Ct. SW1 277 L6
St. James's Ct. SW1 161 DJ76
St. James's Cres. SW9 161 DN83
St. James's Dr. SW12 180 DF88
St. James's Dr. SW17 180 DF88
St. James's La. N10 121 DH56
St. James's Mkt. SW1 277 M1
St. James's Ms. E17 123 DY57
St. James's St.
St. James's Palace SW1 277 L3
St. James's Palace SW1 141 DJ74
St. James's Pk. SW1 277 M6
St. James's Pk. SW1 161 DJ75
St. James's Pk., Croy. 202 DQ101
St. James's Pas. EC3 275 N9
St. James's Pl. SW1 277 K3
St. James's Pl. SW1 141 DJ74
St. James's Rd. SE1 162 DU78
St. James's Rd. SE16 162 DU76
St. James's Rd., Brwd. 108 FW48
St. James's Rd., Croy. 201 DP101
St. James's Rd., Grav. 191 GG86
St. James's Rd., Hmptn. 176 CB92
St. James's Row EC1 274 F4
St. James's Sq. SW1 277 L2

St. James's Sq. SW1 141 DK74
St. James's St. E17 123 DY57
St. James's St. SW1 277 K2
St. James's St. SW1 141 DJ74
St. James's St., Grav. 191 GG86
St. James's Ter. NW8 140 DF68
Prince Albert Rd.
St. James's Ter. Ms. NW8 140 DF67
St. Jeromes Gro., Hayes 135 BQ72
St. Joans Rd. N9 100 DT46
St. John Fisher Rd., Erith 166 EX76
St. John St. EC1 274 F2
St. John St. EC1 141 DN68
St. Johns, Dor. 263 CH140
St. John's, Red. 266 DE136
St. Johns Ave. N11 98 DF50
St. John's Ave. NW10 139 CT67
St. John's Ave. SW15 179 CX85
St. Johns Ave., Brwd. 108 FX49
St. Johns Ave., Epsom 217 CT112
St. John's Ave., Harl. 36 EW11
St. Johns Ave., Lthd. 231 CH121
St. John's Ch. Rd. E9 122 DW64
St. John's Ch. Rd., Dor. 262 BZ139
Coast Hill
St. Johns Clo. N14 81 DJ44
Chase Rd.
St. John's Clo. SW6 160 DA80
Dawes Rd.
St. John's Clo., Guil. 258 AU135
St. John's Rd.
St. Johns Clo., Lthd. 231 CJ120
St. John's Clo., Pot.B. 64 DC33
St. Johns Clo., Rain. 147 FG66
St. John's Clo., Uxb. 134 BH67
St. John's Clo., Wem. 118 CL64
St. John's Cotts. SE20 182 DW94
Maple Rd.
St. Johns Cotts., Rich. 158 CL84
Kew Foot Rd.
St. Johns Ct., Buck.H. 102 EH46
St. Johns Ct., Egh. 173 BA92
St. John's Ct., Islw. 157 CF82
St. Johns Ct., Nthwd. 93 BS53
Murray Rd.
St. Johns Ct., St.Alb. 43 CH19
St. John's Cres. SW9 161 DN83
St. Johns Dr. SW18 180 DB88
St. Johns Dr., Walt. 196 BW102
St. Johns Dr., Wind. 151 AN82
St. John's Est. N1 275 L1
St. John's Est. N1 142 DR68
St. John's Est. SE1 279 P5
St. John's Gdns. W11 139 CY73
St. Johns Gro. N19 121 DJ61
St. Johns Gro. SW13 159 CT82
Terrace Gdns.
St. Johns Gro., Rich. 158 CL84
Kew Foot Rd.
St. John's Hill SW11 160 DD84
St. Johns Hill, Couls. 235 DN117
Canon's Hill
St. Johns Hill, Pur. 235 DN116
St. John's Hill, Sev. 257 FJ123
St. John's Hill Gro. SW11 160 DD84
St. Johns Hill Rd., Wok. 226 AU119
St. John's La. EC1 274 F5
St. John's La. EC1 141 DP70
St. John's La., Ware 33 EA09
St. John's Lye, Wok. 226 AT119
St. John's Ms. W11 140 DA72
Ledbury Rd.
St. Johns Ms., Wok. 226 AU119
St. John's Rd.
St. Johns Par., Sid. 186 EU91
Church Rd.
St. John's Pk. SE3 164 EF80
St. Johns Pas. SE23 182 DW88
Davids Rd.
St. John's Pas. SW19 179 CY93
Ridgway Pl.
St. John's Path EC1 274 F5
St. Johns Pathway SE23 182 DW88
Devonshire Rd.
St. John's Pl. EC1 274 F5
St. Johns Ri., Wok. 226 AV119
St. Johns Rd. E4 101 EB48
St. John's Rd. E6 144 EL67
Ron Leighton Way
St. Johns Rd. E16 144 EG72
St. John's Rd. E17 101 EB54
St. John's Rd. N15 122 DS58
St. Johns Rd. NW11 119 CZ58
St. John's Rd. SE20 182 DW94
St. John's Rd. SW11 160 DE84
St. John's Rd. SW19 179 CY93
St. John's Rd., Bark. 145 ES67
St. John's Rd., Cars. 200 DE104
St. Johns Rd., Croy. 201 DP104
Sylverdale Rd.
St. John's Rd., Dart. 188 FQ87
St. John's Rd., Dor. 262 CC137
St. Johns Rd., E.Mol. 197 CD98
St. John's Rd., Epp. 69 ET30
St. Johns Rd., Erith 167 FD78
St. John's Rd., Felt. 176 BY91
St. Johns Rd., Grav. 191 GK87
St. Johns Rd., Grays 171 GH78
St. John's Rd., Guil. 258 AT135
St. Johns Rd., Har. 117 CF58
St. Johns Rd., Hem.H. 40 BG22
St. Johns Rd., Ilf. 125 ER59
St. John's Rd., Islw. 157 CE82
St. Johns Rd., Kings.T. 197 CJ96
St. Johns Rd., Lthd. 231 CJ121
St. Johns Rd., Loug. 85 EM40
St. John's Rd., N.Mal. 198 CQ97
St. John's Rd., Orp. 205 ER100
St. John's Rd., Red. 266 DF136
St. John's Rd., Rich. 158 CL84
St. Johns Rd., Rom. 105 FC50
St. Johns Rd., Sev. 257 FH121
St. John's Rd., Sid. 186 EV91
St. Johns Rd., Slou. 132 AU73
St. Johns Rd., Sthl. 156 BY76
St. Johns Rd., Sutt. 200 DA103
St. John's Rd., Uxb. 134 BH67
St. Johns Rd., Wat. 75 BV40
St. John's Rd., Well. 166 EV83
St. John's Rd., Wem. 118 CL64
St. Johns Rd., Wind. 151 AN82
St. John's Rd., Wok. 226 AU119
St. John's Sq. EC1 274 F5
St. John's St., Hert. 32 DR09
St. Johns Ter. E7 144 EH65
St. Johns Ter. SE18 165 EQ79
St. Johns Ter. SW15 178 CR91
Kingston Vale
St. Johns Ter. W10 139 CX70
Harrow Rd.
St. Johns Ter., Enf. 82 DR37
St. John's Ter., Red. 266 DF136
St. John's Ter. Rd.
St. John's Ter. Rd., Red. 266 DF136
St. Johns Vale SE8 163 EA82
St. Johns Vill. N19 121 DK61
St. John's Vill. W8 160 DB76
St. Mary's Pl.
St. Johns Way N19 121 DJ61
St. Johns Well Ct., Berk. 38 AV18
St. Johns Well La., Berk. 38 AV18
St. John's Wd. Ct. NW8 272 A3
St. John's Wd. High St. NW8 272 A1
St. John's Wd. High St. NW8 140 DD68
St. John's Wd. Pk. NW8 140 DD67
St. John's Wd. Rd. NW8 140 DD70
St. John's Wd. Ter. NW8 140 DD68
St. Josephs Clo. W10 139 CY71
Bevington Rd.
St. Joseph's Clo., Orp. 223 ET105
St. Joseph's Ct. SE7 164 EH79
St. Josephs Dr., Sthl. 136 BY74
St. Joseph's Gro. NW4 119 CV56
St. Josephs Rd. N9 100 DV45
St. Joseph's Rd., Wal.Cr. 67 DY33
St. Joseph's Vale SE3 163 ED83
St. Jude St. N16 122 DS64
St. Judes Clo., Egh. 172 AW92
St. Jude's Rd. E2 142 DV68
St. Jude's Rd., Egh. 172 AW90
St. Julians, Sev. 257 FL130
St. Julian's Clo. SW16 181 DN91
St. Julian's Fm. Rd. SE27 181 DN91
St. Julian's Rd. NW6 139 CZ66
St. Julians Rd., St.Alb. 43 CD22
St. Justin Clo., Orp. 206 EX97
St. Katharines Prec. NW1 141 DH68
Outer Circle
St. Katharine's Way E1 142 DU74
St. Katherines Rd., Cat. 252 DU125
St. Katherines Rd., Erith 166 EX75
St. Katherine's Row EC3 275 N10
St. Katherines Way, Berk. 38 AT16
St. Keverne Rd. SE9 184 EL91
St. Kilda Rd. W13 137 CG74
St. Kilda Rd., Orp. 205 ET102
St. Kilda's Rd. N16 122 DR60
St. Kildas Rd., Brwd. 108 FV45
St. Kildas Rd., Har. 117 CE58
St. Kitts Ter. SE19 182 DS92
St. Laurence Clo. NW6 139 CX67
St. Laurence Clo., Orp. 206 EX97
Edmunds Ave.
St. Laurence Dr., Brox. 49 DY23
St. Laurence Way, Slou. 152 AU76
St. Lawrence Clo., Abb.L. 59 BS30
St. Lawrence Clo., Edg. 96 CM52
St. Lawrence Clo., Hem.H. 57 BA27
St. Lawrence Clo., Uxb. 134 BJ71
St. Lawrence Dr., Pnr. 115 BV57
St. Lawrence Rd., Upmin. 128 FQ61
St. Lawrence St. E14 143 EC74
St. Lawrence Ter. W10 139 CY71
St. Lawrence Way SW9 161 DN82
St. Lawrence Way, Cat. 236 DQ121
Coulsdon Rd.
St. Lawrence Way, St.Alb. 60 BZ30
St. Lawrence's Way, Reig. 250 DA134
Church St.
St. Leonards Ave. E4 101 ED51
St. Leonards Ave., Har. 117 CJ57
St. Leonards Ave., Wind. 151 AQ82
St. Leonards Clo., Hert. 32 DS07
St. Leonards Clo. (Bushey), Wat. 76 BY42
St. Leonard's Clo., Well. 166 EU83
Hook La.
St. Leonards Ct. N1 275 L2
St. Leonard's Gdns., Houns. 156 BY81
St. Leonards Gdns., Ilf. 125 EQ64
St. Leonards Hill, Wind. 151 AK84
St. Leonards Ri., Orp. 223 ES105
St. Leonards Rd. E14 143 EB71
St. Leonards Rd. NW10 138 CR70
St. Leonard's Rd. SW14 158 CP83
St. Leonards Rd. W13 137 CJ72
St. Leonards Rd., Amer. 55 AS35
St. Leonards Rd., Croy. 201 DP104
St. Leonards Rd., Epsom 233 CW119
St. Leonards Rd., Esher 215 CF107
St. Leonards Rd., Hert. 32 DR07
St. Leonard's Rd., Surb. 197 CK99
St. Leonards Rd., T.Ditt. 197 CG100
St. Leonards Rd., Wal.Abb. 68 EE25
St. Leonards Rd., Wind. 151 AN83
St. Leonards Sq. NW5 140 DG65
St. Leonard's Sq., Surb. 197 CK99
St. Leonard's Rd.
St. Leonards St. E3 143 EB69
St. Leonard's Ter. SW3 160 DF78
St. Leonards Wk. SW16 181 DM94
St. Leonards Wk., Iver 153 BF76
St. Leonards Way, Amer. 55 AS35
St. Leonards Way, Horn. 127 FH61
St. Loo Ave. SW3 160 DE79
St. Louis Rd. SE27 182 DQ91
St. Loy's Rd. N17 100 DS54
St. Luke Clo., Uxb. 134 BK72
St. Luke's Ave. SW4 161 DK84
St. Lukes Ave., Enf. 82 DR38
St. Luke's Ave., Ilf. 125 EP64
St. Lukes Clo. EC1 142 DQ70
Old St.
St. Luke's Clo. SE25 202 DV100
St. Lukes Clo., Dart. 189 FS92
St. Lukes Clo., Swan. 207 FD96
St. Luke's Est. EC1 275 K3
St. Luke's Est. EC1 142 DR69
St. Lukes Ms. W11 139 CZ72
Basing St.
St. Lukes Pas., Kings.T. 198 CM95
St. Lukes Rd. W11 139 CZ71
St. Lukes Rd., Uxb. 134 BL66
St. Lukes Rd., Whyt. 236 DT118
Whyteleafe Hill
St. Lukes Rd., Wind. 172 AU86
St. Lukes Sq. E16 144 EF72
St. Lukes Sq., Guil. 259 AZ135
St. Luke's St. SW3 276 C10
St. Luke's St. SW3 160 DE78
St. Luke's Yd. W9 139 CZ69
St. Malo Ave. N9 100 DW48
St. Margaret Dr., Epsom 232 CN116
Dorking Rd.
St. Margarets, Bark. 145 EQ67
St. Margarets, Guil. 243 AZ133
St. Margarets Ave. N15 121 DP56
St. Margarets Ave. N20 98 DC46
St. Margarets Ave., Ashf. 175 BP92
St. Margarets Ave., Har. 116 CC62
St. Margarets Ave., Sid. 185 ER90
St. Margaret's Ave., Sutt. 199 CY104
St. Margarets Ave., Uxb. 134 BN70
St. Margarets Clo., Berk. 38 AX20
St. Margarets Clo., H.Wyc. 88 AC47
St. Margarets Clo., Iver 133 BD68
St. Margarets Gate
St. Margarets Clo., Orp. 224 EV105
St. Margaret's Ct. SE1 279 K3
St. Margarets Cres. SW15 179 CV85
St. Margaret's Cres., Grav. 191 GL90
St. Margaret's Dr., Twick. 177 CH85
St. Margarets Gate, Iver 133 BD68
St. Margaret's Gro. E11 124 EF62
St. Margaret's Gro. SE18 165 EQ79
St. Margarets Gro., Twick. 177 CG86
St. Margarets La. W8 160 DB76
St. Margarets Pas. SE13 164 EE83
Church Ter.
St. Margarets Rd. E12 124 EJ61
St. Margarets Rd. N17 122 DS55
St. Margaret's Rd. NW10 139 CW69
St. Margarets Rd. SE4 163 DZ84
St. Margarets Rd. W7 157 CE75
St. Margarets Rd., Couls. 235 DH121
St. Margarets Rd. (South Darenth), Dart. 189 FS94
St. Margarets Rd., Edg. 96 CP50
St. Margaret's Rd., Grav. 190 GE89
St. Margarets Rd., Islw. 157 CH84
St. Margarets Rd., Ruis. 115 BR58
St. Margarets Rd., Twick. 177 CH86
St. Margaret's Rd., Ware 33 EA13
St. Margarets Sq. SE4 163 DZ84
Adelaide Ave.
St. Margaret's St. SW1 277 P5
St. Margaret's St. SW1 161 DL75
St. Margaret's Ter. SE18 165 EQ78
St. Margarets Way, Hem.H. 41 BR20
St. Mark St. E1 142 DT72
St. Marks Ave., Grav. 190 GE87
St. Marks Clo. SE10 163 EC80
Ashburnham Pl.
St. Marks Clo. W11 139 CY72
Lancaster Rd.
St. Mark's Clo., Barn. 80 DB41
St. Marks Clo., St.Alb. 44 CP22
St. Marks Cres. NW1 140 DG67
St. Marks Gate E9 143 DZ66
Cadogan Ter.
St. Mark's Gro. SW10 160 DB79
St. Mark's Hill, Surb. 198 CL100
St. Mark's Pl. SW19 179 CZ93
Wimbledon Hill Rd.
St. Marks Pl. W11 139 CY72
St. Marks Pl., Wind. 151 AQ82
St. Marks Ri. E8 122 DT64
St. Marks Rd. SE25 202 DU98
Coventry Rd.
St. Mark's Rd. W5 138 CL74
The Common
St. Marks Rd. W7 157 CE75
St. Marks Rd. W10 139 CX71
St. Marks Rd. W11 139 CY72
St. Marks Rd., Brom. 204 EH97
St. Marks Rd., Enf. 82 DT43
St. Marks Rd., Epsom 233 CW118
St. Marks Rd., Mitch. 200 DF96
St. Mark's Rd., Tedd. 177 CH94
St. Marks Rd., Wind. 151 AQ82
St. Marks Sq. NW1 140 DG67
Regents Pk. Rd.
St. Martha's Ave., Wok. 227 AZ121
St. Martin Clo., Uxb. 134 BK72
St. Martins App., Ruis. 115 BS59
St. Martins Ave. E6 144 EK68
St. Martins Ave., Epsom 216 CS114
St. Martin's Clo. NW1 141 DJ67
St. Martins Clo., Enf. 82 DV39
St. Martins Clo., Epsom 216 CS113
Church Rd.
St. Martins Clo., Erith 166 EX75
St. Helens Rd.
St. Martins Clo., Lthd. 245 BS129
St. Martin's Clo., Wat. 94 BW49
Muirfield Rd.
St. Martin's Clo., West Dr. 154 BK76
St. Martin's Rd.
St. Martin's Ct. WC2 273 P10
St. Martin's Ct., Ashf. 174 BJ92
St. Martins Dr., Walt. 196 BW104
St. Martins Est. SW2 181 DN88
St. Martin's La. WC2 273 P10
St. Martin's La. WC2 141 DL73
St. Martins Meadow, West. 240 EW123
St. Martins Ms., Dor. 263 CG136
Church St.
St. Martin's Pl. WC2 277 P1
St. Martin's Pl. WC2 141 DL73
St. Martins Rd. N9 100 DV47
St. Martin's Rd. SW9 161 DM82
St. Martins Rd., Dart. 188 FM86
St. Martin's Rd., West Dr. 154 BJ76
St. Martin's St. WC2 277 N1
St. Martins Wk., Dor. 263 CH136
St. Martins Way SW17 180 DC90
St. Martin's-le-Grand EC1 275 H8
St. Martin's-le-Grand EC1 142 DQ72
St. Mary Abbots Pl. W8 159 CZ76
St. Mary Abbots Ter. W14 159 CZ76
St. Mary at Hill EC3 279 M1
St. Mary at Hill EC3 142 DS73
St. Mary Ave., Wall. 200 DG104
St. Mary Axe EC3 275 M9
St. Mary Axe EC3 142 DS72
St. Mary Rd. E17 123 EA56
St. Mary St. SE18 165 EN77
St. Marychurch St. SE16 162 DW75
St. Marys, Bark. 145 ER67
St. Marys App. E12 125 EM64
St. Marys Ave. E11 124 EH58
St. Mary's Ave. N3 97 CY54
St. Mary's Ave., Brwd. 109 GA43
St. Mary's Ave., Brom. 204 EE97
St. Mary's Ave., Nthwd. 93 BS50
St. Mary's Ave., Sthl. 156 CA77
St. Mary's Ave., Stai. 174 BK87
St. Mary's Ave., Tedd. 177 CF93
St. Marys Clo. N17 100 DU53
Kemble Rd.
St. Marys Clo., Chess. 216 CM108
St. Marys Clo., Epsom 217 CU108
St. Mary's Clo., Grav. 191 GJ89
St. Marys Clo., Grays 170 GD79
Dock Rd.
St. Mary's Clo., Lthd. 231 CD123
St. Marys Clo., Orp. 206 EV96
St. Mary's Clo., Oxt. 254 EE129
St. Mary's Clo., Stai. 174 BK87
St. Mary's Clo., Sun. 195 BU98
Green Way
St. Mary's Clo., Uxb. 114 BH55
St. Marys Clo., Wat. 75 BV42
St. Marys Ct. E6 145 EM70
St. Mary's Ct. SE7 164 EK80
St. Mary's Ct. W5 157 CK75
St. Mary's Rd.
St. Mary's Cres. NW4 119 CV55
St. Mary's Cres., Hayes 135 BT73
St. Marys Cres., Islw. 157 CD80
St. Marys Cres., Stai. 174 BK87
St. Marys Dr., Felt. 175 BQ87
St. Mary's Dr., Sev. 256 FE123
St. Mary's Gdns. SE11 278 E8
St. Mary's Gdns. SE11 161 DN77
St. Mary's Gate W8 160 DB76
St. Marys Grn. N2 120 DC55
Thomas More Way
St. Marys Grn., West. 238 EJ118
St. Mary's Gro. N1 141 DP65
St. Mary's Gro. SW13 159 CV83
St. Mary's Gro. W4 158 CP79
St. Mary's Gro., Rich. 158 CM84
St. Marys Gro., West. 238 EJ118
St. Mary's La., Hert. 31 DM11
St. Mary's La., Upmin. 128 FN61
St. Marys Mans. W2 140 DD71
St. Mary's Ms. NW6 140 DB66
Priory Rd.
St. Mary's Ms., Rich. 177 CJ90
Back La.
St. Mary's Mt., Cat. 236 DT124
St. Marys Path N1 141 DP67
St. Mary's Pl. SE9 185 EN86
Eltham High St.
St. Mary's Pl. W5 157 CK75
St. Mary's Rd.
St. Mary's Pl. W8 160 DB76
St. Marys Rd. E10 123 EC62
St. Marys Rd. E13 144 EH68
St. Marys Rd. N8 121 DL56
High St.
St. Marys Rd. N9 100 DV46
St. Mary's Rd. NW10 138 CS67
St. Marys Rd. NW11 119 CY59
St. Mary's Rd. SE15 162 DW81
St. Mary's Rd. SE25 202 DS97
St. Mary's Rd. (Wimbledon) SW19 179 CY92
St. Mary's Rd. W5 157 CK75
St. Mary's Rd., Barn. 98 DF45
St. Marys Rd., Bex. 187 FC88
St. Marys Rd., E.Mol. 197 CD99
St. Mary's Rd., Grays 171 GH76
St. Mary's Rd., Green. 189 FS85
St. Mary's Rd., Hayes 135 BT73
St. Mary's Rd., Hem.H. 40 BK19
St. Marys Rd., Ilf. 125 EQ61
St. Marys Rd., Lthd. 231 CH122
St. Marys Rd., Reig. 266 DB135
St. Mary's Rd., Slou. 132 AY74
St. Mary's Rd., S.Croy. 220 DR110
St. Marys Rd., Surb. 197 CK100
St. Marys Rd. (Long Ditton), Surb. 197 CJ101
St. Marys Rd., Swan. 207 FD98
St. Mary's Rd. (Denham), Uxb. 113 BF58
St. Mary's Rd. (Harefield), Uxb. 114 BH56
St. Mary's Rd. (Cheshunt), Wal.Cr. 66 DW29
St. Marys Rd., Wat. 75 BV42
St. Marys Rd., Wey. 213 BR105
St. Mary's Rd., Wok. 226 AX117
St. Mary's Rd., Wor.Pk. 198 CS103
St. Marys Sq. W2 140 DD71
St. Mary's Sq. W5 157 CK75
St. Mary's Rd.
St. Marys Ter. W2 140 DD71
St. Marys Vw., Har. 117 CJ57
St. Mary's Wk. SE11 278 E8
St. Mary's Wk. SE11 161 DN77
St. Mary's Wk., Hayes 135 BT73
St. Mary's Rd.
St. Mary's Wk., Red. 252 DR133
St. Marys Wk., St.Alb. 43 CH16
St. Marys Way, Chesh. 54 AP31
St. Mary's Way, Chig. 103 EN50
St. Marys Way, Ger.Cr. 90 AX54
St. Matthew Clo., Uxb. 134 BK72
St. Matthew St. SW1 277 M7
St. Matthew's Ave., Surb. 198 CL102
St. Matthews Clo., Rain. 147 FG66
St. Matthews Clo., Wat. 76 BX44
St. Matthew's Dr., Brom. 205 EM97
St. Matthew's Rd. SW2 161 DM84
St. Matthews Rd. W5 138 CL74
The Common
St. Matthew's Rd., Red. 250 DF133
St. Matthew's Row E2 142 DU69
St. Matthias Clo. NW9 119 CT57
St. Maur Rd. SW6 159 CZ81
St. Merryn Clo. SE18 165 ER80
St. Michael's All. EC3 275 L9
St. Michaels Ave. N9 100 DW45
St. Michaels Ave., Hem.H. 41 BP22
St. Michael's Ave., Wem. 138 CN65
St. Michaels Clo. E16 144 EK71
Fulmer Rd.
St. Michael's Clo. N3 97 CZ54
St. Michaels Clo. N12 98 DE50
St. Michaels Clo., Brom. 204 EL97
St. Michaels Clo., Erith 166 EX75
St. Helens Rd.
St. Michaels Clo., Harl. 35 ES14
St. Michaels Clo., S.Ock. 148 FQ73
St. Michaels Clo., Walt. 196 BW103
St. Michaels Clo., Wor.Pk. 199 CT103
St. Michael's Ct., Slou. 131 AK70
St. Michaels Cres., Pnr. 116 BY58
St. Michaels Dr., Wat. 59 BV33
St. Michaels Gdns. W10 139 CY71
St. Lawrence Ter.
St. Michael's Grn., Beac. 89 AL52
St. Michaels Rd. NW2 119 CW63
St. Michael's Rd. SW9 161 DM82
St. Michael's Rd., Ashf. 174 BN92
St. Michaels Rd., Brox. 49 DZ20
St. Michaels Rd., Cat. 236 DR122
St. Michaels Rd., Croy. 202 DQ102
St. Michaels Rd., Grays 171 GH78
St. Michaels Rd., Wall. 219 DJ107
St. Michaels Rd., Well. 166 EV83
St. Michael's Rd., Wok. 211 BD114
St. Michaels St. W2 272 A8
St. Michaels St. W2 140 DD72
St. Michaels St., St.Alb. 42 CB20
St. Michaels Ter. N22 99 DL54
St. Michaels Way, Pot.B. 64 DB30
St. Mildred's Ct. EC2 275 K9
St. Mildreds Rd. SE12 184 EF87
St. Mildreds Rd., Guil. 243 AZ133
St. Monica's Rd., Tad. 233 CZ121
St. Nazaire Clo., Egh. 173 BC92
Mullens Rd.
St. Neots Clo., Borwd. 78 CN38
St. Neots Rd., Rom. 106 FM52
St. Nicholas Ave., Horn. 127 FG62
St. Nicholas Ave., Lthd. 246 CB125
St. Nicholas Clo., Amer. 72 AV39
St. Nicholas Clo., Borwd. 77 CK44
St. Nicholas Clo., Uxb. 134 BK72
St. Nicholas Dr., Sev. 257 FJ126
St. Nicholas Dr., Shep. 194 BN101
St. Nicholas Glebe SW17 180 DG92
St. Nicholas Hill, Lthd. 231 CH122
St. Nicholas Mt., Hem.H. 39 BF20
St. Nicholas Rd. SE18 165 ET78
St. Nicholas Rd., Sutt. 218 DB106
St. Nicholas Rd., T.Ditt. 197 CF100
St. Nicholas St. SE8 163 DZ81
Lucas St.
St. Nicholas Way, Sutt. 218 DB105
St. Nicolas La., Chis. 204 EL95
St. Ninian's Ct. N20 98 DF48
St. Norbert Grn. SE4 163 DY84
St. Norbert Rd. SE4 183 DX85
St. Normans Way, Epsom 217 CU110
St. Olaf's Rd. SW6 159 CY80
St. Olaves Clo., Stai. 173 BF94
St. Olaves Ct. EC2 275 K9
St. Olave's Est. SE1 279 N4
St. Olaves Gdns. SE11 278 D8
St. Olaves Rd. E6 145 EN67
St. Olave's Wk. SW16 201 DJ96
St. Olav's Sq. SE16 162 DW75
Albion St.
St. Omer Ridge, Guil. 259 BA135
St. Omer Rd., Guil. 259 BA135
St. Oswald's Pl. SE11 161 DM78
St. Oswald's Rd. SW16 201 DP95
St. Oswulf St. SW1 277 N9
St. Pancras Way NW1 141 DJ66
St. Patrick's Ct., Wdf.Grn. 102 EE52
St. Patrick's Gdns., Grav. 191 GK90
St. Patricks Pl., Grays 171 GJ77
St. Paul Clo., Uxb. 134 BK71
St. Paul St. N1 142 DQ67
St. Paul's All. EC4 141 DP72
St. Paul's Chyd.
St. Paul's Ave. NW2 139 CW65
St. Paul's Ave. SE16 143 DX74
St. Pauls Ave., Har. 118 CM57
St. Pauls Ave., Slou. 132 AT73
St. Paul's Chyd. EC4 274 G9
St. Paul's Chyd. EC4 141 DP72
St. Paul's Clo. SE7 164 EK78
St. Paul's Clo. W5 158 CM75
St. Pauls Clo., Add. 212 BG106
St. Pauls Clo., Ashf. 175 BQ92
St. Paul's Clo., Cars. 200 DE102
St. Pauls Clo., Chess. 215 CK105
St. Pauls Clo., Hayes 155 BR78
St. Paul's Clo., Houns. 156 BY82
St. Pauls Clo., S.Ock. 148 FQ73
St. Pauls Clo., Swans. 190 FY87
Swanscombe St.
St. Paul's Ct. W14 159 CX77
Colet Gdns.
St. Pauls Ctyd. SE8 163 EA80
Deptford High St.
St. Pauls Cray Rd., Chis. 205 ER95
St. Paul's Cres. NW1 141 DK66
St. Pauls Dr. E15 123 ED64
St. Paul's Ms. NW1 141 DK66
St. Paul's Cres.
St. Paul's Pl. N1 142 DR65
St. Pauls Pl., St.Alb. 43 CG20
St. Pauls Pl., S.Ock. 148 FQ73
St. Pauls Ri. N13 99 DP51
St. Paul's Rd. N1 141 DP65
St. Paul's Rd. N17 100 DU52
St. Paul's Rd., Bark. 145 EQ67
St. Paul's Rd., Brent. 157 CK79
St. Paul's Rd., Erith 167 FC80
St. Pauls Rd., Hem.H. 40 BK19
St. Paul's Rd., Rich. 158 CM83
St. Pauls Rd., Stai. 173 BD92
St. Paul's Rd., Th.Hth. 202 DQ97
St. Pauls Rd., Wok. 227 BA117
St. Paul's Rd. E., Dor. 263 CH137
St. Paul's Rd. W., Dor. 263 CG137
St. Paul's Shrubbery N1 142 DR65
St. Pauls Sq., Brom. 204 EG96
St. Paul's Ter. SE17 161 DP79
Westcott Rd.
St. Pauls Twr. E10 123 EC59
St. Pauls Wk., Kings.T. 178 CN94
Alexandra Rd.
St. Paul's Way E3 143 DZ71
St. Paul's Way E14 143 DZ71
St. Paul's Way N3 98 DB52
St. Pauls Way, Wal.Abb. 67 ED33
Rochford Ave.

Sedgewick Ave., Uxb. 135 BP66
Sedgewood Clo., Brom. 204 EF101
Sedgmoor Pl. SE5 162 DS80
Sedgwick Rd. E10 123 EC61
Sedgwick St. E9 123 DX64
Sedleigh Rd. SW18 179 CZ86
Sedlescombe Rd. SW6 159 CZ79
Sedley, Grav. 190 GA93
Sedley Gro., Uxb. 114 BJ56
Sedley Pl. W1 273 H9
Sedley Ri., Loug. 85 EM40
Sedum Clo. NW9 118 CP57
Old Kenton La.
Seeley Dr. SE21 182 DS91
Seeleys, Harl. 36 EW12
Seeleys Clo., Beac. 88 AJ51
Seeleys La., Beac. 89 AK52
Seeleys Wk.
Seeleys Rd., Beac. 88 AJ50
Seeleys Wk., Beac. 88 AJ52
Seelig Ave. NW9 119 CU59
Seely Rd. SW17 180 DG93
Seer Grn. La., Beac. 90 AS52
Seer Mead, Beac. 89 AR51
Seething La. EC3 275 N10
Seething La. EC3 142 DS73
Seething Wells La., Surb. 197 CJ100
Sefton Ave. NW7 96 CR50
Sefton Ave., Har. 95 CD53
Sefton Clo., Orp. 205 ET98
Sefton Clo., St.Alb. 43 CF19
Blenheim Rd.
Sefton Clo., Slou. 132 AT66
Sefton Paddock, Slou. 132 AU66
Sefton Pk., Slou. 132 AU66
Sefton Rd., Croy. 202 DU102
Sefton Rd., Epsom 216 CR110
Sefton Rd., Orp. 205 ET98
Sefton St. SW15 159 CW83
Sefton Way, Uxb. 134 BJ72
Segal Clo. SE23 183 DY87
Segrave Clo., Wey. 212 BN108
Sekforde St. EC1 274 F5
Sekforde St. EC1 141 DP70
Sekhon Ter., Felt. 176 CA90
Selah Dr., Swan. 207 FC95
Selan Gdns., Hayes 135 BV71
Selbie Ave. NW10 119 CT64
Selborne Ave. E12 125 EN63
Walton Rd.
Selborne Ave. E17 123 DZ56
Selborne Ave., Bex. 186 EY88
Selborne Gdns. NW4 119 CU56
Selborne Gdns., Grnf. 137 CG68
Selborne Rd. E17 123 DZ57
Selborne Rd. N14 99 DL48
Selborne Rd. N22 99 DM53
Selborne Rd. SE5 162 DR82
Denmark Hill
Selborne Rd., Croy. 202 DS104
Selborne Rd., Ilf. 125 EN61
Selborne Rd., N.Mal. 198 CS96
Selborne Rd., Sid. 186 EV91
Selborne Wk. E17 123 DY57
High St.
Selbourne Ave., Add. 212 BH110
Selbourne Ave., Surb. 198 CM103
Selbourne Clo., Add. 212 BH110
Selbourne Rd., Guil. 243 BA131
Selbourne Sq., Gdse. 252 DW130
Selby Ave., St.Alb. 43 CD20
Selby Chase, Ruis. 115 BV61
Selby Clo. E6 144 EL71
Linton Gdns.
Selby Clo., Chess. 216 CL108
Selby Clo., Chis. 185 EN93
Selby Gdns., Sthl. 136 CA70
Selby Grn., Cars. 200 DE101
Selby Rd. E11 124 EE62
Selby Rd. E13 144 EH71
Selby Rd. N17 100 DS51
Selby Rd. SE20 202 DU96
Selby Rd. W5 137 CH70
Selby Rd., Ashf. 175 BQ93
Selby Rd., Cars. 200 DE101
Selby St. E1 142 DU70
Selby Wk., Wok. 226 AV118
Wyndham Rd.
Selcroft Rd., Pur. 219 DP112
Selden Hill, Hem.H. 40 BK21
Selden Rd. SE15 162 DW82
Selden Wk. N7 121 DM61
Durham Rd.
Sele Rd., Hert. 31 DP09
Selhurst Clo. SW19 179 CX88
Selhurst Clo., Wok. 227 AZ115
Selhurst New Rd. SE25 202 DS100
Selhurst Pl. SE25 202 DS100
Selhurst Rd. N9 100 DR48
Selhurst Rd. SE25 202 DS99
Selinas La., Dag. 126 EY59
Selkirk Dr., Erith 167 FE81
Selkirk Rd. SW17 180 DE91
Selkirk Rd., Twick. 176 CC89
Sellers Clo., Borwd. 78 CQ39
Sellers Hall Clo. N3 98 DA52
Sellincourt Rd. SW17 180 DE92
Sellindge Clo., Beck. 183 DZ94
Sellon Ms. SE11 278 C9
Sellons Ave. NW10 139 CT67
Sells Rd., Ware 33 DZ05
Sellwood Dr., Barn. 79 CX43
Selsdon Ave., S.Croy. 220 DR107
Selsdon Rd.
Selsdon Clo., Rom. 105 FC53
Selsdon Clo., Surb. 198 CL99
Selsdon Cres., S.Croy. 220 DW110
Selsdon Pk. Rd., S.Croy. 221 DX109
Selsdon Rd. E11 124 EG59
Selsdon Rd. E13 144 EJ67
Selsdon Rd. NW2 119 CT61
Selsdon Rd. SE27 181 DP90
Selsdon Rd., Add. 212 BG111
Selsdon Rd., S.Croy. 220 DR106
Selsdon Rd. Ind. Est., S.Croy. 220 DR107
Selsdon Rd.
Selsdon Way E14 163 EB76
Selsea Pl. N16 122 DS64
Crossway
Selsey Cres., Well. 166 EX81
Selsey St. E14 143 EA71
Selvage La. NW7 96 CR50
Selway Clo., Pnr. 115 BV55
Selwood Clo., Stai. 174 BJ86
Selwood Gdns., Stai. 174 BJ86
Selwood Pl. SW7 160 DD78
Selwood Rd., Brwd. 108 FT48
Selwood Rd., Chess. 215 CK105
Selwood Rd., Croy. 202 DV103
Selwood Rd., Sutt. 199 CZ102
Selwood Rd., Wok. 227 BB120
Selwood Ter. SW7 160 DD78
Neville Ter.
Selworthy Clo. E11 124 EG57
Selworthy Rd. SE6 183 DZ90
Selwyn Ave. E4 101 EC51
Selwyn Ave., Hat. 44 CR19
Selwyn Ave., Ilf. 125 ET58
Selwyn Ave., Rich. 158 CL83
Selwyn Clo., Houns. 156 BY84
Selwyn Ct. SE3 164 EF83
Selwyn Ct., Edg. 96 CP52
Camrose Ave.
Selwyn Cres., Hat. 44 CS18
Selwyn Cres., Well. 166 EV83
Selwyn Dr., Hat. 44 CR18
Selwyn Pl., Orp. 206 EV97
Saxville Rd.
Selwyn Rd. E3 143 DZ68
Selwyn Rd. E13 144 EH67
Selwyn Rd. NW10 138 CR66
Selwyn Rd., N.Mal. 198 CR99
Selwyn Rd., Til. 171 GF82
Dock Rd.
Semaphore Rd., Guil. 258 AY136
Semley Gate E9 143 DZ65
Eastway
Semley Pl. SW1 276 G9
Semley Pl. SW1 160 DG77
Semley Rd. SW16 201 DL96
Semper Clo., Wok. 226 AS117
Semper Rd., Grays 171 GJ75
Semphill Rd., Hem.H. 40 BL23
Senate St. SE15 162 DW82
Senator Wk. SE28 165 ER76
Broadwater Rd.
Send Barns La., Wok. 227 BD124
Send Clo., Wok. 227 BC123
Send Hill Rd., Wok. 243 BC125
Send Marsh Rd., Wok. 227 BE123
Send Par. Clo., Wok. 227 BC123
Send Rd.
Send Rd., Wok. 227 BB122
Seneca Rd., Th.Hth. 202 DQ98
Senga Rd., Wall. 200 DG102
Senhouse Rd., Sutt. 199 CX104
Senior St. W2 140 DB71
Senlac Rd. SE12 184 EH88
Sennen Rd., Enf. 100 DT45
Sennen Wk. SE9 184 EL90
Nunnington Clo.
Senrab St. E1 143 DX72
Sentinel Clo., Nthlt. 136 BY70
Sentinel Sq. NW4 119 CW56
Sentis Ct., Nthwd. 93 BS51
Carew Rd.
September Way, Stan. 95 CH51
Sequoia Clo. (Bushey), Wat. 95 CD46
Giant Tree Hill
Sequoia Gdns., Orp. 205 ET101
Sequoia Pk., Pnr. 94 CB51
Serbin Clo. E10 123 EC59
Sergeants Grn. La., Wal.Abb. 68 EJ33
Sergehill La., Abb.L. 59 BT27
Serjeants Inn EC4 274 E9
Serle St. WC2 274 C8
Serle St. WC2 141 DM72
Sermed Ct., Slou. 132 AW74
Sermon Dr., Swan. 207 FC97
Sermon La. EC4 142 DQ72
Carter La.
Serpentine Ct., Sev. 257 FK122
Serpentine Grn., Red. 251 DK129
Malmstone Ave.
Serpentine Rd. W2 276 D3
Serpentine Rd. W2 140 DF74
Serpentine Rd., Sev. 257 FJ123
Service Rd., The, Pot.B. 64 DA32
Serviden Dr., Brom. 204 EK95
Setchell Rd. SE1 279 P8
Setchell Way SE1 279 P8
Seth St. SE16 162 DW75
Swan Rd.
Seton Gdns., Dag. 146 EW66
Settle Pt. E13 144 EG68
London Rd.
Settle Rd. E13 144 EG68
London Rd.
Settle Rd., Rom. 106 FN49
Settles St. E1 142 DU71
Settrington Rd. SW6 160 DB82
Seven Acres, Cars. 200 DE103
Seven Acres, Nthwd. 93 BU51
Seven Acres, Swan. 207 FD100
Seven Arches Rd., Brwd. 108 FX47
Seven Clo., Cars. 200 DE103
Seven Hills Clo., Walt. 213 BS109
Seven Hills Rd., Cob. 213 BS110
Seven Hills Rd., Iver 133 BB65
Seven Hills Rd., Walt. 213 BS110
Seven Hills Rd. S., Cob. 213 BS113
Seven Kings Rd., Ilf. 125 ET60
Seven Sisters Rd. N4 122 DQ59
Seven Sisters Rd. N7 121 DM62
Seven Sisters Rd. N15 122 DR58
Seven Stars Cor. W12 159 CU76
Goldhawk Rd.
Sevenoaks Business Cen., Sev. 257 FH121
Sevenoaks Bypass, Sev. 256 FC123
Sevenoaks Clo., Bexh. 167 FB84
Sevenoaks Clo., Rom. 106 FJ49
Sevenoaks Clo., Sutt. 218 DA110
Sevenoaks Ct., Nthwd. 93 BQ52
Sevenoaks Ho. SE25 202 DU97
Sevenoaks Rd. SE4 183 DY86
Sevenoaks Rd., Orp. 223 ET105
Sevenoaks Rd. (Green St. Grn.), Orp. 223 ET108
Sevenoaks Rd. (Otford), Sev. 241 FH116
Sevenoaks Way, Orp. 206 EW98
Sevenoaks Way, Sid. 186 EW94
Seventh Ave. E12 125 EM63
Seventh Ave., Hayes 135 BT74
Severalls Ave., Chesh. 54 AQ30
Severn Ave., Rom. 127 FH55
Severn Cres., Slou. 153 BB78
Severn Dr., Enf. 82 DU38
Severn Dr., Esher 197 CG103
Severn Dr., Upmin. 129 FR58
Severn Dr., Walt. 196 BX103
Severn Rd., S.Ock. 148 FQ72
Severn Way NW10 119 CT64
Severn Way, Wat. 60 BW34
Severnake Clo. E14 163 EA77
Severnmead, Hem.H. 40 BL17
Severns Fld., Epp. 70 EU29
Severnvale, St.Alb. 62 CM27
Thamesdale
Severus Rd. SW11 160 DE84
Seville Ms. N1 142 DS66
Seville St. SW1 276 E5
Seville St. SW1 160 DF75
Sevington Rd. NW4 119 CV58
Sevington St. W9 140 DB70
Seward Rd. W7 157 CG75
Seward Rd., Beck. 203 DX96
Seward St. EC1 274 G3
Seward St. EC1 141 DP70
Sewardstone Gdns. E4 83 EB43
Sewardstone Rd. E2 142 DW68
Sewardstone Rd. E4 101 EB45
Sewardstone Rd., Wal.Abb. 83 ED38
Sewardstone St., Wal.Abb. 67 EC34
Sewdley St. E5 123 DX63
Sewell Clo., St.Alb. 44 CL20
Sewell Harris Clo., Harl. 35 ET13
Sewell Rd. SE2 166 EU75
Sewell St. E13 144 EG69
Sewells, Welw.G.C. 29 CY05
Sextant Ave. E14 163 ED77
Sexton Clo., Rain. 147 FF67
Blake Clo.
Sexton Rd., Til. 171 GF81
Seymer Rd., Rom. 127 FD55
Seymour Ave. N17 100 DU54
Seymour Ave., Cat. 236 DQ122
Fairbourne La.
Seymour Ave., Epsom 217 CV109
Seymour Ave., Mord. 199 CX101
Seymour Clo., E.Mol. 196 CC99
Seymour Clo., Loug. 84 EL44
Seymour Clo., Pnr. 94 BZ53
Seymour Ct. E4 102 EF47
Seymour Cres., Hem.H. 40 BL20
Seymour Dr., Brom. 205 EM102
Seymour Gdns. SE4 163 DY83
Seymour Gdns., Felt. 176 BW91
Seymour Gdns., Ilf. 125 EM60
Seymour Gdns., Ruis. 116 BX60
Seymour Gdns., Surb. 198 CM99
Seymour Gdns., Twick. 177 CH87
Seymour Ms. W1 272 F8
Seymour Ms. W1 140 DG72
Seymour Ms., Saw. 36 EX08
Seymour Pl. SE25 202 DV98
Seymour Pl. W1 272 C6
Seymour Pl. W1 140 DE71
Seymour Rd. E4 101 EB46
Seymour Rd. E6 144 EK68
Seymour Rd. E10 123 DZ60
Seymour Rd. N3 98 DB52
Seymour Rd. N8 121 DP57
Seymour Rd. N9 100 DV47
Seymour Rd. SW18 179 CZ87
Seymour Rd. SW19 179 CX90
Seymour Rd. W4 158 CQ77
Seymour Rd., Berk. 38 AS17
Seymour Rd., Cars. 218 DG106
Seymour Rd., Ch.St.G. 90 AW49
Seymour Rd., E.Mol. 196 CC99
Seymour Rd., Grav. 191 GF88
Seymour Rd., Hmptn. 176 CC92
Seymour Rd., Kings.T. 197 CK95
Seymour Rd., Mitch. 200 DG101
Seymour Rd., St.Alb. 43 CE17
Seymour Rd., Slou. 151 AR75
Seymour Rd., Til. 171 GF81
Seymour Rd., W.Mol. 196 CC99
Seymour St. W1 272 D9
Seymour St. W1 140 DF72
Seymour St. W2 272 D9
Seymour St. W2 140 DF72
Seymour Ter. SE20 202 DV95
Seymour Vill. SE20 202 DV95
Seymour Wk. SW10 160 DC79
Seymour Wk., Swans. 190 FY87
Seymour Way, Sun. 175 BS94
Seymours, Harl. 51 EM18
Seymours, The, Loug. 85 EN39
Seyssel St. E14 163 EC77
Shaa Rd. W3 138 CR73
Shacklands Rd., Sev. 225 FB111
Shackleford Rd., Wok. 227 BA121
Shacklegate La., Tedd. 177 CE91
Shackleton Clo. SE23 182 DV89
Shackleton Rd., Slou. 132 AT73
Shackleton Rd., Sthl. 136 BZ73
Shackleton Wk., Guil. 242 AT134
Humbolt Clo.
Shackleton Way, Abb.L. 59 BU32
Lysander Way
Shackleton Way, Welw.G.C. 30 DD09
Shacklewell Grn. E8 122 DT63
Shacklewell La.
Shacklewell La. E8 122 DT64
Shacklewell Rd. N16 122 DT63
Shacklewell Row E8 122 DT63
Shacklewell St. E2 142 DT69
Shad Thames SE1 279 P3
Shad Thames SE1 162 DT75
Shadbolt Clo., Wor.Pk. 199 CT103
Shadwell Dr., Nthlt. 136 BZ69
Shadwell Gdns. E1 142 DW72
Martha St.
Shadwell Pierhead E1 142 DW73
Glamis Rd.
Shadwell Pl. E1 142 DW73
Sutton St.
Shady Bush Clo. (Bushey), Wat. 94 CC45
Richfield Rd.
Shady La., Wat. 75 BV40
Shaef Way, Tedd. 177 CG94
Shafter Rd., Dag. 147 FC65
Shaftesbury, Loug. 84 EK41
Shaftesbury Ave. W1 273 M10
Shaftesbury Ave. W1 141 DK73
Shaftesbury Ave. WC2 277 M1
Shaftesbury Ave. WC2 141 DK73
Shaftesbury Ave., Barn. 80 DC41
Shaftesbury Ave., Enf. 83 DX40
Shaftesbury Ave., Felt. 175 BU86
Shaftesbury Ave., Har. 116 CB60
Shaftesbury Ave. (Kenton), Har. 117 CK57
Shaftesbury Ave., Sthl. 156 CA77
Shaftesbury Circle, Har. 116 CC60
Shaftesbury Ave.
Shaftesbury Ct. N1 142 DR68
Shaftesbury St.
Shaftesbury Cres., Stai. 174 BK94
Shaftesbury Gdns. NW10 138 CS70
Shaftesbury La., Dart. 168 FP84
Shaftesbury Ms. SW4 181 DJ85
Clapham Common S. Side
Shaftesbury Ms. W8 160 DA76
Stratford Rd.
Shaftesbury Pt. E13 144 EH68
High St.
Shaftesbury Rd. E4 101 ED46
Shaftesbury Rd. E7 144 EJ66
Shaftesbury Rd. E10 123 EA60
Shaftesbury Rd. E17 123 EB58
Shaftesbury Rd. N18 100 DS51
Shaftesbury Rd. N19 121 DL60
Shaftesbury Rd., Beck. 203 DZ96
Shaftesbury Rd., Cars. 200 DD101
Shaftesbury Rd., Epp. 69 ET29
Shaftesbury Rd., Rich. 158 CL83
Shaftesbury Rd., Rom. 127 FF58
Shaftesbury Rd., Wat. 76 BW41
Shaftesbury Rd., Wok. 227 BA117
Shaftesbury St. N1 275 J1
Shaftesbury St. N1 142 DQ68
Shaftesbury Way, Twick. 177 CD90
Shaftesbury Waye, Hayes 136 BW71
Shaftesburys, The, Bark. 145 EQ68
Shafto Ms. SW1 276 D7
Shafton Rd. E9 143 DX67
Shaftsbury Rd., Beck. 203 DZ96
Shaftsbury Way, Kings L. 59 BQ28
Shaggy Calf La., Slou. 132 AU73
Shakespeare Ave. N11 99 DJ50
Shakespeare Ave. NW10 138 CR67
Shakespeare Ave., Felt. 175 BU86
Shakespeare Ave., Hayes 135 BU72
Shakespeare Ave., Til. 171 GH82
Shakespeare Cres. E12 145 EM65
Shakespeare Cres. NW10 138 CR67
Shakespeare Dr., Har. 118 CM58
Shakespeare Gdns. N2 120 DF56
Shakespeare Ho. N14 99 DK47
High St.
Shakespeare Rd. E17 101 DX54
Shakespeare Rd. N3 98 DA53
Popes Dr.
Shakespeare Rd. NW7 97 CT49
Shakespeare Rd. SE24 181 DP85
Shakespeare Rd. W3 138 CQ74
Shakespeare Rd. W7 137 CF73
Shakespeare Rd., Add. 212 BK105
Shakespeare Rd., Bexh. 166 EY81
Shakespeare Rd., Dart. 168 FN84
Shakespeare Rd., Rom. 127 FF58
Shakespeare Sq., Ilf. 103 EQ51
Shakespeare St., Wat. 75 BV38
Shakespeare Twr. EC2 142 DQ71
Beech St.
Shakespeare Way, Felt. 176 BW91
Shakspeare Ms. N16 122 DS63
Shakspeare Wk.
Shakspeare Wk. N16 122 DS63
Shalcomb St. SW10 160 DC79
Shalcross Dr. (Cheshunt), Wal.Cr. 67 DZ30
Shaldon Dr., Mord. 199 CY99
Shaldon Dr., Ruis. 116 BW62
Shaldon Rd., Edg. 96 CM54
Shaldon Way, Walt. 196 BW104
Shale Grn., Red. 251 DK129
Bletchingley Rd.
Shalfleet Dr. W10 139 CX73
Shalford Clo., Orp. 223 EQ105
Shalford Rd., Guil. 258 AX138
Shalimar Gdns. W3 138 CQ73
Shalimar Rd. W3 138 CQ73
Hereford Rd.
Shallcross Cres., Hat. 45 CU21
Shallons Rd. SE9 185 EP91
Shalston Vill., Surb. 198 CM100
Shalstone Rd. SW14 158 CP83
Shamrock Clo., Lthd. 231 CD121
Shamrock Rd., Croy. 201 DM100
Shamrock Rd., Grav. 191 GL87
Shamrock St. SW4 161 DK83
Shamrock Way N14 99 DH46
Shand St. SE1 279 N4
Shand St. SE1 162 DS75
Shandon Rd. SW4 181 DJ86
Shandy St. E1 143 DX71
Shanklin Clo., Wal.Cr. 66 DT29
Hornbeam Way
Shanklin Gdns., Wat. 94 BW49
Shanklin Rd. N8 121 DK57
Shanklin Rd. N15 122 DU56
Shanklin Way SE15 162 DT80
Pentridge St.
Shannon Clo. NW2 119 CX62
Shannon Clo., Sthl. 156 BX78
Shannon Gro. SW9 161 DM84
Shannon Pl. NW8 140 DE68
Allitsen Rd.
Shannon Way, Beck. 183 EB93
Shannon Way, S.Ock. 148 FQ73
Shantock Hall La., Hem.H. 56 AY29
Shantock La., Hem.H. 56 AX30
Shap Cres., Cars. 200 DF102
Shapland Way N13 99 DM50
Shardcroft Ave. SE24 181 DP85
Shardeloes Rd. SE14 163 DZ82
Sharland Clo., Th.Hth. 201 DN100
Sharland Rd., Grav. 191 GJ89
Sharman Ct., Sid. 186 EU91
Sharnbrooke Clo., Well. 166 EW83
Sharney Ave., Slou. 153 BB76
Sharon Clo., Epsom 216 CQ113
Sharon Clo., Lthd. 230 CA124
Sharon Clo., Surb. 197 CJ102
Sharon Gdns. E9 142 DW67
Sharon Rd. W4 158 CR78
Sharon Rd., Enf. 83 DY40
Sharp Way, Dart. 168 FM83
Sharpcroft, Hem.H. 40 BK18
Sharpe Clo. W7 137 CF71
Templeman Rd.
Sharpecroft, Harl. 51 EQ15
Sharpes La., Hem.H. 39 BB22
Sharpleshall St. NW1 140 DF66
Sharpness Clo., Hayes 136 BY71
Sharps La., Ruis. 115 BR60
Sharratt St. SE15 162 DW79
Sharsted St. SE17 161 DP78
Shavers Pl. SW1 277 M1
Shaw Ave., Bark. 146 EY68
Shaw Clo. SE28 146 EV74
Shaw Clo., Cher. 211 BC107
Shaw Clo., Epsom 217 CT111
Shaw Clo., Horn. 127 FH60
Shaw Clo., S.Croy. 220 DT112
Shaw Clo. (Cheshunt), Wal.Cr. 66 DW28
Shaw Clo. (Bushey), Wat. 95 CE47
Shaw Ct., Wind. 172 AU85
Shaw Cres., Brwd. 109 GD42
Shaw Cres., S.Croy. 220 DT112
Shaw Cres., Til. 171 GH81
Shaw Dr., Walt. 196 BW101
Shaw Gdns., Bark. 146 EY68
Shaw Rd. SE22 162 DS84
Shaw Rd., Brom. 184 EF90
Shaw Rd., Enf. 83 DX39
Shaw Rd., West. 238 EJ120
Shaw Sq. E17 101 DY53
Shaw Way, Wall. 219 DL108
Shawbridge, Harl. 51 EQ18
Shawbrooke Rd. SE9 184 EJ85
Shawbury Rd. SE22 182 DT85
Shawfield Ct., West Dr. 154 BL76
Shawfield Pk., Brom. 204 EK96
Shawfield St. SW3 160 DE78
Shawford Ct. SW15 179 CU87
Shawford Rd., Epsom 216 CR107
Shawley Cres., Epsom 233 CW118
Shawley Way, Epsom 233 CV118
Shaws, The, Welw.G.C. 30 DC10
Shaws Cotts. SE23 183 DY90
Shaxton Cres., Croy. 221 EC109
Shearing Dr., Cars. 200 DC101
Stavordale Rd.
Shearling Way N7 141 DL65
Shearman Rd. SE3 164 EF84
Shearsmith Ho. E1 142 DU73
Cable St.
Shearwater Way, Hayes 136 BX72
Shearwood Cres., Dart. 167 FF83
Sheath's La., Lthd. 214 CB113
Sheaveshill Ave. NW9 118 CS56
Sheehy Way, Slou. 132 AV73
Sheen Common Dr., Rich. 158 CN84
Sheen Ct., Rich. 158 CN84
Sheen Rd.
Sheen Ct. Rd., Rich. 158 CN84
Sheen Gate Gdns. SW14 158 CQ84
Sheen Gro. N1 141 DN67
Richmond Ave.
Sheen La. SW14 178 CQ85
Sheen Pk., Rich. 158 CL84
Sheen Rd., Orp. 205 ET98
Sheen Rd., Rich. 178 CL85
Sheen Way, Wall. 219 DM106
Sheen Wd. SW14 178 CQ85
Sheendale Rd., Rich. 158 CM84
Sheenewood SE26 182 DV92
Sheep La. E8 142 DV67
Sheep Wk., Epsom 232 CR122
Sheep Wk., Reig. 249 CY131
Sheep Wk., Shep. 194 BM101
Sheep Wk. Ms. SW19 179 CY93
Sheepbarn La., Warl. 222 EF112
Sheepcot Dr., Wat. 60 BW34
Sheepcot La., Wat. 59 BU33
Sheepcote, Welw.G.C. 30 DA12
Sheepcote Clo., Beac. 88 AJ51
Sheepcote Clo., Houns. 155 BU80
Sheepcote Gdns., Uxb. 114 BG58
Sheepcote La. SW11 160 DF82
Sheepcote La., H.Wyc. 110 AG61
Sheepcote La., Orp. 206 EZ100
Sheepcote La., St.Alb. 28 CL07
Sheepcote La., Slou. 110 AF62
Sheepcote La., Swan. 206 FA98
Sheepcote Rd., Har. 117 CF58
Sheepcote Rd., Hem.H. 40 BM20
Sheepcote Rd., Wind. 151 AL82
Sheepcote Rd. (Eton Wick), Wind. 151 AN78
Sheepcotes Rd., Rom. 126 EX56
Sheepfold La., Amer. 55 AR39
Sheepfold Rd., Guil. 242 AT131
Sheephouse Grn., Dor. 262 BZ140
Sheephouse La., Dor. 262 BZ139
Sheephouse Rd., Hem.H. 40 BM22
Sheephouse Way, N.Mal. 198 CR102
Sheeplands Ave., Guil. 243 BC132
Sheepwalk La., Lthd. 245 BT134
Sheering Dr., Harl. 36 EX11
Sheering Lwr. Rd., Harl. 36 EZ09
Sheering Lwr. Rd., Saw. 36 EZ08
Sheering Mill La., Saw. 36 EZ05
Sheering Rd., Harl. 36 EZ10
Sheerwater Ave., Add. 211 BE112
Sheerwater Business Cen., Wok. 211 BC114
Sheerwater Rd. E16 144 EK71
Sheerwater Rd., Add. 211 BE112
Sheerwater Rd., W.Byf. 211 BE113
Sheerwater Rd., Wok. 211 BE112
Sheet St., Wind. 151 AR82
Sheethanger La., Hem.H. 40 BG24
Sheffield Dr., Rom. 106 FN50
Sheffield Gdns., Rom. 106 FN50
Sheffield Rd., Slou. 131 AQ72
Sheffield Sq. E3 143 DZ69
Malmesbury Rd.
Sheffield St. WC2 274 B9
Sheffield Ter. W8 140 DA74
Shefton Ri., Nthwd. 93 BU52
Sheila Clo., Rom. 105 FB52
Sheila Rd., Rom. 105 FB52
Sheilings, The, Horn. 128 FM57
Shelbourne Clo., Pnr. 116 BZ55
Shelbourne Rd. N17 100 DV54
Shelburne Rd. N7 121 DM63

Shelbury Clo., Sid. 186 EU90
Shelbury Rd. SE22 182 DV85
Sheldon Ave. N6 120 DE59
Sheldon Ave., Ilf. 103 EP54
Sheldon Clo. SE12 184 EH85
Sheldon Clo. SE20 202 DV95
Sheldon Clo., Harl. 52 EY15
Sheldon Clo., Reig. 266 DB135
Sheldon Clo. (Cheshunt), Wal.Cr. 66 DS26
Sheldon Ct., Guil. 259 AZ135
Lower Edgeborough Rd.
Sheldon Rd. N18 100 DS49
Sheldon Rd. NW2 119 CX63
Sheldon Rd., Bexh. 166 EZ81
Sheldon Rd., Dag. 146 EY66
Sheldon St., Croy. 202 DQ104
Wandle Rd.
Sheldrake Clo. E16 145 EM74
Newland St.
Sheldrake Pl. W8 160 DA75
Sheldrick Clo. SW19 200 DD96
Shelduck Clo. E15 124 EF64
Sheldwich Ter., Brom. 204 EL100
Shelford Pl. N16 122 DR62
Stoke Newington Ch. St.
Shelford Ri. SE19 182 DT94
Shelford Rd., Barn. 79 CW44
Shelgate Rd. SW11 180 DE85
Shell Clo., Brom. 204 EL100
Shell Rd. SE13 163 EB83
Shellbank La., Dart. 189 FU93
Shellduck Clo. NW9 96 CS54
Swan Dr.
Shelley Ave. E12 144 EL65
Shelley Ave., Grnf. 137 CD69
Shelley Ave., Horn. 127 FF61
Shelley Clo., Bans. 233 CX115
Shelley Clo., Couls. 235 DM117
Shelley Clo., Edg. 96 CN49
Shelley Clo., Grnf. 137 CD69
Shelley Clo., Hayes 135 BU71
Shelley Clo., H.Wyc. 110 AE55
Falcons Cft.
Shelley Clo., Nthwd. 93 BT50
Shelley Clo., Orp. 205 ES104
Shelley Clo., Slou. 153 AZ78
Shelley Cres., Houns. 156 BX81
Shelley Cres., Sthl. 136 BZ72
Shelley Dr., Well. 165 ES81
Shelley Gdns., Wem. 117 CJ61
Shelley Gro., Loug. 85 EM42
Shelley La., Uxb. 92 BG53
Shelley Pl., Til. 171 GH81
Kipling Ave.
Shelley Rd., Brwd. 109 GD45
Shelley Rd., Chesh. 54 AP29
Shelley Way SW19 180 DD93
Shelleys La., Sev. 239 ET116
Shellfield Clo., Stai. 174 BG85
Shellgrove Est. N16 122 DS64
Shellness Rd. E5 122 DV64
Shellwood Dr., Dor. 263 CJ140
Shellwood Rd. SW11 160 DF82
Shellwood Rd., Reig. 264 CQ141
Shelmerdine Clo. E3 143 EA71
Shelson Ave., Felt. 175 BT90
Shelton Ave., Warl. 236 DW117
Shelton Clo., Guil. 242 AU129
Shelton Clo., Warl. 236 DW117
Shelton Ct., Slou. 152 AW76
London Rd.
Shelton Rd. SW19 200 DA95
Shelton St. WC2 273 P9
Shelton St. WC2 141 DL72
Shelvers Grn., Tad. 233 CW121
Shelvers Hill, Tad. 233 CW121
Ashurst Rd.
Shelvers Spur, Tad. 233 CW121
Shelvers Way, Tad. 233 CW121
Shenden Clo., Sev. 257 FJ128
Shenden Way, Sev. 257 FJ128
Shenfield Clo., Couls. 235 DJ119
Woodfield Clo.
Shenfield Cres., Brwd. 108 FY47
Shenfield Gdns., Brwd. 109 GB44
Shenfield Grn., Brwd. 109 GA45
Hutton Rd.
Shenfield Ho. SE18 164 EK80
Shooter's Hill Rd.
Shenfield Pl., Brwd. 108 FY45
Shenfield Rd., Brwd. 108 FX47
Shenfield Rd., Wdf.Grn. 102 EH52
Shenfield St. N1 275 N1
Shenfield St. N1 142 DS68
Shenley Ave., Ruis. 115 BT61
Shenley Hill, Rad. 77 CG35
Shenley La., St.Alb. 61 CG25
Shenley Rd. SE5 162 DS81
Shenley Rd., Borwd. 78 CN42
Shenley Rd., Dart. 188 FN87
Shenley Rd., Hem.H. 40 BN15
Shenley Rd., Houns. 156 BY81
Shenley Rd., Rad. 61 CH34
Shenleybury Cotts., Rad. 62 CL31
Shenstone Clo., Dart. 167 FD84
Shenstone Dr., Slou. 131 AK70
Shenstone Gdns., Rom. 106 FJ53
Shenstone Hill, Berk. 38 AY18
Shepcot Ho. N14 81 DJ44
Shepherd Clo., Abb.L. 59 BT31
Jacketts Fld.
Shepherd Mkt. W1 277 H3
Shepherd St. W1 277 H3
Shepherd St., Grav. 190 GD87
Shepherdess Pl. N1 275 J2
Shepherdess Wk. N1 275 J1
Shepherdess Wk. N1 142 DQ68
Shepherds Bush Grn. W12 159 CW75
Shepherds Bush Mkt. W12 159 CW75
Uxbridge Rd.
Shepherds Bush Pl. W12 159 CX75
Shepherds Bush Rd. W6 159 CW77
Shepherds Clo. N6 121 DH58
Shepherds Clo., Beac. 89 AM54
Shepherds Clo., Lthd. 231 CK124
Shepherds Clo., Orp. 205 ET104
Stapleton Rd.
Shepherds Clo., Rom. 126 EX57
Shepherds Clo., Shep. 195 BP100
Shepherds Clo. (Cowley), Uxb. 134 BJ70
High St.
Shepherds Ct. W12 159 CX75
Shepherds Bush Grn.
Shepherds Ct., Hert. 32 DQ06
Shepherds Grn., Chis. 185 ER94
Shepherds Grn., Hem.H. 39 BE21
Shepherds Hill N6 121 DH58
Shepherds Hill, Guil. 242 AU132
Shepherds Hill, Red. 251 DJ126
Shepherds Hill, Rom. 106 FN54
Shepherds La. E9 143 DX65
Shepherds La., Beac. 89 AM54
Shepherds La., Brwd. 108 FS45
Shepherds La., Dart. 187 FG88
Shepherds La., Guil. 242 AT131
Shepherds La., Rick. 73 BD44
Shepherds Path, Nthlt. 136 BY65
Fortunes Mead
Shepherds Pl. W1 272 F10
Shepherds Rd., Wat. 75 BT41
Shepherds Wk. NW2 119 CU61
Shepherds Wk. NW3 120 DD63
Shepherds' Wk., Epsom 232 CP121
Shepherds Wk. (Bushey), Wat. 95 CD47
Shepherds Way, Chesh. 54 AR33
Shepherds Way, Guil. 258 AY138
Shepherds Way, Hat. 64 DB27
Shepherds Way, Rick. 92 BH45
Shepherds Way, S.Croy. 221 DX108
Shepiston La., Hayes 155 BR78
Shepiston La., West Dr. 155 BP77
Shepley Clo., Cars. 200 DG104
Shepley Clo., Horn. 128 FK64
Chevington Way
Shepley Ms., Enf. 83 EA37
Sheppard Clo., Enf. 82 DV38
Sheppard Clo., Kings.T. 198 CL98
Beaufort Rd.
Sheppard Dr. SE16 162 DV78
Sheppard St. E16 144 EF70
Sheppards, Harl. 51 EM18
Sheppards Clo., St.Alb. 43 CE17
Shepperton Business Pk., Shep. 195 BQ99
Shepperton Clo., Borwd. 78 CR39
Shepperton Ct. Dr., Shep. 195 BP99
Shepperton Rd. N1 142 DQ67
Shepperton Rd., Orp. 205 ER100
Shepperton Rd., Shep. 194 BL98
Shepperton Rd., Stai. 194 BJ97
Sheppey Clo., Erith 167 FH80
Sheppey Gdns., Dag. 146 EW66
Sheppey Rd.
Sheppey Rd., Dag. 146 EV66
Sheppey Wk. N1 142 DQ66
Clephane Rd.
Sheppeys La., Abb.L. 59 BS28
Sheppy Pl., Grav. 191 GH87
Sherard Rd. SE9 184 EL85
Sheraton Business Cen., Grnf. 137 CH68
Sheraton Clo., Borwd. 78 CM43
Sheraton Dr., Epsom 216 CQ113
Sheraton Ms., Wat. 75 BS42
Sheraton St. W1 273 M9
Sherborne Ave., Enf. 82 DW40
Sherborne Ave., Sthl. 156 CA77
Sherborne Clo., Epsom 233 CW117
Sherborne Clo., Hayes 136 BW72
Sherborne Cres., Cars. 200 DE101
Sherborne Gdns. NW9 118 CN55
Sherborne Gdns. W13 137 CH71
Sherborne Gdns., Rom. 104 FA50
Sherborne La. EC4 275 K10
Sherborne Rd., Chess. 216 CL106
Sherborne Rd., Felt. 175 BR87
Sherborne Rd., Orp. 205 ET98
Sherborne Rd., Sutt. 200 DA103
Sherborne St. N1 142 DR67
Sherborne Wk., Lthd. 231 CJ121
Windfield
Sherborne Way, Rick. 75 BP42
Sherboro Rd. N15 122 DT58
Ermine Rd.
Sherbourne, Guil. 260 BK139
Sherbourne Clo., Hem.H. 40 BL21
Sherbourne Clo., Slou. 153 BE81
Sherbourne Cotts., Guil. 260 BL138
Shere Rd.
Sherbourne Cotts., Wat. 76 BW43
Watford Fld. Rd.
Sherbourne Dr., Wind. 151 AM84
Sherbourne Gdns., Shep. 195 BS101
Windmill Grn.
Sherbourne Wk., Slou. 111 AQ63
Sherbrook Gdns. N21 99 DP45
Sherbrooke Clo., Bexh. 166 FA84
Sherbrooke Rd. SW6 159 CY80
Shere Ave., Sutt. 217 CW110
Shere Clo., Chess. 215 CK106
Shere Clo., Dor. 263 CJ140
Shere La., Guil. 260 BN139
Shere Rd., Guil. 260 BG136
Shere Rd., Ilf. 125 EN57
Shere Rd., Lthd. 245 BP130
Sheredan Rd. E4 101 ED50
Sheredes Dr., Hodd. 49 DZ19
Sherfield Ave., Rick. 92 BK48
Sherfield Gdns. SW15 179 CT86
Sherfield Rd., Grays 170 GB79
Sheridan Clo., Hem.H. 40 BH21
Sheridan Clo., Rom. 106 FJ52
Sheridan Clo., Swan. 207 FF97
Willow Ave.
Sheridan Clo., Uxb. 135 BQ70
Alpha Rd.
Sheridan Ct., Houns. 176 BZ85
Vickers Way
Sheridan Cres., Chis. 205 EP96
Sheridan Dr., Reig. 250 DB132
Sheridan Gdns., Har. 117 CK58
Sheridan Ms. E11 124 EG58
Woodbine Pl.
Sheridan Pl. SW13 159 CT82
Brookwood Ave.
Sheridan Pl., Hmptn. 196 CB95
Sheridan Rd. E7 124 EF62
Sheridan Rd. E12 124 EL64
Sheridan Rd. SW19 199 CZ95
Sheridan Rd., Belv. 166 FA77
Sheridan Rd., Bexh. 166 EY83
Sheridan Rd., Rich. 177 CJ90
Sheridan Rd., Wat. 94 BX45
Sheridan St. E1 142 DV72
Watney St.
Sheridan Ter., Nthlt. 116 CB64
Whitton Ave. W.
Sheridan Wk. NW11 120 DA58
Sheridan Wk., Brox. 49 DY20
Sheridan Wk., Cars. 218 DF106
Carshalton Pk. Rd.
Sheridan Way, Beck. 203 DZ95
Turners Meadow Way
Sheridans Rd., Lthd. 246 CC126
Sheriff Way, Wat. 59 BU33
Sheringham Ave. E12 125 EM63
Sheringham Ave. N14 81 DK43
Sheringham Ave., Felt. 175 BU90
Sheringham Ave., Rom. 127 FC58
Sheringham Ave., Twick. 176 BZ88
Sheringham Dr., Bark. 125 ET64
Sheringham Rd. N7 141 DM65
Sheringham Rd. SE20 202 DW97
Sheringham Twr., Sthl. 136 CB73
Sherington Ave., Pnr. 94 CA52
Sherington Rd. SE7 164 EH79
Sherland Rd., Twick. 177 CF87
Sherlies Ave., Orp. 205 ES103
Sherlock Ms. W1 272 F6
Sherman Rd., Brom. 204 EG95
Sherman Rd., Slou. 132 AS71
Shermanbury Pl., Erith 167 FF80
Betsham Rd.
Shernbroke Rd., Wal.Abb. 68 EF34
Shernhall St. E17 123 EC55
Sherrard Rd. E7 144 EJ65
Sherrard Rd. E12 144 EK65
Sherrards Ms., Welw.G.C. 29 CV06
Sherrards Way, Barn. 80 DA43
Sherrardspark Rd., Welw.G.C. 29 CW07
Sherrick Grn. Rd. NW10 119 CV64
Sherriff Rd. NW6 140 DA65
Sherrin Rd. E10 123 EA63
Sherringham Ave. N17 100 DU54
Sherrock Gdns. NW4 119 CU56
Sherwin Rd. SE14 163 DX81
Sherwood Ave. E18 124 EH55
Sherwood Ave. SW16 181 DJ94
Sherwood Ave., Grnf. 137 CE65
Sherwood Ave., Hayes 135 BV70
Sherwood Ave., Pot.B. 63 CY32
Sherwood Ave., Ruis. 115 BS58
Sherwood Ave., St.Alb. 43 CH17
Sherwood Clo. SW13 159 CV83
Lower Common S.
Sherwood Clo. W13 137 CH74
Sherwood Clo., Bex. 186 EW86
Sherwood Clo., Lthd. 230 CC122
Sherwood Clo., Slou. 152 AY76
Sherwood Cres., Reig. 266 DB138
Sherwood Gdns. E14 163 EA77
Sherwood Gdns. SE16 162 DU78
Sherwood Gdns., Bark. 145 ER66
Sherwood Pk. Ave., Sid. 186 EU87
Sherwood Pk. Rd., Mitch. 201 DJ98
Sherwood Pk. Rd., Sutt. 218 DA106
Sherwood Pl., Hem.H. 40 BM16
Turnpike Grn.
Sherwood Rd. NW4 119 CW55
Sherwood Rd. SW19 179 CZ94
Sherwood Rd., Couls. 235 DJ116
Sherwood Rd., Croy. 202 DV101
Sherwood Rd., Hmptn. 176 CC92
Sherwood Rd., Har. 116 CC61
Sherwood Rd., Ilf. 125 ER56
Sherwood Rd., Well. 165 ES82
Sherwood Rd., Wok. 226 AS117
Sherwood St. N20 98 DD48
Sherwood St. W1 273 L10
Sherwood Ter. N20 98 DD48
Green Rd.
Sherwood Way, W.Wick. 203 EB103
Sherwoods Rd., Wat. 94 BY45
Shetland Clo., Borwd. 78 CR44
Percheron Rd.
Shetland Clo., Guil. 243 BB129
Weybrook Dr.
Shetland Rd. E3 143 DZ68
Shevon Way, Brwd. 108 FT49
Shewens Rd., Wey. 213 BR105
Shey Copse, Wok. 227 BC117
Shield Dr., Brent. 157 CG79
Shield Rd., Ashf. 175 BQ91
Shieldhall St. SE2 166 EW77
Shifford Path SE23 183 DX90
Shilburn Way, Wok. 226 AU118
Shillibeer Pl. W1 272 C7
Shillibeer Wk., Chig. 103 ET48
Shillingford St. N1 141 DP66
Cross St.
Shillitoe Ave., Pot.B. 63 CX32
Shillitoe Rd. N13 99 DP50
Shimmings, The, Guil. 243 BA133
Shinfield St. W12 139 CW72
Shingle Ct., Wal.Abb. 68 EG33
Shinglewell Rd., Erith 166 FA79
Shinners Clo. SE25 202 DU99
Stanger Rd.
Ship All. W4 158 CN79
Thames Rd.
Ship and Mermaid Row SE1 279 L4
Ship Hill, H.Wyc. 111 AL60
Ship Hill, West. 238 EJ121
Ship La. SW14 158 CQ83
Ship La. (Sutton at Hone), Dart. 208 FK95
Ship La., Grays 169 FS76
Ship La., Purf. 169 FS76
Ship La., S.Ock. 149 FR74
Ship La., Swan. 208 FK95
Ship St. SE8 163 EA81
Ship Tavern Pas. EC3 275 M10
Ship Yd. E14 163 EB78
Napier Ave.
Ship Yd., Wey. 213 BP105
High St.
Shipfield Clo., West. 238 EJ121
Shipka Rd. SW12 181 DH88
Shipley Bri. La., Horl. 269 DM154
Shipman Rd. E16 144 EH72
Shipman Rd. SE23 183 DX89
Shipton Clo., Dag. 126 EX62
Shipton St. E2 142 DT68
Shipwright Rd. SE16 163 DY75
Shirburn Clo. SE23 182 DW87
Tyson Rd.
Shirbutt St. E14 143 EB73
Shire Clo., Brox. 67 DZ26
Groom Rd.
Shire Ct., Epsom 217 CT108
Shire Ct., Erith 166 EX76
St. John Fisher Rd.
Shire Horse Way, Islw. 157 CF83
Shire La., Ger.Cr. 91 BB48
Shire La., Orp. 222 EL109
Shire La., Rick. 73 BB43
Shire La., Uxb. 91 BD54
Shire Pk., Welw.G.C. 29 CY07
Shire Pl. SW18 180 DC87
Whitehead Clo.
Shirebrook Rd. SE3 164 EK83
Shirehall Clo. NW4 119 CX58
Shirehall Gdns. NW4 119 CX58
Shirehall La. NW4 119 CX58
Shirehall Pk. NW4 119 CX58
Shirehall Rd., Dart. 188 FJ92
Shiremeade, Borwd. 78 CM43
Shires, The, Rich. 178 CL91
Shires Clo., Ash. 231 CK119
Shires Ho., W.Byf. 212 BL113
Eden Gro. Rd.
Shirland Ms. W9 139 CZ69
Shirland Rd. W9 139 CZ69
Shirley Ave., Bex. 186 EX87
Shirley Ave., Couls. 235 DP119
Shirley Ave., Croy. 202 DW102
Shirley Ave., Red. 266 DF139
Shirley Ave., Sutt. 218 DD105
Shirley Ave. (Cheam), Sutt. 217 CZ109
Shirley Ave., Wind. 151 AM81
Shirley Ch. Rd., Croy. 202 DW104
Shirley Clo. E17 123 EB57
Addison Rd.
Shirley Clo., Brox. 49 DZ24
Shirley Clo., Dart. 168 FJ84
Shirley Clo., Houns. 176 CC85
Shirley Clo. (Cheshunt), Wal.Cr. 66 DW29
Shirley Ct., Croy. 203 DX104
Shirley Cres., Beck. 203 DY98
Shirley Dr., Houns. 176 CC85
Shirley Gdns. W7 137 CF74
Shirley Gdns., Bark. 145 ES65
Shirley Gdns., Horn. 128 FJ61
Shirley Gro. N9 100 DW45
Shirley Gro. SW11 160 DG83
Shirley Heights, Wall. 219 DJ109
Shirley Hills Rd., Croy. 221 DX106
Shirley Ho. Dr. SE7 164 EJ80
Shirley Oaks Rd., Croy. 203 DX102
Shirley Pk. Rd., Croy. 202 DV102
Shirley Rd. E15 144 EE66
Shirley Rd. W4 158 CR75
Shirley Rd., Abb.L. 59 BT32
Shirley Rd., Croy. 202 DV101
Shirley Rd., Enf. 82 DQ41
Shirley Rd., St.Alb. 43 CF21
Shirley Rd., Sid. 185 ES90
Shirley Rd., Wall. 219 DJ109
Shirley St. E16 144 EF72
Shirley Way, Croy. 203 DY104
Shirlock Rd. NW3 120 DF63
Shobden Rd. N17 100 DR53
Shobroke Clo. NW2 119 CW62
Shoe La. EC4 274 E8
Shoe La. EC4 141 DN72
Shoe La., Harl. 52 EZ16
Shoebury Rd. E6 145 EM66
Sholden Gdns., Orp. 206 EW99
Sholto Rd., Houns. 174 BM85
Shonks Mill Rd., Rom. 87 FG37
Shoot Up Hill NW2 119 CY64
Shooters Ave., Har. 117 CJ56
Shooters Dr., Wal.Abb. 50 EE22
Shooter's Hill SE18 165 EN81
Shooter's Hill, Well. 165 EQ82
Shooter's Hill Rd. SE3 164 EF81
Shooter's Hill Rd. SE10 163 ED81
Shooter's Hill Rd. SE18 164 EK81
Shooters Rd., Enf. 81 DP39
Shootersway, Berk. 38 AU20
Shootersway La., Berk. 38 AT20
Shootersway Pk., Berk. 38 AT20
Shophouse La., Guil. 260 BK144
Shoplands, Welw.G.C. 29 CX05
Shord Hill, Ken. 236 DR116
Shore, The (Northfleet), Grav. 190 GC85
Shore, The (Rosherville), Grav. 191 GF86
Shore Clo., Felt. 175 BU87
Shore Clo., Hmptn. 176 BY92
Stewart Clo.
Shore Gro., Felt. 176 CA89
Shore Pl. E9 142 DW66
Shore Rd. E9 142 DW66
Shorediche Clo., Uxb. 114 BM62
Shoreditch High St. E1 275 N5
Shoreditch High St. E1 142 DS70
Shoreham Clo. SW18 180 DB85
Ram St.
Shoreham Clo., Bex. 186 EX88
Stansted Cres.
Shoreham Clo., Croy. 202 DW99
Shoreham La., Orp. 224 FA107
Shoreham La., Sev. 256 FF122
Shoreham La. (Halstead), Sev. 224 EZ112
Shoreham Pl., Sev. 225 FG112
Shoreham Ri., Slou. 131 AK70
Lower Britwell Rd.
Shoreham Rd., Orp. 206 EV95
Shoreham Rd., Sev. 225 FH112
Shoreham Rd. E., Houns. 174 BL85
Shoreham Rd. W., Houns. 174 BL85
Shoreham Way, Brom. 204 EG100
Shores Rd., Wok. 210 AY114
Shorncliffe Rd. SE1 279 P10
Shorncliffe Rd. SE1 162 DT78
Shorndean St. SE6 183 EC88
Shorne Clo., Orp. 206 EX98
Shorne Clo., Sid. 186 EV86
Shornefield Clo., Brom. 205 EN97
Shornells Way SE2 166 EW78
Willrose Cres.
Shorrolds Rd. SW6 159 CZ80
Short Gate N12 97 CZ49
Short Hedges, Houns. 156 CA81
Lampton Ave.
Short Hill, Har. 117 CE60
High St.
Short La., Oxt. 254 EH132
Short La., St.Alb. 60 BZ29
Short La., Stai. 174 BM87
Short Path SE18 165 EP79
Westdale Rd.
Short Rd. E11 124 EE61
Short Rd. E15 143 ED67
Short Rd. W4 158 CS79
Short Rd., Houns. 174 BL86
Short St. NW4 119 CW56
New Brent St.
Short St. SE1 278 E4
Short Wall E15 143 ED69
Bisson Rd.
Short Way N12 98 DE51
Short Way SE9 164 EL83
Short Way, Twick. 176 CC87
Shortacres, Red. 251 DM133
Shortcroft Rd., Epsom 217 CT108
Shortcrofts Rd., Dag. 146 EZ65
Shorter Ave., Brwd. 109 FZ44
Shorter St. E1 142 DT73
Shortfern, Slou. 132 AW72
Shortlands W6 159 CX77
Shortlands, Hayes 155 BR79
Shortlands Clo. N18 100 DR48
Shortlands Clo., Belv. 166 EZ76
Shortlands Gdns., Brom. 204 EE96
Shortlands Grn., Welw.G.C. 29 CZ10
Shortlands Gro., Brom. 203 ED97
Shortlands Rd. E10 123 EB59
Shortlands Rd., Brom. 203 ED97
Shortlands Rd., Kings.T. 178 CM94
Shortmead Dr. (Cheshunt), Wal.Cr. 67 DY31
Shorts Cft. NW9 118 CP56
Shorts Gdns. WC2 273 P9
Shorts Gdns. WC2 141 DL72
Shorts Rd., Cars. 218 DE105
Shortway, Amer. 55 AR37
Shortway, Chesh. 54 AP29
Shortwood Ave., Stai. 174 BH90
Shortwood Common, Stai. 174 BH91
Shotfield, Wall. 219 DH107
Shothanger Way, Hem.H. 57 BC26
Shott Clo., Sutt. 218 DC106
Turnpike La.
Shottendane Rd. SW6 160 DA81
Shottery Clo. SE9 184 EL90
Shottfield Ave. SW14 158 CS84
Shoulder of Mutton All. E14 143 DY73
Narrow St.
Shouldham St. W1 272 C7
Shouldham St. W1 140 DE71
Showers Way, Hayes 135 BU74
Shrapnel Clo. SE18 164 EL80
Shrapnel Rd. SE9 165 EM83
Shrewsbury Ave. SW14 158 CQ84
Shrewsbury Ave., Har. 118 CL56
Shrewsbury Clo., Surb. 198 CL103
Shrewsbury Ct. EC1 142 DQ70
Whitecross St.
Shrewsbury Cres. NW10 138 CR67
Shrewsbury La. SE18 165 EP81
Shrewsbury Ms. W2 140 DA71
Chepstow Rd.
Shrewsbury Rd. E7 124 EK64
Shrewsbury Rd. N11 99 DJ51
Shrewsbury Rd. W2 140 DA72
Shrewsbury Rd., Beck. 203 DY97
Shrewsbury Rd., Cars. 200 DE100
Shrewsbury Rd., Red. 250 DE134
Shrewsbury St. W10 139 CW70
Shrewsbury Wk., Islw. 157 CG83
South St.
Shrewton Rd. SW17 180 DF94
Shrimpton Clo., Beac. 89 AK49
Shrimpton Rd., Beac. 89 AK49
Shroffold Rd., Brom. 184 EE91
Shropshire Clo., Mitch. 201 DL98
Shropshire Pl. WC1 273 L5
Shropshire Rd. N22 99 DM52
Shroton St. NW1 272 B6
Shroton St. NW1 140 DE71
Shrubberies, The E18 102 EG54
Shrubberies, The, Chig. 103 EQ50
Shrubbery, The, Hem.H. 39 BE19
Shrubbery, The, Upmin. 128 FQ62
Shrubbery Clo. N1 142 DQ67
St. Paul St.
Shrubbery Gdns. N21 99 DP45
Shrubbery Rd. N9 100 DU48
Shrubbery Rd. SW16 181 DL91
Shrubbery Rd. (South Darenth), Dart. 209 FR95
Shrubbery Rd., Grav. 191 GJ88
Shrubbery Rd., Sthl. 136 BZ74
Shrubhill Rd., Hem.H. 39 BF21
Shrubland Gro., Wor.Pk. 199 CW104
Shrubland Rd. E8 142 DT67
Shrubland Rd. E10 123 EA59
Shrubland Rd. E17 123 EA57
Shrubland Rd., Bans. 233 CZ116
Shrublands, Hat. 64 DB26
Shrublands, The, Pot.B. 63 CY33
Shrublands Ave., Berk. 38 AU19
Shrublands Ave., Croy. 221 EA105
Shrublands Clo. N20 98 DD46
Shrublands Clo. SE26 182 DW90
Shrublands Clo., Chig. 103 EQ51
Shrublands Rd., Berk. 38 AU18
Shrubs Rd., Rick. 92 BM51
Shrubsall Clo. SE9 184 EL88
Shuna Wk. N1 142 DR65
St. Paul's Rd.
Shurland Ave., Barn. 80 DD44
Shurland Gdns. SE15 162 DT80
Rosemary Rd.
Shurlock Ave., Swan. 207 FD96
Shurlock Dr., Orp. 223 EQ105
Shuters Sq. W14 159 CZ78
Sun Rd.
Shuttle Clo., Sid. 185 ET87
Shuttle Rd., Dart. 167 FG83
Shuttle St. E1 142 DU70
Buxton St.
Shuttlemead, Bex. 186 EZ87
Shuttleworth Rd. SW11 160 DD82
Sibella Rd. SW4 161 DK82
Sibley Clo., Bexh. 186 EY85
Sibley Gro. E12 144 EL66
Sibneys Grn., Harl. 51 ES19

Somersby Gdns., Ilf. 125 EM57
Somerset Ave. SW20 199 CV96
Somerset Ave., Chess. 215 CK105
Somerset Ave., Well. 185 ET85
Somerset Clo. N17 100 DR54
Somerset Clo., Epsom 216 CR109
Somerset Clo., N.Mal. 198 CS100
Somerset Clo., Walt. 213 BV106
Queens Rd.
Somerset Clo., Wdf.Grn. 102 EG53
Somerset Est. SW11 160 DD81
Somerset Gdns. N6 120 DG59
Somerset Gdns. SE13 163 EB82
Somerset Gdns. SW16 201 DM97
Somerset Gdns., Horn. 128 FN60
Somerset Gdns., Tedd. 177 CE92
Somerset Rd. E17 123 EA57
Somerset Rd. N17 122 DT55
Somerset Rd. N18 100 DT50
Somerset Rd. NW4 119 CW56
Somerset Rd. SW19 179 CX90
Somerset Rd. W4 158 CR76
Somerset Rd. W13 137 CH74
Somerset Rd., Barn. 80 DB43
Somerset Rd., Brent. 157 CK79
Somerset Rd., Dart. 187 FH86
Somerset Rd., Enf. 83 EA38
Somerset Rd., Har. 116 CC58
Somerset Rd., Kings.T. 198 CM96
Somerset Rd., Orp. 206 EU101
Somerset Rd., Red. 266 DD136
Somerset Rd., Sthl. 136 BZ72
Somerset Rd., Tedd. 177 CE92
Somerset Sq. W14 159 CY75
Somerset Way, Iver 153 BF75
Somerset Waye, Houns. 156 BY80
Somersham, Welw.G.C. 30 DD09
Somersham Rd., Bexh. 166 EY82
Somerswey, Guil. 258 AY142
Somerton Ave., Rich. 158 CP83
Somerton Clo., Pur. 235 DN115
Somerton Rd. NW2 119 CX62
Somerton Rd. SE15 162 DV84
Somertons Clo., Guil. 242 AU131
Somertrees Ave. SE12 184 EH89
Somervell Rd., Har. 116 BZ64
Somerville Rd. SE20 183 DX94
Somerville Rd., Cob. 214 CA114
Somerville Rd., Dart. 188 FM86
Somerville Rd., Rom. 126 EW58
Somerville Rd. (Eton), Wind. 151 AQ78
Sonderburg Rd. N7 121 DM61
Sondes Pl. Dr., Dor. 263 CF136
Sondes St. SE17 162 DR79
Sonia Clo., Wat. 94 BW45
Sonia Ct., Har. 117 CF58
Sonia Gdns. N12 98 DC49
Woodside Ave.
Sonia Gdns. NW10 119 CT63
Sonia Gdns., Houns. 156 CA80
Sonnet Wk., West. 238 EH118
Kings Rd.
Sonnets, The, Hem.H. 40 BH19
Sonning Gdns., Hmptn. 176 BY93
Sonning Rd. SE25 202 DU100
Soothouse Spring, St.Alb. 43 CF16
Soper Clo. E4 101 DZ50
Soper Dr., Cat. 236 DQ121
Coulsdon Rd.
Sopers Rd. (Cuffley), Pot.B. 65 DM29
Sophia Clo. N7 141 DM65
Mackenzie Rd.
Sophia Rd. E10 123 EB60
Sophia Rd. E16 144 EH72
Sophia Sq. SE16 143 DY73
Rotherhithe St.
Sopwell La., St.Alb. 43 CD21
Sopwith Ave., Chess. 216 CL106
Sopwith Clo., Kings.T. 178 CM92
Sopwith Clo., West. 238 EK116
Sopwith Dr., W.Byf. 212 BL112
Sopwith Dr., Wey. 212 BL111
Sopwith Rd., Houns. 156 BW80
Sopwith Way SW8 161 DH80
Sopwith Way, Kings.T. 198 CL95
Sorbie Clo., Wey. 213 BR107
Sorrel Bank, Croy. 221 DY110
Sorrel Clo. SE28 146 EU74
Sorrel Ct., Grays 170 GD79
Salix Rd.
Sorrel Gdns. E6 144 EL71
Sorrel La. E14 143 ED72
Sorrel Wk., Rom. 127 FF55
Sorrel Way, Grav. 190 GE91
Sorrell Clo. SE14 163 DY80
Southerngate Way
Sorrento Rd., Sutt. 200 DA104
Sospel Ct., Slou. 131 AQ68
Sotheby Rd. N5 122 DQ62
Sotheran Clo. E8 142 DU67
Sotheron Rd. SW6 160 DB80
Sotheron Rd., Wat. 76 BW41
Soudan Rd. SW11 160 DF81
Souldern Rd. W14 159 CX76
Souldern St., Wat. 75 BV43
Sounds Lo., Swan. 207 FC100
South Access Rd. E17 123 DY59
South Acre NW9 97 CT54
South Africa Rd. W12 139 CV74
South Albert Rd., Reig. 249 CZ133
South App., Nthwd. 93 BR48
South Audley St. W1 276 G1
South Audley St. W1 140 DG73
South Ave. E4 101 EB45
South Ave., Cars. 218 DG108
South Ave., Egh. 173 BC93
South Ave., Rich. 158 CN82
Sandycoombe Rd.
South Ave., Sthl. 136 BZ73
South Ave., Walt. 213 BS110
South Ave. Gdns., Sthl. 136 BZ73
South Bank, Chis. 185 EQ90
South Bank, Surb. 198 CL100
South Bank, West. 255 ER126
South Bank Rd., Berk. 38 AT17
South Bank Ter., Surb. 198 CL100
South Birkbeck Rd. E11 123 ED62
South Black Lion La. W6 159 CU78
South Bolton Gdns. SW5 160 DB78
South Border, The, Pur. 219 DK111
South Carriage Dr. SW1 160 DE75
South Carriage Dr. SW7 276 B4
South Carriage Dr. SW7 160 DE75
South Clo. N6 121 DH58
South Clo., Barn. 79 CZ41
South Clo., Bexh. 166 EX84
South Clo., Dag. 146 FA67
South Clo., Mord. 200 DB100
Green La.
South Clo., Pnr. 116 BZ59
South Clo., St.Alb. 60 CB25
South Clo., Slou. 131 AK73
St. George's Cres.
South Clo., Twick. 176 CA90
South Clo., West Dr. 154 BM76
South Clo., Wok. 226 AW116
South Clo. Grn., Red. 251 DH129
South Colonnade E14 143 EA74
South Common Rd., Uxb. 134 BL65
South Cottage Dr., Rick. 73 BF43
South Cottage Gdns., Rick. 73 BF43
South Countess Rd. E17 123 DZ55
South Cres. E16 143 ED70
South Cres. WC1 273 M7
South Cres. WC1 141 DK71
South Cft., Egh. 172 AV92
South Cross Rd., Ilf. 125 EQ57
South Croxted Rd. SE21 182 DR90
South Dene NW7 96 CR48
South Dr., Bans. 218 DE113
South Dr., Beac. 110 AH55
South Dr., Brwd. 108 FX49
South Dr., Couls. 235 DK115
South Dr., Dor. 263 CJ136
South Dr., Orp. 223 ES106
South Dr. (Cuffley), Pot.B. 65 DL30
South Dr., Rom. 128 FJ55
South Dr., Ruis. 115 BS60
South Dr., St.Alb. 43 CK20
South Dr., Sutt. 217 CY110
South Dr., Vir.W. 192 AU102
South Ealing Rd. W5 157 CK75
South Eastern Ave. N9 100 DT48
South Eaton Pl. SW1 276 G8
South Eaton Pl. SW1 160 DG77
South Eden Pk. Rd., Beck. 203 EB100
South Edwardes Sq. W8 159 CZ76
South End W8 160 DB76
St. Albans Gro.
South End, Croy. 220 DQ105
South End, Lthd. 246 CB126
South End Clo. NW3 120 DE63
South End Rd. NW3 120 DE63
South End Rd., Horn. 147 FH65
South End Rd., Rain. 147 FG68
South End Row W8 160 DB76
South Esk Rd. E7 144 EJ65
South Gdns. SW19 180 DD94
South Gate, Harl. 51 ER15
South Gate Ave., Felt. 175 BR91
South Gipsy Rd., Well. 166 EX83
South Glade, The, Bex. 186 EZ88
Camden Rd.
South Grn. NW9 96 CS53
Clayton Fld.
South Grn., Slou. 132 AS73
South Gro. E17 123 DZ57
South Gro. N6 120 DG60
South Gro. N15 122 DR57
South Gro., Cher. 193 BF100
South Gro. Ho. N6 120 DG60
Highgate W. Hill
South Hall Clo., Dart. 208 FM101
South Hall Dr., Rain. 147 FH71
South Hill, Chis. 185 EM93
South Hill, Guil. 258 AX136
South Hill Ave., Har. 116 CC62
South Hill Gro., Har. 117 CE63
South Hill Pk. NW3 120 DE63
South Hill Pk. Gdns. NW3 120 DE63
South Hill Rd., Brom. 204 EE97
South Hill Rd., Grav. 191 GH88
South Hill Rd., Hem.H. 40 BJ20
South Huxley N18 100 DR50
South Island Pl. SW9 161 DM80
South Kensington Sta. Arc. SW7 160 DD77
Pelham St.
South Kent Ave., Grav. 190 GC87
South Lambeth Pl. SW8 161 DL79
South Lambeth Rd. SW8 161 DL79
South La., Kings.T. 197 CK97
South La., N.Mal. 198 CR98
South La. W., N.Mal. 198 CR98
South Ley, Welw.G.C. 29 CY12
South Lo. Ave., Mitch. 201 DL98
South Lo. Cres., Enf. 81 DK42
South Lo. Dr. N14 81 DK42
South Mall N9 100 DU48
Plevna Rd.
South Mead NW9 97 CT53
South Mead, Epsom 216 CS108
South Mead, Red. 250 DF131
South Meadow La., Wind. 151 AQ79
South Meadows, Wem. 118 CM64
South Molton La. W1 273 H9
South Molton La. W1 141 DH72
South Molton Rd. E16 144 EG72
South Molton St. W1 273 H9
South Molton St. W1 141 DH72
South Mundells, Welw.G.C. 29 CZ08
South Norwood Hill SE25 202 DS95
South Oak Rd. SW16 181 DM91
South Par. SW3 276 A10
South Par. SW3 160 DD78
South Par. W4 158 CR77
South Par., Wal.Abb. 67 EC33
Sun St.
South Pk. SW6 160 DA82
South Pk., Ger.Cr. 113 AZ57
South Pk., Sev. 257 FH125
South Pk. Ave., Rick. 73 BF43
South Pk. Cres. SE6 184 EF88
South Pk. Cres., Ger.Cr. 112 AY56
South Pk. Cres., Ilf. 125 ER62
South Pk. Dr., Bark. 125 ES62
South Pk. Dr., Ger.Cr. 112 AY56
South Pk. Dr., Ilf. 125 ES61
South Pk. Gdns., Berk. 38 AV17
South Pk. Gro., N.Mal. 198 CQ98
South Pk. Hill Rd., S.Croy. 220 DR106
South Pk. La., Red. 252 DU134
South Pk. Ms. SW6 160 DB83
South Pk. Rd. SW19 180 DA93
South Pk. Rd., Ilf. 125 ER62
South Pk. Ter., Ilf. 125 ES62
South Pk. Vw., Ger.Cr. 113 AZ56
South Pk. Way, Ruis. 136 BW65
South Path, Wind. 151 AQ81
South Penge Pk. Est. SE20 202 DV96
South Perimeter Rd., Uxb. 134 BL69
Kingston La.
South Pier Rd., Gat. 269 DH152
South Pl. EC2 275 L7
South Pl. EC2 142 DR71
South Pl., Enf. 82 DW43
South Pl., Harl. 36 EU12
South Pl., Surb. 198 CM101
South Pl. Ms. EC2 275 L7
South Ridge, Wey. 213 BP110
South Riding, St.Alb. 60 CA30
South Ri., Cars. 218 DE109
South Ri. Way SE18 165 ER78
South Rd. N9 100 DU46
South Rd. SE23 183 DX89
South Rd. SW19 180 DC93
South Rd. W5 157 CK77
South Rd., Amer. 55 AQ36
South Rd., Edg. 96 CP53
South Rd., Egh. 172 AW93
South Rd., Erith 167 FF80
South Rd., Felt. 176 BX92
South Rd., Guil. 242 AV132
South Rd., Hmptn. 176 BY93
South Rd., Harl. 36 EU12
South Rd., Reig. 266 DB135
South Rd., Rick. 73 BC43
South Rd. (Chadwell Heath), Rom. 126 EY58
South Rd. (Little Heath), Rom. 126 EW57
South Rd., S.Ock. 149 FW70
South Rd., Sthl. 156 BZ75
South Rd., Twick. 177 CD90
South Rd., West Dr. 154 BN76
South Rd., Wey. 213 BQ106
South Rd. (St. George's Hill), Wey. 212 BN110
South Rd., Wok. 210 AX114
South Row SE3 164 EF82
South Sea St. SE16 163 DZ76
South Side W6 159 CT76
South Spur, Slou. 153 BC75
South Sq. NW11 120 DB58
South Sq. WC1 274 D7
South Sta. App., Red. 267 DL136
South St. W1 276 G2
South St. W1 140 DG74
South St., Brwd. 108 FW47
South St., Brom. 204 EG96
South St., Dor. 263 CG137
South St., Enf. 82 DW43
South St., Epsom 216 CR113
South St., Grav. 191 GH87
South St., Hert. 32 DR09
South St., Islw. 157 CG83
South St., Rain. 147 FC68
South St., Rom. 127 FE57
South St., Stai. 173 BF92
South St., Ware 33 EC11
South Tenter St. E1 142 DT73
South Ter. SW7 276 B8
South Ter. SW7 160 DE77
South Ter., Dor. 263 CH137
South Ter., Surb. 198 CL100
South Vale SE19 182 DS93
South Vale, Har. 117 CE63
South Vw., Brom. 204 EH96
South Vw. Ave., Til. 171 GG81
South Vw. Ct., Wok. 226 AY118
Constitution Hill
South Vw. Dr. E18 124 EH55
South Vw. Dr., Upmin. 128 FN62
South Vw. Rd. N8 121 DK55
South Vw. Rd., Ash. 231 CK119
South Vw. Rd., Dart. 188 FK90
South Vw. Rd., Ger.Cr. 112 AX56
South Vw. Rd., Grays 169 FW79
South Vw. Rd., Loug. 85 EM44
South Vw. Rd., Pnr. 93 BV51
South Vill. NW1 141 DK65
South Wk., Hayes 135 BR71
Middleton Rd.
South Wk., Reig. 250 DB134
Church St.
South Wk., W.Wick. 204 EE104
South Way N9 100 DW47
South Way N11 99 DJ51
Ringway
South Way, Abb.L. 59 BR33
South Way, Beac. 110 AG55
South Way, Brom. 204 EG101
South Way, Cars. 218 DD110
South Way, Croy. 203 DY104
South Way, Har. 116 CA56
South Way, Purf. 169 FS76
South Way, Wem. 118 CN64
South Weald Dr., Wal.Abb. 67 ED33
South Weald Rd., Brwd. 108 FU48
South W. India Dock Entrance E14 163 EC75
South Western Rd., Twick. 177 CG86
South Wf. Rd. W2 140 DD72
South Woodford to Barking Relief Rd. E11 124 EJ55
South Woodford to Barking Relief Rd. E12 125 EN63
South Woodford to Barking Relief Rd. E18 124 EJ55
South Woodford to Barking Relief Rd., Bark. 125 EN63
South Woodford to Barking Relief Rd., Ilf. 124 EJ55
South Worple Ave. SW14 158 CS83
South Worple Way
South Worple Way SW14 158 CR83
Southacre Way, Pnr. 94 BW53
Southall Clo., Ware 33 DX05
Southall La., Houns. 155 BV79
Southall Pl. SE1 279 K5
Southall Pl. SE1 162 DR75
Southall Way, Brwd. 108 FT49
Southam St. W10 139 CY70
Southampton Bldgs. WC2 274 D7
Southampton Gdns., Mitch. 201 DL99
Southampton Pl. WC1 274 A7
Southampton Pl. WC1 141 DL71
Southampton Rd. NW5 120 DF64
Southampton Rd., Houns. 174 BL86
Southampton Row WC1 274 A6
Southampton Row WC1 141 DL71
Southampton St. WC2 274 A10
Southampton St. WC2 141 DL73
Southampton Way SE5 162 DR80
Southbank, T.Ditt. 197 CH101
Southborough Clo., Surb. 197 CK102
Southborough La., Brom. 204 EL99
Southborough Rd. E9 143 DX66
Southborough Rd., Brom. 204 EL97
Southborough Rd., Surb. 198 CL102
Southbourne, Brom. 204 EG101
Southbourne Ave. NW9 96 CQ54
Southbourne Clo., Pnr. 116 BY59
Southbourne Cres. NW4 119 CY56
Southbourne Gdns. SE12 184 EH85
Southbourne Gdns., Ilf. 125 EQ64
Southbourne Gdns., Ruis. 115 BV60
Southbridge Pl., Croy. 220 DQ105
Southbridge Rd., Croy. 220 DQ105
Southbridge Way, Sthl. 156 BY75
Southbrook, Saw. 36 EY06
Southbrook Dr. (Cheshunt), Wal.Cr. 67 DX28
Southbrook Ms. SE12 184 EF86
Southbrook Rd. SE12 184 EF86
Southbrook Rd. SW16 201 DL95
Southbury Ave., Enf. 82 DU43
Southbury Clo., Horn. 128 FK64
Southbury Rd., Enf. 82 DR41
Southchurch Rd. E6 145 EM68
Southcliffe Dr., Ger.Cr. 90 AY50
Southcombe St. W14 159 CY77
Southcote, Wok. 226 AX115
Southcote Ave., Felt. 175 BT89
Southcote Ave., Surb. 198 CP101
Southcote Ri., Ruis. 115 BR59
Southcote Rd. E17 123 DX57
Southcote Rd. N19 121 DJ63
Southcote Rd. SE25 202 DV99
Southcote Rd., Red. 251 DJ129
Southcote Rd., S.Croy. 220 DS110
Southcroft, Slou. 131 AP70
Southcroft Ave., Well. 165 ES83
Southcroft Ave., W.Wick. 203 EC103
Southcroft Rd. SW16 181 DH93
Southcroft Rd. SW17 180 DG93
Southcroft Rd., Orp. 205 ES104
Southdale, Chig. 103 ER51
Southdean Gdns. SW19 179 CZ89
Southdene, Sev. 224 EZ113
Southdown Ave. W7 157 CG76
Southdown Ct., Hat. 45 CU21
Southdown Cres., Har. 116 CC60
Southdown Cres., Ilf. 125 ES57
Southdown Dr. SW20 179 CX94
Crescent Rd.
Southdown Rd. SW20 199 CX95
Southdown Rd., Cars. 218 DG109
Southdown Rd., Cat. 237 DZ122
Southdown Rd., Hat. 45 CU21
Southdown Rd., Horn. 127 FH59
Southdown Rd., Walt. 214 BY105
Southdowns (South Darenth), Dart. 209 FR96
Skinney La.
Southend Arterial Rd., Brwd. 129 FW57
Southend Arterial Rd., Horn. 128 FL55
Southend Arterial Rd., Rom. 106 FK54
Southend Arterial Rd., Upmin. 128 FP56
Southend Clo. SE9 185 EP86
Southend Cres. SE9 185 EP86
Southend La. SE6 183 EA91
Southend La. SE26 183 DZ91
Southend La., Wal.Abb. 68 EH34
Southend Rd. E4 101 DZ51
Southend Rd. E6 145 EM66
Southend Rd. E17 101 ED53
Southend Rd. E18 102 EF54
Southend Rd., Beck. 183 EA94
Southend Rd., Grays 170 GC77
Southend Rd., Wdf.Grn. 102 EJ54
Southerland Clo., Wey. 213 BQ105
Southern Ave. SE25 202 DT97
Southern Ave., Felt. 175 BU88
Southern Ave., Red. 266 DG142
Southern Dr., Loug. 85 EM44
Southern Gro. E3 143 DZ69
Southern Lo., Harl. 51 EQ18
Southern Perimeter Rd., Houns. 174 BJ85
Southern Pl., Swan. 207 FD98
Southern Rd. E13 144 EH68
Southern Rd. N2 120 DF56
Southern Row W10 139 CY70
Southern St. N1 141 DM68
Southern Way, Harl. 51 EN18
Southern Way, Rom. 126 FA58
Southerngate Way SE14 163 DY80
Southernhay, Loug. 84 EK42
Southerns La., Couls. 234 DD124
Southernwood Clo., Hem.H. 40 BN19
Southerton Rd. W6 159 CW76
Southey Rd. N15 122 DS57
Southey Rd. SW9 161 DN81
Southey Rd. SW19 180 DA94
Southey St. SE20 183 DX94
Southey Wk., Til. 171 GH81
Southfield, Barn. 79 CX44
Southfield, Welw.G.C. 29 CX11
Southfield Ave., Wat. 76 BW38
Southfield Clo., Uxb. 134 BN69
Southfield Clo., Wind. 150 AJ76
Southfield Cotts. W7 157 CF75
Oaklands Rd.
Southfield Gdns., Slou. 130 AH71
Southfield Gdns., Twick. 177 CF91
Southfield Pk., Har. 116 CB56
Southfield Pl., Wey. 213 BP108
Southfield Rd. N17 100 DS54
Southfield Rd. W4 158 CR75
Southfield Rd., Chis. 205 ET97
Southfield Rd., Enf. 82 DV44
Southfield Rd., Hodd. 49 EA16
Southfield Rd., Wal.Cr. 67 DY32
Southfield Way, St.Alb. 43 CK17
Southfields NW4 119 CV55
Southfields, E.Mol. 197 CE100
Southfields, Swan. 187 FE94
Southfields Ave., Ashf. 175 BP93
Southfields Ct. SW19 179 CY88
Southfields Pas. SW18 180 DA86
Southfields Rd.
Southfields Rd. SW18 180 DA86
Southfields Rd., Cat. 237 EB124
Southfleet Rd., Dart. 189 FW91
Southfleet Rd., Grav. 191 GF89
Southfleet Rd., Orp. 205 ES104
Southfleet Rd., Swans. 190 FZ87
Southgate, Purf. 168 FQ77
Southgate Ave., Felt. 175 BR91
Southgate Circ. N14 99 DK46
The Bourne
Southgate Gro. N1 142 DR66
Southgate Rd. N1 142 DR67
Southgate Rd., Barn. 80 DD35
Southgate Rd., Pot.B. 64 DC33
Southholme Clo. SE19 202 DT95
Southill La., Pnr. 115 BV56
Southill Rd., Chis. 184 EL93
Southill St. E14 143 EB72
Chrisp St.
Southland Rd. SE18 165 ET80
Southland Way, Houns. 177 CD85
Southlands Ave., Horl. 268 DG147
Southlands Ave., Orp. 223 ER105
Southlands Clo., Couls. 235 DM117
Southlands Gro., Brom. 204 EL97
Southlands La., Oxt. 253 EB134
Southlands Rd., Brom. 204 EJ99
Southlands Rd., Uxb. 113 BF62
Southlea, Wind. 152 AU84
Southlea Rd., Slou. 152 AV81
Southly Clo., Sutt. 200 DA104
Southmead Cres. (Cheshunt), Wal.Cr. 67 DY30
Southmead Rd. SW19 179 CY88
Southmont Rd., Esher 197 CE103
Southmoor Way E9 143 DZ65
Southold Ri. SE9 185 EM90
Southolm St. SW11 161 DH81
Southover N12 98 DA48
Southover, Brom. 184 EG92
Southport Rd. SE18 165 ER77
Southridge Pl. SW20 179 CX94
Southsea Ave., Wat. 75 BU42
Southsea Rd., Kings.T. 198 CL98
Southside, Ger.Cr. 112 AX55
Southside Common SW19 179 CW93
Southspring, Sid. 185 ER87
Southvale Rd. SE3 164 EE82
Southview Ave. NW10 119 CT64
Southview Clo. SW17 180 DG92
Southview Clo., Bex. 186 EZ86
Southview Clo., Swan. 207 FG98
Southview Clo. (Cheshunt), Wal.Cr. 66 DS26
Southview Cres., Ilf. 125 EP58
Southview Gdns., Wall. 219 DJ108
Southview Rd., Brom. 183 ED91
Southview Rd., Cat. 237 EB124
Southview Rd., Warl. 236 DV119
Southviews, S.Croy. 221 DX109
Southville SW8 161 DK81
Southville Clo., Epsom 216 CR109
Southville Clo., Felt. 175 BS88
Southville Cres., Felt. 175 BS88
Southville Rd., Felt. 175 BS88
Southville Rd., T.Ditt. 197 CG101
Southwark Bri. EC4 279 J1
Southwark Bri. EC4 142 DQ74
Southwark Bri. SE1 279 J1
Southwark Bri. SE1 142 DQ74
Southwark Bri. Rd. SE1 279 H5
Southwark Bri. Rd. SE1 161 DP76
Southwark Gro. SE1 279 H3
Southwark Pk. Est. SE16 162 DV77
Southwark Pk. Rd. SE16 162 DT77
Southwark Pl., Brom. 205 EM97
St. Georges Rd.
Southwark St. SE1 278 G2
Southwark St. SE1 141 DP74
Southwater Clo. E14 143 DZ72
Southwater Clo., Beck. 183 EB94
Southway N20 98 DA47
Southway NW7 97 CU52
Southway NW11 120 DB57
Southway SW20 199 CW98
Southway, Guil. 242 AS134
Southway, Hat. 45 CU22
Southway, Wall. 219 DJ105
Southway Ct., Guil. 242 AS134
Southwell Ave., Nthlt. 136 CA65
Southwell Gdns. SW7 160 DC77
Southwell Gro. Rd. E11 124 EE61
Southwell Rd. SE5 162 DQ83
Southwell Rd., Croy. 201 DN100
Southwell Rd., Har. 117 CK58
Southwest Rd. E11 123 ED60
Southwick Ms. W2 272 A8
Southwick Pl. W2 272 B9
Southwick Pl. W2 140 DE72
Southwick St. W2 272 B8
Southwick St. W2 140 DE72
Southwold Dr., Bark. 126 EU64
Southwold Rd. E5 122 DV61
Southwold Rd., Bex. 187 FB86
Southwold Rd., Wat. 76 BW38
Southwold Spur, Slou. 153 BC75
Southwood Ave. N6 121 DH59
Southwood Ave., Cher. 211 BC108
Southwood Ave., Couls. 235 DJ115
Southwood Ave., Kings.T. 198 CQ95
Southwood Clo., Brom. 205 EM98
Southwood Clo., Wor.Pk. 199 CX102
Carters Clo.
Southwood Dr., Surb. 198 CQ101
Southwood Gdns., Esher 197 CG104
Southwood Gdns., Ilf. 125 EP56
Southwood La. N6 120 DG59
Southwood Lawn Rd. N6 120 DG59
Southwood Rd. SE9 185 EP89
Southwood Rd. SE28 146 EV74
Southwood Smith St. N1 141 DN67
Barford St.
Soval Ct., Nthwd. 93 BR52
Maxwell Rd.
Sovereign Clo. E1 142 DV73
Sovereign Clo. W5 137 CJ71
Sovereign Clo., Ruis. 115 BS60
Sovereign Ct., Brom. 205 EM99
Sovereign Ct., W.Mol. 196 BZ98

Sovereign Cres. SE16 143 DY74
Rotherhithe St.
Sovereign Gro., Wem. 117 CK62
Sovereign Ms. E2 142 DT68
Pearson St.
Sovereign Pk. NW10 138 CP70
Sovereign Pl., Kings L. 58 BN29
Sovereign Rd., Bark. 146 EW69
Sowerby Clo. SE9 184 EL85
Sowrey Ave., Rain. 147 FF65
Soyer Ct., Wok. 226 AS118
Raglan Rd.
Spa Clo. SE25 202 DS95
Spa Dr., Epsom 216 CN114
Spa Grn. Est. EC1 274 E2
Spa Hill SE19 202 DR95
Spa Rd. SE16 279 P7
Spa Rd. SE16 162 DT76
Space Waye, Felt. 175 BU85
Spackmans Way, Slou. 151 AQ76
Spafield St. EC1 274 D4
Spalding Rd. NW4 119 CW58
Spalding Rd. SW17 181 DH92
Spalt Clo., Brwd. 109 GB47
Spanby Rd. E3 143 EA70
Spaniards Clo. NW11 120 DD60
Spaniards End NW3 120 DC60
Spaniards Rd. NW3 120 DC62
Spanish Pl. W1 272 G8
Spanish Pl. W1 140 DG72
Spanish Rd. SW18 180 DC85
Spareleaze Hill, Loug. 84 EL43
Sparepenny La. (Eynsford), Dart. 208 FK103
Sparkbridge Rd., Har. 117 CE56
Sparks Clo. W3 138 CR72
Joseph Ave.
Sparks Clo., Dag. 126 EX61
Sparks Clo., Hmptn. 176 BY93
Victors Dr.
Sparrow Clo., Hmptn. 176 BY93
Sparrow Dr., Orp. 205 EQ102
Sparrow Fm. Dr., Felt. 176 BW86
Sparrow Fm. Rd., Epsom 217 CU105
Sparrow Grn., Dag. 127 FB62
Sparrows Herne (Bushey), Wat. 94 CB45
Sparrows La. SE9 185 EQ87
Sparrows Mead, Red. 250 DG131
Sparrows Way (Bushey), Wat. 94 CC46
Sparrows Herne
Sparrowswick Ride, St.Alb. 42 CC15
Sparsholt Rd. N19 121 DM60
Sparsholt Rd., Bark. 145 ES67
Sparta St. SE10 163 EC81
Spear Ms. SW5 160 DA77
Spearman St. SE18 165 EN79
Spearpoint Gdns., Ilf. 125 ET56
Spears Rd. N19 121 DL60
Speart La., Houns. 156 BY80
Spedan Clo. NW3 120 DB62
Speed Ho. EC2 142 DR71
Silk St.
Speedbird Way, West Dr. 154 BH80
Tarmac Way
Speedgate Hill (Fawkham Grn.), Long. 209 FU103
Speedwell Clo., Guil. 243 BC131
Speedwell Clo., Hem.H. 39 BE21
Campion Rd.
Speedwell Ct., Grays 170 GE80
Speedwell St. SE8 163 EA80
Comet St.
Speedy Pl. WC1 273 P3
Speer Rd., T.Ditt. 197 CF101
Speke Ho. SE5 162 DQ80
Speke Rd., Th.Hth. 202 DR96
Spekehill SE9 185 EM90
Speldhurst Clo., Brom. 204 EG99
Speldhurst Rd. E9 143 DX66
Speldhurst Rd. W4 158 CR76
Spellbrook Wk. N1 142 DQ67
Basire St.
Spelman St. E1 142 DU71
Spelthorne Gro., Sun. 175 BT94
Spelthorne La., Ashf. 195 BQ95
Spence Ave., W.Byf. 212 BL114
Spence Clo. SE16 163 DZ75
Vaughan St.
Spencer Ave. N13 99 DM51
Spencer Ave., Hayes 135 BU71
Spencer Ave. (Cheshunt), Wal.Cr. 66 DS26
Spencer Clo. N3 98 DA54
Spencer Clo. NW10 138 CM69
Spencer Clo., Epsom 232 CS119
Spencer Clo., Orp. 205 ES103
Spencer Clo., Uxb. 134 BJ69
Spencer Clo., Wok. 211 BC113
Spencer Clo., Wdf.Grn. 102 EJ50
Spencer Ct. NW8 140 DC68
Marlborough Pl.
Spencer Dr. N2 120 DC58
Spencer Gdns. SE9 185 EM85
Spencer Gdns. SW14 178 CQ85
Spencer Gdns., Egh. 172 AX92
Spencer Gate, St.Alb. 43 CE18
Spencer Hill SW19 179 CY93
Spencer Hill Rd. SW19 179 CY94
Spencer Ms. W6 159 CY79
Greyhound Rd.
Spencer Pk. SW18 180 DD85
Spencer Pas. E2 142 DV68
Pritchard's Rd.
Spencer Pl. N1 141 DP66
Canonbury La.
Spencer Pl., Croy. 202 DR101
Gloucester Rd.
Spencer Ri. NW5 121 DH63
Spencer Rd. E6 144 EK67
Spencer Rd. E17 101 EC54
Spencer Rd. N8 121 DM57
Spencer Rd. N11 99 DH49
Spencer Rd. N17 100 DU53
Spencer Rd. SW18 160 DD84
Spencer Rd. SW20 199 CV95
Spencer Rd. W3 138 CQ74
Spencer Rd. W4 158 CQ80
Spencer Rd., Brom. 184 EF94
Spencer Rd., Cat. 236 DR121
Spencer Rd., Cob. 229 BV115
Spencer Rd., E.Mol. 197 CD98
Spencer Rd., Har. 95 CE54
Spencer Rd., Ilf. 125 ET60
Spencer Rd., Islw. 156 CC81
Spencer Rd., Mitch. 200 DG97
Spencer Rd. (Beddington), Mitch. 200 DG101
Spencer Rd., Rain. 147 FD69
Spencer Rd., Slou. 153 AZ76
Spencer Rd., S.Croy. 220 DS106
Spencer Rd., Twick. 177 CE90
Spencer Rd., Wem. 117 CJ61
Spencer St. EC1 274 F3
Spencer St. EC1 141 DP69
Spencer St., Grav. 191 GG87
Spencer St., Hert. 32 DS08
Spencer St., St.Alb. 43 CD20
Spencer St., Sthl. 156 BX75
Spencer Wk. NW3 120 DC63
Hampstead High St.
Spencer Wk. SW15 159 CX84
Spencer Wk., Rick. 74 BJ43
Spencer Wk., Til. 171 GG82
Spencer Way, Hem.H. 40 BG17
Spencer Way, Red. 266 DG139
Spencers Cft., Harl. 52 EV17
Spenser Ave., Wey. 212 BN109
Spenser Cres., Upmin. 128 FQ59
Spenser Gro. N16 122 DS63
Spenser Rd. SE24 181 DN85
Spenser St. SW1 277 L6
Spenser St. SW1 161 DJ76
Spensley Wk. N16 122 DR62
Clissold Rd.
Speranza St. SE18 165 ET78
Sperling Rd. N17 100 DS54
Spert St. E14 143 DY73
Spey St. E14 143 EC71
Spey Way, Rom. 105 FE52
Speyside N14 81 DJ44
Spezia Rd. NW10 139 CU68
Sphere Ind. Est., St.Alb. 43 CG21
Spicer Clo. SW9 161 DP82
Spicer Clo., Walt. 196 BW100
Spicer St., St.Alb. 42 CC20
Spicers Fld., Lthd. 215 CD113
Spicers La., Harl. 36 EW11
Wayre St.
Spicersfield (Cheshunt), Wal.Cr. 66 DU27
Spice's Yd., Croy. 220 DQ105
Spielman Rd., Dart. 168 FM84
Spiers Clo., N.Mal. 199 CT100
Spiers Way, Horl. 269 DH150
Spigurnell Rd. N17 100 DR53
Spikes Bri. Rd., Sthl. 136 BY72
Spilsby Clo. NW9 96 CS54
Kenley Ave.
Spilsby Rd., Rom. 106 FK52
Spindles, Til. 171 GG80
Spindlewood Gdns., Croy. 220 DS105
Spindlewoods, Tad. 233 CV122
Spindrift Ave. E14 163 EA77
Spinel Clo. SE18 165 ET78
Spingate Clo., Horn. 128 FK64
Spinnells Rd., Har. 116 BZ60
Spinners Wk., Wind. 151 AQ81
Spinney, Slou. 131 AP74
Spinney, The N21 99 DN45
Spinney, The SW16 181 DJ90
Spinney, The, Barn. 80 DB40
Spinney, The, Beac. 89 AL54
Spinney, The, Brwd. 109 GC44
Spinney, The, Brox. 49 DZ19
Spinney, The, Chesh. 54 AR29
Spinney, The, Epsom 233 CV118
Spinney, The, Hert. 32 DT09
Spinney, The, Horl. 268 DG146
Spinney, The, Lthd. 214 CC112
Spinney, The (Great Bookham), Lthd. 230 CB124
Spinney, The, Pot.B. 64 DD31
Spinney, The, Pur. 219 DP111
Spinney, The, Sid. 186 EY91
Spinney, The, Stan. 96 CL49
Spinney, The, Sun. 195 BU95
Spinney, The, Sutt. 217 CW105
Spinney, The, Swan. 207 FE96
Spinney, The, Wat. 75 BU39
Spinney, The, Welw.G.C. 29 CY10
Spinney, The, Wem. 117 CG62
Spinney, The, Wok. 244 BJ127
Spinney Clo., Cob. 214 CA111
Spinney Clo., N.Mal. 198 CS99
Spinney Clo., Rain. 147 FE68
Spinney Clo., West Dr. 134 BL73
Yew Ave.
Spinney Dr., Felt. 175 BQ87
Spinney Gdns. SE19 182 DT92
Spinney Gdns., Dag. 126 EY64
Spinney Hill, Add. 211 BE106
Spinney Oak, Brom. 204 EL96
Spinney Oak, Cher. 211 BC107
Murray Rd.
Spinney St., Hert. 32 DU09
Spinney Way, Sev. 223 ER111
Spinneycroft, Lthd. 231 CD115
Spinneys, The, Brom. 205 EM96
Spinneys Dr., St.Alb. 42 CB22
Spinning Wk., Guil. 260 BN139
Spinning Wheel Mead, Harl. 52 EU18
Spire Clo., Grav. 191 GH88
Spires, The, Dart. 188 FK89
Spirit Quay E1 142 DU74
Smeaton St.
Spital Heath, Dor. 263 CJ135
Spital La., Brwd. 108 FT48
Spital Sq. E1 275 N6
Spital Sq. E1 142 DS71
Spital St. E1 142 DU71
Spital St., Dart. 188 FK86
Spital Yd. E1 275 N6
Spitalfields Mkt. E1 275 P6
Spitalfields Mkt. E1 142 DT71
Spitfire Est., Houns. 156 BW78
Spitfire Way, Houns. 156 BW78
Splendour Wk. SE16 162 DW78
Verney Rd.
Spode Wk. NW6 140 DB65
Lymington Rd.
Spondon Rd. N15 122 DU56
Spook Hill, Dor. 263 CH141
Spoonbill Way, Hayes 136 BX71
Spooner Wk., Wall. 219 DK106
Spooners Dr., St.Alb. 60 CC27
Sportsbank St. SE6 183 EC87
Spottons Gro. N17 100 DQ53
Gospatrick Rd.
Spout Hill, Croy. 221 EA106
Spout La., Eden. 255 EQ133
Spout La., Stai. 174 BG85
Spout La. N., Stai. 154 BH84
Spratt Hall Rd. E11 124 EG58
Spratts All., Cher. 211 BE107
Spratts La., Cher. 211 BE107
Spray La., Twick. 177 CE86
Kneller Rd.
Spray St. SE18 165 EP77
Spreighton Rd., W.Mol. 196 CB98
Spriggs Oak, Epp. 70 EU29
Palmers Hill
Sprimont Pl. SW3 276 D10
Sprimont Pl. SW3 160 DF77
Spring Ave., Egh. 172 AY93
Spring Bottom La., Red. 251 DN127
Spring Bri. Ms. W5 137 CK73
Spring Bri. Rd.
Spring Bri. Rd. W5 137 CK73
Spring Clo., Barn. 79 CX43
Spring Clo., Borwd. 78 CN39
Spring Clo., Chesh. 72 AX36
Spring Clo., Dag. 126 EX60
Spring Clo., Gdmg. 258 AS143
Spring Clo., Uxb. 92 BK53
Spring Clo. La., Sutt. 217 CY107
Spring Cotts., Surb. 197 CK99
St. Leonard's Rd.
Spring Ct., Guil. 242 AV130
Day Spring
Spring Ct., Sid. 186 EU90
Station Rd.
Spring Ct. Rd., Enf. 81 DN38
Spring Cfts. (Bushey), Wat. 76 CA43
Spring Dr., Maid. 130 AD65
Yew Tree Wk.
Spring Dr., Pnr. 115 BU58
Eastcote Rd.
Spring Gdns. N5 122 DQ64
Grosvenor Ave.
Spring Gdns. SW1 277 N2
Spring Gdns., Dor. 263 CG136
Spring Gdns., H.Wyc. 110 AE55
Watery La.
Spring Gdns., Horn. 127 FH63
Spring Gdns., Orp. 224 EV107
Spring Gdns., Rom. 127 FC57
Spring Gdns., Wall. 219 DJ106
Spring Gdns., Wat. 76 BW35
Spring Gdns., W.Mol. 196 CC99
Spring Gdns., West. 238 EJ118
Spring Gdns., Wdf.Grn. 102 EJ52
Spring Gdns. Ind. Est., Rom. 127 FC57
Spring Glen, Hat. 45 CT19
Spring Grn., Gdmg. 258 AS143
Spring Gro. SE19 182 DT94
Alma Pl.
Spring Gro. W4 158 CN78
Spring Gro., Grav. 191 GH88
Spring Gro., Hmptn. 196 CB95
Plevna Rd.
Spring Gro., Lthd. 230 CB123
Spring Gro., Loug. 84 EK44
Spring Gro., Mitch. 200 DG95
Spring Gro. Cres., Houns. 156 CC81
Spring Gro. Rd., Houns. 156 CB81
Spring Gro. Rd., Islw. 157 CD81
Spring Gro. Rd., Rich. 178 CM85
Spring Hill E5 122 DU59
Spring Hill SE26 182 DW91
Spring Hills, Harl. 35 EN14
Spring Lake, Stan. 95 CH49
Spring La. E5 122 DV59
Spring La. N10 120 DG55
Spring La. SE25 202 DV100
Spring La., Hem.H. 39 BF18
Spring La., Oxt. 253 ED131
Spring La., Slou. 131 AM74
Spring La. (Farnham Common), Slou. 131 AP66
Spring Ms. W1 272 E6
Spring Ms., Epsom 217 CT109
Old Schools La.
Spring Pk. Ave., Croy. 203 DX103
Spring Pk. Dr. N4 122 DQ60
Spring Pk. Rd., Croy. 203 DX103
Spring Pas. SW15 159 CX83
Embankment
Spring Path NW3 120 DD64
Spring Pl. NW5 121 DH64
Spring Ri., Egh. 172 AY93
Spring Rd., Felt. 175 BT90
Spring Shaw Rd., Orp. 206 EU95
Spring St. W2 140 DD72
Spring St., Epsom 217 CT109
Spring Ter., Rich. 178 CL85
Spring Vale, Bexh. 167 FB84
Spring Vale, Green. 189 FW86
Spring Vale Clo., Swan. 187 FF94
Spring Vale N., Dart. 188 FK87
Spring Vale S., Dart. 188 FK87
Spring Vw. Rd., Ware 32 DW07
Spring Vill. Rd., Edg. 96 CN52
Spring Wk. E1 142 DU71
Old Montague St.
Spring Wk., Brox. 48 DW22
Spring Wk., Horl. 268 DF148
Court Lo. Rd.
Spring Way, Hem.H. 41 BP18
Spring Wds., Vir.W. 192 AV98
Springall St. SE15 162 DV80
Springate Fld., Slou. 152 AY75
Springbank N21 81 DM44
Springbank Ave., Horn. 128 FJ64
Springbank Rd. SE13 183 ED86
Springbank Wk. NW1 141 DK66
St. Paul's Cres.
Springbourne Ct., Beck. 203 EC95
Springclose La., Sutt. 217 CY107
Springcopse Rd., Reig. 266 DC135
Springcroft Ave. N2 120 DF56
Springdale Ms. N16 122 DR63
Springdale Rd.
Springdale Rd. N16 122 DR63
Springfarm Clo., Rain. 148 FK69
Springfield E5 122 DV60
Springfield, Epp. 69 ET32
Springfield, Oxt. 253 ED130
Springfield (Bushey), Wat. 95 CD46
Springfield Ave. N10 121 DJ55
Springfield Ave. SW20 199 CZ97
Springfield Ave., Brwd. 109 GE45
Springfield Ave., Hmptn. 176 CB93
Springfield Ave., Swan. 207 FF98
Springfield Clo. N12 98 DB50
Springfield Clo., Chesh. 54 AQ33
Springfield Clo., Pot.B. 64 DD31
Springfield Clo., Rick. 75 BP43
Springfield Clo., Stan. 95 CG48
Springfield Clo., Wind. 151 AP82
Springfield Clo., Wok. 226 AS118
Springfield Dr., Ilf. 125 EQ58
Springfield Dr., Lthd. 231 CE119
Springfield Gdns. E5 122 DV60
Springfield Gdns. NW9 118 CR57
Springfield Gdns., Brom. 205 EM98
Springfield Gdns., Ruis. 115 BV60
Springfield Gdns., Upmin. 128 FP62
Springfield Gdns., W.Wick. 203 EB103
Springfield Gdns., Wdf.Grn. 102 EJ52
Springfield Gro. SE7 164 EJ79
Springfield Gro., Sun. 195 BT95
Springfield La. NW6 140 DB67
Springfield La., Wey. 213 BP105
Springfield Meadows, Wey. 213 BP105
Springfield Mt. NW9 118 CR57
Springfield Pk., Maid. 150 AC78
Springfield Pl., N.Mal. 198 CQ98
Springfield Ri. SE26 182 DV90
Springfield Rd. E4 102 EE46
Springfield Rd. E6 145 EM66
Springfield Rd. E15 144 EE69
Springfield Rd. E17 123 DZ58
Springfield Rd. N11 99 DH50
Springfield Rd. N15 122 DU56
Springfield Rd. NW8 140 DC67
Springfield Rd. SE26 182 DV92
Springfield Rd. SW19 179 CZ92
Springfield Rd. W7 137 CE74
Springfield Rd., Ashf. 174 BM92
Springfield Rd., Berk. 38 AT16
Springfield Rd., Bexh. 167 FB83
Springfield Rd., Brom. 205 EM98
Springfield Rd., Chesh. 54 AQ33
Springfield Rd., Dor. 262 CB137
Springfield Rd., Epsom 217 CW110
Springfield Rd., Grays 170 GD75
Springfield Rd., Guil. 258 AY135
Springfield Rd., Har. 117 CE58
Springfield Rd., Hayes 136 BW74
Springfield Rd., Hem.H. 40 BM19
Springfield Rd., Kings.T. 198 CL97
Springfield Rd. (Colney Heath), St.Alb. 43 CG21
Springfield Rd. (Smallford), St.Alb. 44 CP20
Springfield Rd., Slou. 153 BB80
Springfield Rd., Tedd. 177 CG92
Springfield Rd., Th.Hth. 202 DQ95
Springfield Rd., Twick. 176 CA88
Springfield Rd., Wall. 218 DG106
Springfield Rd. (Cheshunt), Wal.Cr. 67 DY32
Springfield Rd., Wat. 59 BV33
Haines Way
Springfield Rd., Well. 166 EV83
Springfield Rd., Wind. 151 AP82
Springfield Wk. NW6 140 DB67
Springfield Wk., Orp. 205 ER102
Place Fm. Ave.
Springfields, Brox. 49 DZ19
Springfields, Wal.Abb. 68 EE34
Springfields, Welw.G.C. 29 CV11
Springfields Clo., Cher. 194 BH102
Springhall La., Saw. 36 EY06
Springhall Rd., Saw. 36 EY05
Springhaven Clo., Guil. 243 BA134
Springhead Enterprise Pk., Grav. 190 GC88
Springhead Rd., Erith 167 FF79
Springhead Rd., Grav. 190 GC89
Springhill Clo. SE5 162 DR83
Springholm Clo., West. 238 EJ118
Springhurst Clo., Croy. 221 DZ105
Springle La., Hert. 33 DZ12
Springpark Dr., Beck. 203 EC97
Springpond Rd., Dag. 126 EY64
Springrice Rd. SE13 183 ED86
Springs, The, Brox. 67 DY25
Springs, The, Hert. 32 DT08
Springshaw Clo., Sev. 256 FD123
Springside Ct., Guil. 242 AW133
Springvale Ave., Brent. 158 CL78
Springvale Est. W14 159 CY76
Blythe Rd.
Springvale Ter. W14 159 CX76
Springvale Way, Orp. 206 EW97
Springwater Clo. SE18 165 EN81
Springwell Ave. NW10 139 CT67
Springwell Ave., Rick. 92 BG47
Springwell Clo. SW16 181 DN91
Etherstone Rd.
Springwell Ct., Houns. 156 BX82
Springwell La., Rick. 92 BG47
Springwell La., Uxb. 92 BH50
Springwell Rd. SW16 181 DN91
Springwell Rd., Houns. 156 BX82
Springwood (Cheshunt), Wal.Cr. 66 DU26
Springwood Clo., Uxb. 92 BK53
Springwood Cres., Edg. 96 CP47
Springwood Wk., St.Alb. 43 CK17
Springwood Way, Rom. 127 FG57
Sprowston Ms. E7 144 EG65
Sprowston Rd. E7 124 EG64
Spruce Ct. W5 158 CL76
Elderberry Rd.
Spruce Hill, Harl. 51 ES20
Spruce Hills Rd. E17 101 EC54
Spruce Pk., Brom. 204 EF98
Cumberland Rd.
Spruce Rd., West. 238 EK116
Spruce Way, St.Alb. 60 CB27
Sprucedale Clo., Swan. 207 FE96
Sprucedale Gdns., Croy. 221 DX105
Sprucedale Gdns., Wall. 219 DK109
Sprules Rd. SE4 163 DY82
Spur, The, Slou. 131 AK71
Spur, The (Cheshunt), Wal.Cr. 67 DX28
Welsummer Way
Spur Clo., Abb.L. 59 BR33
Spur Clo., Rom. 86 EV41
Spur Dr., Tad. 234 DB121
Spur Rd. N15 122 DR56
Philip La.
Spur Rd. SE1 161 DM75
Lower Marsh
Spur Rd. SW1 277 K5
Spur Rd. SW1 161 DJ75
Spur Rd., Bark. 145 EQ69
Spur Rd., Edg. 96 CL49
Spur Rd., Felt. 175 BV85
Spur Rd., Islw. 157 CH80
Spur Rd., Orp. 206 EU103
Spur Rd. Est., Edg. 96 CM49
Spurfield, W.Mol. 196 CB97
Spurgate, Brwd. 109 GA47
Spurgeon Ave. SE19 202 DR95
Spurgeon Rd. SE19 202 DR95
Spurgeon St. SE1 279 K7
Spurgeon St. SE1 162 DR76
Spurling Rd. SE22 162 DT84
Spurling Rd., Dag. 146 EZ65
Spurrell Ave., Bex. 187 FD91
Spurstowe Rd. E8 142 DV65
Marcon Pl.
Spurstowe Ter. E8 122 DV64
Squadrons App., Horn. 148 FJ65
Square, The W6 159 CW78
Square, The, Berk. 39 BB16
Square, The, Brox. 49 DY23
High Rd. Wormley
Square, The, Cars. 218 DG106
Square, The, Guil. 258 AT136
Orchard Rd.
Square, The (Shere), Guil. 260 BN139
Square, The, Hayes 135 BR74
Square, The, Ilf. 125 EN59
Square, The, Rich. 177 CK85
Square, The, Saw. 36 EY05
Square, The, Sev. 256 FE122
Amherst Hill
Square, The, Swan. 207 FD97
Square, The, Wat. 75 BV37
The Harebreaks
Square, The, West Dr. 154 BH81
Square, The, West. 238 EJ120
Square, The, Wey. 213 BQ106
Square, The, Wok. 228 BL116
Square, The, Wdf.Grn. 102 EG50
Square Rigger Row SW11 160 DC83
York Pl.
Squarey St. SW17 180 DC90
Squerryes Mede, West. 255 EQ127
Squires Bri. Rd., Shep. 194 BM98
Squires Ct. SW19 180 DA91
Squires Ct., Cher. 194 BH102
Springfields Clo.
Squires Fld., Swan. 207 FF95
Squires La. N3 98 DB54
Squires Mt. NW3 120 DD62
East Heath Rd.
Squires Rd., Shep. 194 BM98
Squires Wk., Ashf. 175 BR94
Napier Rd.
Squires Way, Dart. 187 FD91
Squires Wd. Dr., Chis. 185 EM94
Squirrel Chase, Hem.H. 39 BE19
Squirrel Clo., Houns. 156 BW83
Squirrel Wd., W.Byf. 212 BH112
Dartnell Ave.
Squirrels, The SE13 163 ED83
Belmont Hill
Squirrels, The, Hert. 32 DV09
Squirrels, The, Pnr. 116 BZ55
Squirrels, The (Bushey), Wat. 77 CD44
Squirrels, The, Welw.G.C. 30 DC10
Squirrels Chase, Grays 171 GG75
Hornsby La.
Squirrels Clo. N12 98 DC49
Woodside Ave.
Squirrels Clo., Uxb. 134 BN66
Squirrels Grn., Lthd. 230 CA123
Squirrels Grn., Wor.Pk. 199 CU103
The Ave.
Squirrels Heath Ave., Rom. 127 FH55
Squirrels Heath La., Horn. 128 FK56
Squirrels Heath La., Rom. 128 FJ56
Squirrels Heath Rd., Rom. 128 FL55
Squirrels La., Buck.H. 102 EK48
Squirrels Ms. W13 137 CG73
Squirrels Trd. Est., The, Hayes 155 BT76
Squirrels Way, Epsom 232 CR115
Squirries St. E2 142 DU69
Stable Clo., Nthlt. 136 CA68
Stable La., Beac. 89 AQ51
Stable Wk. N2 98 DD53
Old Fm. Rd.
Stable Way W10 139 CW72
Latimer Rd.
Stable Yd. SW1 277 K4
Stable Yd. SW9 161 DM82
Broomgrove Rd.
Stable Yd. SW15 159 CW83
Danemere St.
Stable Yd. Rd. SW1 277 L4
Stable Yd. Rd. SW1 161 DJ75
Stables, The, Buck.H. 102 EJ45
Stables, The, Cob. 214 BZ114
Stables, The, Guil. 242 AX131
Old Fm. Rd.
Stables, The, Swan. 207 FH95
Stables End, Orp. 205 EQ104
Stables Ms. SE27 182 DQ92
Stables Way SE11 278 D10
Stables Way SE11 161 DN78
Stacey Ave. N18 100 DW49
Stacey Clo. E10 123 ED57
Halford Rd.
Stacey Clo., Grav. 191 GL92
Stacey St. N7 121 DN62
Stacey St. WC2 273 N9
Stacey St. WC2 141 DK72
Stack Rd., Dart. 209 FR97
Stackfield, Harl. 36 EU12
Stackhouse St. SW3 276 D6
Stacklands Rd., Welw.G.C. 29 CV11
Stacy Path SE5 162 DS80
Harris St.
Stadium Rd. NW2 119 CW59
Stadium Rd. SE18 165 EM80

Stadium St. SW10 160 DC80
Stadium Way, Dart. 187 FE86
Stadium Way, Wem. 118 CM63
Staff St. EC1 275 L3
Staffa Rd. E10 123 DX60
Stafford Ave., Horn. 128 FK55
Stafford Ave., Slou. 131 AQ70
Stafford Clo. E17 123 DZ58
Stafford Clo. N14 81 DJ43
Stafford Clo. NW6 140 DA69
Stafford Clo., Cat. 236 DT123
Stafford Clo., Green. 189 FT85
Stafford Clo., Maid. 130 AH72
Stafford Clo., Sutt. 217 CY107
Stafford Clo. (Cheshunt), Wal.Cr. 66 DV29
Stafford Ct. W8 160 DA76
Kensington High St.
Stafford Cross Ind. Est., Croy. 219 DM106
Stafford Dr., Brox. 49 EA20
Stafford Gdns., Croy. 219 DM106
Stafford Pl. SW1 277 K6
Stafford Pl. SW1 161 DJ76
Stafford Pl., Rich. 178 CM87
Stafford Rd. E3 143 DZ68
Stafford Rd. E7 144 EJ66
Stafford Rd. NW6 140 DA69
Stafford Rd., Cat. 236 DT122
Stafford Rd., Croy. 219 DN105
Stafford Rd., Har. 94 CC52
Stafford Rd., N.Mal. 198 CQ97
Stafford Rd., Ruis. 115 BT63
Stafford Rd., Sid. 185 ES91
Stafford Rd., Wall. 219 DH107
Stafford Sq., Wey. 213 BR105
Rosslyn Pk.
Stafford St. W1 277 K2
Stafford St. W1 141 DJ74
Stafford Ter. W8 160 DA75
Stafford Way, Sev. 257 FJ127
Staffords, Harl. 36 EY12
Staffords Pl., Horl. 269 DH149
Staffordshire St. SE15 162 DU81
Stag Clo., Edg. 96 CP54
Stag Grn. Ave., Hat. 45 CW16
Stag Hill, Guil. 258 AU135
Stag La. NW9 118 CQ55
Stag La. SW15 179 CT89
Stag La., Berk. 38 AV18
Stag La., Buck.H. 102 EH47
Stag La., Edg. 96 CP54
Stag La., Rick. 73 BC44
Stag Leys, Ash. 232 CL120
Stag Leys Clo., Bans. 234 DE115
Stag Pl. SW1 277 K6
Stag Pl. SW1 161 DJ76
Stag Ride SW19 179 CT90
Stagbury Ave., Couls. 234 DE118
Stagbury Clo., Couls. 234 DE119
Stagg Hill, Barn. 80 DE36
Stagg Hill, Pot.B. 80 DD35
Staggart Grn., Chig. 104 EU51
Stags Way, Islw. 157 CF79
Stainash Cres., Stai. 174 BH92
Stainash Par., Stai. 174 BH92
Stainbank Rd., Mitch. 201 DH97
Stainby Clo., West Dr. 154 BL76
Stainby Rd. N15 122 DT56
Stainer Rd., Borwd. 77 CK39
Stainer St. SE1 279 L3
Stainer St. SE1 142 DR74
Staines Ave., Sutt. 199 CX103
Staines Bri., Stai. 173 BE91
Staines Bypass, Ashf. 174 BK92
Staines Bypass, Stai. 173 BC89
Staines Cen. Trd. Est., Stai. 173 BE91
Staines Grn., Hert. 31 DK11
Staines La., Cher. 193 BF99
Staines La. Clo., Cher. 193 BF99
Staines Rd., Cher. 193 BF97
Staines Rd., Felt. 175 BS87
Staines Rd., Houns. 176 BW85
Staines Rd., Ilf. 125 ER63
Staines Rd., Stai. 174 BG94
Staines Rd. (Wraysbury), Stai. 172 AY87
Staines Rd., Twick. 176 CA90
Staines Rd. E., Sun. 175 BU94
Staines Rd. W., Ashf. 175 BP93
Staines Rd. W., Sun. 175 BT94
Staines Wk., Sid. 186 EW93
Evry Rd.
Stainford Clo., Ashf. 175 BR92
Stainforth Rd. E17 123 EA56
Stainforth Rd., Ilf. 125 ER59
Staining La. EC2 275 J8
Staining La. EC2 142 DQ72
Stainmore Clo., Chis. 205 ER95
Stains Clo. (Cheshunt), Wal.Cr. 67 DY28
Stainsbury St. E2 142 DW68
Royston St.
Stainsby Pl. E14 143 EA72
Stainsby Rd. E14 143 EA72
Stainton Rd. SE6 183 ED86
Stainton Rd., Enf. 82 DW39
Stainton Wk., Wok. 226 AW118
Inglewood
Stairfoot La., Sev. 256 FC122
Staithes Way, Tad. 233 CV120
Stakescorner Rd., Guil. 258 AU142
Stalbridge St. NW1 272 C6
Stalham St. SE16 162 DV76
Stalisfield Pl., Orp. 223 EN110
Mill La.
Stambourne Way SE19 182 DS94
Stambourne Way, W.Wick. 203 EC104
Stamford Brook Ave. W6 159 CT76
Stamford Brook Rd. W6 159 CT76
Stamford Clo. N15 122 DU56
Stamford Clo., Har. 95 CE52
Stamford Clo., Pot.B. 64 DD32
Stamford Clo., Sthl. 136 CA73
Stamford Cotts. SW10 160 DB80
Billing St.
Stamford Ct. W6 159 CT77
Goldhawk Rd.
Stamford Dr., Brom. 204 EF98
Stamford Gdns., Dag. 146 EW66
Stamford Grn. Rd., Epsom 216 CP113
Stamford Gro. E. N16 122 DU60
Oldhill St.
Stamford Gro. W. N16 122 DU60
Oldhill St.
Stamford Hill N16 122 DT61
Stamford Hill Est. N16 122 DT60
Stamford Rd. E6 144 EL67
Stamford Rd. N1 142 DS66
Stamford Rd. N15 122 DU56
Stamford Rd., Dag. 146 EV67
Stamford Rd., Walt. 196 BX104
Kenilworth Dr.
Stamford Rd., Wat. 75 BV40
Stamford St. SE1 278 D3
Stamford St. SE1 141 DN74
Stamp Pl. E2 275 P2
Stamp Pl. E2 142 DT69
Stanard Clo. N16 122 DS59
Stanborough Ave., Borwd. 78 CN37
Stanborough Clo., Borwd. 78 CN38
Stanborough Clo., Hmptn. 176 BZ93
Stanborough Clo., Welw.G.C. 29 CW10
Stanborough Grn., Welw.G.C. 29 CW11
Stanborough Pk., Wat. 75 BV35
Stanborough Pas. E8 142 DT65
Abbot St.
Stanborough Rd., Houns. 157 CD83
Stanborough Rd., Welw.G.C. 29 CV12
Stanbridge Pl. N21 99 DP47
Stanbridge Rd. SW15 159 CW83
Stanbrook Rd. SE2 166 EV75
Stanbrook Rd., Grav. 191 GF88
Stanbury Ave., Wat. 75 BS37
Stanbury Rd. SE15 162 DV81
Stancroft NW9 118 CS57
Standale Gro., Ruis. 115 BQ57
Standard Ind. Est. E16 165 EM75
Standard Pl. EC2 275 N3
Standard Rd. NW10 138 CQ70
Standard Rd., Belv. 166 FA78
Standard Rd., Bexh. 166 EY84
Standard Rd., Enf. 83 DY37
Standard Rd., Houns. 156 BY83
Standard Rd., Orp. 223 EN110
Standen Ave., Horn. 128 FK62
Standen Rd. SW18 179 CZ87
Standfield, Abb.L. 59 BS31
Standfield Gdns., Dag. 146 FA65
Standfield Rd.
Standfield Rd., Dag. 126 FA64
Standingford, Harl. 51 EP20
Phelips Rd.
Standish Rd. W6 159 CU77
Standlake Pt. SE23 183 DX90
Standring Ri., Hem.H. 40 BH23
Stane Clo. SW19 200 DB95
Hayward Clo.
Stane St., Dor. 247 CK128
Stane St., Lthd. 232 CM124
Reigate Rd.
Stane Way SE18 164 EL80
Stane Way, Epsom 217 CU110
Stanfield Rd. E3 143 DY68
Stanford Clo., Hmptn. 176 BZ93
Stanford Clo., Rom. 127 FB58
Stanford Clo., Ruis. 115 BQ58
Stanford Clo., Wdf.Grn. 102 EL50
Stanford Ct., Wal.Abb. 68 EG33
Stanford Gdns., S.Ock. 149 FS74
Stanford Ho., Bark. 146 EV68
Stanford Pl. SE17 279 M9
Stanford Rd. N11 98 DF50
Stanford Rd. SW16 201 DK96
Stanford Rd. W8 160 DB76
Stanford Rd., Grays 170 GD76
Stanford St. SW1 277 M9
Stanford Way SW16 201 DK96
Stangate Cres., Borwd. 78 CR43
Stangate Gdns., Stan. 95 CH49
Stanger Rd. SE25 202 DU98
Stanham Pl., Dart. 167 FG84
Crayford Way
Stanham Rd., Dart. 188 FJ85
Stanhope Ave. N3 119 CZ55
Stanhope Ave., Brom. 204 EF102
Stanhope Ave., Har. 95 CD53
Stanhope Clo. SE16 163 DX75
Middleton Dr.
Stanhope Gdns. N4 121 DP58
Stanhope Gdns. N6 121 DH58
Stanhope Gdns. NW7 97 CT50
Stanhope Gdns. SW7 160 DC77
Stanhope Gdns., Dag. 126 EZ62
Stanhope Rd.
Stanhope Gdns., Ilf. 125 EM60
Stanhope Gate W1 276 G2
Stanhope Gate W1 140 DG74
Stanhope Gro., Beck. 203 DZ99
Stanhope Heath, Stai. 174 BJ86
Stanhope Ms. E. SW7 160 DC77
Stanhope Ms. S. SW7 160 DC77
Gloucester Rd.
Stanhope Ms. W. SW7 160 DC77
Stanhope Par. NW1 273 K2
Stanhope Pk. Rd., Grnf. 136 CC70
Stanhope Pl. W2 272 D9
Stanhope Pl. W2 140 DF73
Stanhope Rd. E17 123 EB57
Stanhope Rd. N6 121 DJ58
Stanhope Rd. N12 98 DC50
Stanhope Rd., Barn. 79 CW43
Stanhope Rd., Bexh. 166 EY82
Stanhope Rd., Cars. 218 DG108
Stanhope Rd., Croy. 202 DS104
Stanhope Rd., Dag. 126 EZ61
Stanhope Rd., Grnf. 136 CC71
Stanhope Rd., Rain. 147 FG68
Stanhope Rd., St.Alb. 43 CF20
Stanhope Rd., Sid. 186 EU91
Stanhope Rd., Slou. 131 AK72
Stanhope Rd., Swans. 190 FZ85
Stanhope Rd., Wal.Cr. 67 DY33
Stanhope Row W1 277 H3
Stanhope St. NW1 273 K3
Stanhope St. NW1 141 DJ69
Stanhope Ter. W2 272 A10
Stanhope Ter. W2 140 DD73
Stanhope Way, Sev. 256 FD122
Stanhope Way, Stai. 174 BJ86
Stanhopes, Oxt. 254 EH128
Stanier Clo. W14 159 CZ78
Aisgill Ave.
Stanier Ri., Berk. 38 AT16
Staniland Dr., Wey. 212 BM111
Stanlake Ms. W12 139 CW74
Stanlake Rd. W12 139 CW74
Stanlake Vill. W12 139 CW74
Stanley Ave., Bark. 145 ET68
Stanley Ave., Beck. 203 EC96
Stanley Ave., Chesh. 54 AP31
Stanley Ave., Dag. 126 EZ60
Stanley Ave., Grnf. 136 CC67
Stanley Ave., N.Mal. 199 CU99
Stanley Ave., Rom. 127 FG56
Stanley Ave., St.Alb. 60 CA25
Stanley Ave., Wem. 138 CL66
Stanley Clo. SW8 161 DM79
Stanley Clo., Couls. 235 DM117
Stanley Clo., Green. 189 FS85
Stanley Clo., Horn. 128 FJ61
Stanley Rd.
Stanley Clo., Rom. 127 FG56
Stanley Clo., Uxb. 134 BK67
Stanley Clo., Wem. 138 CL66
Stanley Cotts., Slou. 132 AT74
Stanley Cres. W11 139 CZ73
Stanley Cres., Grav. 191 GK92
Stanley Dr., Hat. 45 CV20
Stanley Gdns. NW2 119 CW64
Stanley Gdns. W3 158 CS75
Stanley Gdns. W11 139 CZ73
Stanley Gdns., Borwd. 78 CL39
Stanley Gdns., Mitch. 180 DG93
Ashbourne Rd.
Stanley Gdns., S.Croy. 220 DU112
Stanley Gdns., Wall. 219 DJ107
Stanley Gdns., Walt. 214 BW107
Stanley Gdns. Ms. W11 139 CZ73
Stanley Cres.
Stanley Gdns. Rd., Tedd. 177 CE92
Stanley Grn. E., Slou. 153 AZ77
Stanley Grn. W., Slou. 153 AZ77
Stanley Gro. SW8 160 DG82
Stanley Gro., Croy. 201 DN100
Stanley Hill, Amer. 55 AR40
Stanley Hill Ave., Amer. 55 AR39
Stanley Pk. Dr., Wem. 138 CM67
Stanley Pk. Rd., Cars. 218 DE108
Stanley Pk. Rd., Wall. 219 DH107
Stanley Pas. NW1 273 P1
Stanley Rd. E4 101 ED46
Stanley Rd. E10 123 EB58
Stanley Rd. E12 124 EL64
Stanley Rd. E15 143 ED67
Stanley Rd. E18 102 EF53
Stanley Rd. N2 120 DD55
Stanley Rd. N9 100 DT46
Stanley Rd. N10 99 DH52
Stanley Rd. N11 99 DK51
Stanley Rd. N15 121 DP56
Stanley Rd. NW9 119 CU59
West Hendon Bdy.
Stanley Rd. SW14 158 CP84
Stanley Rd. SW19 180 DA94
Stanley Rd. W3 158 CQ76
Stanley Rd., Ashf. 174 BL92
Stanley Rd., Brom. 204 EH98
Stanley Rd., Cars. 218 DG108
Stanley Rd., Croy. 201 DN101
Stanley Rd., Enf. 82 DS41
Stanley Rd., Grav. 190 GE89
Stanley Rd., Grays 170 GB78
Stanley Rd., Har. 116 CC61
Stanley Rd., Hert. 32 DS10
Stanley Rd., Horn. 128 FJ61
Stanley Rd., Houns. 156 CC84
Stanley Rd., Ilf. 125 ER61
Stanley Rd., Mitch. 180 DG94
Stanley Rd., Mord. 200 DA98
Stanley Rd., Nthwd. 93 BU53
Stanley Rd., Orp. 206 EU102
Stanley Rd., Sid. 186 EU90
Stanley Rd., Sthl. 136 BY73
Stanley Rd., Sutt. 218 DB107
Stanley Rd., Swans. 190 FZ86
Stanley Rd., Tedd. 177 CE91
Stanley Rd., Twick. 177 CD90
Stanley Rd., Wat. 76 BW41
Stanley Rd., Wem. 138 CM65
Stanley Rd., Wok. 227 AZ116
Stanley Rd. N., Rain. 147 FE67
Stanley Rd. S., Rain. 147 FF68
Stanley Sq., Cars. 218 DF109
Stanley St. SE8 163 DZ80
Stanley Ter. N19 121 DL61
Stanley Way, Orp. 206 EV99
Stanley Wd., Amer. 55 AS40
Stanley Hill
Stanleycroft Clo., Islw. 157 CE81
Stanmer St. SW11 160 DE81
Stanmore Gdns., Rich. 158 CM83
Stanmore Gdns., Sutt. 200 DC104
Stanmore Hill, Stan. 95 CG48
Stanmore Pl. NW1 141 DH67
Arlington Rd.
Stanmore Rd. E11 124 EF60
Stanmore Rd. N15 121 DP56
Stanmore Rd., Belv. 167 FC77
Stanmore Rd., Rich. 158 CM83
Stanmore Rd., Wat. 75 BV39
Stanmore St. N1 141 DM67
Caledonian Rd.
Stanmore Ter., Beck. 203 EA96
Stanmore Way, Loug. 85 EN39
Stanmount Rd., St.Alb. 60 CA25
Stannard Ms. E8 142 DU65
Stannard Rd.
Stannard Rd. E8 142 DU65
Stannary Pl. SE11 161 DN78
Stannary St.
Stannary St. SE11 161 DN79
Stannet Way, Wall. 219 DJ105
Stannington Path, Borwd. 78 CN39
Warenford Way
Stansfeld Rd. E6 144 EK71
Stansfield Rd. SW9 161 DM83
Stansfield Rd., Houns. 155 BV82
Stansgate Rd., Dag. 126 FA61
Stanstead Clo., Brom. 204 EF99
Stanstead Dr., Hodd. 49 EB15
Stanstead Gro. SE6 183 DZ88
Catford Hill
Stanstead Manor, Sutt. 218 DA107
Stanstead Rd. E11 124 EH57
Stanstead Rd. SE6 183 DZ88
Catford Hill
Stanstead Rd. SE23 183 DX88
Stanstead Rd., Cat. 252 DR127
Stanstead Rd., Hert. 32 DT08
Stanstead Rd., Hodd. 49 EB16
Stanstead Rd., Houns. 174 BM86
Stanstead Rd., Ware 32 DW09
Stansted Clo., Horn. 147 FH65
Stansted Cres., Bex. 186 EX88
Stanswood Gdns. SE5 162 DS80
Sedgmoor Pl.
Stanthorpe Clo. SW16 181 DL92
Stanthorpe Rd. SW16 181 DL92
Stanton Ave., Tedd. 177 CE92
Stanton Clo., Epsom 216 CP106
Stanton Clo., Orp. 206 EW101
Stanton Clo., St.Alb. 43 CK16
Stanton Clo., Wor.Pk. 199 CX102
Stanton Rd. SE26 183 DZ91
Stanton Way
Stanton Rd. SW13 159 CT82
Stanton Rd. SW20 199 CX95
Stanton Rd., Croy. 202 DQ101
Stanton Sq. SE26 183 DZ91
Stanton Way
Stanton St. SE15 162 DU81
Stanton Way SE26 183 DZ91
Stanton Way, Slou. 152 AY77
Stantons, Harl. 51 EN15
Stantons Wf., Guil. 259 BA144
Stanway Clo., Chig. 103 ES50
Stanway Ct. N1 142 DS68
Hoxton St.
Stanway Gdns. W3 138 CN74
Stanway Gdns., Edg. 96 CQ51
Stanway Rd., Wal.Abb. 68 EG33
Stanway St. N1 142 DS68
Stanwell Clo., Stai. 174 BK86
Stanwell Gdns., Stai. 174 BK86
Stanwell Moor Rd., Stai. 174 BH90
Stanwell Moor Rd., West Dr. 154 BH81
Stanwell New Rd., Stai. 174 BH90
Stanwell Rd., Ashf. 174 BL89
Stanwell Rd., Felt. 175 BQ87
Stanwell Rd., Slou. 153 BA83
Stanwick Rd. W14 159 CZ77
Stanworth St. SE1 279 P5
Stanworth St. SE1 162 DT75
Stanwyck Dr., Chig. 103 EQ50
Stanwyck Gdns., Rom. 105 FH50
Stapenhill Rd., Wem. 117 CH62
Staple Clo., Bex. 187 FD90
Staple Hill Rd., Wok. 210 AS105
Staple Inn Bldgs. WC1 274 D7
Staple La., Guil. 244 BK132
Staple St. SE1 279 L5
Staple St. SE1 162 DR75
Staple Tye, Harl. 51 ER18
Parnall Rd.
Staplefield Clo. SW2 181 DL88
Staplefield Clo., Pnr. 94 BY52
Stapleford, Welw.G.C. 30 DD09
Stapleford Ave., Ilf. 125 ES57
Stapleford Clo. E4 101 EC48
Stapleford Clo. SW19 179 CY87
Stapleford Clo., Kings.T. 198 CN97
Stapleford Ct., Sev. 256 FF123
Stapleford Gdns., Rom. 104 FA51
Stapleford Rd., Rom. 87 FB43
Stapleford Rd., Wem. 137 CK66
Stapleford Tawney, Ong. 71 FC32
Stapleford Tawney, Rom. 87 FC35
Stapleford Way, Bark. 146 EV69
Staplehurst Clo., Reig. 266 DC138
Staplehurst Rd. SE13 184 EE85
Staplehurst Rd., Cars. 218 DE108
Staplehurst Rd., Reig. 266 DC138
Staples Clo. SE16 143 DY74
Staples Cor. NW2 119 CV60
Staples Cor. Business Pk. NW2 119 CU60
Staples Rd., Loug. 84 EK41
Stapleton Clo., Pot.B. 64 DE31
Stapleton Cres., Rain. 147 FG65
Stapleton Gdns., Croy. 219 DN106
Stapleton Hall Rd. N4 121 DM60
Stapleton Rd. SW17 180 DG90
Stapleton Rd., Bexh. 166 EZ80
Stapleton Rd., Borwd. 78 CN38
Stapleton Rd., Orp. 205 ET104
Stapley Rd., Belv. 166 FA78
Stapley Rd., St.Alb. 43 CD19
Stapylton Rd., Barn. 79 CY41
Star & Garter Hill, Rich. 178 CL88
Star Hill, Dart. 187 FE85
Star Hill, Wok. 226 AW119
Star Hill Rd., Sev. 240 EZ115
Star Home Ct., Ware 33 DY06
Star La. E16 144 EE70
Star La., Couls. 234 DG122
Star La., Epp. 70 EU30
Star La., Orp. 206 EW98
Star Path, Nthlt. 136 CA68
Brabazon Rd.
Star Pl. E1 142 DT73
Thomas More St.
Star Rd. W14 159 CZ79
Star Rd., Islw. 157 CD82
Star Rd., Uxb. 135 BP70
Star St. E16 144 EF71
Star St. W2 272 A8
Star St. W2 140 DE72
Star St., Ware 33 DY06
Star Yd. WC2 274 D8
Starboard Ave., Green. 189 FV86
Starboard Way E14 163 EA76
Starch Ho. La., Ilf. 103 ER54
Starcross St. NW1 273 L3
Starcross St. NW1 141 DJ69
Starfield Rd. W12 159 CU75
Starkleigh Way SE16 162 DV78
Egan Way
Starling Clo., Buck.H. 102 EG46
Starling Clo., Pnr. 116 BW55
Starling La. (Cuffley), Pot.B. 65 DM28
Starling Ms. SE28 165 ER75
Whinchat Rd.
Starling Wk., Hmptn. 176 BY93
Oak Ave.
Starlings, The, Lthd. 214 CC113
Starmans Clo., Dag. 146 EY67
Starrock La., Couls. 234 DF120
Starrock Rd., Couls. 235 DH119
Starts Clo., Orp. 205 EN104
Starts Hill Ave., Orp. 223 EP105
Starts Hill Rd., Orp. 205 EN104
Starveall Clo., West Dr. 154 BM76
Starwood Clo., W.Byf. 212 BJ111
Starwood Ct., Slou. 152 AW76
London Rd.
State Fm. Ave., Orp. 223 EP105
Staten Gdns., Twick. 177 CF88
Lion Rd.
Statham Gro. N16 122 DQ63
Green Las.
Statham Gro. N18 100 DS50
Station App. E7 124 EH63
Woodford Rd.
Station App. (Snaresbrook) E11 124 EG57
High St.
Station App. N11 99 DH50
Friern Barnet Rd.
Station App. (Woodside Pk.) N12 98 DB49
Holden Rd.
Station App. (Stoke Newington) N16 122 DT61
Stamford Hill
Station App. NW10 139 CT69
Station Rd.
Station App. SE1 278 C5
Station App. SE3 164 EH83
Kidbrooke Pk. Rd.
Station App. (Mottingham) SE9 185 EM88
Station App. (Lower Sydenham) SE26 183 DZ92
Worsley Bri. Rd.
Station App. (Sydenham) SE26 182 DW91
Sydenham Rd.
Station App. SW6 159 CY83
Station App. SW16 181 DK92
Station App. W7 137 CE74
Station App., Amer. 55 AQ38
Station App. (Little Chalfont), Amer. 72 AX39
Chalfont Sta. Rd.
Station App., Ashf. 174 BM91
Station App., Bex. 186 FA87
Bexley High St.
Station App., Bexh. 166 EY82
Avenue Rd.
Station App. (Barnehurst), Bexh. 167 FC82
Station App., Brom. 204 EG102
Station App., Buck.H. 102 EK49
Cherry Tree Ri.
Station App., Chis. 205 EN95
Station App. (Elmstead Wds.), Chis. 184 EL93
Station App., Couls. 235 DK115
Station App. (Chipstead), Couls. 234 DF118
Station App., Dart. 188 FL86
Station App. (Crayford), Dart. 187 FF86
Station App., Dor. 247 CJ134
Station App. (Theydon Bois), Epp. 85 ES36
Coppice Row
Station App., Epsom 216 CR113
Station App. (Ewell E.), Epsom 217 CV110
Station App. (Ewell W.), Epsom 217 CT109
Chessington Rd.
Station App. (Stoneleigh), Epsom 217 CT106
Station App. (Hinchley Wd.), Esher 197 CF104
Station App., Ger.Cr. 112 AY57
Station App., Grays 170 GA79
Station App., Grnf. 137 CD66
Station App., Guil. 258 AY135
Station App., Hmptn. 196 CA95
Milton Rd.
Station App., Harl. 36 EW10
Station App., Har. 117 CE59
Station App., Hayes 155 BT75
Station App., Hem.H. 40 BG23
Station App., Horl. 269 DH148
Station App., Kings.T. 198 CN96
Station App., Lthd. 231 CG121
Station App. (East Horsley), Lthd. 245 BS126
Station App. (Oxshott), Lthd. 214 CC113
Station App., Loug. 84 EL43
Station App. (Debden), Loug. 85 EQ42
Station App., Nthwd. 93 BS52
Station App., Orp. 205 ET103
Station App. (Chelsfield), Orp. 224 EV106
Station App. (St. Mary Cray), Orp. 206 EV98
Station App., Oxt. 254 EE129
Station App., Pnr. 116 BY56
Station App. (Hatch End), Pnr. 94 CA52
Uxbridge Rd.
Station App., Pot.B. 63 CZ32
Wyllyotts Pl.
Station App., Pur. 219 DN111
Whytecliffe Rd. S.
Station App., Rad. 77 CG35
Shenley Hill
Station App., Rich. 158 CN81
Station App., Rick. 73 BC42
Station App., Ruis. 115 BV64
Station App., Shep. 195 BQ99
Station App., Sid. 186 EU89
Station App., S.Croy. 220 DR109
Sanderstead Rd.
Station App., Stai. 174 BG91
Station App., Sun. 195 BU95
Station App. (Belmont), Sutt. 218 DB110
Brighton Rd.
Station App. (Cheam), Sutt. 217 CY108
Station App., Swan. 207 FE98
Station App., Upmin. 128 FQ61
Station App. (Denham Golf Club), Uxb. 113 BD59
Middle Rd.

Station App., Vir.W. 192 AX98
Station App., Wal.Cr. 67 DY34
Station App. (Cheshunt), Wal.Cr. 67 DZ30
Station App., Wat. 75 BT41
Cassiobury Pk. Ave.
Station App. (Carpenders Pk.), Wat. 94 BX48
Prestwick Rd.
Station App., Well. 166 EU82
Station App., Wem. 137 CH65
Station App., W.Byf. 212 BG112
Station App., West Dr. 134 BL74
High St.
Station App., Wey. 212 BN107
Station App., Whyt. 236 DU118
Station App., Wok. 227 AZ118
Station App. E., Red. 266 DF136
Brambletye Pk. Rd.
Station App. Rd. W4 158 CQ80
Station App. Rd., Gat. 269 DH152
London Rd.
Station App. Rd., Tad. 233 CW122
Station App. Rd., Til. 171 GG84
Station App. W., Red. 266 DF136
Earlswood Rd.
Station Ave. SW9 161 DP83
Coldharbour La.
Station Ave., Cat. 236 DU124
Station Ave., Epsom 216 CS109
Station Ave., N.Mal. 198 CS97
Station Ave., Rich. 158 CN81
Station Ave., Walt. 213 BT105
Station Clo. N3 98 DA53
Station Clo., Hmptn. 196 CB95
Station Clo., Hat. 63 CY26
Station Rd.
Station Clo., Pot.B. 63 CZ31
Station Cres. N15 122 DR56
Station Cres. SE3 164 EG78
Station Cres., Ashf. 174 BK90
Station Cres., Wem. 137 CH65
Station Est., Beck. 203 DX98
Elmers End Rd.
Station Est. Rd., Felt. 175 BV88
Station Footpath, Kings L. 59 BP30
Station Gdns. W4 158 CQ80
Station Gro., Wem. 138 CL65
Station Hill, Brom. 204 EG103
Station Ho. Ms. N9 100 DU49
Fore St.
Station La., Horn. 128 FK62
Station Par. E11 124 EG57
Station Par. N14 99 DK46
High St.
Station Par. NW2 139 CW65
Station Par. SW12 180 DG88
Balham High Rd.
Station Par. W3 138 CN72
Station Par., Bark. 145 EQ66
Station Par., Horn. 127 FH63
Rosewood Ave.
Station Par., Lthd. 245 BS126
Ockham Rd. S.
Station Par., Rich. 158 CN81
Station Ave.
Station Par., Sev. 256 FG124
London Rd.
Station Par., Uxb. 114 BG59
Station Par., Vir.W. 192 AX98
Station Pas. E18 102 EH54
Maybank Rd.
Station Pas. SE15 162 DW79
Asylum Rd.
Station Path E8 142 DV65
Amhurst Rd.
Station Path, Stai. 173 BF91
Station Pl. N4 121 DN61
Seven Sisters Rd.
Station Pl., Gdmg. 258 AT144
Summers Rd.
Station Ri. SE27 181 DP89
Norwood Rd.
Station Rd. (Chingford) E4 101 ED46
Station Rd. E7 124 EG63
Station Rd. E10 123 EC62
Station Rd. E12 124 EK63
Station Rd. E17 123 DY58
Station Rd. N3 98 DA53
Station Rd. N11 99 DH50
Station Rd. N17 122 DU55
Hale Rd.
Station Rd. N19 121 DJ62
Station Rd. N21 99 DP46
Station Rd. N22 99 DL54
Station Rd. NW4 119 CU58
Station Rd. NW7 96 CS50
Station Rd. NW10 139 CT68
Station Rd. SE20 182 DW93
Station Rd. (Norwood Junct.) SE25 202 DT98
Station Rd. SW13 159 CT82
Station Rd. SW19 200 DC95
Station Rd. W5 138 CM72
Station Rd. (Hanwell) W7 137 CE74
Station Rd., Add. 212 BJ105
Station Rd., Amer. 55 AQ38
Station Rd., Ashf. 174 BM91
Station App.
Station Rd., Barn. 80 DB43
Station Rd., Beac. 89 AK52
Station Rd., Belv. 166 FA76
Station Rd., Berk. 38 AW18
Station Rd., Bet. 248 CS131
Station Rd., Bexh. 166 EY83
Station Rd., Borwd. 78 CN42
Station Rd., Brom. 204 EG95
Station Rd. (Shortlands), Brom. 204 EE96
Station Rd., Brox. 49 DZ20
Station Rd., Cars. 218 DF105
Station Rd., Cat. 237 DY122
Station Rd., Cher. 193 BF102
Station Rd., Chesh. 54 AQ31
Station Rd., Chess. 216 CL106
Station Rd., Chig. 103 EP48
Station Rd., Cob. 230 BY117
Station Rd. (East Croydon), Croy. 202 DR103
Station Rd. (West Croydon), Croy. 202 DQ102
Station Rd. (Crayford), Dart. 187 FF86
Station Rd. (Eynsford), Dart. 208 FK104
Station Rd. (South Darenth), Dart. 208 FP96
Station Rd., Dor. 263 CG135
Station Rd., Edg. 96 CN51
Station Rd., Egh. 173 BA92
Station Rd., Epp. 69 ET30
Station Rd. (North Weald Bassett), Epp. 71 FB27
Station Rd., Esher 197 CD103
Station Rd. (Claygate), Esher 215 CD106
Station Rd., Ger.Cr. 112 AY57
Station Rd., Gdmg. 258 AT144
Station Rd. (Betsham), Grav. 190 FZ91
Station Rd. (Northfleet), Grav. 190 GB86
Station Rd., Green. 189 FU85
Station Rd., Guil. 258 AY140
Station Rd. (Bramley), Guil. 259 AZ144
Station Rd. (Gomshall), Guil. 261 BQ138
Station Rd., Hmptn. 196 CA95
Station Rd., Harl. 36 EW11
Station Rd., Har. 117 CF56
Station Rd. (North Harrow), Har. 116 CB57
Station Rd., Hat. 45 CW24
Station Rd., Hayes 155 BS77
Station Rd., Hem.H. 40 BH22
Station Rd., Hert. 30 DG12
Station Rd., H.Wyc. 88 AC53
Station Rd., Horl. 269 DH148
Station Rd., Houns. 156 CB84
Station Rd., Ilf. 125 EP62
Station Rd. (Barkingside), Ilf. 125 ER55
Station Rd., Ken. 220 DQ114
Station Rd., Kings L. 59 BP29
Station Rd., Kings.T. 198 CN95
Station Rd. (Hampton Wick), Kings.T. 197 CK95
Station Rd., Lthd. 231 CG121
Station Rd., Loug. 84 EL42
Station Rd., Maid. 130 AF72
Station Rd. (Motspur Pk.), N.Mal. 199 CV99
Station Rd., Orp. 205 ET103
Station Rd. (St. Mary Cray), Orp. 206 EW98
Station Rd. (Cuffley), Pot.B. 65 DL29
Station Rd., Rad. 77 CG35
Station Rd., Red. 250 DE133
Station Rd. (Merstham), Red. 251 DJ128
Station Rd., Rick. 92 BK45
Station Rd. (Chadwell Heath), Rom. 126 EX60
Station Rd. (Gidea Pk.), Rom. 127 FH56
Station Rd. (Harold Wd.), Rom. 106 FM53
Station Rd. (Bricket Wd.), St.Alb. 60 CA31
Station Rd. (Colney Heath), St.Alb. 44 CP19
Station Rd. (Dunton Grn.), Sev. 241 FE120
Station Rd. (Halstead), Sev. 224 EZ110
Station Rd. (Otford), Sev. 241 FH116
Station Rd. (Shoreham), Sev. 225 FG111
Station Rd., Shep. 195 BQ99
Station Rd., Sid. 186 EU91
Station Rd., Slou. 131 AL72
Station Rd. (Langley), Slou. 153 BA76
Station Rd. (Wraysbury), Stai. 173 AZ86
Station Rd., Sun. 175 BU94
Station Rd. (Belmont), Sutt. 218 DA110
Station Rd., Swan. 207 FE98
Station Rd., Tedd. 177 CF92
Station Rd., T.Ditt. 197 CF101
Station Rd., Twick. 177 CF88
Station Rd., Upmin. 128 FQ61
Station Rd., Uxb. 134 BJ70
Station Rd., Wal.Cr. 67 EA34
Station Rd., Ware 33 DX06
Station Rd. (St. Margarets), Ware 33 EA11
Station Rd., Wat. 75 BV40
Station Rd., W.Byf. 212 BG112
Station Rd., West Dr. 134 BK74
Station Rd., W.Wick. 203 EC103
Station Rd., West. 240 EV123
Station Rd., Whyt. 236 DT118
Station Rd., Wok. 210 AT111
Station Rd. E., Oxt. 254 EE128
Station Rd. N., Belv. 167 FB76
Station Rd. N., Egh. 173 BA92
Station Rd. N., Red. 251 DJ128
Station Rd. S., Red. 251 DJ128
Station Rd. W., Oxt. 254 EE129
Station Row, Guil. 258 AY140
Station Sq. (Petts Wd.), Orp. 205 EQ99
Station Sq. (St. Mary Cray), Orp. 206 EV98
Station St. E15 143 ED66
Station St. E16 145 EP74
Station St., Ware 33 EA11
Station Ter. NW10 139 CX68
Station Ter. SE5 162 DQ81
Station Vw., Grnf. 137 CD67
Station Vw., Guil. 258 AW135
Station Way SE15 162 DU82
Rye La.
Station Way (Roding Valley), Buck.H. 102 EJ49
Station Way (Epsom), Epsom 216 CR113
High St.
Station Way (Claygate), Esher 215 CE107
Station Way, St.Alb. 43 CF20
Station Way (Cheam), Sutt. 217 CY107
Station Way, Welw.G.C. 29 CX08
Station Yd., Twick. 177 CG87
Stationers Hall Ct. EC4 141 DP72
Ludgate Hill
Staunton Rd., Kings.T. 178 CL93
Staunton Rd., Slou. 131 AR71
Staunton St. SE8 163 DZ79
Stave Yd. Rd. SE16 143 DY74
Staveley Clo. E9 122 DW64
Churchill Wk.
Staveley Clo. N7 121 DL63
Penn Rd.
Staveley Clo. SE15 162 DV81
Asylum Rd.
Staveley Gdns. W4 158 CR81
Staveley Rd. W4 158 CQ79
Staveley Rd., Ashf. 175 BR93
Staveley Way, Wok. 226 AS117
Staverton Rd. NW2 139 CW66
Staverton Rd., Horn. 128 FK58
Stavordale Rd. N5 121 DP63
Stavordale Rd., Cars. 200 DC102
Stayne End, Vir.W. 192 AU98
Stayner's Rd. E1 143 DX70
Stayton Rd., Sutt. 200 DA104
Stead St. SE17 279 K9
Stead St. SE17 162 DR77
Steadfast Rd., Kings.T. 197 CK95
Steam Fm. La., Felt. 155 BT84
Stean St. E8 142 DT67
Stebbing Way, Bark. 146 EU68
Stebondale St. E14 163 EC78
Stedham Pl. WC1 273 P8
Stedman Clo., Bex. 187 FE90
Stedman Clo., Uxb. 114 BN62
Steed Clo., Horn. 127 FH61
St. Leonards Way
Steedman St. SE17 279 H9
Steeds Rd. N10 98 DF53
Steeds Way, Loug. 84 EL41
Steele Ave., Green. 189 FT85
Steele Rd. E11 124 EE63
Steele Rd. N17 122 DS55
Steele Rd. NW10 138 CQ68
Steele Rd. W4 158 CQ76
Steele Rd., Islw. 157 CG84
Steele Wk., Erith 167 FB80
Sussex Rd.
Steeles Ms. N. NW3 140 DF65
Steeles Rd.
Steeles Ms. S. NW3 140 DF65
Steeles Rd.
Steeles Rd. NW3 140 DF65
Steel's La. E1 142 DW72
Devonport St.
Steels La., Lthd. 214 CB114
Steelyard Pas. EC4 142 DR73
Upper Thames St.
Steen Way SE22 182 DS85
East Dulwich Gro.
Steep Clo., Orp. 223 ET107
Steep Hill SW16 181 DK90
Steep Hill, Croy. 220 DS105
Steeplands (Bushey), Wat. 94 CB45
Steeple Clo. SW6 159 CY82
Steeple Clo. SW19 179 CY92
Steeple Ct. E1 142 DV70
Coventry Rd.
Steeple Gdns., Add. 212 BH106
Weatherall Clo.
Steeple Heights Dr., West. 238 EK117
Steeple Wk. N1 142 DQ67
Basire St.
Steeplestone Clo. N18 100 DQ50
Steer Pl., Red. 266 DG143
Bonehurst Rd.
Steerforth St. SW18 180 DC89
Steers Mead, Mitch. 200 DF95
Steers Way SE16 163 DY75
Stella Rd. SW17 180 DF93
Stellar Ho. N17 100 DU51
Stelling Rd., Erith 167 FD80
Stellman Clo. E5 122 DU62
Stembridge Rd. SE20 202 DV96
Stents La., Cob. 230 BZ120
Stents La., Lthd. 230 BZ120
Cobham Rd.
Stepbridge Path, Wok. 226 AX117
Goldsworth Rd.
Stepgates, Cher. 194 BH101
Stepgates Clo., Cher. 194 BH101
Stephan Clo. E8 142 DU67
Stephen Ave., Rain. 147 FG65
Stephen Clo., Egh. 173 BC93
Stephen Clo., Orp. 205 ES104
Stephen Ms. W1 273 M7
Stephen Rd., Bexh. 167 FC83
Stephen St. W1 273 M7
Stephen St. W1 141 DK71
Stephendale Rd. SW6 160 DB83
Stephens Clo., Rom. 106 FJ50
Stephen's Rd. E15 144 EE67
Stephenson Ave., Til. 171 GG81
Stephenson Dr., Wind. 151 AP80
Stephenson Rd. E17 123 DY57
Stephenson Rd. W7 137 CF72
Stephenson Rd., Twick. 176 CA87
Stephenson St. E16 144 EE70
Stephenson St. NW10 138 CS69
Stephenson Way NW1 273 L4
Stephenson Way NW1 141 DJ70
Stephenson Way, Wat. 76 BX41
Stepney Causeway E1 143 DX72
Stepney Grn. E1 142 DW71
Stepney High St. E1 143 DX71
Stepney Way E1 142 DV71
Sterling Ave., Edg. 96 CM49
Sterling Ave., Wal.Cr. 67 DX34
Sterling Gdns. SE14 163 DY79
Sterling Ind. Est., Dag. 127 FB63
Sterling Pl. W5 158 CL77
Sterling Rd., Enf. 82 DR39
Sterling St. SW7 276 C5
Sterling Way N18 100 DR49
Stern Clo., Bark. 146 EY69
Choats Rd.
Sterndale Rd. W14 159 CX76
Sterndale Rd., Dart. 188 FM87
Sterne St. W12 159 CX75
Sternhall La. SE15 162 DU83
Sternhold Ave. SW2 181 DK89
Sterry Cres., Dag. 126 FA64
Alibon Rd.
Sterry Dr., Epsom 216 CS105
Sterry Dr., T.Ditt. 197 CE100
Sterry Gdns., Dag. 146 FA65
Sterry Rd., Bark. 145 ET67
Sterry Rd., Dag. 126 FA63
Sterry St. SE1 279 K5
Sterry St. SE1 162 DR75
Steucers La. SE23 183 DY88
Steve Biko La. SE6 183 EA91
Steve Biko Rd. N7 121 DN62
Steve Biko Way, Houns. 156 CA83
Stevedale Rd., Well. 166 EW82
Stevedore St. E1 142 DV74
Waterman Way
Stevenage Cres., Borwd. 78 CL39
Stevenage Ri., Hem.H. 40 BM16
Stevenage Rd. E6 145 EN65
Stevenage Rd. SW6 159 CX80
Stevens Ave. E9 142 DW65
Stevens Clo., Beck. 183 EA93
Stevens Clo., Bex. 187 FD91
Steven's Clo., Dart. 189 FS92
Stevens Clo., Epsom 216 CS113
Upper High St.
Stevens Clo., Hmptn. 176 BY93
Stevens Clo., Pnr. 116 BW57
Bridle Rd.
Stevens Grn. (Bushey), Wat. 94 CC46
Stevens La., Esher 215 CG108
Stevens Rd., Dag. 126 EV62
Stevens St. SE1 279 N6
Stevens Way, Chig. 103 ES49
Stevenson Clo., Erith 167 FH80
Stevenson Cres. SE16 162 DU78
Stevenson Rd., Slou. 111 AR61
Steventon Rd. W12 139 CT73
Stew La. EC4 142 DQ73
High Timber St.
Steward Clo. (Cheshunt), Wal.Cr. 67 DY30
Steward St. E1 275 N6
Steward St. E1 142 DS71
Stewards Clo., Epp. 70 EU32
Stewards Grn. La., Epp. 70 EV32
Stewards Grn. Rd., Epp. 70 EU33
Stewards Wk., Rom. 127 FE57
Stewart, Tad. 233 CX121
Stewart Ave., Shep. 194 BN98
Stewart Ave., Slou. 132 AT71
Stewart Ave., Upmin. 128 FP62
Stewart Clo. NW9 118 CQ58
Stewart Clo., Abb.L. 59 BT31
Stewart Clo., Chis. 185 EP92
Stewart Clo., Hmptn. 176 BY93
Stewart Clo., Maid. 150 AD81
Stewart Clo., Wok. 226 AT117
Nethercote Ave.
Stewart Rainbird Ho. E12 125 EN64
Stewart Rd. E15 123 EC63
Stewart St. E14 163 EC75
Stewart's Dr., Slou. 111 AP63
Stewart's Gro. SW3 276 B10
Stewart's Gro. SW3 160 DE78
Stewart's Rd. SW8 161 DJ80
Stewartsby Clo. N18 100 DQ50
Steyne Rd. W3 138 CP74
Steyning Clo., Ken. 235 DP116
Steyning Gro. SE9 185 EM91
Steyning Way, Houns. 156 BW84
Steynings Way N12 98 DA50
Steynton Ave., Bex. 186 EX89
Stickland Rd., Belv. 166 FA77
Picardy Rd.
Stickleton Clo., Grnf. 136 CB69
Stifford Hill, S.Ock. 149 FW73
Stifford Rd., S.Ock. 149 FS74
Stile Hall Gdns. W4 158 CN78
Stile Hall Par. W4 158 CN78
Chiswick High Rd.
Stile Path, Sun. 195 BU97
Stile Rd., Slou. 152 AX76
Stilecroft, Harl. 52 EU17
Stilecroft Gdns., Wem. 117 CH62
Stiles Clo., Brom. 205 EM100
Stiles Clo., Erith 167 FB78
Riverdale Rd.
Stillingfleet Rd. SW13 159 CU79
Stillington St. SW1 277 L8
Stillington St. SW1 161 DJ77
Stillness Rd. SE23 183 DY86
Stilton Cres. NW10 138 CQ66
Stilton Path, Borwd. 78 CN38
Brampton Ter.
Stipularis Dr., Hayes 136 BX70
Stirling Clo. SW16 201 DJ95
Stirling Clo., Bans. 233 CZ117
Stirling Clo., Rain. 147 FH69
Stirling Clo., Uxb. 134 BJ69
Ferndale Cres.
Stirling Clo., Wind. 151 AK82
Stirling Dr., Orp. 224 EV106
Stirling Gro., Houns. 156 CC82
Stirling Rd. E13 144 EH68
Stirling Rd. E17 123 DY55
Stirling Rd. N17 100 DU53
Stirling Rd. N22 99 DP53
Stirling Rd. SW9 161 DL82
Stirling Rd. W3 158 CP76
Stirling Rd., Har. 117 CF55
Stirling Rd., Hayes 135 BV73
Stirling Rd., Houns. 174 BM86
Stirling Rd., Slou. 131 AN71
Stirling Rd., Twick. 176 CA87
Stirling Rd. Path E17 123 DY55
Stirling Wk., N.Mal. 198 CQ99
Green La.
Stirling Wk., Surb. 198 CP100
Stirling Way, Abb.L. 59 BU32
Stirling Way, Borwd. 78 CR44
Stirling Way, Croy. 201 DL101
Stirling Way, Welw.G.C. 30 DE09
Stites Hill Rd., Cat. 235 DP120
Stiven Cres., Har. 116 BZ62
Stoats Nest Rd., Couls. 219 DL114
Stoats Nest Village, Couls. 235 DL115
Stock Fm. Rd., Rick. 92 BK48
Stock Hill, West. 238 EK116
Stock La., Dart. 188 FJ90
Stock Orchard Cres. N7 121 DM64
Stock Orchard St. N7 121 DM64
Stock St. E13 144 EG68
Stockbreach Clo., Hat. 45 CU17
Stockbreach Rd., Hat. 45 CU17
Stockbury Rd., Croy. 202 DW100
Stockdale Rd., Dag. 126 EZ61
Stockdales Rd. (Eton Wick), Wind. 151 AM77
Stockdove Way, Grnf. 137 CF69
Stockers La., Wok. 227 AZ120
Stockfield, Horl. 269 DH147
Stockfield Ave., Hodd. 49 EA15
Stockfield Rd. SW16 181 DM90
Stockfield Rd., Esher 215 CE106
Stockham's Clo., S.Croy. 220 DR111
Stockholm Rd. SE16 162 DW78
Stockholm Way E1 142 DU74
Thomas More St.
Stockhurst Clo. SW15 159 CW82
Stocking La. (Bayford), Hert. 47 DN18
Stockings La. (Little Berkhamsted), Hert. 47 DK18
Stockingswater La., Enf. 83 DY41
Stockland Rd., Rom. 127 FD58
Stockley Clo., West Dr. 155 BP75
Stockley Fm. Rd., West Dr. 155 BP76
Stockley Rd.
Stockley Pk. Business Pk., Uxb. 135 BP74
Stockley Rd., Uxb. 134 BN72
Stockley Rd., West Dr. 155 BP76
Stockport Rd. SW16 201 DK95
Stockport Rd., Rick. 91 BC45
Stocks Clo., Horl. 269 DH149
Stocks Pl. E14 143 DZ73
Grenade St.
Stocksfield Rd. E17 123 EC55
Stockton Gdns. N17 100 DQ52
Stockton Rd.
Stockton Gdns. NW7 96 CS48
Stockton Rd. N17 100 DQ52
Stockton Rd. N18 100 DU51
Stockton Rd., Reig. 266 DA137
Stockwell Ave. SW9 161 DM83
Stockwell Clo., Brom. 204 EH96
Stockwell Clo. (Cheshunt), Wal.Cr. 66 DU27
Stockwell Gdns. SW9 161 DM81
Stockwell Gdns. Est. SW9 161 DL82
Stockwell Grn. SW9 161 DM82
Stockwell La. SW9 161 DM82
Stockwell La. (Cheshunt), Wal.Cr. 66 DV28
Stockwell Ms. SW9 161 DM82
Stockwell Rd.
Stockwell Pk. Cres. SW9 161 DM82
Stockwell Pk. Est. SW9 161 DM83
Stockwell Pk. Rd. SW9 161 DM81
Stockwell Pk. Wk. SW9 161 DM83
Stockwell Rd. SW9 161 DM82
Stockwell St. SE10 163 EC79
Stockwell Ter. SW9 161 DM81
Stockwells, Maid. 130 AD70
Stocton Clo., Guil. 242 AW133
Stocton Rd., Guil. 242 AW133
Stodart Rd. SE20 202 DW95
Stofield Gdns. SE9 184 EK90
Aldersgrove Ave.
Stoford Clo. SW19 179 CY87
Stoke Ave., Ilf. 104 EU51
Stoke Clo., Cob. 230 BZ116
Stoke Common Rd., Slou. 112 AU63
Stoke Ct. Dr., Slou. 132 AS67
Stoke Flds., Guil. 258 AX135
York Rd.
Stoke Gdns., Slou. 132 AS74
Stoke Grn., Slou. 132 AU70
Stoke Gro., Guil. 242 AX134
York Rd.
Stoke Ms., Guil. 258 AX135
Stoke Rd.
Stoke Newington Ch. St. N16 122 DR62
Stoke Newington Common N16 122 DT62
Stoke Newington High St. N16 122 DT62
Stoke Newington Rd. N16 122 DT64
Stoke Pk. Ave., Slou. 131 AQ69
Stoke Pl. NW10 139 CT69
Stoke Pl. Conference Cen., Slou. 132 AU70
Stoke Poges La., Slou. 132 AS74
Stoke Rd., Cob. 230 BW115
Stoke Rd., Guil. 242 AX133
Stoke Rd., Kings.T. 178 CQ94
Stoke Rd., Rain. 148 FK68
Stoke Rd., Slou. 132 AT74
Stoke Rd., Walt. 196 BW104
Stoke Wd., Slou. 112 AT63
Stokenchurch St. SW6 160 DB81
Stokers Clo., Horl. 268 DE151
Stokes Ridings, Tad. 233 CX123
Stokes Rd. E6 144 EL70
Stokes Rd., Croy. 203 DX100
Stokesay, Slou. 132 AT73
Stokesby Rd., Chess. 216 CM107
Stokesheath Rd., Lthd. 214 CC111
Stokesley Ri., H.Wyc. 110 AE55
Wootton Way
Stokesley St. W12 139 CT72
Stoll Clo. NW2 119 CW62
Stomp Rd., Slou. 130 AH71
Stompond La., Walt. 195 BU103
Stoms Path SE6 183 EA92
Sedgehill Rd.
Stonard Rd. N13 99 DN48
Stonard Rd., Dag. 126 EV64
Stonards Hill, Epp. 70 EU29
Stonards Hill, Loug. 85 EM44
Stondon Pk. SE23 183 DY86
Stondon Wk. E6 144 EK68
Arragon Rd.
Stone Bldgs. WC2 274 C7
Stone Bldgs. WC2 141 DM72
Stone Clo. SW4 161 DJ82
Larkhall Ri.
Stone Clo., Dag. 126 EZ61
Stone Clo., West Dr. 134 BM74
Stone Cres., Felt. 175 BT87
Stone Cross, Harl. 35 ER14
Post Office Rd.
Stone Hall Gdns. W8 160 DB76
St. Mary's Gate
Stone Hall Pl. W8 160 DB76
St. Mary's Gate
Stone Hall Rd. N21 99 DM45
Stone Ho. Ct. EC3 275 N8
Stone Ness Rd., Grays 169 FV79

Stone Pk. Ave., Beck. 203 EA98
Stone Pl., Wor.Pk. 199 CU103
Stone Pl. Rd., Green. 189 FS85
Stone Rd., Brom. 204 EF99
Stone St., Croy. 219 DN106
Stone St., Grav. 191 GH86
Stonebanks, Walt. 195 BU101
Stonebridge Common E8 142 DT66
Mayfield Rd.
Stonebridge Fld., Wind. 151 AP78
Stonebridge Flds., Guil. 258 AX141
Stonebridge Pk. NW10 138 CR66
Stonebridge Rd. N15 122 DT57
Stonebridge Rd., Grav. 190 GA85
Stonebridge Way, Wem. 138 CP65
Stonebridge Wf., Guil. 258 AX141
Stonechat Sq. E6 144 EL71
Peridot St.
Stonecot Clo., Sutt. 199 CY102
Stonecot Hill, Sutt. 199 CY102
Stonecourt Clo., Horl. 269 DJ148
Stonecroft Ave., Iver 133 BE72
Stonecroft Clo., Barn. 79 CV42
Stonecroft Rd., Erith 167 FC80
Stonecroft Way, Croy. 201 DL101
Stonecrop Rd., Guil. 243 BC132
Kingfisher Dr.
Stonecross, St.Alb. 43 CE19
Stonecross Clo., St.Alb. 43 CE19
Stonecross
Stonecross Rd., Hat. 45 CV16
Stonecutter Ct. EC4 141 DP72
Stonecutter St.
Stonecutter St. EC4 274 F8
Stonecutter St. EC4 141 DP72
Stonefield Clo., Bexh. 166 FA83
Stonefield Clo., Ruis. 116 BY64
Stonefield St. N1 141 DN67
Stonefield Way SE7 164 EK80
Greenbay Rd.
Stonefield Way, Ruis. 116 BY63
Stonegate Clo., Orp. 206 EW97
Main Rd.
Stonegrove, Edg. 96 CL49
Stonegrove Est., Edg. 96 CL49
Stonegrove Gdns., Edg. 96 CL50
Stonehall Ave., Ilf. 124 EL58
Stoneham Rd. N11 99 DJ50
Stonehill Clo. SW14 178 CR85
Stonehill Clo., Lthd. 246 CA125
Stonehill Grn. Rd., Dart. 187 FC94
Birchwood Rd.
Stonehill Rd. SW14 178 CQ85
Stonehill Rd. W4 158 CN78
Wellesley Rd.
Stonehill Rd., Cher. 210 AY107
Stonehill Rd., Wok. 210 AW108
Stonehill Wds. Caravan Pk., Sid. 187 FB93
Stonehills, Welw.G.C. 29 CX08
Stonehills Ct. SE21 182 DS90
Stonehorse Rd., Enf. 82 DW43
Stonehouse Gdns., Cat. 252 DS125
Stonehouse La., Purf. 169 FS79
Stonehouse La., Sev. 224 EX109
Stonehouse Rd., Sev. 224 EW110
Stoneings La., Sev. 239 ET118
Stonelea Rd., Hem.H. 40 BM23
Stoneleigh Ave., Enf. 82 DV38
Stoneleigh Ave., Wor.Pk. 199 CU104
Stoneleigh Clo., Wal.Cr. 67 DX33
Stoneleigh Cres., Epsom 217 CT106
Stoneleigh Dr., Hodd. 33 EB14
Stoneleigh Pk., Wey. 213 BQ106
Stoneleigh Pk. Ave., Croy. 203 DX100
Stoneleigh Pk. Rd., Epsom 217 CT107
Stoneleigh Pl. W11 139 CX73
Stoneleigh Rd. N17 122 DT55
Stoneleigh Rd., Cars. 200 DE101
Stoneleigh Rd., Ilf. 124 EL55
Stoneleigh Rd., Oxt. 254 EL130
Stoneleigh St. W11 139 CX73
Stoneleigh Ter. N19 121 DH61
Dartmouth Pk. Hill
Stonells Rd. SW11 180 DF85
Chatham Rd.
Stonenest St. N4 121 DM60
Stones All., Wat. 75 BV42
Exchange Rd.
Stones Cross Rd., Swan. 207 FC99
Stones End St. SE1 279 H5
Stones End St. SE1 162 DQ75
Stones La., Dor. 262 CC137
Stones Rd., Epsom 216 CS112
Stoneswood Rd., Oxt. 254 EH130
Stonewall E6 145 EN71
Stonewood, Dart. 189 FW90
Stonewood Rd., Erith 167 FE78
Stoney All. SE18 165 EN82
Stoney Brook, Guil. 242 AS133
Stoney Cft., Hem.H. 40 BG20
Stoney Cft., Welw.G.C. 30 DA08
Stoney Gro., Chesh. 54 AR30
Stoney La. E1 275 P8
Stoney La. SE19 182 DT93
Church Rd.
Stoney La., Hem.H. 57 BB27
Stoney La., Kings L. 57 BE30
Stoney La., Slou. 131 AN67
Stoney Meade, Slou. 131 AP74
Weekes Dr.
Stoney St. SE1 279 K2
Stoney St. SE1 142 DR74
Stoneyard La. E14 143 EB73
Poplar High St.
Stoneycroft, Hem.H. 40 BG20
Long Chaulden
Stoneycroft Clo. SE12 184 EF87
Stoneycroft Rd., Wdf.Grn. 102 EL51
Stoneydeep, Tedd. 177 CG91
Twickenham Rd.
Stoneydown E17 123 DY56
Stoneydown Ave. E17 123 DY56
Stoneyfield Rd., Couls. 235 DM117
Stoneyfields Gdns., Edg. 96 CQ49
Stoneyfields La., Edg. 96 CQ50
Stoneylands Ct., Egh. 173 AZ92
Stoneylands Rd., Egh. 173 AZ92
Stonhouse St. SW4 161 DK83
Stonny Cft., Ash. 232 CM117
Stonor Rd. W14 159 CZ77
Stony La., Amer. 72 AY38
Stony Path, Loug. 85 EM39
Stony Wd., Harl. 51 ES16
Stonycroft Clo., Enf. 83 DY40
Brimsdown Ave.
Stonyrock La., Dor. 246 BY134
Stonyshotts, Wal.Abb. 68 EE34
Stoop Ct., W.Byf. 212 BH112
Stopford Rd. E13 144 EG67
Stopford Rd. SE17 161 DP78
Store Gdns., Brwd. 109 GD43
Store Rd. E16 165 EN75
Store St. E15 123 ED64
Store St. WC1 273 M7
Store St. WC1 141 DK71
Storers Quay E14 163 ED77
Storey Rd. E17 123 DZ56
Storey Rd. N6 120 DF58
Storey St. E16 145 EN74
Storey St., Hem.H. 40 BK24
Storey's Gate SW1 277 N5
Storey's Gate SW1 161 DK75
Stories Ms. SE5 162 DS82
Stories Rd. SE5 162 DS83
Stork Rd. E7 144 EF65
Storks Rd. SE16 162 DU76
Storksmead Rd., Edg. 96 CS52
Stormont Rd. N6 120 DF59
Stormont Rd. SW11 160 DG83
Stormont Way, Chess. 215 CJ106
Stormount Dr., Hayes 155 BQ75
Stornaway Strand, Grav. 191 GM91
Stornoway, Hem.H. 41 BP22
Storr Gdns., Brwd. 109 GD43
Storrington Rd., Croy. 202 DT102
Stort Mill, Harl. 36 EV09
Stort Twr., Harl. 35 ET13
Stortford Rd., Hodd. 49 EB16
Story St. N1 141 DM66
Carnoustie Dr.
Stothard Pl. EC2 142 DS71
Bishopsgate
Stothard St. E1 142 DW70
Colebert Ave.
Stoughton Ave., Sutt. 217 CX106
Stoughton Clo. SE11 278 C9
Stoughton Clo. SW15 179 CU88
Bessborough Rd.
Stoughton Rd., Guil. 242 AU131
Stour Ave., Sthl. 156 CA76
Stour Clo., Kes. 222 EJ105
Stour Clo., Slou. 151 AP76
Stour Rd. E3 143 EA66
Stour Rd., Dag. 126 FA61
Stour Rd., Dart. 167 FG83
Stour Rd., Grays 171 GG78
Stour Way, Upmin. 129 FS58
Stourcliffe St. W1 272 D9
Stourcliffe St. W1 140 DF72
Stourhead Clo. SW19 179 CX87
Castlecombe Dr.
Stourhead Gdns. SW20 199 CU97
Stourton Ave., Felt. 176 BZ91
Stovell Rd., Wind. 151 AP80
Stow, The, Harl. 35 ET13
Stow Cres. E17 101 DY52
Stowage SE8 163 EA79
Stowe Ct., Dart. 188 FQ87
Stowe Cres., Ruis. 115 BP58
Stowe Gdns. N9 100 DT46
Latymer Rd.
Stowe Pl. N15 122 DS55
Stowe Rd. W12 159 CV75
Stowe Rd., Orp. 224 EV105
Stowe Rd., Slou. 131 AL73
Stowell Ave., Croy. 221 ED109
Stowting Rd., Orp. 223 ES105
Stox Mead, Har. 95 CD53
Stracey Rd. E7 124 EG63
Stracey Rd. NW10 138 CR67
Strachan Pl. SW19 179 CW93
Woodhayes Rd.
Stradbroke Dr., Chig. 103 EN51
Stradbroke Gro., Buck.H. 102 EK46
Stradbroke Gro., Ilf. 124 EL55
Stradbroke Pk., Chig. 103 EP51
Stradbroke Rd. N5 122 DQ63
Stradella Rd. SE24 182 DQ86
Strafford Ave., Ilf. 103 EN54
Strafford Clo., Pot.B. 64 DA32
Strafford Gate
Strafford Gate, Pot.B. 64 DA32
Strafford Rd. W3 158 CQ75
Strafford Rd., Barn. 79 CY41
Strafford Rd., Houns. 156 BZ83
Strafford Rd., Twick. 177 CG87
Strafford St. E14 163 EA75
Strahan Rd. E3 143 DY69
Straight, The, Sthl. 156 BX75
Straight Bit, H.Wyc. 110 AC55
Straight Rd., Rom. 105 FH50
Straight Rd., Wind. 172 AU85
Straightsmouth SE10 163 EC80
Strait Rd. E6 144 EL73
Straker's Rd. SE15 162 DV84
Strand WC2 277 P1
Strand WC2 141 DL73
Strand Clo., Epsom 232 CR119
Strand La. WC2 274 C10
Strand on the Grn. W4 158 CN79
Strand Pl. N18 100 DS49
Silver St.
Strand Sch. App. W4 158 CN79
Thames Rd.
Strandfield Clo. SE18 165 ES78
Strangeways, Wat. 75 BS36
Strangways Ter. W14 159 CZ76
Melbury Rd.
Stranraer Gdns., Slou. 132 AS74
Stranraer Rd., Houns. 174 BL86
Stranraer Way N1 141 DL66
Strasburg Rd. SW11 161 DH81
Stratfield Dr., Brox. 49 DY19
Stratfield Pk. Clo. N21 99 DP45
Stratfield Rd., Borwd. 78 CM41
Stratfield Rd., Slou. 152 AU75
Stratford Ave. W8 160 DA76
Stratford Rd.
Stratford Ave., Uxb. 134 BM68
Stratford Cen., The E15 143 ED66
Broadway
Stratford Clo., Bark. 146 EU66
Stratford Clo., Dag. 147 FC66
Stratford Clo., Slou. 131 AK70
Stratford Ct., N.Mal. 198 CR98
Kingston Rd.
Stratford Dr., H.Wyc. 110 AD59
Stratford Gro. SW15 159 CX84
Stratford Ho. Ave., Brom. 204 EL97
Stratford Mkt. E15 143 ED67
Bridge Rd.
Stratford Pl. W1 273 H9
Stratford Pl. W1 141 DH72
Stratford Rd. E13 144 EF67
Stratford Rd. W3 158 CQ75
Bollo Bri. Rd.
Stratford Rd. W8 160 DA76
Stratford Rd., Hayes 135 BV70
Stratford Rd., Houns. 175 BP86
Stratford Rd., Sthl. 156 BY77
Stratford Rd., Th.Hth. 201 DN98
Stratford Rd., Wat. 75 BU40
Stratford Vill. NW1 141 DJ66
Stratford Way, Hem.H. 40 BH23
Stratford Way, St.Alb. 60 BZ29
Stratford Way, Wat. 75 BT40
Strath Ter. SW11 160 DE84
Strathan Clo. SW18 179 CY86
Strathaven Rd. SE12 184 EH86
Strathblaine Rd. SW11 180 DD85
Strathbrook Rd. SW16 181 DM94
Strathcona Ave., Lthd. 246 BY128
Strathcona Clo., H.Wyc. 110 AC56
Strathcona Rd., Wem. 117 CK61
Strathcona Way, H.Wyc. 110 AC56
Strathdale SW16 181 DM92
Strathdon Dr. SW17 180 DD90
Strathearn Ave., Hayes 155 BT80
Strathearn Ave., Twick. 176 CB88
Strathearn Pl. W2 272 B10
Strathearn Pl. W2 140 DE73
Strathearn Rd. SW19 180 DA92
Strathearn Rd., Sutt. 218 DA106
Stratheden Par. SE3 164 EG80
Stratheden Rd.
Stratheden Rd. SE3 164 EG81
Strathfield Gdns., Bark. 145 ER65
Strathleven Rd. SW2 161 DL84
Strathmore Clo., Cat. 236 DS121
Strathmore Gdns. N3 98 DB53
Strathmore Gdns. W8 140 DA74
Palace Gdns. Ter.
Strathmore Gdns., Edg. 96 CP54
Strathmore Gdns., Horn. 127 FF60
Strathmore Rd. SW19 180 DA90
Strathmore Rd., Croy. 202 DQ101
Strathmore Rd., Tedd. 177 CE91
Strathnairn St. SE1 162 DU77
Strathray Gdns. NW3 140 DE65
Strathville Rd. SW18 180 DA89
Strathyre Ave. SW16 201 DN97
Stratton Ave., Enf. 82 DR37
Stratton Ave., Wall. 219 DK109
Stratton Chase Dr., Ch.St.G. 90 AU46
Stratton Clo. SW19 200 DA96
Stratton Clo., Bexh. 166 EY83
Stratton Clo., Edg. 96 CM51
Stratton Clo., Houns. 156 BZ81
Stratton Clo., Walt. 196 BW102
St. Johns Dr.
Stratton Dr., Bark. 125 ET64
Stratton Gdns., Sthl. 136 BZ72
Stratton Rd. SW19 200 DA96
Stratton Rd., Beac. 88 AH53
Stratton Rd., Bexh. 166 EY83
Stratton Rd., Rom. 106 FN50
Stratton Rd., Sun. 195 BT96
Stratton St. W1 277 J2
Stratton St. W1 141 DH74
Stratton Ter., West. 255 EQ127
High St.
Stratton Wk., Rom. 106 FN50
Strattondale St. E14 163 EC76
Strauss Rd. W4 158 CR75
Straw Clo., Cat. 236 DQ121
Coulsdon Rd.
Strawberry Fld., Hat. 45 CU21
Strawberry Flds., Swan. 207 FE95
Strawberry Hill, Twick. 177 CF90
Strawberry Hill Clo., Twick. 177 CF91
Strawberry Hill Rd., Twick. 177 CF90
Strawberry La., Cars. 200 DF104
Strawberry Vale N2 98 DD53
Strawberry Vale, Twick. 177 CF90
Strawfields, Welw.G.C. 30 DB08
Strawmead, Hat. 45 CV16
Cob Mead
Strayfield Rd., Enf. 81 DP37
Streakes Fld. Rd. NW2 119 CU61
Stream Clo., W.Byf. 212 BK112
Stream La., Edg. 96 CP50
Stream Way, Belv. 166 EZ79
Streamdale SE2 166 EU79
Streamside Clo. N9 100 DT46
Streamside Clo., Brom. 204 EG98
Streatfield Ave. E6 145 EM67
Streatfield Rd., Har. 118 CL55
Streatham Clo. SW16 181 DL90
Streatham Common N. SW16 181 DL92
Streatham Common S. SW16 181 DL93
Streatham Ct. SW16 181 DL90
Streatham High Rd. SW16 181 DL92
Streatham Hill SW2 181 DL89
Streatham Pl. SW2 181 DL87
Streatham Rd. SW16 200 DG95
Streatham Rd., Mitch. 200 DG95
Streatham St. WC1 273 P8
Streatham Vale SW16 201 DJ95
Streathbourne Rd. SW17 180 DG89
Streatley Pl. NW3 120 DC63
New End Sq.
Streatley Rd. NW6 139 CZ66
Street, The, Ash. 232 CM118
Street, The, Bet. 248 CS134
Street, The, B.Stort. 37 FB07
Street, The, Dart. 208 FQ98
Street, The (Albury), Guil. 260 BJ139
Street, The (East Clandon), Guil. 244 BK131
Street, The (Shalford), Guil. 258 AX139
Street, The (West Clandon), Guil. 244 BG128
Street, The (Wonersh), Guil. 259 BA144
Street, The, Kings L. 58 BG31
Street, The, Lthd. 231 CD121
Street, The (Effingham), Lthd. 246 BX127
Street, The (West Horsley), Lthd. 245 BP130
Streeters La., Wall. 201 DK104
Streetfield Ms. SE3 164 EG83
Streimer Rd. E15 143 EC68
Strelley Way W3 138 CS73
Stretton Pl., Amer. 72 AT38
Stretton Rd., Croy. 202 DS101
Stretton Rd., Rich. 177 CJ89
Stretton Way, Borwd. 78 CL38
Strickland Ave., Dart. 168 FM83
Strickland Rd., Belv. 166 FA77
Strickland Row SW18 180 DD87
Strickland St. SE8 163 EA81
Strickland Way, Orp. 223 ET105
Stride Rd. E13 144 EF68
Stringers Ave., Guil. 242 AW128
Stringer's Common, Guil. 242 AW129
Stringhams Copse, Wok. 227 BF124
Stripling Way, Wat. 75 BU44
Strode Clo. N10 98 DG52
Pembroke Rd.
Strode Rd. E7 124 EG63
Strode Rd. N17 100 DS54
Strode Rd. NW10 139 CU65
Strode Rd. SW6 159 CY80
Strode St., Egh. 173 BA91
Strodes College La., Egh. 173 AZ92
Strodes Cres., Stai. 174 BJ92
Stroma Clo., Hem.H. 41 BQ22
Stroma Ct., Slou. 131 AK73
Lincoln Way
Strone Rd. E7 144 EJ65
Strone Rd. E12 144 EK65
Strone Way, Hayes 136 BY70
Strongbow Cres. SE9 185 EM85
Strongbow Rd. SE9 185 EM85
Strongbridge Clo., Har. 116 CA60
Stronsa Rd. W12 159 CT75
Stronsay Clo., Hem.H. 41 BQ22
Northend
Strood Ave., Rom. 127 FD60
Stroud Clo., Wind. 151 AK83
Stroud Cres. SW15 179 CU90
Stroud Fld., Nthlt. 136 BY65
Stroud Gate, Har. 116 CB63
Stroud Grn. Gdns., Croy. 202 DW101
Stroud Grn. Rd. N4 121 DM60
Stroud Grn. Way, Croy. 202 DV101
Stroud Rd. SE25 202 DU100
Stroud Rd. SW19 180 DA90
Stroud Way, Ashf. 175 BP93
Courtfield Rd.
Stroude Rd., Egh. 193 BA96
Stroude Rd., Vir.W. 192 AY98
Stroudes Clo., Wor.Pk. 198 CS101
Stroudley Wk. E3 143 EB69
Stroudwater Pk., Wey. 213 BP107
Strouts Pl. E2 275 P2
Strutton Grd. SW1 277 M6
Strutton Grd. SW1 161 DK76
Struttons Ave., Grav. 191 GF89
Strype St. E1 275 P7
Stuart Ave. NW9 119 CU59
Stuart Ave. W5 138 CM74
Stuart Ave., Brom. 204 EG102
Stuart Ave., Har. 116 BZ62
Stuart Ave., Walt. 195 BV102
Stuart Clo., Brwd. 108 FV43
Stuart Clo., Swan. 187 FF94
Stuart Clo., Uxb. 134 BN65
Stuart Clo., Wind. 151 AM82
Stuart Ct. (Elstree), Borwd. 77 CK44
High St.
Stuart Cres. N22 99 DM53
Stuart Cres., Croy. 221 DZ105
Stuart Cres., Hayes 135 BQ72
Stuart Cres., Reig. 266 DA137
Stuart Evans Clo., Well. 166 EW83
Stuart Gro., Tedd. 177 CE92
Stuart Mantle Way, Erith 167 FD80
Stuart Pl., Mitch. 200 DF95
Stuart Rd. NW6 140 DA69
Stuart Rd. SE15 162 DW84
Stuart Rd. SW19 180 DA90
Stuart Rd. W3 138 CQ74
Stuart Rd., Bark. 145 ET66
Stuart Rd., Barn. 98 DE45
Stuart Rd., Grav. 191 GG86
Stuart Rd., Grays 170 GB78
Stuart Rd., Har. 117 CF55
Stuart Rd., Reig. 266 DA137
Stuart Rd., Rich. 177 CH89
Stuart Rd., Th.Hth. 202 DQ98
Stuart Rd., Warl. 236 DV120
Stuart Rd., Well. 166 EV81
Stuart Twr. W9 140 DC69
Stuart Way, Stai. 174 BH93
Stuart Way, Vir.W. 192 AU97
Stuart Way (Cheshunt), Wal.Cr. 66 DV31
Stuart Way, Wind. 151 AL82
Stuarts Clo., Hem.H. 40 BK22
Marriots Way
Stubbers La., Upmin. 149 FR65
Stubbings Hall La., Wal.Abb. 67 EB28
Stubbs Dr. SE16 162 DV78
Stubbs End Clo., Amer. 55 AS37
Stubbs Hill, Sev. 224 EW113
Stubbs La., Tad. 249 CZ128
Stubbs Ms., Dag. 126 EV63
Marlborough Rd.
Stubbs Pt. E13 144 EG70
Stubbs Way SW19 200 DD95
Brangwyn Cres.
Stubbs Wd., Amer. 55 AS36
Stubs Clo., Dor. 263 CJ138
Stubs Hill
Stubs Hill, Dor. 263 CJ138
Stucley Pl. NW1 141 DH66
Hawley Cres.
Stucley Rd., Houns. 156 CC80
Stud Grn., Wat. 59 BV32
Studd St. N1 141 DP67
Studdridge St. SW6 160 DA82
Studholme Ct. NW3 120 DA63
Studholme St. SE15 162 DV80
Studio Ct., Borwd. 78 CQ40
Studio Pl. SW1 276 E5
Studio Way, Borwd. 78 CQ40
Studios, The (Bushey), Wat. 76 CA44
Studios Rd., Shep. 194 BM97
Studland SE17 279 K10
Studland Clo., Sid. 185 ET90
Studland Rd. SE26 183 DX92
Studland Rd. W7 137 CD72
Studland Rd., Kings.T. 178 CL93
Studland Rd., W.Byf. 212 BM113
Studland St. W6 159 CV77
Studley Ave. E4 101 ED52
Studley Clo. E5 123 DY64
Studley Ct., Sid. 186 EV92
Studley Dr., Ilf. 124 EK58
Studley Est. SW4 161 DL81
Studley Gra. Rd. W7 157 CE75
Studley Rd. E7 144 EH65
Studley Rd. SW4 161 DL81
Studley Rd., Dag. 146 EX66
Stukeley Rd. E7 144 EH66
Stukeley St. WC2 274 A8
Stukeley St. WC2 141 DL72
Stumps Hill La., Beck. 183 EA93
Stumps La., Whyt. 236 DS117
Stumpwell La., H.Wyc. 88 AE48
Sturdy Rd. SE15 162 DV82
Sturge Ave. E17 101 EB53
Sturge St. SE1 279 H4
Sturgeon Rd. SE17 161 DP78
Sturges Fld., Chis. 185 ER93
Sturgess Ave. NW4 119 CU59
Sturlas Way, Wal.Cr. 67 DX33
Sturmer Clo., St.Alb. 43 CJ21
Sturmer Way N7 121 DM64
Stock Orchard Cres.
Sturminster Clo., Hayes 136 BW72
Sturrock Clo. N15 122 DR56
Sturry St. E14 143 EB72
Sturt Ct., Guil. 243 BC132
Ashbury Cres.
Sturt St. N1 275 J1
Sturt St. N1 142 DQ68
Sturts La., Tad. 249 CT127
Stutfield St. E1 142 DU72
Stychens Clo., Red. 252 DQ133
Stychens La., Red. 252 DQ132
Stylecroft Rd., Ch.St.G. 90 AX47
Styles End, Lthd. 246 CB127
Styles Gdns. SW9 161 DP83
Styles Way, Beck. 203 EC98
Styventon Pl., Cher. 193 BF101
Succombs Hill, Warl. 236 DV120
Succombs Hill, Whyt. 236 DV120
Succombs Pl., Warl. 236 DV120
Sudbourne Rd. SW2 181 DL85
Sudbrook Gdns., Rich. 178 CL90
Sudbrook La., Rich. 178 CL88
Sudbrooke Rd. SW12 180 DF86
Sudbury E6 145 EN72
Newark Knok
Sudbury Ave., Wem. 117 CJ64
Sudbury Ct. E5 123 DY63
Sudbury Ct. Dr., Har. 117 CF62
Sudbury Ct. Rd., Har. 117 CF62
Sudbury Cres., Brom. 184 EG93
Sudbury Cres., Wem. 117 CH64
Sudbury Cft., Wem. 117 CF63
Sudbury Gdns., Croy. 220 DS105
Langton Way
Sudbury Heights Ave., Grnf. 117 CF64
Sudbury Hill, Har. 117 CE61
Sudbury Hill Clo., Wem. 117 CF63
Sudbury Rd., Bark. 125 ET64
Sudeley St. N1 274 G1
Sudeley St. N1 141 DP68
Sudicamps Ct., Wal.Abb. 68 EG33
Sudlow Rd. SW18 180 DA85
Sudrey St. SE1 279 H5
Suez Ave., Grnf. 137 CF68
Suez Rd., Enf. 83 DY42
Suffield Clo., S.Croy. 221 DX112
Suffield Rd. E4 101 EB48
Suffield Rd. N15 122 DT57
Suffield Rd. SE20 202 DW96
Suffolk Clo., Borwd. 78 CR43
Clydesdale Clo.
Suffolk Clo., Horl. 268 DG149
Suffolk Clo., St.Alb. 61 CJ25
Suffolk Clo., Slou. 131 AL72
Suffolk Ct. E10 123 EA59
Suffolk Ct., Ilf. 125 ES58
Suffolk Dr., Guil. 243 BB129
Suffolk La. EC4 275 K10
Suffolk Pk. Rd. E17 123 DY56
Suffolk Pl. SW1 277 N2
Suffolk Rd. E13 144 EG69
Suffolk Rd. N15 122 DR58
Suffolk Rd. NW10 138 CS66
Suffolk Rd. SE25 202 DT98
Suffolk Rd. SW13 159 CT80
Suffolk Rd., Bark. 145 ER66
Suffolk Rd., Dag. 127 FC64
Suffolk Rd., Dart. 188 FL86
Suffolk Rd., Enf. 82 DV43
Suffolk Rd., Grav. 191 GK86
Suffolk Rd., Har. 116 BZ58
Suffolk Rd., Ilf. 125 ES58
Suffolk Rd., Pot.B. 63 CY32
Suffolk Rd., Sid. 186 EW93
Suffolk Rd., Wor.Pk. 199 CT103
Suffolk St. E7 124 EG64
Suffolk St. SW1 277 N1
Suffolk Way, Horn. 128 FN56
Suffolk Way, Sev. 257 FJ125
Sugar Bakers Ct. EC3 275 N9
Sugar Ho. La. E15 143 EC68
Sugar La., Berk. 39 AZ22
Sugar La., Hem.H. 39 BB22
Sugar Loaf Wk. E2 142 DW69
Victoria Pk. Sq.
Sugar Quay Wk. EC3 142 DS73
Lower Thames St.
Sugden Rd. SW11 160 DG83
Sugden Rd., T.Ditt. 197 CH102
Sugden Way, Bark. 145 ET68
Sulgrave Gdns. W6 159 CW75
Sulgrave Rd.
Sulgrave Rd. W6 159 CW76
Sulina Rd. SW2 181 DL87
Sulivan Ct. SW6 160 DA82
Sulivan Rd. SW6 160 DA83
Sullivan Ave. E16 144 EK71
Sullivan Clo. SW11 160 DE83
Sullivan Clo., Dart. 187 FH86

Sullivan Clo., W.Mol. 196 CA97
Victoria Ave.
Sullivan Cres., Uxb. 92 BK54
Sullivan Rd. SE11 278 E8
Sullivan Rd. SE11 161 DN77
Sullivan Rd., Til. 171 GG81
Sullivan Way, Borwd. 77 CJ44
Sullivans Reach, Walt. 195 BT101
Sultan Rd. E11 124 EH56
Sultan St. SE5 162 DQ80
Sultan St., Beck. 203 DX96
Sumatra Rd. NW6 120 DA64
Sumburgh Rd. SW12 180 DG86
Sumburgh Spur, Slou. 132 AS71
Summer Ave., E.Mol. 197 CE99
Summer Clo., Lthd. 231 CD124
Summer Ct., Hem.H. 40 BK18
Townsend
Summer Gdns., E.Mol. 197 CE99
Summer Gro., Borwd. 77 CK44
Summer Hill, Borwd. 78 CN43
Summer Hill, Chis. 205 EN96
Summer Hill Vill., Chis. 205 EN95
Summer Ho. Rd. N16 122 DS61
Stoke Newington Ch. St.
Summer Rd., E.Mol. 197 CE99
Summer Rd., T.Ditt. 197 CF99
Summer St. EC1 274 D5
Summer Trees, Sun. 195 BV95
The Ave.
Summercourt Rd. E1 142 DW72
Summerdale, Welw.G.C. 29 CX05
Summerdene Clo. SW16 181 DJ94
Bates Cres.
Summerfield, Ash. 231 CK119
Summerfield, Hat. 45 CU21
Summerfield Ave. NW6 139 CY68
Summerfield Clo., Add. 211 BF106
Spinney Hill
Summerfield Clo., St.Alb. 61 CJ26
Summerfield La., Surb. 197 CK103
Summerfield Pl., Cher. 211 BD107
Crawshaw Rd.
Summerfield Rd. W5 137 CH70
Summerfield Rd., Loug. 84 EK44
Summerfield Rd., Wat. 75 BU35
Summerfield St. SE12 184 EF87
Summerfields Ave. N12 98 DE51
Summerhayes Clo., Wok. 210 AY114
Summerhays, Cob. 214 BX113
Summerhill Clo., Orp. 205 ES104
Summerhill Ct., St.Alb. 43 CF19
Avenue Rd.
Summerhill Gro., Enf. 82 DS44
Summerhill Rd. N15 122 DR56
Summerhill Rd., Dart. 188 FK87
Summerhill Way, Mitch. 200 DG95
Summerhouse Ave., Houns. 156 BY81
Summerhouse Dr., Bex. 187 FD91
Summerhouse Dr., Dart. 187 FD92
Summerhouse La., Uxb. 92 BG52
Summerhouse La., Wat. 76 CC40
Summerhouse La., West Dr. 154 BK79
Summerhouse La. Ind. Est., Uxb. 92 BG51
Summerhouse Way, Abb.L. 59 BT30
Summerland Gdns. N10 121 DH55
Summerlands Ave. W3 138 CQ73
Summerlands Rd., St.Alb. 43 CJ16
Summerlay Clo., Tad. 233 CY120
Summerlea, Slou. 131 AP74
Summerlee Ave. N2 120 DF56
Summerlee Gdns. N2 120 DF56
Summerley St. SW18 180 DB89
Summerly Ave., Reig. 250 DA133
Burnham Dr.
Summers Clo., Sutt. 218 DA108
Overton Rd.
Summers Clo., Wem. 118 CP60
Summers Clo., Wey. 212 BN111
Summers La. N12 98 DD52
Summers Rd., Gdmg. 258 AT144
Summers Rd., Slou. 130 AJ69
Summers Row N12 98 DE51
Summersbury Dr., Guil. 258 AY142
Summersby Rd. N6 121 DH58
Summerstown SW17 180 DC90
Summerswood Clo., Ken. 236 DR116
Longwood Rd.
Summerswood La., Borwd. 78 CS35
Summerton Way SE28 146 EX73
Summerville Gdns., Sutt. 217 CZ107
Summerwood Rd., Islw. 177 CF85
Summit, The, Loug. 85 EM39
Summit Ave. NW9 118 CR57
Summit Clo. N14 99 DJ47
Summit Clo. NW9 118 CR56
Summit Clo., Edg. 96 CN52
Summit Ct. NW2 119 CY64
Summit Dr., Wdf.Grn. 102 EK54
Summit Est. N16 122 DU59
Summit Pl., Wey. 212 BN108
Caenshill Rd.
Summit Rd. E17 123 EB56
Summit Rd., Nthlt. 136 CA66
Summit Rd., Pot.B. 63 CY30
Summit Way N14 99 DH47
Summit Way SE19 182 DS94
Sumner Ave. SE15 162 DT81
Sumner Rd.
Sumner Clo., Orp. 223 EQ105
Sumner Est. SE15 162 DT80
Sumner Gdns., Croy. 201 DN102
Sumner Pl. SW7 276 A9
Sumner Pl. SW7 160 DD77
Sumner Pl., Add. 212 BG106
Sumner Pl. Ms. SW7 276 A9
Sumner Rd. SE15 162 DT80
Sumner Rd., Croy. 201 DN102
Sumner Rd., Har. 116 CC59
Sumner Rd. S., Croy. 201 DN102
Sumner St. SE1 278 G2
Sumner St. SE1 141 DP74
Sumners Fm. Clo., Harl. 51 EN20
Sumpter Clo. NW3 140 DC65
Sumpter Yd., St.Alb. 43 CD20
Sun Ct. EC3 275 L9
Sun Ct., Erith 167 FF82
Sun Hill (Fawkham Grn.), Long. 209 FU103
Sun Hill, Wok. 226 AV121
Sun La. SE3 164 EH80
Sun La., Grav. 191 GJ89
Sun Pas. SE16 162 DU76
Frean St.
Sun Pas., Wind. 151 AR81
Peascod St.
Sun Ray Ave., Brwd. 109 GE44
Sun Rd. W14 159 CZ78
Sun Rd., Swans. 190 FZ86
Sun Sq., Hem.H. 40 BK19
High St.
Sun St. EC2 275 L6
Sun St. EC2 142 DR71
Sun St., Saw. 36 EZ06
Sun St., Wal.Abb. 67 EC33
Sun St. Pas. EC2 275 M7
Sun Wk. E1 142 DU74
Mews St.
Sunbeam Cres. W10 139 CW70
Sunbeam Rd. NW10 138 CR70
Sunbury Ave. NW7 96 CR50
Sunbury Ave. SW14 158 CR84
Sunbury Ct., Sun. 196 BX96
Sunbury Ct. Island, Sun. 196 BX96
Sunbury Ct. Ms., Sun. 196 BX96
Lower Hampton Rd.
Sunbury Ct. Rd., Sun. 196 BW96
Sunbury Cres., Felt. 175 BT91
Ryland Clo.
Sunbury Gdns. NW7 96 CR50
Sunbury La. SW11 160 DD81
Sunbury La., Walt. 195 BU100
Sunbury Rd., Felt. 175 BT90
Sunbury Rd., Sutt. 199 CX104
Sunbury Rd. (Eton), Wind. 151 AR79
Sunbury St. SE18 165 EM76
Sunbury Way, Felt. 176 BW92
Suncroft Pl. SE26 182 DW90
Sundale Ave., S.Croy. 220 DW110
Sunderland Ave., St.Alb. 43 CG19
Sunderland Ct. SE22 182 DU87
Sunderland Mt. SE23 183 DX89
Sunderland Rd.
Sunderland Rd. SE23 183 DX88
Sunderland Rd. W5 157 CK76
Sunderland Ter. W2 140 DB72
Sunderland Way E12 124 EK61
Sundew Ave. W12 139 CU73
Sundew Ct., Grays 170 GD79
Salix Rd.
Sundew Rd., Hem.H. 39 BE21
Sundial Ave. SE25 202 DT97
Sundon Cres., Vir.W. 192 AV99
Sundorne Rd. SE7 164 EH78
Sundown Ave., S.Croy. 220 DT111
Sundown Rd., Ashf. 175 BQ92
Sundra Wk. E1 143 DX70
Beaumont Gro.
Sundridge Ave., Brom. 204 EK96
Sundridge Ave., Chis. 184 EL94
Sundridge Ave., Well. 165 ER82
Sundridge Clo., Dart. 188 FN86
Sundridge Ho., Brom. 184 EH92
Burnt Ash La.
Sundridge La., Sev. 240 EV117
Sundridge Pl., Croy. 202 DU102
Inglis Rd.
Sundridge Rd., Croy. 202 DT101
Sundridge Rd., Sev. 240 FA120
Sundridge Rd., Wok. 227 BA119
Sunfields Pl. SE3 164 EH80
Sunflower Way, Rom. 106 FK53
Sunkist Way, Wall. 219 DL109
Sunland Ave., Bexh. 166 EY84
Sunleigh Rd., Wem. 138 CL67
Sunley Gdns., Grnf. 137 CG67
Sunmead Clo., Lthd. 231 CF122
Sunmead Rd., Hem.H. 40 BK18
Sunmead Rd., Sun. 195 BU97
Sunna Gdns., Sun. 195 BV96
Sunning Hill, Grav. 190 GE89
Sunningdale N14 99 DK50
Wilmer Way
Sunningdale Ave. W3 138 CS73
Sunningdale Ave., Bark. 145 ER67
Sunningdale Ave., Felt. 176 BY89
Sunningdale Ave., Rain. 147 FH70
Sunningdale Ave., Ruis. 116 BW60
Sunningdale Clo. E6 145 EM69
Ascot Rd.
Sunningdale Clo. SE16 162 DV78
Ryder Dr.
Sunningdale Clo. SE28 146 EX72
Summerton Way
Sunningdale Clo., Stan. 95 CG52
Sunningdale Clo., Surb. 198 CL103
Culsac Rd.
Sunningdale Gdns. NW9 118 CQ57
Sunningdale Gdns. W8 160 DA76
Lexham Ms.
Sunningdale Ms., Welw.G.C. 29 CY05
Sunningdale Rd., Brom. 204 EL98
Sunningdale Rd., Rain. 147 FG66
Sunningdale Rd., Sutt. 217 CZ105
Sunningfields Cres. NW4 97 CV54
Sunningfields Rd. NW4 119 CV55
Sunninghill Rd. SE13 163 EB82
Sunnings La., Upmin. 128 FQ64
Sunningvale Ave., West. 238 EJ115
Sunningvale Clo., West. 238 EK116
Sunny Bank SE25 202 DU97
Sunny Bank, Warl. 237 DY117
Sunny Cres. NW10 138 CQ66
Sunny Cft., Harl. 51 ET18
Sunny Gdns. Par. NW4 97 CW54
Great N. Way
Sunny Gdns. Rd. NW4 97 CV54
Sunny Hill NW4 119 CV55
Sunny Nook Gdns., S.Croy. 220 DR107
Selsdon Rd.
Sunny Ri., Cat. 236 DR124
Sunny Rd., The, Enf. 83 DX39
Sunny Side, Walt. 196 BW99
Sunny Vw. NW9 118 CR57
Sunny Way N12 98 DE52
Sunnybank, Epsom 232 CQ116
Sunnybank Rd., Pot.B. 64 DA33
Sunnybank Vill., Red. 252 DT132
Sunnycroft Gdns., Upmin. 129 FT59
Sunnycroft Rd. SE25 202 DU97
Sunnycroft Rd., Houns. 156 CB82
Sunnycroft Rd., Sthl. 136 CA71
Sunnydale, Orp. 205 EN103
Sunnydale Gdns. NW7 96 CR51
Sunnydale Rd. SE12 184 EH85
Sunnydell, St.Alb. 60 CB26
Sunnydene Ave. E4 101 ED50
Sunnydene Ave., Ruis. 115 BU60
Sunnydene Clo., Rom. 106 FM52
Sunnydene Gdns., Wem. 137 CJ65
Sunnydene Rd., Pur. 219 DP113
Sunnydene St. SE26 183 DY91
Sunnyfield NW7 97 CT49
Sunnyfield, Hat. 45 CX15
Sunnyfield Rd., Chis. 206 EU97
Sunnyhill Clo. E5 123 DY63
Sunnyhill Rd. SW16 181 DL91
Sunnyhill Rd., Hem.H. 40 BH20
Sunnyhill Rd., Rick. 91 BD51
Sunnyhurst Clo., Sutt. 200 DA104
Sunnymead Ave., Mitch. 201 DJ97
Sunnymead Rd. NW9 118 CR59
Sunnymead Rd. SW15 179 CV85
Sunnymede, Chig. 104 EV47
Sunnymede Ave., Cars. 218 DD111
Sunnymede Ave., Chesh. 54 AS28
Sunnymede Ave., Epsom 216 CS109
Sunnymede Dr., Ilf. 125 EP57
Sunnyside NW2 119 CZ62
Sunnyside SW19 179 CY93
Sunnyside, Wal.Abb. 50 EF22
Sunnyside Cotts., Chesh. 38 AT24
Two Dells La.
Sunnyside Dr. E4 101 EC45
Sunnyside Gdns., Upmin. 128 FQ61
Sunnyside Pas. SW19 179 CY93
Sunnyside Pl. SW19 179 CY93
Sunnyside
Sunnyside Rd. E10 123 EA60
Sunnyside Rd. N19 121 DK59
Sunnyside Rd. W5 137 CK74
Sunnyside Rd., Chesh. 54 AP30
Sunnyside Rd., Epp. 69 ET32
Sunnyside Rd., Ilf. 125 EQ62
Sunnyside Rd., Tedd. 177 CD91
Sunnyside Rd. E. N9 100 DU48
Sunnyside Rd. N. N9 100 DT48
Sunnyside Rd. S. N9 100 DT48
Sunray Ave. SE24 162 DR84
Sunray Ave., Brom. 204 EL100
Sunray Ave., Surb. 198 CP103
Sunray Ave., West Dr. 154 BK75
Sunrise Ave., Horn. 128 FJ61
Sunrise Clo., Felt. 176 BZ90
Exeter Rd.
Sunrise Cres., Hem.H. 40 BM23
Sunset Ave. E4 101 EB46
Sunset Ave., Wdf.Grn. 102 EF49
Sunset Clo., Erith 167 FH80
Sunset Dr. (Havering-atte-Bower), Rom. 105 FH50
Sunset Gdns. SE25 202 DT96
Sunset Rd. SE5 162 DQ84
Sunset Rd. SE28 146 EU74
Sunset Vw., Barn. 79 CY40
Sunshine Way, Mitch. 200 DF96
Sunstone Gro., Red. 251 DL129
Sunwell Clo. SE15 162 DV81
Cossall Wk.
Superior Dr., Orp. 223 ET107
Surbiton Ct., Surb. 197 CJ100
Surbiton Cres., Kings.T. 198 CL99
Surbiton Hall Clo., Kings.T. 198 CL98
Surbiton Hill Pk., Surb. 198 CM99
Surbiton Hill Rd., Surb. 198 CL98
Surbiton Par., Surb. 198 CL100
St. Mark's Hill
Surbiton Rd., Kings.T. 197 CK98
Surlingham Clo. SE28 146 EX73
Surly Hall Wk., Wind. 151 AM81
Surma Clo. E1 142 DU70
Surman Cres., Brwd. 109 GC45
Surr St. N7 121 DL64
Surrendale Pl. W9 140 DA70
Surrey Ave., Slou. 131 AQ71
Surrey Canal Rd. SE14 163 DX79
Surrey Canal Rd. SE15 162 DW79
Surrey Cres. W4 158 CN78
Surrey Dr., Horn. 128 FN56
Surrey Gdns. N4 122 DQ58
Surrey Gdns., Lthd. 229 BU122
Surrey Gro. SE17 162 DS78
Surrey Sq.
Surrey Gro., Sutt. 200 DD104
Surrey Hills, Tad. 248 CP130
Surrey Hills Ave., Tad. 248 CQ130
Surrey La. SW11 160 DE81
Surrey La. Est. SW11 160 DE81
Surrey Lo. SE1 278 D7
Surrey Ms. SE27 182 DS91
Hamilton Rd.
Surrey Mt. SE23 182 DV88
Surrey Quays Rd. SE16 162 DW76
Surrey Rd. SE15 183 DX85
Surrey Rd., Bark. 145 ES66
Surrey Rd., Dag. 127 FB64
Surrey Rd., Har. 116 CC57
Surrey Rd., W.Wick. 203 EB102
Surrey Row SE1 278 F4
Surrey Row SE1 161 DP75
Surrey Sq. SE17 279 M10
Surrey Sq. SE17 162 DS78
Surrey St. E13 144 EH69
Surrey St. WC2 274 C10
Surrey St. WC2 141 DM73
Surrey St., Croy. 202 DQ103
Surrey Ter. SE17 279 N10
Surrey Ter. SE17 162 DS77
Surrey Water Rd. SE16 143 DX74
Surridge Clo., Rain. 148 FJ69
Surridge Gdns. SE19 182 DR93
Hancock Rd.
Susan Clo., Rom. 127 FC55
Susan Rd. SE3 164 EH82
Susan Wd., Chis. 205 EN95
Susannah St. E14 143 EB72
Sussex Ave., Islw. 157 CE83
Sussex Ave., Rom. 106 FM52
Sussex Border Path, Horl. 268 DA152
Sussex Clo. N19 121 DL61
Cornwallis Rd.
Sussex Clo., Ch.St.G. 90 AV47
Sussex Clo., Hodd. 49 EA16
Roman St.
Sussex Clo., Ilf. 125 EM58
Sussex Clo., N.Mal. 198 CS98
Sussex Clo., Reig. 266 DD135
Sussex Clo., Slou. 152 AV75
Sussex Clo., Twick. 177 CH86
Westmorland Clo.
Sussex Cres., Nthlt. 136 CA65
Sussex Gdns. N4 122 DQ57
Sussex Gdns. N6 120 DF57
Great N. Rd.
Sussex Gdns. W2 140 DD72
Sussex Gdns., Chess. 215 CK107
Sussex Keep, Slou. 152 AV75
Sussex Clo.
Sussex Ms. E. W2 272 A9
Sussex Ms. W. W2 272 A10
Sussex Pl. NW1 272 D3
Sussex Pl. NW1 140 DF70
Sussex Pl. W2 272 A9
Sussex Pl. W2 140 DD72
Sussex Pl. W6 159 CW78
Sussex Pl., Erith 167 FB80
Sussex Pl., N.Mal. 198 CS98
Sussex Pl., Slou. 152 AV75
Sussex Ring N12 98 DA50
Sussex Rd. E6 145 EN67
Sussex Rd., Brwd. 108 FV49
Sussex Rd., Cars. 218 DF107
Sussex Rd., Dart. 188 FN87
Sussex Rd., Erith 167 FB80
Sussex Rd., Har. 116 CC57
Sussex Rd., Mitch. 201 DL99
Lincoln Rd.
Sussex Rd., N.Mal. 198 CS98
Sussex Rd., Orp. 206 EW100
Sussex Rd., Sid. 186 EV92
Sussex Rd., S.Croy. 220 DR107
Sussex Rd., Sthl. 156 BX76
Sussex Rd., Uxb. 115 BQ63
Sussex Rd., Wat. 75 BU37
Sussex Rd., W.Wick. 203 EB102
Sussex Sq. W2 272 A10
Sussex Sq. W2 140 DD73
Sussex St. E13 144 EH69
Sussex St. SW1 161 DH78
Sussex Wk. SW9 161 DP84
Sussex Way N7 121 DL61
Sussex Way N19 121 DL60
Sussex Way, Barn. 81 DH43
Sussex Way, Uxb. 113 BF57
Sutcliffe Clo. NW11 120 DB57
Sutcliffe Clo. (Bushey), Wat. 76 CC42
Sutcliffe Ho., Hayes 135 BU72
Sutcliffe Rd. SE18 165 ES79
Sutcliffe Rd., Well. 166 EW82
Sutherland Ave. W9 140 DA70
Sutherland Ave. W13 137 CH72
Sutherland Ave., Guil. 242 AX128
Sutherland Ave., Hayes 155 BU77
Sutherland Ave., Orp. 205 ET100
Sutherland Ave. (Cuffley), Pot.B. 65 DK28
Sutherland Ave., Sun. 195 BT96
Sutherland Ave., Well. 165 ES84
Sutherland Ave., West. 238 EK117
Sutherland Clo., Barn. 79 CY42
Sutherland Clo., Green. 189 FT85
Sutherland Ct. NW9 118 CP56
Sutherland Ct., Welw.G.C. 29 CZ08
Sutherland Dr. SW19 200 DD95
Willow Vw.
Sutherland Dr., Guil. 243 AZ131
Sutherland Gdns. SW14 158 CS83
Sutherland Gdns., Sun. 195 BT96
Sutherland Ave.
Sutherland Gdns., Wor.Pk. 199 CV101
Sutherland Gro. SW18 179 CY86
Sutherland Gro., Tedd. 177 CE92
Sutherland Pl. W2 140 DA72
Sutherland Pt. E5 122 DV63
Tiger Way
Sutherland Rd. E17 101 DX54
Sutherland Rd. N9 100 DU46
Sutherland Rd. N17 100 DU52
Sutherland Rd. W4 158 CS79
Sutherland Rd. W13 137 CG72
Sutherland Rd., Belv. 166 FA76
Sutherland Rd., Croy. 201 DN101
Sutherland Rd., Enf. 83 DX43
Sutherland Rd., Sthl. 136 BZ72
Sutherland Rd. Path E17 123 DX55
Sutherland Row SW1 277 J10
Sutherland Row SW1 161 DH78
Sutherland Sq. SE17 162 DQ78
Sutherland St. SW1 277 H10
Sutherland St. SW1 161 DH78
Sutherland Wk. SE17 162 DQ78
Sutherland Way (Cuffley), Pot.B. 65 DK28
Sutlej Rd. SE7 164 EJ80
Sutterton St. N7 141 DM65
Sutton Ave., Slou. 152 AW75
Sutton Ave., Wok. 226 AS119
Sutton Clo., Beck. 203 EB95
Albemarle Rd.
Sutton Clo., Brox. 49 DY20
Sutton Clo., Loug. 102 EL45
Sutton Clo., Pnr. 115 BU57
Sutton Common Rd., Sutt. 199 CZ101
Sutton Ct. W4 158 CQ79
Sutton Ct. Rd. E13 144 EJ69
Sutton Ct. Rd. W4 158 CQ80
Sutton Ct. Rd., Sutt. 218 DC107
Sutton Ct. Rd., Uxb. 135 BP67
Sutton Cres., Barn. 79 CX43
Sutton Dene, Houns. 156 CB81
Sutton Est. SW3 276 C10
Sutton Est. SW3 160 DE78
Sutton Est. W10 139 CW71
Sutton Est., The N1 141 DP66
Sutton Gdns., Bark. 145 ES67
Sutton Rd.
Sutton Gdns., Croy. 202 DT99
Sutton Gdns., Red. 251 DK129
Sutton Grn., Bark. 145 ES67
Sutton Rd.
Sutton Grn. Rd., Guil. 242 AY126
Sutton Gro., Sutt. 218 DD105
Sutton Hall Rd., Houns. 156 CA80
Sutton Ho., Hem.H. 40 BL16
Sutton La., Bans. 234 DB115
Sutton La., Dor. 261 BV143
Sutton La., Houns. 156 BZ83
Sutton La., Slou. 153 BB79
Sutton La., Sutt. 218 DB111
Sutton La. N. W4 158 CQ78
Sutton La. S. W4 158 CQ79
Sutton Pk., Guil. 243 AZ127
Sutton Pk. Rd., Sutt. 218 DB107
Sutton Path, Borwd. 78 CN40
Stratfield Rd.
Sutton Pl. E9 122 DW64
Sutton Pl., Dor. 261 BT143
Sutton Pl., Slou. 153 BB79
Sutton Rd. E13 144 EF70
Sutton Rd. E17 101 DX53
Sutton Rd. N10 98 DG53
Sutton Rd., Bark. 145 ES68
Sutton Rd., Houns. 156 CA81
Sutton Rd., St.Alb. 43 CH21
Sutton Rd., Wat. 76 BW41
Sutton Row W1 273 N8
Sutton Row W1 141 DK72
Sutton Sq. E9 122 DW64
Urswick Rd.
Sutton Sq., Houns. 156 BZ81
Sutton St. E1 142 DW73
Sutton Way W10 139 CW71
Sutton Way, Houns. 156 BZ81
Suttons Ave., Horn. 128 FJ62
Suttons Gdns., Horn. 128 FK62
Suttons La., Horn. 128 FK64
Sutton's Way EC1 275 J5
Swabey Rd., Slou. 153 BA77
Swaby Rd. SW18 180 DC88
Swaffham Way N22 99 DP52
White Hart La.
Swaffield Rd. SW18 180 DB87
Swaffield Rd., Sev. 257 FJ122
Swain Clo. SW16 181 DH93
Swain Rd., Th.Hth. 202 DQ99
Swains Clo., West Dr. 154 BL75
Swains La. N6 120 DG60
Swains Rd. SW17 180 DF94
Swainson Rd. W3 159 CT75
Swaisland Dr., Dart. 187 FF85
Swaisland Rd., Dart. 187 FH85
Swakeleys Dr., Uxb. 114 BM63
Swakeleys Rd., Uxb. 114 BL63
Swale Clo., S.Ock. 148 FQ72
Swale Rd., Dart. 167 FG83
Swaledale Rd., Dart. 188 FQ88
Swallands Rd. SE6 183 EA90
Swallow Clo. SE14 163 DX81
Swallow Clo., Erith 167 FE81
Swallow Clo., Green. 189 FT85
Swallow Clo., Rick. 92 BJ45
Swallow Clo., Stai. 173 BF91
Swallow Clo. (Bushey), Wat. 94 CC46
Swallow Ct., Hert. 32 DQ09
Swallow Dr. NW10 138 CR65
Kingfisher Way
Swallow Dr., Nthlt. 136 CA68
Swallow End, Welw.G.C. 29 CZ09
Swallow Gdns., Hat. 45 CU20
Swallow La., Dor. 263 CH142
Swallow La., St.Alb. 43 CH23
Swallow Pas. W1 273 J9
Swallow Pl. W1 273 J9
Swallow St. E6 144 EL71
Swallow St. W1 277 L1
Swallow St., Iver 133 BD69
Swallow Wk., Horn. 147 FH65
Heron Flight Ave.
Swallowdale, Iver 133 BD69
Swallowdale, S.Croy. 221 DX109
Swallowdale La., Hem.H. 40 BN17
Swallowfield, Egh. 172 AV93
Heronfield
Swallowfield Rd. SE7 164 EH78
Swallowfield Way, Hayes 155 BR75
Swallowfields, Grav. 190 GE90
Hillary Ave.
Swallowfields, Welw.G.C. 29 CZ09
Swallows, Harl. 36 EW11
Station Rd.
Swallows, The, Welw.G.C. 29 CZ05
Swallows Oak, Abb.L. 59 BT31
Swan & Pike Rd., Enf. 83 EA38
Swan App. E6 144 EL71
Swan Ave., Upmin. 129 FT60
Swan Clo. E17 101 DY53
Swan Clo., Chesh. 54 AP27
Swan Clo., Croy. 202 DS101
Swan Clo., Felt. 176 BY91
Swan Clo., Orp. 206 EU97
Swan Clo., Rick. 92 BK45
Parsonage Rd.
Swan Ct. SW3 160 DE78
Flood St.
Swan Ct., Guil. 242 AX132
Swan Dr. NW9 96 CS54
Swan La. EC4 279 K1
Swan La. N20 98 DC48
Swan La., Dart. 187 FF87
Swan La., Guil. 258 AX135
Swan La., Loug. 102 EJ45
Swan Mead SE1 279 M7
Swan Mead SE1 162 DS76
Swan Mill Gdns., Dor. 247 CJ134
Swan Pas. E1 142 DT73
Cartwright St.
Swan Pl. SW13 159 CT82
Swan Rd. SE16 162 DW75
Swan Rd. SE18 164 EK76
Swan Rd., Felt. 176 BY92
Swan Rd., Iver 133 BF72
Swan Rd., Sthl. 136 CB72
Swan Rd., West Dr. 154 BK75
Swan St. SE1 279 J6
Swan St. SE1 162 DQ76
Swan St., Islw. 157 CH83
Swan Ter., Wind. 151 AP80
Mill La.
Swan Wk. SW3 160 DF79
Swan Wk., Rom. 127 FE57
Swan Wk., Shep. 195 BS101
Swan Way, Enf. 83 DX40
Swan Yd. N1 141 DP65
Highbury Sta. Rd.
Swanage Rd. E4 101 EC52
Swanage Rd. SW18 180 DC86
Swanage Waye, Hayes 136 BW72
Swanbourne Dr., Horn. 128 FJ64
Swanbridge Rd., Bexh. 166 FA81
Swandon Way SW18 160 DB84

Swanfield Rd., Wal.Cr. 67 DY33
Swanfield St. E2 275 P3
Swanfield St. E2 142 DT69
Swanhill, Welw.G.C. 30 DA06
Swanland Rd., Hat. 63 CV25
Swanland Rd., Pot.B. 63 CV33
Swanley Bar La., Pot.B. 64 DB28
Swanley Bypass, Sid. 207 FC96
Swanley Bypass, Swan. 207 FC96
Swanley Cres., Pot.B. 64 DB29
Swanley La., Swan. 207 FF97
Swanley Rd., Well. 166 EW81
Swanley Village Rd., Swan. 207 FH95
Swanns Meadow, Lthd. 246 CA126
Swans Clo., St.Alb. 44 CL21
Swanscombe Rd. W4 158 CS78
Swanscombe Rd. W11 139 CX74
Swanscombe St., Swans. 190 FY87
Swansea Rd., Enf. 82 DW42
Swanshope, Loug. 85 EP40
Swansland Gdns. E17 101 DY53
McEntee Ave.
Swanston Path, Wat. 94 BW48
Swanton Gdns. SW19 179 CX88
Swanton Rd., Erith 167 FB80
Swanwick Clo. SW15 179 CT87
Swanworth La., Dor. 247 CH128
Sward Rd., Orp. 206 EU100
Swaton Rd. E3 143 EA70
Swaylands Rd., Belv. 166 FA79
Swaynes La., Guil. 243 BE134
Swaynesland Rd., Eden. 255 EM134
Swaythling Clo. N18 100 DV49
Sweden Gate SE16 163 DY76
Swedenborg Gdns. E1 142 DU73
Sweeney Cres. SE1 162 DT75
Sweeps Ditch Clo., Stai. 174 BG94
Sweeps La., Egh. 173 AZ92
Sweeps La., Orp. 206 EX99
Sweet Briar, Welw.G.C. 30 DA11
Sweet Briar Grn. N9 100 DT48
Sweet Briar Gro. N9 100 DT48
Sweet Briar La., Epsom 216 CR114
Madans Wk.
Sweet Briar Wk. N18 100 DT49
Sweet La., Guil. 261 BR143
Sweetbriar Clo., Hem.H. 40 BG17
Sweetcroft La., Uxb. 134 BM66
Sweetmans Ave., Pnr. 116 BX55
Sweets Way N20 98 DD47
Swete St. E13 144 EG68
Swetenham Wk. SE18 165 EQ78
Sandbach Pl.
Sweyn Pl. SE3 164 EG82
Sweyne Rd., Swans. 190 FY86
Sweyns, Harl. 52 EX17
Swievelands Rd., West. 238 EH119
Swift Clo. E17 101 DY53
Swift Clo., Har. 116 CB61
Swift Clo., Hayes 135 BT72
Church Rd.
Swift Clo., Upmin. 129 FS60
Swift Clo., Ware 33 EC12
Swift Rd., Felt. 176 BX91
Swift Rd., Sthl. 156 BZ76
Swift St. SW6 159 CZ81
Swiftfields, Welw.G.C. 29 CZ08
Swiftsden Way, Brom. 184 EE93
Swinbrook Rd. W10 139 CY71
Swinburne Ct. SE5 162 DR84
Basingdon Way
Swinburne Cres., Croy. 202 DW100
Swinburne Gdns., Til. 171 GH82
Swinburne Rd. SW15 159 CU84
Swinderby Rd., Wem. 138 CL65
Swindon Clo., Ilf. 125 ES61
Salisbury Rd.
Swindon Clo., Rom. 106 FM50
Swindon Gdns., Rom. 106 FM50
Swindon La., Rom. 106 FM50
Swindon Rd., Houns. 175 BQ86
Southern Perimeter Rd.
Swindon St. W12 139 CV74
Swinfield Clo., Felt. 176 BY91
Swinford Gdns. SW9 161 DP83
Swing Gate La., Berk. 38 AX21
Swingate La. SE18 165 ES80
Swinnerton St. E9 123 DY64
Swinton Clo., Wem. 118 CP60
Swinton Pl. WC1 274 B2
Swinton Pl. WC1 141 DM69
Swinton St. WC1 274 B2
Swinton St. WC1 141 DM69
Swires Shaw, Kes. 222 EK105
Swiss Ave., Wat. 75 BS42
Swiss Clo., Wat. 75 BS41
Swiss Ter. NW6 140 DD66
Swithland Gdns. SE9 185 EN91
Sword Clo., Brox. 49 DX20
Swyncombe Ave. W5 157 CH77
Swynford Gdns. NW4 119 CU56
Handowe Clo.
Sybil Ms. N4 121 DP58
Lothair Rd. N.
Sybil Phoenix Clo. SE8 163 DX78
Sybil Thorndike Ho. N1 142 DQ65
Clephane Rd.
Sybourn St. E17 123 DZ59
Sycamore App., Rick. 75 BQ43
Sycamore Ave. W5 157 CK76
Sycamore Ave., Hat. 45 CU19
Sycamore Ave., Hayes 135 BS73
Sycamore Ave., Sid. 185 ET86
Sycamore Ave., Upmin. 128 FN62
Sycamore Clo. E16 144 EE70
Clarence Rd.
Sycamore Clo. N9 100 DU49
Pycroft Way
Sycamore Clo. SE9 184 EL89
Sycamore Clo. W3 138 CS74
Bromyard Ave.
Sycamore Clo., Amer. 55 AR37
Sycamore Clo., Barn. 80 DD44
Sycamore Clo., Cars. 218 DF105
Sycamore Clo., Ch.St.G. 90 AU48
Sycamore Clo., Felt. 175 BU90
Sycamore Clo., Grav. 191 GK87
Sycamore Clo., Lthd. 231 CE123
Sycamore Clo., Nthlt. 136 BY67
Sycamore Clo., Wal.Cr. 66 DS27
Sycamore Clo., Wat. 75 BV35
Sycamore Clo. (Bushey), Wat. 76 BY40
Sycamore Clo., West Dr. 134 BM73
Whitethorn Ave.
Sycamore Dene, Chesh. 54 AR28
Sycamore Dr., Brwd. 108 FW46
Copperfield Gdns.
Sycamore Dr., St.Alb. 61 CD27
Sycamore Dr., Swan. 207 FE97
Sycamore Fld., Harl. 51 EN19
Broadley Rd.
Sycamore Gdns. W6 159 CV75
Sycamore Gdns., Mitch. 200 DD96
Sycamore Gro. NW9 118 CQ59
Sycamore Gro. SE6 183 EC86
Sycamore Gro. SE20 182 DU94
Sycamore Gro., N.Mal. 198 CR97
Sycamore Hill N11 98 DG51
Sycamore Ms. SW4 161 DJ83
Sycamore Ri., Bans. 217 CX114
Sycamore Ri., Berk. 38 AX20
Sycamore Ri., Ch.St.G. 90 AU48
Sycamore Rd. SW19 179 CW93
Sycamore Rd., Amer. 55 AQ37
Sycamore Rd., Ch.St.G. 90 AU48
Sycamore Rd., Dart. 188 FK87
Sycamore Rd., Guil. 242 AX134
Sycamore Rd., Rick. 75 BQ43
Sycamore St. EC1 275 H5
Sycamore Wk. W10 139 CY70
Fifth Ave.
Sycamore Wk., Egh. 172 AV93
Sycamore Wk., Ilf. 125 EQ56
Civic Way
Sycamore Wk., Reig. 266 DC136
Sycamore Wk., Slou. 132 AY72
Sycamore Way, S.Ock. 149 FX70
Sycamore Way, Tedd. 177 CJ93
Sycamore Way, Th.Hth. 201 DN99
Grove Rd.
Sycamores, The, Hem.H. 39 BF23
Sycamores, The, Rad. 61 CH34
Sycamores, The, S.Ock. 149 FR74
Dacre Ave.
Sydenham Ave. SE26 182 DV92
Sydenham Clo., Rom. 127 FF56
Sydenham Cotts. SE12 184 EJ89
Sydenham Hill SE23 182 DV88
Sydenham Hill SE26 182 DT91
Sydenham Hill Est. SE26 182 DU90
Sydenham Pk. SE26 182 DW90
Sydenham Pk. Rd. SE26 182 DW90
Sydenham Ri. SE23 182 DV89
Sydenham Rd. SE26 183 DX92
Sydenham Rd., Croy. 202 DQ102
Sydenham Rd., Guil. 258 AX136
Sydmons Ct. SE23 182 DW87
Sydner Ms. N16 122 DT63
Sydner Rd.
Sydner Rd. N16 122 DT63
Sydney Ave., Pur. 219 DM112
Sydney Clo. SW3 276 A9
Sydney Clo. SW3 160 DD77
Sydney Cres., Ashf. 175 BP93
Sydney Gro. NW4 119 CW57
Sydney Gro., Slou. 131 AQ72
Sydney Ms. SW3 276 A9
Sydney Pl. SW7 276 A9
Sydney Pl. SW7 160 DD77
Sydney Pl., Guil. 259 AZ135
Sydney Rd. E11 124 EH58
Mansfield Rd.
Sydney Rd. N8 121 DN56
Sydney Rd. N10 98 DG53
Sydney Rd. SE2 166 EW76
Sydney Rd. SW20 199 CX96
Sydney Rd. W13 137 CG74
Sydney Rd., Bexh. 166 EX84
Sydney Rd., Enf. 82 DR41
Sydney Rd., Felt. 175 BU88
Sydney Rd., Guil. 259 AZ135
Sydney Rd., Ilf. 103 EQ54
Sydney Rd., Rich. 158 CL84
Sydney Rd., Sid. 185 ES91
Sydney Rd., Sutt. 218 DA105
Sydney Rd., Tedd. 177 CF92
Sydney Rd., Til. 171 GG82
Sydney Rd., Wat. 75 BS43
Sydney Rd., Wdf.Grn. 102 EG49
Sydney St. SW3 276 B10
Sydney St. SW3 160 DE78
Sykecluan, Iver 153 BE75
Sykeings, Iver 153 BE76
Sykes Dr., Stai. 174 BH92
Sykes Rd., Slou. 131 AP72
Sylvan Ave. N3 98 DA54
Sylvan Ave. N22 99 DM52
Sylvan Ave. NW7 97 CT51
Sylvan Ave., Horn. 128 FL58
Sylvan Ave., Rom. 126 EZ58
Sylvan Clo., Grays 170 FY77
Warren La.
Sylvan Clo., Hem.H. 40 BN21
Sylvan Clo., Oxt. 254 EH129
Sylvan Clo., S.Croy. 220 DV110
Sylvan Clo., Wok. 227 BB117
Sylvan Est. SE19 202 DT95
Sylvan Gdns., Surb. 197 CK101
Sylvan Gro. NW2 119 CX63
Sylvan Gro. SE15 162 DV79
Sylvan Hill SE19 202 DS95
Sylvan Rd. E7 144 EG65
Sylvan Rd. E11 124 EG57
Sylvan Rd. E17 123 EA57
Sylvan Rd. SE19 202 DT95
Sylvan Rd., Ilf. 125 EQ61
Hainault St.
Sylvan Wk., Brom. 205 EM97
Sylvan Way, Chig. 104 EV48
Sylvan Way, Dag. 126 EV62
Sylvan Way, Red. 266 DG135
Sylvan Way, W.Wick. 222 EE105
Sylvana Clo., Uxb. 134 BM67
Sylvandale, Welw.G.C. 30 DC10
Sylverdale Rd., Croy. 201 DP104
Sylverdale Rd., Pur. 219 DP113
Sylvester Ave., Chis. 185 EM93
Sylvester Gdns., Ilf. 104 EV50
Sylvester Path E8 142 DV65
Sylvester Rd.
Sylvester Rd. E8 142 DV65
Sylvester Rd. E17 123 DZ59
Sylvester Rd. N2 98 DC54
Sylvester Rd., Wem. 117 CJ64
Sylvestres, Sev. 241 FD119
London Rd.
Sylvestrus Clo., Kings.T. 198 CN95
Sylvia Ave., Brwd. 109 GC47
Sylvia Ave., Pnr. 94 BY51
Sylvia Gdns., Wem. 138 CP66
Symes Ms. NW1 141 DJ68
Camden High St.
Symons St. SW3 276 E9
Symons St. SW3 160 DF77
Syon Gate Way, Brent. 157 CG80
Syon La., Islw. 157 CF79
Syon Pk. Gdns., Islw. 157 CF80
Syon Vista, Rich. 157 CK81
Kew Rd.
Syracuse Ave., Rain. 148 FL69
Syringa Ct., Grays 170 GD80
Sythwood, Wok. 226 AV117

T

Tabard Gdn. Est. SE1 279 L5
Tabard Gdn. Est. SE1 162 DR75
Tabard St. SE1 279 K5
Tabard St. SE1 162 DR75
Tabarin Way, Epsom 233 CW116
Tabernacle Ave. E13 144 EG70
Barking Rd.
Tabernacle St. EC2 275 L5
Tabernacle St. EC2 142 DR70
Tableer Ave. SW4 181 DJ85
Tabley Rd. N7 121 DL63
Tabor Gdns., Sutt. 217 CZ107
Tabor Gro. SW19 179 CY94
Tabor Rd. W6 159 CV76
Tabrums Way, Upmin. 129 FS59
Tachbrook Est. SW1 161 DK78
Tachbrook Ms. SW1 277 K8
Tachbrook Rd., Felt. 175 BT87
Tachbrook Rd., Sthl. 156 BX77
Tachbrook Rd., Uxb. 134 BJ68
Tachbrook St. SW1 277 L9
Tachbrook St. SW1 161 DJ77
Tack Ms. SE4 163 EA83
Tadema Rd. SW10 160 DC80
Tadlows Clo., Upmin. 128 FP64
Tadmor Clo., Sun. 195 BT98
Tadmor St. W12 139 CX74
Tadorne Rd., Tad. 233 CW121
Tadworth Ave., N.Mal. 199 CT99
Tadworth Clo., Tad. 233 CX122
Tadworth Par., Horn. 127 FH63
Maylands Ave.
Tadworth Rd. NW2 119 CU61
Tadworth St., Tad. 233 CW123
Taeping St. E14 163 EB77
Taffy's How, Mitch. 200 DE97
Taft Way E3 143 EB69
St. Leonards St.
Tagg's Island, Hmptn. 197 CD96
Tailworth St. E1 142 DU71
Chicksand St.
Tait Rd., Croy. 202 DS101
Takeley Clo., Rom. 105 FD54
Takeley Clo., Wal.Abb. 67 ED33
Talacre Rd. NW5 140 DG65
Talbot Ave. N2 120 DD55
Talbot Ave., Slou. 153 AZ76
Talbot Ave., Wat. 94 BY45
Talbot Clo. N15 122 DT56
Talbot Clo., Reig. 266 DB135
Talbot Ct. EC3 275 L10
Talbot Ct., Hem.H. 40 BK22
Crabtree La.
Talbot Cres. NW4 119 CU57
Talbot Gdns., Ilf. 126 EU61
Talbot Ho. E14 143 EB72
Giraud St.
Talbot Pl. SE3 164 EE82
Talbot Pl., Slou. 152 AW81
Talbot Rd. E6 145 EN68
Talbot Rd. E7 124 EG63
Talbot Rd. N6 120 DG58
Talbot Rd. N15 122 DT56
Talbot Rd. N22 99 DJ54
Talbot Rd. SE22 162 DS84
Talbot Rd. W2 140 DA72
Talbot Rd. W11 139 CZ72
Talbot Rd. W13 137 CG73
Talbot Rd., Ashf. 174 BK92
Talbot Rd., Brom. 204 EH98
Masons Hill
Talbot Rd., Cars. 218 DG106
Talbot Rd., Dag. 146 EZ65
Talbot Rd., Har. 95 CF54
Talbot Rd., Hat. 45 CU15
Talbot Rd., Islw. 157 CG84
Talbot Rd., Rick. 92 BL46
Talbot Rd., Sthl. 156 BY77
Talbot Rd., Th.Hth. 202 DR98
Talbot Rd., Twick. 177 CE88
Talbot Rd., Wem. 117 CK64
Talbot Sq. W2 272 A9
Talbot Sq. W2 140 DD72
Talbot St., Hert. 32 DS09
Talbot Wk. NW10 138 CS65
Garnet Rd.
Talbot Wk. W11 139 CY72
Lancaster Rd.
Talbot Yd. SE1 279 K3
Talbrook, Brwd. 108 FT48
Taleworth Clo., Ash. 231 CK120
Taleworth Pk., Ash. 231 CK120
Taleworth Rd., Ash. 231 CK119
Talfourd Pl. SE15 162 DT81
Talfourd Rd. SE15 162 DT81
Talgarth Rd. W6 159 CX78
Talgarth Rd. W14 159 CX78
Talgarth Wk. NW9 118 CS57
Talisman Clo., Ilf. 126 EV60
Talisman Sq. SE26 182 DU91
Talisman Way, Epsom 233 CW116
Talisman Way, Wem. 118 CM62
Forty Ave.
Tall Elms Clo., Brom. 204 EF99
Tall Oaks, Amer. 55 AR37
Tall Trees SW16 201 DM97
Tall Trees, Slou. 153 BE81
Tall Trees Clo., Horn. 128 FK58
Tallack Clo., Har. 95 CE52
College Hill Rd.
Tallack Rd. E10 123 DZ60
Tallents Clo. (Sutton at Hone), Dart. 188 FP94
Tallis Clo. E16 144 EH72
Tallis Gro. SE7 164 EH79
Tallis St. EC4 274 E10
Tallis St. EC4 141 DN73
Tallis Vw. NW10 138 CR65
Mitchellbrook Way
Tallis Way, Borwd. 77 CK39
Tallon Rd., Brwd. 109 GE43
Tally Ho Cor. N12 98 DC50
Tally Rd., Oxt. 254 EL131
Talma Gdns., Twick. 177 CE86
Talma Rd. SW2 161 DN84
Talmage Clo. SE23 182 DW87
Tyson Rd.
Talman Gro., Stan. 95 CK51
Talus Clo., Purf. 169 FR77
Brimfield Rd.
Talwin St. E3 143 EB69
Tamar Clo., Upmin. 129 FS58
Tamar Dr., S.Ock. 148 FQ72
Tamar Grn., Hem.H. 40 BM15
Tamar Sq., Wdf.Grn. 102 EH51
Tamar St. SE7 164 EL76
Tamar Way N17 122 DT55
Tamar Way, Slou. 153 BB78
Tamarind Clo., Guil. 242 AU129
Tamarind Yd. E1 142 DU74
Asher Way
Tamarisk Clo., St.Alb. 43 CD16
New Grns. Ave.
Tamarisk Clo., S.Ock. 149 FW70
Tamarisk Rd., S.Ock. 149 FW69
Tamarisk Sq. W12 139 CT73
Tamarisk Way, Slou. 151 AN75
Tamerton Sq., Wok. 226 AY118
Tamesis Gdns., Wor.Pk. 198 CS103
Tamesis Strand, Grav. 191 GL92
Tamian Est., Houns. 156 BW84
Tamian Way, Houns. 156 BW84
Tamworth Ave., Wdf.Grn. 102 EE51
Tamworth Gdns., Pnr. 93 BV54
Tamworth La., Mitch. 200 DG96
Tamworth Pk., Mitch. 201 DH98
Tamworth Pl., Croy. 202 DQ103
Tamworth Rd., Croy. 201 DP103
Tamworth Rd., Hert. 32 DT08
Tamworth St. SW6 160 DA79
Tancred Rd. N4 121 DP58
Tandridge Ct., Cat. 236 DU122
Tandridge Dr., Orp. 205 ER102
Tandridge Gdns., S.Croy. 220 DT113
Tandridge Hill La., Gdse. 253 DZ128
Tandridge La., Oxt. 253 EA131
Tandridge Pl., Orp. 205 ER101
Tandridge Dr.
Tandridge Rd., Warl. 237 DX119
Tanfield Ave. NW2 119 CT63
Tanfield Clo., Wal.Cr. 66 DV27
Spicersfield
Tanfield Rd., Croy. 220 DQ105
Tangent Rd., Rom. 106 FK53
Ashton Rd.
Tangier La. (Eton), Wind. 151 AR79
Tangier Rd., Guil. 259 BA135
Tangier Rd., Rich. 158 CP84
Tangier Way, Tad. 233 CY117
Tangier Wd., Tad. 233 CY118
Tangle Tree Clo. N3 120 DB55
Tanglebury Clo., Brom. 204 EL98
Tangles Clo., Uxb. 134 BN69
Tanglewood Clo., Cher. 192 AV104
Tanglewood Clo., Croy. 202 DW104
Tanglewood Clo., Stan. 95 CE47
Tanglewood Clo., Wok. 227 BD116
Tanglewood Way, Felt. 175 BV90
Tangley Gro. SW15 179 CT87
Tangley La., Guil. 242 AT130
Tangley Pk. Rd., Hmptn. 176 BZ92
Tanglyn Ave., Shep. 194 BN99
Tangmere Cres., Horn. 147 FH65
Tangmere Gdns., Nthlt. 136 BW68
Tangmere Gro., Kings.T. 177 CK92
Tangmere Way NW9 96 CS54
Tanhouse Rd., Oxt. 253 ED132
Tanhurst Wk. SE2 166 EX76
Alsike Rd.
Tank Hill Rd., Purf. 168 FN78
Tank La., Purf. 168 FN77
Tankerdale Rd., Surb. 198 CM103
Tankerton St. WC1 274 A3
Tankerville Rd. SW16 181 DK94
Tankridge Rd. NW2 119 CV61
Tanner St. SE1 279 N5
Tanner St. SE1 162 DS75
Tanner St., Bark. 145 EQ65
Tanners Clo., St.Alb. 42 CC19
Tanners Clo., Walt. 195 BV100
Tanners Cres., Hert. 32 DQ11
Tanners Dean, Lthd. 231 CJ122
Tanners End La. N18 100 DS49
Tanners Hill SE8 163 DZ81
Tanners Hill, Abb.L. 59 BT31
Tanners La., Ilf. 125 EQ55
Tanners Meadow, Bet. 264 CP138
Tanners Way, Ware 34 EJ06
Tanners Wd. Clo., Abb.L. 59 BS32
Tanners Wd. La.
Tanners Wd. La., Abb.L. 59 BS32
Tannersfield, Guil. 258 AY142
Tannery, The, Red. 250 DE134
Oakdene Rd.
Tannery Clo., Beck. 203 DX99
Tannery Clo., Dag. 127 FB62
Tannery La., Guil. 258 AY144
Tannery La., Wok. 227 BD123
Tannington Ter. N5 121 DN62
Tannsfeld Rd. SE26 183 DX92
Tannsfield Dr., Hem.H. 40 BM18
Tannsmore Clo., Hem.H. 40 BM18
Tansley Clo. N7 121 DK64
Hilldrop Rd.
Tanswell Est. SE1 278 E5
Tanswell St. SE1 278 D5
Tansy Clo. E6 145 EN72
Tansy Clo., Guil. 243 BC132
Tansy Clo., Rom. 106 FL51
Tansycroft, Welw.G.C. 30 DB08
Tant Ave. E16 144 EF72
Tantallon Rd. SW12 180 DG88
Tantony Gro., Rom. 126 EX55
Tanworth Clo., Nthwd. 93 BQ51
Tanyard La., Bex. 186 FA87
Bexley High St.
Tanyard Way, Horl. 269 DH146
Tanys Dell, Harl. 36 EU12
Tanza Rd. NW3 120 DF63
Tapestry Clo., Sutt. 218 DB108
Taplow NW3 140 DD66
Taplow SE17 162 DR78
Taplow Common Rd., Slou. 130 AF65
Taplow Rd. N13 100 DQ49
Taplow Rd., Maid. 130 AG71
Taplow St. N1 275 J1
Taplow St. N1 142 DQ68
Tapners Rd., Reig. 265 CT139
Tapp St. E1 142 DV70
Tappesfield Rd. SE15 162 DW83
Tapster St., Barn. 79 CZ41
Taransay, Hem.H. 41 BP22
Tarbay La., Wind. 150 AH82
Tarbert Rd. SE22 182 DS85
Tarbert Wk. E1 142 DW73
Juniper St.
Target Clo., Felt. 175 BS86
Tarham Clo., Horl. 268 DE146
Tariff Cres. SE8 163 DZ77
Enterprize Way
Tariff Rd. N17 100 DU51
Tarleton Gdns. SE23 182 DV88
Tarling Clo., Sid. 186 EV90
Tarling Rd. E16 144 EF72
Tarling Rd. N2 98 DC54
Tarling St. E1 142 DV72
Tarling St. Est. E1 142 DW72
Tarmac Way, West Dr. 154 BH80
Tarn St. SE1 279 H7
Tarnbank, Enf. 81 DL43
Tarnwood Pk. SE9 185 EM87
Tarnworth Rd., Rom. 106 FN50
Tarpan Way, Brox. 67 DZ26
Tarquin Ho. SE26 182 DU91
Tarragon Clo. SE14 163 DY80
Tarragon Dr., Guil. 242 AU129
Tarragon Gdns. SE14 163 DY80
Southerngate Way
Tarragon Gro. SE26 183 DX93
Tarrant Pl. W1 272 D7
Tarrington Clo. SW16 181 DK90
Tarry La. SE8 163 DY77
Tartar Rd., Cob. 214 BW113
Tarver Rd. SE17 161 DP78
Tarves Way SE10 163 EB80
Tash Pl. N11 99 DH50
Woodland Rd.
Tasker Clo., Hayes 155 BQ80
Tasker Ho., Bark. 145 ER68
Dovehouse Mead
Tasker Rd. NW3 120 DF64
Tasker Rd., Grays 171 GH76
Tasman Rd. SW9 161 DL83
Tasman Wk. E16 144 EK72
Royal Rd.
Tasmania Ter. N18 100 DQ51
Tasso Rd. W6 159 CY79
Tatam Rd. NW10 138 CR66
Tate & Lyle Jetty E16 164 EL75
Tate Clo., Lthd. 231 CJ123
Windmill Dr.
Tate Rd. E16 145 EM74
Newland St.
Tate Rd., Ger.Cr. 91 AZ50
Tate Rd., Sutt. 218 DA106
Tatnell Rd. SE23 183 DY86
Tatsfield App. Rd., West. 238 EH123
Tatsfield Ave., Wal.Abb. 49 ED23
Tatsfield La., West. 238 EL121
Tattenham Cor. Rd., Epsom 232 CS117
Tattenham Cres., Epsom 233 CU118
Tattenham Gro., Epsom 233 CV118
Tattenham Way, Tad. 233 CX118
Tattersall Clo. SE9 184 EL85
Tattle Hill, Hert. 31 DL05
Tatton Cres. N16 122 DT59
Clapton Common
Tatum St. SE17 279 L9
Tatum St. SE17 162 DR77
Tauber Clo., Borwd. 78 CM42
Taunton Ave. SW20 199 CV96
Taunton Ave., Cat. 236 DT123
Taunton Ave., Houns. 156 CC82
Taunton Clo., Bexh. 167 FD82
Taunton Clo., Ilf. 103 ET51
Taunton Clo., Sutt. 200 DA102
Taunton Ct. N17 100 DS52
Taunton Dr. N2 98 DC54
Taunton Dr., Enf. 81 DN41
Taunton La., Couls. 235 DN119
Taunton Ms. NW1 272 D5
Taunton Pl. NW1 272 D4
Taunton Pl. NW1 140 DF70
Taunton Rd. SE12 184 EE85
Taunton Rd., Grav. 190 GA85
Taunton Rd., Grnf. 136 CB67
Taunton Rd., Rom. 106 FJ49
Taunton Vale, Grav. 191 GK89
Taunton Way, Stan. 96 CL54
Tavern Clo., Cars. 200 DE101
Tavern La. SW9 161 DN82
Taverner Sq. N5 122 DQ63
Highbury Gra.
Taverners, Hem.H. 40 BL18
Taverners Clo. W11 139 CY74
Addison Ave.
Taverners Way E4 102 EE46
Douglas Rd.
Taverners Way, Hodd. 49 EA17
Tavistock Ave. E17 123 DX55
Tavistock Ave., Grnf. 137 CG68
Tavistock Ave., St.Alb. 43 CD23
Tavistock Clo. N16 122 DS64
Crossway
Tavistock Clo., Pot.B. 64 DD31
Tavistock Clo., Rom. 106 FK53
Tavistock Clo., St.Alb. 43 CD23
Tavistock Clo., Stai. 174 BK94
Tavistock Cres. W11 139 CZ71
Tavistock Cres., Mitch. 201 DL98
Tavistock Gdns., Ilf. 125 ES63
Tavistock Gate, Croy. 202 DR102
Tavistock Gro., Croy. 202 DR101
Tavistock Ms. E18 124 EG56
Avon Way
Tavistock Ms. W11 139 CZ72
Lancaster Rd.
Tavistock Pl. E18 124 EG55
Avon Way

Tavistock Pl. N14 99 DH45
Chase Side
Tavistock Pl. WC1 273 P4
Tavistock Pl. WC1 141 DL70
Tavistock Rd. E7 124 EF63
Tavistock Rd. E15 144 EF65
Tavistock Rd. E18 124 EG55
Tavistock Rd. N4 122 DR58
Tavistock Rd. NW10 139 CT68
Tavistock Rd. W11 139 CZ72
Tavistock Rd., Brom. 204 EF98
Tavistock Rd., Cars. 200 DD102
Tavistock Rd., Croy. 202 DR102
Tavistock Rd., Edg. 96 CN53
Tavistock Rd., Uxb. 115 BQ64
Tavistock Rd., Wat. 76 BX39
Tavistock Rd., Well. 166 EW81
Tavistock Rd., West Dr. 134 BK74
Tavistock Sq. WC1 273 N4
Tavistock Sq. WC1 141 DK70
Tavistock St. WC2 274 A10
Tavistock St. WC2 141 DL73
Tavistock Ter. N19 121 DK62
Tavistock Wk., Cars. 200 DD102
Tavistock Rd.
Taviton St. WC1 273 M4
Taviton St. WC1 141 DK70
Tavy Bri. SE2 166 EW76
Tavy Clo. SE11 278 E10
Tawney Common, Epp. 70 FA32
Tawney Rd. SE28 146 EV73
Tawneys Rd., Harl. 51 ES16
Tawny Ave., Upmin. 128 FP64
Tawny Clo. W13 137 CH74
Tawny Clo., Felt. 175 BU90
Chervil Clo.
Tawny Way SE16 163 DX77
Tay Way, Rom. 105 FF53
Tayben Ave., Twick. 177 CE86
Taybridge Rd. SW11 160 DG83
Tayburn Clo. E14 143 EC72
Tayfield Clo., Uxb. 115 BQ62
Tayles Hill, Epsom 217 CT110
Taylifers, Harl. 51 EN20
Taylor Ave., Rich. 158 CP82
Taylor Clo. N17 100 DU52
Taylor Clo., Hmptn. 176 CC92
Taylor Clo., Orp. 223 ET105
Taylor Clo., Rom. 104 FA52
Taylor Clo., St.Alb. 43 CG15
Taylor Ct. E15 123 EC64
Taylor Rd., Ash. 231 CK117
Taylor Rd., Mitch. 180 DE94
Taylor Rd., Wall. 219 DH106
Taylors Ave., Hodd. 49 EA18
Taylors Bldgs. SE18 165 EP77
Spray St.
Taylors Clo., Sid. 185 ET91
Taylors Grn. W3 138 CS72
Long Dr.
Taylors La. NW10 138 CS66
Taylors La. SE26 182 DV91
Taylors La., Barn. 79 CZ39
Taylors Rd., Chesh. 54 AR29
Taymount Ri. SE23 182 DW89
Taynton Dr., Red. 251 DK129
Tayport Clo. N1 141 DL66
Tayside Dr., Edg. 96 CP48
Taywood Rd., Nthlt. 136 BZ69
Invicta Gro.
Teak Clo. SE16 143 DY74
Teal Ave., Orp. 206 EX98
Teal Clo. E16 144 EK71
Fulmer Rd.
Teal Clo., S.Croy. 221 DX111
Teal Dr., Nthwd. 93 BQ52
Teale St. E2 142 DU68
Tealing Dr., Epsom 216 CR105
Teardrop Ind. Est., Swan. 207 FH99
Teasel Clo., Croy. 203 DX102
Teasel Way E15 144 EE69
Teazle Wd. Hill, Lthd. 231 CE117
Oaklawn Rd.
Teazlewood Pk., Lthd. 231 CG117
Tebworth Rd. N17 100 DT52
Teck Clo., Islw. 157 CG82
Tedder Clo., Chess. 215 CJ107
Tedder Clo., Ruis. 115 BV64
West End Rd.
Tedder Clo., Uxb. 134 BM66
Tedder Rd., Hem.H. 40 BN19
Tedder Rd., S.Croy. 220 DW108
Teddington Clo., Epsom 216 CR110
Teddington Lock, Tedd. 177 CG91
Teddington Pk., Tedd. 177 CF92
Teddington Pk. Rd., Tedd. 177 CF91
Tedworth Gdns. SW3 160 DF78
Tedworth Sq.
Tedworth Sq. SW3 160 DF78
Tee, The W3 138 CS72
Tees Ave., Grnf. 137 CE68
Tees Clo., Upmin. 129 FR58
Tees Dr., Rom. 106 FK48
Teesdale, Hem.H. 40 BL17
Teesdale Ave., Islw. 157 CG81
Teesdale Clo. E2 142 DU68
Teesdale Gdns. SE25 202 DS96
Grange Hill
Teesdale Gdns., Islw. 157 CG81
Teesdale Rd. E11 124 EF58
Teesdale Rd., Dart. 188 FQ88
Teesdale Rd., Slou. 131 AM70
Teesdale St. E2 142 DV68
Teesdale Yd. E2 142 DV68
Teesdale St.
Teeswater Ct., Erith 166 EX76
Middle Way
Teevan Clo., Croy. 202 DU101
Teevan Rd., Croy. 202 DU102
Teggs La., Wok. 227 BF116
Teignmouth Clo. SW4 161 DK84
Teignmouth Clo., Edg. 96 CM54
Teignmouth Gdns., Grnf. 137 CF68
Teignmouth Rd. NW2 119 CX64
Teignmouth Rd., Well. 166 EW82
Telcote Way, Ruis. 116 BW59
Woodlands Ave.
Telegraph Hill NW3 120 DB62
Telegraph La., Esher 215 CF107
Telegraph Ms., Ilf. 126 EU60
Telegraph Rd. SW15 179 CV87
Telegraph St. EC2 275 K8
Telegraph Track, Wall. 219 DH110
Telemann Sq. SE3 164 EH83
Telephone Pl. SW6 159 CZ79
Lillie Rd.
Telfer Clo. W3 158 CQ75
Church Rd.
Telferscot Rd. SW12 181 DK88
Telford Ave. SW2 181 DK88
Telford Clo. E17 123 DY59
Telford Clo. SE19 182 DT93
St. Aubyn's Rd.
Telford Clo. W3 158 CQ75
Church Rd.
Telford Clo., Wat. 76 BX35
Telford Ct., Guil. 258 AY135
Clandon Rd.
Telford Ct., St.Alb. 43 CE21
Telford Dr., Slou. 151 AN75
Telford Dr., Walt. 196 BW101
Telford Rd. N11 99 DJ51
Telford Rd. NW9 119 CU58
West Hendon Bdy.
Telford Rd. SE9 185 ER89
Telford Rd. W10 139 CY71
Telford Rd., St.Alb. 61 CJ27
Telford Rd., Sthl. 136 CB73
Telford Rd., Twick. 176 CA87
Telford Ter. SW1 161 DJ79
Telford Way W3 138 CS71
Telford Way, Hayes 136 BY71
Telfords Yd. E1 142 DU73
The Highway
Telham Rd. E6 145 EN68
Tell Gro. SE22 162 DT84
Tellisford, Esher 214 CB105
Tellson Ave. SE18 164 EK81
Telscombe Clo., Orp. 205 ES103
Telston La., Sev. 241 FF117
Temeraire St. SE16 162 DW75
Albion St.
Temperance St., St.Alb. 42 CC20
Temperley Rd. SW12 180 DG87
Tempest Ave., Pot.B. 64 DD32
Tempest Rd., Egh. 173 BC93
Tempest Way, Rain. 147 FG65
Templar Dr. SE28 146 EX72
Templar Dr., Grav. 191 GG92
Templar Ho. NW2 139 CZ65
Shoot Up Hill
Templar Pl., Hmptn. 176 CA94
Templar St. SE5 161 DP82
Templars Ave. NW11 119 CZ58
Templars Cres. N3 98 DA54
Templars Dr., Har. 95 CD51
Temple EC4 274 D10
Temple EC4 141 DN73
Temple Ave. EC4 274 E10
Temple Ave. EC4 141 DN73
Temple Ave. N20 98 DD45
Temple Ave., Croy. 203 DZ103
Temple Ave., Dag. 126 FA60
Temple Bank, Harl. 36 EV09
Temple Bar Rd., Wok. 226 AT119
Temple Clo. E11 124 EE59
Wadley Rd.
Temple Clo. N3 97 CZ54
Cyprus Rd.
Temple Clo. SE28 165 EQ76
Temple Clo. (Cheshunt), Wal.Cr. 66 DU31
Temple Clo., Wat. 75 BT40
Temple Ct., Hert. 32 DR06
Temple Ct., Pot.B. 63 CY31
Mimms Hall Rd.
Temple Flds. Ind. Area, Harl. 36 EU11
Temple Fortune Hill NW11 120 DA57
Temple Fortune La. NW11 119 CZ57
Temple Gdns. N21 99 DP47
Barrowell Grn.
Temple Gdns. NW11 119 CZ58
Temple Gdns., Dag. 126 EX62
Temple Gdns., Rick. 93 BP49
Temple Gdns., Stai. 193 BF95
Temple Gro. NW11 120 DA58
Temple Gro., Enf. 81 DP41
Temple Hill, Dart. 188 FM86
Temple Hill Sq., Dart. 188 FM85
Temple La. EC4 274 E9
Temple Mead, Harl. 50 EH15
Temple Mead, Hem.H. 40 BK18
Temple Mead Clo., Stan. 95 CH51
Temple Mill La. E15 123 EA63
Temple Pk., Uxb. 134 BN69
Temple Pl. WC2 274 C10
Temple Pl. WC2 141 DM73
Temple Rd. E6 144 EL67
Temple Rd. N8 121 DM56
Temple Rd. NW2 119 CW63
Temple Rd. W4 158 CQ76
Temple Rd. W5 157 CK76
Temple Rd., Croy. 220 DR105
Temple Rd., Epsom 216 CR111
Temple Rd., Houns. 156 CB84
Temple Rd., Rich. 158 CM82
Temple Rd., West. 238 EK117
Temple Rd., Wind. 151 AQ82
Temple Sheen SW14 158 CP84
Temple Sheen Rd. SW14 158 CP84
Temple St. E2 142 DV68
Temple Vw., St.Alb. 42 CC18
Temple Way, Slou. 111 AQ64
Temple Way, Sutt. 200 DD104
Temple W. Ms. SE11 278 F7
Temple W. Ms. SE11 161 DP76
Temple Wd. Dr., Red. 250 DF131
Templecombe Ms., Wok. 227 BA116
Dorchester Ct.
Templecombe Rd. E9 142 DW67
Templecombe Way, Mord. 199 CY99
Templecroft, Ashf. 175 BR93
Templedene Ave., Stai. 174 BH94
Templefield Clo., Add. 212 BH107
Templefields, Hert. 32 DR06
Templehof Ave. NW2 119 CW59
Templeman Clo., Pur. 235 DP116
Croftleigh Ave.
Templeman Rd. W7 137 CF71
Templemead Clo. W3 138 CS72
Templemere, Wey. 195 BR104
Templepan La., Rick. 74 BL37
Templer Ave., Grays 171 GG77
Templeton Ave. E4 101 EA49
Templeton Clo. N16 122 DS64
Truman's Rd.
Templeton Clo. SE19 202 DR95
Templeton Pl. SW5 160 DA77
Templeton Rd. N15 122 DR58
Templewood W13 137 CH71
Templewood, Welw.G.C. 29 CX06
Templewood Ave. NW3 120 DB62
Templewood Gdns. NW3 120 DB62
Templewood La., Slou. 111 AQ64
Templewood Pk., Slou. 112 AT63
Tempsford, Welw.G.C. 30 DD09
Tempsford Ave., Borwd. 78 CR42
Tempsford Clo., Enf. 82 DQ41
Gladbeck Way
Temsford Clo., Har. 94 CC54
Ten Acre, Wok. 226 AU118
Abercorn Way
Ten Acre La., Egh. 193 BC96
Ten Acres, Lthd. 231 CD124
Ten Acres Clo., Lthd. 231 CD124
Tenbury Clo. E7 124 EK64
Romford Rd.
Tenbury Ct. SW2 181 DK88
Tenby Ave., Har. 95 CH54
Tenby Clo. N15 122 DT56
Hanover Rd.
Tenby Clo., Rom. 126 EY58
Tenby Gdns., Nthlt. 136 CA65
Tenby Rd. E17 123 DY57
Tenby Rd., Edg. 96 CM53
Tenby Rd., Enf. 82 DW41
Tenby Rd., Rom. 126 EY58
Tenby Rd., Well. 166 EX81
Tench St. E1 142 DV74
Tenchleys La., Oxt. 254 EK131
Tenda Rd. SE16 162 DV77
Roseberry St.
Tendring Rd., Harl. 51 EQ17
Tendring Way, Rom. 126 EW57
Tenham Ave. SW2 181 DK89
Tenison Ct. W1 273 K10
Tenison Way SE1 278 C3
Tenison Way SE1 141 DM74
Tennand Clo. (Cheshunt), Wal.Cr. 66 DT26
Tenniel Clo. W2 140 DC72
Porchester Gdns.
Tennis Ct. La., E.Mol. 197 CF97
Hampton Ct. Way
Tennis St. SE1 279 K4
Tennis St. SE1 162 DR75
Tennison Ave., Borwd. 78 CP43
Tennison Clo., Couls. 235 DP120
Tennison Rd. SE25 202 DT98
Tenniswood Rd., Enf. 82 DS39
Tennyson Ave. E11 124 EG59
Tennyson Ave. E12 144 EL66
Tennyson Ave. NW9 118 CQ55
Tennyson Ave., Grays 170 GB76
Tennyson Ave., N.Mal. 199 CV99
Tennyson Ave., Twick. 177 CF88
Tennyson Ave., Wal.Abb. 68 EE34
Tennyson Clo., Enf. 83 DX43
Tennyson Clo., Felt. 175 BT86
Tennyson Clo., Well. 165 ET81
Tennyson Rd. E10 123 EB60
Tennyson Rd. E15 144 EE66
Tennyson Rd. E17 123 DZ58
Tennyson Rd. NW6 139 CZ67
Tennyson Rd. NW7 97 CU50
Tennyson Rd. SE20 183 DX94
Tennyson Rd. SW19 180 DC93
Tennyson Rd. W7 137 CF73
Tennyson Rd., Add. 212 BL105
Tennyson Rd., Ashf. 174 BL92
Tennyson Rd., Brwd. 109 GC45
Tennyson Rd., Dart. 188 FN85
Tennyson Rd., Houns. 156 CC82
Tennyson Rd., Rom. 106 FJ52
Tennyson Rd., St.Alb. 60 CA26
Tennyson Rd., Well. 165 ET81
Tennyson St. SW8 161 DH82
Tennyson Wk., Grav. 190 GD90
Tennyson Wk., Til. 171 GH82
Tennyson Way, Horn. 127 FG61
Tennyson Way, Slou. 131 AL70
Wordsworth Rd.
Tensing Ave., Grav. 190 GE90
Tensing Rd., Sthl. 156 CA76
Tent Peg La., Orp. 205 EQ99
Tent St. E1 142 DV70
Tentelow La., Sthl. 156 CA78
Tenter Grd. E1 275 P7
Tenter Pas. E1 142 DT72
Mansell St.
Tenterden Clo. NW4 119 CX55
Tenterden Clo. SE9 185 EM91
Tenterden Dr. NW4 119 CX55
Tenterden Gdns. NW4 119 CX55
Tenterden Gdns., Croy. 202 DU101
Tenterden Gro. NW4 119 CX55
Tenterden Rd. N17 100 DT52
Tenterden Rd., Croy. 202 DU101
Tenterden Rd., Dag. 126 EZ61
Tenterden St. W1 273 J9
Tenterden St. W1 141 DH72
Tenzing Rd., Hem.H. 40 BN20
Terborch Way SE22 182 DS85
East Dulwich Gro.
Tercel Path, Chig. 104 EV49
Terence Clo., Grav. 191 GM89
Teresa Gdns., Wal.Cr. 66 DW34
Teresa Ms. E17 123 EA56
Teresa Wk. N10 121 DH57
Connaught Gdns.
Terling Clo. E11 124 EF62
Terling Rd., Dag. 126 FA61
Terling Wk. N1 142 DQ67
Britannia Row
Terlings, The, Brwd. 108 FU48
Terminus Ho., Harl. 35 ER14
Terminus Pl. SW1 277 J7
Terminus Pl. SW1 161 DH76
Terminus St., Harl. 35 ER14
Tern Gdns., Upmin. 129 FS60
Tern Way, Brwd. 108 FS49
Terrace, The E4 102 EE48
Chingdale Rd.
Terrace, The N3 97 CZ54
Hendon La.
Terrace, The NW6 140 DA67
Terrace, The SW13 158 CS82
Terrace, The, Add. 212 BL106
Terrace, The, Dor. 263 CJ137
Deepdene Wd.
Terrace, The, Grav. 191 GH86
Terrace, The, Har. 117 CH60
Terrace, The, Maid. 150 AC76
Terrace, The, Sev. 256 FD122
Terrace, The, Wdf.Grn. 102 EG51
Broadmead Rd.
Terrace Gdns. SW13 159 CT82
Terrace Gdns., Wat. 75 BV40
St. Albans Rd.
Terrace La., Rich. 178 CL86
Terrace Rd. E9 142 DW66
Terrace Rd. E13 144 EG67
Terrace Rd., Walt. 195 BU101
Terrace St., Grav. 191 GH86
Terrace Wk., Dag. 126 EY64
Terraces, The, Dart. 188 FQ87
Terrapin Rd. SW17 181 DH90
Terretts Pl. N1 141 DP66
Upper St.
Terrick Rd. N22 99 DL53
Terrick St. W12 139 CV72
Terrilands, Pnr. 116 BZ55
Terront Rd. N15 122 DQ57
Tessa Sanderson Pl. SW8 161 DH83
Heath Rd.
Tessa Sanderson Way, Grnf. 117 CD64
Lilian Board Way
Testard Rd., Guil. 258 AW136
Testers Clo., Oxt. 254 EH132
Testerton Wk. W11 139 CX73
Whitchurch Rd.
Testwood Rd., Wind. 151 AK81
Tetbury Pl. N1 141 DP67
Upper St.
Tetcott Rd. SW10 160 DC80
Tetherdown N10 120 DG55
Tethys Rd., Hem.H. 40 BM17
Tetterby Way SE16 162 DU78
Catlin St.
Tetty Way, Brom. 204 EG96
Teversham La. SW8 161 DL81
Teviot Ave., S.Ock. 148 FQ72
Teviot Clo., Guil. 242 AU131
Teviot Clo., Well. 166 EV81
Teviot St. E14 143 EC71
Tewin Clo., St.Alb. 43 CJ16
Tewin Ct., Welw.G.C. 29 CZ09
Tewin Rd., Hem.H. 41 BQ20
Tewin Rd., Welw.G.C. 29 CZ09
Tewkesbury Ave. SE23 182 DV87
Tewkesbury Ave., Pnr. 116 BY57
Tewkesbury Clo. N15 122 DR58
Tewkesbury Rd.
Tewkesbury Clo., Loug. 84 EL44
Tewkesbury Clo., W.Byf. 212 BK111
Tewkesbury Gdns. NW9 118 CP55
Tewkesbury Rd. N15 122 DR58
Tewkesbury Rd. W13 137 CG73
Tewkesbury Rd., Cars. 200 DD102
Tewkesbury Ter. N11 99 DJ51
Tewson Rd. SE18 165 ES77
Teynham Ave., Enf. 82 DR44
Teynham Grn., Brom. 204 EG99
Teynton Ter. N17 100 DQ53
Thackeray Ave. N17 100 DU54
Thackeray Ave., Til. 171 GH81
Thackeray Clo. SW19 179 CX94
Thackeray Clo., Har. 116 CA60
Thackeray Clo., Islw. 157 CG82
Thackeray Clo., Uxb. 135 BP72
Dickens Ave.
Thackeray Dr., Ilf. 126 EU59
Thackeray Dr., Rom. 126 EU59
Thackeray Rd. E6 144 EK68
Thackeray Rd. SW8 161 DH82
Thackeray St. W8 160 DB75
Thackrah Clo. N2 98 DC54
Thakeham Clo. SE26 182 DV92
Thalia Clo. SE10 163 ED79
Feathers Pl.
Thalmassing Clo., Brwd. 109 GB47
Thame Rd. SE16 163 DX75
Thames Ave. SW10 160 DC81
Thames Ave., Cher. 194 BG97
Thames Ave., Dag. 146 FA70
Thames Ave., Grnf. 137 CF68
Thames Ave., Hem.H. 40 BM15
Thames Ave., Wind. 151 AR80
Thames Bank SW14 158 CQ82
Thames Circle E14 163 EA77
Westferry Rd.
Thames Clo., Cher. 194 BH101
Thames Clo., Hmptn. 196 CB96
Thames Clo., Rain. 147 FH72
Thames Ct., W.Mol. 196 CB96
Thames Dr., Grays 171 GG78
Thames Dr., Ruis. 115 BQ58
Thames Gate, Dart. 168 FN84
St. Edmunds Rd.
Thames Mead, Walt. 195 BU101
Thames Mead, Wind. 151 AL81
Thames Meadow, Shep. 195 BR102
Thames Meadow, W.Mol. 196 CA96
Thames Pl. SW15 159 CX83
Thames Rd. E16 144 EK74
Thames Rd. W4 158 CN79
Thames Rd., Bark. 145 ES69
Thames Rd., Dart. 167 FF82
Thames Rd., Grays 170 GB80
Thames Rd., Slou. 153 BA77
Thames Rd. Ind. Est. E16 144 EK74
Thames Side, Cher. 194 BJ99
Thames Side, Kings.T. 197 CK95
Thames Side, Stai. 194 BH96
Thames Side, Tedd. 177 CK94
Thames Side, Wind. 151 AR80
Thames St. SE10 163 EB79
Thames St., Hmptn. 196 CB95
Thames St., Kings.T. 197 CK96
Thames St., Stai. 173 BE91
Thames St., Sun. 195 BU98
Thames St., Walt. 195 BT101
Thames St., Wey. 195 BP103
Thames St., Wind. 151 AR81
Thames Vw., Grays 171 GG78
Thames Village W4 158 CQ81
Thames Way, Grav. 190 GC88
Thames Wf. E16 144 EF74
Thamesbank Pl. SE28 146 EW72
Thamesdale, St.Alb. 62 CM27
Thamesfield Ct., Shep. 195 BQ101
Thamesgate Clo., Rich. 177 CH91
Locksmeade Rd.
Thameshill Ave., Rom. 105 FC54
Thameside, Tedd. 177 CJ94
Thameside Ind. Est. E16 164 EL75
Thameside Wk. SE28 146 EV72
Thamesmead, Walt. 195 BU101
Thamesmead Spine Rd., Belv. 167 FC75
Thamesmere Dr. SE28 146 EU73
Thamesvale Clo., Houns. 156 CA82
Thamley, Purf. 168 FN77
Thane Vill. N7 121 DM62
Thane Wks. N7 121 DM62
Thane Vill.
Thanescroft Gdns., Croy. 202 DS104
Thanet Dr., Kes. 204 EK104
Phoenix Dr.
Thanet Pl., Croy. 220 DQ105
Thanet Rd., Bex. 186 FA87
Thanet Rd., Erith 167 FE80
Thanet St. WC1 273 P3
Thanet St. WC1 141 DL69
Thanington Ct. SE9 185 ES86
Thant Clo. E10 123 EB62
Tharp Rd., Wall. 219 DK106
Thatcham Gdns. N20 98 DC45
Thatcher Clo., West Dr. 154 BL75
Classon Clo.
Thatchers Clo., Horl. 269 DH146
Wheatfield Way
Thatchers Clo., Loug. 85 EQ40
Thatchers Cft., Hem.H. 40 BL16
Marlborough Ri.
Thatchers Way, Islw. 177 CD85
Thatches Gro., Rom. 126 EY56
Thavies Inn EC1 274 E8
Thaxted Grn., Brwd. 109 GC43
Thaxted Pl. SW20 179 CX94
Thaxted Rd. SE9 185 EQ89
Thaxted Rd., Buck.H. 102 EK45
Thaxted Wk., Rain. 147 FF67
Ongar Way
Thaxted Way, Wal.Abb. 67 ED33
Thaxton Rd. W14 159 CZ79
Thayer St. W1 272 G7
Thayer St. W1 140 DG71
Thayers Fm. Rd., Beck. 203 DY95
Thaynesfield, Pot.B. 64 DD31
The Floats, Sev. 241 FD119
London Rd.
Theatre St. SW11 160 DF83
Theberton St. N1 141 DN67
Theed St. SE1 278 E3
Theed St. SE1 141 DN74
Thele Ave., Ware 33 ED11
Thellusson Way, Rick. 91 BF45
Thelma Clo., Grav. 191 GM92
Thelma Gdns. SE3 164 EK81
Thelma Gdns., Felt. 176 BY90
Thelma Gro., Tedd. 177 CG93
Theobald Cres., Har. 94 CB53
Theobald Rd. E17 123 DZ59
Theobald Rd., Croy. 201 DP103
Theobald St. SE1 279 K7
Theobald St., Borwd. 78 CL39
Theobald St., Rad. 77 CH36
Theobalds Ave. N12 98 DC49
Theobalds Ave., Grays 170 GC78
Theobalds Clo. (Cuffley), Pot.B. 65 DM30
Theobalds Ct. N4 122 DQ61
Queens Dr.
Theobalds La. (Cheshunt), Wal.Cr. 66 DW32
Theobalds Pk. Rd., Enf. 81 DP35
Theobald's Rd. WC1 274 B6
Theobald's Rd. WC1 141 DM71
Theobalds Rd. (Cuffley), Pot.B. 65 DL30
Theodore Rd. SE13 183 ED86
Thepps Clo., Red. 267 DM137
Therapia La., Croy. 201 DK101
Therapia Rd. SE22 182 DW86
Theresa Rd. W6 159 CU77
Theresas Wk., S.Croy. 220 DR110
Sanderstead Rd.
Therfield Ct. N4 122 DQ61
Brownswood Rd.
Therfield Rd., St.Alb. 43 CD16
Thermopylae Gate E14 163 EB77
Theseus Wk. N1 274 G1
Thesiger Rd. SE20 183 DX94
Thessaly Rd. SW8 161 DJ80
Thetford Clo. N13 99 DP51
Thetford Gdns., Dag. 146 EX66
Thetford Rd., Ashf. 174 BL91
Thetford Rd., Dag. 146 EX66
Thetford Rd., N.Mal. 198 CR100
Thetis Ter., Rich. 158 CN79
Kew Grn.
Theydon Bower, Epp. 70 EU31
Theydon Ct., Wal.Abb. 68 EG33
Theydon Gdns., Rain. 147 FE66
Theydon Gate, Epp. 85 ES37
Coppice Row
Theydon Gro., Epp. 70 EU30
Theydon Gro., Wdf.Grn. 102 EJ51
Theydon Pk. Rd., Epp. 85 ES39
Theydon Pl., Epp. 69 ET31
Theydon Rd. E5 122 DW61
Theydon Rd., Epp. 69 ER34
Theydon St. E17 123 DZ59
Thicket, The, West Dr. 134 BL72
Thicket Cres., Sutt. 218 DC105
Thicket Gro. SE20 182 DU94
Anerley Rd.
Thicket Gro., Dag. 146 EW65
Thicket Rd. SE20 182 DU94
Thicket Rd., Sutt. 218 DC105
Thicketts, Sev. 257 FJ123
Thickthorne La., Stai. 174 BJ94
Berryscroft Rd.
Thieves La., Hert. 31 DM10
Thieves La., Ware 32 DW08
Third Ave. E12 124 EL63
Third Ave. E13 144 EG69
Third Ave. E17 123 EA57
Third Ave. W3 139 CT74
Third Ave. W10 139 CY69
Third Ave., Dag. 147 FB67
Third Ave., Enf. 82 DT43
Third Ave., Grays 171 GF79
Third Ave., Harl. 51 EM16
Third Ave., Hayes 135 BT74
Third Ave., Rom. 126 EW58
Third Ave., Wat. 76 BX35
Third Ave., Wem. 117 CK61

Third Clo., W.Mol. 196 CB98
Third Cres., Slou. 131 AQ71
Third Cross Rd., Twick. 177 CD89
Third Way, Wem. 118 CP63
Thirkleby Clo., Slou. 131 AQ74
Thirleby Rd. SW1 277 L7
Thirleby Rd. SW1 161 DJ76
Thirleby Rd., Edg. 96 CR53
Thirlmere Ave., Grnf. 137 CJ69
Thirlmere Ave., Slou. 130 AJ71
Thirlmere Clo., Egh. 173 BB94
Keswick Rd.
Thirlmere Dr., St.Alb. 43 CH22
Thirlmere Gdns., Nthwd. 93 BP50
Thirlmere Gdns., Wem. 117 CJ60
Thirlmere Ho., Islw. 177 CF85
Thirlmere Ri., Brom. 184 EF93
Thirlmere Rd. N10 99 DH53
Thirlmere Rd. SW16 181 DK91
Thirlmere Rd., Bexh. 167 FC82
Thirlstane, St.Alb. 43 CF19
Thirsk Clo., Nthlt. 136 CA65
Thirsk Rd. SE25 202 DR98
Thirsk Rd. SW11 160 DG83
Thirsk Rd., Borwd. 78 CN37
Thirsk Rd., Mitch. 180 DG94
Thirza Rd., Dart. 188 FM86
Thistle Clo., Hem.H. 39 BE21
Thistle Gro. SW10 160 DC78
Thistle Gro., Welw.G.C. 30 DC11
Thistle Mead, Loug. 85 EN41
Thistle Rd., Grav. 191 GL87
Thistle Wd. Cres., Croy. 221 ED112
Thistlebrook SE2 166 EW76
Thistlecroft, Hem.H. 40 BH21
Thistlecroft Gdns., Stan. 95 CK53
Thistlecroft Rd., Walt. 214 BW105
Thistledene, T.Ditt. 197 CE100
Thistledene, W.Byf. 211 BF113
Thistledene Ave., Har. 116 BY62
Thistledene Ave., Rom. 105 FB50
Thistledown, Grav. 191 GK93
Thistlemead, Chis. 205 EP96
Thistles, The, Hem.H. 40 BH19
Thistlewaite Rd. E5 122 DV62
Thistlewood Clo. N7 121 DM61
Thistleworth Clo., Islw. 157 CD80
Thistley Clo. N12 98 DE51
Summerfields Ave.
Thomas à Beckett Clo., Wem. 117 CF63
Thomas Ave., Cat. 236 DQ121
Thomas Baines Rd. SW11 160 DD83
Thomas Clo., Brwd. 108 FY48
Thomas Darby Ct. W11 139 CY72
Thomas Dean Rd. SE26 183 DZ91
Kangley Bri. Rd.
Thomas Dinwiddy Rd. SE12 184 EJ89
Thomas Doyle St. SE1 278 G6
Thomas Doyle St. SE1 161 DP76
Thomas Dr., Grav. 191 GK89
Thomas Hardy Ho. N22 99 DM52
Thomas La. SE6 183 EA87
Thomas More Ho. EC2 142 DQ71
The Barbican
Thomas More St. E1 142 DU73
Thomas More Way N2 120 DC55
Thomas Pl. W8 160 DB76
St. Mary's Pl.
Thomas Rd. E14 143 DZ72
Thomas Rd., H.Wyc. 110 AD59
Thomas Rochford Way, Wal.Cr. 67 DY26
Thomas Sims Ct., Horn. 127 FH64
Thomas St. SE18 165 EP77
Thomas Wall Clo., Sutt. 218 DB106
Clarence Rd.
Thompkins La., Slou. 131 AM66
Thompson Ave., Rich. 158 CN83
Thompson Clo., Ilf. 125 EQ61
High Rd.
Thompson Clo., Slou. 153 BA77
Thompson Rd. SE22 182 DT86
Thompson Rd., Dag. 126 EZ62
Thompson Rd., Uxb. 134 BL66
Thompson Way, Rick. 92 BG45
Thompson's Ave. SE5 162 DQ80
Thompsons Clo., Wal.Cr. 66 DT29
Thompson's La., Loug. 84 EF38
Thomson Cres., Croy. 201 DN102
Thomson Rd., Har. 117 CE55
Thong La., Grav. 191 GM91
Thorburn Sq. SE1 162 DU77
Thorburn Way SW19 200 DD95
Willow Vw.
Thoresby St. N1 275 J2
Thoresby St. N1 142 DQ69
Thorkhill Gdns., T.Ditt. 197 CG102
Thorkhill Rd., T.Ditt. 197 CG102
Thorley Clo., W.Byf. 212 BG114
Thorley Gdns., Wok. 212 BG114
Thorn Ave. (Bushey), Wat. 94 CC46
Thorn Bank, Guil. 258 AU136
Thorn Clo., Brom. 205 EN100
Thorn Clo., Nthlt. 136 BZ69
Thorn Dr., Slou. 132 AY72
Thorn Hill Clo., Amer. 55 AP40
Thorn Ho., Beck. 203 DY95
Thorn La., Rain. 148 FK68
Thorn Ter. SE15 162 DW83
Nunhead Gro.
Thornaby Gdns. N18 100 DU51
Thornaby Pl., H.Wyc. 110 AE55
Wootton Way
Thornash Clo., Wok. 226 AW115
Thornash Rd., Wok. 226 AW115
Thornash Way, Wok. 226 AW115
Thornbank Clo., Stai. 174 BG85
Thornbridge Rd., Iver 133 BC67
Thornbury Ave., Islw. 157 CD80
Thornbury Clo. N16 122 DS64
Truman's Rd.
Thornbury Clo., Hodd. 33 EB13
Thornbury Gdns., Borwd. 78 CQ41
Thornbury Rd. SW2 181 DL86
Thornbury Rd., Islw. 157 CD80
Thornbury Sq. N6 121 DJ60
Thornby Rd. E5 122 DW62
Thorncliffe Rd. SW2 181 DL86
Thorncliffe Rd., Sthl. 156 BZ78
Thorncombe Rd. SE22 182 DS85
Thorncroft, Egh. 172 AW94
Thorncroft, Hem.H. 41 BP22
Thorncroft, Horn. 127 FH58
Thorncroft Clo., Couls. 235 DN120
Waddington Ave.
Thorncroft Dr., Lthd. 231 CH123
Thorncroft Rd., Sutt. 218 DB105
Thorncroft St. SW8 161 DL80
Thorndales, Brwd. 108 FX49
Thorndean St. SW18 180 DC89
Thorndene Ave. N11 98 DG46
Thorndike, Slou. 131 AN71
Thorndike Ave., Nthlt. 136 BX67
Thorndike Clo. SW10 160 DC80
Thorndike St. SW1 277 M9
Thorndike St. SW1 161 DK77
Thorndon Clo., Orp. 205 ET96
Thorndon Gdns., Epsom 216 CS106
Thorndon Gate, Brwd. 109 GC50
Thorndon Rd., Orp. 205 ET96
Thorndyke Ct., Pnr. 94 BZ52
Westfield Pk.
Thorne Clo. E11 124 EE63
Thorne Clo. E16 144 EF72
Thorne Clo., Ashf. 175 BQ94
Thorne Clo., Erith 167 FC79
Thorne Pas. SW13 158 CS82
Thorne Rd. SW8 161 DL80
Thorne St. E16 144 EF72
Thorne St. SW13 158 CS83
Thorneloe Gdns., Croy. 219 DN106
Thornes Clo., Beck. 203 EC97
Thornet Wd. Rd., Brom. 205 EN97
Thorney Cres. SW11 160 DD80
Thorney Hedge Rd. W4 158 CP77
Thorney La. N., Iver 133 BF72
Thorney La. S., Iver 153 BF75
Thorney Mill Rd., Iver 154 BG76
Thorney St. SW1 277 P8
Thorney St. SW1 161 DL77
Thorneycroft Clo., Walt. 196 BW100
Thornfield Ave. NW7 97 CY53
Thornfield Rd. W12 159 CV75
Thornfield Rd., Bans. 234 DA117
Thornford Rd. SE13 183 EC85
Thorngate Rd. W9 140 DA70
Thorngrove Rd. E13 144 EH67
Thornham Gro. E15 123 ED64
Thornham St. SE10 163 EB79
Thornhaugh Ms. WC1 273 N5
Thornhaugh St. WC1 273 N6
Thornhaugh St. WC1 141 DK71
Thornhill, Epp. 71 FC26
Thornhill Ave. SE18 165 ES80
Thornhill Ave., Surb. 198 CL103
Thornhill Bri. Wf. N1 141 DM67
Caledonian Rd.
Thornhill Cres. N1 141 DM66
Thornhill Gdns. E10 123 EB61
Thornhill Gdns., Bark. 145 ES66
Thornhill Gro. N1 141 DM66
Lofting Rd.
Thornhill Ho. N1 141 DN66
Thornhill Rd.
Thornhill Rd. E10 123 EB61
Thornhill Rd. N1 141 DN66
Thornhill Rd., Croy. 202 DQ101
Thornhill Rd., Nthwd. 93 BQ49
Thornhill Rd., Surb. 198 CL103
Thornhill Rd., Uxb. 114 BM63
Thornhill Sq. N1 141 DM66
Thornhill Way, Shep. 194 BN99
Thornlaw Rd. SE27 181 DN91
Thornleas Pl., Lthd. 245 BS126
Station App.
Thornley Clo. N17 100 DU52
Thornley Dr., Har. 116 CB61
Thornley Pl. SE10 164 EE78
Caradoc St.
Thornridge, Brwd. 108 FV45
Thorns, The, Reig. 250 DC131
Thorns Meadow, West. 240 EW123
Thornsbeach Rd. SE6 183 EC88
Thornsett Pl. SE20 202 DV96
Thornsett Rd. SE20 202 DV96
Thornsett Rd. SW18 180 DB88
Thornside, Edg. 96 CN51
High St.
Thornton Ave. SW2 181 DK88
Thornton Ave. W4 158 CS77
Thornton Ave., Croy. 201 DM100
Thornton Ave., West Dr. 154 BM76
Thornton Clo., Guil. 242 AU130
Thornton Clo., Horl. 268 DE148
Thornton Clo., West Dr. 154 BM76
Thornton Ct. SW20 199 CX99
Thornton Cres., Couls. 235 DN119
Thornton Dene, Beck. 203 EA96
Thornton Gdns. SW12 181 DK88
Thornton Gro., Pnr. 94 CA51
Thornton Hill SW19 179 CY94
Thornton Pl. W1 272 D6
Thornton Pl. W1 140 DF71
Thornton Pl., Horl. 268 DE147
Thornton Rd. E11 123 ED61
Thornton Rd. N18 100 DW48
Thornton Rd. SW12 181 DK87
Thornton Rd. SW14 158 CR83
Thornton Rd. SW19 179 CX93
Thornton Rd., Barn. 79 CY41
Thornton Rd., Belv. 167 FB77
Thornton Rd., Brom. 184 EG92
Thornton Rd., Cars. 200 DD102
Thornton Rd., Croy. 201 DM101
Thornton Rd., Ilf. 125 EP63
Thornton Rd., Pot.B. 64 DC30
Thornton Rd., Th.Hth. 201 DN99
Thornton Rd. E. SW19 179 CX93
Thornton Rd.
Thornton Row, Th.Hth. 201 DN99
London Rd.
Thornton St. SW9 161 DN82
Thornton St., Hert. 32 DR09
Thornton St., St.Alb. 42 CC19
Thornton Wk., Horl. 268 DE148
Thornton Pl.
Thornton Way NW11 120 DB57
Thorntons Fm. Ave., Rom. 127 FC60
Thorntree Rd. SE7 164 EK78
Thornville Gro. SW19 200 DC96
Thornville St. SE8 163 EA81
Thornwood Clo. E18 102 EH54
Thornwood Rd. SE13 184 EE85
Thornwood Rd., Epp. 70 EV29
Thorogood Gdns. E15 124 EE64
Thorogood Way, Rain. 147 FE67
Thorold Clo., S.Croy. 221 DX110
Thorold Rd. N22 99 DL52
Thorold Rd., Ilf. 125 EP61
Thoroughfare, The, Tad. 249 CU125
Chequers La.
Thorparch Rd. SW8 161 DK81
Thorpe Bypass, Egh. 193 BB96
Thorpe Clo. W10 139 CY72
Cambridge Gdns.
Thorpe Clo., Croy. 221 EC111
Thorpe Clo., Orp. 205 ES103
Thorpe Cres. E17 101 DZ54
Thorpe Cres., Wat. 94 BW45
Thorpe Hall Rd. E17 101 EC53
Thorpe Ind. Pk., Egh. 193 BC95
Thorpe Lea Rd., Egh. 173 BB93
Thorpe Lo., Horn. 128 FK58
Thorpe Rd. E6 145 EM67
Thorpe Rd. E7 124 EF63
Thorpe Rd. E17 101 EC54
Thorpe Rd. N15 122 DS58
Thorpe Rd., Bark. 145 ER66
Thorpe Rd., Cher. 193 BD99
Thorpe Rd., Kings.T. 178 CL94
Thorpe Rd., St.Alb. 43 CD21
Thorpe Rd., Stai. 173 BD93
Thorpebank Rd. W12 139 CU74
Thorpedale Gdns., Ilf. 125 EN56
Thorpedale Rd. N4 121 DL61
Thorpefield Clo., St.Alb. 43 CK17
Thorpes Clo., Guil. 242 AU131
Thorpeside Clo., Stai. 193 BE95
Thorpewood Ave. SE26 182 DV89
Thorpland Ave., Uxb. 115 BQ62
Thorsden Clo., Wok. 226 AY119
Thorsden Ct., Wok. 226 AY118
Guildford Rd.
Thorsden Way SE19 182 DS91
Oaks Ave.
Thorton Rd. Retail Pk., Croy. 201 DM100
Peall Rd.
Thorverton Rd. NW2 119 CY62
Thoydon Rd. E3 143 DY68
Thrale Rd. SW16 181 DJ91
Thrale St. SE1 279 J3
Thrale St. SE1 142 DQ74
Thrasher Clo. E8 142 DT67
Stean St.
Thrawl St. E1 142 DT71
Threadneedle St. EC2 275 L9
Threadneedle St. EC2 142 DR72
Three Arch Rd., Red. 266 DF138
Three Cherrytrees La., Hem.H. 41 BP16
Three Clo. La., Berk. 38 AW20
Three Colt St. E14 143 DZ72
Three Colts Cor. E2 142 DU70
Weaver St.
Three Colts La. E2 142 DV70
Three Cors., Bexh. 167 FB82
Three Cors., Hem.H. 40 BN22
Three Cups Yd. WC1 274 C7
Three Forest Way, Epp. 51 EM22
Three Forest Way, Harl. 34 EG14
Three Forest Way (Mark Hall N.), Harl. 36 EU10
Three Forest Way, Wal.Abb. 51 EM21
Three Forest Way, Ware 35 EM12
Three Forests Way, Chig. 104 EW48
Three Gates, Guil. 243 BC132
Three Gates Rd. (Fawkham Grn.), Long. 209 FT104
Three Horseshoes Rd., Harl. 51 EP17
Three Kings Rd., Mitch. 200 DG97
Three Kings Yd. W1 273 H10
Three Kings Yd. W1 141 DH73
Three Mill La. E3 143 EC69
Three Oak La. SE1 279 P4
Three Oaks Clo., Uxb. 114 BM62
Three Pears Rd., Guil. 243 BE134
Threehouseholds, Ch.St.G. 90 AT49
Threshers Bush, Harl. 36 FA14
Threshers Pl. W11 139 CY73
Thriffwood SE26 182 DW90
Thrift, The, Dart. 189 FW90
Thrift Fm. La., Borwd. 78 CQ40
Thrift Grn., Brwd. 109 GA48
Knight's Way
Thrift La., Sev. 239 ER116
Cudham La. S.
Thrift Vale, Guil. 243 BD131
Thriftfield, Hem.H. 40 BK18
Thrifts Mead, Epp. 85 ES37
Thrigby Rd., Chess. 216 CM107
Throckmorten Rd. E16 144 EH72
Throgmorton Ave. EC2 275 L8
Throgmorton Ave. EC2 142 DR72
Throgmorton St. EC2 275 L8
Throgmorton St. EC2 142 DR72
Throwley Clo. SE2 166 EW76
Throwley Rd., Sutt. 218 DB106
Throwley Way, Sutt. 218 DB105
Thrums, The, Wat. 75 BV37
Thrupp Clo., Mitch. 201 DH96
Thrupps Ave., Walt. 214 BX106
Thrupps La., Walt. 214 BX106
Thrush Ave., Hat. 45 CU20
Thrush Grn., Har. 116 CA56
Thrush Grn., Rick. 92 BJ45
Thrush La. (Cuffley), Pot.B. 65 DL28
Thrush St. SE17 279 H10
Thruxton Way SE15 162 DT80
Daniel Gdns.
Thumbswood, Welw.G.C. 30 DA12
Thumpers, Hem.H. 40 BL18
Thundercourt, Ware 33 DX05
Thunderer Rd., Dag. 146 EY70
Thundridge Clo., Welw.G.C. 30 DB10
Amwell Common
Thurbarn Rd. SE6 183 EB92
Thurgood Rd., Hodd. 49 EA15
Thurland Rd. SE16 162 DU76
Thurlby Clo., Har. 117 CG58
Gayton Rd.
Thurlby Clo., Wdf.Grn. 103 EM50
Thurlby Rd. SE27 181 DN91
Thurlby Rd., Wem. 137 CK65
Thurleigh Ave. SW12 180 DG86
Thurleigh Rd. SW12 180 DF87
Thurleston Ave., Mord. 199 CY99
Thurlestone Ave. N12 98 DF51
Thurlestone Ave., Ilf. 125 ET63
Thurlestone Clo., Shep. 195 BQ100
Thurlestone Rd. SE27 181 DN90
Thurloe Clo. SW7 276 B8
Thurloe Clo. SW7 160 DE77
Thurloe Gdns., Rom. 127 FF58
Thurloe Pl. SW7 276 A8
Thurloe Pl. SW7 160 DD77
Thurloe Pl. Ms. SW7 276 A8
Thurloe Sq. SW7 276 B8
Thurloe Sq. SW7 160 DE77
Thurloe St. SW7 276 A8
Thurloe St. SW7 160 DD77
Thurloe Wk., Grays 170 GA76
Thurlow Clo. E4 101 EB51
Higham Sta. Ave.
Thurlow Gdns., Ilf. 103 ER51
Thurlow Gdns., Wem. 117 CK64
Thurlow Hill SE21 182 DQ88
Thurlow Pk. Rd. SE21 181 DP88
Thurlow Rd. NW3 120 DD64
Thurlow Rd. W7 157 CG75
Thurlow St. SE17 279 L10
Thurlow St. SE17 162 DR78
Thurlow Ter. NW5 120 DG64
Thurlstone Rd., Ruis. 115 BU62
Thurlton Ct., Wok. 226 AY116
Chobham Rd.
Thurnby Ct., Twick. 177 CE90
Thurnham Way, Tad. 233 CW120
Thurrock Lakeside, Grays 169 FV77
Thurrock Pk. Ind. Est., Til. 170 GD80
Thurrock Pk. Way, Til. 170 GD80
Thursby Rd., Wok. 226 AU118
Thursland Rd., Sid. 186 EY92
Thursley Cres., Croy. 221 EC108
Thursley Gdns. SW19 179 CX89
Thursley Rd. SE9 185 EM90
Thurso Clo., Rom. 106 FP51
Thurso St. SW17 180 DD91
Thurstan Rd. SW20 179 CV94
Thurstans, Harl. 51 EQ20
Thurston Rd. SE13 163 EB82
Thurston Rd., Slou. 132 AS72
Thurston Rd., Sthl. 136 BZ72
Thurtle Rd. E2 142 DT67
Thwaite Clo., Erith 167 FC79
Thyer Clo., Orp. 223 EQ105
Isabella Dr.
Thyme Ct., Guil. 243 BB131
Mallow Cres.
Thyra Gro. N12 98 DB51
Tibbatts Rd. E3 143 EB70
Tibbenham Wk. E13 144 EF68
Whitelegg Rd.
Tibberton Sq. N1 142 DQ66
Popham Rd.
Tibbets Clo. SW19 179 CX88
Tibbets Cor. SW19 179 CX87
Tibbet's Ride SW15 179 CX87
Tibbles Clo., Wat. 76 BY35
Tibbs Hill Rd., Abb.L. 59 BT30
Tiber Gdns. N1 141 DM67
Treaty St.
Ticehurst Clo., Orp. 186 EU94
Grovelands Rd.
Ticehurst Rd. SE23 183 DY89
Tichborne Wd., Rick. 91 BD50
Tichmarsh, Epsom 216 CQ110
Tickenhall Dr., Harl. 52 EX15
Tickford Clo. SE2 166 EW75
Ampleforth Rd.
Tidal Basin Rd. E16 144 EF73
Tidenham Gdns., Croy. 202 DS104
Tideswell Rd. SW15 159 CW84
Tideswell Rd., Croy. 203 EA104
Tideway Clo., Rich. 177 CH91
Locksmeade Rd.
Tidey St. E3 143 EA71
Tidford Rd., Well. 165 ET82
Tidworth Rd. E3 143 EA70
Tidy's La., Epp. 70 EV29
Tiepigs La., Brom. 204 EF102
Tiepigs La., W.Wick. 204 EE103
Tierney Rd. SW2 181 DL87
Tiger La., Brom. 204 EH98
Tiger Way E5 122 DV63
Tilbrook Rd. SE3 164 EJ83
Tilburstow Hill Rd., Gdse. 252 DW132
Tilbury Clo. SE15 162 DT80
Willowbrook Rd.
Tilbury Clo., Orp. 206 EV96
Tilbury Docks, Til. 170 GE84
Tilbury Gdns., Til. 171 GG84
Tilbury Hotel Rd., Til. 171 GG84
Tilbury Mead, Harl. 52 EU17
Tilbury Rd. E6 145 EM68
Tilbury Rd. E10 123 EC59
Tildesley Rd. SW15 179 CW86
Tile Fm. Rd., Orp. 205 ER104
Tile Kiln Clo., Hem.H. 41 BP21
Tile Kiln Cres., Hem.H. 41 BP21
Tile Kiln La. N6 121 DJ60
Winchester Rd.
Tile Kiln La. N13 100 DQ50
Tile Kiln La., Bex. 187 FC89
Tile Kiln La., Hem.H. 41 BP21
Tile Kiln La., Uxb. 115 BP59
Tile Yd. E14 143 DZ72
Commercial Rd.
Tilecroft, Welw.G.C. 29 CX05
Tilegate Rd., Harl. 51 ET17
Tilegate Rd., Ong. 53 FC19
Tilehost, Guil. 242 AU130
Tilehouse Clo., Borwd. 78 CM41
Tilehouse La., Ger.Cr. 91 BE53
Tilehouse La., Rick. 91 BE53
Tilehouse La., Uxb. 113 BE55
Tilehouse Rd., Guil. 258 AY138
Tilehouse Way, Uxb. 113 BF59
Tilehurst La., Dor. 263 CK137
Tilehurst Rd. SW18 180 DD88
Tilehurst Rd., Sutt. 217 CY106
Tilekiln Clo., Wal.Cr. 66 DT29
Tiler's Wk., Reig. 266 DC138
Tiler's Way, Reig. 266 DC138
Tileyard Rd. N7 141 DL66
Tilford Ave., Croy. 221 EC108
Tilford Gdns. SW19 179 CX88
Tilia Rd. E5 122 DV63
Clarence Rd.
Tilia Wk. SW9 161 DP84
Moorland Rd.
Till Ave. (Farningham), Dart. 208 FM102
Tiller Rd. E14 163 EA76
Tillett Clo. NW10 138 CQ65
Tillett Sq. SE16 163 DY75
Howland Way
Tillett Way E2 142 DU69
Gosset St.
Tilley La., Epsom 232 CQ123
Tillgate Common, Red. 252 DQ133
Tilling Rd. NW2 119 CW60
Tilling Way, Wem. 117 CK63
Tillingbourne Gdns. N3 119 CZ55
Tillingbourne Grn., Orp. 205 ET98
Tillingbourne Rd., Guil. 258 AY140
Tillingbourne Way N3 119 CZ55
Tillingbourne Gdns.
Tillingdown Hill, Cat. 236 DU122
Tillingdown La., Cat. 252 DV125
Tillingham Ct., Wal.Abb. 68 EG33
Tillingham Way N12 98 DA49
Tillman St. E1 142 DV72
Bigland St.
Tilloch St. N1 141 DM66
Carnoustie Dr.
Tillotson Rd. N9 100 DT47
Tillotson Rd., Har. 94 CB52
Tillotson Rd., Ilf. 125 EN59
Tillwicks Rd., Harl. 51 ET16
Tilly's La., Stai. 173 BF91
Tilmans Mead (Farningham), Dart. 208 FM101
Tilney Ct. EC1 275 J4
Tilney Dr., Buck.H. 102 EG47
Tilney Gdns. N1 142 DR65
Mitchison Rd.
Tilney Rd., Dag. 146 EZ65
Tilney Rd., Sthl. 156 BW77
Tilney St. W1 276 G2
Tilney St. W1 140 DG74
Tilson Gdns. SW2 181 DL87
Tilson Ho. SW2 181 DL87
Tilson Gdns.
Tilson Rd. N17 100 DU53
Tilstone Ave. (Eton Wick), Wind. 151 AL78
Tilstone Clo. (Eton Wick), Wind. 151 AL78
Tilsworth Rd., Beac. 88 AJ54
Tilsworth Wk., St.Alb. 43 CJ15
Sandringham Cres.
Tilt Clo., Cob. 230 BY116
Tilt Meadow, Cob. 230 BY116
Tilt Rd., Cob. 230 BW115
Tilt Yd. App. SE9 185 EM86
Tilthams Cor. Rd., Gdmg. 258 AV143
Tilthams Grn., Gdmg. 258 AV143
Tilton St. SW6 159 CY79
Tiltwood, The W3 138 CQ73
Acacia Rd.
Timber Clo., Chis. 205 EN96
Timber Clo., Lthd. 246 CC126
Timber Clo., Wok. 211 BF114
Hacketts La.
Timber Hill Rd., Cat. 236 DU124
Timber La., Cat. 236 DU124
Timber Hill Rd.
Timber Mill Way SW4 161 DK83
Timber Orchard, Hert. 31 DN05
Timber Pond Rd. SE16 143 DX74
Timber Ridge, Rick. 74 BJ42
Timber Slip Dr., Wall. 219 DK109
Timber St. EC1 275 H4
Timbercroft, Epsom 216 CS105
Timbercroft, Welw.G.C. 29 CZ06
Timbercroft La. SE18 165 ES79
Timberdene NW4 97 CX54
Timberdene Ave., Ilf. 103 EQ53
Timberham Fm. Rd., Gat. 268 DD151
Timberham Way, Horl. 268 DE151
Timberhill, Ash. 232 CL119
Ottways La.
Timberland Rd. E1 142 DV72
Timberling Gdns., S.Croy. 220 DR109
Sanderstead Rd.
Timbertop Rd., West. 238 EJ118
Timberwharf Rd. N16 122 DU58
Timberwood, Slou. 111 AR62
Time Sq. E8 122 DT64
Times Sq., Sutt. 218 DB106
High St.
Timothy Clo. SW4 181 DJ85
Elms Rd.
Timothy Clo., Bexh. 186 EY85
Timothy Rd. E3 143 DZ71
Timperley Gdns., Red. 250 DE132
Timplings Row, Hem.H. 40 BH18
Timsbury Wk. SW15 179 CU88
Timsway, Stai. 173 BF92
Tindal St. SW9 161 DP81
Tindale Clo., S.Croy. 220 DR111
Tindall Clo., Rom. 106 FM54
Tinderbox All. SW14 158 CR83
Tine Rd., Chig. 103 ES50
Tinkers La., Wind. 151 AK82
Tinniswood Clo. N5 121 DN64
Drayton Pk.
Tinsey Clo., Egh. 173 BB92
Tinsley Rd. E1 142 DW71
Tintagel Clo., Epsom 217 CT114
Tintagel Clo., Hem.H. 40 BK15
Tintagel Cres. SE22 162 DT84
Tintagel Dr., Stan. 95 CK49
Tintagel Gdns. SE22 162 DT84
Oxonian St.
Tintagel Rd., Orp. 206 EW103
Tintagel Way, Wok. 227 BA116
Tintells La., Lthd. 245 BP128
Tintern Ave. NW9 118 CP55
Tintern Clo. SW15 179 CY85
Tintern Clo. SW19 180 DC94
Tintern Clo., Slou. 151 AQ76
Tintern Gdns. N14 99 DL45
Tintern Path NW9 118 CS58
Ruthin Clo.
Tintern Rd. N22 100 DQ53
Tintern Rd., Cars. 200 DD102
Tintern St. SW4 161 DL84
Tintern Way, Har. 116 CB60
Tinto Rd. E16 144 EG70
Tinwell Ms., Borwd. 78 CQ43
Cranes Way
Tinworth St. SE11 278 A10
Tinworth St. SE11 161 DL78
Tippendell La., St.Alb. 60 CA25
Tippetts Clo., Enf. 82 DQ39

Tipthorpe Rd. SW11 160 DG83
Tipton Cotts., Add. 212 BG105
Oliver Clo.
Tipton Dr., Croy. 220 DS105
Tiptree Clo. E4 101 EC48
Tiptree Clo., Horn. 128 FN60
Tiptree Cres., Ilf. 125 EN55
Tiptree Dr., Enf. 82 DR42
Tiptree Est., Ilf. 125 EN55
Tiptree Rd., Ruis. 115 BV63
Tiree Clo., Hem.H. 41 BP22
Tirlemont Rd., S.Croy. 220 DQ108
Tirrell Rd., Croy. 202 DQ100
Tisbury Ct. W1 273 M10
Tisbury Rd. SW16 201 DL96
Tisdall Pl. SE17 279 L9
Tisdall Pl. SE17 162 DR77
Titan Rd., Grays 170 GA78
Titan Rd., Hem.H. 40 BM17
Titchborne Row W2 272 C9
Titchfield Rd. NW8 140 DF67
Titchfield Rd., Cars. 200 DD102
Titchfield Rd., Enf. 83 DY37
Titchfield Wk., Cars. 200 DD101
Titchfield Rd.
Titchwell Rd. SW18 180 DD87
Tite Hill, Egh. 172 AX92
Tite St. SW3 160 DF79
Tithe Barn Clo., Kings.T. 198 CM95
Tithe Barn Clo., St.Alb. 42 CC23
Tithe Barn Ct., Abb.L. 59 BT29
Tithe Barn Dr., Maid. 150 AD78
Tithe Barn Est., St.Alb. 42 CC23
Tithe Barn Way, Nthlt. 135 BV68
Tithe Clo. NW7 97 CU53
Tithe Clo., Maid. 150 AC78
Tithe Ct., Slou. 153 BA77
Tithe Fm. Ave., Har. 116 CA62
Tithe Fm. Clo., Har. 116 CA62
Tithe La., Stai. 173 BA86
Tithe Meadow, Vir.W. 192 AX100
Tithe Meadow, Wat. 75 BR44
Tithe Wk. NW7 97 CU53
Tithebarns La., Wok. 244 BG126
Tithelands, Harl. 51 EN18
Tithepit Shaw La., Warl. 236 DV117
Titian Ave. (Bushey), Wat. 95 CE45
Titley Clo. E4 101 EA50
Titmus Clo., Uxb. 135 BQ72
Titmuss Ave. SE28 146 EV73
Titmuss St. W12 159 CV75
Titsey Hill, Oxt. 238 EF123
Titsey Rd., Oxt. 254 EG128
Tiverton Ave., Ilf. 125 EN55
Tiverton Dr. SE9 185 EQ88
Tiverton Gro., Rom. 106 FN50
Tiverton Rd. N15 122 DR58
Tiverton Rd. N18 100 DS50
Tiverton Rd. NW10 139 CX67
Tiverton Rd., Edg. 96 CM54
Tiverton Rd., Houns. 156 CC82
Tiverton Rd., Pot.B. 64 DD31
Tiverton Rd., Ruis. 115 BU62
Tiverton Rd., Th.Hth. 201 DN99
Willett Rd.
Tiverton Rd., Wem. 138 CL68
Tiverton St. SE1 279 H7
Tiverton St. SE1 162 DQ76
Tiverton Way, Chess. 215 CJ106
Tivoli Ct. SE16 163 DZ75
Tivoli Gdns. SE18 164 EL77
Tivoli Rd. N8 121 DK57
Tivoli Rd. SE27 182 DQ92
Tivoli Rd., Houns. 156 BY84
Toad La., Houns. 156 BZ84
Tobacco Quay E1 142 DV73
Wapping La.
Tobago St. E14 163 EA75
Manilla St.
Tobin Clo. NW3 140 DE66
Toby La. E1 143 DY70
Toby Way, Surb. 198 CP103
Tockley Rd., Slou. 130 AH69
Todd Clo., Rain. 148 FK70
Toddbrook, Harl. 51 EP16
Harberts Rd.
Todds Clo., Horl. 268 DE146
Todds Wk. N7 121 DM61
Andover Rd.
Toft Ave., Grays 170 GD77
Token Yd. SW15 159 CY84
Montserrat Rd.
Tokenhouse Yd. EC2 275 K8
Tokyngton Ave., Wem. 138 CN65
Toland Sq. SW15 179 CU85
Tolcarne Dr., Pnr. 93 BU54
Toley Ave., Wem. 118 CL59
Tollbridge Clo. W10 139 CY70
Kensal Rd.
Tolldene Clo., Wok. 226 AS117
Robin Hood Rd.
Tollers La., Couls. 235 DM119
Tollesbury Gdns., Ilf. 125 ER55
Tollet St. E1 143 DX70
Tollgate, Guil. 243 BD133
Tollgate Ave., Red. 266 DF139
Tollgate Clo., Rick. 73 BF41
Tollgate Dr. SE21 182 DS89
Tollgate Gdns. NW6 140 DB68
Tollgate Rd. E6 144 EK71
Tollgate Rd. E16 144 EJ71
Tollgate Rd., Dart. 189 FR87
Tollgate Rd., Dor. 263 CH139
Tollgate Rd., St.Alb. 44 CR23
Tollgate Rd., Wal.Cr. 83 DX35
Tollhouse La., Wall. 219 DJ109
Tollhouse Way N19 121 DJ61
Tollington Pk. N4 121 DM61
Tollington Pl. N4 121 DM61
Tollington Rd. N7 121 DM63
Tollington Way N7 121 DL62
Tollpit End, Hem.H. 40 BG17
Tolmers Ave. (Cuffley), Pot.B. 65 DL28
Tolmers Gdns. (Cuffley), Pot.B. 65 DM29
Tolmers Ms., Hert. 65 DL25
Tolmers Pk., Hert. 65 DL25
Tolmers Rd. (Cuffley), Pot.B. 65 DK27
Tolmers Sq. NW1 273 L4
Tolpits Clo., Wat. 75 BT43
Tolpits La., Wat. 93 BQ46
Tolpuddle Ave. E13 144 EJ67
Rochester Ave.
Tolpuddle St. N1 141 DN68
Tolsford Rd. E5 122 DV64
Tolson Rd., Islw. 157 CG83
Tolvaddon, Wok. 226 AU117
Cardingham
Tolverne Rd. SW20 199 CW95
Tolworth Clo., Surb. 198 CP102
Tolworth Gdns., Rom. 126 EX57
Tolworth Pk. Rd., Surb. 198 CM103
Tolworth Ri. N., Surb. 198 CQ101
Elmbridge Ave.
Tolworth Ri. S., Surb. 198 CQ102
Warren Dr. S.
Tolworth Rd., Surb. 198 CL103
Tom Coombs Clo. SE9 164 EL84
Well Hall Rd.
Tom Cribb Rd. SE28 165 EQ76
Tom Gros. Clo. E15 123 ED64
Maryland St.
Tom Hood Clo. E15 123 ED64
Maryland St.
Tom Mann Clo., Bark. 145 ES67
Tom Nolan Clo. E15 144 EE68
Tom Smith Clo. SE10 164 EE79
Maze Hill
Tom Thumbs Arch E3 143 EA68
Malmesbury Rd.
Tomahawk Gdns., Nthlt. 136 BX69
Javelin Way
Tomkins Clo., Borwd. 78 CL39
Tallis Way
Tomkyns La., Upmin. 107 FR54
Tomlin Clo., Epsom 216 CR111
Tomlin Rd., Slou. 131 AL70
Tomlins Gro. E3 143 EA69
Tomlins Orchard, Bark. 145 EQ67
Tomlins Ter. E14 143 DZ71
Rhodeswell Rd.
Tomlins Wk. N7 121 DM61
Briset Way
Tomlinson Clo. E2 142 DT69
Tomlinson Clo. W4 158 CP78
Oxford Rd. N.
Tomlyns Clo., Brwd. 109 GE44
Tompion St. EC1 274 F3
Toms Cft., Hem.H. 40 BL21
Toms Fld., Hat. 44 CS19
Toms Hill, Kings L. 58 BJ33
Bucks Hill
Toms La., Abb.L. 59 BS27
Toms La., Kings L. 59 BP29
Tomswood Ct., Ilf. 103 EQ53
Tomswood Hill, Ilf. 103 EP52
Tomswood Rd., Chig. 103 EN51
Tonbridge Clo., Bans. 218 DF114
Tonbridge Cres., Har. 118 CL56
Tonbridge Ho. SE25 202 DU97
Tonbridge Rd., Rom. 106 FK52
Tonbridge Rd., Sev. 257 FJ126
Tonbridge Rd., W.Mol. 196 BY98
Tonbridge St. WC1 273 P2
Tonbridge St. WC1 141 DL69
Tonbridge Wk. WC1 273 P2
Tonfield Rd., Sutt. 199 CZ102
Tonge Clo., Beck. 203 EA99
Tonsley Hill SW18 180 DB85
Tonsley Pl. SW18 180 DB85
Tonsley Rd. SW18 180 DB85
Tonsley St. SW18 180 DB85
Tonstall Rd., Epsom 216 CR110
Tonstall Rd., Mitch. 200 DG96
Tony Cannell Ms. E3 143 DZ69
Maplin St.
Tooke Clo., Pnr. 94 BY53
Took's Ct. EC4 274 D8
Tooley St. SE1 279 L2
Tooley St. SE1 142 DS74
Tooley St., Grav. 190 GD87
Toorack Rd., Har. 95 CD54
Toot Hill Rd., Ong. 71 FF30
Tooting Bec Gdns. SW16 181 DK91
Tooting Bec Rd. SW16 181 DH91
Tooting Bec Rd. SW17 180 DG90
Tooting Gro. SW17 180 DE92
Tooting High St. SW17 180 DE93
Tootswood Rd., Brom. 204 EE99
Tooveys Mill Clo., Kings L. 58 BN28
Top Dartford Rd., Swan. 187 FF94
Top Ho. Ri. E4 101 EC45
Parkhill Rd.
Top Pk., Beck. 204 EE99
Top Pk., Ger.Cr. 112 AW58
Topaz Clo., Slou. 131 AP74
Pearl Gdns.
Topaz Wk. NW2 119 CX59
Marble Dr.
Topcliffe Dr., Orp. 223 ER106
Topham Sq. N17 100 DQ53
Topham St. EC1 274 D4
Topiary, The, Ash. 232 CL121
Topiary Sq., Rich. 158 CM83
Topland Rd., Ger.Cr. 90 AX52
Toplands Ave., S.Ock. 148 FP74
Topley St. SE9 164 EK84
Topp Wk. NW2 119 CW61
Topping La., Uxb. 134 BK69
Cleveland Rd.
Topsfield Clo. N8 121 DK57
Wolseley Rd.
Topsfield Par. N8 121 DL57
Tottenham La.
Topsfield Rd. N8 121 DL57
Topsham Rd. SW17 180 DF90
Tor Gdns. W8 160 DA75
Tor La., Wey. 213 BQ111
Tor Rd., Well. 166 EW81
Torbay Rd. NW6 139 CZ66
Torbay Rd., Har. 116 BY61
Torbay St. NW1 141 DH66
Hawley Rd.
Torbitt Way, Ilf. 125 ET57
Torbridge Clo., Edg. 96 CL52
Torbrook Clo., Bex. 186 EY86
Torcross Dr. SE23 182 DW89
Torcross Rd., Ruis. 115 BV62
Torin Ct., Egh. 172 AW92
Torland Dr., Lthd. 215 CD114
Tormead Clo., Sutt. 218 DA107
Tormead Rd., Guil. 243 AZ134
Tormount Rd. SE18 165 ES79
Toronto Ave. E12 125 EM63
Toronto Dr., Horl. 269 DN148
Toronto Rd. E11 123 ED63
Toronto Rd., Ilf. 125 EP60
Toronto Rd., Til. 171 GG82
Torquay Gdns., Ilf. 124 EK56
Torquay Spur, Slou. 131 AP69
Torquay St. W2 140 DB71
Harrow Rd.
Torr Rd. SE20 183 DX94
Torrance Clo., Horn. 127 FH60
Torre Wk., Cars. 200 DE102
Torrens Clo., Guil. 242 AU131
Torrens Rd. E15 144 EF65
Torrens Rd. SW2 181 DM85
Torrens Sq. E15 144 EF65
Torrens St. EC1 274 E1
Torrens St. EC1 141 DN68
Torrens Wk., Grav. 191 GL92
Torriano Ave. NW5 121 DK64
Torriano Cotts. NW5 121 DJ64
Torriano Ave.
Torriano Ms. NW5 121 DK64
Torriano Ave.
Torridge Gdns. SE15 162 DW84
Torridge Rd., Slou. 153 BB79
Torridge Rd., Th.Hth. 201 DP99
Torridge Wk., Hem.H. 40 BM15
The Dee
Torridon Clo., Wok. 226 AV117
Torridon Rd. SE6 183 ED87
Torridon Rd. SE13 184 EE87
Torrington Ave. N12 98 DD50
Torrington Clo. N12 98 DD49
Torrington Clo., Esher 215 CE107
Torrington Dr., Har. 116 CB63
Torrington Dr., Loug. 85 EQ42
Torrington Dr., Pot.B. 64 DD32
Torrington Gdns. N11 99 DJ51
Torrington Gdns., Grnf. 137 CJ67
Torrington Gdns., Loug. 85 EQ42
Torrington Gro. N12 98 DE50
Torrington Pk. N12 98 DC50
Torrington Pl. E1 142 DU74
Torrington Pl. WC1 273 L6
Torrington Pl. WC1 141 DK71
Torrington Rd. E18 124 EG55
Torrington Rd., Berk. 38 AV19
Torrington Rd., Dag. 126 EZ60
Torrington Rd., Esher 215 CE107
Torrington Rd., Grnf. 137 CJ67
Torrington Rd., Ruis. 115 BT62
Torrington Sq. WC1 273 N5
Torrington Sq. WC1 141 DK70
Torrington Sq., Croy. 202 DR101
Tavistock Gro.
Torrington Way, Mord. 200 DA101
Tortoiseshell Way, Berk. 38 AT17
Torver Rd., Har. 117 CE56
Torver Way, Orp. 205 ER103
Torwood Clo., Berk. 38 AT19
Torwood La., Whyt. 236 DT120
Torwood Rd. SW15 179 CU85
Torworth Rd., Borwd. 78 CM38
Tothill St. SW1 277 M5
Tothill St. SW1 161 DK75
Totnes Rd., Well. 166 EV80
Totnes Wk. N2 120 DD56
Tottan Ter. E1 143 DX72
Belgrave St.
Tottenhall Rd. N13 99 DN51
Tottenham Ct. Rd. W1 273 L5
Tottenham Ct. Rd. W1 141 DJ70
Tottenham Grn. E. N15 122 DT56
Tottenham La. N8 121 DL57
Tottenham Ms. W1 273 L6
Tottenham Rd. N1 142 DS65
Tottenham St. W1 273 L7
Tottenham St. W1 141 DJ71
Totterdown St. SW17 180 DF91
Totteridge Common N20 97 CU47
Totteridge Grn. N20 98 DA47
Totteridge La. N20 98 DA47
Totteridge Rd., Enf. 83 DX37
Totteridge Village N20 97 CY46
Totternhoe Clo., Har. 117 CJ57
Totton Rd., Th.Hth. 201 DN97
Toulmin Dr., St.Alb. 42 CC16
Toulmin St. SE1 279 H5
Toulmin St. SE1 162 DQ75
Toulon St. SE5 162 DQ80
Tournay Rd. SW6 159 CZ80
Toussaint Wk. SE16 162 DU76
John Roll Way
Tovey Ave., Hodd. 49 EA15
Tovey Clo., St.Alb. 61 CK26
Tovey Clo., Wal.Abb. 50 EE23
Tovil Clo. SE20 202 DV96
Towcester Rd. E3 143 EB70
Tower Bri. E1 279 P3
Tower Bri. E1 142 DT74
Tower Bri. SE1 279 P3
Tower Bri. SE1 142 DT74
Tower Bri. App. E1 279 P2
Tower Bri. App. E1 142 DT74
Tower Bri. Piazza SE1 142 DT74
Horselydown La.
Tower Bri. Rd. SE1 279 M7
Tower Bri. Rd. SE1 162 DS76
Tower Clo. NW3 120 DD64
Lyndhurst Rd.
Tower Clo. SE20 182 DV94
Tower Clo., Berk. 38 AU20
Tower Clo., Epp. 53 FD24
Tower Clo., Grav. 191 GL92
Tower Clo., H.Wyc. 110 AC56
Tower Clo., Horl. 268 DF148
Tower Clo., Ilf. 103 EP51
Tower Clo., Orp. 205 ET103
Tower Clo., Wok. 226 AX117
Tower Ct. WC2 273 P9
Tower Ct., Brwd. 108 FV47
Tower Cft. (Eynsford), Dart. 208 FL103
High St.
Tower Gdns. Rd. N17 100 DQ53
Tower Gro., Wey. 195 BS103
Tower Hamlets Rd. E7 124 EF63
Tower Hamlets Rd. E17 123 EA55
Tower Hill EC3 279 N1
Tower Hill EC3 142 DS73
Tower Hill, Brwd. 108 FW47
Tower Hill, Dor. 263 CH138
Tower Hill, Guil. 261 BQ140
Tower Hill, Kings L. 57 BE29
Tower Hill La., Guil. 261 BQ140
Tower Hill
Tower Hill La., St.Alb. 28 CM10
Tower Hill Ri., Guil. 261 BQ140
Tower Hill Rd., Dor. 263 CH138
Tower Hill Ter. EC3 142 DS73
Byward St.
Tower La., Guil. 261 BQ140
Tower La., Wem. 117 CK62
Main Dr.
Tower Ms. E17 123 EA56
Tower Pier EC3 279 N2
Tower Pier EC3 142 DS73
Tower Pl. EC3 279 N1
Tower Pt., Enf. 82 DR42
Tower Ri., Rich. 158 CL83
Jocelyn Rd.
Tower Rd. NW10 139 CU66
Tower Rd., Amer. 55 AN43
Tower Rd., Belv. 167 FC77
Tower Rd., Bexh. 166 FA84
Tower Rd., Dart. 188 FJ87
Tower Rd., Epp. 69 ES30
Tower Rd., Orp. 205 ET103
Tower Rd., Tad. 233 CW123
Tower Rd., Twick. 177 CF90
Tower Rd., Ware 33 DY05
Tower Royal EC4 275 J10
Tower St. WC2 273 N9
Tower St. WC2 141 DK72
Tower St., Hert. 32 DQ07
Tower Ter. N22 99 DM54
Mayes Rd.
Tower Vw., Croy. 203 DX101
Towers, The, Ken. 236 DQ115
Towers Ave., Uxb. 135 BQ69
Towers Pl., Rich. 178 CL85
Eton St.
Towers Rd., Grays 170 GC78
Towers Rd., Hem.H. 40 BL19
Towers Rd., Pnr. 94 BY52
Towers Rd., Sthl. 136 CA70
Towers Wk., Wey. 213 BP107
Towers Wd., Dart. 209 FR95
Towfield Rd., Felt. 176 BZ89
Towing Path, Guil. 242 AW132
Towing Path Wk. N1 141 DK67
York Way
Town, The, Enf. 82 DR41
Town Bri. Ct., Chesh. 54 AP32
Water Meadow
Town Cen., Hat. 45 CU17
Town Ct. Path N4 122 DQ60
Town End, Cat. 236 DS122
Town End Clo., Cat. 236 DS122
Town Fld. La., Ch.St.G. 90 AW48
Town Fld. Way, Islw. 157 CG82
Town Flds., Hat. 45 CU17
Town Hall App. N16 122 DS63
Milton Gro.
Town Hall App. Rd. N15 122 DT56
Town Hall Ave. W4 158 CR78
Town Hall Rd. SW11 160 DF83
Town La., H.Wyc. 110 AD59
Town La., Stai. 174 BK86
Town Meadow, Brent. 157 CK80
Town Path, Egh. 173 BA92
Town Quay, Bark. 145 EP67
Town Rd. N9 100 DV47
Town Sq., Erith 167 FE79
Pier Rd.
Town Tree Rd., Ashf. 174 BN92
Towncourt Cres., Orp. 205 EQ99
Towncourt La., Orp. 205 ER100
Towney Mead, Nthlt. 136 BZ68
Townfield, Chesh. 54 AP32
Townfield, Rick. 92 BJ45
Townfield Cor., Grav. 191 GJ88
Townfield Rd., Dor. 263 CG137
Townfield Rd., Hayes 135 BT74
Townfield Sq., Hayes 135 BT73
Towngate, Cob. 230 BY115
Townholm Cres. W7 157 CF76
Townley Ct. E15 144 EF65
Townley Rd. SE22 182 DS85
Townley Rd., Bexh. 186 EZ86
Townley St. SE17 279 K10
Townmead, Red. 252 DR133
Townmead Rd. SW6 160 DB83
Townmead Rd., Rich. 158 CP82
Townmead Rd., Wal.Abb. 67 EC34
Townsend, Hem.H. 40 BK18
Townsend Ave. N14 99 DK49
Townsend Ave., St.Alb. 43 CE19
Townsend Dr., St.Alb. 43 CD17
Townsend Ind. Est. NW10 138 CQ68
Townsend La. NW9 118 CR59
Townsend La., Wok. 227 BB121
St. Peters Rd.
Townsend Rd. N15 122 DT57
Townsend Rd., Ashf. 174 BL92
Townsend Rd., Chesh. 54 AP30
Townsend Rd., Sthl. 136 BY74
Townsend St. SE17 279 M8
Townsend St. SE17 162 DR77
Townsend Way, Nthwd. 93 BT52
Townsend Yd. N6 120 DG60
Townshend Clo., Sid. 186 EV93
Townshend Est. NW8 140 DE68
Townshend Rd. NW8 140 DE67
Townshend Rd., Chis. 185 EP92
Townshend Rd., Rich. 158 CM84
Townshend St., Hert. 32 DS09
Townshend Ter., Rich. 158 CM84
Townshott Clo., Lthd. 246 CA125
Townslow La., Wok. 228 BK116
Townson Ave., Nthlt. 135 BU69
Townson Way, Nthlt. 135 BU68
Townson Ave.
Towpath, Shep. 194 BM102
Dockett Eddy La.
Towpath Way, Croy. 202 DT100
Towton Rd. SE27 182 DQ89
Toynbec Clo., Chis. 185 EP91
Beechwood Ri.
Toynbee Rd. SW20 199 CY95
Toynbee St. E1 275 P7
Toynbee St. E1 142 DT71
Toyne Way N6 120 DF58
Gaskell Rd.
Tozer Wk., Wind. 151 AK83
Tinkers La.
Tracery, The, Bans. 234 DB115
Tracey Ave. NW2 119 CW64
Tracious Clo., Wok. 226 AV116
Sythwood
Tracious La., Wok. 226 AV116
Tracy Ct., Stan. 95 CJ52
Tracyes Rd., Harl. 52 EV17
Trade Clo. N13 99 DN49
Trader Rd. E6 145 EP72
Tradescant Rd. SW8 161 DL80
Trading Est. Rd. NW10 138 CQ70
Trafalgar Ave. N17 100 DS51
Trafalgar Ave. SE15 162 DT78
Trafalgar Ave., Brox. 49 DZ21
Trafalgar Ave., Wor.Pk. 199 CX102
Trafalgar Business Cen., Bark. 145 ET70
Trafalgar Clo. SE16 163 DY77
Greenland Quay
Trafalgar Ct., Cob. 213 BU113
Trafalgar Dr., Walt. 195 BU104
Trafalgar Gdns. E1 143 DX71
Trafalgar Gdns. W8 160 DB76
South End Row
Trafalgar Gro. SE10 163 ED79
Trafalgar Pl. E11 124 EG56
Trafalgar Pl. N18 100 DU50
Trafalgar Rd. SE10 163 ED79
Trafalgar Rd. SW19 180 DB94
Trafalgar Rd., Dart. 188 FL89
Trafalgar Rd., Grav. 191 GG87
Trafalgar Rd., Rain. 147 FF68
Trafalgar Rd., Twick. 177 CD89
Trafalgar Sq. SW1 277 N2
Trafalgar Sq. SW1 141 DK74
Trafalgar Sq. WC2 277 N2
Trafalgar Sq. WC2 141 DK74
Trafalgar St. SE17 279 K10
Trafalgar St. SE17 162 DR78
Trafalgar Ter., Har. 117 CE60
Nelson Rd.
Trafalgar Way E14 143 EC74
Trafalgar Way, Croy. 201 DM103
Trafford Clo. E15 123 EB64
Trafford Clo., Ilf. 103 ET51
Trafford Clo., Rad. 62 CL32
Trafford Rd., Th.Hth. 201 DM99
Tramway Ave. E15 144 EE66
Tramway Ave. N9 100 DV45
Tramway Path, Mitch. 200 DE98
London Rd.
Tranby Pl. E9 123 DX64
Homerton High St.
Tranley Ms. NW3 120 DE63
Fleet Rd.
Tranmere Rd. N9 100 DT45
Tranmere Rd. SW18 180 DC88
Tranmere Rd., Twick. 176 CB87
Tranquil Dale, Bet. 249 CT132
Tranquil Pas. SE3 164 EF82
Tranquil Vale
Tranquil Ri., Erith 167 FE78
West St.
Tranquil Vale SE3 164 EE82
Transay Wk. N1 142 DR65
Marquess Rd.
Transept St. NW1 272 C7
Transept St. NW1 140 DE71
Transmere Clo., Orp. 205 EQ100
Transmere Rd., Orp. 205 EQ100
Transom Clo. SE16 163 DY77
Plough Way
Transom Sq. E14 163 EB77
Transport Ave., Brent. 157 CG78
Tranton Rd. SE16 162 DU76
Trapps La., Chesh. 54 AR32
Traps Hill, Loug. 85 EM41
Traps La., N.Mal. 198 CS95
Trapstyle Rd., Ware 32 DU05
Trasher Mead, Dor. 263 CJ139
Travellers Clo., Hat. 45 CW23
Travellers La., Hat. 45 CU19
Travellers La. (Welham Grn.), Hat. 45 CV21
Travellers Way, Houns. 156 BW82
Travers Clo. E17 101 DX53
Travers Rd. N7 121 DN62
Travic Rd., Slou. 131 AM69
Travis Ct., Slou. 131 AP69
Treachers Clo., Chesh. 54 AP31
Treacy Clo. (Bushey), Wat. 94 CC47
Treadgold St. W11 139 CX73
Treadway St. E2 142 DV68
Treadwell Rd., Epsom 232 CS116
Treaty Rd., Houns. 156 CB83
Hanworth Rd.
Treaty St. N1 141 DM67
Trebble Rd., Swans. 190 FY86
Trebeck St. W1 277 H2
Trebellan Dr., Hem.H. 40 BM19
Trebovir Rd. SW5 160 DA78
Treby St. E3 143 DZ70
Trecastle Way N7 121 DK63
Carleton Rd.
Tredegar Ms. E3 143 DZ69
Tredegar Ter.
Tredegar Rd. E3 143 DZ68
Tredegar Rd. N11 99 DK52
Tredegar Rd., Dart. 187 FG89
Tredegar Sq. E3 143 DZ69
Tredegar Ter. E3 143 DZ69
Trederwen Rd. E8 142 DU67
Tredown Rd. SE26 182 DW92
Tredwell Clo., Brom. 204 EL98
Tredwell Rd. SE27 181 DP91
Tree Clo., Rich. 177 CK88
Tree Rd. E16 144 EJ72
Tree Tops, Brwd. 108 FW46
Tree Way, Reig. 250 DB131
Treebourne Rd., West. 238 EJ117
Treebys Ave., Guil. 242 AX128
Treelands, Dor. 263 CJ139
Treen Ave. SW13 158 CS83
Treeside Clo., West Dr. 154 BK77
Treetops, Grav. 191 GH92
Treetops, Whyt. 236 DU118
Treetops Clo. SE2 166 EY78
Treetops Clo., Nthwd. 93 BR50
Treeview Clo. SE19 202 DS95
Treewall Gdns., Brom. 184 EH91
Trefgarne Rd., Dag. 126 FA61
Trefil Wk. N7 121 DL63
Trefoil Rd. SW18 180 DC85
Trefusis Wk., Wat. 75 BS39
Tregaron Ave. N8 121 DL58
Tregaron Gdns., N.Mal. 198 CS98
Avenue Rd.
Tregarth Pl., Wok. 226 AT117
Tregarthen Pl., Lthd. 231 CJ121
Tregarvon Rd. SW11 160 DG84

Tregelles Rd., Hodd. 33 EA14
Tregenna Ave., Har. 116 BZ63
Tregenna Clo. N14 81 DJ43
Tregenna Ct., Har. 116 CA63
Trego Rd. E9 143 EA66
Tregothnan Rd. SW9 161 DL83
Tregunter Rd. SW10 160 DC79
Trehearn Rd., Ilf. 103 ER52
Trehern Rd. SW14 158 CR83
Treherne Ct. SW9 161 DN81
Eythorne Rd.
Treherne Ct. SW17 180 DG91
Trehurst St. E5 123 DY64
Trelawn Clo., Cher. 211 BC108
Trelawn Rd. E10 123 EC62
Trelawn Rd. SW2 181 DN85
Trelawney Ave., Slou. 152 AX76
Trelawney Clo. E17 123 EB56
Orford Rd.
Trelawney Est. E9 142 DW65
Trelawney Gro., Wey. 212 BN107
Trelawney Rd., Ilf. 103 ER52
Trellick Twr. W10 139 CZ70
Trellis Sq. E3 143 DZ69
Malmesbury Rd.
Treloar Gdns. SE19 182 DR93
Hancock Rd.
Tremadoc Rd. SW4 161 DK84
Tremaine Clo. SE4 163 EA82
Tremaine Gro., Hem.H. 40 BL16
Tremaine Rd. SE20 202 DV96
Trematon Pl., Tedd. 177 CJ94
Tremlett Gro. N19 121 DJ62
Tremlett Ms. N19 121 DJ62
Tremlett Gro.
Trenance, Wok. 226 AU117
Cardingham
Trenance Gdns., Ilf. 126 EU62
Trench Yd. Ct., Mord. 200 DB100
Green La.
Trenchard Ave., Ruis. 115 BV63
Trenchard Clo., Stan. 95 CG51
Trenchard Clo., Walt. 214 BW106
Trenchard Ct., Mord. 200 DB100
Trenchard St. SE10 163 ED78
Trenches La., Slou. 133 BA73
Trenchold St. SW8 161 DL79
Trenham Dr., Warl. 236 DW116
Trenholme Clo. SE20 182 DV94
Trenholme Ct., Cat. 236 DU122
Trenholme Rd. SE20 182 DV94
Trenholme Ter. SE20 182 DV94
Trenmar Gdns. NW10 139 CV69
Trent Ave. W5 157 CJ76
Trent Ave., Upmin. 129 FR58
Trent Clo., Rad. 62 CL32
Trent Gdns. N14 81 DH44
Trent Rd. SW2 181 DM85
Trent Rd., Buck.H. 102 EH46
Trent Rd., Slou. 153 BB79
Trent Way, Hayes 135 BS69
Trent Way, Wor.Pk. 199 CW104
Trentbridge Clo., Ilf. 103 ET51
Trentham Cres., Wok. 227 BA121
Trentham Dr., Orp. 206 EU98
Trentham Rd., Red. 266 DG136
Trentham St. SW18 180 DA88
Trentwood Side, Enf. 81 DM41
Treport St. SW18 180 DB87
Tresco Clo., Brom. 184 EE93
Tresco Gdns., Ilf. 126 EU61
Tresco Rd. SE15 162 DV84
Tresco Rd., Berk. 38 AT18
Trescoe Gdns., Har. 116 BY59
Trescoe Gdns., Rom. 105 FC50
Tresham Cres. NW8 272 B4
Tresham Cres. NW8 140 DE70
Tresham Rd., Bark. 145 ET66
Tresham Wk. E9 122 DW64
Churchill Wk.
Tresilian Ave. N21 81 DM43
Tresilian Sq., Hem.H. 40 BM15
The Dee
Tressillian Way, Wok. 226 AU116
Tressell Clo. N1 141 DP66
Sebbon St.
Tressillian Cres. SE4 163 EA83
Tressillian Rd. SE4 163 DZ84
Tresta Wk., Wok. 226 AU115
Trestis Clo., Hayes 136 BY71
Jollys La.
Treston Ct., Stai. 173 BF92
Treswell Rd., Dag. 146 EY67
Tretawn Gdns. NW7 96 CS49
Tretawn Pk. NW7 96 CS49
Trevanion Rd. W14 159 CY77
Treve Ave., Har. 116 CC59
Trevelgae Way, Hem.H. 40 BL16
Trevellance Way, Wat. 60 BW33
Trevelyan Ave. E12 125 EM63
Trevelyan Clo., Dart. 168 FM84
Trevelyan Cres., Har. 117 CK59
Trevelyan Gdns. NW10 139 CW67
Trevelyan Rd. E15 124 EF63
Trevelyan Rd. SW17 180 DE92
Trevelyan Way, Berk. 38 AV17
Trevereux Hill, Oxt. 255 EM131
Treveris St. SE1 278 G3
Treverton St. W10 139 CY70
Treville St. SW15 179 CV87
Treviso Rd. SE23 183 DX89
Farren Rd.
Trevithick Clo., Felt. 175 BT88
Trevithick Dr., Dart. 168 FM84
Trevithick St. SE8 163 EA79
Trevone Gdns., Pnr. 116 BY58
Trevor Clo., Barn. 80 DD44
Trevor Clo., Brom. 204 EF101
Trevor Clo., Har. 95 CF52
Kenton La.
Trevor Clo., Islw. 177 CF85
Trevor Clo., Nthlt. 136 BW68
Trevor Cres., Ruis. 115 BT63
Trevor Gdns., Edg. 96 CR53
Trevor Gdns., Nthlt. 136 BW68
Trevor Gdns., Ruis. 115 BU63
Bedford Rd.
Trevor Pl. SW7 276 C5
Trevor Pl. SW7 160 DE75
Trevor Rd. SW19 179 CY94
Trevor Rd., Edg. 96 CR53
Trevor Rd., Hayes 155 BS75
Trevor Rd., Wdf.Grn. 102 EG52
Trevor Sq. SW7 276 D5
Trevor Sq. SW7 160 DE76
Trevor St. SW7 276 C5
Trevor St. SW7 160 DE75
Trevose Ave., W.Byf. 211 BF114
Trevose Rd. E17 101 ED53
Trevose Way, Wat. 94 BW48
Trewarden Ave., Iver 133 BD68
Trewenna Dr., Chess. 215 CK106
Trewenna Dr., Pot.B. 64 DD32
Trewince Rd. SW20 199 CW95
Trewint St. SW18 180 DC89
Trewsbury Rd. SE26 183 DX92
Triandra Way, Hayes 136 BX71
Triangle, The EC1 141 DP70
Goswell Rd.
Triangle, The N13 99 DN49
Lodge Dr.
Triangle, The, Bark. 145 EQ65
Tanner St.
Triangle, The, Hmptn. 196 CC95
High St.
Triangle, The, Kings.T. 198 CQ96
Kenley Rd.
Triangle, The, Wok. 226 AW118
St. John's Rd.
Triangle Ct. E16 144 EK71
Tollgate Rd.
Triangle Pas., Barn. 80 DC42
Station Rd.
Triangle Pl. SW4 161 DK84
Triangle Rd. E8 142 DV67
Trident Gdns., Nthlt. 136 BX69
Jetstar Way
Trident Ind. Est., Hodd. 49 EB17
Trident Ind. Est., Slou. 153 BE83
Trident Rd., Wat. 59 BT34
Trident St. SE16 163 DX77
Trident Wk. SE16 163 DX77
Greenland Quay
Trident Way, Sthl. 155 BV76
Trig La. EC4 275 H10
Trigg's Clo., Wok. 226 AX119
Trigg's La., Wok. 226 AX118
Trigo Ct., Epsom 216 CR111
Blakeney Clo.
Trigon Rd. SW8 161 DM80
Trilby Rd. SE23 183 DX89
Trim St. SE14 163 DZ79
Trimmer Wk., Brent. 158 CL79
Netley Rd.
Trinder Gdns. N19 121 DL60
Trinder Rd.
Trinder Rd. N19 121 DL60
Trinder Rd., Barn. 79 CW43
Trindles Rd., Red. 267 DM136
Tring Ave. W5 138 CM74
Tring Ave., Sthl. 136 BZ72
Tring Ave., Wem. 138 CN65
Tring Clo., Ilf. 125 ER57
Tring Clo., Rom. 106 FM49
Tring Gdns., Rom. 106 FL49
Tring Grn., Rom. 106 FL49
Tring Gdns.
Tring Wk., Rom. 106 FL49
Tring Gdns.
Tringham Clo., Cher. 211 BC106
Trinidad Gdns., Dag. 147 FD66
Trinidad St. E14 143 DZ73
Trinity Ave. N2 120 DD55
Trinity Ave., Enf. 82 DT44
Trinity Ch. Pas. SW13 159 CV79
Trinity Ch. Rd. SW13 159 CV79
Trinity Ch. Sq. SE1 279 J6
Trinity Ch. Sq. SE1 162 DQ76
Trinity Chyd., Guil. 258 AX136
High St.
Trinity Clo. E8 142 DT65
Trinity Clo. E11 124 EE61
Trinity Clo. NW3 120 DD63
Hampstead High St.
Trinity Clo. SE13 163 ED84
Wisteria Rd.
Trinity Clo., Brom. 204 EL102
Trinity Clo., Hert. 32 DW12
Trinity Clo., Houns. 156 BY84
Trinity Clo., Nthwd. 93 BS51
Trinity Clo., S.Croy. 220 DS109
Trinity Clo., Stai. 174 BJ86
Trinity Cotts., Rich. 158 CM83
Trinity Rd.
Trinity Ct. N1 142 DS66
Downham Rd.
Trinity Ct. SE7 164 EK77
Charlton La.
Trinity Cres. SW17 180 DF89
Trinity Gdns. SW9 161 DM84
Trinity Gro. SE10 163 EC81
Trinity Gro., Hert. 32 DQ07
Trinity Hall Clo., Wat. 76 BW40
Trinity La., Wal.Cr. 67 DY32
Trinity Ms. SE20 202 DV95
Trinity Ms. W10 139 CX72
Cambridge Gdns.
Trinity Ms., Hem.H. 41 BR21
Pancake La.
Trinity Path SE26 182 DW90
Sydenham Pk.
Trinity Pl., Bexh. 166 EZ84
Trinity Pl., Wind. 151 AQ82
Trinity Ri. SW2 181 DN88
Trinity Rd. N2 120 DD55
Trinity Rd. N22 99 DL52
Whittington Rd.
Trinity Rd. SW17 180 DF89
Trinity Rd. SW18 180 DD85
Trinity Rd. SW19 180 DA93
Trinity Rd., Grav. 191 GJ87
Trinity Rd., Hert. 32 DW12
Trinity Rd., Ilf. 125 EQ55
Trinity Rd., Rich. 158 CM83
Trinity Rd., Sthl. 136 BY74
Trinity Rd., Ware 33 DY05
Trinity Sq. EC3 279 N1
Trinity Sq. EC3 142 DS73
Trinity St. E16 144 EG71
Vincent St.
Trinity St. SE1 279 J5
Trinity St. SE1 162 DQ75
Trinity St., Enf. 82 DQ40
Trinity Wk. NW3 140 DC65
Trinity Wk., Hem.H. 41 BR21
Pancake La.
Trinity Way E4 101 DZ51
Trinity Way W3 138 CS73
Trio Pl. SE1 279 J5
Tripps Hill, Ch.St.G. 90 AU48
Tripps Hill Clo., Ch.St.G. 90 AU48
Tripton Rd., Harl. 51 ES16
Tristan Sq. SE3 164 EE83
Tristram Clo. E17 123 ED55
Tristram Rd., Brom. 184 EF91
Triton Sq. NW1 273 K4
Triton Sq. NW1 141 DJ70
Triton Way, Hem.H. 40 BM18
Tritton Ave., Croy. 219 DL105
Tritton Rd. SE21 182 DR90
Trittons, Tad. 233 CW121
Triumph Clo., Hayes 155 BQ81
Triumph Ho., Bark. 146 EU69
Triumph Rd. E6 145 EM72
Trivett Clo., Green. 189 FU85
Trodd's La., Guil. 243 BD133
Trojan Ct. NW6 139 CY66
Willesden La.
Trojan Way, Croy. 201 DM104
Trolling Down Hill, Dart. 188 FQ89
Troon St. E1 143 DY72
White Horse Rd.
Troopers Dr., Rom. 106 FK49
Trosley Ave., Grav. 191 GH89
Trosley Rd., Belv. 166 FA79
Trossachs Rd. SE22 182 DS85
Trothy Rd. SE1 162 DU77
Monnow Rd.
Trotsworth Ave., Vir.W. 192 AY98
Trotsworth Ct., Vir.W. 192 AX98
Trott Rd. N10 98 DF52
Trott St. SW11 160 DD81
Trotters Bottom, Barn. 79 CU37
Trotters Gap, Ware 33 ED11
Trotters La., Wok. 210 AV112
Trotters Rd., Harl. 52 EU17
Trotts La., West. 255 EQ127
Trotwood, Chig. 103 ER51
Trotwood Clo., Brwd. 108 FY46
Middleton Rd.
Troughton Rd. SE7 164 EH78
Trout La., West Dr. 134 BH73
Trout Ri., Rick. 74 BH41
Trout Rd., West Dr. 134 BK74
Troutbeck Clo., Slou. 132 AU73
Troutbeck Rd. SE14 163 DY81
Troutstream Way, Rick. 74 BH42
Trouville Rd. SW4 181 DJ86
Trowbridge Est. E9 143 DZ65
Osborne Rd.
Trowbridge Rd. E9 143 DZ65
Trowbridge Rd., Rom. 106 FK51
Trowers Way, Red. 251 DH131
Trowley Ri., Abb.L. 59 BS31
Trowlock Ave., Tedd. 177 CJ93
Trowlock Island, Tedd. 177 CJ92
Trowlock Way, Tedd. 177 CK93
Troy Clo., Tad. 233 CV120
Troy Ct. SE18 165 EP77
Troy Rd. SE19 182 DR93
Troy Town SE15 162 DU83
Truesdale Dr., Uxb. 114 BJ56
Truesdale Rd. E6 145 EM72
Trulock Ct. N17 100 DU52
Trulock Rd. N17 100 DU52
Truman Clo., Edg. 96 CP52
Pavilion Way
Truman's Rd. N16 122 DS64
Trump St. EC2 275 J9
Trumper Way, Slou. 131 AM74
Trumper Way, Uxb. 134 BJ67
Trumpers Way W7 157 CE75
Trumpets Hill Rd., Reig. 265 CU135
Trumpington Dr., St.Alb. 43 CD23
Trumpington Rd. E7 124 EF63
Trumps Mill La., Vir.W. 193 AZ100
Trumpsgreen Ave., Vir.W. 192 AX100
Trumpsgreen Clo., Vir.W. 192 AY99
Trumpsgreen Rd.
Trumpsgreen Rd., Vir.W. 192 AW102
Trundle St. SE1 279 H4
Trundlers Way (Bushey), Wat. 95 CE46
Trundleys Rd. SE8 163 DX78
Trundleys Ter. SE8 163 DX77
Trunks All., Swan. 207 FB96
Trunley Heath Rd., Guil. 258 AW144
Truro Gdns., Ilf. 124 EL59
Truro Rd. E17 123 DZ56
Truro Rd. N22 99 DL52
Truro Rd., Grav. 191 GK90
Truro St. NW5 140 DG65
Truro Wk., Rom. 106 FJ51
Saddleworth Rd.
Truro Way, Hayes 135 BS69
Portland Rd.
Truslove Rd. SE27 181 DN92
Trussley Rd. W6 159 CW76
Trust Rd., Wal.Cr. 67 DY34
Trust Wk. SE21 181 DP88
Peabody Hill
Trustees Way, Uxb. 113 BF57
Trustons Gdns., Horn. 127 FG59
Tryfan Clo., Ilf. 124 EK57
Tryon St. SW3 276 D10
Tryon St. SW3 160 DF78
Trystings Clo., Esher 215 CG107
Tuam Rd. SE18 165 ER79
Tubbenden Clo., Orp. 205 ES103
Tubbenden Dr., Orp. 223 ER105
Tubbenden La., Orp. 223 ER105
Tubbenden La. S., Orp. 223 ER106
Tubbs Rd. NW10 139 CT68
Tubs Hill Par., Sev. 256 FG124
Tubwell Rd., Slou. 132 AV67
Tuck Rd., Rain. 147 FG65
Tucker Rd., Cher. 211 BD107
Tucker St., Wat. 76 BW43
Tuckey Gro., Wok. 227 BF124
Tudor Ave., Hmptn. 176 CA93
Tudor Ave., Rom. 127 FG55
Tudor Ave. (Cheshunt), Wal.Cr. 66 DU31
Tudor Ave., Wat. 76 BX38
Tudor Ave., Wor.Pk. 199 CV104
Tudor Circle, Gdmg. 258 AS144
Tudor Clo. N6 121 DJ59
Tudor Clo. NW3 120 DE64
Tudor Clo. NW7 97 CU51
Tudor Clo. NW9 118 CQ61
Tudor Clo. SW2 181 DM86
Elm Pk.
Tudor Clo., Ashf. 174 BL91
Tudor Clo., Bans. 233 CY115
Tudor Clo., Brwd. 109 FZ44
Tudor Clo., Chess. 216 CL106
Tudor Clo., Chig. 103 EN49
Tudor Clo., Chis. 205 EM95
Tudor Clo., Cob. 214 BZ113
Tudor Clo., Couls. 235 DN118
Tudor Clo., Dart. 187 FH86
Tudor Clo., Grav. 190 GE88
Tudor Clo., Hat. 45 CT21
Tudor Clo., Horl. 269 DP148
Tudor Clo., Lthd. 230 CA124
Tudor Clo., Pnr. 115 BU57
Tudor Clo., S.Croy. 236 DV115
Tudor Clo., Sutt. 217 CY107
Tudor Clo., Wall. 219 DJ108
Tudor Clo. (Cheshunt), Wal.Cr. 66 DV31
Tudor Clo., Ware 34 EK07
Tudor Clo., Wok. 227 BA117
Tudor Clo., Wdf.Grn. 102 EH50
Tudor Ct. E17 123 DZ59
Tudor Ct., Borwd. 78 CL40
Tudor Ct., Felt. 176 BW91
Tudor Ct., Swan. 207 FC101
Tudor Ct. N., Wem. 118 CN64
Tudor Ct. S., Wem. 118 CN64
Tudor Cres., Enf. 82 DQ39
Tudor Cres., Ilf. 103 EP51
Tudor Dr., H.Wyc. 110 AD55
Tudor Dr., Kings.T. 177 CK92
Tudor Dr., Mord. 199 CX100
Tudor Dr., Rom. 127 FG56
Tudor Dr., Walt. 196 BX102
Tudor Dr., Wat. 76 BX38
Tudor Est. NW10 138 CP69
Tudor Gdns. NW9 118 CQ61
Tudor Gdns. SW13 158 CS83
Treen Ave.
Tudor Gdns. W3 138 CN71
Tudor Gdns., Rom. 127 FG56
Tudor Gdns., Slou. 130 AJ72
Tudor Gdns., Twick. 177 CF88
Tudor Gdns., Upmin. 128 FQ61
Tudor Gdns., W.Wick. 203 EC104
Tudor Gro. E9 142 DW66
Tudor Gro. N20 98 DE48
Church Cres.
Tudor La., Wind. 172 AW87
Tudor Manor Gdns., Wat. 60 BX32
Tudor Par., Rick. 92 BG45
Berry La.
Tudor Pk., Amer. 55 AR37
Tudor Pl. W1 273 M8
Tudor Pl., Mitch. 180 DE94
Tudor Ri., Brox. 49 DY21
Tudor Rd. E4 101 EB51
Tudor Rd. E6 144 EJ67
Tudor Rd. E9 142 DV67
Tudor Rd. N9 100 DV45
Tudor Rd. SE19 182 DT94
Tudor Rd. SE25 202 DV99
Tudor Rd., Ashf. 175 BR93
Tudor Rd., Bark. 145 ET67
Tudor Rd., Barn. 80 DA41
Tudor Rd., Beck. 203 EB97
Tudor Rd., Gdmg. 258 AS144
Tudor Rd., Hmptn. 176 CA94
Tudor Rd., Har. 95 CD54
Tudor Rd., Hayes 135 BR72
Tudor Rd., Houns. 157 CD84
Tudor Rd., Kings.T. 178 CN94
Tudor Rd., Pnr. 94 BW54
Tudor Rd., St.Alb. 43 CE16
Tudor Rd. (Wheathampstead), St.Alb. 28 CL07
Tudor Rd., Sthl. 136 BY73
Tudor Sq., Hayes 135 BR71
Tudor St. EC4 274 E10
Tudor St. EC4 141 DN73
Tudor Wk., Bex. 186 EY86
Tudor Wk., Lthd. 231 CF120
Tudor Wk., Wat. 76 BX37
Tudor Wk., Wey. 195 BP104
West Palace Gdns.
Tudor Way N14 99 DK46
Tudor Way W3 158 CN75
Tudor Way, Hert. 31 DN08
Tudor Way, Orp. 205 ER100
Tudor Way, Rick. 92 BG46
Tudor Way, Uxb. 134 BN65
Tudor Way, Wal.Abb. 67 ED33
Tudor Way, Wind. 151 AL81
Tudor Well Clo., Stan. 95 CH50
Tudors, The, Reig. 250 DC131
Tudorwalk, Grays 170 GA76
Thurloe Wk.
Tudway Rd. SE3 164 EH83
Tufnail Rd., Dart. 188 FM86
Tufnell Pk. Rd. N7 121 DK63
Tufnell Pk. Rd. N19 121 DJ63
Tufter Rd., Chig. 103 ET50
Tufton Gdns., W.Mol. 196 CB96
Tufton Rd. E4 101 EA49
Tufton St. SW1 277 P7
Tufton St. SW1 161 DK76
Tugboat St. SE28 165 ES75
Tugela Rd., Croy. 202 DR100
Tugela St. SE6 183 DZ89
Tugmutton Clo., Orp. 223 EP105
Acorn Way
Tuilerie St. E2 142 DU68
Hackney Rd.
Tulip Clo. E6 145 EM71
Bradley Stone Rd.
Tulip Clo., Brwd. 108 FV43
Poppy Clo.
Tulip Clo., Croy. 203 DX102
Tulip Clo., Hmptn. 176 BZ93
Partridge Rd.
Tulip Clo., Rom. 106 FK51
Cloudberry Rd.
Tulip Clo., Sthl. 156 CC75
Chevy Rd.
Tulip Ct., Pnr. 116 BW55
Tulip Dr., Ilf. 125 EP64
Tulip Gdns., Ilf. 145 EP65
Tull St., Mitch. 200 DF101
Tulse Clo., Beck. 203 EC97
Tulse Hill SW2 181 DN86
Tulse Hill Est. SW2 181 DN86
Tulsemere Rd. SE27 182 DQ89
Tulyar Clo., Tad. 233 CV120
Tumber St., Epsom 248 CQ125
Tumbler Rd., Harl. 52 EU16
Tumblewood Rd., Bans. 233 CY116
Tumbling Bay, Walt. 195 BU100
Tummons Gdns. SE25 202 DS96
Tun Yd. SW8 161 DH82
Peardon St.
Tuncombe Rd. N18 100 DS49
Tunfield Rd., Hodd. 33 EB14
Tunis Rd. W12 139 CV74
Tunley Grn. E14 143 DZ71
Burdett Rd.
Tunley Rd. NW10 138 CS67
Tunley Rd. SW17 180 DG88
Tunmarsh La. E13 144 EH69
Tunmers End, Ger.Cr. 90 AW53
Tunnan Leys E6 145 EN72
Tunnel Ave. SE10 163 ED75
Tunnel Gdns. N11 99 DJ52
Tunnel Rd. SE16 162 DW75
St. Marychurch St.
Tunnel Rd., Reig. 250 DA133
Church St.
Tunnel Wd. Clo., Wat. 75 BT37
Tunnel Wd. Rd., Wat. 75 BT37
Tunnmeade, Harl. 36 EU14
Tuns La., Slou. 151 AQ76
Tunsgate, Guil. 258 AX136
Tunsgate Sq., Guil. 258 AX136
Castle St.
Tunstall Ave., Ilf. 104 EU51
Tunstall Clo., Orp. 223 ES105
Tunstall Rd. SW9 161 DM84
Tunstall Rd., Croy. 202 DS102
Tunstall Wk., Brent. 158 CL79
Ealing Rd.
Tunstock Way, Belv. 166 EY76
Tunworth Clo. NW9 118 CQ58
Tunworth Cres. SW15 179 CT86
Tupelo Rd. E10 123 EB61
Tupwood Ct., Cat. 252 DU125
Tupwood La., Cat. 252 DU125
Tupwood Scrubbs Rd., Cat. 252 DU128
Turenne Clo. SW18 160 DC84
Turfhouse La., Wok. 210 AS109
Turin Rd. N9 100 DW45
Turin St. E2 142 DU69
Turkey Oak Clo. SE19 202 DS95
Turkey St., Enf. 82 DU36
Turks Clo., Uxb. 134 BN69
Harlington Rd.
Turk's Head Yd. EC1 274 F6
Turks Row SW3 276 E10
Turks Row SW3 160 DF78
Turle Rd. N4 121 DM60
Turle Rd. SW16 201 DL96
Turlewray Clo. N4 121 DM60
Turley Clo. E15 144 EE67
Turmore Dale, Welw.G.C. 29 CW10
Turnagain La. EC4 274 F8
Turnagain La., Dart. 187 FG90
Turnage Rd., Dag. 126 EY60
Turnberry Clo. SE16 162 DV78
Ryder Dr.
Turnberry Ct., Wat. 94 BW48
Turnberry Dr., St.Alb. 60 BY30
Turnberry Quay E14 163 EB76
Pepper St.
Turnberry Way, Orp. 205 ER102
Turnbull Clo., Green. 189 FS87
Turnbury Clo. SE28 146 EX72
Summerton Way
Turnchapel Ms. SW4 161 DH83
Cedars Rd.
Turner Ave. N15 122 DS56
Turner Ave., Mitch. 200 DF95
Turner Ave., Twick. 176 CC90
Turner Clo. NW11 120 DB58
Turner Clo., Guil. 243 AZ131
Turner Clo., Hayes 135 BQ68
Charville La.
Turner Ct., Dart. 188 FJ85
Wilmot Rd.
Turner Dr. NW11 120 DB58
Turner Rd. E17 123 EC55
Turner Rd., Dart. 189 FV90
Turner Rd., Edg. 96 CL54
Turner Rd., N.Mal. 198 CR101
Turner Rd., Slou. 152 AW75
Turner Rd. (Bushey), Wat. 76 CC42
Turner Rd., West. 222 EJ112
Turner St. E1 142 DV71
Turner St. E16 144 EF72
Turners Clo., Stai. 174 BH92
Turners Gdns., Sev. 257 FJ128
Turners Hill, Hem.H. 40 BL20
Turners Hill (Cheshunt), Wal.Cr. 67 DX30
Turners La., Walt. 213 BV107
Turners Meadow Way, Beck. 203 DZ95
Turners Rd. E3 143 DZ71
Turners Way, Croy. 201 DN103
Turners Wd. NW11 120 DC60
Turners Wd. Dr., Ch.St.G. 90 AX48
Turneville Rd. W14 159 CZ79
Turney Rd. SE21 182 DQ87
Turneys Orchard, Rick. 73 BD43
Turnham Clo., Guil. 258 AW138
Turnham Grn. Ter. W4 158 CS77
Turnham Grn. Ter. Ms. W4 158 CS77
Turnham Grn. Ter.
Turnham Rd. SE4 183 DY85
Turnmill St. EC1 274 E5
Turnmill St. EC1 141 DN70
Turnoak Ave., Wok. 226 AY120
Turnoak La., Wok. 226 AY119
Wych Hill La.
Turnoak Pk., Wind. 151 AL83
Turnpike Clo. SE8 163 DZ80
Amersham Vale
Turnpike Dr., Orp. 224 EW109
Turnpike Grn., Hem.H. 40 BM16
Turnpike Ho. EC1 274 G3
Turnpike La. N8 121 DM56
Turnpike La., Sutt. 218 DC106
Turnpike La., Til. 171 GK78
Turnpike La., Uxb. 134 BL69
Turnpike Link, Croy. 202 DS103
Turnpike Way, Islw. 157 CG81
Turnpin La. SE10 163 EC79
Turnstone Clo. E13 144 EG69
Turnstone Clo. NW9 96 CS54
Kestrel Clo.

Turnstone Clo., S.Croy. 221 DY110
Turnstone Clo., Uxb. 115 BP64
Turnstones, The, Grav. 191 GK89
Turnstones, The, Wat. 76 BY36
Turp Ave., Grays 170 GC75
Turpentine La. SW1 161 DH78
Sutherland St.
Turpin Ave., Rom. 104 FA51
Turpin La., Erith 167 FG80
Turpin Rd., Felt. 175 BT86
Staines Rd.
Turpin Way N19 121 DK61
Elthorne Rd.
Turpin Way, Wall. 219 DH108
Turpington Clo., Brom. 204 EL100
Turpington La., Brom. 204 EL101
Turpins Clo., Hert. 31 DM09
Turpins La., Wdf.Grn. 103 EM50
Turquand St. SE17 279 J9
Turret Gro. SW4 161 DJ83
Turton Rd., Wem. 118 CL64
Turton Way, Slou. 151 AR76
Turville Ct., Lthd. 246 CB125
Proctor Gdns.
Turville St. E2 142 DT70
Old Nichol St.
Tuscan Rd. SE18 165 ER78
Tuskar St. SE10 164 EE78
Tustin Est. SE15 162 DW79
Tuttlebee La., Buck.H. 102 EG47
Tuxford Clo., Borwd. 78 CL38
Twankhams All., Epp. 70 EU30
Hemnall St.
Tweed Clo., Berk. 38 AV18
Tweed Glen, Rom. 105 FD52
Tweed Grn., Rom. 105 FD52
Tweed La., Bet. 264 CP139
Tweed Rd., Slou. 153 BB79
Tweed Way, Rom. 105 FD52
Tweedale Ct. E15 123 EC64
Tweeddale Gro., Uxb. 115 BQ62
Tweeddale Rd., Cars. 200 DD102
Tweedmouth Rd. E13 144 EH68
Tweedy Rd., Brom. 204 EG95
Tweenways, Chesh. 54 AR30
Tweezer's All. WC2 274 D10
Twelve Acre Clo., Lthd. 230 BZ124
Twelve Acres, Welw.G.C. 29 CY11
Twelvetrees Cres. E3 143 EC70
Twentyman Clo., Wdf.Grn. 102 EG50
Twickenham Bri., Rich. 177 CJ85
Twickenham Bri., Twick. 177 CJ85
Twickenham Clo., Croy. 201 DM104
Twickenham Gdns., Grnf. 117 CG64
Twickenham Gdns., Har. 95 CE52
Twickenham Rd. E11 123 ED61
Twickenham Rd., Felt. 176 BZ90
Twickenham Rd., Islw. 177 CG85
Twickenham Rd., Rich. 177 CJ85
Twickenham Rd., Tedd. 177 CG91
Twickenham Trd. Est., Twick. 177 CF86
Twig Folly Clo. E2 143 DX68
Roman Rd.
Twigg Clo., Erith 167 FE80
Twilley St. SW18 180 DB87
Twinches La., Slou. 131 AP74
Twine Clo., Bark. 146 EV69
Thames Rd.
Twine Ct. E1 142 DW73
Twineham Grn. N12 98 DA49
Tillingham Way
Twining Ave., Twick. 176 CC90
Twinn Rd. NW7 97 CY51
Twinoaks, Cob. 214 CA113
Twisden Rd. NW5 121 DH63
Twisleton Ct., Dart. 188 FK86
Priory Hill
Twitchells La., Beac. 90 AT51
Twitton La., Sev. 241 FD115
Twitton Meadows, Sev. 241 FE116
Two Acres, Welw.G.C. 29 CZ11
Two Dells La., Chesh. 38 AT24
Two Waters Rd., Hem.H. 40 BJ24
Twybridge Way NW10 138 CQ66
Twyford Abbey Rd. NW10 138 CM69
Twyford Ave. N2 120 DF55
Twyford Ave. W3 138 CN73
Twyford Cres. W3 138 CN74
Twyford Pl. WC2 274 B8
Twyford Rd., Cars. 200 DD102
Twyford Rd., Har. 116 CB60
Twyford Rd., Ilf. 125 EQ64
Twyford Rd., St.Alb. 43 CJ16
Twyford St. N1 141 DM67
Twyner Clo., Horl. 269 DK147
Twysdens Ter., Hat. 45 CW24
Dellsome La.
Tyas Rd. E16 144 EF70
Tybenham Rd. SW19 199 CZ97
Tyberry Rd., Enf. 82 DV41
Tyburn La., Har. 117 CE59
Tyburn Way W1 272 E10
Tyburns, The, Brwd. 109 GC47
Tycehurst Hill, Loug. 85 EM42
Tychbourne Dr., Guil. 243 BC131
Tydcombe Rd., Warl. 236 DW119
Tye Grn. Village, Harl. 51 ET18
Tye La., Epsom 248 CR126
Headley Common Rd.
Tye La., Orp. 223 EQ106
Tye La., Tad. 249 CT128
Dorking Rd.
Tyers Est. SE1 279 M4
Tyers Est. SE1 162 DS75
Tyers Gate SE1 279 M5
Tyers St. SE11 161 DM78
Tyers Ter. SE11 161 DM78
Tyeshurst Clo. SE2 166 EY78
Tyfield Clo. (Cheshunt), Wal.Cr. 66 DW30
Tykeswater La., Borwd. 77 CJ40
Tyle Grn., Horn. 128 FL56
Tyle Pl., Wind. 172 AU85
Tylecroft Rd. SW16 201 DL96
Tylehost, Guil. 242 AU130
Tylehurst Gdns., Ilf. 125 EQ64
Tyler Clo. E2 142 DT68
Tyler Gdns., Add. 212 BJ105
Tyler Gro., Dart. 188 FM84
Spielman Rd.
Tyler St. SE10 164 EE78
Tyler Way, Brwd. 108 FV46
Tylers Causeway, Hert. 47 DH23
Tylers Clo., Gdse. 252 DV130
Tylers Clo., Kings L. 58 BL28
Tylers Clo., Loug. 102 EL45
Tyler's Ct. W1 273 M9
Tylers Cres., Horn. 128 FJ64
Tylers Gate, Har. 118 CL58
Tylers Grn. Rd., Swan. 207 FC100
Tylers Hill Rd., Chesh. 56 AT30
Tylers Path, Cars. 218 DF105
Rochester Rd.
Tylers Rd., Harl. 50 EJ19
Tylers Way, Wat. 77 CE43
Tylersfield, Abb.L. 59 BT31
Tylney Ave. SE19 182 DT92
Tylney Cft., Harl. 51 EQ17
Tylney Rd. E7 124 EJ63
Tylney Rd., Brom. 204 EK96
Tylsworth Clo., Amer. 55 AR38
King George V Rd.
Tynan Clo., Felt. 175 BU88
Sandycombe Rd.
Tyndale Clo., Dart. 189 FR88
Tyndale Ct. E14 163 EB78
Tyndale La. N1 141 DP66
Upper St.
Tyndale Ter. N1 141 DP66
Canonbury La.
Tyndall Rd. E10 123 EC61
Tyndall Rd., Well. 165 ET83
Tyne Clo., Upmin. 129 FR58
Tyne Gdns., S.Ock. 148 FQ73
Tyne St. E1 142 DT72
Old Castle St.
Tynedale, St.Alb. 62 CM27
Thamesdale
Tynedale Rd., Bet. 264 CP138
Tyneham Rd. SW11 160 DG82
Tynemouth Clo. E6 145 EP72
Covelees Wall
Tynemouth Dr., Enf. 82 DU38
Tynemouth Rd. N15 122 DT56
Tynemouth Rd. SE18 165 ET78
Tynemouth Rd., Mitch. 180 DG94
Tynemouth St. SW6 160 DC82
Tynley Gro., Guil. 242 AX128
Type St. E2 143 DX68
Typelden Clo., Hem.H. 40 BK18
Tyrawley Rd. SW6 160 DB81
Tyrell Clo., Har. 117 CE63
Tyrell Ct., Cars. 218 DF105
Tyrell Gdns., Wind. 151 AM83
Tyrell Ri., Brwd. 108 FW50
Tyrell Sq., Mitch. 200 DE95
Tyrells Clo., Upmin. 128 FP61
Tyrols Rd. SE23 183 DX88
Wastdale Rd.
Tyron Way, Sid. 185 ES91
Tyrone Rd. E6 145 EM68
Tyrrel Way NW9 119 CT59
Tyrrell Ave., Well. 186 EU85
Tyrrell Rd. SE22 162 DU84
Tyrrells Hall Clo., Grays 170 GD79
Tyrrells Wd. Dr., Lthd. 231 CH123
Tyrwhitt Ave., Guil. 242 AV130
Tyrwhitt Rd. SE4 163 EA83
Tysea Clo., Harl. 51 ET18
Tysea Hill, Rom. 105 FF45
Tysea Rd., Harl. 51 ET18
Tysoe Ave., Enf. 83 DZ36
Tysoe St. EC1 274 D3
Tyson Rd. SE23 182 DW87
Tyssen Pas. E8 142 DT65
Tyssen St.
Tyssen Pl., S.Ock. 149 FW69
Tyssen Rd. N16 122 DT62
Tyssen St. E8 142 DT65
Tyssen St. N1 275 N1
Tythebarn Clo., Guil. 243 BB129
Dairyman's Wk.
Tytherton Rd. N19 121 DK62
Tyttenhanger Grn., St.Alb. 43 CK23

U

Uamvar St. E14 143 EB71
Uckfield Gro., Mitch. 200 DG95
Uckfield Rd., Enf. 83 DX37
Udall Gdns., Rom. 104 FA51
Udall St. SW1 277 L9
Udney Pk. Rd., Tedd. 177 CG92
Uffington Rd. NW10 139 CU67
Uffington Rd. SE27 181 DN91
Ufford Clo., Har. 94 CB52
Ufford Rd.
Ufford Rd., Har. 94 CB52
Ufford St. SE1 278 E4
Ufford St. SE1 161 DN75
Ufton Gro. N1 142 DR66
Ufton Rd. N1 142 DR66
Uhura Sq. N16 122 DS62
Ujima Ct. SW16 181 DL91
Sunnyhill Rd.
Ullathorne Rd. SW16 181 DJ91
Ulleswater Rd. N14 99 DL49
Ullin St. E14 143 EC71
St. Leonards Rd.
Ullswater Business Pk., The, Couls. 235 DL116
Ullswater Clo. SW15 178 CR91
Ullswater Clo., Brom. 184 EE94
Ullswater Clo., Hayes 135 BS68
Ullswater Clo., Slou. 130 AJ71
Buttermere Ave.
Ullswater Ct., Har. 116 CA59
Oakington Ave.
Ullswater Cres. SW15 178 CR91
Ullswater Cres., Couls. 235 DL116
Ullswater Rd. SE27 181 DP89
Ullswater Rd. SW13 159 CU80
Ullswater Rd., Hem.H. 41 BQ22
Ullswater Way, Horn. 127 FG64
Ulstan Clo., Cat. 237 EA123
Ulster Gdns. N13 100 DQ49
Ulster Pl. NW1 273 H5
Ulster Ter. NW1 273 H4
Ulundi Rd. SE3 164 EE79
Ulva Rd. SW15 179 CX85
Ravenna Rd.
Ulverscroft Rd. SE22 182 DT85
Ulverston Rd. E17 101 ED54
Ulverstone Rd. SE27 181 DP89
Ulwin Ave., W.Byf. 212 BL113
Ulysses Rd. NW6 119 CZ64
Umberston St. E1 142 DU72
Hessel St.
Umberville Way, Slou. 131 AM69
Umbria St. SW15 179 CU86
Umfreville Rd. N4 121 DP58
Underacres Clo., Hem.H. 40 BN19
Undercliff Rd. SE13 163 EA83
Underhill, Barn. 80 DA43
Underhill Pk. Rd., Reig. 250 DA131
Underhill Pas. NW1 141 DH67
Camden High St.
Underhill Rd. SE22 182 DU85
Underhill St. NW1 141 DH67
Camden High St.
Underne Ave. N14 99 DH47
Underriver Ho. Rd., Sev. 257 FP130
Undershaft EC3 275 M9
Undershaft EC3 142 DS72
Undershaw Rd., Brom. 184 EF90
Underwood, Croy. 221 EC106
Underwood, The SE9 185 EM89
Underwood Rd. E1 142 DU70
Underwood Rd. E4 101 EB50
Underwood Rd., Cat. 252 DS126
Underwood Rd., Wdf.Grn. 102 EJ52
Underwood Row N1 275 J2
Underwood Row N1 142 DQ69
Underwood St. N1 275 J2
Underwood St. N1 142 DQ69
Undine Rd. E14 163 EB77
Undine St. SW17 180 DF92
Uneeda Dr., Grnf. 137 CD67
Unicorn Wk., Green. 189 FT85
Union Cotts. E15 144 EE66
Welfare Rd.
Union Ct. EC2 275 M8
Union Ct., Rich. 178 CL85
Eton St.
Union Dr. E1 143 DY70
Solebay St.
Union Grn., Hem.H. 40 BK19
Union Gro. SW8 161 DK82
Union Rd. N11 99 DK51
Union Rd. SW4 161 DK82
Union Rd. SW8 161 DK82
Union Rd., Brom. 204 EK99
Union Rd., Croy. 202 DQ101
Union Rd., Nthlt. 136 CA68
Union Rd., Wem. 138 CL65
Union Sq. N1 142 DQ67
Union St. E15 143 EC67
Union St. SE1 278 G3
Union St. SE1 142 DQ74
Union St., Barn. 79 CY42
Union St., Kings.T. 197 CK96
Union Wk. E2 275 N2
Unity Clo. NW10 139 CU65
Unity Clo. SE19 182 DQ92
Unity Clo., Croy. 221 EB109
Castle Hill Ave.
Unity Rd., Enf. 82 DW37
Unity Way SE18 164 EK76
Unity Wf. SE1 162 DT75
Mill St.
University Clo. NW7 97 CT52
University Clo., Wat. 76 CA42
University Gdns., Bex. 186 EZ87
University Pl., Erith 167 FB80
Belmont Rd.
University Rd. SW19 180 DD93
University St. WC1 273 L5
University St. WC1 141 DJ70
University Way (Dartford Northern Bypass), Dart. 168 FJ84
Unstead La., Guil. 258 AW144
Unstead Wd., Guil. 258 AW142
Unwin Ave., Felt. 175 BR85
Unwin Clo. SE15 162 DU79
Unwin Rd. SW7 160 DD76
Imperial College Rd.
Unwin Rd., Islw. 157 CE83
Upbrook Ms. W2 140 DC72
Chilworth St.
Upcerne Rd. SW10 160 DC80
Upchurch Clo. SE20 182 DV94
Upcroft, Wind. 151 AP83
Upcroft Ave., Edg. 96 CQ50
Updale Clo., Pot.B. 63 CY33
Updale Rd., Sid. 185 ET91
Upfield, Croy. 202 DV103
Upfield, Horl. 268 DG149
Upfield Clo., Horl. 268 DG150
Upfield Rd. W7 137 CF70
Upfolds Grn., Guil. 243 BC130
Upgrove Manor Way SW2 181 DN87
Trinity Ri.
Uphall Rd., Ilf. 125 EP64
Upham Pk. Rd. W4 158 CS77
Uphill Dr. NW7 96 CS50
Uphill Dr. NW9 118 CQ57
Uphill Gro. NW7 96 CS49
Uphill Rd. NW7 96 CS49
Upland Ave., Chesh. 54 AP28
Upland Ct. Rd., Rom. 106 FM54
Upland Dr., Hat. 64 DB25
Upland Ms. SE22 182 DU85
Upland Rd.
Upland Rd. E13 144 EF70
Sutton Rd.
Upland Rd. SE22 182 DU85
Upland Rd., Bexh. 166 EZ83
Upland Rd., Cat. 237 EA120
Upland Rd., Epp. 69 ER25
Upland Rd., S.Croy. 220 DR106
Upland Rd., Sutt. 218 DD107
Upland Way, Epsom 233 CW118
Uplands, Ash. 231 CK120
Uplands, Beck. 203 EA96
Uplands, Rick. 74 BM44
Uplands, Ware 33 DZ05
Uplands, Welw.G.C. 29 CW05
Uplands, The, Ger.Cr. 112 AY60
Uplands, The, Loug. 85 EM41
Uplands, The, Ruis. 115 BU60
Uplands, The, St.Alb. 60 BY30
Uplands Ave. E17 101 DX54
Blackhorse La.
Uplands Business Pk. E17 123 DX55
Uplands Clo. SW14 178 CP85
Monroe Dr.
Uplands Clo., Ger.Cr. 112 AY60
Uplands Clo., Sev. 256 FF123
Uplands Dr., Lthd. 215 CD113
Uplands End, Wdf.Grn. 102 EL52
Uplands Pk. Rd., Enf. 81 DN41
Uplands Rd. N8 121 DM57
Uplands Rd., Barn. 98 DG46
Uplands Rd., Brwd. 108 FY50
Uplands Rd., Ken. 236 DQ116
Uplands Rd., Orp. 206 EV102
Uplands Rd., Rom. 126 EX55
Uplands Rd., Wdf.Grn. 102 EL52
Uplands Way N21 81 DN43
Uplands Way, Sev. 256 FF123
Upminster Rd., Horn. 128 FM61
Upminster Rd., Upmin. 128 FN61
Upminster Rd. N., Rain. 148 FJ70
Upminster Rd. S., Rain. 147 FG70
Upney Clo., Horn. 128 FJ64
Tylers Cres.
Upney La., Bark. 145 ES65
Upnor Way SE17 279 N10
Uppark Dr., Ilf. 125 EQ58
Upper Abbey Rd., Belv. 166 EZ77
Upper Addison Gdns. W14 159 CY75
Upper Ashlyns Rd., Berk. 38 AV20
Upper Bardsey Wk. N1 142 DQ65
Clephane Rd.
Upper Barn, Hem.H. 40 BM23
Upper Belgrave St. SW1 276 G6
Upper Belgrave St. SW1 160 DG76
Upper Belmont Rd., Chesh. 54 AP28
Upper Berkeley St. W1 272 D9
Upper Berkeley St. W1 140 DF72
Upper Beulah Hill SE19 202 DS95
Upper Bray Rd., Maid. 150 AC77
Upper Brentwood Rd., Rom. 128 FJ56
Upper Bri. Rd., Red. 250 DE134
Upper Brighton Rd., Surb. 197 CK100
Upper Brockley Rd. SE4 163 DZ82
Upper Brook St. W1 276 F1
Upper Brook St. W1 140 DG73
Upper Butts, Brent. 157 CJ79
Upper Caldy Wk. N1 142 DQ65
Clephane Rd.
Upper Camelford Wk. W11 139 CY72
Lancaster Rd.
Upper Cavendish Ave. N3 120 DA55
Upper Cheyne Row SW3 160 DE79
Upper Ch. Hill, Green. 189 FS85
Upper Clabdens, Ware 33 DZ06
Upper Clapton Rd. E5 122 DV60
Upper Clarendon Wk. W11 139 CY72
Lancaster Rd.
Upper Cor. Clo., Ch.St.G. 90 AV47
Upper Cornsland, Brwd. 108 FX48
Upper Ct. Rd., Cat. 237 EA123
Upper Ct. Rd., Epsom 216 CQ111
Upper Culver Rd., St.Alb. 43 CE18
Upper Dagnall St., St.Alb. 43 CD20
Upper Dengie Wk. N1 142 DQ67
Popham Rd.
Upper Dr., Beac. 89 AK50
Upper Dr., West. 238 EJ118
Upper Dunnymans, Bans. 217 CZ114
Basing Rd.
Upper Edgeborough Rd., Guil. 259 AZ135
Upper Elmers End Rd., Beck. 203 DY98
Upper Fairfield Rd., Lthd. 231 CH121
Upper Fm. Rd., W.Mol. 196 BZ98
Upper Forecourt, Gat. 269 DH152
Upper Fosters NW4 119 CW57
New Brent St.
Upper George St., Chesh. 54 AQ30
Frances St.
Upper Gladstone Rd., Chesh. 54 AQ30
Upper Grn. E., Mitch. 200 DF96
Upper Grn. W., Mitch. 200 DF97
London Rd.
Upper Grenfell Wk. W11 139 CX73
Whitchurch Rd.
Upper Grosvenor St. W1 276 F1
Upper Grosvenor St. W1 140 DG73
Upper Grotto Rd., Twick. 177 CF89
Upper Grd. SE1 278 D2
Upper Grd. SE1 141 DN74
Upper Gro. SE25 202 DS98
Upper Gro. Rd., Belv. 166 EZ79
Upper Guildown Rd., Guil. 258 AV137
Upper Gulland Wk. N1 142 DQ65
Clephane Rd.
Upper Hall Pk., Berk. 38 AX20
Upper Halliford Bypass, Shep. 195 BS99
Upper Halliford Grn., Shep. 195 BS98
Holmbank Dr.
Upper Halliford Rd., Shep. 195 BS98
Upper Ham Rd., Rich. 177 CK91
Upper Handa Wk. N1 142 DR65
Clephane Rd.
Upper Harley St. NW1 272 G5
Upper Harley St. NW1 140 DG70
Upper Hawkwell Wk. N1 142 DQ67
Popham Rd.
Upper Heath Rd., St.Alb. 43 CF18
Upper High St., Epsom 216 CS113
Upper Highway, Abb.L. 59 BR33
Upper Highway, Kings L. 59 BQ32
Upper Hill Ri., Rick. 74 BH44
Upper Hitch, Wat. 94 BY46
Upper Holly Hill Rd., Belv. 167 FB78
Upper Hook, Harl. 51 ES17
Upper James St. W1 273 L10
Upper John St. W1 273 L10
Upper Lattimore Rd., St.Alb. 43 CE20
Upper Lees Rd., Slou. 131 AP69
Upper Lismore Wk. N1 142 DQ65
Clephane Rd.
Upper Mall W6 159 CU78
Upper Manor Rd., Gdmg. 258 AS144
Upper Marlborough Rd., St.Alb. 43 CE20
Upper Marsh SE1 278 C6
Upper Marsh SE1 161 DM75
Upper Marsh La., Hodd. 49 EA18
Upper Mealines, Harl. 52 EU18
Upper Montagu St. W1 272 D6
Upper Montagu St. W1 140 DF71
Upper Mulgrave Rd., Sutt. 217 CY108
Upper N. St. E14 143 EA71
Upper Paddock Rd., Wat. 76 BY44
Upper Palace Rd., E.Mol. 196 CC97
Upper Pk., Harl. 35 EP14
Upper Pk., Loug. 84 EK42
Upper Pk. Rd. N11 99 DH50
Upper Pk. Rd. NW3 140 DF65
Upper Pk. Rd., Belv. 167 FB77
Upper Pk. Rd., Brom. 204 EH95
Upper Pk. Rd., Kings.T. 178 CN93
Upper Phillimore Gdns. W8 160 DA75
Upper Pines, Bans. 234 DF117
Upper Rainham Rd., Horn. 127 FF60
Upper Ramsey Wk. N1 142 DR65
Clephane Rd.
Upper Rawreth Wk. N1 142 DQ67
Popham Rd.
Upper Richmond Rd. SW15 159 CY84
Upper Richmond Rd. W. SW14 158 CR84
Upper Richmond Rd. W., Rich. 158 CN84
Upper Riding, Beac. 88 AG54
Upper Rd. E13 144 EG69
Upper Rd., Uxb. 113 BD59
Upper Rd., Wall. 219 DK106
Upper Rose Hill, Dor. 263 CH137
Upper Ryle, Brwd. 108 FW45
Upper St. Martin's La. WC2 273 P10
Upper St. Martin's La. WC2 141 DL73
Upper Sales, Hem.H. 39 BF21
Upper Sawley Wd., Bans. 217 CZ114
Upper Selsdon Rd., S.Croy. 220 DS108
Upper Sheppey Wk. N1 142 DQ66
Clephane Rd.
Upper Sheridan Rd., Belv. 166 FA77
Coleman Rd.
Upper Shirley Rd., Croy. 202 DW103
Upper Shot, Welw.G.C. 30 DA08
Upper Shott (Cheshunt), Wal.Cr. 66 DT26
Upper Sq., Islw. 157 CG83
North St.
Upper Sta. Rd., Rad. 77 CG35
Upper Stonyfield, Harl. 51 EP15
Upper St. N1 141 DN68
Upper St., Guil. 260 BM139
Upper Sunbury Rd., Hmptn. 196 BY95
Upper Sutton La., Houns. 156 CA80
Upper Swaines, Epp. 69 ET30
Upper Tachbrook St. SW1 277 L8
Upper Tachbrook St. SW1 161 DJ77
Upper Tail, Wat. 94 BY48
Upper Talbot Wk. W11 139 CY72
Lancaster Rd.
Upper Teddington Rd., Kings.T. 177 CJ94
Upper Ter. NW3 120 DC62
Upper Thames St. EC4 274 G10
Upper Thames St. EC4 142 DQ73
Upper Tollington Pk. N4 121 DN59
Upper Tooting Pk. SW17 180 DF89
Upper Tooting Rd. SW17 180 DF91
Upper Town Rd., Grnf. 136 CB70
Upper Tulse Hill SW2 181 DM87
Upper Vernon Rd., Sutt. 218 DD106
Upper Wk., Vir.W. 192 AY98
Upper Walthamstow Rd. E17 123 ED56
Upper W. St., Reig. 249 CZ134
Upper Wickham La., Well. 166 EV83
Upper Wimpole St. W1 272 G6
Upper Wimpole St. W1 140 DG71
Upper Woburn Pl. WC1 273 N3
Upper Woburn Pl. WC1 141 DK69
Upper Woodcote Village, Pur. 219 DK113
Upperfield Rd., Welw.G.C. 29 CZ10
Upperton Rd., Guil. 258 AW135
Upperton Rd., Sid. 185 ET92
Upperton Rd. E. E13 144 EJ69
Inniskilling Rd.
Upperton Rd. W. E13 144 EJ69
Uppingham Ave., Stan. 95 CH53
Upsdell Ave. N13 99 DN51
Upshire Rd., Wal.Abb. 68 EF32
Upshott La., Wok. 227 BF117
Upstall St. SE5 161 DP81
Upton, Wok. 226 AV117
Upton Ave. E7 144 EG66
Upton Ave., St.Alb. 43 CD19
Upton Clo., Bex. 186 EZ86
Upton Clo., St.Alb. 61 CD25
Upton Clo., Slou. 152 AT76
Upton Ct. SE20 182 DW94
Blean Gro.
Upton Ct. Rd., Slou. 152 AU76
Upton Dene, Sutt. 218 DB108
Upton Gdns., Har. 117 CH57
Upton La. E7 144 EH65
Upton Lo. Clo. (Bushey), Wat. 94 CC45
Upton Pk., Slou. 152 AS76
Upton Pk. Rd. E7 144 EH66
Upton Rd. N18 100 DU50
Upton Rd. SE18 165 EQ79
Upton Rd., Bex. 186 EZ86
Upton Rd., Bexh. 166 EY84
Upton Rd., Houns. 156 CA83
Upton Rd., Slou. 152 AU76
Upton Rd., Th.Hth. 202 DR96
Upton Rd., Wat. 75 BV42
Upton Rd. S., Bex. 186 EZ86
Upway N12 98 DE52
Upway, Ger.Cr. 91 AZ52
Upwood Rd. SE12 184 EG86
Upwood Rd. SW16 201 DL95
Uranus Rd., Hem.H. 40 BM18
Urban Ave., Horn. 128 FJ62
Urlwin St. SE5 162 DQ79
Urlwin Wk. SW9 161 DN81
Urmston Dr. SW19 179 CY88
Ursula Ms. N4 122 DQ60
Portland Ri.
Ursula St. SW11 160 DE81
Urswick Gdns., Dag. 146 EY66
Urswick Rd.
Urswick Rd. E9 122 DW64
Urswick Rd., Dag. 146 EX66
Usborne Ms. SW8 161 DM80
Usher Rd. E3 143 DZ68
Usherwood Clo., Tad. 248 CP131
Usk Rd. SW11 160 DC84
Usk Rd., S.Ock. 148 FQ71
Usk St. E2 143 DX69

Waldron Gdns., Brom. 203 ED97
Waldron Ms. SW3 160 DD79
Old Ch. St.
Waldron Rd. SW18 180 DC90
Waldron Rd., Har. 117 CE60
Waldronhyrst, S.Croy. 219 DP105
Waldrons, The, Croy. 219 DP105
Waldrons, The, Oxt. 254 EF131
Waldrons Path, S.Croy. 220 DQ105
Bramley Hill
Waleran Clo., Stan. 95 CF51
Chenduit Way
Waleran Flats SE1 162 DS77
Old Kent Rd.
Walerand Rd. SE13 163 EC82
Wales Ave., Cars. 218 DE106
Wales Fm. Rd. W3 138 CR71
Waley St. E1 143 DY71
Walfield Ave. N20 98 DB45
Walford Clo., Harl. 36 EW12
Walford Rd. N16 122 DS63
Walford Rd., Dor. 263 CH140
Walford Rd., Uxb. 134 BJ68
Walfrey Gdns., Dag. 146 EY66
Walham Gro. SW6 160 DA80
Walham Ri. SW19 179 CY93
Walham Yd. SW6 160 DA80
Walham Gro.
Walk, The, Horn. 128 FM61
Walk, The, Oxt. 253 EA133
Walk, The, Pot.B. 64 DA32
Walk, The, Sun. 175 BT94
Walk, The (Eton Wick), Wind. 151 AN78
Walkden Rd., Chis. 185 EN92
Walker Clo. N11 99 DJ49
Walker Clo. SE18 165 EQ77
Walker Clo. W7 137 CE74
Walker Clo., Dart. 167 FF83
Walker Clo., Hmptn. 176 BZ93
Fearnley Cres.
Walkers Ct. E8 142 DU65
Wilton Way
Walkers Ct. W1 273 M10
Walkers Pl. SW15 159 CY83
Felsham Rd.
Walkerscroft Mead SE21 182 DQ88
Walkfield Dr., Epsom 233 CV117
Walkford Way SE15 162 DT80
Daniel Gdns.
Walkley Rd., Dart. 187 FH85
Walks, The N2 120 DD55
Walkwood End, Beac. 88 AJ54
Walkwood Ri., Beac. 110 AJ55
Wall End Rd. E6 145 EN66
Wall St. N1 142 DR65
Wallace Clo. SE28 146 EX73
Haldane Rd.
Wallace Clo., Horn. 127 FH60
Wallace Clo., Shep. 195 BR98
Wallace Clo., Uxb. 134 BL68
Grays Rd.
Wallace Cres., Cars. 218 DF106
Wallace Flds., Epsom 217 CT112
Wallace Gdns., Swans. 190 FY86
Milton St.
Wallace Rd. N1 142 DQ65
Wallace Rd., Grays 170 GA76
Wallace Wk., Add. 212 BJ105
Wallace Way N19 121 DK61
Giesbach Rd.
Wallasey Cres., Uxb. 114 BN61
Wallbutton Rd. SE4 163 DY82
Wallcote Ave. NW2 119 CX60
Walled Gdn., The, Bet. 264 CR135
Walled Gdn., The, Tad. 233 CX122
Heathcote
Wallenger Ave., Rom. 127 FH55
Waller Dr., Nthwd. 93 BU54
Waller La., Cat. 236 DT123
Waller Rd. SE14 163 DX81
Waller Rd., Beac. 89 AM53
Wallers Clo., Dag. 146 EY67
Wallers Clo., Wdf.Grn. 103 EM51
Waller's Hoppit, Loug. 84 EL40
Wallers Way, Hodd. 33 EB14
Wallfield All., Hert. 32 DQ10
Wallflower St. W12 139 CT73
Wallgrave Rd. SW5 160 DB77
Wallhouse Rd., Erith 167 FH80
Wallingford Ave. W10 139 CX71
Wallingford Rd., Uxb. 134 BH68
Wallingford Wk., St.Alb. 43 CD23
Wallington Clo., Ruis. 115 BQ58
Wallington Rd., Chesh. 54 AP30
Wallington Rd., Ilf. 125 ET59
Wallington Sq., Wall. 219 DH107
Woodcote Rd.
Wallis All. SE1 279 J5
Wallis Clo. SW11 160 DD83
Wallis Clo., Dart. 187 FG90
Wallis Ct., Slou. 152 AU76
Nixey Clo.
Wallis Ms. N22 121 DN55
Brampton Pk. Rd.
Wallis Ms., Lthd. 231 CG122
Wallis Pk., Grav. 190 GB85
Wallis Rd. E9 143 DZ65
Wallis Rd., Sthl. 136 CB72
Walliss Cotts. SW2 181 DL87
Wallorton Gdns. SW14 158 CR84
Wallside EC2 142 DQ71
Wood St.
Wallwood Rd. E11 123 ED60
Wallwood St. E14 143 DZ71
Walm La. NW2 139 CW65
Walmar Clo., Barn. 80 DD39
Walmer Clo. E4 101 EB47
Walmer Clo., Orp. 223 ER105
Tubbenden La. S.
Walmer Clo., Rom. 105 FB54
Walmer Gdns. W13 157 CG75
Walmer Ho. N9 100 DT46
Walmer Pl. W1 272 D6
Walmer Rd. W10 139 CW72
Latimer Rd.
Walmer Rd. W11 139 CY73
Walmer St. W1 272 D6
Walmer Ter. SE18 165 EQ77
Walmgate Rd., Grnf. 137 CH67
Walmington Fold N12 98 DA51
Walney Wk. N1 142 DQ65
St. Paul's Rd.
Walnut Ave., West Dr. 154 BN76
Walnut Clo. SE8 163 DZ79
Clyde St.
Walnut Clo., Cars. 218 DF106
Walnut Clo. (Eynsford), Dart. 208 FK104
Walnut Clo., Epsom 233 CT115
Walnut Clo., Hayes 135 BS73
Walnut Clo., Ilf. 125 EQ56
Civic Way
Walnut Clo., St.Alb. 60 CB27
Walnut Ct. W5 158 CL75
Walnut Ct., Welw.G.C. 29 CY12
Walnut Dr., Tad. 233 CY124
Warren Lo. Dr.
Walnut Flds., Epsom 217 CT109
Walnut Gdns. E15 124 EE63
Burgess Rd.
Walnut Grn. (Bushey), Wat. 76 BZ40
Walnut Gro., Bans. 217 CX114
Walnut Gro., Enf. 82 DR43
Walnut Gro., Hem.H. 40 BK20
Walnut Gro., Welw.G.C. 29 CY12
Walnut Ms., Sutt. 218 DC108
Walnut Rd. E10 123 EA61
Walnut Tree Ave., Dart. 188 FL89
Walnut Tree Ave., Mitch. 200 DE97
Dearn Gdns.
Walnut Tree Clo. SW13 159 CT81
Walnut Tree Clo., Bans. 217 CY112
Walnut Tree Clo., Chis. 205 EQ95
Walnut Tree Clo., Guil. 242 AW134
Walnut Tree Clo., Hodd. 49 EA17
Walnut Tree Clo. (Cheshunt), Wal.Cr. 67 DX31
Walnut Tree Cotts. SW19 179 CY91
Church Rd.
Walnut Tree La., W.Byf. 212 BK112
Walnut Tree Pk., Guil. 242 AW134
Walnut Tree Rd. SE10 164 EE78
Walnut Tree Rd., Brent. 158 CL79
Walnut Tree Rd., Dag. 126 EX61
Walnut Tree Rd., Erith 167 FE78
Walnut Tree Rd., Houns. 156 BZ79
Walnut Tree Rd., Shep. 195 BQ96
Walnut Tree Wk. SE11 278 D8
Walnut Tree Wk. SE11 161 DN77
Walnut Tree Wk., Ware 33 DX08
Walnut Way, Buck.H. 102 EK48
Walnut Way, Ruis. 136 BW65
Walnut Way, Swan. 207 FD96
Walnuts, The, Orp. 206 EU102
High St.
Walnuts Rd., Orp. 206 EU102
Walpole Ave., Couls. 234 DF119
Walpole Ave., Rich. 158 CM82
Walpole Clo. W13 157 CJ75
Walpole Clo., Grays 170 GC77
Palmers Dr.
Walpole Clo., Pnr. 94 CA51
Walpole Cres., Tedd. 177 CF92
Walpole Gdns. W4 158 CQ78
Walpole Gdns., Twick. 177 CE89
Walpole Ms. NW8 140 DD67
Queen's Gro.
Walpole Ms. SW19 180 DD93
Walpole Rd.
Walpole Pk. W5 137 CJ74
Walpole Pk., Wey. 212 BN108
Walpole Pl. SE18 165 EP77
Anglesea Rd.
Walpole Pl., Tedd. 177 CF92
Walpole Rd. E6 144 EJ66
Walpole Rd. E17 123 DY56
Walpole Rd. E18 102 EF53
Walpole Rd. (Downhills Way) N17 122 DQ55
Walpole Rd. (Lordship La.) N17 100 DQ54
Walpole Rd. SW19 180 DD93
Walpole Rd., Brom. 204 EK99
Walpole Rd., Croy. 202 DR103
Walpole Rd., Slou. 131 AK72
Walpole Rd., Surb. 198 CL101
Walpole Rd., Tedd. 177 CF92
Walpole Rd., Twick. 177 CE89
Walpole Rd., Wind. 172 AV87
Walpole St. SW3 276 D10
Walpole St. SW3 160 DF78
Walrond Ave., Wem. 118 CL64
Walsh Cres., Croy. 222 EE112
Walsham Clo. N16 122 DU59
Braydon Rd.
Walsham Clo. SE28 146 EX73
Walsham Rd. SE14 163 DX82
Walsham Rd., Felt. 175 BV87
Walshford Way, Borwd. 78 CN38
Walsingham Clo., Hat. 45 CT17
Walsingham Gdns., Epsom 216 CS105
Walsingham Pk., Chis. 205 ER96
Walsingham Pl. SW4 160 DF84
Clapham Common W. Side
Walsingham Rd. E5 122 DU62
Walsingham Rd. W13 137 CG74
Walsingham Rd., Croy. 221 EC110
Walsingham Rd., Enf. 82 DR42
Walsingham Rd., Mitch. 200 DF99
Walsingham Rd., Orp. 206 EV95
Walsingham Wk., Belv. 166 FA79
Walsingham Way, St.Alb. 61 CJ27
Walt Whitman Clo. SE24 161 DP84
Shakespeare Rd.
Walter Rodney Clo. E6 145 EM65
Stevenage Rd.
Walter St. E2 143 DX69
Walter St., Kings.T. 198 CL95
Sopwith Way
Walter Ter. E1 143 DX72
Walter Wk., Edg. 96 CQ51
Walters Ho. SE17 161 DP79
Otto St.
Walters Mead, Ash. 232 CL117
Walters Rd. SE25 202 DS98
Walters Rd., Enf. 82 DW43
Walters Way SE23 183 DX86
Walters Yd., Brom. 204 EG96
Walterton Rd. W9 139 CZ70
Waltham Ave. NW9 118 CN58
Waltham Ave., Guil. 242 AV131
Waltham Ave., Hayes 155 BQ76
Waltham Clo., Brwd. 109 GC44
Bannister Dr.
Waltham Clo., Dart. 187 FG86
Waltham Clo., Orp. 206 EX102
Waltham Dr., Edg. 96 CN54
Waltham Gdns., Enf. 82 DW36
Waltham Gate, Wal.Cr. 67 DZ26
Thomas Rochford Way
Waltham Pk. Way E17 101 EA53
Waltham Rd., Cars. 200 DD101
Waltham Rd., Cat. 236 DV122
Waltham Rd., Sthl. 156 BY76
Waltham Rd., Wal.Abb. 68 EE26
Waltham Rd., Wdf.Grn. 102 EL51
Waltham Way E4 101 DZ49
Walthamstow Ave. E4 101 DY50
Walthamstow Business Cen. E17 101 EC54
Waltheof Ave. N17 100 DR53
Waltheof Gdns. N17 100 DR53
Walton Ave., Har. 116 BZ64
Walton Ave., N.Mal. 199 CT98
Walton Ave., Sutt. 199 CY104
Walton Bri., Shep. 195 BS101
Walton Bri. Rd., Shep. 195 BR100
Walton Clo. E5 123 DX62
Orient Way
Walton Clo. NW2 119 CV61
Walton Clo. SW8 161 DL80
Walton Clo., Har. 117 CD56
Walton Ct., Wok. 227 BA116
Walton Cres., Har. 116 BZ63
Walton Dr. NW10 138 CR65
Mitchellbrook Way
Walton Dr., Har. 117 CD56
Walton Gdns. W3 138 CP71
Walton Gdns., Brwd. 109 GC43
Walton Gdns., Felt. 175 BT91
Walton Gdns., Wal.Abb. 67 EB33
Walton Gdns., Wem. 118 CL61
Walton Grn., Croy. 221 EB109
Walton La., Shep. 195 BR101
Walton La., Slou. 131 AL69
Walton La., Wey. 195 BP103
Walton Pk., Walt. 196 BX103
Walton Pk. La., Walt. 196 BX103
Walton Pl. SW3 276 D6
Walton Pl. SW3 160 DF76
Walton Rd. E12 125 EN63
Walton Rd. E13 144 EJ68
Walton Rd. N15 122 DT56
Walton Rd., E.Mol. 196 BY98
Walton Rd. (Epsom Downs), Epsom 233 CT117
Walton Rd. (Headley), Epsom 232 CQ121
Walton Rd., Har. 117 CD56
Walton Rd., Hodd. 49 EB15
Walton Rd., Rom. 104 EZ52
Walton Rd., Sid. 186 EW89
Walton Rd., Walt. 196 BW99
Walton Rd., Ware 33 DX07
Walton Rd. (Bushey), Wat. 76 BX42
Walton Rd., W.Mol. 196 BY98
Walton Rd., Wok. 227 AZ116
Walton St. SW3 276 C8
Walton St. SW3 160 DE77
Walton St., Enf. 82 DR39
Walton St., St.Alb. 43 CF19
Walton St., Tad. 233 CU124
Walton Ter., Wok. 227 BB115
Walton Way W3 138 CP71
Walton Way, Mitch. 201 DJ98
Walverns Clo., Wat. 76 BW44
Walworth Pl. SE17 162 DQ78
Walworth Rd. SE1 279 H9
Walworth Rd. SE1 162 DQ77
Walworth Rd. SE17 279 H9
Walworth Rd. SE17 162 DQ77
Walwyn Ave., Brom. 204 EK97
Wambrook Clo., Brwd. 109 GC46
Wanborough Dr. SW15 179 CV88
Wanderer Dr., Bark. 146 EV69
Wandle Bank SW19 180 DD94
Wandle Bank, Croy. 201 DL104
Wandle Ct., Epsom 216 CQ105
Wandle Ct. Gdns., Croy. 201 DL104
Wandle Rd. SW17 180 DE89
Wandle Rd., Croy. 202 DQ104
Wandle Rd. (Waddon), Croy. 201 DL104
Wandle Rd., Mord. 200 DC98
Wandle Rd., Wall. 201 DH103
Wandle Side, Croy. 201 DM104
Wandle Side, Wall. 201 DH104
Wandle Way SW18 180 DB88
Wandle Way, Mitch. 200 DF99
Wandon Rd. SW6 160 DB80
Wandsworth Bri. SW6 160 DB83
Wandsworth Bri. SW18 160 DB83
Wandsworth Bri. Rd. SW6 160 DB81
Wandsworth Business Cen., Grnf. 137 CJ68
Wandsworth Common SW12 180 DF87
Wandsworth Common N. Side SW18 180 DC85
Wandsworth Common W. Side SW18 180 DC85
Wandsworth High St. SW18 180 DA85
Wandsworth Plain SW18 180 DA85
Wandsworth Rd. SW8 161 DH83
Wangey Rd., Rom. 126 EX59
Wanless Rd. SE24 162 DQ83
Wanley Rd. SE5 162 DR84
Wanlip Rd. E13 144 EH70
Wanmer Ct., Reig. 250 DA133
Birkheads Rd.
Wannions Clo., Chesh. 56 AU30
Wannock Gdns., Ilf. 103 EP52
Wansbeck Rd. E9 143 DZ66
Wansbury Way, Swan. 207 FG99
Wansdown Pl. SW6 160 DB80
Fulham Rd.
Wansey St. SE17 279 J9
Wansey St. SE17 162 DQ77
Wansford Clo., Brwd. 108 FT48
Wansford Grn., Wok. 226 AT117
Kenton Way
Wansford Pk., Borwd. 78 CR42
Wansford Rd., Wdf.Grn. 102 EJ53
Wanstead Clo., Brom. 204 EJ96
Wanstead La., Ilf. 124 EL58
Wanstead Pk. E11 124 EJ59
Wanstead Pk. Ave. E12 124 EK61
Wanstead Pk. Rd., Ilf. 124 EL58
Wanstead Pl. E11 124 EG58
Wanstead Rd., Brom. 204 EJ96
Wansunt Rd., Bex. 187 FC88
Wantage Rd. SE12 184 EF85
Wantz La., Rain. 147 FH70
Wantz Rd., Dag. 127 FB63
Waplings, The, Tad. 233 CV124
Deans La.
Wapping Dock St. E1 142 DV74
Cinnamon St.
Wapping High St. E1 142 DU74
Wapping La. E1 142 DV73
Wapping Wall E1 142 DW74
Wapseys La., Slou. 112 AS58
Wapshott Rd., Stai. 173 BE93
War Coppice Rd., Cat. 252 DR127
Warbank Clo., Croy. 222 EE110
Warbank Cres., Croy. 222 EE110
Warbank La., Kings.T. 179 CT94
Warbeck Rd. W12 159 CV75
Warberry Rd. N22 99 DM54
Warblers Grn., Cob. 214 BZ114
Warboys App., Kings.T. 178 CP93
Warboys Cres. E4 101 EC50
Warboys Rd., Kings.T. 178 CP93
Warburton Clo., Har. 95 CD51
Warburton Rd. E8 142 DV67
Warburton Rd., Twick. 176 CB88
Warburton St. E8 142 DV67
Warburton Rd.
Warburton Ter. E17 101 EB54
Ward Ave., Grays 170 GA77
Ward Clo., Erith 167 FD79
Ward Clo., Iver 133 BF72
Ward Clo., S.Croy. 220 DS106
Ward Clo. (Cheshunt), Wal.Cr. 66 DU27
Spicersfield
Ward Clo., Ware 32 DW05
Ward Gdns., Rom. 106 FK54
Whitmore Ave.
Ward Gdns., Slou. 131 AL73
Ward Hatch, Harl. 36 EU12
Mowbray Rd.
Ward La., Warl. 236 DW116
Ward Pl., Amer. 55 AP40
Ward Rd. E15 143 ED67
Ward Rd. N19 121 DJ62
Ward Royal, Wind. 151 AQ81
Alma Rd.
Ward St., Guil. 258 AX135
Martyr Rd.
Wardalls Gro. SE14 162 DW80
Wardell Clo. NW7 96 CS52
Wardell Fld. NW9 96 CS53
Warden Ave., Har. 116 BZ60
Warden Ave., Rom. 105 FC50
Warden Rd. NW5 140 DG65
Wardens Fld. Clo., Orp. 223 ES107
Wardens Gro. SE1 279 H3
Wardle St. E9 123 DX64
Wardley St. SW18 180 DB87
Garratt La.
Wardo Ave. SW6 159 CY81
Wardour Ms. W1 273 L9
Wardour St. W1 273 L8
Wardour St. W1 141 DJ72
Wardrobe Pl. EC4 274 G9
Wardrobe Ter. EC4 274 G10
Ward's Pl., Egh. 173 BC93
Wards Rd., Ilf. 125 ER59
Ware Pk. Rd., Hert. 32 DR07
Ware Rd., Hert. 32 DS09
Ware Rd. (Hertford Heath), Hert. 33 EA12
Ware Rd., Hodd. 49 EA15
Ware Rd., Ware 33 EC05
Ware Rd. (Chadwell Springs), Ware 32 DS09
Wareham Clo., Houns. 156 CB84
Warehams La., Hert. 32 DQ10
Waremead Rd., Ilf. 125 EP57
Warenford Way, Borwd. 78 CN39
Warenne Heights, Red. 266 DD136
Warenne Rd., Lthd. 230 CC122
Warepoint Dr. SE28 165 ER75
Warescot Clo., Brwd. 108 FV45
Warescot Rd., Brwd. 108 FV45
Wareside Clo., Welw.G.C. 30 DB10
Warfield Rd. NW10 139 CX69
Warfield Rd., Felt. 175 BS87
Warfield Rd., Hmptn. 196 CB95
Warfield Yd. NW10 139 CX69
Warfield Rd.
Wargrave Ave. N15 122 DT58
Wargrave Rd., Har. 116 CC62
Warham Rd. N4 121 DN57
Warham Rd., Har. 95 CF54
Warham Rd., Sev. 241 FH116
Warham Rd., S.Croy. 219 DP106
Warham St. SE5 161 DP80
Waring Clo., Orp. 223 ET107
Waring Dr., Orp. 223 ET107
Waring Rd., Sid. 186 EW93
Waring St. SE27 182 DQ91
Warkworth Gdns., Islw. 157 CG80
Warkworth Rd. N17 100 DR52
Warland Rd. SE18 165 ER80
Warley Ave., Dag. 126 EZ59
Warley Ave., Hayes 135 BU72
Warley Clo. E10 123 DZ60
Millicent Rd.
Warley Gap, Brwd. 107 FV52
Warley Hill, Brwd. 107 FV51
Warley Mt., Brwd. 108 FW49
Warley Rd. N9 100 DW47
Warley Rd., Brwd. 107 FU53
Warley Rd., Hayes 135 BU72
Warley Rd., Ilf. 103 EN53
Warley Rd., Upmin. 106 FQ54
Warley Rd., Wdf.Grn. 102 EH52
Warley St. E2 143 DX69
Warley St., Brwd. 129 FW56
Warley St., Upmin. 129 FW58
Warlingham Rd., Th.Hth. 201 DP98
Warlock Rd. W9 139 CZ70
Warlters Clo. N7 121 DL63
Warlters Rd.
Warlters Rd. N7 121 DL63
Warltersville Rd. N19 121 DL59
Warltersville Way, Horl. 269 DJ150
Warmark Rd., Hem.H. 39 BE18
Warmington Clo. E5 123 DX62
Orient Way
Warmington Rd. SE24 182 DQ86
Warmington St. E13 144 EG70
Barking Rd.
Warminster Gdns. SE25 202 DU96
Warminster Rd. SE25 202 DU97
Warminster Sq. SE25 202 DU96
Warminster Rd.
Warminster Way, Mitch. 201 DH95
Warndon St. SE16 162 DW77
Warne Pl., Sid. 186 EV86
Westerham Dr.
Warneford Pl., Wat. 76 BY44
Warneford Rd., Har. 117 CK55
Warneford St. E9 142 DV67
Warner Ave., Sutt. 199 CY103
Warner Clo. E15 124 EE64
Warner Clo. NW9 119 CT59
Warner Clo., Hmptn. 176 BZ92
Tangley Pk. Rd.
Warner Clo., Hayes 155 BR80
Warner Clo., Slou. 131 AL74
Warner Par., Hayes 155 BR80
Warner Pl. E2 142 DU68
Warner Rd. E17 123 DY56
Warner Rd. N8 121 DK56
Warner Rd. SE5 162 DQ81
Warner Rd., Brom. 184 EF94
Warner Rd., Ware 33 DX07
Warner St. EC1 274 D5
Warner St. EC1 141 DN70
Warner Yd. EC1 274 D5
Warners Ave., Hodd. 49 DZ19
Warners Clo., Wdf.Grn. 102 EG50
Warners End Rd., Hem.H. 40 BG20
Warners La., Guil. 260 BL141
Warners La., Kings.T. 177 CK92
Warners Path, Wdf.Grn. 102 EG50
Warnford Ind. Est., Hayes 155 BS75
Warnford Rd., Orp. 223 ET106
Warnham Ct. Rd., Cars. 218 DF108
Warnham Rd. N12 98 DD50
Warple Ms. W3 158 CS75
Warple Way
Warple Way W3 158 CS75
Warren, The E12 124 EL63
Warren, The, Ash. 232 CL119
Warren, The, Cars. 218 DD109
Warren, The, Chesh. 54 AL28
Warren, The, Ger.Cr. 91 AZ52
Warren, The, Grav. 191 GK91
Warren, The, Hayes 135 BU72
Warren, The, Houns. 156 BZ80
Warren, The, Lthd. 214 CC112
Warren, The (East Horsley), Lthd. 245 BT130
Warren, The, Rad. 61 CG33
Warren, The, Tad. 233 CY123
Warren, The, Wor.Pk. 216 CR105
Warren Ave. E10 123 EC62
Warren Ave., Brom. 184 EE94
Warren Ave., Orp. 223 ET106
Warren Ave., Rich. 158 CP84
Warren Ave., S.Croy. 221 DX108
Warren Ave., Sutt. 217 CZ110
Warren Clo. N9 101 DX45
Warren Clo. SE21 182 DQ87
Lairdale Clo.
Warren Clo., Bexh. 186 FA85
Pincott Rd.
Warren Clo., Esher 214 CB105
Warren Clo., Hat. 45 CV15
Warren Clo., Hayes 135 BV71
Warren Clo., Slou. 152 AY76
Warren Clo., Wem. 117 CK61
Warren Ct., Chig. 103 ER49
Warren Ct., Sev. 257 FJ125
Warren Ct., Wey. 212 BN106
Warren Cres. N9 100 DT45
Warren Cutting, Kings.T. 178 CR94
Warren Dale, Welw.G.C. 29 CX06
Warren Dr., Grnf. 136 CB70
Warren Dr., Horn. 127 FG63
Warren Dr., Orp. 224 EV106
Warren Dr., Ruis. 116 BX59
Warren Dr., Tad. 233 CZ122
Warren Dr., The E11 124 EJ59
Warren Dr. N., Surb. 198 CP102
Warren Dr. S., Surb. 198 CQ102
Warren Fld., Epp. 70 EU32
Warren Fld., Iver 133 BC68
Warren Flds., Stan. 95 CJ49
Valencia Rd.
Warren Footpath, Twick. 177 CJ88
Warren Gdns. E15 123 ED64
Ashton Rd.
Warren Gdns., Orp. 224 EU106
Warren Grn., Hat. 45 CV15
Warren Gro., Borwd. 78 CR42
Warren Hastings Ct., Grav. 191 GF86
Pier Rd.
Warren Heights, Grays 170 FY77
Warren Hill, Epsom 232 CR116
Warren Hill, Loug. 84 EJ43
Warren Ho. E3 143 EB69
Bromley High St.
Warren La. SE18 165 EP76
Warren La., Grays 169 FW77
Warren La., Guil. 260 BJ139
Warren La., Lthd. 214 CC111
Warren La., Oxt. 254 EG134
Warren La., Stan. 95 CF48
Warren La., Wok. 228 BG118
Warren Lo. Dr., Tad. 233 CY124
Warren Mead, Bans. 233 CW115
Warren Ms. W1 273 K5
Warren Pk., Kings.T. 178 CQ93
Warren Pk., Warl. 237 DX118
Warren Pk. Rd., Hert. 32 DQ08
Warren Pk. Rd., Sutt. 218 DD107
Warren Pl. E1 143 DX72
Pitsea St.
Warren Pond Rd. E4 102 EF46
Warren Ri., N.Mal. 198 CR95
Warren Rd. E4 101 EC47
Warren Rd. E10 123 EC62
Warren Rd. E11 124 EJ58
Warren Rd. NW2 119 CT61
Warren Rd. SW19 180 DE93
Warren Rd., Add. 212 BG110
Warren Rd., Ashf. 175 BS94
Warren Rd., Bans. 217 CW114
Warren Rd., Bexh. 186 FA85
Warren Rd., Brom. 204 EG103
Warren Rd., Croy. 202 DS102

Warren Rd., Dart. 188 FL90
Warren Rd., Gdmg. 258 AS144
Warren Rd., Grav. 190 GB92
Warren Rd., Guil. 259 AZ135
Warren Rd., Ilf. 125 ER57
Warren Rd., Kings.T. 178 CQ93
Warren Rd., Orp. 223 ET106
Warren Rd., Pur. 219 DP112
Warren Rd., Reig. 250 DB133
Warren Rd., St.Alb. 42 CC24
Warren Rd., Sid. 186 EW90
Warren Rd., Twick. 176 CC86
Warren Rd., Uxb. 114 BL63
Warren Rd. (Bushey), Wat. 94 CC46
Warren St. W1 273 J5
Warren St. W1 141 DJ70
Warren Ter., Grays 169 FX75
Arterial Rd. W. Thurrock
Warren Ter., Hert. 32 DR07
Warren Ter., Rom. 126 EX56
Warren Wk. SE7 164 EJ79
Warren Way NW7 97 CY51
Warren Way, Wey. 213 BQ106
Warren Wd. Clo., Brom. 204 EG103
Hillside La.
Warrender Rd. N19 121 DJ62
Warrender Rd., Chesh. 54 AS29
Warrender Way, Ruis. 115 BU59
Warreners La., Wey. 213 BR109
Warrenfield Clo. (Cheshunt), Wal.Cr. 66 DU31
Portland Dr.
Warrengate La., Pot.B. 63 CW31
Warrengate Rd., Hat. 63 CV26
Warrenhyrst, Guil. 259 BA135
Warren Rd.
Warrenne Rd., Bet. 264 CQ136
Warrenne Way, Reig. 250 DA134
Warrens Shawe La., Edg. 96 CP47
Warriner Ave., Horn. 128 FK61
Warriner Gdns. SW11 160 DF81
Warrington Ave., Slou. 131 AQ72
Warrington Cres. W9 140 DC70
Warrington Gdns. W9 140 DC70
Warwick Ave.
Warrington Gdns., Horn. 128 FJ58
Warrington Pl. E14 143 EC74
Yabsley St.
Warrington Rd., Croy. 201 DP104
Warrington Rd., Dag. 126 EX61
Warrington Rd., Har. 117 CE57
Warrington Rd., Rich. 177 CK85
Warrington Spur, Wind. 172 AV87
Warrington Sq., Dag. 126 EX61
Warrington St. E13 144 EG70
Doherty Rd.
Warrior Ave., Grav. 191 GJ91
Warrior Sq. E12 125 EN63
Warsaw Clo., Ruis. 135 BV65
Glebe Ave.
Warsdale Dr. NW9 118 CR57
Mardale Dr.
Warspite Rd. SE18 164 EK76
Warton Rd. E15 143 EC66
Warwall E6 145 EP72
Warwick Ave. W2 140 DC71
Warwick Ave. W9 140 DB70
Warwick Ave., Edg. 96 CP48
Warwick Ave., Egh. 193 BC95
Warwick Ave., Har. 116 BZ63
Warwick Ave. (Cuffley), Pot.B. 65 DK27
Warwick Ave., Slou. 131 AQ70
Warwick Ave., Stai. 174 BJ93
Warwick Clo., Barn. 80 DD43
Warwick Clo., Bex. 186 EZ87
Warwick Clo., Dor. 263 CH144
Warwick Clo., Hmptn. 176 CC94
Warwick Clo., Hert. 32 DQ11
Warwick Clo., Orp. 206 EU104
Warwick Clo. (Cuffley), Pot.B. 65 DK27
Warwick Clo. (Bushey), Wat. 95 CE45
Magnaville Rd.
Warwick Ct. SE15 162 DU82
Warwick Ct. WC1 274 C7
Warwick Ct., Surb. 217 CL103
Hook Rd.
Warwick Cres. W2 140 DC71
Warwick Cres., Hayes 135 BT70
Warwick Deeping Pl., Cher. 211 BC106
Warwick Dene W5 138 CL74
Warwick Dr. SW15 159 CV83
Warwick Dr. (Cheshunt), Wal.Cr. 67 DX28
Warwick Est. W2 140 DB71
Warwick Gdns. N4 122 DQ57
Warwick Gdns. W14 159 CZ76
Warwick Gdns., Ash. 231 CJ117
Warwick Gdns., Ilf. 125 EP60
Warwick Gdns., Rom. 128 FJ55
Warwick Gdns., T.Ditt. 197 CF99
Warwick Gro. E5 122 DV60
Warwick Gro., Surb. 198 CM101
Warwick Ho. St. SW1 277 N2
Warwick Ho. St. SW1 141 DK74
Warwick La. EC4 274 G9
Warwick La. EC4 141 DP72
Warwick La., Rain. 148 FM69
Warwick La., Upmin. 148 FM68
Warwick La., Wok. 226 AU119
Warwick Pas. EC4 141 DP72
Old Bailey
Warwick Pl. W5 157 CK75
Warwick Rd.
Warwick Pl. W9 140 DC71
Warwick Pl., Grav. 190 GB85
Warwick Pl., Uxb. 134 BJ66
Warwick Pl. N. SW1 277 K9
Warwick Pl. N. SW1 161 DJ77
Warwick Rd. E4 101 EA50
Warwick Rd. E11 124 EH57
Warwick Rd. E12 124 EL64
Warwick Rd. E15 144 EF65
Warwick Rd. E17 101 DZ53
Warwick Rd. N11 99 DK51
Warwick Rd. N18 100 DS49
Warwick Rd. SE20 202 DV97
Warwick Rd. SW5 159 CZ77
Warwick Rd. W5 157 CK75
Warwick Rd. W14 159 CZ77
Warwick Rd., Ashf. 174 BL92
Warwick Rd., Barn. 80 DB42
Warwick Rd., Beac. 89 AK52
Warwick Rd., Borwd. 78 CR41
Warwick Rd., Couls. 219 DJ114
Warwick Rd., Dor. 263 CJ144
Warwick Rd., Enf. 83 DZ37
Warwick Rd., Houns. 155 BV83
Warwick Rd., Kings.T. 197 CJ95
Warwick Rd., N.Mal. 198 CQ97
Warwick Rd., Rain. 148 FJ70
Warwick Rd., Red. 250 DF133
Warwick Rd., St.Alb. 43 CF18
Warwick Rd., Sid. 186 EV92
Warwick Rd., Sthl. 156 BZ76
Warwick Rd., Sutt. 218 DC105
Warwick Rd., T.Ditt. 197 CF99
Warwick Rd., Th.Hth. 201 DN97
Warwick Rd., Twick. 177 CE88
Warwick Rd., Well. 166 EW83
Warwick Rd., West Dr. 154 BL75
Warwick Row SW1 277 J6
Warwick Row SW1 161 DH76
Warwick Sq. EC4 274 G8
Warwick Sq. SW1 277 K10
Warwick Sq. SW1 161 DJ78
Warwick Sq. Ms. SW1 277 M9
Warwick St. W1 273 L10
Warwick St. W1 141 DJ73
Warwick Ter. SE18 165 ER79
Warwick Way SW1 277 J10
Warwick Way SW1 161 DH78
Warwick Way, Rick. 75 BQ42
Warwick Wold Rd., Red. 251 DN129
Warwick Yd. EC1 275 J5
Warwicks Bench, Guil. 258 AX136
Warwicks Bench La., Guil. 259 AZ137
Warwicks Bench Rd., Guil. 258 AY137
Warwickshire Path SE8 163 DZ80
Wash, The, Hert. 32 DR09
Wash Hill, H.Wyc. 110 AE59
Wash Hill Lea, H.Wyc. 110 AD59
Wash La., Pot.B. 63 CV33
Wash Rd., Brwd. 109 GD44
Washington Ave. E12 124 EL63
Washington Ave., Hem.H. 40 BL15
Washington Clo. E3 143 EB69
St. Leonards St.
Washington Clo., Reig. 250 DA131
Washington Dr., Slou. 131 AK73
Washington Dr., Wind. 151 AL83
Washington Rd. E6 144 EJ66
St. Stephens Rd.
Washington Rd. E18 102 EF54
Washington Rd. SW13 159 CU80
Washington Rd., Kings.T. 198 CN96
Washington Rd., Wor.Pk. 199 CV103
Washington Row, Amer. 55 AQ40
London Rd. W.
Washneys La., Orp. 224 EU114
Washneys Rd., Orp. 224 EV113
Washpond La., Warl. 237 EC118
Wastdale Rd. SE23 183 DX88
Wat Tyler Rd. SE3 163 EC82
Wat Tyler Rd. SE10 163 EC82
Watchfield Ct. W4 158 CQ78
Watchgate, Dart. 189 FR91
Watchlytes, Welw.G.C. 30 DC09
Watchmead, Welw.G.C. 30 DA09
Watcombe Cotts., Rich. 158 CN79
Watcombe Pl. SE25 202 DV99
Albert Rd.
Watcombe Rd. SE25 202 DV99
Water End Rd., Berk. 39 BB17
Water Gdns., Stan. 95 CH51
Water La. E15 144 EE65
Water La. EC3 142 DS73
Lower Thames St.
Water La. NW1 141 DH66
Kentish Town Rd.
Water La. SE14 162 DW80
Water La., Berk. 38 AW19
Water La., Chesh. 54 AP32
Water La., Cob. 230 BY115
Water La., Dor. 261 BV143
Water La., Guil. 260 BH138
Water La., Harl. 50 EL19
Water La., Hem.H. 57 BA29
Water La., Ilf. 125 ES62
Water La., Kings L. 59 BP29
Water La., Kings.T. 197 CK95
Water La., Lthd. 246 BY126
Water La., Oxt. 254 EG127
Water La., Purf. 168 FN77
Water La., Rich. 177 CK85
Water La., Sev. 225 FF112
Water La., Sid. 186 EZ90
Water La., Twick. 177 CG88
The Embk.
Water La., Wat. 76 BW42
Water La., West. 255 ER127
Water Lily Clo., Sthl. 156 CC75
Navigator Dr.
Water Meadow, Chesh. 54 AP32
Water Mill Way 208 FP96
(South Darenth), Dart.
Water Rd., Wem. 138 CM67
Water Row, Ware 33 DX06
Water St. WC2 274 C10
Water Twr. Clo., Uxb. 114 BL64
Water Twr. Hill, Croy. 220 DR105
Water Twr. Pl. N1 141 DN67
Liverpool Rd.
Water Vw., Horl. 269 DJ148
Carlton Tye
Waterbank Rd. SE6 183 EB90
Waterbeach, Welw.G.C. 30 DD09
Waterbeach Rd., Dag. 146 EW65
Waterbeach Rd., Slou. 131 AR72
Waterbrook La. NW4 119 CW57
Watercress Pl. N1 142 DS66
Hertford Rd.
Watercress Way, Wok. 226 AV116
Watercroft Rd., Sev. 224 EZ110
Waterdale, Hert. 32 DQ11
Waterdale Rd. SE2 166 EU79
Waterdales, Grav. 190 GC89
Waterdell Pl., Rick. 92 BG47
Uxbridge Rd.
Waterden Clo., Guil. 259 AZ135
Waterden Rd. E15 123 EA64
Waterden Rd., Guil. 258 AY135
Waterend La., St.Alb. 28 CQ07
Waterend La., Welw. 28 CS06
Waterer Gdns., Tad. 233 CX118
Waterer Ri., Wall. 219 DK107
Waterfall Clo. N14 99 DJ48
Waterfall Clo., Vir.W. 192 AU97
Waterfall Cotts. SW19 180 DD93
Waterfall Rd. N11 99 DH49
Waterfall Rd. N14 99 DJ48
Waterfall Rd. SW19 180 DD93
Waterfall Ter. SW17 180 DE93
Waterfield, Rick. 91 BC45
Waterfield, Tad. 233 CV119
Waterfield, Welw.G.C. 30 DB08
Waterfield Clo. SE28 146 EV74
Waterfield Clo., Belv. 166 FA76
Waterfield Dr., Warl. 236 DW119
Waterfield Gdns. SE25 202 DR98
Waterfield Grn., Tad. 233 CV120
Waterfields, Lthd. 231 CH119
Waterfields Way, Wat. 76 BX43
Waterford Common, Hert. 31 DP05
Waterford Grn., Welw.G.C. 30 DB09
Waterford Rd. SW6 160 DB80
Watergardens, The, Kings.T. 178 CQ93
Watergate EC4 274 F10
Watergate, Wat. 94 BX47
Watergate St. SE8 163 EA79
Watergate Wk. WC2 278 A1
Waterhall Ave. E4 102 EE49
Waterhall Clo. E17 101 DX53
Waterhead Clo., Erith 167 FE80
Waterhouse Clo. E16 144 EK71
Waterhouse Clo. NW3 120 DD64
Lyndhurst Rd.
Waterhouse Clo. W6 159 CX77
Great Ch. La.
Waterhouse La., Ken. 236 DQ119
Hayes La.
Waterhouse La., Red. 252 DT132
Waterhouse La., Tad. 233 CZ121
Waterhouse Moor, Harl. 51 ET16
Waterhouse Sq. EC1 141 DN71
Waterhouse St., Hem.H. 40 BJ20
Wateridge Clo. E14 163 EA76
Westferry Rd.
Wateringbury Clo., Orp. 206 EV97
Waterloo Bri. SE1 278 B1
Waterloo Bri. SE1 141 DM74
Waterloo Bri. WC2 278 B1
Waterloo Bri. WC2 141 DM73
Waterloo Clo. E9 122 DW64
Churchill Wk.
Waterloo Clo., Felt. 175 BT88
Waterloo Est. E2 142 DW68
Waterloo Gdns. E2 142 DW68
Waterloo Gdns., Rom. 127 FD58
Waterloo Pas. NW6 139 CZ66
Waterloo Pl. SW1 277 M2
Waterloo Pl. SW1 141 DK74
Waterloo Pl., Rich. 178 CL85
Sheen Rd.
Waterloo Pl. (Kew), Rich. 158 CN79
Waterloo Rd. E6 144 EJ66
Waterloo Rd. E7 124 EF64
Wellington Rd.
Waterloo Rd. E10 123 EA59
Waterloo Rd. NW2 119 CU60
Waterloo Rd. SE1 278 D4
Waterloo Rd. SE1 141 DN74
Waterloo Rd., Brwd. 108 FW46
Waterloo Rd., Epsom 216 CR112
Waterloo Rd., Ilf. 103 EQ54
Waterloo Rd., Rom. 127 FE58
Waterloo Rd., Sutt. 218 DD106
Waterloo Rd., Uxb. 134 BJ67
Waterloo St., Grav. 191 GJ87
Waterloo Ter. N1 141 DP66
Waterlow Ct. NW11 120 DB59
Heath Clo.
Waterlow Rd. N19 121 DJ60
Waterlow Rd., Reig. 266 DC135
Waterman Clo., Wat. 75 BV44
Waterman Ct., Slou. 131 AL74
Waterman St. SW15 159 CX83
Waterman Way E1 142 DV74
Waterman's Clo., Kings.T. 178 CL94
Woodside Rd.
Watermans Wk. SE16 143 DY74
Redriff Rd.
Watermans Way, Epp. 70 FA27
Watermark Way, Hert. 32 DT09
Watermead, Felt. 175 BS88
Watermead, Tad. 233 CV121
Watermead, Wok. 226 AT116
Watermead La., Cars. 200 DF101
Watermead Rd. SE6 183 EB91
Watermead Way N17 122 DU55
Watermeadow Clo., Erith 167 FH81
Hollywood Way
Watermeadow La. SW6 160 DC82
Watermen's Sq. SE20 182 DW94
Watermill Clo., Rich. 177 CJ90
Watermill La. N18 100 DS50
Watermill La., Hert. 32 DR06
Watermill La. N., Hert. 32 DQ06
Watermill Way SW19 200 DC95
Watermill Way, Felt. 176 BZ89
Watermint Clo., Orp. 206 EX98
Wagtail Way
Watermint Quay N16 122 DU58
Waterperry La., Wok. 210 AT110
Waters Dr., Rick. 92 BL46
Waters Dr., Stai. 173 BF90
Waters Gdns., Dag. 126 FA64
Sterry Rd.
Waters Rd. SE6 184 EE90
Waters Rd., Kings.T. 198 CP96
Waters Sq., Kings.T. 198 CP97
Watersedge, Epsom 216 CQ105
Watersfield Way, Edg. 95 CK52
Waterside, Beck. 203 EA95
Rectory Rd.
Waterside, Berk. 38 AX19
Holliday St.
Waterside, Chesh. 54 AQ32
Waterside, Dart. 187 FE85
Waterside, H.Wyc. 110 AE56
Waterside, Horl. 268 DG146
Waterside, Kings L. 58 BN29
Waterside, St.Alb. 62 CL27
Waterside, Uxb. 134 BJ71
Waterside, Welw.G.C. 30 DA07
Waterside Clo. E3 143 DZ67
Parnell Rd.
Waterside Clo. SE16 162 DU75
Bevington St.
Waterside Clo., Bark. 126 EU63
Waterside Clo., Nthlt. 136 BZ69
Waterside Clo., Rom. 106 FN52
Waterside Clo., Surb. 198 CL103
Culsac Rd.
Waterside Dr., Slou. 153 AZ75
Waterside Dr., Walt. 195 BU99
Waterside Ms., Guil. 242 AW132
Waterside Pl. NW1 140 DG67
Princess Rd.
Waterside Pl., Saw. 36 FA05
Waterside Pt. SW11 160 DE80
Waterside Rd., Guil. 242 AX131
Waterside Rd., Sthl. 156 CA76
Waterside Trd. Cen. W7 157 CE76
Waterside Way SW17 180 DC91
Waterside Way, Wok. 226 AV118
Winnington Way
Watersmeet, Harl. 51 EP19
Watersmeet Clo., Guil. 243 BA129
Cotts Wd. Dr.
Watersmeet Way SE28 146 EW72
Waterson Rd., Grays 171 GH77
Waterson St. E2 275 N2
Waterson St. E2 142 DS69
Watersplash Clo., Kings.T. 198 CL97
Watersplash La., Hayes 155 BU77
North Hyde Rd.
Watersplash La., Houns. 155 BV78
Watersplash Rd., Shep. 194 BN99
Waterton Ave., Grav. 191 GL87
Waterview Ho. E14 143 DY71
Carr St.
Waterway Rd., Lthd. 231 CG122
Waterworks Cotts., Brox. 49 DY22
Waterworks La. E5 123 DX61
Waterworks Rd. SW2 181 DM86
Waterworks Yd., Croy. 202 DQ104
Surrey St.
Watery La. SW20 199 CZ96
Watery La., Cher. 193 BD101
Watery La., Hat. 44 CS19
Watery La., H.Wyc. 110 AE55
Watery La., Nthlt. 136 BW68
Watery La., St.Alb. 61 CK28
Watery La., Sid. 186 EV93
Wates Way, Brwd. 108 FX46
Wates Way, Mitch. 200 DF100
Wateville Rd. N17 100 DQ53
Watford Bypass, Borwd. 95 CG45
Watford Clo. SW11 160 DE81
Petworth St.
Watford Clo., Guil. 243 AZ134
Watford Fld. Rd., Wat. 76 BW43
Watford Heath, Wat. 94 BX45
Watford Rd. E16 144 EG71
Watford Rd., Borwd. 77 CJ44
Watford Rd., Har. 117 CG59
Watford Rd., Kings L. 58 BN30
Watford Rd., Nthwd. 93 BT52
Watford Rd., Rad. 77 CE35
Watford Rd., Rick. 74 BM44
Watford Rd., St.Alb. 60 CA27
Watford Rd., Wem. 117 CG61
Watford Way NW4 119 CU56
Watford Way NW7 96 CS49
Wathen Rd., Dor. 263 CH135
Watkin Rd., Wem. 118 CP62
Watkinson Rd. N7 141 DM65
Watling Ave., Edg. 96 CQ53
Watling Clo., Hem.H. 40 BL17
Watling Ct. EC4 275 J9
Watling Ct., Borwd. 77 CK44
Watling Fm. Clo., Stan. 95 CJ45
Watling Gdns. NW2 139 CY65
Watling Knoll, Rad. 61 CF33
Watling St. EC4 275 H9
Watling St. EC4 142 DQ72
Watling St., Bexh. 167 FB84
Watling St., Borwd. 77 CH38
Watling St., Dart. 189 FR88
Watling St., Grav. 191 GG92
Watling St., Rad. 61 CF32
Watling St., St.Alb. 61 CD25
Watling St. Caravan Site (Travellers), St.Alb. 60 CC25
Watling Vw., St.Alb. 42 CC23
Watlings Clo., Croy. 203 DY100
Watlington Gro. SE26 183 DY92
Watlington Rd., Harl. 36 EX11
Watney Mkt. E1 142 DV72
Commercial Rd.
Watney Rd. SW14 158 CQ83
Watney St. E1 142 DV72
Watneys Rd., Mitch. 201 DK99
Watson Ave. E6 145 EN66
Watson Ave., Sutt. 199 CY104
Watson Clo. N16 122 DR64
Matthias Rd.
Watson Clo. SW19 180 DE93
Watson Clo., Grays 169 FU81
Watson Gdns., Rom. 106 FK54
Watson Rd., Dor. 262 CC137
Watson St. E13 144 EH68
Watsons Ave., St.Alb. 43 CF17
Watsons Ms. W1 272 C7
Watsons Rd. N22 99 DM53
Watson's St. SE8 163 EA80
Watsons Wk., St.Alb. 43 CE21
Watsons Yd. NW2 119 CT61
North Circular Rd.
Wattendon Rd., Ken. 235 DP116
Wattisfield Rd. E5 122 DW62
Wattleton Rd., Beac. 110 AJ55
Watts Bri. Rd., Erith 167 FF79
Reddy Rd.
Watts Clo. N15 122 DS57
Seaford Rd.
Watts Clo., Tad. 233 CX122
Watts Cres., Purf. 168 FQ77
Watts Fm. Par., Wok. 210 AT110
Barnmead
Watts Gro. E3 143 EB71
Watts La., Chis. 205 EP95
Watts La., Tad. 233 CX122
Watts La., Tedd. 177 CG92
Watts Mead, Tad. 233 CX122
Watts Rd., T.Ditt. 197 CG101
Watts St. E1 142 DV74
Watts Way SW7 276 A6
Wauthier Clo. N13 99 DP50
Wavel Ms. N8 121 DK56
Wavel Ms. NW6 140 DB66
Acol Rd.
Wavel Pl. SE26 182 DT91
Sydenham Hill
Wavell Clo. (Cheshunt), Wal.Cr. 67 DY27
Wavell Dr., Sid. 185 ES86
Wavell Gdns., Slou. 131 AM69
Wavell Rd., Beac. 89 AP54
Wavendene Ave., Egh. 173 BB94
Wavendon Ave. W4 158 CR78
Waveney, Hem.H. 40 BM15
Waveney Ave. SE15 162 DV84
Waveney Clo. E1 142 DU74
Kennet St.
Waverley Ave. E4 101 DZ49
Waverley Ave. E17 123 ED55
Waverley Ave., Ken. 236 DS116
Waverley Ave., Surb. 198 CP100
Waverley Ave., Sutt. 200 DB103
Waverley Ave., Twick. 176 BZ88
Waverley Ave., Wem. 118 CM64
Waverley Clo. E18 102 EJ53
Waverley Clo., Brom. 204 EK99
Waverley Clo., Hayes 155 BR77
Waverley Ct., Wok. 226 AY117
Waverley Cres. SE18 165 ER79
Waverley Cres., Rom. 106 FJ52
Waverley Dr., Cher. 193 BD104
Waverley Dr., Vir.W. 192 AU97
Waverley Gdns. E6 144 EL71
Oliver Gdns.
Waverley Gdns. NW10 138 CM68
Waverley Gdns., Bark. 145 ES68
Waverley Gdns., Grays 170 GA75
Waverley Gdns., Ilf. 103 EQ54
Waverley Gdns., Nthwd. 93 BU53
Waverley Gro. N3 119 CX55
Waverley Ind. Pk., Har. 117 CD55
Waverley Pl. N4 121 DP61
Adolphus Rd.
Waverley Pl. NW8 140 DD68
Waverley Pl., Lthd. 231 CH122
Church Rd.
Waverley Rd. E17 123 EC55
Waverley Rd. E18 102 EJ53
Waverley Rd. N8 121 DL58
Waverley Rd. N17 100 DV52
Waverley Rd. SE18 165 EQ78
Waverley Rd. SE25 202 DV98
Waverley Rd., Cob. 214 CB114
Waverley Rd., Enf. 81 DP42
Waverley Rd., Epsom 217 CU107
Waverley Rd., Har. 116 BY60
Waverley Rd., Lthd. 214 CB114
Waverley Rd., Rain. 147 FH69
Waverley Rd., St.Alb. 42 CC18
Waverley Rd., Slou. 131 AQ71
Waverley Rd., Sthl. 136 CA73
Waverley Rd., Wey. 212 BN106
Waverley Vill. N17 100 DT54
Waverley Wk. W2 140 DA71
Waverley Way, Cars. 218 DE107
Waverton Ho. E3 143 DZ67
Waverton Rd. SW18 180 DC87
Waverton St. W1 277 H2
Waverton St. W1 140 DG74
Wavertree Ct. SW2 181 DM88
Streatham Hill
Wavertree Rd. E18 102 EG54
Wavertree Rd. SW2 181 DL88
Waxlow Cres., Sthl. 136 CA72
Waxlow Rd. NW10 138 CQ68
Waxwell Clo., Pnr. 94 BX54
Waxwell La., Pnr. 94 BX54
Waxwell Ter. SE1 278 C5
Way, The, Reig. 250 DD133
Way Volante, Grav. 191 GL91
Waybourne Gro., Ruis. 115 BQ58
Waycross Rd., Upmin. 129 FS59
Waye Ave., Houns. 155 BU81
Wayfarer Rd., Nthlt. 136 BX69
Wayfarers Pk., Berk. 38 AT19
Wayfaring Grn., Grays 170 FZ78
Curling La.
Wayfield Link SE9 185 ER86
Wayford St. SW11 160 DE82
Wayland Ave. E8 122 DU64
Waylands, Swan. 207 FF98
Waylands Clo., Sev. 240 EY115
Waylands Mead, Beck. 203 EB95
Wayleave, The SE28 146 EV73
Oriole Way
Waylett Pl. SE27 181 DP90
Waylett Pl., Wem. 117 CK62
Wayman Ct. E8 142 DV65
Wayne Clo., Orp. 205 ET104
Wayneflete Twr. Ave., Esher 196 CA104
Waynflete Ave., Croy. 201 DP104
Waynflete Sq. W10 139 CX72
Waynflete St. SW18 180 DC89
Wayre, The, Harl. 36 EW11
Wayre St., Harl. 36 EW11
Wayside NW11 119 CY60
Wayside SW14 178 CQ85
Wayside, Croy. 221 EB107
Field Way
Wayside, Kings L. 58 BH30
Wayside, Pot.B. 64 DD33
Wayside, Rad. 61 CK33
Wayside, The, Hem.H. 41 BQ21
Wayside Ave., Horn. 128 FK61
Wayside Ave. (Bushey), Wat. 77 CD44
Wayside Clo. N14 81 DJ44
Wayside Clo., Rom. 127 FF55
Wayside Commercial Est., Bark. 146 EU68
Wayside Ct., Twick. 177 CJ86
Wayside Ct., Wem. 118 CN62
Oakington Ave.
Wayside Ct., Wok. 226 AS116
Langmans Way
Wayside Gdns. SE9 185 EM91
Wayside Gro.
Wayside Gdns., Dag. 126 FA64
Wayside Gdns., Ger.Cr. 112 AX59
Wayside Gro. SE9 185 EM91
Wayside Ms., Ilf. 125 EN57
Gaysham Ave.
Wayville Rd., Dart. 188 FP87
Weald, The, Chis. 185 EM93
Weald Bri. Rd., Epp. 53 FD24

Weald Clo. SE16 162 DV78
Stevenson Cres.
Weald Clo., Brwd. 108 FU48
Weald Clo., Brom. 204 EL103
Weald Clo., Grav. 190 GE94
Weald Clo., Guil. 258 AY140
Station Rd.
Weald Hall La., Epp. 70 EW25
Weald La., Har. 95 CD54
Weald Pk. Way, Brwd. 108 FS47
Weald Ri., Har. 95 CF52
Weald Rd., Brwd. 106 FM46
Weald Rd., Sev. 257 FH129
Weald Rd., Uxb. 134 BN68
Weald Sq. E5 122 DV61
Rossington St.
Weald Way, Cat. 252 DS128
Weald Way, Hayes 135 BS69
Weald Way, Reig. 266 DC138
Weald Way, Rom. 127 FB58
Wealdon Ct., Guil. 242 AT134
Humbolt Clo.
Wealdstone Rd., Sutt. 199 CZ103
Wealdwood Gdns., Pnr. 94 CB51
Highbanks Rd.
Weale Rd. E4 101 ED48
Weall Grn., Wat. 59 BV32
Wear Pl. E2 142 DV69
Weardale Ave., Dart. 188 FQ89
Weardale Gdns., Enf. 82 DR39
Weardale Rd. SE13 163 ED84
Wearside Rd. SE13 183 EB85
Weasdale Ct., Wok. 226 AT116
Roundthorn Way
Weatherall Clo., Add. 212 BH106
Weatherhill Clo., Horl. 269 DM148
Weatherhill Common, Horl. 269 DM147
Weatherhill Rd., Horl. 269 DM148
Weatherley Clo. E3 143 DZ71
Weaver Clo. E6 145 EP72
Trader Rd.
Weaver St. E1 142 DU70
Weaver Wk. SE27 182 DQ91
Weavers Clo., Grav. 191 GG88
Weavers Clo., Islw. 157 CE84
Weavers La., Sev. 257 FJ121
Weavers Orchard, Grav. 190 GA93
Weavers Ter. SW6 160 DA79
Micklethwaite Rd.
Weavers Way NW1 141 DK66
Webb Clo., Chesh. 54 AP30
Webb Clo., Slou. 152 AX77
Webb Est. E5 122 DU59
Webb Gdns. E13 144 EG70
Kelland Rd.
Webb Pl. NW10 139 CT69
Old Oak La.
Webb Rd. SE3 164 EF79
Webb St. SE1 279 M7
Webb St. SE1 162 DS76
Webber Clo., Borwd. 77 CK44
Rodgers Clo.
Webber Clo., Erith 167 FH80
Webber Row SE1 278 E5
Webber Row SE1 161 DN75
Webber St. SE1 278 F5
Webber St. SE1 161 DN75
Webb's All., Sev. 257 FJ125
Webbs Rd. SW11 160 DF84
Webbs Rd., Hayes 135 BV69
Webbscroft Rd., Dag. 127 FB63
Webster Clo., Horn. 128 FK62
Latimer Dr.
Webster Clo., Lthd. 214 CB114
Webster Clo., Wal.Abb. 68 EG33
Webster Gdns. W5 137 CK74
Webster Rd. E11 123 EC62
Webster Rd. SE16 162 DU76
Websters Clo., Wok. 226 AV120
Wedderburn Rd. NW3 120 DD64
Wedderburn Rd., Bark. 145 ER67
Wedgewood Clo., Epp. 70 EU30
Wedgewood Clo., Nthwd. 93 BQ52
Wedgewood Dr., Harl. 52 EX16
Wedgewood Wk. NW6 120 DB64
Lymington Rd.
Wedgewood Way SE19 182 DQ94
Wedgewoods, West. 238 EJ121
Westmore Rd.
Wedgwood Ms. W1 273 N9
Wedhey, Harl. 51 EQ15
Wedlake Clo., Horn. 128 FL60
Wedlake St. W10 139 CY70
Kensal Rd.
Wedmore Ave., Ilf. 103 EN53
Wedmore Gdns. N19 121 DK61
Wedmore Ms. N19 121 DK62
Wedmore St.
Wedmore Rd., Grnf. 137 CD69
Wedmore St. N19 121 DK62
Wednesbury Gdns., Rom. 106 FM52
Wednesbury Grn., Rom. 106 FM52
Wednesbury Gdns.
Wednesbury Rd., Rom. 106 FM52
Weech Rd. NW6 120 DA63
Weedington Rd. NW5 120 DG64
Weedon Clo., Ger.Cr. 90 AV53
Weedon La., Amer. 55 AN36
Weekes Dr., Slou. 131 AP74
Weekley Sq. SW11 160 DD83
Thomas Baines Rd.
Weigall Rd. SE12 164 EG84
Weighouse St. W1 272 G9
Weighouse St. W1 140 DG72
Weighton Rd. SE20 202 DV96
Weighton Rd., Har. 95 CD53
Weihurst Gdns., Sutt. 218 DD106
Weimar St. SW15 159 CY83
Weind, The, Epp. 85 ES36
Weir Est. SW12 181 DJ87
Weir Hall Ave. N18 100 DR51
Weir Hall Gdns. N18 100 DR50
Weir Hall Rd. N17 100 DR51
Weir Hall Rd. N18 100 DR50
Weir Pl., Stai. 193 BE95
Weir Rd. SW12 181 DJ87
Weir Rd. SW19 180 DB90
Weir Rd., Bex. 187 FB87
Weir Rd., Cher. 194 BH101
Weir Rd., Walt. 195 BU100
Weirdale Ave. N20 98 DF47
Weir's Pas. NW1 273 N2
Weir's Pas. NW1 141 DK69
Weiss Rd. SW15 159 CX83
Welbeck Ave., Brom. 184 EG91
Welbeck Ave., Hayes 135 BV70
Welbeck Ave., Sid. 186 EU88
Welbeck Clo. N12 98 DD50
Torrington Pk.
Welbeck Clo., Borwd. 78 CN41
Welbeck Clo., Epsom 217 CU108
Welbeck Clo., N.Mal. 199 CT99
Welbeck Rd. E6 144 EK69
Welbeck Rd., Barn. 80 DD44
Welbeck Rd., Cars. 200 DE102
Welbeck Rd., Har. 116 CB60
Welbeck Rd., Sutt. 200 DD103
Welbeck St. W1 272 G7
Welbeck St. W1 140 DG71
Welbeck Wk., Cars. 200 DE102
Welbeck Rd.
Welbeck Way W1 273 H8
Welbeck Way W1 141 DH72
Welby St. SE5 161 DP81
Welch Pl., Pnr. 94 BW53
Welclose St., St.Alb. 42 CC20
Welcomes Rd., Ken. 236 DQ116
Welcote Dr., Nthwd. 93 BR51
Weld Pl. N11 99 DH50
Welden, Slou. 132 AW72
Welders La., Beac. 90 AT52
Welders La., Ger.Cr. 90 AV52
Weldon Clo., Ruis. 135 BV65
Weldon Dr., W.Mol. 196 BZ98
Weldon Way, Red. 251 DK129
Welfare Rd. E15 144 EE66
Welford Clo. E5 123 DX62
Denton Way
Welford Pl. SW19 179 CY91
Welham Clo., Hat. 45 CW24
Welham Ct., Hat. 45 CW24
Dixons Hill Rd.
Welham Manor, Hat. 45 CW24
Welham Rd. SW16 181 DH93
Welham Rd. SW17 180 DG92
Welhouse Rd., Cars. 200 DE102
Well App., Barn. 79 CW43
Well Clo. SW16 181 DM91
Well Clo., Ruis. 116 BY62
Parkfield Cres.
Well Clo., Wok. 226 AW117
Well Cottage Clo. E11 124 EJ59
Well Ct. EC4 275 J9
Well Ct. SW16 181 DM91
Well Cft., Hem.H. 40 BH19
Gadebridge Rd.
Well End Rd., Borwd. 78 CQ37
Well Fm. Rd., Whyt. 236 DU119
Well Garth, Welw.G.C. 29 CY10
Well Gro. N20 98 DC45
Well Hall Par. SE9 165 EM84
Well Hall Rd.
Well Hall Rd. SE9 164 EL83
Well Hill, Orp. 225 FB107
Well Hill La., Orp. 225 FB108
Well Hill Rd., Sev. 225 FC107
Well La. SW14 178 CQ85
Well La., Brwd. 108 FT41
Well La., Harl. 35 EN14
Well La., Wok. 226 AW117
Well Pas. NW3 120 DD62
Well Path, Wok. 226 AW117
Well La.
Well Rd. NW3 120 DD62
Well Rd., Barn. 79 CW43
Well Rd., Pot.B. 64 DB28
Well Row, Hert. 47 DM17
Well St. E9 142 DW66
Well St. E15 144 EE65
Well Wk. NW3 120 DD63
Well Way, Epsom 232 CN115
Wellacre Rd., Har. 117 CH58
Wellan Clo., Sid. 186 EV85
Welland Clo., Slou. 153 BB79
Welland Gdns., Grnf. 137 CF68
Welland Ms. E1 142 DU74
Kennet St.
Welland St. SE10 163 EC79
Wellands, Hat. 45 CU16
Wellands Clo., Brom. 205 EM96
Wellbank, Maid. 130 AE70
Rectory Rd.
Wellbrook Rd., Orp. 223 EN105
Wellbury Ter., Hem.H. 41 BQ20
Wellclose Sq. E1 142 DU73
Wellclose St. E1 142 DU73
The Highway
Wellcome Ave., Dart. 168 FM84
Wellcome Chemical Wks., Dart. 188 FM85
Wellcroft Clo., Welw.G.C. 30 DA11
Wellcroft Rd., Slou. 131 AP74
Wellcroft Rd., Welw.G.C. 30 DA10
Welldon Cres., Har. 117 CE58
Wellen Ri., Hem.H. 40 BL23
Weller Clo., Amer. 55 AS37
Weller Rd., Amer. 55 AS37
Weller St. SE1 279 H4
Wellers Clo., West. 255 EQ127
Weller's Ct. N1 273 P1
Wellers Ct., Guil. 260 BN139
Wellers Gro. (Cheshunt), Wal.Cr. 66 DU28
Wellesford Clo., Bans. 233 CZ117
Wellesley, Harl. 51 EN20
Wellesley Ave. W6 159 CV76
Wellesley Ave., Iver 153 BF76
Wellesley Ave., Nthwd. 93 BT50
Wellesley Ct. W9 140 DC69
Maida Vale
Wellesley Ct. Rd., Croy. 202 DR103
Wellesley Cres., Pot.B. 63 CY33
Wellesley Cres., Twick. 177 CE89
Wellesley Gro., Croy. 202 DR103
Wellesley Pk. Ms., Enf. 81 DP40
Wellesley Path, Slou. 152 AU75
Wellesley Rd.
Wellesley Pl. NW1 273 M3
Wellesley Rd. E11 124 EG57
Wellesley Rd. E17 123 EA58
Wellesley Rd. N22 99 DN54
Wellesley Rd. NW5 120 DG64
Wellesley Rd. W4 158 CN78
Wellesley Rd., Brwd. 108 FW46
Wellesley Rd., Croy. 202 DQ102
Wellesley Rd., Har. 117 CE57
Wellesley Rd., Ilf. 125 EP61
Wellesley Rd., Slou. 152 AU75
Wellesley Rd., Sutt. 218 DC107
Wellesley Rd., Twick. 177 CD90
Wellesley St. E1 143 DX71
Wellesley Ter. N1 275 J2
Wellesley Ter. N1 142 DQ69
Welley Ave., Stai. 152 AY84
Welley Rd., Stai. 172 AX85
Wellfield Ave. N10 121 DH55
Wellfield Clo., Hat. 45 CU17
Wellfield Gdns., Cars. 218 DE109
Woodmansterne Rd.
Wellfield Rd. SW16 181 DL91
Wellfield Rd., Hat. 45 CU16
Wellfield Wk. SW16 181 DM92
Wellfields Rd., Loug. 85 EN41
Wellfit St. SE24 161 DP83
Hinton Rd.
Wellgarth, Grnf. 137 CH65
Wellgarth Rd. NW11 120 DB60
Wellhouse La., Barn. 79 CW42
Wellhouse La., Bet. 264 CQ138
Wellhouse Rd., Beck. 203 DZ98
Welling High St., Well. 166 EU83
Welling Way SE9 165 ER83
Welling Way, Well. 165 ES83
Wellings Ho., Hayes 135 BV74
Wellington Ave. E4 101 EA47
Wellington Ave. N9 100 DV48
Wellington Ave. N15 122 DT58
Wellington Ave., Houns. 176 CA85
Wellington Ave., Pnr. 94 BZ53
Wellington Ave., Sid. 186 EU86
Wellington Ave., Vir.W. 192 AV99
Wellington Ave., Wor.Pk. 199 CW104
Wellington Bldgs. SW1 161 DH78
Ebury Bri. Rd.
Wellington Clo. SE14 163 DX81
Rutts Ter.
Wellington Clo. W11 140 DA72
Ledbury Rd.
Wellington Clo., Dag. 147 FC66
Wellington Clo., Walt. 195 BT102
Hepworth Way
Wellington Cotts, Lthd. 245 BS129
Wellington Ct. NW8 140 DD68
Wellington Rd.
Wellington Ct., Stai. 174 BL87
Wellington Cres., N.Mal. 198 CQ97
Wellington Dr., Dag. 147 FC66
Wellington Dr., Pur. 219 DM110
Wellington Dr., Welw.G.C. 30 DC09
Wellington Gdns. SE7 164 EJ78
Wellington Gdns., Twick. 177 CD91
Wellington Hill, Loug. 84 EH37
Wellington Ms. SE7 164 EJ79
Wellington Ms. SE22 162 DU84
Peckham Rye
Wellington Pk. Ind. Est. NW2 119 CU60
Wellington Pas. E11 124 EG57
Wellington Rd.
Wellington Pl. N2 120 DE57
Great N. Rd.
Wellington Pl. NW8 272 A2
Wellington Pl. NW8 140 DD69
Wellington Pl., Brwd. 108 FW50
Wellington Pl., Brox. 48 DW23
Wellington Rd. E6 145 EM67
Wellington Rd. E7 124 EF63
Wellington Rd. E10 123 DY60
Wellington Rd. E11 124 EG57
Wellington Rd. E17 123 DY55
Wellington Rd. NW8 140 DD68
Wellington Rd. NW10 139 CX69
Wellington Rd. SW19 180 DA89
Wellington Rd. W5 157 CJ76
Wellington Rd., Ashf. 174 BL92
Wellington Rd., Belv. 166 EZ78
Wellington Rd., Bex. 186 EX85
Wellington Rd., Brom. 204 EJ98
Wellington Rd., Cat. 236 DQ122
Wellington Rd., Croy. 201 DP101
Wellington Rd., Dart. 188 FJ86
Wellington Rd., Enf. 82 DS42
Wellington Rd., Epp. 70 FA27
Wellington Rd., Felt. 175 BS85
Wellington Rd., Hmptn. 177 CD92
Wellington Rd., Har. 117 CE55
Wellington Rd., Orp. 206 EV100
Wellington Rd., Pnr. 94 BZ52
Wellington Rd., St.Alb. 43 CH21
Wellington Rd. (London Colney), St.Alb. 61 CK26
Wellington Rd., Til. 171 GG83
Wellington Rd., Twick. 177 CD91
Wellington Rd., Uxb. 134 BJ67
Wellington Rd., Wat. 75 BV40
Wellington Rd. N., Houns. 156 BZ83
Wellington Rd. S., Houns. 156 BZ84
Wellington Row E2 142 DT69
Wellington Sq. SW3 276 D10
Wellington Sq. SW3 160 DF78
Wellington St. SE18 165 EN77
Wellington St. WC2 274 A10
Wellington St. WC2 141 DL73
Wellington St., Bark. 145 EQ67
Axe St.
Wellington St., Grav. 191 GJ87
Wellington St., Hert. 31 DP08
Wellington St., Slou. 152 AT75
Wellington Ter. E1 142 DV74
Waterman Way
Wellington Ter. N8 121 DN55
Turnpike La.
Wellington Ter., Har. 117 CD60
Wellington Way E3 143 EA69
Wellington Way, Horl. 268 DF146
Wellington Way, Wey. 212 BM110
Wellingtonia Ave. (Havering-atte-Bower), Rom. 105 FE48
Wellmeade Dr., Sev. 257 FH127
Wellmeadow Rd. SE6 184 EE87
Wellmeadow Rd. SE13 184 EE86
Wellmeadow Rd. W7 157 CG77
Wellow Wk., Cars. 200 DD102
Whitland Rd.
Wells, The N14 99 DK45
Wells Clo., Lthd. 230 CB124
Wells Clo., Nthlt. 136 BW69
Yeading La.
Wells Clo., St.Alb. 42 CC19
Artisan Cres.
Wells Clo., Wind. 151 AN81
Wells Dr. NW9 118 CR60
Wells Gdns., Dag. 127 FB64
Pondfield Rd.
Wells Gdns., Ilf. 124 EL59
Wells Gdns., Rain. 147 FF65
Wells Ho. Rd. NW10 138 CS71
Wells Ms. W1 273 L7
Wells Pk. Rd. SE26 182 DU90
Wells Pl., Red. 251 DH130
Wells Ri. NW8 140 DF67
Wells Rd. W12 159 CW75
Wells Rd., Brom. 205 EM96
Wells Rd., Epsom 216 CN114
Wells Rd., Guil. 243 BC131
Wells Sq. WC1 274 B3
Wells St. W1 273 K7
Wells St. W1 141 DJ71
Wells Ter. N4 121 DN61
Wells Way SE5 162 DS79
Wells Way SW7 160 DD76
Wells Yd. N7 121 DN64
Holloway Rd.
Wellside Clo., Barn. 79 CW42
Wellside Gdns. SW14 178 CQ85
Well La.
Wellsmoor Gdns., Brom. 205 EN97
Wellsprings Cres., Wem. 118 CP62
Wellstead Ave. N9 100 DW45
Wellstead Rd. E6 145 EN68
Wellstones, Wat. 75 BV41
Wellstones Yd., Wat. 75 BV41
Wellstones
Wellswood Clo., Hem.H. 41 BP19
Wellwood Clo., Couls. 219 DL114
The Vale
Wellwood Rd., Ilf. 126 EU60
Welsford St. SE1 162 DU78
Welsh Clo. E13 144 EG69
Welsh Side Wk. NW9 118 CS58
Fryent Gro.
Welshpool Ho. E8 142 DU67
Benjamin Clo.
Welshpool St. E8 142 DV67
Broadway Mkt.
Welsummer Way, Wal.Cr. 67 DX27
Weltje Rd. W6 159 CU77
Welton Rd. SE18 165 ES80
Welwyn Ave., Felt. 175 BT86
Welwyn Ct., Hem.H. 40 BM16
Welwyn Rd., Hert. 30 DG08
Welwyn St. E2 142 DW69
Globe Rd.
Welwyn Way, Hayes 135 BS70
Wembley Commercial Cen., Wem. 117 CK61
Wembley Hill Rd., Wem. 118 CM64
Wembley Pk. Business Cen., Wem. 118 CP62
Wembley Pk. Dr., Wem. 118 CM63
Wembley Pt., Wem. 138 CP66
Wembley Retail Pk., Wem. 118 CP63
Wembley Rd., Hmptn. 176 CA94
Wembley Way, Wem. 138 CP65
Wemborough Rd., Stan. 95 CH53
Wembury Rd. N6 121 DH59
Wemyss Rd. SE3 164 EF82
Wend, The, Couls. 219 DK114
Wend, The, Croy. 221 DY111
Wendela Clo., Wok. 227 AZ118
Wendela Ct., Har. 117 CE62
Wendell Rd. W12 159 CT76
Wendle Ct. SW8 161 DL79
Wendley Dr., Add. 211 BF110
Wendling Rd., Sutt. 200 DD102
Wendon St. E3 143 DZ67
Wendover SE17 279 M10
Wendover Clo., Hayes 136 BY70
Kingsash Dr.
Wendover Clo., St.Alb. 43 CJ15
Highview Gdns.
Wendover Dr., N.Mal. 199 CT100
Wendover Gdns., Brwd. 109 GB47
Wendover Pl., Stai. 173 BD92
Wendover Rd. NW10 139 CT68
Wendover Rd. SE9 164 EK83
Wendover Rd., Brom. 204 EH97
Wendover Rd., Slou. 130 AH71
Wendover Rd., Stai. 173 BC92
Wendover Way, Horn. 128 FJ64
Wendover Way, Orp. 206 EU100
Glendower Cres.
Wendover Way (Bushey), Wat. 76 CC44
Wendover Way, Well. 186 EU85
Wendron Clo., Wok. 226 AU118
Shilburn Way
Wendy Clo., Enf. 82 DT44
Wendy Cres., Guil. 242 AU132
Wendy Way, Wem. 138 CL67
Wengeo La., Ware 32 DV05
Wenham Gdns., Brwd. 109 GC44
Bannister Dr.
Wenlack Clo., Uxb. 114 BG62
Lindsey Rd.
Wenlock Ct. N1 275 L1
Wenlock Gdns. NW4 119 CU56
Rickard Clo.
Wenlock Rd. N1 275 H1
Wenlock Rd. N1 142 DQ68
Wenlock Rd., Edg. 96 CP52
Wenlock St. N1 275 J1
Wenlock St. N1 142 DQ68
Wennington Rd. E3 143 DX68
Wennington Rd., Rain. 147 FG70
Wensley Ave., Wdf.Grn. 102 EF52
Wensley Clo. SE9 185 EM86
Wensley Clo., Rom. 104 FA50
Wensley Rd. N18 100 DV51
Wensleydale, Hem.H. 40 BM17
Wensleydale Ave., Ilf. 102 EL54
Wensleydale Gdns., Hmptn. 176 CB94
Wensleydale Pas., Hmptn. 196 CA95
Wensleydale Rd., Hmptn. 176 CA93
Wensum Way, Rick. 92 BK46
Wentbridge Path, Borwd. 78 CN38
Wentland Clo. SE6 183 ED89
Wentland Rd.
Wentland Rd. SE6 183 ED89
Wentworth Ave. N3 98 DA52
Wentworth Ave., Borwd. 78 CM43
Wentworth Ave., Slou. 131 AN68
Wentworth Clo. N3 98 DB52
Wentworth Clo. SE28 146 EX72
Summerton Way
Wentworth Clo., Ashf. 175 BP91
Reedsfield Rd.
Wentworth Clo., Brom. 204 EG103
Hillside La.
Wentworth Clo., Grav. 191 GG92
Wentworth Clo., Mord. 200 DA101
Wentworth Clo., Orp. 223 ES106
Wentworth Clo., Pot.B. 64 DA31
Strafford Gate
Wentworth Clo., Surb. 197 CK103
Wentworth Clo., Wat. 75 BT38
Wentworth Clo., Wok. 228 BH121
Wentworth Cotts., Brox. 49 DY22
Wentworth Cres. SE15 162 DU80
Wentworth Cres., Hayes 155 BR76
Wentworth Dr., Dart. 187 FG86
Wentworth Dr., Pnr. 115 BU57
Wentworth Dr., Vir.W. 192 AT98
Wentworth Gdns. N13 99 DP49
Wentworth Hill, Wem. 118 CM60
Wentworth Ms. E3 143 DZ70
Eric St.
Wentworth Pk. N3 98 DA52
Wentworth Pl., Grays 170 GD76
Wentworth Pl., Stan. 95 CH51
Greenacres Dr.
Wentworth Rd. E12 124 EK63
Wentworth Rd. NW11 119 CZ58
Wentworth Rd., Barn. 79 CX41
Wentworth Rd., Croy. 201 DN101
Wentworth Rd., Hert. 32 DQ12
Wentworth Rd., Sthl. 156 BW77
Wentworth St. E1 275 P8
Wentworth St. E1 142 DT72
Wentworth Way, Pnr. 116 BX56
Wentworth Way, Rain. 147 FH69
Wentworth Way, S.Croy. 220 DU114
Wenvoe Ave., Bexh. 167 FB82
Wernbrook St. SE18 165 EQ79
Werndee Rd. SE25 202 DU98
Werneth Hall Rd., Ilf. 125 EM55
Werrington St. NW1 273 L1
Werrington St. NW1 141 DJ68
Werter Rd. SW15 159 CY84
Wesley Ave. E16 144 EE72
Silvertown Way
Wesley Ave. NW10 138 CR69
Wesley Ave., Hert. 32 DR10
Hale Rd.
Wesley Ave., Houns. 156 BY82
Wesley Clo. N7 121 DM61
Wesley Clo. SE17 278 G9
Wesley Clo., Har. 116 CC61
Wesley Clo., Horl. 268 DG146
Wesley Clo., Orp. 206 EW97
Wesley Clo., Reig. 265 CZ135
Wesley Clo. (Cheshunt), Wal.Cr. 66 DQ28
Wesley Dr., Egh. 173 BA93
Wesley Hill, Chesh. 54 AP30
Wesley Rd. E10 123 EC59
Wesley Rd. NW10 138 CQ67
Hillside
Wesley Rd. SE17 278 G9
Wesley Rd., Hayes 135 BU73
Wesley Sq. W11 139 CY72
Bartle Rd.
Wesley St. W1 272 G7
Wesleyan Pl. NW5 121 DH63
Gordon Ho. Rd.
Wessels, Tad. 233 CX121
Wessex Ave. SW19 200 DA96
Wessex Clo., Ilf. 125 ES58
Wessex Clo., Kings.T. 198 CP95
Gloucester Rd.
Wessex Dr., Erith 167 FE82
Wessex Dr., Pnr. 94 BY52
Wessex Gdns. NW11 119 CY60
Wessex La., Grnf. 137 CD68
Wessex Rd., Houns. 154 BJ84
Wessex St. E2 142 DW69
Wessex Way NW11 119 CY60
West Acres, Amer. 55 AR40
West App., Orp. 205 EQ99
West Arbour St. E1 142 DW72
West Ave. E17 123 EB56
West Ave. N3 98 DA51
West Ave. NW4 119 CX57
West Ave., Hayes 135 BT73
West Ave., H.Wyc. 88 AC46
West Ave., Pnr. 116 BZ58
West Ave., Red. 266 DG140
West Ave., St.Alb. 60 CB25
West Ave., Sthl. 136 BZ73
West Ave., Wall. 219 DL106
West Ave., Walt. 213 BS109
West Ave. Rd. E17 123 EA56
West Bank N16 122 DS59
West Bank, Bark. 145 EP67
Highbridge Rd.
West Bank, Dor. 263 CF137
West Bank, Enf. 82 DQ40
West Barnes La. SW20 199 CV99
West Barnes La., N.Mal. 199 CV97
West Burrow Fld., Welw.G.C. 29 CX11
West Carriage Dr. W2 276 B1
West Carriage Dr. W2 140 DD73
West Cen. St. WC1 273 P8
West Chantry, Har. 94 CB53
Chantry Rd.
West Clo. N9 100 DT48
West Clo., Ashf. 174 BL91
West Clo., Barn. 79 CV43
West Clo. (Cockfosters), Barn. 80 DG42
West Clo., Grnf. 136 CC68
West Clo., Hmptn. 176 BY93
Oak Ave.
West Clo., Hodd. 49 EA16
West Clo., Rain. 147 FH70
West Clo., Wem. 118 CM60
West Common, Ger.Cr. 112 AX57
West Common Clo., Ger.Cr. 112 AY57
West Common Rd., Brom. 204 EG103
West Common Rd., Uxb. 114 BK64
West Cotts. NW6 120 DA64
West Ct. SE18 165 EM80
Prince Imperial Rd.
West Ct., Wem. 117 CJ61
West Cres., Wind. 151 AM81

West Cres. Rd., Grav. 191 GH86
West Cromwell Rd. SW5 159 CZ77
West Cromwell Rd. W14 159 CZ78
West Cross Route W10 139 CX73
West Cross Route W11 139 CX74
West Cross Way, Brent. 157 CH79
West Dene, Sutt. 217 CY107
Park La.
West Dene Dr., Rom. 106 FK50
West Dene Way, Wey. 195 BS104
West Down, Lthd. 246 CB127
West Drayton Pk. Ave., West Dr. 154 BL76
West Drayton Rd., Uxb. 134 BM72
West Dr. SW16 181 DJ91
West Dr., Cars. 218 DD110
West Dr., Har. 95 CD51
West Dr. (Cheam), Sutt. 217 CX109
West Dr., Tad. 233 CX118
West Dr., Vir.W. 192 AS101
West Dr., Wat. 75 BV36
West Dr. Gdns., Har. 95 CD51
West Eaton Pl. SW1 276 F8
West Eaton Pl. SW1 160 DG77
West Eaton Pl. Ms. SW1 276 F7
West Ella Rd. NW10 138 CS66
West End Ave. E10 123 ED57
West End Ave., Pnr. 116 BX56
West End Ct., Pnr. 116 BX56
West End Ct., Slou. 132 AT67
West End Gdns., Esher 214 BZ106
West End Gdns., Nthlt. 136 BW68
Edward Clo.
West End La. NW6 120 DA64
West End La., Barn. 79 CX42
West End La., Esher 214 BZ108
West End La., Hat. 46 DC18
West End La., Hayes 155 BQ80
West End La., Pnr. 116 BX55
West End La., Slou. 132 AS68
West End Rd., Brox. 48 DS23
West End Rd., Nthlt. 136 BW66
West End Rd., Ruis. 115 BU63
West End Rd., Sthl. 136 BY74
West Fm. Ave., Ash. 231 CJ118
West Fm. Clo., Ash. 231 CJ119
West Fm. Dr., Ash. 231 CK119
West Gdn. Pl. W2 272 C9
West Gdns. E1 142 DV73
West Gdns. SW17 180 DE93
West Gdns., Epsom 216 CS110
West Gate W5 138 CL69
West Gate, Harl. 51 EQ15
West Gorse, Croy. 221 DY112
West Grn. Pl., Grnf. 137 CD67
Uneeda Dr.
West Grn. Rd. N15 121 DP56
West Gro. SE10 163 EC81
West Gro., Walt. 213 BV106
West Gro., Wdf.Grn. 102 EJ51
West Halkin St. SW1 276 F6
West Halkin St. SW1 160 DG76
West Hall Rd., Rich. 158 CP81
West Hallowes SE9 184 EL88
West Ham La. E15 143 ED66
West Ham Pk. E7 144 EF66
West Hampstead Ms. NW6 140 DB65
West Harding St. EC4 274 E8
West Harold, Swan. 207 FD97
West Hatch Manor, Ruis. 115 BT60
West Heath Ave. NW11 120 DA60
West Heath Clo. NW3 120 DA62
West Heath Clo., Dart. 187 FF86
West Heath Rd.
West Heath Dr. NW11 120 DA60
West Heath Gdns. NW3 120 DA61
West Heath La., Sev. 257 FH128
West Heath Rd. NW3 120 DA61
West Heath Rd. SE2 166 EW79
West Heath Rd., Dart. 187 FF86
West Hendon Bdy. NW9 119 CT58
West Hill SW15 179 CX87
West Hill SW18 179 CX87
West Hill, Dart. 188 FJ86
West Hill, Epsom 216 CP113
West Hill, Har. 117 CE61
West Hill, Orp. 223 EM112
West Hill, Oxt. 253 ED130
West Hill, S.Croy. 220 DS110
West Hill, Wem. 118 CM60
West Hill Ave., Epsom 216 CP113
West Hill Bank, Oxt. 253 ED130
West Hill Ct. N6 120 DG62
West Hill Dr., Dart. 188 FJ86
West Hill Pk. N6 120 DF61
Merton La.
West Hill Ri., Dart. 188 FK86
West Hill Rd. SW18 179 CZ86
West Hill Rd., Wok. 226 AX119
West Hill Way N20 98 DB46
West Holme, Erith 167 FC81
West Ho. Clo. SW19 179 CY88
West Hyde La., Ger.Cr. 91 AZ52
West India Ave. E14 143 EA74
West India Dock Rd. E14 143 DZ72
West Kent Ave., Grav. 190 GC86
West Kentish Town Est. NW5 140 DG65
Warden Rd.
West La. SE16 162 DV75
West La., Dor. 262 BX139
West Lo. Ave. W3 138 CN74
West Mall W8 140 DA74
Palace Gdns. Ter.
West Malling Way, Horn. 128 FJ64
West Mead, Epsom 216 CS107
West Mead, Ruis. 116 BW63
West Mead, Welw.G.C. 30 DB12
West Meads, Guil. 258 AT136
West Ms. N17 100 DV51
West Ms. SW1 277 K9
West Mill, Grav. 191 GF86
West Mt., Guil. 258 AW136
The Mt.
West Oak, Beck. 203 ED95
West Palace Gdns., Wey. 195 BP104
West Pk. SE9 184 EL89
West Pk. Ave., Rich. 158 CN81
West Pk. Clo., Houns. 156 BZ79
Heston Gra. La.
West Pk. Clo., Rom. 126 EX57
West Pk. Hill, Brwd. 108 FU48
West Pk. Rd., Epsom 216 CM112
West Pk. Rd., Rich. 158 CN81
West Pk. Rd., Sthl. 136 CC74
West Pier E1 142 DV74
Wapping High St.
West Pl. SW19 179 CW92
West Pt., Slou. 131 AK74
West Poultry Ave. EC1 274 F7
West Quarters W12 139 CU72
Du Cane Rd.
West Quay Dr., Hayes 136 BY71
West Ramp, Houns. 154 BN81
West Ridge Gdns., Grnf. 136 CC68
West Riding, St.Alb. 60 BZ30
West Rd. E15 144 EF67
West Rd. N17 100 DV51
West Rd. SW3 160 DF78
West Rd. SW4 181 DK85
West Rd. W5 138 CL71
West Rd., Barn. 98 DG46
West Rd., Berk. 38 AU18
West Rd., Chess. 215 CJ111
West Rd., Felt. 175 BR86
West Rd., Guil. 258 AY135
West Rd., Harl. 36 EU11
West Rd., Kings.T. 198 CQ95
West Rd., Reig. 266 DB135
West Rd. (Chadwell Heath), Rom. 126 EX58
West Rd. (Rush Grn.), Rom. 127 FD59
West Rd., S.Ock. 149 FU69
West Rd., West Dr. 154 BM76
West Rd., Wey. 213 BP109
West Row W10 139 CY70
West Shaw, Long. 209 FX96
West Sheen Vale, Rich. 158 CM84
West Side, Brox. 67 DY25
High Rd. Turnford
West Side Common SW19 179 CW93
West Smithfield EC1 274 F7
West Smithfield EC1 141 DP71
West Spur Rd., Uxb. 134 BK69
West Sq. SE11 278 F7
West Sq. SE11 161 DP76
West Sq., Iver 133 BF72
High St.
West St. E2 142 DV68
West St. E11 124 EE62
West St. E17 123 EB57
Grove Rd.
West St. WC2 273 N9
West St., Bexh. 166 EZ84
West St., Brent. 157 CJ79
West St., Brom. 204 EG95
West St., Cars. 200 DF104
West St., Croy. 220 DQ105
West St., Dor. 263 CG136
West St., Epsom 216 CQ113
West St. (Ewell), Epsom 216 CS110
West St., Erith 167 FD77
West St., Grav. 191 GH86
West St., Grays 170 GA79
West St., Har. 117 CD60
West St., Hert. 32 DQ10
West St., Reig. 249 CY134
West St., Sutt. 218 DB106
West St., Ware 33 DX06
West St., Wat. 75 BV40
West St., Wok. 227 AZ117
Church St. E.
West St. La., Cars. 218 DF105
West Temple Sheen SW14 158 CP84
West Tenter St. E1 142 DT72
West Thurrock Way, Grays 169 FT76
West Twrs., Pnr. 116 BX58
West Valley Rd., Hem.H. 58 BJ25
West Vw. NW4 119 CW56
West Vw., Chesh. 54 AR29
West Vw., Felt. 175 BQ87
West Vw., Loug. 85 EM42
West Vw. Ave., Whyt. 236 DU118
Station Rd.
West Vw. Ct., Borwd. 77 CK44
High St.
West Vw. Gdns., Borwd. 77 CK44
High St.
West Vw. Ri., Hem.H. 40 BK19
West Vw. Rd., Dart. 188 FM86
West Vw. Rd., St.Alb. 43 CD19
West Vw. Rd., Swan. 207 FG98
West Vw. Rd. (Crockenhill), Swan. 207 FD100
West Wk. W5 138 CL71
West Wk., Barn. 98 DG45
West Wk., Harl. 35 EQ14
West Wk., Hayes 135 BU74
West Warwick Pl. SW1 277 K9
West Warwick Pl. SW1 161 DJ77
West Way N18 100 DR49
West Way NW10 118 CR63
West Way, Beac. 88 AF54
West Way, Brwd. 108 FU48
West Way, Cars. 218 DD110
West Way, Croy. 203 DY103
West Way, Edg. 96 CP51
West Way, Houns. 156 BZ80
West Way, Pnr. 116 BX56
West Way, Rick. 92 BH46
West Way, Ruis. 115 BT60
West Way, Shep. 195 BR100
West Way, W.Wick. 203 ED100
West Way Gdns., Croy. 203 DX103
West Woodside, Bex. 186 EY87
West World W5 138 CL69
West Yoke, Sev. 209 FW103
Westacott, Hayes 135 BS71
Westacott Clo. N19 121 DK60
Westacres, Esher 214 BZ108
Westall Clo., Hert. 32 DQ10
Westall Rd., Loug. 85 EP41
Westanley Ave., Amer. 55 AR39
Westbank Rd., Hmptn. 176 CC93
Westbeech Rd. N22 121 DN55
Westbere Dr., Stan. 95 CK49
Westbere Rd. NW2 119 CY63
Westbourne Ave. W3 138 CR72
Westbourne Ave., Sutt. 199 CY103
Westbourne Bri. W2 140 DC71
Westbourne Clo., Hayes 135 BV70
Westbourne Cres. W2 140 DD73
Westbourne Cres. Ms. W2 140 DD73
Westbourne Cres.
Westbourne Dr. SE23 183 DX89
Westbourne Dr., Brwd. 108 FT49
Westbourne Gdns. W2 140 DB72
Westbourne Gro. W2 140 DA72
Westbourne Gro. W11 139 CZ73
Westbourne Gro. Ms. W11 140 DA72
Westbourne Gro.
Westbourne Gro. Ter. W2 140 DB72
Westbourne Pk. Ms. W2 140 DB72
Westbourne Gdns.
Westbourne Pk. Pas. W2 140 DA71
Westbourne Pk. Rd. W2 140 DA71
Westbourne Pk. Rd. W11 139 CY72
Westbourne Pk. Vill. W2 140 DA71
Westbourne Pl. N9 100 DV48
Eastbournia Ave.
Westbourne Rd. N7 141 DM65
Westbourne Rd. SE26 183 DX93
Westbourne Rd., Bexh. 166 EY80
Westbourne Rd., Croy. 202 DT100
Westbourne Rd., Felt. 175 BT90
Westbourne Rd., Stai. 174 BH94
Westbourne Rd., Uxb. 135 BP70
Westbourne St. W2 140 DD73
Westbourne Ter. SE23 183 DX89
Westbourne Dr.
Westbourne Ter. W2 140 DC72
Westbourne Ter. Ms. W2 140 DC72
Westbourne Ter. Rd. W2 140 DC71
Westbridge Rd. SW11 160 DD81
Westbrook, Maid. 150 AE78
Westbrook Ave., Hmptn. 176 BZ94
Westbrook Clo., Barn. 80 DD41
Westbrook Cres., Barn. 80 DD41
Westbrook Dr., Orp. 206 EW102
Westbrook Rd. SE3 164 EH81
Westbrook Rd., Houns. 156 BZ80
Westbrook Rd., Stai. 173 BF92
South St.
Westbrook Rd., Th.Hth. 202 DR95
Westbrook Sq., Barn. 80 DD41
Westbrooke Cres., Well. 166 EW83
Westbrooke Rd., Sid. 185 ER89
Westbrooke Rd., Well. 166 EV83
Westbury Ave. N22 121 DP55
Westbury Ave., Esher 215 CF107
Westbury Ave., Sthl. 136 CA70
Westbury Ave., Wem. 138 CL66
Westbury Clo., Ruis. 115 BU59
Westbury Clo., Shep. 195 BP100
Burchetts Way
Westbury Clo., Whyt. 236 DS116
Beverley Rd.
Westbury Dr., Brwd. 108 FV48
Westbury Gro. N12 98 DA51
Westbury La., Buck.H. 102 EJ47
Westbury Lo. Clo., Pnr. 116 BX55
Westbury Par. SW12 181 DH86
Balham Hill
Westbury Pl., Brent. 157 CK79
Westbury Ri., Harl. 52 EX16
Westbury Rd. E7 124 EH64
Westbury Rd. E17 123 DZ56
Westbury Rd. N11 99 DL51
Westbury Rd. N12 98 DA51
Westbury Rd. SE20 203 DX95
Westbury Rd. W5 138 CL72
Westbury Rd., Bark. 145 ER67
Westbury Rd., Beck. 203 DY97
Westbury Rd., Brwd. 108 FW47
Westbury Rd., Brom. 204 EK95
Westbury Rd., Buck.H. 102 EJ47
Westbury Rd., Croy. 202 DR100
Westbury Rd., Felt. 176 BX88
Westbury Rd., Ilf. 125 EN61
Westbury Rd., N.Mal. 198 CR98
Westbury Rd., Nthwd. 93 BR49
Westbury Rd., Wat. 75 BV43
Westbury Rd., Wem. 138 CL66
Westbury St. SW8 161 DJ82
Westbury Ter. E7 144 EH65
Westbury Ter., Upmin. 129 FS61
Westbury Ter., West. 255 EQ127
Westbush Clo., Hodd. 33 DZ14
Westcar La., Walt. 213 BV107
Westchester Dr. NW4 119 CX55
Westcombe Ave., Croy. 201 DL100
Westcombe Ct. SE3 164 EF80
Westcombe Pk. Rd.
Westcombe Dr., Barn. 80 DA43
Westcombe Hill SE3 164 EG79
Westcombe Hill SE10 164 EG78
Westcombe Lo. Dr., Hayes 135 BR71
Westcombe Pk. Rd. SE3 164 EE79
Westcoombe Ave. SW20 199 CT95
Westcote Ri., Ruis. 115 BQ59
Westcote Rd. SW16 181 DJ92
Westcott, Welw.G.C. 30 DD08
Westcott Ave., Grav. 191 GG90
Westcott Clo. N15 122 DT58
Ermine Rd.
Westcott Clo., Brom. 204 EL99
Ringmer Way
Westcott Clo., Croy. 221 EB109
Castle Hill Ave.
Westcott Cres. W7 137 CE72
Westcott Rd. SE17 161 DP79
Westcott Rd., Dor. 263 CE137
Westcott St., Dor. 262 CB137
Westcott Way, Sutt. 217 CW110
Westcott Way, Uxb. 134 BJ68
Westcourt, Sun. 195 BV96
Westcroft, Slou. 131 AP70
Westcroft Clo. NW2 119 CY63
Westcroft Clo., Enf. 82 DW38
Westcroft Ct., Brox. 49 EA19
Westcroft Gdns., Mord. 199 CZ97
Westcroft Rd., Cars. 218 DG105
Westcroft Rd., Wall. 218 DG105
Westcroft Sq. W6 159 CU77
Westcroft Way NW2 119 CY63
Westdale Pas. SE18 165 EP79
Westdale Rd.
Westdale Rd. SE18 165 EP79
Westdean Ave. SE12 184 EH88
Westdean Clo. SW18 180 DB85
Westdown Rd. E15 123 EC63
Westdown Rd. SE6 183 EA87
Wested La., Swan. 207 FG101
Westel Ho. W5 137 CJ73
Westerdale, Hem.H. 40 BL17
Westerdale Rd. SE10 164 EG78
Westerfield Rd. N15 122 DT57
Westerfolds Clo., Wok. 227 BC116
Westergate Rd. SE2 166 EY79
Westerham Ave. N9 100 DR48
Westerham Clo., Add. 212 BJ107
Westerham Clo., Sutt. 218 DA110
Westerham Dr., Sid. 186 EV86
Westerham Hill, West. 239 EN120
Westerham Rd. E10 123 EB58
Westerham Rd., Kes. 222 EK108
Westerham Rd., Oxt. 254 EF129
Westerham Rd., Sev. 256 FC123
Westerham Rd., West. 255 EM128
Westerley Cres. SE26 183 DZ92
Westerly Ware, Rich. 158 CN79
Kew Grn.
Western Ave. NW11 119 CX58
Western Ave. W3 138 CN70
Western Ave. W5 138 CM70
Western Ave., Brwd. 108 FW46
Western Ave., Cher. 194 BG97
Western Ave., Dag. 147 FC65
Western Ave., Egh. 193 BB97
Western Ave., Epp. 69 ET32
Western Ave., Grays 169 FT79
Western Ave., Grnf. 137 CE68
Western Ave., Nthlt. 136 BZ67
Western Ave., Rom. 106 FJ54
Western Ave., Ruis. 135 BQ65
Western Ave. (Denham), Uxb. 114 BJ63
Western Ave. (Ickenham), Uxb. 114 BK63
Western Clo., Cher. 194 BG97
Western Ave.
Western Ct. N3 98 DA51
Huntley Dr.
Western Cross Clo., Green. 189 FW86
Johnsons Way
Western Dr., H.Wyc. 110 AE58
Western Dr., Shep. 195 BR100
Western Gdns. W5 138 CN73
Western Gdns., Brwd. 108 FW47
Western Gateway E16 144 EG73
Western Ho. W5 138 CL69
Western La. SW12 180 DG87
Western Ms. W9 139 CZ70
Great Western Rd.
Western Par., Reig. 266 DA137
Prices La.
Western Pathway, Horn. 148 FJ65
Western Perimeter Rd., Houns. 154 BH83
Western Pl. SE16 162 DW75
Canon Beck Rd.
Western Rd. E13 144 EJ67
Western Rd. E17 123 EC57
Western Rd. N2 120 DF56
Western Rd. N22 99 DM54
Western Rd. NW10 138 CQ70
Western Rd. SW9 161 DN83
Western Rd. SW19 200 DD95
Western Rd. W5 137 CK73
Western Rd., Brwd. 108 FW47
Western Rd., Epp. 69 ES32
Western Rd., Mitch. 200 DE95
Western Rd., Rom. 127 FE57
Western Rd., Sthl. 156 BW77
Western Rd., Sutt. 218 DA106
Western Rd., Wal.Abb. 50 EE22
Western Ter. W6 159 CU78
Chiswick Mall
Western Trd. Est. NW10 138 CP70
Western Vw., Hayes 155 BT75
Station Rd.
Western Way SE28 165 ER76
Western Way, Barn. 80 DA44
Westernville Gdns., Ilf. 125 EQ59
Westferry Circ. E14 143 EA74
Westferry Rd. E14 163 EA75
Westfield, Ash. 232 CM118
Westfield, Dor. 261 BT143
Westfield, Harl. 51 ES16
Westfield, Hat. 46 DA23
Westfield, Loug. 84 EJ43
Westfield, Reig. 250 DB131
Westfield, Sev. 257 FJ122
Westfield, Welw.G.C. 30 DA08
Westfield Ave., S.Croy. 220 DR113
Westfield Ave., Wat. 76 BW37
Westfield Ave., Wok. 226 AY121
Westfield Clo. NW9 118 CQ55
Westfield Clo. SW10 160 DC80
Westfield Clo., Enf. 83 DY41
Westfield Clo., Grav. 191 GJ93
Westfield Clo., Sutt. 217 CZ105
Westfield Clo., Wal.Cr. 67 DY31
Westfield Common, Wok. 226 AY122
Westfield Ct., St.Alb. 43 CK17
Westfield Dr., Har. 117 CK56
Westfield Dr., Lthd. 230 CA122
Westfield Gdns., Har. 117 CK56
Westfield Gro., Wok. 226 AY120
Westfield La., Har. 117 CK56
Westfield La., Slou. 132 AX72
Westfield Par., Add. 212 BK110
Westfield Pk., Pnr. 94 BZ52
Westfield Rd. NW7 96 CR48
Westfield Rd. W13 137 CG74
Westfield Rd., Beac. 88 AJ54
Westfield Rd., Beck. 203 DZ96
Westfield Rd., Berk. 38 AS17
Westfield Rd., Bexh. 167 FC82
Westfield Rd., Croy. 201 DP103
Westfield Rd., Dag. 126 EY63
Westfield Rd., Guil. 242 AY130
Westfield Rd., Hert. 32 DQ07
Westfield Rd., Hodd. 49 DZ16
Westfield Rd., Mitch. 200 DF96
Westfield Rd., Slou. 131 AP70
Westfield Rd., Surb. 197 CK99
Westfield Rd., Sutt. 217 CZ105
Westfield Rd., Walt. 196 BY101
Westfield Rd., Wok. 226 AX122
Westfield St. SE18 164 EK76
Westfield Wk., Wal.Cr. 67 DZ31
Westfield Clo.
Westfield Way E1 143 DY69
Westfield Way, Ruis. 115 BS62
Westfield Way, Wok. 226 AY122
Westfields SW13 159 CT83
Westfields, St.Alb. 42 CA22
Westfields Ave. SW13 158 CS83
Westfields Rd. W3 138 CP71
Westgate Clo., Epsom 232 CR115
Chalk La.
Westgate Ct., Wal.Cr. 83 DX35
Holmesdale
Westgate Cres., Slou. 131 AM73
Westgate Rd. SE25 202 DV98
Westgate Rd., Beck. 203 EB96
Westgate Rd., Dart. 188 FK86
Westgate St. E8 142 DV67
Westgate Ter. SW10 160 DB78
Westglade Ct., Har. 117 CK57
Westgrove La. SE10 163 EC81
Westhall Pk., Warl. 236 DW119
Westhall Rd., Warl. 236 DU118
Westhay Gdns. SW14 178 CP85
Westhill Clo., Grav. 191 GH88
Leith Pk. Rd.
Westhill Rd., Hodd. 49 DZ16
Westholm NW11 120 DB56
Westholme, Orp. 205 ES101
Westholme Gdns., Ruis. 115 BU60
Westhorne Ave. SE9 184 EK85
Westhorne Ave. SE12 184 EH86
Westhorpe Gdns. NW4 119 CW55
Westhorpe Rd. SW15 159 CW83
Westhumble St., Dor. 247 CH131
Westhurst Dr., Chis. 185 EP92
Westlake Clo. N13 99 DN48
Westlake Clo., Hayes 136 BY70
Lochan Clo.
Westlake Rd., Wem. 117 CK61
Westland Ave., Horn. 128 FL60
Westland Clo., Stai. 174 BL86
Westland Dr., Brom. 204 EF103
Westland Dr., Hat. 63 CY26
Westland Pl. N1 275 K2
Westland Rd., Wat. 75 BV40
Westlands Ave., Slou. 130 AJ72
Westlands Clo., Hayes 155 BU77
Granville Rd.
Westlands Clo., Slou. 130 AJ72
Westlands Ave.
Westlands Ct., Epsom 232 CQ115
Westlands Est., Hayes 155 BS76
Westlands Ter. SW12 181 DJ86
Gaskarth Rd.
Westlands Way, Oxt. 253 ED127
Westlea Ave., Wat. 76 BY36
Westlea Clo., Brox. 49 DZ24
Westlea Rd. W7 157 CG76
Westlea Rd., Brox. 49 DZ23
Westleas, Horl. 268 DE146
Westlees Clo., Dor. 263 CK139
Wildcroft Dr.
Westleigh Ave. SW15 179 CV85
Westleigh Ave., Couls. 234 DG116
Westleigh Dr., Brom. 204 EL95
Westleigh Gdns., Edg. 96 CN53
Westlinks, Wem. 137 CK69
Alperton La.
Westly Wd., Welw.G.C. 30 DA08
Westlyn Clo., Rain. 148 FJ69
Westmacott Dr., Felt. 175 BT87
Westmead SW15 179 CV87
Westmead, Wind. 151 AP83
Westmead, Wok. 226 AV117
Westmead Cor., Cars. 218 DE105
Colston Ave.
Westmead Dr., Red. 266 DG142
Westmead Rd., Sutt. 218 DD105
Westmeade Clo. (Cheshunt), Wal.Cr. 66 DV29
Westmede, Chig. 103 EQ51
Westmere Dr. NW7 96 CR48
Westmill Ct. N4 122 DQ61
Brownswood Rd.
Westminster Ave., Th.Hth. 201 DP96
Westminster Bri. SE1 278 A5
Westminster Bri. SE1 161 DM75
Westminster Bri. SW1 278 A5
Westminster Bri. SW1 161 DL75
Westminster Bri. Rd. SE1 278 C5
Westminster Bri. Rd. SE1 161 DM75
Westminster Cathedral Piazza SW1 277 K7
Westminster Clo., Felt. 175 BU88
Westminster Clo., Ilf. 103 ER54
Westminster Clo., Tedd. 177 CG92
Westminster Ct., St.Alb. 42 CC22
Westminster Dr. N13 99 DL50
Westminster Gdns. E4 102 EE46
Westminster Gdns., Bark. 145 ES68
Westminster Gdns., Ilf. 103 EQ54
Westminster Rd. N9 100 DV46
Westminster Rd. W7 137 CE74
Westminster Rd., Sutt. 200 DD103
Westmoat Clo., Beck. 183 EC94
Westmont Rd., Esher 197 CE103
Westmoor Gdns., Enf. 83 DX40
Westmoor Rd., Enf. 83 DX40
Westmoor St. SE7 164 EK76
Westmore Grn., West. 238 EJ121
Westmore Rd., West. 238 EJ121
Westmoreland Ave., Horn. 128 FJ57
Westmoreland Ave., Well. 165 ES83
Westmoreland Bldgs. EC1 142 DQ71
Bartholomew Clo.
Westmoreland Dr., Sutt. 218 DB109
Westmoreland Pl. SW1 161 DH78
Westmoreland Pl. W5 137 CK71
Mount Ave.
Westmoreland Rd. NW9 118 CM55
Westmoreland Rd. SE17 162 DR79
Westmoreland Rd. SW13 159 CT81
Westmoreland Rd., Brom. 204 EE99
Westmoreland St. W1 272 G7
Westmoreland St. W1 140 DG71
Westmoreland Ter. SW1 161 DH78
Westmoreland Wk. SE17 162 DR79
Westmoreland Rd.
Westmorland Clo. E12 124 EK61
Westmorland Clo., Epsom 216 CS110
Westmorland Clo., Twick. 177 CH86
Westmorland Rd. E17 123 EA58
Westmorland Rd., Har. 116 CB57
Westmorland Ter. SE20 182 DV94
Hawthorn Gro.
Westmorland Way, Mitch. 201 DK98
Westmount Ave., Amer. 55 AQ39
Westmount Rd. SE9 165 EM82
Westoe Rd. N9 100 DV47
Weston Ave., Add. 212 BG105
Weston Ave., Grays 169 FT78
Weston Ave., T.Ditt. 197 CE101
Weston Ave., W.Mol. 196 BY97
Weston Clo., Brwd. 109 GC45
Weston Clo., Couls. 235 DM120
Weston Clo., Pot.B. 63 CZ32

Whiteleys Cotts. W14 159 CZ77
Whiteleys Way, Felt. 176 CA90
Whitemore Rd., Guil. 242 AX130
Whiteoak Gdns., Sid. 185 ET87
Whiteoaks, Bans. 218 DB113
Whiteoaks La., Grnf. 137 CD68
Whitepit La., H.Wyc. 110 AC56
Whitepost Hill, Red. 250 DE134
Whites Ave., Ilf. 125 ES58
Whites Clo., Green. 189 FW86
Whites Dr., Brom. 204 EF101
Whites Grds. SE1 279 N5
Whites Grds. SE1 162 DS75
Whites Grds. Est. SE1 279 N4
Whites La., Slou. 152 AV79
White's Row E1 275 P7
White's Row E1 142 DT71
White's Sq. SW4 161 DK84
Nelson's Row
Whitestile Rd., Brent. 157 CJ78
Whitestone La. NW3 120 DC62
Heath St.
Whitestone Wk. NW3 120 DC62
North End Way
Whitestone Wk., Hem.H. 40 BG17
Fennycroft Rd.
Whitethorn, Welw.G.C. 30 DB10
Whitethorn Ave., Couls. 234 DG115
Whitethorn Ave., West Dr. 134 BL73
Whitethorn Gdns., Enf. 82 DR43
Whitethorn Gdns., Horn. 128 FJ58
Whitethorn Pl., West Dr. 134 BM74
Whitethorn Ave.
Whitethorn St. E3 143 EA70
Whitewaits, Harl. 35 ES14
Whiteways Ct., Stai. 174 BH94
Pavilion Gdns.
Whitewebbs La., Enf. 82 DS35
Whitewebbs Rd., Enf. 81 DP35
Whitewebbs Way, Orp. 205 ET95
Whitewood Cotts., West. 238 EJ120
Whitfield Clo., Guil. 242 AU131
Whitfield Pl. W1 273 K5
Whitfield Rd. E6 144 EJ66
Whitfield Rd. SE3 163 ED81
Whitfield Rd., Bexh. 166 EZ80
Whitfield St. W1 273 K5
Whitfield St. W1 141 DJ70
Whitfield Way, Rick. 91 BF46
Whitford Gdns., Mitch. 200 DF97
Whitgift Ave., S.Croy. 219 DP106
Whitgift St. SE11 278 B8
Whitgift St. SE11 161 DM77
Whitgift St., Croy. 202 DQ104
High St.
Whiting Ave., Bark. 145 EP66
Whitings, Ilf. 125 ER57
Whitings Rd., Barn. 79 CW43
Whitings Way E6 145 EN71
Whitland Rd., Cars. 200 DD102
Whitlars Dr., Kings L. 58 BM28
Whitley Clo., Abb.L. 59 BU32
Whitley Clo., Stai. 174 BL86
Whitley Rd. N17 100 DS54
Whitley Rd., Hodd. 49 EB15
Whitlock Dr. SW19 179 CY87
Whitman Rd. E3 143 DY70
Whitmead Clo., S.Croy. 220 DS107
Whitmoor Common, Guil. 242 AV127
Whitmoor La., Guil. 242 AX126
Whitmore Ave., Rom. 106 FL54
Whitmore Clo. N11 99 DH50
Whitmore Est. N1 142 DS68
Nuttall St.
Whitmore Gdns. NW10 139 CW68
Whitmore Rd. N1 142 DS67
Whitmore Rd., Beck. 203 DZ97
Whitmore Rd., Har. 116 CC59
Whitmore Way, Horl. 268 DE147
Whitmores Clo., Epsom 232 CQ115
Whitnell Way SW15 179 CW85
Whitney Ave., Ilf. 124 EK56
Whitney Rd. E10 123 EA59
Whitney Wk., Sid. 186 EY93
Whitstable Clo., Beck. 203 DZ95
Whitstable Clo., Ruis. 115 BS61
Chichester Ave.
Whitstable Ho. W10 139 CX72
Silchester Rd.
Whitta Rd. E12 124 EK63
Whittaker Ave., Rich. 177 CK85
Hill St.
Whittaker Rd. E6 144 EK66
Whittaker Rd., Slou. 131 AK70
Whittaker Rd., Sutt. 199 CZ104
Whittaker St. SW1 276 F9
Whittaker St. SW1 160 DG77
Whittaker Way SE1 162 DU77
Lynton Rd.
Whittell Gdns. SE26 182 DW90
Whittenham Clo., Slou. 132 AU74
Whittingstall Rd. SW6 159 CZ81
Whittingstall Rd., Hodd. 49 EB15
Whittington Ave. EC3 275 M9
Whittington Ave., Hayes 135 BT71
Whittington Ct. N2 120 DF57
Whittington Ms. N12 98 DC49
Fredericks Pl.
Whittington Rd. N22 99 DL52
Whittington Rd., Brwd. 109 GC44
Whittington Way, Pnr. 116 BY57
Whittle Clo. E17 123 DY58
Whittle Clo., Sthl. 136 CB72
Whittle Parkway, Slou. 131 AK72
Whittle Rd., Houns. 156 BW80
Whittlebury Clo., Cars. 218 DF108
Whittlesea Clo., Har. 94 CC52
Whittlesea Rd.
Whittlesea Path, Har. 94 CC53
Whittlesea Rd., Har. 94 CC53
Whittlesey St. SE1 278 E3
Whitton Ave. E., Grnf. 117 CE64
Whitton Ave. W., Grnf. 117 CD64
Whitton Ave. W., Nthlt. 116 CB64
Whitton Clo., Grnf. 137 CH65
Whitton Dene, Houns. 176 CB85
Whitton Dene, Islw. 177 CD85
Whitton Dr., Grnf. 137 CG65
Whitton Manor Rd., Islw. 176 CC85
Whitton Rd., Houns. 156 CB84
Whitton Rd., Twick. 177 CE86
Whitton Wk. E3 143 EA69
Whitton Waye, Houns. 176 CA86
Whitwell Rd. E13 144 EG69
Whitwell Rd., Wat. 76 BX35
Whitworth Pl. SE18 165 EP77
Whitworth Rd. SE18 165 EN79
Whitworth Rd. SE25 202 DS97
Whitworth St. SE10 164 EE78
Whopshott Ave., Wok. 226 AW116
Whopshott Clo., Wok. 226 AW116
Whopshott Dr., Wok. 226 AW116
Whorlton Rd. SE15 162 DV83
Whybridge Clo., Rain. 147 FE67
Whymark Ave. N22 121 DN55
Whytebeam Vw., Whyt. 236 DT118
Whytecliffe Rd. N., Pur. 219 DP111
Whytecliffe Rd. S., Pur. 219 DN111
Whytecroft, Houns. 156 BX80
Whyteleafe Hill, Whyt. 236 DS120
Whyteleafe Rd., Cat. 236 DS122
Whyteville Rd. E7 144 EH65
Wichling Clo., Orp. 206 EX102
Wick, The, Hert. 31 DP06
Wick La. E3 143 DZ66
Wick La., Egh. 172 AT92
Wick Rd. E9 143 DX65
Wick Rd., Egh. 192 AU95
Wick Rd., Tedd. 177 CH94
Wick Sq. E9 143 DZ65
Eastway
Wick Way, St.Alb. 43 CH17
Marshalswick La.
Wickenden Rd., Sev. 257 FJ122
Wicker St. E1 142 DV72
Burslem St.
Wickers Oake SE19 182 DT91
Wickersley Rd. SW11 160 DG82
Wicket, The, Croy. 221 EA106
Wicket Rd., Grnf. 137 CG69
Wickets, The, Ashf. 174 BL91
Wickets Way, Ilf. 103 ET51
Wickford Clo., Rom. 106 FM50
Wickford Dr.
Wickford Dr., Rom. 106 FM50
Wickford St. E1 142 DW70
Wickford Way E17 123 DX56
Wickham Ave., Croy. 203 DY103
Wickham Ave., Sutt. 217 CW106
Wickham Chase, W.Wick. 203 ED102
Wickham Clo., Enf. 82 DV41
Wickham Clo., Horl. 268 DF147
Wickham Clo., N.Mal. 199 CT99
Wickham Clo., Uxb. 92 BK53
Wickham Ct., St.Alb. 43 CH18
Wickham Ct. Rd., W.Wick. 203 EC103
Wickham Cres., W.Wick. 203 EC103
Wickham Fld., Sev. 241 FF116
Wickham Gdns. SE4 163 DZ83
Wickham Ho. E1 142 DW71
Jamaica St.
Wickham La. SE2 166 EU78
Wickham La., Egh. 173 BA94
Wickham La., Well. 166 EU78
Wickham Ms. SE4 163 DZ82
Wickham Rd. E4 101 EC52
Wickham Rd. SE4 163 DZ83
Wickham Rd., Beck. 203 EB96
Wickham Rd., Croy. 202 DW103
Wickham Rd., Grays 171 GJ75
Wickham Rd., Har. 95 CD54
Wickham St. SE11 278 B10
Wickham St. SE11 161 DM78
Wickham St., Well. 165 ES82
Wickham Way, Beck. 203 EC98
Wicklands Rd. (Hunsdon), Ware 34 EK07
Wickliffe Ave. N3 97 CY54
Wickliffe Gdns., Wem. 118 CP61
Wicklow St. WC1 274 B2
Wicklow St. WC1 141 DM69
Wicks Clo. SE9 184 EK91
Wicksteed Clo., Bex. 187 FD90
Wicksteed Ho., Brent. 158 CM78
Wickwood St. SE5 161 DP82
Wid Clo., Brwd. 109 GD43
Widbury Gdns., Ware 33 DZ06
Widbury Hill, Ware 33 DZ06
Widdecombe Ave., Har. 116 BY61
Widdenham Rd. N7 121 DM63
Widdin St. E15 143 ED66
Wide Way, Mitch. 201 DK97
Widecombe Clo., Rom. 106 FK53
Widecombe Gdns., Ilf. 124 EL56
Widecombe Rd. SE9 184 EL90
Widecombe Way N2 120 DD57
Widecroft Rd., Iver 133 BE72
Widegate St. E1 275 N7
Widenham Clo., Pnr. 116 BW57
Bridle Rd.
Widford Rd. (Hunsdon), Ware 34 EK05
Widford Rd., Welw.G.C. 30 DB09
Widgeon Clo. E16 144 EH72
Maplin Rd.
Widgeon Rd., Erith 167 FH80
Wallhouse Rd.
Widgeon Way, Wat. 76 BY37
Widley Rd. W9 140 DA69
Widmoor, H.Wyc. 110 AE60
Widmore Dr., Hem.H. 40 BN18
Widmore Lo. Rd., Brom. 204 EK96
Widmore Rd., Brom. 204 EG96
Widmore Rd., Uxb. 135 BP70
Widworthy Hayes, Brwd. 109 GB46
Wieland Rd., Nthwd. 93 BU52
Wigan Ho. E5 122 DV60
Warwick Gro.
Wigeon Path SE28 165 ER76
Wigeon Way, Hayes 136 BX72
Wiggenhall Rd., Wat. 75 BV43
Wiggie La., Red. 250 DG132
Wiggington Ave., Wem. 138 CP65
Wiggins Mead NW9 97 CT52
Wightman Ho., Bark. 145 EQ66
Wightman Rd. N4 121 DN56
Wightman Rd. N8 121 DN56
Wigley Bush La., Brwd. 108 FS47
Wigley Rd., Felt. 176 BX89
Wigmore Pl. W1 273 H8
Wigmore Pl. W1 141 DH72
Wigmore Rd., Cars. 200 DD103
Wigmore St. W1 272 F9
Wigmore St. W1 140 DG72
Wigmore Wk., Cars. 200 DD103
Wigmore Rd.
Wigmores N., Welw.G.C. 29 CX08
Wigmores S., Welw.G.C. 29 CX09
Wigram Rd. E11 124 EJ58
Wigram Sq. E17 101 ED54
Wigston Clo. N18 100 DS50
Wigston Rd. E13 144 EH70
Wigton Gdns., Stan. 96 CL53
Wigton Pl. SE11 161 DN78
Milverton St.
Wigton Rd. E17 101 DZ53
Wigton Rd., Rom. 106 FL49
Wigton Way, Rom. 106 FL49
Wilberforce Rd. N4 121 DP61
Wilberforce Rd. NW9 119 CU58
Wilberforce Way SW19 179 CX93
Wilberforce Way, Grav. 191 GK92
Wilbraham Pl. SW1 276 E8
Wilbraham Pl. SW1 160 DF77
Wilbury Ave., Sutt. 217 CZ110
Wilbury Rd., Wok. 226 AX117
Wilbury Way N18 100 DR50
Wilby Ms. W11 139 CZ73
Wilcot Ave., Wat. 94 BY45
Wilcox Clo. SW8 161 DL80
Wilcox Clo., Borwd. 78 CQ39
Wilcox Gdns., Shep. 194 BM97
Wilcox Pl. SW1 277 L7
Wilcox Rd. SW8 161 DL80
Wilcox Rd., Sutt. 218 DB105
Wilcox Rd., Tedd. 177 CD91
Wild Ct. WC2 274 B8
Wild Ct. WC2 141 DM72
Wild Goose Dr. SE14 162 DW81
Wild Grn. N., Slou. 153 BA77
Verney Rd.
Wild Grn. S., Slou. 153 BA77
Swabey Rd.
Wild Hatch NW11 120 DA58
Wild Oaks Clo., Nthwd. 93 BT51
Wild St. WC2 274 A9
Wild St. WC2 141 DL72
Wildacres, W.Byf. 212 BJ111
Wildbank Ct., Wok. 227 AZ118
White Rose La.
Wildcroft Dr., Dor. 263 CK139
Wildcroft Gdns., Edg. 95 CK51
Wildcroft Rd. SW15 179 CW87
Wilde Clo. E8 142 DU67
Wilde Clo., Til. 171 GJ82
Coleridge Rd.
Wilde Pl. N13 99 DP51
Medesenge Way
Wilde Pl. SW18 180 DD87
Heathfield Rd.
Wilde Rd., Erith 167 FB81
Belmont Rd.
Wilder Clo., Ruis. 115 BV60
Wilderness, The, Berk. 38 AW19
Wilderness, The, Hmptn. 176 CB91
Park Rd.
Wilderness Rd., Chis. 185 EP94
Wilderness Rd., Guil. 258 AT135
Wilderness Rd., Oxt. 254 EE130
Wildernesse Ave., Sev. 257 FL122
Wildernesse Mt., Sev. 257 FK122
Wilders Clo., Wok. 226 AW118
Wilderton Rd. N16 122 DS59
Wildfell Rd. SE6 183 EB87
Wildhill Rd., Hat. 45 CY23
Wild's Rents SE1 279 M6
Wild's Rents SE1 162 DS76
Wildwood NW3 120 DC60
Wildwood, Nthwd. 93 BR51
Wildwood Ave., St.Alb. 60 BZ30
Wildwood Clo. SE12 184 EF87
Wildwood Clo., Lthd. 245 BT125
Wildwood Clo., Wok. 227 BF115
Wildwood Ct., Ken. 236 DR115
Wildwood Gro. NW3 120 DC60
North End Way
Wildwood Ri. NW11 120 DC60
Wildwood Rd. NW11 120 DB58
Wilford Clo., Enf. 82 DR41
Wilford Clo., Nthwd. 93 BR52
Wilford Rd., Slou. 152 AY77
Wilfred Ave., Rain. 147 FG71
Wilfred Owen Clo. SW19 180 DC93
Tennyson Rd.
Wilfred St. SW1 277 K6
Wilfred St. SW1 161 DJ76
Wilfred St., Grav. 191 GH86
Wilfred St., Wok. 226 AX118
Wilfrid Gdns. W3 138 CQ71
Wilhelmina Ave., Couls. 235 DJ119
Wilkes Rd., Brent. 158 CL79
Albany Rd.
Wilkes Rd., Brwd. 109 GD43
Wilkes St. E1 142 DT71
Wilkie Way SE22 182 DU88
Lordship La.
Wilkin St. NW5 141 DH65
Wilkin St. Ms. NW5 141 DH65
Wilkin St.
Wilkins Clo., Hayes 155 BT78
Wilkins Clo., Mitch. 200 DE95
Wilkins Grn. La., Hat. 44 CR19
Wilkins Grn. La., St.Alb. 44 CP20
Wilkins Gro., Welw.G.C. 29 CX10
Wilkins Way, West. 240 EV124
Wilkinson Clo., Dart. 168 FM84
Henderson Dr.
Wilkinson Rd. E16 144 EJ72
Wilkinson St. SW8 161 DM80
Wilkinson Way W4 158 CR75
Southfield Rd.
Wilks Ave., Dart. 188 FM89
Wilks Gdns., Croy. 203 DY102
Wilks Pl. N1 275 N1
Will Crooks Gdns. SE9 164 EJ84
Willan Rd. N17 100 DR54
Willan Wall E16 144 EF73
Victoria Dock Rd.
Willard St. SW8 161 DH83
Willcocks Clo., Chess. 198 CL104
Willcott Rd. W3 138 CP74
Willen Fld. Rd. NW10 138 CQ68
Willenhall Ave., Barn. 80 DC44
Willenhall Dr., Hayes 135 BS73
Willenhall Rd. SE18 165 EP78
Willersley Ave., Orp. 205 ER104
Willersley Ave., Sid. 185 ET88
Willersley Clo., Sid. 185 ET88
Willes Rd. NW5 141 DH65
Willesden La. NW2 139 CW65
Willesden La. NW6 139 CZ67
Willet Way SE16 162 DV78
Egan Way
Willett Clo., Nthlt. 136 BW69
Broomcroft Ave.
Willett Clo., Orp. 205 ES100
Willett Pl., Th.Hth. 201 DN99
Willett Rd.
Willett Rd., Th.Hth. 201 DN99
Willett Way, Orp. 205 ER99
Willetts La., Uxb. 113 BF63
Willey Broom La., Cat. 251 DN125
Willey Fm. La., Cat. 252 DQ126
Willey La., Cat. 252 DR125
William Barefoot Dr. SE9 185 EM91
William Bonney Est. SW4 161 DK84
William Booth Rd. SE20 202 DU95
William Carey Way, Har. 117 CE58
William Clo., Rom. 105 FC53
William Clo., Sthl. 156 CC75
Windmill Ave.
William Cory Prom., Erith 167 FE78
Erith High St.
William Ct., Hem.H. 40 BK24
King Edward St.
William Covell Clo., Enf. 81 DM38
William Dunbar Ho. NW6 139 CZ68
William Ellis Clo., Wind. 172 AU85
William Ellis Way SE16 162 DU76
St. James's Rd.
William Evelyn Ct., Dor. 262 BZ139
William IV St. WC2 277 P1
William IV St. WC2 141 DL73
William Gdns. SW15 179 CV85
William Guy Gdns. E3 143 EB69
Talwin St.
William Margrie Clo. SE15 162 DU82
Moncrieff St.
William Ms. SW1 276 E5
William Morley Clo. E6 144 EK67
William Morris Clo. E17 123 DZ55
William Morris Way SW6 160 DC83
William Moulder Ct., Chesh. 54 AP28
William Nash Ct., Orp. 206 EW97
Brantwood Way
William Pl. E3 143 DZ68
Roman Rd.
William Rd. NW1 273 K3
William Rd. NW1 141 DJ69
William Rd. SW19 179 CY94
William Rd., Cat. 236 DR122
William Rd., Guil. 242 AW134
William Rd., Sutt. 218 DC106
William Russell Ct., Wok. 226 AS118
Raglan Rd.
William Saville Ho. NW6 139 CZ68
William Sq. SE16 143 DY73
Rotherhithe St.
William St. E10 123 EB58
William St. N17 100 DT52
William St. SW1 276 E5
William St. SW1 160 DF75
William St., Bark. 145 EQ66
William St., Berk. 38 AX19
William St., Cars. 200 DE104
William St., Grav. 191 GH87
William St., Grays 170 GB79
William St., Slou. 132 AT74
William St. (Bushey), Wat. 76 BX41
William St., Wind. 151 AR81
William Swayne Pl., Guil. 258 AY135
Station App.
Williams Ave. E17 101 DZ53
Williams Bldgs. E2 142 DW70
Williams Clo. N8 121 DK58
Coolhurst Rd.
Williams Clo., Add. 212 BH106
Monks Cres.
Williams Gro. N22 99 DN53
William's La. SW14 158 CQ83
Williams La., Mord. 200 DC99
Williams Rd. W13 137 CG73
Williams Rd., Sthl. 156 BY77
Williams Ter., Croy. 219 DN107
Williams Wk., Guil. 242 AV130
Grange Rd.
Williams Way, Rad. 77 CH35
Williamson Clo. SE10 164 EF77
Lenthorp Rd.
Williamson Rd. N4 121 DP58
Williamson St. N7 121 DL63
Williamson Way NW7 97 CY51
Williamson Way, Rick. 92 BG46
Willifield Way NW11 119 CZ56
Willingale Clo., Brwd. 109 GE44
Fairview Ave.
Willingale Clo., Loug. 85 EQ40
Willingale Rd.
Willingale Clo., Wdf.Grn. 102 EJ51
Willingale Rd., Loug. 85 EQ39
Willingdon Rd. N22 99 DP54
Willinghall Clo., Wal.Abb. 67 ED32
Willingham Clo. NW5 121 DJ64
Leighton Rd.
Willingham Ter. NW5 121 DJ64
Leighton Rd.
Willingham Way, Kings.T. 198 CN97
Willington Ct. E5 123 DY62
Mandeville St.
Willington Rd. SW9 161 DL83
Willis Ave., Sutt. 218 DE108
Willis Clo., Epsom 216 CP114
Willis Rd. E15 144 EF68
Willis Rd., Croy. 202 DQ101
Willis Rd., Erith 167 FC77
Willis St. E14 143 EB72
Willmore End SW19 200 DB95
Willoughby Ave., Croy. 219 DM105
Willoughby Clo., Brox. 49 DY21
Willoughby Dr., Rain. 147 FE66
Willoughby Gro. N17 100 DV52
Willoughby Ho. EC2 142 DR71
Moor La.
Willoughby La. N17 100 DV51
Willoughby Pk. Rd. N17 100 DV52
Willoughby Pas. E14 143 EA74
West India Ave.
Willoughby Rd. N8 121 DN55
Willoughby Rd. NW3 120 DD63
Willoughby Rd., Kings.T. 198 CM95
Willoughby Rd., Slou. 153 BA76
Willoughby Rd., Twick. 177 CK86
Willoughby St. WC1 273 P7
Willoughby Way SE7 164 EH77
Willoughbys, The SW14 158 CS84
Upper Richmond Rd. W.
Willow Ave. SW13 159 CT82
Willow Ave., Sid. 186 EU86
Willow Ave., Swan. 207 FF97
Willow Ave., Uxb. 114 BJ64
Willow Ave., West Dr. 134 BM73
Willow Bank SW6 159 CY83
Willow Bank, Rich. 177 CH90
Willow Bank, Wok. 226 AY122
Willow Brean, Horl. 268 DE146
Willow Bri. Rd. N1 142 DQ65
Willow Clo. W5 137 CK71
Willow Clo., Add. 211 BF111
Willow Clo., Bex. 186 EZ86
Willow Clo., Brent. 157 CJ79
Willow Clo., Brwd. 109 GB44
Willow Clo., Brom. 205 EM99
Willow Clo., Buck.H. 102 EK48
Willow Clo., Erith 167 FG81
Willow Rd.
Willow Clo., H.Wyc. 110 AC57
Willow Clo., Horn. 127 FH62
Willow Clo., Orp. 206 EV101
Willow Clo., Slou. 153 BC80
Willow Clo., Th.Hth. 201 DN100
Willow Clo. (Cheshunt), Wal.Cr. 66 DS26
Willow Cotts., Mitch. 201 DJ97
Willow Cotts., Rich. 158 CN79
Kew Grn.
Willow Ct. EC2 142 DS70
Willow St.
Willow Ct., Edg. 96 CL49
Willow Ct., Horl. 269 DH145
Willow Ct., St.Alb. 61 CK26
Willow Cres., St.Alb. 43 CJ20
Willow Cres. E., Uxb. 114 BJ64
Willow Cres. W., Uxb. 114 BJ64
Willow Dene, Pnr. 94 BX54
Willow Dene (Bushey), Wat. 95 CE45
Willow Dr., Barn. 79 CY42
Willow Dr., Wok. 228 BG124
Willow Edge, Kings L. 58 BN29
Willow End N20 98 DA47
Willow End, Nthwd. 93 BU51
Willow End, Surb. 198 CL102
Willow Fm. La. SW15 159 CV83
Queens Ride
Willow Gdns., Houns. 156 CA81
Willow Gdns., Ruis. 115 BT61
Willow Grn. NW9 96 CS53
Clayton Fld.
Willow Grn., Borwd. 78 CR43
Ashley Dr.
Willow Grn., Dor. 263 CH140
Holmesdale Rd.
Willow Gro. E13 144 EG68
Libra Rd.
Willow Gro., Chis. 185 EN93
Willow Gro., Ruis. 115 BT61
Willow La., Amer. 72 AT41
Willow La., Guil. 243 BA133
Boxgrove Rd.
Willow La., Mitch. 200 DF100
Willow La., Wat. 75 BU43
Willow La. Ind. Est., Mitch. 200 DF100
Willow Mead, Chig. 104 EU48
Willow Mead, Dor. 263 CG135
Portland Rd.
Willow Mead, Saw. 36 EY06
Willow Mt., Croy. 202 DS104
Langton Way
Willow Pk., Sev. 241 FF117
Willow Pk., Slou. 132 AU66
Willow Path, Wal.Abb. 68 EF34
Mason Way
Willow Pl. SW1 277 L8
Willow Pl. SW1 161 DJ77
Willow Pl., Wind. 151 AQ79
Willow Rd. NW3 120 DD63
Willow Rd. W5 158 CL75
Willow Rd., Dart. 188 FJ88
Willow Rd., Enf. 82 DS41
Willow Rd., Erith 167 FG81
Willow Rd., Gdmg. 258 AT143
Willow Rd., N.Mal. 198 CQ98
Willow Rd., Red. 266 DC137
Willow Rd., Rom. 126 EY58
Willow Rd., Slou. 153 BE82
Willow Rd., Wall. 219 DH108
Willow Side, St.Alb. 62 CL27
Willow St. E4 101 ED45
Willow St. EC2 275 M4
Willow St. EC2 142 DS70
Willow St., Rom. 127 FC56
Willow Tree Clo. E3 143 DZ67
Birdsfield La.
Willow Tree Clo. SW18 180 DB88
Cargill Rd.
Willow Tree Clo., Hayes 136 BW70
Willow Tree Clo., Uxb. 115 BQ62
Willow Tree La., Hayes 136 BW70
Willow Tree Wk., Brom. 204 EH95
Willow Vale W12 139 CU74
Willow Vale, Chis. 185 EP93
Willow Vale, Lthd. 230 CB123
Willow Vw. SW19 200 DD95
Willow Wk. E17 123 DZ57
Willow Wk. N2 98 DD54
Central Ave.
Willow Wk. N15 121 DP56
Willow Wk. N21 81 DM44
Willow Wk. SE1 279 N8
Willow Wk. SE1 162 DS77
Willow Wk., Cher. 194 BG101
Willow Wk., Dart. 188 FK85
Francis Rd.
Willow Wk., Egh. 172 AW92
Willow Wk., Guil. 260 BN139
Willow Wk., Orp. 205 EP104
Willow Wk., Red. 267 DH136
Ash Dr.
Willow Wk., Sutt. 199 CZ104
Willow Wk., Tad. 248 CQ130
Oak Dr.
Willow Wk., Upmin. 129 FS60
Willow Way N3 98 DB52
Willow Way SE26 182 DV90
Willow Way W11 139 CX74
Freston Rd.
Willow Way, Epsom 216 CR107
Willow Way, Gdse. 252 DU132

Willow Way, Guil. 242 AV130
Willow Way, Hat. 45 CT21
Willow Way, Hem.H. 40 BH18
Willow Way, Pot.B. 64 DB33
Willow Way, Rad. 77 CE36
Willow Way, Rom. 106 FP51
Willow Way, St.Alb. 60 CA27
Willow Way, Sun. 195 BU98
Willow Way, Tad. 248 CP130
Oak Dr.
Willow Way, Twick. 176 CB89
Willow Way, Wem. 117 CG62
Willow Way, W.Byf. 212 BJ111
Willow Way, Wok. 226 AX121
Willow Wd. Cres. SE25 202 DS100
Willowbank Gdns., Tad. 233 CV122
Willowbrook (Eton), Wind. 151 AR77
Willowbrook Rd. SE15 162 DT79
Willowbrook Rd., Sthl. 156 CA76
Willowbrook Rd., Stai. 174 BL89
Willowcourt Ave., Har. 117 CH57
Willowdene N6 120 DF59
Denewood Rd.
Willowdene, Brwd. 108 FT43
Willowdene, Wal.Cr. 67 DY27
Willowdene Clo., Twick. 176 CC87
Willowdene Ct., Brwd. 108 FW49
Willowfield, Harl. 51 ER17
Willowhayne Dr., Walt. 195 BV101
Willowhayne Gdns., Wor.Pk. 199 CW104
Willowherb Wk., Rom. 106 FJ52
Clematis Clo.
Willowmead, Hert. 31 DP10
Willowmead, Stai. 194 BH95
Northfield Rd.
Willowmead Clo. W5 137 CK71
Willowmead Clo., Wok. 226 AU116
Willowmere, Esher 214 CC105
Willows, The, Amer. 55 AP35
Willows, The, Buck.H. 102 EK48
Willows, The, Esher 215 CE107
Albany Cres.
Willows, The, Grays 170 GD79
Willows, The, Rick. 92 BG47
Uxbridge Rd.
Willows, The, St.Alb. 43 CH24
Willows, The, Wat. 93 BV45
Brookside Rd.
Willows, The, W.Byf. 212 BL113
Willows, The, Wey. 194 BN104
Willows Ave., Mord. 200 DB99
Willows Clo., Pnr. 94 BW54
Willows Path, Epsom 216 CP114
Willows Path, Wind. 150 AJ81
Willrose Cres. SE2 166 EV78
Wills Cres., Houns. 176 CB86
Wills Gro. NW7 97 CU50
Willson Rd., Egh. 172 AV92
Wilman Gro. E8 142 DU66
Wilmar Clo., Hayes 135 BR70
Wilmar Clo., Uxb. 134 BK66
Wilmar Gdns., W.Wick. 203 EB102
Wilmcote Ho. W2 140 DA71
Wilmer Clo., Kings.T. 178 CM92
Wilmer Cres., Kings.T. 178 CM92
Wilmer Gdns. N1 142 DS67
Wilmer Lea Clo. E15 143 EC66
Wilmer Pl. N16 122 DT61
Stoke Newington Ch. St.
Wilmer Way N14 99 DK50
Wilmerhatch La., Epsom 232 CP118
Wilmington Ave. W4 158 CR80
Wilmington Ave., Orp. 206 EW103
Wilmington Ct. Rd., Dart. 187 FG90
Wilmington Gdns., Bark. 145 ER65
Wilmington Sq. WC1 274 D3
Wilmington Sq. WC1 141 DN69
Wilmington St. WC1 274 D3
Wilmot Clo. N2 98 DC54
Wilmot Clo. SE15 162 DU80
Wilmot Grn., Brwd. 107 FW51
Wilmot Pl. NW1 141 DJ66
Wilmot Pl. W7 137 CE74
Boston Rd.
Wilmot Rd. E10 123 EB61
Wilmot Rd. N17 122 DR55
Wilmot Rd., Cars. 218 DF106
Wilmot Rd., Dart. 187 FG85
Wilmot Rd., Pur. 219 DN112
Wilmot Rd., Slou. 130 AH69
Wilmot St. E2 142 DV70
Wilmot Way, Bans. 218 DA114
Wilmots Clo., Reig. 250 DC133
Wilmount St. SE18 165 EP77
Wilna Rd. SW18 180 DC87
Wilsham St. W11 139 CX74
Wilshaw St. SE14 163 EA81
Wilshere Ave., St.Alb. 42 CC23
Wilsman Rd., S.Ock. 149 FW68
Wilsmere Dr., Har. 95 CE52
Wilsmere Dr., Nthlt. 136 BY65
Wilson Ave., Mitch. 180 DE94
Wilson Clo., Wem. 118 CM59
Wilson Clo., West Dr. 154 BK79
Hatch La.
Wilson Dr., Cher. 211 BB106
Wilson Dr., Wem. 118 CM59
Wilson Gdns., Har. 116 CC59
Wilson Gro. SE16 162 DV75
Wilson La., Dart. 209 FT96
Wilson Rd. E6 144 EK69
Wilson Rd. SE5 162 DS81
Wilson Rd., Chess. 216 CM107
Wilson Rd., Ilf. 125 EM59
Wilson St. E17 123 EC57
Wilson St. EC2 275 L6
Wilson St. EC2 142 DR71
Wilson St. N21 99 DN45
Wilson Way, Wok. 226 AX116
Wilsons, Tad. 233 CX121
Heathcote
Wilsons Pl. E14 143 DZ72
Salmon La.
Wilsons Rd. W6 159 CX78
Wilstone Clo., Hayes 136 BY70
Kingsash Dr.
Wilstone Dr., St.Alb. 43 CJ15
Wilthorne Gdns., Dag. 147 FB66
Acre Rd.
Wilton Ave. W4 158 CS78
Wilton Clo., West Dr. 154 BK79
Hatch La.
Wilton Cres. SW1 276 F5
Wilton Cres. SW1 160 DG75
Wilton Cres. SW19 199 CZ95
Wilton Cres., Beac. 89 AL52
Wilton Cres., Hert. 32 DQ12
Wilton Cres., Wind. 151 AK84
Wilton Dr., Rom. 105 FC52
Wilton Gdns., Walt. 196 BX102
Wilton Gdns., W.Mol. 196 CA97
Wilton Gro. SW19 199 CZ95
Wilton Gro., N.Mal. 199 CT100
Wilton La., Beac. 89 AR52
Wilton Ms. SW1 276 G6
Wilton Ms. SW1 160 DG76
Wilton Par., Felt. 175 BU89
Highfield Rd.
Wilton Pk. Ct. SE18 165 EN80
Prince Imperial Rd.
Wilton Pl. SW1 276 F5
Wilton Pl. SW1 160 DG75
Wilton Pl., Add. 212 BK108
Wilton Rd. N10 98 DG54
Wilton Rd. SE2 166 EW77
Wilton Rd. SW1 277 J7
Wilton Rd. SW1 161 DJ77
Wilton Rd. SW19 180 DE94
Wilton Rd., Barn. 80 DF42
Wilton Rd., Beac. 89 AL51
Wilton Rd., Houns. 156 BX83
Wilton Rd., Ilf. 125 EP62
Ilford La.
Wilton Rd., Red. 266 DF135
Wilton Row SW1 276 F5
Wilton Row SW1 160 DG75
Wilton Sq. N1 142 DR67
Wilton St. SW1 277 H6
Wilton St. SW1 161 DH76
Wilton Ter. SW1 276 F6
Wilton Ter. SW1 160 DG76
Wilton Vill. N1 142 DR67
Wilton Way E8 142 DU65
Wilton Way, Hert. 32 DQ11
Wiltshire Ave., Horn. 128 FM56
Wiltshire Ave., Slou. 131 AQ70
Wiltshire Clo. NW7 97 CT50
Wiltshire Clo. SW3 276 D9
Wiltshire Clo., Dart. 189 FR87
Wiltshire Gdns. N4 122 DQ58
Wiltshire Gdns., Twick. 176 CC88
Wiltshire La., Pnr. 115 BT55
Wiltshire Rd. SW9 161 DN83
Wiltshire Rd., Orp. 206 EU101
Wiltshire Rd., Th.Hth. 201 DN97
Wiltshire Row N1 142 DR67
Wilverley Cres., N.Mal. 198 CS100
Wimbart Rd. SW2 181 DM87
Wimbledon Bri. SW19 179 CZ93
Wimbledon Common SW19 179 CT91
Wimbledon Hill Rd. SW19 179 CY93
Wimbledon Pk. SW19 179 CZ89
Wimbledon Pk. Est. SW19 179 CZ88
Wimbledon Pk. Rd. SW18 179 CZ88
Wimbledon Pk. Rd. SW19 179 CY89
Wimbledon Pk. Side SW19 179 CX89
Wimbledon Rd. SW17 180 DC91
Wimbledon Sta. SW19 179 CZ93
The Bdy.
Wimbolt St. E2 142 DU69
Wimborne Ave., Hayes 135 BV72
Wimborne Ave., Sthl. 156 CA77
Wimborne Clo. SE12 184 EF85
Wimborne Clo., Buck.H. 102 EJ47
Wimborne Clo., Epsom 216 CS113
Wimborne Clo., Saw. 36 EX05
Wimborne Clo., Wor.Pk. 199 CW102
Wimborne Dr. NW9 118 CN55
Wimborne Dr., Pnr. 116 BX59
Wimborne Gdns. W13 137 CH71
Wimborne Gro., Wat. 75 BS37
Wimborne Rd. N9 100 DU47
Wimborne Rd. N17 100 DS54
Wimborne Way, Beck. 203 DX98
Wimbourne Ave., Orp. 205 ET98
Wimbourne Ave., Red. 266 DF139
Wimbourne Ct. N1 142 DR68
Wimbourne St.
Wimbourne St. N1 142 DR68
Wimbrel Clo., S.Croy. 220 DR111
Wimpole Clo., Brom. 204 EJ98
Stanley Rd.
Wimpole Clo., Kings.T. 198 CM96
Wimpole Ms. W1 273 H6
Wimpole Ms. W1 141 DH71
Wimpole Rd., West Dr. 134 BK74
Wimpole St. W1 273 H7
Wimpole St. W1 141 DH72
Wimshurst Clo., Croy. 201 DL101
Winans Wk. SW9 161 DN82
Wincanton Cres., Nthlt. 116 CA64
Wincanton Gdns., Ilf. 125 EP55
Wincanton Rd. SW18 179 CZ87
Wincanton Rd., Rom. 106 FK48
Winch Dells, Hem.H. 40 BN23
Winchcomb Gdns. SE9 164 EK83
Winchcombe Rd., Cars. 200 DD103
Winchelsea Ave., Bexh. 166 EZ80
Winchelsea Clo. SW15 179 CX85
Winchelsea Rd. E7 124 EG63
Winchelsea Rd. N17 122 DS55
Winchelsea Rd. NW10 138 CR67
Winchelsey Ri., S.Croy. 220 DT107
Winchendon Rd. SW6 159 CZ80
Winchendon Rd., Tedd. 177 CD91
Winchester Ave. NW6 139 CY67
Winchester Ave. NW9 118 CM55
Winchester Ave., Houns. 156 BZ79
Winchester Ave., Upmin. 129 FT60
Winchester Clo. E6 144 EL72
Boultwood Rd.
Winchester Clo. SE17 278 G9
Winchester Clo. SE17 161 DP77
Winchester Clo., Amer. 55 AS39
Lincoln Pk.
Winchester Clo., Brom. 204 EF97
Winchester Clo., Enf. 82 DS43
Winchester Clo., Esher 214 CA105
Winchester Clo., Kings.T. 178 CP94
Winchester Clo., Slou. 153 BE81
Winchester Cres., Grav. 191 GK90
Winchester Cres., H.Wyc. 88 AC53
Winchester Dr., Pnr. 116 BX57
Winchester Gro., Sev. 257 FH123
Winchester Ho. SE18 164 EK80
Shooter's Hill Rd.
Winchester Ms. NW3 140 DD66
Winchester Rd.
Winchester Pk., Brom. 204 EF97
Winchester Pl. E8 122 DT64
Kingsland High St.
Winchester Pl. N6 121 DH60
Cromwell Ave.
Winchester Pl. W3 158 CQ75
Avenue Rd.
Winchester Rd. E4 101 EC52
Winchester Rd. N6 121 DH59
Winchester Rd. N9 100 DU47
Winchester Rd. NW3 140 DD66
Winchester Rd., Bexh. 166 EX82
Winchester Rd., Brom. 204 EF97
Winchester Rd., Felt. 176 BZ90
Winchester Rd., Har. 118 CL56
Winchester Rd., Hayes 155 BS80
Winchester Rd., Ilf. 125 ER62
Winchester Rd., Nthwd. 93 BT54
Winchester Rd., Orp. 224 EW105
Winchester Rd., Twick. 177 CH87
Winchester Rd., Walt. 195 BU102
Winchester Sq. SE1 279 K2
Winchester St. SW1 277 J10
Winchester St. SW1 161 DH78
Winchester St. W3 158 CQ75
Winchester Wk. SE1 279 K2
Winchester Wk. SE1 142 DR74
Winchester Way, Rick. 75 BP43
Winchet Wk., Croy. 202 DW100
Medway Clo.
Winchfield Clo., Har. 117 CJ58
Winchfield Rd. SE26 183 DY92
Winchfield Way, Rick. 92 BJ45
Winchilsea Cres., W.Mol. 196 CC96
Winchmore Hill Rd. N14 99 DK46
Winchmore Hill Rd. N21 99 DM45
Winchstone Clo., Shep. 194 BM98
Winckley Clo., Har. 118 CM57
Wincott St. SE11 278 E9
Wincott St. SE11 161 DN77
Wincrofts Dr. SE9 165 ER84
Wind Hill, Ong. 53 FF20
Windborough Rd., Cars. 218 DG108
Windermere Ave. N3 120 DA55
Windermere Ave. NW6 139 CY67
Windermere Ave. SW19 200 DB97
Windermere Ave., Har. 117 CJ59
Windermere Ave., Horn. 127 FG64
Windermere Ave., Ruis. 116 BW59
Windermere Ave., St.Alb. 43 CH22
Windermere Ave., Wem. 117 CJ59
Windermere Clo., Dart. 187 FH88
Windermere Clo., Egh. 173 BB94
Derwent Rd.
Windermere Clo., Felt. 175 BT88
Windermere Clo., Hem.H. 41 BQ21
Windermere Clo., Orp. 205 EP104
Windermere Clo., Rick. 73 BD44
Windermere Clo., Stai. 174 BL88
Viola Ave.
Windermere Ct. SW13 159 CT79
Windermere Ct., Ken. 235 DP115
Windermere Gdns., Ilf. 124 EL57
Windermere Gro., Wem. 117 CJ60
Windermere Ave.
Windermere Ho., Islw. 177 CF85
Windermere Rd. N10 99 DH53
Windermere Rd. N19 121 DJ61
Holloway Rd.
Windermere Rd. SW15 178 CS91
Windermere Rd. SW16 201 DJ95
Windermere Rd. W5 157 CJ76
Windermere Rd., Bexh. 167 FC82
Windermere Rd., Couls. 235 DL115
Windermere Rd., Croy. 202 DT102
Windermere Rd., Sthl. 136 BZ71
Windermere Rd., W.Wick. 204 EE103
Windermere Way, Reig. 250 DE133
Windermere Way, West Dr. 134 BM74
Providence Rd.
Winders Rd. SW11 160 DE82
Windfield, Lthd. 231 CH121
Windfield Clo. SE26 183 DX91
Windgates, Guil. 243 BC131
Tychbourne Dr.
Windham Ave., Croy. 221 ED110
Windham Rd., Rich. 158 CM83
Windhill, Welw.G.C. 30 DA08
Windhover Way, Grav. 191 GL91
Winding Shot, Hem.H. 40 BG19
Winding Way, Dag. 126 EW62
Winding Way, Har. 117 CE63
Windings, The, S.Croy. 220 DT111
Windlass Pl. SE8 163 DY77
Windlesham Gro. SW19 179 CX88
Windley Clo. SE23 182 DW89
Windmere Way, Slou. 130 AJ71
Windmill Ave., Epsom 217 CT111
Windmill Ave., St.Alb. 43 CJ16
Windmill Ave., Sthl. 156 CC75
Windmill Clo. SE1 162 DU77
Beatrice Rd.
Windmill Clo. SE13 163 EC82
Windmill Clo., Cat. 236 DQ121
Windmill Clo., Epsom 217 CT112
Windmill Clo., Horl. 269 DH148
Windmill Clo., Sun. 175 BS94
Windmill Clo., Surb. 197 CJ102
Windmill Clo., Upmin. 128 FN61
Windmill Clo., Wal.Abb. 68 EE34
Windmill Clo., Wind. 151 AP82
Windmill Ct. NW2 139 CY65
Windmill Dr. SW4 181 DH85
Windmill Dr., Kes. 222 EJ105
Windmill Dr., Lthd. 231 CJ123
Windmill Dr., Reig. 250 DD132
Windmill Dr., Rick. 74 BM44
Windmill End, Epsom 217 CT112
Windmill Fld., Ware 33 DX07
Windmill Flds., Harl. 36 EZ11
Windmill Gdns., Enf. 81 DN41
Windmill Grn., Shep. 195 BS101
Windmill Gro., Croy. 202 DQ100
Windmill Hill NW3 120 DC62
Windmill Hill, Amer. 89 AM45
Windmill Hill, Enf. 81 DP41
Windmill Hill, Kings L. 57 BF32
Windmill Hill, Ruis. 115 BT59
Windmill La. E15 143 ED65
Windmill La., Barn. 79 CT44
Windmill La., Epsom 217 CT112
Windmill La., Grnf. 136 CC71
Windmill La., Islw. 157 CE77
Windmill La., Sthl. 156 CC75
Windmill La., Surb. 197 CH100
Windmill La. (Cheshunt), Wal.Cr. 67 DY30
Windmill La. (Bushey), Wat. 95 CD46
Windmill Ms. W4 158 CS77
Chiswick Common Rd.
Windmill Pas. W4 158 CS77
Chiswick Common Rd.
Windmill Ri., Kings.T. 178 CP94
Windmill Rd. N18 100 DR49
Windmill Rd. SW18 180 DD86
Windmill Rd. SW19 179 CW90
Windmill Rd. W4 158 CS77
Windmill Rd. W5 157 CJ77
Windmill Rd., Brent. 157 CK78
Windmill Rd., Croy. 202 DQ101
Windmill Rd., Ger.Cr. 90 AX52
Windmill Rd., Hmptn. 176 CB92
Windmill Rd., Hem.H. 40 BL20
Windmill Rd., Mitch. 201 DJ99
Windmill Rd., Sev. 257 FH130
Windmill Rd., Slou. 131 AR74
Windmill Rd. (Fulmer), Slou. 112 AX64
Windmill Rd., Sun. 195 BS95
Windmill Rd. W., Sun. 195 BS96
Windmill Row SE11 161 DN78
Windmill St. W1 273 M7
Windmill St. W1 141 DK71
Windmill St., Grav. 191 GH87
Windmill St. (Bushey), Wat. 95 CE46
Windmill Wk. SE1 278 E3
Windmill Wk. SE1 141 DN74
Windmill Way, Reig. 250 DD132
Windmill Way, Ruis. 115 BT60
Windmill Wd., Amer. 55 AN37
Windmore Ave., Pot.B. 63 CW31
Windover Ave. NW9 118 CR56
Windridge Clo., St.Alb. 42 CA22
Windridge Rd., St.Alb. 42 BX24
Windrose Clo. SE16 163 DX75
Windrush Ave., Slou. 153 BB76
Windrush Clo. SW11 160 DD84
Maysoule Rd.
Windrush Clo. W4 158 CQ81
Windrush Clo., Uxb. 114 BM63
Windrush La. SE23 183 DX90
Winds End Clo., Hem.H. 40 BN18
Winds Ridge, Wok. 243 BC125
Windsock Clo. SE16 163 DZ76
Windsor & Eton Relief Rd., Wind. 151 AP81
Windsor Ave. E17 101 DY54
Windsor Ave. SW19 200 DC95
Windsor Ave., Edg. 96 CP49
Windsor Ave., Grays 170 GB75
Windsor Ave., N.Mal. 198 CQ99
Windsor Ave., Sutt. 199 CY104
Windsor Ave., Uxb. 135 BP67
Windsor Ave., W.Mol. 196 CA97
Windsor Castle, Wind. 152 AS80
Windsor Cen., The SE27 182 DQ91
Advance Rd.
Windsor Clo. N3 97 CY54
Windsor Clo. SE27 182 DQ91
Windsor Clo., Borwd. 78 CN39
Warenford Way
Windsor Clo., Brent. 157 CH79
Windsor Clo., Chis. 185 EP92
Windsor Clo., Guil. 258 AT136
Windsor Clo., Har. 116 CA62
Windsor Clo., Hem.H. 40 BL22
Windsor Clo. (Bovingdon), Hem.H. 57 BA28
Windsor Clo., Nthwd. 93 BU54
Windsor Clo. (Cheshunt), Wal.Cr. 66 DU30
Windsor Ct. N14 99 DJ45
Windsor Ct., Sun. 175 BU93
Windsor Rd.
Windsor Ct. Rd., Wok. 210 AS109
Windsor Cres., Har. 116 CA62
Windsor Cres., Wem. 118 CP62
Windsor Dr., Ashf. 174 BK91
Windsor Dr., Barn. 80 DF44
Windsor Dr., Dart. 187 FG86
Windsor Dr., Hert. 31 DM09
Windsor Dr., Orp. 224 EU107
Windsor End, Beac. 111 AM55
Windsor Gdns. W9 140 DA71
Windsor Gdns., Croy. 201 DL104
Richmond Rd.
Windsor Gdns., Hayes 155 BR76
Windsor Gro. SE27 182 DQ91
Windsor Hill, H.Wyc. 110 AE58
Windsor La., Slou. 130 AJ70
Windsor Pk. Rd., Hayes 155 BT80
Windsor Pl. SW1 277 L7
Windsor Pl., Cher. 194 BG100
Windsor St.
Windsor Rd. E4 101 EB49
Chivers Rd.
Windsor Rd. E7 124 EH64
Windsor Rd. E10 123 EB61
Windsor Rd. E11 124 EG60
Windsor Rd. N3 97 CY54
Windsor Rd. N7 121 DL62
Windsor Rd. N13 99 DN48
Windsor Rd. N17 100 DU54
Windsor Rd. NW2 139 CV65
Windsor Rd. W5 138 CL73
Windsor Rd., Barn. 79 CX44
Windsor Rd., Beac. 111 AM55
Windsor Rd., Bexh. 166 EY84
Windsor Rd., Brwd. 108 FV44
Windsor Rd., Chesh. 54 AP28
Windsor Rd., Dag. 126 EY62
Windsor Rd., Egh. 172 AW88
Windsor Rd., Enf. 83 DX36
Windsor Rd., Ger.Cr. 112 AW60
Windsor Rd., Grav. 191 GH90
Windsor Rd., Har. 95 CD53
Windsor Rd., Horn. 128 FJ59
Windsor Rd., Houns. 155 BV82
Windsor Rd., Ilf. 125 EP63
Windsor Rd., Kings.T. 178 CL94
Windsor Rd., Maid. 150 AE79
Windsor Rd., Rich. 158 CM82
Windsor Rd., Slou. 152 AS76
Windsor Rd. (Datchet), Slou. 152 AU80
Windsor Rd. (Fulmer), Slou. 112 AU62
Windsor Rd., Sthl. 156 BZ76
Windsor Rd., Stai. 172 AY86
Windsor Rd., Sun. 175 BU93
Windsor Rd., Tedd. 177 CD92
Windsor Rd., Th.Hth. 201 DP96
Windsor Rd., Wat. 76 BW38
Windsor Rd., Wind. 150 AE79
Windsor Rd. (Eton), Wind. 151 AR79
Windsor Rd., Wok. 210 AS109
Windsor Rd., Wor.Pk. 199 CU103
Windsor St. N1 141 DP67
Windsor St., Cher. 194 BG100
Windsor St., Uxb. 134 BJ66
Windsor Ter. N1 275 J2
Windsor Ter. N1 142 DQ69
Windsor Wk. SE5 162 DR82
Windsor Wk., Walt. 196 BX102
King George Ave.
Windsor Wk., Wey. 213 BP106
Windsor Way W14 159 CX77
Windsor Way, Rick. 92 BG46
Windsor Way, Wok. 227 BC116
Windsor Wf. E9 123 DZ64
Windsor Wd., Wal.Abb. 68 EE33
Monkswood Ave.
Windsors, The, Buck.H. 102 EL47
Windspoint Dr. SE15 162 DV79
Ethnard Rd.
Windus Rd. N16 122 DT60
Windus Wk. N16 122 DT60
Alkham Rd.
Windward Clo., Enf. 83 DX35
Windy Hill, Brwd. 109 GC46
Windy Ridge, Brom. 204 EL95
Windycroft Clo., Pur. 219 DK113
Windyridge Clo. SW19 179 CX92
Wine Clo. E1 142 DW73
Wine Office Ct. EC4 274 E9
Winern Glebe, W.Byf. 212 BK113
Winery La., Kings.T. 198 CM97
Winford Dr., Brox. 49 DZ22
Winford Ho. E3 143 DZ66
Jodrell Rd.
Winforton St. SE10 163 EC81
Winfrith Rd. SW18 180 DC87
Wing Way, Brwd. 108 FW46
Geary Dr.
Wingate Cres., Croy. 201 DK100
Wingate Rd. W6 159 CV76
Wingate Rd., Ilf. 125 EP64
Wingate Rd., Sid. 186 EW93
Wingate Trd. Est. N17 100 DT52
Wingate Way, St.Alb. 43 CG21
Wingfield, Grays 170 FZ78
Wingfield Bank, Grav. 190 GC89
Wingfield Clo., Add. 212 BH110
Wingfield Clo., Brwd. 109 GA48
Pondfield La.
Wingfield Gdns., Upmin. 129 FS58
Wingfield Ms. SE15 162 DU83
Wingfield St.
Wingfield Rd. E15 124 EE63
Wingfield Rd. E17 123 EB57
Wingfield Rd., Grav. 191 GH87
Wingfield Rd., Kings.T. 178 CN93
Wingfield St. SE15 162 DU83
Wingfield Way, Ruis. 135 BV65
Wingford Rd. SW2 181 DL86
Wingletye La., Horn. 128 FM61
Wingmore Rd. SE24 162 DQ83
Wingrave Cres., Brwd. 108 FS49
Wingrave Rd. W6 159 CW79
Wingrove Rd. SE6 184 EE89
Wings Clo., Sutt. 218 DA105
Winifred Ave., Horn. 128 FK63
Winifred Gro. SW11 160 DF84
Winifred Rd. SW19 200 DA95
Winifred Rd., Couls. 234 DG116
Winifred Rd., Dag. 126 EY61
Winifred Rd., Dart. 187 FH85
Winifred Rd., Erith 167 FE78
Winifred Rd., Hmptn. 176 CA91
Winifred Rd., Hem.H. 40 BK24
Winifred St. E16 145 EM74
Winifred Ter. E13 144 EG68
Victoria Rd.
Winifred Ter., Enf. 100 DT45
Great Cambridge Rd.
Winkers Clo., Ger.Cr. 91 AZ53
Winkers La., Ger.Cr. 91 AZ53
Winkfield Rd. E13 144 EH68
Winkfield Rd. N22 99 DN53
Winkley St. E2 142 DV68
Winkwell, Hem.H. 39 BD22
Winkworth Pl., Bans. 217 CZ114
Bolters La.
Winkworth Rd., Bans. 218 DA114
Winlaton Rd., Brom. 183 ED91
Winmill Rd., Dag. 126 EZ62
Winn Common Rd. SE18 165 ES79
Winn Rd. SE12 184 EH88
Winnards, Wok. 226 AV118
Abercorn Way
Winnett St. W1 273 M10
Winnings Wk., Nthlt. 136 BY65
Arnold Rd.
Winnington Clo. N2 120 DD58
Winnington Rd. N2 120 DD60
Winnington Rd., Enf. 82 DW38
Winnington Way, Wok. 226 AV118
Winnipeg Dr., Orp. 223 ET107
Winnock Rd., West Dr. 134 BK74
Winns Ave. E17 123 DY55
Winns Ms. N15 122 DS56
Grove Pk. Rd.
Winns Ter. E17 101 EA54
Winsbeach E17 101 ED54
Winscombe Cres. W5 137 CK70
Winscombe St. N19 121 DH61
Winscombe Way, Stan. 95 CG50
Winsford Rd. SE6 183 DZ90
Winsford Ter. N18 100 DR50
Winsham Gro. SW11 180 DG85
Winslade Rd. SW2 181 DL85
Winslade Way SE6 183 EB87
Rushey Grn.
Winsland Ms. W2 140 DD72
London St.
Winsland St. W2 140 DD72
Winsley St. W1 273 K8

Winsley St. W1 141 DJ72
Winslow SE17 162 DS78
Kinglake St.
Winslow Clo. NW10 118 CS62
Neasden La. N.
Winslow Clo., Pnr. 115 BV58
Winslow Gro. E4 102 EE47
Winslow Rd. W6 159 CW79
Winslow Way, Felt. 176 BX90
Winslow Way, Walt. 196 BW104
Winsor Ter. E6 145 EN71
Winstanley Clo., Cob. 213 BV114
Winstanley Est. SW11 160 DD83
Winstanley Rd. SW11 160 DD83
Winstead Gdns., Dag. 127 FC64
Winston Ave. NW9 118 CS59
Winston Clo., Green. 189 FT85
Winston Clo., Har. 95 CF51
Winston Clo., Rom. 127 FB56
Winston Ct., Har. 94 CB52
Winston Dr., Cob. 230 BY116
Winston Gdns., Berk. 38 AT19
Winston Rd. N16 122 DR63
Winston Wk. W4 158 CR77
Acton La.
Winston Way, Ilf. 125 EP62
Winston Way, Pot.B. 64 DA33
Winston Way, Wok. 227 BB120
Winstone Clo., Amer. 54 AP34
Winstre Rd., Borwd. 78 CN39
Winter Ave. E6 144 EL67
Winter Box Wk., Rich. 158 CM84
Winterbourne Ave., Orp. 205 ER104
Winterbourne Gro., Wey. 213 BQ107
Winterbourne Rd. SE6 183 DZ88
Winterbourne Rd., Dag. 126 EW61
Winterbourne Rd., Th.Hth. 201 DN98
Winterbrook Rd. SE24 182 DQ86
Winterdown Gdns., Esher 214 BZ107
Winterdown Rd., Esher 214 BZ107
Winterfold Clo. SW19 179 CY89
Wintergreen Clo. E6 144 EL71
Yarrow Cres.
Winterhill Way, Guil. 243 BB130
Winters Cft., Grav. 191 GK93
Winters Rd., T.Ditt. 197 CH101
Winters Way, Wal.Abb. 68 EG33
Winterscroft Rd., Hodd. 49 DZ16
Wintersells Rd., W.Byf. 212 BK110
Winterstoke Gdns. NW7 97 CU50
Winterstoke Rd. SE6 183 DZ88
Winterton Ho. E1 142 DV72
Winterton Pl. SW10 160 DC79
Park Wk.
Winterwell Rd. SW2 181 DL85
Winthorpe Rd. SW15 159 CY84
Winthrop St. E1 142 DV71
Brady St.
Winthrop Wk., Wem. 118 CL62
Everard Way
Winton App., Rick. 75 BQ43
Winton Ave. N11 99 DJ52
Winton Clo. N9 101 DX45
Winton Cres., Rick. 75 BP43
Winton Dr., Rick. 75 BP44
Winton Dr. (Cheshunt), 67 DY29
Wal.Cr.
Winton Gdns., Edg. 96 CM52
Winton Rd., Orp. 223 EP105
Winton Rd., Ware 33 DZ06
Winton Way SW16 181 DN92
Wintoun Path, Slou. 131 AL70
Winvale, Slou. 152 AS76
Winwood, Slou. 132 AW72
Wireless Rd., West. 238 EK115
Wisbeach Rd., Croy. 202 DR99
Wisborough Rd., S.Croy. 220 DT109
Wisdons Clo., Dag. 127 FB60
Wise La. NW7 97 CU50
Wise La., West Dr. 154 BK76
Wise Rd. E15 143 ED67
Wiseman Ct. SE19 182 DT92
Wiseman Rd. E10 123 EA61
Wisemans Gdns., Saw. 36 EW06
High Wych Rd.
Wise's La., Hat. 63 CW27
Wiseton Rd. SW17 180 DE88
Wishart Rd. SE3 164 EK82
Wishbone Way, Wok. 226 AT116
Wishford Ct., Ash. 232 CM118
The Marld
Wisley Common, Wok. 228 BM117
Wisley La., Wok. 228 BJ116
Wisley Rd. SW11 180 DG85
Wisley Rd., Orp. 186 EU94
Wissants, Harl. 51 EP19
Wisteria Clo. NW7 97 CT51
Wisteria Clo., Brwd. 108 FV43
Wisteria Clo., Ilf. 125 EP64
Wisteria Clo., Orp. 205 EP103
Wisteria Gdns., Swan. 207 FD96
Wisteria Rd. SE13 163 ED84
Wistlea Cres., St.Alb. 44 CP22
Witan St. E2 142 DV69
Witches La., Sev. 256 FD123
Witchford, Welw.G.C. 30 DD09
Witham Clo., Loug. 84 EL44
Witham Rd. SE20 202 DW97
Witham Rd. W13 137 CG74
Witham Rd., Dag. 126 FA64
Witham Rd., Islw. 157 CD81
Witham Rd., Rom. 127 FH57
Withens Clo., Orp. 206 EW98
Wither Dale, Horl. 268 DE147
Witherby Clo., Croy. 220 DS106
Witherfield Way SE16 162 DV78
Egan Way
Witheridge La., H.Wyc. 88 AF48
Witherings, The, Horn. 128 FL57
Witherington Rd. N5 121 DN64
Withers Clo., Chess. 215 CJ107
Coppard Gdns.
Withers Mead NW9 97 CT53
Witherston Way SE9 185 EN89
Withey Clo., Wind. 151 AL81
Withey Meadows, Horl. 268 DD150
Witheygate Ave., Stai. 174 BH93
Withies, The, Lthd. 231 CH121
Withies, The, Wok. 226 AS117
Withy La., Ruis. 115 BQ57
Withy Mead E4 101 ED48
Withy Pl., St.Alb. 60 CC28
Withybed Cor., Tad. 233 CV123
Withycombe Rd. SW19 179 CX87
Withycroft, Slou. 132 AY72
Witley Cres., Croy. 221 EC107
Witley Gdns., Sthl. 156 BZ77
Witley Rd. N19 121 DJ61
Holloway Rd.
Witney Clo., Pnr. 94 BZ51
Witney Clo., Uxb. 114 BM63
Witney Path SE23 183 DX90
Inglemere Rd.
Wittenham Way E4 101 ED48
Wittering Clo., Kings.T. 177 CK92
Wittering Wk., Horn. 148 FJ65
Pembrey Way
Wittersham Rd., Brom. 184 EF92
Wivenhoe Clo. SE15 162 DV83
Wivenhoe Ct., Houns. 156 BZ84
Wivenhoe Rd., Bark. 146 EU68
Wiverton Rd. SE26 182 DW93
Wix Hill, Lthd. 245 BP130
Wix Rd., Dag. 146 EX67
Wixs La. SW4 161 DH83
Woburn Ave., Epp. 85 ES37
Woburn Ave., Horn. 127 FG63
Woburn Ave., Pur. 219 DN111
High St.
Woburn Clo. SE28 146 EX72
Summerton Way
Woburn Clo. SW19 180 DC93
Tintern Clo.
Woburn Clo. (Bushey), 76 CC43
Wat.
Woburn Hill, Add. 194 BJ103
Woburn Pl. WC1 273 N4
Woburn Pl. WC1 141 DK70
Woburn Rd., Cars. 200 DE102
Woburn Rd., Croy. 202 DQ102
Woburn Sq. WC1 273 N5
Woburn Sq. WC1 141 DK70
Woburn Wk. WC1 273 N3
Wodeland Ave., Guil. 258 AV136
Woffington Clo., Kings.T. 197 CJ95
Wokindon Rd., Grays 171 GH76
Woking Business Pk., 227 BB115
Wok.
Woking Clo. SW15 159 CT84
Woking Rd., Guil. 242 AW128
Wold, The, Cat. 237 EA122
Woldham Pl., Brom. 204 EJ98
Woldham Rd., Brom. 204 EJ98
Woldingham Rd., Cat. 236 DV120
Wolds Dr., Orp. 223 EN105
Wolf La., Wind. 151 AK83
Wolfe Clo., Brom. 204 EG100
Wolfe Clo., Hayes 135 BV69
Ayles Rd.
Wolfe Cres. SE7 164 EK78
Wolfe Cres. SE16 163 DX75
Wolferton Rd. E12 125 EM63
Wolffe Gdns. E15 144 EF65
Wolffram Clo. SE13 184 EE85
Wolfington Rd. SE27 181 DP91
Wolfs Hill, Oxt. 254 EG131
Wolf's Row, Oxt. 254 EH130
Wolfs Wd., Oxt. 254 EG132
Wolftencroft Clo. SW11 160 DD83
Wollaston Clo. SE1 279 H8
Wolmer Clo., Edg. 96 CP49
Wolmer Gdns., Edg. 96 CN48
Wolseley Ave. SW19 180 DA89
Wolseley Gdns. W4 158 CP79
Wolseley Rd. E7 144 EH66
Wolseley Rd. N8 121 DK58
Wolseley Rd. N22 99 DM53
Wolseley Rd. W4 158 CQ77
Wolseley Rd., Har. 117 CE55
Wolseley Rd., Mitch. 200 DG101
Wolseley Rd., Rom. 127 FD59
Wolseley St. SE1 162 DU75
Wolsey Ave. E6 145 EN69
Wolsey Ave. E17 123 DZ55
Wolsey Ave., T.Ditt. 197 CF99
Aragon Ave.
Wolsey Ave. (Cheshunt), 66 DT29
Wal.Cr.
Wolsey Clo. SW20 179 CV94
Wolsey Clo., Houns. 156 CC84
Wolsey Clo., Kings.T. 198 CP95
Wolsey Clo., Sthl. 156 CC76
Wolsey Clo., Wor.Pk. 217 CU105
Wolsey Cres., Croy. 221 EC109
Wolsey Cres., Mord. 199 CY101
Wolsey Dr., Kings.T. 178 CL92
Wolsey Dr., Walt. 196 BX102
Wolsey Gdns., Ilf. 103 EP51
Wolsey Gro., Edg. 96 CR52
Wolsey Gro., Esher 214 CB105
Wolsey Ms. NW5 141 DJ65
Wolsey Ms., Orp. 223 ET106
Osgood Ave.
Wolsey Pk., Wat. 93 BR45
Wolsey Rd. N1 122 DR64
Wolsey Rd., Ashf. 174 BL91
Wolsey Rd., E.Mol. 197 CD98
Wolsey Rd., Enf. 82 DV40
Wolsey Rd., Esher 214 CB105
Wolsey Rd., Hmptn. 176 CB93
Wolsey Rd., Hem.H. 40 BK21
Wolsey Rd., Nthwd. 93 BQ47
Wolsey Rd., Sun. 175 BT94
Wolsey St. E1 142 DW71
Sidney St.
Wolsey Wk., Wok. 226 AY117
Church St. W.
Wolsey Way, Chess. 216 CN106
Wolsley Clo., Dart. 187 FE85
Wolstan Clo., Uxb. 114 BG62
Lindsey Rd.
Wolstonbury N12 98 DA50
Wolvens La., Dor. 262 CA140
Wolvercote Rd. SE2 166 EX75
Wolverley St. E2 142 DV69
Bethnal Grn. Rd.
Wolverton SE17 279 M10
Wolverton Ave., Kings.T. 198 CN95
Wolverton Clo., Horl. 268 DF150
Wolverton Gdns. W5 138 CM73
Wolverton Gdns. W6 159 CX77
Wolverton Gdns., Horl. 268 DF149
Wolverton Rd., Stan. 95 CH51
Wolverton Way N14 81 DJ43
Wolves La. N13 99 DN51
Wolves La. N22 99 DN52
Wombwell Gdns., Grav. 190 GE89
Womersley Rd. N8 121 DM58
Wonersh Common, Guil. 259 BB141
Wonersh Common Rd., 259 BB142
Guil.
Wonersh Way, Sutt. 217 CX109
Wonford Clo., Kings.T. 198 CS95
Wonford Clo., Tad. 249 CU126
Wonham La., Bet. 264 CS135
Wonham Way, Guil. 261 BR139
Wontford Rd., Pur. 235 DN115
Wontner Clo. N1 142 DQ66
Greenman St.
Wontner Rd. SW17 180 DF89
Wooburn Common, 110 AF59
H.Wyc.
Wooburn Common Rd., 110 AG59
H.Wyc.
Wooburn Gra., H.Wyc. 110 AD60
Wooburn Grn. La., Beac. 110 AG56
Wooburn Manor Pk., 110 AE58
H.Wyc.
Wooburn Ms., H.Wyc. 110 AE58
Wooburn Town, H.Wyc. 110 AD59
Wood Ave., Purf. 168 FQ77
Wood Clo. E2 142 DU70
Wood Clo. NW9 118 CR59
Wood Clo., Bex. 187 FE90
Wood Clo., Har. 117 CD59
Wood Clo., Hat. 45 CV18
Wood Clo., Red. 266 DG143
Wood Clo., Wind. 151 AQ84
Wood Common, Hat. 45 CV15
Wood Cres., Hem.H. 40 BK21
Wood Dr., Chis. 184 EL93
Wood Dr., Sev. 256 FF126
Wood End, Hayes 135 BS72
Wood End, St.Alb. 60 CC28
Wood End Ave., Har. 116 CB63
Wood End Clo., Hem.H. 41 BQ19
Wood End Clo., Nthlt. 117 CD64
Wood End Clo., Slou. 111 AR62
Wood End Gdns., Nthlt. 116 CC64
Wood End Grn. Rd., Hayes 135 BR71
Wood End La., Nthlt. 136 CB65
Wood End Rd., Har. 117 CD63
Wood End Way, Nthlt. 116 CC64
Wood Fm. Rd., Hem.H. 40 BL20
Wood Grn. Way 67 DY31
(Cheshunt), Wal.Cr.
Holme Clo.
Wood Ho. La., Brox. 48 DT21
Wood La. N6 121 DH58
Wood La. NW9 118 CS59
Wood La. W12 139 CW72
Wood La., Cat. 236 DR124
Wood La., Dag. 126 EW63
Wood La., Dart. 189 FR91
Wood La., Horn. 127 FG64
Wood La., Islw. 157 CE79
Wood La., Iver 133 BC69
Wood La., Ruis. 115 BR60
Wood La., Slou. 151 AM76
Wood La., Stan. 95 CG48
Wood La., Tad. 233 CZ117
Brighton Rd.
Wood La., Ware 33 EA05
Wood La., Wey. 213 BQ109
Wood La., Wdf.Grn. 102 EF49
Wood La. Clo., Iver 133 BB69
Wood La. End, Hem.H. 40 BN19
Wood Lo. Gdns., Brom. 184 EL94
Wood Lo. La., W.Wick. 203 EC104
Wood Meads, Epp. 70 EU29
Wood Pt. E16 144 EG71
Fife Rd.
Wood Pond Clo., Beac. 89 AQ51
Wood Retreat SE18 165 ER80
Clothworkers Rd.
Wood Ride, Barn. 80 DD39
Wood Ride, Orp. 205 ER98
Wood Riding, Wok. 227 BF115
Pyrford Wds. Rd.
Wood Ri., Guil. 242 AS132
Wood Rd., Gdmg. 258 AT144
Wood Rd., Shep. 194 BN98
Wood Rd., West. 238 EJ118
Wood St. E16 144 EH73
Ethel Rd.
Wood St. E17 123 EC55
Wood St. EC2 275 J9
Wood St. EC2 142 DQ72
Wood St. W4 158 CS78
Wood St., Barn. 79 CW42
Wood St., Grays 170 GC79
Wood St., Kings.T. 198 CL95
Wood St., Mitch. 200 DG101
Wood St., Red. 251 DJ129
Wood St., Swan. 208 FJ95
Wood Vale N10 121 DJ57
Wood Vale SE23 182 DV88
Wood Vale, Hat. 45 CV18
Wood Vale Est. SE23 182 DW86
Wood Vw., Hem.H. 40 BH18
Wood Vw. (Cuffley), Pot.B. 65 DL27
Wood Wk., Rick. 73 BE40
Wood Way, Beac. 88 AF54
Wood Way, Orp. 205 EN103
Wood Wf. SE10 163 EB79
Thames St.
Woodall Clo. E14 143 EB73
Lawless St.
Woodall Rd., Enf. 83 DX44
Woodbank Ave., Ger.Cr. 112 AX58
Woodbank Dr., Ch.St.G. 90 AX48
Woodbank Rd., Brom. 184 EF90
Woodbastwick Rd. SE26 183 DX92
Woodberry Ave. N21 99 DN47
Woodberry Ave., Har. 116 CB56
Woodberry Clo., Sun. 175 BU93
Ashridge Way
Woodberry Cres. N10 121 DH55
Woodberry Down N4 122 DQ59
Woodberry Down, Epp. 70 EU29
Woodberry Down Est. N4 122 DQ59
Woodberry Gdns. N12 98 DC51
Woodberry Gro. N4 122 DQ59
Woodberry Gro. N12 98 DC51
Woodberry Gro., Bex. 187 FD90
Woodberry Way E4 101 EC46
Woodberry Way N12 98 DC51
Woodbine Clo., Harl. 51 EQ17
Linford End
Woodbine Clo., Twick. 177 CD89
Woodbine Clo., Wal.Abb. 84 EJ35
Woodbine Gro. SE20 182 DV94
Woodbine Gro., Enf. 82 DR38
Woodbine La., Wor.Pk. 199 CV104
Woodbine Pl. E11 124 EG58
Woodbine Rd., Sid. 185 ES88
Woodbine Ter. E9 142 DW65
Morning La.
Woodbines Ave., Kings.T. 197 CK97
Woodborough Rd. SW15 159 CV84
Woodbourne Ave. SW16 181 DK90
Woodbourne Clo. SW16 181 DL90
Woodbourne Ave.
Woodbourne Dr., Esher 215 CF107
Woodbourne Gdns., Wall. 219 DH108
Woodbridge Ave., Lthd. 231 CG118
Woodbridge Clo. N7 121 DM61
Woodbridge Clo. NW2 119 CU62
Woodbridge Clo., Rom. 106 FK49
Woodbridge Ct., Wdf.Grn. 102 EL52
Woodbridge Gro., Lthd. 231 CG118
Woodbridge Hill, Guil. 242 AV133
Woodbridge Hill Gdns., 242 AU133
Guil.
Woodbridge La., Rom. 106 FK48
Woodbridge Meadows, 242 AW133
Guil.
Woodbridge Rd., Bark. 125 ET64
Woodbridge Rd., Guil. 242 AV133
Woodbridge St. EC1 274 F4
Woodbridge St. EC1 141 DP70
Woodbrook Gdns., 68 EE33
Wal.Abb.
Woodbrook Rd. SE2 166 EU79
Woodburn Clo. NW4 119 CX57
Woodburn Clo., Uxb. 135 BP70
Aldenham Dr.
Woodbury, B.End 110 AC59
Woodbury Clo. E11 124 EH56
Woodbury Clo., Croy. 202 DT103
Woodbury Clo., West. 239 EM118
Woodbury Dr., Sutt. 218 DC110
Woodbury Hill, Loug. 84 EL41
Woodbury Hollow, Loug. 84 EL40
Woodbury Pk. Rd. W13 137 CH70
Woodbury Rd. E17 123 EB56
Woodbury Rd., West. 239 EM118
Woodbury St. SW17 180 DE92
Woodchester Pk., Beac. 88 AJ49
Woodchester Sq. W2 140 DB71
Woodchurch Clo., Sid. 185 ER90
Woodchurch Dr., Brom. 184 EK94
Woodchurch Rd. NW6 140 DA66
Woodclyffe Dr., Chis. 205 EN96
Woodcock Ct., Har. 118 CL59
Woodcock Dell Ave., Har. 117 CK59
Woodcock Hill, Har. 117 CJ57
Woodcock Hill, Rick. 92 BL50
Woodcock Hill, St.Alb. 28 CN14
Woodcock Hill Trd. Est., 92 BL49
Rick.
Woodcocks E16 144 EJ71
Woodcombe Cres. SE23 182 DW88
Woodcote, Guil. 258 AV138
Woodcote, Horl. 269 DJ147
The Fieldings
Woodcote Ave. NW7 97 CW51
Woodcote Ave., Horn. 127 FG63
Woodcote Ave., Th.Hth. 201 DP98
Woodcote Ave., Wall. 219 DH109
Woodcote Clo., Enf. 82 DW44
Woodcote Clo., Epsom 216 CR114
Woodcote Clo., Kings.T. 178 CM92
Woodcote Clo. 66 DW30
(Cheshunt), Wal.Cr.
Woodcote Dr., Orp. 205 ER102
Woodcote Dr., Pur. 219 DK110
Woodcote End, Epsom 232 CR115
Woodcote Grn., Wall. 219 DJ109
Woodcote Grn. Rd., 232 CQ116
Epsom
Woodcote Gro., Cars. 219 DH112
Woodcote Gro. Rd., Couls. 235 DK115
Woodcote Hurst, Epsom 232 CQ116
Woodcote La., Pur. 219 DK111
Woodcote Ms., Wall. 219 DH107
Woodcote Pk. Ave., Pur. 219 DJ112
Woodcote Pk. Rd., Epsom 232 CQ116
Woodcote Pl. SE27 181 DP92
Woodcote Rd. E11 124 EG59
Woodcote Rd., Epsom 216 CR114
Woodcote Rd., Wall. 219 DH107
Woodcote Side, Epsom 232 CP115
Woodcote Valley Rd., Pur. 219 DK113
Woodcrest Rd., Pur. 219 DL113
Woodcrest Wk., Reig. 250 DE132
Woodcroft N21 99 DM46
Woodcroft SE9 185 EM90
Woodcroft, Grnf. 137 CG65
Woodcroft, Harl. 51 EQ17
Woodcroft Ave. NW7 96 CS52
Woodcroft Ave., Stan. 95 CF53
Woodcroft Ave., Ware 33 ED11
Woodcroft Cres., Uxb. 135 BP67
Woodcroft Rd., Chesh. 54 AR28
Woodcroft Rd., Th.Hth. 201 DP99
Woodcutters Ave., Grays 170 GC75
Woodedge Clo. E4 102 EF46
Woodend SE19 182 DQ93
Woodend, Esher 196 CC103
Woodend, Lthd. 247 CJ125
Woodend, Sutt. 200 DC103
Woodend, The, Wall. 219 DH109
Woodend Clo., Wok. 226 AU119
Woodend Gdns., Enf. 81 DL42
Woodend Pk., Cob. 230 BX115
Woodend Rd. E17 101 EC54
Wooder Gdns. E7 124 EG63
Wooderson Clo. SE25 202 DS98
Woodfall Ave., Barn. 79 CZ43
Woodfall Dr., Dart. 167 FE84
Woodfall Rd. N4 121 DN60
Woodfall St. SW3 160 DF78
Woodfarrs SE5 162 DR84
Woodfield, Ash. 231 CK117
Woodfield Ave. NW9 118 CS56
Woodfield Ave. SW16 181 DK90
Woodfield Ave. W5 137 CJ70
Woodfield Ave., Cars. 218 DG107
Woodfield Ave., Grav. 191 GH88
Woodfield Ave., Nthwd. 93 BS49
Woodfield Ave., Wem. 117 CJ62
Woodfield Clo. SE19 182 DQ94
Woodfield Clo., Ash. 231 CK117
Woodfield Clo., Couls. 235 DJ119
Woodfield Clo., Enf. 82 DS42
Woodfield Clo., Red. 250 DE133
Woodfield Cres. W5 137 CK70
Woodfield Dr., Barn. 98 DG46
Woodfield Dr., Hem.H. 41 BR22
Woodfield Dr., Rom. 127 FG56
Woodfield Gdns. W9 139 CZ71
Woodfield Rd.
Woodfield Gdns., Hem.H. 41 BR22
Woodfield Gdns., N.Mal. 199 CT99
Woodfield Gro. SW16 181 DK90
Woodfield Hill, Couls. 235 DH119
Woodfield La. SW16 181 DK90
Woodfield La., Ash. 232 CL117
Woodfield La., Hat. 46 DD23
Woodfield La., Hert. 46 DD23
Woodfield Pk., Amer. 55 AN37
Woodfield Pl. W9 139 CZ70
Woodfield Ri. (Bushey), 95 CD45
Wat.
Woodfield Rd. W5 137 CJ70
Woodfield Rd. W9 139 CZ71
Woodfield Rd., Ash. 231 CK117
Woodfield Rd., Houns. 155 BV82
Woodfield Rd., Rad. 77 CG36
Woodfield Rd., T.Ditt. 197 CF103
Woodfield Rd., Welw.G.C. 29 CZ09
Woodfield Ter., Epp. 70 EW25
High Rd.
Woodfield Ter., Uxb. 92 BH54
Woodfield Way N11 99 DK52
Woodfield Way, Horn. 128 FK60
Woodfield Way, Red. 250 DE132
Woodfield Way, St.Alb. 43 CJ17
Woodfields, Sev. 256 FD122
Woodfields, The, S.Croy. 220 DT111
Woodfines, The, Horn. 128 FK58
Woodford Ave., Ilf. 124 EL55
Woodford Bri. Rd., Ilf. 124 EK55
Woodford Ct. W12 159 CX75
Shepherds Bush Grn.
Woodford Ct., Wal.Abb. 68 EG33
Woodford Cres., Pnr. 93 BV54
Woodford New Rd. E17 124 EE56
Woodford New Rd. E18 102 EE54
Woodford New Rd., 102 EF52
Wdf.Grn.
Woodford Pl., Wem. 118 CL60
Woodford Rd. E7 124 EH63
Woodford Rd. E18 124 EG56
Woodford Rd., Wat. 75 BV40
Woodford Trd. Est., 102 EK54
Wdf.Grn.
Woodford Way, Slou. 131 AN69
Woodgate, Wat. 59 BV33
Woodgate Ave., Chess. 215 CK106
Woodgate Cres., Nthwd. 93 BU51
Woodgate Dr. SW16 181 DK94
Woodgavil, Bans. 233 CZ116
Woodger Clo., Guil. 243 BC132
Kingfisher Dr.
Woodger Rd. W12 159 CW75
Goldhawk Rd.
Woodgers Gro., Swan. 207 FF96
Woodget Clo. E6 144 EL72
Remington Rd.
Woodgrange Ave. N12 98 DD51
Woodgrange Ave. W5 138 CN74
Woodgrange Ave., Enf. 82 DU44
Woodgrange Ave., Har. 117 CJ57
Woodgrange Clo., Har. 117 CK57
Woodgrange Gdns., Enf. 82 DU44
Woodgrange Rd. E7 124 EH64
Woodgrange Ter., Enf. 82 DU44
Great Cambridge Rd.
Woodgreen Rd., Wal.Abb. 68 EH33
Woodhall Ave. SE21 182 DT90
Woodhall Ave., Pnr. 94 BY54
Woodhall Clo., Hert. 32 DQ07
Woodhall Clo., Uxb. 114 BK64
Woodhall Ct., Welw.G.C. 29 CY10
Woodhall Cres., Horn. 128 FM59
Woodhall Dr. SE21 182 DT90
Woodhall Dr., Pnr. 94 BX53
Woodhall Gate, Pnr. 94 BX52
Woodhall La., Hem.H. 40 BL19
Woodhall La., Rad. 78 CL35
Woodhall La., Wat. 94 BX48
Woodhall La., Welw.G.C. 29 CY10
Woodhall Par., Welw.G.C. 29 CZ11
Woodhall Rd., Pnr. 94 BX52
Woodham Ct. E18 124 EF56
Woodham La., Add. 212 BG110
Woodham La., Wok. 211 BB114
Woodham Pk. Rd., Add. 211 BF109
Woodham Pk. Way, Add. 211 BF111
Woodham Ri., Wok. 211 AZ114
Woodham Rd. SE6 183 EC90
Woodham Rd., Wok. 211 AZ114
Woodham Waye, Wok. 211 BB114
Woodhatch Clo. E6 144 EL72
Remington Rd.
Woodhatch Rd., Red. 266 DC137
Woodhatch Rd., Reig. 266 DB137
Woodhatch Spinney, 235 DL116
Couls.
Woodhaven Gdns., Ilf. 125 EQ55
Brandville Gdns.
Woodhaw, Egh. 173 BB91
Woodhayes, Horl. 269 DH147
Woodhayes Rd. SW19 179 CW94
Woodhead Dr., Orp. 205 ES103
Sherlies Ave.
Woodheyes Rd. NW10 118 CR64
Woodhill SE18 164 EL77
Woodhill, Harl. 51 ES19
Woodhill, Wok. 243 BD126
Woodhill Ave., Ger.Cr. 113 AZ58
Woodhill Cres., Har. 117 CK58
Woodhouse Ave., Grnf. 137 CF68
Woodhouse Clo., Grnf. 137 CF68
Woodhouse Clo., Hayes 155 BS76
Woodhouse Eaves, 93 BU50
Nthwd.
Woodhouse Gro. E12 144 EL65
Woodhouse La., Dor. 261 BU143
Woodhouse Rd. E11 124 EF62
Woodhouse Rd. N12 98 DC51
Woodhurst Ave., Orp. 205 EQ100
Woodhurst Ave., Wat. 60 BX34
Woodhurst Dr., Uxb. 113 BF57
Woodhurst La., Oxt. 254 EE131
Woodhurst Pk., Oxt. 254 EE130
Woodhurst Rd. SE2 166 EU78
Woodhurst Rd. W3 138 CQ73

Worton Rd., Islw. 157 CD84
Worton Way, Houns. 157 CD82
Worton Way, Islw. 157 CD82
Wotton Dr., Dor. 262 BZ139
Wotton Grn., Orp. 206 EX98
Wotton Rd. NW2 119 CW62
Wotton Rd. SE8 163 DZ79
Wotton Way, Sutt. 217 CW110
Wouldham Rd. E16 144 EF72
Wouldham Rd., Grays 170 FY79
Wrabness Way, Stai. 194 BH95
Wragby Rd. E11 124 EE62
Wrampling Pl. N9 100 DU46
Wrangley Ct., Wal.Abb. 68 EG33
Wrangthorn Wk., Croy. 219 DN105
Epsom Rd.
Wray Ave., Ilf. 125 EN55
Wray Clo., Horn. 128 FJ59
Wray Common, Reig. 250 DD132
Wray Common Rd., Reig. 250 DC133
Wray Cres. N4 121 DL61
Wray La., Reig. 250 DC130
Wray Mill Pk., Reig. 250 DD132
Wray Pk. Rd., Reig. 250 DB133
Wray Rd., Sutt. 217 CZ109
Wrayfield Ave., Reig. 250 DC133
Wrayfield Rd., Sutt. 199 CX104
Wraylands Dr., Reig. 250 DD132
Wrays Way, Hayes 135 BS70
Balmoral Dr.
Wraysbury Clo., Houns. 176 BY85
Dorney Way
Wraysbury Rd., Stai. 173 BB89
Wrekin Rd. SE18 165 EQ80
Wren Ave. NW2 119 CW64
Wren Ave., Sthl. 156 BZ77
Wren Clo. E16 144 EF72
Ibbotson Ave.
Wren Clo. N9 101 DX46
Chaffinch Clo.
Wren Clo., Orp. 206 EX97
Wren Clo., S.Croy. 221 DX109
Wren Ct., Slou. 153 BA76
New Rd.
Wren Cres., Add. 212 BK106
Wren Cres. (Bushey), Wat. 94 CC46
Wren Dr., Wal.Abb. 68 EG34
Wren Dr., West Dr. 154 BK76
Wren Gdns., Dag. 126 EX64
Wren Gdns., Horn. 127 FF60
Wren Landing E14 143 EA74
Cabot Sq.
Wren Path SE28 165 ER76
Wren Pl., Brwd. 108 FX48
Wren Rd. SE5 162 DR81
Wren Rd., Dag. 126 EX64
Wren Rd., Sid. 186 EW91
Wren St. WC1 274 C4
Wren St. WC1 141 DM70
Wren Wk., Til. 171 GH80
Poynder Rd.
Wren Wd., Welw.G.C. 30 DB08
Wrens Ave., Ashf. 175 BQ91
Wrens Cft., Grav. 190 GE90
Wrens Hill, Lthd. 230 CC115
Wrensfield, Hem.H. 40 BG20
Wrentham Ave. NW10 139 CX68
Wrenthorpe Rd., Brom. 184 EE91
Wrenwood Way, Pnr. 115 BV56
Wrestlers Clo., Hat. 45 CW15
Wrestlers Ct. EC3 142 DS72
Camomile St.
Wrexham Rd. E3 143 EA68
Wrexham Rd., Rom. 106 FK48
Wricklemarsh Rd. SE3 164 EJ81
Wrigglesworth St. SE14 163 DX80
Wright Clo., Swans. 189 FX86
Milton St.
Wright Gdns., Shep. 194 BN99
Laleham Rd.
Wright Rd., Houns. 156 BW80
Wright Sq., Wind. 150 AJ83
Wright Way
Wright Way, Wind. 150 AJ83
Wrights All. SW19 179 CW93
Wrights Clo. SE13 163 ED84
Wisteria Rd.
Wrights Clo., Dag. 127 FB63
Wrights Grn. SW4 161 DK84
Nelson's Row
Wrights La. W8 160 DB76
Wrights Pl. NW10 138 CQ65
Mitchell Way
Wrights Rd. E3 143 DZ68
Wrights Rd. SE25 202 DS97
Wrights Row, Wall. 219 DH105
Wrights Wk. SW14 158 CR83
North Worple Way
Wrightsbridge Rd., Brwd. 106 FN46
Wrigley Clo. E4 101 ED50
Writtle Wk., Rain. 147 FE67
Wrotham Pk., Barn. 79 CZ36
Wrotham Rd. NW1 141 DJ66
Agar Pl.
Wrotham Rd. W13 137 CH74
Mattock La.
Wrotham Rd., Barn. 79 CY40
Wrotham Rd., Grav. 191 GG91
Wrotham Rd., Well. 166 EW81
Wroths Path, Loug. 85 EM39
Wrottesley Rd. NW10 139 CU68
Wrottesley Rd. SE18 165 EQ79
Wroughton Rd. SW11 180 DF85
Wroughton Ter. NW4 119 CV56
Wroxall Rd., Dag. 146 EW65
Wroxham Ave., Hem.H. 40 BK22
Wroxham Gdns. N11 99 DJ52
Wroxham Gdns., Enf. 81 DN35
Wroxham Gdns., Pot.B. 63 CX31
Wroxham Rd. SE28 146 EX73
Wroxton Rd. SE15 162 DV82
Wrythe Grn., Cars. 200 DF104
Wrythe Grn. Rd., Cars. 200 DF104
Wrythe La., Cars. 200 DC101
Wulfstan St. W12 139 CT71
Wyatt Clo. SE16 163 DZ75
Wyatt Clo., Felt. 176 BX88
Wyatt Clo., Hayes 135 BU71
Wyatt Clo., Wat. 95 CE45
Wyatt Dr. SW13 159 CV79
Wyatt Pk. Rd. SW2 181 DL89
Wyatt Rd. E7 144 EG65
Wyatt Rd. N5 122 DQ62
Wyatt Rd., Dart. 167 FF83
Wyatt Rd., Stai. 174 BG92
Wyatt Rd., Wind. 151 AK83
Wyatts Clo., Rick. 74 BG41
Wyatts La. E17 123 EC55
Wyatts Rd., Rick. 73 BF42
Wybert St. NW1 141 DJ70
Stanhope St.
Wyborne Way NW10 138 CQ66
Wyburn Ave., Barn. 79 CZ40
Wych Elm, Harl. 35 EQ14
Wych Elm Clo., Horn. 128 FN59
Wych Elm Dr., Brom. 184 EF94
London La.
Wych Elm Pas., Kings.T. 198 CM95
Wych Elm Ri., Guil. 258 AY137
Wych Elm Rd., Horn. 128 FN58
Wych Elms, St.Alb. 60 CB28
Wych Hill, Wok. 226 AW119
Wych Hill La., Wok. 226 AY119
Wych Hill Pk., Wok. 226 AX119
Wych Hill Ri., Wok. 226 AW119
Wych Hill Way, Wok. 226 AX120
Wyche Gro., S.Croy. 220 DR108
Wycherley Clo. SE3 164 EF80
Wycherley Cres., Barn. 80 DB44
Wychford Dr., Saw. 36 EW06
Wychwood Ave., Edg. 95 CK51
Wychwood Ave., Th.Hth. 202 DQ97
Wychwood Clo., Edg. 95 CK51
Wychwood Clo., Sun. 175 BU93
Wychwood End N6 121 DJ59
Wychwood Gdns., Ilf. 125 EM56
Wychwood Way SE19 182 DR93
Roman Ri.
Wychwood Way, Nthwd. 93 BT52
Wyclif St. EC1 274 F3
Wycliffe Clo., Well. 165 ET81
Wycliffe Ct., Abb.L. 59 BS32
Wycliffe Gdns., Red. 251 DJ130
Wycliffe Rd. SW11 160 DG82
Wycliffe Rd. SW19 180 DB93
Wycliffe Row, Grav. 191 GF88
Alfred Pl.
Wycombe End, Beac. 110 AH55
Wycombe Gdns. NW11 120 DA61
Wycombe La., H.Wyc. 110 AE56
Wycombe Pl. SW18 180 DC86
Wycombe Rd. N17 100 DU53
Wycombe Rd., Ilf. 125 EM57
Wycombe Rd., Wem. 138 CN67
Wycombe Way, St.Alb. 43 CH17
Wyddial Grn., Welw.G.C. 30 DB09
Widford Rd.
Wydehurst Rd., Croy. 202 DU101
Wydell Clo., Mord. 199 CX100
Wydeville Manor Rd. SE12 184 EH91
Wye, The, Hem.H. 40 BN15
Wye Clo., Ashf. 175 BP91
Wye Clo., Orp. 205 ET101
Wye Clo., Ruis. 115 BQ58
Wye Rd., Grav. 191 GK89
Wye Rd., H.Wyc. 110 AD55
Wye St. SW11 160 DD82
Wyedale, St.Alb. 62 CM27
Wyemead Cres. E4 102 EE47
Wyeth's Ms., Epsom 217 CT113
Wyeths Rd., Epsom 217 CT113
Wyevale Clo., Pnr. 115 BU55
Wyfields, Ilf. 103 EP53
Ravensbourne Gdns.
Wyfold Rd. SW6 159 CY81
Wyhill Wk., Dag. 147 FC65
Wyke Clo., Islw. 157 CF79
Wyke Gdns. W7 157 CF76
Wyke Rd. E3 143 EA66
Wyke Rd. SW20 199 CW96
Wykeham Ave., Dag. 146 EW65
Wykeham Ave., Horn. 128 FK58
Wykeham Clo., Grav. 191 GL93
Wykeham Clo., West Dr. 154 BN78
Wykeham Grn., Dag. 146 EW65
Wykeham Hill, Wem. 118 CM60
Wykeham Ri. N20 97 CY46
Wykeham Rd. NW4 119 CW57
Wykeham Rd., Guil. 243 BD133
Wykeham Rd., Har. 117 CH56
Wykeridge Clo., Chesh. 54 AP27
Wylands Rd., Slou. 153 BA77
Wylchin Clo., Pnr. 115 BT56
Wyld Way, Wem. 138 CP65
Wyldes Clo. NW11 120 DC60
Wildwood Rd.
Wyldfield Gdns. N9 100 DT47
Wyldwood Clo., Harl. 36 EW09
Wyleu St. SE23 183 DY87
Wylie Rd., Sthl. 156 CA76
Wyllen Clo. E1 142 DW70
Wyllyotts Clo., Pot.B. 63 CZ32
Wyllyotts La., Pot.B. 63 CZ32
Wyllyotts Pl., Pot.B. 63 CZ32
Wylo Dr., Barn. 79 CU44
Wymering Rd. W9 140 DA69
Wymers Clo., Slou. 130 AH68
Wymerswood Rd., Slou. 130 AG67
Wymond St. SW15 159 CW83
Wynan Rd. E14 163 EB78
Wynaud Ct. N22 99 DM51
Palmerston Rd.
Wyncham Ave., Sid. 185 ES88
Wynchgate N14 99 DK46
Wynchgate N21 99 DL45
Wynchgate, Har. 95 CE52
Wynchlands Cres., St.Alb. 43 CK20
Wyncote Way, S.Croy. 221 DX109
Wyncroft Clo., Brom. 205 EM97
Wyndale Ave. NW9 118 CN58
Wyndcliff Rd. SE7 164 EH79
Wyndcroft Clo., Enf. 81 DP41
Wyndham Ave., Cob. 213 BU113
Wyndham Clo., Orp. 205 EQ102
Wyndham Clo., Sutt. 218 DA108
Wyndham Cres. N19 121 DJ62
Wyndham Cres., Houns. 176 CA86
Wyndham Cres., Slou. 130 AH68
Wyndham Est. SE5 162 DQ80
Wyndham Ms. W1 272 D7
Wyndham Pl. W1 272 D7
Wyndham Pl. W1 140 DF71
Wyndham Rd. E6 144 EK66
Wyndham Rd. SE5 162 DQ80
Wyndham Rd. W13 157 CH76
Wyndham Rd., Barn. 98 DF46
Wyndham Rd., Kings.T. 178 CM94
Wyndham Rd., Wok. 226 AV118
Wyndham St. W1 272 D6
Wyndham St. W1 140 DF71
Wyndham Yd. W1 272 D7
Wyndhams End, Welw.G.C. 29 CZ13
Wyneham Rd. SE24 182 DR85
Wynell Rd. SE23 183 DX90
Wynford Gro., Orp. 206 EV97
Wynford Pl., Belv. 166 FA79
Wynford Rd. N1 141 DM68
Wynford Way SE9 185 EM90
Wyngrave Pl., Beac. 88 AJ50
Wynlie Gdns., Pnr. 93 BV54
Wynndale Rd. E18 102 EH53
Wynne Rd. SW9 161 DN82
Wynns Ave., Sid. 186 EU85
Wynnstay Gdns. W8 160 DA76
Wynnstow Pk., Oxt. 254 EF131
Wynnswick Rd., Beac. 89 AQ50
Wynter St. SW11 160 DC84
Wynton Gdns. SE25 202 DS99
Wynton Gro., Walt. 195 BU104
Wynton Pl. W3 138 CP72
Wynyard Clo., Rick. 74 BG36
Wynyard Ter. SE11 278 C10
Wynyard Ter. SE11 161 DM78
Wynyatt St. EC1 274 F3
Wyre Gro., Edg. 96 CP48
Wyre Gro., Hayes 155 BU77
Wyresdale Cres., Grnf. 137 CF69
Wysemead, Horl. 269 DJ147
Wyteleaf Clo., Ruis. 115 BQ58
Wythburn Pl. W1 272 D9
Wythens Wk. SE9 185 EP86
Wythenshawe Rd., Dag. 126 FA62
Wythes Clo., Brom. 205 EM96
Wythes Rd. E16 144 EL74
Wythfield Rd. SE9 185 EM86
Wyton, Welw.G.C. 30 DD09
Wyvenhoe Rd., Har. 116 CC62
Wyvern Clo., Dart. 188 FJ87
Wyvern Clo., Orp. 206 EV104
Wyvern Gro., Hayes 155 BP80
Wyvern Rd., Pur. 219 DP110
Wyvern Way, Uxb. 134 BH66
Wyvil Est. SW8 161 DL80
Luscombe Way
Wyvil Rd. SW8 161 DL79
Wyvis St. E14 143 EB71

Y

Yabsley St. E14 143 EC74
Yaffle Rd., Wey. 213 BQ110
Yalding Clo., Orp. 206 EX98
Yalding Rd. SE16 162 DU76
Yale Clo., Houns. 176 BZ85
Bramley Way
Yale Way, Horn. 127 FG63
Yarborough Rd. SW19 200 DD95
Runnymede
Yard Mead, Egh. 173 BA90
Yardbridge Clo., Sutt. 218 DB110
Yardley Clo. E4 83 EB43
Yardley Clo., Reig. 250 DB132
Yardley La. E4 83 EB43
Yardley St. WC1 274 D3
Yardley St. WC1 141 DN69
Yarm Clo., Lthd. 231 CJ123
Yarm Ct. Rd., Lthd. 231 CJ123
Yarm Way, Lthd. 231 CJ123
Yarmouth Cres. N17 122 DV57
Yarmouth Pl. W1 277 H3
Yarmouth Rd., Slou. 131 AQ73
Yarmouth Rd., Wat. 76 BW38
Yarnfield Sq. SE15 162 DU81
Clayton Rd.
Yarnton Way SE2 166 EX75
Yarnton Way, Erith 166 EX75
Yarrow Cres. E6 144 EL71
Yarrow Side, Amer. 72 AV40
Yarrowfield, Wok. 226 AX123
Yateley St. SE18 164 EK76
Yates Ct. NW2 139 CX65
Yattendon Rd., Horl. 269 DH148
Yeading Ave., Har. 116 BY61
Yeading Fork, Hayes 136 BW71
Yeading Gdns., Hayes 135 BV71
Yeading La., Hayes 135 BV72
Yeading La., Nthlt. 136 BW69
Yeames Clo. W13 137 CG72
Yeate St. N1 142 DR66
Yeatman Rd. N6 120 DF58
Yeats Clo. NW10 138 CS65
Yeats Clo. SE13 163 ED82
Eliot Pk.
Yeats Clo., Red. 266 DC137
Yeldham Rd. W6 159 CX78
Yellow Hammer Ct. NW9 96 CS54
Eagle Dr.
Yellowpine Way, Chig. 104 EV49
Yelverton Clo., Rom. 106 FK53
Yelverton Rd. SW11 160 DD82
Yenston Clo., Mord. 200 DA100
Yeo St. E3 143 EB71
Yeoman Clo. E6 145 EP72
Ferndale St.
Yeoman Clo. SE27 181 DP90
Yeoman Rd., Nthlt. 136 BY66
Yeoman St. SE8 163 DY77
Yeoman Way, Red. 267 DH139
Yeomanry Clo., Epsom 217 CT112
Dirdene Gdns.
Yeomans Acre, Ruis. 115 BU58
Yeomans Keep, Rick. 73 BF41
Rickmansworth Rd.
Yeomans Meadow, Sev. 256 FG126
Yeoman's Ms., Islw. 177 CE85
Queensbridge Pk.
Yeoman's Row SW3 276 C7
Yeoman's Row SW3 160 DE76
Yeomans Way, Enf. 82 DW40
Yeomans Yd. E1 142 DT73
Chamber St.
Yeomen Way, Ilf. 103 EQ51
Yeoveney Clo., Stai. 173 BD89
Yeovil Clo., Orp. 205 ES103
Yeovil Rd., Slou. 131 AL71
Yeovilton Pl., Kings.T. 177 CK92
Yerbury Rd. N19 121 DK62
Yester Dr., Chis. 184 EL94
Yester Pk., Chis. 185 EM94
Yester Rd., Chis. 184 EL94
Yevele Way, Horn. 128 FL59
Yew Ave., West Dr. 134 BL73
Yew Clo., Buck.H. 102 EK47
Yew Clo., Wal.Cr. 66 DS27
Yew Gro. NW2 119 CX63
Yew Gro., Welw.G.C. 30 DC10
Yew Pl., Wey. 195 BT104
Yew Tree Bottom Rd., Epsom 233 CV116
Yew Tree Clo. N21 99 DN45
Yew Tree Clo., Beac. 89 AM54
Yew Tree Clo., Brwd. 109 GB44
Yew Tree Clo., Chesh. 56 AU30
Botley Rd.
Yew Tree Clo., Couls. 234 DF119
Yew Tree Clo., Hem.H. 40 BG22
Fishery Rd.
Yew Tree Clo., Horl. 268 DG146
Yew Tree Clo., Sev. 256 FD123
Yew Tree Clo., Well. 166 EU81
Yew Tree Clo., Wor.Pk. 198 CS102
Yew Tree Ct., Borwd. 77 CK44
Barnet La.
Yew Tree Dr., Cat. 252 DT125
Yew Tree Dr., Guil. 242 AV130
Yew Tree Dr., Hem.H. 57 BB28
Yew Tree Gdns., Rom. 127 FD57
Yew Tree Gdns. (Chadwell Heath), Rom. 126 EY57
Yew Tree La., Reig. 250 DB131
Yew Tree Rd. W12 139 CT73
Yew Tree Rd., Dor. 247 CG134
Yew Tree Rd., Slou. 152 AU76
Yew Tree Rd., Uxb. 134 BM67
Yew Tree Wk., Houns. 176 BZ85
Yew Tree Wk., Lthd. 246 BX127
Yew Tree Wk., Maid. 110 AC64
Yew Tree Wk., Pur. 220 DQ110
Yew Tree Way, Croy. 221 DY110
Yew Trees, Egh. 193 BC97
Yew Trees, Shep. 194 BM98
Laleham Rd.
Yew Wk., Har. 117 CE60
Yew Wk., Hodd. 49 EA18
Yewbank Clo., Ken. 236 DR115
Yewdale Clo., Brom. 184 EE93
Yewdells Clo., Bet. 249 CU133
Yewfield Rd. NW10 139 CT65
Yewlands, Hodd. 49 EA18
Yewlands, Saw. 36 EY06
Yewlands Clo., Bans. 234 DB115
Yewlands Dr., Hodd. 49 EA18
Yews, The, Ashf. 175 BP91
Yews, The, Grav. 191 GK89
Yews Ave., Enf. 82 DV36
Yewtree Clo. N22 99 DJ53
Yewtree Clo., Har. 116 CB56
Yewtree End, St.Alb. 60 CB27
Yewtree Gdns., Epsom 232 CP115
Yewtree Rd., Beck. 203 DZ97
Yoakley Rd. N16 122 DS61
Yoke Clo. N7 141 DL65
Ewe Clo.
Yolande Gdns. SE9 184 EL85
Yonge Pk. N4 121 DN62
York Ave. SW14 178 CQ85
York Ave. W7 137 CE74
York Ave., Hayes 135 BQ71
York Ave., Sid. 185 ES89
York Ave., Slou. 131 AQ72
York Ave., Stan. 95 CH53
York Ave., Wind. 151 AP82
York Bri. NW1 272 F4
York Bri. NW1 140 DG70
York Bldgs. WC2 278 A1
York Clo. E6 145 EM72
Boultwood Rd.
York Clo. W7 137 CE74
York Ave.
York Clo., Amer. 72 AT39
York Clo., Brwd. 109 FZ45
York Clo., Kings L. 58 BN29
York Clo., Mord. 200 DB98
York Clo., W.Byf. 212 BL112
York Cres., Borwd. 78 CR40
York Cres., Loug. 84 EL41
York Gdns., Walt. 196 BX103
York Gate N14 99 DL45
York Gate NW1 272 F5
York Gate NW1 140 DG70
York Gate, Cat. 236 DR122
York Gro. SE15 162 DW81
York Hill SE27 181 DP90
York Hill, Loug. 84 EL41
York Hill Est. SE27 181 DP90
York Ho., Wem. 118 CM63
York Ho. Pl. W8 160 DB75
York Ms. NW5 121 DH64
Kentish Town Rd.
York Ms., Ilf. 125 EN62
York Rd.
York Par., Brent. 157 CK78
York Pl. SW11 160 DC83
York Pl. WC2 278 A1
York Pl., Dag. 147 FC65
York Pl., Grays 170 GA79
York Pl., Ilf. 125 EN61
York Rd.
York Ri. NW5 121 DH62
York Ri., Orp. 205 ES102
York Rd. E4 101 EA50
York Rd. E7 144 EG65
York Rd. E10 123 EC62
York Rd. E17 123 DX57
York Rd. N11 99 DK51
York Rd. N18 100 DV51
York Rd. N21 100 DR45
York Rd. SE1 278 C4
York Rd. SE1 161 DM75
York Rd. SW11 160 DC84
York Rd. SW18 160 DC84
York Rd. SW19 180 DC93
York Rd. W3 138 CQ72
York Rd. W5 157 CJ76
York Rd., Barn. 80 DC43
York Rd., Brent. 157 CK78
York Rd., Brwd. 109 FZ45
York Rd., Croy. 201 DN101
York Rd., Dart. 188 FM87
York Rd., Epp. 70 FA27
York Rd., Grav. 191 GJ90
York Rd. (Northfleet), Grav. 190 GD87
York Rd., Guil. 258 AX135
York Rd., Houns. 156 CB83
York Rd., Ilf. 125 EN62
York Rd., Kings.T. 178 CM94
York Rd., Nthwd. 93 BU54
York Rd., Rain. 147 FD66
York Rd., Rich. 178 CM85
Albert Rd.
York Rd., St.Alb. 43 CF19
York Rd., S.Croy. 221 DX110
York Rd., Sutt. 218 DA107
York Rd., Tedd. 177 CE91
York Rd., Uxb. 134 BK66
York Rd., Wal.Cr. 67 DY34
York Rd., Wat. 76 BW43
York Rd., W.Byf. 212 BK112
York Rd., West. 238 EH119
York Rd., Wey. 213 BQ105
York Rd., Wind. 151 AP82
York Rd., Wok. 226 AX119
York Sq. E14 143 DY72
York St. W1 272 D7
York St. W1 140 DF71
York St., Bark. 145 EQ67
Abbey Rd.
York St., Mitch. 200 DG101
York St., Twick. 177 CG88
York Ter., Enf. 82 DQ38
York Ter., Erith 167 FC81
York Ter. E. NW1 272 G5
York Ter. E. NW1 140 DG70
York Ter. W. NW1 272 F5
York Ter. W. NW1 140 DG70
York Way N1 141 DL67
York Way N7 141 DK65
York Way N20 98 DF48
York Way, Borwd. 78 CR40
York Way, Chess. 216 CL108
York Way, Felt. 176 BZ90
York Way, Hem.H. 40 BL21
York Way, Wat. 76 BX36
York Way Ct. N1 141 DL67
York Way Est. N7 141 DL65
York Way
Yorke Gdns., Reig. 250 DA133
Yorke Rd., Reig. 249 CZ133
Yorke Rd., Rick. 74 BN44
Yorkes, Harl. 51 ET17
Yorkland Ave., Well. 165 ET83
Yorkshire Clo. N16 122 DS62
Yorkshire Gdns. N18 100 DV50
Yorkshire Grey Pl. NW3 120 DC63
Heath St.
Yorkshire Grey Yd. WC1 274 B7
Yorkshire Rd. E14 143 DY72
Yorkshire Rd., Mitch. 201 DL99
Yorkton St. E2 142 DU68
Young Rd. E16 144 EJ72
Young St. W8 160 DB75
Young St., Lthd. 247 CE125
Youngfield Rd., Hem.H. 39 BF19
Youngmans Clo., Enf. 82 DQ39
Young's Bldgs. EC1 275 J4
Youngs Ri., Welw.G.C. 29 CV09
Youngs Rd., Ilf. 125 ER57
Youngstroat La., Wok. 210 AY110
Yoxley App., Ilf. 125 EQ58
Yoxley Dr., Ilf. 125 EQ58
Yukon Rd. SW12 181 DH87
Yule Clo., St.Alb. 60 BZ30
Yuletide Clo. NW10 138 CS66
Yunus Khan Clo. E17 123 EA57

Z

Zampa Rd. SE16 162 DW78
Zander Ct. E2 142 DU68
St. Peter's Clo.
Zangwill Rd. SE3 164 EK81
Zealand Ave., West Dr. 154 BK80
Zealand Rd. E3 143 DY68
Zelah Rd., Orp. 206 EV101
Zennor Rd. SW12 181 DJ88
Zenoria St. SE22 162 DT84
Zermatt Rd., Th.Hth. 202 DQ98
Zetland St. E14 143 EB71
Zig Zag Rd., Dor. 247 CJ130
Zig Zag Rd., Tad. 247 CK132
Zig-Zag Rd., Ken. 236 DQ116
Zion Pl., Grav. 191 GH87
Zion Pl., Th.Hth. 202 DR98
Zion Rd., Th.Hth. 202 DR98
Zion St., Sev. 257 FM121
Church Rd.
Zoar St. SE1 279 H2
Zoffany St. N19 121 DK61

The following is a comprehensive listing of all the railway stations which appear in this atlas. Bold references can be found within the Central London enlarged scale section (pages 272-279).

INDEX TO LONDON REGIONAL TRANSPORT STATIONS

The following is a comprehensive listing of all London Regional Transport Stations which appear in this atlas. Bold references can be found within the Central London enlarged scale section (pages 272-279). A London Underground map can be found on page 431. Restricted line services are indicated by brackets.

London Undergound Line Abbreviations

Bak.	Bakerloo	*Dist.*	District	*Met.*	Metropolitan
Cen.	Central	*E.L.*	East London	*North.*	Northern
Circ.	Circle	*H. & C.*	Hammersmith & City	*Picc.*	Piccadilly
D.L.R.	Docklands Light Railway	*Jub.*	Jubilee	*Vic.*	Victoria

Acton Town	Dist.; Picc.	158	CN75
Aldgate	**Circ.; Met.**	**275**	**P8**
Aldgate East	Dist.; H. & C.	142	DT72
All Saints	D.L.R.	143	EB73
Alperton	Picc.	138	CL67
Amersham	Met.	55	AQ38
Angel	**North.**	**274**	**E1**
Archway	North.	121	DJ61
Arnos Grove	Picc.	99	DJ49
Arsenal	Picc.	121	DN62
Baker Street	**Bak.; Circ.; H. & C.; Jub.; Met.**	**272**	**E5**
Balham	North.	180	DG88
Bank	**Cen.; D.L.R.; North.**	**275**	**K9**
Barbican	**Circ.; H. & C.; Met.**	**275**	**H6**
Barking	Dist.; (H. & C.)	145	EQ66
Barkingside	Cen.	125	ER56
Barons Court	Dist.; Picc.	159	CY78
Bayswater	Circ.; Dist.	140	DB73
Beckton	D.L.R.	145	EN71
Beckton Park	D.L.R.	145	EM73
Becontree	Dist.	146	EX65
Belsize Park	North.	120	DE64
Bermondsey	Jub. (Opening Autumn1999)	162	DU76
Bethnal Green	Cen.	142	DV69
Blackfriars	**Circ.; Dist.**	**274**	**F10**
Blackhorse Road	Vic.	123	DX56
Blackwall	D.L.R.	143	EC73
Bond Street	**Cen.; Jub.**	**272**	**G9**
Borough	**North.**	**279**	**J4**
Boston Manor	Picc.	157	CG77
Bounds Green	Picc.	99	DK51
Bow Church	D.L.R.	143	EA69
Bow Road	Dist.; (H. & C.)	143	EA69
Brent Cross	North.	119	CX59
Brixton	Vic.	161	DM84
Bromley-by-Bow	Dist.; (H. & C.)	143	EC69
Buckhurst Hill	Cen.	102	EK46
Burnt Oak	North.	96	CQ53
Caledonian Road	Picc.	141	DM65
Camden Town	North.	141	DH67
Canada Water	Jub. (Opening Autumn1999)	162	DW75
Canary Wharf	D.L.R.	143	EA74
Canary Wharf	Jub. (Opening Autumn1999)	143	EB74
Canning Town	D.L.R.; Jub.	144	EE72
Cannon Street	**Circ.; Dist.**	**279**	**K1**
Canons Park	Jub.	96	CL52
Chalfont & Latimer	Met.	72	AW39
Chalk Farm	North.	140	DG66
Chancery Lane	**Cen.**	**274**	**D7**
Charing Cross	**Bak.; Jub.; North.**	**277**	**P2**
Chesham	Met.	54	AQ31
Chigwell	(Cen.)	103	EP49
Chiswick Park	Dist.	158	CQ77
Chorleywood	Met.	73	BD42
Clapham Common	North.	161	DJ84
Clapham North	North.	161	DL83
Clapham South	North.	181	DH86
Cockfosters	Picc.	80	DG42
Colindale	North.	118	CS55
Colliers Wood	North.	180	DD94
Covent Garden	**Picc.**	**273**	**P9**
Crossharbour	D.L.R.	163	EB76
Croxley	Met.	75	BP44
Custom House	D.L.R.	144	EH73
Cutty Sark	D.L.R. (Opening early 2000)	163	EC79
Cyprus	D.L.R.	145	EN73
Dagenham East	Dist.	127	FC64
Dagenham Heathway	Dist.	146	EZ65
Debden	Cen.	85	EQ42
Deptford Bridge	D.L.R. (Opening early 2000)	163	EA81
Devons Road	D.L.R.	143	EB70
Dollis Hill	Jub.	119	CU64
Ealing Broadway	Cen.; Dist.	137	CK73
Ealing Common	Dist.; Picc.	138	CM74
Earls Court	Dist.; Picc.	160	DA77
East Acton	Cen.	139	CT72
East Finchley	North.	120	DE56
East Ham	Dist.; (H. & C.)	144	EL66
East India	D.L.R.	143	ED73
East Putney	Dist.	179	CY85
Eastcote	Met.; Picc.	116	BW59
Edgware	North.	96	CP51
Edgware Road	**Bak.; Circ.; Dist.; H. & C.**	**272**	**B7**
Elephant & Castle	**Bak.; North.**	**278**	**G7**
Elm Park	Dist.	127	FH63
Elverston Road	D.L.R. (Opening early 2000)	163	EB82
Embankment	**Bak.; Circ.; Dist.; North.**	**278**	**A2**
Epping	Cen.	70	EU31
Euston	**North.; Vic.**	**273**	**M3**
Euston Square	**Circ.; H. & C.; Met.**	**273**	**L4**
Fairlop	Cen.	103	ER53
Farringdon	**Circ.; H. & C.; Met.**	**274**	**E6**
Finchley Central	North.	98	DA53
Finchley Road	Jub.; Met.	140	DC65
Finsbury Park	Picc.; Vic.	121	DN61
Fulham Broadway	Dist.	160	DA80
Gallions Reach	D.L.R.	145	EP72
Gants Hill	Cen.	125	EN58
Gloucester Road	Circ.; Dist.; Picc.	160	DC77
Golders Green	North.	120	DA59
Goldhawk Road	H. & C.	159	CW75
Goodge Street	**North.**	**273**	**L6**
Grange Hill	(Cen.)	103	ER49
Great Portland Street	**Circ.; H. & C.; Met.**	**273**	**J5**
Green Park	**Jub.; Picc.; Vic.**	**277**	**K3**
Greenford	Cen.	137	CD67
Greenwich	D.L.R. (Opening early 2000)	163	EB80
Gunnersbury	Dist.	158	CP78
Hainault	(Cen.)	103	ES52
Hammersmith	Dist.; H. & C.; Picc.	159	CW77
Hampstead	North.	120	DC63
Hanger Lane	Cen.	138	CM69
Harlesden	Bak.	138	CR68
Harrow & Wealdstone	Bak.	117	CE55
Harrow on the Hill	Met.	117	CE58
Hatton Cross	Picc.	155	BT84
Heathrow Terminal 4	Picc.	175	BP85
Heathrow Terminals 1,2,3	Picc.	155	BP83
Hendon Central	North.	119	CW57
Heron Quays	D.L.R.	143	EA74
High Barnet	North.	80	DA42
High Street Kensington	Circ.; Dist.	160	DB75
Highbury & Islington	Vic.	141	DP65
Highgate	North.	121	DH58
Hillingdon	Met.; (Picc.)	115	BP64
Holborn	**Cen.; Picc.**	**274**	**A7**
Holland Park	Cen.	139	CZ74
Holloway Road	Picc.	121	DM64
Hornchurch	Dist.	128	FK62
Hounslow Central	Picc.	157	CD83
Hounslow East	Picc.	156	CC82
Hounslow West	Picc.	156	BY82
Hyde Park Corner	**Picc.**	**276**	**F4**
Ickenham	Met.; (Picc.)	115	BQ63
Island Gardens	D.L.R. (Reopening early 2000)	163	EC78
Kennington	**North.**	**278**	**F10**
Kensal Green	Bak.	139	CW68
Kensington (Olympia)	(Dist.)	159	CY76
Kentish Town	North.	121	DH64
Kenton	Bak.	117	CH58
Kew Gardens	Dist.	158	CN81
Kilburn	Jub.	119	CZ64
Kilburn Park	Bak.	140	DA68
King's Cross St. Pancras	**Circ.; H. & C.; Met.; North.; Picc.; Vic.**	**274**	**A1**
Kingsbury	Jub.	118	CN57
Knightsbridge	**Picc.**	**276**	**D5**
Ladbroke Grove	H. & C.	139	CY72
Lambeth North	**Bak.**	**278**	**D6**
Lancaster Gate	Cen.	140	DD73
Latimer Road	H. & C.	139	CX73
Leicester Square	**North.; Picc.**	**273**	**P10**
Lewisham	D.L.R. (Opening early 2000)	163	EC83
Leyton	Cen.	123	EC62
Leytonstone	Cen.	124	EE60
Limehouse	D.L.R.	143	DY72
Liverpool Street	**Cen.; Circ.; H. & C.; Met.**	**275**	**M7**
London Bridge	**North.**	**279**	**L3**
Loughton	Cen.	84	EL43
Maida Vale	Bak.	140	DB68
Manor House	Picc.	122	DQ59
Mansion House	**Circ.; Dist.**	**275**	**J10**
Marble Arch	**Cen.**	**272**	**E10**
Marylebone	**Bak.**	**272**	**D5**
Mile End	Cen.; Dist.; (H. & C.)	143	DZ70
Mill Hill East	North.	97	CX52
Monument	**Circ.; Dist.; D.L.R.**	**275**	**L10**
Moor Park	Met.	93	BR47
Moorgate	**Circ.; H. & C.; Met.; North.**	**275**	**K7**
Morden	North.	200	DB97
Mornington Crescent	North.	141	DJ68
Mudchute	D.L.R. (Reopening early 2000)	163	EB77
Neasden	Jub.	118	CS64
New Cross	E.L.	163	DZ80
New Cross Gate	E.L.	163	DY80
Newbury Park	Cen.	125	ER58
North Acton	Cen.	138	CR71
North Ealing	Picc.	138	CM72
North Greenwich	Jub.	164	EE75
North Harrow	Met.	116	CB57
North Wembley	Bak.	117	CK62
Northfields	Picc.	157	CJ76
Northolt	Cen.	136	CA65
Northwick Park	Met.	117	CG59
Northwood	Met.	93	BS52
Northwood Hills	Met.	93	BU54
Notting Hill Gate	Cen.; Circ.; Dist.	140	DA73
Oakwood	Picc.	81	DJ43
Old Street	**North.**	**275**	**K3**
Osterley	Picc.	157	CD80
Oval	North.	161	DN79
Oxford Circus	**Bak.; Cen.; Vic.**	**273**	**K8**
Paddington	Bak.; Circ.; Dist.; H. & C.	140	DC72
Park Royal	Picc.	138	CN70
Parsons Green	Dist.	160	DA81
Perivale	Cen.	137	CG68
Piccadilly Circus	**Bak.; Picc.**	**277**	**M1**
Pimlico	**Vic.**	**277**	**M10**
Pinner	Met.	116	BY56
Plaistow	Dist.; (H. & C.)	144	EF68
Poplar	D.L.R.	143	EB73
Preston Road	Met.	118	CL60
Prince Regent	D.L.R.	144	EJ73
Pudding Mill Lane	D.L.R.	143	EB67
Putney Bridge	Dist.	159	CY83
Queen's Park	Bak.	139	CY68
Queensbury	Jub.	118	CM55
Queensway	Cen.	140	DB73
Ravenscourt Park	Dist.	159	CU77
Rayners Lane	Met.; Picc.	116	BZ59
Redbridge	Cen.	124	EK58
Regent's Park	**Bak.**	**273**	**H5**
Richmond	Dist.	158	CL84
Rickmansworth	Met.	92	BK45
Roding Valley	(Cen.)	102	EK49
Rotherhithe	E.L.	162	DW75
Royal Albert	D.L.R.	144	EK73
Royal Oak	H. & C.	140	DB71
Royal Victoria	D.L.R.	144	EG73
Ruislip	Met.; (Picc.)	115	BT60
Ruislip Gardens	Cen.	115	BU63
Ruislip Manor	Met.; (Picc.)	115	BU60
Russell Square	**Picc.**	**273**	**P5**
St. James's Park	**Circ.; Dist.**	**277**	**M5**
St. John's Wood	Jub.	140	DD68
St. Paul's	**Cen.**	**275**	**H8**
Seven Sisters	Vic.	122	DS57
Shadwell	D.L.R.; E.L.	142	DV73
Shepherd's Bush	Cen.; H. & C.	139	CW74
Shoreditch	(E.L.)	142	DT70
Sloane Square	**Circ.; Dist.**	**276**	**F9**
Snaresbrook	Cen.	124	EG57
South Ealing	Picc.	157	CK76
South Harrow	Picc.	116	CC62
South Kensington	**Circ.; Dist.; Picc.**	**276**	**A8**
South Kenton	Bak.	117	CJ60
South Quay	D.L.R.	163	EB75
South Ruislip	Cen.	116	BW64
South Wimbledon	North.	180	DB94
South Woodford	Cen.	102	EH54
Southfields	Dist.	179	CZ88
Southgate	Picc.	99	DK46
Southwark	**Jub. (Opening Autumn 1999)**	**278**	**F3**
Stamford Brook	Dist.	159	CT77
Stanmore	Jub.	95	CK50
Stepney Green	Dist.; (H. & C.)	143	DX70
Stockwell	North.; Vic.	161	DL82
Stonebridge Park	Bak.	138	CP66
Stratford	Cen.; D.L.R.; Jub.	143	EC66
Sudbury Hill	Picc.	117	CE63
Sudbury Town	Picc.	137	CH65
Surrey Quays	E.L.	163	DX76
Swiss Cottage	Jub.	140	DD66
Temple	**Circ.; Dist.**	**274**	**C10**
Theydon Bois	Cen.	85	ET36
Tooting Bec	North.	180	DG90
Tooting Broadway	North.	180	DE92
Tottenham Court Road	**Cen.; North.**	**273**	**M8**
Tottenham Hale	Vic.	122	DU55
Totteridge & Whetstone	North.	98	DB47
Tower Gateway	D.L.R.	142	DT73
Tower Hill	**Circ.; Dist.**	**275**	**P10**
Tufnell Park	North.	121	DJ63
Turnham Green	Dist.; Picc.	158	CS77
Turnpike Lane	Picc.	121	DN55
Upminster	Dist.	128	FQ61
Upminster Bridge	Dist.	128	FN61
Upney	Dist.	145	ET66
Upton Park	Dist.; (H. & C.)	144	EJ67
Uxbridge	Met.; (Picc.)	134	BK66
Vauxhall	Vic.	161	DL78
Victoria	**Circ.; Dist.; Vic.**	**277**	**J7**
Walthamstow Central	Vic.	123	EA56
Wanstead	Cen.	124	EH58
Wapping	E.L.	142	DW74
Warren Street	**North.; Vic.**	**273**	**L4**
Warwick Avenue	Bak.	140	DC70
Waterloo	**Bak.; Jub.; North.**	**278**	**C4**
Watford	Met.	75	BT41
Wembley Central	Bak.	118	CL64
Wembley Park	Jub.; Met.	118	CN62
West Acton	Cen.	138	CN72
West Brompton	Dist.	160	DA78
West Finchley	North.	98	DB51
West Ham	Dist.; (H. & C.); Jub.	144	EE68
West Hampstead	Jub.	140	DA65
West Harrow	Met.	116	CC58
West India Quay	D.L.R.	143	EA73
West Kensington	Dist.	159	CZ78
West Ruislip	Cen.	115	BQ61
Westbourne Park	H. & C.	139	CZ71
Westferry	D.L.R.	143	EA73
Westminster	**Circ.; Dist.**	**278**	**A5**
White City	Cen.	139	CW73
Whitechapel	Dist.; E.L.; H. & C.	142	DV71
Willesden Green	Jub.	119	CW64
Willesden Junction	Bak.	139	CT69
Wimbledon	Dist.	179	CZ93
Wimbledon Park	Dist.	180	DA90
Wood Green	Picc.	99	DM54
Woodford	Cen.	102	EH51
Woodside Park	North.	98	DB49

THE LIBRARY
GUILDFORD COLLEGE
of Further and Higher Education

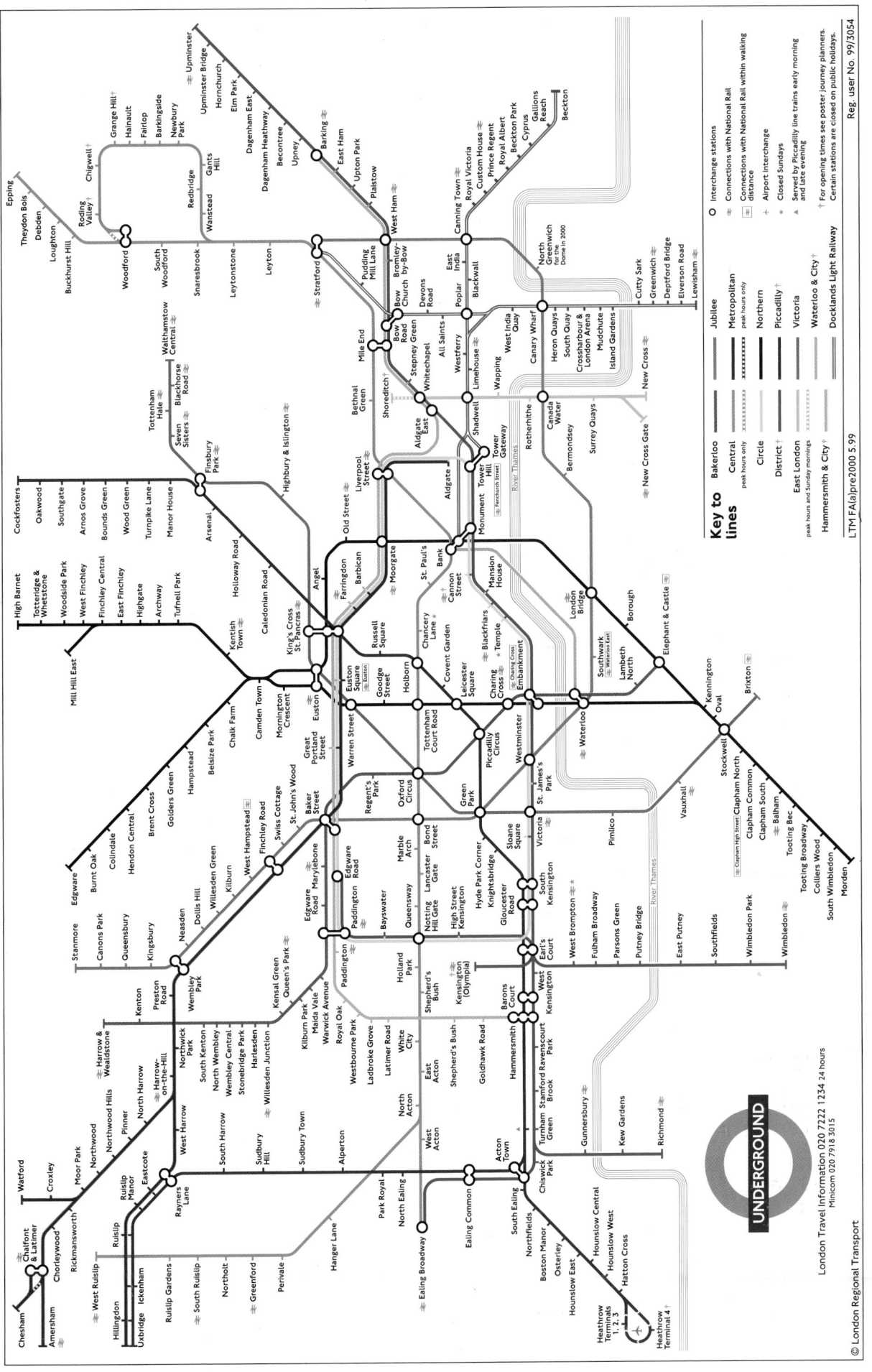

Reg. user No. 99/3054

Key to lines

Bakerloo	Jubilee
Central	Metropolitan peak hours only
Circle	Northern
District †	Piccadilly †
East London peak hours and Sunday mornings	Victoria
Hammersmith & City †	Waterloo & City †
	Docklands Light Railway

○ Interchange stations
⇌ Connections with National Rail
▣ Connections with National Rail within walking distance
✈ Airport interchange
+ Closed Sundays
▲ Served by Piccadilly line trains early morning and late evening
† For opening times see poster journey planners. Certain stations are closed on public holidays.

LTM FA(a)pre2000 5.99

UNDERGROUND

London Travel Information 020 7222 1234 24 hours
Minicom 020 7918 3015

© London Regional Transport

AYLESBURY VALE

D A C O R U M

ST.

WELWYN

28 29 30

ALBANS

HATFIELD

38 39 40 41 42 43 44 45 46

CHILTERN

54 56 57 58 59 60 61 62 63 64

THREE WATFORD HERTSMERE

55 72 73 74 75 76 77 78 79 80

RIVERS

WYCOMBE

88 89 90 91 92 93 94 95 96 97 98

BARNET

HARROW

110 111 112 113 114 115 116 117 118 119 120

SOUTH BUCKS HILLINGDON BRENT CAMDEN

130 131 132 133 134 135 136 137 138 139 140

SLOUGH EALING KENSINGTON & CHELSEA WESTMINSTER

HAMMERSMITH & FULHAM

150 151 152 153 154 155 156 157 158 159 160

WINDSOR & MAIDENHEAD

HOUNSLOW

WANDSWORTH

172 173 174 175 176 177 178 179 180

RICHMOND

UPON THAMES

WOKINGHAM SPELTHORNE

BRACKNELL KINGSTON MERTON

FOREST 192 193 194 195 196 197 198 199 200

RUNNYMEDE UPON THAMES

SUTTON

THE LIBRARY
GUILDFORD COLLEGE
of Further and Higher Education

Author Nicholson

Title Greater London
Street Atlas

Class REF 914.
421 NIC

Accession 95645

95645

FOR
REFERENCE ONLY

SURREY HEATH

210 211 212 213 214 215 216 217 218

ELMBRIDGE EPSOM
& EWELL

HART

WOKING

226 227 228 229 230 231 232 233 234

RUSHMOOR

242 243 244 245 246 247 248 249 250

REIGATE &
BANSTEAD

GUILDFORD

258 259 260 261 262 263 264 265 266

MOLE VALLEY

EAST
HANTS

268

WAVERLEY

CRAWL